THE
SOCIAL
SCIENCE
ENCYCLOPEDIA

THE
SOCIAL
SCIENCE
ENCYCLOPEDIA

Edited by

Adam Kuper and
Jessica Kuper

Routledge & Kegan Paul

London, Boston and Henley

First published in 1985
by Routledge & Kegan Paul plc

14 Leicester Square, London WC2H 7PH, England

9 Park Street, Boston, Mass, 02108, USA and

Broadway House, Newtown Road,
Henley on Thames, Oxon RG9 1EN, England

Set in Baskerville, 9 on 10 pt,
by Input Typesetting Ltd, London
and printed in Great Britain

Library of Congress Cataloging in Publication Data

The social science encyclopedia.
Includes index.
1. Social sciences—Dictionaries.   I. Kuper, Adam.
II. Kuper, Jessica.
H41.S63   1985   300'.3'21   84–27736

British Library CIP data also available

ISBN 0–7102–0008–0

Contents

Editorial preface

This Encyclopedia is intended for a sophisticated but not necessarily specialist readership, including social scientists, students, journalists, planners and administrators, and all those with a serious interest in contemporary academic thinking about the individual in society. Our aim has been to provide a broad, accessible and up-to-date coverage of the social sciences, in a convenient format.

There are well over 700 entries dealing with theories, issues and methods, and dozens more are devoted to the life and work of individual scholars whose contributions to the field have been of exceptional significance. The major social sciences are reviewed in considerable detail. Anthropology, economics, political science and political theory, psychology and sociology are all treated in one (or more) master entries, by scholars of high international reputation. A large number of individual entries written by specialists then cover subfields in these disciplines, and also particular theories and problem areas. Other relevant disciplines are dealt with in a similar though less complete fashion. Though not mainstream social sciences, they belong, at least in part, to the same general field of discourse. These disciplines include demography, development studies, linguistics and semiotics, and psychiatry. Some other intellectual traditions, professions and problem areas have also been given extended attention, notably the biological dimension of the social sciences, business studies and industrial relations, communication and media studies, education, geography, history, law, Marxism, medicine, and women's studies. Special emphasis has been given to methods and to relevant issues in philosophy. The Encyclopedia also deals with the applications of the social sciences – in market research and opinion polls, in therapy, in aptitude testing and the measurement of intelligence, in industrial relations and in management, in economic and financial analysis and in planning, in social work, in criminology and penology.

Yet although the various disciplines and problem areas may form part of a single area of discourse, the very notion of a social science has been repeatedly brought into question in recent years. Outsiders have doubted its pretensions, insiders its internal coherence. (Ralf Dahrendorf discusses the issues in his entry 'social science'.) To a considerable extent this Encyclopedia itself illustrates the extent of interconnectedness, of overlap, if not of cohesion among the intellectual traditions which comprise the social sciences. Even at the level of theory there is less diversity than some specialists might imagine. Edward Shils, in his entry 'sociology', defines the often implicit ideas which are common currency in that apparently extremely diverse field; ideas which, taken together, amount in the end almost to a shared theoretical perspective. A single field of discourse does not necessarily require a single set of theoretical assumptions, but through interchange, by a process of challenge and response, it stimulates the development of shared standards and concerns, and fosters a consensus as to which theoretical approaches should be considered serious contenders. The attentive reader will find that certain themes recur in the most unexpected places, and that an initial enquiry may lead from an obvious starting-point right across disciplinary boundaries to perhaps hitherto unheard of destinations.

Another aspect of this unity in diversity appears from the fact that the 500 contributors to the Encyclopedia are drawn from twenty-five countries. The largest contingents come (in almost equal proportions) from the United States of America and the United Kingdom, but there are also a substantial number of contributors from Australia, Canada, France, The Netherlands, the Scandinavian countries and West Germany. The fluidity of disciplinary boundaries is matched by the international character of the social sciences today.

But we must not exaggerate the convergences and the areas in which a certain degree of consensus reigns. There is certainly more than enough diversity to raise questions about emphasis, or even bias. We have selected our contributors for their individual expertise, but inevitably they represent a very broad cross-section of opinion and a variety of intellectual orientations. Moreover, contributors were encouraged to be controversial where that seemed appropriate. The balance comes from reading further, followed up cross-references, so that one perspective is countered by another. These considerations are especially relevant where political or moral issues arise. One obvious example is sociobiology, and the reader can get an immediate sense of how different points of view are represented by comparing, say, Van den Berghe on 'sociobiology', Feldman on 'population genetics', and 'genetics and behaviour', Grammar on 'ethology' and McHenry on 'evolution'.

It is, of course, precisely this sort of diversity which has led some to query the scientific status of the social sciences (though there is even less agreement as to what constitutes a proper science). Desirable or not, the divergences are real enough, and the Encyclopedia reflects the controversies as well as the common assumptions. Our ambition has been to review the whole gamut of ideas on the individual and society which have emerged from a century of academic research, criticism and discussion.

Adam Kuper
Jessica Kuper

Leiden, July 1984

Contributors

General editors
Adam Kuper and Jessica Kuper

Subject editors

Economics – Phyllis Deane, Emeritus Professor of Economic History, University of Cambridge

Linguistics – Paul Newman, Professor of Linguistics, Indiana University

Psychiatry – Alan A. Stone, Professor of Psychiatry and Law, Harvard University

Sociology and Social Problems – Stanley Cohen, Professor of Criminology, The Hebrew University of Jerusalem

Editorial consultants

Andrew Colman, Reader in Psychology, University of Leicester

Max Coltheart, Professor of Psychology, Birkbeck College, University of London

Kingsley Davis, Fellow, The Hoover Institute, Stanford

Harry Johnson, Professor of Sociology, University of Illinois at Champaign-Urbana

Richard M. Lerner, Professor of Child Psychology, Pennsylvania State University

Gigi Santow, Research School of Social Science, The Australian National University

Alphabetical list of contributors

Aerts, Erik
  State Archives, Brussels
Akeroyd, Anne
  Dept of Sociology, University of York
Alexander, Jeff
  Dept of Sociology, University of California, Los Angeles
Andvig, Jens Christopher
  Norwegian Institute of International Affairs, Oslo
Appelbaum, Paul S., M.D.
  University of Massachusetts Medical School, Worcester, Massachusetts
Apthorpe, Raymond
  Institute of Social Studies, The Hague
Apter, Michael
  Dept of Psychology, University College, Cardiff
Arens, William
  Dept of Anthropology, State University of New York at Stony Brook
Argyle, Michael
  Dept of Experimental Psychology, University of Oxford
Armstrong, A. G.
  Dept of Economics, University of Bristol

Armstrong, David
  Unit of Sociology as Applied to Medicine, Guy's Hospital Medical School, University of London
Arnould, Eric
  American Embassy, Niamey, Niger
Asimakopulos, A.
  Dept of Economics, McGill University, Montreal
Azarya, Victor
  The Harry S. Truman Research Institute for the Advancement of Peace, The Hebrew University of Jerusalem
Baddeley, Alan
  MRC Applied Psychology Unit, Cambridge
Bailey, F.G.
  Dept of Anthropology, University of California, San Diego
Bain, Andrew
  Dept of Economics, University of Strathclyde
Ball, Sir James
  Former Principal, The London Business School
Baltes, Paul B.
  Max Planck Institute for Human Development and Education, Berlin

Bannister, D., M.D.
  High Royds Hospital, Ilkley, W. Yorkshire
Banton, Michael
  Dept of Sociology, University of Bristol
Barnard, Alan
  Dept of Anthropology, University of Edinburgh
Barnett, A. S.
  School of Development Studies, University of East Anglia
Barrell, Ray
  Dept of Economics, University of Southampton
Barron, Frank
  Dept of Psychology, University of California, Santa Cruz
Bart, Pauline B.
  Dept of Psychiatry, University of Illinois at the Medical Center, Chicago
Bartley, W. W. III
  Dept of Philosophy, California State University at Hayward and The Hoover Institution, Stanford
Baum, Alan
  Dept of Social Science, Middlesex Polytechnic, Enfield, Middlesex
Bauman, Zygmunt
  Dept of Sociology, University of Leeds
Beaumont, J. Graham
  Dept of Psychology, University of Leicester
Beer, C. G.
  Institute of Animal Behavior, Newark College of Arts and Sciences, Rutgers, The State University of New Jersey
Beiner, R. S.
  Dept of Politics, University of Southampton and Dept of Philosophy, Queen's University, Kingston, Ontario
Beisser, Arnold R., M.D.
  Los Angeles
Belmont, Nicole
  Laboratory of Social Anthropology, École Pratique des Hautes Études, Paris
Beloff, Lord Max
  Former Principal, University of Buckingham
Bem, Sacha
  Dept of Psychology, University of Leiden
Berkowitz, Marvin
  Dept of Psychology, Marquette University, Milwaukee
Béteille, André
  Centre for Advanced Study in Sociology, Delhi School of Economics
Beyme, Klaus von
  Dept of Political Science, University of Heidelberg
Billig, Michael
  Dept of Psychology, Loughborough University, Leicestershire
Bird, James H.
  Dept of Geography, University of Southampton

Birnbaum, Pierre
  Dept of Political Science, University of Paris 1
Black, R. D. C.
  Dept of Economics, The Queen's University of Belfast
Bliss, Christopher
  Nuffield College and Dept of Economics, Oxford
Bliss, Eugene L., M.D.
  Dept of Psychiatry, University of Utah Medical Center, Salt Lake City
Bloch, Maurice
  Dept of Social Anthropology, The London School of Economics and Political Science
Blondel, Jean
  Pro-Vice-Chancellor, and Dept of Government, University of Essex
Bloor, David
  Science Studies Unit, University of Edinburgh
Boden, Margaret A.
  School of Social Sciences, University of Sussex
Boissevain, Jeremy
  Dept of Anthropology, University of Amsterdam
Boland, Lawrence A.
  Dept of Economics, Simon Fraser University, Burnaby, British Columbia
Bolen, Jean Shinoda
  C. J. Jung Institute, San Francisco
Bowman, Mary Jean
  Dept of Economics, University of Chicago
Bray, Margaret
  Faculty of Economics and Politics, Cambridge
Bredow, Wilfried von
  Dept of Political Science, Philipps University, Marburg, West Germany
Brislin, Richard
  Culture Learning Institute, East-West Center, Honolulu
Brittan, Arthur
  Dept of Sociology, University of York
Bronfenbrenner, Martin
  Dept of Economics, Duke University, Durham, North Carolina and Aoyama Gakuin University, Tokyo
Brown, Archie
  St Antony's College, University of Oxford
Brown, Arthur
  Emeritus Professor of Economics, University of Leeds
Brown, Barrie
  Dept of Psychology, Institute of Psychiatry, University of London
Brown, C. V.
  Dept of Economics, University of Stirling
Brown, Gillian
  Dept of Linguistics, University of Essex
Brown, R. J.
  Social Psychology Research Unit, University of Kent

Brown, Richard K.
Dept of Sociology and Social Policy, University of Durham

Brubaker, Stanley C.
Dept of Political Science, Colgate University

Brunner, Ronald D.
Colorado Center for Public Policy Research, University of Colorado

Buckley, Kerry W.
Northampton, Massachusetts

Bulmer, Martin
Dept of Social Administration, The London School of Economics and Political Science

Burke, Peter
Emmanuel College, University of Cambridge

Burton, Michael
School of Social Sciences, University of California, Irvine

Button, Kenneth
Dept of Economics, Loughborough University, Leicestershire

Caldwell, J. C.
Research School of Social Sciences, Australian National University

Calhoun, Craig
Dept of Sociology, University of North Carolina at Chapel Hill

Calhoun, Lawrence
Dept of Psychology, University of North Carolina at Charlotte

Cann, Arnold
Dept of Psychology, University of North Carolina at Charlotte

Canovan, Margaret
Dept of Politics, University of Keele

Canter, David
Dept of Psychology, University of Surrey

Cartwright, Rosalind
Dept of Psychology and Social Sciences, Rush-Presbyterian-St Luke's Medical Center, Chicago

Carver, Terrell
Dept of Politics, University of Bristol

Casson, Mark
Dept of Economics, University of Reading

Casson, Ronald W.
Dept of Sociology and Anthropology, Oberlin College, Ohio

Cattell, R. B.
Emeritus Professor of Psychology, University of Illinois, Champaign-Urbana

Chamberlain, Mariam
Russell Sage Foundation, New York

Chambliss, William J.
Dept of Sociology, University of Delaware

Cherlin, Andrew
Dept of Sociology, The Johns Hopkins University, Baltimore

Chick, Victoria
Dept of Political Economy, University College London

Chirot, Daniel
School of International Studies, University of Washington, Seattle

Chisholm, Michael
Department of Geography, University of Cambridge

Christie, Nils
Institute of Criminology and Criminal Law, University of Oslo

Clark, J. A.
Science Policy Research Unit, University of Sussex

Claxton, G. L.
Centre for Science and Mathematics Education, Chelsea College, University of London

Coats, A. N.
Dept of Economics, University of Nottingham

Cohen, Brenda
Dept of Philosophy, University of Surrey

Cohen, G.
Human Cognition Research Laboratory, Open University, Milton Keynes

Cohen, Percy
Dept of Sociology, The London School of Economics and Political Science

Cohen, Stanley
Institute of Criminology, The Hebrew University of Jerusalem

Coleman, John C.
The Sussex Youth Trust, Seaford, Sussex

Collard, D. A.
School of Humanities and Social Sciences, University of Bath

Colman, Andrew
Dept of Psychology, University of Leicester

Coltheart, Max
Dept of Psychology, Birkbeck College, University of London

Cook, Karen S.
Dept of Sociology, University of Washington, Seattle

Cornwall, John
Dept of Economics, Dalhousie University, Halifax, Nova Scotia

Cowan, Charles D.
Bureau of the Census, Washington D.C.

Cowell, F. A.
Dept of Economics, The London School of Economics and Political Science

Crump, Thomas
Dept of Anthropology, University of Amsterdam

Currie, J. M.
Dept of Economics, University of Manchester

Curtice, John
Dept of Political Theory and Institutions, University of Liverpool

Dahrendorf, Ralf
Former Director, The London School of Economics and Political Science

Danziger, K.
Dept of Psychology, York University, Downsview, Ontario

Darnell, Regna
Dept of Anthropology, University of Alberta, Edmonton

Davidson, Paul
Dept of Economics, Rutgers, The State University of New Jersey

Davies, S. W.
School of Economic and Social Studies, University of East Anglia

Deane, Phyllis
Emeritus Professor of Economic History, University of Cambridge

Denoon, Donald
Research School of Pacific Studies, Australian National University

Dietz, Elliott, M.D.
School of Law, University of Virginia

Dilnot, Andrew
Institute for Fiscal Studies, London

Domhoff, William
Adlai Stevenson College, University of California, Santa Cruz

Doob, Leonard
Dept of Psychology, Yale University

Doreian, Patrick
Dept of Sociology, University of Pittsburgh

Douglas, Susan P.
Graduate School of Business Administration, New York University

Draguns, Juris G.
Dept of Psychology, Pennsylvania State University

Dubé-Simard, Lise
Dept of Psychology, University of Montreal

Duller, H.
Dept of Development Sociology, University of Leiden

Duncan, John
MRC Applied Psychology Unit, Cambridge

Elbers, Ed
Dept of Psychology, University of Utrecht

Ellen, Roy
Dept of Social Anthropology, University of Kent

Engerman, Stanley
Dept of Economics, University of Rochester

Estrin, Saul
Dept of Economics, University of Southampton

Evans, G. R.
Fitzwilliam College, University of Cambridge

Evans, H. David
Institute of Development Studies, University of Sussex

Ewbank, Douglas
Population Studies Center, University of Pennsylvania

Eysenck, H. J.
Institute of Psychiatry, University of London

Eysenck, Michael W.
Dept of Psychology, Birkbeck College, University of London

Farr, R. M.
Dept of Social Psychology, The London School of Economics and Political Science

Fawcett, Sir James, Q.C.
Former President, European Commission of Human Rights, and Emeritus Professor of International Law, King's College London

Feinberg, Walter
Dept of Education, University of Illinois at Champaign-Urbana

Feiwel, George R.
Dept of Economics, University of Tennessee, Knoxville

Feldman, Marcus W.
Dept of Biological Sciences, Stanford University

Femia, Joseph V.
Dept of Political Theory, University of Liverpool

Fielding, Guy
Dept of Communication Studies, Sheffield City Polytechnic

Fienberg, Stephen E.
Dept of Statistics, Carnegie-Mellon University, Pittsburgh

Fishman, Joshua
Graduate School of Professional Psychology, Yeshiva University, New York

Fitzgerald, E.
Institute of Social Studies, The Hague

Floud, Roderick
Dept of History, Birkbeck College, University of London

Forbes, Duncan
Clare College, and Dept of History, University of Cambridge

Fox, J. Robin
Dept of Anthropology, Rutgers, The State University of New Jersey

Francis, Wayne, L.
Dept of Political Science, University of Missouri-Columbia

Frankel, Fred H., M.D.
Dept of Psychiatry, Beth Israel Hospital, Boston

Fraser, Colin
Social and Political Sciences Committee, University of Cambridge

Freeman, C.
Social Policy Research Unit, University of Sussex

Frey, Bruno
Institute of Empirical Economics, University of Zurich

Friedman, Gary D., M.D.
Dept of Medical Methods Research, The Permanente Medical Group Inc., Oakland, California

Friedman, Jonathan
Dept of Ethnology, University of Copenhagen

Friedman, William J.
Dept of Psychology, Oberlin College, Ohio

Fromkin, Victoria
Dean, Graduate Division, Vice Chancellor Graduate Programs, and Dept of Linguistics, University of California, Los Angeles

Galtung, Johan
International Peace Research Institute, Oslo

Gasper, D. R.
Institute of Social Studies, The Hague

Geary, Dick
Dept of German Studies, University of Lancaster

Gecas, Viktor
Dept of Sociology, Washington State University, Pullman, Washington

Geer, John van de
Dept of Psychology, University of Leiden

Gellner, Ernest
Dept of Social Anthropology, University of Cambridge

Gibbs, Jack
Dept of Sociology, Vanderbilt University, Nashville, Tennessee

Gibson, H. B.
Cambridge

Gieryn, Thomas
Dept of Sociology, Indiana University, Bloomington

Giles, Howard
Dept of Psychology, University of Bristol

Gilgen, Albert R.
Dept of Psychology, University of Northern Iowa, Cedar Falls

Gilhooly, K. J.
Dept of Psychology, University of Aberdeen

Ginneken, Jaap van
Dept of Psychology, University of Leiden

Glickman, Maurice
Dept of Sociology, University of Botswana

Goethals, George W., M.D.
Dept of Psychiatry, Harvard University

Gogel, W. F.
Dept of Psychology, University of California, Santa Barbara

Goldstone, Jack A.
Dept of Sociology, Northwestern University, Evanston, Illinois

Goode, Erich
Dept of Sociology, State University of New York at Stony Brook

Goodwin, Barbara
Dept of Government, Brunel University, Uxbridge, Middlesex

Gorecki, Jan
Dept of Sociology, University of Illinois at Champaign-Urbana

Goyder, John
Dept of Sociology, University of Waterloo, Ontario

Graff, Harvey J.
Dept of History, University of Texas at Dallas

Grammar, Karl
Institute for Human Ethology, Max Planck Institute for Physiology, Seewiesen, West Germany

Grathoff, Richard
Dept of Sociology, University of Bielefeld, West Germany

Green, Jerry
Dept of Economics, Harvard University

Greenberg, Joseph
Dept of Anthropology and Dept of Linguistics, Stanford University

Gregory, Mary B.
St Hilda's College, University of Oxford

Groenewegen, P. D.
Dept of Economics, University of Sydney

Gruchy, Allan G.
Dept of Economics, University of Maryland

Grunebaum, Henry, M.D.
Family Studies, The Cambridge Hospital, Cambridge, Massachusetts

Gudeman, Stephen
Dept of Anthropology, University of Minnesota

Gulliver, Phillip
Dept of Anthropology, York University, Downsview, Ontario

Gutheil, Thomas, G., M.D.
Harvard University and Program in Psychiatry and the Law, Boston

Haddock, B. A.
Dept of Political Theory, University College, Swansea

Hage, Per
Dept of Anthropology, University of Utah

Hagège, Claude
Dept of Linguistics, École Pratique des Hautes Études, Paris

Hall, John R.
Dept of Sociology, University of Missouri-Columbia

Hall, Thomas D.
Dept of Sociology, University of Oklahoma, Norman

Halsey, A. H.
Dept of Social and Administrative Studies, University of Oxford

Hampson, Sarah E.
Dept of Psychology, Birkbeck College, University of London

Hannerz, Ulf
Dept of Social Anthropology, University of Stockholm

Hanson, F. Allan
Dept of Anthropology, University of Kansas
Hansson, Björn
Dept of Economics, University of Lund
Harary, Frank
Institute for Social Research, University of Michigan, Ann Arbor
Harcourt, G.
Faculty of Economics and Politics, University of Cambridge
Hareven, Tamara K.
Center for Population Studies, Harvard University
Hargreaves, David J.
Dept of Psychology, University of Leicester
Harris, Chris
Dept of Sociology and Anthropology, University College, Swansea
Hatch, Elvin
Dept of Anthropology, University of California, Santa Barbara
Hazan, Haim
Dept of Sociology and Anthropology, University of Tel-Aviv
Heald, Suzette
Dept of Sociology, University of Lancaster
Heaven, Patrick
School of Humanities and Social Sciences, Riverina College, Australia
Heer, David M.
Population Research Laboratory, Dept of Sociology, University of Southern California
Heertje, Arnold
Dept of Economics, University of Amsterdam
Hemsley, David
Institute of Psychiatry, University of London
Hepple, L. W.
Dept of Geography, University of Bristol
Herbert, Martin
Dept of Psychology, University of Leicester
Hernandez, Donald
Center for Population Research, Kennedy Institute of Ethics, Georgetown University, Washington, D. C.
Herriot, Peter
Dept of Occupational Psychology, Birkbeck College, University of London
Heusch, Luc de
Dept of Social Anthropology, Free University, Brussels
Hewitt, Cynthia
El Colegio de Mexico, Mexico City
Himmelweit, Hilde
Dept of Social Psychology, The London School of Economics and Political Science
Hirst, Paul
Dept of Political Science, Birkbeck College, University of London
Hodder, Ian
Dept of Archaeology, University of Cambridge

Holmes, Peter
Dept of Economics, University of Sussex
Holy, Ladislaw
Dept of Social Anthropology, University of St Andrews
Hope, Keith
University of Oxford
Horvat, Branko
Dept of Economics, University of Zagreb
Howells, Kevin
Dept of Psychology, University of Leicester
Hudson, Liam
Dept of Psychology, Brunel University, Uxbridge, Middlesex
Hughes, Gordon
Faculty of Economics and Politics, University of Cambridge
Humphreys, Sally
Dept of Anthropology, University of Michigan, Ann Arbor
Humphries, Jane
Faculty of Economics and Politics, University of Cambridge
Hunt, E. K.
Dept of Economics, University of Utah
Ignatieff, Michael
King's College Research Centre, King's College, University of Cambridge
Ingleby, David
Dept of Development Psychology, University of Utrecht
Ingold, Tim
Dept of Social Anthropology, University of Manchester
Israel, J.
Dept of History, University College London
Izard, Michel
Laboratory of Social Anthropology, École Pratique des Hautes Études, Paris
Jackson, Dudley
Dept of Economics, University of Wollongong, New South Wales, Australia
Jahoda, Marie
Science Policy Research Unit, University of Sussex
Jarvie, I. C.
Dept of Philosophy, York University, Downsview, Ontario
Jennings, Jeremy
Dept of Political Theory and Government, University College, Swansea
Johnson, Harry M.
Dept of Sociology, University of Illinois at Champaign-Urbana
Jones, Alan
Dept of Senior Psychologist (Navy), Ministry of Defence (UK)
Jones, Edward E.
Dept of Psychology, Princeton University

Jones, Emrys
Dept of Geography, The London School of Economics and Political Science
Jones, Maxwell, M.D.
Wolfville, Nova Scotia
Jonung, Lars
Dept of Economics, University of Lund, Sweden
Jorion, Paul
Food and Agricultural Organization, Benin
Joshi, Heather
Centre for Population Studies, London School of Hygiene and Tropical Medicine, University of London
Josselin de Jong, P. E. de
Dept of Cultural Anthropology, University of Leiden
Kalberg, Stephen
Center for European Studies, Harvard University
Kanbur, S. M. Ravi
Dept of Economics, University of Essex
Karady, Victor
Centre for European Sociology, CNRS, Paris
Kassiola, Joel
Dept of Political Science, Brooklyn College, City University of New York
Kavanagh, Dennis
Dept of Political Science, University of Nottingham
Keil, Charles
Dept of American Studies, State University of New York at Buffalo
Kellner, Douglas
Dept of Philosophy, University of Texas at Austin
Kelly, Aileen
King's College, University of Cambridge
Kendall, Philip C.
Dept of Psychology, Temple University, Philadelphia
Kenny, Michael
Dept of Anthropology, Catholic University of America, Washington, D.C.
Ketner, Kenneth Laine
Institute for Studies in Pragmatism, Texas Tech University, Lubbock, Texas
Keyfitz, Nathan
Center for Population Studies, Harvard University
Kieser, A.
Dept of Industrial Organization, University of Mannheim, West Germany
Kiiveri, Harry
Division of Mathematics and Statistics, CSIRO Institute of Physical Sciences, Wembley, Western Australia
Kimmel, H. D.
Dept of Psychology, University of South Florida
Kindleberger, Charles, P.
Emeritus Ford International Professor of Economics, Massachusetts Institute of Technology

Kirk, Dudley
Emeritus Dean and Virginia Morrison Professor, Food Research Institute, Stanford University
Kleinman, Arthur
Dept of Anthropology, Harvard University
Kline, Paul
Dept of Psychology, University of Exeter
Klir, George
Dept of Systems Science, State University of New York at Binghampton
Kourvetaris, George A.
Dept of Sociology, N. Illinois University, De Kalb, Illinois
Kramer, Deirdre
Max Planck Institute for Human Development and Education, Berlin
Krathwohl, David R.
School of Education, Syracuse University, Syracuse, N.Y.
Kraynak, Robert
Dept of Political Science, Colgate University, Hamilton, N.Y.
Kregel, J. A.
Dept of Economics, University of Groningen, The Netherlands
Kriesberg, Louis
Dept of Sociology, Syracuse University, Syracuse, N.Y.
Kris Anton, M.D.
Brookline, Massachusetts
Kroeber-Riel, W.
Institute for Behaviour Research, University of Saarlandes, West Germany
Kumar, Krishan
Keynes College, University of Kent
Kuper, Adam
Dept of Human Sciences, Brunel University, Uxbridge, Middlesex
Landy, Frank
Dept of Psychology, Pennsylvania State University
Lass, Roger
Dept of General Linguistics, University of Cape Town
Lassman, P.
Dept of Sociology, University of Birmingham
Lavers, Annette
Dept of French, University College London
Layton, Robert
Dept of Anthropology, University of Durham
Lazare, Aaron, M.D.
Massachusetts General Hospital, Boston
Lecomber, Richard
Formerly of the Dept of Economics, University of Bristol
Lehmann, David
Faculty of Economics and Politics, Cambridge
Leibowitz, Herschel W.
Dept of Psychology, Pennsylvania State University

Leiter, Kenneth C. W.
  Dallas, Texas
Lemert, Charles
  Dept of Sociology, Wesleyan University,
  Middletown, Connecticut
Leonini, Luisa
  Dept of Sociology, University of Milan
Lerner, Richard M.
  College of Human Development, Pennsylvania
  State University
Levy, Bernard, M.D.
  Human Resource Institute, Brookline,
  Massachusetts
Lidz, Victor
  Dept of Sociology and Anthropology, Haverford
  College, Pennsylvania
Lijphart, Arendt
  Dept of Political Science, University of California,
  San Diego
Lipset, David
  Dept of Anthropology, University of Minnesota
Lipsitt, Lewis P.
  Walter S. Hunter Laboratory of Psychology, Brown
  University, Providence, Rhode Island
Llewellyn, David
  Dept of Economics, Loughborough University,
  Leicestershire
Loasby, B. J.
  Dept of Economics, University of Stirling
Lock, Grahame
  Faculty of Social Science, Catholic University of
  Nijmegen, The Netherlands
Long, Norman
  Dept of Rural Sociology, University of
  Wageningen, The Netherlands
Lyons, David
  Cornell Law School, Cornell University
MacCannell, Dean
  Dept of Applied Behavioral Sciences, University of
  California, Davis
McDonald, Peter
  Institute of Family Studies, Melbourne
McGhee, Paul E.
  Dept of Home and Family Life, Texas Tech
  University, Lubbock, Texas
McHenry, Henry M.
  Dept of Anthropology, University of California,
  Davis
Mackenzie, Beryl
  Dept of Psychology, La Trobe University, Victoria,
  Australia
Mackintosh, N. J.
  Dept of Experimental Psychology, University of
  Cambridge
Maclean, Ian
  Queen's College, University of Oxford
McLellan, David
  Eliot College, University of Kent

McQuail, Denis
  Dept of Mass Communications, University of
  Amsterdam
Manis, Melvin
  Dept of Psychology, University of Michigan, Ann
  Arbor
Manstead, Tony
  Dept of Psychology, University of Manchester
Maratsos, Michael
  Institute of Child Development, University of
  Minnesota
Marris, Peter
  Graduate School of Architecture and Urban
  Planning, University of California, Los Angeles
Marsh, D. C.
  Formerly of the University of Nottingham
Marvick, Dwaine
  Dept of Sociology, University of California, Los
  Angeles
Mayes, Andrew
  Dept of Psychology, University of Manchester
Maynard, Alan
  Centre for Health Economics, University of York
Meja, Volker
  Dept of Sociology, Memorial University of
  Newfoundland, St John's, Newfoundland
Melzack, Ronald
  Dept of Psychology, McGill University, Montreal
Mendlewicz, Julien
  Erasmus Hospital, Free University, Brussels
Mensch, Ivan N.
  Dept of Psychiatry and Biobehavioral Sciences,
  School of Medicine, University of California, Los
  Angeles
Menzies, Kenneth
  Dept of Sociology and Anthropology, University of
  Guelph, Ontario
Meyer, Alfred G.
  Dept of Political Science, University of Michigan,
  Ann Arbor
Miller, David
  Nuffield College, University of Oxford
Miller, Gerald
  Dept of Communications, Michigan State
  University, East Lansing
Millward, R.
  Dept of Economics, University of Salford
Minogue, Kenneth
  Dept of Government, The London School of
  Economics and Political Science
Mishan, Ezra J.
  London
Modell, Judith
  Dept of Social Sciences, Carnegie-Mellon
  University, Pittsburgh
Moggridge, Donald
  Royal Economic Society, Toronto

Mollon, J. D.
Dept of Experimental Psychology, University of Cambridge

Monge, Peter R.
Annenberg School of Communications, University of Southern California

Moore, Basil
Dept of Economics, Wesleyan University, Middletown, Connecticut

Moore, Sally Falk
Dept of Anthropology, Harvard University

Moreland, Richard L.
Dept of Psychology, University of Pittsburgh

Morris, Peter
Dept of Psychology, University of Lancaster

Moss, Lawrence S.
Babson College, Wellesley, Massachusetts

Muellbauer, John
Nuffield College, University of Oxford

Muller-Schwarze, Dietland
College of Environmental and Forest Biology, State University of New York, Syracuse

Mullineux, A. W.
Dept of Economics, University of Birmingham

Neale, Sir Alan
London

Neary, J. Peter
Dept of Political Economy, University College Dublin

Nell, Edward J.
Dept of Economics, New School for Social Research, N.Y.

Nelson, Michael
Dept of Political Science, Vanderbilt University, Nashville, Tennessee

Nemiah, John C., M.D.
Beth Israel Hospital, Boston

Newman, Paul
Dept of Linguistics, Indiana University, Bloomington

Newmeyer, F.
Dept of Linguistics, University of Washington, Seattle

Niemi, Richard G.
Dept of Political Science, University of Rochester

O'Brien, D. P.
Dept of Economics, University of Durham

O'Neil, W. M.
Emeritus Professor of Psychology, Sydney University

Odell, Peter
Centre for International Energy Studies, Erasmus University, Rotterdam

Olmsted, D. L.
Dept of Anthropology, University of California, Davis

Oppong, Christine
International Labour Organization, Geneva

Panoff, Michel
CNRS, Paris

Parkes, C. M., M.D.
The London Hospital Medical College, University of London

Parkinson, S. T.
Henley, The Management College, Henley-on-Thames

Parry, Jonathan P.
Dept of Social Anthropology, The London School of Economics and Political Science

Pasquino, Gianfranco
Dept of Political Science, University of Bologna

Payne, Staney G.
Dept of History, University of Wisconsin-Madison

Peach, Terry
Faculty of Economic and Social Studies, University of Manchester

Pearce, David
Dept of Economics, University College London

Peel, John
Dept of Sociology, University of Liverpool

Pen, Jan
Dept of Economics, University of Groningen, The Netherlands

Peplau, Anne
Dept of Psychology, University of California, Los Angeles

Perry, John
Dept of Philosophy, Stanford University

Philp, Mark
Oriel College, University of Oxford

Pinto-Duschinsky, M.
Dept of Government, Brunel University, Uxbridge, Middlesex

Platt, Gerald
University of Massachusetts, Amherst

Plummer, K. J.
Dept of Sociology, University of Essex

Pollack, Alan S., M.D.
Adult Outpatient Clinic, McLean Hospital, Belmont, Massachusetts

Pollock, George H., M.D.
President, American Psychoanalytic Association

Pomorska Jakobson, Krystyna
Foreign Languages and Literatures, Massachusetts Institute of Technology

Poole, Michael
Dept of Business Administration and Accountancy, University of Wales Institute of Science and Technology, Cardiff

Pope, Harrison G., M.D.
The Mailman Research Center, Belmont, Massachusetts

Pouillon, Jean
Editor *L'Homme*, Paris

Prestwich, M.C.
Dept of History, University of Durham

Prins, Gwyn
 Emmanuel College, University of Cambridge
Punch, M. E.
 Nijenrode Business College, The Netherlands
Rabbitt, Patrick
 Dept of Psychology, University of Manchester
Rangell, Leo, M.D.
 Los Angeles
Ray, William J.
 Dept of Psychology, Pennsylvania State University
Rayner, Steve
 Oak Ridge National Laboratory, Tennessee
Reekie, W. Duncan
 Dept of Business Studies, University of the
 Witwatersrand, Johannesburg
Reisman, D. A.
 Dept of Economics, University of Surrey
Revell, J. R. S.
 Institute of European Finance, University College
 of North Wales, Bangor
Reynolds, P. A.
 Vice-Chancellor, University of Lancaster
Rhodes, G. F.
 Dept of Economics, Colorado State University
Ritvo, Edward R., M.D.
 Center for Health Sciences, School of Medicine,
 University of California, Los Angeles
Robertson, Roland
 Dept of Sociology, University of Pittsburgh
Rock, Paul
 Dept of Sociology, The London School of
 Economics and Political Science
Roman, Paul
 Dept of Sociology, Tulane University, New Orleans
Rondinelli, D. A.
 Maxwell School, Syracuse University, Syracuse,
 N.Y.
Rose, Hilary
 Dept of Applied Social Studies, University of
 Bradford
Rosen, F.
 Dept of Politics, The London School of Economics
 and Political Science
Ross, Robert
 Unit for the Study of European Expansion,
 University of Leiden
Roth, Loren, M.D.
 Western Psychiatric Institute and Clinic,
 University of Pittsburgh
Rothschild, Kurt
 Dept of Economics, Johannes Kepler University,
 Linz, Austria
Rubin, Zick
 Dept of Psychology, Brandeis University
Rudra, Ashok
 Dept of Economics, Visva-Bharati, Santiniketan,
 West Bengal, India

Runyan, William McKinley
 School of Social Welfare, University of California,
 Berkeley
Rupp-Eisenreich, B.
 École Pratique des Hautes Études, Paris
Russell, Peter
 Dept of Political Science, University of Toronto
Rushton, J. Philippe
 Dept of Psychology, University of Western Ontario,
 London, Ontario
Saith, Ashwani
 Institute for Social Studies, The Hague
Santow, Gigi
 Dept of Demography, Research School of Social
 Sciences, The Australian National University
Saporta, Sol
 Dept of Linguistics, University of Washington,
 Seattle
Sayers, Janet
 Dept of Psychology, University of Kent
Scaff, Lawrence
 Dept of Political Science, University of Arizona
Schaffer, Bernard
 Formerly of the Institute of Development Studies,
 University of Sussex
Schnabel, P. E.
 Dept of Sociology, University of Bielefeld, West
 Germany
Schröder, Peter
 Ministry of Education, Leidschendam, The
 Netherlands
Schur, Edwin M.
 Dept of Sociology, New York University
Scott, Wolf
 United Nations Research Institute for Social
 Development, Geneva
Self, Peter
 Research School of Social Science, The Australian
 National University, and The London School of
 Economics and Political Science
Seppänen, Paavo
 Dean of the Social Sciences, and Dept of Sociology,
 University of Helsinki
Sexton, Virginia S.
 Dept of Psychology, St John's University, Jamaica,
 N.Y.
Shallice, Tim
 MRC Applied Psychology Unit, Cambridge
Sharaf, Myron, M.D.
 Dept of Psychiatry, Harvard University
Sharp, Derrick
 Dept of Education, University College of Wales,
 Swansea
Shaw, G. K.
 Dept of Economics, University of Buckingham
Shaw, William H.
 Dept of Philosophy and Religious Studies,

Tennessee State University, Nashville
Shils, Edward
Committee on Social Thought, University of Chicago, and Peterhouse College, University of Cambridge
Shone, Ronald
Dept of Economics, University of Stirling
Short, James F.
Social Research Center, Washington State University, Pullman, Washington
Shumaker, Sally Ann
Center for Metropolitan Planning and Research, The Johns Hopkins University, Baltimore
Sillitoe, Paul
Dept of Anthropology, University of Durham
Singer, H. W.
Institute of Development Studies, University of Sussex
Singer, Jerome L.
Dept of Psychology, Yale University
Skinner, Andrew
Dept of Political Economy, University of Glasgow
Sly, David F.
Center for the Study of Population, The Florida State University, Tallahassee, Florida
Smith, Carol
Dept of Anthropology, Duke University, Durham, North Carolina
Smith, James E.
Cambridge Group for the History of Population and Social Structure, University of Cambridge
Smith, N.
Dept of Linguistics, University College London
Smooha, Sammy
Dept of Sociology, University of Haifa
Snow, David A.
Dept of Sociology, University of Texas at Austin
Spanier, Grahame B.
Vice Provost for Undergraduate Studies, State University of New York at Stony Brook
Spector, Malcolm
Dept of Sociology, McGill University, Montreal
Spencer, Paul
Dept of Social Anthropology, School of Oriental and African Studies, University of London
Spiegel, David, M.D.
Dept of Psychiatry, School of Medicine, Stanford University
Spielberger, Charles D.
Center for Research in Behavioral Medicine and Community Psychology, University of South Florida, Tampa, Florida
St John-Stevas, The Right Hon. Norman, M.P.
House of Commons, London
Stack, Steven
Dept of Sociology, Pennsylvania State University
Stansfield, R. G.
Bishop's Stortford, Hertfordshire

Stehr, Nico
Dept of Sociology, University of Alberta, Edmonton
Stone, Alan A., M.D.
Harvard Law School
Stone, Karen
Belmont, Massachusetts
Stone, Mervyn
Dept of Statistical Sciences, University College London
Stoneman, Paul
Dept of Economics, University of Warwick
Stotland, Ezra
Society and Justice Program, University of Washington, Seattle
Strathern, Marilyn
Dept of Social Anthropology, University of Manchester
Strauss, John S., M.D.
Dept of Psychiatry, Medical School, Yale University
Streissler, E.
Dept of Economics, University of Vienna
Stuckey, Sterling
Dept of History, Northwestern University, Evanston, Illinois
Switzky, Harvey
Dept of Learning, Development and Special Education, Northern Illinois University, De Kalb, Illinois
Taeuber, Conrad
Center for Population Research, Georgetown University, Washington, D.C.
Talbott, John A., M.D.
The Payne Whitney Psychiatric Clinic, The New York Hospital
Tarascio, Vincent J.
Dept of Economics, University of North Carolina at Chapel Hill
Tarrow, Sidney
Dept of Government, Cornell University
Tarullo, Louisa B.
Cambridge, Massachusetts
Thayer, H. S.
Dept of Philosophy, City University of New York
Thirlwell, A. P.
Keynes College, University of Kent
Thompson, John B.
Jesus College, University of Cambridge
Thuriaux, Michel, M.D.
Regional Office, World Health Organization, Copenhagen
Timms, Noel
Dept of Social Work, University of Leicester
Tiryakian, Edward J.
Dept of Sociology, Duke University, Durham, North Carolina
Tischler, Gary, M.D.
Yale Psychiatric Institute, New Haven

Tjon Sie Fat, Franklin
Dept of Cultural Anthropology, University of Leiden

Tobias, Phillip, M.D.
Dept of Anatomy, University of the Witwatersrand, Johannesburg

Tournon, Jean
Dept of Political Studies, University of Grenoble

Townsend, Peter
Department of Social Administration, University of Bristol

Toye, John
Centre for Development Studies, University College of Wales, Swansea

Tudor, Andrew
Dept of Sociology, University of York

Tudor, Henry
Dept of Political Science, University of Durham

Turner, Bryan
Dept of Sociology, The Flinders University of South Australia, Bedford Park

Turner, Jonathan H.
Dept of Sociology, University of California, Riverside

Urry, John
Dept of Sociology, University of Lancaster

Vaillant, George, M.D.
Dartmouth Medical School, Hanover, New Hampshire

Valentine, E. R.
Dept of Psychology, Bedford College, University of London

Van den Berghe, Pierre
Dept of Sociology, University of Washington, Seattle

Vansina, Jan
Dept of History, University of Wisconsin-Madison

Van der Ven, A. H. G. S.
Dept of Psychology, Catholic University of Nijmegen, The Netherlands

Verdon, Michel
Dept of Anthropology, University of Montreal

Vines, David
Dept of Applied Economics, University of Glasgow

Vondracek, Fred W.
College of Human Development, Pennsylvania State University

Waddington, Ivan
Dept of Sociology, University of Leicester

Walker, Jack L.
Institute of Public Policy Studies, University of Michigan, Ann Arbor

Walker, Nigel
Institute of Criminology, University of Cambridge

Walker, S. F.
Dept of Psychology, Birkbeck College, University of London

Wallis, Roy
Dept of Social Studies, The Queen's University of Belfast

Ward, Michael
OECD, Paris

Watson, Andrew S., M.D.
Dept of Psychiatry and Dept of Law, University of Michigan, Ann Arbor

Watt, E. D.
Dept of Politics, University of Western Australia, Nedlands

Weale, Martin
Dept of Applied Economics, University of Cambridge

Weale, R. A., M.D.
Institute of Ophthalmology, University of London

Wexler, Kenneth
School of Social Sciences, University of California, Irvine

Whitaker, John K.
Dept of Economics, University of Virginia

Whittington, Geoffrey
Dept of Economics, University of Bristol

Whitworth, John
Dept of Sociology, Simon Fraser University, Burnaby, British Columbia

Wiatr, Jerzy J.
Dept of Political Science, University of Warsaw

Wilson, Deirdre
Dept of Linguistics, University College London

Winter, J. M.
Pembroke College, University of Cambridge

Wolf, Charlotte
Dept of Sociology, Memphis State University, Memphis, Tennessee

Wolff, Janet
Dept of Sociology, University of Leeds

Wong, Normund, M.D.
Director, Karl Menninger School of Psychiatry, Menninger Foundation, Topeka, Kansas

Wortis, Joseph
Editor, *Biological Psychiatry*, Brooklyn, N.Y.

Wunsch, Guillaume
Dept of Demography, Louvain University, Belgium

Yates, Aubrey J.
Dept of Psychology, University of Western Australia, Nedlands

Yolton, John
Dean, Rutgers, The State University of New Jersey

Zaleznik, Abraham
Harvard University School of Business Administration

Entries grouped by discipline and problem area

Note: An alphabetical list of entries is given at the back of the book

ANTHROPOLOGY
BIOLOGY
BUSINESS STUDIES
COMMUNICATION AND
  MEDIA STUDIES
DEMOGRAPHY
DEVELOPMENT STUDIES
ECONOMICS
EDUCATION

GEOGRAPHY
HISTORY
INDUSTRIAL RELATIONS
LAW
LINGUISTICS
MARXISM
MEDICINE
METHODOLOGY

PHILOSOPHY
POLITICAL SCIENCE
POLITICAL THEORY
PSYCHIATRY
PSYCHOLOGY
SOCIAL PROBLEMS AND
  CRIMINOLOGY
SOCIOLOGY

ANTHROPOLOGY

acculturation
age organization
anthropology
archaeology
art, anthropology of
Bateson
Big Man
Boas
cannibalism
cargo cults
caste
cultural anthropology
culture
culture and personality
culture area
descent and descent groups
diffusion
divine kingship
division of labour by sex
Douglas
ecology
economic anthropology
ethnic groups
ethnic relations
ethnographic fieldwork
ethnology
Evans-Pritchard
evolution
evolutionism and progress
exchange
feud

fieldwork *see* Ethnographic
  fieldwork
folklore and myth
Frazer
functional analysis
Geertz
grid/group
hunters and gatherers
incest
incest behaviour
kinship
law
leach
Lévi-Strauss
Lévy-Bruhl
life cycle
magic
Maine
Malinowski
marriage
Mauss
Mead
medical anthropology
money, primitive
Morgan
myth *see* Folklore and myth
participant observation *see*
  Ethnographic fieldwork
pastoralism
peasants
political anthropology
primitive art *see* Art,
  anthropology of

progress *see* Evolutionism and
  progress
race
Radcliffe-Brown
religion and ritual
rites of passage
Rivers
Sapir
social structure: anthropological
  approaches
stateless societies
state, origin of
structuralism
symbolism
taboo
totemism
trade and markets, anthropology
  of
tribe
Tylor
Van Gennep
war, primitive
witchcraft and sorcery
witchhunts
women's studies in social
  anthropology

BIOLOGY

activation and arousal
biological psychiatry
comparative psychology
ecology

EDUCATION

GEOGRAPHY

spatial statistics
time-space analysis
transport, economics and
  planning

HISTORY

Annales school
archaeology
Bloch
Braudel
capitalism
cliometrics
economic history *see* Cliometrics,
  History
evolutionism and progress
feudalism
historical linguistics
history
McNeill
oral tradition
Pirenne
social change
sociocultural evolution
Sombart
Tawney

INDUSTRIAL RELATIONS

capitalism
employment and
  underemployment
employment and unemployment,
  social psychological aspects
entrepreneurship
ergonomics
industrial and organizational
  psychology
industrial democracy
industrialization and
  deindustrialization
industry, sociology of
labour market analysis
labour relations
multinational enterprises
occupational psychology
productivity
trade unions

LAW

arbitration and mediation
constitutions and
  constitutionalism
human rights

judicial process
law
legitimacy
Maine

LINGUISTICS

bilingualism
Bloomfield
Chomsky
Greenberg
historical linguistics
Jakobson
language, social psychology of *see*
  Social psychology of language
language and culture
language development
lexicostatistics
linguistics
Martinet
pragmatics
psycholinguistics
Sapir
Saussure
semantics
semiotics
social psychology of language
sociolinguistics
structural linguistics
transformational generative
  grammar

MARXISM

alienation
Asiatic Mode of Production
capitalism
class, social
communism
Engels
Frankfurt School
Gouldner
Gramsci
Gurvitch
Habermas
ideology
imperialism
labour theory of value
Lukács
Marcuse
Marx
Marxian economics
Marx's theory of history and
  society
socialism
value, labour theory of *see* Labour
  theory of value

MEDICINE

abortion
anxiety
biological psychiatry
epidemiology
fertility
health economics
medical anthropology
medical sociology
mental health
morbidity
mortality
pain
psychiatry
psychoanalysis
psychosomatic illness
public health
stress

METHODOLOGY

Bayes' Theorem
case studies
catastrophe theory
categorical data
census of population
cohort analysis
computer simulation
cost-benefit analysis
cybernetics *see* General systems
  theory
deflation as a statistical device
ethics in social research
ethnographic fieldwork
evaluation
experimental design
Feyerabend
functional analysis
game theory
game theory, economic
  applications
general systems theory
graph theory
index numbers
input-output analysis
interviewing
Kuhn
life-histories
marketing research
mathematical models
measures of central tendency and
  dispersion
multivariate analysis
opinion polls
participant observation *see*
  Ethnographic fieldwork

nationalism
neocolonialism *see* Imperialism
peace
Plato
political theory
populism
power
progress *see* Evolutionism and
    progress
radicalism
representation, political
Rousseau
social contract
socialism
social welfare policy
state
Third World
Tocqueville
utilitarianism
Utopianism
war
war, primitive
welfare state

PSYCHIATRY

Adler
analytical psychology
anorexia nervosa
attachment
autism
aversion therapy
biological psychiatry
Bowlby
character disorders
countertransference
defences
depressive disorders
drugs *see* Drug use,
    Psychopharmacology
drug use
DSM III
electroconvulsive therapy
family therapy
free association
Freud, A.
Freud, S.
genetic aspects of mental illness
group therapy
Horney
hypnosis
hysteria
Jung
Klein, M.
Lacan
Laing

mental disorders
mental health
neuroses
obsessive-compulsive disorder
paranoid reactions
phobia
psychiatry
psychoanalysis
psychopathic personality
psychopharmacology
psychosomatic illness
Reich
Rogers
schizophrenia
separation and loss
Sullivan
super-ego
therapeutic community
transactional analysis
transference
unconscious

PSYCHOLOGY

abnormal psychology
activation and arousal
adolescence
aesthetics
ageing – psychological aspects
aggression and anger
altruism
anxiety
aptitude tests
artificial intelligence
associationism
attachment
attention
attitudes
attribution theory
authoritarian personality
behaviourism
behaviour therapy
bereavement
Bowlby
child psychology *see*
    Developmental psychology
clinical psychology
cognition *see* Intelligence,
    Memory, Sensation and
    perception, Thinking
cognitive-behavioural therapy
cognitive dissonance
cognitive science
colour vision
comparative psychology

conditioning, classical and
    operant
conflict resolution
conformity
consciousness and its disorders
constitutional psychology
creativity
cross-cultural psychology
culture and personality
depth perception
developmental psychology
dreams
Eastern psychology
educational psychology
emotion
employment and unemployment,
    psychological aspects
environmental psychology
ergonomics
ethology
existential psychology
Eysenck
fantasy
friendship
gender studies *see* Women's
    studies, Women's studies in
    psychology
genetics and behaviour
gestalt therapy
group dynamics
group therapy
Hull
humour, psychology of
identity *see* Self-concept, Social
    identity
industrial and organizational
    psychology
infancy and infant development
instinct
intelligence and intelligence
    testing
James
language, social psychology of *see*
    Social psychology of language
language development
learning
Le Play
life-span development
loneliness
loss *see* Bereavement
McCollough effect
memory
mental retardation
mind
moral development
motivation
nervous system

occupational psychology
pain
parapsychology
Pavlov
personal construct theory
personality
personality assessment
physiological psychology
Piaget
play
prejudice
problem solving
projective methods
psychology
reaction times
reinforcement *see* Conditioning,
  Learning
repertory grid analysis *see*
  Personal construct theory
Rorschach test *see* Projective
  methods
self-concept
semantic differential
sensation and perception
sensory and motor development
sexual behaviour
Skinner
sleep
socialization
social psychology
social psychology of language
social skills and social skills
  training
stereotypes
stigma
stress
Thematic Apperception Test *see*
  Projective methods
thinking – cognitive organization
  and processes
time
traits
vision
vocational and career
  development
Watson
women's studies in psychology
Wundt

SOCIAL PROBLEMS
AND CRIMINOLOGY

abortion
alcoholism
bereavement
capital punishment
crime and delinquency

criminology
deviance
divorce
drug use
homosexuality
juvenile delinquency *see* Crime
  and delinquency
labelling theory
mental health
penology
police
pornography
poverty
prostitution
psychopathic personality
public health
punishment
rape
rape avoidance
refugees
rehabilitation
social problems
social welfare
social welfare policy
social work
subculture
suicide

SOCIOLOGY

alienation
anomie
Aron
art, sociology of
Asiatic Mode of Production
Blau
body, sociology of the
capitalism
centre and periphery
Chicago School of Sociology
city
civil religion
class, social
Clausewitz
collective behaviour and crowds
commitment
communal groups
communication networks
communications
community
community development
Comte
conflict, social
criminology
crowds *see* Collective behaviour
  and crowds

cults *see* Sects and cults
death
divorce
Durkheim
Elias
élites
equality
ethnic groups
ethnic relations
ethnomethodology
family
family history
Foucault
Frankfurt School
friendship
functional analysis
futurology
games *see* Play, Sport, sociology of
game theory
gangs
generalized media
gerontology, social
Goffman
Gouldner
groups
Gurvitch
hierarchy
households
human needs
industry, sociology of
institutions
integration
intellectuals
knowledge, sociology of
labelling theory
labour relations
leisure *see* Work and leisure
Le Play
Mannheim
marketing research
marriage
Marx
Marx's theory of history and
  society
mass media
mass society
Mead, G. H.
medical sociology
Merton
military sociology
Mills
modernization
networks
organizations
Park
Parsons
peasants

NOTE ON ARRANGEMENT

(1) To conserve space, only references not given in detail in the text are listed at the end of an entry.

(2) The cross-references provided at the end of most entries are intended only as an initial pointer. The lists of entries grouped under disciplinary and problem-area headings will suggest further relevant entries.

(3) If you cannot find an entry for a particular subject, try the list of entries for possible alternative headings.

Abnormal Psychology

Abnormal psychology may be viewed as the scientific study of abnormalities of behaviour and experience, their determinants and correlates. However, the complexity of any such definition is well illustrated by the instructions for authors in the *Journal of Abnormal Psychology*, which includes as a topic falling within the journal's area of focus 'normal processes in abnormal individuals'. It is apparent that a consideration of the use of the word abnormal in this context is necessary.

It is common to distinguish at least three definitions of psychological abnormality. (1) *The statistical definition*. It is dependent upon a knowledge of the relative frequencies of certain behaviours, experiences, traits, etc., in the population; the extremes of the distributions are defined as abnormal. There are several problems with this approach: (i) Even if one restricts oneself to those dimensions studied extensively in experimental and social psychology, it is apparent that much of the population is likely to be abnormal in at least some respects. (ii) Abnormalities of relevance to adjustment may not lie solely in terms of the absolute levels of particular variables, but also in the way in which different measures covary. (iii) Abnormally high scores on measures such as those of ability would not be regarded as abnormal in the sense of a psychological aberration. (iv) The interpretation placed on statistical abnormality, for example, a high score on an anxiety questionnaire, is highly dependent on context, for example, whether or not the subject faced an identifiable stressful experience. It should be noted that this last point applies equally to the definitions of abnormality discussed below. (2) *The social definition* of psychological abnormality indicates that behaviours seen as violating the rules of social functioning are classified as abnormal. It is clear that standards of social behaviour vary according to the social reference group. There is obviously a partial overlap with statistical definitions of abnormality in that conformity to standards defines normal social behaviour. (3) *The medical definition* of psychological abnormality suggests that it be defined in terms of specific symptoms which indicate the presence of an underlying disordered state. However, the majority of problems of adjustment which result in intervention have no clear organic basis. Although guidelines for what constitutes symptoms have been developed (e.g., Wing *et al.*, 1974) and can result in

their reliable assessment, it is apparent that the designation even of such symptoms as hallucinations as psychological impairment may be dependent on social and cultural factors (Al-Issa, 1977).

Shapiro (1975) has argued that the field of psychopathology consists largely of those psychological phenomena requiring intervention. He suggests that they have at least one of the following four characteristics: they are distressing to the person concerned and/or to his associates; they are disabling; they are socially inappropriate in the context of the patient's subculture; they are inconsistent with reality. Research in abnormal psychology may be viewed as an attempt to describe and explain such phenomena in terms of concepts and theories derived from the scientific investigation of animal and human behaviour. Within abnormal psychology it is common to distinguish several models, or overall ways, of conceptualizing the area of study: the biological, emphasizing the biological bases of abnormality; the cognitive-behavioural; and the social. However, these are best seen as complementary approaches, reflecting different levels of analysis. Most of the phenomena of psychopathology are amenable to, and indeed require, analysis at all three levels.

A number of research strategies in abnormal psychology may be distinguished. (1) Group comparisons based on psychiatric classification. Despite frequent criticisms of this method of classification, the resultant groupings form the basis of much research in abnormal psychology. Such studies aim to test deductions from hypotheses concerning the nature and determinants of the disorder. (2) Studies examining the correlates and properties of an objectively defined aspect of abnormal behaviour or experience. (3) Experimentally induced pathological behaviour: here psychopathology is modelled and reproduced in the laboratory either with animal or human subjects. (4) Analogue studies: these involve the investigation of naturally occurring but non-clinical forms of statistically abnormal behaviour patterns, such as fear of spiders, which are seen as similar on critical dimensions to those phenomena requiring intervention.

David R. Hemsley
Institute of Psychiatry
University of London

References

Al-Issa, I. (1977), 'Social and cultural aspects of hallucinations', *Psychological Bulletin*, 84.

Shapiro, M. B. (1974), 'The requirements and implications of a systematic science of psychopathology', *Bulletin of the British Psychological Society*, 28.

Wing, J. K., Cooper, J. E. and Sartorius, N. (1974), *The Measurement and Classification of Psychiatric Symptoms*, London.

See also: *mental disorders*.

Abortion

The definition of induced abortion has been complicated by a debate about when 'life' can be said to begin. Frequently, however, it is defined as the intentional termination of pregnancy prior to the time at which the foetus attains viability, or capacity for life outside the womb. Cross-cultural evidence indicates that induced abortion is a universal practice (Devereux, 1955). Abortion, as a factor affecting fertility levels, has always interested demographers. The laws governing abortion at various times have reflected governmental population policies – for example, restrictions during the 1930s in the Soviet Union; encouragement of abortion in post-World War II Japan. Prior to the mid-1950s, Western social scientists other than demographers devoted little attention to the problem of abortion, although philosophers and theologians often discussed its moral implications.

Medically, the early termination of pregnancy by a trained physician under proper conditions is in most cases a simple and safe procedure. The legal status of this practice, however, has varied greatly by time and place. Since the beginning of the 1960s, the two major factors heightening social science interest in abortion are (1) concern for the possibly adverse social consequences of restrictive abortion laws; and (2) the growth and influence of the Women's Liberation Movement. Numerous studies (see Schur, 1965) have demonstrated that legal proscription does not significantly deter women from terminating unwanted pregnancies, but merely drives the demand for abortion underground, supporting an illicit market. Abortion seekers are then subject to economic and other exploitation by unscrupulous operators. The illegal operations themselves (and the attempts at self-induced abortion that typically precede them) often carry a high risk of physical as well as psychological harm.

Increasingly, abortion is recognized as a pre-eminent issue for feminists. Restrictive policies are seen to control female sexuality, impose undesired maternity, and impair women's rights to bodily self-determination. Furthermore, as Simone de Beauvoir (1953) has emphasized, abortion policies – the effects of which are felt almost entirely by women – have invariably been enacted and implemented by men (be they legislators or medical practitioners). Feminist political activity on behalf of women's reproductive rights has had a world-wide impact on public policy since the 1960s. Some of the most dramatic developments have occurred in the United States where a process of gradual legal liberalization led to a major US Supreme Court ruling (*Roe v. Wade*, 1973) legalizing abortion in the early months of pregnancy. Since that decision, there has been a sharp crystallization of 'pro-choice' (anti-restriction) and 'right to life' (pro-restriction) advocates – the latter including, but by no means limited to, Roman Catholic opponents. These groups have been actively engaged in collective organization and political action aimed at influencing public policy. Thus, in America and elsewhere the question of abortion has led to a clash of large-scale social and political movements, while the issue has continued to generate debate on a more abstract philosophical level.

Edwin M. Schur
New York University

References

Beauvoir, S. de (1953), *The Second Sex*, New York.

Devereux, G. (1955), *A Study of Abortion in Primitive Societies*, New York.

Schur, E. (1965), *Crimes Without Victims*, Englewood Cliffs, N.J.

Further Reading

Cohen, M., Nagel, T. and Scanlon, T. (eds) (1974), *The Rights and Wrongs of Abortion*, Princeton.

Jaffe, F., Lindheim, B. and Lee, P. (1981), *Abortion Politics: Private Morality and Public Policy*, New York.

Luker, K. (1975), *Taking Chances: Abortion and the Decision Not to Contracept*, Berkeley and Los Angeles.

See also: *fertility*.

Accelerator Principle

In contrast to the (Keynesian) multiplier, which relates output to changes in investment, the accelerator models investment as determined by changes in output. As the principle that investment responds to the changes in output which imply pressure on capacity, the accelerator has a long history, but its formal development dates from the realization that its combination with the multiplier could produce neat models of cyclical behaviour. J. M. Clark originally noted the possibilities inherent in such models, but their first formal development was by Lundberg and Harrod, and subsequently by Samuelson, with Hicks and Goodwin and others providing refinements.

Suppose the optimal capital stock stands in fixed proportion to output, that is, formally:

$$K^* = \alpha Y$$

where K^* is the desired stock of fixed capital

  Y is annual output

  α is the average and marginal ratio of optimal capital to output i.e. $(K^* / Y = \Delta K^* / Y)$

Now let the subscripts t and t-1 refer to the variables in years t and t-1

$$K^*_{t-1} = \alpha Y_{t-1}$$
$$K^*_t = \alpha Y_t$$

so $K^*_t - K^*_{t-1} = \alpha(Y_t - Y_{t-1})$

Assume that the optimal capital stock was achieved in year t-1,

$$K_{t-1} = K^*_{t-1}$$

therefore $K^*_t - K_{t-1} = \alpha(Y_t - Y_{t-1})$

  To understand investment, that is, the flow of expenditure on capital goods, it is necessary to know how quickly investors intend to close any gap between the actual and optimal capital stocks. Let λ be an adjustment coefficient which represents the extent to which the gap between the realized and the desired capital stocks is to be closed.

  Then

$$I_t = \lambda\alpha(Y_t - Y_{t-1})$$
or $I_t = V(Y_t - Y_{t-1})$

The λ and α coefficients together link investment to first differences in output levels and are described as the accelerator coefficient, here V. Even at this elementary level the accelerator has several interesting implications. First, net investment determined by the accelerator will be positive (negative and zero respectively) if and only if $(Y_t - Y_{t-1})$ is positive (negative and zero respectively). Second, such net investment will fall if the *rate* at which output is increasing declines.

  However, even at this simple level the weaknesses of the approach are also apparent. First, the results above relate *only* to investment determined by the accelerator, that is motivated as described above by a desire to expand capacity in line with output. It may well be that while entrepreneurs are influenced by relative pressure on their capital stocks, other factors also act as an inducement/disincentive to investment such as expectations, availability of new technology, and so on. Thus, the accelerator describes only a part of investment which might not stand in any fixed relation to total investment. Furthermore, the capacity argument really only models the *optimal capital stock*. To make the jump to the flow of investment requires the introduction of the λ coefficient which can only be justified by *ad hoc* references to supply conditions in the investment goods industries and/or the state of expectations. In

the absence of such additional assumptions it would only be possible to say that $I \gtrless O$ according to whether $K^*_t \gtrless K_{t-1}$.

  As suggested above, the accelerator has been fruitfully combined with the multiplier in models designed to explicate economic dynamics. Here the problem has been that while such models are useful in understanding the origins of cyclical fluctuation, realistic estimates of V predict an unreasonable degree of dynamic instability. This problem has generally been solved by combining the accelerator with other determinants of investment in more general models, and more specifically by theorizing the existence of 'floors' and 'ceilings' to income fluctuation, hence constraining potentially explosive accelerator multiplier interactions. In addition, generalized accelerator models themselves have provided the basis for empirical investigation of investment behaviour.

Jane Humphries
University of Cambridge

Further Reading
Goodwin, R. M. (1948), 'Secular and cyclical aspects of the multiplier and the accelerator', in *Income Employment and Public Policy: Essays in Honor of Alvin H. Hansen*, New York.
Harrod, R. F. (1936), *The Trade Cycle: An Essay*, Oxford.
Hicks, J. R. (1949), 'Mr Harrod's dynamic theory', *Economica*, XVI.
Hicks, J. R. (1950), *A Contribution to the Theory of the Trade Cycle*, Oxford.
Lundberg, E. (1937), *Studies in the Theory of Economic Expansion*, London.
Samuelson, P. A. (1939), 'A synthesis of the principle of acceleration and the multiplier', *Journal of Political Economy*, 47.
Samuelson, P. A. (1939), 'Interactions between the multiplier analysis and the principle of acceleration', *Review of Economic Statistics*, 21.

Accounting

Accounting deals with the provision of information about the economic activities of various accounting entities, the largest of which is the whole economy, for which national accounts are prepared. However, the traditional province of the accountant is the smaller unit, typically a business firm. Here, a distinction is often made between financial accounting and management accounting.

  (1) *Financial accounting* deals with the provision of information to providers of finance (shareholders and creditors) and other interested parties who do not participate in the management of the firm (such as trade unions and consumer groups). This usually takes the form of a balance sheet (a statement of assets and

claims thereon at a point in time), and a profit and loss account (a statement of revenue, expenses and profit over a period of time), supplemented by various other statements and notes. The form of financial accounting by companies is, in most countries, laid down by statute, and the contents are usually checked and certified independently by auditors. In some countries, there are also accounting standards laid down by the accounting profession or by the independent bodies which it supports, such as the United States Financial Accounting Standards Board, which determine the form and content of financial accounts.

(2) *Management accounting* is concerned with the provision of information to management, to assist with planning, decision making and control within the business. Because planning and decision making are inevitably directed to the future, management accounting often involves making future projections, usually called budgets. Important applications of this are capital budgeting, which deals with the appraisal of investments, and cash budgeting, which deals with the projection of future cash inflows and outflows and the consequent financial requirements of the entity. Management accounting is also concerned with controlling and appraising the outcome of past plans, for example, by analysing costs, and with assessing the economic performance of particular divisions or activities of the entity. Because the demand for management accounting information varies according to the activities, size and management structure of the entity, and because the supply of such information is not subject to statutory regulation or audit, there is a much greater variety both of techniques and of practice in management accounting than in financial accounting.

Both management accounts and financial accounts derive from an accounting system which records the basic data relating to the transactions of the entity. The degree to which management accounting and financial accounting information can both derive from a common set of records depends on the circumstances of the individual accounting entity and, in particular, on the form of its management accounting. However, all accounting systems have a common root in double-entry bookkeeping, a self-balancing system, based on the principle that all assets of the entity ('debits') can be attributed to an owner (a claim on the entity by a creditor or the owners' 'equity' interest in the residual assets of the entity, both of which are 'credits'). This system owes its origin to Italian merchants of the fifteenth century, but it is still fundamental to accounting systems, although records are now often kept on computers, so that debits and credits take the form of different axes of a matrix, rather than different sides of the page in a handwritten ledger. The design of accounting systems to avoid fraud and error is an important aspect of the work of the accountant.

The traditional orientation of accounting was to record transactions at their historical cost, that is, in terms of the monetary units in which transactions took place. Thus, an asset would be recorded at the amount originally paid for it. Inflation and changing prices in recent years have called into question the relevance of historical cost, and inflation accounting has become an important subject. It has been proposed at various times and in different countries that accounts should show current values, that is, the specific current prices of individual assets, or that they should be adjusted by a general price level index to reflect the impact of inflation on the value of the monetary unit, or that a combination of both types of adjustment should be employed. Intervention by standard-setting bodies on this subject has been specifically directed at financial accounting, but it has been hoped that the change of method would also affect management accounting.

Financial accounting has also been affected, in recent years, by an increased public demand for information about business activities often supported by governments. Associated with this has been demand for information outside the scope of traditional profit-oriented accounts, resulting in research and experimentation in such areas as human asset accounting and corporate social reporting. There has also been more interest in accounting for public-sector activities and not-for-profit organizations. Recent developments in management accounting, facilitated by the increased use of computers, include the greater employment of the mathematical and statistical methods of operational research for such uses as the control of stock levels. This development has, however, been matched by a growing interest in behavioural aspects of accounting, for example, studies of the human response to budgets and other targets set by management accountants. The whole area of accounting is currently one of rapid change, both in research and in practice.

Geoffrey Whittington
University of Bristol

Further Reading
Arnold, J., Carsberg, B. and Scapens, R. (1980), *Topics in Management Accounting*, Oxford.
Barton, A. D. (1977), *The Anatomy of Accounting*, St Lucia, Queensland.
Bull, R. J. (1980), *Accounting in Business*, London.
Carsberg, B. and Hope A. (1977), *Current Issues in Accounting*, Oxford.
Edwards, E. O., Bell, P. W. and Johnson, L. T. (1979), *Accounting for Economic Events*, Houston.
See also: *capital consumption; depreciation; stock-flow analysis.*

Acculturation

Acculturation is the process of cultural change which occurs when two people with different cultures come into long and intimate contact. Acculturation studies have focused chiefly on the effects of the dominant Western cultures on subordinate, non-literate ones. The term is used primarily by American anthropologists, whereas British anthropologists normally use the phrase 'cultural contact'. Acculturation studies were a major focus of research among American anthropologists beginning in the 1930s, and continued to be important through the 1950s and early 1960s. The research has moved in several directions. One has been to study the ways in which subordinated peoples have integrated the newly acquired features of Western culture into their own. Thus, through syncretism, the old and new traits are amalgamated to form a system that is different from either of the two original cultures. Another process is compartmentalization, whereby the newly acquired traits are relegated to specific areas of life and so are kept separate and distinct from most of the traditional items of the culture. Comparmentalization is one form of resistance to change. Another direction that acculturation studies have taken has been to investigate the effects that culture contact has had on the personality structures of the members of the subordinate societies. The reactions vary widely according to the circumstances, and range from general personality disintegration to the achievement of effective adjustments to the contact situation.

Elvin Hatch
University of California
Santa Barbara

Further Reading
Linton, R. (ed.) (1940), *Acculturation in Seven American Indian Tribes*, New York.
Spicer, E. H. (1965), 'Acculturation', *International Encyclopedia of the Social Sciences*, London.
See also: *culture; culture and personality.*

Activation and Arousal

The terms activation and arousal have often been used interchangeably to describe a continuum ranging from deep sleep or coma to extreme terror or excitement. This continuum has sometimes been thought of as referring to observed behaviour, but many psychologists have argued that arousal should be construed in physiological terms. Of particular importance in this connection is the ascending reticular activating system, which is located in the brain-stem and has an alerting effect on the brain.

Some question the usefulness of the theoretical constructs of activation and arousal. On the positive side, it makes some sense to claim that elevated arousal is involved in both motivational and emotional states. It appears that individual differences in personality are related to arousal levels, with introverts being characteristically more aroused than extroverts (H. J. Eysenck, 1967). In addition, proponents of arousal theory have had some success in predicting performance effectiveness on the basis of arousal level. In general, performance is best when the prevailing level of arousal is neither very low nor very high. Particularly important is the fact that there are sufficient similarities among the behavioural effects of factors such as intense noise, incentives and stimulant drugs to encourage the belief that they all affect some common arousal system.

On the negative side, the concepts of activation and of arousal are rather amorphous. Different physiological measures of arousal are often only weakly correlated with one another, and physiological, behavioural and self-report measures of arousal tend to produce conflicting evidence. Faced with these complexities, many theorists have suggested that there is more than one kind of arousal. For example, H. J. Eysenck (1967) proposed that the term arousal should be limited to cortical arousal, with the term activation being used to refer to emotional or autonomic arousal.

It may be desirable to go even further and identify three varieties of arousal. For example, a case can be made for distinguishing among behavioural, autonomic and cortical forms of arousal (Lacey, 1967). Alternatively, Pribram and McGuinness (1975) argued for the existence of stimulus-produced arousal, activation or physiological readiness to respond, and effort in the sense of activity co-ordinating arousal and activation processes.

In sum, the basic notion that the behavioural effects of various emotional and motivational manipulations are determined at least in part by internal states of physiological arousal is plausible and in line with the evidence. However, the number and nature of the arousal dimensions that ought to be postulated remains controversial. In addition, there is growing suspicion that the effects of arousal or behaviour are usually rather modest and indirect. What appears to happen is that people respond to non-optimal levels of arousal (too low or too high) with various strategies and compensatory activities designed to minimize the adverse effects of the prevailing level of arousal (M. W. Eysenck, 1982). Thus, the way in which performance is maintained at a reasonable level despite substantial variations in arousal needs further explanation.

Michael W. Eysenck
Birkbeck College
University of London

References

Eysenck, H. J. (1967), *The Biological Basis of Personality*, Springfield, Ill.

Eysenck, M. W. (1982), *Attention and Arousal: Cognition and Performance*, Berlin.

Lacey, J. I. (1967), 'Somatic response patterning and stress: some revisions of activation theory', in M. H. Appley and R. Trumbull (eds), *Psychological Stress*, New York.

Pribram, K. H. and McGuinness, D. (1975), 'Arousal, activation, and effort in the control of attention', *Psychological Review*, 82.

See also: *nervous system*.

Adler, Alfred (1870–1937)

Born in Vienna in 1870, Alfred Adler trained as an ophthalmologist and first practised general medicine before becoming a psychiatrist and a charter member of Freud's inner circle. An energetic, articulate man and a prolific writer, Adler was soon made the titular president of the first Psychoanalytic Society. Unlike Freud, Adler was a political and social activist; in retrospect it seems that at least some of their conflicts were due to this basic difference. Adler is best known for originating the concept of the inferiority complex and of understanding personality in terms of the compensatory struggle to achieve superiority. Although Adler did in fact formulate these reductionistic and mechanistic theories, he also had other, much more subtle, ideas about human nature.

Adler disagreed with Freud's emphasis on biological and sexual factors; instead he gave primary importance to social, interpersonal, and hierarchical relationships. Adler believed that man is motivated by his expectations of the future: 'The final goal alone can explain man's behaviour.' Human behaviour is not determined by childhood experiences themselves, but by the 'perspective in which these [experiences] are regarded'. The final goal of the individual determines the perspective in which he views these important early experiences. This conception of behaviour, motivated by a particular perspective and by ideas about the future, is described as 'idealistic positivism'. It is compatible with, if not identical to, many strands of contemporary psychological, philosophical and social theory (for example, existential theories). Idealistic positivism de-emphasizes the importance of the unconscious and transforms Freud's conception of psychic determinism.

Adler rejected the idea that a human being is simply a product of environment and heredity. He posited a creative self, which makes something of hereditary abilities and interprets environmental impressions, thus constituting a unique individual personality and life-style. While Adler, the first defector from Freud's circle, is today ignored by most psychologists and psychiatrists, in his Individual Psychology can be found the beginnings of contemporary humanistic psychology. Adler's views suggested the great importance of methods of childrearing and education. According to Adler, physical infirmity, rejection, and pampering were the factors most likely to result in a pathological style of life. He helped establish child-guidance clinics in association with the Viennese school system, and became a major advocate of the child-guidance movement.

Alan A. Stone
Harvard University

Further Reading

Adler, A. (1924 [1920]), *The Practice and Theory of Individual Psychology*, London. (Original German edn, *Praxis und Theorie der Individual-Psychologie*, Munich.)

Ansbacher, H. L. and Ansbacher, R. R. (eds), (1956), *The Individual Psychology of Alfred Adler: A Systematic Presentation in Selections from his Writings*, New York.

Hall, C. S. and Lindzey, G. (1978), *Theories of Personality*, 3rd edn, New York.

Orgler, H. (1973), *Alfred Adler, The Man and His Work*, New York.

Sperber, M. (1970), *Alfred Adler, oder das Elend der Psychologie*, Vienna.

Administration

Administration is an aspect of organizational institutionalization or establishment. Its job is to avoid crucial challenges so as to keep institutions going. The administrator can establish and maintain any organization by imposing a process of compartmentalization. This requires the establishment of four sets of rules: the rules of satisficing, simplication, simulation and jurisdiction. Following these rules means that administration keeps things going by finding satisfactory means, by admitting only selected data and labelled categories and case applicants, by not trying to deal with a chaos of raw and unordered life and, finally, by dealing only with certain issues, and then only in particular ways and via specified officials – not with anything by anyone in any way. Overall, there is a departmental line or philosophy, an agenda. In short, the job of administration is to control the agenda, and the formulation of data, and to determine what and who can enter the discussion about policy, and how the discussion is then conducted.

However disguised, administration is political, partly because keeping organizations going demands the management of endogenous relations, legitimation and the creation of loyalty, and more generally because it is an inescapable part of any state apparatus. Administration allows the balance in state politics to be tilted to organization rather than coercion, so that in consequence politicians kill people less often than they might otherwise.

Administration is not confined to modern political organizations but, however common, old and various, administration seems to require certain conditions:
(1) Administration does not work well where decision making is weakly ordered. It requires an interest in keeping the organization going, because of loyalty or organizational slack. The favoured administrative ecology fosters political, constitutional or consensual mutual adjustment, rather than economistic, market-like or warlike adaptations.
(2) The administrator works best where each case needs to be referred through the hierarchy for minuting about precedents. Where this sort of expert supervision is carried out, it creates steep and highly pyramidical organizations.
(3) Another condition of administration is the establishment of a distinction between administrators and political office-holders. The distinction has, not surprisingly, been variously pursued through the history of administrative reforms and administrative sciences and among political systems. The Westminster model is peculiar. It provides for an elected and partisan minister who is at once a member of a collectively responsible cabinet and an amateur and changing extrinsic chief of a specific type of administrative organization. However, there have been politically significant variations in ministerialization, in recruitment and formation, and in the professional and legal status of administrative performances as between the generalistic Oxbridge anglophonic ideal, the Napoleonic codification of schools, service and administrative law, and the American Jeffersonian ambivalence about spoils, appointments and business or academic careers.

Politics and administration, however, are always in a necessary alliance in order to secure resources, foster institutional legitimation, manage conflicts, facilitate the delivery of services, and invent policy themes. Therefore, administration is not quite bureaucracy in Palmerston's sense of government by appointed office-holders. Yet it is bureaucratic in the sort of organizations it institutionalizes, in those peculiar methods of work and, above all, in its justifications by equity of process rather than substantive outcomes.

While it is common, culturally specific and non-cosmopolitan, administrative behaviour always provokes similar concerns: as in the search for other ways of doing it, like pretences that there could be a development administration different from the (colonial) 'hearing cases and collecting taxes', however ill-served development could be if cases were unheard and taxes uncollected; and in sterile discussions about professional, scientific or technical status.

Administration is inescapably present save in the abundance of Utopia, but however instrumentally therapeutic, it is also exclusive, punitive, privileged and dominant. Consequently, it lends itself to a legalistic, depoliticized and reductionist treatment in Marxist, economistic or managerial traditions of analysis.

Bernard Schaffer
University of Sussex

Further Reading
Dunsore, A. (1978), *Implementation in a Bureaucracy: The Execution Process*, Oxford.
Ham, C. and Hill, M. (1983), *The Policy Process in the Modern Capitalist State*, Brighton.
Heclo, H. and Wildavsky, A. (1980), *The Private Government of Public Money*, London.
Schaffer, B. B. (1973), *The Administrative Factor*, London.
Simon, H. A. (1945), *Administrative Behavior*, New York (2nd edn in 1957).
See also: *bureaucracy; decision making; development administration; organizations; policy making; policy sciences.*

Adolescence

Adolescence, that period between puberty and adulthood, is universally acknowledged to be a critical phase in human development, yet psychologists and other social scientists have given it little attention in comparison to other stages of the life cycle. In the last few years, however, more research has been done on the course of normal adolescent development. The results of a number of large-scale studies have begun to appear in the literature, substantially expanding our knowledge of the teenage years and affecting profoundly many widely-held assumptions about young people. In particular, these studies have called into question the belief that the adolescent years are a time of 'storm and stress' and have indicated rather that most young people do not experience serious emotional upheaval. Furthermore, the evidence shows that, contrary to expectation, most people get on well with their parents and select friends who reinforce rather than contradict family values.

Naturally there are some adolescents who have difficulties. In this connection it should be noted that social scientists are increasingly aware that events in the first five years of life are not the only events which have fundamental implications for later development, whereas they used to think that what happened in infancy laid the foundations for later personality development, and that many of the effects of the experiences of these early years were irreversible. They now acknowledge that experiences during other critical phases of development, especially during adolescence, have an equally important bearing on what happens in later life. This realization, that adjustment in adolescence has critical implications for adult development, as well as for the health of society in general, has led to a new surge of interest in the adolescent years.

A further change which has gradually occurred is a preference for viewing adolescence as a transitional process rather than as a stage or a number of stages. To conceptualize the period in this way implies that we must understand adolescence as a time during which the individual passes from one state – childhood – to another – maturity – and the issues and problems that individuals face during this period are predominantly the result of the transitional process. This transition, it is believed, results from the operation of a number of pressures. Some of these, in particular the physiological and emotional pressures, are internal, while other pressures originate from peers, parents, teachers and society and are external to the young person. Sometimes these external pressures hurry the individual towards maturity at a faster rate than he would prefer, while on other occasions they act as a brake, holding the adolescent back from the freedom and independence which he believes to be a legitimate right. It is the interplay of these forces which in the final analysis contributes more than anything else to the success or failure of the transition from childhood to maturity.

John C. Coleman
Sussex Youth Trust

Further Reading
Coleman, J. C. (1980), *The Nature of Adolescence*,
London.
Katchadourian, H. (1977), *The Biology of Adolescence*,
San Francisco.

Advertising

Advertising is a way of drawing attention to goods offered for sale. Its aim may include the enhancing of a reputation as well as inducing immediate purchase, for example, political and charitable advertising, announcement of corporate trading results, and the sponsorship of sports or cultural events. Media employed include journals, newspapers, television, radio, cinema, bill hoardings and direct mail. Advertising grew in importance with the Industrial Revolution, mass production and, later, self-service retailing. As these replaced traditional methods of manufacture and distribution, so salesmen 'pushing' goods to a relatively small number of retailers were gradually and partially displaced by advertising aimed at large numbers of final consumers who, if convinced of a product's merits, would 'pull' it through the marketing channel. Retailers would stock goods which had been 'presold' by manufacturers' advertising.

Since the advent of television and the abolition of newsprint rationing after World War II, the economic importance of advertising has changed little. Total UK expenditure was 1.43 per cent of GNP in 1960; in 1981 1.34 per cent. In the US, the 1981 figure was 1.38 per cent. In the UK in 1981 the press accounted for 65 per cent of all expenditure, television for 28.7 per cent. For the US corresponding figures were 54.7 per cent and 31.3 per cent. The most obtrusive form is MCA (manufacturers' advertising directed at consumers) which excludes financial, employment, trade, classified (or personal), retailer and charitable advertising. The 1981 MCA component was 42 per cent of the UK total.

Advertising presupposes free consumer choice and consequentially provides problems to both practitioners and economists. Businesses must decide what to spend on advertising in terms of results. These are difficult to measure and so unambiguously to link the input with sales or profits. Economists have different concerns, such as advertising's link with competition, resource allocation and choice distortion. The traditional 'informative' and 'persuasive' distinction exemplifies that disquiet. The dichotomy for many is useful but non-operational. J. K. Galbraith (1962) popularized it by awarding the outcome of 'persuasive' advertising the title of the 'Dependence Effect'. Thus, consumer wants depend not on innate human needs but on advertising; producers must 'create' these wants to dispose of their output, and were it not for advertising, people would have no important, unsatisfied desires. However, the argument's force lies in its originator's persuasive semantics and not in empirical proof.

In the last three decades a large amount of empirical work has been conducted. On balance it is indecisive. Advertising has not been found to be conclusively associated or otherwise with a range of economic variables: for example, measures of industrial concentration, entry barriers, competitive mobility, monopoly profits, price-cost margins or aggregate demand. Other controversies have been settled. Advertising appears to be closely linked to technological innovation and diffusion (whether this is to be approved of will vary with the view adopted regarding the Dependence Effect). Advertising also provides a guarantee of quality since a brand name can be relied upon to denote product consistency; conversely, some brand names would indicate products to avoid. An unadvertised product would not be so identifiable. Again, however, consensus is wanting since, unless the assumption is made that persistent purchasing of a brand *vis à vis* a cheaper non-advertised product is free of the Dependence Effect, then no agreement can be reached that branding and advertising guarantee value *vis à vis* quality.

One way out of the theoretical and empirical impasse is the suggestion by economists of the Austrian school that advertising should be seen as part of the total product package bought, or not bought, by the consumer. Without advertising, the product either ceases to exist or is a different product, just as it would if a tangible input was removed. Littlechild (1981) claims that the relevant (practical) alternatives then become the product as it stands or no product at all. The concept of the product with or without advertising is not a real world choice. Although this approach could resolve many of the economic debates and could also bring economists into agreement with practitioners, it seems unlikely to command a consensus.

W. Duncan Reekie
University of the Witwatersrand

Further Reading

Broadbent, S. (1979), *Spending Advertising Money*, 3rd edn, London.
Galbraith, J. K. (1962), *The Affluent Society*, London.
Littlechild, S. C. (1981), 'The social costs of monopoly power', *Economic Journal*.
Reekie, W. D. (1981), *The Economics of Advertising*, London.

See also: *marketing research.*

Aesthetics

The study of aesthetics, which concerns the creation and appreciation of beauty, forms part of philosophy as well as psychology, with points of contact with sociology, biology and anthropology. It could very loosely be described as the scientific study of the arts, although there are two reasons why some might disagree with this description. First, the scientific approach is not one that is universally acceptable; the distinction has been made between 'speculative' and 'empirical' aesthetics, and some areas of philosophy, art history and art criticism come into the former category. Speculative aesthetics is concerned with high-level questions such as the nature of beauty, or the meaning of art works, whereas empirical aesthetics involves the scientific study of the component processes of appreciation. Thus, the second point of disagreement might be about what constitutes a work of art: some of the experimental stimuli used in empirical aesthetics have little in common with real-life music, painting, poetry or sculpture.

Psychologists, along with other social scientists, have adopted the empirical approach; indeed, the field of experimental aesthetics is one of the oldest branches of psychology. One of the founding fathers of the discipline was the German physicist, physiologist and philosopher Gustav Theodor Fechner. Fechner's extensive studies in the field of psychophysics led him towards the problems of aesthetics, and he published his *Vorschule der Ästhetik (Prolegomenon to Aesthetics)* in 1876.

Fechner's explicit aim was to found what he called an 'aesthetics from below'; he was primarily concerned with the elementary mechanisms of likes and dislikes, and he used experimental techniques that have a great deal in common with those employed in modern experimental psychology. One such technique, for example, was the 'method of choice', in which subjects were required to select the stimulus they liked best out of several that were presented to them. Fechner hoped to work up from this fairly rudimentary and basic starting point to the more complex questions of aesthetics.

He attempted, for example, to test the early theory of the 'aesthetic mean', in which beauty was considered to be associated with the absence of extremes, by assessing people's preferences for different colours, visual patterns, and auditory stimuli. He presented subjects with rectangles of different shapes in order to test the famous 'golden section' hypothesis that the ratio of 0.62 between the lengths of the longer and the shorter sides may constitute a 'divine proportion' with special aesthetic properties. Though Fechner's early efforts along these lines gave experimental aesthetics a firm methodological footing, the findings over the next few decades (Valentine, 1962) were generally inconsistent. No conclusive evidence was obtained concerning the 'aesthetic mean' or 'golden section' theories, for example, and interest in experimental aesthetics consequently declined.

In the mid-1960s, however, psychologist Daniel Berlyne coined the term 'new experimental aesthetics' to describe a branch of research that was taking a different approach to the old problems: its theoretical basis is in biology (Berlyne, 1971). Two major features of the new approach are its emphasis on *arousal* as the main determinant of aesthetic response, and on what Berlyne calls 'collative variables'. This theory holds that art objects produce pleasure by manipulating the level of arousal, attention or excitement of the observer; they do this by means of their collative properties, such as their complexity, surprisingness or familiarity. In other words, the observer collates information from different properties of the stimulus, and the resulting level of arousal will determine the likelihood of his exploring that stimulus. Berlyne further proposes that the 'hedonic value', or pleasantness, of a stimulus is related to the subject's level of arousal according to an inverted-U-shaped curve; pleasantness is greatest for stimuli that produce an intermediate level of arousal. It is the emphasis on collative variables of form, and on the potential for integration with other areas of psychology (such as motivation, exploration and play), that distinguishes the new from the old experimental aesthetics. Although some researchers would dispute the details of Berlyne's theoretical formulation, the new experimental aesthetics is nonetheless healthy and flourishing. Three broad lines of development can be distinguished:

(1) This relates directly to Berlyne's concern with collative variables; there is a growing amount of research which manipulates them, as well as considerably greater sophistication in the scaling, grouping and quantification of experimental stimuli. Multidimensional scaling techniques, for example, provide a means of operationalizing the concept of artistic style, such that real-life art works can be scaled for use as experimental stimuli. The application of information theory to aesthetic objects, begun in the 1950s, continues to provide objective measures of properties such as 'information content' and 'redundancy'. Multivariate computer content analysis has been used to assess the melodic originality of themes in classical music, for example. It may well be this kind of advance that will throw most light on questions about the nature of 'goodness of form', which were raised long ago by the Gestalt psychologists.

(2) This involves the investigation of observer characteristics. One area of research, for example, is exploring the relationship between personality factors such as extraversion/introversion and aesthetic judgement. Another concerns variables of cognitive style, such as tolerance for ambiguity. A third growing area of research that comes loosely under this heading is that on the development of aesthetic sensitivity in children. Most prominent in this field is Howard Gardner's *Project Zero* team at Harvard University which has investigated a wide variety of children's reactions to different art forms.

(3) Possibly the most difficult research area concerns the relationship between affect and cognition: that is, how does the emotional aspect of an aesthetic response interact with the thought processes involved? This kind of question was originally addressed by Freud in his psychoanalytic studies of the artistic process, and it is only in the 1980s that researchers such as Pavel Machotka and Robert Zajonc are turning to it once more. Endeavours such as these suggest that empirical research is now beginning to tackle some of the complex problems of speculative aesthetics; a *rapprochement* between the two may one day be possible.

David J. Hargreaves
University of Leicester

References
Berlyne, D. E. (1971), *Aesthetics and Psychobiology*, New York.
Fechner, G. T. (1876), *Vorschule der Ästhetik*, Leipzig.
Valentine, C. W. (1962), *The Experimental Psychology of Beauty*, London.

Further Reading
Gardner, H. (1973), *The Arts and Human Development*, New York.
Winner, E. (1982), *Invented Worlds*, Cambridge, Mass.

See also: *activation and arousal; art, anthropology of; art, sociology of.*

Ageing – Psychological Aspects

The study of age-related changes in cognitive processes has received fresh impetus as the proportion of elderly people in the population of Western societies continues to increase. It is important that these changes should be recognized, understood and taken into account so as to enable the elderly to cope with a modern environment and continue living a full life of work and leisure activities.

The researcher tries to isolate and identify the effects of normal ageing on cognitive abilities. Changes caused by the ageing process are confounded with associated changes in physical health, in life-style, in motivation and personality. Poor performance may be the product of sensory deficits, anxiety or lack of interest rather than mental deterioration. When old and young are compared, tests may be contaminated by cohort effects. Just as intelligence tests may be criticized for not being 'culture-fair', they can also be criticized for not being 'cohort-fair'. The educational and life experience of the generations are different and have shaped different sorts of ability. Experimental research on ageing seeks to disentangle these confounding variables and focus on the effects of age alone.

Many mental abilities do show some deterioration with age, but others are unimpaired. Individual differences tend to increase, with some individuals deteriorating while others preserve their intellect intact. In general, little decline is observable before the mid-sixties. Traditional psychometric testing has yielded age norms for performance on batteries of standard intelligence tests. The results led to a distinction between 'crystallized' (or age invariant) intelligence and 'fluid' (age sensitive) intelligence. Tests which measure intellectual attainment, such as vocabulary, verbal ability and factual knowledge, show little age effect. Tests measuring ability to manipulate or transform information such as backward digit span, or digit-symbol substitution and some tests of spatial reasoning, generally reveal a decline. These tests, however, give little insight into the changes in the underlying mechanisms that cause some abilities to be impaired and others to be preserved.

Psychologists turned, therefore, to the experimental techniques developed in the study of perception, attention, learning and memory, and applied these to the problem of ageing. The information processing approach allows complex tasks to be decomposed so that the defective component can be identified. So, for example, experimental studies of memory indicate that the process of retrieval is relatively more affected by ageing than encoding or storage (Burke and Light, 1981); and studies of mental arithmetic show that the capacity of working memory, the 'holding store', is the vulnerable component (Wright, 1981). Common factors such as a diminished rate of information processing and a diminished capacity of working memory are seen to underlie performance decrements on many tasks. The pattern of deficit can be interpreted in terms of theoretical distinctions, like that between attentional processes (ones that require conscious monitoring) and automatic processes (ones that are highly practised, rapid and unconscious). Attentional processes are more likely to be age-impaired, while automatic processes are often unaffected.

One problem that arises when complex tasks are studied is that of distinguishing between age differences in strategy and in capacity. Defective performance may result from failure to employ the right strategy rather than from reduced capacity. Where strategies are implicated, the age difference may be eliminated by remedial training. When a capacity limitation is the cause, the age difference can only be removed by restructuring the task so as to make it less demanding. The current trend in ageing research is to study performance in real-world situations with emphasis on the practical and applied aspects. For this more applied approach it is clearly very important to discover how far the difficulties old people experience in their daily lives can be overcome by training in appropriate strategies, and how far it is necessary to modify the environment to suit their capacities.

Gillian Cohen
Open University

References
Burke, D. M. and Light, L. L. (1981), 'Memory and aging: the role of retrieval processes', *Psychological Bulletin*, 90.
Wright, R. E. (1981), 'Aging, divided attention and processing capacity', *Journal of Gerontology*, 36.

Further Reading
Kausler, D. H. (1982), *Experimental Psychology and Human Aging*, New York.
See also: *gerontology; intelligence and intelligence testing; life-span development; memory.*

Age Organization

All societies share (up to a point) two components of age organization. These are age itself and the principles that govern seniority within each family, such as birth order and generational differences. In most pre-industrial societies, family position determines status, and age is a moderating factor only when there is an obvious discrepancy. In certain areas, however, and especially among males in East Africa, age is a major principle of social organization reckoned normally from the time at which groups of adolescents are initiated

together into adulthood and share a bond that unites them for the remainder of their lives. Where ranking by age is controlled outside the family, this may inhibit competition between males that might otherwise be generated within the family. In other instances, anomalies between age and generational seniority may be critical and provide essential clues for exploring age organization in the wider social context; in extreme instances this should more accurately be described as a *generational system* rather than an *age system*. In other words, age organization has to be viewed as a principle which may in some way structure the anomalies thrown up by the kinship system.

No age organization can be satisfactorily studied as an entity separated from its wider social context; for this reason many existing accounts of such systems which imply that they are self-contained and self-explanatory do not in fact explain very much, while those that seek to pursue the ramifications of the age system are inevitably daunting in their scope.

In the analysis of age organizations, the term *age-set* (sometimes age group, or *classe d'âge* in French) may be used to refer to all those who are initiated in youth during a definite span of time, and as a group share certain constraints and expectations for the remainder of their lives; and *age grade* (*échelon d'âge* in French) refers to a status through which every individual passes at some period of his life unless he dies first. Each is an institutionalized arrangement governed by an explicit set of rules. The Nuer of the Southern Sudan have age-sets into which boys are initiated, but beyond this point they have no age grades. In our own society, we have age grades relating to infancy, schooling, adulthood and retirement, but (schools apart) we have no age-sets; members pass through these successive grades of their lives as individuals, and alone. In the more formalized instances of age organization, both institutions exist, and members of an age-set pass together through the various age grades, rather like pupils in a school. Using a ladder as an analogy for the system of age stratification, each rung (échelon) would represent an age grade, and successive age-sets would pass up it in procession, with youths climbing onto the lowest rung on initiation.

This procession involves a regulated cycle of promotions with a new age-set formed on the lowest rung once every cycle. The example of our own school system, stratified by year and with mass promotions once a year, is extremely rudimentary and consciously contrived to fulfil a task. In age organizations that span the entire lives of adults, the procession is more complex and the precise span of the periodic cycle is less predictable. A constantly changing configuration of roles occurs as members of each age-set mature and step up the ladder. Spacing tends to be uneven, with a certain jostling between successive age-sets at one point and sometimes a vacant rung elsewhere – an intermediate age grade with no incumbent. Changes in this configuration are predictable, however, and one complete cycle later there will be jostling and unoccupied rungs at precisely the same levels on the ladder, although each age-set meanwhile will have climbed to the position previously held by its predecessor. The anthropologist who normally only sees the system during one phase of the cycle, which may span fifteen years or more in some societies, has to use indirect evidence to piece together the profile of a complete cycle, but the existence of such regularities – the predictability of each successive phase – clearly indicates that this is indeed a system with its own inner logic and feedback mechanisms.

It is probably significant that formalized age systems are especially widespread in Africa, where there is a pronounced respect for older men in the more traditional areas and generally a higher polygyny rate than in any other part of the world. The older men are the polygynists, and the younger men correspondingly often face a prolonged bachelorhood. The existence of an age organization tends to structure the balance of power among men between the young who have reached physical maturity, and the old whose experience and widespread influence remain their principal assets despite failing strength and falling numbers. This may be regarded as a balance between Nature and Culture, and is reflected in much of the symbolism associated with age organization which often emphasizes the depravity of youth and the respect due to old age, and imposes circumcision as a major step in the civilizing process administered by older men. It is they who control the rate at which younger men advance, when they can marry, and what privileges they can enjoy. Unlike the more widely reported opposition between males and females, a dynamic transformation constantly in play is between young and old, and the young have a long-term interest in the status quo which women can never enjoy in male-dominated societies. It is never a question of *if* they will take over from the older men, but when and in what manner. They have to assert themselves to show their mettle, and yet restrain themselves from any flagrant violation of the system that might undermine the gerontocratic system and damage their own reputation when they become older men. In Nature, it is often males at their physical prime who control the females of the herd. In gerontocratic Culture there is a displacement towards the men who are past their physical prime. They are the polygamists, while the younger men must wait as bachelors. The age organization, with its frequent emphasis on ritual and moral values, provides a system which the older men must control if they are to maintain their advantage.

Paul Spencer
School of Oriental and African Studies
University of London

References
Baxter, P. T. W. and Almagor, U. (eds) (1978), *Age, Generation and Time: Some Features of East African Age Organisations*, London.
Spencer, P. (1976), 'Opposing streams and the gerontocratic ladder: two models of age organisation in East Africa', *Man* (NS), 12.
Spencer, P. (1983), 'Homo ascendens et homo hierarchicus', in M. Abélès and C. Collard (eds), *Aînesse et générations en Afrique*, ICAES.
Stewart, F. H. (1977), *Fundamentals of Age-Group Systems*, New York.
See also: *gerontology*; *life-style*; *rites of passage*.

Age-Sex Structure

The age-sex structure of a population is its distribution by age and sex. The classification of the population according to age and sex can be given either in absolute numbers or in relative numbers, the latter being the ratio of the population in a given age-sex category to the total population of all ages by sex or for both sexes. The age distribution is given either in single years of age or in age groups, for example, five-year age groups. Broad age groups such as 0 to 14, 15 to 59, 60 and over are also sometimes used. The grouping of ages depends on the degree of precision desired, and on the quality of the data at hand. If data are defective, as in some developing countries where people do not know their precise age, the classification by age groups is often to be preferred to the distribution by individual year of age, even if this implies a loss of information.

A graphic presentation of the age-sex structure of the population is the so-called *population pyramid*. This is a form of histogram, absolute or relative population figures being given on the axis of the abscissa, and age or age groups being represented on the ordinate. Male data are given on the left-hand side of the axis of ordinates and female data on the right-hand side. The areas of the rectangles of the histogram are taken to be proportional to the population numbers at each age or age group.

Figure 1 presents, as an example, the population pyramid of Algeria in 1966. Population figures at each age are given here per 10,000 persons of all ages and of both sexes. One sees that the population of Algeria is young: the population under 15 years of age, for example, is quite large compared to the rest. One also sees that the classification by age in the Algerian census of 1966 is defective. People tend to round off the age they declare, yielding higher population numbers at ages ending by digits 0 and 5. In the Algerian case, this age-heaping effect is more pronounced for females than for males.

Another useful graph shows the differential distribution of sexes by age, presenting sex ratios by age or age group. Sex ratios are obtained by dividing the

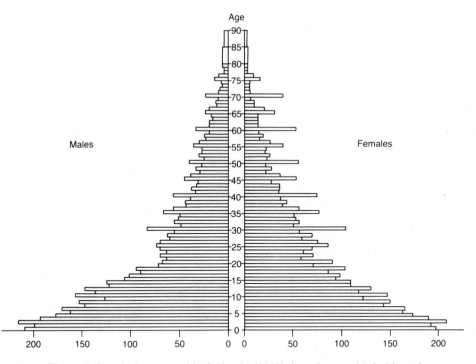

Figure 1 Population pyramid of Algeria (1966) (per thousand inhabitants)

number of males in each age group by the corresponding number of females. The results are often called *masculinity ratios*. Masculinity ratios tend to decrease with age. At young ages there are usually more boys than girls; approximately 105 male births occur per 100 female births. As age increases, masculinity ratios decline and become lower than 1, due to the prevalence of higher age-specific risks of dying for males than for females. On the whole, there are usually more females than males in the total population, due to excess male mortality. Masculinity ratios by age are also dependent on the impact of migration. If migration is sex-specific, masculinity ratios will reflect this phenomenon at the ages concerned.

One often speaks of young or old age structures. In the former case, the proportion of young in the population is high; the opposite is true in the second case. Young population age structures are essentially linked to high fertility. Ageing population structures are observed as fertility declines. The impact of mortality decline on age structure is much smaller than that of fertility decline, as the decrease in risks of dying affects all ages simultaneously. If decreases in risks of dying occur mainly at young ages, lower mortality will actually rejuvenate the population; the converse is true if gains in life expectancy are obtained principally at old ages.

If fertility and mortality remain constant over time and the population is closed to migration, a *stable* age structure will eventually result in the long run: the age distribution becomes invariant and depends solely on the age-specific fertility and mortality schedules. This property has been demonstrated by A. J. Lotka and is known as *strong ergodicity*.

Guillaume Wunsch
University of Louvain

Further Reading

Coale, A. J. (1957), 'How the age distribution of a human population is determined', *Cold Spring Harbor Symposia on Quantitative Biology*, 22.

Coale, A. J. (1964), 'How a population ages or grows younger' in R. Freedman (ed.), *Population: The Vital Revolution*.

See also: fertility; migration; mortality; vital statistics.

Aggression and Anger

Biological/instinctual, psychoanalytic, ethological, social learning and cognitive theorists have all attempted to further our understanding of aggression, often spurred by a stated concern about humans' capacity to inflict suffering on others and by fears for the future of the species. While most would accept that some progress has been made, the actual achievements of social scientists to date are thought by some to be limited. The reasons for these limitations are of interest in themselves. Marsh and Campbell (1982) attribute lack of progress to a number of factors, including the difficulties in studying aggression, both in laboratory and naturalistic settings, and the compartmentaliz-ation of the academic world, such that researchers fail to cross the boundaries dividing psychology from soci-ology, physiology and anthropology, or even the subdivisions within psychology itself.

There are, however, two even more basic problems which have inhibited progress. The first is the difficulty in arriving at any generally acceptable definition of aggression, and the second is the related problem of the over-inclusiveness of the theories themselves. An important starting point in providing an adequate definition is to distinguish aggression from anger and hostility. Anger refers to a state of emotional arousal, typically with autonomic and facial accompaniments. A person may be angry without being behaviourally destructive and vice versa. Hostility refers to the cognitive/evaluative appraisal of other people and events. It would be possible to appraise a particular group in society in very negative terms without their eliciting anger or overt aggression, though in most cases cognition and affect will be intimately linked (see below).

Aggression itself refers to overt behaviour, though precisely what sort of behaviour should be labelled aggressive is controversial. Bandura (1973) proposes cutting through the 'semantic jungle' in this area by restricting the term to acts resulting in personal injury or destruction of property, while accepting that injury may be psychological as well as physical. There then remain problems in defining what is injurious and in dealing with 'accidental' aggression (where injury is inflicted but not intended) and 'failed' aggression (as when a person tries to shoot another person but misses). In general, the definition of an act as aggressive involves a social judgement on the part of the observer. For this reason, injurious acts may not be labelled as aggressive when socially prescribed (for example, capital punishment) or when they support values the observer endorses (for example, a parent beating a child to instil godfearing virtue). In this sense, labelling a behaviour as aggressive inevitably has a social and political dimension to it.

The second difficulty lies in the breadth of activities addressed by most theories. Stabbing another person in a fight, battering a baby, being abusive in a social encounter and waging warfare may all be behaviours that meet the definition of aggression, but they are also disparate activities with little obvious functional unity. This should, but often does not, preclude attempts to provide general theories which would account for them all. Many different theories are likely to be required to account for these different forms of aggressive behaviour.

In recent years the utility of one particular distinc-tion has become apparent – that between 'angry' and 'instrumental' or what some have called 'annoyance-motivated' and 'incentive-motivated' aggression (Zillman, 1979). The former is preceded by affective arousal. The person is in an emotional, physiologically activated state, often induced by environmental frus-tration of some sort. In instrumental aggression, on the other hand , the aggressive act is used as a way of securing some environmental reward and emotional activation may not be present, as in the case of someone using violence to rob a bank. The two classes are not entirely independent in that environmental reinforce-ment is also involved in angry aggression, though the reward obtained is likely to be that of inflicting pain or injury itself.

The many sources of instrumental aggression have been well documented in psychological research. That some aggressive behaviour is indeed learned socially because it is effective in securing environmental rewards or because aggressive models for imitation exist is now widely accepted (for a review see Bandura, 1973). The powerful effects of pressures towards obedi-ence to authority in producing cruelty have also been shown in laboratory investigations. Recent years, however, have witnessed a renewal of interest in angry forms of aggression and it is on this work that I shall focus for the remainder of this article.

Angry aggression is an important feature of much of the violence which causes social concern. Studies of homicide, for example, suggest that the violent act is often a response to intense anger arousal. The violent person is often described as in a 'fury' or a 'rage', directed in many cases at a person with whom they have an intimate relationship (a wife or husband). Anger may also be involved in less obvious forms of violence. There is evidence, for example, that many rapes show features of angry aggression. A substantial number of rapists are in an angry/frustrated state preceding the assault and appear to be motivated to hurt and degrade the victim rather than to obtain sexual relief (Groth, 1979).

Research on Anger

Until very recently much less attention has been directed by social scientists at the affect of anger than at its direct behavioural manifestations. Anger has been widely discussed by philosophers and poets but rarely by the experimental psychologist. The recent renewed interest in this phenomenological aspect of aggression stems in part from a general reconsideration of the emotions within psychology and also from developments in the field of cognition and its relationship to affect.

Anger seems to have four components – the environment, cognition, emotional/physiological arousal, and behaviour itself, and these components interact reciprocally in a complex fashion (Noveco, 1978). The first two of these elements, in particular, have been the focus for recent experimental investigation. Anger and angry aggression are generally preceded by a triggering environmental event. There are a number of theories of what kind of event is likely to be important (the frustration-aggression theory, for example). In a recent review, Berkowitz (1982) has argued persuasively that environmental events elicit aggression to the extent that they are *aversive*. Thus the absence of reward where it is expected or the blocking of goal-directed activity provoke aggression because they are unpleasant. Experiencing failure, being insulted, unjustly treated or attacked share the property of aversiveness and are capable, therefore, of producing anger and aggression. Berkowitz suggests that both humans and animals are born with a readiness to flee or to fight when confronted by an aversive stimulus. Which reaction will occur will depend on learning experiences (flight, for example, may have been found to be more effective) and on the nature of the particular situation (a situation where the person has expectations of control may make fight more likely). Consistent with Berkowitz's thesis that aversiveness is critical are a number of laboratory and naturalistic studies showing, for example, that pain is a potent elicitor of angry aggression. Unpleasant smells, 'disgusting' visual stimuli and high temperatures have also been found to lower the threshold for aggression, though in the latter case the relationship is curvilinear.

Diary studies of what makes people angry in everyday life confirm the importance of aversive/frustrating events but also suggest a feature of anger not always apparent in laboratory studies – that it is predominantly elicited by *interpersonal* events. Other people, rather than things or impersonal occurrences, make us angry. James Averill (1982) found that people reported becoming mildly to moderately angry in the range of several times a day to several times a week and that only 6 per cent of incidents were elicited by a non-animate object. The frustrating person in over half the episodes was someone known and liked – friends and loved ones are common sources of aversive experiences!

The second component of anger currently receiving attention is the cognitive processing of social and internal events. The concerns of cognitive theorists are typically with how people appraise, interpret and construct the social environment. Attribution theory has been a major force in cognitive theorizing and attributional processes are now widely acknowledged to be relevant to angry aggression. Such processes are best viewed as mediating the emotional and behav-ioural responses to the aversive/frustrating events described above. The power of attributions can be appreciated by considering the differing emotional and behavioural consequences of various attributions for an event such as being knocked off one's bicycle on the way home from work. This painful and aversive occurrence might be attributed by the cyclist to his own inadequacies ('not looking where I was going') or to chance ('given the number of cars and bicycles it is inevitable some people are knocked down'). Neither of these attributions is, intuitively, likely to produce an aggressive response. Suppose, however, that the attribution was made that the car driver had deliberately intended to knock me off my bicycle. The threshold for aggression, at least towards the driver, might be expected to be considerably lowered by such an appraisal. Attributions of 'malevolent intent' of this sort have been shown to be important for anger and aggression (see Ferguson and Rule, 1983).

The third and fourth components of anger are affective/physiological arousal itself and the aggressive act which may or may not follow anger arousal. Anger is undoubtedly accompanied by autonomic activation (increases in blood pressure, heart rate, respiration and muscle tension and so on), but it is still unclear whether the pattern of activation can be discriminated from arousal caused by other emotions. Most experiences of anger in everyday life are not followed by physical aggression. Averill (1982) found that less than 10 per cent of angry episodes induced physical aggression. What he called 'contrary reactions', activities opposite to the instigation of anger, such as being very friendly to the instigator, were twice as frequent as physical aggression. Anger may produce a range of other reactions – the previous learning experiences of the individual are clearly important in determining whether frustration and anger are responded to with withdrawal, help-seeking, constructive problem-solving or what Bandura (1973) has called 'self-anaesthetization through drugs and alcohol'.

The reciprocal bi-directional influence between the components of anger is something that has been stressed by Novaco (1978). Cognitions may induce anger and aggression, but behaving aggressively may activate hostile cognitions and also change the environment in such a way as to make the person even more frustrated. Hostile appraisals of other people are often self-fulfilling. Untangling the complex interrelationships between these environmental, cognitive, physiological and behavioural component processes will be the major task for future aggression researchers.

Kevin Howells
University of Leicester

References
Averill, J. R. (1982), *Anger and Aggression: An Essay on Emotion*, New York.

Bandura, A. (1973), *Aggression: A Social Learning Analysis*, Englewood Cliffs.

Berkowitz, L. (1982), 'Aversive conditions as stimuli to aggression', in L. Berkowitz (ed.), *Advances in Experimental Social Psychology* 15, New York.

Ferguson, T. J. and Rule, B. G. (1983), 'An attributional perspective on anger and aggression', in *Aggression: Theoretical and Empirical Reviews Vol. 1*, New York.

Groth, A. N. (1979), *Men who Rape*, New York.

Marsh, P. and Campbell, A. (1982) (eds), *Aggression and Violence*, Oxford.

Novaco, R. W. (1978), 'Anger and coping with stress', in J. P. Foreyt and D. P. Rathjen (eds), *Cognitive Behavior Therapy*, New York.

Zillman, D. (1979), *Hostility and Aggression*, Hillsdale, N.J.

See also: *activation and arousal; attribution theory; conflict; emotion; stress.*

Agricultural Economics

The first formal conceptualization of agriculture within economic theory can be attributed to the Physiocrats or, more specifically, to Quesnay's *Tableau Economique*, which modelled economic flows between different sectors on the eve of industrialization in France. Agriculture was held to be the only productive sector, since it allowed for extended reproduction in terms of grain, while the embryo manufacturing sector was seen merely to transform agricultural produce into other forms of artisanal or manufactured articles, and it was assumed that this latter process did not generate any additional economic value. A contrasting stance was adopted by English classical political economists. The key Ricardian argument was that the rising demand for food would extend the margin of cultivation to inferior lands and raise the price of grain as well as the rents accruing on all non-marginal land. Ricardo's pessimism about technological progress then led inexorably to the deduction that rent would erode the share of profit in the national product. Such a conceptualization of the economic process provided the theoretical underpinnings of the anti-landlord class bias of the classical economists. An exception was Malthus, who argued that agriculture was thus not merely the generator of foodstuffs for the manufacturing sector, but also, crucially, of demand for its products.

From the common roots of classical political economy emerge two divergent systems of economic theorizing of agriculture: the Marxian and the neoclassical. The former focused special attention on the analysis of the role of agriculture in the transition from the feudal to the capitalist mode of production, a process characterized by primitive capital accumulation and surplus transfer from the pre-capitalist, mostly agrarian, sectors to the capitalist, mainly indus-trialist, ones. Both the classical and the Marxian approaches analyse the agricultural sector within a macroeconomic framework dealing with the structural position and functional role of agriculture in terms of intersectoral and national economic linkages; both emphasize the importance of the generation and extraction of agricultural surplus – in the form of industrial crops, food and labour – for industrialization; both treat, though to different degrees, the dynamic intra-rural dimensions of production relations and organization as necessary parts of the analysis. Thus, agriculture and industry are treated as distinct sectors, characterized by different internal technological and production conditions, social and political organization, and by different functional roles in the process of economic development.

The second offshoot of classical economy, neoclassical economics, now forms the disciplinary mainstream, and agricultural economics (as generally defined in the curricula of most universities) is identified closely with the method and schema of neoclassical theory. In sharp contrast to other traditions, neoclassical agricultural economics focuses primarily on microeconomic issues dealing with the static efficiency of resource use in agricultural production. The optimal choice of products, and combinations of inputs to produce these, form virtually its exclusive concerns. The central problem of agricultural economics is then reduced to one of profit maximization by an individual farmer operating with specified resources and technologies in an economic environment marked by perfect competition in all input and output markets. There is no analysis of the structure of agrarian production relations and organization or its transformation *vis-à-vis* the stimulus of economic growth. In general, production relations, for example, sharecropping, are analysed specifically from the vantage point of their impact through implicit (dis)incentive effects on the efficient allocation of available resources by decision makers. Within this framework, there has been a plethora of empirical studies which have asked the question: Are peasants efficient in their resource-use? The methodology has involved assuming perfect competition, and then deriving an econometric estimate – using cross-sectional data on a group of peasants – of a production function, frequently of the Cobb-Douglas type. A simple test for the equality of the estimated marginal productivity of each factor of production with respect to its relative price (with respect to the output) then reveals, within this paradigm, whether this decision maker could be adjudged to be efficient or not.

This framework was amplified initially in debates over sharecropping systems in the American South, but more recently has been advanced further in the contemporary context of rural development in the Third World. If one believes, as some celebrated neoclassical empirical studies argue, that peasants are poor but efficient, then additional agricultural growth is possible either if the relative price and hence the profitability of the agricultural sector is boosted, or if there is technological progress. The recipe is thus an improvement in agriculture's terms of trade alongside the use of improved methods such as those characterizing the recent so-called green revolution. While policies for rural education, health, agricultural extension services and credit are justified as necessary for expediting rapid technological absorption, the prime emphasis is on the role of relative prices in guiding resource allocation. Another crucial corollary is that poor countries should not hesitate to concentrate resources on commercial crops and rely on heavy food imports so long as they enjoy a comparative trade advantage in the former at the going world prices. The validity of this policy package depends crucially on the realism of the fundamental premises underlying the neoclassical edifice. With regard to distribution, the twin assumptions of infinite factor substitution and perfectly competitive markets have been held to imply that growth would tend to increase the incomes of the landless labourers, leading to the contention that the benefits of agricultural growth would trickle down to the bottom echelons, even in highly inegalitarian property ownership structures. As such, neoclassical agricultural economics has provided the intellectual underpinnings for a conservative political programme.

Far from being perfectly competitive, however, agricultural product and factor markets are heavily segmented, interlocked and frequently governed by an unequal and personalized power equation between landed patrons and (near)landless clients; as such, peasants are frequently not independent decision makers. The production system has inherent externalities, for example, in soil conservation and irrigation, and uncertainties arising from information gaps and the elemental unpredictability of the delivery system and a changing technological matrix. A second criticism of the neoclassical approach applies to the behavioural postulates and the notion of efficiency. The economic calculus of rich farmers might be determined considerably by the longer-term objective of maximizing 'power' rather than short-term profits, while that of the poor is influenced by the immediate objective of guaranteeing survival in the face of price and output risks and uncertainty. The method ignores the realistic situation where the pursuit of efficient maximization algorithms of peasant profit-maximizers would lead dynamically to a process of collective deterioration, as in the widely observable illustrations of the vicious circle of ecological destruction. Neither is the question of the efficiency of the production relations themselves considered: alternative forms of production organization, *ceteris paribus*, could provide a powerful source of growth unrecognized by the paradigm of neoclassical

agricultural economics. Finally, there are problems with the neoclassical modelling of agricultural production. For example, when the peasant farm is treated virtually as an industrial firm, the critical importance of the timing and interdependence of sequential cultivation operations is ignored. More significantly, the methodological validity of attempts to test for the economic efficiency of peasants through the use of a cross-sectional production function is highly dubious. The joint burden of these objections is to undermine the theoretical basis of the policy recommendations offered by the neoclassical approach.

Experience of Third-World development in the postcolonial period has stimulated the discipline in several directions:

(1) There has been an empirical enrichment as a result of many lively, theoretically eclectic, debates on questions pivoting on stylized factual observations. What accounts for the inverse relationship between farm-size and land-productivity? Are there economies of scale in agricultural production? Is there surplus labour in agriculture? How is the simultaneous co-existence of different production relations to be understood? Do the benefits of growth actually 'trickle-down' to the poor in the prevalent rural institutional framework? Do prevalent modes of production constitute barriers to technological change and growth in rural areas? Are famines manifestations of production shortfalls, or of failures of exchange entitlements? These debates, focused on the unfolding experience of agrarian change in the underdeveloped countries, have an immediacy which demands that theoretical construction be based unambiguously on verifiable realistic premises about the nature of rural socioeconomic organization. The spotlight has thus shifted away from the tunnel vision of the narrow neoclassical enquiry focusing on issues of static efficiency. Indeed, as a response, this school has widened its terms of reference and begun to include within its scope questions about the efficiency of, and the rationale underlying, alternative production relations. Thus, both the neoclassical and the neo-Marxian schools are currently analysing the nature and implications of interlocking rural markets. Inevitably, fundamental differences in method persist: the former investigates the multiplicity and logic of production relations ahistorically, as a purely economic choice-theoretic game between individual transactors, while the latter poses the problem in class terms within an historically conditioned framework explicitly mediated not only by economic but also by political factors. Nevertheless, this recent emergence of overlapping areas of investigation has invigorated the subject.

(2) The revival or emergence of some institutional nonclass approaches to the analysis of agrarian questions has introduced an overdue element of multidisciplinarity into the arena of conventional agricultural

economics. Notable here are the resuscitation of Chayanov's theory of the demographic differentiation within the pre-1917 Russian peasant economy, Geertz's speculative interpretation of colonial rural Java, using the concept of agricultural involution, and Lipton's attribution of the persistence of rural poverty to the phenomenon of urban bias. However, underlying this multifaceted diversity of agricultural economics are the latent roots of further disagreement and debate.

Ashwani Saith
Institute of Social Studies, The Hague

Further Reading
Bhaduri, A. (1883), *The Economic Structure of Backward Agriculture*, New York.
Bliss, C. J. and Stern, N. H. (1982), *Palanpur: The Economy of an Indian Village*, Oxford.
Rudra, A. (1982), *Indian Agricultural Economics*, Delhi.
Schultz, T. W. (1964), *Transforming Traditional Agriculture*, New Haven.
See also: *peasants*; *rural sociology*.

Aid

The terms aid or development aid (often also foreign aid or development assistance) are not entirely unambiguous and are often used with slightly different meanings by different writers and organizations. However, there is agreement that in essence resource transfers from a more developed to a less developed country (or from a richer country to a poorer country) qualify for inclusion in 'aid' provided they meet three criteria:
(1) The objective should be developmental or charitable rather than military.
(2) The donor's objective should be non-commercial.
(3) The terms of the transfer should have a concessional element ('grant element').
Each of these criteria gives rise to some conceptual difficulty. The first one neglects the factor of 'fungibility', that is, that up to a point the use of resources by the recipient country is somewhat flexible. For example, aid may be given and ostensibly used for developmental purposes, but in fact the recipient country may use its own resources set free by this transaction in order to buy armaments; or the aid may lead to leakages and abuses and result in the building up of bank accounts in Switzerland, rather than to the ostensible developmental objectives. Such frustrations of aid objectives are impossible to allow for statistically.

The second criterion, that the objective should be non-commercial, also presents difficulties. Much of the bilateral aid, that is, aid given by a single government to another government, is 'tied', which means that the proceeds must be spent on classified goods produced in the donor country. Here we clearly have a commercial objective mixed in with the developmental objective; it

is again impossible to decide statistically at what point the transaction becomes a commercial transaction rather than aid. The line of division between export credits and tied aid of this kind is clearly a thin one. Moreover, many acts of commercial policy, such as reduction of tariffs or preferential tariff treatment given to developing countries under the internationally agreed GSP (Generalized System of Preferences) can be more effective aid than many transactions listed as aid – yet they are excluded from the aid concept.

The third criterion – that the aid should be concessional and include a grant element – is also not easy to define. What, for example, is a full commercial rate of interest at which the transaction ceases to be aid? The grant element may also lie in the duration of any loan, in the granting of a 'grace period' (a timelag between the granting of the loan and the date at which the first repayment is due). The DAC (Development Assistance Committee of the OECD, the Organization for Economic Cooperation and Development in Paris) makes a valiant attempt to combine all these different aspects of concessionality into one single calculation of the grant element. However, such calculations are subject to the objection that the grant element in aid from the donor's point of view may differ from that from the recipient's point of view. In DAC aid in 1981, some 75 per cent was direct grants and the loans had a 58 per cent grant element, resulting in an 'overall grant element' for total aid of 89 per cent.

The Development Assistance Committee is the main source of aid statistics, and its tabulations and definitions are generally recognized as authoritative. DAC publishes an Annual Report under the title 'Development Cooperation'; the 1983 volume contains detailed tables and breakdowns of aid flows. The OECD countries (the Western industrial countries including Japan, Australia and New Zealand) and the international organizations supported by them, such as the World Bank, the Regional Development Banks, the UN Development Programme, and so on, account for the bulk of global aid. DAC also provides some data on other aid flows such as from OPEC (Organization of Petroleum Exporting Countries) countries and from the Eastern bloc.

Private investment, lending by commercial banks, and private export credits are by definition treated as commercial and thus excluded from aid. In recent years such private flows have been larger than aid, although this has only been the case since 1974 when some of the big surpluses of the OPEC countries were recycled by commercial banks to developing countries.

One of the main distinctions is between bilateral aid and multilateral aid (contributions of multilateral institutions such as the World Bank, the Regional Development Banks, and so forth). This distinction is also not entirely clear. For example, the Western

European countries give some of their aid through the EEC (European Economic Community). EEC aid is not bilateral nor is it fully multilateral as the World Bank is; it is therefore to some extent a matter of arbitrary definition whether EEC aid should be counted as bilateral or multilateral. Multilateral aid is more valuable to the recipient than tied bilateral aid, because it gives a wider choice of options to obtain the imports financed by aid from the cheapest possible source. Untied bilateral aid would be equally valuable to the recipient – however, on political grounds, the recipient (and some donors, too) may prefer the multilateral route. In recent years multilateral aid has constituted about 25 per cent of total aid.

It has been frequently pointed out that aid donors could increase the value of their aid to the recipients without any real cost to themselves, either by channelling it multilaterally or by mutually untying their aid by reciprocal agreement. However, this might lose bilateral aid some of the political support which it acquires by tying and which gives national producers and workers a vested interest in aid. This is particularly important in the case of food aid.

H. W. Singer
University of Sussex

Reference

OECD (1983), *Development Cooperation in 1983 Review*, Paris.

Further Reading

Bhagwati, J. and Eckaus, R. S. (eds) (1970), *Foreign Aid. Selected Readings*, Harmondsworth.

Brandt Commission (1983), *Common Crisis. North-South Co-operation for World Recovery*, London.

Pincus, J. (1967), *Trade, Aid and Development*, New York.

See also: *development banks; technical assistance.*

Alcoholism

Alcohol use has been a major social problem only since the rise of industrialized, urban societies. The likelihood that social and personal disruption will accompany drinking sharply increases in urban environments and when man–machine interaction becomes fundamental to work. At the same time, technical advances have enhanced the availability of alcoholic beverages in a wide variety of flavours, potencies and forms (Lisansky *et al.*, 1982).

Social scientists became interested in alcoholism after the repeal of Prohibition in the US in 1933. Alcoholism now came to be conceived of not as a moral failing but as a disease. This 'disease model' attributed chronic excessive drinking to a biochemical abnormality in certain individuals which created a 'craving'

for alcohol once their drinking careers began (Jellinek, 1960).

Anthropologists were the first social scientists to make a significant contribution to the study of alcoholism. Documenting the variety of cultural habits related to the use of alcohol, despite the fact that it was universally known, they paved the way for the inclusion of cultural and social structural variables in the study of alcohol use and abuse (Marshall, 1980). Comparable studies of ethnic differences in alcoholism rates brought out the importance of socialization, social definition and social support (Pittman and Snyder, 1962).

Social scientists have, however, been slow to develop aetiological theories of alcohol abuse and alcoholism, and they have been impeded in part by their association with alcoholism interventionists. While this association has been the basis for the increasing commitment of public resources to alcohol-related research, most interventionists are committed to a biological aetiology of alcoholism. This is especially true of those associated with Alcoholics Anonymous. Further, the medically-oriented research establishment routinely presses for increased research allocations to studies which either directly, or by inference, propose biological solutions to alcohol problems.

There are some notable exceptions. Trice (1966) has shown that there are social personalities predisposed to alcoholism, but that their behaviour is influenced also by the 'opportunity structure' provided by drinking groups. Bacon (1973) has drawn attention to the generalized use of alcohol to facilitate social interaction. Mulford (1982) has developed a symbolic interactionist theory which focuses on the reactions of alcoholics to their social environments. Akers's (1977) social learning theory of deviant drinking combines both experiential and group-feedback elements.

Social scientists have been critical of the logic and internal consistency of the disease model of alcoholism (Calahan, 1979), and public policy has increasingly come under their scrutiny. Some of these studies have aroused considerable reaction from the North American 'alcoholism' establishment, which could affect their eventual credibility and utility.

A related body of research explores the consequences of different national and regional policies of alcohol distribution. These studies indicate that distribution policies influence the incidence of alcohol problems and alcoholism (Moore and Gerstein, 1981). Research by historians on the development of alcohol policy provides a valuable back-up to the work of the social scientists (Clark, 1976).

International comparisons have also put in question the view, common in Alcoholics Anonymous and in the treatment community, that abstinence is the only possible solution to alcohol abuse. A reduction of alcohol intake or a routinization of intake may also provide viable solutions (Heather and Robertson, 1981).

In the US, Canada and Australia, the workplace has emerged during the past decade as the primary setting within which alcoholism may be tackled. Studies are providing new insights into the processes of identifying, confronting and rehabilitating the problem drinker (Roman, 1981).

In general, then, research on alcohol abuse and alcoholism by social scientists has shifted from a primary concern with the problems of individuals and with community reaction to problem drinkers to a focus on policy and intervention. Such studies are not necessarily competitive in terms of theory or method with the claims of biomedical science.

Paul Roman
Tulane University

References
Akers, R. (1977), *Deviant Behavior and Social Learning*, Belmont, Cal.
Bacon, S. (1973), 'The process of addiction to alcohol', *Journal of Studies on Alcohol*, 34.
Calahan, D. (1970), *Problem Drinkers*, San Francisco.
Clark, N. (1976), *Deliver Us From Evil*, New York.
Heather, N. and Robertson, I. (1981), *Controlled Drinking*, London.
Jellinek, E. M. (1960), *The Disease Concept of Alcoholism*, New Haven.
Lisansky, E., White, H. and Carpenter, J. (eds) (1982), *Alcohol, Science and Society Revisited*, Ann Arbor, Mich.
Marshall, M. (ed.) (1980), *Beliefs, Behaviors, and Alcoholic Beverages*, Ann Arbor, Mich.
Moore, M. and Gerstein, G. (eds) (1981), *Alcohol and Public Policy*, Washington.
Mulford, H. A. (1982), 'The epidemiology of alcohol and its implications', in E. M. Pattison and E. Kaufman (eds), *Encyclopedic Handbook of Alcoholism*, New York.
Pittman, D. and Snyder, C. (eds) (1962), *Society, Culture and Drinking Behavior*, New York.
Roman, P. (1981), 'From employee alcoholism to employee assistance: de-emphasis on prevention and alcohol problems in work-based programs', *Journal of Studies on Alcoholism*, 42.
Trice, H. M. (1966), *Alcoholism in America*, New York.

Further Reading
Ward, D. A. (1983), *Alcoholism: An Introduction to Theory and Treatment*, Dubuque.

Alienation

Alienation (in German *Entfremdung*), sometimes called estrangement, is a psychological, sociological or philo-sophical-anthropological category, largely derived from the writings of Hegel, Feuerbach and Marx.

In Hegel (1971 [1807]), we find the claim that the sphere of Spirit, at a certain stage in history, *splits up* into two regions: that of the 'actual world . . . of self-estrangement', and that of pure consciousness, which is, says Hegel, simply the 'other form' of that same estrangement. In this situation, self-consciousness is in absolute disintegration; personality is split in two. Here we have the '*entire estrangement*' of reality and thought from one another. This alienation will only be over-come when the division between Nature and Spirit is overcome – when Spirit becomes 'divested of self', that is, itself externalized.

This massive, objective, idealist philosophy of history was challenged by Feuerbach (1936[1841]) whose critique of Hegel centred precisely around a rejection of the latter's conception of the process of alienation. It is not that Feuerbach takes the 'separation' between subject and object to be a philosophical mythology. But this separation, he thinks, is assigned the status of a 'false alienation' in Hegel's work. For while man is real, God is an imaginary projection: 'the consciousness of God is the self-consciousness of man, the perception of God the self-perception of man'. Nor is nature a self-alienated form of the Absolute Spirit. But this reference to a 'false' alienation in Hegel suggests the existence of something like a 'true' – that is, really existing or operative – form of alienation. And Feuerbach does indeed believe in such a form; for it is only in some relation of contact with the objects which man produces – thus separating them off from himself – that he can become properly conscious of himself.

Marx (1975[1844]) seems to disagree. He argues that it is just by creating a world of objects through his practical activity that man proves himself as a conscious species-being. Under capitalism, however, the objects produced by human labour come to confront him as something *alien*. So the product of labour is transformed into an alien object 'exercising power over him', while the worker's activity becomes an alien activity. Marx adds that man's species-being then turns into a being alien to him, estranging him from his human aspect, and that man is thus estranged from man.

Marx's early writings, including the so-called *1844 Manuscripts*, were (re)discovered in the 1930s. Thus it was that some of their themes, including that of 'alienation', found their way into political, sociological and philosophical writings of the following period, including works of a non-Marxist character. A psycho-logical line in alienation theory can also be identified, partially derived from Hegel (see below). The concept also, of course, has an ethical aspect: alienation is generally considered (whatever theory it derives from) a bad thing. It has even been said (Sargent, 1972) to be 'a major or even the dominant condition of contemporary life'. An abundant literature exists on recent uses of the term (see Josephson and Josephson, 1962).

Lukes (1967) has clearly identified the fundamental difference between two concepts which are apparently often confused: that of alienation, and that – introduced by Durkheim – of anomie. For Durkheim the problem of anomic man is that he needs (but misses) rules to live by, limits to his desires and to his thoughts. Marx's problem is rather the opposite: that of man in the grip of a system from which he cannot escape.

Althusser (1969[1965]) developed a powerful critique of the notion of alienation as used by the young Marx, claiming that it was a metaphysical category abandoned by Marx in his later works.

It may finally be noted that the same term has appeared in the psychoanalytical writings of Lacan (1977[1966]), in the context of his theory of the 'mirror stage' in child development. This stage establishes an initial relation between the organism and its environment, but at the cost of a 'fragmentation' of the body. This may sound like a materialist version of Hegel's notion of the divided personality; and Lacan is indeed influenced by Hegel's analyses. It is, according to Lacan, in the relation between human subject and language that 'the most profound alienation of the subject in our scientific civilization' is to be found.

Grahame Lock
Catholic University of Nijmegen

References
Althusser, L. (1969[1965]), *For Marx*, London. (Original French edn, *Pour Marx*, Paris.)
Feuerbach, L. (1936[1841]), *Das Wesen des Christentums*, Berlin.
Hegel, G. W. F. (1971[1807]), *The Phenomonology of Mind*, London. (Original German edn, *System der Wissenschaft: Erster Teil, die Phänomenologie des Geistes*, Leipzig.)
Josephson, E. and Josephson, M. (1962), *Man Alone*, New York.
Lacan, J. (1977[1966]), *Ecrits*, London. (Original French edn, *Ecrits*, Paris.)
Lukes, S. (1967), 'Alienation and anomie', in P. Laslett and W. C. Runciman (eds), *Philosophy, Politics and Society*, Oxford.
Marx, K. (1975[1844]), *Economic and Philosophic Manuscripts of 1844*, in K. Marx and F. Engels, *Collected Works*, vol. 3, London. (Original German edn, *Ökonomisch-philosophische Manuskripte*.)
Sargent, L. T. (1972), *New Left Thought. An Introduction*, Homewood, Ill.

Further Reading
Blauner, R. (1964), *Alienation and Freedom. The Factory Worker and his Industry*, London.

Schaff, A. (1975), 'Alienation as a social and philosophical problem', *Social Praxis*, 3.
Sykes, G. (ed.) (1964), *Alienation. The Cultural Climate of Modern Man*, 2 vols, New York.
See also: *Althusser; anomie; Hegel; Lacan; Marx.*

Althusser, Louis (1918 –)

The French Communist philosopher, Louis Althusser, was a prisoner-of-war in Germany throughout the Second World War, thereafter student, lecturer, and finally Secretary of the Ecole Normale Supérieure, rue d'Ulm, Paris.

In 1965 Althusser published a collection of essays under the title of *Pour Marx* (*For Marx*, 1969) in which he opposes new Marxist 'orthodoxies' and in particular 'humanist' and 'Hegelian' interpretations of Marx. In order to designate the form of causality operating in the social and political sphere, he borrows (from Freud) the concept of 'over-determination', which he glosses by reference to Lenin's and Mao's notion of the uneven development of social contradictions. He also rejects the notion of 'alienation', a term found in certain early writings of Marx (and more rarely in the later works), but which is inconsistent with Marx's later explanatory apparatus (class struggle, the dialectic of relations and forces of production, the dictatorship of the proletariat, and so on).

In the same year (1965), Althusser published a collective volume (co-authors Etienne Balibar, Pierre Macherey, Jacques Rancière, Roger Establet), *Lire le Capital* (*Reading Capital*, 1970), where he expounds a supposed opposition between the 'ideological' and 'scientific' domains – an opposition which he was later, in his *Eléments d'auto-critique*, 1974 (*Essays in Self-Criticism*, 1976), to reject as 'rationalist' in inspiration and content. He also borrows another concept from Freud, that of the 'symptomatic reading' of a text (involving the search for the absence of a concept beneath the presence of a word and vice versa). From Gaston Bachelard he takes, in modified form, the notion of the 'epistemological break' to denote the division between the 'problematic' (ideological or theoretical framework) of Marx's earlier and later works.

In the article 'Ideologie et appareils idéologiques d'état' (1969), Althusser adds to the well-known Marxist notion of the (repressive) State apparatus that of the 'ideological State apparatus(es)', these consisting not only of the political parties, the education system, the legal system and other 'public' organisms, but also of 'private' organisms like the family, the Church, the arts, sport and even the trade unions. The distinction between the 'public' and 'private' spheres is itself, he argues, proper to the 'juridical ideology' dominant in bourgeois society; it is thus the influence of bourgeois, juridical ideology which masks the fact that so-called 'private' institutions can function as State apparatuses, that is, function in the reproduction of capitalist relations of production and of capitalist State power.

In his *Réponse à John Lewis* (1972–73) (*Reply to John Lewis*, 1976) originally published in the journal of the British Communist Party, *Marxism Today*, Althusser maintains his earlier distinction between the early and later Marx (and his preference for the latter), but admits that the break is less clean than he had first suggested. In his *Eléments d'auto-critique* and his Soutenance d'Amiens (1975), entitled 'Est-il simple d'être marxiste en philosophie?' (the answer is 'no'), he attributes his earlier, simplistic account of the break to his adoption of the above-mentioned 'rationalist' distinction between ideology and science. He now believes that these are not opposites, but concepts of different orders (a science may, for example, function as an ideology). There can, he claims, be no *general theory* of science in its opposition to ideology; strictly speaking, there can be no epistemology (or philosophy of science) which is not caught up in the bourgeois juridical practice of adjudging from above the criteria of legitimacy of candidate sciences.

In his *22ème Congrès* – of the French Communist Party – (1977), and his *Ce qui ne peut plus durer dans le parti communiste* (1978), Althusser turns his attention to directly political matters. In the former, he welcomes the opening announced at the Party Congress (the 'Union of the Left', and so on), but criticizes the theoretical arguments used to justify this opening. In the latter, he violently attacks the Party for its organizational forms (half parliamentary, half military – and in any case 'bourgeois') and for its 'fortress' mentality and practices.

From 1965 onwards, when his name became widely known, Althusser was subjected to bitter criticism, both from non-Marxists and from Marxists who had chosen either to defend the old Stalinist line and practices or to attempt to escape from these by adopting humanist positions. Most of these critiques are of little theoretical interest. Notable for its inaccuracies is E. P. Thompson's (1978), which uses *ad personam* invective in order to defame Althusser with the label of 'Stalinist'. (Althusser had, in the *Réponse à John Lewis*, distinguished between a 'right-wing' and a 'left-wing' critique of Stalin, the former being limited to moral indignation and accusations of violations of legality, the latter attempting 'serious historical research into the causes of the Stalinist deviation'.) More interesting, though also of direct political inspiration, is a critical commentary by an ex-pupil, Jacques Rancière (1974).

Althusser's influence on French philosophy, as well as on French Marxism, remains very considerable, though by now it takes mostly indirect forms.

Grahame Lock
Catholic University of Nijmegen

References
Rancière, J. (1974), *La Leçon d'Althusser*, Paris.
Thompson, E. P. (1978), *The Poverty of Theory*, London.

Further Reading
Althusser, L. (1976), *Essays in Self-Criticism*, London. (Contains a bibliography of works by and on Althusser.)
Callinicos, A. (1976), *Althusser's Marxism*, London.
Geras, N. (1972), 'Althusserian Marxism', *New Left Review*, 71.
Kolakowski, L. (1971), 'Althusser's Marx', *The Socialist Register*, London.
See also: *alienation*.

Altruism

For thousands of years philosophers have been intrigued by the problem of altruism, whether considering its status as a virtue, or debating its part in human nature. Seventeenth- and eighteenth-century British philosophers in particular, including Bentham, Hobbes, Locke, Mill, Sidgwick and Smith, argued at length about the psychological genuineness of human benevolence. It was the French philosopher, Auguste Comte, however, who originated the term, placing it in opposition to egoism. He believed the purpose of an advanced society was to foster the love of humanity, and that positivistic science, especially the discipline of sociology (a term he also coined), would produce this new set of values. More recently, behavioural scientists from several disciplines have examined the concept of altruism more objectively (Rushton and Sorrentino, 1981).

The definition of altruism is a matter of controversy. Some define it in terms of underlying motivations such as empathy or intention, while others prefer definitions in terms of behavioural effects such as 'that which benefits others'. One advantage of the behavioural definition is that it finesses the endless and fruitless debate as to whether such a thing as 'true' altruism exists. Defining altruism behaviourally does not, of course, preclude looking for the underlying motivation. It also allows the concept to be applied to animals.

In regard to motives, a number of internal mediators have been suggested. Among these are role-taking ability, empathic emotion, guilt, ideas of justice, personal values and social norms. There has been much research and model building on these hypothesized processes (Rushton and Sorrentino, 1981). Many of these models suggest that there are genuinely altruistic motivations, at the very least in the sense that internal standards prevail over immediate egoism.

Where does altruism originate? Three major developmental theories are (1) sociobiology, (2) cognitive development, and (3) social learning.

(1) Sociobiologists suggest that altruism is part of the inherited nature of human beings, arising from evolutionary history. Evidence for this view comes from studies of (a) animals, and (b) behaviour genetics. In regard to (a), altruism has been found in other species that, like our own, live in social groups. Social insects such as ants, bees and wasps, through to birds, dogs, porpoises and chimpanzees, all demonstrate altruism – in parental care, mutual defence, rescue behaviour, co-operative hunting and food sharing (Wilson, 1975). Sociobiologists view altruism as having evolved to help propagate genes. The altruist is helpful to kin, who share genes and thereby increase the number of reproductively successful offspring they raise. In so doing he helps to propagate his own genes. In this view altruism serves the 'selfish' biological purpose of propagating DNA, and is expected to follow lines of genetic similarity. In regard to (b), twin studies have found that individual differences in altruism, empathy, kindness and nurturance, as measured by paper-and-pencil questionnaires, have a substantial genetic component (Rushton, 1984).

(2) Researchers following in the cognitive developmental tradition of Piaget (1932) have documented the increments with age in children's capacity to (a) roletake the needs and perspectives of others, and (b) make moral judgements concerned with increasing ethical altruism. Both of these are seen as developing in a series of stages over the life span, invariant in sequence, hierarchical in nature, and universal across cultures. Many individuals, however, are said never to reach the higher levels of role-taking or moral reasoning due to 'developmental arrest'. This theory, therefore, essentially sees altruistic behaviour as based on maturationally unfolding cognitive development. In its support are the findings that individual differences in both roletaking ability and level of moral reasoning are predictive of altruistic behaviour, and that all three increase with age.

(3) The social learning theory approach, as its name suggests, stresses the importance of social conditioning in the development of altruism. Four processes in particular have been well researched: (a) classical conditioning; (b) response-contingent reinforcement and punishment; (c) observation of others; and (d) verbal socialization, including attributional labelling. Learning theorists have applied these procedures to understand the way in which socialization occurs through the educational system, the family, the peer group, and the mass media (Rushton, 1980). For example, if one of the main ways in which people learn is by observing others, then it follows that people should learn a great deal from viewing others on television. It is now fairly well documented that television has the power to alter the norms of appropriate behaviour.

A different orientation to altruism has come from personality theorists who have investigated whether there is a 'trait' of altruism, that is, whether some people are consistently more altruistic than others. The answer appears to be 'yes'. Evidence suggests that the likelihood of people being altruistic can be predicted from the manner in which they endorse or respond to items on paper-and-pencil measures of empathy, moral judgement, social responsibility, and moral knowledge. Altruists also appear to be consistently more honest, persistent, and self-controlled than non-altruists, and are likely to have strong feelings of personal efficacy. As already mentioned, some of this individual difference variance is inherited.

The effects on altruism of many social variables have been examined (Rushton and Sorrentino, 1981). One that has been much researched is the size of a group helping in an emergency. It is found that bystanders are more likely to offer help in an emergency if they are alone than if they are with others; the presence of others reduces helping, possibly through diffusing people's sense of responsibility. Another variable related to altruism is mood: good moods increase altruism whereas bad moods decrease it. Perhaps connected both with group size and mood is the apparent negative relation between altruism and population density: altruism is more frequent in small towns than in suburbs and more in the suburbs than in big cities. Finally, altruism has been related to friendship and similarity. In children, altruism and friendship sociograms overlap, and studies of adults have shown that they are more likely to help members of their own race or country than members of other races or foreigners. People also feel more empathic with, and help, those they perceive as similar to themselves.

Altruism has usually been viewed as an unqualified virtue. However, research is beginning to show that this is not always the case. Kindness can have unintended negative consequences. In some circumstances it can lead to a lowered self-concept, a feeling of helplessness and resentment in the recipient. Some have also argued that institutionalized altruism, such as occurs in the social welfare system, robs the individual of feelings of initiative or responsibility.

J. Philippe Rushton
University of Western Ontario

References

Piaget, J. (1932), *The Moral Judgment of the Child*, London.

Rushton, J. P. (1980), *Altruism. Socialization, and Society*, Englewood Cliffs, N.J.

Rushton, J. P. (1984), 'Sociobiology: toward a theory of individual and group differences in personality and social behavior', in J. R. Royce and L. P. Moss (eds), *Annals of Theoretical Psychology* vol. 2, New York.

Rushton, J. P. and Sorrentino, R. M. (eds) (1981), *Altruism and Helping Behavior: Social, Personality and Developmental Perspectives*, Hillsdale, N.J.

Wilson, E. O. (1975), *Sociobiology: The New Synthesis*, Cambridge, Mass.

See also: *empathy and sympathy; social learning theory; sociobiology.*

Analytical Psychology (Jungian Psychology)

C. G. Jung described his approach to psychotherapy as analytical psychology, differentiating it from Freud's psychoanalysis, and Adler's individual psychology. Jung's psychology takes into account a person's age, psychological type, and a 'collective unconscious'. This collective unconscious is distinct from the 'personal unconscious', with its forgotten or repressed contents. It is a common human inheritance, which gives everyone a propensity to respond emotionally to archetypal myths and images, to have dreams with universal symbols, and to respond instinctually.

Jung described four stages in analytical treatment: (1) confession (abreaction or catharsis); (2) elucidation (interpretation); (3) education: and (4) transformation (individuation).

(1) All therapies, the religious confessional, and initiation rituals have in common the first stage, catharsis, which Jung described as 'not merely the intellectual recognition of the facts with the head, but their confirmation by the heart and actual release of suppressed emotion'.

(2) Jung considered the second stage, elucidation or interpretation, as the main emphasis of Freudian psychoanalysis. It is a necessary stage if the patient becomes fixated on the analyst in a transference neurosis. Since transference is an unconscious process, a transference neurosis (or psychosis) can arise in any therapeutic situation. Although Jungian analysis does not foster transference, when it does arise in the analysis, transference interpretations are a necessary stage in the work.

(3) The stage of education, in which the analyst appeals to the patient's understanding of his symptoms and provides social education, was Adler's emphasis in psychotherapy. Jung saw this third stage as an effort by the analyst to help his patient learn how to adapt as a 'normal human being' in the everyday world. If a patient in Jungian analysis has a neurosis or psychosis that has made him unfit for normal life, then the direction of therapy at some point might include this stage.

(4) The fourth stage – transformation or individuation – was Jung's contribution to the analytic process. In this stage, the patient discovers his uniqueness, connects with an inner source of meaning that Jung called the Self, and shifts the centre of his personality from the ego to the Self.

The transformation stage takes place through a dialectical process or dialogue between analyst and patient. The process involves conscious attitudes and unconscious elements in the personalities of both people; as a result, both are deeply affected. A personal analysis is a prerequisite for any analyst undertaking this work.

Jung maintained that,

'The personalities of the doctor and patient are often infinitely more important for the outcome of the treatment than what the doctor says or thinks (although what he says and thinks may be a disturbing or a healing factor not to be uneresti-mated). For two personalities to meet is like mixing two different chemical substances: if there is any combination at all, both are transformed.'

Jean Shinoda Bolen
C.J. Jung Institute
San Francisco

Further Reading

Jung, C. G. (1966), *The Practice of Psychotherapy*, vol. 16 of the Collected Works of C. G. Jung, New York.

Mattoon, M. A. (1981), *Jungian Psychology in Perspective*, New York.

See also: *Jung; unconscious.*

Anarchism

Anarchism is a political philosophy which holds that societies can and should exist without rulers. Anarchists believe that this will not, as is commonly supposed, lead to chaos – 'anarchy' in the popular sense – but on the contrary to an increase in social order. Anarchists see the state as the decisive source of corruption and disorder in the body politic. They point to many examples where people freely co-operate, without coercion, to achieve common purposes. Among traditional societies they find much to interest them in the 'ordered anarchies' of certain African tribes such as the Nuer, as well as in the workings of autonomous peasant communities such as the Russian *mir* and the self-governing cities of medieval Europe. In modern times they have hailed the anarchist experiments of the German Anabaptists of sixteenth-century Münster; the Diggers and Fifth Monarchists of the English Civil War; the popular clubs and societies of the French Revolution; the Paris Commune of 1871; the Russian soviets of 1905 and 1917; and the anarchist ventures in Catalonia and Andalusia during the Spanish Civil War.

Christ and Buddha have been claimed among earlier anarchists; and there were many social movements in both medieval Europe and medieval China which drew a fundamentally anarchist inspiration from Christianity and Buddhism. Religious anarchism continued into modern times with Tolstoy and Gandhi. But the modern phase of anarchism proper opens with the eighteenth-century Enlightenment, and can be traced equally from Rousseau's romanticism and William Godwin's rationalism. An early exponent was Godwin's son-in-law, the poet Shelley. Later advocates included the French socialist Proudhon, the German philosopher of egoism Max Stirner, the American individualist Thoreau, and the Russian aristocratic rebels Michael Bakunin and Peter Kropotkin. Anarchism was a strong current during the Russian Revolution and its immediate aftermath; the suppression of the Kronstadt rising in 1921 and the emasculation of the soviets signalled its defeat. But the ideas lived on, to surface not only in Spain in the 1930s, but in Hungary in 1956, and in Paris in 1968, where the student radicals achieved a dazzling blend of anarchism and surrealism.

Krishan Kumar
University of Kent

Further Reading
Joll, J. (1964), *The Anarchists*, London.
Miller, D. (1984), *Anarchism*, London.
Ritter, A. (1980), *Anarchism: A Theoretical Analysis*, Cambridge.
Woodcock, G. (1963), *Anarchism*, London.
See also: *Kropotkin; stateless societies*.

Annales School

The journal *Annales d'histoire économique et sociale*, long planned, was founded in 1929 by two historians at the University of Strasbourg, Lucien Febvre and Marc Bloch, because they were unhappy with the manner in which history was studied in France and elsewhere, and wished to offer an alternative. They considered orthodox history to be too much concerned with events, too narrowly political, and too isolated from neighbouring disciplines. In their attempt to construct a 'total' history, as it came to be called (total in the sense of dealing with every human activity, not in that of trying to include every detail), Febvre and Bloch were concerned to enlist the collaboration of workers in the social sciences. They were both admirers of the work of Paul Vidal de la Blache in human geography, and interested in the ideas of Lucien Lévy-Bruhl on 'primitive mentality', while Bloch was also inspired by Durkheim's concern with the social and by his comparative method. The first editorial board of *Annales* included the geographer Albert Demangeon, the sociologist Maurice Halbwachs and the political scientist André Siegfried.

The movement associated with the journal can be divided into three phases. In the first phase (to about 1945), it was small, radical and subversive. After the Second World War, however, the rebels took over the historical establishment. Febvre became President of the new interdisciplinary École Pratique des Hautes Études. He continued to edit *Annales: Economies, Sociétés, Civilisations*, as it became in 1946, thus extending its range to the 'history of mentalities' practised by Febvre in his own work on the Reformation. He was aided by Fernand Braudel, whose doctoral thesis on *The Mediterranean and the Mediterranean World in the Age of Philip II* (1949) quickly made him famous. Braudel dominated the second generation of the movement, in which it was most truly a 'school' with distinctive concepts and methods. Braudel himself stressed the importance of the long-term (*la longue durée*), of historical geography, and of material culture (*civilisation matérielle*). Pierre Chaunu emphasized quantitative methods (*L'histoire sérielle*), notably in his vast study of trade between Spain and the New World, *Seville et l'Atlantique*. Pierre Goubert, a former student of Bloch's, integrated the new historical demography, developed by Louis Henry, into a historical community study of the Beauvais region. Robert Mandrou remained close to Febvre and the history of mentalities.

A third phase in the history of the movement opened in 1968 (a date which seems to mark the revenge of political events on the historians who neglected them). Braudel reacted to the political crisis by deciding to take a back seat and confiding the journal to younger men, notably Emmanuel Le Roy Ladurie. Le Roy Ladurie made his reputation with *The Peasants of Languedoc* (1966), a total history from the ground up in the Braudel manner, which used quantitative methods wherever possible, but he has since moved 'from the cellar to the attic', towards the history of mentalities and historical anthropology, as in his bestselling study of a fourteenth-century village, *Montaillou* (1975). The last few years have seen a fragmentation of the former school, which has in any case been so influential in France that it has lost its distinctiveness. It is now a 'school' only for its foreign admirers and its domestic critics, who continue to reproach it for underestimating the importance of political events. Some members of the *Annales* group, notably Le Roy Ladurie and Georges Duby, a medievalist, who has moved, like Ladurie, from rural history to the history of mentalities, are presently concerned to integrate both politics and events into their approach, and to provide narrative as well as analysis.

Since Braudel had a quasi-filial relationship with Febvre and a quasi-paternal relationship with Ladurie, the development of the *Annales* movement into a school and its fragmentation into a loosely-organized group might be interpreted in terms of the succession of three generations. It also illustrates the cyclical process by which the rebels become the establishment and are in turn rebelled against. However, the journal and the people associated with it still offer the most sustained long-term example of fruitful interaction between historians and the social sciences.

Peter Burke
Emmanuel College, University of Cambridge

Further Reading
Stoianovich, T. (1976), *French Historical Method: The Annales Paradigm*, Ithaca.
Review, special issue, (1978), 'The impact of the Annales School on the social sciences', vol. 1.
See also: *Bloch*; *Braudel*; *Pirenne*.

Anomie

Observations on conditions in which dominant norms are questioned or repudiated antedate Durkheim's (1947[1893]), (1951[1897]) anomie concept. Earlier writers had noted the repeated tendency of such periods to lead to diminished social cohesion (for example, Marx, 1968 [1853]) and eventually to new forms of despotism. Durkheim discerned other features: not only economic crisis but also increasing prosperity is accompanied by abeyance of established norms, that is, anomie, which releases unlimited desires and ultimately causes sharp rises in suicide rates, to an extent dependent on a nation's main religious ideology.

Widening its application to various kinds of deviance, Merton (1938) reconceptualized anomie to refer less to normlessness than to disparities between well-defined norms and limited opportunities for fulfilling them. Anomie, therefore, has two principal connotations: a weakening of rules of conduct which maintain social solidarity, and widespread frustration at the inability to achieve cultural goals. Both notions have been heavily criticized (Clinard, 1964). They are unacceptable to perspectives less concerned with emphasizing strict adherence to norms as essential to social life than with exploring how norms are manipulated, constructed, made explicit, juxtaposed, defied, and so on. Unreliability of official statistics and other difficulties in research has cast doubt on the applicability of anomie theory to suicidal behaviour and other forms of deviance. However, even stern critics, for example, Downes and Rock (1982), stop short of condemning anomie theory as otiose. It continues to command the attention of sociologists concerned with identifying sources of disenchantment with the modern world.

Maurice Glickman
University of Botswana

References
Clinard, M. (ed.) (1964), *Anomie and Deviant Behaviour*, London.
Downes, D. and Rock, P. (1982), *Understanding Deviance*, Oxford.
Durkheim, E. (1947[1893]), *The Division of Labour in Society*, New York. (Original French, *De la division du travail social*, Paris.)
Durkheim, E. (1951[1897]), *Suicide*, New York. (Original French, *Le Suicide*, Paris.)
Marx, K. and Engels, F. (1968), *Selected Works*, Moscow.
Merton, R. (1938), 'Social structure and anomie', *American Sociological Review*, 3.
See also: *alienation*; *deviance*; *Durkheim*; *norms*; *suicide*.

Anorexia Nervosa

Anorexia nervosa probably represents a weight phobia – the fear of obesity. Once a rare disorder, it is now common in affluent countries where the cultural mandate for females is a slim figure. Characteristic patterns in families of anorexics include parental expectations of perfection, at least as seen through the eyes of the affected young person.

The average patient – over 90 per cent are female – aged seventeen or eighteen, weighs 123 pounds prior to the onset of the disorder. She begins a voluntary diet, loses control and drops to seventy-nine pounds, although extreme cases go below sixty pounds. To facilitate a loss of weight, patients radically reduce their calorie intake, but many also induce vomiting, over-exercise, or take cathartics. Some periodically go on eating binges when self-control is temporarily lost.

The physiological disturbances resulting from these disordered eating habits lead to physical distress with eating and disruption of the ordinary experience of satisfaction. This situation reinforces the anorexic process. Patients continue to perceive themselves as fat despite the reality; this distortion of body image is probably a function of the phobic process, which magnifies the feared object. The malnutrition leads to an amenorrhea, constipation, hypotension, bradycardia and anaemia. However, some patients display a remarkable energy despite their wasted appearance and in fact engage in compulsive exercise.

Why does a small fraction of the dieting population lose control and develop this syndrome? Many are troubled adolescents, who regard slimness as a key to happiness, attractiveness, and a sense of inner worth. Most are diligent, perfectionist and compliant; these traits may make them more susceptible to cultural mandates for slimness. Finally, as a group they are excellent hypnotic subjects, which may contribute to the phobia. Therapy involves realimentation, usually by behavioural tactics. However, the fear of obesity tends to linger, remaining a formidable problem. Some therapists maintain that comprehensive treatment requires involving the family in an effort to deal with underlying causes of the disorder.

Eugene L. Bliss
University of Utah

Further Reading

Bliss, E. A. and Branch, C. H. H. (1960), *Anorexia Nervosa: Its History, Psychology and Biology*, Hoeber, N.Y.
Dally, P., Gomez, J. and Isaacs, A. J. (1979), *Anorexia Nervosa*, London.
Gross, M. (ed.) (1982), *Anorexia Nervosa*, Lexington, Mass.

Anthropology

I am dealing here with 'anthropology' understood as the holistic 'science of man'. There is confusion in the use of the term since in Europe it usually means simply 'physical anthropology'. However, it is fairly well understood now, especially in the Americas, that 'anthropology' describes a discipline comprising the study of primate and human evolution, prehistoric archaeology, linguistics and social/cultural anthropology, the latter understood as the comparative study of preliterate peoples. This is a minimum definition and the cavils and exclusions would constitute a whole article. This also raises the first question: what is this disparate collection of disciplines doing under one heading, itself claiming to be a discipline? After all, what is *not* the 'science of man'? Earlier versions of 'anthropology' in fact excluded linguistics (the province of comparative philology) while having something to say about language, but they *included* 'technology' or 'material culture', now neglected almost entirely. These inclusions and exclusions are part of the history of the discipline. Since it grew up around museums in large part, 'artifacts' loomed large, and for long stretches of the discipline's history ethnographers 'collected' customs and culture traits much as their museological colleagues 'collected' artifacts. As anthropology eventually developed in many universities independently of museums, artifacts declined in importance. But, for example, in the US, where much work was done for the Bureau of American Ethnology, the 'recording of native languages' became central, and the science of 'descriptive linguistics' was developed almost entirely *within* anthropology. In Britain, again, where the Colonial Office sponsored much research, native languages were learned, but the 'science' was already owned by philology.

Roughly, however, wherever it is found, when anthropology is treated as a holistic science (largely in the US), it recognizes the two major divisions of 'physical anthropology' and 'cultural anthropology',

and even if scholars may specialize wholly in one or the other for research purposes, in the education of an anthropologist these are both 'required' (as are some linguistics and archaeology). 'Survivals' of this remain in the undergraduate curricula of some British universities, but by the postgraduate stage they are totally separated. How did they come to be related, and why are they now only so tenuously linked, and what is the future of this relationship?

As a discipline, anthropology took shape in the 1860s, and was established in the universities by the turn of the century. It developed originally outside the universities: Tylor in England was a Quaker businessman, and Morgan in the US, a lawyer. Indeed, Tylor's nonconformity excluded him from an education at Oxford or Cambridge, but the liberalization of these universities allowed him, later, to teach there and to establish anthropology as 'Mr Tylor's science'. His text, *Anthropology*, of 1881 marks the establishment of the discipline in England, as does Morgan's *Ancient Society* (1877) for the US. Many commentators have taken pains to point out that both writers inherited a tradition of social evolutionism from the French and Scottish Enlightenment thinkers and from Spencer, that owed nothing to Darwin – even vice versa. This has perhaps been exaggerated, and there is no question that the *physical* evolution of man would not have loomed so large in the development of anthropology had it not been for the Darwinian revolution and the need to come to terms with it. For anthropology was born of what Owen Lovejoy (1936) called the 'temporalization' of the idea of the 'great chain of being' in the eighteenth century. The secularized version showed a debatable gap between the 'highest animals' and the 'lowest savages' and a progression upwards to the highest civilizations. Side debates between 'progressivists' (usually secular and anti-clerical) and 'degenerationists' (usually clerical and orthodox) consumed much energy, but the strength of the 'progressive' paradigm was more in tune with the tenor of the times, and Morgan and Tylor embraced it. Anthropology's special brief among the intellectual disciplines emerging in the second half of the nineteenth century, then, concerned the 'lower races' and the variety of explanations for the emergence of the highest civilizations. At this stage the distinction between it and 'sociology' was not all that clear, but as sociology in England took on a more Fabian tinge and in America a concern with the immigrant, the differentiation became clearer: anthropology was primarily to deal with the material and spiritual culture of the 'lower races', with peasant folklore, with the distribution and origin of physical types and, later, when evidence became available, with human evolution, because this bore precisely on that origin.

'Physical anthropology' as such was a slow starter because, despite the impact of Darwin, evidence was scanty, there was at first no genetic theory and then dispute among the geneticists and, also, within the 'liberal progressive' tradition of anthropology, there was a growing opposition to racial thinking led primarily by Boas in America. In England as well the subject was split over race since the early disputes on slavery in the amateur anthropological societies. On both sides of the Atlantic (including the continent) there were those who seized enthusiastically on 'eugenics' – and considered themselves the true progressives – and those who followed Tylor and Boas on 'the psychic unity of mankind' and refused to trace cultural differences to racial sources. The disputation was bitter, and its residue continues to plague anthropology, which was forced to become the science that dealt with racial variation and yet was at the same time concerned to deny its cultural significance.

In Europe this 'split mind' was perhaps somewhat less in evidence, since from the start physical anthropology was never that well integrated with cultural anthropology. It was mostly taught in medical schools in departments of anatomy, and 'ethnology' or 'ethnography' was taught separately – often attached to museums. The concerns of the latter disciplines – such as 'diffusion versus independent invention' and the like – while sometimes invoking racial arguments, were largely unconcerned with what the anatomists were doing; and the latter were very little in touch with the geneticists. Archaeology was still largely 'classical' or 'Egyptological', and so there was no concerted 'physical anthropology'. Where there was, it largely concerned the descriptive typology of races. Meanwhile, 'ethnology' – the concern with 'primitive peoples' – took a decidedly 'sociological' turn in France under Durkheim and his school and in England under Rivers at Cambridge. Thus a 'holistic' anthropology never really got off the ground in Europe.

In the US, however, the nutcracker continued to squeeze. 'Physical anthropology' was firmly established in anthropology proper: Boas (1911) did important work on the head-shapes of immigrants, and Kroeber wrote extensively of fossil man and primate intelligence in his *Anthropology* (1923). But at the same time, Boas was elaborating the theoretical basis of cultural relativism (and training students like Mead and Benedict to produce the 'proof'), while Kroeber took an extreme culturalist position in his doctrine of the 'super-organic' nature of culture. The net result was a firm ideological position in which culture became a prime mover, a reality *sui generis* as was 'society' for Durkheim. In the work, for example, of Leslie White (1949), this was taken to its extreme: culture operated entirely according to its own laws. This was of course the logical extrapolation from Tylor's position, but Tylor would have wanted to lodge this, ultimately, in the natural process. It was symptomatic of the later developments that when White brought out a revised edition

of Tylor's *Anthropology* in 1960, he omitted the 'Darwinian' chapter on 'Man and other animals' as 'not consonant with modern knowledge'.

This general thrust, although plainly ideological in origin, was also sustained 'scientifically' by both positive and negative developments. On the negative side, fossil evidence was thin, disputed (in the case of Dart's *Australopithecus*) or fraudulent (in the case of Piltdown). Genetics was divided, and until the remarkable burst of talent in the 1930s (Huxley, Haldane, Fisher, Sewall Wright), serious evolutionary genetics was retarded – and we must not forget that it was not until the 1950s that the genetic code was broken. Ethological work was being done, but it was not well known. Even if it had been known its significance would have been missed, since the general triumph of behaviourism – the main 'positive' development – would have excluded it. Instinct theory was thought to be thoroughly discredited, and behaviourism, established with equal firmness in the US and USSR, dominated psychology, linguistics, philosophy and anthropology. It was, of course, totally compatible with, and generally welcomed by, the proponents of cultural determinism.

The other major intellectual force that hit anthropology was psychoanalysis. Kroeber was analysed and was a practising lay analyst for a while, but the major impetus came from Linton and Kardiner. Psychoanalysis was married to cultural relativism and produced the 'culture and personality' school which was prominent in the 1930s and 1940s. Even here, however, there was an attempt to translate Freudianism into a behaviouristic system. The epitome of this was probably Murdock's *Social Structure* (1949) in which behaviourism, Freudianism and the 'cross-cultural method' were combined in an attempt to answer traditional questions of kinship theory. 'Culture and personality', as a subfield of anthropology, was comfortably in line with the assumptions of cultural relativism: each culture produced its 'basic personality' which was unique and a result of cultural conditioning. A few 'holistic' anthropologists like Hallowell (1959) tried to keep 'culture and personality' in an evolutionary framework, but theirs were lonely voices.

After the initial Freudian-Behaviourist stage, this movement fragmented into a general 'psychological anthropology'. Fragmentation became characteristic of anthropology from the late 1950s, as we shall see, and 'psychological' anthropology tended to take off after the latest fads in psychology generally. Perhaps the strongest development, and in the long run the most lasting, was the alliance with cybernetics, topology, systems theory, computers and 'cognitive psychology'. This proved prophetic, since there is no question that 'cognitive science' is one of the more durable, coherent and exciting areas of development in the behavioural sciences generally. It moves naturally into strong association with neuroscience, the most obvious growth area in the physiology of behaviour. Already 'neuropsychology' is established, and a field of 'neurosociology' cannot be far behind.

In picking out the trends with durability, as opposed to the fads, it is important to note ecology. This was in danger of being a fad during the 1960s and 1970s, but it had fairly deep roots in anthropology and has survived and flourished. Early on, it was a province of zoology, and attempts to look at ecological systems were confused with 'environmental determinism' and Marxism. Often, as with White (1949), they were grandiose and unsophisticated, but Julian Steward (1955), for example, kept a high standard of ecological thinking to the forefront of the anthropological imagination. The impact of the 'ecological crisis' sent many young anthropologists into this area, and some of the best. The connection again with systems theory was quickly established, and this was excellent in ridding the discipline of antiquated 'cause and effect' thinking. It was also very important that anthropological ecology arose, essentially, out of the 'archaeological' wing of the subject. This revolutionized archaeology which, for example, under Binford (1972) at New Mexico, found a new sophistication and much closer links with 'cultural' anthropology proper.

As is often the case with these internal developments, however, fanatics take them up as causes, attach them to ideologies, and try to claim 'total' explanation of social facts for them. For the cognitive anthropologists this meant a curious version of solipsism – in the case of 'structuralism' a kind of collectivist solipsism, with almost a revival of the idea of a 'group mind'. With the ecologists, on the contrary, it became what early critics had feared – a crude materialistic determinism advanced in the name of 'cultural materialism' and claiming, strangely, to be 'Marxist' in some cases. This fad seems to be passing, and if ecologists can (a) stick to their cybernetic models and (b) expand their models of feedback systems to include other variables – such as cognition and communication – then there is much promise here. The work of people like Rappoport, for example, continues to impress in this area.

The mention of communication points to another strong trend in 'holistic' anthropology. The influence of linguistics, as we have seen, has always been strong in American anthropology, and various linguistic models have been tried as paradigms for examining other areas of culture – by Pike, Kluckhohn, and others. It was this influence that led to the whole 'language and culture' movement that for a while rivalled 'culture and personality' for centre stage. At first this was largely concerned with arguing the 'Sapir-Whorf' hypothesis about – again – the *deterministic* role of language; but this developed into the basis of 'formal analysis' of cultures through set theory and componential analysis. While this ran into difficulties (to do with its solipsistic problems) it did mean that there was a

useful pre-adaptation for the assimilation of French structuralism under Lévi-Strauss, itself a product of de Saussure, Jakobson and European linguistics. The idea that all culture was like language in being an arbitrary 'code' which could be broken, thus 'solving' the messages contained in everything from myths through kinship systems to art, was certainly attractive. It corresponded to a revolution in American linguistics from outside anthropology, but one that had a tremendous impact, namely the Chomskian transformational grammar, which rested on similar premises about universal, rational mental processes. (In structuralism the issue of 'innateness' is skirted; for Chomsky it is central.) This was all rightly opposed by the ecologists, who insisted that cultures were not *just* systems of communication but existed in real adaptational situations. But, as we have seen, the ecologists themselves need to take more note of communication, and ultimately, as Richard Alexander (1979) has said, they have to include the genes, 'since so far no one has found any other way to make a human being'.

This brings us back to what was happening in physical anthropology. We have established the 'split', which was partly ideological but also partly based on the paucity of usable material and theory in biology itself. Even students of animal behaviour, themselves biologists, had little help from genetics, for example. This help existed potentially in the work of Fisher in the 1930s, but it was missed until the 1960s. The growing body of work of the ethologists which studied, after all, the social interactive behaviour of animals, was little known until its popularization in the 1960s. But during those same remarkable and effervescent 1960s there was a positive renaissance of physical anthropology, which dropped its obsession with racial typologies and suddenly turned into a powerful science. Several things contributed. The first was an upsurge in fossil finds. This was not solely due to the Leakeys and Olduvai Gorge, although no one can underestimate their importance. All over the old world crucial finds were made that rapidly filled in the 'gaps' in the fossil record and revolutionized our notions of the age of the hominid line – pushing it back into the pliocene (to 3.5 million years). At the same time, under Washburn at Berkeley and his student DeVore at Harvard, and under Hall at Bristol, there began a fantastic development of primate studies. Although this has now spread to embrace zoologists, psychologists, ethologists, neuroscientists and others, its early inspiration in America (and in Japan where studies got under way after the end of World War II) was anthropological. It wanted to help understand human evolution by looking at the social behaviour of our closest relatives; but at the same time, its methods were borrowed from social anthropology: long-term studies in the field, living in daily contact, and even some kind of 'participant observation' with the animals.

Again cross-referencing began. It was soon obvious that this was close to what ethologists were doing, and thus a new interest in their work was engendered. The ethologists had been concentrating almost entirely on animal *communication*, and the primatologists were able to introduce a healthy measure of ecology. As usual this became a polarized argument on the futile 'nature versus nurture' issue, but there are signs that at long last this tedious debate (which after all was settled by Kant and resettled by William James) is being seen for what it is, and an 'interactionist' set of hypotheses are taking over. Like all these developments, primatology became largely an end in itself for its practitioners, but this over-specialization is perhaps necessary. Most people are not good at synthesis: to use one analogy, there are a million good bricklayers for every good architect. But too much bricklaying can slow down development in a discipline, and can kill it altogether by inducing total fragmentation. Primatology became so popular that most departments have at least a 'token' primatologist. Since they tend to be obsessive about 'data' and basically non-theoretical, they do not threaten, unlike their more theoretically aggressive 'ethological' colleagues. As 'symbolic anthropologists' attest, people are happier with limited categories and firm boundaries. Disruption of these produces reactions of witchcraft, pollution and taboo. (There are of course neural mechanisms which explain why this happens – but 'symbolic' anthropologists would reject such an intrusion of 'other' data as 'reductionism'!)

Other developments were largely technical. Improved methods of dating grew apace. These were again shared with the archaeologists, so cross-boundary ties were possible. Also, primatologists were pushed into being more 'zoological', hence forcing the connection with biology. Studies of chimpanzees in the wild had to be measured against the studies of chimpanzee communication in the laboratory (largely undertaken by psychologists). All this made for a ferment and the rapid development of primatology, but the result was not at all a closing of the physical-cultural gap. If anything, the cultural anthropologists began to close ranks and became even more stridently ideological, denying more forcefully than ever the relevance of these data the more forceful the data became. Attempts like those of Tiger and Fox (1970), for example, to call attention to this relevance, not only for anthropology, but for human survival, were largely sidestepped or attacked as 'reductionist' or 'revivals of Social Darwinism' or reactionary or whatever. Some commentators realized that they were a genuine attempt to be 'true to the broadest mandate' of anthropology (Seigel), but these were few. Of course these attempts did have their problems. They were overly impressed by the ethologists and hence concentrated largely on communication which, as we have seen,

needed the corrective of ecology. The development of primatology made this more possible since much more complex creatures with higher levels of social learning were involved than those popular with the ethologists. There was response, but it was limited. 'Cultural' anthropology, in the 1960s and 1970s, was not moving in that direction.

A lot of this had to do with two factors in the sociology of anthropology itself: the post-Sputnik explosion of the number of departments and professionals, and the turmoil in society itself over civil rights and Vietnam.

The proliferation of academic anthropologists took place, for obvious reasons, largely within 'cultural' anthropology – new departments usually did not have the infrastructure necessary for ambitious physical anthropology programmes – and so largely within its assumptions. This coincided with the upsurge of physical anthropology, as well as exciting developments in neuroscience, endocrinology and genetics, but the fast-developing cultural anthropology departments tended to proliferate in unrelated directions. 'Area' studies were big for a time, since money was available; this was true also of 'medical' and 'urban' anthropology. 'Symbolic' anthropology was popular – it needed little investment of either money or brains, and could pick up on what was happening in structuralism and linguistics ('semiotics' as it soon became). Bold souls like Sebeok tried to initiate 'zoo-semiotics' – recognizing the connection to ethology – but this went nowhere. An almost frantic fragmentation was taking place. This was *not* healthy specialization: that can only take place in a science that already has a central theory within which to specialize. The too-rigid expansion of anthropology in America, combined with the demands of the promotion system and the entrepreneurial nature of academic life, simply led to a proliferation of mini-specialisms and a chasing after every fad to come out of Paris or Frankfurt. Among these the oddest was the revival of 'Marxism'. It was not a Marxism that many of those truly familiar with Marx could easily recognize. Partly, it was highly fashionable to be 'radical' during this period in academic circles, and fashionably daring to be 'Marxist' – in some version or another, usually acquired second hand. Marx was pinned to the social radical mast-head much as Darwin had been to that of the social Darwinists, usually with about the same lack of relevance. The most interesting area of this development was essentially a revival within anthropology of the tradition of the 'sociology of knowledge' – or the 'social construction of reality', as Berger and Luckmann (1966) chose to call it. The 'Marxist' anthropologists behaved as though this was a remarkable discovery and quoted Althusser and 'hermeneutics' a great deal. But, curiously, it sat well with the 'symbolic' and 'cognitive' developments and so got its hearing. As Berger recognized, though, there is a circularity in the argument: the mind is a social construct, but the mind 'constructs' society. The only way out of this is to examine the mind as an evolutionary product (Donald Campbell's 'evolutionary epistemology'); but this, naturally, does not sit well with the current ideology. The other 'radical' impetus came from feminism, but since this was essentially an anti-intellectual movement (at least in America) its relevance was limited to its ability, which was considerable, to harass those it considered opponents. (In Europe there are genuinely interesting developments in this area, but these have not penetrated to North America.) 'Urgent' anthropology spawned a good deal of interesting work on rapidly disappearing hunting and gathering societies, a development further encouraged by the renewed interest in human evolution: many of those engaged in the 'Man the Hunter' movement were also primatologists.

The overall impression of this period is one of chaos. The pressures to 'radicalism', 'urbanism', 'relevance' and so on, together with the sudden affluence of what had always been a small and exclusive discipline, produced not progress but simply a proliferation of fads. It may take many years for the ill effects of this period to work themselves out. Meanwhile, we might ask what has been happening to the classic areas of social anthropology? Where, for example is kinship? This had always been the central topic – the key to anthropological thinking and theory, responsible for more than 50 per cent of publications. Well, it continued to receive 'structural' attention from Lévi-Strauss and a few of his students, and it provided subject matter for the 'componential analysts' – but otherwise it all but disappeared. This is one of the stranger modern developments. It is as though philosophy decided to abandon logic. No history of the period is possible yet, but when one is written this will have to be dealt with. Partly, kinship was simply submerged by the 'urgent' and 'relevant' concerns, which, demanding little intellect and much passion, were more in tune with the times. Partly also, it got bogged down with intricate 'in-house' disputes that simply began to bore people – the 'prescriptive marriage' debate was one. To get out of this impasse, Schneider (1968), for example, led kinship studies into the 'symbolic' camp in America. This was at exactly the time when a combination of 'biosocial' movements were putting kinship back into nature with a vengeance!

This must surely rank as one of the great ironies of intellectual history. For all those years, social anthropologists had been insisting that kinship *was* the heart of social structure, and the study of it was the great strength of anthropology. In the 1960s, Hamilton, picking up on the work of Fisher in the 1930s, re-established the importance of kinship in evolution with his theory of 'inclusive fitness'. One would have thought that social anthropologists would have been

ecstatic, and felt that they were totally vindicated. Some were – a few – and immediately saw that the 'gap' could here be bridged at the more crucial point of theory. But the majority were uninterested or simply hostile. The lack of interest of course stems from the drifting of anthropology into the morass of 'soft' specialisms we have noted – and the concomitant decline of interest in kinship. The hostility is more interesting. Some of it came from the deep-rooted antipathy to evolutionary biology that we have noted, and there were several half thought-out 'rushes to judgement' – Sahlins producing the most notable. Other hostility was more overtly political and was sparked off by the media hype surrounding E. O. Wilson's *Sociobiology* (1975). We live in a social, political and media-dominated world, and ideas do not exist in a vacuum. But it was obvious that Wilson, who combined all the available entomological, ethological, and primatological evidence with the evolutionary theory derived from Hamilton and Trivers, was making a grab for a *total* explanation of *all* social behaviour from insect to man. As early as 1971 Tiger and Fox had recognized that Hamilton's work was important in understanding altruism. But Wilson's ambitions put the social sciences on the defensive. This, combined with a highly touted 'radical' attack, muddled the debate – which simply seemed parochial and confusing to the Europeans. At the same time, the grab by the evolutionary biologists for a *total* explanation was offensive to those physical anthropologists who, through studies of primate behaviour, anatomy, the brain and the endocrine systems, had been labouring to produce *proximate* explanations of behaviour. There is in fact no real conflict. *Proximate* mechanisms must always be referable back to *ultimate* mechanisms, that is, those of natural selection which produced them. But certainly, and again, ironically, the physical anthropologists felt as threatened as the cultural! The media hype (in a nation where being a 'celebrity' is the equivalent of being knighted) hid from intellectual view, for example, the fact that a small group of anthropologists and others were already co-operating to produce a combined ultimate/proximate approach. In the same year as *Sociobiology* (1975), Fox edited *Biosocial Anthropology*, which proposed exactly such a programme and included work from primatology, ethology (Bischof, Blurton Jones, Chance), and endocrinology. It was politely received, but lacking the hype, did not get centre stage, and no one noticed the real alternative it offered.

This recital of the recent history of kinship shows that, within this next decade, it is doubtful that the gap will be closed. But eventually the sheer weight of evidence from the physical sciences is bound to tell. This may mean that, as Wilson has predicted, a new 'biosociology' will emerge that will simply bypass the social sciences. It may be, however, that after the smoke of controversy has cleared, anthropologists in sufficient numbers may realize that for intellectual survival if nothing else, they had better re-tool their skills and accept their natural alliance with the natural sciences in the framework of natural selection (that is, evolutionary biology). At present this is hard to see. The subject is shrinking, not expanding, and once exciting areas, like British social structural analysis, seem to have run into a dead end. French anthropology seems exhausted after the heady popularity of structuralism. If the future is anywhere it is in America, but whether anything viable will emerge from the current chaos and ideological muddle is hard to see. What is more likely – and this is evident from the near collapse and 'reorganization' of the professional association – is that a series of relatively autonomous specialisms will diverge from one another and gravitate towards their nearest relatives in other fields. Thus the 'cognitive' anthropologists, for example, are already part of a 'cognitive science' movement starting its own newsletter and so on, and incorporating psychologists, neuroscientists, linguists, and artificial intelligence experts. Many of the 'physical' specialists already prefer to gravitate to close neighbours like genetics or anatomy. The 'ecologists' likewise are breaking away. This leaves the 'cultural' anthropologists moving if anything closer to the humanities in the pursuit of 'meaning' through 'symbols'. It would appear that 'Mr Tylor's science' is in total disarray.

This does not mean that excellent things are not being done in the various subfields. They are. But I have been concerned here with the ideal of an integrated, holistic field of anthropology proper, and this seems, at the moment, unrealizable. There are glimpses of hope within the field which suggest that some integration is possible. A number of young people do take up research in the 'biology of social behaviour' – but it is not well supported. Some of those, like Laughlin and d'Aquili (1974) who helped to pioneer such an integrative approach (their 'biogenetic structuralism') continue to press the analysis into areas like ritual, which had been the preserve of the social/cultural wing. More significantly, an outstanding practitioner of the 'symbolic' approach, Victor Turner (1983) was affected by the new information, and studied brain mechanisms. If there is any hope for the holistic science it lies in these directions, and the work of Chagnon and Irons (1979), Konner (1982) and Chisholm (1983) combines the best of training in physical and cultural anthropology with a refreshing, integrative approach. The possibilities are there, but it is hard to see their making much headway against the ideological inertia of this sadly fragmented discipline.

Robin Fox
Rutgers University

References

Alexander, R. (1979), *Darwinism in Relation to Social Affairs*, Seattle.

Berger, P. and Luckmann, T. (1966), *The Social Construction of Reality*, Garden City, N.Y.

Binford, L. R. (1972), *An Archaeological Perspective*, New York.

Boas, F. (1911), *The Mind of Primitive Man*, New York.

Campbell, D. (1974), 'Evolutionary epistemology', in *The Philosophy of Karl Popper*, La Salle, Ill.

Chagnon, N. and Irons, W. (1979), *Evolutionary Biology and Human Social Behavior: An Anthropological Perspective*, North Scituate, Mass.

Chisholm, J. (1983), *Navaho Childhood: An Ethnological Study of Child Development*, Chicago.

Chomsky, N. (1957), *Syntactic Structures*, The Hague.

DeVore, I. (ed.) (1965), *Primate Behavior: Field Studies of Monkeys and Apes*, New York.

Fisher, H. A. L. (1930), *The Genetical Theory of Natural Selection*, Oxford. (2nd edn revised and enlarged, New York, 1958.)

Fox, R. (ed.) (1975), *Biosocial Anthropology*, New York.

Hallowell, A. I. (1959), 'Behavioral evolution and the emergence of the self', in B. Hegers (ed.), *Evolution and Anthropology: A Centennial Appraisal*, Washington.

Huxley, J. (1942), *Evolution: The Modern Synthesis*, London.

Kardiner, A., Linton, R. and West, J. *et al.* (1945), *The Psychological Frontiers of Society*, New York.

Konner, M. R. (1982), *The Tangled Wing: Biological Constraints on the Human Spirit*, New York.

Kroeber, A. L. (1923), *Anthropology*, New York.

Laughlin, C. D. and d'Aquili, E. G. (1974), *Biogenetic Structuralism*, New York.

Lévi-Strauss, C. (1958), *Anthropologie Structurale*, Paris.

Lévi-Strauss, C. (1973), *Anthropologie Structurale Deux*, Paris.

Linton, R. (1945), *The Cultural Background of Personality*, New York.

Lovejoy, Arthur O. (1936), *The Great Chain of Being*, Cambridge.

Morgan, L. H. (1877), *Ancient Society*, New York.

Murdock, G. P. (1949), *Social Structure*, New York.

Pike, K. L. (1954), *Language in Relation to a Unified Theory of the Structure of Human Behavior*, Glendale.

Rappoport, R. (1968), *Pigs for the Ancestors*, New Haven.

Sahlins, M. (1976), *The Use and Abuse of Biology*, Ann Arbor.

Schneider, D. (1968), *American Kinship: A Cultural Account*, Englewood Cliffs, N.J.

Steward, J. (1955), *Theory of Culture Change*, Urbana, Ill.

Tiger, L. and Fox, R. (1970), *The Imperial Animal*, New York.

Turner, V. (1983), 'Body, brain and culture', *Zygon*, 18.

Tylor, E. B. (1934 [1881]), *Anthropology*, 2 vols, London.

White, L. (1949), *The Science of Culture*, New York.

Wilson, E. O. (1975), *Sociobiology: The New Synthesis*, Cambridge, Mass.

See also: *archaeology; cultural anthropology; ethnology; kinship; linguistics; social anthropology.*

Antitrust Legislation

Capitalist economies rely primarily on free markets to allocate resources efficiently and make suppliers responsive to consumer preferences. If individual businesses or combinations of suppliers (cartels) are able to restrict output and raise prices, resources will be misallocated and consumer choice may be limited. For these reasons, most countries with free market economies have some form of law or regulation aimed at preventing or curbing undue exercise of monopoly power. In framing such legislation the question arises whether to lay down clear rules of law proscribing monopolistic conduct, or whether to provide that the legality of such conduct should depend on some assessment of its economic effects.

Clear rules of law are best exemplified in the antitrust legislation of the United States of America, reflecting the strong American preference for settling issues through the courts rather than by administrative action. Thus the Sherman Act (1890) declares illegal (Section 1) 'every contract, combination . . . or conspiracy in restraint of trade or commerce among the several States or with foreign nations' and makes it a misdemeanour (Section 2) for any person 'to monopolize or attempt to monopolize . . . any part of the trade or commerce. . .'. The Clayton Act (1914) with later amendments makes illegal exclusive dealing, price discrimination and acquisitions where the effect may be 'to substantially lessen competition or tend to create a monopoly', and the Federal Trade Commission Act (1914) prohibits 'unfair methods of competition in commerce'.

The courts interpret these broad provisions according to a 'rule of reason', but this is concerned only to establish that the purpose of the defendants is truly anti-competitive; it does not permit deliberate restrictions of competition to be defended on the ground that they are economically reasonable. In the 1980s, however, under the influence of the Chicago school of economics, an important section of legal opinion holds that enforcement action should be shown to be in the interests of economic efficiency. A notable feature of antitrust enforcement is that private suits may be undertaken and plaintiffs, if successful, can obtain treble damages, that is three times the damage caused to them by the antitrust offence, as well as their costs.

In economies smaller than the United States and more dependent on international trade, it may appear that the domestic market cannot sustain a number of competitors of adequate strength to compete in world markets, and hence that the exercise of monopoly power should not be condemned without careful analysis of its economic effects. In the United Kingdom, for example, under the Restrictive Trade Practices Act (1976) restrictive agreements and cartels are brought before the Restrictive Practices Court, and there is a presumption that they operate against the public interest; but the presumption is rebuttable if certain economic justifications for them can be established. No such presumption operates against monopolies or proposed mergers, but cases may be referred under the Fair Trading Act (1973) to the Monopolies and Mergers Commission which advises on broad economic grounds whether such arrangements operate or may be expected to operate against the public interest. Where it finds this to be so, the government has powers of remedial action.

The legislation in the European Economic Community lies between these poles. Under Article 85 of the Treaty of Rome, all agreements and concerted practices restricting competition within the common market are prohibited as 'incompatible with the common market', and Article 86 prohibits 'any abuse by one or more undertakings of a dominant position within the common market. . .'. At first sight these provisions look similar to the clear rules of law of the Sherman Act and they are enforced by decisions of the European Court. There are, however, significant differences. Article 85(3) provides that agreements may be exempted from the general prohibition where they promote technical or economic progress and do not affect competition unduly. Article 86 operates against the abuse of dominant positions, not as Section 2 of the Sherman Act against acquiring and taking steps to maintain a monopoly position. Moreover, the operation of the Treaty relies heavily on administrative action by the European Commission which has, for example, promulgated significant exemptions from Article 85 for classes of restrictive agreement, and which has the responsibility with relatively meagre resources for selecting and preparing cases to be brought before the Court. For these reasons the impact of the legislation on business in the Community is markedly less than that of antitrust in the United States, and the main emphasis so far has been on preventing types of restrictive practice which have the effect of re-establishing trade barriers between the member countries.

Alan Neale
London

Further Reading

Neale, A. D. and Goyder, D. G. (1980), *The Antitrust Laws of the USA* (3rd edn), Cambridge.

Hawk, B. E. (1979), *United States, Common Market and International Antitrust: A Comparative Guide*, New York.

See also: *business concentration; cartels and trade associations; competition; monopoly; oligopoly.*

Anxiety

The term anxiety is currently used in psychology and psychiatry to refer to at least three related, yet logically different, constructs. Although most commonly used to describe an unpleasant emotional state or condition, anxiety also denotes a complex psychophysiological process that occurs as a reaction to stress. In addition, the concept of anxiety refers to relatively stable individual differences in anxiety proneness as a personality trait.

Anxiety states can be distinguished from other unpleasant emotions such as anger, sorrow or grief, by their unique combination of experiential, physiological and behavioural manifestations. An anxiety state is characterized by subjective feelings of tension, apprehension, nervousness and worry, and by activation (arousal) and discharge of the autonomic nervous system. Such states may vary in intensity and fluctuate over time as a function of the amount of stress that impinges on an individual. Calmness and serenity indicate the absence of anxiety; tension, apprehension and nervousness accompany moderate levels of anxiety; intense feelings of fear, fright and panic are indicative of very high levels of anxiety.

The physiological changes that occur in anxiety states include: increased heart rate (palpitations, tachycardia), sweating, muscular tension, irregularities in breathing (hyperventilation), dilation of the pupils, and dryness of the mouth. There may also be vertigo (dizziness), nausea, and muscular skeletal disturbances such as tremors, tics, feelings of weakness and restlessness. Individuals who experience an anxiety state can generally describe their subjective feelings, and report the intensity and duration of this unpleasant emotional reaction.

Anxiety states are evoked whenever a person perceives or interprets a particular stimulus or situation as potentially dangerous, harmful or threatening. The intensity and duration of an anxiety state will be proportional to the amount of *threat* the situation poses for the individual and the persistence of his interpretation of the situation as personally dangerous. The appraisal of a particular situation as threatening will also be influenced by the person's skills, abilities and past experience.

Anxiety states are similar to fear reactions, which are generally defined as unpleasant emotional reactions to anticipated injury or harm from some external danger. Indeed, Freud regarded fear as synonymous with 'objective anxiety', in which the intensity of the anxiety reaction was proportional to the magnitude of the external danger that evoked it: the greater the external danger, the stronger the perceived threat, the more intense the resulting anxiety reaction. Thus, fear denotes a process that involves an emotional reaction to a perceived danger, whereas the anxiety state refers more narrowly to the quality and the intensity of the emotional reaction itself.

The concept of anxiety-as-process implies a theory of anxiety as a temporally-ordered sequence of events which may be initiated by a stressful external stimulus or by an internal cue that is interpreted as dangerous or threatening. It includes the following fundamental constructs or variables: stressors, perceptions and appraisals of danger or threat, anxiety state and psychological defence mechanisms. Stressors refer to situations or stimuli that are objectively characterized by some degree of physical or psychological danger. Threat denotes an individual's subjective appraisal of a situation as potentially dangerous or harmful. Since appraisals of danger are immediately followed by an anxiety state reaction, anxiety as an emotional state is at the core of the anxiety process.

Stressful situations that are frequently encountered may lead to the development of effective coping responses that quickly eliminate or minimize the danger. However, if a person interprets a situation as dangerous or threatening and is unable to cope with the stressor, he may resort to intraphsychic manoeuvres (psychological defences) to eliminate the resulting anxiety state, or to reduce its level of intensity.

In general, psychological defence mechanisms modify, distort or render unconscious the feelings, thoughts and memories that would otherwise provoke anxiety. To the extent that a defence mechanism is successful, the circumstances that evoke the anxiety will be less threatening, and there will be a corresponding reduction in the intensity of the anxiety reaction. But defence mechanisms are almost always inefficient and often maladaptive because the underlying problems that caused the anxiety remain unchanged.

While everyone experiences anxiety states from time to time, there are substantial differences among people in the frequency and the intensity with which these states occur. Trait anxiety is the term used to describe these individual differences in the tendency to see the world as dangerous or threatening, and in the frequency that anxiety states are experienced over long periods of time. People high in trait anxiety are more vulnerable to stress, and they react to a wider range of situations as dangerous or threatening than low trait anxiety individuals. Consequently, high trait anxious people experience anxiety state reactions more frequently and often with greater intensity than do people who are low in trait anxiety.

To clarify the distinction between anxiety as a personality trait and as a transitory emotional state, consider the statement: 'Mr Smith is anxious.' This statement may be interpreted as meaning either that Smith is anxious *now*, at this very moment, or that Smith is *frequently* anxious. If Smith is 'anxious now', he is experiencing an unpleasant emotional state, which may or may not be characteristic of how he generally feels. If Smith experiences anxiety states more often than others, he may be classified as 'an anxious person', in which case his average level of state anxiety would generally be higher than that of most other people. Even though Smith may be an *anxious person*, whether or not he is *anxious now* will depend on how he interprets his present circumstances.

Two important classes of stressors have been identified that appear to have different implications for the evocation of anxiety states in people who differ in trait anxiety. Persons high in trait anxiety are more vulnerable to being evaluated by others because they lack confidence in themselves and are low in self-esteem. Situations that involve psychological threats (that is, threats to self-esteem, particularly ego-threats when personal adequacy is evaluated), appear to be more threatening for people high in trait anxiety than for low trait anxious individuals. While situations involving physical danger such as imminent surgery generally evoke high levels of state anxiety persons high or low in trait anxiety show comparable increases in anxiety state in such situations.

Individuals very high in trait anxiety, for example, psychoneurotics or patients suffering from depression, experience high levels of state anxiety much of the time. But even they have coping skills and defences against anxiety that occasionally leave them relatively free of it. This is most likely to occur in situations where they are fully occupied with a non-threatening task on which they are doing well, and are thus distracted from the internal stimuli that otherwise constantly cue state anxiety responses.

Charles D. Spielberger
University of South Florida

Further Reading
Freud, S. (1936), *The Problem of Anxiety*, New York.
Lazarus, R. S. (1966), *Psychological Stress and the Coping Process*, New York.
Levitt, E. E. (1980), *The Psychology of Anxiety*, Hillsdale, N.J.
Spielberger, C. D. (1972), 'Anxiety as an emotional state', in C. D. Spielberger (ed.), *Anxiety: Current Trends in Theory and Research*, 2 vols, New York.
Spielberger, C. D. (1979), *Understanding Stress and Anxiety*, London.

See also: *activation and arousal; emotion; stress.*

Aptitude Tests

Aptitude tests are standardized tasks designed to indicate an individual's future job proficiency or success in training. Some tests have been specifically developed for this purpose (for example, name and number comparison tests for selecting clerical workers, whilst others have been borrowed from educational, clinical and research use (for example, Cattell's 16 Personality Factor Questionnaire). Tests may be administered to an individual or to a group. The main types now in use are of intellectual, spatial, mechanical, perceptual and motor abilities, and of interests and personality traits.

Tests must be shown to be job-relevant, the most persuasive evidence usually being the demonstration of a relationship between pre-entry tests scores and later training or job performance ('predictive validity'). For example, Flanagan (1948) showed in one study that none of the very low scorers (grade 1) on a pilot aptitude test battery graduated from pilot training, as against some 30 per cent of average scorers (grade 5) and over 60 per cent of the very high scorers (grade 9). Ghiselli (1973) concluded that aptitude tests are generally better at predicting training success rather than job proficiency, but that for every type of job there is at least one type of test which gives a moderate level of prediction. Combining tests into a battery would tend to improve prediction.

It was generally accepted until recently that a test had to show predictive validity in each specific instance of use, but many psychologists now believe that validity can be generalized given an adequate specification of the test and of the job. Thus, an organization need no longer rely solely on its own research, since evidence from a number of organizations can be collected to serve as a national or international data-base.

The financial benefit to an organization from test use depends on other factors besides validity, notably on how selective it can be when choosing job applicants and the nature of the job (variation in performance in monetary terms). The reductions in costs or increase in profits can be impressive; Schmidt *et al.* (1979) estimated that the selection of computer programmers using a programmer aptitude test could produce productivity gains of some 10 billion dollars per year for the US economy.

The 1970s saw, particularly in the US, increasing criticism of aptitude tests in personnel selection because of alleged unfairness to minority groups. Some of the specific instances raised in the law courts indicated that the necessary validation research had not been carried out; test use was therefore potentially unfair to all applicants and disadvantageous to the organization. There remains much debate on how fairness can best be estimated and how test use should be modified to maximize it.

Most tests have until now been paper-and-pencil, with only a small proportion involving other types of material or apparatus. Future developments are likely to include the production of computerized versions of existing tests and of new tests designed to benefit from computer technology, for example, tests involving the display of dynamic material on the visual display unit.

Alan Jones
Department of Senior Psychologist (Navy)
Ministry of Defence (UK)

References
Flanagan, J. C. (1948), *The Aviation Psychology Program in the Army Air Forces*, Report No. 1, Washington D. C.
Ghiselli, E. E. (1973), 'The validity of aptitude tests in personnel selection', *Personnel Psychology*, 26.
Schmidt, F. L., Hunter, J. E., McKenzie, R. C. and Muldrow, T. W. (1979), 'Impact of valid selection procedures on work-force productivity', *Journal of Applied Psychology*, 64.
See also: *ergonomics*.

Arbitration and Mediation

Both arbitration and mediation refer to third-party intervention in dispute resolution. Although sometimes confused, they are essentially different, in that arbitration involves a third party who is the decision maker, whilst mediating involves that party as a facilitator and adviser but not a decision maker. The arbitrator helps people by deciding for them, and the mediator helps them decide for themselves.

An arbitrator is one kind of adjudicator who, therefore, has the right and the responsibility to hear a case of dispute and to give his decision. He differs from a judge in that his procedures can be quite informal and may be *ad hoc*: even where some formality is observed, many of the binding rules of procedure of a judicial hearing are absent. There are two major possibilities: (1) The disputing parties agree before the hearing to abide by the arbitrator's decision. This may occur, for example, in some industrial arbitration cases. (2) The alternative occurs more frequently where the disputing parties make no such commitment and are therefore able to ignore an unpopular decision. Nevertheless, depending on the context of the dispute, the status of the arbitrator and the degree to which he represents governmental or public opinion, it may be difficult to repudiate his decision. In any case, disputants, who are otherwise locked in frustrating conflict with each other, may welcome almost any decision which breaks the deadlock and the continuing dispute. The arbitrator may be appointed from outside (for example, by a political authority or the leader of the relevant group) or by agreement between the disputants; or he may intrude himself as someone who has legitimate concern for the dispute and the disputants. He is likely to be a person with expertise and prestige (government official, law professor, judge, local politician or an influential neighbour, kinsman or co-member of the common group). The more marked his prestige, the more likely that his decision will be accepted. However, in some cases an outsider or a stranger or unimportant person within the group is deliberately chosen, thus removing the onus of decision making from the group, gaining a more disinterested arbitrator and making repudiation easier should that be found desirable.

Mediation may occur, though not usually inevitably, in the process of negotiation where the disputants are seeking to reach a joint decision in their dispute. A mediator may intervene in situations of deadlock or where self-help and violence occur, in the hope that peaceful talking may resume or begin. Having succeeded in that endeavour, the mediator may retire, he may remain on hand in case further threat of breakdown occurs, or he may continue as active facilitator. In any case, the mediator is not expected, nor has he the legitimate ability, to make the decision. It must be emphasized that, contrary to some idealistic and ethnocentric assumptions, there is no such thing as *the* role of *the* mediator. The range is wide, both of the statuses of mediators (who they are and why they are so acting) and of the roles they play (the strategies they choose or are forced to adopt).

Like an arbitrator, a mediator may be an expert in the matters in dispute (a trained industrial relations expert, a specialist lawyer, a genealogical expert, and so on), or he may be a person of prestige whose influence and good offices are likely to be helpful. Often the mediator is a structural intermediary – the common kinsman or neighbour, co-member of their group, member of an allied group – who has legitimate concern for both the dispute and the disputants to whom he is linked. Despite cultural ideals in some societies, a mediator is not necessarily neutral or disinterested. Gulliver (1979) argued that he is never wholly so. Every mediator brings interests of his own, together with values, norms and ideas, and therefore potential biases, that need not altogether coincide with those of either disputant. Deliberately or not, his own interests and ideas are most likely to affect the help and advice he gives and, thus, the outcome attained. Even where he may be neutral (as, say, an external expert) he cannot wholly set aside his own interests. He may not try; he may not even be aware of his bias. He always has some interest in attaining an outcome through his mediation: such a result feeds his self-esteem, brings him credit and, in some societies, earns him a fee. He can seldom be merely a catalyst, because he creates a triad where formerly there was a dyad. It can occur that a mediator is known to be partial to one of the disputants: sometimes any mediator, anyone who can help towards an outcome when costly deadlock is the alternative, is preferable to no one at all (Gulliver 1979).

A mediator may be invited to participate by the disputants who recognize their need. He may be suggested, even imposed, from the outside by a political authority (such as the Department of Labour, village headman) or by leading members of the group to which the disputants belong (kin group, trade association, church). In that event, there is some notion of the mediator as representative of the wider public. When he begins to intervene, he can adopt many strategies; and he can change his strategy as the process continues. He may, by choice or virtual compulsion, be rather passive, though merely being there can affect the parties' interaction. Beyond that, a mediator may chair the talking sessions, maintaining order and regularity; he may work at clarifying issues, demands and offers, and suggesting appropriate norms and their application; he may, from the first or later, make creative suggestions for outcomes on various matters in dispute or point the way towards outcomes; he may consult with and advise parties in caucus or in joint sessions. At the extreme of mediation, he may press his own evaluations of the situation and his opinions as to effective outcomes. Beyond that point, the mediator may take control such that, in effect, he becomes an arbitrator, dictating the outcome (just as, in reverse, an arbitrator may turn to mediatory advice rather than decision making). The dividing line here is inevitably blurred as one process merges into the other.

P. H. Gulliver
York University
Downsview, Ontario

Reference

Gulliver, P. H. (1979), *Disputes and Negotiations: A Cross-Cultural Perspective*, New York.

Further Reading

Douglas, A. (1962), *Industrial Peacemaking*, New York.
Eckhoff, T. (1967), 'The mediator, the judge and the administrator in conflict resolution', *Acta Sociologica*, 10.
Edmead, F. (1971), *Analysis and Prediction in International Mediation*, New York.
Fisher, R. J. (1972), 'Third party consultation: a method for the study and resolution of conflict', *Journal of Conflict Resolution*, 16.
Fuller, L. (1963), 'Collective bargaining and the arbitrator', *Wisconsin Law Review*, 18.

Fuller, L. (1971), 'Mediation – its forms and functions', *Southern California Law Review*, 44.
Walton, R. E. (1969), *Interpersonal Peacemaking, Confrontation and Third Party Consultation*, Reading, Mass.
Young, O. (1967), *The Intermediaries. Third Parties in Intervention in International Crises*, Princeton, N.J.
See also: *conflict resolution.*

Archaeology

Archaeology often appears to mean different things, from the particular to the general, in different contexts. At one extreme it can refer to the recovery of ancient remains by excavation, 'digging up pots and bones'. But even field archaeology now includes a wide range of activities from survey, the cleaning and recording of industrial machines (industrial archaeology), underwater archaeology to air photography. Excavation itself involves both archaeological concepts such as context, association and assemblage, and external techniques such as methods of probing below the surface soil with magnetometers, pollen analysis to reconstruct past environments and data processing with computers. More generally, archaeology is often used to refer to what archaeologists do, including what is more properly termed prehistory or history. All reconstruction of the past which is based on material remains other than written records might be termed archaeology. Yet within historical archaeology use is often made of written records as part of the interpretive process. The boundary between archaeology and history (including prehistory) is blurred, because the interpretation of layers on a site is closely dependent on accumulated knowledge about what went on at any particular place and time in the past. Since there are few Pompeiis, and archaeological remains are typically fragmentary and ambiguous, the burden on theory is great. Theories and paradigms often change with little contradiction from the data. There is much scope for historical imagination.

Views differ as to the degree of rigour and certainty that can be obtained in reconstructing the past from archaeological remains, at least partly in relation to whether one thinks archaeology is really an historical or an anthropological science. Unfortunately, the two approaches have normally been opposed. Those who claim that the purpose of archaeology is historical emphasize the particularity of past cultures, the unpredictability of human action, and the role of individuals. They state that each past culture has its own value system which it is difficult for archaeologists to reconstruct with any confidence. Prehistory and archaeology are interpretive by nature. For those who claim that 'archaeology is anthropology or it is nothing', and who believe in the cross-cultural method, allied with positivism and with laws of evolution and systematic relationships, rigorous explanation of events in past societies is feasible. The concern with scientific explanation has been particularly strong in America, but the two views of archaeology, as history or science, have a long tradition in the discipline.

The History of Archaeology

Speculation about the human past began in classical antiquity, but investigation of monuments and artefacts dates back to the Renaissance and increased markedly in the eighteenth and nineteenth centuries as part of national interests, pride and identity. This early archaeology had its origin in (1) the study of oriental and classical antiquities such as Pompeii, (2) the recording of European monuments such as Stonehenge and Carnac, and (3) the interest in human origins as an outcome of developments in geology and biology.

The initial concern was to establish a chronological sequence, and in the early nineteenth century in Denmark C. J. Thomsen grouped antiquities into stone, bronze and iron and gave them chronological significance, while J. J. A. Worsaae provided stratigraphical evidence for the sequence. The scheme was argued on ethnographic grounds to relate to a development from savagery to civilization. This idea of Sven Nilsson was, in the second half of the nineteenth century, developed by Sir Edward Tylor and Lewis H. Morgan, and it influenced Marx and Engels. An evolutionary emphasis in archaeology was, in the debates about the origins of man, also closely linked to Charles Darwin.

In this early period of archaeology, an evolutionary approach was closely allied to a cross-cultural emphasis, scientific optimism, and notions of progress from barbarism to industrial societies. Yet in the early twentieth century, and particularly after the First World War, the main concern in archaeology became the building up of local historical sequences, the identification of cultural differences and the description of the diffusion and origin of styles and types. V. Gordon Childe crystallized earlier German and English uses of the term culture and defined it as a recurring association of traits in a limited geographical area. These spatial and temporal units became the building blocks for the definition of local historical sequences and the diffusion of traits. Childe described the prehistory of Europe as at least partly the result of diffusion from the Near East, 'ex Oriente lux'.

But Childe was already responsible for reintroducing an evolutionary emphasis in European archaeology by taking up Morgan's scheme, while in America Julian Steward and Leslie White embraced similar ideas. Rather than describing sites, processes were to be examined. In particular, attention focused on the econ-omic relationships between a site and its environment. The work of Clark in Europe and Willey and Braidwood in America pioneered this new, functional, integrative approach which owed much to developments in anthropology. The discovery of physical dating methods such as radiocarbon (C^{14}) measurement freed the archaeologist from a reliance on typology, types, cultures and associations in establishing chronologies.

A full mixture of evolutionary theory, anthropology, and science in archaeology was attempted in the 'New Archaeology', a development of the 1960s and 1970s, spearheaded by Lewis Binford in America and David Clarke in Britain. Although there were many differences between these and other New Archaeologists, the overall concern was to introduce scientific, rigorous methods of explanation into archaeology. Rather than describing what happened in the past (the perceived view of earlier, historical approaches in archaeology), they tried to explain why events occurred. Ethnography and anthropology provided the theories for the explanation of past events, and a sub-discipline, 'ethnoarchaeology', developed in order to study more closely the relationship between material culture residues and processes in the living world. From such studies they hoped to build laws of cultural process from which particular archaeological occurrences could be deduced. They frequently referred to positivism and Hempel's hypothetico-deductive method.

The Current Scene

Much archaeology today, particularly in America, remains within the grip of ecological functionalism, evolutionary theory and positivism, in the aftermath of the New Archaeology. The enduring concerns have been with process, the application of systems theory, positivism and scientific methods, including the widespread use of computers for the storing and sorting of field data, statistical manipulations, taxonomy and simulation. Cemeteries are examined in order to identify age, sex and status groupings as part of 'social archaeology', and settlement data are searched for organizational clues. Evolutionary theory is referred to in the definition of bands, tribes, chiefdoms and states and in discussions of the transformation of these categories through time. There are both Neo-Darwinian and Neo-Marxist schools.

Yet for many archaeologists, particularly in Europe, archaeology remains an historical discipline. Many field archaeologists, funded by central or local government or by development contractors, find that the academic rhetoric of their university colleagues has little relevance to their problems and interests. The split between theory and application is widening. Similarly, museum curators are aware that popular interest centres on local and regional historical continuity, and on the material achievements of foreign cultures, rather than on cross-cultural laws of social process. In addition, many academic archaeologists cling to the historical tradition in which they had been taught and reject the claims of the New Archaeology.

An emerging feeling in archaeology is that the old battle between historical and scientific-anthropological views of the past is inadequate. The concern is to allow the particularity of historical sequences, and the individuality of culture, while at the same time focusing on social process and cultural change.

Ian Hodder
University of Cambridge

Further Reading
Binford, L. (1972), *An Archaeological Perspective*, New York.
Childe, V. G. (1936), *Man Makes Himself*, London.
Willey, G. and Sabloff, J. (1974), *A History of American Archaeology*, London.
Wheeler, M. (1954), *Archaeology From The Earth*, Harmondsworth.
See also: *anthropology; evolutionism; history.*

Arendt, Hannah (1906–75)

Hannah Arendt was one of the outstanding students of politics of our century, making major contributions both as a political historian and as a political philosopher. Born in Germany in 1906, she attended the universities of Marburg, Freiburg and Heidelberg, where she completed a doctoral thesis on St Augustine under the supervision of Karl Jaspers. After fleeing Germany in the 1930s she worked with Zionist organizations in France, then moved to the United States where she lectured at many universities, principally the University of Chicago and the New School for Social Research in New York. She was the recipient of many distinguished prizes and honours for her contribution to contemporary thought and culture. She died in New York City in 1975.

Arendt first gained prominence as an analyst of the totalitarian form of government, with the publication in 1951 of her monumental three-part study, *The Origins of Totalitarianism*. Her most important philosophical work is *The Human Condition* (1958), in which she argues that there is a 'hierarchy within the *vita activa* itself, where the acting of the statesman occupies the highest position, the making of the craftsman and artist an intermediary, and the labouring which provides the necessities for the functioning of the human organism the lowest'. On the basis of her division of worldly activities into labour, work and action, Arendt affirms that freedom and autonomy can only be fully realized in the context of a politicized existence, and that only by fulfilling the public dimension of life can we give meaning to human affairs. This comprehensive theoretical understanding of politics is further developed in *On Revolution* (1963) and in the essays in *Between Past and Future* (1961; enlarged edition, 1968).

All of Hannah Arendt's works generated intense controversy, from her early writings on Zionism of the 1940s to her essays on the American republic of the 1960s and 1970s. The fiercest of these controversies was provoked by her book *Eichmann in Jerusalem* (1963), in which she argued that the real evil of Eichmann's deeds lay in the bureaucratic shallowness that allowed the monstrous to appear ordinary – Eichmann's mindless banality. This raises the question of whether thoughtlessness is somehow essential to political evil, or whether the active exercise of man's mental abilities actually makes us abstain from evil-doing, and it is to questions such as these that Arendt devoted her last, unfinished work on *The Life of the Mind* (posthumously published in 1978).

Ronald Beiner
University of Southampton

Further Reading
Canovan, M. (1974), *The Political Thought of Hannah Arendt*, New York.
Hill, M. A. (ed.) (1979), *Hannah Arendt: The Recovery of the Public World*, New York.
Kateb, G. (1983), *Hannah Arendt: Politics, Conscience, Evil*, Totowa, N.J.
Young-Bruehl, E. (1982), *Hannah Arendt: For Love of the World*, New Haven.

Aristotle (384–322 B.C.)

Aristotle was born in Stagira, a small Greek town on the coast of the Chalcidice peninsula in the northern Aegean, close to the Macedonian kingdom. His father was court physician to Amyntas III of Macedon. He studied with Plato in Athens from 367 to 348 B.C., then moved to the court of Hermias of Atarneus, in the Troad, another pupil of Plato, one of whose relatives became Aristotle's wife. After a period in Lesbos, Aristotle joined Philip of Macedon's court as tutor to Alexander in 342. After Philip's death in 335 he returned to Athens and stayed there until Alexander's death in 323 when the anti-Macedonian reaction forced him to withdraw to Chalcis, the Euboean city from which his mother had come.

Aristotle was thus exposed both socially and intellectually to contradictory influences. Socially, he belonged to the Greek polis in the last generation of its struggle to retain autonomy – a limited local autonomy in the case of Stagira, the claim of a fading imperial power in the case of Athens – but at the same time he had firsthand experience of living in the new form of society which was to succeed the polis. Intellectually, his father was part of the empiricist tradition of Greek medicine with its emphasis on careful reporting and observation as the only basis for accurate prediction of the likely future course of a disease, while his teacher Plato believed that the visible world was merely an imperfect reflection of a reality which could only be apprehended intellectually, and thought it the right and duty of the philosopher to reason out the correct course for man and society and then – if only he could – impose his prescriptions on his fellow-citizens.

This second source of tension in Aristotle's life, between opposing epistemologies, was much more productive than the first. It led him firmly to assert the intellectual satisfactions, as well as the practical utility, of studying apparently low forms of animal life and engaging in the messy activity of dissection (Lloyd 1968), and to extend the methods of research developed in medicine to the whole field of biology; it also led him to reflect systematically on logic and processes of reasoning, both human and animal. The characteristics which men shared with animals, instead of being seen in a negative way as inescapable defects (mortality) of a 'lower nature' which had to be subdued, became a basis for understanding, a transformation with particularly far-reaching implications for psychology. At the same time the principles of argument which had been being worked out piecemeal in law courts, assembly debates, medical practitioners' disputes and treatises (see Lloyd 1979), mathematical proofs and philosophical dialectic were drawn together in a systematic way which helped to establish methodology or 'second-order thinking, thinking about thinking' (Elkana, 1981) as a problem in its own right. Aristotelian logic eliminated many of the sophistic puzzles that had perplexed earlier philosophers, extended the idea of 'proof' from mathematics to other areas of scientific and philosophical thought, and even, by implication, anticipated modern concern with the relation between logic and language. Aristotle's comprehensive interests and systematic organization of research provided the first foundations for the idea of a university as a place where students are taught how to extend knowledge in all its branches. Discussion and criticism of earlier views was part of the method.

In principle, Aristotle's procedure of taking earlier opinions, particularly those of Plato, and criticizing them on the basis of observation, coupled with his experience of the Macedonian court, might have produced important transformations in political theory. In practice it hardly did so; Aristotle's political and social thought remained enclosed within the frame of the city-state. His view that *chremastiké*, the art of money-making, was morally wrong prevented him from developing an understanding of the growing importance of trade and commodity production in the economy, and in general his empirical attitude tended to lead to a confusion between the statistically normal and the normative. Since domination of males over females, parents over children and masters over slaves was so widespread, it must be right. Belief in the superiority of Greeks over barbarians led Aristotle to assert that some ethnic groups are naturally fit only for slavery, a view which had a long career in the service of racism, though Aristotle himself thought of culturally rather than physically transmitted qualities. The view that the family, observable in animals as well as humans, is the basic form of society had already been put forward by Plato in the *Laws* (earlier Greek thinkers had pictured primitive human society as a herd rather than a family: Cole, 1967). Aristotle took it up and extended it, producing the model of development from family to *gens* and from *gens* to phratry, tribe and city which was to have such an important influence on anthropological kinship theory in the nineteenth and early twentieth centuries. Possibly the growing importance of private life in fourth-century Greece, particularly for those not directly involved in politics, helped to make this view of kinship ties as the basic bonds of society attractive (see Humphreys, 1983a-b).

The fact that Aristotle lived an essentially 'private' life (whatever his relations with the ruling Macedonian élite may have been) is also responsible for his marked interest in the study of friendship; which plays a large part in his *Ethics*. Friends were the philosopher's reference-group, the people who assured him that the philosophical life was indeed the best life; Aristotle's discussion of friendship supplied the basis for the stoic idea of the 'cosmopolitan' community of wise men. At the same time Aristotle's relations with the Macedonians had given him plenty of experience of patronage and friendship between unequals: his acute remarks here were to prove useful to later Hellenistic philosophers grappling with the problems of royal power and patronage.

There is no doubt that Aristotle was a shrewd observer of human behaviour. He firmly rejected the Socratic view that virtue is knowledge, on the grounds that people often know what they should do but fail to do it; what we call virtues are consistent patterns of behaviour, though conscious thought must also enter into them. How the habit of virtuous behaviour is to be inculcated Aristotle does not really tell us. He accepted social conflict as inevitable; rich and poor have opposed interests and the best way to achieve stability in society is to have a large middle class of intermediate wealth who will hold the balance between them. This emphasis of the middle class as the key element in society is part of his more general belief that virtue and right action is a mean between two extremes, an adaptation of the Delphic maxim *méden agan*, 'nothing to excess'.

Medical theory helped Aristotle fit a much more liberal attitude than Plato's towards the arts into this framework. Though care must be exercised in choosing music and stories for children, adults can benefit from having their emotions stirred by music and tragedy because this purges them of excess emotion. In an important book, Jones (1962) has argued that Aristotle's remarks on tragedy have been misunderstood in the European tradition and, when correctly interpreted, can throw light on the difference between Greek conceptions of the person and of action and those of the modern Western world.

In a sense Aristotle seems to be a consolidator rather than an innovator, a systematizer and synthesizer of ideas originally raised by others. Nevertheless, the new fields of research he opened up, his contributions to methodology and scientific terminology, and the intelligence of his criticisms of earlier views and proposed solutions to philosophical problems make him a founding figure in many branches of research. The works which survive were written for teaching purposes rather than for the general public: their inelegant, rather jerky style gives an attractive impression of an unpretentious thinker who faced difficulties and objections to his own views honestly.

S. C. Humphreys
University of Michigan

References
Cole, T. (1967), *Democritus and the Sources of Greek Anthropology*, Cleveland.
Elkana, Y. (1981), 'A programmatic attempt at an anthropology of knowledge', in E. Mendelssohn and Y. Elkana (eds), *Sciences and Cultures*, 5.
Humphreys, S. C. (1983a), 'The family in classical Athens', in S. C. Humphreys, *The Family, Women and Death*, London.
Humphreys, S. C. (1983b), 'Fustel de Coulanges and the Greek "genos" ', *Sociologia del diritto*, 9.
Jones, H. J. (1962), *Aristotle and Greek Tragedy*, London.
Lloyd, G. E. R. (1968), *Aristotle: The Growth and Structure of his Thought*, Cambridge.
Lloyd, G. E. R. (1979), *Magic, Science and Religion*, Cambridge.

Further Reading
Guthrie, W. K. C. (1981), *History of Greek Philosophy*, VI. *Aristotle: An Encounter*, Cambridge.
Wood, E. and Wood, N. (1978), *Class Ideology and Ancient Political Theory. Socrates, Plato and Aristotle in Social Context*, Oxford.
See also: *Plato*.

Aron, Raymond (1905–83).

Raymond Aron was unquestionably the dominant figure in French sociology since World War I. He was born in Paris in 1905 and from 1955 to 1968 was professor of sociology at the Sorbonne. Most contemporary French sociologists were in one way or another his students; his numerous studies have been widely read, and his frequent articles in the press have influenced politicians as well as a broader public. He was a sociological theorist, and an analyst of industrial society, and he re-evaluated the role of politics in society.

In his thesis *Introduction à la philosophie de l'histoire* (1939) (An Introduction to the Philosophy of History) Aron demonstrated the way in which the objective knowledge of history depended on values, and he rejected the pretensions of Christian and Hegelian theories. He introduced to France the German sociology of Dilthey, Tönnies, Simmel and, above all, Weber (*La Sociologie allemande contemporaine* (1936)) (Contemporary German Sociology) which he had studied at source, and he disseminated this relativistic way of thinking in a domestic context often susceptible to deterministic approaches. In *Les Etapes de la pensée sociologique* (1965) (*Main Currents in Sociological Theory*, 1968), Aron argued for the views of a Tocqueville or a Weber in preference to those of a Marx or a Durkheim. Tocqueville had re-evaluated the role of politics in social change, while Weber had based the sociology of action in the recognition of the multiple values of individuals. Aron took issue with the tenets of Marxism, which plays an important role in France, advocating instead a relativistic position and suggesting that the end of the age of ideologies was approaching.

Aron attempted to analyse the novel features of industrial society, the degree of pluralism, the multiplicity of values, the role of social mobility, anticipating studies which were to be developed on the other side of the Atlantic, such as those of Daniel Bell. However, he rejected the view that there would inevitably be a convergence between the societies of the US and the USSR, which some regarded as identical industrial societies, showing that the point at which the political structure intervenes, as an independent variable, has specific effects (*Dix huit leçons sur la société industrielle* (1963); *18 Lectures on Industrial Society*, 1967); *La Lutte de classes* (1964) (The Class Struggle).

Aron published a great deal on Pareto and on the theory of élites, suggesting a more limited definition of the élite which permitted the differentiation of those situations in which there was an element of pluralism with competing élites, as in France and the US, from those in which a ruling class was formed by the fusion of élites, as in Soviet society. Here again he adopted a comparative approach and insisted, like Weber and Schumpeter, on the specificity of the political élites. He also drew attention to contemporary empirical studies, such as Robert Dahl's, which analysed plural élites.

Given his rediscovery of the weight of the political

factor, Aron was logically drawn to the study of international relations, where the political factor was most evident. In *Paix et guerre entre les nations* (1967), (*Peace and War*, 1967), and then in *Penser la guerre, Clausewitz* (1976), (*Clausewitz, Philosopher of War*, 1983), he analysed power politics as a demonstration of the specificity of politics and, in consequence, of the multiple values of the actors themselves.

Pierre Birnbaum
University of Paris

Further Reading
Many books by Aron have appeared in English translation. These include:

(1957) *The Opium of the Intellectuals*
(1968) *Democracy and Totalitarianism*
(1968) *Progress and Disillusion: The Dialectics of Modern Society*
(1969) *The Elusive Revolution: Anatomy of a Student Revolt*

Dahrendorf, R. (1980), 'The achievements of Raymond Aron', *Encounter*.

Arrow, Kenneth (1921–)

Born in 1921 in New York City, Arrow received his education at the City College of New York and Columbia University. In 1947 he went to the Cowles Commission at Chicago as a research associate, and later served as an assistant professor. He was on the faculty at Stanford University from 1949 to 1968, at Harvard University from 1968 to 1979, and is currently Joan Kenney professor of economics and professor of operations research at Stanford. In 1972, he shared the Nobel Prize for economics with John Hicks.

Arrow has been a major innovator in many areas of economic theory. His Ph.D. thesis (published in 1951 as *Social Choice and Individual Values*) was the seminal work in social choice theory. It showed the general impossibility of designing rules for social decision making that are suitably sensitive to the preferences of the members of society and capable of achieving efficient outcomes. Subsequently, he wrote many papers on moral philosophy and applications of social choice theory to welfare economics.

His second major line of work is in the area of general equilibrium theory. Together with Gerard Debreu (who received a Nobel prize for economics in 1983), he demonstrated the precise circumstances in which a market-clearing price system could be proven to exist. The optimality of this system was also analysed. In the context of this theory, in which the simultaneous and initial interaction among economic agents occurs, Arrow studied the stability of price adjustment processes, the ability of markets to mitigate risks, the departures from optimality when the classical conditions are violated, and the appropriate social policy when these problems arise.

His work has also touched on some applied problems: medical insurance, investment, growth, index numbers and many others. In addition, he has written extensively on the economics of information and uncertainty and has formed some of the central ideas of the subject: measures of risk aversion, the effects of moral hazard, adverse selection and privacy of information on resource allocation in markets and organizations.

Jerry Green
Harvard University

Further Reading
Arrow, K. (1965), *Aspects of the Theory of Risk-Bearing*, New York.
Arrow, K. (1971), *Essays in the Theory of Risk-Bearing*, New York.

Art, Anthropology of

Art in one sense refers to visual representation, as opposed to dance or poetry. In another sense, it refers to principles of harmonious composition and the ordered juxtaposition of images in any medium used to reveal design behind the disorder of sensory experience. Art may be achieved through both the formal qualities of the work, and the ideas represented. While science uses abstract generalizations and mathematical formulae, art uses concrete forms and particular images.

A *style* is identified by the recurrent use of particular formal elements and by the recurrent combination of such elements into characteristic compositions. Styles can be identified in both decorative and representational art. Aesthetic values are often expressed in symmetrical composition or rhythmic repetition. Representational styles reduce the complexity and variety of forms in the real world to a more limited range of motifs and structures. This is most obviously the case in art executed on two-dimensional surfaces. To 'read' such work often requires knowledge of cultural convention; this problem is exemplified by split representation on the northwest coast of North America (Vastokas, 1978). The reduction of complex to simple forms is another means of revealing order in the world of experience. In 'primitive' or tribal art this aim is often more important than attempting to depict appearances as they really seem. Swinton (1978) illustrates this in Inuit (Eskimo) sculpture: the aim of the carver is to be as 'real' as possible, yet this is achieved not by slavishly reproducing the actual proportions of the animal or human figures modelled. Forms are simplified, textures roughened or smoothed, volumes exaggerated, tensions increased. Although it is true to say that in representational art there is always a similarity between the art form and the objects depicted, these similarities are dictated by cultural tradition and are not always apparent to members of other cultures. The art of the Warlpiri of central Australia, based on geometric shapes and footprints, depicts the marks left by people and animals on the ground: an arc often represents a person sitting cross-legged; a circle a camp fire, or holes made by probing in the ground for a lizard's lair.

While representational art often depicts objects of everyday experience, it may also portray legendary and visionary creatures and spirits. Among the Inuit of southern Alaska, for instance, shamans wore masks which represented faces with the distorted features of spirits encountered in trance. Even a carved or painted representation of an everyday object signifies not the object, but the mental construct, the *idea* of that object held by the artist and other members of his culture. The objects depicted in representational art often have many levels of significance within the culture that produces it. Munn (1964) showed how the Warlpiri use simple geometric motifs to express metaphorical equations in their religious philosophy. In following the ancestral law, Warlpiri think of themselves as 'tracking' the ancestors by following their marks, an image literally conveyed by the mode of representation in their art. The simple motifs can also be read in many ways: the Rainbow Snake created water courses, and the wavy line representing a snake may simultaneously represent the creek bed and the mark he left behind him on his journey. At a more basic level, Munn suggests, all Warlpiri motifs can be reduced to variants on circles and lines, representing male and female principles. The 'female' circle, potentially depicting a breast, waterhole, fire, or ancestral camp infused with the ancestor's power, is a basic Warlpiri image of procreation.

It may be tempting to treat such recurrent images as the real meaning of all art traditions. But this is unsatisfactory for two reasons: to suppose that the complex equations of, say, Warlpiri thought are achieved naturally and inevitably does not do justice to the creativity of Warlpiri culture, while to demonstrate that human experience recurrently suggests the appropriateness of certain symbolic equations and visual images does not prove that they are universal. Biebuyck (1969) refers to female figures carved by the Lega of central Africa. Often interpreted as fertility images, they are in fact a reminder of the dangers of committing adultery while pregnant. If art can tell us anything about the universal features of cultural thought, it is more likely to do so at the level of structure: revealing the processes through which meanings are attributed to visible motifs, how parallels are established between levels of thought, and how such understandings are communicated.

Like living species, human cultures have an inherent capacity to develop and change. Art, like language,

provides useful evidence for the nature of human creativity. It can be argued that, like a language, any visual tradition contains a set of units of meaning and rules for combining these into diverse and original compositions or statements. But representational motifs are not like the sounds of language because they are motivated by the appearance of the depicted objects; and redundancy, a useful concept in communication theory, may not be appropriate to the study of art where repetition and inversion satisfy aesthetic impulses.

One of the most vivid demonstrations of human creativity has been the development of new art forms among previously self-contained subsistence cultures, as they have entered national and international markets. Morphy (Morphy and Layton, 1981) showed how Aboriginal clans from northern Australia responded in various ways to the dilemma of marketing ceremonial art. The most successful solutions were to eliminate sacred, geometric forms in favour of animal or plant motifs, or to represent only minor legends. Kimber (1981) showed how at Papunya, in central Australia, the opposite solution was achieved. By increasing the frequency of geometric motifs and painting in a pointillist technique, formal and aesthetically pleasing designs could be sold which concealed any reference to secret legend and ritual.

R. Layton
University of Durham

References

Biebuyck, D. (1969), 'Introduction', in D. Biebuyck (ed.), *Tradition and Creativity in Tribal Art*, Berkeley and Los Angeles.

Kimber, R. (1981), 'Central Australian and western desert art: some impressions', in A. Crocker (ed.), *Mr. Sandman Bring me a Dream*, Alice Springs.

Morphy, H. and Layton, R. (1981), 'Choosing among alternatives: cultural transformations and social change in Aboriginal Australia and French Jura', *Mankind*, 13.

Munn, N. (1964), 'Totemic designs and group continuity in Warlpiri cosmology', in M. Reay (ed.), *Aborigines Now*, Melbourne.

Swinton, G. (1978), 'Touch and the real: contemporary Inuit aesthetics', in M. Greenhalgh and V. Megaw (eds), *Art in Society: Studies in Style, Culture and Aesthetics*, London.

Vastokas, J. M. (1978), 'Cognitive aspects of Northwest Coast art', *Art in Society*, London.

Further Reading

Layton, R. (1981), *The Anthropology of Art*, St Albans.

Ucko, P. J. (ed.) (1977), *Form in Indigenous Art*, Canberra.

See also: *aesthetics*; *art, sociology of*; *semiotics*.

Artificial Intelligence

Workers in artificial intelligence (AI) try to write programs enabling computers to carry out complex information-processing tasks requiring flexibility and context-sensitivity.

Examples of such tasks include: noticing a creature moving in the shadows, attending to it, and recognizing it as a robin (and, sometimes, mistaking it for a chaffinch); understanding speech, even in noisy conditions; having a conversation about people's plans and motives, and interpreting their behaviour in terms of specific purposes; understanding a piece of written text well enough to be able to answer questions about it, or to translate it sensibly into a foreign language; seeing an analogy, and using it to help solve a problem; making a medical diagnosis, and prescribing medicine appropriately; playing chess, backgammon, or poker – and learning to play better; picking up a delicate object and packing it into a box; assembling a structure out of Meccano parts, where the diagrammed instructions have been lost.

Each of these can already be achieved by AI-systems – but only to a limited extent. Intelligence normally requires considerable knowledge, and the ability to locate the relevant items quickly. It is very difficult to make knowledge fully explicit, and to formulate principles of inference that will use it sensibly. Existing AI-systems are restricted to a narrow domain. A program that can see cannot hear, and one that can read cannot play chess; a program that can play chess cannot play draughts, or understand English (except possibly descriptions of chess-moves); and one that can summarize news stories about earthquakes cannot understand letters about the first cuckoo of spring. The robot which can see, hear, touch, speak, plan, move and manipulate *in a wide variety of contexts* is still only science fiction.

AI-workers differ in their aims. Some hope to develop a general theory of intelligence, applicable to Martians, men and machines. Others are primarily interested in human intelligence: they try to write programs that process information in ways like those used by the human mind. Still others see AI as technology: they want computer systems that will be useful to the public (the military, the medic, the man-in-the-street), not caring whether their programs solve problems in the way that we do.

AI has had a short history, but already promises to change everyday life as much as the Industrial Revolution did. It grew out of the work on digital computers in World War II (with anticipations by Turing in the 1930s and Babbage in the nineteenth century). It received its name in 1956 (though many AI-workers prefer to use the blander 'knowledge-engineering'). Through the 1960s and 1970s, interest in AI gradually increased, but even in 1980 most educated people had not heard of it. The media suddenly became aware of it when, in the early 1980s, the Japanese announced their 'Fifth Generation Computer' project. This was an ambitious ten-year national plan, lavishly funded by government and industry. It aimed to develop large parallel-processing machines, and intelligent software, enabling computers of the 1990s to understand Japanese and other natural languages, to interpret the speech of many different individuals, to act as intelligent assistants in a wide variety of tasks, and to provide advanced problem-solving and sensori-motor abilities for mobile domestic and industrial robots.

It remains to be seen whether the plan will succeed. Most people grossly underestimate the difficulties involved: one of the prime lessons of AI is the previously unrecognized richness and subtlety of 'common sense'.

Specialist expertise is a different matter: 'expert systems' are already on the market. They offer consultant advice on technical matters like medical diagnosis, tax laws, oil prospecting and genetic engineering. They are rule-based programs, incorporating the theoretical knowledge and 'rules of thumb' of the experienced person. They can offer explanations of their advice to the user (who may decide to reject it), and can be incrementally improved by accepting new information (for example, that a certain drug should not be prescribed for specific types of patient). A few of these programs already give more reliable advice than all but the very best human experts (and one or two outperform us all).

But 'expert systems' are not infallible, any more than human specialists are. In general, AI programs are not foolproof systems guaranteed to reach the right answer, nor is their reasoning 'objective' in an absolute sense. *Any* finite intelligent system living in a complex and changing world would be liable to mistakes, for intelligence is a matter of making sensible decisions *without* having all the evidence. One can do this only on the basis of one's expectations, or previous knowledge – which will sometimes prove inadequate. Moreover, programs designed to answer similar questions will give different answers if they use different models, or representations, of the world (and of ways of reasoning about the world). These representations – like those inside human heads – can be more or less veridical, more or less sensible. They are subjective and questionable rather than objective and infallible. In principle, the conclusions of a computer program are open to challenge just as a person's are.

It is often remarked that 'a program can do only what the programmer tells it to do'. Certainly, everything the program does is done because of some instruction – either written by the programmer or generated by other instructions written by the programmer. But the chains of inference made by a program can be so complex that a human cannot follow them, and many programs can accept unforeseen information (from teletype, camera or microphone). Consequently, computers can surprise us. A complex program cannot be guaranteed to do *all* and *only* what the programmer had in mind when writing it. This is true even if there are no mistakes in the program.

This points a warning about the social impact of AI. Already there are large programs whose behaviour no one person fully understands. Quite apart from clear misuse (such as 'Big Brother' applications), there is a danger that human responsibility for decisions might be insidiously undermined. And some social effects of changes in employment patterns may be highly unfortunate, at least in the transitional phase.

But AI has a rehumanizing potential also. It could provide many useful tools, and do many boring, dirty or dangerous jobs. It could free our time for interacting with other people (family, friends and the clients of 'service industries'). It could lead to a greater valuation of emotional life, in contrast to the unemotionality of (most) programs. And it could even encourage an 'image of man' that is humanist rather than mechanist: already, it has confirmed the irrelevance of IQ-tests to the understanding of intelligence, and made *mind* respectable again after the arid years of behaviourism.

Margaret A. Boden
University of Sussex

Further Reading
Waltz, D. L. (1982), 'Artificial Intelligence', *Scientific American*, vol. 247.
Boden, M. A. (1977), *Artificial Intelligence and Natural Man*, New York.
Feigenbaum, E. A. and McCorduck, P. (1983), *The Fifth Generation*, Reading, Mass.
Feigenbaum, E. A. and Barr, A. (eds) (1981 and 1982), *The Artificial Intelligence Handbook*, 3 vols, London.
See also: *cognitive science; intelligence and intelligence testing; mind.*

Art, Sociology of

The term 'sociology of art' usually serves as a convenient, if confusing, shorthand for 'sociology of the arts' or, sometimes, 'sociology of art and literature'. In fact, the sociology of the visual arts is probably far less developed than the sociology of literature, drama or even film. The generic nature of the subject-matter of this subdiscipline does unavoidably create difficulties for analysis, since it is not always possible to draw exact parallels between, say, music and the novel, in their social or political contexts.

The sociology of art is an extremely diverse body of work. There is no single, or even dominant, model of analysis or theory of the relationship between the arts

and society. In Britain and in some other European countries, Marxist and neo-Marxist approaches have been particularly influential in the past ten or fifteen years, though there are plenty of studies and contributions by non-Marxist scholars too; in the United States, Marxism is rarely the foundation for a sociology of the arts. It is useful to begin to survey work in this area by starting from these two very different traditions.

The American sociology of art is often referred to as the 'production-of-culture' approach. It is very much in the mainstream of sociological analysis, and focuses on the study of the institutions and organizations of cultural production – (see Coser, 1978; Peterson, 1976; Becker 1982; Kamerman and Martorella, 1983). The interest is on the social relations in which art is produced. Sociologists have looked at the role of 'gatekeepers' (publishers, critics, gallery-owners) in mediating between artist and public; at the social relations and decision-making processes in a college of art, or an opera company; or at the relation between particular cultural products (for example, photographs) and the social organizations in which they are produced (Bystryn, 1978; Adler, 1979; Rosenblum, 1978). The emphasis is often, though by no means exclusively, on the performing arts, where the complexity of social relations merits analysis; in Britain, the performing arts take second place to literature as a central focus for sociologists.

The Marxist tradition. A criticism sometimes levelled at the so-called 'production-of-culture' approach is that it often ignores the cultural product itself, taking it simply as a given object, and paying no attention to its content, symbolic nature, or conventions of representation. Work in the Marxist tradition, on the other hand, has increasingly come to recognize the importance of looking critically and analytically at the novel, or painting, or film, as well as at its conditions of production. Marxist aesthetics has moved away from the simple and misleading metaphor of 'base-and-superstructure', with its constant risk of an economic reductionist account of culture, and of conceiving of literature and art as merely 'reflections' of class or economic factors. Here the earlier work of continental European authors (Gramsci, Adorno, Althusser, Goldmann) has been crucial in refining the model, stressing the mediating levels of social group, individual (authorial) consciousness and experience, and more recently, of textual specificity. In this last case, there has been a fruitful incorporation of structuralist, semiotic, and psychoanalytic insights into a more sociological perspective, which has facilitated an attention to such things as narrative, visual imagery, cinematic techniques and conventions, and televisual codes. Thus, as well as demonstrating that, for example, a television news programme is produced in the particular context of capitalist social relations, governmental or commercial financing, and professional and political ideologies, it is also possible to look at the 'text' itself (the programme, in this case), and to analyse the ways in which meanings (aesthetic, political, ideological) are constituted in a variety of ways – through visual and aural codes, narrative commentary, camera angles and so on.

The strengths of the sociology of art to date, particularly in the United States and in Britain, have been, first, the development of a methodology for the study of the institutions and practices of cultural production and, second, the analysis of culture as part of a wider social and historical framework. The sociology of cultural production and the sociology of the text, as complementary analyses, provide a valuable corrective to the more traditional, uncritical approaches to the arts dominant in art history, literary criticism, and aesthetics. (It is worth noting, however, that a major contribution to the development of the sociology of art, at least in Britain, has come from people working in those disciplines. Concerned to expose the ideological nature of their subject-matter as well as of their disciplines, they have argued that the 'great tradition' and the 'literary canon' are much better perceived as social and historical products, constituted in particular institutions and through specific values, than as presenting any 'natural' or 'transcendent' values (Eagleton, 1976; Widdowson, 1982).

Another area of great importance to the sociology of art is the study of reception – of audiences and their responses. This aspect of culture has so far been neglected, although developments in literary criticism in the United States, in East and West Germany and in Scandinavia (hermeneutics, reception-aesthetics, psychoanalytic approaches) provide the possibility of an approach to the constitution of meaning in the reader/viewer. It is now realized by several sociologists that the critical study of texts needs to be supplemented by a sociology of readers and audiences, their nature, constitution, and modes of reception (Eco, 1980).

The sociological approach to the arts has been able to demonstrate the contingent, and class-related, development and separation of 'high art' from 'popular culture', and thus to render more problematic the élitist conceptions of art which obtain among those involved in support and funding for the arts, as well as in society in general (including, incidentally, among many of its sociologists). The notion of 'cultural capital' (Bourdieu, 1980), suggesting the use made by dominant social groups of specific forms of culture as a way of securing their identity by the exclusion of other groups, is a useful way of demonstrating the historical and continuing production of boundaries and aesthetic judgements in culture.

Recognition of the interdisciplinary character of the sociology of art must also include mention of work by feminist critics and historians, who have noted and challenged the exclusion of women from both the production of art and the history of art (Parker and Pollock, 1981; Pollock, 1982; Moers, 1977). The answer to the question 'why have there been no great women artists?' (Nochlin, 1973) is certainly a sociological or social-historical one, and feminist analysis enables us to comprehend the one-sided nature of the production of culture, in terms of gender, and also the dominance of patriarchal ideology in artistic representation. The way in which women (and men) are represented in art and literature is both a product of their actual position in society and the ideologies which maintain this, and also a contributing factor *to* those ideologies. For culture is not simply a reflection of social structures: it is also the producer of meanings and the determinant and support of ideologies. In this sense, the metaphor of base and superstructure is clearly reversible, since art and culture can also sustain, and in some cases subvert, the existing order.

Janet Wolff
University of Leeds

References

Adler, J. (1979), *Artists in Offices: An Ethnography of an Academic Art Scene*, New Jersey.
Becker, H. (1982), *Art Worlds*, Berkeley and Los Angeles.
Bourdieu, P. (1980), 'The aristocracy of culture', *Media, Culture and Society*, 2.
Bystryn, M. (1978), 'Art galleries as gatekeepers: the case of the Abstract Expressionists', in L. A. Coser (ed.), *The Production of Culture, Social Research*, 45.
Coser, L. A. (ed.) (1978), *The Production of Culture, Social Research*, 45.
Eagleton, T. (1976), *Criticism and Ideology*, London.
Eco, U. (1980), 'Towards a semiotic enquiry into the television message', in J. Corner and J. Hawthorn (eds), *Communication Studies*, London.
Kamerman, J. B. and Martorella, R. (eds) (1983), *Performers and Performances*, New York.
Moers, E. (1977), *Literary Women*, New York.
Nochlin, L. (1973), 'Why have there been no great women artists?' in T. B. Hess and E. C. Baker (eds), *Art and Sexual Politics*, New York.
Parker, R. and Pollock, G. (1981), *Old Mistresses: Women, Art and Ideology*, London.
Peterson, R. A. (ed.) (1976), *The Production of Culture*, Beverley Hills.
Pollock, G. (1982), 'Vision, voice and power: feminist art history and Marxism', *Block*, 6.
Rosenblum, B. (1978), *Photographers at Work: A Sociology of Photographic Styles*, New York.
Widdowson, P. (ed.) (1982), *Re-reading English*, London.

Further Reading
Wolff, J. (1982), *The Social Production of Art*, London.
See also: *aesthetics*; *art, anthropology of*; *hermeneutics*;
  semiotics.

Asiatic Mode of Production

The Asiatic Mode of Production refers to a much debated concept in Marxist social science. In the writings of Marx and Engels, discussions of 'Asiatic forms' appear on numerous occasions although almost never in combination with the term 'mode of production', a concept which was not systematized until after Marx's death. Moreover, they employ the term in reference to two quite different phenomena. In the newspaper articles and correspondence on India, the concept would appear to extend and elaborate a more economic version of older eighteenth and nineteenth century ideas of 'Oriental Despotism', referring here to the great Asiatic empires with their complex political organization. In the justly famous section of the *Grundrisse der Kritik der politischen Ökonomie* (1857–8), called *Pre-Capitalist Economic Formations* (1964), the concept is used to characterize the most primitive form of state society where a collection of self-sufficient agricultural communities are ruled by a higher instance, the theocratic representative of the higher unity of collectivity – sacralized nature, deity or ancestor – of primitive society. Similarly, economic exploitation is a simple extension of a potential already present in primitive society: 'Surplus labour belongs to the higher community, which ultimately appears as a person' (Marx, 1964).

The Oriental Despotic version of the Asiatic Mode concept is that which dominated the intellectual development of the latter nineteenth and early twentieth centuries. The Asiatic empires were conceived of as historically stagnant societies dominated by a state class that controlled the totality of the land and organized supra-local irrigation works, but whose economic base consisted of self-sufficient village communities whose contact with one another was minimal and who supported the state-class by means of the taxation of their surplus product. With the emergence of a formalized historical materialism in the work of Engels and the Second International (Kautsky, Plekhanov), the concept became increasingly linked to a techno-ecological kind of explanation. This tendency reached its climax in the subsequent work of Wittfogel and which emerged finally in the hydraulic hypothesis, which posits a causal relation between the ecologically determined necessity of large-scale irrigation and the emergence of the despotic-bureaucratic state machine (Wittfogel, 1957). The Asiatic Mode was not a particularly welcome concept among the higher echelons of post-revolutionary Soviet society for obvious reasons, and both Wittfogel and the Asiatic Mode of Production were purged from the Third International, whose project for a Chinese revolution was incompatible with the suggestion that Asia was fundamentally different from the West, that it possessed a stagnant mode of production, or that a bureaucracy could in any way constitute a ruling class.

While the work of Wittfogel significantly influenced American neo-evolutionism (Steward, 1955), theoretical discussion of the Asiatic Mode of Production was not again revived until the late 1950s and 1960s, after the Twentieth Congress of the Communist Party officially announced the reopening of Marxist debate. Discussions began first in Eastern Europe and then spread to Paris, where they have played a central role in the development of structural Marxist theory in general, and anthropology in particular (Godelier, 1969; Althusser *et al.*, 1965). The new discussion has been based primarily on Marx's *Pre-Capitalist Economic Formations* and has focused on the problem of early state formation in general, the relation between 'primitive' communal forms and class formation, the symbolism of state power and theocracy, and the specifics of 'Asiatic' social forms in evolutionary as well as concrete historical frames of reference (Krader, 1975; Hindness, and Hirst, 1975; Friedman, 1979).

Jonathan Friedman
University of Copenhagen

References
Althusser, *et al.* (1969 [1965]), *Reading Capital*,
  London. (Original French edn, *Lire le capital*,
  Paris.)
Friedman, J. (1979), *System, Structure and Contradiction
  in the Evolution of 'Asiatic' Social Forms*, Copenhagen.
Godelier, M. (1969), 'La Notion de "mode de
  production asiatique" et les schémas marxistes
  d'évolution des sociétés', in R. Garaudy (ed.), *Sur
  le mode de production asiatique*, Paris.
Hindess, B. and Hirst, P. (1975), *Pre-Capitalist Modes
  of Production*, London.
Krader, L. (1975), *The Asiatic Mode of Production*,
  Assen, Netherlands.
Marx, K. (1964), *Pre-Capitalist Economic Formations*, ed
  E. Hobsbawn, London.
Marx, K. and Engels, F. (1955), *Selected Correspondence*,
  Moscow.
Marx, K. and Engels, F. (1970[1845–6]), *The German
  Ideology*, London. (Original German edn, *Die
  Deutsche Ideologie*.)
Steward, J. (1955), 'Introduction' and 'Some
  implications of the symposium', in *Irrigation
  Civilizations*, Washington, D.C.
Wittfogel, K. (1957), *Oriental Despotism*, New Haven.
See also: *Marx's theory of history and society; state, origin
  of.*

Associationism

The concept of the association of ideas is as old as Aristotle, but its use as the basic framework for a complete account of mental life is essentially British, beginning with John Locke and ending with Alexander Bain. There were some near contemporary continental associationists and some Scottish philosophers who made considerable but subsidiary use of the concept. They were not as thoroughgoing, or perhaps as single-minded, as the group recognized as British Empiricists.

Locke, Berkeley and Hume used associationism to provide support for the empiricist epistemology they were developing in opposition to Descartes's basically rationalist view. They maintained that knowledge and belief derived from, and could only be justified by, reference to sensory experience, as distinct from the innate ideas and necessary truths argued for by Descartes. They also held that such sense-based experience could be divided into elementary units such as sensations (experiences brought about by the impact of external objects on the senses), images (re-evoked or remembered sensations) and feelings (affective values attached to sensations and images). This resort to atomistic elements was probably made in the belief that such experiences were incorrigible and hence beyond dispute; what I experience on one occasion is not corrected by what I experience on comparable occasions, even though the series may build up a web of experience. This web or set of patterned knowledge is built up as the separate ideas become associated or linked in synchronous groups or chronological chains.

British associationism reached its peak as a psychological system when a series of thinkers, David Hartley, James Mill, John Stuart Mill and Bain, concentrated on erecting a free-standing theory of mental life and not just a psychological foundation for an epistemology.

It is important to note the growing positivist sensationism of the three early philosophers. Locke had assumed a mind or self on which external objects made an impact through the senses; Berkeley accepted the mind or self but denied that we could have any direct knowledge of external objects (all we could directly know were our 'ideas'); Hume went further and claimed that the so-called mind or self was no more than the passage of our 'ideas'.

Hartley, a physician rather than a philosopher, tried to give sensations, images, feelings and their associations a neurophysiological basis. He suggested that the impact of external objects on the senses set up vibrations in the sensory nervous apparatus and that these were experienced as sensations. Images were the result of later minor vibrations, which he called 'vibratiuncles', induced by associated sensations or images. James Mill, an historian and political theorist, abandoned Hartley's premature and rather fantastic neurophysiology but developed the psychological thinking

on more systematic and positivistic lines. His treatment was strictly atomistic and mechanical. John Stuart Mill and Alexander Bain softened these tendencies, arguing for 'mental compounds' in the chemical sense as well as for 'mental mixtures' in which the totality was no more than the sum of the associated elements.

There was much disagreement over the 'laws' or conditions of the association of 'ideas'. It was universally accepted that frequency and contiguity (two or more 'ideas' often occurring together or in close succession) constituted a basic condition, for example 'table' and 'chair' are said to be associated because these two 'ideas' are frequently experienced in conjunction. (Some modern learning theories would call this assumption into question.) In addition to this basic law, some associationists added one or more qualitative laws, such as the 'law of similarity' governing the association of 'dark' and 'black', the 'law of contrast' 'dark' and 'light', and the 'law of cause and effect', 'boiling' with sustained 'heat'. Bain added a 'law of effect' which claimed that an experience followed by another became associated if the latter satisfied a need related to the former; this was given a prominent place in later S-R learning theory.

Though claiming to be based on observation or sensory experience, British associationism was based largely on common sense and anecdotal evidence. Later, von Helmholtz, Wundt, Ebbinghaus, Kulpe, G. E. Muller and others developed experimental methods to provide a sounder empirical basis for somewhat revised associationist theorizing.

W. M. O'Neil
University of Sydney

Further Reading
Peters, R. S. (ed.) (1953), *Brett's History of Psychology*, London.
See also: *Hume; Locke; Mill.*

Attachment

Attachment refers to the tie between two or more individuals; it is a psychological relationship which is discriminating and specific and which bonds one to the other in space and over enduring periods of time. Researchers and clinicians have been particularly concerned with two types of attachment: parental attachment (which sadly, in the literature, usually means *maternal*) and infantile attachment.

It is widely agreed that the infants of many vertebrate species become psychologically attached to their parents; human babies first acquire an attachment to their mothers and (usually a little later) significant others during the second half of their first year of life.

Proximity seeking (for example, following) is commonly interpreted as an index of infant-to-parent attachment; other indicators include behaviour in 'strange situations' and activities such as differential smiling, crying and vocalization, as well as protest at separation. Multiple criteria are used to specify attachment phenomena because of individual differences in the way attachment is organized and manifested – differences that seem to be related to variations among mothers in their infant-care practices. Indeed, because the child's attachment system is, in a sense, the reciprocal of the parents', it may be preferable to speak of, say, the mother and young child as forming a single, superordinate attachment system. The delicate and complementary intermeshing of their respective, individual attachment repertoires is such that it is not possible to describe one fully without also describing the other.

There is little agreement on the nature of this powerful motivational process: a plethora of explanatory ideas have been put forward, in the name of learning theory (Gerwitz, 1972; Hoffman *et al.*, 1973), psychoanalysis (Freud, 1946) and ethology (Ainsworth, 1973; Bowlby, 1969). Bowlby – to take one example – sees attachment behaviour as the operation of an internal control system. Children are biologically predisposed to form attachments. It could be said that they are genetically programmed to respond to social situations and to display forms of behaviour (smiling, crying, clinging, and so on) from the beginning of life up to and beyond the point in time when they make a focused attachment to parental figures. What is new, then, when the infant becomes attached is not the display of new forms of behaviour or new intensities of social responses, but a pattern of organization of these responses in relation to one significant person. Virtually all the elements in the child's behaviour repertoire become capable of being functionally linked to a controlling system or plan, which is hierarchical in its organization and target-seeking in its effect. The 'target' is defined as the maintenance of proximity to the care-giver, and the hierarchical nature of the organization is revealed in the fact that a particular response can serve a number of different functions in maintaining this proximity.

Bowlby's conceptualization of attachment seems to offer fruitful ways of looking at the concept; it suggests new ways in which attachment systems can be compared. Instead of thinking of children as simply being more or less attached, their attachment systems can be compared according to the nature of the favoured strategies they employ, how strongly they are established, the degree of elaboration of alternative strategies, and the nature of their setting, that is, the closeness of the proximity they are set to maintain.

The preoccupation with the allegedly decisive influence of the mother on the infant's development, and the foundational significance of the first attachment has had salutary effects: highlighting the psychological needs of the young child and humanizing substitute child-care arrangements. The cost was a professional ideology, particularly rampant in the 1950s, whereby mothers were inculpated in the causation of psychopathology varying from infantile autism to juvenile delinquency. Rutter (1972), among others, has been instrumental in producing a more balanced view of the role of attachment and maternal care in the development of normal and abnormal behaviour.

Mother-to-infant attachment is usually referred to as maternal bonding. The widespread belief that in some mammalian species, including our own, mother-to-infant bonding occurs rapidly through mother-infant, skin-to-skin contact during a short duration, critical period after birth, has been challenged. The ethological support for the bonding doctrine, derived from early experiments with ewes and goats ('olfactory imprinting'), has not stood the test of time. Nor has evidence from human longitudinal studies comparing mothers who, after giving birth to a baby, have either been separated from it or have been allowed extended skin-to-skin contact with it, supported a 'sensitive' period, 'ethological' explanation. The impact of the doctrine upon the thinking of practitioners in obstetric, paediatric and social work fields has been considerable, particularly in relating bonding failures (allegedly due to early separation experiences) to serious problems such as child abuse. These clinical applications have also been challenged. It seems more likely that exposure learning, different forms of conditioning, imitation and cultural factors, all influence the development of mother-to-infant (and, indeed, father-to-infant) attachments and involve a process of learning gradually to love an infant more strongly – a process characterized by ups and downs, and one which is often associated with a variety of mixed feelings about the child.

Martin Herbert
University of Leicester

References

Ainsworth, M. D. S. (1973), 'The development of infant-mother attachment', in B. M. Caldwell and H. N. Ricciuti (eds), *Review of Child Development Research, Vol. III*, Chicago.

Bowlby, J. (1969), *Attachment and Loss*, Vol. I. *Attachment*, New York.

Freud, A. (1946), 'The psychoanalytic study of infantile feeding disturbances', *Psychoanalytic Study of the Child*, 2.

Gerwitz, J. L. (1972), 'Attachment, dependence, and a distinction in terms of stimulus control', in J. L. Gewirtz (ed.), *Attachment and Dependency*, Washington, D.C.

Hoffman, H. S. and Ratner, A. M. (1973), 'A reinforcement model of imprinting: implications for socialization in monkeys and men', *Psychological Review*, 80.

Rutter, M. (1972), *Maternal Deprivation Reassessed*, Harmondsworth.

Further Reading

Klaus, M. H. and Kennell, J. N. (1976), *Maternal Infant Bonding*, Saint Louis.

Rajecki, D. W., Lamb, M. E. and Obmascher, P. (1978), 'Toward a general theory of infantile attachment: a comparative review of aspects of the social bond', *The Behavioural and Brain Sciences*, 3.

Sluckin, W., Herbert, M. and Sluckin, A. (1983), *Maternal Bonding*, Oxford.

See also: *Bowlby; separation and loss.*

Attention

All behaviour is a matter of selecting a particular course of action among many alternatives. In experimental psychology, many different aspects of this selectivity are studied under the heading of 'attention'.

Perhaps the most characteristic example concerns the limit on how much we can see, hear or do at one time. The driver of a car may stop speaking when the demands of the traffic situation increase. A student daydreaming in a lecture may 'wake up' to discover he has taken no notes. Difficulties in doing several things at once, and the associated need to select between competing alternatives ('paying attention'), were already under experimental study in the nineteenth century. Helmholtz showed that if a page of text is briefly illuminated in a dark room, it may be impossible to read more than a small part, but possible to choose *which* part at will (and without moving the eyes). The publication of Broadbent's *Perception and Communication* in 1958 established selective perception of this type as a core topic in the modern development of 'information processing' psychology.

Some workers propose that limits on our ability to do several things at once reflect the existence of a unique psychological resource, limited in supply and called upon (to various extents) by all the different activities we can perform: listening to a conversation, playing the piano, solving a puzzle, and so on. Doing two things at once causes trouble if the total resource demand exceeds the total supply. Connections are often made between the 'attentional' resource and consciousness, since there seem definite limits to the number of things we can be conscious of at one time. A frequent idea is that well-practised activities may require rather little of this resource, in line with the experience that they are sometimes performed unconsciously and with little disturbing influence on whatever else we are doing.

Others take a different view. Many different psychological operations are involved in the control of behaviour: orientation of receptors towards chosen objects; perceptual recognition of visual, auditory and tactile patterns; operations performed upon spatial, verbal and other internal representations; control of speech and other movements, and so on. Such processes are separable in several senses. For example, they may take place in different anatomical areas of the brain. A strong possibility, among the multiplicity of psychological operations involved in the multiplicity of different actions we can perform, is that there are many different ways in which simultaneous tasks can interfere and interact with one another. Thus there may be many different reasons for our limited ability to do several things at once.

Other aspects of selectivity have different bases. A thing may not be done because there are better alternatives for the purpose at hand, because the person is drunk, sleepy or bored, and so on. Though these different aspects of selectivity may all be studied under the heading of attention, it is of course questionable how much they have in common. Sometimes when we say that a person 'paid attention' to one thing and not to another, we mean little more than that, for whatever reason, one thing was done while the other was not. As a whole, experimental psychology attempts to understand the underlying process in the selection of appropriate activity.

John Duncan
MRC Applied Psychology
Unit, Cambridge

Reference

Broadbent, D. E. (1958), *Perception and Communication*, London.

Further Reading

Allport, D. A. (1980), 'Attention and performance', in G. Claxton (ed.), *Cognitive Psychology: New Directions*, London.

Kahneman, D. (1973), *Attention and Effort*, Englewood Cliffs, N.J.

See also: *sensation and perception.*

Attitudes

In a classic article published nearly fifty years ago, Gordon Allport (1935) contended that the attitude concept was 'the most distinctive and indispensable concept in contemporary social psychology'. While this confident assertion may perhaps be more debatable in the 1980s, the study of attitudes continues to occupy the attention of many researchers.

Attitudes are predominantly a matter of affective evaluation. They represent the evaluations (positive or negative) that we associate with diverse entities, for example, individuals, groups, objects, actions and institutions. Attitudes are typically assessed through a direct inquiry procedure in which respondents are essentially asked to indicate their evaluative reaction (like-dislike, and so on) to something or someone. A number of indirect (disguised) measurement procedures have also been developed (Kidder and Campbell, 1970), but these are sometimes difficult to apply and have not been widely utilized.

Some theorists contend that attitudes should not be defined solely in affective (or evaluative) terms, suggesting instead that attitudes are normally found in combination with 'related' cognitive and behavioural components. Thus, people who *like* unions will usually hold characteristic beliefs; they may believe, for example, that union activities have often been treated unfairly in the press. In addition, people with pro-union attitudes will often *act* accordingly, by joining a union, or by purchasing union goods in preference to those produced by non-unionized labour. Despite the plausibility of these assertions, however, they have not gone unchallenged; in particular, the relationship between attitudes and behaviour has often proven to be weak or nonexistent.

Rather than defining attitudes such that associated beliefs and behaviours are included as essential components (by definition), contemporary researchers have preferred to focus on the evaluative aspect of attitudes, to judge from the assessment procedures they have developed, and have gone on to study *empirically* (1) the relationship between attitudes and beliefs, and (2) the relationship between attitudes and behaviour.

(1) *Attitudes and beliefs*. A commonsensical approach suggests that our attitudes, pro or con, derive from our beliefs. For example, if we learn that a newly-opened store offers excellent service, superior goods and low prices, we are likely to evaluate it positively. Advertising campaigns are often based on an implicit model of this type; they may attempt to change our beliefs about a product or institution by telling us of the good qualities it possesses, in the hope that this will ultimately influence our attitudes and buying behaviour.

While it is clear that attitudes can be influenced by changes in belief (as outlined above), there is also evidence for the reverse proposition. That is, attitudes may not only be influenced by beliefs, but they may also contribute to the things that we believe (Rosenberg *et al.*, 1960). In one study, for example, respondents were led (through direct post-hypnotic suggestion) to accept a new position with respect to foreign aid. Subsequent inquiry indicated that these hypnotically-induced attitudes were accompanied by a spontaneous acceptance of new beliefs that had not been mentioned during the induction procedure, beliefs that were supportive of the respondents' new views. Other studies suggest that attitudes may also play a type of filtering role, influencing the extent to which we accept new information that bears on the validity of our attitudes (Lord, Ross and Lepper, 1979).

(2) *Attitudes and behaviour*. Attitudes are generally thought to influence behaviour. People who favour a given candidate or political position are expected to vote for that person, or to provide other concrete support (for example, in the form of donations), in contrast to those who hold relatively negative views. Despite the seeming obviousness of this proposition, however, many studies have found only weak, unreliable relations between attitudes and everyday behaviour. Part of the difficulty here derives from the fact that behaviour is often dependent on situational factors that may override the influence of the individual's preferences. Despite the fact that someone holds extremely positive views towards organized religion, he may nonetheless be unresponsive to requests for financial donations to his church if he has recently lost his job. Similarly, a hotel clerk may override his personal prejudices and politely serve patrons of diverse ethnic origins, if this is what his job requires. On the other hand, there is now persuasive evidence that attitudes may be more substantially associated with everyday actions if we take a broader view of behaviour, tracking the individual's reactions in a wide range of settings rather than just one. For example, although religious attitudes (positive-negative) may be weakly associated with financial contributions to the church, a more clearcut linkage between religious attitudes and religious behaviour may be observed if a composite behavioural index is employed, one that takes account of such matters as weekly religious observance, observance during holiday celebrations, saying Grace before meals, and so on (Fishbein and Ajzen, 1974). Attitudes may also be effectively related to overt actions if they are action-oriented and are measured with appropriate specificity. Thus, church donations may be related to people's attitudes toward the concrete act of 'donating to the church', as contrasted with their general attitude towards 'organized religion'.

One of the most firmly-established phenomena in contemporary attitude research is the fact that behaviours may have a causal impact on attitudes, rather than simply reflecting the actor's previously-held views. This proposition has been supported in a wide range of experiments. In a classic study by Festinger and Carlsmith (1959), some respondents were led to describe a certain laboratory activity as 'interesting', despite the fact that they actually regarded it as rather dull. People who had enacted this form of counter-attitudinal behaviour for a modest (one-dollar) incentive subsequently rated the dull laboratory task in relatively favourable terms, compared to those who had not been required to produce counter-attitudinal statements. Other researchers have employed a procedure in which a person who was supposed to be 'teaching' something to another, seemingly punished the learner with electric shocks whenever he made an error. Subsequent inquiry revealed that people who had served as 'teachers' in this type of situation became increasingly negative to their 'pupils' as a consequence.

The continuing vitality of the attitude construct may derive, in part, from the seemingly universal importance of evaluation (Osgood 1964). We are apparently disposed to respond evaluatively to the people, objects, events and institutions that we encounter. These evaluative (attitudinal) reactions, their origins, correlates and consequences, continue to constitute a fertile domain for academic and applied research.

Melvin Manis
University of Michigan and
Ann Arbor Veterans Administration Medical Center

References
Allport, G. W. (1935), 'Attitudes', in C. Murchison (ed.), *A Handbook of Social Psychology*, Worcester, Mass.
Festinger, L. and Carlsmith, J. M. (1959), 'Cognitive consequences of forced compliance', *Journal of Abnormal and Social Psychology*, 58.
Fishbein, M. and Ajzen, I. (1974), 'Attitudes toward objects as predictive of single and multiple behavioral criteria', *Psychological Review*, 81.
Kidder, L. H. and Campbell, D. T. (1970), 'The indirect testing of social attitude', in G. I. Summers (ed.), *Attitude Measurement*, Chicago.
Lord, C. G., Ross, L. and Lepper, M. R. (1979), 'Biased assimilation and attitude polarization: the effects of prior theories in subsequently considered evidence', *Journal of Personality and Social Psychology*, 37.
Osgood, C. E. (1964), 'Semantic differential technique in the comparative study of cultures', *American Psychologist*, 66.
Rosenberg, M. J., Hovland, C. I., McGuire, W. J., Abelson, R. P. and Brehm, J. W. (1960), *Attitude Organization and Change*, New Haven.

Further Reading
Petty, R. E. and Cacioppo, J. T. (1981), *Attitudes and Persuasion: Classical and Contemporary Approaches*, Dubuque, Iowa.
McGuire, W. J. (1969), 'The nature of attitudes and attitude change', in *The Handbook of Social Psychology*, 2nd edn, vol. 3, Reading, Mass.
See also: *authoritarian personality; cognitive dissonance; prejudice; semantic differential.*

Attribution Theory

Attribution theory is concerned with the study of perceived causation. All developments of this theory stem from Heider's influential work (Heider, 1958) in which he proposed that naive explanations of behaviour distinguish between personal (dispositional) and impersonal (situational) causes, a distinction that has been a central theme in subsequent theorizing.

Early developments of attribution theory emphasized the rational and exhaustive nature of attribution processes. Jones and Davis's (1965) theory of correspondent inferences specified when dispositional or personal attributions will be made: when observed behaviour is considered intentional and corresponds to the inferred disposition, particularly those behaviours which result in distinctive and socially undesirable outcomes. Kelley (1967) proposed that attributions are governed by the principle of covariation: an effect will be attributed to personal or impersonal factors depending on with which of these factors it covaries.

More recently, irrational biases in attribution have been emphasized. Jones and Nisbett (1971) noted the tendency for actors to attribute their behaviour to situational factors, whereas observers attribute behaviour to dispositional factors. For example, if I trip over the cat, it is because the cat got in the way, but if someone else does it is because that person is clumsy. Ross (1977) has proposed a more basic bias, the fundamental attribution error, which refers to the pervasive tendency for people to explain behaviour in dispositional terms, underestimating the importance of situational factors.

The enthusiasm for documenting the naive psychologist's attribution errors rather than accuracies might seem misplaced, but biases in attribution are believed to be evidence of the useful short cuts in human thinking which usually help make people such efficient information processors.

Sarah E. Hampson
Birkbeck College
University of London

References
Heider, F. (1958), *The Psychology of Interpersonal Relations*, New York.
Jones, E. E. and Davis, E. E. (1965), 'From acts to dispositions: the attribution process in person perception', in L. Berkowitz (ed.), *Advances in Experimental Social Psychology*, Vol. 2, New York.
Jones, E. E. and Nisbett, R. E. (1971), *The Actor and the Observer: Divergent Perceptions of the Causes of Behavior*, Morristown, N.J.
Kelley, H. H. (1967), 'Attribution theory in social psychology', in L. Berkowitz (ed.), *Advances in Experimental Social Psychology*, Vol. 10, New York.

Ross, L. (1977), 'The intuitive psychologist and his shortcomings: distortions in the attribution process', in L. Berkowitz (ed.), *Advances in Experimental Social Psychology*, Vol. 10, New York.

Further Reading
Harvey, J. H., Ickes, W. and Kidd, R. E. (eds) (1981), *New Directions in Attribution Research*, Vol. 3, Hillsdale, N.J.
See also: *personal construct theory*.

Augustine of Hippo (354–430)

Brought up in North Africa by a pagan father and a Christian mother, Augustine was converted to Christianity as a young professor of rhetoric in Milan. He spent the greater part of his working life as Bishop of Hippo, in the area where he was born. As a boy and a young man he had been searching for a philosophical or religious system which would satisfy him; he had been a Manichee; he had gone to magicians and astrologers; and he had learned what he could of philosophy. Now, as a Christian, his thinking was further formed by the need to solve practical and political problems which presented themselves to him as a bishop, and by the questions on doctrine and ethics which he was asked by his congregation, and by letters from all over the Roman world as his fame as a preacher and teacher spread.

One root of the difficulty lay in the fact that the late Roman world was dividing into Greek- and Latin-speaking areas. Augustine himself never succeeded in learning Greek properly. His thinking and his formulations of principles of life and doctrine required him to stretch and adapt the Latin language and to work out for himself a position on a number of points. As a result, his writing has an exploratory air; often repetitious, it nevertheless coheres as a whole in a system of immense complexity and fullness. He left few of the major questions of ethics and theology untouched. He thought the human psyche was made up of memory, will and understanding, an image of the Trinity which God had provided to make it easier for man to understand him. He provided a solution of the problem of evil which regarded it as a mere absence of good, and he arrived at an extreme view of man's helplessness to act for the good in his fallen state except when divine grace aids him. He thought man's need for government an unfortunate consequence of his sinful state; in Eden, Adam and his kind would have lived co-operatively in peace. The need for man to concentrate not upon improving life in this world, but upon his eternal destiny in the next was constantly in his thoughts.

His writings were copiously influential in the Middle Ages and beyond. The thinkers of the Reformation returned to him in reaction against late medieval scholasticism.

G. R. Evans
Fitzwilliam College
University of Cambridge

Austrian School

The Austrian School of Economics is one of the branches of economic thought which grew out of the Marginalist or neoclassical revolution (1870–1890). Although basically similar to the teachings stemming from Jevons, Leon Walras and Marshall, the Austrian School's unique ideas were already contained in Menger's relatively slim volume, *Grundsätze der Volkswirtschaftslehre* (1871), thus giving the school its alternative name, the 'Menger School'. Menger was the sole professor of economic theory in the law faculty of Vienna University between 1873 and 1903. Wieser succeeded him in 1904 and held the position until 1922. But from 1904 until 1913, Böhm-Bawerk, too, was an economics professor in the university, which is why the school is also known as the 'Vienna School'.

Menger (1950 [1871]) tried to create a unified theory of prices, encompassing commodity as well as distributional prices. He based this on subjective valuation of the buyers at the moment of purchase, that is, on their direct utility for consumption goods or their indirect utility for productive services. These ideas are similar to other marginalist traditions. But what was unique to Menger's approach was his stress on problems of information in economics (taken up later by Hayek), consequent upon the time structure of production which entails the likelihood of forecasting errors, especially by producers of 'higher order commodities' – those far removed from final demand ('first order commodities'). From this developed the Austrians' concern with both capital and business cycle theory, the two being seen as closely linked (Böhm-Bawerk, Mises, Hayek, Schumpeter). Another unique contribution by Menger was his vision of price formation, with monopolistic pricing or even individual bargains at the fore, and perfect competition only a limiting case. Thus prices are not fully determinate, but subject to bargaining – this approach developed via Morgenstern into the Theory of Games. Menger regarded commodities as typically unhomogeneous; the constant creation of new varieties of final commodities, aside from offering insights into productive possibilities, were to him the most important aspects of development, another idea taken up by Schumpeter. Finally, Menger was the first of many Austrians to be concerned with monetary theory: he saw in money the most marketable commodity, and a medium of reserve held for precautionary reasons, with, consequently, a volatile velocity of circulation.

The best-known contributions of Menger's successors are Böhm-Bawerk's (1959) attempts to measure capital in terms of waiting time, and his determinants of 'the' rate of interest. Wieser (1927 [1914]) should be remembered for his notion that prices are, above all, informative, and therefore necessary for all private and social calculations (an idea which is now usually associated with Mises's strictures on the impossibility of efficient socialist economies without market prices). Wieser also propounded the leadership role of the creative entrepreneur, an idea which Schumpeter (1952 [1912]) expanded into his theory of innovation and economic development. Mises (1949) and Hayek created a monetary ('Austrian') theory of the business cycle: investment booms are caused by bouts of bank credit at a market rate of interest below the rate of return on capital, a credit creation which cannot be prolonged indefinitely without additional saving, so that much new capital formation must be prematurely terminated.

More recently, a new 'Austrian School' has developed, particularly in the US. Taking up the strands of Austrian thought, it stresses the non-static nature of economic processes and the informational uniqueness of entrepreneurial decision taking. It must be noted, however, that both in respect of the full scope of thought and in its personal links, its connection with the now defunct former Austrian School is rather tenuous.

Erich Streissler
University of Vienna

References
Böhm-Bawerk, E. (1890), 'The Austrian economists', *Annals of the American Academy of Political and Social Science*, 1.
Böhm-Bawerk, E. (1959), *Capital and Interest*, 3 vols, South Holland, 1.
Menger, C. (1950 [1871]), *Principles of Economics: First General Part*, ed J. Dingwall and B. F. Hoselitz, Glencoe, Ill. (Original German edn, *Grundsätze der Volkswirtschaftslehre*, Vienna.)
Mises, L. (1949), *Human Action: A Treatise on Economics*, 3rd edn, New Haven.
Schumpeter, J. (1952[1912]), *The Theory of Economic Development: An Inquiry into Profits, Capital, Credit, Interest and the Business Cycle*, 5th edn, Cambridge, Mass. (Original German edn, *Theorie der wirtschaftlichen Entwicklung*, Leipzig.)
Wieser, F. (1927 [1914]), *Social Economics*, New York. (Original German edn, 'Theorie der gesellschaftlichen Wirtschaft' in *Grundriss der Sozialökonomik*, Tübingen.)

Further Reading
Hicks, J. R. and Weber, W. (eds) (1973), *Carl Menger and the Austrian School of Economics*, Oxford.
Streissler, E. (1969), 'Structural economic thought – on the significance of the Austrian School today', *Zeitschrift für Nationalökonomie*, 29.
See also: *Hayek*; *Schumpeter*.

Authoritarianism and the Authoritarian Personality

Soon after the end of the Second World War, a group of social scientists in the US, under the leadership of T. W. Adorno, sought to identify the factors giving rise to anti-Semitism. They hoped that by identifying the causes, they would be in a position to prevent a repetition of the holocaust. Their research led to the publication of the now classic volume, *The Authoritarian Personality* (Adorno et al., 1950). They viewed the concept of authoritarianism as consisting of the following (Sanford, 1956):

(1) Conventionalism: rigid adherence to conventional middle-class values.
(2) Authoritarian Submission: submissive, uncritical attitude toward idealized moral authorities of the in-group.
(3) Authoritarian Aggression: tendency to be on the look out for, and to condemn, reject and punish people who violate conventional values.
(4) Anti-intraception: opposition to the subjective, the imaginative, the tenderminded.
(5) Superstition and Stereotypy: belief in mystical determinants of the individual's fate; the disposition to think in rigid categories.
(6) Power and Toughness: preoccupation with the dominance-submission, strong-weak, leader-follower dimension; identification with power figures; exaggerated assertions of strength and toughness.
(7) Destructiveness and Cynicism: generalized hostility, vilification of the human.
(8) Projectivity: disposition to believe that wild and dangerous things go on in the world; the projection outward of unconscious emotional impulses.
(9) Sex: ego-alien sexuality; exaggerated concern with sexual 'goings on', and punitiveness toward violators of sexual mores.

The publication of *The Authoritarian Personality* generated voluminous social psychological research, which mainly supported the view that authoritarians are raised in homes characterized by strict discipline. Their parents typically endeavour to keep them subordinate, conforming, and dependent, and in later life these same children manifest conservative, domineering, rigid and prejudiced attitudes.

Some research has been critical of *The Authoritarian Personality* (Christie and Jahoda, 1954). Doubts were expressed concerning the validity and reliability of the primary measuring instrument (the F scale). It was noted that the F scale elicits in the respondent the tendency to agree with the items regardless of content (this refers to acquiescence). Perhaps most important of all, it was shown that the F scale was unable to predict actual authoritarian *behaviour*. As such, it is little more than a measure of *attitudes*. If social psychology is to contribute to explaining human behaviour, our measuring instruments must be able to predict the behaviour we are seeking to explain.

More recently Ray (1976) developed the Directiveness Scale, which is well able to predict dominant behaviour, a key characteristic of authoritarianism. Ray's scale is regarded as a starting point for the construction of a behaviour inventory encompassing not only dominance, but rather all aspects of authoritarianism.

Patrick C. L. Heaven
Riverina College, Australia

References

Adorno, T. W., Frenkel-Brunswik, E., Levinson, D. J. and Sanford, N. (1950), *The Authoritarian Personality*, New York.
Christie, R. and Jahoda, M. (1954), *Studies in the Scope and Method of 'The Authoritarian Personality'*, Glencoe, Ill.
Ray, J. J. (1976), 'Do authoritarians hold authoritarian attitudes?', *Human Relations*, 29.
Sanford, N. (1956), 'The approach of the authoritarian personality', in J. L. McCary (ed.), *Psychology of Personality: Six Modern Approaches*, New York.

Further Reading

Altemeyer, B. (1982), *Right-Wing Authoritarianism*, Winnipeg.

See also: *attitudes*; *prejudice*; *political psychology*.

Authority

Six distinctions must be drawn in any account of the concept of authority (Friedman, 1973; Lukes, 1978).

(1) The failure to explain the unity and order of social life and the compliance of subjects solely in terms of coercion and/or rational agreement opens a space for the concept of authority. Authority refers to a distinctive form of compliance in social life (see 2). Three accounts exist of the basis of this special compliance. One sees authoritative institutions as reflecting the common beliefs, values, traditions and practices of members of society (Parsons, 1960; Arendt, 1963); a second sees political authority as offering a co-ordination solution to a Hobbesian state of nature, or a lack of shared values (Hobbes, 1651); and a third view argues that although social order is imposed by force, it derives its permanence and stability through techniques of legitimation, ideology, hegemony, mobilization of bias, false consensus and so on, which secure the willing compliance of citizens through the manipulation of their beliefs (Weber, 1978 [1922]; Lukes, 1978).

(2) What is special about the compliance B renders A which marks off authority from coercion and rational agreement? Coercion secures B's compliance by the use of force or threats; persuasion convinces B by appeal to arguments that an action is in B's interests, is, for example, morally right, or prudent; but B complies with authority when B recognizes A's right to command him in a certain sphere. B voluntarily surrenders the right to make compliance contingent on an evaluation of the content of A's command, and obeys because A's order comes from an appropriate person and falls within the appropriate range. Where authority exists there will be 'rules of recognition' (Hart, 1961) or 'marks' by which to identify those eligible to exercise it.

(3) We must also distinguish between *de facto* and *de jure* authority (Peters, 1967; Winch, 1967). *De facto* authority is evidenced whenever B complies with A in the appropriate manner; *de jure* authority exists where A has a right to B's compliance in a given area which derives from a set of institutional rules. That A has one form of authority in no way entails that he will also have the other.

(4) Many writers have referred to authority as 'legitimate power'. This may mean (i) that coercion is exercised by someone with *de jure* authority, although the coerced agent is not responding to A's authority; or (ii) that A's orders in fact produce this distinctive form of non-coerced deferential obedience (A thus has *de facto* authority) – this being in sharp contrast to cases where compliance is based on fear.

(5) Authority is thus a two-tier concept: it refers to a mode of influence and compliance, and to a set of criteria which identify who is to exercise this influence. For this influence to take effect it must be exercised 'within a certain kind of normative arrangement accepted by both parties' (Friedman, 1973). This normative arrangement may be a common tradition, practice or set of beliefs (Winch, 1967; MacIntyre, 1967), or it may be simply a common acknowledgment that some set of rules is required to avoid chaos. B's compliance with A's authority may take two forms: it may be unquestioning (as with Weber's 'charismatic authority') or B may be able to criticize A's command,

yet still complies because he recognizes A's right to command, even if he privately disagrees with its content.

(6) A further important distinction is that between being *an* authority and being *in* authority. The former concerns matters of belief; the latter concerns A's place in a normative order with recognized positions of *de jure* authority. When A is *an* authority, he is held to have, or successfully claims, special knowledge, insight, expertise, and so on, which justifies B's deference to A's judgement. When A is *in* authority, he claims, and is recognized as occupying, a special institutional role with a co-ordinate sphere of command (as with Weber's legal-rational authority (1978)). When B complies with A's judgement where A is *an* authority, B's compliance involves belief in the validity of A's judgement; whereas, when A is simply *in* authority, B may disagree yet comply because he recognizes A's *de jure* authority. Traditional and charismatic leaders are authoritative over belief and value; leaders in legal-rational systems are granted authority in certain spheres of action for convenience. Where A is *an* authority, his influence over B relies on B's continued belief in A's guaranteed judgement. Where A is *in* authority, he relies on B continuing to recognize that he fulfils a valuable co-ordination function. Both systems may face legitimation crises when B no longer believes A, or no longer believes that A successfully co-ordinates. However, both systems may seek to maintain B's belief through a variety of techniques: ideology, hegemony, mobilization of bias, and so on (Habermas, 1976 [1973]).

Mark Philp
Oriel College, University of Oxford

References

Arendt, H. (1963), 'What is authority', in *Between Past and Future*, New York.

Friedman, R. B. (1973), 'On the concept of authority in political philosophy', in R. E. Flathman (ed.), *Concepts in Social and Political Philosophy*, New York.

Habermas, J. (1976 [1973]), *Legitimation Crisis*, London. (Original German edn, *Legitimationsproblem im Spatkapitalismus*, Frankfurt.)

Hart, H. L. A. (1961), *The Concept of Law*, Oxford.

Hobbes, T. (1651), *Leviathan*, London.

Lukes, S. (1978), 'Power and authority' in T. Bottomore and R. Nisbett (eds), *A History of Sociological Analysis*, London.

MacIntyre, A. (1967), *Secularisation and Moral Change*, London.

Parsons, T. (1969), 'Authority, legitimation, and political action', in *Structure and Process in Modern Societies*, Glencoe, Ill.

Peters, R. S. (1967), 'Authority', in A. Quinton (ed.), *Political Philosophy*, Oxford.

Weber, M. (1978 [1922]), *Economy and Society*, 2 vols, eds G. Roth and C. Wittich, Berkeley and Los Angeles.

Winch, P. (1967), 'Authority', in A. Quinton (ed.), *Political Philosophy*, Oxford.

Autism

In psychiatry generally, the term autism refers to apparent withdrawal from the outside world, self-absorption, and lack of communication with others. In childhood, the syndrome of autism is a severely incapacitating developmental disability which appears prior to thirty months of age. It occurs in approximately five out of every 100,000 births and is four times more common in boys than in girls. It has been found throughout the world in families of all racial, ethnic and social backgrounds. No known factors in the psychological environment of a child have been shown to cause autism.

The symptoms, expressive of neuropathology, include:

(1) Disturbances in the rate of appearance of physical, social and language skills.

(2) Abnormal responses to sensations. Any one or a combination of sight, hearing, touch, pain, balance, smell, taste, and the way a child holds his body are affected.

(3) Speech and language are absent or delayed, while specific thinking capabilities may be present. Immature rhythms of speech, limited understanding of ideas, and the use of words without attaching the usual meaning to them are common.

(4) Abnormal ways of relating to people, objects and events.

Autism occurs by itself or in association with other disorders which affect the function of the brain, such as viral infections, metabolic disturbances (PKU), epilepsy, and Fragile X syndrome. On IQ testing of autistic people, approximately 60 per cent have scores below 50, 20 per cent between 50 and 70, and only 20 per cent greater than 70. Most show wide variations of performance on different tests and at different times. Autistic people live a normal life span. Since symptoms change, and some disappear with age, periodic re-evaluations are necessary to respond to changing needs. Multiple incidences in a family are common. The severe form of the syndrome may include the most extreme forms of self-injurious, repetitive, highly unusual and aggressive behaviours. Such behaviours may be persistent and highly resistant to change, often requiring unique management, treatment or teaching strategies.

Special education programmes using behavioural methods and designed for specific individuals have been shown to be most helpful. Psychotropic medication may be used to reduce temporarily injurious behaviour. Supportive counselling may help families with autistic members, as it helps families who have members with other severe permanent disabilities.

Edward R. Ritvo
University of California
Los Angeles

Further Reading
Ritvo, E. R. (ed.) (1976), *Autism, Current Research and Management*, New York.
Ritvo, E. R. and Freeman, B. J. (1978), 'National Society for Autistic Children definition of the syndrome of autism', *Journal of the American Academy of Child Psychiatry*, 17.

Automation

The key feature of an automated production process is its control, either total or partial, by machines. Although over the years it has been used in widely differing ways (Rezler, 1969), automation can be considered an extension to, although not necessarily an evolution of, mechanization, the application of machines to previously human or animal tasks. Mechanization becomes automation when the human operator is partially or totally replaced by automatic controls. Automation may involve, as general examples, the automatic transfer of materials within a production process; or the automatic provision of information on the state of a production process and automatic reaction to divergences from pre-set norms; or the collection, processing and transmission of data and information either without, or with only limited, human intervention.

Although early embodiments of the automation concept, such as the thermostat, can be found, it now largely concerns the application of computer technology in production (widely defined). Thus present-day examples of automated processes include computer-numerically-controlled machine tools, automatic transfer lines, automated warehousing systems, flexible manufacturing systems, computer-aided design and manufacture (CAD/CAM), robots, word processing, electronic funds transfer and information networks. Given the computer-based nature of most automated processes and the information processing principles embodied in these processes, the current terminology of computerization or information technology is synonymous with automation. Such synonyms have the advantage of correctly suggesting that the technology can be applied to any economic sector, not just manufacturing.

Since the advent of electronic computers in the late 1940s, enormous advances based largely on develop-

ments in the technology of electronic components have generated machines that are physically smaller, more powerful and with greater logic and storage capacity, in many cases the improvements being by factors measured in thousands. Extensive miniaturization and improvements in information-processing ability have opened up the technological possibility of automating processes that it was not previously possible to automate. One must be careful, however. The hardware advances must be matched by suitable software (programming) before their application is possible, and software advances have not in general kept pace with hardware improvements. The improvements in computer technology have also been matched by significant price reductions. These changes make automation economically as well as technologically feasible.

Attitudes to automation vary across a wide spectrum. The potential that automation provides for replacing men by machines conjures up two possible extreme scenarios for the future of industrial society:

(1) A future is envisaged where automation ensures an unlimited growth of labour productivity, man is increasingly dispensable in the production process, goods and services will be supplied in unlimited amounts by machines, and man can devote his efforts to the arts and the higher levels of human experience rather than be tied to machines. It is a vision of a society where most material wants can be satisfied, where there is no poverty and unlimited leisure time.

(2) At the other extreme is the vision of a society of mass unemployment, with wide disparities in income distribution and, consequently, an underlying threat of violence in society. Those who own the machines, or the few still employed, will be the wealthy. The masses will be unemployed and impoverished.

Such science-fiction type visions are probably more fiction than science, at least in a medium-term view. These visions imply such enormous increases in productivity as a corollary to automation that they can really only be extremely long-term projections. In the shorter term, the impact on productivity of extensions to the use of new information technology is much more moderate. If one thinks of automation as something additional to the 'normal' processes leading to productivity increase (which itself is not really certain), rough approximations suggest that labour productivity may only be 10 per cent higher in 1990 than if the potential for automation did not exist (Stoneman *et al.*, 1982). This does not seem particularly revolutionary. This is not to deny, however, the strength of feeling behind the discussions of the impact of automation on society, in particular the fear of potential mass unemployment.

The impact of technological change on employment has been raised many times since Ricardo's original contribution to the subject. The parallel between modern discussions and Ricardo's work suggests that we have not proceeded far in finding an answer to the problem (David, 1982). (For a fuller discussion see Stoneman, 1983.) However the following points are salient to the debate:

(1) The adoption of any new technology will not be instantaneous. Diffusion processes are slow.
(2) Given that the new technology increases labour productivity, the impact on employment depends upon what happens to output. If it increases, then the direct labour demand-reducing effects may be offset.
(3) The impact of new technology in any one economy will depend on what happens in others through the international trading nexus.
(4) New technology may affect the quality of products rather than costs, and the repercussions of product innovation may differ from those of process innovations.
(5) It is clear that most technologies when introduced change the required skill mix of the labour force. Such changes will almost definitely generate at least transitional unemployment.

On the positive side, automation can, although not necessarily will, reduce the need for work in harsh physical environments, increase the potential for leisure in society, generate new products, expand the potential for scientific advance, open up the frontiers of space or help tap new sources of energy (for example, solar power). Here again diffusion is slow, and one cannot expect instantaneous results.

Perhaps one of the most interesting impacts of automation or information technology will be its effect on the industrial structure of the economy. As automation proceeds, the proportion of the work force employed in the information sector will increase further. Moreover, traditional dividing lines between industries will become less distinct. The distinction between telecommunications and computers has almost disappeared. Data networks and electronic fund transfer already integrate data transfer into source industries. Within specific industries the classic phases in the production process of design, development, manufacture and inventory management have already, through CAD/CAM and computerized stock control systems, been shown to be capable of integration. As such changes occur so we should expect changes in both the organization of work and the location of industry.

It is clear that further extensions to computer use, automation and the application of new information technology can potentially, in the long term, affect dramatically the nature of industrial society. A vision of the future depends largely upon one's faith in the automaticity of the economy's responses to disequilibria, and one's view of the degree of inequality in the distribution of the costs and benefits of automation.

P. Stoneman
University of Warwick

References
David, P. A. (1982), 'Comments', in *Micro-Electronics, Robotics and Jobs*, ICCP, No. 7, Paris.
Rezler, J. (1969), *Automation and Industrial Labour*, New York.
Stoneman, P., Blattner, N. and Pastre, O. (1982), 'Major findings on and policy responses to the impact of information technologies on productivity and employment', in *Micro-Electronics, Robotics and Jobs*, ICCP, No. 7, Paris.
Stoneman, P. (1983), *The Economic Analysis of Technological Change*, Oxford.

Further Reading
Gourvitch, A. (1966), *Survey of Economic Theory on Technological Change* and (1940), *Employment*, New York.
Heertje, A. (1977), *Economics and Technical Change*, London.
Jones, T. (ed.) (1980), *Microelectronics and Society*, Milton Keynes.
See also: *technological progress*.

Aversion Therapy

Aversion therapy is an attempt by a clinician to suppress undesirable behaviour by punishing it with unpleasant (aversive) stimulation. Punishment, of course, is also delivered by the natural environment (as in the painful consequences of falling or touching hot objects) and in other social contexts (as in a schoolmaster's use of caning or a mother's painting a bitter substance on her child's hands to inhibit nail-biting or thumb-sucking). But random and arbitrary punishments are not aversion therapy, and the result of such punishments is often paradoxical. In aversion therapy, a trained clinician designs a treatment protocol based on the needs and particular behavioural problem of an individual patient.

Like other behaviour therapy techniques, aversion therapy has ancient antecedents but derives its scientific rationale and some of its technical principles from the experimental psychology of learning. Nonetheless, leading authorities on learning (notably E. L. Thorndike, J. B. Watson and B. F. Skinner) have thought that positive reinforcement would be more effective, and that aversive techniques would have only temporary effects that would not generalize beyond the treatment setting. Subsequent research has shown that the duration of effect can be increased by simultaneously rewarding desired behaviours and through 'booster sessions', and that generalization can be increased by having multiple therapists deliver the aversive stimulation in multiple settings.

The delivery of unpleasant stimulation distinguishes aversion therapy from those punishment techniques that remove a reward, such as 'timeout' (removal to a less rewarding setting) or 'response cost' (removal of money, tokens, points or other sources of pleasure). Aversive stimuli that have been used clinically include reprimands (expressions of disapproval), tastes (for example, concentrated lemon juice, pepper sauce or shaving cream), odours (aromatic ammonia and so on), sounds (loud noises of interrupted music), sights (light, flashes of interrupted television), tactile sensations (tickling, hand-slapping, snaps with a rubber band, spanking or electric shock), and more generalized discomfort (forced exercise, drug-induced nausea and vomiting, or even paralysis with neuromuscular blocking agents). When the form of aversive stimulation is unpleasant mental imagery, the technique is known as covert sensitization.

Many studies have shown that aversion therapy can produce complete suppression of a behaviour. It has been used with partial or apparently complete success in the treatment of tics, bruxism, stuttering, bedwetting, rumination of vomitus, smoking, alcoholism, obsessive thoughts, fetishism, sexual masochism, transvestism, exhibitionism and homosexuality, as well as in treating self-injurious, aggressive and other behaviour problems among autistic children and among schizophrenic and mentally-retarded individuals.

There have also been untoward side effects, for example, with children, expressions of fear or distress, emergence of, or increases in, other undesirable behaviours, suppression of desirable behaviours, and increases in the target behaviour in settings where it is unpunished. In general, adverse reactions have occurred when insufficient attention has been given to rewarding desired behaviour; these reactions have been of brief duration and are quickly responsive to treatment.

Inappropriate, excessive or capricious administration of aversive stimulation has led to scandals, lawsuits and prohibitions. Documented abuses and fear-arousing portrayals (as in Stanley Kubrick's film, *A Clockwork Orange*) have rendered aversion therapy highly controversial and have also fuelled the public's fear of non-aversive behaviour therapies and of electro-convulsive therapy (ECT), which some lay people mistake for an aversive technique.

As with other powerful treatments, a judicious decision to use aversion therapy should take into consideration the possible alternative treatments, the documented effectiveness and risk of the proposed technique for the purpose, the degree of pain or discomfort the treatment would entail, the danger of the target behaviour to the patient (and, in some situations, to others), the ability and freedom of the patient to consent knowingly to this treatment and to terminate its use, and the availability of safeguards against abuse. With incompetent patients and in residential institutions, it is essential that the treatment plan be reviewed, both by other clinicians and by an independent human rights committee, and that the treatment process be monitored continually

Park Elliott Dietz
University of Virginia

Further Reading

Axelrod, S. and Apsche, J. (eds) (1983), *The Effects of Punishment on Human Behavior*, New York.

Rachman, S. and Teasdale, J. (1969), *Aversion Therapy and Behavior Disorders: An Analysis*, Coral Gables, Florida.

B

Bagehot, Walter (1826–77)

Walter Bagehot was perhaps Victorian England's most versatile genius. He was remarkable for his scope and breadth of interest even in an age when men of science and of letters, politicians, philosophers, and economists came together in the Metaphysical Society or the Political Economy Club (Bagehot was an active participant in both); when the discoveries of physical science were absorbed into the poetry of Tennyson, and of sociology into the novels of George Eliot.

Bagehot was a banker by profession, although one with an education (at a non-sectarian Bristol school and University College, London) combining to an unusual degree academic rigour and a wide-ranging curriculum. He was also a great editor of *The Economist*, from 1861 until his death, writing most of the political and many of the financial articles. As an economic theorist with an intimate knowledge of the money market, Bagehot's advice was sought by Gladstone and his successors at the Treasury; in the last year of his life he conceived the short-dated Exchequer Bill, still in use; his *Lombard Street* (1873) convincingly established that England had a single reserve banking system (and through his devoted admirer, President Wilson, inspired its adoption in America). Yet Keynes could say that *Lombard Street* was better psychology than economics, and that lively work is far more like Bagehot's writing in other kinds than any treatise by an economist – even one who wrote as well as his friend Stanley Jevons. Those other kinds ranged far: historical, biographical and critical essays, at the leisurely length possible in the great periodicals, of which one of the most intelligent – the *National Review* – was partly founded and co-edited by Bagehot himself; writings on current politics, including *The English Constitution* (1867), a detached insider's view of how it actually worked which has proved his most influential book; an attempt, in *Physics and Politics* (1872), to explain social structures in terms of national character and of discoveries about development in the natural sciences and ethnology.

Bagehot observed people, and the institutions that they shape and are shaped by, with the eye of a novelist. He had all the creative writer's keen appreciation of the ordinary, of quiet people going about their business, and of the conditions necessary to its continuance – an appreciation nourished by his roots in the Somerset countryside, and giving a conservative dimension to his thought. Politically, he was a reforming Liberal, setting out as the ideal a society in which the 'cake of custom' was broken and a sceptical 'government by discussion' became possible; yet in all he wrote there is a tension between the claims of progress and those of continuity and stability. In the 1860s, when Arnold was demanding more intelligence, and the remodelling of institutions, Bagehot was bringing home the paradox that the necessary condition of parliamentary government and a free society was a certain amount of 'stupidity' in ruled and rulers, and that the reform of an institution, obnoxious to logic but in working order, whether the banking system or the constitution, could not safely be entrusted to impatient theorists and utilitarians. To see this paradox most brilliantly enforced by Bagehot when it had first taken hold on him, one should read the letters he wrote from Paris for the *Inquirer* about the *coup d'état* of 1851. There, and in all that he wrote, one is engaged by a strong, lively mind and a style that brings to prose discourse the raciness and suppleness of a supreme conversationalist.

Norman St John-Stevas
House of Commons, London

Further Reading
Bagehot, W. (1965-78), *The Collected Works of Walter Bagehot*, ed. N. St John-Stevas, I-XI, London.
Buchan, A. (1959), *The Spare Chancellor: The Life of Walter Bagehot*, London.
Keynes, J.M. (1915), 'The works of Bagehot', *Economic Journal*, 25.
St John–Stevas, N. (1959), *Walter Bagehot: A Study of His Life and Thought Together with a Selection from his Political Writings*, London.
Young, G. M. (1948), 'The greatest Victorian', *Today and Yesterday*, London.

Balance of Payments

A balance of payments is an accounting record of a country's international transactions with the rest of the world. Foreign currency receipts from the sale of goods and services are called exports and appear as a credit item in what is termed the current account of the balance of payments. Foreign currency payments for purchases of goods and services are called imports and appear as a debit item in the current account. In addition, there are transactions in capital which appear in a separate capital account. Outflows of capital, to finance overseas investment, for example, are treated as debits, and inflows of capital are treated as credits. A deficit on current account may be offset or 'financed' by a surplus on capital account and vice versa. Since the foreign exchange rate is the price of one currency in terms of another, total credits (the supply of foreign exchange) and debits (the demand for foreign exchange) must be equal if the exchange rate is allowed to fluctuate freely to balance the supply of and demand for foreign currency. If the exchange rate is not free to vary, however, deficits or surpluses of foreign currency will arise. Deficits may be financed by government borrowing from international banks and monetary institutions, such as the International Monetary Fund, or by selling gold and foreign currency reserves. Surpluses may be dissipated by accumulating reserves or lending overseas.

The fact that a flexible exchange rate guarantees a balance in the foreign exchange market does not mean a country is immune from balance of payments difficulties. A country may experience a decline in real income and employment because of the inability of exports to pay for imports on current account. Such a deficit financed by capital inflows will not preserve jobs, nor will a depreciating currency necessarily guarantee that the current account deficit will be rectified. Neither can a country be indifferent to the international value of its currency. Widely fluctuating exchange rates may adversely affect international trade. A rapidly depreciating currency, which raises the domestic price of imports, can be highly inflationary, which necessitates further depreciation, and so on.

In considering measures to adjust the balance of payments, therefore, it is highly desirable that countries should focus on the current account if they are concerned with the functioning of the real economy, and (if in deficit) wish to avoid turbulent exchange rates round a declining trend. Three major approaches to balance of payments adjustment have been developed by economists, corresponding to how deficits are viewed. (1) The elasticities approach sees deficits as a result of distorted relative prices or uncompetitiveness in trade. Adjustment should work through exchange rate depreciation provided the sum of the price elasticities of demand for imports and exports exceeds unity. (2) The absorption approach views deficits as a result of excessive expenditure relative to domestic output, so that favourable adjustment must imply that expenditure falls relative to output. (3) The monetary approach ascribes deficits to an excess supply of money relative to demand, so that adjustment can be successful only if it raises the demand for money

relative to the supply. In many contexts, particularly in developing countries, none of the approaches may be relevant where the problem is one of the characteristics of goods produced and exported, so that the price of balance of payments equilibrium is always slow growth. In this case, there is an argument for structural adjustment through planning and protection. If economic objectives are to be obtained simultaneously, a necessary condition is that the form of adjustment should be related to the initial cause of the disequilibrium.

A. P. Thirlwall
University of Kent

Further Reading
Thirlwall, A.P. (1982), *Balance of Payments Theory and the United Kingdom Experience*, 2nd edn, London.
See also: *devaluation; exchange rate; international monetary system; international trade.*

Banking

The word for a bank is recognizably the same in virtually all European languages, and is derived from a word meaning 'bench' or 'counter'. The bench in question appears to have been that of the money-changer at the medieval fairs rather than that of the usurer, and the link of banking with trade between nations and communities has been maintained. The early banks were often started as a subsidiary business by merchants, shippers, cattle drovers and, more recently, by travel agents. Other banks grew out of the business of the goldsmiths, and some of the earliest were founded for charitable reasons. In the last two centuries, however, banking has become a recognizable trade in its own right, and companies and partnerships have been founded to carry on the specific business of banking.

Each legal system has its own definition of a bank. One common element present in nearly all definitions is the taking of deposits and the making of loans for the profit of the owners of the bank, although in some cases the proviso is made that both the deposits and the loans should be short term. An economist would be more likely to seize on the fact that a banker is able to use a relatively small capital of his own to pass large sums from ultimate lenders to ultimate borrowers, taking a margin on each transaction in the form of higher interest rates for loans than for deposits. Both these approaches credit banks with only one function, the macroeconomic function of intermediation. In reality all banks perform many more functions, while some recognized banks are not particularly active as intermediaries. Many provide payment services, and most act as insurers by giving guarantees on behalf of their customers. Services of this sort could plausibly be regarded as facilitating intermediation, but there are many other services that are purely incidental – investment management, computer services and travel agency are among them. Increasingly important in many countries is the part of the bank's income that comes from fees and commission rather than from the interest margin.

Because the liabilities of banks form a large part of the accepted definitions of the money supply, banks attract government regulation on a scale that is greater than that applying to almost every other sector. This regulation can be divided into two main areas. The first is regulation for the purposes of furthering monetary policy. The other area of regulation covers the prudent behaviour of banks in an effort to ensure the safe and efficient functioning of the banking system.

Monetary policy seeks to influence the behaviour of the real economy by changing various financial variables like interest rates, the stock of money, the volume of credit and the direction of credit. Since bank deposits account for a large part of the stock of money, and since bank loans are a very important part of the total volume of credit, it is only natural that banks should be the most important channel for monetary policy measures. The measures that have been imposed on banks include control of their interest rates, primary and secondary requirements on holdings of reserves with the central bank and of government securities, limitation of the amount of credit extended, and control over the direction of credit. Many of these measures built on constraints that the banks had previously observed on their own initiative for prudential reasons.

Banking is a business that depends completely on the confidence of the public, and for the most part banks have always been very careful not to endanger that confidence. After the banking crisis of the early 1930s, the self-regulation that banks had practised for prudential reasons was supplemented in most countries by an elaborate set of prudential regulations and often by detailed supervision; the same intensification of prudential regulation and supervision occurred after the 1974–5 banking crisis. The various measures adopted are often said to be motivated by a desire to protect the interests of the depositor, but an even more important motive is the need for any government to protect the stability and soundness of the entire financial system. The measures laid down in regulations are designed to prevent bank failures by ensuring that the capital and reserves are adequate to cover all likely risks of loss, and that there are sufficient sources of liquidity to meet cash demands day by day. Many sets of regulations seek to achieve these aims by detailed and rigid balance-sheet ratios, but the real problem is to ensure that no banks indulge in bad banking practices.

Over the past twenty or thirty years the banking systems of most developed countries have changed considerably in several directions. The first major trend has been the internationalization of banking. Until the middle of this century banks conducted most of their international business through correspondent banks in the various countries, but most large and many medium-sized banks now reckon to have branches in all important international financial centres. This move was led by the large banks from the United States, and they and branches of banks from other countries have introduced new techniques and been the catalysts for change in many countries whose banking markets were previously sheltered. Banking has also become internationalized through the establishment of a pool of international bank deposits (the so-called eurodollar market) and through syndicated lending by numbers of large banks to multinational corporations and to governments. During the recession that started in 1978, the inability of many governments and other borrowers to meet the conditions of loan repayments has been a considerable source of instability.

On the domestic scene the methods of operation of the international banking market have been adopted in what is termed 'wholesale' banking, in which banks deal with large organizations. The technique is essentially the mobilization of large deposits through an interbank money market to provide funds for loans of up to ten years, often at rates of interest that change every three or six months.

In 'retail' banking, with households and small businesses, the number of personal customers has increased, especially through the payment of wages into bank accounts rather than by cash. Competition has intensified, and savings banks, building societies and co-operative banks are becoming more like the main banks in their powers and kinds of business. The new electronic technology of payments, using the plastic card, will further increase competition, because it will enable institutions without branch networks to compete successfully with those that have branches.

Jack Revell
University College of North Wales
Bangor

Further Reading
Pecchioli, R. (1983), *The Internationalisation of Banking*, Paris.
Revell, J. R. S. (1973), *The British Financial System*, London.
Revell, J. R. S. (1983), *Banking and Electronic Fund Transfers: A Study of the Implications*, Paris.
See also: *credit; development banks; financial crises; financial systems.*

Barthes, Roland (1915–80)

Roland Barthes, after studies in French and Classics interrupted by tuberculosis, started a career as literary critic and researcher in sociology. These pursuits were soon subsumed in his mind under a common theoretical activity which he identified with semiology, the general science of signs (manifested as words, images, gestures, and so on) postulated by the linguist Saussure at the turn of the century. This realization is enshrined in *Mythologies* (1957–72), a brilliant analysis of the myths perpetrated around consumer goods, sporting events or public figures for conservative purposes by cultural institutions and the media. It determined Barthes's image as a censor, casting over contemporary arts and mores the stern eye of a Marxist and existentialist critic, and seeking to account for all symbolic systems, whether observed in everyday life or in innovating, 'difficult' authors like Brecht or the New Novelists, by means of equally new and difficult theories based on linguistics and psychoanalysis. This impression, confirmed by articles reprinted in *Sur Racine* (1963) *(On Racine,* 1964) and *Essais critiques* (1964) *(Critical Essays,* 1972), led to a violent attack by a Sorbonne specialist of Racine; the resulting 'quarrel of the critics' drove Barthes to define, in *Critique et vérité* (1966), an approach to all sign systems, and especially texts, which came to be known as 'structuralism'. This term, largely derived from Lévi-Strauss's application of Jakobson's linguistics to anthropology but also descriptive of recent trends in psychoanalysis, historiography and Marxism, characteristically stressed unconscious structures, as opposed to the self-knowledge and freedom professed by phenomenologists and existentialists, or to the traditional reverence for creators and characters at the expense of critical discourse in literary studies.

Despite rearguard action in academic circles (Barthes always taught in marginal though prestigious establishments, the École Pratique des Hautes Études, then, from 1976, the Collège de France), structuralism soon played a dominant part in all the social sciences. Barthes then set out to develop semiology thanks to a framework supplied by Saussure's study of the linguistic sign. This made linguistics both the method and the object of the prospective new science, a paradox which looms through his structuralist studies: *Eléments de sémiologie* (1967), *Système de la Mode* (1967), and many articles on narrative. Barthes's own overriding concern with language led him to regard science, its methodological constraints and its ideal of truth, as irrelevant in the literary field (this comes out in S/Z (1970), a commentary on Balzac which shows his own outstanding gift for formal inventiveness) and even in the social sciences, which depend on ordinary language. Other thinkers had come to the same conclusion, a major factor of this disaffection towards science being the disillusionment of French intellectuals with Marxist rationality, where truth is both intelligible and historical. This left the individual as the sole remaining value, and Barthes's lifelong aspirations towards self-expression came to the fore in the semi-autobiographical works like *Le Plaisir du texte* (1973) *(The Pleasure of the Text,* 1975), *Barthes par Barthes* (1975) *(Roland Barthes by Roland Barthes,* 1977), and *Fragments d'un discours amoureux* (1977) *(A Lover's Discourse: Fragments,* 1978). They even saved him from total theoretical nihilism, since his last work, *La Chambre claire* (1980) *(Camera Lucida,* 1982) unites the scientific and the personal, the observed and the observer; this enquiry into the essence of photography where grief is an actual agent of discovery fittingly sums up a career which epitomized the self-consciousness typical of modern science and modern art.

Annette Lavers
University College London

Further Reading
Culler, J. (1983), *Barthes,* London.
Lavers, A. (1982), *Roland Barthes, Structuralism and After,* London.

Basic Needs

The concept of 'basic needs' has played a big part in analysing conditions in poor countries in recent years. In reports produced by international agencies the term has a long history (see, for example, Drewnowski and Scott, 1966). But the term was given particularly wide currency after the International Labour Office's World Employment Conference at Geneva in 1976, where it was formally adopted. Basic needs were said to include two elements:

> Firstly, they include certain minimum requirements of a family for private consumption: adequate food, shelter and clothing, as well as certain household furniture and equipment. Second, they include essential services provided by and for the community at large, such as safe drinking water, sanitation, public transport and health, education and cultural facilities. . . . The concept of basic needs should be placed within a context of a nation's overall economic and social development. In no circumstances should it be taken to mean merely the minimum necessary for subsistence; it should be placed within a context of national independence, the dignity of individuals and peoples and their freedom to chart their destiny without hindrance (ILO, 1976, pp.24–5).

The idea has played a prominent part in a succession of national plans (see, for example, Ghai *et al.,* 1979) and in international reports (see, for example, UNESCO, 1978, and the Brandt Report, 1980).

The term is quite clearly an enlargement of the subsistence concept, the older idea that families could be assessed as to whether their incomes were 'sufficient to obtain the minimum necessaries for the maintenance of merely physical efficiency' (Rowntree, 1901). However, the 'basic needs' formulation differs to the extent that it adds a new emphasis on minimum facilities required by local communities. The arbitrariness of the criteria used to select the items on the list is very evident. Moreover, the needs of populations cannot be defined adequately just by reference to the physical needs of individuals *and* the reference to a few of the more obvious physical provisions and services required by local communities. The exposition of need depends on some assumptions about the functioning and development of societies. The emerging *social* expectations laid upon the citizens of poor countries during periods of development are not adequately acknowledged. The disproportionate poverty and deprivation experienced by tribal groups, ethnic minorities, women, the elderly, children and people with disabilities in such countries is not adequately allowed for in this formulation.

It is important to recognize the function of 'basic needs' in the debates going on about the relationship between the First and Third Worlds. The more that social aspects of need are acknowledged, the more it becomes necessary to accept the relativity of need to the world's and national resources. The more the concept is restricted to physical goods and facilities, the easier it is to argue that economic growth alone, rather than a complex combination of growth, redistribution and reorganization of trading and other institutional relationships, is implied.

Peter Townsend
University of Bristol

References

Brandt, W. (chairman) (1980), *North-South: A Programme for Survival*, London.
Drewnowski, J. and Scott, W. (1966), *The Level of Living Index*, United Nations, Research Institute for Social Development, Research Report No. 4, Geneva.
Ghai, D., Godfrey, M. and Lisk, F. (1979), *Planning for Basic Needs in Kenya*, International Labour Organization, Geneva.
ILO (1976), *Employment Growth and Basic Needs: A One-World Problem*, Geneva.
Rowntree, B.S. (1901), *Poverty: A Study of Town Life*, London.
UNESCO (1978), *Study in Depth on the Concept of Basic Human Needs in Relation to Various Ways of Life and its Possible Implications for the Action of the Organizations*, Paris.
See also: *human needs; poverty; relative deprivation; social indicators.*

Bateson, Gregory (1904–80)

An elusive, Cambridge-trained anthropologist who made his career largely in the United States, Bateson was an interdisciplinary innovator and generalist, with strong interests in philosophy and ecology.

The youngest son of the Cambridge geneticist, William Bateson, his upbringing left him a zoologist by training and marked him as a naturalist by inclination. He was thus well suited to contribute to British social anthropology in the 1920s, when the worth of biological analogies in the social sciences was being debated. Gregory Bateson's awkward classic, *Naven* (1936), a study of ritual among a New Guinea people, broke ground theoretically: its argument was self-referential and focused explicitly on abstracting patterns of conflict in social relations.

During the New Guinea fieldwork, Bateson met the American cultural anthropologist Margaret Mead, whom he later married. In 1936 they did fieldwork together in Bali, resulting in the publication of a unique photographic ethnography, *Balinese Character* (1942). Influenced by the American subdiscipline of culture-and-personality and by cybernetic theories of self-correcting machinery, Bateson became interested in problems posed by theories of learning. He studied communication and learning among aquatic mammals and families of schizophrenics while based in a Veterans Hospital in Palo Alto, California. Following the failure of dolphin research in the 1960s, he turned his attention to global ecological crises and the bearing of cybernetic theory upon Western thinking.

Bateson's most influential post-war work came in 1956. Seeking a theory of communication, he developed an interpretation of schizophrenia in which the concept of a 'double bind' played a central role. Double binds were patterns of paradoxical love/hate messages exchanged in families leading to the psychosis of one of the members. Bateson regarded this theory as an attack upon reductionist learning theory. He was dismayed when his notion and the holistic focus on the family as an integrated unit was taken up for therapeutic purposes by psychiatrists.

It is, as yet, too early to assess Bateson's unique career and his various contributions to the social sciences. His diverse enterprise can be approached best in the anthology *Steps to an Ecology of Mind* (1973). His final book, *Mind and Nature* (1978), returned to an early interest in the analogy between evolutionary change and the structure of mind.

David Lipset
University of Minnesota

Further Reading

Lipset, D. (1982), *Gregory Bateson: The Legacy of a Scientist*, Boston.

Bayes' Theorem

Bayes' Theorem is an elementary result in the theory of probability named after the Reverend Thomas Bayes, an English Presbyterian minister who, in a posthumously published essay (Bayes, 1764), first presented a special case of it, and proposed its use in statistical inference. When viewed as part of probability theory, Bayes' Theorem is a simple rule for computing the conditional probability of each of a set of k mutually exclusive and exhaustive events H_1, H_2, ..., H_k, when an event E is given:

$$Pr(H_i|E) = \frac{Pr(H_i)Pr(E|H_i)}{\sum\limits_{j=1}^{k} Pr(H_j)Pr(E|H_j)} , i = 1,2,...,k .$$

Here $Pr(H_i)$ is the *prior* probability of the event H_i, and $Pr(E|H_i)$ is the conditional probability of the event E given that H_i has occurred or is true. The rule then gives the *posterior* probability of the event H_i given the occurrence of E, $P(H_i|E)$.

When Bayes' Theorem is used as the basis of statistical inference, the occurrence of E might correspond to the results of an experiment or the data from a sample survey, and the events H_i, H_2, ..., H_k might correspond to competing hypotheses or to different values of a parameter in a statistical model. The difficulty that has prevented the use of Bayes' Theorem for virtually all statistical inference purposes is the determination of the *a priori* probabilities, $Pr(H_i)$ for i = 1,2,...,k. The lack of agreement regarding the values of these *a priori* probabilities has led many statisticians to turn to other modes of inference.

Bayesian inference or Bayesian statistics is an approach to inference linked to the theory of subjective or personal probability, based on degrees of belief as opposed to being based only on long-run frequencies. Subject to formal rules of *coherence*, each individual assesses personal, *a priori* probabilities, $Pr(H_i)$, and updates them using the data via Bayes' Theorem to produce personal *a posteriori* probabilities. The rise of current interest in the subjective approach dates to the work of Bruno de Finetti in the 1930s, and Leonard J. Savage in the 1950s. Bayes' Theorem now plays, for many statisticians, the role in inference originally described in Thomas Bayes's historic essay.

Stephen E. Fienberg
Carnegie–Mellon University

Reference
Bayes, T. (1963 [1764]), *Facsimiles of Two Papers by Bayes*, New York.
See also: *statistical reasoning*.

Behaviourism

Behaviourism is mainly a twentieth-century orientation within the discipline of psychology in the United States. The behavioural approach emphasizes the objective study of the relationships between environmental manipulations and human and animal behaviour change, usually in laboratory or relatively controlled institutional settings. Emerging as a discrete movement just prior to World War I, behaviourism represented a vigorous rejection of psychology defined as the introspective study of the human mind and consciousness. Early behaviourists eschewed the structuralism of Wundt and Titchener, the functional mentalism of James, Dewey, Angell and Carr, and the relativism and phenomenology of Gestalt psychology.

John B. Watson is credited with declaring behaviourism a new movement in 1913; but the foundations of the development extend back to the ancient Greeks and include empiricism, elementism, associationism, objectivism and naturalism. The direct antecedents of of behaviourism during the late nineteenth and early twentieth centuries were: the studies of animal behaviour and the functional orientation inspired by Darwin's theory of evolution; the conditioning research of Russian physiologists Ivan Pavlov and Vladimir Bekhterev emphasizing stimulus substitution in the context of reflexive behaviour; and the puzzle box studies of American psychologist Edward Thorndike concerned with the effects of the consequences of behaviour on response frequency. The two predominant and often competing theoretical-procedural models of conditioning research have been classical conditioning derived from the work of Pavlov and Bekhterev, and Skinner's operant conditioning.

While it is generally claimed that behaviourism as a distinct school ceased to exist by the 1950s, behaviourism as a general orientation has gone through the following overlapping periods: classical behaviourism (1900–25), represented by the work of Thorndike and Watson; neo-behaviourism (1920s–40s), an exciting time when the theories of Clark Hull, Edward Tolman, Edwin Guthrie and Burrhus F. Skinner competed for pre-eminence; Hullian behaviourism (1940s–50s) when Hull's complex hypothetico-deductive behaviour theory appeared most promising; Skinnerian behaviourism (1960s–mid-1970s) during which time operant conditioning techniques, emphasizing the control of behaviour implicit in the consequences of behaviour, afforded the most powerful methodologies; and finally cognitive behaviourism (1975–present) when the limits of a purely Skinnerian approach to behaviour change became increasingly apparent, and cognitive perspectives, such as social learning theories, seemed necessary to account for behaviour change.

A behavioural orientation has been central to twentieth-century psychology in the United States primarily because of a strong faith in laboratory research and experimental methodologies; an interest in studying the process of learning; a preference for quantitative information; the elimination from the discipline of ambiguous concepts and investigations of complex and therefore difficult to describe private (subjective) experiences; and, since the late 1950s, a very conservative approach to theory building.

While each of the major behavioural programmes from Thorndike's to Skinner's failed to provide a comprehensive account of behaviour change, the behavioural orientation has led to the development of behaviour-control methodologies with useful application in most areas of psychology. In addition, the movement has inspired precision and accountability in psychological inquiry.

Behavioural methodologies have, of course, been employed by psychologists in countries other than the United States, particularly those with strong scientific traditions such as Britain and Japan. Behavioural assumptions have also influenced other social sciences, especially sociology and political science. But because laboratory animal research is central to the behavioural orientation, behaviourism as a major movement only developed in psychology.

Albert R. Gilgen
University of Northern Iowa

Further Reading

Marx, M. H. and Hillix, W.A. (1979), *Systems and Theories in Psychology*, New York.

See also: *behaviour therapy; cognitive-behavioural therapy; conditioning, classical and operant; Hull; Pavlov; Skinner; Watson.*

Behaviour Therapy

The movement that has come to be known as behaviour therapy (or behaviour modification) arose shortly after the end of World War II, having its origins independently in the United States, Britain and South Africa. In Britain, behaviour therapy developed mainly out of dissatisfaction with the traditional role of the clinical psychologist who worked within a medical model which likened 'mental disease' to 'bodily disease', except that the former was a disease of the mind rather than the body. There was also dissatisfaction with the psychodynamic approach that viewed patients' symptoms as indicators of some underlying conflict requiring for their resolution in-depth analysis, and with the diagnostic (testing) approach resulting in patients being labelled, but without any obvious consequent implications for therapy.

To replace these traditional approaches, it was proposed that psychologists make use of the entire body of knowledge and theory that constituted psychology as a scientific discipline and in which only the psychologist was an expert. In practice, the aim was to be achieved by stressing experimental investigation of the single case (that is, the presenting patient), in which the precise nature of the patient's problem was to be elucidated by systematic investigations. Behaviour therapy was simply the extension of this method to attempts to modify the maladaptive behaviour by similar controlled experimental procedures. In the United States, behaviour therapy developed mainly out of the efforts to apply the principles of operant conditioning to the description and control of human behaviour, especially, in its early stages, the bizarre behaviours of psychotics. In South Africa, the impetus for behaviour therapy came largely from the work of Wolpe. His reciprocal inhibition theory, developed from studies of animal neuroses, underlay the technique of systematic desensitization which was applied to the treatment of phobias with great success, and served more than anything else to bring behaviour therapy to notice as a significant new way of approaching the therapy of maladaptive behaviours.

Between 1950 and 1970 behaviour therapy developed rapidly, its achievements being critically reviewed in three simultaneous publications (Bandura, 1969; Franks, 1969; Yates, 1970). Although Eysenck's definition of behaviour therapy as 'the attempt to alter human behaviour and emotion in a beneficial manner according to the laws of modern learning theory' (Eysenck, 1964) has been very widely accepted, Yates (1970) has stressed that behaviour therapy is a much broader endeavour than Eysenck's definition suggests, since, in principle, the whole body of the knowledge and theory that constitutes psychology is available to the behaviour therapist when dealing with a presenting patient. But for some behaviour therapists, the development of techniques that 'work' is more important than the use of theory and the experimental method, even though the best-known technique of all (Wolpe's systematic desensitization) was based on specific theoretical considerations. Justification for a technique-oriented approach, however, stems in part from the demonstration that flooding, a technique directly contradicting Wolpe's theory, appears to be as effective as systematic desensitization in the therapy of phobias. There are few other standard techniques available, one notable successful example being the bell-and-pad method of treating enuresis (bedwetting).

The rapid growth of behaviour therapy has led to its application to a far wider range of problems than could earlier have been envisaged (Yates, 1981). In its early stages behaviour therapy was mainly concerned with the investigation of individuals, either alone or in hospital settings. Now it is widely used by professional social workers, in marital therapy, in the design of social communities, in crime prevention and the treatment of criminals, to name but a few areas. The approach has been utilized in the control of littering, energy consumption and refuse disposal; in community aid to the disadvantaged (such as persuading low-income parents to have their children accept dental care). A good indication of the vastly expanded range of behaviour therapy can be gained by perusing successive volumes of the *Journal of Applied Behavior Analysis* (1968+), *Progress in Behavior Modification* (1975+) and the *Annual Review of Behavior Therapy* (1969+).

An important development over the past ten years has been the attempt to reconcile behaviour therapy with psychodynamic psychotherapy and even to integrate them. Yates (1970) had argued that the two approaches differed so fundamentally in their theories about the genesis and maintenance of abnormalities of behaviour that any reconciliation and integration was impossible. However, such moves had started as early as 1966 and by 1980 had achieved considerable progress (Yates, 1983). The strength of the movement is indicated by the appearance of a symposium in *Behavior Therapy* (1982, 13: articles by Kendall, Goldfried, Wachtel and Garfield). While admitting the strength of the evidence in favour of a reconciliation and integration, a fundamental difficulty remains, namely, the relationship between theory and therapy which makes it difficult, if not impossible, for agreement to be reached on the appropriate therapy for disorders such as enuresis and stuttering; this consequently undermines the apparent integration achieved in relation to more complex disorders such as anxiety (Yates, 1983).

Behaviour therapy has become as prominent an approach to the explanation and treatment of disorders of behaviour in the second half of this century as psychoanalysis was in the first half. There seems no doubt that it has fundamentally and irrevocably altered the framework within which disorders of behaviour are viewed. Its greatest virtue is perhaps its relative open-endedness and therefore its capacity for change and self-correction in the light of empirical evidence. It seems unlikely that it will suffer the fate of many of its predecessors, which became prematurely frozen within a rigid conceptual and methodological framework.

Aubrey J. Yates
University of Western Australia

References
Bandura, A. (1969), *Principles of Behavior Modification*, New York.
Eysenck, H.J. (1964), 'The nature of behaviour therapy', in H. J. Eysenck (ed.), *Experiments in Behaviour Therapy*, London.
Franks, C. (1969), *Behavior Therapy: Appraisal and Status*, New York.
Yates, A. J. (1970), *Behavior Therapy*, New York.
Yates, A. J. (1981), 'Behaviour therapy: past, present, future – imperfect?', *Clinical Psychology Review*, 1.
Yates, A. J. (1983), 'Behaviour therapy and psychodynamic psychotherapy: basic conflict or reconciliation and integration?', *British Journal of Clinical Psychology*, 22.

Further Reading
Kazdin, A. E. (1978), *History of Behavior Modification: Experimental Foundations of Contemporary Research*, Baltimore.
Wachtel, P. L. (1977), *Psychoanalysis and Behavior Therapy: Toward an Integration*, New York.
Wolpe, J. (1958), *Psychotherapy by Reciprocal Inhibition*, Stanford.
See also: *aversion therapy; behaviourism; cognitive-behavioural therapy; conditioning.*

Bentham, Jeremy (1748–1832)

Jeremy Bentham was undoubtedly one of the most important and influential figures in the development of modern social science. His numerous writings are major contributions to the development of philosophy, law, government, economics, social administration and public policy, and many have become classic texts in these fields. To these subjects he brought an analytical precision and careful attention to detail which, especially in matters of legal organization and jurisprudence, had not been attempted since Aristotle, and he transformed in method and substance the way these subjects were conceived. He combined a critical rationalism and empiricism with a vision of reform and, latterly, radical reform, which gave unity and direction to what became Philosophic Radicalism. Although he was not the first philosopher to use the greatest happiness principle as the standard of right and wrong, he is rightly remembered as the founder of modern utilitarianism. Many of Bentham's writings were never published in his lifetime or were completed by various editors. The new edition of the *Collected Works* (1968 — in progress) will replace in approximately sixty-five volumes the inadequate *Works of Jeremy Bentham* (1838–43), edited by John Bowring, and will reveal for the first time the full extent and scope of Bentham's work.

Bentham is best known for some of his earliest writings. *An Introduction to the Principles of Morals and Legislation* (printed in 1780 and published in 1789) and *Of Laws in General* (not published until 1945) are important texts in legal philosophy and, together with his critique of William Blackstone's *Commentaries on the Laws of England* in the *Comment on the Commentaries* (published first in 1928) and *A Fragment on Government* (1776), represent major landmarks in the development of jurisprudence. The *Introduction to the Principles of*

Morals and Legislation was also intended to serve as an introduction to a penal code, which was an important part of a lifelong ambition, never fully realized, of constructing a complete code of laws (latterly called the *Pannomion*). At this time Bentham also turned to economic questions which were to occupy him in various forms throughout his life. His first publication was the *Defence of Usury* (1787), a critique of Adam Smith's treatment of this subject in *The Wealth of Nations*.

From the outset of his career, Bentham was devoted to reform and especially to the reform of legal institutions. His attitude towards fundamental political reform developed more slowly. Although at the time of the French Revolution he was not part of the radical movement in England, he wrote numerous manuscripts in support of democratic institutions in France. He eventually reacted strongly against the excesses of the revolution, but earlier contacts, largely developed through Lord Lansdowne, and the publication of his *Draught of a New Plan for the Organisation of the Judicial Establishment of France*, led to his being made an honorary citizen of France. One important development of this period was his friendship with Etienne Dumont, the Swiss reformer and scholar, whose French versions of Bentham's works, especially the *Traités de législation, civile et pénale* (1802), were read throughout Europe and Latin America and earned for Bentham a considerable international reputation. Following the French Revolution much of Bentham's practical energies were devoted, in conjunction with his brother Samuel, to establishing model prisons, called Panopticons, in various countries. His main effort in England failed, and this failure, though ultimately compensated by the government, was one factor leading him to take up the cause of radical political reform. The influence of James Mill was perhaps the most important factor (there were many) in his 'conversion' to radicalism in 1809–10, and the publication of *A Plan of Parliamentary Reform* in 1817 launched the Philosophic Radicals in their quest for parliamentary reform. In the 1820s, though now in his seventies, Bentham resumed the task of codification and the construction of the *Pannomion* in response to requests from governments and disciples in Spain, Portugal, Greece and Latin America. In his massive, unfinished *Constitutional Code* (1822–), he set forth a theory of representative democracy which was a grand synthesis of many of his ideas and a classic of liberal political thought.

Frederick Rosen
The London School of Economics
and Political Science

Further Reading

Halévy, E. (1901–4), *La Formation du Radicalisme Philosophique*, 3 vols, Paris.

Hart, H. L. A. (1982), *Essays on Bentham: Jurisprudence and Political Theory*, Oxford.

Hume, L. J. (1981), *Bentham and Bureaucracy*, Cambridge.

Rosen, F. (1983), *Jeremy Bentham and Representative Democracy*, Oxford.

See also: *Mill; utilitarianism.*

Bereavement

The term bereavement covers any situation in which people experience the loss of an object to which they were attached. In a narrow sense it is taken to refer to the loss by death of a loved person, but in its wider sense can cover many other losses.

Bereavement includes grief, the psychological reaction of the individual, and mourning, the social expression of grief (although this term has also been ambiguously used for the process of grieving).

Burton's claim that grief is 'the model, epitome and chief cause of melancholia' (1621) is echoed in Freud's classical paper, 'Mourning and melancholia' (1917), but it was Lindemann's study of 101 bereaved people that gave rise to the first, and arguably the best, systematic description of 'The symptomatology and management of acute grief' (1944). More recently, John Bowlby (1980) and sociologist Peter Marris (1974) have classified the nature of grief and the central place which it must play in our understanding of the human reaction to social change.

Grief is a process of psychological change through which the individual tends to pass from (1) a phase of numbness or disbelief, to (2) pining and yearning for the lost object, to (3) disorganization and despair, and followed by (4) a phase of reorganization and recovery. These phases are not clear-cut and the griever moves back and forth across them as each reminder of the loss evokes another pang of grief (Bowlby and Parkes, 1970).

During this process the individual can be seen as engaging in a struggle between competing motivations:
(a) to search for and recover the lost object;
(b) to find some way of minimizing or avoiding the pain of grief;
(c) to revise and relearn basic assumptions about the world that have been invalidated by the loss.

How these competing urges are expressed depends upon a wide range of individual and social factors, hence the confusing diversity of the manifestations of mourning reported by anthropologists (Rosenblatt *et al.*, 1976). Nevertheless, a common pattern can be discerned and has given rise to ritual observances which often seem to provide social support and a frame of reference for the bereaved, a *rite de passage*.

Because grief is so painful and because some patterns of grieving are more painful than others, it is not surprising to find that many bereaved people come to regard themselves, and to be regarded by others, as sick. While there may be some justification for regarding certain complications of grieving as pathological, the wholesale medicalization of mourning has created fresh problems for the mourner. Some bereaved people readily use alcohol or medically-prescribed drugs in order to suppress the 'symptoms' of grief and cling to mourning as a 'sick role'.

The breakdown in developed countries of extended family networks, together with disillusionment with the belief systems and loss of many of the rituals attending bereavement, has added to the plight of the bereaved, as has the increased mechanization and alienation of our systems of medical care which effectively remove the dying person from his family and deprive the family of the opportunity to care. Consequently, grief is often complicated by bewilderment, avoidance, anger and guilt. But the pendulum is now swinging, with the emergence of hospices, bereavement counselling, self-help (or mutual help) groups and a resurgence of neighbourhood and family support for the bereaved.

Colin Murray Parkes
The London Hospital Medical School
University of London

References
Bowlby, J. (1980), *Loss: Sadness and Depression*, vol. III of *Attachment and Loss*, London.
Bowlby, J. and Parkes, C. M. (eds) (1970), 'Separation and loss', in E. J. Anthony and C. Koupernik (eds), *The Child in his Family*, vol. I, New York.
Marris, P. (1974), *Loss and Change*, London.
Rosenblatt, P. C., Walsh, R.P. and Jackson, D. A. (1976), *Grief and Mourning in Cross-Cultural Perspective*, New Haven.

Further Reading
Lindemann, E. (1944), 'The symptomatology and management of acute grief', *American Journal of Psychiatry*, 101.
Parkes, C.M. (1972), *Bereavement: Studies of Grief in Adult Life*, London.
See also: *attachment; Bowlby; death; separation and loss.*

Big Man

Big Man refers to a person of repute and influence in Melanesian society. The term has probably an indigenous derivation taken over by ethnographers, people in this part of the world referring in Pidgin to adult males in general, and talented respected persons in particular, as *bikpela man*.

A critical feature is that the status of Big Man is achieved, not ascribed, although in some places sons of Big Men are reckoned to be in a better position than others to make the grade. It is an informal standing, not an instituted nor inherited office. It carries no authority. An analogous position in our society would be the respect and admiration accorded to an outstanding all-rounder in a sports club.

Any man endowed with the required qualities can aspire to the status. These qualities vary from one society to another. They range from an above average ability to contribute to festivals and manipulate wealth in ceremonial exchanges, to a fearless warrior reputation backed by an aggressive temperament, from a capacity for oration and persuasion, to specialized ritual knowledge which may extend to a fearsome renown for sorcery. A Big Man's reputation and status decline as these qualities wane with age; the distinction depends on current ability, not previous glories.

The influence that accrues to a person who achieves Big Man status fluctuates from one region to another. In some they reportedly exert considerable political control over the activities of small, varyingly constituted local groups, directing by force of character, proven ability and by putting others in their debt. Some have even referred to despotic Big Men. In other regions, while some influence accrues to esteemed Big Men as first among equals, they cannot be said to achieve positions of leadership.

Paul Sillitoe
University of Durham

Further Reading
Bailey, F. G. (1969), *Strategems and Spoils*, Oxford.
Sahlins, M. (1963), 'Poor man, rich man, big man, chief: political types in Melanesia and Polynesia', *Comparative Studies in Society and History*, 5.
See also: *leadership.*

Bilingualism

A working definition of bilingualism is the use by individuals of two languages in their daily lives. Balanced bilingualism – equal use of and proficiency in two languages – is rare, and so it is possible to speak of degrees of bilingualism according to the level of dominance of one or other language. Multilingualism, the use of three or more languages, should be considered under the same heading, as should bi- and multi-culturalism.

Bilingualism used to be seen as occurring in clearly-defined areas of the world, such as Wales, Canada, Belgium and South Africa, but we now realize that bilingualism is not restricted to such indigenous groups. It occurs in many areas of the world where minority groups live and work within a majority culture, usually as the result of immigration, for general reasons (as in Britain and the US) or to meet specific labour needs (as in Scandinavia and West Germany). The rights and needs of ethnic minorities are now a major concern in many countries.

People are beginning to realize, especially in Canada, that bilingualism may in certain circumstances be an advantage, not only in giving access to two cultures but also in the educational development of children. Many parents are now seeking information and advice on bringing up children bilingually. Earlier attention focused on the disadvantages and handicaps of bilingualism, often because bilingual children were tested in their weaker second language and naturally achieved poor results, or because research failed to take into account socioeconomic background. However, problems associated with bilingualism must not be ignored, because they can be severe in political, religious, cultural and educational spheres, quite apart from the emotional stress an individual may suffer.

The study of bilingualism is interdisciplinary, involving mainly linguistics, psychology, sociology and education. If, in addition, we include biculturalism, the difficulty of bilingualism as an area for study and research can be readily understood. Current issues in bilingualism include theoretical investigations, such as the relationship between diglossia and bilingualism, learning disabilities amongst bilinguals, the fundamental nature of bilingualism, and teaching methodology. Practical considerations cover the many and varied questions of policy, both in the wider language usage in a nation or community and in the development of bilingual education. If a bilingual education policy is implemented, then curriculum development is required to meet the demand for classroom methods and materials, yet most minority languages provide a small, unprofitable market, as in Wales or Friesland. There is increasing emphasis on multicultural education, especially in England and the US. The problems and challenges are clearly seen, but courses for teachers, for example, range from an obsessive concern with the trivia of culture to an inconclusive attempt to explore philosophical fundamentals.

Derrick Sharp
University College of Swansea

Further Reading
Baetens Beardsmore, H. (1982), *Bilingualism: Basic Principles*, Clevedon.
Fishman, J. A. (1976), *Bilingual Education: An International Sociological Perspective*, Rowley.
Lambert, W. E. (1977), 'The effects of bilingualism on the individual: cognitive and sociocultural consequences', in P. A. Hornby (ed.), *Bilingualism: Psychological, Social and Educational Implications*, New York.
Saunders, G. (1982), *Bilingual Children: Guidance for the Family*, Clevedon.
Swain, M. (1980), 'Bilingual education for the English-Canadian: three models of "immersion" ', in L. K. Boey (ed.), *Bilingual Education*, Singapore.
See also: *language and culture; psycholinguistics; sociolinguistics.*

Biological Psychiatry

The long history of psychiatry reflects a constant conflict between philosophical idealism, with its insistence on the primacy of ideas, and materialism, with its emphasis on the biological substrate. In the US a psychological approach – notably in the form of psychoanalysis – was dominant in the 1940s. A counter movement developed to restore the medical, and especially neurological, dimensions of psychiatry. It called itself biological psychiatry, and its basic assumption was that the psychoses reflected actual derangements of brain function, and should be studied and treated by neurological as well as psychological means. The movement was initiated by Johannes Maargaard Nielsen, a Los Angeles neurologist, who founded a Society of Biological Psychiatry in 1946. Though a behavioural scientist like the late Horsley Gantt, a pupil of Pavlov, was a president of the American Society of Biological Psychiatry, that society tended to focus on physiological research and paid relatively little attention to the more general scientific study of behaviour. This has perpetuated and reinforced the notion that biological psychiatry is limited to physiology, but its development has served to stimulate the use of scientific and experimental methods in psychiatric research, and has fostered a preference for systematic data collection and analysis over the use of anecdotal case histories and appeals to unvalidated theories.

Shock treatment. The physiological approach to psychiatric disorder received enormous impetus with the promulgation of the insulin shock treatment of schizophrenia by Manfred Sakel in the 1930s. Sakel, a general physician, had observed that deep insulin coma (due to low blood sugar), if terminated promptly, had a beneficial effect on some forms of psychotic excitement. He then elaborated a systematic application of the principle for the treatment of schizophrenia, with the sponsorship and support of Professor Poetzl of the University of Vienna. Since it was the first effective treatment of schizophrenia, and the most significant advance in psychiatry since the discovery of the fever treatment of general paresis by Wagner-Jauregg, it won wide acclaim: Sakel was invited to the US where he resided until his death in 1957 (Wortis, 1959).

In spite of the initial resistance of the psychiatric establishment, insulin treatment was almost universally accepted, and paved the way for the next big discovery, Meduna's convulsive treatment. Like insulin shock, this treatment was based mainly on empirical observation, and its mode of action, as with insulin shock, is still not understood. Initially Meduna induced convulsions by injection of stimulants, but this was soon superseded by the use of an electrical stimulus applied to the scalp. The term 'shock' was used in connection with the insulin treatment because the occurrence of unconsciousness from insulin overdosage was regarded as a dangerous complication in the treatment of diabetics, and the warning word seemed appropriate. Later, the use of a brief electric stimulus to induce a fit was also called a shock, but the term, however, has unfortunately been unduly alarming, since in neither of these treatments does the patient subjectively experience any shock.

Lobotomy. Another treatment that gained wide acceptance in this period was pre-frontal lobotomy, based on the observation of Moniz in 1936 that brain lesions which interrupted thalamo-cortical pathways relieved anxiety and tension, and ameliorated some psychoses (Freeman and Watts, 1950). The price for this amelioration, however, was a loss of significant brain function, with a blunting of personality and increased impulsivity. As a result the treatment has fallen largely into disfavour.

The new psychopharmacology. Though insulin treatment is time-consuming and expensive, and electroshock causes memory difficulties, all these treatments still have some applicability, especially electroconvulsive therapy. But in the past three decades they have been largely supplanted by a wide range of new psychopharmacological agents. The first of these, chlorpromazine, was developed in 1951 by Laborit, in France, and is a non-hypnotic sedative with a selective action on the lower brain centres that regulate emotion. It proved to be remarkably effective in schizophrenia and related psychoses. A variety of stimulants are now also available to relieve depression: a profusion of new drugs are now used for many minor and major disorders. Most recently nutritional therapy has been added to this armamentarium (Pfeiffer, 1975).

The remarkable technologies that now allow us to explore the chemistry of neurotransmission (Krieger, 1983), to measure metabolism within the human brain by computerized radiography, to insert genes into living cells, and to study ultramicroscopic structures, all hold much promise, and may soon uncover the causes of mental illness.

Psychotherapy. The rigorous experimental methodology that has been demanded of all these new treatments has also affected psychotherapy. The first of the psychotherapeutic schools to publish controlled studies with strict experimental design and statistical analysis was behavioural therapy, derived from Pavlovian conditioning. In the more recent period, however, all schools of psychotherapy, including psychoanalysis, have been made aware of the need to subject their methods and their claims to the same scientific rigour of biological psychiatry. At the same time there is always the danger that a crude and uncritical application of physical treatment modalities can lead to new excesses. Psychiatrists, as always, need to be alert to the whole range of physiological, psychological and social factors involved in psychiatric disorders.

Joseph Wortis
State University of New York, Stony Brook

References
Freeman, W. and Watts, J. W. (1950), *Psychosurgery,* Springfield, Ill.
Krieger, D. T. (1983), 'Brain peptides: what, where and why', *Science,* 222.
Pfeiffer, C. C. (1975), *Mental and Elemental Nutrients,* New Canaan.
Wortis, J. (1959), 'The history of insulin shock treatment', in M. Rinkel (ed.), *Insulin Treatment in Psychiatry,* New York.
Wortis, J. (1983), 'Johannes Maargaard Nielsen', *Biological Psychiatry,* 18.
See also: *electroconvulsive therapy; genetic aspects of mental illness; nervous system; physiological psychology; psychopharmacology.*

Birth Order

The extensive research on birth order may reflect the relative ease with which it can be assessed, or perhaps its intuitive appeal as a source of individual differences in behaviour. For whatever reasons, psychologists have studied the effects of birth order on many variables, including physical and mental health, intelligence and achievement, personality, and social relations. They have been especially interested in the effects on intelligence and personality.

The relationship between birth order and intelligence was first discussed by Sir Francis Galton, who noted that prominent English scientists were usually the first-born or only children in their families. Galton suggested that the special attention that these scientists received from their parents during childhood may have enhanced their intellectual development. Galton's work stimulated many other psychologists to study the effects of birth order on intelligence. Unfortunately, this later research often suffered from serious methodological problems and rarely reflected any clear theoretical perspectives. The observed effects of birth order on intelligence were sometimes positive and sometimes negative, and never very strong. In fact, some of the best research showed that those effects disappeared entirely when other relevant variables such as family size were taken into account. Many psychologists now believe that there is no real relationship at all between birth order and intelligence.

Alfred Adler was the first to discuss the relationship between birth order and personality. On the basis of his clinical experiences, Adler suggested that birth order can influence a child's relationships with other family members and thereby affect his adult personality. For example, the pampering that last-born children often receive from their parents and siblings could cause them to became lazy, unambitious and insecure as adults. Adler's work led other psychologists to investigate the relationship between birth order and personality, but much of this research was also plagued by methodological problems and theoretical ambiguities. Although many significant birth order effects were reported, they were often difficult to interpret and were rarely replicable. Only a few birth order effects were both sensible and reliable, and those seemed to be mediated by other variables. For example, several studies showed that first-borns were more dependent and conforming than others, yet this relationship was severely attenuated when differences in social class were taken into account. These and other research findings persuaded many psychologists that birth order and personality are essentially unrelated.

There are clearly some good reasons to be dismayed by the current status of research on the psychological effects of birth order. Indeed, some experts have recommended that such research be abandoned altogether. An alternative recommendation, more difficult but less extreme, might be to improve the quality of birth order research until it yields more meaningful results. At a methodological level, more attention should be given to such variables as family size, social status, and parental characteristics, all of which may be correlated with birth order and therefore involved in its effects. Birth order itself could also be measured in a more precise way by taking into account not only the ordinal position of the child in the family, but also the ages and sexes of his siblings. At a theoretical level, more formal theories are needed to generate clear and testable hypotheses about birth order effects. Such theories should ideally place birth order within the context of other family variables to which it is related. One approach that seems promising in this regard is the confluence model of intellectual development proposed by Zajonc and his colleagues (Zajonc and Markus, 1975; Zajonc, Markus and Markus, 1979). This theory and others like it should help to clarify the current confusion regarding birth order effects.

Richard Moreland
University of Pittsburgh

References

Zajonc, R. B. and Markus, G. B. (1975), 'Birth order and intellectual development', *Psychological Review*, 82.

Zajonc, R. B., Markus, H. and Markus, G. B. (1979), 'The birth order puzzle', *Journal of Personality and Social Psychology*, 37.

Further Reading

Adams, B. N. (1972), 'Birth order: a critical review', *Sociometry*, 35.

Ernst, C. and Angst, J. (1983), *Birth Order: Its Influence on Personality*, Berlin.

Falbo, T. (1977), 'The only child: a review', *Journal of Individual Psychology*, 33.

Schooler, C. (1972), 'Birth order effects: not here, not now!', *Psychological Bulletin*, 78.

See also: *Adler; intelligence and intelligence testing.*

Black Economy

In the strict sense, the black economy refers to that part of the economy based on illegal transactions, or to economic behaviour that is against the law. This covers income earned through criminal activities or undeclared but legally acquired income. In a broader sense, the black economy encompasses all kinds of economic transactions not reflected in the official statistics. Dealing with the black economy in this broader sense, one must also consider tax evasion, whereby people avoid the intended level of taxation through loopholes in the law. Other terms in use are 'unobserved economy', 'underground economy', and 'secondary economy', which all make clear that the concept is not only concerned with illegal, but also with legal, transactions that may result in a difference between the actual workings of an economy and the picture provided of it by the official data.

Official employment figures do not fully reflect the unemployment situation. People who receive social payments because they are sick or handicapped are not actually part of the labour market, so they contribute to hidden unemployment. Conversely, others who are registered as unemployed are gainfully occupied, in which case there is greater employment than officially registered.

We have similar problems when we investigate private consumption. Those who acquire black money by not declaring their income to the tax authorities also spend part of it. If shops do not invoice purchases, then actual consumption will be higher than registered consumption. Consequently, in many countries the depression seems actually to have been less severe for consumers than one would expect on the basis of reported developments. Real income distribution is also different from what the records suggest. Registered salaries fail to take into account the various fringe benefits such as free telephone, free meals and travel perks, while, at the lower end of the income scale, people often receive unrecorded payments. This also applies to production, national income and the economic growth rate, where official estimates fall below the actual.

The black economy has always existed, but there are strong indications, supported by econometric research in Europe and the US, that it has grown from a marginal phenomenon to a major feature of modern welfare states only since World War II. It is not easy to quantify the significance of the black economy, because this depends largely on what aspects of it are being considered. If one considers only non-declared income and/or hidden production, empirical studies suggest that it amounts to between 20 and 30 per cent of the real national income.

The theoretical economists' explanation of why an individual would choose to participate in the black economy is based on a calculation of expected costs and benefits, rather than on any moral judgements. Looked at from this perspective, it is clear that heavy taxes play a role. Nevertheless, in the US where taxes are lower and the consequences of being caught more severe, the size of the black economy seems to be roughly the same as in Europe. It may be significant that people nowadays are more critical of government spending than in the past. Furthermore, the government may create situations in which both parties benefit if one party were to act illegally. There may also be a tendency for individuals to defer less to the views and decisions of authorities and to place greater reliance on individual opinions and participation in decision making.

If policy makers react by tightening the laws and punishing offenders, export of capital may be stimulated, and people will seek other ways of avoiding taxes. By basing policy measures on an economic analysis of the decision-making process in the black economy, it might be possible to predict individual reactions, and in this way to establish optimal rules and norms. One could, for example, avoid formulating laws that would enable both parties to benefit from illegal behaviour. But as long as governments are not prepared to base policy measures on an analysis of the phenomenon itself, the black economy will continue to grow.

A. Heertje
University of Amsterdam

Further Reading
Heertje, A., Allen, M. and Cohen, A. (1982), *The Black Economy*, London.
Mars, G. (1983), *Cheats at Work*, London.

Black Power

When, in the summer of 1966, Stokely Carmichael of the Student Non-Violent Coordinating Committee (SNCC) called for 'Black Power', it was not the first time that phrase had gained the attention of the Black community. Nor was it the first time that essentials of its meaning were voiced, for the desire of Blacks for self-determination and their insistence on their right to self-defence were expressed at least as early as 1829 in David Walker's *Appeal to the Colored Citizens of the World*. Such principles were affirmed by a succession of Black intellectuals after Walker, including W. E. B. Du Bois and Paul Robeson in the twentieth century. In addition, politician and Baptist minister, Adam Clayton Powell, Jr, used the precise phrase in his 'buy Black' economic campaigns in Harlem in the 1930s, and Richard Wright entitled his study of the independent nation of Ghana *Black Power* (1954).

What was surprising to most students of civil rights was that advocacy of Black Power, in this instance with overtones of hostility toward Whites, came at a time when it appeared America was ridding itself of racism. Even more people were surprised when SNCC asserted that integration is 'an insidious subterfuge' used by Whites to maintain control over Blacks. Despite the passage of the Civil Rights Act of 1964, which ended discrimination in public accommodation, and the Civil Rights Act of 1965, which greatly strengthened voting rights for Blacks, SNCC held that little of a substantive nature had been accomplished for Blacks generally. Not only did the masses, it was argued, lack the money with which to patronize hotels and restaurants in the South but their votes were being channelled into the Democratic Party, which blunted the radical edge of the movement.

Black Power was, in large measure, an attempt to fill a leadership vacuum, to redirect the energy of civil rights activists toward empowerment of the masses. Central to Black Power was the view that Blacks must overcome dependence on Whites and avoid being compromised by a Federal Government that at times collaborated with the worst enemies of freedom, even to the extent of complicity in the assassination of Black leaders. Still, Black Power was more a vaguely but powerfully felt sentiment than a practical plan for transforming the consciousness and condition of Black people. And that, perhaps more than anything else, resulted in its eclipse some time before its spokesmen took cognisance of its previous evolutions in history. Thus, the socialist dimension of the thought of Du Bois and Robeson was missed and, consequently, the connection between class and nationalism was not made.

The Black Power Movement met with a cold reception from the gradualist National Association for the Advancement of Colored People (NAACP) and from

Martin Luther King's more creative Southern Christian Leadership Conference (SCLC), principally because it was thought that Black Power was little more than a disturbing slogan. Nevertheless, self-assertiveness for Blacks and concern for the masses in the Carmichael formulation made Black Power appealing to young Blacks not only in America but elsewhere in the Black World, including the West Indies and South Africa.

References
Du Bois, W. E. B. (1940), *Dusk of Dawn*, New York.
Carmichael, S. and Hamilton, C. (1957), *Black Power*, New York.
Powell, A.C. (1945), *Marching Blacks*, New York.
See also: *ethnic groups; ethnic relations.*

Blau, Peter M. (1918–)

Peter Blau has contributed substantially, both theoretically and empirically, to the scientific analysis of social structure. He was a graduate student in sociology at Colombia University during a revival of Max Weber's theories of bureaucracy. Blau's dissertation, published as *The Dynamics of Bureaucracy* (1952), combined with those by Columbia graduates Philip Selznick and Alvin Gouldner to establish a foundation for the systematic study of formal organizations. His interest in bureaucracies continued for over two decades, although a collection of essays *On the Nature of Organizations* (1974) shows important shifts in theoretical orientation.

Initially, Blau adopted a social psychological perspective focusing on interpersonal relations among workers in bureaucracies. His exploration of how *formal* structures of organizations constrain *informal* social relations of bureaucrats remains a classic of sociological analysis. Blau's early social psychological perspective led to his first contribution to general social theory, *Exchange and Power in Social Life* (1964). Along with work by George Homans, Blau established 'exchange theory' in sociology, which tries to derive theories of social structure from simple processes of social association such as reciprocity and obligation, differentiation of power, bonds of attraction and competition for status.

In the late 1960s, Blau's orientation shifted from social psychological to social structural, from 'micro' to 'macro'. While making this transition, Blau stepped outside the specialty of formal organizations to collaborate with Otis Dudley Duncan on *The American Occupational Structure* (1967), an examination of inter-generational mobility and occupational achievement that initiated sophisticated statistical studies of social stratification and processes of 'status attainment'. His work on bureaucracies went on, but he focused on structural features of organizations, for example, how the size of a bureaucracy affected the proportion of its workers in administrative positions. The social structural perspective led to a second contribution to general social theory, *Inequality and Heterogeneity* (1977). With the elegantly simple definition of 'social structure' as 'the distribution of people among social positions', Blau has offered several (now empirically confirmed) predictions, among them the idea that as a social group increases in size, the proportion of its members who marry outside the group declines.

Blau's theorizing has been consistently rigorous: he defines his terms precisely, announces clearly his assumptions, and states his principles in a way that yields empirical deductions. He once wrote, 'The theorist's aim is to discover a few theoretical generalizations from which many different empirical propositions can be derived.' Few sociologists have done this as often and with as much success.

Thomas F. Gieryn
Indiana University

Bloch, Marc (1886–1944)

One of the most influential medieval historians of the twentieth century, Marc Bloch was a pioneer in broadening the range of historical inquiry. He firmly believed that history was a science, and was a powerful advocate of the value of comparative methods in studying past societies. He was skilled in the use of a wide range of evidence, from chronicles and charters to folklore, and he never lost a keen sense of the value of precise detail even when presenting the most general arguments. His initial work on serfdom in the Ile-de-France led on to his classic study of *Les charactères originaux de l'histoire rurale française* (1931) (*French Rural History: An Essay on its Basic Characteristics*, London, 1966). By the time that was written, he had already displayed the width of his interests with *Les rois thaumaturges* (*The Royal Touch*, London, 1973), a remarkable study of healing powers claimed by the French and English monarchies, which showed his ability to take an apparently limited problem and develop its implications extensively. His aim, above all, was to present a total study of medieval society, and he came nearest to achieving this in his great work *La société féodale* (1939, 1940) (*Feudal Society*, 1961). His work focused not upon individuals and their role, but upon society as a whole, and he laid little stress upon political developments. In 1931 Marc Bloch was, with Lucien Febvre, a founder, of the influential *Annales d'histoire économique et sociale*, a journal which did much to popularize his novel conception of history. He taught for many years at Strasbourg, and moved to the Sorbonne in 1936. He was an ardent, though not uncritical, patriot, and volunteered for active service in 1939. In 1944 he was executed by the Gestapo because of his activities in the Resistance.

Michael Prestwich
University of Durham

Further Reading
Perrin, Ch.–E. (1948), 'L'oeuvre historique de Marc Bloch', *Revue Historique*, 199.
See also: *Annales School; Braudel.*

Bloomfield, Leonard (1887–1949)

Leonard Bloomfield, one of the leaders in structural-linguistics in North America, was born in Chicago in 1887. He graduated from Harvard at nineteen, was converted to linguistics by Eduard Prokosch at the University of Wisconsin, and gained a doctorate from the University of Chicago in 1909. He progressed from research in Germanic and Indo-European to general linguistics and studies of other languages, such as Tagalog and the Algonquian languages. He held academic appointments at a number of universities, ending his career at Yale University (Sterling professor of linguistics, 1940–9). He died in 1949.

At first, Bloomfield was influenced by Wundt's psychology, but he became a behaviourist under the influence of A. P. Weiss. Thus, his book *Language* (1933) broke sharply with the past in concentrating on analysis of sounds and forms with only minimal, replicable use of the meanings of utterances. At one stroke he swept from linguistics all the apparatus of introspectionist psychology. The break with the past was so abrupt that Bloomfield has often been credited with singlehandedly making linguistics into a science, an excessive claim; however, his book was very important. Bernard Bloch (1949) called it a 'work without an equal as an exposition and synthesis of linguistic science'. Though he had few students, his book was so influential as to make several generations of linguists do work that directly derives from his formulation. After half a century, it still serves as the classic version of some aspects of linguistics, because it is so concisely written. His reconstruction of Proto-Central Algonquian is one of the finest examples of the comparative method in linguistics.

D. L. Olmsted
University of California, Davis

Reference
Bloch, B. (1949), 'Obituary of Leonard Bloomfield', *Language*, 25.

Further Reading
Esper, E. A. (1969), *Mentalism and Objectivism in Linguistics: The Sources of Leonard Bloomfield's Psychology of Language*, New York.
See also: *structural linguistics.*

Boas, Franz (1858–1942)

Franz Boas, born in Germany in 1858, naturalized American citizen in 1892, unquestionably dominated both the intellectual paradigm and institutional development of twentieth-century American anthropology until the Second World War, presiding over the emergence of anthropology as a professional discipline based on the concept of culture, and establishing a subdisciplinary scope including cultural, physical and linguistic anthropology as well as prehistoric archaeology.

In spite of his focus on professionalism in science, Boas himself was trained in (psycho)physics in his native Germany, thereby coming into contact with the folk psychology of Wundt and the anthropology of Bastian (European folk cultures) and Virchow (anthropometry). Boas's dissertation at the University of Kiel in 1881 on the colour of sea water led to concern with the inherent subjectivity of observer perception. His work in geography with Fischer initially supported environmental determinism, but his expedition to the Eskimo of Baffin Land in 1882–3 led to a more flexible argument stressing the interaction of culture and environment.

Boas settled permanently in North America only in 1887, recognizing greater opportunities there for an ambitious young Jewish scholar. In the ensuing years, he was crucially involved in the development of American anthropology in all of its early major centres. The institutional framework for the emerging Boasian anthropology was usually collaboration between a university, ensuring the academic training of professional anthropologists, and a museum to sponsor field research and publication. Boas himself settled in New York, teaching at Columbia from 1896 until 1936. He had previously served as Honorary Philologist of the Bureau of American Ethnology, which dominated Washington and government anthropology. Through F. W. Putnam of Harvard, he organized anthropology at the Chicago World's Fair of 1892 and acquired ties to archaeological work centring at Harvard. Boas's own students established programmes elsewhere, particularly Kroeber at Berkeley, Speck at Pennsylvania, and Sapir in Ottawa. By about 1920, Boasian anthropology was firmly established as the dominant paradigm of the North American discipline.

Boas's theoretical position, often characterized as historical particularism, claimed that unilinear evolution was an inadequate model for the known diversity of human cultures. Human nature was defined as variable and learned tradition. Although he was extremely interested in particular historical developments, Boas argued that progress did not necessarily follow a fixed sequence, nor was it always unidirectional from simple to complex. He further parted from evolutionary theorists like E. B. Tylor in his contention that cultural learning is basically unconscious rather than rational. Boas produced particular ethnographic examples to argue the limits of theoretical generalization in anthropology, indeed in social science generally. 'Laws' comparable to those of the natural sciences were possible in principle though usually premature in practice. The ultimate generalizations of anthropology would be psychological (1911b), but Boas's own studies rarely transcended the prior level of ethnographic description. Later students, especially Margaret Mead and Benedict, elaborated these ideas in what came to be called 'culture and personality'.

Particular histories could not be reconstructed in detail for societies without written records. In contrast, Boas stressed the historical dimensions of synchronically observable, particular cultural phenomena. For example, distribution was the primary reconstructive method to trace the diffusion (borrowing) of folklore motifs and combinations on the Northwest Coast. Elements in a single culture had diverse sources rather than a single common origin. Boas applied this same argument to linguistic work, assuming that language was a part of culture. His scepticism about distant genetic relationships of American Indian languages was consistent with his lack of training in Indo-European philology, and brought him into frequent disagreement with his former student Edward Sapir whose linguistic work was far more sophisticated.

On the other hand, Boas made important contributions to linguistics, being the first to establish the theoretical independence of race, language and culture as classificatory variables for human diversity (1911a). He broke with the Indo-European tradition in insisting on the 'inner form' (Steinthal) of each language in its grammatical patterning, developing new analytic categories appropriate to American Indian languages.

Boas insisted on the importance of firsthand fieldwork in living cultures, and he returned again and again to the Kwakiutl and other Northwest Coast tribes. He trained native informants to record their own cultures, and collected native language texts for folklore as well as linguistics. He was particularly concerned to record the symbolic culture of these tribes, focusing on art, mythology, religion and language, and was influential in the development of the disciplines of folklore and linguistics as well as anthropology.

Boas's own research spanned the scope of anthropology in its North American definition. In archaeology, he pioneered in Mexico and the Southwest in developing research programmes to reconstruct the history of particular cultures. In physical anthropology, he demonstrated that the head-form of descendants of immigrants can change in a single generation, thereby illustrating the essential variability and plasticity of the human form. He further developed important statistical methods for human growth studies, using longitudinal studies and family-line variation to show the role of environment in modifying heredity. Moreover, Boas was dedicated to the idea that anthropology had practical consequences for society generally, arguing, particularly in response to events in Nazi Germany at the end of his life, for the essential equality of races (defined in terms of statistical variability) and the validity of each cultural pattern.

Boas is, then, more than any other individual, responsible for the characteristic form which the discipline of anthropology has taken in North America. During his long career, he and several successive generations of students stood for a particular scope, method and theory, applied largely to the study of the American Indians. The increasing diversity of North American anthropology since World War II still has Boasian roots.

Regna Darnell
University of Alberta

References

Boas, F. (1888 [1964]), *The Central Eskimo*, Lincoln, Nebraska.

Boas, F. (1911a), 'Introduction', in *Handbook of American Indian Languages*, Washington, D.C.

Boas, F. (1911b), *The Mind of Primitive Man*, New York.

Boas, F. (1940), *Race, Language and Culture*, New York.

Further Reading

Goldschmidt, W. (ed.) (1959), *The Anthropology of Franz Boas. Memoir of the American Anthropological Association*, 89.

Harris, M. (1968), *The Rise of Anthropological Theory*, New York.

Stocking, G. (1968), *Race, Culture and Evolution*, New York.

See also: *cultural anthropology; culture; evolutionism and progress; Mead, M.; Sapir.*

Bodin, Jean (1530?–96)

Bodin is best remembered for his work in economics, jurisprudence and political science. He was trained in civil law, first at Angers and then at Toulouse, where he also taught for a few years before going to Paris to practise at the bar. In 1571 he joined the household of the Duke of Alençon and became associated with the *Politiques*, an association he maintained until 1588 when he felt constrained to join the League. He died in 1596. His most noteworthy political achievement was to mount a successful opposition to Henry III in the

Estates General at Blois in 1576.

At an early stage, Bodin endorsed the humanist view that Roman law should be treated, not as a universally valid legal system, but as the legal code of a historically specific state. However, he went on to argue that the laws of *all* states should be investigated and then compared with a view to establishing 'the principles of universal jurisprudence'. He made two attempts at this project: his *Methodus* of 1566 and, later, his massive *Six Livres de la République* (1576). The most controversial aspect of the latter work was its theory of sovereignty. By depicting the sovereign as law maker rather than magistrate, and the law as the sovereign's will rather than a product of reason, Bodin broke decisively with tradition. And by arguing that sovereignty is necessarily absolute and cannot be divided or shared, he undermined the prevailing preference for mixed forms of government.

His claim to being a founder of modern economics rests on his earlier *Réponse aux Paradoxes de Malestroict* (1568) in which he attributed inflation to restraints on trade and an increase in the money supply. His two other major works, *Demonamanie des Sorciers* (1580) and *Universae naturae Theatrum* (1596), deserve the oblivion into which they have sunk; but his posthumously published *Heptaplomeres* is a remarkable attack on religious dogmatism.

H. Tudor
University of Durham

Further Reading
Frankin, J. H. (1973), *Jean Bodin and the Rise of Absolutist Theory*, Cambridge.

Body, Sociology of the

While sociology has not developed a coherent approach to the body as the cultural product of social and historical arrangements, there are elements to such a theory in classical sociology and anthropology, and in Marxism (Schmidt, 1971). In mainstream sociology, it was Parsons who came, especially in his later writing, to recognize an implicit sociology of the body in his analyses of the symbolism of blood, the gift of life, death and the transformation of organic existence by medical technology (Parsons 1977; Parsons, 1978). Within an entirely different perspective, Goffman was acutely aware of the importance of the body in the presentation of self in everyday life, in the loss of social face and in stigmatization (Goffman, 1969).

These traditions in social theory point to a major but problematic notion of 'the body' as a socially constructed phenomenon rather than as a physiologically given datum. This view of biology and physiology as the effects of social construction came into sociology via the sociology of knowledge of Berger and Luck-mann (1967) who were developing the philosophical anthropology of Gehlen. Since man's biological equipment is unspecialized and unspecific, human beings inhabit a sociocultural environment which they have to construct. Finally, the sociology of the body has also been developed in a structuralist perspective by the French philosopher Foucault in his studies of medicine, prisons and sexuality (Foucault, 1973; Foucault, 1977; Foucault, 1978).

These developments in modern sociology reflect, to some extent, important social changes in contemporary society which have brought into prominence the ambiguous nature of the human body: (1) Medical advances in the control of fertility, sexuality and longevity have raised complex problems about the legal status of the body, the meaning of parenthood and the nature of life itself. The body has become a central political issue. (2) Changes in the nature of consumption and fashion have made people far more aware of their embodiment in relation to their moral worth and their social status. It has been argued that the new diseases of the twentieth century (especially anorexia nervosa) are products of this ambiguity of embodiment, and others have suggested that this gives rise to a new form of the self (the presentational self) and a modern form of consumerism involving a narcissistic personality (Lasch, 1980).

The sociology of the body would involve the reproduction of bodies in time, the regulation of bodies in space, the restraint of the interior body and the representation of the exterior body. Every human society requires the production of the material means of existence and the reproduction of human beings. The sociology of the body thus draws attention to the importance of sexual regulation in the political stability of societies and hence to the traditional role of household patriarchy in reproduction and regulation. With the emergence of capitalism, the body is subject to extensive restraint of sexuality via religion (Weber, 1930) and this results in a rationalization of the body through diet, cosmetics, physical education, discipline and medicine (Turner, 1981). Finally, with changes in consumption and distribution in modern society, it is the exterior of the body which becomes the focus of social activity; to be slim is to be morally valuable. The sociology of the body is thus a necessary feature of a range of traditional dichotomies (nature/culture, self/society, body/mind) which lies at the root of sociology (Turner, 1984).

Bryan S. Turner
Flinders University of South Australia

References
Berger, P. L. and Luckmann, T. (1967), *The Social Construction of Reality: Everything that Passes for Knowledge in Society*, London.

Foucault, M. (1973), *The Birth of the Clinic, An Archaeology of Medical Perception*, London.

Foucault, M. (1977), *Discipline and Punish, The Birth of the Prison*, London. (Original French edn, *Surveiller et punir*, 1975.)

Foucault, M. (1978), *The History of Sexuality, Vol. I. An Introduction*, London.

Goffman, E. (1969), *Behavior in Public Places. Notes on the Social Organization of Gatherings*, New York.

Lasch, C. (1980), *The Culture of Narcissism*, London.

Parsons, T. (1977), *Social Systems and the Evolution of Action Theory*, New York.

Parsons, T. (1978), *Action Theory and the Human Condition*, New York.

Schmidt, A. (1971), *The Concept of Nature in Marx*, London.

Turner, B.S. (1981), 'The government of the body, medical regimens and the rationalization of diet', *The British Journal of Sociology*, 33.

Turner, B.S. (1984), *The Body and Society, Explorations in Social Theory*, Oxford.

Weber, M. (1930 [1922]), *The Protestant Ethic and the Spirit of Capitalism*, London. (Original German edn, *Die protestantische Ethik und der 'geist' des Kapitalismus*, Tübingen.)

Bowlby, John E. (1907–)

John Bowlby is best known for his pioneering research on the development and nature of mother-child attachment and for his long association with the child family psychiatry service at the Tavistock Clinic in London. Born on 26 February 1907 in London into a medical family, he was educated at Dartmouth and Trinity College, Cambridge. In 1937, he was appointed staff psychiatrist at the London Child Guidance Clinic. Later during the Second World War he served as consultant psychiatrist in the RAMC (1940–5) in the rank of Lieutenant Colonel. In 1946 he joined the Tavistock Clinic as chairman of the Department for Children and Parents, where he remained until his retirement in 1972.

Bowlby is both a prolific writer and controversial figure. His many publications include *Personal Aggressiveness and War* in 1938, *Forty Four Juvenile Thieves* in 1946, *Maternal Care and Mental Health* (written for the World Health Organization) in 1951, *Child Care and the Growth of Love* in 1953 and, perhaps most extensive and authoritative, his three volumes in the series *Attachment and Loss* published between 1969 and 1980.

Bowlby received many academic and national honours in his years of work with disturbed children and their families including an honorary D.Sc at Cambridge in 1977 and the Distinguished Scientific Contribution Award for research into child development in 1981. Well before this latter honour, however, Bowlby's research and clinical work into early separ-

ation, mother-child attachment, and childhood disturbance had had a widespread impact on all the mental health and welfare professions, in particular child psychiatry and social work, although in later years the methodological basis for Bowlby's theory of maternal deprivation was subjected to criticism and debate, with new evidence and more thorough analysis suggesting alternative explanations for his earlier work. His influence on professionals of all kinds working with disturbed children and their families has been acknowledged world-wide.

Barrie J. Brown
Institute of Psychiatry
University of London

See also: *attachment; bereavement; separation and loss.*

Braudel, Fernand (1902–)

Fernand Braudel is one of the most influential historians of this century. The third of the founding fathers of the so-called Annales School of French historians, he followed the lead of such pre-World War II historians as Lucien Fèbvre and Marc Bloch in seeking to revitalize the study of history in the light of the methods and concerns of the social sciences. However, Braudel went considerably further along this path than his predecessors, developing an entirely new concept of, and approach to, historical studies. In a more systematic way than his precursors, Braudel sought to emancipate history from its traditional division into political, economic and cultural history and to achieve a 'total' history of society. The objective was to integrate all aspects of man's past, placing the chief emphasis on the changing environment and lifestyle of the common man and of society as a whole. Inevitably, the new approach involved a marked de-emphasizing and distancing from the political and constitutional history, which had always been the central preoccupation of historians and which Braudel and his followers term 'histoire événementielle'.

Braudel's most famous and important work, on the Mediterranean world in the age of Philip II, was first published in 1949 and was greeted with widespread and eventually almost universal acclaim. A revised and considerably expanded second edition was published in 1966. In this vast undertaking, Braudel transcended all political and cultural borders, as he did in all historical practice and procedure. He sought to reveal the immense scope and implications of the decline of Mediterranean society in the sixteenth century, achieving a majestic and often elegant synthesis of economic, demographic, cultural and political data and interpretation. It was by no means Braudel's intention to disregard political phenomena; rather he wished to tackle these in a new way, within the context of long-

and medium-term socioeconomic trends. Thus one of his principal objectives was to throw new light on the shift in the policy concerns of Philip II of Spain away from the Mediterranean and towards the Atlantic, a change in the direction of Spanish policy making which dates from the 1580s.

Basic to Braudel's approach was his novel categorization of history into simultaneous processes proceeding on different levels at quite different speeds. He envisaged these various trends as taking place on three main levels and, on occasion, compared the processes of historical change to an edifice consisting of three storeys. On the lowest level, he placed the slow, long-term changes in mankind's agrarian, maritime and demographic environment. On the middle level, Braudel placed the medium-term economic and cultural shifts which take place over one or two centuries rather than millenniums. Finally, on his uppermost storey, he located all short-term fluctuations and 'events' in the traditional sense.

This novel approach to history is further developed in Braudel's second major work, an ambitious trilogy entitled *Civilisation matérielle et capitalisme* (1967), (English trans., 1973–82, *Civilization and Capitalism*) which deals with the evolution of the world economy and of society generally from the end of the Middle Ages down to the Industrial Revolution. Despite Braudel's insistence on material factors as the determinants of social change, and his readiness to borrow concepts from Marx, including the term 'Capitalism' which figures prominently in his later work, Braudel's system, like the work of the Annales School more generally, is in essence quite outside the Marxist tradition in that it allocates no central role to class conflict. In the view of some scholars, certain weaknesses evident in the earlier work are much more pronounced in the later study. A less secure grasp of detail, frequent errors both of fact and interpretation of data and, generally, much less convincing evaluations detract considerably from the value of the later work. Certain historians now also see serious defects in Braudel's overall approach, running through his entire *oeuvre* which, besides the two major works, includes a number of noteworthy short books and essays. In particular it is felt that Braudel's method of handling the interaction between socioeconomic and political history is unconvincing and unsatisfactory. Thus, his radical de-emphasizing of political and military power, and the impact of 'events' on socioeconomic development, gives rise in his writing to numerous, often major, distortions.

The influence of Braudel's ideas and the extent to which they have been adopted as the 'modern' approach to historical studies varies from country to country, but is pervasive in several European and many Latin American countries as well as in North America. It has been repeatedly asserted that he is 'indisputably the greatest of living historians', but it must also be said that a tendency towards uncritical adulation of his work has become fashionable in many quarters on both sides of the Atlantic. Some history departments in universities, and a number of collaborative historical research projects and publications, have professed Braudel and his approach as the guiding principle directing their studies.

Jonathan I. Israel
University College London

References
Braudel, F. (1966), *La Méditerranée et le monde méditerranéan à l'époque de Philippe II* (2nd enlarged edn, 2 vols), Paris. (English translation of this edn, *The Mediterranean and the Mediterranean World in the Age of Philip II*, 2 vols, New York.)
Braudel, F. (1967–79), *Civilisation matérielle et capitalisme*, Paris. (English translation, *Material Civilization and Capitalism, 15th–18th Century*, Vol. 1: *The Structure of Everyday Life*, London, 1982; Vol. II: *The Wheels of Commerce*, London, 1983; Vol. III: *The Perspective of the World*, London, 1984.)

Further Reading
Journal of Modern History (1972), Vol. 44: special issue on Braudel with articles by H. R. Trevor-Roper and J. H. Hexter, and Braudel's own 'Personal testimony'.
Israel, J. I. (1983), 'Fernand Braudel – a reassessment', *The Times Literary Supplement*, no. 4, 164.
See also: *Annales School; Bloch.*

Bureaucracy

Agreement as to when and how the word bureaucracy was invented is widespread and precise. 'The late M. de Gornay . . .' notes Baron de Grimm, the French philosopher, in a letter dated 1 July, 1764, 'sometimes used to . . . invent a fourth or fifth form of government under the heading of *bureaucratie*.' Within a very short time, the physiocrat economist's word entered the international language of politics: the Italian *burocrazia*, the German *Bureaukratie* (later *Bürokratie*), and the English 'bureaucracy' (Albrow, 1970).

Agreement about what the word means, however, could hardly be *less* widespread or precise. In political debate, writes Martin Albrow, ' "bureaucracy" has become a term of strong emotive overtones and elusive connotations'. Social scientists have been no more precise. 'Sometimes "bureaucracy" seems to mean administrative efficiency, at other times the opposite. It may appear as simple as a synonym for civil service, or it may be as complex as an idea summing up the specific features of modern organizational structure. It may refer to a body of officials, or to the routines of office administration' (Albrow, 1970).

This confusion may be more apparent than real. From the plethora of definitions, two stand out: bureaucracy as rule by officials, and bureaucracy as a particular form of organization. Even these meanings, though distinct, are not unrelated.

Rule by officials was Vincent de Gornay's intention when, in the style of 'democracy' and 'aristocracy', he attached the Greek suffix for rule to the French word 'bureau', which already included 'a place where officials work' among its definitions. It also was the meaning of Harold Laski when he defined bureaucracy in the 1930 *Encyclopaedia of the Social Sciences* as 'A system of government the control of which is so completely in the hands of officials that their power jeopardizes the liberties of ordinary citizens,' and of Harold Lasswell and Abraham Kaplan (1950), who defined it in *Power and Society* as 'the form of rule in which the élite is composed of officials'.

Twentieth-century heirs to de Gornay's definition of bureaucracy have characteristically shared his observations on 'bureaumania' – the spread of bureaucracy – as well. They regard rule by officials to be the most prevalent form of government in modern society. Some have traced this rise to officials' organized concentration of expert knowledge. Others, such as Robert Michels (1962), have explained it in terms of the imperatives of large-scale organization itself: 'Who says organization, say oligarchy.'

Most modern authors of the de Gornay school have also inherited his displeasure with what he called the 'illness' of bureaucracy. Yet their shared distress belies the polarity of their diagnoses. Sometimes bureaucracy is looked upon as 'intolerably meddlesome', 'a demanding giant', 'an oppressive foreign power', and sometimes as 'timid and indecisive', 'flabby, overpaid, and lazy'. The same critics often seem to regard bureaucracy as both aggressive and passive. Laski, for example, having identified bureaucracy as a form of rule that 'jeopardizes the liberties of ordinary citizens', adds in the next sentence that: 'The characteristics of such a regime are a passion for routine in administration, the sacrifice of flexibility to rule, delay in the making of decisions and a refusal to embark upon experiment.'

In all cases, however, officials tend to be judged by subscribers to this first definition as the real power in any political system in which the ranks of officialdom are large. It was this view that Max Weber (Gerth and Mills, 1946) challenged in the early part of the twentieth century, with arguments that set the stage for the development of bureaucracy's second definition, as a particular form of organization.

To Weber, those who equated large numbers of officials with rule by officials sometimes confused appearance and reality. They saw official orders given and obeyed, and assumed from this that officials were wielding independent power. In truth, Weber argued, orders were more likely obeyed because their recipients believed that it was right to obey. Not power *per se*, but 'authority' – power cloaked with legitimacy – was at play. In modern society, such authority characteristically was 'legal' rather than 'charismatic' or 'traditional' in nature: an official's orders were considered legitimate when he was seen to be acting in accordance with his duties as defined by a written code of laws, including statutes, administrative regulations, and court precedents.

As Weber conceived it, bureaucracy was the form of organization best suited to the exercise of legal authority. If legal authority calls for 'a government of laws and not of men', bureaucracy may be thought of as 'an organization of positions and not of people'. Bureaucratic organizations consist of offices whose powers and duties are clearly defined, whose activities are recorded in writing and retained in files, and whose arrangement in relation to one another is hierarchic. Offices are filled on the basis of 'merit', as measured by diplomas, examinations, or other professional qualifications. Officeholders occupy, but in no sense own, their positions or the powers, duties, and other resources that go with them. Their personal relationships with the organization are defined by contracts that specify salary and career structure.

'Rule by officials' and 'a particular form of organization' are very different understandings of bureaucracy. But they also are related: as this history has shown, one definition was formed in reaction to the other. There may even be grounds for reconciling, if not fusing, the two.

Weber, for example, seemed most provoked by the connotations that were usually attached to the 'rule by officials' definition – the easy assumption that wherever officials proliferated, they governed. He was right in seeing that this assumption was often made, but one would be wrong in thinking it necessarily must be made. One can think of bureaucracy as a form of government without assuming that it is the most prevalent form of government.

Conversely, it is not uncommon for those who define bureaucracy in organizational terms to be concerned about rule by officials, either as dangerously efficient (a 'demanding giant') or as hopelessly inefficient ('flabby, overpaid, and lazy'). For Weber's part, he warned in one of his most widely remembered passages of the potential power of bureaucracy at its most efficient:

Under normal conditions, the power position of a fully developed bureaucracy is always overtowering. The 'political master' finds himself in the position of the 'dilettante' who stands opposite the 'expert', facing the trained official who stands within the management of administration. This holds whether the 'master' whom the bureaucracy serves is a 'people' . . . or a parliament . . . a popularly elected president, a hereditary and 'absolute' or a 'constitutional' monarch (Gerth and Mills, 1946).

Other social scientists who basically accept Weber's definition of bureaucracy direct their concerns about bureaucratic power to the inefficiency of such organizations. Robert Merton (1952), for example, notes the danger, inherent to any rules-bound organization, that the rules will become ends in themselves, blinding officials to the organization's service functions and making them resistant to change. In the same spirit, Michel Crozier (1964) describes bureaucracy as 'an organization that cannot correct its behaviour by learning from its errors'.

Michael Nelson
Vanderbilt University

References
Albrow, M. (1970), *Bureaucracy*, New York.
Crozier, M. (1964), *The Bureaucratic Phenomenon*, London.
Gerth, H. and Mills, C.W. (1946), *From Max Weber: Essays in Sociology*, New York.
Laski, H. (1930), 'Bureaucracy', in *Encyclopaedia of the Social Sciences*, Vol. 3, New York and London.
Lasswell, H.D. and Kaplan, A. (1950), *Power and Society: A Framework for Political Inquiry*, New Haven.
Merton, R. (1952), 'Bureaucratic structure and personality', in R. Merton (ed.), *Reader in Bureaucracy*, Glencoe, Ill.
Michels, R. (1962 [1911]), *Political Parties*, New York.
See also: *administration; authority; organizations; Weber*.

Burke, Edmund (1729–97)

Edmund Burke, the British statesman and political theorist, was born in Dublin in 1729. He came to London in 1750 and soon acquired a reputation as a philosopher and man of letters. In 1765, he was elected to the House of Commons, acting as party secretary and chief man of ideas to the Whig connection led by the Marquis of Rockingham. He wrote voluminously, and the eloquence he brought to expressing a high-minded but by no means unrealistic view of political possibilities has never been surpassed. He could bring out the universal element in the most parochial of issues.

Burke's enduring importance in articulating a political tendency is particularly evident in the *Reflections on the Revolution in France* (1790) and subsequent late works in which he defended his criticism of the Revolution against fellow Whigs who had welcomed it as an act of liberation from an odious Bourbon absolutism. Attacked as one who had betrayed the cause of liberty, Burke agreed (in the *Appeal from the Old to the New Whigs*) that consistency was the highest virtue in politics, but proceeded to theorize its complex nature. In supporting the American colonists, he argued, he was in no way committed to support every movement which raised the banner of liberty, for in his view the Americans 'had taken up arms from one motive only; that is, our attempting to tax them without their consent . . .' (Burke, *Appeal*, Vol. III). Real political consistency must take account of circumstances, and cannot be deduced from principles. And it was in terms of the contrast between historical concreteness and abstract principle that Burke interpreted the challenge posed by the revolutionaries in France.

The revolutionaries were, Burke argued, amateur politicians attempting to solve the complex problems of French society with a set of theories or what he called 'metaphysic rights'. They believed that an ideal rational constitution, in which a republic guaranteed the rights of man, was suitable for all societies. This belief constituted a revelation which stigmatized most existing beliefs as prejudice and superstition, and all existing forms of government as corrupt and unjust. On Burke's historical understanding of the specificity of different societies, the beliefs and practices of any society revealed their character; indeed, properly understood, they revealed a kind of rationality much more profound than the propositional fantasies of revolutionaries. To condemn what whole societies had long believed as merely mistaken was in the highest degree superficial. Society is a delicate fabric of sentiments and understandings which would be irreparably damaged if subjected to the butchery of abstract ideas. Burke judged that, as the revolutionaries discovered that the people were not behaving according to the rationalist prescriptions, they would have increasing recourse to violence and terror. At the end of every prospect would be found a gallows. He predicted that the outcome would be a military dictatorship.

Burke's genius lay in breaking up the conventional antitheses through which politics was then understood. He had never been, he wrote, 'a friend or an enemy to republics or to monarchies in the abstract' (Burke, 1855, *Appeal*, Vol. III), and this refusal to take sides on an abstractly specified principle became a dominant strain in conservatism. The real clue to wisdom in politics lay not at the level of high principle but of low and humble circumstance. This was the level of actual human experience, and at this level, there was not a great deal that governments could achieve, and most of what they could was to prevent evils rather than promote goods. No stranger to paradox, Burke insisted that one of the most important of the rights of man is the right to be restrained by suitable laws. Again, Burke was prepared to agree that society was indeed a contract, but he instantly qualified this conventional judgement by insisting that it was a contract of a quite sublime kind, linking the living, the dead and those yet to be born. It is in these hesitations and qualifications of conventional wisdom to which he was impelled by the excitements of his time that Burke's contribution to political understanding lies.

More philosophically, Burke adapted to political use the empiricist doctrine that the passions, especially as entrenched in and shaped by social institutions, are closer to reality than the speculations of philosophers, and especially of *philosophes*. His defence of prejudice threw down a gauntlet to the superficial rationalism of his opponents, and has sometimes been seen as expressing an irrationalism endemic to conservative thought. It is, however, an argument about the relations between reason and passion similar to that of Hegel, though in a quite different idiom.

Burke's political judgement is a conservative modification of the English political tradition and covers many areas. On the nature of representation, for example, he argued that the House of Commons was not a congress of ambassadors from the constituencies. His defence of the place of parties in British politics contributed to the acceptance and development of party government, however limited in intention it may have been (Brewer, 1971). In the indictment of Warren Hastings, he stressed the trusteeship of power and property which was never far from his thoughts. But in all his political writings, Burke wrote to the occasion, and it is perilous to generalize about him too far. His personal ambitions required manoeuvring in the complex world of late eighteenth-century politics which have led some writers (for example, Namier, 1929, and Young, 1943) to regard him as little more than a silver-tongued opportunist. This is to do less than justice to the suggestiveness of his prose and the momentousness of the occasions to which he so brilliantly responded.

Kenneth Minogue
London School of Economics
and Political Science

References

Burke, E. (1855), *Works*, London.

Brewer, J. (1971), 'Party and the double cabinet: two facets of Burke's thoughts', *The Historical Journal*, XIV.

Namier, L. (1929), *The Structure of Politics at the Accession of George III*, London.

Young, G.M. (1943), *Burke* (British Academy Lecture on a Mastermind), London.

Further Reading

Canovan, F. P. (1960), *The Political Reason of Edmund Burke*, North Carolina.

Cone, C. (1964), *Burke and the Nature of Politics: The Age of the French Revolution,* Lexington, Mass.

Macpherson, C. B. (1980), *Burke*, Oxford.

O'Gorman, F. (1973), *Edmund Burke*, London.

Parkin, C. (1956), *The Moral Basis of Burke's Political Thought*, Cambridge.

Stanlis, P. J. (1958), *Edmund Burke and the Natural Law*, Ann Arbor.

See also: *conservatism*.

Business Concentration

Business seller concentration refers to the extent to which sales in a market, or economy, are concentrated in the hands of a few large firms. At the level of an individual market or industry, *market concentration* is thus an (imperfect) indicator of the *degree of oligopoly*, and measures thereof are widely used by industrial economists in empirical tests of oligopoly theory. The most popular operational measure is the *concentration ratio*, which records the share of industry size (usually sales, but sometimes employment or value added) accounted for by the k largest firms (where, usually, k = 3 or 4 or 5). Its popularity derives more from its regular publication in Production Census reports than from a belief in its desirable properties (either economic or statistical). The multitude of other concentration measures include the Hirschman-Herfindahl index, which is the sum of squared market shares of all firms in the industry, the Hannah-Kay index, a generalization of the former, and various statistical inequality measures borrowed from the study of personal income distribution. While there is general agreement that a respectable measure of concentration should be inversely related to the number of sellers and positively related to the magnitude of size inequalities, these criteria are satisfied by a large number of the alternative indexes, and there is no consensus on what is the ideal measure.

Evidence on market concentration is readily available for most Western economies, and although differences in methods of data collection and definitions make most international comparisons hazardous, some broad facts are indisputable:
(1) The pattern of concentration is similar within most countries, with high concentration prevalent in consumer good and capital-intensive industries.
(2) Typical levels of market concentration are higher in smaller economies.
(3) In-depth studies of the UK and the US suggest that, on average, the 5 firm ratio may be as much as 14 points higher in the UK. Studies of trends over time show a steady and pronounced increase in the UK from 1935 to 1968, with a levelling off in the 1970s. In the US, on the other hand, market concentration has remained fairly constant since World War II.

Theories on the causes of concentration include the technology and entry barrier explanation (emanating from the Structure-Conduct-Performance paradigm), and a range of stochastic models based on Gibrat's Law of Proportionate Effect. The latter are largely (statistically) successful in accounting for the characteristic positive skew observed in most firm size distributions and for the steady increase in concentration ('spontaneous drift'). They do not, however, provide a true economic understanding of the forces at work. Empirically, mergers have also been identified as a major source of concentration increases.

Aggregate concentration is often measured as the share in G.D.P, or aggregate manufacturing of the top 100 corporations. In the UK this rose dramatically from 16 per cent in 1909 to 40 per cent in 1968 and then remained constant up to 1980.

S. W. Davies
University of East Anglia

Further Reading

Curry, B. and George, K. D. (1983), 'Industrial concentration: a survey', *Journal of Industrial Economics*, 31.

See also: *antitrust legislation; competition; corporate enterprise; markets; monopoly; oligopoly.*

Business Cycles

Business cycles are recurring cycles of economic events involving a period of more rapid than normal or average growth (the *expansionary phase*) and culminating in a peak, followed by a phase of slower than average growth (a *recession*), or a period of negative growth (a *depression*) culminating in a trough. In the post-war literature, business cycles are normally assumed to be forty to sixty months in duration, and they are distinguished from various longer cycles that have been discussed in the economics literature, such as the six to eight year Major trade cycle, the fifteen to twenty-five year Kuznets or building cycle and the fifty to sixty year Kondratieff wave.

Business cycles have commonly been viewed as evolving around a long-term growth trend, especially in the post-war period, and this has typically led to a divorce of 'business cycle theory', which attempts to explain the fluctuations around the trend, from 'growth theory', which attempts to explain the trend growth itself. In the 1970s, interest in long waves revived, and an alternative view is that business cycles are short-term fluctuations in economic activity around longer cycles or waves. In this case, business cycles will be analysed as growth cycles, with alternating rapid growth expansionary phases and slower growth contractionary phases (or recessions) during the upswing of the long wave; while during the downswing of the long wave they will involve periods of positive growth in the expansionary phase followed by periods of zero or negative growth in the contractionary phase (or depression).

There has been some debate about whether business cycles are systematic economic fluctuations, or whether they are instead purely random fluctuations in economic activity. It is certainly true that business cycles are not regular, in the sense of a sine wave with constant period and amplitude. But the weight of evidence, largely due to the accumulated studies produced through the National Bureau of Economic Research, indicates that business cycles are sufficiently uniform to warrant serious study.

Business cycle modelling in the post-war period has usually adopted the approach, suggested by the work of Frisch and Slutsky, of regarding the economic system as fundamentally stable but being bombarded by a series of shocks or unexpected events. Thus business cycle models have commonly attempted to devise a 'propagation model' of the economy capable of converting shocks, generated by an impulse model, into a cycle. Using this strategy, many different models have been devised; these vary according to the degree of stability assumed in the 'propagation model', the form of the series of shocks emanating from the 'impulse model', and the sources of the shocks and sectors of the economy described by the propagation model. The various models have commonly involved linear stochastic second order equation systems. The linearity assumption serves both to simplify analysis and to allow an easy separation of business cycle and growth theory, because growth can be represented by a linear or log linear trend. There have been exceptions to this general modelling strategy that have used nonlinear equation systems capable of generating – in the absence of shocks – self-sustaining 'limit cycles'. These can be stable and self-repeating even in the face of shocks, which merely impart some additional irregularity. Such contributions have been relatively rare but may become more common as economists increasingly familiarize themselves with nonlinear techniques of mathematical and statistical analysis. The possibility of modelling the business cycle as a limit cycle, as an alternative to the Frisch-Slutsky approach, raises the general question of whether the business cycle is something that would die out in the absence of shocks, or whether it is endogenous to the economic system.

The nonlinear models have also commonly treated business cycles and growth theory as separable. There is, however, an alternative view, which is that business cycles and growth should be explained together, and that a theory of dynamic economic development is required. This view is most frequently associated with Marxist writings, but other students of the business cycle have suggested that the work of Schumpeter might provide a useful starting point.

In 1975, a series of published papers discussing the political and the equilibrium theories of the business cycle had a major impact. The political theory of the business cycle argues that business cycles are in fact electoral economic cycles which result from governments manipulating the economy in order to win elections. This contrasts with the broad Keynesian consensus view of the mid 1960s that governments, through anti-cyclical demand management policies, had on the whole been successful in reducing the amplitude of the cycle, although it was accepted that at times they may have aggravated it because of the problems involved in allowing for the lag in the effect of policy interventions. The equilibrium theory of the business cycle assumes that economic agents are endowed with 'rational expectations' but must make decisions based on inadequate information about whether price changes are purely inflationary, so that no real response is required, or whether they indicate a profitable opportunity. In models based on this theory, systematic anti-cyclical monetary policy can have no effect, and the only contribution the government can make is to reduce the shocks to the economy by pursuing a systematic monetary policy. The equilibrium theory of the business cycle contrasts with most other theories, which view business cycles as being fundamentally a disequilibrium phenomenon. Although the political and equilibrium theories have many contrasting features, they both raise questions concerning the appropriate treatment of the government in business cycle models. The Keynesian consensus view was that the government could be treated exogenously. In contrast, the political and equilibrium theories of the business cycle indicate that the government should be treated endogenously in business cycle models. A possible route for progress in business cycle modelling might involve game theoretic analyses of government policy making.

Both the political and equilibrium theories of the business cycle have their origins in much earlier literature and the evidence in support of each of them is rather less than conclusive. Nevertheless, these modern theories have revived interest in the controversial subject concerning the nature and causes of business cycles.

Andy Mullineux
University of Birmingham

Further Reading
Hansen, A. H. (1964), *Business Cycles and National Income* (enlarged edn), New York.
Harberler, G. (1964), *Prosperity and Depression* (5th edn), London.
Kuhne, K. (1979), *Economics and Marxism: Vol. II – The Dynamics of the Marxian System*, London.

Mandel, E. (1980), *Long Waves of Capitalist Development: The Marxist Interpretation*, Cambridge.
Mullineux, A. W. (1984), *The Business Cycle After Keynes: A Contemporary Analysis*, Brighton.
See also: *equilibrium; financial crises; stagflation.*

Business Studies

The term business studies is a loose generic title for several related aspects of enterprises and their environments, foremost amongst these being administration and management, accounting, finance and banking, international relations, marketing, and personnel and industrial relations. There is considerable disagreement, however, on the extent to which scholastic, managerial or professional values should predominate in the framing of the curriculum and in research and teaching objectives.

It is usual to trace modern ideas on business studies to formative developments in the United States, where the Wharton School of Finance and Commerce was the first of twenty schools of business administration and commerce to be founded between 1881 and 1910. But it was particularly in the next two decades, when a further 180 schools were established, that the distinctive American style of business education, with a high degree of abstraction and a quantitative approach to the solution of problems, became firmly rooted (Rose, 1970). Management education developed much later in Europe, originally under the tutelage of practitioners from the United States. Indeed, in Great Britain, it was not until 1947 that the first major centre, the Administrative Staff College at Henley, was inaugurated. There are now several leading European institutes for business and management studies. In recent years, too, in both Europe and Japan, there have been active attempts to develop programmes which are distinctive from the original North American model, a change which has been facilitated by the considerable interest in business studies in Third World nations and by the rigorous analytical techniques which have latterly evolved in the United States.

The precise causes of the expansion of business education are open to some doubt, although processes of rationalization in modern societies and the rapid growth in numbers of managerial personnel have been signal influences. Further favourable trends have been increased international competition and investment, major technical changes, a larger scale and greater complexity of modern enterprises and a facilitative role of governments (Poole, Mansfield, Blyton and Frost, 1981).

However, opinion differs on whether business studies should become an empirical social science or whether, to the contrary, it should be founded on a series of prescriptive values (what should be accomplished) and ideas (what can be achieved) in actual employing organizations. A particular problem of internal coherence in business education also stems from the varied subject backgrounds of research workers and teachers, a situation which has militated against an adequate interdisciplinary synthesis.

In principle, the theoretical linkages between the main areas of business studies are examined in business policy, although this has in practice become a highly specialized area dealing primarily with the intertemporal concept of strategy. In substantive terms, organizational behaviour is the most obvious branch of study that connects the disparate approaches within the business field. Nevertheless, its excessive reliance on contingency theory (which implies that whether a particular organizational form is effective depends on the nature of the environmental context) has proved to be an encumbrance, since challenges to this approach have ensured that there is no longer a generally accepted model for conceptualizing business behaviour.

A further critical issue in business studies is the extent to which, regardless of cultural, socioeconomic or political conditions, common administrative practices are appropriate on a world-wide scale. The earliest perspectives tended to assume a considerable uniformity, the various strands being combined in the 'industrial society' thesis in which a basic 'logic of industrialism' was seen to impel all modern economies towards similar organizational structures and modes of administration (Kerr, Dunlop, Harbison and Myers, 1960). This complemented the earlier work on classical organization theory, which postulated universal traits of business management, and on studies of bureaucracy, which arrived at similar conclusions. In this approach, too, a key assumption was that there had been a divorce of ownership from control in the business enterprise that, in turn, had ensured the convergence of decision-making processes between societies with ostensibly irreconcilable political ideologies and economic systems.

More recently, however, the 'culturalist' thesis has emerged as a check-weight to these universalist approaches. This assumes great diversity in business behaviour and ideology occasioned either by variations in the 'task' environment (community, government, consumer, employee, supplier, distributor, shareholder) or, more especially, in the 'social' environment (cultural, legal, political, social). Above all, it emphasizes that each new generation internalizes an enduring strain of culture through its process of socialization, with people in different countries learning their own language, concepts and systems of values. Moreover, such deep-rooted cultural forces are continually reasserted in the way people relate to one another and ensure that organizational structures which are not consonant with culturally derived expectations will remain purely formal (Child and Kieser, 1979).

Divergence in business organization and practice can also stem from temporal as well as spatial differences between societies. Indeed, 'late development' would appear to enhance a mode of industrialization quite distinct from the earliest Western models, with the state being more predominant at the expense of a *laissez-faire* ideology, educational institutions preceding manufacturing, more substantial technical and organizational 'leaps', human relations and personnel management techniques being more advanced, and large-scale enterprises being deliberately constructed as a spearhead for economic advancement (Dore, 1973). In this respect, too, the choices of strategic élites are as important as the constraints of environment and organizational structure in determining which types of business conduct become ascendant in any given society.

Since the Second World War, business studies have also been particularly influenced by notions of 'human resourcing'. This relates to the central issue of whether business managers have wider moral obligations above those of seeking to enhance profitability and efficiency. External social responsibility refers to the interests of the community and wider society, and to various groups and individuals located outside the organization (Ackerman and Bauer, 1976; Davis, Frederick and Blomstrom, 1980). It is particularly examined in the context of marketing policy, where various ethical questions are raised by the strategies and techniques for promoting different types of goods and services. Internal social responsibility concerns employee welfare and satisfaction and interpersonal and inter-group relations in the actual enterprise.

Interest in this latter group of questions has helped to occasion a major expansion in research and teaching in the areas of personnel management and industrial relations. The personnel function relates to the objectives, policies, plans and practices affecting people within work environments and, although the relevant body of knowledge is not settled, the main areas covered are 'employee resourcing', 'employee development' and 'employee relations' (Strauss and Sayles 1980; Thomson, 1981). In industrial relations, too, trade unions have been seen as increasingly influential and legitimate in decision making, while a variety of schemes for employee participation and industrial democracy have been viewed as appropriate for the future organization of internal relationships within the enterprise.

In the curriculum objectives of business studies, however, a principal problem is engendered by differences between professional and managerial approaches. Classical models of professionalism have always emphasized the role of the professional body as a means of social control and as an accrediting agency. This contrasts sharply with the rationale of the modern corporation as a management-directed organization that involves an attempt to ensure control over the specialists carrying out a variety of work functions. Such a tension is manifest particularly in the areas of accounting and law where, traditionally, a professional orientation has been paramount. More recently, though, the former subject in particular has become significantly more 'behavioural' in focus, and its current techniques and information are increasingly allied to conceptions of management control.

In the future, there are thus likely to remain far-reaching differences of view on the appropriate aims of business studies, reflecting professional versus managerial objectives, the extent to which an empirical social science should be developed (if necessary at the expense of consultancy-style links with ongoing enterprises), the diverse disciplinary backgrounds of the practitioners, and the degree of commitment to external and internal social responsibilities. Nevertheless, the expansion of interest in business education is likely to continue and a wide range of new ideas on principles and practices of administration to be formulated. Moreover, the resolution of the various specialist debates is likely to be closely in accord with wider movements in advanced industrial societies, and to reinforce the thesis that there is a wide degree of choice in the framing of the policies of commercial organizations and in the premises guiding the systematic analysis of actual businesses themselves.

Michael Poole
University of Wales Institute
of Science and Technology

References

Ackerman, R. W. and Bauer, R.A. (1976), *Corporate Social Responsiveness*, Reston, Virginia.

Child, J. and Kieser, A. (1979), 'Organization and managerial roles in British and West German companies: an examination of the culture-free thesis', in C. J. Lammers and D. J. Hickson (eds), *Organizations Alike and Unlike: International and Inter-Institutional Studies in the Sociology of Organizations*, London.

Davies, K., Frederick, W. C. and Blomstrom, R. L. (1980), *Business and Society: Concepts and Policy Issues*, New York.

Dore, R. P. (1973), *British Factory-Japanese Factory*, London.

Kerr, C., Dunlop, J. T., Harbison, F. H. and Myers, C. A. (1960), *Industrialism and Industrial Man*, Cambridge, Mass.

Poole, M., Mansfield, R., Blyton, P. and Frost, P. (1981), *Managers in Focus*, Aldershot.

Rose, H. (1970), *Management Education in the 1970's*, London.

Strauss, G. and Sayles, L. R. (1980), *Personnel: The Human Problems of Management*, 4th edn, Englewood Cliffs, N.J.

Thomson, G. F. (1981), *A Textbook of Personnel Management*, London.

See also: *decision making; organizations.*

C

Cambridge School of Economics

In his 1922 Introduction to the Cambridge Economic Handbooks, Keynes defined 'The Cambridge School of Economics' as lecturers in the University of Cambridge (UK) whose 'ideas . . . are traceable to . . . the two economists who have chiefly influenced Cambridge thought . . ., Dr Marshall and Professor Pigou' (successor in Marshall's Chair of Political Economy), and included F. Lavington, H. D. Henderson, D. H. Robertson (Pigou's successor), and G. F. Shove.

A process of rejuvenation and internal criticism started in 1927 when Keynes imported a young Italian, P. Sraffa, who committed 'the sacrilege of pointing out inconsistencies in Marshall', as Joan Robinson put it. Combining work by Shove, E. A. G. Robinson, and R. F. Kahn, Joan Robinson developed these inconsistencies into a 1933 book which launched the 'Imperfect Competition Revolution'. Shortly after, with the help of these young economists (and J. E. Meade, an Oxford visitor who eventually succeeded Robertson), Keynes himself challenged the established views of Marshall and Pigou in his revolutionary *General Theory*.

The new generation, joined by Kaldor in the 1950s, and Pasinetti in the 1960s, propagated and extended Keynes's theory, formulating original approaches to capital, growth and distribution theory. Together with Sraffa's 1960 theory of prices, which built on his earlier work, the process of internal criticism of the 1930s reached maturity in a coherent approach (although Robertson and Meade defended the traditional positions) which superseded traditional marginal analysis and provoked the 'Cambridge Controversies', which dominated economics in the 1960s and 1970s. In the 1980s Cambridge economists exhibit no unified approach, yet the Cambridge tradition is preserved in the post-Keynesian and Surplus approaches in universities around the world.

J. A. Kregel
University of Groningen

References
Keynes, J. M. (1922), 'Introduction' to H. D. Henderson, *Supply and Demand*, vol. I, London.
Keynes, J. M. (1936), *The General Theory of Employment, Interest and Money*, London.
Robinson, J. (1933), *The Economics of Imperfect Competition*, London.
Sraffa, P. (1960), *Production of Commodities by Means of Commodities*, Cambridge.
See also: *capital theory; economic dynamics; Kaldor; Keynes; Keynesian economics; Pigou; Robinson; Sraffa.*

Cannibalism

Cannibalism, as the customary consumption of human flesh in some other time or place, is a worldwide and time-honoured assumption. This pervasive, and in many ways appealing, characterization of others has also found its place in contemporary anthropology, which has tended to accept uncritically all reports of cannibalism in other cultures as ethnographic fact. This propensity has led to the development of a variety of categories for the conceptualization of the pattern and motivation for the purported behaviour. These have included the recognition of endocannibalism (eating one's own kind) as opposed to exocannibalism (eating outsiders), and ritual in contrast to gustatory or nutritional cannibalism. Uncondoned survival cannibalism, under conditions of extreme privation, has also been noted. Yet, despite the uncounted allusions and the elaborate typologies, there is reason to treat any particular report of the practice with caution, and the entire intellectual complex with some scepticism.

This estimation is warranted for a number of reasons. Depending on time or place, written accounts of alleged cannibalism entered the historical record long after the cessation of the purported custom – often after the obliteration of the culture itself and the decimation of its population. Moreover, reporters were representatives of the very society that was then engaged in the subjugation and exploitation of the people in question. Those responsible for our contemporary impressions rarely took an unbiased view of the traditional culture, and at best relied upon informants who claimed that 'others', such as the nobility or priesthood, engaged in such reprehensible practices. Consequently, rather than reliably documenting a custom, between the early sixteenth and late nineteenth centuries the allegation of cannibalism in Western literature often merely legitimized the conquest of foreign cultures by expansionist European states.

These suspect conditions could have been rectified by modern anthropologists actually resident among presumed cannibals in the remoter regions of the world. However, contemporary reports continue to be second-hand; indeed, no anthropologist has ever provided an account of cannibalism based on observation. While reasonable explanations are offered for these circumstances, for example, that the practice has been discontinued or is now hidden, the overall pattern continues to be one of circumstantial rather than direct evidence.

Thus, is it reasonable to assume that cannibalism ever occurred? The answer is yes, but neither as often nor in the context usually assumed. There is as indicated survival cannibalism, but also an antisocial or criminal variety and sometimes subcultural cannibalism practised by a deviant segment of the population (see Parry, 1982). In rare instances, 'inversion' cannibalism has also occurred. The first three types are sporadically noted in every part of the world, where they are frowned upon by the majority. The final instance, of which there are a few accounts, involves rituals in which members of a society are constrained to act for the moment in ways prohibited under ordinary moral circumstances (Poole, 1983). Such occasions of inversion underscore the basic rules of society by intentional violations but should not be construed as custom in the general sense. There is a simplistic and unwarranted tendency to label non-Western societies with such restricted practices of any aforementioned type as cannibalistic. This suggests that the portrayal of others as man-eaters, rather than the deed itself, is the pervasive human trait.

W. Arens
State University of New York
Stony Brook

References

Parry, J. (1982), 'Sacrificial death and the necrophagous ascetic', in M. Bloch and J. Parry (eds), *Death and the Regeneration of Life*, Cambridge.

Poole, F. P. (1983), 'Cannibals, tricksters and witches', in D. Tuzin and P. Brown (eds), *The Ethnography of Cannibalism*, Washington.

Further Reading

Arens, W. (1979), *The Man-Eating Myth*, New York.

Capital Consumption

Understanding capital consumption (that is, the using up of fixed capital) must be based on an understanding of the distinction between fixed capital and circulating capital. In this context, the word 'capital' refers to tangible assets (i.e. as excluding financial assets). Items of circulating capital have only a once-for-all (or 'once-over') use in the process of production; items of fixed capital have a continuing and repeated use in the process of production. A dressmaker has a stock of cloth and a sewing machine: the cloth has a once-for-all use in the process of dressmaking; the sewing machine can be used repeatedly. The cloth is *circulating capital;* the sewing machine is *fixed capital*. The universal feature of items of fixed capital (apart from land) is that, for more than one reason, they have finite working lifetimes and will eventually have to be replaced (as the cloth has immediately to be replaced) if the production process is to continue.

Suppose the working lifetime of a sewing machine is ten years: at the beginning of Year 1 the dressmaker starts business with a (new) sewing machine valued at $1,000 and at the end of Year 10 the sewing machine is worth nothing (assuming it has no residual scrap-metal value). In order to continue in business, the dressmaker has then to spend $1,000 on replacing the sewing machine (abstracting from inflation – a very significant proviso). Now, if over the years the dressmaker has not gathered in from all the customers an aggregate amount of $1,000, then the effect is that those customers have had the free gift of the services of the sewing machine. Therefore, customers should be charged for the use of fixed capital. Suppose the dressmaker makes 200 dresses a year; over ten years 2,000 dresses will have been made and customers should be charged 50 cents per dress, reckoned as: $1,000 (original capital cost of sewing machine) *divided by* 2,000 (dresses) *equals* $0.50 per dress. The 50 cents is the charge for (fixed) capital consumption per dress, and is analogous to the charge made for the cloth used. The price charged must include the cost of capital consumption per dress.

However, most enterprises do not proceed in this direct way to incorporate capital consumption into the price(s) of the item(s) they produce. Instead, the same result may be achieved by making an overall deduction of annual capital consumption from annual gross income (income gross of – including – capital consumption). The dressmaker may deduct from gross income an *annual* charge for capital consumption, reckoned as: $1,000 (original capital cost of sewing machine) *divided by* 10 (years – the lifetime of the sewing machine) *equals* $100 per annum.

If 'income' is to be taxed, then net income rather than gross income is the appropriate tax-base. Hence tax authorities have regulations concerning the deduction of (annual) capital consumption, otherwise known as depreciation provisions.

There are various methods of calculating the flow of depreciation provisions. The formula just given is known as the 'straight-line' method because it gives a linear decline in the depreciated value of the fixed capital stock and a linear increase in the cumulated depreciation provisions (that is, there is a constant annual charge for depreciation), as follows: beginning Year 1, $1,000 capital, $0 cumulated depreciation provisions; end Year 1, $900 depreciated value of capital, $100 cumulated depreciation provisions; end Year 2, $800 depreciated value of capital, $200 cumulated depreciation provisions; and so on until end Year 10, $0 depreciated value of capital, $1,000 cumulated depreciation provisions. Together, the sum of depreciated capital and cumulated depreciation provisions always equal $1,000 and so 'maintains' capital (i.e. wealth) intact.

This arithmetic example illustrates the definitions that: 'Depreciation is the measure of the wearing out, consumption or other loss of value of a fixed asset' (Accounting Standards, 1982); or that capital consumption is the fall in the value of fixed capital between two accounting dates; or that charging depreciation provisions is a method of allocating the (original) cost of a long-lived asset to the time periods in which the asset is 'used up'. It also illustrates how the purpose of charging capital consumption against gross income to arrive at net (true) profit is to prevent an enterprise from 'living off its capital': 'A provision for depreciation reduces profit by an amount which might otherwise have been seen as available for distribution as a dividend' (Pizzey, 1980). It is not essential that the depreciation provisions be re-invested in the same item: it is quite in order for the dressmaker to invest, in an ongoing way, the depreciation provisions in, say, a knitting machine – what is essential is that sufficient capital equipment for production purposes continues to be available.

Dudley Jackson
University of Wollongong, Australia

References

Accounting Standards (1982), *Statements of Standard Accounting Practice 12*, 'Accounting for depreciation', London.
Pizzey, A. (1980), *Accounting and Finance: A Firm Foundation*, London.
See also: *capital theory; depreciation; stock-flow analysis.*

Capitalism

The term capitalism relates to a particular system of socioeconomic organization (generally contrasted with feudalism on the one hand and socialism on the other), the nature of which is more often defined implicitly than explicitly. In common with other value-loaded concepts of political controversy, its definition – whether implicit or explicit – shows a chameleon-like tendency to vary with the ideological bias of the user. Even when treated as a historical category and

precisely defined for the purpose of objective analysis, the definition adopted is often associated with a distinctive view of the temporal sequence and character of historical development. Thus historians such as Sombart, Weber and Tawney, who were concerned to relate changes in economic organization to shifts in religious and ethical attitudes, found the essence of capitalism in the acquisitive spirit of profit-making enterprise and focused on developments occurring in the sixteenth, seventeenth and early eighteenth centuries. Probably a majority of historians have seen capitalism as reaching its fullest development in the course of the Industrial Revolution and have treated the earlier period as part of a long transition between feudalism and capitalism. Marxist historians have identified a series of stages in the evolution of capitalism – for example, merchant capitalism, agrarian capitalism, industrial capitalism, state capitalism – and much of the recent debate on origins and progress has hinged on differing view of the significance, timing and characteristics of each stage. Thus Wallerstein (1979), who adopts a world-economy perspective, locates its origins in the agrarian capitalism that characterized Europe of the sixteenth, seventeenth and eighteenth centuries; while Tribe (1981), who also takes agrarian capitalism as the original mode of capitalist production, sees the essence of capitalism in a national economy where production is separated from consumption and is co-ordinated according to the profitability of enterprises operating in competition with each other.

Whatever the historical or polemical objective of the writer, however, his definition is likely to be strongly influenced by Karl Marx, who was the first to attempt a systematic analysis of the 'economic law of motion' of capitalist society and from whom most of the subsequent controversy on the nature and role of capitalism has stemmed. For Marx, capitalism was a 'mode of production' in which there are basically two classes of producers: (1) the capitalists, who own the means of production (capital or land), make the strategic day-to-day economic decisions on technology, output and marketing, and appropriate the profits of production and distribution; and (2) the labourers, who own no property but are free to dispose of their labour for wages on terms which depend on the numbers seeking work and the demand for their services. This was essentially the definition adopted, for example, by non-Marxist economic historians such as Lipson and Cunningham and by Marxists such as Dobb.

Given this perspective, it is primarily the emergence of a dominant class of entrepreneurs supplying the capital necessary to activate a substantial body of workers which marks the birth of capitalism. In England, and even more emphatically in Holland, it can be dated from the late sixteenth and early seventeenth centuries. Holland's supremacy in international trade, associated with its urgent need to import grain and timber (and hence to export manufactures) enabled Amsterdam to corner the Baltic trade and to displace Venice as the commercial and financial centre of Europe. The capital thus amassed was available to fund the famous chartered companies (Dutch East India Company, 1602, West India Company, 1621) as well as companies to reclaim land and exploit the area's most important source of industrial energy – peat. It also provided the circulating capital for merchants engaged in the putting-out system whereby they supplied raw materials to domestic handicraftsmen and marketed the product. Specialization within agriculture drew the rural areas still further into the money economy, and the urban areas supplied a wide range of industrial exports to pay for essential raw material imports.

Dutch capitalists flourished the more because they were subject to a Republican administration which was sympathetic to their free market, individualist values. In England, where similar economic developments were in progress in the sixteenth and early seventeenth centuries, the rising class of capitalists was inhibited by a paternalistic monarchical government bent on regulating their activities for its own fiscal purposes and power objectives and in terms of a different set of social values. The Tudor system of State control included checking enclosures, controlling food supplies, regulating wages and manipulating the currency. The early Stuarts went further in selling industrial monopolies and concessions to favoured entrepreneurs and exclusive corporations and infuriated the majority whose interests were thus damaged. The English capitalists carried their fight against monopolies to the Cromwellian Revolution. When the monarchy was restored in the 1660s, the climate of opinion had been moulded by religious, political and scientific revolution into an environment which favoured the advancement of capitalism and laid the foundations for its next significant phase – the Industrial Revolution.

Orthodox economic theorists eschew the concept of capitalism – it is too broad for their purposes in that it takes into account the social relations of production. Modern economic historians adhering to an orthodox framework of economic theory also tend to avoid the term. They do, however, recognize a significant aspect of capitalism by emphasizing the rational, profit-maximizing, double bookkeeping characteristics of capitalist enterprise; and in the post-Second World War debates on economic development from a backward starting-point, there has been a tendency to regard the emergence of this 'capitalist spirit' as an essential prerequisite to the process of sustained economic growth in non-socialist countries. (See, for example, Landes, 1969; North and Thomas, 1973; Morishima, 1982.)

The modern debate on capitalism in contemporary advanced economies has revolved around its being an alternative to socialism. Marxist economists follow Marx in seeing capitalism as a mode of production whose internal contradictions determine that it will eventually be replaced by socialism. In the aftermath of the Second World War, when the governments of most developed countries took full employment and faster economic growth as explicit objectives of national economic policy, there was a marked propensity for the governments of capitalist economies to intervene actively and extensively in the process of production. At that stage the interesting issues for most Western economists seemed to be the changing balance of private and public economic power (see Shonfield, 1965), and the extent to which it was either desirable or inevitable for the increasingly 'mixed' capitalist economies to converge towards socialism. In the late 1960s and 1970s, when the unprecedented post-war boom in world economic activity came to an end, Marxist economists were able to point confidently to the 'crisis of capitalism' for which they found evidence in rising unemployment and inflation in capitalist countries; but non-Marxist economists had lost their earlier consensus. The economic debate on capitalism is now taking place in a political context which is relatively hostile to state intervention; and those economists who believe that the 'spirit of capitalism', or free private enterprise, is the key to sustained technological progress and that it is weakened by socialist economic policies, seem to carry more conviction than they did in the 1950s and 1960s.

Phyllis Deane
University of Cambridge

References

Dobb, M. (1946), *Studies in the Development of Capitalism*, London.
Landes, D. (1969), *Prometheus Unbound*, Cambridge.
Morishima, M. (1982), *Why has Japan Succeeded?*, Cambridge.
North, D. C. and Thomas, R. P. (1973), *The Rise of the Western World*, Cambridge.
Shonfield, A. (1965), *Modern Capitalism*, London.
Sombart, W. (1915), *The Quintessence of Capitalism*, New York.
Tawney, R. H. (1926), *Religion and the Rise of Capitalism*, London.
Tribe, K. (1981), *Genealogies of Capitalism*, London.
Wallerstein, I. (1979), *The Capitalist World-Economy*, Cambridge.
Weber, M. (1930), *The Protestant Ethic and the Spirit of Capitalism*, New York. (Original German, 1922, Tübingen.)

See also: *capital theory; feudalism; Marx's theory of history and society; socialism; world-system theory.*

Capital Punishment

Capital punishment is an historical condition. Accompanied by torture, it is widely applied and taken for granted in primitive societies, past and present (see, for example, Diamond, 1971). Cultural progress brings a tendency toward decreasing severity of criminal punishments, and, especially, toward decreasing use of the death penalty (Gorecki, 1983). This pattern has been particularly marked in European history; however, the total abolition of capital punishment only became a publicly articulated demand after the Enlightenment. Today, most liberal democracies do not have the death penalty. The United States is the most conspicuous exception. Following a protracted struggle which they very nearly lost, the American retentionists won, by a crucial Supreme Court decision of 1976; thus a number of the states in the US continue to punish the most abominable cases of murder by death. This development was precipitated by the increasing public anger against high crime rates in America. On the other hand, many authoritarian, especially totalitarian, societies apply capital punishment profusely; in those societies the will of the despots affects criminal law, and the despots are rarely open to abolitionist arguments.

The arguments of both abolitionists and retentionists are many and hotly debated. The most forcefully stressed retentionist plea is utilitarian (or, strictly speaking, teleological): capital punishment is claimed to deter wrongdoing even better than lifelong confinement. There are further utilitarian contentions as well – that capital punishment constitutes the only secure incapacitation, and that it increases respect for criminal law. Non-utilitarian retentionists believe in the ultimate retributive value of capital punishment as the only 'just desert' for the most abhorrent crimes. In rejoinder, the abolitionists question the superior deterrent value of the death penalty. Furthermore, they stress the sanctity of human life and immorality of the state killing anyone. They argue that the penalty brutalizes society, that it is inevitably arbitrarily imposed, and that it endangers the innocent, since judicial errors do occur. They feel that the suffering of convicts led to execution and of those who wait on death row are appalling. Many believe in the re-education of wrongdoers rather than in retribution as the basic goal of criminal justice, and complain that execution is both vindictive and precludes rehabilitation.

The logical status and empirical validity of these arguments vary. The non-utilitarian arguments constitute moral axioms, like any ultimate ethical norms. On the other hand, the utilitarian arguments are questionable on purely empirical grounds. This is particularly true of the deterrence idea, which has stimulated a wealth of statistical inquiries aimed at its testing.

Despite their increasing refinement (especially by Ehrlich, 1975, and his opponents), the inquiries have been inconclusive; we do not know and may never learn whether capital punishment deters most effectively.

With the impact of the death penalty on effective functioning of criminal justice unproved and uncertain, the heat of the capital punishment debate seems hardly justified by practical needs. On the other hand, whether we send criminals to their death presents a moral dilemma of the utmost importance. That is why interest in the issue remains intense, especially in societies which have not yet opted for abolition.

Jan Gorecki
University of Illinois
Champaign-Urbana

References
Diamond, A. S. (1971), *Primitive Law Past and Present*, London.
Ehrlich, I. (1975), 'The deterrent effect of capital punishment: a question of life and death', *American Economic Review*, 65.
Gorecki, J. (1983), *Capital Punishment – Criminal Law and Social Evolution*, New York.
See also: *penology; punishment.*

Capital Theory

Capital's role in the technological specification of production and as a source of income called interest or profit encompasses theories of production and accumulation and theories of value and distribution. The subject has perplexed economists because capital produces a return which keeps capital intact and yields an interest or profit which is thus permanent, while consumption goods produce a unique return (utility) equal to cost and are destroyed in use.

The pre-industrial Classical economists thought of capital as stocks of food and provisions advanced to labour; it was the accumulation of stocks making possible the division of labour which was of importance. This position is reflected in J. S. Mill's (1848) statement that to 'speak of the "productive powers of capital" . . . is not literally correct. The only productive powers are those of labour and natural agents.' Capital was at best an intermediate good determined by technology and thus subject to exogenous or 'natural' laws, rather than human or economic 'laws'.

By Marx's time, factory-labour working with fixed machinery had become widespread, and he was impressed by the increase in the ratio of 'dead' labour, which had gone into producing the machines, to the living labour which operated them. Marx's idea of a 'mode of production' made capital a social, rather than a purely technological, relation; it was not the machinery, but the operation of the laws of value and distribution under capitalism that produced revolutionary implications. This integration of production and distribution challenged Mills's separation and clearly raised the question of the justification for profit or interest as a permanent return to capital.

Jevons was among the first to note the importance of the time that labour was accumulated in stock. Böhm-Bawerk's Austrian theory of capital built on time as a justification for interest in answer to Marx. The Austrians considered human and natural powers as the original productive factors, but 'time', which allowed more 'roundabout' production processes using intermediate inputs, was also productive. Longer average periods of production would produce greater output, but in decreasing proportion. It was the capitalists' ability to wait for the greater product of longer processes, and the workers' haste to consume, which explained the former's profit.

Clark extended Ricardo's Classical theory of differential rent of land to physical capital goods, considering diminishing returns to be a 'natural law' of production. In Clark's explanation it is the capital goods themselves which are considered productive, their return equal to their marginal product. Determination of capital's 'marginal' contribution requires that it be 'fixed' while the amount of labour employed varies, but 'transmutable' into the appropriate technical form when different quantities are used with a 'fixed' quantity of labour.

L. Walras shifted emphasis from physical capital goods to their services as the 'productive' inputs and the return to owning the goods themselves which can then be analysed as the exchange and valuation of the permanent net revenues they produce.

Wicksell was critical of Walras, rejected 'time' as a productive factor, and was sceptical of the application of marginal theory to aggregate capital, for the 'margin' of the capital stock could not be clearly defined. The problem was in the fact that 'land and labour are measured each in terms of their own technical unit' while 'capital. . . is reckoned as a sum of exchange value . . . each particular capital good is measured by a unit extraneous to itself', which meant that the value of capital, equal in equilibrium to its costs of production, could not be used to define the quantity used to calculate its marginal return because 'these costs of production include capital and interest. . . . We should therefore be arguing in a circle' (1934). Wicksell's argument recalls the original Classical view of capital as an intermediate good, a produced means of production, rather than an 'original' productive factor.

Fisher made a sharp distinction between the flow of income and the capital stock that produced it; since discounting future income converts one into the other,

the key to the problem is in the role of individual preferences of present over future consumption, or the 'rate of time preference' in determining the rate of interest. The greater the preference for present goods, the higher the rate of time discount and the lower the present value of future goods represented by the stock of capital.

Keynes's *General Theory* assumption of a fixed stock of capital and the absence of a clear theory of distribution left open the analysis of capital and the determination of the rate of interest or profit to complement the theory. Neoclassical theorists (based in Cambridge, US) added a simplified version of Clark's theory via an aggregate production function relating homogeneous output to the 'productive' factors: labour and aggregate capital, in which the 'quantity' of capital would be negatively associated with its price, the rate of interest. This preserved the negative relation between price and quantity of traditional demand theory. Cambridge (UK) economists rejected capital as a productive factor, arguing that the value of the heterogeneous produced means of production comprising 'aggregate capital' could not be measured independently of its price, which was a determinant of the value used to identify its quantity. These theoretical disputes came to be known as the 'Cambridge Controversies' in capital theory.

A crucial role was played in these debates by Sraffa's 1960 theory of prices, which furnished formal proof of Wicksell's criticisms by demonstrating that changes in the rate of interest (or profit) in an interdependent system could affect the prices of the goods making up the means of production in such a way that the sum of their values representing the aggregate 'quantity' of capital might rise or fall, or even take on the same value at two different rates of interest. These demonstrations came to be known as 'capital reversal' and 'reswitching' and clearly demonstrated that the negative relation between the quantity of aggregate capital and the rate of interest had no general application. Such criticism does not apply to the analysis of individual capital goods, although a general equilibrium in which the rate of return is uniform requires the comparison of competing rates of return and thus ratios of profits to the value of the capital goods that produce them. Modern theorists only agree on the inappropriateness of aggregate capital concepts.

J. A. Kregel
University of Groningen

References
Mill, J. S. (1886 [1848]), *Principles of Political Economy*, London.
Wicksell, K. (1934), *Lectures on Political Economy*, London.

Sraffa, P. (1960), *Production of Commodities by Means of Commodities*, Cambridge.

Further Reading
Harcourt, G. C. (1972), *Some Cambridge Controversies in the Theory of Capital*, Cambridge.
Kregel, J. A. (1976), *Theory of Capital*, London.
See also: *capital consumption; capitalism; human capital; Keynesian economics; Marxian economics; Sraffa; Wicksell.*

Career Development

See Vocational and career development.

Cargo Cults

Cargo Cults is the name given to millenarian movements of Melanesia, which centre on a belief that specified ritual manipulations and observances will soon bring to the people concerned material rewards, notably manufactured goods, and a better, even paradisaical, life. The name originates from the frequent use by participants of the Pidgin word *kago* (derived from the English 'cargo') to describe the returns they intend their activities to bring, although having a wider, and in the cult context uniquely Melanesian, connotation.

These small-scale and intense cults usually have messianic leaders who rise up to direct their activities, using relevant traditional belief, reinterpreting myths and manipulating associated symbols to promulgate their syncretized and appealing message. The activities inspired and directed by these 'prophets' frequently disrupt everyday life, as they divert people from subsistence tasks (at times even forbid them), and encourage the pursuit of preparations for the coming millennium. One example is clearing airstrips, and surrounding them with bamboo landing lights, to receive the prophesied aircraft coming with cargo, sometimes to be piloted by the ancestors.

One cult reported in the late 1970s, from the Vanuatuan island of Tanna, centres on the Duke of Edinburgh and his autographed photograph. The people think the Duke was spirited from their midst at birth, and they have prepared for his return, which they believe is imminent, to cure sickness, rejuvenate the elderly and bring material wealth to all. They have a site ready on a nearby beach where the Duke's boat will berth on arrival.

Early reports interpreted such cults as the actions of irrational and deluded people, even states of temporary collective madness. Sensitive research in post-war years has refuted this dismissive conclusion, showing that cargo cults are a rational indigenous response to traumatic culture contact with Western society. Although

precipitated by familiarity with, and a desire to possess, the goods of the industrialized world, they have a traditional focus and logic. They turn to traditional beliefs and idioms to cope with a bewildering invasion, and although inappropriate, even comical to us in their misunderstanding of our society and their bizarre interpretation of unintelligible aspects of it (like the role of the Royal Family or aircraft technology), they are neither illogical nor stupid.

The newcomers have material wealth and technical capabilities beyond local people's understanding and imagination and – for tribal societies – irresistible political and military power emanating from incomprehensible nation states. Europeans apparently do no physical work to produce these goods, unlike the politically subjugated local population, many of whom they put to hard labour for paltry returns. Neither do Europeans share their fabulous wealth with others, a direct assault on a cardinal Melanesian value, where giving and receiving is an integral aspect of social life.

Clearly Europeans know something, and the problem for the Melanesians is how to gain access to this knowledge. Unable to comprehend Western society and the long-term nature of education, which they interpret as a scheme to dupe them, or the world-wide capitalist economic system and the life of a factory worker, they turn to millenarian cults. A recurring feature in these cults is a belief that Europeans in some past age tricked Melanesians and are withholding from them their rightful share of material goods. In cargo cults the Melanesians are trying to reverse this situation, to discover the ritual formula that will facilitate access to their misappropriated manufactured possessions. They conclude that material goods come from the spirit world and that the wealthy Whites are stealing their share; so it is a case of manipulating rituals to reverse the situation and gain access to them.

An oft-repeated aim is to secure the cargo of the ancestors, who some cultists believe will return at the millennium. They will come to right current injustices. Some cults take on a disturbing racist tone here, probably reflecting the attitudes of the White newcomers, which signal people's discontent with European domination and feelings of impotence. With the coming of the millennium Blacks will become Whites, and the Whites turn Black, and White domination will end.

The relatively frequent pan-Melanesian occurrence of cargo cults in a wide range of disparate cultures, and their recurrence time and again, with modified dogma and ritual, in the same region, testify to their importance to the people concerned. In their expression of tensions, they lend themselves to a range of sociological and psychological interpretations. Although frenetic, short-lived and – to outsiders – disruptive, these cults allow Melanesians who find themselves in a confusing and inexplicable world invaded by technically superior outsiders to cope with the changed situation, even manipulate it, for in some cases their behaviour brings results: desperate governments supply processed food and other provisions to alleviate the resulting, sometimes chronic, food shortages following the disruption of subsistence activities.

Paul Sillitoe
University of Durham

Further Reading
Cohn, N. (1961), *The Pursuit of the Millennium*, 2nd edn, New York.
Lawrence, P. (1965), *Road Belong Cargo*, Manchester.
Worsley, P. (1957), *The Trumpet Shall Sound*, London.
See also: *sects and cults*.

Cartels and Trade Associations

Cartels are a common form of collusion in oligopolistic markets. In a market with many sellers (perfect competition) each seller can take the market price as parametric, but in an oligopolistic market firms will be aware that their pricing decisions will affect the decisions of others. It is commonly agreed that isolated profit maximization in an oligopolistic market will lead all producers to have lower profits than would be possible if they colluded. Cartels and trade associations are descriptions for collusion, the former in markets with a small number of firms, the latter in markets where there are many (100). Cartels vary from gentleman's agreements to legally binding contracts. In most countries they are illegal, but have often also been formed at government behest, as in Germany and the US in the 1930s. The objective of a cartel is to raise price and cut quantity to increase industry profits. Although they are commonly observed (and more commonly exist), they are often unstable, as each firm has an incentive to cheat by offering small discounts to gain increased sales. Because every firm can cheat, many will, and cheating will occur unless the cartel is properly policed. Cartels can take many forms, from overt (or covert) agreements to tacit agreements on price leadership in the market. Agreement appears to be easier to reach when numbers involved are modest, products are homogeneous and government regulation lax. Recent developments in the theory of games, using infinite dynamic game theory with time discounting and plausible retaliation for cheating, have aided our understanding of the topic (see Friedman, 1982), but have only served to emphasize the indeterminateness of possible solutions in cartelized markets.

Ray Barrell
University of Southampton

Reference
Friedman, J. (1982), *Oligopoly Theory*, Cambridge.

Further Reading
Scherer, F. M. (1980), *Industrial Structure and Economic Performance*, 2nd edn, Chicago.
See also: *antitrust legislation; business concentration; markets; monopoly; oligopoly*.

Case Studies

Case studies are detailed perceptions of connected processes in individual and collective experience. They have the following distinctive features:
(1) They contain *cases*, instances of theoretical principles. Not every case need be typical, but 'ideal-typical' cases sometimes provide particularly 'apt illustrations' (Gluckman, 1961).
(2) They discuss *particularities*, including particular individuals (pseudonymized), rather than merely the abstracted roles of, for example, spouses. They carefully follow events such as those preceding particular divorces, particular strikes or particular development schemes before generalizing about incompatible conjugal roles, causes of industrial conflict or achievable policies. Data transcend analysis, inviting alternative interpretations.
(3) They are case *histories*, recording ongoing processes in the relationship between particular individuals, the interaction of particular individuals with particular institutions, the step-by-step transformation of particular institutions, the vicissitudes of particular social movements faced with support or antagonism from particular individuals or groups, and so on. Because the same actors appear in diverse situations, defining or redefining their relationships, pursuing or resolving their conflicts, case studies have not been common in static structural-functional models, which divide the social universe into 'political', 'kinship', 'economic', and so on. However, Turner (1968) used case studies to investigate processes maintaining structural continuity, van Velsen (1967) stressed their indispensability in studying structural change, and Blau (1963) used them to demonstrate 'permanence of change' in bureaucracies regarded as structurally rigid.
(4) They are frequently *social-problem oriented*. Disputes are analysed long before they come to court – if they ever do. Case studies unearth processes which lead to some activities being labelled as social problems but which leave other activities, arguably more harmful, of little public interest. Case studies demonstrate the principle that issues alter as different groups adopt them. Thus, Spector and Kitsuse (1977) delineated how American concern for Soviet dissidents in mental hospitals was replaced by one related issue after another until the 'main' one became *American psychiatrists*' resistance to judicial cross-examination.

Methods
(1) All science involves comparison. Individual

researchers may not arrange case studies comparatively themselves, preferring to detail a few cases. However, their cases and others' must be continually scrutinized for variables on which to base generalizations.

(2) Ongoing dialogue between conjecture and data-gathering attenuates distinctions between deduction and induction.

(3) Detail demands diverse techniques, including analysis of documents, both official and personal, taped interviews and informant feedback. Participant observation is particularly important, for casual conversation and observing people in 'unguarded moments' (Langness, 1970) often suggest fresh lines of investigation. Superficial rapport, however, can impair case-studies. Authenticity also requires cross-checking. Follow-up and replication studies test whether developments in the short term continue in the long term, and whether developments in one set of circumstances are repeated in another.

(4) Writing up case studies itself deepens understanding. Familiar postulates often fail to do justice to complex information, making conceptual refinement necessary. Resulting 'sensitizing concepts', without masquerading as 'grand theory', enable other researchers to apply them to very different sociological problems. Even unconceptualized case studies, however, may bring conventional suppositions into question.

(5) Statistical inferences are derivable from case-study variables, although common sociological failings are absence of case studies *and* of quantitative estimation of variance (Rosenblatt, 1981). Unfortunately many statistical studies dispense with sensitizing concepts. Such studies seem unaware that 'more discoveries have arisen from intense observation than from statistics applied to large groups' (Beveridge, 1951). Eysenck, who once regarded case studies as mere anecdotage, now takes the view that 'We simply have to keep our eyes open and look carefully at individual cases – not in the hope of proving anything, but rather in the hope of learning something' (1976).

Maurice Glickman
University of Botswana

References
Beveridge, W. I. B. (1951), *The Art of Scientific Investigation*, London.
Blau, P. (1963), *The Dynamics of Bureaucracy: A Study of Interpersonal Relations in Two Government Agencies*, London.
Eysenck, H. (1976), 'Introduction', in *Case Studies in Behaviour Therapy*, London.
Gluckman, M. (1961), 'Ethnographic data in British social anthropology', *Sociological Review*, 9.
Langness, L. (1970), 'Unguarded moments', in R. Naroll and R. Cohen (eds), *A Handbook of Cultural Anthropology*, New York.
Rosenblatt, P. (1981), 'Ethnographic case studies', in M. Brewer and B. Collins (eds), *Scientific Enquiry and the Social Sciences*, London.
Spector, M. and Kitsuse, J. (1977), *Constructing Social Problems*, London.
Turner, V. W. (1968), *Schism and Continuity in an African Society: A Study of Ndembu Village Life*, Manchester.
Van Velsen, J. (1967), 'The extended-case method and situational analysis', in A. L. Epstein (ed.), *The Craft of Social Anthropology*, London.
See also: *life histories.*

Caste

Caste systems have been defined in the most general terms as systems of hierarchically ordered endogamous units in which membership is hereditary and permanent (for example, Berreman, 1960). On such a definition a whole range of rigidly stratified societies would be characterized by caste – Japan, for example, or certain Polynesian and East African societies, or the racially divided world of the American Deep South. Hindu India is generally taken as the paradigmatic example. Many scholars would argue, however, that the difference between this case and the others are far more significant than the similarities, and that the term 'caste' should properly be applied only to this context.

The morphology of the Hindu caste system can be described in terms of three key characteristics (Bouglé, 1908), all of which are religiously underpinned by the religious values of purity (Dumont, 1970): (1) There is a *hierarchy* of castes which is theoretically based on their relative degree of purity. As the purest of all the Brahmans rank highest, and are in principle both distinct from and superior to the caste which actually wields politico-economic power. (2) Since the pure can only maintain their purity if there are impure castes to remove the pollution they inevitably incur by their involvement in the natural world, there is a *division of labour* between castes resulting in their *interdependence*. (3) Pollution is contagious, and a caste must therefore restrict its contacts with inferiors in order to maintain its status. This *separation* takes many forms: a rule of endogamy precluding marital alliances with inferiors; restrictions on commensality; the outcasting of those who transgress the rules lest they pollute the rest of the group, and the phenomenon of Untouchability debarring physical contact between 'clean' and 'polluted' groups. (We even have historical reports of theoretically Unseeable castes; while in parts of traditional Kerala the relative status of non-Brahman castes was in theory precisely reflected in the number of paces distant they had to keep from the highest Brahmans.)

While the (upward) mobility of *individuals* is theoretically impossible and empirically rare, the group as a whole may lay claim to a higher status by emulating the customs and practices of its superiors, and may succeed in validating its claims by using a new-found political or economic leverage to persuade erstwhile superiors to interact with it on a new basis (the crucial test being their acceptance of its food and water). As the actors present it, however, this is not a matter of social climbing but of reasserting a traditional *status quo* which was temporarily disrupted. A theory of timeless stasis is thus preserved despite a good deal of actual mobility.

The system is often visualized as being like a layer-cake with each layer as an occupationally specialized group characterized by endogamy and unrestricted commensality. A better image is of a set of Chinese boxes. At the most schematic level (i) contemporary Hindus, following the scriptures, represent the caste order in terms of a fourfold division: Brahman, Kshatriya, Vaishya, Shudra. At the local level (the details vary considerably), the Brahmans may be subdivided into priestly and non-priestly subgroups, the priestly Brahmans into Household-priests, Temple-priests and Funeral-priests (iii); the Household-priests into two or more endogamous circles (iv), and each circle into its component clans and lineages (v) who may be the only people who will freely accept one another's food. The answer to the question 'What is your caste?' will depend on context and might legitimately be phrased in terms of any of these five levels. At each level the group is referred to as a *jati*, a term which is conventionally translated as 'caste' but is more accurately rendered as 'breed' or 'species'. Groups which share a common status in relation to outsiders are internally hierarchized – all Brahmans are equal in relation to non-Brahmans, but non-priestly Brahmans are superior in relation to priestly ones, and Household-priests in relation to Funeral-priests. It will be seen that the occupationally specialized group (iii) is not necessarily coterminous with the endogamous group (iv), which may not coincide with the unit of unrestricted commensality (v). It is therefore impossible to define caste by listing a series of characteristics (e.g. occupation, endogamy etc.) common to all. The universe of caste is a relational universe, rather than one made up of a given number of fixed and bounded units.

J. P. Parry
London School of Economics and Political Science

References
Berreman, G. D. (1960), 'Caste in India and the United States', *American Journal of Sociology*, 66.
Bouglé, V. (1971 [1908]), *Essays on the Caste System*, Cambridge. (Original French edn, *Essais sur le régime des castes*, Paris.)
Dumont, L. (1970), *Homo Hierarchicus: The Caste System and Its Implications*, London.
See also: *hierarchy; stratification.*

Catastrophe Theory

Historically the field of research known as catastrophe theory began with the ideas of the French topologist René Thom in the early 1960s. In purely mathematical terms, elementary catastrophe theory is concerned with the classification of singularities of differentiable mappings on manifolds. A catastrophe is a singularity in a map that arises stably in the following way. Let C be an n-dimensional control or parameter space, let X be a k-dimensional behaviour or state space, and let f be a smooth generic potential-like function on X parametrized by the manifold C. Let M be the set of stationary values of f obtained by setting the partial derivatives of f with respect to the coordinates x_i of X equal to zero. Then M is a smooth surface or hypersurface (the catastrophe manifold). Regions on M represent maximum or minimum values of the potential function f. A catastrophe is a structurally stable singularity of the projection of M onto the control space C.

If the number of dimensions n of the control space is 4 or less, there are only 7 elementary catastrophes.

Elementary catastrophes Family	Name	Dimension of X	Dimension of C
Cuspoids	Fold	1	1
	Simple cusp	1	2
	Swallowtail	1	3
	Butterfly	1	4
Umbilics	Hyperbolic	2	3
	Elliptic	2	3
	Parabolic	2	4

Catastrophe theory provides a coherent framework for modelling the complex dynamics of systems. Points on the catastrophe manifold represent stationary values of the potential-like function associated with the behaviour of the system. The position of the state point on the manifold is determined by combinations of the control variables or factors. Smooth, continuous changes in the control factors can result in qualitatively distinct types of behaviour of the state point. It may move in a smooth, continuous trajectory along the surface of the manifold. However, smooth changes in the control factors may also cause a sudden, discontinuous ('catastrophic') jump of the state point from one region of the catastrophe manifold to another.

Thus by means of catastrophe theory one is able to model the smooth, continuous processes of change and development, as well as the occurrence of phenomena associated with the dynamics of instability within the same framework.

Applications of catastrophe theory divide into two distinct categories. On the one hand, there is an expanding corpus of successful studies concerned with rigorous applications of the formal mathematical theory. The applications are largely in physics and engineering (Poston and Stewart, 1978; Gilmore, 1981, and some of the examples in Zeeman, 1977). The aim is utilitarian and oriented towards the quantitative analysis of specified dynamic systems. On the other hand, the approach exemplified by the work of Thom is essentially hermeneutic and interpretative. The interest is in providing a global, qualitative view of the dynamics of a system. One postulates the applicability of some elementary catastrophe as a model for the system of interest, and analyses its dynamics in terms of the properties of the model. Applications of catastrophe model building are found in biology and the social sciences (Thom, 1976, 1983; Zeeman, 1977).

Franklin E. Tjon Sie Fat
University of Leiden

References
Gilmore, R. (1981), *Catastrophe Theory for Scientists and Engineers*, New York.
Poston, T. and Stewart, I. (1978), *Catastrophe Theory and its Applications*, London.
Thom, R. (1976), *Structural Stability and Morphogenesis. An Outline of a General Theory of Models*, Reading, Mass.
Thom, R. (1983), *Mathematical Models of Morphogenesis*, Chichester.
Zeeman, E. C. (1977), *Catastrophe Theory. Selected Papers 1972–1977*, Reading, Mass.

Further Reading
Behavioral Science (1978), 23, Special issue on applications of catastrophe theory in the behavioral and life sciences.
Deakin, M. A. B. (1980), 'Applied catastrophe theory in the social and biological sciences', *Bulletin of Mathematical Biology*, 42.

Categorical Data

Definition and Notation

Categorical data in its broadest sense is simply a collection of values of discrete variables obtained from a sample of individuals or objects. Here the term discrete variable means a variable which can have only a finite number of values (levels or categories). These levels may also have other features, such as a natural order.

A common type of categorical data arises if the same p variables $X_1, X_2, \ldots, X_p$ (say) are measured on each individual. In this case, a convenient means of summarizing the resulting data is in the form of a p-way contingency table. Such a table gives the number of individuals with any given configuration of values of the p discrete variables. If $n_1, n_2, \ldots, n_p$ denote the number of categories of each of the variables, then the contingency table will have $n_1 \times n_2 \times \ldots \times n_p$ entries (or cells). Table 1, which combines tables 5.3–1 and 5.3–5 in Bishop, Fienberg and Holland (1975), illustrates a three-way contingency table.

Table 1   Social mobility data

Country	Father's status	Son's status				
		1	2	3	4	5
Britain	1	50	45	8	18	8
	2	28	174	84	154	55
	3	11	78	110	223	96
	4	14	150	185	714	447
	5	0	42	72	320	411
Denmark	1	18	17	16	4	2
	2	24	105	109	59	21
	3	23	84	289	217	95
	4	8	49	175	348	198
	5	6	8	69	201	246

As an example, the number 320 in Table 1 shows that there were 320 father-son pairs in the sample who were British and had status levels 5 and 4 respectively. The status categories have a natural order (and are said to be ordinal), whereas the country categories have no natural order (and hence have a nominal scale).

If there are variables measured on some but not all individuals, the data is not representable as a contingency table unless extra categories are invented to denote missing values of variables. (Having said this, the discussion will be restricted to categorical data *naturally* summarized by a contingency table.)

The following notation and conventions will be used throughout: Given a finite number of discrete variables $(X_1, X_2, X_3, \ldots)$ measured on a sample of individuals, the symbol $n_{ijk\ldots}$ stands for the number of individuals with $X_1 = i$, $X_2 = j$, $X_3 = k$, $\ldots$. The corresponding expected count under a given model is denoted by $m_{ijk\ldots}$ and $p_{ijk\ldots}$ = Probability $(X_1 = i, X_2 = j, X_3 = k, \ldots) > 0$. A plus sign (+) used as a subscript denotes summation over an index e.g. $p_{i+k} = \sum_j p_{ijk}$. To avoid technical problems, all divisors in mathematical expressions will be assumed to be positive. Finally, the symbol *ln* is used to denote the natural (base *e*) logarithm.

Sampling Assumptions

Basic to any analysis of categorical data is a consideration of how the data was (or is to be) collected. This is essential in the formulation of an appropriate statistical model for the data.

As an illustration of different sampling schemes and possible models, consider Table 1. One way in which the data could have been collected is by determining *beforehand* the number of father-son pairs in Britain and in Denmark to be surveyed. In this situation, a suitable model for the distribution of the counts n_{ijk} ($X_1 =$ Country, $X_2 =$ Father's status, $X_3 =$ Son's status) might be a product of two multinomials, one for the counts obtained in Britain and one for those obtained in Denmark. These multinomials would have sample sizes n_{i++} and probabilities $p_{ijk} = m_{ijk}/n_{i++}$; $j,k = 1, \dots, 5$ for $i = 1$ (Britain) and 2 (Denmark) respectively.

An alternative way in which the data could have been obtained is by interviewing as many pairs in Britain and Denmark as was possible within a fixed time period or budget. In this case the total sample size in each country would be random, and a suitable model for the counts in Table 1 might be the product of all values of i,j,k of Poisson distributions of the form

$$\left\{ \exp(-m_{ijk}) \ (m_{ijk})^{n}ijk \right\} n/_{ijk}!$$

where exp denotes the exponential function and $n! = n(n-1) \dots 1$.

For further discussion concerning sampling distributions, in particular product multinomial and Poisson models, see Bishop, Fienberg and Holland (1975). It should be emphasized that how closely the data conforms with any distributional assumptions is a matter which requires checking.

Log-Linear Models

Statistical models for contingency tables generally consist of two parts. The first part involves the specification of a probability distribution for the counts in the table, and this has been mentioned in Section 2 above. The second part involves formulating a suitable structure for the expected counts, relating them to the levels of the discrete variables. The suitability of any given structure at this second stage will depend on a knowledge of the sampling scheme and whether some variable(s) is (are) considered *response variables* and the rest *explanatory*. Of the many possibilities, the discussion below is limited to a particular type of *log-linear* model for the expected counts, one which can be used to express hypotheses concerning *interaction* (association) between variables as well as *conditional independence* relations. In doing so, the implicit assumption is made that the table has no *structural zeros*, i.e. there are no cells with zero probability of having a

positive count. It is important to recognize structural zeros in a table if they exist (see Bishop, Fienberg and Holland, 1975; Fienberg, 1977).

The type of log-linear model to be considered here expresses the natural logarithm of the expected counts as a linear function of *interaction* or *association terms*. An example of such a model for Table 1 is

$$\ln m_{ik} = u + u_{1(i)} + u_{2(j)} + u_{3(k)} + u_{12(ij)} + u_{13(ik)} + u_{23(jk)} \quad (1)$$
$$+ u_{123(ijk)}.$$

The term $u_{1(i)}$ denotes the main (or zero order interaction) effect of X_1 when it is at level i, $u_{12(ij)}$ denotes the first order interaction effect of variable X_1 and X_2 when they are at levels i and j respectively, while $u_{123(ijk)}$ denotes the second order interaction effect of variables X_1, X_2, X_3 when they are at levels i,j,k respectively. All the *u*-terms in (1) satisfy the usual analysis of variance type constraints that the sum over any subscript within a bracket is zero e.g. $\Sigma \ u_{23(jk)} = \overset{\text{k}}{\Sigma} u_{23(jk)} = 0$. For an interpretation of the u-parameters in terms of measures of association, in particular cross-product ratios, see Bishop, Fienberg and Holland (1975). In general a *p*-way contingency table can have interaction terms up to order *p*-1.

Equation (1) is an example of a *saturated* log-linear model i.e. one which allows all possible interaction terms. As such it imposes no constraints on the expected counts. An example of a non-saturated model is when $u_{123(ijk)} = u_{12(ij)} = u_{13(ik)} = u_{23(jk)} = 0$ in (1). This corresponds to the hypothesis of no interaction effects or, under a product multinomial sampling scheme for Table 1, the conditional independence of the two status variables given country of origin.

A log-linear model of the type above is said to be *hierarchical* if it has the property that whenever an interaction term involving a set *B* of variables is in the model then so are all the interaction terms involving subsets of *B*. There are difficulties in interpreting these models when they are not hierarchical (see for example Fienberg, 1977).

A shorthand way of specifying a hierarchical log-linear model is by giving its *generating class*, or, in the terminology of Bishop, Fienberg and Holland (1975), the set of minimal sufficient configurations. The generating class identifies the maximal order interaction terms in the model and can be used to write down all the model terms. This is illustrated in Example 1 below.

Example 1. Suppose the generating class of a log-linear model for a four-way table is given to be [123], [24], [34] . This means that $u_{123(ijk)}$, $u_{24(jl)}$ and $u_{34(kl)}$ are in the model and consequently all the terms in Equation (1) as well as u, $u_{(2j)}$, $u_{4(1)}$, $u_{24(jl)}$, and u, $u_{3(k)}$, $u_{4(1)}$, $u_{34(kl)}$. Adding all these, including any term only once, gives us the form of the model.

As has been alluded to earlier, certain log-linear

models can be interpreted in terms of conditional independence constraints imposed on the variables. For multinomial sampling models it is possible to summarize conveniently the conditional independence relations (if any) implied by a given log-linear model by associating it with a graph. Details can be found in Kiiveri and Speed (1982) and Darroch, Lauritzen and Speed (1980).

Additional information can be used to improve the analysis of a contingency table. One form of additional information not utilized in the discussion so far is ordering of the levels of one or more of the discrete variables. (See Fienberg (1977) for an example and discussion of a model incorporating such information.)

Models which explicitly make use of the fact that one variable is a response and the others explanatory can be found in Fienberg (1977) and Haberman (1978; 1979).

Estimation and Goodness-of-Fit

The *u*-parameters in log-linear models or equivalently the expected counts can be estimated using maximum likelihood methods. An important result concerning these estimates is that they are the same for product multinomial and the simpler Poisson likelihoods *provided* all *u*-terms involving variables with margins fixed beforehand are included in the log-linear model. (See Bishop, Fienberg and Holland, 1975.)

To test the goodness of fit of a particular log-linear model either of the following statistics could be used:

$$X^2 = \Sigma_{i,j,k,\ldots}(\hat{m}_{ink}\ldots - n_{ijk}\ldots)2/\hat{m}_{ijk}\ldots \quad (2)$$

$$G^2 = 2\Sigma_{i,j,k,\ldots} \hat{m}_{ijk}\ldots \ln(\hat{m}_{ijk}\ldots/n_{ijk}\ldots) \quad (3)$$

where $\hat{m}_{ijk}\ldots$ is the estimated expected count under the model. Both statistics have an asymptotic chi-square distribution with degrees of freedom equal to the total number of cells in the table minus the total number of parameters in the model. Computation of the degrees of freedom is more difficult if the table has structural zeros (Haberman, 1978). The likelihood-ratio statistic (3) has the attractive property that it can be partitioned into a number of additive components for a nested hierachy of models (see Fienberg, 1977).

Procedures useful for isolating counts with undue influence on estimates, systematic departures from log-linearity and the like can be found in Pregibon (1981) and the reference therein.

Other Topics

Some topics of special interest to social scientists, namely causal models for systems of discrete variables and latent class models, have been omitted. References which can be consulted for further information regarding these are Kiiveri and Speed (1982), Goodman (1978) and Haberman (1979).

H. T. Kiiveri
CSIRO Institute of
Physical Sciences, Australia

References

Bishop, Y.M.M., Fienberg, S.E. and Holland, P.W. (1975), *Discrete Multivariate Analysis: Theory and Practice*, Cambridge, Mass.

Darroch, J.N., Lauritzen, S.L. and Speed, T.P. (1980), 'Log-linear models for contingency tables and Markov fields over graphs', *Annals of Statistics*, 8.

Fienberg, S.E. (1977), *The Analysis of Cross-Classified Categorical Data*, Cambridge, Mass.

Goodman, L.A. (1978), *Analyzing Qualitative Categorical Data: Log-linear Models and Latent Structure Analysis*, ed. J. Magidson, Cambridge, Mass.

Haberman, S.J. (1978), *Analysis of Qualitative Data, Volume 1: Introductory Topics*, New York.

Haberman, S.J. (1979), *Analysis of Qualitative Data, Volume 2: New Developments*, New York.

Kiiveri, H.T. and Speed, T.P. (1982), 'Structural analysis of multivariate data: a review', in S. Leinhardt (ed.), *Sociological Methodology 1982*, San Francisco.

Pregibon, D. (1981), 'Logistic regression diagnostics', *Annals of Statistics*, 9.

See also: *multivariate analysis*.

Census of Population

A Census of Population, as defined in United Nations reports, is the total process of collecting, compiling, evaluating, analysing, and publishing, or otherwise disseminating, demographic, economic, and social data pertaining to all persons in a country, or to a well delimited part of a country at a specified time.

The census of population is the oldest and most widely distributed statistical undertaking by governments throughout the world. Censuses have also been developed to provide information on housing, manufactures, agriculture, mineral industries, and business establishments. Many of the principles applying to the census of population apply equally to these other censuses.

No one knows which ruler first ordered a count of the people in order to assess the numbers potentially available for military service or to determine how many households might be liable to pay taxes. Population counts were reported from ancient Japan and counts were compiled by Egyptians, Greeks, Hebrews, Persians, and Peruvians. Many of these early censuses were limited as to the area covered and in some instances dealt with only a part of the population, such as men of military age. The results were generally treated as state secrets. In Europe, censuses on a city-wide basis were reported in the fifteenth and sixteenth centuries. India reported a census in 1687. Various censuses have been claimed as the first in modern times.

Data collected in a population census have often been used as the basis for the allocation of a territory to one or the other claimant governments. Today census data are widely used by governments for planning and carrying out a variety of governmental functions. In some countries representation in legislative bodies and distribution of funds by the central government are significantly affected by the census results. The powers and duties of many municipalities depend on the size of their population. The private economy makes extensive use of the data for site locations, marketing strategies, and many other activities. Health, education, and welfare programmes depend very heavily on such data.

The oldest continuous census taking is that of the United States where a census has been taken every ten years since 1790. The United Kingdom began taking a census in 1801 and followed the ten-year pattern except in 1941 when wartime requirements led to its cancellation. The ten-year pattern is widely observed. In many countries the census is authorized anew whenever the government finds a need for the data. In a few countries censuses are taken at regular five-year intervals. During the 1970s special efforts by the United Nations and some donor countries were directed to assisting African countries which had not previously taken a census. In 1982 the People's Republic of China completed the largest census ever taken. By 1983 virtually every country in the world had taken at least one census of population.

Early censuses often utilized household lists or similar sources as the basis of their tabulations. A modern census is one in which information is collected separately about each individual. Such practices became common during the last half of the nineteenth century.

The information assembled in a census depends in large part on the needs of the government for such information and on the availability of alternative sources. The United Nations has identified a set of topics which appear most essential. They include: place where found at time of census, place of usual residence, place of birth, sex, age, relationship to head of household, marital status, children born alive, children living, literacy, school attendance, status (employer, employee, etc.). International comparability will be facilitated to the extent that national census offices utilize the standard definitions which have been developed by the United Nations.

A question which needs careful attention prior to a census is who is to be counted as part of the national and local population. Special consideration needs to be given to such persons as members of the Armed Forces, including those stationed outside the home country, migratory workers, university students, technical assistance personnel outside their home countries, long-term visitors, and guest workers.

Having determined who is to be included in the census, it becomes necessary also to determine in which part of the national territory they are to be counted. The classic distinction is that between a *de facto* and a *de jure* census. In a *de facto* census people are generally counted as a part of the population of the place where they encountered the census enumerator. This differs from the practice in a *de jure* census where an effort is made to ascertain where the person 'belongs'. This may be a usual residence, a legal residence, or an ancestral home. Persons who spend part of the time in one place and the remainder in one or more other places, and persons in long-stay institutions (prisons, hospitals, etc.) need to be recorded in a uniform manner within the country. Special procedures may need to be developed for persons who have no fixed place of residence, such as persons who live on the streets, nomads, refugees, or illegal aliens.

Customarily two basic methods of taking the census are recognized – direct enumeration and self enumeration. Under the former method the enumerator collects information directly from the household. Self enumeration means that the household members are given a questionnaire with the request that they enter the appropriate information and deliver the completed form to the designated census office or to an enumerator who comes by for the completed forms.

The law establishing the census normally makes provision for the authority of the census office and its employees to conduct the census and establishes the obligation of the residents to provide the answers to the best of their ability. There are normally legal penalties for refusal or for providing false information.

An important part of the legal provision for the census is the guarantee that the individually identifiable information will be held in strict confidence and will be used only for statistical purposes, and violation of pledge of confidentiality is a punishable offence.

The almost universal availability of computers for the processing, tabulation and printing of the data collected in the census has greatly facilitated the work of census offices. A more complete and thorough review of the raw data as well as of intermediate and final tabulations is possible, and where the research community also has access to computers the provision of summary tapes and of public use micro-data sample tapes has enabled them to use the data more effectively.

The improved access of the public to the census products has greatly increased the concern over errors in the census from whatever source, whether in coverage of the population, errors by the respondents, errors in recording the information supplied by respondents, or errors made in the processing of the data, and census officials are alerted to this problem.

Sampling procedures are increasingly being used in connection with the census. In many cases, samples have been drawn for use in pre-tests. A part of the questionnaire may be asked of a sample of the population, thus reducing the total response burden and reducing the work load for processing and tabulation. Samples may be drawn for advance tabulations, thus speeding up the availability of the census results to the public. Samples of the data may be drawn for special tabulations. Public use of micro-data samples may be drawn to make the census data more readily available to the research community, provided that no individually identifiable information is released. Sample surveys may be used to secure specialized information as a follow-up to the census itself. An important use of sampling has been to facilitate internal analysis of the raw census data and in carrying out post-census studies of the quality of the data. Sampling procedures are effective tools in quality control of all operations, including preparatory work for the census: the distribution of supplies; recruitment, training, and supervision of the field staff; receipt and control of the completed census schedules; editing and coding; tabulation; and preparation and distribution of the reports. The integration of census procedures applying to the entire population and of sampling methods at various stages of the census operations has already demonstrated its effectiveness and promises significant gains for future censuses and surveys.

Conrad Taeuber
Georgetown University

References
National Academy of Sciences, Committee on Population and Demography (1981), *Collecting Data for the Estimation of Fertility and Mortality*, Washington DC.
Shryock, H. S. and Taeuber, C. (1976), *The Conventional Population Census*. Chapel Hill, NC.
United Nations (1980), *1979 Demographic Yearbook*, New York.
United Nations (1980), *Principles and Recommendations for Population and Housing Censuses*, New York.
See also: *households; population; sample surveys.*

Centre and Periphery

The two concepts centre and periphery form part of an attempt to explain the processes through which capitalism is able to affect the economic and political structure of 'underdeveloped' or 'developing' societies. Drawing on the Marxist tradition, this view assumes that in the central capitalist countries there is a high organic composition of capital, and wage levels approximate the cost of reproducing labour. By contrast, in the peripheral countries, there is a low organic composition of capital, and wages are likely to be low, hardly meeting the cost of reproducing labour. This happens because in peripheral areas reproduction of labour is often dependent on some degree of non-capitalist production, and the wages paid to workers are subsidized by subsistence production. In some cases, such as with plantation workers, smallholder plots may contribute as much as the actual money wage paid, or in mining, the migrant male wage labourer may receive a wage which supports him but not his family, who depend on subsistence production elsewhere. In the centre, wages are determined largely by market processes, whereas at the periphery nonmarket forces, such as political repression or traditional relations of super- and subordination (as between patrons and clients), are important in determining the wage rate.

The use of the concepts centre and periphery implies the world system as the unit of analysis, and 'underdevelopment' as an instituted process rather than a mere descriptive term. Underdevelopment is the result of contradictions within capitalist production relations at the centre. It is the outcome of attempts to solve these problems and is a necessary part of the reproduction of capitalism on a world scale.

Attempts to analyse the processes of surplus extraction, together with the claim that the world economy had become capitalist, gave rise to two major interrelated debates. One concerned the precise definition of capitalism and whether it is to be satisfactorily characterized by a specific system of production or of exchange relations. The other tried to identify the links between centre and periphery, and thus the nature of the system, in terms of the relations or articulations between different modes of production. In trying to clarify these theoretical issues together with their political implications, the use of the terms centre and periphery was elaborated and empirically researched. This gave rise to various forms of world-system theory, represented in the writing of Wallerstein (1974), Frank (1978) and Amin (1976); it also revived interest in theories of national and global economic cycles, for example in the work of Mandel (1980). In addition, in attempting to explain the position of countries such as Brazil, Argentina and Mexico, the concept of the semi-periphery was developed. This concept involves the idea that their particular political cultures and the mixed nature of their industrialization places these countries in a 'buffer' position, particularly in their international political stance, between central capitalist countries and those of the true periphery.

Tony Barnett
University of East Anglia

References
Amin, S. (1976), *Unequal Development*, New York.
Frank, A. G. (1978), *Dependent Accumulation and Underdevelopment*, London.
Mandel, E. (1980), *Long Waves of Capitalist Development*, Cambridge.
Wallersein, I. (1974), *The Modern World System*, New York.

Further Reading
Hoogvelt, A. M. (1982), *The Third World in Global Development*, London.
See also: *dependency theory; world-system theory.*

Chamberlin, Edward Hastings (1899–1967)

Born in La Conner, Washington, 18 May 1899, Chamberlin received his education in the public schools of Iowa City, Iowa, and took a BSc from the University of Iowa in 1920. He earned postgraduate degrees from the University of Michigan (MA 1922), and Harvard University (MA 1924 and PhD 1927). He began his teaching career at the University of Michigan and later joined the faculty at Harvard in 1922 where he remained until his retirement in 1966.

Chamberlin's major contribution to economic theory is his book *Theory of Monopolistic Competition* (1933), which, for him, represented a reconstruction of value theory and a departure from the neoclassical theory of the firm. The neoclassical theory, which recognized only two types of market structures – competition and monopoly – was not exhaustive, in the sense that it was not general enough to account for the behaviour of certain prices and outputs in the 'real world'. Chamberlin set out to close this gap. He extended the theory of duopoly (two-seller markets) which had been familiar to earlier writers to include what he termed oligopoly – a market consisting of more than one seller but where the actions of any single seller can influence price. Every seller was assumed to take account of his total influence on price, indirect and direct. The resulting equilibrium price and output would be similar to that of a monopolist, since firms would combine to maximize joint profits as a single seller.

The introduction of advertising and product differentiation to his theory represented a significant contribution in adjusting economic theory to the realities of the real world. It was also an attack on the concept of consumers' sovereignty characteristic of neoclassical theory. Through his work, Chamberlin opened the door for an entirely new field known as Industrial Organization.

Vincent J. Tarascio
University of North Carolina
Chapel Hill

Reference
Chamberlin, E. H. (1933), *Theory of Monopolistic Competition*, Cambridge, Mass.

Further Reading
Chamberlin, E. H. (1961), 'The origins and early development of monopolistic competition theory', *Quarterly Journal of Economics*, 75.

Character Disorders

Although omitted from the latest diagnostic and statistical manual of the American Psychiatric Association (APA), the term character disorder is used mainly by dynamic psychiatrists to describe a situation in which elements of a person's character interfere with his everyday functioning. We must first examine character to understand its disorders.

Character may be described as that durable and persisting set of defences used by the individual in adapting to the world. Of central importance in character formation are the internalization of the parents and other identifications with moral precepts and codes. Analytically-trained psychiatrists refer to the embodiment of the person's parentally-inspired internal code as the super-ego or conscience.

A second essential element of the concept of character is that it is considered 'the way one is', or 'that's who I am'; in dynamic terms, character is experienced as ego-syntonic (consistent with one's self-concept) as opposed to ego-alien (inconsistent with one's self-concept). The term ego-alien can describe neurotic symptoms. For example, a person with a compulsive character may accept, even take pride in, the description of himself as meticulous, while a person with the neurotic compulsion to wash his hands constantly may chafe against this symptom, wish to be free of it, be ashamed of it, and see it as definitely not a part of his rational self.

The step from character to character disorder involves the impact of character traits or character structure on a person's daily life functioning; when the elements of the person's character become an interference, or take a destructive form, we speak of character disorders. A troubling psychiatric confusion is that the terms 'character' and 'personality' are often used as though synonymous. However, some use the term personality to refer to the outward presentation of an individual, his 'face' towards the world, rather than referring to the intrapsychic structure. (The psychopath or sociopath, which many consider the most significant 'character disorder', is discussed separately.)

Among the other commonly recognized character disorders is depressive character, not uncommonly seen in persons for whom the depressed state is a way of life. Chronic pessimism, decreased self-esteem and pervasive sadness are its hallmarks.

Besides meticulousness, the compulsive character is marked by an addiction to orderliness, cleanliness, and scrupulousness, as well as a tendency to adhere to the 'letter of the law'. A frequent concomitant is isolation of affect which constricts the range of emotional responsivity, often compensated by prominence of intellectual functioning.

The passive-aggressive character is most readily identified through understanding of his most common habitat, the bureaucracy. In this character structure, deep hostility is expressed through delay, passivity, obstructionism and procrastination. The French refer to the passive-aggressive bureaucrat as a '*petit fonctionnaire*', the minor functionary whose power is both realized and expressed by his capacity to keep one waiting.

The narcissistic character is recognized by an extreme love of and need for adulation and admiration from those around him, coupled with what the layman terms egotism, a self-obsessed attitude. The craving for applause is addictive in its power and pervasiveness; this entity is thus not uncommonly seen in professional performers.

The schizoid character, in contrast, might be described as the withdrawn, 'cool' loner who has approached the problem of dealing with the world by withdrawing from it, at least in emotional attachments and investments. The subject's emotional inaccessibility, which may be frustrating to others, is used to defend the individual from the anxiety that might otherwise attend social interaction.

Thomas G. Gutheil
Harvard University
Program in Psychiatry and the Law, Boston

Further Reading
Cleckley, H. (1955), *The Mask of Sanity*, St Louis, Missouri.
McCord, W. and McCord, J. (1964), *The Psychopath*, Princeton.
Reich, W. (1945), *Character Analysis*, New York.
Vaillant, G. (1975), 'Sociopathy as human process', *Archives of General Psychiatry*, 32.
See also: *depressive disorders; neuroses; obsessive compulsive disorders; personality; psychopathic personality; psychosis.*

Charisma

Charisma is one of the more contentious sociological concepts, in part because it has been absorbed into popular, or at least mass-media, usage in a considerably adulterated form. The term derives from a theological conception which referred to the divine gift of grace. Max Weber developed its sociological use by extending it to refer to the recognition in an individual leader by his followers of supernatural or superhuman powers or qualities of an exemplary kind or of transcendental origin.

Weber's formulation gave rise to ambiguities. On the one hand, it could be argued that the nature of charisma inhered in the powers or qualities displayed by the individual, and thus was to be explained primarily in terms of the personal psychological attributes of the leader. On the other hand, it could be argued that the character of charisma lay in the recognition extended by the following, and thus was to be explained primarily in terms of the social psychological features of the interpersonal relationship between leader and followers. Common usage bears elements of both approaches, identifying the charismatic figure as one who displays personal attractiveness or forcefulness of a kind which leads to great popularity or popular devotion. However, this is quite antithetical to Weber's central thrust.

Weber sharply contrasts charisma with forms of authority deriving from tradition and from rationalistic or legal considerations. The charismatic leader is one who breaks with tradition or prevailing legal norms, and demands obedience on specifically irrational grounds of devotion as God's Prophet, the embodiment of transcendental forces, or as possessor of supernatural powers. Conventionally elected leaders, or heirs of an established tradition, cannot therefore be construed as charismatic because of their attractiveness or popularity or even both.

The following of a charismatic leader offers its obedience and devotion in virtue of the mission upon which it believes the leader to be engaged and the transcendental forces which he manifests. But it may require periodically to be reassured of the possession of those powers, demanding signs of the miraculous as the price of commitment.

The charismatic leader operates through a body of disciples or other personally devoted inner circle rather than an established administrative staff. Often – especially in the case of religious charisma – it may consist of members of the leader's immediate household, living in an intimate and emotionally-laden communal relationship with him. They receive their appointment not on the basis of technical expertise, but rather because of the intensity of their devotion or willingness to subordinate themselves to the leader's will. They are commissioned to carry out that will on an *ad hoc* basis. There is no administrative routine, or any such routine is short-lived, constantly disrupted by the intervention and revelation of the leader. The economic basis of the movement is irregular and founded on booty or free-will offerings. Decision making is erratic and inspirational.

Charisma is inevitably a precarious form of authority. Max Weber maintained that it could exist in its pure form for only a relatively brief period. In the course of time it tends to become transformed into a less spontaneous or less unpredictable form of leadership, toward traditionalism or rational-legal authority. Such a development appears to be an ineluctable consequence of perpetuating the movement's mission or of spreading it beyond an immediate, local band of disciples. Endurance over time or wider spread is likely to introduce the need for mechanisms of co-ordination, supervision and delegation. In consequence there will arise increasing impersonality and routine and the desire for greater stability and predictability on the part of officials.

The problem of succession often accelerates the process of routinization. The charisma of the founder is vested in another by virtue of hereditary succession or a ritual of consecration. Thus, such forms as 'hereditary charisma' or 'charisma of office' become an intervening step in the transformation of authority in a traditionalistic or rational-legal direction.

Roy Wallis
Queen's University of Belfast

Further Reading
Weber, M. (1947 [1922]), *The Theory of Social and Economic Organization*, London. (Part 1 of *Wirtschaft und Gesellschaft*, Tübingen.)
Willner, A. (1984), *The Spellbinders: Charismatic Political Leadership*, New Haven.
Wilson, B. (1975), *The Noble Savages: The Primitive Origins of Charisma and its Contemporary Survival*, Berkeley and Los Angeles.
See also: *sects and cults; Weber.*

Chicago School of Economics

The so-called Chicago School of economics, chiefly American, is a neoclassical counter-revolution against institutionalism in economic methodology, against Keynesian macroeconomics, and against 'twentieth-century liberalism', i.e. interventionism and *dirigisme*, in economic policy generally. Its centre has been the University of Chicago, where it first achieved prominence in the 1930s. Its intellectual leaders until about 1950 were Frank H. Knight in matters of theory and methodology and Henry C. Simons in matters of economic policy. During the next generation, the leaders have been Milton Friedman, George Stigler and Gary Becker. Many economists not trained at Chicago have aligned themselves with many 'Chicago' positions, and many members of the Chicago economics faculty, to say nothing of its graduates, have dissociated themselves from 'Chicago' doctrine.

Some characteristic Chicago School views have been:
(1) Methodological positivism. The validity of a theory depends neither upon its generality nor upon the plausibility of its initial assumptions, but exclusively upon the confirmation or disconfirmation (primarily statistical) of such of its implications as diverge from the implications of alternative theories.
(2) Acceptance of market solutions for economic problems, not in any Utopian or optimal sense but in aid of political and intellectual freedom. Chicago School economists see the market economy as a *necessary* condition for free societies generally. It is not, however, a *sufficient* condition.
(3) Distrust of administrative discretion and *ad hoc* intervention in economic policy. Preference for 'rules versus authorities' in matters of monetary and fiscal policy.
(4) Monetarism rather than fiscalism in macroeconomic regulation.
(5) The use of fiscal measures to alleviate poverty, but distrust of redistributionism above the poverty line.
(6) Disciplinary imperialism, by which is meant the applicability of economic analysis by economists to problems normally restricted to other disciplines, particularly law and sociology.

The school's positions with regard to a number of topics, especially trade regulation and monetary policy, have changed over the years. Simons, for example, believed in the active maintenance of competition by a strong anti-monopoly or 'trust-busting' policy, while Friedman and Stigler thought monopoly and oligopoly to be only short-term problems of minor long-term significance. Simons also believed that monetary policy should be guided by a price-level rule – expansionary when the price level was falling and contractionary when it was rising. Friedman, impressed by the long and variable time lags involved in price-level reactions to monetary change, has favoured a constant rate of monetary growth.

The two best summaries of Chicago doctrine are Simons's *Economic Policy for a Free Society* and Friedman's *Capitalism and Freedom*.

Martin Bronfenbrenner
Duke University
and Aoyama Gakuin
University, Tokyo

Further Reading
Patinkin, D. (1981), *Essay On and In the Chicago Tradition*, Durham, N.C.
See also: *Friedman; monetarism; Stigler.*

Chicago School of Sociology

The Chicago School of sociology flourished between about 1915 and the early 1930s in the Department of Sociology at the University of Chicago. Its principal inspirational figures were William Isaac Thomas (up to 1918, when he left the university), and particularly Robert Park, with a subsidiary role played by Ernest Burgess. Its major works were Thomas and Znaniecki's monograph *The Polish Peasant in Europe and America* (1918–20), Charles Johnson's study *The Negro in Chicago*

(1922), a series of monographs produced by Park and Burgess's students including *The Hobo, The Gold Coast and the Slum, The Gang,* and *The Taxi-Dance Hall,* and several major criminological studies supervised by Burgess. Theoretical underpinning was provided by Park's wide-ranging essays and the teachings of social psychologist, George Herbert Mead.

The work of the Chicago School had several distinctive characteristics. It sought to study society empirically, using a variety of observational, documentary, historical and statistical methods, focusing particularly upon the city of Chicago, which was viewed through the framework of ecological theory. A series of notable monographs resulted, which remain landmarks in the study of urban structure, race relations, social problems and crime and deviance. The theoretical approach emphasized the point of view of the actor and the need to interpret social behaviour in terms of the subjective meaning attached to it by the actor. Park placed great emphasis upon the significance of social process and collective behaviour through the study of social control, mass communications, the crowd and social movements. The theory of social disorganization was an embryonic sociological explanation of the genesis of social problems. The origins of sociological social psychology and symbolic interactionism are often traced to the Chicago School.

The fertility of this period and place owed a great deal to the strong collective sense of purpose developed by Chicago sociologists. The main research was done by the graduate students of Park and Burgess who received close supervision and lived and worked sociology. Most staff and students lived on or near the university campus. Various student and departmental societies brought them together in leisure time. Park provided the intellectual leadership and integrating vision which fashioned a series of unrelated studies into a School. Financial support from the Laura Spelman Rockefeller Memorial to the Local Community Research Committee provided the institutional underpinning for the programme. Chicago became the centre of a national network spread over the middle west and the west. Between 1920 and 1935 Chicago was the leading sociology department in the world.

The significance of the Chicago School lay in its successful pursuit of empirical research informed by theory. It turned American sociology away from armchair theorizing toward firsthand and empirical inquiry. The focus upon the city and its social problems demonstrated the utility of sociology and helped to institutionalize it in the American university.

The Chicago School of political science was the creation of Charles E. Merriam. It flourished between 1923 and 1940 and embodied a behaviourist approach to the study of politics. The Chicago School of economics, which crystallized around 1950 under the influence of Milton Friedman, is associated with an approach to economic analysis and management emphasizing the free market and monetary control.

Martin Bulmer
London School of Economics and Political Science

Further Reading
Bulmer, M. (1984), *The Chicago School of Sociology,* Chicago.
Faris, R. E. L. (1967), *Chicago Sociology 1920–1932,* San Francisco.
See also: *Chicago School of economics; city; Mead, G. H.; Park; symbolic interactionism.*

Child Psychology

See Developmental psychology.

Chomsky, Noam (1928–)

Noam Chomsky, born 1928 in Philadelphia, the son of a Hebrew scholar, has achieved eminence both as a linguist and as a political activist and writer. His linguistic research, conducted for the last 30 years at MIT, has revolutionized the study of language, has been profoundly influential in psychology and philosophy, and has had repercussions in mathematics, anthropology, sociology and the study of literature. His political work is less original but, in reflecting his adopted role of conscience of the West, has been important in focusing attention on the perceived injustices of the American social and political system.

Twentieth-century linguistics prior to Chomsky (e.g. Bloomfield) was preoccupied with cataloguing and describing the facts of language, and was largely limited to phonology (sound structure) and morphology (word structure). Chomsky reoriented the discipline in two ways: on the one hand he initiated a technical breakthrough which for the first time made possible a rigorous account of syntax; on the other he moved beyond the description of data to concentrate on those human mental properties which underlie our observable linguistic abilities. The ability to speak and understand a language entails having a certain body of linguistic knowledge, usually referred to as our *competence.* This knowledge is conceived as being embodied in a set of mentally represented rules which interact with other cognitive systems (memory, logic) to determine our linguistic behaviour or *performance.* Chomsky's claim that these rules and the principles which govern their operation are in part innate rather than learned has been instrumental in reopening the philosophical debate on innate ideas.

That our use of language is rule-governed is clear from the infinite *creativity* of language (our ability to produce and understand any of an indefinitely large number of sentences we have never heard before); from *over-generalization* of the sort indulged in by children who remark that 'the sheeps comed'; and from the identifiability of *mistakes* in speaking (how else would you know that this sentence wrong was?). Part of Chomsky's contribution has been to provide a formalism in which many of these rules (phonological, syntactic and semantic) can be satisfactorily couched. The best known of these rule types is the *transformation*, a device which has given its name to the theory of Transformational Grammar, and which encodes the claim that the syntax of human languages is optimally described by reference to (at least) two levels of representation: deep structure and surface structure. One of the hallmarks of Chomsky's formal work, however, has been its continual unpredictability and innovativeness. As descriptive problems arise, theoretical constructs of a novel kind are drawn in to deal with them. The status of such constructs is a matter of endless and fruitful debate within linguistics, but whether the grammars of all human languages necessarily contain transformations is of secondary importance, as even a demonstration that they were not the optimal descriptive device would leave untouched the philosophical and psychological speculations that are his prime concern. Part of Chomsky's argument is that the complexity of our linguistic knowledge and the relative poverty of the data we are exposed to as children make implausible any form of inductive learning of the rules involved. Hence, whatever formal properties the rules may have, we must postulate a rich innate component to our linguistic knowledge if we are to explain our mastery of them. It follows, moreover, that if our knowledge is in part innately determined, then universal properties of language can be investigated by tapping the linguistic intuitions of the speakers of just one language, for example, English. Claims of universality must obviously then be tested against other languages, but it is both unnecessary (and impossible) to document the totality of facts about all languages first.

In this desire to *explain* (some of) the data, rather than describe all of them, Chomsky has devoted much of his recent work to developing a theory with a deductive structure rich enough to provide explanatory principles showing *why* linguistic phenomena have the form they do, and not merely that they have this form. For instance, the possibility of construing *themselves* as referring to *the girls* but not *the boys* in 'the boys think the girls admire themselves', and of construing *them* as referring to *the boys* but not *the girls* in 'the boys think the girls admire them) follows from principles of considerable abstractness: principles which are so general that the child has only to learn that *them* is a pronoun and *themselves* a reflexive pronoun for these and a number of other facts to follow without further stipulation. The conclusion Chomsky draws is that these principles can be neither learnt piecemeal nor

motivated by considerations of the communicative function of language, but are part of Universal Grammar: the innate endowment which controls the growth of language in each individual.

Chomsky's contribution to philosophy and his impact on psychology – both by his demolition of Skinner's behaviourism and by his emphasis on linguistics as a branch of cognitive psychology – are incontestable. His influence on other fields is less direct, but it is a measure of his stature and pre-eminence in linguistics that even those who disagree with him are forced to argue in terms of the concepts and idealizations he has propounded.

Chomsky's linguistics and politics are intellectually unconnected. He brings the same devastating analytic ability to both; he displays the same unflagging persistence in putting forth his ideas and correcting his opponents in both, but only his linguistic ideas with their philosophical and psychological ramifications have the originality of genius, and it is these which will still be discussed in future centuries.

N. V. Smith
University College London

Further Reading
D'Agostino, F. (1985), *Chomsky's System of Ideas*, Oxford.
Chomsky, N. (1957), *Syntactic Structures*, The Hague.
Chomsky, N. (1969), *American Power and the New Mandarins*, Harmondsworth.
Chomsky, N. (1973), *For Reasons of State*, London.
Chomsky, N. (1975), *The Logical Structure of Linguistic Theory*, New York.
Chomsky, N. (1980), *Rules and Representations*, Oxford.
Smith, N. and Wilson, D. (1979), *Modern Linguistics: The Results of Chomsky's Revolution*, Harmondsworth.
See also: *language development; transformational grammar.*

City

Terms like the city, urban and urbanism relate to a wide range of phenomena, which have varied greatly through history and between world regions. Different disciplines also develop their own perspectives toward urban phenomena – there is an urban anthropology, an urban economics, an urban geography, an urban sociology, etc. Conceptions of the urban community are not congruent between different languages either – the English town/city distinction does not have direct counterparts even in closely related languages.

We may regard a reasonably large and permanent

concentration of people within a limited territory as the common characteristic of all cities and other urban places. Scholarship has focused on the one hand on the role of such communities within the wider society, and on the other hand on the particular characteristics of their internal life.

The beginnings of urbanism are now usually identified with a broad type of ritual-political centre which developed apparently independently in six areas: Mesopotamia, the Nile and Indus Valleys, North China, Mesoamerica, the Andes, and Yorubaland in West Africa (Wheatley, 1971). In these centres divine monarchs and priesthoods, with a corps of officials and guards, controlled the peasants of the surrounding region and extracted a surplus from them. What may have begun as modest tribal shrines were elaborated as complexes of monumental architecture: temples, pyramids, palaces, terraces and courts. We find here not only the early history of the city, but also of civilization and the state. The Yoruba towns, last of the kind to emerge independently, but the only ones still existing as ongoing concerns in a form at all resembling the original, have not exhibited the complexity of architecture and other technology of the earlier and more famous cases but show similarities of social form.

The early centres were urban especially through their capacity to organize the countryside around them, evidently mostly through symbolic control. Yet they might have small residential populations, and most of the people under their rule came to them only for major ritual events. In this sense, one may see the centres as marginally urban. Over time, however, warfare and other factors tended to lead to more secular forms of political control, as well as to greater population concentrations at the centres themselves. The same development can be discerned in European antiquity. In *La Cité antique* (1864) *(The Ancient City)*, Fustel de Coulanges has described its urban beginnings as once more a complex of ritual politics, but at the height of their power, the cities of the Graeco-Roman world had élites of landowners and warriors, in control of enormous slave work forces.

These were cities of power, and cities of consumers. Commerce and industry played a minor part within them. But the ancient empires and their cities would decline, and in the Middle Ages, a new urbanism came into being in Western Europe. It was mostly commercially based, and with business as the dominant element, the cities developed a considerable autonomy and independence from the feudal social structures surrounding them. The Belgian historian Henri Pirenne is one of the scholars who have been concerned with these medieval European cities. Another is Max Weber, who developed an ideal type in *The City* (1958 [1921]): an urban community must have a market as its central institution, but also a fortification, an at least partially autonomous administrative and legal system, and a form of association reflecting the particular features of urban life (the guild was a conspicuous example).

This frequently quoted formulation constituted a very restrictive definition of urbanism. The distinctiveness of the town in relation to the surrounding countryside is clear, but the institutional apparatus belonged in a particular phase of European history. Weber also contrasted this occidental city with its oriental counterparts. The latter were more internally fragmented and at the same time more closely integrated into imperial administrations. As cities of power rather than of commerce, often with some emphasis on the symbolic expression of pre-eminence, the great urban centres of the East as seen by early European travellers may appear more related to the first urban forms.

Industrialism, of course, has given shape to yet other kinds of cities. One important account of the misery of the huge new concentrations of labouring people in rapidly growing cities is Friedrich Engels's in *The Condition of the Working Class in England* (1969 [1845]), based on his experience in Manchester. Another classic set of studies of urban life under industrialism were carried out by the Chicago school of sociologists – Robert E. Park, Louis Wirth and others – in the 1920s and 1930s. The Chicago sociologists drew attention to the spatial organization of the industrial city and its apparently orderly changes, and thus launched an 'urban ecology'. At the same time, they located a series of smaller-scale ethnographies of particular 'natural areas' within the wider spatial order. Thus they simultaneously pioneered the study of many topics now central to urban anthropology – ethnic quarters, youth gangs, occupations, deviant groups and public places.

In a well-known formulation, Louis Wirth (1938) described urban social contacts as 'impersonal, superficial, transitory, and segmental', and the Chicago sociologists were generally pessimistic about the possibilities of achieving a satisfying human life under urban conditions, as a great many other thinkers have also been. (Yet, on the other hand one celebrates the contribution of urbanism to intellectual life.) On the whole, they concerned themselves more with the internal characteristics of the city, rather than with its place in society. This probably contributed to their tendency to generalize about urbanism on the basis of their Chicago experience, instead of emphasizing that this city was a product of a particular American context, including expansive industrial capitalism as well as ethnic diversity in a somewhat unsettled state.

Partly in response to such generalizations, a considerable body of ethnographically inclined research has emphasized the great variety of forms of life which can be found under urban conditions, and not least the fact that informal social organization may indeed be quite different from the type summarized by Wirth's phrase. William F. Whyte's *Street Corner Society*

(1943), describing a close-knit Italian-American neighbourhood in Boston, was a noteworthy early study in this vein, and it is by now generally understood that while city life may have its share of impersonality and anonymity, it also contains a web of friendship, kinship, and occupational linkages; in part, it may be a mosaic of 'urban villages'. With the growth of new subcultures and life styles in recent times, and a new appreciation for cultural diversity in the city, urban ethnography has been further revitalized in North America and Europe.

Similar perspectives have also been important in the study of contemporary urbanism in the Third World. Especially as the process of urbanization accelerated greatly in Africa, Asia and Latin America in the mid-twentieth century, there was first a tendency by commentators to emphasize 'disorganization', 'detribalization', and the weakening of traditional social ties generally. Later studies have tended to point to the security still provided by kinship and ethnicity, the economic and political uses to which they may be put, and the ability of urbanites to evolve new adaptations, even without significant economic means. Research on squatter settlements, especially in Latin American cities, has thus often made the point that such 'informal housing' is often superior in its efficiency to large-scale public housing projects, and a wave of studies of the 'informal sector' of the urban economy has recently shown that a very large number of people in Third World urban centres make some kind of living through self-employment or less formal employment arrangements, without occupational training in formal educational structures, and with very limited material resources. This sector includes artisans, petty traders, rickshaw drivers, ice cream vendors, shoe shiners, truck pushers and a multitude of other more or less legitimate ways of supporting oneself, as well as a variety of illicit occupations.

One must not exaggerate the capacity of informal modes of organization to solve the problems of urban living, however, in Third World countries or elsewhere, and the debate on such issues is not yet concluded. What is clear is that generalizations about cities and city life must almost always be qualified. There are in fact a great many types of urban centres, each city has many kinds of inhabitants, and every urbanite engages in social contacts and activities of multiple sorts.

This diversity obviously depends to a great extent on the varying relationships between cities and society. Several different research perspectives thus concern themselves with setting urban centres in a wider context. In economic geography and regional science, different models have been developed to deal with the spatial distribution of urban functions within larger areas. 'Central place theory' as first constructed by Walter Christaller in the 1930s, and since then gradually modified, is a prominent example, dealing with the

location of commercial, administrative and transport centres. Geographers have also concerned themselves with the problem of classifying cities according to their major societal functions, and analysing their internal structure as determined by these functions. Among early well-known classifications, for example, is one showing eight types of urban communities in the United States: retail, wholesale, manufacturing, mining, transport, resort and retirement, university, and diversified. Beginning in the 1960s, there has been a strong interdisciplinary trend to view urban processes especially in Western Europe and North America within the framework of the political economy of industrial capitalism. This trend, under Marxist inspiration, relates urbanism more closely to issues of class, power and social movements (Castells, 1977).

In the years since Max Weber drew his contrast between occidental and oriental cities, there have also been numerous further attempts at delineating various regional urban types, such as the 'Middle Eastern City' or the 'Latin American City'. Cultural historians and other area specialists have played an important part in evolving such constructs, and they have not always been guided by a desire to arrive at a comprehensive comparative understanding of world urbanism. Because of colonialism and other kinds of Western expansion, of course, the urban forms of different regions have not all been equally autonomous in their development. Often they must be seen within the context of international centre-periphery relationships. In Africa, Asia and Latin America the large port cities which grew with Western domination – Dakar, Bombay, Calcutta, Shanghai, Buenos Aires and others – are an example of this. A recurrent pattern in the colonial and post-colonial Third World has also been the growth of 'primate cities', which through a strong concentration of the commercial, administrative, industrial, cultural and other functions of a country or a territory become much larger and more important than any other urban centre there. Yet colonialism has also created other kinds of urban communities – mining towns, small administrative centres, 'hill stations' for resort purposes, and so forth – and its products may have coexisted with more indigenous urban traditions. Due to such variations, it would seem wiser to look at regional forms of urbanism not always as single types but as typologies in themselves, generated through an interplay of international influences and local forces of social and spatial differentiation.

As for present and future changes in urbanism, these depend in complex ways on demographic, economic, technological and other factors. The twentieth century has witnessed urban growth on an unparalleled scale. 'Megalopolis' and 'conurbation' are new concepts applicable to phenomena of both the Western and the non-Western world. Yet new modes of transport and communication tend to make human beings less dependent on crowding themselves in limited spaces. 'Counterurbanization' is thus another modern phenomenon.

Ulf Hannerz
University of Stockholm

References

Castells, M. (1977), *The Urban Question*, London.
Engels, F. (1969 [1845]), *The Condition of the Working Class in England*, London.
Fustel de Coulanges, N. D. (n.d. [1864]), *The Ancient City*, Garden City, NY. (Original French edn, *La Cité antique*, Paris.)
Weber, M. (1958 [1921]), *The City*, New York.
Wheatley, P. (1971), *The Pivot of the Four Quarters*, Edinburgh.
Whyte, W. F. (1943), *Street Corner Society*, Chicago.
Wirth, L. (1938), 'Urbanism as a way of life', *American Journal of Sociology*, 44.
See also: *Chicago School of Sociology; Park; urbanization; urban planning.*

Civil Religion

Durkheim's *Elementary Forms of the Religious Life* (1915 [1912]) showed that some kind of constitutive symbolism, treated as sacred, is necessary to whatever stability and continuity a society may have. Religion always involves something transcendent and legitimating, whether it be a supernatural order or a purely secular utopian vision that is to be fully realized in the distant future.

In the pluralistic society of the United States, institutionalized values of freedom and equality serve as a resource that partially excluded minorities can activate in their struggle to be 'included' in the societal community (Raboteau, 1982). These values are certainly grounded in a relatively this-worldly ('secularized') version of the Judaeo-Christian tradition. Nevertheless, interwoven with Christianity and Judaism, the civil religion of the United States (Bellah, 1967, reprinted in Richey and Jones, eds, 1974) has its own quasi-mythological history and heroes and its quasi-sacred national holidays and public rituals (see also Hayes, 1926, on the United States and France, and Shils and Young, 1953, on Great Britain).

As far as separation of church and state is concerned, the civil religion is to some extent in tension with humanists as well as with so-called religionists. Some critics of Bellah's thesis protested because they feared that the nation was being set above God. Other critics of the concept of civil religion (applied more generally) object to categorizing secular ideologies such as Communism as religions, because they view religion as inherently unjust and static. Still other critics implicitly acknowledge the essential correctness of Bellah's civil religion thesis but object to some of the civil religions themselves. They are inclined to focus on the prevalence of social conflict and to 'demystify' ideologically the occasional existence of a modicum of social integration. (But is there any sociologist anywhere who thinks that any society anywhere is the Peaceable Kingdom?)

Many societies with ethnic regional divisions lack a firm national identity. The somewhat exceptional case of modern Switzerland depends on complex balances and on 'eternal vigilance' to maintain unity (McRae, 1964). A vigorous civil religion does contribute, however, to Swiss identity and solidarity, as anyone must feel who witnesses the complex of 'sacred' ceremonies of the First of August.

Comparison of nations with a strong civil religion (for example, Poland, Sweden, Japan) with nations less fortunate in this respect (for example, Lebanon, Cyprus, Uganda, Nigeria, the Soviet Union), suggests that among the important variables are the extent to which a traditional religion has come to be at the same time a symbolic focus of national identity,thus a civil religion as well; successful historical national struggles, or unifying episodes of foreign domination, which can serve as the basis of 'mythology'; *continuing* external pressures that help to form and then highlight the national identity by contrast; whether or not national boundaries can plausibly be viewed as natural in the sense of predestined; and presence/absence of large ethnic minorities that resist being included or are relentlessly excluded by a dominant group (not necessarily a numerical majority). A civil religion, like any other religion, partly crystallizes from within some crescive solidarity in which it has been crescively involved; but the process varies in extent and depth.

Harry M. Johnson
University of Illinois
Champaign-Urbana

References

Bellah, R. N. and Hammond, P. E. (1980), *Varieties of Civil Religion*, New York.
Durkheim, E. (1915 [1912]), *Elementary Forms of the Religious Life*, London. (Original French edn, *Formes élémentaires de la vie religieuse*, Paris.)
Hayes, C. J. H. (1926), *Essays on Nationalism*, New York.
McRae, K. D. (1964), *Switzerland: Example of Cultural Coexistence*, Toronto.
Raboteau, A. J. (1982), Review of *Public Religion in American Culture*, by J. F. Wilson, *Religious Studies Review*, 8.
Richey, R. E. and Jones, D. G. (eds) (1974), *American Civil Religion*, New York.
Shils, E. and Young, M. (1953), 'The meaning of the coronation', *Sociological Review*, 1.
See also: *secularization.*

Class, Social

In the course of the first three decades of the nineteenth century the term class gradually replaced 'estates', 'ranks' and 'orders' as the major word used to denote divisions within society. The change of vocabulary reflected the diminishing significance of rank and ascribed or inherited qualities in general, and the growing importance of possessions and income among the determinants of the social position. Taken over by social theory from its original context of political debate, class came to refer to large categories of population, (1) distinct from other categories in respect of wealth and related social position, (2) deriving their distinctive status mainly from their location in the production and distribution of social wealth, (3) sharing accordingly in distinctive interests either opposing or complementing other group interests, and (4) consequently displaying a tendency to a group – distinctive political, cultural and social attitudes and behaviour. At the very early stage of the debate, class was given a pronounced economic meaning, arguably under the influence of David Ricardo, who identified the social category of labourers with the economic category of labour, understood as one of the factors of capitalist production. Political economists of the 'Ricardian socialist' school (William Thompson (1824), Thomas Hodgskin (1825) and others) developed Ricardo's suggestions into a comprehensive economic theory of class division, which was then adopted and elaborated upon by Karl Marx.

The many usages of class in social-scientific theory and research are invariably influenced by Marx's magisterial vision of class division as, simultaneously, the principal source of social dynamics and the main principle of its interpretation. Even if historiosophic aspects of Marx's class theory (all history is a history of class struggle; social change occurs through class revolutions; the conflict between capitalists and workers, arising from the capitalist form of production, is bound to lead to a proletarian revolution and to a new, socialist form of production) are questioned or rejected, the enduring interest in class and, indeed, the unfaltering centrality of the category of class in social-scientific discourse are due to Marx-inspired belief in a high predictive and explanatory value of (primarily economic) class in respect of both individual and collective behaviour.

The resilience of this latter aspect of Marx's theoretical legacy is in no small part due to its overall harmony with the dominant liberal world view, which interprets individual action as, by and large, rational pursuit of interests, and assigns to 'gain' the role of the central motive of human conduct. The continuous popularity of Marx's class theory has been helped by the incorporation of these tacit premises of common sense and the resulting strategy of interpreting social antagonisms as conflicts of economic interests (that is, incompatibility of goals rationally pursued by various groups differently located within the economic process).

Defining classes as large groups united by their common location within the economic process and aspiring, against efforts of other classes, to an increased share of the surplus product, was a habit firmly established inside the classic political economy before Marx. The fateful contribution of Marx consisted in the reading into the class conflict of another dimension – the struggle for the management of social surplus. Since, within the capitalist order, the right to the surplus was the prerogative of the managers of the productive process, rational effort to amplify a class share in the surplus product must be aimed at the management of production; since, again in the capitalist system, the right to manage productive process was a prerogative of the owners of capital (or means of production), a class barred from access to the surplus can defy its deprivation only through dissociating the right to manage from the right of ownership – through the expropriation of the owners of the capital. In the succession of historical forms of class struggle, the conflict between capitalists and their workers was thus presented by Marx as the modern equivalent of *both* the conflict between precapitalist landlords and their serfs *and* the conflict between landowning aristocracy and industry-owning capitalists. Indeed, the specifically Marxist approach to class analysis of industrial society consists in conflating the two dimensions of class conflict and the tendency to interpret the first (the redistribution of surplus) as an immature manifestation, or an early stage, of the second (the management of the production of surplus).

In consequence, the Marx-inspired study of class and class conflict focuses its attention on the combat between owners of capital and industrial workers. More specifically, in this conflict, considered central for the current historical era, this study is interested in the progression of industrial workers from their objective situation as a factor in the process of capitalist production ('class in itself') to the acquisition of a consciousness of their situation and, finally, to the appropriation of a political strategy aimed at radically overcoming their subordination to capital by abolishing the capitalist mode of production itself ('class for itself').

For the Marx-inspired class theory, therefore, the major difficulty arises from the evident failure of industrial workers to make any notable advance along the line of anticipated progression. A century and a half after the essential historiosophical assumptions of Marx's class theory had been made public in the *Communist Manifesto* (1980 [1848]), the workers of the industrialized world seem to come nowhere near the threshold of the socialist transformation of society.

The gap between predictions generated by class theory and the actual tendency of historical development was brought into sharp relief in the wake of the October Revolution in Russia: a revolution claiming to fulfil the Marxist promise of socialist transformation occurred in a society little advanced in its capitalist development, while all the timid attempts at socialist revolution in truly capitalist countries with a large industrial working population failed. What, from the theoretical perspective, appeared a bewildering incongruity of historical praxis, triggered off recurring attempts among Marxist thinkers to provide auxiliary theories accounting for the failure of the anticipated historical tendency to materialize.

The first, and tone-setter, in the long chain of such auxiliary theories was Lukacs's (1967 [1923]) 'false consciousness' theory. Lukács distinguished 'consciousness of class' from 'class consciousness'; the first was the empirically ascertainable state of ideas and motives of the class members arising from the experience accessible within their daily business of life, while the second could be arrived at only through a bird's-eye survey of the total situation of the society, and a rational study of the totality of the information related to the social system (Lukács was here influenced by Weber's method of 'ideal types'). In Lukács's view, there was no automatic passage from the first to the second: the information necessary to construct ideal-typical 'class consciousness' was not available within the individual experience constrained by the tasks of daily survival. The empirical consciousness of class displayed a tendency, therefore, to remain a 'false consciousness', misguided and misled as it were by the narrow horizons of individual experience – unless assisted by scientific analysis filtered into the minds of the workers through the channels of their political organizations. In Lukács's subtle revision of the original model, the passage from 'class in itself' to 'class for itself', far from being an automatic process guaranteed by the logic of capitalist economy, has now become a matter of ideological struggle. Without such battle of ideas the passage would not be probable, let alone inevitable.

As indicated, Lukács's shifting of the behaviourally relevant aspects of class theory from the economic to the cultural and ideological sphere set the tone for the later search for updated versions of auxiliary theories attempting to salvage the long-term predictive validity of Marx's class model in the face of a continuing, and ever more salient, absence of a potent socialist opposition to capitalism in the ranks of industrial workers. The most radical recent expression of this trend can be found in Althusser's (1971) concept of 'Ideological State Apparatuses' – an elaborate network of cultural and political institutions stretching from the Church through the school to the family – which effectively prevents the proletariat, however deprived,

from embracing the scientific truth of its situation and historical task.

Numerous suggestions have been made in the sociological literature of the last two decades to render the discrepancy between the objective deprivation of the workers, and the apparent lack of radical opposition to the system responsible for it, amenable to empirical study, leading eventually to the location of factors either furthering the persistence of deprivation or prompting opposition to it. An early attempt was made by Dahrendorf (1959) to analyse the problem in terms of the passage from 'quasi-groups', united only by 'latent interests', to 'interest groups', whose consciousness of the common fate renders their interests 'manifest'. Sharing of latent interests is a necessary, but insufficient, condition of the passage; the latter demands that a number of additional factors must be present. Developing this insight, Morris and Murphy (1966) suggested that class consciousness should be seen as 'a processual emergent', and that from 'no perception of status difference' to a 'behaviour undertaken on behalf of the stratum interests and ideology' lead a number of stages, each subject to a somewhat different set of factors. In a highly influential collective study of *The Black-Coated Worker*, Lockwood (1958) departed from the 'stages' or 'progression' framework heretofore dominant in post-Marxian study of class consciousness and proposed that depending on the technologically determined type of employment, presence or absence of communal living and other cultural aspects of the mode of life, different types of consciousness ('traditional', 'deferential' or 'privatized') may develop among workers, each acquiring a degree of permanence grounded in its congruence with specific conditions of life. The early study of class consciousness by Parkin (1974) prompted similar conclusions: Parkin singled out, as an attitudinal type most likely to arise from life experience of the workers, a 'subordinate' ideology, taking either a 'deferential' or 'aspirational' form, but in both cases inducing the workers to make peace with the system responsible for their subordinate position.

These auxiliary theories all assume that the life situation of the workers within the capitalist mode of production necessarily produces an anti-capitalist tendency in their consciousness. It is this assumption, and this assumption only, which renders the evident absence of anti-capitalist action problematic and gives both meaning and urgency to the study of factors responsible for the empirical departure from a theoretically-grounded expectation.

Not so in the case of another large family of class theories, tracing its origin to Max Weber. Weber revised Marx's theory of class in three important respects. First, having accepted Marx's notion of class as a category articulated first and foremost within the network of economic relations, he denied to these relations the determining role in respect of the articulation of society on its sociocultural and political planes. Status groups (the nearest equivalent of the Marxist idea of class consciousness) as well as political groupings (the nearest equivalent of the Marxist idea of class action) are categories in their own right, parallel to but not necessarily overlapping with economically determined classes, and subject to their own constitutive rules and developmental logic. In short, Weber denied that economic divisions were necessarily mirrored in the cultural and political articulation of the society. Then, having related class, as an economic phenomenon, to the market (specifically, to the chances of access to marketable goods), Weber questioned the possibility of determining *a priori* which of the many conflicts of interests the market may generate at various times should be assigned a paramount role. And in contrast to Marx, Weber argued that interests vary with respect to different goods and market chances. Consequently they divide the population exposed to the market in more than one way, each individual belonging in principle to a number of classes whose boundaries need not overlap. (The concept of 'housing classes', recently advanced by Rex, is a good example of a category of economic classes articulated in relation to just one, though highly important, marketable commodity.) The relative importance attached by a given individual to each of the classes to which they belong is not, therefore, determined in advance. It may change, depending on the structure of the market situation, and no one class can be credited in advance with a capacity to command an overwhelming allegiance, displacing all other classes as the major determinant of action.

Weber's insight into the multiplicity of classes and the role of the market in their articulation has been applied, particularly by British sociologists, in a novel analysis of the self-perception of classes and their responses to class inequality. Theoretical models emerging from these analyses refuse to be constrained by the idea of a structurally-assigned class consciousness organizing the field of class attitudes and opinions, and instead attempt to gear themselves, with some success, to the empirically accessible evidence of actual ideologies, policies and actions of labour. Among these developments two are perhaps most seminal. One is W. G. Runciman's (1966) concept of 'relative deprivation' (akin to Moore's concept of 'outraged justice'), according to which groups, in their effort to assess their own social position, tend to 'compare with comparable' only: that is, they do not perceive as inequality, at least not as an 'unjust' inequality, the differences between their situation and that of groups distant on the scale of possessions – but they keenly guard their parity with groups they consider their equals, and are goaded into collective action when overtaken by those occupying a lower rung of the ladder. A somewhat similar analysis of class conflicts has been advanced by Parkin (1979)

in his later study, drawing on the little used concept of 'closure', introduced but left largely undeveloped by Weber. According to Parkin, the mechanism of class behaviour can best be understood in terms of a tendency to preserve, and if possible enhance, whatever privileged access to coveted market commodities a given class may possess. Subject to this tendency, rational action would consist in the policy of either 'closure by exclusion' (to prevent dilution of the privilege by an influx of those below), or 'closure by usurpation' (to acquire a share in the privileges of those above). In the light of both analyses, organized labour's notorious lack of concern with the extremes of the social distribution of surplus, the paramount importance attached in the practice of trade unions to the preservation of 'differentials', or the puzzling indifference of the same unions to the conditions of the unemployed poor (as distinct from the defence of members' jobs), are all manifestations of a sociological regularity, rather than aberrations calling for special explanations in terms of unusual factors.

The American reception of Weberian ideas pointed in a somewhat different direction. It was guided by the Weberian image of the essential multidimensionality of social differentiation, and was concerned above all with the investigation of correlation (or lack of correlation) between wealth, prestige and influence. In practice most American sociology (particularly until the 1960s) tended to assign a central role to the dimension of prestige (as exemplified by the widespread studies of social deference in relation to occupations). In the context of these practices, however, the term 'class' was employed but rarely (when used outside the Weberian current, for example by Warner or Centers, the term was given a primarily psychological meaning). The specifically American approaches to the question of socially-induced inequality are not an exact equivalent (or an alternative to) class theory, and are better analysed in their own framework, as theories of stratification (based on the master-image of gradation, rather than division).

As for class theory proper, both post-Marxian and post-Weberian approaches remain faithful to the ground premises articulated early in the nineteenth century: class is first and foremost an economic phenomenon, and class conflict is above all about the defence or the improvement of economic position, that is, of the share in the distribution of social surplus. One can say that the discursive formation of class has been shaped in its present form in the period of reinterpretation, in economic terms, of social conflicts spanning the course of West-European history between the French Revolution and the 'Spring of Nation' of 1848. It was only quite recently that the rethinking of the class model of society has developed sufficiently to put in question the very premises on which the discourse of class is grounded. One of the important lines of questioning comes from the work of Foucault (1980) which revealed a close association of the modern social system, not so much with the invention of machine technology or the spread of the capitalist form of labour, as with the establishment of a new type of 'disciplinary' power, aimed directly at the control of the human body and using surveillance as its main method. From this perspective the intense social conflicts of the early nineteenth century, later interpreted as manifestations of the inchoate labour movement, are seen as the last stage of the defensive struggle against new forms of controlling power; while the economically-oriented organizations of factory workers, portrayed within class theory as specimens of a mature labour movement, are seen as a product of displacing the original conflict, centred around control, onto the field of distribution.

Whatever the view of the applicability of class theory to the understanding of the past two centuries, other doubts are raised about its usefulness in the study of the current stage in social development. Habermas (1978), Offé (1964), Gorz (1982) and Touraine (1971) among others drew attention, each in a slightly different way, to the rapidly shrinking size of the industrial labour force, to the diminishing role of bargaining between owners of capital and industrial workers in organizing the distribution of surplus, and to the growing mediation and, indeed, initiative of the state in reproducing the essential conditions of the social production of surplus. In view of these developments, it is increasingly difficult to maintain that class membership remains a major key to the mechanism of reproduction of societally-inflicted deprivations (and, more generally, social differentiation as such) or, for that matter, a major explanatory variable in the study of individual and group behaviour. Thus far, however, no alternative concept of similar comprehensiveness and cogency has been proposed to replace class in the description and interpretation of socially produced inequality.

Zygmunt Bauman
University of Leeds

References

Althusser, L. (1971 [1968]), *Lenin and Philosophy and Other Essays*, London. (Original French edn, *Lénine et la philosophie*, Paris.)
Dahrendorf, R. (1959), *Class and Conflict in Industrial Society*, London.
Foucault, M. (1980), *Power and Knowledge*, ed. C. Gordon, Brighton.
Gorz, A. (1982), *Farewell to the Working Class*, London.
Habermas, J. (1978 [1973]), *Legitimation Crisis*, London. (Original German edn, *Legitimationsprobleme in Spatkapitalismus*.)
Hodgskin, T. (1825), *Labour Defended Against the Claims of Capital*, London.
Lockwood, D. (1958), *The Black-Coated Worker*, London.
Lukács, G. (1967 [1923]), *History and Class Consciousness*, London. (Original German edn, *Geschichte und Klassenbegrips*, Berlin.)
Offé, K. (1964), 'Political authority and class structures', in D. Senghaas (ed.), *Politikwissenschaft*, Frankfurt.
Parkin, F. (1974), *Class Inequality and Political Order*, London.
Parkin, F. (1979), *Marxism and Class Theory*, London.
Rex, J. (1967), *Race, Community and Conflict*, Oxford.
Runciman, W. G. (1966), *Relative Deprivation and Social Justice*, London
Thompson, W. (1824), *An Inquiry into the Principles of the Distribution of Wealth most Conducive to Human Happiness*, London.
Touraine, A. (1971), *The Post-Industrial Society*, New York.

Further Reading

Bauman, Z. (1982), *Memories of Class*, London.
Bottomore, T. (1965), *Classes in Modern Society*, London.
Giddens, A. (1973), *Class Structure of the Advanced Societies*, London.
See also: *caste; equality; hierarchy; Marx's theory of history and society; prestige; status; stratification; Weber.*

Classical Economics

The term Classical Economics, although sometimes given the rather broader meaning of any economics which is not Keynesian, is generally taken to refer to the body of economic ideas stemming from the work of David Hume, whose most important work was published in 1752, and Adam Smith whose great *Wealth of Nations* was published in 1776. These ideas came to dominate economics particularly, but far from exclusively, in Britain throughout the last quarter of the eighteenth and the first three quarters of the nineteenth century.

Hume's contributions principally concerned money and the balance of payments. But Smith's work is a virtual compendium of economics, focusing on the key question of economic growth, and covering division of labour, distribution, capital accumulation, trade and colonial policy, and public finance. Amongst their successors was T. R. Malthus; though chiefly famous for his writings on population, he covered the whole field of economic inquiry. A major impetus to the development of Classical economics was provided by David

Ricardo. He read Smith's work critically and from it constructed a 'model' which, unlike Smith's work, produced fairly clear and definite predictions. Ricardo succeeded initially in attracting disciples, notably J. Mill and – though he later drifted away from Ricardo's influence – J. R. McCulloch as well as Thomas De Quincey. But his influence waned after his death and the work of J. Mill's son, J. S. Mill, is much closer to Smith in range, reliance upon empirical material, and the avoidance of precise predictions.

Classical economics covered the whole field of economic enquiry, but with an emphasis on questions dealing with large aggregates – economic growth, international trade, monetary economics, public finance – rather than with the analysis of the behaviour of the maximizing individual which came to be of dominant interest after 1870. (In the field of value theory, in particular, the Classical economists generally made do with various sorts of production theories emphasizing, in varying degrees, the importance of labour cost in total cost.) At the same time a fundamental premise lying behind the analysis of aggregates, and stemming from Smith, was that individuals were motivated by the pursuit of self-interest, and that their pursuit had to be limited by a framework of law, religion and custom, to ensure coincidence of private and social interest. This in turn meant that in the field of economic policy Classical economics, while predisposed against government interference (partly because of the way in which such interference could be used for purely sectional interest, and partly because of a belief that decentralized individual knowledge was superior to State knowledge), was pragmatic – the necessary legislative framework could only be learnt by experience and enquiry.

At the heart of the Classical vision is the idea of economic growth occurring through the interaction of capital accumulation and division of labour. Capital accumulation made it possible to postpone the sale of output, permitting the development of specialization and division of labour. Division of labour in turn increased total output, permitting further capital accumulation. Economic growth would be increased by allowing capital to flow to where it was most productive; thus, other things being equal, it was desirable to remove restraints on the free allocation of resources. Division of labour itself was limited by the extent of the market. The extent of the home market depended on population and income per head. As capital was accumulated, the available labour supply found itself in greater demand and wages rose above the necessary minimum – 'subsistence' which could be either psychological or physiological. Population responded to the rise in wages by increasing; this in turn increased the labour supply which pushed wages back towards subsistence, though, if subsistence was a psychological variable – as it was with many Classical

writers – population growth might well stop before wages had fallen to the old level of subsistence. As wages rose, profits fell; this might check capital accumulation, but as long as profits were above a necessary minimum, capital accumulation would continue. Output, population, and capital thus all grew together. However, a brake on growth was provided by the shortage of a third input, land. With the progress of economic growth, food became more and more expensive to produce, while landlords enjoyed the benefit of an unearned rent arising from ownership of this scarce but vital resource – this aspect was particularly stressed by Malthus and Ricardo. The rising cost of food also meant that the floor below which subsistence could not fall – the minimum wage necessary to procure basic physical necessities of life – rose; and Ricardo in particular emphasized that such a rise would depress profits and might eventually stop capital accumulation and growth altogether. (Smith had believed that growth would only stop when investment opportunities were exhausted.) He then argued that repeal of the Corn Laws (restricting food imports) was urgent, since subsistence could be obtained more cheaply abroad. (Later Classical economists such as McCulloch and J. S. Mill were, however, optimistic about technical progress in agriculture which could postpone any slowdown in economic growth by lowering the cost of agricultural output.)

The argument for repeal of the Corn Laws provided one part of a general Classical case for freedom of trade; the desire to widen the market to maximize possible division of labour provided another. However, a more general and sophisticated argument for freedom of trade was provided by R. Torrens and Ricardo, in the form of the theory of comparative costs (later refined and developed by J. S. Mill) which showed that a country could gain from importing even those commodities in which it had a competitive advantage if it had an even greater competitive advantage in the production of other commodities – it should concentrate its scarce resources on the latter.

Balance of payments equilibrium was ensured by a mechanism which was due to David Hume, and which was also basic to Classical monetary theory, the price-specie-flow mechanism. A balance of payments deficit would, through gold outflow, reduce the money supply, and thus the price level, making exports competitive and imports less attractive, and this equilibrating mechanism would continue until the gold outflow stopped and payments came into balance. The price level was thus dependent on the money supply: and the predominant Classical view from Ricardo to Lord Overstone was that the note issue, as part of the money supply, should be contracted if gold was flowing out, since the outflow was a symptom of a price level which was too high. Monetary control was also necessary to dampen the effects of an endogenous trade cycle, an element introduced into Classical economics, chiefly by Overstone, from the late 1830s. (A minority of Classical economists however viewed the money supply as demand-determined.)

Classical economics represented a major intellectual achievement. The foundations which it laid in the fields of monetary and trade theory, in particular, are still with economics today. Eventually however it lost some of its momentum; it was always policy-orientated, and as the policy questions were settled – usually along the lines indicated by the Classical analyses – and as economists came to take continuing economic growth for granted, they turned their attention to different questions requiring different techniques of analysis.

D. P. O'Brien
University of Durham

Further Reading
Blaug, M. (1958), *Ricardian Economics*, New Haven.
O'Brien, D. P. (1975), *The Classical Economists*, Oxford.
See also: *Hume, Malthus; Mill; Ricardo; Smith.*

Clausewitz, Karl von (1780–1831)

A rather quiet and reflective character, Clausewitz was not in the front rank of Prussian military reformers despite his friendship and intellectual contact with Scharnhorst and, later, with Gneisenau. He began his military career as a boy soldier in the war of 1793–4, and spent some years in Russian service after 1812. After 1815 he was involved for a long period in routine service, during which time he worked on his monumental book, *On War*. The book was never completed and was published posthumously in 1832–4. In several more modest studies, Clausewitz had shown himself an informed patriot and an intelligent observer of the military. *On War*, however, represents the fruits of many years of systematic reflection on the theory of war and it conduct.

The fundamental principle of Clausewitz's theory of war is surprisingly simple. It is that war should always be purposefully related to political aims. His views about the relationship between war and politics, and between the politician on the one hand and the commander-in-chief on the other, had an even greater impact than his more narrowly proposed military theories. The latter reflected the conditions at the time, of a transition from the feudal army of the past to modern mass armies. Nevertheless, his influence in Germany was slight, and his reputation reached a nadir with Ludendorff's rather arrogant rejection of his ideas. But he did profoundly influence Lenin and Mao Tse-tung, and today there is something of a renaissance of his reputation in the West, particularly in the context of thinking about nuclear strategy.

Wilfried von Bredow
Philipps University, Marburg

Further Reading
Aron, R. (1983 [1976]), *Clausewitz: Philosopher of War*, London. (Original French edn, *Penser la guerre: Clausewitz*, Paris.)
Howard, M. (1983), *Clausewitz*, London.
Paret, P. (1976), *Clausewitz and the State*, Oxford.
See also: *military sociology; war.*

Clinical Psychology

Clinical psychology is one of the speciality areas of applied psychology, together with such other specialities as industrial, physiological, measurement and developmental psychology. The science and profession of clinical psychology, as one of the mental health disciplines, utilizes the principles of psychology to: (1) understand, diagnose and treat psychological problems; (2) teach and train students in these principles and their applications; and (3) conduct research in human behaviour as well as function as consumer of research advances as a means of upgrading the delivery of health care.

The two World Wars and the major development of public schools in the United States between the wars vastly accelerated the growth of clinical psychology, first as purely a psychological or 'mental' test application in assessing intellectual and other psychological responses and capabilities, and then, after the Second World War, expanding into other roles, in the psychotherapies as well as in research and training and in formal graduate programmes in clinical psychology. In the US alone, it has been estimated that during the Second World War 16 million military candidates and recruits were given psychological tests for classification and assignment to duties. In the First World War psychologists did psychometric assessment only; in the Second World War they also carried out treatment responsibilities for mentally ill personnel, together with psychiatrists, social workers, nurses, and technicians.

Two major developments after the Second World War furthered the growth of clinical psychology in the US – the establishment of the National Institute of Mental Health and its support for training and research; and the decision of the Veterans Administration to fund training for clinical psychology as one of the disciplines in mental health, to assess and treat veterans with psychological illness. There followed the accreditation, by the American Psychological Association (APA), of doctoral training programmes (130 in 1982) and internship programmes (211 in 1982) in professional psychology (clinical, counselling, school and, more recently, professional-scientific psychology); and certification and licensing by states.

Two other standards organizations developed, the first in 1947 and thus growing during the great 'spurt' years of the past 35 years; and the second initially an outgrowth of the former. The American Board of Professional Psychology (ABPP) was established in 1947 by the Council of Representatives of the American Psychological Association 'to define the standards, conduct examinations, grant diplomas, and encourage the pursuit of excellence in professional psychology' (1980). The four fields of specialization are clinical, counselling, industrial and organizational, and school; and shortly, neuropsychology.

In 1957, there were in the APA 15,545 Life Members, Fellows and Associates, of whom 1,907 Fellows and Associates were in the Division of Clinical Psychology. A quarter century later there were 52,440 Fellows, Members and Associates; nearly 4,600 of whom were in the Division of Clinical Psychology and more than 7,400 in four closely related Divisions – Community, Psychotherapy, Health and Clinical Neuropsychology (however, many APA members belong to several Divisions so that there is considerable overlap among these members). At the present time there are over 2,600 ABPP Diplomates of whom more than 1,800 are in the speciality of Clinical, and nearly 14,000 registrants in the National Register.

Two recent directions have both moved clinical psychology toward a reintegration with other fields of psychology and have created new specialities within clinical psychology. Health psychology has drawn to it scientists and professionals from other domains of psychology, principally clinical, social, physiological and learning or cognitive areas. This field was initially a research area and increasingly has become an applied field. The second direction represents an interesting cycle in the history of clinical psychology. As noted above, psychological or 'mental' tests have had a prominent 90-year role in the history and development of clinical psychology. After the Second World War, primarily in the US, graduate programmes decreased their commitment to teaching assessment methods, and their graduates increasingly turned to psychotherapy as a principal activity. Then, research training support, litigation over the effects upon individuals of toxic and other industrial and environmental pollutants, and mounting interest in psychological changes in disease and accident victims and in the elderly all contributed to bringing assessment again into prominence, especially neuropsychological assessment; and there now are local, state, regional, national and international societies of neuropsychologists.

Ivan N. Mensh
University of California, Los Angeles

Further Reading
American Board of Professional Psychology (1980), *Directory of Diplomates*, Washington DC.
Cattell, R. B. (1983), 'Let's end the duel', *American Psychologist*, 38.
Council for the National Register of Health Science Providers in Psychology (1981), *National Register of Health Service Providers in Psychology*, Washington DC.
Mensh, I. N. (1966), *Clinical Psychology: Science and Profession*, New York.

Cliometrics

The term cliometrics (a neologism linking the concept of measurement to the muse of history) was apparently coined at Purdue University, Indiana, US, in the late 1950s. Originally applied to the study of economic history as undertaken by scholars trained as economists (and also called, by its practitioners and others, the 'new economic history', 'econometric history', and 'quantitative economic history'), more recently cliometrics has been applied to a broader range of historical studies (including the 'new political history', the 'new social history', and, most inclusively, 'social science history').

The historians' early interest in cliometrics partly reflects the impact of two important works in United States economic history. The detailed estimates by Conrad and Meyer (1958) of the profitability of slavery before the Civil War and the quantitative evaluation of the role of the railroads in economic growth by Fogel (1964) triggered wide-ranging debate, with much attention to questions of method as well as substance. While these two works, combining economic theory and quantitative analysis, attracted the most attention, two other books published at about the same time also highlighted the quantitative aspect, although in a more traditional (and less controversial) manner. A National Bureau of Economic Research conference volume, edited by Parker (1960), presented a number of important studies (by, among others, Easterlin, Gallman, Lebergott, and North) pushing back many important times series on economic variables to the early nineteenth century, an effort complemented by the publication, several years later, of another NBER conference dealing mainly with nineteenth-century economic change (1966). North (1961) combined his new estimates of pre-1860 foreign trade with a familiar regional approach to describe the basic contours of United States economic growth from 1790 to the Civil War. These works had important implications for discussions of economic growth in the United States, particularly in the period before the Civil War. The concentration of major publications within a short time period, together with the start of an annual conference of cliometricians at Purdue University (which, with several changes of venue, still continues), generated the momentum which led to major shifts in the nature of the writing of American economic history, as well as revisions of many interpretations of past developments. The late 1950s and 1960s saw similar changes in other subfields of history, particularly political and social history, although it was in economic history that the concentration on theory, quantitative data, and statistical methods was most complete.

The most general characteristics of cliometric work (in economic history) have been the systematic use of economic theory and its concepts to examine economic growth in the past, and the widespread preparation and formal statistical analysis of quantitative material. While none of this may seem to provide a new approach in historical studies (as is often pointed out in criticizing claims of novelty), the more explicit attention to theory and the more frequent reliance on quantitative materials and statistical procedures have had an important impact upon the manner in which historical questions have been approached and interpreted. However, cliometricians still differ in how they make use of quantitative and statistical methods. To some, the major work is the preparation of quantitative data, either of detailed information for a particular time period (e.g., the samples of population, agriculture, and manufacturing records drawn from the decadal federal census) or of long-period time series (e.g., national income and wealth, wages, labour force) to be used in measuring and understanding past economic changes. These estimates require imaginative reconstructions from the available samples of past data, but do not often involve sophisticated statistical tools. Others emphasize the use of more formal statistical methods, most frequently regression analysis, to test hypotheses. And some cliometricians restrict themselves to the use of economic theory to analyse institutional and economic changes, which are not described quantitatively.

Continued interest in economic (and political and sociological) theory has led to a more frequent attempt to find historical generalizations based upon social science concepts and methods than some, more traditionally-trained, historians seem comfortable with. Nevertheless, the ability to collect and examine data, from archival and published sources, furthered by the development of the computer, has permitted a considerable expansion in the amount of material relevant to questions of interest to historians, as well as better methods of organizing, analysing, and testing data. In recent years, the heat of earlier debates on method has apparently declined as the use of quantitative methods and theoretical constructs has become a part of the standard 'tool-kit' of historians, while cliometricians have broadened the range of questions they have discussed and the varieties of evidence utilized.

While the first cliometric studies were done principally by North American scholars and, for reasons of data availability, most frequently concerned the United States in the nineteenth century, over the past two decades the temporal and geographic scope has widened, as has the types of questions to which cliometric analysis is applied. Much work has been done on the colonial period, as well as the twentieth century, in the United States. And, not only have the interests of American cliometricians expanded to include studies of other parts of the world, but cliometric work has developed in a number of other countries, most particularly in Britain and in Western Europe. Although, as with most attempts at categorization, a sharp dividing line is often difficult to draw, cliometric history continues to emphasize the systematic application of social science theory and the use of quantitative data and statistical analysis to understand the historical past.

Stanley L. Engerman
University of Rochester

References
Conrad, A. H. and Meyer, J. R. (1958), 'The economics of slavery in the ante-bellum South', *Journal of Political Economy.*
Fogel, R. W. (1964), *Railroads and American Economic Growth: Essays in Econometric History*, Baltimore.
National Bureau of Economic Research, Conference in Research in Income and Wealth (1960), *Trends in the American Economy in the Nineteenth Century*, Princeton.
National Bureau of Economic Research, Conference on Research in Income and Wealth (1966), *Output, Employment, and Productivity in the United States after 1800*, New York.
North, D. C. (1961), *The Economic Growth of the United States, 1790–1860*, Englewood Cliffs, NJ.

Further Reading
Engerman, S. L. (1977), 'Recent developments in American economic history', *Social Science History.*
Kousser, J. M. (1980), 'Quantitative social-scientific history', in M. Kammen (ed.), *The Past Before Us*, Ithaca.
McCloskey, D. N. (1978), 'The achievements of the cliometric school', *Journal of Economic History.*
McCloskey, D. N. and Hersh, G. (1985), *The Bibliography of Historical Economics, 1957–1980*, Cambridge.
See also: *history.*

Coalitions

Coalitions are collections of people who band together to accomplish some goal. As such, they are the stuff of which group decision making – especially what we think of as politics – is made.

Work on coalitions is both empirical and theoretical, two traditions which are now merging, each one informing the other. The empirical approach consists of establishing which individuals or groups work together, usually in some institutional setting. Thus, for example, there are studies of coalition making in the formation of cabinet governments, in electorates, legislatures, the judiciary, the military and so on, as well as in non-governmental structures. The formation of alliances – though usually not referred to as coalitions – is yet another example. All forms of government require coalitions to obtain and retain power – whether the coalitions are groups who supported the election of those in power or groups that support the suppression of those who are not. Coalitions are ever changing, very quickly in some circumstances and more slowly in others.

Theoretical work on coalitions deals with the following: (1) the size of winning coalitions; (2) the basis on which coalitions form; (3) the distribution of 'pay-offs' among members of the winning coalition; and (4) the duration of the coalition.

Some of the most exciting work focuses on the size of winning coalitions. William Riker argued that in cases of complete information, coalitions would form that were of minimal winning size such that subtraction of one member would result in the coalition losing. The logic is simply that the pay-off to the coalition needs to be split up among fewer members. In situations with incomplete information, coalitions would be somewhat larger but would still tend toward minimal size.

A considerable volume of work has followed up on Riker's ideas. Some of it has expanded the theory, showing, for example, that in threatening situations there may be incentives for forming large coalitions. Similarly, the theory has been altered slightly to take account of situations in which actors (e.g., political parties) are of unequal sizes. Extensive empirical work has been done to try to support or refute the 'size principle'. Not surprisingly, the great uncertainty in social situations makes it difficult to know how small coalitions must be to confirm the minimal winning theory. Thus no one can agree about whether or not the theory is confirmed. What can be said is that Riker clearly recognized a force – that towards minimizing the size of coalitions just so long as they remain winning – that is of fundamental importance, even though in the real world it does not always operate to the same degree that it does in abstract situations.

Other work attempts to specify coalition formation by the characteristics of various possible outcomes, for example, those that are undominated, in the sense that the players in the winning coalitions could not guarantee that they would be better off by defecting from them. As with Riker's work, such theories often do not predict that a particular coalition will form but only that one of a set of coalitions will form. Experimental evidence has not shown one solution to be uniformly superior to another.

Coalition theories have been less successful in predicting exactly which coalitions will form and the basis on which co-operation will be established. In a three-person situation, it is usually apparent why two should coalesce against one (the minimal winning size idea), but it is less readily apparent why any particular pair would join together. The most frequent hypothesis is probably that the specific coalitions that form depend on shared values. Thus, for example, if there are three political parties – one liberal, one moderate, and one conservative – one might well predict that the liberal and moderate parties, or the moderate and conservative parties, would more readily coalesce than the liberal or conservative parties. But a variety of other factors such as friendship or past experiences may also contribute to which individuals or groups coalesce.

One reason that prediction of specific coalitions is difficult is that it is not always clear just what the pay-off is to coalition members. Indeed, it may very well be that different coalition members are rewarded with different kinds of pay-offs. In a cabinet situation, for example, one party may obtain legislation that it thinks is important, another will receive visibility that will help it in the next election campaign, and yet another will achieve useful recognition for one of its leaders.

Coalition theory is also less successful with respect to specifying how pay-offs are divided among members of a winning coalition. That is, theories are often quite explicit about pay-offs, but in experiments players sometimes use simple rules such as equal pay-offs to all members. Most studies, however, find that pay-offs are weighted in favour of the larger coalition members.

A criticism of most coalition theories is that they are relatively static rather than dynamic. Simple observation and reasoning tells us that notions like trust ought to be very important when the same situation is faced repeatedly, as in legislative voting situations. Yet these notions are the most difficult to specify theoretically. Therefore, perhaps the weakest area of coalition theory is with respect to repeated 'plays'.

Richard G. Niemi
University of Rochester

Reference
Riker, W. H. (1962), *The Theory of Political Coalitions*, New Haven.

Further Reading

Holler, M. (ed.) (1983), *Coalitions and Collective Action*, Würzburg.

See also: *committees; decision making.*

Cognition

See Intelligence, Memory, Sensation and Perception, Thinking.

Cognitive-Behavioural Therapy

Cognitive-behavioural interventions are an attempt to preserve the demonstrated efficiencies of behavioural therapy within a less doctrinaire context and to incorporate the cognitive activities of the client in the efforts to produce therapeutic change (Kendall and Hollon, 1979). Based upon current data (Smith, 1982), cognitive-behavioural therapy is a dominant force in psychotherapy, ranking with psychoanalysis and just behind eclecticism as a major theoretical and applied framework.

Basic to the cognitive-behavioural approach is a set of principles captured briefly as follows: (1) Client and therapist work together to evaluate problems and generate solutions (e.g., collaborative empiricism). (2) Most human learning is cognitively mediated. (3) Cognition, affect, and behaviour are causally interrelated. (4) Attitudes, expectancies, attributions and other cognitive activities are central in producing, predicting, and understanding behaviour and the effects of therapy. (5) Cognitive processes can be integrated into behavioural paradigms, and it is possible and desirable to combine cognitive treatment strategies with enactive and contingency management techniques (Kendall and Bemis, 1984; Mahoney, 1977).

Within the boundaries of these fundamental principles, the actual implementation of the cognitive-behavioural therapies varies. The major strategies within cognitive-behavioural therapy include: (1) Cognitive-behaviour therapy of depression; (2) Rational-emotive therapy; (3) Systematic rational restructuring; (4) Stress inoculation, and (5) Self-control training with children.

(1) Cognitive-behavioural therapy of depression (Beck, Rush, Shaw and Emery, 1979) is structured, active, and typically time-limited. Learning experiences are designed to teach clients to monitor their negative thinking, to examine the evidence for and against their distorted (negative) thinking, to substitute more reality-oriented interpretations for negative thinking, and to begin to alter the dysfunctional beliefs and life style associated with negative thinking. Behav-

ioural strategies such as self-monitoring of mood, activity scheduling, graduated task assignments, and role-playing exercises are integrated with more cognitive procedures such as focusing on changing negative thinking, reattribution, and decentering.

(2) Rational-emotive therapy (RET) offers both a theoretical and therapeutic system consistent with cognitive-behavioural therapy (Ellis, 1980). In RET, events do not cause emotional and behavioural consequences; private beliefs do. When the individuals' beliefs (salient assumptions) are inaccurate/irrational and are framed in absolutistic or imperative terms, maladjustment is likely to result. RET teaches clients to identify and change the illogical notions that underlie their distressing symptoms.

(3) Systematic rational restructing (SRR) is a derivative of RET which offers a clear description of the procedures of treatment. SRR offers specific techniques for modifying anxiety and irrational beliefs and is implemented in four stages: (a) presenting the rationale for the treatment to the clients; (b) reviewing the irrationality of certain types of beliefs and assumptions; (c) analysing the client's problems in terms of irrational thinking and undesirable self-talk; (d) teaching the client to modify self-talk and irrationality (e.g., Goldfried, 1979).

(4) Stress-inoculation (Meichenbaum, 1977) is a three-stage intervention which focuses on teaching cognitive and behavioural skills for coping with stressful situations. In the educational phase, clients are taught a conceptual framework for understanding stress in cognitive terms. The second phase, skills training, teaches clients cognitive (imagery, changing irrational self-talk) and behavioural (relaxation, breathing) skills. In the final stage, clients practise the new skills in stressful situations.

(5) Focusing on children, self-instructional training is designed to teach thinking skills (Kendall and Braswell, 1985). Especially relevant for children who lack foresight and planning (e.g., impulsive, nonself-controlled, hyperactive/attention disorder), self-instructional procedures involve rehearsal of overt, then covert, self-guiding verbalizations. Using tasks and role-plays, the therapist and child practise thinking out loud. Behavioural contingencies are also implemented.

Cognitive-behavioural therapies are consistent with therapeutic integration, where varying resources are tapped as sources of effective treatment. In one sense they are prototypic of integration: performance-based behavioural treatments with a focus on the cognitive representation/meanings of events and the merits of thinking — in other words, thought and action in psychotherapy.

Philip C. Kendall
Temple University

References

Beck, A. T., Rush, A. J., Shaw, B. F. and Emery, G. (1979), *Cognitive Therapy of Depression*, New York.

Ellis, A. (1980), 'Rational-emotive therapy and cognitive behaviour therapy: similarities and differences', *Cognitive Therapy and Research*, 4.

Goldfried, M. R. (1979), 'Anxiety reduction through cognitive-behavioral intervention', in P. C. Kendall and S. D. Hollon (eds), *Cognitive-Behavioral Interventions: Therapy, Research, and Procedures*, New York.

Kendall, P. C. and Bemis, K. M. (1984), 'Thought and action in psychotherapy: the cognitive-behavioral approaches', in M. Hersen, A. E. Kazdin and A. S. Bellack (eds), *The Clinical Psychology Handbook*, New York.

Kendall, P. C. and Braswell, L. (1984), *Cognitive-Behavioral Therapy for Impulsive Children*, New York.

Kendall, P. C. and Hollon, S. D. (eds) (1979), *Cognitive-Behavioral Interventions: Theory, Research and Procedures*, New York.

Mahoney, J. M. (1977), 'Reflections on the cognitive-learning trend in psychotherapy', *American Psychologist*, 32.

Meichenbaum, D. (1977), *Cognitive-Behavior Modification: An Integrative Approach*, New York.

Smith, D. (1982), 'Trends in counseling and psychotherapy', *American Psychologist*, 37.

See also: *behaviour therapy*.

Cognitive Dissonance

The theory of cognitive dissonance, which gained prominence in social psychology during the 1960s and 1970s, was first proposed by Leon Festinger (1957) and later refined and elaborated by Brehm and Cohen, Aronson, and Wicklund and Brehm (1976). The elements in the theory are the cognitions (items of knowledge or belief) that a person may hold at a given time. Between any pair of cognitions, one of the following relations is assumed to exist: consonance (one of the cognitions follows from the other), dissonance (one cognition follows from the negation of the other), or irrelevance (neither cognition follows from the other or from its negation). The 'follows from' criterion refers to psychological, rather than to logical, implication. Thus, for example, the pair of cognitions *I voted for a socialist candidate in the last election* and *I believe in socialism* are consonant because the second follows psychologically from the first; this is evident from the fact that, given the first cognition, an observer would normally expect the second rather than its negation to be more likely.

The dissonance relation, which is of special importance in the theory, is held to be a motivating state of tension, in many ways like hunger or thirst, and the theory's main assumption is that dissonance tends to generate dissonance-reducing behaviour. Three methods of reducing dissonance are possible: changing one of the dissonant cognitions, decreasing the perceived importance of the dissonant cognitions, and adding further (justifying) cognitions. A familiar example is the dissonance normally experienced by people who hold the cognitions *I smoke cigarettes* and *cigarette smoking damages one's health*. It may be difficult to change the first cognition, which is behaviourally anchored, but research has confirmed that many smokers reduce the dissonance by changing the second – that is, by debunking the evidence linking cigarette smoking with health risks – and by adding further (justifying) cognitions, such as *I smoke only mild brands* and *there will soon be a cure for lung cancer*.

Despite its almost tautological simplicity, cognitive dissonance theory has been shown to generate non-obvious predictions across a wide range of human behaviour. The attitudinal consequences of making free choices, of stating opinions at variance with one's true beliefs, and of resisting temptation have been illuminated by dissonance theory, and empirical research in these areas has yielded results that are broadly in line with predictions from the theory. The behaviour of end-of-the-world cultists after their prophecies have failed has also been investigated in the light of the theory.

Though undoubtedly successful, cognitive dissonance theory has been criticized for its conceptual fuzziness and for the ambiguity of the predictions that can sometimes be derived from it. The most sustained critique has come from Daryl Bem (1967) who has attempted, not altogether convincingly, to reinterpret dissonance effects in terms of a self-perception theory based on radical Skinnerian behaviourism.

Andrew M. Colman
University of Leicester

References

Bem, D. J. (1967), 'Self-perception: an alternative interpretation of cognitive dissonance phenomena', *Psychological Review*, 74.

Festinger, L. (1957), *A Theory of Cognitive Dissonance*, Stanford.

Wicklund, R. A. and Brehm, J. W. (1976), *Perspectives on Cognitive Dissonance*, Hillsdale, NJ.

See also: *attitudes; sensation and perception*.

Cognitive Science

Cognitive science is an interdisciplinary field, originally formed around shared interests in *cognitive* psychology and computer *science*, that has recently expanded to include related research in cognitive anthropology and cognitive linguistics. Cognitive scientists are interested in conceptual structures that mediate between stimuli received by the sense organs and behavioural responses. These knowledge structures, which are most often termed 'schemata' (singular 'schema'), are the building blocks of cognition – the fundamental elements in all human information processing, e.g., perception and comprehension, recognition and recall, categorizing and planning, and problem-solving and decision making (Rumelhart, 1980).

Schemata

A schema is both a structure and a processor. It is a framework comprised of a network of nodes and relations that represents knowledge about a concept, its constituents, and their interrelationships. At the same time, it is also an active process that operates to construct interpretations of experience; it is a procedure capable of accessing its own goodness-of-fit to elements in the environment and, thus, of accounting for them. Schemata have variables, or 'slots', that must be filled, or 'bound', by specific instances of data, i.e., elements in the environment in particular instantiations. 'Instantiation' refers to the binding of elements to particular variables on particular occasions. This binding of elements to variables is restricted by conditions, known as 'variable constraints', that are associated with variables. Binding is constrained by the typical values of variables and by the interrelationships holding among variables (Minsky, 1975; Rumelhart, 1980). The schema underlying commercial events in American culture may be described to illustrate 'schema', 'variable', and 'variable constraint'.

The commercial event schema, a repeatedly discussed example in the cognitive science literature (see Fillmore, 1977; Rumelhart, 1980; Casson, 1983), has the variables BUYER, SELLER, MONEY, GOODS, and EXCHANGE. An event is understood as a commercial transaction when persons, objects, and sub-events in the environmental situation are bound to appropriate schema variables. Binding of these variables is constrained by typical variable values (BUYER and SELLER are normally persons, MONEY is generally currency, GOODS are usually inanimate objects, and an EXCHANGE typically involves a transfer of objects between participants) and by variable interrelationships (the value of the MONEY variable covaries with the value of the GOODS variable).

A schema is most often a complex structure that includes a number of embedded subschemata as constituent parts. Schema structure is generally hierarchical: schemata at higher levels represent general concepts, while those at successively lower levels represent more and more specific concepts. Compre-hended in general terms, a commercial event involves a BUYER who EXCHANGES a sum of MONEY with a SELLER for equivalently valued GOODS. But the schematic representation of EXCHANGE contains subschemata for CAUSE and TRANSFER, i.e., it represents a sub-event in which (simplifying somewhat) the BUYER CAUSES two TRANSFERS of possession, one of MONEY from the BUYER to the SELLER and another of GOODS from the SELLER to the BUYER. So a commercial event may be understood generally in terms of the major schema alone, or more specifically in terms of these embedded sub-schemata (See Rumelhart, 1980).

Types of Complex Schemata

Three types of complex schemata may be distinguished (Casson, 1983): (1) Object schemata are the complex schemata underlying classification systems of concrete objects. Among the object classifications that have been studied are classifications of plants, animals, manufactured objects (e.g., vehicles, tools, clothing, furniture, and containers), persons, kinsmen, occupations, ethnic identities, illnesses, and emotions.

(2) Orientation schemata are complex schemata that represent knowledge about spatial orientations. Often termed cognitive maps, schemata of this type represent knowledge of environments, of the position of the self in environments, and of processes for moving the self through environments. Studies have been done of cognitive maps for small-scale spaces, such as offices and apartments, as well as for large-scale spaces, such as cities and seas.

(3) Event schemata represent a wide range of activities and interactions, varying from simple actions to sequences of scenes. To cite another example widely discussed in the cognitive science literature (see especially Schank and Abelson, 1977), the schematic representation underlying the event 'eating in a restaurant' is comprised of a sequence of linked sub-schemata: ENTERING, ORDERING, EATING, and EXITING. These sequentially ordered subschemata, which are called 'scenes', comprise a 'script'. As Schank and Abelson, who originated this notion, have defined it, a script is a 'predetermined, stereotyped sequence of actions that defines a well-known situation'. Subschemata for scenes represent the specific chains of actions that constitute scripts. The ORDERING scene in the restaurant script, for example, includes EXAMINING the menu, CHOOSING food items, SUMMONING the waitress, and so on.

Topics in Cognitive Science

Two currently popular topics in cognitive science are: (1) Metaphor: Lakoff and Johnson (1980) have recently explored metaphor using schema theory. The principal aim of their research is to show that everyday experience is conceptualized metaphorically by means of 'experiential gestalts', i.e., complex schemata. In essence, Lakoff and Johnson argue that abstract concepts not clearly delineated in experience are understood metaphorically in terms of concepts that are experientially more concrete. The TIME IS MONEY metaphor is an example. TIME is an abstract concept that is understood, experienced, and talked about in terms of MONEY, a concept more concrete in experience. Lakoff and Johnson argue that linguistic expressions provide insight into and evidence for conceptual metaphors. Example expressions for TIME IS MONEY include: How do you *spend* your time these days? This gadget will *save* you hours. I've *invested* a lot of time in her. You need to *budget* your time. He's living on *borrowed* time.

(2) Narrative: Schank and Abelson's (1977) work on scripts, which has been a major force in this development, can be used to illustrate this line of research. The restaurant script, for example, is invoked in comprehending the simple story, 'John went to a restaurant. He ordered chicken. He left a large tip.' Because mention in this story of a *restaurant* and of *ordering* and *tipping* instantiates the restaurant script, the full sequence of actions in the event is filled in on the basis of knowledge represented in the script, and the story is interpreted as 'John went to a restaurant. He sat down. He read the menu. He ordered chicken. He ate the chicken. He left a large tip. He paid the check. He left the restaurant.'

Discussions of topics covered here and detailed bibliographies can be found in Minsky (1975), Rumelhart (1980), Casson (1983), and Johnson-Laird (1983).

Ronald W. Casson
Oberlin College, Ohio

References

Casson, R. W. (1983), 'Schemata in cognitive anthropology', *Annual Review of Anthropology*, 12.

Fillmore, C. J. (1977), 'Topics in lexical semantics', in R. W. Cole (ed.), *Current Issues in Linguistic Theory*, Bloomington.

Johnson-Laird, P. N. (1983), *Mental Models*, New York.

Lakoff, G. and Johnson, M. (1980), *Metaphors We Live By*, Chicago.

Minsky, M. (1975), 'A framework for representing knowledge', in P. H. Winston (ed.), *The Psychology of Computer Vision*, New York.

Rumelhart, D. E. (1980), 'Schemata: the building blocks of cognition', in R. J. Sprio, B. C. Bruce and W. F. Brewer (eds), *Theoretical Issues in Reading Comprehension*, Hillsdale, NJ.

Schank, R. C. and Abelson, R. (1977), *Scripts, Plans, Goals, and Understanding*, Hillsdale, NJ.

Cohort Analysis

Cohort analysis (also known as longitudinal analysis) refers to studies measuring characteristics of cohorts throughout their lives, a cohort being a group of persons who have experienced the same life event during a specified period of time (usually one year). If the life event is birth, one speaks of a birth cohort or generation. One may similarly speak of marriage cohorts, divorce cohorts, educational cohorts, etc., life events respectively being in these cases marriage, divorce, or attaining a certain level of education, during a particular period of time. For example, one may follow over time a cohort of marriages in order to see how many couples eventually divorce, and to determine the risk of divorcing at each duration of marriage.

Cohort data are usually obtained by comparing the characteristics of a cohort at two or more points in time, using census or sample survey data. When the *same* individuals are thus compared, the term 'panel study' is often used. Demographic and epidemiologic data on cohorts can frequently be derived from records or registers, such as vital statistics or cancer registers. Other important sources of cohort data are retrospective studies, where respondents are asked to give information concerning past characteristics and events.

All cohort data are affected by possible selection effects: people die or move between censuses or surveys; similarly, retrospective questions can only be answered by those who survive! If people who are lost to follow-up have other characteristics from those who are interviewed, biased results may occur. Retrospective studies are, moreover, influenced by recall lapses: one may forget to declare events which happened many years ago.

Cohort measures may relate to characteristics of the cohort, or to events experienced by the cohort. For example, one may make a comparison between cohorts in an inter-cohort study, the proportions ultimately single, bachelor- or spinsterhood being the characteristics considered, birth being the event under study. One may also be interested, in an intra-cohort study, in changes in characteristics during a lifetime or in the distribution of events by age, e.g. changes in proportions surviving by age, or the distribution of deaths or risks of dying by age.

Cohort studies are often performed in order to distinguish cohort effects, i.e. effects particular to each cohort, from age (or duration) effects and period effects. This distinction cannot be reached using ordinary statistical methods, due to the so-called *identification problem*. Age, period, and cohort are not independent variables: knowing two yields the third. One may not, therefore, use all three variables simultaneously in statistical methods requiring linear independence between variables. One way out is to place constraints on the model, for example, to suppose that there is no period effect, or that age, cohort, and period effects are additive. Another solution is to consider that the period variable (such as the year), is used as an indicator of an underlying variable, for example, yearly income per capita. If data are available, one may then substitute the underlying variable for the year; this is a simple resolution of the identification problem, as the underlying variable is not a linear construct of age and cohort. It should be stressed that the choice between alternatives cannot be made on purely statistical grounds; the choice of the procedure or constraint must rest on supplementary information or on the use of theory.

Guillaume Wunsch
University of Louvain

Further Reading
Glenn, N. D. (1977), *Cohort Analysis, Quantitative Applications in the Social Sciences*, Beverly Hills.
Ryder, N. B. (1965), 'The cohort as a concept in the study of social change', *American Sociological Review*, 30.

Collective Behaviour and Crowds

Historical Origins of Collective Behaviour Studies
The nineteenth-century 'founding fathers' of collective behaviour studies were mainly Italian (Ferri, Sighele) and French (Tarde, Fournial, Le Bon). They are usually grouped together as the Roman (or Latin) school. Ferri, Sighele and Tarde were criminologists, interested in the problem of individual accountability for collective crimes committed by crowds and sects. Fournial and Le Bon were physicians, interested in the mechanisms of mutual influence, which they likened to those operating in hypnotic suggestion. A later Anglo-Saxon school proposed the existence of a 'herd instinct' (Trotter) and the development of a 'group mind' (McDougall) in collectivities. The major German-language contributions of the Freudians and, later, of the Frankfurt School centred on the authoritarian (or narcissistic) personalities of leaders and followers, and on the libidinal ties between them. The major American tradition (Park, Blumer) tried to understand the 'natural history' of collective behaviour patterns, and 'the way in which a new social order arises'. Most of the earlier European authors were psychologists, emphasizing psychic regression to emotional and irrational states. Most of the subsequent American authors were sociologists, emphasizing social progress through the emergence of new norms and values.

Jaap van Ginneken
University of Leiden

Modern Approaches to the Study of Collective Behaviour
Broadly conceived, collective behaviour refers to group problem-solving behaviour that encompasses crowds, mass phenomena, issue-specific publics, and social movements. The concept of crowd traditionally refers specifically to the more ephemeral and episodic kinds of collective behaviour.

The term crowd usually brings to mind a relatively large gathering of people in close physical proximity who attend to a common object. Although much collective behaviour occurs within a limited spatial area, it can also occur among a set of people who are not in one another's immediate vicinity. It is thus useful to reserve the term crowd or, more appropriately, compact crowd for any collectivity of individuals who can monitor one another by being visible to, or within earshot of, one another. Examples include protest demonstrations, riots, victory celebrations, the gatherings that congregate around fires and accidents, and the panic associated with flight from a burning building. In contrast to these compact types of crowd behaviour are those which occur among a set of individuals who are not physically proximate, but who share a common focus of attention without developing the debate characteristic of the public or the organization of the social movement, and who are linked together by social networks, the media, or both. Variants of this form of collective behaviour, referred to as the diffuse crowd (Turner and Killian, 1972) or the mass (Lofland, 1981), include rumour, fads, crazes, mass panic, deviant epidemics, mass hysteria, and collective blaming.

Understanding these two forms of collective behaviour requires consideration of three questions: (1) How do these forms of collective behaviour differ from everyday behaviour? (2) Under what conditions does such collective behaviour emerge? (3) What accounts for the co-ordination of collective behaviour?

(1) *Distinguishing between collective behaviour and everyday behaviour*
Although in recent years there has been increasing awareness of the continuity between collective behaviour and everyday behaviour, the existence of collective behaviour as a field of sociology still rests in large part on the assumption of significant differences between collective behaviour and everyday institutionalized

behaviour (Aguirre and Quarantelli, 1983; Killian, 1980). One of the key distinctions lies in the normative and relational basis of each. Both forms of behaviour are predicated on social norms and social relationships, but collective behaviour is characterized by either emergent norms, or emergent relationships, or by both. In contrast, everyday behaviour is usually based on established relationships and enduring norms that have the force of tradition, and frequently legal sanctions, behind them (Turner and Killian, 1972; Weller and Quarantelli, 1973).

Compact crowd phenomena can be further distinguished from everyday behaviour temporally and spatially. The predictability and stability of everyday behaviour derives in part from the fact that it is scheduled and enacted in spatial areas (streets, parks, malls) or physical structures (office buildings, theatres, stadiums) that were designed and are used for such behaviours. Compact crowd phenomena, excluding conventional audiences and queues, are neither temporally nor spatially routinized. Instead, they are 'more likely to be unscheduled and staged in spatial areas and structures that were designed and are currently used for purposes other than crowds – that is, for so-called institutional or everyday behavior' (Snow et al., 1981).

Since the diffuse crowd or mass is not confined to a limited spatial area, these temporal and spatial considerations do not distinguish it from everyday behaviour. What does make it distinctive, however, is that it is characterized by an almost obsessive preoccupation with a particular behaviour, viewpoint or object – as in the case of fads; with something that is experienced – as in the case of hysterical contagion; with flight and escape – as in the case of mass panic; with the acquisition of a scarce commodity – as in the case of craze; and with the attribution of responsibility – as in the case of collective blaming. To indicate preoccupation as a distinguishing mark of the diffuse crowd or mass is not to suggest that some compact crowd phenomena may not be similarly characterized. But this intense, albeit short-lived, preoccupation is not characteristic of all variants of the compact crowd.

These observations go beyond the recent contention that collective behaviour is typified in large part by the sense that 'something unusual is happening' (Lofland, 1981). But what it is that gives rise to the sense that something 'outside the ordinary' is occurring is not specified. The conceptualization offered here suggests two possibilities. In the case of the compact crowd, it is the collective appropriation of space or structures for purposes other than intended at a particular point in time that indicates that something unusual is happening. In the case of the diffuse crowd, it is a collective preoccupation that diverts attention from everyday routines that alerts us to some out-of-the-ordinary occurrence.

(2) Emergence of collective behaviour

Three sets of factors underlie the emergence of collective behaviour: (a) conditions of conduciveness; (b) situational precipitants or strains; and (c) conditions for mobilization. Each set of conditions is necessary but not sufficient for the emergence of collective behaviour.

(a) Conditions of conduciveness refer to sociocultural factors that 'permit or encourage episodes of collective behavior' (Smelser, 1982). These include ecological factors that affect the arrangement of people in space so as to facilitate communication and interaction, as exemplified by malls on college campuses and high-density residential areas; technological innovations that similarly enhance communication and interaction, as with the telephone, radio, and television; policies and actions of social control agents, which can expand or contract opportunities for interaction and communication; and daily routines and interactional patterns that can influence structural and psychological availability for participation in collective behaviour, such as degree of class or cultural heterogeneity among a population, discretionary or unscheduled time, and the extent of schedule congruence among potential participants (McPhail and Wohlstein, 1983; Smelser, 1962; Turner and Killian, 1972).

(b) Situational precipitants refer to specific conditions or strains that, given a relatively high rate of conduciveness, enhance the possibility of some form of collective behaviour occurring (Smelser, 1962; Turner and Killian, 1972). The specific kinds of conditions typically associated with the emergence of collective behaviour include unanticipated events, such as car accidents on residential streets and fires in night clubs and theatres; disruption of interdependent networks of institutionalized roles as in the typical disaster situation, in large-scale police strikes, for example, in Montreal in 1969, and in large-scale power blackouts, as in New York city in 1977; and conflicting values and definitions of reality, as in the case of most lynchings, riots, and protest demonstrations.

(c) A situational precipitant coupled with a high degree of conduciveness is seldom sufficient to produce an episode of collective behaviour. Conditions for mobilization also have to be met. That is, people have to be assembled or put into contact with one another, and attention must be focused. On some occasions in everyday life the condition of assemblage is already satisfied, as in the case of the conventional audience, queue, or pedestrian crowd. More often than not, however, assemblage is contingent on the rapid convergence of people in time and space. The importance of this and related processes, such as collective locomotion, to the emergence of collective behaviour have been amply demonstrated (McPhail and Wohlstein, 1983). The focusing of attention can occur spontaneously, as when someone yells 'Fire!' It can also be an unintended consequence of media broadcasts, or it can be accompanied by prior planning and organization, which often implies the operation of a social movement. But however it occurs, it is a necessary condition for the emergence of collective behaviour.

(3) Co-ordination of collective behaviour

Close inspection of the varieties of collective behaviour reveals that in each instance the behaviour in question is co-ordinated and patterned rather than random and individualistic. Identification of the sources of co-ordination has thus been one of the major research tasks confronting students of collective behaviour.

Early researchers and theorists tended to view this co-ordination as the result of either the rapid spread of emotional states and behaviour in a contagion-like manner due to the presumed suggestibility of crowd participants (LeBon, 1895; Blumer, 1951) or the convergence of individuals who are predisposed to behave in a similar manner because of common background characteristics and latent tendencies (Allport, 1924; Dollard et al., 1939; Hoffer, 1951). Both views are seriously flawed. They assume that collective behaviour is characterized by uniformity of action and thereby gloss over the existence of various categories of actors, the ongoing interaction between them, and the role interaction plays in determining the direction and character of collective behaviour. These oversights are primarily due to the perceptual trap of taking the behaviour of the most conspicuous element of the episode as typifying all categories of actors, thereby giving rise to the 'illusion of unanimity' (Turner and Killian, 1972). In the case of the compact crowd, attention is directed away from the less dramatic segments and their contributions to the direction and character of the collective episode. As a consequence, the range of interactions that occur within episodes of collective behaviour are ignored (McPhail and Wohlstein, 1983).

An alternative and sociologically more palatable view holds that collective behaviour is co-ordinated by a definition of the situation that functions in a normative manner by encouraging behaviour in accordance with the definition (Turner and Killian, 1972). As noted earlier, the collective definition of the situation may be emergent or pre-established. In either case, behaviour may vary considerably depending on the extent to which it is tightly regulated, as in the case of many non-violent protests, or loosely regulated, as in the case of most victory celebrations.

Today it is generally conceded that most instances of collective behaviour are normatively regulated. Accordingly, the focus of recent research has shifted from identifying the source of co-ordination to detailing the process by which normative definitions emerge and to examining the interactional dynamics underlying that process (McPhail and Wohlstein, 1983; Snow et al., 1981; Wright, 1978). Distinctive to this research is the view that crowd-specific interaction, rather than the background characteristics and cognitive states of individuals, is the key to understanding the direction and character of collective behaviour.

David A. Snow
University of Texas, Austin

References

Aguirre, B. E. and Quarantelli, E. L. (1983), 'Methodological, ideological, and conceptual-theoretical criticisms of collective behavior: a critical evaluation and implications for further studies', Sociological Focus, 16.
Allport, F. H. (1924), Social Psychology, Boston.
Blumer, H. (1951), 'Collective behavior', in A. M. Lee (ed.), Principles of Sociology, New York.
Dollard, J., Doob, L. W., Miller, N. E., Mower, O. H. and Sears, R. R. (1939), Frustration and Aggression, New Haven.
Hoffer, E. (1951), The True Believer, New York.
Killian, L. M. (1980), 'Theory of collective behavior: the mainstream revisited', in H. Blalock (ed.), Sociological Theory and Research, New York.
Le Bon, G. (1960 [1896]), The Crowd: A Study of the Popular Mind, New York. (Original French edn, Psychologie des Foules, Paris.)
Lofland, J. (1981), 'Collective behavior: the elementary forms', in M. Rosenberg and R. Turner (eds), Social Psychology: Sociological Perspectives, New York.
McPhail, C. and Wohlstein, R. T. (1983), 'Individual and collective behaviors within gatherings, demonstrations, and riots', in R. Turner (ed.), Annual Review of Sociology, Palo Alto.
Smelser, N. J. (1962), Theory of Collective Behavior, New York.
Snow, D. A., Zurcher, L. A. and Peters, R. (1981), 'Victory celebrations as theater: a dramaturgical approach to crowd behavior', Symbolic Interaction, 4.
Turner, R. H. and Killian, L. M. (1972), Collective Behavior, 2nd edn, Englewood Cliffs, NJ.
Weller, J. M. and Quarantelli, E. L. (1973), 'Neglected characteristics of collective behavior', American Journal of Sociology, 79.
Wright, S. (1978), Crowds and Riots: A Study in Social Organization, Beverly Hills.
See also: Le Bon; mass society; social movements.

Colonialism

See Imperialism.

Colour Vision

In sunlit woodland or at a thronged racecourse we may experience an apparently endless variety of hues, tints and lightnesses. Yet our colour vision is subject to a fundamental limitation, a limitation that is expressed in the fact of *trichromacy*. Suppose that we present to an observer a circular illuminated area divided into two halves and suppose we illuminate one half with a mixture of three fixed wavelengths, our reference lights. Suppose next that we illuminate the other side of the field with an unknown wavelength or mixture of wavelengths. Then, merely by adjusting the radiances of our three reference lights, it will always be possible to make the two sides of the field look alike. Sometimes, when matching a very saturated, monochromatic, light, we shall need to transfer one of our reference lights to the other side of the field; but we always need only three adjustments. The fact of trichromacy strongly suggests that at some stage in our visual system information about colour is carried by only three, unidimensional signals. In fact, it is now known that the limitation occurs at the first stage of the visual process, the cone cells of the retina, which contain photosensitive pigments. There are just three kinds of cone receptor with peak sensitivities in different spectral regions, at approximately 420, 530 and 560 nm (Dartnall, Bowmaker and Mollon, 1983). See Figure 1.

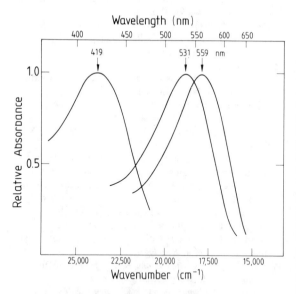

Figure 1 This graph shows how the absorption of each of the three classes of retinal cone varies with the frequency of light. (Frequency is inversely related to wavelength, and a wavelength scale has been added to top of the graph.) The data are taken from Dartnall *et al.* (1983) and were obtained by microspectrophotometric measurements of individual receptor cells in human retinal tissue.

An individual cone cell cannot discriminate colours. As the wavelength of a stimulating light is varied, all that changes is the magnitude of the electrical signal generated by the cone, and the same change could be generated by varying the radiance of the stimulating light. So, if it is to extract information about wavelength, independently of radiance, the visual system must compare the signals generated by different classes of cone. Early in the visual system, there exist cells that appear to receive neural signals of opposite sign (excitatory or inhibitory) from different classes of cone (see Gouras and Zrenner, 1981). Such cells are 'chromatically opponent': over a large range of radiances, they will always be excited by one portion of the spectrum and inhibited by another part. The most common type of chromatically opponent cell receives signals of opposite sign from the long- and middle-wave cones of Figure 1. The short-wave (violet-sensitive) receptors are rare in the retina (accounting for less than 10 per cent of all cones) and only a minority of chromatically opponent cells receive inputs from them; this is probably why our spatial resolution is so poor when it depends only on signals from the violet-sensitive cones.

There is more to colour vision, however, than the analysis of wavelength in a local region of the scene. Our perception of the colour of a given object is remarkably stable, despite large changes in the wavelength composition of the ambient illumination and thus in the wavelength composition of the light reflected to us by the object. The mechanism that ensures this *colour constancy*, and its site within the brain, are not known for certain; but it is clear that the visual system must be taking into account the pattern of illumination over a more than local region of the retina. Some non-spectral colours, such as brown and olive green, and the metallic colours, such as gold and silver, are indeed seen only in complex scenes, and there is no mixture of wavelengths that will generate them when a spatially homogeneous patch of light is viewed in isolation. There is little mystery about the physical properties of surfaces that yield such colours: thus a brown surface is a surface that predominantly reflects light of long wavelength (light that would look yellowish or orange if viewed in isolation) but nevertheless reflects less light overall than do nearby yellow and orange surfaces; and a surface will appear metallic if it is *specular*, if, that is, it reflects light predominantly at one angle (equal to the angle of incidence) rather than scattering it at many angles as does a matt surface. But how the visual system extracts these properties of surfaces is little understood. Nor do we know why most people judge that a brown surface differs from a yellow one in a more qualitative way than a dark red surface differs from a bright red one.

Colour blindness. In Caucasian populations, about 8 per cent of men and 0.5 per cent of women exhibit a hereditary deficiency or anomaly of colour vision (for a review, see Pokorny *et al.*, 1979). Some are *dichromatic*, that is, in a colour-matching experiment they require only two variables instead of the three required by a normal observer (see above). The most natural explanation of dichromacy is that one of the three types of retinal cone is absent; this hypothesis was first advanced in 1781 by von Gentilly and is now widely accepted. Another, milder form of colour-deficiency is *anomalous trichromacy*: observers of this type require three variables in a colour-matching experiment, but the matches they make differ from those of a normal observer. The most likely explanation of anomalous trichromacy is that one of the three photopigments of the retina is displaced from its normal position in the spectrum and has its wavelength of peak sensitivity close to that of one of the other photopigments.

The colour sense is a delicate one and impairments of colour discrimination can accompany a variety of diseases. Curiously, while it is the long- and middle-wave receptors that are most commonly affected in genetic deficiencies, it is the short-wave receptors that are most vulnerable to diseases (such as diabetes mellitus) that affect the retina. Diseases that affect the optic nerve (such as multiple sclerosis) produce a general elevation in thresholds for discriminating hue, although the patient may pass tests designed to detect the genetically colour-deficient. Very rarely, a central lesion may produce a total loss of colour vision while yet leaving unimpaired the patient's ability to read small print; in one such case, examined by the present writer, it was possible to show that all three classes of cone were present and that each could control verbal responses in a psychophysical experiment, but the patient had apparently lost some crucial part of the machinery that allows the outputs of different cones to be compared (Mollon *et al.*, 1980). The existence of such cases argues for some independence in the central analysis of colour and spatial detail.

J. D. Mollon
University of Cambridge

References
Dartnall, H. J. A., Bowmaker, J. K. and Mollon, J. D. (1983), 'Human visual pigments: microspectrophotometric results from the eyes of seven persons', *Proceedings of the Royal Society*, Ser. B.
Gouras, P. and Zrenner, E. (1981), 'Color vision: a review from a neurophysiological perspective', *Progress in Sensory Physiology*, 1.
Mollon, J. D., Newcombe, F., Polden, P. G. and Ratcliff, G. (1980), 'On the presence of three cone mechanisms in a case of total achromatopsia', in G Verriest (ed.), *Colour Vision Deficiencies V*, Bristol.
Pokorny, J., Smith, V. C., Verriest, G. and Pinckers, A. J. L. G. (eds) (1979), *Congenital and Acquired Color Vision Defects*, New York.
von Gentilly, G. (1781), *Magazin für das Neueste aus der Physik und Naturgeschichte (Gotha)*, 1.

Further Reading
Barlow, H. B. and Mollon, J. D. (eds) (1982), *The Senses*, Cambridge.
Boynton, R. M. (1979), *Human Color Vision*, New York.
Mollon, J. D. and Sharpe, L. T. (eds) (1983), *Colour Vision: Physiology and Psychophysics*, London.

See also: *depth perception; McCollough effect; vision.*

Commitment

Parsons saw commitment, varying in extent, as normative attachment to religious, economic or other social arrangements (Parsons, 1960). Becker (1960), however, presented commitment to 'a consistent line of activity' as based less on attachment to that activity itself than on attachment to connected but 'extraneous' activities. Thus, 'the "normal" person, when he discovers a deviant impulse in himself, is able to check that impulse in thinking of the manifold consequences acting on it would produce for him' (Becker, 1963). Similarly, a person may become disenchanted with his career but continue in it because of past investment of effort and money or expected future status and security. Because of sanctions or desired approval, however, he must maintain a display, termed 'situational adjustment', of normative commitment.

Matza (1964) divorced normative commitment from normative activity by arguing that delinquents were committed to law-abiding values but continued to be delinquent because they believed that friends, equally silent about their true attitudes, had deviant values.

Stebbins (1971), instead of asking how the deviant 'manages to avoid the impact of conventional commitments', analysed 'commitment to deviance' in terms of manifold problems in returning to a normal life.

Glickman (1983), focusing on a project for rehabilitating ex-prisoners through an ('extraneous') educational programme, found varied client commitment from 'undercommitment' to 'overcommitment', accompanied, however, by situational adjustment to the project. Overcommitted clients, intensely attached to it, yet fearful of academic and personal failure, were prone to invite arrest by renewed criminal activity.

Maurice Glickman
University of Botswana

References
Becker, H. (1960), 'Notes on the concept of commitment', *American Journal of Sociology*, 66.

Becker, H. (1963), *Outsiders: Studies in the Sociology of Deviance*, New York.
Glickman, M. (1983), *From Crime to Rehabilitation*, Aldershot.
Matza, D. (1964), *Delinquency and Drift*, London.
Parsons, T. (1960), 'Durkheim's contribution to the theory of integration of social systems', in K. Wolff (ed.), *Emile Durkheim 1858–1915*, Columbus.
Stebbins, R. (1971), *Commitment to Deviance*, Westport, Connecticut.
See also: *conformity*; *integration*; *norms*.

Committees

The most notable committees are those that help govern nations – cabinet committees, legislative assemblies, party committees, and higher courts. But there are also boards of directors of corporations, labour union councils, state or provincial assemblies, and city councils, all of which are involved in governance. The term committee normally refers to a face-to-face group of people who arrive at a decision through some means of polling member opinions. The types of committees mentioned above have a firm institutional grounding and will have well-defined means of voting the issues that come before them. Their decisions have a semi-binding nature to them, perhaps subject to appeals or approvals elsewhere.

In contrast, there are many committees that are no more than advisory in nature, acting as a source of information for an administrator, a supervisor, or even a larger organization. For a larger organization, advisory committees offer a division of work, specialization, and economies of scale. For a single administrator or supervisor, advisory committees offer balanced judgement and a diversification of information sources beyond the ordinary chain-of-command. The growth of the seemingly infinite variety of committee organization and function has in many ways marked a decline in the traditional efficient chain-of-command method of conducting business. In a purely practical sense, technology has made it easier for committees to function effectively. Duplicating services and electronic transmission have made it more convenient to share information and communication and to arrange for meetings. Transportation advances have also facilitated the convening of committees.

The study of committees has progressed in two directions: in the study of single committees and in the study of committee systems. The study of single committees has concentrated on the justification of their use and voting strategies of members (for example, Black, 1958), or on the substantive decision-making norms of very important groups. Recently there has been increased attention given to committee systems, primarily in relation to legislatures. An eight-nation study of committee systems in national legislatures was completed in 1979 by Lees and Shaw which tried to determine the significance of the various committee systems in relation to other decision-making foci. The study confirmed, for example, as others suspected, that committee systems have the most central role in US legislatures, while political parties have a weaker role.

The organizers of committee systems are faced with several decisions – how to divide up the subject matter; how many committees; how many members on each committee; how many committee assignments per member; how much authority to delegate; and whether or not to have subcommittees within committees. In representative bodies, small committees sacrifice representativeness, yet they may be necessary under a heavy agenda. The US Congress and state legislatures legislate through committees, and in Congress, the committees legislate through subcommittees. In other words, in the latter case, the subcommittees debate the subject before the committees deal with it. In Britain, India, and Canada, the issues are debated on the floor before they are assigned to committee. In essence, committee systems are becoming complex forms of organization, and serve as an ample challenge in future theories of decision making.

Wayne L. Francis
University of Missouri, Columbia

References
Black, D. (1958), *The Theory of Committees and Elections*, Cambridge.
Lees, J. D. and Shaw, M. (eds) (1979), *Committees in Legislatures*, Durham, NC.

Further Reading
Barber, J. (1966), *Power in Committees*, Chicago.
Francis, W. L. (1982), 'Legislative committee systems, optimal committee size, and the costs of decision-making', *Journal of Politics*, 44.
See also: *decision making*; *organizations*.

Commodity Stabilization Schemes

Schemes for the stabilization of primary commodity prices have always been an important item on the agenda of international policy discussions. This is because the prices of these commodities are volatile, and because exports of them are large sources of revenue for many countries, particularly those of the Third World. One of the most famous schemes was proposed by Keynes in 1942, as a companion to his International Clearing Union (which later became the IMF). Keynes's argument for commodity price stabilization led to political opposition from those opposed to market intervention and had to be shelved. More recently the same fate has befallen the Integral Program for Commodities put forward by UNCTAD (the United Nations Conference on Trade and Development). Those schemes which exist have developed in a piecemeal fashion. 'Only [schemes for] wheat, sugar, tea and coffee have lasted a number of years, and few appear to have achieved much before their demise' (MacBean and Snowden, 1981).

Price stabilization is usually put forward as a means of stabilizing the incomes of producers and consumers. It could also be used as a means of raising the average incomes of producers, but would then need to be buttressed by quota schemes to restrict production.

Price stabilization will normally succeed in stabilizing revenues to producers in the face of shifts in demand for commodities of the kind which occur because of the world business cycle. The managers of the scheme need to operate some kind of buffer stock. When demand is high, the extra can be satisfied by sales from the buffer stock: producers' revenue is unaltered by the demand increase. The reverse is true when demand falls. Stabilization of prices will, it is true, allow fluctuations in producers' incomes to remain in the face of fluctuations in the quantity produced, as a result, say, of changes in harvests. However, without stabilization of prices, producers' incomes might be even more unstable, if good harvest produced very large falls in prices (and vice versa). Price stabilization will also isolate consumers of primary commodities from shocks to the purchasing power of their incomes in a wide variety of circumstances.

Economists differ in their assessment of the benefits to be obtained from such stabilization of prices. Newbery and Stiglitz (1981) have argued, in a powerful modern study, that the benefits to producers are small. Newbery and Stiglitz would clearly be correct if producers could adjust their spending in line with fluctuations in their income. However, they ignore the great hardships which could arise when primary commodity producers (both individuals and nations) have to make unexpected cuts in expenditures. Such hardships will indeed arise when average incomes are not much above subsistence or when the revenue from sales of primary commodities is used to pay for development projects which are hard to stop and start at will. Newbery and Stiglitz also argue that the potential benefits to consumers would be small. But they largely ignore the inflationary difficulties for consumers which primary-commodity-price instability creates, and it was those which concerned Keynes. It must be admitted that contemporary proponents of primary commodity price stabilization schemes have been slow

to produce good evidence about the size of those effects which Newbery and Stiglitz ignore.

There are fundamental difficulties in the way of setting up any stabilization scheme. It is necessary to choose (1) the price level at which stabilization is to take place, and (2) the optimum size for the buffer stock. An obvious candidate for the price level is that one which would balance supply with demand, averaging over the normal fluctuations in both supply and demand. But the amount of information required accurately to determine this price would be formidable for most commodities. As for the buffer stock, it should presumably be able to deal with the normal fluctuations in supply and demand. But in order to avoid running absurdly large stocks the objective of *complete* price stabilization would need to be abandoned, at least in extreme circumstances. Even so, the cost of operating the required buffer stock might be very large for many commodities. It is thus easy to see why those stabilization schemes which have been established have always been on the verge of breaking down.

David Vines
University of Glasgow

References
Newbery, D. M. G. and Stiglitz, J. E. (1981), *The Theory of Commodity Price Stabilization: A Study on the Economics of Risk*, Oxford.
MacBean, A. I. and Snowden, P. N. (1981), *International Institutions in Trade and Finance*, London.
See also: *cartels and trade associations*.

Communal Groups

Communal groups are collective households of three or more individuals, at least some of them unrelated by blood or marriage, brought together by shared values. Often deemed threatening to an established order, communal groups challenge 'sacred' institutions – e.g. capitalism, the nuclear family, Christianity – by providing alternative pathways of life. Typically, communal groups are 'outside' the society. Societal controls are limited, and do not impinge on the 'inner' commitments of members. Censure therefore can result in reactive solidarity of members who see themselves as 'persecuted' *because* their cause is just (e.g. the Peoples Temple at Jonestown). Even without persecution, diminished external controls promote the emergence of a 'state within a state'. Indeed, the founders of communal groups often seek to create a total institution, to nurture a shared utopian, but socially deviant, way of life.

Sometimes social conditions spawn great numbers of communal groups, as with the counterculture during the 1960s (Zablocki, 1980; Berger, 1981). Different groups share a critique of an established order and a broad ethic of communal association, but they are best understood as alternative ways out of the established order: (1) 'communes' of friendship and family-like solidarity; (2) 'warring sects' struggling against an established order; (3) 'other-worldly sects' of true believers living in heavens-on-earth; (4) rationalistic 'intentional associations' based on pluralism, equality, and justice; (5) 'communities' embracing an egalitarian solidarity of the 'many who act as one'; and (6) 'ecstatic associations' dedicated to transcending ordinary reality through orgy or meditation (Hall, 1978).

Where do the ways out lead? Most groups fail to survive over a generation. Kanter (1972) has shown that, among nineteenth-century American groups, surviving groups are likely to have solved commitment problems of continuity, cohesiveness, and control. The communal groups structured to resolve commitment problems are not communes and intentional associations, but communities – which sustain cohesiveness through ethnic boundaries – and other-wordly sects, which maintain social control through spiritual hierarchies.

But organizational persistence is not the only measure of effectiveness. Communal groups engage in cultural innovation, serving as seedbeds of alternative ways of life. If the alternatives resolve cultural dilemmas of a wider society, they may be adopted among various social strata whose material and spiritual interests make them receptive to the new ways. The classic case is Protestant inner-wordly asceticism, with its origins in Christian monasticism (Hall, 1978).

But the utopian dream of a communal society-at-large remains elusive. Communalism does not align well with the imperatives of the capitalist world economy, much less with prevailing political and social interests. Nonetheless, as was the case with the rise of modern capitalism, an ethic diffused from communal groups could transform the world, by providing a new basis of social and economic life. Certain modern tendencies toward collectivist institutions should leave us to ponder whether Karl Marx may have been right to anticipate communism as a logical outgrowth of capitalist rationalization. If communalism becomes 'scientific' (that is, rational) rather than 'utopian', it may become the order of the day.

John R. Hall
University of Missouri, Columbia

References

Berger, B. M. (1981), *The Survival of a Counterculture: Ideological Work and Everyday Life among Rural Communards*, Berkeley and Los Angeles.
Hall, J. R. (1978), *The Ways Out; Utopian Communal Groups in an Age of Babylon*, London.
Kanter, R. M. (1972), *Commitment and Community: Communes and Utopias in Sociological Perspective*, Cambridge, Mass.
Zablocki, B. D. (1980), *Alienation and Charisma: A Study of Contemporary American Communes*, New York.
See also: *sects and cults; utopianism.*

Communication Networks

A network can be defined as a particular type of relation that links a set of people or objects, called the 'nodes' of the network (Mitchell, 1969). The communication relation is defined as the channels through which messages are transmitted by people who comprise a social system (Farace *et al.*, 1977). Sometimes researchers are interested in examining multiple relations among the same set of nodes. These 'multiplex' relations will produce unique networks, since different types of relations define different networks. For example, the relation 'seeks advice from' will probably create a quite different network among the same set of people than the relation 'flirts with'.

The communication relation has been studied in various social systems and at differing levels of analysis. In the area of interpersonal relations, Parks and Adelman (1983) have examined the role of a friend and family communication networks on the development of romantic relations, and Bott (1971) has explored the implications of different communication patterns developed by husbands and wives. In the context of small group behaviour, a long series of studies has focused on the effects of differing network structures on the performance and satisfaction of group members engaged in problem solving (Collins and Raven, 1969; Shaw, 1964). Considerable research has been conducted on communication and information flow in production, innovation, and informal social networks within large organizations. For instance, Monge, Edwards and Kirste (1983) showed that proximity, propensity to communicate, and commitment to the organization were important antecedents to the involvement of individuals in organizational networks. There is likewise a rapidly growing literature on the communication linkages among inter-organizational systems. This research examines such phenomena as interlocking corporate directorates, interdependent health care delivery systems, and community development projects (Eisenberg *et al.*, 1983). At the broader societal and cultural levels, Rogers and Kincaid (1981) describe the uses of network analysis for the diffusion of ideas. Typical of this approach is their analysis of the communication patterns for the diffusion of family planning among 69 women in the Korean village of Oryu Li. These examples all employ 'people' as the nodes of the communication network, but this need not be the case. For example, Reeves and Borgman (1983) used communication network analysis to demonstrate the influence and show the citation patterns among nine core journals in the field of communication.

Farace and Mabee (1980) indicate that two major objectives of network analysis are structural articulation and network metrics. In structural articulation, individuals are assigned to various network role classifications such as clique member, liaison, and isolate. Liaisons do not belong to particular groups but have information linkages with people in two or more groups; they frequently figure importantly in linking groups together. As the name implies, isolates have few, if any, connections within the network. Research has shown that liaisons, isolates, and group members have different characteristics and function quite differently in communication networks (Roberts and O'Reilly, 1978). Network metrics refers to quantitative indices of various aspects of the network. The most frequently studied indices include reachability, density, centrality, and dominance.

Techniques for observing communication networks are many and varied. Often people are asked to recall their interactions with all other network members and to report the frequency, duration, and importance of these contacts. In some studies, participants have been asked to keep diaries of their interactions during a given time period. In other research, participant-observers have logged the frequency of interactions among people in an organization. In one interesting series of studies, Milgram (1967) asked people to send a message to an unknown target by sending it through someone they knew personally. That process was repeated at each step until a person was eventually found who knew the target and delivered the message. In yet another study, Bernard and Killworth (1980) collected data about the communication networks among ham radio operators by recording their public dialogue on the radio waves. A final example is the work of Rice (1982), who used a computer to record the frequency and duration of communication linkages among a group of scientists utilizing a teleconferencing system.

Analysis of communication network data, whether network articulation or network metrics, is laborious, especially if undertaken by hand. Consequently, most network data are analysed by computer. Several good programs are currently available at major computing centres around the world, and the interested reader is directed to Rice and Richards (1983) and Rogers and Kincaid (1981) as starting points for comparing alternatives. The programs differ considerably in terms of the assumptions they make about network data, objectives of the analysis, computational algorithms, efficiency, and cost.

Peter R. Monge
University of Southern California
Gerald R. Miller
Michigan State University

References

Bernard, H. R. and Killworth, P. D. (1980), 'Informant accuracy in social network data IV: a comparison of clique-level structure in behavioral and cognitive network data', *Social Networks*, 2.

Collins, B. E. and Raven, B. H. (1969), 'Group structure: attraction, coalitions, communication, and power', in G. Lindzey and E. Aronson (eds), *The Handbook of Social Psychology* (2nd edn), Reading, Mass.

Eisenberg, E. M., Farace, R. V., Monge, P. R., Bettinghaus, E. P., Kurchner-Hawkins, R., Miller, K. I. and White, L. (1983), 'Communication linkages in interorganizational systems: review and synthesis', in B. Dervin and M. Voight (eds), *Progress in Communication Science*, Vol. 6, Norwood, NJ.

Farace, R. V. and Mabee, T. (1980), 'Communication network analysis methods', in P. R. Monge and J. N. Cappella (eds), *Multivariate Techniques in Human Communication Research*, New York.

Farace, R. V., Monge, P. R. and Russell, H. M. (1977), *Communicating and Organizing*, Reading, Mass.

Milgram, S. (1967), 'The small world problem', *Psychology Today*, 1.

Mitchell, J. C. (1969), 'The concept and use of social networks', in J. C. Mitchell (ed.), *Social Networks in Urban Situations*, Manchester.

Monge, P. R., Edwards, J. A. and Kirste, K. K. (1983), 'Determinants of communication network involvement: connectedness and integration', *Group and Organization Studies*, 8.

Parks, M. R. and Adelman, M. B. (1983), 'Communication networks and the development of romantic relationships', *Human Communication Research*, 10.

Reeves, B. and Borgman, C. L. (1983), 'A bibliometric evaluation of core journals in communication research', *Human Communication Research*, 10.

Rice, R. E. (1982), 'Communication networking in computer conferencing systems: a longitudinal study of group roles and system structure', in M. Burgoon (ed.), *Communication Yearbook 6*, Beverly Hills.

Rice, R. E. and Richards, W. D. (1983), 'An overview of network analysis methods and programs', in

B. Dervin and M. Voight (eds), *Progress in Communication Sciences*, vol. 6, Norwood, NJ.

Roberts, K. H. and O'Reilly, C. A. (1978), 'Organizations as communication structures: an empirical approach', *Human Communication Research*, 4.

Rogers, E. M. and Kincaid, D. L. (1981), *Communication Networks: Toward a New Paradigm for Research*, New York.

Shaw, M. E. (1964), 'Communication networks', in L. Berkowitz (ed.), *Advances in Experimental Social Psychology*, vol. 1, New York.

Communications

The social scientific study of human communication began during the late 1930s in the United States. Schramm (1983) attributes the birth of this movement to four fathers: the political scientist, Harold Lasswell; the sociologist, Paul Lazarsfeld; and the social psychologists, Kurt Lewin and Carl Hovland. Though the parentage of any scholarly movement is bound to be ambiguous, many communication researchers would doubtless concur with Schramm's attribution, for these four pioneers not only authored much of the early influential communication research; they also were responsible for training a second generation of scholars who carried on their work.

The work of two of these founding fathers, Lasswell and Lazarsfeld, centred almost exclusively on the impact of mass media on public information and attitudes, with some of Hovland's (1949) work at Yale University focusing on the same problem. At the time, considerable apprehension was being voiced about the possible manipulative power of the media; the 'hypodermic needle' model of medial effects metaphorically posited that the media could 'inject' new information and attitudes into individual citizens in much the same way as a doctor could inject serum into a patient. As a result of the classic election studies conducted in the 1940s by Lazarsfeld and his colleagues (1948), a different, less communicatively hegemonous view of the mass media emerged, one positing that the media transmitted information to opinion leaders who, in turn, employed it to influence others in face-to-face settings – a process labelled 'the two-step flow hypothesis'. Although later research revealed that both the hypodermic-needle model and the two-step flow hypothesis were oversimplified explanations of the impact of mass media on individual attitudes and behaviours, these two notions exerted a strong influence on the thinking of mass communication researchers for several decades.

During roughly the same time period, Lewin was conducting his famous studies at the University of Iowa concerning the effects of group decision making (1958) and group leadership (Lewin, 1939; Lippitt and White, 1943) on the productivity and morale of group members, studies motivated at least partially by his repugnance for the Fascist regimes emerging in Germany and Italy. With the advent of the Second World War, concern for ways of mounting effective public information campaigns against these Axis powers spawned the remarkably fruitful programme of research on communication and persuasion carried out by Hovland and his associates at Yale, a programme which produced an influential set of volumes which began appearing around the mid-1900s (Rosenberg *et al.*, 1960; Sherif and Hovland, 1961).

As the preceding chronicle suggests, most groundbreaking early work was problem-oriented and was conducted by scholars of varying disciplinary commitments. Communication did not emerge as an academic discipline until the 1950s, one of the earliest signs of its emergence being the establishment of a Communication Research Institute at the University of Illinois under the directorship of Wilbur Schramm. In 1955, Michigan State University established a College of Communication Arts and Sciences which eventually included one of the first formal departments dedicated to the social-scientific study of communication. Chaired by David Berlo, whose book *The Process of Communication* (1961) exerted a strong influence on the contemporary scene, the Department of Communication was staffed by faculty whose degrees were from departments of journalism, speech, sociology, psychology, and political science; all shared a common commitment to studying human communication scientifically.

The growth of communication as a discipline accelerated rapidly in the 1960s and 1970s. Two Annenberg Schools of Communication were founded, the first at the University of Pennsylvania and the second at the University of Southern California. Schools of Communication were also established at such institutions as Ohio University, the University of Texas, and the University of Kentucky. Finally, while retaining other traditional scholarly and professional components, numerous departments of journalism and speech communication made valuable contributions to the social-scientific study of human communication.

As with most fledgling academic enterprises, consensus regarding conceptual delineation of the field has emerged slowly and equivocally. One approach to defining the field has focused on the various situational contexts in which communication may occur (Miller, 1978). This category system has produced researchers interested in mass communication, organizational communication, small-group communication, interpersonal communication, and, most recently, even intrapersonal communication. A second approach has focused on various functions of communication, with persuasion or social influence receiving the lion's share of attention. Indeed, until the last 10 or 15 years, most of the theoretical, methodological, and empirical literature was devoted to the persuasion process. McGuire's (1969) ambitious summary of attitude and attitude-change work through the late 1960s has 42 pages of references dealing with the topic.

Though persuasion research is certainly not a dead issue (Miller and Burgoon, 1978), students of communication have diversified their interests considerably. Spurred by several important educational and scholarly occurrences, including the growth of interpersonal classes in the universities and the publication of Watzlawick, Beavin and Jackson's (1967) *Pragmatics of Human Communication*, a number of researchers have turned to the study of symbolic transactions in more intimate, face-to-face settings. A lively interest has developed in examining message exchanges from a transactional, relational perspective (Ericson and Rogers, 1973; Millar and Rogers, 1976; Rogers and Farace, 1975). Rather than using individual communicators as the unit of analysis, this approach uses the relationship: 'the focus of analysis is on the systemic properties that the participants have collectively, not individually' (Rogers and Farace, 1975). Furthermore, greater emphasis has been placed on investigating communication relationships developmentally, that is, in looking at the evolution of relationships over time. During initial encounters, communicators relate to each other primarily as undifferentiated role occupants; should the relationship continue, they may be motivated to seek information which distinguishes other relational partners as individuals (Miller and Sunnafrank, 1982). 'To achieve *interpersonal understanding*, the persons must be engaged in a symbolic exchange which both sets the knowledge generation processes in motion and serves to verify a considerable number of mutual descriptions, predictions, and explanations' (Berger, Gardner, Parks, Schulman and Miller, 1976). This approach can be tested adequately only by studies which examine communication relationships across relatively extended time periods.

Two major paradigmatic alternatives have emerged to the established approaches: (1) The systems perspective (Monge, 1977; Watzlawick, Beavin and Jackson, 1967) stresses the structure and organization of all components of a system, rather than focusing on one or more underlying elements as would a reductionist approach. Moreover, systems theory is not grounded in one 'monolithic logical framework' but rather lends itself to at least three alternative logics (Monge, 1977). (2) The major paradigmatic alternative, the rules perspective (Cronen, Pearce and Harris, 1982; Cushman, Valentinsen and Dietrich, 1982;

Pearce and Cronen, 1980), places the communicator, as *actor*, theoretically centre-stage, and asserts the theoretical import of notions such as 'intention', volition', 'motive', and 'choice'. Communicators themselves both negotiate new rules and abandon old ones – processes involving intent and choice.

As the study of communication moves toward the year 2000, these paradigmatic debates, buttressed, one hopes, by more durable research foundations, will doubtless continue. In addition, the burgeoning communication technology is likely to generate more intensive efforts to identify the interfaces between mediated and face-to-face communication systems. Technological developments probably exert more basic, profound influences on people's daily interpersonal transactions than were ever envisioned by proponents of the hypodermic-needle and two-step flow interpretations of media effects (Miller, 1982). The precise nature of these influences constitutes an important priority for future communication research.

Gerald Miller
Michigan State University

References
Berger, C. R. *et al.* (1976), 'Interpersonal epistemology and interpersonal communication', in G. R. Miller (ed.), *Explorations in Interpersonal Communication*, Beverly Hills, Cal.
Berlo, D. K. (1961), *The Process of Communication*, New York.
Cronen, V. E., Pearce, W. B. and Harris, L. M. (1982), 'The coordinated management of meaning: a theory of communication', in F.E.X. Dance (ed.), *Human Communication Theory*, New York.
Cushman, D. P., Valentinsen, B. and Dietrich, D. (1982), 'A rules theory of interpersonal relationships', in F.E.X. Dance (ed.), *Human Communication Theory*, New York.
Ericson, P. M. and Rogers, L. E. (1973), 'New procedures for analysing relational communication', *Family Process*, 12.
Hovland, C. I., Lumsdaine, A. A. and Sheffield, F. D. (1949), *Experiments on Mass Communication*, Princeton.
Lazarsfeld, P., Berelson, B. and Gaudet, H. (1948), *The People's Choice*, New York.
Lewin, K. (1958), 'Group decision and social change', in E. E. Maccoby, T. M. Newcomb and E. E. Hartley (eds), *Readings in Social Psychology*, New York.
Lewin, K., Lippitt, R. and White, R. K. (1939), 'Patterns of aggressive behavior in

experimentally created social climates', *Journal of Social Psychology*, 10.

Lippitt, R. and White, R. K. (1943), 'The social climate of children's groups', in R. G. Barker, J. Kounin and H. Wright (eds), *Child Behavior and Development*, New York.

McGuire, W. J. (1969), 'The nature of attitudes and attitude change', in G. Lindzey and E. Aronson (eds), *Handbook of Social Psychology*, vol. 3, Reading, Mass.

Millar, F. E. and Rogers, L. E. (1976), 'A relational approach to interpersonal communication', in G. R. Miller (ed.), *Explorations in Interpersonal Communication*, Beverly Hills, Cal.

Miller, G. R. (1982), 'A neglected connection: mass media exposure and interpersonal communicative competency', in G. Gumpert and R. Cathcart (eds), *Intermedia: Interpersonal Communication in a Media World*, 2nd edn, New York.

Miller, G. R. and Burgoon, M. (1978), 'Persuasion research: review and commentary', in B. D. Ruben (ed.), *Communication Yearbook 2*, New Brunswick, N.J.

Miller, G. R. and Sunnafrank, M. J. (1982), 'All is for one but one is not for all: a conceptual perspective of interpersonal communication', in F.E.X. Dance (ed.), *Human Communication Theory*, New York.
theoretical basis for the study of human communication', *Communication Quarterly*, 25.

Pearce, W. B. and Cronen, V. E. (1980), *Communication, Action, and Meaning: The Creation of Social Realities*, New York.

Rogers, L. E. and Farace, R. V. (1975), 'Analysis of relational communication in dyads: new measurement procedures', *Human Communication Research*, 1.

Rosenberg, M. J. *et al.* (1960), *Attitude Organization and Change*, New Haven, Conn.

Schramm, W. (1983), 'The unique perspective of communication: a retrospective view', *Journal of Communication*, 33.

Sherif, M. and Hovland, C. I. (1961), *Social Judgment: Assimilation and Contrast Effects in Communication and Attitude Change*, New Haven, Conn.

Watzlawick, P., Beavin, J. and Jackson, D. D. (1967), *Pragmatics of Human Communication*, New York.

See also: *attitudes; communication networks; generalized media; mass media*.

Communism

Communism connotes any societal arrangement based on communal ownership, production, consumption, self-government, perhaps even communal sexual mating. The term refers both to such societies and practices and to any theory advocating them. Examples of the former can be found in religious orders throughout history and in radical communities, from the sixteenth-century Anabaptists to the contemporary 'counterculture'; and the most famous example of advocacy of communism may well be the regime proposed for the guardian caste in Plato's *Republic*.

In the middle of the nineteenth century, the most radical schools of the growing socialist movement, including that of Marx and Engels, called themselves communists in order to dissociate themselves from other, allegedly less consistent, socialist groups. Hence when reference is made to that period, communism often is synonymous with the system of ideas developed by Engels and Marx, even though they often used the terms 'communism' and 'socialism' interchangeably. Communism in this sense connotes the sum-total of Marxist doctrines; hence it is the Marxist critique of capitalism and liberal theory and the project for the proletarian revolution, though at times it connotes specifically the ultimate goal of that revolution – the society visualized as emerging out of it, which is dimly foreseen as a society without property, without classes or a division of labour, without institutions of coercion and domination. The precise features of this society are not delineated in the writings of Marx and Engels, and among Marxists there are controversies about the degree of residual alienation and oppression (if any) that one ought to expect in the communist society of the future. Some of the hints Marx and Engels themselves gave come from their notion of a primitive communism allegedly prevailing among the savage early ancestors of the human race.

Among the earliest followers of Engels and Marx, the term fell into disuse; most Marxists around the turn of the century called themselves Social-Democrats. The term was revived after the Russian Revolution of 1917 by V. I. Lenin, who renamed his faction of the Russian Marxist movement the 'Communist Party' and compelled all those parties who wished to join the newly-created Third (or Communist) International to adopt the same designation, so as to dissociate themselves from the Social-Democratic parties. As a consequence, communism since then connotes that interpretation of Marxism which considers the ideas and actions of Lenin and his Bolshevik faction to be the only correct interpretation of Marxism, and the sum-total of parties that subscribe to this interpretation.

Leninism is characterized by the insistence that meaningful social change can come only through revolution, while reforms threaten to corrupt the oppressed. Further, it implies the application of Marxism to countries where capitalism is underdeveloped, hence the development of flexible political strategies, including the mobilization of peasants and ethnic minorities for revolution. Foremost, it insists on the need for a 'vanguard party' of revolutionaries-by-profession to whom correct knowledge of the laws of history and politics ('consciousness') is attributed. Within the party and its numerous auxiliary organizations designed to mobilize the working class and its presumed allies, the vanguard is expected to ensure the prevalence of enlightened 'consciousness' over blind passion by a combination of mass initiative and bureaucratic control that Lenin called 'democratic centralism'. Finally, Leninism implies the accumulated experience of the Russian Communist Party in governing their country. Communism thus connotes the theory and practice of rule by communist parties.

Although the leaders of ruling communist parties have generally refrained from claiming that the systems they were ruling were communist, it has become customary in the Western world to refer to them as communist systems. Communism thus refers to any society or group of societies governed by communist parties.

The mature form of communist rule was developed in the USSR under the rule of J. V. Stalin. Hence Communism since the 1930s has become synonymous with Stalinism or Neo-Stalinism. This is a system in which the communist party proclaims itself the enlightened leadership and claims authority to speak for the entire nation. It enforces this claim through control over all organizations and associations, all forms of communication, education, and entertainment, individual appointments and careers. The chief aim of these systems is rapid economic growth through crash programmes of industrialization, carried out through a centralized command economy. Communism in its Stalinist form thus is a species of entrepreneurship.

Contemporary communist societies thus bear no resemblance to the vision of communism sketched by Marx and Engels or even to that provided by Lenin in his unfinished work, *The State and Revolution*. Yet the memory of that vision lingers and has repeatedly led to attempts within communist parties to define alternatives to Leninist and Stalinist theories and practices. Contemporary communism therefore is not one single orthodoxy, but an ever growing cluster of orthodoxies and heresies, all of them backing up their arguments by reference to Engels and Marx, yet fiercely contending with each other.

Alfred G. Meyer
University of Michigan

Further Reading
Claudin, F. (1975), *The Communist Movement: From Comintern to Cominform*, London.
Daniels, R. V. (ed.) (1965), *Marxism and Communism: Essential Readings*, New York.
Kolakowski, L. (1978), *Main Currents of Marxism*, 3 vols, Oxford.
Meyer, A. G. (1984), *Communism* (4th edn), New York.
Rosenberg, A. (1967), *A History of Bolshevism*, New York.
See also: *socialism*.

Community

The term community relates to a wide range of phenomena and has been used as an omnibus word loaded with diverse associations. In 1955, Hillery unearthed no less than 94 definitions of community (Hillery, 1955), and its definition has continued to be a thriving intellectual pastime of sociologists.

A preliminary confusion arises between community as a type of *collectivity* or social unit, and community as a type of *social relationship* or sentiment. The root of the problem could be traced to Tönnies's *Gemeinschaft*, which uses the term to describe both a collectivity and a social relationship. Subsequently, most scholars have used community to connote a form of collectivity (with or without *Gemeinschaft* ties), but some, such as Nisbet (1953), have kept the community-as-sentiment approach alive in their emphasis on 'the quest for community' and their concern with the loss of community in modern life. These approaches are clearly mixed with some nostalgia for a glorious past in which people were thought to be more secure, less alienated and less atomized. But, as Schmalenbach (1960) pointed out, Tönnies's *Gemeinschaft* implied a spontaneous, taken-for-granted relationship. Fellowship ties which are consciously sought and are more emotionally-laden better fit what he called communion (*bund*) ties, such as those found in religious sects or ideological groups. Communion ties are often created by precisely those people who are dissatisfied with the routinization (hence loss of meaning and involvement) of the extant community ties.

Community, in the sense of type of collectivity, usually refers to (1) a group sharing a defined physical space or geographical area such as a neighbourhood, city, village or hamlet; (2) a group sharing common traits, a sense of belonging and/or maintaining social ties and interactions which shape it into a distinctive social entity, such as an ethnic, religious, academic or professional community. The differences are between what may be called territorial and non-territorial approaches. For some scholars (Park, 1929; Hawley, 1950) the most important basis of commonality is common territory. While they do not dismiss the essential element of common ties, these ties are not sufficient in themselves to constitute a community. The non-territorial approach stresses the common ties at the expense of territory. Community still denotes a *social entity* with common ties and not the ties themselves, but territory is not a necessary ingredient of commonality.

Common ties and a sense of belonging may derive from beliefs in a common past or a common fate, common values, interests, kinship relations and so on, none of which presuppose living together, as illustrated by ethnic or religious communities whose members might be geographically dispersed. But this approach stresses social ties without indicating what is distinctive about community ties compared to ties of other collectivities. Since locality is not the distinctive feature in this approach, one looks for distinctiveness elsewhere, most plausibly in the type of ties. This may in turn recreate the confusion between community as a form of collectivity or community as a form of human bond. The non-territorial approach has gained force as a result of modern advances in communication which have reduced the importance of territorial proximity as a basis for human association, increasingly creating what Webber (1964) called 'community without propinquity'. A related non-territorial approach is found among social network theorists, some of whom also object to treating communities as social entities in their own right, regarding this a legacy of Durkheimian corporationist tendencies as opposed to Simmel's interactionist approach (Boissevain, 1968).

Hillery (1968) and Gottschalk (1975) have made the most systematic attempt to differentiate between formal organization and community (or rather communal organization). The formal organization's primary orientation towards a specific, defining goal is contrasted with the communal organization's primarily diffuse goal orientation. In their goal-related activities, members of formal organizations relate to one another as specific role-bearers, while relations among members of communal organizations are more diffuse, encompassing a larger aspect of one another's life. Corporations, schools, churches, armies, political movements, professional associations are all formal organizations, while families, ethnic groups and neighbourhoods are communal organizations. Communal and formal organizations can, of course, include subunits of the opposite kind, as for example informal community-like friendship groups among workers of an industrial plant, or, by contrast, voluntary associations created within a neighbourhood or an ethnic community.

Delineating the boundaries of communities is one of the greatest difficulties hampering their proper identification. The lack of clear boundaries is indeed one of the major properties of communities as compared to formal organizations (Hillery, 1968). In non-territorial communities, clear boundaries and sharp differentiation between members and non-members are signs of association formation within the community, which brings it closer to the formal organizaton pole. In territorial communities, if no size limitations are set on 'the people living together' which the community is said to represent, the concept may be stretched to include an entire nation or even the world at large (Warren, 1973). Some scholars (Hawley, 1950) prefer to limit community to a size which enables the inhabitants to have a diffuse familiarity with the everyday life of the area. While one knows about special events that occur outside the community, familiarity with one's own community includes ordinary events which would not draw attention elsewhere. This would exclude global, national and metropolitan areas from being called communities.

However a measure of maximal size may be specified, what would be the minimal size of a territorial community? The smaller the community, the greater its members' familiarity with routine life, but would that make a single house (or an apartment building) a community? According to Warren, some basic functions have to be performed in each community, including the provision of basic economic needs, socialization, social control, social participation and mutual support (Warren, 1973). The community might depend on external organizations in performing these functions, and community members do not have to prefer locally offered services to external ones, but some activity has to take place in the community in each of these spheres. This would exclude an apartment building or a modern nuclear family from being a community in its own right, though not necessarily the pre-modern extended family household. A related feature of community stressed in the literature is its being a microcosm of society. The community, unlike other collectivities, is a social system in itself, including such subsystems as government, economy, education, religion, and family found in a larger society. A certain size has to be attained for these institutional spheres to manifest themselves. It is also possible that the community loses some of its multifaceted characteristics in more developed societies, becoming less differentiated as societies become more so (Elias, 1974).

The conceptual disarray of social science regarding community has not prevented an abundance of community studies, some of which are among the best-known pieces of social science literature. The various urban studies of the Chicago School in the 1920s and 1930s, Warner's *Yankee City*, Redfield's *Tepotzlan: A Mexican Village*, Whyte's *Street Corner Society*, Gans's *Urban Villagers* and *Levittowners* are just a few examples of a much longer list. Scholarly interest in community has included units of greatly different size, autonomy, demographic composition, technological, economic or cultural traits. Community characteristics have been used to explain other phenomena – inequality, deviance, transformative capacity. Special attention has focused on the extent to which urban-rural differences can explain variations in community structure and interactions (Wirth, 1938). Doubts have been raised about the narrative style and idiosyncratic methodology of most community studies which make them irreproducible and hard to compare. Ruth Glass called them 'the poor sociologist's substitute for the novel' (Bell and Newby, 1971), but perhaps this concrete quality and the 'story' that they carried has been their greatest advantage.

Victor Azarya
Hebrew University, Jerusalem

References

Bell, C. and Newby, H. (1971), *Community Studies*, London.
Boissevain, J. (1968), 'The place of non-groups in the social sciences', *Man*, 3.
Elias, N. (1974), 'Towards a theory of communities', in C. Bell and H. Newby (eds), *The Sociology of Community*, London.
Gottschalk, S. (1975), *Communities and Alternatives*, Cambridge, Mass.
Hawley, A. (1950), *Human Ecology: A Theory of Community Structure*, New York.
Hillery, G. A. Jr (1955), 'Definitions of community: areas of agreement', *Rural Sociology*, 20.
Hillery, G. A. Jr (1968), *Communal Organizations*, Chicago.
Nisbet, R. A. (1953), *The Quest for Community*, New York.
Park, R. E. and Burgess, E. W. (1929), *Introduction to the Science of Sociology*, 2nd edn, Chicago.
Schmalenbach, H. (1961), 'The sociological category of communion', in T. Parsons *et al.* (eds), *Theories of Society*, 2 vols, New York.
Warren, R. (1973), *The Community in America*, Chicago.
Webber, M. M. (1964), 'The urban place and the nonplace urban realm', in M. M. Webber *et al.* (eds), *Explorations into Urban Structure*, Philadelphia.
Wirth, L. (1938), 'Urbanism as a way of life', *American Journal of Sociology*, 44.

See also: *city; networks; Tönnies.*

Community Development

In the context of public policy, the phrase community development has most often been used to describe projects initiated by, or with the active participation of, the inhabitants of a locality, which are intended to benefit them collectively. The projects may concern education, social welfare, health, infrastructure such as roads, wells or irrigation, farming, manufacture or commerce. While much of the benefit may accrue to individual families, the projects are intended to enhance the community as a whole, in self-confidence and political skills, for instance, even if not more tangibly.

This conception of community development was widely adopted by British, French and Belgian colonial administrations in Africa and Asia, especially after the Second World War, as a social and political as much as economic strategy for rural areas. In British Africa, for example, Departments of Community Development were created with Community Development Officers trained according to increasingly self-conscious principles of professional community development practice (du Sautoy, 1968; Batten, 1962). The stimulation of local leadership, the growth of capacity to initiate projects and organize self-help, and the learning of skills were characteristically considered more important than the achievements of any particular project. The ideal Community Development Officer was therefore a facilitator, adviser and sensitive guide, who sought to encourage a collective capacity for initiative and organization that would then continue independently.

In practice, the Community Development Officer's role was more ambivalent than this ideal allowed. As a government employee, he was bound to favour local initiatives which corresponded with national policy and discourage others. His intervention was often crucial in drawing local factions into co-operation and in securing resources. Hence community development remained essentially an aspect of government policy, although a variety of mutual aid and village development associations evolved independently of government – as for instance in Eastern Nigeria.

After independence, community development was seen as a means of mobilizing rural people for such endeavours as mass literacy or education, as for instance in the movement for self-reliance in Tanzania, or the Harambee movement in Kenya. But the inherent ambiguity remains of a strategy intended both to encourage self-help and initiative while implementing national government's goals.

In the 1960s, the term community development came to be applied to projects in predominantly urban neighbourhoods of America and later Britain, where poverty and social pathologies were believed to concentrate. Like their colonial predecessors, these projects were intended both to provide practical benefits, such as improved social services, more relevant vocational training, legal aid, low-cost housing and more jobs, and in doing so, to increase the community's sense of its collective competence. In the United States, this approach became national policy under Title II of the Economic Opportunity Act of 1964, following earlier experiments by the Ford Foundation and the President's Committee on Juvenile Delinquency (Marris and Rein, 1980) and was continued in many subsequent policies, such as the Model Cities Program and Community Development Block Grants from the federal to local governments. Besides community action agencies, largely concerned with social welfare and educational programmes, community development corporations were funded to promote housing and commercial enterprises, especially in neighbourhoods of high unemployment. The Watts Labor Community Action Coalition, for instance, has, at various times, developed produce markets, a bus service, a large shopping centre, and housing in a Black district of Los Angeles (Hampden-Turner, 1974). Apart from housing, Development Corporations have experienced great difficulties in sustaining viable commercial enterprises in their communities. In most instances, the attempt to fulfil social purposes, such as employment opportunities for local residents, in market settings which more experienced commercial enterprises have already judged unprofitable, proves too difficult even with the help of subsidies. Over time, therefore, the Corporations tend either to withdraw from commercial endeavours or to defer many of their original social reasons for starting them.

The British Community Development Project, modelled on American Community Action agencies, was initiated in 1969 by the Home Office with a similar hope of stimulating self-help and innovative solutions in neighbourhoods of concentrated social problems, choosing for the experiment twelve mostly urban neighbourhoods in Britain (Marris, 1982). Over time, as concern shifted from social pathology – which was neither as apparent nor as concentrated as had been assumed – to unemployment, the project had to confront the difficulty of applying very localized resources to remedy the effects of large-scale changes of economic structure.

Both the British and American projects were regarded as experimental by the governments which initiated them. Community development, in this context, was intended to discover inexpensive solutions to problems of poverty and unemployment, through self-help and innovative, more relevant and efficient use of resources already allocated. It has therefore never received funding on a scale commensurate with the problems it addressed. Its most lasting achievement, especially in the United States, probably lies in the growing sophistication and organizational capacity of neighbourhood groups in dealing with economic and physical changes which affect them.

Peter Marris
University of California
Los Angeles

References

Batten, T. R. (1962), *Training for Community Development*, London.

du Sautoy, P. (1958), *Community Development in Ghana*, London.

Hampden-Turner, C. (1974), *From Poverty to Dignity: A Strategy for Poor Americans*, Garden City, N.Y.

Marris, P. and Rein, M. (1980), *Dilemmas of Social Reform*, 3rd edn, Chicago.

Marris, P. (1982), *Community Planning and Conceptions of Change*, London.

Comparative Politics

'I think, consequently I am comparing,' began a recent text in comparative politics (Dogan and Pelassy, 1984). Students of politics through the ages have used the comparative method and some – like J. S. Mill – have even theorized about it. However, the universality of comparison in political science has led to no real unity on *how* to compare, *what* to compare, and *how much* to compare. There are three main traditions in the field: (1) the study of foreign governments; (2) the comparison of whole political systems; (3) the use of comparative materials to analyse problems within political systems.

(1) *The study of foreign governments* can be divided between studies which cover the same ground for a number of countries – but with little or no theoretical framework – and studies which, while less superficially rigorous, often contain gems of insight or theory. The emphasis of the first type is usually on institutions and can be seen at its best in the work of Bryce (1963) and Friedrich (1950); the emphasis of the second is more often on politics and is at its best in the hands of a Tocqueville (1945 [1835–40]). At first limited to the great Western democracies, work in this tradition has more recently come to comprehend the study of totalitarian systems and of the Third World as well, usually in the form of teaching texts which select one or two countries for examination from among each type of state.

(2) *The comparative analysis* of whole systems dates back to the constitutional typologies of the classical tradition, but took on new life in a different form after the Second World War, especially in the United States. Though the classical theorists were most interested in legal forms, contemporary analysts try to comprehend in their concept of 'system' political inputs into the government and policy outputs as well (Almond and Powell, 1966). A strong impetus in this direction came from functionalist sociology in the 1960s. More recently, whole system analysis has been encouraged by the revival of the concept of the state and by a growing interest in political economy.

(3) *The use of comparative materials* to analyse within-system problems is the least well-defined tradition, but the most vital part of the field. Its subject matter is as broad as politics itself, from comparative elections and voting behaviour to parties and interest groups, parliaments and executives, to public policy, political economy and planning. Methodological approaches are equally diverse, leading to a fragmentation of research effort that hampers both communication and cumulation of findings. For example, the dominant

form of voting analysis in France until recently has been electoral geography, which makes comparison immensely difficult with the largely survey-based tradition of voting research in Britain and the United States.

Comparative politics has been peculiarly open to influence from other disciplines, ranging from law and history to anthropology and sociology and, most recently, economics. Among the three main traditions, the country-by-country approach has been the most legalistic and historical, the comparative analysis of whole systems more influenced by macrosociology or economics, and the study of intrasystemic problems through the use of comparative materials the most diverse in its disciplinary influences. This too has contributed to the richness of the field, but has hampered communication and cumulation of research findings.

Though comparative theorists have from time to time proposed overall paradigms for the field, area specialization, methodological diversity, and changing political conditions have inhibited these efforts. The idea of 'development' in the 1960s and that of 'dependency' in the 1970s are illustrative. The evolutionary model behind the former and the world-system perspective driving the latter were not shared by most comparativists and appeared inappropriate or inadequate to the experiences of many countries.

Comparativists also differ regarding the optimal spread of countries for comparison. Theorists like Przeworski and Teune (1970) argue powerfully for 'most different systems' designs whose logic – like that of statistical analysis – is to maximize the measurable variance in independent variables. Others prefer 'most similar systems' designs, in order to minimize the unmeasured variance in intervening variables. While the first approach leads naturally to statistical analysis of a large number of countries, the latter is more congenial to paired comparisons of similar nations.

With so fragile a theoretical or methodological unity, comparative politics has been particularly vulnerable to fads and fashions. In the 1960s, it seemed as if the field would share in the behavioural revolution that was sweeping American political science; that it would become more explicitly comparative and macrosystemic in character: and that research would more and more shift to the developing areas and away from the old parliamentary democracies of Western Europe and North America.

But these innovations – even had they been as irresistible as they seemed at the time – pulled in different directions. The behavioural revolution had individual and group political behaviour as its subject, while comparative macro-theory focused on the political system as a whole. Generalizing about whole political systems on the basis of group or individual data could be hazardous in the extreme. At the same time, the attempt to integrate the Third World into comparative politics was discouraged by the shifting and volatile regimes in those countries, by growing resentments against Western 'cultural imperialism', and by the difficulty of finding conceptual common denominators between these countries and the parliamentary democracies of the West. As for the Socialist systems of the East, they have never been adequately integrated within comparative politics, particularly as the internal diversity of the Socialist world increased in the 1960s and 1970s.

Surveying British and American journals which cover comparative politics over the past two decades shows that the majority of research published in them is still made up of single country studies; that the dominant methodology remains the configurative case study; and that the kind of political system that is best represented there is the parliamentary democracy. Neither the behavioural revolution, multi-country comparative study nor a shift to the Third World have become dominant in comparative politics, if the content of these scholarly journals is a reliable guide.

Sidney Tarrow
Cornell University

References

Almond, G. and Powell, G. B. Jr (1966), *Comparative Politics*, Boston.

Bryce, J. (1963), 'Modern democracies', in H. Eckstein and D. Apter (eds), *Comparative Politics; A Reader*, New York.

Dogan, M. and Pelassy, D. (1984), *How to Compare Nations; Strategies in Comparative Politics*, Chatham, N.J.

Friedrich, K. (1950), *Constitutional Government and Democracy*, New York.

Przeworski, A. and Teune, H. (1970), *The Logic of Comparative Social Inquiry*, New York.

Tocqueville, A. de (1945 [1835–40]), *Democracy in America*. (Original French edn, *De la démocratie en Amérique*, 4 vols, Paris.)

Further Reading

Lijphart, A. (1971), 'Comparative politics and the comparative method', *American Political Science Review*, 65.

Merritt, R. L. (1970), *Systematic Approaches to Comparative Politics*, Chicago.

Verba, S. (1967), 'Some dilemmas in comparative research', *World Politics*, 20.

See also: *Tocqueville: world-system theory*.

Comparative Psychology

Comparative psychology is a term applied nowadays only to the study of animals, and not to comparisons made between or within human cultures. There are several issues involved in the psychological study of animals, some of them resolvable by evidence, and others more questions of the purposes and strategies of the enterprise itself. It is partly a strategic question whether to try to list the peculiarities of individual species, or to search for general principles which apply to large groups of species. Cutting across this distinction is the question of whether to be satisfied with descriptions or whether to look more deeply for explanations of known or as-yet-unknown facts.

Descartes dissected animals, and had a positive influence in arguing from his knowledge of the sensory nerves that the brain is the organ of all sensation and feeling. However, he also started a mechanistic trend in the explanation of animal behaviour, by inventing the concept of the sensory-motor reflex, and he unfortunately effectively split off discussion of human psychology, seen as the experience of a uniquely human soul, from animal psychology, seen as collections of reflexes. A return to Aristotle's idea of a natural scale of life, which had persisted up until Descartes, and in which there are clear continuities between human and animal psychology, was promoted by, among others, Darwin, his collaborator Romanes, and Herbert Spencer.

In the twentieth century, several branches of comparative psychology have been influenced by the Darwinian theory of evolution. Behaviourists such as Watson and Skinner and learning theorists such as Pavlov and Thorndike reflect Darwinian theory in so far as results obtained in experiments with animals are held to have relevance for human psychology. On the other hand, these theorists and their followers ignore evolution to the extent that they neglect species differences. The inheritance of characteristics, whether physical or mental, was an axiom of Darwin's theory, and therefore it is acceptably Darwinian to propose that each animal species comes equipped with a different set of capacities, or a different set of 'species-specific behaviours'. This last term was introduced by ethologists including the 1973 Nobel Laureates, Tinbergen and Lorenz, who approached animal behaviour as biologists rather than psychologists, and catalogued such items as 'fixed action patterns' of courtship behaviour in birds, which take particular stereotyped forms in a given species. Another zoologist, E. O. Wilson, in 1975 coined the term 'Sociobiology', intended to cover complex social behaviour (even, controversially, in the human species) in relation to biological variables.

The nature-versus-nurture debate continues. It is plain that animal behaviour is not so determined by education, culture and history as is that of the human species, and that inherited and instinctual influences must play a correspondingly greater role in animal psychology. But it is a matter of factual evidence, from both field observations and laboratory experiment, that local traditions and individual accomplishments have considerably more importance in the life of birds and mammals than the inherited-clockwork-reflexes view would suggest.

Much factual data about many animal species is continually being collected, but agreed theories do not necessarily flow from the increased volume of facts. One theoretical trend in biology, which serves as a very remote level of explanation in psychology, is statistical treatment of various genetical possibilities – as applied to social behaviour this had been popularized as the 'selfish gene' theory. It has had some success in accounting for such things as the breeding strategies adopted by particular animal species – including, for example, the inbreeding avoidance which has been discovered in many wild populations. Within more strictly psychological theories, there has been a trend in the second half of the twentieth century to move away from the extreme scepticism and behaviourism of the first half. Elaborate and painstaking laboratory testing has added weight to theories which presume that psychological capacities under the headings of perception, expectancy, emotion and memory are present in at least the higher vertebrates, the mammals and birds. Specialized experimentation with monkeys and chimpanzees has confirmed that intellectual abilities of some description are present in these species, although attempts to train chimpanzees in the social and syntactical complexities of human language have had successes so limited that they would be better called failures.

Animals are widely used for investigating physiological mechanisms rather than psychological theories: for instance, for investigating the details of the eye and brain which allow for vision, or for studying the brain biochemistry which accounts for the emotional effects of tranquillizing or addictive drugs. For this and other reasons an important comparison in comparative psychology is between the human species and the rest. It was Aristotle's view that perception, memory, passion, appetite and desire, as well as pleasure and pain, belong to almost all living creatures. Modern studies would place greater restrictions on the generality of these psychological components, but for a full understanding of human youth and age, sleep and dreams, and human passion and perception, biological comparisons remain essential.

S. F. Walker
Birkbeck College, University of London

Further Reading
McFarland, D. (ed.) (1980), *The Oxford Companion to Animal Behaviour*, Oxford.
Walker, S. F. (1983), *Animal Thought*, London.
See also: *ethology; evolution; instinct; sociobiology.*

Compensation Principle

The compensation principle is an ingenious device for getting around the view that interpersonal comparisons of utility are unscientific. If everyone gains, real income has unambiguously increased and so has economic welfare. There has been a Pareto-improvement. But suppose, as is usually the case, that some gain and some lose. What has happened to real income and to economic welfare? It was to deal with this problem that Kaldor (1939), endorsed by Hicks, formulated the compensation principle: there will be a potential improvement if the gainers from a change are able to compensate the losers and yet still be better off – i.e. they can 'over-compensate' the losers. Without some such rule one is powerless to make judgements about change, even when it makes almost everyone much better off. There were early technical criticisms and suggestions for improvement by Scitovsky, who noticed that losers might at the same time be able to bribe gainers to return to the initial situation, and the principle has continued to be controversial because of its ambiguous status. It has long been recognized that either compensation is hypothetical only – in which case it is contentious – or it is actual – in which case it is anodyne. Further is it a *test* for increases in real income or a *criterion* of policy? As a criterion of policy it forms the basis, though in simplified form, for much of cost-benefit analysis. The debate among cost-benefit analysts about whether distributional weights should be included, exactly reflects the ambiguities of the compensation principle itself.

David Collard
University of Bath

Reference
Kaldor, N. (1939), 'Welfare propositions of economic and interpersonal comparisons of utility', *Economic Journal*, 49.

Further Reading
Mishan, E. J. (1981), *Introduction to Normative Economics*, Oxford.
See also: *cost-benefit analysis; welfare economics.*

Competition

Competition and its different aspects have maintained a central place in economic reality and economic theory for well over two hundred years. Competition – always to some extent a motivating force in economic affairs (as in other fields of human endeavour) – rose to prominence when the static and regulated world of medieval and feudal days, with its guilds and restrictions, began to decline and gave way to the dynamics of the Industrial Revolution bringing division of labour, capital accumulation, free markets and mobile workers.

When the foundations of economic theory were built in eighteenth-century Britain – above all with the publication of Adam Smith's pathbreaking work *Wealth of Nations* (1776) – competition in the leading capitalist country was already so pronounced that it could not escape the attention of any realistic economist. But from the very beginning competition was not only seen as a real-world phenomenon whose working had to be explained ('positive' economics). It also rapidly acquired the status of a norm, a standard of efficiency to which economic systems should aspire ('normative' economics). This was already true for Adam Smith. He tried to analyse the working of competitive markets – the formation of demand, supply, and prices. At the same time, he was intrigued by the moral problem of how the multitude of isolated actions of egotistic, profit-seeking individuals could result in a common good, the growing wealth of nations. He saw competition as the force, the hidden hand, which brings about this socially desirable transformation.

This double vision of competition has remained typical for all so-called classical and neo-classical schools of economic theory. They try to *explain* the variations in demands, supplies and relative prices through increasingly sophisticated theories of competitive processes, and they *advocate* the adoption of competitive policies by pointing out the alleged advantages of competition: efficient allocation of resources through prices signalling the desires of consumers and producers (if backed by purchasing power); pressure on producers to lower production costs and prices in order to be able to compete; dynamic efficiency, because competition enforces a constant search for new products and marketing opportunities.

While real world competition is a complex phenomenon and always coexisted with other economic mechanisms (as Smith clearly saw), economic *theory* tended more and more towards a highly formalistic and abstract model of 'perfect competition' which soon became the basic standard for both 'positive' and 'normative' investigations of economic processes. 'Perfect competition' denotes a market situation where large numbers of fully informed ('transparent markets') producers and consumers meet in order to sell or buy clearly defined and uniform goods and services ('homogeneous markets'). The very large number of economic agents implies that a single seller or buyer is such a small fraction of the market that his individual action (purchase or sale – entry or withdrawal) is so infinitesimal that it cannot noticeably affect the market situation and the market price ('atomistic competition').

Full information means that no seller will sell below the going (equilibrium) price and no buyer will be prepared to pay more than that price. There will thus be at any moment just one price for a given commodity ('Law of One Price') and this price will serve as a basis for the decision-making process of economic agents. If we assume a general network of such 'perfect markets', and add a general competitive search for high profits (in the case of firms) and low costs of provisioning (in the case of households), we obtain a picture of the efficiency of a 'perfectly competitive' system. Suppose, for instance, that the demand for commodity A increases. More buyers enter the A-market and this causes a shortage of supplies. As a consequence prices rise (flexibility of market prices being another assumption of perfect competition). The ensuing super-profits attract firms from other branches. Supplies in the A-market increase, price and profits fall until the super-profits are wiped out. Perfect competition and its price system has brought about a rearrangement of the production structure to suit a changed demand and has at the same time – by permitting free entry of new firms – forced a return to lower prices and 'normal' profits.

The 'idyllic' features of perfect competition – a theoretical construct – lie behind the age-old advocacy of free markets, free competition, and free trade by members of the economic profession. Monopoly, where the producer can raise prices by keeping out competitors and keeping goods in short supply, was to be fought with all means. But the forces making for monopolistic inroads on competition are very strong. It was already becoming clear in the nineteenth century that technological changes leading to extensive capital equipment and mass production methods involved a concentration process in many industries, reducing the number of firms. In the place of 'atomistic' (perfect) competition there is a steadily growing trend towards 'oligopolistic competition', the 'Competition among the Few' (Fellner, 1949). Here prices and profits are no longer regulated by competition alone, but also by conventions and agreements between powerful agents. The chance for higher profits is a strong urge – apart from technological factors – towards concentration, and this urge has proved more effective than the anti-monopoly legislation that was started approximately one hundred years ago in the US (Sherman Act 1890) and later spread to other countries.

But the 'ideal' of perfect competition is not only threatened by concentration and oligopoly. Even where markets are characterized by a large number of firms, the conditions of perfect competition are frequently missing because products are not homogeneous and information is incomplete. In many markets, *technically* similar goods (e.g. motor cars, toothpastes, and so on) are markedly differentiated through trademarks, make-up, advertising. The heterogeneous goods are no longer perfect substitutes. Their prices can differ, and although there is competition between them, it is by no means perfect. Each firm has some influence on the sales, prices and profits of its 'own' product. This fragmentation of markets is intensified by the insufficient information of consumers regarding prices and quality differences. As a consequence 'perfect competition' gives way to 'imperfect' or 'monopolistic competition' (Robinson, 1933; Chamberlin, 1932) which no longer 'guarantees' efficient allocation and low costs.

The gap between the idealized model of 'perfect competition' and real-world developments has led to various criticisms of the 'normative' bias towards competitive rules in traditional theories. One line of reasoning, the 'Theory of the Second Best' (Lipsey and Lancaster, 1956), has shown that once perfect competition is not the *general* rule, non-competitive measures in other fields may turn out to be preferable. An example is the 'Theory of Countervailing Power' (Galbraith, 1952), which discusses the creation of big units as effective answer to already existing monopolies. The 'Theory of Market Failures' has shown that while competition for high profits may be efficient within the framework of a single market, it may lead to 'external effects', i.e. to positive or negative developments in other fields which are not sufficiently taken into account in a purely competitive adjustment process. This factor, which has acquired important dimensions in the ecological context, indicates that public intervention and collective action might be advantageous. They become imperative in the case of the so-called Public Goods (e.g. public security, law courts, etc.) which by their very nature cannot be regulated in a competitive manner. Finally, we have to mention the socioeconomic reform movements, like some Christian social theories and – above all – the socialist movements, which criticize the uneven distribution of income resulting from private capital and competitive markets. They would prefer to replace – at least partly – the competition-plus-profit mechanism of economic regulation by more collective and solidaric methods, both for economic and general humanitarian reasons.

Kurt W. Rothschild
Johannes Kepler University, Linz

References
Chamberlin, E. H. (1932), *The Theory of Monopolistic Competition*, Cambridge, Mass.
Fellner, W. (1949), *Competition among the Few*, New York.
Galbraith, J. K. (1952), *American Capitalism. The Concept of Countervailing Power*, Oxford.

Lipsey, R. G. and Lancaster, K. (1956/57), 'The general theory of the second best', *Review of Economic Studies*, 24.

Robinson, J. (1933), *The Economics of Imperfect Competition*, London.

See also: *markets; Smith.*

Computer Simulation

Computer simulation is a methodology for building, testing, and using computer programs which imitate (latin *simulare*, to imitate) system behaviour. Numbers or symbols representing a system and its parts are stored in computer memory and are manipulated by a *simulation program* written in a suitable computer programming language.

A useful approach to simulation modelling is the so-called *entity-attribute-relationship* approach. A system is thought of as a collection of one or more entities each of which has one or more attributes. In addition, various relationships exist between the entities. As time passes, activities or events occur in the system to cause entities to be created or destroyed, or to undergo changes in their attributes or relationships to other entities. Most simulation models in the social sciences can be formulated using the entity-attribute-relationship approach.

When the entire system is treated as a single entity, the simulation model is called a *macro-simulation*. For example, an entire population might be simulated as one entity with attributes representing the numbers of people in various categories within the population. The simulation program would change these numbers from one simulated time period to the next in order to imitate the processes of birth, death, marriage, migration, etc., in the real population. Macro-simulation models can usually be represented by systems of equations which are solvable by traditional mathematical methods, but which require computer simulation for practical reasons.

When a system is treated as a collection of many entities which, taken as a whole, make up the system, then the simulation model is called a *micro-simulation*. For example, each person in a population might be modelled as an entity with attributes of age, sex, marital status, and so on. The simulation program would cause each entity (person) to experience events such as birth, marriage, and death at appropriate times during the course of the simulation. At any time during the simulation, features of the population, such as the number of people with a given age and marital status could be obtained by simply counting the appropriate entities. Micro-simulation models are often difficult to represent with traditional mathematical notation, and it is for these types of models that computer simulation methods are most often used in the social sciences.

Most micro-simulation models are *stochastic* models in the sense that some degree of randomness is allowed in the behaviour of individual entities. In a simulation program *pseudo-random numbers* are used to simulate randomness. Strictly speaking, computers cannot generate truly random numbers, but methods for generating pseudo-random numbers with most of the important properties of true random numbers are well developed. By using the *inverse transform method*, pseudo-random numbers representing a wide range of probability distributions can be generated as needed during the course of a simulation. Stochastic micro-simulations are also called *monte-carlo simulations* because of their reliance upon random numbers.

A critical and often slighted task in computer simulation modelling is that of program *verification*. This is the process of determining that the simulation program does not contain logical errors which could lead to meaningless results. Verification of stochastic simulations is especially difficult, since some logical errors may be evident only when certain rare events, or rare combinations of events, occur during the course of a simulation. But by keeping simulation models as simple as possible, by testing with fixed extreme values in place of pseudo-random numbers, and by spending ample time verifying the program, reliable stochastic simulation programs can be produced.

Validation is the process of comparing simulation results to empirical data in order to determine whether the simulation program imitates the real system closely enough for its intended purposes. Standard statistical procedures are used to determine whether results from stochastic simulations differ from empirical data by a significant amount. *Tuning* a simulation model involves making necessary adjustments to achieve a desired degree of validity. Like any scientific model, a simulation model is a simplified representation of reality and is not intended to match perfectly the behaviour of the real system. Therefore, model validity can only be judged relative to the particular research context.

Sometimes the emphasis in simulation modelling is on *prediction*, while at other times it is on *sensitivity analysis*. The former involves interpreting simulation results as statements about actual past, present, or future system behaviour. Predictions derived from computer simulation models are prone to the same errors as other types of predictions, and in most social science, applications have proven less than adequately accurate. Sensitivity analysis refers to the use of a simulation model to explore the response of selected output variables to specified changes in system parameters or input variables. The emphasis is on understanding the behavioural dynamics of a system rather then upon predicting its behaviour. The general trend is toward this use of computer simulation.

Because they include a random component, stochastic simulations yield information about *variances* as well as *expected values* of simulation results. Each repeated execution of a simulation program, or *repli-*

cation, produces results that differs from the results of other replications due to the random component. All of the replications necessary to answer a particular research question constitute a *simulation experiment*, and the principles of experimental design apply to the design of efficient and informative simulation experiments with the added advantage that the nature of the random component can be controlled by the experimenter.

The practice of computer simulation is closely tied to the technology of computing. The early micro-simulation experiments of Orcutt *et al.* (1961) consumed vast amounts of computer time on a large computer that was slower and had less memory than today's inexpensive microcomputers. But even with advanced technology, computer simulation typically requires large amounts of computing resources, largely due to the need for many replications in most simulation experiments. The task of simulation programming is greatly simplified by specialized programming languages which provide for automatic memory management for large numbers of entities, the timing of events during the course of the simulation, and the generation of pseudo-random numbers. Many elementary texts (for example, Mitrani 1982; Payne 1982) introduce the concepts, issues, and programming languages relevant to computer simulation.

James E. Smith
Cambridge Group for the History
of Population and Social Structure

References

Mitrani, I. (1982), *Simulation Techniques for Discrete Event Systems*, Cambridge.

Orcutt, G. H., Greenberger, M., Korbel, J. and Rivlin, A. M. (1961), *Microanalysis of Socioeconomic Systems: A Simulation Study*, New York.

Payne, J. A. (1982), *Introduction to Simulation: Programming Techniques and Methods of Analysis*, New York.

Comte, Auguste (1798–1857)

Auguste Comte, philosopher of science and social visionary, is perhaps best known for giving a name to a subject he outlined rather than practised: sociology. As the Comtist motto 'Order and Progress' suggests, the keynote of his thought is his search, in chaotic times, for principles of cultural and political order that were consistent with the forward march of society. Born at Montpellier in southern France of a conservative, middle-class family, Comte received a good scientific education at the École Polytechnique in Paris, a centre of advanced liberal thought. From 1817 to 1824 he was closely associated with the radical prophet of a new industrial order, Henri de Saint-Simon, to whom he owed a considerable (and largely disavowed) intellectual debt. At the same time, despite the loss of his Catholic faith, he was drawn to some of the ideas of the conservative thinker, Joseph de Maistre, and eventually based much of the 'religion of humanity' on medieval, Catholic models.

Comte's writings fall into two main phases, which express different aspects of a single, unified vision of knowledge and society, rather than a change in fundamental emphasis. Of the first, the major work is the six-volume *Cours de philosophie positive* (1830–42) (*The Positive Philosophy of Auguste Comte*, 1896), which sets forth a developmental epistemology of science. In his later writings, especially the *Discours sur l'esprit positif*, (1844) (*Discourse on the Positive Spirit*), the *Système de politique positive* (1848–54) (*System of Positive Polity*, 1875–77), and the *Catechism of Positive Religion* (1858), Comte gives the blue-print of a new social order, including the 'religion of humanity' which was to provide its ethical underpinning. For Comte, 'positivism' was not merely the doctrine that the methods of the natural sciences provide the only route to a knowledge of human nature and society (as it has latterly come to mean), but also a source of value for social reorganization. 'Sociology' is, in fact, the specific knowledge requisite to this task.

In the *Cours* Comte sets forth the famous 'Law of the three stages'. In its origins, human thought is 'theological', making use of an idiom of spiritual forces; later, in a phase which culminates in the Enlightenment, it moves to a 'metaphysical' stage, which is conjectural and largely negative; finally, when it is able to grasp real causal relations between phenomena, it achieves the scientific or 'positive' stage. To these stages there also correspond characteristic social and political institutions. Individual sciences develop in the same manner, emerging at the positive stage in the order of their complexity: mathematics, astronomy, physics, chemistry, biology and, finally, sociology. Comte's view of sociology is highly programmatic: he argues for an analytic distinction between social 'statics' and 'dynamics', and for society to be analysed as a system of interdependent parts, based upon a consensus.

Despite his religious eccentricities, Comte exercised an immediate influence on his comtemporaries. J. S. Mill introduced his work to the English-speaking world, where the positive philosophy appealed as a check to the extremes of liberal individualism, and even Spencer adopted the name 'sociology'. Though he is little read today, the functionalist and natural scientific paradigms which Comte advocated have remained in sociology's mainstream.

J. D. Y. Peel
University of Liverpool

Further Reading
Lenzer, J. (ed.) (1975), *Auguste Comte and Positivism: The Essential Writings*, New York.
Thompson, K. (1975), *Auguste Comte: The Foundation of Sociology*, London.
See also: *positivism; Saint-Simon.*

Conditioning, Classical and Operant

The Russian physiologist, Ivan Pavlov, was not the first scientist to investigate how animals learn, but he was certainly one of the first to undertake a systematic series of experiments intended to provide precise quantitative information on the subject, and it is to his work that we owe the term 'conditioning' to describe one form of that learning. In the course of his work on the digestive system of dogs, Pavlov had found that salivary secretion was elicited not only by placing food in the dog's mouth but also by the sight or smell of food, and that eventually a dog might start to salivate at the sight or sound of the attendant who usually provided the food. These 'psychic secretions', although initially interfering with the planned study of the digestive system, provided the basis for the study of conditional reflexes for which Pavlov is now far more famous.

Pavlov's experimental arrangement was simple. A hungry dog is restrained on a stand; every few minutes, the dog receives some meat powder, the delivery of which is signalled by an arbitrary stimulus, such as the ticking of a metronome or the flashing of a light. The food itself elicits copious salivation, which is measured by diverting the end of the salivary duct through a fistula in the dog's cheek. After a number of trials on which the delivery of food is always preceded by the ticking of the metronome, the dog does not wait for the food, but starts to salivate as soon as the metronome is sounded. Food is referred to as an unconditional stimulus because it unconditionally elicits salivation; the metronome is a conditional stimulus which comes to elicit salivation conditional on its relationship to the food. By similar reasoning, salivation to food is an unconditional response, but when the dog starts salivating to the metronome, this is a conditional response, strengthened or reinforced by the delivery of food whenever the metronome sounds, and weakened or extinguished whenever the metronome occurs without being followed by food. In translation from the original Russian, 'conditional' and 'unconditional' became 'conditioned' and 'unconditioned' and the verb 'to condition' was rapidly introduced to describe the procedure which brought about this change in the dog's behaviour.

At about the same time as Pavlov was starting his work on what is now called classical conditioning, a young American research student, Edward Thorndike, was undertaking an equally systematic series of experiments which are now regarded as providing the first analysis of operant conditioning. Thorndike was more catholic in his choice of animal to study than was Pavlov, using cats, chickens and monkeys impartially. And the impetus for his work was also different. While Pavlov was a physiologist who saw himself as studying the brain and how it controlled not only inborn but also acquired reflexes, Thorndike was concerned to study how animals learned in an objective and scientific manner in order to dispel the myths that he thought had arisen about the amazing feats of intelligence of which animals were capable, myths that owed much to a post-Darwinian desire to prove the mental continuity of man and other animals.

In a typical experiment, Thorndike would place a cat in a 'puzzle box' from which the animal could escape, and so get access to a dish of food, only by performing some arbitrary response such as pressing a catch or pulling on a piece of string. Thorndike recorded the time it took the animal to perform the required response on successive trials, and observing a gradual decline in this time, interpreted the learning in terms of his celebrated 'law of effect': the reward of escaping from confinement and obtaining food strengthened the one response that was successful in achieving this, while all other responses, being followed by no such desirable effects, were weakened.

The term 'operant conditioning' was introduced by the American psychologist, B. F. Skinner, who refined Thorndike's procedure by the simple device of delivering food to the animal (via, for example, an automatic pellet dispenser) while it remained inside the box. In this apparatus, a rat could be trained to perform hundreds of responses, usually pressing a small bar protruding from one wall, in order to obtain occasional pellets of food. The response of pressing the bar was termed an 'operant' because it operated on the animal's environment, and the procedure was therefore operant conditioning, which was reinforced by the occasional pellet of food, and extinguished if pressing the bar was no longer followed by food.

Although Skinner, unlike Thorndike, took over much of Pavlov's terminology, he interpreted the learning he observed in a way much more closely related to Thorndike's analysis. For Skinner, as for Thorndike, the central feature of learning and adaptation is that an animal's behaviour should be modified by its consequences. The rat presses the bar because this response produces a particular outcome – the delivery of food; when it no longer does so, the rat stops pressing the bar, just as it will also stop if pressing the bar produces some other, less desirable outcome such as the delivery of a brief shock. And the schedules according to which the experimenter arranges these outcomes have orderly and appropriate effects on the animal's behaviour.

The law of effect, which summarizes these observations, is entirely in accord with common sense: parents hope and believe that rewarding children for good behaviour or punishing them for bad will also have appropriate effects, and when they are mistaken or disappointed we are more inclined to look for other sources of reward or to question the efficacy of their punishment than to question the underlying logic of the argument. Operant conditioning, therefore, although no doubt only one, rather simple form of learning or way of modifying behaviour, is surely an important and pervasive one. It is not so immediately obvious that the process of classical conditioning identified by Pavlov is of such importance. Why does the dog start salivating at the sound of the metronome? The experimenter delivers the food regardless of the dog's behaviour (this, of course, is the precise distinction between classical and operant conditioning, for in Skinner's experiments the rat only gets food *if* it presses the bar). It has been argued that salivation does actually achieve something – for example, it makes dry food more palatable and this is why the dog learns to salivate in anticipation of food. The explanation attempts to interpret classical conditioning in operant terms, for it seeks to identify a desirable consequence of salivation responsible for reinforcing the response. But the explanation is probably false. Another popular example of classical conditioning is that of blinking by a rabbit to a flash of light which signals the delivery of a puff of air to the rabbit's eye. Since this is a classical experiment, the puff of air is delivered on every trial regardless of the rabbit's behaviour. Just as in the case of the dog's salivary response, however, it seems reasonable to argue that the rabbit's eye blink serves to protect the eye from the puff of air and is therefore reinforced by this desirable consequence. The argument implies that if the experimenter arranged that on any trial on which the rabbit blinked in anticipation of the puff of air, the experimenter cancelled its delivery altogether, the rabbit would learn to blink even more readily. Here, after all, blinking has an even more beneficial consequence than usual: it completely cancels an aversive consequence. But in fact such a procedure significantly interferes with the conditioning of the rabbit's eye blink.

A more plausible interpretation, then, is that classical conditioning simply reflects an animal's anticipation of a particular consequence, not necessarily an attempt to obtain or avoid that consequence – this latter being the provenance of operant conditioning. Classical conditioning probably has its most important application in the area of emotions and attitudes: the anticipation of an unpleasant event may generate a variety of emotional changes, such as fear or alarm which are not necessarily under voluntary control. Voluntary behaviour, i.e., that directly affected by its consequences, is the sphere of operant conditioning.

N. J. Mackintosh
University of Cambridge

Further Reading
Davey, G. (1981), *Animal Learning and Conditioning*, London.
Gray, J. A. (1979), *Pavlov*, London.
Mackintosh, N. J. (1983), *Conditioning and Associative Learning*, Oxford.
Pavlov, I. P. (1927), *Conditioned Reflexes*, Oxford.
Schwartz, B. (1978), *Psychology of Learning and Behavior*, New York.
Skinner, B. F. (1938), *The Behavior of Organisms*, New York.
Thorndike, E. L. (1911), *Animal Intelligence*, New York.

See also: *behaviourism*; *learning*; *Pavlov*; *Skinner*.

Conflict, Social

Social scientists are interested in two aspects of conflict: how conflict relations permeate and shape all aspects of human interaction and social structure (that is, a conflict perspective to social life), and how a conflict or other theoretical perspective helps elucidate the genesis, escalation, de-escalation, and outcome and consequences of wars, revolutions, strikes and uprisings.

Conflict Perspective
Stated at a necessarily high level of generality, writers using the conflict approach (as opposed to, say, a functionalist, exchange, or systems approach) seek to explain not only how social order is maintained, but how it is maintained despite great inequalities, and also how social structures change. They view societies, organizations and other social systems as arenas for personal or group contests. (Complementary and common interests are not excluded, but the competitive and incompatible character of interests are emphasized.) Coercion is a major way in which people seek to advance their interests. It is assumed that humans generally do not want to be dominated or coerced, and therefore resist attempts at coercion, and struggles ensue.

Conflict theory has a long tradition going back to the beginnings of cynical counsel to rulers and naturalistic history, as can be seen in the writings of Thucydides, Machiavelli and Hobbes. Marx stressed the material conditions underlying conflict, especially class struggles based upon property relations. Other conflict theorists such as Gumplowitz, Ratzenhofer and Novicow worked in the context of evolutionary thought and posited a group struggle for existence; they variously stressed military power in conflict, and interests – for example, ethnic differences – as bases for conquest. Simmel was another classical sociologist concerned with the forms and consequences of conflict.

Interest in the conflict perspective revived, at least in English-speaking countries, in the 1960s. In preceding decades the dominant social-science theories portrayed societies as based on consensus and consent, but the political turmoil of the sixties, both domestic and international, directed attention to social conflicts and to the conflict approach.

Recent conflict theorists have emphasized different combinations of elements from the rich conflict tradition. Many contemporary social scientists regard themselves as Marxists, but they differ a great deal in their interpretations of Marx and in the way they have developed elements of dialectical materialism in analysing contemporary social life. Some stress the clash of immediate economic interests, others the divisions based on ideological structures, while still others focus on the role of nonclass divisions such as ethnicity and sex in shaping conflicts. Many conflict theorists stress their differences with Marxism, or they simply emphasize certain factors and processes which Marxists do not. The work of Dahrendorf (1959) and Collins (1975) are illustrative. Dahrendorf argued that authority relations, not property relations, underlie social conflict. Collins considered coercion, including violence, as important means of control, and he drew from the symbolic-interaction tradition to stress the importance of meanings in the organization of people for struggle, both at the interpersonal and the social-structural levels.

The study of economic development provides one example of how the conflict perspective has become important in all branches of the social sciences, and in many topics of inquiry. The conflict approach in this context stresses the use of power (economic, political and military) to impose unequal exchanges which lead to a world-system marked by dependency; several economists and sociologists have sought to account for underdevelopment in the Third World using this perspective.

Social Conflicts

Social scientists have recently looked for a comprehensive explanation of all social conflicts, for, despite their differences, they all have important similarities:
(1) As a form of social interaction, adversary groups, or persons purporting to represent contending groups, take each other into account in waging the conflict.
(2) Collectivities based upon social categories and divisions develop a sense of group consciousness partly out of their antagonistic interaction with each other.
(3) The adversaries believe that what each seeks from the other is at least partly incompatible.
(4) The interacting parties engage in a series of exchanges or encounters, so that we can recognize a struggle with a course of development.

Types of Social Conflict

Variations in types of social conflicts affect the way they emerge, escalate, and de-escalate. Among the many variations are three particularly significant and interrelated factors: the character of the parties, the nature of the goals, and the means used in the struggle.

(1) Conflicting parties differ in their degree of organization and boundedness. At one extreme are governments, trade unions and other entities with membership rules and generally recognized roles for forming and executing policy towards adversaries. At the other extreme are more nebulous entities such as social classes and believers in a common ideology where boundaries of adherence may be disputed or in flux, and which generally lack recognized roles for contending with adversaries. Moreover, every social conflict is likely to include many sets of adversaries; some overlap and cross-cut, or one encompasses some entities and is encompassed by others. For example, heads of governments may claim to speak for a government, a state, a people, an ideology, a political party faction, and a social class. Each such claim helps constitute a corresponding adversary. Herein lies one of the bases for the interlocking character of conflict.

(2) Social conflicts are about incompatible goals, and the nature of these goals are another basis for distinguishing different kinds of conflicts. Adversaries may contest control over land, money, or other resources which they all value: such disputes over resources are *consensual* conflicts. Alternatively they may come into conflict about differently held values, for example, ideology or religion. These are *dissensual* conflicts. Of course, in specific conflicts both consensual and dissensual components are likely to be present. In addition, goals differ in the degree to which the adversaries consider the issue in contention to be important or even vital.

(3) Conflicts are waged in a variety of ways. Conflict analysts are particularly interested in struggles involving great coercion, whether employed or threatened, and coercion which is relatively uninstitutionalized. In many conflicts, the adversaries adhere to well-developed and highly-institutionalized rules; indeed, these are often not regarded as social conflicts at all. This may be the case, for instance, in electoral campaigns, where different parties seek to control the government. Certain kinds of conflicts may become increasingly institutionalized and regulated over time, and that transformation is a matter of paramount significance. We can recognize such a change in labour-management conflicts in many countries during the nineteenth century (Dahrendorf, 1959).

Aside from the theoretical issues, the value orientations of the investigators are also crucial in the study of conflicts. Some tend to approach social conflict from a partisan perspective, trying to learn how to advance the particular goals of their side. This is the case for military strategists and many advocates of national liberation. Others are concerned to minimize violence and look for alternative ways of defending or attaining sought-for goals. Still others are primarily interested in attaining a new social order, justified in terms of universal claims for justice or equity; they may see conflicts as the natural process towards this end. Finally, the intellectually curious adopt a disinterested, relativistic view of social conflicts.

Origins of Social Conflict

Social scientists mostly look for the origins of social conflicts in social, political and economic relations and do not reduce them to the innate biological nature of humans. (Such factors seem inadequate to explain the variations in conflicts.) But conditions and processes internal to one party in a conflict may be stressed in accounting for a fight or for the means used in waging the struggle. For example, resentments arising from dissatisfaction from one source may be displaced upon easily targeted scapegoats. This produces an unrealistic conflict, in the sense that it is not based on any objective condition, or that the means employed are disproportionate to the issues at stake. It is difficult to assess the objective basis and appropriate means for solving a conflict, although recent work is contributing something in this direction, as noted below.

Most conflict theorists stress inequality as the underlying basis for conflict: if it appears to one party that the other is gaining at their expense, this is the basis for consensual conflict. Other conflicts may relate to disagreements about desired goals – when groups have different values and wish to impose their own upon the other, the objective conditions for a dissensual conflict exist. Functionalist theorists emphasize the dissensual bases of social conflicts, particularly dissensus resulting from unequal rates of social change in the social system. Concentrating on the functional integration and consensual character of social systems, they tend to view conflicts as flowing from their disruption (Johnson, 1966). This focus helps to account for behaviour which analysts regard as expressive rather than instrumental.

Awareness by adversaries that they are in conflict is necessary for a conflict to exist – analysts do not agree about how such awareness comes about. Some argue that absolute deprivation is a major factor, while others regard relative deprivation as more important – that is, how deprived people feel compared to their expectations based on past experience, or relative to comparative groups (Gurr, 1970). In any event, the group members' beliefs that they are able to improve their conditions are crucial, and these beliefs vary with developments in each contesting party and in their relations with each other. Groups must also be able to mobilize to pursue their goals (Tilly, 1978). Pre-existing linkages of persons and groups help to channel mobilization, while leadership and the shared ideologies of possible recruits are also key factors.

The fact that relatively dominant groups are able to attain their goals helps to explain why they may initiate further demands leading to overt conflict. And if the subordinate group should believe that they can effectively challenge the status quo, the dominant group may react by attempting to meet the challenge and by persuading others to regard the status quo as legitimate.

Conflict Management

Most studies of social conflicts have focused on the emergence of conflict behaviour and its escalation, but recently there is greater interest shown in de-escalation and conflict management. The means used in waging a conflict can vary greatly in intensity and extent. Inducements in a conflict are also noncoercive. While coercion encompasses a variety of violent and nonviolent means, noncoercion includes efforts at persuasion and positive sanctions, such as promised benefits (Kriesberg, 1982; Ebert, 1981). Escalation and de-escalation are affected by (1) the internal developments in each of the adversary groups; (2) the interaction between them, and (3) the conduct of actors not initially involved in the conflict.

(1) Internal factors include various social-psychological processes and organizational developments which lead to an increasing commitment to the cause of the struggle. Sub-units engaged in the conflict may derive power, status and economic gains by building up their fighting resources (Senghaas, 1972), while those who suffer in the struggle, especially if they are much more severely affected than their adversaries, may become less committed.

(2) The manner in which the two sides interact is significant: adversary actions can be strong, provocative and escalating, or successfully intimidating and de-escalating; or the actions can be conciliatory and thus de-escalating, or appeasing and thereby encouraging escalation. Evidence suggests that if both sides are more or less equally antagonistic, then the conflict is less likely to escalate.

(3) Parties not initially involved in the conflict can affect the course of conflict by joining in later in order to advance their own interests, or by setting limits to the conflict. Intermediaries can also mitigate the undesired aspects of conflicts by mediation, thus facilitating communication and providing face-saving options.

Adversaries in conflicts generally evaluate the outcomes in terms of victories and defeats, wins or losses. In addition, there are possible mutual losses and gains because of the interlocking character of conflicts. Functionalists will examine the functions of social conflicts for the parties and the larger system in which the conflicts occur. But analysts adopting a conflict perspective are also likely to observe that not only are conflicts endemic, but they are ways of bringing about needed changes.

Louis Kriesberg
Syracuse University

References
Collins, R. (1975), *Conflict Sociology*, New York.
Dahrendorf, R. (1959), *Class and Class Conflict in Industrial Society*, London.
Ebert, T. (1981), *Gewaltfreier Aufstand*, Waldkirch.
Gurr, T. R. (1970), *Why Men Rebel*, Princeton, N.J.
Johnson, C. (1966), *Revolutionary Change*, Boston.
Kriesberg, L. (1982), *Social Conflicts* (2nd edn), Greenwich, Conn.
Senghaas, D. (1972), *Rüstung und Militarismus*, Frankfurt/Main.
Tilly, C. (1978), *From Mobilization to Revolution*, Reading, Mass.

Further Reading
Boulding, K. E. (1962), *Conflict and Defense*, New York.
Burton, J. W. (1969), *Conflict and Communication: The Use of Controlled Communication in International Relations*, London.
Galtung, J. (1980), *The True Worlds: A Transnational Perspective*, New York.
Schelling, T. C. (1980), *The Strategy of Conflict*, Cambridge, Mass.
See also: *conflict resolution; game theory; Marx's theory of history and society; war.*

Conflict Resolution

Conflicts are inevitable because resources and time are limited or because alternative courses of action are usually numerous. The individual, acting by himself, decides to express or repress an impulse. Together with other persons in a group, he competes with another group to capture honours or to improve a common status. As a member of a tribe, an ethnic grouping, or a nation, he and his compatriots believe they are compelled to struggle with a rival or enemy to secure or maintain what they consider to be their sovereign or justifiable rights. Undoubtedly some conflicts are desirable: the spice they add to living provides an incentive to achieve personal or group goals (Coser, 1956). But many, perhaps most, conflicts are painful or non-productive; hence conflict resolutions are consciously or unconsciously, whole- or halfheartedly pursued. If there were a magic formula or procedure for resolving conflicts, as there is not, modern societies would have, for example, fewer psychiatric institutes, riots, and wars.

To simplify the present exposition, a value judgement is explicitly made: a person or some persons in conflict seek a 'favourable' resolution. Conflicts are assumed to be resolvable – if a hedge be tolerated – at least in the long run. Resolutions result either from an external constraint or from a somewhat prolonged interaction between competing impulses or individuals. In the first category would be a person who, wishing to be counter-aggressive toward an insulting stranger, curbs his hostility in accordance with a rigid convention in that social situation; representatives of management and labour who have agreed to submit disputes to binding arbitration; or a small, relatively powerless country like Belgium which could not repel invading German armies in both World Wars. We consider here interactions leading or not leading to challenging resolutions: the smoker cannot resist the urge to smoke, but would avoid lung damage; workers strike and the plant shuts down; two great powers idiotically strengthen their nuclear arsenals.

, Apparently intractable conflicts may be resolvable when and if it is possible to peer beneath the ostensible reasons for their existence and thus to uncover the 'real' objectives. A conflict betwen two persons seeking an advantage only one of them can attain may lead to a compromise or a zero-sum solution with a winner and a loser. The verbal, emotional phrasing of demands, however, does not necessarily reflect 'real' desires which, if ascertainable, could be integrated into a creative resolution. For a holiday a wife would go to Place A, her husband to Place B; after coolly determining the underlying goal of each, they select Place C which provides the wife with the natural beauty she seeks and the husband with the sports attainable at B. This oversimplified, hypothetical analogy may indeed function as a guiding model to creative resolutions of conflict, in spite of the sceptical assertion that only a compromise has been achieved, since Place C may not be as satisfying as A would have been to the wife and B to the husband.

In real life and in the absence of external constraints, therefore, three sometimes insuperable difficulties must be overcome to achieve a resolution of a conflict:

(1) The party or parties must seek a resolution and be willing and able to interact within himself or with others. The disturbed person who cannot decide whether to be or not to be faces the cosmic or trivial alternatives, or seeks aid from a friend, clergyman, or psychiatrist. Contending parties in an industrial or international dispute agree to negotiate or refer their differences to a third party such as an arbitration board, a court, or the United Nations Security Council. Traditional societies have often evolved standardized procedures to resolve internal disputes (Gulliver, 1979).

(2) Problems that can plague interactions are legion. In psychoanalysis and some other non-physiological therapies, the patients' repressed or significant impulses do not readily emerge from their unconscious or unverbalizable cages; or relevant behaviour modific-

ation is elusive. During negotiations the parties in conflict are likely to mistrust each other and quite naturally seek to win as many concessions as possible from an opponent, evidence for which abounds and is ever discoverable at every international confrontation especially, to our sorrow, in modern times. As each party caucuses before and during the negotiation, its members who are not supermen are prone to exhibit all imaginable human frailties: misperceptions, projections upon others, stereotypes, defective information, selective exposure, exaggerated vigilance, defensive avoidance, impatience, feigned conformity in the interest of in-group morale, in fact all the shortcomings that make ordinary and extraordinary decision making considerably less rational than some classical economists, theoretical political scientists, and logicians perforce assume (Janis, 1982; Jervis, 1976).

On the basis of well-controlled experiments with atypical subjects under artificial conditions (Abelson and Levi, 1983; Collins and Guetzkow, 1964), of conferences or workshops arranged by private organizations such as Friends and Pugwash (Doob, 1975), of labour-management confrontations (Vroom and Yetton, 1973), and a pathetically small number of international meetings employing the non-shuttle diplomacy of Trieste (Campbell, 1976) and Camp David, a dash of optimism can be injected into comtemporary gloom. Under specified conditions conflicts can be creatively resolved to the satisfaction of all parties, or at least progress toward that end is possible. Non-neurotic persons of good will, capable of participating and striving to reach a novel resolution, assemble for some period of time, probably many days or weeks, at a neutral site where they feel detached and comfortable. Mass media are excluded. Under the auspices of a third party, whether an arbitrator, intervener, or mediator, the participants are taught to recognize their own psychological and social strengths and weaknesses and to improve the ways in which they communicate with others. Preaching and lecturing are not likely to be efficacious; instead new insights and methods are actually experienced both intellectually and emotionally (Burton, 1969). The phrasing of propositions (Fisher and Ury, 1981); the subtle use of experiential devices like simulation (direct or reverse role-playing); and the implementation of deliberate training programmes such as those provided by T-Groups (Bradford, Gibb, and Benne, 1964), Tavistock (Miller and Rice, 1967), and other practitioners (e.g., Delbecq, Van de Ven, and Gustafson, 1975) facilitate understanding and promote the kind of consensus contributing to a conflict's resolution.

(3) These obstacles appear after the participants leave the intimate, face-to-face situation and re-enter their normal milieu. Even if they themselves are important policy-makers, they must convince their followers that the achieved resolution is desirable; or as official or unofficial representatives they must effectively communicate that resolution to their superiors. They may have grown to love one another and their opponents while momentarily detached from the conflict, but now they face suspicion and hostility from non-participants. Unanticipated changes in conditions may occur. The resolution realized at a distance, in short, may turn out to be unrealizable in the workaday arena (Doob and Foltz, 1974). On the other hand, the transition from dreams to reality need not always be tortuous or impossible. Perhaps the basis for a resolution at a more opportune time in the future may have been created.

Leonard W. Doob
Yale University

References

Abelson, R. P. and Levi, A. (1983), 'Decision-making and decision theory', in G. Lindzey and E. Aronson (eds), *Handbook of Social Psychology* (3rd edn), Reading, Mass.

Bradford, L. P., Gibb, J. R. and Benne, K. (1964), *T-Group Theory and Laboratory Method*, New York.

Burton, J. (1969), *Conflict and Communication*, London.

Campbell, J. C. (ed.) (1976), *Successful Negotiation: Trieste, 1954*, Princeton.

Collins, B. E. and Guetzkow, H. (1964), *A Social Psychology of Group Processes for Decision-Making*, New York.

Coser, L. (1956), *The Functions of Social Conflict*, New York.

Delbecq, A. A., Van de Ven, A. H. and Gustafson, D. H. (1975), *Group Techniques for Program Planning*, Glenview, Ill.

Doob, L. W. (1975), 'Unofficial intervention in destructive social conflicts', in R. W. Brislin, S. Bochner, and W. J. Lonner (eds), *Cross-Cultural Perspectives on Learning*, New York.

Doob, L. W. and Foltz, W. J. (1974), 'The impact of a workshop upon grass-roots leaders in Belfast', *Journal of Conflict Resolution*, 18.

Fisher, R. and Ury, W. (1981), *Getting to Yes*, Boston.

Gulliver, P. H. (1979), *Disputes and Negotiations*, New York.

Janis, I. L. (1982), *Groupthink* (2nd edn), Boston.

Jervis, R. (1976), *Perception and Misperception in International Politics*, Princeton.

Miller, E. J. and Rice, A. K. (1967), *Systems of Organization*, London.

Vroom, V. H. and Yetton, P. W. (1973), *Leadership and Decision Making*, Pittsburgh.

See also: *conflict*; *decision making*.

Conformity

Early attempts to explain the many uniformities observable in human social behaviour in terms of either a limited number of instincts (McDougall) or some general principle of learning such as imitation or suggestion (Tarde, Le Bon) proved to be unsatisfactory because they were essentially circular explanations. Research on conformity *per se* did not commence until the question of accounting for regularities in behaviour was tackled experimentally in the laboratory.

In the 1930s Sherif investigated, under laboratory conditions, the formation and functioning of social norms. He chose a task, based on the autokinetic effect, for which there were no pre-established norms or standards which might aid his subjects in making their judgements. When a fixed point of light is viewed in an otherwise totally darkened room it will appear to move. Sherif's subjects had to estimate, in inches, the extent of this apparent movement. Individuals, making a series of such judgements alone, established their own particular norm. When several such individuals subsequently performed the task in each other's presence, a convergence in their estimates was noted, i.e. the emergence of a group norm. Other individuals, who made their initial estimates under group conditions, subsequently maintained the group norm when responding alone. It was Durkheim who had first identified the state of 'anomie' or normlessness. Sherif, by selecting the autokinetic effect, was able to investigate scientifically this social phenomenon, and he demonstrated how a social norm acts as a frame of reference to guiding individual action.

Enlightened liberals, who value the autonomy of the individual, disliked a possible implication of Sherif's findings: that humans are gullible. Asch, in the early 1950s, hoped to demonstrate individual autonomy by removing the ambiguity in the stimuli to be judged. Naive subjects in his experiment found themselves, on certain critical trials, in a minority of one when making simple judgements about the equivalence of length of lines. They were unaware of the fact that the other participants were, in reality, stooges of the experimenter who, on the pre-selected trials, were unanimous in making a wrong choice. On each trial the naive subject responded either last or last but one. On approximately two-thirds of the occasions when this conflict occurred, the naive subject remained independent. So Asch had proved his point. Or had he? It was the minority response in the Asch situation, however, that riveted people's attention i.e. yielding to the opinion of the false majority. Individuals differed quite widely in the extent to which they conformed. That naive subjects should conform on as many as a third of such occasions deeply shocked many Americans and also, one suspects, Asch himself.

The experiment had an immediate impact outside of Asch's own laboratory. Much was written, of a popular nature, about the prevalence of conformity in social life. By varying both the size and the unanimity of the false majority Asch showed that the effect depended crucially upon the majority being unanimous and that it was maximal in strength with a majority of four. Crutchfield mechanized the Asch procedure by standardizing on a group of five and substituting 'electronic' for live stooges. All five were naive subjects, each believing himself to be subject number five. This greatly increased the efficiency of data collection without significantly reducing the level of conformity. Deutsch and Gerard increased the individual's independence in the Asch situation by either increasing the salience of self to self (by requiring subjects to note down their own responses *before* hearing the responses of the others) or by decreasing the salience of self to others (with anonymous responding).

Milgram's experimental studies of obedience were as controversial in the mid 1960s as Asch's studies had been in the early 1950s. Milgram identified the conditions conducive to the carrying out of instructions coming from a legitimate source of authority (i.e. the experimenter). In response to Asch's studies, Moscovici has developed a theory of minority influence. He is concerned with identifying how it is that minorities, over time, come to influence the majority. Whilst his theory is based on laboratory evidence, Moscovici is more broadly interested in how creative individuals (like Freud, Einstein or Darwin) manage to convert the majority to their own way of thinking. He is thus more interested in studying creativity and change than in studying the maintenance of the status quo.

Robert M. Farr
London School of Economics and Political Science

References
Asch, S. E. (1956), 'Studies of independence and submission to group pressure: 1. A minority of one against a unanimous majority', *Psychological Monographs*, 70.
Crutchfield, R. S. (1955), 'Conformity and character', *American Psychologist*, 10.
Deutsch, M. and Gerard, H. B. (1955), 'A study of normative and informational social influences upon individual judgment', *Journal of Abnormal and Social Psychology*, 51.
Milgram, S. (1974), *Obedience to Authority: An Experimental View*, London.
Moscovici, S. (1976), *Social Influence and Social Change*, London.
Sherif, M. (1935), 'A study of some social factors in perception', *Archives of Psychology*, 27.
See also: *commitment*.

Consciousness and its Disorders

The behaviourists took the view that science must ignore reports of conscious experience as unreliable, and deal only with publicly observable phenomena.

'Consciousness' was, accordingly, no more amenable to scientific investigation than concepts like 'ghost' and 'soul'. Latterly a cognitive approach has become increasingly influential in psychology, and in consequence the explanation of the existence and function of consciousness is no longer a taboo subject.

A variety of empirical phenomena indicate that if there is to be a scientific understanding of human thought, consciousness cannot be dismissed as a mere epiphenomenon. On the contrary, it relates to some very central aspect of the human information-processing system. The most dramatic of these phenomena are neuropsychological observations. Thus a syndrome called blindsight has been discovered which can arise with lesions to the occipital lobe of the brain. In this condition the patient can remain completely unaware of visual stimuli presented within a certain part of the field of vision. Yet if asked to 'guess', the patient can point very accurately to where a faint light has been flashed, or to discriminate a cross from a circle. One patient, when pressed, described the experience as a 'feeling' that it was 'smooth' (the O) or 'jagged' (the X), yet he stressed that he did not 'see' anything at all (Weiskrantz et al., 1974). This syndrome indicates that whatever systems are responsible for consciousness, they are not required in the performance of a task like pointing to a visual stimulus. Such a deduction would be difficult to make from phenomenological analysis of normal experience.

A better-known neurological condition, which is also relevant, is the so-called 'split brain' syndrome resulting from a rarely performed operation which attempts to control epilepsy. This involves the sectioning of the corpus callosum – the primary fibre tract joining the two cerebral hemispheres. After this operation, processing in the two separate hemispheres is relatively independent. It appears that at times each of the two processes can be sufficiently complex such that if normal people were to carry it out one would assume that they would be aware of doing so (see Levy, Trevarthen and Sperry, 1972). It is therefore plausible that in the split-brain patient the two hemispheres can give rise to two different conscious experiences at the same time.

Turning to normal human experimental psychology, it has been shown that if a meaningless pattern of jumbled lines is presented a very short time after a brief visual stimulus ('visual masking'), an observer may be unable to distinguish consciously anything about the stimulus. Yet a masked stimulus may facilitate the detection of a second stimulus, semantically related to it, which follows a second or so later (see Marcel, 1983). Thus semantic processing must be occurring without the subject being aware of it.

This third phenomenon, like the first one, shows that the relation between conscious awareness and types of cognitive operation can be intuitively surprising. A satisfactory explanation must, however, specify the relation between consciousness and the operation of the nervous system. The second phenomenon suggests that an attempt to explain awareness as some property of the physics or chemistry of the brain's material constituents is unlikely to be successful. Such phenomena have rather encouraged psychologists to attempt to explain consciousness not as a property of the cellular composition of the brain, but of the functional system of information-processing operations upon which thought is based. Consciousness, within a phenomenological conceptual framework, is thought to correspond to certain types of information-processing operations, within a mechanistic conceptual framework. But there has been no agreement at all over what these particular information-processing operations are. One view popular in the early 1970s was that a central working memory is used in most major cognitive operations and that consciousness corresponded to its content (for example, Atkinson and Shiffrin, 1971). However, most workers in the field now believe that there are in fact a variety of temporary holding stores, and no good explanation exists as to why the diverse totality of their contents should have any special ontological status. A second alternative position is that a number of cognitive operations are occurring in parallel in normal thought, but one dominates in its ability to control future cognitive and motor operations and because it can be spoken about and remembered (Shallice, 1972). In this approach the existence of a unitary conscious experience corresponds to the functional necessity for a single dominant mainstream of thought. Yet a third approach is that the human cognitive system contains a subsystem which oversees and modulates the operation of the more routine over-learned processes whereby thought and action are basically carried out. Awareness in some sense corresponds to what occurs in the supervisory modulating system (for example, Marshall and Morton, 1978).

In these types of explanation the phenomenal distinction between conscious experience and unconscious cognitive acts is explained through differences in the underlying processing operations. Properties of conscious experience – for example, the fact that the contents in some sense control action, that they can be spoken about, or that they can be remembered – are assumed to correspond to the properties of some rather special processing system which has developed in evolution. These types of functionalist explanations are, however, still not free of philosophical problems. For instance, Block (1980) has argued that as a thought experiment one could simulate the neuronal interactions within a brain by communication between people. Each person would be instructed that if he received certain signals from a set of other people he should send a signal to yet further people. Thus the acts of an individual person would mimic the operation of an individual neuron. Of course an enormous number of people would be required – Block uses the example of the population of China – and the process would be far slower than in the brain processes being simulated. It is highly implausible that the whole population involved would acquire a unitary awareness, and so Block argues that consciousness cannot just be a property of the system of processing operations since these are isomorphic in the two situations. Yet a processing system of sufficient power could presumably develop a set of 'concepts' to describe its own internal states. If a system with a particular functional architecture tended to develop the same set of such concepts, even given a wide variety of 'environments', and if these were isomorphic with those we attribute to consciousness, this would make the functionalist approach plausible despite paradoxes like Block's. The information processing approaches discussed earlier are attempts to characterize the essence of such a system. Therefore, despite undoubted philosophical difficulties, information-processing theorizing provides for the first time a research programme through which a theory of consciousness could be produced which is solidly linked to scientific findings.

Tim Shallice
MRC Applied Psychology Unit, Cambridge

References

Atkinson, R. C. and Shiffrin, R. M. (1971), 'The control of short-term memory', *Scientific American*, 224.
Block, N. (1980), *Readings in Philosophy of Psychology*, vol. 1, Cambridge, Mass.
Levy, J., Trevarthen, C. and Sperry, R. W. (1972), 'Perception of bilateral chimeric figures following hemispheric disconnection', *Brain*, 95.
Marcel, A. J. (1983), 'Conscious and unconscious perception', *Cognitive Psychology*, 15.
Marshall, J. C. and Morton, J. (1978), 'On the mechanics of Emma', in A. Sinclar *et al.* (eds), *The Child's Conception of Language*, Berlin.
Shallice, T. (1972), 'Dual functions of consciousness', *Psychological Review*, 79.
Weiskrantz, L., Warrington, E. K., Saunders, M. D. and Marshall, J. (1974), 'Visual capacity in the hemianopic field following a restricted occipital ablation', *Brain*, 97.

Further Reading

Maudler, J. (1984), *Mind and Body: Psychology of Emotion and Stress*, New York.
Shallice, T. (1978), 'The dominant action system; an information-processing approach to consciousness', in K. S. Pope and J. L. Singer (eds), *The Stream of Consciousness*, New York.
See also: *memory*; *nervous system*.

Conservation

Conservation is essentially a stockholding activity. Holding back today allows greater use tomorrow or perhaps 100 years hence. Economists' attention, and ours, is generally focused on natural phenomena – fish, oil, environmental quality, and suchlike – although machines, literature, culture may also be conserved and many of the same principles apply.

The earth is finite, its resources and its ability to carry population and absorb pollution are limited. Some economists believe that continued growth in output and population will bring the world to these limits perhaps rather quickly. According to this view both nonrenewable stocks (such as oils and metals) and renewable resources (for example, fish and land) will come under increasing and perhaps irreparable strain. Environmental damage (through erosion, build-up of carbon dioxide) will likewise become excessive, and habits of high consumption, once built up, will be difficult to break. Radical and Marxist economists often blame such problems on capitalism, even if the Eastern bloc appears to have fared equally badly.

A more characteristic view among economists is that *markets* provide adequate incentives to conservation. Resource use will be determined mainly by expected price movements and the discount rate. Scarcity involves high prices, expected scarcity expected high prices, increasing the advantage both of conserving the resource and of taking other resource-saving measures such as recycling and appropriate technical change. Only where market failure occurs is there perhaps cause to worry, and even then such failure may tend to excessive conservation. Moreover, market failure can generally be recognized and alleviated. Occasionally the view emerges that such difficulties present a challenge, which mighty man must and will overcome. Wise use of resources to build up capital and develop new techniques and skills may be a crucial part of this fight.

The 1973 oil crisis exhibited vividly the possibilities and dangers of a resource crisis. The sudden fourfold rise in oil prices caused worldwide disruption; the ensuing slumpflation (though doubtless partly due to earlier causes) has been an obvious disaster, economically, medically, and socially, Even an oil-rich country like Britain has been depressed. Recent econometric studies have indicated great responsiveness to price, but building up slowly over decades as capital, technologies and habits change. It is the slowness of these changes that has created the current crisis, while in the longer run technological changes may bring unwelcome side effects.

Renewable resources (like fish) are constantly replenished by nature, hence permitting (up to a point) continued use without depletion. There is a maximum sustainable yield, although it may be desirable to hold yield below this level because of harvesting cost, or above it because of discounting. With nonrenewable resources (like oil), use now precludes use later, although reserves can be extended by improved extraction techniques and by exploration. Metals are normally considered nonrenewable, although recycling can extend their use.

The natural environment is another kind of resource. To some extent it is the concern of the rich, for example, as a source of landscape and recreational experiences. However, in this it differs little from other parts of market and indeed non-market systems. But not all environmental problems are of this type. Water pollution and air pollution damage those who live in the areas concerned – often the poor, as the rich can afford to move away (into 'Conservation Areas' perhaps). Erosion, flooding and pesticides will affect everyone. There are also international problems, such as global overheating and the excessive build-up of carbon dioxide leading to difficult-to-reverse melting of the polar ice caps and very extensive flooding. Problems associated with nuclear radiation are widely feared.

There are two reasons for including population in this discussion: (1) Population size and growth are major determinants of problems of resources and environment; (2) Childbearing involves the characteristic externality problem of unpaid burdens on others, especially if fiscal help is given to large families. Currently the world's population is doubling every 40 years. In some countries, such as China and Taiwan, dramatic downward shifts in birthrate are occurring. But elsewhere, as in India and most Muslim and Roman Catholic countries, signs of change are very weak. Even in most developed countries population growth continues, with particularly strong resource effects. The causes are complex and poorly understood, although cost has been found relevant.

Many factors underlie inadequate conservation (see Pearce, 1976), for example, difficulties of prediction and the appropriate treatment of uncertainty. Particularly important are common access problems, applying not only to fishing, but to forestry, hunting, extraction of oil and deep sea nodule mining, and to population growth. Tax regimes can be strongly anti-conservationist - childbearing and US mining are important examples. Another possible problem is that the discount rate used is too high, giving undue favour to the present; the difficulties here are: (1) that this is an economy-wide problem, by no means confined to resources, and indeed some writers have used it to justify greater investment and faster growth; (2) governments may hesitate to override the preferences of the current generation; and (3) more radical authors suggest that growth itself uses resources and damages the environment, although this is disputed.

Remedies are difficult to summarize. Characteristic-ally those used (and supported by most non-economists) are regulations, whereas much of the economic debate is over the superiority of taxes. Regulations include net size, limited seasons and outright bans in fishing, limits or bans for pollution, including pesticides, and planning regulations for building and land use. The objection is that lack of discrimination leads to inefficiency; sometimes extreme inefficiency, as when limited fishing seasons invite the multiplication of boats, which stand idle over the rest of the year. Direct controls also tend to be narrowly specific, leaving no incentive to achieve more than the specified cut-back or to undertake R & D to improve control. Fiscal measures are occasionally used but with little finesse, and subsidies or tax concessions (as for airlines, heavy industries, children) are generally preferred to taxes. More promising examples, such as fuel-saving subsidies and also the emerging systems of penalizing pollution in several European countries, incidentally (and unlike controls) generating substantial revenue. There are many other possible remedies, such as nationalization, diversification (often favoured by ecologists) indirect measures (recycling, durability and curbs on advertising and so on), auctioned rights (for example to cull a resource or to pollute), public expenditure (on sewage or agricultural infrastructure and so on), provision of information, including forecasts, and attempts to influence attitudes. As Baumol and Oates (1979) emphasize, each of these methods, or indeed various combinations, will be appropriate in particular circumstances.

Richard Lecomber
University of Bristol

References

Baumol, W. J. and Oates, W. E. (1979), *Economics, Environmental Policy and the Quality of Life*, Englewood Cliffs, N.J.

O'Riordan, T. (1976), *Environmentalism*, London.

Pearce, D. W. (1976), *Environmental Economics*, London.

Schultz, T. P. (1981), *Economics of Population*, Reading, Mass.

See also: *energy*; *population and resources*.

Conservatism

Conservatism is the doctrine that the reality of any society is to be found in its historical development, and therefore that the most reliable, though not the sole, guide for governments is caution in interfering with what has long been established. Clearly distinctive conservative doctrine emerged in the 1790s, in reaction to the rationalist projects of the French revolutionaries, and its classic statement is to to found in Edmund Burke's *Reflections on the Revolution in France* (1790). Burke's historical emphasis was itself the outcome of deep currents in European thought, currents rejecting abstract reasoning as a method for understanding the human world. The sheer flamboyance of Burke's rhetoric was necessary to bring conservatism into the world, however, since the doctrine in its purest form consists of a few maxims of prudence (concerning the complexity of things and the wisdom of caution) which, in the intellectualist atmosphere of the last two centuries, make a poor showing against the seductive philosophical pretensions of modern ideologies. These competing doctrines claim to explain not only the activity of politics, but man and his place in the universe. Burke himself thought that this wider picture was supplied for us by religion, and thus he was prone to extend the reverence appropriate to divine things so that it embraced the established institutions of society. This fideist emphasis, however, ought not to conceal the fact that conservatism rests upon a deep scepticism about the ability of any human being, acting within the constraints of a present consciousness, to understand the daunting complexities of human life as it has developed over recorded time.

Conservatism construes society as something that grows, and conservatives prefer pruning leaves and branches to tearing up the roots. The latter view is taken by radicals who believe that nothing less than a revolutionary transformation both of society and of human beings themselves will serve to save us from what they believe to be a deeply unjust society. Generically, then, all are conservative who oppose the revolutionary transformation of society. Specifically, however, conservatism is one of three doctrinal partners, each of which may plausibly claim centrality in the European political tradition. One of these is liberalism, constituted by its allegiance to liberty and the values of reform, and the other is constitutional socialism, whose fundamental preoccupation with the problem of the poor leads it to construe all political problems as issues of realizing a truer community. Modern politics is a ceaseless dialogue between these three tendencies and movements.

Conservatism in this specific sense emerged from a split in the Whig party in late eighteenth-century Britain, and it was only in the 1830s, when the present nomenclature of each of the three doctrines crystallized, that Tories began calling themselves 'conservatives'. This name failed to catch on in other countries, most notably perhaps the United States, where 'conservative' until recently connoted timidity and lack of enterprise. From the 1960s onwards, however, the tendency of American liberals (predominantly but not exclusively in the Democratic Party) to adopt socialist policies has provoked a reaction which calls itself 'neo-conservative' in testimony to its adherence to many classical liberal positions.

Since it is conservative doctrine that political parties must respond to changing circumstances, it would be not merely futile but paradoxical to discover a doctrinal essence in the changing attitudes of any particular Conservative party. Nevertheless, conservatism is not merely a doctrine but a human disposition, and many conservative temperaments have influenced the British Conservative Party, whose response to the successive problems of the modern world may give some clue to conservatism. Under Disraeli it organized itself successfully to exploit successive nineteenth-century extensions of the franchise, and its electoral viability has since largely depended upon the allegiance of the figure known to political scientists as the 'Tory workingman'. In the latter part of the nineteenth century, it rode a tide of imperial emotion and economic protection and stood for the unity of the United Kingdom against attempts to grant self-government to Ireland. Between the two World Wars, Baldwin saw it as the task of the Party to educate an electorate, now enjoying universal suffrage, in the responsibilities of power. After Attlee's creation of the Welfare State from 1945 to 1951, Churchill and Macmillan found conservative reasons for sustaining a welfarist consensus, but since 1976, Mrs Thatcher and a dominant wing of the Party identified the expense of the welfare state in its present form as one of the emerging problems of politics.

A principle of conservation offers little substantive guide to political action, and is vulnerable to the objection brought by F. A. Hayek: 'By its nature, it cannot offer an alternative to the direction we are moving' (*The Constitution of Liberty*, 1960). It is a mistake, however, to identify conservatism with hostility to change; the point is rather, the *source* of change. It is characteristic of all radicals to seek one big change, after which a perfected community will be essentially changeless. On this basis, they often seek to monopolize the rhetoric of change. Liberals consider it the duty of an active government to make the reforms that will dissipate social evils. While refusing to erect limitation of government into an absolute principle, conservatives tend to think that, within a strong framework of laws, society will often work out for itself a better response to evils than can be found in the necessary complexities of legislation, and worse, of course, in the simple *dictat* of the legislator. Conservatism is, in this respect, a political application of the legal maxim that hard cases make bad law. It is thus a central mistake to think of conservatism as mere hostility to change. It poses, rather, the issue of where change should originate.

Like all political doctrines, conservatism is loosely but importantly associated with a particular temperament, a view of the world. It is characteristic of the conservative temperament to value established identities, to praise habit and to respect prejudice, not because it is irrational, but because such things anchor the darting impulses of human beings in solidities of custom which we often do not begin to value until we are already losing them. Radicalism often generates youth movements, while conservatism is a disposition found among the mature, who have discovered what it is in life they most value. The ideological cast of contemporary thought has provoked some writers to present conservatism as if it contained the entire sum of political wisdom; but this is to mistake the part for the whole. Nevertheless, a society without a strong element of conservatism could hardly be anything but impossibly giddy.

Kenneth Minogue
London School of Economics and Political Science

Reference
Hayek, F. A. (1960), *The Constitution of Liberty*, London.

Further Reading
Kirk, R. (1953), *The Conservative Mind*, Chicago.
Oakeshott, M. (1962), *Rationalism in Politics*, London.
Scruton, R. (1980), *Meaning of Conservatism*, London.
See also: *Burke; liberalism; radicalism.*

Constitutional Psychology

Constitutional psychology is, at the same time, an obvious and widely accepted feature of psychological thinking, and a controversial view held by relatively few psychologists. It may be defined as the study of the relation between, on the one hand, the morphological structure and the physiological functioning of the body and, on the other hand, psychological and social functioning. Few psychologists would disagree with the idea that bodily structure and functioning are related to one's psychosocial functioning, and in fact considerable data support this relation (see Sorell and Nowak, 1981, for a review).

The early work of Kretschmer (1921) and the later, more comprehensive research of Sheldon (1940, 1942) were criticized on conceptual, methodological, and data analytic grounds (Humphreys, 1957). The scientific community had little confidence in the strengths of association between physique type and temperament reported in this work (e.g., correlations on the order of +.8 between theoretically related physique and temperament types; Sheldon, 1941). However, more methodologically careful work has established that significant associations do exist between: (1) somatotypes (endomorphs, mesomorphs, and ectomorphs) and/or other features of the body (such as its physical attractiveness); and (2) personality or temperament characteristics theoretically related to these somatotypes (for example, viscerotonic traits, somatotonic traits, and cerebrotonic traits, respectively) or to the other bodily features (e.g., physically attractive children are more popular with peers than are physically unattractive children). But, the strengths of the association are considerably less than

that reported by Sheldon; for example, correlations more typically cluster around +.3 (Walker, 1962). Moreover, research relating pubertal change (such as early, on-time, and late maturation) to psychosocial functioning has established also that significant relations exist between physiological (such as hormonal) changes or morphological characteristics and psychosocial functioning (Petersen and Taylor, 1980).

The controversy involved in constitutional psychology surrounds the explanation of the empirical relations between bodily characteristics and psychosocial functions. These explanations involve the well-known nature-nurture controversy. Only a minority of psychologists working in this area subscribe to nature-based interpretations of body-behaviour relations. Such interpretations stress that hereditary and/or other biological variables provide a common source of morphology, physiology, and psychosocial functioning. For example, the biological variables thought to provide the source of one's mesomorphic somatotype are thought also to provide the source of one's aggressive or delinquent behaviours (Hall and Lindzey, 1978). Nurture-based explanations of body–behaviour relations, which have been most popular among American psychologists (for example, McCandless, 1970), stress that environmental events (for example, socialization experiences) influence both one's bodily and one's behavioural characteristics. An example of this type of interpretation is that the socialization experiences that lead one to have a chubby body build will lead one to be dependent and/or self-indulgent (Hall and Lindzey, 1978). Finally, some interpretations propose that biological and experiential variables interact to provide a basis of one's physical, physiological, and psychosocial characteristics (see, for example, Lerner, 1982; Petersen and Taylor, 1980). A representative idea here is that children with different physical characteristics evoke differential reactions in significant others, and that these reactions feed back to children and provide a differential basis for their further psychosocial functioning; this functioning includes personality and social behaviour and also self-management behaviours (e.g., in regard to diet and exercise) which may influence their physical characteristics.

There are still no crucial or critical tests of key hypotheses derived from any of the extant interpretative positions. Indeed, data in this area, although increasingly more often theoretically-derived, are still typically open to alternative explanations. It is likely that in this area of psychology descriptive advances will continue to exceed explanatory ones for some time.

Richard M. Lerner
Pennsylvania State University

References

Hall, C. S. and Lindzey, G. (1978), *Theories of Personality* (3rd edn), New York.

Humphreys, L. G. (1957), 'Characteristics of type concepts with special reference to Sheldon's typology', *Psychological Bulletin*, 54.

Kretschmer, E. (1921), *Körperbau und Charakter*, Berlin.

Lerner, R. M. (1982), 'Children and adolescents as producers of their own development', *Developmental Review*, 2.

McCandless, B. R. (1970), *Adolescents*, Hinsdale, Ill.

Petersen, A. C. and Taylor, B. (1980), 'The biological approach to adolescence: biological change and psychological adaptation', in J. Adelson (ed.), *Handbook of Adolescent Psychology*, New York.

Sheldon, W. H. (1940), *The Varieties of Human Physique*, New York.

Sheldon, W. H. (1942), *The Varieties of Temperament*, New York.

Sorell, G. T. and Nowak, C. A. (1981), 'The role of physical attractiveness as a contributor to individual development', in R. M. Lerner and N. A. Busch-Rossnagel (eds), *Individuals as Producers of Their Development*, New York.

Walker, R. N. (1962), 'Body build and behavior in young children. I: Body build and nursery school teachers ratings', *Monographs of the Society for Research in Child Development*, 27.

Constitutions and Constitutionalism

The constitution of a state is the collection of rules and principles according to which a state is governed. In antiquity the most important function of a constitution was to determine who should rule. The criterion which served as the basis for assigning political power reflected the ethos of the society. Thus each constitutional form exercised a moulding influence on virtue; the good citizen was a different being in an oligarchy, a democracy and an aristocracy (Aristotle). Although modern constitutions are far more complex, still the rules they establish for acquiring and exercising governmental power will usually embody the underlying norms and ideology of the polity.

The constitution of the modern nation state contains three main elements: (1) It establishes the principal institutions of government and the relationships among these institutions. These institutions may be structured on traditional Western lines of a division of executive, legislative and judicial responsibilities. The constitutions of one-party states gives greater emphasis to the structures of the governing party, while those based on theocratic principles assign a dominant position to religious offices and institutions. (2) Constitutions provide for a distribution of governmental power over the nation's territory. In a unitary state, local units of government are established as agencies of the central government. The constitution of a federal state assigns power directly to central and local levels of government. (3) Constitutions provide a compendium of fundamental rights and duties of citizens including their rights to participate in the institutions of government. Some constitutions emphasize economic and social rights as much, if not more, than political and legal/procedural rights.

In most countries there is a single document called 'The Constitution' which contains most of the significant elements of the constitutial system. But this is not the only form in which the rules of a constitution may be expressed. They may also take the form of ordinary laws such as statutes or decrees, judicial decisions or well-established customs and conventions. The United Kingdom is distinctive in that it does not have a document known as the Constitution; all of its constitutional rules are expressed more informally as statutes, judicial opinions, customs and conventions. Since the American Revolution the worldwide trend has been very much towards the codification of constitutional norms. New states established in the aftermath of revolution, the withdrawal of empire and world war have relied on a formal constitutional text to set out their basic governmental arrangements. However, even in these new nations, statutes, judicial decisions and conventions usually supplement the formal constitution.

A country may have a constitution but may not enjoy constitutionalism. Constitutionalism is a political condition in which the constitution functions as an effective and significant limit on government. Where constitutionalism characterizes a regime, the constitution is 'antecedent' to government, and those who govern are constrained by its terms. The constitutional rules of such a regime are not easily changed – even when they are obstacles to policies supported by leading politicians. Thus, constitutional government is said to be 'limited government' (Sartori, 1956). The limits imposed by a constitution are sometimes said to embody a 'higher law' – the enduring will of a people – which constitutes the basis of a legitimate check on the will of governments representing transient majorities (McIlwain, 1947; Corwin, 1955).

Constitutionalism may be maintained by the practice of judicial review, whereby judges with a reasonable degree of independence of the other branches of government have the authority to veto laws and activities of government on the grounds that they conflict with the constitution. Constitutionalism may also be manifest in a formal amendment process that requires much more than the support of a dominant political party or a simple majority of the population to change the formal constitution. The British situation demonstrates, however, that neither of these practices is a necessary condition for constitutionalism. In that country the most important constitutional precepts are maintained and enforced more informally through well-established popular attitudes and the restraint of politicians (Dicey, 1959).

The reality of constitutionalism depends on whether there are political forces genuinely independent of the government of the day powerful enough to insist on the government's observance of constitutional limits. Critics of those liberal democracies that claim to practise constitutionalism contend that in reality the constitutions imposing constitutional limits (e.g. the judiciary or the opposition party) are not independent of government, because they are controlled by social or economic interests aligned with the government. On the other hand, defenders of these regimes may point to occasions on which the maintenance of constitutional rules has forced political leaders to abandon major policies or even to abandon office (e.g. US President Nixon in the Watergate affair).

In countries that have formal 'written' constitutions, whether or not they practise constitutionalism, the constitution may serve an important symbolic function. Constitutions are often employed as instruments of political education designed to inculcate public respect for political and social norms. A constitution may also be a means of gaining legitimacy, both internally and externally, for a regime. This is a primary function of constitutions in communist states (Brunner, 1977). The development of codes of fundamental human rights since the Second World War has prompted many states to include such rights in their domestic constitutions in order to ingratiate themselves in the international community.

Peter H. Russell
University of Toronto

References

Andrews, W. G. (1961), *Constitutions and Constitutionalism*, Princeton.

The Politics of Aristotle (1948), trans. by E. Barker, Oxford.

Brunner, G. (1977), 'The functions of communist constitutions', *Review of Socialist Law*, 2.

Corwin, E. S. (1955), *The 'Higher Law' Background of American Constitutional Law*, Ithaca, N.Y.

Dicey, A. V. (1959), *Introduction to the Study of the Law of the Constitution*, 10th edn, London.

Friedrich, C. J. (1950), *Constitutional Government and Democracy*, New York.

McIlwain, C. H. (1947), *Constitutionalism: Ancient and Modern*, revised edn, Ithaca, N.Y.

Sartori, G. (1956), 'Constitutionalism: a preliminary discussion', *American Political Science Review*, 56.

See also: *human rights*.

Consumer Behaviour

In his authoritative review of the development of utility theory, Stigler (1950) wrote, 'If consumers do not buy less of a commodity when their incomes rise, they will surely buy less when the price of the commodity rises. This was the chief product – so far as the hypotheses on economic behaviour go of the long labours of a very large number of able economists . . . [who] had known all along that demand curves have negative slopes, quite independently of their utility theorizing.' So what use is utility theory, the reigning paradigm among economists interested in consumer behaviour?

Thirty-five years on, data on consumer behaviour have expanded enormously, computing costs have plummetted, statistical numeracy has spread and the range of applied studies has multiplied. Simultaneously more content has been put into choice theory and more accessible links forged via the cost and other 'dual' functions between the structure of preferences and behaviour. A comprehensive modern treatment of choice theory and its application to most types of consumer behaviour can be found in Deaton and Muellbauer (1980).

The existence of an ordinal utility function defined on bundles of goods implies that certain axioms of choice are fulfilled, the key ones being transitivity or consistency of choice, continuity (small differences matter only a little) and nonsatiation. Preferences can also be represented through the cost function. This defines the minimum cost of reaching a given utility level for a consumer facing given prices. Among its properties: it is concave in prices and its price derivatives give purchases as functions of prices and the utility level i. e., compensated demands. The great advantage is that a simple step – differentiation – leads from a representation of preferences to a description of the behaviour of a consumer faced with a linear budget constraint. Concavity then immediately implies the law of demand described above. In fact, considerably more is implied: the matrix of compensated price derivatives is symmetric negative semidefinite. A great deal of econometric effort has gone into applying and testing these very considerable restrictions on behaviour.

Systems of demand equations are usually estimated for annual or quarterly observations on aggregate consumer spending on such categories as food, clothing, housing, fuel, etc. More is now understood about the links between individual and aggregate behaviour. For example, under quite restrictive conditions, average behaviour is like that of a single consumer so that then one can say a 'representative consumer' exists. Specific assumptions on the structure of preferences yield further implications. Thus an additive utility function strongly restricts the cross-price responses of demands. These and many other properties are analysed in Gorman (1976) who makes elegant use of cost and profit functions. Almost invariably, some kind of separability assumptions are made in applied work: thus, preferences for current period goods need to be separable from the allocation of leisure and of consumption in other periods if demands are functions only of current prices and total expenditure on these goods. On the other hand, such static demand functions are, by most empirical evidence, mis-specified. A widely applied hypothesis which can explain why is that preferences are conditioned by past behaviour, not only of the consumer but of others, so that demand functions are dynamic (more on this below).

By assuming the consumer can lend or borrow at the same interest rate, the utility maximizing consumer's intertemporal choices are subject to a linear budget constraint. In this life-cycle theory of consumption, developed by Modigliani and his co-workers, the budget is life-cycle wealth consisting of initial asset holdings, income and discounted expected income, and relative prices depend on real interest rates. Extensions to the demand for money and durables have yielded interesting insights into, for example, the role of interest rates.

The treatment of income expectations has been the most controversial issue for empirical workers using this theory. The simple treatment by Friedman in his book on the permanent income hypothesis of consumption, as well as his suppression of a separate role for assets, is now seen as less than satisfactory. Hall (1978) has shown that, under certain conditions, the life-cycle model together with rational expectations implies that consumption follows a random walk which seems not a bad empirical approximation for some countries.

One of the major criticisms of life-cycle theory is that the budget constraints are not in fact linear for credit constrained consumers, though the implications are hard to model on aggregate data. Much attention has been paid to non-linear budget constraints in the analysis of behaviour from household surveys. Labour supply decisions are the major example; others are the choice of housing tenure and transport models where choice has discrete elements. An integrated statistical framework with rational and random elements for such decisions now exists. In this context too, restrictions on preferences have major empirical content, for example, additive preferences allow great simplifications in the analysis of repeated surveys of the same households. A more traditional use of household budget surveys collected to derive weights for cost of living indices and to analyse inequality has been the derivation of Engel functions which link expenditures on different goods with the total budget and household demography. A major use has been derivation of equivalence scales used to standardize budgets in studies of poverty and inequality for variations in household size and structure.

Another way to put more content into the theory is to regard the household as a producer using market goods and time of utility yielding commodities. This household production approach has proved useful, for example, in the measurement of quality change, in welfare measurement of the provision of public leisure facilities, and in the economics of fertility and other aspects of family life. There has been little work, however, on how decisions by individual family members are co-ordinated, an important lacuna.

Most decisions are, of course, made under uncertainty and the expected utility approach has been widely used by economists. Under the axioms assumed here, subjective probabilities are themselves defined and this gives rise to a theory of learning founded on Bayes' Theorem. The intuitive notion of risk averting behaviour here has a formal basis and applications to the behaviour of financial markets have proved particularly popular. In recent years, evidence against some of the axioms has accumulated from laboratory experiments on volunteers. So far no agreement exists on a better set of axioms.

There have been many criticisms of the utility maximizing approach ranging from 'it is tautologous' to the introspective doubt that anyone could be so good at absorbing and storing information and then computing consistent decisions. H. A. Simon's notion of bounded rationality has much intuitive appeal. Certainly one can interpret the role of costs of adjustment or habits based on own or others' behaviour in this light. The implication of a stimulus response smaller in the short run than in the long is suggestive. Psychologists have suggested models such as that of 'cognitive dissonance' which appeal in particular contexts but do not yield a general behavioural theory. Market researchers have developed distinct approaches of their own based on the interpretation of attitude surveys used as marketing tools and with the major focus on brand choice, repeat buying and the introduction of new varieties. They have drawn relatively little out of the utility maximizing hypothesis, though not all these approaches are necessarily inconsistent with it.

John Muellbauer
Nuffield College, University of Oxford

References
Deaton, A. and Muellbauer, J. (1980), *Economics and Consumer Behavior*, New York.
Gorman, W. M. (1976), 'Tricks with utility functions', in M. Artis and R. Nobay (eds), *Essays in Economic Analysis*, Cambridge.
Hall, R. E. (1978), 'Stochastic implications of the life cycle-permanent income hypothesis: theory and evidence', *Journal of Political Economy*, 86.

Stigler, G. (1950), 'The development of utility theory', *Journal of Political Economy*, 58.
See also: *consumer surplus; consumption function; marketing research; maximization.*

Reference
Deaton, A. and Muellbauer, J. (1980), *Economics and Consumer Behavior*, New York.
See also: *consumer behaviour; consumption function.*

Consumer Surplus

There can be few areas of economics where more ink has been spilled in obfuscating an essentially simple idea. The basic idea of the change in consumer surplus is to measure the loss or gain to a consumer from a change in consumption or from a change in one or more prices. The early formulation by Dupuit in 1844 was justified by Marshall in 1880. It consists of taking the area under the demand curve which traces out the effect of changes in the good's price, holding constant the budget in order to measure the change in utility in money terms. Already in 1892 Pareto criticized Marshall's assumption of a constant marginal utility of the budget. Indeed, there are only two circumstances where Marshall's formulation is correct: either the proportions in which goods are consumed are independent of the budget, which is grossly untrue empirically, or, for the particular good whose price is changing, the demand is unaffected by changes in the budget.

Hicks in 1939 recognized that the correct measure is to take the change in area under the compensated demand curve. However, as Samuelson remarked in l947, consumer surplus was essentially a superfluous concept since there was already an established theory of economic index numbers. The modern theory of index numbers is based on the cost or expenditure function which gives the minimum cost of reaching a given indifference curve at a specified set of prices. The money value of a change in utility is then given by the change in cost at some reference prices. When the change in utility is caused by some price changes, Hicks's 'compensating variation' can be viewed as the measure which uses the new prices as reference and his 'equivalent variation' as that which uses the old prices as reference.

There is a widespread impression that the computation of such correct concepts is intrinsically harder or requires more information than computing Marshallian consumer surplus. However, simple and accurate approximations to the correct measures are available, and straightforward algorithms exist to calculate them with any required degree of accuracy. Finally, it should be noted that *aggregating* utility changes over different consumers raises a new issue: is a dollar to the poor worth the same in social terms as a dollar to the rich? Consumer surplus as such does not address this question, though it is an inescapable one in cost benefit analysis.

John Muellbauer
Nuffield College, University of Oxford

Consumption Function

The consumption function expresses the functional dependence of consumption on variables thought to influence the level of consumption expenditure by individuals, such as income, wealth and the rate of interest. The consumption function was an important innovation introduced into economic theory by J. M. Keynes in his *General Theory of Employment, Interest and Money* (1936), to undermine the classical orthodoxy that the rate of interest acts to equilibrate savings and investment at the full employment level of income. Keynes made consumption, and therefore saving, a function of income, and by doing so divorced the savings function from the investment function. He then showed that if plans to invest fall short of plans to save out of the full employment level of income, there will be a tendency for the level of income (not the rate of interest) to fall to bring saving and investment into equilibrium again, the extent of the fall being given by the value of the income multiplier which is the reciprocal of the marginal propensity to save. By means of the consumption function, Keynes had apparently demonstrated the possibility that an economy may find itself in an equilibrium state at less than full employment. This demonstration was part of the Keynesian revolution of thought which undermined the idea that there are macroeconomic forces at work which automatically guarantee that economies tend to long run full employment. This is the theoretical importance of the consumption function.

The practical interest in the consumption function relates to the relation between consumption and income through time. Keynes seemed to suggest that the long run consumption function was non-proportional, so that as societies became richer they would spend proportionately less on consumption, implying that a higher proportion of income would have to be invested if economies were not to stagnate. Fears were expressed that mature economic societies might run out of profitable investment opportunities. The international cross section evidence reveals an interesting pattern. The savings ratio does rise with the level of development but at a decreasing rate, levelling off in maturity at about 25 per cent of national income. There is a voluminous literature concerning why this should be the case. It is as if saving is a luxury good which then loses its appeal. James Duesenberry (1949) developed the relative income hypothesis, which predicts that the savings-income ratio will remain unchanged through time if the personal distribution of income remains unchanged. Ando and Modigliani (1963) developed the life-cycle hypothesis of saving, which predicts a constant savings ratio if the rate of growth of population and per capita income are steady. Milton Friedman (1957) developed the permanent income hypothesis, arguing that individuals wish to maintain a constant relation between their consumption and a measure of permanent income determined by wealth and other factors. To discriminate between the hypotheses is virtually impossible. As societies develop, both growth and income inequality first increase and then decelerate and stabilize, which would explain the historical savings behaviour observed. Other factors that might be important relate to the increased monetization of an economy, which then yields diminishing returns. However, the fears of a lack of investment opportunities to match growing saving, owing to the saturation of markets, seems to be unfounded.

A. P. Thirlwall
University of Kent

References

Ando, A. and Modigliani, F. (1963), 'The life cycle hypothesis of saving: aggregate implications and tests', *American Economic Review*.
Duesenberry, J. (1949), *Income, Saving and the Theory of Consumer Behavior*, Cambridge, Mass.
Friedman, M. (1957), *A Theory of the Consumption Function*, Washington.

See also: *consumer behaviour; consumer surplus.*

Co-operatives

Co-operatives are economic organizations run by their members on the basis of one person, one vote, with their trading surplus being distributed among the membership in an agreed manner. Membership can therefore be seen as an extention of corporate shareholding except that, in co-operatives, decision making is based on democratic principles, and a capital stake is not necessarily the crucial element in joining. Indeed, the return on capital holdings is generally fixed at a low level, leaving the bulk of the surplus to be allocated according to member transactions. For example, in consumer co-operatives, membership derives from the act of purchase and profits are distributed according to the amount spent. In agricultural co-ops, the members are private farmers who join forces for production, retailing and services. Other important co-operative forms include credit unions and housing co-operatives, in which the membership are borrowers and lenders and tenants respectively, and producer co-operatives, in which the workers control the business through some democratic process and jointly share the profits as income.

The first co-operative was opened by twenty-eight Lancashire workers in Toad Lane, Rochdale, in 1844, who developed the seven 'Co-operative Principles' which still form the basis of the international co-operative movement. These are open membership; one member, one vote; limited return on capital; allocation of surplus in proportion to member transactions; cash trading; stress on education; and religious and political neutrality. They were reviewed by the International Co-operative Alliance (ICA), the world-wide organization of all co-ops, in 1966, and the latter two principles were dropped in favour of a new one supporting inter-co-operative collaboration. The international co-operative movement has now grown to enormous proportions, with the more than 700,000 co-operatives affiliated to the ICA in 1980 containing some 350 million members in 65 countries. The largest number of societies were agricultural and credit co-operatives, with a quarter of a million each world-wide covering some 180 million members between them. However, the largest number of members are in consumer co-operatives, containing some 130 million in around 60,000 societies. There are also some 45,000 industrial co-operatives with a labour force in excess of five and a half million workers.

Inspired by the Yugoslav system of workers' self-management of industry and following the seminal work of Ward (1958) and Vanek (1970), these producer co-operatives, or labour-managed firms as they have become known, have been studied extensively in recent years (see Ireland and Law (1982) for a survey). Analysts interested in how enterprise decisions change when the interests of workers replace profitability as the corporate objective, have focused on four main areas: the possibility of sluggish or even 'perverse' production responses to shifts in demand and cost conditions, of insufficient investment, of managerial deficiencies and unwillingness to bear risks, and of a boost to performance due to higher worker morale. The latter prospect has stimulated interest in schemes for worker participation in management as a way of obtaining the positive incentive effects without the presumed deficiencies of full workers' control.

There are producer co-operative sectors in most Western economies, the largest and most successful being the Mondragon group in the Basque area of Spain. Since its formation in the mid-1950s, an integrated productive, retail, financial and educational structure has emerged providing around 16,000 industrial jobs. Empirical work establishes the group to be relatively more productive and profitable than comparable capitalist firms, as well as being better able to meet social goals (see Thomas in Jones and Svejnar, 1982). Other studies isolate a positive productivity effect in the 20,000 Italian producer co-operatives, the 700 French ones and the 800 societies in the United States (see Jones and Svejnar, 1982). However, apart from Mondragon, producer co-operatives have tended to be relatively small, under-capitalized, concentrated in traditional sectors like textiles and processing, and short-lived. The co-operative form has probably failed to displace joint stock companies despite their democratic structure and the productivity benefits because of difficulties with risk-bearing; entrepreneurial workers cannot spread their risks by working in a number of activities in the way that capital owners can spread theirs by holding a diversified portfolio of assets. Hence capital has historically hired workers rather than labour hiring capital, but recently many new producer co-operatives have been founded as a way of maintaining employment – some 400 in the UK between 1975 and 1980 – and if risk-bearing problems can be solved this may prove to be an important type of enterprise in the future.

Saul Estrin
University of Southampton

References

Ireland, N. J. and Law, P. J. (1982), *The Economics of Labour-Managed Enterprises*, London.
Jones, D. C. and Svejnar, J. (1982), *Participatory and Self-Managed Firms*, Lexington, Mass.
Vanek, J. (1970), *The General Theory of Labour-Managed Market Economics*, Ithaca, N.Y.
Ward, B. (1958), 'The Firm in Illyria; market syndicalism', *American Economic Review*, 55.

See also: *industrial democracy*.

Corporate Enterprise

Corporations as an important business form appeared in large numbers after the institution of limited liability. Prior to that, and still numerically important today, most businesses were conducted by sole traders (that is, generally owner-managers) and unlimited partnerships of two or more people. Incorporation encouraged firm growth and as a corollary, except in the smallest corporations, shareholders participated less in day-to-day management. In the UK this growth continued well into the twentieth century resulting in an increasing concentration of industry. In 1949, 22 per cent of manufacturing net output emanated from the 100 largest firms, and by 1976, 42 per cent. This trend levelled elsewere, and in the US the share of value added by the 100 largest manufacturing firms remained at around one-third from the early 1950s. Small firms (under 200 employees) are still important in the UK, accounting for 95 per cent of firms in manufacturing and around 20 per cent of net output

and employment. Their prominence is even greater in service sectors of the economy.

Firms initially grew to obtain the advantages of scale economies and of monopoly power. The latter was perceived to be especially true in the US where men like Rockefeller and Carnegie built industrial empires in the oil and steel industries. Congress, fearful of the consequences of industrial size, passed the Sherman Anti-trust Act in 1890, and firms such as Standard Oil and American Tobacco were ordered to divest themselves of assets and split into separate firms. In the next three-quarters of a century many American firms took alternative growth routes, partly to minimize their visibility to 'trust-busters' and partly to obtain the benefits of diversification. Risk-avoidance was obtained by spreading the company's efforts over a range of domestic markets for different products, or by expanding abroad with the original product range. These activities were mirrored elsewhere by British, German, Dutch and Swiss firms such as ICI, Hoechst, Philips, and Nestlé respectively.

Many students of industrial structure are concerned at the levels of concentration now ruling. They argue that as a consequence prices are uncompetitively high, that very large firms become inefficient and reluctant to change and innovate. Others argue that concentration varies industry by industry and is determined by technology or is a reward for innovation and efficiency. Large firms only become large by winning the consumer's approval. The identities of the leading firms are also changing, and the leading 100 firms of 1900 are different in both identity and in ranking from the leading 100 in 1980. Thus firms must either change as demand and supply conditions change or forfeit any position they have won through previous successful responsiveness to market conditions. This school believes that provided entry to and exit from an industry are easy, concentration levels need not be a cause for concern. The issue of whether industrial structure determines firm conduct and performance, or whether firm performance and conduct determines industrial structure is still unsettled. If there are barriers to entry imposed by regulations, the truth may embody both theses.

A further area of debate is the degree to which incorporation and what Berle and Means (1968) called the consequential 'divorce of ownership from control' has resulted in managers pursuing goals different from the maximization of profit which the owner-manager is presumed to do in the standard theory of the firm. Alternative theories have been put forward suggesting that managers pursue sales or asset growth, size *per se*, or maximize utility functions containing both financial and psychic variables. In most cases these alternative goals are subject to a minimum profit constraint which, if not met, would result in a takeover by another firm, loss of managerial job security and a return to a profit target closer to that of maximization. Proponents of these views argue that these alternative goals result in different patterns of firm behaviour if the external environment changes (for example, a tax on profits does not affect a profit maximizer's behaviour, but a sales maximizer subject to a minimum profits constraint would reduce output and raise price). Defenders of the traditional theory argue that efficient stock markets, *via* the takeover mechanism, ensure that managers depart but little from profit maximization. To the extent that they do, this is a cost borne willingly by owners to achieve the net benefits of specialization of function between the risk-capital providers and the more risk-averse providers of managerial expertise.

W. Duncan Reekie
University of the Witwatersrand, Johannesburg

Reference
Berle, A. A. and Means, G. C. (1968), *The Modern Corporation and Private Property* (rev. edn), New York.

Further Reading
Brozen, Y. (1982), *Concentration, Mergers and Public Policy*, New York.
Reekie, W. D. (1978), *Industry, Prices and Markets*, Oxford.
Scherer, F M. (1980), *Industrial Market Structure and Economic Performance* (2nd edn), Chicago.
See also: *business concentration; monopoly.*

Corporatism

Corporatism, whether corporate, clerical or Fascist in origin, is an ideology of organization which assumes that a variety of parties will co-operate on the basis of shared values. Corporatism (also called neo-corporatism or liberal corporatism) presupposes, on the contrary, the existence of fundamental conflicts which, however, need not produce organizational disruption but can be mediated with the help of the state. The concept first appeared in Scandinavian writings after the Second World War (Heckscher, St Rokkan), but was only made generally known by Schmitter (1979, 1981). However, functional equivalents of the concept, labelled 'organized capitalism', can be traced back to Hilferding (1915) in the social democratic debate in Germany and Austria. The concept was thus developed in countries where state sponsorship of trade unions had a certain tradition, but where unions had achieved positions of considerable power.

In recent years, corporatism has been greatly extended. Left-wing theorists invoke it to explain how – despite expectations – through successful manipulation, crises did not come to a head, and class struggles were not exacerbated. More conservative scholars embraced neo-corporatism as a solution to what was termed the problem of 'ungovernability' (Schmitter, 1981). Ungovernability in modern democracies was widely thought to be a consequence of the over-burdening of the system of communication. There was also said to be a weakening of legitimacy, from the point of view of the citizen. Schmitter pointed rather to the inadequate co-ordination of interests and of demands by state agencies. Corporatism offered itself as an alternative to the syndicalist view that a multitude of uncoordinated and sharply antagonistic groups confronted one another. In countries where the ideas of a social contract is undeveloped – as in Italy – or where a kind of 'bargained corporatism' is beginning to crystallize – as in Britain (Crouch, 1977) – the notion of corporatism has been rejected by the unions.

Where strategies of negotiation and conflict are in a more differentiated fashion, it is often apparent that the possibilities of neo-corporatism have been overestimated. Great strides have been made in spatial planning, health policies and to some extent in education (Cawson, 1978); but where many economic interests are involved, it seems that pluralist market models are more effective in articulating interests. Where ideologically founded alternatives are in question, as in environmental policy, negotiated settlements and compromise proposals tend to meet with strong opposition.

Klaus von Beyme
University of Heidelberg

References
Cawson, A. (1978), 'Pluralism, corporatism, and the role of the state', *Government and Oppositions*, 13.
Crouch, C. (1977), *Class Conflict and Industrial Relations Crisis. Compromise and Corporatism in the Policies of the British State*, London.
Schmitter, P. C. (1979), 'Still the century of corporatism?' in P. C. Schmitter and G. Lehmbruch (eds), *Trends Towards Corporatist Intermediation*, Beverly Hills.

Further Reading
von Beyme, K. (1983), 'Neo-corporatism. A new nut in an old shell', *International Political Science Review*.
Lehmbruch, G. and Schmitter, P. C. (eds) (1982), *Pattern of Corporatist Policy-Making*, Beverly Hills.
See also: *trade unions.*

Corruption

In its most general sense, corruption means the perversion or abandonment of a standard. Hence it is common to speak of the corruption of language or of moral corruption. More narrowly, corruption refers to the abandonment of expected standards of behaviour by those in authority for the sake of unsanctioned personal advantage. In the business sphere. a company director is deemed corrupt if he sells his private property to the company at an inflated price, at the expense of the shareholders whose interests he is supposed to safeguard. Lawyers, architects and other professionals are similarly guilty of corruption if they take advantage of their clients to make undue personal gains.

Political corruption can be defined as the misuse of public office or authority for unsanctioned private gain. Several points about the definition should be noted. (1) Not all forms of misconduct or abuse of office constitute corruption. An official or a government minister who is merely incompetent or who betrays government secrets to a foreign power for ideological reasons is not generally considered corrupt. (2) Legislators and public officials in most countries are entitled to salaries and other allowances. Corruption occurs only when they receive additional *unsanctioned* benefits, such as bribes. In practice, it is frequently hard to draw the line between authorized and unauthorized payments and, in any case, this will change over time and will be drawn differently in different countries. A benefit regarded as a bribe in one country may be seen as normal and legitimate in another. Legal definitions of corrupt practices are only an imperfect guide since benefits forbidden by law are often sanctioned by social custom, and vice versa. The boundaries of accepted behaviour can be especially difficult to determine in countries affected by rapid political and social change. (3) *Electoral corruption* needs to be defined differently from other forms. Whereas most political corruption involves the abuse of public office, electoral corruption is the abuse of the process by which public office is won.

Common forms of corruption are bribery, extortion (the unauthorized extraction of money by officials from members of the public) and misuse of official information. Bribery need not consist of a direct payment to a public official. 'Indirect bribery' may take the form of a promise of a post-retirement job, the provision of reduced-price goods, or the channelling of business to a legislator or to members of his family.

Corruption was a serious problem in biblical and classical times, and was found in most periods of history. Cases of judicial corruption were particularly frequent. By the 1960s, an influential school of 'revisionist' political scientists nevertheless presented an optimistic view about the decline of corruption in advanced Western democracies (see Heidenheimer, 1970). Some of the 'revisionists' maintained that corruption did not present as grave a problem as previous writers had suggested. In many newly independent nations, where corruption was supposedly rampant, the practices condemned by Western observers as corrupt (for example, making payments to low-level officials for routine services) were accepted as normal by local standards. Moreover, some forms of corruption, far from damaging the process of social and economic development, could be positively beneficial. Bribery enabled entrepreneurs (including foreign companies) to cut through red tape, thereby promoting the economic advance of poor nations. Corruption was seen as a transitory phenomenon, which was likely to decline as economic and social progress was achieved. The general trend was to be seen, it was argued, in the history of Britain and the United States. In Britain, electoral corruption, the sale of titles and government jobs, and corruption relating to public contracts had been rife until the nineteenth century. The introduction of merit systems of appointment to the civil service, the successful battle against electoral corruption and a change in public attitudes towards the conduct of government had led to a dramatic decline in corruption – a decline which coincided with the nation's economic development. Similarly, in the United States, corruption had been rampant in the late nineteenth and early twentieth centuries. This had been a period of intense economic and social change. As suggested by Robert Merton, the corrupt urban party machines, such as the Democratic Party organization in New York City (Tammany Hall) had provided avenues for advancement for underpriviliged immigrant groups. After the Second World War, full employment, the advance of education, the decline of political patronage and the growth of public welfare benefits combined to eliminate the deprivation that had previously led to corruption. A new civic culture replaced the former loyalties to family and to ethnic group. According to a common view, the party machine and the corruption that had accompanied it withered away.

This interpretation has recently come under challenge. Corruption is neither so benign in underdeveloped countries, nor is it so rare in advanced ones as previously thought. It is unrealistic to suppose that advances in education or in techniques of public administration, the development of a 'public-regarding ethos' or economic development can lead to the virtual disappearance of corruption. The growth of governmental activity and regulation in the modern state increases the opportunities and the temptations for corruption. Improvements in education need not lead to the elimination of corruption but to its perpetuation in new, sophisticated forms.

Revelations since the 1970s have led scholars to give increased attention to the contemporary problems of corruption in advanced democracies and in communist countries. In the United States, the Watergate affair of 1972–4 led to a wave of investigations that resulted in hundreds of convictions for corruption, including that of Vice-President Spiro Agnew. Others convicted included the governors of Illinois, Maryland, Oklahoma and West Virginia. Rampant corruption was uncovered in a number of states including Florida, New Jersey, Pennsylvania and Texas. In Britain, the conventional view about the virtual elimination of corruption was shattered by several major scandals in the 1970s. The far-reaching Poulson scandal, involving local government corruption in the north of England as well as members of Parliament, erupted in 1972. Local government corruption was proved in South Wales, Birmingham and in Scotland, while in London senior police officers were imprisoned. Japan, Italy and Israel are among other economically developed coutries where there have been recent revelations about corruption. In the communist sphere, there have been academic studies as well as official campaigns against corruption in the Soviet Union, China and Poland. The wide scope of governmental activity and control in these countries leads to a correspondingly wide scope for practices to evade this control. Forms of corruption that have been the focus of attention in a number of countries include police corruption and bribery involving multinational corporations (for example, in the arms trade).

The definition, causes and effects of corruption and techniques of reform continue to be matters of controversy among sociologists and political scientists. What has been established beyond dispute is that political corruption is a widespread, pervasive and potentially serious phenomenon.

M. Pinto-Duschinsky
Brunel University, Uxbridge

References

Clarke, M. (ed.) (1983), *Corruption: Causes, Consequences and Control*, London.

Heidenheimer, A. J. (ed.) (1970), *Political Corruption: Readings in Comparative Analysis*, New York.

Cost-Benefit Analysis

In terms of its practical application, cost-benefit analysis (CBA) is usually regarded as having its origins in the United States Flood Control Act of 1936. Without reference to the body of welfare economics that had already arisen by then, and before the introduction of compensation criteria into the literature, the Act argued that flood control projects had their social justification in a weighing up of the costs and benefits, with the latter being summed regardless of to whom they accrued. It is this reference to the *social* dimension of investment appraisal that distinguishes CBA from the more orthodox techniques which deal with the cash flow to a firm or single agency.

Oddly, CBA grew in advance of the theoretical foundations obtained from welfare economics that subsequently provided its underpinning. The notion that the benefits to individuals should be measured according to some indicator of consumer's surplus was well established by nineteenth-century writers especially Dupuit and Marshall, but Hicks's work (1943) established the exact requirements for such measures. Similarly, the notion of a *shadow price* is crucial to CBA since, even if a project's output is marketed, CBA does not necessarily use market prices as indicators of value. Rather, reference is made to the marginal cost of providing the extra output in question. Despite the ambiguous relationship between marginal cost pricing in an economy where some sectors have unregulated pricing policies which force price above marginal cost, CBA and shadow pricing has flourished as an appraisal technique. It secured widespread adoption in US public agencies in the 1950s and 1960s, and was both used and advocated in Europe in the 1960s. It suffered a mild demise in the early 1970s in light of critiques based on the alleged fallacy of applying monetary values to 'intangible' items such as peace and quiet, clean air and the general 'quality of life'. Significantly, post-1973 recession revived its use as governments sought 'value for money' in public expenditure. Unease with the monetization of many unmarketed costs and benefits has, however, remained, resulting in a proliferation of alternative techniques such as environmental impact assessment, cost-effectiveness analysis (in which only resource costs are expressed in money and benefits remain in non-monetary units), and some 'multi-objective' approaches. CBA retains its strength because of its ability potentially to identify optimal expenditures (where net benefits are maximized) and to secure a well-defined project ranking. However, few practitioners would argue that it has a role outside the ranking of expenditures within a given budget. That is, it has a highly limited role in comparing the efficiency of expenditures across major budget areas such as defence, education, health and so on.

As generally formulated, CBA operates with the efficiency objectives of welfare economics. The maximization of net social benefits is formally equivalent to securing the largest net welfare gain as defined by the Kaldor-Hicks compensation principle. Academic debate in this respect has centred on the appropriate choice of the measure of consumer's surplus, with the dominant advocacy being of the use of the 'compensating variation' measure introduced by Hicks (1943). It seems fair to say, however, that the philosophical basis of CBA remains a source of professional confusion. Use of social prices based on consumer valuations implicitly assumes that the distribution of market power within the relevant economy is itself optimal. Since this is a value judgement, it is open to anyone to substitute it with an alternative distributional judgement. Some would argue that this apparent arbitrariness defines the inadequacies of CBA, while others suggest that no society has ever operated with disregard for distributional criteria and that distributional judgements are no less arbitrary than efficiency judgements.

Much of the practical effort in CBA has gone into actual mechanisms for discovering individuals' preferences in contexts where there is no explicit market. The most successful have been the hedonic price technique and the use of bidding techniques. Hedonic prices refer to the coefficients defining the relationship between property prices and changes in some unmarketed variable affecting property prices. An example would be clean air which should raise the price of a property, other things being equal. Bidding techniques involve the use of questionnaires which ask directly for consumers' valuations of the benefits.

Since costs and benefits accrue over time, CBA tends to adopt a discounting approach whereby future cash and non-cash flows are discounted back to a present value by use of a discount rate. The determination of the discount rate has occupied a substantial literature. In theory, one would expect consumers to prefer the present to the future because of impatience ('myopia') and expectations of higher incomes in the future (thus lowering their marginal valuation of a unit of benefit in the future). In turn, the resulting rate of time preference should be equal to interest rates ruling in the market which also reflect the productivity of capital. In practice, time preference rates and cost of capital estimates can vary significantly because of imperfections in capital markets. Moreover, the rate of discount relevant to *social* decisions can differ from the average of individual valuations, because choices made as members of society will differ when compared to choices made on an individualist basis. Further controversy surrounds the issue of intergenerational fairness since positive discount rates have the potential for shifting cost burdens forward to future generations. Thus the risks of, say, storing nuclear waste appear small when discounted back to the present and expressed as a present value. Conversely, zero discount rates may discriminate against projects which offer the highest potential for leaving accumulated capital for the use of future generations. To pursue the nuclear power example, non-investment because of the waste disposal problem could reduce the inherited stock of energy availability to future generations, by forcing a rapid depletion of finite stock resources such as coal or oil. The intergenerational issue is thus complex and raises the fundamental issue of just how far into the future CBA should look. Because of its foundations in consumer sovereignty, there is a temptation to argue that the time horizon is set by the existing generation and, at most, the succeeding one or two generations.

CBA remains a controversial appraisal technique. As an aid to rational thinking its credentials are higher than any of the alternatives so far advanced. That it cannot substitute for political decisions is not in question, but social science has a duty to inform public choice, and it is in this respect that CBA has its role to play.

David Pearce
University College London

Reference
Hicks, J. (1943), 'The four consumer's surplus', *The Review of Economic Studies*, LL.

Further Reading
Mishan, E. J. (1975), *Cost Benefit Analysis*, 2nd edn, London.
Pearce, D. W. (1983), *Cost Benefit Analysis*, 2nd edn, London.
See also: *Hicks; project analysis; welfare economics.*

Countertransference

Countertransference represents one of the most subtle and complex concepts in dynamic psychiatry. Alas for consistency, however, it is used in two quite distinct ways, each of which will be reviewed here.

(1) In the first category of definition, the term 'countertransference' refers to those feelings in the *therapist* that are stirred up unconsciously during the therapeutic process and fasten on the patient, who is thus understood to represent an important figure from the therapist's past life. In this meaning, 'counter' merely describes a vector. The issue is still transference, but since that term usually describes feelings flowing from patient to therapist, 'counter' refers here to the reverse flow. For example, the older patient might remind the younger therapist of the therapist's father, thus inhibiting the therapist from confronting the patient (where such intervention would ordinarily be necessary for the patient's good).

(2) The second major usage of the term refers to the therapist's *reaction* to the *patient's* transference. In this model, the 'counter' indicates that the therapist is responding in reaction to the stimulus provided by the patient's transferring feelings on to him. An example of this last might be that the patient transfers hostile feelings on to the therapist, and the latter, not detecting the transferential origin of these feelings, feels himself to be the subject of genuine anger and becomes angry in response.

As may be inferred from the above examples, countertransference feelings pose a problem for achievement of the realistic perceptions so essential to therapy. Because these feelings are almost unavoidable, however, they do not represent, as many novices believe, failures of technique or attitude, but rather problems requiring ongoing attention on the therapist's part. The therapist must permit their identification and resolution through introspection, self-analysis, and reality-testing.

Thomas G. Gutheil
Harvard University
Program in Psychiatry and
The Law, Boston

Further Reading
Kernberg, O. F. (1965), 'Notes on countertransference', *Journal of the American Psychoanalytic Association*, 13.
Little, M. (1951), 'Countertransference and the patient's response to it', *International Journal of Psychoanalysis*, 32.
Reich, A. (1951), 'On countertransference', *International Journal of Psychoanalysis*, 32.
Winnicott, D. W. (1949), 'Hate in the countertransference', *International Journal of Psychoanalysis*, 30.
See also: *psychoanalysis; transference.*

Cournot, Antoine Augustin (1801–77)

During a prosperous career in the French civil service and academic establishment, Cournot contributed to three related branches of knowledge: probability theory, foundations of knowledge (broadly, epistemology), and economics. Of these, his contributions to economics (recorded in *Recherches sur les principes mathématiques de la théorie des richesses*, 1838) have been most enduring, even though his works in probability theory and philosophy of science met with more immediate acclaim. Cournot himself apparently regarded the works in probability theory and epistemology more favourably, despite the fact that they do not adduce new results still bearing his name, as do his essays in economics.

Cournot's application of mathematics to economic reasoning was both novel and elegant. Indeed, his main success consisted in giving rigorous mathematical statement to economic concepts and propositions that already existed, but only in confusing and fuzzy form. Cournot's analysis is one of the mainsprings that turned economics from literary discourse to formal logic and mathematical exposition.

Cournot provided a rigorous formulation of the Law of Demand. Prior to his performance, literary economists had experienced considerable difficulty in formulating this simple relationship between price and quantity demanded. After the appearance of *Recherches*, the debate, which still continues today, focused on whether Cournot regarded the price-quantity schedule as primarily empirical or mainly theoretical. Cournot's exposition of the Law of Demand was apparently used as foundation by Alfred Marshall in his famous *Principles of Economics* (1890).

The theory of the monopoly firm attributed to Cournot also found its way into Marshall's *Principles*. To this original contribution Cournot added works on bilateral monopoly, competitive and oligopolistic markets, and the theory of costs. His theories of bilateral monopoly and oligopoly have often provided either target straw men or gambit points for the extensive literature on market behaviour, including game theory. While the ideas in *Recherches* were not novel, the precise formulation, together with extensive deductive exploration that Cournot offered, showed the way to improved clarity and precision in an infant social science. In all of his writing Cournot urged a marriage between theoretical formulation and empirical testing that has become popular in many of the sciences.

G. F. Rhodes, Jr
Colorado State University

Further Reading
Cournot, A. A. (1960 [1838]), *Researches into the Mathematical Principles of the Theory of Wealth*, New York. (Original French edn, *Recherches sur les principes mathématiques de la théorie des richesses*, Paris.)
Cournot, A. A. (1956 [1851], *An Essay on the Foundations of Our Knowledge*, New York. (Original French edn, *Essai sur les fondements de nos connaissances*, 2 vols, Paris.)

Creativity

Creativity is the ability to bring something new into existence. It shows itself in the acts of persons. Through the creative process taking place in a person or group of persons, creative products are born. Such products may be quite diverse: mechanical inventions, new chemical processes, new solutions or new statements of problems in mathematics and science; the composition of a piece of music, or a poem, story or novel; the making of new forms in painting, sculpture, photography; the forming of a new religion or philosophical system; an innovation in law, a general change in manners, a fresh way of thinking about and solving social problems; new medical agents and techniques; even new ways of persuasion and of controlling the minds of others.

Implicit in this diversity is a common core of characteristics that mark creative products, processes, and persons. Creative products are distinguished by their originality, their aptness, their validity, their usefulness, and very often by a subtle additional property which we may call aesthetic fit. For such products we use words such as fresh, novel, ingenious, clever, unusual, divergent. The ingredients of the creative process are related functionally to the creative forms produced: seeing things in a new way, making connections, taking risks, being alerted to chance and to the opportunities present by contradictions and complexities, recognizing familiar patterns in the unfamiliar so that new patterns may be formed by transforming old ones, being alert to the contingencies which may arise from such transformations. And in creative people, regardless of their age, sex, ethnic background, nationality, or way of life, we find certain traits recurring: an ability to think metaphorically or analogically as well as logically, independence of judgement (sometimes manifesting itself as unconventionality, rebellion, revolutionary thinking and acting), a rejection of an insufficient simplicity (or a tendency to premature closure) in favour of a search for a more complex and satisfying new order or synthesis. A certain *naïveté* or innocence of vision must be combined with stringent requirements set by judgement and experience. The act of verification is a final stage in the creative process, preceded by immersion in the problem, incubation of the process subliminally, and illumination or new vision.

The Birth of 'Creativity'
The creative aspects of Mind and of Will engaged the attention of all the major philosopher-psychologists of the late nineteenth and early twentieth centuries. Alfred Binet, the famed constructor of intelligence tests, was known first through the pages of *L'Année Psychologique* in the 1880s and 1890s as the author of widely ranging empirical studies of creativity (including research by questionnaire and interview of leading French writers) and the originator of dozens of tests of imagination (devised first as games to play with his own children). The fateful decision to exclude such occasions for imaginative play from his compendium of tasks protoypical of needed scholastic aptitudes has led to much mischief in educational application and to continuing confusion about the relationship of 'intelligence' to 'creativity'. The former as generally measured is important to certain aspects of the latter, but people of equal intelligence have been found to vary widely in creativity; and, alas, some notably creative persons have also been found notably lacking in whatever it takes to get on successfully in school.

Of the two most famous psychoanalysts, Carl Jung made the greater contribution in this field, developing especially the notions of intuition and of the collective unconscious as the sources of creation. Henri Bergson,

in *Creative Evolution*, distinguished intuition from intellect as the main vehicle of the creative process in mind-in-general and in what, in retrospect, is more than mere vitalism he attributed to will, as *élan vital*, the chief motivating force of the creative process in nature. Nearly a century after Bergson's initial formulations, Gregory Bateson was writing in that same tradition, and his gradual development of 'an ecology of mind' found expression in his 1979 volume, *Mind and Nature: A Necessary Unity*.

The Modern Empirical Study of Creativity
New methods of observation and measurement have produced a marked proliferation of articles and books about creative persons, processes, and products since the Second World War. A commonly recognized milestone in the systematic research effort is an address in 1950 by J. P. Guilford who, as president of the American Psychological Association, pointed out that up to that time only 186 out of 121,000 entries in *Psychological Abstracts* dealt with creative imagination. In the following decades there was a surge of publications in the field. Studies at the University of California of highly creative contemporary writers, architects, artists, mathematicians and scientists by intensive methods of personal assessment contributed important impetus to the study of personality and creativity (work funded mostly by foundations such as Carnegie, Ford, Rockefeller, and Richardson), while the US Office of Education gave significant support to research on creativity in education. A bibliography published in the late 1960s by the Creative Education Foundation contains 4,176 references, nearly 3,000 of them dated later than 1960.

Yet this abundance of effort also produced a mixed picture of results based on psychological measurement, due mainly to inconsistencies in the choice of measures, their relative unreliability, and the equally inconsistent, somewhat unreliable, and factorially and definitionally complex criteria. Psychologists generally have restricted the term creativity to the production of humanly *valuable* novelty in an effort to exclude from consideration the relatively mundane expressions of creativity in everyday life, but this introduction of value to the definition of creativity, and the consequent invocation of historically-bound and subjective judgements to assess such value, necessarily raise theoretical and methodological questions which have bedevilled and divided students of creativity for decades. *Whose* values, for example, must be met for an act to be 'creative' – the values of the creative agent alone, or the values of a social group? And if so, which group?

Further, should the term creative be restricted to novel activities valued by connoisseurs of achievement in the 'classically creative' domains of literature, music, and the arts, or can it be applied also to novel behaviour valued by those able to recognize achievement in mathematics, science, and technology? While most creativity scholars and investigators extend 'creative' to these latter domains with few qualms, they do not generally assume that the creative processes involved in producing good literature, good music, good art and good science are the same, or that the personality and intellectual characteristics associated with creative achievement in these various domains are highly similar. And whether the term creative can be extended to novel activities of value in domains such as business, sports, teaching, therapy, parenting, and homemaking is an even more controversial question among creativity scholars.

Nor can the issue of values and standards be resolved simply by accepting as legitimate a particular domain of activity, for even within a specific domain, such as art, the question remains: whose values or standards are to be met – the values and standards of the artist who produced the piece, of other artists, of art critics, of art historians, or the audience in general? And if other artists, *which* artists; if art critics, *which* art critics; and if art historians, *which* art historians – from which schools and what eras? And if behaviour in less public domains (for example, therapy and parenting) is considered, who is to assess the novelty and effectiveness of the behaviour and how is scholarship and investigation to proceed?

Intimately related to the question of values and standards are questions concerning the nature or form of the act's impact. Several theorists, for example, have drawn distinctions between acts of 'primary' creativity – acts whose values derive from their power to transform in a basic way our perception of reality or our understanding of the universe of human experience and possibility – and acts of 'secondary' creativity – acts which merely apply or extend some previously developed meaning, principle, or technique to a new domain or instance.

While it would be comforting to be able to report that the definitional differences and distinctions reviewed here are relatively trivial compared to the core of common meaning contained within them, it is not at all clear that this is so. Whether creative individuals are identified on the basis of their achievements, or their skills and abilities, or their activities, or their personality characteristics, shapes answers to frequently asked substantive questions about creativity (for example, can creativity be taught or fostered? Can creativity be predicted? How are creativity and intelligence related?). Definitional differences and variations in emphasis have led, and will continue to lead, to many misunderstandings, misreadings, and confusions in the study of creativity. Readers of the psychological literature on creativity are therefore well advised to ascertain the conceptual perspectives and operational definitions of the scholars and investigators whose works they are examining. Thus, not only measurement unreliability in both predictors and criteria but basic definitional questions as well as the genuine role of chance itself in both the genesis and the recognition of creativity also have served to confound results. Overall, none the less, a strong impressionistic consensus of the sort reported at the outset of this article prevails today. And the research enterprise continues undeterred.

A critical review of the professional literature on creativity in the decade 1970–80 by F. Barron and D. Harrington in the *Annual Review of Psychology* (1981) turned up an additional 2,500 studies, produced at a steady rate of about 250 per year during that decade. Emerging new themes are creativity in women, creativity and altered states of consciousness, creativity throughout the lifespan with emphasis on the continuation of creativity in late maturity, and finally, somewhat belatedly, the social psychology of creativity: the influence of social climates and conditions facilitating creativity in the home, the classroom, the work place, and the culture itself with its enormous diversity of micro-climates and its intersection with historical and economic forces.

Frank Barron
David M. Harrington
University of California, Santa Cruz

References
Barron, F. and Harrington, D. M. (1981), 'Creativity, intelligence, and personality', *Annual Review of Psychology*, 32.
Bergson, H. (1911[1907]), *Creative Evolution*, London. (Original French edn, *L'Evolution créative*, Paris, 1907.)

Further Reading
Albert, R. S. (1983), *Genius and Eminence: The Social Psychology of Creativity and Exceptional Achievement*, Oxford.
Barron, F. (1969), *Creative Person and Creative Process*, New York.
Ghiselin, B. (1952), *The Creative Process*, Berkeley and Los Angeles.
Koestler, A. (1964), *The Act of Creation*, New York.
Simonton, D. K. (1984), *Genius, Creativity and Leadership*, Cambridge, Mass.

Credit

'Credit', derived from the Latin *credere* (to believe), has several meanings, many of which are outside the field of finances. Even in finance it can be used to indicate a positive accounting entry, an increase in wealth or income, but the main use, with which we are concerned here, involves an element of deferred payment. It thus covers not only formal loans but also the multitude of informal arrangements whereby payment for a transaction is made some time after the physical transfer of the goods or services, and by extension it is also used where payment is made in advance. In accounting terms it refers not only to trade credit between businesses but also to the various items known as accruals. Examples of such accruals are the payment of salaries after a person has worked for a week or a month and, on the other side, the advance payment of a year's premium for insurance.

In macroeconomics the term is used with a special meaning to refer to those items of credit that are measurable for the economy as a whole; in practice this restricts it to credit extended by the banking system. As bank loans are made, the proceeds are used to pay for goods and services, and the recipients of these payments pass the cheques to the credit of their own bank deposits: bank loans can be said to create bank deposits. By controlling the volume of bank credit, the monetary authorities can thus indirectly control the volume of bank deposits, which are the most important element in the money supply. The control of bank credit, both in total volume and in the selection of favoured and unfavoured borrowing sectors, is thus often a weapon of monetary policy.

Credit plays an important part in the theory of financial intermediation. The first stage of development of a financial system can be taken as the move from barter to the use of commodity money. Although this move frees the exchange of commodities from the restrictions of barter, by itself it does nothing for the growth of business enterprises because the only funds available for capital investment come from the current income or the previously accumulated money balances of the entrepreneur himself. The development of credit, in the form of direct lending and borrowing, enables the accumulated money balances of others to be transferred to the entrepreneur, who can thus put to profitable use the savings of many other people. Because this development was associated with the levying of interest, it faced religious and social obstacles; these still persist in Muslim countries, where an alternative form of banking (Islamic banking) has been developed on the basis of profit-sharing by the depositor.

For several centuries, credit, both as formal loans and as trade credit, was restricted to businesses and the wealthier households, but in the past 50 years all but the poorest households have obtained access to formal and informal credit. This extension of credit has been achieved by a number of innovations in the forms in which credit is granted. Few of these forms were completely new; the innovations came in the use to which they were put and in the ways in which they were combined.

All lenders need to satisfy themselves on two points before granting credit: these are the ability of the borrower to repay and his willingness to do so. Traditionally, the ability to repay was assured by requiring the borrower to give the lender a mortgage or charge on assets to a value greater than that of the loan, and willingness to repay was assessed on the past record of the borrower and personal knowledge of his character. Unless the loan is for the purchase of a house, the problem raised in giving credit to the ordinary household is that there are no suitable assets to pledge as security. The solution has taken several forms. The first was to obtain a mortgage on the asset (car or television set, for example) that was being purchased with the loan; where the legal system did not permit this (as under English law), the asset was hired to the 'borrower', with a final nominal payment to transfer ownership – hire purchase. Even where this legal subterfuge was not necessary, there was a growth in leasing and straight hiring to households to overcome many of the credit problems.

The key change in this form of consumer lending was a realization that current income rather than accumulated assets was the real security for a loan. In lending on consumer durables this came about because there is a poor second-hand market, but even with houses lenders prefer to avoid the trouble of auctioning the property to secure repayment. During the 1960s this change of attitude towards the nature of the security for a loan was also adopted in corporate lending; it came to be known as lending on the cash flow. For large corporate loans, banks often use their computers for simulating the cash flows of prospective borrowers under a number of hypothetical conditions.

It is obvious from the previous analysis that the key point in granting credit is the assessment of the creditworthiness of the borrower. In the past much of this depended on the personal judgement of local bank managers and on adequate collateral. With the growth in the number of customers, no branch manager can now claim a close knowledge of all his customers, and more formal methods of assessment have become necessary. This is particularly necessary when loans can be obtained by post through the filling in of a simple questionnaire or even through answering questions posed by an electronic terminal. Most of the methods used are based on credit scoring, which uses a statistical technique known as multivariate discriminant analysis (MDA) or one of its variants. Applicants are scored according to such characteristics as ownership of their home, steady employment, and possession of a telephone, and the loan is granted if the score exceeds a predetermined level based on past experience of bad debts.

Jack Revell
University College of North Wales, Bangor

Further Reading
Beckman, T. N. (1969), *Credits and Collections: Management and Theory*, 8th edn, New York.
Gurley, J. G. and Shaw, E. S. (1960), *Money in a Theory of Finance*, Washington, D.C.
See also: *banking*.

Crime and Delinquency

The study of crime and delinquency is an interdisciplinary inquiry which brings together the theoretical and methodological insights of sociology, economics, political science, psychology and law. The field consists of two interrelated but separable areas of concern: the development and implementation of laws which define acts and people as criminal or delinquent, and the social, psychological and biological forces that cause people to commit acts of crime and delinquency.

Much of the work of social scientists studying crime and delinquency leads to the debunking of commonplace myths. For example, historical research on the process whereby acts come to be defined as crime (murder, theft, vagrancy, assault, and so on) contradicts the commonsensical view that the customary beliefs of the people or a society's 'moral consensus' determines which acts are defined as criminal. Most acts are defined as criminal precisely because there is little consensus that they should be. It is the political struggles taking place at the time that culminate in one interest group succeeding in getting their ideas enshrined in law. Thus, murder was defined as an offence against the state in early England in the Crown's struggle against the power of the Church and the feudal aristocracy; by removing their control over disputes amongst the citizens, the Crown greatly enhanced its power. The theft of wood, killing of game and poaching of fish from 'common grounds' was incorporated into the criminal law and deemed so serious that violators could be put to death, at a time when the Crown sought to reward loyal nobles by giving them private hunting and fishing grounds.

In a field as diverse and politically sensitive as the study of crime and delinquency, there are few incontrovertible facts and theories. High on the list of accepted truths, however, is the fact that in most societies people in all social classes and in all groups commit crimes at some time in their lives. Thus a theory of why people commit crimes must account for what is defined in law as criminal or delinquent but what is in fact normal, in the sense of being almost universal amongst the population. A further fact generally agreed upon is that while everyone commits some acts of crime in almost every society, the age from fifteen to twenty-five is the period in life when people are most apt to engage in delinquent and criminal acts. Indeed, even people who

engage in some types of crime with regularity during this age period tend to stop committing criminal acts after the age of twenty-five.

It is also clear that the definition of acts and actors as criminal, as well as the way crime is depicted in a society, are politically determined events. For example, officially published crime rates in most countries of the world show a marked increase in the incidence of criminal and delinquent behaviour in the past century. Criminologists have been sceptical about these statistics, since a decision to report an incident as a crime is a bureaucratic one which is heavily influenced in every country by the politics of crime reporting.

Police departments and governments manipulate statistics to serve the interests of the bureaucracy and the political desires of the government. Furthermore, the way in which the statistics are gathered, even when they are not intentionally manipulated, renders them useless as an index of the amount and type of crime taking place. Crimes of the upper classes are rarely represented by official statistics, and crimes of the lower classes are usually exaggerated in the direction of appearing much more serious than they in fact are (Chambliss and Seidman, 1971). Criminologists therefore rely more heavily on carefully conducted research for a picture of the quality and quantity of crime than they do on official statistics. In recent years population surveys asking whether a person has been the victim of a crime provide a better, although far from perfect, picture of the incidence and distribution of crime. But even these surveys tend to be biased by not including categories of crime typical of upper class and business criminality.

The enforcement of criminal law reflects the class system of the society. In Western capitalist democratic societies the enforcement of criminal laws against the upper classes for business crimes and political corruption are rare in comparison with the enforcement of criminal laws against minor offences of the lower classes such as gambling, drug taking, vagrancy and being disorderly in public. In every Western society most of the arrests (usually over 80 per cent) made every year by the police are of lower class persons accused of committing minor offences. The arrest rate for more serious offences, whether committed by lower, middle or upper class persons, is quite low.

In the history of the study of crime and delinquency, four overarching, general paradigms have dominated research and theory: (1) the social psychological, (2) sociological, (3) biological and (4) Marxian.

(1) The social psychologists see crime and delinquency as emanating from the life experiences of individuals. There are many different theories in this tradition including (a) the psychoanalytic theory which stresses the importance of family relations and interpersonal conflicts as the source of criminal or delinquent actions; (b) the cultural approach which postulates the

existence of criminal and delinquent subcultures which are learned by some people in the same fashion that non-criminal actions are learned by others; (c) the 'societal reaction' or 'labelling' approach which postulates that people become delinquent because they are caught and labelled by parents, peers, teachers or police; and (d) the anomie theory that argues that it is a failure of some people to internalize consensually held norms that leads them to be delinquent or criminal.

(2) Although biological theories have largely been in disrepute since the 1900s, there has been a resurgence of interest in these theories in the last few years. In general they argue that a certain combination of genetic and biological predispositions increases the likelihood that delinquent acts will occur if social and personal experiences are such as to exacerbate these tendencies.

(3) The sociological tradition focuses on different propensities towards crime by people located in different social classes in the society. Opinions differ, however, about what characteristics of social class are most fundamental in determining the likelihood that people will commit crime. Some sociologists argue that the cause of crime is cultural, and therefore social class membership makes it more likely that people will learn criminal behaviour from people who value crime as a way of life (Sutherland and Cressey, 1984). Other sociologists argue that social class restricts opportunities for success and therefore some members will possibly resort to crime as an alternative means of achieving success. Most sociologists agree that social class is a starting point for an understanding of crime. People in the upper, middle and lower classes commit crimes that are a reflection of their class position; this does not mean that crime is necessarily limited to those in the lower classes.

(4) The Marxian tradition accepts the legitimacy of the sociological emphasis on social class but argues that crime is a reflection of structural contradictions in the political economy and class struggle. There are several theoretical traditions within the Marxian framework; especially important are the instrumentalist and dialectical theories. (a) The instrumentalist theory argues that the ruling class defines lower class behaviours as criminal in an effort to maintain control over them; the lower classes protest against ruling class control by committing criminal acts. (b) A more sophisticated Marxian approach involves the idea that the contradictions of a period's political and economic systems generates pressure towards criminal behaviour on members of different social classes. The capitalist class resorts to crime in an effort to maintain and enhance the accumulation of capital, where illegal means are more effective than legal ones (the conspiring to restrain trade, engaging in the importation and distribution of illegal commodities such as

drugs, etc). The lower class resorts to crime so that they are able to purchase the commodities which they, along with everyone else, are encouraged to want in a system that depends on commodity consumption for its economic survival.

Criminologists believe that research and critical appraisal will resolve these differences of theory. The faith is, alas, not based on past experience. Yet, there are certain facts which any theory must fit, and it is a failure to meet this criteria which renders many of the existing traditions untenable. For example, it is well established that in the course of a lifetime *most* people – probably almost 100 per cent – commit a large number of criminal acts. Any theory that postulates some unique set of social, personal or biological experiences differentiating criminals from non-criminals is therefore suspect. If everyone commits crime, then it is nonsense to suppose that we can explain why some people commit crime while others do not. Thus theories of crime that do no recognize the universality of criminal behaviour are necessarily faulted from the start.

Connected to this observation is the fact that even if one limits the problem of explanation to those who commit 'serious' crimes or those whose criminality is ongoing and part of a 'way of life', there is the second pillar of established fact: both the upper and lower classes produce large numbers of people in both of these categories. Thus any theory that argues for differences in the seriousness or incidence of crime as a result of differences in social class position must also be wanting. The modern world institutionalized the use of illegal means by one government to overthrow unfriendly political forces in another, including assassination and illegal supplying of military equipment. These and other crimes of the powerful are fundamental facts which any explanation of crime must fit.

William J. Chambliss
University of Delaware

References
Chambliss, W. J. and Seidman, R. B. (1971), *Law, Order and Power*, Reading, Mass.
Sutherland, E. H. and Cressey, D. R. (1984), *Principles of Criminology*, Philadelphia.

Further Reading
Chambliss, W. J. (1984), *Criminal Law in Action*, New York.
Christie, N. (1981), *The Limits of Pain*, Oxford.
Clinard, M. B. and Yeager, P. C. (1981), *Corporate Crime*, New York.
Leonard, E. B. (1982), *Women, Crime and Society*, New York.

Sutherland, E. H. (1983), *White Collar Crime: The Uncut Version*, New Haven.

Taylor, I., Walton, P. and Young, J. (1973), *The New Criminology*, London.

See also: *criminology; deviance; labelling theory; punishment.*

Criminology

There are two scriptural beginnings to the history of criminology, each marking out a somewhat different fate for the study of crime and its control. The first dates from the mid-eighteenth century and tells of the revolutionary contribution of Enlightenment thinkers like Beccaria and Bentham in breaking with a previously 'archaic', 'barbaric', 'repressive'. or 'arbitrary' system of criminal law. This was the classical school.

For these reformers, legal philosophers and political theorists, the crime question was dominantly the punishment question. Their programme was to prevent punishment from being, in Beccaria's words, 'an act of violence of one or many against a private citizen'; instead it should be 'essentially public, prompt, necessary, the least possible in given circumstances, proportionate to the crime, dictated by laws'. Classicism presented a model of rationality: on the one side, the free 'sovereign' individual acting according to the dictates of reason and self interest; on the other, the limited liberal state, contracted to grant rights and liberties, to prescribe duties and to impose the fair and just punishment that must result from the knowing infliction of social harm.

This 'immaculate conception' account of the birth of classicism has been challenged by revisionist histories of law and the state. Dates, concepts and subjects have been reordered. Classicism is now to be understood in terms of the broader rationalization of crime control associated with the emergence of the free market and the new capitalist order. But the preoccupations of classicism – whether they appear in utilitarianism, Kantianism, liberalism, anarchism or indeed any political philosophy at all – have remained a constant thread in criminology. This is where the subject overlaps with politics, jurisprudence and the history and sociology of the law.

A century after classicism, though, criminology was to claim for itself another beginning and another set of influences. This was the positivist revolution – dated in comic-book intellectual history with the publication in 1876 of Lombroso's *Delinquent Man*. This was a 'positivism' which shared the more general social-scientific connotations of the term (the notion, that is, of the unity of the scientific method) but which acquired in criminology a more specific meaning. As David Matza suggests in his standard sociologies of criminological knowledge (Matza, 1964 and 1969), criminological positivism managed the astonishing feat of separating the study of crime from the contemplation of the state. Classicism was dismissed as mere metaphysical speculation. The new programme was to focus not on the crime (the act) but the criminal (the actor); it was to assume not rationality, free will and choice, but determinism (biological, psychic or social). At the centre of the criminological enterprise now was the notion of causality. No longer a sovereign being, subject to more or less the same pulls and pushes as his fellow citizens, the criminal was now a special person or member of a special class.

The whole of the last century of criminology can be understood as a series of creative, even brilliant, yet eventually repetitive variations on these late nineteenth-century themes. The particular image conjured up by Lombroso's criminal type – the atavistic genetic throwback – faded away, but the subsequent structure and logic of criminological explanation remained largely within the positivist paradigm. Whether the level of explanation was biological, psychological, sociological or a combination of these ('multifactorial' as some versions were dignified), the Holy Grail was a general causal theory: why do people commit crime? This quest gave the subject its collective self definition: 'the scientific study of the causes of crime'.

At each stage of this search, criminology strengthened its claim to exist as an autonomous, multidisciplinary subject. Somewhat like a parasite, criminology attached itself to its host subjects (notably, law, psychology, psychiatry and sociology) and drew from them methods, theories and academic credibility. At the same time – somewhat like a colonial power landing on new territory – each of these disciplines descended on the eternally fascinating subjects of crime and punishment and claimed them as its own. In this fashion, criminological theories and methods draw on Freudianism, behaviourism, the Chicago school of sociology, functionalism, anomie theory, interactionism, Marxism and much else. Each of these traces can be found in any current criminology textbook; it would be difficult to think of a major system of thought in the social sciences which would not be so represented.

All the time this positivist trajectory was being established, criminologists retained their interest in the question of punishment. If, in a sense, all criminology became positivist, then also all criminology remained concerned with 'classical' matters. But instead of speculation about the limits and nature of the criminal sanction, this side of criminology (sometimes called penology) took this sanction as politically given. True, there was (and still is) an important debate about whether the subject matter of criminology should be confined to conventional legal definitions of crime or shifted to include all forms of socially injurious conduct. The punishment question, however, was largely resolved in empirical terms: describing, analysing and evaluating the workings of the criminal justice system. Research findings were built up about the police, courts, prisons and various other agencies devoted to the prevention, control, deterrence or treatment of crime. This remains today the major part of the criminological enterprise.

Little of this, however, was 'pure' empiricism. The classical tradition was alive in another sense: modern criminologists became the heirs of the Enlightenment beliefs in rationality and progress. Their scientific task was carried along by a sense of faith: that the business of crime and delinquency control could be made not only more efficient, but also more humane. As reformers, advisers and consultants, criminologists claim for themselves not merely an autonomous body of knowledge, but the status of an applied science or even a profession.

It is this simultaneous claim to knowledge and power which links the two sides of criminology: causation and control. In positivism, this is an organic link: to know the cause is to know the right policy. Recently, however, both this link and its justification in the immaculate-conception history of positivism have been questioned. Histories of the emergence of the prison in the late eighteenth and early nineteenth century have shown the dependence of control systems on theories of rehabilitation, behaviour modification and anomie well before their supposed 'discovery' by scientific criminology. To critics like Foucault (1977) criminological knowledge has always been wholly utilitarian: an elaborate alibi to justify the exercise of power.

In the general climate of radical self-scrutiny which descended on the social sciences in the 1960s, criminology, too, began to fragment a little. There were three major attacks against the positivist hegemony – each in its peculiar and quite distinct way representing a return to classical questions.

(1) Labelling theory – a loose body of ideas derived from symbolic interactionism – restated some simple sociological truths about the relative nature of social rules and the normative boundaries which they mark. Crime was one form of that wider category of social action, deviance; criminology should be absorbed into the sociology of deviance. Beyond such conceptual and disciplinary boundary disputes, the very nature of the conventional quest for causality was regarded with scepticism. In addition to the standard behavioural question (why do some people do these bad things?) there were a series of definitional questions: Why are certain actions defined as rule breaking? How are these rules applied? And what are the consequences of this application? At times, these definitional questions

seemed to attain causal primacy: it was not that control led to deviance, but deviance to control. Social control agencies – with their organized systems of labelling, stigmatizing and isolation – were meddlesome busybodies, making matters worse for society and its underdogs and outsiders. And behind the pretentions of scientific criminology was a simple-minded identification with middle-class values.

(2) This liberal criticism of liberalism was to become harder and tighter in the second onslaught on mainstream criminology. This came from what has been labelled variously as 'conflict', 'new', 'critical', 'radical', or 'Marxist' criminology. Drawing initially on some strands of labelling theory and conflict sociology and on the classical Marxist writing about law, class and the state, these theories moved even further from the agenda of positivism. Traditional causal questions were either dismissed or made subservient to the assumed criminogenic features of capitalism. Legalistic definitions were either expanded to include crimes of the powerful (those social harms which the state licences itself to commit), or else subjected to historicist and materialist enquiry. Labelling theory's wider notion of deviance was abandoned. Law was the only important mode of control, and the focus of criminology had to be shifted to the power of the state to criminalize certain actions rather than others. The analytical task was to construct a political economy of crime and its control. The normative task (that is, the solution to the crime problem) was to eliminate those economic and political systems of exploitation which gave rise to crime. The goal was a crime-free society, possible only under a different social order and impossible with the conceptual tools of bourgeois criminology.

(3) Another critique of the positivist enterprise came from a quite different theoretical and political direction. Impressed by the apparent failure of the causal quest and of progressive policies such as treatment, rehabilitation and social reform, a loose coalition of intellectuals appeared under such rallying calls as 'realism', 'back to justice' and 'neo-classicism'. Some of them are neo-liberals – and theirs is a note of sad disenchantment with the ideas and policies of progressive criminology. Some of them are conservatives (or neo-conservatives) – and theirs is a note of satisfaction about the supposed failures of liberalism. Both these wings harken back to classical questions; the notion of justice (or 'just deserts') allows liberals to talk of rights, equity and fairness, while it allows conservatives to talk about law and order, social defence, deterrence and the protection of society. In neither case – but particularly for conservatives – is there much interest in traditional questions of causation.

Criminology is a subject with a complicated past and a polemical present. Most criminologists are employed at the core of the enterprise: busy either describing, classifying and explaining crime or else analysing, evaluating and advocating policy. At the periphery, are various fascinating intellectual disputes about the subject's true content and justification. As Jock Young has recently shown (1981), the major schools of criminological thought are divided on quite basic issues: the image of human nature, the basis of social order, the nature and extent of crime, the relationship between theory and policy. And if we move out of the Anglo-American cultures in which contemporary criminology has mainly flourished, even more fundamental differences appear (a major – and belated – recent development has been the serious comparative analysis of crime and its control).

But whether positivist or neoclassical, radical or conservative, detached intellectuals or disguised policemen, criminologists confront the same questions. All this diversity is a manifestation of a single tension: crime is behaviour, but it is behaviour which the state is organized to punish.

Stanley Cohen
Hebrew University of Jerusalem

References
Foucault, M. (1977 [1975]), *Discipline and Punish*, London. (Original French edn, *Surveiller et punir*, Paris.)
Matza, D. (1964), *Delinquency and Drift*, New York.
Matza, D. (1969), *Becoming Deviant*, Englewood Cliffs, N.J.
Young, J. (1981), 'Thinking seriously about crime' in M. Fitzgerald *et al.* (eds), *Crime and Society*, London.

Further Reading
Christie, N. (1981), *Limits to Pain*, Oxford.
Sutherland, E. and Cressey, D. (1984), *Principles of Criminology*, Philadelphia.
Sykes, G. (1978), *Criminology*, New York.
See also: *crime and delinquency; labelling theory; penology; punishment; social control.*

Cross-Cultural Psychology

Cross-cultural psychology refers to the collective efforts of scholars in all parts of the world who do research among people who speak different languages, live in societies ranging from technologically unsophisticated to highly industrialized, and who submit to various forms of political organization. Many of the activities of these psychologists are similar to those of anthropologists, especially the emphasis on fieldwork, sensitivity to the point of view of people in the cultures under investigation, and the development of broad theories which incorporate observations made by individual researchers. Psychologists have also borrowed from anthropologists' definitions of culture. From hundreds of treatments of 'culture', key elements which have proved useful include people's conceptions about the world and the values attached to those conceptions; subjective reactions to people's view of their man-made world in the form of roles, status hierarchies, and attitudes; and symbols which provide meaning to life and which are transmitted from generation to generation.

Psychologists who undertake cross-cultural research must be willing to bear additional hardships above and beyond the difficulties of any research endeavour. Cross-cultural research involves language or dialect differences between investigator and participants, creating special problems in assuring (a) adequate and accurate communication and (b) equivalence of meaning of measuring instruments across different samples. The demands of fieldwork, including adjustment to life in another culture and time to establish one's identity among people often unfamiliar and perhaps hostile to research studies, force the development of effective skills to cope with the resulting stress.

The benefits, however, are substantial (Triandis *et al.*, 1980–1): (1) The range of independent variables available for study can be increased. For example, if a researcher is interested in the relationship between age of weaning and adult development, there is a very limited range *within* any one culture, since the norm for 'proper' weaning age is widely shared among people who have frequent contact. However, *across* cultures, the age of weaning varies widely, up to a maximum of five years. Since one variable can be related to another only if there is sufficient range in both, some studies can be done only with cross-cultural data.

(2) Variables which naturally occur together in one culture can be unconfounded, or taken apart, in another. In highly industrialized nations, it is difficult to separate the effects of age and schooling on cognitive development since virtually all children of a certain age are in school. But in other societies, some children of a given age attend school and others do not, and consequently a study of the relative contribution of the two factors can be undertaken.

(3) It is possible to test theories which are based on a clear distinction between people's competencies and their performance. One reason why researchers may not observe a competency is that people may never have had a *latent* competency challenged by a task in their everyday lives. There is the danger that the lack of behavioural evidence for the competency will be misdiagnosed as a deficit, leading to unfair charges of 'less able or intelligent'. The problem can be overcome if psychologists develop training studies in which people perform tasks that challenge their latent, but rarely used, competencies. Specifying the nature of the

tasks should also be a benefit to more precise theory development, as well as to various intervention programmes, such as formal schooling.

Measurement is central to all psychological research. Probably the most central concern in measurement as applied to cross-cultural investigations is the demand for evidence that instruments are measuring relevant variables in the cultures under investigation. The demand is becoming widely accepted as a methodological *sine qua non*. The era of giving standardized tests in other cultures, without attention to cross-validation and to the construct validity of measures, is blessedly coming under intense challenges and is, one hopes, coming to an end. An alternative is the development of measures for research in another culture which assess aspects of a concept meaningful *within* that culture. For instance, Miller and her colleagues (1981), not satisfied with administering the same questionnaire in two countries and calculating mean differences, developed new measures in their investigations of the meaning of authoritarianism-conservatism in the United States and Poland. They could have administered the F-scale or the dogmatism scale in the two countries and then compared results; instead, they devised these new measures which tapped meaning unique to the United States or Poland, and they also identified a core meaning common to both countries. They found, for example, that an aspect more central to the general concept of authoritarianism-conservatism in Poland than the United States consists of items measuring a deference to hierarchical authority which is bureaucratically or legally legitimized. One of the newly-designed United States item sets focused on the endorsement of public intervention in matters ordinarily addressed elsewhere (for example, in the family or in the courts). A complete analysis of any concept, then, demands treatment of both shared aspects across cultures as well as unique aspects within each culture under investigation.

Another measurement principle in cross-cultural psychology is that direct comparisons across cultures on single measures are rarely warranted. There are too many methodological reasons why one group may score higher or lower, such as translation and/or conceptual equivalence problems, to warrant direct comparisons. An important point is that many substantive conclusions of both theoretical and practical interest can be made without direct comparison across cultures. Theoretical and practical conclusions are better made by examining the antecedents, correlates, and consequences of phenomena within cultures. Direct cross-cultural comparisons often lead to a set of score-keeping, derogatory charges of one culture high, another low on some variable. If it *is* theoretically interesting to make comparisons, it is essential to compare results consisting of patterns of multiple variables, the variables ideally measured by more than one method. Plausible rival explanations based on methodological difficulties are far more difficult to formulate, given patterns of results in contrast to single data points. Of course, substantive reasons for the patterns of variables should be specified.

Cross-cultural research has always been under threat of becoming a fringe area, separated from the mainstream of general psychology. This should not happen provided that cross-cultural researchers are careful to draw from general principles when possible and to contribute to the development of those same principles based on their data. Distinctions between cross-cultural and general psychology should diminish as more research facilities are established in various parts of the world, and as they become staffed by indigenously-trained psychologists.

Richard W. Brislin
East-West Center, Honolulu, Hawaii

References
Miller, J., Slomczynski, K. and Shoenberg, R. (1981), 'Assessing comparability of measurement in cross-national research: authoritarianism-conservatism in different sociocultural settings', *Social Psychology Quarterly*, 44.
Triandis, H. C., Lambert, W., Berry, J., Lonner, W., Heron, A., Brislin, R. and Draguns, J. (eds) (1980–1), *Handbook of Cross-Cultural Psychology* (vols 1–6), Boston.
See also: *culture; culture and personality.*

Crowding Out

The concept of the crowding out of private sector activity by expansions of government sector has become increasingly important in recent political/academic debates. All participants in the debate accept that if the economy is at full employment, then an increase in government spending will reduce private sector spending. The debate is concentrated on the effect of increases in government spending away from full employment. If government spending rises by $100 million and national income increases by less than $100 million, then crowding out is said to have occurred. In other words, crowding out is associated with a *multiplier* of less than unity. Even if national income rises by more than $100 million, it would normally be the case that the higher interest rates associated with higher borrowing will reduce productive private sector investment and so 'crowd out' some elements of national income.

The resurgence of interest in crowding out has been associated with the monetarist critique of macroeconomic policy and has received its main theoretical (Carlson and Spencer, 1975) and empirical (Anderson and Jordan, 1968) support from work undertaken at the Federal Reserve Bank of St Louis in the US. Although much of this work has been discredited (see Goldfeld and Blinder, 1972), the political impact has been increasing. Apart from the interest rate effect on investment, a number of other possible sources for crowding out have been suggested. Increased government expenditure may have a depressing effect on people's expectations about the future possible productivity of the economy, and so causing them to reduce investment. Alternatively, investment could be so interest sensitive that even a small rise in the interest rate will reduce investment fully in line with the increase in government spending (this is sometimes known as the Knight case after the Chicago economist Frank Knight).

The major case emphasized by monetarist economists comes from an analysis of the financing of a government deficit. To have an impact on the economy a deficit has to be sustained for a number of years, but each year that deficit has to be financed by borrowing or printing money. Continual financing by borrowing will raise interest rates as the government competes for funds, and the gradual increase in interest rates will reduce investment. As well as this effect, it may be stressed that government debt is safer than private debt, so dollar for dollar substitution will increase the liquidity of the economy and reduce the impulsion to save (and therefore reduce investment funds).

However lacking in persuasiveness these arguments may be, there is strong empirical support for the proposition that multipliers are very low in the UK at least (see Taylor in Cook and Jackson, 1979). In versions of the Treasury Model and the Keynesian National Institute model, long run multipliers vary from 1.1 to .4 giving considerable credence to the arguments in favour of crowding out. This does not demonstrate that fiscal policy is impossible, but that it is just difficult to sustain.

Ray Barrell
University of Southampton

References

Anderson, L. C. and Jordan, J. L. (1968), 'Monetary and fiscal actions: a test of their relative importance in economic stabilisation', *Federal Reserve Bank of St Louis Review*.

Carlson, K. M. and Spencer, R. W. (1975), 'Crowding out and its critics', *Federal Reserve Bank of St Louis Review*.

Cook, S. T. and Jackson, P. M. (eds), *Government Issues in Fiscal Policy*, London.

Goldfeld, S. and Blinder, A. (1972), 'Some implications of endogenous stabilisation policy', *Brookings Papers on Economic Activity*.

See also: *fiscal policy; monetarism*.

Crowds

See Collective Behaviour and Crowds.

Cults

See Sects and Cults.

Cultural Anthropology

The term cultural anthropology is used mainly in the United States to define the branch of anthropology which is concerned with man as a social being, and with learned rather than genetically-transmitted forms of behaviour. Some authors prefer to use the term ethnology. In either case the concept covers social organization, but in the American tradition the emphasis has been rather on technology, language, myth, history and religion.

Boas and many of his students employed a diffusionist, historical approach to culture. Later, Mead and others developed an interest in the relationship between 'culture' and 'personality'. Some authors emphasized the material basis of culture, stressing the interplay between technology and environment. For some, like Benedict, culture was a whole, a closed system; for others it was rather a loosely-integrated set of traits which were only related by historical accident. Notwithstanding such variations, all these authors shared the fundamental postulate that culture, a learnt, historically-variable tradition, was the main determinant of behaviour.

The implication was that man was malleable. Cultural adaptation was possible, even normal, either through borrowing and innovation or, at the individual level, through learning. It was also generally agreed that cross-cultural judgements of value were difficult to make, and that a relativistic moral position was justified, at least within wide limits. These implications of cultural anthropology may have been significantly related to the liberal vision of the United States as a melting-pot, in which people of various races and cultures were transformed into Americans.

In the last generation, under the influence of the writings of Talcott Parsons, 'culture' was marked off as a subject of study distinct from 'society' in American anthropology. In this context, culture is defined as a system of symbols. The most influential of the Parsonian cultural anthropologists, Clifford Geertz and David Schneider, argue that cultural systems must be distinguished from social systems and analysed, in the first instance, as internally coherent wholes. Their work has led in the direction of hermeneutics and semiology, and away from cross-cultural comparison. This version of cultural anthropology is sometimes described as 'symbolic anthropology' or 'cognitive anthropology'.

Adam Kuper
Brunel University, Uxbridge

Further Reading

Geertz, C. (1973), *The Interpretation of Cultures*, New York.
Herskovits, M. J. (1947), *Man and His Works*, New York.
Schneider, D. M. (1968), *American Kinship: A Cultural Account*, Chicago.
Silverman, S. (ed.) (1981), *Totems and Teachers: Perspectives on the History of Anthropology*, New York.
See also: *anthropology; Boas; culture; culture and personality; Geertz; Mead, M.; social anthropology.*

Culture

Culture is the way of life of a people. It consists of conventional patterns of thought and behaviour, including values, beliefs, rules of conduct, political organization, economic activity, and the like, which are passed on from one generation to the next by learning – and not by biological inheritance. The concept of culture is an idea of signal importance, for it provides a set of principles for explaining and understanding human behaviour. It is one of the distinguishing elements of modern social thought, and may be one of the most important achievements of modern social science, and in particular of anthropology.

The modern culture concept entails several principles for understanding behaviour:

(1) The patterns which both guide and define thought and behaviour are learned. For example, we sometimes hear the admonition to 'act yourself', or 'to behave naturally', and not to copy someone else. The notion of culture makes this a specious distinction, inasmuch as all thought and behaviour are modelled on cultural patterns that we learn. To behave 'naturally' for a middle-class Englishman is to behave according to a particular cultural style, and an American or Australian who follows that style would be considered quite odd. The view of human thought and behaviour as culturally patterned assumes that human beings are by nature very malleable, for they exhibit a wide variety of behavioural forms as a result of the process of socialization or enculturation.

(2) A large component of culture is below the level of conscious awareness. Language – which is a subsystem of culture – is an example. All people employ complicated systems of linguistic rules, such as phonological and grammatical rules, that provide the code by which individuals are able to understand one another's utterances. Neither listener nor speaker can fully express what these rules are, and typically the individual is no more than dimly aware that they even exist. The same is true for other spheres of culture, in that the members of a society share a large body of implicit conceptions about nature, moral values, property ownership, and the like.

(3) Cultural patterns structure both thought and perception. For instance, the colour spectrum is a continuous gradation of hue, yet by cultural convention it is broken up into distinct segments. English speakers distinguish between blue and green, for example, which is to say that at a certain point along the spectrum, by convention, a category distinction is made. Hues which fall to one side of this point are referred to as blue, and the other as green. Different languages make distinctions between colours at different places along the continuum. The categorization of colour in this fashion has implications for perception of the real world: for instance, a rainbow is a continuous gradation of colour, yet it is thought of as a series of distinct bands. Values also influence thought and perception. For example, a landscape is not perceived in a purely neutral fashion, inasmuch as values are projected onto it. A virgin forest is conceived by Western peoples very differently from a hillside that has been eroded as a result of industrial excavations, and this difference is in part a matter of aesthetic values.

The term culture has been an important part of the anthropologist's vocabulary since about the mid-1800s, yet the meaning of the term underwent an important change at around the turn of this century. The nineteenth-century usage, which characterized the works of such Victorian anthropologists as Sir Edward B. Tylor and Lewis Henry Morgan, viewed culture or civilization as the conscious creation of rational minds for the purpose of improving the lives of society's members. For example, moral values were thought to have been invented to promote human happiness. Past experiences with laziness, thriftlessness, unchastity, and the like, prompted the establishment of Victorian values about sex, work, and 'proper' behaviour in general. Similarly, the parliamentary form of government, monogamy, capitalism, modern clothing styles, and so on, were thought to have arisen as a result of rational reflections upon human experiences and needs.

The Victorian anthropologists assumed that some societies had done a better job than others of thinking through the issues confronting them and so had achieved higher levels of culture, and that Western civilization ranked highest of all. This is not to say that the Victorian anthropologists believed that Western society had no room for improvement: further reflection upon even the most intelligent institutions can produce progressively better ways of life. Yet it was thought that the world's cultures can be arranged according to a single hierarchy, from the least cultured to the most, and that Western civilization stands at the progressive end of the scale. The Victorian anthropologists also had an explanation for the inferior position of the lower societies: these people were less intelligent. Race, intelligence, and culture were thought to vary along the same continuum. However, they did not assume that the lower races would necessarily remain behind forever. One common assumption was that the human mind can be improved from one generation to the next according to Lamarckian principles of inheritance. If a person lives in a more intelligent and stimulating environment than his parents, his mind will be slightly improved over theirs, and this improvement will be passed on to his children; his children's minds in turn may be slightly improved further by having been raised in an even more intelligent environment, and so on. All people are gradually moving toward higher and higher levels of culture.

The modern culture concept emerged at about the turn of the century, and it did so largely in opposition to the Victorian ideas just described. A number of people contributed to these changes, perhaps the most significant being Franz Boas, a German scientist who emigrated to the United States in the 1880s and eventually became the dean of American anthropology. A main thrust of these writers was that culture is governed by its own principles and not by the raw intellect, and that the differences among peoples do not reflect differences in levels of intelligence. Emile Durkheim, the turn-of-the-century French sociologist, is illustrative. Durkheim did not use the term culture in his work, yet his notion of 'collective representations' had much the same meaning. He argued that collective representations express certain properties concerning the way society is organized: if the physical arrangement of the members of society is changed, then the collective representations will change accordingly. Consequently, raw intellect simply is not the guiding force behind cultural institutions. Similarly, to Boas, what explains the occurrence of a cultural item among certain people and not others is historical accident. Once a trait is created it is borrowed and modified to fit its new cultural context, and then it is borrowed again by another society and modified further, and so on. Boas argued that it is impossible to trace a cultural item back to the original intellectual impulse which gave rise to it, for there are too many intervening historical events. The development of a trait has less to do with the intellect than with the principles of culture history.

With the development of the modern culture concept the intellect itself came to be viewed differently: instead of being the guiding principle behind culture, it was now seen to be largely constituted by culture. It was now understood that people acquire the ideas, beliefs, values, and the like, of their society, and that these cultural features provide the basic materials by which they think and perceive. In addition, a significant implication of the modern culture concept is that race does not provide an adequate explanation for differences among societies. Cultures vary independently of race, and members of all races acquire whatever cultural patterns are available to them. The notion of cultural superiority itself is called into question with the modern culture concept, which contains a degree of cultural relativism. The evaluation of superior or inferior rests upon a cultural point of view, and the attempt to use the Western point of view as the basis for judging others should be treated with great caution.

Culture is an explanatory concept in two senses: (1) It has the potential for explaining why specific institutions occur when and where they do. For example, it has been suggested that certain types of religious patterns are associated with specific types of social structure, and that certain forms of ecological adaptation entail the development of specific kinds of social and political organization. In other words, certain features of the cultural system explain other features of that system. (2) Culture contains principles for interpreting behaviour and institutions. To interpret is not to explain *why* an institution occurs when and where it does, but to make sense of it. An interpretive explanation is one which gives an account of an institution or behaviour by explicating the values, beliefs, symbols, and so on, which are behind it, and which make an enigmatic pattern (say, the couvade) intelligible. Interpretation in this sense is roughly analogous to literary criticism, which attempts to achieve progressively deeper levels of understanding of a creative work.

Most social scientists today employ some variation of the modern culture concept in their research, and while they agree about the essential features of culture, they still disagree fundamentally about how culture works, the factors governing it, and the full extent of its influence on behaviour, thought, and perception.

Elvin Hatch
University of California, Santa Barbara

Further Reading

Hatch, E. (1973), *Theories of Man and Culture*, New York.

Kroeber, A. L. and Kluckhohn, C. (1963), *Culture: A Critical Review of Concepts and Definitions*, New York.

Stocking, G. W. Jr (1968), *Race, Culture, and Evolution*, New York.

See also: *Boas; cultural anthropology; Durkheim.*

Culture and Personality

Culture and Personality was a psychoanalytically-oriented subdiscipline of American cultural anthropology which sought to relate traits of individual personality and symbolic aspects of culture to socialization variables, that is, peculiarities of parent-child relationships. How was individual character influenced by culture? What were the observable processes of behaviour by which individuals became members of their own culture? Such questions gained prominence in the 1930s and 1940s, when leading contributors included Bateson, Gorer, Hallowell, Kardiner, and Kluckhohn.

The anti-eugenic and pro-relativist teaching of Franz Boas, the immigrant German Jew and father of modern American anthropology, is perhaps one origin of the subdiscipline. Human behaviour was the provenance of culture and not race. The goal was to distinguish varying cultural and psychological processes from universal ones. Was the Oedipus complex, for example, merely a construction whose validity was limited to European family relationships or had it wider relevance?

Under the influence of Boas, two students, Mead and Benedict, used vocabulary and models from developmental and learning theories to discuss personality formation. Dubois, in addition, employed personality assessment techniques such as the Rorschach and word associations in her fieldwork.

Following the big wartime study of enemy national character at Columbia University, *Research in Contemporary Cultures* (1953), activity in this subfield began to change. Allied subfields – medical, psychological, and cognitive anthropologies – arose and interest in culture and personality questions was diverted into new forums.

David Lipset
University of Minnesota

Further Reading

Hsu, F. L. K. (1961), *Psychological Anthropology: Approaches to Culture and Personality*, Homewood, Ill.

See also: *Mead, M.*

Culture Area

The phrase culture area refers to a geographical region which encompasses a cluster of societies possessing similar customs and social institutions, or similar material culture. The concept grew largely out of the comparative ethnography of North American Indians by American anthropologists at the time of Franz Boas. It reached its peak as a theoretical interest about the 1920s in the work of Clark Wissler, though Wissler himself (1927) modestly denied that the development of the idea should be attributed to any one individual.

Early versions of culture area theory centred on the mapping of environmental zones and subsistence techniques, a practice which led directly, if not immediately, to Julian Steward's notion of 'cultural ecology' (1955). Culture areas frequently were equated with environmental zones, each having a centre from which 'culture traits' were believed to have diffused. Marginal areas, far from a culture centre, would have traits of more than one culture area. Sets of functionally related traits were known as 'trait complexes', and much debate in American anthropology in the 1920s and 1930s focused on defining these complexes and the various levels of 'grand areas', 'culture areas' and 'sub-areas' which possessed them.

Paralleling the culture area approach in North America, and to some extent foreshadowing it, was the *Kulturkreis* (culture circle) school in Europe. Building on the work of earlier German and Austrian diffusionists, Fritz Graebner and Father Wilhelm Schmidt tried to map the history of the world according to supposed expanding and overlapping 'circles' of culture, spread by migration and diffusion.

In contrast, the American culture area school had more modest goals. Its adherents concentrated on the history of particular continents and even particular culture areas. The historical aspect of their work was exemplified by Wissler's hypothesis that traits diffused from the centre to the periphery of a culture area, and consequently that the oldest traits were those on the periphery rather than those of the everchanging centre. This idea both grew from and had influence upon the archaeology of aboriginal North America.

A modern, loosely, 'structuralist' form of culture area theory was developed independently in Holland (Josselin de Jong, 1977 [1935]) and is now providing new insights, particularly in studies of kinship and cosmological systems.

Alan Barnard
University of Edinburgh

References

Josselin de Jong, J. P. B. de (1977 [1935]), 'The Malay Archipelago as a field of ethnological study', in P. E. de Josselin de Jong (ed.), *Structural Anthropology in the Netherlands*, The Hague.

Steward, J. H. (1955), *Theory of Culture Change*, Urbana, Ill,

Wissler, C. (1927), 'The culture-area concept in social anthropology', *American Journal of Sociology*, 32.

Further Reading
Kluckhohn, C. (1936), 'Some reflections on the method and theory of the *Kulturkreislehre*', *American Anthropologist*, 38.

See also: *diffusion*.

Cybernetics

See: General Systems Theory.

D

Death

In almost any culture, death provides a unique occasion for specialized ritual and symbolic representation. The most common underlying theme is that order, represented by life, becomes, with death, disorder. Cosmos is replaced by chaos. The purpose of the ritual is the restoration of order, a process sometimes so protracted that a whole generation can pass before it is completed (Hertz, 1960 [1928]). Two factors tend to determine both the duration and the elaboration of the ritual: (1) The social status of the deceased. The ritual for children and strangers will be simple and short, involving only a few people, while that for a king will be complex and protracted, involving the whole society; (2) This factor depends upon the manner of disposal and decomposition of the corpse. The rites which close the funeral cycle generally await the completion of this process. The deliberate destruction of the body, as found in the cremation practices of Hinduism, is relatively uncommon, but even in these cases there is a period of intense ritual immediately following death. In any case the period closes with the corpse reaching its final destination, which may vary from commitment to a mausoleum to being washed away, as ashes, by a sacred river such as the Ganges. The possibilities are endless. The process may be the responsibility of a special class, or caste, of priests, who at the same time will be the official guardians of the system of beliefs according to which the eventual fate of everyone, on the other side of death, is determined.

The general theme here is the regeneration of life (Bloch and Parry (eds), 1982). It is in the first place critical that the ordinary life of society, or at least of those members of it who were in the deceased's immediate circle, can only be fully resumed at the termination of the funeral ritual – which may therefore be a festive occasion. At the same time there is a clear parallel with the rites of initiation by which a child is recognized as having become a full member of society. The Christian requirement, fulfilled by baptism, that the child must be 'born again of water and the Holy Spirit' has its parallel in almost every religion, but in death Christianity is almost unique in its preoccupation with the destiny of the individual soul. The contemporary Christian idea of a paradise, in which one is reunited with one's 'nearest and dearest', dates only from the nineteenth century (Ariès, 1983), and has no more theological justification than the curious idea of purgatory – first appearing in the late Middle Ages – which represents the ultimate in protracted *rites de passage*.

The cognitive basis of the ritual and symbolism surrounding death is to be found in different forms of eschatology, literally the science of the *last* things. Eschatology, which is concerned with the ultimate destiny of both mankind and the individual, may, but need not, combine with theodicy and reincarnation. The former is primarily an ethical judgment, based upon the earthly life, which in some way determines its future destiny. This, in Buddhism and Hinduism, takes the form of reincarnation, and the judgment decrees the form in which this will take place. In other types of eschatology, the fate of the deceased may depend upon the manner of death, so that homicide and, even more, suicide are likely to be special cases. Euthanasia, the deliberate ending of a life of suffering, is a special case in the modern world, but the eschatological implications tend to be underplayed, and the question is debated in terms of earthly morality. The socio-legal consequences of death primarily concern the succession to the property and authority of the deceased, whose scale tends to determine the elaboration of the ritual process. Law and tradition usually lay down the mode of succession according to prescribed rules: the right of the living to determine these matters by a testamentary disposition, which is particularly characteristic of the Anglo-American law, is by no means universal. The *ultimate* disposal of the bodies of the deceased according to tradition may itself establish and perpetuate a palpable model of the social order, as Bloch (1971) has demonstrated for the Merina of Madagascar. Here the special provisions made for kings are again noteworthy.

The economic significance of death is not confined to the succession to property and authority: the celebration of the ritual may – at least in part – provide for the maintenance of particular institutions and their officeholders. In our own age, undertaking, particularly in the United States, has become big business, largely by transforming the ritual and symbolism of death in conformity with the ethic of the consumer society.

Thomas Crump
University of Amsterdam

References

Ariès, P. (1983), *The Hour of Our Death*, Harmondsworth.

Bloch, M. and Parry, J. (eds) (1982), *Death and the Regeneration of Life*, Cambridge.

Hertz, R. (1960 [1928]), *Death and the Right Hand*, London (original French edn, *Mélanges de la sociologie religieux et folklore*, Paris).

Humphreys, S. C. and King, H. (1981), *Mortality and Immortality*, London.

See also: *rites of passage*.

Debreu, Gérard (1921–)

A mathematical economist *par excellence*, Gérard Debreu was born in 1921 in Calais, France. Early in his studies he was attracted to mathematics and only later was drawn to economics, more specifically to the Walrasian mathematical theory of general economic equilibrium in the exposition of Allais (1943). In 1949 a Rockefeller Fellowship enabled him to broaden his horizons as an economist. He joined the Cowles Commission, a centre for mathematical economics, where he devoted his research to Pareto optima, the existence of a general economic equilibrium, and utility theory. In 1962 Debreu was appointed professor of economics (and later mathematics) at the University of California, Berkeley – a continuing happy association.

The purpose of Debreu's 1959 monograph was an axiomatic analysis of the theory of general economic equilibrium, and in 1962 he provided the complex proof of a more general theorem on the existence of an economic equilibrium. Essentially, Debreu's most notable achievement (together with Arrow and others) was not only to demonstrate that a coherent and orderly economic allocation can be theoretically achieved, but to specify the necessary conditions to reach this result. By elucidating the requisite conditions, Debreu helped to show not only what the world would have to be like for the results to be achieved, but also allowed us to focus on the absence of these conditions in the real world. Also important is his treatment of uncertainty.

Thereafter Debreu turned his attention to the core of an economy, the theory of measure spaces of economic agents (with the related problem of topologizing the set of preference relations), and the question of regular economies. His most recent interests lie in studies of differentiable utility functions, the characterization of the excess demand function of an economy, the rate of convergence of the core of an economy to its set of competitive equilibria, the question of least concave utility functions, and the problem of decomposed quasi-convex functions.

In 1983 Debreu was awarded the Nobel Memorial Prize in Economic Sciences 'for having introduced new analytical methods into economic theory and for his rigorous reformulation of the theory of general equilibrium'. His approach to economics is characterized by rarefied purity and abstraction. His work is never 'contaminated' by the 'impurities' of applied economics or data. He finds that the logical rigour, the generality, and the simplicity of his theories satisfy deep personal intellectual needs. Debreu epitomizes the new breed of somewhat narrow technically sophisticated economists. He knows and exercises his comparative advantages and limits his contributions to fields in which he excels.

George R. Feiwel
University of Tennessee

Reference

Allais, M. (1943), *A la recherche d'une discipline économique*, Paris.

Further Reading

Debreu, G. (1959), *Theory of Value*, New York.

Debreu, G. (1982), 'Existence of competitive equilibrium', in K. J. Arrow and M. D. Intriligator (eds), *Handbook of Mathematical Economics*, vol. 2, Amsterdam.

Debreu, G. (1983), *Mathematical Economics: Twenty Papers of Gérard Debreu*, Cambridge.

See also: *equilibrium*.

Decision Making

There are three definitions of decision making, each of which is associated with a specific analytical approach. (1) Decision making is a rational, cognitive process by which a choice is made among several alternatives. The assumption is that the individual is capable of ranking alternatives in a rational manner, and choosing accordingly. This definition is associated with normative decision-making theory. (2) Decision making is concerned with the behaviour involved in making a choice even if such behaviour is spontaneous, impulsive or habitual. Here decision making is not treated as a cognitive process. This view of decision making is associated with behavioural decision theory. (3) Decision making is the actual process of making a choice. Various phases are distinguished: the recognition of the problem; the search for information; the processing of information and consideration of alternatives; and the formulation of the final choice. This procedural view is associated with the theory of collective decision making.

There are two sorts of theories concerning decision making. One set seeks logical, non-behavioural explanations, provides a formal analysis, and portrays decision making in terms of axiomatic models (Raiffa, 1968). Empirical theories, in contrast, describe actual decision-making behaviour, and explain it with reference to behavioural hypotheses.

Decision Making in Social Science Theories

Individual decision making is generally analysed in terms of psychological or social-psychological approaches. The researcher must consider and distinguish two types of psychological variables. The A-variable relates to the human arousal system (emotions, motivations, goals, etc.). The K-variable is the cognitive system, which is concerned with the perception, processing and storage of information.

Some decision-making theories are weighted in favour of the A-variable – for example, the conflict decision-making model of Janis and Mann (1977), who argue that the decision-making process is determined by the extent of conflict, whether emotional or motivational. Stronger conflicts induce insecurity and distress, and may interrupt or delay the decision-making process, while the individual searches for alternative, less threatening, solutions. Other theories restrict themselves to the K-features, and analyse decision making as the outcome of human information processing. These cognitive approaches neglect the influence of emotional factors (Kozielecki, 1981). The key element of cognitive theory is the notion that human beings have a limited capacity to recognize and digest information presented to them, and that decision making follows subjective, 'psycho-logical' rules that are considerably different from the rules of objective logic (Nisbet and Ross, 1980). Given his cognitive limitations, the individual is obliged to simplify the complexities of decision making. He uses various strategies to this end, including the identification of key pieces of information, the application of stereotypes, and simple rules of elimination.

Personality traits and personal self-image are key variables in individual decision making. Willingness to take risks is significant. While many people have internalized standards of 'rational decision making', their actual behaviour frequently diverges from this ideal standard, although they may present rational explanations of non-rational behaviour. This illustrates one of the pitfalls of using verbal methods to uncover the processes of decision making.

Currently, cognitive approaches are usually preferred for the analysis and measurement of decision-making processes. The researcher tries to understand the way in which individuals process information and make decisions, using various methods, including information display matrices, and the observation and measurement of visual and other sensory cues. These methods have not, however, yielded a satisfactory account of the 'psycho-logic' involved in decision making.

Collective decisions made by groups or within organizations have been of particular interest to sociologists, political scientists and economists. The early economic approach was normative, and favoured an axiomatic theory of rational decision making (corresponding to definition 1, above). Social scientists of other kinds preferred a more complex and descriptive approach (corresponding rather to definition 3). Recent studies tend to combine these approaches, economists now distancing themselves from the use of a simple monetary calculus and input-output models, and paying more attention to descriptions of decision-making behaviour.

Collective decisions are produced by the interaction of several individuals, whose personal qualities and views affect the final outcome. Yet collective decision making is more than the sum of a series of individual decision-making processes. Collective decisions are necessary where one individual is not competent to make a decision alone (K-explanation), or when several people are in conflict about the desired goals (A-explanation). The participants in the decision-making process may have specialized functions, which enhance productivity, but since the co-ordination of these specialists requires planning and adjustment, collective decision making may be a long drawn-out process.

Ideal-types of various kinds can be found in the literature on decision making, but there is little empirical research concerning the kinds of decisions made by groups of interacting individuals, nor is it at all clear whether individual or collective decisions are the more efficient. Contingency theory does deal with this issue, and suggests that collective decision making is more likely to be successful when the issue is very complex. Conversely, less complicated decisions are more efficiently made by individuals. Complexity is measured with reference to relevance, risk, problems of conflict, the existence of precedents, time pressures, and so on.

Collective decision making is complicated by a number of problems that are absent from individual decision making:

(1) *Deciding upon the actual goal.* People may collaborate and yet have different goals, because of different motivations (A-variable), or different cognitive approaches (K-variable), or different roles and statuses. If a solution is to be agreed upon, goal conflict must first be reduced (by a goal formation process).

(2) *Problems of communication.* Communication is the key to gaining information about goals, contexts, and strategies. While the process of communication may lead to distortion and delay, it can also increase rationality.

(3) *Co-ordination efforts.* Participants may make different types of contributions, and offer different perspectives on the issues. Some individuals take more initiatives, while others are more reserved. Information must be collected from various quarters and evaluated. Alternatives must be considered. A co-ordinator must steer the decision-making process, to ensure that it can be completed efficiently, effectively, and within a reasonable time.

(4) *Power problems*. Some individuals are more powerful and consequently more influential. Others will, to a greater or lesser extent, concur in the goals and methods of the more influential members of the group. (5) *Negotiation difficulties*. Decisions are normally made after a process of negotiation has been completed. The outcome of these negotiations depends on collective learning over time, especially by key members of the group. The process is influenced by personality factors, communications, the formation of coalitions, techniques of negotiation and arbitration, and the tactics employed by the actors, including, for example, the use of threats or deception.

While empirical research into all forms of decision making is still limited, insights have been won which already suggest ways of improving the efficiency and effectiveness of decision making in general.

Werner Kroeber-Riel
University of the Saarland

Jürgen Hauschildt
Christian-Albrechts University, Kiel

References

Janis, I. L. and Mann, L. (1977), *Decision Making, A Psychological Analysis of Conflict, Choice, and Commitment*, New York.
Kozielecki, J. (1981), *Psychological Decision Theory*, Dordrecht.
Nisbet, R. and Ross, L. (1980), *Human Inference: Strategies and Short-Comings of Social Judgment*, Englewood Cliffs, N.J.
Raiffa, H. (1968), *Decision Analysis*, Reading, Mass.

Further Reading

Hill, P. H., Bedau, H. A. *et al.* (1979), *Making Decisions. A Multi-disciplinary Introduction*, Reading, Mass.

See also: *committees*; *organizations*; *policy sciences*.

Defences

The conceptualization of ego mechanisms of defence presents one of the most valuable contributions that Sigmund Freud and psychoanalysis have made to psychology. Modern psychiatrists, including non-Freudians, define defence mechanisms in a more generic sense, as innate coping styles which allow individuals to minimize sudden, often unexpected, changes

in internal and external environment and to resolve cognitive dissonance (psychological conflicts). Defences are deployed involuntarily, as is the case in physiological homeostasis, and in contrast to so-called 'coping strategies'. Evidence continues to accumulate that differences in how individuals deploy defences – their unconscious coping styles – are a major consideration in understanding differential responses to environmental stress. For example, some people respond to stress in a calm, rational way, whereas others become phobic or sarcastic or emotional. These different responses are intelligible in terms of different defences.

In 1894, Sigmund Freud suggested that psychopathology was caused by upsetting affects, or emotions, rather than disturbing ideas. Freud observed that the ego's defence mechanisms can cause affects to become 'dislocated or transposed' from particular ideas or people, by processes which Freud later called dissociation, repression, and isolation. However, affects could be 'reattached' to other ideas and objects through displacement, projection and sublimation.

Freud identified four significant properties of the defences: (1) they help manage instincts and affects; (2) they are unconscious; (3) they are dynamic and reversible; and (4) although the hallmarks of major psychiatric syndromes, in most people they reflect an adaptive, not a pathological, process.

The use of defence mechanisms usually alters the individual's perception of both internal and external reality. Awareness of instinctual 'wishes' is often diminished; alternative, sometimes antithetical, wishes may be passionately adhered to. While ego mechanisms of defence imply integrated and dynamic – if unconscious – psychological processes, they are more analogous to an oppossum playing dead in the face of danger than to a reflexive eye-blink or to conscious tactics of interpersonal manipulation.

Some inferred purposes of ego mechanisms of defence are: (1) to keep affects within bearable limits during sudden changes in one's emotional life (for example, following the death of a loved one); (2) to restore psychological homeostasis by postponing or deflecting sudden increases in biological drives (such as heightened sexual awareness and aggression during adolescence); (3) to create a moratorium in which to master critical life changes (for example, puberty, life-threatening illness, or promotion); and (4) to handle unresolved conflicts with important people, living or dead.

In 1936, Freud advised the interested student: 'There are an extraordinarily large number of methods (or mechanisms, as we say) used by our ego in the discharge of its defensive functions . . . my daughter, the child analyst, is writing a book upon them.' He was referring to his eightieth-birthday present from Anna Freud; her monograph, *The Ego and the Mechan-*

isms of Defense (1937), is still the best single reference on the subject.

George E. Vaillant
Dartmouth Medical School, Hanover,
New Hampshire

Further Reading
Freud, S. (1964 [1894]), 'The neuro-psychosis of defence', *The Complete Works of Sigmund Freud*, vol. 3, London.
Vaillant, G. E. (1977), *Adaptation to Life*, Boston.
See also: *psychoanalysis*; *unconscious*.

Deflation as a Statistical Device

Economists are interested in abstracting from the effects of price changes when studying movements in economic variables. Deflation is the division of a value variable by an appropriate price index so as to obtain a quantity variable. When the value variable represents a purchase of goods or services the problem is relatively straightforward. A price index can be clearly identified and, although the result will depend on the choice of index, the question is relatively uncontroversial.

But the problem of deflating a variable which does not have any clearly identified flow of goods as its counterpart is much harder to solve. This has arisen particularly from attempts to measure the effect on national income of a change in the terms of trade. If the price of imports rises a country's income must fall, although there may be no change in the volume of its output measured (as output volume usually is) by a Laspeyres quantity index. If a country goes into trade deficit because of a rise in the price of oil, it is little comfort to observe that in base period prices it would still be in surplus. Following from work of Stuvel (1959), it has been pointed out that if one deflates all goods flows by their appropriate price index and all other flows in the national accounts by the ratio of GDP/deflated GDP, then a set of national accounts will be obtained which add up and in which terms like the 'real trade balance' and 'real profit' can be given some meaning.

Martin Weale
University of Cambridge

Reference
Stuvel, G. (1959), 'Asset revaluation and terms of trade effects in the framework of the national assets', *Economic Journal*.

Further Reading
Hibbert, J. (1975), 'Measuring changes in the nation's real income', *Economic Trends*.
See also: *index numbers*; *national income analysis*.

Democracy

In the classical Greek *polis*, democracy was the name of a constitution in which the poorer people (*demos*) exercised power in their own interest as against the interest of the rich and aristocratic. Aristotle thought it a debased form of constitution, and it played relatively little part in subsequent political thought, largely because Polybius and other writers diffused the idea that only mixed and balanced constitutions (incorporating monarchic, aristocratic and democratic elements) could be stable. Democracies were commonly regarded as aggressive and unstable and likely to lead (as in Plato's *Republic*) to tyranny. Their propensity to oppress minorities (especially the propertied) was what Burke meant when he described a perfect democracy as the most shameless thing in the world.

Democracy as popular power in an approving sense may occasionally be found in early modern times (in the radical thinkers of the English Civil War, the constitution of Rhode Island of 1641, and in the deliberations of the framers of the American Constitution), but the real vogue for democracy dates from the French Revolution. The main reason is that 'democracy' came to be the new name for the long-entrenched tradition of classical republicanism which, transmitted through Machiavelli, had long constituted a criticism of the dominant monarchical institutions of Europe. This tradition had often emphasized the importance of aristocratic guidance in a republic, and many of its adherents throughout Europe considered that British constitutional monarchy with an elected parliament was the very model of a proper republic. This idea fused in the nineteenth century with demand to extend the franchise, and the resulting package came generally to be called 'democracy'.

It is important to emphasize that democracy *was* a package, because the name had always previously described a source of power rather than a manner of governing. By the nineteenth century, however, the idea of democracy included representative parliaments, the separation of powers, the rule of law, civil rights and other such liberal desirabilities. All of these conditions were taken to be the culmination of human moral evolution, and the politics of the period often revolved around extensions of the franchise, first to adult males, then to women, and subsequently to such classes as young people of 18 (rather than 21) and, recently in Great Britain, to voluntary patients in mental hospitals.

Democracy proved to be a fertile and effervescent principle of political perfection. Inevitably, each advance towards democracy disappointed many adherents, but the true ideal could always be relocated in new refinements of the idea. The basis of many such extensions had been laid by the fact that 'democracy' was a Greek term used, for accidental reasons, to describe a complicated set of institutions whose real roots were medieval. The most important was representation, supported by some American founding fathers precisely because it might moderate rather than reflect the passions of an untutored multitude. The Greekness of the name, however, continually suggests that the practice of representation is not intrinsic to modern democracy, but rather a contingent imperfection resulting from the sheer size of modern nations by comparison with ancient city states. In fact, modern constitutional government is quite unrelated to the democracy of the Greeks.

Although modern democracy is a complicated package, the logic of the expression suggests a single principle. The problem is: what precisely is the principle? And a further question arises: how far should it extend? So far as the first question is concerned, democracy might be identified with popular sovereignty, majority rule, protection of minorities, affability, constitutional liberties, participation in decisions at every level, egalitarianism, and much else. Parties emphasize one or other of these principles according to current convenience, but most parties in the modern world (the fascist parties between 1918 and 1945 are the most important exception) have seldom failed to claim a democratic legitimacy. The principle of democracy was thus a suitably restless principle for a restless people ever searching for constitutional perfection.

Democracy is irresistible as a slogan because it seems to promise a form of government in which rulers and ruled are in such harmony that little actual governing will be required. Democracy was thus equated with a dream of freedom. For this reason, the nationalist theories which helped destroy the great European empires were a department of the grand principle of democracy, since everybody assumed that the people would want to be ruled by politicians of their own kind. The demographic complexities of many areas, however, were such that many people would inevitably be ruled by foreigners; and such people often preferred to be ruled on an imperial principle – in which all subjects are, as it were, foreigners – rather than on a national principle, which constitutes some as the nation, and the rest as minorities. In claiming to be democratic, rulers might hope to persuade their subjects that they ruled in the popular interest.

Democracy is possible only when a population can recognize both sectional and public interests, and organize itself for political action. Hence no state is seriously democratic unless an opposition is permitted to criticize governments, organize support, and contest elections. But in many countries, such oppositions are likely to be based upon tribes, nations or regions, which do not recognize a common or universal good in the state. Where political parties are of this kind, democratic institutions generate quarrels rather than law

and order. In these circumstances, democracy is impossible, and the outcome has been the emergence of some other unifying principle: sometimes an army claiming to stand above 'politics', and sometimes an ideological party in which a doctrine supplies a simulacrum of the missing universal element. One-party states often lay claim to some eccentric (and superior) kind of democracy – basic, popular, guided and so on. In fact, the very name 'party' requires pluralism. Hence, in one-party states, the party is a different kind of political entity altogether, and the claim to democracy is merely window-dressing. This does not necessarily mean, however, that such governments are entirely without virtue. It would be foolish to think that one manner of government suited all peoples.

Democracy as an ideal in the nineteenth century took for granted citizens who were rationally reflective about the voting choices open to them. Modern political scientists have concentrated their attention upon the actual irrationalities of the democratic process. Some have even argued that a high degree of political apathy is preferable to mass enthusiasm which endangers constitutional forms.

Kenneth Minogue
London School of Economics and Political Science

Further Reading
Macpherson, C. B. (1973), *Democratic Theory: Essays in Retrieval*, Oxford.
Plamenatz, J. (1973), *Democracy and Illusion*, London.
Sartori, G. (1962), *Democracy*, Detroit.
Schumpeter, J. (1943), *Capitalism, Socialism and Democracy*, London.
See also: *elections*; *parties*; *representation, political*.

Demographic Transition

Demographic transition, also known earlier as the demographic cycle, describes the movement of death and birth rates in a society from a situation where both are high to one where both are low. In the more developed economies, it was appreciated in the nineteenth century that mortality was declining. Fertility began to fall in France in the late eighteenth century, and in northwest and central Europe, as well as in English-speaking countries of overseas European settlement, in the last three decades of the nineteenth century. Fertility levels were believed to have approximated mortality levels over much of human history, but the fact that fertility declined later than mortality during demographic transition inevitably produced rapid population growth. In France this situation appeared to have passed by 1910, as birth and death rates once again drew close to each other, and by the

1930s this also seemed to be happening in the rest of the countries referred to above.

In 1929, Thompson categorized the countries of the world into three groups according to their stage in this movement of vital rates (later to be termed also the vital revolution). This process was to be carried further by C. P. Blacker, who in 1947 discerned five stages of which the last was not the reattainment of nearly stationary demographic conditions but of declining population, a possibility suggested by the experience of a range of countries in the economic depression of the 1930s. However, it was a paper published in 1945 by Notestein, the Director of Princeton University's Office of Population Research, which introduced the term demographic transition. This paper implied the inevitability of the transition for all societies and, together with another paper published seven years later, began to explore the mechanisms which might explain the change. Notestein argued that the mortality decline was the result of scientific and economic change, and was generally welcomed. On the other hand, fertility had been kept sufficiently high in high-mortality countries to avoid population decline only by a whole array of religious and cultural mechanisms which slowly decayed once lower mortality meant that they were no longer needed. He also believed that the growth of city populations, and economic development more generally, created individualism and rationalism which undermined the cultural props supporting uncontrolled fertility.

Demographic transition theory is less a theory than a body of observations and explanations. Coale (1973) has summarized research on the European demographic transition as indicating the importance of the diffusion of birth control behaviour within cultural units, usually linguistic ones, with diffusion halting at cultural frontiers. Caldwell (1976) has argued that high fertility is economically rewarding in pre-transitional societies to the decision makers, usually the parents, and that, if subsequent changes in the social relations between the generations mean that the cost of children outweighs the lifelong returns from them, then fertility begins to fall. The Chicago Household Economists (see Schultz, 1974) place stress on the underlying social and economic changes in the value of women's time as well as on the changing marginal value of children.

After the Second World War doubt was cast as to whether the transition necessarily ended with near-stationary population growth because of the occurrence in many industrialized countries of a 'baby boom', but by the 1970s this was regarded as an aberrant phenomenon related largely to a perhaps temporary movement toward early and universal marriages. By this time the demographic transition's claim to be globally applicable had received support from fertility declines (usually assisted in developing countries by government family planning programmes) in most of the world with the major exceptions of Africa and the Middle East.

John C. Caldwell
Australian National University

References
Blacker, C. P. (1947), 'Stages in population growth', *Eugenics Review*, vol. 39.
Caldwell, J. C. (1976), 'Toward a restatement of demographic transition theory', *Population and Development Review*, vol. 2 (3 and 4).
Coale, A. J. (1973), 'The demographic transition', in *International Population Conference, Liege, 1973. Proceedings*, vol. 1, Liege.
Notestein, F. W. (1945), 'Population: the long view', in T. W. Schultz (ed.), *Food for the World*, Chicago.
Schultz, T. W. (ed.) (1974), *Economics of the Family: Marriage, Children, and Human Capital. A Conference Report of the National Bureau of Economic Research*, Chicago.
Thompson, W. S. (1929), 'Population', *American Journal of Sociology*, vol. 34.
See also: *fertility*; *population*; *population and resources*; *population policy*.

Demography

Demography is the analysis of population variables. It includes both methods and substantive results, in the fields of mortality, fertility, migration and resulting population numbers. Demographers collect data on population and its components of change, and construct models of population dynamics. They contribute to the wider field of population studies that relate population changes to non-demographic – social, economic, political, or other – factors. In so far as it reaches into population studies, demography is inter-disciplinary: it includes elements of sociology, economics, biology, history, psychology and other fields. Its methods include parts of statistics and numerical analysis. Public health officials and actuaries have had their part in its development. Most demographers have professional knowledge of one or more of these disciplines.

Population variables are of two kinds – stock and flow. The important source of information on stock variables is national censuses, whose modern form goes back to the seventeenth century in Canada, Virginia, Sweden, and a few other places, and which are now carried out periodically in nearly all countries of the world. Among the cross-sectional information collected in censuses are age and sex distribution, labour force status and occupation, and birthplace.

The flow variables, the components of population change, include birth and death registrations, initiated before the nineteenth century in Sweden and in Britain, and now routine in all industrial countries. Efforts to attain completeness are slowly making their way elsewhere. Migration statistics, collected at national frontiers, are less available and less reliable than birth and death registrations. Much additional information, including statistics of birth expectations, is collected by sample surveys.

These four sources (censuses, vital registration, migration records, and sample surveys) differ in the ease with which they may be instituted in a new country. Censuses and surveys are the easiest to initiate. With care the completeness of a census can reach 97 per cent or more. It is true that a large number of enumerators have to be mobilized (over 100,000 in the United States in 1980, over 5 million for China's 1982 census), but that is easier to arrange than the education of the entire population to the need for birth registration. The United States first attained 90 per cent complete birth records in the first quarter of the twentieth century; contemporary poor countries are unlikely to reach this level of completeness until their residents come to have need for birth certificates. Migration statistics will not be complete as long as many of those crossing international borders can conceal their movement from the immigration authorities. Apart from illegal crossings there is the difficulty that migrants are a small fraction of those passing national boundaries, the majority being tourists, persons travelling on business, commuters, and other non-immigrants. American sentiment that people ought to be able to leave their country of residence without hindrance is so strong that outgoing residents are not even stopped at the border to be asked whether they intend to return.

What especially characterizes demography are the quantitative and empirical methods that it uses. Once data in the form of censuses and registrations are available, demographic techniques are needed for valid comparisons among these. In today's terms, Mexico has a death rate of 6 per thousand, against France's 10; this does not signify that Mexico is healthier, but only that it has a younger age distribution as a result of recent high fertility; standardized comparison consists in finding what Mexico's death rate would be if it had France's age distribution but retained its own age-specific rates.

Partly for purposes of comparing mortality, but originally more for the conduct of pension and insurance business, life tables were developed in the Netherlands and in Great Britain during the course of the eighteenth century. The first technical problem that actuaries and demographers solved was how to go from statistics of deaths and of populations exposed to probabilities of dying. With data in finite age intervals the probabilities are not uniquely ascertainable, and a variety of methods for making life tables are currently in use.

The concerns of public health have led to the improvement of mortality statistics along many lines, including drawing up the International List of Causes of Death, now in its ninth revision. Unfortunately uniformity in applying the classification among physicians in all countries is still a distant goal. One object of the International List is the making of cause-related tables. The expectation of life in the United States at the time of writing is 75 years. If all deaths from cancer were eliminated this would be increased by about 3 years; elimination of all heart disease would increase the expectation by over 15 years.

Increasing populations have lower proportions of deaths than stationary populations. In effect the age distribution pivots on the middle ages as population growth slows. A sharp drop in the birth rate does not show its full effect immediately; births remain high as the large cohorts of children already born themselves come into childbearing; population growth thus has a kind of momentum. Replacement is the condition where each child is replaced in the next generation by just one child, so that ultimately the population is stationary. After birth rates fall to bare replacement a population can still increase by 60 per cent or more.

Births are not as sensitive to the pivoting of age distribution as are deaths, since the fertile ages, intermediate between childhood and old age, are a relatively constant fraction of a population. Fast-growing countries have more children below reproductive age but fewer old people. But births are greatly affected by a bulge of individuals in the reproductive ages; births in the United States have risen from about 3.1 million in the early 1970s to about 3.6 million currently, almost entirely due to change in age distribution as the large cohorts of the 1950s reach reproduction.

The pioneer in demographic methods and models was Alfred J. Lotka, who in a series of papers extending from 1907 to 1948 showed how to answer a number of questions that are still being asked. A central one was, 'How fast is a given population really growing, as determined by its age-specific birth and death rates in abstraction from its age distribution?' Any population that grows at a fixed rate for a long period develops a stable or fixed age distribution which Lotka showed how to calculate, and its increase when it reaches this stage is its intrinsic rate.

After a long period of neglect, Lotka's work came to be applied and further developed during the 1960s. It turned out that his approach could help the estimation of birth and death rates for countries of known age distribution but lacking adequate registration data.

The techniques of birth and death analysis have been carried over to migration, especially in the form of Markov chains that describe movement or transition between countries, and other areas, just as they describe transition between life and death. Such Markov chains are capable also of representing transitions between the married and single condition, among working, being unemployed, and leaving the labour force, and many other sets of states. A literature has now been built up in which changes of state, including migration, are represented by matrices, particularly easy to handle on a computer. The first extensive calculation of this kind was due to P. H. Leslie in the 1940s.

Communities living under 'primitive' conditions grow slowly; their high birth rates are offset by high deaths. The movement of a community from this condition to one of low birth and death rates as it modernizes is known as the demographic transition. Since the fall in the birth rate lags behind the fall in the death rate, very large increases can be recorded during the transition. Britain's population multiplied fourfold between the censuses of 1801 and 1901. Contemporary less-developed countries are increasing even more rapidly.

This effect of rising income is contrary to what has often been thought: that people want children and will have as many as they can afford – a view commonly attributed to Malthus, although Malthus's writings, after the first edition of his *Essay*, are much more subtle than this. Apparently at a certain point the causal mechanism flips over: for very poor people a rise of income results in a faster rate of increase; once people are better off a further rise slows their increase.

The modernization that brings down the birth rate affects subgroups of national populations at different times. In consequence the demographic transition shows itself as differential fertility: the rich, the urban, the educated have for a time lower birth rates than the poor, the rural, and the illiterate in cross sections taken during the transition. Such differentials close up as incomes generally rise and income distributions narrow.

Some of the most puzzling questions concern the causal mechanisms that lie behind contemporary demographic changes. In what degree the fall of fertility is due to education, in what degree to income, cannot yet be answered in a way that applies to all countries. Less developed countries today have far greater rates of increase than did the countries of Europe when these were at a comparable stage of development. To what extent is the difference due to higher birth rates among presently poor countries than among the poor countries of the eighteenth century, and to what extent to lower death rates? Population models can provide answers to such questions; they show that birth differences are much more influential than death differences.

More difficult are questions on the direction of causation between two variables clearly related to each other. In most advanced countries more women are working outside the home now than 30 years ago, at a time when their husbands are for the most part earning higher real wages; at the same time their fertility has diminished, when the income of their spouses would permit them to have more children if they wanted. Is the fall in fertility the result of women seeking jobs, and so finding it inconvenient to have children, the wish to work being primary, or, on the other hand, do they no longer wish to have children and so take jobs to fill their time? A wealth of data exists, but the techniques for answering such questions are elusive. Again, are the present low birth rates a cohort or a period phenomenon? Do they result from present generations intending to finish up with fewer births, or are they a conjunctural phenomenon due, say, to the world recession of the past decade?

A task that demographers are often called on to perform is population forecasting. Professional demographers describe their statements on future population as projections, the working out of the consequences of a set of assumptions. Users believe that the assumptions are chosen by the demographers because they are realistic, and they accept the results as forecasts. Forecasting has gone through many styles, starting with extrapolation of population numbers by exponential, logistic, or other curves. More acceptable is extrapolating the components of population – birth, death, and migration – and assembling the population from the extrapolated values of these. Sampling to ascertain childbearing intentions of women has been extensively tried. Demographers have no illusions about the predictability of the long-term future, but on the other hand estimates made by those who have studied the past are more worthy of attention than the simple-minded extrapolations that are the alternative. Some numbers on future population are indispensable for virtually any kind of economic planning, whether by a corporation or a government.

The richness of demography today is in part due to the commitment of scholars from many disciplines. Actuaries developed much of the early theory, and statisticians and biostatisticians today add to their work the techniques of numerical analysis and determination of error. Sociologists see population change as both the cause and the result of major changes in social structures and attitudes; they study the increase of labour-force participation by women, of divorce, of single-person households, the apparently lessening importance of marriage, and the decline in fertility rates. Economists see fertility rising and falling as people try to maximize utility. Biologists employ an ecological framework relating human populations to the plant and animal populations among which they live and on which they depend. Psychologists have brought their survey and other tools to the study of preferences of parents for number and sex of children. Historians, in a particularly happy synthesis with demography, are putting to use the enormous amount of valuable data in parish and other records to gain new insights on what happened to birth and death rates during the past several centuries.

Nathan Keyfitz
Harvard University
and the International Institute
for Applied Systems Analysis

Further Reading
Coale, A. J. (1972), *The Growth and Structure of Human Populations*: *A Mathematical Investigation*, Princeton, N.J.
Keyfitz, N. (1977), *Applied Mathematical Demography*, New York.
Petersen, W. (1969), *Population*, 2nd edn, Toronto.
Pressat, R. (1969), *L'Analyse demographique*, 2nd edn, Paris.
Shryock, H. S. and Siegel, J. S. (1971), *The Methods and Materials of Demography*, 2 vols, Washington, D.C.

Dependency Theory

The dependency paradigm, which gained currency within the social sciences during the 1960s and continued to be very influential in the 1970s, can be characterized as an eclectic, historical structuralist perspective on spatially-bounded socioeconomic and political inequality. The concept of *dependence*, lying at the heart of the paradigm and implying a constant concern for elements of social interaction precluding autonomous development within certain subunits of a wider system, is sufficiently broad to allow application to a number of general problem areas, within varying disciplines, and to be utilized within somewhat dissimilar ideological parameters. One can therefore speak of dependency in several forms: (1) The dialogue on neo-colonial dependence developed by European and African social scientists from the 1950s onward, as they dealt with the continued lack of autonomy of recently freed colonial peoples through reference to the social and psychological legacy of colonial rule. (2) The analysis of unequal terms of international trade through which Latin American economists explained the continued underdevelopment of their region in the early post-war period, later supplemented by a more comprehensive treatment of the phenomenon of unequal exchange within a world capitalist system. (3) The elucidation of complexities in relations among classes and within state formations shaped by the specific requirements of interaction during an era of international monopoly capitalism, which, in contrast to interpretations by economists, placed primary emphasis not on understanding the nature of external domination, but rather on clarifying distinctive *internal* patterns of response. (4) The presentation of a comprehensive historical explanation for the development of capitalism in Europe, positing the systematic transfer toward hegemonic centres from societies whose form of insertion in the wider system assured the 'development of underdevelopment' outside core areas of capitalist accumulation, and the extension of this argument into the field of intranational socioeconomic relations, where underdeveloped regions were considered 'internal colonies' of more developed ones.

All of these approaches had in common a rejection of earlier liberal or functionalist 'dualism', which had posited the coexistence of two theoretically unrelated types of societies (whether 'traditional' and 'modern' or 'developed' and 'underdeveloped'), and a consequent insistence upon the dynamic interaction of all subunits within a world system. All also exhibited certain points of disagreement with earlier Marxist treatment of imperialism, which was considered too rigid a projection of the European experience. Specifically, dependency theories appended an additional concern to the Marxist emphasis on exploitation as a transfer of surplus value from one class to another, during the process of production. This was a concern with territorially-based transfers of surplus product from one geographical unit to another during the process of circulation. The way was thus left open for consideration of exploitative or asymmetrical relations within modern socialist or communist society (Nerfin, 1977), although analytical priority was consistently granted to explaining the unequal development of capitalism.

Theoretical heterogeneity within the paradigm was reflected in varying prescriptions for policy and conflicting predictions of the future course of world development. One current of thought upheld the possibility that an alliance between working class and bourgeoisie within peripheral societies could encourage autonomous development. A second discarded the viability of such an alliance, given the strategic international ties of any supposedly 'national' bourgeoisie, yet saw the likelihood of 'dependent development' in association with international capital. And a third predicted the development of the periphery only upon the qualitative transformation of socioeconomic relations brought about by proletarian revolution on a world-wide scale.

Cynthia Hewitt de Alcántara
El Colegio de México

Reference
Nerfin, M. (ed.) (1977), *Another Development*: *Approaches and Strategies*, Uppsala.

Further Reading
Chilcote, R. (ed.) (1981), *Dependency and Marxism*: *Toward a Resolution of the Debate*, Boulder, Co.
Roxborough, I. (1979), *Theories of Underdevelopment*, London.
See also: *centre and periphery*; *world-system theory*.

Depreciation

Depreciation has two specific meanings in economics. The first of these relates to the depreciation of a currency and the second to a decline in the value of an asset.

Currency depreciation involves a decline in the value of a currency, as measured by a fall in its rate of exchange with one or more other currencies. It is usually applied to falls in exchange rates that occur in a floating exchange-rate system. The corresponding term used for falls in exchange rates that take place in a fixed exchange-rate system is devaluation. A currency will depreciate if there is a fall in the demand for that currency relative to its supply.

The assets to which the term depreciation is normally applied are fixed capital assets, or investment goods, such as plant and machinery. In this case depreciation is the decline in the value of the capital stock due to wear and tear during the life of the investment project. It is not the loss of value due to technological obsolescence, since this should be allowed for in determining the life of the project and in the estimation of the scrap value of the capital asset. Depreciation allowances are deductions from the income of a business. They are made prior to the calculation of profit because they represent an allowance for the consumption of capital, which may be regarded as a cost of production. Depreciation allowances are not subject to taxation, provided they are calculated in accordance with statutory guidelines, and need not necessarily be accumulated to replace worn-out plant and machinery.

Andy Mullineux
University of Birmingham

Further Reading
Group of Thirty (1982), *The Problem of Exchange Rates*, New York.
Grubel, H. (1984), *The International Monetary System*, 4th edn, Harmondsworth.
See also: *devaluation*.

Depressive Disorders

Depressive disorders are a heterogeneous group of conditions that share the common symptom of dysphoric mood. Current psychiatric classification divides major depressive disorders into bipolar and non-bipolar categories, depending on whether there is evidence of associated manic episodes. Less severe depressive states are categorized as dysthymic, cyclothymic, and atypical depressive disorders.

The diagnosis of a depressive disorder is made only when the intensity and duration of depressive symptoms exceed those usually provoked by the stresses of normal life. Major depressive episodes are characterized by a pervasive dysphoric mood, which may be associated with feelings of worthlessness, suicidal ideation, difficulty with concentration, inability to feel pleasure, and neurovegetative changes in appetite, sleep patterns, psychomotor activity and energy levels. In severe cases, psychotic symptoms such as hallucinations and delusions with evident depressive themes may also be present. Dysthymic disorders are conceptualized as chronic, non-psychotic conditions, of at least two years' duration, with similar symptomatology but of lesser intensity. Cyclothymic disorders involve alternating periods of dysthymic and mildly manic moods. Depressive conditions that do not clearly fit into any of these categories are designated as atypical.

Current classificatory tendencies are to group depressive disorders on the basis of their phenomonology, thus eschewing conclusions as to aetiology. Nonetheless, many experts continue to find value in differentiating between endogenous (or autonomous) and reactive, or psychotic and neurotic, conditions. However defined, the prevalence of depressive disorders is relatively high; most estimates are in the range of 7 per cent of the population suffering from a diagnosable depression each year. Lifetime incidence is thought to be 15–30 per cent, with women affected twice as often as men.

Conclusions as to aetiology remain controversial. A minority of cases have clearcut origins in medical conditions, such as viral infections, central nervous system diseases (for example, multiple sclerosis, tumours), endocrine disorders, post-partum states and nutritional deficiencies, or in the side-effects of medications, such as steroids and antihypertensives. For cases without an obvious organic basis, most experts would endorse a diathesis-stress model of causation. Some factor is believed to predispose the depressed person to experiencing the disorder, but this latent diathesis only leads to overt symptomatology when a precipitating stress occurs.

A large number of factors have been posited as inducing both the diathesis and the acute episode. Given that symptomatic depression is probably the final common pathway for a number of distinct disorders, many of these theories may be correct for separate sub-populations. The role of genetic endowment as a predisposing factor has been identified in studies that have shown a clustering of cases within families. There is evidence to suggest that pure unipolar and bipolar illnesses run in separate clusters, and that a form of dysthymic disorder may segregate in families with high incidences of alcoholism and anti-social personality disorder. Recent work has claimed to show linkage between depression and cellular antigens located on a particular chromosome.

Other theories of causation focus on the following potentially interactive factors: failures in normal personality development, losses in early life (especially death of a parent before age 17), and learned dysfunctional patterns of cognition and interpersonal behaviour.

Precipitating factors for acute episodes are often easily identifiable events, such as the loss of a parent or divorce from a spouse. In other cases, external stresses seem to be absent. Psychodynamic theorists maintain that even in these patients a seemingly minor event has been idiosyncratically interpreted as a major loss, or that something has led patients to recognize the dysfunctional nature of their existence. Freud postulated that the loss of an ambivalently regarded person is particularly likely to induce a depression because of associated difficulties in resolving grief. More biologically oriented investigators believe that some physiologic dysfunction precipitates most episodes.

Whether the cause or the result of a depressive disorder, a number of physiologic abnormalities have been associated with subgroups of depressed patients. Neurotransmitter metabolism is altered in many cases of depression. The early 'catecholamine hypothesis' pointed to evidence that a deficiency of the neurotransmitter norepinephrine was responsible for depression, but the picture is clearly more complex than that. Various groups of depressed patients may have high, low or normal amounts of norepinephrine metabolites in blood or urine. The transmitters serotonin and acetylcholine have also been implicated in some studies. Although many of these findings have been replicated, a consistent theory to account for them has yet to emerge.

Other physiologic changes identified in depression include alterations in the architecture of brain-wave patterns during sleep (especially the REM phase), and in normal secretion patterns of pituitary hormones. A promising way of linking many of these abnormalities points to disturbances of the circadian rhythm generator in the brain-stem as a crucial defect in depression. Norepinephrine is implicated in control of the generator, which in turn can affect sleep patterns and hormone secretion rates. The peculiar observation that cases of severe depression can be successfully treated by sleep deprivation confirms the importance of this system as a locus for further study.

The natural history of depression is variable, again suggesting that we are considering a number of disorders under this general rubric. Onset of major depressive disorders can occur at any time in the life cycle, although bipolar disorders usually appear in the second or third decades of life. Untreated, these acute episodes may last for several months or even years, or may moderate somewhat and develop into dysthymic disorders. Acute episodes may be single or recurrent, and there is evidence that recurrent episodes become lengthier, with shorter intervening periods, as the person ages. Dysthymic disorders, especially those that appear to be related to characterologic difficulties, often begin before the age of 30. Epidemiologic studies suggest that the majority of depressive episodes are untreated, either resolving on their own, or developing into chronic disorders. An additional danger for inadequately treated patients is the risk of suicide.

Treatment of depression is as diverse as theories of aetiology. Traditional or modified forms of psychoanalysis and psychoanalytically oriented psychotherapy are often employed, although without more than anecdotal evidence of success. Enthusiasm for short-term psychotherapies in depression has been stirred by recent studies demonstrating success with time-limited interpersonal and cognitive therapies. The latter attempts to change the guilt-ridden and hopeless patterns of thought seen so frequently in depressed patients, conceptualizing the basic disorder as one of cognition rather than of mood.

The real revolution in the treatment of depression in the last generation has occurred as a result of the development of anti-depressant medications. The tricyclic antidepressants and the monoamine oxidase inhibitors have been shown to be effective in as many as 80 per cent of major depressions, and often to be effective in dysthymic conditions. New classes of non-tricyclic drugs are now being introduced, with a major effort being made to correlate responses to particular medications with symptomatology and biochemical changes. The development of techniques for measuring blood levels of antidepressants and their metabolites has already made more precise treatment possible. Maintenance medication with antidepressants, or in the case of bipolar (and some unipolar) disorders with lithium, demonstrably decreases the frequency and intensity of recurrent episodes.

Electroconvulsive therapy (ECT) remains an important treatment, although these days it is largely reserved for life-threatening conditions, depressions refractory to drug therapy, and delusionally depressed states. Effectiveness of ECT may be as high as 90 per cent in major depressions.

In the next decade, one can look for continued changes in nomenclature of depression, as more precise ideas of aetiology are developed, and for a more careful tailoring of types of treatment to subtypes of depressive disorders.

Paul S. Appelbaum
University of Massachusetts
Medical School, Worcester, Massachusetts

Further Reading

Arieti, S. and Bemporad, J. (1978), *Severe and Mild Depression*, New York.
Klein, D. F., Gittelman, R., Quitkin, F. and Rifkin, A. (1980), *Diagnosis and Drug Treatment of Psychiatric Disorders: Adults and Children*, 2nd edn, Baltimore.

Klerman, G. L. (1980), 'Overview of affective disorders', in H. I. Kaplan *et al.* (eds), *Comprehensive Textbook of Psychiatry III*, Baltimore.

Kovacs, M. and Beck, A. T. (1978), 'Maladaptive cognitive structures in depression', *American Journal of Psychiatry*, 135.

Vogel, G. W., Vogel, F., McAbee, R. S. and Thurmond, A. J. (1980), 'Improvement of depression by REM sleep deprivation: new findings and a theory', *Archives of General Psychiatry*, 37.

Weissman, M. M., Myers, J. K. and Thompson, W. D. (1981), 'Depression and its treatment in a US urban community – 1975–1976', *Archives of General Psychiatry*, 38.

how the different cues are put together to help determine the perception of a unified visual world.

Walter C. Gogel
University of California, Santa Barbara

References

Hochberg, J. (1972), 'Perception II. Space and movement', in J. W. Kling and L. A. Riggs (eds), *Woodworth and Schlosberg's Experimental Psychology*, 3rd edn, New York.

Ogle, K. N. (1962), 'Spatial localization through binocular vision', in H. Davson (ed.), *The Eye*, vol. 4, *Visual Optics and the Optical Space Sense*, New York.

See also: *colour vision*; *sensation and perception*; *vision*.

Depth Perception

A classical problem in visual perception is understanding how an observer can perceive the world as extended in three dimensions from information registered on the two-dimensional retinas of the eyes. Unlike horizontal and vertical extensions in the world which are represented by proportional retinal extents, information or cues regarding the dimension of distance are coded indirectly in the visual system. There are two kinds of distance cues. One kind, called egocentric cues, provides information as to the distance of objects from the observer. The other, termed exocentric cues, indicates the depth between objects. Two instances of egocentric cues to distance involve motor adjustments of the eyes. In one of these (the cue of vergence), the two eyes turn in opposite directions in order to position the image of the object being viewed on the most sensitive portion of each retina (the fovea). In the other (the accommodative cue), the curvature of the lens of the eye is adjusted in order to focus clearly the image on the retina. These oculomotor cues are ineffective for objects beyond about three metres from the observer. A possible egocentric cue that by definition is learned and can apply to both near and distant objects is the known size of familiar objects. In general, exocentric cues are more precise than egocentric cues and help to extend the perception of distance to far distances from the observer. Among the exocentric cues that have been identified is the cue of binocular disparity, which is a consequence of the two eyes being laterally separated in the head and thus receiving slightly different views of scenes extended in depth (Ogle, 1962). Another exocentric cue occurs between different successive views of the world as the head is moved laterally, and is called relative motion parallax (Hochberg, 1972). Although the contribution and limitations of these and other sources of distance information have been examined in many studies, less is known about

Descent and Descent Groups

To most nineteenth-century anthropologists, kinship, descent and consanguinity were synonymous. Kinship, or descent, was reducible to the physiological fact of consanguinity which in turn reflected marriage practices. In this perspective, matrilineal descent could have evolved only in societies ignorant of paternity, and where sexual encounters were probably promiscuous, for in such conditions only links between mother and child could be ascertained. (Patrilineal descent, however, was not thought to imply ignorance of maternity.) Consequently, the evolutionists believed that matrilineal descent must have appeared first. Some even thought that women originally wielded political power; the most 'primitive' societies would thus have been both matrilineal and matriarchal. With the development of personal property, however, men took over political control from the women in order to transmit their property to their own children, thereby instituting patrilineal descent.

But anthropologists failed to find any 'matriarchal' societies, and evolutionism in general fell into disrepute. The evolutionists, for instance, had argued that the family, being bilateral, had evolved only recently; 'primitive' societies only knew of groups formed on the basis of unilineal descent (such groups were usually described as clans). However, it was soon demonstrated that both families and clans were to be found in the most 'primitive' societies. Malinowski also argued that some societies acknowledged the existence of 'fathers' without recognizing any consanguineal connection between the 'father' and the children of his wife.

Rivers (1924) refined the terms of the debate on descent. Clans differed from families in two major ways: (1) through their mode of recruitment – bilateral for the family, unilateral for clans; and (2) through their functions – domestic for the family, political and ritual for clans. The term 'descent' should be used only to denote the criterion for membership of clans or other unilateral groups.

Inspired by Maine, Radcliffe-Brown (1935) defined descent groups as corporations, which own estates. The estate owned by a descent group is composed partly of the statuses (that is, the sum of rights and duties) of its members. Descent could thus also be viewed as a means whereby rights and duties are distributed *within* groups, or as the mechanism regulating interaction within descent groups.

Fortes and Evans-Pritchard (1940) later stressed that a special mechanism is needed to ensure the peaceful coexistence of corporate groups within a given political community, in order to regulate their relationships. The 'lineage system', itself based on descent, appeared as one of these mechanisms. In their model, a series of descent groups are ordered hierarchically, contraposed at every level to equivalent groups. Descent thus became a mechanism for the regulation of intergroup (political) relations. A variety of African societies were described in these terms, most notably the Nuer (Evans-Pritchard, 1940).

More recent writers have described descent as a metaphor of group continuity, or as symbolic patrifiliation. As definitions proliferate, the analytical usefulness of the concept diminishes. Verdon (1980) has suggested that we should restrict the meaning of descent to one specific phenomenon (group aggregation). Kuper (1982) seems to deny that the concepts evolved in the framework of 'lineage theory' have any analytical validity at all and urges that we do away with lineage or descent theory altogether.

Michel Verdon
University of Montreal

References
Evans-Pritchard, E. E. (1940), *The Nuer*, Oxford.
Fortes, M. and Evans-Pritchard, E. E. (1940), 'Introduction', in M. Fortes and E. E. Evans-Pritchard (eds), *African Political Systems*, London.
Kuper, A. (1982), 'Lineage theory: a critical retrospect', in *Annual Review of Anthropology for 1982*, Palo Alto, Calif.
Radcliffe-Brown, A. R. (1935), 'Patrilineal and matrilineal succession', *Iowa Law Review*, 20.
Rivers (1924), *Social Organization*, London.
See also: *kinship*.

Devaluation

The reduction in the official rate of exchange of one currency for another is called devaluation. The term is used in connection with exchange-rate reduction, in a fixed exchange-rate system, and corresponds to the depreciation of a currency in a floating exchange-rate system.

A fixed exchange-rate system operated between 1944, following the 'Bretton Woods Agreement', until 1973, when a floating exchange-rate system took its place, following the collapse of the 1971 'Smithsonian Agreement'. Under the Bretton Woods Agreement, member countries agreed to stabilize their exchange rates within a 1 per cent band around the agreed per exchange rate against the dollar. This band was widened to 2.25 per cent, following the Smithsonian Agreement. Countries in 'fundamental balance of payments disequilibrium' could apply to the International Monetary Fund for permission to devalue or revalue their currencies. Revaluation involved the raising of the official exchange rate against the dollar.

Britain devalued its currency twice in the period of the Bretton Woods Agreement: in September 1949 the rate of exchange against the US dollar was reduced from $4.03 to $2.80; and in November 1967 it was reduced to $2.40. In 1982, the French franc and the Italian lira were devalued within the European Monetary System, which incorporates a fixed exchange-rate system called the Exchange Rate Mechanism.

Devaluation (or depreciation) has the effect of reducing the price of exports, in terms of foreign currencies, and raising the price of imports in the home market. If this results in a rise in exports and a fall in imports, in value terms, then it will help to overcome a country's trade deficit with the rest of the world. There has been considerable debate concerning the likelihood that the domestic and foreign markets will respond in the desired manner and about the inflationary effects of devaluation, following the rise in import prices.

Andy Mullineux
University of Birmingham

Further Reading
Group of Thirty (1982), *The Problem of Exchange Rates*, New York.
Grubel, H. (1984), *The International Monetary System*, 4th edn, Harmondsworth.
See also: *depreciation*.

Development

See Development Studies, Economic Development.

Development Administration

The concept of development administration has changed drastically over the past three decades. During the 1950s, development administration was concerned primarily with transferring the techniques of public management applied in Western industrial countries to developing countries. The aim was to create rational, politically impartial, efficient bureaucracies in the Weberian tradition. In the 1960s, the emphasis shifted from improving administrative procedures to political modernization and administrative reform. Political modernization theorists viewed development administration as a process of social engineering in which national governments assumed the primary role in stimulating economic growth, promoting social change and transforming traditional societies. Both approaches came under increasing criticism during the 1970s for being ethnocentric and for attempting to impose Western concepts and values that were often irrelevant, inappropriate or adverse in poor countries. Moreover, the 'tools' of administration transferred to developing countries usually were those that sought to increase efficiency in carrying out repetitive and routine maintenance tasks and did little to help policy makers or administrators cope with the complex and uncertain problems of change in their own political and cultural environments.

Institution-building and project planning and management became the focus during the early 1970s. Concern with project management was a consequence of the growing role of international lending and aid organizations in providing funding and technical assistance to developing countries, and of their insistence that governments adopt systems methods of analysing and managing development projects. The institution-building approach evolved from widespread dissatisfaction with Weberian models of administration. Developing countries needed institutions that would help administrators deal creatively with complex and uncertain problems and promote innovation and change. Esman (1972) defined institution-building as 'The planning, structuring and guidance of new or reconstituted organizations which (a) embody changes in values, functions, physical and social technologies; (b) establish, foster and protect new normative relationships and action patterns, and (c) obtain support and complementarity in the environment.' Management training and organizational design were used to pursue these goals. Institution-building was concerned not only with strengthening the administrative capacity of individual organizations, but also with forging co-operative relationships among them.

The focus of development administration shifted again in the mid-1970s to expanding the capacity of organizations not only to manage development projects and programmes efficiently, but also to bring about more equitable distribution of the benefits of development activities. Greater attention was given to ways in which governments might alleviate the high levels of poverty in rural areas, elicit participation of the poor in development planning and management, and deliver essential public services to those groups who had previously been by-passed or neglected. Emphasis was

on improving the capacity of public agencies to respond more effectively to the needs of the poor, to provide for basic human needs, to stimulate productivity and raise the incomes of disadvantaged groups, to create conditions in which community, private and voluntary organizations could take a stronger role in 'bottom-up' processes of development planning, and to cope more effectively with the complexity and uncertainty of development activities (Rondinelli, 1983). Decentralized processes of planning and implementation were of greater concern than centralized control and management (Cheema and Rondinelli, 1983).

The emerging challenges of development administration have been of finding ways of improving the capacity of both public and private institutions in developing countries to anticipate, plan for, and cope with social and economic change, and to structure their administrative procedures more efficiently and effectively in order to bring about more equitable economic growth.

Dennis A. Rondinelli
Syracuse University

References

Cheema, G. S. and Rondinelli, D. A. (eds) (1983), *Decentralization and Development: Policy Implementation in Developing Countries*, Beverly Hills, Calif.

Esman, M. (1972), 'The elements of institution building', in J. Eaton (ed.), *Institution Building and Development*, Beverly Hills, Calif.

Rondinelli, D. A. (1983), *Development Projects as Policy Experiments: An Adaptive Approach to Development Administration*, London.

See also: *administration*; *aid*; *development studies*.

Developmental Psychology

Developmental psychology studies growth and change in psychological processes from before birth, through childhood, adolescence and adulthood, to old age. In its nineteenth-century origins it was strongly influenced by evolutionary theory, which saw childhood as a phase in which the transition from 'animal' to 'human' nature could be studied *in vivo*, rather than through fossils. The growth of the discipline was also stimulated by the notion – itself a bone of contention among developmentalists – that the conditions of early development strongly influence adult potential, and therefore contain the key to many social problems. As an applied science, it mainly addresses itself to practical interventions and social policy concerning the care and education of children, and has considerable overlap with experimental and clinical psychology, psychiatry, and the study of personality.

To a large extent the theoretical ideas of developmental psychology have been borrowed or adapted from other branches of psychology, and much research on development has accordingly been merely an application of whatever approaches were currently dominant in the rest of psychology. Psychoanalytic principles, for example, informed the pre-war work of Anna Freud, Melanie Klein and others on the stages of emotional development and the role of fantasy and play, and the influential post-war work of John Bowlby on attachment and the need for security. In turn, psychoanalysis came to be overshadowed by the behaviourist 'social learning' approach, which sought to explain development in terms of external contingencies, invoking general laws of learning rather than stage-related 'inner processes'.

Another major theme of developmental psychology – the development of intelligence – has been largely divorced from the study of emotional growth, and reflects social concern with sorting and grading individuals and maximizing their cognitive potential. Intellectual development has been studied from both quantitative and qualitative angles. The main instrument of quantitative study has been the IQ test, and a veritable industry has grown up around the refinement of such tests and the question of whether performance on them reflects innate endowment or environmental influences. Indeed, the construction of norms of all kinds has been a major activity of developmental psychology, through which it helps to propagate social values and regulate individual conduct.

It is in the qualitative study of cognitive development that most of developmental psychology's original contributions to the rest of psychology are to be found. Within mainstream American and British psychology, the behaviourist emphasis on studying observable stimuli and responses discouraged interest in mental processes for several decades, but a major breach in this position was made in 1959 by Chomsky, who demonstrated that the child's ability to learn language could not possibly be explained on stimulus-response principles. With mental activities once again accepted as a proper object of study, Piaget's 'cognitive-developmental' approach to the child's active structuring of the world – developed several decades earlier – was widely adopted, along with his more sensitive and detailed methods of observation. The particular theories of both Chomsky and Piaget have been heavily criticized, but their emphasis on the distinctively human activities of language and thought – to which behaviourism could not do justice – helped to displace mechanistic and biologistic thinking from psychology.

Since the 1960s, the study of linguistic and cognitive development has become one of the most fertile areas of psychology. The renewed influence (after half a century) of the Russian psychologist Vygotsky, who saw cognitive structures as rooted in social interaction, reflects growing discontent with the study of development in a social vacuum, and gradual recognition of its cultural and historical variability.

David Ingleby
University of Utrecht, The Netherlands

Further Reading
Bee, H. (1981), *The Developing Child* (3rd edn), New York.
Bower, T. G. R. (1979), *Human Development*, San Francisco.
Sants, J. and Butcher, H. J. (eds) (1975), *Developmental Psychology: Selected Readings*, Harmondsworth.

See also: *language development*; *Piaget*; *psychoanalysis*.

Development Banks

Development banks (DBs) perform a key role in providing investment finance for less-developed countries (LDCs). There is wide recognition of the huge shortfall between funds required and funds available for financing economic development. DBs have the formidable task of increasing the supply of credit for productive investment projects, both by mobilizing domestic savings, and by channelling international development aid. Virtually all LDCs now have their own DB or Development Finance Corporation (DFC).

In spite of the powerful arguments for increased aid to developing countries, based on mutual self-interest as well as altruism, the developed countries have increasingly fallen behind their own target aid figure of 0.7 per cent of GDP. The aggregate figure for aid in 1980 was below 0.3 per cent. International DBs, in addition to their subscribed paid-in capital from developed donor countries, borrow in international capital markets to on-lend for project and programme lending, at rates derived from their cost of borrowing. The most important international DBs are the International Bank for Reconstruction and Development (IBRD) (World Bank); International Finance Corporation (IFC); Inter-American Development Bank (IDB); Asian Development Bank (ADB); African Development Bank (AFDB); Caribbean Development Bank (CDB); European Investment Bank (EIB); and the International Investment Bank (IIB).

An important feature of World Bank lending is its project-oriented character. In recent years a greater emphasis has been placed on combating poverty directly, which has resulted in increased assistance to small-scale enterprises, labour-intensive projects, and agriculture, as opposed to major projects such as steel mills. The financing of national DBs has been the World Bank's major mechanism for assisting small- and medium-scale enterprises. The Bank has attempted to enhance DB professional skills to ensure that loans are made for projects with high economic rates of return and substantial job-creation prospects. Financial liberalization has been encouraged to permit DBs to charge differential lending rates, so that more risky (smaller) borrowers are not rationed out of the market by high collateral requirements. The record of most DBs in mobilizing domestic resources has to date been distinctly unimpressive, due essentially to the unwillingness of their governments to ensure the payment of sufficiently positive real interest rates to potential lenders.

Basil J. Moore
Wesleyan University

See also: *aid*.

Development Studies

The concept of development, like its kindred notions of growth and modernization, has its historical and intellectual roots in the period of major social changes associated with the Industrial Revolution, or what Kumar (1978) has called the 'Great Transformation', when industrial and social change in Europe became synonymous with social progress. Throughout the century that followed, and often in the face of strong countercurrents challenging this simple orthodoxy (Kitching, 1982), development in the eyes of most people (experts and laymen alike) came to be identified with some kind of stage-by-stage movement towards more 'modern', technologically and economically 'advanced' forms of society such as the industrial nations.

By the mid-twentieth century the dominant image of social change was modernization, the process by which so-called traditional social structures are transformed into those of a more modern type, along the lines of what happened at an earlier stage in Europe (Smelser, 1963; Smith, 1973). Following the Second World War, the industrial nations, and especially those with colonies or ex-colonies, were increasingly confronted with the economic and political problems of the poorer nations. This led to a greater awareness of the need to devise strategies aimed at alleviating the poverty and raising the living standards of the populations of these more 'backward' countries. Development policies therefore stressed the importance of expanding production and modernizing the physical and social infrastructure. Development aid, of course, often indirectly benefited the Western nations as much as it did the recipients.

This interest in modernization was quickly translated into a new field of study gradually calling itself development studies, an interdisciplinary grouping of subjects focusing upon the analysis and solution of problems of development, particularly those faced by the poorer, so-called developing countries. The types of disciplines brought together in this way included economics, geography, political science, public administration, sociology, and anthropology; and they were sometimes joined by more technical subjects, such as agronomy and irrigation or civil engineering. Despite their differences in scientific interest and specific policy recommendations, they all, in the 1950s and early 1960s, shared a general belief in the efficacy of Western technological, economic and managerial practice for solving development problems. Even the anthropologists, whose professional expertise rested upon the elucidation of non-Western modes of behaviour and rationality, accepted, explicitly or implicitly, the modernization model when they sought to identify sociocultural obstacles or facilitating factors that might block or promote technological and economic change (Foster, 1962; Long, 1977).

By the mid-1960s, the stage was set for the establishment of a number of departments and special institutions which would provide the main scientific arena within which relevant development issues would be debated and investigated from both a theoretical and policy point of view. For example, the Institute of Development Studies at Sussex was founded in 1966, and the Overseas Development Group (later to form part of the School of Development Studies) at the University of East Anglia in the following year. However, almost as soon as development studies, with much promise, gained a foothold in academia, so it entered a period of growing uncertainty in development-policy thinking and in existing theories of development and social change (Myrdal, 1968; Seers, 1969). The credibility of simple growth and modernization models was shaken by the evident high environmental and human costs of such policies and by the widening gap in per capita incomes between the rich and poor nations and between classes within the developing countries.

Hence, by the late 1960s and early 1970s, the field had become a rather untidy collection of competing theoretical paradigms and policy objectives. This situation resulted in part from the devastating critiques of modernization theory mounted by the 'dependency' and 'underdevelopment' writers (Frank, 1967; Dos Santos, 1973) who argued that it was impossible to understand the processes and problems of development without locating them within the wider sociohistorical context of the expansion of mercantile and industrial capitalism to the poorer, more 'peripheral', countries. They sought to demonstrate that the fundamental problems facing the developing countries were a consequence of the emergence of this international system of economic and political domination. Genuine solutions to the problems of 'underdevelopment', then, would only come when the basic social contradictions inherent in structures of dependency were resolved 'in favour of the popular forces' (Salinas, 1977). At the same time, certain 'liberal' planners injected into the discussions of policy and strategy questions of income redistribution, equity and participation. Many development specialists now argued that the transfer of technology and organizational structures, together with economic growth strategies, were inadequate for tackling the fundamental problems of poor economic performance coupled with maldistribution of income and resources (Chenery *et al.*, 1974).

These radical and liberal criticisms of modernization theory and policy destroyed the earlier coherence of development studies. By the 1980s, we find no real consensus about the major analytical issues to be explored, nor how to go about solving practical problems of development. A healthy scepticism prevails about the idea of progressive development, a scepticism which is reinforced by the global ecological and military threat and by the world economic recession. Development can no longer be regarded as a relatively self-generating process set off by the implantation of modern technology and values. There is also, nowadays, a more explicit awareness of the essentially political and ideological nature of development: formulating goals and means for societal change (whether from the point of view of the central planner or citizen) necessarily entails value commitments and choice. Development studies therefore can no longer be monopolized by economic, technological and administrative types of argument but must take serious account of opposing ethical, political and cultural evaluations.

Development, then, is a concept with different implications depending upon the point of view of the user. It is possible, because of its association with ideas of developmentalism and evolutionist thought, that it may be replaced by some other concept (Nisbet, 1970). However, the kind of problematic it deals with – namely the analysis of societies at critical junctures of social transition – will remain an important area for enquiry, reflection and social action. Development studies will continue to play a role in providing an important arena within which this debate can take place.

Development studies remains torn between, on the one hand, relatively detached (though possibly policy-relevant) scientific analysis and, on the other hand, a commitment to engaging in the practical business of solving concrete problems. It also faces the problem of bringing together disciplines whose theoretical interests, methodologies, epistemologies, and scientific milieux are strikingly different. It frequently gives insufficient emphasis to understanding what different development processes mean to individuals in the pursuit of their everyday lives: there is a tendency to concentrate upon macrostructural aspects to the neglect of microprocesses that provide important

insights into the changing human condition in the contemporary world.

Norman Long
Agricultural University, Wageningen

References
Chenery, H. *et al.* (1974), *Redistribution with Growth*, London.
Dos Santos, T. (1973), 'The crisis of development theory and the problem of dependence in Latin America', in H. Bernstein (ed.), *Underdevelopment and Development*, Harmondsworth.
Frank, A. G. (1969), 'Sociology of underdevelopment and underdevelopment of sociology', in *Latin America: Underdevelopment or Revolution*, New York.
Foster, G. M. (1962), *Traditional Cultures and the Impact of Technological Change*, New York.
Kitching, G. (1982), *Development and Underdevelopment in Historical Perspective. Populism, Nationalism and Industrialization*, London.
Kumar, K. (1978), *Prophecy and Progress*, London.
Long, N. (1977), *An Introduction to the Sociology of Rural Development*, London.
Myrdal, G. (1968), *Asian Drama: An Inquiry into the Poverty of Nations*, 3 vols, New York.
Nisbet, R. A. (1970), *Social Change and History: Aspects of the Western Theory of Development*, London.
Salinas, P. W. (1977), 'A paradigmatic view of development strategies', *Cornell Sociology Bulletin Series*, 89.
Seers, D. (1969), 'The meaning of development' in D. Lehmann (ed.), *Development Theory: Four Critical Studies*, London.
Smelser, N. J. (1963), 'Mechanisms of change and adjustments to change', in B. F. Hoselitz and W. E. Moore (eds), *Industrialization and Society*, The Hague.
Smith, A. D. (1973), *The Concept of Social Change: A Functionalist Theory of Social Change*, London.

Deviance

Although the word *deviance* has been employed for over three hundred years, its sociological meanings are rather recent and distinct. In the main, sociologists and criminologists have taken deviance to refer to behaviour that is banned, censured, stigmatized or penalized. It is often portrayed as a breaking of rules. It is considered more extensive than crime, crime being no more than a breach of one particular kind of rule, but it includes crime and its outer margins are unclear and imprecise. What exactly deviance comprises, what it excludes, what makes it interesting, and how it should be characterized, are not settled. There have been studies of very diverse groups in the name of the sociology of deviance. There have been descriptions of the deaf, the blind, the ill, the mad, dwarves, stutterers, strippers, prostitutes, homosexuals, thieves, murderers, nudists and drug addicts. Sociologists are not in accord about whether all these roles are unified and what it is that may be said to unify them. They can appeal to no common convention within their own discipline. Neither can they turn to lay definitions for guidance. On the contrary, commonplace interpretations are often elastic, contingent and local. What is called deviant can shift from time to time and place to place, its significance being unstable.

Common sense and everyday talk do not seem to point to an area that is widely and unambiguously recognized as deviant. It is not even evident that people *do* talk about deviance with any great frequency. Instead, they allude to specific forms of conduct without appearing to claim that there is a single, over-arching category that embraces them all. They may talk of punks, addicts, glue-sniffers, extremists, thieves, traitors, liars and eccentrics, but they rarely mention *deviants*. It may only be the sociologist who finds it interesting and instructive to clump these groups together under a solitary title.

The apparent elusiveness and vagueness of the idea of deviance has elicited different responses from sociologists. Some have refrained from attempting to find one definition that covers every instance of the phenomenon. They have used *ad hoc* or implied definitions that serve the analytic needs of the moment and suppress the importance of definition itself. Others, like Liazos, have questioned the intellectual integrity of the subject, alleging that it may amount to little more than an incoherent jumble of 'nuts, sluts and perverts'. Phillipson has actually described the analysis of deviance as 'that antediluvian activity which sought to show oddities, curiosities, peccadilloes and villains as central to sociological reason'.

A number of sociologists have chosen to represent 'that antediluvian activity' as important precisely because its subject is so odd: the inchoate character of deviance becomes a remarkable property of the phenomenon rather than a weakness in its description. Matza, for example, held that 'plural evaluation, shifting standards, and moral ambiguity may, and do, coexist with a phenomenal realm that is commonly sensed as deviant'. His book, *Becoming Deviant* (1969), proceeded to chart the special contours of that realm by following the passage of an archetypal deviant into its interior. In such a guise, deviance is taken to offer a rare glimpse of the fluid and contradictory face of society, showing things in unexpected relief and proportion. Garfinkel, Goffman and others have taken to repairing to the deviant margins because they offer new perspectives through incongruity or strain, perspectives that jolt the understanding and make the sociologist 'stumble into awareness'. Deviants are required to negotiate problems of meaning and structure that are a little foreign to everyday life. The study

of their activity may force the sociologist to view the world as anthropologically strange. Indeed, some sociologists have implicitly turned the social world inside out, making deviance the centre and the centre peripheral. They have explored the odd and the exotic, giving birth to a sociology of the absurd that dwells on the parts played by indeterminacy, paradox and surprise in social life.

Absurdity is perhaps given its fullest recognition in a number of essays by structuralists and phenomenologists. It is there asserted that deviance is distinguished by its special power to muddle and unsettle social reality. Deviation is described by its ability to upset systems of thought and methods of classification. Deviant matters are things out of place, things that make no sense. As Scott argued, 'The property of deviance is conferred on things that are perceived as being anomalous . . .' The meaninglessness of deviance is thus forced to become substantially more than a simple lack of intellectual coherence in sociology. People are thought to find it disturbing, and phenomenologists have replied by turning their gaze towards the problems which disturbance can raise. The phenomenologists' difference with Marxist and radical sociologists probably turns on their emphasis on flux and disorder. Radical sociologists tend to stress the solidity of the social world and the importance of what Gouldner called 'overpowering social structures'. Phenomenologists and others tend to stress the openness and plasticity of things, arguing that social structure is actually rather delicate and negotiable.

What *is* certain is that the analysis of deviance echoes many of the unities and disunities of sociology at large. Sociological definition is not neutral and independent. It will refract wider debates, problems and pursuits. It is in this sense that sociologists do not necessarily mean the same thing when they talk of deviance. Their ideas sometimes contradict one another, although contradiction is often no more than a trick of language, an effect of the different vocabularies that have become attached to theories.

A list of examples should reveal a little of that diversity.

Probably the most elementary definition of deviance describes it as behaviour that is *statistically infrequent*. A contrast is traced between the normal, which is common, and the abnormal or deviant, which is uncommon. That definition is deployed characteristically in clinical or psychological analysis that relies on counting: normal distribution curves are drawn, and the deviant is that which falls at the poles. Those who wet their beds with unusual frequency, who are very tall or very short, who read obsessively or not at all are deviant for practical numerical purposes. It is a definition that serves well enough in certain settings, but it can sometimes fail to make sense of deviance as it is presented in everyday life. Thus, the statistically infrequent may be socially unremarked and inconsequential. The statistically frequent may be exposed to control, disapproval and stigma. What is *assumed* to be infrequent, acquiring some of its identity from that assumption, may actually be quite common. (Homosexuality, adultery and chastity are all rather more abundant than many people suppose, but they are *taken* to be unusual.) It may indeed be *beliefs* about statistical incidence that are occasionally more significant than the incidence itself. Statistical analysis can then be rephrased to produce a commentary about the interplay between ideas about deviance and convention.

A second major strand of sociological thought is *Marxism*, but many Marxists have relegated deviance to the margins of analysis. Its pettiness has been emphasized both in the explicit arguments of some sociologists and in the practical neglect of deviance by others. Deviation is commonly thought to be a process that is relatively trivial in a world that is dominated by the massive structures of political economy. It has been maintained that little can be gained from studying deviance that cannot be achieved more directly, efficiently and elegantly from the analysis of class and state. Some, like Hirst, Bankowski and Mungham, have actually reproached Marxist and radical sociologists of deviance for discussing inappropriate and minor problems. Marxists, they claim, should concentrate on the class struggle.

When Marxists *do* explore deviance, they tend to stress its bearing on the class struggle and the state. Thus Hill, Thompson and Hobsbawm have developed a social history of crime that emphasizes the scale of popular opposition to the emergence of capitalism in England. Hall, Cohen and Willis have talked of youthful deviance as 'resistance through ritual', a fleeting and probably doomed act of refusal to accede to the authority of institutions that oppress the working class. Sumner has taken the unity of deviance to stem from the censures that reside in the core of capitalist ideology; Taylor has lodged the origins of deviance in the contradictions of the ailing political economy of late capitalism in crisis; Platt and Quinney cast deviants as those who have been defeated in the class war; Box and Pearce present them as the scapegoats who divert the gaze from the major pathologies of capitalism; and so it goes on. Marxists deposit deviation in a world made up of resistance, protest and conflict. Few have occupied themselves with processes outside that world. After all, that is the world of Marxism. Lea and Young *have* ventured outside but their place within Marxism may have become a little unsure in consequence.

A third major representative strand is *functionalism*, and Talcott Parsons is the pivot of functionalism. Parsons typified one version of deviance as the disorganized phenomena that can attend institutions and individuals that have become out of joint. He argued that, as the social world changes, so its parts may move with unequal velocities and in different directions, straining against one another and creating problems of cohesion. Deviance then became activity that sprang from defective integration. It could evolve to become a new conformity; persist as a source of stress within the social system; or disappear altogether as coherence returned to society.

Parsons also focused on a very special form of deviance in his essay on the 'sick role'. He depicted illness as the status of those who should not be rewarded for occupying what could become a dangerously seductive and useless position. The sick are pampered and, without discouragement, people might learn to malinger. Illness had to be controlled by the threat of stigma.

Almost all other functionalists have diverged from Parsons's insistence on the dysfunctions of deviance. Instead, they have elected to illustrate the surprising fashion in which deviation has unintentionally buttressed the social order. Durkheim pointed to the solidarity conferred by collective sentiments outraged by the breaking of rules. Erikson wrote of how dramatized encounters between deviants and agents of social control beat the bounds of the moral community. Deviance was to be described as a dialectical foil to themes that infuse the moral centre of society. Without a vividly reproduced deviance, it was held, the centre would lose its structure and integrity. Good requires the bad, God Satan, and morality immorality. Within the borders of society, too, deviance was to be depicted as a kind of dangerous but necessary zone between major regions and classes of phenomena. The revulsion said to surround the homosexual and the hermaphrodite enforces morally charged divisions between the genders. Deviance then supports convention, and it does so in numerous ways. Bell and Merton talked of the part played by organized crime in repairing economic and political defects in America, suggesting that the criminal offers power, influence and services where none is provided by the respectable order. Davis remarked how prostitution supports monogamy and bastardy primogeniture. Most functionalist essays on deviance are brief and unsystematic. Yet their recurrent theme is that deviance upholds what it seems to disrupt. Their paradox is the interesting symbiosis of rule-making, rule-enforcement and rule-breaking.

There are other postures: feminists writing about the rooting of deviation in patriarchy; control theorists taking deviance to be the wildness that erupts when social disciplines become weak; and ecologists charting the interlacing of deviance and conformity in the lives of people who live in the same territory. Each gives rule-breaking a place in a distinct theoretical environment. Each imparts a distinctiveness that is sometimes quite marked and sometimes a little superficial. Without much effort, it is quite possible to transcribe some of those definitions so that they begin to resemble one another more closely. Thus functionalism resonates the assertions made by Marxists about the interdependence of crime and capitalism, by feminists about the links between patriarchy and rule-breaking, and by phenomenologists about the work done in the social regulation of anomaly.

The sociology of deviance has probably been allied most prominently to the symbolic interactionism, labelling theory and phenomenology that came to the fore in the 1960s. So intimate is that connexion that the sociology of deviance is often taken to be a wholly interactionist undertaking, bearing with it a crowd of unstated assumptions about methods, history and focus. *Deviance* is then held to refer not only to rule-breaking but also to a special method of interpreting rule-breaking. Those who chose to explore deviance in the late 1950s, 1960s and 1970s sought to advertise their distance from criminologists described as 'positivist' and 'correctionalist'. They took their task to be the symbolic reconstruction of deviance, learning how rule-breaking had become possible, what meanings it attained, and how it progressed from stage to stage. The cast of performers was enlarged to include all those who significantly affected critical passages in the evolution of deviant histories. The influence of people and events was held to change with each new phase, being interpreted and reinterpreted by participants. Developments were thought to be intelligible only within the emergent logic of an unfolding career. The importance of interpretation, the processual character of·social life and the centrality of deviant identity led interactionists to redefine deviation as a moving transaction between those who made rules, those who broke rules and those who implemented rules. Deviance was held to be *negotiated* over time, its properties reflecting the practical power and assumptions of those who propelled it from phase to phase. At the very core of the negotiating process are deviants themselves, and their conduct responds to the attitudes which are taken towards them at various junctures. Becoming deviant entails a recasting of the self and a redrafting of motives. It entails a supplying of accounts, meanings, purposes and character. In that process, deviant and conventional identities are manufactured, and the interactionist sociologists of deviance furnished portrait after portrait of hustlers, police officers, prostitutes, delinquents and drug users. Their work continues although it has become a little overshadowed by more recent models of conduct.

Paul Rock
London School of Economics and Political Science

References

Bankowski, Z., Mungham, G. and Young, P. (1977), 'Radical criminology or radical criminologist?', *Contemporary Crises*, 1.

Becker, H. (1963), *Outsiders*, New York.

Bell, D. (1960), *The End of Ideology*, New York.

Cohen, P. (1972), 'Working class youth cultures in East London', in *Working Papers in Cultural Studies*, Birmingham.

Davis, K. (1961), 'Prostitution' in R. Merton and R. Nisbet (eds), *Contemporary Social Problems*, New York.

Downes, D. and Rock, P. (1982), *Understanding Deviance*, Oxford.

Durkheim, E. (1933), *The Division of Labour in Society*, New York *(De la Division du travail social*, 1893, Paris).

Erikson, K. (1966), *Wayward Puritans*, New York.

Garfinkel, H. (1967), *Studies in Ethnomethodology*, Englewood Cliffs, N.J.

Goffman, E. (1963), *Stigma*, Englewood Cliffs, N.J.

Gouldner, A. (1970), *The Coming Crisis in Western Sociology*, New York.

Hall, S. *et al.* (eds) (1976), *Resistance Through Ritual*, London.

Hill, C. (1961), *The Century of Revolution*, Edinburgh.

Hirst, P. (1975), 'Marx and Engels on law, crime and morality', in I. Taylor *et al.* (eds), *Critical Criminology*, London.

Hobsbawm, E. (1965), *Primitive Rebels*, New York.

Lea, J. and Young, J. (1984), *What Is To Be Done About Law and Order?*, London.

Merton, R. (1957), *Social Theory and Social Structure*, New York.

Parsons, T. (1951), *The Social System*, New York.

Platt, A. (1978), '"Street Crime" – A view from the Left', *Crime and Social Justice*, 9.

Quinney, R. (1975), 'Crime control in capitalist society', in I. Taylor *et al.* (eds), *Critical Criminology*, London.

Scott, R. (1972), 'A proposed framework for analyzing deviance as a property of social order', in R. Scott and J. Douglas (eds), *Theoretical Perspectives on Deviance*, New York.

Scott, R. and Douglas, J. (eds) (1972), *Theoretical Perspectives on Deviance*, New York.

Smart, C. (1977), *Women, Crime and Criminology*, London.

Sumner, C. (1976), 'Ideology and deviance', Ph.D. Dissertation, Sheffield.

Taylor, I. (1980), 'The law and order issue in the British General Election and the Canadian Federal Election of 1979', *Canadian Journal of Sociology*.

Taylor, I., Walton, P. and Young, J. (1973), *The New Criminology*, London.

Thompson, E. (1975), *Whigs and Hunters*, London.

Willis, P. (1977), *Learning to Labour*, Farnborough.

See also: *symbolic interactionism*.

Diffusion

The problem of diffusion is linked to some perennial and still puzzling questions of culture history – where do cultures come from, what are the conditions of their rise and decline, how are they preserved and transmitted and, above all, how is it that similar forms of culture can be observed in different places? Do they arise independently among different peoples and converge because they are expressions of a common human nature (parallelism); or are there one or more centres of invention from which culture elements or systems have spread over the earth – as the result of contact – by way of borrowing, imitation, infiltration or acculturation?

In some formulations, diffusionism offered a theory of cultural development which competed with unilineal evolutionism. Broadly diffusionist theories were developed in American cultural anthropology by Boas and his followers, but in a narrower sense diffusionist assumptions were associated especially with the Austro-German school of ethnology which flourished from the end of the nineteenth century until about 1930, when functionalist, structuralist and dynamic movements within social anthropology presented themselves as new paradigmatic alternatives, reacting to overly schematic and speculative historical reconstructions.

The founding father of both the American and the European diffusionist traditions was the geographer Ratzel. He took over the concept of 'diffusion' (Gerland) and the 'theory of migration' (Wagner), and analysed the geographical distribution of culture elements (such as African bows and arrows), operating with the criterion of 'form'. He used the term *Kulturkreis* to describe supposedly organic relations between constituent elements. These methods were adopted by the Viennese school of culture-historical ethnology, founded by Schmidt, and by two museum ethnographers in Cologne, Ankermann and, most notably, Gräbner, who focused on smaller culture provinces, each of which had to be understood first 'in all its expressions as a lived totality' (Gräbner and Ankermann, 1905).

Although they collected an enormous quantity of data, often on the basis of field-studies, the diffusionists were later criticized for their conjectural reconstructions and for underplaying human inventiveness. The modern renewal of interest in ethnohistory may, however, gain them fresh attention, for their ultimate goal was to enquire 'whether the so-called "peoples without history" are amenable to historical representation' (Gräbner and Ankermann, 1905).

Britta Rupp-Eisenreich
École des Hautes Études en Sciences Sociales
Paris

Reference

Gräbner, F. and Ankermann, B. (1905), 'Kulturkreise und Kulturschichten in Ozeanien', and 'Kulturkreise und Kulturschichten in Afrika', in *Zeitschrift für Ethnologie*, 37.

Further Reading

Boas, F. (1924), 'Evolution or diffusion', *American Anthropologist*, 26.
Koppers, W. (1955), 'Diffusion: transmission and acceptance', in W. L. Thomas, Jr (ed.), *Yearbook of Anthropology*, New York.
Marett, R. R. (1927), *The Diffusion of Culture*, London.
See also: *culture*; *culture area*.

Distribution of Incomes and Wealth

The distribution of income is usually understood by economists in two main senses: (1) the distribution of income amongst *factors* (sometimes known as the *functional* distribution of income), and (2) the distribution of income amongst *persons* (alternatively known as the *size* distribution of income).

(1) The distribution of income amongst factors is an integral part of the economic analysis of relative prices, output and employment. In this sense there are several 'Theories of Income Distribution' corresponding to different theoretical and ideological stances on these central issues. However these various analyses usually focus on the same basic economic concepts: employment of the 'factors of production' – land, labour and capital – and the rates of remuneration of their services – rent, wages and profit. It should be understood that this tripartite classification is by no means the only functional decomposition which is useful in economic theory; in some analyses, for example, a finer subdivision is attempted, distinguishing specifically between interest and profits as rewards to 'waiting' and 'entrepreneurship' respectively, or distinguishing between rewards to different types of labour. Moreover, in many practical applications the characteristics of national data make it expedient to subdivide the functional categories simply as income from work and income from property. Note that when these categories are applied to the income of an individual, household or subgroup of the population, a third type must be added, transfer income, although items in this category, such as welfare payments and alimony, net out when the economy as a whole is considered. Some macroeconomists gave much attention to the supposed constancy or stability of the share of wages in national income. This interest now appears to have been somewhat misplaced, since it is clear that over long periods this share does change significantly. In many industrialized countries during the present century it has

been increasing, and now stands at about three-quarters (UK) to four-fifths (USA).

(2) The distribution of income amongst persons – the size distribution – and the distribution of wealth may both be thought of as particular applications of a statistical frequency distribution, although they are often represented by other statistical devices such as the Lorenz curve (which in the case of income distribution graphs cumulative proportions of income received against cumulative proportions of income receivers). The frequency distribution of each quantity is generally positively skewed with a long 'upper tail' indicating the presence of relatively small numbers of very well-off people. The dispersion of these frequency distributions, which can be measured in a number of ways, is taken as an indicator of the inequality of the size distributions of income and of wealth.

The size distribution of income is noted almost everywhere for two remarkable qualities: the great inequality of personal incomes that is revealed, and the stability of the distribution over time. This is true even though the exact shape of the size distribution is significantly affected by the particular definition of income one employs (for example whether one includes transfer incomes and incomes received in 'kind' rather than cash, and deducts personal taxes), and the definition of the income-receiving 'unit' (for example, whether one looks at the distribution of income amongst households, or incomes amongst persons). In the case of the US, the top one-fifth of income receivers in 1947 received about 45.5 per cent of total personal income before tax and the bottom fifth then received about 3.5 per cent of total income; in 1977 the shares in total personal income of these two groups were about 45 and 4 per cent respectively (although there was some variation in intervening years) (Blinder, 1980). Whilst the composition of personal incomes in the lower tail of the distribution has changed substantially as the scope of government transfers has altered, it is still true to say that in most Western-style economies the component of personal income that comes from various forms of property is primarily associated with the upper tail of the distribution. In order to understand the size distribution of *incomes* in the upper tail, therefore, it is important to examine the size distribution of wealth.

One of the most difficult problems in analysing the wealth distribution within any community with reasonably extensive holdings of private property is to decide exactly what one means by wealth. This is not a point of semantics, nor is it one of purely arcane, theoretical interest. While *marketable* wealth – including financial assets such as stocks and cash balances, and physical assets such as land, houses and jewellery – is fairly readily recognizable for what it is, other forms of wealth may also need to be taken into account in estimating the people's effective command over economic resources. These include various pension rights, which represent substantial *future* claims against economic goods (and are thus in that sense substitutes for cash or negotiable securities that have been held as a precaution against old age), but which may have little or no immediate surrender value. As is the case with the size distribution of incomes, estimates of the distribution of wealth are sensitive to assumptions one makes about the definition of wealth itself and the 'units' of population amongst whom the wealth is distributed. Moreover, parts of the wealth distribution are also very sensitive to different methods of valuing the components of wealth and to short-term changes in the prices of assets. However, it is virtually incontestable that the size distribution of wealth is much more unequal than the size distribution of income. For example, in the UK in 1976 the top 1 per cent of wealth holders possessed at least 14 per cent of personal wealth (this is on the most generous assumptions which include state and occupational pension rights as personal wealth; were these to be excluded the figure would have been 25 per cent), but the top 1 per cent of income recipients received about 5.5 per cent of personal income before tax (3.5 per cent after tax). Furthermore, it is clear that a substantial proportion of this implied inequality in the distribution of wealth is attributable to the effects of inheritance, rather than to the process of wealth accumulation that takes place during the course of people's lives (Harbury and Hitchens, 1979).

Finally if one switches one's attention from the analysis of the size distribution of income (or wealth) within national economies to the size distribution in the world as a whole, not only do the problems of measurement and comparison become much greater, so also does the dispersion. However one resolves the difficult practical questions of defining and quantifying personal or household incomes on this inter-country basis, it is clear that income inequality within national economies is usually much smaller than the income inequality that persists between countries.

Frank A. Cowell
London School of Economics and Political Science

References
Blinder, A. S. (1980), 'The level and distribution of economic well-being', in M. Feldstein (ed.), *The American Economy in Transition*, Chicago.
Harbury, C. and Hitchins, D.M.W.N. (1979), *Inheritance and Wealth Inequality in Britain*, London.

Further Reading
Atkinson, A. B. and Harrison, A. J. (1978), *Distribution of Personal Wealth in Britain*, Cambridge.
Pen, J. (1971), *Income Distribution*, London.
See also: *distributive justice; income distribution, theory of.*

Distributive Justice

The term distributive justice has a long history reaching back to Aristotle (*Nicomachean Ethics*). More recent philosophical treatments of the topic abound and are mostly concerned with specifying just or fair principles of distribution within a collectivity, typically a society. Whenever valued goods or resources exist some mechanism of distribution arises, and the concern of philosophers has been to examine the 'justness' of the resulting distribution (and sometimes, the fairness of the distribution procedure itself). Rawls (1971), in a major philosophical treatise on justice, identifies principles by which members of a society properly distribute the 'benefits and burdens of social cooperation'. For Rawls, the 'primary subject of justice is the basic structure of society'.

All social systems evolve mechanisms for distributing valued resources and for allocating rights, responsibilities, costs and burdens. Theories of distributive justice specify the conditions under which particular distributions are perceived to be just or fair. The various conceptions of distributive justice proposed by philosophers and social scientists include the conceptualizations identified by Eckhoff (1974): (1) *objective equality* – equal amounts to each recipient; (2) *subjective equality* – equal amounts based on perceived need or 'deservingness'; (3) *relative equality* – allocation based on the 'fitness' or 'deservingness' of the recipient; (4) *rank order equality* – allocation according to the status or positional rank of the recipient in the social system; and (5) *equal opportunity* – the allocation of equivalent opportunities to obtain the valued outcome to each recipient. A further distinction is often made between distributive justice and retributive justice, which is identified most frequently as involving judgements of the fairness of the allocation of punishments for activity not condoned by the collectivity.

Social scientists in the past three decades have conducted empirical research to investigate commonly held conceptions of distributive justice, and to examine the reactions of individuals and groups to perceived injustice. Findings suggest that perceptions of inequity are linked to lower levels of productivity, morale, and satisfaction, as well as to the formation of 'revolutionary' coalitions. In some experimental settings actors even attempt to redistribute outcomes in a more equitable fashion, but the generality of these results has not been established. Recent survey research attempts to examine the perceived fairness of the distribution of income in various countries. Robinson and Bell (1978), for example, report that in Great Britain and in the United States, those who benefit from the system of distribution define objective inequality as just, while those who do not benefit (the 'underdogs') define objective inequality as unjust. More research identifying the impact of general cultural, social and economic conditions on justice-related attitudes and behaviour is needed. Contributors to a recent volume by Lerner and Lerner (1981) attempt to specify how economic conditions of demand and supply affect preferences for particular distribution principles and the perceived justness of these principles. Greenberg (1981) has examined the impact of scarcity. Both the theoretical and policy implications of different distributions and distributional procedures for collective action and social change must be specified in subsequent research.

Karen S. Cook
University of Washington

References

Eckhoff, T. (1974), *Justice: Its Determinants in Social Interaction*, Rotterdam.

Greenberg, J. (1981), 'The justice of distributing scarce and abundant resources', in M. J. Lerner and S. C. Lerner (eds), *The Justice Motive in Social Behavior*, New York.

Lerner, M. J. and Lerner, S. C. (eds) (1981), *The Justice Motive in Social Behavior*, New York.

Rawls, J. (1971), *A Theory of Justice*, Cambridge, Mass.

Robinson, R. V. and Bell, W. (1978) 'Equality, success and social justice in England and the United States', *American Sociological Review*, 43.

See also: *distribution of incomes and wealth; relative deprivation*.

Divine Kingship

It was Frazer (1890) who first perceived that political power in archaic societies was intimately related to ritual functions, to the control which political leaders exercised over nature and, especially, rainfall. The sacred leader had to be put to death when his strength waned, since it was feared that his physical decline would result in a parallel weakening of the cosmic forces mysteriously associated with his person.

Evans-Pritchard denied the ritual character of regicide, seeing in it no more than the disguised expression of political conflict between rival factions. Recent studies in Africa have shown, however, that the putting to death of the sovereign forms an integral feature of the symbolic complex of sacred kingship (which Frazer called 'divine kingship').

This mystical institution, which was supposed to assure fecundity and prosperity, is characterized by a set of traits which are constant, though more or less developed in particular instances. The sacred king or chief commits fundamental transgressions: during his investiture he breaks the law of exogamy and commits real or symbolic incest (as among the Kuba, Lunda, Rwanda and Swazi) or even a sort of cannibalism, which consists in eating the flesh of his clan totem (for example, Rukuba). A formidable and august figure, the sacred chief is hedged about by interdictions which regulate his conduct. This extraordinary being is potentially dangerous, and he may himself be contaminated. If he is regarded as an ambiguous creature, outside culture, this is because he has responsibility for the natural order. The Kuba identify their sovereign at once with a good natural spirit and with a powerful sorcerer.

Very often the king's body, isolated from the group, cannot fulfil its magical function when it begins to age. In some cases he must disappear after an arbitrarily fixed period, at least unless a substitute can be sacrificed to regenerate him. This is, for example, the Swazi conception (see Kuper, 1947). Every year, during the summer solstice, the naked king, proclaimed 'bull of the nation', is seated on the principal ox of the herd and then thrown to the ground beside another beast, which has been stolen from a commoner, and which is tortured and sacrificed. The Mundang of Chad put their king himself, the master of the rain, to death at the end of a reign which may not exceed ten years (Adler, 1982).

Sacred chiefship is based on a radical separation of political power (ritual in essence) and the society over which it is exercised. It is no accident that many African myths represent the founder of the sacred kingship not as a powerful warrior but as a foreign hunter who possesses powerful magic and bears the stigma of his outsider's status (de Heusch, 1972, 1982). This symbolic structure, which recurs in the most diverse historical contexts, is not a mystifying ideological representation of the state. One finds the same elements in tiny Rukuba polities no larger than a single village. The sacred chief here is the prisoner of the group which depends on his magical power to guarantee general prosperity. One cannot assume that this is the primitive form of kingship, but many African examples do show that various state institutions may develop from this representation of power. The state, in so far as it implies the existence of a system of coercion, requires the emergence of magico-religious institutions which do not fall within the domain of the kinship system, and which are in fact capable of breaking the monopoly of kinship institutions in the field of social organization.

Luc de Heusch
Free University of Brussels

References

Adler, A. (1982), *La mort est le masque du roi*, Paris.
Frazer, J. G. (1890), *The Golden Bough*, London.
Heusch, L. de (1972), *Le roi ivre ou l'origine de l'état*, Paris (English trans., *The Drunken King*, Bloomington, 1982).
Kuper, H. (1947), *An African Aristocracy*, London.
See also: *Frazer; political anthropology; state, origin of.*

Division of Labour by Sex

The sexual division of labour is a basic structural element in human social organization. Interest in this topic began in the nineteenth century, but understanding was clouded by major misconceptions. These concerned the original human division of labour by sex, changes in this division of labour in the course of human evolution, and consequences for the relations between the sexes. A widespread view was that primitive subsistence was based mainly on tasks performed by males: hunting, fishing and herding. Marx and Engels (1947 [1932]), for example, inferred from this premise that masculine economic superiority was the order of nature, with slavery latent in the human family. Engels (1972 [1884]) compounded this misconception by assuming relative constancy of the sexual division of labour over time. He attributed a decline in female status to the larger societal division of labour and the rise of private property, with monogamy a corollary of property relations. A different misconception, found in Durkheim (1933 [1893]), is that the original sexual division of labour was minimal. He viewed differentiation between the sexes as increasing with time, moving towards organic solidarity and strong marriage ties.

Bias towards under-reporting women's contribution to subsistence is common across studies of many types of societies. Reporting biases will be reviewed where relevant in discussion of evidence on the following topics: (1) the original human division of labour; (2) ethnological variability in sexual division of labour; (3) changes in sexual division of labour with societal complexity; and (4) consequences of the sexual division of labour.

(1) Evidence for the original human division of labour comes from two sources: primate ethology and the ethnology of foragers. Male specialization in hunting is consistent with the tendency of male terrestrial primates to specialize in defence. The latter specialization gives a selective advantage to larger males. Sexual dimorphism is a consequence of this original division of labour. Humans are alone among the primates in having a marked sexual division of labour in food production and in having food sharing on a regular basis. Early studies of foragers, while noting that men tend to hunt and women to gather, greatly underestimated the importance of female gathering, and in so doing fostered a view of the human family which overemphasizes the dependence of wives on their husbands. Recent studies of foragers (Lee and DeVore, 1968) show that women's gathering often contributes more than half of the subsistence calories.

(2) Variability in sexual division of labour is also much greater than commonly assumed for both preindustrial and industrial societies. The rise of cross-cultural and cross-national research makes it possible

to estimate the relative frequencies of allocations of male and female effort to various tasks. As a result of Murdock's work, (Murdock and Provost 1973) we now have cross-cultural codes on sexual division of labour for fifty tasks. These codes confirm earlier generaliz-ations about near-universals. Tasks done by males in more than 95 per cent of the sample societies include hunting large land animals, metal-working, wood- and bone-working, boatbuilding, and trapping. Tasks done by females in more than 95 per cent of the sample include only cooking and care of infants. Patterns of sexual division of labour appear to have only a partial basis in biology, and most tasks exhibit high varia-bility. This is especially true of the important food production tasks pertaining to agriculture and the care of domesticated animals.

These variations, however, fall within constraints of a relative rather than universal nature. Many researchers have sought rules of consistency in the variable allocation of tasks. While earlier researchers emphasized the male strength advantage, current research places more emphasis on constraints due to the reproductive specialization of women. Brown (1970) emphasizes the compatibility of women's tasks with simultaneous child-care responsibilities. Women's tasks are likely to be relatively close to home, not dangerous, and interruptible. Burton, Brudner and White (1977) propose that these relative constraints produce entailments within production sequences. Women will tend to take on additional tasks within production sequences in an order which begins with tasks closer to the home and ends with tasks farther afield. Men take on additional tasks in the opposite order, from the more distant to those closer to home. Burton, Brudner and White find entailment chains for the following production sequences: animal tending, animal products, textiles, fishing and agriculture. An example from agriculture: if women clear the land, then they also prepare the soil; if the latter, then they also plant, tend crops, and harvest. If they tend crops, they also fetch water, and if they plant, they also prepare vegetables for cooking.

(3) In preindustrial societies female participation in many tasks declines with societal complexity. For example, women build houses in nomadic societies but not in sedentary societies; and female participation in pottery-making declines with increasing population density. For crafts, the explanation for these changes seems to be the evolution of occupational specializ-ation, which displaces craft activity from the domestic arena to the workshop. Agricultural intensification is accompanied by dramatic decreases in female contri-butions to farming. For Boserup (1970) agricultural intensification results from population pressure and introduction of the plough, and pulls men into agricul-ture to meet the increased demand for labour. Ember (1983) suggests a second mechanism in the shift to male farming: women are pulled out of farming into the household economy by increased time spent on food processing, household chores, and child care. Burton and White (1984) carry this work further with a model of four factors – population density, a short growing season, presence of the plough, and high dependence on domesticated animals – which lead to the displacement of women's labour from agriculture to the domestic and less economically visible activities.

The four-factor intensification model accounts for many empirical observations concerning female subsistence participation: that it is higher in tropical climates and in horticultural societies and that it is higher with root crops than with cereal crops, for these attributes are correlated with a long rainy season, low dependence on domesticated animals, absence of the plough, and low population density.

(4) Recently, several researchers following Boserup (1970) have hypothesized that agricultural intensific-ation has a negative impact on female control of econ-omic resources. This research suggests that high female subsistence contributions are a necessary prerequisite to female control of economic resources, and to women's freedom of choice in life events. In searching for other consequences of the sexual division of labour, Heath (1958), and several recent researchers find that low female subsistence contributions lead to monogamy. Such studies shed new light on puzzles such as the rise of monogamy and decline in women's status, originally noted by nineteenth-century theorists.

Michael L. Burton
Douglas R. White
University of California, Irvine

References
Boserup, E. (1970), *Woman's Role in Economic Development*, New York.
Brown, J. K. (1970), 'A note on the division of labor by sex', *American Anthropologist*, 72.
Burton, M. L. and White, D. R. (1984), 'Sexual division of labor in agriculture', *American Anthropologist*, 86.
Burton, M. L., Brudner, L. A. and White, D. R. (1977), 'A model of the sexual division of labor', *American Ethnologist*, 4.
Durkheim, E. (1933 [1893]), *The Division of Labor in Society*, New York. (Original French edn, *De la division du travail social: étude sur l'organization des sociétés supérieures*, Paris.)
Ember, C. R. (1983), 'The relative decline in women's contribution to agriculture with intensification', *American Anthropologist*, 85.
Engels, F. (1972 [1884]), *The Origin of the Family, Private Property and the State*, New York. (Original German edn, *Der Ursprung der Familie, des Privateigentums und des Staats*.)

Heath, D. (1958), 'Sexual division of labor and cross-cultural research', *Social Forces*, 37.

Lee, R. B. and DeVore, I. (1968), *Man the Hunter*, Chicago.

Marx, K. and Engels, F. (1947 [1932]), *The German Ideology*, London. (Original German edn, *Die deutsche Ideologie*, Moscow.)

Murdock, G. P. (1937), 'Comparative data on the division of labour by sex', *Social Forces*, 15.

Murdock, G. P. and Provost, C. (1973), 'Factors in the division of labor by sex: a cross-cultural analysis', *Ethnology*, 12.

Divorce

Divorce is an institutionalized way of voluntarily ending a marriage. There are other forms of voluntary marital dissolution, such as desertion or a mutually-agreed-upon separation; but divorce differs in that it is officially sanctioned by the state or the ruling group, and it allows both partners to remarry. The institution of divorce was present in many preindustrial societies and exists in most countries today. As Goode (1956) noted, '*All* family systems have *some* kinds of escape mechanisms built into them, to permit individuals to survive the pressures of the system, and one of these is divorce.'

Nevertheless, the levels of divorce and the reasons for divorce have varied widely from society to society. In some traditional Islamic societies, divorce was easy to obtain (at least for males) and quite common; in other traditional societies, such as China before the twentieth century, divorce was rather rare. Social and economic development has often brought a lowering of divorce levels in societies where it was quite common, and an increase in societies where it was quite uncommon (Goode, 1963).

In the West, the divorce rate has risen from a relatively low level in the preindustrial era to the current high level. This process accelerated in the 1960s and 1970s, leading to widespread concern about the future of marriage, but, since the mid-1970s, the rate of increase in divorce appears to have slowed down. In the US, which has the highest divorce rate of the developed nations, about one out of two marriages will end in divorce if current rates continue.

The reasons for Western divorce are different now from the past. Previously, a divorce was granted when one partner failed to fulfil an important responsibility: sexual fidelity, economic support, and so forth. But in many Western countries, divorces are now granted on the basis of incompatibility, without the need for either partner to be legally at fault. This shift toward 'no-fault' divorce reflects a changing view of marriage from an 'institution to a companionship' in the famous phrase of Burgess and Locke (1945). Marriage is defined less as a contractual arrangement in which each partner must carry out certain tasks, and more as a partnership in which both partners primarily seek emotional gratification. When that gratification is lacking, either partner may feel justified in seeking a divorce. The Western view of marriage and divorce has changed because of rising standards of living, the greater economic independence of women from men, the higher expectations couples have about marriage, and the decrease in the stigma of being divorced.

Because of the rise in divorce in the West, three family forms are becoming dominant: families of first marriages, single-parent families (usually a mother and children), and families formed by remarriages after divorce. Divorce remains a traumatic event, at least in the short run, for those who experience it. Much current research is directed at the effects of parental divorce on children. It is clear that the short-run effects are quite traumatic (Wallerstein and Kelly, 1980); but the long-term effects are not yet clear.

Andrew Cherlin
Johns Hopkins University

References

Burgess, E. W. and Locke, H. J. (1945), *The Family: From Institution to Companionship*, New York.

Goode, W. J. (1956), *Women in Divorce*, New York.

Goode, W. J. (1963), *World Revolution and Family Patterns*, New York.

Wallerstein, J. S. and Kelly, J. B. (1980), *Surviving the Breakup: How Children and Parents Cope with Divorce*, New York.

Further Reading

Cherlin, A. J. (1981), *Marriage, Divorce, Remarriage*, Cambridge, Mass.

Chester, R. (ed.) (1977), *Divorce in Europe*, The Hague.

Levinger, G. and Moles, O. C. (eds) (1979), *Divorce and Separation: Context, Causes, and Consequences*, New York.

See also: *marriage*.

Douglas, Mary (1921–)

A British anthropologist, Mary Douglas established her reputation as an Africanist with fieldwork among the Lele of the Belgian Congo (Zaire) in 1949–50 and 1953. In *The Lele of the Kasai* (1963) and subsequent articles, she describes Lele notions of social accountability, especially in the manipulation of raffia cloth debts by which polygamous older men restrict their juniors' access to women.

Her early work already displays the insight (which she attributes to her teacher and colleague E. E. Evans-Pritchard) that society consists of actively negotiating moral agents, rather than role-playing automata following functionalist social rules or the dictates of childhood conditioning (*Evans-Pritchard*, 1980).

Douglas's view of culture being created afresh each day runs through her writings on both preindustrial and industrial societies. She particularly emphasizes the active use of consumable commodities, especially food, as media of communication in a wide range of interactions (*The World of Goods*, 1980).

Douglas's comparative studies of ritual and of pollution beliefs in preindustrial as well as contemporary Western society have systematically related religion and ethical beliefs to social behaviour. *Natural Symbols* (1973), *Purity and Danger* (1966), and *Risk and Culture* (1982) all emphasize the universal use of appeals to nature to justify political and moral orders. For example, Douglas argues that where people use the body as a symbol of society, with strong concern over what is edible and how bodily wastes are disposed of, they are carefully maintaining the boundary around their social group; this is one vital dimension of social control. Her interpretations of the dietary restrictions of Leviticus as taxonomic anomalies, and of the structure of British working-class meals, point to the importance of cultural classification as another means of defining social order. She brings both dimensions together in an explanatory typology of social accountability called grid/group analysis (*Cultural Bias*, 1978, and *Essays in the Sociology of Perception*, (ed.) 1982). In 1977, Douglas moved to the United States and was appointed Avalon Professor of the Humanities at Northwestern University in 1980.

Steve Rayner
Oak Ridge National Laboratory, Tennessee
See also: *grid/group*.

Dreams

Despite their power to bewilder, frighten or amuse us, dreams remain an area of human behaviour little understood and typically ignored in models of cognition. As the methods of introspection were replaced with more self-consciously objective methods in the social sciences of the 1930s and 1940s, dream studies dropped out of the scientific literature. Dreams were neither directly observable by an experimenter nor were subjects' dream reports reliable, being prey to the familiar problems of distortion due to delayed recall, if they were recalled at all. More often dreams are, of course, forgotten entirely, perhaps due to their prohibited character (Freud, 1955 [1900]). Altogether, these problems seemed to put them beyond the realm of science.

The discovery that dreams take place primarily during a distinctive electrophysiological state of sleep, Rapid Eye Movement (REM) sleep, which can be identified by objective criteria, led to a rebirth of interest in this phenomenon. When REM sleep episodes were timed for their duration and subjects woken to make reports before major editing or forgetting could take place, it was determined that subjects accurately matched the length of time they judged the dream narrative to be ongoing to the length of REM sleep that preceded the awakening. This close correlation of REM sleep and dream experience was the basis of the first series of reports describing the nature of dreaming: that it is a regular nightly, rather than occasional, phenomenon, and a high-frequency activity within each sleep period occurring at predictable intervals of approximately every 60 to 90 minutes in all humans throughout the life span. REM sleep episodes and the dreams that accompany them lengthen progressively across the night, with the first episode being shortest, of approximately 10–12 minutes duration, and the second and third episodes increasing to 15 to 20 minutes. Dreams at the end of the night may last as long as 45 minutes, although these may be experienced as several distinct stories due to momentary arousals interrupting sleep as the night ends. Dream reports can be retrieved from normal subjects on 50 per cent of the occasions when an awakening is made prior to the end of the first REM period. This rate of retrieval is increased to about 99 per cent when awakenings are made from the last REM period of the night. This increase in ability to recall appears to be related to an intensification across the night in the vividness of dream imagery, colours and emotions. The dream story itself in the last REM period is farthest from reality, containing more bizarre elements, and it is these properties, coupled with the increased likelihood of spontaneous arousals allowing waking review to take place, that heighten the chance of recall of the last dream. The distinctive properties of this dream also contribute to the reputation of dreams being 'crazy'. Reports from earlier dreams of the night, being more realistic, are often mistaken for waking thoughts.

Systematic content analysis studies have established that there are within-subject differences between dreams collected from home versus laboratory sleep periods, with home dreams being on the whole more affect-laden. This calls into question the representativeness of laboratory-collected dreams, particularly when subjects have not been adapted to the laboratory and the collections are carried out only for a limited period. More often, between-group comparisons are being made. Here clear differences have been reported between the home-recalled dreams of males and females, old and young, rich and poor, and between those of different ethnic groups living in the same geographical area. These differences reflect the waking sex-role characteristics, personality traits, and sociocultural values and concerns of these groups. These findings raise the question of whether dreams make some unique contribution to the total psychic economy, or merely reflect, in their distinctive imagistic, condensed language and more primitive logic, the same mental content available during wakefulness by direct observation or interviewing techniques.

The question of uniqueness of dream data and function may well be answered differently for home and laboratory retrieved dreams. Home dreams are so highly selected, whether from dream diaries or those recalled in response to questionnaires, that they yield culturally common material much like the study of common myths. In the laboratory, where the data base includes all of the dreams of a night in sequence and where experimental controls can be instituted to ensure uniform collection, the yield is more individual and varied. Despite this, the question of dream function has continued to be an area of controversy over the past thirty years of modern sleep research. It has been approached empirically through studies of the effects of dream deprivation with little progress. Neither awakenings at REM onset to abort dreams nor nights of drug-induced REM sleep deprivation have been followed by reliable deficits in waking behaviour or the appearance of dream-like waking hallucinations.

It is possible that these studies have not been carried out long enough or that the dependent measures have not been appropriately designed. Other studies have proceeded by manipulating the pre-sleep state to heighten a specific drive, such as thirst or sex, or to introduce a problem requiring completion such as a memory task and testing for the effects on dream content or subsequent waking behaviour. Again, effects have been small and rarely replicable. The laboratory setting and experimenter effects have been implicated in masking the very phenomenon the studies were designed to reveal, being more powerful stimuli than the experimental manipulation itself (Cartwright and Kaszniak, 1978).

Seldom have theoretical models of dream function been tested. These have varied widely in the psychological processes implicated. Learning and memory have been prominent, as in the Hughlings Jackson (1932) view that sleep serves to sweep away unnecessary memories and connections from the day. This was recently revised by Crick and Mitchison (1983) and stated as a theory that dream sleep is a period of reversed learning. However, the opposite view that dreaming has an information-handling, memory-consolidating function (Hennevin and Leconte, 1971) is also common. Other writers stress an affective function. Greenberg and Pearlman (1974) and Dewan (1970) hold that during dreaming, reprogramming of emotional experiences occurs, integrating new experiences and updating existing programmes. The modern psychoanalytically oriented view is an adaptation of Freud's conception of dreams as safe ways for unconscious drive discharge to take place (Fisher, 1965; French and Fromm, 1964). Beyond the issue of what psychological process is involved is the further problem posed by those who deny that studies of dream content can make any headway without taking into account their latent as well as their manifest content. This requires obtaining waking associations to each dream to plumb their function fully. Such a design would produce confounding effects on subsequent dreams.

Despite the theoretical morass and methodological problems rife in this field, systematic headway in understanding dreams has been made. One such advance came from a ground-breaking longitudinal collection of home and laboratory dreams of boys and girls by Foulkes (1982). These were analysed to explore the age- and sex-related changes in dream structure and content in terms of the cognitive and other aspects of the developmental stages of these children. Another advance came in the area of methodology with the development of standardized content analysis systems (Foulkes, 1978) and rating scales (Winget and Kramer, 1979). Another recent improvement in design combines the advantages of the methods of the laboratory with the reality of a field study by predicting dream-content differences in the laboratory-retrieved dreams among groups of persons differing in response to a major affect-inducing life event.

The study of dreams is ready to move beyond the descriptive. Many facts have been amassed about this distinctive mental activity without any clear understanding of its basic nature. How is a dream put together into a dramatic format without the contribution of any voluntary intent of the dreamer? How are the new perceptions formed that often express in such highly economical terms a coming together of old memories and current waking experiences? Do dreams have effects despite the fact that they are forgotten? What do these processes tell us about how the mind works? Dreams are a difficult challenge. They deserve our best response.

Rosalind D. Cartwright
Rush-Presbyterian-St Luke's Medical Center, Chicago

References

Cartwright, R. and Kaszniak, A. (1978), 'The social psychology of dream reporting', in A. Arkin et al. (eds), The Mind in Sleep, Hillsdale, N.J.

Crick, F. and Mitchison, G. (1983), 'The function of dream sleep', Nature, 304.

Dewan, E. (1970), 'The programming "P" hypotheses for REM sleep', in E. Hartmann (ed.), Sleep and Dreaming, Boston.

Fisher, C. (1965), 'Psychoanalytic implications of recent research on sleep and dreaming. II. Implications of psychoanalytic theory', Journal of American Psychoanalytical Association, 13.

Foulkes, D. (1978), A Grammar of Dreams, New York.

Foulkes, D. (1982), Children's Dreams, New York.

French, T. and Fromm, E. (1964), Dream Interpretation: A New Approach, New York.

Freud, S. (1955 [1900]), *The Interpretation of Dreams*, ed. J. Strachey, New York.

Greenberg, R. and Pearlman, C. (1974), 'Cutting the REM nerve: an approach to the adaptive role of REM sleep', *Perspectives in Biology and Medicine*.

Hennevin, E. and Leconte, P. (1971), 'La fonction du sommeil paradoxal: faits et hypotheses', *L'Ann. Psychologique*, 2.

Jackson, J. H. (1932), *Selected Writings of John Hughlings Jackson*, ed. J. Taylor, London.

Winget, C. and Kramer, M. (1979), *Dimensions of Dreams*, Gainesville.

Further Reading

Cartwright, R. (1977), *Night Life: Explorations in Dreaming*, Englewood Cliffs, N.J.

Cohen, D. (1979), *Sleep and Dreaming*, New York.

Fishbein, W. (1981), *Sleep, Dreams and Memory*, New York.

See also: *fantasy; sleep.*

Drugs

See Drug Use, Psychopharmacology.

Drug Use

The ingestion of mind-altering substances is very nearly a human universal; in practically every society, a sizeable proportion of its members take at least one drug for psychoactive purposes (Weil, 1972). This has been true for a significant stretch of history. Fermentation was one of the earliest of discoveries, predating the fashioning of metal; humans have been ingesting alcoholic beverages for some 10,000 years. Several dozen plants contain chemicals that influence the workings of the mind, and have been smoked, chewed or sniffed by members of societies all over the world. These plants include coca leaves, the opium poppy, marijuana, the psilocybin mushroom, the peyote cactus, quat leaves, nutmeg, tobacco, coffee beans, tea leaves, and the cocoa bean. During the past century or more, hundreds of thousands of psychoactive chemicals have been discovered, isolated or synthesized by scientists or physicians. Thousands have been marketed for medicinal purposes. According to the journal, *Pharmacy Times*, approximately 1.5 billion medical prescriptions for drugs are written each year in the United States alone. Although most of these drugs are not psychoactive, roughly one out of six of these prescriptions is written for a substance that significantly alters the workings of the human mind. Drug-taking is one of the more widespread of human activities.

Most of the time that psychoactive chemicals are ingested, they are used 'in a culturally approved manner' (Edgerton, 1976), with little or no negative impact on the user or on society. However, in a significant minority of cases, drugs are taken in a culturally unacceptable or disapproved fashion: a condemned drug is taken instead of an approved one, it is taken too frequently or under the wrong circumstances, for the wrong reasons, or with undesirable consequences. With the establishment of the modern nation-state and, along with it, the elaboration of an explicit legal code, certain actions came to be deemed illegal or criminal. The use, possession or sale of certain kinds of drugs, taking drugs in certain contexts, or the ingestion of drugs for disapproved motives, have been regarded as crimes in nearly all countries, punished with a fine or imprisonment of the offender. The catch-all term 'abuse' is commonly used to refer to somewhat different types of drug use: (1) any use of an illegal drug for non-medical purposes, or (2) any use of a drug, legal or illegal, to the point where it becomes a threat to the user's physical or mental well-being, or interferes with major life goals or functioning, such as educational or occupational achievement, or marriage. 'Misuse' is the term that is commonly used to refer to the inappropriate use of a legal prescription drug for medical purposes.

It must be emphasized that drug use is not a unitary phenomenon. There are, to begin with, different types of drugs, classified according to their action. Drugs are commonly categorized on the basis of their impact on the central nervous system (the CNS) – the brain and spinal cord. Some drugs speed up signals passing through the CNS; they are called *stimulants* and include cocaine, the amphetamines, caffeine, and nicotine. Other drugs retard signals passing through the CNS, and are called *depressants*. Depressants include *narcotics* (such as opium, heroin, and morphine), which dull the sensation of pain, *sedatives* (such as alcohol, the barbiturates, and mathaqualone) and 'minor' *tranquillizers* (such as Valium), which reduce anxiety, and 'major' tranquillizers or *antipsychotics*, which inhibit the manifestation of symptoms of psychosis, especially schizophrenia. Hallucinogens (such as LSD) and marijuana do not fit neatly into this stimulant-depressant continuum.

Psychoactive drugs, even of the same type, are taken for a variety of reasons: to attain religious or mystical ecstasy, to suppress fatigue, hunger, or anxiety, to enhance hedonism and pleasure, to heal the body or the mind, to facilitate socializing or interpersonal intimacy, to follow the dictates of a particular group or subculture, and to establish an identity as a certain kind of person. A drug's psychoactive properties may be central to the user's motive for taking it, or incidental to it; the intoxication may be experienced for intrinsic reasons (that is, the drug is taken by the user to get 'high') or the drug taken for instrumental purposes (that is, to attain a specific goal, such as alleviating pain). Of the many varieties of drug use, perhaps the three most common and important are:

(1) legal recreational use, (2) illegal recreational use, and (3) legal medical use. Each of these modes of use will attract strikingly different users and will have strikingly different consequences. Even the same drug will be used by a different set of individuals for entirely different purposes with different effects. It is a fallacy to assume that the pharmacological properties of a drug dictate the consequences following its use; factors such as the motives for its use, the social context in which use is embedded, social norms surrounding use, methods of use, and so on, all play a major role in a drug's impact on the individual and on society. It is misleading, therefore, to assume that the use of even the same drug in different cultural settings will result in the same effects, consequences or impact. In parts of India, for example, holy men (*sadhus*) smoke cannabis to quell their appetite for food and sex; in the West, the same drug is successfully used to enhance precisely the same appetites.

(1) *Legal recreational use* refers to the attempt to alter one's consciousness by ingesting a psychoactive substance whose possession is not against the law. For the most part, in Western nations, this refers mainly to alcohol consumption. When the term 'drug' is used to apply to substances consumed outside a medical context, it usually connotes those whose use is illegal and/or strongly condemned and disvalued. It rarely refers to substances such as alcohol. Although not generally perceived or regarded as a drug, alcohol qualifies for the term in a pharmacological and a physiological sense: not only is it psychoactive, and widely used for this reason, but it can produce a physical dependence, or 'addiction', in heavy, long-term, chronic users, and it causes or is associated with a wide range of medical maladies. Many estimates place the proportion of alcoholics at roughly one drinker in ten, and argue that alcoholism is the West's most serious drug problem. In short, alcohol is 'a drug by any other name' (Fort, 1973).

(2) Of all types of drug use, *illegal recreational use* attracts the most public attention and interest. In the two decades following the early 1960s, Western Europe and North America experienced an unprecedented rise in the recreational use of illegal psychoactive drugs. The most widely used of these drugs are marijuana and hashish, products of the plant *Cannabis sativa*. In most countries, there are as many episodes of cannabis use as episodes of the use of all other illegal drugs combined. And of all illegal drugs, cannabis is the one that users are most likely to continue using regularly, and least likely to abandon or use extremely episodically. Of all illegal drugs, marijuana is the one with the highest ratio of current to lifetime users. In one study, 52 per cent of all at least one-time marijuana users had taken this drug one or more times in the past month; for cocaine, this was 34 per cent, for the other stimulants, 19 per cent, for the hallucinogens, 18

per cent, and for the sedatives, 16 per cent (Fishburne *et al.*, 1980). Cannabis is the illegal drug that people most frequently 'stick with'. As with alcohol, the majority of users take the drug in a fairly moderate, controlled fashion. Approximately 10 per cent of all cannabis users become so involved with their drug of choice that it becomes an obsession or a psychological dependency, threatening their health and occupational or educational attainment. While the recreational use of more dangerous drugs, such as heroin, cocaine, and barbiturates, is considerably less than for cannabis, the potential for abuse of these substances is far greater. It is estimated that there are as many as half a million heroin addicts in the United States alone (Goode, 1984).

(3) The *medical use* of psychoactive chemicals in the Western world has undergone dramatic changes over the past century. Late in the nineteenth century, over-the-counter preparations containing psychoactive substances such as morphine and cocaine were freely available and were widely used to treat or cure medical ailments. Legal controls on what these nostrums contained were practically non-existent. When authorities became aware of widespread abuses of these drugs, dispensing them became tightly controlled, and medical prescriptions became necessary to obtain them. In the United States, the number of prescriptions written for psychoactive drugs rose steadily until the early 1970s when, again, misuse and abuse of these substances was publicized. Since that time, there has been a steep decline in the number of psychoactive drug doses dispensed by physicians. For instance, in the United States in 1975, 61.3 million prescriptions were written for Valium, that nation's number one prescription drug; in 1980, this figure had dropped to 33.6 million (Rosenblatt, 1982). The number of prescriptions written for morphine in 1981 was half the number for 1976. Benzedrine, a once popular stimulant, was prescribed one-sixth as often in 1981 as in 1976 (Goode, 1984). There has been a dramatic downward trend in the use of psychoactive prescription drugs between the 1970s and the 1980s; the trend continues unabated. With some of these drugs, such as the barbiturates, this cut-back has translated into a decline in illegal recreational or 'street' usage; with other drugs, such as methaqualone and amphetamine, this has not taken place.

In contrast, the treatment of psychotic disorders, mainly schizophrenia, with the use of anti-psychotic drugs such as Thorazine, has been increasing dramatically since their discovery in the 1950s. The impact of the medical use of anti-psychotic drugs, also called 'major' tranquillizers, can be measured by the dramatic decline in the number of resident patients in mental hospitals. Between 1945 and 1955, in the United States, there was a yearly average increase of 13,000 patients residing in state mental hospitals; in the latter year, the total was just under 560,000. Between 1954 and 1955, psychoactive agents were introduced as treatment for psychosis. Because of the success of this modality in controlling the symptoms of schizophrenia, patients who were previously confined in hospitals were released as outpatients. By 1978, the number of resident state mental hospital patients in the United States had plummeted to under 150,000 (Ray, 1983). The average length of hospitalization dropped from six months in 1955 to 26 days in 1976. The decline in the number of mental patients in hospitals can be traced directly to the use of anti-psychotic or phenothiazine drugs, the 'major' tranquillizers.

Erich Goode
State University of New York at Stony Brook

References
Edgerton, R. B. (1976), *Deviance: A Cross-Cultural Perspective*, Menlo Park, Calif.
Fishburne, P. M. *et al.* (1980), *National Survey on Drug Abuse: Main Findings, 1979*, Rockville, Maryland.
Fort, J. (1973), *Alcohol: Our Biggest Drug Problem*, New York.
Goode, E. (1984), *Drugs in American Society*, 2nd edn, New York.
Ray, O. (1983), *Drugs, Society, and Human Behavior*, 3rd edn, St Louis.
Rosenblatt, J. (1982), 'Prescription-drug abuse', *Editorial Research Reports*, 1.
Weil, A. (1972), *The Natural Mind: A New Way of Looking at Drugs and the Higher Consciousness*, Boston.

Further Reading
Abel, E. L. (1982), *Marihuana: The First Twelve Thousand Years*, New York.
Grinspoon, L. and Bakalar, J. B. (1979), *Psychedelic Drugs Reconsidered*, New York.
Judson, H. F. (1974), *Heroin Addiction in Britain*, New York.
Young, J. (1971), *The Drugtakers: The Social Meaning of Drug Use*, London.
See also: *alcoholism*; *psychopharmacology*.

DSM III

DSM III is the third edition of the American Psychiatric Association's *Diagnostic and Statistical Manual of Mental Disorders*, published in 1980. It is a guide for diagnosis of mental illnesses, whether for clinical, administrative or legal purposes.

Historically, classification systems for mental disorders are relatively recent. In 1863, Kahlbaum proposed the first classification system based on observation rather than theory. In 1892, Kraepelin published such a classification, that separated for the first time those serious illnesses with a deteriorating course (such as, dementia praecox) from those that

might be serious and episodic, but did not result in progressive dysfunction (for example, cyclic insanity). These conditions, now better understood, are referred to respectively as schizophrenia and manic-depressive disorder. In the United States, the first complete nomenclature, *The Standard Classified Nomenclature of Disease*, was printed in 1933. In 1952, the American Psychiatric Association issued the first DSM, and in 1968, the second. Both of these manuals used the traditional trichotomization of mental disorders: psychosis, neurosis and personality disorders.

DSM III makes a further attempt to specify and to clarify mental disorders, to avoid any implication of aetiology (for example, neuroses stemming from unconscious conflict) by using a 'descriptive approach', and to delimit sharply some diagnoses (such as schizophrenia) while moving toward a spectrum concept for others (for example, manic-depressive illness, now called affective disorders). While it is not explicitly stated, the fact that affective disorders and anxiety states can now be treated much more effectively, while schizophrenia remains more problematic, leads to exclusionary criteria favouring the spectrum approach to these more treatable illnesses.

DSM III defines five axes: (1) those illnesses previously considered neurotic or psychotic; (2) only the personality disorders – so that one may diagnose both a non-personality disorder (such as schizophrenia) and personality disorder (for example, schizoid); (3) physical disorders, some of which might previously have been considered 'psychosomatic'; (4) indicating the severity of the pre-illness stressors; and (5) the highest level of recent functioning. Since Axes 1 and 2 contain all the mental disorders, they will be the focus of further discussion.

DSM III begins with conditions that usually start in childhood, including mental retardation, and attention deficit, conduct, anxiety, eating, stereotyped movement (such as tics), and pervasive developmental disorders (for example, infantile autism). Next, the manual lists the organic mental disorders, whether acute (deliria) or chronic (dementias), and whether of unknown (primary degenerative dementia) or known (for example, alcohol or other abused substances) cause. Substance abuse itself is diagnosed separately. The schizophrenic disorders are divided into disorganized, catatonic, paranoid and undifferentiated types. Paranoid disorders, as well as several other psychotic conditions (such as, schizophreniform, brief reactive, and schizo-affective), are listed separately. The affective disorders group contains those illnesses which are major (previously considered manic-depressive), other (previously neurotic or characterological), and atypical (such as present with hypersomnia rather than insomnia). The anxiety disorders emcompass phobias (with or without panic attacks), anxiety states (including obsessive-compulsive disorders) and post-traumatic stress disorders. An entirely new concept, that of somatoform disorders, incorporates somatiz- ation, conversion, psychogenic pain and hypochon- driacal disorders. Then there are the dissociative (amnesia, fugue, and so on) and psychosexual disorders – the latter divided into paraphilias (for example, transvestism, voyeurism, sadism) and dysfunctions (for example, inhibited orgasm). Finally there are separate categories for factitious, impulse control and adjustment disorders. As mentioned previously, the personality disorders are all classified in Axis 2 and include paranoid, schizoid, schizotypal, histrionic, narcissistic, antisocial, borderline, avoidant, dependent, compulsive, passive-aggressive, and mixed personality disorders.

John A. Talbott
Cornell University Medical College
The Payne Whitney Psychiatric Clinic
The New York Hospital

References

American Psychiatric Association (APA) (1952), *Diagnostic and Statistical Manual of Mental Disorders*, 1st edn, Washington, DC.
APA (1968), *Diagnostic and Statistical Manual of Mental Disorders*, 2nd edn, Washington, DC.
APA (1980), *Diagnostic and Statistical Manual of Mental Disorders*, 3rd edn, Washington, DC.
Commonwealth Fund (1933), *The Standard Classified Nomenclature of Disease*, New York.
Kahlbaum, K. L. (1973 [1862]), *Catatonia*, Baltimore.
Kraepelin, E. (1921 [1892]), *Manic Depressive Insanity and Paranoia*, Edinburgh.

See also: *mental disorders*.

Dual Economy

The term dual economy has at once a technical academic meaning and a broader, more general meaning. In the former sense it relates to the simul- taneous coexistence within the same economy of two different sectors, divided by different culture, different laws of development, different technology, different demand patterns, and so on. In certain models or theories of development, such a two-sector division, and the interaction between the two sectors, that is, a dual economy is taken as a foundation for theoretical analysis.

The best-known of such models is the Arthur Lewis model, based on his famous article 'Economic develop- ment with unlimited supply of labour' (1954). Lewis distinguishes between a rural low-income subsistence type sector in which there is surplus population (zero or very low marginal productivity of labour), and a developing urban capitalist sector in which wages are held down by the pressure of rural surplus population with resulting rapid development, ultimately exhausting the labour surplus. A considerable litera- ture has followed in the wake of the Lewis model. The main modification of this model has been through Harris and Todaro (1970), who pointed out that the transfer of the labour surplus from rural to urban sectors could lead to urban unemployment and the development of an urban 'informal sector' rather than a reduction in wages in the capitalist sector to subsist- ence level.

The concept of the dual economy was originally developed by Boeke (1953), to describe the coexistence of modern and traditional sectors in a colonial economy. Today the term dual (or more frequently dualistic) economy is applied more broadly to the coexistence of rich and poor sectors (either rich and poor countries in the global economy or rich and poor people in the national economy), where there is often a tendency for the 'rich to become richer, while the poor remain poor or become poorer'. For a discussion and literature survey of the concept in this broader sense see Singer (1970).

H. W. Singer
Institute of Development Studies
University of Sussex

References

Boeke, J. H. (1953), *Economics and Economic Policy of Dual Societies*, New York.
Harris, J. R. and Todaro, M. P. (1970), 'Migration, unemployment and development: a two-sector analysis', *American Economic Review*.
Lewis, W. A. (1954), 'Economic development with unlimited supply of labour', *The Manchester School*.
Singer, H. W. (1970), 'Dualism revisited: a new approach to the problems of dual society in developing countries', *Journal of Development Studies*, 7.

See also: *Lewis*; *plural society*.

Durkheim, Émile (1858–1917)

Émile Durkheim was the founding father of academic sociology in France and the most influential early theoretician of archaic or primitive societies. A Jew from north-east France, Durkheim followed the educational and ideological path of the positivist gener- ation of great Republican academics. He was educated at the *École Normale Supérieure*, taking a teacher's degree in philosophy and a doctorate (1893). After a short period as a *lycée* teacher, he spent a year in German universities studying social theory. On his return, he was appointed the first ever lecturer in 'social science and pedagogy' in a French university, at Bordeaux

(1887). In 1902 he transferred to the Sorbonne, where he held a chair for the rest of his life.

Durkheim's seminal teaching and publications, included *De la Division du travail social* (1893) (*The Division of Labor in Society*, 1933), *Les Règles de la méthode sociologique* (1894) (*The Rules of Sociological Method*, 1938), *Le Suicide* (1897) (*Suicide*, 1952), and work on socialism, family organization, the scope and development of German social theories. He attracted a cluster of gifted young scholars – mostly philosophers but also historians, economists and jurists (including Mauss, Hubert, Simiand, Fauconnet, Richard and Bouglé) – with whom he founded the *Année sociologique* (1898). This was an essentially critical journal intended to cover the whole range of emerging social disciplines (social geography, demography, collective psychology, social and economic history, history of religion, ethnology and sociology proper). It was to become instrumental in developing and promoting a synthetic theory of social facts which overrode earlier disciplinary divisions.

Durkheim's later work included studies and lecture courses on the sociology of education, morality and moral science, pragmatism, family sociology, history of the social sciences, vital statistics and several other topics, but after the birth of the *Année* he was primarily concerned with the study of archaic societies, and especially with primitive religion and social organization. The problem of social cohesion in so-called polysegmentary societies which, according to Durkheim, were based on mechanical solidarity (as against the organic solidarity of modern societies, based on a division of labour) had been a major theme in his doctoral thesis (1893), but there it lacked any significant ethnological underpinning. Durkheim developed an intense interest in primitive society much later, after reading contemporary British 'religious anthropologists', above all, Robertson Smith and Frazer. This resulted in a reorientation of his work towards the study of 'collective representations' and, more specifically, of religion, from 1896 onwards.

There were two sets of reasons, theoretical and methodological, for this shift: (1) Religion was considered to serve an essential social 'function', creating a strong community of beliefs and providing a basis for social cohesion. The 'sacred' and the 'profane' became the two essential categories in Durkheim's sociology, which ordered the system of social facts. (2) Primitive religion, either because it was believed to be more simple and consequently easier to study, or because it appeared to be functionally interconnected with most other 'social facts' (like economy, law, technology and so on, which had gained a measure of functional autonomy in the course of later development) seemed to provide the key to a theory of social order. The religious system of archaic societies thus became a privileged topic of research for Durkheim

and some of the most gifted scholars of his cluster, notably Mauss, Hubert and Hertz. One out of four review articles published in the *Année* was dedicated to social anthropology, and primitive societies now supplied, for the first time in French intellectual history, a central topic in public philosophical debate, which soon engaged other leading academics (like Bergson and Lévy-Bruhl) as well.

In his anthropological work, Durkheim never surmounted the basic ambiguity of his approach to 'primitives', who were regarded either as prototypes, or as exemplifying the simplest imaginable occurrences of observable social types, or both at the same time. Moreover, he was initially sceptical about the heuristic utility of ethnographic data, and believed that preference should be given to historical documents over ethnographic information. His attitude changed, however, especially with the publication of more 'professional' ethnographies, like Spencer and Gillen (on the Australian aborigines), Boas (on the Kwakiutl Indians), and the Cambridge scholars of the expedition to Torres Straits. He discussed all these new studies in painstakingly detailed critical reviews. They also supplied the data for his own contributions in the contemporary international debate concerning archaic societies. These fall broadly under two thematic headings: social organization and belief systems (and various combinations of the two).

The essay on 'La Prohibition de l'inceste et ses origines' (1898) (*Incest: The Nature and Origin of the Taboo*, 1963) obeyed to the letter his own prescription, 'Explain the social fact by other social facts.' Social institutions could not be explained by invoking instinctive behaviour. They must be accounted for purely in terms of social causes. Incest and exogamy derived from the nature of the elementary, that is, uterine, clan. Respect for the clan's totem manifested itself by a religious aversion to the blood of fellow clanspeople and, by extension, to sexual contact with the clan's women. The prohibition of incest was accompanied by prescriptions concerning interclan marriage. Some modern writers on kinship (for example, Lévi-Strauss, 1949) recognize their debt to Durkheim, though they have submitted his theory to substantial criticism. Similarly, in his essays on totemism (1902) and Australian kinship (1905a), Durkheim seemed clearly to anticipate much later structuralist approaches. He identified, beyond the social categories of kinship, truly logical categories which, he suggested, could be understood as 'mathematical problems' (Durkheim, 1905a). He went further in the exploration of such logical categories in a famous study, written together with Mauss, 'De quelques formes primitives de classification: contribution à l'étude des représentations collectives' (1903) (*Primitive Classification*, 1963). This essay related ideas about space among some Australian and North-American tribesmen to their social organizations. Durkheim and Mauss argued that men 'classified things because they were divided into clans'. The model of all classification (especially of spatial orientation) is the society, because it is the unique whole (or totality) to which everything is related, so that 'the classification of things reproduces the classification of men'. Primitive classifications generated the first concepts or categories, enabling men to unify their knowledge. They constituted the first 'philosophy of nature'. Durkheim and Mauss suggested that in these classifications could be discerned 'the origins of logical procedure which is the basis of scientific classifications'. Durkheim would systematize these intimations in his last great work which focused on the social functions of religion proper.

Les Formes élémentaires de la vie religieuse (1912) (*The Elementary Forms of Religious Life*, 1915) was the culmination of Durkheim's anthropological studies. His focus upon Australians (and to some extent on American Indians) was grounded on the methodologically essential (and still ambiguous) assumption that their clan system was the most 'elementary' observable. The 'elementary' religion is that of totemic clans. It contains the germ of all essential elements of religious thought and life.

Durkheim starts from the proposition that religious experience cannot be purely illusory and must refer to some reality. The reality underlying religious practice is society itself. Religion is 'above all a system of ideas by which individuals represent the society they belong to'. Moreover, 'metaphorical and symbolic as it may be, this representation is not unfaithful'. Certain types of 'collective effervescence' produce religious beliefs, or help to reconfirm beliefs and values of religious relevance. The type of religion is also determined by social structure. For example, the cult of the 'great god' corresponds to the synthesis of all totems and to the unification of the tribe.

Religion also helps to interpret or 'represent' social realities by means of their projection in a special symbolic language. Thus, mythologies 'connect things in order to fix their internal relations, to classify and to systematize them'. They represent reality, as does science. The function of religion is ultimately social integration, which is effected, by 'constantly producing and reproducing the soul of the collectivity and of individuals'. Symbolism is the very condition of social life, since it helps social communication to become communion, that is, 'the fusion of all particular sentiments into one common sentiment'.

Durkheim's religious anthropology has been severely criticized by field researchers, yet without ceasing to inspire scholars concerned with archaic religions. At the time, his sociology of religion had an immediate public appeal in consequence of the conflict then raging between the Church and the Republican State. The study of primitive religion allowed Durkheim to adopt a purely scientific posture, while offering an historical criticism and a sociological evaluation of contemporary religious institutions. (He once described the Catholic Church as a 'sociological monster' (1905b).)

Ethnographic evidence drawn from primitive societies also led to heuristic generalizations concerning the nature of social cohesion, its agents and conditions. Ethnology, moreover, lent itself more easily than other established disciplines (like history or geography) to Durkheimian theorizing, because it was an intellectually weak and institutionally marginal branch of study (see Karady, 1981). Durkheim's theoretical anthropology, together with the work of his followers and debating partners (such as Lévy-Bruhl, Mauss, Hubert and Hertz) contributed decisively to the birth of French academic field anthropology between the two world wars. A later generation of French anthropologists, including Griaule, Métraux, Dumont and Lévi-Strauss, continued to exploit Durkheim's heritage, while critically re-evaluating it. As a consequence of its Durkheimian roots, French social anthropology never broke with the other social sciences, and retained a penchant for high-level generalization.

Victor Karady
Centre National de la Recherche Scientifique
Paris

References

Durkheim, E. (1902), 'Sur le totémism', *L'Année Sociologique*, 5.

Durkheim, E. (1905a), 'Sur l'organisation matrimoniale des sociétés australiennes', *L'Année Sociologique*, 8.

Durkheim, E. (1905b), 'Conséquences religieuses de la séparation de l'Eglise et de l'Etat', republished in E. Durkheim (1975), *Textes*, Paris.

Karady, V. (1981), 'French ethnology and the Durkheimian breakthrough', *Journal of the Anthropological Society of Oxford*, XII.

Lévi-Strauss, C. (1949), *Les Structures élémentaires de la parenté*, Paris. (English edn, *The Elementary Structures of Kinship*, London, 1969.)

Further Reading

Besnard, P. (ed.) (1983), *The Sociological Domain: The Durkheimians and the Founding of French Sociology*, Cambridge.

Lukes, S. (1972), *Émile Durkheim: His Life and Work. A Historical and Critical Study*, London.

Pickering, W. S. F. (ed.) (1975), *Durkheim on Religion. A Selection of Readings with Bibliographies and Introductory Remarks*, London.

See also: *anomie*; *Lévi-Strauss*; *Lévy-Bruhl*; *Mauss*; *social anthropology*; *social structure*; *totemism*.

Dynamics

See Economic Dynamics.

Dyslexia

The general meaning of dyslexia is an impairment of the ability to read. Such impairments can arise in either of two ways: (1) There are cases of people who learned to read normally and reached a normal level of skill in reading, and who subsequently suffered some form of damage to the brain, a consequence of which was a reduction or even loss of their reading ability. This is often referred to as acquired dyslexia. (2) There are cases of people who fail to learn to read adequately in the first place and who never reach a normal level of skill in reading. The condition from which they suffer is known as developmental dyslexia. (An alternative terminology is to use the words *alexia* for acquired dyslexia, and *dyslexia* for development dyslexia.) These are two rather different conditions.

A parallel term is dysgraphia, the general meaning of which is an impairment of the ability to spell (in writing or aloud). This too can be an acquired or a developmental disorder, so that acquired and developmental dysgraphia are distinguished. The terms agraphia and dysgraphia are sometimes used to express this distinction.

A child's intelligence is strongly related to the likelihood that an adequate level of reading will be attained. Therefore there will be children whose reading ability is less than would be expected for their age but is what would be expected for their level of intelligence. In contrast, however, there are also children who are of normal intelligence but who read less well than would be expected for their age and intelligence. The first kind of dyslexia might be thought of as a non-specific concomitant of below-normal intelligence, whilst the second kind is specific to reading and associated abilities, since other intellectual abilities are at a normal level. It has been argued by Rutter and Yule (1975) that this distinction is important. Hence they proposed the term *reading backwardness* to refer to a condition in which poor reading is accompanied by similarly poor performance in other, unrelated, intellectual spheres, and the term *specific reading retardation* to refer to a condition in which only reading and closely related abilities are impaired.

Current progress in understanding the nature of acquired and developmental dyslexia and dysgraphia is being achieved largely through taking seriously the obvious fact that neither reading nor spelling is an indivisible mental activity: each relies on the correct functioning of a considerable number of independent cognitive subsystems. It follows that impairment of any one of the various cognitive subsystems involved in reading will produce some form of dyslexia. The particular form of dyslexia which will be seen will depend upon the particular cognitive subsystem which is imperfect. Theories about which cognitive subsystems actually underlie reading and spelling thus permit one to offer interpretations of the different sets of symptoms manifest in different varieties of dyslexia and dysgraphia.

Max Coltheart
Birkbeck College, University of London ·

Reference
Rutter, M. and Yule, W. (1975), 'The concept of specific reading retardation', *Journal of Child Psychology and Psychiatry*, 16.

Further Reading
Coltheart, M. (1982), 'The psycholinguistic analysis of acquired dyslexias', *Philosophical Transactions of the Royal Society*, B298.
Ellis, A. W. (1984), *Reading, Writing and Dyslexia*, London.
Jorm, A. F. (1983), *The Psychology of Reading and Spelling Disabilities*, London.

E

Eastern Psychology

Eastern psychology is the widely used, though rather unfortunate, label for a rapidly growing field of study that is concerned to translate the insights and techniques of various spiritual and mystical traditions into the languages and mechanisms of contemporary psychology. These traditions are to be found in Europe (mystical Christianity) and the Middle East (Hasidism and Sufism) as well as in India (Buddhism), China (Taoism) and Japan (Zen). And the geographical distinction becomes even more inappropriate as increasing numbers of practitioners from these 'schools' come to settle and to teach in Western Europe and America.

Spiritual traditions are best seen neither as systems of belief nor as codes of conduct, but as practical psychologies and psychotherapies of considerable depth, sophistication and subtlety. Their goal is not to inform but to transform the serious student. Man lives, they all agree, under an almost universal misapprehension – that there is such a thing as an individual Self, and that we all 'have' one, or 'are' one. While to most people it is second nature that 'I' exist as something *separate* from other things, *persisting* through space and time, and at least partially *autonomous* in what 'I' choose and think and do, nevertheless this creation of a boundary is an error. Or rather it is an error if we take it as referring to a 'real' discontinuity in nature rather than as a convention that exists only within thought and speech. Contour lines convey useful information about mountains, but we should not fear lest we trip over them as we climb, nor do we expect Everest to ascend in neat hundred metre steps. The illusion of the Self is of the same sort, and it leads to the same kinds of bizarre actions and expectations – which we do not see as strange only because everybody else is under the same spell. 'The (Self) is an imaginary, false belief which has no corresponding reality . . . It is the source of all the troubles in the world from personal conflicts to wars between nations' (Rahula, 1967). This is what Buddha, Lao Tsu, Rinzai, Jesus, Muhammad and all other disillusioned masters have taught.

Where Eastern psychology goes beyond much of humanistic psychology and psychotherapy, therefore, is that it focuses on what is seen as the *root* of all misery, rather than on its many forms; and its goal is not improvement but insight. Liberation and integration occur not as a result of the effort and intention to change, but simply and automatically through inspecting clearly what is the case and what is not. When one observes closely the conjurer's sleight-of-hand, the magic is dispelled. This unbiased wide-eyed scrutiny of the details of life is *meditation*.

Eastern psychology's fascination lies in its bringing together of the theoretical and the experimental with the experiential. Conceptual advances are being made. Empirical research about the physical and neurophysiological effects of meditation is accumulating. And at the same time the only real proof of the pudding is in the eating: the student is his or her own subject, and what could be of greater interest to me than my self?

Guy Claxton
Chelsea College
University of London

Reference
Rahula, W. (1967), *What the Buddha Taught*, Bedford.

Further Reading
Claxton, G. L. (Swami Anand Ageha) (1981), *Wholly Human: Western and Eastern Visions of the Self and its Perfection*, London.
Wilber, K. (1977), *The Spectrum of Consciousness*, Wheaton, Ill.

Ecology

The concept of ecology finds its immediate historical origins in Darwin's 'web of life', although such a non-Aristotelian view of the relationship between entities had been increasingly common since the eighteenth century. The term itself *(ökologie)* we owe to Ernst Haeckel (1834–1919). By the opening years of the twentieth century, crude generalizations and theory had been translated into empirical studies, beginning with the natural history of plants.

Ecology might briefly be described as the study of relations between living species, associations of different species, and their physical and biotic surroundings through the exchange of calories, material and information. As such it has been centrally concerned with the concept of adaptation and with all properties having a direct and measurable effect on the demography, development, behaviour and spatiotemporal position of an organism. Within this frame-work, the main preoccupations of contemporary biological ecology have been with population dynamics, energy transfer, systems modelling, nutrient cycles, environmental degradation and conservation.

In the social sciences, the concept of ecology in the strict sense was introduced first into human geography, via biogeography, and many geographers soon came to redefine their subject in explicitly ecological terms. By the 1930s, the Chicago school of urban sociology under the tutelage of R. E. Park and E. W. Burgess was describing its conceptual baggage as human ecology. Such an epithet was claimed to be justified on the grounds that analogies were drawn directly from the biological lexicon to explain spatial relationships, such as 'succession' for the movement of different class groups through urban areas. For a short time Chicago ecology was extremely influential, but it finally floundered on its own naive analogies, crude empiricism and functionalist inductivism.

A number of the most fruitful applications of ecological approaches in the human and social sciences have been associated with anthropology, This has been so despite the dual intellectual dominance of Emile Durkheim (1858–1917) and Franz Boas (1858–1942) during the first three decades of the present century which had thoroughly crushed a nineteenth century concern with environmental determinism. But although environmental issues were considered for the most part peripheral, and the environment not accorded a determinant role, there have been a number of studies dealing with environmental interactions in this tradition. Boas's own work on the central Eskimo might be mentioned, as well as that of Mauss and Beuchat on the same subject. The British school also provides us with a few studies of environmental interaction (e.g. Evans-Pritchard, 1940), although, in line with the Durkheimian viewpoint, environmental variables are characteristically regarded as setting only the outer limits to the ways in which humans might manipulate resources. The general theoretical position is set out clearly in Forde's (1934) *Habitat, Economy and Society*.

The first really explicit use of the concept of ecology in anthropology is found in the work of Julian Steward during the thirties (Steward and Murphy, 1977). In Steward's theory the concept of cultural adaptation becomes paramount, and the key adaptive strategies of a particular culture are located in an infrastructural core of social institutions and technical arrangements directly concerned with food-getting activities. The recognition of distinctive adaptive strategies provided the basis for the delineation of cultural types, which Steward maintained evolved multilineally, rather than in the unilinear fashion subscribed to by many nine-teenth-century thinkers. Steward's work has been very influential (and has found admirers in other disci-

plines), but his theory of cultural ecology entailed an interpretation of the concept of adaptation, together with a fundamental division between organic and super-organic levels of explanation and between a core of key adaptive traits and a neutral periphery, which more recent writers have been inclined to reject.

Advances within biological ecology linked to the notion of ecosystem, the empirical measurement of energy flow and the employment of the language of cybernetics and systems theory, led during the 1960s to a new formulation of ecological problems in the social sciences; in archaeology (Clarke, 1972), geography (Stoddart, 1965), and also in anthropology. The prominence given by Steward to the superorganic level of organization was passed over in favour of a view of human behaviour in many respects functionally equivalent to that of other animals. The description of ecological interactions became more sophisticated, involving computations of carrying-capacity, estimates of energy intake, output and efficiency for different groups and activities. There also developed an interest in the way in which cultural institutions might serve to regulate certain systems of which human popu-lations are part. All of these trends are demonstrated in the seminal work of Rappaport (1968), undertaken on a Maring clan from Highland New Guinea.

Sustained interest in the theoretical problems of systems approaches, plus an increasing number of detailed empirical analyses of particular cases has, however, bred scepticism concerning simplisitic notions of adaptation and the more extreme prop-osition that certain kinds of small-scale society have built-in mechanisms for maintaining environmental balance through homeostasis (Bennett, 1976). Recent work has paid more attention to how societies actually cope with environmental hazards, to detailed descrip-tions of overall subsistence strategies, to the perception of environmental resources, and to the articulation between economic and ecological organization. It has also tended to stress positive (rather than negative) feedback, rekindled an interest in the evolution of social and ecological systems, and generally moved towards more explicitly historical approaches. In this latter area it has drawn in particular on demography and on the French Annales school. For a review of the literature see Ellen (1982).

The other major (and somewhat independent) impact of ecological concepts in the social sciences has been in relation to political environmentalism. Under the influence of people such as Garrett Hardin and Kenneth Boulding, economic thinking has been placed in a broader biospheric context, and the 'growth model' rejected both in relation to advanced industrial soci-eties (capitalist and collectivist) and underdeveloped ones. Practical concern for environmental degradation, the profligate use of finite resources, the calculated advantages of 'alternative' technologies and worries for genetic conservation have spawned theories of under-development which draw upon the conceptual apparatus of modern ecology and focus on environmental interactions. Some writing in this vein is distinctively utopian, some is concerned with practical matters of implementing specific controls, and some with seeking to modify the existing world-system through retaining capitalist relations of production. Others seek a rapprochement between Marxism and environmentalism (Riddell, 1981; Sandbach, 1980).

R. F. Ellen
University of Kent

References

Bennett, J. W. (1976), *The Ecological Transition: Cultural Anthropology and Human Adaptation*, New York.

Clarke, D. L. (1972), 'Models and paradigms in contemporary archaeology', in D. L. Clarke (ed.), *Models in Archaeology*, London.

Ellen, R. F. (1982), *Environment, Subsistence and System: The Ecology of Small-Scale Social Formations*, Cambridge.

Evans-Pritchard, E. E. (1940), *The Nuer*, Oxford.

Rappaport, R. A. (1968), *Pigs for the Ancestors: Ritual in the Ecology of a New Guinea People*, New Haven.

Riddell, R. (1981), *Ecodevelopment*, London.

Sandbach, F. (1980), *Environment, Ideology and Policy*, Oxford.

Steward, J. C. and Murphy, B. E. (eds) (1977), *Evolution and Ecology: Essays in Social Transformation*, Urbana, Ill.

Stoddart, D. R. (1965), 'Geography and the ecological approach; the ecosystem as a geographic principle and method'. *Geography*, 50.

See also: *geography; population and resources.*

Econometrics

As the main concern of economics has shifted away from description and institutional analysis, economists have sought to quantify the relationships underpinning their models more precisely. In part this concern has been prompted by the desire to forecast the future behaviour of economic variables – for example, the response of aggregate consumption expenditure to changes in disposable income, or the effect of income tax changes on labour supply and the willingness of individuals to participate in the labour market. For such quantitative forecasts to have any value, it is essential that the empirical relationships on which the predictions rest should be relatively stable, both in terms of their structural characteristics and their coefficient values. On the other hand, it is less important that the empirical relationships should conform to the specification of a fully articulated economic model of the phenomenon under consideration,

since, in practice, 'naive' models may yield good forecasts and it may be quite impossible to observe the variables or to estimate the parameters in an elaborate model. There is, however, another reason for quantifying economic relationships which necessarily implies that careful model specification is essential if the resulting empirical estimates are to be of any value. This arises when the economist wishes to use the estimates to test hypotheses about the relative importance of different factors or economic variables which simultaneously determine some particular aspect of economic behaviour.

These distinct uses of quantitative economic relationships – i.e. forecasting and the investigation of economic hypotheses – have meant that econometrics, which is the branch of economics and statistics devoted to the empirical estimation of economic models, has developed in a number of quite separate directions. This tendency has been encouraged by the nature of the data available to econometricians. Much of classical statistical theory was developed for the purpose of making inferences from data collected in controlled experiments, typically involving some kind of randomized design in which all combinations of variables have an equal – or, at least, a known – probability of occurring. Economists must be satisfied either with time series data produced by governments or other bodies, or with responses to sample surveys of a cross-section of the population during some period of time. Because their data is not experimentally generated, econometricians have been obliged to develop special techniques to deal with the characteristics of different types of data. For example, the user of aggregate time series data must always check for the possibility that the errors about a particular equation are systematically correlated over time – this is called serial correlation. For the user of cross-section data, there is the consistent problem that the sample of observations may be non-random because, for example, self-selection means that certain types of individuals either refused to answer the questions or were excluded from the sample.

These and many other similar considerations mean that it is never simple to interpret data concerning economic relationships. Since the classical statistical assumptions rarely hold, the econometrician is unable to separate questions concerning the validity of his statistical assumptions from issues relating to the specification of the model which he is estimating. As a result, the progress of empirical economic work has been characterized by interlocking disputes about econometric methodology and the relevance of the equations modelling aspects of economic behaviour. This means that it is often difficult to set up decisive econometric tests of particular hypotheses, especially as the underlying theoretical models may be specified in terms of variables which can, at best, only be approximately measured in practice. Nonetheless, econometric work has frequently prompted economists to reformulate or extend their models, either because the estimated equations had a poor forecasting record or because their explanatory power was rather low.

Historically, the development of econometric techniques has run parallel with changes in the availability of economic data and in the amount of computing power. Econometrics began to establish itself as a distinct discipline in the late 1920s and early 1930s – the Econometric Society was founded in 1931 with help from Alfred Cowles who was interested in forecasting stock market price movements – but it grew most rapidly in the years after the Second World War. This was because the political commitment to full employment using Keynesian policies prompted governments to monitor macroeconomic developments much more closely. The availability of time series data on aggregate economic variables, and interest in forecasting aggregate demand encouraged econometric work on the relationships which comprise a simple Keynesian model of the economy. Two elements of such a model attracted particular attention: (1) the consumption function in which consumption (or saving) is linked to disposable income, and (2) the investment function which expresses aggregate investment in terms of the growth of aggregate demand (or production), interest rates, and other variables. While there are a number of competing formulations of the consumption function, econometric work on this has always appeared to be much more successful than that dealing with the investment function. It was found to be very difficult to forecast aggregate investment reliably, and estimated relationships differ significantly between time periods so that even after more than thirty years of work there is no general agreement on the best specification for this relationship.

Interest in making forecasts of individual components of effective demand gradually evolved into the estimation of large macroeconometric models designed to forecast the overall macroeconomic behaviour of particular economies, as well as to investigate the implications of changes in aggregate variables for specific sectors of the economy or categories of expenditure. Work of this kind was initiated by Klein in the early 1950s, but by the late 1960s advances in data and computing power had allowed econometricians to compile and simulate large-scale macroeconometric models. Despite considerable scepticism about the reliability of the forecasts produced by these models, their use has become an indispensable part of the process of making macroeconomic policy in all developed countries, so that argument tends now to revolve around the merits of competing models rather than about the value of making such forecasts. As macroeconomic models have become larger and more specialized, it has also become increasingly difficult to

understand the factors which determine the way in which they behave as a whole. Hence, during the 1970s, econometricians started to focus more on the properties of complete models rather than on the performance of individual equations within the model.

Another application of econometrics that has been developing since the 1950s combines the interest in forecasting with the scope provided by econometric models for testing propositions derived from theoretical models. This is the estimation of single, or systems of, demand equations using either aggregate data on prices and consumption patterns or information collected in surveys of household expenditure. Initially, the main purpose of this work was to estimate income and price elasticities of demand for specific goods. This remains an important consideration, but theoretical work on consumer behaviour has shown that, if consumer expenditure decisions are derived from some kind of maximizing model, it is necessary to impose quite stringent conditions on the specification and parameter values of systems of demand equations. These restrictions include homogeneity in income and prices, symmetry of cross-price effects, and negative substitution effects. The results of testing these restrictions illustrate the difficulties of using econometric work to test theoretical models. Most studies have found that some or all of these restrictions are rejected by the data, but the response of economists has not been to discard the maximizing model of consumer behaviour but rather to investigate more elaborate specifications of the demand equations until the restrictions are not rejected. It is never possible to test the general restrictions implied by theoretical analysis except by adopting specific functional forms for the equations under investigation, so that statistical evidence against some hypothesis may be interpreted as implying either that the functional specification is inadequate, or that the basic theoretical model is wrong. In cases such as demand analysis, where the underlying theory is highly developed, econometricians have inevitably tended to regard their results as tests of specification rather than of general theoretical propositions. Only by the accumulation of negative evidence for a wide range of specifications is it possible to regard such work as undermining prior theoretical assumptions.

The availability of large-scale cross-section surveys – and of panel data sets in which individuals/households are interviewed at regular intervals over a period of years – has prompted the recent development of econometric techniques to deal with qualitative or limited dependent variables. These are variables which take on discrete values – e.g. 0 or 1 corresponding to 'no' or 'yes' responses to certain choices – or for which the range of permissible values is limited – e.g. it is not possible to work for a negative number of hours. The estimation of such microeconometric models is typically much more expensive than for classical regression models, and in most cases the amount of data to be handled is many times greater than for macroeconometric work. Hence, this work would have been impossible without the great improvements in computer hardware and software since the late 1960s. The principal applications of these techniques have been in the area of labour economics to the analysis of choices concerning labour supply and participation, education, job movement, retirement and migration. The results of this work have generated much interest among economists working on other topics so that the range of applications may be expected to continue to increase rapidly as also will the techniques of analysis and estimation.

Econometrics has developed to the extent that it dominates applied work in most branches of economics. Indeed, even economic historians use econometric analysis – often under the title 'cliometrics' – in discussing issues such as the impact of railways on US or British economic growth, and of technical change in both agriculture and industry. The major improvements in the volume and quality of economic statistics and in the availability of large-scale sample surveys which stimulated many econometric developments during the period 1950–80 are not likely to be repeated. Thus, future developments in the subject will necessarily focus on methods of extracting more information from the data which is available. In practice, this will mean that applied economists and econometricians will have to devote more attention to the theoretical and statistical specification of their models in order to clarify the assumptions underpinning tests of particular hypotheses. Fortunately, the speed of technical change in computing is such that the cost of investigating more complex models, which has been prohibitive in the past, will not be a significant consideration in the future.

Gordon Hughes
University of Cambridge

Further Reading

Griliches, Z. (1983), *Handbook of Econometrics*, vols I and III, Amsterdam.

Harvey, A. C. (1981), *The Econometric Analysis of Time Series*, Oxford.

Maddala, G. S. (1983), *Limited–Dependent and Qualitative Variables in Econometrics*, Cambridge.

Pindyck, R. S. and Rubinfeld, D. (1981), *Econometric Models and Economic Forecasts*, 2nd edn, New York.

See also: *cliometrics; macroeconomics; microeconomics*.

Economic Anthropology

The field of economic anthropology falls somewhere between economic history and economics proper. Like economic history, it is a descriptive discipline in which other economies and their transformations are carefully documented; like economics proper, it is a field in which competing theories of human behaviour are elaborated and intensely debated.

The substantive differences among exotic economies have been recorded by anthropologists for more than sixty years. Systems of production, for example, exhibit great variation. Considerable attention has been given to hunting and gathering, but anthropologists also have examined forms of pastoralism and patterns of agriculture, including slash-and-burn, terrace, and irrigation systems. Trade, exchange and distribution take many forms. For example, in capitalist economies distribution occurs through market pricing of wage, profit and rent, but this is not a universal custom. In some societies distribution is carried out by dividing animals joint by joint and allocating each to specific social roles. The link between economic processes and social formations also is highly variable. In the simplest case all economic functions may be performed within a single household unit; but usually larger groupings such as lineages, bands and villages are involved. Sometimes production will involve units at one level of the society, but property control, distribution and consumption may bring into play other social aggregations. A descriptive and analytic task for economic anthropologists, therefore, is to show how the several economic functions are fitted together within the social organization of a particular society.

Most exotic economies are now undergoing change due to penetration by the world market system. In recent years, therefore, anthropologists have been studying shifting conceptions of wealth, labour and gender, as well as the ways nonmonetary economies become reorganized when brought into contact with systems based on the use of cash and arranged according to different principles.

The very fact that differences exist in the ways people gain and use their livelihood poses questions about the economic models that anthropologists employ. Can we, for example, extend Western economic categories to the analysis of other cultures? What assumptions are involved? Is anthropology a testing ground for the development of universal theories of the economy?

Many economic anthropologists use theories derived from neoclassical economics. Their central assumption is that actors choose among alternatives to maximize preferences or utility; the model has a rationalist basis. For example, input-output or production functions are sometimes employed to show how pastoralists produce cattle or foragers select game. Similarly, a neoclassical analysis of bridewealth transactions will focus on the exchange rate of women and cattle and the ways in which it is responsive to conditions of supply and demand.

Institutionalists, whose approach is more empiricist, pay greater attention to the organizational differences that are found among economies. Karl Polanyi (1968) suggested that land and labour comprise the bedrock for all economies; but these underlying elements, he argued, are institutionally organized according to different patterns of exchange. Polanyi isolated three such patterns: reciprocity, redistribution and market haggling. According to the Polanyi view, the analyst should try to reveal the connection between the substratum of land and labour and the visible but differing modes of exchange. In the case of bridewealth, an institutionalist might attempt to show how the exchange is linked to land and labour, yet is unlike other transactions in society. In nonmarket economies, each exchange is embedded in a distinct social context; different patterns of exchange are not reducible, one to another, through the solvent of the market.

Marxists commence with the assumption that the human is a material maker, that he produces things of value only through labouring. The organization of this capacity provides the base for the superstructural parts of social life. On this view, there exists a relation between modes of exploiting labour and other sectors of society, such as religion, ideology or kinship. In the case of bridewealth, for example, neo-Marxists have emphasized that control of cattle by elder males sustains their position of power and their ability to extract labour from younger males as well as females.

Despite their differences, the three models resemble one another in a crucial respect. Each starts from a supposed core feature of human behaviour and attempts to show how the ethnographic data can be fitted to or derived from it. The three models continuously reproduce their own assumptions in the exotic materials.

One alternative to this style of analysis is to assume that a people model their own actions just as Western economists model our behaviour. Exotic lives and thoughts, which are a residue of the past and a plan for the future, constitute a model for ethnographers to examine. Exotic economic actions have their own meanings. According to this view the task is to 'understand' other economic patterns rather than 'explain' how well they fit a supposed pan-cultural characteristic. For example, in many societies where bridewealth is found, women and cattle are constructed as metaphors of one another; cattle both are and are not women. Because both are constructed as being like each other but unlike other 'goods', they are mutually and exclusively exchanged. Similarly, other wealth items and economic practices have their particular formulations. According to such a constructivist view, the economy is a symbolic sphere filled with cultural information. Therefore, Western assumptions and categories such as maximization, exploitation, production and consumption must be put in abeyance in favour of the particular constructions which the ethnographer encounters and tries to translate to his

Western audience. This final approach is more distinctly anthropological than the other three, which derive from one or another form of modern economics; it is not, however, widely used.

Stephen Gudeman
University of Minnesota

Reference
Polanyi, K. (1968), *Primitive, Archaic and Modern Economies*, Boston.

Further Reading
Sahlins, M. (1972), *Stone Age Economics*, Chicago.
See also: *division of labour by sex*; *exchange*; *hunters and gatherers*; *money, primitive*; *pastoralism*; *peasants*; *trade and markets, anthropology of*.

Economic Development

The central question in the study of economic development has turned out to be 'in what *precisely* does the economic development of a society consist?' For many years, the accepted view was that the prolonged and steady increase of national income was an adequate indicator of economic development. This was held to be so because it was believed that such an increase could only be sustained over long periods if specific economic (and social) processes were at work.

These processes, which were supposed to be basic to development, can be briefly summarized as follows:
(1) The share of investment in national expenditure rises, leading to a rise in capital stock per person employed;
(2) The structure of national production changes, becoming more diversified as industry, utilities and services take a larger relative share, compared with agriculture and other forms of primary production;
(3) The foreign trade sector expands relative to the whole economy, particularly as manufactured exports take a larger share in an increased export total;
(4) The government budget rises relative to national income, as the government undertakes expanded commitments to construct economic and social infrastructure.

Accompanying these structural changes in the economy, major changes of social structure also occur:
(5) The population expands rapidly as death rates fall in advance of birth rates. Thereafter, a demographic transition occurs in which improved living conditions in turn bring the birth rate down, to check the rate of overall population increase;
(6) The population living in urban areas changes from a small minority to a large majority;
(7) Literacy, skills and other forms of educational attainment are spread rapidly through the population.

This conceptualization of economic development as the interrelation of capital accumulation, industrialization, government growth, urbanization and education can still be found in many contemporary writers. It seems to make most sense when one has very long runs of historical statistics to look back over. Then the uniformities which this view implies are most likely to be visible. One doubt has always been whether generalizing retrospectively from statistics is not an ahistorical, rather than a truly historical, approach. It almost always presupposes some 'theory of history' which links the past to the future in an unsubtly mechanistic and deterministic manner.

Another major doubt about the adequacy of the view of development described in 1–7 above centres around the question of income distribution. If the basic development processes described above either do not make the distribution of income more equal, or actually worsen the degree of inequality for more than a short period, some theorists would argue that economic development has not taken place. They prefer to distinguish economic growth from economic development which, by their definition, cannot leave the majority of the population as impoverished as they originally were. For them, measures of growth and structural change must be complemented by measures of improvement in the quality of everyday life for most people.

Such measures can be of various kinds. They can focus on the availability of basic needs goods – food, shelter, clean water, clothing and household utensils. Or they can focus on life expectation tables and statistics of morbidity. The availability and cost of educational opportunities are also relevant. Although the distribution of income may be a good starting point, the distribution of entitlements (to use a concept expounded by A. K. Sen (1981)) to consume of all kinds is the terminus. The difficulty here is clearly with weighting all of the different indices involved to arrive at a single measure of the degree of development in this extended sense. Perhaps it cannot be done; and perhaps, if policy rather than international league tables is our main concern, this failure is not very important.

Similar kinds of consideration arise when one examines the role of political liberty in economic development. Is rapid growth and structural change induced by an oppressive, authoritarian regime true development? Those who object to the 'costs' of the development strategies of the USSR or the People's Republic of China do not think so. From a libertarian standpoint, they refuse to accept the standard account of 'economic development' as sufficiently comprehensive.

These wider concerns with the meaning of 'development' inevitably influence the many debates about how economic development can be actively promoted. Disagreement has focused on the following issues:
(1) Whether the government should confine itself to its so-called 'traditional functions' and the creation of incentives for development by private enterprise, or whether some overall co-ordination through economic planning, plus an expanded sphere for government investment in manufacturing industry is required.
(2) How much emphasis should be placed on the creation of physical capital, compared with human capital – the education and good health of the labour force. Where physical capital is involved, how should the investments be phased? In a single big push, so that they create demand for each other (as recommended by Rosenstein-Rodan, 1943)? Or, as shortages and bottlenecks reveal the need for each (Hirschman's (1958) unbalanced growth)?
(3) Should greater priority in investment be given to a particular sector of the economy – the capital goods sector (suggested by Maurice Dobb, 1955) or agriculture (as argued by Lipton, 1977)? Or should investments be selected, regardless of sector, solely in accordance with a calculation of their social profitability, the criterion for the appraisal of projects devised by Little and Mirrlees (1974)?
(4) What role should the foreign sector play in development? Has isolation from the world economy triggered off economic development, as is argued of Meiji Japan (by Baran, 1973) and Latin America during the Depression of the 1930s (by Frank, 1969)? Or do countries like Taiwan and South Korea, which deliberately organize their economy to be competitive in world markets, develop faster? The utility of foreign financial and technical assistance from governments and international agencies and foreign private investment through multinational companies is also debated in this context, with strong views being held both for and against, often on flimsy empirical evidence.

Somewhat greater agreement exists on the facts of recent economic development than on the methods of bringing it about. That many poor countries have experienced much economic growth and structural change since 1945 is widely accepted. A few still claim that growth in developed countries actually causes increased poverty in other, poorer countries. This suggests a trend of global polarization of income and wealth, combined with the immiserization of the poorest people/countries. A weaker version of this thesis is that there is an ever-widening gap between richest and poorest, which can arise when the welfare of the poorest is constant or rising. Even this weaker version is controversial, on the grounds that countries are ranged evenly along a spectrum of wealth/poverty, and thus to split this spectrum into two groups of 'rich' and 'poor' in order to compare group statistics of economic performance can be somewhat arbitrary. In fact, the measured growth rates of 'developed' and 'developing' countries over the last thirty odd years show relatively small differences and ones that may well lie within the margins of error that attach to such estimates.

But, although the overall record of economic growth at least need not give cause for deep gloom, certain geographical regions do appear to have markedly unfavourable development prospects. Such regions include sub-Saharan Africa and South Asia, and parts of Central and South America. The reasons for their poor prospects vary from place to place. Some are held back by severe pressure of population on cultivable land; some by inability to generate indigenous sources of appropriate technical progress; some by the persistence of intense social and political conflict; some by unenlightened policy making; and some by the continuing failure to evolve a world-wide financial system which does not tend to amplify the inherent unevenness (over place and time) of economic development.

J. F. J. Toye
University College of Swansea
University of Wales

References
Baran, P. (1973), *The Political Economy of Growth*, Harmondsworth.
Dobb, M. (1955), *On Economic Theory and Socialism*, London.
Frank, A. G. (1969), *Latin America: Underdevelopment or Revolution?*, New York.
Hirschman, A. (1958), *The Strategy of Economic Development*, New Haven.
Lipton, M. (1977), *Why Poor People Stay Poor*, London.
Little, I. M. D. and Mirrlees, J. A. (1974), *Project Appraisal and Planning for Developing Countries*, London.
Rosenstein-Rodan, P. N. (1943), 'Problems of industrialisation of Eastern and South-Eastern Europe', *Economic Journal*, June-September.
Sen, A. K. (1981), *Poverty and Famines; An Essay on Entitlement and Deprivation*, Oxford.

Further Reading
Kitching, G. (1982), *Development and Underdevelopment in Historical Perspective*, London.
Little, I. M. D. (1983), *Economic Development: Theory, Policy and International Relations*, New York.
See also: *aid; development studies; economic growth; technical assistance.*

Economic Dynamics

Comte's 'social dynamics' appears to have stimulated J. S. Mill's original distinction between statics, the theory of equilibrium, and dynamics, the theory of the laws of the progress of society. On this definition the classical theories of Smith, Ricardo and Marx represent the first economic dynamics. By 1890, however, J. M. Keynes reported that 'the main body of economic science' was concerned with statics. Analogy with physical mechanics displaced Comte's ideas, and the great neoclassical economists (Clark, Marshall, Walras) all promised, but never produced, dynamic theories. Marshall even suggested a biological analogy might be more appropriate for dynamics. The problem was important, for the mechanical analogy not only implied use of deduction in place of the induction of the evolutionary (or biological) approach; it also implied a new definition of dynamics (as in Samuelson's 'correspondence principle') as the stability properties of equilibrium.

Keynes's *General Theory* (1936) interrupted development of the dynamic implications of lagged relationships in quantitative business cycle models (Kalecki, Tinbergen, Frisch), while von Neumann's theory of an expanding general economic equilibrium did not create interest until its post-war publication in English. Hicks (1939) defined dynamics as the study of 'dated' quantities and 'the way changes in these dates affect the relations between factors and products', but his static 'temporary equilibrium' created most interest. Harrod's (1939) 'fundamental relation': $G = s/C$ (where s is the ratio of saving to income and C the ratio of an extra pound invested to the additional income it generates), used to explain trend growth rates had more success. If s, determined by households, generates growth in demand which satisfies entrepreneurs' expected returns on new investment, G is a 'warranted' rate, for it will be maintained (provided it does not exceed a maximum, 'natural' rate given by population and productivity growth). Comparison of its actual and warranted rates indicates an economy's future movement. Domar's post-war analysis of whether short-run Keynesian demand management could assure full employment over time produced a similar equation.

In the 1950s Harrod-Domar theory was extended by the Cambridge School (e.g. Robinson, Kaldor, Pasinetti) who suggested that if s were an average of savings propensities from wages and profits, then the distribution of income adjusts to make saving equal to the rate of investment implied by the rate of growth, which thus determined distribution and the rate of return to capital. Neoclassical economists (e.g. Swan, Solow, Meade) argued that if relative prices affect the proportions of capital to labour used in production, C will be affected, via an aggregate production function linking output to aggregate capital and labour inputs. Here input prices adjust capital intensity to the available savings given the rate of growth. The differences in the explanation of distribution and in the role of aggregate capital in the two approaches reflected different conceptions of dynamics which surfaced in the 'Cambridge Controversies'.

In the mid-1970s both Hicks and Lowe attempted, without success, to bridge these differences by specifying a 'traverse' adjustment path in terms of an 'Austrian' time-pattern of inputs. These debates suggest that economics still has no accepted definition or theory of dynamics.

J. A. Kregel
University of Groningen

References
Domar, E. D. (1946), 'Capital expansion, rate of growth and employment', *Econometrica*, 14.
Harrod, R. F. (1939), 'An essay in dynamic theory', *Economic Journal*, 49.
Hicks, J. R. (1939), *Value and Capital*, Oxford.
Hicks, J. R. (1973), *Capital and Time*, Oxford.
Keynes, J. M. (1890), *The Scope and Method of Political Economy*, London.
Keynes, J. M. (1936), *The General Theory of Employment, Interest and Money*, London.
Lowe, A. (1976), *The Path of Economic Growth*, London.
Marshall, A. (1925), 'Mechanical and biological analogies in economics', in A. C. Pigou (ed.), *Memorials of Alfred Marshall*, London.
Mill, J. S. (1848), *Principles of Political Economy*, London.
Samuelson, P. A. (1947), *Foundations of Economic Analysis*, Cambridge, Mass.
Von Neumann, J. (1945–6), 'A model of general economic equilibrium', *Review of Economic Studies*, 13.

Further Reading
Jones, H. (1975), *Modern Theories of Economic Growth*, London.
Kregel, J. A. (1972), *Theory of Economic Growth*, London.
See also: *economic growth*; *equilibrium*.

Economic Efficiency

A machine is more efficient if it generates more power or more product for a given amount of fuel or input. Although this more obvious notion of efficiency is contained within the concept of economic efficiency, it plays only an intermediate role inasmuch as the latter addresses itself broadly to the goal of bringing the limited resources of society into proper relation with the desired ends. The ends themselves are expressed through the pattern of social valuation or demand for finished goods, which pattern is determined in part through the market mechanisms of the private sector of the economy and in part through the political mechanisms that control expenditures in the public sector.

There are heuristic advantages in decomposing the concept of economic efficiency into three components, the first two being subsidiary to and subsumed in the third.

(1) *Exchange Efficiency* is increased if, beginning with a collection of goods divided arbitrarily among a number of persons, the exchange of goods between them makes at least one person better off and nobody worse off (hereafter abridged to '"everyone" better off'). Such an economic change is said to meet an actual Pareto improvement.

Provided the exchange of goods incurred no costs, the process of exchange would culminate in a set of relative prices that were common to all. This resulting situation, one in which no opportunity remains for making 'everyone' better off, is described as an 'exchange optimum'.

(2) *Production Efficiency* is increased if, with given supplies of the factors of production, the factor proportions used in the various goods are altered so as to produce more of 'every good'. Once all such opportunities are exhausted, a 'production optimum' obtains.

An economy where each firm minimizes the production costs of its goods in the presence of a common set of factor prices is sufficient to realize a production optimum.

(3) *Top-Level Efficiency*: Allowing that exchange and production optima are met, as a result of which society is faced with a 'production frontier' of alternative collections of goods – each collection associated with a particular set of goods and factor prices – a movement from an existing collection of goods to another, in consequence of which 'everyone' *could* be made better off (by a costless redistribution of the goods), identifies an increase in top-level efficiency. Such increase in efficiency may properly be described as a *potential* Pareto improvement.

A sufficient condition for a movement from an existing goods collection (I) to a new collection (II) to meet a potential Pareto improvement (or increase in top-level efficiency) is that, valued at the goods prices of the I collection, the goods contained in the II collection have a higher aggregate value.

A situation in which all opportunities for top-level efficiency increases are exhausted is one described as a 'Top-Level Optimum'. A sufficient condition for the existence of top-level optimum is that at the prevailing set of goods prices no other collection of goods (producible with the given supplies of factors) has a higher aggregate value.

It must be borne in mind, however, that there can be any number of possible top-level optimum collections, each associated with a particular set of goods prices, which in general alter with changes in taste and with redistributions of purchasing power. Thus an existing top-level optimum assumes given tastes and a given distribution of purchasing power.

One last point in this connection: since the range of alternative collections of goods along a large part of the production frontier qualify – in virtue of all conceivable patterns of distribution of purchasing power – as potential optima, some economists have embraced the notion of a 'social welfare function' in order to rank these alternative possible optima and, consequently, to identify a 'best' optimum or 'optimum optimorum'. While the idea has formal appeal, it has no 'operational value' – no acceptable way having been discovered for identifying such a position.

Ezra J. Mishan
London

Further Reading

Graaf, J. de V. (1957), *Theoretical Welfare Economics*, Cambridge.

Mishan, E. J. (1981), *Introduction to Normative Economics*, Oxford.

Winch, D. M. (1971), *Analytic Welfare Economics*, Harmondsworth.

See also: *welfare economics*.

Economic Externalities

Economic externalities are (positive or negative) goods or services generated by an economic activity whose costs or benefits do not fall upon the decision-taking agent. Pollution is a leading and important example. They may, alternatively, be thought of as residuals, the difference between 'social' and 'private' costs and benefits. The divergence was first popularized and elaborated by Pigou in *The Economics of Welfare* (1920) and is believed to be a major reason for market failure: for example, the market will over-produce goods with high external costs. For that reason a main principle of cost-benefit analysis is that *all* costs and benefits, no matter to whom they accrue, should be included. Popular discussion rightly emphasizes external costs associated with production, but one should not entirely ignore positive production effects (apples and honey) or effects on the consumption side, either positive (attractive dress) or negative (radio noise).

Various policies are, in principle, available for dealing with externalities. For example, the extent of an activity may be *regulated*, as in the case of the discharge of industrial effluent into estuaries. Using partial equilibrium analysis the regulation should set the amount of discharge at an 'optimum', that is, where marginal social cost and benefit are equal to one another. This is, of course, very difficult to calculate, so rough rules of thumb are used instead. Economists often argue for the direct use of *pricing*: the agent is charged a tax (or paid a subsidy) equal to the value of the externality at the margin. The congestion tax is an example of this. Such taxes and subsidies are referred to as Pigouvian: they are intended to intern-

alize the externality. Internalization may also come about spontaneously by the *merger* of two units inflicting large externalities upon one another (as in industrial integration).

The tax-subsidy solution is often objected to on the ground that it is open to injured parties to bring an action in tort against the offending agent. If agents know this to be the case, they will take expected compensation for damages into account and externalities will automatically be internalized. On this view not only would Pigouvian taxes not be needed but they would, if imposed, lead to an over-restriction of activity (Coase, 1960). Property rights are seen to be crucial, as they define rights to compensation: defenders of the market system therefore argue that externalities do not constitute market failure provided that property rights are adequately delineated. The direction of compensation naturally depends on the initial distribution of legal rights.

The alternative solutions are closely related to one another. Take the case of a major oil spillage which fouls beaches and destroys fishing and wildlife. If spillages are to be 'banned' the fine must be at least equal to the Pigouvian tax. If there is to be a legal contest, it will have to be fought between states and oil companies rather than through improvised groups of holiday-makers, fishermen and wildlife enthusiasts. And fines/compensation must not give an outcome which is totally unreasonable in relation to the optimum (possibly, though not certainly, zero) amount of spillage.

David Collard
University of Bath

Reference

Coase, R. H. (1960), 'The problem of social cost', *Journal of Law and Economics*, 3.

Further Reading

Pearce, D. W. (ed.) (1978), *The Valuation of Social Cost*, London.

Economic Geography

Economic geography is a discipline that deals with economic phenomena in a spatial context, examining the interrelationships of man and the environment as mediated by the economic processes of production, exchange, and consumption.

Modern economic geography is a fusion of three strands of scholarship. The oldest of these is the compilation of factual accounts of where useful commodities are produced and how they are traded, information that was widely regarded as of major importance in the nineteenth-century days of colonial empire. *The Handbook of Commercial Geography* by G. G. Chisholm, first published in 1889 and running to many editions over almost a century, is probably the best known of these writings; much of the work of Stamp was in the same tradition. These and other authors pioneered the systematic collation of descriptive data about the distribution of economic activities, primarily the production of agricultural, mineral and industrial goods. The second and third strands represent attempts to provide explanatory frameworks for the mass of descriptive data. In 1935 Buchanan applied the tools of formal economic analysis to the dairy industry of New Zealand, but it was not until 1966 that the first geographical text was published which systematically applied neoclassical economic ideas to the explanation of geographical patterns of production and exchange. The third strand can be described as the discovery by geographers of the locational models for agriculture, published by von Thünen in 1826, A. Weber's 1909 systematization of industrial location decisions, and seminal work in the same idiom by the geographer Christaller on models of central places, published in 1933.

Economic geography came of age in the 1950s and 1960s. The single most important problem addressed has been the analysis of industrial and office location and especially changes in the distribution of firms. What causes some regions to specialize in the manufacture of steel, vehicles, textiles or electronic goods? To answer this question, it is necessary to examine the manufacturing requirements – raw materials, fuel, labour, research information, etc. – and the markets for the products, as well as the transport needs. If entrepreneurs were fully rational 'economic men', they would compile the relevant cost surfaces and calculate the location which would maximize their profits. In practice, other considerations necessarily carry some weight. A first question, therefore, is to determine what the optimal location pattern should be, and several practical algorithms have been devised for this purpose. Real-world patterns diverge from this ideal, and a major theme has been to examine the reasons for this divergence. This leads to an examination of the actual decision process for location choices and the factors that weigh with managers. Empirical evidence shows that larger firms are more 'rational' in their location choices and are willing to move longer distances than small firms, which have fewer resources to devote to a careful evaluation of opportunities. In the last decade or two, a widespread trend has been observed for manufacturing firms to leave the larger conurbations in favour of smaller cities and even rural areas. Problems of space and traffic congestion in big cities provide one reason for this trend; another reason lies in the nature of new industrial and office businesses and their greater need to locate where their workers like to live.

The location decision of any one firm is taken in the light of the existing distribution of firms and facilities, and expectations about the future decisions of others. Actual or expected external economies of scale play an important part in this decision process, providing a major reason for the agglomeration of activities into growth centres. The same mechanism provides the justification for using growth poles as an instrument of policy in the development of less prosperous regions within countries. However, it now appears that diseconomies arising from congestion, etc., are beginning to outweigh the advantages of agglomeration in the more developed nations, though not yet in Third-World countries. At the wider regional scale within nations, the progressive concentration of activity is now often less evident than the development of new regions, suitable for the new generation of industries.

The primary sector continues to receive attention, but proportionately less than hitherto – reflecting the declining proportion of the work-force engaged in primary activities in most developed nations. On the other hand, the interplay of environmental conditions, technological change and economic circumstances is more clearly seen in the agricultural, forestry and mining industries than in much modern manufacturing, making it easier to maintain the geographer's traditional interest in man/land relationships. To accommodate changes in farming practice, major changes in the settlement pattern and layout of farms has been necessary in much of Europe and elsewhere, effecting a drastic alteration of the rural landscape.

At the international level, economic geographers have contributed major studies to the processes of agrarian change and industrialization, in a context of changing comparative advantage. A theme of considerable interest is the interrelationships of the world 'core' and the 'periphery' (often called the North and South respectively). Debate focuses around questions such as: Does the core drain resources from the periphery? What has been the impact of the core on the nature and scale of development in the periphery? Economic geographers approach questions such as these through aggregate data and also by means of national and intra-national case studies.

Commercial production depends on transport. Therefore, transport systems deserve study in their own right and as part of wider studies of the economy. In the less developed world, the close association of transport and development is readily apparent; it is harder to disentangle in more advanced nations. Indeed, in a small country such as Britain geographical differences in the cost of transport seem to be too small significantly to affect location choices. The movement of people, intra-regionally and inter-regionally, has been assuming greater significance and provides the basis for many firms to locate near international airports. Studies of freight and passenger movements show a very clear decline of inter-action as distance increases.

Governments have become major agents shaping the geography of nations, through their policies of redistribution, of direct involvement in production and the provision of services, and through procurement. Some policies have an explicitly spatial purpose, and it is important to evaluate their success or otherwise; other policies have unintentional spatial consequences which need to be recognized.

Two areas are emerging as important foci of enquiry. Economic geographers are interested in the functioning of cities and city systems, especially the processes by which land uses change and cities grow or decline, both in the more advanced nations and the Third World. Secondly, as the pressure on natural resources grows, so does the need for rational management – of energy resources and recreational facilities, of minerals and agricultural land, and so on.

Michael Chisholm
University of Cambridge

Further Reading

Abler, R., Adams, J. S. and Gould, P. (1971), *Spatial Organization. The Geographer's View of the World*, Englewood Cliffs, N.J.

Blunden, J., Brook, C., Edge, G. and Hay, A. (eds) (1973), *Regional Analysis and Development*, London.

Chisholm, M. (1970), *Geography and Economics*, 2nd edn, London.

Cox, K. (1972), *Man, Location and Behavior*, New York.

Hodder, B. W. and Lee, R. (1974), *Economic Geography*, London.

Lloyd, P. E. and Dicken, P. (1977), *Location in Space: A Theoretical Approach to Economic Geography*, 2nd edn, New York.

Morrill, R. L. (1974), *The Spatial Organization of Society*, Belmont, Calif.

Paterson, J. H. (1972), *Land, Work and Resources*, London.

Smith, R. H. T., Taaffe, E. J. and King, L. J. (eds) (1968), *Readings in Economic Geography. The Location of Economic Activity*, Chicago.

See also: *energy; geography; time-space analysis; transport, economics and planning.*

Economic Growth

Economic growth can be measured and defined in various ways. One of the most common is the rate at which aggregate production and spending, i. e., GNP or GDP grows. Alternatively, the rate of growth of per capita GNP or GDP is used because of its closer proximity to the growth of living standards and economic welfare. The recognition of growth so measured as a natural part of the economic history of a nation is fairly new, dating more or less from the Industrial Revolution. By the First World War enough countries had experienced periods of sustained growth that its achievement had become a goal of highest priority in those countries yet to experience a 'take-off' into modernity. During the quarter of a century following the Second World War many economies, capitalist and communist alike, experienced historically high rates of economic growth. A comparison of relative growth rates between capitalist and communist countries became a standard practice in determining the relative worth of alternative economic systems.

With the recognition of economic growth as a natural part of the evolution of an economy came the desire to explain differences in growth patterns and growth rates. Attempts to discern differences and similarities in patterns of growth have merged with efforts to discover 'stages of growth' common to countries that have experienced growing per capita incomes. Marx was one of the earliest to see distinct historical processes and stages in the growth process. His vision was so comprehensive as to encompass distinct changes in the legal, social and economic systems that would evolve as a natural part of the growth process. Less sweeping have been the more recent writings of Schumpeter and Svennilson who, nevertheless, saw economic growth largely in terms of a 'transformation' in which the unbalanced nature of growth leads to changing patterns of output, resource allocation and regional development. For example, those economies experiencing rising per capita incomes have at the same time undergone a relative decline in agriculture accompanied by the rise of industry and manufacturing employment and output. The increasing importance of the service sector was also apparent.

The immediate causal factor behind this transformation has been rising per capita incomes and affluence. As living standards rise, households rearrange their expenditures towards 'luxuries' and away from 'necessities'. For example, the demand for food and clothing declines relatively as living standards rise, while consumer durable goods become a more important item in consumer budgets. Moreover, the more rapidly that per capita incomes rise, the more rapidly has been the rate at which the economy transforms itself. Thus, more rapid growth should be viewed as a more rapid rate of transformation of an economy.

Until very recently, economists wishing to explain why growth and transformation rates differed have stressed the importance of capital formation. The development of new processes, goods, industries and regions was seen to require new plant and equipment of a qualitatively different kind. The more rapid was this rate of capital formation (as measured typically by the rate of investment to GNP) the more rapid was growth and transformation. With the increased popularity of mathematics in economic theory, highly abstract models of growth have been developed. By their very structure they downplay the importance of investment. The influence of this kind of theorizing on policy has been slight.

The Keynesian revolution, as well as the stagnation of the capitalist economies in more recent times, has led to an interest in the relative importance of demand and supply in the determining rates of growth. The important issue today, of whether economies can ever resume the growth performance of the 1950s and 1960s while unemployment is so high and capital utilization so low, is very much a part of this debate. For example, a currently popular view about growth, supply-side economics, argues that even under conditions of depressed aggregate demand and stagnation, policies can be implemented that stimulate the rate of growth of capital and productivity and somehow also cause demand to grow rapidly. Modern Keynesians, by contrast, find little hope in ever ending the current stagnation of growth rates without first greatly reducing the slack in the economy.

Rising per capita incomes, while conferring benefits such as the reduction of poverty, have also led to new problems. As Keynes pointed out over a half century ago, when incomes have risen enough to allow savings to become a significant portion of incomes, problems of effective demand arise. If these are not handled through government intervention, widespread unemployment becomes a distinct possibility.

The prolonged period of full employment and sustained growth following the Second World War permitted rapidly rising living standards, increased savings and expanded public welfare programmes including unemployment insurance. One result was to increase vastly the power of labour, thereby intensifying the conflict between capital and labour over the distribution of incomes. This has led to a marked acceleration of inflation rates in the post-war period compared to earlier 'normal' periods. It has also resulted in governments in capitalist countries repressing aggregate demand in the interests of fighting inflation. Unfortunately, this has caused stagnation and the virtual end to economic growth. Unless new policies can be devised to stabilize wages and prices when the economy reaches full employment, it is unlikely that stimulative policies will be pursued with any vigour. The result may be little or no economic growth for some time to come.

John Cornwall
Dalhousie University

Further Reading
Duesenberry, J. (1958), *Business Cycles and Economic Growth*, New York.
Kaldor, N. (1967), *Strategic Factors in Economic Development*, Ithaca.

Schumpeter, J. (1961), *The Theory of Economic Development*, New York.
Svennilson, I. (1954), *Growth and Stagnation in the European Economy*.
See also: *business cycles; planning, economic; stagflation.*

Economic History

See Cliometrics, History.

Economics

The Ancient Greeks who gave to us the name of this subject lacked the concept of what we now call economics. *Oeconomicus* would be 'Household management' in modern English, the domain of Mrs Beeton rather than J. S. Mill. Of course what we would now recognize as economic questions are certainly ancient, but such questions and particular answers to them amount to less than the kind of knowledge that in Schumpeter's elegant description, '. . . has been the object of conscious efforts to improve it'. In that sense, which is of a science in the broad and generous use of that term, economics is a young discipline. The term now usually employed is even younger than the modern form of the subject itself. Earlier writers described themselves as '*political economists*'. Too much can be and has been made of this distinction. In an age in which the educated knew Greek, it was pertinent to remind the reader what the term did not mean. However, any terminological distinction between economics and political economy must be questioned. The unadorned 'economic' had long been in use, and was frequently employed by Marx, while 'political economy' has continued in use into the twentieth century and has enjoyed something of a revival lately from writers wishing to advertise that their work has not treated its subject in isolation from the political system.

It is customary to associate the beginning of modern economics with the publication of Adam Smith's *The Wealth of Nations*. As this attribution sets aside more than a thousand years of economic writing, ancient, Christian and Islamic, it calls for justification. However, a study of the earlier literature will not leave the reader long in doubt concerning the claim that a radical shift of method had taken place. What we recognize in Adam Smith's work, and what sets it apart from that which had gone before, is the characteristic imprint of the eighteenth century in which the Grand Idea finds its expression in the language of exact scholarship. We recognize the same spirit in reading Gibbon's *History*.

Adam Smith's writing represents the source of a stream which runs to the present day. This is true of modern economics in general but more particularly of a style of approaching the subject which was his own. Its distinguishing characteristic is its limited use of the method of simplification and abstraction. The strengths of the method are obvious, but experience has revealed its weaknesses. Description needs a strong guiding principle if it is not to deteriorate into the unenlightening elaboration of a mass of incoherent fact. One could illustrate this point from *The Wealth of Nations* itself, where illustrations are sometimes developed to the point of tedium, but that would do less than justice to a writer whose genius generally enabled him to surmount this problem. Better illustrations of the point might be provided from much later work by the Institutionalist School which made its influence felt in Germany and in the United States in the late nineteenth and early twentieth centuries.

A problem inherent in Adam Smith's method is that it provides no guidance concerning the resolution of disagreements. The arguments make use of persuasive reasoning and examples to back them up. If the number and quality of these is overwhelming there will clearly be no difficulty, but such cannot always be the case, and as economics grew the triumph of ideas by acclamation was far from being the rule. What was required were more refined methods of economic reasoning and more powerful methods of evaluating the kinds of claim to which that reasoning gave rise. The first development preceded the second but they were ultimately seen to be closely related.

The method of studying economic questions by means of simplification and abstraction was developed, and even taken to extremes, by David Ricardo. So important was his innovation of method that writers for two generations acknowledged his influence even when they propounded conclusions quite contrary to his own. The kind of abstraction that Ricardo developed took the form of what today would be called an 'economic model'. This consists in a formal, more or less simple, invented economy which is claimed to illustrate a point or to capture the essence of the true, and of course more complicated, economy of real life. One illustration would be a numerical example. Another would be the stylized story, such as the Tribe of Hunters by means of which Adam Smith illustrated his theory of the division of labour. The numbers of an example are not taken by their inventor to be the values of real life, while stories can be taken to be schematic accounts of true history. For the present purpose, however, this distinction is less important than the fact that both are examples of model building.

Ricardo was not the first or the only economist to employ a model in his work. What makes him stand out is that model-building was not a method to which he had occasional recourse: it was his typical and usual method of reasoning. Moreover, an examination of his arguments will show that the model is essential to the argument; it is not there to add colour or verisimilitude.

Thus Ricardo's work sometimes reveals an almost mathematical quality, being concerned with the development of the logical implications of certain postulates. The apparent power and objectivity of this kind of reasoning could not fail to impress those who came to it anew.

From the beginning of the modern subject, then, certain important distinctions are already apparent, notably that between realism and abstraction, and between description and model building. The method of economics for another hundred years was to be very largely historical, historical, that is, in the sense that the kind of evidence employed and the manner in which it was made use of were both the same as would characterize historical enquiry. Ricardo used invented numbers, partly because his argument was general and not dependent upon the particular values selected, but also because the availability of statistics in his time was extremely limited and haphazard. But it would be wrong to suppose that this made economics a non-empirical subject. Malthus, for example, was certainly influenced by the observation that population was growing at an unprecedented rate in the England of his time, and the correctness of that observation cannot be questioned. He estimated that population unchecked by restraints would double every 25 years, which corresponds to an annual rate of increase of 2.8 per cent per annum. The latter estimate has stood up well for a population which is balanced in age composition at the start and then accelerates in its growth.

The work of Petty in gathering statistics is frequently cited, but it stands out more for being pioneering than for being representative. It was government that was to collect statistics, and government was still exceedingly small by later standards. A growing science normally demands measurement, if not experiment, as a young child calls for food. Economics, however, was nourished for a long time by such observations as were available to the informed citizen and chiefly by its own ideas. In this respect it resembled Greek science or modern physics when the latter has outreached the possibility of experiment. Most of all, it resembled philosophy to which its close affinity was recorded in the term 'moral sciences' for long in use in the ancient universities of Britain. One could characterize the 150 years and beyond following the publication of *The Wealth of Nations* as having been preoccupied with working out the logical implications of certain assumptions about economic reality, while at the same time those assumptions themselves were in the process of being changed and influenced by far-reaching alterations in economic institutions. This was no small task. The logical implications of economic assumptions can be rich and complex, and they readily give rise to controversy. Some have attributed these problems to the inherent difficulty of the subject, others to the powerful ideological content of the questions involved – both are partly correct.

The difficulties of economic theory do not consist simply of the intellectual demands that it makes, which do not compare with those of physics or pure mathematics. It is rather that economics requires a body of analytical tools and a technique of reasoning without which even simple questions cannot be accurately answered. The uninitiated constantly demonstrate the truth of that claim. However, the development of these tools and methods took some considerable time. One need only compare the writings of John Stuart Mill with those of some indifferent economist of the turn of the century to see what a difference the accumulation of technique had made. In Mill we see one of the finest intellects of the nineteenth century struggling to cut his way through a jungle. In the plain economist of the later years we would see an unskilled craftsman no doubt, but one working with what by then had become a thoroughly useful box of tools. There are even tasks for which the latter would be better employed.

The ideological problem is ever present. Economists have sometimes seen it as a distraction, as a diversion from the important questions on which economics could speak, but there is no justification for such a simple separation. Through experience and through the application of the same apparatus that he uses to resolve other matters, the economist is uniquely placed to say useful things about the type of political conflict which is concerned with the division of economic goods. That does not mean, of course, that he should play God, or pretend to more expertise than he has, but equally he cannot push such questions aside and say that because they are not all to do with him, they are therefore not at all to do with him.

The problem is naturally not peculiar to economics. It arises in any field in which the expert must address himself to issues concerning which people, including the practitioners themselves, their students, their employers and others, have strong feelings. Certain principles are obvious if economics is not to be sucked into the political whirlpool. The pursuit of objectivity and scholarly integrity clearly belong among them. These principles are under attack from two sides. On the one side will be some who will argue that there is no detachment, no standing apart, and that science should serve progressive forces in society, however those may be defined at the time. On the other side will be those who claim to accept these principles, only to discredit them by advancing under the guise of the objective and the detached what is patently the ideological.

Economics has been assaulted to its foundations during its still-short history by the claim that its doctrines are no more than 'false ideology'. Marx attacked what he called 'bourgeois political economy' as mere apologetics for the existing social order. He said the most wounding thing that can be said about a science – that his opponents were concerned only with the superficial, the surface appearance of things. The importance of Marx's contribution will ultimately be judged by what he put in the place of the economics which he attacked, and not by the attacks as such, memorable though their invective may be to anyone who has read them. It was Marx's political activity, and his political writing, that changed the world, as indeed they did, and not his economic theory. This is to insist on making a distinction to which the master would have strongly objected, but make it we must. Within the narrow field of economic theory he retains his followers to the present day, but Marxist economics, recent revivals notwithstanding, remains a backwater and a curiosum beside mainstream economics. The fact that it has failed to propose an alternative system to orthodoxy with anything like the same reach and the same richness, and probably could not as it is formulated, may alone explain this fact.

The last third of the nineteenth century witnesses a huge burgeoning of economic theory and the beginnings of systematic empirical investigation. The theoretical movement has been unhappily named 'neoclassical'. It was not 'neo' if that prefix means a revival of an earlier period, and it is difficult to see what meaning of the term 'classical' would usefully connect it with the early writers. Naturally, however, no movement is unconnected with the past. The use of abstraction and model-building was now freely employed, sometimes again to excess, but more fruitfully, generally speaking, than ever before. Most importantly, perhaps, the ultimately inescapable, mathematical character of economic reasoning was becoming clear. Diagrams were employed, not without resistance at first, and the concept of 'elasticity of demand' made its appearance. The 'marginalism' sometimes taken to characterize the period was more the result of the new approach than its generator. It may nevertheless be the most powerful single organizing principle that economics has yet seen.

These developments which established economics as we know it today began to change the appearance of the discipline. It came to stand apart from its neighbouring fields, not in every respect or in every part of the field to be sure, but noticeably all the same. Its employment of mathematics in particular, or mathematical-like reasoning, sometimes made it resemble physics more than it resembled law, philosophy, politics, history or sociology. On closer examination, however, economics did not seem to resemble any other discipline at all closely. The quantification of its theoretical relations, for example, without which a 'natural' science was not counted as having established itself, was still at a primitive stage of development. Still more, it was far from clear that the theoretical relationships of economics would ever attain to the status of those of physics or chemistry. The latter had arrived at powerful 'laws' which seemed to hold without exception and to a degree of approximation defined by the resolving power of the measuring instruments. True amendments to these laws were later shown to be necessary, but they were corrections and often unimportant ones. In economics few 'laws' worth stating could be expected to hold except as tendencies. Science certainly could investigate weak effects or tendencies but it liked to have a great deal of preferably reliable data to undertake this task. But reliable data was in short supply and often small in quantity.

Had economists reached the point at which they demanded a testable implication of every new theory, they would undoubtedly have become completely discouraged by the formidable difficulties which confront the testing of economic hypotheses. Fortunately, perhaps, they have not yet arrived at that point. Many economic models are seen as following in the tradition established by Ricardo and illustrated by his model of comparative advantage. They are not designed to produce a hypothesis to be compared with the observation of reality, so much as they aim to explore the implications of making a set of assumptions, simplified by intention but equally meant to be realistic enough to capture something of reality. The ultimate aim of such an exercise is to influence the way in which people think about the world. There are so many examples of what such reasoning might be doing that it is not easy to find an instance that stands for more than its own type. However, the following case is certainly encountered rather frequently. An economist, drawing on observation formal or informal, says to himself: 'I think that people behave in such and such a way. What would follow if I was right in that belief?'

Why should the economist worry about the subsidiary question, which may very well involve him in a lot of work? The answer is that it is a check on the reasonableness of his initial assumption. It is no different in kind, though surely less monumental in import, than Newton asking himself what would happen if bodies moved in straight lines at constant velocity unless acted upon by a force. Interesting assumptions need to have their plausibility tested in a throughgoing manner. Otherwise people who believe that the wealth of a nation is measured by its balance of payments surplus, have too much influence.

Economic theory in the twentieth century has been altered by a major intellectual revolution, associated with the name of Keynes, of which more will be said below. However, the effect of the Keynesian revolution, important though it has been, should not be allowed to detract from certain advances which have gone on more or less continually, and not directly influenced by the new ways of thinking. Nineteenth-century economic theory was based on abstraction and on bringing economic concepts to bear on practical questions.

These tendencies were continued in the twentieth century which has witnessed some of the greatest successes of formalization and generalization which the subject has known, at the same time as it has seen a growing interest in bringing economic theory to bear directly on important real matters. In an age in which econometrics was increasingly available as a research tool, the old presumptions about realism and unrealism have sometimes been upset. Mathematically rich models have sometimes, though not always, lent themselves better to empirical implementation than have homely and realistic ones. An important example of this is the new mathematical method of linear programming which has made complex maximization problems, even of large size, highly soluble.

Nineteenth-century economic theory borrowed from ethics the notion of 'utility' as measuring or representing the level of satisfaction or well-being of the household or consumer. It no doubt struck the students of the time as reasonable and sensible, as did Marshall's assumption that the marginal utility of income would be approximately constant, and it was useful in deriving simply the so-called 'law of demand'. Eventually this was too out of touch with reality for the twentieth-century taste, which had become more positivistic. How was utility to be measured? The outcome of these doubts was the realization that utility could only be an ordinal quantity, that this was all that was required to derive the consumer's behaviour, and the eventual understanding of income and substitution effects in a general framework.

The implication of this change of view did not stop with demand theory. Economic policy, or welfare economics, had previously been conceived as an application of utilitarian principles to economic questions. The application concerned, however, was a quantitative one; it supposed the measurability of utility. If that was now called into question, how were policy recommendations to be justified? A radical sceptical view said that they could only be justified as value judgements, that any claimed scientific basis to economic recommendations was unfounded. A more constructive approach set out to delineate which properties a recommendation would have to fulfil so as not to require value judgements for its validation. It was not so much that many interesting recommendations could be value-free that made this exercise of importance; rather the whole investigation greatly clarified how value judgements enter into economic reasoning and for the first time put welfare economics on a sound basis.

The earlier welfare economics of the nineteenth century was now seen to be, to a great extent, the economics of efficiency. The problem of distribution, of equity, one could say, had been treated as something separate, independent of efficiency. One of the major advances of the twentieth century, particularly the period following the Second World War, has been the development of a theory of economic policy, much closer to reality in its conception and in its method than traditional welfare economics. Efficiency has not been shown to be an irrelevant consideration – far from it – but the role that efficiency plays in a system constrained by perhaps a bad distribution of incomes, or constrained to depart from efficiency in certain directions, has been clarified. Economic policy has become the art of maximizing the possible, second-best optimization in the jargon of today's economics.

A settled interpretation and assessment of the contribution of Keynes is still elusive nearly fifty years after the publication of his great work, *The General Theory*. That this should be so is a measure partly of problems and obscurities in that work, and partly of the value which has been conceded to its ideas even by those who have undertaken to attack them. Only recently have wholehearted rejections arisen in the main countries of economic research, rejections not based simply on ideological revulsion. Many earlier critiques, notably that associated with Milton Friedman's monetarism, were more revisionist than completely counter to Keynes's method as well as to his conclusions. One reason is that Keynes posed some sharp and important questions to the then orthodoxy which it was at the time wholly unable to answer. To these questions Keynes provided answers. There are no more potent ingredients for an intellectual revolution and its rapid dissemination.

Keynesian ideas found their expression in a new field, macroeconomics. This division of economic theory into separate and largely non-communicating sectors was readily accepted at the time but was later felt to be unhealthy. While setting itself apart from much existing theory, the new ideas very easily connected with applied economics and econometrics, and the new macroeconomics was an applied subject from the outset. Economic forecasting models were constructed, sometimes of huge scale, and governments and private users began to pay for their results. Just as it was applied in spirit, so was the new theory interventionist in outlook. According to Keynesian doctrine a wise government could stabilize the economy close to full employment and avoid fluctuations and inflation. Later the numerous problems associated with such a programme became apparent. From early optimism there has been a pessimistic reaction in which stress has been laid on the powerlessness of governments to have any useful influence in a world whose individual actors have become more sophisticated and far-seeing. It is too early yet to forecast where these latest ideas themselves will lead, but one may note a development which is unlikely to be harmful in the end. The apparently well-established division between macroeconomics and microeconomics is breaking down. On the one hand, macro-theorists

are no longer willing to accept that agents act in not very intelligent rule-of-thumb ways when it comes to determining employment and wages and asset prices, or assessing the influence of government policies on their futures, while attributing considerable sophistication to those agents when discussing price determination in individual markets. On the other hand, microeconomic theorists are more interested in building models of the price rigidities and rationing that sometimes seem to characterize markets, rather than dismissing such cases as freaks.

Meanwhile, at the practical level, economists are in a state of intellectual ferment, which manifests itself to the outsider as chaotic disunity, concerning fundamental questions of macroeconomic management. On the basic question of the consequences of a large government deficit, for example, reputable spokesmen can be found to claim that the deficit as such is unimportant, that only the supply-side, somehow defined, matters; that the deficit matters only if translated to excessive growth in the money supply; or that the deficit is expansionary, if not perhaps in the most healthy manner. The world and the profession must derive what comfort it can from the fact that such widespread disagreements tend to resolve themselves, usually as the result of the accumulation of new evidence, but sometimes of new ideas as well. Modern economics has huge resources in its techniques and in its methods of evaluating empirical evidence. These should eventually enable it to emerge from the present 'crisis of confidence' stronger and in better shape. If, as seems likely, the public never quite recovers an excessive confidence which it may have placed in the pronouncements of economists, there will be no harm in that.

Economics began as a British subject and remained so for many years. Today it is an international discipline including scholars from most countries of the world and from all regions. Its chief centre is in the US, and papers originating from there account for a sizeable proportion of those appearing in the major journals. Economists everywhere advise governments and private institutions, and they frequently write in newspapers and appear on the radio and on television. Another important development, particularly since the Second World War, has been the use of economics in new and unexpected fields. Thus the economics of medicine, to cite one example, has now become a specialism with its own practitioners and its own journals. Through optional courses at universities, more people now have some exposure to economics than ever before. While co-operating well with workers from other disciplines in applied work, economists still stand apart when it comes to theory, and fruitful cross-disciplinary co-operation, while it happens, is not at all common. A growing tendency towards specialization within the field has been evident. Few scholars are economists and econometricians, for example, and many define their field of interest surprisingly narrowly. In part this state of affairs is imposed by the huge amount of literature now appearing in every field which demands the attention of the serious worker. While it would be rash to predict the future of the subject very far ahead, it is interesting to note that the loss of an excessive confidence in economists' abilities to pronounce the truth has not been accompanied by a loss of interest in employing them. Although academic openings in the 1980s compare unfavourably with the rich possibilities of the 1960s, many other employment opportunities continue to attract economists.

Christopher Bliss
University of Oxford

Further Reading
Blaug, M. (1980), *The Methodology of Economics, or How Economists Explain*, Cambridge.
Friedman, M. (1969), *The Optimal Quantity of Money and Other Essays*, Chicago.
Keynes, J. M. (1931), *Essays in Persuasion*, London.
Keynes, J. M. (1936), *The General Theory of Employment, Interest and Money*, London.
Koopmans, T. C. (1957), *Three Essays on the State of Economic Science*, New York.
Little, I. M. D. (1982), *Economic Development: Theory, Politics and International Relations*, New York.
Luce, R. D. and Riaffa, H. (1967), *Games and Decisions*, New York.
Meade, J. E. (1975), *The Intelligent Radical's Guide to Economic Policy: The Mixed Economy*, London.
Robinson, J. (1966), *An Essay on Marxian Economics*, London.
Samuelson, P. A. (1958), *Economics: An Introductory Analysis*, 4th edn, New York.
Schumpeter, J. S. (1952), *Ten Great Economists*, London.
Schumpeter, J. S. (1954), *History of Economic Analysis*, Oxford.
Sen, A. K. (1982), *Choice, Welfare and Measurement*, Oxford.
Shackle, G. L. S. (1967), *The Years of High Theory*, Cambridge.

Economies of Scale

The term economies of scale refers to the situation in which, at a given and unchanging set of input prices, the unit cost of production is lower in a plant of larger scale of (annual) output than in a plant of smaller scale. This is sometimes called 'real economies of scale' and is contrasted with 'pecuniary economies of scale' in which the plant of larger scale may obtain inputs,

including finance for investment, at a lower price. Economies of scale usually obtain in unit labour cost and unit capital costs, but scarcely ever in unit materials cost. An example of economies of scale may be given for ethylene production (Jackson, 1982).

Scale of ethylene plant, thousand tons per annum	100	200	300
Operating cost per ton of ethylene			
Feedstock costs, chemicals, and utilities, £ per ton	41.2	41.2	41.2
Labour costs, £ per ton	3.5	2.7	2.1
Capital cost (depreciation and interest), £ per ton	15.1	12.3	10.1
Total operating costs, £ per ton	59.8	56.2	53.4
Index of operating costs (59.8 taken as 100)	100	94	89

In this real-world example (c. 1970), unit operating costs are 6 per cent lower in a plant of capacity 200 thousand tons per annum than in a plant of capacity 100 thousand tons per annum, and 11 per cent lower in a plant of capacity 300 thousand tons per annum; while there is no alteration in unit feedstock etc, costs, unit labour costs are 40 per cent lower in the 300 thousand ton plant, and unit capital costs are 33 per cent lower.

The main reason for lower unit labour costs is that an increase in the scale of this process plant does not require an equi-proportionate increase in the number of workers. In manufacturing plants, a larger scale of output may facilitate changes in the organization and/or mechanization of work which makes labour more productive. The introduction by Henry Ford of assembly-line mass-production techniques and matching organization of work is a famous example. Between 1909 and 1911, Ford moved from its original small Piquette Street plant to the much larger Highland Park plant and introduced the moving assembly-line. As Ford (1926) remarked of this change: 'You will note that men were not employed in proportion to the output.'

	1908	1911
Factory output, number of cars	6,181	34,528
Number of employees	1,908	4,110
Labour productivity, cars per employee per annum	3.2	8.4
Unit labour cost (estimated at annual earnings in 1910 of $651 per full-time employee in manufacturing), $ per car	201	77

The main reason for lower unit capital cost is likewise that an increase in the scale of output does not require an equi-proportionate increase in the initial investment. For the ethylene plants, the initial capital costs were, respectively, £8.4 million, £13.5 million, and £16.6 million; as the scale of output doubles the fixed capital cost rises by 61 per cent, and as it increases by a further 50 per cent the capital cost rises by a further 23 per cent. The investment cost per ton capacity thus declines from £84 to £67.5 to £55.3. The reasons for declining investment cost per unit of capacity are many and complex. One commonly cited reason is that much capital equipment takes the general form of a container, the cost of which is related to surface area while production capacity is related to volume: e.g. a box 1m x 1m x 1m has a surface area of 6 square metres and a volume of 1 cubic metre; a box 2m x 2m x 2m has an eightfold increase in volume (in production capacity) for only a fourfold increase in surface area (in cost). Such relationships explain economies of scale in, for example, steel-making. Or to take another example, increasing the carrying capacity of a goods vehicle is unlikely to require an increase in the cost of gearbox, axles, electrics, and so on, so that the capital cost of the vehicle will not rise commensurately with the increase in its carrying capacity.

The economic implications of economies of scale are considerable and reasonably obvious: plants of bigger scale will tend to have a price/profitability advantage over smaller plants, which have to seek a specialized niche in the market if they are to survive.

Dudley Jackson
University of Wollongong
Australia

References
Ford, H. (1926), *My Life and Work*, London.
Jackson, D. (1982), *Introduction to Economics: Theory and Data*, London.
US Department of Commerce, Bureau of the Census (1975), *Historical Statistics of the United States: Colonial Times to 1970*, Washington.

Education

Although recently dominated by psychology, the field of educational research was once largely restricted to the general discipline of philosophy. Today other disciplines such as anthropology, economics, political science and sociology have been increasingly prominent.

The status of education as an applied field makes it difficult to identify any specific method or conceptual domain which would single it out from other fields. For most scholars and researchers, however, the study of education has meant investigating activities related to learning, usually within the context of the schools. The problems studied and the method employed vary a great deal, depending largely on the training and background of the researchers. However, in contrast to the earlier, philosophical, studies which focused on the *aims* of education, the prominence of the behavioural and social sciences has signalled a shift in concern to questions of *means*.

As an applied field of study, the problems investigated in the area of education tend to follow closely the concerns articulated by leaders in business, government and the media. For example, in the late 1950s and early 1960s when American political leaders were primarily concerned with the space race with the Soviet Union and the so-called missile gap, a series of reports by the well-known educator, James B. Conant (1959) focused on the lagging academic quality of education in the United States. Educational research in that country then turned towards developing curriculum units, teaching strategies, school procedure and design that would produce more scientists and engineers. In this period, for example, the 'New Math' flourished, and influential educators, such as the psychologist Jerome Bruner, proposed the teaching of science, mathematics and other academic programmes in the lower grades (Bruner, 1960).

In the mid-1960s, social pressure built up over the civil rights issue, and the concern of much of the educational research community again shifted towards issues related to equality of opportunity. The work of Jean Piaget provided the intellectual basis for curriculum researchers in Britain and the US who argued for relaxing the structure of the curriculum by allowing more room for the individual expression of interests. Some opposed these moves because they were too permissive, but the intention was to create a fruitful interaction between the developmental patterns found among children and the structure and pacing of curriculum knowledge. However, the apparently reduced emphasis on a hierarchy of knowledge (with science, maths and other college preparatory subjects at the top and vocational subjects at the bottom), and the renewed recognition of the importance of the interest of the individual child as a major factor in the learning process, appeared to be consistent with the wider concern for equality of opportunity.

Equality has continued to be a major issue in educational research and debate in a number of different areas. For example, James Coleman's (1968) analysis of data from thousands of American schools explored the extent to which different variables affect school achievement across racial lines. His finding that the class and racial characteristics of the student body had an important influence on individual achievement was rapidly used as intellectual support for the busing of children across racially distinct neighbourhoods in an effort to achieve greater racial balance. At the same time other studies explored the effectiveness of pre-school programmes in raising the achievement levels of Blacks and other children from lower socio-economic classes.

At the time that educational research was exploring the pedagogical factors involved in maintaining inequality, the traditional meaning of equality of opportunity was first challenged. Coleman (1973), in an important article on equality of educational opportunity, suggested that the extent to which this ideal has been realized should be measured not in terms of equality of input – the resources spent on different children – but rather in terms of equality of results – whether or not the pattern of achievement is similar among different racial groups and minorities. Had this conception of equal opportunity been widely accepted, it would have significantly changed the rules of the game. This proposal would thus have mandated the allocation of unequal resources in some cases in order to achieve equal results.

Coleman's proposed conception was never fully accepted (Coleman, himself, only offered it tentatively). However, educational policy makers and politicians in the US did begin to assign federal resources to special groups, such as the handicapped, Blacks, women and non-native speakers of English; legal efforts were increased to redress racial imbalance in schools; and affirmative action programmes tried to increase the opportunities for minority students and women in universities and professional schools.

Even prior to Coleman's attempt to redefine the concept of equal opportunity, there had been other challenges to compensatory policies. The most publicized was an article in 1969 by Arthur Jensen which claimed that most compensatory programmes had failed, and therefore children of different intellectual ability should be taught differently. Children with high IQ scores, Jensen argued, should be taught conceptually by problem-solving methods. Children with low IQ scores should be taught through associative or rote methods. Jensen's article was controversial because of three propositions. These were: IQ tests measure intelligence; in a population intelligence is eighty percent explained by genetic factors; and Blacks as a population score on the average consistently lower than Whites on both standard IQ tests and culture-fair tests. Jensen concluded that environmental enrichment programmes were severely limited in their ability to raise IQ scores, and that educators would better spend their time and resources identifying conceptual and associative learners and teaching them through the methods appropriate to their learning style. Jensen himself believed that when IQ tests were appropriately refined to identify the two types of learners, Blacks and other minority students would be more fairly treated. He also believed that teaching style would become more consistent with learning style and that conceptual

learners from these groups would be less likely to fall victim to the prejudicial judgement of a few teachers. However, he also strongly implied that because of genetic factors Blacks would continue to achieve at a lower rate than Whites.

An uproar followed the publication of Jensen's article. The twin studies on which he had built much of his case for the prominence of genetic over environmental factors were discredited. Questions were raised about the whole concept of measurement as applied to intelligence and about the appropriateness of such tests for culturally distinct, minority children. In addition, Jensen's argument traded on the ambiguity of the claim that 'IQ tests measure intelligence'. The claim could mean that a conceptual limit exists beyond which an individual cannot reach and an IQ test measures it, or it could mean that IQ tests measure the speed at which different individuals learn. This ambiguity is especially significant when it is understood that Jensen's view of associative and conceptual learning is inaccurate in at least one important respect. He believes that children can learn essentially the same basic material either through associative or conceptual methods, depending upon the learning style of the child. But, in fact, the children would be learning the same skills in only the most superficial sense. They might be learning how to translate symbols on a page into oral sounds, or learning to repeat number facts, thus giving the *appearance* of learning the same thing. However, each group also would be learning something about learning. One group would be learning that learning is a rote affair, while the other would be learning that it is essentially a conceptual and problem-solving activity. Jensen's article provides no evidence to support the view that such learning styles were irreversible, even though his own proposal seemed to rest upon this assumption.

The debate over Jensen's article was significant for a number of reasons. One of these went to the very heart of the question of equality of opportunity. For if equality of opportunity means that everyone is to be given the same chance, then presumably ability differences should be the sole determinant of outcomes. However, if the major measure of ability, that is, IQ tests, is put into question, so too is the justification for different outcomes.

Some scholars, while dismissing the significance of IQ tests, continued to justify differential outcomes and to argue against 'extraordinary' measures to achieve educational equality. These arguments were often based on the view that governmental intervention creates unrealistic expectations and increases frustration and, possibly, violence. Environmental factors were considered important, but the most significant aspect of environment, the habits, discipline and foresight developed through class culture were thought extremely difficult to change. Because these studies took 'class-culture' and the habits and attitudes associated with it an an independent variable, they failed to examine the relationship between a student's habits, attitudes and achievement, and the work structures that were available to children from certain social classes.

This enlarged focus came only with a renewed interest in Marxist scholarship and, especially, with the work of two economists, Bowles and Gintis (Bowles and Gintis, 1976). Their study concluded that schooling provided very little mobility, even when research controlled for IQ scores, and that schools largely served to reproduce and legitimize the personality characteristics required by the hierarchical relations found in advanced capitalistic countries.

The findings of Bowles and Gintis were challenged on a number of methodological grounds. However, one of the more significant effects of their work for educational scholarship was to reintroduce a Marxist perspective into the study of education in the US. This perspective continued a tradition that was already established in England, Western Europe, Australia, and in a number of Third-World countries. In effect Marxists have shifted some of the focus of educational research from the individual to the larger social, historical, cultural and political context of schooling (Apple, 1982).

There is no uniform Marxist perspective. For example, the Brazilian educator, Paulo Freire, draws on Marxist literature for many of his insights, but he also draws on French existentialism, phenomenology, and upon Christian theology (Freire, 1973). Some analysts have adopted a structural approach and have examined the limits placed on the educational system by a hierarchical mode of production. Others, utilizing an ethnographic methodology, have explored the way in which a critical working-class consciousness is both developed and blunted in schools. There have been insightful studies on the reproduction of classroom knowledge for different social classes, on the production of educational materials and texts, and on the dilemmas created by radical educational thought for teacher education (Apple, 1982; Giroux, 1981).

While Marxist-oriented research represents a significant redefinition of the problem of education, it has remained a largely critical movement which only occasionally penetrates mainstream thinking about education. When inequality was a major issue for the educational community and the wider public, Marxism was able to gain a reasonable hearing. However, as unemployment rates in the United States, Britain and Western Europe hit post-depression records, educational policy makers steered the agenda away from the issue of equality and towards the educational needs of the 'high technology revolution'. Educational research is following suit as more concern is expressed about developing 'computer literacy', and about increasing the pool from which future scientists and engineers can be drawn. There have been calls to tighten up the curriculum, increase standards for admission into and matriculation out of higher education, and to reduce the 'frills' in the public schools. These concerns seem to signal a return to the era dominated by Conant. However, the applied nature of educational research and its inability to develop a reasonably independent research programme makes any prediction about the future direction of educational scholarship dependent upon uncertain political and economic developments.

This point raises a deeper issue about the nature of educational research and its potential for developing a research programme that involves more than simply the application of methods drawn from other disciplines to problems as they are defined by immediate political forces. The last attempt to provide an independent focus for the study of education was developed by the American philosopher, John Dewey. Since Dewey, educational philosophy has taken a different turn, one that emphasizes the anaylsis of concepts and linguistic clarity. Yet the deeper questions about education involve the understanding of intergenerational continuity and change and the normative concerns that guide the process of social and cultural reproduction. While little systematic effort has been undertaken to explore the process and patterns of social identity, it is possible to specify some of the factors that such a research programme would involve. They would include an analysis of the kind of knowledge that is prized by a given society, the institutional arrangements to protect and carry on such knowledge, the methods used to identify and train those who will bear that knowledge in the future, and the way in which knowledge is distributed among different groups in the society. Such a programme would maintain the interdisciplinary character of educational studies but would provide a focus that has been lacking. It would also provide a critical point from which to appraise present educational practice.

Walter Feinberg
University of Illinois
Champaign-Urbana

References

Apple, M. (1982), *Education and Power*, London.
Bowles, S. and Gintis, H. (1976), *Schooling in Capitalist America: Educational Reform and the Contradictions of Economic Life*, New York.
Bruner, J. (1960), *The Process of Education*, Cambridge, Mass.
Coleman, J. S. (1968), 'The concept of equality of educational opportunity', *Harvard Educational Review*, 38.
Coleman, J. S. (1973), 'Equality of opportunity and equality of results', *Harvard Educational Review*, 43.

Conant, J. B. (1959), *The American High School Today*, New York.

Freire, P. (1973), *Pedagogy of the Oppressed*, New York.

Giroux, H. A. (1981), *Ideology, Culture and the Process of Schooling*, Philadelphia.

Jensen, A. R. (1969), 'How much can we boost I. Q. and scholastic achievement?', *Harvard Educational Review*, 39.

Further Reading

Bourdieu, P. and Passeron, J.-C. (1977), *Reproduction in Education, Society and Culture*, London.

Feinberg, W. (1983), *Understanding Education: Toward a Reconstruction of Educational Inquiry*, Cambridge.

Sharp, R. and Green, A. (1975), *Education and Social Control; A Study in Progressive Education*, London.

See also: *educational psychology; intelligence and intelligence testing; Piaget*.

Educational Psychology

Educational psychology covers two related, but distinguishable, fields. One is a branch of academic psychology that seeks to understand the processes of teaching and learning. The other is a profession – specifically that which is concerned to diagnose and to treat those handicaps and lacks that impede or impair a person's ability to learn. To aid this distinction the academics tend to refer to themselves as 'psychologists of education' while the professionals are more generally known as 'educational psychologists'.

In practice both the descriptions given above are too general. Academic educational psychology has focused almost exclusively on specific *contexts* of teaching and learning, and specific *types of knowledge* that are acquired. The contexts are formal institutions of education – schools, colleges and universities. The types of knowledge are predominantly conceptual, symbolic, verbal and rational.

These overemphases arise because psychologists have been as guilty as anyone of confusing 'schooling' with 'education', and thereby assuming that what is important in school reflects what is important psychologically. The best example of this is the fact that there is still no integrative framework for viewing human learning. There are many *cognitive* theories (e.g. Smith, 1975) but they neither contain, nor are readily coupled to, ways of construing feeling, need, intuition, physical skill, social demeanour or personality. Yet, while intellect forms the *de jure* matter of schools, these other domains are central parts of its *de facto* curriculum, at least for the young people.

This links to a second underlying assumption of the psychology of education, namely that because teachers are important in schools they are important in learning. Many people would agree with Ausubel (1968) that it is the teachers's prime task to 'ascertain what the learner knows and teach him accordingly'. But this demand has unsettled generations of student teachers, for it is clearly impossible to keep tabs on the shifting states of knowledge and readiness of twenty or thirty other people. The best way to ascertain what the learner already knows is to feed him and let him spit out what he doesn't want. But teachers acquire from psychologists a lack of trust in the learner's ability to chew and to choose, and from the examination boards the assumption that the menu has been so well designed that to wish to leave some on the plate is a symptom of either ill-health or sacrilege. In general, psychologists of education are beginning to suspect that teaching is neither necessary nor sufficient to produce learning, and that it can have many unintended, unacknowledged, conflicting and counterproductive effects.

The relationship of the 'psychology of education' to 'educational psychology' is similar to that of physiology to medicine: the former generates knowledge which the latter adapts and uses to remedy disabilities of learning (though, like medicine, educational psychology generates and conducts its own applied research as well). In practice, educational psychologists concern themselves mostly with the problem of school-age children, although their statutory responsibility in England and Wales is for the 2 to 19-year-old range. Most educational psychologists in the UK are employed by local Education Authorities, and work within the School Psychological Service. They may also have responsibilities within Child Guidance Clinics.

The work in academic psychology on which educational psychologists can draw is extensive. They tend, however, to make use of any or all of three main areas: (1) psychometrics, from which come the specialist tests, diagnostic tools and measuring instruments which are the stock-in-trade of many educational psychologists; (2) psychotherapy, which provides methods of treatment, particularly for emotional and neurotic problems, that are based on empathic conversation (though play and fantasy may be used as well) with the child and/or his family; (3) behaviourism or 'learning theory', which has generated the principles and techniques of behaviour modification. There is sometimes acrimony between those who favour one or the other of these approaches to behavioural and learning problems. The testers are said to use their tests in mechanical and insensitive ways. The behaviourists, it is claimed, degrade and dehumanize their clients by treating them simply as faulty machines to be fixed. And those of a therapeutic or humanistic persuasion are accused of being romantic and ineffective. These criticisms have some force when levelled – in less crude terms – at *abuses* of the methods: they are not valid comments on the methods as such.

Trained educational psychologists help to ensure that the best possible decisions are made in respect to children who are having trouble at school. To this end they will spend time talking with, and perhaps administering tests to, the child in question; consulting with teachers, parents and other professionals (education welfare officers, social workers, remedial teachers, child psychiatrists and psychotherapists); finding out what suitable provisions (special schools, tutorial centres, residential homes) are available, and writing detailed reports and recommendations. This latter activity is an increasingly prominent and time-consuming part of the work, In addition to this, educational psychologists may work directly with parents or teachers to help them set up and monitor programmes of training or other conditions that will be helpful to the child. And they act too in an advisory and consultative capacity to schools, local authorities and other interested parties. Senior members of the profession will also be involved in formulating policy on how to deal with the various types of child in need of special educational help. Whether children with such 'special education needs' (Warnock, 1978) are best helped within normal schools, or whether they do better in specially designed schools, is such an issue, the preferred solution to which alternates from gener-ation to generation.

The educational psychologist's clients fall into three main groups – the physically handicapped (those with serious impairments to vision, hearing or co-ordination, for example); the mentally handicapped (those with learning or other predominantly intellectual problems that have some clearly identifiable and usually irre-medial physical basis); and those whose problems are seen as primarily emotional or social. Some of the latter children are labelled 'maladjusted' or as having 'behavioural problems', though the questions of to whom the behaviour is a problem, and whether it is healthy for a particular young person to adjust to a school system that may be damaging his dignity and denying him a sense of worth or purpose, are some-times not explored as fully as they might be (Hargreaves, 1982). It is currently thought to be an advance to dispense with labels for different kinds of client, and to categorize instead the types of educational provision that they are deemed to require.

Guy Claxton
Chelsea College, University of London

References

Ausubel, D. (1968), *The Psychology of Meaningful Verbal Learning*, New York.

Hargreaves, D. H. (1982), *The Challenge for the Comprehensive School*, London.

Smith, F. (1975), *Comprehension and Learning*, New York.

Warnock, M. (1978), *Special Educational Needs*, London.

Further Reading

Chazan, M., Moore, T., Williams, P., Wright, J. and Walker, M. (1974), *The Practice of Educational Psychology*, London.

See also: *education*; *learning*.

Efficiency

See Economic Efficiency.

Elasticity

Many propositions in economics are in the form of a relationship between two variables. We may write the relationship in general as $y = f(x)$, which reads 'y is a function of x'. 'Quantity consumed (y) is a function of price (x)' is an example of such a proposition. One important feature of any such relationship is how y responds to a change in x. If we let Δx be the change in x and Δy the corresponding change in y, then the sign of $\frac{\Delta y}{\Delta x}$ tells us whether y increases or decreases for a given increase in x. Thus 'quantity consumed falls when price rises' would be represented by a negative sign of $\frac{\Delta y}{\Delta x}$.

For many purposes, it is not enough simply to know the *direction* of the response of y to a given change in x – we also need to know the *magnitude* of this response. How is this to be measured? One candidate is the absolute value of $\frac{\Delta y}{\Delta x}$. The problem with this measure is that it is not free of the units in which y and x are measured, since Δx, and Δy are both measured in their respective units. However $\frac{\Delta x}{x}$ and $\frac{\Delta y}{y}$ are unit free measures of the change in x and the corresponding change in y. Hence

$$\frac{\frac{\Delta y}{y}}{\frac{\Delta x}{x}}$$

is a unit free measure of the responsiveness of y to a change in x. The absolute value of this is known as the *elasticity* of y with respect to x. The expression can be rewritten as $\left(\frac{\Delta y}{\Delta x}\right)\left(\frac{x}{y}\right)$ and, for a small change in x it becomes $\frac{dy}{dx} \cdot \frac{x}{y}$, where $\frac{dy}{dx}$ is the derivative of y with respect to x.

It is not surprising that elasticity – the responsive-ness of one variable to another – has widespread uses in economics. To take just two examples, 'Price elasticity of demand' and 'Income elasticity of demand' are central concepts in consumer theory; 'Price elasticity of Imports' and 'Price elasticity of Exports' are used, for example, in the famous Marshall-Lerner conditions in International Trade Theory.

S. M. Ravi Kanbur
University of Essex

Elections

In politics elections are a device whereby popular preferences are aggregated to choose an officeholder. Choice by elections is now almost inseparable from representative democracy. Some see the opportunity for choice at periodic elections as the key element of Western democracy (Schumpeter, 1942; Lipset, 1960). As of 1975, 33 states did not hold elections to choose political leaders. For other states the crucial question is: what sort of elections? A further 33 states allowed only one candidate for each office. These are 'consent' elections (Mackenzie, 1958). States which allow competitive elections and the possibility of replacing the government are largely Western.

Election systems provide guidelines on such matters as who votes and how, frequency of election, how votes are counted, who stands for office and so on. In the twentieth century, most states have granted the vote to all (with a few exceptions) adult resident citizens. Over time, the suffrage has been extended from estates to individuals, and in the twentieth century to large categories formerly excluded on grounds of race, sex and property qualifications. The change has also been to equality or 'one man one vote one value' (Rokkan, 1970).

In most states, responsibility for registering eligible voters lies with the government. A significant exception is the United States, where states leave registration to individuals. This partly explains why the turn-out in presidential elections since 1960 has averaged 60 per cent, compared to over 80 per cent in many Western states. But American voters have more opportunities to cast votes, in federal, state, local and primary elections, and in long ballots. At the other extreme, political and cultural pressures may produce remarkable turn-outs and verdicts, for example 99.9 per cent turn-out in East Germany in 1964.

Elections have several functions (Rose and Mossawir, 1967). These include: (1) designating, directly or indirectly, the government; (2) providing feedback between voters and government; (3) demonstrating public support for or repudiation of a regime: (4) providing a means for the recruitment of political leaders, and (5) making the government answerable to the electorate. Functions may differ in states which have elections without choice, where a party's hegemonic or monopolistic position makes the outcome a foregone conclusion (Hermet et al, 1978).

In some countries (Belgium, Italy, Denmark and the Netherlands, for example) it is not the election but the inter-party bargaining following the election which determines the composition of government. Where the party system provides a choice between alternative potential majorities, voters do have such a choice. The impact of elections on policies depends in part on a programmatic disciplined majority party being in government. Until recently, the British two-party system was admired for providing a model of 'responsible party government'. More direct popular verdicts on issues may be made through referendums.

The nature of the electoral choice in each state is shaped by three sets of factors. (1) The *object* of election, for example, to choose a constituency representative, party list or President. (2) The *party system*, or pattern of voting alignments (Lipset and Rokkan, 1967). In turn this is shaped by cleavages in society, the electoral system, and the manœuvres of élites. (3) The *electoral system*, particularly those provisions which aggregate votes and translate them into seats, that is, rules for counting and weighing votes.

A distinction may be drawn between the absolute majoritarian system, as in France, in which the 'winner' has to achieve at least half the votes; the plurality (first past the post) system in many English-speaking countries; the various forms of proportionalism, including the pure Proportional Representation in the Netherlands (where 0.67 per cent of the vote gives a group a seat in the legislature); and those that combine different elements of different systems (for example, West Germany has P. R. for half the seats, subject to a party gaining at least 5 per cent of the vote).

Proportionalism was introduced at the turn of the century in divided societies to provide guarantees to minorities which felt threatened by universal suffrage or majority rule. Proportionalism furthers the goals of representativeness but, in the absence of a clear party majority, makes the choice of government less certain.

The British plurality system has usually achieved certainty in choice of the government while sacrificing representativeness. In October 1974 Labour had 51 per cent of the seats in the House of Commons with 39 per cent of the votes. The two systems maximize different values; most Western states have opted for proportionalism, subject to qualifications.

We lack a good typology of elections. One may distinguish between degrees of choice, which in turn depends on the number of effective parties and the prospects of turnover in government. The United States has two parties, the Netherlands and Denmark a dozen. Italy, Sweden and Norway have had very long spells of dominant one-party rule, and there has been only one change in France since 1958. In the

United States, Key (1955) distinguished between elections which were *maintaining* (reflecting normal party loyalties), *deviating* (in which short-term factors produced a short-term surge or decline in support for the parties), and *realigning* (in which there is a long-term change in the balance of party strengths).

There are limits on the decisiveness of elections as authoritative arbiters of policy. Incumbents of the bureaucracy and judiciary, and leaders of powerful interests, who are not elected by the voters, constitute checks. At present 'votes count, resources decide' (Rokkan, 1966). The debate about the relative influence of socioeconomic factors or party political factors (and therefore elections) has not been conclusive. The influence of the government depends on the power centralization in society. In pluralist and market societies the government is only one decision maker among others, and competitive elections and majority rule are only two elements in representative democracy. Competitive elections do not ensure the political responsiveness of an élite; they have to operate in favourable conditions. There are alternative methods of facilitating popular choice and eliciting and demonstrating popular consent (for example, acclamation, seniority, rotation, and élite bargaining), but election is still the birthmark of a government claiming to be democratic.

Dennis Kavanagh
University of Nottingham

References
Hermet, G. *et al.* (1978), *Elections Without Choice*, Paris.
Key, V. O. Jr (1955), 'A theory of critical elections', *Journal of Politics*.
Lipset, S. (1960), *Political Man*, London.
Lipset, S. and Rokkan, S. (eds) (1967), *Party Systems and Voter Alignments*, New York.
Mackenzie, W. J. M. (1958), *Free Elections*, London.
Rokkan, S. (1966), 'Norway: numerical democracy and corporate pluralism', in R. Dahl (ed.), *Political Oppositions in Western Democracies*, New Haven.
Rokkan, S. (1970), *Citizens, Elections, Parties*, New York.
Rose, R. and Mossawir, H. (1967), 'Voting and elections: a functional analysis', *Political Studies*.
Schumpeter, J. A. (1942), *Capitalism, Socialism and Democracy*, New York.
See also: *democracy; parties, political; voting.*

Electroconvulsive Therapy

Electroconvulsive therapy (ECT) is essentially the induction of a cerebral seizure by application of an electrical stimulus to the scalp. The convulsive procedure was introduced after clinical observations suggested sudden improvement in psychiatric patients after spontaneous convulsions. The use of electricty to induce seizures was first introduced by two Italian psychiatrists, Cerletti and Bini, in 1938. Today the use of muscle relaxants almost entirely avoids the actual physical convulsion, which was similar to an epileptic seizure. The physiological reaction in the brain, however, which is like that associated with an epileptic seizure, is unaffected by the relaxing drugs, and is the essential therapeutic event in the treatment. The usual therapeutic course involves a total of eight to twelve treatments administered at the rate of two or three per week.

From the outset, clinical improvement was noted when the treatment was administered to patients with severe depressive illness or psychosis. Because of dramatic clinical improvement following the use of ECT in some patients, and with new control over adverse side-effects such as fractures and dislocations, some psychiatrists tended to use ECT for conditions other than depression. However, although ECT is occasionally of benefit to patients with other conditions, its continued use is in the main justified by the positive response of depressed patients for whom other treatments may be less effective; it has also led to improvement in catatonic states and in other cases of schizophrenia.

One of the concerns about ECT regards possible loss of memory. Memory loss following ECT varies. Some patients return to intellectually demanding jobs with no sense of impairment. Others complain of problems with memory. When both electrodes are placed over the non-dominant hemisphere, memory complaints are fewer. Almost all memory difficulties disappear over days or weeks, although occasionally memories of the treatment period itself may be persistently lost.

It has been postulated that the efficacy of ECT as an antidepressant results from the increased release and distribution of hypothalamic peptides in the brain. Understanding the therapeutic effect of ECT in this and other conditions will require further investigation.

Fred H. Frankel
Harvard University
Beth Israel Hospital, Boston

Further Reading
American Psychiatric Association Task Force on Electroconvulsive Therapy (1978), *Report no. 14.* APA, Washington, D.C.
See also: *biological psychiatry; depressive disorders.*

Elias, Norbert (1897–)

The sociologist, Norbert Elias, was born in Wroclaw, in 1897. He studied medicine, philosophy and psychology at the universities of Wroclaw and Heidelberg, and later worked with Karl Mannheim in Frankfurt. In 1933 he fled Germany, going first to Paris and then to London. After the Second World War, Elias was appointed to a lectureship at the University of Leicester (1954–1962), then became professor at the University of Ghana (1962–1964), and finally returned to Germany as visiting professor at Zentrum für Interdisziplinare Forschung in Bielefeld. He now lives in Amsterdam.

Elias's *magnum opus*, *Ueber der Prozesz der Zivilisation* (1939) (*The Civilizing Process*, 2 vols, 1978–1982), is a historical sociological study of European civilization between the end of the Middle Ages and the nineteenth century. It shows the interdependence of the developments in the structure of European societies and in the personality of their citizens. Processes of state-formation, characterized by ever-increasing state control of violence and taxation, are accompanied by increasing self-restraint on the part of their citizens. The progressive stylization of the elementary (corporal, emotional) activities of life is vividly illustrated, successive contemporary guides to etiquette serving as sources. In *Die Höfische Gesellschaft* (1969) (*The Court Society*, 1984), Elias deals specifically with the transformation of France from a regional system governed by a warrior aristocracy, to a centralized state under the court nobility of Louis XIV.

In these two works, Elias succeeds in integrating macrosociological conceptualizations of command structures, reminiscent of Max Weber, with Freudian ideas of self-control on the individual level. He argues that man's deepest feelings are social, and that individuals have no nonsocial identity. The theoretical implications of this interpenetration of individuals and their society, which is called figurational sociology, are worked out in *Was ist Soziologie?* (1970) (*What is Sociology?* 1978).

Goudsblom has formulated the basic principles of figurational sociology as follows:

(1) Human beings are interdependent, in a variety of ways: their lives evolve in, and are significantly shaped by, the social figurations they form with each other. (2) These figurations are continually in flux, undergoing changes of different orders – some quick and ephemeral, others slower but perhaps more lasting. (3) The long-term developments taking place in human social figurations have been and continue to be largely unplanned and unforeseen. (4) Development of human knowledge takes place within human figurations, and form one important aspect of their overall development: as an aspect of the largely unplanned and unforeseen development of industrial state societies.

The publication of *Ueber der Prozesz der Zivilisation* just before the outbreak of The Second World War went almost unnoticed by the profession, and Elias's English publications of the 1950s met with the same fate. Only after his retirement, with the support of Goudsblom, did he found something of a school, starting in Amsterdam and spreading first to Germany and France, where he met a favourable reception from the *Annales* historians, and then to England and the United States.

Peter Schröder
Ministry of Education, The Netherlands

Reference
Goudsblom, J. (1977), *Sociology in the Balance*, Oxford.

Élites

The term élite is part of a tradition which makes modern social scientists uneasy. At the same time, its use facilitates historical and contemporary analysis by providing an idiom of comparison that sets aside institutional details and culture-specific practices, and calls attention instead to intuitively understood equivalencies. Typically, an adjective precedes the word 'élite', clarifying its aim (oligarchic élite, modernizing élite), or its style (innovating élite, brokerage élite), or its institutional domain (legislative élite, bureaucratic élite), or its resources base (media élite, financial élite), or the decisional stage it dominates (planning élite, implementing élite), or its eligibility grounds (birth élite, credentialed élite).

Two quite different traditions of inquiry persist. In the older tradition, élites are treated as exemplars: fulfilling some historic mission, meeting a crucial need, possessing superior talents, or otherwise demonstrating qualities which set them apart. Whether they stabilize the old order or transform it into a new one, they are seen as pattern setters.

In the newer approach, élites are routinely understood to be incumbents: those who are collectively the influential figures in the governance of any sector of society, any institutional structure, any geographic locality or translocal community. Idiomatically, élites are thus roughly the same as leaders, decision makers or influentials, and not too different from spokesmen, dignitaries, or central figures. This second usage is more matter-of-fact, less normative in tone.

Still, élites are seen by many as selfish people in power, bent upon protecting their vested interests, contemptuous of the restraints on constitutional order, callous about the needs of larger publics, ready to manipulate opinion, to rig elections, to use force if necessary to retain power. A conspiratorial variant worries those who fear revolutionary subversive élites: fanatical, selfless, disciplined, competent, and devoted to their cause, equally contemptuous of political democracy, constitutional order, or mass contentment, willing to exploit hatred and misery, to misrepresent beliefs and facts, and to face personal degradation and social obloquy. Whether to preserve old patterns of life or to exemplify new ones, élites are those who set the styles.

When most social scientists talk about élites, they have in mind 'those who run things' – that is, certain key actors playing structured, functionally understandable roles, not only in a nation's governance processes but also in other institutional settings – religious, military, academic, industrial, communications, and so on (Czudnowski, 1982, 1983).

Earlier formulations lacked this pluralist assumption. Mosca and Pareto (see Meisel, 1965) both presumed that a ruling class effectively monopolized the command posts of a society. Michels insisted that his 'iron law of oligarchy' was inevitable; in any organization, an inner circle of participants would take over, and run it for their own selfish purposes. By contrast, Lasswell's formulation in the 1930s was radically pluralistic. Élites are those who get the most of what there is to get in any institutionalized sector of society and not only in the governing institutions and ancillary processes of organized political life. At every functional stage of any decision process – indeed, in any relevant arena – some participants will be found who have sequestered disproportionate shares of those values, whether money, esteem, power, or some other condition of life which people seek and struggle for. They are the élite at that stage and in that context. For Lasswell (1977), the question whether a situation is fully egalitarian – that is, extends élite status to every participant – is an empirical question, not a conceptual one. Nor is there necessarily any institutional stability. Macro-analysis of history shows periods of ascendancy for those with different kinds of skills, such as in the use of violence, propaganda, organization, or bargaining strategy.

The social formations – classes, communities, movements – from which élites derive are not fixed, either. Élites are usefully studied by asking which communities they represent or dominate, which classes they are exponents or products of, which interests they reflect or foreshadow, which personality types they are prone to recruit or to shunt aside, which circumstances of time and place (periods of crisis, tranquility, or transition) seem to provide missions and challenges for them.

Élites may change their character. Élite transformation has often been traced. Pareto saw vitality and decay as an endless cycle. Students of Third-World modernization often note the heightened tensions within a governing élite that accompany the shift in power from a revolutionary-agitational generation to a programmatic-executive generation. Specialized élites – engineers, soldiers, priests – have often served as second-tier élites, recruited in the service of a ruling class that continues to set a governing style but whose members lack the skills to cope with new and pressing problems. Some scholars hold that a true élite emerges when those who perform the historic mission – whether to bring change, adapt to change, or resist to the end – become convinced that only they can carry out the mission properly. Self-consciously, they come to think of themselves as superior by nature – for example, able to think like scientists or soldiers, willing to take risks like capitalists or revolutionaries (Thoenes, 1965).

For some centuries, the historical forces that have been shaping the institutions of modern, urban, industrial, interdependent, institutionally-differentiated societies have had a net effect that enlarges, democratizes and equalizes the life-chances for élitehood. Everywhere the political stratification system typically resembles a pyramid, reflecting the striking cross-national uniformity that only tiny fractions of a country's citizens have more than an infinitesimal chance of directly influencing national policy or even translocal policies. At the same time, fewer disadvantages linked to social status, educational attainment, geographic residence, cultural claims, age and sex attributes, or institutional credentials appear to operate nowadays as conclusively or comprehensively as in the past.

Viewed as incumbents, those who hold key positions in the governing institutions of a community are, collectively, the élite. They are the custodians of the machinery for making policy. Once a sector of society becomes institutionally differentiated, its ability to adjust to conditions on its own terms is likely to be seriously constrained. Even within its semi-autonomous domains, a custodial élite finds it hard to sustain a liaison network or co-ordinate sector-wide efforts (Field and Higley, 1980). Medical élites are typically locality-rooted. Military services feud with one another. Scientists are engrossed with specialized lines of inquiry. Commercial élites are fragmented. Industrial giants are rivals.

In the modern world, when élites are seen as housed within conventionally recognized establishments such as military, diplomatic, legislative, or party organizational structures, mid-élites and cadres are linked hierarchically to top élites and specialized to implement the specific public and system goals of their domains. When élites are viewed as the top talent in a vocational field – lawyers, academics, entrepreneurs, and so on – the élite structure is much more disjointed. Mid-élites are the source of eligible talent, engaged in tasks having no necessary articulation with what top élites do, but nonetheless tasks that train and test, groom and screen individuals who may in due course reach top élitehood in their field (Putnam, 1976).

Top élites in a custodial structure do not necessarily work well together. The structural complexity of legislatures is such that they typically have rather segmented power structures. In characterizing a military élite, the rivalries of services and branches, the geographic deployment and the generational gaps between echelons all must be acknowledged (Janowitz,

1960). The illusion of homogeneity about the administrative élite is dispelled when one looks closely (Dogan, 1975). Career services give some coherence to relatively autonomous fields, like police, fire, diplomacy, health. But in specific policy domains, clientele élites often dominate the picture (Armstrong, 1973).

Especially when talking about élites in rather amorphous fields of endeavour, the implications of structural disjunctions on the perspectives of those in top positions seem far reaching. Most communications élites are set at working odds with one another in the various media where their contacts and skills apply. At community levels, civic leaders rarely sustain close contacts with their counterparts in other localities.

Élites are studied both in context, in what can be called élite characterization work, and out of context, in what is referred to as élite survey work. There are two main genres of the former – namely, those in which élites are characterized by their mission or function, and those in which élites are seen in a custodial capacity, and characterized by the performance of the institutional processes they control. In a corresponding way, élite surveys – in which élites are taken out of context – also have two main genres: those in which the investigator is mainly interested in what élites think, in the acumen, loyalty, and ideological bent of mind typical of certain élite perspectives; and those which explore the recruitment of élite figures by looking at the changing opportunity structure, at social credentials, screening criteria, processes of sponsorship, grooming and socialization, and at those who are the gatekeepers, brokers, mentors who affect the *corsus honorum* of a career. In modern systematic survey work, it is customary at the outset to say how, when and where the élite status of those studied has been established, whether by reputation, position held, or process participated in. Interviews are then held, often rather long interviews, to learn their beliefs, perceptions, preferences and appraisals. Necessarily, in survey work, élites are not studied 'in action'.

Dwaine Marvick
University of California, Los Angeles

References
Armstrong, J. A. (1973), *The European Administrative Elite*, Princeton.
Czudnowski, M. N. (ed.) (1982), *Does Who Governs Matter?*, DeKalb, Ill.
Czudnowski, M. N. (ed.) (1983), *Political Elites and Social Change*, DeKalb, Ill.
Dogan, M. (ed.) (1975), *The Mandarins of Western Europe*, New York.
Eulau, H. and Czudnowski, M. (eds) (1979), *Elite Recruitment in Democratic Polities*, New York.
Field, G. L. and Higley, J. (1980), *The Professional Soldier*, Glencoe, Ill.
Lasswell, H. D. (1977), 'The study of political elites', in D. Marvick (ed.), *Harold D. Lasswell on Political Sociology*, Chicago.
Mosca, G. (1939 [1896]), *The Ruling Class*, ed. A. Livingston, New York. (Original Italian edn, *Elementi di Scienza parlamentare*.)
Putnam, R. D. (1976), *The Comparative Study of Political Elites*, Englewood Cliffs, N.J.
Thoenes, P. (1966), *The Elite in the Welfare State*, Glencoe, Ill.
See also: *leadership*; *Mill, C.W.*; *Mosca*; *Pareto*; *political recruitment and careers*.

Emotion

William James wrote that he would 'as lief read verbal descriptions of the shapes of the rocks on a New Hampshire farm' as toil again through the classic works on emotion, which lacked a 'central point of view, a deductive or generative principle'. Since then, many theories of emotion have been advanced, but none has succeeded in gaining widespread acceptance. Indeed, one hundred years after James's famous essay in *Mind* (1884), 'What is an emotion?', we are hardly better placed than James to answer the question he posed – a situation which is partly attributable to the neglect of emotion by psychologists during the behaviourist era. Recently, however, there has been a notable resurgence of interest from psychologists and other social scientists in the study of emotion. Most theories of emotion adopt a biological or psychological level of analysis, although more emphasis is also given nowadays to social and cultural factors.

The issues that preoccupy modern emotion theory are remarkably similar to those that arose from James's (1884) theory of emotion and its subsequent rebuttal by Cannon. Briefly, James advocated what has come to be called a *peripheral* theory of emotion, in which he argued that the perception of an arousing stimulus causes changes in peripheral organs such as the viscera (heart, lungs, stomach, and so on) and the voluntary muscles, and that emotion is quite simply the perception of these bodily changes. To use James's own example, it is not that we run because we are afraid; rather, we are afraid because we run. This view clearly implies that there should be as many discrete patterns of physiological activity accompanying emotion as there are discernible emotional states. Cannon (1927) published what was widely regarded as a devastating critique of James's theory, although later research has shown that some, if not all, of Cannon's objections were ill-founded.

The essence of Cannon's critique was that the visceral changes that occur during emotion are too non-specific to serve as the basis for differentiated emotional experience. This point led later researchers to abandon the search for an explanation of emotion couched exclusively in terms of bodily changes, and to consider more carefully the role played by cognitive factors – the individual's interpretation of external and internal events. Two cognitive theories of emotion have attracted some attention. The more complex theory is the one proposed by Lazarus and his associates (Lazarus *et al.*, 1970), basic to which is the notion that emotion is based on the individual's *appraisal* of his circumstances. Thus the appraisal of a stimulus as 'threatening' instigates various responses (cognitive, expressive and instrumental) which together comprise the experience of fear. One limitation of Lazarus's theory is that it was developed with specific reference to the understanding of stress, and it is by no means clear how easily it generalizes to other emotions.

The other influential cognitive theory of emotion is Schachter's (1964) two-factor theory. One of Cannon's objections to James's theory was that the artificial induction (by adrenaline injection) of bodily changes characteristic of emotion does not result in emotional experience. Schachter reasoned that this is because the individual knows the bodily changes to be the product of the injection, rather than an emotional stimulus. Therefore, emotion is the joint product of *two* factors, namely a general state of physiological arousal, and the cognition that this arousal is caused by an emotional stimulus. The arousal creates the conditions necessary for *any* emotion to be experienced, while the cognition determines which emotion is actually experienced. Thus the same physiological arousal could, in principle, be experienced as any of a variety of emotions, depending on cognitive factors. Although this theory has an appealing elegance and simplicity, there is little evidence to support it (Manstead and Wagner, 1981).

Whereas Schachter treats bodily changes accompanying emotion as undifferentiated arousal, recent research findings support the Jamesian notion that discrete patterns of physiological change accompany emotion. For example, Ekman, Levenson and Friesen (1983) found that flexing the facial muscles into emotional expressions has effects on measures such as heart rate and skin temperature, and that anger and fear expressions have different effects from those produced by happiness, surprise and disgust. It would therefore seem that the facial musculature is intimately related to the autonomic nervous system, which controls functions such as heart rate. It seems likely that future research on bodily changes in emotion will take emotion theory away from Schachter's view that cognitive factors are solely responsible for differentiating emotional experience into qualitatively distinct states such as anger and joy, and towards the type of view advocated by theorists such as Izard (1971), who argues that (for some emotions, at least) there are discrete, innate patterns of neural, facial-postural, and

motor activity, awareness of which generates the subjective experience of emotion.

Apart from work aimed at elucidating the roles played by cognitive and physiological processes in the generation of emotion, there are two other notable lines of research on emotion. One is concerned with facial expression. More specifically, some investigators have examined whether the way in which emotion is expressed in the face is the same across diverse cultures (Ekman, 1982), while others have studied individual differences, both in facial expressiveness during emotional experience and in the ability to recognize from facial expressions what emotions others are experiencing (Rosenthal, 1979). A second line of research, much of it conducted by sociologists, is concerned with what is referred to as the 'socialization of the emotions'. Here the focus is on how social and cultural factors influence 'feeling rules' (Hochschild, 1979), that is, rules concerning how to express emotions, when to express emotions, how emotions are managed, how emotions are labelled, and how emotions are interpreted (Lewis and Michalson, 1982).

A. S. R. Manstead
University of Manchester

References
Cannon, W. B. (1927), 'The James-Lange theory of emotions: a critical examination and an alternative theory', *American Journal of Psychology*, 39.
Ekman, P. (1982), *Emotion in the Human Face* (2nd edn), New York.
Ekman, P., Levenson, R. W. and Friesen, W. V. (1983), 'Autonomic nervous system activity distinguishes among emotions', *Science*, 221.
Hochschild, A. R. (1979), 'Emotion work, feeling rules, and social structure', *American Journal of Sociology*, 85.
Izard, C. E. (1971), *The Face of Emotion*, New York.
Lazarus, R. S., Averill, J. R. and Opton, E. M. (1970), 'Toward a cognitive theory of emotion', in M. B. Arnold (ed.), *Feelings and Emotions*, New York.
Lewis, M. and Michalson, L. (1982), 'The socialization of emotions', in T. Field (ed.), *Emotion and Early Interaction*, Hillsdale, N.J.
Manstead, A. S. R. and Wagner, H. L. (1981), 'Arousal, cognition and emotion: an appraisal of two-factor theory', *Current Psychological Reviews*, 1.
Rosenthal, R. (1979), *Skill in Nonverbal Communication: Individual Differences*, Boston.
Schachter, S. (1964), 'The interaction of cognitive and physiological determinants of emotional state', in L. Berkowitz (ed.), *Advances in Experimental Social Psychology* (vol. 1), New York.

Further Reading
Izard, C. E. (1977), *Human Emotions*, New York.
Mandler, G. (1975), *Mind and Emotion*, New York.
See also: *activation and arousal; aggression and anger; empathy and sympathy.*

Empathy and Sympathy

Empathy has been conceived as being a cognitive process or an emotional-cognitive one. The former conception relates primarily to an individual's intellectual understanding of another's ideation and feelings, and has led to studies of the accuracy of predicting another's responses to questionnaire items and of other adjustments about others. These studies have been fraught with methodological difficulties.

The emotional-cognitive conception has focused on a person's perceiving – veridically or not – that another is experiencing an emotional state and, as a consequence, experiencing the same type of emotion. The degree of similarity of the two emotional states is in some dispute. Furthermore, the other's state can be inferred from the situation, from direct observation, or from other information. This conception does not include the trivial case in which the other's emotional state is a precursor of an affect causing experience for the 'empathizer'.

Emotional-cognitive empathy has been found to be an outcome definitionally required of 'taking the role of the other', although it may also be based on learned associations between one's own and other's experiences. Emotional-cognitive empathy has been found to be related to helping the other person, when such help appears to be a means of reducing negative affect in the other; and it also appears to be related to moral behaviour. However, recent research has suggested that if the empathizer is motivated only to free himself from the empathized negative emotion, then he may do so by escaping the situation as well as by helping the other, whichever is less costly and more effective. In fact, if the empathized negative emotion is very strong, the individual may flee from the other person.

On the other hand, if the empathizer also has a positive attitude toward the other and is motivated to help him, then his empathy becomes a form of sympathy. Sympathy may be viewed as a state in which a person is concerned about another's welfare. Whether or not empathy is a necessary correlate of sympathy is undetermined as yet, since a person may sympathize with another even when the latter is not experiencing any relevant emotion.

Ezra Stotland
University of Washington

Further Reading
Hoffman, M. L. (1977), 'Empathy, its development and prosocial implications', in C. B. Keasey (ed.), *Nebraska Symposium on Motivation: 1977 Social Cognitive Development*, Lincoln.
Stotland, E., Mathews, K., Hansson, R., Richardson, B. and Sherman, S. (1978), *Fantasy, Empathy and Help*, Beverly Hills.
Stotland, E., Sherman, S. and Shaver, K. G. (1971), *Empathy and Birth Order: Some Experimental Explorations*, Lincoln.
See also: *emotion.*

Employment and Underemployment

Most generally, employment is the process of devoting human time and energy to production. It is the labour input to the economy, the performance and organization of work by people in an economic system. In economics the term is normally used in a restricted sense, to describe the creation of goods and services that fall within whatever convention is in use to define the National Product. Economists conventionally exclude unpaid domestic or voluntary services and remunerated activities such as crime, gambling or prostitution which are not considered 'productive'.

The term employment, strictly speaking, derives from the capitalist and wage-labour mode of production. On a narrower definition, it refers to the contractual arrangements which bring workers together with materials and equipment which are not their own property. The term is extended by analogy to other modes of production to cover self-employment, people working in collective enterprises and – at a stretch – family-based production and other pre-capitalist institutions like sharecropping.

The corollary of employment being a productive activity is that it entitles the performer to income – wages in the capitalist mode. Sen (1975) draws attention to these production and income aspects of the notion of employment, to which he adds a third perspective, that it entitles the worker to recognition, or self- and social-esteem, as doing something worthwhile. There is thus a threefold cause for concern if an economy is deemed to have an 'employment problem': production is unnecessarily low, some incomes are unnecessarily low and some people may be deprived of the recognition, or status, that employment would give them.

For wage-labour economies, where employment is organized on a regular full-time basis, 'employment' can be roughly measured as the number of people holding jobs. The suitability of this simplification for any actual situation will depend on how much the quantity of work actually varies between workers. The following exposition also abstracts from heterogeneity in the quality of workers and employment. Employment is the minimum of labour supply and labour demand. On a head-count measure, it is the numbers required by employers or the numbers available for work (at the going wage rate), whichever is smaller. Labour supply in this context is equivalent to the 'labour force' – the total numbers willing to perform paid work, consisting of people in employment plus those available for employment but unable to find it, that is, the unemployed. The classic criterion for unemployment is therefore unsuccessful job search.

The Keynesian notion of 'full employment' in such a labour market is that the effective demand for labour is at a level where productive capacity is fully utilized and unemployment is at a minimum. This minimum consists of at least one element, 'frictional unemployment', people spending a relatively short time finding a suitable job where labour market information is, perhaps inevitably, not good enough to match all vacancies and job seekers instantaneously. Under some circumstances, keeping employment at this frictional minimum would satisfy another definition of full employment as that level of demand for labour which does not aggravate inflation. This level of employment will, however, only ensure maximal utilization of the labour force if there is enough material capital to equip each job. Ideally, capital would accumulate embodying techniques (capital: labour ratios) which utilize available labour resources. But in the short run the stock of capital is fixed, and often the techniques by which it can be operated are also virtually fixed. This sets an upper limit to the amount of labour an economy can absorb in the short run. If available labour supplies exceed this limit there is said to be 'structural' unemployment, as it could only be eliminated by changes in the structure or size of the capital stock. 'Structural unemployment' also arises when the quality of labour required differs from the quality of the labour on offer in respects such as skill, education or location.

In economies not dominated by the simplified sort of labour market postulated above, underemployment (or the underutilization of labour) and its attendant problems need not take the form of 'open unemployment'. Indeed, unless there are institutions (such as social insurance or the family) which transfer resources to the jobless, open unemployment is a luxury which few can afford. Unemployment may be hidden in various ways.

(1) Potential workers may drop out of the labour force altogether, labelling themselves as 'retired', 'housewife', or 'student', though they might be available for employment should the demand arise.

(2) Work and income may be shared by members of the labour force working fewer hours, fewer days or less intensively than they would otherwise.

(3) The 'underemployed' may actually work hard and long in inferior, low productivity occupations for want of access to employment in well equipped and well paid sectors of the economy.

The first type of hidden unemployment (or 'discouraged workers') avoids the recognition aspect (if people really do think of themselves in the social accountant's mutually exclusive categories), and is sometimes regarded as none too pressing a social problem, particularly as it is certainly problematic to discover how many people fall into this category at any given time.

The second, work sharing, version typically arises in family-run modes of production such as peasant agriculture when faced either by deficiencies of market demand for output, or, in the classic 'surplus labour' situation, by limited availability of land.

The third type of underemployment is characteristic of 'informal' employment in the urban sectors of developing countries, though it was an example from a mature economy – match selling on the streets of London – that Joan Robinson (1937) used when advancing the idea of disguised unemployment in the 1930s. The notion of dual or segmented labour markets harbouring sectors where underprivileged participants labour at a disadvantage and form an underutilized reserve to a more productive part of the labour market has found applications for both rich and poor countries in the current economic literature. 'Discouraged' housewives might also be regarded as a subset of the third type if their domestic work were a less productive use of their time than their potential market employment.

'Employment policies' are interventions designed to alleviate 'employment problems'. They comprise a very wide set of measures, just as the diagnosis can cover a very wide range of circumstances. Macroeconomic policy can alleviate (or exacerbate) the part of underemployment attributable to deficient aggregate demand. Then there are measures to improve labour market information, to assist labour and employer mobility and to train and retrain the available manpower. In the long run, labour demand can be affected by interventions in the wage formation process, development planning, international trade policy and fiscal policy which favours either capital or labour intensive techniques. From the classic job-creation measure of public works, the list of employment policies now extends to those which redistribute earning opportunities, promote or protect the employment of special groups, encourage work-sharing and develop intermediate techniques.

Heather Joshi
London School of Hygiene and Tropical Medicine

References
Robinson, J. (1937), *Essays on the Theory of Employment*, London.

Sen, A. K. (1975), *Employment, Technology and Development*, Oxford.

Further Reading
Garraty, J. (1979), *Unemployment in History*, New York.
Greenhalgh, C. A., Layard, P. R. G. and Oswald, A. S. (eds) (1983), *The Causes of Unemployment*, Oxford.
I.L.O. (1984), *World Labour Report 1: Employment, Incomes, Social Protection, New Information Technology*, Geneva.
Squire, L. (1981), *Employment Policy in Developing Countries: A Survey of Issues and Evidence*, New York.
See also: *employment and unemployment – social psychological aspects; labour market analysis; productivity.*

Employment and Unemployment: Social Psychological Aspects

Employment as the dominant institution through which people earn their living is largely the result of the Industrial Revolution. Since then social scientists of all kinds have thought about its impact on individuals and society. Their powerful ideas influenced the climate of thought about industrialism long before social psychology came of age. Karl Marx and Max Weber had proposed conflicting ideas on work motivation: alienation versus the Protestant work ethic. Frederick Taylor (curiously acclaimed by Lenin) concentrated on productivity through changes in work organization. Few social psychologists based their work explicitly on these forerunners, but when they began systematic study they adopted their themes: work motivation and productivity.

A considerable number of early studies were based on a combination of both themes and searched for ways to improve morale in the expectation that increase in productivity would follow. The results of these efforts are ambiguous. On the positive side, an enormous amount has been learned about how to improve morale: job enrichment and enlargement, flexible working hours, group organization, participation in decision making, profit-sharing and co-operative organization have all been demonstrated as capable of strengthening morale, even though less effectively for workers in the most routinized jobs. The expectation that productivity would increase correspondingly, however, was not universally fulfilled: it happened in some cases, not in others, and in a few instances improved morale occurred even with lowered productivity. The reasons for these inconclusive results have so far not been identified (see Klein, 1976, for a full discussion).

Recently it has become recognized that productivity is more a function of technology, less of morale. Continuing studies of morale and motivation are undertaken in the belief that improvement in these matters is a legitimate goal in its own right, even if it does not increase productivity.

The current wave of mass unemployment in Western societies has induced many social psychologists to switch from their concern with these issues to the study of the psychological impact of unemployment. For the second time in this century the tragic opportunity has arisen to elucidate the taken-for-granted meaning of employment by the systematic study of its absence.

During the Great Depression of the 1930s the psychological impact of unemployment was documented in over 100 studies (summarized in Eisenberg and Lazarsfeld, 1938). They showed the suffering of the unemployed through abject poverty and lack of work; they were often without public support and depended on charity. Many felt depressed and bored, time had lost its meaning, voluntary activities that previously could be accommodated after a long working day were abandoned, self-respect was undermined, people felt thrown on the scrap-heap. Of course there were individual differences, but the general picture was one of resignation or deeply felt frustration.

Was this response due more to living in extreme poverty or more to the absence of employment? A comparison with the impact of unemployment in the 1980s, when economic deprivation is as a rule relative and not absolute, suggests the answer: the current response to unemployment shows many similarities to those in the 1930s. The majority of unemployed suffer from depressive moods, boredom and loss of time orientation, feel socially useless and abandoned by the larger community.

This similarity, notwithstanding the enormous social changes that have occurred since the 1930s, suggests that the meaning of employment has remained relatively constant. Like every other institution, employment has not only conscious, manifest purposes but also latent consequences that inevitably enforce, for better or worse, experiences within certain categories on those who participate in it. These enforced categories of experience (more fully discussed in Jahoda, 1982) are: a specific organization of time, an enlarged horizon through contact with others, a demonstration of the need for collective effort, and an assignment of social identity and regular activity.

The frustrations of the unemployed (also of many housewives whose children have left home and of many retired people) suggest that some experiences within these general categories are needed to make sense of one's daily life, and that the majority of those who were used to the social support provided by the organization of employment in meeting these needs feel deprived when this support is withdrawn. In the 1980s, as was also the case in the 1930s, those few unemployed who manage out of their own initiative and against the norms of society to meet these needs in voluntary work do not suffer psychologically, even if they do economically, when they lose their jobs. But it is unrealistic to expect that most of the unemployed – consisting of unskilled workers and young people without any work experience – could manage.

Social psychological thought and research thus support the notion that people need work beyond economic considerations, though not necessarily under conditions of employment, to make sense of their daily lives. For the foreseeable future, economic necessity will, however, continue to make employment the central institution through which most people satisfy their often unrecognized psychological needs as well as their aspirations for a high material standard of living. The identification of the five basic needs helps not only to understand why the unemployed suffer, but also provides a concrete agenda for the humanization of employment. While all employment is psychologically preferable to unemployment, there exist some employment conditions where the time experience, the quality of the social contact, the collective purpose, the social identity and the actual activity are deeply unsatisfactory. There is great scope for future research-based changes in all these areas.

Marie Jahoda
University of Sussex

References

Eisenberg, P. and Lazarsfeld, P. F. (1938), 'The psychological effects of unemployment', *Psychological Bulletin*, 35.

Jahoda, M. (1982), *Employment and Unemployment*, Cambridge.

Klein, L. (1976), *New Forms of Work Organisation*, Cambridge.

See also: *employment and underemployment*.

Energy

Any society's ability to survive depends on its continued access to energy in appropriate quantities and at acceptable costs. The relationship over time between the level of development in an economy and the use of energy is illustrated in Figure 1. Given this relationship, then the transformation of the world over the last 150 years, from a world which consisted mainly of peasant economies largely subsistent in their organization to one consisting of post-industrial, industrial and industrializing economies, has produced a global use of energy which is now over twenty times greater than it is estimated to have been in 1860. Figure 2 shows what a remarkably consistent rate of growth in energy use there has been over the whole of this period

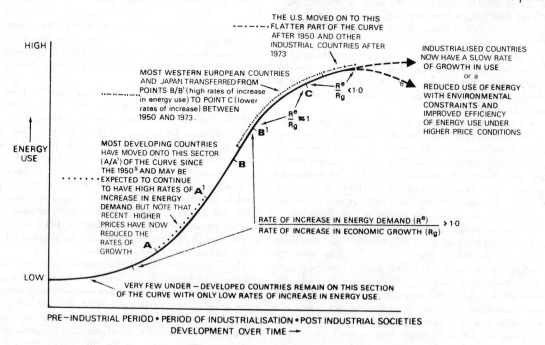

Figure 1   The relationship between energy use and economic development over time
This figure demonstrates how the ratio between the rate of increase in energy use and the rate of economic growth in developing countries remains higher than in the industrialized world. As developing countries depend mainly on oil for their energy this means that their importance as participants in the international oil industry will steadily increase.

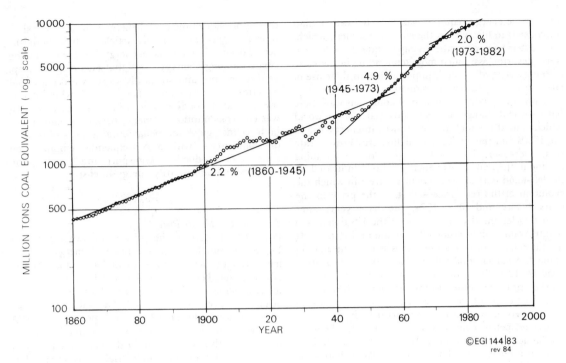

©EGI 144|83
rev 84

Figure 2   World energy use 1860–2000

(at about 2.2 per cent per annum), except for the years between 1950 and 1973 when the rate of growth was almost 5 per cent per annum.

The Demand for Energy

As current attitudes to the world energy situation and outlook are heavily dependent on the idea that this exceptional period of rapid energy growth represents the 'norm', so that the future energy supply potential is evaluated in the context of a 'required' ±5 per cent per annum growth in energy use, it is important to show that it was a unique combination of time-coincident factors which produced an energy growth rate so much higher than the long-term trend (to which, incidentally, Figure 2 shows that the world has returned since 1973).

Between 1950 and 1973 virtually all the world's nations were on the steepest part of the curve in Figure 1, in a situation, that is, in which their economies were in the most highly energy intensive period of development. Thus, the rich countries of the Western economic system were going through the later stages of the industrialization process with an emphasis on products with high energy inputs – such as motor vehicles, household durable goods, petrochemical products. As a result, the use of energy on the production side of the economy greatly increased. On the consumption side the increase in energy use was even more dramatic as a result of the mass use of motor

cars, the suburbanization of cities, the switch from public to private transport, the expanded availability of leisure time and the 'annihilation of space' in the public's use of such time, the mechanization of households by the use of electricity-intensive equipment, and the achievement of much higher standards of comfort (by heating and/or cooling) in homes and other buildings.

Many of the same factors positively influenced the rate of growth in energy use in the centrally planned economies of the Soviet Union and Eastern Europe. This was particularly the case in respect of those countries' industrialization, with its special emphasis on the rapid expansion of heavy, intensive industry. And to a smaller, but nevertheless a still significant, extent, consumers in the centrally planned economies have also increased their levels of energy use as a result of higher living standards and changes in lifestyle.

Meanwhile, in the Third World most countries moved off the lowest part of the curve shown in Figure 1, as policies of industrialization, accompanied by urbanization, were deliberately pursued in the search for higher living standards. Again the sort of industry which was established was either energy-intensive heavy industry, such as iron and steel and cement, or relatively energy-intensive industry, such as textiles and household goods. The urbanization process meant that peasants and other rural inhabitants were transferred from their low-energy ways of living (in which most of the energy required was collected rather than purchased) to lifestyles in the city environment which, no matter how poor the living standards achieved, were, nevertheless, much more demanding in their use of energy generally – and, in particular, in their use of electricity and petroleum products.

It was essentially the temporal coincidence of these basic societal change factors in most parts of the world which caused the high rate of growth in energy use in the 1950s and the 1960s. The high energy growth rate was, moreover, increased by the long continuing decline in the real price of energy. This is indicated by the left-hand part of the curve in Figure 3 in which the evolution of the real price – that is, the price in the years before and after 1974, the base year, after adjusting for the declining value of the US dollar – of Saudi Arabian light crude oil over the period 1950–81 is illustrated. From this one can see that the market value of a barrel of oil fell by almost 60 per cent from 1950 to 1970. This decline brought about a falling market price for other forms of energy during this period throughout the world, and most especially in the Western industrial countries with their open – or relatively open – economies. In these areas local energy production (such as coal in Western Europe and oil and natural gas in the United States) either had to be reduced in price to enable it to compete, or it went out of business. (This phenomenon was also important for the supply side of the global energy situation. We shall return to this later in this article.) Thus, both the actual decline in the price of energy and the perception created amongst energy users that energy was cheap, getting cheaper and so hardly worth worrying about in terms of the care and efficiency with which it was used, created conditions in which the careless and wasteful consumption of energy became a hallmark of both technological and behavioural aspects of societal developments – with a consequential emphasis on systems of production, transport and consumption which were unnecessarily energy-intensive.

The Impact of Higher Prices

Post-1970 changes in the price of oil (also shown in Figure 3), and hence in the price of energy overall, have brought these attitudes to an end, so that the use of energy has been curbed. The results of this change have, as shown in Figure 2, been dramatic. The rate of increase over the last decade has fallen right back to the historic rate of ±2 per cent per annum, with the most important element in the reduction in the rate of growth being the fall in the energy-intensity of economic activities in the industrialized countries. For Western European countries, for example, the energy-intensity of economic growth from 1973–82 was less than half that of the preceding ten years, and since 1982 the ratio has fallen still further. There have been both technological and behavioural components in this change; the latter include consumers' decisions to save energy through the expenditure of effort and money on insulating their homes and on living with lower temperatures; and on their more efficient use of their motor cars by driving more carefully and by combining trips to save mileage. It is, however, the technological improvements that have been the more important in saving energy – through more efficient processes in factories, more efficient lighting in offices, the development of motor vehicles, planes and ships which give more kilometres per litre (ton) of fuel, and the expansion of inherently more energy efficient systems of electricity production. The combined production of heat and power (CHP) enables at least 70 per cent of the energy value of the input fuels to be made available to users. In conventional power stations, from which most of the heat is lost to the atmosphere and/or cooling water, only 40 per cent, at best, of the energy of the fuel used is made available as electricity. Both the behavioural and the technological aspects of more effective energy use still have a long way to go before the existing energy inefficient systems of the period of low and decreasing-cost energy are finally replaced – even in the richer countries where the required investment funds and other inputs (of knowledge, managerial and technical expertise and so on) are available to

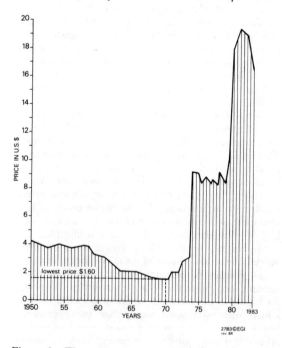

Figure 3   The price of oil, 1950–1983 (shown in 1974 $ terms: in current dollars the 1981 price was $34 per barrel)

make the changes simply a matter of time. The diffusion of more effective energy-using systems to the modern sectors of most Third-World countries will be a slower process because of the scarcity of the inputs involved. Such diffusion is, however, taking place, under the stimulus of the very high foreign exchange cost of energy (particularly oil) imports to the economies concerned. Thus, enhanced levels of energy-use efficiency will eventually be achieved in the Third World – an important consideration for the longer-term evolution of global energy demand, as the percentage of world energy use in these countries steadily increases under the joint impact of expanding populations and of economies which are going through the most energy intensive period of development (see Figure 1). The countries with centrally planned economies lie somewhere in between the industrialized and the Third-World countries in respect of energy use and prospects patterns; so far they have not done as well as the market economies in saving energy, but the importance of energy conservation has now become generally recognized by the governments concerned so that, given the nature of these 'command' economies, the implementation of measures to save energy will now be given a high priority.

The Supply of Fossil Fuels
Meanwhile, on the supply side a search for energy self-sufficiency by nations in all parts of the world has become a key element in energy policy making. This is because of widely shared fears for the repetition of the kinds of supply problems that emerged from the undue dependence on oil from the Middle East and a few other OPEC countries. This development has caused a reversal of the increasingly concentrated geography of energy production of the post-World War II period, during which the prolific and extremely low-cost resources of the Middle East and other areas undermined the economic production of most energy sources in most other parts of the world. Thus, not only did hitherto important energy-producing regions such as Western Europe (where the economy had been built on the use of indigenous coal) become dependent on oil imports from the low-cost countries, but so did much of the developing world, where the required rapidly increasing supply of energy was easier to secure on the basis of oil imported through the aegis of the international oil companies than through efforts to expand the indigenous production of energy – even where resources were known to exist. It was only in the case of the few countries, including the United States, which protected their indigenous energy-supply industries to a high enough degree that the contribution of low-cost imported oil was restricted to a relatively small part of total energy supply. By the early 1970s even the United States, with its wealth of energy resources, finally had to reduce the degree to

which it protected its indigenous production in order to reduce the energy cost disadvantage it had come to suffer, compared with competing industrial nations where energy costs were related to the cheap oil available from the Middle East.

This situation changed drastically once OPEC determined to increase the price of oil – as shown in Figure 3. The approximately fivefold real price increase of OPEC oil between 1970 and 1975 and the subsequent further doubling of the price by 1981 removed the economic restraints on investment in locally available sources of energy, and there was thus a general reappraisal of the prospects for indigenous energy production in most countries. Some developments were possible in the short term, notably in the United States where under-utilized capacity in already established energy-supply industries could quickly be brought into production. In Western Europe a massive stimulus was given to the efforts to exploit North Sea oil and gas, and the hitherto deteriorating prospects for the continent's coal industry were reversed. Similar developments occurred elsewhere in the non-communist world and produced the changes, shown in Table 1, in the relative importance of OPEC exports and non-OPEC energy use by 1982.

Table 1

Oil exports from OPEC compared with other energy used in the rest of the non-communist world in 1973 and 1982 (in million of tons of oil equivalent)

	1973		1982	
	m.t.o.e	% of total	m.t.o.e.	% of total
(a) OPEC oil exports	1480	36.5%	850	21.0%
(b) Other energy use in rest of non-communist world	2565	63.5%	3200	79.0%
of which Oil	810	20.0%	1170	29.0%
Natural Gas	795	19.5%	790	19.5%
Coal	825	20.5%	1015	25.0%
Other	135	3.5%	225	5.5%
(c) Total of (a) and (b)	4045	100%	4050	100%

Sources: Derived from UN Energy Statistics (Series J) and BP's Statistical Review of World Energy

This shows how dramatically OPEC's contribution to the non-communist world's energy supply has fallen – compared with total energy production elsewhere in the non-communist world. The latter's oil production now exceeds its imports of oil from OPEC by a very comfortable margin. OPEC's 1982 oil exports, moreover, were little more than natural gas production elsewhere and well below the production of coal.

World energy supplies have thus become geographically more dispersed, and this is a process which will continue as long as the price of OPEC oil remains so far above the cost of alternatives, and so long as oil supplies from most OPEC countries are perceived to be unreliable. In essence, the low-cost, but high-price, oil reserves of the OPEC countries have become 'the energy source of last resort'. This involves real economic costs for the world economy as a result of the higher-than-necessary costs of energy inputs to both production and consumption activities – so reducing the potential for economic growth in the system.

Alternative Energy Sources
The prospects for the exploitation of renewable energy sources – to supplement and replace the use of fossil fuels – has attracted much attention over the last decade. Thus, there are enthusiastic lobbies for the rapid expansion of benign energy systems based on solar, wind, water, wave and biomass energy potential. There has been but a modest response to this enthusiasm by energy policy-makers in most parts of the world, mainly as an increased availability of necessary research and development funds. However, apart from the continued expansion of hydroelectricity production (a long-established source of energy), relatively little progress has been made in 'commercializing' the potential contribution of the benign energy sources, partly because of the long gestation period required for technical innovation, partly because their successful utilization depends on locating appropriate physical geographical conditions, and partly because their use also depends on changes in the structure of societies and the reorganization of national energy supply networks. These are formidable problems. Thus the relative contribution of such sources of energy to the world's now slowly rising total energy needs is unlikely to grow very much at all until well after the turn of the century.

By contrast, nuclear power has secured the support of many governments as a means of reducing dependence on imported oil. Its expansion has thus been generously, even extravagantly, funded (partly, at least, because it is linked to the development of the major powers' nuclear arsenals). There has been a fourfold expansion in nuclear electricity production over the last decade, but this was from a very small initial level of output. In spite of all the efforts and money devoted to it, nuclear power remains globally less than half as important as water power, and it still contributes less then one quarter of 1 per cent to the world's total energy use. Some governments and other authorities remain convinced of nuclear power's potential, but cost escalation, public concern for the safety of the reactors and of the irradiated waste products

from the power stations, and, most important of all, the lack of adequate growth in the demand for electricity in those countries where nuclear power is a practicable proposition from the standpoints of available finance and technology, have severely undermined the prospects for nuclear power. It, too, seems destined to make little additional contribution to world energy supplies over the rest of the century. Figures 4 and 5 summarize the outlook for world energy over the period up to 2010. Growth in use will be modest compared with experience between 1948 and 1973, but the contribution of fossil fuels will remain dominant – though oil will lose part of its share of the market to natural gas and coal.

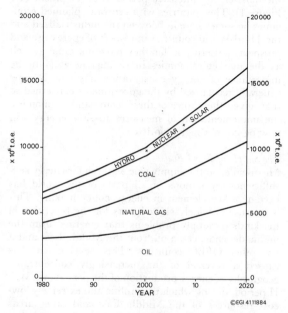

Figure 4　Growth in total world energy use 1980–2020 showing the contributions of individual main sources of energy

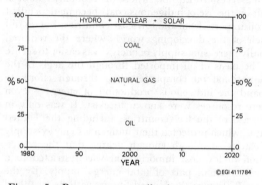

Figure 5　Percentage contributions of the various energy sources to total energy use 1980–2020

The Poor World's Energy Problem

Outside the framework of the discussion of energy presented in this article is one element that remains important for large parts of the world; that is, the supply of locally available energy in societies which remain largely or partly subsistent in their economic organization. The *per capita* use of energy in such societies is small (see Figure 1), as it depends on the immediately available supply of combustible materials (such as wood and dung) which can provide for cooking and heating needs. Collectively, however, this pattern of energy use in the world is still large given the numbers of people involved in such societies. Overall, it is estimated to account for about 20 per cent of total world energy use – ranging from near zero in the industrialized countries, to 15 per cent in Latin America, to over 95 per cent in some of the poorest countries of Africa. In almost all of the latter areas the local scarcity of wood is becoming an increasingly difficult problem. The solution requires 'energy-farming' and new, albeit simple, technological developments which bring improved efficiencies in the use of the combustible materials. This is a world energy problem of which little is known and about which even less is being done – compared, that is, with the attention which is given to the problems of oil and the other energy sources required for intensive use in the developed world and in the modernized sectors of the developing countries' economies.

Peter R. Odell
Erasmus University, Rotterdam

Further Reading

Adelman, M. A. (1972), *The World Petroleum Market*, Baltimore.

Anderer, J. *et al.* (1981), *Energy in a Finite World*, Cambridge, Mass.

Darmstadter, J. *et al.* (1977), *How Industrial Societies Use Energy*, Baltimore.

Dienes, L. and Shabad, T. (1974), *The Soviet Energy System*, Washington.

Dunkerley, J. (1981), *Energy Strategies for Developing Nations*, Baltimore.

Hoffman, T. and Johnson, B. (1981), *The World Energy Triangle*, Cambridge, Mass.

Lovins, A. B. (1975), *World Energy Strategies*, New York.

Odell, P. R. (1983), *Oil and World Power*, Harmondsworth.

Odell, P. R. and Valenilla, L. (1978), *The Pressures of Oil*, London.

Smil, V. and Knowland, W. E. (1980), *Energy in the Developing World: The Real Energy Crisis*, New York.

Schurr, S. and Netschert, B. (1977), *Energy in the American Economy 1850–75*, Baltimore.

World Energy Conference (1978), *World Energy Resources 1985–2020*, Guildford.

See also: *population and resources*.

Engel, Ernst (1821–96)

Ernst Engel was director of the Prussian Bureau of Statistics (1861–82) who discovered Engel's Law, while director of the statistical bureau of Saxony (1850–8). He studied at the École des Mines in Paris after an academic training in mining in Germany.

In 1857 he published his paper, 'Die Produktions- und Consumtionsverhältnisse des Königreichs Sachsen', in which he demonstrated the existence of an inverse proportional relationship between consumer income and food expenditures. In other words, the income elasticity of the demand for food is less than 1. This relationship became known as Engel's Law, and was among the first quantitative 'laws' in economics established on empirical grounds. Engel's Law seems to have withstood the test of time.

The significance of his discovery is that it stimulated the search for other empirical laws, among the most notable being Pareto's 'Law of income distribution'. Unfortunately, the search for empirical laws in economics, which are invariant in space and time, has not been successful and Engel's Law is the exception which proves the rule.

Vincent J. Tarascio
University of North Carolina

Reference

Engel, E. (1857), 'Die Produktions-und Consumtionsverhältnisse des Königreichs Sachsen', *Zeitschrift des statistischen Büreaus des Königlich Sächsischen Ministeriums des Innern.*

Further Reading

Stigler, G. J. (1954), 'The early history of empirical studies of consumer behavior', *Journal of Political Economy*, 62.

Engels, Friedrich (1820–95)

Friedrich Engels was born into a family of mill-owners in the Rhineland with business interests in Manchester. He took employment in the family firm at sixteen and never formally attended university. When he was eighteen, he published an attack on industrial poverty and middle-class philistinism in his home town, launching a career for himself as social critic. While on national service in Berlin the young Engels joined liberal and radical Young Hegelians in attacking the conservatism encouraged by the Prussian state. His first meeting in November 1842 with Karl Marx, then editor of a liberal newspaper in Cologne, was cool because Marx found the Young Hegelians amateurish. In August 1844 they met again in Paris and established a lifelong partnership.

The works produced by Engels during the intervening two years' residence in England were his most substantial independent efforts: *Umrisse zu einer Kritik der Nationalökonomie* (1844) (*Outlines of a Critique of Political Economy*, 1930), and *Die Lage der arbeitenden Klasse in England* (1845) (*The Condition of the Working Class in England*, 1958). Both were praised by Marx, the former as an anticipation of his own critique of political economy and the latter for its adumbration of the proletarian revolution which he considered inevitable. In partnership, Marx and Engels produced only three major works: *Die heilige Familie* (1845) (*The Holy Family*, 1956) with separately signed contributions; *Die deutsche Ideologie* (1845–46) (*The German Ideology*, 1939), and *Manifest der Kommunistischen Partei* (1848) (*The Communist Manifesto*, 1963) where Engels's analysis of industrialization and Marx's rhetorical gifts contributed equally to a masterpiece.

Engels's later career as Marx's chief interpreter began with his 1859 review of Marx's *Zur Kritik der politischen Ökonomie* (1859) (*A Contribution to the Critique of Political Economy*, 1971), in which he set the standard canons of interpretation for Marx: a similarity with Hegel as a systematic theorist, an inversion of Hegel's idealist premises, a demystification of Hegel's dialectical method, and the discovery of laws within a unified and comprehensive materialist science. These themes were developed subsequently in *Herrn Eugen Dührings Umwälzung der Wissenschaft* (1878) (*Anti-Dühring*, 1959) and in *Socialism: Utopian and Scientific* (1880) (first published in French) which were powerfully influential in attracting adherents to socialism.

The mature Engels was the first Marxist historian ('Der deutsche Bauernkrieg', 1850) (*The Peasant War in Germany*, 1956), and *Germany: Revolution and Counterrevolution* (1851–52) (first published as newspaper articles in English), anthropologist (*Der Ursprung der Familie, des Privateigentums und des Staats*, 1884) (*The Origin of the Family, Private Property and the State*, 1942) and philosopher (*Ludwig Feuerbach und der Ausgang der klassischen deutschen Philosophie*, 1886), (*Ludwig Feuerbach and the Outcome of Classical German Philosophy*, 1941 [1886]), and the posthumously published *Dialektik und Natur* (1935) (*Dialectics of Nature*, 1954). He was the first commentator on the early Marx, became his first biographer, and after Marx's death, his literary executor, editor of Volumes 2 and 3 of *Das Kapital* and the author of more than twenty introductions to Marx's works. He also coined the phrases 'materialist interpretation of history' and 'false consciousness', and formulated three dialectical laws: the transformation of quality into quantity and *vice versa*, the interpenetration of opposites, and the negation of the negation.

Throughout his life Engels was in no doubt that his own writings agreed exactly with Marx's and even expanded their scope, but it is now widely accepted that discrepancies between the two men's works are at the root of many of the debates in contemporary Marxist theory and practice.

Terrell Carver
University of Bristol

Further Reading

Carver, T. (1981), *Engels*, Oxford.
Carver, T. (1983), *Marx and Engels: The Intellectual Relationship*, Brighton.
Henderson, W. O. (1976), *The Life of Friedrich Engels*, 2 vols, London.
Lichtheim, G. (1964), *Marxism: An Historical and Critical Study*, London.
McLellan, D. (1977), *Engels*, Glasgow.
Marcus, S. (1974), *Engels, Manchester and the Working Class*, New York.
See also: *Marx*; *Marx's theory of history and society*.

Entrepreneurship

The term entrepreneur seems to have been introduced into economic theory by Cantillon (1755), and was first accorded prominence by Say (1803). It was variously translated into English as 'merchant', 'adventurer', or 'employer', though the precise meaning is the undertaker of a project. John Stuart Mill (1848) popularized the term in England.

In the neoclassical theory of the firm, entrepreneurial ability is analogous to a fixed factor endowment because it sets a limit to the efficient size of the firm. The static and passive role of the entrepreneur in the neoclassical theory reflects the theory's emphasis on perfect information – which trivializes management and decision-making – and on perfect markets – which do all the co-ordination that is necessary and leave nothing for the entrepreneur.

According to Schumpeter (1934), the entrepreneur is the prime mover in economic development, and his function is to innovate, or 'carry out new combinations'. Five types of innovation are distinguished: (1) the introduction of a new good (or an improvement in the quality of an existing good); (2) the introduction of a new method of production; (3) the opening of a new market – in particular an export market in new territory; (4) the 'conquest of a new source of supply of raw materials or half-manufactured goods'; (5) the creating of a new type of industrial organization – in particular the formation of a trust or some other type of monopoly.

Schumpeter is also very clear about what the entrepreneur is *not*: he is not an inventor, but someone who decides to allocate resources to the exploitation of an invention; nor is he a risk-bearer: risk-bearing is the function of the capitalist who lends funds to the entrepreneur. Essentially, therefore, Schumpeter's entrepreneur has a managerial or decision-making role.

This view receives qualified support from Hayek (1937) and Kirzner (1973), who emphasize the role of the entrepreneur in acquiring and using information. The entrepreneur's alertness to profit-opportunities, and his readiness to exploit them through arbitrage-type operations, makes him the key element in the 'market process'. Hayek and Kirzner regard the entrepreneur as responding to change – as reflected in the information he receives – whilst Schumpeter emphasizes the role of the entrepreneur as a source of change. These two views are not incompatible: a change effected by one entrepreneur may cause spill-over effects, which alter the environment of other entrepreneurs. Hayek and Kirzner do not insist on the novelty of entrepreneurial activity, however, and it is certainly true that a correct decision is not always a decision to innovate; premature innovation may be commercially disastrous. Schumpeter begs the question of whether someone who is the first to evaluate an innovation, but decides (correctly) not to innovate, qualifies as an entrepreneur.

Knight (1921) insists that decision making involves uncertainty. Each business situation is unique, and the relative frequencies of past events cannot be used to evaluate the probabilities of future outcomes. According to Knight, measurable risks can be diversified – or 'laid off' – through insurance markets, but uncertainties cannot. Those who take decisions in highly uncertain environments must bear the full consequences of those decisions themselves. These people are entrepreneurs: they are the owners of businesses and not the salaried managers that make the day-to-day decisions.

Leibenstein (1968) regards the entrepreneur as someone who achieves success by avoiding the inefficiencies to which other people – or the organizations to which they belong – are prone. Leibenstein's approach has the virtue of emphasizing that, in the real world, success is exceptional and failure is the norm.

Casson (1982) defines the entrepreneur as someone who specializes in taking decisions where, because of unequal access to information, different people would opt for different strategies. He shows that the evaluation of innovations, as discussed by Schumpeter, and the assessment of arbitrage opportunities, as discussed by Hayek and Kirzner, can be regarded as special cases. He also shows that if Knight's emphasis on the uniqueness of business situations is used to establish that differences of opinion are very likely in all business decisions, then the Knightian entrepreneur can be embraced within his definition as well. Because the definition identifies the *function* of the entrepreneur, it is possible to use conventional economic concepts to discuss the valuation of entrepreneurial services and many other aspects of the market for entrepreneurs.

Perhaps the aspect of entrepreneurship that has attracted most attention is the motivation of the entrepreneur. Hayek and Kirzner take the Austrian view that the entrepreneur typifies purposeful human action directed towards individualistic ends. Schumpeter, however, refers to the dream and will to found a private dynasty, the will to conquer and the joy of creating, whilst Weber (1930) emphasizes the Protestant Ethic and the concept of calling, and Redlich (1956) the role of militaristic values in the culture of the entrepreneur. Writers of business biographies have ascribed a whole range of different motives to people they describe as entrepreneurs. For many students of business behaviour, it seems that the entrepreneur is simply someone who finds adventure and personal fulfilment in the world of business. The persistence of this heroic concept suggests that many people do not want a scientific account of the role of the entrepreneur.

Successful entrepreneurship provides an avenue of social advancement that is particularly attractive to people who are denied opportunities elsewhere. This may explain why it is claimed that immigrants, religious minorities and people denied higher education are over-represented amongst entrepreneurs. Hypotheses of this kind are difficult to test without carefully controlled sampling procedures. The limited evidence available suggests that, in absolute terms, the most common type of entrepreneur is the son of an entrepreneur.

Mark Casson
University of Reading

References
Cantillon, R. (1755), *Essai sur la nature du commerce en générale* (ed. H. Higgs, London, 1931).
Casson, M. C. (1982), *The Entrepreneur: An Economic Theory*, Oxford.
Hayek, F. A. von (1937), 'Economics and knowledge', *Economica* (N.S.), 4.
Kirzner, I. M. (1973), *Competition and Entrepreneurship*, Chicago.
Knight, F. H. (1921), *Risk, Uncertainty and Profit* (ed. G. J. Stigler), Chicago.
Leibenstein, H. (1968), 'Entrepreneurship and development', *American Economic Review*, 58.
Redlich, F. (1956), 'The military enterpriser: a neglected area of research', *Explorations in Entrepreneurial History* (series 1), 8.
Schumpeter, J. A. (1934), *The Theory of Economic Development* (trans. R. Opie), Cambridge, Mass.
Weber, M. (1930), *The Protestant Ethic and the Spirit of Capitalism* (trans. by T. Parsons), London.
See also: *economic growth*; *Schumpeter*.

Environmental Psychology

Canter and Craik (1981) define environmental psychology as: 'That area of psychology which brings into conjuction and analyses the transactions and inter-relationships of human experiences and actions with pertinent aspects of the socio-physical surroundings.' This approach emphasizes that although the 'environment' of environmental psychology is usually regarded as essentially physical (typically the designed architectural environment or the natural environment), it is always treated as part of the socio-physical matrix. The field of environmental psychology emerged from the collaboration of perceptually oriented psychologists and design decision makers, but it now overlaps considerably with many aspects of social psychology, especially the developments in situational theory (Canter, 1985).

In Europe the initial impetus for environmental studies came from the practical problems produced by the devastation of World War II. The need to build quickly on a vast scale for unidentified individuals and large groups led to user requirement studies and surveys, which tried to establish recurring patterns and preferences to be considered in design. In the 1960s these studies extended to the evaluation of existing buildings, social scientists being called upon to provide 'feedback' about psychological successes and failures. It was paralleled in the design professions by an examination of the nature of the design process. This examination gave rise to the consideration of various forms of systematic design which clearly required as a basis some scientific underpinnings concerned with the ways in which the built environment influenced behaviour.

In North America, pressures from the design professions, whilst present, have not been so strong. The consideration of psychological implications of environmental design has grown out of developing interests (and the search for social relevance) of university-based psychologists. In general, the pioneering environmental psychologists such as Ittelson et al. (1974) have emphasized the need to consider perceptual problems on an environmental scale, given the advances in perceptual psychology, and social psychologists such as Sommer (1983) have seen the need to take into account the physical setting.

Measurement techniques in environmental psychology have concentrated on standardized questionnaire procedures on the one hand and detailed observations of actions in situ on the other. The relative efficacy of these two forms of measurement was debated in the late 1960s, but the emerging consensus is that both are necessary for a full account of action and experience in relation to the physical environment.

Research design has taken many forms, with the laboratory experiment being dominant only in studies dealing with heat, light and sound. Questionnaires and observational studies of users of existing facilities have attempted to highlight the strengths and defects of the particular environment under study, and findings are consequently difficult to generalize. More novel field experiment techniques have been developed which appear to offer the possibility of both minimizing interference with the environment under study while at the same time testing hypotheses and providing results of general applicability. A further method is to represent the environment in some form and then to modify these representations in order to produce environments which differ in controlled ways.

Most of the laboratory research following in the footsteps of classical psychophysics has explored the human correlates of design variables such as temperature, noise level and luminance, although also increasingly considered are issues such as air pollution and other hazards and environmental risks. In general, two separate sets of psychological variables have been examined: the effects upon task performance and the relationship to comfort or satisfaction. These studies have been fruitful in establishing meaningful relationships and providing information for design decision makers.

The relationship between satisfaction and performance has been found to be quite complex (Canter, 1983). Another growing area of investigation considers the consequences for general health and well-being of a combination of environmental features (Evans, 1983).

From the variety of studies of institutional environments, a number of themes have emerged: (1) It is essential to examine the institution and its setting over time in order to reveal the effects of the physical surroundings. (2) The institutional administration is a crucial influence in modifying the interaction between environment and behaviour. It follows from these two points that the way in which a person makes use of, or is affected by, his physical surroundings relates to a marked degree to his role in the organization.

Within the theoretical approaches underlying all the research two distinct trends have emerged. One set of researchers draws its impetus from the formulations of the ecological psychologists and learning theorists. They assign a deterministic role to the environment, which influences behaviour. They are concerned with detailed descriptions based upon observations of ongoing behaviour and with describing the physical environment as one aspect of the general ecological system (Kaminski, 1983).

The alternative trend has its roots in cognitive and phenomenological psychology. These studies attempt to understand the ways in which people experience and understand their environments, relating these processes to the built forms involved. The emphasis here is on the interactions which occur between people and places (Canter, 1977). Increasingly, however, these two approaches complement one another, and a variety of hybrid theories are emerging which will contribute both to the development of academic psychology and to real world decision making.

David Canter
University of Surrey

References

Canter, D. (1977), *The Psychology of Place*, London.

Canter, D. (1983), 'The physical context of work' in D. J. Oborne and M. M. Ginsburg (eds), *The Physical Environment at Work*, Chichester.

Canter, D. (1985), 'Putting situations in their place', in A. Furham (ed.), *Social Behavior in Context*, New York.

Canter, D. and Craik, K. H. (1981), 'Environmental psychology', *Journal of Environmental Psychology*, 1.

Evans, G. W. (ed.) (1983), *Environmental Stress*, London.

Ittelson, W. H., Proshansky, H. M., Rivlin, L. G. and Winkel, G. H. (1974), *An Introduction to Environmental Psychology*, New York.

Kaminski, G. (1983), 'The enigma of ecological psychology', *Journal of Environmental Psychology*, 3.

Sommer, R. (1983), *Social Design*, Englewood Cliffs, N.J.

See also: *ergonomics*.

Epidemiology

The most widely accepted definition of epidemiology is probably that of Brian MacMahon *et al.* (1960): 'Epidemiology is the study of the distribution and determinants of disease prevalence in man.' In contrast to clinical medicine, in which attention is focused on individual patients, epidemiology is primarily concerned with populations, or large groups of persons. Epidemiology is the basic science on which preventive medicine is based. Epidemiologists investigate how disease occurs in the population – who gets the disease and who does not – and what are the reasons or causal factors that explain the patterns of occurrence. In the analysis of population data, statistical methods, both simple and complex, are used extensively. The underlying assumption of epidemiology, that diseases do not occur randomly in populations, has been repeatedly verified.

Although epidemiology did not become a relatively organized and self-conscious scientific profession until the twentieth century (particularly the last few decades), epidemiologic reasoning and investigation go back to antiquity. The ancient Greek physician, Hippocrates, wrote in 'On Airs, Waters and Places' that anyone who wished to investigate medicine properly should consider the climate and geographic situation of a locality, the waters that the inhabitants use 'and the mode in which the inhabitants live, and what are their pursuits, whether they are fond of drinking and eating to excess, and given to indolence, or are fond of exercise and labour'.

Epidemiologic investigations of various sorts have been carried out in more recent centuries. A classic example in the nineteenth century was John Snow's investigations of cholera epidemics in London. Although other explanations had been offered for the occurrence of cholera epidemics (e.g. climatic conditions), Snow and others believed that person-to-person transmission was responsible, because cholera epidemics spread in the direction of, and never faster than, human travel; because persons in contact with cholera victims frequently developed cholera themselves, and because the disease was associated with filth, poverty, and crowded living conditions. Snow hypothesized that cholera was frequently transmitted through the water supply and that this explained why some parts of London were much more affected than others. His careful investigation and determination of the rates of occurrence of disease in defined subgroups of Londoners showed that cholera was frequent in persons who obtained water from the Broad Street pump and in persons living in homes that obtained water from a particular company whose water supply came from a contaminated section of the Thames River. These findings led to control measures for the disease even before the specific causal agent, the cholera vibrio, was identified. While some scientists are not satisfied that they have identified a cause of disease until the detailed mechanism down to the molecular level has been elucidated, epidemiologists often take a more global and pragmatic view: if a factor can be identified, which if reduced will lead to a reduction in the occurrence of a disease, the factor can be assumed to be causal while we await a fuller explanation of the biochemical details. Of course, epidemiologists would not accept a supposed cause of disease if it is inconsistent with biological knowledge.

Until the mid-twentieth century most epidemiologic studies were directed at infectious diseases, which had been the main causes of death until modern times. The work 'epidemic' from which 'epidemiology' is derived, means the occurrence of a disease in a proportion of the population of a community or geographic area far in excess of the usual or expected proportion. Now that many infectious diseases have been brought under control in relatively affluent industrialized societies, epidemiologic attention is being increasingly paid to chronic non-infectious diseases that are now the leading killers, such as heart disease and cancer. It is clear that some societies are experiencing epidemics of such diseases as coronary heart disease (heart attacks) and cancer of the lung, in that these diseases are occurring far in excess of what is observed in other societies. Thus, epidemiologic attention is directed at explaining the nonrandom distribution of these conditions in the world in the hope that methods of prevention and control will be found.

Epidemiological studies may be subdivided into the descriptive and the analytic. Descriptive studies measure the occurrence of disease in various major subgroups of the population. (The commonest epidemiological measures of disease occurrence are prevalence – the proportion of a group with the disease at a given moment, and incidence – the proportion developing the disease per unit of time.) So, for example, a descriptive study might compare the incidence of a disease in men and women, in persons of various ages, races and occupations, in one geographic area against another, or in one time period against another. These exemplify the major axes of classification found in descriptive studies, that is, person (who, or what type of person, is more apt to get the disease?), place (where does it occur more frequently?), and time (when does or did it occur more frequently?). For example, an interesting descriptive observation about place concerns Japanese who have migrated to the United States compared to those living in Japan. The migrants experience a higher incidence of breast cancer and a lower incidence of stomach cancer than their non-migrant counterparts. This has suggested hypotheses concerning dietary and other environmental factors that might play a role in causing these two types of cancer.

Investigation of specific hypotheses is the purpose of analytic studies. In these one attempts to determine whether persons exposed to a particular suggested causal factor (for example, dietary fat intake, cigarette smoking, exposure to X-rays or to a chemical at work, infection by a particular micro-organism, crowding, intense sunlight, and so on) have a higher incidence of disease than those not so exposed. For practical reasons, epidemiologists sometimes will not tackle this question directly by following up persons through time, but will conduct a backward-looking 'retrospective' or 'case-control' study in which they determine whether persons with the disease under study were more often exposed to the factor in question than those free of the disease.

A special form of analytic study is the experiment. An experiment involves some intervention on the part of the investigator rather than simply collecting and analysing data as is done in the usual observational study. For example, an experimental field trial may be carried out in which an active vaccine is administered to one group of people while another, otherwise comparable, group receives a 'dummy' or placebo. The object is to determine whether the incidence of the disease to be prevented is lower in the group receiving vaccine. Most analytic epidemiological studies are observational because of the practical difficulties involved in conducting controlled experiments on free-living humans. Sometimes ethical considerations rule out an experiment, particulary when exposure to a suspected disease-causing agent or substance is involved. But experiments are generally accepted as being more rigorous and believable demonstrations of cause-and-effect than can be achieved through observational studies. The findings of the latter are sometimes suspected of entailing guilt by association. When an exposed group has a higher incidence of a disease, it may be some characteristics of the group other than the exposure itself that is responsible. Epidemiologists devote considerable effort to investigating whether associations between proposed causal factors and diseases may really be due to other 'confounding' factors.

Recent major accomplishments of epidemiology include the demonstration that cigarette smoking is the main cause of lung cancer and that several personal characteristics, such as serum cholesterol level, blood pressure, cigarette smoking and obesity, are highly predictive of who will develop ischemic heart disease, the leading killer of adults in industrialized societies. The field of epidemiology continues to broaden as it did in the past, when non-infectious diseases became as important to society as infectious diseases. Now the analytic skills of epidemiologists are becoming involved in other pressing health-related matters, such as improving the delivery of medical care while limiting its economic costs.

Gary D. Friedman
Kaiser-Permanente Medical Care Program
Oakland, California

Reference

MacMahon, B., Pugh, T. F. and Ipsen, J. (1960), *Epidemiologic Methods*, Boston.

Further Reading

Friedman, G. D. (1980), *Primer of Epidemiology*, 2nd edn, New York.
Lilienfeld, A. M. and Lilienfeld, D. E. (1980), *Foundations of Epidemiology*, 2nd edn, New York.
MacMahon, B. and Pugh, T. F. (1970), *Epidemiology: Principles and Methods*, Boston.
Morris, J. N. (1975), *Uses of Epidemiology*, 3rd edn, Edinburgh.
Roueché, B. (1982), *The Medical Detectives*, New York.
See also: *medical sociology*; *morbidity*; *public health*.

Equality

'We hold,' wrote Thomas Jefferson (1747–1826), 'these truths to be sacred and undeniable; that all men are created equal and independent . . .' No natural scientist *qua* scientist could do other than dismiss such a statement as either meaningless or empirically false. Equality for a mathematician is a concept of some complexity in relation, for example, to identity or correlation, but one of no moral significance. Social scientists by contrast are latecomers to a debate about equality which is unresolved because it adds to the mathematician's complexity the further complications of moral argument. Equality refers to the principles on which human society ought, as well as might, be based. Jefferson's was a moral declaration, not an empirical description. Social science attempts to explore the empirical validity of such declarations. The question is whether, and in what sense, social, political, and economic equalities are possible. The answer is tentative, requiring the determination of the origins of inequality, the significance of inequality, and the viability of action intended to establish equality. All three aspects are disputed.

Traditional discussion of the origins of inequality turned on a crude distinction between nature and society. Modern recognition of cultural evolution complicates that distinction and tends to substitute a more elaborate matrix out of the consequences of interaction between genetic and environmental influences. But in neither simple nor sophisticated discussion is there denial of natural inequalities, the Jeffersonian declaration notwithstanding. Men are not clones, and Mendelian genetics guarantees variation. Dispute, however, continues in important areas of scientific ignorance. For example, there is not adequate scientific evidence to settle the dispute between those who believe in the genetic basis of differences between ethnic or racial or class groups in educational attainment or performance in intelligence tests, and those who hold such differences to be socially created. Resolution of such disputes is, in principle, possible through the further advance of empirically tested theories of the interaction between heredity and environment.

Meanwhile dispute about the significance of natural differences continues its long history. Plato confidently argued from natural to political inequalilty. Hobbes in *Leviathan* (1934 [1651]), expressed the opposite view:

Nature hath made man so equall, in the faculties of body, and mind; as that though bee found one man sometimes manifestly stronger in body, or of quicker mind than another; yet when all is reckoned together, the difference between man, and man, is not so considerable, as that one man can thereupon claim to himself and benefit, to which another may not pretend, as well as he.

Hobbes's formulation still defines the debate. Egalitarian claims, especially with respect to race and gender, are more strident now than they were in the seventeenth century, and we would now say that Hobbes was making empirical propositions from both genetics and sociology, the one referring to natural differences and the other (about claiming and pretending) referring to the social psychology of man's perceptions of social rights. But the central assertion is fundamentally about the values which ought to be reflected in the actual relations of men and women in society.

In this sense the debate, turning as it does on ethical priorities between such values as equality, liberty, and fraternity, may never be finally resolvable. There have been, to be sure, notable recent contributions to greater conceptual clarity as to the meaning of terms. John Rawls (1971) adopts the device of the 'original position' – an 'if so' story of the rational choices that might be expected from an individual contemplating different societies with known different equalities or inequalities of positions but an unknown placement for the contemplator – to illuminate the problems of value choice. Brian Barry (1973) takes the discussion further to demonstrate how a small adjustment to Rawls's social and psychological assumptions opens the possibility of a crucial shift of preference towards egalitarian rather than liberal forms of society. But no amount of conceptual clarification, sophisticated or erudite, solves the problem of evaluation.

The social sciences can, however, note the provenance of different priorities. One mundane but momentous perspective recurs down the ages – the recognition of mortality. Thus Horace (65–8 BC) wrote: 'Pale death kicks his way equally into the cottages of the poor and the castles of kings.' And James Shirley (1596–1666) reminds us that:

Death lays his icy hand on kings
    Sceptre and crown
    Must tumble down
And in the dust be equal made
With the poor crooked scythe and spade.

This attitude is integral to Christian social teaching, which dominated the evaluation of equality at least until the eighteenth century. It was not that natural inequalities between individuals were denied so much as deemed irrelevant in discussing the rights and wrongs of dictatorship or democracy, freedom or slavery. Christians were not only 'equal before the Cross' but, as the early Church Fathers insisted, would, if they eschewed sin, live like brothers without inequalities of property and power. Sin, since the fall of Adam, had created earthly inequality. Political inequality might be necessary to protect order and restrain evil, but it did not arise, as Plato had imagined, from natural inequality. Political inequality in Christian tradition must be endured but by no means implied a necessary respect or admiration for the rich and the powerful. On the contrary, position in the next world was typically held to be threatened by privilege in this. 'He hath put down the mighty from their seat and hath exalted the humble and meek,' says the Magnificat.

The break with Christian attitudes of submission to inequality dates from the eighteenth century, with the decline of religious belief and the beginnings of a secular optimism with respect to the possibility of social transformation. Egalitarianism as a movement is commonly associated with Rousseau. But Rousseau, though believing that the evils of unfreedom and inequality were socially created, was a remorseless pessimist. He held that freedom was impossible except in a community of equals, but held out no hope of social transformation towards equality. In this sense he was a child of Christianity, and if the early socialists (Fourier, Proudhon, Saint-Simon, Robert Owen, William Thompson) were his intellectual children they were also crucially different in entertaining the hope of progress. Modern egalitarianism derives from this form of sociological optimism, and it was encouraged by, if by no means identical with, either the Hegelian idealist or Marxist materialist theories of the inevitability of social transformation. Hegel's elaborate analysis of the relation between masters and slaves, and Marx's development of it into a prediction of the future history of the working class hold out the possibility of a community of equals.

However, egalitarianism does not presuppose either the Hegelian or the Marxist theory of history. Its more fruitful contemporary discussion in the social sciences proceeds on assumptions of openness or voluntarism as opposed to necessitous history. These debates are the substance of the third aspect of the equality problem – the viability of deliberate social action aimed at reducing inequality. One theoretical approach deserves mention here because it avoids both liberal evolutionist determinism and the alternative Marxist historicism. This is T. H. Marshall's interpretation of the development of citizenship in advanced industrial societies (Marshall, 1950). He shows in the case of Britain how the basic equality of membership in a society, which is rooted in the civil rights established in the eighteenth century, was extended to include political rights in the nineteenth century and certain social rights in the twentieth century, when citizenship and class have been at war as opposing principles of social distribution. Marshall's analysis also brings out the important truth that the forces which influence the distribution of life chances are neither mechanical nor irreversible. Class displaced feudal status with formal equality of market relations, as well as ushering in new inequalities of social condition. Citizenship promotes unequal rewards as well as equal rights, for example, state scholarships to selective university admission and universal political franchise. More generally, it may be noted that no social goal, equality, efficiency, liberty, order or fraternity may be regarded as absolute. Public policies are perforce compromises aiming at optimal balance between desired ends.

Three illustrations of the limits to egalitarianism are prominent in recent writing in the form of arguments against the viability of egalitarian theory:

(1) This concerns the immutability of occupational hierarchy, postulating a *de facto* necessity for some jobs to be more distasteful, unrewarding, and injurious to health than others. Given that life chances are largely determined by the individual's occupation, a hierarchy of social advantage seems to be inescapable, and equality, as opposed to equality of opportunity, therefore unobtainable. But, egalitarians reply, a less inegalitarian society is not sociologically impossible. It is not difficult to imagine a wide range of counteracting social policies. Apart from progressive taxation and levies on wealth, there could be national service specifically designed to direct the advantaged to a period of distasteful labour. The obvious rejoinders are lodged in the name of liberty and economic efficiency, again emphasizing the relativist character of claims for any social principle. Value choice is always the nub of the issue.

(2) An illustration may be had from Christopher Jencks's *Inequality* (1972) which essentially argues the importance of educational reform as an instrument of egalitarianism and stresses the role of chance or luck in the unequal distribution of income and occupational status. Schooling explains only 12 per cent of the variance in American incomes. But Jencks's argument is flawed in that his evidence is about the distribution of individuals over a given structure of occupations and wages. The explanation of inequality of income accruing to jobs is not what would explain who happens to hold those jobs. Whether the inequality of the job structure is immutable remains an open question.

(3) Finally, there is the alleged obstacle of genetic differences between races and classes of which Jensen has been an outstanding proponent (Jensen, 1972). As to classes, and against Jensen's marshalling of the evidence from studies of twins reared apart, there is the opposed conclusion of Schiff (1982) from his studies of cross-class adopted children in France. As to race, it has to be said that we do not yet have the techniques or the data to measure definitively the genetic and environmental influences on race-IQ differences. Nor does the answer really matter, for there are more important issues of equality and justice in present-day society which do not have to wait upon further advances in the social sciences.

A. H. Halsey
University of Oxford

References
Barry, B. (1973), *The Liberal Theory of Justice*, Oxford.
Hobbes, T. (1934 [1651]), *Leviathan* (London Everyman edn, 1934).
Jencks, C. (1972), *Inequality*, New York.
Jensen, A. (1972), *Genetics and Education*, London.
Marshall, T. H. (1950), *Citizenship and Social Class*, Cambridge.

Rawls, J. (1971), *A Theory of Justice*, Cambridge, Mass.

Schiff, M. (1982), *L'Intelligence Gaspillée*, Paris.

Further Reading

Letwin, W. (ed.) (1983), *Against Equality: Readings on Economic and Social Policy*, London.

Runciman, W. G. (1966), *Relative Deprivation and Social Justice*, London.

Tawney, R. H. (1952), *Equality*, (4th rev. edn), London.

See also: *distributive justice; hierarchy; stratification*.

Equilibrium

Ever since philosophers replaced divine intervention with rational man, economists have been intrigued that uncoordinated individual decision making does not produce economic anarchy. Adam Smith (1776) was among the first to posit free will based in self-interest, but he also noted that the specialization associated with the division of labour implied co-ordination among individuals. Quesnay's (1766) earlier physiocratic system of circulation reflected a particular form of economic interdependence centred on the surplus net product of agricultural land.

General equilibrium theory attempts to explain how the price mechanism in a free market operates to resolve this seeming paradox of increasing independence in decision making requiring increased co-ordination of economic decisions to produce coherent economic behaviour.

Although the Classical economists were aware of the paradox, the origins of the modern treatment of the problem had to await the marginal revolution in economics associated with Leon Walras's (1874) *Elements*, which along with Jevons's (1871) *Theory of Political Economy* and Menger's (1870) *Principles of Economics*, attempted to provide the analysis of individual market demand absent in Classical theory. Only when demand was treated on an equal footing with supply could equilibrium be conceived as the combination of prices and quantities at which the 'forces' of supply just offset those of demand.

A general equilibrium system provides a sufficiently complete description of individuals' decisions concerning supply and demand to determine the quantities and prices of all goods and services produced and exchanged. Given the complexity of analysing an economy with a multiplicity of individuals and goods and services, a high level of abstraction is required and most authors appeal to the aide of mathematics. To a large extent, advances in the theory have been linked to advances in mathematical techniques. Leon Walras, generally considered the father of equilibrium theory, envisaged a system composed of households, endowed with specific quantities of factors and preferences over the available consumption goods, facing a budget constraint limiting expenditures to the market value of

the factor endowment, and firms who earned zero profit from the entrepreneurial activity of combining factors in fixed proportions (later made to depend on prices) to produce consumption goods. Firms' receipts were thus exhausted by payments for factor services. The desired combination of consumption goods by households was thus determined by preferences and the prices at which endowments could be sold and consumption goods purchased. An equilibrium was constituted by the balance of supply and demand in each market for goods and factor services.

Since the prices considered were relative prices, ratios of quantities exchanged, there could be no more than n-1 such ratios for any number, n, of goods considered; one of them might serve as numeraire to give a common expression to all prices, its ratio equal to unity. The supply and demand relations were thus independent of the measure or level of prices expressed in numeraire, for its absolute quantity had no effect on the ratios of the other goods or its own price equal to unity (that is, the relations are homogeneous of degree zero in prices). Together with the budget constraint on household expenditure, and firms' zero profits, this produces what has come to be known as 'Walras' Law': since the market value of all goods and services sold is by definition equal to the market value of all goods and services purchased irrespective of prices, the (n) supply-demand relations comprising the system cannot be linearly independent. If supply equals demand in the markets for all but one (n-1) good, then supply must also equal demand in the market for the remaining (nth) good; equilibrium in the markets for any n-1 goods determines prices and quantities exchanged over all n goods' markets.

The use of the idea of an equilibrium or a balance of forces reflected the influence of classical mechanics and the belief that market forces, like those acting on a pendulum, would naturally lead the system to an equilibrium state. Walras describes this process of 'tâtonnement' (groping) by starting from a random set of prices for each good or service, called out in succession by an 'auctioneer', to which households and firms respond with non-binding offers of the quantities they wish to buy or sell at those prices. The auctioneer follows a simple rule of raising prices when buy offers exceed offers to sell, and vice versa. Although the offers for any good are influenced by the price of every other, if its own offers are more influenced by its own price than others (that is, if goods are gross substitutes so that the rise in the price of a good produces excess demand for all others), then the system will converge by successive rounds of price adjustments, or by 'groping', to an equilibrium of prices and quantities at which everyone independently deciding how much to buy or sell at those prices succeeds in completing desired transactions without external direction or control. These adjustments were thought in practice to occur simultaneously in all markets as the result of the forces of household utility maximization and firms' profit maximization.

An alternative formulation of this process was put forward at about the same time by Edgeworth (1881) who emphasized individual bargaining. Letting the length of the two legs of the lower left and upper right corners of an 'Edgeworth box' represent the quantities available of two goods to two traders, and using the corners as the origin of each trader's indifference map for the two goods, a 'contract curve' may be drawn up connecting the tangency points of the two indifference systems. Combinations of the two goods represented by the curve will be preferred by both individuals to any other. A bargaining process over combinations which provides either trader with the possibility of 'recontracting' if a preferable combination of goods (representing a new relative price) which makes the other trader no worse off is discovered, will lead the traders to a combination on the curve. Once the curve has been reached, improved combinations can only be achieved at the expense of the other trader (the combinations on the curve are Pareto optimal) so that further bargaining is blocked. The contract curve thus represents a 'core' of competitive equilibrium combinations, for once one is reached any attempt to change it is blocked. Edgeworth argued that as the number of goods and the number of traders increases, the number of combinations in the core decreases to a limit of a single combination which replicates the price and quantity equilibrium of Walrasian theory. This method of approach was virtually ignored until Shubik (1959) reintroduced it to modern debate.

Neither was Walras's work much studied in his lifetime, except by his successor in Lausanne, Pareto (1896–7); a similar equilibrium formulation in Cassel's Theory of Social Economy (published in German in 1918, in English in 1923) gained wider audience, however. Contemporary theory can be traced to elaborations of Cassel's book in the 1930s when Wald, and then von Neumann, both writing in German, proposed the first mathematically satisfactory solutions for the equilibrium of a Walrasian system (see Weintraub, 1983).

Interest in Walras in the English-speaking world had to wait for Hicks's Value and Capital (1939) which used general equilibrium theory to recast economic statics in order to build a new theory of dynamics. At about the same time work by Samuelson which was published later in his Foundations of Economic Analysis (1947) also sought a theory of dynamic adjustment in support of comparative static stability properties of equilibrium in his 'correspondence principle'. These insights were eventually used as the basis for modern Hicksian IS-LM representations of Keynes's relation to traditional theory and the subsequent 'Neoclassical synthesis' propounded in Samuelson's influential textbook Economics. Ironically, it is the descendants of these early general equilibrium formulations of Keynes that have been criticized for their lack of microfoundations.

By the early 1950s knowledge of the earlier work of Wald and von Neumann amongst others had become known, and a number of economists in the United States took up the formal problems of the existence of equilibrium. Against the background of developments in game theory and linear systems analysis, a series of articles by Debreu, Arrow, and, in an international context, by McKenzie were published nearly simultaneously, providing definitive proofs using modern mathematical methods (see Weintraub, 1983). The theory reached the maturity of textbook treatment in Arrow and Hahn's General Competitive Analysis (1971).

Current investigations have returned to the earlier concerns with the stability and the dynamic adjustment process underlying the comparative static analysis. If equilibria are multiple, comparative statics must analyse not only the stability of the new equilibrium, but which one will be established. This extension of stability analysis has grown out of non-tâtonnement analysis initiated by Hahn and is known as the 'disequilibrium' foundations of equilibrium economics (Fisher, 1983); it seeks to investigate 'hysterisis' effects, the possibility that the past history of adjustment affects the set of potential competitive equilibria. Such concerns encompass the analysis of sequential monetary exchange and price setting without an auctioneer.

J. A. Kregel
University of Groningen

References

Arrow, K. J. and Hahn, F. H. (1971), General Competitive Analysis, Edinburgh.
Cassel, G. (1923), The Theory of Social Economy, trans. J. McCabe, London.
Edgeworth, F. Y. (1881), Mathematical Psychics, London.
Fisher, F. M. (1983), Disequilibrium Foundations of Equilibrium Economics, London.
Hicks, J. R. (1939), Value and Capital, Oxford.
Pareto, V. (1896–7), Cours d'Economique politique, Lausanne.
Samuelson, P. A. (1947), Foundations of Economic Analysis, Cambridge, Mass.
Shubik, M. (1959), Game Theory, Cambridge, Mass.
Smith, A. (1976 [1776]), Wealth of Nations, Oxford.
Walras, M. (1954 [1874]), Elements of Pure Economics, trans. W. Jaffe, London.
Weintraub, E. R. (1983), 'On the existence of competitive equilibrium: 1930–1954', Journal of Economic Literature, 21.

Further Reading

Weintraub, E. R. (1973), General Equilibrium Theory, London.
Weintraub, E. R. (1975), Conflict and Co-operation in Economics, London.

Weintraub, E. R. (1979), *Microfoundations*,
  Cambridge.
See also: *Arrow*; *Debreu*; *economic dynamics*; *Hicks*;
  Walras, L.

Ergonomics

Ergonomics is that area of applied science which
studies the characteristics of individuals with special
reference to the tools, machines and other equipment
which they use, and to the effects on them of the
physical environment. It tries to help people perform
more easily, effectively, comfortably and safely. The
word 'ergonomics' was coined in 1949 to identify the
area where the interests of human anatomy, physiology
and experimental psychology meet with engineering
and physics. Researchers from these fields had worked
together during World War II investigating the practical problems of military equipment and military operations. In order to build on this experience in post-war
reconstruction and in industry, they met in the UK and
founded a society now called the Ergonomics Society.
Three areas of interest were: (1) display of information;
(2) controls to be operated; (3) physical characteristics
of the operator and the effects of the environment.

(1) Display raised questions for experimental
psychology in designing instrument scales as well as
lettering and diagrams, and in assessing the relative
merits of moving-pointer and digital displays. Other
practical problems concerned the grouping of instruments on control panels and presenting information so
that the user could best grasp its meaning. 'Display'
takes account of information received by senses other
than visual; of what is heard and what is obtained from
the kinaesthetic sense of position and force.

(2) Study of the psychology of processing (and
storing) information leads on to the study of controls.
Simple issues are the layout of buttons and keys, or
the design of knobs and control-levers to enable a plant
operator to keep moving indicators at the proper
positions. We control the tools we use; a knife used for
delicate work needs a handle providing a precision grip
and is shaped quite differently from one which is used
for heavy cutting.

(3) The size and strength of the user are important
for the design of controls – whether they can be
reached, or are too stiff to move – and calls for anatomical and physiological knowledge. These disciplines are
even more prominent in the third area of ergonomics
– concern with environmental factors. Posture and
seating are important here; other factors include the
effects of heat and cold, illumination and noise.

The relevance of ergonomics outside the industrial
and military fields soon became apparent. Early studies
related to transport were of the design of cars, so as to
help drivers of any height and build to reach the
controls and to see clearly both road and dashboard

displays. After considerable delay, the results of these
studies are now widely and increasingly applied by
car manufacturers. In medicine, ergonomics has been
applied to the design of tools and equipment for
doctors, surgeons and dentists, and particularly to help
handicapped people. The able-bodied in their sports,
the worker in the kitchen provided with sinks and
work-tables of appropriate height and with safe cooker
controls, likewise now benefit from the efforts of ergonomics. The importance of the man-machine interface
in computing and information technology has recently
been recognized; since about 1980, there has been a
sudden and increasing demand for ergonomics specialists, as producers of equipment and 'software' have
realized the unfortunate consequences of neglecting
ergonomic principles and data.

The sociologist of science will be interested by ergonomics. Its rapid evolution from an interdisciplinary
collaboration to a fully-fledged discipline, established
worldwide, is unusually well-documented. The International Ergonomics Association was founded in 1959
to federate national societies; there are journals devoted
to the subject, and universities offer degrees in ergonomics. Ergonomics' applied science origin has been
reflected in uneasy co-operation with technologists,
especially production engineers, who deal with similar
problems but have different attitudes. However, its
commitment to experimental science has hampered
communication with social scientists, and it has taken
insufficient account of the effects of other human beings
in the individual's working environment. In Eastern
Europe, 'ergonomia' is coming to embrace areas of
occupational psychology, sociology of the workplace,
and industrial hygiene and safety. In the US, a development parallel to ergonomics called 'Human Factors'
puts relatively more emphasis on experimental
psychology and engineering and less on anatomy and
physiology.

Ronald G. Stansfield
Bishop's Stortford

Further Reading
Grandjean, E. (1980), *Fitting the Task to the Man: An
  Ergonomic Approach*, 3rd edn, London.
Stansfield, R. G. (1979), 'The origins of the
  International Ergonomics Association', *Ergonomia*,
  3, Krakov and Warsaw.
See also: *environmental psychology*; *industrial and
  organizational psychology.*

Ethics in Social Research

Social research ethics involve the consideration of the
moral implications of social science inquiry. Ethics is
a matter of principled sensitivity to the rights of others,
in such a way that human beings who are being studied
by social scientists are treated as ends rather than
as means. Such ethical issues frequently also lead to

consideration of the politics of research, the place of the investigator in the power structure, and the wider social impact of research. Those conducting social research need increasingly to be aware of the ethical and political implications of their actions.

The protection of human subjects is enshrined in the doctrine of informed consent, first developed in biomedical research. This stipulates that the voluntary consent of the human subject is essential, and this should be freely given without duress, and knowing and understanding what the research involves. Most social research, whether by experimental, social survey or observational methods, respects this principle, but there have been occasional sharp controversies where experimental or observational subjects have been left in ignorance of research, or have had research misrepresented to them. In observing the principle, most social scientists do not follow the formal procedures used in medical research such as signed consent forms.

A related controversy has concerned the use of deception in social research. The majority of social scientists are open about their purposes and aims, but in rare cases deception has been used on the grounds that, because of practical methodological or moral considerations, research could not otherwise be carried out. (Such studies include research on obedience to authority, and sexual deviance.) Objections to deception include its degrading and false character, its harmful social consequences, harm to the investigator, the creation of suspicion among subjects, and the breach of informed consent.

Research may in certain circumstances impinge upon the privacy of research subjects (that is, the freedom of the individual to decide how much of the self to reveal to others, when and to whom). Some information about the individual may be sensitive. Some settings (for example, jury rooms, Cabinet meetings) may be entirely closed to outsiders. The wider dissemination of research results may affect subjects adversely. Such problems may be handled by obtaining informed consent or by various forms of making data anonymous. In the latter case, for example, the location in which research was carried out may be concealed and the identities of particular individuals hidden under pseudonyms. A distinction may be made between the circumstances under which data are collected, and their subsequent storage, dissemination, analysis and re-analysis. Issues of confidentiality are raised by the latter, though also impinging upon collection. What will happen to data once collected? To whom will they be available? What repercussions might there be for the individual in providing certain data to a social researcher?

The importance of these questions has been intensified by the advent of the electronic computer, with immensely powerful means of large-scale data storage and retrieval. This has a major impact upon census data and large-scale social survey data. Various techniques have been developed to ensure that individual identities cannot be linked to published information. These include the deletion of individual identifiers such as name, address or local area of residence; the suppression of tables containing small numbers of cases; and processes of random error injection. In addition to physical security, technical means exist for making anonymous the data held in computer files, including the separation of identifiers from the main body of data and their linkage by suitable codes. Randomized response is a method of ensuring the confidentiality of data while it is being collected.

The ethical issues raised by research go wider than the treatment of research subjects and handling of data once collected. The social impact of research has been of concern and controversy both within particular societies (as in the Moynihan Report on Black families in the US) and internationally (as in Project Camelot in Chile in the 1960s). There is increasing concern about the sponsorship of research (who pays? for whom, and in whose interest, is research conducted?), the negotiation of research access (especially the role played by gatekeepers, who may give or withhold permission), and about the possible adverse effects of the publication of research results on certain weaker groups or lower status sections of society. The investigator can rarely control any of these factors, but awareness of them can help to produce more effective work. Particular care is also required to review the ethical implications of action research and applied research leading to social intervention (for example, of some of the large-scale social experiments for social policy). Consideration of these broader issues leads on to an examination of the political role of social science research and its place in the society in which it is carried out.

There is no agreed theory of research ethics with which to evaluate the merits of undertaking particular pieces of research. It is difficult to determine whether, and if so to what extent, research subjects may be harmed by particular research practices. One widespread approach is in terms of a utilitarian risk/benefit calculus, but this leaves several issues unresolved. Both risks and benefits are difficult to predict and to measure, harm to the individual can only with difficulty be weighted against societal benefits, and the investigator is usually the judge in his own case. Another approach is in terms of situational ethics, where the investigator weighs up the morally appropriate course of action in the actual research context. A different approach is in terms of absolute moral principles to be followed in all situations. No approach receives universal approval, and ethical decision making in research remains ultimately a matter of individual judgement as well as professional controversy.

One practical consequence both of the societal impact of research and the indeterminacy of ethical decision making about research has been a move toward greater regulation. Many professional associations of social scientists have their own ethical codes, to which members are expected to adhere. Various forms of peer review by a researcher's own department or institution are a more rigorous and direct form of oversight. The Institutional Review Boards now established by universities in the United States are one example of efforts to prevent unethical behaviour by social researchers.

Martin Bulmer
London School of Economics and Political Science

Further Reading
Barnes, J. A. (1980), *Who Should Know What? Social Science, Privacy and Ethics*, Cambridge.
Beauchamp, T. L. *et al.* (eds) (1982), *Ethical Issues in Social Science Research*, Baltimore.

Ethnic Groups

Segments of a population form ethnic groups by virtue of sharing the combination of (a) common descent (real or supposed), (b) a socially relevant cultural or physical characteristic, and (c) a set of attitudes and behaviours.

On this definition, people are usually born to an ethnic group rather than acquiring their ethnic status through a special act. Most marry within and remain part of the ethnic group of origin throughout their entire lives even if mobility is feasible (as in the case of religious conversion). Since ethnic group members are actually or putatively related to one another by blood ties, an ethnic group is a kind of a super-extended family.

A primary basis for differentiation between ethnic groups can be either cultural – such as a language, a nationality and a religion – or physical – such as skin pigmentation and body shape – or both. The distinguishing feature is considered significant in the society, and people use it in differentiating themselves from others.

Members of an ethnic group also share certain feelings, ideas and behaviours. To form a real ethnic group and not just a mere ethnic collection of people, people must, at least to some degree, perceive themselves as a distinct ethnic group ('we' and 'they' feelings), sense a common fate, interact more among themselves than with outsiders, and think and behave similarly.

Ethnicity is not presumed to exist when any of these defining criteria is missing. Lacking an idea of common descent, women, the disabled, the sane, or nonbelievers, should not be regarded as ethnic groups although each of these categories of people is distinguished by evident cultural or biological traits, and even by certain attitudes and behaviours.

Furthermore, a distinct characteristic becomes ethnically relevant only when people apply it to mark themselves off from others or when it is used to impose an identity by outsiders. In India, for instance, for centuries speakers of different languages intermingled freely. Linguistically based ethnic groups emerged there only after the British established administrative divisions, which in 1948 turned into provincial states, along linguistic lines, so creating linguistic majorities and minorities. To cite another example, in Nazi Germany Jews were forced into a status of a racial group.

Ethnic groups should also be distinguished from social classes. A social class is a group of people who share the same level of resources, such as education, income, prestige and power, or work in the same occupational category (such as blue-collar jobs). According to another view, a social class is constituted by persons who hold similar positions in the process of production (workers, employers). Since social classes are groups of unequal statuses and ethnic groups are descent groups, they can cross-cut each other. A social class may include members of different ethnic groups, and an ethnic group may include members of different social classes. Commonly, however, ethnic groups and social classes overlap appreciably.

Formation
Ethnicity crystallizes only in situations where people of different backgrounds come into contact or share the same institutions or political system. Villagers or tribesmen in isolated areas, or citizens in homogeneous states like Portugal, are not members of ethnic groups.

Ethnic divisions are evident throughout human history, yet they became more pervasive in recent times because technological advances multiplied intergroup contacts and brought together hitherto separate peoples. The great historical forces that fashioned the world ethnic mosaic are colonialism, imperialism, annexation, involuntary migration, free emigration and nationalism. European expansion into overseas colonies formed a division between the white settlers and the indigenous population and in certain cases engendered coloured, mixed-blood groups, as in South Africa and throughout Latin America. Since the boundaries of many ex-colonial states in Asia and Africa were artificially drawn for reasons of colonial expediency, they do not correspond to 'ethnic boundaries'. An ethnic group (for example, the Kurds) might be split among several states, or hitherto separate societies might be thrown together into a single deeply divided state (such as the Sudan). Within Europe, conquest and annexation were regular events until the 1950s.

New ethnic divisions are regularly formed as the result of involuntary population movements, including mass expulsions, flows of refugees, indentured or contracted labourers and large-scale enslavement. Armenians outside Turkey, Bengalis in India, Indians in East and Southern Africa and Blacks in the United States are several of the numerous cases. Free immigration also played a crucial role in the construction of ethnically split societies. The Americas and Australia were settled heavily by poor immigrants from Europe. They sought better economic and other opportunities and succeeded in forging new ethnic entities and identities.

In the post-World War II era, 'uneven development' has become a powerful push for the steady migration of the unemployed, the impoverished, or rather the relatively mobile in the developing countries, to the Western world. The flow of legal and illegal 'guest workers' to states such as the United States (mostly from Mexico), Israel (from the occupied territories) and Central and Western Europe (mostly from the Mediterranean countries) adds new ethnic groups and problems.

The rise of nationalism has stimulated the crystallization of ethnicity in many parts of the world. Nationalism is the claim of ethnic groups to self-determination. When an ethnic group achieves sovereignty in a certain state, it will become a nation which then excludes the other ethnic groups. The excluded ethnic groups are then forced to get organized and to seek a national minority status and an ethnic autonomy (Smith, 1981).

Diversity

The huge variety of formative processes make for enormous differences among ethnic groups on criteria of affiliation, relative size, geographical concentration, socio-economic standards, political dominance, social separateness, identity, goals, collective consciousness and degree of organization.

One significant distinction is between race and ethnicity (van den Berghe, 1978). A racial group is composed of people who are believed to share the same biological make-up, while a non-racial ethnic group is identified by a cultural marker. Racial differentiation tends to be more visible, hierarchical, stigmatizing and mutually exclusive and allows less passing and mobility than non-racial differentiation. For this reason, subordinate racial groups like the Blacks in the United States tend to redefine their racial status in ethnic (cultural) terms. This is also why the South African government has switched recently from racial to ethnic terminology in presenting its *apartheid* policy.

A further fundamental distinction is between assimilating and non-assimilating ethnic (or racial) groups. The non-French immigrants to Canada, European immigrants to the United States and Jewish immigrants to Israel are predominantly assimilating ethnic groups. They wish and are allowed (or even pressured) to assimilate into the mainstream. On the other hand, in the same societies the French of Quebec, non-Whites in the United States and Arabs in Israel either insist on preserving their separate identity or are barred from assimilation. In due course assimilation reshapes ethnic boundaries and affiliations.

Yet dominance provides the best criterion to classify ethnic groups. There are certain societies where ethnic groups are more or less equal in their relative status and power. The Flemish and Walloons in Belgium, and the Germans, French and Italians in Switzerland are of this type. Most ethnic groups are, however, either dominant or subordinate. In such cases ethnic origin is embedded in the class and power structure of the society, producing an ethnic hierarchy. The extreme cases are the classic Indian caste system and the modern racial pyramid in South Africa. In an era when equality is spreading as an acceptable world norm, dominance is difficult to tolerate, and hence non-dominant ethnic groups tend to reject their subordinate position and to struggle for change.

Approaches

Social scientists disagree appreciably on the best way to conceive of ethnic groups. The debate hinges upon which of the defining characteristics of ethnicity is the most decisive: is it common descent, or rather shared culture or consciousness of kind? According to the 'ascriptive' (or 'primordialist') approach, members of an ethnic group are bound together by their common descent. Primary blood ties instil immutable emotional attachments and allegiances. Being 'given' and rigid, ethnicity transcends individual perceptions and changing circumstances. It is thus easier to activate people's sense of ethnic loyalty than their loyalty to such 'rational' organizations as trade unions.

The opposing view, known as the 'situational' ('subjectivist' or 'instrumental') approach, posits that what really matters is people's definition of themselves as culturally or physically distinct from others. Their shared descent is secondary and, if necessary, may be manufactured and manipulated (Cohen, 1974). Ethnicity is, therefore, flexible, adaptable and capable of taking different forms and meanings depending on the situation and perceptions of advantage. Consequently ethnic groups emerge, merge, and split constantly.

The contrast between the two viewpoints can be illustrated by asking, Who is a Palestinian? According to the ascriptive approach, all Arab inhabitants of Palestine until 1947 and their descendants were, are and will be Palestinians, regardless of their present place of residence, behaviours and attitudes. In contrast, the situational approach presents a much more complicated picture: up to the 1920s, the Palestinians were 'Syrian Arabs'; then, in the period up to the 1940s, they emerged as 'Palestinian *Arabs*'; during the 1950s and the 1960s they became 'Arab refugees'; and since the 1970s they have defined themselves as 'Palestinian Arabs'. Second-generation Palestinians in the United States, Jordan and Israel differ in cultural traits, identity and manner from Palestinians in the West Bank, Gaza Strip and refugee camps. Further nuances in Palestinian identity and nationalism are generated by the differential and changing positions of significant outsiders – non-Palestinian Arabs, Israelis and others.

The situational view of ethnicity seems more valid and realistic. It is also in line with the shift in focus of the scientific study of ethnicity from a single ethnic group to *relations* between groups.

Sammy Smooha
University of Haifa

References

Cohen, A. (ed.) (1974), *Urban Ethnicity*, London.
Francis, E. K. (1976), *Interethnic Relations*, New York.
Smith, A. (1981), *The Ethnic Revival*, Cambridge.
Van den Berghe, P. L. (1978), *Race and Racism*, 2nd edn, New York.

Further Reading

Banton, M. (1967), *Race Relations*, London.
Mason, P. (1970), *Race Relations*, London.
van den Berghe, P. L. (1981), *The Ethnic Phenomenon*, New York.

See also: *Black Power*; *caste*; *ethnic relations*; *plural society*; *race*; *stratification*.

Ethnic Relations

Ethnic groups are groups which differ in descent, in cultural or physical traits, and in collective identity. The term 'ethnic relations' refers to the interactions between ethnic groups, relations that are very often replete with intolerance, hostility and violence.

The most common terms used to convey the troubled substance of ethnic relations are the social psychological concepts of prejudice and discrimination (Simpson and Yinger, 1972). 'Prejudice' is a set of preconceived rigid beliefs, emotions and preferences of one ethnic group towards another (for example, the idea that all Blacks are lazy), whereas 'discrimination' is a denial of equal treatment on ethnic grounds (thus, refusing a person a job for being Black). It is thus assumed that if prejudice and discrimination were eliminated, relations between the ethnic groups would cease to be problematic.

These concepts have proved, however, to be of limited value in understanding ethnic relations. It has become clear, for instance, that the present Black-White inequality in occupational achievements in the United States would not vanish if White Americans as individuals start to think of and treat Blacks and Whites in the same way. Neither could one adequately describe or explain the Nazi holocaust in terms of prejudicial beliefs and discriminatory actions of German individuals.

To overcome such difficulties, it is necessary to shift to *institutional terms*, such as ethnic ideology and institutional discrimination. 'Ethnic ideology' is a system of beliefs regarding existing and desirable ethnic relations. Nationalism, racism, Nazism, *apartheid*, assimilation and cultural pluralism are important ethnic ideologies that are institutionalized in certain countries, transmitted through the media, schools, churches, and families, made into state policies, and allocated appreciable resources for implementation. They are much more consequential for ethnic relations than individual prejudices.

Similarly, discrimination is more effective in its institutional than in its personal form. Institutional discrimination is evident when the normal functioning, whether intended or not, of a given institution (such as education or the economy) results in the unequal distribution of benefits or deprivations to different ethnic groups. For instance, when unemployment disproportionately hits the lower classes in which Blacks are over-represented, one may talk of institutional discrimination regardless of whether economic policy makers are aware of it or not (Wilson, 1978).

Institutional analysis, which is made possible by these broader concepts, is superior to interpersonal analysis because it treats ethnic relations as part of the structure and processes of the whole society and not in terms of individual responses. Ethnic relations are not determined by the irrational behaviours, ignorance and bigotry of some 'bad' people, but rather constitute a system of institutionalized behaviour, norms, sanctions, organizations, vested interests, tensions, conflicts, and so on evolving from fairly continuous contacts between ethnic groups.

Main Types of Ethnic Relations

Although ethnic relations take a wide variety of forms, the major ones are: (1) assimilation, (2) consociationalism, (3) domination and other, mostly mixed or transient, situations.

(1) In assimilationist situations, ethnic groups merge by adopting common cultural patterns, sharing the same institutions, intermarrying, and eventually they lose their distinctiveness. States which allow or push (but do not impose by force) assimilation are quite tolerant. They tend (a) to incorporate ethnic members as equal citizens, making little or no ethnic distinction in their laws or practices, and (b) to have a multi-ethnic élite or at least an élite fairly open to members of the subordinate groups. Universalistic treatment makes ethnic solidarity redundant; open élite structure legitimizes the ethnic status quo, and both encourage ethnic assimilation.

Assimilation rarely takes the form of a true melting pot which produces a genuinely new nation. Mexico is one of these extraordinary cases where the Spanish, Indians and Blacks were amalgamated to such an extent that a new mestizo Mexican culture, people, and identity emerged, to which each constituent group made a recognizable contribution. More commonly, the subordinate group assimilates into the dominant group. Van den Berghe (1981) characterizes the group most likely to assimilate as follows: 'An immigrant group similar in physical appearance and culture to the group to which it assimilates, smaller in proportion to the total population, of low status and territorially dispersed.' This profile applies to the 32 million immigrants from Europe to the United States during 1820–1930 who were largely assimilated into the Anglo-Saxon mainstream. Assimilation also succeeded because it was a common goal and a channel of social mobility for the poor European immigrants.

Assimilation in Mexico and the United States has not phased ethnicity out entirely but rather reduced it to such a level that it no longer regulates everyday life. Nor does it shape such cardinal decisions as which job to enter and whom to marry. As Gans (1979) puts it, 'real' immigrant ethnicity was so diluted over generations as to become 'symbolic' only.

At the same time it should be emphasized that Anglo-Saxon qualities in the United States and Spanish features in Mexico have remained the most cherished values and continue to figure significantly in status attainment.

(2) The course of ethnic relations is quite different in 'consociational' states such as Switzerland, Canada, Belgium, Austria, Yugoslavia, Nigeria and Lebanon (Lijphart, 1977). Far from assimilating, ethnic groups in these states keep their distinct cultures, institutions and identities and interact on a more or less equal footing ('consociationalism' literally means 'association between equals'). They are politically organized, and a mechanism for their proportional representation in key positions is set up. Their élites that join together to form the national élite are intensively engaged in the politics of accommodation and bargaining. Since every constituent ethnic group has a veto power on questions of vital interest to it, no decision can be made unless consensus is reached, a situation that quite often leads to a deadlock. While the vested interests of every group are carefully guarded, conflicts are difficult to resolve and problems are not satisfactorily settled. The largest or most powerful group has no choice but to share proportionately resources and decisions with the other ethnic groups which are unassimilable but sufficiently powerful to disrupt the system if they are not accorded their due share. Hence, consociationalism evolves as a compromise or parity situation when none of the other options – assimilation, domination and total separation – is feasible.

The contrast between Switzerland and Lebanon demonstrates the strengths and weaknesses of consociationalism. In Switzerland the division into predominantly homogeneous cantons enables each of the three major linguistic groups to exercise full cultural and territorial autonomy, while the federal institutions supply a shared framework with proportional representation, and the internationally recognized neutrality insulates the system from external pressures. This successful Swiss consociational democracy emerged and developed gradually over the last seven centuries.

Lebanon, in contrast, failed to develop the essential national consensus over its identity as a separate Arab state, without a Moslem dominant majority, and without being a party to the Israeli-Arab conflict. Proportional representation, which is the core of consociationalism, also became controversial as a result of the shifting demographic ratios and the rise of traditionally undeveloped groups (for example, the Shi'ites). Furthermore, the Lebanese did not enjoy the time and freedom available to the Swiss to work out their internal problems; they were instead continuously subjected to foreign rule or interventions. Indeed, the civil war in 1975 was the direct outcome of the crucial role played by non-Lebanese (the Palestinians, Syrians and Israelis).

(3) *Dominant* patterns of ethnic relations are more commonly found. Here one ethnic group clearly controls the other ethnic groups, monopolizes decision making, establishes its own culture as the prevalent one, appropriates to itself the lion's share of resources, and exacts from the subordinate groups various services and benefits. Compliance is achieved by a series of measures including economic dependence, political regulation, élite co-optation and segregation, that decrease the subordinate groups' capacity to resist. Domination may be made acceptable to the subordinate groups as the price of living in a stable society and receiving protection against persecution, deportation and bloodshed.

Dominance appears in many variations, the most important being slavery, indentured labour, caste systems, conquest, empires, colonialism, and their legacies in modern states such as South Africa and Israel (for Arabs). The most relevant brand of slavery, for instance, is 'chattel slavery', which prevailed in the New World. It was, indeed, a dominant pattern of race relations where Whites controlled Blacks, exploited them economically and sexually, deprived them of human rights, atomized them to the extent that they could not build a community and resist, and let them absorb their masters' culture but not assimilate. Slavery was accompanied by racism in the United States, but was much less racist in Latin America where Blacks, to a large extent, penetrated into and assimilated to the dominant White group.

After the demise of colonialism all over the world and especially in Black Africa, the rule of the White minority in South Africa stands out as the most blatant contemporary modern system of domination (Adam and Giliomee, 1979). The prospects for democratization in the foreseeable future are slim because of the following combination of conditions: (a) since Whites feel as native as the Africans do and regard South Africa as their only homeland, they will not depart, as did White settlers elsewhere; (b) Whites depend on non-White labour for their exceedingly high standard of living; (c) the liberal alternatives of assimilation, majority rule, consociational democracy, or negotiated partition are less advantageous for Whites than the status quo, and (d) Whites are strong enough to withstand internal unrest and external pressures. To sustain White domination, the South African government removed, in the late 1970s, superfluous economic and segregationist restrictions.

There are other situations which do not fit neatly into any of the above three patterns. One is the warfare frontier setting involving the large-scale liquidation of the widely dispersed and 'useless' natives by the technologically superior overseas settlers (for example, the Aborigines in Australia, the Indians in the Americas). The number of transient and mixed situations in our era of rapid change is also increasing. Cases in point are Black-White relations in the United States and the Catholic-Protestant relations in Northern Ireland, both following the collapse of domination in the 1960s.

Approaches to the Study of Ethnic Relations
Three major approaches have emerged in the social sciences to account for the tremendous variation in ethnic relations, particularly in industrial societies: the (1) cultural, (2) class and (3) pluralist.

(1) The cultural perspective sees cultural differences as the prime factor shaping ethnic relations. Modernization and the building of national institutions such as mass media, schools, political parties, industrial plants and trade unions gradually replace the ethnic traditional cultural and primordial ties by new overarching values and identities. Greater ethnic equality and assimilation will also result from modernization. This school of thought takes the Western experience as a model for other countries, forecasting the decline of ethnicity in the long run despite temporary digressions (Deutsch, 1966; Eisenstadt and Stein, 1973).

(2) The class theorists, on the other hand, expect rather a continuous revival of ethnicity caused by the exacerbation of internal contradictions in the world capitalist economy (Bonacich, 1980; Wallerstein, 1979). They regard comtemporary ethnic situations as by-products of capitalism which necessitated large-scale population movements (slaves, indentured labourers, guest workers, poor immigrants), colonialism (colonies as economic enterprises) and imperialism (cheap raw materials, new markets). The subordinate groups suffer from both class and ethnic deprivation, but they are slowly rising to liberate themselves from dependence, economic exploitation and ethnic discrimination.

(3) In contrast to the cultural and class approaches, the pluralist one assumes no *a priori* universal factor or trend in ethnic relations (Kuper and Smith, 1969; van den Berghe, 1973). It rather takes the vast diversity of ethnic relations as its vantage point, claiming that the dynamics vary appreciably from one situation to another. Thus the main determinant of ethnic relations is ethnicity in Black Africa, as compared to class in Latin America (van den Berghe, 1981). The pluralists also deny that Western development necessarily leads to assimilation or to non-ethnic liberal democracy, and point to a number of Western consociational democracies in which ethnicity is institutionalized, and to the spread of ethnic strife in some Western countries (Esman, 1977). Modernization may have various consequences for ethnicity, depending on other features of the ethnic situation (for example, industrialization encouraged the assimilation of European immigrants but not Blacks in the United States).

Strategies of Change
Policy makers and social scientists are hard pressed to formulate strategies to tackle the mounting ethnic problems. One general strategy is to ensure equality of rights and to create opportunities for contact between ethnic groups. The United Nations adopted several declarations on these lines, and many states enacted laws whose aim was to provide individual members of different ethnic groups with equal rights and protection against discrimination. Prejudice is combated through dissemination of information on minorities and the overall upgrading of the educational standard of the general population. Intergroup contact in schools, workplaces, armed forces and in experimental settings has also been used to promote ethnic tolerance (Katz, 1976).

While such a strategy is geared to removing barriers to assimilation, a competing strategy is to improve the conditions conducive for the retention and equalization of ethnic groups. Some of these measures include provision of ethnic group rights, cultural and territorial autonomy, and the extension of the principle of proportional representation to various posts and benefits. Most of them are embodied in the constitution or structure of many multi-ethnic states with federal or confederal structures. The idea is that through these measures, systems of ethnic domination can be transformed into consociational democracies.

The cases of Northern Ireland and South Africa reveal the difficulties inherent in the process. The British programme to resolve the ethnic dispute in Northern Ireland through power-sharing was blocked in the mid-1970s by the Protestant majority. More calculating and hesitant is the government of South Africa's attempt to harness consociational arrangements for alleviating its racial tensions. In the early 1980s it proposed a constitutional reform aptly branded by critics 'sham consociationalism', that aimed to broaden its racial base by co-opting the Coloureds and Asians into the White system (Hanf, Weiland and Vierdag, 1981).

A radical strategy is to reduce or eliminate ethnic relations by territorial and physical means. One possibility is secession or partition, like the successive divisions of the Indian sub-continent into India, Pakistan and Bangladesh. Another related method calls for population transfers, successfully completed in the early 1920s between Turkey, Greece and Bulgaria. The extremist variations – which are by no means infrequent – are mass deportations and genocidal attempts (Kuper, 1981). Peaceful reconstitution of state boundaries and voluntary population exchanges are not generally a practical solution, however, because they would require, in view of the present ethnic mess, a virtual revamping of the world political map and immense population movements.

Ethnic problems will endure, and, like all other social problems, there are no overall stock solutions. What could be more realistically expected is some reduction in ethnic conflict if the principle of negotiated conflict regulation gains greater acceptance.

Sammy Smooha
University of Haifa

References
Adam, H. and Giliomee, H. (1979), *Ethnic Power Mobilized*, New Haven.
Bonacich, E. (1980), 'Class approaches to ethnicity and race', *The Insurgent Sociologist*, 10.
Deutsch, K. W. (1966), *Nationalism and Social Communication*, Cambridge, Mass.
Eisenstadt, S. N. and Stein, R. (eds) (1973), *Building States and Nations*, Beverly Hills.
Esman, M. J. (ed.) (1977), *Ethnic Conflict in the Western World*, Ithaca.
Gans, H. J. (1979), 'Symbolic ethnicity: the future of ethnic groups and cultures in America', *Ethnic and Racial Studies*, 2.
Hanf, Th., Weiland, H. and Vierdag, G. (1981), *South Africa: The Prospects for Peaceful Change*, London.
Katz, P. A. (ed.) (1976), *Towards the Elimination of Racism*, New York.
Kuper, L. (1981), *Genocide*, Harmondsworth.
Kuper, L. and Smith, M. G. (eds) (1969), *Pluralism in Africa*, Berkeley and Los Angeles.
Lijphart, A. (1977), *Democracy in Plural Societies*, New Haven.
Simpson, G. E. and Yinger, J. M. (1972), *Racial and Ethnic Minorities*, New York.
van den Berghe, P. L. (1973), 'Pluralism', in J. J. Honigman (ed.), *Handbook for Social and Cultural Anthropology*, Chicago.
van den Berghe, P. L. (1981), *The Ethnic Phenomenon*, New York.
Wallerstein, E. (1979), *The Capitalist World-Economy*, Cambridge.
Wilson, W. J. (1978), *The Declining Significance of Race*, Chicago.

Further Reading
Glazer, N. and Moynihan, D. P. (eds) (1975), *Ethnicity: Theory and Experience*, Cambridge, Mass.
Hechter, M. (1975), *Internal Colonialism*, London.
Rex, J. (1970), *Race Relations in Sociological Theory*, London.
See also: *Black Power*; *caste*; *ethnic groups*; *plural society*; *prejudice*; *stratification*.

Ethnographic Fieldwork

The modern field researcher has the double task of collecting data and analysing it. He must first describe events and customs from within, in order to search for patterns and to explore the cognitive maps of his subjects. This is ethnography. He has also to trace developments over time and to compare his findings with data in other societies. He must then provide insights into the factors influencing similarities, differences and developments. Basic to his task, however, is the quality of his own field data. His primary research method is participant observation, supplemented by a growing arsenal of research instruments.

Participant observation basically involves living for an extended period alongside the people being studied. This period can vary from several months to more than a year, depending among other things on the research problem and available funds. (In Eastern Europe short research expeditions are more common.) To get to know the people he is studying the ethnographer must as far as possible share their experiences. It is obviously essential for him to learn the local language.

Participant observation in a foreign culture is a deeply emotional, sometimes even a traumatic, experience. The hardships of fieldwork can be extreme, but so can the rewards. For months the ethnographer lives in close contact with his subjects. He shares pleasures and griefs, hardships and victories. He often becomes involved in their personal and group conflicts. He also has to face and solve the myriad problems of daily life in new strange surroundings, to learn to give new content to such familiar roles as friend, neighbour, husband and father, and to act these out in public under the critical eyes of his new neighbours. He must always be fair, pleasant and, above all, constantly available. He will be subject to pressure to take sides in personal disputes between close informants, to express openly his preference for a particular faction, political party or class. Unless his introduction into the community has been carefully prepared through high-status persons, he may have a marginal position. He then becomes fair game for other marginals in the community who seek him out. Since he is eager for friendship and contact, he reciprocates these advances and may thus become identified with the community's eccentrics and outcasts, thereby jeopardizing his own status and credibility. The pressure of new roles, experiences and conflicts can become intense. Energy and time are usually also in short supply. The ethnographer must spend up to a third of his time writing up his data.

Fieldwork is often a lonely experience. The fieldworker's own family, if they are with him, can provide warmth and companionship. It is a little island to which the researcher can withdraw to regain a measure of objectivity and distance from neighbours and informants. For a male, his family may be the only way he can gain some access to the world of women. Nonetheless, many fieldwork locations are unhealthy and dangerous. Has an ethnographer the right to expose members of his family to such risks in order to enhance his scientific effectiveness and/or to meet his own need for affection and comfort? Many ethnographers have taken such risks and have profited by them, while others have suffered.

The ethnographer often faces other moral dilemmas. In the field the first is how to explain his presence. If he is researching a sensitive subject, he may be obliged to use a cover story that 'stretches' the truth somewhat. For example, in the early 1960s I carried out research in Sicily into the failure of a community development project. In the process I hoped to achieve an understanding of Mafia activities. Because the project itself was highly controversial and because it is unhealthy in Sicily to advertise an interest in Mafia, I told people I was studying the impact of emigration, a critical issue at the time. People were very helpful, but their enthusiasm for the subject constrained me since they did not take seriously my interest in community development and Mafia. The ethnographer, if he can, should thus avoid 'cover stories'. But if he must adopt one, he should stick as close to the truth as he can. Still, operating under a cover he is not being honest and is deceiving people who have given him their trust.

Informants become friends. This creates another dilemma, for it leads to a very instrumental, and often dishonest, approach to friendship. The interest of science demands that you milk your informants. You do this by making them your friends, by exchanging confidences, giving presents, talking for hours about subjects which bore you. Are these friends or scientific objects? The subjects themselves often realize that they are being used. For some fieldworkers the scientific ends justify the means. They have no moral problem. For many others, however, the dilemma remains.

By no means all informants are friends. Many are crude manipulators, unpleasant at best and uncompromisingly untrustworthy. Some informants, even those the researcher regards as friends, may steal, cheat and lie. They may ridicule him in public in a way he does not fully comprehend, in order to enhance their own status.

Later an ethnographer will be faced with publishing data essential to his analysis which, if published, could damage persons who befriended him and trusted him with their confidences. To delete or alter events does violence to science; to publish is a betrayal of trust and may, in an extreme case, lead to injury, imprisonment or death. This is a moral problem which many ethnographers have had to face. The solutions range from 'publish and be damned' to production of fiction.

Participant observation is thus a many-sided research instrument. While it is the anthropologist's primary research tool, his toolbag is more extensive. Most anthropologists also spend much of their time analysing archives, taking village censuses and holding surveys. They may carry out comparative research in other communities. They ask informants not only to submit to formal interviews, but occasionally also to a battery of tests, to write down their own experiences and attitudes and to categorize animate and inanimate objects, including their kin and neighbours, the supernatural beings they worship and the vegetables they eat.

All ethnographers are obliged to spend a great deal of time writing up their diaries, notebooks, interviews. The consolidation, classification and filing of the volume of data is essential. It has been demonstrated that unless information gleaned from informants is written up immediately, it is soon forgotten.

In general male and female fieldworkers have similar experiences. However, some problems they face are specific to their gender. It is very difficult for a male ethnographer to obtain intimate information from female informants, or even to observe their daily life. On the other hand, women researchers often encounter difficulties if they pursue their investigation in such typical male reserves as the South European coffee bars and cafes. Although they encounter problems and barriers, female ethnographers are able to operate among men far more successfully then male researchers can among women.

Ethnographic fieldwork is challenging, fascinating and hard work. For many it is an emotional experience of the same order as a psychoanalytical encounter. But the task is not finished when the researcher returns from the field. Fieldwork is but a first step. His task ends only when he has completed the much more difficult and time-consuming chore of digesting his material, analysing it and presenting it in a readable and convincing form to his readers.

Jeremy Boissevain
University of Amsterdam

Further Reading
Boissevain, J. (1970), 'Fieldwork in Malta', in G. D. Spindler (ed.), *Being an Anthropologist: Fieldwork in Eleven Cultures*, New York.

Epstein, A. L. (ed.) (1967), *The Craft of Social Anthropology*, London.

Golde, P. (ed.) (1970), *Women in the Field: Anthropological Experiences*, Chicago.

Pelto, P. J. (1970), *Anthropological Research. The Structure of Inquiry*, New York.

Spradley, J. P. (1980), *Participant Observation*, New York.

See also: *ethics in social research*; *interviews and interviewing*.

Ethnology

Ethnology has been variously defined in different national traditions. The term itself seems to have been coined in Switzerland by Chavannes in the late eighteenth century. In the nineteenth century the study of ethnology included 'moral and physical' aspects of man, the observation, classification and explanation of cultural phenomena only gradually being separated from biological anthropology. Today in Central Europe and the USSR 'ethnology' remains historically oriented, and in general the term is often used to denote the study of vanished or primitive societies. It also means a synthetic fusion of ethnographic field data as a preliminary to more theoretical analysis. Elsewhere it has become a synonym for 'cultural anthropology' or even 'folklore'.

Britta Rupp-Eisenreich
École des Hautes Études en Sciences Sociales, Paris

Further Reading

Bromley, Y. (1974), *Soviet Ethnology and Anthropology Today*, Paris.

Cresswell, R. (1975), *Eléments d'ethnologie*, Paris.

Gadamer, H. and Volger, P. (eds) (1972), *Neue Anthropologie*, vol. 4, *Kulturanthropologie*, Stuttgart.

Lowie, R. (1937), *The History of Ethnological Theory*, New York.

Voget, F. W. (1975), *A History of Ethnology*, New York.

Ethnomethodology

The subject matter of ethnomethodology is common sense knowledge, which consists of three interrelated phenomena: (1) The stock of knowledge at hand consisting of the social typifications, rules of thumb, maxims and recipes for getting things done. (2) The sense of social structure, which is our experience of the world as an object possessing the properties of typicality, predictability, causality, perceptual independence, pragmatic relevance and historical givenness. (3) The practices of common sense reasoning which are the methods people use to apply the stock of knowledge to concrete situations and to create the concrete character of situations.

Common sense knowledge is the bedrock of social interaction. Through the use of the practices of common sense reasoning, people experience their inter-

actions with other people as founded upon the 'same' meaning and addressing the 'same' environment. Common understanding and the intersubjective environment are viewed as practical accomplishments that are continually worked at by people, who rely on common sense reasoning to assemble ethnographic contexts of interpretation. These contexts consist of bits and pieces of information of everyday life which are brought together to form a perceptual aide for interpreting other people's talk and behaviour, objects, events and one's own behaviour. Anything can be used as a contextual particular, and the particulars themselves can have different meanings when assembled in different ways. Furthermore, people do not have to assemble the same substantive context in order to understand each another. Skinner found that while doctors and their patients assembled contexts that were different in content, they nevertheless experienced their interaction as mutually understandable. Ethnomethodologists use this theory of 'meaning by context' (Leiter, 1980) to study the interpretive methods people rely on.

Early formulations of these methods are found in Husserl (1960; 1965) and in Schutz (1962; 1964). Among the methods Husserl described are the 'assumption that things are always accessible again', and the reciprocity of perspectives. Schutz's 'natural attitude of everyday life' is a description of the properties of a factual environment of objects as perceived by a person within that environment and is synonymous with the 'sense of social structure' (Cicourel, 1973). Schutz viewed the natural attitude of everyday life as a product of ongoing interpretation through the use of four common sense idealizations: (1) The interchangeability of perspectives. (2) The temporary irrelevance of biographical differences. (3) The assumption that knowledge is social. (4) The assumption that people possess specialized knowledge. These idealizations are the basis of Cicourel's (1973) 'interpretive procedures', and Garfinkel's (1967) practices of the documentary method of interpretation.

Cicourel's interpretive procedures are analytical descriptions of the different ways in which people create and sustain a sense of social structure. They are: (1) The reciprocity of perspectives: people assume that if they exchange places each will see what the other sees, and that their experiences are congruent enough to treat differences of interpretation as minor. (2) Normal forms: they assume that others will talk in a way that is recognizable, intelligible and embedded within a body of common knowledge. (3) Et cetera principle: (a) the talker assumes that as he talks others fill in the unstated intended meanings of what he is saying, and (b) the listeners assume that the speaker will say something later that will serve to clarify ambiguous expressions. (4) Descriptive vocabularies as indexical expressions: people assume that to understand each other they must go beyond formal meanings and embed talk and behaviour within an ethnographic context. In his empirical work Cicourel had provided ethnographic descriptions of how the interpretive procedures are used (a) by high school counsellors to interpret students' behaviour and create types of students and student careers (Cicourel and Kitsuse, 1963); (b) by police, to decide appropriate interrogation practices and construct 'delinquent careers' from vague and truncated entries in official records (Cicourel, 1968), and (c) how researchers use interpretive procedures to assemble ethnographic contexts to interpret data (Cicourel, 1974).

Harold Garfinkel (1967) designed a method of capturing the practices of common sense reasoning in use. Subjects asked advice of a 'psychotherapist'. The advice was in the form of yes-no responses given at random which the subjects were to interpret before asking for more advice. The practices Garfinkel describes are similar to those described by Cicourel (1973): (1) Perceiving the yes-no responses as motivated by questions. (2) Using retrospective-prospective review to form questions. (3) Awaiting later answers to decide the meaning of previously unclear or contradictory answers. (5) Managing the truthful character of the advice by using practices 1–4 to assign the properties of a factual environment to the advice.

Later research by students of Cicourel and Garfinkel has clarified and refined the earlier theoretical perspective. Zimmerman (1974) noted that social workers treated official documents as part of a natural order independent of any one person's action or perception. Mehan (1974) found that students employed interpretive procedures to make sense of the teacher's instructions, which otherwise remained vague and incomplete even when the teacher supplied his own interpretive contexts. This does not mean that the teacher is doing a bad job; rather it indicates that the teacher and students continually negotiate the meaningful character of the lesson. The assembling of contexts for supplying meaning to the lesson relied on: (1) Imitation: copying verbal and nonverbal examples provided by the teacher and other students. (2) Cohort production: putting together fragments of interaction into an answer. (3) Searching: following the teacher's question with a question instead of an answer, thereby eliciting clarifying details from the teacher which are then used to answer the original question. Ethnographic particulars like nonverbal actions of the teacher, physical setting, clarifications, fragments of other students' answers are also assembled into contexts in order to make sense of the lesson and answers.

Kenneth C. W. Leiter
Locke, Purnell, Boren, Laney and Neely, Dallas

References
Cicourel, A. V. (1968), *The Social Organization of Juvenile Justice*, New York.
Cicourel, A. V. (1973), *Cognitive Sociology*, Harmondsworth.
Cicourel, A. V. (1974), *Theory and Method in a Study of Argentine Fertility*, New York.
Cicourel, A. V. and Kitsuse, J. (1963), *The Educational Decision Makers*, Indianapolis.
Garfinkel, H. (1967), *Studies in Ethnomethodology*, Englewood Cliffs, N.J.
Husserl, E. (1960 [1931]),*Cartesian Meditations*, The Hague. (Original German edn, *Cartesianische Meditationen*, Paris.)
Husserl, E. (1965), *Phenomenology and the Crisis of Philosophy*, New York.
Leiter, K. (1980), *A Primer on Ethnomethodology*, New York.
Mehan, H. B. (1974), 'Accomplishing classroom lessons', in A. V. Cicourel *et al.* (eds), *Language Use and School Performance*, New York.
Schutz, A. (1962), *Collected Papers I: The Problem of Social Reality*, The Hague.
Schutz, A. (1964), *Collected Papers II: Studies in Social Theory*, The Hague.
Zimmerman, D. H. (1974), 'Fact as practical accomplishment', in R. Turner (ed.), *Ethnomethodology*, Harmondsworth.
See also: *phenomenology*; *Schutz*.

Ethology

Konrad Lorenz defined ethology as 'the discipline which applies to the behaviour of animals and humans all those questions asked and those methodologies used as a matter of course in all other branches of biology since Charles Darwin's time'. Ethology is concerned with causality and the functions of behaviour, and it tries to establish the influence on behaviour of genetic, physiological and ecological variables. Ethologists also ask how and why forms of behaviour develop in interaction with the environment in the ontogeny of the individual, as well as how behaviour could have developed phylogenetically. Behaviour is thus interpreted as a contribution to adaptation to a particular environment. The methods of ethology involve primarily observation of a species in their natural environment. Having collected the data, ethologists then develop an 'ethogram', an inventory of behaviour of a species. This step is followed by systematic experiments and interspecific comparisons.

The origins of ethology can be traced back to Darwin. His book, *On the Origin of Species* (1859), established the basis for the concept of instinct, while even more important was his theory that natural selection underlies the behaviour of an animal as well as its morphology and physiology. In 1898 Whitman also claimed that an evolutionary perspective on behaviour was necessary, and independently of Whitman, Heinroth (1910) discovered the existence of 'patterns of movements' which, like morphological structures, are comparable between species. Through such comparisons, particular behaviours could be called homologous and could be traced back to a common ancestor.

Another antecedent of ethology is 'purposive psychology' developed by McDougall in *An Outline of Psychology* (1923) and later by Tolman in *Purposive Behavior in Animals and Man* (1932). Both postulated a factor called 'instinct' and noted that the behaviour of animals follows a 'purpose' governed by this instinct. Craig (1918) differentiated the end of a chain of behaviours (the consummatory act) from its beginning (appetitive behaviour). Appetitive behaviour is a specific seeking behaviour for a stimulus situation in which the consummatory act can begin.

Modern ethology dates back to 1931 with Lorenz's 'Contributions to the study of the ethology of social *corvidae*'. This article and others that followed represented a synthesis of previously isolated efforts in ethology and led to a new model of animal behaviour. Lorenz stressed that the interpretation of animal behaviour is only possible after detailed observation of the animal in its natural environment, and that it is necessary to compare behaviours of different species.

Lorenz used a hydraulic model to describe the interaction between internal and external factors, and he redefined Craig's 'consummatory act' as the 'fixed action pattern' (F.A.P.); the preliminary 'appetitive behaviour' was the phase leading to the performance of the F.A.P. Appetitive behaviour causes the animal to look for a configuration of stimuli which release the F.A.P. These stimuli are recognized innately according to a hypothetical mechanism, the 'innate releasing mechanism'. These signals are not only objects in the environment but also signals emitted by other members of the species, in which case signals serve a social function and are called 'releasers'. Releasers are not always equally efficient: this is because the efficiency is modulated by an 'action specific energy' which is diminished by the execution of an F.A.P. If only a little of the action specific energy is present, then the F.A.P. can only be executed incompletely and thus becomes an intention movement. When the F.A.P. has not been executed for a long stretch of time, the threshold for the execution decreases and the F.A.P. can be released even by a weak or inadequate stimulus; Lorenz termed this a 'vacuum activity'.

Lorenz's model was often criticized because it was so simple. Niko Tinbergen elaborated on Lorenz's original model. He expanded the techniques of observation through simple but ingenious experiments, and he evolved more sophisticated notions of releasers and instincts. He defined instinct as 'a hierarchical organized nervous mechanism which reacts to priming, releasing and directing stimuli of either endogenous or exogenous character. The reaction consists of a co-ordinated series of movements that contribute to the preservation of the individual and species'. Tinbergen worked mainly on the reproductive behaviour of the stickleback and through his findings expanded our understanding of the hierarchical organization of instincts. His experiments were mostly concerned with motivational conflicts, redirected activities, ambivalent behaviour and displacement.

Following Lorenz's and Tinbergen's seminal work, ethology spread rapidly all over Europe and, at a slower rate, to the US. Progress was halted during World War II and commenced again the the 1950s with the first international publication of Tinbergen's *The Study of Instinct* (the first ecology textbook) in 1951, and Lorenz's *King Solomon's Ring*, a popularized account of ethology, in 1952.

With the growth of ethology came a major conflict between two opposing views of behaviour. American experimental psychology adopted a behaviourist orientation that stressed the influence of environment and learning factors; they carried out laboratory experiments using rats, cats, dogs and apes as models for humans. On the other hand, ethology, with its systematic observation of species in their natural setting, tried to discover evolutionary and adaptive mechanisms underlying animal behaviour – the genetic basis for behaviour. Unlike experimental psychologists, ethologists studied many and diverse species, thus strengthening their case for innateness and instinct. The neglect of learning by ethologists provoked a strong reaction against the discipline from members of the opposing camp, notably by Lehrman (1953) who based his criticisms on the work of Kuo (1932).

The innate versus acquired dichotomy resulting from the debate seems somewhat sterile and false today. Innate and learned are no longer regarded as exclusive categories. Contemporary ethologists would agree that behaviour develops ontogenetically through the interaction between genetic information and environment. This does not imply that an apparently innate characteristic is really learned, or that every phylogenetically pre-programmed behaviour must be adaptively modifiable through learning. But everything learned must have as its foundation a phylogenetically provided programme if appropriate and adaptive behaviour patterns are to be produced. It seems logical to postulate that certain behaviour elements – those which conduct learning processes – should never be modifiable through learning. Learned behaviour does contain genetic information, to the extent that the basis of learning is a physiological apparatus which evolved under the pressure of selection. Lorenz termed this mechanism the 'innate school-marm'. Thus the question is not whether behaviour patterns are innate or acquired but rather how behaviour can be modified, or what can be learned, and when.

From the beginning, ethology was also interested in aspects of social behaviour such as territorial behaviour, group structure, and communication. A milestone in the ethological study of communication was the development of the concept of 'ritualization' (Huxley, 1966), referring to the modification of a behaviour pattern by natural selection in order to serve a communicative function. Such expressive movements mostly occur in courtship and in displays of aggression or submission. Their social function is largely to channel aggression – thus ritualized fighting or submissive behaviour hinders escalation of a fight. Bonding is another function of ritualized behaviour.

Ethologists also investigated ranking as an aspect of social behaviour. Schielderup-Ebbe (1935) found that among a flock of hens a few enjoyed privileges during feeding and had first access to the feeding site and pecked at other, lower-ranking, hens. This led on to the study of dominance, defined as having priority access to scarce resources, and measured by the number of conflicts won. This concept is now generally limited to description of relationships, while other forms of behaviour are referred to in the construction of social hierarchies where high-ranking individuals are the focus of attention of other group members.

Other areas of interest to ethologists are the relationship between social organization and ecology (DeVore, 1965); play behaviour; 'imprinting', or how individuals become attached to other members of the group, first observed by Lorenz in birds and studied by Hess (1973) and others. Ethologists have also considered the link between behaviour and the nervous system. Holst and St Paul (1963) elicited different behavioural reactions in hens through electrical stimulation of the brain, and Delgado (1967) was able to control aggressive behaviour using similar techniques. Neurophysiological research led to the discovery of neurons in the brain that are responsible for the control of different aspects of behaviour (Ewert, 1976).

A new development in ethology is sociobiology. Sociobiologists propose a global theory of behaviour which derives from the 'selfish interest' of the gene to reproduce itself; this selfishness leads to the concept of kin-selection, for related individuals share a determinable number of genes. Sociobiology's primary tools are intriguing mathematical models that consider phylogenetic adaptation and ecological pressures. When, in certain situations, different possible behaviours exist, pressures result in the development of evolutionary stabile strategies (E.S.S.) of behaviour. Sociobiology tries to include the social sciences in a modern synthesis of evolutionary theory, arguing that all forms of social organization – in animals ranging from termites to primates, including man – can be described using the same parameters and the same quantitative theory. They are criticized for their overemphasis on genetic determinism and for their analytical models which are strongly reminiscent of the Social Darwinism of the early twentieth century. Nevertheless they can provide

new insights into the structure and organization of individuals and their behaviour, and their importance is acknowledged in the study of insects, fish and birds. But the general applicability of sociobiological laws to primates and humans has yet to be proved.

The originality of the ethological approach in the study of human behaviour was in its methods of systematic observation and qualitative description, its considerations of phylogenetic roots, and the functions of behaviour deduced from a comparative approach. Human ethology in turn influenced areas of anthropology, psychology and sociology. However, the construction of an appropriate theoretical framework still remains a problem for the human ethologist.

Development of speech is a distinguishing primary characteristic of human behaviour. This made it possible to transmit information between generations by non-genetic means. Cultural evolution then assumed a major role in the adaptation of the species. It is possible that cultural evolution follows rules comparable to those which govern phylogenetic evolution, and also leads to the modification in behaviour. Moreover, humans are capable of altering their environment, thus changing selective pressures. These possibilities make it more difficult to determine the genetic adaptive value of a behaviour, and blur the distinction between phylogenetic and cultural traits. Finally, human ethologists have tended to neglect the adaptive modification of behaviour, that is, learning processes.

Several popular books on human ethology – Ardrey's *The Territorial Imperative* (1966), Lorenz's *On Aggression* (1963), Morris's *The Naked Ape* (1967) and Wilson's *On Human Nature* (1978) – brought the subject to the attention of a wider public. These authors tried to present a biological explanation for human behaviour, but they often worked with naive analogies and simplistic comparisons. At the same time, however, an authentic human ethology was being developed. Research focused on human-ethological interpretations of child development (child ethology), as in the work of Blurton-Jones (1972) and McGrew (1972); others described children's relationships and resulting group structures. Intercultural comparisons were made in the work of Eibl-Eibesfeldt on non-verbal behaviour (1972), who also observed the expressive behaviour of children born deaf and blind (1973). These studies have shown the complexities and the multidimensional nature of ontogeny, as well as confirmed the existence of invariant transcultural traits in human behaviour, such as expressive behaviour and its ritualization.

Human ethology has moved away from its descriptive beginnings and no longer restricts itself to investigating phylogenetic adaptations in behaviour: cultural patterns are also studied in relation to adaptation, and already a number of universal social interaction strategies have been observed through cross-cultural comparison. Their apparent variation can be attributed to the fact that phylogenetic and cultural patterns can be substituted as functional equivalents for one another, or they can be verbalized. Nevertheless, the underlying structural rules remain the same. This opens the way for the study of a grammar of human social behaviour encompassing verbal and nonverbal strategies. Such an approach could provide a theoretical framework and together with the empirical research in progress could give human ethology the refinement of animal ethology.

The results of human ethological studies could have an important impact on social questions, and the dangers arising from the neglect of human nature should be clear. While the modifiability of human behaviour, especially through educational programmes, is limited, this knowledge should not be used to justify a freeze on social changes, as extreme conservatives have already suggested. Indeed, this view was only possible because of the oversimplification of the field by popular writers. Rather, the universals identified by human ethology, especially in communication and in mechanisms of group cohesion and seclusion, could be the basis for shared concern and a common understanding and could provide a means to overcome ethnocentric political strategies.

Karl Grammer
Max-Planck Institut für Verhaltensphysiologie
Forschungsstelle für Humanethologie, West Germany

References

Blurton-Jones, N. G. (1972), *Ethological Studies of Child Behaviour*, Cambridge.

Bowlby, J. (1969), *Attachment and Loss: Vol. I Attachment*, London.

Craig, W. (1918), 'Appetites and aversions as constituents of instincts', *Biological Bulletin*, 34.

Dawkins, R. (1976), *The Selfish Gene*, London.

Delgado, J. M. R. (1967), 'Aggression and defense under cerebral radio control', in C. D. Clemente and D. B. Lindsley (eds), *Aggression and Defense*, Berkeley and Los Angeles.

DeVore, I. (1965), *Primate Behavior: Field Studies of Monkeys and Apes*, New York.

Eibl-Eibesfeldt, I. (1972), 'Similarities and differences between cultures in expressive movements', in R. A. Hinde (ed.), *Non-Verbal Communication*, London.

Eibl-Eibesfeldt, I. (1973), 'The expressive behaviour of deaf and blindborn', in M. von Cranach and I. Vine (eds), *Non-Verbal Behaviour and Expressive Movements*, London.

Ewert, J. P. (1976), *Neuro-Ethologie*, Berlin.

Heinroth, O. (1910), 'Beitrage zur Biologie, insbesondere Psychologie und Ethologie der Anatiden', *Verh. J. Int. Orthin. Kong.*, Berlin.

Hess, E. H. (1973), *Imprinting: Early Experience and the Development of Attachment*, New York.

Holst, E. V. and St Paul, U. V. (1963), 'On the functional organization of drives', *Animal Behaviour*, 11.

Huxley, J. S. (1966), 'A discussion on ritualization of behaviour in animals and man', *Philosophical Transactions of the Royal Society*, London, 251.

Kuo, Z. Y. (1932), 'Ontogeny of embryonic behavior in Aves I and II', *Journal of Experimental Zoology*, 61.

Lehrman, D. S. (1953), 'A critique of Konrad Lorenz's theory of instinctive behaviour', *Quarterly Review of Biology*, 28.

McGrew, W. C. (1972), *An Ethological Study of Children's Behavior*, New York.

Schielderup-Ebbe, T. (1935), 'Social behavior of birds', in A. Murchinson (ed.), *A Handbook of Social Psychology*, New York.

Tinbergen, N. (1942), 'An objective study of the innate behavior of animals', *Biblioth. Biotheor.*, 1.

Whitman, C. C. (1898), 'Animal behavior', *Biol. Lect. Mar. Lab.*, Woods Hole, Mass.

Further Reading

Bateson, P. P. G. and Hinde, R. A. (eds) (1976), *Growing Points in Ethology*, London.

Eibl-Eibesfeldt, I. (1975), *Ethology: The Biology of Behavior*, 2nd edn, New York.

Lehner, P. N. (1979), *Handbook of Ethological Methods*, New York.

See also: *altruism*; *comparative psychology*; *evolution*; *instinct*; *sociobiology*.

Evaluation

Evaluation as a distinct professional area refers to the assessment of projects, programmes or policies which are or have been in operation – as opposed to 'appraisal' of activities before initiation. Formerly both were called 'evaluation', since their formal logics are similar. They fit into an overall cycle: diagnosis-design-appraisal – (initiation and operation) – (monitoring and evaluation) – (adjustment of operation or design, or diagnosis). A separate formal evaluation stage is part of the attempt to rationalize policy making. It derives a special interest and flavour from its critical feedback and regulatory role, thus a close involvement with both decision and experience. Evaluation findings usually differ from appraisals, for they cover unexpected and unintended effects and are typically, though certainly not always, less favourable.

Standardization of terms is still limited, but the following distinctions are common: (1) Times: 'ongoing' (as opposed to '*ex post*') evaluation is while an activity is still continuing. 'Monitoring', as data-collection and reporting, occurs during the operation but serves both ongoing and *ex post* work; data is also collected before and after the operation. (2) Roles: the rationale for 'formative' evaluation is to improve a programme which will continue. 'Summative' evaluation considers total effect and whether a programme should have been undertaken or be continued. (3) Loci: evaluation may be 'internal', that is, done within a programme, or 'external'. (4) Foci: if, following Scriven (1967), all 'evaluation' is about performance ratings, then 'process evaluation' concerning lower-level outcomes, in the detailed terms of the programme processes, may be contrasted with 'impact evaluation' of effects on higher level goals. (The latter term is sometimes reserved for such studies done several years after programme implementation, when effects have matured and emerged, as opposed to immediate studies with more 'audit'-type intentions.)

Process, ongoing and formative evaluation in the above senses typically go together; but their occasional conflation, labelled as 'constructive'/'not backward-looking' (or conversely, as 'soft', afraid to pass judgement), misses the point that all studies are *both* about 'results' (what happened) *and* about trying to improve future action. However, since there are many levels of results and many stages of the future, the planning process contains many types of feedback and correspondingly many types of study (and much terminological confusion!) – not just the two or few types suggested by conflation. With a broader view than Scriven's, process studies on how and why effects are being or not being achieved are then also called 'process evaluation'.

The counterposing of impact and process studies reflects the historical preoccupation with impact studies, followed by some reaction. The 'classical'/'agricultural-botany' model was influenced by work in psychology, drug-testing and agriculture on determining the impacts of specified treatments. Programme goals, control and implementation were not deemed problematic: attention focused on the statistical assessment of effects. Forms of this approach were widely promoted in programme management, notably in the US in the 1960s, and were also prominent as formal evaluation units and studies spread into less developed countries (LDCs) via international aid programmes. Experience has been difficult in many contexts due to: (1) the multiplicity of effects; (2) a common inability to control closely the causal factors through experiments or quasi-experiments, so that data often have limited discriminatory power; (3) disputes over what were relevant alternatives; (4) problems in specifying goals in manageable form, reflecting a programme's internal conflicts, the goals' obscure and evolving nature in complex changing environments, or the expressed goals' functions in winning resources and avoiding criticism rather than guiding performance. Common outcomes – more so with social/innovatory/LDC/rural programmes – are then that findings are open to interpretation and dispute, conflicts occur between evaluators and programme practitioners, and there is a disappointing utilization of findings.

Besides attempts to advance research methods and to order programme goals better (for example, in 'logical frameworks'), reactions to evaluation studies include reflection on such studies' role when their results are not decisive and figure as only one influence amongst others. First, studies can still provide another set of checks and constraints on an *ad hoc* approach and sectional interest in resource allocation, as imperfect-yet-useful as other planning processes. Second, with studies as forms of influence rather than absolute arbiters, attention may turn to the range of areas and channels for influence, and hence the many types of study that can be valuable, for example, both internal and external evaluations, and studies on implementation and understanding programme processes. In that perspective (see, for example, Patton, 1978) evaluation studies are less a separate specialism and merge into the spectrum of studies of programme experiences and effects.

D. R. Gasper
Institute of Social Studies, The Hague

References
Patton, M. (1978), *Utilization-Focused Evaluations*, Beverly Hills.
Scriven, M. (1967), 'The methodology of evaluation', in R. Tyler, R. Gayne and M. Scriven (eds), *Perspectives of Curriculum Evaluation*, Chicago.

Further Reading
Guttentag, M. and Struening, E. (eds) (1975), *The Handbook of Evaluation Research*, 2 vols, Beverly Hills.
See also: *planning, economic*.

Evans-Pritchard, Edward Evan (1902–73)

Edward Evan Evans-Pritchard was the most eminent social anthropologist in the English tradition since Malinowski and Frazer. In 1946 he succeeded his distinguished teacher A. R. Radcliffe-Brown as professor of social anthropology at Oxford University, a post he held until his retirement in 1970. Evans-Pritchard's abundant writings reflect a fruitful tension between a native tradition of empiricist historical scholarship – his first degree was in history – and an adopted allegiance to the French tradition of sociological holism as exemplified in the *Année Sociologique* school founded by Émile Durkheim. He rejected Radcliffe-Brown's view of anthropology as a natural science of society, seeing it rather as an art, akin to historiography (1950). He was generally wary of 'grand theory', regarding himself as 'first an ethnographer and secondly as a social anthropologist' (1963). He saw social anthropology as primarily concerned with the task of translation from one culture to another, an idea he owed to Malinowski. But Evans-Pritchard had no equal in his ability at rendering in sensitive and often beautiful prose, the meaning of alien modes of thought and life.

This ability is outstandingly exemplified in his studies of witchcraft and other magical beliefs among the Azande people of Africa (1937), and of the religion of the Nuer, another African people (1956). Evans-Pritchard's account of the lineage and political systems of the Nuer (1940) profoundly influenced a generation of social anthropologists, but its conceptual basis has recently attracted radical criticism from several quarters (see Kuper, 1982). For general assessments of Evans-Pritchard see Bidney (1953), Hatch (1973) and Douglas (1980).

Roy Willis
University of Edinburgh

References
Bidney, D. (1953), *Theoretical Anthropology*, New York.
Douglas, M. (1980), *Evans-Pritchard*, London.
Evans-Pritchard, E. E. (1937), *Witchcraft, Oracles and Magic among the Azande*, Oxford.
Evans-Pritchard, E. E. (1940), *The Nuer*, Oxford.
Evans-Pritchard, E. E. (1950), 'Social anthropology: past and present', *Man*, 50, 198.
Evans-Pritchard, E. E. (1956), *Nuer Religion*, Oxford.
Evans-Pritchard, E. E. (1963), 'The comparative method in social anthropology' (Hobhouse Memorial Lecture), London.
Hatch, E. (1973), *Theories of Man and Culture*, New York.
Kuper, A. (1982), 'Lineage theory: a critical retrospect', *Annual Review of Anthropology*, 11.

Evolution

The term evolution implies transformation through a sequence of stages. Although the term is a general one which is used in many fields of study (Lewontin, 1968), in biology it is a fundamental unifying theory. Biological evolution specifically refers to *genetic* transformation of populations through time which results primarily from changes in the interactions between organisms and their environment (Dobzhansky *et al.*, 1977). The fact that life evolved is accepted by almost all modern biologists, although the exact mechanisms by which organic evolution occurs are the subject of intense research today.

Principles
The bench mark for the beginning of research on biological evolution is the 1859 publication of Charles Darwin's *The Origin of Species*, although evolutionary ideas were common before that date. Darwin and Alfred Russel Wallace independently developed the idea of natural selection as the chief mechanism of causing life to evolve. The key feature of natural selection is that it is indirect: inherited variability exists in all species and the best adapted variants tend to leave more offspring, so that through time there is gradual change. In this view, evolution is not directed by the processes that create the inherited variability, but rather by how that variability is shaped or pruned through time by natural selection.

Natural selection is a major feature of the synthetic theory of evolution, a term used to describe the modern view of the mechanisms of organic evolution. This synthesis was forged in the first half of this century by combining the theory of natural selection, Mendelian genetics, and other features to explain how life evolves. There has never been complete agreement on all aspects of the synthetic theory, however, with current controversy centring on topics such as the importance of random processes, the mechanisms of speciation, and the extrapolation from observable genetic changes over a short time span to patterns of phylogeny (Gould, 1982).

At the core of the synthetic theory of evolution are the processes that result in genetic transformation from generations to generation. These processes occur in two phases: (1) The production and arrangement of genetic variation by gene mutation, chromosomal changes, genetic recombination, and gene migration. (2) The reduction of genetic variation by natural selection and genetic drift. Genetic variability is ultimately produced by gene mutation, which is a chemical change in the DNA molecule. Most mutations are deleterious or relatively neutral to the survival of the organism. Mutations with small effects probably accumulate and eventually have a greater role in evolution than macromutations. Mutation rate has little relationship with evolutionary rate. Genetic recombination is also a source of genetic variation, but at a different level. Whereas gene mutation is a change in the DNA molecule, genetic recombination is the formation of different combinations of genetic factors that occur during the sexual cycle from the formation of the sex cells to fertilization. Theoretically, this process can create nearly an infinite number of different organisms simply by reshuffling the immense amount of genetic differences between the DNA of any two parents. Gene migration or flow is a source of new variability at the population level. A local population, for example, can undergo profound genetic change by the introduction of genes from other populations.

The second phase of genetic transformation is the reduction of genetic variation which is done primarily by natural selection. Since far more sex cells are fertilized than can possibly survive and reproduce, there is immense loss of potential life at each generation. In humans it is estimated that only about 12 per cent of all fertilized eggs survive, grow to adulthood and reproduce. The loss is probably mostly selective: genetic variants that do not survive to reproduce are lost because of deleterious mutations or combinations of genetic factors that tend to decrease vitality. Even resistance to disease often has a genetic component that can be selected. Simple chance may also be a factor in loss of genetic variability from generation to generation, a process called genetic drift. The importance of this random factor in evolution has been controversial ever since Sewall Wright proposed it in the 1930s.

The formation of new species involves mechanisms which reproductively isolate populations that were once part of the same species. In animals this usually requires physical isolation and no gene flow between populations that then undergo divergent genetic change. Naturalistic studies show that this can occur relatively rapidly in small isolated populations. Alternatively, changes in chromosomal structure between local populations may lead to their reproductive isolation and speciation.

A common misunderstanding of evolution is that it occurs because of mutations that arise and directly change the genetic composition of a species through the generations. This view, called the mutation theory of evolution, was common in the early part of theory, but is now discredited for complex organisms. Genetic variability in species is immense, and recent biochemical research has shown that a large percentage of genetic loci have one or more mutant variants. According to the synthetic theory, the direction of genetic change is determined by the selection and random loss of this vast store of existing genetic variability.

Another common misunderstanding of the synthetic theory of evolution is that it explains why the organic world evolved in the way it did. The *pattern* of evolution revealed in the fossil record and, by inference, from living organisms cannot be predicted by the processes of production and reduction of genetic variation any more than human history can be explained by the processes by which individuals learn from birth to death.

Human Evolution

There are eighteen living orders of mammals. The one in which humans are classified (Primates) may have originated in the late Cretaceous (roughly 70–65 million years ago) but only by Eocene times (54 to 35 million years) do primates of the modern aspect appear (Szalay and Delson, 1979). These Eocene forms resemble modern lemurs and tarsiers. By Oligocene times (35 to 24 million years) there are primates which share some derived characteristics seen in the group containing modern monkeys, apes and people (Anthropoidea). Not until the Miocene (24 to 5 million years) are there fossils which have traits shared uniquely with the superfamily containing apes and people (Hominoidea). Although some middle to late Miocene (roughly 16 to 8 million years) hominids have a chewing apparatus that looks like early members of the human family (Hominidae), the resemblance is probably due to the fact that the common ancestor of the great apes and

people also shared these traits. The earliest fossils that can be linked unequivocally and uniquely to modern humans are grouped in the genus *Australopithecus* and date back at least to 3.7 and probably to 5 or 5.5 million years (McHenry, 1982). The earlier date is from a fragment of jaw which appears to share unique characteristics with later and better-known members of *Australopithecus*. All members of this genus are confined to Africa.

The earliest fossil species that is undoubtedly a member of the human family is *Australopithecus afarensis* known in East Africa from geological strata dating between 3.7 and 3.0 million years ago. Its dentition shows many derived traits in common with later hominids, but it also retains numerous generalized characteristics of the ape-human common ancestor, such as distally worn upper canine teeth, obliquely set lower first premolars with small inside cusps, sloping chin, and a space between the upper incisors and canines. It had relatively very large cheek teeth and well developed chewing muscles like later species of *Australopithecus*. The brain size relative to body size is much closer to modern apes than to modern people, being less than one half the relative size of *Homo sapiens*. The body below the head (postcranium) is completely reorganized away from the common plan seen in all other primates and shares the uniquely human bipedal pattern. Some primitive traits are retained in the postcranium such as long and curved toes, which may imply a retention of greater tree climbing ability than that seen in *Homo sapiens*. By about 2.5 million years ago many of the primitive dental and cranial features of *A. afarensis* are lost and another species is recognized, *A. africanus*. Relative cheek tooth size remains large and relative brain size remains diminutive. The postcranial skeleton is only partly known, but appears to be very similar to *A. afarensis*. By about 2 million years ago two species of hominid appear in the fossil record, *A. robustus* and *Homo habilis*. The former (*A. robustus*) continues and exaggerates the trend to heavy chewing adaptation with an emphasis on grinding. The latter (*H. habilis*) shows the first signs of relative brain size increase and dental reduction. Stone tools first appear at about this time. In African strata dated to about 1.6 million years ago hominids appear which resemble very closely the well-known Asian *H. erectus*. Relative brain size is further increased and stone tool technology becomes much more elaborate.

The first appearance of human populations outside of Africa may precede 1 million years, but certainly by about 0.9 million years ago *H. erectus* occupied parts of tropical Asia. The exact chronology is still uncertain, but some time after this and before 0.5 million years ago some populations had adapted to life in the temperate climatic zone of Asia and Europe. The appearance of *H. sapiens* depends on the definition, but by 0.3 million years ago the fully modern brain size had evolved, although the skull still retained many *H. erectus*-like traits. These archaic *H. sapiens* persisted in most areas of Eurasia until about 35,000 years ago. The earliest traces of anatomically modern *H. sapiens* are in Africa perhaps as early as 130,000 years ago, although in Eurasia this form becomes abundant only after 35,000. By at least 30,000 years ago Australia was inhabited by anatomically modern *H. sapiens* (yet archaic forms persisted until at least 10,000). America was settled by immigrants from Asia who migrated across a landbridge connecting Siberia and Alaska perhaps at 20,000 to 15,000 years ago. People first reached some of the Pacific islands several thousand years ago from the east, reaching the Marquesas Islands by about AD 300 and New Zealand by about AD 900.

Technological development in human evolution appears to be erratic in pace, but it certainly shows a pattern of acceleration. Relatively crude stone tools persist for over 1.5 million years. Finely worked blade tools are much more recent. Humans have had agriculture, cities, and writing for less than one quarter of one per cent of their evolutionary development as a separate mammalian lineage.

Behaviour

Human locomotor behaviour probably evolved from an ape-like ancestor with a short back, a flat chest, and a highly mobile shoulder and forelimb adapted to climbing and suspending the body below tree branches (McHenry, 1982). Like modern apes (but unlike monkeys) this hypothetical ancestor was relatively awkward and energetically inefficient at walking on the ground either quadrupedally or bipedally. But as has happened to many other primate groups, terrestrial travel was increasingly adopted. Why our ancestors took up bipedality instead of quadrupedality is unknown, but certainly the unique ape-like body plan made either gait equally efficient in terms of energetic cost at normal speeds. Free hands for carrying makes bipedality more advantageous. Fossil evidence at about 3.5 million years ago shows that bipedality had been established in the human evolutionary lineage, but before that time the paleontological record is not yet complete enough.

The evolutionary history of human feeding behaviour is documented by fossil dental remains spanning millions of years. The earliest hominids were quite different from modern African apes, having thick molar enamel, exceptionally large cheek teeth, and powerful chewing muscles. Microscopic studies of dental scratches show that these early humans were probably not eating seeds and grass, nor were they crushing bones. By about 2 million years ago meat eating was certainly practised, as evidenced by bone remains with stone tool cut marks. Relative cheek tooth size reduces fairly gradually from 2 million years ago to the present which may be because extra-oral food preparation to some extent took over the function of the grinding teeth.

Many other aspects of human behavioural evolution are related to the fact that absolute brain size tripled and relative brain size more than doubled over the last 2.5 million years of human evolution. Human fossils dating between about 3.5 and 2.5 million years ago have endocranial volumes the size of modern chimpanzees, although relative to body size they are slightly larger.

The biological evolution of most aspects of human behaviour are much more difficult to document. The basic method of inquiry involves comparisons with other living animals. From this perspective it is clear that spoken symbolic language is the most unique human attribute in the organic world. Recent field studies of monkeys reveal that they possess a form of vocal symbolic communication, but there is a vast quantitative gap in speech capabilities between human and nonhuman primates.

The chief difficulty of studying the biological evolution of human behaviour is determining the genetic component of behaviour. Often the only genetic component is genetically conditioned developmental plasticity. There is a genetic basis for the development of the neurophysiology required for speech, for example, but a great deal of plasticity in the kind of language that is learned. There is a genetic basis for most aspects of human sexuality, but an enormous flexibility in how it is expressed. One method for approximating the extent of genetic contribution to specific behaviours is by comparing differences between identical twins (and hence genetically identical individuals) with the differences among unrelated individuals. Twin studies are complicated by the fact that most twins are raised in the same environment and that the sample of identical twins raised apart is still very small.

One theoretical breakthrough in the study of behavioural evolution came in 1964 with the publication of W. D. Hamilton's 'The genetical theory of social behavior'. He suggested that even genetically controlled behaviours that were detrimental to an organism's survival could be favoured by natural selection because of what has become known as kin selection. Kin selection refers to the '. . . selection of genes because of their effect in favouring the reproductive success of relatives other than offspring' (Barash, 1982). Kin selection theory has been successfully employed to explain several aspects of the social behaviour of nonhuman animals, especially social insects, but application of this and other sociobiological theories to the evolution of human social behaviour has not yet resulted in universally accepted principles. The enormity of human behavioural plasticity makes the search for evolutionary principles difficult, but a great deal of research on this topic is currently being pursued. Even more difficult, if not impossible, is the search for any behavioural evolutionary divergence between human groups that have a genetic basis.

Henry M. McHenry
University of California, Davis

References
Barash, D. P. (1982), *Sociobiology and Behavior*, New York.
Darwin, C. (1859), *On the Origin of Species by Means of Natural Selection*, London.
Dobzhansky, T., Ayala, F. J., Stebbins, G. L. and Valentine, J. W. (1977), *Evolution*, San Francisco.
Gould, S. J. (1982), 'Darwinism and the expansion of evolutionary theory', *Science*, 216.
Hamilton, W. D. (1964), 'The genetical theory of social behavior', *Journal of Theoretical Biology*, 12.
Lewontin, R. C. (1968), 'Concept of evolution', *International Encyclopedia of the Social Sciences*, New York.
McHenry, H. M. (1982), 'The pattern of human evolution: studies on bipedalism, mastication, and encephalization', *Annual Review of Anthropology*, 11.

Further Reading
Futuyma, D. J. (1979), *Evolutionary Biology*, Sunderland, Mass.
Nelson, H. and Jurmain, R. (1982), *Introduction to Physical Anthropology*, 2nd edn, St Paul.
See also: *evolutionism and progress*; *genetics and behaviour*; *population genetics*; *race*; *sociobiology*; *sociocultural evolution*.

Evolutionism and Progress

Evolutionism is the label now commonly used for a current of thought which was strongly represented in the anthropology and sociology of the nineteenth century. Although it fed on biological analogies, it must be clearly distinguished from Darwinian thinking. Its inspiration came rather from the older tradition of Lamarckian evolutionary theory, which provided the main rival to Darwinian theory until well into the twentieth century. Key elements in this tradition were the beliefs that organisms were intrinsically bound to improve themselves, that changes were progressive and often radical and sudden, and that acquired characters could be transmitted genetically. Typically, the 'stages' of ontogeny, or the individual life history, were taken to exemplify the 'stages' of phylogeny, the development of a species.

Herbert Spencer, one of the most consistent exponents of the organic analogy in the social sciences, was perhaps the leading evolutionist in sociology, but these general ideas were taken for granted by authors as diverse as Marx, Freud and Durkheim, and they survived in some modern theories in anthropology (for example, Childe, 1951), in the psychological theory of Piaget, in 'Whig' history, and so on. The 'evolutionist' assumptions were, however, directly in contradiction to the Darwinian theory of evolution by variation and natural selection, which did not assume the existence of any progressive line of change. On the contrary, Darwin (1859) stated emphatically that 'I believe in no fixed law of development' (*On the Origin of Species*).

Evolutionist theory in the social sciences should perhaps be regarded as part of a broader tradition of theories of 'progress', which represents the most deeply entrenched way of conceptualizing social history in the West. It has a particular appeal to 'progressive' radicals and utopians, while the mirror-image theory, that the trend of history is towards social and cultural decadence, is, on the other hand, associated rather with right-wing political theories and with religious revivalism. Whether the unit of perfectibility was assumed to be humanity or a particular civilization or 'race', the theory was so abstract and value-laden as almost to defy empirical reference. Nisbett (1980), nevertheless, argues that the faith in progress has been eroded by a widespread scepticism about the unique superiority of contemporary Western civilization.

Adam Kuper
Brunel University, Uxbridge

References
Childe, G. (1951), *Social Evolution*, London.
Nisbett, R. (1980), *History of the Idea of Progress*, New York.

Further Reading
Mayr, E. (1982), *The Growth of Biological Thought*, Cambridge, Mass.
Peel, J. D. Y. (ed.) (1972), *Herbert Spencer on Social Evolution*, Chicago.
Stocking, G. (1968), *Race, Culture and Evolution*, New York.
See also: *evolution*; *social change*; *sociocultural evolution*.

Exchange

In both exotic and modern societies people exchange a variety of items: shells, religious icons, axes, secret spells, greeting cards, dances and even humans themselves. The study of such exchange systems has assumed a prominent place in modern anthropology. The most well-known example, called the *kula* and found off the coast of New Guinea, was described by Malinowski (1922). In the *kula*, armbands and necklaces flow in opposite directions along circular tracks that serially unite a number of islands and societies. This institution typifies many nonmarket exchange systems: *kula* debts among partners remain outstanding and are liquidated, if ever, only in the long run; direct haggling over exchange rates is not found; and the items exchanged have no immediate practical use. Participation in the *kula*, however, brings great prestige.

A catalogue of exchange systems is overwhelming in its diversity. Among foraging groups, for example, a successful hunter usually distributes his kill to the entire community; over time he may or may not receive an equal return from other members. The exchange of feasts has been reported for the northwest coast of America, and in many rural areas of the world, peasants offer festal food and drink to secure the labour of others. Very complex exchange systems have been found in Papua New Guinea. For example, the *tee* consists of a series of branching paths, oriented in an East-West direction, along which pearl shells and other items are passed. The goods first move in one cardinal direction, and then the entire flow is reversed. Throughout Africa, the exchange of bridewealth for wives was common; more generally, Lévi-Strauss (1969) has tried to demonstrate that marriage everywhere represents an exchange of women between men.

Anthropological theories of exchange are as varied as the ethnography, but there are two principal positions: (1) Some theories are situated within the tradition of Hobbes, Adam Smith and Bentham. Society is viewed as a collection of self-interested actors, and exchange between them is said to be a *means* for gaining personal utility or satisfaction. The *kula*, for example, has been viewed as a kind of peace pact; under its cover the trade of useful goods can be carried out. Some exchange patterns, it is argued, serve to build up 'political' followings and thereby to secure territory and access to needed resources; participation in them also can be a means for gaining social prestige. (2) According to an alternative theory, deriving from Malinowski, Mauss and Lévi-Strauss, exchange itself is an *end*, for it both establishes and mediates the distinction between self and other. Material exchanges express the moral order of society. In this view, exchange is a fundamental condition of social life and is not reducible to self-interest. Thus, Malinowski insisted that the *kula* was based solely upon reciprocity, and Lévi-Strauss has made similar claims about marriage.

In fact, both theories are equally essentialist; society is said to be built up from self-contained, interacting units or from patterned relationships. Each theory has implications about the 'origin' of society as well as the functions of exchange.

In recent years some anthropologists have attempted to circumvent this Western debate by considering the meaning which actors themselves attribute to exchange. This perspective provides a different form of explanation. Consider the following scheme, which is a simplification of several instances from Africa and New Guinea: goods are divided into two classes, alpha and beta, while humans are divided into three categories – our group, groups with whom amicable relations are established, and unrelated persons. Within a group, alpha and beta goods are shared; between groups, alpha goods are exchanged to begin, continue or restore a relationship; between unrelated persons, beta goods are traded. A metaphoric relation, we may say, is established between humans and goods; material exchanges are modelled or seen through the perspective of social relationships, and in reverse. Goods both *are* and *are not* equivalent to human bonds. A homicide, for example, may be repaired by a flow of alpha goods. In strict terms, a homicide can be rectified only by offering a human replacement; the goods are a metaphoric substitution. The 'magic' of such an exchange of goods consists in its capacity to do one thing (repair a human relationship) by doing another (offering a material item). To see what an exchange accomplishes, therefore, requires an examination of the cultural metaphors on which it is founded. Exchange in exotic contexts is an intentional act that has effects, but anthropologists are increasingly wary of reducing its meaning to a means-ends framework or the postulate of primal human bonding. These are Western explanations which miss the imaginative and rich metaphors found in other cultures.

Stephen Gudeman
University of Minnesota

References
Lévi-Strauss, C. (1969), *The Elementary Structures of Kinship*, London.
Malinowski, B. (1922), *Argonauts of the Western Pacific*, London.
See also: *economic anthropology*; *markets*; *trade and markets, anthropology of.*

Exchange Rate

The exchange rate is a price: the price of one currency in terms of another. A distinction is made between the *nominal, effective* and *real* exchange rate. The *nominal* rate is a bilateral price expressed and quoted either as the number of units of the domestic currency per unit of another, or vice versa.

The *effective* exchange rate is an index of a currency's value in terms of a weighted basket of other currencies. Movements in this index show how a currency has moved, not against a single currency, but against the group of currencies in the basket. Movement in the effective rate is a weighted average of divergent changes in nominal rates.

The exchange rate (nominal or effective) determines the competitive position of domestic output in international markets. At constant domestic prices it gives the foreign currency price of a country's exports and hence influences foreign demand for domestically produced goods. Similarly, at constant foreign currency prices, the exchange rate determines the domestic currency price of imports and hence influences the demand for imports. Movements in the exchange rate can, therefore, have a powerful influence on the competitive position of goods and services produced in different countries and thereby influence the pattern of international trade flows.

The *real* exchange rate calculation adjusts movements in either a nominal or effective exchange rate for relative changes in the domestic price of goods in the country of production. Thus, if a currency depreciates by 10 per cent while its rate of inflation is 4 per cent more than its competitors, the real exchange rate has declined by 6 per cent.

The theory and empirical evidence about the determination of the exchange rate are far from settled. Flow theories tend to concentrate on the current account of the balance of payments and therefore on the factors (such as relative price and income movements between countries) influencing trade flows. The exchange rate is viewed as an equilibrating mechanism for the current account. Portfolio theories, or the asset-market approach (of which the monetary theory of the exchange rate is one of many variants), concentrate on the required conditions for equilibrium in wealth-holders' portfolios. In these models, movements in the exchange rate reflect an excess supply or demand for financial assets as between countries. A depreciation is viewed as a sympton of an excess supply of domestic financial assets. Stability in exchange rates requires, in these models, consistent monetary policies as between countries.

Governments have an interest in the level and stability of exchange rates. As movements influence the domestic price of imports, they have an effect on the domestic price level and, dependent upon how wage bargainers respond, the rate of inflation also. Through the same mechanism the exchange rate affects the level of real income and wages at each level of output. To the extent that the international competitive position of domestic goods is affected, movements in the exchange rate have implications for the level of output and employment. Thus governments might resist an appreciation because of its adverse employment effects, but also a depreciation because of the prices effect.

David T. Llewellyn
Loughborough University

Further Reading
Isard, P. (1978), *Exchange Rate Determination*, Princeton.
Llewellyn, D. T. (1981), *International Financial Integration*, London.
See also: *balance of payments*; *devaluation*; *international monetary system*; *trade, international*.

Existential Psychology

Existential psychology developed in Europe between World Wars I and II and gradually spread to America in the 1950s. The seeds of existentialism were found in the writings of Kierkegaard, the Danish philosopher, but the principal founders of existential philosophy were two Germans, Heidegger and Jaspers. In France its leading protagonists were Marcel, Sartre and Merleau-Ponty.

Existential psychology did not claim to be a new branch of psychology, nor even a new theory. It viewed itself as a new orientation, essentially idiographic, as opposed to the nomothetic tendencies of other forms of psychology, such as behaviourism.

The general characteristics of existential psychology are as follows:
(1) It is not a school, but a *movement* which focuses its inquiry on the individual person as being-in-the-world.
(2) Several basic tenets underlie this movement: (a) every man is unique in his inner life, perceptions and evaluations of the world, and in his reactions to it; (b) man as a person cannot be understood in terms of functions of elements within him. He cannot be explained in terms of physics, chemistry, or neurophysiology; (c) psychology, if patterned after physics, cannot fully understand human nature; (d) neither the behaviouristic nor psychoanalytic approach is totally satisfactory.
(3) As a *human* psychology, it attempts to complement, not to replace or suppress, other existing orientations in psychology.
(4) It attempts to develop a comprehensive concept of man and an understanding of man in his total existential reality. It concerns itself with the person's consciousness, feelings, moods, and experiences relating to his individual existence in the world and among other humans. Its ultimate goal is to discover the basic force in human life that would provide a key to understanding human nature in its entirety.
(5) Its themes are person-to-person relationships, freedom and responsibility, individual scales of values, the meaning of life, suffering, anxiety, and death.
(6) Its principal method is phenomenological, including *intuiting* (or intense concentration on the phenomena of consciousness), *analysing* (or focusing on aspects of consciousness and how they relate to each other), and *describing* (or rendering an intelligible account to others). Existential psychology seeks to grasp the essence of whatever appears in consciousness and to describe what is perceived, imagined or felt.
(7) Its contributions have been primarily to personality theory, psychotherapy, and counselling.

In Europe one of the leading existential psychologists, Ludwig Binswanger, developed *Daseinsanalyse* (existential analysis). This method seeks to describe an individual's relationship with the world (*Umwelt*), with his fellow-men (*Mitwelt*) and with himself (*Eigenwelt*) in order to help the person become his own authentic self.

Two important American existential psychologists are Carl Rogers and Rollo May. Stressing the developmental aspect of *becoming*, Rogers seeks to help the person achieve greater self-actualization. Like Rogers, May has been concerned with existential psychotherapy. He emphasizes understanding the basic nature of man and insists that through existential psychology man will be able to understand the characteristics that make him human.

Existential psychology has been criticized by behaviourists and rigorous experimentalists for its lack of verifiable data, subjectivism and strong attachment to philosophy.

Virginia Staudt Sexton
St John's University, New York

Further Reading
Binswanger, L. (1963), *Being-in-the-World: Selected Papers by Ludwig Binswanger*, New York.
May, R. (1969), *Existential Psychology*, 2nd edn, New York.
Misiak, H. and Sexton, V. S. (1973), *Phenomenological, Existential, and Humanistic Psychologies: A Historical Survey*, New York.
Rogers, C. (1961), *On Becoming A Person*, Boston.
See also: *phenomenology*; *Rogers*; *Sartre*.

Experimental Design

The Function of Experimental Design
Experiments involve introducing a planned intervention (usually referred to as a 'treatment') into a situation, in order to associate the treatment with resulting change. Experimental design facilitates this process in several ways:
(1) It translates all aspects of one's hypothesis – the statement of expected relation of changes to the intervention – into operational terms: subjects, behaviours, situation, equipment, procedures, and so on. These permit the hypothesis to be tested empirically.
(2) It rules out those alternative explanations which provide the most serious challenge to the treatment as *the* explanation for the change.
(3) It facilitates relating the changes to other variables, thus permitting better understanding of the relationship.

The Logic of Experimental Design
(1) The first step in experimental design is to translate expectations expressed in one's hypothesis into operational terms. The accuracy of this translation is critical. Misleading conclusions are likely to result from a treatment that inadequately represents that intended, or an insufficiently sensitive measure of change.
(2) Following stage 1, one must create a situation in which changes can be sensed. Sometimes one compares the pre- with the post-intervention condition of the experimental subjects. In other instances, experimental subjects may be compared with an untreated comparable group, a 'control group'. In still other instances, post-treatment condition is compared with estimates of the untreated state, for instance, test norms or regression estimates made from previous data or comparable groups.
(3) One then rules out whatever alternative explanations may be important rivals to that intended. For example, if a control group is used, the groups may not have been equivalent to begin with, or drop outs may make them non-equivalent at the end. Alternative explanations common to many studies have been identified (see below) but some may be unique to a study. For example, if subjects are allowed to complete a test at home, their score may reflect more their ability to seek help than their own achievement.
(4) Assuming the data support one's expectations, these steps in the logic follow:
  (a) since the results were as predicted;
  (b) and since there is no reasonable explanation for the phenomenon other than the treatment (others having been ruled out by one's design);
  (c) then the hypothesis escaped disconfirmation. While one cannot test the hypothesis in every situation, one infers from this one that similar predictions would prove accurate in like instances. With each such confirmation, confidence in the hypothesis increases, but a single disconfirmation, without a reasonable explanation, is sufficient to disprove it.

Experimental Control
It is difficult to provide sufficient experimental control to protect against every possible alternative explanation. Further, one typically buys protection at a price. For example, a laboratory gives more complete control, but laboratory circumstances are rarely like those to which one hopes to generalize. Yet, natural circumstances may provide too little control. Zimbardo, Anderson and Kabat (1981) supply an interesting example of this dilemma and its solution. They hypothesized that the paranoid behaviour frequent in elderly people was due to the gradual unnoticed loss of hearing common in old age. An expensive longitudinal design following subjects over time would have been inconclusive because of the subjects' varying social experiences. In addition, it would involve the ethical problem of withholding hearing loss information to see if paranoid behaviour developed.

The researchers devised a creative experimental design. Post-hypnotic suggestion produced a temporary unnoticed hearing loss in college student volunteers with resulting increase in paranoid behaviour. To eliminate rival alternative explanations, two control groups of similar subjects were established: one received post-hypnotic suggestion of a hearing loss of which they would be *aware* and another a neutral post-hypnotic suggestion in order to show that the hypnotic process itself did not induce paranoid behaviour. The paranoia was shown to follow only unnoticed induced hearing loss, and all subjects were exposed to controlled similar social experiences following the loss.

Altogether, this is a clever use of experimental design for an otherwise difficult problem.

But using a laboratory-like setting is not without costs. Impressed by the scientific laboratory, subjects may have tried to please the researcher; here, the researchers, knowing which was the experimental group, may have unintentionally cued subjects to appropriate behaviour (Rosenthal, 1976). The verisimilitude of the hypnotically induced hearing loss to that which occurs in older people may be questioned, as may the use of college students.

Nearly every design choice involves trade-offs in the use of resources which might have been used to control something else. Part of the 'art' of design is finding a suitable middle ground, one realistic enough to generalize but permitting sufficient control.

The Criteria of Good Design

A good design reduces one's uncertainty that the variables are linked with some generality as hypothesized. Showing they are linked requires a combination of internal, statistical conclusion and construct validity as defined by Cook and Campbell (1979). Internal validity assures that variables are linked in the form in which they were manipulated or measured. Statistical conclusion validity assures appropriate use and interpretation of statistics. Construct validity assures that the form in which the variables were manipulated or measured is that hypothesized.

Similarly, demonstrating generality requires a combination of external and construct validity. External validity assures the applicability of the results to other persons, places and times; construct validity, to other ways of operationalizing the variables.

Good designs accomplish the above with the best use of all available resources, time and energy. They fit an appropriate formulation of the problem rather than one cut to fit design requirements. They accurately anticipate those alternative explanations most reasonable to one's audience. Finally, ethical standards and institutional and social constraints are observed – altogether, a complex but manageable set of criteria.

Common Alternative Explanations

Some common conditions provide as plausible explanations as the treatment. Called 'threats to validity', they have been most recently redefined by Cook and Campbell (1979). A sampling of these includes:

(1) *Testing* – Pre-treatment testing may affect post-treatment's, especially if the same test is used. A control group provides protection since its post-test would be equally affected.

(2) *Selection* – Those selected for the experimental group differ from their controls, for example, when the experimental group consists of all volunteers and the control group comprises the remainder. Remedy? Use only volunteers randomly assigned to experimental and control groups.

(3) *Testing by treatment interaction* – Subjects sensitized to aspects of a treatment by pre-testing react differently on post-testing. A post-test only design provides protection.

Common Designs

(1) *Single group designs* – These are often called time series designs; relations are inferred from the pattern of treatment and response over time:
  - (a) For static situations: pre-measure, treat, post-measure.
  - (b) For situations with a regular pattern: observe it, treat, and determine if the pattern is disturbed.
  - (c) With either an irregular pattern or for an especially conclusive demonstration, relate the pattern of change to that of treatment, intentionally varying the latter's timing, length, strength and such factors.

Also referred to as AB, ABA, or ABABA designs (A is the untreated condition, B the treated), ABA and more complex designs are useful only where the change under the 'B' condition is impermanent. (For information on such designs see Kratochwill, 1978).

(2) *Multiple group designs* – These designs may involve both multiple experimental and control groups (Zimbardo used two control groups). Groups are unlike as far as possible except for the conditions to which change is to be attributed. But, only one condition can be different between groups being compared. Assuring group equivalency is usually achieved by randomly assigning subjects. *On the average* this will equate them for everything, from length of eyelashes to motivation.

The simplest, yet a very effective, design involves post-testing only. Let 'R' indicate random assignment of subjects to groups, 'O' a test or observation, and 'X' treatment. Then it is diagrammed as:

$$R \qquad X \qquad O$$
$$R \qquad \qquad O$$

To assure that the groups were equivalent at the outset, a pre-test may be added:

$$R \qquad O \qquad X \qquad O$$
$$R \qquad O \qquad \qquad O$$

But this introduces both testing and testing by treatment interaction as alternative explanations. For better control, the Solomon four group design combines the previous two:

$$R \qquad \qquad X \qquad O$$
$$R \qquad \qquad \qquad O$$
$$R \qquad O \qquad X \qquad O$$
$$R \qquad O \qquad \qquad O$$

Designs in which groups are not created by random assignment of subjects (same designs as above without the 'R') are designated quasi-experimental designs. Their strengths and weaknesses are explored in

Campbell and Stanley (1963) and in Cook and Campbell (1979).

Blocking equates groups by the individual's random assignment from within a relatively homogeneous 'block'. Blocks are created by subdividing subjects into levels on a characteristic such as intelligence where non-equivalence is a serious threat to design validity. The matched pairs design is an extreme form of blocking.

(3) *Factorial designs* – Factorial designs permit analysis of the simultaneous effects of two or more treatments or related variables by providing a group for each possible combination. For instance, to study the effect on speed of prose memorization of (a) no emphasis, (b) italics and (c) underlining of important parts, and of printing them in (1) black or (2) red would require six groups – a 2×3 factorial design:

	No emphasis	Italics	Underlining
Black type			
Red type			

From this design one could learn which emphasis treatment or colour was best alone, and, if these factors interact, what combination of emphasis and colour is best. The latter is called an interaction effect. If a pre-test were given this would be a 'repeated measures 2×3 factorial design'.

(4) *Other designs* – As may be anticipated, the variety of designs is limited mainly by one's ingenuity. A number of designs have been borrowed from agriculture, such as the Latin and Graeco-Latin square and the split plot designs. These and others are described in Bow *et al.* (1978), Cochran and Cox (1957), Fisher (1966), Kirk (1982), and Winer (1971).

David R. Krathwohl
Syracuse University

References

Bow, G. E. P., Hunter, W. G. and Hunter, J. S. (1978), *Statistics for Experimenters: An Introduction to Design, Data Analysis and Model Building*, New York.
Campbell, D. T. and Stanley, J. C. (1963), 'Experimental and quasi-experimental designs for research on teaching', in N. L. Gage (ed.), *Handbook of Research on Teaching*, Chicago.
Cochran, W. G. and Cox, G. M. (1957), *Experimental Design*, 2nd edn, New York.
Cook, T. D. and Campbell, D. T. (1979), *Quasi-Experimentation*, Chicago.
Fisher, R. A. (1966), *Design of Experiments*, 8th edn, New York.
Kirk, R. (1982), *Experimental Design*, 2nd edn, Belmont, Calif.
Kratochwill, T. R. (1978), *Single Subject Research: Strategies for Evaluation Change*, New York.
Rosenthal, R. (1976), *Experimenter Effects in Behavioural Research*, New York.
Winer, B. S. (1971), *Statistical Principles in Experimental Design*, 2nd edn, New York.
Zimbardo, P. G., Anderson, S. M. and Kabat, L. G. (1981), 'Induced hearing deficit generates experimental paranoia', *Science*, 212.

Externalities

See Economic Externalities.

Eysenck, Hans J. (1916–)

A voluntary expatriate from Germany in 1933, Eysenck studied at University College, London, and thus in the psychometric tradition of Galton, Spearman and Burt; he was later to extend the methodology of the study of intellectual ability to the study of human personality, and so to create one of the major schools of personality theory. The war forced him into the clinical field, and he was eventually to found the first university-based course in clinical psychology, a profession in Britain that owes much to his early initiative and scientific approach. He is quite unusual in his literary output, being the author or joint author of well over 50 books and 600 journal articles: many of the layman's modern concepts of psychology as a scientific discipline owe much to his popular writings. He has been at the centre of the longstanding debate concerning the role of genetic factors in determining individual differences in intellectual ability, with its strong overtones of political controversy, and he appears to enjoy controversy. Although reputed to be a hard-nosed scientist, and having been a leading figure in the critical onslaught against the vagaries of psychoanalytic theory, Eysenck has shown a surprising fondness for treating seriously such fringe topics as astrology and psychic research. Retiring from the chair of Psychology at the age of 67 in 1983, he is still a man of remarkable intellectual and physical vigour, and in terms of citations in learned journals, he proves to be quite the most influential of living British psychologists.

H. B. Gibson
Cambridge

Further Reading

Broadbent, D. E. (1981), 'Introduction', in R. Lynn (ed.), *Dimensions of Personality: Papers in Honour of H. J. Eysenck*, Oxford.
Eysenck, H. J. (1979), 'Autobiographical sketch', in G. Lindzey (ed.), *A History of Psychology in Autobiography*, vol. VII, San Francisco.
Gibson, H. B. (1981), *Hans Eysenck: The Man and His Work*, London.

F

Factions

A faction is a coalition of individuals personally recruited by, or on behalf of, an individual in competition with another individual or coalition with whom he was formerly united. Factions compete for honour and/or the control of resources. The central focus of a faction is the leader who has recruited it. Ties between leader and followers are usually personal, although followers sometimes recruit others on behalf of their leader. Factionalism – the competition between factions for scarce resources or power – can take many forms and has been recorded in all parts of the world, although the most numerous and detailed descriptions come from India. Factions are fundamental political units and factionalism the most elementary political process.

The earliest interest in factions came from political scientists (Lasswell, 1931), while social anthropologists only became aware of their significance during the past few decades. Firth (1957) was the first to attempt to set out systematically some of their functions and structural characteristics. He treated them as informal counterparts of more formal political groupings, and noted that members were recruited according to structurally diverse principles. This approach was elaborated by Nicholas a decade later (1965), who viewed factions as essentially symmetrically organized conflict groups in balanced opposition to each other. Factionalism occurred in situations of rapid social change and was one of the processes of adjustment leading to a situation of dynamic equilibrium (Siegel and Beals, 1966). The study of factionalism during the following decades reflected more general theoretical changes in the social sciences. Those interested in factions abandoned notions of dynamic equilibrium and balanced opposition, fundamental to the structural-functional mode of analysis (Silverman and Salisbury, 1978).

Competing factions are asymmetrical, and recruitment of members, while structurally diverse, is not random. Sometimes it manifests a definite class bias. Factionalism can bring about change. It is not exclusively a product of changes in the wider society. Rival factions, far from being in balanced opposition, differ in respect to access to resources and strategy, internal organization, ideology, social composition and symbolism. Although the number of competing factions can vary, there are usually two. Often one is associated with the dominant power configuration in the community, focusing on the headman, chief, or dominant landlord. This coalition forms the establishment. It is usually conservative; it has access to a range of resources, including the most important cultural symbols, and it tends to be defensive and concerned with protecting its superior position. Aligned against this power bloc is a category of persons who are dissatisfied with the way in which those with superior power wield it. Although initially they may be merely disgruntled, they may later organize a rival coalition and compete for resources. They form the opposition faction. Opposition factions, if they persist over time, tend to develop a more tightly-knit organizational structure in order to compete effectively against their more powerful rival.

Because factionalism takes place in a social framework in which unity and consensus is generally regarded as an ideal, it is seen as divisive, a temporary unpleasantness, the details of which should not be discussed with outsiders. Factionalism is basic to most communities and an intrinsic part of political life. In many societies factions have become permanent ritual moieties or political parties, embellished with a range of cultural and symbolic trappings.

Jeremy Boissevain
University of Amsterdam

References
Firth, R. (1957), 'Introduction: factions in Indian and overseas societies', *British Journal of Sociology*, 8.
Lasswell, H. D. (1931), 'Faction', *Encyclopedia of the Social Sciences*, New York.
Nicholas, R. W. (1965), 'Factions: a comparative analysis', in M. Banton (ed.), *Political Systems and the Distribution of Power*, London.
Siegel, B. J. and Beals, A. R. (1966), *Divisiveness and Social Conflict: An Anthropological Approach*, Stanford.
Silverman, M. and Salisbury, R. S. (1978), *A House Divided? Anthropological Studies of Factionalism*, Dalhousie.
See also: *coalitions*; *leadership*.

Family, The

Like kinship and marriage, family is a term used in everyday language whose meaning is cognate with the culturally and historically specific social practices to which it refers. Unlike kinship and marriage the term is specifically associated with European and American cultures and societies and their historical antecedents. In consequence, while some social scientists have seen 'the family' as a universal social institution, others have used the term to refer to a distinctive characteristic of the social life of particular cultures and epochs. Whereas American functionalist sociology has tended to regard the family as 'universal', historians and Marxists tend to speak of the emergence of 'the family' or to envisage its eventual abolition. However much these views are the result of differing political commitments, each of them represents a tenable intellectual position provided one assumes (as each view does) that 'the family' is the name of an entity. Whether the entity is held to be found universally or only in particular locations will depend upon the way the term family is defined. Sociological, historical and Marxist work on 'the family' has not been distinguished by its conceptual and definitional clarity.

Functionalist thought adopts a definition of 'the family' in terms of its activities and their effects on the maintenance of the social structure of the society of which it is part, concentrating on biological and demographic features. This definitional strategy allows it to claim near-universality for the 'nuclear family' defined as a residential group composed of parents and immature children, though it has to admit that 'the nuclear family' is often 'submerged' in larger residential groups – particularly in descent-group societies.

The use of the term 'family' to refer to entities of a specific type, that is, to use it as the name of an empirical type, may be contrasted with the *analytic* use of the term. Used in this way, 'family' is not the name of an entity which is universally found but of a concept which has a universal application. Since all individuals have male and female genitors, the existence of human individuals presupposes the existence of biological relations involving mating, filiation and sibship. It is always possible to define sets of persons who stand in these biological relations to one another, and then to enquire as to the social recognition of these relationships and as to the rights, duties and activities that subsist between the persons so related. A given individual may belong to two such sets, being a child in his parents' set and a parent in his own set. Any population will necessarily be composed of a series of overlapping sets of this kind. Such sets may be termed 'elementary' or 'immediate' in that they include the basic elements of any kinship system and the relationships involved are unmediated.

The term 'family' carries the implication not merely of *set* membership but of *group* membership. Hence it is necessary to enquire also as to whether, and in what sense, set members in a given population constitute social groups whose membership is identical with set membership. At this point it is customary to distinguish groups composed of parents and immature (that is, dependent) children and those composed of parents and mature (independent) children. Within the category of groups whose composition is elementary or immediate may be distinguished two subcategories: groups including only mature children and those including immature children. The latter are termed 'nuclear families', a term arising from the doubtful belief that groups with this composition constitute the smallest possible kin group. Nuclear and post-nuclear families are elementary or immediate families at different stages of their development cycle.

It is also necessary to enquire as to the extent to which such groups (if found) are bounded and as to the composition of other larger kin groups of which they may form part.

It is apparent that such an analysis of kin-group formation in a given population is directed by a concern with the relation between mating and procreation and group formation. It can now be seen that the study of families involves a set of questions which are universally applicable since mating and procreation are universal activities, but it does not follow that the elementary sets of relationships to which these activities give rise constitute the chief principle of kin-group formation in every society. It is therefore possible to distinguish a class of societies in which they do, in which 'family' predominates over 'kinship' as a principle of social organization. The sign 'family' points both to a universal set of questions and to particular forms of social organization.

The terms 'nuclear family' and 'elementary family' enable us to classify actual groups of people. This use of these terms must be sharply distinguished from their employment to classify types of family system. 'Family system' refers to the principles of group formation employed by a given population. Because elementary sets necessarily overlap and the typical individual belongs to two such sets, it is impossible to use set membership as a principle of exclusive group formation. Primacy must therefore be given either to ties of filiation or to those of marriage. Where primacy is given to *marriage*, the result is the formation of exclusive kin groups corresponding in composition to that of nuclear elementary sets: the group formed is composed of spouses and dependent children. Such a family system is termed 'nuclear', but it may also, therefore, be termed 'conjugal', since it is upon the conjugal relation that the solidarity of the group depends.

'Nuclear' family systems have been opposed in sociological writing to 'extended' family systems. It is, perhaps, more precise to oppose 'conjugal' to 'filial' systems: to contrast groups composed of spouses and dependent children with groups composed of parents and adult children, their spouses and offspring. If primacy is given to ties of *filiation*, it is necessary to introduce a further principle determining which children or category of children remain members of the group on maturity, the remainder leaving to become members of other groups.

The existence of a given family system must be rigorously distinguished from the incidence of different types of family group. In a nuclear system there will necessarily be 'denuded' elementary families, some or all of the children of which have founded their own nuclear families; there may also be 'extended families', in other words, elementary families who have incorporated the spouses and offspring of their children.

In an extended or filial system there will be found nuclear families, the parents of whose spouses have died before the arrival of the spouses' children, and post-nuclear elementary families, none of whose mature children has married. The incidence of types of actual family is not the result of the operation of the type of family system alone but of the interaction of that operation with demographic factors, chiefly age at marriage and expectation of life, or (more generally) is a result of the engagement in structured activity under particular social and material conditions.

Whichever system of group formation is employed, the actual incidence of family types will be the result of the movement of family groups through different stages of a developmental cycle whose exact shape will be determined by other factors.

Nothing has so far been said about the type of group constituted by families except to refer to the activities of mating and procreation. These activities do not require, but tend to result in, the co-residence of the parties. Hence nuclear families are normally residential groups. Since mating, procreation and the associated activity of childrearing require close proximity, residence is frequently in the same dwelling, and this in turn is frequently associated with the co-operation of the members in the provision of domestic services to the whole group – that is to say, that families frequently constitute households. Families may also be the possessors or owners of property, be engaged in economic production on their own account or through working as a group for others.

It is, however, not helpful from the analytic standpoint to define the family in terms of these activities, though it is customary in sociological work to regard families as residential and domestic groups, which, as a matter of fact, they usually are. For such a definition forecloses on the issue of why, and under what social conditions, familial groups perform what acitivities.

The debate on 'the family and industrial society' (for an account see Harris, 1983) taught sociologists to locate family systems within the structure of the society in which they are found, a lesson which has been emphasized by Marxian contributors to the study of the family. Feminist writers, often also Marxian (for a review see Rushton in Harris et al., 1979) have made it difficult to assume either the universality or necessity

of the fusion of domestic and childrearing activities in residential familial groups. In so doing they have rightly drawn attention to the differentiation of members of familial households in terms of power and authority, and have therefore related such differentiation to the different relations in which family members stand to the system of production *via* their differential participation in the labour market.

The result of these shifts in perspective has been for 'the family' to be seen no longer as a 'universal social institution' but rather as a set of constructions or types of construction built around the activities of biological and ideological reproduction, an emphasis which closely parallels functionalist emphases on replacement and socialization as two of 'the family's' distinctive features.

Empirical work is increasingly concentrating on households rather than family systems. Whatever the merits of this concentration as a research strategy (and they are considerable), the tendency for the 'household' to eclipse any concern with family systems and their operation is to be deplored. For if families in contemporary societies can only be understood in terms of their relation to societal structure, household composition and functioning is not fully intelligible without reference to the family system which is one of the chief determinants of household formation.

C. C. Harris
University College of Swansea
University of Wales

References
Harris, C. C. (1983), *The Family and Industrial Society*, London.
Harris, C. C. *et al.* (eds) (1979), *The Sociology of the Family*, Keele.

Further Reading
Anderson, M. (ed.) (1980), *The Sociology of the Family*, Harmondsworth.
Goode, W. J. (1982), *The Family*, 2nd edn, Englewood Cliffs, N.J.
See also: *descent and descent groups*; *family history*; *households*; *kinship and marriage*.

Family History

Research in the history of the family has progressed from a narrow view of the family as a household unit at one point in time to considering it as a process over the entire lives of its members; from a study of discrete domestic family or household structure to one of the nuclear family's interaction with the wider kinship group; and from a study of the family as a separate domestic unit to an examination of its interaction with social processes and institutions, such as the worlds of work, education, correctional and welfare institutions and such processes as migration. On a more global level, research has focused on the family's interaction with the processes of industrialization and urbanization.

Family and Household Structure

Over the past decade and a half, historical research on the family has successfully demolished prevailing myths about family behaviour in the past. Sociologists had commonly assumed that 'modern' family and population behaviour (earlier age at marriage, family limitation, and population mobility) were innovations resulting from industrialization, and that the predominant household form in preindustrial society had been the extended family, in many cases involving the co-residence of three generations. It was argued that industrialization destroyed a three-generation co-resident family structure, and led to the emergence of the isolated nuclear family – a structure more compatible with the demands of the modern industrial system.

The French *Annales* historians and, later, Peter Laslett and his Cambridge Group firmly established the predominance of a nuclear household structure in preindustrial Western Europe, and its persistence over at least the past three centuries. A critical distinction was made between family and household, the household often including non-relatives in addition to the members of the nuclear family (Laslett and Wall, 1972).

In Western societies most men and women have expected to live out their lives in familial or surrogate familial settings, and the household has traditionally been the basic economic unit as well as the locus of vocational training and welfare. The most important conclusion emerging from the first wave of historical research was that industrialization did not break down the traditional extended family and lead to the emergence of an isolated nuclear family. In many respects the household continued to function as an economic unit even after it had been stripped of its major functions in production. A flexible unit, the household expanded and contracted in response to the family's needs.

Kinship

Households and families were connected by a network of kinship ties, and kin networks formed the base of social security prior to the emergence of the welfare state. More recently, historians have documented the continuity of kinship ties in the process of migration and the important role of kin in the adaptation to new environments. The tendency overall was to include non-relatives in the household rather than kin outside the nuclear family, but to engage in relations of mutual assistance with kin outside the household (Anderson, 1971; Hareven, 1982).

Family Development

In the nineteenth century, later marriage, higher fertility, and shorter life expectancy generated family configurations different from those characterizing contemporary society. Especially in large families, there would be children in the home throughout the lifetime of the parents. Young and almost adult children interacted, and socialized one another. Most important, the nest was rarely empty, since under conditions of economic insecurity, one adult child usually remained at home throughout the parents' lives. The most marked modern change has been the isolation of the parents at home in middle age. The combination of earlier marriage and fewer children, born while the parents are young, has made the 'empty nest' a common pattern (Glick, 1977).

Demographic factors account only in part for recent changes, however. There is less feeling of obligation to parents than was the case in the past, and today the usual pattern is for children to require parental support, whereas, earlier in the century, at least one child was expected to remain at home in order to support ageing parents.

The Family and Social Change

While rejecting the assumption that industrialization generated a new type of family structure, historians agree that industrialization has had an impact on changes in family functions, values, and developmental processes. The most crucial changes were the transfer of functions from the family to other social institutions, and the transformation of the household from a place of production to a place of consumption and the nurturing of children (Demos and Boocock, 1978). The home is increasingly viewed as a retreat from the outside world, its ideals and its major features being domesticity, intimacy and privacy. The privacy of the home and its separation from the work-place are emphasized.

Some historians have stressed the rise of affective individualism, representing the 'modern' family as private, nuclear, domestic and child-centred. The sentimental bond between husband and wife and parents and children is the crucial base of family relations. Stone (1977) and to some extent Degler (1980) see the weakening of bonds with kin as an inevitable consequence of this type of family.

Tamara K. Hareven
Clark University
Center for Population Studies, Harvard University

References
Anderson, M. (1971), *Family Structure in Nineteenth-Century Lancashire*, Cambridge.
Degler, C. N. (1980), *At Odds: Women and the Family in America from the Revolution to the Present*, New York.

Demos, J. and Boocock, S. (eds) (1978), *Turning Points: Historical and Sociological Essays on the Family*, Chicago.

Glick, P. (1977), 'Updating the life cycle of the family', *Journal of Marriage and the Family*, 39.

Hareven, T. K. (1982), *Family Time and Industrial Time*, New York.

Laslett, P. and Wall, R. (eds) (1972), *Household and Family in Past Time*, Cambridge.

Stone, L. (1977), *The Family, Sex and Marriage in England 1500–1800*, New York.

Further Reading

Ariès, P. (1962), *Centuries of Childhood*, London.

Hareven, T.K. (ed.) (1978), *Transitions: The Family and the Life Course in Historical Perspective*, New York.

Shorter, E. (1976), *The Making of the Modern Family*, New York.

Stone, L. (1981), 'Family history in the 1980's', *Journal of Interdisciplinary History*, XII.

See also: *family; household.*

Family Therapy

Family therapy is both a theory of family functioning and a treatment technique for troubled couples or families. The theory maintains that the family is a functioning and cohesive system with rules or patterns, which it maintains when faced with stress. Thus, the family system is different from and greater than the sum of its parts and must be observed as a whole in action. Malfunctioning or pathological family systems often lead to individual symptomatology.

To understand and change the family, the therapist requires certain information, including details about its culture, ethnicity and socioeconomic status, the facts about each member, and the family's history and life-cycle phase. Each family has its own traditions, marital contracts, myths, secrets and loyalties to the past. Each individual in the family has his own dynamics, expectations, hopes and life experiences. Direct observations are necessary in order to assess the roles, coalitions, hierarchies and alliances between members, the communicational patterns and their clarity, the patterns of rewards and punishments, and the distribution of power. Finally, the experimental and ethical aspects must be ascertained. This last step involves assessing the empathic experience of the family from the perspective of each member, learning whether they have been treated fairly and justly and what debts and credits they have *vis-à-vis* other family members.

The family therapist uses these observations to form a therapeutic alliance and meets with the appropriate family members to design appropriate interventions in order to change family functioning. In maximally distressed families, interventions should initially be aimed at preventing physical harm to members, strengthening the parental-marital coalition, appropriately controlling the children, and promoting suitable distance between over-involved pairs. Other goals include encouraging clear and open communication, exploring mistaken attributions made of members, particularly as these are related to the past, and rebalancing the family towards fairness and justice.

Techniques commonly employed include: (1) The exploration of projective identification, where disowned aspects of the self are attributed to others, who are both related to as though the attribution was correct, and are often pressured to act in accordance with it. (2) The assignment of tasks to the family with the purpose of altering behavioural reinforcements, interrupting malfunctioning aspects of the family system, particularly when the family resists change, and providing a new and novel experience. (3) Helping the family to find ways of redressing past injustices and finding new and fairer ways of functioning.

Family therapy is considered more effective than individual treatment when the problems involve a dysfunctional marriage, and at least as effective in the treatment of disturbed children and adolescents – particularly if the problems are neurotic or psychosomatic. Psycho-educational work with families has recently been found valuable in preventing relapse in schizophrenia. The family is educated about the disease, its course and treatment, and is helped to attend to and comment on the patient's behaviour rather than to criticize thoughts and feelings. Finally, meetings with the families of individual psychotherapy patients have been found to be a useful adjunct to the treatment of adults in marital difficulties.

Henry Grunebaum
Harvard University

Further Reading

Grunebaum, H. and Glick, I. (1983), 'The basics of family treatment', in L. Grinspoon (ed.), *Psychiatry Update: The American Psychiatric Association Annual Review*, vol. II.

McFarlane, W. R., Beels, C. C. and Rosenheck, S. (1983), 'New developments in the family treatment of the psychotic disorders', in L. Grinspoon (ed.), *Psychiatry Update: The American Psychiatric Association Annual Review*, vol. II.

Fantasy

Fantasy is a form of human thought characterized by a freedom from the thinker's ordinary concerns about evaluating such activity in terms of its relevance to specific problem solutions, or about responding to objects or tasks in the immediate environment. Modern psychological investigators generally use 'fantasy' as an alternative to the term 'daydreaming'. Fantasy reflects a shift of one's attention away from an immediate task set for oneself, mental or physical, towards the sometimes almost effortless unfolding of a sequence of images or interior monologues typified by a mixture of playful consideration of often improbable or at least 'as if' occurrences (Singer, 1981), and story-like projections in which the thinker or others may serve as protagonists. Fantasies are most often thought sequences involving interpersonal transactions, but they may also take the form of juxtapositions of unlikely or unexperienced natural events, as in the case of scientists or engineers using 'thought experiments' – such as imagining the consequences of men flying faster than the speed of light, or of 'big bangs' which initiate the structures and dynamics that characterize our solar system or galaxy.

Fantasy thought or daydreaming has often been regarded as primitive, regressive or as a distraction or escape from directed, logical problem-solving thought (except when it is turned into the socially-approved product of a work of literature). Recent systematic research suggests that it may essentially be a normal feature of human cognition and that, properly employed, it can serve a variety of adaptive functions, from self-entertainment in dull situations to the effective use of mental rehearsal for later social interaction or even athletic performances (Richardson, 1969; Singer, 1981). Fantasy thought is often also used loosely in connection with terms like mental or imagination imagery. The human imagery capacity, which involves the private reduplication in some roughly analogous form of objects or persons in one's environment, is certainly a common feature of fantasy and daydreaming. The latter processes may be viewed as ongoing or continuous, in William James's phrase 'a stream of thought' in which sequences of images, for example, sights, sounds and tastes, are linked along with interior self-conversations.

Psychological Research on Fantasy and Daydreaming

Our knowledge of fantasy processes rests largely on personal experience and introspection or on the verbal reports of other persons, as well as on the observations of children's play and their often unlimited verbalizations during make-believe play (Piaget, 1962; Singer, 1973). There is some research evidence of various physiological processes that accompany fantasy or daydream-like thought. But we cannot as yet infer private fantasy activity in other persons solely from such physiological processes, and must therefore depend ultimately on written or verbalized reports or, at least, on the same pre-agreed-upon signal from the research participants that such fantasy thought is under way. Important advances have occurred, however, in the elaboration of a number of methods for studying patterns of fantasy and the behavioural correlates of such activity from verbal reports.

Projective Techniques in Personality Assessment

Clinical methods such as the Rorschach inkblots or the Thematic Apperception Test have been employed to infer characteristic fantasy activities for individuals or groups of subjects. Persons who respond to Rorschach inkblots by reporting associations involving human figures or persons in action (M responses) have been shown in various studies to be more prone to imaginative or creative thought on other measures, as well as more likely to be more planning, controlled, deliberate and restrained in overt action. The extensive studies of stories told to the ambiguous pictures of the Thematic Apperception Test indicate that recurrent themes of achievement, power-striving or affiliation in a respondent's verbalized fantasies are predictive of diverse behavioural activities such as entrepreneurial endeavours, alcohol abuse or marital relationships (McClelland, 1966).

Questionnaire Methods

Direct questions of people about the forms and content on their daydreams and fantasies in the form of psychometrically sophisticated questionnaires have yielded evidence that daydreaming and various aspects of fantasy are common phenomena. Normative data for a wide variety of persons from various age and social-class cohorts have been emerging, although cross-national data from non-English-speaking countries remain sparse. Factor analyses of questionnaires for large numbers of respondents repeatedly identify three general clusters of self-reported inner activity: (1) Positive-constructive daydreaming, which involves acceptance and enjoyment of fantasy and constructive use of one's imagery; (2) Guilty-dysphoric fantasies; (3) Poor attentional control with little elaboration of fleeting, often fearful, fantasies (Segal, Huba and Singer, 1980). Only the third of these patterns has been consistently linked to measures of anxiety or emotional disturbance. Behavioural or psychometric correlates of questionnaire reports of fantasy suggest some congruent validity for such self-report measures.

Laboratory Studies Using Signal Detection

By training individuals to an agreed-upon definition of task-irrelevant thought and imagery, it is possible to study the occurrence of fantasy activities – by having them signal periodically while they are engaged in a variety of continuous absorbing mental or perceptual tasks such as auditory or visual signal detection watches. Such procedures make it possible to estimate the conditions conducive or detrimental to the occurrence of spontaneous fantasy or daydreaming, the extent to which such activities occur concurrently with (parallel processing) or during interruptions in signal detections (sequential processing) and so on (Antrobus, Singer, Goldstein and Fortgang, 1970). Data indicate that some fantasy activity is a regular feature of almost all circumstances in which attention is chiefly being paid to processing external stimulation. Content reports suggest that such daydreaming often involves (playful or fearful) attention to and elaboration of recurrent unfulfilled intentions or 'current concerns', as well as wishful or aesthetic elaborations of recent experiences or anticipated social encounters.

Thought-Sampling

Although psychoanalysts and other clinicians have long relied heavily on fantasies reported during psychotherapy sessions, recent approaches have used continuous talking or intermittent report methods throughout several days (using randomly-generated portable electronic 'beepers' to alert participants to report on thoughts) in order to obtain more reliable samples of 'natural-occurring' fantasy. Such methods further demonstrate the extent to which fantasy is a recurring feature of normal human thought and may reflect a major way in which humans orient themselves toward a variety of potential futures and keep track of previously established intentions or goals (Klinger, Barta, and Maxeiner, 1981).

Psychophysiological Measurement

Fantasy or daydream-like thought has been found in various studies to be associated with reduced ocular motility in the waking state, or to leftward eye-shifting preceding reflection (presumably reflecting greater right brain hemispheric involvement). Imagery involving events that evoke different emotions have been found to yield differential blood pressure patterns or brainwave activity.

Psychotherapeutic Uses of Fantasy

A wide variety of behaviour modification and psychotherapeutic or stress reduction procedures rely on our human capacity for producing fantasies. These range from the transference and dream interpretation procedures of psychoanalytically-derived therapies through the guided imagery approaches increasingly prevalent in Germany and France. Behavioural techniques such as covert modelling, covert aversive conditioning or symbolic elaboration all can be shown to rely on the client's capacity to generate vivid or detailed daydreams (Singer and Pope, 1978; Singer, 1974). Research findings in these spheres further point to the value of regarding our capacity to travel mentally to potential futures, or to take an 'as if' stance in our thought, as an inherently adaptive feature of our evolutionary development, even with the misuse we may often make of 'the vanity of human wishes'.

Jerome L. Singer
Yale University

References

Antrobus, J. S., Singer, J. L., Goldstein, S. and Fortgang, M. (1970), 'Mindwandering and cognitive structure', *Transactions of the New York Academy of Science*, Series II, 32.
Klinger, E., Barta, S. and Maxeiner, M. (1981), 'Current concerns: assessing therapeutically relevant motivation', in P. Kendall and S. Hollon (eds), *Assessment Strategies for Cognitive-Behavioral Interventions*, New York.
McLelland, D. (1966), 'Longitudinal trends in the relation of thought to action', *Journal of Consulting Psychology*, 30.
Piaget, J. (1962), *Play, Dreams and Imitation in Childhood*, New York.
Richardson, A. (1969), *Mental Imagery*, New York.
Schwartz, G., Weinberger, D. and Singer, J. L. (1981), 'Cardiovascular differentiation of happiness, sadness, anger and fear, following imagery and exercise', *Psychosomatic Medicine*, 43.
Segal, B., Huba, G. J. and Singer, J. L. (1980), *Drugs, Daydreaming and Personality: A Study of College Youth*, Hillsdale, N.J.
Singer, J. L. (1973), *The Child's World of Make-Believe*, New York.
Singer, J. L. (1981), *Daydreaming and Fantasy*, London.
Singer, J. L. and Pope, K. S. (1978), *The Power of Human Imagination*, New York.
See also: *dreams*; *projective methods*; *thinking – cognitive organization and processes*.

Fascism

Of all the major terms in twentieth-century political usage, fascism has tended to remain one of the most vague. At the popular level, it has become during the past two generations little more than a derogatory epithet employed to denigrate a bewildering variety of otherwise mutually contradictory political phenomena. It has been applied at one time or another to virtually every single form of twentieth-century radicalism or authoritarianism, as well as many more moderate phenomena. More specifically, in terms of political regimes, there has developed since the 1930s a broad tendency to refer to any form of right-wing authoritarian system that is not specifically socialist as fascist. In this usage the Italian regime of Benito Mussolini is used as terminological prototype for all non-Marxist or non-socialist authoritarian systems, however they may differ from Italian Fascism or among themselves.

Rigorous scholarly and historical definition of fascism, however, refers to the concrete historical phenomena of the European fascist movements that emerged between the two World Wars, first in the Italian Fascist and German National Socialist movements founded in 1919–20 and then among their numerous counterparts in many European countries.

An adequate political and historical definition of fascism must define common unique characteristics of all the fascist movements in Europe during the 1920s and 1930s while at the same time differentiating them from other political phenomena. Such a criterial definition must specify (1) the typical fascist negations; (2) fascist doctrine and goals, and (3) the uniqueness of fascist style and organization.

The uniqueness of fascism lay in its opposition to nearly all the existing political sectors, left, right, and centre. It was antiliberal, anticommunist (as well as antisocialist in the social democratic sense), and anticonservative, though willing to undertake temporary alliances with other groups, primarily rightist.

In their ideology and political goals, fascist movements represented the most intense and radical form of nationalism known to modern Europe. They aimed at the creation of a new kind of nationalist authoritarian state that was not merely based on traditional principles or models. Though fascist groups differed considerably among themselves on economic goals, they all hoped to organize some new kind of regulated, multiclass, integrated national economic structure, diversely called national corporatist, national socialist or national syndicalist. All fascist movements aimed either at national imperial expansion or at least at a radical change in the nation's relationship with other powers to enhance its strength and prestige. Their doctrines rested on a philosophical basis of idealism and voluntarism, and normally involved the attempt to create a new form of modern, self-determined secular culture.

Fascist uniqueness was particularly expressed through the movements' style and organization. Great emphasis was placed on the aesthetic structure of meetings, symbols, and political choreography, relying especially on romantic and mystical aspects. Fascist movements all attempted to achieve mass mobilization, together with the militarization of political relationships and style and with the goal of a mass party militia. Unlike some other types of radicals, fascists placed strong positive evaluation on the use of violence, and strongly stressed the masculine principle and male dominance. Though they espoused an organic concept of society, they vigorously championed a new élitism and exalted youth above other phases of life. In leadership, fascist movements exhibited a specific tendency toward an authoritarian, charismatic, personal style of command (the *Führerprinzip*, in German National Socialist parlance).

Radical rightist groups shared some of the fascists' political goals, just as revolutionary leftist movements exhibited some of their stylistic and organizational characteristics. The uniqueness of the fascists, however, lay in their rejection of the cultural and economic conservatism, and the particular social élitism of the right, just as they rejected the internationalism,

nominal egalitarianism and materialist socialism of the left. The historical uniqueness of fascism can be better grasped once it is realized that significant political movements sharing all – not merely some – of these common characteristics existed only in Europe during the years 1919–45.

Fascists claimed to represent all classes of national society, particularly the broad masses. Marxists and some others, conversely, claimed that they were no more than the tool of the most violent, monopolistic and reactionary sectors of the bourgeoisie. Both of these extreme interpretations are not supported by empirical evidence. In their earliest phase, fascist movements drew their followers from among former military personnel and small sectors of the radical intelligentsia, in some cases university students. Though some fascist movements enjoyed a degree of backing from the upper bourgeoisie, the broadest sector of fascist support, comparatively speaking, was provided by the lower middle class. Since this was one of the largest strata in European society during the 1920s and 1930s, the same might also have been said for various other political groups. In both Italy and Germany, a notable minority of party members were drawn from among urban workers. In Hungary and Romania primary social backing came from university students and poor peasants, and there was also considerable agrarian support in some parts of Italy.

A bewildering variety of theories and interpretations have been advanced since 1923 to explain fascism. Among them are (1) theories of socioeconomic causation of various kinds, primarily of Marxist inspiration; (2) concepts of psychocultural motivation related to social psychology and personality and social structures; (3) the application of modernization theory, which posits fascism as a phase in modern development; (4) the theory of totalitarianism, which interprets fascism as one aspect of the broader phenomenon of twentieth-century totalitarianism; and (5) historicist interpretations, which attempt multicausal explanation in terms of the major dimensions of central European historical development in the early twentieth century.

The only fascist movements to establish independent regimes of their own were those of Benito Mussolini (1922–43) and Adolf Hitler (1933–45), and only in the latter case did the movement's leader achieve complete power over the state. The other countries in whicl. fascist movements were strongest were Austria (Austrian National Socialists), Hungary (Arrow Cross), Romania (Iron Guard), and Spain (Spanish Phalanx). In general, fascism had most appeal in countries defeated or destabilized by the effects of World War I. Though fascist movements appeared in every single European country during these years (and also, very faintly, in the countries of the western hemisphere and Japan, paralleled by more vigorous expression in South Africa), very few of them enjoyed any degree of success. In nearly all countries antifascists were generally much more numerous than fascists. The extreme radicalism and calls to war and violence of the fascists limited their appeal, as did the nonrationalist, voluntarist nature of their doctrines. The great expansion of military power by Hitler's Germany was mainly responsible for the broader influence and historical importance achieved by fascism for a few years. Similarly, the complete defeat of Germany and Italy in the war condemned fascism to such total political destruction and historical discredit that all attempts at revival have enjoyed only miniscule support since 1945.

Stanley G. Payne
University of Wisconsin

Further Reading
Laqueur, W. (ed.) (1976), *Fascism: A Reader's Guide*, Berkeley and Los Angeles.
Larsen, S. U. *et al.* (eds) (1980), *Who were the Fascists: Social Roots of European Fascism*, Bergen-Oslo.
Payne, S. G. (1980), *Fascism: Comparison and Definition*, Madison.
See also: *nationalism*; *radicalism*.

Federalism

Federalism is a way of organizing a state so that there is a division of powers between general and regional governments each independent within a sphere (Wheare, 1946). The territory of a federal state is divided into units (for example, states, cantons, provinces, republics) which often coincide with distinctive geographic, cultural or historic divisions of the country. Many of the institutions of government are duplicated at the national and local levels with both levels of government exercising effective control over the same territory and population. Thus, the citizens of a federal state belong simultaneously to two political communities: for those functions which are constitutionally assigned to the local level of government the relevant community is the citizen's particular state, canton, province or republic; for functions assigned to the national government, the entire nation is the relevant community.

In a true federal state, both levels of government derive their powers directly from the constitution and neither is able to eliminate the other's jurisdiction. In this way a federal state is distinguished from a unitary state with territorial sub-units, (such as counties, departments, districts) that receive all of their powers by delegation from a central government. At the other extreme, a federal system of government should be distinguished from a confederation, or league of states, in which the central level of government receives all its powers from the member states and has no autonomous powers of its own.

The United States of America was the first modern nation-state to adopt a federal constitution. In the nineteenth century some of the new states of South and Central America (for example, Venezuela, Colombia, Argentina, Brazil and Mexico) were organized on federal lines. But federal constitutions have been of less enduring significance there than in Switzerland (1848); Canada (1867) and Australia (1901) which, along with the United States, are the countries which have been practising federal constitutionalism without interruption for the longest time. In the twentieth century many of the constitutions established in the process of worldwide political reorganization following the two World Wars have incorporated the federal principle. Federalism has been a feature of constitutions adopted by many of Britain's former colonies (among them, India, Pakistan, Malaysia, and Nigeria) (Watts, 1966). In Europe, it is prominent in the constitution of the Federal Republic of Germany and is provided for in the constitution of two communist states, Yugoslavia and the USSR.

The balance of power and of citizens' allegiance between the two levels of government is a dynamic element in the politics of a federal state. In some federations, the forces of centralization, especially when fostered by a single unified political party, may be so strong as to negate the autonomy of the local level of government. In others the forces of decentralization may be such that they lead to the break-up of the federal state (as in the case of British West Indian Federation). For a federal system to endure, there must be significant independent political forces supporting each level of government.

Peter H. Russell
University of Toronto

References
Watts, R. L. (1966), *New Federations: Experiments in the Commonwealth*, Oxford.
Wheare, K. C. (1946), *Federal Government*, Oxford.

Further Reading
Bowie, R. R. and Friedrich, C. J. (1954), *Studies in Federalism*, Boston.
MacMahon, A. W. (ed.) (1962), *Federalism – Mature and Emergent*, New York.
Riker, W. H. (1964), *Federalism: Origin, Operation, Significance*, Boston.
See also: *constitutions and constitutionalism*; *plural society*.

Fertility

Fertility (also referred to as natality) always refers in demographic usage to the achievement of live births. This is in keeping with its Latin etymological derivation from *ferre*, to bear, but in contrast to the verb, fertilize, which relates to conception. In English-language social science, the capacity to bear children is described as fecundity and the fact of giving birth as fertility. This is the reverse of the usage in French and other Romance languages. It also conflicts with much popular, medical and biological usage where infertility means not childlessness but infecundity or sterility (confusingly, the last can be employed in both senses even by demographers).

Fertility has long been identified with fruitfulness and productiveness, not only in terms of human reproduction but also with regard to the availability of game for hunters and the yield of crops. Indeed, the perceived relationship has played a major role in religion since palaeolithic times. The dependence of fertility upon preceding sexual relations has meant that both fertility and coitus play a central role in much of human culture and morality. In some cultures, particularly in the Middle East, the fact of pregnancy or childbirth to a married woman is usually the cause of pleasure, but should she not be married the reaction of her relatives might be so antagonistic as to result in her death and in great problems in securing the marriage of her siblings.

In spite of the biblical advice to 'be fruitful and multiply', and its mirroring in the adages of many pre-industrial societies, the maximization of fertility is usually constrained by other competing social objectives. Fertility is usually not favoured outside marriage partly because it may interfere with achieving the desired marriage. It may be discouraged soon after the birth of another child, because of the risk to health and life of both mother and children, or by grandmothers, because of the conflict between grandmaternal and maternal duties. Traditionally these constraints have been embedded in religion and mores rather than being expressed solely in terms of conflicting roles and danger to health.

Fertility may be expressed as a measure of the behaviour of a society, a couple or an individual. In theory, reproductive measures are just as valid for individual males as females, but estimates for the former are rarely attempted because the fact of a man's fathering a child is less obvious to the community and may be unknown to the progenitor himself. The most meaningful measures of a woman's reproduction is the number of births she experiences between menarche (or puberty) and menopause. For the whole society, the average for all women is known as completed fertility. However, this measure can be determined only in retrospect, a quarter of a century after the peak in fertility for most women completing their reproductive spans, and societies frequently demand more immediate measures which are necessarily those for aggregate populations of different ages for a specified period (usually one year and hence described as an annual rate). The most

common aggregate measure is the crude birth rate or the number of live births per year per thousand population. For national populations, this varied in 1980 from 51 in Niger to 10 in West Germany. The crude birth rate can prove to be an unsatisfactory measure in a society where immigration or some other social change has distorted the distribution of the population by sex or age, and more statistically refined measures relate births only to women of specified age or marital condition. The general fertility rate is the ratio of the births during a year to the total number of women 15–49 years of age. The relating of births to women of a specific age, or age range, for a specified period (usually one year), is termed the age-specific birth rate (or fertility rate) and its sum over the whole reproductive age range is the total fertility rate, which, in a society characterized by constant fertility over several decades, is an annual measure of the same magnitude as completed fertility. The total fertility rate ranged in 1981 from 8.2 in Kenya to 1.4 in West Germany. Attention may be confined to married women so as to determine marital age-specific birth rates and the total marital fertility rate. If only female births are related to mothers of each age, then the cumulative measure is known as the gross reproduction rate. Because for societies the effective measure of reproduction is not live births but surviving children, a measure known as the net reproduction rate has been devised. This may be defined as the ratio of female births in the next generation to those in this generation in conditions of constant fertility and mortality, and hence measures the eventual multiplication of societies' numbers from one generation to the next, once the age structure changes so as to conform with these stable conditions. If the society maintains a rate of unity for a considerable period (half a century or more in societies which were previously growing rapidly) it will become stationary, while a lower rate will imply eventually declining population size, and a higher rate, a growing population. In 1980, levels below unity were recorded by 18 European countries as well as the US, Canada, Australia, Japan, Cuba and Singapore. However, only West Germany also exhibited a marked decline in numbers (East Germany, Austria and Denmark being stationary), because such rates have been achieved so recently that there are still disproportionately more women in the potentially most fertile ages than would be the case in a population which had exhibited a net reproduction rate at or below unity for many years. Births within marriage may be described as nuptial or legitimate and those outside as exnuptial or illegitimate.

The female reproductive span varies between women and between societies (or the same society at different dates), but approximately spans ages from around 15 years to the late 40s. If fertility were in no way constrained, not even by the institution of marriage or by the practice of breast-feeding which tends to depress fertility, completed family size would be around 15 (Bongaarts (1982) employs 15.3 in his model). The total marital fertility rate of the Hutterites, a religious community opposed to deliberate fertility control, was in the western United States in the late 1920s at least 12.4 (a level employed by Coale (1967) in his model), but this figure was almost certainly rising because of the reduction of the period of breast-feeding. Where breast-feeding is of traditional duration (two years or more) the following completed family sizes are found if deliberate control of marital fertility is not practised: (1) Where female marriage is early and widow remarriage is common, as among the Ashanti of West Africa (who practise only short periods of postpartum abstinence), around 8. (2) Where female marriage is early and widow remarriage is discouraged, as in India prior to the family planning programme, around 6. 5. (3) Where female marriage is late and there are no strong feelings about widow remarriage, as in Western Europe before the Industrial Revolution, around 6. The term natural fertility has been employed to describe the level of fertility, and its structure by female age, found in societies which do not deliberately restrict marital fertility (but in which sexual abstinence may be practised after childbirth and terminal sexual abstinence after becoming a grandmother).

However, contemporary interest in fertility largely arises from the decline in fertility in all industrialized and many other societies and the possibility of further reduction in developing countries. The latter has been assisted by family planning programmes which have now been instituted by a majority of Third World governments (beginning with India in 1952). The determinants of fertility have been classified (by Davis and Blake in a 1956 paper) as: (1) Intercourse variables (age at first entrance to sexual union; the proportion of women never entering a union; the period spent after or between unions; voluntary and involuntary abstinence, and frequency of intercourse). (2) Conception variables (subfecundity or infecundity; contraception, and sterilization). (3) Gestation variables (spontaneous or induced abortion). The list does not separately identify the duration of breast-feeding, which was undoubtedly in most traditional societies the major determinant of marital fertility, or sexual activity outside stable unions. Bongaarts (1982) has demonstrated that only four factors – the proportion of the female reproductive period spent in a sexual union (in many societies the period of marriage), the duration of postpartum infecundability (that is, the period without menstruation or ovulation plus any period beyond this of postpartum sexual abstinence), the practice of contraception and its effectiveness, and the extent of induced abortion – provide 96 percent of the explanation of the variance in fertility levels in nearly all societies.

Beginning in France in the late eighteenth century, and becoming more general in industrialized countries from the late nineteenth century, fertility has fallen in economically developed countries so that most appear likely to attain zero population growth. This has been achieved largely through the deliberate control of marital fertility, in most countries by contraception (before the 1960s by chemical or mechanical means as well as rhythm, abstinence, and withdrawal or coitus interruptus and subsequently increasingly by the use of the pill, intra-uterine devices and sterilization), supplemented by different levels of abortion. By 1980 fertility was clearly low or declining in every major world region except Africa and the Middle East. Increasingly the relationship between the sexual act and conception has been weakened, and this has allowed a weakening in the relation between sexual activity and marriage.

John C. Caldwell
Australian National University

References
Bongaarts, J. (1982), 'The fertility-inhibiting effects of the intermediate fertility variables', *Studies in Family Planning*, 13.
Coale, A. J. (1967), 'Factors associated with the development of low fertility: An historic summary', in *Proceedings of the World Population Conference, Belgrade, 1965*, Vol. II, New York.
Davis, K. and Blake, J. (1956), 'Social structure and fertility: An analytical framework', *Economic Development and Cultural Change*, 4.

Further Reading
United Nations (1965), *Population Bulletin of the United Nations, No. 7 – 1963, with Special Reference to Conditions and Trends of Fertility in the World*, New York.
Wrong, D. H. (1977), *Population and Society*, 4th edn, New York.
See also: *abortion*; *demographic transition*; *nuptiality*; *population projections*.

Feud

In pre-industrial societies, there tend to be three levels of homicide. At the most intimate level, killing within the family or local descent group is felt to bring the threat of permanent mystical misfortune, because it violates the most fundamental bonds of kinship. At the most remote level, like warfare, it lies outside the boundaries of society and social order, in an amoral cosmos beyond. Between these two levels, any homicide tends to mobilize groups that work towards some resolution. *Feud* may be said to exist where the principle of blood-debt between groups is the expected response to homicide. It tends to be associated with societies in which local agnatic descent forms the basis of corporate grouping. Ideally, a feud is strictly limited by the convention that hostilities should be discriminating and that ultimately there should be a negotiated settlement with compensation. Those that are not directly involved in the feuding have an interest in ensuring that the conventions are upheld, or society itself is threatened. In practice, a satisfactory settlement may be evasive and the state of feud may persist indefinitely as the tally of injury mounts on both sides and resistance to any negotiated compromise increases.

It is revealing to compare feud with marriage alliance. Both are middle-range institutions, incompatible with close blood-ties, where the possibility of fratricide or incest evokes horror. Feud goes beyond the immediate relationship between killer and killed, just as marriage alliance goes beyond the union of husband and wife. The asymmetry of both may lead to further incidents of the same kind: retaliatory killings and exchange marriages. In other respects, they are neatly inverted. A marriage is initiated in the same manner as a feud may be terminated through a negotiated agreement which is confirmed by the payment of compensation (bride-wealth and blood-wealth). A feud is initiated in the same manner as a marriage may be terminated: through precipitate action between the principals (homicide and divorce). Permanence of the relationship is an ideal in marriage and a threat in feud; and *vice versa*. It is this structural transformation between them that accounts for their frequent association. It is the complementarity between one institution that fosters the reproduction of kin groups and of the wider society, and another that poses a threat to this reproduction. This has been summarized by Black-Michaud (1975): 'They are two aspects of precisely the same process. The ambiguities inherent in marital alliance often cause feuds, just as feuds are also frequently the "cause" of the marriages contracted to "conclude" hostilities.' In practice, any marriage to perpetuate the dead man's line is as likely to perpetuate the feud as to resolve it. In such circumstances, it is the blood-debt that has the binding force of a contract, and any settlement emerges as little more than a truce.

Paul Spencer
School of Oriental and African Studies
University of London

Reference
Black-Michaud, J. (1975), *Cohesive Force: Feud in the Mediterranean and the Middle East*, New York.
See also: *war, primitive*.

Feudalism

There is no agreement on a definition of feudalism. The word can be used in very general terms to describe the totality of the economic and political relationships of medieval European society and of similar societies elsewhere. If such a view is taken, stress is normally laid upon the exploitation of the peasantry by the exaction of labour services in a closed, or natural, economy. The institution of the manor is of great importance; the main social relationships are seen in terms of lordship exercised both over men and land. Frequently such a definition becomes so wide as to be little more than synonymous with 'medieval', and so loses any real value, but even when used more carefully, there are still considerable problems.

During the medieval period, the economy underwent such transformations as to make the application of a single model of feudalism very dangerous. Money was far more important than was once thought, and production for the market more widespread. There were wide variations, both chronological and geographical, in the degree of the subjection of the peasantry. In England many labour services were commuted in the twelfth century, when feudalism could be thought to have been at its apogee, only to be reimposed in the thirteenth century. At best, society was only partly feudal, and it is significant that in his definition of feudalism one of its greatest historians, Marc Bloch (1961 [1939–40]), allowed for 'the survival of other forms of authority, family and state', alongside the structures of feudal lordship. Attempts at redefinition of the broad concept of feudalism, seeing small-scale peasant production under the political constraints of aristocratic lordship as the key element, have not proved satisfactory.

The alternative tradition to that which seeks a general model of feudalism is one which centres upon a specific type of landholding in return for military service. The word feudalism itself is derived from the latin *feudum*, or fief, the land held by a knight in return for service usually performed on horseback for forty days. It is possible to provide a much more satisfactory description and explanation for feudalism in such terms. The system had its origins in the collapse of public authority in the ninth century as the Carolingian Empire declined. Men commended themselves to lords, who granted them lands as fiefs. The knight and the castle were central to this feudalism, in which lordship resulted from the man, or vassal, performing a specific ceremony known as homage to his lord. The system evolved gradually, save in countries such as England and Southern Italy, where it was imported by the Normans in the eleventh century. Fiefs came to be held in primogeniture, and the rights of the lord to certain dues, or feudal incidents, were given increasing definition. A lord could, for example, demand aid from his vassals to help pay for the knighting of his eldest son, and payment was expected when the son of a vassal succeeded his father in his estates. A complex legal system developed: the jurisdictional rights of lords over their tenants were an important element in a feudal society.

Such a definition is largely satisfactory, provided that it is understood that no society was ever wholly feudalized. In the case of England, the king was never solely dependent upon his feudal cavalry, but relied extensively upon mercenaries and infantry levies. The last effective feudal summons was issued in 1327, but in the first half of the previous century the levels of service had been radically reduced, so that the quotas of knights came to bear little relationship to the feudal landholding structure. Castles were initially an integral part of the feudal organization of the country, but when Edward I came to build his great castles in Wales in the late thirteenth century, he used paid workmen and employed paid troops as garrisons. Such castles can hardly be described as feudal. The system of hiring soldiers by means of contracts and the issue of livery in the later Middle Ages has been described as 'bastard feudalism', but the true feudal elements of landed fiefs, heritability and homage were all absent. Yet the legal aspects of feudalism in England long outlasted the military utility of the system; there was even a revival of feudal techniques of money-raising in the early seventeenth century.

If it is only with care that the term feudalism in a strict sense can be applied to a Western European country in the Middle Ages, then it is only with great difficulty that it can be used with reference to different regions and periods. Medieval Byzantium and Islam, with the *pronoia* and *iqta* respectively, had types of land grants which were not entirely dissimilar to fiefs. The *iqta* could only exceptionally be passed on by a holder to his children, but by the twelfth century the Byzantine system was moving towards the heritability which characterized Western feudalism. The legal structure of European feudalism was largely lacking in these parallel systems. Japan is frequently cited as developing something very akin to the military feudalism of Western Europe, but an economy based on rice production, and a wholly different cultural and legal tradition, made for contrasts as well as similarities. For those who are influenced by Marxist theories, however, feudalism represents a stage through which most societies must pass in the course of their development. Such a view involves using an extremely general definition of feudalism, with its attendant difficulties.

Many of the arguments of scholars over feudalism have been the result of a failure to agree upon definitions. No one word, no single model, can ever sum up the complex and varying structures of medieval societies. As a term describing a very specific set of relationships within the noble and knightly classes of medieval Europe, feudalism is convenient, but the word should only be used with great circumspection.

Michael Prestwich
University of Durham

Reference
Bloch, M. (1961 [1939 and 1940]), *Feudal Society*, trans. L. A. Manyon, London. (Original French edn, *La Société féodale*, Paris.)

Further Reading
Brown, R. A. (1973), *Origins of English Feudalism*, London.
Ganshof, F. (1961), *Feudalism*, New York.
Postan, M. M. (1983), 'Feudalism and its decline: a semantic exercise', in T. H. Aston *et al.* (eds), *Social Relations and Ideas: Essays in Honour of R. H. Hilton*, Cambridge.
See also: *Bloch.*

Feyerabend, Paul K. (1924–)

Paul K. Feyerabend, a leading philosopher of science, has fundamentally challenged the logical positivist account of the scientific method and, in addition, advocated an anarchistic theory of knowledge, relying on the works of such political theorists as J. S. Mill, Marx, Lenin and Trotsky. He emphasizes the significance of political action, propaganda and political thought for the study and practice of science.

Born in Vienna, Feyerabend was induced into the Austrian army during the Nazi occupation, and at the end of World War II he read history, physics and astronomy at the University of Vienna. He received his doctorate in 1951 and then went to England to study with fellow Austrian philosopher, Ludwig Wittgenstein. But Wittgenstein's untimely death resulted in Feyerabend studying with the philosopher of science, Karl Popper – whose ideas about the nature and significance of science Feyerabend has been criticizing for many years. For the past 25 years he has taught at the University of California at Berkeley, and during this time has held several teaching positions at European universities as well.

Following numerous philosophical articles on the nature of scientific inquiry, Feyerabend published in 1975 his well-known and provocative volume, *Against Method: Outline of an Anarchistic Theory of Knowledge*, which contains his vehement attack on the mainstream rationalist theory of scientific methodology. Feyerabend's thought becomes most relevant to social scientists in his conception of the traditional philosophical fields of logic, epistemology, and the philosophy of science as empirical inquiries requiring historical, sociological, psychological, anthropological and political data.

Some of Feyerabend's characteristic positions include his passionate rejection and fear of the stultifying consequences of one method of doing science which demands conformity on the part of scientists: 'Science is an essentially anarchistic enterprise: theoretical anarchism is more humanitarian and more likely to encourage progress than its law-and-order alternatives' (*Against Method*); and his corresponding deep commitment to fostering the conditions of maximum scientific creativity even to the point of claiming the creative value of violence! 'Violence . . . is *beneficial* for the individual, for it releases one's energies and makes one realize the powers at one's disposal' (*Against Method*). His admonition not to stifle scientists' creativity because of a dominant methodology is reflected in his renowned methodological credo for science of 'Anything Goes': 'All methodologies have their limitations and the only "rule" that survives is "anything goes"' (*Against Method*).

Feyerabend argues for the democratic control of science by the lay public and replies to the critics of *Against Method* in his *Science in a Free Society* published in 1978.

Joel Kassiola

Brooklyn College of the City University of New York
See also: *Popper*.

Fieldwork

See Ethnographic Fieldwork.

Financial Crises

Financial crises are a form of economic difficulty more general than commercial crises, which is what they were called in the nineteenth century, but less so than the more pervasive economic crisis envisaged by Marxist economic thought. The typical financial crisis comes after a period of speculation, called 'overtrading' in classical economics, using borrowed money, and occurs when speculators, investors, lenders or depositors try to liquidate all at once. Prices of the asset which had been bid up are driven down, risking bankruptcy of firms and failure of banks.

A typical financial crisis can be divided into several stages. First is an exogenous shock to the economic system, some unexpected change that alters profit opportunities and induces changes in investment. It may be outbreak of war, the end of a war, political revolution. It may be more narrowly economic, such as discovery of a new resource, a major innovation, good crops, bad crops. It can be narrowly financial – the unexpected success of a security issue, conversion of debt to lower interest rates, leading holders to try to maintain their returns in new investments. Whatever the event that perturbs the system, it alters profit opportunities and leads to new patterns of investment and usually to speculation for capital gains.

If the change is sufficiently pervasive, euphoria and overtrading are likely. The objects traded depend on the nature of the shock, and may consist of many things: commodities, stocks, bonds (foreign or domestic), railroads, factories, mines, office buildings, houses, land, virtually anything substantial in value. Rising prices leading to further price increases – called 'bubbles' – occur in isolated cases, like the Florida land boom of 1925, without causing financial crisis outside the group of participants. The most recent example of significant excessive lending has been loans by international syndicates of banks, notably to Mexico, Brazil and Argentina. This was initiated by easy money in the United States beginning in 1970, and accelerated by increases in oil prices in 1973 and 1979 that increased both the need for loans by non-oil producing countries and the capacity to borrow of oil producers.

In the typical pattern of overtrading followed by financial crisis, success of early investors induces others to participate. As more and more join with borrowed funds, credit becomes distended, interest rates rise, and some marginal buyers may be forced to liquidate. Some, who anticipate that the assets in question have risen as far as they are likely to, cash in their gains. Prices stop rising, may level off or may start to slip. There follows a period called 'financial distress', as the confident expectation that prices will continue to climb gives way to doubt. If expectations of a price rise are replaced by expectations of a fall, a financial crisis is likely. A rush from real or financial assets into money drives down the prices of those assets and in acute cases leads to bankruptcy of individuals or concerns still holding them with borrowed funds, and even to bank failures.

Whether financial crises are serious or ephemeral depends to a considerable extent on how they are handled by monetary authorities. The eighteenth century developed a doctrine of supporting a market in crisis by a 'lender of last resort' which stood ready to halt the panicky liquidation and render it orderly by making money available to concerns with debts to pay, and to banks facing deposit withdrawals. The concept was understood by Henry Thornton as early as 1802, but found fuller rationalization in Walter Bagehot's *Lombard Street* in 1873. Other devices to provide the same assurance have been guarantees of a bank's liabilities by other banks, as in the Hamburg crisis of 1857, or the Baring crisis in England in 1890, or mere suspension of a central bank's legal limit on the right of note issue. The crises of 1847, 1857 and 1866 in London were quickly quieted by a letter of indemnity from the Chancellor of the Exchequer to the Bank of England, undertaking to make good to the Bank any hurt it might suffer by reason of violating the limits imposed by the Bank Act of 1844. In 1847 and 1866, so effective was the lifting of the limit that it did not in fact have to be exceeded. When the market in panic found it could get all the money it might want, it wanted less.

If there is no lender of last resort, deflation of asset prices may spread from one type of asset to another, leading to bankruptcies, bank failures and prolonged depression. The leading examples are 1873 and 1929.

There is a disability in using a lender of last resort: the more a financial market knows it will be helped in emergency, the more likely it is to take the chances that will land it in one. This is the 'moral hazard' principle in insurance, that the more insurance one has, the less motivated one is to be careful. It is on this ground that monetary authorities usually leave some doubt as to whether they will rescue markets and banks in difficulty.

A widespread English view holds that financial crises in that country ended with 1866 as the Bank of England learned how to use its policy instruments, particularly the rate of rediscount, so as to prevent overtrading. In 1873, when the Continent and the United States shared a crisis, the Bank of England undertook 24 changes of bank rate and England remained outside the difficulty. This belief tends to overlook the Baring crisis of 1890, the share collapse of 1921 following the overtrading of 1919–20, a potential crisis in foreign lending in 1914 diverted by the outbreak of war, and a 1974 crisis in London real estate which ruined the so-called 'fringe banks'.

A financial crisis may be confined to a single country, such as the series of troubles in France from the crash of the Union générale in 1882, the collapse of the copper corner engineered by the Comptoir d'escompte in 1889, and the bankruptcy and subsequent scandal of the Panama company from 1889 to 1893; or they may be widely shared in several countries. Propagation of the boom takes place through the rise of internationally traded commodities or securities, through capital flows which increase the recipient's monetary base and induce credit expansion, or through the mere communication of euphoria. The boom of 1885 to 1889 occurred simultaneously in South Africa, Latin America and Australia, stimulated by diamond and gold discoveries in South Africa, and rising commodity prices leading to land clearing in Latin America and Australia, and fed by an outflow of capital from London to all three areas. This outflow of capital, in turn, was partly a consequence of the Goschen conversion of national debt from 3 to 2.5 per cent, inducing investors to seek higher returns in brewery shares and foreign mortgage bonds. The financial crisis was precipitated by the halt in British lending which made it impossible for the countries to continue expanding investment.

Writers or various nationalities typically regard financial crises that affect their country strongly as of local origin. In particular, many American economists and economic historians believe that the 1929 depression started primarily in the United States. A more complete view suggests that it is difficult to disentangle the complicated skein of international causality in such a crisis as the Anglo-American one of 1836,

the New York-Liverpool-Stockholm-Hamburg crisis of 1857, and, without enumerating, several others, especially the world crisis of 1929. Crisis started in Germany and the temperate developing countries when the United States, in its fascination in 1928 with the rising New York stock market, cut off long-term lending to those areas. The stock market crash in 1929 itself was precipitated by short-term capital withdrawals from London in response to the Hatry crisis of September 1929.

International financial crisis requires an international lender of last resort. In the nineteenth century the City of London was the major financial centre from which other centres in trouble borrowed. When London itself faced crisis, it was helped on a number of occasions by the Bank of France (1825, 1836, 1839, 1890 and 1907), by Hamburg (1839) and by the State Bank of Russia (1890). Even so, Britain did not respond to the 1873 crisis in Central Europe and the United States. The classic case, however, seems to have been the 1929 depression when Britain, financially weakened by World War I, had ceased to act as the international lender of last resort, and the United States (and France) were unwilling to take on the role on an adequate scale.

The United States undertook to stabilize the world economy from World War II to about 1971. When the boom in syndicated bank loans to developing countries encountered difficulties in 1981 and 1982 and reached the stage of distress, the world turned not to the United States but to the International Monetary Fund created at Bretton Woods in 1944. The IMF successfully organized rescue operations from Mexico, Argentina and Brazil on a temporary basis by using its own resources, those of the Bank for International Settlements, and advances from the United States Federal Reserve System, and by persuading commercial banks not to halt lending, but in fact to lend more. The resources of the IMF are limited, however, and it is generally recognized that they need to be increased against any further relapse that would lead to financial crisis.

Charles P. Kindleberger
Massachusetts Institute of Technology

Further Reading

Evans, D. M. (1849), *The Commercial Crisis, 1847–48*, London.

Kindleberger, C. P. (1973), *The World in Depression, 1929–1939*, London.

Kindleberger, C. P. (1978), *Manias, Panics and Crashes*, London.

Kindleberger, C. P. and Laffargue, J. P. (eds) (1982), *Financial Crises: Theory, History and Policy*, Cambridge.

Lauck, W. J. (1907), *The Causes of the Panic of 1893*, Boston.

Wirth, M. (1890), *Geschichte der Handelskrisen*, 4th edn, Vienna.

See also: *banking*; *financial system*; *international monetary system*; *securities markets*.

Financial System

Financial systems provide society with a mechanism for facilitating trade, a machinery for transferring resources from savers to investors, and a means of holding wealth in a convenient form. Their origin lies in the need for a satisfactory payments system; further development has had more to do with the requirements of savers and investors, of wealth-owners and those who control the use of physical capital assets.

It is these physical assets – lands, buildings, equipment and other assets comprising the 'physical' capital stock – which form the foundation on which the superstructure of the financial system is created. Financial 'instruments' are claims whose value depends ultimately on physical resources (including human capital) or the income derived from them. The institutions within the financial system attempt to divide up or combine these ultimate claims in ways which match their clients' needs. The result in a sophisticated system is a great variety of instruments, handled by a broad and diverse range of institutions and financial markets.

The provision of notes and coins as generally acceptable means of payments has usually been regarded as a duty (or profitable right) of the state – the sovereign, government or central bank. These suffice only for small payments and are nowadays supplemented in even the most rudimentary financial system by banks, which take deposits and make payments by effecting transfers between accounts. Allied to this function is the provision of finance for trade – short-term loans to bridge the gap between the despatch of goods and the receipt of payment for them. Though important, activities associated with trade and payments now tend to comprise only a small part of the activities of financial systems.

Much more significant are activities associated with saving, investment, and the ownership of wealth. The financial system enables society to separate the ownership of wealth from the control of physical capital and to ensure that savers and wealth-holders have access to financial assets whose characteristics are attractive to them and differ from those of the physical assets which underpin their value. For example, savers frequently seek safety and liquidity in the assets they hold, whereas physical assets are durable, liable to lose their value, and difficult to turn into cash quickly; and the scale of investment is often of an order which dwarfs the amount available from individual savers.

Financial systems thus facilitate effective capital accumulation. By *intermediating* between savers and investors, financial institutions enable surplus resources to be transferred to those who are able to use them. By *mobilizing* saving from many savers, they provide finance for large-scale investment projects. And by *transforming* securities, the system allows the risk inherent in productive activity to be concentrated on wealth-holders who are prepared to take it, while others obtain the safe and liquid assets that they want. In a properly functioning system these activities can be expected both to increase the saving which is available for investment, and to raise the productivity of the investment that takes place.

Most financial systems consist largely of *intermediaries* – institutions which issue their own liabilities, and hold as assets the liabilities of ultimate borrowers or of other intermediaries. They fall into three broad groups: banks and other deposit-taking institutions, such as building societies, savings and loan associations, or credit unions; long-term investing institutions, such as life assurance companies, pension funds and investment companies or trusts; and special credit institutions, usually set up by governments to provide long-term finance for particular purposes. These institutions often compete with each other in the 'market' for savings, loans, or both. In addition most sophisticated financial systems, and some that are not yet highly developed, contain organized markets. These are security markets, such as the Stock Exchange, where long-term securities are issued and traded, and money markets, where short-term deposits and loans are made.

Economic and political conditions are the principal factors governing the evolution of financial systems. Goldsmith (1969) has suggested that three broad categories of system can be identified, distinguished according to the scale and composition of the economy's financial superstructure: (1) The systems found in Europe and North America up to the middle of the nineteenth century: the total value of financial instruments was low, financial institutions accounted for a low share of the outstanding assets, and commercial banks were pre-eminent. Risk-capital was predominantly in the hands of the owners of (comparatively small-scale) enterprises, and did not play a large part in the financial system. (2) The structure is similar to the first one, and was found in nonindustrialized countries in the first half of the century. But in this case governments and government-supported institutions played a larger part, thanks to the mixed nature of the economies. A similar situation can be found in many developing countries today, with government-supported institutions supplying capital for particular purposes. (3) This category, common amongst industrial countries in this century, shows a considerably greater degree of financial development, a higher proportion of risk-assets, and increased diversity amongst financial institutions. Some (for example,

Netherlands, UK, US) have strong long-term institutions supplying risk capital; others (among them, France and Italy) rely more heavily on special credit institutions. Socialist countries might be thought to form a fourth category: their financial systems are generally less highly developed than in market economies, with banks dominant amongst financial institutions.

While the tendency for financial and economic development to proceed in tandem is well-documented, the direction of causation is still the subject of controversy. Some argue that financial development is a response to economic growth, others (such as Drake, 1980), that improved financial facilities act as an independent stimulus. There is probably some truth in both views: financial innovation, in the form of new instruments or institutions, often results from changes in the economy; but, once created, new facilities are made available to others and help to stimulate further growth. Thus, even if financial development seldom sparks off economic growth, there is a positive feedback from the financial to the economic system.

A.D. Bain
University of Strathclyde

References

Drake, P. J. (1980), *Money, Finance and Development*, Oxford.
Goldsmith, R. W. (1969), *Financial Structure and Development*, New Haven.
See also: *banking*; *financial crises*; *securities markets*.

Firm, Theory of

The role of specialization in economic progress was emphasized by Adam Smith. Now specialized activities need to be co-ordinated, either by conscious integration within an organization or through market relationships; and the effects of both organizational forms and market structures on economic performance are topics which date back at least to Smith. But economists rarely try to treat the firm simultaneously as an organization and as a component of an industry or market, and so one can distinguish two major kinds of theory of the firm.

The problems of business enterprise were last treated comprehensively by Marshall (1919, 1920), whose carefully explained decision to give preference to detailed empirically based analyses over further refinement of theoretical structures was rejected by his successors. For Marshall, the problems of the firm were problems of acquiring (or generating) and using knowledge: knowledge of production methods, knowledge of existing and potential markets, knowledge of the ways to construct an organization and to motivate its

members to create opportunities for profit. The firm's environment – its customers and its competitors, including potential competitors – at once constrained its actions and provided opportunities to those who had the wit to perceive and the ability to exploit them. (That such ability might be destructive rather than constructive, or perhaps both together, did not escape Marshall's consideration.) For the analysis of this complex evolutionary process the methods of static equilibrium offered some useful guidance, but could be misleading if rigorously pressed; there was no substitute for the detailed investigation of particular organizational and market arrangements, in relatiion to the technical conditions and demand characteristics of each case.

After Marshall, the study of the firm distintegrated. Economists chose to develop static models of resource allocation in which the major activities of firms were defined away by the assumption of fully specified demand and cost functions, and the firm itself became a unitary decision maker whose actions were completely determined by its situation. Firms as organizations had no reason for existence. The 'theory of the firm' was the label given to a set of exercises in constrained optimization, by which equilibrium price and output were derived for a series of market structures – perfect and imperfect competition, oligopoly and monopoly – and the effects of change read off from shifts in demand or cost curves. Though this style of theorizing began with perfect competition, it was Joan Robinson's *Economics of Imperfect Competition* (1933) which epitomized the triumph of the formal model. (Her diagrams are to be found in many textbooks.) It epitomized too the dominance of problems generated within the theoretical structure; for the origins of imperfect competition theory lay in the logical impossibility of reconciling increasing returns (statically defined) with perfectly competitive equilibrium. Both were concepts which Marshall had avoided.

Though often regarded as an alternative presentation of this model, Chamberlin's (1933) conception of monopolistic competition was very different. Whereas Marshall had insisted that elements of competition and monopoly were usually blended in practice, Chamberlin set out to blend them in theory. In so doing, he tried to incorporate both product variation and selling costs within a formal analysis which used the method (though often not the language) of static equilibrium. Despite his limited success, he provided the primary inspiration for the strong American tradition in industrial economics (even though some of its practitioners borrowed their welfare criteria from Robinson). Chamberlin's approach was also distinguished by the attention he gave to oligopoly, attention which steadily increased over the years. His insistence that oligopolistic behaviour (like all behaviour) depends on expectations, and that there could be no general theory of oligopoly because there could be no general theory of expectations, has haunted theorists ever since.

There are many specific models of oligopoly, though it is noteworthy that most restrict themselves either to relationships within the group (as, for example, the dominant firm and kinked demand models) or to the barriers, natural or artificial, against new entrants, and do not attempt to deal with both issues together – another example of economists' aversion to multi-level analysis. (Andrews (1949) exceptionally tried to argue, significantly in a non-formal way, that the threat of cross-entry and the desire of managers to show themselves worthy of promotion might combine to ensure good value for the customer's money – especially if the customer was another firm.) But the kind of situational determination which is apparently so effective in producing general solutions for other market structures will not work for oligopoly.

This failure was exploited by Baumol, who founded an alternative, though closely related, line of analysis. Instead of varying the environment around a standard firm, why not vary the firm within a standard environment? Baumol's (1959) variation was to assume that a firm's decision makers sought to maximize not profit, but sales revenue; his lead was followed by Williamson (1963), who proposed a managerial utility function, and Marris (1964), who favoured growth. In all three models, the decision makers were constrained not only by the market opportunities but also by their shareholders: in the first two directly by the need to provide an acceptable profit, and in the third by the risk of takeover when share prices were depressed by the low earnings associated with unprofitable growth. Each model generated some plausible contrasts to the results of profit maximization; yet all three were open to a double attack. Although claiming to apply to oligopolistic firms, none attempted to deal seriously with interdependence; and, though they invoked the firm as an organization to justify their choice of managerially oriented objectives, none offered any analysis of organizational influences on behaviour. They consider neither the firm as a system nor the firm within a system.

Williamson has since turned (1975) to firms as organizations, pursuing a research programme adumbrated by Coase (1937), who argued that firms came into existence where they offered a cheaper alternative to the use of costly market transactions, and that the organization of industry could be explained by the comparative advantages, for varying classes of activity, of management and the market. Williamson has extended the costs of transactions to include those arising from differentiated knowledge, which may be exploited by opportunism and guile, but has provided no explanation of the kind of co-operative interdependence between complementary organizations which has been persuasively analysed by Richardson (1972).

Complementary to the allocation of activities between markets and firms is the allocation of activities within the organization; here the transactions cost approach converges with the historical studies of organizational structure by Chandler (1962, 1977).

It is perhaps significant that the unit of analysis is called a transaction, for the economics of organization has rather little to say about price and output decisions. Nor is it much concerned with the actual problems and processes of decision making, which are the focus of what is usually called (in economics) behavioural theory. This kind of theory is characterized by its emphasis on the inadequacy of knowledge, and on the limited ability of people to make use even of what knowledge they think they have. Simon's (1976) proposal to substitute procedural for substantive rationality makes obvious sense at a time of much concern over control systems, information systems, techniques of planning, and the machinery of government. So far, such studies of organizational processes and their implications (for example, by Cyert and March, 1963) have centred on short-term decision making, whereas transactions cost theorists write about an organization's structure and scope. Each might borrow from the other, perhaps building on Penrose's (1959) explanation of the growth of firms through the activities of managers who have developed effective decision procedures through their experience of management.

The firm as an agent of discovery and progress has received little attention during the last sixty years. It was a key element in Schumpeter's (1943) theory of economic development through 'creative destruction', but Schumpeter is not usually thought of as a theorist of the firm. There has been some recent interest in the concept of the entrepreneur as the agent of change; and though neo-Austrians have so far studied the entrepreneur only as an individual in the market, Casson (1982) depicts him as the creator of an organization, facing some of the problems discussed by Marshall. Meanwhile, studies of innovation and technical change have increasingly recognized the need to investigate how organizational form as well as market structure influences the generation, transmission and exploitation of knowledge, and also the effects of these processes on markets and organizations. The problems of substance and of method thereby raised are well displayed by Nelson and Winter (1982). There seems no early prospect of any formal apparatus that will handle simultaneously the issues identified by Smith; there may be increasing awareness of the limitations of present models.

Brian J. Loasby
University of Stirling

References
Andrews, P. W. S. (1949), *Manufacturing Business*, London.

Baumol, W. J. (1959), *Business Behavior, Value and Growth*, New York.

Casson, M. (1982), *The Entrepreneur: An Economic Theory*, Oxford.

Chamberlin, E. H. (1933), *The Theory of Monopolistic Competition*, Cambridge, Mass.

Chandler, A. D. (1962), *Strategy and Structure*, Cambridge, Mass.

Chandler, A. D. (1977), *The Visible Hand*, Cambridge, Mass.

Coase, R. H. (1937), 'The nature of the firm', *Economica* (N.S.), 4.

Cyert, R. M. and March, J. G. (1963), *A Behavioral Theory of the Firm*, Englewood Cliffs, N.J.

Marris, R. L. (1964), *The Economics of 'Managerial' Capitalism*, London.

Marshall, A. (1919), *Industry and Trade*, London.

Marshall, A. (1920), *Principles of Economics*, 8th edn, London.

Nelson, R. R. and Winter, S. G. (1982), *An Evolutionary Theory of Economic Change*, Cambridge, Mass.

Richardson, G. B. (1972), 'The organisation of industry', *Economic Journal*, 82.

Robinson, J. V. (1933), *The Economics of Imperfect Competition*, London.

Schumpeter, J. A. (1943), *Capitalism, Socialism and Democracy*, London.

Simon, H. A. (1976), 'From substantive to procedural rationality', in S. J. Latsis (ed.), *Method and Appraisal in Economics*, Cambridge.

Williamson, O. E. (1963), *Economics of Discretionary Behavior: Managerial Objectives in a Theory of the Firm*, Englewood Cliffs, N.J.

Williamson, O. E. (1975), *Markets and Hierarchies: Analysis and Anti-Trust Implications*, New York.

See also: *competition*; *markets*; *Marshall*; *organizations*.

Fiscal Policy

Book V of J. S. Mill's *Principles of Political Economy* (1848) was labelled 'The Influence of Government', a very apt description of what we mean by fiscal policy. Clearly most important, and the areas which have attracted most attention, are government tax and expenditure policy, and the consequent overall financial impact on the economy. Until the publication of J. M. Keynes's *General Theory* in 1936 it was the impact of individual taxes and expenditures which had been most studied. Keynes's belief that it was not merely the level of tax and expenditure that was important, but that they could be used to bring the economy more quickly to an acceptable equilibrium which it would otherwise only slowly or never achieve, and that active manipulation of the government's budget was vital to the maintenance of a stable economy, revolutionized the analysis of public policy.

In the post-war years, discussion of the impact of government policy on the overall level of economic activity became a recognized part of the debate on economic policy in most of the Western world. With hindsight, it seems clear that much of the fine tuning indulged in by many governments had effects which were at best very small and, in some cases, counter-cyclical. The use of fiscal policy for short-term stabilization of the economy was substantially undermined by the economic problems of the early 1970s, which combined spiralling rates of inflation with levels of unemployment unprecedented in the post-war years, and marked the flowering of the so-called monetarist versus Keynesian debate.

Questionmarks over the use of fiscal policy for macroeconomic stabilization have perhaps helped to heighten the interest in the microeconomic impact of government tax and expenditure policy. Much work has recently been done in the areas of individual responses to taxes; their effect on work effort, investment decisions, risk taking, pricing behaviour, and consumption patterns. The analysis of public expenditure raises questions about the nature of public goods, and the optimum size of the public sector. The latter has recently caused a good deal of controversy, with something of a backlash against the very rapid recent growth in the size of the public sector in many Western countries.

Andrew Dilnot
Institute for Fiscal Studies, London

Reference

Keynes, J. M. (1936), *The General Theory of Employment, Interest and Money*, London.

Further Reading

Bluider, A. S. and Solow, R. M. (1974), 'Analytical foundations of fiscal policy', in A. S. Bluider and R. M. Solow (eds), *The Economics of Public Finance*, London.

Kay, J. A. and King, M. A. (1983), *The British Tax System*, 3rd edn, Oxford.

See also: *public goods*; *taxation*.

Fisher, Irving (1867–1947)

Irving Fisher is widely regarded as the outstanding American economist of his day. During his lifetime, however, he was underestimated: 'His career was marked by neglect at its inception and ridicule at its close'.

Fisher's professional life was centred on Yale University, first as a student, then as a member first of the mathematics and later the economics departments. As an undergraduate, Fisher was advised by Willard Gibbs, the great Yale physicist, to combine his talents in mathematical economics – becoming the first American to achieve distinction in this field. His Yale doctoral dissertation, *Mathematical Investigations in the Theory of Value and Prices* (1892), presented a general equilibrium system, which carried the notions of complementarity and indifference surfaces well beyond the work of Leon Walras, which he had not known as a student.

The earlier period of Fisher's subsequent career at Yale (apart from an elementary *Principles of Political Economy* (1910)) was devoted to capital theory. It began with a monograph, 'Appreciation and Interest', to which we owe the distinction between real and nominal interest rates and the statistical testing of the theory that the real rate is independent of the price level. Then came two major books, *The Nature of Capital and Income* (1906) and *The Rate of Interest* (1907). (Fisher's *Theory of Interest* (1930) expands *The Rate of Interest*. His *Constructive Income Taxation* (1942) draws the public-finance implications of *The Nature of Capital and Income*.) The first of these is known for Fisher's identification of income with consumption (a flow of utility), and for the distinction between income and additions to capital. The second Fisher volume bases interest on 'the impatience to spend income and the opportunity to invest it'. For the first of these, Fisher follows Böhm-Bawerk; as for the second, he does not take 'the next step' of associating investment opportunity with the productivity of capital.

Fisher is best known for his later research on monetary economics. This developed in a series of works from *The Purchasing Power of Money* (1911) and *Stabilizing the Dollar* (1920) through *Booms and Depressions* (1932) and *100% Money* (1938). He began as a strict quantity theorist; the 'Fisherine' equation of exchange ($MV = PT$) is the best-known formulation of that equation. (M is a quantity of money, V is its velocity of circulation, P is a general price level, and T is an estimate of the volume of transactions (*not* income) evaluated at base-period prices.) His initial plan for price-level stabilization proposed a gold bullion standard. The computed 'weight' of the dollar would vary directly with the price level, meaning that the money value of a gold bar or ingot would vary inversely with it.

Fisher believed that price-level stabilization was important, not only as a matter of justice between debtors and creditors but because he saw the business cycle as primarily 'a dance of the dollar'. This theory eventually led Fisher astray. Since the general price level had not risen in the 1920s, Fisher underestimated the severity of the depression which followed the crash of 1929. Like President Hoover, he continually saw prosperity as 'just around the corner'.

Later, however, Fisher formulated a 'debt-deflation' cycle theory, and made two proposals to avert future depressions. The first of these involved stamped money as a carrying charge on hoarding and an indirect encouragement to investment. The second was a proposal for 100 per cent reserves on bank deposits, to avoid what later writers have called the innate 'fragility' of a fractional-reserve banking system faced with a crisis of confidence. Neither of these proposals was original with Fisher; both were regarded, probably unjustly, as mere crank schemes.

Fisher made major contributions to economic statistics; *The Making of Index Numbers* (1927) is a classic. As a mathematical economist and economic statistician, he was a founder of the Econometric Society in 1933.

In other fields than economics, Fisher was a general-purpose reformer. His bestselling book, *How to Live* (1915) dealt primarily with nutrition. He was a eugenicist, a prohibitionist, an internationalist, and a pacifist. He made a fortune from a visible card-index filing system of his own invention, but lost much of it in the stock-market crash. His total output includes 30 books and hundreds of scientific papers. He was outstanding for expository clarity; Fisher often illustrated his points with mechanical models of his own construction. He left no single major work, however, to combine and summarize his contributions to economics.

Martin Bronfenbrenner
Duke University

Further Reading
Allais, M. (1958), 'Irving Fisher', in D. Sills (ed.), *International Encyclopedia of the Social Sciences*, New York.

Folklore and Myth

The discipline of folklore was given its name by William Thoms only in 1846, but its origins go back to the beginning of the nineteenth century. It was a product of an intellectual movement opposed to the philosophy of the Enlightenment and associated with pre-Romanticism and, especially in Germany, with *Sturm und Drang*.

The publication in 1760 of James MacPherson's *Fragments of Ancient Poetry Collected in the Highlands of Scotland and Translated from the Gaelic or Erse Language* caused shock-waves throughout Europe. The Celtic bard Ossian was regarded as a Nordic Homer. The modern sensibility welcomed a poetry which, while ignorant of formal rules, was original, authentic and bursting with energy. The success of Ossian's poems was both profound and enduring, although it was gradually established that they were the work of MacPherson himself.

J. G. Herder, the spokesmen for *Sturm und Drang* in Germany, provided the conceptual basis for the academic study of folklore. Popular poetry was an emanation of the popular spirit. Various cultures, which were 'equal in necessity, equal in originality, equal in value, equal in happiness' functioned in an organic manner.

The next generation developed these ideas. For the brothers Grimm, there was no question but that popular cultural products, stories, legends, *lieder*, beliefs, customary law, shared the same source as mythology itself. They were various forms, perhaps modified in the course of history, of natural poetry (*Naturpoesie*). This poetry was born and evolved in an organic unconscious fashion in the human spirit. Its creation and functioning was controlled by the same mechanisms as those which ordained living organisms or natural phenomena, or, more to the point, human language. This ancient poetry was the product not of invention but of divine revelation. In time it generated a variety of epics, legends and stories. While it may sometimes be convenient to distinguish these genres of popular literature, they may equally legitimately be merged with each other since their content is the same – they all participate in the nature of myths. In the preface to the 1819 edition of *Kinder-und Hausmärchen*, the Grimms suggested that the ancient German myths could be recognized in the surviving folktales. In the postscript to the 1857 edition, Wilhelm Grimm expressed the same idea with greater precision. The stories were survivals, the debris, of ancient beliefs which are figuratively expressed in them, and which are to be identified, however fictionalized, in the motifs of a performance. The mythical content fragments, because the story is a living organism. Continually evolving, it sheds beliefs which are no longer comprehensible, and integrates new elements. However, the further back one goes in time, the more the mythical element (*das Mythische*) predominates, until it constitutes the essence, the 'sole foundation'. This mythical context, which is retained in a fragmentary form in the stories, satisfies our taste for the extraordinary, the marvellous. It accounts for a certain category of stories (nos 300–749 in Aarne-Thompson's typology), in which 'mythical' features are presented in a figurative fashion, in and through the narrative.

This conception of the nature of the popular story and of folklore more generally was accepted by scholars in the nineteenth and early twentieth centuries. Stories developed out of ancient myths and tended to erode as, with the passage of time, they were distanced from their ancient source in natural poetry. The scholars of the nineteenth century regarded folklore as a product of the degeneration of myths, which eroded and degenerated over the centuries. One had to trace them back in order to discover their pure and noble structure.

The concern of scholars was consequently with the mode of degeneration (or 'devolution', to use the expression of Dundes, 1975) 'from myth to folklore'. The English school, represented by Tylor (1871) and Lang (1884, 1887) developed the idea of 'survivals' in an evolutionist perspective. Survivals were the remains of dead civilizations which persisted in a living culture in the form of beliefs, practices, rituals or tales. The idea was accepted in France, where Sébillot (1908) wrote of 'contemporary paganism' and Saintyves (1923) congratulated the anthropologists for providing scholars with 'the historico-scientific notion of survivals', permitting them to recognize in popular stories commentaries on rituals which had fallen into disuse. As late as 1928, V. Propp took the view that rites, myths, the forms of primitive thought, and certain social institutions were anterior to particular stories and provided the means for their interpretation.

Modern scholars have abandoned this 'archaic illusion', which is ideological in nature, but without investigating its rationale or its origin. In consequence, they have instituted a radical distinction between myth and folklore, limiting themselves to the collection of items of folklore or to the study of their social function, and applying both to myths and to popular stories formalist methods which pass over questions of content. Yet it is surely the case that folkloric products may have a mythic content, even though this may be masked by superficial and formal features. This presence of the 'mythic' is not the consequence of what Lévi-Strauss (1952) called 'historical viscosity'. Folklore retains its functions, especially the permanent necessity of transmitting myth, by whatever means.

Nicole Belmont
École des Hautes Études en Sciences Sociales, Paris

References

Dundes, A. (1975), *Analytic Essays in Folklore*, The Hague.

Grimm, J. and Grimm, W. (1819 and 1857), *Kinder-und Hausmärchen*, Berlin.

Lang, A. (1884), *Custom and Myth*, London.

Lang, A. (1887), *Myth, Ritual and Religion*, London.

Lévi-Strauss, C. (1952), 'Le Père Noël supplicié', *Les Temps Modernes*, 77.

Propp, V. (1908 [1928]), *Morphology of the Folktale*, Austin, Texas.

Saintyves, P. (1923), *Les Contes de Perrault et les récits parallèles*, Paris.

Sebillot, P. (1908), *Le Paganisme contemporain chez les peuples celto-latins*, Paris.

Tylor, E. B. (1871), *Primitive Culture*, London.

Further Reading

Dorson, R. M. (1968), *The British Folklorists: A History*, London.

Dundes, A. (1965), *The Study of Folklore*, Englewood Cliffs, N.J.

See also: *Lévi-Strauss*; *Van Gennep*.

Force

One must distinguish between the use of force within an organization and the use of force to attain collective goals at the expense of other collectivities. Thus, in virtually every war each side tends to regard its own goals as legitimate and those of the other side as illegitimate.

As a generalized symbolic medium, power is the capacity to gain compliance with binding decisions ('political' obligations), where compliance is presumptively important to collective goal attainment and where failure to comply is liable to be punished by negative situational sanctions (Parsons, 1969). In the paradigmatic case, the negative sanctions symbolize particular collective interests and the general value of collective effectiveness. Power and, therefore, obligatory compliance with binding decisions are found in all organizations, public and private.

Force, as earlier noted, has often been used *by* organizations in dealing with non-members (individual or collective). As the 'ultimate' negative situational sanction of power within organizations, force is characteristically used if necessary by duly elected or appointed representatives of independent states and their subdivisions; however, more informally, force is also used sometimes by parents and others. More or less secret illegal organizations, being in danger of dissolution if exposed, also tend to rely on force or the threat of force to keep rank-and-file members in line, whereas the political systems of legal private organizations use less drastic negative situational sanctions, such as fines and loss of membership status. The use of force by an individual who has no collective authority is a limiting case and not typical, although it is fairly common.

Mobilization of collective force requires some degree of willingness to co-operate, as well as technology and material resources. Legitimacy is general; authority is relatively specific, normatively confining binding decisions to particular functional aspects of collective action, to territorial or departmental limits, or to a combination of both.

Legitimacy of government is seldom, if ever, perfect and seldom lacking entirely. Virtually by definition, a one-party system is not completely legitimate within its territory, yet in some one-party systems the collective goals of modernization and national glory do somewhat legitimate them even for many who must submit to a great deal of coercion.

Vilfredo Pareto said that 'lions' are often more willing to use force than 'foxes', because lions have deep moral conviction while foxes, being less moralistic and more expedient, may be unable to use force and tend to rely to a greater extent on rhetoric and deceit. This famous generalization, while broadly true, requires qualification. Apparently deep moral conviction may conceal doubt and ambivalence. We may cite the attempt by the US Confederacy in the nineteenth century to maintain slavery in the South by force, against the Union government, and the attempt by the present government of South Africa to enforce *apartheid* and 'White' supremacy. Even solidly legitimate governments must seek to justify particular binding decisions. In waging war against Nazi and Japanese imperialism, the United States government gained widespread willing compliance with its binding decisions, but in the Vietnamese war the government encountered a great deal of resistance and noncompliance among American citizens.

Harry M. Johnson
University of Illinois, Champaign-Urbana

Reference
Parsons, T. (1969), *Politics and Social Structure*, Glencoe, Ill.
See also: *authority*; *legitimacy*; *power*.

Forecasting

See Prediction and Forecasting.

Foreign Aid

See Aid.

Foucault, Michel (1926–84)

Michel Foucault, the French philosopher, was successively a university teacher, professor at Clermont-Ferrand, Paris-Vincennes, and from 1970, professor of the history of systems of thought at the Collège de France.

At first sight – and on account of the title of his chair – one might take Foucault to be engaged in a kind of history of ideas. In fact, he refuses any such definition of his work. His *L'Archéologie du savoir* (1969) (*The Archaeology of Knowledge*, 1972) is directed against the discipline called 'the history of ideas', which he takes to be something like a totalizing overview that rewrites the past in order to produce a unified object of study. In the same book he criticizes certain aspects of his own earlier work: for example, the presupposition of the existence of a 'general subject of history' contained in *Histoire de la folie à l'âge classique* (1961) (*Madness and Civilization*, 1967). In *Les Mots et les choses* (1966) (*The Order of Things*, 1970) Foucault claims that man is a modern invention and destined to disappear. Such an opinion might lead us to call him a 'structuralist', for he takes the idea of *man*, in any sense recognizable to the contemporary reader, to be a product of nineteenth-century structures (in fact, of structures of knowledge or *savoir*). But in *L'Archéologie du savoir* he had also turned against the structuralist leanings of his earlier writings.

The problem appears to have lain in the use made in those writings of the concept of an *episteme*: roughly, a structure of knowledge or – in his own terms – a 'discursive formation', which determines the manner in which the world is experienced in a given epoch. Can a study of the history of the appearance and disappearance of epistemic formations itself make use of the concept of episteme as an *explanatory* tool? If not, what does explain epistemic ruptures and eruptions? Foucault insists that the explanation must lie in 'the regime of materiality', which he then interprets as consisting in the *institutions* in which the material relations structuring discursive events are embodied.

Knowledge therefore has to be explained in terms of institutions, and of the events which take place in the latter – events of a technical, economic, social and political nature. But institutions cannot function without the exercise of *power*. Foucault therefore turns to an examination of the question of power, which, being institutional, is not and cannot be personal in origin or character. Unlike Marxists, however, he wants to study not some mechanistic process whereby power in general is explained in terms of economic ownership, but rather what he calls the 'strategies' of power. And, in order to avoid any semblance of anthropocentrism, he explains that he means by the term 'strategy' not the conscious plan or design of some human individual or group but 'the effect of a strategic position'.

The merely descriptive – and structuralist – notion of the *episteme* is now subordinated to a genuinely historical conception of the eruption of new epistemic configurations, including new sciences, a conception which – as mentioned – is avowedly materialist.

Power, he says, is located in strategies which are operative at every level: they cannot be reduced to the power of, for example, the State, or of a ruling class. Power is productive (and in particular productive of knowledge). He talks about a 'microphysics of power', power disseminated throughout the whole of society. There are of course clashes between the multifarious and multi-levelled strategies of power. What is not clear is how the outcome of such clashes and similar processes is to be explained, given that no general mechanism of the generation of power is provided. Foucault has thus been criticized for offering, at the theoretical level, no more (nor less) than a *metaphysics* of power.

This critique does not detract from the interest of the detailed studies carried out by him (often in collaboration with pupils): for instance, his study of prisons and imprisonment (*Surveiller et punir*, 1975) (*Discipline and Punish*, 1977) and of the history of sexuality (*La Volonté de savoir*, 1976) (*The History of Sexuality*, vol. I, 1979).

Foucault's metaphysics of power – if such it is – is in any case, as we have seen, a microphysics. This point is worth underlining in the light of the exploitation made of his work by the so-called 'nouveaux philosophes' (André Glucksmann and others), who have drawn on some of its themes or vocabulary in order to produce a violently anti-Marxist metaphysics of the State – otherwise called a theory of totalitarianism – which reintroduces the idea, rejected by Foucault, of a single centre of power (see Glucksmann, 1977).

Grahame Lock
Catholic University, Nijmegen

Reference
Glucksmann, A. (1977), *Les Maîtres penseurs*, Paris.

Further Reading
Dreyfus, H. and Rabinow, P. (1982), *Michel Foucault: Beyond Structuralism and Hermeneutics*, Brighton.
Foucault, M. (1977), *Language, Counter-Memory, Practice*, ed. D. Bouchard, Oxford.
Foucault, M. (1979), *Power, Truth, Strategy*, ed. M. Morris and P. Patton, Sydney.
Foucault, M. (1980), *Power/Knowledge*, ed. C. Gordon, Brighton.
Sheridan, A. (1981), *Michel Foucault: The Will to Truth*, London.
White, H. (1979), 'Michel Foucault', in J. Sturrock (ed.), *Structuralism and Since*, Oxford.

Frankfurt School

The Frankfurt School refers to the work of members of the *Institut für Sozialforschung*, which was established in Frankfurt, Germany, in 1923 as the first Marxist-oriented research centre affiliated with a major German University. Under its director, Carl Grunberg, the Institute's work in the 1920s tended to be empirical, historical, and oriented towards problems of the European working-class movement, although theoretical works by Karl Korsch, Georg Lukács and others were also published in their journal, *Archiv für die Geschichte des Sozialismus und der Arbeiterbewegung*.

Max Horkheimer became director of the Institute in 1930, and gathered around him many talented theorists, including Erich Fromm, Herbert Marcuse, and T. W. Adorno. Under Horkheimer, the Institute sought to develop an interdisciplinary social theory which could serve as an instrument of social transformation. The work of this era was a synthesis of philosophy and social theory, combining sociology, psychology, cultural studies, and political economy. The results appeared in their own journal, *Zeitschrift für Sozial forschung* (1932–1941), which contains a rich collection of articles and book reviews still worth reading.

The first major Institute project in the Horkheimer period was a systematic study of authority, an investigation into individuals who submitted to irrational authority in authoritarian regimes. This culminated in a two-volume work, *Studien über Autorität und Familie* (1936). Fascism was a major interest during the 1930s. Most members were both Jews and Marxist radicals and were forced to flee Germany after Hitler's ascendancy to power. The majority emigrated to the United States, and the Institute became affiliated with Columbia University from 1934 until 1949, when it returned to Frankfurt.

From 1936 to the present, the Institute referred to their work as the 'critical theory of society'. For many years, 'critical theory' stood as a code word for the Institute's Marxism and was distinguished by its attempt to found a radical interdisciplinary social theory rooted in Hegelian-Marxian dialectics, historical materialism, and the Marxian critique of political economy and theory of revolution. Members argued that Marx's concepts of the commodity, money, value, exchange and fetishism characterize not only the capitalist economy but also social relations under capitalism, where human relations and all forms of life are governed by commodity and exchange relations and values.

Horkheimer claimed in a key article 'Traditional and critical theory' (1937) that since 'the economy is the first cause of poverty, theoretical and practical criticism has to direct itself primarily at it'. Institute members were convinced that the capitalist economy was driving bourgeois society to catastrophe through its underlying cycle of production, anarchy, depressions, unemployment and wars. They believed that increasing tendencies toward bureaucratization and social rationalization were destroying the features of individuality and freedom which the capitalist system extolled as its prize creation.

Horkheimer (1937) wrote that critical theory's 'content consists of changing the concepts that thoroughly dominate the economy into their opposites: fair exchange into a deepening of social injustice; a free economy into monopolistic domination; productive labour into the strengthening of relations which inhibit production; the maintenance of society's life into the impoverishment of the people's'. The goal of critical theory is to transform these social conditions, and provide a theory of 'the historical movement of an epoch that is to come to an end'.

Critical theory produced aspects of a theory of the transformation of competitive capitalism into monopoly capitalism and fascism, and hoped to be part of a historical process through which capitalism would be replaced by socialism. Horkheimer claimed that, 'The categories which have arisen under its influence

criticize the present. The Marxist categories of class, exploitation, surplus value, profit, impoverishment, and collapse are moments of a conceptual whole whose meaning is to be sought, not in the reproduction of the present society, but in its transformation to a correct society.' Critical theory is thus motivated by an interest in emancipation and is a philosophy of social practice engaged in 'the struggle for the future'. Critical theory must remain loyal to the 'idea of a future society as the community of free human beings, in so far as such a society is possible, given the present technical means'.

In a series of studies carried out in the 1930s, the Institute for Social Research sketched out theories of monopoly capitalism, the new industrial state, the role of technology and giant corporations in monopoly capitalism, the cultural industries and the decline of the individual. They articulated theories which were to occupy the centre of social theory for the next several decades. Rarely, if ever, has such a talented group of interdisciplinary workers come together under the auspices of one institute. They managed to keep alive radical social theory during a difficult historical era and provided aspects of a neo-Marxian theory of the changed social reality and new historical situation in the transition from competitive capitalism to monopoly capitalism.

During World War II, the Institute tended to split up due to pressures of the war. Adorno and Horkheimer moved to California, while Lowenthal, Marcuse, Neumann and others worked for the US government as their contribution in the fight against fascism. Adorno and Horkheimer worked on their collective book *Dialectic of Enlightenment* (1947), which contains implicit critiques of Marxism, as well as fascism and consumer capitalism. Departing from the Marxian theory of history, they presented a philosophy of history that traced the fate of the enlightenment from the beginning of scientific thought with the Greeks to fascist concentration camps and the cultural industries of US capitalism. They showed how Western rationality served as instruments of domination and how 'enlightenment' turned into its opposite, mystification and oppression. The book criticized enlightenment scientism and rationalism, and implicitly implicated Marxism within the 'dialectic of Enlightenment'.

After World War II, Adorno, Horkheimer, and Pollock returned to Frankfurt to re-establish the Institute in Germany, while Lowenthal, Marcuse, and others remained in the United States. In Germany, Adorno, Horkheimer, and their associates published a series of books and became a dominant intellectual current in Germany. At this time, the term 'Frankfurt School' became widespread as a characterization of their version of interdisciplinary social research and of the particular social theory developed by Adorno, Horkheimer, and their associates. They engaged in frequent methodological and substantive debates with other social theories, most notably, the 'positivism dispute' where they criticized more empirical and quantitative approaches to social theory and defended their own more speculative and critical brand of social theory. The German group around Adorno and Horkheimer was also increasingly hostile toward orthodox Marxism and were in turn criticized by a variety of types of 'Marxism-Leninism' and 'scientific Marxists' for their alleged surrender of revolutionary and scientific Marxian perspectives.

The Frankfurt School eventually became best known for their theories of 'the totally administered society', or 'one-dimensional society', which theorized the increasing power of capitalism over all aspects of social life and the development of new forms of social control. During the 1950s, however, there were divergences between the work of the Institute relocated in Frankfurt and the developing theories of Fromm, Lowenthal, Marcuse and others who did not return to Germany which were often at odds with both the current and earlier work of Adorno and Horkheimer. Thus it is misleading to consider the work of various critical theorists during the post-war period as members of a monolithic 'Frankfurt School'. Whereas there was both a shared sense of purpose and collective work on interdisciplinary social theory from 1930 to the early 1940s, thereafter critical theorists frequently diverge, and during the 1950s and 1960s the term the 'Frankfurt School' can really only be applied to the work of the Institute in Germany.

It is thus impossible to characterize the 'Frankfurt School' as a whole, since their work spanned several decades and involved a variety of thinkers who later engaged in sharp debates with one another. Rather one should perceive various phases of Institute work: (1) The empirical-historical studies of the Grunberg era. (2) Attempts in the early to mid-1930s to establish a materialist interdisciplinary social theory under Horkheimer's directorship. (3) Attempts to develop a critical theory of society during the exile period from about 1937 to the early 1940s. (4) The dispersion of Institute members in the 1940s and new directions sketched out by Adorno and Horkheimer. (5) The return of the Institute to Germany and its work in Frankfurt during the 1950s and 1960s. (6) The development of critical theory in various ways by Fromm, Lowenthal, Marcuse, and others who remained in the US. (7) The continuation of Institute projects and development of critical theory in Germany by Jurgen Habermas, Oskar Negt, Alfred Schmidt, and others in the 1970s and 1980s. (8) Contributions to critical theory by younger theorists and scholars currently active in Europe and the United States.

In surveying the field of critical theory, one observes a heterogeneity of theories, theorists, and projects loosely connected by commitment to interdisplinary social theory, and an interest in social critique and transformation, all influenced by the work of theorists like Adorno, Horkheimer, Marcuse, Habermas, or others. Critical theorists tend to be critical of empirical and quantitative social theory and more sympathetic to theoretical construction, social critique, and social transformation. It continues to be an active, though frequently marginal, tendency of social theory today; thus the legacy of the Frankfurt School endures.

Douglas Kellner
University of Texas, Austin

Further Reading
Adorno, T. W. and Horkheimer, M. (1972), *Dialectic of Enlightenment*, New York.
Bottomore, T. (1984), *The Frankfurt School*, London.
Horkheimer, M. (1937), 'Philosophie und kritische Theorie', *Zeitschrift für Sozialforschung*, 6.
Horkheimer, M. (1972), *Critical Theory*, New York.
Jay, M. (1973), *The Dialectical Imagination*, Boston.
Jay, M. (1984), *Adorno and the Frankfurt School*, London.
Marcuse, H. (1984), *One-Dimensional Man*, Boston.
See also: *authoritarian personality*; *Habermas*; *Marcuse*.

Frazer, James George (1854–1941)

Educated in Glasgow University, Frazer proceeded in 1879 to Trinity College Cambridge, where he spent the rest of his long career. He started off as a classicist, but became increasingly engaged with anthropological questions, under the influence of the orientalist W. Robertson Smith, and the anthropologist E. B. Tylor.

Robertson Smith had adopted the theory that the original religion of mankind was 'totemism': members of a clan worshipped an animal from which they believed themselves to be descended. The sacrifice of an animal totem prefigured more developed religious beliefs (including Christian beliefs) about Gods which were sacrificed for the sakes of their followers. Frazer published two authoritative reviews of totemism, *Totemism* (1887) and *Totemism and Exogamy* (1910), and investigated the meaning of divine sacrifice in his most famous study, *The Golden Bough*, which first appeared in 1890 and was regularly republished thereafter. Frazer compulsively added more and more documentation, bringing together classical and biblical myths, European folklore and ethnographic materials published in a number of European languages.

Frazer also drew on Comte's theory that the intellectual development of mankind was marked by a progression from magical thinking to religious thinking and, finally, to scientific thinking. Magical thought was based on an erroneous theory of causality. Objects were thought to influence one another because they were in contact (contagious magic) or because of some superficial similarity between them (sympathetic magic).

The implication of his work was that Christianity was just another primitive cult (though Frazer was circumspect about drawing such conclusions). This may explain the enormous influence of *The Golden Bough* on twentieth-century literature, but its reputation within anthropology was short-lived.

Frazer was extraordinarily prolific if never particularly original; but his greatest long-term contribution was perhaps his stimulation of ethnographers all over the world. He maintained a huge correspondence with amateur scholars in the tropics, and developed questionnaires to guide ethnographic research. He consistently argued that ethnographic studies had a far greater permanent value than any theories, and was always ready to abandon old hypotheses when confronted with awkward new information.

Adam Kuper
Brunel University, Uxbridge

Further Reading
Downie, R. A. (1979), *Frazer and the Golden Bough*, London.
See also: *divine kingship*.

Free Association

The requirement for free association is often referred to as the fundamental rule of psychoanalysis. The patient in psychoanalytic treatment attempts to express in words all thoughts, feelings, wishes, sensations, images, and memories without reservation, as they spontaneously occur. Originally, Sigmund Freud introduced free association to assist in the abreaction of traumatic experiences. Later it served him especially well in deciphering the language and grammar of dreams and in describing the vicissitudes of human passion, emotion, and motivation. Gradually, as psychoanalysis progressed, free association became the vehicle for elucidation of unconscious conflicts and of the history of their formation in the life of the individual.

Free association replaced hypnosis in Freud's early investigative and psychotherapeutic work in the 1890s. The approach was consonant with his general conviction about the determinism of mental life and the importance of unconscious influences. It served and continues to serve as the principal method of psychoanalysis and of psychoanalytic psychotherapy. The word 'free' in this term indicates relative freedom from *conscious* determination. Unconscious determinants, both those that seek expression and those that oppose it (resistance), can be inferred from the many varieties of sequence, content and form of the free associations. The analyst's interventions, based on a grasp of conscious and unconscious determinants, aim at expansion of the patient's *freedom* of association mainly through clarification and interpretation, with a concomitant development of the patient's insight. The analyst is guided by his own associations and by the requirement of maintaining a non-judgemental attitude characterized by personal anonymity, neutrality and abstinence.

Free association can be seen to promote continuity in mental functioning – the continuity, for example, of thought, feeling, memory, styles of loving, and sense of self. Discontinuities in these functions and corresponding restrictions in the freedom of association are characteristic of the psychopathology which may be expected to respond favourably to psychoanalytic treatment. In a narrower sense, free association aims to make conscious what is unconscious, to revive lost experience, to expand what is condensed, to express the components of inner conflict, and to put thought and feeling, as much as possible, into words. Although not all of mental life can be put into words, emphasis on the intimate connection between language, reason, consciousness, and the capacity for decision and resolution has been an explicit feature of the psychoanalytic method from the beginning. The considerable variety of perspectives and theoretical formulations with which psychoanalysts perform their work can regularly be shown to relate to these features of the free association method.

Anton O. Kris
Boston Psychoanalytic Institute

Further Reading
Kris, A. O. (1982), *Free Association: Method and Process*, New Haven.
See also: *psychoanalysis*; *unconscious*.

Freedom

Freedom is the constitutive value of European political life, in that slaves, lacking freedom, must submit to a master, while free men, being equal in respect of being free, constitute for themselves a government which secures order by law, and not by the unchecked will of a master. It is on this basis that Europeans have always distinguished their civil societies from the despotisms of the Orient, in which (according to the account commonly given in Western political thought) all submit to a master.

Among the ancient Greeks, *eleutheria* was the adult condition in which a free male left behind the tutelage of childhood and took his place among fellow citizens in the public life of the *agora*, ruling and being ruled in turn. For the Romans, *libertas* was the quality of the free plebeian and corresponded to the *dignitas* of the patrician. The concrete reality of freedom for the Romans lay in their intense constitutionality, and their aversion, for many centuries after the expulsion of the Tarquins, to submitting themselves to a king. When the civic humanists of the medieval Italian cities revived the republican ideal, Julius Caesar stood as the man who extinguished freedom and gave Rome at last a master.

Medieval Europe, however, had its own indigenous sources of freedom, derived from both Christianity and from the practices of the barbarians who replaced the Romans. Regarding the situation in which one man rules another as sufficiently unusual to require justification (*omne potestas est a deo* was a common statement of the sentiment), they explored the forms of consent and the constitution of authority with great inventiveness: parliaments, juries, inquests, the principle of representation and much else in what we call 'democracy', descend from the civil experience of that period.

In early modern Europe, these monarchical institutions and the classical republican tradition of freedom supplied a joint inheritance, and by no means a harmonious one. In the monarchical tradition, freedom was essentially a condition sustained by public life but enjoyed within the private realm. It came to be defined as a set of rights, which could be distinguished as the civil rights of the subject and the political rights of the citizen. Freedom, argued Thomas Hobbes, is 'the silence of the law', and, in this tradition, freedom has always resided in the ability of individuals, as judges of their own best interests, to order their lives within a structure of rules which are clear, predictable and known to all. The republican tradition, by contrast, took freedom as the moral ideal which identified being fully human with participation in public life. The active citizen, thus understood, was self-determining in that he participated in making the laws under which he lived. This view ultimately rested upon ideal memories of the virtuous and public-spirited cities of the ancient world. From Montesquieu onwards, many writers have judged that modern freedom, which is individualistic, is quite different from the civic freedom of those earlier times, but the ideal of a truly participatory community has never lost its power to influence European thought.

It was Rousseau who most notably elaborated this latter view of freedom, with a clarity of mind which led him to the paradoxical implication that the citizen who has been compelled to abide by a law for which he is in principle responsible is being 'forced to be free'. In the extreme development of this view, a man can only properly be described as free when he acts virtuously, which seems, in terms of the modern view of freedom, to be self-contradictory. These two views of freedom are often discussed today, following Isaiah Berlin (1969), as the negative and positive view of freedom. The negative view tends to be strongly associated with Anglo-Saxon societies, while continental life is more receptive to the positive view.

The issue is important because the ideal of freedom has become the ratchet of European social and political development, Philosophers and politicians alike make use of slogans and images developed from the contrast between slave and freed. 'Man is born free and everywhere he is in chains' begins Rousseau's *Social Contract* (1762), while Marx and Engels end the *Communist Manifesto* (1848) by telling workers that they have nothing to lose but their chains. Hegel argued in his *Philosophy of History* (1837) that a universal freedom has been the great achievement of the modern Germanic world. In the despotisms of the East, he argued, one was free; among the Greeks and Romans, some were, but in modern Europe, all were free. And indeed, within a few decades of Hegel's death in 1831, slaves had been freed throughout European possessions, and also in the United States. Paradoxically, it was in exactly this period that a new type of politician arose – communist, anarchist, nationalist and so on – to proclaim that modern Europe was, contrary to all appearances, the most cunningly contrived system of domination the world had ever seen. This doctrine launched the idea of liberation. But whereas freedom and liberty refer to the removal of arbitrary interferences with the way an individual governs his life, liberation was the project of removing *all* conditions thought to frustrate human satisfaction. It stands for a vision of human life in which desire flows freely and uninterruptedly into satisfying action. This is a vastly more ambitious project than that of liberty, and has appealed to a correspondingly less sophisticated audience.

Kenneth Minogue
London School of Economics and Political Science

Reference
Berlin, I. (1969), *Four Essays on Liberty*, London.

Further Reading
Cranston, M. (1953), *Freedom: A New Social Analysis*, London.
Mill, J. S. (1859), *On Liberty*, London.
See also: *democracy; human rights.*

Free Trade

Free international trade became the dominant theory, ideology and trade policy of mid-nineteenth-century Britain. It commanded the support of classical political economists from Adam Smith to David Ricardo and Karl Marx. The theoretical justification was Ricardo's theory of comparative advantage, which assumed internal mobility and international immobility of labour and capital. At the peak of its support free trade implied international mobility of capital and labour.

Free trade was also associated with *laissez-faire*, that is, the freedom of enterprise from regulation by the state, although with a commanding British navy this hardly meant the end of state intervention in the struggle for dominance in international trade.

Challenges to the idea of free trade came from Britain's nineteenth-century rivals, the United States and Germany. Hamilton (1957) and List (1904) argued that new industrialized nations required protection before free trade became desirable. By the 1930s, free trade had been abandoned, even in Britain, and international trade theorists acknowledged the case for protection to assist infant industries (sometimes infant nations) or to exploit national monopoly power. But beggar-my-neighbour protectionism in the 1930s crisis gave way in the post-World War II period to a new wave of political and theoretical support for free trade and free international capital mobility, embodied in the institutions of the post-war settlement. Free trade and international capital mobility was embraced by the dominant *pax Americana*, and there was a substantial dismantling of protection between industrial countries.

The theory of international trade was extended to allow for the international mobility of factors and the link between free trade and *laissez-faire* was broken. Protectionist arguments have been rejected by those who use the theory of domestic market distortions as a framework for the analysis of government intervention in the market mechanism. Within this context, protection through intervention in trade is likely to be worse than subsidies or other policies aimed more directly towards policy objectives. Increasingly, it is argued that development of dynamic comparative advantage is better served by imperfect markets than imperfect government policies.

As in the nineteenth century, such ideas have not gone unchallenged. The modern-day counterparts of List and Hamilton successfully argued for protected import-substituting industrialization in many less-developed parts of the world economy in the early post-war period. In Eastern Europe, in spite of considerable integration of their national economies, drives towards import substitution and self-sufficiency, both nationally and as a trading bloc, remained powerful tendencies in their economic mechanisms.

Since the 1960s import substitution policies have been widely questioned. Many developing countries switched to export orientation and benefited from access to world markets and freer trade policies. However, in all twentieth-century late developers, the state has had a strategic and pervasive role in the development process. The export orientated Newly Industrializing Countries (NICs) are no exception, relying on pervasive regulation and control of labour, capital and also trade. With at least 20 per cent of OECD trade directly controlled by multinational corporations (MNCs) as intra-firm trade, freer trade

in the twentieth century is a far cry from nineteenth-century free trade of *laissez-faire*.

With a new crisis in the world economy, protectionism is again on the march. New tensions and contradictions are evident in the Western industrial countries, the existing socialist countries and the debt-ridden developing countries. Freedom of exchange, if not free trade, will be a central dimension of political and economic debate for the foreseeable future.

H. David Evans
Institute of Development Studies
University of Sussex

References
Hamilton, A. (1957), 'Encouragement of trade', and 'Encouragement of manufactures', in R. B. Morris (ed.), *Alexander Hamilton and the Founding of the Nation*, New York.
List, F. (1904), *The National System of Political Economy*, London.

Further Reading
Corden, W. M. (1974), *Trade Policy and Economic Welfare*, Oxford.
Evans, H. D. and Alizadeh, P. (1984), 'Trade, industrialisation and the visible hand', *Journal of Development Studies*, October.
Kenen, P. B. and Jones, R. W. (eds) (1984), *Handbook of International Economics*, Vol. I, Amsterdam.
Roemer, J. E. (1982), *A General Theory of Exploitation and Class*, Cambridge, Mass.
See also: *international trade*; *laissez-faire*.

Freud, Anna (1895–1982)

The youngest of Sigmund Freud's six children, Anna Freud was born in Vienna in 1895. As the only one of his children to follow her father's profession, she referred to psychoanalysis as a sibling. She was for many years her father's caretaker and confidante, and she promulgated his theories during the generation after his death. Her own work focused on child analysis and adolescence.

Beginning her career as a teacher of young children, Anna Freud presented her first paper to the Vienna Psychoanalytic Society in 1922 and joined the Society soon after. One of her first and most important works was *The Ego and the Mechanisms of Defense* (1936). In it she stressed that for psychoanalytic understanding of ego development, the defences are as important as the instincts. This insight was a major contribution not only to psychoanalytic theory, but to psychoanalytic therapy as well. She also focused on adolescence as a crucial period of ego and super-ego transformation.

Among her other notable publications are two monographs derived from her wartime experience: *Infants*

Without Families (1943) and *War and Children* (1943). These studies marked the beginning of detailed and systematic psychoanalytic observation of children and its relation to the reconstruction of childhood in the psychoanalysis of adults. *Normality and Pathology in Childhood: Assessments in Development* (1965) brought a new, developmental direction to the so-called psychoanalytic meta-psychology. *Beyond the Best Interests of the Child* (1973), written with collaborators from the Yale School of Law, was an attempt to apply psychoanalytic theories to legal policy affecting children.

Anna Freud escaped with her father to London following the Nazi occupation of Austria in 1938. There, in order to advance the study and treatment of children, she established a nursery school which evolved into the Hampstead Child Therapy Course and Clinic. Anna Freud died in London in 1982.

Leo Rangell
University of California, Los Angeles
University of California, San Francisco

Further Reading
Freud, A. (1936), *The Ego and the Mechanisms of Defense*, New York.
Freud, A. (1965), *Normality and Pathology in Childhood*, New York.
See also: *Freud, Sigmund.*

Freud, Sigmund (1856–1939)

Ernest Jones, the foremost biographer of Freud, comments that Freud gave the world an incomplete theory of mind, but a new vista on man (Jones, 1953–57). The insights Freud arrived at and shared with the world changed and developed as he expanded his knowledge and understanding of himself, pursued his clinical work with patients, and broadened his interest in the world of science and letters. The perilous times in which he lived had a profound impact on his personal and professional life.

Freud was born on 6 May 1856, in Schlossergasse, Moravia, a small town in what is now Czechoslovakia (Freud, 1959 [1925]). His parents were Jewish, and though he was an agnostic he always maintained his identity as a Jew. The family moved to Vienna when Freud was four, and he lived there until 1938, when he and his family fled the Nazis to London (Hampstead). He died a year later, on 23 September 1939.

Although the family was not well off, no pressure was put on Sigmund, the oldest child, to seek a career that would be economically advantageous. Stimulated by Darwin's theories, he saw new hopes for under-standing human nature. An essay by Goethe, 'On Nature', read at a popular lecture, sparked his interest in becoming a natural scientist and strengthened his desire to go to medical school. Freud's interests in social sciences, human interactions, developmental processes and ancient history were already evident during his childhood and youth; they were later to give richness to the discipline he founded: psychoanalysis.

At the university, he experienced serious disappointments. Yet the fact that his Jewishness made him an outsider seemed to strengthen his independence of mind. In Ernst Brücke's physiological laboratory, where he *was* allowed to work, he found role models he could respect, not only Brücke himself but his assistants, Sigmund Exner and Ernst Fleischl von Marxow. Brücke asked him to work on the histology of the nervous system, which he did before undertaking his own independent research. In 1882, when he had been at the laboratory for six years, Brücke strongly advised him, in view of his 'bad financial position', to abandon his research and theoretical career for a clinical one.

Freud entered the General Hospital in Vienna, where he pursued his neurohistological interests at the Institute of Cerebral Anatomy, published several short papers, and was encouraged by Professor Theodore Meynert to devote himself to the study of the anatomy of the brain.

In 1882 Freud's friend Josef Breuer told him about his work with a patient suffering from hysterical symptoms. After putting the patient into deep hypnosis, Breuer had asked her to tell him what was on her mind. In her awakened state she could not repeat what she had revealed under hypnosis. The major contribution of the case of Anna O. (whose real name was Bertha Pappenheim) was the discovery of a technique that was a precursor to psychoanalytic treatment – free association.

In 1885 Freud won a travelling grant and went to Paris, where he became a student at the Saltpêtrière of the eminent neurologist, Jean-Martin Charcot. Freud's interest in Breuer's work had made him eager to find out more about Charcot's studies on hysteria. Charcot demonstrated quite convincingly the genuineness of hysterical phenomena and their conformity to laws, the frequent occurrence of hysteria in men (contrary to current theories), the production of hysterical paralyses and contractures by hypnosis, and the finding that artificially induced states showed features similar to those of spontaneous attacks that were initiated traumatically. Freud determined to study neuroses in greater depth. Before returning to Vienna, he spent a few weeks in Berlin in order to gain more knowledge of childhood disorders. During the next few years he published several monographs on unilateral and bilateral cerebral palsies in children.

In 1886 he settled in Vienna as a physician, married Martha Bernays, to whom he had been engaged for several years, and became known as a specialist in nervous diseases. He reported to the Vienna Society of Medicine on his work with Charcot, an account which the medical society did not receive with favour. Some of his critics doubted that there could be hysteria in males. In response to their scepticism he found a male with a classical hysterical hemianesthesia, demonstrated it before the medical society, and was applauded – but ultimately ignored. Once again he was an outsider. He was excluded from the laboratory of cerebral anatomy, had no place to deliver his lectures, withdrew from academic life, and ceased to attend meetings of the professional societies.

Freud's therapeutic armamentarium was limited. He could use electrotherapy or hypnotism. Since it became known that the positive effects of electrotherapy were in fact the effects of suggestion, Freud turned his sole attention to hypnosis. With this shift he thus became more firmly committed to psychological rather than organic treatment. He had observed in Paris how hypnotism could produce symptoms similar to hysteria and could then remove them again. In 1889 he went to Nancy where he observed the technique developed by Liébeault and Bernheim which used suggestion, with or without hypnosis, for therapeutic purposes. As he wrote in his autobiographical study (1925), '[I] received the profoundest impression of the possibility that there could be powerful mental processes which nevertheless remained hidden from the consciousness of men.' This was one of the first statements presaging Freud's monumental discovery of the unconscious.

In the early 1890s, Freud attempted to persuade Breuer to renew his interest in the problems of hysteria and to share with the world the discoveries he had made in the case of Anna O. *Studien über Hysterie* (1895) (*Studies on Hysteria*) was the result – a collaborative effort in which Breuer and Freud presented their ideas on the origin and treatment of hysterical symptoms. Freud described the unconscious in detail and introduced two key concepts: that a symptom arises through the restraining of a conflictful affect, and that it results from the transformation of a quantum of energy which, instead of being used in other ways, was converted into the symptom. Breuer described the way in which the technique he used with Anna O. allowed for the cathartic discharge of feelings (abreaction) with symptom relief. Although subsequent clinical research has questioned the universality of the effectiveness of this technique, it was *Studies on Hysteria* that introduced psychoanalysis to the world.

Breuer ultimately left the field of psychological treatment, but Freud, undeterred by the unfavourable reception given to the *Studies* by the experts of the day, pursued his studies of patients. He discovered that what was strangulated in neurosis was not just any kind of emotional experience but those that were primarily sexual in nature. Freud then began to study the so-called neurasthenics as well as the hysterics. As a consequence of these investigations, he believed at that time that the neuroses, without exception, resulted from disturbances in sexual function.

Freud's study of Breuer's patient, Anna O., led to the discovery of the concept of 'transference', a key to clinical and applied psychoanalysis. In a patient's relationship with his analyst, Freud thought, the patient re-experiences the early emotional relations that he had with his parents. It is the analysis of this transference that becomes the most fruitful instrument of analytic treatment. As a result of his discovery of transference, Freud abandoned hypnotism and began to use other procedures that evolved into the technique used in psychoanalysis today. The patient lies on a couch with the analyst sitting behind. The patient associates freely, and the analyst listens for patterns of transference, linkages, feelings, dreams, and other products of the associative process.

Once he had abandoned the use of hypnosis, Freud came to understand that there were forces which he called resistances which kept certain patterns, linkages, and connections from awareness. An impulse barred from access to consciousness was in fact retained and pushed into the unconscious (that is, repressed), from which it was capable of re-emerging when the counter-forces were weakened or the repressed impulses strengthened. Freud considered repression a mechanism of defence, comparable to the flight mechanism used to avoid external conflict. In order to keep the debarred impulse repressed in the unconscious, the mental apparatus had to deploy 'energy'. The amount of energy available for other nonconflicted activities was thereby depleted, and as a result symptoms appeared. The theory of repression became the cornerstone of the newer understanding of the neuroses, which in turn affected the task of therapy.

Freud's early 'topographic model' of the mind separated the unconscious into the preconscious and the unconscious proper. The topographic model was later to evolve into the 'structural model' of the mind, which consisted of the id, the ego, and the ego ideal or super-ego.

As Freud investigated his patients' lives, he was struck by the significance of events that had seemingly occurred during the first years of childhood. The impressions of that early period of life, though buried in the unconscious, still played a significant role in the individual's personality and vulnerability to later emotional disturbance. Freud's assertion that sexuality is present from the beginning of life and has a subsequent course of development was a pivotal concept of psychoanalysis and one that evoked a good deal of controversy.

At the time of this discovery, Freud believed that experiences of sexual seduction in childhood were universally the basis of neurosis. The evidence for this was derived from his clinical work. Subsequently, however, he came to realize that the seductions had not actually taken place but were fantasies. That such wishful fantasies were of even greater importance than actual external reality, however, was one of Freud's most significant discoveries.

Freud's ideas of infantile and childhood sexuality became the basis of his developmental theory of sexual progression. Initially, he believed that sexuality is connected with what he called 'component instincts', i. e., instincts which are connected with erotogenic zones of the body but which have an independent wish for pleasure. These are usually connected with the vital biological activities necessary for survival. For example, oral activities involve sucking and feeding as well as oral pleasures; anal activities involve excretion as well as anal pleasures; and genital pleasures are related to reproduction and conception. Freud called the energy of sexual instincts libido. In the course of psychosexual development, fixations of libido may occur at various points which may be returned to when later threats force a withdrawal to an earlier level. Freud called this process 'regression'. Freud also noted in *An Autobiographical Study* (1925) that, 'The point of fixation is what determines the *choice of neurosis*, that is, the form in which the subsequent illness makes its appearance.'

The first object of libidinal gratification and fulfilment is the mother. Her breasts serve as the source of oral pleasure, and she takes on the significance of the external source from which later confidence, self-esteem, and self-regulation are derived. This relationship with the mother plays a pivotal role in a developmental stage that Freud named the Oedipus complex, after the famous Greek tragic hero. Using the male child as an illustration, and reducing this developmental stage to a simple formulation that did not take into account variations, complexities and consequences, Freud noted that boys focus their sexual wishes upon their mothers and become hostile to and rivalrous with their fathers. This incestuous object choice and its feared and fantasied consequences of genital damage and retaliation give rise to a stage of latency during which the conscience (super-ego) becomes evident through feelings of morality, shame and disgust. At puberty, the earlier conflicts, including the Oedipus complex, may become reanimated. Although Freud's discoveries of the sexuality of children were made from the psychoanalyses of adults, direct observation of children as well as the analyses of children and adolescents have confirmed, extended, detailed and modified his ideas.

Freud also made a major contribution to the study of dreams – their meaning and their use in the therapeutic situation. In one of his major works, *Die Traumdeutung* (1900) (*The Interpretation of Dreams*, 1913), Freud described his researches on dreams, dream work and formation, symbolism, and his wish-fulfilment theory of the function of dreams.

In *Zur Psychopathologie des Alltagslebens* (1904) (*The Psychopathology of Everyday Life*), Freud turned his attention to slips and lapses of memory. Such symptomatic acts, so common in everyday life, he believed, have meaning, can be explained and interpreted, and indicate the presence of conflicting impulses and intentions. The study of dreams and of symptomatic acts has applicability to both pathological situations and normal healthy mental functioning.

For ten years after he and Breuer parted (1895–96 through 1906–7) Freud worked in isolation, rejected by the German-Austrian establishment. In 1900–1902, however, Bleuler and Jung, working at the Burghölzli, a large hospital near Zurich, became interested in psychoanalysis and began to extend the application of Freudian theories beyond the confines of upper-middle-class Vienna.

In 1909, Freud, Jung, and Sandor Ferenczi, a member of Freud's circle in Vienna, gave lectures at Clark University in Worcester, Massachusetts. James J. Putnam, a neurologist at Harvard, and William James were among those present. The trip was a success, and marked the beginning of international recognition. In 1910 the International Psycho-Analytic Association was founded, an organization that still exists. Several journals, institutes, and societies were organized in Vienna, Berlin, Moscow, New York, Zurich and London.

Although many of the earlier pioneers remained loyal to Freud and to psychoanalysis, some of his followers ultimately left him to found their own movements (for example, Adler, Jung, Reich, Rank, and Stekel).

Freud's research continued at an intense pace, but gradually his students and colleagues took over increasingly from him. In 1923 he became ill with a malignancy of the jaw which was to give him pain and anguish for the rest of his life. His contributions to our understanding of art and artists, literature and writers, jokes, the psychology of religion, anthropology, myths and fairy tales, rituals, the emotional aspects of group psychology, philosophy, education, child care and rearing, and the question of educating nonphysicians to be psychoanalysts were some of the by-products of his lifelong struggle to penetrate the science of the mind.

Freud was a brilliant and a learned man, a researcher, clinician, theoretician, and writer. Psychoanalysis allowed us to understand what previously was seen as irrational human behaviour from a new perspective. His contributions to psychiatry, psychology, sociology, and biology are monumental. The science of psychoanalysis has moved on since Freud's time, correcting some of his errors and expanding into areas that he did not develop. One can only do so much in a lifetime, and Freud gave us so much that it will be many lifetimes before we have fully understood him.

George H. Pollock
Institute for Psychoanalysis, Chicago

References
Freud, S. (1953–74), *Standard Edition of the Complete Psychological Works of Sigmund Freud*, 24 vols, ed. J. Strachey, London.
Included are: Vol. XX: *An Autobiographical Study, Inhibitions, Symptoms, Anxiety, Lay Analysis and Other Works* (1925–6).
Vol. II: *Studies on Hysteria* (1893–5) (with J. Breuer).
Vol. IV and V: *The Interpretation of Dreams* (I) and (II) (1900–1).
Vol. VI: *The Psychopathology of Everyday Life* (1901).
Jones, E. (1953–7), *The Life and Work of Sigmund Freud*, 3 vols, London.

Further Reading
Schur, M. (1972), *Freud: Living and Dying*, London.
Sulloway, F. J. (1979), *Freud: Biologist of the Mind*, New York.
Wollheim, R. (1971), *Sigmund Freud*, London.
See also: *psychoanalysis*.

Friedman, Milton (1912–)

Since 1950, Milton Friedman has been a leader of international monetarism, methodological positivism, and traditional liberalism, as well as of the so-called 'Chicago School' which embodies these ideas. He was Nobel Laureate in 1976; his presidencies include the American Economic Association and the Mont Pelerin Society. His best-known book among the general public remains probably *Capitalism and Freedom* (1962), followed by selections from his *Essays in Positive Economics* (1953) and his *Monetary History of the United States* (1963, with Anna J. Schwartz).

Born in New Jersey of immigrant parents, Friedman was trained almost simultaneously in mathematics, economics, and statistics (AB Rutgers University, MA University of Chicago, Ph.D. Columbia University). He was initially known primarily as a mathematical statistician specializing in decision theory. His broader interests in economic theory, history, and methodology became apparent in university teaching at the Universities of Wisconsin (1949–50), Minnesota (1945–7) and Chicago (1947–77), and dominate his later work. Since his retirement from Chicago, Friedman has been affiliated with the Hoover Institute on the Stanford University campus in California.

Friedman the methodologist believes that the widely ridiculed differences of opinion and advice among economists relate primarily to questions of *what is* (positive economics) rather than of what *should be* (normative economics), and that once the 'positive' questions are satisfactorily answered the 'normative' ones will be manageable. Friedman maintains that questions in positive economics can in principle be answered at least tentatively by comparing (evaluating) the quantitative predictions, which themselves result from alternative, 'models' of how the world – or the economy – works. It makes no difference to him whether the basic assumptions underlying these models are or are not themselves intuitively realistic; also, any 'general case' theory, into which wide ranges of alternative results fit equally well as 'special cases', is untestable and thus of little value.

Friedman's monetarism and his 'modernized' quantity theory of money illustrate his methodological position. He interprets the quantity theory as a theory of nominal income, and as maintaining only that the quantity of money in a country (however defined) is a more accurate determinant of both the levels and changes of that country's nominal income than is the country's 'autonomous' expenditures, in the sense of Keynesian theory. As for the division of nominal-income effects between real income and the price level, and, also, as for the precise structure relating money and income, the quantity theory (in Friedman's version) has little to say. We should also note that Friedman has favoured exchange-rate flexibility, whereas most 'international monetarists' prefer a fixed-rate system.

In their *Monetary History of the United States* and related works, Friedman and Schwartz apply their monetary insights to the period since the American Civil War, tracing changes in both price levels and business activity to monetary uncertainties – fluctuations of monetary growth above and below any smooth relationship with the long-term growth rate of the real economy. It contains two disconcerting results: (1) The inauguration of the Federal Reserve System in 1914 seems to have made things worse rather than better than they were previously – Friedman favours 'rules', including the pre-1914 gold standard, over 'authorities', like the Federal Reserve Board, as regulators of the money supply. (2) The main explanation for the depth and the persistence of the Great Depression of the 1930s is a series of errors in Federal Reserve policy, whose fears of 'going off gold' permitted the American money supply to fall by approximately one-third over the 3-year period following the stock-market collapse of October 1929, without preventing America's departure from the gold standard.

Friedman's overall liberal faith in the market as an economic regulator is a matter of 'second best' and does not regard market determinations as utopian. This liberalism arises primarily from Friedman's understanding and interpretation of the record of intervention, extending even to attempts like the American

Anti-Trust Laws at enforcement of closer approaches to 'pure and perfect competition' upon an imperfectly competitive market-place. Friedman's negative judgement embraces both the errors of well-intentioned voting majorities and of well-intentioned intellectual meritocrats, along with the errors of tyrants, dictators, and despots. A secondary Friedman argument for the market is the shelter its anonymity offers to social, religious, racial, and ideological minorities doomed to failure so long as success requires employment of licensure by the majority or by the Establishment. At the same time, Friedman's liberal individualism does not go so far as the 'libertarianism' of some other American writers for whom the State is illegitimate and taxation, in particular, is robbery. Friedman's major concession to the contemporary (twentieth-century) concept or distortion of liberalism has been his advocacy of a minimum income below which individuals and families should not be required to fall, but which should replace the myriad of social services programmes embodied in the contemporary 'Welfare State'.

Martin Bronfenbrenner
Duke University

Further Reading
Breit, W. and Ransom, R. (1982), *The Academic Scribblers*, rev. edn, Chicago.
Thygessen, N. (1975), 'The scientific contributions of Milton Friedman', *Scandinavian Journal of Economics*.
Tobin, J. (1972), 'Friedman's theoretical framework', *Journal of Political Economy*, 80.
See also: *Chicago School of economics; monetarism.*

Friendship

The term friend appears to be applied very loosely by most Americans. In a survey of a random sample of 1,050 residents of Northern California, the average respondent called 11 people 'friend' – comprising fully 83 per cent of his associates who were not relatives. Many more people were called 'friends' than were called 'close' (an average of 7 people and 25 per cent of non-kin associates were 'close') (Fischer, 1982). Rather than denoting any special intimacy or camaraderie, friend often seems to be a catch-all category for a wide range of associates.

Although I know of no directly comparable data for Europeans, the impression persists that Americans tend to have superficial friendships with many people, while Europeans tend to have deeper friendships with fewer people (see Lewin, 1948). In non-Western cultures, friendship sometimes takes on special meanings, such as the obligations of blood brotherhood (Brain, 1976).

People's conceptions of friendship change as they move through the years of childhood. Robert Selman (1980) finds that preschool children (from about age 3 to 5) characteristically view friends as 'momentary playmates' – whoever one is playing with at a particular time. When asked what sorts of people make good friends, the preschool child is likely to provide such answers as 'Someone who plays a lot' or 'Someone who lives in Watertown'. By the age of 11 or 12, the child comes to view close friendships as involving 'intimate and mutual sharing'. The actual conduct of children's friendships does not necessarily correspond to these developing conceptions, however. Preschool children often have unique and enduring friendships, even if they explain them only in terms of momentary interaction (Rubin, 1980). And older children – like adults – may have friends who are hardly more than temporary acitivity partners.

Friend is not only a category of relation but also a label that people apply at particular times for particular reasons. Children often employ the label of friend as part of a strategy to gain entry into a group or activity ('We're friends, right?') (Corsaro, 1979). Similarly, adults may refer to a certain acquaintance as a friend when they are concerned with getting something from him ('I'll call my friend at the Ford Foundation'). David Jacobson (1975) observed that in a sample of unemployed engineers, the label of friend was applied to those associates who helped the men find jobs and was withheld from those who did not provide such help. (The latter sort are sometimes termed 'fair-weather friends'.) Distinctions are also made between different sorts of friends – for example, 'best friends', 'old friends', and 'just friends' – and people sometimes reclassify their associates from one category to another.

The ambiguity of friendship has not deterred social scientists in recent years from launching many investigations of its antecedents, correlates, and consequences. Many of these studies are motivated by the current interest in people's network of social support, as important props for mental and physical health. In this connection, many questions about friendship are being asked: Are close friends essential to people's health or happiness? How do men's and women's friendships differ? How does marriage affect a person's friendships? How do friendships develop and change through the span of life?

For all of these general questions, which may in some cases be susceptible to general answers, it must also be acknowledged that friendships are highly individual matters. Friendships tend to be less encumbered by specific social expectations than are other social relationships (such as parent-child, marital, or work relationships) (see Suttles, 1970). Thus, the most revealing descriptions of friendship have come less often from social scientists than from novelists, biographers, and journalists (for example, Michaelis, 1983) who have portrayed individual friendships in all their uniqueness and idiosyncrasy.

Zick Rubin
Brandeis University

References
Brain, R. (1976), *Friends and Lovers*, New York.
Corsaro, W. A. (1979), '"We're friends, right?":
  Children's use of access rituals in nursery school',
  Language in Society, 8.
Fischer, C. S. (1982), 'What do we mean by friend?',
  Social Network, 3.
Jacobson, D. (1976), 'Fair-weather friend: label and
  context in middle-class friendships', *Journal of
  Anthropological Research*, 31.
Lewin, K. (1948), 'Some social-psychological
  differences between the U. S. and Germany', in
  K. Lewin, *Resolving Social Conflicts*, New York.
Michaelis, D. (1983), *The Best of Friends*, New York.
Rubin, Z. (1980), *Children's Friendships*, Cambridge,
  Mass.
Selman, R. L. (1980), *The Growth of Interpersonal
  Understanding: Developmental and Clinical Analyses*,
  New York.
Suttles, G. D. (1970), 'Friendship as a social
  institution', in G. J. McCall *et al.* (eds), *Social
  Relationships*, Chicago.

Further Reading
Brenton, M. (1974), *Friendship*, New York.

Frisch, Ragnar (1895–1973)

Ragnar Frisch, the Norwegian economist and Nobel Laureate, was one of the leaders of the strong 'mathematization' of economics that took place during the 1930s and 1940s. The son of a jeweller, Frisch himself completed his apprenticeship as a jeweller in the same year as he was awarded the degree in economics in Oslo in 1919. He received his Norwegian doctorate in 1926 for a study in mathematical statistics, but had been educated mainly in France. He was appointed full professor at the University of Oslo in 1931.

Frisch's scientific contributions extended to most fields of economics, but a few basic ideas run through most of his work. He strongly believed that economic theory should be formulated mathematically, and that economics should become a quantitative science using measurable concepts only. How these ideals were reflected in Frisch's own work may be illustrated by his contributions to demand theory. In 'Sur une problème d'économie pure' (1926), Frisch constructed an axiom system from which the existence of a (cardinal) utility function was derived – probably the first of its kind in economics. On this basis he derived testable implications for consumer behaviour that he explored in greater detail in *New Methods of Measuring Marginal Utility* (1932). Here Frisch demonstrated that utility theory did not have to remain at the speculative level. Finally, in 'A complete scheme for computing all direct and cross demand elasticities in a model with many sectors' (1959) he showed how utility theory might be helpful in the construction of empirical demand functions for planning purposes. Other fields where Frisch's contributions have been of particular importance are mathematical theory of production, economics of planning, and econometric methodology. In the last field one should mention his confluence analysis ('error in variables' approach) and his study of identification and multicollinearity problems. With the exception of the studies in the economics of planning, his major contributions were made in the 1920s and 1930s.

Together with Jan Tinbergen, Frisch was awarded the first Nobel Prize in Economics in 1969. His contribution to economic dynamics was emphasized, and, in this field, his 'Propagation problems and impulse problems in dynamic economics' (1933) was very important. In addition, he showed how macroeconomic ideas could be formulated mathematically and how stochastic assumptions should be fed into the models. The last development was extremely important for making models testable.

Aside from his own scientific contributions, Frisch influenced the direction of economic research through talks, discussions and organizational activities. He was a member of the small group that founded the Econometric Society in 1930, and edited *Econometrica* from its start in 1933 until 1955.

Jens Chr. Andvig
Norwegian Institute of International Affairs

Further Reading
Arrow, K. J. (1960), 'The work of Ragnar Frisch,
  econometrician', *Econometrica*. 28.
Johansen, L. (1969), 'Ragnar Frisch's contributions
  to economics', *The Swedish Journal of Economics*,
  LXXI.

Functional Analysis

The terms functional analysis and functionalism are often equated, yet to equate them is to beg a number of questions, is misleading and perhaps even mistaken.

Functionalism is a doctrine which asserts that the principal task of sociology and social anthropology is to examine the contribution which social items make to the social and cultural life of human collectivities; it may additionally assert that to examine social phenomena in this way is to explain why those items occur at all, and/or why they have persisted.

Functional analysis is a method of sociological or anthropological enquiry which consists in examining social and cultural items by locating them in a wider context. This usually means showing how these items affect and are affected by others with which they coexist over time.

From these descriptions it is clear why the doctrine is named functionalism: it claims that cultural phenomena either have uses, and otherwise would not endure, or that they come into being, and then persist, because they are useful. But it is not initially clear why a method of examining cultural phenomena within the context of other such items should be called functional, in the sense of 'useful'. The most obvious reason is that functional analysis has been seen as so necessary to functionalism that the two have been treated almost as one. To explain the function(s) of a social item does itself require locating it within the context of a wider system or subsystem. For example, in order to show that the function of kinship terminology is to express the shared recognition of a set of kinship categories, which are necessary to sustain rules of co-operation, alliance, marital eligibility, succession, inheritance, and so on, one has to examine kinship terms of reference and address in the contexts of rules governing different degrees and directions of kinship interaction. So much is obvious. What is not at all obvious is that the practice of functional analysis also presupposes that the doctrine of functionalism is true: in short, from the decision to locate the use of kinship terminology within the context of its various uses, it does not follow that that terminology owes its existence to those uses; it might be equally plausible to argue that the usages are consequent upon linguistic rules.

Here we encounter a second article of faith endorsed, unquestioningly in some cases, by earlier functionalist anthropologists: that, in the absence of written histories, or other reliable clues to the past, one must assume that some features of the here-and-now must be taken as given and as accounting for others; and that both sets of features are readily identifiable. For example, it would be assumed that the level of technology, the system of ordering economic and political relations through kinship, and the form of that kinship system could be taken as given, and that certain other practices, such as linguistic and ritual norms (symbolic representations) could be explained as functioning to maintain those given features of social and cultural life.

Furthermore, it seems also to have been assumed that the effectiveness of the method of functional analysis attested to the strength of the theory, and that the theory justified the method.

Whether or not the theory could have justified the method, what did justify it were two sets of circumstances in which ethnographers of preliterate societies worked: (1) They dealt with societies with no written records and, it was often believed, with no other clear evidence which could illuminate the past and, consequently, the processes whereby the societies' existing features could have developed. Thus is seemed that all that ethnographers could do well was to examine certain existing practices and beliefs in their context, so as to make sense of them in comparison with the practices and beliefs of the societies in which ethnographic reports would be read. (2) They dealt with societies which, unlike their own, were relatively simple and slow-changing and, therefore, in which there appeared to be a high degree of interdependence of the different features of social and cultural life (Cohen, 1968).

To qualify the first point: the absence of evidence for recounting reliable histories of certain societies had not inhibited the anthropological precursors of functionalists from constructing histories that were informed either by the theory of evolutionary parallelism or by that of diffusionism. Functionalism and functional analysis emerged in reaction to these so-called histories. And, given the reaction against these seemingly untestable theories of pseudo-history and, moreover, their distracting effect on the examination of the here-and-now, it is likely that the commitment to functionalist doctrine was regarded not only as a necessary justification of the method, but as a rationalized refutation of the two doctrines of 'conjectural' history.

To qualify the second point, it should not be thought that functionalists explicitly acknowledged the greater interdependence of different features of social life to be found in the technologically simpler and smaller-scale societies. Rather, it can be said that the significant degree of functional autonomy possessed by different features of social life in most complex societies is expressed in a language which treats different areas of social and cultural activity as separable, even when they are not altogether separate. This language, fashioned not for self-conscious social scientific discourse, but, rather, for everyday use, was imposed on societies within which such categories were for the most part foreign. Thus, certain activities were separated out by the use of the ethnographers' taken-for-granted language and then shown to be more or less strongly interrelated. But few, if any, such ethnographers recognized that the degree of interconnectedness which constitutes a social and cultural system might itself vary from one such system to another. Moreover, some interpretations of the method encouraged an undue emphasis on the degree and nature of the interconnectedness of social and cultural phenomena in even the simplest societies, and, also, promoted an even greater error in the excessive search for it in more complex societies.

The almost casual equation of method and doctrine by some social anthropologists was highly misleading: the doctrine that functional analysis could also yield explanations of the existence of social and cultural phenomena was in many instances not even demonstrated, and was, in any case, at worst erroneous and at best confusing.

But what use of functional analysis of the here-and-now has ever explained why the Bemba are matrilineal, why the Tallensi have no centralized political authority, why the Nuer have a form of monotheism, or why some Australian aboriginal societies have moeities and others, in almost the same physical environment, do not? While a functional analysis of Nuer feuds might be thought to account for their forms by showing how these forms serve to maintain particular patterns of kin-based alignments, it could hardly account for the segmentary structure of that society. Of course, if one knows that the Nuer have a particular type of segmentary structure, characterized by particular processes of alignment and division, that knowledge might help explain why, if certain other conditions remain constant, that structure tends to perpetuate and to resist transformation into a more centralized type of society. Such an explanation of social reproduction – which could be called an equilibrium analysis, since it shows that the processes which inhere in this type of structure are self-correcting with regard to the non-centralization of power – does not itself rest on any part of the functionalist doctrine.

As philosophical critics, followed in turn by social scientists, have long shown, those explanations of social phenomena which are truly and simply functionalist are seriously flawed: they are teleological in that they account for items by examining their positive consequences in maintaining a wider system of which they are a part; and they reify such systems by treating them as though they were either mechanical or organic wholes (Nagel, 1956).

The only reply to such critics is to argue that functional analysis may demonstrate a continuous, circular flow of causes and effects – that is, of so-called feedback processes – which show how a system persists, and therefore explains why particular items are to be found at a particular time and place. But even if this can be done convincingly – and it requires empirical confirmation, not simply an intuitive judgement that coexisting phenomena must interrelate in this self-maintaining way – it hardly attests to the value of a functionalist doctrine. Rather, it illustrates the point that social and cultural persistence may in some cases be explained in terms of 'systemic feedback' or, if one prefers, in terms of benign chains of cause and effect which are at some points recursive.

But, of course, the outcome of such causal chains may not be benign, at least to some sections of a society. For example, the educational systems of (most) industrial societies favour the children of the advantaged, whose environments not only facilitate educational performance but may also strengthen and channel motivations to succeed in it. But, since structured inequalities of performance contradict the principle of equality of opportunity, it could be argued that while the system 'functions' for the advantaged it does not do so for the disadvantaged and, especially, not where the latter are aware of the discrepancy between principle and reality. However, ardent functionalists might show that the system works effectively at creating only a low level of motivation among those who are least likely to succeed and, thus, in this way *does* function to maintain both itself and a degree of wider social stability. On the other hand, it could be said that the symbols of alienation with which the disadvantaged young adorn themselves signify an ill-contained and, perhaps, ill-defined discontent which they occasionally express in more overt fashion. But then one could also argue that those expressive symbols also serve the wider system; and so on (Merton, 1949).

But what of those situations in which the working of the system benefits no one? In some circumstances of low, or even zero, economic growth, the institutionalized forms of conflict over income levels and differentials could become so intensified as to contribute to a negative growth rate and to an uneven but overall fall in real incomes. One could argue even here that the seeming dysfunctions of the systems are, after all, functional for it: since the contending parties cannot unite to change a system which no one wants in its existing form, their inactions contribute to its persistence.

What such an example demonstrates is that the term functional, meaning 'useful', pertains only to those circumstances in which the gratification of the conscious or unconscious motives of social actors is (intentionally or unintentionally) facilitated by certain enduring practices, which sustain those motives, and which in turn contribute to the continuation of the practices themselves. No other use of the term can be permitted. Certainly, to refer to social practices as functioning to maintain a system, regardless of whether any groups or collectivities have an interest in maintaining it, is either to state the obvious – that a system persists – or it is to beg the very question that needs to be answered. And if the answer is negative, then either the use of the term function creates a self-contradiction or it is meretriciously redundant.

What has been called functional analysis should, in fact, be seen as a particular form of the systems approach in the social sciences. To state that there is a system is to imply that discernibly separable processes interact so as to endure in this state over a period of time. To enquire as to why particular features of that system persist is to locate those features in the wider system. To establish that some social practice, which is part of a system, gratifies the motives of some social members, is to ascribe a function to that practice.

Percy S. Cohen
London School of Economics and Political Science

References
Cohen, P. S. (1968), *Modern Social Theory*, London.
Merton, R. K. (1949), 'Manifest and latent functions', in *Social Theory and Social Structure*, Glencoe, Ill.
Nagel, E. (1956), 'A formalization of functionalism', in *Logic Without Metaphysics*, Glencoe, Ill.

Further Reading
Davis, K. (1959), 'The myth of functional analysis as a special method in sociology and anthropology', *American Sociological Review*, 24.
See also: *Malinowski; Merton; Radcliffe-Brown; social structure.*

Futurology

Futurology is not so much a social science as a social movement that sprang up in Europe and North America in the late 1950s and has since spread throughout the world. Its pretensions are scientific: to predict future developments in society by an intensive study of past and present trends. In this it follows the lead given by the first systematic futurological exercise, H. G. Wells's *Anticipations* (1901). From Wells, too, it takes its strongly technological bias, as reflected in the *chef d'oeuvre* of the movement, Herman Kahn and Anthony Wiener's *The Year 2000* (1967) and *The United Kingdom in 1980* (1974). But beyond this general orientation there is no agreement on scientific method, as revealed by the variety of techniques practised by its numerous acolytes. These range from imaginative, one-off shots, like Michael Young's satirical *The Rise of the Meritocracy* (1958) and Dennis Gabor's *Inventing the Future* (1963), through the civilized speculations of Bertrand de Jouvenel's *The Art of Conjecture* (1967), to the solemn computer-based team reports such as the EEC's *Europe 2000* projections, and the Club of Rome's *The Limits to Growth* (1972). A notable contribution from Eastern Europe in the latter vein is the report of Radovin Richta's Czech team, *Civilization at the Crossroads* (1967). Somewhere in the middle come the projections and speculations of experts working from their home disciplinary bases, as in the collections edited by Daniel Bell, *Towards the Year 2000* (1968), and Robert Jungk and Johan Galtung, *Mankind 2000* (1969). The centrality of technology in futurological thinking is underlined by the movement's frequent reference to Erich Jantsch's *Technological Forecasting in Perspective* (1967), which is for many the Old Testament, if not the Bible, of futurology. Other popular techniques include a kind of team game known as 'Delphi' forecasting, where experts revise their initial forecasts in the light of forecasts by other members of the team. The results are understandably not usually very exciting.

Most products of futurology, again following Wells, breathe a spirit of confidence, not to say complacency. They look forward to a 'post-industrial society' or even a 'super-industrial society', where the fruits of applied science have produced an era of leisure and abundance. The basic expectation seems to be that the future will be the present writ large. Some form of extrapolation is the method common to most futurologists, and given that the movement received its main impetus in the prosperous years of the 1960s, it is hardly surprising that the future appears largely as a bigger and better version of the 1960s, above all in the technological sphere. Differences of ideology and values are played down, in the belief that the technological imperative largely commands social systems. Here futurology shows its kinship with certain kinds of science fiction and utopianism; but an added and somewhat spurious dimension of serious science is given by the team and 'think-tank' basis of much of its activities. This has made it attractive to governments, the more especially as it appears to offer the materials for long-range planning, and also because much of the thinking has been about 'the unthinkable', namely the prospect and possibility of nuclear war. Large private corporations have shown interest for the same reasons, and some, such as Shell, Unilever, and Xerox have themselves gone in for large-scale exercises in futurology.

In the wake of the oil crisis of 1973, and the world recession of the later 1970s, something of the gloss has gone off futurological speculation. There has been greater readiness to include the thinking of 'alternative' and radical futurologists, especially those of an ecological persuasion. Groups such as Friends of the Earth, and magazines like *The Ecologist*, can see many of their ideas taken up in mainstream futurological journals such as *Futures* and *The Futurist*. In addition to the physical limits to growth indicated by the Club of Rome report, there has been a new awareness of the 'social limits to growth', as persuasively discussed in Fred Hirsch's book of that name (1977). The world no longer seems quite so amenable to Western patterns of development, nor indeed so open to Western or Soviet penetration. Fears about nuclear war have revived. The rosy glow that hovered over the millennial year 2000 now carries a more apocalyptic connotation. Futurology has not given up all the hopes implicit in its supposedly neutral scientific enterprise; but it has come to balance these with a greater realization of the limited historical and cultural context that inspired it in the heady days of the 1960s.

Krishan Kumar
University of Kent

Further Reading
Clarke, I. F. (1979), *The Pattern of Expectation 1644–2001*, New York.
Toffler, A. (1970), *Future Shock*, New York.
See also: *planning, economic; post-industrial society; prediction and forecasting; Utopianism.*

G

Galbraith, John Kenneth (1908–)

Galbraith, as a student first of agricultural science (in his native Ontario) and then of agricultural economics (at Berkeley), was struck by the apparent failure of the market mechanism to correct the large-scale unemployment of the 1930s, and was impressed by the success of the New Deal. In the Second World War he was in charge of price controls for the whole of the United States, an experience which deepened his confidence in the interventionist State.

It was not until 1952, when he was 44, that Galbraith wrote the first of the multidisciplinary social science bestsellers which have made him the most famous political economist of his generation. In that book, *American Capitalism*, he accepted (following Schumpeter and not the textbook approach of Marshallian perfect competition) that power does arise in the economy, but maintained that fortunately it develops in pairs – as where a large union and/or a large retailing chain countervails and neutralizes the power of a large corporation. This was followed, in 1958, by *The Affluent Society*, with its diagnosis of 'private affluence, public poverty', and its warnings against manipulative advertising and the underprovision of public goods.

The New Industrial State in 1968, delayed by a two-year spell as American Ambassador to India under President Kennedy (a close friend), provides Galbraith's most ambitious synthesis. It describes how the 'technostructure' will eventually be brought to heel by the intelligentsia. (They are a group of highly-trained experts working together in committees in pursuit of organizational goals such as security and growth and utilizing techniques such as defence contracts with fellow bureaucrats in defence ministries – a phenomenon he calls 'bureaucratic symbiosis' in *Economics and the Public Purpose*, 1973). His view of the ideal future society is somewhat vague but obviously includes, alongside the Welfare State, Keynesian demand management techniques and environmental planning, a liberal use of wage and price controls and some nationalization (especially of defence contractors).

Galbraith is a prolific, if also occasionally a repetitive, writer whose books cover many subjects, even including Indian art. He spent virtually the whole of his professional career at Harvard University, and retired in 1975.

D. A. Reisman
University of Surrey

Further Reading
Hession, C. H. (1972), *John Kenneth Galbraith and his Critics*, New York.
Reisman, D. A. (1980), *Galbraith and Market Capitalism*, London.

Games

See Play, Sport, Sociology of.

Game Theory

The theory of games is a branch of mathematics devoted to the study of interdependent decision making. It applies to any social situation in which: (1) there are two or more decision makers, called *players*, each with a choice of two or more courses of action, called *strategies*; (2) the outcome depends on the strategy choices of all the players; and (3) each player has well-defined preferences among the possible outcomes, so that numerical payoffs reflecting these preferences can be assigned. Games such as chess and poker, together with many social, economic, political and military conflicts which are not commonly thought of as games, possess these properties and are therefore amenable in principle to game theory analysis. The primary goal of the theory is to determine, through formal reasoning alone, what strategies the players ought to choose in order to pursue their interests rationally, and what outcomes will result if they do so.

Although some progress was made by Zermelo in 1912, and by Borel during the early 1920s, the theory was not firmly established until John von Neumann proved the fundamental minimax theorem in 1928. This theorem applies to two-person, strictly competitive (zero-sum) games, in which one player's payoffs are simply the negatives of the other player's. If the number of strategies is finite, and the players are permitted to use randomizing devices to 'choose' weighted averages of their strategies, then each player can adopt a strategy that yields the best payoff given the most damaging counter-strategies available to the adversary. The minimax theorem asserts that these payoffs are equal, and that every game of this type therefore has a well-defined solution.

Applications of game theory in the social sciences have focused chiefly on non-zero-sum games. A famous example is the two-person *Prisoner's Dilemma*, identified in 1951 by Merrill Flood and later explicitly formulated and named by Albert W. Tucker. This game has the paradoxical property that whereas each player has a *dominant* strategy that yields the best payoff against both of the opponent's available counter-strategies, each player obtains a better payoff if both choose *dominated* strategies. A multi-person generalization of this, the *N-Person Prisoner's Dilemma*, was discovered in the early 1970s; in this game, every player is better off if all choose dominated strategies than if all choose dominant strategies. The N-Person Prisoner's Dilemma is a model of many familiar social problems, including resource conservation, wage inflation, environmental pollution, and arms races.

Experimental games have been used by psychologists to study co-operation and competition in two-person and multi-person groups, and economists have applied game theory to the study of bargaining and collective choice. In political science and sociology, game theory has been used to analyse voting behaviour and coalition formation, and numerous other applications of the theory in social anthropology and other fields have been attempted. During the 1970s, applications of the theory to the study of the evolution of social behaviour began to flourish in sociobiology.

Andrew M. Colman
University of Leicester

Further Reading

Colman, A. M. (1982), *Game Theory and Experimental Games: The Study of Strategic Interaction*, Oxford.
Von Neumann, J. and Morgenstern, O. (1953), *Theory of Games and Economic Behavior*, 3rd edn, Princeton.
See also: *game theory; economic applications; Von Neumann*.

Game Theory, Economic Applications

The popularity of game theory has varied considerably since its introduction into economics by J. von Neumann and O. Morgenstern in their 1944 classic *The Theory of Games and Economic Behavior*. Game theory is an attempt to analyse rational strategic behaviour in situations of uncertainty. The initial applications of the theory were to oligopoly theory, and in the 1950s this strand of development seemed to come to an end. After a lull game theory was applied to general equilibrium theory and has given some fruitful insights into the structure of competitive equilibria through concepts such as 'the core'. Game theorists were able to show that competitive equilibrium was only possible if rational agents could not form blocking coalitions to improve their own position at the expense of the non-coalition actors in the situation. Recently there has been a new wave of interest in game theory. This has

had three dimensions, all associated with attempts to analyse economic and social institutions. The three areas are: (1) the analysis of markets and monetary institutions; (2) the analysis of planning processes; and (3) in the area of social choice and welfare economics. Game theory has been used for both analytical and normative problems in all these areas.

One major advance has been the introduction of the concept of incentive compatibility as a constraint on action. The idea is simple: any agent, when designing his strategy, should take account of the fact that the other players will only act in their own best interests. If a player wants others to act, then he should only undertake actions that give others incentives to comply. This analytical concept has been extremely useful in aiding our understanding of bargaining and contracting in labour markets in franchising contracts, and in the analysis of the impact of taxes. It is not so much a new behavioural concept as a recognition of the obvious constraints a rational actor will face. A related set of ideas has been used in the public-choice literature where researchers have been trying to design games where individuals will reveal their true preferences. These ideas have been particularly useful in looking at feasible public utility pricing schemes and in looking at the properties of voting schemes.

Some recent developments in the theory of games have aided our understanding of the market process. The concept of a game can be applied to a process that repeats itself over time. For instance the problem of oligopolistic pricing can be seen as a repeated game problem. Standard tools can be applied, and it has been discovered that if the length of the game is finite, then in the last period the analysis to apply is that of the one-period game. But if this is known in the period before last, then the same applies to the period before last (this is sometimes known as the chainstore paradox). If one period analysis applies, then the development of 'reputation' and 'reliability' are not possible. It is possible to analyse these concepts in the concept of an infinite (or never-ending) game, where reputation effects change solutions. These concepts have usefully been adopted in the analysis of monetary institutions, in the study of oligopoly, and, most recently, in the analysis of general economic equilibrium.

Often in game theory the results are much less impressive than the techniques used, and new concepts, such as discounted games, are often more useful for telling us where the blind alleys are rather than where they are not. Despite this, clear advances have recently been made in the application of game theory based on agents whose expectations are in some sense 'rational' (in perfect equilibrium games) and whose actions are incentive compatible. After several false starts game theory now appears to be an indispensable part of the economists tool-kit. An excellent recent survey may be found in *The Journal of Economic*

Literature, June 1981, by A. Schotter and G. Schwodjauer.

Ray Barrell
University of Southampton

Gangs

The term gang is at once commonplace and controversial. It is necessary to distinguish gangs and subcultures, on the one hand, and gangs and youth groups, on the other. Reduced to the simplest terms, (youth) gangs are *non-adult sponsored adolescent groups*, that is, groups whose members meet together somewhat regularly, and over time, on the basis of *self-defined* criteria of membership and with some sense of territoriality (Miller, 1974). It is improper to include *behaviour* in defining gangs, for that is often what we wish to explain or understand. Similarly, organizational characteristics do not define gangs, for these vary among gangs as among other youth groups.

Territoriality is important in defining gangs and in explaining differences between gangs, as well as other youth collectivities. Identification with a 'hanging' or 'ranging' *area* typifies gangs, while adult-sponsored groups typically identify with an institution, such as a school, church, or agency. In any case, the adult world context is important. In Northern Ireland, for example, the Catholic-Protestant conflict has intruded on the traditional, territorially-based identity of some youth gangs.

Subcultures are shared systems of values, artifacts, and reference, among individuals and groups. The existence of a local gang culture is indicated, for example, when younger boys (and girls) aspire to become members of a local gang. In general, however, age grading is not so rigid – nor are age distinctions so fine – among gangs as among other youth groups, especially those that are adult-sponsored. When rivalries develop between gangs, the subculture may take on a *conflict* character with implications for gang organization (roles, performance criteria, valued artifacts and skills). Gang subcultures emerge from interaction within and between groups, and between groups and institutions of the larger society, such as police, schools, the economic sector (Short, 1974).

Most members of even the most delinquent gang are not delinquent most of the time. Typically, a few members will take part in any given delinquency episode, while most do not. Delinquent episodes may erupt when a gang leader's status, or the status of an entire gang, is challenged or threatened. What is considered threatening varies among gangs with differing subcultural orientations.

Delinquency committed by gangs may be very serious, yet most often it is trivial. Gangs are responsible for much serious crime in some localities, but for most gang members, violence and other serious crime is rare and quite incidental.

The existence and continuity of a gang may be determined by forces external to the gang. Paradoxically, the youth-oriented quality of troublesome gangs results from the exclusion of young people from large areas of adult institutional life. Social separation produces cultural differentiation, and when separation is categorical – based on categories such as age, sex, race, ethnicity, or class – subcultural differentiation is likely to develop along these lines. Persons who share the characteristics which are the basis of separation develop their own status systems, beliefs, and ways of meeting problems among themselves and in relationships with the rest of the world.

James F. Short, Jr
Washington State University

References
Miller, W. B. (1974), 'American youth gangs: past and present', in A. S. Blumberg (ed.), *Current Perspectives on Criminal Behavior: Original Essays on Criminology*, New York.
Short, J. F., Jr (1974), 'Collective behavior, crime, and delinquency', in D. Glaser (ed.), *Handbook of Criminology*, Chicago.
See also: *subculture*.

GDP/GNP

See National Income Analysis.

Geertz, Clifford (1926–)

Clifford Geertz, the American cultural anthropologist, was born in San Francisco, received his BA in Philosophy from Antioch College (1950) and his Ph.D. in Anthropology from Harvard (1956). His teaching appointments at the University of California, Berkeley (1958–60), the University of Chicago (1960–70) and at Princeton (1970–present) have been in conjunction with a constant programme of research and writing that have helped to define a more open, experimental and interpretive approach to ethnography focused upon meaning more than action (Marcus and Cushman, 1982).

Extensive fieldwork by Clifford and Hildred Geertz in Java (1952–4) and Bali (1957–8) generated a series of books on religion, agriculture, economy, social history, ecology and kinship; five field trips to Morocco over the past two decades have further developed a comparative approach to religion (in books and articles that extend Max Weber's work) and to processes of social change in the Third World as viewed from culturological or interpretative, rather than a Marxist or partisan, perspective.

Geertz's main influence has been through his eloquent theoretical essays (1973, 1983) on religion, ideology, art and common sense as cultural systems, on charisma, law, politics, nationalism in the new states, and on the major themes of ethnography as epistemology – world-view, relativism, genre, translation. Taking inspiration from Kenneth Burke's earlier 'dramatistic' syntheses of literary criticism and social analyses (1969), Geertz builds bridges between disciplines, points up the convergence of theories from a variety of fields, and has, thereby, encouraged philosophers and humanists to take anthropology seriously while guiding anthropologists to approach philosophy, literature and culture, if not more playfully, at least with fewer scientific pretensions.

Charles Keil
State University of New York at Buffalo

References
Burke, K. (1969a), *A Grammar of Motives*, Berkeley and Los Angeles.
Burke, K. (1969b), *A Rhetoric of Motives*, Berkeley and Los Angeles.
Burke, K. (1970), *The Rhetoric of Religion: Studies in Logology*, Berkeley and Los Angeles.
Geertz, C. (1973), *The Interpretation of Cultures*, New York.
Geertz, C. (1983), *Local Knowledge*, New York.
Marcus, G. E. and Cushman, D. (1982), 'Ethnographies as texts', *Annual Review of Anthropology*.
See also: *thick description*.

Gender Studies

See Women's Studies.

Generalized Media

A familiar instance of a generalized medium is money. In essence, money is a complex symbolic mechanism. As circulating currency, it facilitates the exchange of economic goods over markets that bring together buyers and sellers. As a measure of value, it enables actors to assign degrees of economic worth to extremely diverse objects. By relating specific economic decisions to a general nexus of exchanges and evaluations, the monetary institution constrains actors to follow norms of rational calculation (Keynes, 1936). High levels of efficiency in combining factors of production cannot be maintained without money and market institutions.

Talcott Parsons suggested that subsystems of society other than the economy also use generalized media to gain flexibility and rationality of social process (Parsons, 1969). Thus, political power, defined as a capacity to command or bind others to specific performances, can be viewed as a medium of the polity. Influence can be regarded as a symbolic means for invoking social solidarity and, hence, as a medium of social integration. Commitment based on shared values can be treated as a medium sustaining common cultural frameworks and traditions in social life. The general equilibrium of a society might then be analysed dynamically in terms of exchanges and transfers of the four media: money, power, influence and commitments.

Parsons later proposed that mental, personal and cultural as well as social processes might be analysed in terms of symbolic media (Parsons, 1970). His insights on intelligence, affect and collective representations were not as well codified as his analyses of the social media, but they did draw media theory deeply into the overall study of human communication.

In situated uses, the media appear as 'pragmatic operators' imparting special effects to particular uses of language. An overtone of affect indicates the emotional status of an expression, just as spending money brings a purchase into effect or a use of power gives binding capacity to a command. Study of the media as pragmatic communicators presents a special opportunity to integrate structural and dynamic, microscopic and macroscopic aspects of social analysis (Lidz, 1981).

Victor Lidz
Haverford College, Pennsylvania

References
Keynes, J. H. (1936), *The General Theory of Employment, Interest and Money*, London.
Lidz, V. (1981), 'Transformational theory and the internal environment of action systems', in K. Knorr Cetina and A. Cicourel (eds), *Advances in Social Theory* and *Methodology: Toward an Integration of Micro- and Macrosociologies*, London.
Parsons, T. (1969), *Politics and Social Structure*, New York.
Parsons, T. (1970), 'Some problems of general theory in sociology', in J. McKinney and E. Tiryakian (eds), *Theoretical Sociology*, New York.
See also: *symbolism*.

General Systems Theory

General Systems Theory in the broadest sense refers to a collection of general concepts, principles, tools, problems and methods associated with systems of any kind. As such, it is not a theory in the usual sense, but rather a field of study. To avoid confusion, it is often referred to as General Systems Research.

The terms general system and general systems theory were first used by Ludwig von Bertalanffy in the early 1930s, although the first written presentations appeared only after the Second World War (von Bertalanffy, 1950).

Von Bertalanffy was not only the originator of general systems theory, but also one of the major organizers of the general systems movement, represented initially by the Society for General Systems Research (established in 1954, originally under the name 'Society for the Advancement of General Systems Theory'), and extended later to the other organizations and activities (Cavallo, 1979). The Society was founded with the following objectives:

(1) To investigate the isomorphy of concepts, laws and models from various fields, and to help in useful transfers from one field to another.
(2) To encourage development of adequate theoretical models in fields which lack them.
(3) To minimize the duplication of theoretical effort in different fields.
(4) To promote the unity of science through improving communication among specialists.

System is typically defined as 'a set or arrangement of things so related or connected as to form a unity or organic whole' (*Webster's New World Dictionary*). To follow this common definition, a system consists of a set of some things, say set T, and some sort of relation among the things, say relation R. That is, a system is an ordered pair S= (T,R), where S denotes a system. The term 'relation' is used here in a broad sense to encompass the whole set of kindred terms such as constraint, structure, information, organization, interaction, dependence, correlation, cohesion, coupling, linkage, interconnection, pattern, and the like.

The common sense conception of systems as ordered pairs (T,R) is too general and, consequently, of little pragmatic value. To make it useful it must be refined in the sense that specific classes of the ordered pairs are introduced. Such classes can basically be introduced by (i) restricting set T to certain kind of things, or (ii) by restricting relation R to certain kind of relations.

Classification criteria (i) and (ii) are independent of each other. Criterion (i) is exemplified by the traditional classification of science and technology into disciplines and specializations, each focusing on the study of certain kinds of things (physical, chemical, biological, political, economical, etc.) without committing to any particular kind of relations. Criterion (ii) leads to fundamentally different classes of systems, each characterized by a specific kind of relation but not committed to any particular kind of things for which the relation is defined.

Since different kinds of things require different experimental (instrumentation) procedures for data acquisition, the classification of systems based on criterion (i) is essentially *experimentally based*. Criterion (ii), on the other hand, is primarily relevant to data processing

of all kinds rather than data acquisition; as such, it is predominantly *theoretically based*.

The largest classes of systems based on criterion (ii) are those which characterize various *epistemological types of systems*, that is, types of knowledge regarding the phenomena under consideration. These types are naturally ordered. This ordering, which is often referred to as an *epistemological hierarchy of systems*, is vital to a comprehensive characterization of systems problems and the development of methodological tools to deal with them (Klir, 1979, 1985; Zeigler, 1974, 1976).

Each class of systems defined by a particular epistemological type is further refined by various *methodological distinctions*. Problems that are associated with systems characterized by the same epistemological type and methodological distinction can be handled by the same kind of methods. These classes of systems are further divided into still smaller classes. Each of these classes consists of systems that are equivalent with respect to *some* specific, pragmatically significant aspects of their relations.

The smallest classes of systems are reached when systems in each class are required to be equivalent in *all* aspects of their relations. Such equivalence is usually called *isomorphism* between systems, and classes based on it are called *isomorphic classes of systems*.

While systems in each isomorphic equivalence class are totally equivalent in their relations, they may be based on completely different kinds of things. To deal with relational aspects of systems, it is sufficient to replace each isomorphic class of systems by a single system as its representative. Although the choice of these representatives is arbitrary, in principle, it is important that the same selection criteria be used for all isomorphic classes.

When systems representing the individual equivalence classes are required to be defined on some purely abstract (interpretation-free) entities and their relations are described in some convenient standard form (for example, in a specific mathematical or programming language), they are called *general systems*. Hence, a general system is a standard and interpretation-free system chosen to represent a class of systems equivalent (isomorphic) with respect to all relational aspects that are pragmatically relevant in a given context. *General systems theory* (or research) is the study of the full scope of relational phenomena conceptualized as various types (epistemological and methodological) of general systems.

George J. Klir
State University of New York, Binghamton

References
Bertalanffy, L. von (1950), 'An outline of general systems theory', *British Journal of the Philosophy of Science*, 1.

Cavallo, R. E. (ed.) (1979), 'Systems research movement: characteristics, accomplishments, and current developments', *General Systems Bulletin*, 9.

Klir, G. J. (1979), 'General systems problem solving methodology', in B. Zeigler *et al.* (eds), *Modelling and Simulation Methodology*, Amsterdam.

Klir, G. J. (1985), *Architecture of Systems Problem Solving*, New York.

Zeigler, B. P. (1974), *Theory of Modelling and Simulation*, New York.

Zeigler, B. P. (1976), 'The hierarchy of system specifications and the problem of structural inference', *PSA 1976*, East Lansing, Michigan.

Further Reading
Ashby, W. R. (1956), *An Introduction to Cybernetics*, New York.

Bertalanffy, L. von (1968), *General Systems Theory*, New York.

Cavallo, R. E. (1979), *The Role of Systems Methodology in Social Science Research*, New York.

Mesarovic, M. D. and Takahara, Y. (1975), *General Systems Theory: Mathematical Foundations*, New York.

See also: *mathematical models*.

Genetic Aspects of Mental Illness

Differences in the prevalence of mental illnesses may be partly explained by genetic factors (breeding effects and higher consanguinity rates), or by differences in ethnic backgrounds. However, environmental factors may also be implicated, while some divergences could be a result of sampling errors.

Affective Disorders
One may conclude from the more reliable lifetime-risk studies that at least 1 per cent of the population suffers from manic-depressive illness. If one were to include milder forms of bipolar illness and unipolar illness, where a considerable number of subjects are being treated as outpatients, the general prevalence may well be as high as 10 per cent. Most studies have reported an appreciable difference between the sexes in the distribution of manic-depressive illness. The sex ratio generally accepted is two females to one male. The interpretation of this excess of females is still controversial. It is conceivable that for cultural reasons, women are more likely to be hospitalized for manic-depressive illness than men. If this were true, one would expect to find the same phenomenon for schizophrenia, and this is yet to be proved. Another possible explanation is the fact that male suicides outnumber female suicides by a ratio of about 2 to 1. Finally, one could also invoke the hypothesis of sex-limited factors, for example, hormonal fluctuations or sex-linked genetic factors which increase the express-

ivity of manic-depressive illness in females predisposed to this disorder (Mendlewicz and Fleiss, 1974).

The twin method allows comparison of concordance rates for a trait between sets of monozygotic (MZ) and dizygotic (DZ) twins. Both types of twins share a similar environment, but whereas monozygotic twins behave genetically as identical individuals, dizygotic twins share only half of their genes and thus behave as siblings. Most twin studies show that the concordance rate for manic-depressive illness in MZ twins is significantly higher than the concordance rate for the disease in DZ twins (Zerbin-Rüdin, 1969). This observation is taken as evidence in favour of a genetic factor in manic-depressive illness.

Price reviewed the twin studies literature in order to locate pairs of identical twins, reared separately since early childhood, where at least one had been diagnosed as having an affective disorder (Price, 1968). Price was able to find twelve such pairs of MZ twins. Among these pairs, eight were concordant for the disease, an observation suggesting that the predisposition to manic-depressive illness will usually express itself regardless of the early environment.

The complex interaction between hereditary and environmental factors underlying the aetiology of manic-depressive illness cannot be elucidated by the twin method, nor can it tell us anything about the type of genetic mechanisms that may be involved in the transmission of manic-depressive illness.

Most of the early studies on manic-depressive illness have shown that this illness tends to be familial (Kallmann, 1954). The lifetime risk for the disease in relatives of manic-depressive probands is significantly higher than the risk in the general population.

Most of the early family studies were influenced by Kraepelin's classification. As a result, the investigators included among their subjects patients suffering from mania and depression (bipolar) and patients presenting depression only (unipolar) without distinguishing between these. Thus, the samples investigated in the various studies are relatively heterogeneous. Leonhard (1959) was one of the first investigators to make a clinical distinction between bipolar and unipolar forms of affective disorders on genetic grounds. This genetic distinction between unipolar and bipolar illness has recently been confirmed in the United States (Winokur *et al.*, 1969).

When correction has been made for age, diagnoses, and statistical procedures, the morbidity risks for manic-depressive illness in different types of first-degree relatives (parents, siblings, children) are similar. This observation is consistent with a dominant mode of transmission for this disease. Mendlewicz and Fleiss (1974) were able to demonstrate close linkage between bipolar illness and both deutan and protan colour blindness in seventeen pedigrees, suggesting that an X-linked dominant factor is involved in the transmission of the manic-depressive phenotype in at least some families. The linkage studies conducted so far on manic-depressive illness are of great value, since they are able to discriminate between sex-linked and sex-influenced types of inheritance, and they provide an estimate of the significance of the results. They all point to the presence of an X-linked dominant factor in the transmission of manic-depressive illness. This methodological approach has great potential and should be extended to the study of other psychiatric conditions, such as schizophrenia, using other genetic markers.

A recent study of adoption showing more psychopathology of the affective spectrum in biological parents of manic-depressive adoptees as compared to their adoptive parents is further evidence in favour of the genetic hypothesis of affective illness (Mendlewicz and Rainer, 1977).

Schizophrenia

Family risk studies, twin surveys, the model of adoption, and longitudinal investigations of high-risk children have been used successively to approach the numerous problems at issue in the area of schizophrenia. These special problems are (1) diagnosis; (2) the separation, at least conceptually, of heredity and environment; (3) the forms of inheritance; and (4) the developmental expression of genetic predisposition.

Despite the absence of hard data on the heritability of schizophrenia, the genetic-oriented approach has been valuble in that it has facilitated the distinction between schizophrenia and other psychotic illnesses, particularly manic-depressive psychosis, and the correlation of schizophrenia with such syndromes as involutional psychosis. The schizophrenic spectrum is a group of disorders exhibited, for example, by the biological children of schizophrenics reared in adoptive homes (Rosenthal and Kety, 1968). It encompasses various disorders, including schizophrenia itself and borderline states, schizoid disorders, and inadequate personality.

Roberts (1963) believes that 'genetic advice on mental disease must be left to psychiatrists. Some of those interviewed, and the histories they give, need psychiatric appraisal. What is even more important is the difficulty to anyone not a psychiatrist of interpreting and assessing psychiatric reports.' A second contribution of psychiatry to genetic counselling concerns ways of presenting material and discussing it with persons who need help. Marriage choice, family planning, child rearing, adoption, and foster care are all questions that fall under the wider sphere of genetic counselling.

Empirically, risks run from about 40 per cent for the children of two schizophrenic parents, to about 15 per cent in children of one schizophrenic parent. Risks of 100 per cent in the former case (theoretical recessive)

or 50 per cent in the latter (theoretical dominant) have not been observed. Since most people do not consider risks below 10 per cent to be serious, the clearest indication for a warning of caution is in the case of dual matings; with one parent affected, the empirical risk for the offspring is low, though not negligible. It is necessary in such cases to help the family to consider also the possible effect of having a child on the course of illness in the disabled parent, and, second, the effect of a possibly disrupted home on the development of the child regardless of genetic considerations. In all cases, the psychiatrically trained genetic counsellor will have the opportunity to utilize all of his diagnostic abilities, psychological understanding, clinical experience, and biological sophistication in dealing with the many family problems presented by schizophrenia. This multidisciplinary approach can best be utilized in longitudinal studies of high-risk children.

Julien Mendlewicz
University Clinics of Brussels
Department of Psychiatry
Erasme Hospital

References

Kallmann, F. J. (1954), 'Genetic principles in manic-depressive psychoses', in P. Hoch and J. Zubin (eds), *Depression*, New York.

Leonhard, K. (1959), *Aufteilung der Endogenen Psychosen*, Berlin.

Mendlewicz, J. and Fleiss, J. L. (1974), 'Linkage studies with X-chromosome markers in bipolar (manic-depressive) and unipolar (depressive) illness', *Biological Psychiatry*, 9.

Mendlewicz, J. and Rainer, (1977), 'Adoption study supporting genetic transmission in manic depressive illness', *Nature*, 268.

Price, J. (1968), 'The genetics of depressive behaviour', in A. Coppen and A. Walk (eds), *Recent Developments in Affective Disorders, British Journal of Psychiatry*, Special Publication, no. 2.

Roberts, J. A. F. (1963), *An Introduction to Medical Genetics*, London.

Rosenthal, D. and Kety, S. (eds) (1968), *Transmission of Schizophrenia*, Oxford.

Winokur, G., Clayton, P. J. and Reich, T. (1969), *Manic-Depressive Illness*, St Louis.

Zerbin-Rüdin, E. (1969), 'Zur Genetik der depressiven Erkrankungen', in H. Hippius and H. Selbach (eds), *Das Depressive Syndrome*, Munich.

See also: *biological psychiatry; genetics and behaviour.*

Genetics and Behaviour

In the late nineteenth century, Sir Francis Galton collected information on accomplishments, physical traits and occupational status of members of families and began the correlational approach to behaviour genetics. In agreement with the prevailing sentiment of the British establishment, the finding that these characters aggregated in families was used as a biological justification for the social class structure of the time and even for the predominance of the British Empire. Kamin (1974) points out that similar reasoning by American psychologists responsible for the administration of intelligence tests to immigrants to the United States led to Congressional passage of the Immigration Act of 1924 which restricted immigration to the US from southern and eastern Europe. Thus over the past hundred years the issues involved in the relationship between genetics and behaviour have had serious political ramifications.

R. A. Fisher's 1918 paper reconciled particulate Mendelian transmission genetics with the continuously varying phenotypes that interested the biometricians. This paper led to the variance-analysis approach to familial data on continuously varying traits, in particular, behavioural characters. The idea is that overall phenotypic variance, P, can be partitioned into contributions due to variation in gene action, G, those due to environmental variation, E, and interactions between genes and environment. Later, animal breeders termed the ratio of G to P the 'heritability' of the trait. The sense in which animal breeders used heritability was as an index of amenability to selective breeding. Of course, this is inappropriate in the context of human behaviour, and in this context it unfortunately developed the connotation of an index of biological determination and refractivity to environmental intervention.

The use of heritability in situations where experimental controls are lacking has been criticized by geneticists, who prefer to think in terms of the 'norm of reaction'. The norm of reaction for a given genotype is the graph of the phenotype against the environment. It emphasizes the dependence of gene action on the particular environment; a genotype that performs better than another in one environment may do worse in a second. An example is the human genetic disease phenylketonuria, PKU, in which sufferers accumulate toxic concentrations of phenylalanine resulting in extreme mental retardation. Under a diet that restricts intake of phenylalanine from birth, normal mental function occurs. The norm of reaction approach informs us that even if the heritability of IQ were 100 per cent, this would say nothing about its potential for environmental manipulation.

Fisher's approach to the genetics of continuous variation produces expected values for correlations between relatives of all degrees which can then be compared to observed correlations and heritability estimated. In principle the most powerful data of this kind uses adoptions and, in particular, identical twins

reared apart. Such twins are extremely difficult to find and unfortunately the largest sample, that published by Burt in his analysis of the heritability of IQ, has since been shown to be fraudulent. The remaining samples of this kind normally suffer from nonrandomness in the adoption procedure. Nevertheless, until about 1970 the estimates obtained using data that included Burt's produced the widely accepted statistic that genes accounted for about 80 per cent of variation in IQ.

In the past ten years Wright's (1934) method of path analysis has become the predominant one for estimating heritability. In 1974 this method produced an estimate of genetic heritability of 67 per cent. The latest path-analytic treatments make allowances for assortative mating and for the transmission of environments within families, that is, cultural transmission. The most recent estimates by Rice et al. (1980) and Rao et al. (1982) suggest that genetic and cultural transmission each account for about one-third of the variance in IQ. As with Fisher's variance analysis, the path-analysis approach is based on linear models of determination and has been criticized for that reason. Among the other criticisms are that most adoptions are not random, that the increase in mean IQ of adoptive children over that of their biological parents is ignored, and that the estimates of genetic and cultural heritability depend on how the environment is defined and its transmission modelled.

It has frequently been claimed that a high heritability of a trait within a group makes it more likely that average differences between groups, for example, races, are genetic. This is false since heritability is strictly a within-group measure strongly dependent on the range of environments in which it is measured.

In studies of the distribution of human behaviours within families, where the data base is not as large as that used for IQ and where the trait in question is a clinically defined disorder, the twin method and the method of adoptions have been widely used. In the twin method the fraction of identical (monozygous or MZ) twin pairs in which both members are affected is compared to that in fraternal (dizygous or DZ) twin pairs. A significant margin in favour of the former is taken as evidence of genetic aetiology. Numerous studies of these concordance rates for criminality, neuroses, homosexuality, drinking habits, affective disorders such as manic depression, and schizophrenia have generally shown greater agreement among MZ than DZ twins. In these studies the twins are usually not reared apart and the role of special environmental influences, especially on MZ twins, cannot be discounted. Other problems such as the mode of ascertainment of the proband, heterogeneity in syndrome definition and variation among the concordance rates in different studies also raise doubts about the efficacy of the twin method.

In the adoption method, the incidence of a trait in the adoptive relatives of an affected adoptee is compared with that in the biological relatives. If the latter is higher than the former the inference is usually drawn that there is some genetic aetiology to the disease. Adoption studies of behavioural disorders from among those mentioned above have generally produced higher agreements between biological than between adoptive relatives. Again the interpretation of a genetic basis for the behavioural abnormality must be viewed with circumspection since truly random adoption is extremely rare and frequently adoption occurs relatively late in childhood. In none of the behavioural disorders mentioned above has any biochemically distinguishable genetic variant been identified, although research directed at the role of variation in properties of catecholamine and indole metabolism still continues.

The evolution of social behaviour has provided something of a puzzle to natural historians since Darwin. This field of study was subsumed under ethology and behavioural ecology, and until recently was relatively immune to the developments in evolutionary population genetics by Fisher, Wright (1934) and Haldane (1932; 1955). 1975 saw the publication of E. O. Wilson's book *Sociobiology* in which he not only stressed that social behaviours were similar across the animal kingdom from termites to humans, but also claimed that these behaviours were genetically determined. Ethology and much of behavioural ecology were then subsumed under a new name, 'sociobiology'.

J. B. S. Haldane had speculated in 1932 as to how alarm calls in birds might have evolved genetically but concluded that a simple genetic basis for the evolution of self-sacrifice might only apply to the social insects. In 1955 he foreshadowed sociobiology by asking for how many cousins should one's self-sacrifice be equivalent to that for a brother. These speculations were formalized in 1964 by Hamilton, who modelled the evolution of a single gene one allele of which conferred 'altruistic' behaviour on its carrier. Altruism here means that the fitness of the altruistic individuals is reduced by their performance of a behaviour which increases the fitness of others in the population. Hamilton arrived at conditions on the degree of relatedness between the donor and recipient of the behaviour that would enable 'altruistic' genotypes to increase in the population. The condition is usually stated in the form $\beta r > \gamma$ where β and γ measure the gain in fitness to recipients and loss in fitness to donors and r is a coefficient of relatedness. Hamilton noted that in the haplodiploid insects like the hymenoptera his measure of relatedness between sisters is higher than for any other relationship. Since the above inequality is then easier to satisfy than in species where both sexes are diploid, this could explain on a simple genetic basis the evolution in the social hymenoptera

of the social caste system with sterile workers. This theory of the evolution of the kin-directed behaviours is now called 'kin selection'.

Hamilton's theoretical analysis was made using a mathematical approximation that allows the allele frequency of the 'altruistic' variant, the 'altruistic gene' frequency, to play the central role. With this approximation the mathematics gives the impression that it is possible to add fitness contributions from all relatives affected by the altruism to produce the 'inclusive fitness' of the allele. It has recently been shown that inclusive fitness is an unnecessary concept and that the theory of kin selection can be developed in terms of classical population genetic models with frequency-dependent Darwinian fitness differences. Hamilton's formulation contains many assumptions, but when these are removed his theory remains qualitatively true: the closer is the degree of the relatedness between the donor and recipient of an individually disadvantageous behaviour (controlled by a single gene), the easier it is for that behaviour to evolve.

In *Sociobiology*, E. O. Wilson extrapolated from Hamilton's theory to posit that the evolution of social behaviour throughout the animal kingdom including *Homo sapiens* has followed these rules of kin selection. Of course this position ignores the general criticism that none of the social behaviours discussed have been shown to have a genetic basis and are certainly not under simple genetic control. Although many behavioural ecologists took Wilson's position in the years immediately following the publication of his book, the difficulty of empirical measurement of relatedness, and fitness gains and losses, as well as technical criticism by population geneticists, have had a moderating effect. Kinship still plays a central role in behavioural ecology, but the explanatory limitations of the simple kin selection theory are now more widely appreciated.

In *Homo sapiens* the position of sociobiology is to minimize the role of learning and cultural transmission of social behaviours. In particular, the human sociobiologists have taken the position that such phenomena as aggression, incest taboos, sex-differentiated behaviours, sexual preferences, conformity and spite have largely genetic antecedents. There is clear political danger in acceptance of this assertion that such human behaviours have a genetic basis. We have the precedent of the politics of IQ based on erroneous inferences drawn from data of dubious quality. Sociobiology adopts a position of pan selectionism in which the terms adaptive and genetic are interchangeable. Cultural transmission, under which the properties of evolution are obviously different from those under genetic transmission, is ignored. Clearly sociobiology tried to claim too much: 'Sooner or later, political science, law, economics, psychology, psychiatry and anthropology will all be branches of sociobiology' (Trivers in *Time*, 1 August 1977). Fortunately, we are all biologists enough to tell the tail from the dog.

Marcus W. Feldman
Stanford University

References

Fisher, R. A. (1918), 'The correlation between relatives on the supposition of Mendelian inheritance', *Transactions of the Royal Society*, 52.

Haldane, J. B. S. (1932), *The Causes of Evolution*, New York.

Haldane, J. B. S. (1955), 'Population genetics', *New Biology*, 18.

Hamilton, W. D. (1964), 'The genetical evolution of social behaviour, I and II', *Journal of Theoretical Biology*, 7.

Kamin, L. (1974), *The Science and Politics of IQ*, Hillsdale, N.J.

Rao, D. C., Morton, N. E., Lalouel, J. M. and Lew, R. (1982), 'Path analysis under generalized assortative mating, II, American IQ', *Genetical Research Cambridge*, 39.

Rice, J., Cloninger, C. R. and Reich, T. (1980), 'The analysis of behavioral traits in the presence of cultural transmission and assortative mating: application to IQ and SES', *Behavior Genetics*, 10.

Wilson, E. O. (1975), *Sociobiology*, Cambridge, Mass.

Wright, S. (1934), 'The method of path coefficients', *Annual of Mathematical Statistics*, 5.

Further Reading

Cavalli-Sforza, L. L. and Feldman, M. W. (1978), 'Darwinian selection and altruism', *Theoretical Population Biology*, 14.

Cavalli-Sforza, L. L. and Feldman, M. W. (1981), *Cultural Transmission and Evolution*, Princeton.

Feldman, M. W. and Lewontin, R. C. (1975), 'The heritability hangup', *Science*, 190.

See also: *altruism; ethology; evolution; intelligence; population genetics; race; sociobiology.*

Geography

The range and internal diversity of geography make definition problematic. I suggest two definitions, one elaborated, the other concise. Long definition: Geography seeks and refines deductive laws concerning the changing spatial patterns and relationships of terrestrial phenomena viewed as the world of man at varying scales of study. Short definition: Geography is the scientific study of changing relationships of terrestrial phenomena viewed as the world of man (Bird, 1973).

Geography is a social science, but it is also more than a social science. Within 'physical geography' fall such fields as cartography, climatology, parts of biogeography, and geomorphology (the study of the nature and processes of the evolution of earth surface features). These treat phenomena that can be expected to obey the cause and effect laws of physics. The subject has perhaps a dangerously diverse agenda, but geography derives its unity from its constant attempt to see *zusammenhang* between the spatial relationships of terrestrial features. Here are four different dimensions of the subject.

(1) Geographers have been driven to seek ever more profound description of the world of man in maps, numbers and words, and in that endeavour they have naturally wanted to know how contemporary spatial patterns evolved. Why not look at past patterns (historical geography) to seek an explanation not only of these, but perhaps also of the present in their light via a true scientific cause and effect sequence over time? Any success in this search must lead to an understanding of processes. So why not let that process run on beyond the present, leading to possibilities of prediction, perhaps as an aid to planning?

But planning for whom? The world perceived by whom? As soon as man is studied as a vital constituent of earth-space patterns, we encounter all the problems of perception. The actions taken by man in shaping his environment (physical and social) are so taken in the light of his behavioural values and attitudes. That is the subject matter of behavioural geography. The guiding view is that man's actions are not determined directly by the environment, but rather by what he thinks the environment (again physical and social) constrains him to do. He then modifies his view of the world as he perceives the results of his actions.

(2) A second dimension is made by dividing the subject in two different ways: there is the worldwide study of a narrow range of phenomena – systematic geography; and there is regional, 'total' geography of manageable areas, treated as variations upon regional models. This twofold division, supported by courses in techniques, particularly in the physical geography laboratory, in computation, and in cartography, is often used as the framework for the undergraduate curriculum. A key problem related to these subjects is that of scale. The study of one world implies the ability to slide from one scale to another appropriate scale in view of the study objective. The 'appropriate' scale is where the phenomena under study deviate most from randomness.

(3) A third dimension of the subject has to do with its relation to other environmental and regional sciences. In university curricula geography is often combined with other environmental sciences (commonly geology and biology), or it may form part of a training in regional science, when it is taught together with mathematics (statistics) and economics. This integrated approach is particularly useful at post-

graduate level, where there is a greater emphasis on problem-orientation than on 'discipline servitude'. Three broad headings for geography's contribution to an integrated attack on problems are spatial analysis, ecological analysis and regional complex analysis.

(4) A fourth dimension of geography has to do with the internal tension between its natural science and social science poles. This contrast occurs *within* geography (as it does in medicine) as either a basic weakness or a source of strength. If geographers are able to allow one method to act as a continual critique of the other, it may provide deeper insights. Areas of the subject tending towards the 'harder' pole are more likely to use some form of positivistic thinking; areas tending towards the other pole are likely to employ some form of behaviouralism.

A useful umbrella phrase to describe what the geographer seeks in both his desk and field studies is a 'search for spatial relationships', bearing in mind that this includes physical as well as man-made modifications of the earth surface, the spatial relationships of these modifications and man himself, and the spatial relationships of man with man. If these are difficult objectives, they are nevertheless vital questions for a modern society attempting to manage the distribution of resources: land-use planning (*aménagement de la territoire, Raumordnung*), is practised in some form everywhere, as competing claims turn spaces into places exhibiting environmental pressures. Planning becomes at once more sophisticated, as the citizens on whose behalf plans are promulgated become more environmentally informed, and also more difficult as expectations rise.

Having emphasized that research in geography is problem-oriented, I turn to one or two problems that preoccupy geographers today. In physical geography there is an emphasis on process-landform relationships, with time seen as an important variable. The tendency for pioneer geomorphologists to see landform shaping in a 'compartmented' sequence of mountain building, followed by discrete periods of degradational erosion, has given way to a perspective which sees change in the landscape as more continuous, with perhaps contemporaneous mountain-building and erosion. There is continual refinement of mathematical modelling principles in order to understand and predict the changes in the landscape, an objective with obvious applied importance.

In physical and in human geography, there is the constant striving to produce concepts, models and laws. (For a list of fifty 'basic concepts' in behavioural geography worked on by geographers see Hurst, 1974.) Geographers have moved away from regarding areal differentiation as a prime objective and have begun to worry less that the scientific rigour of the natural sciences has never been approached (will never be?) by the social sciences aspects of geography. In the face of many possible research strategies in human geography, from micro case studies to macro aggregate models, from positivistic to humanistic geography, a current response has been to suggest that what is believed to be the most appropriate strategy for the problem in question (in itself a subjective choice, but to be more objectively judged by its results) should be made subject to the critique of alternative strategies.

Since 1954 there have been behavioural geography theories that the causal sequence of spatial relationships is basically as follows: political idea, decision, leading to movement over a designated field of operation or political area, giving the projection of ideas on to space, as power in the political field and as property in the economic field. Behavioural geography also grew because of progressive dissatisfaction with the fruits of the positivistic locational analysis school of human geography of the 1960s. It was even realized that physical environmental hazards were best studied in the light of the way the decision maker on the ground perceived the hazard, rather than via the perspective of some supposed objective principles from within physical geography. The supplantation of optimizing economic men by satisficers was accompanied by an interest in the spatial diffusion of innovations and, more broadly, by the time-space geography of the Swedish school of geographers led by Torsten Hagerstrand, where time and space are seen as scarce resources and their attempted optimum allocation by individuals builds up to the spatial relationships of societies.

Geographers have tried to keep abreast of work by psychologists as to whether perceptions are hypotheses and only hypotheses, or whether the relationship between perceiver and perceived is something like the symbiotic relationship between predator and prey. A celebrated tool of the geographer, the map, is now seen as a perceptual filter imposed upon our observation of space that is too large to be individually observed at one moment of time. A whole sub-subject of mental maps has arisen wherein questionnaire fieldwork survey compares individuals' ideas of spatial patterns with some external standard representation.

J. H. Bird
University of Southampton

References

Bird, J. H. (1973), 'Desiderata for a definition: or is geography what geographers do?', *Area*, 6.

Hurst, M. E. E. (1974), *A Geography of Economic Behaviour*, London.

Further Reading

Holt-Jensen, A. (1981), *Geography: Its History and Concepts*, London.

Johnston, R. J. (1979), *Geography and Geographers: Anglo-American Human Geography Since 1945*, London.

See also: *economic geography; social geography; time-space analysis.*

Gerontology, Social

Gerontology is the scientific study of biological, psychological and sociocultural aspects of the ageing process. Social gerontology is concerned only with its sociological-anthropological component. Although public interest in old age commonly stems from the association of ageing with 'social problems', such considerations will be excluded from the present discussion.

Social gerontology emerged in the late 1950s, and has become established as a recognized subject of study and research in academic institutes throughout the world, most especially in the United States. The conceptual approaches and methodologies applied in this new field reflect a wide gamut of theoretical frameworks and techniques. None the less, three core issues in the study of behavioural phenomena in later life can be identified: (1) the relative importance in ageing of universal human processes and specific cultural factors; (2) the dialectic between stability and change in later life; (3) questions concerning the place of the elderly in a social structure, and in the symbolic worlds of both the aged and non-aged.

(1) The quest for universal, generic characteristics of ageing has taken several theoretical forms. Some anthropologists have imputed common needs and aspirations to all old people, such as the desire for a prolonged life and dignified death, and they have tried to identify general role features, such as a shift from active participation in economic production to sedentary advisory roles. Similarly, 'disengagement theory' states that there is a gradual process of mutual disengagement between the aged person and his society in all cultures. Critics have cited cross-cultural and cross-sectional data to show that there have been a variety of context-bound, behavioural responses to old age. It has also been argued that patterns of active behaviour among the elderly, as well as manifestations of retreatism and inertia, are conditioned by environmental constraints and cultural configurations. More recently, however, some psychologists with a similar universalist bias have maintained that the process of ageing is governed by an increased concentration on the inner self, and especially on a retrospective life-review.

(2) Ageing is a dynamic process of concurrent transformations in various spheres of life. In a complex, changing society, where life transitions are generally equated with social mobility and progress within a given career opportunity structure, the changes associated with old age engender a paradoxical perception of later life. In a social structure which allocates statuses and prestige according to mastery of information, control of wealth and command of physical resources and mental faculties, the aged are conceived of as a stagnant, marginal social category. This stereotype persists, in spite of the growing numbers of elderly persons whose life expectancy is increasing and whose functioning capacities are improving relative to previous generations. Such incongruity between social definition and personal experience generates ambivalence and ambiguity. In the experience of the temporal universe of the aged, long-term planning becomes problematic, if not impossible. The past is recalled selectively, and is mined in order to construct a meaningful present. The struggle of old people for continuity in identity is often expressed through their review and reinterpretation of life-histories, as well as through their reorganization of social relationships and systems of meaning. Temporal asynchrony and disorganization of this kind usually does not exist in so-called simple societies, where the position of the aged accurately reflects the balance between their control of valuable resources and their diminishing ability to protect their interests. In some economically 'hand-to-mouth' preliterate societies, an aged person whose presence becomes a burden may be abandoned, or ritually killed. In agricultural societies, however, knowledge and spiritual powers are attributed to the aged. Elders have social and ritual roles entailing a honourable place in society.

(3) Social roles are often associated with age categories. Passage through a series of age grades represents an important organizing principle of social life in most simple societies. In modern societies, age is less significant than occupational specialization. Yet the phases of 'childhood' and 'old age' are, by definition, social categories circumscribed by age norms, which are decisive in shaping individuals' social identities. The very fact that age alone is enough to define the 'old' reflects the disappearance of the normally decisive occupational and other roles and values, which in turn generates negative images and stereotypes of the elderly. This phenomenon has led a number of scholars to consider the potential development of subcultural or countercultural social units made up exclusively of the aged. Research on such groups, mainly in age-homogeneous communities, day centres and residential settings, shows that in many cases a new alternative system of social relationships and symbolic meanings is developed to supersede those of the prior, stigmatizing and alienating social milieu.

Social gerontology is currently in a transitional phase. Many aspects of ageing can be analysed and explained by other disciplines, but the growing reservoir of data and theory on old age encourages social research into such specific issues as the politics of ageing, ageing and the law, and the existential problems connected with old age. Much research is also directed to the aged as a 'social problem' and the object of public social concern. The central problems have been defined, but there is as yet no adequate theoretical treatment of them.

Haim Hazan
Tel-Aviv University

Further Reading
Binstock, R. H. and Shanes, E. (eds) (1976), *Handbook of Aging and the Social Sciences*, New York.
Hareven, T. K. and Adams, K. J. (eds) (1982), *Ageing and Life Course Transitions*, London.
Holmes, L. (1983), *Other Culture, Elder Years*, St Paul.
Myerhoff, B. G. and Simic, A. (eds) (1978), *Life's Career and Aging: Cultural Variations on Growing Old*, Beverly Hills.
See also: *age organization; ageing, psychological aspects; life-cycle.*

Gestalt Therapy

Gestalt therapy is a particular approach to psychological growth and change rooted in psychoanalysis and existentialism. It was developed in the 1940s by Laura and Fritz Perls, trained psychoanalysts who had worked with Kurt Goldstein (developer of the holistic 'organismic approach') and with Karen Horney and Wilhelm Reich. Gestalt therapy and Gestalt perceptual theory are not directly related but do share a few similar ideas, such as the whole being greater than the parts and the notion of a constantly shifting figure-ground relationship (our awareness of the world is always shifting, so that one aspect will become important at one moment and then move into the background as another replaces it).

The goal of Gestalt therapy is to make someone responsible for his own life. It resembles Eastern approaches to growth, for example, Theravada Buddhism and insight meditation. The therapist begins by concentrating on what a person is attending to at that moment: by focusing on the present it is possible to articulate better the rules and assumptions that govern a person's life. The therapy emphasizes not so much change *per se* but an awareness of what choices the person is making. With awareness comes freedom, and with freedom responsibility.

A second common theme in Gestalt therapy is behavioural integration. People are assumed to have both tacit rules and inconsistent sets of behaviours, ideas and feelings. A person may express one idea intellectually and, at the same time, just the opposite idea with his body – facial expression, muscle tension and so on. (The man who says, 'I am not mad at my wife' in a loud voice while beating on the table would be an example of this situation.) The aim in therapy would be to integrate these modes of expression. The therapist might merely draw his patient's attention to his voice and pounding fist, or he might use the technique of getting the patient to exaggerate his movements or tone of voice. There are, in fact, no required techniques in Gestalt therapy, although in the past Perls did utilize certain specific modes of therapy. The therapist is more or less free to use any process that will help to increase awareness.

Many of the people who came to Perls for therapy were not sensitive to bodily sensations and compensated through overintellectualizing. To Perls, bodily and emotional expressions were positive, natural processes, not to be feared or kept under control, and the techniques he used were directed at eliciting these processes. Many critics treated his views as anti-intellectual – which they were to the extent that Perls regarded overintellectualizing as a barrier to full self-awareness.

Three other notions inform Gestalt therapy: (1) The patient knows all he needs to know for change to occur – he just does not know that he knows it. The therapist must try to increase awareness and through therapy help the patient to see, feel, function and relate better. (2) Life and change take place in the present. From this derives the Gestalt focus on 'what is going on now', and the emphasis on how one feels, thinks and what one does right now. This is not to deny the capacity to remember or be influenced by the past, but the effects of the past are in the present. Therefore important past events will be manifested now, at this moment, in therapy. (3) Everything is personal. Whatever a person says or does expresses his own consciousness and internal processes; in everything he does, he is talking about himself. This leads to the various techniques used by Gestalt therapists to elicit from the patient his statements concerning others and the world, and to help him to see them as part of his own psyche.

The therapy examines, brings forth, and explores ways in which people stop themselves from functioning properly. The techniques of Gestalt borrow from Freud (for example, free association) and Jung (for example, active imagination), but these are carried a step further by stressing the patient's active participation – motor, emotional, intellectual and spiritual – in the course of therapy.

William Ray
Pennsylvania State University

Further Reading
Perls, F. (1972), *Gestalt Therapy Verbatim*, New York.
See also: *Eastern psychology; existential psychology; Horney; Reich.*

Goffman, Erving (1922–82)

A Canadian-born social scientist, Goffman graduated from the University of Toronto, and received his MA (1949) and Ph.D. (1953) from the University of Chicago. He taught at the Universities of Edinburgh, Berkeley and Pennsylvania, and carried out field research in the Shetland Islands, and in a public mental hospital in Washington DC. Among his many books are: *The Presentation of Self in Everyday Life* (1959), *Asylums* (1961), *Encounters: Essays on the Social Situation of Mental Patients and Other Inmates* (1961), *Stigma: Notes on the Management of Spoiled Identity* (1963), *Frame Analysis* (1974), and *Gender Advertisements* (1979).

Goffman took as his focus the microanalysis of everyday behaviour, in a variety of contexts. He analysed social situations in terms of the linkage between sociocultural frames of meaning and the ability of the actor to manage and interpret his environment. His topics were aspects of social behaviour such as games, public gatherings, stigmatizing behaviour, the interaction of 'staff' and 'inmates', and so on. In interpreting these phenomena, Goffman used theoretical constructs such as 'ritual', 'the management of impression', 'social encounters', 'role distance', and others, designed to formulate the principles whereby social situations and relationships were constituted. He was often linked to the tradition of social interactionism, but especially in his later work he appeared to be taking a different path. He emphasized that human interaction is structured by the position of actors in a wider social setting, governed by a symbolic code which defines its boundaries, rules of conduct and universe of meaning. Like Simmel, Goffman was more interested in the structure of social situations than in their content.

In Goffman's world, the actor is assumed to be aware of his role, and to interpret it. The individual is allowed to manœuvre within the web of interactional contingencies which constitute the frame of action. The actor responds to shifting involvements and breaches in communication. Failure to sustain an acceptable performance in social encounters is liable to lead to embarrassment, self-reproach and sanctions. Here, perhaps, Goffman's perspective is grounded in a structural model rather than in a social-psychological approach, but (perhaps because he was working in a complex society) his analyses exhibit a flexibility and subtlety which mute any tendency to functionalist analysis.

Methodologically, Goffman is open to criticism. His work is rife with cultural preconceptions, and he depends on unsystematic observations. This limits the force of his work, and diminishes its value as a model for further research and thought.

Haim Hazan
Tel-Aviv University

Further Reading
Gonos, G. (1977), 'Situation versus frame: the "interactionist" and the "structuralist" analysis of everyday life', *American Sociological Review*, 42.
Perry, N. (1974), 'The two cultures and the total institution', *British Journal of Sociology*, 24.
Psathas, G. and Waksler, C. (1973), 'Essential features of face to face interaction', in G. Psathas (ed.), *Phenomenological Sociology: Issues and Implications*, London.
See also: *institutions*.

Gouldner, Alvin Ward (1920–80)

Alvin Gouldner, born in New York in 1920, was both a Marxist and a sociologist, yet neither. Gouldner's *The Coming Crisis in Western Sociology* (1971) is the classic interpretation of the social basis for the failure of post-Second World War sociological functionalism in the West and of Marxism in the East. This book was broadly influential, especially among those who turned to sociology in response to their disappointment with the political radicalism of the 1960s.

Coming Crisis was also a major work in his life's project – the critical interpretation of the history of social theory. *Enter Plato* (1966) was the first in this series. It turned social scientists' attention to Greek thought. (Classicists were annoyed that an outsider would dare to enter their scholarly domain.) After *Coming Crisis*, *The Dialectic of Ideology and Technology* (1976) and *The Future of Intellectuals and the Rise of the New Class* (1979) examined the fate of critical thinking and political action in late industrial society. The latter made the controversial claim that the new class, comprising intellectuals, managers, and the technical intelligentsia, was the best hope for revolution in light of the failure of the industrial proletariat. He thus challenged the central political and theoretical premise of Marxism. But in *The Two Marxisms* (1980) he carefully distinguished scientific and critical Marxisms and clearly identified himself with the latter, more humanistic, course. *Against Fragmentation: The Origins of Marxism and the Sociology of Intellectuals* (posthumous, 1985) is an extension of his historical theory of intellectuals to Marxism – thus completing a twenty-year project that began with Greeks and ended with twentieth-century Marxism.

Of his fourteen books, *Patterns of Industrial Bureaucracy* (1954) stands with *Coming Crisis* as a sociological classic. The former is a *locus classicus* of American industrial sociology, just as the latter became the manifesto of post-1960s social scientists seeking a third way between their academic disciplines and the political visions of Marxism. *Theory and Society*, the international journal which he founded in 1974 and edited until his death, was the institutionalization of this third-way strategy.

Charles Lemert
Wesleyan University, Connecticut

Further Reading
Theory and Society II (1982) (issue devoted to the comprehensive assessment of Gouldner's life and work).

Government

The study of government lies at the heart of political science, but there is little unanimity within the discipline as to how it should be studied or as to the types or forms that exist. Indeed, the term itself has a multiplicity of distinct, if related, meanings. Only an overview of the confusion and controversy can be given here.

Following Finer (1974) we can discern four different meanings of the term 'government': (1) Government refers to the process of governing, that is, the authoritative exercise of power. (2) The term can be used to refer to the existence of that process, to a 'condition of ordered rule'. (3) By 'the government' is often meant the people who fill the positions of authority in a society or institution, that is, the offices of government. (4) The term may refer to the manner, method or system of government in a society, that is, to the structure and arrangement of the offices of government and the relationship between the government and the governed.

The existence of some institution of sovereign government is a distinguishing feature of the 'state'. The study of such sovereign governments has been a major preoccupation of political scientists. But not all governments are sovereign; any institution, such as a trade union, a church group or a political party, which has a formal system of offices endowed with the authority to make binding decisions for that organization, can be said to have a government. Equally, government (in the sense of ordered rule) may exist in the absence of the state. A number of anthropological studies have revealed the existence of 'primitive' societies in which conflict is resolved by various social processes without resort to the coercive powers of a formalized state. Indeed, in any society there are many social situations (such as a bus or theatre queue) where potential conflict over an allocative decision is avoided by a non-coercive social process.

Sovereign government in advanced societies is normally regarded as consisting of three distinct sets of offices, each set having a particular role: (1) The role of the *legislature* is to make the law. (2) The *executive* (also sometimes confusingly referred to as the government) is responsible for the implementation of the law and in most advanced polities has come to play a predominant role in the formulation of proposals for new laws. (3) The *judiciary*, meanwhile, is responsible for the interpretation of the law and its application in individual cases.

Classification Schemes: The precise arrangement of the offices of government varies from state to state. Ever since Aristotle, the study of government attempted to classify the varieties of governments according to different types. The purpose of such classification exercises has varied, and has included both a desire to make normative statements about the best type of government and positive statements concerning the behavioural implications of different governmental structures. But all the classification exercises have in common an attempt to produce conceptual categories that make it possible to make meaningful generalizations about government in the face of a bewildering variation in the ways governments are organized.

Classifications of government are legion, yet some common threads can be discerned. Classifications have tended to concentrate on two criteria: (1) The arrangement of offices, which is more narrow in conception. (2) The relationship between the government and the governed.

(1) The first criterion has produced two classification schemes which are in wide currency amongst political scientists, particularly amongst students of democratic government. (a) The first of these classification schemes is based on the relationship between the executive and the legislature. In a parliamentary system, the executive is dependent for its continuance in office upon maintaining the support of the legislature. Members of the executive are commonly also members of the legislature. While a prime minister may be the most powerful member of the executive, important decisions within the executive are usually made collectively by a group of ministers. In a presidential system, on the other hand, the executive is independent of the legislature. Members of the executive are not normally also members of the legislature, while the ultimate source of decision-making authority within the executive lies with one man – the president. (b) The second classification concentrates on the distribution of power between different levels of government. In a unitary state all authority to make laws is vested in one supreme legislature whose jurisdiction covers the whole country. While it may permit local legislatures to exist, they do so only on the sufferance of the main legislature. In a federal state, on the other hand, there exist local legislatures which have at least a measure of guaranteed autonomous decision-making authority. Both forms of government can be distinguished from a confederation, where a group of

states combine for certain purposes but with each state retaining its sovereignty.

(2) Classifications based on the second criterion – the relationship between the government and the governed – have commonly concentrated on the extent to which governments attempt to achieve their aims by coercion of their citizens rather than persuasion, and on the extent to which limits are placed on the legitimate authority of government. The precise formulation of classification schemes based on this criterion varies widely, but not uncommonly a distinction is drawn between, at one extreme, liberal democratic government and, at the other, totalitarian governments. Under liberal democratic government, government is seen as primarily responsive to the wishes of society, and clear limitations are placed upon its ability to coerce society or to mould it in any particular way. Totalitarian governments, on the other hand, have few limits placed upon them and are seen as instruments whereby society may be changed.

New Approaches
The study of government has changed considerably since the Second World War. Historically, the study of government grew out of the study of constitutional law. It was characterized by a concentration on the formal institutions of government and upon constitutional provisions, while individual countries tended to be studied in isolation rather than in comparative framework. However, under the influence of the behavioural revolution, scholars have paid increasing attention to how governments actually operate, to institutions outside the formal apparatus of the state but which play a vital role in its operation (such as political parties and pressure groups), and to explicitly comparative study. Particularly influential in the development of comparative study have been approaches derived from systems theory, especially structural-functionalism. These approaches have attempted to develop a conceptual language, based upon the functions that are performed within any society, that could be applied to the study of government in any country, including developing as well as advanced societies.

John Curtice
University of Liverpool

Reference
Finer, S. E. (1974), *Comparative Government*, Harmondsworth.

Further Reading
Almond, G. A. and Coleman, J. S. (eds) (1960), *The Politics of the Developing Countries*, Princeton.
Easton, D. (1965), *A Systems Analysis of Political Life*, New York.
See also: *administration; authority; constitutions and constitutionalism; power; state.*

Gramsci, Antonio (1891–1937)

Antonio Gramsci, a native of Sardinia, was one of the outstanding Marxist thinkers of this century. After leaving Turin University, he became a leading activist and journalist in the Italian Socialist Party (PSI). During Italy's *biennio rosso* of 1919–20, a period of great unrest, he championed the cause of factory councils, and he developed his theory of councils in *L'Ordine Nuovo*, a weekly review which he co-edited. The network of councils was seen as both the main agency of revolutionary change and the embryonic structure of the future society. After the rise of Fascism, however, Gramsci abandoned this theory – denounced as 'syndicalist' by his more orthodox comrades – and turned his attention to the co-ordinative and educational role of the party. In 1921, he, along with fellow left-wing dissidents, split off from the PSI to form the *Partito comunista d'Italia*, an organization which he led from 1924 to 1926, the year he was imprisoned by Mussolini's regime.

While in prison Gramsci composed his *Prison Notebooks*, a massive, disordered, and unfinished work which is nevertheless a classic of our time. The *Notebooks*, elaborating ideas which had often been implicit in his earlier newspaper articles, put forward a humanist conception of Marxism, focusing on human subjectivity – on beliefs, values, aspirations and theories. Influenced by Croce's brand of idealist philosophy, and with scant regard for orthodoxy, Gramsci challenged crucial theoretical elements of classical Marxism: the reductive physicalism which denied reality to anything but matter; the passive, or contemplative, conception of knowledge; the attempt to extend the methods of the natural sciences to the study of man; the belief that history obeys universal causal laws similar to those of the physical sciences; the dismissal of cultural and political activities as pale reflections of economic practices; the assumption that capitalism is a conflict-ridden system precariously held together by coercion; and the optimistic conviction that the downfall of capitalism is guaranteed by its inherent contradictions. In Gramsci's view, conventional Marxism had disastrously imposed a metaphysical, or transcendent, design on history, independent of human will and action – though the 'hidden God' was no longer Hegel's 'Spirit' but an equally abstract and impersonal 'Nature'.

Gramsci is best remembered for his doctrine of 'hegemony', or moral/spiritual supremacy, according to which the ascendancy of a class or group rests, essentially, on its ability to translate its own worldview into a pervasive dominant ethos, guiding the patterns of daily life. Because of bourgeois hegemony, Marxists should, in his opinion, adopt a non-Bolshevik strategy, whereby the revolutionary party effects a mental transformation of the masses *before* seizing power. The emphasis shifts from political to cultural revolution, to the long-term task of scraping away 'the muck of ages'. This patient, 'gradualist' approach was, as Gramsci realized, incompatible with the Leninist conception of the party as a monolithic, quasi-military structure, aloof from the everyday concerns of the people. His version of Marxism, with its stress on persuasion, culture and mass participation, has given inspiration to the 'Eurocommunists', in their efforts to distance themselves from Moscow. Gramsci himself, however, remained a committed revolutionary, though he wanted a 'majority' not a 'minority' revolution.

Joseph V. Femia
University of Liverpool

Reference

Gramsci, A. (1975), *Quaderni del Carcere*, 4 vols, ed. V. Gerratana, Turin (trans. Q. Hoare and G. Nowell Smith, *Selections from the Prison Notebooks*, London 1971).

Further Reading

Adamson, W. L. (1980), *Hegemony and Revolution: Antonio Gramsci's Political and Cultural Theory*, Berkeley and Los Angeles.
Femia, J. V. (1981), *Gramsci's Political Thought: Hegemony, Consciousness, and the Revolutionary Process*, Oxford.

Graph Theory

Graph theory (Harary, 1969) is a branch of topology and the cornerstone of combinatorics. It studies patterns of relationships among pairs of abstract elements. Represented pictorially, a graph consists of a point set with some points joined by lines (see Figure 1). Common empirical interpretations of graphs are social networks and genealogical trees where the points represent persons and the lines relations of communication and descent respectively. Leonhard Euler began the formal study of graph theory in 1736 when he resolved the celebrated Königsberg Bridge Problem. There have been numerous rediscoveries of graph theory since then. Thus, Cayley utilized tree-graphs to

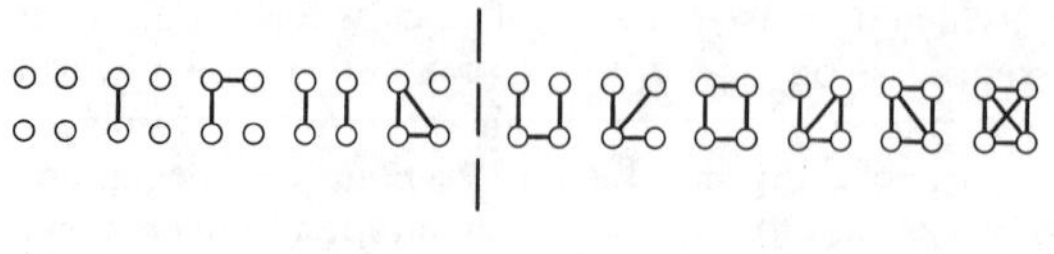

Figure 1 The graphs with four points (G59)

enumerate organic chemical isomers, and the physicist Kirchhoff initiated electrical engineering, modelling the topology of an electrical network by its abstract graph.

Firmly established in the natural sciences, graph theory has become the essential model for structural analysis in the social sciences. First explicitly applied in social psychology – for example, to the analysis of balance in cognitive structures, and status in organizations (Harary, Norman and Cartwright, 1965) – it was the natural model for social network studies concerning the effects of direct and indirect connections on individual and group behaviour (Barnes, 1972). The current multidisciplinary interest in graph theory in computer and social science is reflected in the new journal, *Social Networks*.

The expanding range of real world applications of graph theory is shown by recent results in anthropology (Hage and Harary, 1983) which draw on all adjacent disciplines. The distance between points in a graph is essential for studying the relative centrality of communities in trade networks and for articulating the interaction between mediated communication and power in informal political systems. A signed graph has positive and negative values on its lines; here the concepts of balance and clustering serve to explicate folk theories of consistency in kinship relations, and they model the evolution of political alliances. Directed graphs or digraphs (those with arrows on the lines) give highly intuitive representations of logical relations and thus facilitate the purely formal, comparative approach to social structure originally proposed by Lévi-Strauss. The concept of structural duality in graphs – dual operations applied to each type of graph, ordinary, signed and directed – yields transformation rules for myths and disentangles the variety of meanings of 'opposite' in structural analysis. The interactions between graphs and groups make explicit the permutational models evoked in structuralism. Finally, networks (graphs or digraphs with numerical values on the lines) enable the analysis of group processes such as fission and fusion. The probabilistic theory of Markov chains provides models for simulating subsistence practices where the ethnographic record is weak or absent.

The attractions of graph theory for the practising social scientist (whether anthropologist, archaeologist, economist, geographer, historian, political scientist, psychologist or sociologist) are fourfold: (1) The models are iconic and intuitively meaningful. (2) The language is rich as well as exact and thus is just as applicable to the analysis of efficacy in primitive mnemonics as connectivity in social networks. (3) There are techniques for the calculation of quantitative aspects of structure through the application of matrix algebra. (4) Finally, graph theory contains theorems which enable one to draw conclusions about certain properties of a structure from knowledge of other properties.

Per Hage
University of Utah

Frank Harary
University of Michigan

References

Barnes, J. A. (1972), *Social Networks*, Reading, Mass.
Hage, P. and Harary, F. (1983), *Structural Models in Anthropology*, Cambridge.
Harary, F. (1969), *Graph Theory*, Reading, Mass.
Harary, F., Norman, R. Z. and Cartwright, D. (1965), *Structural Models: An Introduction To the Theory of Directed Graphs*, New York.

See also: *networks*.

Greenberg, Joseph H. (1915–)

Joseph H. Greenberg, distinguished American linguist and anthropologist, was born in Brooklyn, New York, on 28 May 1915. He took his bachelor's degree at Columbia University in 1936 and his Ph.D. (anthropology) at Northwestern University in 1940. He taught at the University of Minnesota from 1946 to 1948 and Columbia University from 1948 to 1962; since 1962 he has been professor of anthropology and linguistics at Stanford University.

Greenberg is a versatile scholar who has made major contributions in the areas of kinship, traditional religion, poetics, culture history, language contact, and linguistic reconstruction. His most important, best-known work has been concerned with language classification and language universals.

(1) *Language Classification*: Greenberg's major work in this area (Greenberg, 1963a) is his comprehensive classification of the languages of Africa. As presented in revised form in 1963, the classification assigned all of the thousand or so languages of Africa to four large stocks: Niger-Kordofanian, Nilo-Saharan, Afroasiatic (formerly 'Hamito-Semitic') and Khoisan. Significant departures from earlier classifications of African languages included the following: (a) The Bantu languages were treated as a closely knit family related to the languages of West Africa rather than as an independent stock. (b) The 'Hamitic' family was rejected *in toto* as a racially inspired concept having no linguistic reality. Languages previously classified as 'Hamitic', such as Fulani, Maasai, Hausa and Nama (Hottentot) were assigned as appropriate to the four established stocks. (c) The sub-Saharan Chadic languages were placed within the Afroasiatic stock alongside languages of North Africa and the Near East such as Berber,

Ancient Egyptian, Hebrew and Somali.

Greenberg has also provided substantive classifications of Oceanic and American Indian languages. In addition, he has done important work on the theory and methodology of language classification, typological as well as historical/genetic (Greenberg, 1957).

(2) *Language Universals*: Greenberg's innovative approach to language universals, dating from the early 1960s (Greenberg, 1963b; 1966; 1978), represented a revolutionary break from the then dominant ethos in American linguistics and anthropology, namely the extreme relativistic, particularistic view that the structure of each language was unique and potentially completely different from that of every other language. Greenberg demonstrated that from the comparative study of large numbers of languages, one could draw significant empirical generalizations about languages as a whole, the so-called 'language universals'. For example, given the three categories Subject (S), Verb (V) and Object (O), six word orders are logically possible, whereas in fact only three (SOV, SVO, VSO) commonly occur (and these in very unequal numbers) while the others are exceedingly rare. Greenberg further developed the concept of implicational universals, that is, generalizations of the form, 'If a language has X, then Y holds,' there being no universal requirement that a language must have X. For example, if a language has nasalized vowels (and many do not) it holds universally that the number of such vowels will not exceed the number of non-nasal vowels in the same language.

A live question spawned by Greenberg's work has been to explain why the universals exist. Greenberg himself has shown that some universals at least are a natural consequence of known processes of language change. Other scholars have continued to seek explanations in terms of formal grammar, pragmatics or psychology.

Paul Newman
Indiana University, Bloomington

References

Greenberg, J. H. (1957), *Essays in Linguistics*, Chicago.
Greenberg, J. H. (1963a), *The Languages of Africa*, Bloomington.
Greenberg, J. H. (ed.) (1963b), *Universals of Language*, Cambridge, Mass.
Greenberg, J. H. (1966), *Language Universals*, The Hague.
Greenberg, J. H. (ed.) (1978), *Universals of Human Language*, 4 vols, Stanford.

Further Reading

Juilland, A. (ed.) (1976), *Linguistic Studies Offered to Joseph Greenberg on the Occasion of his Sixtieth Birthday*, Saratoga, California.

Grid/Group

A grid/group is a typological paradigm for the comparative analysis of cultures and the forms of social organization that support them. Introduced by Mary Douglas in *Natural Symbols* (1970), and developed by her in *Cultural Bias* (1978) and by Gross and Rayner in *Measuring Culture* (1985), grid and group are each polythetic variables that describe the social organization of the units to be compared.

The *group* variable represents the extent to which people are restricted in their social transactions by their commitment to a social unit larger than the individual. Using measures loosely based on network theory, high or low values may be assigned to group strength. It is low when people negotiate their way through life on their own behalf as individuals, neither constrained by nor reliant upon a single group of others. Group strength is highest when people devote their available time to interacting with other members of a social unit to which they owe allegiance and which they count on for support.

The *grid* variable consists of a complementary bundle of constraints on social interaction; constraints on how people interact rather than with whom. In common with multiple hierarchy analysis, grid is designed to provide a composite index of the constraints upon peoples' behaviour by categorical distinctions such as gender, class, colour, age, descent in a certain clan or lineage, and the like.

Grid is high strength whenever roles are distributed on the basis of these explicit social classifications. A low-grid organization is one in which there is less differentiation of distinctive social roles dependent on ascribed characteristics. Access to roles at low grid is achieved rather than ascribed, and may even depend on formal rules for taking turns.

When the grid and group variables are represented as a pair or orthogonal co-ordinates, simultaneous consideration of high or low strength of each co-ordinate gives rise to four prototype possibilities of social life (ideal types) to which any social unit, thus measured, may conform. These four social contexts have been given animal mnemonics by Gerald Mars in *Cheats at Work* (1982): (1) Low-grid/low-group *hawks* are competitive entrepreneurs. (2) High-grid/high-group *wolfpacks* form bureaucratic or hierarchical corporate systems. (3) Low-grid/high-group *vultures* constitute egalitarian small-groups. (4) High-grid/low-group *donkeys* are atomized individuals with limited scope for determining their destiny and for forming alliances.
social organization. Grid/group proposes the hypothesis that, in each social context, shared cultural ideas about such things as nature, time and space, morality, human nature, and so on will be structured in such a way that individuals within it can steer their way through the constraints they experience in daily life – to make sense of the world they live in. This structuring of culture is shared by all social units in any single grid/group context, irrespective of whether they are African villages or London law firms.

The grid/group typology is a useful tool both for comparing different social units at a fixed time, and for charting changes in a single unit over a period of time. However (as in all comparisons) for reliable results care must be taken that the social units chosen for comparison are comparable in other respects, and scale variables held constant. The level of analysis is that of face-to-face interactions, and although it is not necessary to obtain grid/group scores for every member of a social unit (standard sampling techniques may be employed), grid/group analysis works best when the social units being compared are of similar scale.

Steve Rayner
Oak Ridge National Laboratory, Tennessee

See also: *Douglas*.

Group Dynamics

'Group Dynamics' was originally the term used, from the 1930s to the early 1950s, to characterize the study of changes in group life by Kurt Lewin and his followers (Lewin, 1948). Gradually, however, the term lost its restricted reference and came to be more or less synonymous with 'the study of small groups'. It is in this broader, second, sense that it will be used here.

A small group consists of from three to about three dozen persons, every one of whom can recognize and react to every other as a distinct individual, and the members are likely to manifest sustained interaction, perception of group membership, shared group goals, affective relations, and norms internal to the group which may be organized around a set of roles. These are amongst the most commonly invoked criteria of groups.

According to Hare (1976), by end of the first decade of this century about twenty social scientific articles on small groups had appeared, and many of the subsequent concerns of small-group research had been identified. Triplett (1898) posed questions and conducted experiments investigating the effect of the group on individual performance. Within the next half-dozen years, Cooley had written about the importance of the primary group, Simmel had discussed some of the consequences of group size, Taylor, the apostle of 'scientific management' techniques, had started to examine pressures on individuals to conform to group norms regarding productivity, and Terman (1904) had studied group leaders and leadership. From about 1920 onwards the rate at which relevant publications appeared started to increase. The 1930s saw the appearance of three classic lines of research: the work of Lewin *et al.* on different styles of leadership, parts of the programme of research at the Western Electric Company's Hawthorn plant, together with the beginnings of Mayo's misleading popularization of its findings (see Rose, 1975), and reports by Moreno and others of sociometric techniques designed to represent choices, preferences or patterns of affect in a group.

By the late 1930s, the developing study of group processes, in the United States at any rate, was seen as part of the defence of conventional democratic practices in the face of authoritarian threats, and these hopes and expectations continued through the 1940s to the heyday of small-group research, the 1950s and early 1960s. During that period Bales produced his category system for the relatively detailed description of group interaction processes, the sensitivity or experiential group appeared on the scene (Hartman, 1979) and those not preoccupied with experiential groups increasingly studied laboratory experimental ones. From the mid-1950s onwards, Hare calculated that about 200 articles or books on groups were appearing each year. The quantity of work has not abated, but the sense of excitement and enthusiasm has. Mainly via laboratory experiments, a variety of delimited issues, often refinements of earlier topics, have provided successive foci for attention, including co-operation and competition, aspects of group cohesion, leadership styles, social influence processes including minority influences, group decision making and group polarization, personal space and density, and interpersonal attraction. Increasing methodological sophistication has been claimed and the absence of major theoretical advances bemoaned (Zander, 1979; McGrath and Kravitz, 1982).

Let us examine some of the field's achievements in the four major areas of (1) group structure; (2) leadership; (3) processes; and (4) products, before turning to a brief critique.

(1) Various aspects of the structure of groups have been studied. Of these the most common have been the affective or liking structures, communication networks, power relations and role structures. Rather less attention has been paid to the interrelations of conceptually distinguishable types of group structures.

(2) Hierarchically organized structures may suggest the existence of leaders, and from Terman (1904) onwards considerable effort was invested in attempts to specify recurring personality and social correlates of individuals who were leaders, but with only limited success. After a brief flirtation with the opposite strategy of attempting to relate the emergence of leaders to features of specific situations, in recent decades the emphasis has been on increasingly sophisticated attempts to understand leadership, which may or may not be concentrated in a particular individual leader. Leadership functions, roles and styles have all been examined in some detail (for example, Fiedler, 1967).

(3) A major part of the study of group processes has been concerned with social influence processes. Classic laboratory studies by Sherif and Asch demonstrated the powerful impact on group members of internal groups norms and led to a continuing emphasis on conformity within groups. More recent work from Europe, however, has shown that conformity need not always be on the part of a minority towards a majority (Moscovici, 1976) and that a group consensus or decision need not represent a mere averaging of individuals' views (Fraser and Foster, 1984).

(4) From Triplett onwards, the outcomes or effectiveness of groups has been a major issue. It has become conventional to distinguish two sets of criteria of group effectiveness. (a) Criteria such as quantity, quality, economy and speed measure success on the extrinsic task and can be regarded as assessing a group's productivity. (b) Measures of interpersonal pleasure, socio-emotional effectiveness and group stability are assessments of group satisfaction. While productivity and satisfaction are often assumed to go together, there have been many empirical demonstrations that they need not, so that a strong relationship between productivity and satisfaction is better seen as an ideal to aim at rather than a fact of life. Attempts to specify the determinants of group effectiveness are virtual summaries of research on group dynamics (see Hare, 1976).

Initially the study of group dynamics was held to offer answers to a number of democracy's problems (Zander, 1979), but the group dynamics movement's most tangible legacy was the spawning of, first, group-centred training groups and then individual-centred existential groups. This move from a concern with the world's problems to the soothing of personal anxieties is perhaps symptomatic of the failure, as yet, of the study of groups to fulfil its potential (Steiner, 1974). All too often narrow questions have been studied by increasingly restricted methods, leading, at best, to mini-theories which have failed to sustain interest in the issues. Some of the reasons for this reflect North American experimental social psychology more generally. But the nature of the 'groups' studied, particularly in recent decades, must be a prime contributing factor. In practice, the study of small groups has not been primarily concerned with families, friends, committees, and the multitude of naturalistic groups that mediate between individuals and the societies they live in. Instead it has examined small collectivities of student strangers meeting for no more than an hour at a time; it is possible that a majority of 'groups' studied have manifested few, if any, of the defining properties of actual groups. In an analogy with 'nonsense syllables', Fraser and Foster (1984) have dubbed them 'nonsense groups', and if group dynamics is to regain its position as a major field in the social sciences, the rediscovery of real social groups would appear to be a necessity.

Colin Fraser
University of Cambridge

References
Fiedler, F. E. (1967), *A Theory of Leadership Effectiveness*, New York.
Fraser, C. and Foster, D. (1984), 'Social groups, nonsense groups and group polarization', in H. Tajfel (ed.), *The Social Dimension: European Developments in Social Psychology*, vol. II, Cambridge.
Hare, A. P. (1976), *Handbook of Small Group Research*, 2nd edn, New York.
Hartman, J. J. (1979), 'Small group methods of personal change', *Annual Review of Psychology*, 30.
Lewin, K. (1948), *Resolving Social Conflicts: Selected Papers on Group Dynamics*, New York.
McGrath, J. E. and Kravitz, D. A. (1982), 'Group research', *Annual Review of Psychology*, 33.
Moscovici, S. (1976), *Social Influence and Social Change*, London.
Rose, M. (1975), *Industrial Behaviour: Theoretical Development since Taylor*, London.
Terman, L. M. (1904), 'A preliminary study of the psychology and pedagogy of leadership', *Pedagogical Seminary*, 11.
Triplett, N. (1898), 'The dynamogenic factors in pacemaking and competition', *American Journal of Psychology*, 9.
Zander, A. (1979), 'The psychology of group processes', *Annual Review of Psychology*, 30.

Further Reading
Steiner, I. D. (1974), 'Whatever happened to the group in social psychology?', *Journal of Experimental Social Psychology*, 10.
 See also: *communication networks; conformity; group therapy; groups; leadership; social psychology.*

Groups

The concept group features prominently in sociology and anthropology because of their interest in social relationships that are habitual, institutionalized and relatively enduring. Group has been used in many different ways, but it commonly refers to a plurality of individuals bounded by some principle of recruitment and by a set of membership rights and obligations. Everyone fulfilling the recruitment criteria is a member of the group and occupies a specific status in the group, and every group member automatically has the rights and discharges the obligations of membership. Groups are, in turn, the main elements of the social structure.

Recent critics of such a conceptualization of groups stress the fact that the notion of a society as consisting of permanent discrete groups is not a generalization from the observable social processes, but is either the analyst's model or a model that the members themselves have of their own society. When the object of the analysis is not to explain actual social processes, but rather the actors' cultural notions, or the cognitive structure of a given society, then the group can be defined simply in terms of the ideology of group membership.

Reference group (Merton and Kitt, 1950) refers to a collection of persons with which an individual identifies, or which he uses as a point of reference for his aspirations; it is a typical example of a group as a notional entity. But the manifestation of groups in actual interactional situations cannot be assumed to follow automatically from their existence as notional phenomena. Instead, the interactions of specific individuals are seen to derive from their decisions about which of their numerous statuses or group memberships, or which of their interpersonal relationships, they wish to activate. In turn, these decisions cannot be generalized in terms of permanent groups but only in terms of cultural preferences. The distinction between the cognitive model of the society as consisting of permanent discrete groups, and the actual social processes in which the society's members are involved, led to the conceptual distinction between the social structure and social organization (Firth, 1951) and to the development of network analysis. It also led to a more rigorous conceptualization of a group and to the analytical distinction between social groups and social categories.

A *social category* is a collection of individuals grouped conceptually because of some shared socially relevant features or characteristics (age, sex, occupation, religious beliefs, common ancestry, mutual genealogical relationship, and so on). A *social group* consists of individuals who interact in an interconnected set of roles (such as economic, political, ritual, occupational). While membership of a specific category usually defines eligibility for membership in a group, taking up group membership is not an automatic process; whether an eligible person will activate his group membership depends on many contingent factors other than belonging to the category. Depending on the nature of the interaction of its members, it is customary to distinguish *primary* groups whose members interact face to face (for example, a household or family) from *secondary* groups all of whose members do not necessarily interact directly and personally with one another (for example occupational or political groups). Some groups have the character of corporations in that they control a body of property or estate which may be either material (such as land or capital equipment) or immaterial (such as skills, privileges, ritual names, titles). Ownership of this property is held by the group as a single entity, and all its members acquire certain rights in the joint property. In consequence, corporate groups typically exhibit greater continuity than non-corporate groups: they retain their identity as groups over time although their personnel changes.

At the other extreme is an action group or task group. It consists of individuals who assemble in some organized fashion to perform jointly a specific task. Action groups have only a limited existence in time, and they dissolve once the task for which they organized themselves has been completed. What distinguishes most groups from a task group and other units like crowds, or gatherings whose existence is also temporary, is their more or less permanent existence deriving from the fact that their members interact recurrently and that they have a more or less enduring internal organization and discreteness, though these characteristics may be variously defined and stressed by different analysts.

Ladislav Holy
University of St Andrews

References
Firth, R. (1951), *Elements of Social Organisation*, London.
Merton, R. K. and Kitt, A. (1950), 'Contributions to the theory of reference group behavior', in R. K. Merton and P. Lazarsfeld (eds), *Continuities in Social Research*, Glencoe, Ill.

Further Reading
Bales, R. F. (1951), *Interaction Process Analysis*, Reading, Mass.
Homans, G. C. (1950), *The Human Group*, New York.
Hare, A. P., Borgatta, E. and Bales, R. F. (eds) (1955), *Small Groups*, New York.
See also: *networks; social structure*.

Group Therapy

Group therapy implies a group of people who, in an optimal environment with a leader or leaders skilled in psychodynamics, interact for the purpose of conflict resolution and social maturation. For such a process to occur, regularly scheduled meetings over an extended period of time are usually regarded as essential. This is the stand taken by most group psychotherapists whose basic training includes an extensive knowledge of Freudian psychodynamics and/or object relations theory.

As with any relatively new discipline, universal standards of training and practice have not yet been formulated, but most agree that a mix of didactic and experiential experiences is essential. Until we understand the details of group process more fully, it is inevitable that psychoanalytic theory remains the basis of didactic training and, also, that some form of exposure to actual group process is part of a group therapist's 'apprenticeship' (Roman and Porter, 1978).

Intellectual understanding of group phenomena is not enough, and the therapist must, among other things, be able to empathize with his clients' anxieties and gauge their stress tolerance if he is to help them grow. At the same time he must be acutely aware of his own subjective responses to the clients; it is here that a personal psychoanalytic training is often considered to be invaluable.

Perhaps the most intriguing part of group therapy is the way it forces one to recognize nuances of interpersonal behaviour that are usually missed (for a detailed discussion of therapy, see Yalom, 1970). In fact, it amounts to a depth perspective where the spoken word is no longer the pre-eminent aspect of communication but only a part. A subtle process is at work in the group where members begin to identify themselves with the group and place increasing trust in it. This build-up of trust is partly the result of the group's performance in assuming responsibility for its members and partly due to other more intangible factors, for example, man's need for a family or social support system. Little is as yet understood about intuition but it is linked with philosophy and religion in many cultures. Further research in this area is needed if we are to understand better the nature of evolution and change which are an integral part of group process. At a more tangible level we know that the wisdom of the group can amount to more than the total inputs of the individuals concerned – this synergism is part of a creative process and links group therapy with education and growth.

A training in group therapy can be invaluable in many areas of ordinary life where interpersonal conflict is seldom turned into a learning or growth experience. This is particularly true in our educational system where teachers lacking skills in group dynamics, tend to rely on punishment to redress deviant behaviour and thus lose an invaluable opportunity for learning at a formative age. Similar skills would seem to be called for in all walks of life, from arbitration in trade disputes, prison reform, or consumer advocacy to holistic issues world-wide.

Maxwell Jones
Nova Scotia

References
Roman, M. and Porter, K. (1978), 'Combining experiential and didactic aspects in a new group therapy training approach', *International Journal of Group Psychotherapy*, 28.
Yalom, D. (1970), *The Theory and Practice of Group Psychotherapy*, New York.
See also: *group dynamics; therapeutic community*.

Gurvitch, Georges (1894–1965)

Georges Gurvitch, following his return to France from America in the aftermath of the Second World War, became the central figure in French-speaking sociology right to the time of his death. Founder in 1946 of the *Cahiers Internationaux de Sociologie* and co-founder in the 1950s of the International Association of French-speaking Sociologists, his seminars at the Sorbonne in Paris and his various writings and edited volumes (*La Sociologie au vingtième siècle*, 2 vols, 1947; *La Vocation actuelle de la sociologie*, 2 vols, 1950; *Traité de sociologie*, 2 vols, 1958 and 1960; *The Spectrum of Social Time*, 1964) provided interdisciplinary bridges between sociology, history, anthropology and social psychology. His rejection of systemic, static analyses of social reality led him to bitter intellectual disputes with the 'social system' approach of Talcott Parsons and the 'structuralism' of Lévi-Strauss. It is hard to pinpoint the crux of his sociological ideas (see Bosserman, 1968; Swedberg, 1982) which reflect as much philosophical influences (Fichte, Bergson and Husserl, among others) and socialist currents (Saint-Simon, Proudhon and Marx) as sociological ones (Weber, Durkheim and, particularly, Mauss). He delineated various types of social groups and bonds, various types of 'global societies' and various 'depth levels' of social reality. He characterized his sociology as a 'dialectical hyper-empiricism', and felt particularly close to P.-J. Proudhon (*Proudhon, sa vie, son oeuvre*, 1965) not only for his radical dialectics (viewing society as progressing only by means of conflict) but also for his political views stressing decentralization and workers' control of the means of production ('autogestion').

Gurvitch was certainly a person committed to sociological praxis. He took an active part in the Russian Revolution, and had to flee after criticizing Lenin. He denounced early the Hitler regime, and in the 1950s bitterly opposed the Algerian War, as well as tendencies towards the centralization of power in modern technico-bureaucratic society.

Edward A. Tiryakian
Duke University

References

Bosserman, P. (1968), *Dialectical Sociology: An Analysis of the Sociology of George Gurvitch*, Boston.

Swedberg, R. (1982), *Sociology as Disenchantment: The Evolution of the Work of Georges Gurvitch*, Atlantic Heights, N.J.

H

Habermas, Jürgen (1929–)

Jürgen Habermas has been the most prolific and influential representative of the 'second generation' of the Frankfurt School. He has both continued the theoretical tradition of his teachers Adorno and Horkheimer and his friend Marcuse, and has also significantly departed from 'classical' critical theory and made many important new contributions to contemporary philosophy and social theory. In particular, he has opened critical theory to a dialogue with other philosophies and social theories such as the hermeneutics of Gadamer, systems theory and structural functionalism, empirical social sciences, analytic and linguistic philosophy, and theories of cognitive and moral development. In recent years, he has been synthesizing these influences into a theory of 'communicative action', which presents the foundation and framework of a social theory that builds on the tradition of Marx, Weber and classical critical theory, but which also criticizes his predecessors and breaks new theoretical ground.

Habermas was born on 18 June 1929 in Dusseldorf, and grew up in Gummersbach, Germany. His father was head of the Bureau of Industry and Trade, and his grandfather was a minister and director of the local seminary. He experienced the rise and defeat of Fascism, and was politicized by the Nuremberg trials and documentary films of the concentration camps shown after the war. Habermas began his university studies in Göttingen in 1949 and finished a dissertation of *Das Absolute und die Geschichte* in 1954. In the 1950s, Habermas studied – and was strongly influenced by – Lukács's *History and Class Consciousness* and Adorno and Horkheimer's *Dialectic of Enlightenment* which he first read in 1955. He studied the young Marx and the young Hegelians with Karl Löwith, one of Germany's great scholars and teachers.

Habermas resolved to work with Adorno and Horkheimer because he believed that they were establishing a dialectical and critical theory of society from within a creative and innovative Marxist tradition. He thus went to Frankfurt and continued his studies in the Institute for Social Research. In this context, he wrote his first major book *Strukturwandel der Öffentlichkeit* (1962). Combining historical and empirical research with the theoretical framework of critical theory, Habermas traced the historical rise and decline of what he called the 'bourgeois public sphere' and its replacement by the mass media, technocratic administration, and societal depoliticization. This influential work continues to animate discussion concerning problems of representative democracy in contemporary capitalist societies and the need for more participatory, democratic and egalitarian spheres of sociopolitical discussion and debate.

In the 1960s, Habermas taught at the Universities of Heidelberg (from 1961–4) and Frankfurt (from 1964–71). At this time he also became more interested in politics and published *Student und Politik* with others in 1961 which called for university reforms, and *Protestbewegung und Hochschulreform* in 1969 which continued his concern with university reform and also criticized what he saw as the excesses of the German student movement in the 1960s. Habermas was also engaged in intense theoretical work during this period. His *Theorie und Praxis* appeared in 1963 (*Theory and Practice*, Boston, 1973), which contained theoretical papers on major classical and contemporary social and political theorists, as well as anticipations of his own theoretical position; *Zur Logik der Sozialwissenschaften* in 1967 contained a detailed and critical summary of contemporary debates in the logic of the social sciences; *Erkenntnis und Interesse* in 1968, (*Knowledge and Human Interests*, Boston, 1971) traced the development of epistemology and critical social theory from Kant to the present; and several collections of essays: *Technik und Wissenschaft als Ideologie* (1968); *Arbeit-Erkenntnis-Fortschritt* (1970); and *Philosophische-politische Profile* (1971).

During the 1970s Habermas intensified his studies of the social sciences and began restructuring critical theory as communication theory. Key stages of this enterprise are contained in a collection of studies written with Niklas Luhmann, *Theorie der Gesellschaft oder Sozialtechnologie* (1971); *Legitimationsprobleme im Spätkapitalismus* (1973); *Zur Rekonstruktion des Historischen Materialismus* (1976); and essays collected in several other books. In these works, Habermas sharpened his critique of classical Marxism and his critical theory predecessors. He attempted to develop his own reconstruction of historical materialism, a critical theory of society, and a philosophical theory rooted in analyses of communicative action. During much of this period, since 1971, Habermas was director of the Max Planck Institute in Starnberg where he involved himself in various research projects and was in close touch with developments in the social sciences. After a series of disputes with students and colleagues, he resigned in 1982 and returned to Frankfurt where he is now Professor of Philosophy and Sociology.

In 1981, Habermas published his two volume magnum opus, *Theorie des kommunikativen Handelns*. This impressive work of historical scholarship and theoretical construction appraises the legacies of Marx, Durkheim, Weber, Lukács and 'Western Marxism', including critical theory, and criticizes their tendencies towards theoretical reductionism and their failure to develop an adequate theory of communicative action and rationality. Habermas also contributes his own analysis of the importance of communicative action and rationality for contemporary social theory. The book points both to his continuity with the first generation of the Frankfurt school and his significant departures. *Theorie des kommunikativen Handelns* also manifests Habermas's continued interest in the relationship between theory and practice with his discussion of new social movements. The concluding section is a testament to his interest in systematic social theory with a practical intent in his summation of the status of critical theory today. The work as a whole thus sums up Habermas's last decade of theoretical work and points to some issues and topics that will probably constitute future projects. Habermas's legacy thus remains open to new theoretical and political developments and is an important part of contemporary discussions within social theory and science.

Douglas Kellner
University of Texas, Austin

Further Reading

Horster, D. and von Reijen, W. (1979), 'Interview with Jürgen Habermas', *New German Critique*, 18.
McCarthy, T. (1978), *The Critical Theory of Jürgen Habermas*, London.
See also: *Frankfurt School*; *Marcuse*.

Harrod, H. R. F. (1900–78)

Sir Roy Harrod, born in 1900 and schooled in an era when J. S. Mill was still one of the most revered of English philosophers and political economists, became Lecturer in Modern History and Economics at Christ Church, Oxford, in 1922, where he was to teach for the new joint honours course in Politics, Philosophy and Economics. To broaden his economic horizons his college released him for two terms intensive instruction by J.M. Keynes at Cambridge and also sent him to Berlin for several months; in Oxford he learnt much from F.Y. Edgworth, the mathematical eonomist then Drummond Professor. It was Keynes who had the greatest influence on him, however, and the powerful *Life of John Maynard Keynes* which he produced in 1951

owes its unassailable authority to the fact that he was writing of a master, colleague and friend, whose economic system of ideas he knew intimately, and who also valued highly his critical comments on the *Treatise on Money* and *The General Theory of Employment, Interest and Money*. Harrod himself was an original and independent thinker on philosophy as well as economics and made a series of individual pioneer contributions to both theoretical and applied economics in areas where the economics of the inter-war period was breaking loose from neoclassical orthodoxy.

Apart from his early articles in the area of production theory (for example, those published in the *Economic Journal* of 1928 and 1931), Harrod is best known to modern theorists for his distinctive textbook on *International Economics* (1933), his monograph on *The Trade Cycle* (1936), and his famous 'Essay on dynamic theory' (*Economic Journal*, 1939) which became the launch-pad for the post-war theory of economic growth. Meanwhile he maintained an active interest in new directions for applied economic research and in current policy problems. For example, he was a member of the Oxford group of economists which revealed that businessmen preferred to base their pricing policies on a calculation of cost of production plus conventional mark-up (the full cost principle) rather than on the rational profit-maximizing considerations attributed to them by orthodox economic theory; he was a member of Professor Lindemann's wartime group of advisers directly serving Churchill; and he wrote a steady stream of newspaper articles, particularly for the *Financial Times* and particularly on questions of international monetary policy, on which he was a leading authority. Surprisingly, in view of the high respect in which he was held by his fellow economists, he did not achieve the Oxford Professorship and remained Nuffield Reader in International Economics from 1952 to his retirement in 1967.

Phyllis Deane
University of Cambridge

Further Reading

Phelps-Brown, E. H. (1980), 'Sir Roy Harrod: a biographical memoir', *Economic Journal*.

Hayek, Friedrich A. (1899–)

Recipient of the Nobel Prize in Economic Science (together with Gunnar Myrdal) in 1974, Friedrich August von Hayek was born in Vienna on 8 May 1899. He earned two doctorates at the University of Vienna – Dr. jur. (1921) and Dr. rer. pol. (1923) – and became Privatdozent in Political Economy in 1929. He was director of the Austrian Institute for Economic Research from 1927 to 1931. In 1931 he accepted an appointment at the University of London as Tooke Professor of Economic Science and Statistics. He was awarded a D.Sc. degree by that institution in 1944. He remained at London until 1950, when he accepted a position at the University of Chicago. He returned to Europe in 1962 as Professor of Economic Policy at the University of Freiburg, and upon retirement from that institution in 1967 he accepted a position as honorary professor at the University of Salzburg, from which he received an honorary doctor's degree in 1974.

Hayek was instrumental in the founding of the Mont Pelerin Society in April 1947, a society whose aims were to contribute to the preservation and improvement of the free society. He served as president of the Society for twelve years.

Hayek's broad scope of inquiry is reflected in his contributions to economic science. These include: the theory of economic fluctuations; the pure theory of capital; the theory of economic planning under socialism and competitive capitalism; and the methodology of economics.

In addition to many articles, his theory of economic fluctuations was presented in two books: *Monetary Theory and the Trade Cycle* (1926 and 1933) and *Prices and Production* (1931). Beginning with Wicksell's theory of the 'cumulative process', Hayek expanded and modified Wicksell's theory and then proceeded to develop his own theory of economic fluctuations which included such elements as how changes in the quantity of money affect relative prices, rather than general price levels, as well as allocation of resources, especially between producer and consumer goods; the related disturbances in investment period and voluntary saving, as well as 'forced saving'; bank credit and its effects on 'forced saving' and capital deepening; a model of the price mechanism and its operation in the context of fluctuations.

In 1941, Hayek published the *Pure Theory of Capital*, a treatise on capital theory. Among the topics treated and which represented a contribution to the theory of capital were: the concept of 'intertemporal equilibrium'; physical productivity of investment; the phenomenon of natural growth; 'period of investment', the idea of the 'force of interest'; and finally, 'durable goods'.

In spite of his contributions to economic theory, Hayek was never accorded the recognition of his contemporary J. M. Keynes, whose *General Theory* (1936) was accepted as the standard paradigm of economic fluctuations in economics. Also, the Austrian theory of capital had fallen out of fashion by the time his *Pure Theory of Capital* appeared, and his work in this area was largely ignored. The later period of his career was devoted to political and social philosophy and methodology, the most popular of these being *The Road to Serfdom* (1944) and *The Counter-Revolution in Science* (1952).

Vincent J. Tarascio
University of North Carolina

References
Hayek, F. A. (1928), *Geldtheorie und Konjunkturtheorie*, Vienna. (English edn, *Monetary Theory and the Trade Cycle*, London, 1933.)
Hayek, F. A. (1931), *Price and Production*, London.
Hayek, F. A. (1941), *The Pure Theory of Capital*, London.
Hayek, F. A. (1952), *The Road to Serfdom*, London.
Hayek, F. A. (1952), *The Counter-Revolution in Science*, Glencoe, Ill.

Further Reading
Machlup, F. (1974), 'Friedrich von Hayek's contribution to economics', *Scandinavian Journal of Economics*, 76.
Machlup, F. (ed.) (1976), *Essays on Hayek*, New York.
See also: *Austrian school*.

Health Economics

Health economics is concerned with the analysis of health care inputs such as expenditure and employment, and an appraisal of their impact on that desired outcome, the health of society.

Clearly, many imputs may affect an individual's health. In a world of scarce resources it is necessary to ensure that these resources are used efficiently – that the cost of producing care and health is minimized and the benefits are maximized. At the individual level, this can be modelled in a human capital framework (Grossman, 1972). Grossman's model permits an exploration of the links between inputs (such as education, income, wealth, health care and nutrition) and their impact on health status; this work indicates that the relative importance of income and nutrition on health is greater than that of health care.

The evaluation of health care is seriously deficient. Cochrane (1971) has argued that most health care therapies in use today have not been evaluated scientifically. By 'scientifically', he means the application of randomized controlled trials which administer the therapy under investigation to a randomly selected (experimental) group of patients, and a placebo or alternative therapy (a control) to another randomly selected group of patients. The difference, if any, between the therapeutic results for the experimental and control groups gives an indication of the relative impact of the therapies. Such results require replication to ensure validity, and such methods are noticeable by their relative absence (as documented in Bunker, Barnes and Mosteller, 1977).

Such clinical evaluation informs decision makers about the benefits of health care, but an economic component is needed to assess costs. The economist's role is to elicit the social opportunity costs of the alternative therapies, that is, the costs to all decision makers, both public (the government) and private (for example, the individual and his family). A guide to the application of such techniques and an appraisal of over a hundred case studies is provided by Drummond (1980; 1981).

The dominant (monopolist) role of the medical profession in the health care market-place has resulted in an investigation of physicians' capacity to create demand for their own and other people's services (Department of Health and Human Services, 1981). This, together with the fact that third parties (governments and insurance companies, rather than patients or producers) usually pay for health care, has led to cost containment problems (McLachlan and Maynard, 1982). To control such inflation, user charges (prices) can be introduced, a policy that has both costs and benefits (Maynard, 1979; Newhouse *et al.*, 1981); or more effective incentives must be devised to encourage producers (doctors) to economize, for example, through health maintenance organizations (Luft, 1981).

The inefficient use of health care resources is clearly unethical; it deprives patients of care from which they could benefit. The aim of health economists is to generate information about the costs and benefits of alternative ways of achieving health and health goals. It is hoped that such information will improve the efficiency and equity of health care systems across the world.

Alan Maynard
University of York, England

References

Bunker, J. P., Barnes, B. A. and Mosteller, F. (eds) (1977), *The Costs, Benefits and Risks of Surgery*, New York.

Cochrane, A. L. (1971), *Effectiveness and Efficiency*, London.

Department of Health and Human Services (1981), *Physician Induced Demand for Surgical Operations*, Washington D.C.

Drummond, M. F. (1980), *Principles of Economic Appraisal in Health Care*, Oxford.

Drummond, M. F. (1981), *Case Studies in Economic Appraisal in Health Care*, Oxford.

Grossman, M. (1972), *The Demand for Health*, New York and London.

Luft, H. (1981), *Health Maintenance Organisation*, New York.

McLachlan, G. and Maynard, A. (eds) (1982), *The Public Private Mix for Health*, London.

Maynard, A. (1979), 'Pricing, insurance and the National Health Service', *Journal of Social Policy*, 8.

Newhouse, N. P. *et al.* (1981), 'Interim results from a controlled trial of cost-sharing in health-insurance', *New England Journal of Medicine*, 305.

Hegel, Georg Wilhelm F. (1770–1831)

Probably no other philosophy dominates the modern European consciousness to the same extent as Hegel's. Yet few great thinkers have been so consistently misunderstood and their teaching so distorted by friend and foe alike, even today, in spite of the work of specialist Hegel scholars, who in the last decade or two have swarmed as never before. The old stereotypes still persist: the allegedly 'tender-minded' reality-behind-appearance Idealist; the arch-rationalist; the professional historian's *bête noire* with his *a priori* philosophy of history; the apologist of Prussian authoritarianism and the conservatism of the Restoration, the apostle of *Machtpolitik* and totalitarianism, if rarely in their cruder shapes yet often nowadays in more subtle and sophisticated kinds of criticism. Scholars are reluctant, even timid, to start at the other end of the spectrum: to accept Hegel without reserve as the thoroughly down-to-earth realist that he always was, interested especially in what we would call sociological phenomena (and Hegel's *Volksgeist*, for instance, is to be seen in this light and not that of Romantic nationalism); or to see him as the lifelong enthusiast for the ideals of the French Revolution, in many ways closer to Benthamite radicalism than Burkian conservatism, who tried to use philosophy to expound the logic of the claim of modern man to self-realization and freedom and therefore the rationale of the modern democratic state as such, a thinker who is not outside the liberal democratic tradition, but sociologically realistic within it.

It is a strange paradox that Marx did accept much of this, precisely because in his critique of Hegel's political philosophy he was attacking the idea of the state as such, in its most plausible form, and wanted to show that it was self-contradictory, because it was an illusion of the alienated false consciousness of bourgeois society or, rather, non-society, which could not possibly become a reality in the modern world. Marx admired the detail and clarity of Hegel's account of modern society and its sociological realism – only it was 'upside down', like a photographic negative. And for modern Marxists it is an unshakeable dogma that Marx 'demystified' Hegel, removed the centre of gravity from *Geist* to man, and so on. In fact they have created a new myth: not the state, but what in Hegel is one of its 'moments', namely, 'civil society', is all-in-all, and the state is powerless to intervene and correct the self-destructive evils of this sphere of rampant economic liberalism that he analysed so acutely, especially the production of an alienated 'pöbel' or proletariat. Hegel is said to be describing something on its way out. Although this sort of interpretation involves too much looking down the wrong end of the telescope, it does come closer to the real Hegel than traditional liberal distortions, for example, that Hegel 'equated' state and society, in so far as Hegel's view of modern industrial and commercial civilization was not only profoundly critical but closely related to a dialectic designed to develop fully the inherent self-contradictions in all partial truths, and which applies not only to thinking but to the reality that is thought.

An interpretation which spotlights the theme of alienation generally and the need for community need not be Marxist, and in England and America especially this has recently been fashionable. The influence of the *Zeitgeist* seems fairly obvious in this concentration on community rather than state in Hegel, a concentration which is inclined to lean heavily on certain aspects of his immature thought, especially his enthusiasm for the 'beautiful wholeness' of the life-style of the ancient Greeks. The mature Hegel is then interpreted in this light.

All these interpretations suffer from failure to understand the meaning and significance of the religious dimension of Hegel's philosophy, his claim that philosophy is the fully rational truth of Christianity, and how this is reflected in the Hegelian 'concept' or 'notion', the concrete universal that is the tool of Reason, as opposed to the scientific 'Understanding' which knows its objects by separating and dividing. This means accepting the reality and necessity of continuing division and conflict for true harmony and unity in the human spirit and society, and rejecting all belief in a 'beyond' as a pathological symptom of alienation. A true unity is a unity of differences, unlike the primitive undifferentiated wholeness of the Greek *polis*, and a 'rational' state, as understood by philosophy, will be the reverse of totalitarian: it must in fact be pluralistic, since the universal needs the particular as much as the particular needs the universal. It is the 'prodigious strength' of the modern state that it is able to contain its negation: the world of self-seeking particularity that destroyed the primitive unity of the Greek *polis*. This is the fully developed freedom (fully developed in every relevant objective sense, ethical, legal, political and social), of the modern state that makes sense of history, and whose development the philosopher can trace in history. Beyond history and the state is the timeless 'absolute freedom' of art, religion and philosophy; the state and its freedom is not an end in itself. Hegel was in fact 'describing' something on its way in: the *Geist* of modern man, his claim to freedom and the institutions necessary to make that claim real; in many ways he anticipated Max Weber in his account of the modern rational state as an essentially public impersonal institution that belongs to no one but which everyone recognizes as his own in so far as it is seen to uphold his own particular interests, and which generates a perpetual tension between freedom and control, liberty and order.

In the *Grundlinien der Philosophie des Rechts*, 1821 (*Philosophy of Right*, 1942) Hegel spells this out in meticulous detail far surpassing anything to be found in most philosophers who call themselves empirical, and in this he was unnecessarily and dangerously extending his lines into matters that were contingent and time-bound. But it is a superficial view that writes off this sort of thing as 'out-of-date': it is more rewarding to seek the rationale that underlies such obvious anachronisms. And this is in accordance with the Hegelian dialectic, which is not a strict and logically brittle deduction of 'thesis, antithesis and synthesis', but a way of thinking concretely and multi-dimensionally about human experience and of exhibiting such thought, which is one reason why Hegel is 'difficult'. The only test is trueness to life. But anyone who approaches the *Philosophy of Right* in the correct spirit, a book which it should be remembered is not a 'book', but a compendium for a course of lectures, will be repeatedly struck by his soundness and common sense and be able to appreciate the force of his criticism of all abstract thinking about freedom and the state in purely legal or purely ethical or, for that matter, purely sociological modes. But a proper understanding of Hegel requires a sound knowledge of the historical background (which most critics do not have), so that one can make the necessary adjustments in order to arrive at its relevance. The beginner, however, should start with the lectures on the philosophy of history, which Hegel himself designed for beginners, though this too has its dangers. There is simply no short cut to this philosophy, which is a circle, whose end is its beginning. Hegelian dialectic was able to bring home the bacon of sociological realism, as Marx in his own way realized, and political liberalism would have been a lot sounder and healthier if its exponents had realized it too, and not been so busy hunting 'totalitarian' and 'conservative' hares, in country for which they did not possess an adequate map.

Duncan Forbes
University of Cambridge

Further Reading
Avineri, S. (1972), *Hegel's Theory of the Modern State*, Cambridge.
Fleischmann, E. J. (1964), *La Philosophie politique de Hegel*, Paris.
Hegel, G. H. (1975), *Reason in History*, Cambridge.
Knox, T. M. (1967), *Hegel's Philosophy of Right*, London.
Marcuse, H. (1941), *Reason and Revolution*, New York.
Plant, R. (1973), *Hegel*, London.
Pöggeler, O. (ed.) (1977), *Hegel: Einführung in seine Philosophie*, Munich.
Reyburn, H. A. (1921), *Hegel's Ethical Theory*, Oxford.
Rosenzweig, F. (1920), *Hegel und der Staat*, Munich.
Verene, D. P. (ed.) (1980), *Hegel's Social and Political Thought*, New York.
Weil, E. (1950), *Hegel et l'état*, Paris.

Hermeneutics

Hermeneutics is a term used to describe the views of a variety of authors who have been concerned with problems of 'understanding' and 'interpretation'. Some of the themes of hermeneutics were introduced to English-speaking social scientists by the writings of Max Weber. As a participant in the methodological debates which occurred in Germany during the late nineteenth and early twentieth centuries, Weber was familiar with the views of philosophers and historians such as Wilhelm Dilthey, Heinrich Rickert and Wilhelm Windleband, who all argued that the study of the social and historical world requires the use of methods which are different from those employed in the investigation of natural phenomena. These arguments were reflected in Weber's own emphasis on the concept of understanding or *verstehen*.

While Weber played an important role in introducing many social scientists to the ideas of hermeneutics, the latter tradition stretches back to a period well before Weber's time. Hermeneutics derives from the Greek verb *hermēneuein*, which means to make something clear, to announce or to unveil a message. The discipline of hermeneutics first arose, one could say, with the interpretation of Homer and other poets during the age of the Greek Enlightenment. From then on, hermeneutics was closely linked to philology and textual criticism. It became a very important discipline during the Reformation, when Protestants challenged the right of tradition to determine the interpretation of the holy scriptures. Both classical scholars and theologians attempted to elaborate the rules and conditions which governed the valid interpretation of texts.

The scope of hermeneutics was greatly extended by Wilhelm Dilthey (in the nineteenth century). An historian as well as a philosopher, Dilthey was aware that texts were merely one form of what he called 'objectifications of life'. So the problem of interpretation had to be related to the more general question of how knowledge of the social-historical world is possible. Such knowledge is based, in Dilthey's view, on the interrelation of experience, expression and understanding. Cultural phenomena, such as texts, works of art, actions and gestures, are purposive expressions of human life. They are objectified in a sphere of conventions and values which are collectively shared, in the way that a person's attitude may be objectified in the medium of language. To understand cultural phenomena is to grasp them as objectified expressions of life; and ultimately it is to re-experience the creative act, to relive the experience of another. While reorienting hermeneutics towards a reflection on the foundations of the *Geisteswissenschaften* or 'human sciences', Dilthey's writings preserved a tension between the quest for objectivity and the legacy of Romanticism.

The key figure in twentieth-century hermeneutics is Martin Heidegger. Whereas in Dilthey's work the hermeneutical problem is linked to the question of *knowledge*, in Heidegger's it is tied to the question of *being*: problems of understanding and interpretation are encountered while unfolding the fundamental features of our 'being-in-the-world'. For Heidegger, 'understanding' is first and foremost a matter of projecting what we are capable of. This anticipatory character of understanding is a reformulation, in ontological terms, of what is commonly called the 'hermeneutical circle'. Just as we understand part of a text by anticipating the structure of the whole, so too all understanding involves a 'pre-understanding' which attests to the primordial unity of subject and object. We are beings-in-the-world, familiar with and caring for what is ready-to-hand, before we are subjects claiming to have knowledge *about* objects in the world.

Heidegger's work has implications for the way that the human sciences are conceived, as Hans-Georg Gadamer has attempted to show. In *Truth and Method* (1975), Gadamer establishes a connection between the anticipatory character of understanding and the interrelated notions of prejudice, authority and tradition. The assumption that prejudices are necessarily negative is itself an unjustified prejudice stemming, in Gadamer's view, from the Enlightenment. It is an assumption which has prevented us from seeing that understanding always requires pre-judgement or 'prejudice', that there are 'legitimate prejudices' based on the recognition of authority, and that one form of authority which has a particular value is tradition. We are always immersed in traditions which provide us with the prejudices that make understanding possible. Hence there can be no standpoint outside of history from which the totality of historical effects could be grasped; instead, understanding must be seen as an open and continuously renewed 'fusion' of historical 'horizons'.

Gadamer's provocative thesis was challenged in the mid-1960s by Jürgen Habermas and other representatives of 'critical theory'. While acknowledging the importance of Gadamer's hermeneutics for the philosophy of the human sciences, Habermas attacked the link between understanding and tradition. For such a link underplays the extent to which tradition may *also* be a source of power which distorts the process of communication and which calls for critical reflection. Appealing to the model of psychoanalysis, Habermas sketched the framework for a 'depth-hermeneutical' discipline which would be oriented to the idea of emancipation.

The debate between hermeneutics and critical theory has been reappraised by Paul Ricoeur. As a hermeneutic philosopher concerned with critique, Ricoeur has tried to mediate between the positions of Gadamer and Habermas by re-emphasizing the concept of the text. In contrast to the experience of belonging to a tradition, the text presupposes a distance or 'distanciation' from the social, historical and psychological conditions of its production. The interpretation of a text, involving both the structural explanation of its 'sense' and the creative projection of its 'reference', thus allows for the possibility of establishing a critical relation *vis-à-vis* 'the world' as well as 'the self'. Ricoeur shows how the model of the text and the method of text interpretation can be fruitfully extended to the study of such varied phenomena as metaphor, action and the unconscious.

As recent debates indicate, the issues which for centuries have been discussed under the rubric of hermeneutics are still very much alive. The appreciation of texts and works of art, the study of action and institutions, the philosophy of science and social science: in all of these spheres, problems of understanding and interpretation are recognized as central. While few contemporary hermeneutic philosophers would wish to draw the distinction between the natural sciences and the *Geisteswissenschaften* in the way that their nineteenth-century predecessors did, many would nevertheless want to defend the peculiar character of social and historical inquiry. For the *objects* of such inquiry are the product of *subjects* capable of action and understanding, so that our knowledge of the social and historical world cannot be sharply separated from the subjects who make up that world.

John B. Thompson
Jesus College, Cambridge

References

Gadamer, H.-G. (1975), *Truth and Method*, London. (Original German edn, *Wahrheit und Methode*, Tübingen, 1960.)

Palmer, R. E. (1969), *Hermeneutics: Interpretation Theory in Schleiermacher, Dilthey, Heidegger, and Gadamer*, Evanston, Ill.

Ricoeur, P, (1981), *Hermeneutics and the Human Sciences: Essays on Language, Action and Interpretation*, ed. and trans. J. B. Thompson, Cambridge.

See also: *Habermas*; *Weber*.

Hicks, John (1904–)

John Hicks, who was the first Englishman to receive the Nobel Prize in Economics (a joint award with Kenneth Arrow in 1972), has made original contributions to many areas of economics – labour and wages, value, capital, trade cycle theory, growth theory, methodology, ecomomic history, welfare theory and, especially, general equilibrium and monetary theory. He started his intellectual life at Oxford as a mathematician but switched to PPE.

His first job was as a labour economist at the London School of Economics with Lionel Robbins (Hicks had written a thesis on wage differentials at Oxford). Partly as a result of a spell in South Africa in his second year at the LSE, where he analysed the white trade unions in terms of monopoly theory, he became a free market enthusiast. At LSE he was required to lecture on the contributions of the continental economists, and he wrote his first two books, *The Theory of Wages* (1932) and *Value and Capital* (1939), the latter also after a spell of four years at Cambridge in the second half of the 1930s. There, too, he reviewed *The General Theory* for the *Economic Journal* (1936) and wrote 'Mr Keynes and the "Classics" ' (1937), every schoolboy's crib to *The General Theory*. These were preceded by his 'A suggestion for simplifying the theory of money' (1935), and 'Wages and interest: the dynamic problem' (1935), which marked the end of his free market phase as he began to sense the causes of a lack of overall co-ordination in the economic system and the need for intervention. He also wrote some seminal articles on the new welfare economics.

In the post-war period, as an Official Fellow of Nuffield and then as Drummond Professor of Political Economy at Oxford (1952–65) after a period at Manchester, he continued to work on capital and growth theory, on the trade cycle (stimulated by Harrod's dynamics), and on a revision of demand theory, a sequel to his early work with R. G. D. Allen on indifference curves in *Economica* (1934) and his own early chapters in *Value and Capital*.

In all of his work, but especially in the trilogy, *Value and Capital* (1939), *Capital and Growth* (1965), and *Capital and Time* (1973) and their sequels, he has continued to develop his views on how time should be modelled. Hicks modified his approach to this problem in *Value and Capital* when he received the Nobel Prize in 1972 for his 'pioneering contributions to general equilibrium theory and welfare theory', because it did 'deliberate violence to the *order* in which in the real world . . . events occur'. Hicks has been a sturdy self-critic, publicly announcing in 1975 that he needed to change his name – J. R. Hicks, a 'neoclassical economist' and author of *Value and Capital*, was 'now deceased' and 'John Hicks, a non-neoclassic [and the author of *Capital and Time*] . . . is quite disrespectful towards his uncle' (Hicks, 1975). He has also paid generous tributes to the abiding influence of Kaldor (who was his close friend at the LSE in the early 1930s) and to Joan Robinson.

Hicks has continued his studies in monetary theory and waged a determined war against the encroachment in theory and policy of the Monetarists. He has become progressively more radical in his attitudes to government intervention in order to cope with the scourges of unemployment and inflation, but especially of the former. Finally, on a theoretical plane, he has thought deeply on the microeconomic foundations of macroeconomics, eventually, in his *Causality in Economics*

(1979), wondering whether or not he has been chasing a Will o' the Wisp.

G. C. Harcourt
Jesus College, Cambridge

References
Hicks, J. R. (1975), 'Revival of political economy: the old and the new', *Economic Record*, 51.
Hicks, J. R. and Allen, R. G. D. (1934), 'A reconsideration of the theory of value: parts I and II', *Economica*, 1.

Further Reading
Baumol, W. J. (1972), 'John R. Hicks' contribution to economics', *Swedish Journal of Economics*, 74.
Hicks, J. R. (1979), 'The formation of an economist', *Banca Nazionale del Lavoro Quarterly Review*, 130.

Hierarchy

Hierarchy is an organization in grades or orders or ranks of descending power, authority or prestige. In this general meaning, the concept has been absorbed into the social sciences and into common use. But its etymological reference is ecclesiastic. It refers to priestly government, usually to the Roman Catholic Church, but more widely to the graded organization of either angels or clergy. In classical enumeration there were nine functions or orders of the heavenly host subdivided into triads (also called hierarchies) in descending order: Seraphim, Cherubim, Thrones; Dominations, Virtues, Powers; Principalities, Archangels, Angels. The clerical hierarchy reflects the heavenly orders. Its highest triad is formed by baptism, communion and chrism (anointing). Second come the three orders of the ministry, bishops, priests and deacons. Third is the lowest triad of monks, 'initiated' and catechumens (those being prepared for baptism).

The celestial hierarchy is presumably of marginal interest to social scientists, but the earthly hierarchy is part of the complicated history of human organizations. But in its modern secular usage, the word hierarchy has lost, or at least obscured, its connotation of sacredness and function as denoted in the triads described above. Yet these were essential aspects of the organization of the early Christian churches. St Paul appointed bishops at local churches with the pre-eminently spiritual function and spiritual authority of reproducing the Last Supper. As this duty became ritualized into the symbolic ceremony of the Eucharist the bishop was thought of as the representative of the Apostles. It may be that the original churches were collegiate, and therefore almost the opposite of the modern conception of hierarchical, in their organization, holding the authority of Christ collectively. But if so, collegial authority was soon superseded by power vested in a bishop with the presbyters as his council, and deacons appointed by him as administrative assistants. The theory thus emerged of the transmission of authority through the laying on of the bishop's hands.

Further development of the priestly hierarchy followed when Constantine made Christianity the state religion of Rome, willing that the Church be coextensive with his empire. Civil and ecclesiastical administration became standardized, the areas of civil administration being formed to coincide with the ecclesiastical diocese, larger civil regions with patriarchal regions, and the whole Church centred on the supreme patriarchate at Rome. Papal authority thus became supreme in the Church and survived the fall of the Roman Empire.

The hierarchy was challenged at various times in the Middle Ages, notably as a result of the widespread inconsistency between the personal lives of local priests and the official claims of the priesthood to authority over their parishioners. The Lutheran revolt and the ensuing Protestant Reformation challenged the evolved theory of priestly hierarchy as it had developed in imperial and medieval Rome. Luther revived the medieval concept of the secular monarch as the vicar of God on earth in opposition to papal autocracy. The monarch provided the external or secular authority of the Church; internal authority was provided by religious dedication and spiritual grace among the Church members. Calvinism, while also rejecting the Roman hierarchy, gave greater power to its ministers and did not accord supremacy to the state. Calvin's ministers were held to be recipients of divine authority, but it was a collegiate authority vested not in Pope or bishop, but in the representatives chosen from a single united order. In the Church of England the reformed hierarchy is best described as the continuation of Catholicism without the Pope.

Thus the forms of authority and the division of powers and functions between state and church, ministry and laity, vary considerably within Christendom. But all remain hierarchical in the original sense of organizing a divine spiritual authority.

The use of the term hierarchy in modern social science typically lacks this religious reference. Dumont (1970) defines it as 'a ladder of command in which the lower rungs are encompassed in the higher ones in regular succession'. He has in mind here a version of the *Shorter Oxford Dictionary* definition – 'a body of persons or things ranked in grades, orders or classes one above another'. And he refers to Talcott Parsons's (1954) conception of social stratification as a system of ranking based on *evaluation*, which fundamental process of human interaction tends to differentiate individuals and groups into a rank order. From this starting point Dumont develops a comprehensive analysis of the caste system as a hierarchical order.

Caste systems, viewed as a special case of status systems, are essentially hierarchical in the Parsonian sense. Hierarchy can be detached from its religious context and used to describe systems of rank where the elements or strata are judged in relation to the whole. Hierarchy then takes its place as a special form of what is treated in modern sociology and anthropology under the heading of social stratification.

A. H. Halsey
University of Oxford

References
Dumont, L. (1970), *Homo Hierarchicus*, London.
Parsons, T. (1954), 'A revised analytical approach to the theory of social stratification', in T. Parsons, *Essays in Sociological Theory*, Glencoe, Ill.

Further Reading
Tocqueville, A. de (1875), *Democracy in America*, London.
Tocqueville, A. de (1952–3), *L'Ancien Régime et la Révolution*, 2 vols, Paris.
Bendix, R. (1978), *Kings or People*, London.
Bendix, R. and Lipset, S. M. (eds) (1967), *Class, Status and Power*, 2nd edn, London.
See also: *caste*; *equality*; *stratification*.

Historical Linguistics

Historical linguistics, as opposed to History of Linguistics, is the study, reconstruction, theoretical explication and modelling of language change over time. It is the linguistic counterpart of (diachronic) cultural anthropology, cultural or social history, or evolutionary biology.

In the nineteenth century, linguistics *was* predominantly historical: it was the study of evolution and change, not of structure. Following Saussure's radical dichotomy of linguistics into synchronic and diachronic studies as mutually exclusive pursuits (1916), there was a reversal of interest, a period lasting for the most part well into the 1960s, when (in the English-speaking world at least) 'prestige' linguistics was synchronic ('structural'), and historical linguistics was either a minority pursuit of 'general' linguists, or, from the linguist's point of view, an autonomous backwater institutionalized in the universities and journals as 'comparative philology', or 'history of English/German . . .', and so on. (There are notable European exceptions, for example the work of the Prague School, and American exceptions in the work of Sapir, Bloomfield, Hockett, and others – but the generalization holds overall.)

As interest shifted from primary concern with data-processing to 'deeper' theoretical concerns, often with 'explanatory' pretensions (See Lass, 1980), historical linguistics gradually became integrated as a subfield of general linguistics. Each succeeding or competing school ('paradigm') developed a synthesis, in which

techniques of synchronic description and analysis and explanatory claims were applied to historical data, and often (partly at least) validated by their diachronic success. (This assumed, perhaps reasonably, that theories of what something *is* ought to bear on theories of its mutations over time: this could be compared to the largely successful wedding of synchronic genetics and evolutionary theory in biology.)

Current historical linguistics follows three main lines of enquiry:

(1) 'Factual'/'Reconstructive': (i) Reconstructing unattested *états de langue* on the basis of comparison of descendant forms in different languages (for example, Proto-Indo-European *yúg-o-m* 'yoke' on the basis of Latin *jug-u-m*, Greek *zúg-o-n*, Sanskrit *yúg-a-m*, and so on; (ii) construction of 'chronicle' histories of languages or language families (including reworkings of older histories on the basis of new evidence or interpretation); (iii) etymology: constructing phonological and semantic histories of particular words or groups, often showing up relations among forms that seem at first unrelated (such as the connection between *feather*, Greek *pétros* 'rock', and Latin *petere* 'strive' established by Maher, 1973).

These traditional activities, which were the foundation of the discipline, are still practised, applied in some cases to unwritten or 'exotic' language families (see Dixon, 1980 on Australian), or to microhistories of unexplored aspects of familiar languages (see Lass, 1976 on neglected pieces of the history of English).

(2) 'Theoretical'/'interpretive': The reinterpretation of known histories of languages in terms of current (often competing) research paradigms, and the use of historical data to make general theoretical points or validate particular models. An early example is the 'structuralist' synthesis in Hoenigswald (1960); a later one is the generativist synthesis in King (1969). More recently, Lightfoot (1979) attempts to reinterpret aspects of the history of English syntax in the light of a 'restrictive' transformational theory, and Harris (1979) has produced a history of French syntax drawing on recent work in word-order typology and theories of syntactic 'universals'.

(3) 'Sociolinguistic': Contemporary quantitative methods of studying linguistic variation in speech communities, especially the covariation of linguistic and social variables, have led to apparent observations of change 'in progress' (something formerly thought impossible). These studies (for example, Labov *et al.*, 1972; Trudgill, 1974), while not strictly 'historical', have none the less had a profound impact on historians, as they have for the first time made clear the primary mechanism of historical change – variation, cumulatively weighted in particular directions.

More recently, sociolinguistic theory has been projected into history to form a new subdiscipline, 'sociohistorical linguistics', which promises to be a major synthesis of these two directions, and is perhaps the most important contemporary development in the field (see Romaine, 1980).

Roger Lass
University of Cape Town

References

Dixon, R. M. W. (1980), *The Languages of Australia*, Cambridge.

Harris, M. (1979), *The Evolution of French Syntax: A Comparative Approach*, London.

Hoenigswald, H. (1960), *Language Change and Linguistic Reconstruction*, Chicago.

King, R. D. (1969), *Historical Linguistics and Generative Grammar*, Englewood Cliffs, N.J.

Labov, W., Yeager, M. and Steiner, R. (1972), *A Quantitative Study of Sound Change in Progress*, 2 vols, Philadelphia.

Lass, R. (1976), *English Phonology and Phonological Theory: Synchronic and Diachronic Studies*, Cambridge.

Lass, R. (1980), *On Explaining Language Change*, Cambridge.

Lightfoot, D. (1979), *Principles of Diachronic Syntax*, Cambridge.

Maher, J. P. (1973), 'Neglected reflexes of Proto-Indo-European *pet* – 'fly': Greek *pétros* 'stone'/*pétra* 'cliff'; with notes on the role of syntax (IC structure) in polysemy and semantic change, and the situational motivation of syntax', *Lingua e Stile*, 8.

Romaine, S. (1980), *Sociohistorical Linguistics*, Cambridge.

Saussure, F. de (1916), *Cours de Linguistique Générale*, Paris.

Trudgill, P. (1974), *The Social Differentiation of English in Norwich*, Cambridge.

Further Reading

Antilla, R. (1972), *An Introduction to Historical and Comparative Linguistics*, New York.

Bynon, T. (1977), *Historical Linguistics*, Cambridge.

Pedersen, H. (1962), *The Discovery of Language*, tr. J.W. Spargo, Bloomington.

See also: *lexicostatistics; linguistics; sociolinguistics.*

History

History has long had an uneasy relationship with the social sciences. It is the natural tendency of an historian to think first of what has been, rather than what now is. Few historians can ignore the world in which they live, just as few economists or sociologists can ignore the way in which past events have determined the economy and society which they study; nor would most wish to do so. Yet historians turn first to the past, to seek precedents or to examine the evolution of ideas and institutions, and they see such an examination as an essential preliminary to serious study, whether of an event in the past or of an event in the present.

History is, as Marc Bloch put it, 'le science des hommes dans le temps' (Bloch, 1949), and it is the sense of time and of the apparently infinite variety of human experiences in time which creates much of the uneasiness which has characterized the relationship between history and the contemporary sciences of man. To Bloch, one of the founders of the French *Annales* school of historians, which has been the most coherent and most influential force on historical writing since the Second World War, the enormous amount of information that survives to us from the past was a challenge and a boon; time has given to us a range of knowledge which, if our vision is broad enough and our analysis thorough enough, can reveal the 'structures' and 'conjunctures' underlying the 'events' which have been the concern of most historians of past generations. Such a revelation can come only through the use in historical study of the methods or insights of the other social sciences and, in its turn, the study of history is fundamental to the future development of those methods.

The confident assertion by the *Annales* school of the unity and interdependence of history and the social sciences was a reaction to earlier views of history that had been sceptical of newer disciplines. These doubts were based on two contradictory beliefs; the first, held by many historians in the late nineteenth century, was that history was pre-eminent in its ability to give an objective account of the past which would be useful in the present and the future; the second, characteristic of the German historicist school, was that history was concerned, as Barraclough has put it, with 'the realm of the unique, of the spirit and of change' (Barraclough, 1979). In other words, the very diversity of human experience which to the *Annales* school was a source of strength, led earlier historians to reject generalizations and to exalt intuition in the study of individual action.

Of these two views, the historicist emphasis on the study of individual experience and the rejection of generalization from such experience was the more influential in driving a wedge between history and the emergent social sciences. If generalization was impossible, then history was there to be studied for its own sake, evaluated and re-evaluated as more facts came to light, but serving no purpose other than that of satisfying curiosity or, perhaps, training the mind. Moreover, the exercise of the historian's intuition, his empathy with people in the past, could not be based explicitly on knowledge of how people behave in the present, since by definition events and people's reactions to them are unique. The historian could not, therefore, approach his subject with questions or hypotheses, but had to allow the documents to speak for themselves.

Historicism thus narrowed the scope of history, for its emphasis on intuition in the close study of individual experience prevented historians from taking account of many economic and social phenomena, or from studying the behaviour of crowds or groups. Kings and generals might make fascinating subjects, but, particularly to an age which had experienced the Russian Revolution and the rise of Fascism, a wider historical view seemed necessary.

Such a wider view came both from the *Annales* school and from the increasing influence in the years around the Second World War of Marxist history. While some early Marxists exhibited an extreme economic determinism that was as stultifying as the individualism of their fiercest opponents, this extremism was soon modified both by the influence of *Annales* and by historians such as E. J. Hobsbawm, E. P. Thompson and Christopher Hill who had been trained in a British empirical tradition. Thus Marxist history in Britain, and its counterpart, 'radical history' in the United States, developed a blend of the Marxist categorization of historical and particularly economic forces, with an emphasis on social, intellectual and cultural forces.

This widening of the scope and the methods of historical investigation enlarged the impact of the social sciences upon history. The process was encouraged by the increasing tendency of historians, in the 1950s and 1960s, to develop subdisciplines with their own organizational structures. Economic history had been such a distinct entity in some countries since the 1930s, but it was followed by social history, cultural history, and by many smaller groupings. Although, with the principal exception of the 'new' economic historians in the United States, most of the members of these new disciplines had been trained as generalist historians, they naturally tended to look for ideas and methods to the cognate social science disciplines. The closest links which were forged in this way, mainly during the 1960s and 1970s, were in the fields of economic history, historical demography, social history and historical geography. In all these cases, there was an increased awareness of the potential of social science theory and quantitative methods and a consequent desire to borrow whatever seemed useful.

The 'new' history, as it was called with arrogance by its proponents and derision by its opponents, was first manifest in economic history. There have always been close links between economics and economic history, particularly in Britain and the United States. Marx, Marshall, Keynes, Kuznets and many other economists have used historical material or written works of economic history, while economic historians such as Clapham, as early as 1926, emphasized the reliance of economic history on economic theory and on statistics; Clapham, too, saw the need for historians

to fill the 'empty boxes' of the economists (Clapham, 1922), The 'new economic history' which developed in the 1960s, beginning with two studies of the impact of the building of the railways on the economy of the United States (Fogel, 1964; Fishlow, 1965), was thus within an old tradition, but it was new in its emphasis on the quantitative evaluation of hypotheses based on neoclassical economics

The 'new' economic history was accepted with ease by most economists, particularly in the United States – most of its early adherents had been trained there as economists – but was viewed with suspicion or outright hostility by most historians. Suspicion sprang from wariness about the use of methods of multivariate statistics, in particular, regression analysis; hostility sprang from the behavioural assumptions which underlay the economic models and from an apparent innovation in historical study, the 'counterfactual'.

Students of history had long been warned of the danger of hypothetical history, of imagining what would have happened if Cleopatra's nose had been less beautiful; they were aghast to discover that the most striking of the first studies in the 'new' economic history was based on asking the question: what would have happened to the American economy if the railways had not been built? It was even more alarming that Robert Fogel, the author, should argue that discussion of historical causation must be based, explicitly or implicitly, on 'hypothetico-deductive models'. That is, the historian must construct a model of the interaction of the variables that determine the outcome which he is studying, the historical 'fact', and examine its causation by imagining changes in the independent or determining variables.

The 'new' economic history expanded very rapidly in the late 1960s and soon became the predominant form of economic history in the United States. The expansion was marked by controversy, particularly after the publication of Fogel and Engerman's *Time on the Cross* in 1974. The arguments surrounding this discussion of the economics of American Negro slavery took place among 'new' economic historians, as well as between them and more traditional historians, and they were fuelled by the availability of computer tapes containing the data on which Fogel and Engerman had worked. This was paradoxical, since one of the earliest criticisms of the 'new' history had been that its findings were impossible to check just because they were quantitative and based on computer-held data. Moreover, the arguments about the findings of *Time on the Cross* were widely misunderstood by historians who professed to see the 'new' historians falling out and discrediting themselves; in fact, the arguments were based on a shared assumption of the superiority of the 'new' methods.

Despite the arguments, the 'new' economic history is now firmly established as the predominant method within the subject, even if many doubts still remain about its adherence to neoclassical economic assumptions. A similar success for new methods derived from the social sciences has been achieved in the field of demographic history, although in this field opposition was less intense. French scholars working in the 1960s, in particular Louis Henry, developed new methods for the analysis of population history, of which the most novel was 'family reconstitution' – the reconstruction of family trees for entire communities. This method, followed in Britain by the Cambridge Group for the History of Population and Social Structure, and by others in Scandinavia, has not yet justified its immense cost, but other new methods of 'aggregative' analysis of records of baptisms, marriages and deaths have done so. Most notably, Wrigley and Schofield's *Population History of England* (1981) has rewritten the demographic history of England over four centuries.

Perhaps because so much effort has gone into describing population change, demographic history is still weak in analysing the causes of that change. However, it is the area of history in which most progress has been made with computer simulation of historical processes, in particular those concerned with family and household formation (Wachter, 1978). This topic has also been of particular interest to the growing number of social historians who now increasingly interact with a once derided group, genealogists or family historians; it is now recognized that many social processes can only be understood by attention to micro-level data, tracing and linking families or other social groups over long periods. A notable example of such work has been the study conducted by Alan MacFarlane, an historian and social anthropologist, of the many different records of an English village over four centuries (1980–1); but social historians have also studied social and geographical mobility through microlevel data – as in the work of the social and urban historians in the Philadelphia Social History Project.

The methods of political science have contributed to the 'new' political history. The pioneer in this field was W. A. Aydelotte (1971), but he has been succeeded, particularly in the United States and in West Germany, by historians who have made especially good use of the voluminous voting records of the two countries (Kousser, 1980).

In political as in economic and social history, much innovative historical research during the last two decades has been quantitative in method and has relied on the collection of large quantities of data. Contemporary social scientists are often ignorant of the enormous volumes of evidence which lie unused in archives, evidence which can provide sample sizes far larger than are dreamed of in current studies. The effort to use this material has produced new problems and enforced new methods of work for historians. Group research, once almost unknown in a profession where the individual scholar reigned supreme, has now become commonplace. Historical research has become much more expensive, as armies of research assistants are marshalled to tackle archives. Computer terminals are now to be seen in archives. Most strikingly, the use of quantitative methods from the social sciences has changed the vocabulary of history. Books and journals are now replete with regression coefficients and factor scores, where hitherto intuition and the telling quotation had prevailed.

The initial tendency of the 'new' history was fissiparous; economic, social and demographic historians emphasized their separate skills and interests. Recently, however, researchers have begun to realize that such divisions are stupid; consequently, there has been a new emphasis on the uniting qualities of the new methods, leading to the foundation in the United States of the Social Science History Association.

Yet social science history does not have a monopoly of new styles of history. French historians, led by Emmanuel le Roy Ladurie, have been particularly successful in developing the history of 'mentalités', the evocation of past modes of thought and behaviour. Ladurie's most famous and popular book, *Montaillou* (1978), described the life of a medieval French village through the records of the Inquisition. The work of Philippe Ariès has also shown the potential of psychological investigation of the past (1962).

Most striking, however, has been the growth in many countries, particularly in Western Europe, of 'people's history'. In reaction both to the concentration of traditional historians on élite behaviour and to the apparently arcane methods of the new social science historians, 'people's historians' such as the History Workshop group in Britain or the adherents of 'Alltagsgeschichte' in Germany emphasize the history of working people written by and for working people. These groups of historians have been particularly successful in drawing a large number of nonprofessionals into historical study.

These new methods, and those of the social science historians, are still challenged. The most popular English text on historical method, G. R. Elton's *The Practice of History* (1967), argues in traditional vein, for example, that the historian must be 'the servant of his evidence of which he will, or should, ask no specific questions until he has absorbed what it says . . . . The mind will indeed soon react with questions, but these are the questions suggested by the evidence . . .' Many also agree with another leading historian, Lawrence Stone, that the time has come to revive narrative history and to reject the expensive model building of the social science historians (1979).

In spite of these disagreements and in spite of its use of new methods, history retains its identity, part science and part art, its coherence stemming from its role as discoverer and interpreter of the past. Its power to stir and even to inflame is constantly shown by the use and misuse of historical parallels in political argument; the most emotive of academic disciplines, its passion and rhetoric disturb and confuse social scientists. The power of social science to simplify and generalize is its greatest gift to the historian. Yet the lesson of the variability and unpredictability of human behaviour is perhaps the greatest lesson that social science has to learn from history.

Roderick Floud
Birkbeck College, University of London

References
Aydelotte, W. A. (1971), *Quantification in History*, New York.
Ariès, P. (1962), *Centuries of Childhood*, London.
Barraclough, G. (1979), *Main Trends in History*, New York.
Bloch, M. (1949), *Apologie pour l'histoire*, Paris. (English translation, *The Historian's Craft*, New York, 1964.)
Clapham, J. H. (1922), 'On empty economic boxes', *Economic Journal*, 32.
Elton, G. R. (1967), *The Practice of History*, London.
Fishlow, A. (1965), *American Railroads and the Transformation of the Ante-Bellum Economy*, Cambridge, Mass.
Fogel, R. W. (1964), *Railroads and American Economic Growth*, Baltimore.
Fogel, R. W. and Engerman, S. L. (1974), *Time on the Cross*, New York.
Kousser, J. M. (1980), 'Quantitative social science history', in C. Kammen (ed.), *The Past Before Us: Contemporary Historical Writing in the United States*, Ithaca, N.Y.
MacFarlane, A. (1980–1), *Records of an English Village: Earls Colne 1400–1750*, Cambridge.
Ladurie, E. le Roy (1978), *Montaillou*, Paris.
Stone, L (1979), 'The revival of narrative', *Past and Present*, 85.
Wachter, K. W. (1978), *Statistical Studies of Historical Social Structure*, New York,
Wrigley, E. A. and Schofield, R. S. (1981), *The Population History of England, 1541–1871*, London.

Further Reading
Landes, D. S. and Tilly, C. (eds) (1971), *History as Social Science*, Englewood Cliffs, N.J.
Lorwin, V. R. and Price, J. M. (eds) (1972), *The Dimensions of the Past*, New Haven.
Marwick, A. (1970), *The Nature of History*, London.
Tilly, C. (1981), *As Sociology Meets History*, New York.

Hobbes, Thomas (1588–1679)

Thomas Hobbes is one of the most important figures in the development of modern science and modern politics. As a contemporary of Bacon, Galileo and Descartes, he contributed to the radical critique of medieval Scholasticism and classical philosophy that marked the beginning of the modern age. But he alone sought to develop a comprehensive philosophy – one that treated natural science, political science and theory of scientific method in a unified system. He published this system in three volumes, under the titles *Body* (1655), *Man* (1657), and *Citizen*, (1642). In the course of his long career, Hobbes also published treatises on mathematics, on free will and determinism, on the English common law system, and on the English Civil War. Although his work covered the whole of philosophy, Hobbes made his greatest contribution to modern thought in the field of political philosophy. On three separate occasions, he presented his theory of man and the state; the most famous of his political treatises, the *Leviathan* (1651), is generally recognized as the greatest work of political philosophy in the English language.

In all branches of knowledge, Hobbes's thought is characterized by a pervasive sense that the ancient and medieval philosophers had failed to discover true knowledge, and that a new alternative was urgently needed. It is this sense that defines Hobbes as a modern thinker and gives his work its originality, verve and self-conscious radicalism. In natural science (metaphysics and physics), he rejected the Scholastic and Aristotelian ideas of 'abstract essences' and immaterial causes as nothing more than vain and empty speech. The nature of reality is 'matter in motion', which implied that all phenomena of nature and human nature could be explained in terms of mechanical causation. In the theory of science, Hobbes dismissed the disputative method of Scholasticism and classical dialectics as forms of rhetoric that merely appealed to the authority of common opinion and produced endless verbal controversies. The correct method of reasoning combined the resolutive-compositive method of Galileo and the deductive method of Euclidean geometry. By combining these, Hobbes believed that every branch of knowledge, including the study of politics, could be turned into an exact deductive science.

In political science proper, Hobbes was no less radical in his rejection of the tradition. He opposed the republicanism of classical antiquity, the ecclesiastical politics of medieval Europe, and the doctrine of mixed-monarchy prevalent in seventeenth-century England. All these doctrines, Hobbes claimed, were seditious in intent or effect, because they were derived from 'higher' laws that allowed men to appeal to a standard above the will of the sovereign. Hobbes blamed such appeals, exploited by ambitious priests and political demagogues, for the political instability of his times, culminating in the English Civil War. The solution he proposed was political absolutism – the unification of sovereignty in an all-powerful state that derived its authority not from higher laws but from *de facto* power and the consent of the people.

With these three teachings – mechanistic materialism, exact deductive science, and political absolutism – Hobbes sought to establish science and politics on a new foundation that would produce certain knowledge and lasting civil peace.

From the first, Hobbes's philosophical system generated controversy. In the seventeenth century, Hobbes was treated as a dangerous subversive by all who believed in, or had an interest in, the traditional order. Christian clergymen condemned his materialist view of the world as atheistic and his mechanistic view of man as soulless; legal scholars attacked his doctrine of absolutism for placing the sovereign above the civil laws; even kings, whose power Hobbes sought to augment, were wary of accepting the teaching that political authority rested on force and consent rather than on divine right (Mintz, 1962). In the eighteenth and nineteenth centuries his defence of absolute and arbitrary power ran counter to the general demand for constitutional government. Hobbes has been treated more favourably in this century then ever before. Although some scholars have seen certain parallels between Hobbes's Leviathan state and twentieth-century tyrannies (Collingwood, 1942), most clearly recognize that Hobbes's 'enlightened despot', whose primary goal is to secure civil peace, is vastly different from the brutal and fanatical heads of totalitarian states (Strauss, 1959).

Such studies can be divided into several groups, each reflecting the perspective of a contemporary school of philosophy as it probes the origins of modernity. (1) Guided by the concerns of contemporary analytical philosophy, one group argues for the primacy of method and formal logic in Hobbes's system and views his politics as a set of formal rules which serve as utilitarian guidelines for the state (McNeilly, 1968; Watkins, 1965). (2) Another group has examined Hobbes's theory of 'political obligation' from a Kantian point of view. According to this interpretation, Hobbes's argument for obedience goes beyond calculations of utility by appealing to a sense of moral duty in keeping the social contract, and by requiring citizens to have just intentions (Taylor, 1938; Warrender, 1957). (3) Developed by Marxist scholars, a third interpretation uses Hobbes to understand the ideological origins of bourgeois society and to provide a critical perspective on bourgeois liberalism by exposing its Hobbesian roots (Macpherson, 1962; Coleman, 1977). (4) The fourth interpretation reflects the concerns of the natural law school. According to the foremost scholar of this school, Hobbes is the decisive figure in transforming the natural law tradition from classical natural right to modern natural 'rights'; Hobbes accomplished this revolution by asserting that the right of self-preservation, grounded in the fear of violent death, is the only justifiable moral claim (Strauss, 1936).

Robert P. Kraynak
Colgate University

References

Coleman, F. M. (1977), *Hobbes and America: Exploring the Constitutional Foundations*, Toronto.

Collingwood, R. G. (1942), *The New Leviathan*, Oxford.

Macpherson, C. B. (1962), *The Political Theory of Possessive Individualism*, Oxford.

McNeilly, F. S. (1968), *The Anatomy of Leviathan*, London.

Mintz, S. I. (1962), *The Hunting of Leviathan*, Cambridge.

Strauss, L. (1936), *The Political Philosophy of Hobbes*, Chicago.

Strauss, L. (1959), 'On the basis of Hobbes's political philosophy', in *What Is Political Philosophy?*, New York.

Taylor, A. E. (1938), 'The ethical doctrine of Hobbes', *Philosophy*, 13.

Warrender, H. (1957), *The Political Philosophy of Hobbes: His Theory of Obligation*, Oxford.

Watkins, J. W. N. (1965), *Hobbes's System of Ideas: A Study in the Political Significance of Philosophical Theories*, London.

Homosexuality

Although same-sex erotic experiences exist across cultures and throughout history with varying degrees of acceptability and frequency, it was not until the nineteenth century in Europe and America that homosexuality was invented as an object of scientific investigation. The term itself was introduced by a sympathetic Hungarian doctor, Benkert, in 1869 amidst a flurry of attempts at classifying sexuality (Ulrich's term 'Uranians' indicating a kind of third sex was popular, as was the concept of 'invert'). From this time until the 1970s, the dominant mode of thinking about homosexuality was clinical – it was primarily viewed as a pathology, its causes were located in biological degeneracy or family pathology, and treatments, ranging from castration to psychoanalysis, were advocated. Although such an approach continues (for example in the work of Socarides, 1978), since 1973 the American Psychiatric Association has officially removed homosexuality from its clinical nomenclature, seeing it as nonpathological in itself (Bayer, 1981). Ironically, some of the leading clinicians, and notably Freud, had never viewed it as a pathology: in 1935 Freud could write in a famous 'letter to a mother' that whilst 'homosexuality is assuredly no advantage, it is nothing to be classified as an illness; we consider it to be a variation of the sexual development . . .'

While the nineteenth century saw the ascendancy of the clinical model of homsexuality, it also saw the growth of writing and campaigning which challenged the orthodox heterosexual assumptions. Thus Magnus Hirschfield established the Scientific Humanitarian Committee and the Institute for Sexual Science in Germany in 1897 and campaigned through scientific research for the acceptance of homosexuality up until the 1930s, when the Nazi movement stopped such advocacies and started a policy of extermination instead. Others, such as Carpenter in England and Gide in France, pursued a more literary defence (Lauritsen and Thorstad, 1974). It was not, however, until the period after the Second World War that a substantial body of published research suggested the ubiquity and normality of homosexual experience. Pivotal to this enterprise was the publication of the Kinsey Report in 1948 and 1953 containing the findings of interviews with well over 12,000 American men and women. Amongst the former, Kinsey found that 37 per cent had some post-adolescent homosexual orgasm and 4 per cent had a preponderance of such experience; amongst the latter, the figures were around 13 per cent and 3 per cent respectively. When Kinsey added that such responses were to be found amongst all social groups and in all walks of life, he created a social bombshell; when he concluded that homosexual behaviour was neither unnatural nor neurotic in itself but an 'inherent physiologic capacity', he established an outrageous view that was later to be turned into something of an orthodoxy in the research of others like Hooker in America and Schofield in England (Freedman, 1971).

Throughout this period, however, homosexuality was strongly condemned by law in most European countries and in all American states. It was not until the 1960s – and a decade or so after proposals for change in the British Wolfenden report and the American New Model Code – that the legal situation changed. (See Crane, 1982, for the current legal situation.) Despite the progressive build-up of homosexual groups during the 1950s, it is the New York 'Stonewall Riots' of 1969 which are generally taken to symbolize the birth of the modern international 'Gay Movement' (Weeks, 1977; D'Emilio, 1983). The scientifically imposed term 'homosexual' was shifted to the self-created one 'gay'; medical rhetoric was converted to political language; organizations for gays became widespread in most large cities, and millions of gay men and women started to 'come out' and identify positively with the term 'gay'. The 1970s therefore demonstrated a real change in gay experiences – a change well documented in Dennis Altman's *The Homosexualisation of America and the Americanisation of the Homosexual* (1982).

All of this has left its impact upon research. Although there are still those who study causes and cures, it is noticeable that social scientists have largely left this question behind and turned to new areas. Thus, the history of homosexuality has started to be unearthed in much the same ways as women's history has been explored by feminist social scientists. This has meant not just the discovery of the documents of the recent past – as in Katz's *Gay American History* (1976) – but also excavations into the more distant past such as ancient Greece (Dover, 1978), the Middle Ages (Boswell, 1980) and the Renaissance (Faderman, 1981). Far from being universally condemned, homosexual experiences have been reacted to in very different ways throughout history, and indeed, have been experienced as something very different at different times. Closely related to this historical research has been a concern to understand why groups and societies have condemned same-sex experience and how such stimatizing perceptions have had a profound and sometimes negative impact upon them. This has meant that some social psychologist have turned to the analysis of 'homophobia' – the morbid fear of homosexuals (Weinberg, 1972) – some have been interested in studying the labelling of homosexuality (Plummer, 1981), whilst still others have seen homosexuality as constituted by a discourse which embodies power relationships (Foucault, 1979).

Another significant shift in research interests has developed from modern feminism. Arguing that lesbianism should be approached within the framework of women's studies rather than that of male homosexuality, it has directed attention to concerns like child custody problems and the growth of political lesbianism as an explicit rejection of male sexuality (see Ettore, 1980).

Perhaps the most significant change in research has been the sheer range of studies to show the diversity of homosexual experience. The noun 'homosexual' has been replaced by the term 'homosexualities' to signpost as much diversity as is found behind the label 'heterosexual' – there are many ways of becoming gay, and there are many ways of being gay. Amongst these concerns are such features as the different age structures (from being a child to being 'gray and gay'); the different relationships (from gay couples and gay parents to elaborate friendship networks); the different institutions (from gay 'pick-up' places to gay counselling), and the different life cycles that surround gayness (most notably the problems of 'coming out' and choosing a particular lifestyle (Levine, 1979). These studies, perhaps more than any others, have indicated the full range of humanity behind the straitjacketing label of homosexuality.

Ken Plummer
University of Essex

References

Altman, D. (1982), *The Homosexualisation of America and the Americanisation of the Homosexual*, New York.

Bayer, R. (1981), *Homosexuality and American Psychiatry: The Politics of Diagnosis*, New York.

Boswell, J. (1980), *Christianity, Social Tolerance and Homosexuality*, Chicago.

Crane, P. (1982), *Gays and the Law*, London.

D'Emilio, J. (1983) *Sexual Politics, Sexual Communities: The Making of a Homosexual Minority in the United States, 1940–1970*, Chicago.

Dover, K. (1978), *Greek Homosexuality*, London.

Ettore, E. (1980), *Lesbians, Women and Society*, London.

Faderman, L. (1981), *Surpassing the Love of Men: Romantic Friendships among Women from the Renaissance to the Present Day*, London.

Foucault, M. (1979), *The History of Sexuality: Vol. 1 –An Introduction*, London.

Freedman, M. (1971), *Homosexuality and Psychological Functioning*, California.

Katz, J. (1976), *Gay American History: Lesbians and Gay Men in the U.S.A.*, New York.

Lauritsen, J. and Thorstad, D. (1974), *The Early Homosexual Rights Movement* (1864–1935), New York.

Levine, M. P. (ed.) (1979), *Gay Men: The Sociology of Male Homosexuality*, New York.

Plummer, K. (ed.) (1981), *The Making of the Modern Homosexual*, London.

Socarides, C. (1978), *Homosexuality*, New York.

Weeks, J. (1977), *Coming Out: Homosexual Politics in Britain from the 19th Century to the Present*, London.

Weinberg, G. (1972), *Society and the Healthy Homosexual*, New York.

feelings of isolation and helplessness. A particular strategy can become characteristic, causing the person to develop and present a false or neurotic self to others. The goal of Horney's therapy was to help the patient to recognize his true self and to foster its growth.

Horney constructed a typology of the styles of the false self: the expansive, the perfectionist, and others. Her descriptions of these types are intriguing portraits filled with 'aperçus'. Horney anticipated many of the ideas in contemporary psychology: Laing's theory of the divided self, notions of self-actualization and authenticity, the emphasis on the division between the public and the private self, and the focus on self-esteem.

Like many other European psychoanalysts, Horney emigrated to the United States when Hitler came to power. She eventually developed her own 'school' of psychoanalysis in New York. More optimistic about human nature than Freud, Horney believed that neurotic conflict could be avoided and was not an inevitable consequence of civilization. Horney told her women patients who wanted to be good mothers and homemakers to lead lives more like men, counselling that modern women invest too much of themselves in love and thus leave themselves too vulnerable to rejection and loss of self-esteem. A generation of women has taken Karen Horney's advice.

Alan A. Stone
Harvard University

Further Reading

Horney, K. (1937), *The Neurotic Personality of Our Time*, New York.

Horney, K. (1939), *New Ways in Psychoanalysis*, New York.

Horney, Karen (1885–1952)

Born in Germany in 1885, Karen Horney trained as a Freudian psychoanalyst and was the first important 'feminist' critic of Freud's biological and mechanistic theories. Freud, as has often been noted, created a male-oriented psychology which stressed the psychological consequences of anatomical differences. Horney rejected his notion of penis envy as crucial to female psychology and emphasized instead the role of social and cultural factors in producing in women a lack of self-confidence and an overemphasis on the love relationship. Although her own theoretical ideas were not coherent or fully worked out, her psychological insights, her interpretations and her criticisms of Freud are none the less brilliant. Abandoning Freud's ego, id. and super-ego, she replaced them with a theory of the true and the false self. Central to her work is the idea that because of basic anxieties and insecurities, the person begins to develop strategies to cope with

Households

Households are task-oriented social units larger than the individual but smaller than the neighbourhood, community or town. Within the household, many decisions are taken regarding production, pooling and distribution, transmission, reproduction and coresidence. Unlike kin groups (including families), households are localized and enumerable. Nevertheless, their boundaries are permeable. 'Household' is not a universal category but a culturally relative term.

The 1972 Hammel-Laslett classification of households shown in Table 1 is commonly used (Laslett, 1972). A limited number of household forms are recognized for reporting and comparing census-type data. This typology emphasizes genealogical criteria because they are the common denominator in household studies. However, since census data may be ambiguous when detached from their historical context, these

Table 1: *The structure of households: categories and classes*

Category	Class
1 Solitaries	(a) widowed
	(b) single, or unknown marital status
2 No family	(a) coresident siblings
	(b) coresident relatives of other kinds
	(c) persons not evidently related
3 Simple family households	(a) married couples alone
	(b) married couples with child(ren)
	(d) widows with child(ren)
4 Extended family households	(a) extended upwards
	(b) extended downwards
	(c) extended laterally
	(d) combinations of 4a–4c
5 Multiple family households	(a) secondary units(s) Up
	(b) secondary units(s) Down
	(c) units all on one level
	(d) *frérèches*
	(e) other multiple families
6 Indeterminate 'stem families'	5a
	5b and 5a
	5b + 5a + 4a
'Frérèches, alternative definitions	5d
	5d + 5c
	5d + 5c + 4c
	5d + 5c + 4c + 2a

data are supplemented wherever possible by other documentary and oral evidence.

Five spheres of activity are consistently associated with households:

(1) People in every society have definite ideas of what households should produce and how household labour, including 'domestic' labour, should be mobilized. The form of the household is related to man/land and man/animal ratios, timing, sequencing, necessary simultaneity, and diversity of productive tasks. Households can alter in size and composition over time in response to changes in productive requirements, or they may preserve their form albeit at the expense of productivity.

(2) Household members contribute to a common fund. Spatial and temporal clustering of resources affects the rules regulating the members' contributions and allocations to the fund, which in turn affect household form. The distribution and exchange of household resources define the household and subunit boundaries, and patterns of authority between and among house-

holds. Ongoing negotiation of exchange and consumption may modify household composition.

Household form is also affected by the time and manner in which resources are transmitted, especially through inheritance. Degree of restriction and formalization of transmission determines the corporate character of households. Restrictions, such as primogeniture, vary with ecology and productive emphases.

(3) Social reproduction – the care of dependants, maintenance of the work force, socialization and emotional support – will modify the demands made of other household tasks. It may also affect how people are recruited to households and how household boundaries are maintained. Some of the most significant variations in household form, both within and between societies, relate to when biological reproduction begins and the timing of marriage, and the association between these variables and the transmission and inheritance of goods.

(4) There are cross-cultural variations in the desire to maintain household form and function, especially a particular ideal of a household. Indians and Chinese have over generations idealized multiple family households, whereas the Anglo-Saxon tradition idealizes the simple family household. But notions of what constitutes a household can also change rapidly.

(5) Household membership and coresidence are often, but not always, synonymous. Thus, migrants may retain rights to reside and to share in and contribute to resources of households while living elsewhere. Pooling and co-operation between coresidents also varies between households and household systems.

There is no single criterion which defines *the* household. Form is often a compromise among demographic processes, cultural ideals and often contradictory behaviour patterns. The frequency of a particular household type in one single society may also vary according to differential access to resources, stage of domestic cycle, and sex-gender systems. Those activities which determine household form seem to follow broad evolutionary paths – pooling and distribution in simple band societies, to transmission in modern European peasantries. But in defining households, ecologically similar societies and ethnic groups may nevertheless emphasize different cultural criteria and activities. Thus the relationship between form and activity is complex and diachronic. Moreover, different meaning may attach to similar forms, while similar meanings may cling to different forms of household organization.

Household morphology has been of interest to demographers and social historians, who have tried to identify and reconstruct household forms. Ethnologists and archaeologists are now also involved in this type of research. Recently, cross-sectional comparisons and longitudinal analyses have tried to explain why various forms persist, analysed variations, and studied how household forms, for example, affect individuals' choices. Such studies have disproved the thesis that declining household size and corporateness is inevitably associated with industrialization. Finally, in emphasizing process and negotiation, the study of households is linked to the study of systems of power and stratification.

Eric Arnould
United States Embassy, Niamey, Republic of Niger

Reference
Laslett, P. (ed.) (1972), *Household and Family in Past Time*, Cambridge.

Further Reading
Netting, R. McC., Wilk, R. R. and Arnould, E. J. (eds) (1983), *Households: Comparative and Historical Studies of the Domestic Group*, Berkeley and Los Angeles.
Yanagisako, S. (1979), 'Family and household: the analysis of domestic groups', *Annual Review of Anthropology*, 8.
See also: *census of population; family; family history.*

Hull, Clark L. (1884–1952)

An American neobehavioural psychologist whose influence within psychology was most profound during the 1940s and 1950s, Clark L. Hull was himself influenced by Darwin's theory of evolution, Pavlov's concept of delayed or trace-conditioned reflexes, and Thorndike's law of effect. Hull firmly believed that psychology is a true natural science concerned with the 'determination of the quantitative laws of behaviour and their deductive systematization', and set out during his years at Yale University (1929–52) to develop a comprehensive general theory of behaviour constructed of variables linked systematically to experimentally derived data. An extensive study of rote learning led to the publication in 1940 of a monograph entitled *Mathematico-Deductive Theory of Rote Learning*. This work served as a prelude to a more general behaviour system first detailed in *Principles of Behavior* (1943) and later, with modifications, in *A Behavior System*, published posthumously in 1952. The system was based on the assumption that most response sequences leading to the reduction of bodily tension associated with need reduction are learned or reinforced. Hull proposed that the tendency for an organism to make a particular response when a stimulus is presented is a multiplicative function of habit strength (reflecting the number of previous reinforcements) and drive (based on bodily needs), minus certain inhibitory tendencies (associated with previous conditioning trials). These, along with other factors such as stimulus intensity and momentary behavioural oscillation, were seen as variables relating to response acquisition in the context of reinforced trials. Through careful experimentation, much of it with laboratory rats in mazes, Hull sought to quantify the functional relationships among these variables. While he failed to construct a comprehensive behaviour system, his theory led to important studies in the areas of motivation and conflict, frustration and aggression, manifest anxiety, social learning theory, and biofeedback. Early in his career Hull also made contributions in the areas of concept formation, hypnosis and aptitude testing. In the late 1930s and early 1940s, he conducted seminars to explore the congruencies between psychoanalytic and behavioural theories. These seminars did much to bring Freudian ideas to the attention of experimental psychologists.

Albert R. Gilgen
University of Northern Iowa

Further Reading
Hilgard, E. R. and Bower, G. H. (1975), *Theories of Learning*, New York.
See also: *behaviourism.*

Human Capital

Human capital is the stock of acquired talents, skills and knowledge which may enhance a worker's earning power in the labour market. A distinction is commonly made between *general* human capital – which is considered as affecting potential earnings in a broad range of jobs and occupations – and *specific* human capital, which augments a person's earning power within the particular firm in which he is employed but is of negligible value elsewhere. An example of the former would be formal education in general skills such as mathematics; an example of the latter would be the acquired knowledge about the workings of, and personal contacts within, a particular firm. In many cases human capital is of an intermediate form, whether it be acquired 'off the job', in the form of schooling or vocational training, or 'on the job' in terms of work experience.

In several respects the economic analysis of human capital raises problems similar to that of capital as conventionally understood in terms of firms' plant and equipment. It is likely to be heterogeneous in form; it is accumulated over a substantial period of time using labour and capital already in existence; futher investment usually requires immediate sacrifices (in terms of forgone earnings and tuition fees); its quality will be affected by technical progress; the prospective returns to an individual are likely to be fairly uncertain, and the capital stock will be subject to physical deterioration and obsolescence. Nevertheless there are considerable differences. Whereas one can realize the returns on physical or financial capital either by receiving the flow of profits accruing to the owner of the asset or by sale of the asset itself, the returns on human capital usually can only be received by the person in whom the investments have been made (although there are exceptions, such as indentured workers), and usually require further effort in the form of labour in order to be realized in cash terms. The stock of human capital cannot be transferred as can the titles to other forms of wealth, although the investments that parents make in their children's schooling and in informal education at home are sometimes taken as analogous to bequests of financial capital.

While the idea of investment in oneself commands wide acceptance in terms of its general principles, many economists are unwilling to accept stronger versions of the theory of earnings determination and the theory of income distribution that have been based on the pioneering work of Becker (1964) and Mincer (1958). This analysis generally assumes that everywhere labour markets are sufficiently competitive, the services of different types of human capital sufficiently substitutable and educational opportunities sufficiently open, such that earnings differentials can be unambiguously related to differential acquisition of human capital. On the basis of such assumptions estimates have been made of the returns (in terms of increased potential earnings) to human investment (measured in terms of forgone earnings and other costs) by using the observed earnings of workers in cross-sectional samples and in 'panel studies' over time. The rates of return to such investment has usually been found to be in the range of 10 to 15 per cent. However it should be emphasized that such estimates often neglect the impact of other economic and social factors which may affect the dispersion of earnings.

Frank A. Cowell
London School of Economics and Political Science

References
Becker, G. S. (1964), *Human Capital*, New York.
Mincer, J. (1958), 'Investment in human capital and personal income distribution', *Journal of Political Economy*, 66.

Further Reading
Mincer, J. (1974), *Schooling, Experience and Earnings*, New York.
Schultz, T. W. (1972), *Investment in Education*, Chicago.
See also: *capital theory*.

Human Needs

Most of the authors who sought to use human need as a political norm during the 1960s and early 1970s wrote with frankly polemical intent, rejecting the notion that politics is about who gets what, when and how, and that the proper task of government is to meet people's wants, reconciling them in so far as they can be reconciled. In that account of politics, responsiveness is the chief virtue, and paternalism the corresponding vice; each person normally knows best what his wants are; expert knowledge is confined to the most effective *means* of satisfying demands, because nobody can speak with authority on the merits of the various demands; all wants *must* be considered equal, and pushpin must be as good as poetry.

It was in answer to such a 'politics of wants' that Fromm (1955) Marcuse (1964, 1969), Macpherson (1966, 1973), Bay (1965, 1968) and others proposed a 'politics of needs'. Need, not want, was to be the norm: politics was to be the pursuit of justice, and justice was seen as the meeting of human needs. All these writers agreed that it can be shown objectively what human needs are – indeed, human need could not serve as a political norm unless it were believed to have the status of ascertainable fact. And all of these writers held that, though in principle each person may be capable of recognizing his own needs, in present circumstances most people are so indoctrinated as to be incapable of seeing what their true needs are, or of distinguishing them from false needs, or mere wants (Fitzgerald, 1977). Consequently, for the time being knowledge of human needs will be unevenly distributed; some people will know much more about them than others do, and most people's ideas about their needs will be confused, incomplete, even mistaken. Important needs are related to important objectives, and not all objectives are important. Some, like burglary, are not even licit. The proponents of a politics of needs did not advocate the indiscriminate satisfaction of all needs, but only of those needs which they believed to be related to human fulfilment, to the actualization of human potential as they understood it. Their approach, then, like that of Marx (to whose ideas about human needs most of them referred with approval), was teleological. They identified and evaluated human needs, as Marx did, by reference to a model of man, a conception of human excellence which they held, in some sense, to be the sole valid one (Fitzgerald, 1977).

One attack made on the politics of needs position is an attack on its teleological structure: models of man are many, not one, and the attackers asserted that a reasoned choice among models of human excellence is impossible, for any attempt would necessarily fall into the 'naturalistic fallacy'. Hence, there can be no such things as knowledge of human needs or experts on human needs. Another line of attack was to argue that among human *wants* no reasoned choice is possible, and that *needs* are simply what we require to meet our wants; accordingly, there can be knowledge of needs, and experts on needs, but these experts (architects or lawyers, for instance) can only advise us about what we need after *we* have told *them* what we want. Accordingly, the critics held that the politics of needs position is conceptually confused. They also held that its practical tendency is politically despotic, since it may be used to justify extensive coercion over those who are said to know less about their own needs than some group of needs-experts know (Fitzgerald, 1977).

The politics of needs protagonists have clearly expressed their admiration for the governments of such countries as Cuba and Vietnam, so there is nothing conjectural about the association of needs-theory with political despotism (Fitzgerald, 1977). But their critics have not succeeded in showing that needs-theory is *necessarily* despotic in tendency. Nor have they been able to show that needs-theory is conceptually confused. Statements about needs are not, as they say, dependent upon statements about wants. Nor have they shown that between models of excellence there can be no reasoned choice, so that any choice must be arbitrary. It is true that statements about the needs of an organism are related to notions of what constitutes a *good specimen* of that kind of organism and of how a specimen can be recognized as *flourishing*; but it is not true that these notions are arbitrary, and can express nothing more than the personal tastes of observers. That a plant is flourishing is a *fact* about it, no less than its height or its colour. It is, moreover, quite independent of wants. Plants cannot have wants, and human beings, who can have wants, are not expressing those wants in recognizing a plant to be a good specimen. The drug squad, the growers, and any competent person may agree in recognizing a cannabis plant as a flourishing specimen, though they do not all agree in wanting it to flourish.

The *needs* of a plant are the conditions which will enable it to fulfil its potential and become a flourishing specimen. These needs, too, are a matter of fact, not in the least subjective, though to establish what they are may be a more difficult procedure than to recognize a good specimen (Anscombe, 1958).

Some *human* needs would seem to be very closely comparable with the needs of animals and plants. In matters of nutrition and exercise we may speak of needs which must normally be met if a human being is to fulfil his (physical) potential and become a good (physical) specimen. These are objective statements about matters of fact; they are not statements about wants, nor do they depend upon statements about wants. I may need a vitamin I have never heard of, and so cannot possibly want. And other people, such as dieticians and gym instructors, may know more about my needs for nutrition and exercise than I do. To accept these statements is not, of course, to advocate a despotism of dieticians and gym instructors over everyone else's nutrition and exercise. Nor is it necessary, for fear of endorsing such a despotism, to fall into the absurdity of denying that some people may know more than we do about some of our needs.

Human non-physical needs, if there are any, will depend upon the possiblity of similarly clear and sufficiently objective knowledge of what constitutes a flourishing specimen of the human *psyche*. The politics of needs writers have certainly propounded their notions of human excellence, though usually only in outline, and often in a crudely tendentious form, excluding, for instance, such 'socially harmful' activities as watching American films and making profits (Fromm, 1955). They have, then, done little to engender confidence in their own capacity to make reasoned choices among models of human excellence and related human needs. But it has not been shown that what they failed to do cannot be done. In Bowlby's account of the process of attachment in infancy, there is scarcely more subjectivity or arbitrariness in saying of people in whom such needs have not been met that they are (psychologically) handicapped specimens of humanity, than in saying that people whose nutritional needs have not been met are (physically) handicapped specimens of humanity (Bowlby, 1969). In both areas, it is a case of grave deprivation that is most readily recognizable. And whatever physical, psychological or moral needs there may be reason to recognize in human beings, those needs will still have no *political* significance unless it can also be shown that there is something in the public forum that can be done, and ought to be done, to meet them.

E. D. Watt
University of Western Australia

References
Anscombe, G. E. M. (1958), 'Modern moral philosophy', *Philosophy*, 33.
Bay, C. (1968), 'Politics and pseudopolitics', *American Political Science Review*, 59.
Bay, C. (1968), 'Needs, wants and political legitimacy', *Canadian Journal of Political Science*, 1.
Bowlby, J. (1969), *Attachment and Loss*, vols I and II, London.
Fitzgerald, R. (ed.) (1977), *Human Needs and Politics*, Sydney.
Fromm, E. (1955), *The Sane Society*, New York.
Macpherson, C. B. (1966), *The Real World of Democracy*, Oxford.
Macpherson, C. B. (1973), *Democratic Theory: Essays in Retrieval*, Oxford.
Marcuse, H. (1964), *One-Dimensional Man*, London.
Marcuse, H. *et al.* (1969), *A Critique of Pure Tolerance*, London.

Further Reading
Flew, A. G. N. (1977), 'Wants or needs, choices or commands', in R. Fitzgerald (ed.), *Human Needs and Politics*, Sydney.
Minogue, K. R. (1963), *The Liberal Mind*, London.
See also: *human rights*.

Human Rights

Human rights are the rights and freedoms of all human beings, for 'les droits de l'homme' and 'die Rechte des Menschen' embrace women too.

I

Human rights are often called fundamental and universal. Fundamental can mean that there are rights which are inalienable in that there are no circumstances whatever in which they are to be denied; but, as we shall see, the number of rights of this character can be counted on the fingers of one hand: fundamental in this sense, then, is little more than rhetorical. A more realistic use of the term is to describe rights which are given priority in social policy, administration, and enactment of law: they are fundamental in a particular community because, often embodied in constitutional provisions, they not only can guide policy, but in fact override any administrative act or legislative enactment contrary to them. Those rights might also be loosely described as fundamental, which are in general practice to be exercised and respected – there is a presumption in favour of that – but they may still be restricted in special circumstances if that is in the common interest. Examples of these three kinds of fundamental rights may be given: of the first, prohibition of slavery; of the second, the equality of all before the law; and of the third, the freedom of the press.

Universality expresses an ideal, a goal, and not the present character of human rights. It is obvious that the recognition of particular rights and freedoms, and their observance, have varied greatly between cultures and over time, and they still vary; however, the growing interdependence of countries has led to the emergence of a common political objective: the gradual realization of minimum rules and standards of conduct and administration throughout the world.

But Edmund Burke (1729–97) expressed an important truth when, as a member of the British Parliament in 1775, he was pleading for conciliation with the American colonies, and said, 'All government, indeed every human benefit and enjoyment, every virtue and every prudent act, is founded on compromise and barter.' The European Convention on Human Rights adopts this balancing of rights. So Article 8 provides that:

(1) Everyone has the right to respect for his private and family life, his home and his correspondence.

(2) There shall be no interference *(ingérence/Eingriff)* by a public authority in the exercise of this right except such as is in accordance with the law *(prévue par la loi/gesetzlich vorgesehen)* and is necessary in a democratic society in the interests of national security, public safety *(la sûreté publique/die öffentliche Ruhe und Ordnung)*, or the economic well-being of the country, for the prevention of disorder or crime, for the protection of health or morals, or for the protection of the rights and freedoms of others.

Further, the requirements of emergency are recognized, so Article 15 says:

(1) In time of war or other public emergency threatening the life of the nation any High Contracting Party may take measures derogating from its obligations under this Convention *(dérogeant aux obligations prévues . . ./welche die . . . vorgesehenen Verpflichtungen . . . ausser Kraft setzen)*, to the extent strictly required by the exigencies of the situation *(dans la stricte mesure où la situation l'exige/den die Lage unbedingt erfordert)* provided that such measures are not inconsistent with its other obligations under international law.

(2) No derogation from Article 2 except in respect of deaths resulting from lawful acts of war or from Articles 3, 4(1) and 7 shall be made under this provision.

Article 15(3) requires that the Secretary General of the Council of Europe be kept fully informed of such measures.

Similar provisions are to be found in the International Civil and Political Rights Covenant.

II

Rights that are fundamental in the first sense suggested above, being inalienable in any circumstance, including national emergency, are limited in the European Convention to the prohibition of 'torture or inhuman or degrading treatment or punishment': Article 3, and of 'slavery or servitude': Article 4(1). While the right to life, and the principle of non-retroactivity of penalties and offences, are also not to be derogated from even in emergency, they are subject to specific exceptions in the Convention and so cannot be fundamental in the first sense. Rights and freeedoms that can be called fundamental in the second sense are protected in many national systems by constitutional provisions and procedures; while both national systems and the international instruments cover those that are fundamental in the third sense – in reality, with a balancing of rights: for example, how irresponsible can the press be in exercising its freedom of information; how far can a drunken father claim access to his children as a right of family life; are there limits to the right to strike; does the right to property protect the possession of assets acquired for the purpose of tax evasion? It is issues like these that are raised in individual applications to the European Commission of Human Rights and the UN Human Rights Committee.

III

In the balancing of human rights, there may be, first, permissible restrictions, illustrated above, the test of which is that they must be necessary for one or more of the stated purposes. Secondly, there is the principle of responsibility, stated, for example, in the Universal Declaration, Article 29(1): 'Everyone has duties to the Community in which alone the free and full development of his personality is possible.' There is a marked difference, in applying this principle, between what may be called the individualist and the collective approaches. If the European Convention is taken as expressing human rights, as conceived in Western Europe, individual rights predominate; the burden lies always on public authority to justify any restriction of them, and responsibilities are mentioned only for the press. The collective approach is vividly expressed in the USSR Constitution (1977). It contains a 'bill of rights', which is comprehensive and by any standards adequate, if read alone, for the exercise and protection of the rights of the citizen. But there follow statements of overriding social responsibilities: so 'Exercise of rights and freedoms shall be inseparable from the performance by a citizen of his duties . . .' and these include the duty 'to respect the rules of socialist society' (Article 59); 'to safeguard the interests of the Soviet state and contribute to the strengthening of its might and prestige' (Article 62); and 'to work conscientiously in his chosen socially useful occupation, and strictly to observe labour discipline' (Article 60). More generally it is 'for the purpose of strengthening and developing the socialist system' that citizens 'shall be guaranteed freedom of speech, the press, assembly, meetings, street processions and demonstrations' (Article 50).

IV

The exercise, observance and achievement of human rights and freedoms depends in the end on domestic arrangements in each country, though the international processes have influence.

There is first a distinction between means of direct enforcement, and progressive achievement of rights and freedoms, between what are sometimes called 'legal rights' and 'programme rights'. So under the Civil and Political Rights Covenant,

> Each State Party . . . undertakes to respect and ensure (*à respecter et à garantir/zu achten . . . und zu gewährleisten*) to all individuals within its territory and subject to its jurisdiction, the rights recognized . . . .

While in the Economic, Social and Cultural Covenant,

> 'Each State Party . . . undertakes to take steps individually and through international assistance and cooperation . . . to the maximum of its available resources with a view to achieving progressively the full realization of the rights recognized . . . by all appropriate means (*en rue d'assurer progressivement le plein exercise des droits/um nach und nach . . . die volle*

Verwiklichung der . . . Rechte zu erreichen).

The Indian Constitution (1949) makes an analogous distinction between enforceable rights and directive principles. The international processes take many forms, but the principal alternatives are (1) the investigation and reporting of general situations, a method employed in the UN system; (2) the investigation of particular complaints brought by individuals or states with efforts to achieve a settlement: the European Commission of Human Rights deal with great numbers of individual applications (all but Greece, Malta, Cyprus and Turkey have recognized the right of individual petition) and some inter-state complaints, making a factual investigation and possibly a settlement; failing settlement it reports the case to the Committee of Ministers, expressing its *opinion* whether there has been a breach of the Convention. The Committee of Ministers has then to *decide* this issue, unless either the Commission or a Contracting Party involved refer the case to the European Court of Human Rights. The functions of the UN Human Rights Committee are similar but its area of action is rather more limited than that of the European Commission; (3) the judicial process of determination in national courts, the European Court of Human Rights, and possibly other international courts.

James Fawcett
Member of the European Commission of
Human Rights (1962–84)

Further Reading

Bailey, S. (1972), *Prohibitions and Restraints in War*, Oxford.

Drzemczewski, A. (1983), *European Human Rights Convention in Domestic Law*, Oxford.

Lillich, R. and Newman, F. (eds) (1979), *International Human Rights and Problems of Law and Policy*, Boston.

Robertson, A. H. (1977), *Human Rights in Europe*, 2nd edn, Manchester.

Sieghart, P. (1983), *The International Law of Human Rights*, Oxford.

United Nations (1980), *UN Action in the Field of Human Rights*, New York.

Hume, David (1711–76)

Though it is now a cliché that Hume's philosophy is a 'Newtonian' science of man, and that all through this century students of it have noticed such things as the role played by sympathy as a mechanism of communication and factor in the development of self-consciousness and attacked the view of its allegedly atomistic, unhistorical individualism, it seems fair to say that Hume has not occupied a particularly important place in the history of social science, except perhaps negatively. His friends Ferguson and A. Smith have attracted more attention as founding fathers of a truly sociological method and outlook, and there are some good reasons for this: Hume's social theory, compared with theirs, was in many ways 'backward'. Its negative side has attracted those who value it as a useful political hygiene. There has been too much use of hasty generalizations and abridgements of a philosophy which is controversial and difficult to interpret. His social and political thought is no less complex and many-sided, as anyone knows who has tried to make sense of it as a whole. Those determined to place him in the tradition of conservative politics ignore his 'republicanism'; those who collect evidence of his 'civic humanism', or the 'politics of nostalgia' of the country gentlemen, neglect what is forward-looking and 'sociologically' positive in him.

Hume's contribution to 'politics', which he defined as the science of 'men united in society and dependent on each other', can be divided roughly into three main sections or phases: (1) a theory of justice and government as such, as part of a naturalistic ethics; (2) essays covering a wide range of topics in economics and politics; and (3) a *History of England*. All can be seen as parts of a programme not only of political 'moderation' but also of modernization, an attempt to give the Revolution and Hanoverian regime a proper, that is, 'philosophical' or scientific and empirical foundation, and to understand the nature of modern European political civilization.

The natural law that Hume accepted as the ground of political science was, in its contemporary modes, open to the attacks of sceptics, moral relativists and Hobbists, but what Hume provided in his account of 'Justice' – the three 'natural laws' concerning property without which settled society is impossible and which government is instituted to uphold – was wholly secular and too avant-garde for his contemporaries. It was regarded, as was Hume's philosophy generally, as sceptical in a wholly destructive sense, a socially dangerous virus, not a healthy vaccine producing 'moderation', and the view that it destroyed the rational foundations of natural law became canonical in the text-book histories of jurisprudence and political thought. Even when Hume was praised for the sociological realism of his account of the origin of justice and government, allegedly doing away with the 'state of nature' and the social contract, this was usually misunderstood, and Hume's real contribution to social science was overlooked: an empirical, secular and 'one-dimensional' idea of society as the exclusive locus of justice and all moral obligation and social ties and rules. Hume had no use for the idea of a God-governed 'society' of men *qua* rational agents as such; his philosophy could not accommodate it.

Hume's 'philosophical' approach to politics had little more success in the other parts of his programme. Contemporaries in England did not appreciate his ability both as a cosmopolitan Scotsman and a 'Newtonian' scientist, to take a detached view of the British government and political scene or its history, and to compare them, not altogether favourably, with the 'civilized' absolute monarchies of Europe. And the *History* became notoriously the 'Tory' apologia for the Stuarts: its broader theme, the development of 'regular' government in Europe, was invisible through the key-hole of English party politics.

A broader-based, more thorough and intensive study of Hume's 'politics' is a comparatively recent development.

Duncan Forbes
Clare College, University of Cambridge

Further Reading
Forbes, D. (1975), *Hume's Philosophical Politics*, Cambridge.
Miller, D. (1981), *Philosophy and Ideology in Hume's Political Thought*, Oxford.
Stewart, J. B. (1963), *The Moral and Political Thought of David Hume*, New York.

Humour, Psychology of

Humour, a 'serious' field of research only since the 1970s, should be viewed as a cognitive experience which has characteristic physiological and emotional by-products. When humourous insights are achieved, arousal increases and then decreases. These arousal changes are associated with the positive emotion of joy, and are accompanied by varying degrees of laughter and smiling. Widespread individual differences exist in both the disposition to see humourous aspects of events and to respond with laughter when the humour is perceived. For example, on measures of reflection-impulsivity, impulsives generally laugh more than reflectives at jokes – even when they don't fully understand the point. Reflectives tend to comprehend better, but laugh less. It remains unclear which type of person has a 'better' sense of humour.

Researchers of the cognitive aspects of humour agree that most humour contains some element of distortion of one's knowledge of the world. To appreciate humour, we must first detect an incongruity resulting from this distortion, and then resolve it by utilizing other information which makes the incongruous elements meaningfully 'fit' in some unexpected way. In the case of 'nonsense' humour, incongruities may be funny in their own right, apart from any resolution. The following joke shows the importance of incongruity and resolution: One prostitute said to another, 'Can you lend me $10 until I get back on my back?' (The humour here requires familiarity with the American expression 'getting back on your feet'.)

Disparagement or put-down humour is one of the most common forms. People enjoy jokes in which individuals or groups they like or identify with put down those they dislike. Humour is interfered with when these roles are reversed. This applies to political, religious and racial-ethnic humour, as well as humour which focuses on occupational or gender roles.

A long-standing popular belief suggests that a strong sense of humour is good for one's health. This view is generally supported both for physical and mental health. In the latter case, psychoanalysts have long claimed that humour helps one cope with stress and emotional conflict. It helps to substitute a positive (and playful) frame of mind for a negative one.

Infants begin to experience humour at about one year, and developmental changes in the humour they understand and produce closely follow underlying changes in cognitive development. Chimpanzees and gorillas who have been taught sign language also show strong evidence for humour (for example, distorting familiar signs or 'playfully' mislabelling objects whose names are well known). Evidence from stroke victims who have suffered brain damage suggests that the right hemisphere plays a central role in the ability to understand and enjoy humour.

Paul E. McGhee
Texas Tech University, Lubbock

Further Reading
McGhee, P. E. (1979), *Humor: Its Origin and Development*, San Francisco.
McGhee, P. E. and Goldstein, J. H. (eds) (1983), *Handbook of Humor Research*, vols 1 and 2, New York.

Hunters and Gatherers

Hunters and gatherers, hunter-gatherers, gatherer-hunters and foragers are all more or less synonymous terms, and are usually applied only to those populations who live entirely by these two means of subsistence. Sometimes they are used more loosely to refer to populations who obtain most of their subsistence by hunting and gathering, or to populations who subsist entirely by hunting, gathering and/or *fishing*. In order to avoid such problems of definition, some anthropologists employ yet another near-synonym, band societies, which is intended to designate the typical social organization of these peoples.

In 10,000 BC, the world's population consisted solely of hunters, gatherers and fishermen. By AD 1500, with the spread of pastoralism and agriculture, this total was down to 1 per cent. By AD 1900 it was a mere 0.001 per cent (Lee and DeVore, 1968). Today's hunter-gatherers include small, scattered groups in, for example, the Philippines, Malaysia and India; the Pygmies, Bushmen and Hadza in Africa; and, in their traditional lifestyle, the aboriginal inhabitants of Australia and northern North America. Full-time hunting and gathering is dying out, though many modern members of these groups, as well as South American horticulturalists and African pastoralists, engage in part-time hunting and gathering. Throughout the world the sexual division of labour is the same: the men do the hunting and the women do most of the gathering.

In spite of their numbers, 'pure' hunter-gatherers are of great theoretical significance to anthropology and related disciplines.

Evolutionary anthropologists and human ethologists emphasize that the overwhelming part of cultural man's 2,000,000-year existence has been spent in hunting and gathering societies. Some argue as a consequence that man's 'natural' biological and psychological make-up is to be found more readily in foraging societies than in agricultural or industrialized ones. The counter-argument is that present-day foragers are fully 'cultural' and biologically modern, and therefore their means of subsistence bear no necessary relation to man's primeval mentality.

Prehistoric archaeologists also use studies of present-day foragers, in this case as aids to interpreting the archaeological record. Yet the difficulty is that contemporary foragers, who are confined largely to remote deserts and jungles and surrounded by non-foraging peoples, may be quite different from the ancient hunter-gatherers who inhabited the archaeological sites of Europe and temperate North America.

Another area of theoretical interest is in economic anthropology, and, in particular, substantivist theory. According to Sahlins, hunters and gatherers quite possibly represent 'the original affluent society' (Sahlins, 1974). If affluence is measured in free time rather than in accumulated wealth, hunters and gatherers are not infrequently far more affluent than their agricultural and industrialized neighbours. Except in times of scarcity, hunter-gatherer populations need spend only a few hours per day in subsistence-related activities.

Yet despite all this theoretical interest in hunter-gatherers, some specialists have recently come to question the utility of 'hunter-gatherers' as a meaningful category, even for economic anthropology. Ellen argues that there is little difference between the subsistence pursuits of many so-called hunter-gatherers and so-called horticulturalists who also hunt and gather for a large part of their food supply (Ellen, 1982). Likewise, Ingold considers the case for a fuzzy boundary between hunting and herding (Ingold, 1980). More radically still, Arcand suggests that not only can we not easily define hunting and gathering, but, having defined them in some idealized fashion, we can still only say very little about their relation to other aspects of culture. He suggests that we abandon the term 'hunters and gatherers' (Arcand, 1981).

A number of writers still point implicitly to the 'purity' of hunter-gatherers. In ecological writings foragers are seen as more 'natural', and therefore, but contradictorally, more 'human' than other peoples. Part-time foragers are seen as tainted by exposure to post-foraging culture and less worthy of study.

Woodburn has suggested a way out of these impasses (Woodburn, 1980). He draws the line not between hunter-gatherers and others, but between 'immediate-return hunters and gatherers' and others. Immediate-return economies are characterized by a hand-to-mouth existence, that is, lack of time-investment in activities designed to pay off later, such as making fishing nets, keeping horses for use in hunting, or full-time or part-time cultivation of crops. One of the few peoples who qualify as immediate-return is the Hadza, studied by Woodburn himself. In contrast, all other societies, including hunter-gatherers who invest in horses, nets, etc., the Australian Aborigines (who 'farm out' their women), and all non-hunting-and-gathering peoples, have 'delayed-return' economies.

Alan Barnard
University of Edinburgh

References

Arcand, B. (1981), 'The Negritos and Penan will never be Cuiva', *Folk*, 23.

Ellen, R. F. (1982), *Environment, Subsistence and System*, Cambridge.

Ingold, T. (1980), *Hunters, Pastoralists and Ranchers*, Cambridge.

Lee, R. B. and DeVore, I. (1968), 'Problems in the study of hunters and gatherers', in R. B. Lee and I. DeVore (eds), *Man the Hunter*, Chicago.

Sahlins, M. (1974), *Stone Age Economics*, London.

Woodburn, J. (1980), 'Hunters and gatherers today and reconstruction of the past', in E. Gellner (ed.), *Soviet and Western Anthropology*, London.

Further Reading

Barnard, A. (1983), 'Contemporary hunter-gatherers: current theoretical issues in ecology and social organization', *Annual Review of Anthropology*, 12.

Winterhalder, B. and Smith, E. A. (eds) (1981), *Hunter-Gatherer Foraging Strategies*, Chicago.

See also: *pastoralism*.

Hypnosis

Hypnosis is an altered state of mind, usually accompanied by some or all the following:

(1) Increases in the intensity of focal concentration as compared with peripheral awareness.
(2) Changes in perception, memory and temporal orientation
(3) Alternations in the sense of control over voluntary motor functions

(4) Dissociation of certain parts of experience from the remainder.
(5) Intensification of interpersonal relatedness, with an increase in receptivity and suspension of critical judgement.

Individuals capable of experiencing some or all of these changes associated with a shift into the hypnotic-trance state may learn to employ them as tools in facilitating therapeutic change. This applies especially to people with disorders which involve the psychosomatic interface.

Hypnosis is not sleep but rather a shift in attention which can occur in a matter of seconds, either with guidance or spontaneously. Highly hypnotizable individuals are more prone to intensely absorbing and self-altering experiences, for example when reading novels or watching good films. All hypnosis is really self-hypnosis. Under guided conditions, a hypnotizable individual allows a therapist or other person to structure his own shift in attention. However, not everyone can be hypnotized. Recent research using a variety of standardized scales indicates that hypnotizability is highest toward the end of the first decade of life, and declines slowly through adulthood and more rapidly late in life. Approximately two-thirds of the adult population is at least somewhat hypnotizable, and about five per cent are extremely hypnotizable. Among psychiatric patients, this capacity for hypnotic experience has been shown to be higher in certain disorders such as hysterical dissociations, and lower in others such as schizophrenia. In general, the capacity to experience hypnosis is consistent with good mental health and normal brain function. Neurophysiological studies of hypnotized subjects indicate brain electrical activity consistent with resting alertness and some special involvement of the right cerebral hemisphere.

Hypnosis has been used successfully as an adjunctive tool in the treatment of a variety of psychiatric and medical conditions, including the control of pain; anxiety and phobias; habits, especially smoking; and in the treatment of traumatic neurosis. When used in treatment, the hypnotic state provides a receptive and attentive condition in which the patient concentrates on a primary treatment strategy designed to promote greater mastery over the symptom. Some individuals with hysterical fugue states and multiple-personality syndrome are treated with hypnosis because their high hypnotizability becomes a vehicle for the expression of symptoms. Hysterical amnesias can be uncovered, and shifts between different personality states can be facilitated with the goal of teaching the patient greater control over these transitions in states of mind.

All psychotherapies are composed of interpersonal and intrapsyphic components which facilitate change. Hypnotic trance mobilizes· focused concentration, demonstrates the ability to change both psychological and somatic experience, and intensifies receptivity to input from others. This makes the hypnotic state a natural tool for use in psychotherapy and a fascinating psychobiological phenomenon.

David Spiegel
Stanford University

Further Reading
Hilgard, E. R. and Hilgard, J. R. (1975), *Hypnosis in the Relief of Pain*, Los Altos, California.
Spiegel, H. and Spiegel, D. (1978), *Trance and Treatment: Clinical Uses of Hypnosis*, New York.

Hysteria

Known to Hippocrates, hysteria is one of the very earliest psychiatric entities to be recognized. Yet the passage of time has produced more confusion than clarity and more diversity than unanimity as to its meaning.

For the ancients, hysteria was the result of the extravagant wanderings of the uterus (*hysteron* being Greek for womb) which, having broken loose from its moorings, was thought to career about the innards causing various stoppages, effluxions and diverse symptoms of disorder. Latent in this rather mythical formulation are two central ideas, still noteworthy in modern conceptualizations: (1) the tendency of the disorder to be more prevalent in women than men; and (2) the possibility of a multi-symptom clinical picture. Although the multiplicity of symptoms brought the disorder within the compass of medicine, the problem was poorly understood, highly resistant to the non-specific treatments of former times, and complicated by the sexist perspective in which it was considered.

Sigmund Freud's work led to a major breakthrough. His careful analyses of these patients, long considered to be untreatable or malingering, revealed the underlying unconscious residues of past emotional conflicts, usually sexual, that led to the puzzling clinical picture. Hysterics, Freud discovered, suffered from reminiscences.

Since that time, other conflictual issues, such as aggression, have been found to gain expression in hysterical symptoms. To understand hysteria one must grasp a closely related concept, the idea of conversion: the tendency for intrapsychic conflict to express itself through 'conversion' into somatic symptomatology. These symptoms usually involve the voluntary nervous system and its organs, sturctures and actions. In addition, the symptom usually contains within itself, in symbolic fashion, both of the elements of the unconscious conflict. An example might be a person who has an unconscious sexual conflict about masturbation and whose symptom is paralysis of the right forearm which keeps the arm from movement. The conversion symptoms – here, paralysis – afflicts the organ that would express the impulse (the arm) and prevents the feared action (masturbation): both impulse and prohibition are thus captured in the symptom.

Unfortunately for conceptual clarity, the term hysteria is used in several different ways today:
(1) Internists and neurologists commonly use the designation to refer to a multiplicity of non-organically based disorders, including conversion, psychosomatic illness, somatopsychic illness and simple malingering.
(2) Dynamic psychiatrists and psychoanalysts, in contrast, designate by hysteria those neurotic conflicts that stem from the Oedipal stage of development. This conceptualization implies primarily sexual conflicts and a tendency to see nonsexual issues in sexual terms (and therefore to deny or avoid them). A common concurrent finding is the tendency to have relationships that are triangular in configuration, or to experience existing relationships as if they were triangular.
(3) Descriptive psychiatrists may use the term to refer to dramatizing, histrionic and seductive patients, mostly women, who tend to somatize their emotional difficulties; such clinicians may speak of an hysterical personality rather than of hysterical conflicts.

The latest diagnostic and statistical manual of the American Psychiatric Association (DSM-III) deals with this dilemma by eliminating the term entirely. Instead, the historically accrued elements of hysteria are dispersed under a number of headings including somatoform disorders, conversion disorders, histrionic personality disorders, and dissociative disorders (the last relating to a tendency among patients with hysteria toward dissociative states, one dramatic but rare example of which is multiple personality).

Thomas G. Gutheil
Harvard University
Program in Law and Psychiatry, Boston

Further Reading
Breuer, J. and Freud S. (1947 [1895]), *Studies in Hysteria*, New York.
Chodoff, B. and Lyons, H. (1958), 'The hysterical personality and "hysterial" conversion', *American Journal of Psychiatry*, 114.
Marmor, J. (1956), 'Orality in the hysterical personality', *Journal of the American Psychoanalytic Association*, 1.
Veith, I. (1965), *Hysteria: The History of a Disease*, Chicago.

I

Ideology

The concept of ideology is commonly traced back to the European Enlightenment and especially to Destutt de Tracy who is thought to be the first to use the term in print. There are, of course, earlier forms of the notion in, for example, Bacon's concept of 'idola' meaning 'impediment to knowledge'. The eighteenth-century development of the concept is closely linked to the French Encyclopedists' struggle against all forms of religious and otherwise traditional thought in the name of the new secular truth of science. But even if the term ideology is of modern European origin, the concept is quite probably more ancient. It appears, for instance, in the fifth-century Greek equivalent of the struggle between the 'Ancients and the Moderns', when representatives of the latter, champions of science and civilization, attacked the old traditions and religion, in some cases attempting to explain scientifically the origin of ancient religious beliefs.

The concept of ideology reached its florescence in the great philosophical and social scientific systems of the nineteenth century. Comte criticized the negativism of the Enlightenment ideologists' attack on tradition and metaphysics, arguing that the forerunners of science had an important ordering function in society that would of necessity be maintained in the evolution of new mental systems (1901). What is reserved for the domain of purely intellectual activity in Comte is generalized to the entirety of mental production in society in Marx. Developing a line of thought descended from a group of critical students of Hegel referred to as the German ideologists, and especially well articulated in Feuerbach's materialist inversion of Hegel, Marx theorized that society's consciousness of itself was an ethereal self-mystification. Feuerbach's inversion of Hegel consisted in attempting to demonstrate the earthly foundations of metaphysics and religion. This he accomplished in his famous *The Essence of Christianity* (1957) in which he reduced the existence of religion to the fundamentally estranged character of human nature *in general*. Marx's critique of Feuerbach stressed the historicity of the so-called material basis of ideology as well as the notion that human nature is itself a historical product just as much as its ideological correlatives. He argued further that the estranged or alienated forms of consciousness were not mere intellectual reflections but forms of human practice that play an active role in the functioning and transformation of society itself. The practical aspects of ideology were seen to be directly associated with the structure of class domination.

Marx – and Engels – (1970) generalized the question of ideology from the realm of science versus tradition to that of real versus mystified social processes, thus encompassing questions of theory and questions of political control within the same framework. In this way the function as well as the content of the idea systems might be critically scrutinized.

Throughout the nineteenth and early twentieth centuries, the two aspects of the concept of ideology were elaborated upon. A broad array of terms seem to have been used in similar fashion: *Weltanschaung*, collective representation, sometimes even culture, all to capture the idea of the total mental life of society. In the work of Lukács and Mannheim there emerged a tradition of the sociology of knowledge that has been developed throughout the century, its most recent advocate being Habermas. This approach, heavily represented in the Frankfurt School of German sociology, has concentrated much of its effort on understanding the ideological basis of all forms of social knowledge including the natural sciences. In France, Durkheim and the *Année Sociologique* school elaborated the analysis of the relation between social structure and the organization of collective representations (religious, intellectual and otherwise) that are meant to reflect the former (Durkheim, 1965; Durkheim and Mauss, 1963). Their wide-reaching ethnological ambitions had important influences on the development of anthropology in France and Holland and more recently among British symbolists (Turner, 1967; Douglas, 1975). In the work of British functionalists there has been a concentration on the way in which ideology (religion and ritual) maintains social solidarity (Radcliffe-Brown), provides a 'charter' (Malinowski) for the social order, or otherwise prevents social disintegration (Gluckman).

In the more recent work of structural Marxists (for example, Althusser, 1971) a more extreme functionalism is evident, one where ideological 'apparatuses' are conceived as instruments that exist to maintain the coherence of a mode of production, a system of economic exploitation that itself generates its own self-maintenance by way of the production of appropriate mentalities, political structures and socialized subjects who are no more than the agents of the system.

Among both materialist and social determinist theoreticians, ideology has usually been assumed to be a locus in societal structure corresponding to patterns of thought and cognition, systems of values, religious organization, and so on, whose content is supposed in some way to reflect or, at the very least, to be a discourse upon a logically prior social structure.

Among cultural determinists and value determinists, often referred to as idealists, the system of cultural categories or value orientations are said to determine or in some way provide the foundation for social action and organization.

Discussions of ideology have in classical social science been characterized by a pervasive dualism of idea/reality, ideology/practice, idealism/materialism. This mind/body dualism which has systematically conflated ideology and ideas, thought and meaning, has more recently been criticized. Theories of symbolic action (for example, Dolgin, Kemnitzer and Schneider, 1977); praxis theory (Bourdieu, 1977; Giddens, 1979), theories of ideo-logic (Augé, 1975), and theories of the imaginary construction of reality have all in different ways tried to overcome the dualism inherent in sociological and anthropological discourse (Berger and Luckmann, 1966). These approaches elaborate on the recognition that the organization of material praxis is symbolically constituted, just as the structure of meaning is the product of social practice. Works on the symbolism of power, the social functions of knowledge, the relation between culture and class (Foucault, 1977) have focused on the way in which symbolic practice organizes material realities. Anthropological analysis of the logic of category systems and their complex interpenetration with material practices has become an important area of theoretical discussion (Friedman, 1974; Barnett and Silverman, 1979).

Jonathan Friedman
University of Copenhagen

References

Althusser, L. (1971), 'Ideology and ideological state apparatuses', in *Lenin and Philosophy*, New York.

Augé, M. (1975), *Théorie des pouvoirs et idéologie*, Paris.

Barnett, D. and Silverman, M. (1979), *Ideology and Everyday Life*, Ann Arbor, Michigan.

Berger, P. and Luckmann, T. (1966), *The Social Construction of Reality*, New York.

Bourdieu, P. (1977), *Outline of a Theory of Practice*, Cambridge.

Comte, A. (1901 [1877]), *Cours de philosophie positive*, Paris.

Dolgin, J., Kemnitzer, D. and Schneider, D. (1977), 'As people express their lives, so they are . . .', 'Introduction', *Symbolic Anthropology*, New York.

Douglas, M. (1975), *Implicit Meanings*, London.

Durkheim, E. (1965 [1912]), *Elementary Forms of Religious Life*, New York (*Les Formes élémentaires de la vie religieuse*, Paris).

Durkheim, E. and Mauss, M. (1963), *Systems of Primitive Classification*, Chicago.

Feuerbach, L. (1957), *The Essence of Christianity*, New York.

Foucault, M. (1977 [1975]), *Discipline and Punish: The Birth of the Prison*, New York (*Surveiller et punir*, Paris).

Friedman, J. (1974), 'The place of fetishism and the problem of materialist interpretations', *Critique of Anthropology*, 1.

Giddens, A. (1979), *Central Problems in Social Theory*, Cambridge.

Marx, K. (1964), *Economic and Philosophic Manuscripts of 1844*, New York.

Marx, K. (1967 [1867]), *Capital*, vol. I, London.

Marx, K. and Engels, F. (1970), *Selected Works*, Moscow.

Turner, T. (1967), *The Forest of Symbols*, Ithaca, New York.

Further Reading

Feuer, L. (1975), *Ideology and the Ideologists*, Oxford.

Geertz, C. (1973), 'Ideology as a cultural system', in *The Interpretation of Cultures*, New York.

Gouldner, A. (1976), *The Dialectic of Ideology and Technology*, London.

Litchtheim, G. (1967), *The Concept of Ideology and Other Essays*, New York.

See also: *Althusser; Frankfurt School; Marx's theory of history and society.*

Identity

See Self-Concept, Social Identity.

Illich, Ivan (1926–)

Ivan Illich is the 'leading contemporary exponent of the romantic anarchist tradition' (Thomas, 1983). He was born in Vienna in 1926 and grew up in Europe, obtaining degrees in natural sciences, history, philosophy and theology. In 1950 he went to New York where he worked for five years as a parish priest in an Irish and Puerto Rican neighbourhood. Between 1956 and 1960 he was vice-rector of the Catholic University of Puerto Rico. In 1962 he founded the Centre for Intercultural Documentation in Cuernavaca, Mexico, where he is now based, dividing his time between his writing and teaching medieval history in West German universities. His chief works are *Celebration of Awareness* (1971); *Deschooling Society* (1971); *Tools for Conviviality*

(1973); *Energy and Equity* (1974); *Medical Nemesis* (1976); *Toward a History of Need* (1978); *Shadow Work* (1981); and *Gender* (1983).

His work can be understood as a sustained historical polemic against the logic of modern economic development, especially in the Third World. Instead of seeing economic growth as the progressive mastery of need and scarcity, he argues that it is a process in which previously self-subsistent peasant peoples are dispossessed of their own 'vernacular' skills and made to depend on doctors for their health, teachers for their schooling, automobiles for their transport, television for their entertainment, and wage labour for their subsistence. Development is enslavement to need, not liberation from scarcity. His latest work, *Gender*, extends this analysis to women, arguing that economic development has freed them from the segregated domain of 'gender' only to enslave them to the violence and inequality of modern 'sex'.

Illich underestimates the extent to which the new needs created by the modern division of labour actually do correspond to what people desire, but he has made an extremely effective critique of the assumption that economic progress means greater freedom. His writing has had a major influence on post-1968 critiques of Western consumer affluence and, more importantly, on Third World development strategies, which seek to protect the 'vernacular' skills and self-subsisting capacities of indigenous populations from the false needs engendered by capitalist economic development.

Michael Ignatieff
King's College, Cambridge

Reference
Thomas, K. (1983), 'Review of *Gender* by Ivan Illich', *New York Review of Books*, 12 May.

Imperialism

Imperialism has acquired so many meanings that the word ought to be dropped by social scientists, complained Professor Hancock (1950) several decades ago. 'Muddle-headed historians in Great Britain and America use this word with heaven-knows how many shades of meaning, while Soviet writers are using it to summarize a theory and wage a war.' Alas, these errors continue. Autocratic rule over a diversity of otherwise roughly equal peoples goes back in time at least as far as the Indo-European Empire of Alexander the Great, but nowadays imperialism also means to Marxists the triumph of (mostly Western-European) monopoly finance capital over a still larger array of non-European peoples at the end of the nineteenth century, a very different kind of empire indeed. For some 'underdevelopment theorists', the term is simply synonymous with

capitalism in general, not just its monopolistic stage. Demythologizing imperialism is therefore a rather slippery task.

Marxist theories of imperialism were first fleshed out during the first two decades of the century, principally in order to explain why the expected final collapse of capitalism was taking so long to happen. Later the outbreak of the First World War and the promptness with which European working peoples attacked one another rather than their bosses, added fresh urgency to thought. Nationalism, in retrospect, seems to have had something to do with this, as well as the autonomy of political choice at the time of outbreak of war from anything approaching economic rationality. But Marxist writers mostly looked elsewhere for explanations and for ammunition with which to pursue more sectarian concerns. Just before the war, Rosa Luxemburg provided in *Die Akkumulation des Kapitals* (1913) an analysis of imperialism which is still read respectfully today because of its pioneer probing of articulations between expanding capitalism and pre-capitalist social formations outside Europe. But during and after the 1914–18 War it was her advocacy of the mass revolutionary strike in order to speed up the final collapse of capitalism, otherwise given a new lease of life by imperialist expansion, that excited more immediate attention.

Marx himself had seen the expansion of capitalism outside its original heartlands as both a less important phenomenon and a more benign one than Luxemburg: it was a marginal matter, in at least two senses. Luxemburg, however, considered that capitalism could only survive if it continually expanded its territory. One problem with this view, as Mommsen (1981) has pointed out, is that 'Rosa Luxemburg's basic adherence to Marx's complicated and controversial theory of surplus value, which by definition accrued to capitalism alone, prevented her from considering whether, if the consumer capacity of the masses were increased, internal markets might not afford suitable opportunities for the profitable investment of "unconsumed" i.e. reinvestable, surplus value.' Another defect was that Luxemburg undoubtedly misunderstood the significance of the enormous rise in overseas investment at the start of the twentieth century. Along with Hobson before and Lenin subsequently, she assumed that it was closely associated with colonial annexations. In fact, as Robinson and Gallagher (1961) have reminded us, it diverged widely from it. Hilferding had taken a slightly different view. In *Das Finanzkapital* (1910), he was more concerned to explain why capitalist crises had recently become less frequent (there had not been one since 1896), and he argued that free trade had been replaced by finance capital, whose dominance and ability to intervene with state help anywhere in the world had temporarily delayed the final catatrophe. But it was the British journalist and free-trader

Hobson, with his wide array of attacks upon overseas investment and colonial annexations in *Imperialism* (1902), whom Lenin used most extensively in his own famous study of *Imperialism, The Highest Stage of Capitalism* (1917). This was written in order not only to explain the First World War but also to attack the reformism of Karl Kautsky, who had suggested that the coming final collapse of capitalism might be still further delayed by the emergence of an 'ultra-imperialism' stopping for the time being further intra-imperialist wars. In retrospect, Lenin's work on imperialism reads more like a tract than a treatise, but its subsequent importance was of course vastly increased by the success of Lenin's faction in seizing power in Russia in 1917; for many years afterwards it retained unquestionable status as unholy writ.

Shortly after the Russian Revolution, Lenin also latched onto one of the greatest uses of imperialism as political ideology, namely, as a weapon against non-communist empires. This tendency was continued by Stalin, who told the Twelfth Congress of the Russian Communist Party in 1923: 'Either we succeed in stirring up, in revolutionizing, the remote rear of imperialism – the colonial and semi-colonial countries of the East – and thereby hasten the fall of imperialism; or we fail to do so and thereby strengthen imperialism and weaken the force of our movement.' Such statements reversed Marx's original view that imperialism was good for capitalism but only of marginal importance in its development, and substituted a new conventional wisdom that (1) imperialism was bad news for all backward areas of the world, and (2) imperialism was of utterly central importance to the development of capitalism itself.

View (1) has been further popularized in recent years by the underdevelopment school associated with André Gundar Frank, and attacked recently by Warren (1981). View (2), on the other hand, has led to an oddly focused debate among historians over the colonial partition of Africa at the close of the nineteenth century, the 'theory of economic imperialism' being something of a straw man in this debate, as imperialism (on most Marxist views) did not arise until after the Scramble for Africa had taken place; and even after this date Lenin was clearly wrong about the direction of most overseas investment, let alone its political significance. Only in the case of South Africa (and possibly Cuba) is there even a plausible case for economic imperialism being identical with colonial annexation: the South African War indeed was popularly called 'les Boers contre la Bourse' in continental Europe at the time.

Other difficulties with Marxist views of imperialism derive from Lenin's use of Hobson's *Imperialism* (1902). Hobson was a very bitter critic of British overseas investment, but for very un-Marxist reasons. He was a free-trade liberal who saw colonial annexations and wars as a hugely expensive way of propping up the power and profits of a very small class of *rentier* capitalists, who pursued profit abroad to the detriment of investment at home. Only by manipulating the masses by appealing to their patriotism did this small class of capitalists get away with this (in his view) huge confidence trick and, ideally, social reform should increase the purchasing powers of the masses and thereby render 'imperialism' powerless. Lenin ignored Hobson's theories and simply used his facts. In retrospect, the 'facts' about the coincidence of overseas investment with colonial annexation appear very wrong-headed, his 'theories' much less so. Hobson's views on 'under-consumption' were later taken up and given some seminal twists by John Maynard Keynes, while his intuitions about connections between overseas annexations and metropolitan social structures were later taken up by Joseph Schumpeter and Hannah Arendt (for her analysis of the origins of Fascism).

Schumpeter wrote his essay *Zur Soziologie der Imperialismen* (1919) as an explicit attack upon Marxist theories of imperialism. Capitalism itself he considered to be essentially anti-imperialist in nature, and such monopolistic and expansionist tendencies characterizing pre-1914 capitalism he put down to the malevolent influence of an anachronistic militarism surviving from the European feudal past. Schumpeter defined imperialism as 'the objectless disposition on the part of a state to unlimited forcible expansion' (Schumpeter, 1951). The basic trouble with this particular formulation is that while the European colonial annexations of the late nineteenth and early twentieth centuries were certainly sometimes this, they were not always so. Similarly, while much European overseas investment in the late nineteenth century did not go to areas of European colonial annexation, sometimes it did. Furthermore, while 'the theory of economic imperialism' may well be a straw man as far as the debate about the causes of the Scramble for Africa is concerned, it would be absurd to suggest that the partitioners did not believe that there was *something* economically useful about Black Africa. Imperialism needs to be demythologized, not simply wished away.

Probably imperialism is best defined in some median manner. As the etymology of the word itself denotes, imperialism is closely concerned with empires and colonialism, but this is not necessarily always the case. In the Americas the Monroe Doctrine (1823) vetoed new formal empires by European countries – but not subsequent 'dollar diplomacy' by the US, sometimes supported by the overt use of force, sometimes with mere threats and unequal financial practices. Capitalism, too, is not necessarily linked with non-communist imperialism, but sometimes has been, especially in the many African and Asian colonial dependencies established during the second half of the nineteenth century. In these circumstances, imperialism is probably best separated analytically from both 'capitalism' and 'colonialism' and treated principally as the pursuit of intrusive and unequal economic policy in other countries supported by significant degrees of coercion.

Thus defined, imperialism as formal empire (or 'colonialism') may well be largely a thing of the past, except for strategic colonies (*colonies de position*). But imperialism as informal empire (or 'neocolonialism', to employ Nkrumah's terminology) probably has an assured future ahead of it – in both the non-communist and the communist-dominated worlds.

Michael Twaddle
Institute of Commonwealth Studies
University of London

References

Hancock, W. K. (1950), *Wealth of Colonies*, Cambridge.

Mommsen, W. J. (1981), *Theories of Imperialism*, New York.

Robinson, R. and Gallagher, J. (1961), *Africa and the Victorians: The Official Mind of Imperialism*, London.

Schumpeter, J. A. (1951 [1919]), *Imperialism and Social Classes*, Oxford. (Includes translation of *Zur Soziologie der Imperialismen*.)

Warren, B. (1981), *Imperialism: Pioneer of Capitalism*, London.

See also: *dependency theory; Third World; world-system theory.*

Incest

'Sexual commerce of near kindred', says the Concise Oxford Dictionary of 'incest'. Accordingly, the *prohibition* of incest refers to rules forbidding sexual intercourse – and *a fortiori* marriage – between kin who are regarded as too closely related. The precise specification of when a relationship is too close to allow commerce varies with cultures, and, in our own Christian culture, has varied historically.

In the modern Western idiom, incest refers to sex in the nuclear family – between brother and sister, father and daughter, or mother and son; sometimes incest refers to sex within the residential unit of the household, somewhat independently of considerations of kinship.

Because of these cultural variations in the definition of incest, the notion is difficult to use for analysis. One alternative would be to restrict the use to the common and universal core of mother-son sex, but the more popular choice has been to apply the word sex regarded (within a specific culture) with horror and often awe because of the kinship relationship between the persons involved. This establishes a clear distinction between incest and a variety of other forms of prohibited sexual behaviour such as adultery, rape and bestiality.

This emphasis on the sentiment of 'natural' repulsion draws attention to the fact that we are dealing not with a law-enforced social prohibition but with a *taboo* – a prohibition with sacred undertones which is observed not out of fear of getting caught and punished but out of an inner and powerful feeling of inappropriateness. In other words, incest is more of a sin than a crime. Accordingly, in many societies there are no social sanctions attached to incest: punishment is supposed to be automatic, taking the form of death, or, more often, conspicious stigma such as skin complaints or taints on children stemming from an incestuous union. This latter belief is shared by our culture where it is widely supposed to be validated by science.

The unconscious nature of incest avoidance makes its rationale difficult to discern. Hence the large range of explanations that have been offered of the incest taboo. Biological explanations are increasingly popular, and they seem to be supported by behavioural evidence from species related to our own. Incest avoidance would contribute to optimal reshuffling of the genetic pool, and would be assured by making body odours of close kin unattractive. Cultural variety would then be accounted for by the extension, first observed by Brenda Seligman (1950), to classificatory equivalents of mother and sister for men, and father and brother for women.

Fortune (1932) and Lévi-Strauss (1969) argued that the incest prohibition is culturally indispensable for the articulation of allied exogamous units into a vast social tissue. This explanation, however, only explains the brother-sister prohibition, and while it is a convincing explanation of incest avoidance in classificatory kinship systems, it leaves descriptive systems – for which there is even evidence of actual brother and sister marriage – untouched. Other types of explanation account essentially for the mother-son prohibition seen as the hard core of the incest taboo. In Freud's (1950) view, the son is refused sexual access to his mother in order to alleviate the potentially murderous confrontation of father and son. For Leach (1976) the prohibition operates to circumvent the classificatory confusion of mother and wife, which could be fatal to any cultural construction. The clear separation of close kin is indeed central to any purpose of classification. (The Old Testament reminds us that the 'confounding of generations' is destructive of the entire social order.) Cultures also remind us that mother-son incest can only be seen as a futile attempt to escape the cycle of living and dying, a childish quest for the lost paradise. This is expressed exquisitely by the Lovedu when they say that 'the only place one never returns to is the womb'.

Paul Jorion
Food and Agriculture Organization, Benin

References

Fortune, R. W. (1932), 'Incest', in E. R. A. Seligman
(ed.), *Encyclopaedia of the Social Sciences*, London.

Freud, S. (1950 [1912–13]), *Totem and Taboo*, London.
(Original German edn, *Totem und Tabu*.)

Leach, E. R. (1976), *Culture and Communication*,
Cambridge.

Lévi-Strauss, C. (1969 [1949]), *The Elementary
Structures of Kinship*, London. (Original French edn,
Les Structures élémentaires de la parenté, Paris.)

Seligman, B. Z. (1959), 'The problem of incest and
exogamy: a restatement', *American Anthropology*, 52.

Further Reading

Fox, R. (1980), *The Red Lamp of Incest*, London.

Incest Behaviour

Most writings on incest by social scientists deal with
theoretical aspects of incest avoidance and prohibition,
while neglecting the incidence and implications of the
act itself. The two issues are obviously related but not
identical, and a complete grasp of the problem requires
an integrated understanding of both phenomena which
is presently lacking.

The classic approach to the prohibition question has
been to assume that, at some unspecified point in the
past, human beings instituted a rule against intra-
familial sex, and hence marriage, in recognition of
the potential biological, social and/or psychological
effects of inbreeding. Such an argument, which has
been espoused by Freud (1950) and most past and
present social scientists, implies that humans have an
inclination toward incest which is constrained by
explicit rules. The lack of historical evidence for the
actual institutionalization of such a prohibition, and
the absence of an explicit injunction against incest in
many societies which nevertheless do not condone it,
has argued against this approach. In contrast, Edward
Westermarck (1926) argued that human beings
evolved with an avoidance of incest; some societies
then promulgated rules which supported this inclination. For supporters of this notion, this would
explain why inbreeding has never been the pattern for
any society, including those without apparent rules
against it. Circumstantial evidence from natural ethnographic settings which prevailed in traditional China
(Wolf and Huang, 1980) and on contemporary Israeli
kibbutzim (Shepher, 1971) has been interpreted as
support for the conclusion that humans tend to avoid
sexual contact with people with whom they have been
raised in close contact from early childhood. Moreover,
animal ethologists have demonstrated that all nonhuman primate species tend to avoid inbreeding by a
variety of social arrangements. Thus, the position that
mankind evolved with what is also a biologically
advantageous impulsion to outbreed has gained
ascendancy in recent years. Today, adherents of such
a view disagree on whether or not such a pattern is
genetically programmed, or the result of behavioural
imprinting or negative reinforcement at an early age.

A major problem of this sociobiological approach,
as with the preceding cultural one, is accounting for
why incest itself takes place in both Western and some
non-Western societies, In response, Robin Fox (1962)
has suggested that in some societies, including our
own, household arrangements and the socialization
process, which involve a lack of physical contact among
siblings when young, lead both to availability and
attraction when they reach sexual maturity. This, he
argues, would account for both the prohibition against
and the incidence of incestuous contacts. An implication of this argument is that cultural arrangements
can either fail to produce or fail to overcome natural
tendencies to avoid sexual relations among those reared
together.

The existence of institutionalized incest, in the form
of father/daughter or, more commonly, brother/sister
marriage among royalty in a variety of ancient states,
including Egypt, Peru, Persia, Thailand, Hawaii,
Japan, and possibly many others, presents another
problem with the avoidance theory. Moreover. it has
been recently suggested that, during the three centuries
of Roman rule in Egypt, incestuous marriages were
also prevalent among the propertied middle class
(Hopkins, 1980). Sociobiologists have taken the
position that the royal marriages can be explained in
terms of the concept of 'inclusive fitness', that is, they
are a means of ensuring the maximum chance of continuity of one's genes into the next generation. This
interpretation is undermined by the erroneous
historical assumption that such marriages had reproduction as their practical end. This was not the case,
even for the oft-cited example of Cleopatra, who was
not an offspring of her father's marriage to his sister
(Bixler, 1982). Marriages of this sort had cultural strategies related to indigenous perceptions of the nature
of royalty and the right to rule, rather than reproductive ones. None the less, these unions, as well as
the yet not fully understood case of Egyptian middle-
class marriages, suggest, as is also the case for noninstitutionalized incest, that cultural conditions can
generate incest in different contexts and for different
purposes. This also implies that if there is a sociobiological basis for incest avoidance, then the subsequent
evolution of the human capacity for cultural innovation
overcomes this inherent inclination. In other words,
the human species may be responsible for creating
the concept of incest and its practice, rather than the
prohibition. Evaluating such a proposition will require

a more detailed and systematic study of incest in its various forms.

W. Arens
State University of New York
Stony Brook

References
Bixler, R. (1982), 'Sibling incest in the royal families of Egypt, Peru, and Hawaii', *The Journal of Sex Research*, 18.
Fox, R. (1962), 'Sibling incest', *British Journal of Sociology*, 13.
Freud, S. (1950), *Totem and Taboo*, New York.
Hopkins, R. (1980), 'Brother-sister marriage in Roman Egypt', *Comparative Studies in Society and History*, 22.
Shepher, J. (1971), 'Mate selection among second generation kibbutz adolescents and adults', *Archives of Sexual Behaviour*, 1.
Westermarck, E. (1926), *A Short History of Human Marriage*, London.
Wolf, A. and Huang, C. (1980), *Marriage and Adoption in China, 1845–1945*, Stanford, California.

Further Reading
Arens, W. (1985), *The Original Sin*, New York.
Shepher, J. (1983), *Incest: A Biosocial View*, New York.
See also: *incest*.

Income Distribution, Theory of

Whilst economists have not always given such primacy to an explicit discussion of distributional questions, income distribution theory has almost always been central to the analysis of economic systems. The theory deals not only with the 'functional distribution of income' but also with the 'size distribution of income'.

Orthodox economic theory treats questions of income distribution as an integral part of the neoclassical analysis of prices, output mix and resource allocation. Briefly, each competitive firm takes the price it can get for its output and the prices it must pay for inputs as given in the market: it selects its level of output and adjusts its demand for inputs so as to maximize profits at those prices. Each household like-wise takes as given the prices it must pay for goods and services, and the prices paid to it for goods and services (for example the labour services supplied by members of the household): it adjusts the quantities of the goods and services demanded or supplied in the market so as to maximize satisfaction within the limitations imposed by its budget. All these prices adjust so as to clear the markets: aggregate supply is at least as great as aggregate demand for every good and service. The reward to any factor of production – whether it be a particular type of labour, a natural resource, or the services of capital equipment – is deter-

mined by its market clearing price. If the technology changes, or the stock of natural resources alters, or if there is a shift in the preference patterns of households, this will shift the pattern of supply and/or demand in one or more markets, and in general prices of goods and factors alter accordingly to clear the markets anew. The functional distribution of income is thus apparently automatically determined by the market mechanism, Moreover, the details of the distribution of income between persons or between households can be readily worked out within this framework: the time pattern of consumption and saving by households, and the educational investments which people make in themselves or in their offspring – each of which plays a significant role in the size distribution of incomes that is realized – can each be analysed as particular cases of the household's optimization problem.

However, one other piece of information is required for a complete theory of income distribution within this framework: the system of property rights that prevails within the community. The importance of this as regards the size distribution of income, is obvious: the question of who owns which natural resources, of who owns the capital equipment and of who is entitled to a share in the profits of the firms is central to the determination of household incomes. Household budgets are determined jointly by these property rights and the market prices and may be dramatically affected by a change in the pattern of ownership, or by a shift in the *system* of ownership (for example from a system of private property to one of state ownership). But this system of ownership will *also* affect the market prices and thus the functional distribution of income. For if households' rights of ownership are changed, the consequent change in household budgets will change the pattern of demand for goods and services, and hence the market prices of consumption goods and of labour and other resources. Thus orthodox theory might be criticized for evading one of the principal issues of income determination, by passing the question of property rights on to the historian or the political philosopher.

However, the neoclassical orthodoxy has been challenged not only because of such shortcomings, but also on account of its restrictive assumptions concerning the economic processes involved. Because these assumptions lie at the heart of the theory rather than being merely convenient simplifications, many economists have questioned the relevance of various aspects of the standard account of income distribution. We may cite three particular examples which have led to the construction of useful alternative theories.

(1) Note that the orthodox theory neglects barriers to competition and the exercising of monopoly power as being of secondary or transitory importance in the competitive market story. It has been argued that restraints on competition – in the form of segmentation

of the labour market and outright discrimination – are of major importance in analysing the lower tail of the size distribution of earnings; and monopoly power may be particularly important in the upper tail, for example in the determination of earnings in professions with restricted entry. Monopolistic pricing by firms has also been seen as of prime importance in the *functional* distribution of income – see for example Kalecki (1939). Indeed such power has an important part to play in the Marxian concept of exploitation and of theories of distribution that are based on 'struggle' between the classes representing different factors of production. The assumption of pure competition is also likely to be inadequate in analysing economics that have a substantial public sector.

(2) Another feature of the orthodox approach which many theorists find unsatisfactory is the assumption of perfect information by individuals and firms. Indeed it is argued that uncertainty is itself a potent force generating inequality in both earned and unearned income alike, in that the rich are not only better able to bear risk but may have superior information which can be exploited in the stock market and the labour market. Moreover, some of the barriers to competition may have been erected by firms in response to such uncertainty. Hence considerable interest has developed in the distributional implications of recent theories of output, employment and the structure of wages that explicitly incorporate imperfect information.

(3) The last point arises from the second: the predominant interest of the neoclassical orthodox theory of income distribution in smooth adjustments to market clearing equilibria is considered by some writers to be inappropriate to a theory of the functional distribution of income. As a response to this, economists who are strongly influenced by J. M. Keynes's approach to macroeconomics have developed a number of alternative theories of the functional distribution of income using components of the Keynesian system: for example the work of Kaldor (1956) and Pasinetti (1961). Key features of such alternative theories are rule-of-thumb savings decisions by capitalists and workers and a rigid technique by which labour and capital are combined to produce output.

Frank A. Cowell
London School of Economics and Political Science

References
Kaldor, N. (1956), 'Alternative theories of distribution', *Review of Economic Studies*, 23.
Kalecki, M. (1939), *Essays in the Theory of Economic Fluctuations*, London.
Pasinetti, L. L. (1961), 'Rate of profit and income distribution in relation to the rate of economic growth', *Review of Economic Studies*, 29.

Further Reading
Atkinson, A. B. (1983), *The Economics of Inequality*, 2nd edn, London.
Phelps Brown, E. H. (1977), *The Inequality of Pay*, London.
See also: *distribution of incomes and wealth; firm, theory of; prices, theory of.*

Indexation

Indexation represents an attempt to adjust contracts specified in monetary terms for changes in the value in money. It obviously becomes topical at times when prices are rising fairly rapidly. Kendall (1969) refers to the fact that some American states indexed paper during the War of Independence. More recently the French Government has issued loan stocks linked to the price of particular commodities such as electricity or gold, and after some experimental indexed borrowing, in 1981 the UK Government issued indexed loan stocks, whose redemption value and interest payments were indexed to the Retail Price Index. In so far as the index is a good indicator of the value of money, the implication is that it is possible to lend on terms which guarantee a real return.

One might think that indexation is more important for long-term contracts than for short-term ones, because the importance of it depends on the magnitude of movements in prices during the life of the contract. Thus indexation of wages might be seen as unimportant because wages can always be renegotiated. But this argument ignores the link between wages and prices. If wage and salary earners can be persuaded to accept low pay increases because they are also to be compensated for changes in the price level, it may be possible to move smoothly from a state of rapid to one of low inflation. Indexation of wages could therefore form an important part of a policy of disinflation. However, because it has the effect of introducing extra rigidity into real wages, and because it institutionalizes inflation, some authors are highly critical of any form of indexation. A general survey of the topic is provided by Dornbusch and Simonsen (1983).

Martin Weale
University of Cambridge

References
Dornbusch, R. and Simonsen, M. H. (1983), *Inflation, Debt and Indexation*, Cambridge, Mass.
Kendall, M. G. (1969), 'The early history of index numbers', *Journal of the International Statistical Institute*, 37.
See also: *index numbers.*

Index Numbers

Index numbers are constructed essentially as a way of representing a vector of variables by means of a single scalar variable. Clearly there is no uniquely correct way of accomplishing this transformation, and thus a considerable discussion on the implications of different approaches has developed. Economic statisticians have been particularly concerned with two types of scalar representation of vectors: (1) attempts have been made to represent changes in prices by a single price index, and (2) to reduce movements in quantities to a single quantity index, although of course on occasions one may want to reduce other variables to a simple scalar form.

Historically the problem of measuring price movements preceded the quantity analog. The former have always been a more sensitive issue. Early discussion on the subject tended to consider the price of just one commodity, often that of gold. A reduction in the gold content of coinage achieved through debasement of the currency was regarded as the same thing as an increase in the price level. In the last decade of the eighteenth century, the United Kingdom suspended the convertibility of paper money into gold. The subsequent debate on the inflation of prices was then focused on the price of gold bullion in terms of paper money.

The measurement of the price level with reference to one particular price may have been a useful way to determine the magnitude of a sudden marked debasement, and it is still used under circumstances where the value of currency is falling rapidly. (The tendency in Israel to fix prices in US dollars can be seen as an example of this.) However, it is scarcely satisfactory for comparisons over a longer period in which relative prices can change a great deal. It is in order to cope with this problem that the theory of price indices has been developed.

A price index attempts to compare the price level at one time with that of another period, or to compare relative prices in two different places. It is thus always measured relative to a base level (usually 100) and is not absolute in any sense. Early price indices relied on the simple sum of prices divided by the sum of prices in the base period $\Sigma p_t/\Sigma p_0$, or the simple arithmetic average of relative prices $^1/_n\Sigma(p_t/p_0)$ (p_t represents current prices and p_0 base prices). Neither of these is very satisfactory because some commodities are clearly more important than others. If one is trying to measure the change in price of national consumption, it is not very sensible to give the same importance to items which occupy only a small part in the consumption basket as to those which feature prominently. Although the idea of weighting so as to reflect relative importance can be traced back to the early nineteenth century, it is the mid-nineteenth century proposals of Laspeyres

and Paasche which remain of great practical importance to the present day. Laspeyres suggested that one should observe the quantities bought in the base period, and derive the price index, I_t^L, as the ratio of their cost in the current period to that in the base period. $I_t^L = \Sigma p_t q_0/\Sigma p_0 q_0$, where p_t, p_0 are as defined above and q_0 are base period quantities. Paasche proposed current rather than base period weights yielding the price index I_t^P as $I_t^P = \Sigma p_t q_t/\Sigma p_0 q_t$.

Most countries which publish consumer price indices adopt the Laspeyres index because, although the prices have to be measured on each occasion an index is calculated, the quantities used as weights only need to be calculated once, usually from an expenditure survey. In any case the time needed to process an expenditure survey means it is not possible to produce a timely Paasche price index. However it is clear that the weights used in a Laspeyres index can become stale. Expenditure will tend to shift towards goods which become relatively cheaper, and thus a Paasche price index will normally be lower than a Laspeyres index and the gap will tend to increase over time as the Laspeyres weights become increasingly outdated. This problem is usually resolved by updating the weights periodically. A link can be made by calculating indices for one period based on both old and new weights. The United Kingdom is perhaps unusual in updating the weights in its Retail Price Index every year, based on the average consumption pattern in the three previous years. But even here the Laspeyres weights can be very unsuitable if, for example, a seasonal food becomes scarce, with a high price in one particular year.

Quantity indices are constructed in a similar fashion to price indices. When measuring quantities of goods which are broadly similar, simple aggregation is often used. (Steel output is measured by tonnes of steel produced and car output by number of cars, despite the fact that a Mini is very different from a Rolls Royce.) But where very different items are aggregated, some form of weighting is needed. The most common systems used are again derived from Laspeyres and Paasche. The Laspeyres quantity index, J_t^L, is constructed by weighting the quantities by base period prices, $J_t^L = \Sigma q_1 p_0/\Sigma q_0 p_0$, while the Paasche index is calculated using current prices as weights, $J_t^P = \Sigma q_1 p_1/\Sigma q_0 p_1$. Since the quantities will tend to be largest for those goods whose prices have risen least, if one is constructing an index of national output for example, the Laspeyres index will again exceed the Paasche index.

But neither index is completely satisfactory. For multiplying a Laspeyres price index by the same quantity index does not yield the ratio of current to base period values. Instead one must multiply the Paasche price index by the Laspeyres quantity index to obtain the ratio of values. In order to remedy this and a number of other defects, various combinations of the two have been proposed, although these are not greatly used in practice.

Nevertheless the theoretical development of index numbers has continued. Thus Barnett (1981) deals with the problem of constructing a quantity index of monetary aggregates. Allen (1975) provides a detailed reference on index numbers, while the work of Diewert (1976) and Afriat (1977) contributes further theoretical development of the subject.

Martin Weale
University of Cambridge

References
Afriat, S. N. (1977), *The Price Index*, Cambridge.
Allen, R. D. G. (1975), *Index Numbers in Theory and Practice*, Chicago.
Barnett, W. A. (1981), 'Economic monetary aggregates: an application of index number theory', *Journal of Econometrics (Supplement)*.
Diewart, W. E. (1976), 'Exact and superlative index numbers', *Journal of Econometrics*.

Indifference Curves

Indifference curve analysis is now a standard part of the economist's diagrammatic tool kit. Alongside an indifference curve a consumer is equally satisfied with the different bundles of goods available to him. These curves are normally drawn with quantities of goods on each axis and they are derived from the utility function, say

$$u = u(x, y)$$

by taking the total differential and setting the change in utility equal to zero:

$$du = \frac{\partial y}{\partial x} dx + \frac{\partial u}{\partial y} \partial y = 0$$

The slope of the indifference curve:

$$\frac{dy}{dx} = \frac{\partial u / \partial x}{\partial u / \partial y}$$

This is the ratio of the marginal utilities of the two goods and is known as the marginal rate of substitution. It is normally also assumed that the marginal rate of substitution declines as the quantity of a good consumed increases, giving the indifference curves their normal convex to the origin shape. Indifference curve analysis was first introduced by Edgeworth (1881) and was popularized by John Hicks (1937). Although indifference curves are deeply rooted in the theory of utility maximization, attempts were made to demonstrate that they could be derived directly from the axiom of revealed preference without mention of the concept utility. It is now agreed that the existence of indifference curves implies the existence of a utility function. This means that indifference curve analysis must be seen as a teaching tool to illustrate the much wider and deeper results of consumer theory based on utility maximization.

Ray Barrell
University of Southampton

References
Edgeworth, F. Y. (1881), *Mathematical Psychics*, London.
Hicks, J. R. (1937), *Value and Capital*, Oxford.

Industrial and Organizational Psychology

Industrial and organizational psychology (IO) is the application of psychological principles to commerce and industry. It is defined in terms of where and how it is practised rather than according to distinct principles or propositions. There are three clear areas within IO psychology: (1) personnel psychology, (2) industrial/social or industrial clinical psychology, and (3) human factors or engineering psychology.

(1) Personnel Psychology

Every organization has to make decisions about personnel selection, training, promotion, job transfer, lay-off, termination, compensation, and so on. In each case, the characteristics of both workers and jobs must be assessed. In job selection, for example, the personnel psychologist must be able to determine what are the demands of the job in question and which human abilities are required to meet these demands, and then find the most suitable candidate. Similarly, training (or retraining) requires knowledge of the job demands and the current skills levels of an employee. The personnel psychologist's task is to minimize the discrepancy between demands and skills levels. Other decisions, such as promotion or changes in amount of compensation, represent the same basic challenge for the personnel psychologist: to match the environmental characteristics with the individual's.

The personnel psychologist uses various tools, the two most common being job analysis and psychological aptitude testing. Job analysis helps to determine the most important and/or frequently occurring tasks in a particular job. It may involve surveys, observations, interviews, or combinations of these techniques, and data from current incumbents and supervisors are an important source of information. Psychological aptitude testing tries to identify the capacities amd limitations of the candidates in meeting the demands of the job in question. In the past, popular methods were short tests of intellectual ability, particularly verbal and arithmetic skills. Two of the most popular tests of this kind are the Wonderlic Personnel Test and the Otis Intelligence Test. More prominent in recent years are the special ability tests, such as the Bennett Mechanical Aptitude Tests, and Multi-ability test batteries, such as the Differential Aptitude Test Battery and the

Flanagan Aptitude Classification Tests. Psychological testing implies a standardized sample of behaviour. The sample may be gathered by means of a standardized paper-and-pencil test with specific questions and limited alternative answers. Alternatively the sample might include broad questions and open-ended answers, with structure imposed by the respondent rather than by the test or test administrator. The sample could also include motor performance, interview behaviour, and even physiological measures, for example, colour vision tests of vulnerability to stress factors in the work environment.

(2) Industrial/Social or Industrial/Clinical Psychology
This area of IO concerns the reciprocal adjustment between the person and the environment, the emotional capacities of the individual and the environmental climate being the key factors under investigation. The individual worker is assessed on the following criteria: adjustment, motivation, satisfaction, level of performance, tendency to remain within the organization and absenteeism rates. The organizational characteristics which are looked at include, for example, efforts to facilitate a positive emotional climate, reward systems used, leadership styles, and the actual structure and operation of the organization. Most adjustment strategies involve real or imagined others – this is the province of industrial social psychology. The industrial/clinical aspect considers the employee's psychological well-being, and the fact that poor adjustment often creates stress and occasionally transient abnormal behaviour.

(3) Human Factors or Human Engineering Psychology
This area makes assumptions which are just the opposite to those of the personnel psychologist. The problem is still the same: accomplishing a match between the individual and the job. But the human factors psychologist assumes that the person is constant and the job is variable. He must arrange or design the environment in such a way that it is more compatible with the capacities and limitations of human operators. In order to effect a better match, the job must be changed, which usually involves modifications in operations or equipment according to the capacities of the operators. These capacities could be sensory (for example, visual acuity), or cognitive (for example, information processing time). The information input and output system is emphasized: display devices (digital read-out devices, gauges or dials, and so on) and control devices (such as knobs, levers, and switches) are examined and modified if found to have a negative effect on performance. The three areas of IO are seldom, if ever, independent of one another. They are all components of an interrelated system. Selection strategies will define the capacities and shortcomings of the operators. This will yield a range for

equipment design and modification. Similarly available equipment will determine desirable capacities and characteristics of applicants. Finally, the interaction of worker characteristics, equipment and task design, and administrative practices will influence adjustment.

Frank J. Landy
Pennsylvania State University

Further Reading
Dunnette, M. D. (1976), *The Handbook of Industrial and Organizational Psychology*, New York.
Landy, F. J. (1985), *The Psychology of Work Behavior*, 3rd edn, Homewood, Ill.
See also: *aptitude tests; ergonomics; occupational psychology.*

Industrial Democracy

Industrial democracy may be best understood as a generic term for the exercise of power by workers or their representatives over decisions within their places of employment, coupled with a modification in the locus and distribution of authority within the workplace. The principal debates concern the precise characteristics of participatory organizations, the theories of the genesis of this movement and the conditions which ensure effective outcomes within the enterprise. In recent years, industrial democracy has interested politicians and scholars and has become the mainstay of several legislative programmes for the reform of industrial relations.

Classifactory schemes take several forms: some use geographical location, others initiating agents (Poole, 1978), or underlying ideologies, or internal structure properties. The main types are: *workers' self-management* (this involves substantial workers' participation in the main decision-making bodies together with either workers' ownership or the rights to use the assets of the enterprise); *participation of workers' representatives in management organs* (for example, codetermination or worker-director schemes); *trade union action* (including *disjunctive* types based on conceptions of conflicting interests and *integrative* or harmonious practices); and *shop floor experiments* (such as job enrichment and quality of working life programmes).

The advocates of the so-called 'evolutionary' and 'cyclical' approaches are theoretically at odds. The 'evolutionary school' argues that structural movements in modern societies (especially advances in technology and the growth of complex and interdependent roles in modern industry), changes in values (including the increasing concern for social justice) and a redistribution of power in favour of working people and their associations have led to durable institutional procedures for industrial democracy. Further evidence in support of this view is the considerable interest shown by developing countries in schemes of this type.

But 'cyclical' theorists observe that waves of institutional advance have been followed by periods of decline or decay and even of the abandonment of previously well-established participatory forms. Latterly, comparative approaches which focus on international similarities and differences of type have tried to transcend these divisions.

Views about actual outcomes also diverge, but existing research suggests that a relatively democratic enterprise possesses an elaborate and integrated system of formal representation covering a number of levels (such as board room and shop floor). It has carefully drawn-up rules for participation that prescribe employees' involvement in decision making over a wide range of issues, and that grant representatives strong powers. It applies a democratic style of leadership and has a high level of unionization, and also recruits young and female supervisors. Moreover, while opportunities for individual involvement are superior in fairly small businesses, a relatively more egalitarian distribution of power is normally found in large organizations. And finally, a democratic leadership style would appear to be closely correlated with positive attitudes towards work and feelings of involvement in the job on the part of the labour force, regardless of country.

Michael Poole
University of Wales Institute of Science
and Technology, Cardiff

Reference
Poole, M. (1978), *Workers' Participation in Industry*,
London.
See also: *labour relations*.

Industrialization and Deindustrialization

The term industrialization is meant to denote a phase in economic development in which capital and labour resources shift both relatively and absolutely from agricultural activities into industry, especially manufacturing. The rise in the factory system, increasing urbanization, and movement from rural areas partly describe the nature of the process. Agricultural employment undergoes an absolute decline as the rapid growth of productivity, coupled with the relatively slow growth in demand for agricultural output, generate 'surplus labour' in the agricultural sector. The expanding industrial sector, in turn, pulls in the surplus agricultural employment as the output of industry takes on increasing importance. W. Arthur Lewis (1954) was one of the first economists to conceptualize the process of growth and development as the rise of industry made possible by an abundance of cheap labour in agriculture prepared to move to industry when jobs opportunities became available.

Industrialization was a noticeable feature of many economies as early as the second half of the nineteenth century and became a post-Second World War feature of almost all the mature capitalist economies until the late 1960s. Employment in industry and manufacturing in these countries rose both as a share of total employment and absolutely. By the early 1970s, industrial manufacturing employment as a share of total employment began to fall almost everywhere, and in some mature capitalist economies there was a decline in levels of employment. In terms of employment patterns, it can be said that a process of 'deindustrialization' had set in in capitalist (and many communist) countries, even before the period of stagnation and recession of the 1970s and 1980s.

Accompanying these movements in industrial employment has been the rise, both absolutely and relatively, of employment in the service sector. Here the pattern has been universally consistent and pronounced. Relative and absolute employment in the service sector has risen steadily over a period when industrial employment first rose and then fell.

A clue to understanding these employment patterns is found in the relative growths of sectoral outputs and productivities during the growth process. Contrary to the predictions of many, the distribution of final output between goods and services has not shifted appreciably towards services. Nor has the distribution of consumer expenditures shifted noticeably towards the consumption of services. The rates of growth of demand and output for all final goods has been only slightly less than that for final services, and consumer expenditures on goods has grown with expenditures on consumer services. The shifting distribution of employment away from industry towards the service sector can be attributed to lower rates of growth of productivity in the service sector than in the goods-producing industrial sector.

Thus, the process of economic growth in mature capitalist economies can be characterized as one of deruralification and industrialization followed by deindustrialization. Both the shift of labour resources out of agriculture and that eventually out of industry have been caused by very similar underlying forces. Rates of growth of demand for what labour produced in each sector, relative to the rates of growth of productivity, reduced labour requirements, first in agriculture and then in industry.

Much discussion in economics surrounds the question of whether deindustrialization should be a cause of concern. Often those concerned cite the slow rate of growth of labour productivity in the service sector, arguing that as a larger share of the labour force takes employment in this sector, the overall rate of growth of productivity must slow down.

A more serious concern has been voiced by those who distinguish between a slowing down in the rate of employment of labour in industry because of an acceleration in productivity growth, and a similar retardation due to a slowing down in the rate of growth of demand for industrial output. This distinction is considered important by economists who focus on a possible balance of payments constraint that acts to prevent full employment.

Thus, the lower the rate of unemployment in an economy, the higher will be the demand for imports from abroad. If the rate of growth of exports of this economy is less than the growth of imports at full employment, measures must be taken to reduce import demand. The most effective response is to create unemployment through restrictive demand policies.

If the slow rate of growth of employment in industry is due to an abnormally low growth of demand for industrial output, this will likely be due in part to a slow growth in demand for the country's exports of industrial goods. A payments constraint is likely to be in effect in this case, and high unemployment is the result. In contrast, if productivity growth is abnormally high, contributing to a slow growth in employment, then the growth of demand of industrial output both in the home market and abroad may, and indeed is likely to be, high, allowing the economy to pursue full employment goals. Deindustrialization need not be a cause for concern in this case, as full employment can be maintained at the same time as labour is released from industry for employment in the service sector.

Since the early 1970s deindustrialization has speeded up as a result of world-wide stagnation. This has to a large extent been due to the slowing down in the growth of world trade ultimately caused by the restrictive demand policies pursued almost everywhere. Obviously this source of deindustrialization is also a cause for concern as it too is accompanied by the existence of widespread unemployment. Slowing down world-wide deindustrialization is dependent upon ending the current world-wide recession and reducing unemployment in all sectors.

John Cornwall
Dalhousie University

Reference
Lewis, W. A. (1954), 'Economic development with unlimited supplies of labour', *The Manchester School*.

Further Reading
Blackaby, F. (ed.) (1979), *Deindustrialization*, London.
See also: *economic growth*.

Industry, Sociology of

There is no agreed definition of the focus and scope of the sociology of industry. In a review of university teaching of the subject, Smith (1961) reported definitions which ranged from the possibly rather narrow ('the study of the social system of the factory, and of the influences external to the factory which affect that system') to the potentially almost unlimited ('the study of social relations as they influence and are influenced by economic activity'). Typically, however, the sociology of industry has been concerned with the social structure of work organizations, with the roles and social relations within such milieux, and with the ways in which these roles and relations influence and are influenced by 'external' factors. Such concerns have often properly been seen as necessitating consideration of the distinctive characteristics of industrial society and 'industrialism' more generally, so that the boundaries of the subject must inevitably be drawn very broadly (see Burns, 1968).

The interests of the founding fathers of sociology were clearly in these more general issues: the forms and functions of the division of labour, the nature and experience of industrial work, the characteristics of large-scale bureaucratic organizations, and the changing nature of society under continuing industrialization. Indeed the sociology of industry as a distinctive and more specialized field of study only emerged during the 1920s and 1930s, and its development has been largely a feature of the last forty years.

There were two crucially important contributions to the early development of industrial sociology: (1) The Hawthorne Experiments, a programme of research at the Chicago plant of the Western Electric Company between 1927 and 1932, highlighted the importance of so-called 'informal' social relations at work for understanding workers' attitudes and behaviour, and showed the inadequacy of individualistic explanations which emphasized economic incentives or physical conditions of work as simple causative factors. (2) Elton Mayo (1949) popularized these findings and drew conclusions from them about the need for better human relations in industry. His writings were very influential and provided the stimulus for much subsequent research, especially concerning the effects on work-place satisfaction and behaviour of leadership styles, participation, incentives and social relations in small work groups. This 'human relations' tradition in industrial sociology has been extensively criticized for the tendency to define problems in managerial terms, the inadequate conception of conflict as pathological rather than inherent and structural, and the failure in many cases to pursue analysis beyond the confines of the work-place to the wider society. Nevertheless its historical importance in initially identifying problems and demarcating an area of study is very clear.

In the period immediately after the Second World War, the theoretical basis for the sociology of industry broadened and drew particularly on the perspectives of structural-functionalism and the insights of Max

Weber on bureaucracy. Among a number of impressive studies influenced by these approaches was the work of Gouldner (1955 a and b) who explored the intended and unintended functions, or consequences, of bureaucratic rules in a small gypsum plant and used this analysis to provide the basis for an explanation of management-worker conflict which eventually resulted in a 'wild-cat' strike. Many of the same theoretical assumptions guided the work of researchers in Britain, France and the US who subsequently explored the ways in which an industrial organization's technology (that is both machines and equipment and the knowledge and ideas which make possible and guide their use) structures both the organization generally (Woodward in Burns, 1968) and the particular roles and patterns of social relations within it, leading to differing typical experiences of and attitudes towards work (Blauner, 1964).

Whereas the perspective of functionalist sociology had led to the conceptualization of industrial organizations as 'social systems', the emphasis on the importance of technology contributed to the development of the notion of the organization as an 'open socio-technical system', seen as having interdependent social, technological, economic and psychological dimensions. The specific features of any such system were a more or less satisfactory compromise between the demands and limitations deriving from all these different dimensions. Related developments in the study of industrial organizations have placed less emphasis on technology but have elaborated other aspects of what has come to be known as 'contingency theory'. The characteristics of organizational structure and process, if the organization is to survive and be successful, are seen as determined, or at least constrained, by the need to meet the exigencies of its environment (such as the product market, rates of technical or market change, or government legislation). Though large-scale comparative studies of organization have demonstrated that variations between organizations can be related to such environmental factors, a crucial question remains: how far do those in power within organizations, the 'dominant coalition', have possibilities of 'strategic choice' as to organizational size, structure and technology, and indeed as to the environment within which to operate?

This issue in the study of industrial organizations is an example of the more general debate in sociology regarding the role of human agency, the weight to be given to 'action' as against 'structure' in social analysis. The same theoretical issues were also reflected in debates concerning the explanation of industrial attitudes and behaviour. In a very influential study, Goldthorpe and his colleagues (1968) criticized both the 'human relations' and what they called the 'technological implications' approaches to such questions. Both these approaches assumed that industrial workers had stable patterns of needs; the 'human relations'

tradition emphasized that such needs could, and should, be met by appropriate social organization of work, whilst the 'technology' tradition argued that the production system could greatly limit what forms of work organization and patterns of social relations were possible in given situations. In contrast, the 'action approach' advocated by Goldthorpe and his colleagues emphasized the importance of 'the definition of the situation' of those involved. Wants and expectations regarding work were to be seen as culturally determined variables, not psychological constants; and workers' attitudes and behaviour could only be understood in the light of these varying 'orientations to work'. In the case of the groups of 'affluent' workers studied by these investigators, orientations to work were seen as varying independently of the work situation so that analysis necessarily extended beyond the enterprise to take account of the workers' family, community and class situations. Systems of production, such as the assembly line, which other investigators had described as inevitably 'alienating', were willingly tolerated by these affluent workers because they provided the relatively high pay which was their predominant expectation from work.

Though it has generally been accepted that 'orientations to work' must be taken into account, subsequent research has shown that their significance in any explanation of work-place attitudes and behaviour is far less clearcut than was initially suggested. This is also true of explanations of behaviour in the labour market. In contrast to the suggestions made concerning the affluent workers, Blackburn and Mann (1979) have shown that only very rarely do manual workers have both strong simple orientations to work, and adequate knowledge of and opportunities for choice in the labour market which enable them to select jobs which match their expectations. In so far as labour markets are segmented, for example into primary and secondary sectors, and include many job opportunities only available to those already employed in the organization (internal labour markets), the possibilities of choice, guided by 'orientations to work', are correspondingly restricted.

A continuing ground for criticism of much work in industrial sociology conducted within a 'systems' framework is that it is unable to account satisfactorily for conflict. The 'action approach' advocated by Goldthorpe and his colleagues had the merit of conceiving of conflict as a normal rather than a pathological feature of industrial situations, such as management-worker relations, if the actors concerned had differing and conflicting expectations of that situation and of one another. Many sociologists, however, perhaps especially in Europe, wished to go further to assert that conflicting interests were inherent in the social relations of employment in industry: conflicting interests over the relative shares of the earned income of the enterprise which formed wages or profits (Baldamus, 1961) and/or over the exercise of authority to control the activities of subordinates in the interests of owners and managers. Such assumptions are certainly a more satisfactory starting point for the explanation and understanding of many of the issues of importance in the sociology of industry: the growth and activities of trade unions as organizations to represent employees' interests; the emergence and development of arrangements for collective bargaining between management and unions, and for conciliation and arbitration, so that industrial conflict becomes institutionalized; shop-floor struggles over the 'effort bargain', and over differentials for skill and/or responsibility – the 'fair' relationship between pay and work; and the role and activities in these conflicts of shop stewards, shop-floor trade union representatives (Beynon, 1973). Of course, such a starting point for analysis means that although manifestations of conflict, such as strikes, can be explained more easily, other phenomena become problematic: the very uneven spread of trade-union membership and in particular the reluctance of many white-collar workers to join unions or take collective action; the development of conflicts between union leaders and their members, which raise the question of whether and under what circumstances trade unions can be really 'democratic' organizations; and the more or less deep-rooted 'industrial peace' which characterizes most industrial enterprises most of the time. Among the questions raised by these issues are how to account for the absence of an awareness of conflicting interests and of class consciousness; whether divisions within the labour force prevent the effective representation of workers' interests; and what role the ideas (ideology) of those in power may have in maintaining stability in situations of potential conflict (Nichols and Benyon in Nichols, 1980).

These issues have of course been a major preoccupation of writers in the Marxist tradition, though attempts to resolve them have not been regarded as altogether satisfactory. Within the sociology of industry the more distinctive recent contribution of this tradition has been its emphasis on the 'capitalist labour process' as the central point of reference (Nichols, 1980). The labour process refers to the application of 'labour power' to materials and equipment to produce new value in the form of commodities. Within a capitalist economy, it is argued, workers do not receive the full value of their labour and the 'surplus value' is appropriated by their employers, though this is concealed by the payment of wages which appear to represent a 'fair day's pay for a fair day's work'. Capitalist employers are forced by the competitive system of which they are a part constantly to try to increase levels of surplus value. Thus attention is focused on the ways in which this is done in different societies and at different times, and on the ways in which workers

resist such exploitation. In addition, attention is directed to previously generally neglected topics such as the creation of the labour force (including the use of migrant labour), means of intensifying work such as shift-work, and the possible consequences of this intensification such as industrial accidents (Nichols, 1980).

In a major and extremely influential contribution to such debates, Braverman (1974), for example, argued that within the capitalist mode of production there was a continuing process of fragmentation and 'deskilling' of work by employers in order both to cheapen the cost of labour power and to give the employer greater control over the labour process. His argument concerning this degradation of work has not gone unchallenged and has had the valuable result of stimulating historical investigations of the ways in which the organization of work has developed and changed. In contrast to Braverman's initial formulation, much of this research has shown that the form of the labour process must be seen as the result of struggles between capital and labour in which workers' resistance, for example to work simplification or reorganization, can materially affect the outcome. An approach to the sociology of industry which concentrates on analysis of the labour process also raises the question of whether the same analytical framework can be used to investigate social relations in public-sector employment or where the means of production are state-owned and controlled. The account by Haraszti (in Nichols, 1980) of work in a Hungarian factory, for example, reflects many similarities with the capitalist West.

Finally, any approach, Marxist or not, which treats conflict as inherent in the social relations of employers and employees in conventional enterprises must regard attempts to transform that relationship through workers' ownership or workers' control as of particular theoretical interest and significance. The evidence about such 'experiments' is as yet far from conclusive. In so far as they are viable, however, such 'democratic' enterprises provide both a valuable comparative point of reference for a critique of existing forms of work organization, and an indication of alternatives which could materially increase men's range of choice in organizing the world of work.

Richard K. Brown
University of Durham

References
Baldamus, W. (1961), *Efficiency and Effort*, London.
Beynon, H. (1973), *Working for Ford*, Harmondsworth.
Blackburn, R. M. and Mann, M. (1979), *The Working Class in the Labour Market*, London.
Blauner, R. (1964), *Alienation and Freedom*, Chicago.
Braverman, H. (1974), *Labor and Monopoly Capital*, New York.

Burns, T. (ed.) (1968), *Industrial Man*, Harmondsworth.

Goldthorpe, J. H., Lockwood, D., Bechhofer, F. and Platt, J. (1968), *The Affluent Worker: Industrial Attitudes and Behaviour*, Cambridge.

Gouldner, A. W. (1955a), *Patterns of Industrial Bureaucracy*, London.

Gouldner, A. W. (1955b), *Wildcat Strikes*, London.

Mayo, E. (1949), *The Social Problems of an Industrial Civilization*, London.

Nichols, T. (ed.) (1980), *Capital and Labour*, Glasgow.

Smith, J. H. (1961), *The University Teaching of the Social Sciences: Industrial Sociology*, Paris.

Further Reading

Berg, I. (1979), *Industrial Sociology*, Englewood Cliffs, N.J.

Hill, S. (1981), *Competition and Control at Work*, London.

Hyman, R. (1977), *Strikes*, Glasgow.

Rose, M. (1975), *Industrial Behaviour: Theoretical Development since Taylor*, London.

Salaman, G. (1979), *Work Organisations: Resistance and Control*, London.

See also: *industrial and organizational psychology; labour relations; organizations.*

Infancy and Infant Development

Infancy is variously defined from time to time and in different cultures, although technically it is the period from birth to the onset of walking or, put more poetically, the time of life prior to the emergence of independent behaviour. In humans, the onset of walking without support and the beginning of definable 'speech' appear almost simultaneously. Among the significant issues surrounding the nature of development from infancy onward have been: (1) The question of the relative influence of organic or biogenic factors, on the one hand, and environmental, psychogenic, or learned factors, on the other. (2) The role of early experience in the determination or control of later behaviour and development, a concern which includes questions about the durability of early influences, the reversibility of effects of infantile trauma, and the effects of educational interventions on the behavioural maturation of the young. (3) The ever-present reality of individual differences in psychological characteristics paralleling those like height, eye-colour, and hair texture in the biological realm. (4) The mechanisms and processes by which behaviour change and emotional development occur in the early months of life.

(1) This issue is sometimes known as the nature-nurture controversy. Many studies have sought to establish how much of our life destinies and our characteristics (like intelligence level) can be accounted for by genetic factors, and how much by environment. Both domains of influence are relevant and, in fact, affect one another. The assumption of a dichotomy, therefore, is misguided and, as Anastasi (1958) has suggested, developmentalists should be studying how genetics and the environment work their wonders instead of trying to assign numerical weights to represent the relative importance of congenital and experiential determinants.

(2) The role of early experience in the determination of later behaviour and development goes directly to the problem of the plasticity of the young. The assumption that there is a primacy effect of early experience – which is significantly more enduring and influential than the effects of the same experience later in life – has a long tradition and has strong supporters among both psychodynamic and behaviouristic theorists and researchers. The early-experience proposition derives some of its strength from neurobiological data, and from studies of lasting influences of severe deprivational conditions (nutritional and experiential). Both the psychodynamic and the behavioural views allow, of course, for later alteration of patterns of behaviour acquired early; their derivative therapeutic intervention procedures require the further assumption that behaviour patterns acquired even under traumatic conditions must be alterable.

(3) The last concern, that of human individual differences in behaviour and development as in more strictly biological characteristics, has occupied much of the research time of developmental psychologists. The study of mental age in relation to chronological age, or the documentation of behaviour change as a function of age, has yielded the developmental quotient, similar to the IQ (a ratio of mental age and chronological age) by providing standards of capabilities at successive ages, including assessments of variability. Such norms have enabled refinements in the classification of infants with developmental aberrations or disabilities. An unfortunate consequence of the construction of behaviour norms from the examination of large numbers of infants, however, was the unwarranted tendency to assume that a developmental quotient was descriptive of an organic verity and, hence, a stable attribute of the infant. A decided constitutional bias inhered in labelling of an infant as developmentally delayed or behaviourally precocious.

(4) The last issue has occupied theorists the most, from Freud to Piaget to Erikson to Lewin to all others who would understand early development as gradual accommodation or adaptation of behavioural functioning, resulting from both biological and experiential inputs. This latter group includes, of course, those committed to an understanding of child behaviour in terms of learning theory principles and known processes by which new behaviours are acquired through social controls and incentives.

Often seemingly at odds but none the less fuelling one another's empirical defences, the developmentalists concentrating on learning processes include those whose orientation stems from Pavlov, and flows through Thorndike to John B. Watson. The group includes Hull, Spence, Spiker, Skinner, and Bijou, and insists upon the importance of learning processes, as in classical conditioning and operant learning, and the importance of reward events in the production of behaviour change and, thus, memory processes. An often unstated but ever-present presumption is that the promotion of pleasure and the thwarting of annoyance are critical incentives for the occurrence of psychological development.

Those who favour cognitive interpretations of development in the first year of life (emphasizing reorganizations of informational inputs as the hallmark of development) rely heavily, like the learning theorists, on explanations of behaviour change in terms of gradually accruing complexities of function. The capacity for object permanence, for example, is a talent of humans not present at birth but usually seen by eight months. It involves the manifest refusal to believe that something is 'gone' when it has disappeared. Appreciation of object permanence, an obvious prerequisite for attachment by infants to those who nurture them, requires the ability to perceive multiple continuous events, retain memory of the succession of at least some of these events, and express surprise when the prediction of subsequent events from the continuity of earlier events has been violated. It is not clear in such instances how this series of capacities unfolds, although it is plain that the process is both developmental and gradual, and that the eventual talent is dependent upon the earlier acquisition of subroutines. Observers of infants who are in the process of acquiring, or are first manifesting, object permanence behaviour are aware that positive affective expression almost invariably accompanies the infant's appreciation that the object has reappeared or been rediscovered. Little is known, however, of the psychobiological mechanisms inherent in the curiosity behaviour or hypothesis-formation underlying the search, or about the reward mechanisms inherent in the infant's ultimate satisfaction with the search and confirmation of the hypothesis. A fair appraisal of our present level of sophistication must acknowledge enormous gaps in our understanding of even such relatively simple mechanisms of behaviour change with increasing age in young children. Infant development specialists are far more expert in describing infantile behaviour and in noting correlated changes in behaviour with age than in explaining those behaviour changes.

All of the foregoing comments lead to an appreciation of infant behaviour in terms of principles espoused by Harriet L. Rheingold (1963): the infant is an active organism responsive to environmental stimu-lation, and is thus capable of learning. Moreover, infants are shaped by their environments, but they also control their shapers. This reciprocity between the developing child and the childrearing milieu has been cited by Sameroff and Chandler (1975) as requiring a 'transactional' model for an understanding, which, on the one hand, honours the complex interplay of constitutional and environmental factors, and on the other hand, acknowledges the *cumulative nature* of human experience and its lasting effects.

At birth the normal human infant is able to hear, see, smell, taste, and feel touch. Much of the baby's behaviour can be characterized in terms of approach and avoidance tendencies. The baby turns towards and prepares itself to receive substances, objects, and events that are pleasing, as in feeding, and avoids stimulation that is clearly unpleasant. Even the newborn child is capable of behavioural self-regulation, as is evident when something sweet is placed in its mouth. The same baby will resist 'smothering' with head shakes and hand swipes when, as often inadvertently happens, the head falls into a position, even at the breast, that causes or threatens blockage of the respiratory passages. Infants also manifest conflict behaviour, as when both approach and avoidance behaviours are simultaneously elicited. All of these rudimentary psychobiological processes, initially gifts of the species, are shaped by subsequent environmental events to dispose the child towards increasingly complex, 'socialized' behaviour.

Human infants double in weight in the first three months of life and triple in the first year. Behavioural gains during these periods are equally astonishing. Over this time, the infant undergoes numerous transitions, not the least important of which involves development from a largely subcortical status to a system of behavioural and social interaction requiring extensive cortical mediation, autonomic nervous system organization, and memory based upon learning. The very rapid growth of myelin tissue in the first year of life, along with the proliferating maturation of dendrites characteristic of this neuronal super-growth period, are doubtlessly responsible in part for the infant becoming capable so quickly of taking in such vast amounts of information, selecting salient stimulation, acquiring simple associations between events, and performing psychomotor acts necessary to enhance further development.

Lewis P. Lipsitt
Brown University

References

Anastasi, A. (1958), 'Heredity, environment, and the question "How"', *Psychological Review*, 65.
Rheingold, H. L. (1963), *Maternal Behavior in Mammals*, New York.

Sameroff, A. J. and Chandler, M. J. (1975), 'Reproductive risk and the continuum of caretaking casualty', in F. D. Horowitz (ed.), *Review of Child Development Research*, Vol. 4, Chicago.

Further Reading

Bower, T. G. R. (1982), *Development in Infancy*, 2nd edn, San Francisco.

Bowlby, J. (1969), *Attachment and Loss* (vol. I), New York.

Field, T. M., Huston, A., Quay, H. C., Troll, L. and Finley, G. E. (eds) (1982), *Review of Human Development*, New York.

Garmezy, N. and Rutter, M. (eds) (1983), *Stress, Coping, and Development in Children*, New York.

Kagan, J., Kearsley, R. B. and Zelazo, P. R. (1978), *Infancy: Its Place in Human Development*, Cambridge, Mass.

Lipsitt, L. P. and Reese, H. W. (1979), *Child Development*, Glenview, Ill.

Stratton, P. (ed.) (1982), *Psychobiology of the Human Newborn*, Chichester.

See also: *attachment; Bowlby; conditioning; intelligence.*

Inflation and Deflation

Inflation is generally taken to be the rise of all or most prices, or, put the other way round, the fall of the general purchasing power of the monetary unit. For almost fifty years inflation had been continuous in the United Kingdom, and nearly continuous in the United States, consumers' prices having, in that time, risen more than twentyfold in the former country and more than eightfold in the latter. Only the official prices in some of the centrally planned economies have escaped the worldwide trend.

The corresponding sense of deflation – the general fall of prices – is less familiar because it has not been experienced for some time, though deflation prevailed in most countries from the early 1920s to the mid-1930s, and in many for long periods in both the earlier and the later nineteenth century. At present, deflation is perhaps more often used to refer to a fall in total money income or in the total stock of money, or, more loosely, to falls in their rate of growth. Inflation is sometimes used in corresponding, looser, senses.

The idea that the value, or purchasing power, of money depends simply on the amount of it in relation to the amount of goods goes back in a fairly clear form at least to the mid-eighteenth century. So long as money consisted wholly, or mainly, of gold and/or silver coins, the application of this doctrine was easy. A reasonably convincing account of the main changes in price-trend even in the nineteenth century can be given in terms of the gold discoveries of the mid-century and those (together with the ore-processing innovations) of its last decade, set against the

continuous rise of physical output of goods. From early on, however, paper claims on trusted debtors began to constitute further means of payment, and such claims, in the form of liabilities of banks and quasi-banking institutions, have now replaced 'commodity money' (coined gold or silver, circulating at virtually its bullion value) almost completely. This makes the definition of money harder – inevitably somewhat arbitrary. Moreover, the supply of 'money', though subject also to other influences, has always been to a considerable extent responsive to the demand for it, so that it cannot be taken as independently given.

The simplest kind of modern inflationary process is that where a government, perhaps for war purposes, needs to acquire an increased flow of goods and services, and pays at least partly for it with newly printed money (in practice, borrowed from the banking system). If the economy was fully employed to start with, and if we exclude the possibility of the need being met by imports, the effect is to raise prices in proportion to the increase in total (government and non-government) expenditure. Since the money spent by the government goes into private hands, private expenditure rises, and the government can get an increased share of the national real output only by printing money faster and faster to keep ahead in the race. In the absence of complications from price rigidities and taxation, an indefinite, exponential inflation is generated. In practice, such complications exist and slow the process down; governments often try to increase price-rigidity by price control, which has usually to be supplemented by rationing. Inflation can, however, become completely explosive in the extreme cases of 'hyperinflation', like that in Germany in 1923, and the even bigger one in Hungary in 1946, when prices eventually doubled (or more) each day. These hyperinflations were assisted by special circumstances; their very speed made revenue collection ineffective, so that nearly all government expenditure had to be financed by new money, expectations of their continuation made for very rapid adjustment of wages and salaries to the rate of inflation, and the disruption of the economy (by a general strike in one case, foreign occupation in the other) reduced the real flow of goods for which the government and other spenders were competing. True hyperinflation has occurred only where something like this last condition has been present.

More usually, inflation has to be considered in the light of the fact that prices are formed in different ways. The prices of many raw materials and foodstuffs, in the world market, are flexible and strongly and quickly influenced by supply and demand conditions. The great upward surge of these prices in 1972–4 was induced partly by the boom in industrial production and demand (which, however, was no greater in relation to trend than the one of four or five years earlier), partly by particular conditions affecting mainly cereals – the breakdown a few years earlier of the World Wheat Agreement, the widespread running down of stocks thereafter, and the failure of the harvest in the USSR. Petroleum, the price of which quadrupled, is a special case; its price is 'administered' rather than formed in the market, but the administration of it had passed from the international oil companies to the Organization of Petroleum Exporting Countries (OPEC). In addition, the outlook both for future discoveries of oil and for alternative sources of energy (on which a rational pricing of oil largely depends) had worsened. The immediate occasion for the biggest oil price increase, of course, was the Arab-Israeli war of 1973. (Events in Iran caused another increase in 1979.)

In contrast, the prices of manufactures, though also largely administered rather than determined on 'auction' principles in free markets, seem to be governed fairly closely by costs of production, which depend on wages, raw material and fuel costs, and labour productivity.

The determination of wages is more complex. They are hardly anywhere formed on the 'market-clearing' principle that unemployed workers will underbid current rates until they get jobs; labour solidarity and the need for a minimum of security and trust in the relations of employers with existing employees are too great for that. In fact, collective bargaining determines most wages in some countries (three-quarters of them in the UK), and even where the proportion is lower, as in the US, the main collective agreements exercise widespread influence as 'price-leaders'. The result is that wage claims – and settlements – show considerable sensivity to rises in the cost of living, but that they also show a tendency to creep upward in response to the natural ambitions of trade unionists and their leaders, and sometimes as a result of jockeying for relative position between different trades.

The most noteworthy attempt to generalize about wage-inflation was that of A. W. Phillips (1958), who derived empirically, from British data, a negative relation between the level of unemployment and the rate of wage increases, which was for a time thought by some to be practically usable evidence of a possible policy 'trade-off'. Unfortunately, within ten years of its formulation current data began to show that the 'Phillips Curve' in the UK (and also in the US, though the same is not true, for instance, of Germany) was shifting rapidly upwards – the unemployment rate needed to keep wage-inflation down to a given level was rising. At the same time, Milton Friedman (1968) argued that such a relation was inherently implausible; experience of wage-inflation would lead people to expect more of the same, and so raise bids and settlements. The curve would become vertical, only one rate of unemployment (the 'natural' rate) being consistent with a rate of wage-

inflation that was not either accelerating upwards or accelerating downwards. Examination of evidence from a number of countries suggests that the extent to which experience leads to expectations which have this effect varies greatly, and the time taken to convince people that inflation will continue, rather than subside, is also variable, but has often been a matter of years or even decades rather than months. Attempts to explain the formation of wages econometrically have been only partially successful.

From early in the post-war years, various governmental attempts were made to curb the tendency towards inflationary wage increases in conditions of low unemployment. Exhortation, informal agreements with trade unions or employers' organizations, legislative limits, temporary wage freezes, conferences in which potential negotiators were confronted with the average increases the economy was estimated to be able to bear without inflation, have all been tried somewhere, singly or in combination, sometimes in succession, in the United States and the countries of Western Europe. The results have been mixed. The more drastic policies have sometimes been successful, but only temporarily, and there has been some rebound afterwards. Nevertheless, some countries, notably Austria and Germany, have achieved relatively high degrees of wage-restraint and low average levels of inflation over a long period with the help of their institutional arrangements. Japan has also been successful (with one or two lapses), largely because in the large firms, guarantees of employment reconcile employees to arrangements which make their earnings sensitive to conditions in the product markets.

It is important to distinguish between inflation which arises from demand for a country's final output ('demand-pull') and that which comes, immediately at least, from rises in its import prices or in its labour costs of production ('cost push'). The former tends to increase output, the latter to depress it.

It is natural to ask how 'cost-push' can raise prices in a country without a concomitant rise in the supply of money; indeed, some writers do not recognize cost-push as a useful concept in explaining inflation, and the monetarist school, associated with Milton Friedman (but with many and various subdivisions) holds, generally, that the price level varies with the supply of money, and could be controlled, without detriment to the level of real output and employment, by increasing the money supply uniformly in line with the estimated physical capacity of the economy.

The relevant facts are complex. Controlling the supply of money is not easy; money is created by commercial bank lending, which will normally respond in some degree to demand, and central banks cannot fail to act as lenders of last resort to the commercial banks without risking collapse of the monetary system. The need for increased money payments, whether created by a rise in import prices or by an increase in physical output, can be and normally is met, to a substantial extent, by more rapid turnover of money (increase in the velocity of circulation) rather than by increase in the stock of money – though this a short-term accommodation, normally reversed eventually. 'Tightness' in the supply of money curtails spending plans, and normally reduces physical output and employment before (and usually more than) it reduces prices, at least in the short run of two to four years. In the longer run, tightness of money tends to induce a proliferation of 'quasi-monies', the liabilities of institutions outside the banking system as for the time being defined.

Since the mid-1970s, control of the growth of the money stock as a means of controlling inflation has been much in vogue. Experience has shown the difficulty of hitting the target rates of increase, for the reasons just stated, and has demonstrated, not for the first time, that monetary stringency, sometimes combined with parallel fiscal policies, reduces inflation only at the cost of severe unemployment and the reduction of growth in real living standards.

In contrast with the damage to output which seems to be inseparable from deflationary policies (though its severity varies greatly with the institutional arrangements in the country concerned), it is hard to demonstrate any comparable material damage from, at all events, moderate demand-pull inflation (or moderate cost-push inflation which is 'accommodated' by sufficient creation of purchasing power). It can cause arbitrary changes in income distribution, but they are not normally of a kind to depress output (rather the contrary) and they are mostly avoidable by suitable indexing arrangements. The worst aspect of any prolonged inflation is its tendency to accelerate, through the conditioning of expectations, and this is a serious problem, even though, as already noted, the extreme phenomenon of hyperinflation has occurred only where the economy has been disrupted by some external cause. Inflation is, however, unpopular even with those to whom it does no material harm; it is certainly inconvenient not to be able to rely upon the real value of the money unit, and it may create an illusion of impoverishment even when money incomes are periodically and fairly closely adjusted to it.

In the present writer's view, some, at least, of the main market economies can avoid inflation without the depressing concomitants of deflationary policies only if they are able to develop permanent incomes policies, or modify their wage- and salary-fixing institutions, so as to enjoy reasonably full employment without upward drift of labour costs such as became established in them at least by the end of the 1960s. But it must be remembered that the severest general peacetime inflation on record, that of the 1970s, was also largely propelled by supply and demand maladjustments in the world economy, plus special circumstances in the oil industry. This experience points to the need for better co-operation between the main industrial countries to stabilize the growth rate of their total activity, and for some co-ordinated forward planning of aggregate supplies of the main raw materials, fuels and foodstuffs. This would require a programme of international co-operation perhaps even more ambitious than that which, from the end of the Second World War, made possible a generation of unparalleled economic progress.

A. J. Brown
University of Leeds

References
Friedman, M. (1968), 'The role of monetary policy', *American Economic Review*, 58.
Phillips, A. W. (1958), 'The relationship between unemployment and the rate of money wage-rates in the United Kingdom, 1861–1957', *Economica*, 25.

Further Reading
Bosworth, B. P. and Lawrence, R. Z. (1982), *Commodity Prices and the New Inflation*, Washington.
Brown, A. J. (1955), *The Great Inflation 1939–51*, Oxford.
Brown, A. J. (1985), *World Inflation Since 1950*, Cambridge.
Fleming, J. S. (1976), *Inflation*, Oxford.
Organization for Economic Co-operation and Development (1977), *Towards Full Employment and Price Stability* (the 'McCracken Report'), London.
Trevithick, J. A. (1977), *Inflation: A Guide to the Crisis in Economics*, Harmondsworth.
See also: *monetarism; Phillips Curve; stagflation.*

Informal Economy

See Black Economy.

Innovation

The rather specialized meaning given to innovation in economics and other social science disciplines does not correspond precisely to the everyday use of the term. Since Schumpeter, economists generally use innovation to describe the first introduction of any new product, process or system into the economy. In Schumpeter's terminology these include *managerial* and *organizational* innovations as well as *technical* innovations, but in practice the emphasis of most innovation studies has been on technical innovations,

Schumpeter distinguished sharply between *invention* and *innovation*. Many inventions, both patented and non-patented, never reach the point of commercial application. Although Schumpeter's usage is widely accepted, an element of ambiguity remains: the expression 'innovation' is used to describe the whole process of development of an invention and launch of a new product or process (as in the 'management of innovation'); it is also used to identify the precise date of introduction of such new products and processes.

Schumpeter's taxonomy extended beyond the stage of first commercial introduction to the whole process of *diffusion* of innovations through a population of potential adopters. As with all such distinctions, the separation of the three stages (invention, innovation and diffusion) can be overemphasized. Attempts to develop and launch a new product, based on one or several inventions, may lead to still further inventions: the diffusion of any innovation generally involves further improvement, inventions and innovations. Nevertheless, the usefulness of Schumpeter's threefold classification is generally recognized and has been adopted in most social science research which attempts to understand the process of technical change.

All schools of economic theory and sociology have recognized the importance of technical and social innovation for the long-term growth and efficiency of firms and of nations, but in practice only Schumpeter and his followers have placed it at the centre of their analysis. Schumpeter insisted that technological competition through new and improved products and processes was an order of magnitude more important than 'normal' price competition between firms, which was the subject of most orthodox theory. This fundamental insight of Schumpeter's has led ultimately to a drastic revision of the traditional theory of the firm in the work of Nelson and Winter (1982).

An equally important consequence of the recognition of the central importance of innovation in the competitive process is the revision of conventional theories of international trade. Since Posner's first revisionist assault on the factor proportions theory in 1959, empirical research has increasingly confirmed the role of technology innovation in explaining the pattern of international trade. Hufbauer (1966) and Soete (1981) have demonstrated that technological gap theories of foreign trade have far greater explanatory power, both for individual product groups and generally for the greater part of OECD trade in manufactured goods.

The greatly increased emphasis on the management of innovation within firms and of innovation and technology policies at government level is another consequence of the recognition of the role of innovation in effective competition, both at firm level and at international level.

Finally neo-Schumpeterian innovation studies have sought to demonstrate a relationship between the introduction of major innovations (new technology systems) and long-term cyclical developments in the world economy.

Innovation studies remain an active and rapidly developing research area pursued by all branches of the social sciences and technologists as well as by interdisciplinary groups, such as those at MIT, Sussex, Karlsruhe, Lund and Aalborg.

C. Freeman
University of Sussex

References
Hufbauer, G. (1966), *Synthetic Materials and Theory of International Trade*, Cambridge, Mass.
Nelson, R. R. and Winter, S. (1982), *An Evolutionary Theory of Economic Change*, Cambridge, Mass.
Posner, M. (1961), 'International trade and technical change', *Oxford Economic Papers*, 13.
Soete, L. (1981), 'A general test of technological gap trade theory', *Weltwirtschaftliches Archiv*, Band 117.

Further Reading
Freeman, C. (ed.) (1982), *The Economics of Industrial Innovation*, London.
See also: *Schumpeter*.

Input-Output Analysis

An input-output table records transactions between industries, and input-output (I-O) analysis uses these data to examine the interdependence between sectors and the impact which changes in one sector have on others. This can be seen as a quantitative development of neoclassical general equilibrium analysis used by economists such as L. Walras. Its origins can be traced back to Quesnay's 'Tableau Économique' in 1758. Presently, and for almost half a century, the key figure has been Wassily Leontief who completed the first I-O table in the US in 1936 and has done much pioneering development work.

An I-O table, such as that shown in figure 1 records in its columns the purchases by each industry, A, B, and C (that is, the inputs into the production process), and in the rows the sales by each industry. Also

Payments to \ Payments by	Industry A	B	C	Final demand	Total output
Industry A		20	45	35	100
Industry B	30		30	140	200
Industry C		80		70	150
Factors of production	70	100	75		
Total input	100	200	150		

Figure 1

included are sales to final purchasers and payments for factors of production (labour and capital) thus showing the necessary integration into the rest of the national accounts.

The production of a commodity requires inputs from other industries, known as *direct inputs*, and from the I-O table a matrix of *technical coefficients* can be derived which shows direct inputs per unit of output, for example, in matrix A below .1=20/200. In turn the production of each of these commodities used as inputs requires inputs from the other industries, and this second round of production then imposes demands on other industries, and so on. All these subsequent inputs are known as *indirect inputs*. Tracing all these ramifications is a laborious process in a large I-O system, but it can be shown mathematically that the solution lies in the matrix $(I-A)^{-1}$ where I is the unit matrix and A is the matrix of direct input coefficients. Such a matrix, known as the *Leontief Inverse*, shows in its columns the total direct plus indirect inputs required per unit of output of the column industry (see figure 2). This matrix is the key to I-O analysis as it encapsulates the interdependence of industries in the economy. For instance, a demand from, say, consumers for 1000 units of A requires the production of 1077 units of A, 351 of B and 141 of C, (using col. A of matrix $(I-A)^{-1}$). The extra 77 units of A are needed by B and C to produce the inputs which A takes from them and which they take from each other.

Matrix A				Matrix $(I-A)^{-1}$		
	Ind A	Ind B	Ind C		Ind A	Ind B	Ind C
A	—	0.1	0.3	A	1.077	.257	.375
B	0.3	—	0.2	B	.351	1.171	.340
C	—	0.4	—	C	.141	.468	1.136

Figure 2

Using such a model it is possible to calculate the effect of a change in demand in an economy on the output in all industries. The analysis can be extended to cover the inputs of factors of production which are closely related to the output levels, and in this way the precise effect which a change in demand for one product has on employment in that industry and in all others can be calculated with perhaps additional information on types of skill. The I-O table can be extended to include purchases of imports, thus enabling the import requirements of any given level of demand to be calculated; of particular interest to the balance of payments is the import content of exports.

Just as the production of a commodity has ramifications back through the chain of production, so a change in the price of an input has effects forward on to many other products, both directly and indirectly. The price of any product is determined by the prices of its inputs, and these can all in turn be traced back to the 'price' of labour, capital and imports, using the formal Leontief Inverse. It is thus possible to calculate the effects on final prices of, for example, an increase in wages in one industry or of a change in import prices due perhaps to changes in the exchange rate or changes in foreign prices.

All the above aspects of input-output analysis can be combined into a planning model which will give a comprehensive and internally consistent picture of the economy 5–10 years ahead. This enables policy makers to see the implications which, say, a certain growth in the economy has for particular industries, employment, prices, the balance of payments and so on, and to locate key sectors. Most countries compile I-O tables, usually identifying fifty or more industries, although models have recently lost some of their popularity in Western Europe. They are, however, extensively used in the USSR and Eastern Europe and in developing economies. Here they are well suited to measuring the impact of marked changes in demand and supply patterns which are expected. Further refinements of I-O analysis include disaggregation by region and making a dynamic model so that investment needs are incorporated.

A. G. Armstrong
University of Bristol

Further Reading
Leontief, W. (1966), *Input-Output Economics*, New York.
United Nations (1973), *Input-Output Tables and Analysis*, *Studies in Methods*, New York.
See also: *Leontief; Walras, L.*

Instinct

In common parlance instinct has a variety of meanings. For example, it can refer to an impulse to act in some way that is purposeful yet 'without foresight of the ends and without previous education in the performance' (James, 1890); to a propensity, aptitude, or intuition with which an individual appears to be born, or a species naturally endowed; to motives, compulsions, or driving energies instigating behaviour serving some vital functions. This multiple meaning seldom causes a problem in everyday conversation. However, a tendency to assume that evidence for one of the meanings entails the others as well has been a cause of confusion in scientific contexts.

Darwin

Most scientific uses of instinct derive from Darwin, He dodged the question of definition, in view of the fact that 'several distinct mental actions are commonly embraced by the term' (Darwin, 1859). He used the word to refer to impulsions such as that which drives a bird to migrate, dispositions such as tenacity in a dog, feelings such as sympathy in a person, and in other senses. However he frequently argued as though 'instinct' stood for something that combined its several meanings into a single concept, licensing inference from one meaning to another. For example, when there was reason to think that some behaviour pattern was genetically inherited, he would assume its development to be independent of experience; and, conversely, he took opportunity for learning as a reason to doubt that he was dealing with an instinct, as though what is instinctive must be both hereditary and unlearned. But the relationship between hereditary transmission and ontogenetic development admits of all sorts of combination between the inborn and the acquired. To take one of Darwin's examples, there is no contradiction between a bird's having an inborn migratory urge, and its having to learn the flypath to follow.

In *The Descent of Man* (1871) Darwin focused on instinct as the underlying source of feeling, wanting and willing. Construed thus as impulse to action, instinct manifests itself as behaviour directed towards a goal. However, if the only evidence for an instinct in this sense is the goal-directed behaviour that it is supposed to account for, the account will be uninformative. Unless there are independently identifiable correlates, such as physiological variables, the inventory of an animal's instincts will amount to an inventory of the goals towards which the animal's behaviour can be seen to be directed. However, observers can differ about what and how many kinds of goal govern an animal's behaviour; and it is an open question whether all the behaviour directed at a particular kind of goal is internally driven and controlled by a single and unitary motivational system. For Darwin these difficulties did not greatly affect his argument for psychological continuity between man and beast. They have been a bother to more recent theories of instinct, as those of Freud, McDougall, and 'classical' ethology, will illustrate.

Freud

Freud held several theories about instinct. In an early version he viewed the psyche as subject to biologically based instinctive drives for self-preservation and reproduction; later a single supply of psychic energy was envisaged as giving rise to and becoming dispersed between the psychic structures of the id, ego, and super-ego, with their rival imperatives of appetite, accommodation, and moral value; and finally this trio incorporated contending instincts of life (*eros*) and death (*thanatos*). For Freud the manifest goals of overt behaviour were false guides to the underlying instincts, since experience works through the ego to suppress or distort their natural expression, in accordance with social constraints. Only by the techniques of psychoanalysis, such as those using word associations and dream

descriptions, can true inner dynamics of human action and preoccupation be revealed.

However, Freud made little attempt to get independent empirical validation of his findings. Also he wrote at times as though instinct were a kind of blind energy, at least analogous to the energy of physics, and at other times as though instinct were an intentional agent employing strategies in the pursuit of ends. Consequently, to some critics, psychoanalysis lacks sufficient empirical anchorage and conceptual consistency to count as science, its instinct theory having more the force of a myth than of a material account. Psychoanalysis itself has come to question the usefulness of its instinct theories. Without denying the existence of biologically grounded factors affecting behaviour and mental life, analysts such as Horney (1937) have emphasized the roles of society and culture in the development, differentiation, and dynamics of the psyche.

McDougall

In his *Introduction to Social Psychology* (1908) William McDougall defined an instinct as '. . . an inherited or innate psycho-physical disposition which determines its possessor to perceive, and to pay attention to, objects of a certain class, to experience an emotional excitement of a particular quality upon perceiving such an object, and to act in regard to it in a particular manner, or, at least, to experience an impulse to such action'.

He thought of the connections between the three aspects of instinct as neural, yet insisted that the system is psycho-physical, by which he meant that perception, emotion and impulse, as mentally manifested, are essential to and active in the instigation, control and direction of instinctive action.

Although McDougall, being an instinctivist, is often represented as ignoring effects of experience, he did allow that instincts are capable of modification through learning. But he held that such modification could occur only in the cognitive and conative divisions; the emotional centre was supposed to be immune. Accordingly he argued that identification of the distinct primary emotions is the way to discover what and how many instincts there are, and that this is a necessary preliminary to understanding of the derived complexes and secondary drives patterning behaviour and mental life. He gave a list of the primary emotions and hence principal instincts in man, together with speculation about their probable adaptive significance and hence evolutionary basis.

The plausibility of this analysis led to a fashion for instinct in psychology and adjacent fields (for example Veblen, 1914; Trotter, 1919). However, as the lists of instincts multiplied so did their variety. Different people parsed their emotions differently, and there was no agreed way of deciding between them. Also McDougall's conception of the psycho-physical nature of instincts led him to vacillate between accounts in terms of causes and effects and accounts in terms of intentions and actions; and his theory and speculation gave little purchase for empirical correlation or experimental test.

Behaviourist critics were provoked into mounting an 'anti-instinct revolt'. This was instigated by Dunlap (1919), who argued that McDougall's theory was scientifically vitiated to unobservable subjective purposiveness. Other attacks struck at the prominence given to innateness, contending that wherever evidence was available it supported the view that all behaviour, apart from the simplest reflexes, is shaped by experience. By and large the behaviourists got the better of the fight in their insistence on the priority of hard facts and the requirement of experimental testability. McDougall's theory has little following today (however, see Boden, 1972).

Ethology

Ethology's 'classical' phase covers the period begining with Lorenz's publications in the thirties (for example, Lorenz, 1937) and culminating with N. Tinbergen's (1951) *The Study of Instinct*. Lorenz began with animal behavioural characteristics that are like certain anatomical features in being correlated with taxonomic relatedness in their distribution and variation. This evidence of genetic basis implied for Lorenz the other instinctive attributes: such behaviour must also be independent of experience in its development, independent of peripheral stimulation in its motor patterning, and internally driven by endogenous sources of 'action specific energy', which also causes 'appetitive behaviour' leading to encounter with 'sign stimuli' necessary to "release' the instinctive act, and to which the mechanism controlling the act is innately tuned (Lorenz, 1950). N. Tinbergen (1951) built the components of this conception into a more comprehensive theory in which each of the major functional classes of behaviour – feeding, reproduction, and so forth – is organized hierarchically, the underlying machinery consisting of control centres receiving motivational energy from above and distributing it to others below, depending on the sequence of alternative releasing stimuli encountered through the associated appetitive behaviour. For Tinbergen, the whole of such a functional system constituted an instinct, and to it he connected his conceptions of sensory and motor mechanisms, behavioural evolution, development, function and social interaction to make the classical ethological synthesis.

However, the next phase of ethology's history was given largely to criticism of the Lorenz-Tinbergen instinct theories. Both within and without ethology, critics pointed to lack of agreement between the quasi-hydraulic properties of the theory, and what was known about how nervous systems actually work; the inadequacy of unitary motivational theories in general and ethological instinct theories in particular to deal

with the full complexity of behavioural fact (for example, Hinde, 1960); the fallacy of arguing from evidence of hereditary transmission to conclusions about individual development and motivational fixity (Lehrman, 1953, 1970). Tough-minded reaction to what was perceived as tender-minded speculation led to conceptual reform to meet empirical demands, and methodological refinement to bring experimental test to theoretical implications and quantitative rigour to behavioural analysis. Even Tinbergen (1963) emphasized the importance of distinguishing between different kinds of questions applying to behaviour. The general trend in later ethology has been division of 'the study of instinct' among the several distinct kinds of problem it encompasses. Indeed ethologists now rarely talk of 'instinct', except to reflect on past uses and abuses, and on the present ambiguity of the word.

The ambition to arrive at an overall theory of animal and human behaviour persists, as some of the claims of sociobiologists demonstrate (see, for example, Wilson, 1975). A reconstituted concept of instinct remains a likely possibility for incorporation in any future synthesis. But unless history is to repeat itself yet again, anyone deploying such a concept would do well to heed the lesson of its forerunners: they thrived on blurred distinctions, but to their ultimate undoing.

C. G. Beer
Rutgers University

References

Boden, M. (1972), *Purposive Explanation in Psychology*, Cambridge, Mass.

Darwin, C. (1964 [1859]), *On the Origin of Species*, Cambridge, Mass.

Darwin, C. (1948 [1871]), *The Descent of Man*, New York.

Dunlap, K. (1919), 'Are there instincts?', *Journal of Abnormal Psychology*, 14.

Hinde, R. A. (1960), 'Energy models of motivation', *Symposia of the Society for Experimental Biology*, 14.

Horney, K. (1937), *The Neurotic Personality of Our Time*, New York.

James, W. (1890), *The Principles of Psychology*, New York.

Lehrman, D. S. (1953), 'A critique of Konrad Lorenz's theory of instinctive behaviour', *Quarterly Review of Biology*, 28.

Lehrman, D. S. (1979), 'Semantic and conceptual issues in the nature-nurture problem', in L. R. Aronson, E. Tobach, D. S. Lehrmann and J. S. Rosenblatt (eds), *Development and Evolution of Behavior*, San Francisco.

Lorenz, K. (1937), 'Über die Bildung des Instinktbegriffes', *Naturwissenschaften*, 25.

Lorenz, K. (1950), 'The comparative method in studying innate behaviour patterns', *Symposia of the Society for Experimental Biology*, 4.

McDougall, W. (1908), *An Introduction to Social Psychology*, London.

Tinbergen, N. (1951), *The Study of Instinct*, Oxford.

Tinbergen, N. (1963), 'On the aims and methods of ethology', *Zeitschrift für Tierpsychologie*, 20.

Trotter, W. (1919), *Instincts of the Herd in Peace and War*, New York.

Veblen, T. (1914), *The Instinct of Workmanship and the State of the Industrial Arts*, New York.

Wilson, E. O. (1975), *Sociobiology*, Cambridge, Mass.

See also: *ethology; sociobiology*.

Institutional Economics

Institutional economics became prominent in the United States in the late nineteenth and early twentieth centuries after the science of anthropology had become an established scientific discipline. For unlike orthodox economists, who patterned their science after the physical sciences, Thornstein Veblen and later institutionalists patterned their science after anthropology. Insitutionalists define economics as a study of a particular aspect of culture concerned with the supplying or provisioning of society with the flow of goods and services needed by individuals to make adjustments to the problems met in the non-social and social environments. In short, institutional economics is the science of social provisioning.

Besides adopting an anthropological approach supported by a pragmatic philosophy, institutionalists have made a basic paradigmatic change. This change involves substituting their concept of process for the orthodox economists' concept of equilibrium as a way of grasping the nature of the real economic world. This substitution relates the current economic situation to a future state of the economy. When the institutionalists take the economic system to be an evolving open-ended process, they explain the nature of this process, the factors that cause it to evolve, and the directions in which it may be moving.

The institutionalists consider the economic system to be a cultural entity that changes its structural and functional features over historical time, and that exhibits considerable social coherence. While this processual entity is not itself a static equilibrium, at any one point in historical time a cross-section of it may be partially analysed from an equilibrium viewpoint. Consequently institutionalists do not dispense with the equilibrium analyses of orthodox economists. Instead they place these inherited analyses in the larger framework of an evolving process.

Institutionalists explain the nature of economic evolution by developing a theory of technological interpretation. They are well aware that many other factors than scientific advance and technological change contribute to economic evolution, but they nevertheless assign special importance to these latter two developmental factors. The institutionalists avoid the charge of excessive technological determination by adopting a multiple factor theory of change, in which scientific advance and technological developments are only two factors leading to structural and functional change.

Since the economic system is an open-ended process, there is the question of the direction in which this process may be moving. It is at this point that the institutionalists introduce the value problem. According to their interpretation the values of the participants in economic activities play a major role in the course of economic evolution. Rather than imposing their own values on the nation's economy, institutionalists analyse objectively the value systems of individuals and groups which influence economic activities.

Institutionalists view economics as an interdisciplinary cultural science that borrows not only from other social sciences, but also from other types of econo'mics. It draws upon their contributions in the larger cultural framework of an evolving open-ended process.

Allan G. Gruchy
University of Maryland

Further Reading

Veblen, T. (1919), *The Place of Science in Modern Civilisation*, New York.

Clark. J. M. (1936), *Preface to Social Economics*, New York.

Ayres, C. E. (1944), *The Theory of Economic Progress*, Chapel Hill, North Carolina.

See also: *Veblen*.

Institutions

Many, perhaps most, sociological concepts are derived from an existing commonsensical image, adapted to meet the requirements of the discipline. In common sense usage the term institutions has various meanings. Most commonly it is used to refer to organizations which *contain* people, as in the case of hospitals, prisons, mental hospitals, homes for the mentally handicapped and the like. This sense of the term has been taken up by Erving Goffman in his work on *total institutions*.

Goffman (1961) describes the total institution as an environment in which a large number of like-situated individuals reside, cut off from the wider society and subjected to a common regime, often for the purpose of effecting a transformation in their identities. Apart from the examples above, Goffman includes such cases as boarding schools, monasteries, army training camps and deep-water naval vessels. He shows that such environments possess a number of common features including the stripping away of former supports to the individual's identity through the use of institutional dress, limitations on personal possessions and appearance, strict timetabling of activities, and common subjection to the staff of the institution.

However, although Goffman's concept provides considerable insight into a wide range of organizations, it also blurs a fundamental distinction between those in which the lower members come to the setting already committed to its values and ethos (such as a monastery, a religious commune, or an officer training academy), and those in which they are involuntarily committed to the institution and largely reject its aims and methods (such as prisons, concentration camps, or some mental hospitals). The latter may generate a countervailing culture among inmates which often inhibits the achievement of the organization's goals in the long-term transformation of individual identity. Prisons are relatively unsuccessful in permanently changing the identities of their inmates, as is demonstrated by the high level of recidivism.

A second commonsensical use of the concept institution refers to widespread or large-scale entities which deal with major interests and problems of social concern: the family, the law, the state, the church. It is this sense of the term which has been most vigorously taken up by the discipline of sociology. The functionalist tradition from Herbert Spencer to Talcott Parsons drew a basic distinction between the structures and the processes of a society – analogous to the physical and organic structures of an organism and the activities which these perform. Thus social institutions were seen as the structural components of a society through which essential social activities were organized and social 'needs' were met. They could take the form of organizations, groups or practices of an enduring kind, to which there was a high level of social commitment which integrated, ordered and stabilized major areas of social life, providing approved procedures and forms for the articulation of relationship and interests.

This use of the term remained of theoretical and analytical significance only as long as the functionalist approach to understanding society carried conviction. (There is no space here to detail the decline in persuasiveness of functionalism as an explanatory theory.) However, once the case for construing society as a complex organism had lost its force, so the importance of a sharp distinction between structure and process, institution and function, diminished.

Indeed, it became clearer that institutions were always in the course of formation, negotiation and decline, and that this process was itself of major significance as a focus of analysis. In this account, institutions are simply patterns of behaviour which persist and crystallize in the course of time and to which people become attached as a result of their role in the formation of identity, or through investments of energy or social interests. Thus social activities or patterns of behaviour are *more or less* institutionalized, that is, involve greater or lesser degrees of formalization, infusion of value and emotional attachment, and, therefore, of resistance to change and orientation to their survival.

Entirely new patterns of behaviour or relationship may emerge – as under the authority of a charismatic leader, or through innovations by political, social or cultural rebels. While people may embrace change, they also strive to render their environment relatively predictable and permanent. Thus, they may grow attached to a particular innovation and seek to perpetuate it, repeating the same pattern in an increasingly routine manner. This development of social habits or highly recognized patterns of behaviour changing little over the course of time, and valued intrinsically, is what is now commonly understood by *institutionalization*, a use of the term which draws upon the commonsensical usage that identifies as *institutions The Times*, the two-martini lunch, or even an admired figure whose highly predictable eccentricities render him endearing. Thus, curiously, while institution was once *contrasted with process*, now the emergence of institutions (institutionalization) *as a process* is more the focus of attention. How do new forms of behaviour or styles of life gain a foothold or following in our society, how do they spread and gain respectability and become integrated with other features of the culture and social structure? This forms a major focus of the sociology of collective behaviour and the sociology of social movements, often the vehicles for such changes.

The functionalist account of institutions saw them as essentially a 'good thing' assisting society to perform its necessary activities, but both Goffman's concept of the 'total institution' and the more recent focus upon institutionalization as a process point up a greater moral ambivalence in the term. While routine and predictability, stability and persistence are features without which social life would be largely impossible, and thus are sought after and valued by human beings, the structures thus engendered come to possess a life of their own; they impose themselves upon social actors and may constrain their choices. A once helpful routine may become an inflexible requirement; a formerly instrumental pattern of action may become an empty formalism; once meaningful expressions of sentiment or value may become a rigid dogma. As they become institutionalized, ideas, actions and relationships may lose their excitement, their vitality, their idealism, and come to be valued simply because thay are familiar. This may be no bad thing in some cases (many a marriage survives usefully and happily despite the disappearance of the heady euphoria of first love). But it may sometimes act as a mechanism of control over innovation, repressing the human spirit beneath powerful institutional structures which have long outlived their usefulness.

Roy Wallis
The Queen's University of Belfast

Reference

Goffman, E. (1961), *Asylums: Essays on the Social Situation of Mental Patients and other Inmates*, New York.

Further Reading

Berger, P. L. and Luckmann, T. (1966), *The Social Construction of Reality*, New York.

See also: *Goffman; groups; organizations.*

Integration

In social science, as in public policy, integration may be valued as a means or as an end, either as a means of achieving a desired state of affairs, which may or may not be described as integration, or as a desired state of affairs for the attainment of which integration may or may not be the preferred method. At the same time, there is another dimension of complexity, namely, whether, in respect of either means or ends where such a distinction can be maintained, integration is sought as something that would be both wholly true and true of the whole (or either of these) or with some lesser, more qualified, connotation. Therefore, it is often easier to be clear about what is deemed to be a lack of the desired degree or form of integration, again whether in part or whole, at some or all levels, rather than the desired state itself. Furthermore, as with 'mutuality of interests' and indeed 'partnership' as public policy, so with 'integration': parties may differ as to either what substantively would be equally integrative for all, or, given that what it means for one party may not be the same for another, whether integration is desirable at all. Some partnerships are those of the rider and the horse. Some integrations are, or involve, new forms of imposed and therefore selective controls, new cleavages imposed on old, additions and permeations rather than combinations. So, whether as an attribute of method or as a desired end in itself, integration may be envisaged in this theory or that policy sometimes as a passive, hidden or latent condition, and sometimes as – or as the product of – an active agent or principle.

In the first case, a gestalt sense of meaningful pattern or even 'deep structure' may be meant, namely, a singular if multiplex and static or rather everlasting quality that is *there* in an essentialist sort of way, merely awaiting discovery and correct identification. In relation to active agents or principles, there is less certainty. Integration in this case is subject to a variety of forces, including competition, struggle and conflict, co-operation, hierarchy and identity which may either destroy or promote it.

Another plane of variation further to all of those thus far mentioned has to do with what the integration in question is integration of. For instance, it may be of culture, society, polity, nation, economy, personality or space, with say, planning, policy, analysing, building, negotiating and other avenues of endeavour, together or separately. The approaches and indicators preferred vary too. They may, for example, be historical or traditional, philosophical, logical, pragmatic. To an extent, too, philosophical approaches in, say, sociology or social anthropology may differ from, say, logical approaches in, say, economics, but at the same time there are also many examples of, some, institutionalist and transactionalist discourses being cultivated across such methodological and disciplinary divisions.

So the entire subject is a miasma, a minefield, which one would be well advised to be wary to enter.

Raymond Apthorpe
Institute of Social Studies, The Hague

Further Reading

Hoyt, E. (1961), 'Integration of culture: a review of concepts', *Current Anthropology*, 2.

Wiener, M. (1965), 'Political integration and political development', *The Annals of the American Academy of Political and Social Science*, 358.

See also: *anomie; commitment; conflict, social; conflict resolution; norms.*

Intellectuals

A strict definition of intellectuals would be that they are persons whose role is to deal with the advancement and propagation of knowledge, and with the articulation of the values of their particular society. In that sense all societies have their intellectuals, since even the most so-called 'primitive' will maintain priests or other interpreters of the divine will and natural order. For most of history, intellectuals have of necessity been supported by the political and religious institutions of their societies, so that rebels against accepted institutions and mores have tended to be critical of what they regarded as the over-intellectual approach of the recognized teachers of their time.

The role of intellectuals was altered in major respects by the advent of printing, and consequently of a public for a wide variety of reading matter including freer discussion of basic problems in science, morals, politics and even religion. The French *philosophes* of the eighteenth century, later to be saddled by some historians with responsibility for the advent of the great Revolution, gave a precedent for the modern idea that intellectuals stand somehow outside the power structure and are, by definition, critical of existing social arrangements.

In the nineteenth century, the concept and its resonance differed in different societies. In France and the other advanced countries of Western Europe, intellectuals were distinguished from scientists and scholars who depended upon institutions and academies funded by the state, and from those practitioners of literature whose appeal was strictly aesthetic. To be an intellectual was to claim a degree of independence of outlook; and the word in general parlance implied respect and approval. In Central Europe, where the state was more suspicious of radical ideas, intellectuals, while courted by the political parties, were looked upon with suspicion by the authorities especially if they were recruited largely from minority groups. Nationalist (and later Fascist) movements appealed to populist anti-intellectual prejudice against the 'Jewish intellectuals' of Vienna at the turn of the century, and in the German Weimar Republic.

Britain differed from her neighbours in that, although there were eminent social critics in the Victorian age, the interaction between the world of the intellect and the political and administrative worlds was very close. Intellectuals could preach reform and hope to have an influence. For this reason the word intellectuals was held to represent a foreign rather than an English reality and was given a slightly scornful edge, as implying a lack of contact with everyday life. Few Englishmen would have wished or would now wish to be called intellectuals. In the United States the similar role of intellectuals was diminished after their triumph in the success of the anti-slavery movement. Towards the end of the nineteenth century, a new movement of radical social criticism did develop among what can be seen as the American equivalent of European intellectuals, and this was renewed after the First World War and Woodrow Wilson's temporary mobilization of some of them in pursuit of his domestic and international ideals. So great was their alienation in this second phase that they became susceptible to Communist penetration and influence to a greater extent than was common in Europe in the 1930s, although Marxism was to enjoy an efflorescence in liberated Europe after the Second World War, notably in the Latin countries.

In Tsarist Russia the differentiation between intellectuals and the members of learned professions was narrower, and they were grouped together as members of the intelligentsia. Faced with an absolutist regime, to be a member of the intelligentsia was almost by definition to be a critic of the social order and an opponent of the regime, although on occasion from a right-wing rather than a left-wing angle. In the Soviet Union, and subsequently in Eastern Europe as well, the monopoly of the Communist Party in defining and expounding the ruling doctrine, and the monopoly of state and Party in access to the media, forced intellectuals seeking to follow their own bent to go 'underground' so that, as under Tsarism, to be intellectual is to be classed as an opponent of regimes whose instruments of repression are greater and used with less scruple than those of earlier times.

In the overseas European Empires of the nineteenth and twentieth centuries, a class of intellectuals influenced by their Western-style education came into being alongside the more traditionally educated and motivated intellectuals of the indigenous tradition. The ideas to which they were exposed, combined with the limited roles available to them, produced a similar effect to that noted in relation to Tsarist Russia, predisposing them towards political opposition. Another similarity was the extension of the concept to include more than the small minority who were full-time intellectuals in the Western sense. What was created was again an intelligentsia. This important aspect of the prelude to independence of the countries of the so-called Third World has had strong repercussions. Ingrained habits of criticism and opposition proved difficult to discard when these intelligentsias took power. Intellectuals, when called upon to rule, rarely perform well and usually have to give way to more disciplined elements such as the military.

More recently, a reaction against the adoption of Western values and attitudes by intellectuals in Third-World countries has produced a revival of a traditional, largely religious-oriented leadership, notably in parts of the Islamic world, and a specific repudiation of intellectuals thought to be tarnished by Western liberal or Marxist contacts.

Intellectuals whose mission is to examine everything are naturally prone to examine their own roles. And this self-consciousness has been heightened by the anti-intellectualism of some populist movements, an anti-intellectualism which has surfaced more than once on the American political scene. There are a number of recurring problems for intellectuals generally. Should they seek solitude to produce and develop their own ideas, or does the notion itself imply a constant commerce between intellectuals such as took place in the salons of eighteenth-century Paris and Regency London, or later in the cafés of Paris and Vienna, or as it now takes place in the many international congresses and seminars supported by American foundations? Should intellectuals engage directly in current controversies or content themselves with publishing their own ideas, leaving the arena to others? Should they accept public office or even seek the suffrages of the people for themselves? Should philosophers be kings?

Max Beloff
University of Buckingham

Further Reading
Beloff, M. (1970), *The Intellectual in Politics and Other Essays*, London.
Benda, J. (1927), *La trahison des Clercs*, Paris.
Hofstadter, R. (1963), *Anti-Intellectualism in American Life*, New York.
Joll, J. (1969), *Three Intellectuals in Politics*, London.
Lasch, C. (1966), *The New Radicalism in America: The Intellectual as a Social Type*, New York.

Shils, E. (1972), *The Intellectuals and the Powers and Other Essays*, Chicago.

Intelligence and Intelligence Testing

The testing of intelligence has a long history (for psychology) going back to the turn of the century when Binet in Paris attempted to select children who might profit from public education. Since that time the notion of intelligence has been the subject of considerable scrutiny, especially by Spearman in Great Britain in the 1930s, and of much and often bitter controversy.

The Meaning of Intelligence

Intelligence is defined as a general reasoning ability which can be used to solve a wide variety of problems. It is called general because it has been shown empirically that such an ability enters into a variety of tasks. In job selection, for example, the average correlation with occupational success and intelligence test scores is 0.3. This is a good indication of how general intelligence is, as an ability.

This general intelligence must be distinguished from other abilities such as verbal ability, numerical ability and perceptual speed. These are more specific abilities which, when combined with intelligence, can produce very different results. A journalist and engineer may have similar general intelligence but would differ on verbal and spatial ability. The illiterate scientist and innumerate arts student are well-known stereotypes illustrating the point.

Intelligence Tests

Most of our knowledge of intelligence has come about through the development and use of intelligence tests. In fact, intelligence is sometimes defined as that which intelligence tests measure. This is not as circular as it might appear, since what intelligence tests measure is known from studies of those who score highly and those who do not, and from studies of what can be predicted from intelligence test scores. Indeed the very notion of intelligence as a general ability comes about from investigations of intelligence tests and other scores. Well-known tests of intelligence are the Wechsler scales (for adults and children), the Stanford-Binet test and the recent British Intelligence Scale. These are tests to be used with individuals. Well-known group tests are Raven's Matrices and Cattell's Culture Fair test.

The IQ (intelligence quotient) is now a figure which makes any two scores immediately comparable. Scores at each age group are scaled such that the mean is 100 and the standard deviation is 15 in a normal distribution. Thus a score of 130 always means that the individual is two standard deviations beyond the norm, that is, in the top 2½ per cent of his age group.

Modern intelligence tests have been developed through the use of factor analysis, a statistical method that can separate out dimensions underlying the observed differences of scores on different tests. When this is applied to a large collection of measures, an intelligence factor (or, strictly, factors, as we shall see) emerges which can be shown to run through almost all tests. Factor loadings show to what extent a test is related to a factor. Thus a test of vocabulary loads about 0.6, that is, it is correlated 0.6 with intelligence. Such loadings, of course, give a clear indication of the nature of intelligence.

The results of the most modern and technically adequate factor analysis can be summarized as follows (for a full description see Cattell, 1971). Intelligence breaks down into two components.

(1)g_f *Fluid ability*: This is the basic reasoning ability which in Cattell's view is largely innate (but see below) and depends upon the neurological constitution of the brain. It is largely independent of learning and can be tested best by items which do not need knowledge for their solution. A typical fluid ability item is:
0 is to $\boxed{0}$ as ▽ is to ... with a multiple choice of five drawings. An easy item (correct answer: $\boxed{▽}$).

(2)g_c *Crystallized ability*: This is a fluid ability as it is evinced in a culture. In Cattell's view crystallized ability results from the investment of fluid ability in the skills valued by a culture. In Great Britain this involves the traditional academic disciplines, for example, physics, mathematics, classics or languages. In later life professional skills, as in law or medicine, may become the vehicles for crystallized ability. A typical Crystallized Ability Item is: Sampson Agonistes is to Comus as the Bacchae are to .... A difficult item (correct answer: The Cyclops).

Many social class differences in intelligence test scores and educational attainment are easily explicable in terms of these factors especially if we remember that many old-fashioned intelligence tests measure a mixture of these two factors. Thus in middle-class homes, where family values and cultural values are consonant, a child's fluid intelligence becomes invested in activities which the culture as a whole values (verbal ability, for example). Performance in education is thus close to the full ability, as measured by gf, of the child. In children from homes where educational skills are not similarly encouraged there may be a considerable disparity between ability and achievement. On intelligence tests where crystallized ability is measured, social class differences are greater than on tests where fluid ability is assessed.

Thus a summary view of intelligence based on the factor analysis of abilities is that it is made up of two components: one a general reasoning ability, largely innate, the other, the set of skills resulting from investing this ability in a particular way. These are the two most important abilities. Others are perceptual speed, visualization ability and speed of retrieval from memory, a factor which affects how fluent we are in our ideas and words.

We are now in a position to examine some crucial issues in the area of intelligence and intelligence testing, issues which have often aroused considerable emotion but have been dealt with from bases of ignorance and prejudice rather than knowledge.

The Heritability of Intelligence

Positions on this controversial question polarize unfortunately around political positions. Opponents of the hereditary hypothesis were heartened by the evidence now generally accepted, that Sir Cyril Burt had manufactured his twin data which supported this hypothesis. However, the fact is that there are other more persuasive data confirming this position – data coming from biometric analyses.

First, what is the hereditary hypothesis? It claims that the variance in measured intelligence in Great Britain and America is attributable about 70 percent to genetic factors, 30 percent to environmental. It is very important to note that this work refers to variance within a particular population. If the environment were identical for individuals, variation due to the environment would be nought. This means that figures cannot be transported from culture to culture or even from historical period to period. This variance refers to population variance; it does not state that 70 percent of the intelligence in an individual (whatever that means) is attributable to genetic factors. Finally, a crucial point is that interaction takes place with the environment; there is no claim that all variation is genetically determined.

These figures have been obtained from biometric analysis (brilliantly explicated by Cattell, 1982) which involve examining the relationship of intelligence test scores of individuals of differing degrees of consanguinity, thus allowing variance to be attributed to within-family and between-family effects, as well as enabling the investigator to decide whether, given the data, assortative mating, or other genetic mechanisms, can be implicated. Work deriving from this approach is difficult to impugn.

Racial Differences in Intelligence

This is an even more controversial issue with potentially devastating political implications. Some social scientists feel that this is a case where research should be stopped, as for example with certain branches of nuclear physics and genetic engineering. Whether suppression of the truth or the search for it is ever justifiable is, of course, itself a moral dilemma.

The root of the problem lies in the inescapable fact that in America Blacks score lower on intelligence tests than any other group. Fascists and members of ultra right-wing movements have immediately interpreted

this result as evidence of Black inferiority. Opponents of this view have sought the cause in a variety of factors: that the tests are biased against Blacks, because of the nature of their items: that Blacks are not motivated to do tests set by Whites; that the whole notion of testing is foreign to Black American culture; that the depressed conditions and poverty of Black families contributes to their low scores; that the prejudice against Blacks creates a low level of self-esteem so that they do not perform as well as they might; that verbal stimulation in the Black home is less than in that of Whites.

Jensen (1980) has investigated the whole problem in great detail and many of these arguments above are refuted by experimental evidence, especially the final point, for Blacks do comparatively worse on nonverbal than verbal tests. But to argue that this is innate or biologically determined goes far beyond the evidence. Motivational factors and attitudes are difficult to measure and may well play a part in depressing Black scores. What is clear, however, is that on intelligence tests American Blacks perform markedly less well than other racial or cultural groups, while these tests still predict individual success in professional, high-status occupations.

Importance of Intelligence

Intelligence as measured by tests is important because in complex technologically advanced societies it is a good predictor of academic and occupational success. That is why people attach great value to being intelligent. Cross-cultural studies of abilities in Africa, for example, have shown that the notion of intelligence is different from that in the West and is not there so highly regarded. Many skills in African societies may require quite different abilities. Thus as long as, in a society, it is evident that a variable contributes to success, that variable will be valued; and even though intelligence is but one of a plethora of personal attributes, there is, in the West, little hope that more reasoned attitudes to intelligence will prevail.

Two further points remain to be made. First, the fact that there is a considerable genetic component does not mean that the environment (family and education) do not affect intelligence test scores. It has clearly been shown that even with 80 percent genetic determination, environmental causes can produce variations of up to 30 points.

Finally, the rather abstract statistically defined concept of intelligence is now being intensively studied in cognitive experimental psychology in an attempt to describe precisely the nature of this reasoning ability. Sternberg's (1977) analyses of analogous reasoning are good examples of this genre – the blending of psychometric and experimental psychology.

Paul Kline
University of Exeter

References

Cattell, R. B. (1971), *Abilities: Their Structure, Growth and Action*, New York.

Cattell, R. B. (1982), *The Inheritance of Personality and Ability*, New York.

Jensen, A. R. (1980), *Bias in Mental Testing*, Glencoe, Ill.

Sternberg, R. J. (1977), *Intelligence, Information Processing and Analogical Reasoning: the Componential Analysis of Human Abilities*, Hillsdale, N.J.

Further Reading

Kline, P. (1979), *Psychometrics and Psychology*, London.

Resnick, R. B. (ed.) (1976), *The Nature of Intelligence*, Hillsdale, N.J.

Vernon, P. E. (1979), *Intelligence: Heredity and Environment*, San Francisco.

See also: *genetics and behaviour*.

Interest

The charge made (or price paid) for the use of loanable funds is called interest. The rate of interest is the amount payable, usually expressed as a percentage of the principal sum borrowed, per period of time, usually per month, quarter or year. Financial intermediaries will commonly both borrow and lend funds, their profitability being dependent on the difference between the rate which they are willing to pay depositors and the rate they charge borrowers. Interest rates may be calculated on a simple or a compound basis. Simple interest involves a percentage return on the principal per period, whereas compound interest involves a return based on both the principal and accumulated interest, already paid in previous periods. Interest rates may be fixed, in which case they stay constant throughout the period of the loan, or they may be variable, in which case they may be changed during the period of the loan.

The supply of loanable funds will depend on: the level of savings in the private sector; the rate of growth of bank lending; and, less commonly, on the size of the public financial surplus, which depends on the excess of government revenue over its expenditure. Demand for loanable funds can come from consumers, businesses and the government, due to the need to finance the Public Sector Borrowing Requirement.

The charging of interest may be rationalized in a number of ways:

(1) The lender is entitled to a share of the profit resulting from the productive use of the loaned funds.

(2) Savers should be rewarded for abstaining from present consumption, which will probably be worth more to them than future consumption.

(3) Lenders should receive a fee for allowing someone else to borrow an asset which provides the service of liquidity.

(4) Lenders should be entitled to a risk premium, because they face the risk of nonrepayment. These factors may also be used to explain the difference between lending and borrowing rates and the fact that different types of financial asset bear different interest rates. In general the shorter the term of the loan and the lower the risk, the lower the rate of interest.

There have been criticisms of the morality of charging interest in the form discussed above. Marx, for example, regarded interest as an element of surplus value, together with rent and profit, which accrued to finance capitalists and as such it stemmed directly from the exploitation of labour by capitalists. Marxist-Leninist regimes have typically had low interest rates; nominally to cover some of the costs of running banks and the payments mechanism. The charging of interest has also been condemned, at times, by followers of various religions, for example, Christianity and Islam, the most reviled practices being those linked to private money lenders, usurers, or 'Shylocks'. Marxist objections, however, stem from social, rather than religious, ethics.

The present revival of Islamic fundamentalism, in Iran, Pakistan and Sudan, for example, has revived criticism of Western-style interest charges. Islam clearly condemns usury, but there is some theological debate concerning whether this means that interest rate charges in general should be prohibited. It would appear that the fundamentalist interpretation has dominated in Pakistan and, more recently, Sudan. The reasons for condemning interest rate charges, given by the fundamentalists, include: their role in reinforcing the accumulation of wealth in the hands of the few, and thereby reducing man's concern for fellow man; the fact that Islam does not permit gain from financial activity unless the beneficiary is also subject to risk of potential loss; and that Islam regards the accumulation of wealth through interest as selfish compared with that accumulated through hard work. These objections, especially the second, would rule out legally guaranteed regular interest payments. It would not, however, rule out equity investment, since this is subject to a return that varies with profit, and equity holders are subject to loss, although they are commonly protected through limited liability. In Pakistan attempts have been made to develop an Islamic banking system in which returns are based on a profit and loss sharing principle, rather than regular guaranteed interest payments, and which are, therefore, akin to the returns on equities.

We have noted that in Western economies with numerous financial assets there is a whole array of interest rates. These do, however, tend to move up and down together, and so it is possible to consider, in the abstract, the determination of the level of the rate of interest. Keynesian economists regard the interest rate as being determined by the equation of the demand for and supply of money. Classical economists claimed that it was determined by the interaction of the demand for funds, by investors, and the supply of funds, by savers. Keynes criticized this view, arguing that changes in national income were primarily instrumental in bringing about an equilibrium between savings and investment through their influence on the supply of, and demand for, loanable funds.

A distinction is often made between the nominal and the real interest rate. The real rate is the nominal rate less the expected rate of inflation; although it is sometimes approximated by subtracting the actual rate of inflation from the nominal rate. The concept of the natural rate of interest is also often used. It is the rate of interest that would hold in an economy which was in a noninflationary equilibrium. The rate of interest, being the contractual income expressed as a percentage of the nominal value of the security, is to be differentiated from the yield of a security, which is a percentage relationship of its income to its current market price.

Andy Mullineux
University of Birmingham

Further Reading

Bain, A. D. (1981), 'Interest rates', in *The Economics of the Financial System*, Oxford.

Karsten, I. (1982), 'Islam and financial intermediation' *IMF Staff Papers*, vol. 29.

Wilczynski, J. (1978), *Comparative Monetary Economics*, London.

See also: *credit; financial systems.*

Interest Groups and Lobbying

Interest groups have been a part of political life in all the industrial societies of the Western world for more than a century, but the modern system began to take shape only in the late nineteenth century. The rapidly developing industrial economy spawned a great many new commercial and scientific specialties that served as the foundations for trade and professional societies. These new associations were meant to exercise control over unruly competition, provide forums for the exchange of information and the development of professional reputations, create knowledge about the latest methods or techniques in the field, and represent the occupational interests of their members before legislative committees or government bureaus. Membership in these groups waxed and waned with the fluctuations of the economy, and there were spurts of development during or immediately after wartime. A new set of linkages between government and the citizenry emerged, based squarely upon the rapidly growing occupational structure of the industrial society.

The number of interest groups has grown steadily throughout the twentieth century in all industrial societies, and the rate of increase has accelerated during the past twenty years. Most group theorists prior to the 1960s assumed that once individual citizens began to experience some social or economic problem, and became aware that they shared their difficulties with others, it would be perfectly natural for them to create a formal organization that would represent their joint interests before government. Individuals might be too poor or isolated from one another to act upon their shared beliefs, or they might not be sufficiently aroused to take the necessary pains. If they cared deeply enough, however, and events produced a sufficient amount of interaction with other affected individuals, theorists believed that eventually 'formal organization or a significant interest group will emerge and greater influence will ensue' (Truman, 1951). The process was thought to be more or less spontaneous, propelled by social disturbances arising from the growing complexity of the urban-industrial economy. Societies that did not impose unreasonable legal constraints upon the formation of associations could be expected to spawn interest groups in waves of mobilization and counter-mobilization until a form of equilibrium was achieved, only to be disturbed by further social or economic developments, setting off another round of mobilization.

A serious challenge to the idea that groups would organize spontaneously came in 1965 from Mancur Olson, who directly attacked the commonsensical assumptions at the heart of group theory about the natural inclination of citizens to take joint action in their collective interest. Olson showed that it would not be rational for self-interested individuals to take part in securing a collective benefit for a large group, even if they were aware they would be better off if the benefit were secured. It is the nature of collective benefits, like health insurance or public education, that they must be provided to everyone who meets universal standards of eligibility, so that any individuals out to maximize their own self-interest would refrain from making any contribution to the common effort, knowing that they would receive as much as everyone else in the group once the government began providing the benefit.

Olson believed that small groups might be able to induce their members to contribute to common objectives through peer pressure, but large groups could not be expected to act in their collective self-interest in most cases. The problem of the 'free rider' could be solved only if groups were able to provide tangible benefits as inducements directly to those who contributed to the common effort, or unless sanctions were employed, sometimes enforced by the courts – as with union shop agreements – that forced all potential group members to contribute to the common effort, whether they wanted to or not.

Olson's theory of public goods and individual incentives highlights the great obstacles facing those who wish to organize deprived elements of society. A balanced representation of group interests cannot be achieved from entirely voluntary political action when the marginal costs of participation differ so greatly among social groups, and where individual incentives to contribute to common goals are so weak. Some of these obstacles are lifted during periods of great political stress (Moe, 1980), and some can be overcome through the efforts of organizational entrepreneurs (Salisbury, 1969; Wilson, 1973), but there are limits to the impact individual leaders can have, no matter how energetic or clever they may be. Groups with large memberships that do not provide exclusive benefits or employ coercion to hold their members, usually attract mainly those with good educations and ample incomes for whom, presumably, the annual dues represent a painless way of amplifying their ideological views and of gaining a sense of involvement in the national political process (Berry, 1977; McFarland, 1976). A great many new associations representing socially disadvantaged elements of the society have appeared in recent years in most Western democracies, but most have managed to remain in existence not through an outpouring of financial support from their members, but through the financial patronage of foundations, wealthy individuals, trade unions, or government agencies (Walker, 1983). Associations representing large social groupings, like consumers or the poor, that depend entirely on support from their members in response to mainly ideological appeals, typically have been short-lived.

Even though there has been an increase during the past two decades in the number of associations claiming to represent disadvantaged minorities, women, the mentally ill, children, or the elderly in most Western democracies, there is a natural tendency in democratic political systems for small, privileged economic or social minorities to present their case more effectively before government than large, unwieldy, disadvantaged groups pursuing broad collective interests. This imbalance in the system of advocacy provides intense minorities with an advantage when highly technical policy problems are being dealt with, when there is little conflict among the interests most directly involved in a policy area, or when policy problems are being resolved away from the glare of publicity mainly within public bureaucracies or government regulatory agencies (Hayes, 1982). Elected legislators can be relied upon to provide the representation required by large, vulnerable groups when there is a reasonable prospect that supporters of these interests can be reached through the mass media and convinced to vote in subsequent elections (Bauer *et al.*, 1963), but the problem of protecting the public interest from the selfish scramble of advocates for narrow interests remains one of the most pressing problems of democracy.

Democratic systems draw their legitimacy from widespead public acceptance of the procedures by which policy decisions are made. Citizens need not accept every rule or regulation, but they must remain convinced that the system is reasonably open, that legislators are striving to represent all the people equally, and that opportunities exist for citizens to organize and petition their leaders to reverse unfavourable decisions. Interest groups, therefore, perform an essential function in democratic government, but ironically, they also pose one of the most serious threats to the maintenance of public trust in democratic institutions. If large numbers of citizens become convinced that elected officials are incapable of advancing the public interest because of unreasonable pressures from advocates for narrow, special interests, the democratic system itself may begin to lose the essential legitimacy it requires to maintain peaceful debate and compromise. In order to manage this unavoidable dilemma of democracy, interest groups must be allowed to engage in vigorous forms of advocacy. But somehow enough balance must be maintained in the system – either through increasing the resources available to elected officials or by creating a balance of forces through subsidies for groups that are inherently difficult to mobilize – so that the public will remain convinced that its system of government is both representative and fair.

Jack L. Walker
University of Michigan

References

Bauer, R. A., Pool, I. de Sola and Dexter, L. A. (1963), *American Business and Public Policy: The Politics of Foreign Trade*, New York.

Berry, J. M. (1977), *Lobbying for the People: The Political Behavior of Public Interest Groups*, Princeton.

Hayes, M. T. (1981), *Lobbyists and Legislators: A Theory of Political Markets*, New Brunswick.

McFarland, A. S. (1976), *Public Interest Lobbies: Decision Making on Energy*, Washington.

Moe, T. M. (1980), *The Organization of Interests*, Chicago.

Olson, M. Jr (1965), *The Logic of Collective Action*, Cambridge, Mass.

Salisbury, R. H. (1969), 'An exchange theory of interest groups', *Midwest Journal of Political Science*, 8.

Truman, D. B. (1951), *The Governmental Process*, New York.

Wilson, J. Q. (1973), *Political Organizations*, New York.

Walker, J. L. (1983), 'The origins and maintenance of interest groups in America', *American Political Science Review*, 77.

International Monetary System

The international monetary system encompasses the arrangements and mechanisms governing monetary and financial relationships between countries. Under alternative 'systems' these may be either precise and reasonably well defined (as under the Gold Standard and, to a lesser extent, the Bretton Woods arrangements in the period 1944–73) or flexible, as has generally been the case since 1973. The monetary relationships between countries are different from those between regions of a country, and raise different issues of analysis and policy. This is because: (1) countries have degrees of policy autonomy (particularly with respect to monetary policy) not conferred upon regions of a nation-state; (2) different currencies are involved and their exchange values may change in such a way as to alter the economic and financial relationship between countries; (3) there is no automatic financing of countries' payments imbalances unlike between regions within a country, and, for this reason; (4) there is pressure on nation states to adjust balance of payments imbalances.

The arrangements within the international monetary system cover six main areas. In various ways, either explicitly or implicitly, it is these six issues that have dominated developments in the international monetary system and the various debates over reform of prevailing systems:

(1) Central to any system or set of arrangements are *exchange rates* and the extent to which, either because of agreed rules of behaviour or because *ad hoc* decisions are made, central banks intervene in the foreign exchange market to influence the level of exchange rates.

(2) Coupled with the exchange rate is the question of *settlement obligations* when a deficit country's currency is purchased by other central banks. This became a major issue in the early 1970s with the break-down of the Bretton Woods system following the substantial accumulation of United States dollars by European and Japanese central banks.

(3) A further element in the monetary relations between countries relates to the linked issues of the balance of pressures that exist as between balance of payments *financing and adjustment*, and the extent to which the pressure for adjustment is symmetrical between surplus and deficit countries. Balance of payments adjustment imposes costs on a deficit country both through the particular mechanism adopted, but also because it usually implies a smaller net absorption of real resources from the rest of the world.

(4) The way in which balance of payments *financing* is conducted is a significant issue for international monetary arrangements. In particular, whether financing is undertaken by transferring reserve assets or by borrowing has implications for the growth of international debt and confidence in the international monetary system. One of the factors behind the eventual breakdown of the Bretton Woods system was that a dominant country (the United States) had its persistent payments deficit financed by the central banks of surplus countries purchasing dollars in the foreign exchange market which were not converted by the American authorities into gold or other reserve asset. A *confidence problem* arose as by the early 1970s the volume of such American liabilities came to exceed the value of the American gold stock. A notable feature of the international monetary system of the 1970s was the financing of balance of payments deficits through borrowing from banks.

(5) The arrangements for satisfying the requirements of central banks to hold *international liquidity* is a significant element. Central in this is the form in which international liquidity is held (and in particular whether certain national currencies are held for this purpose) and the extent to which there are arrangements for the conscious control of the volume of international liquidity, as against conditions where it is largely demand-determined.

(6) Pervading all of the issues identified, there is the question of *management* of the international monetary system and the extent to which it is based upon the acceptance by governments and central banks of agreed rules of behaviour. The 'management' role of supranational organizations (such as the International Monetary Fund) is subject to considerable controversy given its potential implications for the perceptions of national sovereignty.

The several key issues arise because countries (monetary unions) have trade and financial links with one another. This in turn means that policy developments in one country can affect economic conditions in partner countries and, similarly, that the attainment of domestic policy targets can be thwarted by external developments. In practice, most of the problem issues in the international monetary system relate to the consistency of policy targets between countries.

International interdependence necessarily implies that in one way or another *ex post* compatability is secured between countries with respect notably to the balance of payments, the exchange rate and the rate of growth of the money supply. However, these may be secured *ex post* at the expense of some *ex ante* plans not being achieved. This is obvious with respect to the balance of payments, as the sum of separate *ex ante* targets might imply an aggregate world surplus or deficit. In various ways *ex post* these inconsistencies are eliminated. But unless all central banks refrain from foreign exchange market intervention (or can successfully sterilize the monetary effects of such intervention), the same is also true of monetary policies. It is relevant, therefore, to consider how potential conflicts of policy and targets between countries might be minimized through various arrangements for ensuring either *ex ante* consistency, or minimizing the resistance to *ex post* equilibrating mechanisms. Logically, five broad mechanisms or options may be identified: (1) automatic market mechanisms such as floating exchange rates or nonsterilization of balance of payments induced by changes in the money supply; (2) the $(n - 1)$ approach, whereby one country in the system agrees not to have an external target; (3) *ex ante* policy co-ordination designed to ensure consistent targets and compatible means of securing them; (4) an agreement to a precise set of policy rules which indicate what is required of policy makers in specified circumstances; or (5) a multilateral approach, whereby some supranational authority indicates (and possibly enforces) policy measures which have been calculated to ensure consistency and stability in the system. In practice, the mechanisms are likely to be a composite of several.

The Bretton Woods system as it developed in practice was based essentially upon the $(n - 1)$ arrangement with the passive role being played by the United States. Such a system presupposes that the central country agrees not to have an external target, and partners are prepared to accept the hegemony of that country, particularly with respect to monetary policy. It was the latter that proved to be a major weakness in the final years of the Bretton Woods system. The major potential weakness of this mechanism is the moral hazard confronted by the key country, which can largely determine its own policy and targets and in the process impose costs (in terms of nonattainment of targets) on partner countries. For instance, in the monetary sector, with a fixed exchange rate, the rate of growth of the money supply in an integrated group can be determined by the dominant country if, like the United States in the 1960s, it chooses to sterilize the monetary effects of its balance-of-payments position.

For close on thirty years, arrangements in the international monetary system were those outlined in the Bretton Woods agreement of 1944, though the system was operated in practice very differently from the intentions at the outset. The main elements were fixed, but adjustable, exchange rates, with most countries maintaining exchange rates fixed against the United States dollar which became the pivotal currency. International liquidity was held predominantly in dollars which were supplied through a persistent American balance-of-payments deficit.

But the international monetary environment became considerably less certain and predictable over the 1970s, and early in the decade the Bretton Woods arrangements finally disintegrated after almost thirty years. At various times, the fixed-exchange-rate system came under strain as the volume of funds that could move between countries and currencies grew markedly after the general moves towards convertibility in the late 1950s. Towards the end of the 1960s it became increasingly apparent that fixed exchange rates, freedom of international capital flows and independent national control over domestic money supplies were incompatible. The adoption of floating exchange rates in the early 1970s was partly associated with a desire on the part of governments in Europe and elsewhere to determine their monetary policy independently of the United States.

In itself, the Bretton Woods system was potentially stable and had much to commend it. It became, in effect, a dollar standard, and this could have proved durable had Europe been prepared to accept the permanent monetary dominance of America.

Since the breakdown of the Bretton Woods arrangements the international monetary system has operated in an *ad hoc* manner. Attempts at reform in the middle of the 1970s failed to produce a Grand Design new structure similar to that achieved in 1944 which was at the time a response to the turbulance of the 1930s. In the early 1980s, a new 'confidence problem' was emerging and related to the external debt position of a few developing countries. This was a reflection of the shift in the balance of pressures between balance-of-payments financing and adjustment towards the former which had been a notable feature of the previous decade.

David T. Llewellyn
Loughborough University

Further Reading
Tew, J. H. B. (1982), *Evolution of the International Monetary System 1945–81*, London.
Williamson, J. (1977), *The Failure of World Monetary Reform 1971–74*, London.
See also: *balance of payments; devaluation; exchange rate; international trade; reserve currency.*

International Relations

In the most general sense international relations have existed ever since men formed themselves into social groups, and then developed external relations with groups like themselves. Relationships were most frequently conflictual or warlike, although occasionally they were co-operative; but they took place in a system of anarchy and not within the framework of any political or legal or customary rules. These peculiar relationships were little considered by writers in the Western world before Machiavelli, but from the seventeenth century onwards international law (Grotius, Pufendorf, Vattel), and the problems of war and peace (Rousseau, Kant) began to attract attention. These historical origins, combined with the horror of the First World War, led to the subject's emergence as a policy-making, prescriptive and normative study: war was an intolerable evil, its recurrence must forever be prevented, and the duty of international relations scholars was to show how to achieve this. It was assumed that nobody could want war, so if states were democratic and governments were accountable to their peoples, and if the system's anarchy were ended (hence the League of Nations), war might be banished.

The diagnosis was too simple. The aspirations and actions of Hitler, Mussolini, the Japanese, and the Bolsheviks in Moscow showed the truth of the dictum of Morgenthau (1948) that peace and security is the ideology of satisfied powers. Scholars now turned their minds away from study of ways to achieve a supposedly universal goal to study of how things in the international arena in fact were. The modern subject of international relations was born. From the outset, though at first not explicitly, the subject was approached by different scholars from two different points of view. The first sought to establish why the significant units (or actors) on the international stage behaved in the ways they did: most such scholars saw states as the significant actors, and this branch of the subject became foreign policy analysis. The second group focused on the arena within which relations occurred, and was concerned to identify the mechanisms by which patterned relationships with a fair degree of stability and order were able to be maintained in conditions which, formally at least, were anarchical. The 1950s and 1960s saw a burgeoning of methodological experimentation and quasi-theoretical speculation, and a proliferation of journals. The behaviouralist revolution in the United States invaded international relations, as it did other social sciences, and a great debate with the so-called traditionalists raged through the 1960s and early 1970s, and is not yet concluded. But in the last decade, disappointment at the relative lack of success in the creation of theories with explanatory power for real-world problems has led to some redirection of attention towards substantive questions, to smaller-scale analyses and to theorizing over limited ranges of phenomena.

Foreign policy analysis is the branch of the subject in which most practical advances have occurred. Many conceptual frameworks have been developed, the most comprehensive probably being that of Brecher *et al.* (1969), but the central components of such frameworks are now widely agreed. States are conceived as having objectives of various kinds – political/security, economic, ideological. Objectives are not consistently compatible one with another, and a short-term objective may be inconsistent with a long-term goal. Objectives are ranked differently by different groups, organizations, and political leaderships within states, and rankings change over time. Explanation of policy-decisions thus requires understanding of political interplay and bureaucratic process. But the determination

of policy is conditioned also by states' capabilities – economic, demographic, political, military – and by decision makers' perceptions of the comparative efficacy of their own capabilities as against those of the other state(s) with which they are dealing, all in the context of support relationships (alliances, economic aid) and of respective commitments elsewhere in the system. Most, if not all, relationships have elements of conflict and common interest, and are essentially of a bargaining character; but the conflictual element usually predominates, and the concept of power is thus central to the analysis. A check-list of such considerations affecting foreign policy decisions enables rudimentary comparisons of foreign policies to be made, but also makes possible greater awareness among policy makers of the likely consequences of their decisions.

The purposes of studies at the second or system level are to determine the factors that make the stability of the system more or less probable, and the effect on international outcomes of the system's structure. Essential structural components are the number of significant units (or actors) in the system, the nature, quality and quantity of interactions among the units, the distribution of capabilities among them, and the degree to which realignment of relationships is easy or is constrained (a system that is ideologically highly polarized, for example, is relatively inflexible). Analysis at the system level is commonly more highly abstract than analysis of state behaviour: this makes possible theory construction of a more rigorous kind, but by the same token makes application of theory to the real world more difficult.

At both levels statistical and mathematical techniques are used, as well as more traditional methods relying on historical and verbally described data. The distinction between the levels is, of course, analytical only. To take just one example of interdependence: at the unit behaviour level the extent to which states are economically, militarily or ideologically interdependent will very greatly affect the policy choices that are open; at the system level the extent to which the realignment of units is impeded by their interdependence will fundamentally affect both outcomes and the stability of the system. Mention of interdependence calls attention to the fact that while states are widely accepted as still the most significant actors in the international arena, there are now many other actors, including intergovernmental organizations (the International Monetary Fund), and nongovernmental organizations (guerrilla groups, multinational corporations). The roles of these, in interplay with the behaviour of states, and as components of international systems, all form part – and some would say an increasingly important part – of the study of international relations.

P. A. Reynolds
University of Lancaster

References

Brecher, M., Steinberg, B. and Stein, J. (1969), 'A framework for research in foreign policy behaviour', *Journal of Conflict Resolution*, 13.

Morgenthau, H. J. (1948), *Politics Among Nations*, New York.

Further Reading

Carr, E. H. (1939), *The Twenty Years' Crisis 1919–1939*, London.

Holsti, K. J. (1977), *International Politics*, Englewood Cliffs, N.J.

Reynolds, P. A. (1980), *An Introduction to International Relations*, London.

Rosenau, J. N. (1971), *The Scientific Study of Foreign Policy*, Glencoe, Ill.

Smith, M., Little, R. and Shackleton, M. (1981), *Perspectives on World Politics*, London.

Waltz, K. N. (1979), *Theory of International Politics*, Reading, Mass.

See also: *conflict resolution; peace; war.*

International Trade

International trade is not intrinsically different from transactions in which commodities do not cross national boundaries. Nevertheless, the study of international trade has traditionally constituted a separate branch of microeconomics. It may be distinguished from other branches by its focus on situations where some but not all goods and factors are mobile between countries; and from international macroeconomics by its focus on real rather than nominal variables (trade flows and relative prices rather than exchange rates and money supplies), and by a tendency to examine medium-run issues using equilibrium analysis rather than short-run positions of disequilibrium.

One of the first and most durable contributions to the analysis of international trade is the doctrine of *comparative advantage* due to Ricardo. This is the antecedent of both the normative and positive strands of international trade theory. On the one hand, it postulates that an absolutely inefficient country will nevertheless gain from trade; on the other hand, it predicts the direction of trade: each country will tend to export those goods which it produces relatively cheaply in the absence of trade. As a positive explanation, the principle has met with some success. However, in its classical form it is open to the objections that it unrealistically assumes production costs are independent of the scale of output, and that it fails to explain why they differ between countries in the first place.

In an attempt to overcome these deficiencies, the Swedish economists Heckscher and Ohlin developed a theory which stressed international differences in *factor endowments* as the basis for comparative advantage and trade. Thus a country which is relatively capital-abundant will tend to export goods which are produced by relatively capital-intensive techniques. Largely through the influence of Samuelson, a highly simplified version of this theory, assuming only two goods and two factors in each country, has come to dominate the text-books. In this form it is a useful teaching device for introducing some basic concepts of general equilibrium theory but, not surprisingly, it is overwhelmingly rejected by the data. The most notable example of this is the so-called *Leontief Paradox*, an early application by Leontief of his technique of input-output analysis, which found that the presumably capital-abundant United States exported labour-intensive commodities, thus contradicting the theory.

Nevertheless, probably the preferred explanation of trade patterns for most economists is an eclectic theory of comparative advantage along Heckscher-Ohlin lines, allowing for many factors of production, some of them (such as natural resources) specific to individual sectors, as well as for the international differences in technology. Even this theory fails to account adequately for certain features of contemporary international trade, and a variety of special models has been developed to explain different aspects of real-world transactions. Thus, the growth of trade in intermediate goods (as opposed to goods for final consumption) has inspired the theory of *effective protection*, which builds on the insight that an industry benefits from tariffs on its outputs but is harmed by tariffs on its inputs. Attention has also focused on the increased international mobility of factors (in part through the medium of multinational corporations) which in different circumstances may act as a substitute for or a complement to trade. Finally, considerable attention has been devoted to the study of *intra-industry trade*, meaning trade in differentiated products within a single industry category, typically produced by noncompetitive firms under conditions of increasing returns, and traded between countries with similar technology and factor endowments.

As well as attempting to explain the pattern of trade, positive trade theory also makes predictions about many aspects of open economies. Most notorious of these is the implication of the Heckscher–Ohlin model known as the *factor price equalization theorem*, which predicts that free trade will bring about the equalization of the prices of internationally immobile factors. The empirical irrelevance of this theorem is matched only by the implausibility of the many assumptions required for it to hold. Of greater interest are the predictions of international trade theory concerning such issues as the effects of tariffs and international transfers on foreign and domestic prices, the effects of trade policy on domestic income distribution and the consequences of structural change.

Turning to normative trade theory, its traditional focus has been the merits of free trade relative to autarky, stemming from increased specialization in production and increased efficiency and diversity of choice in consumption. Similar arguments favour partially restricted trade relative to autarky, although the benefits of selective trade liberalization (such as the formation of a customs union) are not as clear-cut. The persistence of protectionist sentiment, despite these theoretical arguments, may be explained by the fact that gains from trade accruing to the economy as a whole are not inconsistent with losses to individual groups, especially owners of factors specific to import-competing sectors.

Two other exceptions to the case for free trade are normally admitted. The *optimal tariff argument* states that a country with sufficient market power can gain by behaving like a monopolist and restricting the supply of its exports. The *infant industry argument* defends transitional protection to enable a new industry to benefit from learning and scale economies. As with many arguments for trade restriction, the latter on closer examination is less an argument against free trade than against *laissez-faire*. Finally, it should be noted that tariffs have declined in importance since the Second World War, due largely to international agreements such as the General Agreement on Tariffs and Trade (GATT) and the formation of free-trade areas and customs unions such as the European Economic Community (EEC). As a result, many countries now make much greater use of *non-tariff barriers* (such as quotas, health and safety regulations and government procurement policies) as methods of restricting trade.

J. Peter Neary
University College, Dublin

Further Reading
Jones, R. W. and Kenen, P. B. (eds)(1984), *Handbook of International Economics*: *Volume I*, Amsterdam (see especially Chapter 1: 'The positive theory of international trade', by R. W. Jones and J. P. Neary, and Chapter 2: 'The normative theory of international trade', by W. M. Corden).
See also: *laissez-faire; terms of trade.*

Interviews and Interviewing

The use of surveys in social science research has expanded considerably in the last three decades, and with it the practice of interviewing. The interview is one of the most central parts of the survey-taking process: it is the source of information for the researcher who has carefully designed and integrated the components of a survey. A well-designed survey starts with an overall study design, a sample that fits the needs of the survey, a carefully drafted questionnaire, editing and coding rules to summarize the data

collected, and an analysis plan. But even if these pieces are executed flawlessly, any survey can be a failure if the interviewing is poorly handled. The increased use of interviews has led to the development of multiple interviewing techniques, an improvement in methods used by interviewers, and the establishment of trained permanent staffs to conduct interviews.

Types of Interviews
In survey research, there are essentially three techniques for gathering information from respondents: mail, telephone, and personal interviews. The choice between these techniques depends on the money and time available for collecting information, the types of questions being asked, and concerns about data quality. Mail interviews are usually conducted with a small to moderate length questionnaire; questions asked in a mail questionnaire should not be especially difficult and there should be relatively few places in the questionnaire where the respondent has to 'skip' to a different series of questions. Mail interviews are the cheapest of the methods used for interviewing, but in using them the researcher gives up control over the interview process. In a carefully designed study, research should be conducted under controlled conditions so that no factors extraneous to the topic being studied can intrude on the data collection. In the case of a mail interview, the researcher cannot determine who will fill out the questionnaire if sent to a home or business, nor can he use probing type statements to obtain more detailed answers to complex questions.

Telephone interviews resolve some of these problems. The interviewer can to some degree control who responds to the questions and can probe to obtain clarification of ambiguous responses. These interviews can be more detailed than mail interviews and more complicated questionnaire designs are possible, since the telephone interviewer can be trained in how the questionnaire should be completed. One disadvantage is that telephone interviews must be kept somewhat short, usually one-half hour or less, to avoid respondent fatigue; they also cost more than mail interviews – interviewers must be paid, and there are capital costs for telephone equipment and use.

As in the case of mail and telephone interviews, personal interviews have their trade-offs. Personal interviews can be substantially more expensive than telephone interviews because of the travel costs. But there are advantages: a much more detailed and lengthy interview can be conducted with a respondent; the personal interview allows the interviewer to use printed materials like flash cards to elicit responses; the interviewer is also able to see and interact with the respondent, which can be a help in determining whether the respondent is confused by, or bored with, the questions being asked. This mode allows the interviewer the most control over the interview process.

Ranking the three methods by cost, the mail interview is least expensive, followed by telephone and then personal interviews. There are exceptions to this ordering that depend on the circumstances of the survey. But in terms of the quality of the data, the interviewer has more control of and can ask more detailed questions in a personal interview. Telephone interviews offer some control of the interview, though less than the personal, and mail interviews offer the least control and the least opportunity for asking detailed questions. Again, this ranking will not always hold true, as there are circumstances and types of questions where the respondent will be more comfortable in responding by telephone or mail because of embarrassment or discomfort in talking to a stranger.

Another factor affecting the choice between the three interviewing modes is response rates. Responses to mail surveys have traditionally been lower than those obtained for telephone or personal interview surveys. This has led to the practice of mixed mode surveys, with an initial or multiple attempts to contact respondents by mail, followed by telephone and personal contacts to increase response.

Methods of Interviewing
As in any area of scientific inquiry, the data collected in a survey need to be of the highest quality to enable the researcher to draw from them. Errors in the data, especially biases due to flaws in the collection process, can lead to erroneous conclusions in analysis. To improve further the quality of survey data, several modifications to the interview process have been introduced that increase response and enhance quality.

Two examples of these types of modifications will illustrate such improvements. The first is the use of diaries; in a broad range of surveys, from consumer behaviour to epidemiological studies, diaries have been introduced to improve the quality of the data gathered. Surveys that ask retrospective questions about behaviour frequently have problems with recall loss, that is, the respondent cannot remember all instances of a given action. To help the respondent, it is now a common practice to have an interviewer collect demographic and attitudinal information during a personal visit interview, and to leave a diary to be filled out by the respondent on a daily basis which would describe the type of behaviour being studied over a week or longer. This methodology has been especially useful in consumption studies and research on time usage.

A second method used for interviewing is an enhancement to the telephone interview. Traditional methods for interviewing have used paper questionnaires with the interviewer transcribing responses. The new method, computer-assisted telephone interviewing (CATI), uses the computer to give the interviewer questions on a display screen, and the interviewer types in the respondent's answers to be stored in computer memory. The computer controls the interview, using the responses to determine how to branch through skip patterns and providing some editing of data for inconsistent responses. Although the initial investment can be high, CATI allows for better control of the survey and leads to better quality in the data collected.

The Interviewer
General survey practice for large and moderate-sized survey organizations has been to hire and train permanent interviewing staffs. The interviewer is recognized as a skilled professional who contributes to the survey effort through his experience in contacting respondents, conducting interviews, and understanding what the researcher is attempting to study. In most survey organizations, the interviewer as a permanent staff member receives training in these skills, in methods for asking and coding questions, and in general principles of the conduct of a survey interview. For particular studies, the interviewer will receive training as to the intent of each question and the study as a whole, how to deal with difficult skip patterns, and other information relevant to the study. Many organizations have two interviewing staffs, one trained exclusively for telephone interviewing from a central location, the other a geographically dispersed group of interviewers who conduct personal interviews. These would be trained and supervised differently, since the interviewing techniques would be different.

Charles D. Cowan
Bureau of the Census
United States Department of Commerce

Further Reading
Bradburn, N. M. and Sudman, S. (1979), *Improving Interview Method and Questionnaire Design*, San Francisco.
Cannell, C. F., Oksenberg, L. and Converse, J. M. (1979), *Experiments in Interviewing Techniques*, Ann Arbor.
Gorden, R. (1975), *Interviewing: Strategy, Techniques and Tactics*, Homewood, Ill.
Hoinville, G., Jowell, R. and Associates (1978), *Survey Research Practices*, London.
Smith, J. M. (1972), *Interviewing in Market and Social Research*, London.
See also: *questionnaires; sample surveys.*

Investment

Investment can be defined as the change in the capital stock over a period of time – normally a year for accounting purposes. It is not to be confused with financial investment, which involves the purchase of financial assets, such as stocks and shares, and is, therefore, more closely connected with the analysis of saving. It is also commonly distinguished from inventory investment, which involves changes in stocks of finished goods, work in progress and raw materials.

Capital investment goods differ from consumption goods in that they yield a flow of services, over a period of time, and these services do not directly satisfy consumer wants but facilitate the production of goods and services, or consumer goods. Although some consumer goods are perishable, a large number provide services over a period of time and are, therefore, akin to investment goods. Such goods are called consumer durables. The existence of various goods that provide flows of services over time presents problems for national income accounting. This is because it is not always clear whether such goods should be classified as investment or consumer goods. Expenditure on land and dwellings, by households, is an example. In the UK such expenditures are treated as investment. Expenditure on plant and machinery is, however, clearly part of (capital) investment, since it either replaces worn-out machinery or adds to productive capacity. Gross investment is total expenditure on capital goods per year and net investment is gross investment net of depreciation – which is the decline in the capital stock due to wear and tear.

A distinction is often drawn between public investment, which is undertaken by the public sector, and private investment. Foreign, or overseas, investment involves the purchase of financial or productive assets in other countries.

A number of theories have been developed to explain the determination of investment demand. These commonly relate to private sector investment demand, since public sector investment may involve other considerations. The importance of investment lies in the fact that a rise in the capital stock of an economy may increase its productive capacity and potential for economic growth. It should be noted that the capital stock is one of a number of factors of production, along with labour and raw materials, which contribute to production and, therefore, that investment is not the sole determinant of growth. Additionally, investment is a major route through which technical progress can be made.

Public investment may be guided by principles other than narrow profit maximization, since the government should take account of social costs and benefits as well as pecuniary ones. Public investment might, consequently, be undertaken to alleviate unemployment in depressed areas or to encourage technical change. Keynesian economists have argued that public investment can be an important catalyst to economic development and may have a significant role to play in leading an economy out of recession.

Economic literature postulates that there are two major determinants of private investment demand: the rate of interest, and the increase in national income. Other factors clearly influence investment as well: these include wage and tax rates, which affect the relative cost of capital and labour. Assuming that these other influences are constant, however, it is postulated that changes in the rate of interest or national income will cause a change in the desired capital stock and that this will lead to investment.

A change in the rate of interest will influence the desired capital stock by altering the expected profitability of various potential investment expenditures. This can be seen in various ways. Firms may be viewed as forecasting the revenues and costs over the life of the project in which the capital good is to be employed. To do this they must forecast the expected life of the project, the sales volumes and prices and various costs, in each year of the project. The expected project life will depend on both the physical life and the technological life of the capital good. A firm will not wish to operate with obsolete capital goods, since it will be at a cost disadvantage relative to its competitors. Having estimated the expected future flow of profits, and any scrap value that capital good might have at the end of the project's life, the firm will then *discount* this expected income stream. If it discounts it using the market rate of interest, then it will discover the gross present value of the project, and after subtracting the cost of the capital good it will have calculated the net present value. If this is positive, then the profit is acceptable given the risk involved and the attractiveness of alternative projects. A fall in the rate of interest will lead to a rise in the net present value of various projects and will, other things being equal, lead a number of firms to want to buy additional capital goods. In aggregate, the desired capital stock will rise. Keynes explained the influence of the interest rate on investment in a slightly different manner, based on the internal rate of return, or what he called the marginal efficiency of capital. This alternative suggests that firms will find the rate of discount which equates the (discounted) expected flow of returns to the cost of the capital good. If this rate is less than the market rate of interest, then the project is potentially profitable. A fall in the interest rate should, therefore, increase the number of potentially profitable projects and hence the aggregate desired capital stock. If a firm is borrowing funds to finance investment, the interest rate represents the cost of borrowing. If it is financing investment from internal funds, the interest rate represents the *opportunity cost*, since it represents the revenue the firm could, alternatively, receive from financial investment. Such explanations of the determination of investment demand are based on an assumption of fixed interest rates, throughout the life of the project. Financial institutions are, however, increasingly lending at variable rates, and this will further complicate the investment decision by requiring firms to form expectations of interest rates throughout the project's life. It is to be noted that expectations play a major role in determining investment demand, according to this analysis, and that, consequently, a government policy of trying to stimulate investment, by reducing the interest rate, might not have the desired effect in times of worsening expectations of future profits.

A second major influence on investment demand is believed to be the change in national income. A rise in national income might increase expected sales and lead to a desire to increase productive capacity. The accelerator theory is a more formal explanation of the influence of a rise in national income on investment. It postulates a fixed ratio of capital to output, based on technological considerations, so that output growth should lead to an increase in the desired capital stock. It seems unlikely that an economy's capital to output ratio is fixed over time, since many factors will influence this ratio, such as the relative cost of capital and labour, technical progress, and changes in the relative importance of various sectors of the economy, which may have different capital/output ratios. In its crude form the accelerator theory does not perform well empirically, but in more flexible forms it is more successful at explaining investment.

It is, therefore, clear that a change in the rate of interest or in national income might influence the demand for capital goods and change the aggregate desired capital stock for the economy as a whole. The actual net investment that occurs each year in any economy depends on the rate of depreciation of capital stock, and on the extent to which the increased demand for capital stock is satisfied. This will in turn depend on the ability of the capital goods-producing industry to meet the increased demand; the extent to which the price of capital goods rises in response to the increased demand, thus raising the cost of capital goods and reducing the net present value of investment projects; and the extent to which suitable capital goods can be purchased from abroad.

Andy Mullineux
University of Birmingham

Further Reading
Hawkins, C. J. and Pearce, D. W. (1971), *Capital Investment Appraisal*, London.
Junanker, P. N. (1972), *Investment: Theories and Evidence*, London.
Maurice, R. (ed.) (1968), *National Accounts Statistics: Sources and Methods*, London.
See also: *capital theory; national income analysis.*

J

Jakobson, Roman Osipovič (1896–1982)

Roman Jakobson was born in Moscow in 1896, the son of a chemical engineer and prominent industrialist. He was educated at the renowned Lazarev Institute of Oriental Languages from which he graduated *cum laude* in 1914, and at Moscow University. His academic training predisposed him to treat language as a *functional system* rather than advocating the historical-comparative approach characteristic of the traditional neogrammarian doctrine. Moreover, following the Russian scholarly tradition, he was prepared to link the study of language with that of literature and folklore.

No less important than his formal training was the artistic milieu in which the young Jakobson grew up. As early as 1913–16 he associated with the most avant-garde painters and poets, including K. Malevich and V. Majakowskij. With other students he formed the Moscow Linguistic Circle which had an impact on the famous Russian Formalist School – and paid especial attention to the analysis of poetry as the most marked, semioticized form of discourse.

Jakobson lived and taught in Czechoslovakia from 1920 to 1939, a period which, as Morris Halle (1979) has said, 'saw the full development of his scientific genius'. In 1939, fleeing the Nazi occupation, he went to Scandinavia, and then in 1941 to the United States. He held chairs in Slavic and General Linguistics at Columbia and Harvard Universities and at MIT.

The main areas that had always captivated Jakobson's mind were: (1) the general theory of language (including poetics); (2) neurolinguistics, and (3) Slavic studies. Each of these areas he either totally reshaped or enriched with fundamental contributions.

(1) Jakobson's principal contribution to the science of language – and a turning point in the development of both modern linguistics and the science of man – is his theory of phonology. He developed his new approach in close collaboration with N.S. Trubetzkoy, and forced a revision of the concept of the phoneme, which until then was assumed to be the smallest component of language. He showed that the phoneme could be further resolved into a set of specific properties – *distinctive features*. These properties, defined in articulatory/motor/acoustic terms, are *relative* in character and form *binary oppositions* which make up the phonemic *system* of language. A phoneme as a global unit does not stand in any clear relation to another phoneme, but sets of distinctive features (such as strident vs. non-strident, voiced vs. voiceless, and so on) are the necessary and sufficient components for the specification of the phonemes of a given language. This reduction provides 'the minimum number of the simplest operations that would suffice to encode and decode the whole message' ('Phonology and phonetics', with M. Halle, *Selected Writings*, vol. I). His phonological theory contains another important principle, the principle of *markedness*. The marked member of an opposition is the member that carries more information than its partner. In this way he established the *hierarchical* nature of phonemic oppositions and of phonemic system as a whole. Another concept elaborated in this framework concerns the relation of the *invariant* to *variation*, an idea Jakobson adapted from topology in mathematics. Thus the distinctive features retain their invariant properties amidst the continuous stream of contextual variations.

These principles, which were first developed and refined in the field of phonology, were subsequently applied by Jakobson to all other levels of language, in particular to morphology, resulting in studies of the Russian case system, of the structure of the Russian verb, and of the nominal and pronominal inflections (*Russian and Slavic Grammar: Studies 1931–1981*).

Jakobson revised the doctrine of F. de Saussure and reassessed the Saussurean opposition between synchrony, that is language as a static system, and diachrony – its dynamic, developmental aspect. Jakobson regarded this opposition as false because it excluded the role of the time factor in the present moment of the language state. While Saussure considered the linguistic sign to reflect an arbitrary connection between sound and meaning, Jakobson insisted upon the close and intricate ties between the two parts of the sign. These and other aspects of Jakobsonian theory were guided by semiotic considerations. He worked also to develop semiotics as a discipline of its own, and he contributed pivotal studies to the classification and typology of semiotic systems, with special attention to language ('Language in relation to other communication systems', *Selected Writings*, vol.II). His main inspiration in semiotics came from the works of Charles Sanders Peirce, whom Jakobson considered the greatest American philosopher.

Jakobson worked on poetics all his life and found new insights into its development in the mathematical theory of information. Within this framework he built a model of language in operation in which he showed the integration of poetry and the poetic function into the speech event, and the specific role of language in poetry. He also pointed out the particular role that grammatical categories play in poetry.

(2) Jakobson's most significant contribution to neurolinguistics is reflected in the title of his study 'Two aspects of language and two types of aphasic disturbances' (*Selected Writings*, vol. II). Basing himself on the pioneering work of the Polish linguist Mikołaj Kruszewski, Jakobson showed that our entire linguistic activity gravitates around the axis of selection and the axis of combination. The two axes in question are connected respectively with the metaphoric and metonymic poles, since a process of selection underlies the metaphoric operation, while combinatorial procedures are related to the metonymic operation. The structure and function of the brain are thus reflected in the two types of discourse, poetry and prose, the metaphoric tendency being typical of the former and the metonymic of the latter.

(3) In his research in Slavic studies, Jakobson followed the same integrated approach he displayed in every area of his scientific endeavour. He held that Slavic unity is defined most importantly by the common language patrimony. This patrimony in turn determines the stock of poetic (literary) devices common to all Slavic peoples. These factors permit the reconstruction and thus the explanation of changes in national literary borrowings, convergences and coincidences. His main efforts were focused on reconstructing the archaic forms of Slavic oral and written tradition.

Jakobson's methodology, rooted in linguistics, influenced such disciplines as social anthropology, psychology, psychiatry and biology. Internationally recognized, he received honorary degrees from twenty-six universities. Several *Festschriften* all over the world were devoted to him.

Krystyna Pomorska
Massachusetts Institute of Technology

Reference
Halle, M. (1979), 'Roman Jakobson', in D. L. Sills (ed.), *International Encyclopedia of the Social Sciences*, *Biographical Supplement*, 18, New York.

Further Reading
I. Works of Roman Jakobson
(1962), *Selected Writings*, 7 vols; vol I: *Phonological Studies* (1962); (2nd, expanded edn, 1971); vol. II: *Word and Language* (1972); vol. III: *Poetry of Grammar and Grammar of Poetry* (1981); vol. IV: *Slavic Epic Studies* (1966); vol. V: *On Verse, Its Masters and Explorers* (1979); vol. VI: *Early Slavic Paths and Crossroads* (1985); vol. VII: *Contributions to Comparative Mythology. Recent Studies in Linguistics and Philology. Retrospections. Bibliography* (forthcoming); The Hague-Paris-Berlin-New York.
(ed.) (1975), *N. S. Trubetzkoy's Letters and Notes*, The Hague.
(1978), *Six Lectures on Sound and Meaning*, Cambridge, Mass.
(1979) [With L. R. Waugh], *The Sound Shape of Language*, Bloomington.
(1980), *Brain and Language: Cerebral Hemispheres and Linguistic Structure in Mutual Light*, Columbus, Ohio.
(1980), *The Framework of Language*, Ann Arbor.
(1982) [With K. Pomorska], *Dialogues*, Cambridge, Mass.
(1983), *Russian and Slavic Grammar: Studies 1931–1981*, Berlin.

II Works on Roman Jakobson
Armstrong, D. and van Schooneveld, C. H. (1977), *Roman Jakobson: Echoes of His Scholarship*, Lisse, Holland.
Holenstein, E. (1976), *Roman Jakobson's Approach to Language*, Bloomington.
Holenstein, E. (1983), *A Tribute to Roman Jakobson*, Berlin.
Waugh, L. R. (1976), *Roman Jakobson's Science of Language*, Lisse, Holland.
See also: *linguistics*; *Peirce*; *Saussure*; *semiotics*; *structural linguistics*.

James, William (1842–1910)

William James, eminent psychologist and philosopher, was born in New York City. He, his novelist brother, Henry, and his sister were the main recipients of an unusually unsystematic education supervised by their father which consisted largely of European travels and private tutors. After an interval in which he studied painting, James enrolled in the Lawrence Scientific School at Harvard in 1861. In 1864 he entered Harvard Medical School and received the MD in 1869. His life was marked by periods of acute depression and psychosomatic illnesses which occasioned solitary trips to Europe for rest and treatment. These periods, however, produced two benefits: they gave James firsthand experience of abnormal psychological states concerning which he was later to be a pioneer investigator; and they provided opportunities for extensive reading of science and literature in French, German and English. His marriage in 1878 appears to have been an important factor in improving his health and focusing his concentration on teaching and writing. His academic life was centred at Harvard where he became an Instructor in psychology in 1875 and taught anatomy and physiology. Subsequently he offered courses in philosophy until his retirement in 1907.

James's work in psychology and philosophy was interfused and is not completely separable. His greatest effort and achievement was *The Principles of Psychology* (1890) which, some ten years in writing, made him world-famous and is now regarded a classic in both fields of study. James stated his intention to establish psychology as a natural science. By this he meant that metaphysical questions would be avoided and, wherever possible, explanations in psychology should be based on experimental physiology and biology rather than on introspective procedures which had dominated philosophic psychology since Locke and Hume. In contrast to a widely prevailing conception of mind as composed of ideas, like atoms, ordered and compounded by association, James proposed that mentality is a 'stream of consciousness' including in it feelings and interests. For James, the mental is to be construed in evolutionary and teleological forms: mental activity is evidenced where there are selections of means to achieve future ends. Darwinian theory had an important influence on James's psychological and philosophical views. Ideas and theories are interpreted as instruments enabling us to adapt successfully to and partly transform reality according to our interests and purposes of action.

In an address of 1898, 'Philosophical Conceptions and Practical Results', James inaugurated the theory of pragmatism which soon became the major movement in American philosophy. He also drew attention to the neglected work of Charles S. Peirce whom he credited with having originated pragmatism. The main thesis is that the value and significance of concepts, their meaning and truth, is determined not by their origins but by their future practical consequences. An application of this view is found in 'The Will to Believe' (1896) and in James's Gifford Lectures (1901–2); 'The Varieties of Religious Experience'; it is argued explicitly in *Pragmatism* (1907) and *The Meaning of Truth* (1909). In his later writings and lectures, James refined and defended his metaphysical doctrines of the pluralistic character of reality, indeterminism, and 'radical empiricism' according to which the world is conceived as a growing continuous structure of experience.

H. S. Thayer
The City College of The City
University of New York

Further Reading

James, W. (1975–), *The Works of William James*, ed. F. Burkhardt and F. Bowers, Cambridge, Mass.

Perry, R. B. (1935), *The Thought and Character of William James*, 2 vols, Boston.

Jevons, William Stanley (1835–82)

William Stanley Jevons, logician and economist, was born in Liverpool and educated at University College London. In 1854 he emigrated to Australia to become assayer at the Royal Mint in Sydney. After his return to England in 1859 he turned to an academic career as a social scientist and held the professorship of political economy first at Owens College, Manchester, and later at University College London. His early death was the result of a swimming accident.

In the development of modern symbolic logic, Jevons had a significant part, improving on Boole's system and constructing (in 1869) a 'logical machine' which in some respects anticipated the design of modern computers. His views on scientific method, emphasizing the importance of the hypothetico-deductive approach, were set out in his *Principles of Science* (1874).

In economics, Jevons's best-known work is his *Theory of Political Economy* (1871) which earned him a place alongside Menger and Walras as one of the pioneers of the 'marginal revolution'. In it he attempted to 'trace out the mechanics of self-interest and utility', the basic elements of microeconomics, stressing that the subject required the use of mathematical techniques. But Jevons was also a notable contributor to applied economics, making pioneer studies on the effects of gold discoveries on the price level, on the possible exhaustion of British coal supplies and on the nature and causes of the business cycle. In economic policy as in economic theory Benthamite utilitarianism supplied the unifying principle for his work.

R. D. Collison Black
The Queen's University of Belfast

References

Jevons, W. S. (1871), *The Theory of Political Economy*, London.

Jevons, W. S. (1874), *The Principles of Science: A Treatise on Logic and Scientific Method*, 2 vols, London.

Further Reading

Könekamp, R. (1972–81), 'Biographical Introduction', in R. D. Collison Black (ed.), *Papers and Correspondence of William Stanley Jevons*, 7 vols, London.

Judicial Process

As studied by contemporary social scientists, focusing primarily on liberal democracies, the judicial process is the complex of formal and informal operations by which tribunals adjudicate claims based on rules putatively authorized by the regime. The tribunals are differentiated and relatively autonomous from the rest of the polity, and typically do not initiate action, but respond when a claim fit for adjudication is presented to them through an adversarial presentation of evidence and argument. So defined, the judicial process is a relatively modern inquiry, dependent upon two intellectual developments: (1) The emergence of the ideal concept of a distinct judicial function performed by a distinct institution; and (2) the rise of a science of politics that emphasizes the informal processes over formal procedures of government and which, as applied to the study of the judiciary, questions the reality, attainability and intellectual sophistication of this conceptual ideal.

Although ancient and medieval political philosophers did distinguish a judicial function from other governmental functions, these distinctions were subordinated to a more fundamental one, that between legislation and politics. 'Legislation' was regarded by the ancients as an extraordinary event, subject at most to rare and cautious amendment, while politics encompassed deliberations and actions within the framework of this legislation. Viewing God as the ultimate legislator, medieval thinkers regarded virtually all governmental functions as aspects of the judicial function. Because the law was regarded as everlasting, yet the situations to which it was to be applied were ever-changing, the judicial function, both in ancient and medieval thought, included generous elements of practical wisdom and equity as essential supplements to the more literal terms of the law.

The more carefully defined and tightly circumscribed contemporary judicial function, performed by a specialized agency, arises concomitantly with the idea of law as the enactment of a sovereign legislator, or what students of political development call the shift of authority from a traditional to a constitutional basis. With authority to make law vested in a present institution having the capacity to change the law to meet new situations, the quasi-legislative character of the ancient and medieval judicial function would threaten to derange legislative authority and offend individual rights by effecting burdens and punishments retroactively. Ironically, this rigorous subordination of judgment to legislation also required the autonomy of the judiciary from the legislature, so that courts could be impartial to the parties before it and free from pressure to interpret the law other than as the legislature intended it at the time of enactment. From these conceptual and institutional developments there emerges, then, the idealized modern judicial function as one presupposing the existence of right answers at law, performed by a tribunal with sufficient autonomy to discern these answers in the resolution of disputes. We find numerous expressions of this ideal among theorists and jurists of liberal democracy; perhaps the most frequently quoted is that of Montesquieu, who held that judges were to be 'no more than the mouth that pronounces the words of the law, mere passive beings, incapable of moderating either its force or rigour'.

Influenced by evolutionary theory, jurists and social scientists during the late nineteenth and early twentieth centuries began shifting their focus from institutional forms and idealized purposes to the 'live forces' that were claimed to constitute the underlying reality. Those who called themselves 'realists' provided the most radical onslaught on the ideal judicial function by dismissing the ontological claim of 'right answers'. In most instances, within wide boundaries, they maintained, there was no right answer to be discovered, no measure by which to assess the claims of one judge's opinion over another; what really constituted the law were the psychological traits of the judge. A distinct but related movement, 'sociological jurisprudence', emphasized not only the creative character of the judicial function, but the need to consider both law and courts in the context of their larger political and social environments.

From this odd marriage of a judicial ideal, which is implicit in the theory and institutions of liberal democracy, and this realist assessment of that standard, is born the modern study of the judicial process. Bearing a greater likeness to its realist parent, it is predominantly an empirical inquiry. Central to its study are the following: the processes by which courts are staffed, the conditions of judicial tenure, and the effect of these on judicial decisions; how rules of procedure, both formal and informal, affect the definition and disposition of issues; the decision-making patterns of individual judges, the dynamics of collective decision making in juries and on appellate courts, patterns of interaction among the courts in appellate and federal systems; the impact and implementation of judicial decisions; and the comparative competence of judicial and nonjudicial branches of government for effecting social change. Normative inquiries focus on modes of legal interpretation and, especially regarding constitutional law, the propriety of judicial activism and restraint. A long promising, but as yet underdeveloped, area is the comparative study of the judicial process, including the study of systems other than those in liberal democracies.

Stanley C. Brubaker
Colgate University

Further Reading

Abraham, H. J. (1980), *The Judicial Process*, 4th edn, New York.

Horowitz, D. (1977), *The Courts and Social Policy*, Washington, DC.

Murphy, W. F. and Tanenhaus, J. (1972), *The Study of Public Law*, New York.

See also: *law*.

Jung, Carl Gustav (1875–1961)

Carl Gustav Jung was a Swiss psychiatrist whose theories form the basis of Analytical or Jungian psychology. Concepts that Jung introduced to psychology include: the stages of life with age-related tasks, psychological types with differing attitudes (extraversion-introversion) and functions, the collective unconscious, archetypes, individuation or transformation as an aim of analysis, feminine and masculine principles, and synchronicity (meaningful coincidence).

Jung's depth psychology considers spirituality important. It is considered especially suitable for people in the second half of life, who may be well adapted but plagued by a sense of the meaninglessness of life. His psychology is also of particular value in working with psychosis, since his insights into symbolic material help make delusions and hallucinations, as well as dreams, intelligible.

Jung was a prolific writer; his *Collected Works* (1953–79) contains eighteen volumes. His theories have also had a major impact on literature, history and anthropology.

Training centres in Jungian analysis exist in Europe and the United States. Certified analysts are members of local or regional Societies of Jungian Analysts and the International Association for Analytical Psychology.

Jung's life and his theories are intertwined, as he emphasized in his autobiography, *Memories, Dreams, Reflections*, (1961): 'My life is a story of self-realization of the unconscious. Everything in the unconscious seeks outward manifestation, and the personality too desires to evolve out of its unconscious conditions and to experience itself as a whole.'

Jung was born in 1875 in Kesswil, Switzerland. A sensitive child who played alone in his early years, he mulled over questions raised by his dreams and by observations of himself and others. As a student, he was powerfully drawn to science, especially zoology, paleontology, and geology. His other fascinations were comparative religion and the humanities, especially Graeco-Roman, Egyptian and prehistoric archaeology. These interests represented his inner dichotomy: 'What appealed to me in science were the concrete facts and their historical background, and in comparative religion the spiritual problems, into which philosophy also entered. In science I missed the factor of meaning; and in religion, that of empiricism.' Later in his psychology, he would attempt to bridge the distance between these two poles.

Jung's medical studies were at the Universities of Basel (1895–1900) and Zurich (MD, 1902). At that time psychiatry was held in contempt, mental disease was considered hopeless, and both psychiatrists and patients were isolated in asylums. Jung had no interest in psychiatry, until he read the introduction to Krafft-Ebing's textbook. It had a galvanizing effect; 'My excitement was intense, for it had become clear to me, in a flash of illumination, that for me the only possible goal was psychiatry. Here alone the two currents of my interest could flow together and in a united stream dig their own bed. Here was the empirical field common to biological and spiritual facts, which I had everywhere sought and nowhere found. Here at last was the place where the collision of nature and spirit became a reality.' Jung became an assistant at the Burghölzli Mental Hospital in Zurich in 1902, which alienated him from his medical colleagues.

At Burghölzli, Jung concerned himself with the question: 'What actually takes place inside the mentally ill?' He developed the word association test, which provided insight into emotion-laden complexes, discovered that a patient's secret story is a key in treatment, and found that delusions are not 'senseless'. He became a lecturer in psychiatry at the University of Zurich, senior physician at the Psychiatric Clinic, and acquired a large private practice.

In 1903, Jung discovered the convergence of Freud's *The Interpretation of Dreams* with his own ideas. Jung had frequently encountered repressions in his experiments in word association. In 1907, he published *Über die Psychologie der Dementia Praecox* (*The Psychology of Dementia Praecox*, 1953) which led to a meeting with Freud. Jung considered Freud the first man of real importance he had encountered; Freud believed he had found in Jung his spiritual son and successor.

An idealized father-son relationship betwen Freud and Jung ended over theoretical differences. Jung could not agree with Freud that all neuroses are caused by sexual repression or sexual traumata. Freud considered Jung's interest in religion, philosophy and parapsychology as 'occultism'. The final personal and theoretical divergence concerned mother-son incest; Jung considered incest symbolically, in opposition to Freud's literal, sexual interpretation.

After the break with Freud in 1914, Jung was professionally alone. Then followed a four-year period of uncertainty that Jung called his 'confrontation with the unconscious'. In his private practice, he resolved not to bring any theoretical premises to bear upon his patient's dreams, instead asking them, 'What occurs to you in connection with that?' This method, which arose from theoretical disorientation, became the basis of the 'amplification' approach to dreams in analytical psychology.

This period was characterized by intense inner confusion and discovery for Jung. As he groped to understand himself, he became emotionally engaged in building a small villa out of stones and sticks at the lakeshore. Going about this project with the intensity of a participant in a rite released a stream of memories, fantasies and emotion. (This experience would later influence the development of sandplay therapy.)

Jung had vivid and frightening dreams, fantasies and visions, and feared that he was menaced by a psychosis. Despite his fear of losing command of himself, and motivated in part by 'the conviction that I could not expect of my patients something I did not dare to do myself', Jung committed himself to the 'dangerous enterprise' of plummeting down to the 'underground'. He kept a record of his fantasies and dreams, and painted and conversed with the figures populating his inner world. (This technique would lead to 'active imagination' as a therapy tool.) Jung's effort to understand and assimilate the meaning of his inner reality proved to be a germinal period for ideas that he would develop and write about for the rest of his life.

In 1918, the phase of Jung's intense journey inward ended, and a period of writing followed. The first major work, *Psychologische Typen*, was published in 1921 (*Psychological Types, Collected Works* vol.6). In it, he introduced his concepts of introversion and extraversion as fundamental differences in attitude, and the four functions by which experience is assessed and perceived: thinking, feeling, intuition and sensation. Through this work, he came to understand why he, Freud and Adler could have such divergent theories about human nature.

He continued to write prolifically until his death in Zurich in 1961. Everything he wrote about began as an inquiry into a subject that was personally relevant. He sought empirical data, read widely and travelled considerably. Jung remains of continuing interest to students of religion, literary criticism and humanities. There has been some controversy about Jung's supposed racial theories of the collective unconscious and his alleged sympathies with ideologies of racial superiority.

Jean Shinoda Bolen
Training Analyst, C. G. Jung Institute, San Francisco

References

Jung, C. G. (1961), *Memories, Dreams, Reflections*, recorded and edited by A. Jaffe, New York.
Jung, C. G. (1953–79), *Collected Works of C. G. Jung*, 20 vols, eds, H. Read, M. Fordham and I. Adler, Princeton, N.J.

Further Reading

Jacobi, J. (1969), *The Psychology of C. J. Jung*, London.
Storr, A. (1973), *C. G. Jung*, London.
See also: *analytical psychology*.

Juvenile Delinquency

See Crime and Delinquency.

K

Kaldor, Nicholas (1908–)

Nicholas Kaldor, Professor Emeritus at Cambridge, resembles Keynes in the breadth of his interests in theory and policy, his involvement in government (in the 1960s and the 1970s) and, of course, his membership of the House of Lords. Kaldor has made important contributions across the whole range of economic theory – capital, value, welfare, employment, trade cycle, distribution and growth. Possibly more than any other living economist, he has developed an integrated system, a vision of his own, not only of how individual economies work but also of how the world economy works. He is a genuine eclectic in that there may be discerned in his own vision the insights of Smith, Ricardo, Marx, Keynes and Kaldor's mentor at the LSE, Allyn Young. In particular, Kaldor's stress on cumulative causation – once economies get a run on (or off) they keep it up rather than revert to the pack, as orthodox economists are inclined to argue – and the importance of manufacturing industry and its dynamic effects on the growth of overall productivity developed initially from Young's influences.

Born in Hungary, Kaldor came to the LSE from Berlin to complete his postgraduate studies. He remained to teach there until 1947 when, after two years in Geneva as Head of the Research and Planning Division of the UN Economic Commission for Europe, he was made a Fellow of King's College, Cambridge in 1949 and appointed to the Cambridge Faculty as a Reader in 1952. In the early 1930s, he wrote a seminal article on the equilibrium of the firm (1934), made significant contributions to the new imperfect competition 'revolution', the new welfare economics and, in his celebrated survey in *Econometrica* in 1937, to capital theory. He contributed important papers on speculation (1939) and the trade cycle (1940) and wrote a crucial appendix (C) to Beveridge's *Full Employment in a Free Society* (1944).

In the post-war period he has been a prolific writer. First, there was his book on an expenditure tax (1955), which arose out of his membership of the Royal Commission on Taxation, Second, there is his best-known paper, 'Alternative theories of distribution' (1956), noted for his version of a 'Keynesian', that is to say, macroeconomic, theory of distribution, and for his paradoxical assumption, as a Keynesian economist, of full employment. He has also produced a series of growth models (1957, 1959, 1961, 1962) in which he examines possible relationships between investment, saving, distribution and technical advances in order to produce models which 'explain' the 'stylized' facts of capitalist economic development. His theoretical ideas have since changed 'fairly drastically' and the resulting speculations formed for many years the basis of his lectures to undergraduates at Cambridge, though he himself has 'not yet been able to present the results in the comprehensive form of a "model" ' (Kaldor, 1980). When formulated, such a model will take 'account of the crucial differences, in terms of behavioural assumptions, between the primary, secondary and tertiary sectors of the economy' (Kaldor, 1978–80).

His contributions in government, both as adviser to developing countries and his two spells in British Labour governments as adviser to the Chancellor of the Exchequer, saw a succession of ingenious schemes of taxation which were designed to restructure and revitalize the economy; for example, his emphasis on the importance of manufacturing industry as the mainspring of dynamic growth lay behind his design of a selective employment tax designed to move resources into manufacturing. Kaldor's sustained and effective critique of the Monetarists has been conducted in banter, in letters to *The Times*, speeches in the House of Lords, a selection of which has been published as *The Economic Consequences of Mrs Thatcher* (1983), and in evidence to the Radcliffe Report on the working of the monetary system (1959) and to the House of Commons Select Committee on the Treasury and the Civil Service (1980). Finally, Kaldor has played an important role in the Cambridge (England) critique of neoclassical theory.

G. C. Harcourt
Jesus College, Cambridge

References

Kaldor, N. (1955), *An Expenditure Tax*, London.
Kaldor, N. (1978–80), *Collected Economic Essays*: (1) *Essays on Value and Distribution*; (2) *Essays on Economic Stability and Growth*; (3) *Essays on Economic Policy I*; (4) *Essays on Economic Policy II*; (5) *Further Essays on Economic Theory*; (6) *Further Essays on Applied Economics*; (7) *Reports on Taxation I*; (8) *Reports on Taxation II*, London.
Kaldor, N. (1980), 'Monetarism and U.K. monetary policy', *Cambridge Journal of Economics*, 4.

Kaldor, N. (1982), *The Scourge of Monetarism*, Oxford.

Kaldor, N. (1983), *The Economic Consequences of Mrs Thatcher*, London.

Young, A. 'Increasing returns and economic progress', *Economic Journal*, 38.

Further Reading

Pasinetti, L. L. (1979), 'Kaldor, Nicholas', in D. L. Sills (ed.), *International Encyclopedia of the Social Sciences, Biographical Supplement*, vol. 18, New York and London.

See also: *Cambridge School of economics*.

Kalecki, Michał (1899–1970)

Michał Kalecki was a humble and self-taught Polish economist who worked outside the mainstream of economic theory. A most original and independent thinker, his seminal ideas have had a lasting imprint on diverse branches of modern economics. He not only anticipated the Keynesian revolution and contributed significantly to the theoretical foundations and explanation of modern capitalism in motion, but also developed the subtle device of general (expenditure) rationing to improve the range of economic choice under trying conditions of a war economy, laid the foundations for a theory of economic growth under socialism, achieved a breakthrough in perspective economic planning and in planning methodology in general, contributed to the measurement of efficiency of investment and foreign trade, and advanced research on the problems of industrializing developing nations. The range of his interests embraces the economics of capitalist, socialist and mixed economies.

Kalecki's theory of dynamics and fluctuations of national income and its partition between profits and wages is in many respects superior and more truly general than Keynes's; it is relevant to the contemporary scene and avoids many of the pitfalls of macroeconomic theory and policy. Kalecki avoided the fragmentation of economic theory into macro and micro compartments, thus providing, for instance, a critical starting point for understanding the contemporary problem of simultaneous occurrence of inflation and recession. In addition, he elucidated the dynamic properties of the economic process, incorporated imperfect competition and income distribution as integral parts of his analysis, and dealt with an open economy.

On the surface, Kalecki's economic writings appear to be dispassionate exercises in economic analyses of a highly technical nature. All of his major contributions, however, have their social and ethical underpinning. If one wanted to identify the main line of his life's work, it would surely be full employment and its composition. He was not impressed with huge sacrifices of the present generation for future ones. He was outraged at high employment contrived by means of armaments build-up. He was disturbed by the blunders of socialist planners at the cost of the worker-consumer.

George R. Feiwel
University of Tennessee

Further Reading

Feiwel, G. R. (1975), *The Intellectual Capital of Michał Kalecki: A Study in Economic Theory and Policy*, Knoxville.

Kalecki, M. (1971), *Selected Essays on the Dynamics of the Capitalist Economy 1933–1970*, Cambridge.

Kalecki, M. (1972), *Selected Essays on the Economic Growth of the Socialist and Mixed Economy*, Cambridge.

McFarlane, B. J. (1971), 'Michał Kalecki's economics: an appreciation', *Economic Record*, 47.

Kantorovich, Leonid V. (1912–)

L. V. Kantorovich, the only Soviet citizen to have been awarded the Nobel Memorial Prize in Economics, was distinguished for his contributions to the theory of optimum resource allocation. Born in 1912 in St Petersburg, he graduated in mathematics in 1930 at the University of Leningrad where he was appointed professor in 1934. His distinctions include the Stalin prize for mathematics in 1949 and the Lenin prize for economics in 1965. In 1975 he was awarded the Nobel prize along with the Dutch-born American econometrician T. C. Koopmans. It was no accident that he achieved international renown in the 1960s, for it was in that decade that Western economists were deeply fascinated by the technical problems of planning in developed and developing countries. When Kantorovich showed how the analytical techniques of linear programming could be used to improve methods of economic calculation and planning in the Soviet Union, he produced results of particular interest to the rising generation of Western econometricians and mathematical economists researching in the same field. His linear programming model, originally adumbrated in a paper first published in 1939 (and translated into English in the American journal *Management Science* in 1962), was further developed in a book on *The Best Use of Economic Resources* which appeared in 1959 in the USSR and in an English edition in London and New York in 1965. In recommending the use of a shadow price system for major products and resources as a basis for national investment strategy, and in illustrating the practical applications of his model to a variety of concrete resource allocation problems, Kantorovich made fundamental contributions to scientific economics and provided Soviet planners with a practically useful analytical framework.

His publications in English since the award of the Nobel prize include: (1976) 'Economic problems of science and technical progress', *Scandinavian Journal of Economics*, 5; (1979), 'Mathematical economic modelling of science and technical progress', in *Optimisation and Technical Progress*, 9th IFIP Conference.

Phyllis Deane
University of Cambridge

Further Reading

Johansen, L. (1976), 'L. V. Kantorovich's contribution to economics', *Scandinavian Journal of Economics*, 78.

Keynes, John Maynard (1883–1946)

The son of John Neville Keynes, a Cambridge economist, philosopher and administrator, and Florence Ada (Brown), Cambridge's first woman town councillor and later its mayor, Maynard Keynes made contributions that extended well beyond academic economics. After an education at Eton and King's College, Cambridge (BA in Mathematics 1905), his first career was that of a Civil Servant in the India Office (1906–8). Although he soon returned to Cambridge to lecture in economics (1908–20) and be a Fellow of King's (1909–46), he never lost his connection with the world of affairs. He served as a member of the Royal Commission on Indian Finance and Currency (1913–14), was a wartime Treasury official eventually in charge of Britain's external financial relations (1915–19), a member of the Macmillan Committee on Finance and Industry (1929–31), a member of the Economic Advisory Council (1930–9), an adviser to the Chancellor of the Exchequer (1940–6) and a director of the Bank of England (1941–6). After 1919, he also had an active career in the world of finance as a company director, insurance company chairman and bursar of King's College, Cambridge. Moreover, under the influence of his Bloomsbury friends, Vanessa Bell and Duncan Grant, as well as Lydia Lopokova of the Diaghilev Ballet whom he married in 1925, he played an active and important role in the cultural life of his time as a patron of the arts, founder of the Arts Theatre, Cambridge (which he gave to the City and University in 1938), Trustee of the National Gallery, chairman of the Council for the Encouragement of Music and the Arts, and initiator and first chairman of the Arts Council of Great Britain.

Keynes's reputation as an academic economist arises from work that he started after his fortieth year and published after he was 47. Prior to that, he was much better known as a publicist and commentator on economic affairs, a career he began in 1919 after his resignation as the senior Treasury official at the Paris Peace Conference with his bestselling and influential indictment of the negotiation and terms of the Peace Treaty in *The Economic Consequences of the Peace* (1919). He continued in this popular vein with *A Revision of the Treaty* (1922), *A Tract on Monetary Reform* (1923), *The Economic Consequences of Mr Churchill* (1925), *The End of Laissez-Faire* (1926) and prolific journalism, notably for the liberal *Nation and Athenaeum* (1923–31) and the more socialist *New Statesman and Nation*, for both of which he was chairman of the board. This does not mean that he was unknown as an academic: he was editor of the Royal Economic Society's *The Economic Journal* (1911–45) and the author of *A Treatise on Probability* (1921), a philosophical examination of the principles of reasoning and rational action in conditions of incomplete and uncertain knowledge, the earliest ideas of which date from 1904 when Keynes was strongly influenced by G. E. Moore. Nevertheless, it would be fair to echo Sir Austin Robinson's comment (1947): 'If Maynard Keynes had died in 1925 it would have been difficult for those who knew intimately the power and originality of his mind to have convinced those who had not known him of the full measure of Keynes' ability.'

The bases for Keynes's academic reputation as an economist were his *Treatise on Money* (1930) and *The General Theory of Employment, Interest and Money* (1936). Both were stages in the development in theoretical terms of the principles which should underlie attempts by governments to achieve economic stability. In the *Treatise*, as in the more popular *Tract*, the main concern was with monetary and price stability and the role that monetary policy alone could play in achieving them. As was common in contemporary monetary economics, Keynes dichotomized the economy into its monetary and real sectors and, on the assumption that money was neutral in the long run, looked for the principles of monetary practice which would ensure price stability, in the *Treatise* case a monetary policy which made the long-term market rate of interest equivalent to the 'natural rate' at which savings equalled investment. This initial approach to the problem was found to be inadequate by Keynes's critics, who included R. G. Hawtrey, F. A. Hayek and D. H. Robertson, as well as a group of younger economists in Cambridge (R. F. Kahn, James Meade, Joan and Austin Robinson, and Piero Sraffa). When convinced of the inadequacies of the *Treatise*, Keynes began reformulating his ideas. The major breakthrough came in 1933 when, contrary to traditional theory, Keynes hit on the crucial role of changes in output and employment in equilibration savings and investment, thus providing the basis for a more general theory than his own or his predecessors' previous work. The new theory seemed to offer the possibility of equilibrium at less than full employment, something missing in previous work. From his 1933 breakthrough, which hinged on the consumption-income relationship implicit in the multiplier, after considerable further work, everything fell into place.

During the last ten years of his life, although his activities were inhibited by a severe heart condition after 1937, Keynes devoted less time to defending and somewhat refining his theoretical views than to seeing them implemented. Even before the outbreak of war in 1939, he had started to influence Treasury thinking in Britain, while his students and his writings were becoming influential in such places as Washington and Ottawa. However, the problems of war finance and post-war planning appear to have been crucial in the spread of his ideas into day-to-day policy making, for as he demonstrated in *How to Pay for the War* (1940) the new ideas when married to another contemporary development – national income and expenditure accounting – provided a powerful new way of thinking about the economy and its management. The resulting 'new economics' put less emphasis than Keynes would have done on the roles of monetary policy and the control of public investment in the achievement of full employment, yet, along with a political determination to avoid the wastes of the inter-war years, it led to widespread official commitments to post-war policies of high or full employment. By then, however, Keynes was less involved in such matters: the last years of his life saw him devoting much more of his efforts to shaping other aspects of the post-war world, most notably the international monetary order of the International Monetary Fund and the World Bank, and to securing Britain's post-war international economic position. Gaining these, or at least a semblance of them, finally exhausted him.

Donald Moggridge
University of Toronto

Reference
Robinson, E. A. G. (1947), 'John Maynard Keynes, 1883–1946', *Economic Journal*, 57.

Further Reading
Harrod, R. F. (1951), *The Life of John Maynard Keynes*, London.
Keynes, J. M. (1971–), *The Collected Writings of John Maynard Keynes*, ed. E. Johnson and D. Moggridge, 30 vols, London and New York. (Those approaching Keynes's ideas for the first time are advised to look at volume 9, *Essays in Persuasion*.)
Moggridge, D. E. (1980), *Keynes*, 2nd edn, London.
See also: *Cambridge School of economics*; *Keynesian economics*.

Keynesian Economics

Keynesian economics comprises a body of theory and ways of thinking about the functioning of the aggregate (macro) economy that derives its inspiration from J. M. Keynes's *General Theory of Employment, Interest and Money* (1936), and from the work of Keynes's younger contemporaries such as Sir Roy Harrod, Lord Kaldor, Lord Kahn, Joan Robinson and Michał Kalecki, who extended Keynes's analysis to the growing economy and to the question of the functional distribution of income between wages and profits which Keynes himself had neglected.

There was no formal macroeconomics before Keynes. The prevailing orthodoxy was that economic systems tend to a full employment equilibrium through the operation of the price mechanism, with the distribution of income determined by the payment to factors of production according to their marginal productivity. Growth was assumed to be a smooth continuous process. The twin pillars of classical employment theory were that savings and investment were brought into equilibrium at full employment by the rate of interest, and that labour supply and demand were brought into equilibrium by variations in the real wage. Anyone wanting to work at the prevailing real wage could do so. Keynes's *General Theory* was written as a reaction to the classical orthodoxy. The debate is still very much alive. Keynesians take issue with pre-Keynesian modes of thought relating to such issues as: the tendency of economies to long-run full employment equilibrium; the functioning of aggregate labour markets; the distribution of income, and to other matters such as the relation between money and prices.

There are at least four major differences between Keynesian and pre-Keynesian economics.

(1) In pre-Keynesian economics, investment is governed by decisions to save. Variations in the rate of interest always ensure that whatever saving takes place can be profitably invested. There is no independent investment function. By contrast, Keynesian economics emphasizes the primacy of the investment decision for understanding the level of employment and growth performance. Investment determines output which determines saving, through a multiple expansion of income (called the multiplier process) at less than full employment, and through changes in the distribution of income between wages and profits at full employment. It is capitalists, not savers, that take the investment decision, and they live in historical time with their present actions determined by past decisions and an uncertain future. By the changing 'animal spirits' of decision makers, capitalist economies are inherently unstable. Keynes brought to the fore the role of expectations in economic analysis, and emphasized their key role in understanding capitalist development.

(2) In pre-Keynesian theory there is a divorce between money and value theory. Money is a 'veil' affecting only the absolute price level, not the relative prices of goods and services in the economic system. There is no asset demand for money. Money is demanded for transactions only, and increases in the money supply affect only the price level. In Keynesian economics, money is demanded as an asset, and in the *General Theory* itself, the rate of interest is determined solely by the supply of and demand for money for speculative purposes, with the effect of money on prices depending on how interest rates affect spending relative to output. Keynesian economics attempts to integrate money and value theory. Keynesian inflation theory stresses the strong institutional forces raising the price level to which the supply of money adapts in a credit economy.

(3) In pre-Keynesian economics, the aggregate labour market is assumed to function like any micro market, with labour supply and demand brought into equality by variations in the price of labour, the real wage. Unemployment is voluntary due to a refusal of workers to accept a lower real wage. Keynes turned classical voluntary unemployment into involuntary unemployment by questioning whether it was ever possible for workers to determine their own real wage since they have no control over the price level. Unemployment is not necessarily voluntary, due to a refusal to accept real wage cuts, if by an expansion of demand both labour supply and demand at the current *money* wage would be higher than the existing level of employment. There are still many economists of a pre-Keyne- 'sian persuasion who believe that the major cause of unemployment is that the aggregate real wage is too high and that workers could price themselves into jobs by accepting cuts in money wages to reduce real wages without any increase in the demand for output as a whole.

(4) Keynesian economics rejects the idea that the functional distribution of income is determined by factors of production being rewarded according to the value of their marginal product derived from an aggregate production function. This assumes a constant return to scale production function, otherwise factor income would not equal total output. More serious, since capital goods are heterogeneous they can only be aggregated once the price, the rate of interest or profit, is known. Therefore the marginal product cannot be derived independently. Keynesian distribution theory (as pioneered by Kalecki and Kaldor) shows the dependence of profits on the investment decision of firms and the savings propensities attached to wages and profits. This insight can be found in Keynes's earlier work, *The Treatise on Money* (1930), the story of the widow's cruse.

One unfortunate aspect of Keynes's economics was that, for the most part, it assumed a closed economy.

A Keynesian approach to the functioning of capitalist economies cannot ignore the balance of payments, or more precisely the export decision relative to the propensity to import. This is the notion of the Harrod trade multiplier recently revived by Kaldor and Thirlwall. Keynesian economics now embraces analysis of the functioning of the world economy, recognizing the mutual interaction between countries. What unites Keynesian economists, however, is the rejection of the facile belief that we live in a world in which the functioning of markets guarantees the long-run full employment of resources, and even if we did, that it would have any relevance. As Keynes said in his *Tract on Monetary Reform* (1923), 'Economists set themselves too easy a task if in tempestuous seasons they can only tell us that when the storm is long past the ocean is flat again.'

A. P. Thirlwall
University of Kent

Further Reading
Coddington, A. (1983), *Keynesian Economics; The Search for First Principles*, London.
Eichner, A. (ed.) (1979), *A Guide to Post-Keynesian Economics*, London.
Leijonhufvud, A. (1968), *On Keynesian Economics and the Economics of Keynes*, Oxford.
Patinkin, D. and Clarke Leith, J. (1977), *Keynes, Cambridge and the General Theory*, London.
See also: *Cambridge School of economics; capital theory; employment and underemployment; Keynes; monetary policy; money.*

Kinship

Despite the conclusion of one author that 'there is no such thing as kinship' (Needham, 1971), kinship occupies a prominent place both in the theoretical discourse of social anthropologists and in the lives of the peoples they study. Kinship is often thought to be the most difficult subfield of social anthropology, largely because of the extra effort it takes to master its specialized vocabulary, the complex arguments of its practitioners, and the intricacies of kinship systems so different from those of Western societies.

Kinship comprises that which, among other things, is initiated by marriage, is ascribed by birth, is explained or justified in terms of a biological idiom, includes the nurture and upbringing of small children, involves the use of relationship terms in a systematic way, and/or pertains to a variety of social conventions commonly thought of as aspects of kinship. Its essential characteristics are seen as primarily social rather than biological (Barnard and Good, 1984).

Most authorities agree that kinship as a branch of modern social anthropology and sociology can have little in common with the theoretical interests within psychology which emphasize biological factors in human behaviour, and even less in common with the branches of natural sciences which deal with genetics and human reproduction, although one area of overlap currently being pursued by a few scholars is in the study of incest avoidance.

Conventional anthropological approaches to kinship divide the field into three general areas: relationship terminologies, social institutions (including the family, descent groups, and aspects of residence), and marital alliance. These three areas of interest are often interrelated.

Relationship Terminologies

The study of relationship (or kinship) terminologies can be traced to Lewis Henry Morgan, an American lawyer who was the father of kinship studies. Morgan (1871) distinguished two types of kinship terminology, the 'classificatory' and the 'descriptive'. A 'classificatory' terminology, in Morgan's sense, is one such as Iroquois, which fails to distinguish all direct relatives (direct ascendants, descendants and siblings) from collateral relatives (those related through a sibling link). A 'descriptive' terminology is one such as English, which does make this distinction.

Later attempts to classify relationship terminologies added further distinctions and narrowed the frame of reference. Lowie (1929), for example, distinguished four types on the basis of classification of consanguineal relatives of the parents's generation. Systems such as our own, which distinguish direct relatives (father and mother) from collaterals (uncle and aunt), are classified as 'lineal'. Systems which distinguish parallel relatives (direct relatives and their same-sex siblings) from cross-relatives (those related through an opposite-sex sibling link) are classified as 'bifurcate merging'. 'Bifurcate collateral' systems are those which make both distinctions simultaneously, thus calling each of these six genealogical points of reference within one's parents' generation by a different term. Finally, 'generation' or 'generational' systems are those which fail to make these distinctions: they classify all these relatives by the same term or by terms distinguished only according to sex.

In perhaps the best-known attempt, Murdock (1949) took ego's generation ('ego' being the person from whom relationship is traced) as the basis for terminological classification. He came up with six types, to which he gave ethnic or geographical labels: (1) 'Hawaiian' terminologies classify siblings and cousins alike by one term (or two terms distinguished only by sex). This system is the ego's-generation equivalent of Lowies's generation system. The Hawaiians and other Polynesians, for example, do not distinguish direct relatives from collaterals, or cross-relatives from parallel, either in ego's own generation or in the generation of ego's parents. (2) 'Eskimo' terminologies, such as our

English one, distinguish siblings from cousins and are structurally similar to Lowie's lineal type. (3) 'Sudanese' terminologies, like Lowie's birfurcate collateral, give different labels to each genealogical postion. (4) 'Iroquois' terminologies, including Morgan's 'classificatory' paradigm case, distinguish parellel cousins from cross-cousins. (5) 'Crow' terminologies resemble Iroquois, but further classify father's sister's daughter by the same term as father's sister. (6) 'Omaha' terminologies similarly classify mother's brother's son by the same term as mother's brother.

At this point the uninitiated reader might reasonably ask 'Why?' Why should the Omaha of Nebraska, the Samo of Upper Volta, or the Purum of Manipur call both a particular class of cousins and a particular class of uncles by the same word? Why should anthropologists make so much fuss about the fact that they do?

The answers depend on how one sees the nature of relationship terms. The classic debate on the subject was between Kroeber and Rivers. Kroeber (1909, 1917) accused Rivers and his evolutionist predecessors of overemphasizing the sociological importance of relationship terms, which since Morgan had been assumed to reflect ancient and sometimes extinct social facts. To Kroeber, terminology was an aspect of language, not society, and reflected 'psychology' rather than sociology. Kroeber's notion of psychology comprised what would now be called the formal or structured aspects of human thought. Classes of relatives could be distinguished by sets of criteria such as generation, relative age within a generation, direct/collateral, and so on, and these criteria could be analysed independently of the system of kinship and marriage as a whole. Rivers (1914) replied with an argument that was less evolutionist than that of his predecessors or of his own earlier work, but which retained the assumption that classification was *determined* by social behaviour.

Subsequently, Radcliffe-Brown (1952) entered the debate. Like Rivers, he maintained that relationship terminology should be analysed in the context of social structure, but he did not accept Rivers's determinist explanation. Radcliffe-Brown postulated instead a functional interconnectedness between relationship terminologies and existing social facts. In his view, the Omaha call a mother's brother's son by the same word as a mother's brother because their respective social relationships to ego are similar. Both are members of ego's mother's patrilineal group, and ego behaves in a similar way towards them. Though Radcliffe-Brown is rarely given the credit, his assumptions about the nature of relationship terminology are today more or less taken for granted in the analysis of specific kinship systems.

The exception is in the field of formal analysis. Proponents of formal analysis, often refugees from linguistics, trace their intellectual descent from

Kroeber. Their concern is with the structure of relationship terminologies, rather than with their sociological implications. A number of methods have been proposed, the most enduring of which are componential analysis, as formulated by Goodenough (1956), and transformational analysis, for which the paradigm is the work of Lounsbury (1964). Goodenough's method remains more faithful to the spirit of Kroeber. It emphasizes what are variously called the components, distinctive features or significata (for example, generation, relative age, direct/collateral) which define a class of relatives. Transformational analysis, in contrast, posits the existence of primary genealogical foci to which more distant members of the designated class of relatives can be 'reduced' by the application of transformation rules. Application of one such rule, for example, allows the Omaha mother's brother's son to be 'reduced' to the genealogical position of the mother's brother. Recent work in both semantics and anthropology has debated the psychological, as well as the formal, validity of these methods.

Social Institutions

Those who study kinship in terms of social institutions take a rather different point of view. Traditionally, this area has been particularly prominent in British anthropology, but it has its American adherents as well. British interest, through men such as Radcliffe-Brown, Evans-Pritchard (in his Nuer studies), Fortes and Goody, was at least until the 1960s concentrated in the domain of 'descent theory'. Descent groups can be structured by a patrilineal principle, a matrilineal one, both simultaneously ('double', 'dual' or 'bilineal' descent), or neither ('cognatic' or 'bilateral' descent). In given societies institutions such as the inheritance of property and succession to office may or may not be directly related to descent group structure. Other notions of significance to British descent theorists have been the developmental cycle of domestic groups, complementary filiation (the relationship of a person to the opposite side of the family from which he traces unilineal descent), and the avunculate (the peculiarly close relationship, found in many patrilineal societies, between a man and his mother's brother).

In America, Murdock (1949), following earlier work by Lowie, stressed residence rules. Though he is not usually classified as a descent theorist, his work has a direct bearing on descent theory. In Murdock's view, particular environmental and cultural influences favour the establishment of particular post-marital residence rules (for example, virilocality, uxorilocality, and viri-avunculocality), which in turn lead to the formation of descent groups (respectively patrilineal, female-localized matrilineal, and male-localized matrilineal). Descent group structure, according to Murdock, is itself a determinant of relationship terminology.

Alliance

The third major area of approach of interest to kinship specialists is *alliance* (this technical term is from a French word for 'marriage'). 'Alliance theory' emerged as a major interest in the 1950s and 1960s, sparked off by Lévi-Strauss's difficult and often misunderstood book, *Les Structures élémentaires de la parenté*, first published in 1949 (revised English edition, 1969). In part, it had been anticipated by various ethnographers such as the Dutch Indonesianists of the 1920s and 1930s who had realized that the repeated practice of marriage to certain classes of kin could, and did, generate elegant structures of interrelationship between social groups and categories. Lévi-Strauss himself (1968), with apparent seriousness, has suggested that such models might well have been invented two or three hundred thousand years ago by men of the calibre 'of a Plato or an Einstein', who presumably had little else with which to occupy their minds. Today men and women of lesser genius are left to reconstruct the models in their ethnographic descriptions of Aboriginal Australian, Asian and South American kinship systems.

But what are these models? Alliance theory is centrally concerned with 'elementary structures'. These are found in societies which prescribe marriage with a certain category of relative, for example, that of cross-cousins, or often specifically that of a man's matrilateral cross-cousins (mother's brothers' daughters). This does not necessarily, or even usually, imply marriage to the actual cross-cousin or matrilateral cross-cousin, but merely that marriage is 'prescribed' to someone of such a category, a category which could include any woman of a given lineage or other unit (alliance is customarily expressed from the point of view of a male ego). Repeated marriages according to such rules create, with mathematical precision, a two-way or one-way 'flow of wives' from one unit to the next.

For over two decades after the publication of Lévi-Strauss's book, debate raged about what in fact the term 'prescription' does, or ought to, mean. Needham (1973) argued that alliance theory really involves not two levels of analysis (preference and prescription, or practice and ideology), but three – *behaviour, jural rules*, and *categories*. Whereas 'prescription' had previously been taken to refer to either or both of the last two, it should be taken to mean only the formal relationship between categories of people classified by a relationship terminology.

Alan Barnard
University of Edinburgh

References

Barnard, A. and Good, A. (1984), *Research Practices in the Study of Kinship*, London.

Goodenough, W. (1956), 'Componential analysis and the study of meaning', *Language*, 32.

Kroeber, A. L. (1909), 'Classificatory systems of relationship', *Journal of the Royal Anthropological Institute*, 39.

Kroeber, A. L. (1917), 'California kinship terms', *University of California Publications in American Archaeology and Ethnology*, 12.

Lévi-Strauss, C. (1968), 'The concept of primitiveness', in R. B. Lee and I. DeVore (eds), *Man the Hunter*, Chicago.

Lévi-Strauss, C. (1969 [1949]), *The Elementary Structures of Kinship* (translation of the 1967 French edn, London).

Lounsbury, F. G. (1964), 'A formal account of the Crow- and Omaha-type kinship terminology', in W. Goodenough (ed.), *Explorations in Cultural Anthropology*, New York.

Lowie, R. H. (1929), 'Relationship terms', *Encyclopaedia Britannica*, 14th edn.

Morgan, L. H. (1871), *Systems of Consanguinity and Affinity of the Human Family*, Washington, DC.

Murdock, G. P. (1949), *Social Structure*, New York.

Needham, R. (1971), 'Remarks on the analysis of kinship and marriage', in R. Needham (ed.), *Rethinking Kinship and Marriage*, London.

Needham, R. (1973), 'Prescription', *Oceania*, 43.

Radcliffe-Brown, A. R. (1952 [1941]), 'The study of kinship systems', in *Structure and Function in Primitive Society*, London.

Rivers, W. H. R. (1914), *Kinship and Social Organisation*, London.

Further Reading

Fox, R. (1967), *Kinship and Marriage*, Harmondsworth.

Goody, J. (ed.) (1971), *Kinship*, Harmondsworth.

See also: *descent and descent groups*; *family*; *family history*; *households*; *marriage*.

Klein, Lawrence R. (1920–)

Lawrence Klein was born in Omaha, Nebraska, in 1920. He completed his undergraduate degree at the University of California at Berkeley, and his Ph.D. at the Massachusetts Institute of Technology. After a period on the faculty of the University of Chicago, he went to the National Bureau of Economic and Social Research. He spent five years at the University of Michigan, after which – in protest against the academic implications of the McCarthy era – he crossed to England, taking a readership in Economics at the University of Oxford. He returned to the United States to take up a professorship at the University of Pennsylvania, which he has held to the present day. He was awarded the Nobel Prize for Economics in 1980.

Following the early pioneering work of Jan Tinbergen, Lawrence Klein must be regarded as the major influence on large-scale economic model building in the world over the last forty years. While that represents the peak of his achievement, he is distinguished by the breadth of his contribution to economic statistical theory, to survey work in economics and issues relating to the conduct of economic policy.

Klein's most outstanding early success was the publication of his doctoral thesis, *The Keynesian Revolution*, which provided for many the paradigm for understanding the significance of Keynes's *General Theory*. It followed in the footsteps of his tutor Samuelson in applying more rigour to the presentation and logical consequences of what were seen to be the basic Keynesian assumptions. It emphasized the properties of inhomogeneity which created the link between the financial and real sectors of the economy in the Keynesian framework.

His second phase of work in the 1950s was associated with a variety of activities reflected in his published work. In 1950 he published a major analysis of economic fluctuations in the United States, drawing on the theoretical advances associated with the golden age of the Cowles Foundation. His *A Text Book of Econometrics* was published in 1953. It was the standard work in the field for many years. But his work in the 1950s is perhaps best associated with the publication of the Klein-Goldberger model of the United States which set the standard approach to econometric model building and influenced all model builders in subsequent years. In the late 1950s when he worked in the United Kingdom he played a major role with others in developing the first econometric model of the United Kingdom.

In the 1960s Klein's formidable experience led to the first major model of the United States forecasting on a regular basis using quarterly data. Around this model and its subsequent developments and offshoots, he founded the Wharton School Forecasting Group which provided not only intellectual leadership in the model building field but also an educational base from which many forecasters and model builders world-wide started their careers. He also played a leading role in the development of the Brookings Model of the US economy, which included leading academics from several fields in the United States. In the late 1960s and early 1970s he devoted a substantial part of his time to the development of a worldwide system of analysis and forecasting based on the development of forecasting models in individual countries. This project, so-called Project LINK, resulted in a wide variety of publications by Klein and others, and its basis was described in the volume *The National Linkage of National Economic Models* which was published in 1973. Since then Klein has continued to devote himself to a wide variety of interests in economics and statistics. It is interesting to compare his starting point in

Keynesian economics in the *Keynesian Revolution* with his Presidential address to the American Association in 1970.

James Ball
London Business School

Further Reading
Ball, R. J. (1981), 'On Lawrence Klein's contribution to economics', *Scandinavian Journal of Economics*, 83.
Klein, L. (1983), *Economics of Supply and Demand*, Oxford.

Klein, Melanie (1882–1960)

Born to an intellectual Jewish Viennese family, Melanie Klein had intended to study medicine until an early engagement and marriage intervened. Then, in her thirties, when she was a housewife and mother of three, she discovered Freud's writing. Entering analysis with Ferenczi, she began an analytic career. Ferenczi encouraged her interest in analysing children, virtually an unknown procedure. In 1921, she accepted Abraham's invitation to continue her work in Berlin, and began publishing her observations on child development. After Abraham's death in 1925, she took up permanent residence in London, where she became doyenne of a distinct psychoanalytic school and the centre of a still active, and sometimes passionate, theoretical controversy.

Klein began her psychoanalytic career by developing a technical innovation – play therapy – which permitted the analysis of very young children. Klein came to believe that two broad formations successively organize the child's inner world: 'the paranoid-schizoid position' and the 'the depressive position'. While she ascribes them initially to the first and second half-year of life (an inference which has occasioned considerable criticism), Klein views these 'positions' as constellations of anxieties, defences, and object relations which are reactivated continually throughout development.

The paranoid-schizoid position is established before the achievement of object constancy. During this period, the real external mother contributes a number of quite separate figures to the child's inner world, via introjection of aspects of her in different situations. Thus there come to be 'good objects', introjected during gratifying experiences with the real mother, and eventually these images develop temporal continuity and merge. Moments of deprivation and pain are experienced by the infant as wilful persecution by his care-givers, so introjection during these states establishes sadistic, 'bad objects' in the inner world. The child's anxieties in this stage are that the persecutory objects will succeed in annihilating either the self or the good objects.

In normal development, this fantasy structure is gradually modified so that the various separate internal images of the real mother coalesce into a single object, with aspects both gratifying and frustrating, good and bad. But when the 'bad mother' begins to coalesce with the beloved mother in the child's internal psychic reality, the child comes to feel that his own (fantasized) attacks against the persecutor also damage the adored, essential good object. Guilt and mourning now develop. A new inner constellation, 'the depressive position', gradually emerges.

In addition to defensive regression ('splitting' of the internal object), the pain of the depressive position can also be temporarily assuaged through denial of the effects of one's own aggression (the 'manic defences'). But resolution of the depressive position depends on a different response: acceptance of responsibility, with attempts to repair the damaged objects. The cement for internal integration is the child's growing confidence in the reparative powers of his love.

While Klein's play therapy technique became universally accepted, her conclusions generated intense controversy and led to a schism within the psychoanalytic community. Most of the controversy concerns not the descriptive theory summarized above, but subsidiary issues – such as the timing of psychic phases in development, and the relative influence of constitutional versus environmental factors. Currently, as psychoanalysis struggles to conceptualize more primitive mental states, Klein's formulations are increasingly being integrated into the main body of analytic thought.

Alan S. Pollack
McLean Hospital, Belmont, Massachusetts
Harvard University

Further Reading
Klein, M. (1975), *Love, Guilt, and Reparation and Other Works 1921–1945*, New York.
Segal, H. (1964), *Introduction to the Work of Melanie Klein*, New York.

Knowledge, Sociology of

The sociology of knowledge, although a recognized speciality since the late 1920s, is often regarded as a rather atypical and in some respects unique sociological field, which, to a greater degree than perhaps any other area of sociology, has interested scholars in other social and human sciences.

The philosophers of the French and Scottish Enlightenment were among the first to recognize that all social differences also had social origins and were thus the result of factors subject to human control. They were aware that a wide range of social, economic and political factors shape the genesis, structure and content of human consciousness. In general, however, philosophers have attempted rather to demonstrate that a sociology of knowledge is neither possible nor desirable. Kant, for example, argued that while there cannot be perception without conception, the constitutive components of conception remain *a priori*. Similarly, empiricists of various persuasions have maintained that (scientific) knowledge is warranted by direct experience unaffected by social conditions. At best, these philosophies maintain that extratheoretical factors influence the genesis of ideas but not the structure and the content of thought. Otherwise quite different philosophies of thought shared an often explicit rejection of sociological relativism and attempted to overcome doubts by placing knowledge on a firm foundation, even outside the realm of sociohistorical experience.

Marx was a significant precursor of the field, with his theory that at least under certain historical conditions economic realities ultimately determined the 'ideological superstructure' by ways of various socioeconomic processes. This conception remains a central issue in the sociology of knowledge, and it has directly inspired some exemplary sociological analyses of problems of cultural production, for example in the works of Lukács.

Durkheim is another pioneer of the sociology of knowledge, even though he failed to develop a general model of the classificatory process. He argues that the basic categories which order perception and experience (space, time, causality, direction) derived from the social structure, at least in simpler societies. Durkheim, Mauss and Lévy-Bruhl examined the forms of logical classification of 'primitive' societies and concluded that the basic categories of cognition have social origins. But they were not prepared to extend this kind of analysis to more complex societies. Their basic assumptions have been heavily criticized, but some sociological work continues to take as its starting-point the Durkheimian proposition that the classification of things reproduces the classification of men.

Scheler is another major figure in the field. He appears to have introduced the term *Wissenssoziologie* ('sociology of knowledge') in the early 1920s. He extended the Marxist notion of substructure by identifying different 'real factors' (*Realfaktoren*) which, he believed, condition thought in different historical periods and in various social and cultural systems in specific ways. These 'real factors' have sometimes been regarded as institutionalized instinctual forces, and as representing an ahistorical concept of substructure. Scheler's insistence on the existence of a realm of eternal values and ideas limits the usefulness of his notion of 'real factors' for the explanation of social and cultural (that is, historical) change.

It was Mannheim who provided the most elaborate and ambitious programmatic foundation for a sociological analysis of cognition. Like Scheler, he extended the concept of substructure, suggesting that biological factors (such as 'race'), psychological elements (such as a 'drive for power') and spiritual and even supernatural phenomena might take the place of primary economic relations in the substructure. He conducted research into the social conditions associated with different forms of knowledge, and some of his studies are still considered first-rate examples of the kind of analysis of which the sociology of knowledge is capable. These include his studies of competition as a cultural form, of conservative thought, of the problems of generations, and of economic ambition. Mannheim believed that the sociology of knowledge was destined to play a major role in intellectual and political life, particularly in an age of dissolution and conflict, by examining sociologically the conditions which give rise to competing ideas, political philosophies, ideologies and diverse cultural products.

Nico Stehr
University of Alberta
Volker Meja
Memorial University of Newfoundland
St John's, Halifax

Further Reading

Frisby, D. (1983), *The Alienated Mind: The Sociology of Knowledge in Germany 1918–33*, London.
Meja, V. and Stehr, N. (eds) (1985), *The Sociology of Knowledge Dispute*, London.
Scheler, M. (1980 [1924]), *Problems of a Sociology of Knowledge*, London. (Original German edn, *Die Wissensformen und die Gesellschaft*, Leipzig.)
Stark, W. (1958), *The Sociology of Knowledge: An Essay in Aid of a Deeper Understanding of the History of Ideas*, London.
Stehr, N. and Meja, V. (eds) (1984), *Society and Knowledge: Contemporary Perspectives in the Sociology of Knowledge*, London.

See also: *Mannheim*; *science, sociology of.*

Koopmans, Tjalling C. (1910–)

Tjalling C. Koopmans (born in 1910 in the Netherlands; professor at Chicago and Yale) belongs to the group of pioneer econometricians who gave economics a quantitative twist. He received the Nobel Prize for this contribution (1975). Like his friend Jan Tinbergen, Koopmans studied physics at Leiden University and did statistical business cycle research at the League of Nations secretariat in Geneva. His doctoral thesis (1937) made him an authority on regression analysis. Koopmans and Tinbergen's idea is that the economy, or parts of it, can be understood by using models:

systems of equations with constant parameters that can be determined empirically. When J. M. Keynes voiced his scepticism concerning the new art, Koopmans replied with a confident article (1940) which still makes heartening reading for the friends of econometrics.

Koopmans also dealt with the rationalization of decision making. Together with G. B. Dantzig and others he developed what is called 'activity analysis' or 'operations research'. The scientist looks for systematic relationships in production, but the upshot is lower costs, a better allocation and better planning. Even the greatest sceptic must concede that this technique has great practical relevance. One characteristic example is the efficient use of a given fleet of freighters on the high seas: Koopmans played a role in solving this wartime problem. His calculations also contributed to the prompt and effective air-bridge to Berlin in 1948. Nowadays the technique is widely used, for example, in process industries, car manufacturing, shipbuilding and supplies for the military.

Some of Koopmans's articles are classics. His restatement of Paretian welfare economics in terms of activity analysis (1957), for instance, is a must for those interested in the subject, provided that they can cope with the mathematics (the theory of linear spaces). The mathematician's language may sometimes sound forbidding, but there is always great wisdom in these essays.

J. Pen
University of Groningen

References

Koopmans, T. C. (1940), 'The logic of econometric business cycle research', *Journal of Political Economy*.
Koopmans, T. C. (1957), *Three Essays on the State of Economic Science*, New York.

Further Reading

Werin, L. and Jungenfelt, K. G. (1976), 'Tjalling Koopmans' contribution to economics', *Scandinavian Journal of Economics*, 78.

Kropotkin, Peter (1842–1921)

After Bakunin's death in 1876, Kropotkin became the leading anarchist theorist in Europe. Born in Moscow into an ancient princely family, and educated at the élite Corps of Pages in St Petersburg, he served from 1862 to 1867 as an army officer in Siberia, where his geographical and geological explorations and research won him immediate acclaim. In 1871, his social conscience having been awakened, he abandoned a scientific career of great promise to devote himself to revolutionary activity. Kropotkin was imprisoned in 1874 and escaped two years later to the West, where he became greatly respected in radical circles. He spent three years in prison in France on spurious charges of sedition, and on his release in 1886 settled in England, where he remained until the Revolution of 1917 allowed him to return to Russia.

Kropotkin attempted (as Bakunin had never done) to construct a coherent 'scientific' theory of society. He argued that mutual aid, not Darwinian competition, was the fundamental law of evolution in nature and society, and that the centralized state with its large-scale production, specialization of function and coercive powers, was a temporary aberration which social revolution would sweep away. In several books (notably *The Conquest of Bread* (1892), *Fields, Factories and Workshops* (1899), and *Mutual Aid* (1902)), and numerous articles, Kropotkin outlined his ideal: a society of small communities based on voluntary co-operation, in which integration of industry and agriculture, replacing the division of labour, would give full scope to the individual's mental and manual capacities.

Kropotkin's faith in man's inherent virtue, founded on an idealization of primitive communities, seems naively optimistic in our century; but his belief in the dehumanizing effects of centralized mass production now seems prescient, and he anticipated some modern solutions to these problems in arguing for 'integral' education and small-scale economic units: hence a recent revival of interest in his works, after half a century of neglect.

But Kropotkin deserves to be remembered most as a moralist: for his inflexible opposition to the principle that the end justifies the means, his belief (exemplified by his life) that the revolutionary's personal conduct should reflect his humanist ideals, and his prophetic warnings of the dangers of despotism inherent in revolutions made for, but not by, the majority.

Aileen Kelly
King's College, Cambridge

Further Reading

Miller, M. (1976), *Kropotkin*, Chicago.
Miller, M. (ed.) (1970), *P. A. Kropotkin, Selected Writings on Anarchism and Revolution*, Cambridge, Mass.
Woodcock, G. and Avakumović, I. (1950), *The Anarchist Prince*, London.
See also: *anarchism*.

Kuhn, Thomas Samuel (1922–)

Thomas Kuhn, born in Cincinnati, Ohio in 1922, was trained as a theoretical physicist, but it was his experience teaching a course in the theory and practice of science for non-scientists that first undermined his preconceptions about science and the reasons for its special success. Under the influence of J. B. Conant at Harvard (where Kuhn took his degree), Kuhn began to explore the divergence between the idealized accounts of science produced by philosophers and the reality unearthed by research into its historical development. His subsequent work can be seen as a consistent attempt to bring the former into line with the latter. It is therefore clear why, with these preoccupations, Kuhn is one of the few historians of science to produce a general model of science.

His most influential book is *The Structure of Scientific Revolutions* (1970), first published in 1962, in which science is portrayed as an activity bound by precedent and tradition. Scientific contributions are modelled on past achievements. These exemplary achievements Kuhn calls 'paradigms'. Paradigms are not simply theories but pieces of work which embody all the elements of scientific practice within some specialized area of inquiry. They exhibit the important parameters to be measured, define required standards of accuracy, show how observations are to be interpreted, and the kind of experimental methods to be used. An example is John Dalton's *New System of Chemical Philosophy*, published in 1808, which showed how to understand chemical reactions in terms of atom to atom linkages, and how to make inferences about atoms by measuring the relative weights of combining substances. Paradigms leave many problems unsolved, and hence allow the growth of research traditions in which their concepts are refined to account for new results and applications. Kuhn calls this process of articulation and exploitation 'normal science', because it is what most scientists do most of the time. Normal science is a creative form of puzzle solving, whose difficulties are seen as tests of the ingenuity of the scientist rather than tests of the truth of the paradigm. Kuhn then argues that it is this very commitment of scientists to their paradigm that eventually brings about its overthrow. As it is pressed into service in ever more detail, the expectation of success sensitizes scientists to failures. If experimental results continue to resist explanation in terms of the accepted paradigm, a crisis of confidence may ensue. A new approach based on a new paradigmatic achievement may gain favour if it appears to resolve the difficulty and opens up new lines of puzzle solving activity. This constitutes a revolution, but the rejected paradigm will not have been decisively proven false, because no one knows what greater persistence with it might have revealed. The cycle of paradigm, normal science and revolution then repeats itself.

Kuhn's picture has two important consequences:
(1) Scientific knowledge cannot be simply 'read-off' from nature: it is always mediated by historically specific and culturally shared paradigms. This challenges our intuitions about scientific truth and progress.
(2) Neither continuity nor change in science can be understood by means of abstract rules. The coherence of normal science derives from the family resemblances between work modelled on a paradigm, and the change

of paradigm requires an intuitive judgement that cannot be fully justified by abstract and independent principles. Not surprisingly Kuhn has been charged with 'irrationalism', though he is really only challenging certain philosophical preconceptions about rationality. His position has affinities with Wittgenstein's, because we can say that each paradigm gives rise to a particular 'language-game'. In conjunction with Kuhn's stress on tradition, commitment and precedent, this explains why his work has proved an important stimulus and resource for studies in the sociology of science.

In 1961, Kuhn took up a professorship in the history of science at the University of California, Berkeley, and in 1964 he moved to Princeton University.

David Bloor
University of Edinburgh

Reference
Kuhn, T. S. (1977), *The Structure of Scientific Revolutions*, 2nd edn, Chicago.

Further Reading
Barnes, B. (1982), *T. S. Kuhn and Social Science*, London.
Fleck, L. (1979), *Genesis and Development of a Scientific Fact*, Chicago. (First published in German in 1935.) (A pioneering book in the sociology of knowledge which anticipated many of the themes in Kuhn's work and to which Kuhn was himself indebted.)
Kuhn, T. S. (1957), *The Copernican Revolution*, Cambridge, Mass.
Kuhn, T. S. (1977), *The Essential Tension: Selected Studies in Scientific Tradition and Change*, Chicago.
Kuhn, T. S. (1978), *Black Body Theory and the Quantum Discontinuity, 1894–1912*, Oxford.

Kuznets, Simon (1901–)

In 1971 Simon Kuznets was awarded the Nobel Memorial Prize in Economic Science for 'his empirically founded interpretation of economic growth which has led to new and deepened insight into the economic and social structure and process of development'. In 1977 the American Economic Assoiation bestowed on him its highest distinction – the Walker Medal – for making a real difference to the development of economics and more than once at that. He was cited as 'founder of modern national income and product measurement; designer of new systems of seasonal and cyclical measurement; discoverer of Kuznets cycles; frontiersman in economic demography; pioneer in quantitative studies of the economic growth of nations;

explorer of income distribution' (*American Economic Review*, 68, May 1978).

Born in Kharkov, Russia in 1901, educated at Columbia University, Kuznets was for many years a leading light of the National Bureau of Economic Research. He taught at the University of Pennsylvania, the Johns Hopkins University and Harvard University.

Initially Kuznets contributed to the analysis of economic time series movements (identifying fluctuations of fifteen to twenty years – the Kuznets cycles). He then concentrated on measurement of national income and product – a pivotal contribution that became the point of reference in national income accounting. His development of measures of the national income components provided the empirical counterparts of Keynesian concepts. After the war Kuznets focused on a comparative study of economic growth built on historical series of national income and product for the largest possible number of countries. In a real sense, he is the father of modern national income estimates throughout the world.

Basically Kuznets's approach to economics was influenced by his teacher, Wesley C. Mitchell. Kuznets believes that social problems can be better understood through quantitative research, but not without economic theory (see Kuznets, 1972). A meticulous and cautious scholar, his analysis of statistical data abounds with insights and wisdoms. He harbours grave doubts about formal mathematical and econometric models, owing primarily to his view of the historical relativity of economics. And he points to the failings of economics in its restricted coverage of social reality and calls for interdisciplinary research, especially in the study of economic growth.

George R. Feiwel
University of Tennessee

Reference

Kuznets, S. (1972), *Quantitative Economic Research*, New York.

Further Reading

Abramovitz, M. (1971), 'Nobel Prize for Economics: Kuznets and economic growth', *Science*, 174.

Easterlin, R. A. (1979), 'Kuznets, Simon', in D. L. Sills (ed.), *International Encyclopedia of Social Sciences*, vol. 18, New York.

Kuznets, S. (1941), *National Income and Its Composition, 1919–1938*, 2 vols, New York.

Kuznets, S. (1966), *Modern Economic Growth*, New Haven.

Kuznets, S. (1979), *Essays in Growth, Population, and Income Distribution*, New York.

Lundberg, E. (1971), 'Simon Kuznets' contribution to economics', *Scandinavian Journal of Economics*, 73 (4).

L

Labelling Theory

Durkheim declared of criminal activities that 'what confers this character upon them is not the intrinsic quality of a given act but the definition which the collective consciousness lends them' (1938 [1895]; see Becker, 1973). Most labelling theorists, however, trace their intellectual lineage to G. H. Mead (1928), although his ideas about societal definition of crime are not very different from Durkheim's. In 1931, Shaw entitled his first chapter about a delinquent, 'Labelling a Moron', but his intention was to indicate how delinquents are *mislabelled*.

The Chicago School of Sociology, of which Mead and Shaw were members, stimulated numerous studies of both the structural and interactional aspects of deviance. In Tannenbaum's (1938) study, data and analysis combined to produce the first major example of modern labelling theory. He argued that a young person's leisure activities are given opposite 'definitions of the situation' by the actor and his community. For the former, they constitute play, adventure, excitement, and so on; for the latter, they are evil. Gradually there is a shift from the definition of specific acts as evil to the definition or 'tagging' of the actor himself as evil. The actor accepts this classification and, in the company of a gang of youths similarly classified, behaves accordingly. The idea that societal reaction to deviance worsens matters was taken up by Wilkins (1964), with his concept of 'deviance amplification', while Lemert (1967) propounded the famous dictum, 'Older sociology tended to rest heavily upon the idea that deviance leads to social control. I have come to believe that the reverse idea, i.e., social control leads to deviance, is equally tenable and the potentially richer premise for studying deviance in modern society.'

The development of labelling theory has had an impact on research. Schur (1964) hypothesized that a heroin subculture was less prominent in Britain than in America, because America stamped addicts as criminals, forcing them to resort to crime, rather than physicians, in order to obtain supplies. Cohen (1972) noted how insignificant battles between 'mods' and 'rockers' were exaggerated by the media, causing other young people to seek publicity and reputation by identifying themselves as members of these groups.

Conventional criminologists denied that deviance as a consequence of societal reaction was significant.

'Radical' criminologists also attacked labelling theory, remonstrating that it distracted attention from the capitalist system, which created criminal conditions in the first place. In response, Becker (1973) discarded the term labelling, of which he had been the main disseminator, declaring himself in the mainstream of interactionist theory, which, he argued, in no way ruled out analysis of the interaction between the powerful and the oppressed.

The present state of labelling theory is confused. One group of statistical criminologists (Gove, 1975) claims to have disproved the existence of labelling effects, whereas another such group (West and Farrington, 1977) claims the opposite. Ericson (1975) and Ditton (1979) cogently suggest that more precise identification of the various mechanisms which might lie behind labelling effects is called for, rather than merely iterating rejoinders (for example Downes and Rock, 1979) to denunciatory critics.

Maurice Glickman
University of Botswana

References
Becker, H. (1973), *Outsiders: Studies in the Sociology of Deviance*, 2nd edn, London.
Cohen, S. (1972), *Folk Devils and Moral Panics: The Creation of the Mods and Rockers*, London.
Ditton, J. (1979), *Controlology: Beyond the New Criminology*, London.
Downes, D. and Rock, P. (eds) (1979), *Deviant Interpretations*, Oxford.
Durkheim, E. (1938 [1895]), *The Rules of Sociological Method*, London. (Original French edn, *Les Règles de la méthode sociologique*, Paris.)
Ericson, R. (1975), *Criminal Reactions: The Labelling Perspective*, Farnborough.
Gove, W. (ed.) (1975), *The Labelling of Deviance*, London.
Lemert, E. (1967), *Human Deviance, Social Problems and Social Control*, Englewood Cliffs, N.J.
Mead, G. H. (1928), 'The psychology of punitive justice', *American Sociological Review*, 23.
Schur, E. (1964), 'Drug addiction under British policy', in H. Becker (ed.), *The Other Side: Perspectives on Deviance*, London.
Shaw, C. (1931), *The Natural History of a Delinquent Career*, Chicago.

Tannenbaum, F. (1938), *Crime and the Community*, New York.

West, D. and Farrington, D. (1977), *The Delinquent Way of Life*, London.

Wilkins, L. (1964), *Social Deviance*, London.

See also: *Chicago School of Sociology; deviance; Mead, G. H.; stigma; symbolic interactionism.*

Labour Market Analysis

The traditional approach to the demand for labour has been marginal productivity theory, that the firm will demand labour up to the point at which the value of the additonal output attributable to its employment just equals the wage paid. With production subject to diminishing returns, the demand for labour will vary inversely with the wage. The conditions determining its elasticity with respect to the wage were formalized by Alfred Marshall: for any increase in the wage, the demand for labour will fall by less (1) the less easily it can be substituted by other inputs in production; (2) the less price-sensitive the demand for the final product; (3) the lower the proportion of labour costs in the total costs – 'the importance of being unimportant'; and (4) the less elastic the supply of other factors of production.

But in contemporary conditions the cost of labour to the employer is not simply the wages paid, even when redefined to include social insurance levies. In recruiting a new employee the firm incurs once-for-all costs in the form of agency fees, or advertising and interview expenses, plus the diversion of managerial time for his selection and introduction to the new job. The expected value of the new employee's contribution to the firm's output must cover these as well as wage-related costs. The termination of employment, moreover, is increasingly likely to involve the payment of financial compensation, making changes in the firm's work-force not only costly to effect but costly to reverse; labour is increasingly becoming a 'quasi-fixed' factor of production.

However, employees are not passive agents in the production process. In carrying out their duties they acquire familiarity with these and more widely with procedures within the firm; their productivity rises with job-experience, a process which the firm may reinforce by formal or informal training. As a consequence a current employee, particularly one with greater experience, is more valuable to the firm than a new recruit from outside.

The implications of turnover costs and on-the-job training for the employer's demand for labour give rise to a number of special features in the operation of labour markets. Faced with a change in demand of uncertain duration, the efficient strategy for the firm may be to adjust the hours of work of existing employees to avoid the expensive process of recruitment or discharge, even when the extension of hours beyond the standard work-week involves payment at premium rates. In certain contexts, therefore, the demand for hours of work and the demand for workers are separate components of the demand for labour, reflected in the tendency for fluctuations in overtime and short-time working to precede, and be proportionally greater than, changes in the numbers employed.

Additionally, the firm may engage in 'labour-hoarding', retaining experienced or skilled employees, though the fall in market demand means little current need for their services. This reinforces the widely observed tendency for employment to vary much more sluggishly than output, and consequently for labour productivity (output per worker) to rise as output increases, through fuller utilization of the work-week of existing employees, and fall with output as hoarding is renewed.

The importance of turnover costs and experience with the firm varies across groups of employees, tending to rise with level of skill and scope of responsibilities. The greatest care, and expense, in recruitment typically occurs at managerial level, where poor appointments are most damaging. These differences in costs are reflected in the greater stability of employment among managerial and skilled personnel, and the greater frequency of discharges among the less skilled.

Employers have developed a variety of arrangements to minimize turnover by making the employee's experience and seniority directly valuable to him, for example, job ladders with promotions only from among existing workers and with seniority a major criterion; holiday and pension entitlements based on years of service; a redundancy policy of last-in-first-out. These practices have been widely discussed as the 'internal labour market'.

Since the development of demography as a separate discipline, economists' analysis of labour supply tends to start not with population but with participation, the numbers out of any population who are members of the labour force. Unlike labour demand, where economic factors dominate, labour supply is also importantly influenced by wider aspects of the structure of society.

Economic analysis of participation sets the decision in the context of household choice in the use of members' time, where the main alternatives are paid employment outside the home ('market time') and household duties or leisure ('non-market time'). A rise in the wage has two effects on the household supply of labour: it raises the level of income obtained from any given number of hours of work, encouraging an increased demand for leisure as an expression of the higher standard of living (the income effect on labour supply); on the other hand, a rise in the return to market time raises the opportunity cost, in terms of foregone earnings, of non-market time, making this less attractive (the substitution effect). The net effect of a rise in wages on household labour supply is thus ambiguous. Moreover, the changing profile of labour supply over recent decades has been dominated by variations in participation among women which are largely influenced by the greatly reduced burden of work in the home, the smaller size of families, the extension of education among women and evolving social attitudes.

The incidence of formal education contributes an important qualitative dimension to labour supply. Education constitutes 'investment in human capital' undertaken partly by the state and partly by the individual. Unlike on-the-job training which tends to be firm-specific, formal education provides a general training which is highly transferable between employers, requiring public provision for collective social benefit. Where an individual chooses to continue formal education beyond compulsory schooling, he incurs tuition-related costs and, more importantly, the loss of potential earnings over the period; these costs constitute an investment in himself, to be recouped from his enhanced earnings potential over the remainder of his working life. The impact of education is most marked on the relative supply of labour to different occupations, and hence on pay differentials; the reduction in the overall inequality of earnings is a striking labour-market consequence of the expansion of education in the course of this century.

The level and structure of wages play a central role in balancing demand and supply in labour markets, but the limited flexibility of wages and the complexity of the relationships bring further adjustment processes into play. Typically unemployment and unfilled vacancies coexist. Even at a given wage rate, jobs offered by employers differ in many dimensions – security of employment, promotion prospects, the work environment – the 'net advantages' originally discussed by Adam Smith. Similarly, individuals seeking jobs differ in personal attributes sought by employers, as well as in their own preferences. Hence the process of search, seeking an acceptable match of worker with job, is conducted on both sides. Some of the unemployment among younger-age workers in particular takes the form of repeated spells of short duration, reflecting a process of job-sampling. Longer duration unemployment, however, represents a more profound labour market disequilibrium.

The operation of labour markets has also created the trade union. In most countries, labour has sought to redress the inequality of power between the employer and the individual employee by forming trade unions for the purpose of collective bargaining over wages and working conditions.

Mary B. Gregory
St Hilda's College, Oxford

Further Reading
Rees, A. (1973), *The Economics of Work and Pay*, New York.
King, J. E. (ed.) (1980), *Readings in Labour Economics*, Oxford.
See also: *employment and underemployment*; *productivity*.

Labour Relations

Labour relations, or industrial relations, are the terms most commonly used to refer to study of the social relations between employers and employees, management and workers, or their representatives. These relations have attracted the interest of those with a variety of disciplinary backgrounds – economics, history, law, political science, psychology and sociology, as well as students of business and management or of labour movements; consequently the study of labour relations has always been multidisciplinary. Each of these disciplines has tended to see different aspects of labour relations as problematic: economists, for example, have been interested particularly in the determination of the price of labour, lawyers in the possibilities and limitations of legal regulation, and sociologists in the nature and consequences of industrial conflict. Much of the research and writing on labour relations, however, has been descriptive, concerned with elucidating often very complex social situations, and drawing on and contributing to the various disciplines in a fairly atheoretical way.

The most notable attempts to establish the study of labour relations as an intellectual discipline in its own right have been those within a 'systems' framework (Dunlop, 1958). In an important contribution, Flanders (1970), for example, argued that the system of industrial relations constituted 'a system of rules' (legislation, collective agreements, custom and practice, and so on), regulating the relations between the enterprise and its employees, and among employees; and that the study of industrial relations could be described as 'the study of the institutions of job regulation'. Such claims to disciplinary independence have not been widely accepted, though industrial or labour relations is often the concern, and title, of separate university departments or research institutes; but in a more descriptive sense the notion of an industrial relations 'system' has been very influential.

The ways in which labour relations are analysed and interpreted depend in crucial respects on the 'frame of reference' adopted (Fox, 1966, 1973). A *unitary* perspective conceives of the industrial enterprise as a team in which all have the same underlying interests in commercial success. Symptoms of conflict, such as strikes or grievances, are attributed to inadequate management and/or to workers' irrationality, and there is no agreed place for trade unions or other interest groups. A *pluralist* perspective acknowledges that different sectional groups within the enterprise have legitimately conflicting interests, particularly in the outcome of the market relations which determine wages and in the exercise of managerial authority over employees. These conflicts of interest are manifest in a variety of ways, through 'organized' action (strikes, lock-outs, working to rule) and 'unorganized' individual behaviour (absence, sabotage); but such conflicts can be contained within procedures for negotiation and bargaining which produce acceptable compromises. A *radical* perspective, which draws heavily on Marxist social theory (Hyman, 1975), emphasizes that the relations between capital and labour are inherently asymmetrical and exploitative; labour relations are class relations and the interests of the subordinate, working, class can only be realized by a fundamental transformation of the whole pattern of ownership and control of industry. Few social scientists now adopt a unitary perspective, but debates between adherents of the other two approaches continue unabated.

Richard K. Brown
University of Durham

References

Dunlop, J. T. (1958), *Industrial Relations Systems*, New York.

Flanders, A. (1970), *Management and Unions*, London.

Fox, A. (1966), 'Industrial sociology and industrial relations', *Research Paper* no. 3, Royal Commission on Trade Unions and Employers' Associations, London.

Fox, A. (1973), 'Industrial relations: a social critique of pluralist ideology', in J. Child (ed.), *Man and Organisation*, London.

Hyman, R. (1975), *Industrial Relations: A Marxist Introduction*, London.

Further Reading

Clegg, H. A. (1979), *The Changing System of Industrial Relations in Great Britain*, Oxford.

Hyman, R. (1977), *Strikes*, Glasgow.

Nichols, T. (ed.) (1980), *Capital and Labour*, Glasgow.

See also: *industry, sociology of; industrial democracy; labour market analysis*.

Labour Theory of Value

The labour theory of value is one of the two main intellectual traditions concerned with the issues of the social nature of, as well as the magnitude of prices, in a market, capitalist economy. The other tradition is the utility (or subjective) theory, in which prices are seen as reflecting peoples' subjective feelings of utility, or strengths of subjective preferences. In contrast to the subjective or utility approach, theorists in the labour theory of value tradition see prices as reflecting the social production process generally, and more specifically as reflecting the role of labour in the production process.

Some version or another of the labour theory was espoused by most of the classical economists, who dominated economic thinking from the last quarter of the eighteenth century through the first half of the nineteenth century. Among the classical economists, Adam Smith and David Ricardo were particularly important in developing the theory. From the 1840s until his death, Karl Marx espoused and significantly developed the labour theory of value, and since his death, it has been primarily, although not exclusively, associated with Marxian economics.

Adam Smith argued that in a market society where workers owned their own means of production, prices of commodities would tend to be proportional to the quantities of labour required to produce the commodities. If the price of a particular commodity rose to a level higher than proportional to this labour input, then producers of other commodities could gain by switching to the production of the commodity in question. This self-interested switching of producers would soon create an excess supply of the commodity in question and a shortage of all other commodities. Market competition would lead to a reduction of the price of the commodity in excess supply and to increases in the prices of the other commodities for which shortages existed. This process would continue until the prices were proportional to the quantities of labour. At that point, there would be no incentive for producers to switch to the production of other commodities and therefore no market pressures for prices to change.

Smith noted, however, that all of this would change when a class of people who do not produce acquired ownership of the means of production, and workers without such means were hired to do the producing. Competition among capitalists would tend to establish a general, average, society-wide rate of profit. By abandoning low profit industries and gravitating toward high profit industries, capitalists' competitive, self-interested behaviour would push the rates of profit in each industry towards this general average profit rate. Therefore, prices would tend to that level at which the capitalist could pay his workers' wages and have enough remaining profit to yield the social average return on his fund of capital. For such prices to be proportional to quantities of labour involved in production, it would be necessary that for any given industry the ratio of the value of capital on which profit is received to the quantity of labour expended in production be identical to that same ratio in every other industry. Otherwise, a profit mark-up that yielded equal rates of return on all capital among all industries would render prices disproportional to labour expended. Smith observed that the ratios of capital to labour are very different from industry to industry. He concluded that private ownership of the means of production by an unproductive capitalist class rendered the labour theory of value a relatively poor approximation of reality.

David Ricardo accepted the fact that unequal ratios of capital to labour would yield prices that were not strictly proportional to quantities of labour. He argued, however, that (1) the deviations from proportionality would be slight and of little importance, and (2) the direction as well as the magnitude of the deviations could be scientifically explained. Therefore, he defended the labour theory of value as a scientific explanation of prices in a capitalist, market society.

Karl Marx argued, however, that the deviation of prices from proportionality could be quite substantial. He believed that this accounted for the inability of most businessmen as well as most economic theorists to see the connections between labour and prices. There were, he asserted, two separate connections: qualitative and quantitative.

The 'qualitative connection' referred to Marx's conception of labour in capitalism. Wage labour was seen as private and not social, thus reflecting the fact that in capitalism there was no conscious, rational control of human productive interdependence. This interdependence was controlled by the blind forces of market supply and demand. Private labour therefore became social labour, Marx argued, only when it appeared in the form of the exchange value of the commodity produced by the labour. Prices were the external visible form of social labour in capitalism in Marx's view.

With this conception of prices Marx was able to prove that surplus value was created by surplus labour. Surplus labour was defined as that labour performed in excess of the amount of labour embodied in the goods and services the worker purchases with his wages, and surplus value equalled the value of the product created by labourers minus the value of the commodities labourers could purchase with their wages. When labourers produced surplus value they were said to be exploited. Profit, interest and rent were all the outcome of the exploitation of labour.

The 'quantitative connection' between labour and prices in Marxian economics has come to be known as the 'transformation problem' or the problem of transforming quantities of labour into prices.

The labour theory of value remains today the principal alternative to the dominant orthodoxy of the subjective or utility theory of value.

E. K. Hunt
University of Utah

Further Reading
Meek, R. (1973), *Studies in the Labour Theory of Value*, London.

Hunt, E. K. (1979), *History of Economic Thought, A Critical Perspective*, Belmont, California.
See also: *Marx's theory of history and society*; *Marxian economics*.

Labour Unions

See Trade Unions.

Lacan, Jacques (1901–83)

Jacques Lacan has been called the 'French Freud'. He was probably the most original and certainly the most controversial European psychoanalyst of the post-Second World War era. Lacan was a scathing critic of the 'American' developments in psychoanalysis which moved away from Freud's unconscious to what was called 'ego psychology'. In America, psychoanalytic therapy focused on forming an alliance with the healthy ego, interpreting pathological defences, and promoting the growth of conflict-free adaptation. Lacan entirely rejected this approach. There was, in his view, no conflict-free sphere: the 'ego' was hostile to the unconscious and the essential analytic process. Analysis was an inquiry, not a cure. Lacan, in his characteristic play-on-words style, described American empirical research intended to make psychoanalysis an experimental science as 'ex-peri-mental' (that is, ex-mental and peri-mental). To Lacan, such research with animals left out the mental, because the mental has to do with language, meaning and signification.

Lacan regarded Freud's early and introspective works such as *The Interpretation of Dreams* (1913) as the essence of psychoanalysis. Lacan theorized that the unconscious is structured as a natural language; psychoanalysis, as a theory and as a therapy, was the discovery of this other language by recapturing associative chains of signification. An example of Lacan's theoretical emphasis on linguistics is his reinterpretation of the Oedipal complex. In greatly oversimplified terms, he believed it encompasses the child's movement from the order of images to the order of polysemic symbols. Lacan describes the infant's mental life as beginning in a mirror phase, like Narcissus by the stream seeing reflected images. When language and symbols are acquired, these images are mediated, their signification changes, and the infant becomes a divided subject. The unconscious is 'The Other' and the other language. The hydraulic and mechanistic theories of Freud are replaced in Lacan by a linguistic theory, for example, repression as metaphor formation.

Lacan's writing is arcane, convoluted, technical, poetic and difficult. Existentialist, neo-Hegelian and linguistic theories all influenced Lacan as much as did Freud. Lacan's later work became even more difficult as he emphasized the centrality of topology and mathematics to his theories.

Lacan became a central figure in French intellectual and radical thought, and was of particular interest to literary and social criticism in the West. Whatever Lacan's place may be in the history of modern thought, he was rejected by organized psychoanalysts because of his clinical methods. Most notable was his practice of dismissing patients after 5- or 10-minute sessions because, he said, they had nothing interesting to say or they were getting into a routine which silenced the unconscious. Lacan, in turn, attacked the psychoanalytic establishment which sought to 'authorize' those who would be analysts. Lacan claimed that analysis was a calling and the analyst must authorize himself.

Alan A. Stone
Harvard University

Further Reading
Bär, E. S. (1974), 'Understanding Lacan', in *Psychoanalysis of Contemporary Science*, vol. 3, New York.
Lacan, J. (1966), *Ecrits*, Paris. (English translation, *Ecrits*, London, 1977.)
Schneiderman, S. (1983), *Jacques Lacan: The Death of an Intellectual Hero*, Cambridge, Mass.

Laffer Curve

The Laffer curve, named after Arthur Laffer, an economic adviser to President Reagan, is a relationship between the tax rate and total tax receipts received by the tax authority. It arises from the fact that if the tax rate is zero then the government will receive no tax revenue; if the tax rate is one hundred per cent then there is no incentive at all for people to work and earn, and so the tax base is zero and again the government will receive no tax revenue. These observations indicate that there is some intermediate tax rate, t^* say (between zero and one hundred per cent), at which tax receipts will be a maximum. Laffer and others drew the implication that if the tax rate were below t^* then lowering tax rates would reduce government tax receipts, but if the tax rate were above t^* then reducing the tax rate would lead to a rise in tax receipts. This became the basis for arguing in favour of reducing tax rates. The incentive effect of so doing, so it is argued, would raise tax revenue. To date, the Laffer curve has very little foundation in economic theory and is more of an *ex post* observation. Any such relationship between tax rates and tax receipts will depend on the tax structure, the tax base and the progressivity of the tax system. Furthermore, there is no basis for assuming the curve has only one maximum and that it has a regular shape. Even so, it has been invoked in policy discussion as an essential element in 'supply-side economics'.

Ronald Shone
University of Stirling

Further Reading
Hemming, R. and Kay, J. A. (1980), 'The Laffer curve', *Fiscal Studies*, 1.

Laing, Ronald David (1927–)

The philosopher Kant wrote, 'The only general characteristic of Insanity is the loss of a sense of ideas that are common to all and its replacement with a sense for ideas peculiar to ourselves.' The question remains, however, how does one decide which *peculiar ideas* are delusions? R. D. Laing, born in Glasgow in 1927, began his career as a psychiatrist by attempting to make the *peculiar ideas* of schizophrenic patients (which he assumed were delusions) comprehensible. But in his subsequent work as a psychiatrist-philosopher he concluded that normality, 'the ideas that are common to all', is madness and, therefore, a psychiatry founded on such ideas was unable to declare any beliefs delusions.

Laing, his critics would say, went further than this epistemological relativism; he romanticized insanity and particularly schizophrenia. Madness became a breakthrough, a way of being in the world that rejects the 'pseudo-social' reality, the most awesome psychedelic trip.

Laing's early writings are both psychoanalytic and existential in character, as he attempted to portray the subjective experience of the schizophrenic. There are brilliant descriptions of the divided self unable to be a 'whole person with the other'. Perhaps most powerful are his descriptions of the family interactions out of which comes 'schizophrenic disorder'. It is the family that seems mad in Laing's description, and the patient's delusions and 'bizarre communication' are explained as a symbolic and visionary commentary on that family's madness (Laing and Esterson, 1964). His subsequent writings are less detailed, more prophetic in tone. The schizophrenic experience becomes a divination of the madness of society, not to be cured by drugs or to be interfered with by psychiatrists but perhaps to be learned from. As one of Laing's critics noted, 'Schizophrenia became a State of Grace.' Laing's writings were seized upon by the radical critics of psychiatry and by other radicals seeking liberation during the late 1960s and the 1970s. Laing's influence in psychiatry was short-lived. He turned to mysticism and poetry as his own liberation. In *The Politics of Experience* (1967) he wrote, 'True sanity entails in one way or another the dissolution of the normal ego, that false self competently adjusted to our alienated social reality: the emergence of the "inner" archetypal mediators of divine power, and through this death a rebirth, and the eventual re-establishment of a new king of ego-functioning, the ego now being the servant of the divine, no longer its betrayer.'

Alan A. Stone
Harvard University

References
Laing, R. D. (1967), *The Politics of Experience*, London.
Laing, R. D. and Esterson, A. A. (1964), *Sanity, Madness and the Family*, London.

Further Reading
Laing, R. D. (1959), *The Divided Self*, London.

Laissez-Faire

According to one careful commentator, 'one man's *laissez-faire* is another man's intervention. . . . *Laissez-faire* is in the eye of the beholder: it depends on who he is and where he looks' (Taylor, 1972). Unfortunately this variety of standpoints and interpretations can be found among scholars as well as propagandists. The origin of the concept is usually traced to a seventeenth-century French businessmen's protest against state interference, and it flourished most vigorously among nineteenth-century French, British and American liberals. As a general notion, *laissez-faire* connotes distrust and hostility to government intervention, but it is frequently employed indiscriminately as a description of economic, social and administrative ideas and policy, even of a specific historical era.

The French physiocrats and British classical economists, from Adam Smith onwards, are usually viewed as the leading intellectual spokesmen for *laissez-faire*, whose ideas directly shaped and even dominated nineteenth-century British and American economic and social policy. However, modern historians of economics (for example, Viner, 1927, 1960; Gordon, 1968; Robbins, 1952; Coats, 1971; Samuels, 1966) have conclusively demonstrated that this view is erroneous. Smith and his successors were by no means doctrinaire opponents of state intervention, although Martineau, Wilson, Spencer, and Sumner, and, more recently, von Mises and Friedman, do fall into this category. The classical economists' anti-interventionism was carefully qualified, and increasingly so as time passed. With respect to practice, for example in 1830s England, 'the generation reared in *laissez-faire* doctrines' was systematically engaged in laying 'the foundations of modern collectivism' (Taylor, citing Deane, 1965).

In this century the *laissez-faire* concept is anachronistic, despite a recent revival of anti-interventionist sentiment, for the most important issues concerning the economic and social role of government are questions of degree, not of kind.

A. W. Coats
University of Nottingham
Duke University

References
Coats, A. W. (ed.) (1971), *The Classical Economists and Economic Policy*, London.
Deane, P. (1965), *The First Industrial Revolution*, Cambridge.
Gordon, H. S. (1968), 'Laissez-faire' in *International Encyclopedia of the Social Sciences*, vol. 8, London and New York.
Robbins, L. C. (1952), *The Theory of Economic Policy in Classical Political Economy*, London.
Samuels, W. (1966), *The Classical Theory of Economic Policy*, Cleveland.
Taylor, A. J. (1972), *Laissez-Faire and State Intervention in Nineteenth-Century Britain*, London.
Viner, J. (1927), 'Adam Smith and laissez-faire', reprinted in J. Viner (ed.), *The Long View and The Short, Studies in Economic Theory and Policy*, Glencoe, Ill., 1958.
Viner, J. (1960), 'The intellectual history of laissez-faire', *Journal of Law and Economics*, vol. 3.

Further Reading
Fine, S. (1956), *Laissez-Faire and the General-Welfare State: A Study of Conflict in American Thought, 1865–1901*, Ann Arbor.
See also: *free trade*; *physiocratic thought*; *Smith*.

Land

Economists traditionally classify factors of production into land, labour and capital. The classical economists – notably, Adam Smith, David Ricardo and John Stuart Mill – attached particular significance to land, as, indeed, the pre-eminence of agriculture at the time warranted. They devoted considerable attention to the implications for the growth and distribution of income of a limited supply of land, combined with diminishing returns in agricultural production. The legitimacy of rents accruing to landowners was also challenged. In particular, Mill, accusing landowners of growing rich as a result of the general progress of society rather than as a result of their own efforts, proposed a scheme for taxing such 'unearned increments'.

The tripartite classification of productive factors, whilst possessing the attraction of expositional convenience, is an uneasy one. Ricardo defined land as 'the original and indestructible powers of the soil'. However, few of the productive powers of land are unambiguously free gifts of Nature; most land has physical and human capital improvements inseparably embodied in it. Moreover, the productive properties of the soil can be, and in places have been, eroded by inappropriate forms of cultivation.

Under neoclassical economics, land has lost the special significance it previously enjoyed. A major reason for this is that land has declined in relative importance as a factor of production in developed economies. Nevertheless, there are still many countries where the ownership of land confers extensive economic, social and political powers. Moreover there has in recent years been renewed pessimism over the possible limits to growth in all countries implied by finite natural resources.

J. M. Currie
University of Manchester

Further Reading
Barlowe, R. (1978), *Land Resource Economics*, 3rd edn, Englewood Cliffs, N.J.
Mill, J. S. (1886 [1848]), *The Principles of Political Economy*, London.
Ricardo, D. (1951), *The Principles of Political Economy and Taxation*, in P. Sraffa and M. H. Dobb (eds), *The Works and Correspondence of David Ricardo*, vol. 1, Cambridge.
See also: *land tenure*; *Ricardo*

Land Tenure

The broad term, land tenure, refers to the relationships betwen individuals and groups in respect of land. The basic rights over land enjoyed by individuals or groups involve rights to use, to exclude others from use, to lease, and to alienate by gift, bequest or sale. However, systems of land tenure differ significantly from society to society; certain types of property rights familiar in one society may be meaningless in another. Moreover, whether based on customary practice, on contract or on legislation, systems of proprietary rights and obligations are usually extremely complex, with several individuals or groups frequently having rights over the same tract of land.

The system of land tenure in a society invariably depends both on the scarcity of land and on the predominant forms of land use. Rights and obligations are much more explicit when land is scarce and where more time is required to reap the fruits of labour expended on the land. In 'primitive' societies practising shifting cultivation, there is seldom any concept of individual 'ownership' of land. An individual household has an inalienable right of access to a share of the community's land and an exclusive right to use whatever land is allocated to it, a use-right which, however, is conditional on actual use.

Even in societies where individuals can own land, rights are typically conditional, not absolute. Indeed, during the present century, there has been in most Western economies a proliferation of statutory controls over changes in land use. Furthermore, freedom of contract has increasingly been restricted by legislation defining in considerable detail the respective rights and obligations of landlords and tenants.

J. M. Currie
University of Manchester

Further Reading
Becker, L. C. (1977), *Property Rights: Philosophic Foundations*, London.
Currie, J. M. (1981), *The Economic Theory of Agricultural Land Tenure*, Cambridge.
See also: *agricultural economics*; *land*.

Language

Language is the most human of all human abilities. It may be the defining characteristic of *Homo sapiens*. Wherever humans exist, language exists. Although no one knows the precise number of languages in the world today, there are at least 3,000 and as many as 8,000 according to different estimates and depending on one's definition of 'language' and 'dialect'. Considering that the world is populated by billions of people, the number is actually rather small. One half of the world's population (approximately 2,100,000,000) speak only fifteen of these thousands of languages. Of these, more of the world's population speak Mandarin Chinese than any other language (about 387,000,000). There are just a few speakers of languages like Apache, an Athabaskan language, or Menomini, an Algonquian language. These languages seem very different from each other and from Zulu, Lapp, Hebrew, Uzbek or English. Yet, despite these 'surface' differences, all human languages are governed by universal properties and constraints, a fact that was understood as early as the thirteenth century by Roger Bacon who pointed out that, 'He that understands grammar in one language, understands it in another as far as the essential properties of grammar are concerned.' The similarities of human languages go beyond the spoken languages and include the sign languages used by deaf persons throughout the world. Research on these sign languages show that although gestures instead of sounds are utilized, and the visual perceptual system instead of the auditory system for comprehension, their systems of units, structures and rules are governed by the same underlying principles as are spoken languages.

All human languages are equally complex and equally capable of expression. There are no so-called primitive languages. If one can say something in one language, the same thought can be expressed in another although the form of expression may differ. The vocabulary, that is, the inventory of sound (or gesture)/meaning units of every language, can be expanded to include new words or concepts through borrowing words from another language, through combining words to form compounds such as *bittersweet* or *pickpocket*, through blending words together, such as *smog* from *smoke* and *fog*, through neologisms or the coining of new words, a common practice of manufacturers of new products, by the use of acronyms – words derived from the initial of several words such as *radar* from *Radio Detecting And Ranging*. Abbreviations of longer words or phrases may also become lexicalized as exemplified by *ad* for *advertisement*, and proper names may be used as common terms, such as *sandwich*, named from the fourth Earl of Sandwich in England who, it is reported, ate his food between slices of bread so that he need not take time off from gambling to eat in normal fashion. Although these examples are all from English, all languages can expand vocabularies in similar fashion, as is shown by compounds such as *cure-dent* ('toothpick') in French, *Panzerkraftwagen* ('armoured car') in German, or *četyrexetažnyi* ('four-storied') in Russian. In Akan, a major language spoken in Ghana, the word meaning 'son' or 'child – *Ɔba* – is combined with *Ɔhene* which means 'chief' to form the compound *Ɔheneba* meaning 'prince'.

One common or universal characteristic of all languages is that the form of vocabulary items is for the most part arbitrarily related to its referent or meaning. Thus, the word meaning 'house' in English is *house*, in French is *maison*, in Spanish is *casa*, in Russian is *dom* and in Akan is *Ɔdaŋ*.

All human languages utilize a finite set of discrete sounds (or gestures) like 'c', 'm', 'a' and 't' which can be defined by a finite set of phonetic (or gestural) properties or features. The vowel and consonant sound segments combine to form meaningful units like *cat* or *mat* called *morphemes*. Some words consist of just one morpheme; others are complex 'morphological' units. That is, simple morphemes can be combined to form words like *cats* or *catlike*. Each language has specific constraints on word formation. In English one can add *un-* as a prefix to negate the meaning of a word, as in *unlikely* or *unfortunate*, but cannot add it at the end as a suffix; *likelyun* and *fortunateun* are not words in English, nor are the units formed by prefixing the suffixes *-ly* or *-ate* as in *lylike* or *atefortune*.

Just as in word formation, there are constraints or rules which determine how words can be combined to form sentences. *The cat is on the mat* means something different from *The mat is on the cat*, and *cat the on is mat the* means nothing since the words are not combined according to the syntactic rules of English.

The syntactic rules in every language are similar kinds of rules although they may differ in specific constraints. Thus, in English, adjectives usually precede the nouns they modify (as in *the red house*) whereas in French they usually follow (as in *la maison rouge*). But in all languages these rules of syntax include

a principle of recursion which permits the generation of an infinite set of sentences. We know that this is so since any speaker of any language can produce and understand sentences never spoken or heard previously. This recursive aspect is also revealed by the fact that, in principle, there is no longest sentence in any language; one can keep adding additional words or phrases or conjoin sentences with words like *and* or *but* or relative clauses, such as *The cat is on the mat and the mat is on the floor*, or *The cat is on the mat that is on the floor*, or *The cat is on the mat and the mat is on the floor and the floor is made of wood which comes from the forest in the north of the country near the border*.

Speakers of a language know these rules; the system of knowledge which underlies the ability to speak and understand the infinite set of sentences constitutes the *mental grammar* of a language which is acquired by a child and is accessed and used in speaking and understanding. This linguistic knowledge is not identical to the processes used in speaking and understanding. In actual linguistic performance, however, we must access this mental grammar as well as other non-linguistic systems (motor, perceptual, cognitive) in order to speak and understand. This difference between the knowledge of language (the grammar) and linguistic performance accounts for why in principle there is no longest sentence and language is infinite, whereas in performance each sentence is finite and the total number of sentences produced and understood in any one lifetime is finite.

The universality of language and of the grammars which underlie all languages suggests that the human brain is uniquely suited for the acquisition and use of language. This view is receiving increasing support from research on child language acquisition.

Further support for the view that the human brain is a 'language-learning' organ is provided by neurological studies of language disorders such as aphasia. No one today questions the position put forth by Paul Broca in 1861 that language is specifically related to the left hemisphere. Furthermore, there is converging evidence that focal damage to the left cerebral hemisphere does not lead to an across-the-board reduction in language ability, and that lesions in different locations in the left brain are quite selective and remarkably consistent in the manner in which they undermine language. This selectivity reflects the different parts of the grammar discussed above; access to and processing of the phonology (sound system), the lexicon (inventory of morphemes and words), the syntax (rules of sentence formation), and the semantics (rules for the interpretation of meanings) can all be selectively impaired. There is also strong evidence showing that the language faculty is independent of other mental and cognitive faculties. That is, language appears to be not only unique to the human species but also does not appear to be dependent on general intelligence.

Severely retarded individuals can learn language; persons with brain lesions may lose language abilities and retain other cognitive abilities.

Victoria A. Fromkin
University of California, Los Angeles

Further Reading
Akmajian, A., Demers, R. A. and Harnish, R. M. (1979), *Linguistics: An Introduction to Language and Communication*, Cambridge, Mass.
Chomsky, N. (1975), *Reflections on Language*, New York.
Farb, P. (1974), *Word Play: What Happens When People Talk*, New York.
Fromkin, V. and Rodman, R. (1983), *An Introduction to Language*, 3rd edn, New York.
Klima, E. and Bellugi, U. (1979), *The Signs of Language*, Cambridge, Mass.
Lyons, J. (1981), *Language and Linguistics: An Introduction*, Cambridge.
See also: *language and culture; language development; linguistics.*

Language and Culture

There are three major ways in which language is related to culture: (1) language itself is a *part* of culture; (2) every language provides an *index* of the culture with which it is most intimately associated; (3) every language becomes *symbolic* of the culture with which it is most intimately associated.

(1) Languages as a Part of Culture

Most human behaviours are language-embedded, thus language is an inevitable part of culture. Ceremonies, rituals, songs, stories, spells, curses, prayers and laws (not to mention conversations, requests and instructions) are all speech acts or speech events. But such complex cultural arenas as socialization, education, barter and negotiation are also entirely awash in language. Language is, therefore, not only part of culture but a major and crucial part. All those who seek fully to enter into and understand a given culture must, accordingly, master its language, for only through that language can they possibly participate in and experience the culture. On the other hand, language shift, or loss of a culture's intimately associated language, is indicative of extensive culture change, at the very least, and possibly, of cultural dislocation and destruction, although a *sense* of cultural identity may, nevertheless, persist, as a conscious or unconscious attitudinal level.

(2) Language as an Index of Culture

The role of language as an index of culture is a by-product (at a more abstract level) of its role as part of culture. Languages reveal the ways of thinking or of organizing experience that are common in the associated cultures. Of course, languages provide lexical terms for the bulk of the artifacts, concerns, values and behaviours recognized by their associated cultures. But, above and beyond such obvious indexing, languages also reveal the native clusters or typologies into which the above referents are commonly categorized or grouped. Colours, illnesses, kinship relationships, foods, plants, body parts and animal species are all culture-bound typologies and their culturally recognized systematic qualities are revealed by their associated culture-bound languages. This is not to say that speakers of particular languages are inescapably forced to recognize only the categories encoded in their mother tongues. Such restrictions can be counteracted, at least in part, via cross-cultural and cross-linguistic experience, including exposure to mathematical and scientific languages which provide different categories from those encountered in ethnocultures and their associated mother tongues.

(3) Language as Symbolic of Culture

Since language is the most elaborate symbol system of humankind, it is no wonder that particular languages become symbolic of the particular ethnocultures in which they are embedded and which they index. This is not only a case of a *part* standing for the whole (as when Yiddish stereotypically 'stands for' or evokes Eastern-European derived ultra-Orthodox Jewish culture when we hear it spoken or even mentioned), but also a case of the part becoming a rallying symbol for (or against) the whole and, in some cases, becoming a cause (or a target) in and of itself. Language movements and language conflicts utilize languages as symbols to mobilize populations to defend (or attack) and to foster (or reject) the cultures associated with them.

Joshua A. Fishman
Yeshiva University, New York

Further Reading
Fishman, J. A. (1982), 'Whorfianism of the third kind: ethnolinguistic diversity as a worldwide societal asset (the Whorfian hypothesis: varieties of validation, confirmation and disconfirmation II)', *Language and Society*, 11.
See also: *culture; language.*

Language Development

Learning a language is probably the stellar intellectual achievement across the species. It is robust. Children will learn a normal language right down to an IQ of around 50, before what they learn suffers appreciably. People try to teach children things about language in school, but the real bulk of language is learned in the preschool years, and is learned without anything resembling tutoring. We know now, for example, that parents do not reward children differentially on the basis of how well they put words together to make sentences, even though they may think they do. Nor do less correct sentences seem to communicate appreciably less well than accurate ones. Yet children inexorably learn the complexities of language – the arbitrary noun gender systems of Indo-European languages, the seventeen noun classifications of Bantu, the complex vocabulary of mental terms and modal verbs ˙or particles that seem to be present in all languages.

In doing this, we now know, what they abstract is an underlying system of *rules*, rules for which the utterances they hear only provide examples. It is as though children induced physics from hanging around physics labs. We know they induce such rules partly because of the necessary nature of language, and partly because such rules show themselves in children's acquisition in utterances like *he feeled good*, or *where we should put this*? These show, respectively, application of a rule which happens not to cover all the terms it should (an irregularity), or overgeneralization of a rule from one context of use to another, slightly inappropriate one. Their learning of grammar – the sentence structure of language – is probably no more impressive than their ability to figure out word meanings, or to learn how to communicate to others. It can be estimated, for example, that the average child is learning nine new word meanings a day from the age of 2 to 6.

How do they do this? Chomsky (1980), whose linguistic work was the cause of the modern resurgence of language development work, argues that all these things – the complexity of language, the robustness of its learning, its relative ease of acquisition without tutoring or correction, the child's choice of some rules over others that should be justified by the same examples – all argue that the child approaches the problem with a rich, innately given biological programme for what languages can be like or are likely to be like. This position recently finds some empirical support in the work of Bickerton, who has studied creole languages, the languages that presumably children create out of the fragmentary and conflicting pidgins they are exposed to. Bickerton (1981) finds that these creoles have more in common than the pidgins the children built them from, and this argues they have strong ideas about what languages should be. On the other hand, many, perhaps a large majority in the field of normal acquisition, still think language is constructed by the child using what must be a very rich system of general intelligence. If this is so, the preschool child is far more intellectually powerful than has seemed so in the past, but this is turning out to be true in many areas besides language development.

Michael Maratsos
University of Minnesota

References
Bickerton, D. (1981), *Roots of Language*, Ann Arbor, Mich.
Chomsky, N. (1980), *Rules and Representations*, New York.

Further Reading
Maratsos, M. (1983), 'Some current issues in the study of the acquisition of grammar', in P. Mussen (ed.), *The Handbook of Child Psychology*, 4th edn, New York.
Brown, R. (1973), *A First Language: The Early Stages*, Cambridge, Mass.
Carey, S. (1982), 'Semantic acquisition: the state of the art', in E. Wanner and L. Gleitman (eds), *Language Acquisition: The State of the Art*, Cambridge, Mass.

See also: *Chomsky*; *language*; *psycholinguistics*.

Language, Social Psychology of

See Social Psychology of Language.

Law

Conceptions of what law is are culturally and historically specific. But legal 'theories' often claim for themselves a universalism that they do not really have. When scholars from the Western European legal tradition study the laws and legal institutions of other cultures, what they look for are norms and institutions that are either in form or function analogous to those in their own heritage. The category 'law' they proceed from is a Western cultural construct (Berman, 1983).

Many of the arguments about what law is or should be are organized around a single dichotomy: whether the basis of law is a moral consensus or a matter of organized domination. Law is sometimes interpreted as an expression of cultural values, sometimes as a rationalized framework of power. In ethnographic fact it is usually both. Separating the two absolutely creates a false opposition. Friedman (1975) has argued that 'the function of the legal system is to distribute and maintain an allocation of values that society feels to be right . . . allocation, invested with a sense of rightness, is what is commonly referred to as *justice*'. Society is thus anthropomorphized as a consensual entity having common values. But Friedman's more extended discussion indicates a clear awareness of social stratification, and sharp differences of interest and power. His social science approach tries to embrace both consensus and domination in the same analysis.

In the jurisprudence of the West there have been a number of competing scholarly paradigms of law. The four principal schools of thought with roots in the nineteenth century (and earlier) are conventionally designated: (1) natural law theory; (2) analytical juris-

prudence (or legal positivism); (3) historical jurisprudence (or legal evolutionism); and (4) sociological
jurisprudence. The various modern social science
perspectives on law have been shaped by this intellectual history, as have modern works on jurisprudence
and legal history. Current work is best understood in
the light of earlier ideas.

(1) Natural Law Thinking

In its various forms this dominated Western ideas
about justice through the eighteenth century, and has
not fully disappeared, being perhaps most evident
today in current arguments about universal human
rights. It was once closely associated with the idea of
divine law. Natural law theory postulates the existence
of a universal, underlying system of 'justice' and 'right',
which is distinguishable from mere human enactments,
norms and judgements. The content of this natural
law was thought to be discoverable by human beings
through the exercise of reason. To be just, human laws
should conform to natural law, but they do not always
do so. Human law can be unjust.

(2) Legal Positivism

This was a nineteenth-century development that
continues in new forms to the present, and attacked
natural law thinking on the ground that it was
unscientific, that it was grounded on a mythical entity,
and that it confused law with morality. The notion was
that only *law as it is* can be the subject of scientific
inquiry, that the province of what law ought to be
was not a matter for science, but for philosophers and
theologians. It was Bentham's follower, John Austin,
who first generated 'the science of positive law'.
Austin's science was a 'conceptual jurisprudence' occupied with discovering the key doctrines and ideas actually used in the existing formal legal system.

Austin's most cited formulation is one in which law
is treated as command, the source of law as 'the sovereign person or body' that sets it within a particular
'political society'. And, consistent with this position,
Austin argued that international law was 'improperly
so-called' because it was neither set nor enforced by a
political superior. He invented a category, 'positive
morality' to contrast with 'positive law' to accommodate the law-like quality of international law without
having it disturb his model that associated law with
sovereignty.

Later positivists were critical of Austin, and
developed modifications. Hans Kelsen generated an
analysis which he called 'the pure theory of law' in
which he asserted that law consists of a hierarchy of
norms to which sanctions are attached. The validity of
lower-level norms is derived from higher norms, until
ultimately at the top of the hierarchy is the 'basic
norm' on which the whole structure depends. The effect
of that basic norm is to require people to behave in
conformity to the legal order. It defines the limits of
that order.

Another major positivist critic of the Austinian
perspective is H. L. A. Hart who also has reservations
about the artificiality of Kelsen's idea of the basic
norm, and proposes an alternative. Hart (1961) rejects
a conception of law based on coercive order as one too
much derived from the model of criminal law. He
argues that in fact law does many more things than
prohibit or command and punish. It also can empower
persons to act, and can define the conditions under
which such actions are legally effective. Hart points to
three troublesome issues that frequently recur in the
attempt to define the specifically legal and distinguish
it from other domains: the relationship between law
and coercive orders, between legal obligation and
moral obligation, and the question whether law is to be
understood as a set of rules. Plainly there are coercive
orders, binding obligations and rules that are not
matters of law, yet all three elements also are central
to legal systems. How are these to be distinguished?
Hart's resolution of this problem is to describe law as
a set of social rules divided into two types: primary
rules of obligation and secondary rules of recognition,
change and adjudication. The secondary rules sort the
legal from other rule orders. Since legal validity is
established by formal criteria, according to Hart's
definition, an immoral law can be legally valid. Original and elegantly formulated as Hart's discussion is
widely acknowledged to be, it has been criticized for
its exclusive focus on rules at the expense of other
important dimensions of legal systems, particularly the
fact that it is a formal internal definition that turns
away from questions about the socioeconomic context,
the institutional framework and cultural ideas that
inform law in action. His is very much a formalist
lawyer's definition, and emphatically not a sociological
one. Much of the sociological perspective has emerged
as a reaction against this kind of legal positivism.

(3) The So-Called Historical School

Here renamed evolutionist, this developed as another
nineteenth-century reaction to natural law thinking. It
is much more society-conscious and culture-conscious
than positivism. In Germany this took the form of an
almost mystical conception of the cultural unity of a
people. This was coupled with the idea that there was
an organic mode in which a people's inherent destiny
unfolded over time. For Savigny, law was the
expression of the spirit (*Volksgeist*) of a particular
people, the notion of *Volksgeist* being ambiguously
associated with race as well as culture. In this
interpretation, custom was the fundamental form of
law since it originated in the life of the people. Legislated law was only significant when grounded in
popular awareness, a kind of codification and refine-

ment of legal ideas already in the popular consciousness.

In England, Maine (1861) constructed a very different historical approach. He rejected Savigny's idea of the *Volksgeist* special to each people, and tried to generalize about the evolution of law and legal ideas in universal terms. Using comparative examples of the legal institutions of a few peoples, he endeavoured to show the sequential steps in the legal development of 'progressive' societies. His idea was that in the shift from kin-based to territorially-based polities, collective family property faded out and private individual property came in, that there was a change in the conception of certain wrongs which ceased to be treated as torts and came to be treated as crimes, and that much of the law affecting persons shifted from status to contract. Many of these generalizations have been criticized in later work, but the questions they raise remain issues of importance.

Marx, though only peripherally concerned with law, has had such a profound effect on social thought that his ideas about law must be taken into account in any review of these matters. He resists compartmentalization, but could be suitably placed within the historical school as his is a theory of sequential developments. Since in his model of history, class struggle is the principal dynamic of change, law is a dependent variable, not an independent force. In Marx's thought, the mode and relations of production constitute the 'base' of any social formation, and politics, law and ideology are part of the 'superstructure' of ideas and practices which maintain a given set of class relations. The state and law are seen essentially as instruments of class domination, and reflections of it. In the twentieth century, the expansion of the Welfare State, largely the product of legislation, has often been referred to in order to call into question some of these ideas of Marx's about law, but some Marxists see no contradiction in the matter and argue that what has happened is simply that class domination has taken new forms.

Marxist and neo-Marxist ideas are extremely important in the development of current critical legal theory. Marxist themes can be seen in the work of Abel (1982), Kennedy (1980), and Balbus (1977) among others. They interpret law as a mode of maintaining the inequalities inherent in capitalist economies, however seemingly ameliorative reformist laws sometimes appear on their face.

(4) The Sociological School

By contrast, from the start, this school was wedded to the idea that progress could be made to occur through legal reform. Today, a major species of legal sociology interprets law as the means of solving social problems. Jhering thought of society as an arena of competing interests, and that the function of law was to mediate among them. The purpose was to produce 'the security of the conditions of social life' as a whole. The good of the whole was to come above special interests. Pound (1911–12) came to be very much influenced by Jhering's ideas as he considered the function of law in a democracy. He added his own conception that the task of law was one of 'social engineering'. In order that law achieve a scientifically informed efficacy in this role, he urged that sociological studies be made of any social field to be regulated, and also of the actual impact of existing legal institutions, precepts and doctrines.

Ehrlich, another member of the sociological school, stressed the gap between law on the books and the 'living law', the actual conventional practices of a people. For Ehrlich (1926 [1913]) social practice was the true source of viable law. This 'living law' could come to be embodied in formal statutes and decisions, but law that did not have that anchoring lacked the social vitality to be just and effective. Consequently Ehrlich exhorted lawyers and jurists to make themselves aware of existing social conditions and practices in order to bring formal law into harmony with society. This explains Ehrlich's broad definition of law as 'the sum of the conditions of social life in the widest sense of the term'. 'Law' included rules made and enforced by private associations. His was not a definition focused on 'government', but on 'society'.

Ehrlich's contemporary, Weber (1954 [1922]), conceived of law equally broadly. Law, he said, involved a 'coercive apparatus', the purpose of which was norm-enforcement within a community, corporate organization or an institution. Thus law-like norms could be 'guaranteed' by a variety of social bodies, not only by the state, although the state differed from the others in having a monopoly on 'coercion by violence'. Weber made it clear that, despite the coercive apparatus, the motive for obedience to norms was not necessarily the existence of such a system of physical coercion. The motive could be 'psychological'.

In his models of government and society, his 'ideal types', Weber identified the bureaucratic state with a 'legal order' of 'rational' rules. As he saw it, the evolution of law was marked by a movement from formal and substantive irrationality to rationality. In this sense rationality meant a logically coherent system of principles and rules. Legal irrationality was the use of means other than logic or reason for the decision of cases. Ordeals and oracles were examples of formal irrationality. Arbitrary decisions in terms of the personal predilections of the judge constituted substantive irrationality. In his ideal types Weber postulated a consistency between the type of overall political organization of a society (its mode of 'imperative co-ordination'), its values and ideology, and its type of legal system.

Weber's ideas continue to influence the work of theorists of law. One of the recent revisionist writers is Unger (1976), who borrows 'ideal types' from Weber and postulates a multiplicity of them in historical sequence. But not only do his types differ from Weber's, but he sees as the principal impetus to change an awareness of the dissonance between ideal and real in a particular social order. His is a very orderly, very personal vision. In his view, the problem of our time is the reconciliation of freedom and community.

Like Weber's, Durkheim's (1960 [1893]) legal theory had an evolutionary theme. He thought that primitive societies were held together by 'mechanical solidarity', a coherence produced by a homogeneity of culture and a sameness of all social units, while the cohesion of complex societies was one of 'organic solidarity' founded on the division of labour in society and a system of complementary differences. Associated with each of these was a type of law. He regarded punitive retribution as the mode of dealing with wrongs in primitive society, while restitutive justice was appropriate to repair many wrongs under conditions of 'organic solidarity'. While Durkheim's interpretation of law in primitive societies was quite wrong, as the anthropologist Malinowski (1926) later showed, the direction of his inquiry, the question to what extent law is an aspect of social cohesion, remains cogent.

Today, social scientists approach law with a distilled and selective recombination of many of these classical ideas of nineteenth-century and early twentieth-century scholars. They use these transformed paradigms in combination with new methods, new information and new preoccupations. These have been generated in a very much altered politico-economic setting. Statistical studies have become an essential concomitant in many analyses of law and its effect in mass society. Quantitative methods have also been applied to the study of legal institutions themselves, to the behaviour of courts, lawyers, and administrative agencies. Legal arguments and rationales are not taken at face value, but are studied as texts, both as they reveal and as they obscure values and interests. Economic dimensions and consequences have loomed increasingly large in the study and evaluation of legal norms. The costs of 'justice' and the nature of access to 'justice' have become major issues. The high-flown values that legal principles express are examined by legal economists in the light of their 'efficiency' and their social effect, not just their self-defined moral content.

Anthropologists have substantially enlarged the existing body of knowledge regarding the social order of non-Western societies, simple and complex. Ethnographic materials collected through direct observation have made plain the ways in which order is maintained without government in small-scale systems, and the way disputes are negotiated in oral cultures. These works are pertinent to the operation of subsections of large-scale, complex societies. A knowledge of such subsystems illuminates the peculiar relation between national laws and local practices in many parts of the world.

The importance and widespread existence of plural legal systems has been acknowledged in the post-colonial world as never before. All the theories founded on a notion that consensus and common values necessarily underlie all effective legal systems have been brought into question in the many instances in which power, rather than consensus, underpins particular laws. The role of law in relation to dissensus and conflict, cultural pluralism and class stratification is an increasingly urgent question for social theorists. The difference between the way law is conceived in the West and elsewhere has also become important as the greater interdependence of all countries is manifest. The question whether there are overarching commonalities that are or could be embodied in international law bears on everything from international commerce to the rights of refugees.

Variously conceived by the professions that generate, apply and enforce it, law is obviously quite differently approached by those who observe, analyse and teach it. Thus there is the law of lawyers and judges, of governments, of legislators and administrators, the formal legal system, its concepts and doctrines, its institutions and workings. In a related, but not identical, territory is the law of legal theorists and legal scholars and social scientists, many of them teachers. Beyond that is the way that the legal order impinges on ongoing social life.

Social scientists study all of this wide range, with a great variety of purposes and perspectives. Some are occupied with assembling information which will be the basis for proposed reforms. Others are engaged in trying to understand the relation between the actual workings of legal institutions and the self-explanations that form its ideology, without any immediate application in mind, rather with the idea of enlarging knowledge, and refining theory. In the broadest sense, one might say that there are two general streams of modern research. One is a social problems/social engineering approach that proceeds from the assumption that law is a consciously constructed instrument of control which has the capacity to shape society and to solve problems, an instrument which can itself be reformed and perfected towards this end. Research is seen to serve these practical purposes. In contrast is the social context approach which assumes that law is itself a manifestation of the existing structure (or past history) of the society in which it is found, and tries to know, understand or explain its form, content and institutions by showing contextual connections. Instead of just one 'social science approach' to law, there are many.

Sally Falk Moore
Harvard University

References

Abel, R. (1982), 'The contradictions of informal justice', in R. Abel (ed.), *The Politics of Informal Justice, Vol. I: The American Experience*, New York.

Balbus, I. D. (1977), 'Commodity form and legal form: an essay on the "relative autonomy" of the law', *Law and Society Review*, 571.

Berman, H. J. (1983), *Law and Revolution; The Formation of the Western Legal Tradition*, Cambridge, Mass.

Durkheim, E. (1960 [1893]), *The Division of Labour in Society*, Glencoe, Ill. (Original French edn, *De la Division du travail social*, Paris.)

Ehrlich, E. (1936 [1913]), *Fundamental Principles of the Sociology of Law*, tr. Walter L. Moll, Cambridge, Mass. (Original German edn, *Grundlegung der Soziologie des Rechts*, Munich.)

Friedman, M. (1975), *The Legal System, A Social Science Perspective*, New York.

Hart, H. L. A. (1961), *The Concept of Law*, New York.

Kennedy, D. (1980), 'Toward an historical understanding of legal consciousness: the case of classical legal thought in America 1850–1940', *Research in Law and Sociology*, 3.

Maine, H. (1861), *Ancient Law*, London.

Malinowski, B. (1926), *Crime and Custom in Savage Society*, London.

Pound, R. (1911–12), 'The scope and purpose of sociological jurisprudence', *Harvard Law Review*, 24 and 25.

Unger, R. (1976), *Law in Modern Society*, New York.

Weber, M. (1954 [1922]), *Max Weber on Law in Economy and Society*, ed. M. Feinstein, Cambridge, Mass. (Original German edn, *Wirtschaft und Gesellschaft*, Tübingen.)

Further Reading

Black, D. (1976), *The Behavior of Law*, New York.

Cain, M. and Hunt, A. (1979), *Marx and Engels on Law*, London.

Friedman, L. M. and MacCaulay, S. (eds) (1977), *Law and The Behavioral Sciences*, 2nd edn, Indianapolis.

Nader, L. and Todd, H. F. (eds) (1975), *The Disputing Process – Law in Ten Societies*, New York.

Nonet, P. and Selznick, P. (1978), *Law and Society in Transition*, New York.

See also: *arbitration and mediation; judicial process.*

Leach, Edmund R. (1910–)

Many of Edmund Leach's creative contributions to social anthropology emerged from his opposition to orthodox views. But the targets were well chosen, and in his later years Leach received numerous honours, including knighthood (1975) and election to the British Academy. He gave the 1967 Reith Lectures (*A Runaway World?*) and served as Provost of King's College, Cambridge (1966–78).

Leach is usually regarded as a 'structuralist' and is best known for his technical studies in the fields of kinship, marriage, ritual and myth; however, he has moved rapidly from one topic to another. The touchstone of his work, first elaborated in *Political Systems of Highland Burma* (1954), is the notion of 'verbal categories'. Because Leach's analyses start from labelled concepts, his form of 'structuralism' is more empirically based than the intellectualist versions of it offered on the Continent. The word 'verbal' also means for Leach that categories are used; he is, paradoxically, a 'contextual structuralist'. Initially, he emphasized that there is a dynamic relation between individual choice and social rules which themselves may be inconsistent; later, he examined the ways humans use categories to draw distinctions between the self and the other, we and they, culture and nature. But Leach has been most interested in the patterning of verbal concepts themselves; for example, he holds that 'tabooed' objects and behaviour are found at the points of overlap or boundaries between categories. Leach has also applied the notion of verbal categories to the work of anthropologists. He has attacked the studies of Radcliffe-Brown and his successors who claim to construct typologies and infer social laws directly from ethnographic data. Such taxonomies, argues Leach, are only the verbal concepts of the anthropologist who has been steeped in the traditions of positivism and empiricism.

Leach has had an important impact on several generations of students, not only for his ideas but also his charismatic teaching and provocative writing style.

Stephen Gudeman
University of Minnesota

Further Reading

Leach, E. R. (1961), *Rethinking Anthropology*, London.

Leach, E. R. (1969), *Genesis as Myth and Other Essays*, London.

Leach, E. R. (1976), *Culture and Communication*, London.

Leach, E. R. (1982), *Social Anthropology*, London.

Leadership

Machiavelli, so Bertrand Russell said, produced in *The Prince* a 'handbook for gangsters'. That remark illuminates a fundamental confusion in studies of leadership. An objective analysis should describe and explain how leaders control their followers. Whether they use that control to achieve fame or infamy is, although obviously an important question, one that should be left to historians and other commentators.

There is in fact a mass of *apparently* dispassionate scientific investigation of the subject in sociology, social psychology and books about management. Most of these studies are limited. The effective leader is said to be 'group-oriented', 'fulfils group needs' and oils the wheels of human interaction. But that is only one style of leadership: it is egalitarian in its assumptions, manipulative at its strongest, and sometimes no more than the hypocritical claim of a leader to be only the mouthpiece for his followers. There are also leaders who do not read a consensus, but impose it: remote majestic men and women, objects of fear and reverence. Moreover, these small-group quasi-scientific investigations are often shallow. They rely too much on questionnaires and too little on behaviour. They are blind not only to deceit and bluff, but also to the essential characteristic of leadership, which is its mystique.

Followers can be bought, but the purchaser is not a leader; he is an employer. Domination can also be achieved by force. That can be one element in effective leadership; but not that alone, if only because the required concentration of sustained force is an impossibility. The right to dominate is voluntarily given to one who has the 'gift' of leadership; what Max Weber called 'charisma'. Weber saw charisma as one among other styles of domination, but in fact all effective leaders command some measure of devotion. In one way or another a leader must seem to be superhuman.

Sometimes leaders are officially declared gods, as with all Roman emperors from Augustus onwards. Sometimes the deification is a matter of image and metaphor, as when Nkrumah was called the 'Redeemer'. Sometimes it is no more than human attributes expanded beyond the normal: courage, perseverance, endurance and the like. One essential capacity combines ideas of effectiveness with flair, intuition or luck; an ability to come to the right decision in a manner that transcends rationality. In case after case, leaders, even those not overtly anti-intellectual, make clear that reason has its limits, that leadership is an art (not a science), and is a talent which some people have and others do not.

Since leaders in fact cannot work miracles, the study of leadership becomes the examination of strategies (including institutional arrangements) (1) for maintaining in the followers the illusion of a unique talent in the leader, and (2) for solving problems which the real world presents, or, failing solution, for imposing on the situation a definition which leaves unhurt the image of the leader's effectiveness.

F. G. Bailey
University of California, San Diego

Further Reading
Burns, J. M. (1978), *Leadership*, New York.
Gibb, C. A. (ed.) (1969), *Leadership*, London.
Machiavelli, N. (1950 [1513]), *The Prince*, New York.
See also: *Big Man*; *charisma*; *decision making*; *organizations*.

Learning

For hundreds of years, learning meant the formation of associations, and was considered the means by which society transmitted its acquired cultural capital. Learning was the cliché which lay behind almost every explanation in the social sciences. Increasingly, however, the study of learning has been transformed into the study of the human mind. Nowadays when one speaks of learning one must speak of representations, of knowledge, of modularity, of innate and specific structures of mind. While the new view of learning is still mostly restricted to the cognitive sciences – the social sciences as a whole have not been affected – one would expect that it will ultimately have a powerful impact on the social sciences.

In philosophy and psychology, learning has traditionally been regarded as a potential solution to the problem of knowledge. How is it that a human being comes to have knowledge of the world? In this context, the study of learning has long been central to the study of the human mind. Empiricist philosophers, such as Locke and Hume, conceived of knowledge as a system of association of ideas. Hume invoked principles which explained how these associations were formed. For example, the principle of contiguity said that if two ideas occurred near each other in time, then it was likely that an association was formed between these ideas. In the latter part of the nineteenth century these principles became the focus of experimental study. With the behaviourist revolution in American psychology in the twentieth century, association theory was modified so that it no longer was ideas that were associated. Rather, a stimulus was associated with a response. But the basic underlying notions of association theory persisted: that human knowledge is to be represented as a system of associations and that these associations are learned.

The study of learning thus became the experimental study of the learning of associations. To make these associations experimentally testable, the learning of arbitrary associations was studied, for example, the associations between nonsense syllables, like *dax* and *gep*. From this emerged the famous learning curve, showing the probability of a person's forming an association as a function of the number of times the associated items were shown to him simultaneously. Not surprisingly, it was discovered that the more practice a person has on an association, the better he learns it.

Grand theoretical schemes developed to explain learning, for example, those of Hull. These envisioned learning as a unitary phenomenon. In essence, human and animal learning were conceived to be the same thing, though there might be a quantitative difference. And within a species what appeared to be different kinds of learning really were not. In short, the principles of learning remained unchanged across species and content of what was learned. A number of theoretical disputes arose over the precise character of these principles, but the different theories shared many underlying assumptions of breathtaking simplicity and elegance. These were that all learning was the same and that there were a few general principles of learning. The theory must have had simplicity and elegance, for what else could explain the fact that learning theory in this form lasted for so long? For the matter, plain and simple, was that learning theory did not work. If one actually considered real domains of human knowledge, it quickly became apparent that learning theory could not explain how that knowledge was acquired. The nonsense syllables of the laboratory, like the 'ideas' of the philosophers (or the 'quality spaces' of Quine), were abstractions which lost the essence of the problem.

The ideas which have replaced association theory are rich and interconnected. There is no way here even to hint at the extensive justification that has been developed for them. We will simply list some of the themes of the new study.

(1) Language and Innate Principles
Perhaps the major critique of the adequacy of association theory, as well as the most extensive development of an alternative theory for human learning, has come from the field of linguistics, namely from Chomsky (1965, 1975). Chomsky argues that the structure of language is such that there is no way that a human could learn language given any of the traditional notions of learning (call these 'learning theory'). Since every normal person masters a natural language, learning theory could not possibly be correct. Chomsky argues that the only way that these structures could develop is if there is an innate basis for them in the human mind.

(2) Conscious Awareness
We are not aware of most of the knowledge that we possess. For example, most of the principles of language are beyond our conscious awareness. In broad terms, the modern innatist position is very much like that of the rationalist philosophers (Descartes, Leibniz). Probably the biggest single difference (besides the extensive detailed technical developments in the modern period) is that the philosophers generally seem to have believed that the principles of mind were available to conscious introspection. It also does not seem unreasonable to claim that even behaviourists would only invoke principles of explanation of which they were consciously aware, although they did not explicitly state this. According to the modern view, although principles of knowledge are not necessarily available to consciousness, they are still in the mind, and thus a matter of individual psychology. Giving up the assumption of the necessity of conscious awareness

of principles of mind is a liberating force in learning theory, for it makes possible the development of theoretical constructs which traditionally would have been immediately ruled out on the basis of introspection.

(3) Domain-Specific and Species-Specific Principles
The modern view violates the cardinal principle of the traditional view, that all knowledge except for some simple principles of association is learned. But it also violates the two subsidiary principles, that learning principles do not depend on the species or on the domain of knowledge. Principles of learning differ from species to species. Animals do not learn language, because the principles of language only occur in humans. Some scholars are quite willing to accept the innate character of principles of learning, but believe that these principles operate in all domains of knowledge. That is, the principles are some kind of complicated hypothesis-formation ability. But the modern view holds that there are different principles in different domains of knowledge. Thus those which underlie our ability to recognize objects are different from those which enable us to use language. This latter view has come to be called the *modular* view of cognition. In the entire history of learning theory, there are really only two general kinds of ideas about learning: the formation of associations, and some kind of hypothesis-formation. With the development of the modern view of domain-specific principles, it is possible to have a much more delineated learning theory with particular principles for particular domains of knowledge. Of course it is an open and empirical question whether more general principles of cognition and learning underlie the specific principles which have been discovered. On the evidence to date, it appears unlikely that the domains will be completely unified. For example, visual perception and language just *look* different.

(4) Reinforcement
In many traditional views of learning, an organism could only learn if properly reinforced. For example, a child was supposed to learn a response better if given a piece of candy when he made the correct response. The modern view, based on considerable evidence, is that reinforcement appears much less necessary for learning, although it may still be an effective motivator. Skinner (1957) argued that children learned to speak grammatically by being positively reinforced for correct sentences and negatively reinforced for incorrect sentences. But Brown and Hanlon (1970) and other investigators have shown that parents do not differentially reinforce grammatical and non-grammatical utterances of young children in the language learning period. Thus reinforcement does not appear to play a significant role in language learning, from the stand-

point of giving information to the child. Its role as a motivator is more difficult to assess precisely.

(5) Instruction

One of the surprising discoveries of the modern period is the degree to which children spontaneously develop cognitive abilities, with no special arrangements of the environment. The field of language acquisition, and cognitive development more generally, is replete with examples. It is clear that the rules of language, for example, are not taught to children. People in general do not know the rules, although they use them implicitly, so how could they teach them? Some scholars believe that although parents do not teach the rules of language, they nevertheless provide special instruction by presenting children with a particular simplified language that is 'fine-tuned' to their levels of ability (Snow and Ferguson, 1977). But the best evidence (Newport, Gleitman and Gleitman, 1977) seems to show that there is no such fine-tuning.

Certain abilities unfold naturally, with no special instruction. Language appears to be one of these. Principles of visual perception also follow this outline. The same may be true for certain basic principles of counting, although not for the learning of the names of numbers (Gelman and Gallistel, 1978). Other abilities seem to stretch the ordinary limits of the human mind, and seem to demand instruction in the usual case. The learning of advanced mathematics, or many other subjects, seems to follow this pattern.

(6) Learnability and Feasibility

It has proved possible to define mathematically the question of the possibility of learning. Gold (1967) provided one of the first useful formalizations. Wexler and Culicover (1980) investigated the question of learnability for systems of natural language and showed that linguistic systems could be learned if language-specific constraints were invoked. They further investigated the problem of feasibility, that is, learnability under realistic conditions. Specific constraints can be invoked which allow for feasible learning systems, specifically, very complex systems which can nevertheless be learned from simple input. This would seem to mirror the situation for a child, who learns an essentially infinite system (say language) from exposure to only a fairly small part of the system.

(7) Animal Research

We have concentrated on learning in humans, especially the learning of language, the ability most centrally related to the human species. However, extensive modern research on animal learning also questions the traditional assumptions. It appears that traditional learning theory is not an adequate theory for animals.

(8) Social Implications

The assumption of innate principles of human cognition does *not* imply that there are innate differences between individuals or races. The central idea of the modern view is that the innate principles are part of the shared human endowment, just as the innate existence of a heart is. In fact, the existence of the innate principles of mind may be thought of as helping to define human nature, an old concept generally out of favour in the social sciences. Contemporary social scientists in general founded their theories of society and politics on a psychology closely associated with traditional learning theory. Thus, children are 'socialized' into the values of their society. But it is conceivable that there are principles of mind (of human nature) which relate to the structure of society (or to interpersonal relations, or ethics). If so, the modern view of learning might one day be expanded to include these principles, and there may conceivably be a social science founded on the modern view of learning.

Kenneth Wexler
University of California, Irvine

References
Brown, R. and Hanlon, C. (1970), 'Derivational complexity and the order of acquisition of child speech', in J. R. Hayes (ed.), *Cognition and the Development of Language*, New York.
Chomsky, N. (1965), *Aspects of the Theory of Syntax*, Cambridge, Mass.
Chomsky, N. (1975), *Reflections on Language*, New York.
Gelman, R. and Gallistel, C. R. (1978), *The Child's Understanding of Number*, Cambridge, Mass.
Gold, E. M. (1967), 'Language identification in the limit', *Information and Control*, 10.
Newport, E., Gleitman, H. and Gleitman, L. R. (1977), 'Mother I'd rather do it myself: some effects and non-effects of maternal speech style', in C. E. Snow and C. A. Ferguson (eds), *Talking to Children*, Cambridge.
Skinner, B. F. (1957), *The Behavior of Organisms*, New York.
Snow, C. E. and Ferguson, C. A. (eds) (1977), *Talking to Children: Language Input and Acquisition*, Cambridge.
Wexler, K. and Culicover, P. W. (1980), *Formal Principles of Language Acquisition*, Cambridge, Mass.

Further Reading
Piatelli-Palmarini, M. (ed.) (1980), *Language and Learning*, Cambridge, Mass.
See also: *associationism*; *behaviourism*; *conditioning*; *Hull*; *language*; *language development*.

Le Bon, Gustave (1841–1931)

Gustave Le Bon, a French physician who applied psychopathology to a wide variety of topical subjects, is best known for his work on the crowd and collective behaviour. He was born in a small village near Chartres, studied medicine in Paris, and then embarked on a career as a synthesizer and vulgarizer. He set up a private laboratory to do scientific experiments, and later claimed to have anticipated Einstein's theory of relativity. He travelled abroad to study cultural history, and claimed also to have foreshadowed Nietzsche's theory of eternal recurrence.

Le Bon achieved fame only when he started applying a kind of Social-Darwinian psychology to political questions. His first bestseller, *Lois psychologiques de l'évolution des peuples* (1894) (*Psychological Laws of the Evolution of Peoples*, 1924), discussed the mental development of 'inferior and superior' races in relation to national identity and colonial conquest.

His second, and best-known, success was *Psychologie des foules* (1895), (*The Crowd*, 1896). In it, he tried to apply the principles of early dynamic psychology to the functioning of popular movements, and concluded that they always showed pathological traits such as impulsiveness, mobility, irritability, credulity, suggestibility, emotionality, intolerance, authoritarianism, conservatism and amorality. Statesmen of his time, he argued, should acquaint themselves with these principles if they did not want to be ruled by the masses. The book was translated into at least sixteen languages, and reprinted more than forty-five times in French alone.

Le Bon developed his ideas further in *Psychologie du socialisme* (1898) (*The Psychology of Socialism*, 1899), a fierce polemic against the labour movement; and in *Psychologie de l'education* (1901), which favoured the introduction of drilling methods in schools and army. His later works, *La Psychologie politique et la défense sociale* (1910) and *La Révolution française et la psychologie des révolutions* (1912) (*The Psychology of Revolutions*, 1913), rehearsed the same themes, but were among the very first to apply them to these subjects.

Le Bon's thinking was closely related to that of his French contemporaries, including Barrès and Sorel, and Italians such as Mosca and Pareto. He was powerfully influential in his own time: the total circulation of his forty volumes approached half a million copies in French alone. His ideas were taken up not only by social theorists, but also by practising politicians, mostly from the radical right (Mussolini and Hitler), but also from the moderate centre (Theodore Roosevelt and De Gaulle), and even from the radical left (Kautsky and Lenin). Recently several of his books have been reprinted in France and the US, through the efforts of both social science historians and conservative political admirers.

Jaap van Ginneken
University of Leiden

Further Reading
Barrows, S. (1981), *Distorting Mirrors – Visions of the Crowd in Late Nineteenth Century France*, New Haven, Conn.
Nye, R. (1975), *The Origins of Crowd Psychology – Gustave Le Bon and the Crisis of Mass Democracy in the Third Republic*, London.

Legitimacy

The discussion of legitimacy in social and political theory seems to confirm Hegel's dictum that theoretical reflection begins only when a practice has completed its development and become problematic. Questions about the moral worth or rightness of different forms of rule were present at the very beginning of systematic thinking about society. In *The Politics*, for instance, Aristotle held that some constitutions were 'right' (those promoting the common interest of citizens), while others were 'perverted' (those serving only the particular interest of rulers), a distinction grounded in a teleological metaphysics. However, classical theory lacked an explicit language of legitimacy. That was to be an invention of modern thought, represented best in Rousseau's promise in the *Social Contract* to demonstrate how political authority could be rendered 'legitimate'. Rousseau's hypothetical argument resting on the *volonté générale* served as both an epitaph for the Aristotelian tradition and a warning about the contestability of legitimacy in the modern age. This shift from a metaphysical to a voluntaristic account prepared the way for the contribution of Max Weber, the greatest modern theorist of legitimacy.

All modern theory starts from the assumption that legitimacy has to do with the quality of authoritativeness, lawfulness, bindingness, or rightness attached to an order; a government or state is considered 'legitimate' if it possesses the 'right to rule'. Unfortunately, the definition begs the most crucial question: in what does 'right' consist, and how can its meaning be determined? Generally speaking, this question has been answered in two ways. One school of thought has argued with Weber (1968 [1922]) that, 'It is only the probability of orientation to the subjective *belief* in the validity of an order which constitutes the valid order itself.' According to this view, 'right' reduces to belief in the 'right to rule'. The presence of objective, external or universal standards for judging rightness grounded in natural law, reason or some other transhistorical principle is typically rejected as philosophically impossible and sociologically naive. In his sociology of legitimacy, Weber attempted to guard against the 'relativistic' consequences of such a conception by identifying four *reasons* for ascribing 'legitimacy' to any social order: tradition, affect, value-rationality and legality. This classification then served as the basis for his famous analysis of the 'pure types' of 'legitimate domination' (*legitime Herrschaft*): traditional, charismatic and legal-rational.

Recent scholars have argued about the logic, meaning and application of Weber's views. Some writers have sharply criticized the sociological approach generally for subverting a rational distinction between legitimate and illegitimate forms of rule; for failing to distinguish legitimacy from legality; and for confusing a distinction among belief elicited through coercion, habit or rational choice. (In what sense Weber may be guilty of these charges is a matter of dispute.) Underlying these criticisms from the second school of thought is the conviction, expressed particularly in the work of Jürgen Habermas, that a satisfactory theory of legitimacy must be philosophically grounded in such a way as to render possible a 'rational judgement' about the 'right to rule'. For Habermas (1975), grounds have been sought in a rather complex 'consensus theory of truth', where 'truth' signifies 'warranted assertability' under conditions of *ideal* 'communicative competence'.

Whether Habermas or others sharing his assumptions have provided a coherent philosophical grounding for the theory of legitimacy remains an open question. One difficulty with their attempt is that it comes at an awkward time, philosophically considered, for under the influence of Dewey, Wittgenstein and Heidegger, philosophy itself has begun to challenge the project of identifying foundations of knowledge which can be used to achieve definitive criteria of rationality. If this challenge succeeds, then it will become difficult to imagine any viable philosophical alternative to the Weberian typological approach.

In light of this impasse, the most recent work on legitimacy has proceeded in three directions: (1) Some theorists have moved towards developing a theory of *il*legitimacy, arguing that the real problems of the modern state lie with its essential lack of legitimacy. (2) Social scientists attracted to empirical theory have often dropped the term legitimacy altogether, hoping to avoid troublesome normative issues, and have instead looked only for quantifiable 'regime support'. (3) Probably the most innovative direction has been taken by those investigating processes and strategies of legitimation used by the state (particularly in the domains of science, technology, education and communication) to shore up sagging belief in its right to rule. Such diversification, whatever its eventual results, is a firm indication that the problem of legitimacy will remain centrally important in social and political theory, at least as long as the modern state-system remains intact.

Lawrence A. Scaff
University of Arizona

References
Habermas, J. (1975 [1973]), *Legitimation Crisis*, Boston. (Original German edn, *Legitimationsprobleme im Spätkapitalismus*, Frankfurt.)
Weber, M. (1968 [1922]), *Economy and Society*, New York. (Original German edn, *Wirtschaft und Gesellschaft*, Tübingen.)

Further Reading
Rogowski, R. (1974), *Rational Legitimacy: A Theory of Political Support*, Princeton, N.J.
Schaar, J. H. (1981), *Legitimacy in the Modern State*, New Brunswick.
See also: *authority; social contract; state; Weber.*

Leisure

See Work and Leisure.

Leontief, Wassily (1906–)

Input-output analysis is unquestionably the crowning achievement of Wassily Leontief for which he was awarded the 1973 Nobel Memorial Prize in Economic Sciences. With its roots in Quesnay's *Tableau Économique* and in Walrasian general equilibrium (though Leontief is highly critical of general equilibrium theories since they offer little insight into operational propositions about the measureable properties of specific economic systems), input-output provides a comprehensive breakdown of macroeconomic aggregates, as it is a useful tool for studying the quantitative interdependence among interrelated economic activities, and is a valuable device for national economic planning. Leontief, a prophet enjoying greater honour outside his own country, is a strong advocate of the use of input-output for democratic economic planning.

Originally elaborated to analyse and measure the flows among the different producing and consuming sectors of a national economy, input-output has been sucessfully used in studying more compact economic systems, such as regions or very large enterprises. It was later extended to the analysis of international economic relations and, in its most ambitious form, to the structure of the world economy. Whatever needs to be said about Leontief's pioneering effort (and its subsequent refinements), it was a major *tour de force* in posing the problems of mutual compatibility and accommodation between theoretical formulation and observational capability (development of the empirical data base), and the difficulties in analysing and describing in concrete numerical magnitudes the specific operational features of the modern economy characterized by supercomplexity of the intersectoral links.

Born in 1906 in St Petersburg, the son of an economics professor, Leontief studied at the Universities of Leningrad and Berlin. He began his research career at the Institute for World Economics (University of Kiel), moving in 1931 to the National Bureau of Economic Research. From 1932 he taught at Harvard University from which he resigned in 1975 to become Professor of Economics and Director of the Institute of Economics Analysis, New York University.

Though many Harvard students first learned mathematical economics at Leontief's knees, he is very critical of abstract economic theorizing. He warns that in interpreting the models, all too often we forget their restrictive assumptions, and he underlines that the usefulness of the exercise really depends on the empirical validity of these assumptions. Throughout his research he has taken this warning to heart; there runs an overwhelming current of empirical relevance.

George R. Feiwel
University of Tennessee

Further Reading
Dorfman, R. (1973), 'Wassily Leontief's contribution to economics', *Scandinavian Journal of Economics*, 75.
Leontief, W. (1951), *The Structure of the American Economy, 1919–1939*, New York.
Leontief, W. (1977), *Essays in Economics*, 2 vols, New York.
Leontief, W. *et al.* (1977), *The Future of the World Economy*, New York.
Miernyk, W. H. (1979), 'Leontief, Wassily', in D. L. Sills (ed.), *International Encyclopedia of the Social Sciences*, Vol. 18, New York.

Le Play, Frédéric (1806–82)

The French social scientist Frédéric Le Play was a nineteenth-century pioneer of the direct observation of social reality. Before becoming a professional sociologist, he was a mining engineer, and as professor of metallurgy at the École des Mines he travelled frequently to European metal works and mines, developing a keen eye for the connection between technical innovation and social change. His official reports covered management and manufacturing methods as well as conditions of work and life of the industrial workers. In 1844, Le Play was commissioned to investigate mines and works in the Ural Mountains which employed about 45,000 serfs, and was even persuaded to take over the management of the enterprise.

After an initial enthusiasm for the 1848 Revolution and the Republic, he became disillusioned, and moved to the right on political issues. From then on he gave priority to social studies. He was appointed to the Conseil d'État by Emperor Napoleon II, partly as a result of his work as head of the organization of the 1855 World Exhibition in Paris. In the same year he published his first book of social studies, *Les Ouvriers Européens* (Paris, 1855).

The social data collected on his early travels formed a basis for his later numerous case studies. 'Study the facts,' he urged, advocating a thoroughgoing inductivism; laws as well as suggestions for social reform will emerge from empirical study. For the six volumes on European workers, he and his collaborators wrote 'monographs' consisting largely of the budgets of working-class family expenditures, collected through interviews whose use he pioneered.

Le Play argued that the family was the basic social unit. The patriarchal family was the most stable; the two-generation family with its individualism was the most unstable. It was by the material well-being and the stability of the family that the condition of society could be measured. Technological and industrial innovations did not automatically require social innovations. Customs and traditional values, stable families and the commands of the Decalogue had to set bounds to social change. Constantly referring to the 'original sin', he strongly opposed Rousseau and his optimistic views about human nature.

Among his other works are: *La réforme social en France*, Paris, 1864; *L'Organisation du Travail*, Tours, 1870; *L'Organisation de la famille*, Paris, 1871; and *La Méthode de la science sociale*, Tours, 1879.

Sacha Bem
University of Leiden

Further Reading
Brooke, M. Z. (1970), *Le Play: Engineer and Social Scientist*, London.
Le Play, F. (1982), *Frédéric Le Play on Family, Work and Social Change*, ed. C. B. Silver, Chicago.

Lévi-Strauss, Claude (1908–)

Claude Lévi-Strauss was born in Brussels, of French parents. After attending the Lycée Janson de Sailly in Paris he studied at the Faculty of Law in Paris, where he obtained his license, and at the Sorbonne, where he received his teacher's qualification in philosophy (*agrégation*) in 1931. After teaching for two years at the lycées of Mont-de-Marsan and Laon, he was appointed to the French university mission in Brazil, serving as professor at the University of Sao Paulo from 1935 to 1938. Between 1935 and 1939 he organized and directed several ethnographic expeditions in the Mato Grosso and the Amazon. Returning to France on the eve of the war, he was mobilized. After the armistice, in June 1940, he succeeded in reaching the United

States, where he taught at the New School for Social Research in New York. Volunteering for the Free French forces, he was attached to the French scientific mission in the United States, and founded with H. Focillon, J. Maritain, J. Perrin and others the École Libre des Hautes Études in New York of which he became secretary-general. In 1945 he was appointed cultural counsellor of the French Embassy to the United States, but resigned in 1948 in order to devote himself to his scientific work.

Lévi-Strauss's doctoral thesis, submitted at the Sorbonne, was made up of his first two studies, *La Vie familiale et sociale des Indiens Nambikwara* (1948) and *Les Structures élémentaires de la parenté* (1949) (*The Elementary Structures of Kinship*, 1969). In 1949 he became deputy director of the Musée de l'Homme, and later director of studies at the École Pratique des Hautes Études, chair of the comparative religion of non-literate peoples, in succession to Maurice Leenhardt. In 1959 he was appointed to the Collège de France, establishing a chair in social anthropology. He taught there until his retirement in 1982.

The name of Claude Lévi-Strauss has become linked indissolubly with what later came to be called structural anthropology. Reading his first articles, such as 'Structural analysis in linguistics and in anthropology' (1963 [1945]), one is struck by the clarity with which from the first he formulated the basic principles of structuralism. As the title of the essay suggests, he found his inspiration in the linguistics of Saussure and above all in the phonological method developed by Trubetzkoy and by Jakobson (with whom he was associated in New York during the war). He drew from them rules of procedure: concentrate not on conscious phenomena but on their unconscious infrastructure; do not attribute an independent value to the elements of a system but rather a positional meaning, that is to say, the value of the elements is dependent upon the relations which combine and oppose them, and these relations must be the foundation of the analysis; recognize at the same time that these relations also have a merely positional significance within a system of correlations whose structure must be extracted.

Lévi-Strauss applied this method first to the study of kinship systems, demonstrating their formal analogy with phonetic systems. His article of 1945 paid especial attention to the problem of the avunculate, sketching some of the central themes of his *Elementary Structures*, which he was then elaborating. These included the central role of marriage exchange, which implies a prohibition on incest (of which exchange is, in a sense, the other, positive, side of the coin). Marriage exchange is the condition of kinship: 'Kinship is allowed to establish and perpetuate itself only through specific forms of marriage.' He also stressed the social character of kinship, which has to do not with 'what it retains from nature', but rather with 'the essential way in which

it diverges from nature' (1963). Finally, Lévi-Strauss proposed the definition of kinship systems, and of social systems more generally, as systems of symbols.

Another influence which is also apparent, and which Lévi-Strauss has always acknowledged, is the work of Marcel Mauss. His sympathy for the thought of Mauss is apparent when he compares the method of analysis in Mauss's *Essai sur le don* with the approach of structural linguistics, or when, in the same essay, he charges anthropology with the task of studying 'the unconscious mental structures which one may discern by investigating the institutions, or better still the language', and which render intelligible the variety and apparent disorder of appearances (Lévi-Strauss, 1983 [1950]).

This was the goal which had been set by the author of *The Elementary Structures of Kinship*:

> The diversity of the historical and geographical modalities of the rules of kinship and marriage have appeared to us to exhaust all possible methods for ensuring the integration of biological families within the social group. We have thus established that superficially complicated and arbitrary rules may be reduced to a small number. There are only three possible elementary kinship structures; these three structures are constructed by means of two forms of exchange; and these two forms of exchange themselves depend upon a single differential characteristic, namely the harmonic or disharmonic character of the regime considered. Ultimately, the whole imposing apparatus of prescriptions and prohibitions could be reconstructed *a priori* from one question, and one alone: in the society concerned, what is the relationship between the rule of residence and the rule of descent? (1969 [1949], p. 493)

Furthermore, these kinship structures rest upon universal mental structures: the force of the rule as a rule, the notion of reciprocity, and the symbolic character of the gift.

Lévi-Strauss returned to deal with one unanswered question fifteen years later, in *The Raw and the Cooked*. Are these kinship structures really primary, or do they rather represent 'the reflections in men's minds of certain social demands that had been objectified in institutions'? Are they the effect of what one might term an external logic? His *Mythologiques*, of which this was the first volume, put this functionalist hypothesis out of court, demonstrating that in mythology, which, in contrast to kinship, 'has no obvious practical function . . . is not directly linked with a different kind of reality', processes of the same order were to be found. Whether systems were actually 'lived', in the course of social life, or like the myths, simply conceived in an apparently spontaneous and arbitrary manner, they led back to the same sources, which one might legitimately describe as 'mental'. This answer had in fact been given earlier, in 1962, in *Le Totémisme aujourd'hui* (*Totemism*, 1962) and *La Pensée sauvage* (*The Savage Mind*, 1966), the latter book asserting, in opposition to Lévy-Bruhl's notion of a 'prelogical mentality', that 'savage' forms of thinking are to be found in us all, providing a shared basis which is domesticated by our various cultures.

The issue was whether the structuralist method applied only to kinship structures, and moreover only to those Lévi-Strauss termed 'elementary', which are not universal, even among those societies which traditionally are called traditional. The re-examination of totemism demonstrated how successfully this method could be applied to the symbolic systems with the aid of which people structure their representations of the world. The analysis of myths demonstrated, further, that the method worked not only for closed systems, like kinship systems, but applied also to open systems, or at least to systems whose closure could not be immediately established and whose interpretation could be developed only in the manner of a 'nebula' in the absence of 'the general appearance of a stable and well-defined structure' (*The Raw and the Cooked*).

In his last lectures at the Collège de France, between 1976 and 1982, Lévi-Strauss took up problems of kinship once more, but moved on from the systems based on unilineal descent and preferential alliance, concerning which he had developed his theory of elementary structures in 1949. He now investigated societies whose fundamental grouping brought together 'either cognates and agnates, or else cognates and maternal kin', and which he termed the 'house', borrowing a term which was used in medieval Europe. These studies are described in his latest book, *Paroles données*, published in 1984. Here he demonstrates that structuralism is by no means disqualified from the study of 'a type of institution which transcends the traditional categories of ethnological theory, combining descent and residence, exogamy and endogamy, filiation and alliance, patriliny and matriliny' and can analyse the complex matrimonial strategies which simultaneously or in succession employ principles 'which elsewhere are mutually exclusive'. What is the best alliance? Should one seek a spouse in the vicinity, or far away? These are the questions which dominate the myths. But they are not posed by savages alone. At a conference held in 1983 (whose proceedings were published in *Annales*, November-December, 1983) Lévi-Strauss cited materials from Blanche de Castille, Saint-Simon and the peasant populations of Japan, Africa, Polynesia and Madagascar to show that 'between societies which are called "complex" and those which are wrongly termed "primitive" or "archaic", the distance is less great than one might think'.

It is therefore mistaken to criticize anthropologists, certainly if they are structuralists, for ignoring history and considering the societies they study as though they were static, despite the fact that, like our own, they exist in time, even if they may not situate themselves in time in the same fashion. This criticism rests upon a misunderstanding which Lévi-Strauss, however, tried to forestall very early. It is significant that it was in 1949 – the year in which his *Elementary Structures* appeared – that he published an essay with a title – 'History and Ethnology' – which he was to use again for his conference paper in 1983. In his article of 1949 he emphasized that the difference between the two disciplines was a consequence of their very complementarity, 'history organizing its data with reference to conscious characterizations, ethnology with reference to the unconscious conditions of social life'. In 1983, taking into account what has come to be called the 'nouvelle histoire', this complementarity is restated, but at another level. In fact 'it was through their contact with ethnology that the historians recognized the importance of those obscure and partly submerged facets of life in society. In return, as a consequence of the renewal of its field of study and its methods, history, under the name of historical anthropology, has become a source of considerable assistance to ethnologists'. Thus anthropology and history can serve each other, at least if the historian does not concern himself only with the succession of kings and queens, with wars, with treaties and with the conscious motives of actors, but studies customs, beliefs, and all that which is covered by the vague term 'mentalité', in a given society at a given time; especially if the anthropologist recognizes that the past of so-called complex societies increases 'the number of social experiments which are available for the better knowledge of man'.

It is true that in his inaugural lecture at the Collège de France in 1960 Lévi-Strauss opposed 'cold' societies – those which chose to ignore their historical aspect, and which anthropologists had traditionally preferred to study – and 'hot' societies – those which, on the contrary, valued their historicity and which were of especial interest to historians. Nevertheless, this opposition did not put in question the historicity of one or other type of society, but rather their attitude to their respective pasts. Every society presents a double aspect: structural and historical. But while one aspect might be especially favoured, this does not lead to the disappearance of the other. And in truth, the 'cold' societies do not deny the past: they wish to repeat it. For their part, 'hot' societies cannot totally deny their 'coldness': the history that they value is theirs only by virtue of a certain continuity which guarantees their identity. This explains the paradox that the very peoples who are most concerned with their history see themselves through stereotypes. And recognizing, or desiring, a history, does not prevent them from thinking of others, and especially their neighbours, in a static mode. One might instance the set fashion in which, for example, the French and the English represent each other. Thus structuralism does not put history in question, but rather an idea of history which is so common: the idea that history can concern itself only with flux, and that change is never-ending. Yet although nature does not, apparently, make jumps, history does not seem to be able to avoid them. Certainly one might interest oneself in the moments of transition. One might equally interest oneself in the intervening periods, and is history not in essence constituted by such periods? The times within which different states of society succeed each other are not less discontinuous than the space within which societies contemporary in time but equally different, often ignorant of each other, share a border. It matters little whether the distancing – which appears to the ethnologist to be the condition of his research, since it is the other as such which is the object of his research – is temporal or spatial.

Obviously it is not necessary to accept the notion of a possible fusion between anthropology, as conceived by Lévi-Strauss, and history. The historian strives to surmount discontinuity, his goal being to establish genealogical connections between one social state and another. The anthropologist, on the contrary, tries to profit from discontinuity, by discovering, among distinct societies (without concerning himself as to whether or not they figure in the same genealogical tree) homologies which attest to the reality of a shared foundation for humanity. Lévi-Strauss has always striven to recognize this 'original logic' beneath a diversity of expressions which have often been judged to be absurd, explicable only by positing the priority of affect over intellect, but which are 'a direct expression of the structure of the mind . . . and not an inert product of the action of the environment on an amorphous consciousness' (*Totemism*, 1962).

If one might talk of a Kantian aspect to structuralism (and Lévi-Strauss has never denied it), one should note that its course inverts that of Kant in two ways. First, instead of positing a transcendental subject, it tries to detach, from the variety of concrete systems of representations, collective modes of thought. Secondly, from among these systems it selects those which diverge most from ours. Kantianism without a transcendental subject thus, although the ambition of discovering in this way 'a fundamental and communal matrix of constraints', or in other words invariants, would seem nevertheless at the least to evoke its shade.

Such an enterprise appears to dispose of subjectivity, or at least to put it within parentheses, and this has indeed been one of the reproaches directed at structuralism: that it does not deal with man as a subject. There is a misapprehension here. As Lévi-Strauss, indeed, remarked in his 'Introduction à l'oeuvre de Marcel Mauss' (1983):

Every society different from ours is an object; every group in our society, apart from our own, is an object; indeed, each usage, even of our own group, which we do not share, is an object. Yet this unlimited series of objects, which together constitute the object of the ethnographer, whatever its historical or geographical features, is still, in the end, defined in relation to himself. However objective in analysis, he must in the end achieve a subjective reintegration of them.

And again, in the same text: 'In the last analysis, the ethnological problem is a problem of communication.' That is to say, communication between subjects, between 'the Melanesian of whatever island', as Mauss put it, and the person who observes him, listens to him . . . and interprets him. A similar point was made in *La Pensée sauvage*, published twelve years later, which ended with a consideration of the convergence between the laws of 'savage thought' and modern theories of information, that is, of the transmission and reception of messages. Thus the subject is not neglected or denied, but (while avoiding a solipsism which would obviously be the negation of anthropology) one might say that there is always a plurality of subjects, without which indeed the problem of communication would not present itself, and it is their relations which are significant. This remains a constant principle of Lévi-Strauss's structuralism: it is the relations which matter, not the terms.

That is also the principle which has guided this brief review. It has been concerned less with the analysis of texts, each considered in itself, than with their relations – from a point of view as much synchronic as diachronic – the aim being to abstract the invariant features of a body of work which is at once complete yet always open.

Jean Pouillon
Laboratory of Social Anthropology, Collège de France,
Paris

References
Lévi-Strauss, C. (1963), 'Structural analysis in linguistics and anthropology', *Structural Anthropology*, New York. (Originally published in French as 'L'analyse structurale en linguistique et en anthropologie', *Word*, 1, 1945.)
Lévi-Strauss, C. (1969), *The Elementary Structures of Kinship*, London. (Original French edn, *Les Structures élémentaires de la parenté*, Paris, 1949.)
Lévi-Strauss, C. (1983), *Introduction to Marcel Mauss*, London, 1983. (Originally published in French as 'Introduction à l'oeuvre de Marcel Mauss', in Marcel Mauss, *Sociologie et anthropologie*, Paris, 1950.)
Lévi-Strauss, C. (1984), *Paroles données*, Paris.

Further Reading
Hayes, E. N. and Hayes, T. (eds) (1970), *Claude Lévi-Strauss: The Anthropologist as Hero*, Cambridge, Mass.

Lévi-Strauss, C. (1961), *A World on the Wane*, New York. (Original French edn, *Tristes Tropiques*, Paris, 1955.)

Lévi-Strauss, C. (1963), 'History and ethnology', *Structural Anthropology*, New York. (Originally published in French as 'Histoire et ethnologie', *Révue de Métaphysique et de Morale*, 1949.)

Lévi-Strauss, C. (1963), *Structural Anthropology*, New York. (Original French edn, *Anthropologie structurale*, Paris, 1958.)

Lévi-Strauss, C. (1970), *The Raw and the Cooked*, London. (Original French edn, *Le Cru et le cuit* ([vol. 1 of *Mythologiques*]), Paris, 1964.)

Lévi-Strauss, C. (1972), *From Honey to Ashes*, London. (Original French edn, *Du Miel aux cendres* ([vol. 2 of *Mythologiques*]), Paris, 1966.)

Lévi-Strauss, C. (1978), *The Origin of Table Manners*, London. (Original French edn, *L'Origine des manières de table* ([vol. 3 of *Mythologiques*]), Paris, 1968.)

Lévi-Strauss, C. (1981), *The Naked Man*, London. (Original French edn, *L'Homme nu* ([vol. 4 of *Mythologiques*]), Paris, 1971.)

Lévi-Strauss, C. (1977) 'The scope of anthropology', *Structural Anthropology*, II. (Inaugural lecture, Collège de France, 1960; published in *Anthropologie structurale*, II, Paris, 1973.)

Lévi-Strauss, C. (1983), *Le Regard éloigné*, Paris.

Steiner, G. (1966), 'A conversation with Claude Lévi-Strauss', *Encounter*, 26.

See also: *kinship*; *Mauss*; *structuralism*.

Lévy-Bruhl, Lucien (1857–1939)

Lucien Lévy-Bruhl, anthropologist and philosopher, belonged to the Republican generation of French academics, which, strongly influenced by positivist philosophy and imbued with the ideals of lay (anti-clerical) democracy, took command of the new Sorbonne around the turn of the century. He was educated at the École Normale Superieure and following a rapid university career was appointed to a chair in the history of modern philosophy at the Sorbonne in 1904.

The nomination represented a turning point in his intellectual development: from then on most of his work was dedicated to problems of cultural relativity and, specifically, to the theory of 'primitive mentality'. His first major statement in this area, which was formulated in *La Morale et la science des mœurs* (1903) (*Ethics and Moral Science*, 1905), referred to the variability of morals in space and time, and suggested that a rational art of human conduct (ethics) should follow the observed laws of morality and be only applicable to local social circumstances.

His later books, starting with Les *Fonctions mentales dans les sociétés inférieures* (1910) (*How Natives Think*, 1926) and ending with *L'Expérience mystique et les symboles chez les primitifs* (1938), are based largely upon ethnological evidence from secondary sources. The main focus of this work is the study of mental functions in modern and archaic societies. Lévy-Bruhl postulated a basic difference in mental functions in the two forms of society. Primitive mentality, as expressed in collective representations, ignored the rules of logic, particularly the law of contradiction – hence its definition as 'prelogical'. The principle of contradiction was replaced by a notion of mystical participation. Affective elements supplemented logical generalizations, and no clear-cut distinction was made between ordinary and mystical experience. Lévy-Bruhl's theory altered over time. In his later years he argued that the two types of mentality coexisted, rather than postulating two separate socio-mental structures. Indeed, in his posthumous *Les Carnets de Lucien Lévy-Bruhl* (1949) (*The Notebooks on Primitive Mentality*, 1975), he largely repudiated his original notion of the fundamental differences between modern and archaic mentalities.

Lévy-Bruhl significantly influenced structuralist cultural anthropology and Jungian psychoanalysis. Though he was consistently criticized by Durkheim and Mauss, his teaching provided a powerful impetus to the renewal of anthropological studies in France. He was co-founder, together with Marcel Mauss and Paul Rivet, of the Ethnological Institute of Paris University in 1925.

Victor Karady
Centre National de la Recherche Scientifique, Paris

Further Reading

Cazeneuve, J. (1963), *Lucien Lévy-Bruhl, sa vie, son oeuvre, avec un exposé de sa philosophie*, Paris. (English translation, *Lucien Lévy-Bruhl*, Oxford, 1972.)

Lewis, William Arthur (1915–)

Sir Arthur Lewis, who was awarded the Nobel Memorial Prize in Economics in 1979 for his distinguished contributions to the history, theory and analysis of economic development has had a major influence on scientific debate and practical policy formulation, with particular reference to developing countries since the mid-1950s.

Born in 1915 on St Lucia (British West Indies), Lewis studied at the London School of Economics where he also taught for several years, moving later to Manchester. He played both administrative and advisory roles in the West Indies, many African countries, the UN and the World Bank. Since 1963 he has taught political economy at the Woodrow Wilson School, Princeton University.

Lewis approaches economics as a philosopher, political economist, economic historian and development designer – a clue to his great influence. A further clue is his focus on less developed countries within the context of the world economy. Another is that his models are built along sweeping classical lines that interweave basic relationships and ideas in bold strokes – models for the less imaginative but technically more gifted to develop. Still another is that the models have been subjected to empirical testing to verify general validity. But Lewis is not without critics.

In a nutshell, Lewis's first model focuses on the dual nature of an underdeveloped economy: there are two sectors, one traditional employing no capital and one modern. In a number of economies there is unlimited labour supply available at a subsistence wage. As economic development proceeds, subsistence agriculture offers to the more progressive industrial sector a large pool of additional labour force at such subsistence wages. Employment in the industrial sector grows as capital formation occurs. The latter does not raise wages but rather the share of profits in national income. With the expansion of the industrial sector, an increasing share of national income is reinvested. The second model shows that under specific conditions the terms of trade between developed and underdeveloped countries are determined by the relationship between labour productivity in agriculture in these countries. Whereas comparative costs favour free trade in developed countries, in the underdeveloped ones they offer valid arguments for protection. Generally, Lewis doubts the efficacy of trade as a growth propeller and favours planning through the market as contrasted with planning by direction.

Throughout Lewis's work and policy advice there runs a strong current of concern for the poor and underprivileged. A scholar and statesman, he is a man of courage, insight, and great humanity.

George R. Feiwel
University of Tennessee

Further Reading

Findlay, R. and Bowman, M. J. (1980), 'The Nobel Memorial Prize in Economics 1979: On W. Arthur Lewis' and Theodore W. Schultz's contributions to economics', *Scandinavian Journal of Economics*, 82.

Gersovitz, M. *et al.* (eds) (1982), *The Theory and Experience of Economic Development: Essays in Honour of Sir W. Arthur Lewis*, London.

Lewis, W. A. (1949), *The Principles of Economic Planning*, London.

Lewis, W. A. (1955), *The Theory of Economic Growth*, London.

Lewis, W. A. (1969), *Aspects of Tropical Trade, 1883–1965*, Stockholm.

Lewis, W. A. (1978), *Growth and Fluctuations, 1870–1913*, London.

Lewis, W. A. (1983), *Selected Economic Writings of W. Arthur Lewis*, ed. M. Gersovitz, New York.

Lexicostatistics

Lexicostatistics, also referred to as glottochronology, is a method intended to provide dates for earlier stages of languages on the basis of vocabulary change. It was originated around 1950 by Morris Swadesh, an American linguist, on the model of carbon 14 dating.

The technique is based on the notion that all languages have a basic, core vocabulary that is impervious to the linguistic and sociocultural factors that normally affect language change. Unlike vocabulary as a whole, the words in the basic list (common words such as 'drink', 'foot', 'red', 'three') are claimed to be lost – actually, replaced by other forms – at a relatively constant rate. This replacement rate, or its corresponding retention rate, is assumed to apply equally to all words in the list, to be constant through time, and to be the same for all languages of the world. On the basis of a pilot study of thirteen languages (eleven of which belonged to the Indo-European family) the retention rate was calculated to be approximately 86 per cent per millennium using a 100-word list and 81 per cent using a 200-word list. To illustrate, starting with a basic 100-word list, after 1,000 years approximately 86 of the original words would still be found; after 2,000 years the number would be 74 (= 86 × 86 per cent); after 3,000 years the number would be 64 (= 74 × 86 per cent); and so on.

Given the assumption that basic vocabulary changes independently in separate languages at a fixed rate, it follows naturally that if one can determine the number of words from the list that two related languages have in common (true 'cognate' items), one can calculate the time of separation of the daughter languages from their common ancestor. This is the essence of lexicostatistic (glottochronologic) dating. It is given by the formula

$$t = \frac{\log C}{2 \log r}$$

, where t is time in thousands of years, C the percentage of matching cognates, and r the retention rate per millennium. For example, the nearest common ancestor of two languages with 60 per cent cognates (using the 100-word list) would be dated 1,693 years ago; with 30 per cent cognates the date would be 3,991 years ago; while with 18 per cent cognates the date would be 5,684 years ago.

When lexicostatistics was first proposed, it excited anthropologists and linguists, as it represented the first ever technique that would enable scholars to derive absolute dates from linguistic materials. Studies since then, however, have indicated that the assumptions on which the method depends are all of questionable validity, if not totally invalid, and that the dates calculated are so unreliable and subject to such large margins of error as to be worthless. While the idea of vocabulary 'decaying' in a clock-like fashion may have seemed reasonable to Swadesh at the time, it now appears far-fetched and completely at odds with currently accepted views about the nature of language change and the systemic relationship of vocabulary to grammar and phonology.

A second use of lexicostatistics is for subclassifying languages, where closeness of relationship is established directly in terms of the percentage of cognates that languages share. This use does not require that the presumed retention rate be the same for all language families nor that an exact mathematical rate be ascertainable; but it does depend on the fundamental lexicostatistic assumption that languages undergo basic vocabulary change at a constant rate. The great attraction of this method of subclassification as opposed to traditional non-quantitative methods is its extreme simplicity and its amenability to machine-assisted handling of large numbers of languages. Subgrouping by lexicostatistics thus continues to be used to the present day even though it has not been verified empirically nor have its results proved reliable.

Paul Newman
Indiana University, Bloomington

Reference
Swadesh, M. (1952), 'Lexicostatistic dating of prehistoric ethnic contacts', *Proceedings of the American Philosophical Society*, 96.

Further Reading
Bergsland, K. and Vogt, H. (1962), 'On the validity of glottochronology', *Current Anthropology*, 3.
Hymes, D. (1960), 'Lexicostatistics so far', *Current Anthropology*, 1.
Kruskal, J. B., Dyen, I. and Black, P. (1973), 'Some results from the vocabulary method of reconstructing language trees', in I. Dyen (ed.), *Lexicostatistics in Genetic Linguistics*, The Hague.
Rea, J. A. (1973), 'The Romance data of the pilot studies for glottochronology', in T. A. Sebeok *et al.* (eds), *Current Trends in Linguistics*, vol. II, The Hague.
See also: *historical linguistics*.

Liberalism

The belief that people can and that they should be free to determine their own destiny is certainly ancient and widely diffused. So widespread and vague an idea – a sentiment rather than a dogma – is almost impossible to study in time and space; all that can be observed is the variety of specific social propositions which arise from it.

Contemporary liberalism, in the sense of a series of social ideas belonging to a political tradition, often seeks its roots in the ideas of Levellers in Cromwell's coalition during the English Civil War of the seventeenth century; in the revolt of the American colonists a century later; and in Jacobin revolutionaries in France soon afterwards. Present-day liberals find the clear articulation of a range of liberal propositions in the philosophical writings of Rousseau and Locke, in the propaganda of Tom Paine, and in the economic analysis of Adam Smith. These classic expressions were antagonistic towards the essentially feudal political structures, which had more or less successfully administered agrarian societies in Western Europe but which floundered in the attempt to regulate increasingly urban and non-agricultural peoples and processes. Because of the structure of these historic conflicts, liberalism came to be rationalist and humanist, rejecting hereditary authority and supernatural sanctions on behaviour. Naturally, these ideas appealed most powerfully to individuals and groups who were themselves in conflict with the agrarian order, and to mercantilist regulation of trade. In the long run, as emergent capitalists and their allies took up the classic ideas, general arguments for freedom were transformed into specific requests for equality of economic opportunity.

In the two centuries since liberal ideas were most forcibly expressed, feudal state structures and social relationships have almost entirely disappeared and – at least in fully capitalist societies – many items of a formal liberal programme have been implemented. That list would include the election of legislators by adults, the control of the executive either by popular vote or by legislative supremacy, and a judiciary independent in day-to-day matters from intervention by other arms of government. If the mechanics of government have become more liberal, however, the spirit which animates these modern structures is very much more oppressive than Rousseau, or Paine, or Smith expected. With the logic of capitalist accumulation established as the most promising strategy for creating employment and revenue, the opinions of owners and managers of enterprises naturally carry heavy weight. Equality of political rights restrains, but it does not obliterate the unequal political, cultural and social influence of holders of economic power. In fully industrial societies, therefore, liberalism is close to the point of sterile exhaustion, defending (in the name of ancient revolutions against extinct oppressions) as great a degree of inequality as feudal states ever enjoyed. The actual justification for inequality is not the liberal procedures which restrain it, but rather the relatively high standards of health, education, income and consumption which have prevailed.

Outside the fully capitalist societies, the liberal sentiment confronts and is shaped by quite different circumstances. The French Revolution itself helped to clarify an alternative theory of liberation in the minds of some thoughtful revolutionaries. The alternative theory was less concerned with the survival or revival of feudal structures than with the significance of privately owned property as the source of inequality and oppression. If private ownership of productive property were the core problem, then collective ownership might represent a solution. These socialist ideas, gathered together and restated and developed by Marx and Engels later in the nineteenth century, provided an ideology of liberation – until they were taken over by successful revolutionary movements in Russia, Eastern Europe and China. Like liberalism, socialism could be applied as an ideology of government just as much as an ideology of revolt.

The great ideological struggles of the twentieth century have been dominated by liberal and socialist dogmas. Where capitalist development had not already occurred on a massive scale, socialist ideas have been more successful as ideologies of government than their liberal rivals. In those societies, therefore, liberal ideas retain their pristine revolutionary force, threatening to undermine party and bureaucratic controls.

However, most of the world's population live in societies which are neither fully capitalist nor controlled by socialist administrations. Like socialist societies, most Third-World governments are heavily bureaucratic; and the national bureaucracies are often directed by military officers or by narrow oligarchies. In these oppressive situations, even the formal programme of liberalism – equality before the law, a genuinely independent judiciary, regular elections on a wide franchise – would be revolutionary. In such circumstances, however, the prevalence of a grinding poverty and the daily struggle for survival leave little room even in the imagination for such seemingly abstract notions. For precisely the reasons which would render liberal procedures a revolution, they are unlikely to be realized.

In a programme of procedures, then, liberalism has probably run its course by the late twentieth century, almost as completely as anarchism. Where the programme has been implemented, it has grown sterile; elsewhere it seems unrealizable. But as a sentiment, infinitely adaptable to evolving oppressions and always opposed to them, it is still an idea which is cherished in every corner of the world. To look (and work) for the time where it becomes obsolete is not an unworthy aspiration.

Donald Denoon
Australian National University, Canberra

Further Reading
Brausted, E. K. and Melhuish, K. J. (eds) (1978), *Western Liberalism*, London.
Gaus, G. (1983), *The Modern Liberal Theory of Man*, London.
Minogue, K. R. (1963), *The Liberal Mind*, London.
See also: *conservatism*; *equality*; *Mill*; *socialism*.

Life Cycle

The way in which the life cycle is divided up, and how its phases are represented, varies greatly between cultures. Culture imposes its own pattern on biological events and the process of maturation; and it is society, not physiology, which through its rituals makes men of boys, or ancestors of elders. In many cultures an individual's progress through the sequence of life stages is represented as a series of jumps rather than as a steady undifferentiated flow. It may also be seen as a progress toward the acquisition of full personhood.

Very often the infant is not a person at all until named some weeks after birth; and its death does not therefore occasion any public ritual or mourning. Weaning commonly marks the transition from infancy to childhood – the duration of which is culturally highly variable, as is the extent to which children are represented as inhabiting a separate sphere with needs and requirements quite different from those of adults (see Ariès, 1962). In many traditional societies child labour has a significant role to play in the production process, and in some towards the reproduction of the symbolic order of the adult world. It may, for example, be crucial to the maintenance of purdah restrictions, for female seclusion could not be sustained without children to run errands and carry messages to other houses which adults cannot freely enter, and to market women's home production. While in contemporary Western culture, adolescence is often represented as a phase of rebellious insubordination, experimentation and emotional turmoil, Wilder (1970) describes it as a time during which the rural Malay youth exhibits an extreme passivity amounting almost to suspended animation; and, in a now classic study, Mead (1928) argued that the 'crisis of adolescence' does not exist in Samoa (a conclusion for which the ethnographic basis has been forcefully – if inconclusively – contested by Freeman (1983)).

The cultural definition of adult maturity is highly relative; but in many societies marriage marks the crucial transition for both sexes. Amongst certain groups of Australian Aborigines a woman reverts to the status of 'girl' regardless of her chronological age as soon as her marriage is dissolved. In the age-set systems of East Africa a man's marriage, which confers full adult status, may be delayed until he is 30 or 40 years old. After a Samburu boy's age-set have been circumcised they become *moran* or 'warriors' who will live for a decade or more in the bush away from the settlements of the elders and their polygynous households (Spencer, 1965). Gerontocratic polygyny clearly depends on the prolonged bachelorhood of the warriors. Elsewhere a married man remains a jural minor so long as his father is alive (Fortes, 1949).

Old age is an honoured condition in many traditional societies, and there appears to be a strong correlation between ancestor worship and reverence for the elderly. In many cases the authority of male elders is sustained by their monopoly over rights in women, and/or over the items required for marriage payments (Douglas, 1958). In preliterate cultures the elderly are also the repositories of tradition and of the sacred knowledge which ensure the abundance of the harvest, the fertility of the women and the health of the community. Sometimes the old are expected to withdraw progressively from practical life in order to devote themselves to spiritual matters. In the final phase of his life, the Hindu male should renounce the world and become a wandering ascetic (though it might be argued that the chief effect of this theory is to promote a thoroughly this-worldly ethic during the earlier 'householder' stage on the grounds that there will be time enough for other-worldliness in one's dotage). Elsewhere the old are routinely neglected and treated with some callousness (see Ortner, 1978 on the Sherpas). Amongst the pastoral Fulani of north-eastern Nigeria, each son owns a specified share of the herd managed by his father, from which he withdraws his cattle when he sets up an independent domestic unit after the birth of his first child. At the marriage of his youngest son a man's herd is finally completely dispersed, and he and his wife (or wives) each go to live with their eldest son (which, given high rates of divorce and polygyny, will probably mean that they go to different places). There the old man sleeps on the periphery of the homestead where he will eventually be buried. Socially he is already dead, and he makes his bed over his own grave (Stenning, 1958).

J. P. Parry
London School of Economics and Political Science

References
Ariès, P. (1962), *Centuries of Childhood*, New York.
Douglas, M. (1958), 'Raffia cloth distribution in the Lele economy', *Africa*, 28.
Fortes, M. (1949), *The Web of Kinship Among the Tallensi*, Oxford.
Freeman, D. (1983), *Margaret Mead and Samoa: The Making and Unmaking of an Anthropological Myth*, Cambridge, Mass.
Mead, M. (1928), *Coming of Age in Samoa*, London.
Ortner, S. (1978), *Sherpas Through Their Rituals*, Cambridge.
Spencer, P. (1965), *The Samburu: A Study of Gerontocracy in a Nomadic Tribe*, London.
Stenning, D. (1958), 'Household viability among the Pastoral Fulani', in J. Goody (ed.), *The Developmental Cycle in Domestic Groups*, Cambridge.
Wilder, W. (1970), 'Socialization and social structure in a Malay village', in P. Mayer (ed.), *Socialization: The Approach From Social Anthropology*, London.

See also: *age organization*; *death*; *gerontology, social*; *life-span development*.

Life Histories

A life history may be defined as the sequence of events and experiences in a life from birth until death. Life histories can be studied not only with the 'life history method' of having a respondent recount the story of his or her life, but also with the full range of social scientific and historical methods, including archival research, participant observation, experimental methods, and longitudinal research.

Within the social sciences, it is possible to identify roughly three periods in the study of life histories: (1) From approximately 1920 to the Second World War, there was a substantial and growing interest in life histories, much of it associated with the study of personal documents such as autobiographies, letters and diaries (Thomas and Znaniecki, 1920; Murray, 1938; Allport, 1942). (2) From the Second World War to the mid-1960s, interest declined and instead increased attention was given to more structured quantitative and experimental methods. (3) However, within the last two decades, there has been an enormous outpouring of work in the study of lives associated with developments in fields such as life-history research in psychopathology (Roff and Ricks, 1970), adult development (Levinson *et al.*, 1978; White, 1975), sociological studies of the life course (Elder, 1974), oral history and life stories (Bennett, 1981; Bertaux, 1981), and psychobiography (Erikson, 1975; Runyan, 1982).

Critics argue that life-history studies are ineffective in ruling out competing causal explanations and that it is unsafe to generalize from the study of a single case. Studies of individual life histories are, however, appropriately evaluated not on their effectiveness for testing causal generalizations (a criterion most appropriate for experimental studies), but rather on their ability to present and interpret information about the life of a single individual. Such studies can usefully be evaluated through a 'quasi-judicial' methodology (Bromley, 1977), analogous to procedures in courts of law, where evidence, inferences and interpretations in a life-history study are critically assessed by those with competing points of view who are free to present their own evidence, interpretations and conclusions.

The goals of psychology can be thought of as existing on three distinct levels: learning (1) what is true of persons-in-general; (2) what is true of groups of persons, distinguished by sex, race, social class, culture and historical period; and (3) what is true of individual human beings. These three levels of analysis inform one another, but are also partially independent. The study of individual life histories is a necessary complement to the study of group differences and the search for universal generalizations.

William McKinley Runyan
University of California, Berkeley

References
Allport, G. W. (1942), *The Use of Personal Documents in Psychological Science*, New York.
Bennett, J. (1981), *Oral History and Delinquency: The Rhetoric of Criminology*, Chicago.
Bertaux, D. (ed.) (1981), *Biography and Society: The Life History Approach in the Social Sciences*, Beverly Hills, Calif.
Bromley, D. B. (1977), *Personality Description in Ordinary Language*, New York.
Elder, G. H., Jr (1974), *Children of the Great Depression*, Chicago.
Erikson, E. H. (1975), *Life History and the Historical Moment*, New York.
Levinson, D. *et al.* (1978), *The Seasons of a Man's Life*, New York.
Murray, H. A. *et al.* (1938), *Explorations in Personality*, New York.
Roff, M. and Ricks, D. (eds) (1970), *Life History Research in Psychopathology*, vol. I, Minneapolis.
Runyan, W. M. (1982), *Life Histories and Psychobiography: Explorations in Theory and Method*, New York.
White, R. W. (1975), *Lives in Progress*, 3rd edn, New York.
Thomas, W. I. and Znaniecki, F. (1920), *The Polish Peasant in Europe and America*, Boston.
See also: *case studies*; *life-span development*.

Life-Span Development

Life-span development is the study of individual change (ontogeny) throughout the course of life, in an effort to obtain knowledge about both general principles and individual variation. Although life-span considerations have enjoyed a long history, it is only during the last two decades that researchers have begun to take this approach seriously, following the lead of twentieth-century psychologists such as Bühler, Erikson, Hall and Jung (Baltes, Reese and Lipsitt, 1980; Featherman, 1983).

Life-span development is less a theory than an orientation, containing several unique propositions about development. These are: (1) There is considerable inter-individual variation in development. Whereas child developmentalists have sought unidirectional, universally applicable laws, adult developmentalists have noted greater diversity and plasticity (adapta-

bility) of developmental patterns. (2) Historical changes affect the path development takes. The role of historical change has been studied, for example, with the use of age/cohort sequential methodology, where individuals from two or more cohorts (generations) are followed over a long period of time (Schaie, 1979). (3) Interdisciplinary collaboration is necessary in order to describe fully individual development within a changing world. Featherman (1983) illustrates the usefulness of such an interdisciplinary approach in the fields of psychology, sociology and economics. Jointly considered, these three propositions advanced in life-span research have necessitated an emphasis on the interactive relationships between individual development and historical change, resulting in a dialectical (Riegel, 1976) and contextualist (Lerner *et al.*, 1983) conception of human development.

Life-span researchers propose several frameworks for conceptualizing the direction and patterning of development. One framework emphasizes generalized (normative) patterns of development, as illustrated in Havighurst's work on developmental tasks and Erikson's on life-long sequences of personality themes and goals. Another framework considers variability and plasticity in human development (for example, Brim and Kagan, 1980; Schaie, 1979). To account for such variability, Baltes and his colleagues have described three interacting systems of influences on development: age-graded, history-graded, and non-normative (Baltes *et al.*, 1980). All these systems take into account both biological and environmental factors.

Age-correlated factors have been the major focus of mainstream developmental psychology, particularly child-developmental. History-graded influences refer to biocultural changes in the conditions (for example, health status, resources, tasks, roles, expectations) that may influence the development of particular subgroups, as evidenced, for example, in generation or cohort membership; these have been a hallmark of sociological work on the life course (Elder, 1975; Riley, 1984). Finally, non-normative influences refer to unique biological and environmental events that are not representative of the experiences of the majority of individuals of a given cohort or time period (for example, winning a lottery, contracting a serious illness at an early age, immigrating to a new culture). Explication of the combined operation of age-graded, history-graded, and non-normative life events permits the specification of both commonalities (for example, age-graded) and differences (such as history-graded, non-normative) in life-span development.

Let us consider the development of intelligence across the life span as a substantive example (Labouvie-Vief, 1984; Schaie, 1979). Research has pointed to inter-individual differences in the patterns of growth, maintenance and/or decline of intellectual skills. On the one hand, such variability is the result of differences in life history such as those associated with educational and occupational status. More highly educated individuals, for example, maintain their intellectual skills into old age better than less educated individuals. On the other hand, such variability also involves differences between abilities. For example, measures of fluid intelligence (an index of basic information processing and reasoning presumably independent of specific learning) are more susceptible to deterioration with age, while those of crystallized intelligence (an index of acquired knowledge) may even improve into old age. Furthermore, there is much plasticity in life-long development since, depending on which cognitive processes are exercised or not, the level and rate of intellectual development can vary widely. Even in old age, intellectual capacity remains plastic to some extent.

Life-span developmental research forces us to consider the plurality of factors involved in development. It has provided us with a more dynamic view of human development, and has re-evaluated the more traditional ideas of development across the course of the life which largely depicted behaviour as deterministic and unchanging. The emphasis on flexibility inherent in this view is another important perspective (Featherman, 1983). Such flexibility has implications for child development as well, where the traditional view of childhood as the major determining force in later behaviour has been challenged (Brim and Kagan, 1980). We now know that childhood does not necessarily set the stage for irreversible behaviour patterns in adulthood. A key task of future work on life-span development is to sort out conditions for both universal and particular laws and phenomena of development.

Deirdre A. Kramer
Rutgers University, New Brunswick
Paul B. Baltes
Max Planck Institute for Human Development and
Education, Berlin

References

Baltes, P. B., Reese, H. W. and Lipsitt, L. P. (1980), 'Life-span developmental psychology', *Annual Review of Psychology*, 31.
Brim, O. G., Jr and Kagan, J. (1980), *Constancy and Change in Human Development*, Cambridge, Mass.
Elder, G. H., Jr (1975), 'Age-differentiation in life course perspective', *Annual Review of Sociology*, 1.
Featherman, D. L. (1983), 'The life-span perspective in social science research', in P. B. Baltes and O. G. Brim, Jr (eds), *Life-Span Development and Behavior*, vol. 5, New York.
Labouvie-Vief, G. (1984), 'Intelligence and cognition', in J. E. Birren and K. W. Schaie (eds), *Handbook of the Psychology of Aging*, 2nd edn, New York.
Lerner, R. M., Hultsch, D. F. and Dixon, R. A. (1983), 'Contextualism and the characteristic of developmental psychology in the 1970's', *Annals of the New York Academy of Sciences*.
Riegel, K. F. (1976), 'The dialectics of human development', *American Psychologist*, 31.
Riley, M. W. (1984), 'Age strata in social systems', in R. H. Binstock and E. Shanas (eds), *Handbook of Aging and the Social Sciences* (revised edn), New York.
Schaie, K. W. (1979), 'The primary mental abilities in adulthood: an exploration in the development of psychometric intelligence', in P. B. Baltes and O. G. Brim, Jr (eds), *Life-span Development and Behavior*, vol. 2, New York.

See also: *adolescence*; *ageing – psychological aspects*; *developmental psychology*; *life cycle*.

Limited Liability

The most common form of capitalist business enterprise, the limited liability company, has a legal status of a *persona* separate from owners or shareholders. Three features arise: (1) debts incurred are the firm's, not the shareholders', whose maximum liability is restricted to their original financial outlay; (2) the identity of the firm is unchanged should one shareholder transfer his ownership title to a third party; (3) the firm's contractual relationships are entered into by its officers (for example, directors or managers).

These characteristics were not originally coexistent. By the fifteenth century, English law had awarded limited liability to monastic communities and trade guilds for commonly held property. In the seventeenth century, joint stock charters were awarded by the Crown as circumscribed monopoly privileges to groups such as the East India and Hudson's Bay Companies.

By the early nineteenth century, a joint stock company could be formed simply by registration, and no monopoly privileges were awarded. The merging of the features was completed by mid-century when incorporation with full limited liability became permissible and common in the UK and the US, and in Europe a decade or so later.

It is widely agreed that the move to large-scale industrial enterprise was facilitated, and indeed made possible, by limited liability. The threat of potential confiscation of an individual's total wealth should he invest part of it in an unsuccessful company was removed. Moreover, his risk could be further reduced if he invested in several and not just one firm. Large sums of untapped personal financial capital became available. Transferability of shares permitted continuity of business operation not present in other forms of enterprise. The existence of the firm as a separate contracting *persona* permitted a productive division of labour between risk-bearing capitalists and business administrators.

Schumpeter (1950) criticized this latter development as having pushed 'into the background all . . . the institutions of property and free contracting . . . that expressed the needs . . . of economic activity'. Hessen (1979)has taken the contrary view: limited liability is a creature of private agreement, not the state. Freely negotiated contractual specialization is a device for greater efficiency in meeting private wants, not a shirking of responsibility, not a Schumpeterian 'absentee ownership' which because nobody is 'left . . . to stand for it' must evolve into a state controlled bureaucracy.

W. Duncan Reekie
University of the Witwatersrand, Johannesburg

References
Hessen, R. (1979), *In Defense of the Corporation*, Stanford, California.
Schumpeter, J. (1950), *Capitalism, Socialism and Democracy*, New York.

Linguistics

Linguistics can be defined as the science of language. Language, however, may be approached from a number of different perspectives, and it plays such a central role in human life that many disciplines are concerned with language in one way or another. Indeed every science contains one linguistic component at the very least, the language of its theory and observations with which it may at times be concerned. What then distinguishes linguistics from other sciences?

There is one field which is particularly close to linguistics, and that is the study of literature, since its very material is verbal. However, even in this case the preoccupation with linguistic matters is different from that of linguistics itself. In all other fields, language is a means to an end; only in linguistics is it studied as an end in itself.

Like so many other sciences, linguistics took its modern form as a separate academic discipline in the nineteenth century, although, it has a long prehistory. In particular it was preceded by national philologies, which arose in literate societies such as those of India, China and Greece. Modern linguistics developed in Europe on the basis of the Graeco-Roman tradition with minor contributions from Semitic sources in the Renaissance. The most theoretically sophisticated of these national philologies was that of India, and yet it only became known to Europe in the nineteenth century while an appreciation of its significance is even more recent.

Although the philological studies of the grammarians is the chief source for linguistics in the Classical tradition, two other pursuits are worthy of mention.

One is the philosophical concern with the nature of language. The main question was whether the relation between sound and meaning is natural or conventional and the most important discussion is Plato's *Cratylus*. The second source is rhetoric, the effective use of language in public speaking and writing. Some of the earliest analyses of linguistic phenomena, such as Protagoras' distinguishing of the various moods of the verb, grew out of this applied interest.

The most important, though, was the philological tradition of the grammarians which developed in the Alexandrian period. In common with other national philologies it displayed the following features. The study of languages has as its goal the understanding of certain highly valued texts, sacred or, in the case of the Greeks, profane, namely the Homeric poems. It involves concentration on a single language and a valuation of it as superior to all other forms of speech including the contemporary spoken language which inevitably, in the course of linguistic change, has come to differ from it. It views historic change not as a rational process but as a haphazard degeneration from a formerly ideal state. This in turn involves the notion of prescriptivism, an attempt to restore a particular norm which is contrary to existing usage. The concentration on written texts also makes the written form primary *vis-à-vis* the spoken, since sounds are merely the momentary realizations of the apparently stable and fixed written norms. That language is not here studied for its own sake is very strikingly expressed in the *Technē Grammatikē* (attributed to Dionysius Thrax around 100 BC), itself the model of numerous subsequent grammars. After enumerating the various subdivisions of grammar, the last mentioned is 'the appreciation of literary composition which is the noblest part of grammar'.

Nevertheless this tradition made lasting contributions. It provided a comprehensive model for describing language which was well suited to Latin and Greek and is the source of a large part of current linguistic terminology. It may be called the word-paradigm model. The sentence consists of words which are divisible on the basis of form and function into a small number of classes, the parts of speech. Further, each part of speech can be considered from two points of view, internal variabililty of form (morphology) and functional relation to other words in the speech chain (syntax). In the area of morphology the lasting achievement was the discovery of the paradigm, literally 'example'. Inflectional parts of speech such as the noun vary according to a set of categories, for example, case and number, and the number of distinct models is very small. For instance, all Latin nouns of the first declension have similar variations of form and any one noun, such as *puella*, 'girl', can be viewed as an example to follow for the rest. This was no mean achievement and grew out of the dispute in the Alexandrian period between the analogists, who stressed regularity in language, and the anomalists, who denied it. It was the search for regularities by the analogists that revealed the existence of comprehensive patterns, namely paradigms.

In syntax, there was the classification of types of relationship among words such as government, as when a verb requires and hence 'governs' a particular case, and agreement, as when two words agree in having the same categories, for example, the adjectives agreeing with nouns in gender, number and case.

One further feature of this model should be mentioned. It involved a hierarchy of levels. Sounds made up words; words made up sentences. On this basis there were two main levels, the phonological and grammatical, the latter divided, as has been seen, into morphology and syntax. Such a notion of levels has remained as part of linguistic theory. In particular the existence of phonological and grammatical levels, even though there are relationships between them, seems to be fundamental to any theory of language.

The model just described was not all discovered at once by the Greeks. It developed considerably in the Roman, medieval and the post-medieval periods. In particular the rise of *grammaire générale*, largely but not exclusively French, in the seventeenth and eighteenth century (though without medieval predecessors) deserves mention. It employed the word-paradigm model but sought to explain its structure by reference to universal reason and the very nature of the world and of thought as shown by metaphysics and logic. Thus the difference between nouns and adjectives mirrored the difference between substances and their qualities. Moreover, a number of languages were often compared on the assumption that such categories, inherent in human reason, must exist in all languages.

The nineteenth century was not marked merely by the rise of linguistics as a separate discipline but involved a revolution in the conception of language. As a result of exploration and colonization, Europe became acutely aware of the vast number and diversity of human languages. The traditional explanation was the biblical story of the Tower of Babel, and at first the main question was what language was spoken before the confusion of tongues, the *lingua Adamica*. However, it began to be noticed that the differences in language were not haphazard; they fall into groupings such as the Romance, Germanic and Semitic languages.

The basic explanation which developed about the turn of the nineteenth century was that just as Spanish was like Italian because they were both changed forms of an originally homogeneous language, Latin, so where the original language was not recorded, the explanation had to be similar. There must have been a 'Proto-Germanic' and a 'Proto-Semitic' and so on. Moreover this process of differentiation of an ancestral

language was not confined to the most obvious groupings. In particular the discovery of Sankrit, the sacred language of India, with its obvious resemblance to Latin, Greek and other European languages, led to the hypothesis of an original Indo-European language which had branched into Latin, Greek, Indo-Iranian, Germanic, Slavic and so on, which then in most instances differentiated once more in a more recent period. The metaphor was that of a family tree.

The historical-comparative method that dominated nineteenth-century linguistics had as its goal the reconstruction of the original ancestral language and of the subsequent changes in it, which gave rise to later language. It was mainly applied to Indo-European but was also employed in the study of other language families. This way of looking at language was in many ways diametrically opposed to the traditional one inherited from Classical philology. Change is not a haphazard degeneration but follows rational patterns, indeed, becomes the central object of linguistic science. Changes on the phonological level are understandable in terms of articulatory and auditory similarity. Hence the written form is equally valuable since change is not degeneration, and the logical basis for linguistic prescriptivism is destroyed.

During the nineteenth century and up to about 1920, the inherited pattern of grammatical description, though often modified, continued its sway because the focus of interest was historical change. However, in the late 1920s another basic revolution in linguistics occurred, which we may call the structural. The first articulation of this was in 1915 in the posthumous *Cours de linguistique générale* (English translation, *Course in General Linguistics*, 1959) of Ferdinand de Saussure of Geneva. De Saussure, himself a historical linguist by training, introduced a terminology which has become general in the social sciences. Language can be studied diachronically in its aspect of historical process, or synchronically in terms of the internal relations within a state as abstracted from change. There were a number of structural schools, differing in many respects but united in finding in the synchronic structure of language the central object of linguistic science. An important factor was the work of anthropologists on non-Western languages where both the profound differences from Western languages and the usual absence of historical records combined to concentrate attention on synchronic structure.

The nature of these new methods can be most easily illustrated from phonology, which was in fact the earliest area of interest for the structuralists. A mere enumeration of the sounds of the language without regard to their functional relations was unenlightening. Thus two languages might both have *p* and *b* sounds which were phonetically identical but, if a rule could be formulated that told us when *p* occurs and when *b* in terms of other sounds, there could never be a functional meaning contrast. This is the case for the Algonkian languages. In English, on the other hand, *pat* and *bat* are different words. For the Algonkian languages *p* and *b* belong to the same phoneme or functional unit, while in English they are two contrasting units.

Similarly, methods were extended to the grammatical level leading to the positing of functional units like the morpheme. Thus the English phonemic variants of the plural *-s*, *-z* and *-əz* are predictable on the basis of the final phoneme, the stem, and hence are members of the same functional unit.

In 1957, Chomsky's *Syntactic Structures* ushered in the period of generative grammar. The basic concept uses not functional units but rules. Moreover, grammar was constructed not as in the American structural school of observation by induction from the bottom up, morphemes consisting of phonemes and so on, but from top down – from syntax, particularly relations among whole sentence patterns (transformations) with appeals to native intuitions of grammaticality. The whole grammar was not unlike an axiomatic system. The basic formulas often called deep structure such as Subject + Predicate occurred first and by rule-governed substitutions, and transformations ended up as strings which would then be realized as actual utterances by phonological rules. After some years it became apparent that describing languages with this basic approach also leads to differing theories as in structuralism, and at the time of writing no one version holds the field.

A basic question raised by both the structuralist and generative revolution was the role of interlinguistic comparisons. Historical linguistics was essentially comparative, but was it possible to compare structures ahistorically? Did one just end up with an indefinitely large number of non-comparable individual descriptions? The American structuralist school seemed on the whole content with these results. The only universals of the dominant view were those of methodology. Languages could differ to any degree so that no cross-linguistic generalization was possible. The Prague school stressed the possibility of comparing structures and made some beginnings, especially in phonology. Chomsky had by 1965 (*Syntactic Structures*) moved to the notion of universal grammar and indeed hailed *Grammaire générale* as a predecessor. All grammars had identical deep structures and these reflected a universal genetically based human endowment. This viewpoint ultimately had to be abandoned to be replaced by universal constraints on the forms of grammars. Finally there were those who approached language universals by noting the existence of recurring and limited sets of types based on observations close to the surface, for example, in word order. Such constraints were frequently in the form of implicational relationships. For instance, language of the VSO type (with basic order verb-subject-object) always had the dependent

genitive after the noun, but not necessarily *vice versa*. There were also non-restricted universals, such as that all sound systems have at least two vowel levels and two series of stop sounds based on the point of articulation.

Linguistics is at present divided into a considerable number of subfields, some of which are interdisciplinary. Some linguists pursue historical comparison whose legitimacy has never been seriously questioned by structuralists, usually specializing in some particular historical family, or subfamily, of languages. Others, particularly anthropological linguists, concentrate on the synchronic description of unwritten languages often with an areal specialization and some historical-comparative interests. On the basis of linguistic structure, some specialize in phonology frequently involving laboratory phonetics. Others work on grammatical level, particularly the syntactic, and may have connections with computer science. Still others are chiefly interested in semantics, often in alliance with philosophy. More purely interdisciplinary fields include psycholinguistics involving an analysis of the psychological processes at work in language use, acquisition of language by the child or second-language learning. A further important interdisciplinary area is sociolinguistics, commonly divided into macro-sociolinguistics, for example, language in relation to ethnicity with its accompanying social, political and education problems, and micro-sociolinguistics, which is concerned with conversational interaction as related, for example, to situational factors and the relative social status of the participants.

Since the 1950s linguistics, usually a minor speciality in other departments, has had an almost explosive growth, particularly in the United States, with a corresponding expansion in the number and size of independent departments and reflecting both the intellectual development of the field itself and its numerous connections with other disciplines.

Joseph Greenberg
Stanford University

Further Reading
Greenberg, J. H. (1977), *New Invitation to Linguistics*, Garden City, New York.
Greenberg, J. J. (ed.) (1978), *Universals of Human Language*, 4 vols, Stanford, Calif.
Lyons, J. (1968), *Introduction to Theoretical Linguistics*, 2 vols, London.
Newmeyer, F. J. (1980), *Linguistic Theory in America*, New York.
Robins, R. H. (1968), *A Short History of Linguistics*, Bloomington, Ind.
Sampson, G. (1980), *Schools of Linguistics*, Stanford, Calif.
Vachek, J. (1964), *A Prague School Reader in Linguistics*, Bloomington, Ind.

Liquidity

Keynes's discussion of the incentives to and consequences of *liquidity* is arguably one of the major innovations of *The General Theory*. Assets are said to be more or less liquid according to the ease and certainty with which they can be converted into money, the ultimate liquid asset. There is no absolute standard of liquidity, as Keynes said, but merely a scale of liquidity, and even the latter is 'a partly vague concept' changing 'from time to time depending on social practices and institutions'. Thus today, for example, building society deposits which are fixed in money terms and convertible on demand or at short notice might be regarded as highly liquid, in contrast to fixed property which might be difficult to sell and the market price of which may vary. In the past, however, land and fixed property have been considered very liquid assets due to their well-developed markets. Thus, while objective standards of liquidity may be difficult to gauge given the essentially *subjective* nature of judgements about liquidity, the latter can be inferred from the liquidity premia which wealth holders require to tempt them into various assets. In general terms interest is the reward for parting with liquidity, and the less liquid an asset the greater the reward must be, that is, the higher the liquidity premium. Given a positive interest rate the problem is to explain why people hold any money at all, that is, what motivates 'liquidity preference'.

Keynes identified three motives: (1) The so-called *transactions motive* has strong roots in classical monetary theory deriving as it does from the need to finance current net expenditures, and is usually modelled along classical lines as a function of (often assumed proportional to) the level of income. (2) Not all transactions can be anticipated with certainty, hence the need for incremental liquidity to insure against the possibility that unforeseen transactions might be necessary and might therefore impose substantive costs as illiquid assets have to be converted into cash at short notice. This Keynes called the *precautionary motive* and it too is usually related to income levels. (3) The *speculative motive* develops the Keynesian theme of uncertainty and breaks away from the classical identification of money holdings as fixed in relation to income by the prerequisites of the structure of transactions.

The speculative motive for holding money derives from uncertainty as to the future rate of interest and therefore differential expectations about the future prices of fixed interest-bearing assets. This raises the possibility of making capital gains/losses by out-/underguessing the market. Thus, if an investor anticipates a fall (rise) in the interest rate, then capital gains (losses) could be made (avoided) by moving out of cash (bonds) and into bonds (cash) ahead of the market.

Assuming that expectations relate to the current interest rate relative to some 'long-run normal level', and that the latter is subjectively determined so that we have a distribution of expectations, then the quantity of money that the general public prefer to hold will vary smoothly and inversely with the rate of interest. This identification of the speculative motive breaks the link between income and money holding which underpins the classical belief in the neutrality of money with far-reaching implications.

In addition, the Keynesian insistence on liquidity as a generalized concept, typified but not exhausted at one extreme by money, has two additional important consequences. First, and less well developed in the literature, is Keynes's deprecation of the speculative motive to hold cash as an obstacle to accumulation and therefore wealth. Second, is the post-Keynesian position that the line between money and debts can be drawn only arbitrarily, and that in an advanced industrial economy they are increasingly close substitutes, with the result that monetary constraint must be widened to encompass the disintermediation into non-monetary but still effectively liquid assets that would follow traditional control. While theoretically convincing, the practical problems involved in this approach are enormous and have contributed to the post-Keynesian mistrust of monetary policy as an important component of demand management.

Jane Humphries
University of Cambridge

Further Reading
Goodhart, C.A.E. (1984), 'The importance of money', in *Monetary Theory and Practice*, London.
Keynes, J. M. (1964 [1936]), *The General Theory of Employment, Interest and Money*, London.
The Committee on the Working of the Monetary System (Radcliffe Report) (1969), Cmnd 827, HMSO, London.
See also: *investment*; *money*.

Literacy

Less than two decades ago, the place and meaning of the concept and the fact of literacy in the social sciences was a simple and secure one. Tied closely to the 'liberal', post-Enlightenment synthesis of modernization theory, literacy was seen as a central variable among that complex of factors that distinguished modern, developed or developing, and advanced societies *and* individuals, from the lesser developed areas and persons of the world. Literacy, moreover, was typically conceptualized more as an independent variable than a dependent factor. Support for this set of propositions was drawn, on one hand, from a set of once commonsensical assumptions and expectations, rooted in a special view of the nature of (historical) development that emphasized the linearity and certainty of progress and, on the other hand, from a number of aggregate macrolevel ecological correlations that saw literacy levels relatively highly associated with many of the other indicators of social development, ranging from fertility rates to measures of economic development. Although literacy itself was at best vaguely defined and variously measured, a diffuse positivism and functionalism undergirded the prominence accorded to it in many formulations. But despite strong assumptions, there were surprisingly few empirical or critical studies. Important questions were few: expectations of literacy's key contribution to social and economic development, political democratization and participant citizenship, widening awareness and identification, seizure of opportunities, and action orientations dominated. As such, promotion of literacy often featured as a central element in plans for the development of underdeveloped areas, especially by North American and Western European social scientists, governments and foundations.

Such an understanding no longer maintains its hegemony. In fact, in the mid-1980s, no central theory governs expectations about the roles and meanings of literacy, and its very nature has itself become problematic and arouses contention and increasingly critical attention. From its formerly secure status as critical independent variable, literacy is now conceptualized more as a dependent factor; the linearity of its contributions is also debated. Ironically, as the status – so to speak – of literacy as an independently determinative, necessary if not always sufficient, variable has declined, its place on the agenda of social science research and discussion has risen. There are lessons in that transformation.

Many sources account for this change. Among them are the discovery of the limits of modernization theory and the theoretical synthesis on which it was based; greater awareness of the differences (and different effects) among literacy, schooling and education – terms too often used interchangeably and confused conceptually; recognition of the problematic nature of literacy, and the conceptual and empirical difficulties that the subject represents. For example, by the 1960s, the severe problems of measuring literacy, comparing measures and resulting rates for different places and periods, and assessing associations and contributions, were frequently noted; a variety of measures and definitions, with a trend towards their inflation, proliferated. Whether literacy's impacts were attitudinal and ideational, cognitive, skill-linked, concrete or more abstract, all-pervasive or more selective, sparked further discussion and weakened common bases of understanding. In addition, the conservative functions and consequences of literacy and, indeed, certain 'noneffects' received renewed attention. Empirical studies became more sensitive to weak and contradictory findings; discussions of literacy 'gaps' and time 'lags' in association with other expected aspects and concomitants of development punctuated the literature. International attention increased: from the twin sources of UNESCO's calls for action and analysis and pathbreaking national literacy campaigns in the Third World. The discovery of persisting *il*literacy in the advanced societies led to the identification of *il*literacy, and sometimes literacy, too, as a 'social problem', and a late-twentieth-century threat to national security, economic productivity, national welfare and the promise of democratic life. Rapid changes in communications technology, especially of nonprint and nonalphabetic forms (in contrast to the traditional bases of literacy) not only led to sometimes frenzied questions about the 'future' and 'decline' of literacy and print, but also stimulated more questions about definitions, measures and levels of individual and national skills requisite for survival and advancement in late modern societies. Whereas literacy was seldom deemed *unim*portant or nonconsequential, or *il*literacy *not* an obstacle or liability, its precise contributions and impacts could no longer be assumed.

The challenge of a number of revisionist 'critical theories' was also important. So too was the development of a historical analysis of literacy and illiteracy, much of which aimed specifically at testing the literacy-modernization linkages. In a number of careful, often statistical, studies, historians throughout Europe and North America sharply qualified traditional expectations of a series of direct connections tying rising levels of literacy to developments in societies, economies, polities and cultures. This is one area in which historians and social scientists have had much of importance to contribute to one another. In part, historians discovered relatively high levels of literacy in advance of 'modernization'; they simultaneously located important 'take-offs' prior to 'mass' or even moderately high literacy rates. Literacy's linkages to the spread of modern attitudes and its relationship to individual advancement have been questioned. Notions of stages or 'threshold levels' have also been criticized. Many macrolevel correlations seem to break down in disaggregated testing.

There are, however, a number of critical points at which recent historical and social scientific analyses reflect one another conceptually and empirically. These include: the nature of literacy as a *dependent* variable; its dependence on *context*; the *limits* of universal impacts and generalized consequences (which have major implications for literacy's place in social science theories); the epistemological complications of *defining and measuring* literacy levels at the societal plane or literacy abilities at the individual level; the weakness of the traditional literacy-illiteracy *dichotomy*; and the fact that changes in literacy levels may often *follow from*, rather than precede, basic social, economic, political or cultural transformations. Literacy, increasingly, is connected to the larger network of communicative competencies (the oral, for example), not contrasted dichotomously and developmentally from them; it is also conceptualized more as a *continuous, widely varying, and nonlinear* attribute. Its importance as shaper of attitudes and as a symbol and symbolic influence stands beside, in partial independence from, its role in cognitive and skill determination. To speak of literacy in the abstract is now considered hazardous, if not quite meaningless.

Among the most critical of contemporary research approaches to literacy are the emerging social psychology of literacy. Scribner and Cole (1979) document the limits of literacy by itself and the theoretical assumptions that link it universally to higher forms of thought and practice; they point towards a formulation of literacy as *practice and context* determined and determining. Recent anthropological studies move toward ethnographies of literacy in use and nonuse (Whiteman, 1981; Tannen, 1982; Heath, 1983). Historical studies continue their pathbreaking relevance (Graff, 1979, 1981 a and b, 1984; Lockridge, 1974; Furet and Ozouf, 1977). By contrast, the sociology and economics of literacy find their theoretical presuppositions and empirical methods challenged and seek new paradigms (*Harvard Educational Review*, 1981; Stanley, 1978; Bataille, 1976). The future of literacy studies is an exciting and vastly important one.

Harvey J. Graff
University of Texas, Dallas

References
Bataille, L. (ed.) (1976), *A Turning Point for Literacy*, Oxford.
Furet, F. and Ozouf, J. (1977), *Lire et écrire: l'alphabétisation des français de Calvin à Jules Ferry*, 2 vols, Paris. (English translation of vol. 1, Cambridge, 1983.)
Graff, H. J. (1979), *The Literacy Myth: Literacy and Social Structure in the Nineteenth-Century City*, New York.
Graff, H. J. (ed.) (1981a), *Literacy in History: An Interdisciplinary Research Bibliography*, New York.
Graff, H. J. (ed.) (1981b), *Literacy and Social Development in the West: A Reader*, Cambridge.
Graff, H. J. (1984), *The Legacies of Literacy: Continuities and Contradictions in Western Society and Culture*, Bloomington, Indiana.
Harvard Educational Review (1981), 51, no. 1, 'Education as transformation: identity, change, and development' (entire issue).
Heath, S.B. (1983), *Ways with Words*, Cambridge.
Lockridge, K. (1974), *Literacy in Colonial New England*, New York.
Scribner, S. and Cole, M. (1979), *The Psychology of Literacy*, Cambridge, Mass.
Stanley, M. (1978), *The Technological Conscience*, Glencoe, Ill.
Tannen, D. (ed.) (1982), *Spoken and Written Language: Exploring Orality and Literacy*, vol. 9, *Advances in Discourse Processes*, Norwood, N. J.
Whiteman, M. F. (ed.) (1981), *Writing: The Nature, Development, and Teaching of Written Communication*, vol. 1, *Variations in Writing*, Hillside, N. J.

Further Reading
Martlew, M. (ed.) (1983), *The Psychology of Written Languages*, Chichester.

Lobbying

See Interest Groups and Lobbying.

Local Politics

Modern systems of local government emerged in the eighteenth and nineteenth centuries. Their units were the administrative units of former monarchies which were being transformed into modern nation-states. In the twentieth century, two new types of local political systems developed, both resulting from major political upheavals. The Soviet system of local government, based on the unification of representative and executive functions, and also on the leadership of the Communist party on all levels of government, was first introduced in the USSR and then adopted in several other Socialist states. In the newly independent states of Asia and Africa, various forms of local government emerged, based on the adaptation of the administrative structures of former metropolitan countries, as well as on the precolonial local political institutions.

Because of the diversity of existing patterns of local government, it is difficult to find a common definition for all forms of local politics. Countries differ in the extent to which local politics are autonomous in relation to national government, in the degree to which local government controls economic and other aspects of life within the territorial limits of its jurisdiction, in the internal organization of local politics, the size of local subdivisions, and so on. Nevertheless, the basic characteristic of local politics is that it consists of political activities (1) conducted within territorially delimited units of subnational administration and (2) directed at meeting the needs of such communities.

Relations between national and local politics vary from strictly federal patterns, in which local political units can determine their own destinies, to strictly unitary systems, in which local units of administration are simply extensions of the national government, wholly subordinated to and dependent on it. In practice, existing local political systems occupy various places on this continuum, but the growing complexity of politics in the twentieth century has resulted in closer national-local linkages (Kjellberg and Teune, 1980).

Social science research on local politics has its roots in early twentieth-century American studies on local communities, some of which covered questions of political participation and local political power (see especially Lynd and Lynd, 1929; Lynd and Lynd, 1937). After the Second World War, local politics became one of the most fashionable subjects of political science (Robson, 1948; Banfield and Wilson, 1963). New empirical studies published in the US originally focused on the composition of local ruling elites (Hunter, 1953; Dahl, 1961), but the emphasis soon shifted to the broader issues of 'Who governs, where, when and with what effects?' (Clarke, 1968). This stimulated collaboration with sociologists and encouraged the uses of statistical methods.

After 1960, there was a growth in cross-national comparative research. A notable example was a comparison of local politics and local leadership patterns in India, Poland, the US and Yugoslavia in the late 1960s (Jacob et al., 1971). In 1970, the International Political Science Association established a Research Committee on Comparative Study of Local Government and Politics in an effort to stimulate interest in comparative studies with special reference to participation and local government outputs. Interest in cross-national collaboration in this field is also evident in the activities of other international bodies. Today local politics studies can provide cross-national findings on the relationship between governmental structures and patterns of leadership and community performance and development.

Jerzy J. Wiatr
University of Warsaw

References

Banfield, E. C. and Wilson, J. Q. (1963), *City Politics*, Cambridge, Mass.

Clark, T. N. (ed.) (1968), *Community Structure and Decision-Making: Comparative Analyses*, San Francisco.

Dahl, R. A. (1961), *Who Governs?*, New Haven, Conn.

Hunter, F. (1953), *Community Power Structure*, Chapel Hill, North Carolina.

Jacob, P. E. *et al.* (1971), *Values and the Active Community*, New York.

Kjellberg, F. and Teune, H. (eds) (1980), 'Recent changes in urban politics: national-local linkages', *International Political Science Review*, 1.

Lynd, R. S. and Lynd, H. M. (1929), *Middletown*, New York.

Lynd, R. S. and Lynd, H. M. (1937), *Middletown in Transition*, New York.

Robson, W. A. (1948), *The Development of Local Government*, London.

Locke, John (1632–1704)

John Locke was born in 1632 at Wrington in Somerset. He entered Christ Church College, Oxford in 1652 where he received his MA in 1658. In that same year he was elected student of Christ Church; in 1660 he became lecturer in Greek; lecturer in Rhetoric in 1662, and censor of Moral Philosophy in 1664. From 1667 to 1681 Locke was physician and secretary to Anthony Ashley Cooper, Lord Ashley (later, First Earl of Shaftesbury). He was elected fellow of the Royal Society in 1668, and was secretary to the Lords Proprietors of Carolina from 1668 to 1675. In 1684, he was deprived of his appointment to Christ Church by royal decree. He lived in Holland from 1683 to 1689; was Commissioner on the Board of Trade from 1696 to 1700, and died at Otes (Oates) in the parish of High Laver, Essex in 1704.

Locke's *Essay Concerning Human Understanding* (1690) made a major contribution to psychology and to philosophical psychology. That work offered the outlines of a genetic epistemology, and a theory of learning. Locke's interest in children is reflected not only in his pedagogical work, *Some Thoughts Concerning Education* (1693), but in many passages of the *Essay* where he traced the development of awareness in children. The oft-quoted metaphor used by Locke to characterize the mind as a blank tablet should not blind us to the fact that the Lockean mind comes equipped with faculties, that the child has specific 'tempers' or character traits which the educator must learn to work with, and that human nature for Locke has basic self-preserving tendencies to avoid pain and seek pleasure. These tendencies were even called by Locke 'innate practical principles'. The innate claim his psychology rejected was for truths (moral and intellectual) and specific ideational contents.

Much of the *Essay* is occupied with discussing how we acquire certain ideas, with showing how a combination of physical and physiological processes stimulate and work with a large number of mental operations (for example, joining, separating, considering, abstracting, generalizing) to produce the ideas of particular sense qualities and many complex notions, such as power, existence, unity. One such complex notion is the idea of self or person.

The account of the idea of self – or rather, *my* idea of *my* self, for Locke's account of this notion is a first-person account – emerges out of a discussion of the question, 'Does the soul always think?' That question had been answered in the affirmative by Descartes. For Locke, not only was it empirically false that the soul always thinks; that question suggested wrongly that something in me (my soul), not me, thinks. *I* am the agent of my actions and the possessor of my thoughts. Moreover, all thinking is reflexive; when I think, I am aware that I am thinking, no matter what form that thinking takes (sensing, willing, believing, doubting or remembering). It is the awareness of my act of thinking which also functions in awareness of self. Consciousness appropriates both thoughts and actions. The self or person for Locke consists in that set of thoughts and actions which I appropriate and for which I take responsibility through my consciousness.

Appropriation is a fundamental activity for Locke. I appropriate my thoughts and actions to form my concept of self. The *Essay* details the appropriation by each of us of ideas and knowledge. Education is also an appropriation of information, but more importantly of habits of good conduct. Education is a socializing process. It takes place usually within the family, with a tutor (for Locke writes about the education of a gentleman's son). But the account of the socialization process extends to Locke's political writings, *Two Treatises on Government* (1690), where he discusses the family, duties parents have to their children and to each other (a marriage contract is part of his account of the family), and the rights and duties of citizens in a political society. The appropriation of land, possessions and eventually money by the activities of the person constitutes an early stage in Locke's account of the movement from the state of nature to a civil (political) society.

The political society, as the pre-political state of nature, is grounded in law and order; order is respect and responsibility to each other and ultimately to God whose law of nature prescribes these duties. Locke's law of nature is a Christianized version of that tradition. The individual laws which he cites on occasion prescribe and proscribe the actions sanctioned or denied by the liberal religion of his day. These laws differed little in content from those innate moral truths Locke attacked; it was not the truths he rejects, only the claim that they were innate. Locke's society is fairly slanted in favour of the individual: preservation of the person, privacy of property, tacit assent, the right of dissent. At the same time, the pressures towards conformity and the force of majority opinion are also strong. The structure of his civil society, with its checks and balances, its separation of powers, its grounding on the law of nature is designed to achieve a balance between the rights and needs of the individual and the need for security and order. His views on toleration (which were expressed in a series of tracts), while directed mainly against religious intolerance, match well with his insistence that government does not have the right to prescribe rites, rituals, dress and other practices in religion. Locke's toleration did not, however, extend to unbelief, to atheism.

The methodology for acquiring knowledge recommended by Locke and illustrated in his *Essay* stressed careful observation. Both in the physical sciences and in learning about ourselves and others, it was the 'plain, historical method' (that is, experience and observation) which holds the promise of accurate knowledge, or sound probability. Knowledge was not limited to demonstrative, deductive processes. Truth claims were always open to revision through further reports and observations. These concepts of knowledge and this experiential method were extended by Locke to what was later termed (for example, by Hume) 'the science of man' or 'of human nature'. His detailed attention to his own thought processes enabled him to map the wide variety of mental operations and to begin the development of a cognitive psychology. His interest in children, throughout his life, led to observations and descriptions of their behaviour. He had many friends who had children, and lived for several years on different occasions with families who had several young children. The *Essay* uses some of these observations as the basis for a brief genetic learning theory, and his *Some Thoughts* contains many remarks and recommendations for raising children based upon his firsthand experience with children in their natural environment.

Locke's social theory grew out of his reading and (more importantly) out of these habits of observing people in daily life. In his travels in France and Holland, he often recorded details of activities and practices, religious, academic and ordinary. Where direct observation was not possible, he used the new travel literature for reports on other societies, other customs and habits. He had his own biases and preferences, to be sure, but with his dedication to reason and rationality, he seldom allowed emotions to affect his observation or his conclusions. He was an articulate representative of the Royal Society's attitudes in the sciences, including what we know as the social sciences.

John W. Yolton
Rutgers College

Locke's Writings:
Epistola de Tolerantia, Gouda, 1689.
Essay Concerning Human Understanding, London, 1690.
Further Considerations Concerning Raising the Value of Money, London, 1695.
Letter Concerning Toleration, London, 1689.
A Letter to Edward Lord Bishop of Worcester, London, 1697.
The Reasonableness of Christianity, as Delivered in the Scriptures, London, 1695.
A Second Letter Concerning Toleration, London, 1690.
Short Observations on a Printed Paper, Intituled 'For Encouraging the Coining Silver Money in England, and After, for Keeping it Here', London, 1695.
Some Considerations of the Consequences of the Lowering of Interest and Raising the Value of Money, London, 1692.
Some Thoughts Concerning Education, London, 1693.
A Third Letter for Toleration, London, 1692.
Two Treatises of Government, London, 1690.
Works, London, 1714, 3 vols.

Further Reading
Aaron, R. I. (1971), *John Locke*, 3rd edn, Oxford.
Colman, J. (1983), *John Locke's Moral Philosophy*, Edinburgh.
Cranston, M. (1957), *John Locke, A Biography*, New York.
Dunn, J. (1969), *The Political Thought of John Locke*, Cambridge.
Tully, J. (1980), *A Discourse on Property. John Locke and his Adversaries*, Cambridge.
Yolton, J. W. (1956), *John Locke and the Way of Ideas*, Oxford.
Yolton, J. W. (1970), *Locke and the Compass of Human Understanding*, Cambridge.

Loneliness

Loneliness can range from fleeting moods to severe and chronic states; it is the more extreme forms of loneliness that concern social scientists and the general public. A distinction can be made between emotional loneliness that occurs when an individual lacks an intimate relationship with one special person such as a spouse or parent, and social loneliness that occurs when an individual lacks friends or has no sense of belonging to a community (Rubenstein and Shaver, 1982; Weiss, 1973).

It is useful to distinguish loneliness from other, related, concepts. Loneliness is a subjective experience that is not identical to objective social isolation. Solitude is not invariably accompanied by loneliness. Although lonely people often report having fewer social ties than the non-lonely, many exceptions to this pattern occur. It is also useful to distinguish the psychological loneliness studied by most researchers from the philosophical concept of existential loneliness. From the existential view, loneliness refers to an individual's awareness that we are ultimately separate from others and must confront life challenges on our own (Moustakas, 1972).

In the past decade, research on loneliness has expanded rapidly, spurred in part by the development of reliable paper-and-pencil instruments to assess loneliness (see review by Russell, 1982). Studies in the United States, Europe and Britain (reviewed by Peplau and Perlman, 1982) indicate that loneliness is quite common, with perhaps 20 per cent of adults having felt at least moderately lonely in the past few weeks. Although no social group is immune to loneliness, some people are at greater risk than others. Loneliness is most common among adolescents and young adults, and is less often reported by people in older age groups. Married people report less loneliness than the unmarried. The newly divorced and widowed are at high risk, although this tends to diminish over time. Like other forms of psychological distress, loneliness is more common among lower socioeconomic groups. Possible gender differences in loneliness have not been firmly established.

Several personal characteristics increase the risk of loneliness. These include shyness and introversion, low self-esteem and inadequate social skills. There is some evidence that parental rejection and/or divorce may dispose individuals to loneliness. Features of the social environment can also foster loneliness by limiting opportunities for satisfying social relations.

The immediate cause of loneliness is typically some event that produces a significant deficit in a person's social relations. Common precipitating factors include moving to a new school or community, ending a relationship through death or divorce, or being physically separated from loved ones. Although social transitions such as these can be very distressing, most people appear to cope with them effectively by re-establishing satisfactory social relations. In a minority of cases, however, severe loneliness persists over time and can have disturbing consequences. In adults, chronic loneliness has been linked to depression and suicidal tendencies. In adolescents, loneliness has been associated with school problems, delinquency and running away from home. Therapeutic approaches to helping the severely lonely are currently being developed (Rook and Peplau, 1982; Young, 1982).

Letitia Anne Peplau
University of California, Los Angeles

References
Moustakas, C. E. (1972), *Loneliness and Love*, Englewood Cliffs, N. J.
Peplau, L. A. and Perlman, D. (eds) (1982), *Loneliness: A Sourcebook of Current Theory, Research and Therapy*, New York.
Rook, K. S. and Peplau, L. A. (1982), 'Perspectives on helping the lonely', in L. A. Peplau and D. Perlman (eds), *Loneliness: A Sourcebook of Current Theory, Research and Therapy*, New York.
Rubenstein, C. M. and Shaver, P. (1982), *In Search of Intimacy*, New York.
Russell, D. (1982), 'The measurement of loneliness', in L. A. Peplau and D. Perlman (eds), *Loneliness: A Sourcebook of Current Theory, Research and Therapy*, New York.
Weiss, R. S. (1973), *Loneliness: The Experience of Emotional and Social Isolation*, Cambridge, Mass.
Young, J. (1982), 'Loneliness, depression and cognitive therapy: theory and applications', in L. A. Peplau and D. Perlman (eds), *Loneliness: A Sourcebook of Current Theory, Research and Therapy*, New York.

See also: *friendship*.

Lukács, George Szegedy von (1885–1971)

Born the son of a wealthy Jewish banker, the Hungarian Georg (Gyorgy) Lukács became internationally famous as a literary critic and as an interpreter of Marx. He was additionally a man of action who played a major role in the revolution of 1919, was a member of the Hungarian, Austrian and German Communist Parties between the wars, and was Minister of Culture in the abortive uprising of 1956.

After moving in Budapest literary circles after the turn of the century, Lukács was increasingly influenced by the Heidelberg neo-Kantians and studied first in Berlin under Simmel, and then in Heidelberg, where he met Lask and Weber. His first major work of literary criticism, *Die Seele und die Formen* (1911) (*Soul and Form*, 1971) aimed at a 'philosophy of art in order to pinpoint the ultimate questions of life' and maintained that the critic's role was to relate particular artistic forms to various mental states, or ways of understanding the world. However, tiring of the ahistorical nature of neo-Kantian argument and increasingly influenced by the work of Hegel, Lukács sought in his next major work, *Die Theorie des Romans* (1916) (*The Theory of the Novel*, 1971) to historicize aesthetic categories and already employed that concept which was to become crucial to his later work, the concept of *totality*. It has to be said of this early work, of his subsequent criticism of modernism while living in exile in Russia from 1933 to 1944, and of his account of irrationalism in German intellectual history (*Die Zerstörung der Vernunft*, 1954) (*The Destruction of Reason*, 1954) that it is often crude and omits those events, thinkers or literary works which fail to match Lukács's crassly manipulated schemata. (It is an odd theory of the novel indeed which cannot embrace Stendhal or Dostoevsky.) However, the later *Wider den misverstandenen Realismus* (1958) (*Meaning of Contemporary Realism*, 1963) and especially *Die Eigenart des Aesthetischen* (*The Peculiarity of Aesthetics*, 1963) have to a large extent made good the deficit, proved much more open-minded towards modernism and writers such as Kafka, and have sought to prove that there is such a thing as a *Marxist* aesthetics which does not – *pace* Mehring – require borrowings from other intellectual traditions.

It is none the less in his interpretation of Marx that Lukács has probably been most influential. Lukács had always loathed the autocratic politics of pre-1914 Hungary, had been influenced by the anarchic-syndicalist ideas of Erwin Szabó and had never been attracted to the 'positivism' of the Western democracies. The crude materialism of 'orthodox' Second-International Marxism, represented above all by Kautsky, appalled his neo-Kantian and Hegelian inheritance. The solution to this dilemma Lukács found in Lenin, in the Russian Revolution, and in an interpretation of Marx which was all the more remarkable for the fact that the so-called *Paris Manuscripts* of 1844 had not yet been discovered. Rediscovering the concepts of alienation and praxis in the writings of the mature Marx, Lukács argued that scientist interpretations of Marxism failed to recognize the transitory nature of the capitalist mode of production, reduced man to a cog in an economic machine and thus reduced the world-historical actor, the proletariat, to a fatal impotence, as was only too clear from the history of Social Democracy. What the proletariat required was not a pseudo-scientific theory of economic evolution but an awareness of the *historical* nature of capitalist society, a *total* view. But this could only come through the self-liberation of the proletariat. Thus Lukács initially identified the workers' council as *the* form of proletarian revolution, in which the worker would reappropriate his own fate and become the subject, no longer merely the object, of history. These views, expressed in a series of essays published in 1923 as *Geschicht und Klassenbewusstsein* (*History and Class Consciousness*, 1971), however, stand in a certain tension to Lukács's increasingly Leninist identification of the Communist Party with working-class consciousness and his difficulty, which remained with him to the end of his days, in accepting that there could be a distinction between the interests of the party and those of the working class. Although Lukács subsequently disowned *History and Class Consciousness*, it is perhaps to its image of working-class self-liberation that Lukács owes his fame, at least among the Western intelligentsia.

Dick Geary
University of Lancaster

Further Reading
Lichtheim, G. (1970), *Lukács*, London.
Meszaros, I. (1972), *Lukács' Concept of Dialectics*, London.
Parkinson, G. H. R. (ed.) (1970), *Georg Lukács: The Man, His Work and His Ideas*, London.

M

Machiavelli, Niccolo (1469–1526)

Machiavelli was a Florentine patriot, civil servant and political theorist. Entering the service of the Council of Ten which ruled republican Florence in 1498, he was sent abroad on diplomatic missions which provided much of the experience later to be distilled as advice on political and military skill. In 1512 the republic crumbled and the Medici family, who had long dominated Florentine politics, returned to power. Accidentally and unjustly implicated in a plot against them, Machiavelli was arrested and tortured. On his release he was exiled from the city, and retired to a small farm in Sant' Andrea, seven miles south of the city. The remainder of a disappointed life was devoted to writings, some of them intended to persuade the new rulers to restore him to the centre of affairs which he so dearly loved.

The Prince (1513), written soon after his downfall, was a short work of advice to princes, focused in its last chapter on the local problem of liberating Italy from foreign domination. Some writers (Spinoza and Rousseau most notably) have taken the work as a satire on monarchy, but it seems evidently a piece of self-advertisement in the service of ingratiation. Settling in to a life of exile, Machiavelli farmed, and wrote the *Discourses on the First Ten Books of Titus Livius* ([1532] 1950), a sequence of reflections on political skill, largely as exemplified in the Roman republic. His republican sympathies are evident in this work, but the frank discussion of ruthless and immoral options, for which he is notorious, is no less to be found here than in *The Prince*. By 1520 he had written on *The Art of War* and commenced *The History of Florence*. His comedy *Mandragola* is one of the classics of Italian literature. In 1525, the Medici regime was overthrown and a republic restored, but the new regime failed to employ him. He died in 1526.

Machiavelli criticized previous writers on politics for dealing with ideal and imaginary states, and claimed himself to deal with the 'effective truth' (*verita effettuale*) of politics. Situated firmly within the tradition of civic humanism, he was deeply preoccupied with the constitution of cities and the glory of heroes. His contribution to the unblinking realism of the period was to recognize that the heroes of statesmanship had not invariably followed the moral advice current in a Christian community, and indeed that some of the maxims conventionally pressed upon princes might well lead directly to their ruin. A prince must therefore know, he argued, how not to be good, and to use this knowledge according to necessity. Beyond that, however, he thought that those rulers who are in the process of consolidating their power must know how to dominate the imaginations of men. One who did was Cesare Borgia, a prince with whom Machiavelli dealt while serving the Florentine republic. Borgia had used one of his lieutenants, Ramirro da Orca, to pacify, with all necessary brutality, the newly conquered Romagna; he then had da Orca killed, and his body cut in two, and left in the piazza at Cesena, to satisfy the grievances and no doubt dominate the imaginations of the people. The ferocity of this spectacle, he wrote in chapter VII of *The Prince*, 'caused the people both satisfaction and amazement'. It is often said that Machiavelli believed in one kind of morality for private life, another for statesmen. Yet for all his cynicism, there is nothing actually relativist to be detected in his straightforward recognition of good and evil. Rulers are not accorded a different morality; they are merely construed as the guardians of morality itself and accorded a licence to violate moral norms when necessary. Transposed out of the idiom of advice to princes and into a characterization of the emerging modern state (of which Machiavelli was an acute observer) this became the idea of reason of state.

Machiavelli was very far from encouraging any sort of enormity. Statesmen are the creators of civilization, and their ambitions are without glory unless they serve the public good. Machiavelli talked with some diffidence of the proper use of cruelty in politics. The test of necessary cruelty is that it is economical, and this combination of utility with an ethic of honour was highly distinctive of his attitude. 'When the act accuses him, the outcome should excuse him,' wrote Machiavelli, in a passage often translated as 'the end justifies the means'. But Machiavelli is concerned not with moral justification but with the proper judgement to be made by subjects, and historians. From this technical point of view, religion is important because it binds men to commitments and intensifies their virtue. Machiavelli is deeply anticlerical in a Latin style, and often directly hostile to Christianity because its ethic of humility weakens governments and discourages a serious military ferocity. His admiration goes to the heroic actor in this world rather than to the pious devotee of the next.

The Machiavelli of the *Discourses* is less well-known but more enduring. Here we find a conflict theory of society, with men struggling to hold states together against the tendencies of dissolution. Machiavelli bequeathed to later thinkers the classical idea that any enduring constitution must balance monarchic, aristocratic and democratic elements. To create and sustain such a state, in which mere private and familial preoccupations are transcended in the public realm of citizenship, is the supreme human achievement, but contains its own ultimate doom. For states create peace, and peace allows prosperity, and when men grow accustomed to peace and prosperity, they lose their civic virtue and indulge private passions: liberty, to use Machiavelli's terms, gives way to corruption. This tradition of thought, with its emphasis on citizenly participation never ceased to be cultivated even in the absolute monarchies of early modern Europe, and became dominant from the time of the French Revolution onwards. It composes much of what the modern world calls 'democracy'.

The Machiavelli of popular imagination, however, has always been the exponent of the pleasures of manipulation, the supreme pornographer of power. Many revolutionary adventurers have found in him conscious formulae to cover what they were inclined to do by instinct. And in this role, Machiavelli has been remembered by social psychologists constructing a questionnaire to measure the manipulative tendencies of personality. Those who score high are called 'high machs', while less manipulative people are called 'low machs'.

Kenneth Minogue
London School of Economics and Political Science

Further Reading
Chabrol, F. (1958), *Machiavelli and the Renaissance*, London.
Hale, J. R. (1961), *Machiavelli and Renaissance Italy*, London.
Skinner, Q. (1981), *Machiavelli*, London.
Pocock, J. (1975), *The Machiavellian Moment*, Oxford.

Macroeconomics

Macroeconomics is concerned with explaining and assessing the performance of the economy in the *aggregate*. Accordingly, it focuses attention upon such magnitudes as the national income, the extent of unemployment, the general level of prices and its rate of change, the rate of economic growth and the overall balance of payments. It is, therefore, to be contrasted with microeconomics which is concerned more with *individual* decision making as, for example, the output decision of a particular firm and with *relative* prices of competing goods and factors of production.

There is almost universal agreement that modern macroeconomics dates from the publication of Keynes's *General Theory of Employment, Interest and Money* in 1936 and which, of course, reflects the experience of the great depression. Prior to this time, economists believed that the economy would naturally tend to approximate the full employment level of income if left to its own devices and if competition was allowed free play. Moreover, it was argued that the governing authorities could do little or nothing to speed up the process towards full employment, since any attempt to promote public works programmes would necessarily draw resources away from the private sector so that the *net* employment impact of such policies would be minimal. This view, the so-called 'treasury view', Keynes sought to deny. The Keynesian revolution produced the theoretical rationale to justify government intervention in the economy and argued that expansionary monetary and fiscal policies could generate increased output and employment. In these Keynesian-oriented *demand management* strategies, changes in government expenditure and taxation became the dominant instrument of control, and accordingly interventionist fiscal policy became strongly identified with Keynesianism.

Despite the apparent success of Keynesian policies in the post-war period, this philosophy was increasingly subject to attack. Monetarist critiques, emphasizing the budgetary consequences of such policies, pointed to the inflationary consequences of budget deficits and suggested that any beneficial stimulus to the economy would be of short duration only. Much of this critique emphasized the inadequate treatment of expectations formation, especially in labour markets, which characterized earlier Keynesian-oriented models. In recent years, a more radical brand of monetarism has emerged which, stressing *rational expectations* formation, has suggested that demand management policies are completely ineffective *even in the short run* in influencing real variables such as output and employment. Accordingly, the *new classical macroeconomics* suggests that macroeconomic policy should be supply-oriented. Supply-side economics argues that the economy will tend to its own 'natural' full employment level of output and that attention should be directed to increasing this natural level by promoting incentives to work effort, risk taking, innovation and so forth. Supply-side strategies are aided by the absence of inflation which generates uncertainty and raises interest rates. Accordingly, attention is focused upon the control of the money supply and fiscal policy becomes subordinate to the required money supply targets. The new classical macroeconomics is thus, in large measure, a return to pre-Keynesian orthodoxy, albeit in a far more sophisticated guise.

G. K. Shaw
University of Buckingham

Further Reading

Dornbusch, R. and Fischer, S. (1984), *Macroeconomics*, 3rd edn, New York.

Greenaway, D. and Shaw, G. K. (1983),
Macroeconomics: Theory and Policy in the UK, Oxford.

See also: *Keynesian economics*; *monetarism*.

Magic

'Magick,' says Aleister Crowley, its foremost modern exponent, 'is the Science and Art of causing Change to occur in conformity with Will.' This is possible because 'there is nothing in the universe which does not influence every other thing' (Crowley, 1929). But for E. B. Tylor, generally considered the founding father of British anthropology, magic was 'one of the most pernicious delusions that ever vexed mankind' (Tylor, 1871).

Tylor's study began the first phase in the modern scientific history of magic, which viewed magical ideas and practices as mistaken attempts by ignorant savages and backward and superstitious persons in European society to manipulate physical reality by non-physical means. Tylor's approach was taken up and elaborated by J.G. Frazer, who devoted two volumes of his masterwork *The Golden Bough* (1890) to the analysis of a global range of magical material. Frazer concluded that magic was a mistaken application to the material world of the laws of thought so as to constitute 'a spurious system of natural law'. This 'pseudo-science' (a term first employed by Tylor) could everywhere be reduced to two basic principles: that like produced like, and that things which had once been in contact continued to act on each other at a distance. These two principles resulted respectively in *homeopathic* or *imitative* magic, and *contagious* magic. The two branches could finally be comprehended under the name *sympathetic magic*, 'since both assume that things act on each other at a distance through a secret sympathy, the impulse being transmitted from one to the other by means of what we may conceive as a kind of invisible ether' (Frazer, 1932).

Frazer also saw the magical as the first of three great stages in the evolution of human thought. Magic, according to Frazer, was succeeded by religion, which in turn gave way to science, the characteristic mode of thought of modern times. When, in the early 1920s, anthropology abandoned the evolutionary approach to the study of society which had dominated nineteenth-century theorizing, it also turned aside from the Frazerian ambition of giving a universal account of magic. Instead of seeking for the general characteristics of

magical thought, each local magical system was seen as being like a language, specific to a particular society and culture. The linguistic parallel was explicitly drawn by Marcel Mauss (Mauss, 1972). The functionalist Bronislaw Malinowski devoted two thick volumes of ethnography to the magical practices of the Trobriand islanders of Melanesia, and suggested that magic was always encountered where man's technical resources were inadequate to attain his aims. Magic, he thought, would disappear with technological advance (Malinowski, 1935). This plausible generalization has been shown to be invalid in the case of post-Renaissance England where, according to the historian Keith Thomas, echoing Max Weber, 'magic lost its appeal before the appropriate technical solutions had been devised to take its place'. In the home of the Industrial Revolution the rationalist tradition of classical antiquity had blended with the Christian doctrine of a single all-directing Providence to produce the conception of an orderly and rational universe, in which effect followed cause in a predictable manner (Thomas, 1971).

An important exception to the functionalist particularism that dominated the post-Malinowski era in social anthropology was the work of Lucien Lévy-Bruhl (1857–1939). This French philosopher and scholar sought to show that non-empirical behaviour in tribal societies reflected a general mode of thought which he called *pre-logical* (though he recanted this pejorative term in his posthumous *Carnets*). In a massively documented critique of Lévy-Bruhl, Malinowski's student, E.E. Evans-Pritchard, demonstrated in the case of the Zande people of Central Africa that their 'magical' thought followed logical paths, even though embedded in non-rational premises, such as belief in witchcraft (Evans-Pritchard, 1937).

The functionalists shared with Tylor and Frazer the presumption that magic, and also religion (the two domains being often lumped together under the label 'magico-religious') were intrinsically delusions, however much they might be shown to contribute to the functioning of specific societies. This presumption of a basic nonsensicality in the magical has been challenged by some anthropologists, who see it as merely a symptom of scientistic, arrogant ethnocentricity in Western scholarship. This novel willingness to credit the claims of magicians appears to herald an emergent third phase in the social-scientific approach to magic, one which also appears to mark a return to the universalism of Tylor and Frazer. The most influential contribution to this new genre is that of Carlos Castaneda, who in a series of unprecedentedly popular books has purported to describe his initiation into the paranormal world of experts in sorcery among the Yaqui Indians of Mexico, a world startlingly different from the 'reality' the author's Western education had conditioned him to accept without question. The veracity of Castaneda's account of his bizarre odyssey has been challenged by some scholars, particularly de Mille (1978). But as a reaffirmation from a repressed Third World culture of a magical vision of the world which has disappeared from the cultural mainstream of Western civilization since the Enlightenment, Castaneda's work has the symbolic truth of authentic myth. A comparable though more modest report from Africa is the young archaeologist and ethnographer Adrian Boshier's description of his initiation into the world of Zulu magic (eds Angoff and Barth, 1974). In a similar and more general vein, Drury (1982) has traced interesting parallels between anthropological accounts of tribal shamanism and ritual magic in Europe. This rehabilitation of the 'pseudo-science' of tribal peoples may also be associated with a new convergence between the ideas of some Western scientists and those of the European magical tradition. Experimental evidence has been taken to prove that subatomic particles that have once interacted can instantaneously respond to each other's motions thousands of years later when they are light-years apart. Considering this and other disconcerting results, the physicist David Bohm of London University has suggested that the apparent separation of objects in the universe may conceal an invisible 'implicate' order of a mental kind in which everything is intimately connected with everything else (Bohm, 1980). Magic may be about to recover a scientific respectability lost since the Renaissance.

Roy Willis
University of Edinburgh

References

Bohm, D. (1980), *Wholeness and the Implicate Order*, London.

Boshier, A. (1974), 'African apprenticeship', in A. Angoff and D. Barth (eds), *Parapsychology and Anthropology*, New York.

Crowley, A. (1929), *Magick in Theory and Practice*, Paris.

Drury, N. (1982), *The Shaman and the Magician*, London.

Evans-Pritchard, E. E. (1937), *Witchcraft, Oracles and Magic among the Azande*, Oxford.

Frazer, J. G. (1932), *The Magic Art and the Evolution of Kings*, 2 vols, London.

Malinowski, B. (1935), *Coral Gardens and Their Magic*, 2 vols, London.

Mauss, M. (1972), *A General Theory of Magic* (trans. R. Brain), London.

de Mille, R. (1978), *Castaneda's Journey: the Power and the Allegory*, London.

Thomas, K. (1971), *Religion and the Decline of Magic*, London.

Tylor, E. B. (1871), *Primitive Culture*, 2 vols, London.

See also: *Frazer*; *Lévy-Bruhl*; *Tylor*.

Maine, Henry Sumner (1822–88)

Henry Maine had a distinguished career in academic jurisprudence, and fostered Roman law studies in Britain. He enjoyed a second career as a colonial civil servant, acting as Legal Member of the Viceroy's council in India from 1862–9. He was also an active conservative political journalist. His subsequent reputation, however, has rested largely on the theory of 'ancient society' set out initially in his first and most famous book, *Ancient Law* (1861). It established Maine as one of the most important figures in the generation of legal theorists who founded the comparative study of 'early' or 'primitive' social institutions.

Maine assumed that all the Indo-Germanic-speaking peoples had begun their development with the same social forms. Early Roman law and contemporary Hindu custom preserved primitive Indo-European institutions, notably the patriarchal family and the communal organization of property rights. Maine's method, based on the comparison of the presumed 'stages' of Indo-European social development, was derived from German philology and legal history, but his work also had a political dimension. He was concerned especially with the political development of India, and his books can be read, to some degree, as exotic variants of the Whig model of constitutional history.

In Maine's view, a primitive society was constituted by a series of extended patrilineal and patriarchal family corporations, each holding its property in common. Only after many generations, and then only in the 'progressive societies', did kinship in blood give way to local contiguity as a basis for political aggregation. This movement from kinship to territory, from family relationship to citizenship, also encompassed a movement from communal ownership to private property, from 'status' to 'contract', and from despotism to liberty. The empirical basis of the model was sketchy, despite the comparative and ethnographic flourishes, and his model is perhaps best understood as a direct inversion of the Utilitarian – and French radical – belief that contract had provided the original basis of the social order, and that social inequalities and injustices were a late and perverted distortion.

Adam Kuper
Brunel University, Uxbridge

Further Reading

Feaver, G. (1969), *From Status to Contract: A Biography of Sir Henry Maine*, London.

See also: *social contract*.

Majority Rule

Majority rule as a political slogan was used effectively as a rallying cry in a very few societies, especially

British colonies in Africa during the era of decolonization from the 1950s to the 1970s. Wherever entrenched interests sought to delay full independence or to build minority interests into the independence constitution, the slogan 'majority rule' mobilized popular (and populist) demands for the erosion of those interests. This usage reflected a short-term tactical need, rather than a strategic commitment, to a particular style or substance of government. Accordingly, once the particular obstacles had been removed, the term disappeared from political rhetoric.

Outside this particular context, majority rule has been used surprisingly seldom. In other times and in other places, a popular struggle against foreign control has been expressed in nationalist terms, or in the language of class conflict. It may therefore be a measure of the fragile national sentiment, and the inchoate class configurations of British African colonies, which led to the use of this term in those situations. The precise ethnic character, and the class orientation, of the presumptive independent government, were not yet entirely clear while the process of decolonization was in train: accordingly, the populace was commonly mobilized for independence by populist and ill-defined appeals. Once the successor government was securely installed in office, and governing on behalf of the whole population with more or less credibility, continued use of the term 'majority rule' was either subversive or otiose. Conceivably, it could be resurrected in those countries where the military have superseded civilian administrations, or in South Africa where the White minority retains political power; but in these contexts popular political rhetoric is more commonly couched in terms of ethnicity or of social class, than of majority rule. In general, therefore, it is reasonable to consider the term exclusively as the relic of a quite specific era, and of narrowly defined social and political circumstances. Its essential vacuity has prevented it from making the transition from political slogan to the language of social analysis.

Donald Denoon
Australian National University
Canberra

See also: *democracy.*

Malinowski, Bronislaw Kaspar (1884–1942)

Malinowski was born in Cracow in Poland, the son of a distinguished linguist and folklorist. His parents apparently belonged to the landed gentry. After reading exact sciences at the Jagellonian University (receiving his doctorate in 1908), he moved to the University of Leipzig, where he spent two crucial years, studying psychology with Wundt and economic history with Bücher. In 1910 he left Leipzig for the London School of Economics, where he worked under Westermarck. He was in Australia when war broke out in 1914, and as an Austrian subject was considered an enemy alien. However, he was permitted to do fieldwork in New Guinea, and even granted an official subsidy to do so. After preliminary work among the Mailu he went on to the Trobriand Islands. He spent two years there, from 1915–16 and from 1917–18, and invented modern anthropological fieldwork methods. He began lecturing at The London School of Economics in 1920, and was appointed Reader in 1924. He remained at the LSE until 1938 when he went to the United States, teaching at Yale. He died in New Haven in 1942 at the age of fifty-eight. Although he never did further intensive fieldwork after his Trobriand studies, he spent a few months in Africa, as a consultant and visiting students in the field, and he carried out collaborative research on Mexican markets (See Drucker-Brown (ed.), 1982).

Malinowski is regarded as one of the founders of scientific anthropology. He transformed the 'field' into a laboratory, in which the entire social life of the community provided a sort of experiment from which data were collected. The 'field' was no longer just a place where one met individuals and questioned them about their strange lives and ideas. Previously the classic resource of the anthropological armchair scholar was the questionnaire, circulated among missionaries, traders, planters and travellers. Malinowski revolutionized the relationship between theory and ethnography; henceforth only the man in the field himself could perhaps aspire to be a theorist (Kuper, 1983). Another facet of the same breakthrough is that it now became interesting and valid to study a living 'primitive' people *per se*, instead of as a mere token of ages past, or as the repository of survivals of interest to a prehistorian. The day-to-day life of exotic communities came to the fore as a scientific object, which in turn demanded from the anthropologist both proficiency in the vernacular and a full involvement in the lives of the tribesmen. Malinowski's special talent for 'participant observation' helped demonstrate the value of a method which had been proposed but never previously applied. His diary, published after his death, reflects the hardships he had to suffer, and so perhaps suggests why the advent of participant observation was so long delayed.

The results yielded by participant observation were impressive. No tribal community had ever been described as thoroughly as Malinowski described the Trobrianders. In part, however, his success was due also to his literary talent. His model was his great Anglo-Polish predecessor, Joseph Conrad, and he strove for something of the insight of a sensitive novelist into the minds of the Trobrianders. His discovery that Melanesian gardens were works of art, and that labour and magic spent on subsistence agriculture cannot be separated from aesthetic considerations (*Coral Gardens and Their Magic*, 1935), reflect the same spirit.

Argonauts of the Western Pacific (1922) was his most characteristic achievement. Besides providing an enduring lesson (and object-lesson) in an ethnographic methodology, the monograph offers a now classic description of a Melanesian exchange and trading system, the *kula*, which was to serve as the starting-point for most future debates on economic anthropology. At the same time it demonstrates Malinowski's literary skills and exemplifies his functionalism in action. One might even argue that in this case functionalism and literary form are virtually one and the same thing (Panoff, 1972).

At the LSE, Malinowski occupied a position somewhere between the ethnologist Seligman and the sociologists Westermarck and Hobhouse. He held joint seminars with them, but his charismatic personality impelled him to go his own way, attack the establishment, and recruit his own students for 'functionalism'. Though he wrote and lectured much on functionalism, he never succeeded in formulating a comprehensive theory (see *A Scientific Theory of Culture*, 1944). Instead he oscillated between crude biological platitudes (basic needs must be met) and absurdities (in a society everything necessarily operates). In fact Malinowski's theory was fortunately to remain immanent in his ethnography. Its main theme here was that cultures are integrated wholes which should not be dismembered for comparative purposes, any single aspect or institution being a riddle forever unless it is illuminated by its cultural context. His analysis of the complex *kula* exchange system was the crucial vindication of this rule, and it has even been argued that Malinowski's functionalism was generated by the peculiarities of this Melanesian institution (see Jarvie, 1964). *Argonauts* had a seminal influence on Mauss (*Essai sur le don*, 1925), and it inspired many anthropologists, but it failed to establish a functionalist school of anthropology.

Given his views on culture and social change, Malinowski was inevitably opposed to both historical and diffusionist approaches, at least at the theoretical level. His insistence that cultures were working wholes laid him open to the charge that he neglected the disruptive impact of colonial rule and the collapse of tribal societies, and even that he was an accomplice of colonialism. While his missionary zeal for functionalism led him to advise a few colonial officials, his work eventually had a very different impact, as is evident today. It shook European certainties about the pre-eminence of Western civilization, and (as citizens of now-independent New Guinea have repeatedly told contemporary anthropologists), it helped Melanesians regain a sense of dignity and identity, after the humiliations inflicted by their oppressors.

Michel Panoff
Centre National de la Recherche Scientifique, Paris

References

Drucker-Brown, S. (ed.) (1982), *Malinowski in Mexico*, London.

Jarvie, I. C. (1964), *The Revolution in Anthropology*, London.

Kuper, A. (1983), *Anthropology and Anthropologists: The Modern British School*, London.

Malinowski, B. (1922), *Argonauts of the Western Pacific*, London.

Malinowski, B. (1935), *Coral Gardens and their Magic*, London.

Malinowski, B. (1944), *A Scientific Theory of Culture*, Chapel Hill, North Carolina.

Malinowski, B. (1967), *A Diary in the Strict Sense of the Term*, London.

Mauss, M. (1954 [1925]), *The Gift*, London.

Panoff, M. (1972), *Bronislaw Malinowski*, Paris.

Further Reading

Firth, R. (ed.) (1957), *Man and Culture; An Evaluation of the Work of Bronislaw Malinowski*, London.

Uberoi, S. (1962), *Politics of the Kula Ring*, London.

Weiner, A. (1976), *Women of Value, Men of Renown: New Perspectives on Trobriand Exchange*, Austin, Texas.

Young, M. (ed.) (1979), *The Ethnography of Malinowski*, London.

See also: *functional analysis*; *participant observation*; *social anthropology*.

Malthus, Thomas Robert (1766–1834)

Thomas Robert Malthus, one of the leading figures of the English classical school of political economy, was born near Guildford, Surrey. He entered Jesus College, Cambridge in 1784, graduated in mathematics in 1788 and was a fellow of his college from 1793 until his marriage in 1804. From 1805 until his death he served as professor of history and political economy at Haileybury College, then recently founded by the East India Company for the education of its cadets. The tranquillity of his life and the gentleness of his personality contrasted sharply with the harshness of his doctrines and the fierce controversies which they evoked.

Malthus's most famous contribution to classical political economy was the theory stated in 1798 in his *Essay on the Principle of Population* – 'Population, when unchecked, increases in a geometrical ratio. Subsistence increases only in an arithmetical ratio .... By that law of our nature which makes food necessary to the life of man, the effects of these two unequal powers must be kept equal. This implies a strong and constantly operating check on population from the difficulty of subsistence.'

In the first edition of his *Essay*, Malthus identified the checks to population as either preventive (keeping new population from growing up) or positive (cutting down existing population); hence followed the bleak conclusion 'that the superior power of population cannot be checked without producing misery or vice'. In the second, much enlarged, edition (1803) he extended the category of preventive checks to include 'moral restraint', thus admitting the possibility of population being contained without either misery or vice as necessary consequences. Even when thus modified, Malthus's doctrine still seemed to impose narrow limits on the possibilities of economic growth and social improvement. Idealists and reformers consequently railed against the implications of the theory, but his fellow economists accepted both its premisses and its logic, and for most of the nineteenth century it remained one of the accepted 'principles of political economy'.

Malthus was also one of the first economists to state (in 1815) the theory of rent as a surplus, generally associated with the name of his friend and contemporary, David Ricardo. Both were followers of Adam Smith but Malthus's development of Smith's system differed significantly from Ricardo's, notably in his use of demand and supply analysis in the theory of value as against Ricardo's emphasis on labour-quantities, and his explanation of the 'historical fall' of profits in terms of competition of capitals rather than by the 'necessity of resort to inferior soils' which Ricardo stressed.

Since the time of Keynes the difference between Malthus and Ricardo which has attracted most attention relates to 'the possibility of a general glut'. In a lengthy debate Ricardo argued the validity of Say's Law, that 'supply creates its own demand', while Malthus asserted the possibility of over-saving (and investment) creating an excess supply of commodities. Ricardo's superior logic won acceptance for Say's Law for over a century, but modern economists now see Malthus's *Principles of Political Economy* as containing many insights which anticipate twentieth-century theories of investment and employment.

R. D. Collison Black
Queen's University of Belfast

References

Malthus, T. R. (1798), *An Essay on the Principle of Population*, London. (Second edn, 1803.)

Malthus, T. R. (1820), *The Principles of Political Economy, considered with a View to their Practical Application*, London. (Second edn, 1836.)

Further Reading

James, P. (1979), *Population Malthus, His Life and Times*, London.

Petersen, W. (1979), *Malthus*, London.

Mannheim, Karl (1893–1947)

Karl Mannheim, one of the founders of the sociology of knowledge (*Wissensoziologie*), was born in Budapest in 1893, and held academic posts at the universities of Heidelberg and Frankfurt and The London School of Economics and Political Science. He died in London in 1947. His biography, which is one of intellectual and forced geographical migration, falls into three phases: Hungarian (to 1920), German (1920–33) and British (1933–47). Among the important intellectual influences on Mannheim are Georg Lukács, Georg Simmel, Edmund Husserl, Karl Marx, Alfred and Max Weber, Max Scheler and Wilhelm Dilthey. Through these and other writers, German historicism, Marxism, phenomenology, sociology and, later, Anglo-Saxon pragmatism became decisive influences on his work.

The writings of Mannheim's Hungarian phase – primarily on literary and philosophical themes – demonstrate a first attempt to go beyond the German idealist view of history and society. The German phase was Mannheim's most productive; he gradually turned from philosophy to sociology (although he never completely abandoned philosophical questions), inquiring into the possible social roots of culture and knowledge. Many of his essays on the sociology of knowledge have become classics. Mannheim's most influential work, *Ideologie und Utopie*, Bonn, 1929 (English translation, *Utopia*, London, 1936), was also written during this period. These writings became the focus of a vigorous intellectual dispute in Germany towards the end of the Weimar Republic, in part because of what many critics regarded as the 'relativistic' implications of Mannheim's sociology. Mannheim, however, claimed that his ideas prepared the ground for a new comprehensive perspective capable of transcending the fragmented and partial social and political views held up till then. He maintained that the 'socially unattached' intelligentsia had an instrumental role in developing such a synthesis.

Mannheim's British phase was in some ways foreshadowed by the more practical orientation already evident in his work prior to his emigration from Germany. Applied sociology should be concerned with the comprehensive analysis of the structure of modern society, especially through democratic social planning, in which education should occupy a central role.

The original themes of the sociology of knowledge were formulated in Germany during a period of major social crisis, and may be seen, as Mannheim himself saw them, as the product of one of the greatest social, political and economic dissolutions and transformations, accompanied by the highest form of reflexivity, self-consciousness and self-criticism. The renewed interest in the problems posed by the sociology of knowledge reflects a similar crisis in our own period and may therefore be said to owe more to the course of events than to analytical progress.

Volker Meja
Memorial University
St John's, Newfoundland

Nico Stehr
University of Alberta, Edmonton

Further Reading
A.
Other Works by Mannheim in translation include:
Man and Society in an Age of Reconstruction, London, 1941.
Essays on Sociology and Social Psychology, London, 1953.
Essays on the Sociology of Culture, London, 1956.
Systematic Sociology: An Introduction to the Study of Society, London.
B.
Kettler, D., Meja, V. and Stehr, N. (1984), *Karl Mannheim*, London.
Loader, C. (1985), *Culture, Politics and Planning: The Intellectual Development of Karl Mannheim*, London.
Simonds, A. P. (1978), *Karl Mannheim's Sociology of Knowledge*, Oxford.
Wolff, K. H. (ed.) (1971), *From Karl Mannheim*, London.
See also: *knowledge, sociology of.*

Marcuse, Herbert (1898–1979)

A German-American philosopher and social theorist, Herbert Marcuse was associated with the Frankfurt School. He developed his own version of 'critical Marxism' which attempted to update the Marxian theory in response to changing historical conditions from the 1920s through to the 1970s. Marcuse gained notoriety as 'father of the New Left' in the 1960s when he was perceived as both an influence on and defender of the so-called 'New Left' in the United States and Europe.

Marcuse's first published article in 1928 in Weimar Germany attempted a synthesis of phenomenology, existentialism and Marxism which decades later would be carried out again by various existential and phenomenological Marxists. He also published in 1932 the first major review of Marx's *Economic and Philosophical Manuscripts of 1844* and anticipated the tendency to revise interpretations of Marxism from the standpoint of the works of the early Marx. His study of *Hegel's Ontology and Theory of Historicity* (1932) contributed to the Hegel renaissance taking place in Europe.

In 1934 Marcuse fled from Nazism and emigrated to the United States where he lived for the rest of his life. His first major work in English, *Reason and Revolution* (1941), traced the genesis of the ideas of Hegel, Marx and modern social theory. It demonstrated the similarities between Hegel and Marx, and introduced many English-speaking readers to Hegel, Marx and dialectical thinking. Marcuse worked for the US government from 1941–50 and claimed that his involvement was motivated by a desire to struggle against fascism. He later returned to intellectual work and in 1955 published *Eros and Civilization* which attempted an audacious synthesis of Marx and Freud and sketched the outlines of a non-repressive society.

Marcuse next published a critical study of the Soviet Union in 1958 (*Soviet Marxism*) and a wide-ranging critique of both advanced capitalist and communist societies in *One-Dimensional Man* (1964). This book theorized the decline of revolutionary potential in capitalist societies and the development of new forms of social control. It was severely criticized by orthodox Marxists and theorists of various political and theoretical commitments. Despite its pessimism, the book influenced many in the New Left as it articulated their growing dissatisfaction with both capitalist societies and Soviet communist societies. *One-Dimensional Man* was followed by a series of books and articles which articulated New Left politics and critiques of capitalist societies in 'Repressive Tolerance' (1965), *An Essay on Liberation* (1969), and *Counterrevolution and Revolt* (1972). Marcuse also dedicated much of his work to aesthetics, and his final book, *The Aesthetic Dimension* (1979), briefly summarizes his defence of the emancipatory potential of aesthetic form in so-called 'high culture'. His work in philosophy and social theory generated fierce controversy and polemics, and most critical studies of his work are highly tendentious and frequently sectarian. Although much of the controversy involved his critiques of contemporary capitalist societies and defence of radical social change, in retrospect, Marcuse left behind a complex and many-sided body of work comparable to the legacies of Ernst Bloch, Georg Lukács, T. W. Adorno and Walter Benjamin.

Douglas Kellner
University of Texas, Austin

Further Reading
Kellner, D. (1984), *Herbert Marcuse and the Crisis of Marxism*, Berkeley and Los Angeles.
See also: *Frankfurt School; Habermas.*

Marginal Analysis

Marginal analysis in economics attempts to explain the determination of prices and quantities on the basis of the comparisons of rewards and costs 'on the margin', that is, the rewards and costs of extending economic activity by small incremental amounts. It is an approach that follows naturally from the view that economic agents try to maximize some economic goal, such as utility or profits. They are assumed to possess the information that relates their activities to their goals, for example, the extent to which an increase in consumption increases their utility, or the effects of an increase in output on their profits. This is the cornerstone of neoclassical analysis, which dates from the marginal revolution of the 1870s set in motion by the writings of Jevons, Menger and Leon Walras. As opposed to classical analysis, which concentrated on questions of capital accumulation and growth, neoclassical analysis was concerned with the optimal allocation of given resources, and marginal techniques, with their accompanying mathematics of differential calculus, proved to be a fruitful way of dealing with these questions and appeared to provide economics with 'scientific' precision.

Marginal analysis, although it assumed a central role in economic theory from the 1870s, appeared in economics writings in earlier periods. It was prominent in the work of Thünen, whose theory of distribution was based on the marginal productivity of the factors of production. Cournot discussed the behaviour of firms under the assumption of profit maximization, and he made use of marginal revenue and marginal cost to deduce the positions of equilibrium. Dupuit distinguished between the total and marginal utility of goods when he examined the social benefits derived from public goods such as bridges, and on this basis he arrived at measures of consumers' surplus from the existence of such goods. Gossen enunciated the principle of diminishing marginal utility, which he termed his 'First Law'. He went on to state what has been called Gossen's 'Second Law', that the maximization of an individual's satisfaction from any good that can be used in different ways, requires that it be allocated among these uses in such a way that its marginal utility be the same in all its uses.

The marginal approach was also not unknown in classical economics. In Ricardo's theory the rent of land is price-determined, not price-determining, since it is the price of corn, given the wage and interest rates, that determines the extent of cultivation and the rent that can be extracted from the cultivators. His treatment of this question is an example of marginal analysis, since this decision is based on considerations of the effects on the output of corn of incremental changes in inputs. The combined doses of labour and capital on land that is being cultivated are increased until the output from the final, or marginal, dose is just sufficient to cover the wage and interest costs of that dose. Rent can only be extracted from the products of the intramarginal inputs of labour-capital. Similarly, the extent to which less fertile, or more distant, land will be cultivated depends on the marginal product of labour-capital on this land. No-rent land is that land where output is just sufficient to compensate the labour

and capital employed. Wicksteed, Wicksell, and J. B. Clark generalized Ricardo's approach to cover the case where all factors of production would be treated as being potentially variable, to arrive at a marginal productivity theory of distribution, and thus Blaug (1978) believes that Ricardo should be credited with 'having invented marginal analysis'.

The independent discovery by different theorists of the marginal productivity theory of distribution can be taken as a high point of marginal analysis, since it appeared to complete the marginal revolution by showing that not only are the prices of goods determined by marginal utility, but the prices of the inputs used to produce these goods are determined in a similar manner by their marginal products. This theory of distribution can, however, also be used to show the limitations of marginal analysis. In order to apply marginal techniques exclusively, it is necessary that there exists a known function linking the variable whose value is to be determined (output of a good in this case) to *all* the variables (inputs of the elements of production in this case) on which its value depends. This function should be continuous and differentiable so that the marginal products of the inputs can be derived. These inputs must be measured in physical units, rather than in terms of money values, if their marginal products are to be taken as independent determinants of their prices. In general, however, these conditions are not all satisfied. If the inputs in any specific production process, whose number will be very large, are measured in physical units, then they are often connected by a relationship of complementarity, and separate marginal products cannot be calculated for them. If these inputs are combined to form the aggregate factors of production, labour and capital, as was done by Clark, then capital can only be measured in money-value terms. This means that the marginal analysis begins with the prices of capital goods, and cannot provide an explanation of their determination. In addition, some essential inputs into the productive activity of firms, such as business organization and ability whose importance was emphasized by Marshall, cannot be measured in physical units and placed in a production function. Even though Marshall made extensive use of marginal analysis, and is often erroneously credited with having a marginal productivity theory of distribution, he was aware of the limitations of marginal productivity as the sole explanation of distribution (Marshall, 1920).

Marginal analysis cannot deal fully with situations where future conditions are not known with certainty, or where they cannot be represented by some well-defined probability distribution, since the effects on the variables of interest of marginal changes cannot be determined. Questions having to do with capital accumulation cannot be handled adequately by these techniques, since investment depends on expectations of future conditions that in a fundamental sense cannot be known in a context of historical time. Those wedded to marginal analysis thus tend to assume conditions that permit marginal techniques to be employed, even though they represent serious departures from the reality the analysis is supposed to illuminate. This may be one reason for the predominance given in neoclassical theory to perfect competition despite the fact that modern manufacturing industry is imperfectly competitive. Only in the case of perfect competition is profit maximization, which is concerned with maximizing the present value of the stream of profits over time, synonymous with short-period profit maximization, the maximization of the current period's profits.

A. Asimakopulos
McGill University

References
Blaug, M. (1978), *Economic Theory in Retrospect*, 3rd edn, Cambridge.
Marshall, A. (1920), *Principles of Economics*, 8th edn, London.

Further Reading
Black, R. D., Coats, A. W. and Goodwin, C. D. W. (eds) (1973), *The Marginal Revolution in Economics*, Durham, North Carolina.
Howey, R. S. (1960), *The Rise of the Marginal Utility School 1870–1889*, Lawrence, Kansas.
Schumpeter, J. A. (1954), *History of Economic Analysis*, New York.
See also: *Jevons; maximization; Walras, L.*

Marketing Research

The purpose of marketing research is to provide information which will aid in management decision making. A marketing manager in a large consumer goods company, for example, may want to collect information to assess whether or not to launch a new product or to determine why sales of a product are declining. In collecting this information, five major steps may be identified: (1) establishment of research objectives; (2) development of a research plan; (3) implementation of the research plan; (4) data analysis; and (5) presentation of research findings (Churchill, 1983; Green and Tull, 1978; Lehmann, 1983).

(1) Establishment of Research Objectives
This is the first step, and it requires clear and precise definition by management of the decision problem. This should be expressed not only in terms of problem symptoms such as a decline in market share, but also possible contributing factors such as changes in competitors' strategies or in consumer interests, as well as the actions management might take based on research findings. Otherwise, much irrelevant information may be collected.

(2) Development of a Research Plan
This stage requires determining what data are to be collected, what research techniques and instruments are to be used, how the sample is to be selected, and how information is to be collected from this sample.
(i)   *Data sources*: The required information may already be available in *secondary* sources such as government or trade reports, company records, or sales-force reports. This will not, however, have been collected with this particular problem in mind. Consequently, *primary* data collection may be required, in other words, collection of information specifically for this purpose.
(ii) *Research techniques*: Where primary data are collected, observational or other qualitative techniques, experimentation or survey research may be conducted. *Observational* and other qualitative techniques, such as projective techniques (word association or sentence completion tasks, and focus or group interviewing) are most appropriate in the initial stages of research, where little is known about the problem (Webb, Campbell, Schwartz and Sechrest, 1966). The onus of interpretation is, however, placed on the researcher, and, consequently, such techniques are open to criticisms of subjectivity. *Experimental* techniques are also potentially applicable, but they are rarely used except in in-store experiments, studying, for example, the impact of in-store promotions on sales. Test marketing can also be viewed as field experiments. *Survey* research is the technique most commonly used in marketing research. A standard questionnaire can be administered to large samples, and systematically analysed using computerized techniques.
(iii) *Research instruments*: In observational or qualitative research, instruments such as coding schema, recording sheets and other tests may need to be designed. Mechanical devices such as instruments to measure a subject's eye movements or pupil dilation, or optical scanner equipment are also increasingly used. But more common is the questionnaire. For unstructured interviews and focus groups, only an interview guide indicating the topics to be covered may be required. A crucial aspect of survey research is, however, the design of a questionnaire carefully worded to elicit desired information from respondents (Oppenheim, 1966; Payne, 1951). Attention to question form and sequencing is also often essential in order to avoid biased responses.
(iv) *Sampling plan*: This should specify the sample population, its size and sampling procedures to be adopted. The relevant sample population and

sample size will depend on the purpose of the research, and the research budget. In qualitative research, small samples are common, but more extensive surveys often require a large sample size. A choice has also to be made between probabilistic sampling techniques, such as random or stratified sampling, and non-probabilistic sampling techniques such as judgemental, quota or convenience sampling (Cochran, 1977). Probability sampling is the only way to obtain a representative sample but requires the availability of a sampling list and entails high costs. Convenience, judgemental or quota sampling techniques are thus often used, particularly where qualitative techniques are applied, or a specific target segment is to be studied.

(v) *Data collection procedures*: Three principal methods of data collection may be considered: telephone, mail or personal interviewing. *Telephone* interviewing, which is commonly used in the US, is quick and can be conducted from a central location where interviewers are controlled by a supervisor. However, only those with telephones can be interviewed, and a limited number of questions asked. *Mail* questionnaires are the cheapest method of survey administration, but suffer from low response rates, and also assume that the respondent clearly understands and can respond to questions. *Personal* interviewing is the most flexible method since the interviewer can select the sample by judgement or convenience sampling, and is able to explain questions to the respondent. It is, however, an expensive method of data collection, and susceptible to interviewer bias.

(3) Implementation of the Research Plan
This is where major sources of data inaccuracy and unreliability often arise. In the case of surveys, for example, respondents may bias findings by refusal to co-operate, by providing inaccurate answers, for example, on income, or by giving socially desirable responses. Interviewers may also bias results by encouraging a specific response, by inaccurate recording of responses or, in extreme cases, by falsifying responses.

Current developments in telecommunications and computer technology are rapidly changing data collection procedures and improving their efficiency. For example, in both centralized telephone interviewing and in mobile field units, computer terminals can be used by interviewers or interviewees to record responses, thereby eliminating editing and coding errors. The results can also be analysed and updated with each successive response, thus considerably reducing research time and costs.

(4) Data Analysis
The next step is to tabulate, classify, and interpret the information collected. Here, the complexity of the analysis will depend to a large extent on management needs. In many cases, tabulation or cross-tabulation of results with averages and other summary statistics may suffice. In other cases, more sophisticated multivariate techniques such as factor or cluster analysis or multidimensional scaling may be required, if more complex interactions in the data are to be examined (Green, 1978).

(5) Presentation of Research Findings
Presentation of research findings may be verbal and/or written. In either case, the main focus should be on clear presentation of key research findings and their implications for the decisions to be made by management.

Susan P. Douglas
New York University

References
Churchill, G. (1983), *Marketing Research*, 3rd edn, Hinsdale, Ill.
Cochran, W. G. (1977), *Sampling Techniques*, 3rd edn, New York.
Green, P. E. (1978), *Analyzing Multivariate Data*, Hinsdale, Ill.
Green, P. E. and Tull, D. S. (1978), *Research for Marketing Decisions*, 4th edn, Englewood Cliffs, N.J.
Lehmann, D. (1983), *Market Research and Analysis*, 2nd edn, Homewood, Ill.
Oppenheim, A. N. (1966), *Questionnaire Design and Attitude Measurement*, New York.
Payne, S. (1951), *The Art of Asking Questions*, Princeton.
Webb, E., Campbell, D. T., Schwartz, R. D. and Sechrest, L. (1966), *Unobtrusive Measures*, Chicago.

Further Reading
Baker, M. J. (ed.) (1983), *Marketing: Theory and Practice*, 3rd edn, London.
See also: *opinion polls; sample surveys.*

Markets

The term markets can be used in a wide variety of settings from a physical location, for example, Covent Garden market in London, to an intangible set of transactions, such as those associated with currency exchange, where the real market-place lies somewhere in the electronic signals which pass from one country to another between different currency exchanges. However, all markets share the same basic characteristic: they are a medium for exchange between buyer and seller where transactions between the two parties can be conducted to the satisfaction of both.

The concept of mutually satisfying exchange suggested by this definition lies at the heart of decisions taken in the market-place. The activity of marketing which has been given increasing attention in recent years is based upon making and sustaining relationships with customers. Conversely, the activity of purchasing or consumption is making and sustaining relationships with suppliers.

There are several different views of markets depending upon the perspective chosen. To the early economist, markets were determined in terms of a balance between supply and demand, and the result of market transactions was a price which was agreed between buyer and supplier. This price reflected the supplier's willingness to supply and the intensity of demand, which were influenced respectively by the relative cost of the item to manufacture, and the number and relative attraction of competing alternatives that were available to the buyer. This situation persists in some markets where the number of suppliers and the number of potential buyers has remained large and the product itself is relatively standard, for example, the major commodity markets such as grain, foreign currency or metals.

In many markets this situation has changed, largely as a result of technological innovation. There are two dimensions to such innovation: (1) new manufacturing processes which favour large-scale manufacturing operations and require a large share of the market to remain viable; and (2) new products or processes which confer a temporary (sometimes enduring) monopoly on the manufacturer, for example, the Polaroid Corporation with instant photography.

The effect of new technology on markets has been considerable. For example, in the late nineteenth and early twentieth century, the discovery of new manufacturing processes and the development of new materials caused radical product innovation. In order to produce economically, such processes frequently have to be operated at considerable volume (for example, flat glass manufacture). At the most economical volumes the process could frequently supply a large proportion of the market's needs. While this initially expands the size of the market, at the same time the absolute size of the market relative to the optimum size of the production facility puts an upper limit on the number of companies which can supply the market.

As markets have changed, so companies have increasingly turned to non-price factors as the basis of competition. New product development and advertising have become major influences on the pattern of supply and demand in the market-place. Companies which have failed to respond to changes in the market-place, by introducing new products or services which match new needs, find themselves left behind by competitors who have made such changes.

The concept of buyer and seller meeting as partners to exchange in the market-place can be extended to a broader view of markets which many people hold. The simple buyer-seller pairing can be replaced by a view of individual markets as part of an overall system of buyer-seller relationships running from the extraction of raw materials to the production and distribution of the finished product or service.

In this view the relationships between individual buyers or sellers are influenced by other parts of the system, and each member of the system has an impact on other members of the chain of supply and demand. For example, the demand for capital equipment is frequently referred to as 'derived' demand, since the sale of products such as machine tools depends ultimately upon the sale of the items which the machine tool manufactures (for example, car components).

In some economies these vertical relationships are centrally controlled through a planning system which attempts to co-ordinate the volume and type of production and consumption activity. In other economies such vertical relationships have evolved gradually, without a high degree of formal planning. Nevertheless, in such situations there is a high degree of vertical integration which strongly influences market behaviour such as in the Japanese electronics industry, where component manufacturers, equipment manufacturers and the ultimate users of the equipment are likely to meet on a regular basis and co-operate in co-ordinating their production and consumption activities. This perspective of market behaviour is a long way from the original economists' view of markets which stressed competition rather than co-operation between buyer and seller. There is a wide variation in types of market between the two extremes.

S. T. Parkinson
Henley – The Management College

See also: *trade and markets, anthropology of.*

Marriage

Defining Marriage

Cross-cultural comparison of a number of institutions which may be termed marriage has shown that it is a social phenomenon with a great variety of forms and a considerable number of functions. Attempts have been made both to define the intrinsic nature of the institution and to enumerate the purposes it serves. Thus marriage has been defined as a culturally approved relationship of one man and one woman (*monogamy*); or of one man and two or more women (*polygyny/polygamy*), in which sexual intercourse is usually endorsed between the opposite sex partners, and there is generally an expectation that children will be born of the union and enjoy the full birth status rights of their society. These conditions of sexual intercourse between spouses and reproduction of legitimate and socially recognized offspring are not, however, always fulfilled. *Woman to woman marriage* has been documented in African societies, to provide barren women with heirs (in which the sexual partner of the child-bearer is not a partner to the conjugal relationship); *ghost marriages* are known to raise seed to the dead or to provide a partner in the next world; and marriage rites in contemporary industrial societies have been performed for homosexual and lesbian partners purporting to constitute marriage, or between heterosexual couples incapable of sexual intercourse.

Leach (1955) proposed that it is necessary to include under the category marriage several institutional subtypes which perform certain functions. Of these, he enumerated ten, none of which is common to every known society, nor in any one society does marriage establish all simultaneously. The functions included:

(1) to establish the legal father of a woman's husband;
(2) to give the husband a monopoly of his wife's sexuality;
(3) to give the wife a monopoly of her husband's sexuality;
(4) to establish the legal mother of a man's children;
(5) to give the husband partial or monopoly rights to his wife's domestic services;
(6) to give the wife partial or monopoly rights to her husband's economic services;
(7) to give the husband rights to property accruing to his wife;
(8) to give the wife rights over property accruing to her husband;
(9) to establish a joint fund of property for the benefit of the children;
(10) to establish a socially significant relationship of affinity between the husband and the wife's brothers.

Many anthropological studies in the past have pursued this kind of jural approach, in the sense that marriage has been seen as a bundle of rights and duties and also as entailing significant changes in the structuring of rights and duties between linked individuals and groups, whereby new affinal statuses are created. Such approaches have been analytically useful in that they have demonstrated the necessity of separating out the different elements which form a complex relationship, and which are themselves capable of separation, delegation and joint ownership. For example, sexual rights may be delegated in the case of a sterile or impotent husband, distributed between several, as in the case of *polyandry* or *polygyny*, or split up into ritual,

symbolic elements and a physical element. As well as being jointly owned or shared, such rights may also be subject to strict rules of inheritance or ownership, may be considered to continue *post mortem*, while heirs may only gain usufruct, as in the case of *leviratic widow inheritance*, in which the heir raises up seed to the dead husband. Again, analysis of individual marital rights and duties illustrates clearly that they are of varying duration. A husband's duty to maintain his wife or vice versa may endure beyond divorce. A wife's duty to bear offspring for her husband and his kin group may last beyond death.

Marriage Ceremonies and Payments
A study of the marriage ceremonies practised, the prestations, prayers and rituals performed or omitted are likely to be very illuminating as regards the actors involved in the transactions, the rights transferred and retained, and the changes of status and relationships which occur. The whole process of establishing a socially and legally acceptable form of marital relationship may last any length of time, from a few minutes or hours or days to several months or years, or more than a lifetime in the extreme instance. Indeed, the actual point in time at which a marriage comes into being may be very difficult, if not impossible, to distinguish from the events in a diffuse and protracted social process.

On the other hand, the rituals performed at divorce and funeral ceremonies, such as the purification of widows, may reveal beliefs held in some societies about the enduring nature of marital bonds and the special nature of marriage as irrevocably changing an individual's social status.

Similar considerations direct attention to the symbolic acts and prestations involved in these transfers of rights and duties, and status changes. The major forms of marriage transaction have been diagrammatically represented as shown in Figure 1 (Goody, 1973). Dowry has been seen as a sort of *pre-mortem* inheritance to the bride, and *bridewealth* (sometimes termed *brideprice*) as a transaction between the kin of the groom and bride. Fortes (1962) usefully distinguished two elements in the *bridewealth* payments: a *prime prestation*, which is normally fixed and is the jural instrument for

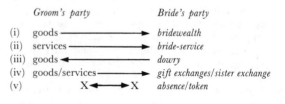

Figure 1: Marriage Transactions

the transfer of marital rights and may be returnable at divorce; and *contingent prestations*, which contain an element of barter and are considered to be the medium for the establishment of affinal relations, being often spread over time and variable according to the status, wealth and cordiality of the people involved. These may permit the husband to gain extra rights and privileges *vis à vis* the wife and her kin. Thus the quantity and value of goods transferred as *bridewealth* have been partly viewed as a function of the degree of jural authority and number of rights gained by the husband.

Such exchanges of valued goods and services, or even people for rights in spouses and their procreative powers, are significant features of the marriage systems of small-scale, preindustrial societies, in which people, in terms of followers, dependents and especially kin and affines, are the main source of political power, economic gain, social prestige and personal pleasure. In such contexts human fertility is at a premium and so highly valued that access to offspring is only made available in return for an equivalent consideration, and often one which will also enable the donor to achieve the same ends of reproductive increase.

Feminist Studies
In the past ten years of feminist studies there has been a reaction to what has been perceived as the legalistic and viricentric approach of many earlier descriptions and discussions of sexual relations and marriage transactions and conjugal rights and duties. Thus, for example, Rosaldo and Lamphere (1974) argued that much of the previous literature had been the outcome of a male perspective, contending that little was recorded of women's views and strategies within domestic power structures; rather the stress was upon the rights over women transferred from one set of men to another and the control over women and their offspring exercised by the male members of kin groups. However, in the past decade, with the expansion of women's studies, increasing attention has been paid to women's sources of power and authority within the family, and to sexual divisions of labour and resources rather than the more legalistic discussion of rights and duties. In particular, more attention has been paid to women's changing access to resources and influence and authority through the life cycle and with maturation of children and achievement of asexual, postmenopausal status. Moreover, there has been more emphasis on domestic decision making, sexual bargaining, control and conflict (for example, Oppong, 1983; Scanzoni, 1979). In addition both contemporary cross-cultural and historical studies have shown an interest in the emotional aspects of marital relations.

Marriage Choice
In all societies there are socially recognized limits to the range of potential marriage partners. Rules of *exogamy* are regulations prescribing selection of spouses outside a specific group, such as a neighbourhood or lineage. At the same time, rules of *endogamy* define the boundary of the wider group within which a husband or wife should be selected, such as a caste, ethnic or racial group, nation or social class. A basic distinction which has been drawn is that between the *status endogamy* and related forms of in-marriage characteristic of the major Euroasian societies, in which like tends to marry like (parents trying to arrange the marriage of their offspring to spouses of equal or superior standing – *hypergamy*), and open systems, in which different strata are bound together by a network of intermarriages (Goody, 1976).

In some culture areas, the proportion of couples formally married with the full range of wedding celebrations has been relatively small, for example, in the Caribbean. Thus, for instance, evidence on marital careers of lower-class Trinidadians showed that friendly relationships were most frequent followed by living together and marriage, and that over a lifetime the movement appeared towards more stable relationships (Voydanoff and Rodman, 1978). Earlier, Rodman (1971) had argued that when economic conditions make it difficult or impossible for people to meet the societal goal of legal marriage, many stretch their values so that alternative marital unions also become normatively acceptable.

Emotional gratification or love is relevant in industrialized and post-industrial cultures to the process of individual mate selection and the associated process of rating and dating potential spouses. It has been widely assumed that with modernization the incidence of love as a basis for individual choice of spouses and marriage has become more widespread (for example, see Goode, 1963). Adams (1979) argued that achievement in society and personal choice of mate seem to go together, and that the historical drift has been towards greater emphasis upon individual achievement in society and increasingly towards individual choice in mate selection.

While some see in the growing numbers of single parents and rising divorce statistics in Europe and North America proof that marriage is on the wane in post-industrial societies, evidence from a number of studies has indicated association between marriage and physical and psychological well-being (see, for example, Veenhoven, 1983).

Christine Oppong
International Labour Organization, Geneva

References
Adams, B. N. (1979), 'Mate selection in the United States: a theoretical summarization', in Burr *et al.* (eds), *Contemporary Theories about the Family: Research Based Theories*, vol. I. New York.

Fortes, M. (ed.) (1962), *Marriage in Tribal Societies*, Cambridge.

Goode, W. J (1963), *World Revolution and Family Patterns*, New York.

Goody, J. R. (1973), 'Bridewealth and dowry in Africa and Eurasia', in J. Goody and S. J. Tambiah (eds), *Bridewealth and Dowry*, Cambridge.

Goody, J. R. (1976), *Production and Reproduction. A Comparative Study of the Domestic Domain*, Cambridge.

Leach, E. R. (1955), 'Polyandry, inheritance and the definition of marriage', *Man*, 54.

Oppong, C. (ed.) (1983), *Female and Male in West Africa*, London.

Rodman, H. (1971), *Lower Class Families*, New York.

Rosaldo, M.Z. and Lamphere, L. (eds) (1974), *Women, Culture and Society*, Stanford.

Scanzoni, J. (1979), 'Social processes and power in families', in Burr *et al.* (eds), *Contemporary Theories about the Family: Research Based Theories*, New York.

Veenhoven, R. (1983), 'The growing impact of marriage', *Social Indicators Research*, 12.

Voydanoff, P. and Rodman, H. (1978), 'Marital careers in Trinidad', *Journal of Marriage and the Family*, February.

See also: *divorce*; *family*; *family history*; *nuptiality*; *women's studies in social anthropology*.

Marshall, Alfred (1842–1924)

The English economist Alfred Marshall was one of the dominant figures in his subject during the late nineteenth and early twentieth centuries. His 1890 masterwork, the *Principles of Economics*, introduced many of the tools and concepts economists use in price theory even today. The book also presented an influential synthesis of received theories of value and distribution.

Marshall was born on 26 July 1842 at Bermondsey, a London suburb, his father William being at the time a clerk at the Bank of England. Alfred was educated at Merchant Taylors' School, revealing there his aptitude for mathematics. Somewhat against his father's wishes, he entered St John's College, Cambridge, to embark on the mathematics tripos, graduating in 1865 as Second Wrangler. He was then elected to a Fellowship at St John's. Soon abandoning mathematics for ethics and psychology, his growing interest in social questions led him to economics, which by 1870 he had chosen as his life's work. He took a prominent part in the teaching for the moral sciences tripos until leaving Cambridge in 1877 on marriage to his one-time student, Mary Paley.

Although Marshall published little, these early years were the formative ones for his economic views. He mastered the classical tradition of A. Smith, D. Ricardo and J. S. Mill and was encouraged towards a math-ematical approach by early acquaintance with the works of A. A. Cournot and J. H. von Thünen. Priority for the marginal 'revolution' of the early 1870s clearly goes to W. S. Jevons, L. Walras and C. Menger, but Marshall had been working on similar lines before 1870. However, his attitude towards these new developments remained somewhat grudging, and he was always reluctant to publish merely theoretical exercises. More general influences significant in this early period were those of H. Sidgwick (perhaps more personal than intellectual), H. Spencer and G. W. F. Hegel. The last two, in tune with the spirit of the age, led Marshall towards an organic or biological view of society. He found the early socialist writers emotionally appealing, but unrealistic in their views as to evolutionary possibilities for human nature. Somewhat later, he saw merit in the programme of the German Historical School of economics, but deplored its anti-theoretical stance. It was from these and other varied sources, including energetic factual enquiry, that he distilled and long pondered his subtle, complex and eclectic approach to economic questions.

Marshall returned to Cambridge in 1885, from exile in Bristol and Oxford, as professor of political economy and the acknowledged leader of British economists. He had already commenced work on his *Principles*. His first two significant publications had appeared in 1879. One was a selection of theoretical chapters from a never-completed book on foreign trade, printed by Sidgwick for private circulation under the title *The Pure Theory of Foreign Trade: The Pure Theory of Domestic Values*. These superb chapters did much to establish Marshall's reputation among British economists. The other was an ostensible primer, the *Economics of Industry*, co-authored by his wife, which foreshadowed many of the ideas of the *Principles*. It was this work that first brought Marshall's views to the attention of foreign economists.

Marshall resided in Cambridge for the rest of his life, resigning his chair in 1908 to devote all his energies to writing. The years were externally uneventful and dominated by the internal struggle to give vent and adequate expression to his vast store of knowledge. The first volume of what was intended as a two-volume work on *Principles of Economics* appeared in 1890 and cemented his international reputation. Although this first volume went through eight editions, little progress was made with the second volume, which had been intended to cover money, business fluctuations, international trade, labour and industrial organization. Among the famous concepts introduced in the *Principles*, as it soon came to be known, were consumer surplus, long and short-period analysis, the representative firm, and external economies. The elucidation and criticism of these and related concepts were to occupy English-speaking economists for many years.

In 1903, under the influence of the tariff agitation, Marshall embarked on a tract for the times on national industries and international trade. This too grew vastly in his hands and, when it eventually appeared in 1919, *Industry and Trade* realized his earlier intentions only incompletely. The book's tone, historical and descriptive rather than theoretical, has made it better known among economic historians than among economists. The years that remained were devoted to a last-ditch effort to salvage some of his unpublished earlier work. Some important early contributions to the theories of money and international trade at last saw the light in *Money, Credit and Commerce* in 1923, but the book remains an unsatisfactory pastiche. Marshall died on 13 July 1924 at the age of eighty-one having failed to do much that he had wished, yet still having achieved greatness.

During his years as professor, Marshall was instrumental in establishing the specialized study of his subject at Cambridge, which eventually became a leading centre for economic study and research. As teacher and adviser he inspired his students with his own high and unselfish ambitions for his subject. Among the several students who were to attain professional prominence and influence, A. C. Pigou and J. M. Keynes should especially be mentioned. Nationally, Marshall was a public figure and played an important role in government inquiries and in the professionalization of economics in Britain. Internationally, he was cosmopolitan in outlook and kept close contact with economists and economic events abroad.

Marshall was anxious to influence events and deeply concerned for the future of Britain, and especially of its poorer and less privileged citizens. Yet he preferred to remain above the fray of current controversy, whether scientific or concerned with policy, trusting that 'constructive' work and patient study would provide the surer if slower route towards the desired goals. His desire for historical continuity and the avoidance of controversy led him frequently to underplay the novelty of his ideas and to exaggerate their closeness to those of his classical forebears.

John K. Whitaker
University of Virginia

Further Reading

Guillebaud, C. W. (ed.) (1965), *Marshall's Principles of Economics, Variorum Edition*, London.
Pigou, A. C. (ed.) (1925), *Memorials of Alfred Marshall*, London.
Whitaker, J. K. (ed.) (1975), *The Early Economic Writings of Alfred Marshall, 1867–1890*, London.
See also: *neoclassical economics*.

Marshall-Lerner Criterion

This criterion is named after the English economist Alfred Marshall and the American economist Abba Lerner. It is a simple condition which shows whether a devaluation of a country's currency will improve the country's balance of trade. Such an improvement need not necessarily follow, since a devaluation will normally cheapen the value of each unit of the country's exports in world currency and may not cheapen the value of each unit of its imports. If the balance of trade is to improve following the devaluation, export sales must increase enough, and/or import purchases diminish enough, to offset any such relative cheapening of exports. The relative cheapening of exports is called a 'worsening of the country's terms of trade'.

The Marshall-Lerner criterion states that 'a country's trade balance will improve following a depreciation of its currency if the (positive value of) the elasticity of foreign demand for its exports and the (positive value of) its elasticity of demand for imports together sum to more than unity'. (An elasticity of demand for a commodity shows the percentage increase in the quantity demanded following a 1 per cent fall in the commodity's price.) The Marshall-Lerner criterion is appropriate if the following simplifying assumptions are applicable: the country's exports are in infinitely elastic supply (export prices are constant in home currency); the world supply of imports to the country is infinitely elastic (import prices are constant in foreign currency); and the balance of trade is initially neither in surplus nor in deficit. In such circumstances an x per cent worsening devaluation will cause an x per cent reduction in the foreign currency revenue from each unit of exports, and no change in the foreign currency revenue for each unit of imports, in other words, it will cause an x per cent worsening of the terms of trade. But it will also cause an increase in export volume and reduction in import volume which together sum to more than x per cent and so outweigh this worsening of the terms of trade.

Qualifications to the Marshall-Lerner criterion are required if the assumptions mentioned in the previous paragraph do not hold. If, for example, the prices of exports in foreign currency are in part tied to foreign competitors' prices in foreign currency, then the terms of trade loss following a devaluation will be smaller, and an improvement in the balance of trade will be easier to obtain. By contrast, a devaluation starting from an initial position of deficit will in general require larger volume responses if it is to improve the trade balance. The export and import elasticities then need to add up to more than unity for a devaluation to be successful.

Modern balance of payments theory, developed since World War II, has suggested some more fundamental modifications to the Marshall-Lerner criterion. Firstly, a devaluation will normally lead to increases in domestic costs and prices. This domestic inflation may partly or fully upset the stimulus to export promotion and import reduction. The second modification is suggested by the techniques of Keynesian 'multiplier' analysis: any improvement in the trade balance will increase domestic incomes and expenditures, sucking in more imports, so partly or fully undoing the initial improvement. The third amendment has been suggested by the 'monetary theory of the balance of payments'. Any improvement in the trade balance may lead to monetary inflow, a stimulus to expenditures at home, and further increases in imports which may undo the initial improvement. These three developments have made it clear that the success of a devaluation depends not only on the size of export and import elasticities, as suggested by the Marshall-Lerner criterion, but also upon the domestic inflationary process, upon domestic income expansion, and upon what happens to domestic monetary conditions.

David Vines
University of Glasgow

Further Reading
Stern, R. M. (1973), *The Balance of Payments: Theory and Policy*, London.
See also: *balance of payments*; *international trade*.

Martinet, André (1908–)

The French linguist, André Martinet, born in 1908 in St-Alban-des-Villards, Savoy, is the main French representative of the Prague school of structural linguistics. He taught phonology in Paris, and from 1946–55 in the United States. He returned to France in 1955 to become professor at the University of Paris, and in 1957 moved to a post at the École Pratique des Hautes Études.

In an important book, *Economie des changements phonétiques* (1955), Martinet shows the importance of system pressures in the explanation of phonetic changes. He has also provided an example of phonological description (*La description phonologique, avec application au parler franco-provençal d'Hauteville (Savoie)* (1956), which many have used as a model. In his best-known work, *Eléments de linguistique générale* (1960), Martinet defines a language as doubly articulated: the experience is mapped onto linguistic utterances analysable into minimal units, the *monemes*, whose sound shape is itself analysable into phonemes. He shows how to establish the phonological ('phonemic' in the American usage) system of a language and how to tell phonemes from variants and archiphonemes appearing in contexts of neutralization. Then he explains how morphological analysis should be conducted: monemes can either have clear boundaries, or they can be discontinuous (for example, French *ne . . . pas*), or blend in unanalysable segments (this phenomenon he refers to as *amalgame*).

The need to reinforce his theory in the face of other models, such as Transformational Grammar, has led

Martinet to develop a recent version which he calls functional linguistics, in which the syntax is more deeply handled (1975), the study of meaning being itself reorganized into a domain labelled *axiology*. At the same time, the development of Labovian sociolinguistics has also led Martinet to extend a study which he had undertaken fairly early on (1945), and which is concerned with linguistic variation as reflecting social differentiations. Many of Martinet's disciples have published work along these lines (see, for example, Walter, 1977).

Claude Hagège
University of Paris

References
Martinet, A. (1945), *La prononciation du français contemporain. Témoignages recueillis en 1941 dans un camp d'officiers prisonniers*, Paris.
Martinet, A. (1975), *Studies in Functional Syntax*, Munich.
Walter, H. (ed.) (1977), *Phonologie et société*, Montreal.

Further Reading
Martinet, A. (1965), *La linguistique synchronique*, Paris.
Martinet, A. (ed.) (1968), 'Le langage', *Encyclopédie de la Pléiade*, Paris.
Martinet, A. (ed.) (1969), *La Linguistique. Guide alphabétique*, Paris.
Mounin, G. (1972), *La linguistique du XXe siècle*, Paris.

Marx, Karl Heinrich (1818–83)

Marx was a German social scientist and revolutionary, whose analysis of capitalist society laid the theoretical basis for the political movement bearing his name. Marx's main contribution lies in his emphasis on the role of the economic factor – the changing way in which people have reproduced their means of subsistence – in shaping the course of history. This perspective has had a considerable influence on the whole range of social sciences.

Karl Heinrich Marx was born in the town of Trier in the Moselle district of the Prussian Rhineland on 5 May 1818. He came from a long line of rabbis on both his father's and his mother's sides. His father, a respected lawyer in Trier, had accepted baptism as a Protestant in order to be able to pursue his career. The atmosphere of Marx's home was permeated by the Enlightenment, and he assimilated a certain amount of romantic and early socialist ideas from Baron von Westphalen – to whose daughter, Jenny, he became engaged in 1835 and later married. In the same year he left the local gymnasium, or high school, and enrolled at the University of Bonn. He transferred the following year to the University of Berlin, where he soon embraced the dominant philosophy of Hegelianism. Intending to become a university teacher, Marx obtained his doctorate in 1841 with a thesis on post-Aristotelian Greek philosophy.

From 1837 Marx had been deeply involved in the Young Hegelian movement. This group espoused a radical critique of Christianity and, by implication, a liberal opposition to the Prussian autocracy. Finding a university career closed to him by the Prussian government, Marx moved into journalism. In October 1842 he became editor, in Cologne, of the influential *Rheinische Zeitung*, a liberal newspaper backed by Rhenish industrialists. Marx's incisive articles, particularly on economic questions, induced the government to close the paper, and he decided to emigrate to France.

Paris was then the centre of socialist thought and on his arrival at the end of 1843, Marx rapidly made contact with organized groups of emigré German workers and with various sects of French socialists. He also edited the shortlived *Deutsch-französische Jahrbücher*, which was intended to form a bridge between nascent French socialism and the ideas of the German radical Hegelians. It was also in Paris that Marx first formed his lifelong partnership with Friedrich Engels. During the first few months of his stay in Paris, Marx rapidly became a convinced communist and set down his views in a series of manuscripts known as the *Ökonomisch-philosophische Manuskripte* (*Economic and Philosophic Manuscripts of 1844*). Here he outlined a humanist conception of communism, influenced by the philosophy of Ludwig Feuerbach and based on a contrast between the alienated nature of labour under capitalism and a communist society in which human beings freely developed their nature in co-operative production. For the first time there appeared together, if not yet united, what Engels described as the three constituent elements in Marx's thought – German idealist philosophy, French socialism, and English economics. It is above all these Manuscripts which (in the West at least) reorientated many people's interpretation of Marx – to the extent of their even being considered as his major work. They were not published until the early 1930s and did not attract public attention until after the Second World War; certain facets of the Manuscripts were soon assimilated to the existentialism and humanism then so much in vogue, and presented an altogether more attractive basis for non-Stalinist socialism than textbooks on dialectical materialism.

Seen in their proper perspective, these Manuscripts were in fact no more than a starting-point for Marx – an initial, exuberant outpouring of ideas to be taken up and developed in subsequent economic writings, particularly in the *Grundrisse* (1857–8) and in *Das Kapital* (1867). In these later works the themes of the '1844 Manuscripts' would certainly be pursued more systematically, in greater detail, and against a much more solid economic and historical background; but the central inspiration or vision was to remain unaltered: man's alienation in capitalist society, and the possibility of his emancipation – of his controlling his own destiny through communism.

Because of his political journalism, Marx was expelled from Paris at the end of 1844. He moved (with Engels) to Brussels, where he stayed for the next three years. He visited England, then the most advanced industrial country in the world, where Engels's family had cotton-spinning interests in Manchester. While in Brussels, Marx devoted himself to an intensive study of history. This he set out in a manuscript known as *The German Ideology* (also published posthumously); its basic thesis was that 'the nature of individuals depends on the material conditions determining their production'. Marx traced the history of the various modes of production and predicted the collapse of the present one – capitalism – and its replacement by communism.

At the same time that he was engaged in this theoretical work, Marx became involved in political activity and in writing polemics (as in *Misère de la Philosophie* (1847) (*The Poverty of Philosophy*) against what he considered to be the unduly idealistic socialism of Pierre Joseph Proudhon. He joined the Communist League, an organization of German emigré workers with its centre in London, for which he and Engels became the major theoreticians. At a conference of the league in London at the end of 1847, Marx and Engels were commissioned to write a *Manifest der kommunistischen Partei* (1848) (*Manifesto of the Communist Party*), a declaration that was to become the most succinct expression of their views. Scarcely was the *Manifesto* published when the 1848 wave of revolutions broke in Europe.

Early in 1848, Marx moved back to Paris, where the revolution had first erupted. He then went on to Germany where he founded, again in Cologne, the *Neue Rheinische Zeitung*. This widely influential newspaper supported a radical democratic line against the Prussian autocracy. Marx devoted his main energies to its editorship, since the Communist League had been virtually disbanded. With the ebbing of the revolutionary tide, however, Marx's paper was suppressed. He sought refuge in London in May 1849, beginning the 'long, sleepless night of exile' that was to last for the rest of his life.

On settling in London, Marx grew optimistic about the imminence of a fresh revolutionary outbreak in Europe, and he rejoined the rejuvenated Communist League. He wrote two lengthy pamphlets on the 1848 revolution in France and its aftermath, entitled *Die Klassenkämpfe in Frankreich 1848 bis 1850* (1850) (*The Class Struggles in France*) and *Der achzehnte Brumaire des Louis Bonaparte* (1852) (*The Eighteenth Brumaire of Louis Bonaparte*). But he soon became convinced that 'a new revolution is possible only in consequence of a new crisis', and devoted himself to the study of political economy to determine the causes and conditions of this crisis.

During the first half of the 1850s the Marx family lived in three-room lodgings in the Soho quarter of London and experienced considerable poverty. The Marxes already had four children on their arrival in London, and two more were soon born. Of these, only three survived the Soho period. Marx's major source of income at this time (and later) was Engels, who was drawing a steadily increasing income from his father's cotton business in Manchester. This was supplemented by weekly articles he wrote as foreign correspondent for the *New York Daily Tribune*. Legacies in the late 1850s and early 1860s eased Marx's financial position somewhat, but it was not until 1869 that he had a sufficient and assured income settled on him by Engels.

Not surprisingly, Marx's major work on political economy made slow progress. By 1857–8 he had produced a mammoth 800-page manuscript – a rough draft of a work that he intended should deal with capital, landed property, wage-labour, the state, foreign trade, and the world market. This manuscript, known as *Grundrisse*(or 'Outlines') was not published until 1941. In the early 1860s he broke off his work to compose three large volumes, entitled *Theorien über den Mehrwert* (1861–3) (*Theories of Surplus Value*), that discussed his predecessors in political economy, particularly Adam Smith and David Ricardo.

It was not until 1867 that Marx was able to publish the first results of his work in Volume One of *Das Kapital*, devoted to a study of the capitalist process of production. Here he elaborated his version of the labour theory of value, and his conception of surplus value and exploitation that would ultimately lead to a falling rate of profit and the collapse of capitalism. Volumes Two and Three were largely finished in the 1860s, but Marx worked on the manuscripts for the rest of his life. They were published posthumously by Engels. In his major work, Marx's declared aim was to analyse 'the birth, life and death of a given social organism and its replacement by another, superior order'. In order to achieve this aim, Marx took over the concepts of the 'classical' economists that were still the generally accepted tool of economic analysis, and used them to draw very different conclusions. Ricardo had made a distinction between use-value and exchange-value. The exchange-value of an object was something separate from its price and consisted of the amount of labour embodied in the objects of production, though Ricardo thought that the price in fact tended to approximate to the exchange-value. Thus – in contradistinction to later analyses – the value of an object was determined by the circumstances of production rather than those of demand. Marx took over these concepts, but, in his attempt to show that capitalism was not static but an historically relative system of class exploitation, supplemented Ricardo's

views by introducing the idea of surplus-value. Surplus-value was defined as the difference between the value of the products of labour and the cost of producing that labour-power, that is, the labourer's subsistence; for the exchange-value of labour-power was equal to the amount of labour necessary to reproduce that labour-power and this was normally much lower than the exchange-value of the products of that labour-power.

The theoretical part of Volume One divides very easily into three sections. The first section is a rewriting of the *Zur Kritik der politischen Ökonomie* (1859) (*Critique of Political Economy*) and analyses commodities, in the sense of external objects that satisfy human needs, and their value. Marx established two sorts of value – use-value, or the utility of something, and exchange value which was determined by the amount of labour incorporated in the object. Labour was also of a twofold nature according to whether it created use-values or exchange-values. Because 'the exchange-values of commodities must be capable of being expressed in terms of something common to them all', and the only thing they shared was labour, then labour must be the source of value. But since evidently some people worked faster or more skilfully than others, this labour must be a sort of average 'socially necessary' labour time. There followed a difficult section on the form of value, and the first chapter ended with an account of commodities as exchange values, which he described as the 'fetishism of commodities' in a passage that recalls the account of alienation in the *Pariser Manuskripte* (1844) (Paris Manuscripts) and (even more) the *Note on James Mill*. 'In order,' said Marx here, 'to find an analogy, we must have recourse to the mist-enveloped regions of the religious world. In that world the productions of the human brain appear as independent beings endowed with life, and entering into relation both with one another and the human race. So it is in the world of commodities with the products of men's hands.' The section ended with a chapter on exchange and an account of money as the means for the circulation of commodities, the material expression for their values and the universal measure of value.

The second section was a small one on the transformation of money into capital. Before the capitalist era, people had sold commodities for money in order to buy more commodities. In the capitalist era, instead of selling to buy, people had bought to sell dearer: they had bought commodities with their money in order, by means of those commodities, to increase their money.

In the third section Marx introduced his key notion of surplus value, the idea that Engels characterized as Marx's principal 'discovery' in economics. Marx made a distinction between *constant* capital which was 'that part of capital which is represented by the means of production, by the raw material, auxiliary material and instruments of labour, and does not, in the process of production, undergo any quantitative alteration of value' and *variable* capital. Of this Marx said: 'That part of capital, represented by labour power, does, in the process of production, undergo an alteration of value. It both reproduces the equivalent of its own value, and also produces an excess, a surplus value, which may itself vary, may be more or less according to the circumstances.' This variation was the rate of surplus value around which the struggle between workers and capitalists centred. The essential point was that the capitalist got the worker to work longer than was merely sufficient to embody in his product the value of his labour power: if the labour power of the worker (roughly what it cost to keep him alive and fit) was £4 a day and the worker could embody £4 of value in the product on which he was working in eight hours, then, if he worked ten hours, the last two hours would yield surplus value – in this case £1.

Thus surplus value could only arise from variable capital, not from constant capital, as labour alone created value. Put very simply, Marx's reason for thinking that the rate of profit would decrease was that, with the introduction of machinery, labour time would become less and thus yield less surplus value. Of course, machinery would increase production and colonial markets would absorb some of the surplus, but these were only palliatives and an eventual crisis was inevitable. These first nine chapters were complemented by a masterly historical account of the genesis of capitalism which illustrates better than any other writing Marx's approach and method. Marx particularly made pioneering use of official statistical information that came to be available from the middle of the nineteenth century onwards.

Meanwhile, Marx devoted much time and energy to the First International – to whose General Council he was elected on its foundation in 1864. This was one of the reasons he was so delayed in his work on *Das Kapital*. He was particularly active in preparing for the annual congresses of the International and in leading the struggle against the anarchist wing of the International led by Mikhail Bakunin. Although Marx won this contest, the transfer of the seat of the General Council from London to New York in 1872 – a move that Marx supported – led to the swift decline of the International. The most important political event during the existence of the International was the Paris Commune of 1871, when the citizens of Paris, in the aftermath of the Franco-Prussian war, rebelled against their government and held the city for two months. On the bloody suppression of this rebellion, Marx wrote one of his most famous pamphlets – entitled *Address on The Civil War in France* (1871) – which was an enthusiastic defence of the activities and aims of the Commune.

During the last decade of his life Marx's health declined considerably, and he was incapable of the sustained efforts of creative synthesis that had so obviously characterized his previous work. Nevertheless, he managed to comment substantially on contemporary politics in Germany and Russia. In Germany he opposed, in his *Randglossen zum Programm der deutschen Arbeiterpartei* (1875) (*Critique of the Gotha Programme*), the tendency of his followers Wilhelm Leibknecht and August Bebel to compromise with the state socialism of Ferdinand Lassalle in the interest of a united socialist party. In Russia, in correspondence with Vera Sassoulitch, he contemplated the possibility of Russia's bypassing the capitalist stage of development and building communism on the basis of the common ownership of land characteristic of the village council, or *mir*. Marx, however, was increasingly dogged by ill health, and he regularly travelled to European spas and even to Algeria in search of recuperation. The deaths of his eldest daughter and of his wife clouded the last years of his life, and he died in London on 13 March, 1883.

The influence of Marx, so narrow during his lifetime, expanded enormously after his death. This influence was at first evident in the growth of the Social Democratic Party in Germany, but reached world-wide dimensions following the success of the Bolsheviks in Russia in 1917. Paradoxically, although the main thrust of Marx's thought was to anticipate that a proletarian revolution would inaugurate the transition to socialism in advanced industrial countries, Marxism was most successful in developing or Third World countries, such as Russia or China. Since the problems of these countries are primarily agrarian and the initial development of an industrial base, they are necessarily far removed from what were Marx's immediate concerns. On a more general level, over the whole range of the social sciences, Marx's materialist conception of history and his analysis of capitalist society have made him probably the most influential figure of the twentieth century.

David McLellan
University of Kent

Further Reading

Avineri, S. (1968), *The Social and Political Thought of Karl Marx*, Cambridge.
Cohen, G. (1978), *Karl Marx's Theory of History: A Defence*, Oxford.
Marx, K. (1977), *Selected Writings*, ed. D. McLellan, Oxford.
McLellan, D. (1974), *Karl Marx: His Life and Thought*, New York.
Ollman, B. (1971), *Alienation, Marx's Conception of Man in Capitalist Society*, Cambridge.
Plamenatz, J. (1975), *Karl Marx's Philosophy of Man*, Oxford.
Suchting, W. (1983), *Marx: An Introduction*, Brighton.

See also: *alienation*; *Engels*; *Marx's theory of history and society*; *Marxian economics*.

Marxian Economics

Marxian economics traditionally begins from a general statement of the labour theory of value (GLTV): that value in commodity exchange is grounded on exploitation in production. This leads to an account of the labour process, showing how exploitation takes place and how it can be measured by a rate of exploitation – the hours worked for the employers – divided by the hours worked to support the labourer. From this, a special labour theory (SLTV) is developed: prices, or ratios of exchange between commodities, are proportioned to the hours of direct and indirect labour that went to produce them. These prices are easily calculable from input-output data, and have the important property that they are independent of the distribution of the surplus between the social classes. But, except in special cases, they are not consistent with a uniform rate of profit in capital, such as free competition would tend to establish (Steedman, 1977). (The question of the relation between prices based on labour values and prices based on a uniform rate of profit is known as 'the Transformation Problem'.)

Important as they are, the theories of exploitation and labour value are foundations. The edifice itself centres upon the General Law of Capitalist Accumulation (GLCA), that the accumulation of capital is accompanied, *pari passu*, by an increase in the proletariat, maintaining, therefore, an 'industrial reserve army' of the unemployed, proportioned in size to the total capital. The arguments for this proportion require a way of expressing prices which is independent of distribution (since, for example, when capital accumulates faster than the proletariat grows, wages rise and profits fall, slowing down accumulation), but do not otherwise depend on the SLTV. Having established the GLCA, Marx turned to the theory of circulation, the tendency of the rate of profit to fall, the behaviour of rents, the theory of crises, and the role of money, credit, and interest.

In the last twenty years there has been a great revival of Marxian economics, due chiefly to the work of Piero Sraffa (1960). Sraffa's construction of the 'Standard Commodity' which solves Ricardo's problem of 'the invariable measure of value', provides a way of expressing prices both consistent with a uniform rate of profit and invariant to changes in distribution. Hence, the SLTV can be discarded; the GLTV, on the other hand, remains unaffected, since the rate of exploitation, and the connection between exploitation and profits can be shown more clearly than ever in equation systems based on Sraffa (Morishima, 1973). Thus, the GLCA can be established on a firm foundation, permitting an analytical treatment of the effects of class conflict on wages and exploitation, although modern work normally gives much greater scope to demand factors than Marx did.

However, the very system of equations which establishes the validity of the basic Marxian scheme – the GLTV and the GLCA – undermines the Marxian argument for the tendency of the rate of profit to fall simply as a result of a rise in the organic composition of capital. For firms will not adapt a new technique unless it is cheaper than the old, at current prices. But it can be shown that if it is cheaper, then when adapted and the new prices are established, the new rate of profit will never be less than the old (Roemer, 1981). Thus, the Marxian theory of crisis needs another foundation. This has led to interesting work on the theory of circulation, money and credit, bringing the Marxian tradition into contact with the work being done by the post-Keynesian school. In particular, Marxists and neo-Ricardians have been concerned with whether the rate of profit determines the rate of interest, or vice versa, or whether they are both determined together.

Questions of circulation and money lead to a re-examination of competition, and the tendency to greater centralization and concentration. Competition has been conceptualized as a form of strategic conflict, but there is as yet no generally accepted theory of the development and behaviour of the corporation. However, this is a rapidly developing field.

Marxian economics has greatly benefited from the Classical Revival instigated by Sraffa. But Marx founded his economic thinking on a critique of the Classics, basically contending that they took relations of social power for the natural order of things, and attributed to mere tokens – money, capital, commodities – power which really resided in class relationships. Modern Marxian economics likewise both learns from the post-Keynesian and modern Classical tradition, and establishes its separate identity through a critique of these schools. Its critique is essentially that of Marx: the economic system works according to laws, but these laws in turn depend on the nature of the political and social system, and cannot be fully understood apart from the whole. This critique has particular force when it comes to the theory of economic policy, for the post-Keynesians, in particular, tend to attribute to the State power and a degree of neutrality which Marxists do not believe possible under capitalism.

Edward J. Nell
The New School for Social Research, New York

References

Morishima, M. (1973), *Marx's Economics: A Dual Theory of Value and Growth*, Cambridge.

Roemer, J. (1981), *Analytical Foundations of Marxian Economic Theory*, Cambridge.

Sraffa, P. (1960), *Production of Commodities by Means of Commodities*, Cambridge.

Steedman, I. (1977), *Marx after Sraffa*, London.

See also: *labour theory of value; Marx's theory of history and society*.

Marx's Theory of History and Society

Marx's general sociohistorical theory, often known as 'the materialist conception of history' or 'historical materialism', seeks, in the words of Engels,

> the ultimate cause and the great moving power of all important historic events in the economic development of society, in the changes in the modes of production and exchange, and in the consequent division of society into distinct classes, and in the struggles of these classes against one another.

Marx first elaborated his theory, which became the 'guiding thread' of his subsequent studies, in *Die deutsche Ideologie* (*The German Ideology*) of 1845–6. A famous, but very compact, statement of it appears in Marx's 'Preface' to *Zur Kritik der politischen Ökonomie* (1859) (*A Contribution to the Critique of Political Economy*).

There Marx contends that the economic structure of society, constituted by its relations of production, is the real foundation of society. It is the basis 'on which rises a legal and political superstructure and to which correspond definite forms of social consciousness'. On the other hand, society's relations of production themselves 'correspond to a definite stage of development of [society's] material productive forces'. In this manner 'the mode of production of material life conditions the social, political and intellectual life process in general'. As society's productive forces develop, they clash with existing production relations, which now fetter their growth. 'Then begins an epoch of social revolution' as this contradiction rifts society and as people become, in a more or less ideological form, 'conscious of this conflict and fight it out'. This conflict is resolved in favour of the productive forces, and new, higher relations of production, whose material preconditions have 'matured in the womb of the old society itself', emerge which better accommodate the continued growth of society's productive capacity. The bourgeois mode of production represents the most recent of several progressive epochs in the economic formation of society, but it is the last antagonistic form of production. With its demise the prehistory of humanity will come to a close.

According to Marx, the expansion of the productive forces (that is, of the means of production and of the skill and expertise of human labour power) determines society's relations of production because, as he wrote to Annenkov, 'Men never relinquish what they have won.' In order to retain 'the fruits of civilization' they will change their way of producing to accommodate the acquired productive forces and facilitate their continued advance. The relations of production, though, influence the momentum and qualitative direction of the development of the productive forces; capitalism in particular is distinguished by its tendency to raise society to a productive level undreamt of before. Still, Marx's materialist conception assigns explanatory primacy to the development of the productive forces, envisioning, for instance, the emergence of capitalism as a response to the level of the productive forces existing at the time of its origin.

The development of society's productive capacity thus determines the main contours of its socioeconomic evolution, while the various economic structures that result shape, in turn, society's legal and political institutions, or superstructure. Which other social institutions are properly part of the superstructure is a matter of debate, but Marx certainly thought that all the various spheres and realms of society reflect the dominant mode of production and that the general consciousness of an epoch is shaped by the nature of its production. The Marxist theory of ideology contends, in part, that certain ideas originate or are widespread because they sanction existing social relations or promote particular class interests. The economy's determination of legal and political forms, however, will tend to be relatively direct, while its influence over other social realms, culture, and consciousness generally is more attenuated and nuanced.

Because a superstructure is needed to organize and stabilize society, the economic structure brings about those institutions that are best suited to it. Law, in particular, is necessary to 'sanction the existing order' and grant it 'independence from mere chance and arbitrariness'. This function itself gives the legal realm some autonomy, since the existing relations of production are represented and legitimated in an abstract, codified form, which in turn fosters the ideological illusion that the law is entirely autonomous with respect to the economic structure. In addition, under capitalism the '*fictio juris* of a contract' between free agents obscures the real nature of production, in particular, the 'invisible threads' that bind the wage-labourer to capital. In precapitalist societies, for example in feudalism, tradition and custom perform a similar stabilizing function and may also win a degree of autonomy from the economic realm. There the true nature of the social relations of production is obscured by entanglement with the relations of personal domination which characterize the other spheres of feudal life.

In the social organization of production, people stand in different relations to the forces and products of production, and in any given mode of production these relations will be of certain characteristic sorts. One's economic position, as that is understood in terms of the existing social production relations, gives one certain material interests in common with others and determines one's class. Hence follow the familiar definitions of the bourgeoisie and proletariat by reference to the purchase and sale, respectively, of labour power (and the underlying ownership or non-ownership of the means of production).

A central thesis of Marx is that class position, so defined, determines the characteristic consciousness or world view of its members. For example, Marx's discussion of the Legitimists and Orleanists in *Der achzehnte Brumaire des Louis Bonaparte* (1852) (*The Eighteenth Brumaire of Louis Bonaparte*) emphasizes that on the basis of its socioeconomic position each class creates 'an entire superstructure of distinct and peculiarly formed sentiments, illusions, modes of thought and views of life'. The differing material interests of classes divide them and lead to their struggle. Classes differ in the extent to which their members perceive themselves as a class, so that antagonisms between classes may not be discerned by the participants, or may be understood only in a mystified or ideological manner.

The ultimate success or failure of a class is determined by its relation to the advance of the productive forces. In the words of *The German Ideology*, 'The conditions under which definite productive forces can be applied are the conditions of the rule of a definite class of society.' That class which has the capacity and the incentive to introduce or preserve the relations of production required to accommodate the advance of the productive forces has its hegemony ensured. Marx's theory views class rule, hitherto, as both inevitable and necessary to force the productivity of the direct producers beyond the subsistence level. The productive progress brought by capitalism, however, eliminates both the feasibility of, and the historical rationale for, class rule. Since the state is primarily the vehicle by which a class secures its rule, it will wither away in post-class society.

Marx's 'Preface' designates the Asiatic, ancient, feudal, and modern bourgeois modes of production as the major epochs in humanity's advance, but these mark the general stages of socioeconomic evolution as a whole – not the steps which history obliges every nation without exception to climb. In a famous letter of November 1877, Marx characteristically denied propounding 'any historic-philosophic theory of the *marche générale* imposed by fate upon every people', but this oft-quoted remark does not amount to a rejection of historical determinism. Although Marx's theory permits countries to lag behind or even skip steps, their course must still be accounted for within the overarching pattern of socioeconomic evolution, and that development is due to the productive forces. Marx could consistently believe in a necessary, productive-force-determined evolution of history without holding that every social group is preordained to follow the same course. It seems likely, in addition, that Marx would have been willing to revise his particular tabulation of historical periods (or at least the pre-feudal ones), since he did not analyse in detail humanity's early modes of production. Modification of Marx's schema, as well as of his analysis of capitalism (and the projected transition to socialism), is in principle compatible with his basic theory of society and history.

It should be borne in mind that Marx's theory does not pretend to explain every last detail of history and society. Certain social and cultural phenomena are beyond its explanatory range, and from its broad purview, many historical events, and certainly the specific forms they take, are accidental. Nor does the theory seek to explain fully and scientifically individual behaviour, though it attempts to situate that behaviour within its sociohistorical confines. In so far as there are ineluctable tendencies in history, these result from, not despite, the choices of individuals.

Marx's ideas have had an influence on the social sciences, the significance of which it is hard to exaggerate. Not only has his work inspired, to various extents, countless writers, but even those who reject Marx frequently find themselves obliged to define their own thought in relation to his. Despite the perennial attractions of Marx's approach and the fertility of his insights, controversy continues over the basic concepts and theorems of his theory, the relative importance of its various components, and the specific features that characterize his sociohistorical methodology. Given Marx's far-reaching claims and the lack of an interpretative consensus, a conclusive assessment of the viability of his general theory of society and history is exceedingly difficult.

William H. Shaw
Tennessee State University

Further Reading
Cohen, G. A. (1978), *Karl Marx's Theory of History: A Defence*, Oxford.
Shaw, W. H. (1978), *Marx's Theory of History*, Stanford.
Wood, A. (1981), *Karl Marx*, London.
See also: *Engels*; *Marx*; *Marxian economics*.

Mass Media

Mass media together comprise a new social institution, concerned with the production and distribution of knowledge in the widest sense of the word, and have a number of salient characteristics, including: the use of relatively advanced technology for the (mass) production and dissemination of messages; the systematic organization and social regulation of this work; the direction of messages at potentially large audiences who are unknown to the sender and free to attend or not. The mass media institution is essentially open, operating in the public sphere to provide regular channels of communication for 'messages' of a kind determined by what is culturally and technically possible, socially permitted and in demand by a large enough number of individuals.

It is usual to date the beginnings of mass media from the first recognizably modern newspaper, in the early seventeenth century, which in turn was a new application of the technology of printing, already in use for over 150 years for the multiple reproduction of book manuscripts. The audiovisual forms which have subsequently been developed, mainly since the end of the nineteenth century, have caused existing media to adapt and have enlarged the total reach of media, as well as extended the diversity of their social functions.

This history of media development is, nevertheless, more than a record of technical advance and of increasing scale of operation. It was a social innovation as much as a technological invention, and turning points in media history are marked, if not caused, by major social changes. The history of the newspaper, still the archetypal as well as the first, mass medium, illustrates the point very well. Its development is linked to the emergence to power of the bourgeois (urban-business-professional) class, which it served in cultural, political and commercial activities. It became an essential instrument in subsequent economic and political struggles, a necessary condition for economic liberalism, constitutional democracy and, perhaps, also, revolution and bureaucratic centralism. Its development thus reflects political and economic forces on the one hand and major social and cultural changes on the other. The latter include: urbanization; rising living standards and the growth of leisure; the emergence of forms of society which are, variously, democratic, highly organized, bureaucratic, nationalistic and committed to gradual change. Consideration of newer media, especially film, radio and television, would not greatly modify this assessment, and these media have not greatly widened the range of functions already performed by the newspaper as advertiser, entertainer and forum for the expression of opinion and culture.

Early social science views of mass media reflect some of these historical circumstances. Commentators were struck by the immense popular appeal of the new media and by the power which they might exert in society. Beyond that, views divided sharply on whether to welcome or regret the new instruments of culture and information, and a division between pessimists and optimists has been an enduring feature of assessments of mass media, only starting to fade as the inevitability and complexity of the media are accepted. The pessimistic view stems partly from the pejorative connotations of the word 'mass', which includes the notions of vast scale, anonymity, impersonality, uniformity, lack of regulation, mindlessness. At the extreme, the media were regarded, sometimes by conservative and radical critics alike, as instruments for manipulation, a threat to existing cultural and spiritual values and to democracy. But optimists saw the mass media as a powerful means of disseminating information, education and culture to the previously excluded classes and of making feasible a genuine participatory democracy. By the 1930s some circumstantial evidence

and enough theory supported both 'sides', but there was little systematic investigation.

The first period of scientific investigation of mass media undertaken between the mid 1930s and the late 1950s resulted in a much more modest estimate of media effects than was previously assumed, even a new 'myth' of media powerlessness. The earlier stimulus-response model of influence was replaced by a model of indirect influence, according to which the media were seen to be subject to mechanisms of selective attention, perception and response, such that any effects would be more likely to reinforce existing tendencies than to cause any major change. Further, the working of media was seen to be subordinate to the existing patterns of social and personal influence and thus not well conceived of as an 'external' influence. While the evidence reassured many critics and discomfited prophets of doom, it seemed to lead to no slackening of efforts to use media, in ever more subtle ways, for political and commercial ends. Since the 1960s there has been further development in the assessment of mass media effects in the direction of a renewed belief in their potency.

The earlier research, despite its reassuring message, left open the possibility that media effects could be considerable under certain conditions: (1) where there exists a monopoly or uniformity of message content; (2) where the messages seem to concern matters beyond immediate experience or direct relevance; (3) where there is a cumulation over a long period of time of similar messages. Research attention has thus shifted from the search for direct, short-time, effects on individuals and towards the following: structures of ownership and control of media; patterns of ideology or culture in messages and texts; professional and organizational contexts in which media knowledge is 'manufactured'. Experts assessing the influence of mass media nowadays emphasize what people 'learn' from the media, thus cognitive effects in the widest sense. We may learn from the media what is normal or approved, what is 'right' or 'wrong', what to expect as an individual, group or class, and how we should view other groups or nations. Aside from the nature and magnitude of media effects on people, it is impossible to doubt the enormous dependence of individuals, institutions and society as a whole on mass media for a wide range of information and cultural services.

If the mass media play an essential part in mediating a wide range of relationships within societies, they have also come to be seen as playing a comparable part in mediating relations between nation states and world blocs. The flow of information and culture by way of mass media does much to establish and confirm patterns of perception, of hostility and attraction and also the relations of economic dependence and latent conflict between the different 'worlds' of East and West, North and South. While mass media still largely consist of separate national systems, the increasing internationalization of networks and content is now interesting researchers.

The history of mass media has so far been fairly short and very eventful, but it already seems on the point of a new and significant departure which may change the essential character of mass communication. The most important developments are of smaller-scale, point-to-point and potentially interactive media, employing cable, satellite or computer technology. It is likely that there will be a move away from centralized and uniform media of distribution towards a more abundant and functionally diversified provision of messages based on receiver demand. The boundaries between mass communication and the emerging new forms of information transfer are likely to become even more blurred in what is being hailed as an emerging 'information society'. Nevertheless, the issues which shaped early debates about mass media are still somewhat relevant in the new conditions, especially those which concern the contribution of mass communication to equality or inequality, order or change, unity or fragmentation.

Denis McQuail
University of Amsterdam

Further Reading
McQuail, D. (1983), *Mass Communication Theory, An Introduction*, London.
Curran, J., Gurevitch, M. and Wollacott, J. (eds) (1977), *Mass Communication and Society*, London.
See also: *communications; Marcuse; mass society; McLuhan.*

Mass Society

The mass society thesis has fallen out of fashion in recent times, but it had a strong appeal in the years after the World War II when it was associated with totalitarianism.

At the 'objective' level, a mass society is an alternative way of talking about industrial societies with a relatively high urban population. In its simplest form, it refers to the concentration of masses of people in urban conglomerations. However, a concentration of population does not by itself qualify a society to be called a mass society. After all, there have been large populations in India and China for a very long time. Crucially, a mass society is characterized by the features discoverable in those societies which were exposed to the consequences of industrialization. In particular, it refers to the incorporation of the entire population of a society within a common culture which has been made possible by the development of sophisticated communication techniques.

The objective features of mass society are not controversial. But what is controversial and problematic are the presumed pathological and social consequences of 'massification'. For a number of social critics, industrial society has produced a situation in which human beings have lost their sense of individuality and have become manipulated units. Mass man is a pathetic isolated atom without any sense of autonomy, whose mental and spiritual life is a carbon copy of other human beings. Indeed, it is this notion of uniformity and standardization that gives rise to the pessimistic prognostications of commentators. Mass society produces a mass culture which is morally and intellectually barren. In particular, 'popular' music, cinema, advertising, and television are seen as constituting a collective form of delusion in which the masses lose any capacity for creativity or originality (Adorno and Horkheimer, 1979).

In addition, mass society is supposedly anti-democratic and authoritarian: in its extreme form, a ruling élite controls and manipulates masses of people – both National Socialist Germany and Stalinist Russia have been seen as examples of totalitarian societies with all the worst features of mass societies (Selznick, 1960). From this point of view, mass society is one in which the masses are continuously indoctrinated by the mass media in the interests of the élite. But not only totalitarian societies control and coerce the masses: the same criticism is directed against liberal democracies. In these societies we surrender our freedom to those who we believe are politically competent, or who have manipulated us into believing that they are. Hence, moral or political action in a liberal democracy is not a result of informed rational reflection, but is a function of the operation of unconscious ideological conditioning. We pay lip-service to freedom, but are incapable of accepting the full consequences of acting as free agents. Marcuse, for example, has argued that 'unfreedom' characterizes the behaviour of 'mass man'. The rhetoric of freedom in Western society is an ideological gloss, a form of 'false consciousness' (Marcuse, 1964).

Accordingly, mass man has no resources to fight the intrusion of bureaucracy and the state into the very depths of his being – he is defeated, empty, neurotic, and psychologically disoriented. Behind this defeat is the feeling that somehow or other capitalism, industrialism, bureaucracy, the state, have betrayed the individual whose essential humanity has been engulfed by mass society.

Mass society is part of that tradition in social thought which dichotomizes societies into categories like *Gemeinschaft* and *Gesellschaft*. In general, mass society theorists regret the decline of community and intimacy associated with our non-industrial past. In this respect left-wing theorists point to the alienation of contemporary society, whereas right-wing theorists stress the disastrous results of mass education and political democracy on the quality of life. Thus, like other typifications, the mass society thesis is, to a large extent, a reflection of ideological commitment, rather than a picture of social reality.

Arthur Brittan
University of York, England

References
Adorno, T. and Horkheimer, M. (1979), *Dialectic of Enlightenment*, London. (Original German, *Die Dialektik der Aufklärung*, Amsterdam, 1974.)
Selznick, P. (1960), *The Organizational Weapon*, Glencoe, Ill.
Marcuse, H. (1964), *One-Dimensional Man*, London.

Further Reading
Giner, S. (1976), *Mass Society*, London.
See also: *Marcuse*; *mass media*.

Mathematical Economics

Mathematical economics has developed from being a relatively small branch of economic theory in 1950 to become almost coextensive with mainstream economic theory. Its success has been such that economists out of sympathy with the basic assumptions and models of so-called neoclassical economic theory have found themselves obliged to provide increasingly mathematical formulations of radical economic theory derived from the Marxian and Ricardian traditions. The reasons for the rapid expansion of mathematical economics after 1950 lie partly in the influx of ex-mathematicians to academic economics – Kenneth Arrow, Gérard Debreu, Frank Hahn, Werner Hildenbrandt – and partly in the increasing concern in all branches of economics with formal rigour and with the establishment of economics as a 'scientific' discipline. Prior to the mathematical formalization of economic theory and the introduction of advanced techniques of mathematical analysis, economic theorists had relied primarily on graphical techniques of analysis and presentation. Up to a point these can be very effective, but they are inherently limited by the two-dimensional character of a piece of paper. More subtly, graphical techniques can introduce implicit assumptions whose significance may be neglected or very difficult to understand.

Historically, among the first applications of mathematical analysis in economics were Leon Walras's use of the theory of simultaneous equations to discuss the problem of equilibrium in several interrelated markets and Edgeworth's use of calculus to analyse consumer behaviour. These subjects remain at the heart of modern mathematical economics, though the mathematical techniques applied have changed totally. They also illustrate the increasingly close relationship between advances in certain areas of mathematical economics and pure mathematics. Walras's problem has stimulated the development of general equilibrium analysis which focuses on the conditions for the exist-

ence of a set of prices, or other instruments, which ensure that supply and demand are equal in all markets simultaneously when the resources, technological possibilities and consumer preferences that determine supply and demand are specified in quite general terms. If a unique general equilibrium can be shown to exist, one may then use comparative statistics to examine how the character of the equilibrium is altered if some of the initial conditions are changed. From such comparisons it may – or may not – be possible to infer the response of prices and quantities to a variety of changes in the world. General equilibrium analysis has come to depend heavily on modern developments in topology and functional analysis, so that the dividing line between the more abstract type of mathematical economics and pure mathematics has almost vanished.

The theory of individual consumer – or producer – behaviour has both benefited from and stimulated advances in the theory of mathematical programming and of convex analysis. As a consequence, familiar results derived by the application of calculus have been subsumed within a much more general theory which is based upon the concept of a maximum/minimum value function – that is, a profit or cost function for a producer, an indirect utility or expenditure function for a consumer. This theory exploits a number of powerful duality results which characterize interrelated maximization and minimization problems and can be given straightforward economic interpretations, such as the association of 'shadow prices' with the constraints which limit the set of feasible choices. This approach to consumer and producer theory has important empirical implications which can in principle be tested. For example, the theory of optimal consumer choice implies that compensated price responses must be symmetric – in other words, the change in the consumption of good i with respect to the price of good j must equal the change in the consumption of good j with respect the price of good i – and that the compensated substitution effect must be negative – an increase in the price of good i should reduce the consumption of i. In both cases the compensated effect refers to the change after income has been adjusted so as to hold utililty constant. This compensation is obviously difficult to measure so that it is not possible to test these predictions directly in experiments, but indirect tests of the hypothesis of maximizing behaviour have been devised. The results have been mixed, but the mathematical developments have stimulated much fruitful empirical work and have provided the basis for modern welfare economics.

The assumptions of equilibrium and maximization which underpin most of economic theory are controversial, especially as descriptions of short-run behaviour. As a result, mathematical economists have sought to construct theoretical models which weaken or dispense with these assumptions. Unfortunately, though these can provide useful insights into particular problems or phenomena, the models are always open to the criticism that they are 'ad hoc' in the sense that they rely upon specific types of behavioural response, and that their results are not robust to even quite small changes in the characterization of these responses. At present there seem to be no powerful simplifying principles which enable economists to analyse models of disequilibrium or non-maximizing behaviour – or even to agree on what these models should look like. Hence most of the current effort of mathematical economists is devoted to modifying standard equilibrium and maximizing models by incorporating considerations of uncertainty and differential information in the hope that this approach will provide the basis for reconciling the more obvious disparities between observed economic behaviour and theoretical predictions. Nonetheless, the basic philosophical problem of how far useful economic models can be developed without the fundamental assumptions of maximization and equilibrium remains unanswered. What, for instance, does it mean to describe someone as 'choosing' a course of action which *he* judges inferior to some other feasible alternative? Until a convincing solution to this problem is found, mathematical economists are likely to continue to rely upon equilibrium models of maximizing behaviour.

Gordon Hughes
University of Cambridge

Further Reading
Arrow, K. J. and Intriligator, M. D. (eds) (1981, 1983, 1984), *Handbook of Mathematical Economics, Vols I–III*, Amsterdam.
Cassels, J. W. S. (1981), *Economics for Mathematicians*, Cambridge.
Varian, H. R. (1978), *Microeconomic Analysis*, New York.
See also: *Arrow*; *Debreu*; *equilibrium*; *mathematical models*.

Mathematical Models

As mathematics is a powerful, flexible language and models are representations, mathematical models are representations framed in mathematical terms. A good metaphor for a mathematical model is a map. A map is a simple device for representing a complex geographical locality. Much of the 'richness' of the locality is removed in the representation but enough remains for it to be recognized. Whether the map is a good one depends not only on its properties but also on the use to which it is put. If you want to get through a city quickly, a simple map of the arterial routes suffices. For a walking tour of a city centre, a detailed map of the city centre is enough, and if you are hiking in open country a geological survey map works fine – if you know how to use it. Much the same applies to

mathematical models: they are representations for a purpose and some knowledge is required to build and use them.

First, the purposes: construction of social science theory entails a concern with, among other things, generality, precision, and parsimony. In place of scattered ideographic propositions, a concern for generality pushes us towards nomothetic propositions that link into coherent and powerful theories of social phenomena. Mathematics has a role in both the formulation of these propositions and their linkage. Given a concern for precision we need to know what we measure, the error bounds of our tools, that our measurement produces high-quality data good enough to support propositions, and that our propositions say exactly what we mean and not some vague approximation. Mathematics can help the construction of measurement tools, the analysis of the properties of these measurement tools and the statement of precise propositions. Parsimony implies a concern for theoretical efficiency: if a simple theory adequately explains phenomena, there is no need for a complex one. Mathematical formulations facilitate the construction of simple theories and make clear the assumptions underlying the construction of theories (which are very important, even if unacknowledged, components of a theory).

Just as it would be folly to claim that generality, precision, and parsimony are all that matter in theory construction, so would it be folly to claim that mathematics is the only way, or even the best way, to achieve these ends. It is one way: a language with tools and techniques that may prove useful.

Second, the knowledge (skill) required for mathematical model building is easily stated. It includes good intuitions, and ability to abstract, some knowledge of a range of models, some facility with the manipulation of the mathematical representations (that is, derivation of logical consequences), an ability to assess critically the models, some flair, and modesty.

We now consider model building which is done within some broad methodology (Doreian and Hummon, 1976) having epistemological, substantive, technical and purposive components. Within the epistemological component, criteria for the construction and evaluation of models are set forth. Within the substantive component, the nature of the theory, its theoretical terms and the nature of relevant data are formulated. The technical component deals with the nuts and bolts of modelling – the mathematical systems used, their properties, measurement and estimation. Within the purposive component we can discuss the goals of the modelling effort. These include explanation, description and explication. They also include a consideration of the uses of a model. Of course, these components are highly interrelated. A model must have a clear set of criteria for evaluating its knowledge claims, make substantive sense, and be technically adequate. Additionally, the model may lead to identification of modes of implementation and intervention.

Discussions of mathematical models are frequently co-ordinated by at least two of the following distinctions. The first differentiates process models from structural models, the second deterministic models from probabilistic (stochastic) models, and the third differentiates models using discrete variables from those using continuous variables. In principle, an eight-cell table can be constructed using these three criteria and each cell filled with mathematical models sharing the criteria defining the cell.

Models of processes explicitly attempt to model change and provide an understanding of the mechanisms of change. Among the frequently used tools are differential equations and difference equations. Models of structure attempt to represent and understand the structure of social relations. Frequently used mathematical tools include graph theory and matrix algebra; in addition, modern algebraic tools such as groups, semi-groups and Boolean algebras find applications in these structural analyses, as well as category theory and algebraic topology.

Stochastic models are used to model processes whose outcomes are governed by a probabilistic mechanism(s). Many types of stochastic models are available to social scientists (see Bartholomew, 1982). Deterministic models eschew stochastic mechanisms in favour of deterministic mechanisms and relations. The process models of social change can be deterministic or stochastic. The structural models tend to be deterministic. If the models are discrete they use variables that can only take one of the small number of states, whereas continuous models use variables that are, or can be, treated usefully as if they are continuous. For the process models, a further distinction can be made concerning the representation of time: it, too, can be taken as discrete or continuous.

Mathematical models have wide-ranging applications in the social sciences. (For many examples see Fararo (1973), Rapoport (1983) and Sørensen (1978).) A modeller selects the mathematical model best suited for a substantive problem where skill shows in knowledge of alternative model candidates and selection of the most fruitful one(s). Mathematical modellers tend to draw on mathematics already developed using models formulated in other disciplines. This is unproblematic if the model captures the crucial theoretical aspects, and critical empirical components, of the substantive problem. Indeed, mathematical models draw their power from being devoid of substantive content: a mathematical model can be used fruitfully in different areas of one field or even in different fields. Seldom have mathematics been invented because of social science needs, which contrasts with the physical science tradition exemplified by the invention of the

differential-integral calculus by Newton and Leibniz. Exceptions include game theory, decision theory and some areas of artificial intelligence research. So much for models, but what is a good model?

Good models must be adequate in all components of its methodology. The Theory-Model-Data triangle of Leik and Meeker (1975) provides a way of discussing this. There are three pairs of mappings – between theory and model; between model and data; and between theory and data – and all are important (although different model builders may place differential emphasis on them).

The theory-model linkage is concerned with expressing a congruence between a theory and its representation in a mathematical model. The theory has to map into the model with little distortion or loss. Deductively, there is a mathematical formalization of the theory while, inductively, this can be a formal generalization of the theory. The mathematical model then has to be useful. Useful, here, means the machinery of the mathematical system has to be mobilized to derive or establish mathematical results. These results can be mapped to the theory and to the data. Deductively, the model maps to the (empirical) data by specifying, or predicting, empirical outcomes. The model is truly predictive if it makes predictions that can be checked empirically. Sometimes models are not predictive in this sense. Instead they lead to the construction of descriptions based on data. Also deductively, the mathematical results (theorems) map to the theory by specifying the theoretical implications of the derivations through the mappings linking theory and model.

When the empirical predictions and specifications stemming from the model are confronted with data, several outcomes are possible: (1) The predictions made on the basis of the theory and the model may be borne out providing support for the model. The results are filtered back through the mappings and interpreted substantively. (2) If a model calls only for empirical descriptions, these by themselves are not, at face value, too important. However, they must make sense when interpreted theoretically. (3) The model may lead to predictions that are disconfirmed, calling the model into question. The model builder then has to establish if the model should be rebuilt or discarded. This requires skill. Further, this decision has other important implications: measurements must be good and empirical evidence is decisive. Which brings us to statistical methodology.

The frequently made distinction between mathematical models and statistical analysis is a very blurred one. Formal approaches can, and do, incorporate error specification (a theory of error) – which other approaches generally do not. This informs estimation. Second, the properties of the statistical tools are stated and established mathematically. Finally, new mathematical models and their uses generate estimation problems and statistical questions.

Space precludes discussion of the rest of the Theory-Model-Data triangle but each does constrain the others. The theory, the model, and the data have to make sense and be consistent with one another – which is the nub of evaluating models.

The charge is often made that mathematical models overlook much of the richness and texture of social life. They do, and this is a virtue (which is not to say the richness and texture are irrelevant). The claim that social phenomena are incredibly complex and that this complexity cannot be captured via mathematical models need not detain us. While the basic laws of physics are simple, for example Newton's laws of motion, they generate behaviours that are, and appear to observers as, very complex. Note also that complex mathematical formulae are generated from 'simple' start points. A direct attempt to model the complexity, for example, to predict the exact trajectory of a snowflake in a storm or a leaf in a wind, would appear bizarre and fruitless. Yet in the social sciences there are many attempts to 'model', in one way or another, the surface phenomena of human life. Following the distinction between noise and true signals, the modeller and the critic need to evaluate the model on the basis of (good) measurement of signals rather than of noise. While empirical evidence is decisive, not all measurements count. That social behaviour is complex cannot be denied, but the principles governing this behaviour need not be complex. They may even permit a mathematical description (which does not mean we have slavishly to follow the mathematical antics of the natural sciences – or even use the same mathematics). In this context, computer simulation models are used fruitfully.

It does not follow that all social scientists should use mathematics, only that some do. While mathematical models are used quite frequently, only a minority of social scientists create and use them. Yet, even so, we can point to a powerful drive towards mathematical expression of and solutions to disciplinary, and, more strongly, interdisciplinary problems. Social science publications like *The Journal of Mathematical Sociology* and *The Journal of Mathematical Psychology* find counterparts among the natural sciences in *The Journal of Mathematical Physics* and *Mathematical Geology*. Of course, neither set validates the other. There are many publications without mathematics in their title but which, nevertheless, carry a heavy mathematical imprint. These include *Psychometrika*, *Sociological Methodology*, *Social Networks*, *Geographical Analysis*, *Econometrica* and *Environment and Planning*. Within all of these journals good mathematical social science can be found. What is less clear is whether all of this activity stems from an intrinsic need for the use of mathematics in a discipline at a certain stage, or crude imitation between

fields, or even the carving out of a niche by the mathematically inclined. Probably a bit of each is involved, but while imitation and niche creation are not intellectually illegitimate, only the first provides the continuing basis and context for significant work.

The mathematically inclined members of the social science tribe talk largely to themselves, primarily because they have learned the language, but also because many other tribe members do not care to listen. To the extent that the mathematical folk are concerned only to build their models for the sake of building them, they will remain in their intellectual niche. This will change only with the construction of powerful and relevant (hence successful) mathematical models. Then, perhaps, the niche will expand to form the ecosystem.

Patrick Doreian
University of Pittsburgh

References
Bartholomew, D. J. (1982), *Stochastic Models for Social Processes*, 3rd edn, New York.
Doreian, P. and Hummon, N. P. (1976), *Modelling Social Processes*, New York.
Fararo, T. (1973), *Mathematical Sociology: An Introduction to Fundamentals*, New York.
Leik, R. K. and Meeker, B. F. (1975), *Mathematical Sociology*, Englewood Cliffs, N.J.
Rapoport, A. (1983), *Mathematical Models in the Social and Behavioural Sciences*, New York.
Sørensen, A. (1978), 'Mathematical models in sociology', *Annual Review of Sociology*, 4.

Further Reading
Coleman, J. S. (1964), *An Introduction to Mathematical Sociology*, New York.
See also: *catastrophe theory; computer simulation; game theory; graph theory; path analysis*.

Mauss, Marcel (1872–1950)

Marcel Mauss, the French sociologist, trained originally as an academic philosopher at the Universities of Paris and Bordeaux. He never took a doctorate or had a normal teaching career, but was one of the first professional researchers in the social sciences. In 1898, his uncle, Émile Durkheim, founded the journal, *Année Sociologique* and put Mauss in charge of religious studies for the publication. Mauss's focus extended to all religious practices, especially those of ancient and contemporary archaic societies, but he later shifted to problems of comparative social anthropology in general. Although an armchair scholar himself, he is regarded as the founder of the French school of field ethnology whose later members included Marcel Griaule, Louis Dumont and Claude Lévi-Strauss. Mauss was appointed to a lectureship on the 'religions of peoples without a civilization' at the École Pratique des Hautes Études in 1901, and later taught at the Ethnological Institute of Paris University, which he co-founded in 1925. He moved to the Collège de France in 1931.

Mauss's published work included no books but a large variety of essays and critical studies. It can be divided roughly into two periods – before and after World War I. In the first period (when Durkheim was still alive), Mauss's contributions were mainly on comparative religion and included studies (with Hubert) on sacrifice (*Essai sur la nature et la fonction du sacrifice*, 1899; *Sacrifice: Its Nature and Function*, 1964); magic (*Equisse d'une théorie générale de la magie*, 1904; *A General Theory of Magic*, 1972), and an introductory essay on primitive religion (*Mélanges d'histoire des religions*, 1909). He also produced an unfinished doctoral thesis on prayer (*La Prière*, 1909). His most famous studies of this period were (with Durkheim) *De quelques formes primitives de classification: contribution à l'étude des représentations collectives*, 1903 (*Primitive Classification*, 1963), and *Essai sur les variations saisonnières des sociétés Eskimos: étude de morphologie sociale*, 1950 (*Seasonal Variations of the Eskimo: A Study in Social Morphology*, 1979). These two studies foreshadowed major theoretical insights developed in his later work about the functional interrelations between the material conditions of societies (seasons, climate, physical organization of camps) and the 'collective representations' (as expressed in religious practice and mental categories).

After World War I, Mauss was invested with the dual task of safeguarding Durkheim's scholarly heritage (aiming at the organization of a unified social science) while continuing his own specialized research, which focused on problems of social cohesion in archaic societies. A number of preliminary enquiries culminated in his famous *Essai sur le don*, 1925 (*The Gift*, 1954). In it, he analysed the exchange of gifts, whether utilitarian or symbolic, as a 'total social phenomenon' with economic, religious and moral implications. Systems of reciprocities secure peace among neighbours, maintain the stability of the social structure, and legitimate social hierarchies. Other major statements in his later work stress the dominance of social patterns in the expression of individual feelings. In an article about civilization (1929), he stated clearly the arbitrary nature of collective values and representations, an essay which was markedly prestructural in flavour.

Victor Karady
Centre National de la Recherche Scientifique, Paris

Further Reading
Mauss, M. (1966), *M. Mauss, Sociologie et anthropologie*, 3rd edn, ed. G. Gurevitch and introduction by C. Lévi-Strauss, Paris.

Mauss, M. (1968–9), *Oeuvres*, 3 vols, introduction by V. Karady, Paris.
(These volumes contain the majority of Mauss's work.)

Maximization

According to an oft-quoted view, economics is about 'doing the best one can in a situation of scarcity'. Many, if not most, problems in economics fall under this heading. For example, the consumer is assumed to choose the best bundle of commodities out of the range possible given his income constraint. The government is assumed to choose its policies to do the best it can for society as a whole, again given the constraints it faces. Such optimization may be said to be at the heart of economic analysis. The mathematical counterpart of this essentially economic problem is the maximization of an objective function subject to constraints on the choice variables.

The general maximization problem may be written as

Max W $(\underline{x})$ subject to $\underline{x} \in X$

where W $(\cdot)$ is the objective function, $\underline{x}$ is the vector of control (or choice) variables. These are shown to be restricted to the set X, which therefore specifies the constraints of the problem. The *economics* of the problem lies in the specification of the objective function W $(\cdot)$ and the constraint set $\underline{X}$. However, once these are specified, we still have to solve the problem in order to derive further economic results of interest. This is where the mathematical theory of maximization comes in.

If $\underline{x}^*$ satisfies

W$(\underline{x}^*) \geq$ W $(\underline{x})$ for all $\underline{x} \in X$

then $\underline{x}^*$ is said to be a *global* solution to the problem. On the other hand, if the inequality holds only for $\underline{x}$ in a neighbourhood of $\underline{x}^*$, then $\underline{x}^*$ is said to be a *local* solution to the problem. *The Weierstrass Theorem* in mathematics says that, if the set X is compact and non empty, and if the objective function W$(\underline{x})$ is continuous on X, then a global solution exists for the above problem. Most economic problems satisfy these conditions. However, can we say more about the nature of the solution $\underline{x}^*$? The answer is that we can, if we define the set $\underline{X}$ in greater detail.

For many economic problems the constraint set $\underline{X}$ can be specified implicitly as a series of inequalities which the control variable has to satisfy. Consider, therefore, the problem

Max W$(\underline{x})$ subject to $g(\underline{x}) \leq \underline{b};\ \underline{x} \geq O$

where $\underline{x}$ is a n × 1 vector. The $\underline{b}$ and the m × 1 vector of functions g define the constraints on $\underline{x}$. Consider now the following function

$$\mathcal{L}(\underline{x}, \underline{\lambda}) = W(\underline{x}) + \underline{\lambda}_z(\underline{b} - g(\underline{x}))$$

where $\underline{\lambda}$ is a m × 1 vector of non-negative auxilliary variables. The m elements of $\underline{\lambda}$ are known as Lagrange multipliers and $\mathcal{L}(\underline{x}, \underline{\lambda})$ is known as the Lagrangian of the problem. The *Kuhn-Tucker theorem* in nonlinear programming then provides the conditions which characterizes the solution to the problem. These conditions are

$$\frac{\partial \mathcal{L}}{\partial \underline{x}}(\underline{x}^*, \underline{\lambda}^*) \leq 0; \quad \frac{\partial \mathcal{L}(\underline{x}^*, \underline{\lambda}^*)}{\partial \underline{x}} \cdot \underline{x}^* = 0; \quad \underline{x}^* \geq 0$$

$$\frac{\partial \mathcal{L}}{\partial \underline{\lambda}}(x^*, \underline{\lambda}^*) \geq 0; \quad \underline{\lambda}^*_z \frac{\partial \mathcal{L}}{\partial \underline{\lambda}}(\underline{x}^*, \underline{\lambda}^*) = 0; \quad \underline{\lambda}^* \geq 0.$$

The first part of the Kuhn-Tucker theorem says that if there exist $\underline{x}^*$, $\underline{\lambda}^*$ satisfying the above conditions, then $\underline{x}^*$ is a solution to the problem. The second part say that if $W(\cdot)$ is concave, $g(\cdot)$ are convex and there is some point $\hat{\underline{x}}$ for which the constraint is satisfied with strict inequality, then, for $\underline{x}^*$ to be a solution to the problem, there must exist $\underline{\lambda}^*$ such that $\underline{x}^*$, $\underline{\lambda}^*$ satisfy the Kuhn-Tucker conditions.

The Kuhn-Tucker conditions provide the basis for characterizing the optimum in nost economic models. For example, if $\underline{x}^* \geq 0$, then we must have that

$$\frac{\partial \mathcal{L}}{\partial \underline{x}}(\underline{x}^*, \underline{\lambda}^*) = 0$$

or

$$\frac{\partial W(\underline{x}^*)}{\partial x_i} = \underline{\lambda}^* \cdot \frac{\partial g(\underline{x}^*)}{\partial x_i} \quad \text{for } i = 1, 2, \ldots, n.$$

In the case where the problem is the consumer's problem of choosing quantities x_i to maximize his utility function $U(\underline{x})$ subject to a single budget constraint

$$\sum_{i=1}^{n} p_i x_i \leq y$$

these conditions become

$$\frac{\partial U(\underline{x}^*)}{\partial x_i} = \lambda p_i \quad i = 1, 2, \ldots, n$$

or

$$\frac{\partial U(\underline{x}^*)}{\partial x_i} \quad \frac{\partial U(\underline{x}^*)}{\partial x_j} = \frac{p_i}{p_j}$$

that is, the marginal rate of substitution between any pair of goods must equal the price ratio of those two goods. Similar conditions can be derived and interpreted for other problems. In fact the $\underline{\lambda}^*$ have interpretation in terms of 'shadow prices' which tell us the values to the agent of releasing each constraint at the margin.

S. M. Ravi Kanbur
University of Essex

Further Reading

Baumol, W. (1965), *Economic Theory and Operations Analysis*, 2nd edn, Englewood Cliffs, N.J.

Dixit, A. K. (1975), *Optimization in Economic Theory*, London.

Intriligator, M. D. (1971), *Mathematical Optimization and Economic Theory*, Englewood Cliffs, N.J.

McCollough Effect

The McCollough effect is the most celebrated of a remarkable class of perceptual phonemena called 'contingent after-effects'. To obtain the McCollough effect the observer inspects alternately two stimuli that differ in colour and in orientation, for example, a red and black grating of vertical bars and a green and black grating of horizontal bars. If, after several minutes of this alternating adaptation, he examines a black and white vertical grating it will look pale green, whereas a black and white horizontal grating will look pink. The after-effect is contingent, in that the illusory hue that is seen depends on a second attribute of the visual stimulus, its orientation. There are analogous colour after-effects that are contingent on direction of movement or on the density of the bars of the grating; and there are after-effects of orientation and movement that are contingent on colour.

There are two dominant theories of contingent after-effects. The first classes them with other sensory after-effects and attributes them to selective adaptation of a subset of feature-detecting neurons. Thus, in the case of the McCollough effect, we are to suppose that a vertical black and white grating produces a response in a variety of cells in the visual cortex of the brain, all of which respond to the same orientation but some of which have biases for particular colours. If now the observer adapts to a vertical red grating, a subset of the population of detectors – those that respond best to vertical red bars or edges – are selectively fatigued. When afterwards the observer examines a black and white grating, this subset of detectors give less than their normal response. The overall response of the full population of detectors then resembles that produced by a pale green vertical grating; and this is the percept that the observer reports.

An alternative theory treats the McCollough effect as a form of Pavlovian conditioning, and indeed there are several ways in which it does not resemble short-term sensory adaptation: an adaptation period of 15 minutes may produce an after-effect that lasts for days or even months; the rate of decay of the effect depends on the frequency of extinction trials (of exposure to the black and white test grating); and if a series of extinction trials are followed by a delay, then spontaneous recovery of an extinguished McCollough effect may occur. But if the McCollough effect is a form of associative conditioning, why is it negative, why is the illusory hue approximately complementary to that associated with a given grating during the adaptation period? We must suppose that the unconditional response to an excess of redness in the world is a reduction in the gain of red-sensitive channels in the visual system. During the adaptation period this response is associated with the conditional stimulus, say, a vertical grating. When, later, a black and white grating is presented, the conditional response is evoked and the red-sensitive channels contribute less to the overall response than they normally would.

J. D. Mollon
University of Cambridge

Further Reading
Stromeyer, C. F. (1978), 'Form-color aftereffects in human vision', in R. Held, H. W. Leibowitz and H. L. Teuber (eds), *Handbook of Sensory Physiology, Vol. VIII: Perception*, Berlin.
See also: *conditioning; sensation and perception; colour vision.*

McLuhan, Marshall (1910–80)

McLuhan was for a time one of the most cited authors in the field of study of mass communication, following the publication of his two main books, *The Gutenberg Galaxy* (1962) and *Understanding Media* (1964). Moreover, he was probably as well known outside the circle of academic media specialists as within it. After a fairly conventional career as a teacher of literature, he became a spinner of theory and publicist for his ideas about the consequences for culture and society of changes in communication technology – from writing to print and from print to electronic media. Although his assessment of television happened to be especially topical in the 1960s, he was also continuing a North American (perhaps especially Canadian) tradition of interest in technology, communication and the new. He owed much of his central thesis to a forerunner and colleague at the University of Toronto, the economic historian Harold J. Innis, who had traced the connection between changes in communication technology in the ancient and medieval world and changing forms of political and social power. Innis argued that each medium had a 'bias' towards a certain kind of application, message and effect and thus, eventually, a bias towards a certain kind of society. A similar version of 'communication determinism' was elaborated by McLuhan, with particular stress on the difference between the pictorial medium of television, which involves the spectator imaginatively and sensorily, and the medium of print, with its linear, sequential logic and its bias towards rationalism and individualism.

McLuhan's dicta are often best remembered summarily by his own catch-phrase 'the medium is the message'. He was a controversial figure and it is

impossible in a few words to strike an adequate balance in assesssing his work. On the positive side were: a lively imagination; a striking and aphoristic turn of phrase; an ability to cross academic boundaries and synthesize his eclectic finds. Furthermore, he seems to have exerted charm as a person and influence as a teacher. The principal entry on the debit side is that he lacked any discernible system of thought or adherence to an established tradition of research method, so that his many ideas are often both questionable and untestable. It is still not clear whether or not he made a valid or original contribution to any precise understanding of media, yet he did call attention to the need to do this, at a good moment and in a way which could not be ignored. This may well remain his most lasting achievement after reality has overtaken his more fanciful predictions about the age of electronic communication. In respect of his own message, the manner of delivery may well have been more significant than the content.

Denis McQuail
University of Amsterdam

Further Reading
Miller, J. (1971), *McLuhan*, London.
See also: *mass media.*

McNeill, William Hardy (1917–)

Born in Vancouver, Canada, McNeill studied at the Universities of Chicago and Cornell, where he took his doctorate in 1947. He is Robert A. Milikan Distinguished Service Professor at the University of Chicago, and editor of *The Journal of Modern History*.

McNeill must be one of the last historians who will ever attempt, singlehanded, a comprehensive history of the world since the agricultural revolution. The great interest of his *The Rise of the West, A History of the Human Community* (1963) is his conceptualization of the social dimension of the major civilizations. Attuned, as a historian, to the dynamic processes of human societies, McNeill was nevertheless impressed by the static, synchronic approach of such anthropologists as Robert Redfield. This led him to enquire into the sources of development in relatively stable societies. McNeill identified intercultural contact as the crucial factor in social change, and defined some of its modalities. He traced various patterns of expansion, including frontier movements and migrations, competition between civilizations, and the conflict between nation-states characteristic of the West.

In *Plagues and Peoples* (1976), McNeill analyses the interrelations between human societies and the populations of micro-organisms (bacteria, viruses) which live on man, and shows the decisive role played by epidemic diseases in Western expansion. The social superstructures which permit some men to play the part of macro-parasites with respect to other men are treated in *The Pursuit of Power* (1982).

Peter Schröder
Ministry of Education, The Netherlands

Further Reading
McNeill, W. H. (1967), *A World History*, Chicago.
McNeill, W. H. (1980), *The Human Condition*, Chicago.

Mead, George Herbert (1863–1931)

George Herbert Mead was an American philosopher whose works have had an enduring impact on sociological research and theory. He studied under William James at Harvard, and taught at the Universities of Michigan and Chicago. His posthumously published lectures from the University of Chicago on social psychology, collected in *Mind, Self and Society* (1934), represent his most critical social scientific work. Here, Mead presents a conceptual view of human action, interaction, and organization. This conceptualization represents a blending of general philosophical traditions, including utilitarianism, behaviourism, Darwinism and pragmatism, with specific concepts borrowed from such thinkers as Wilheim Wundt, William James, Charles Peirce, Charles Horton Cooley, and John Dewey (with whom he founded the 'Chicago School' of pragmatism). In this synthesis, Mead argues that social life is a process of adaptation and adjustment to ongoing patterns of social organization, and that human capacities for symbol use, covert reflection, self-awareness, and self-control are learned responses to environmental pressures for regularized interaction. For Mead, the critical 'conditioned responses' among humans are the behavioural capacities for gesturing, role taking, self and mind. Through conventional gestures, humans signal their course of action; through reading these gestures, humans can mutually assume each others' perspective as well as more 'generalized communities of attitudes' associated with a social context; through minded deliberations, humans can 'imaginatively rehearse' alternative lines of conduct and select the most appropriate response; through the capacities for self, humans can see themselves as objects of evaluation in a situation; and through such self-awareness and self-evaluation, they can control and regulate their responses.

Mead's view of human action, interaction, and organization is the conceptual basis for most modern formulations of interaction in the social sciences, including those in such diverse schools of thought as role theory, ethnomethodology, symbolic interactionism, interactionism, cognitive sociology, action theory, dramaturgy, phenomenology, and ethnoscience.

Jonathan H. Turner
University of California, Riverside

Reference
Mead, G. H. (1932), *Mind, Self, and Society from the Standpoint of a Social Behaviourist*, ed. C. Maris, Chicago.

Further Reading
Mead, G. H. (1938), *The Philosophy of the Act*, Chicago.
Natanson, M. (1956), *The Social Dynamics of George H. Mead*, Washington.
See also: *ethnomethodology*; *symbolic interactionism*.

Mead, Margaret (1901–78)

The 'favoured child' and eldest of an academic family, Margaret Mead was born in 1901 near Philadelphia, and was encouraged by her parents to believe that anyone could accomplish whatever he or she set out to do. She did her first degree at Barnard College, New York, and as a graduate student in anthropology at Columbia University, was greatly influenced by Franz Boas and Ruth Benedict. In anthropology she discovered the vehicle for critical, optimistic revisions of accepted conventions. From studies of child-rearing in the Pacific, through pioneering discussions of gender, into studies of culture change, cultural pluralism, complex societies, race relations, and 1960s drug culture, Mead regarded disciplinary findings in terms of usefulness to the ordinary individual facing everyday problems.

Mead entered the nature-nurture debate, on the side of nurture, learning and custom (see *Coming of Age in Samoa*, 1925). Recently her work has been criticized for an overemphasis on culture, and a need to prove a point that prevented her from doing effective fieldwork. Derek Freeman (*Margaret Mead and Samoa*, 1983), impugns her methods, her view of Samoa, and her argument for cultural determinism. He fails both to understand her purposes and her position; Mead did not neglect biology and in the nature-nurture debate emphasized the extent to which human beings are tied to 'rhythms of the body'. *Sex and Temperament* (1935) and *Male and Female* (1949) argued against universal sex-role stereotypes, while recalling the significance of gender distinctions.

Her confidence that people could choose alternative individual paths and create wiser sociocultural arrangements remained firm. During return trips to the Pacific, Mead monitored the passage of the Manus into a modern capitalist world; she urged that continuities be part of change (*Growing up in New Guinea*, 1930; *New Lives for Old*, 1956). Mead's anthropologist was observer, advocate and adviser, and she readily adopted new strategies for each – tape-recorders and film for the field, introspection for the fieldworker (*Blackberry Winter*, 1972; *Letters from the Field*, 1977). World War II forced a concentration on complex nations and international problems. She commented on disarmament, feminism and iconoclastic youth culture. She died in 1978, having altered anthropology, revised the outlook of her country, and affected the fate of people around the world.

Judith Modell
Carnegie-Mellon University, Pittsburgh

Further Reading
American Anthropologist (1980), *In Memoriam Margaret Mead*, 82.
Brady. G. (ed.) (1983), 'Speaking in the name of the real: Freeman and Mead on Samoa', *American Anthropologist*, 85.
Mead, M. (1953), *The Study of Culture at a Distance*, Chicago.
Mead, M. (1959), *An Anthropologist at Work*, Boston.

Meade, James (1907–)

Meade is one of only three English economists to receive the Nobel Prize in Economics (in 1977, jointly with Bertil Ohlin). He was awarded it for his work in international economics – *The Theory of International Economic Policy*, Vol. I, *The Balance of Payments*; Vol. 2, *Trade and Welfare* (1951–5) are already classics. In his Nobel lecture, Meade (1978) returned to one of the themes of these volumes, the relationship between internal and external balance, giving it a new twist in order to cope with the problems of stagflation.

Since then he has been working on a vast theoretical and policy-orientated project, advocating institutional reform in wage bargaining and the use of model simulations and techniques of control engineers in demand management. He remains the civilized Lib-Lab person who emerged in the 1930s, burrowing away at night with other like-minded Fabians on how to make Britain a better, more equitable society. He has always retained his belief in the price mechanism, in so far as it allowed people to express freedom of choice in their consumption patterns, but he objects strongly to the unequal distribution of property and income which the free market throws up: hence the number of schemes which over the years he has devised to allow us all a more equal start in the economic race.

Meade started as a classicist at Oxford but soon turned to economics. For a year at Cambridge in the early 1930s he was a member of the famous 'circus' which argued out *The Treatise* and helped Keynes considerably in the development of the embryonic *General Theory*. After teaching at Oxford as a fellow of Hertford College (1930–7), he had a spell at the League

of Nations (1937–40). During the war years he joined the Economic Section of the Cabinet Offices (of which he was appointed Director for 1946–7) and made a notable contribution with his lifelong friend, Richard Stone, Nobel prizewinner in Economics, 1984, to the development of a system of national accounting. He worked closely with Keynes, both on problems of the wartime economy and on post-war reconstruction, including the commitment to full employment. Of Keynes, Meade says: 'I admired him beyond measure; he has been the decisive influence in the formation of my ideas about, and attitudes towards, economic policies and institutions.'

In 1947 he was appointed to a chair at the London School of Economics where he wrote his works on international economics. When he was elected in 1957 to Marshall's chair of Political Economy at Cambridge, he changed direction in order to contribute to growth theory in a neoclassical framework. He made some elegant contributions to pure theory. Meade retired early, in 1968, in order to work on his projected volumes of economic principles, *Principles of Political Economy* (1965–76). In recent years, he has greatly influenced thinking about taxation reform, principally through the Meade Report (1978). From his prodigious output, his superbly written articles on policy in the bank journals stand out as the thoughts of a civilized, rational and compassionate English gentleman. Our world would not be in the mess it is if its inhabitants were all James Meades, a fact which he himself has never fully taken into account in his policy prescriptions.

G. C. Harcourt
Jesus College, Cambridge

References
Meade, J. E. (1951–5), *The Theory of International Economic Policy*, 2 Vols, Vol. 1: *The Balance of Payments* (1951); Vol. 2: *Trade and Welfare* (1955), Oxford.
Meade, J. E. (1965–76), *Principles of Political Economy*, 4 Vols, Vol. 1: *The Stationary Economy* (1965); Vol. 2: *The Growing Economy* (1968); Vol. 3: *The Controlled Economy* (1971); Vol. 4: *The Just Economy* (1976), London.
Meade, J. E. (1978), 'The meaning of "Internal Balance" ', *Economic Journal*, 88.
Meade, J. E. *et al.* (1978), *The Structure and Reform of Direct Taxation*, London.

Further Reading
Corden, W. M. and Atkinson, A. B. (1979), 'Meade, James E.', in D. L. Sills (ed.), *International Encyclopedia of the Social Sciences. Biographical Supplement*, Vol. 18, New York.
Johnson, H. G. (1978), 'James Meade's contribution to economics', *Scandinavian Journal of Economics*, 80.

Measures of Central Tendency and Dispersion

(1) Suppose n observations – or measurements – are collected on some variable, such observations could be characterized by a measure of their *central tendency*. It is defined as follows: replace all observations by an identical number $\bar{x}$. Obviously, this implies loss of information. Therefore $\bar{x}$ must be chosen in such a way that loss is minimized. This, in turn, requires a definition of loss. One possibility is to define loss as the average absolute difference between $\bar{x}$ and all individual observations:

$$s = \Sigma |x_i - \bar{x}| n \qquad (i = 1, \ldots, n)$$

Obviously, this measure of loss is a measure of *dispersion*: its value is small if all observations are close to $\bar{x}$, and becomes larger to the extent individual observations have a greater distance from $\bar{x}$. With loss defined in this way, it becomes minimized by setting $\bar{x}$ equal to the *median* (that is, $\bar{x}$ must be chosen in such a way that there are as many individual observations larger than $\bar{x}$ as smaller than $\bar{x}$). A simple example (see also Table 1) is that n = 5 observations are collected with values (1 1 2 4 7). The median equals 2 (there are two observations larger than 2, and also two observations smaller than 2). Absolute differences between the five observations and $\bar{x} = 2$ are equal to (1 1 0 2 5), with average s = 9/5 = 1.8. This value is smaller than for any other choice of $\bar{x}$.

Table 1

	x_i	1	1	2	4	7	15
	$|x_i - \bar{x}|^0$	0	0	1	1	1	3
$\bar{x} = 1$	$|x_i - \bar{x}|^1$	0	0	1	3	6	10
	$|x_i - \bar{x}|^2$	0	0	1	9	36	46
	$|x_i - \bar{x}|^0$	1	1	0	1	1	4
$\bar{x} = 2$	$|x_i - \bar{x}|^1$	1	1	0	2	5	9
	$|x_i - \bar{x}|^2$	1	1	0	4	25	31
	$|x_i - \bar{x}|^0$	1	1	1	1	1	5
$\bar{x} = 3$	$|x_i - \bar{x}|^1$	2	2	1	1	4	10
	$|x_i - \bar{x}|^2$	4	4	1	1	16	26
	$|x_i - \bar{x}|^0$	1	1	1	0	1	4
$\bar{x} = 4$	$|x_i - \bar{x}|^1$	3	3	2	0	3	11
	$|x_i - \bar{x}|^2$	9	9	4	0	9	31

The table shows powers (p=0,1,2) of absolute differences between observed values x_i and $\bar{x}$, with $\bar{x}$ running from 1 to 4.

For $\bar{x} = 1$ (mode) the sum of the powers with p=0 is minimized.

For $\bar{x} = 2$ (median) the sum of the powers with p=1 is minimized.

For $\bar{x} = 3$ (mean) the sum of the powers with p=2 is minimized.

For $\bar{x} = 4$ (midrange) the pth root of the sum of the powers with $p \to \infty$ would become minimized at the value 3 (not shown in table).

Another possibility is to define loss as the average squared difference between $\bar{x}$ and all individual observations:

$$s = \Sigma (x_i - \bar{x})^2 / n$$

To minimize this loss function, $\bar{x}$ must be set equal to the (arithmetic) *mean* of the observations. In the example above, the mean equals 15/5 = 3. Squared differences between individual observations and the mean are equal to (4 4 1 1 16) with average s = 26/5 = 5.2. This is smaller than for any other choice of $\bar{x}$. Again, the average squared distance between mean and individual observations is a measure of dispersion; it is called the *variance*.

A third possible choice for the measure of central tendency is the *mode*. It is defined as the value with the largest frequency. In the example above the mode is equal to 1. Loss now must be defined as the proportion of observations not in the category with largest frequency. In the example this proportion is equal to 3/5 = .6; it is smaller than for any other choice of $\bar{x}$ And, again, this proportion is a (crude) measure of dispersion.

(2) Results obtained above can be unified by defining loss as

$$s = \{\Sigma |x_i - \bar{x}|^p / n\}^{1/p}$$

With p = 0, s is minimized by taking $\bar{x}$ equal to the mode. With p = 1, s is minimized by setting $\bar{x}$ equal to the median. With p = 2, s is minimized by taking $\bar{x}$ equal to the mean. With p very large ($p \to \sim$) it can be shown that s is minimized by setting $\bar{x}$ equal to the *mid-range* (the average of largest and smallest observation; in the example the mid-range is equal to (7 + 1)/2 = 4). In that case s becomes equal to half the *range*, where the range is defined as the difference between largest and smallest observation (in the example, the range equals 7 − 1 = 6, so that s, with very large p, becomes equal to 3).

(3) The choice between mode, median, or mean is related to the level of *measurement* of the observations. At the *nominal* level, numbers are used only as labels for different categories, such as in a hardware shop where box 1 contains nails, box 2 contains screws, box 3 bolts, and box 4 tacks. The mode makes sense: it identifies the category with largest frequency. The median makes sense if observations are on an *ordinal* level: numbers not only label categories but also impose a certain order upon them. The mean requires *interval scale* level of measurement – it assumes that differences between numerical values have meaningful interpretation. On *ratio scale* level – where ratio's between numerical values have meaningful interpretation and where it is assumed that all numerical values are nonnegative – another measure of central tendency might make sense: it is the *geometric mean*, defined as the nth root of the product of all observations. In the example

above the geometric mean would be equal to (56) $1/5 = 2.24$.

(4) For symmetric distributions, mode, median, and mean will have identical value. A distribution is said to be skewed to the right if mode<median<mean, and skewed to the left if mode>median>mean.

(5) If the n observations can be interpreted as a random sample from some population with mean equal to μ, the sample mean $\bar{x}$ is said to be an *estimate* of μ. Moreover, $\bar{x}$ is an *unbiased* estimate, which just says that with n very large, the sample mean approximates the population mean. If the population has symmetric distribution, sample median and sample mode also are unbiased estimates of the population mean. However, sample means then fluctuate around the population mean with less variance than sample medians, or sample modes. Therefore the sample mean is said to be an *efficient* estimate of the population mean, whereas sample median or sample mode are not efficient estimates.

(6) The argument in sections (1) and (2) above imply that choice of a measure of central tendency is intimately related to choice of a measure of loss, or dispersion. But in economics and sociology another measure of dispersion was popular, called the *Gini-index*. It is defined as the average of the absolute differences between all pairs of observations:

$$G = \Sigma|x_i - x_j|/n^2.$$

In this definition, differences between each observation and itself are included – such differences are zero, of course. Sometimes the Gini-index is defined with $n(n-1)$ in the denominator instead of n^2; differences between each observation and itself are then not counted.

The Gini-index is seemingly independent of the choice of a measure of central tendency, as if it measures 'intrinsic' dispersion. This is not true, however. The Gini-index concentrates on absolute differences, and has the same 'philosophy' about loss as the median. This becomes more clear if a revised Gini-index is defined as the average of the squared differences between all pairs of observations. The index then becomes equal to twice the variance. Although it looks as if dispersion is measured 'intrinsically', there is no escape: a measure for dispersion implies a measure for central tendency, and vice versa.

John van de Gier
University of Leiden

See also: *multivariate analysis*; *statistical reasoning*.

Medical Anthropology

The anthropology of medicine is that subfield of anthropology that takes as its subject matter the cultural content of health, illness and healing. Its several distinctive areas of research include cross-cultural comparisons of medical systems (for example, in small-scale preliterate, post-traditional, ethnic and mainstream Western societies), the anthropology of nutrition, population problems, birthing, ageing, and substance abuse, ethnopsychiatry, social epidemiology, clinically applied anthropology, biocultural research on sociosomatic interactions in health and illness and, most recently, cultural analysis of biomedicine itself. Both social and biological wings of anthropology actively contribute to the field; so do, to a lesser extent, ethnohistorical studies of disease and paleopathology.

Since a number of the scholars who contributed to the development of anthropology in the late nineteenth and early twentieth centuries were physicians (such as Rudolph Virchow, Paul Broca, W. H. R. Rivers), it is not surprising that ethnographers have a long and abiding interest in illness and healing. The creation of a subfield has given these concerns, which were frequently a marginal interest in general field studies, a central place. Contemporary medical anthropology took its origin from the work of Clements in the 1930s on presumed universal categories of disease aetiology, from Ackerknecht's reviews of 'primitive surgery', 'primitive prevention', 'primitive psycho-therapy' in the 1940s and from Sigerist's effort in the 1940s and 1950s to construct an historical anthropology of ancient systems of medicine. Other important contributions were the study of ritual healing in the anthropology of religion, fieldwork in ecological anthropology that examined cultural-biology interactions, and applied anthropological contributions to international health research.

Over the past decade the field underwent a period of explosive growth in America so that at present nearly one out of five anthropologists there regards himself as working in this subfield, and more recently it has been actively pursued in Britain, Australia, France and Germany. Medical anthropologists have begun to occupy research and teaching positions in schools of medicine and public health, and in hospitals and clinics. A small but increasing number of physicians, nurses and health administrators have taken advanced degrees in anthropology.

Among the conceptual and methodological achievements of medical anthropologists are: (1) various analytic frameworks for describing and comparing medical systems in non-Western and Western societies; (2) a practically useful distinction between *illness* (learned and shared patterns of perceiving, experiencing and coping with symptoms) and *disease* (the understanding of illness within the system of beliefs and practices of particular groups of practitioners); (3) the analysis of social influences on illness onset in terms of the *production* and *construction* of disease/illness; (4) the assessment of culture-specific and universal aspects of the help-seeking process, practitioner-patient relationships and healing; and (5) applied strategies that can be employed by clinicians in cross-ethnic and cross-cultural settings to reduce cultural miscommunication. The data base has also expanded enormously, so that at present we possess extremely rich ethnographic accounts of illness beliefs and healing practices from much of the world from Amerindians to Zulus. Findings for lay health care in urban Euro-American society, which provide the scientific foundation for understanding popular health practices and responses to sickness, as well as lay reactions to orthodox medicine in the West, are just beginning to be systematically gathered and still lag well behind findings for the non-Western world.

Neither idealist nor materialist anthropological theories have been found to be as illuminating of the medical dimensions of society as have interactionist frameworks that take into account biocultural bridges between psychophysiology, social relations and meanings. Both ecological and culturalist models of these interactions have thrown useful and divergent light on a number of key questions. These include: how cultural meanings and social uses of chronic sickness amplify symptoms and disability in oscillating cycles of sociosomatic amplification and damping; how symptom terms form culturally constituted idioms of distress that conceal core societal symbols and psychosocial problems; how culture-bound disorders are caused; how efficacy is constituted and assessed in healing relationships, and how symbols heal. We now possess, for example, systematic outcome studies of indigenous healing practices that disclose how these practices produce their effects and how effective (and toxic) those effects are. We are increasingly sophisticated in understanding problems in the integration of these practices and their practitioners with orthodox biomedicine. And we are making headway on both psychobiological and social levels in understanding the antecedents and consequences of sorcery, shamanism and religious healing cults.

The anthropology of medicine has disclosed that the orthodox profession of Euro-American medicine is as pluralistic as folk healing; that certain of its categories and practices are as 'magical' and ritualized as traditional therapies; that its system of manufacturing knowledge and passing it on to trainees is infiltrated with cultural norms, and that its *diseases* and *clinical realities* of practice are socially constituted and negotiated. Starting with psychiatry, such studies have moved on to primary care and to other core biomedical institutions. Moreover, information has been forthcoming on how biomedical practice is indigenized in non-Western settings as a complement to more extensive materials gathered on the modernization of traditional healing systems. These data have advanced anthropological efforts to improve physician recognition and treatment of psychosocial and cultural problems in patient care.

Medical anthropology is one of several medical social sciences: others include medical sociology, medical psychology, medical history, medical geography, medical ethics, medical economics. Together these disciplines situate human sickness in its particular moral and political contexts and confirm its inseparability from particular languages and categories of medicine. They – and especially medical anthropology – also convincingly demonstrate that, contrary to the reductionist and empiricist epistemology of biomedicine, clinical work is social praxis, and sickness is embedded in networks of interpersonal communication and institutions of social control. Not the least of their contributions is the creation of an interactionist biopsychosocial model of (and for) health care that, at least in primary care, offers a challenge to the orthodox biomedical model. Having moved into clinics and health science schools, the future of medical anthropology as an applied science will in large part be the future of the biopsychosocial approach to health care. That future will also deeply affect medical anthropology as a basic science. Now that therapeutics and preventive actions are as central a problematic for the discipline as are illness beliefs, medical anthropologists are finding unavoidable the domain of practice as a highly appropriate setting to test anthropological theory and methods that in turn feed back to influence anthropology itself. The case for interactionist theory and for a dialectic between ethnographic and quantitative methods in field research are two illustrations of the fruitfulness of that feedback.

Arthur Kleinman
Harvard University

Further Reading

Chrisman, N. and Maretzki, T. (1982), *Clinically Applied Anthropology*, Dordrecht, Holland.

Eisenberg, L. and Kleinmen, A. (eds) (1981), *The Relevance of Social Science for Medicine*, Dordrecht, Holland.

Fabrega, H. (1974), *Disease and Social Behavior*, Cambridge, Mass.

Hahn, R. and Kleinman, A. (1984), 'Anthropological theories and biomedical practice', *Annual Review of Anthropology*.

Janzen, J. (1878), *The Quest for Therapy in Lower Zaire*, Berkeley and Los Angeles.

Kleinman, A. *et al.* (eds) (1978), *Culture and Healing in Asian Societies*, Cambridge, Mass.

Kleinman, A. *et al.* (1980), *Patients and Healers in the Context of Culture*, Berkeley and Los Angeles.

Lewis, G. (1976), *Knowledge of Illness in a Sepik Society*, London.

Leslie, C. (ed.) (1976), *Asian Medical Systems*, Berkeley and Los Angeles.

Lieban, R. (1977), 'The field of medical anthropology', in D. Landy (ed.), *Culture, Disease and Healing*, New York.
See also: *medical sociology*.

Medical Sociology

Medical sociology is that branch of sociology concerned with the broad preserve of medicine in modern society. The subject has expanded so rapidly in the last three decades that it is now one of the largest (if not the largest) specialized areas of sociology. This growth is undoubtedly partly due to the realization that many of the problems contained within modern health care are essentially social in nature; however, it also reflects the growing interest of medicine itself in the social aspects of illness, particularly in relation to psychiatry, paediatrics, general practice (or family medicine), geriatrics and community medicine. Thus, while medical sociology has had general sociology as an intellectual parent, it has under the patronage of medicine enjoyed funding, appointments, an extended teaching role and ease of access for research which has arguably underpinned much of the expansion of the subject in recent years. But it has probably had to pay a price for this alliance (and reliance) on medicine in terms of a distortion of emphasis in the problems, methods and theories judged appropriate for the new discipline.

Medical sociology as a distinct area of study is first recognizable in the 1950s and, if journals might be used as disciplinary markers, then perhaps the founding of *Journal of Health and Human Behaviour* (later amended to *Journal of Health and Social Behaviour*) in 1960 represents the subject's first claim to autonomy. In these early years, despite the ascendancy of structural-functionalism, it seemed to be medical, psychological and, at best, psychosocial perspectives which predominated. The new post-war interest in social epidemiology, for example, which sought to identify the role of social factors in the causation of disease, was pursued by both interested physicians and sociologists. Early studies showed the influence of social structure, in particular of social class, in the aetiology of both psychiatric and organic disease, though identification of the relevant specific components of social structure proved more difficult.

The failure to establish the 'intervening' variables between social structure and disease led many sociologists to explore aetiology at the more microlevel of stress. Although more the province of the psychologist, stress was seen to offer the possibility of bridging the gap between the social and the biological especially when refined to encompass life events and notions of loss. In early studies research tended to concentrate on those illnesses, such as psychiatric disturbances, which seemingly lacked biological correlates and hence the possibility of a wholly biological aetiology. However,

in recent years the net has widened considerably to embrace organic diseases with supposed biological causes, as it is now recognized that this does not preclude an often important role for social factors in either establishing susceptibility or in actually triggering the onset.

The interest in social factors in illness together with the contemporary findings (through morbidity surveys) by both sociologists and physicians of a symptom iceberg in the community led to another important area in the early development of medical sociology, namely illness behaviour. Given that symptoms were so prevalent in the community, the traditional medical model which viewed symptoms as a simple stimulus to seek help seemed inappropriate. Why people consulted the doctor was therefore more complex, and successive studies set out to explore the particular patterns of behaviour and reactions to stress and illness which affected the decision to seek medical help.

If social epidemiology and illness behaviour were subjects which emerged directly at the interface between medical sociology and medicine, other areas such as labelling, the sociology of the hospital and professions were obviously more closely drawn from general sociology. Thus labelling theory and stigma, while developed within general sociology, were applied at an early stage to particular diagnostic groups such as the physically handicapped and the mentally ill; likewise students of institutions, bureaucracies and organizations found, in the hospital, an ideal model through which to test and illustrate their arguments; and in similar fashion the medical profession provided an archetypal occupational organization for those sociologists intent on exploring the role of professions in the occupational division of labour.

In time many of these various areas of general sociology became the specific province of medical sociology, though again, because of the early close alliance with medicine, these issues tended to be explored in a medicocentric way. Thus the medical profession with its supposed esoteric knowledge and altruistic service was seen as an ideal for the aspiring paramedical occupations, hospital structure was examined in terms of improving efficiency, and labelling in terms of treatment regimes and rehabilitation. If there is one contemporary slogan which sums up the early years it is the now classic difference between sociology *in* medicine and sociology *of* medicine, though arguably the latter was by far the weaker partner. Even so, by 1967 the field of medical sociology was sufficiently well expanded for the appearance of another journal, *Social Science and Medicine*, which in its title steered a neutral course between the conflicting claims of the two medical sociologies.

If it were possible to identify a year or a particular text as marking a watershed in medical sociology, there might well be agreement that the publication of Freidson's *Profession of Medicine* in 1970 was a significant event. It offered a synthesis of earlier studies on professions, labelling, medical organization, patient perceptions and so on, and it was to be marked out as a key text in establishing the formal identity of medical sociology; yet, as its subtitle – 'a study of the sociology of applied knowledge' – implied, it was the form of the analysis which underpinned that synthesis which pointed to a new direction. At root, both illness *and* disease were social constructs, reflections of social organization, professional interests, power relations and so on. Freidson's achievement was to liberate medical sociology from the confines of medically-defined categories, whether it was in the profession's beneficent view of itself or in the supposed biological and objective nature of illness, and in so doing opened up patient experience and medical knowledge to more penetrating and systematic analysis.

Thus during the 1970s, and increasingly during the 1980s, the health care system and health policy has been subjected to a more critical theoretical approach, particularly from those sociologists of a Marxist persuasion. Patients' views, which had been studied only as an adjunct to illness behaviour, are investigated in their own right as internally coherent. On the one hand this manifested itself in the growth of ethno-methodological studies which took as their focus the validity of patient experience, and on the other hand it has involved a critical evaluation of medical knowl-edge as a means by which patient experience has been depoliticized, alienated, controlled or constructed.

Medical sociology remains with its dual parentage. Many medical sociologists are employed by medical institutions or on medically defined tasks; indeed many are themselves directly concerned to ameliorate patient suffering within a medical context. On the other hand, over the last decade a more critical sociology has succeeded in widening the agenda such that the title of a new journal, *Sociology of Health and Illness*, first published in 1979, perhaps reflects the interests of this recent branch of sociology more accurately than the term medical sociology.

David Armstrong
Guy's Hospital Medical School, University of London

Reference
Freidson, E. (1970), *Profession of Medicine: A Study of the Sociology of Applied Knowledge*, New York.

Further Reading
Armstrong, D. (1983), *An Outline of Sociology as Applied to Medicine*, Bristol.
See also: *epidemiology; medical anthropology; morbidity; public health.*

Memory

Memory involves the storage of information and its subsequent retrieval. Despite being referred to by a single term, memory comprises a collection of subsys-tems rather than a single faculty. It can be divided into three components: sensory memory, short-term or working memory, and long-term memory, each of which can be further subdivided.

(1) *Sensory memory.* Part of the process of perception involves the brief storage of sensory information. In the case of vision the term 'iconic memory' is used to refer to this temporary store. The cinema is dependent on such a system. Without it we would see a film as a series of briefly presented still pictures rather than as a continuous image. Similarly, a brief auditory memory, sometimes termed 'echoic memory' is involved in perceiving speech.

(2) *Short-term or working memory.* If one is required to multiply 27 by 5 in one's head, one needs to make use of a good deal of temporary storage, not only of the sum itself but of the intervening steps such as carrying. Such temporary storage is also involved in reasoning, in learning and comprehending, where one may, for example, need to retain a relatively precise record of the beginning of a sentence in order to interpret the end. The term 'working memory' is used for this system which in turn comprises a number of subcomponents. For instance, if asked to remember a postal code long enough to copy it on an envelope, one is likely to use some form of verbal coding, probably repeating it under one's breath. In contrast, if A asks B to remember how many windows there are in B's present house, B will probably create in his 'mind's eye' a temporary image of his house, and perhaps imagine himself wandering around and counting the windows. This type of imagery appears to involve a rather separate component of working memory. These and other components are integrated by an attentional system that selects and manipulates information from the subsystems.

(3) *Long-term memory.* In contrast to the two previous systems, long-term memory is concerned with the rela-tively permanent storage of information. It can be regarded as analogous to a library, in which infor-mation is entered, stored and subsequently retrieved. Like a good library, organization is essential, and organization on the basis of the meaning of the material to be remembered is particularly important. Forgetting occurs over time, although whether this is due to memory traces being destroyed, or simply becoming mislaid, is a matter of some controversy.

It is certainly the case that some forgetting is due to difficulties in locating a memory trace rather than its destruction. Most people have the experience of knowing a name which is on 'the tip of their tongue' but cannot be recalled. Typically such a name would be recognized immediately from a list of plausible alternatives, indicating that the information had been mislaid rather than destroyed.

In general, reinstating the conditions operating during learning is likely to enhance retrieval (the *encoding specificity principle*). For example, material that is learnt in one physical environment or mood is best recalled in that same environment, hence deep-sea divers who learnt something underwater were best able to recall it underwater, while in another experiment, subjects who were presented with a list of words when sad recalled more of them on a subsequent occasion when sadness was induced than when they were happy, and vice versa.

A further distinction within long-term memory is between semantic and episodic memory. The term semantic memory refers to knowledge of the world. It comprises the sort of memory that is needed to answer questions such as 'What is the capital of France?', 'What is the chemical formula for salt?' and 'How many legs does a crocodile have?'. Episodic memory is the ability to remember specific personally experienced events such as what one had for breakfast or whom one met on holiday last year.

There is general agreement that the distinction between semantic and episodic memory is useful theoretically, but there is disagreement on whether the two rely on separate parts of the brain. The distinction between working memory and long-term memory, on the other hand, does appear to reflect different areas of the brain. Studies of brain-damaged patients indicate that a deficit of long-term memory can occur in a patient with normal working memory, and vice versa.

Alan Baddeley
MRC, Applied Psychology Unit, Cambridge

Further Reading
Baddeley, A. D. (1983), *Your Memory: A User's Guide*, Harmondsworth.
See also: *sensation and perception*; *thinking*; *time*.

Mental Disorders

Descriptions of psychological behaviour and intellectual disturbances have existed in the literature of Western civilizations since ancient times. Disturbances associated with the ageing process were among the first to be recorded. There are also descriptions of alcoholic deterioration, as well as phenomena which today would be called delirium, affective disorder, or psychoses. Depending upon the *Zeitgeist*, however, the phenomena were interpreted in many ways. Galen's Doctrine of the Four Humours was invoked as an explanation of psychological and behavioural disturbances well into the seventeeth century, while theories of the occult strongly influenced views of mental disturbances throughout the eighteenth century and into the early nineteenth century.

The origin of modern scientific psychiatry can be traced to the Enlightenment. During this era, the notion of mental disturbances as illnesses began to take hold with some intellectual force. By creating a climate which encouraged people to look upon the mental illnesses as natural phenomena, the rationalism of the age made the phenomena more accessible to systematic inquiry through observation, experimentation, and classification. As with any scientific endeavours to study the human condition, efforts to delineate the mental disorders were influenced by: (1) the dominant intellectual assumptions and attitudes which determine what data will receive attention and how the data will be ordered; (2) the technologies and methodologies available for gathering the data; and (3) the setting or social context delimiting the universe of phenomena accessible to study.

(1) Organic Versus Functional Mental Disorders
In the early nineteenth century, the care of the mentally disturbed gradually became the responsibility of the medical rather than the law enforcement or religious arms of society. Asylums and mental hospitals of the day became the primary sites for the conduct of scientific inquiry. As a result, the phenomena under study represented the most severe examples of behavioural or psychological disturbances. A materialistic philosophical orientation dominated medical thinking. Research in the fields of physiology, bacteriology and pathology were quite productive in delineating the pathophysiology and aetiology of physical illnesses. The philosophical perspective and technological advances tended to promote a view of mental disorder as the expression of physical disease or biological disease processes.

The notion of biological causality was, and remains, a major orienting principle in efforts to understand the nature of mental illness. Then, as today, the existing technology was not adequate to the task of defining an invariable relationship between the behavioural and psychological phenomena under study and either anatomical lesions or pathophysiological processes. A useful convention was adopted, however, by segregating the organic from the functional mental disorders. This dichotomy is based upon an aetiological distinction – the presence or absence of a biological abnormality or dysfunction that fully accounts for the condition.

(2) Psychotic Versus Non-Psychotic Functional Disorders
Since an aetiological distinction based on biological causality could not be used as the basis for differentiating the functional mental disorders, a phenomenological approach was used. Essentially qualitative, the approach involved the careful observation of a clinical

picture on a case-by-case basis. From the observations, relatively unique configurations of symptoms and symptom clusters were identified that suggested natural groupings of phenomena. In this manner, conditions where the dominant feature was a profound disturbance of mood were segregated from those where the dominant feature was a disturbance in the process and content of thought. This distinction between disorders of mood and disorders of thought received further corroboration when longitudinal data indicated that the course of the disorders also differed. Disorders of mood were more likely to remit, while those of thought were associated with progressive deterioration. For many years, these characteristics formed the primary basis for a distinction between what we today call the schizophrenic and the manic depressive disorders.

Regardless of the characteristics differentiating the disorders of thought and mood, individuals with both disorders shared three characteristics: (a) behaviour that grossly violated social norms; (b) the incorrect valuation of the accuracy of thoughts or perceptions; and (c) the marked tendency to draw false inferences about external reality even in the face of incontrovertible evidence to the contrary. These latter two features constitute what is referred to as impaired reality testing. This impaired reality testing, together with bizarre, disorganized behaviour well beyond the pale of social acceptability became the cardinal features for designating functional disorders as psychotic rather than non-psychotic. The utility of this dichotomy as the basis for classification is currently a major source of debate within psychiatry; nevertheless, it still remains a useful convention for differentiating the most severe mental disorders – the schizophrenic disorders, the major affective disorders, and the paranoid disorders – from the other non-organic psychological and behavioural phenomena that constitute the functional mental disorders.

(3) Neurotic Personality and Stress-Related Disorders

The further elaboration of conditions constituting the functional mental disorders was stimulated by two occurrences of particular importance in the field of psychiatry: the shift of the centre of academic inquiry from the asylum to the university psychiatric clinic, and the emergence of psychoanalysis. The former made an increasingly broad range of phenomena acceptable and accessible to study; the latter brought a conceptual framework and methodology for studying the psychogenic origins of disordered behaviour. In addition, the growing interaction among the clinical, behavioural, social and biological sciences that began at the end of the nineteenth century and has carried through to the present, generated a number of useful paradigms. While facilitating an examination of the psychological and social origins of the mental disorders, these para-

digms contributed to the demarcation of three major clusters of non-psychotic functional mental disorders: the neurotic, the personality, and the stress-related disorders.

(a) The neurotic disorders

Just as the invention of the microscope expanded the scope of biology, so the techniques of medical hypnosis and free association opened new avenues for exploring mental functioning and rendered the unconscious accessible to scientific inquiry. An important corollary of these methodological advances was the identification of psychological process. This process is characterized by the existence of conflict within an individual, perceived as a potential threat or danger, which calls into play response patterns called defence mechanisms. These three events occur outside of the individual's conscious awareness. When the events lead to the formation of symptoms or symptom complexes that are distressing, recognized as unacceptable, and experienced as unhealthy or foreign, the outcome is a neurotic disorder.

Not everyone accepts the scientific validity of evidence derived through applying the psychoanalytic method. They question the aetiologic paradigm described above and have offered other models, frequently based on learning theory, to explain the neuroses. Even so, few dispute the importance of psychological mechanisms in the genesis of these disorders. Further, evidence from the clinical and epidemiologic literature indicates that the neurotic disorders can be found in very different cultures, findings which support the view of the phenomena as a discrete class of mental disorders.

The neurotic disorders are identified primarily in terms of their mode of symptomatic or behavioural expression (for example, anxiety disorder, hypochondriasis, dissociative state). While some of the behaviours at times appear bizarre, as in the case of the obsessive, compulsive or phobic disorders, they do not grossly violate social norms. This circumstance, together with the absence of impaired reality testing, provides a basis for distinguishing the neurotic from the psychotic functional mental disorders.

(b) The personality disorders

Originally, personality disorders were identified on the basis of overt behaviour that was associated with, or could lead to, frank violations of the formal rules and conventions established within a society to maintain social order. Criminal, sexually perverse and addictive behaviours fell most easily under this rubric, particularly in those instances where the individual manifesting the behaviours was not psychotic or neurotic, and did not suffer significant subjective distress.

The delineation of personality disorders solely on the basis of rule-breaking behaviour seemed well off the mark as more came to be understood about the social, cultural and psychological processes shaping personality development. Personality came to be viewed as a product of social interaction and individual experiences in a cultural environment. This notion led to a definition of personality as deeply ingrained patterns of behaviour that determine how individuals relate to, perceive, and think about themselves and the environment. Personality disorder, on the other hand, was defined as the existence of persistent, inflexible and maladaptive patterns of behaviour that consistently and predictably were (i) in violation of the rights of others; (ii) denigrating to oneself or others; (iii) destructive to interpersonal and social relationships or vocational performance; or (iv) undermining of the ability to meet day-to-day obligations or achieve life goals. Although conditions characterized primarily by socially deviant behaviour (such as the perversions or anti-social personality disorder) are still considered personality disorders, so too are conditions where interpersonal relationships are significantly compromised (such as the schizoid or explosive personality disorders), or where personality absorption is the dominant feature (such as the aesthenic or inadequate personality disorders).

(c) The stress-related disorders

The interest in the relationship between stress and mental illness, an outgrowth of the experience of military psychiatry in World War I, has been sustained throughout the twentieth century. In the social sciences, research has focused on natural disasters; in the epidemiologic and clinical sciences, on life events and mental disorder; in the behavioural sciences, the emphasis is on coping and adaptation, and in the biological sciences, on homeostasis. A firmer understanding has developed about psychological vulnerability occurring during transitional states as well as normal developmental phases. In turn, the general systems theory has facilitated an examination of psychological factors as stressors that generate pathophysiological responses.

A related group of clinical phenomena was identified, not on the basis of their symptomatic manifestations (which are legion in their variations) but on the basis of the precipitants. These stress-related disorders include: (i) acute catastrophic stress reactions with clear environmental precipitants, such as war or natural disaster; (ii) post-traumatic stress disorders characterized by a re-experiencing of the trauma, reduced involvement with the external world, and a variety of autonomic, dysphoric or cognitive symptoms; (iii) the adjustment disorders precipitated by an array of life events, family factors, developmental crises and the like, which act as psychosocial stressors; (iv) psychophysiological malfunctions of psychogenic origin which occur in the absence of tissue damage or a demonstrable disease process (for example, hyperventilation, neurocirculatory aesthenia or dysmenorrhoea); and (v) psychic factors associated with physical disease – a category which conveys the notion that psychologically meaningful environmental stimuli can initiate or exacerbate certain physical disorders such as asthma, rheumatoid arthritis or ulcerative colitis.

Conclusion

By any criteria, the past century and a half has witnessed enormous strides in the delineation of the mental disorders. With the exception of the organic mental disorders, however, a knowledge of aetiology remains quite primitive. Behavioural, social and neuroscientists are searching for aetiologic factors. To the extent that the demonstration of aetiology allows us to make sharper distinctions among the mental disorders than does a strictly descriptive approach, these efforts, if successful, would undoubtedly lead to further modification of our definitions of the mental disorders.

Gary L. Tischler
Yale University

Further Reading

Alexander, E. S. and Selasnick, S. T. (1966), *The History of Psychiatry*, New York.
American Psychiatric Association (1980), *DSM-III: Diagnostic and Statistical Manual of Mental Disorders*, 3rd edn, Washington D.C.
Brenner, C. (1973), *An Elementary Textbook of Psychoanalysis*, New York.
Gunderson, E. K. E. and Rahe, R. H. (1974), *Life Stress and Illness*, Springfield, Ill.
Kraepelin, E. (1909), *Psychiatrie*, 8th edn, Leipzig.
Levy, R. (1982), *The New Language of Psychiatry*, Boston.
Nichols, A. M. (1978), *The Harvard Guide to Modern Psychiatry*, Cambridge, Mass.
Paykel, E. S. (1982), *Handbook of Affective Disorders*, New York.
Wang, J., Cooper, J. and Sartorius, N. (1974), *The Measurement and Classification of Psychiatric Symptoms*, Cambridge, Mass.
Woodruff, R. A., Goodwin, D. W. and Guze, S. B. (1974), *Psychiatric Diagnosis*, New York.
See also: *character disorders*; *DSM-III*; *mental health*; *neurosis*.

Mental Health

The categories of mental health and mental illness have to be understood against the backdrop of the social institutions and practices which gave rise to them; and to do this, we need to set the whole in historical context.

Mental illness replaced earlier nineteenth-century concepts of 'madness' or 'insanity'. This was not primarily because of changing beliefs about the cause of mental disturbances, but because the medical profession had gained control of their management. Psychiatry arose hand in hand with the asylum system, but at the outset the latter was conceived as a social remedy for a social problem: if anything, doctors captured this territory *despite* their association with physical theories and treatments, not because of it. Thus, the concepts of mental health and illness were not closely tied to a physical approach to mental disorders. In the nineteenth century, indeed, the most significant feature of mental illness was not its cause but its treatment – incarceration in an asylum. Mental patients, at this time, were defined as a group primarily by the danger they were seen to pose to themselves or others, a danger which could not be contained in any other way.

The asylum became in practice a last resort when no hope remained for the patient, but in this century the fight against mental illness was taken outside its walls and into the home, work-place and school, where interventions could be made before problems had become intractable. The invention of psychological theories and treatments, in which Freud played a key role, greatly facilitated this spread. Treatment moved from the asylum to the consulting-room, and the meanings of mental illness and mental health shifted accordingly. A new range of illnesses (most importantly, the neuroses) was recognized, and a new range of professions – social work, psychotherapy and the various branches of psychology – arose alongside psychiatry.

Rather than being seen as dangerous, the mental patient was now primarily someone who could not cope with his allotted tasks in life: mental illness was seen as partial and reversible (Armstrong, 1980). Mental health, in the rhetoric of the influential 'mental hygiene movement' founded in America in 1909, became equated with productiveness, social adjustment, and contentment – 'the good life' itself.

The promise of this approach as a panacea for all human ills, coupled with the enormous potential market it opened up to professionals, led to a huge increase in mental health services by the middle of this century. A key factor in the creation of this 'therapeutic state' was the adoption by the mental health professions of a 'scientific' image: in this way, their interventions came to be seen as applications of a value-free, ideologically neutral technology, after the fashion of Comte's 'positivism'.

Social scientists have approached mental health in two main ways. The first is to explore the connection between mental illnesses and aspects of the social environment. Classic studies in this mould are those of Hollingshead and Redlich (1958), who found an increased incidence of mental illness in lower social classes; Brenner (1973), who associated mental illness and economic cycles; and Brown and Harris (1978), who identified predisposing and precipitating factors in women's depression. Though this approach can be seen as merely an extension of the psychiatric enterprise, it nevertheless suggests that to treat environmentally-related conditions as cases of individual malfunctioning may be a form of 'blaming the victim' (Ryan, 1972). In this light, the role of psychiatrists emerges as a fundamentally conservative one: to alleviate the stresses inherent in the social order, while removing any threat to that order itself. It is implicit in the psychiatric concept of 'maladjustment' that it is the individual who has to adapt to society, and not the other way round.

Nevertheless, in the heyday of psychiatric expansionism in the US (the 1950s and early 1960s), some psychiatrists argued that the reform of adverse social conditions was a valid part of psychiatry's mandate after all. Yet financial cutbacks, professional inhibitions, and a political shift to the right soon nipped this 'preventive' psychiatry in the bud.

The second approach adopted by social scientists challenges the very notion of mental illness, and questions the motives that lie behind professional interventions. (Such questioning is invited by the seemingly arbitrary variations in psychiatric nosology, diagnosis and treatment between different times, places and practitioners.) One line of argument focuses on the way in which the field has been shaped by professional self-interest and financial or political factors (for example, profiteering by the drug companies); this critique runs parallel to that made by Illich (1977) and Freidson (1970) of physical medicine. Such an approach has been adopted by historians who have set out to correct the 'triumphalist' picture which professions tend to present of their own history – a picture in which the cumulative victories of reason and humanity culminate inevitably in the achievements of the present.

Other commentators, however, take the argument a step further: they treat mental health as an ideological concept, concealing highly problematic notions about how people should live, and regard the professions that deal with it as agencies of social control. This critique came to the fore in the 1960s, via the work of Foucault (1961), Szasz (1961), Goffman (1961), Scheff (1966) and 'anti-psychiatrists' such as Laing (1960). These writers were not simply claiming that the labelling of certain conditions as 'pathological' was value-laden and culture-bound, for, as Sedgwick (1982) pointed out, the same is true of physical conditions. The critique of psychiatry went further, in claiming the so-called 'symptoms' to be meaningful, freely-chosen acts.

This criticism seems warranted when psychiatry stops people from doing what they want, by means of physical or chemical intervention – for example, political dissidents in the Soviet Union, homosexuals in the West, or (according to Shrag and Divoky, 1975) the million or so American schoolchildren kept under permanent sedation to prevent 'hyperactivity'. Such an analysis seems inapplicable, however, when treatment is actively sought by people anxious to get rid of their 'symptoms'. Moreover, some treatments (especially psychotherapy) claim to increase autonomy, not to diminish it. To treat mental illness as deviance pure and simple is to ignore essential distinctions between 'mad' and 'bad' behaviour – chiefly, the fact that the former is regarded as not making sense, and not under the control of the individual. A straightforward social control model of the mental health professions is therefore limited in its applications.

This is not to say, however, that the remaining instances lack any political significance and are purely therapeutic in character. Behind the concept of mental health lie numerous presuppositions about norms of work, education and family life; and the mental health professions are probably instrumental in maintaining these norms, by influencing not just problem cases but our way of making sense of the world. (Feminists, for example, have argued that psychiatry powerfully reinforces women's traditional role in society (Chessler, 1972).) But if this is a social control mechanism, it is one which has been largely internalized by the population itself. Foucault (1980) goes further, arguing that the power of this mechanism is not 'repressive' but 'productive', since it actually *creates* forms of subjectivity and social life.

Plenty of instances still remain of repression in the name of mental health – as the activities of civil rights organizations and patients' groups testify – and the most convincing analysis is perhaps that of Castel *et al.* (1982), who see the 'hard' and 'soft' methods of treatment as an ensemble, each depending on the other to be fully effective. Although this idea has obvious validity, it is doubtful whether an adequate understanding of the place of mental health in modern society will ever be achieved by trying to impose the same model on such diverse phenomena as lobotomy, forcible incarceration, marital counselling, psychoanalysis and encounter groups.

David Ingleby
University of Utrecht

References

Armstrong, D. (1980), 'Madness and coping', *Sociology of Health and Illness*, 2.

Brenner, H. (1973), *Mental Illness and the Economy*, Cambridge, Mass.

Brown, G. and Harris, T. (1978), *Social Origins of Depression*, London.

Castel, F., Castel, R. and Lovell, A. (1982), *The Psychiatric Society*, New York.

Chessler, P. (1972), *Women and Madness*, New York.

Foucault, M. (1971), *Madness and Civilization*, New York. (Original French, *Histoire de la folie*, Paris, 1961.)

Foucault, M. (1980), 'Truth and power', in *Power/Knowledge: Selected Interviews and Other Writings 1972–1977*, Hassocks.

Freidson, E. (1970), *Professional Dominance*, New York.

Goffman, E. (1961), *Asylums: Essays on the Social Situation of Mental Patients and Other Inmates*, New York.

Hollingshead, A. B. and Redlich, F. C. (1958), *Social Class and Mental Illness*, New York.

Illich, I. (1977), *Disabling Professions*, London.

Laing, R. D. (1960), *The Divided Self*, London.

Ryan, W. (1972), *Blaming the Victim*, New York.

Scheff, T. (1966), *Being Mentally Ill: A Sociological Theory*, London.

Sedgwick, P. (1982), *Psycho Politics*, London.

Shrag, P. and Divoky, D. (1975), *The Myth of the Hyperactive Child and Other Means of Child Control*, New York.

Szasz, T. (1961), *The Myth of Mental Illness*, New York.

Further Reading

Ingleby, D. (ed.) (1980), *Critical Psychiatry: The Politics of Mental Health*, New York.

See also: *mental disorders*; *psychiatry*; *stigma*.

Mental Retardation

Mental retardation is identified by intellectual subnormality, which is associated with deficits in adaptive behaviour originating during the developmental period. It is a joint product of the individual's biological make-up and successive encounters with his physical and social-psychological environments.

Intelligent behaviour depends both on an intact and developed central nervous system and on facilitating and supportive environmental interactions. There is a continuum of disability in intelligent behaviour, ranging from those who manifest neurological impairments and other components of organic disease, including severe forms of intellectual impairment, to persons with no recognizable underlying organic disease but who nevertheless manifest some intellectual impairment and find it difficult to master academic activities in school situations. The phenotypic trait of intelligence is due in part to many genes, each of which adds a little to the development of the trait of intelligence (Haywood and Wachs, 1981; Scarr-Salapatek, 1975).

Lewis (1933), Penrose (1963) and Zigler and Balla (1981) categorize two subpopulations with reduced intelligence: (1) The 'pathological' or organically-retarded who show demonstrable disease and pathology. These represent the organically-diseased variants of the general population. (2) The 'subcultural' or psychosocially retarded with no demonstrable diseases. These represent the lower end of the nonpathological variation in intelligence found in the general population.

Many categories of severe retardation involve biological syndromes that disfigure the whole body. Gargoylism, anencephaly, meningomyelocele and hydrocephaly are examples, as are many types of brain damage resulting from such adverse prenatal influences as undernutrition, rubella, cytomegalic inclusion disease, radiation and lead poisoning. Organically-retarded persons usually have IQ scores under 50 (American Association on Mental Deficiency, 1977). These cases occur almost equally in all social classes and constitute nearly 25 per cent of the mentally-retarded population (Clarke and Clarke, 1977). The psychosocially retarded are primarily from the lower social classes and usually have IQs of between 50 and 70. They constitute about 75 per cent of the mentally-retarded population (Clarke and Clarke, 1977; Zigler, 1967).

Evidence has been accumulating (Weisz and Zigler, 1969) that the mentally retarded go through the same stages of cognitive development as the nonretarded. However, the mentally retarded develop at a much slower rate, and ultimately reach a lower level of cognitive development. The more severe the mental retardation, the slower the rate and ultimate level of cognitive development. Within a Piagetian model of cognitive development, the mildly retarded might attain the concrete operation stage, the moderately retarded the preoperation stage, the severely retarded the fringes of the preoperation stage, while the profoundly retarded might approach the limits of the sensorimotor stage.

Mentally-retarded persons perform more poorly on a wide variety of tasks than would be predicted from their general level of cognitive ability, as defined by their mental ages. One might expect that retarded and younger nonretarded persons matched on mental age should perform at about the same level and use similar cognitive processes on a wide variety of tasks that require intelligent behaviour. However, the retarded members of such matches do less well than do their nonretarded, but younger, peers. They manifest a mental-age deficit. This mental-age deficit in performance between retarded and nonretarded groups has been interpreted as partly the result of differences in motivation between the two groups.

Haywood and his students (Haywood et al., 1982) have identified a broad trait variable, task-intrinsic motivational orientation, that is associated with individual differences in the efficiency of learning and performance. They define 'intrinsically-motivated' persons as those who characteristically seek their principal satisfactions through task achievement, learning, responsibility, creativity, and aesthetic aspects of tasks. Extrinsically-motivated persons, rather than seek satisfactions, concentrate on avoiding dissatisfactions through nontask aspects of the environment such as ease, comfort, safety, security, practicality, material gain, and avoidance of effort. Mildly and moderately-retarded children who are relatively intrinsically motivated, have significantly higher school achievement scores than extrinsically-motivated children of the same age, sex and IQ. They can learn a visual-size discrimination problem in fewer trials and more efficiently; they persist longer and work more vigorously at a simple motor task for a 'task-intrinsic' incentive – merely the opportunity to do more work; they can work harder under self-monitored than under externally-imposed reinforcement, and they set 'leaner' reinforcement schedules for themselves than under the self-monitored condition. The mental-age deficit often observed in mentally-retarded groups may be due in part to decreased task-intrinsic motivation.

Zigler and his students (Zigler and Balla, 1981) have conceptualized the motivational problems of retarded persons as being due partly to deficient effectance motivation, and a lack of concern for the intrinsic motivation that is inherent in being correct, regardless of whether or not an external agent dispenses the reinforcer. Ziglar believes that the socially-depriving life histories of psychosocially-retarded children, their cognitive deficiencies, and their related failure experience all lead to an attenuation of effectance motivation with a concomitant increase in extrinsically-motivated behaviour.

Harter and Zigler (1974) constructed measures of several aspects of effectance motivation including variation seeking, curiosity, mastery for the sake of competence, and preference for challenging as compared to nonchallenging tasks. Intellectually average, noninstitutionalized retarded, and institutionalized retarded children of comparable mental age were tested. On all components of effectance motivation measured, the intellectually-average children showed more effectance motivation than did the retarded children. Institutionalized retarded children also displayed less curiosity than did noninstitutionalized retarded children.

However, it has been demonstrated that the motivational systems of retarded persons can be improved and their performances facilitated by various early educational intervention programmes such as Project Head Start (Gray et al., 1981; Seitz et al., 1981), the Milwaukee Project (Garber and Heber, 1977) and the Abecedarian Project (Ramey and Hawkins, 1981). Suggestions for changing 'task-extrinsic' motivational orientations into 'task-intrinsic' ones are to be found in Harter (1981).

Harvey N. Switzky
Northern Illinois University, DeKalb, Illinois

References

American Association on Mental Deficiency (1977), *Manual on Terminology and Classification in Mental Retardation*, Washington.

Clarke, A. B. D. and Clarke, A. M. (1977), 'Prospects for prevention and amelioration of mental retardation: a guest editorial', *American Journal of Mental Deficiency*, 81.

Garber, H. and Heber, R. (1977), 'The Milwaukee Project', in P. Mittler (ed.), *Research to Practice in Mental Retardation*, Baltimore.

Gray, S. W., Ramsey, B. K. and Klaus, R. A. (1981), *From 3 to 20: The Early Training Project*, Baltimore.

Harter, S. (1981), 'A model of intrinsic mastery motivation in children: individual differences and development change', in W. A. Collins (ed.), *Minnesota Symposium on Child Psychology*, 14, Hillsdale, N.J.

Harter, S. and Zigler, E. (1974), 'The assessment of effectance motivation in normal and retarded children', *Developmental Psychology*, 10.

Haywood, H. C. (1968), 'Motivational orientation of overachieving and underachieving elementary school children', *American Journal of Mental Deficiency*, 72.

Haywood, H. C. and Wachs, T. (1981), 'Intelligence, cognition, and individual differences', in M. J. Begab *et al.* (eds), *Issues and Theories in Development*, Baltimore.

Haywood, H. C., Meyers, C. E. and Switzky, H. N. (1982), 'Mental retardation', *Annual Review of Psychology*, Palo Alto.

Lewis, E. O. (1933), 'Types of mental deficiency and their social significance', *Journal of Mental Science*, 79.

Penrose, L. S. (1963), *The Biology of Mental Deficiency*, London.

Ramey, C . T. and Hawkins, R. (1981), 'The causes and treatment of school failure; insights from the Carolina Abecedarian Project', in M. J. Begab *et al.* (eds), *Prevention of Retarded Development in Psychosocially Disadvantaged*, Baltimore.

Scarr-Salapatek, S. (1975), 'Genetics and the development of intelligence', in F. P. Horowitz, *Review of Child Development Research*, 4.

Seitz, V., Aptel, N. H. and Rosenbaum, L. (1981), 'Projects Headstart and Follow Through: a longitudinal evaluation of adolescents', in M. J. Begab *et al.* (eds), Baltimore.

Weisz, J. R. and Zigler, E. (1969), 'Developmental versus difference theories of mental retardation', *American Journal of Mental Deficiency*, 73.

Zigler, E. (1967), 'Familial mental retardation: a continuing dilemma', *Science*, 155.

Zigler, E. and Balla, D. (1981), 'Issues in personality and motivation in mentally retarded persons', in M. J. Begab *et al.* (eds), Baltimore.

Further Reading

Ellis, N. R. (ed.) (1979), *Handbook of Mental Deficiency*, 2nd edn, Hillsdale, N.J.

Haywood, H. C., Meyers, C. E. and Switzky, H. N. (1982), 'Mental retardation', *Annual Review of Psychology*, Palo Alto, CA.

Inhelder, B. (1968), *The Diagnosis of Reasoning in the Mentally Retarded*, New York.

Kavoly, P. and Kanfer, F. H. (1982), *Self-Management and Behavior Change*, New York.

Sternberg, R. J. (ed.) (1982), *Handbook of Human Intelligence*, New York.

Switzky, H. N. and Haywood, H. C. (1984), 'A biosocial ecological perspective on mental retardation', in N. Endle and J. M. V. Hunt (eds), *Personality and Behaviour Disorders*, 2nd edn, New York.

See also: *developmental psychology; intelligence; learning; nervous system.*

Mercantilism

The term mercantilism may refer to a sizeable collection of economic literature, as in 'mercantilist economic thought', or it may refer to an extended, historical period from about 1550 to 1750, during which time the then emerging nation states of Europe embarked upon policies designed to promote economic development. The mercantilist writers, almost without exception, identified a healthy 'circulation of money' with low interest rates for business loans. Low interest rates were linked to national prosperity, and national prosperity was essential to success in war. This explains the urgency the mercantilists attached to reshaping economic policy.

The early English mercantilist writer, Gerard Malynes, advocated exchange controls to keep the coins (gold specie) from being exported. Malynes believed the self-interest of merchants, combined with the despicable greed of the bankers, interfered with the national prosperity. The export of English coins would work to the advantage of England's major trading rivals, Holland and Spain. Their 'circulation would improve' at the expense of England's, thereby ominously shifting the balance of power.

After 1620, other mercantilist writers recommended more subtle and indirect means of improving 'circulation'. Rather than holding onto every coin in the realm, both Edward Misselden and Sir Thomas Mun looked at international trade as an interrelated whole (Misselden, 1971; Mun, 1959). The overall balance of trade and, more generally, the balance of payments was the proper object of policy analysis. To improve that national balance might require subsidizing exports and discouraging imports, constructing roads and harbours, lowering wages and raw materials prices, encouraging population growth to keep both wages low and staff armies, and promoting the importation of foreign know-how and technology. The more 'favourable' the balance of trade, the better the circulation and the lower the interest rates. The lower the interest rates, the more commerce and the stronger the nation.

It is now well established that the mercantilists were part of a drama in which the kingdoms of Europe made the transition from local medieval commerce to New World exploration and then the powerful nation state with its standing armies and public credit (Heckscher, 1955). As active participants, the mercantilists often secured privileges for themselves such as exclusive trading rights with different regions of the world. These privileges were monopolies which injured the larger number of consumers. The strange coincidence between their personal avarice and the counsel that they offered kings in the public interest produced definitions that enhanced their private fortunes (Ekelund and Tollison, 1981).

After 1750, enlightenment thinkers, D. Hume and Adam Smith, rejected mercantilism. Smith accused the mercantilists of 'extort[ing]' laws from the legislature 'written in [the] blood' of their fellow citizens. Starting, however, with the German historical school (Schmoller, 1884) and including J. M. Keynes (1936), many later writers have taken a more sympathetic view of the policies of the mercantilists. Sir Dudley North, celebrated for his deductive forms of argument anticipating modern economics, supported high wages for the poor without concern that it might discourage exports. After the Restoration of the English monarch in 1688, a number of mercantilists such as North, D. Thomas and J. Houghton, favoured an 'economy of consumption', that is, an economic system exposed to a large variety of imported goods that would whet the palates of the masses and encourage their more active participation in the economy.

After the Restoration, mercantilists began to develop liberal notions about the advantages of economic freedom. What was required was the clear rejection of the idea that, if one nation gains more 'circulation', there is less opportunity for the other nations to prosper. As eighteenth-century thought made clear, the basis for exchange was mutual gain, and, with free trade, results in a homeostatic balancing of buyers and sellers in the market through the price system. The nineteenth-century classical school followed Smith in rejecting mercantilism. In their view, the surest path to national prosperity was an international division of labour based on the pursuit of private interest within the framework of the law. Today the term Mercantilist is often used to describe those who propose to promote economic development by subsidizing the business community.

Laurence S. Moss
Babson College, Massachusetts

References

Appleby, J. Q. (1978), *Economic Thought and Ideology in Seventeenth-Century England*, Princeton.

Ekelund, R. B., Jr and Tollison, R. D. (1981), *Mercantilism as a Rent-Seeking Society*, College Station, Texas.

Heckscher, E. F. (1955), *Mercantilism*, revised edn, ed. E. F. Soderlund, 2 vols, New York.

Keynes, J. M. (1936), *The General Theory of Employment Interest and Money*, London.

Misselden, E. (1971 [1623]), *The Circle of Commerce or the Balance of Trade*, New York.

Mun, T. (1959 [1664]), *England's Treasure by Forraign Trade*, Oxford.

Schmoller, G. (1884), *The Mercantile System and Its Historical Significance*, London.

Merton, Robert King (1910–)

Merton's reputation rests most securely on his having established the sociology of science as a field, with help, of course, from colleagues and students at Columbia (where he has taught since 1941) and elsewhere. His doctoral dissertation at Harvard, first published in 1938, made him famous. He took for granted that scientific theories develop to some extent by exploration of 'immanent' implications and problems, but he showed that science in the great seventeenth century developed in part from technological and economic interests and, beyond that, from the congruence that existed at several points between Puritan *religious* orientation and *positive* interest in science in general. His later work on priority disputes and multiple independent discoveries is also notable. Concerning his functional theory, he stresses that it draws particular attention to the different consequences of social structure for different segments of the population ('multiple manifest and latent functions and dysfunctions'). Some of his other concepts and terms have become widely known (for example, self-fulfilling prophecy, role set). In supposed opposition to the 'general' theory of Parsons, Merton has insisted on what he calls 'theoretical pluralism' – the inevitable and desirable co-existence of many theories in a field. (This misunderstanding is unfortunate). Parsons was trying to relate to one another, explicitly and systematically, *analytically different types* of empirical system, cultural, social, and so on, as well as he could, of course, but *not* in the only possible way. In any case, Merton has contributed much to 'theories of the middle range' such as reference-group theory. He is the most frequently-cited living sociologist.

Harry M. Johnson
University of Illinois, Champaign-Urbana

Further Reading
Coser, L. A. (ed.) (1975), *The Idea of Social Structure. Essays in Honor of R. K. Merton*, New York.
Merton, R. K. (1935), *Science, Technology and Society in Seventeenth Century England*, reprinted 1970, New York.
Merton, R. K. (1968), *Social Theory and Social Structure*, enlarged edn, New York.
Merton, R. K. (1973), *The Sociology of Science: Theoretical and Empirical Investigations*, edited and with an Introduction by N. W. Storer, Chicago.

Michels, Robert (1876–1936)

Robert Michels made important contributions to the social sciences, especially to the sociology of organizations and political sociology. Born in Cologne in 1876 of a bourgeois-patrician family, Michels studied at the Sorbonne in Paris and at the Universities of Munich, Leipzig, and Halle, where he graduated in 1900 with a dissertation in history. Following his passionate political ideals, he soon joined the German Social Democratic Party and actively participated in the party congresses of 1903, 1904 and 1905. But he later became disillusioned with social democratic policies and leaders and resigned from the party. In the 1920s he showed some sympathy for the Fascist movement. Political activity in socialist quarters excluded Michels from an academic career in Germany, despite the support of influential friends such as Max Weber. In 1914 he thus moved to Basle, where he became professor of political economy; eventually in 1928 he was appointed professor of economics at the University of Perugia in Italy.

Michels wrote a number of books on subjects as different as democracy, socialism, revolution, class conflict, mass society, imperialism, intellectuals, élites, eugenics, sex and morality. But his most important and long-lasting work is the monograph *Zur Soziologie des Parteiwesens in der modernen Demokratie*, first published in 1911 (English translation, *Political Parties*, New York, 1949). In his classic study of political parties, largely based on firsthand knowledge of the German and Italian socialist parties, Michels formulated his famous 'iron law of oligarchy'. According to it, strong oligarchic tendencies inevitably arise in any political organization, notwithstanding its democratic ideology and commitment. Organizational needs – initially the preservation and growth of the organization – in fact produce selection of leadership and development of specialized knowledge and skills. This in turn leads to the emergence of stable and self-perpetuating leaders,

which gives birth to the 'domination of the elected over the electors, of the mandatories over the mandators, of the delegates over the delegators'. Michels's work has inspired and influenced later empirical research on organizations and political parties. The theories and insights of the German sociologist have been generally confirmed, though improved and specified more precisely.

Luisa Leonini
University of Milan

Further Reading
Linz, J. J. (1966), 'Michels e il suo contributo alla sociologia politica', in R. Michels, *La sociologia del partito politico nella democrazia moderna*, Bologna.
May, J. D. (1965), 'Democracy, organization, Michels', *American Political Science Review*, 59.

Microeconomics

Microeconomics is that portion of economic theory concerned with the economic behaviour of individual units in the economy, and the factors determining the prices and quantities exchanged of particular goods and services. It can be contrasted with *macroeconomics* which is concerned with the determination of values for aggregates for the economy. For example, microeconomics examines the determination of the price of wheat, or the relative prices of wheat and steel, or employment in the steel industry, while macroeconomics deals with the determination of the level of employment in a particular economy, or with the level of prices of all commodities. Although this distinction between two areas of economic analysis is useful for many purposes, and economic theory textbooks are usually devoted either to microeconomics (also known as 'price theory') or to macroeconomics, it should not be taken to imply that these two levels of analysis are independent. Micro questions, such as those concerning the relative prices produced in competitive and monopolistic industries, cannot be answered without reference to the level of aggregate demand in the economy, while macroeconomics is built on micro-foundations that specify the nature of competition in different industries, for example, competitive or oligopolistic.

The development of microeconomics as a distinct area was part of the marginal or neoclassical approach that came to dominate economic theory after the 1970s. In contrast to classical economics that was concerned with the economic growth of nations due to the growth of their productive resources, and which explained the relative prices of goods on the basis of the 'objective' conditions of their costs of production, neoclassical theory turned its attention to the efficient allocation of given resources (under the implicit assumption of full employment) and to the 'subjective' determination of individual prices based on marginal utility.

The topics dealt with by microeconomic analysis are often presented under the following headings: (1) theory of consumer behaviour; (2) theory of exchange; (3) theory of production and cost; (4) theory of the firm; (5) theory of distribution; and (6) welfare economics. The common theme underlying these topics is the attempt of individual actors to achieve an optimal position, given the values of the parameters constraining their choices. Consumers try to maximize satisfaction (or utility) given their tastes, incomes and prices of all goods; firms try to maximize profits, and this means, among other things, that any rate of output is produced at least cost. The conditions for maximization are expressed in terms of marginal equalities. For example, for profit maximization a firm's rate of output should be such that marginal revenue is equal to marginal cost. In traditional approaches to microeconomics it is assumed that the self-seeking actions of individual units result in equilibrium positions where, given the values of the parameters, all participants are making the best of the situations facing them. They can be concerned either with partial equilibrium analysis (developed by Marshall) that concentrates on the determination of equilibrium values in a particular industry, assuming that the values in other industries are determined independently of these particular values, or with general equilibrium analysis (developed by Leon Walras) that provides full scope for the interdependence of all sectors of the economy, and deals with the simultaneous determination of all prices and quantities in the system. This generality is obtained at some cost, with the treatment being formal and mathematical, and important aspects of economic processes that occupy time are ignored.

A. Asimakopulos
McGill University

Further Reading
Asimakopulos, A. (1978), *An Introduction to Economic Theory: Microeconomics*, Toronto.
Mansfield, E. (1982), *Microeconomics*, 4th edn, New York.
See also: *consumer behaviour; cost-benefit analysis; firm, theory of; welfare economics.*

Migration

Migration is a generic term used to refer both to immigration (or in-migration) and to emigration (or out-migration). Formally, these terms may refer to various types of change of residence, but we customarily speak of immigration and emigration when the change of residence is between nations, and of in-migration and out-migration when the change of residence is between subunits of a nation. The term 'net migration' is used to denote the difference between the number of in-migratory events and the number of out-migratory events with respect to a particular geographic unit during a given time period.

Events of immigration (in-migration) and emigration (out-migration) constitute two of the four components of population change: the other two components are births and deaths. For large areas population change is generally determined predominantly by the balance of births and deaths (natural increase). However, for small areas the net migration is often larger than the natural increase.

A migration stream is defined as the total number of migratory events from Place A to Place B during a given time period. The counterstream is defined as the total number of migratory events from Place B to Place A. The sum of events in the stream and counterstream is termed the gross interchange between A and B. The effectiveness of migration is defined as the ratio of the net migration between A and B and the gross interchange between the two places. Logically, therefore, the effectiveness of migration can vary from a low of 0 to a high of 1. For most pairs of geographic units the effectiveness of migration tends to be much closer to 0 than to 1.

Certain types of migration are commonly distinguished. Petersen (1975) made useful distinctions between the concepts of free, impelled and forced migration. In free migration the will of the migrant is the main factor. In impelled migration the will of the migrant is subordinated to the will of other persons. In forced migration the will of other persons is paramount, and the will of the migrant of no weight at all. Return migration is defined as migration back to a place in which one had formerly resided. For most individuals who have migrated several times during their lifetime, return migrations are an important component of the total number of movements. Chain migration refers to the common pattern whereby a given individual migrates to a particular destination in which he already has kin or friends who have previously migrated from his own area of origin.

Migration Differentials

It is universally observed that the propensity to migrate is strongest among young adults. Other differentials in migration tend to be limited to particular cultures or locales.

Determinants of Migration

The determinants of migratory behaviour may conveniently be analysed in terms of: (1) a preference system; (2) a price system; and (3) the total amount of resources available for all goals (Heer, 1975).

(1) *The preference system* describes the relative attractiveness of various places as goals for the potential

migrant, compared to other goals which his resources would allow him to pursue. An area's attractiveness is the balance between the positive and negative values which it offers.

Among the most important of the positive values is the prospect of a better-paying job. Other advantages achieved by migration include the chance to live in a more favourable climate, freedom from persecution, marriage and the continuation of marital ties, and the desire for more adequate housing, a factor particularly important with respect to central-city to suburb movements.

However, migration also creates negative values. A major disincentive to migration is that it involves a disruption of interpersonal relationships with kin and old friends. Chain migration is so attractive precisely because it mitigates this disruption of relationships. Other negative aspects of migration are the necessity to learn new customs and sometimes a new language. Laws restraining legal entry or departure are also, of course, important deterrents to migration.

(2) *The price system* describes costs in money, energy and time (which cannot be used in the pursuit of other goals) imposed by a given migration decision. Since the cost of migration generally varies in direct proportion to the distance travelled, the number of migrants to a given place tends to vary inversely with the distance.

(3) *The total resources available* for all goals also affects the decision to migrate. If the only drawback to migration is the expense of the move, then an increase in monetary income should increase the probability of migration. The secular increase in monetary income during the last century or more in the developed nations should have increased rates of migration, provided that the value and price of migration had remained constant. However, to the extent that regional differences in job opportunities may also decline, the factor of increasing resources may be offset.

Consequences of Migration

Migration has consequences for the area of net out-migration, the area of net in-migration, as well as for the larger social system, which includes both the area of out-migration and the area of in-migration.

(1) *Net out-migration* may have several important consequences for an area. It may relieve population pressure and cause the average level of wage and salary income to rise. On the other hand, it may cause the value of land and real estate to decline. Moreover, areas of net out-migration incur the loss of the investments made to raise and educate those children who spend their productive years elsewhere.

(2) *Net in-migration* may also have important consequences. If the area is definitely underpopulated, the resultant population increase may help the area achieve economies of scale and thus raise the general standard of living. Under other circumstances, net in-migration may result in decline in average wage and salary income. In either case, a net flow of in-migrants will tend to raise the price of land and real estate. It is also possible that a high rate of in-migration fosters social disorganization, since social-control networks are not easily established among persons who are strangers to one another.

(3) *For the system comprising both the areas of net inflow and of net outflow*, migration promotes a redistribution of population. If migrants have been responsive to differences in job opportunities, this redistribution will further the economic development of the total system. Usually, migration also has consequences for the degree of regional homogeneity within the total system. Since migrants tend to move from low to high income areas, regional income inequalities are generally reduced by migration. Moreover, migration often helps to reduce regional disparities in racial, ethnic and religious composition.

Migration Policies and Legislation Affecting Migration

It is useful to distinguish between migration policies, which are intentionally designed to influence migratory flows, and legislation affecting migration which in fact influences the flow of migrants even though it is designed to serve some other major goal or goals. Almost all nations have adopted policies with respect to international migration. Currently, most such policies severely restrict immigration, so that the actual stream of legal immigrants is much smaller than it would have been if no barriers had been imposed (Davis, 1981). As a result, many nations, particularly the US, have a large number of illegal immigrants. However, certain nations have actively encouraged immigrants of a particular type. Australia, for example, in the twenty-year period following World War II, actively sought to increase its population through subsidizing immigration from Europe while at the same time discouraging immigration from Asia. Although most governments proclaim the right of their citizens to emigrate, many of them place restrictions on emigration of selected persons for reasons of national security. Moreover, restrictions on emigration can be very severe, as exemplified currently in the USSR.

The stream of rural to urban migration has marked every nation, both developed and less developed, since the beginning of the Industrial Revolution. In the now developed nations, the net stream of rural to urban migration has in most cases ceased; in many of the less-developed nations at the present time it is still of considerable magnitude.

Explicit policies concerning internal migration are less common than with respect to external migration; on the other hand, in most nations there is a large body of legislation which affects internal migration either negatively or positively. Nations which do have explicit policies regarding internal migration have generally tried either to discourage the growth of their largest cities or to encourage settlement of scarcely populated regions with important natural resources.

David M. Heer
University of Southern California

References

Davis, K. (1981), 'Emerging issues in international migration', *International Population Conference, Manila, 1981*, Vol. 2, Liège.
Heer, D. M. (1975), *Society and Population*, 2nd edn, Englewood Cliffs, N.J.
Petersen, W. (1975), *Population*, 3rd edn, New York.
See also: *refugees; residential mobility; urbanization.*

Military Sociology

Military sociology is mainly concerned with the armed forces as a special type of organization with specific social functions. These functions flow from the purpose of the organization, namely security, and from the organizational means, force or violence. These matters have been the subject of discussion for centuries and were considered by the pioneer sociologists Comte and Spencer. An empirically grounded and theoretically informed military sociology only became established, however, during World War II. Pioneering studies were carried out by the Research Branch of the Information and Education Division of the US Armed Forces between 1942–5, and later published (Stouffer *et al.*, 1949). The discipline is still most developed and differentiated in the US, though there are institutions for research in military sociology in other countries.

The main fields of research are the following:

(1) Internal Organizational Problems in Daily Military Life
Processes within small groups and military rituals are analysed in order to identify problems of discipline and motivation, and also to elucidate the way in which the military subculture is ordered.

(2) Internal Organizational Problems in Combat
Studies in this area concern the criteria for the selection of military leaders, including the lower ranks, and evaluate combat motivation.

(3) The Armed Forces and the Society
Military sociologists are interested in the image of the profession with respect to the impact of social and technological change, the recruitment profile of the armed forces, the broader structure of defence, problems of training and educating soldiers and, more recently, the role of women in the army.

(4) The Military and Politics
The traditional question of the causes and functions of militarism has been broken down into more specific issues, and there is now a clear difference between the West and other parts of the world in the emphases chosen. In Western democracies, research has come to focus on the political control of the military and the web of military, economic and administrative interests, which are difficult to disentangle. The sparse analyses of armed forces in the socialist countries address the political balance between the army and the party. In contrast, numerous studies devoted to the military in developing countries are concerned with the causes and consequences of military coups, with the ability of the armed forces to contribute to development, and with 'Praetorianism', the form typically taken by militarism in underdeveloped countries.

(5) Armed Forces in the International System
These studies deal with national and international aspects of security, with armaments and armament control, and with international peacekeeping operations. A proper sociology of war exists in only a rudimentary form.

This brief survey clearly indicates the interdisciplinary nature of the field. Military sociology is also in a special position because of widespread concern with its applied orientation, and with the 'conservative' views of its main client, the armed forces. It is seldom taught in university departments of sociology, and most research is concentrated in extra-university institutions, often within the armed forces. Nevertheless, the best studies in the field have profitably explored this very tension between academic and 'liberal' commitments and the applications of the research. Exemplary studies are Andreski (1954), Huntington (1957), Janowitz (1960), Finer (1962), and Moskos (1970).

The key issues for research in the immediate future relate to the most urgent problems of military organization. Such problems include the consequences of current technological developments and of changes in the civilian view of the military in industrial countries, as well as the growing importance of military and paramilitary violence, especially in developing countries.

Wilfried von Bredow
Philipps University, Marburg

References

Andreski, S. (1954), *Military Organization and Society*, London.
Finer, S. E. (1962), *The Man on Horseback*, London.
Huntington, S. P. (1957), *The Soldier and the State*, Cambridge, Mass.

Janowitz, M. (1961), *The Professional Soldier*, Glencoe, Ill.

Moskos, C. C. Jr (1970), *The American Enlisted Man*, New York.

Stouffer, S. A. *et al.* (1949), *The American Soldier*, Princeton, N.J.

See also: *war*.

Mill, John Stuart (1806–73)

John Stuart Mill, the classic exponent of liberalism, was brought up in utilitarian principles by his father, James Mill, a close friend and associate of Bentham. His rigorous childhood education, described in his *Autobiography* (1873), involved a brilliant and precocious mastery of classical languages by the age of seven. For most of his working life he was a clerk at India House in London, though briefly a Member of Parliament. He married Harriet Taylor whom he always claimed as his inspiration and intellectual partner.

Mill was a many-sided thinker and writer – a philosopher, social scientist and humanist. Amongst the subjects he treated were politics, ethics, logic and scientific method. Particular topics on which he wrote included the position of women (*The Subjection of Women*, 1869), constitutional reform (*Considerations on Representative Government*, 1861), and economics (*Principles of Political Economy*, 1848).

In *Utilitarianism* (1861) Mill expounded and defended the principle that the tendency of actions to promote happiness or its reverse is the standard of right and wrong. His version of utilitarianism was from a logical point of view flawed, and from a moral point of view enhanced, by the notion that some forms of happiness are more worthwhile than others. *On Liberty* (1859) is the classic argument for the claims of the individual against the state, and in it Mill makes an impassioned defence of the principles of liberty and toleration. This is sometimes seen as inconsistent with his basic utilitarianism, but Mill believed that principles like liberty and justice were themselves important social instruments for utility. This follows from his view of human nature, and in particular from his belief that self-determination and the exercise of choice are themselves part of a higher concept of happiness. Regarding toleration, Mill argued in favour of liberty of thought, speech and association, as well as for freedom to cultivate whatever lifestyle one chooses, subject only to the constraint of not harming others. It is often disputed whether there are any actions which do not affect other people in some way, but the distinction between other-regarding and self-regarding actions is an essential element of liberalism.

Mill applied these principles to education, defending a liberal and secular education. He considered compulsory education not an invasion of liberty but essential to it. However, he believed strongly that there should not be a 'state monopoly of education' but that state education should be one amongst a number of competing systems.

In *A System of Logic, Ratiocinative and Deductive* (1843), Mill defended a classical view of induction as empirical generalization and held that this can supply a model for both logical deduction and scientific method. In some respects this may be seen as a classic version of British empiricism, but because Mill was prepared to accept the uniformity of nature as a basic postulate, it is free from the sceptical consequences that this position sometimes seems to involve. Mill extended his discussion of methodology to cover the application of experimental method to social science and set out to provide 'a general science of man in society'. His argument is to be found in Book VI of *A System of Logic*, which has been called the most important contribution to the making of modern sociology until Durkheim's *Rules of Sociological Method*.

Brenda Cohen
University of Surrey

Further Reading
Gray, J. (1983), *Mill on Liberty: A Defence*, London.
Ryan, A. (1974), *J. S. Mill*, London.
Ten, C. L. (1980), *Mill on Liberty*, Oxford.

Mills, Charles Wright (1916–62)

C. Wright Mills, born in Texas in 1916 and dead at the age of forty-six of a heart attack in 1962, was the most controversial social scientist of the post-war era and the first sociologist ever to gain a large public following. Best known and remembered in the discipline for such works as *White Collar* (1951), *The Power Elite* (1956) and *The Sociological Imagination* (1959), he also reached out to wider audiences with such works as *The Causes of World War Three* (1958) and *Listen Yankee* (1960), the latter a spirited polemic that tried to persuade the American people to live with the Cuban Revolution as a hopeful possibility between communism and capitalism. His emphasis on the importance of reason and his call for moral commitment and political action on the part of intellectuals made him one of the heroes of the New Left of the 1960s, which embraced him as an independent leftist who had not ended up rigidly tied to either the pro-communist or anti-communist camp.

Mills is not an easy sociologist to classify in terms of theoretical orientation. He was greatly influenced by the American pragmatist Peirce, but also by the German sociologists Weber and Mannheim. His training as an undergraduate at the University of Texas in the 1930s was in both philosophy and sociology, and he received his Ph.D. in the interdisciplinary graduate programme at the University of Wisconsin.

Usually thought of as a radical or a socialist, he read Marx early in his career but did not consider himself a Marxist until he adopted the label 'plain Marxist' for his book *The Marxists* (1962). Although a critic of capitalism, he considered the Marxian belief in an inevitable proletarian revolution arising inexorably out of the class struggle to be a mere 'labor metaphysic'. His stratification schema in terms of an élite of power based in corporations, the military, and the government bureaucracy; a middle level that corresponds to the interest groups and veto groups of the pluralists, and a large mass at the bottom that is increasingly manipulated by the bureaucratic élites and mass media certainly owes little to Marxism.

Mills portrayed himself as a rough-hewn rural Texan who believed in one gun and one vote, but he was in fact raised in a Catholic white-collar family in Dallas. He was in many ways marginal sociologically, and he always felt like an outsider at the University of Maryland, where he taught in the early 1940s, and Columbia University, where he worked from 1945 until his death. He was difficult as a colleague and at times casual toward his teaching duties at Columbia which contributed more to his professional difficulties than is realized by those who claim he was disliked only for his ideas. If his personality was a big factor in how he was regarded during his lifetime, however, it is by now clear that he was above all an enormously hard-working and insightful sociologist who will be remembered for his passionate devotion to reason and ringing concepts such as 'the power élite', as well as for his polemics against the 'grand theorists' and 'abstracted empiricists' within his discipline.

G. William Domhoff
University of California, Santa Cruz

Further Reading

Domhoff, G. W. and Ballard, H. B. (eds) (1968), *C. Wright Mills and the Power Elite*, Boston.
Gillam, R. (1975), 'C. Wright Mills and the politics of truth: the power elite revisited', *American Quarterly*, XXVIII.
Gillam, R. (1981), 'White collar from start to finish: C. Wright Mills in transition', *Theory and Society*, 10.
Horowitz, I. L. (1983), *C. Wright Mills: An American Utopian*, New York.

Mind

'Mind' is derived from old Teutonic *gamundi* meaning to think, remember, intend. These various senses are apparent in current phrases such as: to bear in mind, remind, give one's mind to, make up or change one's mind. Most verbal forms are now obsolete or dialectal but remain in such phrases as 'never mind' or 'mind how you go' in the sense of attend. Traditionally 'mind' has been used to refer collectively to mental abilities such as perceiving, imagining, remembering, thinking, believing, feeling, desiring, deciding, intending. Sometimes an agent is implied: 'Mind is the mysterious something which feels and thinks' (Mill, 1843); sometimes not: 'What we call mind is nothing but a heap or collection of different perceptions, united together by certain relations' (Hume, 1740).

In classical Greece, questions about the mind were interwoven with those about the soul or spirit, as was the case in medieval Europe, where theological concerns predominated. Plato's tripartite division of the mind into cognitive, conative and affective functions lasted at least until the nineteenth century. Numerous classifications of mental faculties were offered in the eighteenth and nineteenth centuries. Although these were generally speculative, artificial and non-explanatory, they laid the ground for later work in psychometrics and cortical localization of function (McFie, 1972).

Diverse criteria have been offered for distinguishing the mental from the physical (Feigl, 1958). According to the first, mental phenomena are private whereas physical phenomena are public. However, public evidence is in fact intersubjective. Descartes (1641) claimed that body occupied space and was subject to deterministic laws, whereas mind was nonspatial and free. Neither of these criteria are without problems. Quantum mechanics and relativity cast doubt on space as a simple concept in physics. Mental phenomena such as images have spatial properties, and if mind-brain identity theory is accepted, the denial of spatial properties to mental phenomena may become an outmoded convention. Indeterminism has been found to apply to physical phenomena at the subatomic level and it is assumed by psychologists that mental phenomena are determined. Criteria in terms of mnemic properties (Russell, 1921) or purposiveness (McDougall, 1912) are probably too weak. Fairly simple machines are capable of memory and goal direction. Whether purpose implies conscious agency is more difficult to decide. Brentano (1874) suggested intensionality as characteristic of the mental: perceiving, thinking and desiring imply objects which may have no objective existence. This feature of symbolic representation is central to artificial intelligence. Contrasts betwen qualitative and quantitative, holistic and atomistic, or emergent and compositional are inadequate. They represent alternative descriptions rather than distinctions of substance. Attempts have been made to distinguish mental and physical in terms of different logics, for example, intensional and extensional (Chisholm, 1967), or linguistic conventions (Ryle, 1949). The current view is that mental descriptions are compatible with, but logically irreducible to, physical descriptions (Boden, 1972).

Traditionally the mind has been identified with conscious experience: 'Consciousness . . . is the condition or accompaniment of every mental operation' (Fleming, 1858); 'No proposition can be said to be in the Mind which it was never yet conscious of' (Locke, 1690). However, this proposition seems to be patently false. Neurophysiologists and clinicians in the nineteenth century recognized different levels of functioning in the nervous system and acknowledged unconscious mental activity, although the idea has a much more venerable history dating back at least to classical Greek times. William James (1890) pointed out that it is only the perchings and not the flights of thought that are available to consciousness. The majority of mental processes take place outside awareness, for instance, large parts of perception, retrieval, skills and creative thinking. This fact is made even more obvious by consideration of such phenomena as hypnosis, subliminal perception, learning without awareness, split personality and blindsight (a clinical condition in which patients with damage to the occipital lobes may report no experience of seeing and yet be able to make correct discriminations in a forced choice situation).

In Western philosophy a distinction has generally been drawn between mind and body, largely as a result of the influence of Descartes. If such a distinction is made (dualism) the problem of their relation arises, to which various solutions have been offered. Psychophysical parallelism asserts that mental and physical events are correlated but causally independent. This is somewhat unparsimonious and leaves the correlation unexplained. Interaction postulates two-way causal dependence. This accords with common sense, but the problem is how there could be causal relations between two systems so distinctively different; for example, how could bodily causes produce mental effects if the latter are defined as nondetermined? The principles of conservation of energy and matter are contravened: if physical causes are sufficient, mental causes can hardly be necessary. Epiphenomenalism posits causal dependence of mental on physical events but not vice versa. This is an extrapolation, possibly unwarranted, from cases where conscious processes are inefficacious. It is difficult, if not impossible, to test because conscious processes are always accompanied by physical ones. Monist solutions attempt to reduce one set of events to the other or assert that both are aspects of some fundamental neutral stuff (double aspect theory). This last is superficially attractive but vague, and leaves the fundamental stuff unknowable. Idealism claims that all physical events can be reduced to mental: matter is the 'permanent possibililty of sensation' (Mill, 1843). Prima facie this is compelling but encounters difficulties when trying to account for the consistency of experience. Materialism attempts to reduce mental

events to physical and has been held in many different forms. Logical behaviourism claims that mental descriptions can be analysed in terms of physical ones such as dispositions to behave. It is false because mental descriptions are not identical in meaning to physical descriptions. Experiences cannot be identified with the behavioural and physiological evidence for them. Thus, supporters of the mind-brain identity theory claim that the identity which holds between conscious experiences and brain states is contingent rather than conceptual: it is a matter for empirical discovery. This is a parsimonious theory which has the advantage that mental states can be assigned a genuinely causal role. However, there are difficulties in specifying the level at which the identity holds. Functionalism is based on the recognition that mental processes are independent of a particular physical realization: what characterizes the mental is its functional organization rather than its material constitution. According to the computer analogy, mind is the program of software, and brain is the hardware. Mental states are defined in terms of the operations of a Turing machine. Functionalism cannot provide a satisfactory analysis of qualitative differences in experience, for example, where experiences of red and green are interchanged (the 'inverted spectrum') but behaviour remains the same.

Nevertheless the computer analogy has been extremely fruitful in cognitive science. The underlying assumption is that theories of the mind can be expressed in computational terms. Complex operations can be broken down into simple ones, such as composition, primitive recursion and minimization (Johnson-Laird, 1983). The contribution of artificial intelligence is to enable the specification of possible mechanisms at an appropriate level of abstraction and to examine their feasibility.

The mind can be modelled by a hierarchy of multiple parallel processors, enabling speed and flexibility, with interactions and dependencies within and between levels. At the lowest level they govern sensory and motor interactions with the external world. At the highest level overall goals are monitored. Some modules may be fairly general in function; the majority are probably relatively specialized. The evidence suggests a broad division of labour between those specialized for verbal processing and those specialized for spatial processing. A small subset of results, but not the inner workings, are available to consciousness in a limited capacity serial processor which interrelates products of parallel processors. The system can construct models of the external world (including one of itself), which influence its input and output. The contents of the mind appear to be images, propositions, models and procedures for carrying out actions. It is clear that 'mind' is a term which is too vague to be useful. The tools are now becoming available for the detailed specification of its functions, which will require the combined efforts of work in artificial intelligence, empirical psychology and neurophysiology.

E. R. Valentine
Bedford College, University of London

References

Boden, M. (1972), *Purposive Explanation in Psychology*, Cambridge, Mass.

Brentano, F. (1874), *Psychologie vom empirischen Standpunkt*, Leipzig.

Chisholm, R. M. (1967), 'Intentionality', in P. Edwards (ed.), *The Encyclopaedia of Philosophy IV*, New York.

Descartes, R. (1953 [1641]), *Discourse on Method*, trans., London.

Feigl, H. (1958), 'The "mental" and the "physical" ', in H. Feigl *et al.* (eds), *Concepts, Theories and the Mind-Body Problem*, Minneapolis.

Fleming, W. (1858), *The Vocabulary of Philosophy*, London.

Hume, D. (1740), *Treatise of Human Nature*, London.

James, W. (1890), *Principles of Psychology*, New York.

Johnson-Laird, P. N. (1983), *Mental Models*, Cambridge.

Locke, J. (1690), *Essay Concerning Human Understanding*, London.

McDougall, W. (1912), *Psychology; The Study of Behaviour*, London.

McFie, J. (1972), 'Factors in the brain', *Bulletin of the British Psychological Society*, 25.

Mill J. S. (1843), *A System of Logic*, London.

Russell, B. (1921), *The Analysis of Mind*, London.

Ryle, G. (1949), *The Concept of Mind*, London.

Further Reading

Valentine, E. R. (1982), *Conceptual Issues in Psychology*, London.

See also: *artificial intelligence*; *nervous system*; *sensation and perception*; *thinking*.

Mitchell, Wesley Clair (1874–1948)

Wesley Clair Mitchell was a well-known member of the American Institutional School whose reputation was established more in the field of business cycles than institutional economics. He studied at the University of Chicago in the 1890s. His *Business Cycles* (1913) opened the door to an empirical approach that supplemented the work of Thorstein Veblen, his teacher. In the years 1913–29 Mitchell developed a theory of the money economy based upon Veblen's distinction between goods making and money making. After 1929 Mitchell shifted from his concept of a recurring four-phase business cycle to an interpretation of the course of economic events in terms of an irregular economic expansion and contraction, which were greatly influenced by the government's role in economic life. In the 1930s Mitchell turned to indicative democratic national planning as a solution for chronic depression.

Mitchell found the orthodox economics of his time to be too abstract and burdened by an unsatisfactory theory of human nature. His strong empirical bent led him to disagree with much of orthodox economics, but he never proposed to dispense with it entirely. His aim was to improve upon the work of his orthodox predecessors by analysing the economic system as an evolving process, and by drawing attention to the habitual basis of economic activity.

Mitchell never tied together the various elements of his economic analyses in a comprehensive theory of the evolving economic system. Also, he wrote no general treatise on institutional economics, and he failed to lay a foundation for a Columbia University School of Institutional Economics.

Allan G. Gruchy
University of Maryland

Further Reading

Burns, A. F. (ed.) (1952), *Wesley Clair Mitchell, the Economic Scientist*, New York.

Mitchell, W. C. (1927), *Business Cycles: The Problem and Its Setting*, New York.

Mitchell, W. C. (1937), *The Backward Art of Spending Money and Other Essays*, New York.

Moore, G. H. (1978), 'Wesley Mitchell in retrospect', *Journal of Economic Issues*, 12.

Mixed Economy

A purely private right to a resource may be said to exist when an individual can select any use for that resource including the option of sale. This may be contrasted with other specifications of property rights like communal access to roads, state ownership of railways or, indeed, when any privately-owned resource is subject to restrictions in the range of its use. The degree to which purely private rights prevail in an economy would reflect the degree to which an economy is mixed, but a precise measure has yet to be devised.

There are two broad ways of thinking about the mixed economy. One is to ask how and why the public sector has increased its share of property rights. The other way is to ask why the economy should be mixed, and this has been the main focus of debate in the post-war period up to about the late 1960s. It has been a debate partly about aims, but perhaps more about whether certain economic and social aims are better achieved by non-private rights to resources. In this sense, the mixed economy is the outcome of policies consciously espoused by parties, supported by a majority of voters and executed by governments. To understand the post-1945 growth of the public sector, one needs, in this light, firstly to emphasize the effect of the inter-war years of large-scale unemployment. For many people, the low income levels and social tragedies seemed damning evidence of the inefficiencies and injustices of capitalism, to be remedied in part by public ownership of the means of production. Doubts that resources would be efficiently allocated in such a system disappeared for some by the demonstration that public ownership was consistent with the use of a price system (see, for example, Lange, 1936). The efficient allocation of resources which was theoretically obtainable in a perfectly competitive world was obtainable also by public firms adjusting output levels to the point where prices equalled marginal costs, but with the key difference that, with capital publicly owned, profits accrued to the nation rather than to a select few. Similarly, the Keynesian demonstration that unemployment could be an equilibrium feature of capitalism pointed to an enhanced role for the state. While an expansion of private investment would have beneficial effects on income and employment levels comparable to increased public spending, Keynes had stressed the role of pessimistic expectations in preventing a sufficiently low level of interest rates or in inhibiting a business investment expansion independently of interest-rate levels.

In the two decades from 1945, these arguments gradually lost some of their force. Rising living standards in economies where over 60 per cent of GDP still emanated from the private sector, financial losses in public enterprises, waiting-lists for certain public services together with some embryonic doubts, especially by American economists, about whether government deficit manipulation was actually the source of full employment, undermined some of the support for government economic activity. That support was, however, largely sustained, at least intellectually, by several strands of earlier thought receiving increased emphasis. It is clear, for example, that the analysis of public goods has a wider applicability than law, order and defence. In so far as the issue is one of spill-over effects in consumption and production, then, in a world of continuing urbanization, government corrective action for transport congestion, air pollution and safety regulation seemed vital. In a similar technical vein, while public ownership was no longer seen as the best vehicle for improving income distribution, a strand in the early support for such government intervention was to prevent private monopolistic exploitation of economies of scale common in fuel, transport and general infrastructure development. The arguments for public provision of education, health and even housing had never relied solely on the issue of income distribution; rather there were questions about the access to information, to capital markets and to the speed with which the price system could deal

fairly with shortages. Finally, though perhaps least convincingly, the differential growth experience of the post-1945 economies entered the economist's agenda in the 1960s with government again seen as an important catalyst.

There has, however, always been the view that the above is a misconception both of how the private competitive system works and how public ownership works. Private monopoly 'in the field' is quite consistent with competiton for the field so that auction bidding for franchises for refuse collection, electricity supply and such services could eliminate monopoly profits. How, secondly, will private decision takers react to the existence of spill-over effects? If there are net gains to be exploited by public action on the height of chimneys or on river pollution by up-stream firms how can we be sure that private decision takers have not already entered economic dealings to their joint satisfaction? And if the argument is that, especially with large groups, there are transaction costs in private exchange relations, so also are there costs to the government in acquiring information, casting doubt on whether its solution will be any better. More generally, why should the analysis of utility-maximizing behaviour stop at the door of the public sector? Civil servants, public industry managers and politicians are the relevant decision takers. In the Austrian tradition the cost of an activity is the value of the alternative foregone by the decision taker, not by some vague entity like the state. In summary, there is no guarantee on this line of thought that government action will yield a superior solution to the private sector solution with all its warts (see, for example, Demsetz, 1982). Such doubts mounted in the 1970s and 1980s fuelled in part by the increasing growth of government and the part this might have played as the source of monetary expansion in the late 1960s and early 1970s. By the mid 1970s, moreover, Keynesianism as a theoretical framework for analysing unemployment and inflation was under strong attack, precisely because of its deficient analysis of the micro behaviour of agents in the economy.

While such debates on policy have been continually supported by positive studies of how economic systems work, they have not fully confronted the basic question of why the public sector has grown. Indeed, much of the debate has treated the state as an autonomous force, as something separate from the features of the rest of the economy. Doubts about such a characterization should arise when it is recognized that the pre-nineteenth century, early modern European absolutist states had interventionist bureaucracies and armies where the attenuation of private rights, if we could only measure it, might bear comparison to modern state sectors. Many Marxists would certainly want to locate the characterization of the modern state in the capitalist mode of production, in the sense of the state being another form of monopoly capital or a collective form to secure for capitalism what private capital on its own cannot secure – legal system, control of trade unions, and so on. A longer-term view is also developing in other quarters (North, 1982; Olson, 1982). The industrialization which started in the late-eighteenth century meant a rapidly increasing division of labour, thereby enhancing the role of transaction costs and the supply of organized interest groups. The same forces which have advanced the middleman, the white-collar worker and those engaged in banking, accounting, law, insurance, property and trade are also important in prompting the provision of transasction cost reducing services by government, that is, basic transportation, justice, police, fire, defence, postal services, licensing, quality inspection and measurement standards. The attenuation of purely private rights usually requires group or collective action; there are in-built disincentives to such action which, in democracies, take a long time to overcome. It was in the latter part of the nineteenth century that the significant changes became observable. In 1869–1970 the percentage of the US labour force in government grew from 3.5 per cent to 18.1 per cent matching rises from 7.8 per cent to 19.1 per cent in retail trade, 0.4 per cent to 4.0 per cent in finance, insurance and real estate, and ll.1 per cent to 17.4 per cent in other services. It is probably only by a further analysis of such long-run trends that we shall fully understand the mixed economy.

Robert Millward
University of Salford

References

Demsetz, H. (1982), *Economic, Legal and Political Dimensions of Competition*, Amsterdam.
Lange, O. (1936/7), 'On the economic theory of socialism', *Review of Economic Studies*, 4.
North, D. C. and Wallis, J. J. (1982), 'American government expenditures: a historical perspective', *American Economic Association: Papers and Proceedings*.
Olson, M. (1982), *The Rise and Decline of Nations*, New Haven.

Further Reading

Lord Roll of Ipsden (ed.) (1982), *The Mixed Economy*, London.
See also: *crowding out; markets; nationalization; planning, economic; public goods.*

Modernization

In academic development economics and related disciplines, and also in actual public policy on development, the word modernization slips and slides, alludes and obtrudes, both as a key or code term as well as a perfectly ordinary word meaning updating, upgrading renovation, reconstruction or stabilization in the face of adverse social, physical or economic structures. In this ordinary usage, sometimes a particular history, political approach or ideology is intended, sometimes not. Often all that is meant is professionalism, rationalilty, planning or progress in general. Where no particular history or episode of development is taken to be at issue, probably any implied allusion to, say, the Russian Debate about industrialization, or peasant participation in policy, will be sovietized, sanitized, populist perhaps, and certainly depoliticized. Where some particular historical reference *is* intended, such as to congeries of changes which included economic and demographic developments in Western Europe from the sixteenth to the nineteenth centuries, unfortunately there is similarly likely to be much ellipsis and little historiography. As a result, the model matters alluded to tend in this literature to be more misunderstood than understood. For instance, 'industrialization' as in 'Western industrial revolution' will be bandied about as if, for example, English, French and Dutch history in this regard had been the same, as if the Rochdale pioneers in the 'co-operative movement' had not been nonagricultural, not engaged in political protest against a regime from which they felt excluded, not an urban class or class segment with a distinctive religious zeal.

Turning now to its other sense, before modernization as a technical and emotive key or code term or discourse emblem can do for one what it does already for others, some special initiation may be necessary. For example, modernization as a policy remedy for rural or some other backwardness problem may be proposed essentially as an alternative 'paradigm' or option to another policy remedy: self-reliance (understood in a special sense) is the answer for another policy problem, dependency. Modernization theory and dependency theory are constantly pitted in the development studies literature as exclusive and hostile rivals. In development economics since Bretton Woods, this has served indeed as the principal polarization in this literature. Undoubtedly there are some striking contrasts between them with regard, for example, to the consequences for international relations, with each favouring recourse to its own pivotal terms about development problems and solutions. Exponents of modernization will preach dualism, diffusion of innovations, economies of scale, development administration, human resources development, financial and foreign aid. Believers in dependency theory will talk about core and periphery, world-system, unequal exchange, 'small is beautiful', delinking, or adjustment. Yet there are also some equally important, if seldom identified, similarities. Both schools of thought adopt comparable concepts of what one calls traditional, and the other precapitalist society and economy. Both are preoccupied with crises and turning-points and stages of development. Both put a heavy stress on First and Second World determinisms on the Third (and Fourth). Both tend to prefer structuralist analyses and to look for structural change.

Neoclassical economic studies of growth and development say they are or ought to be 'unadulterated by sociological, political and other non-economic variables'. Is modernization neoclassical in the way in which *dependentia* often claim it is (and dependency is not)? Much will depend on the degree to which distinctions are drawn in each as regards dogma and actual practice, and one area or sector compared with another. Lack of stated institutional (as in institutional economics, comparative social institutions, and so on) analysis is not necessarily and equally a matter of implicit default as well, at least to the same extent or form. In modernization (and dependency) theory and practice, some institutional analysis goes – erroneously or otherwise – by omission as well as commission. For instance, nothing could be more institutionalist – and attitudinalist – than modernization's (and again dependency's) ideas of traditional society and economy (and underdevelopment). There is nonetheless much useful truth in the complaint that – in its coded sense – modernization 'crudely foreshortens the historical development of society . . . is a technocratic model of society, conflict-free and politically neutral [which dissolves] genuine social conflict and issues in the abstractions of "the scientific revolution" [and] "productivity" [presuming] that no group in the society will be called upon to bear the costs of the scientific revolution'.

Modernization (like dependency yet again, so really there is very much similarity indeed) tends to self-correct its policies in the light of its disappointments with the actual development record as it unfolds: that is, it self-adjusts within its own shell of epistemological and other assumptions as further challenges present themselves. Thus, unfortunately, the historical perspectives and changes in the development studies are seldom those of the economies and policies to which they say they are addressed. So, and again as with dependency no less, modernization can often be best understood not as a particular development – or development theory or method for the study of development and development theory – but rather as a recurring pattern of perennial speech about such development, theory and method, and would-be practical action. In many development studies and policies this tends to be discourse about solutions which are more likely to be in search of, than for, problems. Whose discourse is this? On the whole this is the perennial speech *of* modernizing élites as well as *about* modernizing élites (neither of which, as most notably in Iran of late, might on empirical investigation turn out in effect to be modernizing). These are the writers and actors who align their own best efforts with state-building, but in the name of nation-building.

Raymond Apthorpe
Institute of Social Studies, The Hague

Further Reading
Adams, A. (1979), 'Open letter to a young researcher', *African Affairs*.
Sunkel, O. (1979), 'The development of development thinking', in J. J. Villamil (ed.), *Transactional Capitalism and National Development*, Hassocks, Sussex.
Wrigley, E. A. (1972), 'The process of modernization and the industrial revolution in England', *Journal of Interdisciplinary History*, I.
See also: *dependency theory; development studies*.

Monetarism

Although there are probably as many varieties of economic doctrine called 'monetarism' as there are economists who call themselves 'monetarist', there is an agreed central postulate: that the money supply is the most important determinant of the level of aggregate money-income.

The development of monetarism, which began in the 1950s with some articles by Milton Friedman and his associates (Friedman, 1956, 1959), can be seen as a reassertion of the importance of money against a simplified form of Keynesian economics which denied money any significant role.

Monetarism's main postulate has its roots in the quantity theory of money. It shares with older quantity theory the belief that the supply of money is determined 'exogenously', that is, independently of the demand for money, even though the bulk of what we now think of as money consists of bank deposits. In an economy with a relatively small international sector like the United States (where monetarism arose), the supply of money is assumed to be determined by the monetary authorities; implicitly their ability to control bank-created money is not questioned.

Changes in this exogenously-determined money supply affect the economy through the behaviour of those who receive the money, codified in a 'demand-for-money function'. Monetarists see the holding of money as an alternative to holding other assets, but since 'other assets' include all consumption and investment goods, a rise in the quantity of money causes prices to rise and stimulates output, thus preserving the link between money and income which is the hallmark of quantity theory. Direct effects of monetary changes on interest rates are treated as unimportant or transitory, though rises in nominal interest rates to cover for inflation (the 'Fisher effect') figure prominently.

Except at full employment, when there is no scope for raising output, it is always an open question how a change in aggregate income is distributed between price changes and altered levels of production and employment. Monetarists explain this distribution in terms of labour's demand for a wage which embodies their expectations of its purchasing power (the 'real wage'): it is only when labour begins to 'catch on' to the fact that economic activity has risen and to expect rising prices that they make higher wage claims; by thus raising costs the balance between price and output changes shifts towards prices. (This is precisely the argument of Hume in 1752.)

Unless the monetary authorities accommodate the increased prices with more money, the wage rise will also tend to offset previous gains in employment. If the authorities *do* accommodate, labour will once again adjust its expectations and an inflationary situation is set up, no more favourable to employment in the end.

The possibility of permanent gains in employment and output by purely monetary means is thus denied. The level of employment to which the economy tends to return through wage and price rises of the kind described is called the 'natural rate of unemployment', although the air of inevitability that the phrase conveys is misleading. The level of unemployment to which it corresponds is determined jointly by producers, workers and the monetary authorities – human agents, not natural forces. The natural rate of unemployment corresponds to an absence of Keynesian involuntary unemployment, bearing in mind that unemployment at the going money wage due to agreement, open or tacit, amongst workers not to work for less is accounted voluntary.

Monetarists are sceptical of government demand-management policies even as a temporary stimulus to employment and output. They argue that the economy is 'financially constrained' (that is, money is exogenous) and that attempts by government to finance expansionary spending programmes by increasing the public debt will push up interest rates and 'crowd out' intended private expenditure similarly based on borrowing. Financing by means of a monetary expansion is admitted to be efficacious as long as prices are not expected to rise, provoking the wage response explained above, and as long as the existing level of unemployment is above the 'natural rate'.

The more quickly expectations adjust, the less likely is any real benefit, in terms of output and employment, from money-financed expansion. Substantial and prolonged monetary expansion results almost entirely in inflation.

Some monetarists believe that expectations adjust very rapidly even without prolonged experience of a particular rate of monetary change, provided the monetary authorities announce their intentions. These monetarists (often called 'New Classical economists') discount both the potential for short-term expansion and the output and employment costs of monetary contraction. They assume that adjustment will fall chiefly on prices and wages.

Under fixed exchange rates the money supply is not under the control of the monetary authorities of open economies. The money supply can be made to adjust to home demand for money through expenditure on imports or may be determined by events abroad. Most monetarists welcomed flexible exchange rates on the grounds that they afforded some insulation of the home economy.

Victoria Chick
University College London

References

Friedman, M. (1956), 'The quantity theory of money – a restatement', in M. Friedman (ed.), *Studies in the Quantity Theory of Money*, Chicago. (Also in Friedman, M. (1969), *The Optimum Quantity of Money and Other Essays*, London.)

Friedman, M. (1959), 'The demand for money: some theoretical and empirical results', *Journal of Political Economy*, 67. (Reprinted in Friedman 1969, cited above.)

Hume, D. (1752), *Of Money*, in E. Rotwein (ed.) (1955), [*David Hume's*] *Writings on Economics*, London.

Further Reading

Laidler, D., Tobin, J., Matthews, R. C. O. and Meade, J. E. (1981), 'Conference: "Monetarism – An Appraisal" ', *Economic Journal*, 91.

Stein, J. L. (ed.) (1976), *Monetarism*, Amsterdam.

See also: *Friedman*; *monetary policy*; *money*; *money, quantity theory of*.

Monetary Policy

Monetary policy can be broadly construed to include virtually all aspects of a country's monetary and financial system, or much more narrowly, taking the institutional background as given. Taking the broader perspective first establishes a rationale for monetary policy.

The central question of monetary policy used to be that of the monetary standard – the choice of the monetary metal and the metallic content of the coinage. The purpose of policy was to establish stability and uniformity of the coinage and thus inspire confidence in it and gain general acceptability for it, to the benefit of sovereign and state.

Although obscured by the enormous institutional changes that have taken place, the maintenance of confidence in money and monetary institutions is still the main purpose of monetary policy. Hence the concern, at various points in history, with the maintenance of convertibility (into gold domestically and gold or a 'key currency' internationally), the prevention of 'over-issue' of credit, the avoidance of financial crises and banking panics, and the stability of the price level.

Though monetary policy in the broadest sense is a government matter, many issues of policy and virtually all responsibility for implementation rest with central banks (for example, the Bank of England, the Federal Reserve System). Since 1946, most Western governments have accepted some responsibility for their country's economic performance, and monetary policy became a tool of 'stabilization policy': the promotion of economic growth without severe recession or inflation. Price stability and a 'healthy' balance of payments remained important as contributions to this end. Until the 1970s it was accepted that the burden of stabilization policy should fall on fiscal policy, monetary policy playing a subordinate role. The interrelation between monetary and fiscal policy is now better appreciated.

The distinctive contribution of monetary policy lies in the influence the central bank can exert on the availability of credit, interest rates and the liquidity of the economy, as measured by the money supply or some broader aggregate. The links between these variables and the broader goals of stabilization policy is complex. There are conflicting theories as to which links are important. Keynesians stress interest rates and the availability of credit, because of their influence on expenditures made with borrowed funds. Monetarists favour a money supply target because they see a strong connection between the money supply and aggregate expenditure (income). Monetarists also favour a 'rule' of stable monetary growth rather than discretionary policy, on the grounds that policy-induced variations in the money supply are a source of instability rather than a contribution to stabilization policy.

The instruments used to influence whatever target is chosen vary from country to country according to the structure of their banking systems and financial markets. In countries with developed markets, central bank purchases and sales of securities ('open market operations') are perhaps the most important instruments. These operations may influence both interest rates and the liquidity, and hence the lending capacity, of banks.

Monetary policy is fraught with conflict. There are potential conflicts between the goals of stabilization policy (for example, domestic expansion and balance-of-payments or exchange rate stability) which monetary policy cannot resolve with the limited instruments at its command. In addition the central bank's responsibility for managing the government debt, given the desire of governments to borrow cheaply, may be inconsistent with its stabilization role. Fundamentally,

however, both of these roles at times conflict with responsibility, once the sole focus of monetary policy, for the stability of the financial structure. Concern for financial stability limits the amount of pressure which may be exerted on the banks or financial markets at any time, and the central bank must stand ready to provide liquidity when the pressure threatens default on commitments. This role, called 'lender of last resort', was urged on central banks by Bagehot (1873) to avert banking panics.

It has come to be realized that Bagehot's principle has much wider application. Pressure on the financial system will raise interest rates as the affected institutions compete for liquid funds. High interst rates have many undesirable features, and they can even rise high enough to contribute further to instability. Thus central banks have to exercise the lender-of-last-resort function more frequently. An expansionary bias is thereby imparted to the system and also derives from the fact that the financial system is not static but is perpetually growing in complexity and sophistication. Attempts to curb the activities of the financial system are a considerable incentive for those involved in it to find ways round the constraints (Minsky, 1957). Monetary policy's stabilization role must be seen as secondary and limited by the need to maintain confidence in the monetary system.

Victoria Chick
University College London

References
Bagehot, W. (1873), *Lombard Street*, London.
Minsky, H. P. (1957), 'Central banking and money market changes', *Quarterly Journal of Economics*, 71. (Reprinted in H. P. Minsky (1952), *Inflation, Recession and Economic Policy*, Brighton.)

Further Reading
Chick, V. (1977), *The Theory of Monetary Policy*, Oxford.
Goodhart, C. A. E. (1975), *Money, Information and Uncertainty*, London.
See also: *banking*; *monetarism*; *money*; *money, quantity theory of*.

Money

Most of the disputes among various schools of thought on the role of money in an economy are due to differing conceptualizations of the functions and properties of money and its relations to the passage of time. Money can only be defined by its essential functions and properties.

In all neoclassical theories (for example, monetarism, general equilibrium theory, neo-Walrasian theory, rational expectations theory, neoclassical synthesis Keynesianism), historical time is treated as if it is irrelevant; all present and future activities are logically determined and paid for at the initial instant. Such theories assume that future events are either known with perfect certainty or known as statistically predictable according to the mathematical laws of probability. Consequently, the sole function of money is as a *numeraire*, that is, a yardstick upon which to measure the relative prices (and therefore scarcities) of the various goods that are produced. In the long run, real output, employment and economic growth are solely determined by the exogenous factors of technology and preferences, in other words, money can not affect long-run real outcomes. Thus while in the short run in neoclassical theory money may have a transient effect on employment, in the long run Say's Law prevails so that supply creates its own demand.

Keynes's revolution against neoclassical theory requires that a monetary economy operate quite differently from a nonmonetary system so that in the short as well as the long run, real output, employment and growth are *not* determined solely (or even mainly) by technology and preferences. For Keynes and post-Keynesians, time is a device that prevents everything from happening at once. Production takes time; and money and forward contracts are human institutions created to organize (efficiently) production processes which will operate over an uncertain (not statistically predictable) future. (A forward contract is one that specifies the future date(s) for delivery and payment.) In such a monetary, contractual economy the concept of money requires two concomitant features, which in turn require two necessary properties.

These features were spelled out at the very beginning of Keynes's *Treatise on Money* (1930) 'Money . . . [is] that by delivery of which debt-contracts and price-contracts are *discharged*, and in the shape of which a store of General Purchasing Power is held', that is, money is (i) *the means of contractual settlement*, and (ii) *a store of value*, a vehicle for moving purchasing power over time – a time machine.

This second feature is known as *liquidity*. Liquidity can be possessed in various degrees by some, but not all, durables. Since any durable besides money can *not* (by definition) settle a contract, then for durables other than money to be a liquidity time machine they must be resaleable in well-organized, orderly spot markets. The degree of liquidity of any durable asset depends on its prompt resaleability in such markets. A fully liquid asset is always resaleable for a fixed quantity of money. A liquid asset is always resaleable, but its exact market price is uncertain. An illiquid asset is not readily resaleable at any money price.

For Keynes (1936) money (and all liquid assets) possess two 'essential properties' which are inexorably tied to money's two features. These properties are: (1) the elasticity of production is zero (or negligible) and (2) the elasticity of substitution is zero (or negligible). The meaning of these elasticity properties is that (1)

'Money [and other liquid assets] do not grow on trees' and hence cannot be harvested by the use of labour in the private sector whenever workers are made idle by a lack of effective demand for all other producible goods; and (2) anything that is easily producible is not a good substitute for money for settling contracts or for use as a liquidity time machine. Consequently, when, in the aggregate, people want to spend some portion of the income they would earn at full employment levels of production on money or other liquid assets, that is, people do not want to commit themselves contractually to buy all the full employment output of industry but instead want to maintain purchasing power to have freedom of future choice while facing an uncertain future, then there will be an insufficient aggregate demand for the full employment output. Firms will not be able to market their full employment production flow profitably, and some workers will be involuntarily unemployed. These unemployed can not be allocated to meeting the public demand for liquidity by being put to work by private entrepreneurs to harvest money from liquidity trees.

In sum, in a world of uncertainty, the existence of a nonproducible money and the fact that goods are priced via contacts 'in terms of money' is highly significant. Of all the various schools of economic thought, only Keynes (and his post-Keynesian followers) possess a conceptualization of money which reflects its role as a store of value in an uncertain world.

Paul Davidson
Rutgers University

References
Keynes, J. M. (1930), *A Treatise on Money*, London.
Keynes, J. M. (1936), *The General Theory of Employment, Interest and Money*, London.

Further Reading
Davidson, P. (1978), *Money and the Real World*, 2nd edn, London.
Friedman, M. (1974), 'A theoretical framework for monetary analysis', in R. J. Gordon (ed.), *Milton Friedman's Monetary Framework: A Debate With His Critics*, Chicago.
Keynes, J. M. (1973), 'A monetary theory of production', in *The Collected Writings of John Maynard Keynes*, XIII, London.
See also: *Keynesian economics; monetarism; money, primitive; money, quantity theory of.*

Money, Primitive

If money is defined in terms of the indefinite circulation of a very large quantity of small, uniform, durable objects for the purpose of maintaining certain recognized social and economic institutions, a number of factors will then distinguish primitive from modern money, even though there is no definitive dividing line between the two. Primitive money *stuff* consists of a range of recognized objects generally with no other use, whose relative *natural* scarcity ensures a stable money *stock*. The range is remarkably narrow, and the cowrie, a small shell found along the shores of the Indian Ocean, has proved to be much the most successful primitive money (Crump, 1981). Primitive money tends to be found in societies in which there is no market in land or labour, where no goods are produced for exchange, and its uses are generally noncommercial, excluding, at least in part, the function of any modern money as a means of exchange. The sphere of payment may be restricted to certain classes, and in one society there may even be different spheres relating to different classes of transaction, each with their own distinctive money stuff, with no possibility of conversion. The Kapauku of New Guinea, however, know no such distinctions, and use shell-money for all possible transactions, commercial and noncommercial. Even in this case, there is no centralized state control over the supply of money such as distinguishes any modern money. Monetary institutions dependent upon any form of bookkeeping, such as modern banking, are perforce absent in primitive systems, although this by no means prevents the widespread use of credit.

Thomas Crump
University of Amsterdam

Reference
Crump, T. (1981), *The Phenomenon of Money*, London.

Further Reading
Dalton, G. (1967), 'Primitive money', in *Tribal and Peasant Economies*, Garden City, New York.
Melitz, J. (1974), *Primitive and Modern Money*, Reading, Mass.
See also: *economic anthropology*; *money*; *trade and markets, anthropology of*.

Money, Quantity Theory of

The quantity theory of money is a rather curious way of referring to the connection between the quantity of money and the general level of prices. The connection was well established by the middle of the seventeenth century: 'It is a common saying that plenty or scarcity of money makes all things dear or good cheap' (Thomas Mun, 1664). A modern version is 'Inflation is too much money chasing too few goods.' In its strongest version, money is not only the cause of price changes but prices are supposed to change in proportion to the monetary change, in the long run.

In the sixteenth and seventeenth centuries discussion of the relation between money and prices could scarcely pass for a *theory*, because there was no articulation of the causal connection. Its status was more that of shrewd observation, the causal role of money made clear by the influx of precious metals from the New World.

The proportionality doctrine was stated by John Locke (1691). His purpose was to refute the mercantilist equation of money with national wealth by showing that money's value varied inversely with its quantity. His reasoning was based on an abstract comparison of the same economy with two different stocks of money (allowing for the velocity of money's circulation). Hume (1752), however, asserted that proportionality applied to ordinary monetary increases and decreases in the long run. It is a plausible enough doctrine in a static, preindustrial society but it is quite unsupported by any reasoning by Hume or anyone since, though it is still widely asserted (as the 'neutrality of money').

Hume's treatment of the short-run effects of monetary changes was, in contrast, good theory – indeed the first *explanation* of the relation between money and prices. (In today's language he explained the 'transmission mechanism'.) An increase of money (from abroad, in exchange for exports) encourages greater output and employment, without, at first, any increase in wages. If workers become scarce, wages will increase (though Hume remarks that the manufacturer will also expect greater productivity). At first, prices of wage-goods are stable and production rises to meet demand. But gradually all prices rise and the situation prior to the monetary increase is restored. This line of reasoning is both congruent with Keynesian export-led growth and similar to the theory put forward by Milton Friedman (1969).

J. S. Mill provides the bridge to modern theory in two ways: he makes clear that the medium-of-exchange function of money is crucial to quantity theory and he deals with nonmetallic, credit money (bank notes, cheques). The older theorists allowed for hoarding, but the advent of credit money, which could not be hoarded in ways which served an alternative purpose, such as plate, simultaneously made hoarding more difficult to justify and gave rise to the possibility that purchases could be made without possessing money (coin).

These problems were new. Irving Fisher (1911) formalized them, but did not solve them, by separating currency from bank-deposit money and postulating a different velocity of circulation for each. It is not obvious which should be the larger, or by how much.

An approach to the hoarding problem is provided by the development, in 'Cambridge quantity theory' (Marshall, 1923), of the concept of a demand for money based chiefly on transactions needs. Expected expenditure levels were indicated by one's income and wealth. It was considered plausible that some money might be held idle (hoarded) if one had so little wealth that lending at interest was not open to one. This would affect the velocity of circulation but probably not substantially.

Friedman (1956), though beginning from the antithetical proposition that money is an asset to be held, contrives in the end to arrive at a similar formulation. It is implied that an exogenous change in money will affect aggregate money-income, but the division between price and quantity in the long run is no more resolved than it was in Hume's time and in the short run somewhat less resolved.

Keynes, although originally an adherent of the quantity theory (1923), broke with it in 1936 by providing a rationale for substantial hoarding of money when interest rates were expected to rise.

The problem of credit raised by Mill is not amenable to analysis in the demand-for-money framework and remains an unresolved part of monetary theory generally.

Victoria Chick
University College London

References
Fisher, I. (1911), *The Purchasing Power of Money*, New York.
Friedman, M. (1956), 'The quantity theory of money – a restatement', in M. Friedman (ed.), *Studies in the Quantity Theory of Money*, Chicago.
Friedman, M. (1969), 'The role of monetary policy', *American Economic Review*, 58.
Hume, D. (1955 [1752]), *Of Money*, in E. Rotwein (ed.), [*David Hume's*] *Writings on Economics*, London.
Keynes, J. M. (1923), *A Tract on Monetary Reform*, London.
Keynes, J. M. (1936), *The General Theory of Employment, Interest and Money*, London.
Locke, J. (1823 [1691]), *Some Considerations of the Lowering of Interest and Raising the Value of Money*, *Works of John Locke*, Vol. V, London.
Marshall, A. (1923), *Money, Credit and Commerce*, London.
Mill, J. S. (1857), *Principles of Political Economy*, 2 Vols, London.
Mun, T. (1928 [1664]), *England's Treasure by Foreign Trade*, Oxford.

Further Reading
Blaug, M. (1978), *Economic Theory in Retrospect*, 3rd edn, London.
See also: *Friedman*; *monetarism*; *money*.

Monopoly

Monopoly in the strictest sense refers to a market where there is only one seller facing a multitude of buyers. Monopoly always attracted the attention of economists, being the exact opposite of the market form which they regarded as normal in capitalist societies: full competition. In competition, with many sellers in the market, each firm has to accept the going price and will try to produce at low costs as far as possible. Output will tend to be high and prices low. The monopolist can influence the price by keeping supplies short. Monopoly, therefore, leads to lower output, higher prices, and higher profits. The exact analysis of this strategy was provided by the French nineteenth-century economist Antoine Augustin Cournot.

Monopoly and full competition are two extreme cases. They are rarely found in pure form in the real world. Pure monopoly is hardly possible, because substitute commodities will exert competitive pressures on monopolists. Alfred Marshall recognized in the nineteenth century that in reality we normally find various mixtures of monopoly and competition. This was incorporated into economic theory in the 1930s through the work on 'monopolistic competition' by E. H. Chamberlin and Joan Robinson.

'Normative' economics has usually condemned monopoly because it leads to an inefficient allocation of resources. Some economists have pointed to possible dynamic advantages of monopoly. In J. A. Schumpeter's theory, adventurous entrepreneurs can establish temporary monopolies by creating new products, and this is seen as the source of economic progress. Also, large-sized firms with safe monopolistic profits may be more research-oriented. Against this has to be set the room for inaction and inefficiency (through lack of competitive pressure). Empirical work on these questions has not led to definite results.

Kurt W. Rothschild
Johannes Kepler University, Linz

Further Reading
Hunter, A. (1969), *Monopoly and Competition. Selected Readings*, Harmondsworth.
Machlup, F. (1952/67), *The Political Economy of Monopoly*, Baltimore.
See also: *cartels and trade associations*; *competition*; *markets*; *oligopoly*.

Montaigne, Michel de (1533–92)

Michel de Montaigne, an independent French thinker on moral and psychological matters and author of *Les Essais* (1580–92), was, until 1571, a minor magistrate in Périgueux near Bordeaux: in that year he retired from public life (although he was still to serve two terms of office as Mayor of Bordeaux, and take an active part in internal diplomatic negotiations during the Religious Wars), and devoted himself to private study. Initially he concentrated on ancient moral philosophy and history, but increasingly was attracted to the study of himself in a way strongly influenced by sceptical doctrines. It is for this self-study and for its political, religious and philosophical consequences that he is best known.

A firm opponent of systematic thought (and especially the still dominant neo-Scholasticism of his day), Montaigne set out to evolve a mode of acquiring knowledge about himself and about the world through an attentive form of introspection and self-examination. This led him to formulate a number of audacious propositions about politics and human psychology: political action, like human action, is seen by him to be a product of chance as well as design; vice and virtue are necessary components in both individuals and in the state (it is significant that Montaigne was one of the few sixteenth-century writers to recognize the acumen of Machiavelli); justice is conventional, not absolute; indeed, as the world consists in mutable beings set in a mutable environment, absolute principles can have no status in human affairs. This thoroughgoing relativism is combined at important points in the *Essais* (notably II,12) with quietism; Montaigne does not himself realize the subversive potential of his own thought, but remains throughout a political conservative and a strong proponent of Roman Catholicism.

Especially in Book III and in late additions to the *Essais*, Montaigne elaborates this relativistic and sceptical stance. Man is conceived of as an individual whose being (*'forme maîtresse'*) is never static and can only be perceived intuitively by others; but all men share the same rational and corporeal nature. A knowledge of one's corporeality is fundamental to self-understanding, and can also provide a means to the understanding of others. The body's functions and states are thus a matter of constant and uninhibited enquiry. Man exists in a world of conventions (*'coutumes'*), to which he attributes a moral or natural character which they do not intrinsically possess; these conventions can be transformed into dogma and lead to repression and tyranny. In two famous chapters of the *Essais* (I,31 and III,6) Montaigne draws attention to the treatment of the Amerindians by the Spaniards as an example of unjustifiable repression in the name of religion. Thus, for both negative and positive reasons, Montaigne comes to stress the need for tolerance in a new version of humanism which transcends education, class, nation and race.

The *Essais* are famous also for their unconstrained form and vigorous style. Montaigne's use of metaphor and free association as an antidote to formal rhetoric and systematic philosophy has left its mark on a number of subsequent thinkers (notably Diderot and Nietzsche); but his relativism, scepticism and project of self-study have also influenced later writers such as Descartes, Pascal and Rousseau.

Ian Maclean
The Queen's College, Oxford

Further Reading
Friedrich, H. (1967), *Montaigne*, 2nd edn, Berne.
Sayce, R. A. (1972), *The Essays of Montaigne. A Critical Exploration*, London.
Starobinski, J. (1982), *Montaigne en mouvement*, Paris.

Montesquieu, Charles Louis de Secondat (1689–1755)

Charles Louis de Secondat, Baron de Montesquieu was one of the major precursors of sociological thought. Born at La Brede near Bordeaux, he inherited the family vineyard estates and was able to use his wealth and training as a lawyer to travel widely both in France and abroad, and to ingratiate himself with the influential Parisian intellectual society of the first half of the eighteenth century. He became a major figure of Enlightenment thought and a perceptive critic of the society of the time.

His major works, the *Lettres Persanes* (1721), the *Considérations sur les causes de la grandeur des Romains et de leur décadence (1734) and the De l'esprit des lois* (1748) ostensibly deal with very different topics, but beneath the surface these can be shown to have a seriousness of purpose and concatenation of subject matter not easily detected. The *Lettres Persanes*, a novel about two Persian princes visiting Paris in the early years of the eighteenth century are, on closer examination, also a critical investigation into the major institutions of *ancien régime* society. The *Considérations*, a study which foreshadows Gibbons's *Decline and Fall of the Roman Empire*, is important in the history of ideas for its revolutionary historical methodology – *histoire raisonnée*, as it was called – making use of an embryonic ideal-type construct.

His third work, and by far his most important, the *De l'esprit des lois* is best known for its contribution to political thought. It continues the critique first developed in the *Lettres Persanes* of the social structure of the *ancien régime*: Montesquieu makes a powerful case for strengthening the role of the nobility and commercial interests as 'intermediate powers' between the absolutist monarchy and the mass of the people. Together with the argument for a 'separation of powers' which Montesquieu adapted from the British constitution, this provided a formula which, if it had been heeded, might have helped save France from the cataclysm that was to occur later in the century.

However, there has been perhaps too great an emphasis on the political aspects of the *Esprit*. Montesquieu, in the Preface to the work, asks the reader to 'approve or condemn the work as a whole', and if one reads beyond the introductory chapters, one finds a wealth of comparative data on all the major institutions of society – economic, belief and value systems, family and kinship systems – with evidence drawn both from his and others' researches on a wide range of societies, plus considerable historical and anthropological material. In this sense, it is true to say that the *De l'esprit des lois* is the first major essay in comparative sociology. Montesquieu brought to the fore the idea that each society, each social system, has its own natural law of development, and it follows that the objective of every student of society is to discover the real nature of that law. By viewing society as a set of interrelated elements, Montesquieu was putting forward an holistic interpretation of social structure akin to contemporary functionalism.

Functionalism is essentially a conservative doctrine, and Montesquieu is remembered as a founder of the conservative tradition in sociological thought. Through the works of Ferguson and Robertson, Bonald and de Maistre, Fustel de Coulanges and Durkheim, his ideas have passed into the mainstream of sociological thought.

John Alan Baum
Middlesex Polytechnic

Further Reading
Baum, J. A. (1979), *Montesquieu and Social Theory*, Oxford.
Shackleton, R. (1961), *Montesquieu: A Critical Biography*, Oxford.

Moral Development

While the psychological study of morality has been explored from a variety of perspectives, the term moral development has predominantly been associated with the cognitive-developmental (structural) approach of Jean Piaget and Lawrence Kohlberg. This approach describes the universal development of an invariant sequence of cognitive structures of understanding. These structures represent increasingly adequate and veridical ways of conceptualizing and adapting to the moral world.

Piaget's (1932) pioneering work, *The Moral Judgment of the Child*, was the impetus for Kohlberg's subsequent work which today serves as the focus of moral development research and theory. Piaget described a number of transitions in childhood representing the development of moral judgement, for example, a shift from an objective, or consequence-based, sense of responsibility and punishment to a subjective, or intention-based, conception. Understanding of rules was described as shifting from a sense of indelible, authority-generated phenomena to consensually-created and changeable phenomena. Piaget, however, did not claim to have identified true structures of moral thinking and did not pursue morality as a topic of study any further.

Kohlberg completed his dissertation in 1958 and for the next twenty-five years refined and expanded a synthesis of psychology, philosophy, education, sociology and theology that attracted a large following of supporters and critics who spawned a wealth of both theoretical and empirical studies of moral development. Kohlberg defines morality as justice and respect for intrinsic human rights, influenced largely by the thinking of Piaget, Dewey, Kant, Socrates and Rawls. He describes six stages of the development of thinking about morality. These stages span from childhood to adulthood. The first two stages determine the morally right by instrumental calculations of the benefits and losses for the individual. Right is what leads to personally valued consequences. The next two stages shift from the focus on consequences to the individual to consequences to members of the social unit. Here right and wrong are determined by conformity to social expectations, consequences to members of the social unit, and maintenance of the social unit. The last two stages shift from a within-system perspective to a prior-to-the-system perspective where right is determined by social contracts, inherent human rights, and universal principles of morality and justice.

Kohlberg has developed a system for assessing moral stages. Research has demonstrated the validity of the cognitive-developmental model of moral development as well as the relationship of the scheme to a broad variety of psychological phenomena such as values, behaviour, personality, and logical, social, religious and political thinking.

Many of Kohlberg's students and colleagues have expanded the model. William Damon has explored stages of early childhood moral development. James Rest (1983) has placed the stage scheme in a broader model of human morality. Others have drawn parallels from Kohlberg's model to other aspects of development.

Kohlberg and others have also demonstrated the (limited) malleability of moral development through education and laboratory interventions. Moral education programmes using techniques such as peer discussion and institutional governance manipulations have demonstrated positive effects from early childhood to adult professional life.

Marvin W. Berkowitz
Marquette University

References
Piaget, J. (1932), *The Moral Judgment of the Child*, London.
Rest, J. R. (1983), 'Morality', in J. H. Flavell and E. M. Markham (eds), *Carmichael's Manual of Child Development: Cognitive Development*, 4th edn, New York.

Further Reading
Colby, A., Kohlberg, L., Gibbs, J. C. and Lieberman, M. (1983), 'A longitudinal study of moral judgment', *Monographs of the Society for Research in Child Development*, 48.

Kohlberg, L. (1981), *Essays on Moral Development. Volume 1. The Philosophy of Moral Development*, New York.

Morbidity

Morbidity is illness or lack of good physical or mental health. Some researchers distinguish 'illness' (the perceived lack of health) from 'sickness' (the behaviour associated with illness), and the 'disease' (the objectively or medically observable condition). This approach stresses the cultural element in the definition of health and the social implications of ill-health.

Parsons has emphasized the sick person's role in society and related this to the social definition of illness. He points out that often the sick person is exempted from some normal responsibilities, is eligible for special considerations such as being taken care of, and is under an obligation to seek technically competent help in trying to 'get well' (Parsons, 1951).

In the United States and Europe, measurement of morbidity is often based on such measures as perceived health, lost days of work or school, bed days, physician visits and disabilities. Although data on these matters do not solve the problem of reliance on a social definition of illness, they do provide a reasonable basis for health planning. In 1981 the US National Health Interview Survey estimated that the incidence of acute conditions was 212 per 1000 population which was associated with 959 days of restricted activity (National Center for Health Statistics, 1982). This survey and most similar surveys in European populations show that although women have substantially lower mortality than men, they report more episodes of illness and more days of restricted activity. In the 1981 survey, women reported 11 per cent more acute conditions and 21 per cent more days of restricted activity for causes not related to reproduction. This difference raises many questions about self-definition of health and the social element in the definition of health. Efforts to distinguish social from biological differences are hampered by weaknesses in both the social and the biological models of disease (Waldron, 1983).

In developing countries, recent social research has focused on the treatment of illness in children and the aetiology of child malnutrition. This involves research on breast-feeding and weaning practices, feeding during illness, sanitary practices, use of modern medical facilities, and the kinds of illnesses treated and the mode of treatment used by traditional healers. This research has direct implications for the design of health education programmes aimed at changing child-care practices.

Douglas Ewbank
University of Pennsylvania

References
National Center for Health Statistics (1982), *Current Estimates from the National Health Interview Survey: United States, 1981*, Series 10, No. 141, Washington.
Parsons, T. (1951), *The Social System*, Glencoe, Ill.
Waldron, I. (1983), 'Sex differences in illness incidence, prognosis and mortality: issues and evidence', *Social Science Medicine*, 17.

Further Reading
Schwartz, H. D. and Kart, C. S. (1978), *Dominant Issues in Medical Sociology*, Reading, Mass.
Fuchs, V. R. (ed.) (1982), *Economics Aspects of Health*, Chicago.
See also: *epidemiology*; *medical sociology*; *public health*.

Morgan, Lewis Henry (1818–81)

Morgan's reputation rested, in his day, on his contributions to American ethnography. After his death, his conjectural history of the evolution of the family was adopted – and vulgarized – by Engels. In this form it later became part of communist historical dogma.

As a lawyer in upstate New York. Morgan became interested in local Iroquois communities, and he published a useful account of Iroquois culture. The unfamiliar form of Iroquois kinship classification caught his attention, and when he discovered similar systems of classification among Indian tribes speaking different languages, he initiated a broader study, which grew into a world-wide comparison.

Morgan's initial interest in the origin of the Indian groups also gradually gave way to a concern with the development of civil institutions. He came to the conclusion that all kinship systems could be divided into two basic types – those based on monogamous marriage and the family, with appropriate 'descriptive' kinship terminologies; and those based on some form of 'group marriage', with appropriate 'classificatory' terminologies, in which members of the nuclear family were, logically enough, not distinguished from other kin. He developed a 'conjectural history' to account for this development from original promiscuity to modern monogamy. The underlying progressive impulse was, in his view, of a moral nature. This argument was developed at great length and with a wealth of illustrations in his *Systems of Consanguinity and Affinity of the Human Family* (1871).

At this stage Morgan came under the influence of the British school of anthropology, which was concerned especially with the development of political institutions from an original condition of kin-based anarchy to the modern state. In *Ancient Society* (1877) Morgan proposed a series of developments from the one pole to the other, which he linked to his conjectures on the evolution of the family. His notion of progress remained fundamentally moral and idealistic, and, *pace* Engels, he did not greatly emphasize property relations, though (like the writers of the Scottish Enlightenment, from whom he took so much) he believed that the final emergence of private property precipitated the move to a civilized culture, complete with monogamous marriage, the family, and a state organization. His historical conjectures were without foundation, but he collected valuable ethnographic materials, and greatly stimulated research on kinship systems.

Adam Kuper
Brunel University, Uxbridge

Mortality

While individuals are born and die only once, populations experience a series of births and deaths of individuals. Social scientists study the rate of mortality, the social and economic determinants of mortality rates, and the ways in which societies deal with the death of an individual.

Mortality in a population is measured by the Crude Death Rate (the number of deaths per year per thousand population), age-specific death rates (annual deaths per thousand population in a specific age group), and the expectation of life at birth (life expectancy). The latter is defined as the average age at death for a group of newborns if the current age-specific mortality rates do not change during their lifetime.

Substantial mortality declines during the past 150 years in European populations and the more recent declines in non-European populations have been caused by other social and economic changes taking place in those populations. The mortality declines have in turn encouraged changes in social structures. For example, declines in mortality imply reduced rates of widowhood and orphanhood and increases in the proportion of families with three living generations. In societies in which widowhood and orphanhood are frequent, there are generally strong social mechanisms for ensuring the welfare of widows and orphans. These often include rapid remarriage of widows, a sharing of the financial responsibility for children among the father's or the mother's brothers, and other risk-sharing practices. In more modern societies with low mortality, these mechanisms become less important. In modern societies the support of elderly parents during a potentially long period of ill-health and low economic productivity is a more significant problem.

The age distribution of dying persons is also important. In a typical developing country with a life expectancy of about 50 years and relatively high fertility, 15 per cent of the population and 40 per cent of the deaths are under age 5. In the United States in 1980 with a life expectancy of 73.6 years and low fertility, only 7 per cent of the population and 3 per cent of the deaths are under age 5. Most deaths in the United States are over age 75 (44 per cent) while only

ll per cent of the deaths in a typical developing country are to persons in this age group. This distribution has implications for cultural attitudes towards death. For example, common customs relating to the naming of children only after they have survived several days may be related to the high frequency of infant and child death.

In most societies mortality rates vary with indicators of social status such as education, income and occupation. These differences are related to differences in nutrition, housing, access to and use of health services, and such behavioural differences as child feeding practices, smoking and alcohol consumption (United Nations, 1982; Kitagawa and Hauser, 1973).

Douglas Ewbank
University of Pennsylvania

References
United Nations (1982), *Levels and Trends of Mortality Since 1950*, Department of International Economic and Social Affairs (ST/ESA/SER.S/74), New York.
Kitagawa, E. M. and Hauser, P. M. (1973), *Differential Mortality in the United States*: *A Study of Socioeconomic Epidemiology*, Cambridge, Mass.
See also: *death*; *demographic transition*; *epidemiology*; *morbidity*.

Mosca, Gaetano (1858–1941)

Gaetano Mosca, the founding father of Italian political science, was born in 1858 in Palermo, Sicily where he graduated in law in 1881. He met with difficulties in his academic career and for ten years was editor of the proceedings of the Chamber of Deputies in Rome. Eventually, in 1896, he became professor of constitutional law at the University of Turin, and in 1923 he was appointed to the chair of political institutions and doctrines in Rome. Mosca also took an active part in political life: between 1908 and 1919 he was a conservative member of the Chamber of Deputies. From 1914 to 1916 he served as under-secretary for the colonies, and in 1919 he became a Senator of the Kingdom. Already in his first work (*Teorica dei governi e governo parlamentare*, 1884), Mosca, while strongly criticizing the Italian parliamentary system, exposed the myth of democracy and democratic institutions and put forward his rather sombre vision of the process of government. These themes were expanded and elaborated in his major work, the *Elementi di scienza politica* (English translation, *The Ruling Class*, New York, 1939), first published in 1896. In this book he systematically worked out his well-known theory of the ruling class, thus anticipating Pareto's similar (but not identical) theory of élites and their circulation developed a few years later; and influencing Michels's thinking on political parties. According to the theory, in every political regime the rulers are always an organized minority who are able, thanks to the close links among its members, to dominate the unorganized majority. Furthermore, the ruling class tries to justify and legitimate its power on the basis of abstract, moral and legal, principles, the so-called 'political formula', which must be consonant with the values of the community that is governed. In Mosca's view, the theory of the ruling class was intended to make the analysis and classification of political regimes less formalistic, more rigorous and, above all, empirically-grounded, since it based them on the characteristics of such a ruling class, the way it formed and changed.

Luisa Leonini
University of Milan

Further Reading

Meisel, J. H. (1962), *The Myth of the Ruling Class*: *Gaetano Mosca and the Elite*, Ann Arbor.
Sola, G. (1982), 'Introduzione', in G. Mosca, *Scritti politici*, Turin.

Motivation

Motivation, as the word implies, is what *moves* people. If most of psychology deals with 'How' questions, like 'How do people perceive?' or 'How do people learn habits?' the field of motivation is concerned with more fundamental 'Why?' questions. The most basic of these include: 'Why does the organism behave at all?'; 'Why does this behaviour lead in one direction rather than another at a particular time?'; and 'Why does the intensity or persistence of the behaviour vary at different times?'

The main types of answers which have been given to these sorts of questions in the last hundred years or so can be listed roughly chronologically in terms of when they were first proposed. Although each approach was developed to some extent in reaction to what went before, and was seen by its adherents as superior in some respect to its predecessors, proponents of all these approaches will be found in one form or another in present-day psychology.

(1) The earliest approach was that of *hedonism*, which said simply that people behave in such a way as to maximize pleasure and minimize pain. From this perspective man was seen as being an essentially rational being, making sensible decisions about what courses of action to take in the light of their likely consequences in relation to pleasure or pain.

(2) The development of *psychoanalysis* from the turn of the century onwards marked a break with this 'commonsense' view. Freud argued that man is irrational and that his behaviour is largely determined by the outcome of the continual struggle between the powerful unconscious urges of the id (especially the

sexual drive, or eros) and the individual's conscience, or super-ego, representing the dictates of society (see especially, Freud, 1933). Every subsequent form of depth psychology has had at least this in common with Freud's original version: that man is seen as being to some extent at the mercy of psychological forces which are outside his conscious control, and that he is usually unaware of the real reasons for his actions.

(3) *Instinct* theorists, like William McDougall (1908), also emphasized the nonrational side of human nature, bringing out the continuity between animal and human motivation, and answering the 'Why' questions in the context of Darwinian biology. This general approach has been adopted again more recently by ethologists like Tinbergen (1951), although the research techniques and interests of ethologists are remote from those of McDougall.

(4) As laboratory experimental work with animals came to dominate psychology, so another motivational concept began to hold sway: that of *drive*. This concept was introduced by Woodworth (1918) to describe the strength of internal forces which impel the organism into action. The main advantage of this concept was that drive could be defined operationally, for example by the number of hours of food deprivation; in this way motivation could be quantified and made more amenable to rigorous scientific investigation. There was broad agreement that such biological drives existed as a hunger drive, a thirst drive and a sexual drive, and later some theorists added various social drives and even such drives an an exploratory drive. The use of the concept probably reached its high point in the elaborate learning theory of Clark Hull (1943), one of the basic ideas of which was that the aim of all behaviour is 'drive-reduction', this being 'reinforcing' to the organism.

(5) A major problem with the notion of drive-reduction was that the organism, especially the human organism, often seems to be engaged in attempts to increase its stimulation and to present itself with challenges, rather than always to maintain drive at as low a level as possible. This problem was overcome with *optimal arousal theory*, originally proposed by Hebb (1955), which suggested that the organism is seeking to attain, and maintain, some level of arousal which is intermediate on the arousal dimension. Thus, the organism is provoked into action not just when arousal is too high but also when it is too low (the latter being experienced, for example, by feelings of boredom). A further advantage of this theory was that the arousal concept provided a way of linking psychological and physiological research.

(6) A completely different approach to motivation was taken by Maslow (1954), with his notion of *self-actualization*, a concept which has subsequently become one of the mainstays of humanistic psychology. The general idea is that people have a fundamental need

to grow psychologically in such a way that they become fully individual and fulfil their own potentials. According to Maslow there is a need hierarchy which ascends from physiological and safety needs, up through the need to belong and love and the need for self-esteem, to the highest level which is that of self-actualization itself. Living involves a kind of snakes-and-ladders course up and down this hierarchy, but the aim is always to reach the top, success in which is marked by so-called 'peak experiences'.

(7) A recent theory, known as 'reversal theory' (Apter, 1982), makes a radical challenge to the basic assumption on which all the other theories of motivation are based: namely, that of homeostasis (in its broadest systems-theory sense). This implies that there is some single preferred state which the organism attempts at all times to achieve, and to maintain once achieved. This may be, for example, low drive, intermediate arousal or the top of a need hierarchy. However it is defined, it remains a relatively unchanging end-point for the organism to strive towards. Reversal theory argues that this is an absurd oversimplification and that, at least in the human case, people want quite contrary things at different times and are in this respect inherently inconsistent. To give just one example, sometimes people want extremely low arousal (for example, when very tired), and at other times they want extremely high arousal (such as during sexual intercourse, or while watching sport). The end-point, therefore, is dynamic rather than static, and the overall situation is better characterized as one of multistability than homeostasis.

Michael J. Apter
University College Cardiff

References
Apter, M. J. (1982), *The Experience of Motivation: The Theory of Psychological Reversals*, London.
Freud, S. (1933), *New Introductory Lectures on Psychoanalysis*, New York.
Hebb, D. O. (1955), 'Drives and the C.N.S. (Conceptual Nervous System)', *Psychological Review*, 62.
Hull, C. L. (1943), *Principles of Behavior*, New York.
Maslow, A. H. (1954), *Motivation and Personality*, New York.
McDougall, W. (1908), *An Introduction to Social Psychology*, London.
Tinbergen, N. (1951), *The Study of Instinct*, London.
Woodworth, R. S. (1918), *Dynamic Psychology*, New York.

Further Reading
Franken, R. E. (1982), *Human Motivation*, Monterey, Calif.

Jung, J. (1978), *Understanding Human Motivation: A Cognitive Approach*, New York.
See also: *instinct*; *learning*; *psychoanalysis*.

Multinational Enterprises

A multinational enterprise owns and controls productive activities located in more than one country. It owns the outputs of these activities even though it may not own the assets used – these may be hired locally in each country. The multinational does not necessarily transfer capital abroad: finance can often be obtained locally as well. The multinational is thus first and foremost an *international producer*, and only secondarily a *foreign investor*.

The activities of the multinational enterprise form an integrated system; they are not usually a mere portfolio of unrelated operations. The rationale for integration is that managerial control within the enterprise co-ordinates the activities more profitably than would arm's length contractual relations (Buckley and Casson, 1976).

The antecedents of the modern multinational enterprise are found in the late nineteenth century, in British direct investments in the colonies, and in the merger movement in the US from which the modern corporation evolved. In the interwar period, multinational operations focused upon backward integration into minerals (especially oil). Horizontal integration was effected through international cartels rather than multinational firms. After World War II, many US enterprises began to produce in Western Europe, particularly in high-technology industries producing differentiated products. They transferred to Europe new US technology, together with improved management and accounting practices, and the experience of selling to a multicultural market of the kind that was developing within the European Community. In the 1970s European firms began to produce in the US on a larger scale than before, often in the same industries in which US firms were producing in Europe. At the same time, Japanese firms began to produce abroad on a large scale in low-wage South-East Asian countries, particularly in low-technology industries such as textiles.

The value added by some of the world's largest multinationals now exceeds the gross national products of some of the smaller countries in which they produce. On the other hand, there are increasing numbers of very small multinational firms: not all multinationals conform to the popular image of the giant corporation.

Multinational operations provide firms with a number of benefits in addition to the operating economies afforded by integration. Intermediate products transferred between the parent company and its overseas subsidiaries – or between one subsidiary and another – can be valued at 'transfer prices' which differ from those prevailing in arm's length trade. The transfer prices can be set so as to minimize *ad valorem* tariff payments, to reallocate profits to subsidiaries in low-tax countries, and to allow the enterprise to bypass exchange controls by disguising capital transfers as income. Transfer prices are particularly difficult for fiscal authorities to detect when the resources transferred are inherently difficult to value: this is particularly true of payments for technology and management services which are very common in firms in high-technology industries. Reliable evidence on transfer pricing is difficult to obtain, though there are some proven instances of it.

Multinational operations also give the enterprise access to privileged information through membership of producers' associations in different countries, and enable it to co-ordinate internationally the lobbying of government for favourable changes in the regulatory environment. Multinationals are often accused of enlisting the support of powerful governments in the pursuit of their interests in foreign countries, though once again reliable evidence is difficult to obtain. The United Nations actively monitors the behaviour of multinationals through its Centre on Transnational Corporations.

Mark Casson
University of Reading

Reference
Buckley, P. J. and Casson, M. C. (1976), *The Future of the Multinational Enterprise*, London.

Further Reading
Caves, R. E. (1982), *Multinational Enterprise and Economic Analysis*, Cambridge.
Dunning, J. H. and Pearce, R. D. (1981), *The World's Largest Industrial Enterprises*, Farnborough, Hants.
Stopford, J. M., Dunning, J. H. and Haberich, K. O. (1980), *The World Directory of Multinational Enterprises*, London.
See also: *business concentration*; *cartels and trade associations*; *international trade*.

Multiplier

A multiplier is a coefficient which relates the change brought about in one variable, considered endogenous, to the change in another variable considered determinant. A large number of multipliers have been defined in modern economics: the bank credit multiplier, which relates the change in total bank deposits to a change in the high-powered money base; the export multiplier, which relates a change in equilibrium real income to a change in exports; and so on. The term was originally used by Richard Kahn and John Maynard Keynes to refer to the coefficients relating ultimate employment and equilibrium real income to an exogenous change in primary employment in the investment goods industries or investment demand respectively.

The concept of the investment multiplier can easily be illustrated:
Given a consumption function:

$$C = a + by \dots 1$$

Where C = aggregate consumption
a = autonomous consumption i.e. consumption that is independent of income
b = the marginal propensity to consume (mpc)
y = income

and an investment function:

$$I_p = \bar{I} \dots\dots 2$$

Where I_p = planned investment
$\bar{I}$ = exogenously determined investment

and characterizing equilibrium by the realization of all plans, then in equilibrium planned savings must equal planned investment

i.e. $S_p = I_p \dots\dots 3$
or $Y = C_p + I_p \dots\dots 4$

substituting 1 and 2 into 4 and solving for Y

$$Y = a + b_y + \bar{I}$$
$$Y(1 - b) = a + \bar{I}$$
$$Y = [a + I] \times \frac{1}{1-b}$$

The expression in square brackets is all spending which is independent of income, and equilibrium income is the product of this expression and a second term: $\frac{1}{1-b}$ i.e. $\frac{1}{1-mpc}$. As the marginal propensity to consume is assumed a positive fraction the value of the whole expression exceeds unity, and as the mpc and the marginal propensity to save, mps, must, by definition, sum to one the expression can be rewritten as $\frac{1}{mps}$.

Now consider an increase in exogenously given investment, ΔI_p. Denote the derived change in equilibrium income by Δy. We define $\frac{\Delta Y}{\Delta I_p}$ as the multiplier.

Using equation 5. for the initial equilibrium income now called y_0:

$$y_0 = [a + I]\frac{1}{1-b} \dots\dots\dots 5a$$

If $\bar{I}$ increases by $\Delta\bar{I}$ the new equilibrium, y_1, is given by

$$y_1 = [a + I + \Delta I]\frac{1}{1-b} \dots\dots 6$$

so that $\Delta y = y_1 - y_0 = \Delta I \frac{1}{1-b}$ 7

and $\frac{\Delta y}{\Delta I} = \frac{1}{1-b}$ 8

Thus $\frac{1}{1-mpc}$ is the multiplier. As it exceeds unity and change in investment spending (or indeed in autonomous spending of any kind in the current simple model) has an amplified or '*multiplier*' effect. To give this algebra an intuitive interpretation, consider the effects of the rise in investment: incomes will be created for the producers of the investment goods who in turn will allocate this incremental income according to their propensities to consume and save, hence generating new income for yet other groups who produce the goods and services purchased. This interpretation of the multiplier emphasizes the underlying practical proposition that one person's expenditure constitutes another person's income and that a change in exogenous spending will precipitate a cycle of income creation and expenditure. Given the marginal propensity to consume b, we know consumer demand at each round of income creation and therefore the income which is passed on:

Summing up we obtain an estimate of ΔY thus:
$\Delta y = \Delta I_p + b \Delta I_p + b^2 \Delta I_p + b^3 \Delta I_p \ldots + b^n \Delta I_p$.
The sum of such an expansion, that is, Δy, is given by $\Delta I_p \times 1-b^{n+1}/1-b$ which in the limit becomes $\Delta I_p \cdot \times 1/1-b$ which confirms our earlier result.

It now becomes clear that the restoration of equilibrium requires that the new income level be large enough that, given the savings propensity, just enough new savings will be forthcoming so that the equilibrium condition $\Delta S_p = \Delta I_p$ is satisfied.

The underlying rationale of a multiplier relationship, although worked out here in a specific context, is readily generalized to the other cases identified above.

Jane Humphries
University of Cambridge

References
Kahn, R. F. (1931), 'The relation of home investment to unemployment', *Economic Journal*, June.
Keynes, J. M. (1964 [1936]), *The General Theory of Employment*, London.

Multivariate Analysis

(1) Multivariate analysis (MVA) is defined here as the analysis of data collected in a matrix with n rows and m columns, in such a way that columns refer to m variables, whereas rows refer to the objects measured. For example, the columns might stand for economic variables (GNP, export/import trade balance, percentage unemployed, and so on) and the row for different countries for which the economic measurements have been collected.

MVA may serve many purposes, the most general of which is to obtain *clarification* of the data, usually in the form of *data reduction*. More specific purposes are the analysis of *dependence* (whether variance of some variables can be 'explained' by co-variance with other variables), and *classification* of objects into subgroups.

(2) The simplest example of dependence analysis is *multiple regression* where the variance of a single variable y is related to that of a number of variables $x_1, x_2, \ldots, x_m$. The basic objective of the analysis is to identify regression weights for the variables x_t, in such a way that their weighted sum has maximum correlation with y. This correlation is called the *multiple correlation coefficient*. A generalization is that there are two or more dependent variables $y_1, y_2, \ldots$. In this case one should also solve for weights for these dependent variables, in such a way that their weighted sum has optimal correlation with a weighted sum of the independent variables $x_1, x_2, \ldots$. Such correlations are called *canonical correlations*.

Dependence analysis may appear in many different guises. One of these is *analysis of variance*, where observations on a single dependent variable y are collected under a variety of experimental conditions. These conditions divide objects into subgroups. They can be coded in an *indicator matrix*. The first column x_1 of this matrix will have entries 1 for all objects in the first condition, and entries zero otherwise. The second column x_2 will have entries 1 for all objects in the second condition, zero otherwise, and so on. Formally, the problem to be solved then becomes the same as in multiple correlation: to find out to what extent y depends on the variables $x_1, x_2 \ldots$, or combinations of them. In *multivariate analysis of variance* there are two or more dependent variables $y_1, x_2, \ldots$. The problem then becomes formally the same as in canonical correlation analysis.

Another guise is *discriminant analysis*. Again objects are categorized in subgroups, in this case not so much on the basis of conditions created by an experimenter as on the basis of categories of an observed variable (such as ethnic groups, political preferences). Subgroups again can be coded in an indicator matrix, and the problem again becomes the same as in canonical analysis. The direction of the dependence could be in either way. One may, for example, want to find out whether political preference depends on such variables as y_1 = age, y^2 = income. Conversely, one might be interested to see to what extent economic variables like y_1 = income, y_2 = house rent, etc., depend on ethnic identification. Discriminant analysis may also serve the purpose of classification. The typical example is that patients with brain disease can be classified into specific types of disease with certainty only on the basis of autopsy. Suppose that patients with different types of disease were found to have shown different patterns of performance on a number of perceptual or psychomotor tests during an early stage of their illness. This then makes it possible to make a tentative diagnosis during the early stages.

(3) Whereas dependence analysis assumes that variables can be divided into two subsets of variables, other types of MVA focus on interrelations between variables belonging to one and the same set. This sometimes is called analysis of *interdependence*. A typical example is *principal components analysis*. 'Components' are defined here as weighted sums of the observed variables, with the requirement that such weighted sums must be highly correlated with all individual observed variables. Conversely, it will then become possible to express observed variables as weighted sums of components. If this is feasible for a data matrix with many variables and only a few components, we have a clear case of *data reduction*. Let us suppose that one has collected performance scores for a number of children of age ten on a number of mental tests. Suppose one finds a component highly correlated with all tests which can be characterized as 'numerical', and another component highly correlated with all 'verbal' tests. Individual scores on the numerical component can then be identified as a certain weighted sum of the 'numerical tests', and individual scores on the verbal component as a weighted sum of the 'verbal tests'. Conversely, an individual's score on some observed test could be expressed as a weighted sum of this individual's 'numerical score' and 'verbal score'.

A variety of principal components analysis is *principal factor analysis*. The basic difference is that in factor analysis it is assumed that observed variables are subject to random measurement error, with the consequence that a weighted sum of observed variables will also be subject to random error, and therefore can only be an approximation of the 'true' underlying component. Factor analysis has been developed mainly in psychology, since 1900. There is a huge literature on factor analysis, in which very many varieties are discussed (Mulaik, 1972).

(4) Thus far we have discussed *linear* MVA. This means that in interdependence analysis all of the variables are numerical, and that in dependence analysis at least one of the two sets contains numerical variables. Linear MVA prescribes that observations on numerical variables may be transformed only by linear transformation – the usual type of linear transformation is that one takes deviations from the mean instead of raw scores, or that one changes the unit of measurement.

A variable is treated as *nominal* or *categorical* if it just sorts objects into different categories, without concern about how these categories might be ordered, or how differences between categories might be scaled.

Examples are political preference, or ethnic identification. Multivariate analysis of such categorical data has been developed along its own lines, more or less independently from linear MVA. Usually, the basic data are in the format of a frequency table – the characteristic example is that rows of such a table sort persons by colour of hair, and columns sort persons by colour of eyes. (Specific solutions for such type of data are described in Goodman, 1978.) However, observations on nominal variables can also be brought within the framework indicated above, in that each nominal variance is coded in the format of an indicator matrix. For example, with two nominal variables, we obtain two indicator matrices, and we are back once again to the canonical analysis situation. Solutions of this kind are proposed by Benzécri (1973), under the name 'correspondence analysis'. With more than two categorical variables, one enters the field of *non-linear* MVA, meaning that categories of a variable can be quantified in any suitable way – the subject is dealt with extensively in Gifi (1982).

(5) An intermediate variety of MVA is *ordinal* MVA, where it is prescribed that categories of variables may be quantified with the restriction that this quantification has a certain prescribed order. The subject is treated in Gifi (1982), where the mixed case (some variables numerical, other variables nominal, and again other variables ordinal) is also discussed.

(6) The history of MVA shows a bifurcation. Linear MVA has been developed mainly in relation to statistical assumptions; in particular that data were sampled from a multinormal population. Applications of MVA then focus on statistical tests. Kshirsagar (1978) is a typical example of this approach. It implies that very severe restrictions are put upon population parameters, and that sample characteristics must either refute such restrictions, or not. In recent years another approach to MVA came into focus. It is often called the 'data theorist' approach (as contrasted to that of the 'statistician'). Whereas the statistician's approach evaluates observed data on the basis of very specific assumptions about the population from which data are sampled (such assumptions might very well be wrong), the data theorist pays more attention to the 'intrinsic appeal of the data themselves'. The statistician's approach makes generalization possible, at the cost of perhaps unrealistic assumptions about a population, whereas the data theorist is not so much concerned about generalization beyond the sample. Obviously, this controversy is somewhat exaggerated: data theorists should be prepared to consider that sample fluctuations must be taken seriously, whereas statisticians should realize that the multinormal model, although convenient from the point of view of statistical theory, might be far too restrictive from the point of view of how observed data can be generalized. Whereas Kshirsagar (1978) emphasizes the statistician's point

of view, Gnanadesikan (1977) or Green and Carroll (1976) emphasize the intrinsic appeal of the data themselves.

John van de Geer
University of Leiden

References
Benzécri, J. P. *et al.* (1973), *Analyse des données* (2 vols), Paris.
Gifi, A. (1982), *Non-Linear Multivariate Analysis*, Leiden.
Gnanadesikan, R. (1977), *Methods for the Statistical Analysis of Multivariate Observations*, New York.
Goodman, L. A. (1978), *Analyzing Qualitative Categorical Data, Loglinear Models, and Latent Structure Analysis*, Reading, Mass.
Green, P. E. and Carroll, J. D. (1976), *Mathematical Tools for Applied Multivariate Analysis*, New York.
Kshirsagar, A. M. (1978), *Multivariate Analysis*, New York.
Mulaik, S. A. (1972), *The Foundation of Factor Analysis*, New York.
See also: *categorical data*; *measures of central tendency and dispersion*; *regression*; *statistical reasoning*.

Myrdal, Gunnar (1898–)

Born in 1898, Gunnar Myrdal, the Swedish economist and a leading member of the Stockholm School, has held a variety of positions during his long and distinguished career. He was professor of economics at the University of Stockholm (1933–50); general secretary of the United Nations Economic Commission for Europe (1947–57); professor of international economics at the University of Stockholm (1960–7), and director of the Institute for International Economic Studies at the University of Stockholm (1962–7). In 1974 he was awarded the Nobel Memorial Prize in Economics for 'pioneering work in the theory of money and economic fluctuations and penetrating analysis of the interdependence of economic, social and international phenomena'.

Early on in his career, Myrdal concentrated on pure theory. His doctoral dissertation on price formation and change (1927) constructs a long-run equilibrium model, where anticipations are a datum alongside the given preferences, endowments and techniques. The ideas from his dissertation were applied in his subsequent works on monetary equilibrium where the notions of *ex ante* and *ex post* are used in the analysis of equilibrating factors. Myrdal also contributed to the methodological debates, emphasizing the normative elements implicit in classical and neoclassical theory. His analysis of the government economic policy explored the multiplicative effects of public works within a cumulative process, giving due consideration to leakages through import, and so on.

In the late 1930s, Myrdal embarked on his classic study of the Black minority in the United States (*An American Dilemma*, 1944). In it he argued that the inferior status of Blacks depended not only on economic factors but also on political and sociological ones interacting with one another in a cumulative fashion. Then, in the 1950s, he turned his attention to South Asia, the research there culminating in another famous study, *Asian Drama* (1968). Here he criticized the view that an increase in physical capital would inevitably lead to self-sustained growth, and again he argued that it was necessary to examine the interrelated factors of human capital, physical capital and institutions.

Björn Hansson
University of Lund

References
Myrdal, G. (1927), *Prisbildningsproblemet och föränderligheten* (*Price Formation and the Change Factor*), Uppsala.
Myrdal, G. (1944), *An American Dilemma. The Negro Problem and Modern Democracy*, New York.
Myrdal, G. (1953), *The Political Element in the Development of Economic Theory*, London.
Myrdal, G. (1968), *Asian Drama. An Inquiry into the Poverty of Nations*, New York.

Further Reading
Bohrn, H. (1977), *Gunnar Myrdal: A Bibliography*, Stockholm.
Reynolds, L. G. (1977), 'Gunnar Myrdal's contribution to economics, 1940–1970', *Scandinavian Journal of Economics*, 74.
See also: *Stockholm School*.

Myth

See Folklore and Myth.

N

National Income Analysis

In any economy millions of transactions take place each year which combine to give the overall level of economic activity. It is the classification, presentation and study of statistics relating to such transactions which is the concern of national income analysis. Such information is vital to policy-makers in assessing what changes are needed in short-term economic policy and in assessing long-term performance of the economy, the latter being of particular interest to developing economies. International organizations may use national income as a basis for allocating aid or demanding contributions to their budget.

The first works in national income were by Sir William Petty and Gregory King in England in the seventeenth century. Modern pioneers include Kuznets in the US and Bowley, Stamp and Clark in the UK. The development and use of Keynesian economics gave a great impetus to national income analysis during and after the Second World War with Richard Stone, Nobel Laureate 1984, as the leading figure (Stone and Stone, 1965).

The central point of national income analysis is the measurement of the amount of economic activity or national product: that is, the value of all goods and services crossing the production boundary. There are three methods of arriving at this aggregate figure: (1) The *income method* totals all incomes earned in economic activity in the form of wages, rent and profits (including undistributed amounts). Old-age pensions and similar transfer payments are excluded as not representing economic activity. (2) The *expenditure method* totals all items of final expenditure – private and government expenditure on current consumption and industrial and government purchases of capital equipment. Payments by one firm to another for raw materials or components or other inputs must be excluded. Such items of *intermediate expenditure* are 'used up' in the production process and do not cross the production boundary. (3) The *production method* looks at each firm and industry and measures its *value added* – the value of its output less the value of intermediate purchases from other firms. This represents an individual firm's contribution to the national product.

When due allowance is made for imports and exports, these three methods will, in principle, yield identical estimates of national income. In practice this is not always the case due to a less than perfect supply of information to government statisticians who are required often to reconcile three slightly differing estimates.

It is generally agreed that national income is a measure of economic activity. Unfortunately there is no general agreement about what constitutes economic activity, that is, where to draw the production boundary. Transfer payments and intermediate expenditures have been noted as transactions which are excluded because they do not cross the production boundary. Many countries follow the UN System of National Accounts (S.N.A.) and include all goods and services (including the services of government employees) for which there is a payment, either in money or in kind. The principal difference occurs in the Soviet Material Product System (M.P.S.) which emphasizes material output and excludes government services and many personal services such as entertainment and hairdressing.

Whatever definition is adopted, there are three different pairs of concepts of national income which can be used: (1) A measure of *gross national product* makes no allowance for depreciation – wear and tear of capital equipment. *Net national product* subtracts an estimate of depreciation from the gross measure, and is a more accurate reflection of the achievement of the economy. (2) If expenditures are valued at the prices paid by purchasers, they will include indirect taxes and will yield a measure of national income at *market prices*. For many purposes of comparison, both internally and externally, it is desirable to deduct indirect taxes (and add on any subsidies) and obtain a measure at *factor cost*, which is the essential costs of production. Such a measure is obtained automatically using the income or production methods. (3) The third pair are measures of gross *domestic* product (GDP) and gross *national* product (GNP). The former relates to all economic activity taking place within the geographical limits of the economy. The latter measures economic activity carried out by the resources – labour and capital owned by national members of the economy. In many developing countries dependent on foreign capital, the outflow of profits means that GDP can exceed GNP by up to 20%. These pairs of concepts can be combined in various ways, the most common being gross domestic product at factor cost.

Table 1 *Social accounting matrix UK 1982 (£ billion)*

Payments by:- \ Payments to:-	PRODUCTION		CONSUMPTION		CAPITAL ACCUM-ULATION	REST OF THE WORLD	TOTALS
	Goods & Services	Taxes on goods & services	Private Sector	Public Sector			
PRODUCTION Goods & services	–	–	136.5 CH	55.6 CG	37.8 V	67.8 X	299.7
Taxes on goods & services	–	–	30.6	4.5	3.2	3.3	41.6
CONSUMPTION (INCOME AND OUTLAY) Private Sector	192.3 YH	–	–	50.4 HG	–	1.6 E	244.3
Public Sector	7.2 YG	41.6	58.4 GH	–	–		107.2
CAPITAL ACCUMULATION	33.0 D	–	18.5 SH	–5.1 SG	–	–	46.4
REST OF THE WORLD	67.2 M	–	0.3 TH	1.8 TG	5.4 B	–	74.7
TOTALS	299.7	41.6	244.3	107.2	46.4	74.7	

CH – Household consumption; CG – Government consumption; HG – Transfers from government to private sector (including Social Security benefits) E – Net income from abroad; YH – Private sector incomes (wages, profit, rent); HG – Transfers from government to private sector (including Social Security benefits) E – Net income from abroad; YG – Public sector trading surplus; GH – Payments by private sector to government (taxes on income; social security contributions); D – depreciation or capital consumption; SH – private sector saving; SG – public sector saving; M – imports of goods and services; TH – private transfers abroad (net); TG – government transfers abroad; B – net investment abroad (= balance of payments on current account)

Gross domestic product at factor cost = YH + YG + D = 232.5

The three methods of measuring national income serve as a focus for different analyses of the aggregate. The income accounts can be used to analyse the shares of wages and profits in total national income and the equality, or otherwise, of the distribution of this income to individuals. The details of the production accounts enable one to examine the relative importance of different industries (for example, manufacturing and services), of different regions in the country, or of privately and publicly-owned production. On the expenditure side, much attention has focused in Western Europe on the split between private and public spending. In general economists are interested in the division between consumption and investment (the purchase of new capital equipment). Here national income analysis is very closely related to macroeconomics and the study of what determines the size of these items and how changes in them affect the overall level of national income.

All transactions are measured in money terms and give national income in *current prices*, but it is necessary to allow for price changes when making comparisons between years. Values at current prices are adjusted by an appropriate index of prices in order to obtain estimates in *constant prices*. Any observed changes will then reflect only changes in quantity and not in price.

National income analysis originated in the measurement of production, income and expenditure aggregate flows, but gradually more and detailed transactions have been included. The analysis of transactions between firms and industries known as *input-output analysis* is a separate topic. Borrowing and lending, that is, transactions in financial assets, are analysed in a *flow-of-funds table*, and the accounting system can be extended to include stocks as well as flows. *National balance sheets* record the value of assets, financial and physical, held by members of the economy at the end of each accounting period. The presentation and analysis of this more complicated system of accounts is greatly facilitated by showing the data in a large square table (see Table 1) recording transactions between sectors of the economy in the columns and those in the rows. Known as a social accounting matrix, this is the most recent methodological development in this field.

A. G. Armstrong
University of Bristol

Reference
Stone, R. and Stone, G. (1965), *National Income and Expenditure*, 7th edn, London.

Further Reading
Abraham, W. I. (1969), *National Income and Economic Accounting*, Englewood Cliffs, N.J.

Beckerman, W. (1976), *An Introduction to National Income Analysis*, London.
See also: *deflation as a statistical device*; *national wealth*.

Nationalism

Nationalism is the belief that each nation has both the right and the duty to constitute itself as a state. There are many difficulties in specifying what a nation is – in Europe, for example, the candidates range from the Welsh and the Basques to Occitanians and Northumbrians – but some common culture is indispensable and a shared language highly desirable. The Swiss have so far got by without a common language, but its lack has sorely tried the rulers of Belgium. Nationalist theory usually attributes conflict to cross-national oppression, and thus offers a promise of world peace when self-determination has become a global reality.

Nationalism emerged in the hatred of cosmopolitanism which registered the resentment of Germans and other Europeans who were coming to feeling marginal in terms of the universalistic rationalism of the French Enlightenment. The romantic idea that true humanity must be mediated by a deep involvement in one's own unique culture led to an admiration for songs, poems, stories, plays and other creations understood as emanations of the national soul. The language of a people was accorded a unique value, no less as the medium of cultural self-expression than as a practical rule of thumb about how far the boundaries of a putative nation might stretch. The conquests of Napoleon turned these particularistic passions in a practical direction, and Fichte's *Addresses to the German Nation* delivered at Berlin in 1807–8 struck a responsive chord throughout Germany. Italy and Germany were both plausible candidates for state creation and both duly became states, though Italy remains imperfectly national to this day, while German unity owed more to Bismarck than to popular passion for nationhood.

The spread of nationalist ideas to Eastern Europe and beyond, where very different peoples were inextricably intertwined, was bound to create difficulties. Doctrinal diffusion was facilitated by the growth of industry, and of cities. Teachers, journalists, clergymen and other intellectuals found in nationalist ideas an identity for the present and a vision for the future. Some set to work writing down languages previously purely oral; others constructed a literature and elicited a suitable history. Opera and the novel were favourite vehicles of nationalist feeling. The politics of these endeavours triumphed with the Treaty of Versailles in 1918, which settled Europe in terms of the principle of national self-determination.

Throughout Africa and Asia, nationalist ideas fuelled the campaigns to replace the old European empires with home grown rulers, but since there were few plausible nations in this area, successor states which had been constructed on a variety of principles claimed freedom in order to *begin* the process of cultural homogenization which might lead to nationhood. Pakistan, based upon the religious identity of Islam, attempted to hold together two separated areas inherited from the British raj, and could not be sustained in that form; the eastern region broke off as Bangladesh in 1971. The artificial boundaries of imperial Africa have, however, been a surprisingly successful container of the often chaotic mixture of tribes they contained, though virtually all have had to compensate for lack of homogeneity by centralizing and frequently tyrannizing governments.

Political scientists often find in nationalism an attractive form of explanation because it promises to explain the hidden causes of conflict between different ethnic groups. In this usage, nationalism is not a belief, but rather a force supposed to move people to both action and belief. Such a concept provokes a search for the conditions under which the force is triggered. The promise of this research programme, like many another in political science, far exceeds the performance. Nationalism is better treated as a complex of ideas and sentiments which respond flexibly, decade by decade, to new situations, usually situations of grievance, in which peoples may find themselves.

Kenneth Minogue
London School of Economics and Political Science

Further Reading
Hertz, F. (1944), *Nationality in History and Politics*, London.
Kedourie, E. (1960), *Nationalism*, London.
Minogue, K. R. (1963), *Nationalism*, London.
Smith, A. D. (1971), *Theories of Nationalism*, London.

Nationalization

At the heart of the term nationalization is the act of converting a privately-owned resource into one owned by the central government (or local government in the case of 'municipalization'). One might then ask how the use and development of the resource and the economic organization of production may be predicted to change. Instead of exploring this issue, many economists in both Europe and North America have taken an essentially prescriptive stance. What advice can one give about the use of the resources? they have asked, invariably on the presumption that the managers, civil servants and ministers are disinterested recipients of that advice. Since no one would want to deny that resources should be used efficiently, economists have translated their own concept of efficiency into guidelines of behaviour. Publicly-owned industries should, as a first approximation, set user prices and extend the use of resources up to the point where the marginal cost of output equals price. The rationale for this is that no gains could then be made by switching resource usage in or out of the industry, since consumer valuation of the marginal dose of resources is just equal to its valuation in other activities. The implications of such a rule are quite striking, suggesting, for example, different electricity tariffs for different times of day, high fares and tariffs for transport, gas and electricity to high-cost rural areas, low fares and freight rates for bulky, long-distance rail journeys. Much work has been undertaken on the detailed implementation of these policy proposals, in terms of identifying short and long-run marginal costs, demand elasticities and time-stream aspects of investment projects. While many economists have not felt that the price at marginal cost rule should be modified to take into account questions of income distribution – on the grounds that the tax system is the way to handle that – they have not advocated the simple rule when spill-over effects exist or when information flows have been regarded as deficient. Health and education are therefore viewed as areas raising other considerations.

The forgotten question about how the use of resources would actually change under public ownership re-emerged in the 1970s, partly as a product of the growing influence of a persistent element in American economic thinking – the study of institutional behaviour – and partly because the economists' policy prescriptions were either ignored or found too difficult to implement. The restriction of a private interest to the end of promoting a public interest can be achieved in a variety of ways. Such 'regulation' has a long history in Britain embracing areas like the factory inspectorate and the control of private railway and fuel companies in the inter-war period. The shift in the immediate post-1945 period to public ownership of strategic industries may itself be a reflection of the siege mentality of the 1930s and 1940s. Study of such issues is still awaited. Instead the main thrust of 'positive' theories has come from American thinking on the property rights characteristics of public firms. For example, one approach stresses that citizen-owners can dispose of their rights in publicly-owned activities only by engaging in high-cost activities like migration or concerted political action. This is contrasted with private ownership, where each owner has the unilateral ability to buy and sell shares, an act viewed as a capitalization of the expected results of current management action. A significant wedge between owner and management therefore arises in public firms, the nearest approximation to which for private firms is the cost to owners of monitoring management behaviour. In the former case the wedge permits scope for discretionary behaviour by civil servants, management and politicians. The precise outcome in each public firm would depend on the way in which property rights are specified and the constraints on the various parties in the pursuit of their own utility maximizing position. But the broad expectation is that productivity will be lower and unit costs higher in public than in private firms. Testing such theories is difficult, for when public firms have product monopolies there is no contemporaneous private firm to act as benchmark, and in the absence of monopoly one has to separate the effects of competition from the effects of ownership. Because of the wide variety of institutional types within many of its industries, America is proving a fruitful data source with comparisons between publicly-owned firms (municipal rather than national) and private firms, some of which are regulated. The evidence on productivity and unit costs shows a very varied pattern, with public firms coming out better in electricity supply, private firms in refuse collection and water supply, and with no clear-cut differences in transport. Pricing structures in public firms seem unambiguously to be less closely geared to the supply costs of particular activities, though whether this is due to electoral influences, empire building or a disinterested pursuit of fairness is not yet clear. Little work has yet been done on explaining why some activities are taken into public ownership whilst others are not.

Robert Millward
University of Salford

Further Reading
Chester, N. (1975), *The Nationalisation of British Industry 1945–51*, London.
Millward, R. and Parker, D. (1983), 'Public and private enterprise: relative behaviour and efficiency', in R. Millward and M. T. Sumner (eds), *Public Sector Economics*, London.
See also: *mixed economy; public goods.*

National Wealth

The wealth of a nation comprises a wide range of assets including both physical capital and net claims on other countries. The physical capital itself is not easily quantified. The United Nations System of National Accounts (1968), however, provides conventional guidelines for building up an inventory of physical assets. Broadly, vehicles, plant and machinery, and buildings are entered at their market value, after allowing for depreciation. Land is valued at its improved value, but no allowance is made for unextracted minerals or growing crops and forests. Equally, and perhaps most importantly, no allowance is made for the human capital possessed by the nation, despite the fact that the productive skills of its people may be its most important resource. Wealth estimates for the United Kingdom are to be found in Revell (1967),

while for the United States they are provided by Goldsmith (1982). In both cases annual statistical estimates are provided of some of the components of national wealth.

In an attempt to measure national wealth, net claims on other nations represent real resources available to the home country, and thus net fixed and portfolio investment must be counted together with foreign currency reserves and other lending to the rest of the world, net of borrowing from the rest of the world. But the network of financial claims within a country has no direct bearing on its national wealth. A country is not richer because the government has borrowed a large national debt from the private sector (although it may be if the government has invested the money it has borrowed more productively than the private sector would have). Individual holders of the national debt are, however, richer because they hold the debt, and in a full analysis of national wealth the economy is broken up into institutional sectors. The wealth of each sector includes not only its physical assets and its net claims on the rest of the world but also its net claims on the other sectors in the economy. Because only net claims are included, the sum of the net wealth of each institutional sector will equal the national wealth, in the same way as transfer payments have to be netted out when adding up institutional income to arrive at national income.

Just as some physical assets are conventionally omitted in the estimation of national wealth, so some financial claims are omitted in the compilation of estimates of sectoral wealth. Buiter (1983) presents a more general accounting framework which includes the capitalized value of social security and national insurance benefits as a liability of central government, and the capitalized value of future tax receipts as an asset, although such an approach can be criticized because future tax rates can change, and there is no obvious reason to capitalize these flows on the basis of any particular future path of tax and payment rates.

Martin Weale
University of Cambridge

References
Buiter, W. M. (1983), 'Measurement of the public sector deficit and its implications for policy evaluation and design', *International Monetary Fund Staff Papers*.
Goldsmith, R. W. (1982), 'The National Balance Sheet of the United States, 1953–1980', NBER.
Revell, J. L. (1967), *The Wealth of the Nation*, Cambridge.
United Nations (1968), *System of National Accounts*, New York.
See also: *national income analysis.*

Neoclassical Economics

The term neoclassical economics refers to the enhanced version of classical economics that was promoted and developed in the late nineteenth century, primarily by Alfred Marshall and Leon Walras. The most familiar versions were developed in the twentieth century by John Hicks and Paul Samuelson. Despite what 'neoclassical' might usually imply, neoclassical economics differs from the classical only in matters of emphasis and focus. Unlike classical methods of explaining the state of any economy in terms of seemingly mysterious forces like the 'invisible hand', neoclassical economics tries to provide a complete explanation by focusing on the actual mechanisms which lead to the explained state.

The pure world that neoclassical economists attempt to explain consists of independently-minded individuals making decisions which can be completely rationalized in terms of aims and means, interacting with one another only by means of market competition, and all the while being limited only by the constraints provided by Nature. It is important to note what is omitted from this world view. There is no necessary role for social institutions such as churches or governments, except those that can be explicitly explained as the consequences of individual market choices. Likewise, there is no role for authorities. The individual or the decision-making unit such as a firm always knows what is best for him, her or it.

In the neoclassical world, whenever any individual is not satisfied with current affairs (say, not consuming enough bread), he allegedly enters the market and competes with other buyers by bidding up the price (of bread), thereby creating an incentive for at least one producer to sell to him rather than anyone else. This process of increasing the going market price raises the average selling price and thereby indicates to producers that more is wanted, and to other buyers that they should consider cheaper substitutes (for bread). If a sufficient amount of time is allowed for all such market activity to be worked out, eventually all individuals will be satisfied relative to what they can afford (to afford any more may mean that they would have had to work more than what they considered optimal). The market process is worked out to a point where one individual can gain only by causing others to lose and thereby leaving them unsatisfied. In other words, in the long run everyone is happy relative to their own personal aims and to their natural givens (for example, to their inherited resources or skills).

Over the last fifty years, formal analyses of this very special neoclassical world have frequently demonstrated that any attempt to interfere with its preconceived free market mechanism – either by manipulating prices or by restricting market trading – can only lead to a world where some people are not being allowed to choose what they want and thus lead to a non-optimal state of affairs. Nevertheless, it has often been pointed out by critics, such as John Maynard Keynes, that the amount of time necessary for the market activity to be worked out is unrealistic. Other critics, such as Thorstein Veblen, merely claimed that the neoclassical world was fundamentally unrealistic as some individuals do not act independently, and thus there is no guarantee, even if there were enough time, that everyone will be satisfied. While there are a few exceptions, most neoclassical economists have been concerned with either the formal analytics of the special neoclassical world or the applicability of its many formal theorems to everyday world problems.

Few of the economists who focus on the analytical aspects of economic theory are actually attempting to answer their critics. Rather, most neoclassical economic theorists have been concerned with other equally important questions. Can we really confidently rely on a world view that allows only independent decision making and only free competition? How can one specify the details of the formal neoclassical world so as to justify such confidence? Critics still question the sufficiency of any purely competitive, individualist world and ask whether other details are necessary. Does this world require that there be numerous individuals participating as buyers and as sellers? Does it require an infinity of time for the 'long run' and thus by doing it so render an impossible world? While the necessity of such additional conditions remains somewhat in doubt, a few logically sufficient views of a world of individual decision makers have been worked out in great, yet tedious, detail.

Since, by methodological commitment, all events are ultimately to be explained in neoclassical economics as being the logical consequences of individual decision making guided by market events, the elements of individual decision making have had to yield to extensive formal analysis. Unfortunately, despite the many impressive displays of mathematical agility and prowess, not much has been accomplished beyond what can be learned from any elementary calculus textbook. Every individual is thought to be maximizing with respect to some particular quantitative aim (for example, utility, profit, net income) while facing specified natural constraints (such as technical knowledge or capabilities, personal skills). It follows, then, whenever utility (the quantity representing the level of satisfaction achieved by consuming the purchased goods) is maximized, the formal relationship between the quantity of any good and the utility (the 'utility function') must be one where, over the relevant range of choice, each additional unit of the good must add slightly less to the total utility than did any previous unit. This is termed 'diminishing marginal utility' and it (or some multidimensional version such as 'diminishing marginal rates of substitution') is a necessary condition for each individual's utility function. Why any individual's marginal utility is diminishing has never been adequately explained using economics principles alone. It only can be asserted that it is a necessary condition for the viability of any neoclassical world. Similar analysis has been provided for the other aims that individuals might have (such as profit, wealth, welfare), although virtually all other aims can be reduced to the analytics of utility maximization (see Samuelson, 1947).

Other neoclassical economists have been trying indirectly to answer the critics by showing that, even without assurances that the neoclassical world is realistic or possible, it can be used to provide detailed explanations of current economic events. Countless academic articles have been written which demonstrate the 'robustness' of neoclassical theories. All are of a form that implies that any desirable economic event must be the logical consequence of the aims and choices of individuals and any undesirable event must be the result of unforeseen natural events or the consequence of interference in the market by 'well-meaning' governments or corporations. So far, few critics have been convinced by the tedious formalities or even by the number of allegedly successful demonstrations.

Lawrence A. Boland
Simon Fraser University

References
Hicks, J. (1939/1946), *Value and Capital*, 2nd edn, Oxford.
Samuelson, P. (1965 [1947]), *Foundations of Economic Analysis*, New York.

Further Reading
Boland, L. (1982), *Foundations of Economic Method*, London.
See also: *Hicks*; *Marshall*; *Samuelson*; *Walras, L.*

Neocolonialism

See Imperialism.

Nervous System

The nervous system has long been recognized as the locus of the control of human action, but the nature of its contribution and the mechanisms by which this is achieved are still a matter of active debate. The main thrust of investigation has been empirical, and has been initiated from two fields within psychology – physiological psychology and human neuropsychology.

(1) *Physiological Psychology* has investigated the influence of general physiological systems upon the fundamental aspects of behaviour, and has concentrated on affective and conative mechanisms rather than cognitive processes. Because the site of these mechanisms is in the central subcortical parts of the head, and in lower brain systems, they have generally been studied in animal preparations, for the survival of human cases with damage to these areas is relatively poor. Research has identified three major functional systems: (i) The limbic system, which includes the cingulate gyrus, the septal region, the fornix, the hippocampus and the amygdala, is involved in the evaluation of experience as punishing or rewarding. It also maintains a memory of these evaluations, so that behaviour can be adaptive and appropriate to its context. Rage and fear, taming, flight and attack are all associated with this region, as is the regulation of psychological mood. (ii) The medial forebrain bundle, grouped around the hypothalamus, is involved in the basic motivational systems for hunger, thirst and sexual behaviour. It can be convenient to think of subsystems within the hypothalamus which turn such drives 'on' or 'off', although the system is in reality more complex. Related structures subserve the effects of reward and punishment, and also exert control on the endocrine system of hormones, and on the autonomic nervous system involved in emotion and anxiety. If pleasure is generated anywhere within the brain, it is here. (iii) The system in the brainstem governs the operation of reflex responses and maintains the general level of alertness and attention within the rest of the nervous system.

(2) The other, and more recently prominent, field is that of *Human Neuropsychology*. This has mainly investigated cognitive functions, and in the cerebral cortex of human subjects. Its origins are in clinical neuropsychology, the study of patients with damage to the central nervous system. From the latter half of the nineteenth century, investigators recognized that fairly discrete behavioural defects could be associated with relatively localized injuries to the surface of the brain. This study of focal brain lesions, promoted by the observation of those injured in both World Wars, laid the basis of modern neuropsychology as both a research area and an applied clinical discipline. The most widely adopted functional model derived from this work is that of regional equipotentiality within an interactionist theory. Interactionist theory, originating with Hughlings Jackson and more recently developed by Luria and Geschwind, proposes that higher abilities are built up from a number of more basic component skills which are themselves relatively localized. Regional equipotentiality argues for localization only within certain rather loosely defined regions. That higher functions appear incompletely localized in the brain may be due to the flexibility of cognitive systems in employing basic components in complex performance.

Three main approaches are adopted in modern clinical neuropsychology: (i) Behavioural neurology, derived from the work of Luria and most widely practised in the Soviet Union, is individual-centred and aims at a qualitative analysis and description of the patient's problems rather than a quantitative assessment. The focus of interest is not only the level of performance, but also the way in which a given task is performed. (ii) An approach, popular in the United States, concentrates on the use of test batteries. The two currently most important are the Halstead-Reitan and the Luria-Nebraska Neuropsychological Batteries. Such batteries, composed of a large number of standard tests, seek to give a complete description of the patient's level of performance across the whole spectrum of abilities, and use statistical methods. Diagnostic indicators are also usually a feature of the results. (iii) The individual-centred, normative approach is most commonly practised in Britain. It relies to some extent upon formal psychometric assessment, but emphasizes the need to tailor the assessment to the nature of a particular patient's difficulties. The aim is an accurate description of the dysfunction being investigated, going beyond a simple diagnostic classification to an understanding in cognitive psychological terms. This approach is more efficient in terms of time and resources, but makes greater demands upon professional skill and clinical insight. The approaches are, of course, rather less distinct in clinical practice.

The clinical tradition in neuropsychology has developed in the past two decades through important contributions from cognitive experimental psychology. The stimulus for this development was undoubtedly the study of the commissurotomy or 'split-brain' patients by Sperry and Gazzaniga in the early 1960s. These patients, in whom the two lateral hemispheres of the cortex had been surgically separated for the treatment of epilepsy, provided a unique opportunity to study the functions of each hemisphere operating alone. It was demonstrated that each was capable of perceiving, learning and remembering, and that there were in addition relative specializations characteristic of each hemisphere: the left subserved speech and verbal, symbolic, logical and serial operations, while the right undertook spatial-perceptual, holistic and parallel processes. The split-brain patients also provided a milieu for the empirical investigation of the seat of consciousness, although the conclusions to be drawn are still very much a matter of debate. However, apart from the research findings directly derived from the split-brain patients which are sometimes difficult to interpret, this work demonstrated that methods already employed in a different context in experimental psychology could be used to investigate brain organization in normal intact human adults. These methods all rely upon presenting information to the nervous system so that by virtue of the arrangement of sensory pathways it is projected initially to only one hemisphere. This may be in vision (divided visual field presentation), in hearing (dichotic listening), or in touch (haptic presentation). Subsequent human performance, in terms of speed or accuracy of response, can then be analysed as a function of which hemisphere received the information. An enormous literature has now built up around these techniques, and the results, although far from unanimous, broadly support the conclusion derived from the split-brain patients. This is that the hemispheres possess relative specializations for cognitive function. While it was at one time thought that this might relate to the type of material processed, or the response mechanisms employed, it is now thought that the nature of the processing determines the relative proficiency of each hemisphere. No one specification of the relevant processing characteristics has yet been widely accepted.

Alongside these developments in experimental neuropsychology has been a renewed interest in electrophysiological processes. The new technology of averaged evoked response recording, and new ways of looking at the ongoing electrical activity of the brain (EEG), have both produced significant advances in directly linking cognitive events in the psychological domain to observable concurrent events in the physiological domain. While this research is difficult in technological and methodological terms, it holds the promise of being able to identify accurately, with good temporal resolution, the concomitants of cognitive processes within the physiological activity of the brain. Despite inventive research, this promise is some way from being fulfilled. At the same time, psychophysiological studies, which have a longer history, have continued into the psychological correlates of autonomic nervous system functions. Much has been learned of the peripheral changes in heart rate, electrodermal response, respiration, blood pressure and vascular changes which accompany changes in emotion and mood, but the problems of individual and situational variability, and the poor temporal association between mental and physiological states because of the slow response of the autonomic processes, have led to a decline in interest in recent years.

A number of fundamental problems face the apparently successful study of brain-behaviour relationships: (1) The philosophical issue of the mind-body problem. Most neuroscientists adopt a position of psychoneural monism, assuming that some identity can be established between mental and physiological events. This, of course, may be a conceptual error. It is possible that developments in electrophysiology may provide a means for the empirical investigation of this issue, till now primarily the domain of philosophers. (2) Much of experimental neuropsychology proceeds by inference to, rather than direct observation of, physiological processes, so placing great importance upon methodological rigour. (3) It has to be admitted that we still have no real idea of how the brain operates to produce high-level cognition. A rather vague cybernetic-electronic model is often assumed, but there is no real certainty that this in any way reflects the actual principles of operation within the brain. (4) The nervous system is a very complex set of highly integrated subsystems. It is unlikely that significant progress will be made in our understanding of it until more adequate models can be developed, both of the physiological performance of large neural systems and of the psychological structure of cognitive abilities.

J. Graham Beaumont
University of Leicester

Further Reading

Beaumont, J. G. (1983), *Introduction to Neuropsychology*, Oxford.
Bradshaw, J. L. and Nettleton, N. C. (1983), *Human Cerebral Asymmetry*, Englewood Cliffs, N.J.
Carlson, N. R. (1981), *Physiology of Behavior*, 2nd edn, Boston, Mass.
Dimond, S. J. (1980), *Neuropsychology*, London.
Heilman, K. M. and Valenstein, E. (eds) (1979), *Clinical Neuropsychology*, New York.
See also: *biological psychiatry*; *mind*; *physiological psychology*; *vision*.

Networks

One of the perennial problems social scientists face is to relate such abstract concepts as society, institution, and group to the activities and relations of actual people. One approach to this problem is to view the circles of relatives and friends, groups and institutional complexes as social networks that link people at various levels.

The concept of social network was first introduced by Radcliffe-Brown in 1940 and used by Barnes (1954) and Bott (1957) in the mid-1950s. Many anthropologists continued to develop network analysis over the next fifteen years, after which sociologists and political scientists took over from them. The enthusiasm for network analysis was related to the theoretical shift away from structural-functional analysis which by 1960 had dominated social sciences in Britain and the United States for thirty years. The network concept permitted the entry on a systematic basis of interacting people engaged in actions that could alter the institutions in which they participated. This introduced a new dimension into the self-regulating structural-functional edifice of corporate groups, systems and moral order seen as impinging upon people, moulding their character and determining their behaviour. Network analysis provided down-to-earth data.

Social networks have been observed to have a definite structure which influences behaviour and aspects of personality. They are influenced, in their turn, by biological factors, physical environment, residence and climate, but also by ideology.

The patterned characteristics of social networks can be divided into interactional and structural criteria. There are four important interactional criteria: (1) Multiplexity: this is the degree to which relations between persons are single or multiple. (2) The transactional content of a relation: the nature of the goods and services, the degree of emotional involvement, the confidences which are exchanged between people who are linked to one another. (3) The directional flow of the things exchanged: most relations are uneven. Asymmetry in the transactions between two people is an indication of the differences in social status and relative power. (4) The frequency and duration of interaction can also be an important indication of the quality in the content of the relation.

There are also at least four significant structural criteria: (1) *Size*: A person can come into contact with many more people than those to whom he is directly linked. Through his direct contacts, sometimes referred to as his first-order zone, he can come into contact with other persons. These form second-order zones. These friends-of-friends form an important category. (2) *Density*: This is the degree to which members of a person's network are in touch with one another independently of him. Density can be expressed as the extent to which links which could possibly exist among persons do in fact exist. This can be calculated by means of a simple formula: $\frac{100\,NA}{\frac{1}{2}N(N-1)}$ where NA = the total number of actual relations and N = the total number of persons in the network. The density of a network is an indication of the potential communication between members of a network. It is usually assumed, although this must be carefully investigated, that where the density of a network is high, there is considerable social communication and thus increased social pressure for conformity. (3) *Centralilty*: This is an index of the accessibility to one another of members of the network. The more central a person is, the better able he is to bring about communication. (4) *Clustering*: This is the degree to which members of a network form clusters of persons who are more closely linked to one another than they are to the rest of the network. The presence of such clusters, if perceived by a person, influences his behaviour. A person linked to several clusters in his own personal network, each of which has slightly different norms, will have to adjust his behaviour accordingly.

Network analysis complements other research techniques in a number of ways: it focuses systematically on interlinkages and interdependences between units of analysis. This focus embraces micro and macro levels in one analytical framework. It provides a systematic framework for analysing tension and asymmetry in social relations and consequently highlights their inherent dynamics. By concentrating on interrelation, interdependency, and interaction, it yields insights into forms of social organization that emerge from interaction, such as patron-client chains, cliques, factions and other coalitions which, until the network revival, had generally been ignored. It provides a means of relating formal, abstract sociological analysis to everyday experience, for it links interpersonal relations to institutions. Finally, it brings into socio-logical focus the ill-defined but important category of friends-of-friends.

Network analysis has offered important insights into urban/rural contrasts, male/female relationships, kinship in industrialized societies, the way leaders recruit and manipulate support, and the way in which gossip circulates. It has also been used to combat organized crime and to delineate overlapping positions from which power is exercised through interlocking company directorships.

There are some problems and difficulties associated with this type of analysis: (1) Methodological invol-ution. Network analysis has borrowed heavily from mathematical graph theory. Analytical rigour in this field easily leads to methodological refinements remote from human beings. (2) The danger in regarding network as an object of study in its own right, which is sterile, rather than using the analysis to answer questions. (3) Attributing specific contents to relations between people who are shown to figure in the same network. Network analysis, for example, can plot the linkage between businessmen via overlapping director-ships, or between *mafiosi* and politicians. This suggests collusions, but it does not demonstrate it. To do that, the actual exchange content of the relations must be studied. (4) The researcher may be trying to explain too much by network analysis. While it can provide insights into, for example, the movement and location of migrants, it cannot explain the long-term social processes that underlie migration (Boissevain, 1979).

Basically, however, network analysis is very uncom-plicated: it asks questions about who is linked to whom, the nature of that linkage, and how the nature of the linkage affects behaviour. These are relatively straight-forward questions, the resolution of which is fairly simple. They should form part of the basic research tool kit of every fieldworker.

Jeremy Boissevain
University of Amsterdam

References
Barnes, J. A. (1954), 'Class and committees in a Norwegian island parish', *Human Relations*, 7.
Boissevain, J. (1979), 'Network analysis: a reappraisal', *Current Anthropology*, 20.
Bott, E. (1957), *Family and Social Network*, London, 2nd edn, 1971.
Radcliffe-Brown, A. R. (1940), 'On social structure', *Journal of the Royal Anthropological Institute*, 70.

Further Reading
Barnes, J. A. (1972), *Social Networks*, Reading, Mass.
Boissevain, J. (1974), *Friends of Friends: Networks, Manipulators and Coalitions*, Oxford.
See also: *communication networks*; *graph theory*.

Neumann, John von (1903–57)

The originator of the theory of games and an innovator in several other branches of pure and applied math-ematics, von Neumann studied in his home town of Budapest and in Zürich and Berlin before settling in the United States, where he became a professor at the Institute for Advanced Study in Princeton in 1933.

In 1928 von Neumann published the first proof of the fundamental minimax theorem of game theory. He later claimed priority as the founder of game theory on the grounds that, although Émile Borel had already done useful preliminary work, there was nothing worth publishing on this subject until the minimax theorem was proved. Von Neumann developed his ideas on game theory at length in *Theory of Games and Economic Behavior* (1944), written in collaboration with the econ-omist Oskar Morgenstern. The second edition of this treatise, published in 1947, contains an axiomatic treat-ment of utility which did much to rehabilitate this concept in economics.

Von Neumann's work on the mathematical foun-dations of quantum theory, which he considered to be among his most important scientific contributions, was set forth in *Mathematische Grundlagen der Quantenmechanik* (1932) [The Mathematical Basis of Quantum Mech-anics]. He was invited to join the atomic bomb project at Los Alamos in 1943, and his mathematical study of shock waves was used in determining the height of the explosions over Hiroshima and Nagasaki in 1945. During the 1940s and 1950s he made pioneering contri-butions to the theory of computers, and developed a new branch of cybernetics concerned with self-repro-ducing machines.

Von Neumann's papers have been collected by Taub (1961), and a review of his life and work can be found in Ulam (1958).

Andrew M. Colman
University of Leicester

References
Taub, A. H. (ed.) (1961), *Collected Works of John von Neumann*, New York.
Ulam, S. (1958), 'John von Neumann, 1903–1957', *Bulletin of the American Mathematical Society*, 64.
See also: *game theory*.

Neuroses

Historically, the neuroses or psychoneuroses have constituted a major category of mental disorders in psychiatry and psychoanalysis. The term neuroses evolved from the belief that the symptoms of these disorders originate in neural disturbances. Later the term psychoneuroses came into being to reflect the understanding that most neurotic symptoms have psychic or emotional origins. The two terms are nowadays used interchangeably. In fact, the *Diagnostic and Statistical Manual of Mental Disorders* (DSM–III) of the American Psychiatric Association – the organization's official manual for nomenclature published in 1980 – omits the classification of 'neuroses'; instead, the neuroses are included under the affective, anxiety, somatoform, dissociative, and psychosexual disorders.

Traditionally, the neuroses have been categorized according to the symptoms or manifestations of anxiety, which is considered their common source. In these illnesses, the predominant disturbance is a symptom or a group of symptoms which cause distress to the individual and are recognized as unacceptable and alien. However, reality testing remains grossly intact and there is no demonstrable organic aetiology. Thus, a neurotic individual's behaviour remains largely normal. Without treatment, these conditions are relatively enduring or recurrent.

Because the definition of normality or health is difficult, one can assume that everyone is a potential neurotic. A person may be considered neurotic when his ego defences are quantitively excessive and disruptive to usual patterns of adaptive functioning. The neurotic process hinders one's freedom to change, limits the capacity to sustain effort, and reduces flexibility in the areas of thinking, behaviour and emotions. Neuroses can be circumscribed, affecting only one of these areas, or they may be more widespread, touching on several areas in the individual's life.

Psychoanalysts and dynamically-oriented psychiatrists believe that the neuroses are caused by conflicts between the sexual and aggressive id drives and ego forces that are attempting to control and modify the drives. Neuroses may also arise from conflicts between the super-ego, or conscience, and the ego. Object relations theorists contend that neurotic conflicts may arise from incongruous self-representations within the ego and super-ego and their internal interactions, as well as from their interactions with the external environment.

According to the classic dynamic formulation, symptom formation is a consequence of the emergence into consciousness of the instinctual derivatives and memory traces producing anxiety. A danger is created, calling forth repression and other defensive mechanisms to ward off the anxiety. If these mechanisms are unsuccessful in containing anxiety, symptoms emerge which represent substitute expressions of the instinctual drives. The symptoms can be understood as compromise formations or attempts of the ego to integrate ego drives, super-ego, and reality.

The appearance of a neurosis in a person usually indicates a fixation or regression to an earlier phase of infantile development. These illnesses may be precipitated by realistic situations that correspond to earlier traumatic life experiences. Unconscious fantasies and feelings are stirred up, activating the original conflict. While there is no definite evidence of biogenetic factors in the production of neurotic disorders, constitutional differences may be contributory.

Originally, Freud classified hysteria, phobias, and the obsessive-compulsive neuroses under the heading 'transference neuroses', because patients with these conditions repeat childhood neurotic patterns within the transference during treatment. Since patients with melancholia and schizophrenia did not exhibit the same tendency in treatment, these entities were termed *narcissistic neuroses*. The term *symptom neuroses* corresponds to the present-day neurotic disorder, while *character neuroses* is roughly equivalent to the concept of personality disorder.

Freud's classification of neuroses was based both on his psychoanalytic understanding of the condition and his experience of those patients' responses to the treatment situation. The psychiatric establishment, unwilling to accept Freud's approach, found a compromise and classified the neuroses as different patterns for dealing with anxiety. Thus, hysterical neurosis, conversion type, implied that anxiety had been converted into a physical symptom, for example, a paralysis. Phobia assumed that anxiety was compartmentalized, and so on.

The more recent psychiatric classification, DSM III has moved still further away from any theory of the underlying dynamics. Instead, the focus is descriptive and behavioural. The current diagnosis of what were once designated neuroses are: panic disorder, generalized anxiety disorder, conversion disorder, psychogenic pain disorder, psychogenic amnesia, psychogenic fugue, multiple personality, sleepwalking disorder (in childhood), simple phobia, social phobia, agoraphobia with panic attacks, agoraphobia without panic attacks, separation anxiety disorder (in childhood), obsessive compulsive disorder, depersonalization disorder, and hypochondriasis. As this list demonstrates, the emphasis is not on the theory of aetiology; rather, classification depends on careful description of the symptoms of the disorder. In addition, two new classifications have been introduced: somatization disorder, and acute and chronic post-traumatic stress disorders.

Nevertheless, it is still true that in these conditions the individual experiences anxiety, directly or indirectly, in addition to one or several recognizable defence mechanisms that serve to identify the disorder. An example would be an obsessive-compulsive disorder in which the person is troubled by involuntary recurrent, persistent ideas, thoughts, images, or impulses that are ego-dystonic (obsessions) and engages in repetitive and seemingly purposeful behaviours performed according to certain rules, or in a stereotyped fashion (compulsions). The individual recognizes that these obsessions and compulsions are senseless or unreasonable, but mounting tension ensues when he attempts to resist the compulsion or to ignore the obsession. Common obsessions include thoughts of violence, contamination, and doubt, while common compulsions are hand-washing, checking, counting, and touching.

The neuroses have responded well to psychoanalysis and other forms of dynamic psychotherapy such as individual reconstructive psychotherapy, supportive therapy, and psychoanalytic group psychotherapy. Other modalities used in treatment of neuroses include behaviour modification, hypnosis, psychotropic medications, and various nondynamic approaches.

Normund Wong
Menninger Foundation
University of Kansas

References
Freud, S. (1959 [1926]), *Inhibitions, Symptoms and Anxiety* (Standard edition of *Complete Psychological Works of Sigmund Freud*, Vol. xx), London. (Original German, *Hemmung, Symptom und Angst.*)
Shapiro, D. (1965), *Neurotic Styles*, New York.
See also: *anxiety*; *hysteria*; *obsessive-compulsive disorder*; *phobia*.

Norms

Norms are mental models or guidelines by which, ideally, we control and evaluate our action and that of others. Normative order is central because upon it largely depends the possibility of mutual co-operation, which should be taken here to include mutual noninterference of action units that are engaged in distinct activities not directly related. Sociology is to a large extent concerned with the functional evaluation, comparison, and explanation of different kinds of normative order – including study of cases of relative failure to achieve integration and inclusive solidarity and study of processes of breakdown, as well as processes by which some kind of normative order comes to be established, is maintained, or re-established. In this article, we are dealing with norms in the generic sense; actually, in complex social systems

the normative order has several types of components of which 'norms' in a more specific sense are only one.

In the generic sense, norms are one of four types of element in the basic frame of reference common to the sciences concerned with symbolic interaction (Parsons, 1937): (1) 'Action' in the technical sense is *goal*-directed. (In a limiting case, the expression of affect may be regarded as a kind of goal-attainment.) (2) Goal attainment is possible only if certain *conditions* are met. (3) Actors seek and often find more or less adequate *means* for attaining their goals. ('Conditions' cannot always be met. The difference between means and conditions is analytical, not concrete. The two types of element are always correlative.) (4) In principle, action is always constrained by *norms*.

Conformity with norms is itself a goal (again, in principle), but this goal is general and relatively nonexpedient; it operates as a constraint or set of constraints on the choice of means that might otherwise serve to reach more variable short- or medium-range goals. In another aspect, however, conformity to norms is also itself a means for goal attainment, especially in the long run. Social norms are the main components of what Emile Durkheim called the *internal* environment of action, which is cultural, social, and psychological. Therefore, in relatively well-integrated systems of social interaction, conformity to norms on the part of acting units is both a means and a condition of goal attainment. The conditions of the *external* environment consist of causal relations that work independently of human orientation.

The commonality of norms is a matter of degree. Further, action is never determined solely by the mental orientations actors *bring* to situations but always takes account (to some extent, of course) of situational aspects they *find*. Therefore, conformity to norms is also a matter of degree and can be a complex question of judgement. Finally, it should be remarked that although norms are constraining to the acting unit, they are often voluntarily accepted as legitimate and need not be imposed by coercion alone.

Harry M. Johnson
University of Illinois, Champaign–Urbana

Reference
Parsons, T. (1937), *The Structure of Social Action*, New York.
See also: *anomie*; *conformity*; *deviance*.

Nuptiality

In the field of demography, the study of nuptiality refers to the study of the marital status composition of the population and the components of change of marital status, that is, first marriage, divorce (and separation), widowhood, and remarriage. Defined in this way, a strict, legal interpretation of marital status is implied. However, in many societies, a person's actual or *de facto* status is frequently different from his legal status. For example, in Latin America and the Caribbean and increasingly in the West, couples begin their partnership in a consensual union which may not later be formally legalized. In other places, several systems of marriage law, such as civil law, religious law, and tribal or customary law, operate simultaneously. The decision to study legal status, *de facto* status, or both must therefore depend on the circumstances prevailing in the particular society.

At a broader level of conception, nuptiality may also cover the study of the balance of the sexes available for marriage (the marriage market), polygamy, and the relative characteristics of husbands and wives (assortive mating). At this point, it becomes apparent that patterns of nuptiality are merely a subset of the totality of a society's marriage customs. This recognition has directed research on nuptiality away from demography in isolation to the place or function of nuptiality patterns within the prevailing social structure. Particular attention has focused on nuptiality in relation to familial organization and religion.

Strongly patrilineal societies, as found in Africa, the Middle East, South Asia, and East Asia, have traditionally been characterized by universal marriage for both sexes, early marriage for women but a relatively wide age difference between the sexes, and low rates of divorce and remarriage. A young girl was seen as a visitor in her parents' household, a person who would soon leave to join her husband's household. As such, her value to her parents was in the alliance with another family that her marriage effected, rather than in any direct services that she would provide to the household economy of her parents. Also, because at marriage she became the property of her husband's household, divorce and remarriage were difficult. In the Middle East and South Asia and in parts of Africa, these patterns are also reinforced by Islam and Hinduism, which place great significance on virginity at marriage for women and on the duty of parents to see their children married. In these religions, marriage is not regarded as a purely individual decision.

Where family structure is more loosely organized or is bilateral, as in European cultures, the Caribbean, Latin America and South-East Asia, marriage has tended to be less than universal and age at marriage somewhat later for women. There has been a smaller age difference between the sexes, and divorce, remarriage and informal unions have been more frequent. These patterns are reinforced by the individualism more prominent in the major religions of these areas, Christianity and Buddhism. On the other hand, Islamic societies in South-East Asia have universal and early marriage for women emphasizing the pre-eminence of religion in this regard.

These more traditional patterns are, of course, changing in many parts of the world. Most spectacularly, age at marriage for women in East Asia has risen substantially and has been accompanied by a major shift of single women into the paid, non-agricultural labour force. Alliance marriages have lost their force in the shift of power to the national level, and in the face of the growing earning potential of single women. In the West, age at marriage for both sexes has fluctuated violently in the twentieth century in relation to economic swings and societal changes in life-course expectations. Age at marriage is also rising slowly in Africa, the Middle East and South Asia mainly because girls spend a longer period in school. However, the chances of any increase of women's age at marriage very much beyond age 20 in these countries are still fairly remote, because a change in the role of single women, similar to that which has occurred in East Asia, is likely to be more strongly resisted.

Peter McDonald
Australian Institute of Family Studies, Melbourne

Further Reading
Dupâguier, J., Hélin, E., Laslett, P., Livi-Bacci, M. and Sogner, S. (1981), *Marriage and Remarriage in Populations of the Past*, London.
Goode, W. J. (1963), *World Revolution and Family Patterns*, Glencoe, Ill.
McDonald, P. (1984), 'Social organisation and nuptiality in developing societies', in J. Cleland and J. Hobcraft (eds), *Reproductive Change in Developing Countries*, Oxford.
See also: *divorce; marriage*.

O

Obsessive-Compulsive Disorder

It is common human experience to have an idea or an image come to mind seemingly of its own accord. When this happens repeatedly and the ideas and images are disturbing, they are called obsessions. Paradoxically, ordinary language describes as obsessed a person who voluntarily fixes on some single idea or goal. Thus, the concept of obsession expresses a dialectical opposition of voluntary and involuntary preoccupation. Adding to the semantic confusion is the practice of using the phrase compulsive (that is involuntary) thoughts interchangeably with obsessions.

The simple technical rule is to limit obsessions to mental events, and compulsions to behaviour. Symptomatic compulsive behaviours are repetitive and stereotyped irrational attempts to produce or prevent some imagined result. The diagnostic term obsessive-compulsive disorder captures a typical pattern. Some obsessive thought comes to mind which is magically prevented by some compulsive ritual. The essence of the obsessive-compulsive disorder is captured in the children's rhyme, 'step on a crack, break your mother's back'. The child then may have a momentary compulsion to avoid stepping on cracks.

Psychoanalysts interpret obsessive phenomena as unconscious ideas coming into consciousness. Typical obsessional ideas have to do with violence, as in the children's rhyme. Another common theme is contamination, leading to hand-washing compulsion. Freud emphasized the similarities between obsessive-compulsive phenomena, superstition, and religious ritual.

Severe obsessive-compulsive disorders can be quite disabling. They are often associated with obvious depression or are thought to mask an underlying depression. French psychiatrists have described a related condition, '*Folie du doute*', the madness of doubting. This condition suggests yet another sense of obsession. The person endlessly ruminates about the remote consequences of any action and becomes immobilized by indecision and uncertainty. Although obsessive-compulsive disorder is not ordinarily associated with actual violence, in rare cases the person acts out the violence or other impulse. Compulsive ritual activity in very young children is often an indication of extreme psychopathology.

Alan A. Stone
Harvard University

See also: *depressive disorders*; *neuroses*; *phobia*.

Occupational Psychology

Occupational psychology is a somewhat catch-all title for an area which has variously been called industrial psychology, organizational psychology, vocational psychology and personnel psychology. Industrial psychology perhaps carries a hint of psychology in the interests of management; organizational psychology limits the field to a particular context; vocational psychology tends to deal with individual careers outside the organizational context in which they are usually conducted, while personnel psychology possibly ignores the non-organizational context. Thus occupational psychology is a useful label, since it incorporates all of these emphases.

Historically, we can view the development of occupational psychology as a product of the social, economic, and cultural changes in Western industrial society. Sometimes, these effects were mediated through parallel developments in mainstream psychology. A few examples may make these relationships clearer.

The biological determinism of the nineteenth century, exemplified in Galton's researches into the supposed hereditary basis of outstanding intellectual ability, coincided with the growth of 'scientific management'. As expounded by F. W. Taylor, this approach assumed that work could be broken down into tasks for which specific abilities were required. The First World War led to the development of psychometric tests to select for military functions, so the ideological justification and the practical tools were available for the growth of the psychometric testing movement for purposes of occupational selection. That this tradition lives on is evident from the following quotation from the doyen of American applied psychologists, Marvin Dunnette (1976): 'Human attributes do indeed exist to a sufficiently consistent degree across situations so that the prediction of human work performance can realistically be undertaken on the basis of tested aptitudes and skills apart from situational modifiers.' This statement clearly implies the assumptions that individuals possess lasting characteristics; that these characteristics hold true across situations; that they are related to particular aspects of jobs, and that jobs are definable in terms of the tasks they involve.

A second influence upon occupational psychology has been the emphasis during the first half of the twentieth century on the importance of the small group. Again, the evidence of the Second World War indicated the value of group cohesiveness in achieving certain sorts of objectives. The military idea of leadership and the post-war emphasis upon skills of man-management led to increased study of work groups. The concept of the working group as dependent for its success upon easy interpersonal relationships gained credence, and managers were seen as oriented towards the maintenance of these relationships as well as towards the achievement of organizational goals. Hence the leadership theories of Fred Fiedler, and the theory x and theory y typology of management propounded by David McGregor fitted in well with the current *zeitgeist*.

The third wave of development in occupational psychology related to the strong cultural influence of humanism in the 1960s, exemplified in the popular text *The Greening of America* (1970) by Theodore Reich. Self-actualization, the reaching of one's full potential, and other slogans gained support of such mainstream psychologists as Carl Rogers and Abraham Maslow. Their influence spilled over into occupational psychology in the form of various types of group training in management development programmes. The objective of many of these programmes was to help individuals to get in touch with their 'real selves' and as a consequence realize more of their true potential as individuals.

The history of occupational psychology can cynically be seen as a response to the opportunity to make the most out of each current ephemeral cultural fad. An alternative point of view might suggest that psychologists have been used for practical purposes when it was thought by the authorities that they could be of use.

Social psychology has much to say about the relationship between organizations and individuals in the theory of roles; about the meaning of work in the phenomenological approaches to cognition; about life careers in the life-span theories of human development; and about the relationships between organizations and between nation states in the theories of conflict and negotiation. The focus today is less upon individuals in isolation from their context, and also less upon the primary working group. The organizational context of work, together with the values and image it implies, are much more to the fore. So too is the environment of organizations, to which they must continuously adapt if they are to survive. In particular, labour relations and economic and technological change are being brought into psychological focus. Cross-cultural studies are beginning to demonstrate how ethnocentric our theories have hitherto been, and how irrelevant they are to the needs of developing nations. Only if a broad perspective proves stronger than a parochial professionalism will occupational psychology come into its own.

Peter Herriot
Birkbeck College, University of London

Reference

Dunnette, M. (ed.) (1976), *Handbook of Industrial and Organizational Psychology*, Chicago.

Further Reading

Bass, B. M. and Barrett, G. V. (1981), *People, Work and Organizations*, 3rd edn, Boston.
Katz, D. and Kahn, R.L. (1978), *The Social Psychology of Organizations*, 2nd edn, New York.
See also: *aptitude testing*; *ergonomics*; *industrial and organizational psychology*; *organizations*; *vocational career and development*.

Ohlin, Bertil (1899–1979)

Bertil Ohlin, the Swedish economist, received the Nobel Prize in Economics in 1977 (jointly with James Meade) for his contributions to the theory of international trade. Bertil Ohlin had two outstanding careers, one as an economist and one as the political leader of Sweden's Liberal Party, 1944–67. He was professor of economics at the University of Copenhagen 1924–9 and at the Stockholm School of Economics 1929–65.

Ohlin made important contributions in a number of fields. The publication of *Interregional and International Trade* in 1933 (a revised version of his doctoral dissertation in Swedish of 1924), reshaped the theory of international trade by giving it a price-theoretical basis. Here Ohlin developed and formalized ideas and insights presented earlier by the Swedish economist Eli Heckscher. The approach constructed by Ohlin, often summarized as the Heckscher-Ohlin model, has been the source of inspiration for the bulk of theoretical as well as empirical work in international economics since the 1930s.

In the late 1920s Ohlin was engaged in an exchange with J. M. Keynes on the effects of the German reparations as a consequence of the Treaty of Versailles. Ohlin's analysis of the 'transfer problem', superior to that of Keynes, inspired later research in this field. During the world-wide depression of the 1930s Ohlin focused his work on the causes of unemployment. He became one of the most prominent members of the Stockholm School or the Swedish School, sometimes claimed to be a forerunner of the Keynesian revolution in macroeconomics.

Ohlin played an important role in Swedish political life for roughly three decades as the leader of the Liberal Party, which became the largest opposition party to the ruling Social Democrats. He developed his own brand of liberalism, which he termed social liberalism. The role of government was to maintain a stable framework for private economic activity using suitable stabilization policies and by income redistribution. He was extremely prolific as an economic journalist, publishing approximately 1,200 newspaper articles and columns. He also published two volumes of his memoirs in the 1970s.

Lars Jonung
University of Lund

Reference

Ohlin, B. (1933), *Interregional and International Trade*, Cambridge, Mass.

Further Reading

Caves, R. (1978), 'Bertil Ohlin's contribution to economics', *Scandinavian Journal of Economics*, 80. (This article also contains a bibliography of his work compiled by Ohlin.)

Samuelson, P. (1981), 'Bertil Ohlin (1899–1979)', *Scandinavian Journal of Economics*, 83.

Oligopoly

Oligopoly is defined as an industry or market in which there are only a few sellers. Evidence on levels of market concentration suggests it to be the prevailing market structure in most Western industrial economies. The central feature of oligopoly is the *interdependence* of firms' activities. Thus any action by one oligopolist will significantly affect the sales, profitability and so on, of its rivals, who might therefore be expected to react or retaliate. Correspondingly, most oligopoly theory posits behaviour in which the oligopolist sets his decision variables (including advertising, research and innovation, as well as the traditional price or quantity decision) on the basis of specific conjectures about rivals' reactions. At one extreme lies the Cournot model, in which zero reactions are assumed, and at the other is the view, most persuasively articulated by Chamberlin, that a recognition of mutual independence will lead oligopolists to maximize their joint profits (thus making oligopoly virtually indistinguishable from monopoly). A major post-war development was the Structure-Conduct-Performance paradigm which extended traditional oligopoly theory to incorporate the effects of entry barriers and product differentiation. A multitude of empirical studies ensued, usually with results pointing to a need for strong antitrust policies. The theoretical basis of much of this work was, however, *ad-hoc*, and only recently have significant developments been added (for example, on strategic entry deterrence and contestable markets) to our theoretical understanding of oligopoly. Dissenting voices to the mainstream include Schumpeter and the Austrians, viewing competition as a dynamic process,

and, latterly, Chicago economists, doubting the general existence of significant entry barriers.

S. W. Davies
University of East Anglia

See also: *antitrust legislation*; *business concentration*; *cartels and trade associations*; *monopoly*.

Opinion Polls

Opinion polls ascertain public opinion via direct enumeration, as distinguished from reliance upon secondary sources such as content analysis of documents or consultation with influential public figures. The sample survey is the usual technique employed by pollsters, though conceivably a tiny population might be polled in its entirety. Polling traditionally is associated with commercial organizations, rather than with academic research. The importance of the distinction lies more in the style of analysis than in the form of opinion data. The commercial poll taker's interest rests largely with the face-value meaning of opinion questions, illustrated for example when a newspaper reports the percentage of a population approving of a prominent politician. The academic researcher is more likely to treat opinion poll items as indicators of a more abstract underlying concept, and seek to identify the factors accounting for how people score on the concept.

As the term itself suggests, polling is closely associated with the measurement of political opinion, though the pollster's interests embrace more than politics alone. Polling of opinion in any sphere can be controversial, but it is in the political arena that the issues appear in particularly sharp relief and prominence in the public consciousness. Much debated, both among the public and among professional social scientists, is the *impact* of polling on opinion formation. Polling results, particularly when receiving the wide publicity characteristic of election poll data, may in an ironic inversion become active ingredients in the formation of opinion. Thus, the very polls which are championed as valuable servants of the public – the 'pulse of democracy', as George Gallup (1940) phrased it – may also hold sway as masters of public opinion. If polls determine opinion, there is the irresistible temptation for benefactors of a favourable poll result – a candidate for political office, for example – to load question wordings.

This latter concern brings us to questions of the *accuracy* of polling. Opinion polls tarnished their image through faulty methods of sampling in the 1930s days of sample surveying. Today, much progress has been registered over the technical difficulties of gathering random samples of human populations. Assuming impeccable ethics by pollsters and their customers, the best of sampling procedures, and perfect response rates, however, more fundamental doubts about the accuracy of polls may be entertained. The superficial probes necessary for an enumeration of several hundreds of citizens dispersed over a wide area cannot, it is sometimes argued, capture some fundamental attitudes. The relentless counting of surface opinion – views hastily offered on sometimes trivial events – ungrounded in either the context of surrounding circumstances or in some basic psychological attitude-set, debases the exercise in the view of some students of mass communications and political sociology.

Justifiably or not, opinion polling has grown into a thriving commercial industry and is part of the institutional landscape of modern industrial societies. At their best, the polls inform, entertain, and, arguably, indeed do lubricate public discourse.

John Goyder
University of Waterloo

Further Reading
Gallup, G. and Rae, S. F. (1949), *The Pulse of Democracy*, New York.
Wheeler, M. (1976), *Lies, Damn Lies, and Statistics: The Manipulation of Public Opinion in America*, New York.
See also: *marketing research*; *sample surveys*.

Oral Tradition

Oral traditions are accounts, which may or may not be historical in content, transmitted verbally from one generation to another. Their peculiarity lies in their particular mode of transmission by hearsay, as opposed to writing, objects or gestures. Their major characteristics are: (1) They testify both to *the past* and to *the present* during which they are recounted; a corpus of oral tradition forms the 'collective memory' of a community, and cultures reproduce themselves mainly through oral tradition and traditional motor behaviour. (2) Oral tradition is made up of a welter of testimonies forming a corpus. Each tradition tends to deal with a small sequence of events or a single situation only, and is linked to particular institutions, activities or speculations. The various accounts may conflict with one another. (3) Oral traditions are couched in all varieties of oral art forms from prayer or song to *obiter dicta*, to poetry, genealogy, narrative or epic. As expressions of culture, such data interest all social scientists as well as historians, linguists and literary critics.

Any oral tradition is a product in a process, a stream of orality that begins with the recollection of an incident or a situation either by an eye witness or as a rumour. Thereupon human memory takes over and recreates the event or the situation, providing logical links between the items observed and making the whole intelligible by the attribution of continuity and motivation. At this stage, testimony is oral history. It

becomes tradition only after transmission from one generation to a following one. Memory apart, the contents are already moulded by audience reaction, consciousness of self-identity, practical social goals and the art form chosen to express the experience, which need not be in narrative form. The contents can be anecdotal or generalizations of the type 'we do this', often with normative overtones. This last type is the stuff informants feed to ethnographers, and its critical evaluation is crucial to anthropology.

Oral tradition proper begins when the accounts are transmitted over generations. They then become family history, history specific to certain institutions (village, chiefdom, age group, court of law and so on) or genres of fictional art. Contents of narratives, particularly, change according to various influences. Homeostasis occurs as accounts tend to be adjusted to existing social or cultural practice, audience response remodels the expressions, and the goals pursued become more specific. Moreover, other accounts in the corpus, especially in the same genre, produce fusions, rebuttals or further mnemonic streamlining. Family history lasts only two or three generations and then dies out or is absorbed into other more official traditions.

Official traditions and fiction can last much longer. Practically all the accounts are now closely tied to specific institutions and serve their ends. This function remodels their contents. Specialists in tradition appear, and where a tradition is felt to be of great importance formal teaching can occur. Distinctions between esoteric and common traditions often appear. Knowledge of esoteric accounts becomes an attribute and sometimes a basis for power, while 'secrets' are used to bind groups together. The contents of narratives or genealogies or epics change again, as a corpus of 'old tradition' becomes better defined. Further mnemonic streamlining introduces anachronisms by sharpened opposition, inclusion in hierarchical subsets and stressing co-occurence, while very stable anecdotes (called clichés) emerge, made up of part fiction and part relevance to a past historical situation. These become paradigms of past events or processes, especially repetitive ones. The impact of symbolic reasoning becomes stronger, using the same processes as mnemonic streamlining, reducing sets of messages to new, simpler and more general messages. At this stage traditions last perhaps two centuries, sometimes more, with elements that may be much older. Their life spans are determined by the stability of the institutions to which they are linked. Once the institutions disappear, or are greatly altered, tradition is erased.

Traditions of origin form a separate class. They are often only very partially inspired by earlier tradition. They represent the outcome of speculation about the nature of the world and of mankind. They account for the categories of space, time, number, creation and the world as it is perceived. They are the equivalent to cosmology, and such data are a prime source for the study of world-views.

All these types of traditions coexist in a single community at a single time. Moreover the stages outlined apply mainly to narratives. Traditions, learned by rote, such as songs, poetry and prayers tend to be more stable, although textual variants can creep in. The glosses on the text vary, however, and since such sources are highly allusive, their message does change as well. Such traditions die out when fashion changes or when their content becomes too obscure for easy understanding.

The usual canons of evidence hold for oral traditions. The necessary data for critical appraisal must be gathered when the traditions are collected. The problems concern variants, transmission, the influence of performance and genre on content, homeostatic adaptation or outright falsification to serve social ends, mnemonic or symbolic streamlining, the interpretation of clichés or metaphors, feedback from other (written or oral) sources and chronology. *Ex post facto* conjecture (structuralist or otherwise) is ordinarily useless. The value of a body of tradition depends very much on the quality of their collection and study in the field.

Oral traditions are most studied by literary critics, folklorists and historians. The latter use them in historical reconstruction, preferably along with cross-cutting data, as oral tradition by itself gives a very ethnocentric view of a society's past. Anthropologists and sociologists are beginning to discover how much light 'distortions' shed on social and cultural processes. Moreover, oral traditions are a major source for the study of how memory and the human brain function.

Jan Vansina
University of Wisconsin

Further Reading

Bernardi, B., Poni, C. and Triulzi, A. (1978), *Fonti orali – Oral Source – Sources orales*, Milan.
Henige, D. (1982), *Oral Historiography*, London.
Vansina, J. (1985), *Oral Tradition as History*, Madison.

Organizations

Organizations can be defined as resource pools (Buchanan, 1977). They come into existence when individuals place the resources available to them (such as skills, money or prestige) under some sort of central control, rather than using them individualistically. Organizations must establish certain rules for the use and distribution of their resources. These rules may be based on an autocratic-hierarchical principle, whereby one person assumes the role of central co-ordinator, or they may be co-operative-democratic, in which case all members participate on equal terms in co-ordinating and distributing decision making. Most organizations fall somewhere between these two extremes, and in reality an organization may combine 'hierarchical' and 'market' features.

A number of basic problems have to be solved in organizations: (1) The division and allocation of work tasks. (2) The co-ordination of work. (3) The recruitment of members. (4) Motivating workers to work more than the minimum. (5) The use and distribution of resources to survive as an organization.

Formalized enforceable rules assign tasks to jobs, specify how tasks should be done, and determine the decisions a job holder is allowed to make, and to whom he is allowed to give orders. Rules control recruitment, promotions and remuneration. The sum of formal rules constitutes the organizational structure, which orders the ways in which individual skills and technology are used to realize organizational goals. Various organizations have at different historical periods offered special solutions to the problems of pooling resources, ranging, in the West, from the medieval guild to the modern corporation. Organizational forms which were especially successful tended to be diffused.

The design of organizational structures, and the achievement of improvements in efficiency, require a consideration of the following principles.

(1) *Division of labour*. A job is defined which compromises several tasks. By constructing such jobs, a number of advantages can be realized. Training for the job, both inside and outside the organization, can be kept within limits. Not everyone need possess the skills, say, to build a car, and yet – with the help of organization rules – workers and employees can co-operate to produce high-quality cars. When jobs are created so that they correspond largely to qualifications available on the labour market, a choice of workers is possible. For example, all electricians with certain qualifications are, in general, suited to work in electrical departments. Recruitment becomes easier, and only a minimal amount of training is necessary before those recruited are able to do the job adequately.

Within a certain range, the efficiency of organizations can be increased by greater division of labour and specialization. Each worker does a specified task for which few techniques are necessary; trained on the job, the worker can thus be expected to achieve a high degree of skill in a short time. One problem with this, however, is that highly-specialized jobs can reduce motivation, increase boredom, and lead to absenteeism, rapid turnover and a high failure rate. It also requires a high degree of co-ordination.

(2) *Co-ordination by the standardization of operating procedures*. This is a very powerful co-ordination instru-

ment, increases in co-ordination reducing the need for communication. If one simply follows the rules, one need not understand the rationale behind the rule and can still achieve a high standard of problem solving. For example, a warehouse employee can successfully apply a re-ordering rule, incorporating a complicated re-order formula without understanding the formula. On the basis of standardized operating procedures, it is possible to delegate decisions and still maintain control at the top; but the disadvantage with such procedures is that they have a tendency to persist when any environmental change requires modifications in the rules. For example, when the environment poses new problems for the organization, those executing standard operating procedures are likely to be criticized because the usual procedures no longer resolve the problems adequately. But adherence to rules is also a very effective means of blocking such a critique. Consequently, standardized operating procedures are often kept, and followed even more rigidly, just when they should be changed (Crozier, 1964, calls this effect the *circulus vitiosus* of bureaucracy).

(3) *Co-ordination by hierarchy.* Assuming that a problem arises on the production floor of an industrial organization – a machine breaks down, the number of rejects rises, or delays occur in the schedule. At first the foreman will try to solve the problem. If he lacks the necessary competence, he will go to his superior. This process of feedback-co-ordination in hierarchies enables the organization to resolve problems at the appropriate level, that is, the level at which all the interdependencies with other organizational units can be taken into consideration. Very big problems are taken right to the top of the organization. In solving such problems, new policies are formulated which apply to the whole organization. But decision makers at all levels do not just wait passively for problems to emerge. They also set targets and make plans for the future. In hierarchies, feedback and also forward co-ordination is possible. Hierarchies are very flexible co-ordinating instruments. But they are also very expensive ones, for managers demand high salaries. Hierarchies can be augmented by staff whose main task is to support decision making in the hierarchical line by providing information. A special form of hierarchy is the matrix system in which multiple-command systems interact in order to achieve co-ordination. For example, one command system may be predominantly concerned with the progress of a specific project, while another co-ordinates functional operations across projects.

(4) *Co-ordination by teams.* This is another mechanism to support hierarchies. A number of experts from different hierarchical positions come together for specific tasks. They exchange information or engage in collective decision making. If certain conditions are met, teams are an effective co-ordination instrument.

Approaches or Paradigms

Organization theory, being a rather young discipline, is characterized by a multitude of approaches or paradigms. They can be classified into:

(1) *The bureaucracy approach.* Max Weber (1968 [1922]), portrayed bureaucracies as manifestations of the rationalization process which took place in Western societies. He used an ideal type of bureaucracy as an analytical tool, to demonstrate how organizations function and how they can be more efficient than other forms of control. However, he also pointed out the negative effects which organizations may have on their members, who are imprisoned by bureaucratic rules, and on clients, who are in many ways dependent on the power of bureaucracies.

(2) *How-to-do-it approaches.* Prescriptions for the design of organizations have a long history. Ptah-hotep wrote the first known guide on running an organization, on papyrus, in 2700 BC. From the beginning of industrialization, practitioners tried to encapsulate effective organizational solutions – good business practice – in the form of design principles, for example, Ure and Babbage in England, both in 1835, Fayol in France in 1916, and Roesky in Germany in 1878.

Design principles published in these early management books were supposed to be valid under all conditions. A higher form of rationalization in designing organizations was reached with Taylor's (1903 and 1911) 'Scientific Management' approach, which applied experimental engineering methods to such problems as assigning tasks to jobs, standardizing of work, optimizing work tools and work flows, and selecting workers. Taylor's methods are still widely followed.

Many design problems, such as choosing between functional, divisional or matrix structures, determining the number of departments, or choosing co-ordination systems, continue to defy attempts to quantify and optimize. The kind of decision support which decision makers can expect for these problems from organization theory requires that they consider the decision alternatives and weigh up the pros and cons on the basis of empirical case studies (see articles in Nystrom and Starbuck, 1981).

(3) *Studies in organizational behaviour.* The early 'how-to-do-it' approaches were based on a machine model of organizations. Most of the authors were engineers. Their aim was to design organizational rules and payment systems so that organization members would function like parts of a machine. The Hawthorne Experiments proved scientifically (or, better, scientifically legitimized) an idea that had been discussed in management journals some time earlier – that individuals also act as social beings. The Human Relation movement can be seen as a countermovement to Scientific Management, and it encouraged many studies of such problems, such as socializing new

members of organizations and motivating them by payments systems, career systems, leadership styles, and work which allowed for self-fulfilment (see Dunnette, 1976 and Dubin, 1976). Some critiques are rather sceptical about the contribution of these studies to the solution of practical problems (see Perrow, 1979).

(4) *Studies of organization decision making.* A number of researchers concentrate on how decisions are made within organizations and how organizations, on the basis of these decisions, adapt to their environments. Rationality in organizations is 'bounded' (March and Simon, 1958); the organization member has a limited capacity to identify alternative actions and to predict and evaluate the consequences of these alternatives. Individuals equipped with bounded rationality can achieve more when they act together in highly complex organizations, because the organizational structure routinizes the wisdom gained by experience in standard operating procedures.

In more recent studies, decision situations in organizations are portrayed as garbage cans into which changing participants dump problems and problem solutions (March and Olsen, 1976). The role of ideologies, myths, sagas, or culture in organizational decision making is attracting much research interest (Starbuck, 1982).

If the development of organizations is seen as the result of an evolutionary process, as some researchers see it (Aldrich, 1979), the degree of rationality which can be achieved in organizational decisions becomes less important. The environment selects those organizations which are well adapted, regardless of whether the organizational change leading to adaptation is the result of clever management or pure chance. New organizational forms evolve and spread when they solve co-ordination problems more efficiently, or when their transaction costs are lower, a point which is stressed in the transaction cost approach (Van de Ven and Joyce, 1981).

The contingency approach, in which variations in organization structure are explained on the basis of correlations between structural variables and context factors such as size of organizations, technology, or dependence on other organizations, also assumes – at least implicitly – that those structures prevail which are best adapted to their environments (Pugh and Hickson, 1976).

Alfred Kieser
University of Mannheim

References
Aldrich, H. E. (1979), *Organizations and Environments*, Englewood Cliffs, N.J.
Buchanan, J. M. (1977), *Freedom in Constitutional Contract, Perspective of a Political Economist*, London.
Crozier, M. (1964), *The Bureaucratic Phenomenon*, London.
Dubin, R. (ed.) (1976), *Handbook of Work, Organization, and Society*, Chicago.
Dunnette, M. D. (ed.) (1976), *Handbook of Industrial and Organizational Psychology*, Chicago.
March, J. G. and Simon, H. A. (1958), *Organizations*, New York.
March, J. G. and Olsen, J. P. (1976), *Ambiguity and Choice in Organizations*, Bergen.
Nystrom, P. C. and Starbuck, W. H. (eds) (1981), *Handbook of Organizational Design*, 2 vols, Oxford.
Perrow, C. (1979), *Complex Organizations. A Critical Essay*, 2nd edn, Glenview.
Pugh, D. S. and Hickson, D. J. (eds) (1976), *Organizational Structure in Its Context. The Aston Programme I*, Westmead.
Starbuck, W. H. (ed.) (1982), 'Organizations as ideological systems', Special Issue, *Journal of Management Studies*, 19.
Van de Ven, A. H. and Joyce, W. F. (eds) (1981), *Perspectives on Organization Design and Behavior*, New York.
Weber, M. (1968), *Economy and Society*, New York.
See also: *bureaucracy; decision making.*

P

Pain

Pain research and therapy have long been dominated by specificity theory, which proposes that pain is a specific sensation subserved by a straight-through transmission system from skin to brain, and that intensity of pain is proportional to the extent of tissue damage. Recent evidence, however, shows that pain is not simply a function of the amount of bodily damage alone, but is influenced by attention, anxiety, suggestion, prior conditioning, and other psychological variables (Melzack and Wall, 1982). Moreover, the results of neurosurgical operations which cut the so-called pain pathway – a natural outcome of specificity theory – have been disappointing, particularly for chronic pain syndromes. Not only does the pain tend to return in a substantial proportion of patients, but new pains may appear. The psychological and neurological data, then, refute the concept of a simple, straight-through pain transmission system.

In recent years the evidence on pain has moved in the direction of recognizing the plasticity and modifiability of events in the central nervous system. Pain is a complex perceptual and affective experience determined by the unique past history of the individual, by the meaning of the stimulus to him, by his 'state of mind' at the moment, as well as by the sensory nerve patterns evoked by physical injury or pathology.

In the light of this understanding of pain processes, Melzack and Wall (1965) proposed the gate-control theory of pain. Basically, the theory states that neural mechanisms in the dorsal horn of the spinal cord act like a gate which can increase or decrease the flow of nerve impulses from peripheral fibres to the spinal cord cells that project to the brain. Somatic input is therefore subjected to the modulating influence of the gate *before* it evokes pain perception and response. The theory suggests that large-fibre inputs tend to close the gate while small-fibre inputs generally open it, and that the gate is also profoundly influenced by descending influences from the brain. It further proposes that the sensory input is modulated at successive synapses throughout its projection from the spinal cord to the brain areas responsible for pain experience and response. Pain occurs when the number of nerve impulses that arrives at these areas exceeds a critical level.

Melzack and Wall (1982) have recently assessed the present-day status of the gate-control theory in the light of new physiological research. The theory is clearly alive and well despite considerable controversy and conflicting evidence. Although some of the physiological details may need revision, the concept of gating (or input modulation) is stronger than ever.

The subjective experience of pain has well-known sensory qualities, such as burning, shooting and sharp. In addition, it has a distinctly unpleasant, affective quality. It becomes overwhelming, demands immediate attention, and disrupts ongoing behaviour and thought. It motivates or drives the organism into activity aimed at stopping the pain as quickly as possible. On the basis of these considerations, Melzack and Casey (1968) proposed that there are three major psychological dimensions of pain: sensory-discriminative, motivational-affective, and cognitive-evaluative. Recent physiological evidence suggests that each is subserved by a physiologically specialized system in the brain. Recognition of the multidimensional nature of pain experience has led to the development of a paper-and-pencil questionnaire (the McGill Pain Questionnaire) to obtain numerical measures of the intensity and qualities of pain (Melzack, 1975).

Many new methods to control pain have been developed in recent years (Melzack and Wall, 1982). Sensory modulation techniques such as transcutaneous electrical nerve stimulation and ice massage are widely used in the attempt to activate inhibitory neural mechanisms to suppress pain. Psychological techniques have also been developed which allow patients to achieve some degree of control over their pain. These techniques include biofeedback, hypnosis, distraction, behaviour modification, and the use of imagery and other cognitive activities to modulate the transmission of the nerve-impulse patterns that subserve pain. A large body of research demonstrates that several of these techniques employed at the same time – 'multiple convergent therapy' – are often highly effective for the control of chronic pain states, particularly those such as low back pain which have prominent elements of tension, depression and anxiety.

Ronald Melzack
McGill University

References
Melzack, R. (1975), 'The McGill Pain Questionnaire: major properties and scoring methods', *Pain*, 1.

Melzack, R. and Casey, K. L. (1968), 'Sensory, motivational and central control determinants of pain: a new conceptual model', in D. Kenshalo (ed.), *The Skin Senses*, Springfield, Ill.

Melzack, R. and Wall, P. D. (1965), 'Pain mechanisms: a new theory', *Science*, 150.

Melzack, R. and Wall, P. D. (1982), *The Challenge of Pain*, Harmondsworth.

See also: *nervous system*.

Paranoid Reactions

Paranoid reactions are a group of pathological responses to emotional stress. They may stand alone, be mixed with other psychopathological states, and even be found in everyday life.

The core of the paranoid reaction is the psychological defence of projection. The essence of this defence is the attribution to the external world of those wishes, impulses, feelings and thoughts that are unacceptable to the individual, though emerging from within him. For example, a person experiencing unacceptable hostility towards other people may project (attribute outward) this feeling and believe himself to be the *object* of hostility or persecution from without.

These reactions, like many mental symptoms, have a restitutive function; that is, they serve a reparative purpose in the mental economy of the individual. An example might be a person suffering from intolerable depression through loneliness, who may project his wish for company in a disguised way by viewing himself as the object of a great deal of attention (though not necessarily benign attention) from others, thus: 'The FBI is following me everywhere, tapping my phone, reading my mail and sending signals through the TV.' As this last example shows, paranoid reactions may become extreme and elaborate, encompassing hallucinations and delusions, which may occasionally be grandiose.

The example also hints at a very common form of paranoid reaction, the false belief that one is the subject of an interaction that has no actual relation at all to oneself; formally, this delusion that a neutral event refers to oneself is termed an 'idea of reference'. Other hallmarks of paranoid reactions are suspicion, mistrust, and guardedness of manner, understandable as reflections of a person's mistrust of his *own* feelings, projected onto others.

Thomas G. Gutheil
Harvard University
Program in Psychiatry
and Law, Boston

Further Reading

Freud, S. (1911), 'Psychoanalytic notes upon an autobiographical account of a case of paranoia', *Collected Papers, Volume III*, ed. J. Strachey, London.

Knight, R. (1940), 'The relationship of latent homosexuality to the mechanism of paranoid delusions', *Bulletin of the Menninger Clinic*, 4.

Waelder, R. (1951), 'The structure of paranoid ideas', *International Journal of Psychoanalysis*, 32.

Parapsychology

Parapsychology in general is concerned with paranormal events – events which cannot be explained according to the usual laws of science. Such events range widely, from the Lochness monster to UFOs (unidentified flying objects), astrological predictions and ghosts. However, the term parapsychology is usually employed in a rather more limited sense, to refer to four major phenomena. These are: (1) *telepathy*: the acquisition of information about another person, at a distant place, by means not involving the known senses or logical inference; (2) *clairvoyance*: similar to telepathy, clairvoyance involves the acquisition of information about an object or event, rather than a person; (3) *precognition*: this refers to a similar kind of information acquisition, but of information which will only exist in the future, such as knowledge about a person's death two weeks ahead, or an accident to take place in the future; (4) *psychokinesis*: the influence of the human mind, by direct action of will, on another person, or event, not mediated by any physical force yet known.

Spontaneous parapsychological phenomena have been reported over centuries, but in the nature of things are hard to submit to scientific scrutiny. This is due to the impossibility of treating the data statistically. A person may dream that a particular horse would win the Derby, or a particular team the cup final; if the horse, or the team, actually succeeds, this might be interpreted as indicating precognition. However, it is not known how many people may have dreamed about the wrong horse, or team, coming out in front, nor do we know much about the actual probability of the given horse, or team, winning. Such stories are intuitively convincing to some people, but have no scientific value. Another difficulty is that such stories are usually only publicized after the event; there is no guarantee that the dream predicting the event actually happened. It would require written notification before the event in order to take the dream seriously as evidence of precognition.

Such reports do exist. Consider the Aberfan disaster in 1966, when 128 children and adults died in a cataclysm, a coal tip sliding down the mountain side and engulfing a South Wales mining town. A number of people reported precognitively, and in the presence of witnesses, having had dreams or other premonitions accurately describing the disaster. Many other authenticated cases have been described in the literature, making spontaneous parapsychological events acceptable to scientific study.

Much more convincing scientifically would of course be experimental evidence collected in the laboratory. The first to do this on any large scale was an American biologist, Joseph Banks Rhine, who started the first parapsychological laboratory at Duke University. Most of his work was done using packs of twenty-five cards, each bearing one of five different symbols (circle, star, wavy line, plus sign and square). Subjects were asked to guess the symbol on each card, under many different kinds of conditions. The probability of guessing correctly is of course one in five, and it is possible statistically to evaluate the chances of guessing at a higher rate than that. Conditions of testing might be with the experimenter looking at a given card, and the subject guessing (telepathy); or the stack of cards lying in front of the subject, but with no one looking at the faces of the cards, and the subject calling out the sequence (clairvoyance). In precognition trials the subject might have to call out the sequence of the twenty-five cards, as this would be after shuffling; having recorded the subject's calls, the experimenter would then shuffle the cards, and compare the resulting sequence with the calls made by the subject before the shuffle. There are many combinations and subtle changes in these procedures, but on the whole there is much evidence that extra-chance results can be obtained, particularly by a small number of specially gifted subjects.

Psychokinesis was tested by Rhine and his associates by means of a dice, either thrown by the experimenter or in an automatically revolving box. Subjects would try to influence the dice to come at either with a high or a low (6 or 1) number, and again the data published in the literature suggest that extra-chance results have been obtained in many cases. These data might be called the *direct* evidence in favour of parapsychological events, also sometimes called ESP (extrasensory perception), or PSI.

There are indirect types of evidence showing phenomena predictable from well-known psychological laws. Thus it has been found that a general tendency exists for scoring rates in all these types of test to decline over time; in other words, a kind of fatigue effect. Motivational factors have been shown to be important, as has personality and attitude. Extroverts tend to do better than introverts, and people who believe in the existence of PSI tend to do better than people who disbelieve it.

A tremendous amount of research has been done since the days of Rhine's early pioneering work, and much of this has been concerned with devising automating procedures and making them foolproof. Thus, to take one example, Helmut Schmidt generated random targets, registered subject's guesses and recorded all relevant data in a computerized manner.

The radioactive decay of the isotope strontium-90 was used to generate random targets for use in PSI-testing, and with the help of his machine Schmidt showed that many people were able to guess when such emissions would or would not take place. The completely automatic nature of the data-gathering and analysing precluded any accidental or wilful errors which might have caused departures from chance.

Critics of parapsychological beliefs have pointed out the ever-present possibility of fraud, the lack of foolproof laboratory procedure that always generates positive data; the possibilities of errors in transcription and analysing; the difficulties inherent in statistical analysis of such data; and the apparent waxing and waning of the parapsychological abilities of even the best subjects. Recent advances have overcome many of these criticisms, and there is now no doubt about the statistics used by parapsychologists, the experimental controls exerted, or the abolition of errors through automation. Fraud is an ever-present danger in all scientific experiments, and there certainly have been cases where fraud has been proved to have occurred in parapsychological experiments. However, it seems unlikely that hundreds of well-known scientists, with a reputation to consider, would risk their good standing in order to fabricate meaningless data, or intentionally defraud the public. On this point, of course, every student of the subject must decide for himself.

H. J. Eysenck
Institute of Psychiatry
University of London

Further Reading
Eysenck, H. J. and Sargent, C. (1982), *Explaining the Unexplained*, London.

Pareto, Vilfredo (1848–1923)

Vilfredo Pareto, born in Paris in 1848, is principally known today for his work on the theory of élites; but his contribution to sociology and political science was both more general and more profound. His approach to the social world was decisively influenced by his early training as an engineer. Throughout his career he championed the application of the methods of the natural sciences to the social studies. The idea of 'equilibrium', which he originally tackled in relation to mechanics, became the *idée maîtresse* of his social theories.

Between 1870 and 1893, Pareto devoted himself to business, politics and journalism. He was a vigorous champion of free trade. After 1876, with the fall from power of the party of moderates which originally formed around Cavour (the *destra storica*), he became progressively more disillusioned with both the protectionist policies and the general conduct of political life in Italy. Observing the practice of fashioning governmental majorities from different facts (*trasformismo*) at close hand furnished him with some of the materials for his later critique of parliamentary democracy. He made a name for himself in these years as an economist, and in 1893 became professor of political economy at Lausanne. He died in Geneva in 1923.

Pareto's first important work, the *Cours d'économie politique* (1896), [Course of Political Economy], formed the bridge between his economic and sociological studies. His contention was that the question of economic utility could not be considered in isolation from wider social and psychological forces. Protectionism is roundly condemned as simply a form of legal spoliation. Stress is upon the degree of social differentiation in a society rather than upon constitutional forms. And Marx's account of class struggles as an expression of economic interests is endorsed, though with the proviso that not all struggles between different interests should be reduced to the same schematic form.

In *Les Systèmes socialistes* (1902) [Socialist Systems] Pareto turned the theory of interests against the socialists themselves. The conflict in the modern age should not be seen in terms of a bourgeois élite and the proletariat but between two élites trying to pursue their own advantage through the manipulation of mass support. In parliamentary democracies, no less than in other forms of polity, leadership is by the few at the expense of the many. In the last resort, it is force which sustains a regime. Pareto's comments on 'humanitarians' who forget this sombre truth are scathing.

Pareto's achievement was to shift attention away from the ideological sphere and towards the nonlogical actions which predominate in social life. In his major work, the *Trattato di sociologia generale* (1916) (English translation, *The Mind and Society: Treatise on General Sociology*, 4 Vols, London, 1936), he distinguished two dimensions in nonlogical actions: 'residues' (the uniform tendencies which determine the pattern of conduct) and 'derivations' (the rationalizations which men advance in justification of a particular course of action). Equilibrium in a society is the product of a balance of 'residues'. An élite will always rule; but (contrary to the practice of classical political theory) an explanation of the form which that rule takes (whether force or persuasion predominates) should be sought in the dominant 'residues' and not in the prevalent ideology.

The *Trattato* is a cumbersome and confused work. No one would accept its conclusions today. The shift from a description of the rule of élites to a justification of authoritarian government is especially questionable. But it served to delineate a sphere for sociology which still finds support in some quarters.

B. A. Haddock
University College of Swansea

Further Reading
Borkenau, F. (1936), *Pareto*, London.
Bucolo, P. (ed.) (1980), *The Other Pareto*, London.
Cirillo, R. (1979), *The Economics of Vilfredo Pareto*, London.
Finer, S. E. (ed.) (1966), *Vilfredo Pareto: Sociology Writings*, London.

Park, Robert Ezra (1864–1944)

Robert E. Park the sociologist was the son of a businessman, and was brought up in Red Wing, Minnesota. After studying with John Dewey at the University of Michigan, he was a newspaper reporter for ten years. He then studied philosophy with William James at Harvard, and sociology in Germany, where he gained a doctorate. From 1905 to 1913 he assisted Booker T. Washington, the Black leader, at Tuskegee Institute in Alabama. In 1913 Park began teaching in the department of sociology at the University of Chicago, where he remained until his retirement in 1934.

Park was the dominant figure in the Chicago School (of Sociology) and the most influential American sociologist during the 1920s. His main writings consist of two studies of the assimilation of immigrants, a major textbook *Introduction to the Study of Sociology* (1921) and three posthumously published volumes of collected essays. His main influence, however, was exercised upon and through his students, who produced notable studies of race relations, collective behaviour, urban structure and urban milieux, and social control. Park sought to adumbrate a theory of social process, in which public opinion played a significant role, hence his continuing interest in the role of the press. He also developed, with Ernest Burgess, an ecological theory of the city which had a lasting impact upon urban sociology.

Park's major significance was as the leader of a fruitful school of empirical sociology and as a scholar whose sociological vision blended acute observation with the capacity to draw out its general significance and conceptualize at an abstract level. He demonstrated the capacity of sociology to grasp and comprehend the phenomena of modern urban society in a way which his American sociological predecessors had not.

Martin Bulmer
London School of Economics and Political Science

Further Reading
Matthews, F. H. (1977), *Quest for an American Sociology: Robert E. Park and the Chicago School*, Montreal.
See also: *Chicago School of Sociology*.

Parsons, Talcott (1902–79)

Talcott Parsons, the son of a Congregational minister in Colorado, became the most important American sociologist. He did an undergraduate degree in biology and philosophy at Amherst College and then did graduate work in social science at The London School of Economics and at Heidelberg. In 1927, he joined the Harvard economics department and in 1931 switched to the sociology department, which had just been created. He became chairman of the sociology department in 1944 and then chairman of the newly formed department of social relations in 1946, a position he retained until 1956. He officially retired in 1973 but continued writing until his death (in Munich) in 1979. His self-image was that of a theoretical synthesizer of social science in general and sociology in particular. Seeing sociocultural forces as the dominant ones shaping human activity, he assigned sociology the role of integrating the analyses of psychology, politics and economics into a science of human action. Sociology also had the role of providing other social sciences with their boundary assumptions (such as specifying what market imperfections exist).

Parsons's first book, *The Structure of Social Action* (1937), assesses the legacy to sociology of Marshall, Pareto, Durkheim and Weber. These thinkers, Parsons argues, converged from different directions on a solution to the problem of why society is not characterized by a Hobbesian war of all against all. According to Parsons, their solution is that people share common values and norms. Parsons's subsequent work, particularly *The Social System* (1951), *Towards a General Theory of Action* (1951), and *Family, Socialization and Interaction Process* (1955), develops the importance of the integration of a shared normative structure into people's need-dispositions for making social order possible. Structure, for Parsons, comprises the elements with greatest permanence in a society. These elements he identifies as the society's values, norms, collectivities and roles. The concern with people being socialized into a society's structure gives a conservative flavour to Parsons's thought.

Parsons argues that for a social structure to persist, four functions must be performed. These are adaptation, goal-attainment, integration and pattern-maintenance or tension-management. Societies tend to differentiate functionally to produce separate institutions specializing in each of these functions. The economy is adaptive, the polity specializes in goal-attainment, the stratification system is integrative, while education and religion are both concerned with pattern-maintenance. The most important social change in human history has been a gradual evolution of more functionally differentiated societies. For the evolution of a more differentiated structure to be successful there must be adaptive upgrading, inclusion and value generalization. The increased specialization produced by functional differentiation makes adaptive upgrading possible. Inclusion refers to processes (such as extension of the franchise) that produce commitment by people to the new more specialized structures. Finally, values must be generalized or stated more abstractly in order to legitimize a wider range of activities.

Parsons sees money, power, influence and commitment as generalized symbolic media that mediate the interchanges among the differentiated sectors of society. Power is defined as the capacity to achieve results. He develops an analysis of power based on its being the political system's equivalent of money. Force is the equivalent of the gold backing of a currency – it provides a back-up to power, but if it has to be resorted to frequently then the political system is breaking down. Inflation can ruin power just as it may destroy a currency.

Parsons's substantive concerns have ranged from Nazi Germany to Ancient Greece to modern school classes. Many of his specific analyses have proved highly influential. Particularly noteworthy are: his analysis of illness as legitimated deviance; of McCarthyism as a response to strains in American society resulting from the American assumption of the responsibilities of being a world power; of the pressures in American society pushing towards full citizenship for Black Americans; and of secularization as a result of increasing functional differentiation. Parsons's analysis of business and the professions involves the use of one of his best-known classifications, the pattern variables. The four pattern variables which can be used to describe any role relationship are affectivity v. neutrality, specificity v. diffuseness, universalism v. particularism, and quality v. performance. The relationship of business people to their clients is identical to professionals to their clients when this relationship is classified using the pattern variables. Each group relates neutrally, specifically, universalistically and in terms of the expected performance of the client. Understood this way, business people and professionals are similar, and their roles mesh easily together. Thus this analysis is better than one that sees professionals as altruistic and radically different from egotistical business people.

Parsons's influence on American sociology is immense. His *The Structure of Social Action* was the first major English-language presentation of the works of Weber and Durkheim and helped make their ideas central to American sociology's heritage. Many of Parsons's specific analyses and concepts are widely accepted, though few people accept his overall position. In the 1940s and 1950s, he was the dominant American theorist. In the 1960s his ideas came under increasing attack for being incapable of dealing with change. Since then, this criticism has come to be seen as simplistic. His work is increasingly being examined in terms of the solutions it offers to various dilemmas about how to theorize about society.

Kenneth Menzies
University of Guelph, Ontario

Further Reading
Bourricaud, F. (1981 [1977]), *The Sociology of Talcott Parsons*, Chicago. (Original French, *L'Individualisme institutionel: essai sur la sociologie de Talcott Parsons*, Paris.)
Menzies, K. (1977), *Talcott Parsons and the Social Image of Man*, London.
See also: *generalized symbolic media; social structure; sociology.*

Participant Observation

See Ethnographic Fieldwork.

Parties, Political

Scholars who have specialized in the study of political parties have found it difficult to agree on a definition of the term. The oldest definition, which emerged in the nineteenth century, may still be the best one: political parties are organizations that try to win public office in electoral competition with one or more similar organizations. The problem with this definition is that it is a narrow one. As Schlesinger (1968) points out, it excludes several kinds of organizations that are also usually referred to as parties: (1) those that are too small to have a realistic chance to win public office, especially executive office, but that do nominate candidates and participate in election campaigns; (2) revolutionary parties that aim to abolish competitive elections; and (3) the governing groups in totalitarian and other authoritarian one-party states. However, the inclusion of these three additional categories makes the definition overly broad. This difficulty may be solved partly by distinguishing two very different types of parties: the governing parties in one-party states and the competitive parties in two-party and multiparty democracies or near-democracies (that is, countries that are not fully democratic but that do allow free electoral competition).

The principal problem that remains is how to draw a distinction, in two-party and multiparty systems, between political parties and interest groups. Interest groups may sometimes also nominate candidates for public office without *ipso facto* changing their character from interest group to political party. Hence two further criteria have been proposed. One concerns the breadth of the interests represented by parties and interest groups. The typical function of interest groups is to 'articulate' interests, whereas political parties serve the broader function of 'aggregating' the articulated interests (Almond, 1960). This distinction is obviously one of degree rather than of a sharp dividing line. It also applies more clearly to two-party systems with broadly aggregative parties than to multiparty situations.

The second criterion, suggested by Blondel (1969), entails a combination of the kinds of goals that parties and interest groups pursue and the types of membership that they have. Interest groups tend to have either a 'promotional' or 'protective' character. Promotional associations tend to advance specific points of view (such as environmentalism or the abolition of capital punishment) and are in principle open to all citizens. Protective associations (such as trade unions or veterans' associations) defend certain groups of people; their membership is therefore more limited, but their goals are broader and may extend over the entire range of public policy issues. Political parties can now be distinguished from both promotional and protective groups: their goals are general (like those of protective associations), but their membership is open (like that of promotional groups). The borderline cases are single-issue parties, which resemble promotional groups, and cultural or ethnic minority parties, which are similar to protective groups.

Parties can be classified according to three principal dimensions: (1) Their form of organization, which distinguishes between 'mass' and 'cadre' parties. The former have relatively many formal members and are centralized, disciplined, and highly oligarchical. The latter have a much smaller formal membership and lower degrees of centralization, discipline, and oligarchy. (2) The parties' programmes, which may be ideological or pragmatic, and which may reflect a leftist, centrist, or rightist outlook. (3) The parties' supporters: these may be mainly working class or mainly middle class, or they may be defined in terms other than the socio-economic spectrum, such as religion and ethnicity.

Duverger (1963) has shown that these dimensions are empirically related: socialists and other parties of the left tend to be based on working-class support, and are ideological mass parties; conservative and centre parties tend to be supported more by middle-class voters, and are pragmatic cadre parties. The link between party organizations and programmes in Western democracies was stronger in the period before the Second World War than in the post-war era. The general post-war trend has been for parties to assume the character of mass parties but also to become more pragmatic. The relationship between programmes and supporters has also grown somewhat weaker, but it is still true that the parties of the left tend to be supported by working-class voters to a greater extent than the parties of the right. Social class is a good predictor of party choice in virtually all democracies, but in religiously or linguistically divided countries voting behaviour is more strongly determined by religion and language (Lijphart, 1979).

The way in which a political party operates in a democracy depends not only on its own characteristics but also on its interaction with other parties. In this respect, the literature on political parties has emphasized the difference between two-party and multiparty systems. Here another definitional problem arises. How should we determine the number of parties in a party system? For instance, Britain is usually said to have a two-party system, although no less than ten different parties were elected to the House of Commons in the 1979 election. The usual practice is to count only the large and 'important' parties and to ignore the small parties. But how large does a party have to be in order to be included in the count?

Sartori (1976) has proposed that only those parties should be counted that have either 'coalition potential' or 'blackmail potential'. A party possesses coalition potential if it has participated in cabinet coalitions (or in one-party cabinets) or if it is regarded as a possible coalition partner by the other major parties. A party without coalition potential may have 'blackmail' potential: it may be ideologically unacceptable as a coalition partner, but it may be so large that it still exerts considerable influence (such as a large Communist party). Sartori's counting rules therefore appear to be based on the two variables of size and ideological compatibility, but it should be pointed out that the size factor is the crucial one. A very small party with only a few parliamentary seats may be quite moderate and ideologically acceptable, but it will generally not have coalition potential simply because the support it can give to a cabinet is not sufficiently substantial. Hence the parties that Sartori counts are mainly the larger ones, regardless of their ideological compatibility. Moreover, although size is the dominant factor, he does not use it to make further distinctions among larger and smaller parties: they are all counted equally.

Blondel (1969) has tried to use both the number of parties and their relative sizes in classifying party systems. His four categories are two-party systems, 'two-and-a-half' party systems, multiparty systems with a dominant party, and multiparty systems without a dominant party. Two-party systems, like those of Britain and New Zealand, are dominated by two large parties, although a few small parties may also have seats in parliament. A two-and-a-half party system consists of two large parties and one that, although considerably smaller, does have coalition potential and does play a significant role, such as the German Free Democrats and the Irish Labour Party. Multiparty systems have more than two-and-a-half significant parties. These may or may not include a dominant party. Examples of the former are the Christian Demo-

crats in the Italian multiparty system and the Social Democrats in the Scandinavian countries. The French Fourth Republic offers a good example of a multiparty system without a dominant party.

The concepts of a 'dominant' party and a 'half' party serve the useful function of distinguishing between parties of different sizes, but they only offer a rough measurement. A more precise index has been developed by Laakso and Taagepera (1979). This 'effective number of parties' index is calculated according to a simple formula that takes the exact share of parliamentary seats of each party into consideration. For a pure two-party system with two equally strong parties, the effective number of parties is 2.0. If the two parties are highly unequal in size – for instance, if they have 65 and 35 per cent of the seats – the effective number of parties is 1.8. This is in agreement with the view that such a party system deviates from a pure two-party system in the direction of a one-party system. If there are three parties of equal strength, the index is 3.0. In a two-and-a-half party system in which the parliamentary seats are distributed in a 45:43:12 ratio, the effective number of parties is exactly 2.5.

Party systems have a strong empirical relationship with electoral systems and with cabinet coalitions and cabinet stability (Lijphart, 1984). In four countries using plurality methods of election (Canada, New Zealand, the United Kingdom, and the United States), the average effective number of parties in the 1945–1980 period was 2.1; in fifteen, mainly West-European, countries with proportional representation, the average effective number of parties was 3.8, almost twice as many. Moreover, as the effective number of parties increases, the probability that a coalition cabinet will be formed also increases, but the longevity of cabinets decreases.

Arend Lijphart
University of California, San Diego

References

Almond, G. A. (1960), 'Introduction: a functional approach to comparative politics', in G. A. Almond and J. S. Coleman (eds), *The Politics of the Developing Areas*, Princeton.

Blondel, J. (1969), *An Introduction to Comparative Government*, London.

Duverger, M. (1963), *Political Parties: Their Organisation and Activity in the Modern State*, trans. B. and R. North, New York.

Laakso, M. and Taagepera, R. (1979), 'The "effective" number of parties: a measure with application to West Europe', *Comparative Political Studies*, 12, 1.

Lijphart, A. (1979), 'Religious vs. linguistic vs. class voting: the "crucial experiment" of comparing Belgium, Canada, South Africa, and Switzerland', *American Political Science Review*, 73.

Lijphart, A. (1984), *Democracies: Patterns of Majoritarian and Consensus Government in Twenty-One Countries*, New Haven.

Sartori, G. (1976), *Parties and Party Systems: A Framework for Analysis*, Vol. 1, Cambridge.

Schlesinger, J. A. (1968), 'Party units', in D. L. Sills (ed.), *International Encyclopedia of the Social Sciences*, 11, New York.

Further Reading

Butler, D., Penniman, H. R. and Ranney, A. (eds) (1981), *Democracy at the Polls: A Comparative Study of Competitive National Elections*, Washington, DC.

Epstein, L. D. (1980), *Political Parties in Western Democracies*, 2nd edn, New Brunswick, N.J.

Merkl, P. H. (ed.) (1980), *Western European Party Systems: Trends and Prospects*, New York.

Janda, K. (1980), *Political Parties: A Cross-National Survey*, New York.

La Palombara, J. and Weiner, M. (eds) (1966), *Political Parties and Political Development*, Princeton.

Lipset, S. M. and Rokkan, S. (eds) (1967), *Party Systems and Voter Alignments: Cross-National Perspectives*, New York.

Von Beyme, K. (1982), *Parteien in westlichen Demokratien*, Munich.

See also: *coalitions; democracy; elections; voting.*

Pastoralism

Pastoralism is a form of livelihood based upon the management of herds of domestic animals, including, in the Old World, cattle, sheep, goats, horses, camels, yak and reindeer; and, in the New World, llamas and alpacas. It is well adapted to semi-arid, mountainous or subarctic environments which are unsuited to agriculture. However, most pastoralists either cultivate a little themselves, or obtain part of their food from agricultural neighbours in exchange for animal produce. Not much is known about the historical origins of pastoralism, but in most parts of the world it has probably arisen as a by-product of agricultural intensification. Only in the Eurasian subarctic and the Peruvian Andes did pastoral economies follow directly on the hunting of wild herds of the same species.

Pastoralists are commonly supposed to be nomadic. Though the grazing requirements of their herds often necessitate frequent shifts of location, the nature and extent of this movement varies considerably from one region to another. Sometimes it takes the form of a regular seasonal migration, but in other cases the movement appears most irregular, though in fact it is conditioned by the erratic incidence of local rainfall. Some pastoralists spend much of their lives in settled communities, or move in order to combine the husbandry of flocks and herds with that of crops or orchards. Since domestic animals may provide not only

food and raw materials, but also a means of transport, many pastoral peoples are heavily involved in long-distance trade. Their nomadic movement may also have political significance, as a strategy to escape domination by an encompassing state organization. People who move about are hard to tax and administer, and for this reason central governments have always had an interest in the settlement of nomads.

Most pastoral societies are markedly egalitarian. Local groups or 'camps' are fluid in composition, and disputes are solved by the parties going their separate ways. However, the recognition of living animals as moveable, self-reproducing property opens up possibilities not only for their accumulation but also for their functioning as a medium of exchange. The transfer of animals from household to household as gifts, loans or marriage payments serves to cement enduring social relations. The possession of animal property further structures relations within, as well as between, domestic groups, allowing men to control their juniors who stand to inherit, and who may need animals in order to marry with bridewealth. Relations between men and women depend critically on whether women can own animals or can only mediate transactions of animal wealth between men.

Pastoral peoples are among the most vulnerable in the modern world. In the past they have often held the key to power in the regions they traversed, by virtue of their military superiority and control over trade. Today their presence is generally considered an embarrassment by the administrations of the territories they inhabit. Restrictions on movement, enforced settlement and commercialization have undermined traditional strategies of security, so that occasional ecological crises – previously endured – have turned into human disasters of catastrophic proportions.

Tim Ingold
University of Manchester

Further Reading

Equipe écologie et anthropologie des sociétés pastorales (1979), *Pastoral Production and Society*, Cambridge.

Ingold, T. (1980), *Hunters, Pastoralists and Ranchers*, Cambridge.

Path Analysis

Path analysis is a suite of techniques for estimating and interpreting simultaneous linear equation systems. The model is interpreted by decomposing total effects into direct, indirect, and joint effects. Every model is accompanied by a heuristic diagram.

If y denotes a vector of dependent variables, x a vector in independent variables, and ϵ a vector of disturbance terms, the equation system can be written as $By = \Gamma x + \epsilon$ with B and Γ as coefficient matrices.

The variance-covariance matrix for the disturbance terms is φ. Path analysis provides estimates of elements of B, Γ, and φ which are viewed as parameters of the model. These estimates form the basis for an interpretation of the estimated model which is provided by the analyst.

As there has to be enough information, in terms of the number of variances and covariances in the data, all such equation systems confront the identification problem – a logical problem – forcing the prior setting of some elements in the three matrices being estimated. In the simplest (and majority) of path analyses, B is assumed triangular and φ diagonal. For these recursive systems, ordinary least squares (OLS) is the optimal estimation procedure.

Path analysis has been extended to deal with reciprocal effects, feedback loops, and correlation between disturbances. For such models and those with unmeasured variables, and/or multiple indicators of variables, OLS is no longer optimal, and a variety of methods exist for estimating single equations in the system or the entire system. However, with the recognition of system estimation, path analysis has given way to LISREL, a powerful full information maximum likelihood method.

Patrick Doreian
University of Pittsburgh

Further Reading
Duncan, O. D. (1966), 'Path analysis: sociological examples', *American Journal of Sociology*, 72.
Sobel, M. E. (1982), 'Asymptotic confidence intervals for indirect effects in structural equation models', *Social Methodology*.

Pavlov, Ivan Petrovich (1849–1936)

The great Russian physiologist and founder of the study of conditioned reflexes, I. P. Pavlov, was the great-grandson of a freed serf and son and grandson of village priests. His sixty-two years of continuous and active research on what he came to call 'Higher Nervous Activity' profoundly and immutably altered the course of scientific study and conceptualization of the behaviour of living organisms, and for the first time established appropriate contact between philosophical empiricism and associationism and laboratory science. The young Pavlov won a gold medal for his second experiment ('The nerve supply of the pancreas'), one of eleven publications before his graduation in 1879 from the Imperial Medico-Surgical Academy in St Petersburg. After completing his doctoral dissertation ('Efferent nerves of the heart') in 1883, he was appointed lecturer in physiology, spent two years in postdoctoral research with Ludwig in Leipzig and Haidenhain in Breslau, became professor of pharmacology in the Academy and director of the Physiological

Laboratory of the new St Petersburg Institute of Experimental Medicine in 1890, and, in 1895, professor of physiology in the Academy. In 1924 he was appointed director of a new Institute of Physiology, created by the Soviet Academy of Sciences especially for his burgeoning research enterprise. He remained in this post until his death, in Leningrad, in 1936.

Pavlov was fifty-five when in 1904 he won the Nobel Prize for his work on neural regulation of digestive secretion – the first given to a Russian and to a physiologist. A special surgical technique he developed during this period, the Pavlov Pouch, is still used. This technique exemplifies a cardinal principle in his work – he disdained the artificiality of 'acute' preparations used by his contemporaries in their stimulation and extirpation research, preferring to study an intact and physiologically 'normal' animal whose life need not be 'sacrificed' after the experiment. Not long after receiving the Nobel award, Pavlov abruptly shifted to the topic for which we remember him, conditioning. Here, too, he emphasized the chronic preparation, studying some dogs for many years, yet always maintaining sound physiological standards (Rule 1. Control of all stimulation, experimental as well as surrounding; Rule 2. Reliable quantitative measures).

Then, already over seventy and famous, he again shifted his emphasis, this time to the study of psychopathology, beginning with laboratory-produced experimental neurosis but also including work with actual patients in mental hospitals and psychiatric clinics.

The basic terminology and research strategies employed today in research on animal conditioning and human behaviour modification originated mainly in Pavlov's laboratory. Modern psychiatry and clinical psychology depend substantially upon ideas and methods, not to mention the myriad of facts, growing out of his work. From behaviour therapy to biofeedback, from the study of how worms and fish learn to the theory and treatment of neurotic anxiety, Pavlov's stubbornly objective and pervasively materialistic application of the scientific method in the study of the nervous system's control of all of the functions of life, including its most adaptive feature – its plasticity – have continued to prove fruitful if not essential.

H. D. Kimmel
University of South Florida

Further Reading
Babkin, B. P. (1949), *Pavlov: A Biography*, Chicago.
Gray, J. A. (1979), *Pavlov*, London.
Pavlov, I. P. (1960 [1927]), *Conditioned Reflexes: An Investigation of the Physiological Activity of the Cerebral Cortex*, New York.
Pavlov, I. P. (1940–9), *Polnoe Sobranie Trudov [Complete Works]*, Moscow.
See also: *behaviourism*; *conditioning*.

Peace

Historically a number of peace concepts can be identified. They are carriers of different ideas, which could be joined together to yield a richer concept of peace than that usually found. Most important in the Western tradition is the Roman 'pax', *absentia belli* – in other words, a negative concept of peace, defined as the absence of war among countries. The Greek *eirene*, the Arabic/Hebrew *sala'am/shalom* and the Japanese/Chinese *heiwa/chowa* point in another direction which can be better understood by such terms as 'justice' and 'harmony'. In the Hindu, Gandhian and Jainist/Buddhist traditions, *shanti* would be more of a harmony concept, while *ahimsa* (the negation of *himsa*, violence) would emphasize the element of nonviolence. These differences are important, for in all cultures 'peace' (or that which tends to be translated into 'peace') stands for something positive, the name of a goal, perhaps one of the deepest and highest goals.

The concept of 'peace' becomes a part of social ideology, embraced by everybody. As such it will also attain a class character. Who benefits from 'absence of war'? Not those with just grievances, fighting for a more just world, but possibly merchants and others who can profit from peaceful relations among states. 'Peace' becomes that which makes inter-state trade possible. And who is served by 'harmony', if not precisely those at the top of a structure which distributes power and privilege very unequally? Moreover, 'nonviolence' may mean pacification rather than peace in a more positive sense. 'Harmony' may also be interpreted as 'justice' – but that may be a synonym for equality, or it may mean giving more to the more worthy, the aristocrats or meritocrats.

In peace research, as it took shape at the end of the 1950s, the debate about the meaning of that very concept proved to be fruitful. It was evident from the beginning that there were two classes of meanings: 'negative peace', meaning absence of war and violence (any type of destruction); and 'positive peace', coming closer to integration, or union – with connotations of harmony and justice. But then violence, destruction, that which should be absent for a peace certificate to be issued (as a minimum condition) also has to be subdivided. On the one hand there is the *direct* violence most people think of: violence which destroys quickly and which is usually directed by a person who intends that destruction. On the other hand there is *structural* violence, built into the social structure, which is also capable of killing, but then usually slowly (through hunger, misery, and disease), but which is as a rule not steered by some clear intention – it just *is*. Structural violence is not the same as institutionalized violence – that is, direct violence which has become an institution, like the vendetta. It is very closely linked to social hierarchy in general, and to the class structure of a society in particular. It can be measured, much as direct violence is measured, by counting casualties. Structural violence can be measured in numbers of years not lived relative to the potential, given the knowledge, technology and resources at our disposal, on the assumption that all parts of the population can benefit fully from them. A life destroyed at the age of thirty through malnutrition is at least half a murder. One might add qualitative measures, to cope with the effect of morbidity on the quality of life. Other measures might be devised to deal with the cost of repression and/or alienation, tying freedom and identity to the concept of peace – in the tradition of non-Western peace theories.

The concept of negative peace is extended through the concept of structural violence. 'Absence of violence' is more than absence of direct violence; it also implies the absence of repression and alienation and exploitation, and other forms of verticality in the social structure. These considerations suggest the two main strategies for a peace process: policies based on maintaining distance (dissociation) and fostering closeness (association), or the pursuit of peace by positive and negative approaches.

Best known in the theory of peace is the policy of dissociation, whose aim it is to achieve 'security' (another word for negative peace), or the absence of direct violence, through the maintenance of distance. This may be achieved by securing natural borders (rivers, mountain chains), keeping great distances (oceans, deserts) between oneself and potential enemies, or fostering social distance (by prejudice and discrimination), and social borders, protected by force. Combining these four approaches, we arrive at the nation-state, built into a balance-of-power system. The system can be said to date from the Peace of Westphalia in 1648. Today its weaknesses are manifold: natural borders and distances become ludicrous in the age of rockets; nationalist prejudices tend to break down in the age of extended interaction; and the balance of power may break down in the age of multidimensional weapon systems, where there is no agreement as to how much of this weapon is equivalent to how much of that, and because weapons that can be potentially used for an attack look offensive, although the intention behind their deployment may be purely defensive – and consequently, they are inevitably provocative.

The closeness, or associative, approach is based on exactly the opposite idea: that a peace structure can be built by bringing the parties together, not by keeping them apart. Such a policy can succeed only when the parties are relatively equal, bound together in a relationship not only of interdependence but also of equity, and where ties proliferate in all directions and at all levels (governmental, public, private, élite, and popular), and so on. The difference between the two strategies is starkly evident if one compares the relation between Germany and France before the Second World War, and today.

For structural violence, there are also dissociative and associative approaches. Distance may be created through 'decoupling', selective or more complete, for example, by means of a violent or nonviolent struggle for liberation. The closeness approach, 'recoupling', is again only possible on the basis of equality. The history of the Nordic countries illustrates a relatively solid and equitable process of recoupling. Recoupling has not so far been achieved successfully inside a society, reducing to zero structural violence between classes within a country. This is possibly because decoupling easily leads to separatism and the formation of a new state.

Johan Galtung
International Peace Research Institute, Oslo

Further Reading
Galtung, J. (1975–80), *Essays in Peace Research*, vols I–V, Copenhagen.
See also: *conflict*; *conflict resolution*; *force*; *war*.

Peasants

The basic problem arising from social scientists' use of the term peasants is this: should it be used, as in everyday parlance, to refer to a 'social type', or should it rather be used as an adjective to describe certain features of varying rural productive systems? In the absence of agreement on this (rarely discussed) point, discussion of substantive issues is clouded by arguments about 'what is a peasant' and about what distinguishes peasants from either proletarians or capitalist producers. The definitional arguments tend in particular to concentrate on an 'all or nothing' type of question, assuming that either a producer is a peasant or he is not, and as a result the substantive discussions resort to hybrid formulations such as 'semi-proletariat', 'petty bourgeoisie', 'petty commodity production', in their attempts to fit an account of rapidly changing social and economic structure into a rigid framework of mutually exclusive social categories and productive systems.

The usage of the term in contemporary social science derives from the experience of eastern Europe in the late nineteenth and early twentieth centuries: peasants are defined as people who organize production almost exclusively on the basis of the unpaid labour of a nuclear family or close kinship group: they are therefore assumed to be autarchic as far as labour is concerned. Furthermore, they either only produce for their own consumption or sell some of their product on the market solely in order to meet their culturally defined consumption requirements, which assumes them to be almost self-sufficient in production and consumption. This is the image of the peasantry developed by Russian populism during the nineteenth century and elaborated in an elegant economic theory of noncapitalist production systems by A. V. Chayanov (1966), whose work remains the classic in the field. Chayanov started out by assuming (implicitly) the existence of a peasant family production and consumption unit with common objectives and rationality, working and eating under the direction of an implicitly male head. He then combined this with a second assumption that wage labour was almost entirely absent from peasant farms. This yielded the immediate conclusion that therefore they could not be profit-seekers, because the category of profit implies, by definition, the use of wage-labour, which was absent. This was reinforced by the implicit assumption that the labour of the family members had no alternative use, and therefore was cost-free as well as unpaid. From this basis, he reached the generalization that peasant farms produced only up to the point where the drudgery of an extra unit of labour was greater than the marginal utility of the corresponding extra unit of output – in other words, that once a family had produced enough to satisfy its subsistence needs its labour input would level off. The categories 'drudgery' and 'utility' are essentially subjective in his model, which refers to a natural economy, and therefore unquantifiable – which makes the theory difficult to test. This in turn led him to interpret the inequalities observed in Russian peasant society in the period just before and after 1917 as an optical illusion, reflecting the movement of households through a life cycle rather than abiding class divisions: as the households were formed at marriage and passed through successive stages until old age and death, the ratio of consumers to workers (mouths-to-feed to arms-to-work) changed, and so did their requirements and therefore ownership of land. This process of 'demographic differentiation' was reinforced by the practice of periodic redistributions of land according to need within the Russian peasant communities (*mir*).

Subsequently, the study of the peasantry has confronted two major areas of inquiry which have gradually forced a rethinking of these relationships and of those between peasantries and the wider society. These areas are: (1) the effects of capitalist development on peasantries in poor and middle-income countries (commonly known as the 'Third World') and (2) the identity of farming populations in advanced capitalist countries.

The central analytical question posed by the expansion of capitalism in the Third World, as far as this subject is concerned, is whether the peasantries in those countries merit the name at all. Vast numbers of studies have revealed the disintegration of the peasantry as defined above, and have shown that they frequently engage in the employment of wage labour, and/or that they depend significantly on income from wage labour in their – often unsuccessful – attempts to meet their subsistence requirements. Some people have seized on this as evidence which confirms the position adopted by the young Lenin (1896) that the penetration of the money economy leads inexorably to 'social differentiation' – the rise of opposing classes of capitalists and proletarians. Others, in particular writers who have taken a feminist view, have begun to question the standard model even more fundamentally: they question the image, assumed even by Lenin, of an arcadian, precapitalist 'peasant family' with common interests and a single central rationality and objectives which existed everywhere 'once upon a time'. In particular they have pointed out that the dominant position of the male head of the household, assumed in the standard definition, may be more a consequence arising from capitalist development than a reality of precapitalist society (Young *et al.*, 1981). Yet the stark reality of mass poverty and proliferating tiny plots of land in poor countries has prevented the abandonment of the term, despite the evidence of rapid proletarianization. To cope with this inconsistency some writers (de Janvry, 1982; Vergopoulos, 1978) have tried to show that this only undermines Lenin's thesis in a superficial sense. For them one main difference between 'dependent' capitalism in contemporary peripheral countries and in advanced capitalism is that, while the latter destroys the peasantry, the former actually benefits from and assures their perpetuation. Theirs is an essentially functionalist model: impoverished rural populations are forced into high fertility by their poverty and by their uncertain expectation of life. This then ensures the reproduction of a mass of cheap potential migrant labour at little cost to capital in education or welfare; capital will further benefit from the cheapness of food produced by the surplus rural population, which applies vast amounts of labour to small plots of land and thus obtains high yields from it. This view is analytically controversial in many ways, but represents an interesting adaptation of the standard concept of peasants to a framework of analysis of class and exploitation. The problem which remains is whether the term peasantry as traditionally defined, with its strong implicit assumptions about family labour and self-consumption, should be used to describe these populations.

Further difficulties arise for the standard view from the contemporary experience of advanced countries of Western Europe, North America and Australia, and even in some of the more developed agricultural regions of the Third World. Here, although farming is largely a family concern and uses very little wage labour, it does use vast amounts of fixed and liquid capital. These units resemble the standard image of peasant units in some ways, but seem to fly in the face of the usual assumption that peasants are impoverished and oppressed and possess hardly any capital base.

In conclusion, it seems best to discard the term 'peasant' as a comprehensive descriptor of rural populations of any sort and to use it instead as an adjective describing features of rural production systems – without pretensions to exhaustive definition.

David Lehmann
University of Cambridge

References

Chayanov, A. V. (1966), *The Theory of Peasant Economy*, ed. D. Thorner *et al.*, Homewood, Ill.
De Janvry, A. (1982), *The Agrarian Question in Latin America*, Baltimore.
Lenin, V. I. (1964 [1896]), *The Development of Capitalism in Russia*, Moscow.
Vergopoulos, K. (1978), 'Capitalism and peasant productivity', *Journal of Peasant Studies*, 4.
Young, K., McCulloch, R. and Wolkowicz, C. (1981), *Of Marriage and the Market*, London.

Further Reading

Harriss, J. (1982), *An Introduction to Rural Development*, London.

Peirce, Charles Sanders (1839–1914)

Although considered by many as the founder of serious philosophical study in the United States, and America's greatest philosopher, Peirce thought of himself as a 'man of science' and a student of logic, conceived broadly as the science of scientific method. The son of Benjamin Peirce, then the leading American mathematician, and Sarah Mills Peirce, daughter of US Senator Mills (founder of a law school in Northampton), he was raised in a circle of physicists, naturalists, and lawyers, the intellectual élite of mid-century Boston. His father trained him in mathematics and in intellectual discipline. After study at Harvard, in order to deepen his understanding of 'logic', he resolved to acquire firsthand experience in methods of physical science. He became a senior staff scientist with the US Coast and Geodetic Survey, then the premier government scientific bureau, and by 1880 was an internationally recognized expert in gravity measurement, having travelled widely in Europe on scientific duties. In 1891 he resigned his government post, and retired to a quiet region of rural Pennsylvania in order to study logic. There he developed and wrote his mature works. He left a tremendous *nachlass* which is just now being edited and published (Fisch, Ketner, Kloesel, 1979).

The range of his interests, in each of which he invariably made original research contributions, reads like that of Da Vinci, if one omits art. Here is a description of them he prepared for Cattell's *Men of Science*: 'Logic, especially logic of relations, probabilities, theory of inductive and retroductive validity and of definition, epistemology; metrology; history of science; multiple algebra; doctrine of the nature and constitution of numbers; gravity; wave-lengths; phonetics of Elizabethan English; great men; ethics; phaneroscopy; speculative cosmology; experimental psychology; physical geometry; foundations of mathematics; classification of science; code of terminology; topical geometry.'

In order to grasp his thought, the fundament of which is methodology, one must remember that he was basically a scientist and a mathematician, thoroughly imbued with the lore and method of laboratories. He described his work as 'the attempt of a physicist to make such conjecture as to the constitution of the universe as the methods of science may permit, with the aid of all that has been done by previous philosophers'. His classification of the sciences is the key for following his thinking. He regarded Mathematics as the most fundamental science. Below that is the science of Philosophy, including Phaneroscopy (phenomenology), Aesthetics, Ethics, and Logic. Logic, which is equivalent to Semiotic, the science of signs, was composed of Speculative Grammar (definitions), Critic (logic in the present-day sense), and Methodeutic (methodology). The last branch of philosophy is Metaphysics. Then comes Special Sciences – Physics and Psychics with their various subdivisions. The informing idea of this classification, and of Peirce's system of scientific philosophy, is that each science requires principles and methods from that which is prior to it.

His work is a rich intellectual legacy which is attracting widespread interest from a number of disciplines. His influence, both acknowledged and unacknowledged, upon contemporary thought is strong and is increasing.

Kenneth Laine Ketner
Texas Tech University

Reference
Fisch, M. H., Ketner, K. L. and Kloesel, C. J. W. (1979), 'The new tools of Peirce scholarship, with particular reference to semiotic', *Peirce Studies*, No.1, Institute for Studies in Pragmaticism, Lubbock.

Further Reading
Eisele, C. (1979), *Studies in the Scientific and Mathematical Philosophy of Charles S. Peirce: Essays by Carolyn Eisele* (ed. R. M. Martin), The Hague.
Fisch, M. H. *et al.* (eds) (1982–), *Writings of Charles S. Peirce: A Chronological Edition*, Vols 1– , Bloomington.
Ketner, K. L. *et al.* (eds) (1981), *Proceedings of the C. S. Peirce Bicentennial International Congress*, Lubbock.
Ketner, K. L. (ed.) (1983), 'Peirce's semiotic and its audiences', special issue of *American Journal of Semiotics*.

Penology

Penology is the study of penalties (from the Greek ποινή: penalty), although in its broadest sense it is also concerned with the consequences and merits of attempting to deal with various kinds of conduct by criminal prohibition ('criminalizing'). It includes the study of penal codes of law, but also investigation of the ways in which such penal codes are applied by courts in practice, and the manner in which each type of penal measure is applied. For example, even when a penal code appears to oblige courts to pronounce a sentence (such as imprisonment for 'life' in the case of murder), there are ways of avoiding this (such as convicting the offender of a less serious charge of homicide); and most penal systems provide legal devices by which a sentence of imprisonment can be terminated before its nominal end. Penologists are interested in all such expedients, and in the criteria which are used by courts, administrators and other personnel to make distinctions between offenders, whether for such purposes or for other reasons. Other reasons may include the belief that certain types of offender are more likely than others to respond to certain regimes, or on the other hand that some prisoners are so 'dangerous' that they must be given special sentences, detained longer than is normal for the offence, or given freedom only under specially strict conditions.

An important task of penologists is to provide answers to the question 'How effective is this (or that) measure?' Effectiveness is usually assessed by reconvictions or rearrests, although this is not without problems. For example it cannot take account of offences of which the offender is not suspected; the follow-up period must be substantial; in some jurisdictions rearrests or reconvictions for minor offences are not recorded centrally. The most serious problem, however, is the difficulty of being sure that offenders who remain free of rearrests during the follow-up period would not have remained free if otherwise dealt with: for example, if merely discharged without penalty. In consequence, follow-up studies must usually be content with *comparing* the reconviction rates after different measures. Even so, they have to take into account the fact that courts are selective, and do not allocate offenders randomly to different measures (a few 'random allocation studies' have been achieved, but only for rather specific groups of offenders or offences: see Farrington, 1983). The criteria used to allot offenders to different measures may themselves be associated with higher or lower reconviction rates. For instance, the more previous convictions in a man's record, the more likely he is to be reconvicted, quite apart from any effect which a sentence may have on him. Again, offenders whose offences usually involve theft, burglary, drunkenness or exhibitionism are more likely to be reconvicted than those who commit serious sexual offences or personal violence. Statistical devices have to be used to allow for this, for example, by subdividing samples into 'high-' 'medium- ' and 'low-risk groups'. It is often said that when such precautions are taken the differences between reconviction rates following such different measures as imprisonment, fines and probation tend to disappear, and that the choice of sentence therefore makes no difference to a person's likelihood of reconviction, or not enough difference to justify expensive measures: but this is probably an oversimplification (as was eventually conceded by the chief exponent of the 'nothing works school' in the 1970s, Martinson, 1974, 1979).

In any case, other possible aims of penal measures have to be taken into account. Psychiatrists, for example, usually regard themselves as primarily concerned with the mental health of those committed to their charge by criminal courts; and social workers – including many probation officers – regard their clients' financial and family problems as more important than their legal transgressions.

Whether these views are accepted or not, some penal measures are valued as general deterrents, in the belief that·even if they do not often affect the conduct of those who have experienced them, they discourage potential offenders who have not yet committed offences (Beyleveld, 1980). The efficacy of general deterrents has been exaggerated, for example, by the supporters of capital punishment: statistical comparisons of jurisdictions which have abolished or retained the death penalty, or of decades in the same jurisdiction preceding and following abolition, suggest that the substitution of long periods of imprisonment for the death penalty does not affect rates of intentional homicide. In plain terms, potential murderers who think before they kill are as likely to be deterred by 'life' as by death. Whatever the penalty, however, its deterrent efficacy depends to a great extent on people's own estimates of the probability of being detected and punished. For some people this seems immaterial; but they tend to be those who commit impulsive or compulsive crimes.

Another aim of some penal measures is simply to protect other people against a repetition of the offence by the offender concerned, usually by some degree of incapacitation. Incapacitation may take the form of long detention, disqualification from certian activities (such as driving or engaging in certain occupations), or surgery (for example, castration for rapists). The more severe types of incapacitating measure are controversial, the chief objection being that the probability of the offender's repeating his offence seldom approaches certainty, and is often less than 50:50 (Floud and Young, 1981).

This illustrates a more general tendency in recent years to acknowledge the relevance of jurisprudence for penology. Scepticism about the efficacy of corrective or deterrent measures, together with the excessive use of very long detention in the name of therapeutic treatment, has revived the classical emphasis on the need for penalties to reflect the culpability of the offender. The underlying Kantian morality of this was never quite abandoned by jurists in West Germany; but the revival of it in the US and Scandinavia is an important phenomenon, although lacking the sophistication of German jurists (Von Hirsch, 1976).

English judges – and, quite independently, Durkheimian sociologists – have contributed yet another notion. Without necessarily accepting the retributive view (which has both difficulties and dangers) they hold that penalties have an important 'expressive' or 'symbolic' function, declaring publicly the moral disapproval with which most people regard harmful offences (Walker, 1978). Some English judges have even stated that an important task of sentencers is to lead public opinion, although this seems to exaggerate the attention and respect which the public pay to sentences (Walker and Marsh, 1984). More tenable is the proposition that sentences *reflect* people's disapproval: the question is whether sentencers are selected or trained so as to be sure of reflecting the views of the law-abiding public, particularly in societies with heterogeneous moralities.

Other subjects in which penologists have interested themselves are the rights of offenders, especially those recognized by conventions (such as those of the United Nations or European Economic Community); the protection of offenders against avoidable stigma; and the rights of victims to compensation,whether from the State or the offender, and to other forms of care.

Nigel Walker
University of Cambridge

References
Beyleveld, D. (1980), *A Bibliography on General Deterrence Research*, Westmead.
Farrington, D. P. F. (1983), 'Randomised experiments on crime and justice', in M. Tonry and N. Morris (eds), *Crime and Justice*, Vol. IV, Chicago.
Floud, J. and Young, W. (1981), *Dangerousness and Criminal Justice*, London.
Martinson, T. (1974), 'What works?', *Public Interest*, 35.
Martinson, T. (1979), 'New findings, new views', *Hofstra Law Review*, 7.
Von Hirsch, A. (1976), *Doing Justice, the Choice of Punishments: Report of the Committee for the Study of Incarceration*, New York.

Walker, N. (1978), 'The ultimate justification', in C. F. H. Tapper (ed.), *Crime, Proof and Punishment: Essays in Memory of Sir Rupert Cross*, London.

Walker, N. and Marsh, C. (1984), 'Do sentences affect public disapproval?', *British Journal of Criminology*.

See also: *capital punishment; criminology; punishment.*

Personal Construct Theory

Personal construct theory appeared on the psychological scene unheralded but complete in Kelly (1955). What distinguished it from traditional psychological theories was its central model of *person-as-scientist*. Historically, psychology has mimicked the natural sciences in distinguishing between the purposeful and understanding scientist and the scientist's ignorant and mechanical subject matter. Kelly insisted that all people are scientists/psychologists in that they theorize about their own nature and the nature of the world: their behaviour is a continuous experiment based on expectations they derive from their theories, and they modify their theories in the light of the relationship between their expectations and unfolding events.

People's theories take the form of personal construct systems. 'Personal' indicates that since we cannot directly apprehend reality, we must interpret it, and no two persons have identical ways of interpreting their world. Though we may communicate our experience and society provides a common interpretative base, we still live in unique personal worlds. 'Construct' refers to the *bipolar discrimination* we use to make sense of the world (nice-nasty, east-west, plus-minus, expensive-cheap, coloured-plain and myriads more). Our constructs are neither all conscious nor verbally labelled but they are part of a 'system'. They are organized hierarchically and, since they are linked, every act of construing is an act of prediction (if, for you, the construct female-male is positively linked to the construct gentle-harsh then you will anticipate gentle behaviour from females).

Kelly's fundamental postulate argued that 'a person's processes are psychologically channelized by the ways in which he or she anticipates events'. Since to construe is to anticipate, then unfolding events may prove you to be right or wrong or perhaps irrelevant. It is in terms of such varying validational fortunes that a person's construct system will change, both in its organizational structure and in its content.

Kelly made a further radical break with traditional psychology in refusing to distinguish between 'thought' and 'emotion'. The affect-cognition distinction is ancient in human culture and has dominated modern psychology to the extent of producing not one psychology but *psychologies of thought* and *psychologies of feeling*. Kelly integrated the two by arguing that 'feeling' is our awareness that our construct system is in transition; it is elaborating or breaking down or

threatened by movement. Thus we may be resisting movement and showing hostility which is defined as 'an attempt to extort validational evidence from a kind of social prediction which is already proving a failure'; we may be anxious, that is 'aware of being confronted by elements which lie mostly outside the range of convenience of our construct system'; we may feel guilty, 'aware of imminent dislodgement from core role construing' (our construing of self) and so forth. In spite of Kelly's clarity on this issue his theory is often wrongly categorized as a *cognitive* theory of personality and criticized as 'mentalistic'.

Kelly demonstrated the practical value of his theory in the field of psychotherapy and, up to his death in 1967, clinical psychology remained its primary field of application. Since then the theory has been vigorously taken up in broad professional fields such as educational and industrial psychology and applied to areas as diverse as architecture, child development, politics, cross-cultural differences, personal relationships, religion, language and so forth. Much research has made use of instruments developed by Kelly directly from construct theory, such as self-characterization, fixed-role therapy and repertory grid technique (Kelly, 1979). A repertory grid is a series of judgements made by a person, using his constructs, on some aspect of the world. The pattern of judgements is statistically analysed so as to show how the person's constructs are defined, related and changing.

D. Bannister
Medical Research Council
External Scientific Staff

References
Kelly, G. A. (1955), *The Psychology of Personal Constructs*, vols I & II, New York.
Kelly, G. A. (1979), *Clinical Psychology and Personality: the Selected Essays of George Kelly*, ed. B. A. Maher, New York.

Further Reading
Bannister, D. and Fransella, F. (1985), *Inquiring Man*, Beckenham.

Personality

Personality can be defined behaviourally as *that which predicts what a person will do in any defined situation*. Equation (1) below gives this more precision in the most promising of several available models.

Virtually all research on personality is now behaviouristic, in Comte's (not Watson's) sense, of dispensing with introspection. Within this experimental phase, most at first followed the Wundtian 'brass instrument', bivariate model (one stimulus, one dependent variable), which proved relatively fruitless until multivariate experiment, mainly manipulative and nonmanipulative factor analysis, teased out from a holistic setting the vital entities for bivariate and multivariate further experiment.

Part of the bivariate approach was reflexological (too frequently misnamed 'behaviouristic', since the latter actually covers much more). This led to a concept, most courageously raised by Mischel (1968) that personality was an atomistic aggregate of personal past conditionings. This theory, as Mischel later recognized, could not stand for a moment against the factor-analytic evidence of (a) definite unitary structures, and (b) substantial genetic components in at least half of them.

The strategy of multivariate research has followed the logical and economical course of (a) finding what unitary trait structures exist (in a given culture), from factoring in the media of (1) life observation (L-data), (2) questionnaire responses (Q-data) and (3) objective (behavioural) tests (T-data). Between 40 and 50 such unitary traits (expressed in all three media) have been confirmed across the three modalities – abilities, temperament, and dynamic (interest) structures – and test batteries now measure them with good reliability and validity, (b) determining by twin and MAVA methods the heritability, H, of each (H ranges from 0 to 1.0), (c) using the measures to plot normal life curves, sex and cultural differences, and relations to life criteria in school, family, occupation, clinical-pathological behaviour and the behaviour of groups (Cattell, Eber and Tatsuoka, 1970). These findings have become extensive in the last 20 years, permitting (a) much more precision in applied psychology, for example, regarding factors for predicting school achievement; behaviour in groups (such as leadership); the understanding of anxiety neurosis, alcoholism, and criminal behaviour; the prediction of group performance from the personality of populations (Cattell and Brennan, 1981), and so on; (b) firmer theoretical advance regarding concepts of the structures themselves, such as of fluid intelligence, the ego (C), the self sentiment (Q₃), surgency (F), the super-ego (G), and schizothymia (A). This, incidentally, has brought a development beyond reflexology, into *structured learning theory*, in which learning is (i) predicted not only from reward (means-end or instrumental conditioning [CR II] learning) but from the influence of existing structures, and (ii) learning laws beyond Skinner's (1969) CR I and CR II are perceived to account for the rise of *structures* (rather than a formless atomicity of reflexes).

Considerable technical advances in factor analytic techniques and concepts, plus the lucky advent of the computer, have enlarged the concepts of structure as primary personality factors to include a hierarchical structure of second-order (secondaries) and tertiary (Royce and Mos, 1979) role factors, psychological

states, the interaction of dynamic traits with other modalities, and the modulation model. Eysenck (1973) has done much to clarify the natural history of two major secondaries: extroversion, and anxiety; Hakstian and Cattell (1974) have brought high resolution to the structure of ability traits, Loehlin (1965) has thrown light on trait inheritances, Nesselroade and Baltes (1979) have brought sophisticated models to bear on the developmental study of personality, and Birkett and Cattell (1978) have shown how longitudinal, P-technique analysis of motivational trait change can reveal the bases of conflicts with which clinical psychology is concerned. Good graduate-level surveys of these developments, along with the less scientifically verifiable theories from the clinical phase, from Freud to Rogers, are to be found in Cartwright (1979), and Smith and Vetter (1982).

Presentations at a controversial closeness to the advancing frontier of personality study are to be found in Cattell and Dreger's *Handbook of Modern Personality Theory* (1977) and Cattell's two-volume *Personality and Learning Theory* (1979, 1980). These use the model of the factor specification equation, which is simply a regression equation using unitary traits as predictors. Because it embraces more meaning than the mathematical skeleton alone it has been called by Cattell the *behavioural equation*. Thus:

$$^{a}h_{ijk} = {}^{x=m}\sum{}^{b}h_{jkx}{}^{T}x_i + {}^{y=n}\sum {}^{b}h_{jky}{}^{R}y_i + {}^{y=p}\sum {}^{b}j_{hjkz^{s}}h_{kz}{}^{L}z_i \quad (1)$$

Here T_{xi} is individual i's score on trait x, of which m are covered. R_{yi} is i's score on role trait y, for example, being a teacher in the classroom, of which there are n. L_{zi} is i's liability to getting excited on state z, for example, anxiety proneness. The b's are *behavioural indices* showing how much the trait is involved in the act, performance or symptom, aj, in response to focal stimulus h in ambient situation k. The comparatively recent statement of *modulation theory* (Cattell and Brennan, 1983), is embodied in the third term in (1), which recognizes that the state a person is in may explain the conduct quite as much as the person's trait scores. The modulation index, shk, is peculiar to the total situation, hk, and to the individual's liability to a particular emotional state, L_{zi}. One would write instead, in (1) the state level itself S_{zhki} which would then be as on the left in:

$$^{z}{}^{b}h_{ijkz^{s}}z_{hki} = {}^{b}h_{ijkz^{s}}hkz{}^{L}zi \quad (2)$$

which is a statement of modulation theory. It has been shown to hold quite well for anxiety and for depression (Cattell, 1984).

The behavioural equation accounts, of course, for all kind of behavioural measures. aj may be a long-term performance, or a momentary response; the strength of a symptom, or the gain from a learning experience. Theoretically one hesitates, naturally, at the equation always making the simplest assumption – that relations are *linear* for each factor trait and *additive* among traits. But in the majority of areas of application its fit to the facts has been so good as to have discouraged most investigators from setting out to try product and curvilinear relations.

This does not mean that more attention should not be paid to qualitative differences in the nature of the factors. In immediate statistical terms all factors are just evidences of some unitary influences. But already in (1) a distinction is drawn between *ordinary traits* (in three modalities), *role traits* and *state proneness factors* liable to modulation. The forms of age trends, of genetic maturation and environmental learning action, and so on will also be among the properties which make any projection of a prediction into a more remote future or a very different situation subject to epi-formulae attached to the simple behavioural equation.

The main theory around this model has occasionally been singled out as a 'trait theory'. This makes sense only in distinguishing from the reflexological atomistic theory. For any science dealing with any object, be it the element magnesium or the star alpha centauri, describes it by traits. If it cannot, it is talking about nothing – or chaos. A second misunderstanding that has reached print is that in speaking of traits the theory neglects the environment. The modulator index, $^s hk$, above (1) and (2) is a quantitative statement about the provocative power of a particular environmental situation. There is, of course, an environmental specificity in each term, for example, $^b hjkx^T xi$, in equation (1) as in estimates of any specific 'bit' of behaviour. It is represented, in the reasonitude of its environmental effect, by the b's in those terms. Just as a profile of T's (R's and L's) gives the pattern of the given *personality*, so the vector of b values (experimentally obtained as factor loadings), gives the character of the *environmental situation*. On the basis of such profiles many interesting things can be done, as in psychologically classifying life situations, and other analyses (See Sells, 1963).

The scientific personality study of the last 50 years, characterized by quantitative psychometric advances, and the statement of theories in testable models has only in the last 25 years invaded the field of motivation and dynamic structure hitherto left to clinical theories, generally too intuitive and speculative to be checked. It has done so only by developing more subtle and flexible methods (such as P-technique and differential R-technique) and particularly by finding measures of human motivation strengths more objective than questionnaires and such-like tests. The outcome has been, first, the discovery of the number and nature of human 'instincts'. Because these are on a more objective basis than such lists of 'drives', 'instincts', and 'needs' as Murray's, McDougall's and even Freud's, they have been distinguished by the term *ergs*. Besides the ergic (rhymes with allergic) structures, factor analysis yields evidence of unitary acquired sentiments, for example,

to home, religion, job, which for brevity have been called *sems*.

Research with controlled experiment on the effect of various influences on ergic tension and semic activation levels, and upon the course of clinical treatments, has yielded a number of generalizations about conflict, ergic investment in sems, the dynamic lattice, integrated and unintegrated components. Collectively these findings and principles have been called the *dynamic calculus*. In essence the dynamic calculus permits calculations on most of the personality phenomena discussed by clinicians, as well as those of group dynamics, for example, on morale, as discussed in Cattell and Child's (1975) *Motivation and Dynamic Structure*, and in the writings of Barton and Dielman (1983), and others. However, empirical research has been slow to exploit the theory, seemingly because of the combination of complex experimental design, demands for adequate samples, and certain skills in multivariate analysis that are indispensable.

Although the social sciences have tended, like materialist theories in history, to deal with super-individual patterns and concepts, a different reality is becoming evident, as in the UNESCO phrase 'Wars begin in the minds of men'. Actually they begin in the guts of men, and a personality is the living intersection point between a physiology, as known in medicine, and a culture, as known in social science. Probably the social sciences would progress faster if they *began* at that intersection point.

Raymond B. Cattell
University of Illinois

References

Barton, K. and Dielman, T. (1983), *Child Personality Structure and Development*, New York.

Birkett, H. and Cattell, R. B. (1978), 'Diagnosis of the dynamic roots of a clinical symptom by P-technique: a case of episodic alcoholism', *Multivariate Experimental Clinical Research*, 3.

Cartwright, D. S. (1979), *Theories and Models of Personality*, Dubuque, Iowa.

Cattell, R. B. (1979, 1980), *Personality and Learning Theory*, vol. 1, *The Structure of Personality and Environment*, vol. 2, *A Systems Theory of Maturation and Structured Learning*, New York.

Cattell, R. B. (1984), 'Handling prediction from psychological states and roles by modulation theory', in J. Demaree (ed.), *A Festschrift for Saul B. Sells*, New York.

Cattell, R. B. and Brennan, J. (1981), 'Population intelligence and national syntality', *Mankind Quarterly*, 21.

Cattell, R. B. and Brennan, J. (1983), 'An experimental test of modulation theory on anxiety and depression states', *Psychological Review*.

Cattell, R. B. and Dreger, R. M. (1977), *Handbook of Modern Personality Theory*, Washington.

Cattell, R. B. and Child, D. (1975), *Motivation and Dynamic Structure*, Eastbourne.

Cattell, R. B., Eber, H. W. and Tatsuoka, M. (1970), *Handbook for the Sixteen Personality Factor Questionnaire*, Savoy, Ill.

Eysenck, H. J. (1973), *Eysenck on Extraversion*, London.

Hakstian, A. R. and Cattell, R. B. (1974), 'The checking of primary ability structure on a broader basis of performance', *British Journal of Educational Psychology*, 44.

Loehlin, J. C. (1965), 'A heredity-environment analysis of personality inventory data', in A. G. Vandenberg (ed.), *Methods and Goals in Human Behaviour Genetics*, New York.

Mischel, W. (1968), *Personality and Assessment*, New York.

Nesselroade, J. R. and Baltes, P. B. (1979), *Longitudinal Research in the Study of Behavior and Development*, New York.

Royce, J. R. and Mos, L. P. (eds) (1979), *Theoretical Advances in Behavior Genetics*, Alphen.

Royce, J. R. and Powell, A. (1983), *Theory of Personality and Individual Differences*, Englewood Cliffs, N.J.

Sells, S. B. (1963), *Stimulus Determinants of Behavior*, New York.

Skinner, B. F. (1969), *Contingencies of Reinforcement*, New York.

Smith, B. D. and Vetter, H. J. (1982), *Theoretical Approaches to Personality*, Englewood Cliffs, N.J.

Further Reading

Buss, A. R. and Poley, W. (1976), *Individual Differences: Traits and Factors*, New York.

Cattell, R. B. (1982), *The Inheritance of Personality and Ability*, New York.

Gorsuch, R. L. (1974), *Factor Analysis*, London.

See also: *multivariate analysis; personality assessment; traits*.

Personality Assessment

There is little agreement among psychologists concerning the meaning of personality. However, one definition which underpins this article is that personality is the sum of an individual's attributes. The task of personality assessment is, therefore, to measure these attributes.

There are two basic approaches to the measurement of personality – the nomothetic and the idiographic. The former is concerned with the measurement of traits that are to be found in more or less degree among all individuals; the latter seeks to measure that which is specific to the individual concerned. Cutting across the nomothetic and idiographic distinction are the different methods of personality measurement. There are three basic methods which we shall discuss separately below, together with some more general procedures which are, sometimes unwisely, used in personality assessment. The three types of personality test are (1) the inventory or questionnaire; (2) the projective technique, and (3) the objective test. Good measurement demands of tests high reliability (the capability of giving the same scores to individuals on repeated testing, and also internal consistency) and high validity (that is, the test clearly measures what it claims to measure). In addition to these methods, it is possible to use interviews, rating-scales, semantic differentials and repertory grids, although these are not common in personality assessment.

(1) *Personality inventories* consist of items, phrases or sentences about behaviour, to which subjects have to respond Yes/No, True/False, Like/Dislike, for example. The items are selected by two methods. In the first, criterion keying, items are selected if they can discriminate one group from another, for instance, schizophrenics from normals. A well-known test thus constructed is the MMPI, the Minnesota Multiphasic Personality Inventory. The second method uses factor analysis to select the items. Factor analysis is a statistical technique which can evaluate dimensions underlying correlations (in this case between test items). Thus a factor analytic test, *ipso facto*, measures a dimension. The best-known examples of these are Cattell's 16PF test, Eysenck's EPQ and the Personality Inventories constructed by Guilford. Personality inventories are reliable and reasonably valid, and have been found useful in industrial and educational psychology for guidance and selection. From these nomothetic tests two variables stand clear: extraversion and anxiety.

(2) *Projective tests* generally consist of ambiguous stimuli to which subjects have to respond more or less freely. There is much argument over their reliability and validity. Essentially idiographic techniques, the Rorschach test, consisting of series of inkblots, is perhaps the most famous example.

(3) *Objective tests* are a recent development in personality assessment stemming mainly from Cattell. They are defined as tests which can be objectively scored and whose purpose cannot be guessed, thus making them highly useful in selection. However, as yet there is little evidence concerning the validity of these nomothetic measures and thus they are definitely at the experimental stage only. Typical tests are: the fidgeto-meter, a chair which measures movement, for example, during an interview, the slow line drawing test, hand-writing pressure test and a balloon blowing measure.

Finally, rating scales and interviews and other methods as mentioned above are usually shown to be lacking in both reliability and validity. Personality tests are much to be preferred, allowing quantification for applied and research purposes.

Paul Kline
University of Exeter

Further Reading
Cattell, R. B. and Kline, P. (1977), *The Scientific Analysis of Personality and Motivation*, London.
Kline, P. (1979), *Psychometrics and Psychology*, London.
Vernon, P. E. (1964), *Personality Assessment*, London.
See also: *personality*; *projective methods*.

Phenomenology

As a philosophical movement, phenomenology was founded by Edmund Husserl, the German philosopher. Its main concern is to provide philosophy with a foundation that will enable it to be a pure and autonomous discipline free from all presuppositions. Its method is essentially descriptive, and its aims are to uncover the fundamental structures of intentionality, consciousness and the 'life-world' (*Lebenswelt*) of man. The idea of the 'life-world' of 'lived experience' that is always 'taken for granted', even by the empirical sciences, is one of the main concepts of phenomenology which has interested many social scientists, including psychologists and psychiatrists. Nevertheless, critics have argued that when phenomenological concepts are transferred from their original domain to the context of social science, their meaning is radically transformed.

The key figure in the transition from pure phenomenology to modern sociology is undoubtedly Alfred Schutz. Schutz, with a background in law and social science, and also personally acquainted with Husserl, arrived in America from Austria in 1939, and from then on considerably influenced successive generations of philosophers and social scientists at the New School for Social Research in New York. In his major work, *Der sinnhafte Aufbau der sozialen Welt*, 1932 (*The Phenomenology of the Social World*, 1967), Schutz examines Max Weber's ideas about the methodology of the social sciences. Central to Weber's account is the view that sociology is concerned with an 'interpretive understanding' of human 'social action'. Although this is essentially correct, in Schutz's opinion, Weber's ideas require further clarification which is best achieved through a phenomenological analysis of the structure of social reality and of the interpretation of that reality.

Schutz's ideas are clearly set out – although his position remains unchanged – in his *Collected Papers* (3 vols, 1962–66). A central argument is that

the thought objects constructed by the social scientist refer to and are founded upon the thought objects constructed by the common sense thought of man living his everyday life among his fellow-men. Thus the constructs used by the social scientist are, so to speak, constructs of the second degree, namely constructs of the constructs made by the actors on the social scene, whose behaviour the scientist observes and tries to explain in accordance with the procedural rules of his science.

The relationship between the social scientist and his subject matter is totally unlike that between the natural scientist and his subject matter. The social world is an 'interpreted world', and the facts of the social sciences are 'interpreted facts'. According to Schutz, this essential characteristic of social reality provides social science with its central problem: attempting to construct objective accounts of a subjective reality.

In contemporary sociology, the use of Schutz's ideas has taken several directions. But common to all is an effort to clarify the philosophical and methodological foundations of sociological knowledge. These different trends are to be found in P. Berger and T. Luckmann's *The Social Construction of Reality* (1966) which is primarily concerned with how a phenomenological approach can redirect the traditional sociology of knowledge towards an investigation of the taken-for-granted world of common sense 'knowledge'; in A.V. Cicourel's *Method and Measurement in Sociology* (1964), a critique of the research methods of conventional social science, which fails to recognize the implicit use of commonsense knowledge; and in H. Garfinkel's *Studies in Ethnomethodology* (1967), the most radical use of phenomenological ideas resulting in fundamental scepticism of the achievements of conventional social science.

Inevitably, all who claim to be working within the broadly defined phenomenological tradition have radicalized or reinterpreted many of the original ideas of phenomenology. Most phenomenological sociologists have concentrated upon relatively small-scale problems and have been sceptical of the achievements of mainstream sociology and its concern with the macroanalysis of social structures. In part, this can be traced back to Schutz's analysis of Weber's work in which he discusses Weber's methodological essays without looking at Weber's own substantive sociology; but it also mirrors an underlying failure of the whole phenomenological project to understand the nature of science.

In a wider context, phenomenology has influenced philosophers interested in the nature of the 'human sciences', many of whom have tried to combine phenomenological ideas with those from other traditions such as, for example, Marxism. Representative figures here are M. Merleau-Ponty, J. P. Sartre, and H. Arendt.

Peter Lassman
University of Birmingham

Further Reading
Luckmann, T. (ed.) (1978), *Phenomenology and Sociology*, Harmondsworth.

Piucevic, E. (1970), *Husserl and Phenomenology*, London.
Wagner, H. R. (ed.) (1970), *Alfred Schutz: On Phenomenology and Social Relations*, Chicago.
See also: *ethnomethodology*; *Sartre*; *Schutz*.

Phillips Curve

The Phillips curve, named after its originator A. W. Phillips in 1955, depicts an inverse relationship between wage inflation and unemployment – usually extended to link price inflation and unemployment. This relationship has attracted more attention and generated more economic discussion than any other simple macroeconomic hypothesis. There has been research into its theoretical foundations, its empirical validity, its policy implications and its estimation problems. As originally set forth by Phillips, it was no more than a statistical relationship based on weak historical data. But so pervasive was its attraction that a theoretical foundation was soon sought, although without much success. The main attraction of the Phillips curve was in indicating that policy makers can choose lower unemployment only at the cost of higher inflation, and in suggesting that it could be possible to calculate the terms of the trade-off between the policy objective of full employment and stable prices. A series of articles trying to estimate such a relationship for various countries demonstrated not only the indeterminate foundations of the relationship, but also the many methodological problems involved in estimating it. As a policy tool, however, it is useful only to the extent that it is a stable relationship, and the relationship was evidently highly unstable for most countries from the late 1960s through the 1970s. This instability was then attributed to the revision of price expectations upwards as governments persisted in running economies at high levels of aggregate demand.

Ronald Shone
University of Stirling

Further Reading
Phillips, A. W. (1958), 'The relationship between unemployment and the rate of change of money wage rates in the United Kingdom, 1861–1957', *Economica*, 22.
Frisch, H. (1983), *Theories of Inflation*, Cambridge Surveys of Economic Literature, Cambridge.
See also: *inflation and deflation*; *employment and underemployment*.

Philosophy of the Social Sciences

Philosophy of the social sciences is, in the bureaucratic jargon of academe, the study of the aims and methods of the social sciences (sociology, anthropology, political science, psychology, sometimes economics; borderline cases are history, geography, demography and linguistics); it constitutes a subspecialty within philosophy of science – the study of the aims and methods of science in general. Standard anthologies organize their material around such questions as: are natural things fundamentally different from social things; must then the sciences of social things use different methods from the sciences of natural things; are then sciences of the social at all possible; alternatively, are social things mere aggregates; do social things mix facts and values; are values a social product? From this list it is apparent that the subject is engaged with traditional philosophical concerns: ontological, epistemological and normative.

Rarely is there a perfect fit between a subject as defined by academic bureaucracy and what its practitioners actually do. And when place is found for transcendental arguments to the effect that the 'subject' is an impossibility, this cannot but affect an encyclopaedia article. All alternative frameworks have their limitations. An Aristotelian matrix approach, dividing the subject up into orderly categories and concepts, conceals unruly and disorderly elements. The historical approach, treating it as a story with a beginning, a middle and, possibly, an end, risks identifying the subject with present preoccupations. The kinship approach, tracing all present elements to a common ancestor, risks merging and simplifying descent. The map-making approach, trying to give an overall picture, has to ignore continental drift. My choice is a metaphysical sketch map, supplemented by a little history. The result will be a trifle untidy, but the reader should be aware this is because the terrain itself is mountainous, dotted with mists, and we are forced to map from sea-level, without radar.

Nature and Convention
The phrase 'philosophy of the social sciences' itself suggests that there is scientific study of the social (denied by phenomenologists and some followers of Wittgenstein, see below), and that the aims and methods of such study may differ from those of science in general (denied by the logical positivists and others, see below). The very distinction between the natural and the social, between nature and convention, is deeply rooted in our thinking. It was not always so, but it is the notion of impersonal nature that is recent. Once, mankind took itself as the measure of all things and explained nature anthropomorphically; the result of the scientific revolution (in ancient Greece and post-Renaissance Western Europe – we concentrate on the latter) was to overthrow anthropomorphism, to depersonalize nature and explain it by postulating orderly and law-like processes unfolding mechanically (Dijksterhuis, 1961). Such was the flush of seventeenth- and

eighteenth-century enthusiasm for the new science that even man himself was to be treated as part of nature, a machine, his works by 'social physics', his aims and desires as motive forces – or motives for short – and his actions as movements, including social movements and social revolutions akin to the revolving of the heavens.

Such euphoria came to grief over problems like how to maximize the creation of wealth; how to realize moral and political aims in social institutions; how to prevent suicide; which seemed to demand, if not anthropomorphism, then, at least, laws of human convention. If nature is taken to be those aspects of things that are more or less given, the laws and motive forces governing which we cannot alter, then convention covers all forms of orderliness that we attribute to human efforts, orderliness that is not constant from place to place and time to time, and which is humanly alterable. This division of our environment into unchanging and changing parts affects our efforts to explain it. It makes it our first task when facing a problem to decide whether it belongs to nature or to convention – usually a far from uncontroversial allocation.

Controversy over what is natural and what is conventional is heightened by the presence of established sciences of nature. A metaphysical issue is given a methodological twist. This comes about as follows: the rise and success of natural science is, it is widely held, to be explained as the application of a particular method, the empirical method. Thus, if a problem is identified as natural, the methods of the natural sciences are appropriate; but having been so successful with nature perhaps they are appropriate for problems of convention also. To the ancient Greeks this might have seemed absurd. But as European society under industrialization changed from *Gemeinschaft* to *Gesellschaft*, more systematic thought had to be given to altering current conventions and making them work better. As such social thought grew in cognitive power and practical importance, debates about the boundary between nature and convention, and hence the appropriate methods with which to approach convention, took on a life of their own. Some philosophers of social science, greatly exercised over questions of method, are unaware that they debate a disguised metaphysical issue. One example of this is those who push the empirical method because they hold that nature is real and observable, whereas conventions are abstract unobservables (Kaufman, 1944). A relic of this thinking is the individualism/holism dispute over what is more and what is less real among conventions. One party, the individualists, holds that only individual human beings are real and larger-scale social entities are aggregates which can be, for explanatory purposes, reduced to theories about individuals. The other party, the holists, questions the reality of individuals when

they can be explained as creatures of society. Although there is some purely philosophical debate of such issues, under the influence of positivism they are usually joined in methodological form: which is more empirically observable – the individual or the whole? A convincing case can be made for either side.

Awkwardly cutting across all attempts to map this field are Marxist variants of each set of issues. Marx could be said to hold that there was only nature, not convention, and that his 'dialectical materialism' should be seen as part of natural science. The cross-cutting occurs because Marxists will not permit him to be treated as just one of a succession of social scientists; hence they dispute the interpretation of Marx's writings, while others advance positions they claim are in the spirit of his work, if not within the letter. As a result almost every issue in the philosophy of the social sciences is duplicated within Marxism, but in a manner that exaggerates the importance of Marx. Mainstream philosophers of social science often mention Marx, but he is a pivotal figure only for Marxists.

Positivism and its Legacy
Empiricist methodology always had its a priorist opponents, but the triumph of Newton's physics over Descartes was taken to be a triumph of empiricism over a priorism. From then, despite Kant's valiant attempt at reconciliation, a priorist methodologies have grown increasingly estranged from science. That left humane studies and social studies as fields to continue the struggle between the rivals. Simmel (1950), Durkheim (1938) and Weber (1949) all wrote their classics on the philosophy of the social sciences when the anti-science tendencies in German academic philosophy were at their peak. History done on Hegelian lines was the model for humanities and their a priorism was now known as hermeneutics. Both empiricism and a priorism are present in these classics.

The twentieth-century high tide of militant empiricism was the logical positivism movement that began in the 1920s. It appropriated all cognition into science, the success of which was attributed to the use of the empirical method. Theories not empirically verifiable were declared nonscientific and merely metaphysical. The battle line the positivists drew in social studies was, could the social sciences live up to their name by producing verifiable theories? If so, then the unity and identity of science and cognition could be upheld. In face of this challenge the a priorists took some time to regroup. Some, amazingly, retreated to the rather unpromising ground of Marxism (the Frankfurt School), which they tried to Hegelianize and a priorize (Frisby, 1976).

The primary interests of the logical positivists were in the natural sciences, but their predilection for a hodgepodge of logic, economics, statistics, Marx (note again how he confuses all issues), psychoanalysis and linguistics ensured that attempts were made to give a positivist account of them that would secure their place in unified science.

So long as logical positivism flourished within philosophy (down to the early 1960s), intense debates took place over the degree to which the empirical method could be utilized in what were now unselfconsciously called 'the social sciences'. The limits of mathematical and quantitative methods and simplicity were explored, as was the problem of whether facts could be separated from values. If social phenomena resisted measurement and quantification, and if they were permeated by values, the verifiable empirical basis of the social sciences was undermined. Along with the classics, the literature generated in this period is the core of most readers and courses in philosophy of the social sciences.

Meanwhile, the regrouped opponents of logical positivism engaged with precisely the same problems. They considered the limits of empiricism to be much more severe, and the problem of values to be much more pervasive, however, than did the logical positivists. Indeed it was argued that the limits of empiricism were the limits of natural science. As for values, these were the tip of the iceberg. As soon as the conscious, self-conscious, meaning-generating, and reflexive activities of human beings were under study, a totally different order of things was involved, demanding a totally different approach. That approach involved historical imagination – *Verstehen* – which requires the scrutiny of texts (hermeneutics) and some phenomenological rather than any empirical method (Natanson, 1963; Schutz, 1962; Dallmayr and McCarthy, 1977).

Disguised under the dispute about method was another about aims. Social things being unlike natural things, it was possible that attempting to explain and predict them was not only erroneous but inappropriate. Followers of the later Wittgenstein went even further than the continental a priorists and used the patron saint of logical positivism's later work to develop a transcendental argument against the very possibility of a science of the social. Winch (1958) and Louch (1966), despite differences, converge on the idea that what makes social things social as opposed to inert are the meaning-generating activities of human beings which show themselves in rules of behaviour. Language, for example, is not random noises but patterns that make sense. Clearly such rules are not natural; rather they are activities that define and constitute human life together. We cannot then explain human conduct in the way we offer mechanical causal explanation in science, but only by mastering from the inside the rules in use and their degrees of freedom. People do social things for reasons, not in obedience to laws. The vast literature on Winch and on whether reasons are causes can be traced through *The Philosopher's Index*.

Methodological Differences, Rationality, Relativism

The logical positivists and their opponents agree in translating metaphysical and epistemological issues into methodology. They also agree on the pivotal role played for method by the possibility of human intervention, in particular that intervention which is an unintended consequence of having thoughts about society that alter people's behaviour. (Popper (1945) labels this the Oedipus effect, Merton (1957) labels it the self-fulfilling prophecy.) Both Marxists and conservatives like to play down the desirable or effective scope for intervention in society, but this argument traps them with their own theories. What is the purpose of theorizing about society if the best we can do to improve it is to let it alone? Moreover, how is that view to be sustained when adequate theorizing itself improves society? One reaction to this is to attribute a privileged status to theorizing, to see it as somehow underdetermined by the general processes of determinism in society. Efforts were made first by Marx and Durkheim, and then, under the label 'sociology of knowledge', by Mannheim, to connect forms of putative cognition with social forms, class interest and the like, meanwhile exempting from such determination the natural sciences and that theorizing itself (Mannheim, 1936). The 'strong programme' of the sociology of knowledge – first proposed by Merton, although he attributes it to Mannheim – embraces science and exempts nothing. This is supported by the idea that reality, especially what people take reality to be, is itself a social construction – an idea that may be ascribed to the school of phenomenology but which goes specifically to Berger and Luckmann (1966). This issue, however, gets debated directly rather than methodologically, with the marshalling of comparative evidence to show how reality can be constructed very differently in different times and places. (Radical psychological theorists – labelling theory, so-called – extended the argument to the boundary between normal and abnormal psychological states, suggesting that psychopathology too is a matter of convention.) Much of the evidence came from anthropology, which had described societies where world-views, counting, the very categories of language and hence of reality, were different from ours. Reality seemed socially relative. Winch (1964) extended his earlier work in this direction, arguing that Evans-Pritchard's classic study of Azande witchcraft (1937) was conceptually confused in comparing magic to science. Battle was joined by the anthropologist Horton (and Finnegan, 1973) who had upheld the validity of such comparisons. He thus followed Gellner, the leading critic of the various sociological idealisms.

Anthropology also stimulated the overlapping and so-called rationality debate, another treatment of the issue of relativism. The search for a characterization of what constituted man's rationality stemmed from

Aristotle's suggestion that it was rationality that set the human animal apart from other animals. Rationality was for long taken to mean reasoning, ratiocination, logic. Mill (1843) took it for granted that logic was the laws of the human mind. Anthropologists had once held that uncivilized peoples lacked the ability to reason, were incapable, even, of coherent speech. In our century they reversed themselves and found primitive peoples to be as rational, if not in some ways more rational, than us. Yet their societies were without science and full of superstition, making them by positivist standards (logic and empiricism) not rational. Relativists argued that standards of rationality were embodied in differing social arrangements and hence differed. Absolutists argued that a necessary minimum for rationality – logic – was a necessary minimum for social life to function at all, therefore no societies were not rational. Still others tried to model degrees of rationality (Wilson, 1970; Jarvie, 1984). Recent developments, as we shall see, reveal new vigour among the relativists.

Logical positivism in philosophy petered out in the 1960s. The social sciences lagged a little behind. Political science and psychology experienced in the 1950s the 'behavioural revolution' (hence 'behavioural sciences' was a briefly fashionable name), in which positivist notions of aims and methods came to dominate – just as the positivist hegemony over philosophy was crumbling. More subtly, in sociology and anthropology the early positivism and empiricism of Durkheim had been blended in the 1940s into structural-functionalism, a way of going about thinking about society that, despite serious logical flaws (Gellner, 1973), survives in a modified form as the mainstream account of aims and methods. Although there was much debate about functionalism, it was endorsed as a method, perhaps because, stemming from a richer positivism, the extreme naturalism and inductivism of logical positivism rarely infected the work of sociologists and anthropologists – even if, sometimes, they echoed the rhetoric (Jarvie, 1964).

Already in the 1940s there had been intervention in the debates about the aims and methods of the social sciences from another quarter. An economist, Hayek, and an anti-positivist philosopher, Popper, in articles that became new classics as books (Hayek, 1952; Popper, 1957), argued that social scientists harboured mistaken views about the natural sciences. Hayek stressed that in science there were elements of a priori model building; Popper said that scientific method was trial and error. They thus criticized the identification of science with the positivist description of it. Both attacked the search for historical laws. Positivism was declared caricature and labelled 'scientism', then diagnosed as underlying the spurious claims not only of Marxists and positivists, but also as being what the continental a priorists were against.

Drawing primarily on the neglected example of economics, Hayek and Popper argued that the test of methods was results: by that test the freedom economists excercised to invent simplified models and work out their implications before complicating the models with real-world additions was one used generally in common sense and professional social thought. Their work was part of a vigorous methodological debate within economics stemming from Robbins (1932) and Hutchison (1938), later pressed further by Friedman (1953), Klappholz and Agassi (1959), and others. Alas, to the other social sciences economics is like mathematics to the nonscientist: a basic subject everyone knows they should be conversant with, and about which they feel guilty because they are ignorant of it. Moreover, there is ambivalence: economics has high status, yet whether economic theories are testable has been repeatedly questioned and still is. Hence the debates about model-building, rationality, realistic assumptions, whether theories should aim at truth or predictive success, and the value of mathematization that go on in economics (Boland, 1982) are scarcely referred to in discussions of the aims and methods of the other social sciences. This is especially poignant, because the debates within economics presuppose that economic behaviour is conventional and hence that the methods of economics are free to be different from those of natural science.

The very important point about false images of science shared by positivists, Marxists and anti-science a priorists had little impact. With the correction made, Hayek and Popper argued that simple modifications of method would allow the social sciences to belong to unified science. Moreover, the same modifications have to be made in cybernetics, which belongs to hard science – mathematics and engineering. Instead, the most controverted point was an ontological one. First, do humans act rationally – do they act at all? In opposition to the Hegelian tendency in Marx to reify abstractions and endow them with causal force (relations of production, classes, and so on), Hayek and Popper side-stepped ontology and proposed the principle of rational action or methodological individualism as more fruitful and in better conformity to the actual practice of the social sciences. This was the principle to attribute aims only to individuals and not to social wholes. Social institutions, they held, were real, but they were built, sustained and given aims only by individuals. A lively and extended debate continues (O'Neill, 1973).

To a large extent Popper and Hayek did not carry the day, as positivist and behavourist and holistic social science flourished through the 1960s. Early in that decade an essay on the history of science was published that was destined finally to purge logical positivism from the social sciences and yet which, like Popper, Hayek and the positivists, continued to urge the unity of science, while explicitly patronizing the social sciences as underdeveloped and hence not yet admissible. Its author, a physicist, was a self-taught historian utterly innocent of economics, sociology or any of the social sciences. The book was *The Structure of Scientific Revolutions*, the author, Thomas Kuhn (Barnes, 1982).

Kuhn argued that what distinguished a science from a prescience or a nonscience was its domination by a paradigm, that is, a recognized piece of work in the field that people copy in method, style and substance. In science such paradigms are fully in place when they are incorporated in current standard textbooks and imposed on novices. Noticing the incessant warring about fundamentals in the social sciences, the existence of rival textbooks, Kuhn could not but characterize them as presciences. There is some irony in the way social scientists have seized on Kuhn's ideas and reversed them, arguing that since the social sciences have textbooks they have paradigms, therefore they are sciences. But Kuhn specifically says there must be agreement amongst the leadership of a field on a single paradigm if that field is to count as scientific. Conclusion: there are as many social sciences, or branches of the social sciences, as there are paradigmatic works; once we declare that Freud and Piaget do not contest child psychology but that there are two fields, developmental psychology and cognitive psychology, a prescientific field is transformed into two paradigm-dominated and scientific fields.

Once again the debate has been vigorous. Kuhn's critics have argued that textbooks are also possessed by pseudoscience (astrology), nonscience (theology) and doubtful cases (psychoanalysis). More telling, Kuhn provides a legitimation-procedure for the boundary-drawing of academic bureaucrats who wish to conceal debate, controversy and confusion and give the impression of the orderly march of progress in 'fields', 'subjects', 'areas', and so on. Yet the categories of natural and conventional, not to mention physical, chemical, biological, or mathematical, may themselves stem from problems and hotly-debated theories (Hattiangadi, 1978/9).

A more relativist reading of Kuhn is that no special aims or methods characterize natural science, which is a subject much like any other, distinguishable if at all by its social status. Hence comparison with the social sciences was an empirical matter *for the social sciences* and the 'strong programme' of the sociology of knowledge vindicated itself (Bloor, 1976). Whether the results point to identity or contrast, they belong to the sociology of knowledge, which thus is the truly comprehensive discipline. Social studies of science, then, under whatever rubric, have implications in all directions, in sociology as well as philosophy, in meta-theory as well as theory.

I. C. Jarvie
York University, Toronto

References

Barnes, B. (1982), *T. S. Kuhn and Social Science*, London.

Berger, P. and Luckmann, T. (1966), *The Social Construction of Reality*, New York.

Bloor, D. (1976), *Knowledge and Social Imagery*, London.

Boland, L. A. (1982), *The Foundations of Economic Method*, London.

Dallmayr, F. and McCarthy, T. (1977), *Understanding Social Inquiry*, Washington.

Dijksterhuis, E. J. (1961), *The Mechanization of the World Picture*, New York.

Durkheim, E. (1938 [1895]), *Rules of Sociological Method*, Glencoe, Ill. (Original French, *Les Règles de la méthode sociologique*, Paris.)

Evans-Pritchard, E. E. (1937), *Witchcraft, Oracles and Magic Among the Azande*, Oxford.

Friedman, M. (1953), *Essays in Positive Economics*, Chicago.

Frisby, D. (ed.) (1976), *The Positivist Dispute in German Sociology*, London.

Gellner, E. (1973), *Cause and Meaning in the Social Sciences*, London.

Hattiangadi, J. N. (1978/9), 'The structure of problems: I and II', *Philosophy of the Social Sciences*, 8 and 9.

Hayek, F. A. (1952), *The Counter-Revolution of Science*, Glencoe. Ill.

Horton, W. R. and Finnegan, R. (eds) (1973), *Modes of Thought*, London.

Hutchison, T. W. (1938), *The Significance and Basic Postulates of Economic Theory*, London.

Jarvie, I. C. (1964), *The Revolution in Anthropology*, London.

Jarvie, I. C. (1984), *Rationality and Relativism*, London.

Kaufmann, F. (1944), *Methodology of the Social Sciences*, Oxford.

Klappholz, K. and Agassi, J. (1959), 'Methodological prescriptions in economics', *Economica*, 26.

Kuhn, T. S. (1962), *The Structure of Scientific Revolutions*, Chicago.

Louch, A. R. (1966), *Explanation and Social Action*, Berkeley and Los Angeles.

Mannheim, K. (1936 [1929]), *Ideology and Utopia*, London. (Original German, *Ideologie und Utopie*, Bonn.)

Merton, R. (1957), *Social Theory and Social Structure*, Glencoe, Ill.

Mill, J. S. (1843), *A System of Logic*, London.

Natanson, M. (ed.) (1963), *Philosophy of the Social Sciences: A Reader*, New York.

O'Neill, J. (ed.) (1973), *Modes of Individualism and Collectivism*, London.

Popper, K. R. (1945), *The Open Society and Its Enemies*, London.

Popper, K. R. (1957), *The Poverty of Historicism*, London.

Robbins, L. (1932), *Essay on the Nature and Significance of Economic Science*, London.
Schutz, A. (1962), *Collected Papers*, Vol. I: *The Problem of Social Reality*, The Hague.
Simmel, G. (1950), *The Sociology of Georg Simmel*, ed. K. H. Wolff, Glencoe, Ill.
Weber, M. (1949), *Methodology of the Social Sciences*, ed. E. Shils, Glencoe, Ill.
Wilson, B. (ed.) (1970), *Rationality*, Oxford.
Winch, P. (1958), *The Idea of a Social Science*, London.
Winch, P. (1964), 'Understanding a primitive society', *American Philosophical Quarterly*, 1.

Further Reading
Agassi, J. (1960), 'Methodological individualism', in O'Neill (1973).
Agassi, J. (1975), 'Institutional individualism,' *British Journal of Sociology*, 26.
Aggasi, J. (1977), *Towards a Rational Philosophical Anthropology*, The Hague.
Bhaskar, R. (1979), *The Possibility of Naturalism: A Philosophical Critique of the Contemporary Social Sciences*, Brighton.
Borger, R. and Cioffi, F. (1970), *Explanation in the Behavioural Sciences*, Cambridge.
Brodbeck, M. (ed.) (1968), *Readings in the Philosophy of the Social Sciences*, New York.
Brown, R. (1963), *Explanation in Social Science*, London.
Brown, S. C. (ed.) (1979), *Philosophical Disputes in the Social Sciences*, Brighton.
Collingwood, R. G. (1946), *The Idea of History*, Oxford.
Dixon, K. (1973), *Sociological Theory: Pretence and Possibility*, London.
Durkheim, E. (1915 [1912]), *Elementary Forms of the Religious Life*, London. (Original French, *Les Formes élémentaires de la vie religieuse*, Paris.)
Emmet, D. and MacIntyre, A. (1970), *Sociological Theory and Philosophical Analysis*, London.
Feigl, H. and Brodbeck, M. (1953), *Readings in the Philosophy of Science*, New York.
Gellner, E. (1964), *Thought and Change*, London.
Gellner, E. (1980), *Spectacles and Predicaments*, Cambridge.
Giddens, A. (1976), *New Rules of Sociological Method*, New York.
Hollis, M. and Lukes, S. (eds) (1982), *Rationality and Relativism*, Oxford.
Hookway, C. and Pettit, P. (eds) (1978), *Action and Interpretation*, Cambridge.
Jarvie, I. C. (1972), *Concepts and Society*, London.
Krimerman, L. (ed.), *The Nature and Scope of Social Science. A Critical Anthology*, New York.
Simmel, G. (1959), *Essays on Sociology, Philosophy and Aesthetics*, New York.
Simmel, G. (1980), *Essays on Interpretation in Social Science*, Totowa.

See also: Althusser; Comte; Habermas; James; Kuhn; Peirce; phenomenology; Popper; positivism; relativism; Wittgenstein.

Phobia

A phobia is a pathological fear of a situation, object or living thing; the fear is understood to be out of proportion, or inappropriate, to the fear-inspiring properties inherent in the external focus. Phobias tend to promote avoidance of the object of the fear.

Phobias may range from mild and non-impairing (for example, a person with a flying phobia may continue to travel by air, although feeling anxious), to totally immobilizing (for example, someone with a very common fear, agoraphobia – fear of going outdoors alone – may be totally house-bound). Phobias may exist within, or in conjunction with, other psychopathological states.

At present, three major explanatory theories and three major treatment approaches pertain to phobias:

(1) Dynamic psychiatrists view phobias as symbolic expressions of feared unconscious neurotic material (internal) which is magically warded off by avoidance of the phobia's (external) target. For example, a person disturbed by sexual impulses and resultant guilt may develop a germ phobia and take elaborate sanitary measures to avoid (ward off) 'contamination' (here to be understood symbolically as representing sexual guilt). This phobia, by the way, may be distinguished from a close psychological cousin, a cleanliness compulsion, by noting that the phobia is usually aimed at self-protection; the compulsion is aimed at protection of others from infection. Stekel, one of the earliest psychoanalysts, expressed this as, 'The phobic is self-ill, the compulsive is object-ill.' Clinicians of this school treat phobias with dynamic psychotherapy.

(2) Behaviourists see phobic avoidance as a learned response that may develop in reaction to extremely subtle cues, and they treat it with a variety of behavioural techniques, including desensitization.

(3) Recently, a pharmacotherapy of phobias has emerged, featuring use of so-called 'minor tranquillizers', anti-depressants, and drugs that block the beta-adrenergic nervous system. Based on the effectiveness of anti-depressant treatments, biologically-oriented psychiatrists now understand certain phobias as symptoms of an underlying depression.

Thomas G. Gutheil
Harvard University
Program in Psychiatry and Law, Boston

Further Reading
Birk, L. (1978), 'Behavior therapy and behavioral psychotherapy', in A. M. Nicholi (ed.), *Harvard Guide to Modern Psychiatry*, Cambridge, Mass.

Marks, I. N. (1978), *Living with Fear*, New York.

Nemiah, J. C. (1978), 'Psychoneurotic disorders', in A. M. Nicholi (ed.), *Harvard Guide to Modern Psychiatry*, Cambridge, Mass.

Sheehan, D. V. (1979), 'The efficient treatment of phobic disorders', in T. C. Manschreck (ed.), *Psychiatric Medicine Update, Massachusetts General Hospital Review for Physicians*, New York.

See also: *obsessive-compulsive disorders*.

Physiocratic Thought

Physiocratic thought, which flourished in France and other parts of Europe mainly during the 1760s and 1770s, embodied the economic, social and political ideas of a school founded by Quesnay and Mirabeau in 1757. The essence of this new social science was a belief in a natural order of society, founded on private property and the authority of government, and designed to be the most advantageous order for securing human welfare. In the history of economics, the only field where physiocratic thought is now discussed, it is confined to the economic theory and policy by which the school tried to improve living conditions and the wealth of the state.

With agriculture still the dominant form of economic activity in Europe, the school concentrated on developing strategies for raising agricultural productivity and hence national output. These included the reorganization of the traditional farming by sharecropping on more capitalist lines as practised in the north of France and England; improved transport and communications as well as free trade in agricultural produce to raise farmers' profits and facilitate capital accumulation; abolition of encumbrances on manufactures to lower farmers' costs; and a fiscal reform concentrating on the single tax on land rent (their net product of agriculture). This concept of surplus, explained in physical and value terms, was seen by them as the source of expanded reproduction of wealth, the power of the state and the people's well-being. In developing these policies, their founder Quesnay constructed a coherent theoretical system of political economy which exerted considerable influence on the systems of Adam Smith and Karl Marx. With current recognition of such influence, their reputation as economists has been enhanced and they are no longer regarded as a peculiar sect, of importance only because of their *laissez-faire* views.

Peter Groenewegen
University of Sydney

Further Reading
Meek, R. L. (1962), *The Economics of Physiocracy*, London.

Weulersse, G. (1910), *Le Mouvement physiocratique en France*, Paris.

See also: *laissez-faire*; *Quesnay*.

Physiological Psychology

Before 1879, when Wundt founded his psychological laboratory in Germany and initiated the contemporary era of scientific psychology as a distinct academic discipline, psychological issues had been investigated within the framework of physiology by pioneering sensory physiologists such as Helmholtz. Even Wundt – and many of his European and American followers – primarily regarded themselves as physiological psychologists, in that they were concerned with elucidating how the human brain and mind are related. Modern physiological psychology, however, relies heavily on the application of physiological measures and manipulations of animals (and particularly animal models of human psychology). For this reason, Thompson (1967) traces the subject's origins as a distinct psychological subdiscipline to Shepherd Franz's 1902 publication on the effects of frontal lobe lesions on simple animal learning tasks, devised by Thorndike at the turn of the century.

Then, as now, the subject was construed as the study of how the brain and endocrine system control those behaviours associated with perception, emotion, motivation, attention, thinking, language, learning and memory. For many years, because of the influence of Watsonian behaviourism, it suffered from a general unwillingness to postulate psychological processes mediating observable behaviour. This neglect, which arose from a justified mistrust of introspection as the royal road to the mind, has been criticized by Hebb (1980), who argued that mental operations are essentially unconscious and can only be inferred from patterns of behavioural and related brain activity. As such inferences are hard to make, there exists an opposing tendency among physiological psychologists, in which, instead of making no theoretical postulates, they explain brain–mind relationships in terms of overly general intuitive psychological concepts, like attention. Success in the enterprise therefore requires both an adequate technology for influencing and measuring brain processes, and also methods for measuring and interpreting behaviour. Exciting developments in techniques for exploring brain processes over the past thirty years have not yet been matched by improvements in analysing behavioural processes, although these may come as artificial intelligence research has increasing impact.

The central issues of physiological psychology concern the extent to which the control of psychological functions is localized in the brain, how these functions are mediated, and how this control emerges in phylogeny and ontogeny. The first two of these issues have been polemical since the late eighteenth century with the emergence of phrenology, over a century before Franz began his research. The phrenologists believed that the control of complex psychological functions, such as philoprogenitiveness, was highly localized in the brain and that their degree of development was indicated by bumps on the overlying skull. Some nineteenth-century researchers, like Flourens (who lesioned pigeon brains to see what functions were lost), adopted a holistic position and argued that functional control was distributed, not localized. Others, such as the neurologists Broca and Wernicke, who found that specific left cortical lesions causes selective verbal impairments, argued that complex functions are indeed controlled by small brain regions. The controversy continued into this century when Karl Lashley formulated an influential holistic viewpoint, based on studies of the effects of lesions on learning in the rat, defined by his principles of mass action (efficiency of a given function depends on the amount of available brain tissue) and equipotentiability (widely distributed brain regions have equivalent function).

The longevity of the holistic v. localized dispute depended partly on an inadequate analysis of the nature of complex psychological functions, such as memory, and partly on the crudeness of physiological techniques before World War II. As Luria (1973) indicated, psychological goals, like remembering, may be achieved through a variety of routes, each using somewhat different subprocesses. Blocking a preferred route by a specific brain lesion may cause a less preferred one to be adopted and different (spared) subprocesses used. How the brain controls these subprocesses is the key issue. Componential analysis of complex behaviours into their functional atoms is based on criteria lacking universal agreement. This uncertainty permits the existence of a range of views about the reasons why partial recovery may occur after brain damage. Some propose that there is always functional loss so that 'recovered' behaviours are performed differently, whereas others argue that functions genuinely recover and are mediated by surviving brain tissue (Stein, Finger and Hart, 1983). The uncertainty also explains the inchoate state of understanding of three other major issues: (1) It relates to why early brain lesions sometimes have different effects than adult lesions. For example, does the fact that early left hemisphere lesions disturb verbal behaviour much less than adult lesions mean that certain processes have not yet been irreversibly assigned to that hemisphere, or that in early life verbal behaviour is achieved differently? (2) It relates to the issue of how different is the organization of people's brains. For example, Ojemann (1983) has reported that the ability to name things is disturbed by electrically stimulating different cortical regions in distinct individuals. Are their subprocesses differently located, or do they name in different ways? (3) The

same question arises with the last issue, cross-species comparisons. Do species with radically differing brains, who can perform similar complex tasks, do so by using distinct systems of subprocesses?

The use of improved physiological techniques have, however, made clear that functions are more localized than Lashley believed. The brain is now seen as an enormous interlinked set of modules, each acting as a special-purpose computer. Roughly, the neocortex comprises a functional mosaic of modules, which process distinct aspects of sensory information in series and in parallel so that meaning can be extracted and spatial representations constructed by cross-modal integration. This information is stored mainly in the neocortex when further subcortical systems are activated. Further neocortical and subcortical modules programme appropriate behaviour, based on such sensory analysis and a determination (made largely subcortically) of the motivational significance of the information.

Detailed parts of this framework have sprung from the application of physiological techniques. These techniques are now sophisticated. Animal lesions can be precisely placed and identified, and accidental human lesions can now be better located in life using computed axial tomography, cerebral blood flow measurement and positron-emission computed tomography. The last technique, in particular, makes it possible to measure a lesion-induced disturbance of apparently healthy tissue. This bears on a major problem with lesion studies: a function may be lost either because it was controlled by destroyed tissue or because the destruction makes healthy tissue act abnormally. The difficulty can only be resolved by the supplementary use of other techniques like electrical or chemical stimulation of tissue, or recording electrophysiological, metabolic or biochemical activity of neurons whilst an animal (or human) subject is performing a selected task. If the use of these techniques yields consistent and convergent implications, an interpretation can be made of the function of a given brain region. Confidence in such interpretations can be further increased by improved knowledge of the brain's microanatomy and connections. Modern techniques have led to a massive surge in this knowledge, giving rise to the hope that by the turn of the century it will be possible to make detailed computer simulations of how activity in well-described brain regions mediates complex psychological abilities, such as the visual perception of objects.

Andrew Mayes
University of Manchester

References
Hebb, D. O. (1980), *Essay on Mind*, Hillsdale, N.J.
Luria, A. R. (1973), *The Working Brain*,
    Harmondsworth.

Ojemann, G. A. (1983), 'Brain organization for language from the perspective of electrical stimulation mapping', *The Behavioral and Brain Sciences*, 6.

Stein, D. G., Finger, S. and Hart, T. (1983), 'Brain damage and recovery: problems and perspectives', *Behavioral and Neural Biology*, 37.

Thompson, R. (1967), *Foundations of Physiological Psychology*, London.

Further Reading

Carlson, N. R. (1981), *Physiology of Behavior*, 2nd edn, Boston.

Carlson, N. R. (1979), *The Brain: A Scientific American Book*, Oxford.

Kolb, B. and Whishaw, I. Q. (1980), *Fundamentals of Human Neuropsychology*, San Francisco.

Oatley, K. (1978), *Perceptions and Representations*, London.

See also: *biological psychiatry*; *nervous system*.

Piaget, Jean (1896–1980)

Jean Piaget, the Swiss psychologist, biologist and philosopher, was professor of experimental psychology at the University of Geneva (1940–1971) and of developmental psychology at the Sorbonne in Paris (1952–1963). As a psychologist, Piaget was influenced by Freud, Janet, J. M. Baldwin and Claparède. Piaget's theories and experiments, which he published in innumerable books and articles, place him among the foremost psychologists of the century.

Piaget's lifelong quest was for the origins of knowledge. Trained as a biologist, and initially influenced by Bergson's evolutionary philosophy, he sought to explain the conditions of knowledge by studying its genesis. Evolutionary theory, the developmental psychology of children's intelligence and the history of science were to provide the scientific underpinnings of this epistemological project.

In his early work (1923–36), Piaget tried to gain insight into children's logic by studying their verbally expressed thought. Using a free method of interrogation, the 'clinical method', Piaget investigated children's reasoning about everyday phenomena, causality and moral problems. A leading idea expressed in Piaget's early books is that of egocentrism in early childhood and its gradual replacement by socialized, and therefore logical, thinking. Young children's egocentrism is revealed in their incapacity to differentiate between their own point of view and that of another. Neither experience nor the influence of adults are sufficient grounds for the attainment of logical thinking. Instead, Piaget explained the abandonment of egocentrism by the child's desire and need to communicate with children of the same age.

In the late 1920s and early 1930s Piaget made extensive observations of his own children as babies and elaborated his theory of sensorimotor intelligence in infancy. Contrary to contemporary conceptions, he considered babies as actively and spontaneously oriented towards their environment. As they 'assimilate' things to their action patterns, they at the same time have to 'accommodate' these patterns to the exigencies of the external world. In this process of interaction with the environment the child's innate reflexes and patterns of behaviour are altered, differentiated and mutually co-ordinated. The organization of action patterns gives rise to a 'logic of actions'. In his account of the development of the object concept, Piaget states that initially children do not appear to recognize a world existing independently of their actions upon it. A baby playing with a toy does not search for it when it is covered; according to Piaget, it ceases to exist for the baby. The concept of an independently existing world is gradually constructed during infancy and is attained only at about 18 months when the child becomes capable of representing things mentally.

The existence of a logic in action, demonstrated in the baby studies, made Piaget revise his earlier theories of the origins of logical thinking in early and middle childhood. Logical operations are prepared in sensorimotor intelligence and the former are the result of internalization of the latter. The attainment of logical thinking, therefore, is not the result of verbal interactions with other children, but of the child's reconstruction of the action logic on a new, mental plane. Piaget now viewed cognitive development as resulting in stages, characterized by a dynamic equilibrium between the child's cognitive structures and the environment. Development is the result of a process of equilibration, in which equilibria of a progressively more stable kind are sought and attained. Piaget distinguished three stages: the sensorimotor stage (0–about 18 months), the stage of concrete operations (about 7–11 years) and the stage of formal operations (from about 11 years). In each of these three stages children's thinking is characterized by its own kind of logic: an action logic in the sensorimotor stage, a logic applied to concrete situations in the concrete operational stage, and a logic applied to statements of a symbolic or verbal kind in the formal operational stage.

In the period between the sensorimotor and the concrete operational stage (which Piaget called the preoperational period) the child's thinking lacks the possibility to carry out operations, that is, reversible mental actions. Piaget and his collaborators demonstrated in many simple yet elegant experiments the transition from preoperational to concrete thinking about concepts such as number, velocity, space, and physical causality. In these experiments they no longer restricted themselves to verbal interaction, but introduced materials which the child could manipulate. In the famous conservation task, the child must judge whether the amount of fluid poured into a glass of different proportions changes or does not change. Preoperational children are characteristically misled by the perceptual appearance of the situation. Only concrete operational children can reverse the transfer in thought and give the correct answer.

From 1950 onward Piaget wrote his great epistemological studies, in which he rejected empiricism and rationalism. Consequently he opposed behaviourism, maturational theories of development and nativist ideas in Gestalt psychology. The newborn child is neither a *tabula rasa*, ready to receive the impression of the environment, nor endowed with a priori knowledge about the world. Piaget showed himself a pupil of Kant by assuming that our knowledge of the world is mediated by cognitive structures. But, unlike Kant, he did not consider these as fundamental ideas given at birth: he showed them to be the products of a lengthy process of construction in the interaction of subject and environment. He therefore coined his epistemology a *genetic* epistemology.

The aim of genetic epistemology is to reconstruct the development of knowledge from its most elementary biological forms up to its highest achievements, scientific thinking included. Psychology has a place in this project, in so far as it studies the development of biological structures in the human baby into sensorimotor and operational intelligence. But the enterprise is essentially a biological one, as the development of intelligence is conceived of as an extension of biological adaptation. Intelligence is the specific product in humans of the same biological principles applying to all living nature: adaptation resulting in structural reorganizations and in equilibria of increasing stability.

Piaget saw psychology as a necessary but limited part of his epistemology, and he always regretted the exclusive interest for the psychological component of his work. In the International Centre for Genetic Epistemology, which he founded at the University of Geneva in 1955 and to which he attracted specialists in all fields of study, he stimulated the interdisciplinary study of epistemology. But the acclaim for his epistemological ideas was never more than a shadow of the universal enthusiasm for the *psychologist* Piaget.

Piaget's influence on developmental psychology can hardly be overestimated. His ideas were seen as a help in supplanting behaviouristic and psychoanalytic theories in psychology. He set the margins for discussions in cognitive developmental psychology from the 1960s up to the present time. But his ideas and methods have always been the object of sharp criticism. Many developmental psychologists think that Piaget underrated the cognitive capacities of young children, and he is reproached for neglecting in his later studies the social context of development in favour of an isolated epistemic subject. Therefore, many now go beyond the mature Piaget and find inspiration in his early works.

Ed Elbers
University of Utrecht

Further Reading

(A) Works by Piaget

Piaget, J. (1923), *Le Langage et la pensée chez l'enfant*, Neuchâtel. (*The Language and Thought of the Child*, London, 1926.)

Piaget, J. (1932), *Le Jugement moral chez l'enfant*, Paris. (*The Moral Judgment of the Child*, London, 1932.)

Piaget, J. (1936), *La Naissance de l'intelligence chez l'enfant*, Neuchâtel. (*The Origin of Intelligence in the Child*, London, 1952.)

Piaget, J. and Inhelder, B. (1948), *La Représentation de l'espace chez l'enfant*, Paris. (*The Child's Conception of Space*, London, 1956.)

Piaget, J. (1950), *Introduction à l'épistémologie génétique*, Vols 1–3, Paris.

Piaget, J. and Inhelder, B, (1959), *La Génèse des structures logiques élémentaires*, Neuchâtel. (*The Early Growth of Logic in the Child*, London, 1964.)

Piaget, J. and Inhelder, B. (1966), *La Psychologie de l'enfant*, Paris. (*The Psychology of the Child*, London, 1969.)

Piaget, J. (1967), *Biologie et connaissance*, Paris. (*Biology and Knowledge*, London, 1971.)

Piaget, J. (1974), *La Prise de conscience*, Paris. (*The Grasp of Consciousness*, London, 1976.)

Piaget, J. (1975), *L'Equilibration des structures cognitives*, Paris. (*The Development of Thought: Equilibration of Cognitive Structures*, Oxford, 1977.)

(B) General

Boden, M. (1979), *Piaget*, London.

Flavell, J. H. (1963), *The Developmental Psychology of Jean Piaget*, Princeton.

Gruber, H. E. and Vonèche, J. J. (eds) (1977), *The Essential Piaget: An Interpretive Reference and Guide*, London.

Rotman, B. (1977), *Jean Piaget: Psychologist of the Real*, Hassocks.

See also: *developmental psychology; moral development*.

Pigou, Arthur Cecil (1877–1959)

Arthur Cecil Pigou was appointed to Marshall's chair of political economy at Cambridge in 1908. While best known for his contributions to welfare economics and for his opposition to Keynes's *General Theory*, he made creative contributions to a wide range of economic questions over five decades. His most famous work is *The Economics of Welfare* (1920) in which he examined the relationship between national income and economic welfare. Economic policy was to be judged on the basis of a double criterion, reformulated from Sidgwick, using income and its distribution. His distinction between social and private costs due, for instance, to pollution formed the basis for 'Pigouvian' taxes and subsidies and for cost-benefit analysis. From his very earliest publications up to his alleged recantation of 1950, Pigou took a major interest in the analysis of unemployment. *Industrial Fluctuations* (1927) was an attempt to disentangle the various causes of fluctuations and the *Theory of Unemployment* (1933) was (as Keynes acknowledged) almost the only coherent statement of neoclassical employment theory. It is highly characteristic of Pigou that in his sixties he produced a carefully worked out analysis in *Employment and Equilibrium* (1941) in which Keynes's multiplier was a special case. The two points most commonly associated with his criticisms are connected on the one hand with the so-called 'Pigou effect', whereby price level changes affect real balances which in turn affect consumption, and on the other hand with wage rigidity in the Keynesian system. Pigou was not a great economist, but his corpus of work represents a major contribution to the working out of post-Marshallian economics, and much of it is still of current interest.

D. A. Collard
University of Bath

Further Reading

Collard, D. A. (1981), 'A. C. Pigou 1877–1959', in D. P. O'Brien and J. R. Presley (eds), *Pioneers of Modern Economics in Britain*, London.

Pigou, A. C. (1932), *The Economics of Welfare*, 4th edn, London.

Pirenne, Henri (1862–1935)

The Belgian scholar, Henri Pirenne, one of the greatest historians of his day, took his doctorate at the University of Liége in 1883, and then studied in Paris, Leipzig, and Bonn. In 1889 he was appointed to a chair at the State University of Ghent. An enormously productive author, Pirenne's bibliography lists more than 300 items. He excelled in synthesis, but never neglected meticulously detailed analysis, the editing of sources, and bibliographic research.

Pirenne first won international attention with his book *Les villes du Moyen Age* (1927) (*Medieval Cities: Their Origins and the Revival of Trade*, 1956), in which he argued that the cities of the eleventh century were settlements of a new kind that owed their origin to the

commercial activities of the *homines novi*, wandering merchants and tradesmen.

In 1917, as a prisoner of war in Germany, Pirenne started his *Histoire de l'Europe* (*A History of Europe: From the Invasions to the 16th Century*, New York (1956 [1936])), a general history of Europe from the end of the Roman world in the fourth century to the Renaissance and Reformation in the middle of the sixteenth century. Many ideas first broached here were later developed in his *Mahomet et Charlemagne* (published posthumously in 1937) (*Mohammed and Charlemagne*, 1958). Pirenne argued that the barbarian invaders did not profoundly alter the unity of the ancient world around the Mediterranean. He tried to prove that the social, cultural and economic structures of A.D. 600 were – roughly speaking – the same as those 200 years earlier. He placed the disintegration of Roman civilization and the transition to the Middle Ages in the seventh century, when the rapid expansion of militant Islam broke the traditional linkages between North and South, and East and West. Later research has shown that he overestimated the impact of Islam in this area.

In his own country, Pirenne's name will be linked forever with his famous *Histoire de Belgique* (7 volumes, 1900–1932), in which he offered a logical explanation for the historical development of the Belgian state. By providing his country with a scientific *raison d'être* he won public honour but incurred severe criticism from historians such as Pieter Geyl, who stressed the differences between Flemish and Walloon culture, and the common destiny of the Flemish and Dutch people.

Pirenne's elegant prose, his powerful use of hypotheses, the multidisciplinary and comparative nature of his work and his *goût de synthèse* recall the work of the *Annales* historians, and in fact he was closely associated with Bloch and Febvre between 1920 and 1935.

Erik Aerts
Archives Générales du Royaume, Brussels

Further Reading

(A) *Other works by Pirenne available in English translation*
Belgian Democracy: Its Early History, London, 1915.
Economic and Social History of Medieval Europe, London, 1936.

(B) *General*
Ganshof, F. L. and Sabbe, E. *et al.* (1938), 'Bibliographie des travaux historiques d'Henri Pirenne', in *Henri Pirenne, Hommages et souvenirs*, vol. 1, Brussels.

Havighurst, E. F. (ed.) (1976), *The Pirenne Thesis: Analysis, Criticism and Revision*, Toronto.

Lyon, B. (1974), *Henri Pirenne: A Biographical and Intellectual Study*, Ghent.

See also: *Annales school*; *Bloch*.

Planning, Economic

Economic planning is the use of a systematic alternative method of allocating economic resources either to replace or supplement the market mechanism. Its main justification is when the market mechanism fails to supply the right signals to decision-makers; this may be because economies of scale render the atomistic market mechanism ineffective, or because the market is incapable of taking into account the long-run needs of the economy. The state may possess knowledge which the market does not, whether about general economic uncertainties, the preferences of the community as a whole, or the longer run future. Alternatively, the state may simply reject the validity of the individual preferences which underlie the market system. Critics of planning have focused on the insuperable quantities of information that must be processed if the entire economy is to be organized by one body, and the undemocratic implications of the state's overruling individuals' choices.

In common usage 'planning' can mean either 'control' or 'forecasting', and 'economic planning' can be anything from consultation to coercion. It is possible in principle to distinguish three types of economic planning: (1) 'Directive planning' involves administrative regulation from a central body entirely replacing autonomous profit-seeking behaviour in the market. (2) 'Incentive planning' – the state attempts to achieve a desired outcome by using monetary rewards without coercion. (3) 'Indicative planning' – the state confines itself to forecasting or consultation, hoping that persuasion and the provision of superior economic information will lead to better economic performance.

In reality no single system falls into one only of the above categories. The Soviet system is in principle 'directive' with respect to enterprises, but the market mechanism is in fact allowed considerable sway in the USSR. Consumer goods are not administratively distributed and enterprise managers actually have considerable freedom of manoeuvre which the state tries to manipulate by incentives schemes. In practice the state gives instructions to firms in annual operating plans rather than the Five Year Plan which is very general. The Soviet state cannot in practice direct the whole of the production side of the economy because of the vast amount of information that it would need to handle even if there were no uncertainty.

Many proposals have been made and continue to be made for reforming planning in the USSR and Eastern Europe (most of which copied the Soviet model after 1945) in order to replace the directive element by incentive-based systems. But despite continuing discussions the only major result has been Hungary's 'market socialism'. A major problem with such reforms is that if the price incentives are set wrongly the decentralization may lead to undesirable actions by enterprises. Other schemes involving the use of computers and mathematical techniques have foundered on the computational complexity and the difficulty of coping with uncertainty.

After World War II the idea of incentive or indicative planning was favoured by many in the West as a way of obtaining the benefits of the co-ordinating powers of both the market and the plan. But actual attempts at planning often lacked the coherence of policy instruments both among one another and between them and desired objectives which would have to exist for real planning. State intervention in many countries and periods has been entirely *ad hoc*. Indicative planning was attempted in France. In principle the planners simply calculated what amounted to an optimal balanced growth path for the economy, the mere revelation of which was supposedly sufficient to induce people to follow it. French planning appears to have had some real success before 1965, but it has atrophied since then. In practice it always involved far less coherence and considerably more compulsion than the pure model of indicative planning. A misunderstanding of French experience led to total failure of the UK National Plan (1965–70); too much weight was placed on the idea that a plan could be virtually self-fulfilling merely by being highly optimistic. Planning as forecasting continues in a number of countries, notably the Netherlands and Scandinavia, and was hotly debated in the US during the mid–1970s. Planning in Western industrial economies (outside wartime) typically does not try to forecast or control every micro-economic variable but rather to regulate the major aggregates such as inflation, overall investment, etc. Incomes policies are a form of macro-economic planning where the free play of market forces in the labour market is held to be socially undesirable.

Economic planning may be carried out at a lower level than the national economy. There is regional and sectoral planning, which may or may not be made consistent with national planning. Large corporations also engage in planning, and there have been suggestions that the planning activities of large corporations can be building blocks for the creation of national plans. Critics of this view point out that usually corporate 'plans' are speculative scenarios rather than fully worked out operational programmes.

Less developed countries have often engaged in development planning. This has rarely attempted to follow the directive model, because agriculture does not lend itself well to central planning and because the political and bureaucratic preconditions are such as to make it very hard to manage. India in the 1950s announced an intention to combine Western parliamentary democracy with Soviet-type planning. In the end planning became little more than a system of forecasting designed to clarify national economic priorities alongside a widely criticized system of bureaucratic regulations. Some countries have been more successful (e.g. South Korea or Tunisia) though attempting less than India did initially.

Probably the most fruitful use that can be made of economic planning lies in attempts to simulate the likely consequences of alternative future scenarios for the economy, and discussing and negotiating on the likely responses of major economic actors. Rigid plans are much more easily overturned by events than ones which constitute strategic reflection and consultation.

Peter Holmes
University of Sussex

Further Reading

Bornstein, M. (ed.) (1979), *Comparative Economic Systems*, 4th edn, Homewood, Ill.
Cave, M. E. and Hare, P. G. (1981), *Alternative Approaches to Economic Planning*, London.
See also: *mixed economy; prediction and forecasting.*

Plato (428/7–348/7 B.C.)

Plato was born into a wealthy, well-connected family of the old Athenian aristocracy (Davies, 1971). He and his elder brothers Adeimantos and Glaukon (both of whom figure in the *Republic*) belonged to the circle of young men attached to Socrates, as did his cousins Kritias and Charmides, who played a leading part in the oligarchic junta of the Thirty which seized power at the end of the Peloponnesian War in 404/3. In the seventh Letter (a sort of *apologia pro vita sua* by Plato himself or a disciple) Plato claims to have been quickly shocked by the tyrannous behaviour of the Thirty, and equally disgusted with the restored democracy when it condemned Socrates to death in 399; but his chances of playing any prominent part in Athenian politics had in any case been fatally compromised by his close connections with the junta. He settled down to the 'theoretical life' of a philosopher and teacher which he praises (for example, *Theaetetus* 172–6) as the highest form of human activity. In 367, however, after thirty years of highly productive theoretical activity, he attempted to put some of the political ideas of the *Republic* into practice by training the young ruler of Syracuse, Dionysius II, for the role of philosopher-king. Not surprisingly, he failed; one of Plato's most obvious weaknesses as a political analyst was his neglect of external factors and relations with other powers, which in the fourth century B.C. constituted in fact the main problem for the Greek cities. While there are problems of detail in dating Plato's dialogues, one can perhaps say that in his work before the Sicilian episode he is still engaged in a vivacious debate with ideas current in the Athens of his youth, whereas in his later works (*Sophist, Statesman, Philebus, Timaeus, Critias, Laws*) he is addressing himself more specifically to

fellow-philosophers, present and future. The philosophical centre he founded in the Academy – a sort of Institute for Advanced Studies in rural surroundings – continued after his death.

The influences which shaped Plato's thought are thus the aristocratic milieu in which he grew up and the political events of his lifetime, the personality of Socrates, and the standards of systematic reasoning associated with the role of philosopher. His contributions to social thought as we would now define it lie mainly in the fields of political and moral philosophy, psychology and education; but these aspects of his thought cannot be detached from his epistemology and cosmology.

Part of the fascination of reading Plato comes from the dialogue form in which he presented his ideas. He was no doubt influenced in this choice by Socrates, who communicated his own ideas solely through argument and left no written works; more generally, the Athenians were used to hearing different points of view upheld by opposing speakers in political assemblies, in law courts and in drama. Socrates takes the leading part in Plato's earlier dialogues, and this enabled the author both to acknowledge his debt to his teacher and, perhaps, to avoid taking full responsibility for the ideas he was putting forward. Plato never figures in his own dialogues. The dialogue form also suited his gifts as a brilliantly natural and graceful writer, a skilful parodist and master of characterization and light-hearted conversation. The introductory scenes of his dialogues provide the historian with lively sketches of upper-class manners and mores in the late fifth century B.C.

The key element in Plato's thought as it concerned social life was a widening of the gap between body and spirit. This enabled him to preserve an essential core of religious belief from the criticisms which had been directed against traditional religion, to ground Socrates' argument that virtue is a kind of knowledge in a general theory of epistemology which offered solutions to logical problems raised by earlier philosophers, and to provide a foundation for belief in the immortality of the soul; at the same time it formalized a psychological split between lower and higher elements in the personality, and linked this to a justification of social hierarchy, and to a theory of education in which censorship played an essential part.

Plato's early dialogues show Socrates attacking a traditional, unreflective upper-class practice of virtue as a routine response of the gentleman to predictable situations. When asked to define courage (*Laches*), piety (*Euthyphro*), or moderation (*Charmides*), his interlocutors give specific examples of brave, pious or self-controlled behaviour, and Socrates then proves to them that such acts would not in all circumstances be considered virtuous. Echoes of the same attitude can be found in Xenophon and Euripides.

Some of Plato's contemporaries went on from this criticism of traditional conceptions of virtue to deny its existence altogether: in the *Republic*, Thrasymachus argues that values and virtues are defined by the ruling class to suit their own interests, and Glaukon argues that they represent the interests of the majority. Plato therefore needed a concept of virtue which was flexible and abstract enough to satisfy Socratic criticism but nevertheless safe against relativist attack. His response was the theory of Forms or Ideas, existing at a level of ultimate, abstract reality which was only imperfectly reflected in the material world but of which the human mind could gradually acquire better knowledge through philosophical training.

Coming closer to the world of Ideas thus becomes both the highest aim of human life and the standard by which all kinds of knowledge are judged; it follows that human societies should be directed by philosophers or by laws formulated by philosophers. The human personality is divided into three elements: intelligence, *amour-propre* (*Thumos*) and the physical appetites. Education aims to train the first to dominate the other two.

Thumos refers to a set of qualities regarded somewhat ambiguously in Plato's culture (Dover, 1974). It was the basis of man's pursuit of prestige and honour and thus – like the appetites – beneficial when exercised in moderation but dangerous when obsessive. Too eager a pursuit of honour led to tyranny or to a tendency to take offence for no reason. Thus there was a popular basis for the view that even ambition for what the ordinary man in the street considered the supreme good had to be controlled. This point was particularly important for Plato, because his belief that the good society was a society ruled by good and wise men meant that the essential problem of political organization was to prevent the ruling élite from becoming corrupted. This led him to formulate the idea of the 'mixed constitution', later to influence Polybius, Montesquieu and the Constitution of the United States.

Because a philosophical education involved training in subjects like astronomy and mathematics for which not all had equal interest or aptitude, and because the philosopher had to detach himself from activities and preoccupations likely to strengthen the influence of his *Thumos* and bodily appetites, the hierarchy of faculties in the psyche led to a hierarchy of groups in the ideal city. Philosophers would have supreme authority, semi-educated 'watch-dogs' would act as a military and police force on their behalf, and those who supplied the economic needs of the city would have the lowest status of all. Education was to be carefully adjusted to the reproduction of the system; the lower class were to be trained to obedience and persuaded by a political 'myth' that their status was due to natural causes; poets should only represent socially commendable

behaviour; knowledge of alternative forms of society was to be carefully suppressed, except in the case of selected members of the ruling élite.

Such views have in our century led to attacks on Plato as a proto-Fascist or -Stalinist (Crossman, 1937; Popper, 1945). In the *Laws* the more extreme proposals of the *Republic* (in particular, the abolition of private property and the family) were dropped; it is interesting to see Plato grappling here with detailed problems of law-drafting, and the text is a key piece of evidence on Greek legal thought. Return to law as a source of authority was a capitulation to the rigid type of definition of virtue which Socrates had attacked (see the *Statesman*); but the argument which had seemed valid when applied to individuals would not work for collectivities. There was something wrong with the analogy between parts of the city and parts of the human psyche.

S. C. Humphreys
University of Michigan

References
Crossman, R. H. (1937), *Plato Today*, London.
Davies, J. K. (1971), *Athenian Propertied Families*, Oxford.
Dover, K. J. (1974), *Greek Popular Morality in the Time of Plato and Aristotle*, Oxford.
Popper, K. (1945), *The Open Society and its Enemies*, London.

Further Reading
Gouldner, A. W. (1966), *Enter Plato: Classical Greece and the Origins of Social Theory*, New York.
Guthrie, W. K. C. (1975–8), *A History of Greek Philosophy*, vols IV–V, Cambridge.
Ryle, G. (1966), *Plato's Progress*, Cambridge.
Shorey, P. (1933), *What Plato Said*, Chicago.
Taylor, A. E. (1926), *Plato. The Man and his Work*, London.
Wood, E. M. and Wood, N. (1978), *Class Ideology and Ancient Political Theory: Socrates, Plato and Aristotle in Social Context*, Oxford.
See also: *Aristotle*.

Play

Easily recognized in children or young domestic animals, play has been impossible to define clearly. It is most frequent in immature creatures and consists of motor patterns belonging to feeding, agonistic, sexual, fleeing or comfort behaviours, but without leading to their usual biological ends. Sequences in play may be highly unlikely, such as fleeing, reclining, and fleeing following one another.

Solitary, parallel, and social play can be distinguished. In parallel play an animal or child observes, copies or is influenced by another playing individual without direct interaction, which is characteristic of social play. Object play can be solitary or social.

Some definitions of play are descriptive: 'Play behavior consists of elements drawn from other types of behavior and rearranged in new patterns of timing and sequence' (Marler and Hamilton, 1966). Others infer processes of behaviour development: 'In mammals, play is comprised largely of rehearsals performed in a nonfunctional context of the serious activities of searching, fighting, courtship, hunting, and copulation' (Wilson, 1971). Assumed proximate causation may be part of a definition: '[Play is] any action which is performed as an outlet for surplus energy which is not required by the animal for its immediate vital activities . . .' (Bolwig, 1963). Similarly, play has been seen as 'behavioural fat' engineered into the behaviour repertoire of a growing animal. It can be dropped without harm to other activities in times of energetic stress (Muller-Schwarze, 1978).

Many short- and long-term *functions* of play have been postulated. These range from general exercise of the cardiovascular and neuromuscular-skeletal systems to learning of specific, especially social, skills such as effective communication or handling of agonistic interactions. Motor development in preambulatory infants has been accelerated by rotational vestibular stimulation as would occur in vigorous play (Clark *et al.*, 1977).

The *evolution* of play clearly parellels that of brain size and function. Primates play more and in more diverse ways than other mammals, and those in turn more than birds. Among birds, play is most prevalent in the larger-brained corvids, whose behaviour is more generalized. Antecedents of play may be found in lower vertebrates but defy recognition and definition.

Sex differences in play have been clearly demonstrated (reviewed by Fagen, 1981). Fagen proposes the study of play in the context of life-history strategies, a confluence of evolutionary and development considerations. Its importance can be measured by the price an animal pays in terms of time, energy and risk to be able to play at certain ages. This price can be viewed as investment in delayed benefits – ultimately improved inclusive fitness.

The occurrence and quality of play can be evaluated in terms of mental and physical health. Social play has been used for rehabilitation of socially isolated rhesus monkeys (Cummins and Suomi, 1976). Hospitalized children benefit from object play, supervised by a play specialist (Jolly, 1968).

Dietland Muller-Schwarze
State University of New York, Syracuse

References

Bolwig, N. (1963), 'Bringing up a young monkey (*Erythrocebus patas*)', *Behaviour*, 21.

Clark, D. L., Kreutzberg, J. R. and Chee, F. K. W. (1977), 'Vestibular stimulation influence on motor development in infants', *Science*, 196.

Cummins, M. S. and Suomi, S. J. (1976), 'Longterm effects of social rehabilitation in rhesus monkeys', *Primates*, 17.

Fagen, R. (1981), *Animal Play Behavior*, New York.

Jolly, H. (1968), 'Play and the sick child: a comparative study of its role in a teaching hospital in London and one in Ghana', *Lancet*, 2.

Marler, P. and Hamilton, W. J. III (1966), *Mechanisms of Animal Behavior*, New York.

Muller-Schwarze, D. (ed.) (1978), *Evolution of Play Behavior*, Stroudsburg, Pennsylvania.

Wilson, E. O. (1971), *The Insect Societies*, Cambridge, Mass.

See also: *ethology*; *sport, sociology of*.

Pluralism, Political

Political pluralism is a normative perspective in modern politics that emphasizes the importance for democracy and liberty of maintaining a plurality of relatively autonomous political and economic organizations. The political pluralist believes that in large-scale societies competing economic interests and differences of political opinion are unavoidable. In opposition to Marxists, the political pluralist does not believe that these significant political cleavages are primarily or necessarily related to class. Nor does he believe that these sources of political conflict can be eliminated by bringing the means of production under public ownership. For the governmental system of large-scale societies to be democratic, the political pluralist insists that there must be institutions through which divergent interests can articulate their views and compete for power. A system of competitive political parties is a hallmark of pluralist democracies. Such democratic polities are often referred to as liberal democracies.

Some political pluralists recognize that inequality in the distribution of political resources may mean that some social interests or groups in a liberal democracy have much more power and influence than others. Thus a political pluralist may advocate redistributive policies to reduce political inequalities (Dahl, 1982). However much inequalities are reduced, the democratic pluralist is still faced with the dilemma of how much autonomy should be extended to groups whose views differ from those of the majority. Federalism is one solution to this dilemma where significant societal differences coincide with territorial divisions. Another approach is consociational democracy in which national policy is arrived at through a consensus of élites drawn from the country's major cultural or ideological segments (Lijphart, 1977).

Peter H. Russell
University of Toronto

References
Dahl, R. A. (1982), *Dilemmas of Pluralist Democracy*, New Haven.
Lijphart, A. (1977), *Democracy in Plural Societies*, New Haven.

Further Reading
Connolly, W. E. (ed.) (1969), *The Bias of Pluralism*, New York.
Lipset, S. M. (1960), *Political Man: The Social Bases of Politics*, Garden City, New York.

Plural Society

In the last quarter century, the term plural society has been used to describe societies, usually at the level of independent states or colonial territories, characterized by sharp internal cleavages between ethnic, racial, religious, or linguistic groups. By the criterion of 90 per cent or more of the population speaking the same language, at best 10 per cent of the 150–odd states represented at the United Nations are genuine nation-states. The remainder exhibit various degrees of cultural and social pluralism, ranging from the extreme fragmentation of countries like Nigeria, Zaire, India, and the Soviet Union, with scores of ethnic groups, often unrelated to each other, to less heterogeneous states like Belgium, Switzerland, or Canada, made up of two or three related language groups.

That broad spectrum of societies has, of course, been studied from a wide variety of perspectives, each with its own vocabulary. Marxists have generally preferred the term 'multi-national states', and the thrust of their analysis has been to explain the cleavages and conflicts of these societies by reference to a combination of internal class cleavages and unequal exchanges between the 'core' and 'periphery' of the 'Capitalist world-system' (Frank, 1967; Lenin, 1969; Wallerstein, 1974). They have treated ethnic, linguistic, racial or religious differences as either residues of past epochs with vanishing significance, or as labels of false consciousness masking class differences.

A number of liberal scholars, on the other hand, when dealing with 'bourgeois democracies' of Western Europe and North America have dealt with pluralism as a condition of the political give-and-take of competition and conflict between contending interest groups (Kornhauser, 1960; Lipset, 1963). By pluralism, however, they have meant not so much ethnic or racial cleavages. Indeed, they often ignored these. Rather, they referred principally to the diversity of political views and of specialized interest groups competing for resources in the political arena of parliamentary democracies.

Yet another tradition has dealt with the accommodation of ethnic conflicts in what it called 'consociational' or 'proportional' democracies (Lijphart, 1977). Scholars in this tradition worked mostly in the advanced industrial countries of Europe (such as Belgium, the Netherlands, Switzerland, and Austria), characterized by only a moderate degree of pluralism and a high degree of equality between the constituent linguistic or religious collectivities.

Most closely associated with the label plural society is a group of social scientists who have studied principally the highly fragmented societies of Asia, Africa, the Caribbean, and Latin America, societies generally characterized by a history of violent conquest, followed by colonialism, slavery, indenture, and other forms of highly institutionalized segmentation and inequality between ethnic or racial groups (Furnivall, 1948; Kuper and Smith, 1969; Schermerhorn, 1970; van den Berghe, 1974). Not unexpectedly, these scholars stress conflict and the coercive role of the state in maintaining a system of social inequality and economic exploitation. Although their analysis shares a number of features with that of the Marxists, they tend to emphasize cultural and racial lines of cleavage more than class lines, and to ascribe causal priority to political relations over economic relations. That is, they tend to regard unequal relations to the means of production as derivative of unequal power relations, rather than vice versa. They also generally insist on treating class and ethnicity as two distinct bases of social organization, which in practice overlap, but which can also vary independently.

Pierre van den Berghe
University of Washington

References
Frank, A. G. (1967), *Capitalism and Underdevelopment in Latin America*, New York.
Furnivall, J. S. (1948), *Colonial Policy and Practice*, London.
Kornhauser, W. (1960), *The Politics of Mass Society*, London.
Kuper, L. and Smith, M. G. (eds) (1969), *Pluralism in Africa*, Berkeley and Los Angeles.
Lenin, V. I. (1969 [1916]), *Imperialism, the Highest Stage of Capitalism*, Peking.
Lijphart, A. (1977), *Democracy in Plural Societies*, New Haven.
Lipset, S. M. (1963), *The First New Nation*, New York.
Schermerhorn, R. A. (1970), *Comparative Ethnic Relations*, New York.
van den Berghe, P. L. (1974), 'Pluralism', in J. J. Honigmann (ed.), *Handbook of Social and Cultural Anthropology*, Chicago.

Wallerstein, I. (1974), *The Modern World-System*, New York.
See also: *ethnic groups; ethnic relations; federalism; imperialism; world-system theory.*

Polanyi, Karl (1886–1964)

Polanyi, a charismatic teacher and original thinker whose ideas cut across both academic and political boundaries, grew up in the intellectual milieu of revisionist socialism in Hungary which also produced Georg Lukács and Karl Mannheim. To escape authoritarian regimes he moved in 1919 from Budapest to Vienna, where he worked as an economic journalist through the years of the depression, and again in 1933 from Vienna to England. His lectures in England for the Workers' Educational Association (he had earlier pioneered workers' education in Hungary with the Galilei Circle) grew into *The Great Transformation* (1944), an analysis of the rise and fall of economic Liberalism and the world economy from Ricardo's England to Hitler's Germany.

In 1947 Polanyi moved to Columbia University; the results of his seminars on the comparative study of economic institutions were outlined in *Trade and Market in the Early Empires* (1957). Through this volume and his influence on collaborators such as Paul Bohannan, George Dalton, Marshall Sahlins, A. L. Oppenheim and M. I. Finley, Polanyi's views have exerted a decisive influence both on economic anthropology and on the economic anthropology and the economic history of the ancient world.

Polanyi's belief that in precapitalist societies the economy (defined as institutionalized provision for man's material needs) is 'embedded' in social relationships governed by values other than concern for profit has clear affinities with the functionalism of Malinowski and Talcott Parsons. His views generated a heated but ephemeral debate between 'Substantivists' and 'Formalists' in economic anthropology in the 1960s; they also, however, aided Marxist anthropologists in their struggle to free themselves from crude economism (Godelier, 1975). His work is rich in detailed insights into the working of money, trade and exchange centres in precapitalist economies; his Weberian typology of exchange systems (reciprocity, householding, redistribution, market exchange) has particularly stimulated research and criticism among historians of ancient Mesopotamia (Gledhill and Larsen, 1982).

For Polanyi, the central problem of modern society was to combine socialist economic planning with individual freedom (Dumont, 1983); in retirement, he worked to found the journal *Co-Existence* as a forum for truly international and intercultural discussion of such questions.

S.C. Humphreys
University of Michigan

References
Dumont, L. (1983), 'Preface' to K. Polanyi, *La Grande Transformation*, Paris.
Gledhill, J. and Larsen, M. T. (1982), 'The Polanyi paradigm and a dynamic analysis of archaic states' in C. Renfrew *et al.* (eds), *Theory and Explanation in Archaeology*, London.
Godelier, M. (1975), 'Introduction' to K. Polanyi, *Les Systèmes économiques dans l'histoire et dans la théorie*, Paris.

Further Reading
Humphreys, S. C. (1969), 'History, economics and anthropology: the work of Karl Polanyi', *History and Theory*, 8.
Polanyi, K. (1977), *The Livelihood of Man*, New York.
See also: *economic anthropology; trade and markets, anthropology of.*

Police

To police is to control some people in the interests of more powerful people. In a sense police are 'the state made flesh'. They are unique in being armed, uniformed, legal representatives of government and the judiciary, visibly present in society and empowered to interfere directly in citizens' daily lives. The police organization is closely associated with crime; yet much police work is not related to crime, while many other agencies also investigate and sanction crimes (such as customs, tax, postal, military, and other regulatory authorities).

In small, homogeneous societies the police function of controlling deviance tends to be adopted by the entire community, whereas in more differentiated societies specific officials are appointed to maintain order. In England there exists a line of functionaries, first formalized in the offices of 'constable' and 'sheriff' under the Normans, who performed a policing role but then largely in a manner that was voluntary, local, and restricted in powers. The formation of nation states in Europe witnessed the development of recognizable police organizations employed to control and manipulate politics and the opponents of the state. Napoleon imposed a dual model in Western-European countries comprising a centralized semi-military force, primarily for public order, and local forces for the general police function. In contrast, the formation of the 'new police', with the founding of the Metropolitan Police in London in 1829, ushered in an alternative style: based on local units and ostensibly local control (with policemen not carrying firearms and answerable to the courts, *not* the state), it shaped a model for Britain, its colonies, and the United States. But there still exists enormous variety across cultures in terms of police structure, powers and performance.

Police in Western societies generally concern themselves with maintaining public order, preventing crime, regulating traffic, performing a range of services, collecting political intelligence, and apprehending (and sometimes also prosecuting) criminals. Theories on the police differ widely: a Marxist would see them as pawns of ruling-class hegemony aimed at oppressing the working class, whereas a functionalist might emphasize the integrative role they play in promoting social solidarity. This diversity can partly be explained by the ideological content of policing, which is intimately related to the legal control of the state and to moral values (as in enforcement related to vice, gambling, and alcohol), and about which opinions vary radically, and partly • by the dubious reputation of specific agencies (for example, the Gestapo, KGB, CIA, South African Police), in terms of conducting political repression. These negative associations are reinforced by the fact that police form something of a problem profession and have frequently been accused of brutality, corruption, racial prejudice and abuse of citizens's rights. A perennial debate surrounding police relates to restrictions on their power and their ability to undermine effective control of their conduct (Punch, 1983): in short, who controls the controllers?

Research on the police commenced some thirty years ago, and has not led to a coherent subfield within the social sciences (Manning, 1977). Most projects are confined to low-level, urban policing in a few Western countries, but the results fairly consistently reveal that policemen rarely use violence; rarely deal with crime (that is, patrol officers); focus predominantly on 'petty', visible, street-crime (and infrequently on élite or 'white-collar' crime); engage in a wide range of welfare functions; employ wide discretion in enforcement, and that enforcement has little impact on patterns of crime. Various sources also indicate that police work can support practices where laws are systematically bent or broken, where prisoners are abused and denied their rights, where perks and venality are institutionalized, and where judicial guidelines are undermined (Rubinstein, 1973). Two influences have promised improvements in some traditional defects of policing: external pressure has sponsored norms of accountability and responsibility, while fiscal and manpower constraints have imposed more efficient managerial styles. There remains a degree of friction between prescriptions for the police as either a decentralized, broad, social agency responsive to the immediate community, or as a sophisticated, professional, technologically equipped instrument for tackling serious crime (some departments manage to unite both in a pattern of antagonistic co-operation).

Imagery and debate on the police is polarized and contradictory: they are the thin-blue line protecting society from a wave of rapacious criminality, or else they are a bunch of prejudiced, head-cracking sadists. An understanding of the world of the police reveals that it itself is ambivalent, and we should remain alive to the differences *between* policemen and not exaggerate the extent to which agencies are monolithic and views within them unanimous. Police work is imbued with moral symbolism and laudable aims, but the dilemmas of the work can promote a culture that is bawdy, blasphemous, and hedonistic and a style that is posited on lies, falsification, deception, and manipulation of evidence, suspects and informants. The police are forced to engage in 'dirty work' and they can become 'schizophrenic', flitting between good and evil, the commendable and the reprehensible. Policemen have to cope with the discrepancy between legally defined work presented to outsiders and the messy confused reality of working the street.

At the macro level there is no doubt that the police form a crucial, powerful, and potentially sinister element of control within the state apparatus. At the micro level, however, work may be characterized by boredom, sloth, frustration, horseplay and two-finger typing. Discrepant expectations and the nature of the work (witnessing violence and suffering, and, for the detective, the potentially polluting and seductive web of underworld connections) can lead to feelings of bitterness and betrayal, with the danger of occupational paranoia where policemen feel isolated and aggrieved. At both levels, macro and micro, the police are potentially dangerous and clearly need to be subject to constant vigilance, while their reputation and performance are significant indicators of the moral health of a society (Goldstein, 1977). Perhaps everyone concerned with the police should strive to undermine the fatalistic notion that society gets the police it deserves.

Maurice Punch
Nijenrode, The Netherlands School of Business

References
Goldstein, H. (1977), *Policing a Free Society*, Cambridge, Mass.
Manning, P. K. (1977), *Police Work*, Cambridge, Mass.
Punch, M. (ed.) (1983), *Control in the Police Organization*, Cambridge, Mass.
Rubinstein, J. (1973), *City Police*, New York.
See also: *crime and delinquency; criminology; penology.*

Policy Making

Policy itself has three senses. In one sense it refers to the purposes for which men associate in the polis. A second sense has to do with the review of information and the determination of appropriate action. The third sense concerns the securing and commitment of resources.

Over the last century a distinction has been constructed between policy (in all these senses) and policy making, a dualism which has sundered the inclusive Baconian view of policy as reason of state. In consequence policy making itself has come to be conceived of as one peculiar process, while policy is something else: a symbolic entity 'out there' merely uttered, chosen or promised. 'We have galaxies of policies' (David Steel, UK General Election 1983).

Two factors determine this dichotomy. One has been the association of the modern state with nationalism, mobilization and elections and therefore with a mandate or platform. The second factor is that the modern state is 'not an enormous coercive power, but a vast and conscious organization' (Durkheim). Concomitant institutional developments provided bases for the classic dualistic formulations of Woodrow Wilson, opposing politics and administration, and of J. S. Mill, who contrasted politics and policy arguments from administrative practices, and of Bagehot, who envisaged a political minister who would be above the dirty business of policy making. The dichotomy was completely established between the philosophical radical decade and the mid-Victorian era.

This rationalistic estrangement of policy and policy making has been inescapable, but ultimately pernicious. It is necessarily premised on a nonpolitical and technical model of policy making as an optimalizing search for the best means to realize a given platform. This has fostered in turn a peculiarly influential and dangerous dichotomy, between policy and implementation.

These dichotomies would have been impossible without the development of such social sciences as scientific management and 'classical' public administration, and without the emergence of vocational rather than political social sciences. At the same time the dichotomous model has provided the conditions for the development of the social sciences, and, in government machines themselves, for a distinction between policy and management, and so for a technologizing of policy making and of social science involvement, for example, in economic and welfare and other policy sectors.

However recent its involvement in policy making may be, these disciplines have managed to suppress any historical consciousness of what has happened, and argue for a favoured role, sector by sector, as though it were unproblematic, scientific, and unique. In truth, the role of specific social sciences in policy making is a consequence of recent political accidents. They share, however, a common subservience to the privileging of the politics of policy.

The dualistic concept of policy making as policy and implementation has, then, been the breeding ground for a dangerous dichotomizing with consequences for the data, problems and agendas of modern policy, and for the strategies and the highly sectoral constructions of modern policy, each with its dutifully innocent social science enshrined in techniques like social cost-benefit analysis, casework and extensions, and within hived-off devices for sectoral improvements like planning cells, or separate foundations such as the many imitators of the RAND corporation.

This splitting up of policy making into policy and implementation also led inevitably to the search for explanations of the unhappy differences between the experience of implementation and the policies which had been promised. Such explications are at once banal and erroneous, since policy is actually about securing and maintaining office, as it always has been. It is also dangerous, since the dichotomy between policy and implementation makes it difficult to determine responsibilty. Decision makers blame implementers, the outside advisers blame insiders, and the policy agencies even blame the poor intended target group members themselves.

The dominant record of the policy-making social sciences thus far has been to participate in the construction and enjoyment of these conveniently escapist dualisms. There have been some institutional descriptions and some survey work on public opinions of familiar policy themes. There has also been an effort to depoliticize the social science of public policy outright by treating policy making as a simulacrum of individual market choice.

Alternative approaches, which are concerned with the whole of policy-making practice, face two difficulties. One is that access to the inner institutional materials often requires acceptance of the fashions and legitimation of the politics of policy. The second difficulty is that an alternative social science of policy making must, at one and the same time, manage to see policy fashions, headlines or technologies for what they are and avoid the apparently harmless policy v. implementation dichotomy.

The alternative policy-making social science would also need to construct a grid for handling all the zones of policy practice. It could then expose the establishment and presentation of policy in terms of objective and unavoidable problems, like deficits and gaps, and in therapeutic and unobjectionable strategies, with heavily disguised favours or exclusions, costs and controls in the actual deliveries.

Such a social science would be a confrontational account of what is involved in policy making, not a co-opted, false or mythologizing discourse. However inconvenient for some social science relationships, it would challenge the unchallengeable, reveal what is hidden, and insist on considering precisely those effects, data, victims and possibilities which are ignored in orthodox social science discourse about policy making.

Bernard Schaffer
Institute of Development Studies
University of Sussex

Further Reading

Appleby, P. (1949), *Policy and Administration*, Alabama.
Ballard, J. (ed.) (1981), *Policy Making in a New State*, St Lucia, Queensland.
Lindblom, C. E. (1968), *The Policy-Making Process*, Englewood Cliffs, N.J.
Self, P. (1975), *The Econocrats and the Policy Process*, London.

See also: *administration*; *policy sciences*.

Policy Sciences

The policy sciences are concerned with understanding the decision processes of public and private institutions, and with assessing the significance of all knowledge for purposes of decision. The term policy sciences was introduced after World War II (Lerner and Lasswell, 1951) to refer to the emergence of this common frame of reference among specialists in many disciplines. Subsequent development of the policy sciences has been marked by the refinement of conceptual tools, their application to a variety of policy problems, and by the establishment of policy-sciences centres in universities, government agencies and the private sector. Policy scientists in the aggregate have only begun to develop a distinctive professional identity and an understanding of the roles they may play in the evolution of our civilization.

Policy scientists are traditionally graduates from academic schools or departments of public or business administration, political science, political economy, jurisprudence, and the like. In recent decades, the physical and natural sciences, as well as the cultural sciences, have also produced policy scientists. These disciplines have had little contact with traditional policy theory but a great deal to do with the policy problems of our time. In a typical career pattern, a scientist in a laboratory or research institute discovers latent interests and talents in an initial attempt to relate his specialized knowledge to the broader environment. The political and social environment may nurture and reinforce these initiatives to the extent that knowledge is expected to pay. The budding policy scientist soon learns to sustain this expectation through delivery of partial results, and to justify further science and scholarship in terms that the environment rewards: security, profits, political advantage, health and social welfare, prestige and many other objectives. This career pattern broadens the attention frame and the circle of contacts beyond one's disciplinary origins.

Policy scientists tend to converge on a common outlook, despite their diversity of origins. One element of the common outlook is contextuality. Scholarship that restricts considerations of realism and worth to those of a single discipline may be acceptable to manuscript editors who enforce disciplinary standards. However, it is less likely to be acceptable to a decision maker who must grapple with a broader range of considerations and is unimpressed by the traditional academic division of labour. In the search for knowledge pertinent to the decision process and problem at hand, partial approaches tend to become more contextual. A second element is a problem-orientation, which includes all the intellectual tasks logically entailed in the solution of any problem. For example, a choice among policy alternatives entails the postulation of goal values. The 'value free' connotation of 'science', as propagated in some disciplines, gradually becomes attenuated as policy scientists discover the value implications of their research and develop competence in normative analysis. (The connotation of 'science' as the 'pursuit of verifiable knowledge' is retained.) Conversely, philosophers and other specialists in normative analysis learn to describe trends, to clarify factors conditioning trends, and to project future possibilities in the process of relating normative principles to specific decisions. A third element is the synthesis of diverse methods. Each method of observation or analysis tends to divert attention from some potentially important aspects of the problem at hand. The use of multiple methods is an important means of compensating for such blind spots.

Evidence of convergence can be found in the development of concepts for contextual, problem-oriented, and multi-method research. Lasswell (1956; 1971) and his collaborators (Lasswell and Kaplan, 1950; Lasswell and McDougal, 1971) have refined the most comprehensive set of conceptual tools, but approximate equivalents are persistently rediscovered, often independently, by others. A contextual approach leads to an explicit conception of the decision process as a whole. Among other things, it identifies the multiple points at which decision outcomes might be affected, and thereby facilitates the rational allocation of analytical and political resources. Workable conceptions have been proposed by Anderson (1975), May and Wildavsky (1978), and Brewer and deLeon (1983). A contextual approach also leads to an explicit conception of the broader social process. Among other things, it directs attention to the otherwise unnoticed or discounted costs and benefits of decisions that impact on society. The social indicator movement (Bauer, 1966) and general systems theory (Isard, 1969) have spawned a number of social process models. The intellectual tasks entailed in problem-oriented research have been conceptualized in nearly equivalent ways by Simon (1968), Allison (1971), and many others. Finally, conceptions of 'economic man' and invariant 'behavioural laws' have turned out to be limited for purposes of the policy sciences. The explanation or interpretation of human acts requires attention to the simplified cognitive 'maps' used by the actors in question to respond to their environments. Essentially equivalent concepts for this purpose are Lasswell's 'maximization postulate' and Simon's (1957) elaboration of the 'principle of bounded rationality'.

Such conceptual tools ideally formulate and conveniently label the principal distinctions that have turned out to be useful across broad ranges of experience. They do not provide general answers to particular problems, as theory is sometimes purported to do. Rather, they provide principles of procedure (or heuristics) to guide a systematic search for data and insights pertinent to a specific decision problem; and they provide principles of content that outline elements of a satisfactory solution and help bring to bear the knowledge cumulated from different times, places, and cultural contexts. As short lists of interrelated concepts, they anticipate or implement findings of cognitive psychology showing how information can be processed efficiently (Simon, 1969; 1979). Command of these conceptual tools enables a policy scientist to maximize the potential for rational decision within the constraints of time, resources and the nature of the situation.

Applications of the policy sciences approach are numerous and diverse. Good examples illustrating the range of applications have addressed problems of administration and governance in a psychiatric hospital; public services for handicapped children; social development at the community level; defence analysis; income redistribution at the national level; public order of the world community, and global political transformations. Among authors of these studies alone, the disciplinary origins include anthropology, economics, law, medicine, political science, public administration and psychiatry.

The professional identity of the policy scientist tends to be in flux. Ideally, the policy scientist perceives himself as an integrator of knowledge and action. Complications arise, however, when other scientists perceive him as an ex-scientist and current politician. Moreover, decision makers may not know what to make of a scientist who nevertheless appears to know how to operate in the policy arena. Further complications arise from the question of whose interests are served. The rich and powerful are in a position to acquire his services, but knowledge may also be used to improve the position of the weak, the poor, and others who are disadvantaged. The situation is complex, and the policy scientist may share the ambivalences he perceives in his relationships with others.

From a broader perspective, there is little doubt that the scientific revolution has failed to modify the political structure of a militant and divided world, or to abolish zones of poverty amidst prosperity. In principle, the fruits of knowledge are available to all. In practice, knowledge is often selectively introduced and used for the benefit of the few. One of the continuing tasks of the policy sciences is to appraise its own impact on policy and society. The search for authoritative criteria can be guided by the Universal Declaration of Human Rights.

Ronald D. Brunner
University of Colorado, Boulder

References
Allison, G. (1971), *Essence of Decision: Explaining the Cuban Missile Crisis*, Boston.
Anderson, J. E. (1975), *Public Policy-Making*, New York.
Bauer, R. A. (ed.) (1966), *Social Indicators*, Cambridge, Mass.
Brewer, G. D. and deLeon, P. (1983), *The Foundations of Policy Analysis*, Homewood, Ill.
Isard, W. (1969), *General Theory: Social, Political, and Regional with Particular Reference to Decision-Making Analysis*, Cambridge, Mass.
Lasswell, H. D. (1956), *The Decision Process: Seven Categories of Functional Analysis*, College Park, Maryland.
Lasswell, H. D. (1971), *A Pre-View of Policy Sciences*, New York.
Lasswell, H. D. and Kaplan, A. (1950), *Power and Society*, New Haven.
Lasswell, H. D. and McDougal, M. S. (1971), 'Criteria for a theory about law', *Southern California Law Review*, 44.
Lerner, D. and Lasswell, H. D. (eds) (1951), *The Policy Sciences*, Stanford.
May, J. V. and Wildavsky, A. B. (eds) (1978), *The Policy Cycle*, Beverly Hills.
Simon, H. A. (1957), 'Rationality and administrative decision making', in H. A. Simon (ed.), *Models of Man*, New York.
Simon, H.A. (1968), 'Research for choice', in W.R. Ewald (ed.), *Environment and Policy: The Next Fifty Years*, Bloomington.
Simon, H. A. (1969), *The Sciences of the Artificial*, Cambridge, Mass.
Simon, H. A. (1979), *Models of Thought*, New Haven.
See also: *decision making*; *policy making*.

Political Anthropology

Politics begin with the idea that people live lives which are not 'solitary, poor, nasty, brutish and short'. They do so by finding ways to regulate competition for power but not always by appointing a Leviathan. They may centralize power in a person or a class, or, valuing equality, they may instead disperse it. They may tie the power struggle into other institutions – religious or familial or economic; alternatively, they may insulate those institutions from the disruptive effects of political competition. They may have law courts and bureaucracies; or they may not. In short, different cultures find different solutions to the problem of living together without excessive conflict over power. Political anthropology is the comparative study of those solutions.

The solution familiar to us is a government with exclusive control over force in its own territory – in other words a state. This is not, however, the only solution. Order may be achieved without a central political authority, by allocating rights and duties (including those concerning power) according to placement in a kinship system. The earliest phase of political anthropology consisted of evolutionary speculation about the manner in which such kinship-based politics gave way to states.

From the 1930s until the 1950s (a time in which intensive fieldwork in 'primitive' or exotic cultures became the norm), political anthropology continued, almost exclusively, to examine political activities in the context of social and religious activities. This stage – best exemplified in *African Political Systems* (Fortes and Evans-Pritchard, 1940) – had certain characteristics. Whether writing about acephalous societies (those in which political interaction was regulated by the rights and obligations of kinsmen) or about the more familiar centralized states, the framework of explanation was the same: the task was done when one had identified groups and (where they existed) offices, and had set out the rights and duties attached to them, and had specified what institutions came into play when someone violated the rules. Why anyone broke the rules was rarely asked: it was enough to explain how offenders were brought back into line. These studies were more like statements of a constitution than accounts of people struggling over power. They paid little attention (at least, analytic attention) to individual initiatives, to strategies, to processes (other than those concerning deviance and – in some cases – succession) or to change – which is strange since most of them were done in the relatively short-lived and by then disintegrating colonial empires.

The reaction to this intellectual fashion (known as structural-functionalism) has taken political anthropology in two directions:

(1) With a slender root in evolutionary speculation and a stronger root in Marxist ideas and in a concern for the world's underprivileged, this direction has produced histories of, for example, agrarian unrest, peasant revolutions, or the effects of colonial rule on subject peoples. These studies combine – sometimes successfully – a close understanding of indigenous cultures with systematic attention (absent in structural-functionalist studies) to political and economic events in the larger world. They are thus centred upon change. But for the most part these studies are not concerned with political initiatives. They are *macro*-studies;

studies, for example, of how an expanding industrial capitalist economy transforms a peasantry into a proletariat. In its own way, this framework is as 'faceless' as structural-functionalism. 'Men make their own history, but they do not make it just as they please' (Marx, 1977 [1869]). Somehow the first part of that sentence escapes attention.

(2) The other direction appears to take account of individual initiatives. However, it does not describe the actions of particular individuals (as certain historians might) but rather examines the repertoire of strategies available in particular cultures, and the contexts which make one rather than another strategy appropriate. This framework is a development out of structural-functionalism, rather than its direct denial. It starts from the indisputable fact that rules for behaviour are general, while situations are particular. Therefore it is not always clear how the rules are to be applied, and there may ensue a contest to define the situation. Moreover, there is often no single overarching set of rules (as structural-functionalists imply in the phrase '*the* structure'): to be a good businessman may require being a bad family man (which implies conflict). Finally, besides the rules which say what is the moral thing to do, there are others which say what is pragmatic – that is, practical and advantageous. All this does no more than supplement the idea of conscience with the idea of interests.

The framework is still designed to describe rules which in a particular culture guide political behaviour, but the concept of 'rules' is brought down from a relatively abstract moral or jural level to one which is much closer to behaviour. Moreover, it produces a different kind of study, one which describes the neglected arenas of political life – factions, brokers, leadership and the like – which help understand process and change.

F. G. Bailey
University of California, San Diego

References
Fortes, M. and Evans-Pritchard, E. E. (eds) (1940), *African Political Systems*, London.
Marx, K. (1973 [1869]), *The Eighteenth Brumaire of Louis Bonaparte*, New York. (Original German, *Der achtzehnte Brumaire des Louis Bonaparte*, Hamburg.)

Further Reading
Bailey, F. G. (1969), *Stratagems and Spoils*, Oxford.
Swartz, M. J. (ed.) (1968), *Local-Level Politics*, Chicago.
See also: *Big Man; divine kingship; factions.*

Political Culture

Though some of the themes evoked by the concept of political culture were not unknown to classical political thought, the term political culture appears to have been first used in the late eighteenth century by Herder (Barnard, 1969) and its elaboration and development as a concept of modern political science dates from the 1950s (especially Almond, 1956). Substantive empirical research organized around the concept began to appear in the 1960s (for example, Almond and Verba, 1963; Pye and Verba, 1965). These early applications of the concept were linked to questionable theories of 'political development', but more recent studies have demonstrated that the value of the concept of political culture in no way depends upon its incorporation in a particular type of developmental, structure-functionalist or systems analysis.

There have been numerous definitions of political culture, but they can be classified into two broad categories: (1) those which confine the scope of political culture to the subjective orientation of nations, social groups or individuals to politics; and (2) those which broaden the concept to include patterns of political behaviour. Most political scientists have favoured the more restrictive category. Representative definitions in this first group include those which see political culture as 'the system of empirical beliefs, expressive symbols, and values which defines the situation in which political action takes place' (Verba, 1965), or as 'the subjective perception of history and politics, the fundamental beliefs and values, the foci of identification and loyalty, and the political knowledge and expectations which are the product of the specific historical experience of nations and groups' (Brown, 1977).

Scholars who prefer the second, and broader, type of definition of the concept have suggested that in characterizing political culture in subjective or psychological terms, 'political scientists have parted company with the great majority of anthropologists' (Tucker, 1973), although that view has recently been questioned (Brown, 1984). There is a minority of political scientists employing the concept who prefer the more anthropological approach, whereby political culture can be defined as 'the attitudinal and behavioural matrix within which the political system is located' (White, 1979).

Those who favour a 'subjective' definition argue that quite enough has already been brought under the umbrella of political culture and that to broaden its scope further reduces its analytical usefulness. Specifically, it makes it difficult, if not imposible, to examine what part the particular perceptions, beliefs and values to be found in different societies may play in explanation of political conduct if no clear conceptual distinction is made between behaviour and subjective beliefs. Accepting that this criticism has some force, a prominent proponent of the 'anthropological' approach has questioned whether the scholarly value of the concept of political culture actually depends upon its 'explanatory potency' and suggests that its central importance lies rather in the fact that 'it assists us to take our bearings in the study of the political life of a society ... to describe and analyse and order many significant data, and to raise fruitful questions for thought and research – *without explaining anything*' (Tucker, 1973).

The study of the political cultures and subcultures of societies ruled by authoritarian governments brings out acutely the definitional dilemma. On the one hand, political behaviour (for instance, voting behaviour in Communist systems) may – as a result of coercion or more subtle pressures – bear only a tenuous relationship to citizens' real beliefs and values. Thus, a more restrictive definition may, in principle, permit useful investigation of lack of congruence between the 'dominant' (as distinct from 'official') political culture and the political system. On the other hand, it is precisely in authoritarian regimes that it is hardest to get reliable quantified data on fundamental political beliefs and values, political knowledge and expectations, and so on, because of the difficulties not only of conducting surveys on such politically sensitive themes but also of getting honest answers from respondents. Behaviour, including deviant behaviour, may be more readily observable.

Yet, whereas early political culture studies concentrated on the First World and the Third World (where the frequent failure of transplanted Western-style political institutions to work in anything like the manner expected by the constitution-writers was a stimulus to the study of political culture), more recently increasing attention has been paid to the Second, or Communist, world (Brown and Gray, 1977; White, 1979; Almond and Verba, 1980). The special interest of these societies lies in the fact that unusually elaborate and conscious efforts have been made by the political power-holders to effect a radical transformation of political culture. Recent evidence indicates a much more limited success in this endeavour than might have been predicted, given Communist leaders' substantially tighter control over most of the major agencies of political socialization than that wielded by their counterparts in more pluralistic political systems. This, in turn, is now leading political scientists to examine more carefully the transmission and evocation of political beliefs and values, and to treat with equal seriousness both the psychological and historical dimensions of the study of political culture.

Archie Brown
St Antony's College, Oxford

References
Almond, G. A. (1956), 'Comparative political systems', *Journal of Politics*, 18.
Almond, G. A. and Verba, S. (eds) (1963), *The Civic Culture: Political Attitudes and Democracy in Five Nations*, Princeton, N.J.

Almond, G. A. and Verba, S. (eds) (1980), *The Civic Culture Revisited*, Boston.

Barnard, F. M. (1969), 'Culture and political development: Herder's suggestive insights', *American Political Science Review*, LXIII.

Brown, A. (ed.) (1984), *Political Culture and Communist Studies*, London.

Brown, A. and Gray, J. (eds) (1977), *Political Culture and Political Change in Communist States*, London.

Pye, L. W. and Verba, S. (eds) (1965), *Political Culture and Political Development*, Princeton, N.J.

Tucker, R. C. (1973), 'Culture, political culture, and Communist society', *Political Science Quarterly*, 88.

White, S. (1979), *Political Culture and Soviet Politics*, London.

Political Economy

Economic science was first called political economy by an unimportant mercantilist writer, Montchrétien de Watteville, in 1615 (*Traicté de l'oeconomie politique*). The word 'economy' dates back to ancient Greeks for whom it meant principles of household management (οἰκος = house, νόμος = law). Montchrétien argued that 'the science of wealth acquisition is common to the state as well as the family' and therefore added the adjective 'political'.

The term had not been accepted immediately, and it was only in 1767 that it reappeared in the *Inquiry into the Principles of Political Economy* by James Steuart, the last precursor of classical economists. With the advent of classical economics, the term came into general use and remained so throughout the entire nineteenth century. It meant economics as it had just emerged as one of the social sciences. English and French authors used the term almost exclusively, while German authors vacillated between *Staatswirtschaft* (Schlözer, 1805–7; Hermann, 1832), *Nationalökonomie* (von Soden, 1804: Hildebrand, 1848) or *Volkswirtschaft* (Eiselen, 1843; Roscher, 1854–94; Menger, 1871; Schmoller, 1900–4), *Politische Ökonomie* (Rau, 1826; List, 1840; Knies, 1855) and *Sozialökonomie* (Dietzel, 1895; M. Weber).

Like any new discipline, political economy included both theoretical principles and practical policies, scientific proofs and political advocacies; it was a combination of science, philosophy and art. In his *Wealth of Nations* (1776, Book IV) Adam Smith wrote: 'Political economy, considered as a branch of the science of a statesman or legislator, proposes two distinct objects: first, to provide a plentiful revenue or subsistence for the people . . . and secondly, to supply the state . . . with a revenue sufficient for the public services.' The titles of some of the later treatises reflect similar ideas (Hufeland, *Neue Grundlagen der Staatswirtschaftskunst*, 1807–13; J. S. Mill, *Principles of Political Economy with Some of Their Applications to Social Philosophy*,

1848). Also, like many other sciences in the nineteenth century, political economy passed through a process of catharsis: it gradually liberated itself from the political and ideological baggage, the concepts used became more rigorously defined, the analysis and proofs imitated procedures in exact sciences, and art (which advises, prescribes and directs) was separated from science (which observes, describes and explains). Commenting a century later (1874) on Smith's definition, Leon Walras observed that 'to say that the object of political economy is to provide a plentiful revenue . . . is like saying that the object of geometry is to build strong houses . . .'.

This development proceeded in two different directions: towards pure economic theory unrelated to social relations, and towards social economics stressing production relations as the main task of analysis. The former is sometimes (very conditionally) denoted as bourgeois economics, the latter (equally conditionally) as Marxist economics. Both were equally critical of inherited doctrines, but from different perspectives. Bourgeois economists took capitalism as an established social order (as data exogenously given) and tried to develop economic science by reducing the immense complexity of social phenomena to some manageable proportions. Marx and the socialists, on the other hand, questioned the established social order itself (and treated production relations as endogenous variables).

Nasau Senior (*An Outline of Political Economy*, 1836) was probably the first to stress explicitly the abstract and hypothetical character of economic theory and to distinguish theoretical economics from policy advice useful for the statesmen. J. B. Say provided the definition of political economy in the title of his book *Traité d'économie politique, ou simple exposition de la manière dont se forment, se distribuent et se consomment les richesses* (1803). While Smith's definition referred to an art, 'from Say's definition it would seem that the *production*, *distribution* and *consumption* of wealth take place, if not spontaneously, at least in the *manner* somehow independent of the will of man' which means treating political economy as a 'natural science' (Walras). Marx also talks of natural laws in economics, though, unlike Say, he also subsumes production relations under the governance of these laws. Although the econometricians – as Schumpeter calls them – of the seventeenth and eighteenth century, Petty, Boisguillebert, Cantillon and Quesnay, tried to measure economic phenomena, it was only Cournot (*Recherches sur les principes mathématiques de la théorie des richesses*, 1838) who successfully introduced mathematics into economics. And 'a science becomes really developed only when it can use mathematics' (Marx). The marginalist revolution of the 1870s gave the purification tendencies full swing. In the last great work under the title of political economy – *Manuale di economia politica* by Pareto, 1906 – the author scorns 'literary economists and metaphysicians' and defines his discipline by enumerating its three component parts: the study of tastes, the study of obstacles and the study of the way in which these two elements combine to reach equilibrium. This type of reasoning led to the most popular definition of economics in the first of the two intellectual traditions: economics as the study of the allocation of scarce resources among competing uses. Starting from this definition, it is logical to conclude, as L. Robbins did, that 'the generalizations of the theory of value are applicable to the behaviour of isolated men or the executive authority of a communist society as they are to the behaviour of men in an exchange economy' (*An Essay on the Nature and Significance of Economic Science*, 1932). Economics has thus become applied praxiology (study of rational behaviour). Most of what goes for the contemporary economic theory is in fact not theory but analysis. The difference between the two consists in economic analysis being *identically* true: if the rules of logic are observed, the conclusions follow with certainty and cannot be refuted. Economic theory, like any other theory, cannot be proved but can be refuted. As a result of these developments, political economy disappeared from the titles of economic treatises and also from Western encyclopaedias.

The Marxist tradition uses the following definition: political economy is the science of the laws governing the production, exchange and distribution of material means for living in the human society (Engels, *Anti-Dühring*, 1878). Since the conditions under which people produce and exchange are different in different epochs, there must be different political economies. Political economy is basically an historical science. Marx's chief work, *Das Kapital. Kritik der Politischen Oekonomie* (1867), was a critique of bourgeois society and was intended to 'discover the law of economic development' of this society. In an earlier work he links political economy with the dominant class in a particular society and draws attention to the 'blind laws of demand and supply, of which consists the political economy of bourgeoisie, and social production governed by social forecast, of which consists the political economy of the working class' (1864). Political economists of Marxist persuasion start from the observation that means of production together with appropriately skilled labour power make up the forces of production. The latter, together with the corresponding relations of production, determine modes of production which represent the proper subject of study for political economy. Marxist economists have preserved the term and the approach, but have not contributed much to the development of political economy after the master's death.

After the Second World War, the emergence of many new nations, substantial political and social changes, and widening gaps in economic development made the usefulness of pure economic theory rather questionable.

Models that implied Western *Homo economicus* proved inapplicable in many parts of the world and, increasingly so, in the West itself. The interest in political economy was revived. The subject was reintroduced into curricula, and studies bearing the title began to reappear (A. Lindbeck, *The Political Economy of the Left*, 1971; H. Sherman, *Radical Political Economy*, 1972). The current tendency is to bridge the gap between the two strands of thought: the most sophisticated analytical techniques are applied to analyse social relations. The term 'political economy' came to denote that part of economic theory which deals with the functioning of entire socioeconomic systems. In a somewhat looser sense it is also used to denote political-economic doctrines or comprehensive sets of economic policies such as liberal, conservative and radical. The increasing exactness of economics and the development of other social sciences make it possible to extend the task of political economy from merely explaining the functioning of economic systems to the design of basically new economic systems. In order to achieve this, an attempt has been made to integrate economic and political theory into one single theory of political economy (Horvat, 1982).

Branko Horvat
University of Zagreb

Reference
Horvat, B. (1982), *Political Economy of Socialism*, New York.

Further Reading
Lange, O. (1963), *Political Economy*, New York.

Political Participation

In earlier studies of political participation the focus was on *psephology*, or the study of electoral behaviour. However, since the 1960s the emergence and rise of political sociology has contributed not only to the study of conventional politics but to unconventional forms of political participation as well, such as protests, movements, revolutions, power and the like.

Every citizen can, theoretically, participate and influence the political process; in reality, however, there is an unequal degree of political participation and influence. Alford and Friedland (1975) note that participation without power is more characteristic of the poor and working classes, while power with or without participation is characteristic of the rich and upper classes.

Political participation includes all those activities by private citizens that seek to influence or to support the government and politics, including the selection of governmental personnel and/or actions they take

(Milbrath and Goel, 1977; Verba and Nie, 1972). Booth and Seligson (1978) define it in terms of 'behaviour influencing the distribution of public goods'.

The empirical indicators include voluntary actions and/or behaviour by citizens in support of the regime; intentionality of participants that these activities are political and efficacious; the element of conventionality or legality, and efforts to oppose the policies of government as a matter of right and privilege.

Most citizens are spectators of politics. In the US, about one-third are politically apathetic, and only a small percentage are activists. In most of the studies of why people do or do not participate in the political process, political sociologists and psychologists have pointed to the various agents of political socialization, including family, socioeconomic status, school, mass media, group/organizational identity, political and civic culture and the like. Lasswell (1951) lists eight reasons for participation: power, wealth, well-being, skill, enlightenment, affection, rectitude, and respect. Likewise, Lane (1959) thinks that a number of conscious and unconscious needs and motives are served by participation in politics, including economic and material gain, friendship and affection, relief from intrapsychic tensions, a need to understand the world, power, and self-esteem.

Any theory of political participation must consider both the individual action (motivation, needs, goals) and the constraints of participation (variable resource, psychological/cognitive and the contextual/environmental) (Booth and Seligson, 1978).

George Kourvetaris
Northern Illinois University

References

Alford, R. R. and Friedland, R. (1975), 'Political participation and public policy', *Annual Review of Sociology*, Palo Alto, Calif.

Booth, J. A. and Seligson, M. (1978), 'Images of political participation in Latin America', in J. A. Booth, M. A. Seligson *et al.* (eds), *Political Participation in Latin America*, New York.

Kourvetaris, G. and Dobratz, B. (1982), 'Political power and conventional political participation', *Annual Review of Sociology*, Palo Alto, Calif.

Lane, R. (1959), *Political Life*, Glencoe, Ill.

Lasswell, H. D. (1951), 'Psychopathology and politics', in *The Political Writings of Harold D. Lasswell*, Glencoe, Ill.

Milbrath, L. W. and Goel, M. L. (1977), *Political Participation*, Chicago.

Verba, S. and Nie, N. (1972), *Participation in America*, New York.

See also: *elections; political recruitment and careers; political representation; social movements; voting.*

Political Psychology

Political psychology considers the psychological, personal or subjective aspects of political behaviour, and draws on a wide variety of disciplines. Applications of political psychology are in the analysis of national political behaviour (from electoral routines to revolutionary upheavals) and international behaviour (from diplomatic accommodation to military conflict).

Early in the century, political psychology was primarily inspired by a common fear of mass irrationality. However, different national traditions reflect somewhat different preoccupations. The French scholars – Taine, Boutmy (*Psychologie politique du peuple anglais*, 1900) and Le Bon (*La Psychologie politique et la défense sociale*, 1910) – were conservatives interested in the threat of revolution and socialism; British scholars – Wallas (*Human Nature in Politics*, 1908) and Rivers (*Psychology and Politics*, 1923) – were socialists and more concerned with the threat of war and nationalism. An American classic is Lasswell's *Psychopathology and Politics* (1930).

Political psychology has developed to cover a large number of subjects. A prominent area of interest is politically relevant aspects of individual personality, particularly the psychobiography of leaders. Many such studies draw heavily on Freud, the Freudians, and psychoanalysis. (Freud himself collaborated with William Bullitt on a study of President Woodrow Wilson.)

Another area in political psychology is the relationship between political views and personality type. Wilhelm Reich's *Massenpsychologie des Faschismus* (1933) was primarily inspired by the apparent connection between the rise of fascism and widespread authoritarianism within Central-European family life and childrearing patterns. Later, in 1936, three members of the Frankfurt School, Horkheimer, Fromm and Marcuse, published *Autorität und Familie*. As refugees in the US from Nazi Germany, they developed their ideas and inspired scholars of the so-called Berkeley or California Group. From this emerged the classic study, *The Authoritarian Personality* (Theodor Adorno *et al.*, 1950), based on the F(ascism)-scale measurement.

Although the F-scale was criticized for its methodological as well as ideological shortcomings – including the fact that it measured only right-wing, and not left-wing, authoritarianism (a contentious issue since publication coincided with the Cold War) (Eysenck, *The Psychology of Politics*, 1954), it nevertheless provided the basis for extended and improved alternative scales. These measured other (political) personality attributes – dogmatism (Rokeach), Machiavellianism (Christie) and others. This particular area of political psychology was dominated by the psychologists.

Political scientists in the field have focused on different issues – political participation and party preference. Survey techniques showed marked improvements from the early studies (P. Lazarsfeld *et al.*, *The People's Choice*, 1944) to later ones (for example, A. Campbell *et al.*, *The American Voter*, 1960). Electoral behaviour was studied in relation to variables such as age, gender, social position, ethnic group, and religion. Similarly, sophistication of opinion polls has facilitated in-depth analyses of belief systems, another interest of political scientists. Neo-Marxists have considered the issue of class and ideology.

Only in the past two decades has political psychology taken shape as an interdiscipline in its own right: an International Society of Political Psychology was established in 1977 which holds annual scientific meetings and publishes a quarterly journal, *Political Psychology*. Many relevant studies still appear within the framework of other related disciplines – anthropology (national character), education (socialization), communication (propaganda), group psychology and organizational sociology (decision making), conflict studies, and so on.

Jaap van Ginneken
University of Leiden

Further Reading
Greenstein, F. I. (1975), *Personality and Politics – Problems of Evidence, Inference and Conceptualization*, 2nd edn, New York.
Knutson, J. N. (ed.) (1973), *Handbook of Political Psychology*, San Francisco.
Long, S. L. (ed.) (1981), *The Handbook of Political Behavior*, 5 vols, New York.
See also: *authoritarian personality*; *voting*.

Political Recruitment and Careers

To study recruitment is to look at political events with an eye to how the participants got there, where they came from and by what pathways, and what ideas, skills, and contacts they acquired or discarded along the way. Knowing their abilities, sensitivities, aims and credentials, one is better able to anticipate and interpret what they say and do. In turn, better evaluations can be made of the key consideration: performance, by élites and by the institutions and systems they run.

Everywhere political recruitment is a system maintenance process that is only partly institutionalized. The trade of politics is largely learned through an apprenticeship system. The career perspectives of each generation are moulded both by new priorities placed on skills and knowledge appropriate to meet changing needs and by the performance examples, good and bad, of men and women ahead of them on the political ladder. It is not uncommon to note that, even at early stages in their careers, tomorrow's leaders are being screened for capacities their elders never had to

possess. At the same time, élites persistently search for successors who are like themselves in style, judgement, temperament, beliefs and outlook. Élites are self-perpetuating.

The classic theorists, Mosca, Pareto and Michels, each explored the stultifying implications of incumbency. Governing élites are not necessarily adequate to the task. Too often, incumbency is a brake on efforts to update an institution's functional rationality, since performance norms and leadership objectives tend to be set by incumbents themselves.

Patterns of incumbency are called careers. Subjectively, career perspectives are moving vantage points from which men and women in politics appraise their duties and opportunities, whether they treat public life as a calling or as a livelihood, or both. Objectively, an individual's life path through the communal and corporate infrastructure of his society never ceases to be an apprenticeship that equips him with crucial skills and typical attitudes as well as with material resources and organizational sponsors – which are often necessary as credentials at subsequent major career thresholds.

Opportunities in politics are almost inevitably characterized by elements of co-optation. Aspirants for political careers cross an unmarked threshold when they are taken seriously for a given job by those who control the necessary political resources to get it and keep it. The intramural screening system for a neophyte legislator, official, or party functionary is often a searching and unnerving process. Formal recruitment processes in politics – whether by election, examination, sponsorship, or other credentialing procedures – seldom bestow much interpersonal influence; rather, such influence comes when one can show special prowess, rally a following, claim inside knowledge, or otherwise impress one's colleagues.

Schlesinger (1966) has stressed the notion of a political opportunity structure. In different polities, the realistic routes to significant office can be identified, and both traffic flow and casualty rates can be calculated. For Seligman (1971) it is not offices but roles that define the opportunity structure. Both the supply of eligibles and the demand for people to fill political roles must be considered. Not only one's birth chances but one's access to education, wealth, or other avenues of mobility affect eligibility. Eligibles for any given role are those with appropriate resources and skills who are socialized, motivated, and certified to fill it.

Careers also depend on the kind of sponsorship available and credentialing mechanisms involved. A minor position can often be seized successfully with no more than makeshift and temporary team efforts. To sustain a significant career of office-holding, on the other hand, implies sustained organizational support. Political career opportunities, as contrasted with *ad hoc* chances to play roles or even briefly to hold formal posts, tend to be controlled by parties; cliques may help one start a career, or may cut it short, but rarely can they suffice to sustain one.

Typically, political parties control the high-risk thresholds that distinguish a local notable from a trans-local functionary, a legislative career from a ministerial one. Once those who control the jobs and roles available at a given organizational node, in a given institutional setting, or at a given geographic locale, have taken an eligible aspirant seriously enough to invest organizational resources by sponsoring him formally, the aspirant is probably certified for at least a modest career in the same orbit. To put the same person in transit to a different career orbit, however, takes venture capital – party resources more difficult to secure and more jealously husbanded.

If a number of rivals contend for a party's nomination, the pattern of risks – financial, programmatic, organizational, and personal – for each contender is a function of the field against him. Some candidates change the risks significantly for others but not for themselves; they may need the exposure and experience, and they and their backers may view the effort as a long-term investment rather than a demonstrable loss.

Using an opportunity structure/political risk schema prompts certain key questions. Who are the gatekeepers? What selection criteria do they use? What quasi-automatic credentialing practices narrow the field? Is self-promotion encouraged? Are aspirants sometimes conscripted? Is a job sought for its own sake, or as a stepping stone, or as a seasoning experience? Career opportunities are probably more agglutinated, more commingled and more presumptively closed to outsiders than the opportunity-structure schema suggest.

Motivations have been much studied also. Lasswell's displacement formula (1930) (see Marvick, 1977) is concerned with personality dynamics: private motives are displaced onto public objects and rationalized in terms of public purposes. Eldersveld (1964) has demonstrated the labile and complex patterns of activist motivations. Wilson (1962) argues that leaders can grant or withhold various incentives, and thus nurture distinctive kinds of organizations. The political pros in 'machine politics' are accommodationist and success-minded. Quite different are the amateur volunteers, whose participation is principled and programmatic.

Dwaine Marvick
University of California, Los Angeles

References
Eldersveld, S. J. (1964), *Political Parties: A Behavioral Analysis*, New York.
Marvick, D. (ed.) (1977), *Harold D. Lasswell on Political Sociology*, Chicago.
Schlesinger, J. (1966), *Ambition and Politics*, Chicago.
Seligman, L. (1971), *Recruiting Political Elites*, Morristown, N.J.
Wilson, J. Q. (1962), *The Amateur Democrat*, Chicago.

Further Reading
Aberbach, J., Putnam, R. and Rockman, B. (1982), *Bureaucrats and Politicians*, Cambridge, Mass.
Eulau, H. and Czudnowski, M. (eds) (1976), *Elite Recruitment in Democratic Polities*, New York.
Eulau, H. and Prewitt, K. (1973), *Labyrinths of Democracy*, New York.
Prewitt, K. (1970), *The Recruitment of Political Leaders*, New York.
Putnam, R. (1976), *The Comparative Study of Political Elites*, Englewood Cliffs, N.J.
See also: *élites; political participation; parties, political*.

Political Science

Although the study of politics is an ancient pursuit, it is only in the last few decades that the discipline of political science became truly established, not perhaps so much because the fundamental problems which had intrigued the authors of the past have been superseded or even radically changed, but because new political processes, new techniques of government and, above all, a greater variety of studies have broadened markedly the fields of inquiry.

Traditionally, political science was essentially concerned with the purpose, character, and organization of the State. The great classics, Hobbes and Locke in the seventeenth century, Rousseau in the eighteenth, for instance, were primarily preoccupied with determining the goals of civil society and describing the institutions which appeared best-suited to achieving these goals. In the nineteenth century, the tradition was developed and amplified as new political institutions were set up in most Western-European countries and in America: the main preoccupation of some of the most prominent political scientists of the period, the constitutional lawyers, was to elaborate the ways in which these institutions could be firmly established and thus give the modern State a stable organization.

While political science analysis was thus focusing on the organization of the State, it was doing so on the basis of a twofold concern which remains a fundamental distinction to the present day. On the one hand, thinkers had a normative or prescriptive purpose: they wished to present the general principles on which the organization of government *should* be based. For political science is in large part born out of the desire to 'improve' political life and thus to reflect on the goals of government which would be most appropriate to bring about the 'good life'. Of course, this type of inquiry necessarily reflects the values of the thinkers themselves. Most political scientists of the past undertook their inquiries because of deeply felt views about human nature in politics; these views consequently differed profoundly from one thinker to another, with the result that the models of society are often in sharp contrast. Hobbes, for example, started from the hypothesis that man is a beast to man, and that the function of political organization is to make more liveable a society which would otherwise be 'nasty, brutish, and short'; Locke and Rousseau, on the contrary, had a more optimistic view of human nature and basically believed that the ills of society came from malorganization rather than from defects inherent in individuals.

On the other hand, alongside a desire to present the goals for a better society, political scientists had also to devote their attention to the examination of the 'facts'; they had to assess what was wrong with a situation they wished to alter and explain why their proposals would achieve the desired results. Political science has thus always included a study of the 'objective' characteristics of government, as well as a prescriptive or normative inquiry. The great classical writers often described in detail the existing arrangements and their drawbacks; they compared institutions in one country with those of another. Similarly, nineteenth-century constitutional lawyers looked for workable arrangements relating to elections, the structure and procedures of parliaments, the relationships between executive and legislature, thereby relating the political goals to the reality.

Political science is, consequently, both concerned with what should be and with what is. This is one reason why some believe that the term 'science' should not be taken too literally in the context of the study of politics, as political science is more than a science in the normal sense of the word: it is both descriptive examination and prescriptive philosophy. Improvements are studied and presented in the form of arguments, rather than by the analysis of data alone.

Naturally enough, although political science does incorporate both aspects, some political scientists are more inclined in one direction than in the other. Especially in recent years, when the discipline grew rapidly and became increasingly specialized, the political philosophers (sometimes known, albeit wrongly, as political 'theorists' – because there are also other political theorists) and the students of the 'facts' of political life (occasionally referred to as empirical political scientists) have often clashed, each group claiming to be superior.

The Problem of Definition

For a very long period, extending to the end of the nineteenth century, political science studied the State. There seemed little need to go beyond this simple definition of the scope of the subject, as the State appeared paramount and other organizations seemed to depend on it; indeed, as years went by, the involvement of the State in the daily life of citizens appeared to be on the increase.

Yet, while the State was becoming more pervasive, governmental decisions were increasingly subjected to the pressure of many groups operating within the State. The growth of political parties, of trade unions, of employers' organizations and, indeed, of large numbers of other associations, was challenging, if not the legal sovereignty of the State, at least its practical supremacy. Political scientists in this century could clearly not confine their analyses to State institutions and to the goals of these institutions; they had to broaden their inquiries to include the bodies which were involved in the many pressures brought upon the State. Moreover, 'political' activities similar to those taking place within the State were occurring within other groups – in the life of the parties, of trade unions, and of pressure groups in general.

Thus political science ceased being concerned exclusively with the State and became more broadly conceived. For this to happen, the subject-matter of the discipline had to shift from a specific area of inquiry – the State – to an activity – politics. But what, then, is politics? From the 1920s, many political scientists tried to establish the basic features of the activity which they were studying. In the 1930s and 1940s, especially under the influence of Lasswell, the operative concept was power, as politics does indeed appear to be closely related to the ability of some men to induce others to act (Lasswell and Kaplan, 1950; Barry, 1976).

But this approach gradually gave way to a more flexible and wider definition, as the scope of politics seemed to go beyond power and include many instances of 'natural' obedience which could not easily be defined as uses of power, at least in the normal sense of the concept. Politics thus became viewed as the activity concerned with the elaboration and implementation of collective decisions, through a variety of mechanisms involving power, to be sure, but also legitimacy, automatic acceptance, and basic loyalty. The definition proposed by Easton in the 1950s was widely adopted and suggests that political activity relates to the 'authoritative allocation of resources' in a community (Easton, 1953).

Such a definition of politics is intellectually more satisfying than the one which relates the field of study to the activities of the State. The effect was to enable political scientists to broaden markedly the scope of their analyses. If, for instance, the study of politics is concerned with the pressures on the government to take a particular decision, it follows that political scientists should also be concerned with examining the features of such pressures and, in particular, with the bodies involved in these pressures. While constitutional lawyers mainly studied assemblies, executives or courts, modern political scientists found it natural, indeed necessary, to look at groups of all kinds, not only political parties, but also other pressure groups in the decision-making process such as trade unions, churches, employers' organizations and others.

The Concern with the Systematic Analysis of Reality and the Development of Behaviourism

In the course of their inquiries, political scientists became increasingly aware of the gap between what constitutions proclaimed and what actually occurred. For example, it was simply not the case that parliaments and even governments were able to exercise the 'sovereignty' which was said to be theirs in liberal democratic systems: that sovereignty was in fact shared by the various groups involved in the decision process. Thus, not only was the scope of empirical inquiries broadened, but there was a disaffection from – and at times a rejection of – the analysis of legal and institutional devices; in its place the emphasis was on the 'true' reality of political life. The new school of thought which pressured for greater realism was called *behaviourism* (Dahl, 1963; Storing, 1962; Meehan, 1971).

The behavioural approach in political science, started in the United States, was widely adopted in the 1950s and 1960s, and later extended to many other academic centres. This approach seemed particularly appropriate at a time when, both in Eastern Communist States and in many parts of the Third World, the gap was increasing between constitutional formulas and the reality of government. Even in Western liberal democracies, the constitutional approach appeared inadequate since parties and interest groups had strikingly modified the characteristics of political life. Thus one major area of political science – the comparative analysis of political systems pioneered by Aristotle over 2500 years ago – benefited from the behavioural approach at a time when so many new systems of government emerged throughout the world.

Quantification, 'Positivism' and the Crisis of Behaviourism

Behaviourism was not only a demand for a more realistic approach to the study of politics: it also included two other claims that were to lead to many controversies and ultimately contributed to its decline in the 1970s. First, behaviourism became closely associated with a desire, in itself eminently justifiable, but in practice often difficult to bring about, to give empirical studies a 'truly' scientific basis. It tried to ensure that conclusions were not drawn merely from a few examples or from impressionistic remarks, but were the result of systematic examination of facts. This new trend in political science was indeed paralleled by similar developments in other social sciences, especially in economics, psychology, and, though to a somewhat lesser extent, sociology. It advocated a systematic presentation of the facts and the testing of hypotheses, in particular, the use of quantitative techniques. Many

political scientists anxiously sought indicators that could be expressed numerically, and they achieved significant results in a variety of fields in which large masses of numerical data could be used. This was obviously the case in electoral studies, which for at least a decade was to be the leading area of development of quantitative political science. Helped by the increased sophistication of survey techniques, political scientists were able to do complex analyses of the relationship between voting patterns and social, economic, and psychological characteristics of electors, both at a given moment and over time.

But there were problems. Not all aspects of political life were as readily quantifiable as electoral behaviour: much of the life of governments and groups appeared at least *prima facie* to have to be described in a less 'rigorous' manner. Moreover, an undue emphasis on quantification might lead to an exaggerated reliance on some types of indicators, because they were quantified, and to the neglect of other aspects, such as cultural factors, not as easily amenable to mathematical treatment. Nevertheless, the quantification process increased in political science during the 1960s and 1970s: parties, interest groups, legislative activity, governmental structures, court pronouncements and certain aspects of the decision-making process were examined more rigorously; but it also became clear that the goal of general quantification was very distant.

Meanwhile, interest began to shift from the problem posed by quantification to the underlying philosophical implications of behaviourism. The supporters of the behavioural approach did not only wish to be more factual and realistic; they also wanted political science to become more scientific. They hoped to develop theories that could be tested systematically through hypotheses; these, in turn, needed the backing of a 'general theory'. This suggested a move towards a positivistic type of inquiry, which was to cause major controversies. Behaviourists pointed out that political science had so far been concerned almost exclusively with normative theories and with the detailed examination of specific situations. They argued that what was needed was a systematization of the data through the search for overall explanatory frameworks which would account for the wide range of political phenomena hitherto presented in an unconnected manner.

Such a goal was logical in the context of a move designed to improve the scientific character of the discipline. But it was at best premature, and it proved to be contentious. It was clearly impossible to elaborate general theories, akin to those in the natural sciences, that could effectively explain all varieties in political life. Some models were advanced, such as systems analysis or structural-functionalism, but these had at best the status of frameworks which might guide the scholar in his inquiries; they were not testable theories accounting for reality. But these models pointed to the interconnection between the many political institutions present in a 'system'; they showed the need to look for the role (or functions) of the various institutions (structures), as this role was not necessarily the same from 'system' to 'system'. But this scarcely amounted to a general theory.

The models also proved contentious as soon as they claimed to be more than a 'guide for research': they tended to emphasize – even overemphasize – the need for 'stability' and 'system maintenance' in the development of political life. Critics argued that, far from being 'scientific' and 'objective', these models were truly ideological in the manner of the normative theories of the classical writers of the past. Marxists were not alone in stressing the part played by values in the analyses which scholars undertake in a field such as political science where the ideas of the 'good society' cannot easily be disentangled from the examination of the 'facts'.

As a result of this conflict, fewer scholars believed it possible to establish rapidly (if at all) a body of general theory from which one could deduce characteristics of political life.

The nature of reality is too complex. This is one reason why in the 1970s more emphasis came to be placed on 'middle-range' analyses of political phenomena, that is, studies of one particular aspect of the political system such as party development, legislative behaviour, or governmental structure and activity. If a general theory is to emerge, this can only be after a long process, especially since political science is not, and cannot be, merely the study of what is, however this is defined: it is also the study of what ought to be. Norms and prescription are part of the study of politics, whether this is consciously recognized or not.

Such a recognition does not make political science 'unscientific'; but it has the effect of leading to the conclusion that political science has to develop, alongside the other social sciences, in its own special way. Ideology and values will always play a part in the analysis of politics. Perhaps a new form of scientific methodology needs to emerge if all aspects of the discipline are to be fully interconnected; meanwhile, progress will have to take place both through normative and through empirical analyses, with, where it proves useful, the help of quantitative techniques.

J. Blondel
University of Essex

References

Barry, B. (1976), *Power and Political Theory*, London.
Dahl, R. A. (1963), *Modern Political Analysis*, Englewood Cliffs, N.J.
Easton, D. (1953), *The Political System*, New York.
Lasswell, H. D. and Kaplan, A. (1950), *Power and Society*, New Haven.
Meehan, E. J. (1971), *The Foundations of Political Analysis*, Homewood, Ill.
Storing, H. (1962), *Essays on the Scientific Study of Politics*, New York.

Further Reading

Blondel, J. (1981), *The Discipline of Politics*, London.
Jouvenal, B. de (1963), *A Pure Theory of Politics*, Cambridge.
Sabine, G. J. and Thorson, T. L. (1973), *A History of Political Theory*, New York.
Seliger, M. (1976), *Ideology and Politics*, London.
See also: *political theory*.

Political Theory

Political theory is a subject which is more easily defined ostensively than formally. It is simple enough to point to the intellectual tradition which runs from Plato and Aristotle through to Marx, Mill and beyond, but less simple to point to the common elements in their thought which enable us to say that they were all in some sense engaged in the same enterprise. Perhaps the best approximation is to say that political theory is an attempt to understand political and social relationships at a high level of generality, and in the light of that understanding to advocate a certain practical stance towards them. At one extreme, a theory may portray existing relationships as the perfect embodiment of rationality and consequently recommend conserving them in their entirety; at the other extreme, a theory may highlight the gulf between existing institutions and rational principles, and describe in some detail an alternative social and political order which would better realize the principles in question. The way in which this common project has been carried out, however, has varied a great deal. Some theories have started from a conception of the human individual, and asked what political and social arrangements would best satisfy his needs and desires. Others have interpreted existing institutions as part of an overall pattern of historical development – either as the culmination of that pattern, or as a transient stage destined to be replaced by something higher. Others again have begun by asking what kind of knowledge is possible in political matters, and gone on to defend institutional arrangements which give people tasks in proportion to their capacity to carry them out. Political theorists have been just as diverse in their methods as they have in their practical conclusions.

Because political theory aims to be prescriptive as well as explanatory, questions inevitably arise about its relationship to the practical outlooks of ordinary men and women, especially those relatively systematic world-views often referred to as ideologies. Political theory is best seen as an attempt to render these outlooks more adequate by reflecting on their underlying assumptions – discarding assumptions that are untenable, and providing more solid foundations for those that remain valid. It is differentiated from ideology by the fact that ideologies take for granted beliefs that political theory puts in question. Thus an ideology might incorporate the belief that social inequalities were the proper result of differences in individual merit. A political theorist would need to ask both about the extent to which the distribution of benefits in society actually corresponded to personal merit, and about the meaning of the notion of merit itself – say about the features in virtue of which one person could be described as more meritorious than another. It would be wrong, however, to harden this contrast into a rigid distinction. No political theorist is able to subject all of the beliefs that enter his theory to critical examination; some he has simply to take for granted. We may therefore refer to the ideological components of political theories, and say of a theory such as Locke's that it embodies elements of liberal ideology, or of Marx's that it embodies elements of socialist ideology. Indeed, we may wish to think of political theory as an activity that can be carried on at different levels, according to the extent to which received ideological beliefs are put in question. At the lowest level, there will be theories that are little more than the systematic expression of an ideology; at the highest level, theories that are very much more reflective, in the sense that a high proportion of their component beliefs have been subjected to critical examination.

In our own century, the very idea of political theory has been called into question by the widespread acceptance of positivism as a philosophical standpoint. Positivism denies that there is any logical connection between empirical propositions describing the world as it is and normative propositions telling us how we ought to act. Acceptance of this view implies that political theory as traditionally conceived rested on a mistake. The mistake was to combine explanations of social and political relationships with recommendations about how those relationships should be carried on. On the positivist view there are two distinct enterprises: political science, which aims at the empirical explanation of political phenomena, and political philosophy, which starts from certain political values such as democracy and equality and draws out their practical implications. Although, as we shall see later, this view is open to challenge, its popularity has been such that a distinction is often now drawn between three types of political theory:

(1) *Empirical political theory.* This term is commonly used to refer to the theoretical parts of political science. Political scientists are interested in describing and explaining particular political events, but they are also interested in developing broader explanatory theories which draw together a wide range of phenomena under a single heading. They have, for instance, tried to explain in general terms why revolutions occur, or why some democracies are dominated by two large parties while others generate many small ones. The issues that are considered are often similar to those addressed in the older tradition of political theory, but much greater use is typically made of quantifiable evidence. Thus someone seeking to produce a theory about the causes of revolution would characteristically begin by looking for correlations between the outbreak of revolutions and other phenomena, such as the extent of economic inequality in the societies under consideration.

(2) *Formal political theory.* This burgeoning field overlaps considerably with 'social choice theory', 'public choice theory', and so on. The approach here is to model a political system by assuming certain procedural rules and actors with designated goals, and then to investigate formally (on the assumption that each actor pursues his goals rationally) what the final configuration of the system will be. Two major applications are to collective decision procedures and to party competition in a representative democracy. In the first case, the theorist postulates a population each of whom has his own preferences as between a number of policies, and looks at how these preferences will be amalgamated into a 'collective choice' by various decision rules (such as majority voting). One well-known result of these investigations is Arrow's (1963) theorem, according to which *no* decision rule can simultaneously meet a number of reasonable-sounding conditions (such as that if each person prefers x to y, y should not be collectively chosen in preference to x). In the second case, the theorist again assumes a population with given policy preferences, and looks at how parties will behave under a democratic electoral system on the assumption that each party's aim is to win the election and each voter's aim is to secure policies that correspond as closely as possible to his preferences. This application was originally developed by Antony Downs (1957), and has since been considerably elaborated.

(3) *Normative political theory.* In this branch of the subject, the theorist is directly interested in the justification of political standpoints and policies. There is, however, disagreement about how strong a form of justification is possible. For some theorists, influenced by positivism, justification ultimately ends in a commitment to one or other basic political value. The theorist's room for manœuvre is created by the fact that such values cannot be translated simply or immediately into policy. Thus someone may believe that his underlying commitment is to individual freedom, but this commitment does not, of itself, tell him whether he should be in favour (say) of a night-watchman state or an interventionist welfare state. The

theorist's job, on this view, is to explore what the idea of freedom means, and then to apply it to practical issues, such as whether redistributive taxation reduces the freedom of the wealthy, or increases the freedom of the poor, or does both. The alternative view maintains that it is possible to go beyond this minimum programme and provide rational foundations for the basic values themselves. An important recent attempt in this direction can be found in the work of John Rawls (1972) who has tried to show that principles of distributive justice can be derived from the choices that rational individuals would make if they were ignorant of their personal characteristics and place in society. Although this attempt has not been judged a success on all sides, it has served as a landmark in the English-speaking world for those who believe that the more ambitious version of normative theory is feasible.

This distinction betwen types of political theory is useful as a labelling device, and it corresponds to a real division of labour in the academic community; but it is much more doubtful whether a rigid separation between the three enterprises can be sustained intellectually. Consider each pairing in turn:

(1) Normative theories necessarily rely on empirical research whenever they move from the most abstract kind of conceptual analysis to consider what various concepts and principles imply for the design of institutions and policies. It is impossible to say, for instance, whether democracy can be achieved through a scheme of parliamentary representation without having some understanding of how electoral systems operate. On the other hand, every empirical theory embodies normative assumptions. This is so because the concepts that are used to group phenomena together for explanatory purposes – concepts such as 'revolution', 'democracy' and 'social inequality' – embody assumptions about what is significant in human affairs, and which occurrences are relevantly similar and dissimilar. Thus a theory that attempts to specify the social conditions under which revolutions are likely to occur presupposes that the term 'revolution' picks out a set of events which are interesting to the social scientist and have important features in common.

(2) Formal and empirical theory also feed off each other. Although those engaged in formal analysis frequently deny that their assumptions are meant to be empirically realistic, the undertaking itself would not be worth engaging in unless there was some connection between the assumptions made and behaviour in the real world. Thus Downs's theory of democracy would be little more than an intellectual conceit if political parties were not as a matter of fact sometimes prepared to alter their policies in order to attract voters. Conversely, the models developed in formal analysis are an important source of explanatory theory. A full theory of party competition will almost certainly need to incorporate Downsian mechanisms – that is, it will need to recognize that parties are driven by their interest in winning elections to adopt policies that correspond to voters' preferences – alongside other factors in explaining party behaviour.

(3) Finally, formal theory both borrows from and contributes to normative theory. This can be seen most easily in the case of the theory of collective choice. The conditions that a theorist will lay down for an acceptable decision procedure will reflect his normative commitments. One such condition might be political equality: each person's preference should have an equal chance of determining what the collective choice will be. Conversely, the results of formal analysis may have important normative implications. An upshot of Arrow's theorem, for instance, is that there is in general no simple 'best' procedure for making social choices; instead societies should be prepared to use different procedures in different areas of decision, depending on such factors as the likely configuration of individual preferences on a given issue.

All of this suggests that the older political theorists were right to see political explanation and political prescription as integrally related. It does not, however, mean that it is now easy to do political theory in the traditional way. Academic specialization has meant that most practitioners currently work in one small corner of the field; and those who try to present a synoptic view of political life are liable to be denounced as amateurs. But since political theory responds to a permanent intellectual need – the need to subject our everyday political attitudes and assumptions to critical questioning – one can safely predict that, in one form or another, the enterprise will continue.

David Miller
Nuffield College, Oxford

References

Arrow, K. (1963), *Social Choice and Individual Values*, New Haven.

Downs, A. (1957), *An Economic Theory of Democracy*, New York.

Rawls, J. (1972), *A Theory of Justice*, Oxford.

Further Reading

Barry, B. (1965), *Political Argument*, London.

Berlin, I. (1964), 'Does political theory still exist?', in P. Laslett and W. G. Runciman (eds), *Philosophy, Politics and Society*, Second Series, Oxford.

Connolly, W. (1974), *The Terms of Political Discourse*, Lexington, Mass.

Miller, D. and Siedentop, L. (eds) (1983), *The Nature of Political Theory*, Oxford.

Riker, W. H. and Ordeshook, P. C. (1973), *An Introduction to Positive Political Theory*, Englewood Cliffs, N.J.

Runciman, W. G. (1969), *Social Science and Political Theory*, Cambridge.

Weldon, T. D. (1953), *The Vocabulary of Politics*, Harmondsworth.

See also: *political science*.

Popper, Karl Raimund (1902–)

Sir Karl Popper is one of the most creative, wide-ranging and controversial philosophers of the twentieth century. Sir Peter Medawar, Nobel laureate in physiology and medicine, has called Popper 'incomparably the greatest philosopher of science that has ever been'. Yet virtually every one of Popper's many contributions – to logic, probability theory, methodology, evolutionary epistemology, quantum physics, social and political philosophy, and intellectual history – is heatedly disputed by professional philosophers.

Popper was born in Vienna in 1902, studied physics, philosophy and music at the University of Vienna, and left Vienna in January 1937 to become senior lecturer in philosophy at Canterbury University College in Christchurch, New Zealand. He was appointed to the staff of The London School of Economics and Political Science in 1945, and became professor of logic and scientific method there in 1949, and remained there until his retirement in 1969. He was knighted in 1965 and made a Companion of Honour in 1982.

His first and most important work is *Logik der Forschung* (1934), published in English translation as *The Logic of Scientific Discovery* (1959), which challenged the main tenets of the positivist philosophers of Popper's native Vienna. An ardent advocate of reason and the scientific spirit, Popper nonetheless denied the very existence of scientific induction, argued that probability (in the sense of the probability calculus) could not be used to evaluate universal scientific theories, disputed the importance of the verification (as opposed to falsification) of hypotheses, denied the importance of meaning analysis in most branches of philosophy and in science, and introduced his famous falsifiability criterion of demarcation to distinguish science from ideology and metaphysics.

This early clash with positivism has set the tone and the underlying themes for much of the later controversy over Popper's ideas: at a time when most physicists and philosophers of physics are inductivist, subjectivist, positivist, instrumentalist, Popper remains deductivist, realist, anti-positivist, anti-instrumentalist.

The chief ideas of Popper's philosophy all relate to the basic anti-reductionist theme – first announced explicitly in *The Self and Its Brain* (1977) (written with Sir John Eccles) – that 'something can come from nothing'. Scientific theories introduce new forms into the universe and cannot be reduced to observations, contrary to proponents of induction. The future is not contained in the present or the past. There is indeterminism in physics, and also in history – not only because of physical indeterminism, but also because new scientific ideas affect history and thus the course of the physical universe. There is genuine emergence in biology. Value cannot be reduced to fact; mind cannot be reduced to matter. Descriptive and argumentative levels of language cannot be reduced to expressive and signal levels. Consciousness is the spearhead of evolution, and the products of consciousness are not determined. Nonetheless, the Copenhagen interpretation of quantum mechanics – which is often used to introduce consciousness or the 'observer' into the heart of physics – is rejected by Popper, who maintains that quantum physics is just as objective as classical physics.

Although Popper is first and foremost a physicist, all of his thought is nonetheless permeated by an evolutionary, Darwinian outlook; and biology has come to dominate his later thinking, particularly his *Objective Knowledge* (1972). His most important contributions to social and political philosophy are *The Open Society and Its Enemies* (1945) and *The Poverty of Historicism* (1957), works both in intellectual history and in the methodology of the social sciences, which dispute the main themes of Marxism and of social planning. The idea of 'piecemeal social engineering' which Popper introduced in these works has had an important influence on practical politicians in the West, particularly in England, Germany, and Italy.

W. W. Bartley, III
The Hoover Institution, Stanford University

Further Reading

Other Works by Popper:
Conjectures and Refutations, 1963.
Unended Quest, 1974.
The Open Universe, 1982.
Quantum Theory and the Schism in Physics, 1982.
Realism and the Aim of Science, 1983.

Works about Popper:
Bartley, W. W. III (1976–82), 'The Philosophy of Karl Popper' (3 parts), *Philosophia*.
Bunge, M. (ed.) (1964), *The Critical Approach to Science and Philosophy*, Chicago.
Schilpp, P. A. (ed.) (1974), *The Philosophy of Karl Popper*, la Salle, Ill.

Population

The size and growth of world population are enormously larger than at any previous epoch of human history. The recent rate of growth, 1.7 to 2.0 per cent per year, is not large by many standards. But continued over any long historical period it leads to population growth of astronomical proportions. Even with slowing rates of growth, the Population Division of the United Nations projects a rise of world population from 4.4 billion in 1980 to 6.1 in the year 2000 and 8.2 billion in the year 2025. This is within the lifetime of the majority of persons alive today.

The following discussion briefly reviews: (1) the major sources of information on population size and demographic characteristics; (2) the major world trends in births, deaths, and migration; and (3) major changes occurring in the more quantifiable characteristics of the world population.

(1) The main sources of information on population are (i) national censuses; (ii) vital statistics from the registration of births and deaths; (iii) sample surveys.

(i) The modern census is a human inventory of the numbers and more measurable characteristics of a national population at a given date. The characteristics usually include place of residence, age, sex, marital status, education, and economic activity by employment, industry and occupation. In fact, censuses are often incomplete, especially in the enumeration of infants and small children and of young and mobile adult males. While such problems are more serious and more common in less developed areas, more developed countries are not immune. Thus in the United States the 1980 census enumerated some five million more people than were estimated from the 1970 census and intercensal information on births, deaths and migration.

(ii) Usable vital statistics are more limited than census data. The registration of births and deaths is generally so incomplete in the less developed world that birth and death rates so derived are not usable for demographic analysis. In the more developed world these provide annual information on birth rates and death rates as well as more sophisticated measures of fertility and mortality.

Migration data are the weakest link in demographic information. Most countries obtain information on legal immigration but, as in the United States, lack data on undocumented (illegal) immigration; also, few maintain adequate records on emigration. Internal migration is usually not identified except in census information on changes in place of residence. This is particularly serious as migration becomes an increasingly important determinant of population change.

(iii) A third type of population data comes from sample surveys. These are undertaken to obtain more accurate information or information not available from census or vital statistics. A prominent example is the World Fertility Survey conducted in some 20 countries by the International Statistical Institute in the 1970s. These studies, undertaken jointly with the statistical offices of the countries concerned, attempted to establish levels and trends of fertility on an internationally comparable basis. Sample surveys of this type have the advantage of more skilled interviews made in a manner and for specific purposes not feasible in censuses. They often suffer from limitations imposed by samples too small for detailed cross-tabulations and for reliable data for local areas.

Methods of population analysis have achieved a high level of mathematical sophistication, notably in extracting reasonable estimates of fertility and mortality from the limited data available for less developed areas. By contrast, population analysis has failed to find (or indeed generally to seek) statistically sophisticated measures of migration.

(2) What do these sources and methods tell us about contemporary trends in world population? First, the world population has been and is experiencing what is commonly called the demographic transition or the 'vital revolution'. This is a transition from wastefully high birth and death rates observable in almost all traditional societies to the low birth and death rates that now prevail in all industrialized and urbanized countries. Most of the latter are in an advanced stage of the transition, in which population approaches the more or less stationary population presumably existing through much the greater part of human history.

However, some projections, including the 'medium' projection of the United Nations, do not foresee this occurring in the total world population before the year 2100.

Population growth derives from an excess of births over deaths, aside from migration. National differences in rates of population growth today are largely determined by levels and trends in the birth rate.

Up to World War II there was a clear dichotomy between those countries that had experienced major fertility declines and those that had not. The former included Europe and Europe overseas (North America, Australasia, and temperate South America). The remainder continued to have high fertility, the levels varying with cultural differences.

This dichotomy has broken down as non-European populations have modernized, conspicuously led by Japan. Today East-Asian and Latin-American countries are experiencing rapid fertility declines consonant with their 'modernization' and/or their break with traditional institutions, as in the People's Republic of China. Less rapid fertility reductions are generally observable in India and other countries in South and South-East Asia. Moslem nations and tropical African countries have not yet experienced major fertility reductions, though these have begun in several Moslem countries such as Turkey, Tunisia, Egypt and Indonesia.

Major progress in reducing mortality has been made in almost every country in the world. Commonly, countries in the less developed world gained 5–10 years in life expectancy between 1960 and 1980. Future gains in reducing mortality will of course slow reductions in the rate of population growth, but in a major way only in Africa, in Moslem South-West Asia and in the most impoverished countries of South Asia such as India, Pakistan and Bangladesh, where death rates are still high. In the most developed countries there is continuing success in reducing infant deaths and new successes in postponing deaths in the older ages. However, these have little impact on long-range population trends; in most developed countries death rates are so low that elimination of *all* deaths prior to age 45 would have a trivial effect in increasing birth rates.

The combined result of these trends in fertility and mortality is that the 1970s witnessed the reversal of the consistently rising rates of world population growth that had prevailed for at least a century. The number, as contrasted with the rate, of population growth, is probably now, in the mid-1980s, passing its peak. It is reasonable to assume that the downward trend will persist if the presently less developed world continues to make socioeconomic progress as much as it has since World War II.

However, there is little ground for complacency about the size of population growth for at least a generation ahead. At best, the inertia of past growth, reflected in the continuing rapid increase in the number of young adults, means continuing huge population growth, notably in the labour force ages, well into the next century.

(3) The role of population policies intended to promote smaller families is disputed. Advocates of such policies often assert their effectiveness even in the absence of major socioeconomic progress. Both socioeconomic development and population control policy jointly contribute to declining fertility, even though the specific contributions of each are difficult to unravel.

Avowed policies intended to promote birth control and family limitation are now in effect in the majority of less developed countries (LDCs) outside of Africa; but a pronouncement is not itself a policy, a policy is not in itself a programme, and the latter may be quite limited in its effectiveness. Relatively few countries have programmes that provide contraceptive services for a statistically large segment of the population. However, the fact of legitimation and publicized support by the government may well in itself have important effects. Most noteworthy in this regard is the case of the People's Republic of China where government-induced social pressure, perhaps as much as formal legislation, has brought about a remarkable acceptance of a two-child, or even one-child, norm.

Among the major cultural regions and continents, Europe, the Soviet Union, Australasia and North America collectively have reached a level of replacement or below (that is, a total fertility of two children or less per woman). Other regions, led by Japan and other countries of East Asia, are moving along a continuum in the demographic transition at different stages roughly consonant with the level of socioeconomic development. Tropical Africa remains the sole large cultural area with as yet no marked fertility declines and with still rising rates of population growth. It is the poorest and least developed region, with the most gains to be made in mortality reduction as well as in fertility reduction.

Prospective population growth will be concentrated in the 'South', the tropical and subtropical countries, as opposed to the 'North', primarily in the temperate zones. According to the 'medium' projections of the United Nations, the presently more developed regions would increase some 250 millions or 22 per cent by the year 2025. In the same period, 1980–2025, the less developed regions, excluding China, are projected to increase well over 3.1 billion or 136 per cent.

With these projections the present and projected future populations for the larger nations for the years 1980, 2000, and 2025 are shown in Table 1.

Table 1

United Nations 'Medium' Population Projections
(in millions)

	1980	2000	2025
China	995	1257	1469
India	684	961	1234
USSR	265	310	355
United States	227	264	306
Indonesia	148	199	247
Brazil	122	187	291
Japan	117	129	131
Bangladesh	88	148	222
Pakistan	87	140	206
Nigeria	77	150	285
Mexico	70	116	174
W. Germany	61	59	54
Italy	57	59	57
United Kingdom	56	55	54
France	54	56	57
Vietnam	54	79	106
Philippines	49	77	108
Thailand	47	69	90
Turkey	45	70	100
Egypt	42	64	95
Iran	38	65	99

Source: United Nations, *World Population Prospects as Assessed in 1980, Population Studies*, 78, 1981

The first four countries will presumably remain in the same order but with the massive populations of China and India even further in the lead than now. By 2025 two presently less developed countries, Brazil and Nigeria, would be on the way to equal or pass the United States and perhaps later the Soviet Union. With these projections, the countries of Western Europe will by 2025 be smallish countries among giants rising in the now less developed world. To the extent that population size weighs in international affairs, the less developed South (the tropics and subtropics) will be gaining very much on the more developed North (the temperate zones). At the same time the enormous prospective population in these poorer and poorest countries will create a massive burden to supply adequate food and jobs for their additional billions.

A caution is in order. These projections may well be no more trustworthy than their predecessors. It is quite possible that birth rates in major less developed countries may fall more rapidly (or indeed less rapidly) than projected. In most of these countries family limitation is encouraged by government policy and promoted by effective means of communication now reaching much larger parts of the population than heretofore. In historical European experience, birth control was opposed by the government, by the church, by social pressure and by the media. In most less developed countries, aside from tropical Africa, all of these forces appear to be promoting rather than inhibiting the spreading practice of later marriage and birth control. In Asia, notably in countries of Chinese culture, and in more advanced countries of Latin America, fertility reduction is occurring at a pace never experienced in Europe. It seems quite unlikely that the momentum of present fertility reductions will be checked before reaching modest levels now existing in temperate South America (2.8 per woman) or even that of Cuba, Hong Kong and Singapore (2.2 children per woman). The inertia of huge numbers entering the reproductive years, barring war or other holocaust, inevitably means large population growth; but with the continuation of rapid fertility declines now observable in the more advanced LDCs the population growth

might well be less than that indicated in Table 1. To take a specific example, with continued fertility declines at rates of reduction experienced in the last decade, Mexico in 2000 will have a population of some 105 million instead of the 116 million forecast by United Nations 'medium variant' and a corresponding lower population in 2025.

Within phenomenal population growth in the modern world there are equally important changes in ways of life indicated by changes in measurable population characteristics and illustrated in Table 2.

Most salient in LDCs is the phenomenal growth of cities and urban patterns of life, albeit at very different levels of urbanization in different parts of the world.

Literally every country in the world experienced an increase in urbanization or metropolitanization between 1960 and 1980. In the world, generally, peasant and pastoral life is giving way to the more stimulating, more mobile and more frenetic life of the town and the metropolis. What may well become the largest metropolises are emerging in Mexico City, in Sao Paolo, in Shanghai, in Calcutta and in Djakarta. The majority of humankind is clearly entering a way of life formerly only experienced by a small minority.

The official figures are of course deceptive in comparing the more and the less developed areas. Urbanization means something different in the two areas of an established metropolitan population as against one growing rapidly from unassimilated rural migrants. But in each case the change in way of life and of human relationships is profound. Despite many cultural differences, universal urban values and material environment are bringing about a convergence in the way of life throughout the world of the upper and middle classes if not yet of the poor.

Table 2
Selected Population Characteristics
1982 and 1960–1980

Number of Countries	Population[a] 1982	Income Range[b] 1982	% Urban		Life Expectancy[c]		Adult Literacy(%)		Per Capita Food Supply[d] 1980
			1960	1980	1960	1980	1960	1980	
Low Income (34)	2267	400	17	21	42	57	34	52	97
China (1)	1008	310	18	21	41	64	43	69	107
India (1)	717	260	18	24	43	52	28	36	87
Others (32)	541	80–390	12	20	40	48	23	40	92
Middle Income (60)	1158	440–6840	33	46[e]	51	60	48	65	110
Lower (38)	670	440–1610	24	34[e]	45	57	39	59	106
Upper (22)	489	1680–6840	45	63[e]	57	65	61	76	115
High Income/Oil Exporters (4)	17	6090–23770	30	66	44	57	9	32	127
Industrial Market Economics (19)	723	5150–17010	68	78	70	74	96	99	134
East European Non-market Economies (8)	383	3900–7180[e]	49	62	68	71	97	99	133

[a] In thousands [b] Average per capita income in 1982 dollars [c] Life expectancy at birth (years)
[d] Daily per capita supply as percent of minimum requirements defined by the United Nations Food and Agricultural Organization
[e] 1982

Other major changes in population characteristics suggest comparable changes in life style. As noted above, there have been major gains in reducing mortality almost everywhere, though a great deal remains to be done in the poorer countries. Socially these achievements in reducing mortality mean less early widowhood, less orphanhood and less loss of work time to illness, especially from infectious diseases. It also means lower infant mortality and less need for having many children in order for some to survive.

Primary education, once the monopoly of the privileged few, is now becoming almost universal for children and young adults in many of the countries still classified as 'less developed', and all countries are moving in this direction.

Gains in economic characteristics, such as food consumption, employment and income have made less progress. Apparently, average food consumption is still below estimated requirements in many countries (chiefly African), but despite setbacks the average daily calorie supply has risen in the LDCs as a group. Of course, even in countries of adequate *average* food supply lower income groups fall below requirements. Obviously a herculean task remains to provide an adequate diet for the many millions of the hungry in the world. While average per capita real incomes have risen over the past 20 years in the great majority of countries, it is unhappily the poorest that have made the least progress (excluding China, 1.2 per cent average annual rise) v. 3.8 per cent in middle-income less developed countries and 3.6 per cent in industrial market economies.

In short, the world, especially the less developed world, is progressing in health, in education, in communication and, unhappily, more slowly in adequacy of diet, in jobs and in income. This socioeconomic development, supplemented and promoted by family limitation programmes, is bringing about general reductions in fertility more than compensating for the welcome reductions in mortality. The result is declining rates and now lower absolute numbers of population growth. These give hope of an ultimate solution of problems associated with population growth, perhaps in the middle of the twenty-first century. But at best the world will have to contend with vast population size and growth along the way.

Dudley Kirk
Stanford University

Further Reading
International Institute of Statistics (1972–), *World Fertility Survey*, numerous country and subject reports.
United Nations, Department of International Economic and Social Affairs (1981), *World Population Prospects as Assessed in 1980*, Population Studies, No. 78, New York.

United Nations (1982), *World Population Trends and Policies, 1981 Monitoring Report*, Population Studies, No. 79, 2 vols, New York.
See also: *census of population; demographic transition; population and resources; population policy; population projections.*

Population and Resources

Great concern is commonly expressed about the impact of huge population size and growth, combined with affluence, on the world's sources of energy and nonrenewable resources. Major issues include the extent to which (1) shortages are market shortages or real; (2) resources are indeed finite, nonrenewable and nonreplaceable; and (3) present and prospective shortages are due to growth in affluence or to population growth. What follows does not attempt to answer these difficult questions but only to comment very briefly on the broad picture.

Perhaps most dramatic among resource shortages has been that of energy. All economies have been profoundly affected by periods of market shortages in fossil fuels, specifically oil and gas. The price rise in these fuels, partly imposed by the OPEC cartel, has shaken the economies of the more industrialized countries, but has had an even worse effect on the less favoured developing areas that must devote much of their scarce foreign exchange to oil purchases. Population growth intensified such shortages, but the market demands of rising world affluence (for example, in use of motor cars) is surely as important and probably much more so. Economists point to the fact that there is no shortage of energy sources, even of some nonrenewable resources, such as coal. However, there is a shortage of cheap and clean sources. Cheap gasoline and fuel have seduced us into undue dependence on a limited source of energy, specifically petroleum. The real price of gasoline (adjusted for inflation) is generally as cheap as it was fifty years ago, when the motor car was first becoming ubiquitous in more industrialized countries and heating was being transferred from coal to oil. In other words, the shortage of oil and gas is not yet reflected in high enough market prices to make it economic to employ other sources of energy for the internal combustion engine (such as alcohol or fuels derived from coal), much less to abandon it in favour of steam, electricity, or other sources of power and, in the industrial countries, to use public transport instead of the economically wasteful private car.

Other natural resources, such as metals, are commonly nonrenewable or, strictly speaking, are converted by human use into nonusable forms. Economists are fond of pointing out that technology has achieved remarkable success in supplanting scarce and more expensive materials by less expensive ones. In sum, the real cost of basic natural resources, again adjusted for inflation, has declined. Of course this has not occurred without some economic costs and price distortions. But in the market place there is little evidence of acute shortages except in isolated instances. For the future, predictions range from those of Cassandras prophesying disastrous shortages, to economists and technologists who predict that the market and new technology will minimize the effect of possible shortages even for a much larger world population in the next century. Thus far the latter have proved more accurate, since technology has far outdistanced resource use, enabling the general rise in material standard of living. However, in no way does this argue for the wasteful and profligate use of resources which deprives our descendants of these cheap and easily accessible sources. These will be sorely needed to aid in providing a higher level of living to the vastly larger world population foreseeable in the all-too-near future.

Dudley Kirk
Stanford University

Further Reading

Goeller, H. E. and Zucker, A. (1984), 'Infinite resources: the ultimate strategy', *Science*, 223.

Kahn, H. *et al.* (1976), *The Next Hundred Years*, New York.

Meadows, D. *et al.* (1972), *The Limits to Growth*, New York.

Simon, J. (1981), *The Ultimate Resource*, Princeton.

See also: *energy; population policy.*

Population Genetics

Population genetics is that branch of science concerned with the description of genetic variation in populations and probable causes of this variation. The former is usually called empirical or experimental and the latter theoretical population genetics.

Inherited variation had been studied in a formal way in the latter half of the nineteenth century, notably by Sir Francis Galton. The modern form of the subject originates with the rediscovery of Mendel's rules of genetic transmission and the enunciation by G. H. Hardy and W. Weinberg in 1908 of the famous Hardy-Weinberg law. This law relates allele frequencies to genotype frequencies at a single genetic locus in large populations that are not subject to natural selection on the gene in question.

The subsequent development of theoretical population genetics was led by R. A. Fisher and J. B. S. Haldane in the UK and Sewall Wright in the US. Fisher's 1918 paper provided a far-reaching connection between simple Mendelian genetic variation and phenotypic variation whose description is essentially statistical. Fisher's approach, in terms of variance analysis, was adopted by agricultural researchers and later by behaviour geneticists. Although Fisher continued to work in all areas of theoretical population genetics, a split developed between the biometrically oriented agricultural geneticists and evolutionary theorists, a split which persists to this day. Fisher's 1930 book, *The Genetical Theory of Natural Selection*, outlines his way of applying mathematics to Darwin's concepts while incorporating genetic discoveries and field observations made up to that time. The book is still widely referred to and stands not only as one of the most significant biology books but as one of the great scientific achievements of this century.

Haldane shared Fisher's interest in the construction and analysis of mathematical models of the evolutionary process. Haldane's series of papers in the Proceedings of the Cambridge Philosophical Society studied the changes in gene frequencies in populations subject to various forms of natural selection, inbreeding, mutation and migration. His 1932 book, *The Causes of Evolution*, is a brilliant survey of the issues in evolution raised by theoretical population genetics and foreshadows the theory of kin selection.

Sewall Wright began his career working on the genetics of coat colour in guinea pigs. His first contributions to theoretical population genetics were made in the 1920s. Much of his subsequent work is summarized in his four-volume treatise *Evolution and the Genetics of Populations* published between 1969 and 1978. Initially Wright was interested in the effect of regular inbreeding on the amount of genetic variability in a population. His classic 1931 paper demonstrated that stochastic effects due to small population size must be considered in evolutionary theory. He termed these effects random genetic drift and showed that the quantitative analysis of the consequences of genetic drift could best be accomplished using a class of parabolic differential equations. Mathematicians such as William Feller became interested and subsequently developed an important part of probability theory in order to solve these equations. Although Wright's main contributions to theoretical population genetics were concerned with population structure, he also made fundamental contributions to statistics. He originated the idea of path analysis now widely used in sociology and econometrics as well as behaviour genetics.

Fisher, Haldane and Wright laid the foundations for theoretical population genetics. The tradition of building mathematical models whose aim is to clarify the populational and evolutionary significance of each newly discovered genetic phenomenon has continued. During the last twenty years, theory has addressed the roles of recombination, meiotic drive, sexual selection and assortative mating, as well as gene-gene interaction in fitness. Phylogenetic techniques have been developed that use genetic rather than phenotypic variation. Evolutionary changes occurring simultaneously at multiple loci can now be studied mathematically, as can the joint effects of genetic and cultural transmission. Much of the recent theory has been developed in response to changes that have occurred in the past twenty years in the picture of genetic variability that exists in nature.

That there is inherited variation in plants and animals has been known, at least implicitly, since agriculture originated. Empirical population genetics is concerned with the genetic basis for inherited variation and how the genes contributing to the observed variation vary among the members of a population. It is also concerned with how well explanations from theoretical population genetics fit these observations. For example, the ABO blood group is determined by antigens on the red blood cells and antibodies in the sera of humans. That the ABO genotype is inherited was known in 1911, but until 1924 it was thought to be controlled by two genes. Only when the mathematician Felix Bernstein compared population data on the frequencies of the ABO genotypes to expectations from theory was it proven that there was a single gene involved.

There are many human genes now known to control antigens on the red cells, and the frequencies of the genotypes vary across the world. In the last twenty years even more variation has been shown to exist for antigenic determinants on the white blood cells. In 1966 the technique of gel electrophoresis made it possible for H. Harris, working with humans, and R. C. Lewontin and J. Hubby, working with Drosophila, to exhibit variation for genes which determine enzymes. There followed an explosion of information on the level of genetically based enzyme variation present in almost 2000 species of plants and animals. In man, for example, about 23 per cent of enzyme genes show population level variability while about 43 per cent are variable in Drosophila.

In these past two decades the amount of genetic variability that exists in man, either in blood groups or in enzyme determinants, has been shown to be great. While on the face of it some of this variation might be ascribed to racial differences, careful statistical examination has shown that this is misleading. In fact, about 85 per cent of human genetic variation (measured by any of a number of common statistics) is between individuals within a population (that is, a nation or tribe). Only about 5 per cent is between races.

Ultimately, all genetic variation is due, of course, to mutation. But what causes the variation to be maintained at a given level in a given population? It is here that the quantitative theory of population genetics is invoked, and it is here that major conceptual disagreements have occurred. On the one hand, Th. Dobzhansky and his students in the US, and the British ecological geneticists following E. B. Ford, believe that most of the observed genetic variation is a direct response to natural selection acting on these variants.

This position has been called the *selectionist* school. The followers of the great geneticist H. J. Muller – most notably M. Kimura from Japan – hold that the genetic variants we see are transient and their frequencies are primarily the result of the interaction between mutation and random genetic drift. This is the *neutralist* school.

We are not yet at the stage where a definitive numerical resolution between these philosophies can be made. In a few cases, most notably the case of the sickle cell haemoglobin in man, the connection between an observed genetic polymorphism and natural selection has been established. For most observed polymorphisms, however, the physiological and fitness differences between genotypes have not been established.

Modern biochemical techniques have enabled examination of variation in the DNA itself. The resulting patterns of variation appear to be very difficult to reconcile with any mode of natural selection acting at this molecular level, although this type of data is still actively being collected.

Among the most active research areas at present, both empirical and theoretical, are the relationship between molecular variation and disease, statistical methodology related to behaviour genetics, the processes of speciation and the significance of molecular variation for classical evolutionary theory. In all of these the tendency over the past ten years has been to move away from earlier considerations of single genes acting in isolation, to genes in a milieu of other genes, of genotypes interacting with environments and towards the evolutionary basis of social structures.

Marcus W. Feldman
Stanford University

References
Fisher, R. A. (1918), 'The correlation between relatives on the supposition of Mendelian inheritance', *Transactions of the Royal Society* (Edinburgh), 52.
Fisher, R. A. (1958) [1930]), *The Genetic Theory of Natural Selection*, 2nd edn, New York.
Haldane, J. B. S. (1924), 'A mathematical theory of natural and artificial selection', *Proceedings of the Cambridge Philosophical Society*, 23.
Haldane, J. B. S. (1932), *The Causes of Evolution*, New York.
Harris, H. (1966), 'Enzyme polymorphisms in man', *Proceedings of the Royal Society B.*, 164.
Kimura, M. (1983), *The Neutral Theory of Molecular Evolution*, Cambridge.
Wright, S. (1968–78), *Evolution and the Genetics of Populations*, 4 vols, Chicago.

Further Reading
Cavalli-Sforza, L. L. and Bodmer, W. F. (1971) *The Genetics of Human Populations*, San Francisco.

Hubby, J. L. and Lewontin, R. C. (1966), 'A molecular approach to the study of genic heterozygosity in natural populations. I. The number of alleles at different-loci in *Drosophila pseudoobscura*', *Genetics*, 54.

Lewontin, R. C. (1974), *The Genetic Basis of Evolutionary Change*, New York.

See also: *evolution; genetics and behaviour.*

Population Policy

A population policy can be defined as a set of governmental actions intended to influence at least one of the demographic components of population change – fertility, mortality, or migration. Population policies are justified by the social, economic, political, or biological consequences expected to result from the intended demographic change. Unintended consequences may also occur, and policies instituted for nondemographic reasons may have important demographic effects.

Because population policies seek to enhance the collective welfare of the community as a whole, policy goals may be consistent with personal goals of some individuals. An effective population policy rests upon knowlege about the demographic trend, its likely future course, and its causes and consequences, and upon a valid theory of how the policy will influence the trend to produce desirable collective consequences.

Nearly universal individual and societal goals include longer life and lower mortality. Hence, nineteenth-century industrializing countries introduced sanitary sewers, pure water, and mass inoculations when they learned that these public health measures would reduce mortality from infectious diseases. Additionally, developed countries have recently pursued partially successful policies directed toward chronic diseases, the major causes of death in these countries. Developing countries have implemented public health measures, with external financial and technical assistance, producing sustained mortality declines of unprecedented speed and magnitude.

Fertility goals vary greatly across individuals and communities because of diverse social, economic, and familial circumstances. In developed countries, despite the absence of antinatalist policies, industrialization brought fundamental institutional changes that dramatically altered individual childbearing goals with consequent fertility declines. Developed countries sometimes pursue pronatalist policies, apparently with little effect.

In developing countries, continued high fertility and rapid mortality declines have produced unprecedented, unintended population growth and severe social and economic problems. Many developing countries responded with family planning programmes which have had little independent effect, because they take individual childbearing goals as given, simply providing services for realizing these goals. In more effective policies to stimulate aggregate fertility declines, several developing countries, including China and Singapore, are introducing incentives, disincentives, and institutional changes in their societies, economies, and families.

Extensive rural to urban migration has characterized most industrializing countries. Without migration policies, eary industrial cities grew because in-migration more than replaced high mortality losses. In currently developing countries, cities with much lower mortality and massive in-migration suffer problems that have prompted policies to slow or redirect such migration.

Forced international migration increased sharply after World War I, as did national controls on immigration. Free international migration, flowing mainly from Europe to America during the hundred years preceding World War II, is now dominated by moves from less developed countries with rapid population growth to more developed countries with greater economic opportunities.

Although a paucity of empirical research limits conclusions regarding the effectiveness of many migration policies, the great prevalence in currently developing countries of potential migrants and of internal migration policies, and the universality of national immigration controls, suggest inconsistencies between the goals of various national policies and many individuals.

Donald J. Hernandez
Georgetown University

Further Reading

Scientific American Book (1974), *The Human Population*, San Francisco.

United Nations (1982), *World Population Trends and Policies: 1981 Monitoring Report* (vols I & II), New York.

See also: *demographic transition; migration; population and resources; urbanization.*

Population Projections

Population projections are calculations that illustrate the development of populations when certain assumptions are made about the course of future population growth. Projections can be made for the country as a whole, for major geographical or political subdivisions of a country, or for particular classes of a population. The assumptions of the projection may mirror patterns of growth observed in the past, may be based on an extrapolation of past trends, or may be conjectural, speculative or illustrative. The length of the projection period may vary from a few years to many decades, depending on the needs being served, the population in question and the availability of resources.

Several procedures for projecting populations can be distinguished. A total population can be projected forward in time by means of a balancing equation, whereby future population size is estimated by adding to a previously enumerated population changes over the intervening period due to natural increase (births less deaths) and net migration. The method demands a satisfactory initial population count and reliable estimates of the components of population growth, and is warranted only for fairly short projection periods.

A slightly different approach can be taken by projecting an initial population by reference to a rate of annual increase under the assumption of a mathematical model for the form of population growth. The most commonly used model is that of exponential growth. The technique also permits calculations of a population's doubling time, or the rate of growth that must have been operating to produce a particular population size after a certain number of years. Variants of the method incorporate other patterns of growth, such as the logistic, but have the common feature that future population size is estimated without regard to the components of growth.

If a population's age structure is not constant, because of past fluctuations in vital rates or age-selective migration, it is greatly preferable to extrapolate from a known age structure on the basis of age-specific fertility and mortality rates. This is known as the component method of population projection, and is performed in several steps. The first is to calculate the survivors of the initial population on the basis of an assumed or underlying life table, and the second is to calculate the children born and surviving over the projection period. Thus, for example, with a projection period of five years, one would calculate the survivors of people initially aged 0–4 years, 5–9 years, and so on, to give the numbers aged 5–9, 10–14 and so on, in the projected population, and then apply age-specific fertility rates to women in the childbearing years to derive the number of children whose survivors will go to make up the 0–4 age group in the projected population. A final refinement might be to adjust for known or assumed rates of immigration and emigration.

Demographers are perhaps best known for making population projections. Nevertheless, there is a considerable difference of opinion within the profession as to the role of the demographer in this regard, and even as to the function of a projection. According to Brass (1974), 'the forecasting of future populations would seem to many people the main practical justification for the science of demography'. Opposing this view Grebenik (1974) declared that, 'it is perhaps salutary to remind ourselves that there is only one feature that all demographic predictions have had in common, and that is that they have all been falsified by events'. We can go some way towards reconciling these points of view by distinguishing, as does Keyfitz, between a prediction of what will actually happen in the future, and a projection, which is merely the numerical consequence of a series of assumptions. A projection is bound to be correct (barring arithmetic error), while a single forecast is nearly certain to be invalidated by subsequent events. For example, a forecast might be based on current mortality which is subject to change, or on an assumed future level of mortality which proves to have been incorrect.

Whatever limitation or qualifications a demographer places on his projections, he cannot prevent their being used as forecasts. The most he can do is to state his assumptions clearly, or perhaps even prepare a range of projections from a range of extreme assumptions, and leave the user to decide whether any sort of forecast is feasible.

Michael Bracher
Australian National University, Canberra

References
Brass, W. (1974), 'Perspectives in population prediction: illustrated by the statistics of England and Wales' (with discussion), *Journal of the Royal Statistical Society, Series A*, 137(4).
Grebenik, E. (1974), 'Discussion', in W. Brass, *Journal of the Royal Statistical Society, Series A*, 137(4).
Keyfitz, N. (1972), 'On future population', *Journal of the American Statistical Association*, 67.

Further Reading
Dorn, H. F. (1950), 'Pitfalls in population forecasts and projections', *Journal of the American Statistical Association*, 45.
Hajnal, J. (1955), 'The prospects for population forecasts', *Journal of the American Statistical Association*, 50.
Shyrock, H. S., Siegal, J. S. and Associates (1973), *The Methods and Material of Demography*, U.S. Bureau of the Census, Washington DC.
See also: *demography; futurology; population; prediction and forecasting.*

Populism

Populism is one of the least precise terms in the vocabulary of social science. It is used to refer to a wide variety of political phenomena, and students of these populisms continue to disagree about what, if any, features they share. It is possible to identify at least seven different types of political phenomena, each considered populist by some political scientists. Three of these are radical movements based on or oriented towards the countryside:

(1) Radical farmers' movements, of which the paradigm case is the US People's Party of the 1890s. This

movement, whose adherents coined the label 'Populist', grew out of the economic grievances of farmers in the Western and Southern states, and for a time appeared to threaten the American two-party system. The Populists, whose manifesto declared, 'We seek to restore the government of the Republic to the hands of "the plain people"', demanded a variety of reforms, including monetary inflation by increased coinage of silver. The movement collapsed after the defeat in the 1896 Presidential election of W. J. Bryan, a Democrat who fought on a largely Populist platform. Other examples of a comparable 'farmers' radicalism' include the rise of Social Credit in Alberta and of the Co-operative Commonwealth Federation in Saskatchewan.

(2) Movements of radical intellectuals, aiming at agrarian socialism and romanticizing the peasantry. The type-case here is *Narodnichestvo* (Populism), a phase of the nineteenth-century Russian revolutionary movement during which disaffected intellectuals 'went to the people' to try to provoke them to revolution. At the height of the movement, in 1874, thousands of young people, girls as well as young men, risked imprisonment by flocking to the countryside to preach the gospel of agrarian socialism. They believed that since communal cultivation of land still survived in the Russian village, a new socialist society could be constructed upon this rural foundation once the state was destroyed. The peasantry proved unresponsive, however, and some of the *Narodniki* took to terrorism instead, even managing to assassinate Tsar Alexander II.·

(3) Spontaneous grassroots peasant movements, aimed at control of the land and freedom from élite domination. Unlike the two previous categories, in this case there is no acknowledged paradigm movement, but examples include the Zapatistas in the Mexican Revolution, the Peasant Parties of Eastern Europe after the First World War, and the Russian Revolution before its capture by the Bolsheviks. Third-World revolutionary movements with a peasant base, such as Maoism, are often thought of as a fusion of Marxism with populism.

While these three categories all relate to political movements, and are all more or less agrarian, the term populism is also applied to several other diverse phenomena.

(4) Populist dictatorship – cases in which a charismatic leader appeals beyond conventional politicians to the masses, and gains unconstitutional power by giving them 'bread and circuses'. Juan Peron, who (with the help of his wife Eva) built up a loyal popular following in Argentina in the 1940s, is an obvious case; 'Southern Demagogues' in the US, such as Huey Long of Alabama, provide other examples. It is sometimes suggested that this kind of populist leader can gain a mass following only where the masses in question are either rural or else recent migrants from the country-side (like many of the first generation of *Peronistas*).

(5) If populism can be used to describe mass-based dictatorship, it can also indicate a form of democracy. 'Populist democracy' is hostile to representation, and seeks to keep as much power as possible in the hands of the people. Its characteristic institutional devices are the popular referendum on legislation passed by the representative assembly; popular initiative, whereby voters can bypass the assembly and initiate legislation to be voted on in a referendum; and the recall, whereby representatives can be forced to undergo an extra election in the course of their term of office if a certain number of voters express dissatisfaction with their performance. Populist democracy is taken to its furthest extreme in Switzerland, but, as a result of its adoption by American Progressives in the early years of this century, many US states (notably California) have constitutional procedures for referenda.

(6) A further sense of populism, which one might call 'reactionary populism', is its use to describe politicians who play to the reactionary prejudices of the masses against the enlightened views of the political élite in democratic countries. Politicians who gain popularity by playing on ethnic hostilities or right-wing views about law and order are particularly liable to the charge of 'populism' in this sense.

(7) Finally, the term is also applied to a particular political style. 'Politicians' populism' is the style of politicians who avoid ideological commitments and claim to speak for the whole people rather than for any faction; of 'catch-all people's parties' that are short on principles, eclectic in their policies and prepared to accept all comers.

Although different social scientists apply the label populism to all these seven types, these types are obviously too diverse to be regarded as different varieties of a single political phenomenon. The only feature all of them share is a rhetoric making great use of appeals to 'the people'. However, since 'the people' can mean either the whole nation or some lower section of it (such as the peasants or the urban masses) this rhetoric is highly versatile and does not in itself indicate any particular programme or constituency.

Theorists who wish to explain 'populism' as a social phenomenon are necessarily selective, focusing on certain of the types listed above and denying that the others are really populist. Many theorists make their selection on sociological grounds, relating populist radicalism to the strains of modernization, and seeing populist movements as a kind of alternative to socialism, either in rural areas or among urban masses recently drawn from the countryside. According to these theories, populists, though politically radical, are characteristically traditionalist in their values and concerned to resist modernization. Many students of politics in the Third World find this type of theory illuminating. Attempts to interpret other populist phenomena (such as the US Populist movement) in these terms are highly controversial.

M. Canovan
University of Keele

Further Reading
Canovan, M. (1981), *Populism*, New York.
Ionescu, G. and Gellner, E. (eds) (1969), *Populism: Its Meanings and National Characteristics*, London.

Pornography

A succession of 'moral panics' has dictated the form and focus of much pornographic research. The pattern has typically been one of violent dipute between those for whom pornography constitutes a fundamental threat and those who seek to combat censorship and repressive legislation in the name of rights and freedoms of expression. Social science played a central role in such arguments – which dominated the scene until the late 1970s – yet, paradoxically, without having any real effects on public debate or legislative action.

The traditional combatants in the pornography debate may be loosely grouped into 'moral' and 'liberal' camps. The moral camp take the initiative, proposing both a general and a specific argument. Most broadly they claim that pornography is damaging to the moral fabric of society, undermining family life, basic values, and the quality of our culture. Social scientists have remained conspicuously silent on most of such general issues, other than to observe occasionally that what is 'moral decline' from one point of view may look like acceptable social change from another. Modern society, after all, is hardly characterized by a consensus on matters moral. But social science has had more to say about the moral camp's more specific claims. The typical argument here is that evidence shows the following: that rising trends in the statistics of violent and/or sexual crimes are associated with a 'rising tide of pornography'; and that specific individuals are demonstrably harmed, directly or indirectly, by the consumption of pornography. However, in support of such claims, the moral campaigners make highly selective use of social-science research – the British NVLA, for example, refer constantly to the work of John Court, while ignoring criticisms of it and alternative research findings.

The essentially defensive response of the liberal camp has been to emphasize the massive inconsistency of research findings in the 'effects' area, and to underline the well-known difficulties of developing a coherent causal interpretation of trend statistics. At the heart of their case lies the claim that unless harmful consequences be clearly demonstrated, there is no justification for curtailing an adult individual's freedom to consume privately whatever cultural materials he wishes. This is most lucidly expressed in the Williams Committee report on *Obscenity and Film Censorship*, the most refined example of the liberal position. The committee rejects both the widely publicized claims of the moral camp, as well as the less familiar case that defends pornography because of its alleged beneficial or cathartic effects: in both cases, they conclude, the evidence is insufficient.

One important consequence of public debate having taken this particular form has been an overwhelming focus of research attention in the area of *individual* effects and harms. This has made it difficult to introduce less individualistic alternative conceptualizations of the effects of pornography. In recent years, however, some feminist writers and researchers have sought to shift the terms of the debate. While conceding that it may not be possible to demonstrate satisfactorily the harmful effects on individuals, they argue that the damaging consequences of pornography are real enough. Inasmuch as pornographic materials articulate and express demeaning, antagonistic, and violent attitudes to women, they serve both to diffuse beliefs and to legitimate actions which are unjust and practically damaging to the interests of women. At its clearest, this way of approaching the question extends the concept of 'effects' into a more macroscopic cultural domain in which it is the legitimation and diffusion of sexism which is at issue. Interestingly, this has the consequence of restricting the notoriously vague term pornography to those cultural materials that express particular kinds of views about women; offensiveness, obscenity, and eroticism cease to be central questions. Though this conceptual transition is as yet incomplete, and much of the current literature confusing, there is now some reason to hope for research that will transcend the restrictive terms imposed by past public debate.

Andrew Tudor
University of York, England

Further Reading
Cline, V. B. (1970), *Where Do We Draw the Line?*, Provo, Utah.
Wilson, W. and Goldstein, M. (eds) (1973), 'Pornography: attitudes, use and effects', *Journal of Social Issues*, 29.

Positivism

Although the explicit postulates of logical positivism are not accepted by most practising social scientists today, there remains an amorphous and implicit self-consciousness, a self-perception, that pervades contemporary social science practice which may be called the 'positivist persuasion'. The major postulates of this persuasion follow.

(1) A radical break exists between empirical observations and non-empirical statements. This seems like a simple and rather commonsensical position, but it is actually a fundamental, specifically intellectual principle that has enormous ramifications.

(2) Because of this assumed break between general statements and observations, it is widely believed that more general intellectual issues – philosophical or metaphysical – are not fundamentally significant for the practice of an empirically oriented discipline.

(3) Since such an elimination of the non-empirical (purely intellectual) reference is taken to be the distinguishing feature of the *natural* sciences, it is believed that any objective study of society must assume a natural 'scientific' self-consciousness.

(4) Questions which are of a theoretical or general nature can correctly be dealt with only in relation to empirical observations. There are three important corollaries of this fourth point: (a) Regarding the *formulation* of scientific theories, the positivist persuasion argues that the process of theory formation should be one of construction through generalization, a construction consisting of inductions from observation. (b) Regarding the problem of theoretical *conflict*, the positivist persuasion argues that empirical tests must in every case be the final arbiter between theoretical disputes. It is 'crucial experiments' rather than conceptual dispute that determine the outcome of competition between theories. (c) If the formulation of theories and the conflict between them can be entirely reduced to *empirical* material, there can be no long-term basis for structured kinds of scientific *disagreement*. Social-scientific development is viewed as a basically progressive one, that is, as linear and cumulative, and the segmentation or internal differentiation of a scientific field is viewed as the product of specialization rather than the result of generalized, non-empirical disagreement. It is viewed, in other words, as the result of focusing on different aspects of empirical reality rather than of seeking to explain the same element of empirical reality in different ways.

The ramifications of these beliefs about social science have been enormous: everywhere they have had an impoverishing effect on the social-scientific imagination, in both its empirical and theoretical modes.

By unduly emphasizing the observational and verificational dimensions of empirical practice, the positivist impetus has severely narrowed the range of empirical analysis. The fear of speculation has technicalized social science and driven it toward false precision and trivial correlational studies. This flight from generality has only contributed further to the inevitable atomization of social-scientific knowledge.

This positivist impetus has also led to a surplus of energy devoted to methodological rather than conceptual innovation, for the scientific challenge is increasingly understood to be the achievement of ever more pure forms of observational expression.

Finally, but perhaps most significantly, the positivist persuasion has crippled the practice of theoretical sociology as well. It has sharply reduced the quantity of discussion that directly concerns itself with the generalized elements of social-scientific thought. But it has also unmistakably reduced the quality. This has occurred because under the rubric of the positivist persuasion, it is much more difficult for theoretical analysis to achieve an adequate self-understanding. The positivist persuasion has caused a widespread 'failure of nerve' in theoretical sociology.

What might an alternative position look like? Clearly, even in the American social science of the last few decades, there has been some alternative put forward. What is usually proposed is some kind of humanistic as compared to scientific approach to empirical study: there is humanistic geography, sociology, political science, psychology, and even, most recently, the humanistic narrative approach in contrast to the analytic approach in history. These humanist alternatives have in common their anti-scientific stances, a position which is held to imply the following: a focus on people rather than external forces; an emphasis on emotions and morality rather than instrumental calculation; interpretive rather than quantitative methods; the ideological commitment to a 'moral' society, one which fights the dangers of technology and positivist science. In the European tradition this purportedly vast dichotomy was formalized by Dilthey as the distinction between *Geisteswissenschaft* and *Naturwissenschaft*, between hermeneutics and science. In its most radical form, the hermeneutical position argues that the uniquely subjective topic of the 'human studies' makes generalizations impossible; in more moderate form it argues that even if some generalizations are possible, our effort must aim only at understanding rather than explanation, hence that casual analysis is the monopoly of natural science.

This distinction between social and natural sciences, which is at the heart of such a humanist position, is an invidious one. Such an alternative to the positivist persuasion is too timid, too self-effacing before the power of the 'big sciences'. It also implies a much too rigid connection between epistemology, method, and ideology. Finally, and this of course is the important point, it is plainly wrong.

The humanistic or hermeneutical alternative to positivism suffers from a misunderstanding of natural science. The post-empiricist philosophy, history, and sociology of science in the last twenty years has conclusively demonstrated that the positivist persuasion has been vastly and irrevocably wrong, not just about the usefulness of the natural science guide to social science, but about natural science itself. From the wide range of this discussion there are certain basic points upon which most of the participants in this movement are agreed. These are the fundamental postulates of the 'post-positivist persuasion', and they all point to the rehabilitation of the theoretical.

(1) First, all scientific data are theoretically informed. The fact/theory distinction is not concrete, does not exist in nature, but is analytic. Calling statements 'observational' is a manner of speech. We use some theories to provide us with the 'hard facts', while we allow others the privilege of 'tentatively' explaining them.

(2) Empirical commitments are not based solely on empirical evidence. The principled rejection of evidence is often the very bedrock upon which the continuity of a theoretical science depends.

(3) The elaboration of general scientific theory is normally dogmatic rather than sceptical. Theoretical formulation does not proceed, as Popper would have it, according to the law of the fiercest struggle for survival: it does not adopt a purely sceptical attitude to generalizations, limiting itself only to falsifiable positions. To the contrary, when a general theoretical position is confronted with contradictory empirical evidence which cannot be simply ignored (which is often the first response), it proceeds to develop *ad hoc* hypotheses and residual categories which allow these anomalous phenomena to be 'explained' in a manner that does not surrender a theory's more general formulations.

(4) Fundamental shifts in scientific belief will occur only when empirical challenges are matched by the availability of alternative theoretical commitments. This background of theoretical change may be invisible, since empirical data give the *appearance* of being concrete (as representing external reality) rather than analytic (representing thought as well). But this appearance is not correct. The struggle between general theoretical positions is among the most powerful energizers of empirical research, and it must be placed at the heart of major changes in the natural sciences.

These insights take us beyond the hermeneutics-versus-science dichotomy. We can see that science itself is a hermeneutical, subject-related activity. Social studies need not, therefore, withdraw itself from the greater ambitions of science. What they must do is to understand the nature of social science in a radically different way, as a science that must be, from the beginning, explicitly concerned with *theoretical* issues. No doubt this much more subjective understanding of the post-positivist position is depressing to those who hope for, and believe in, an objective science; positivists, indeed, might well view such a position as surrender or defeat. I would strongly disagree. As Raymond Aron once wrote in his elegy to the great positivist philosopher Michael Polanyi: 'To recognize

the impossibility of demonstrating an axiom system is not a defeat of the mind, but the recall of the mind to itself.'

Jeffrey C. Alexander
University of California, Los Angeles

Further Reading
Alexander, J. C. (1983), *Theoretical Logic in Sociology*, 2 vols, London.
Frisby, D. (ed.) (1976), *The Positivist Dispute in German Sociology*, London.
Halfpenny, P. (1982), *Positivism and Sociology*, London.
See also: *hermeneutics; philosophy of the social sciences; Popper.*

Post-Industrial Society

The term post-industrial society seems to have originated with Arthur Penty, a Guild Socialist and follower of William Morris, at the turn of the century. Penty looked forward to a 'post-industrial state' based on the small craft workshop and decentralized units of government. The concept was not taken up again until the 1950s, when it was given an entirely new twist. It owes its present meaning largely to the writings of the Harvard sociologist, Daniel Bell.

In numerous works, especially *The Coming of Post-Industrial Society* (1973), Bell has argued that modern industrial societies are entering into a new phase of their evolution, a post-industrial phase. Post-industrial society is as different from classic industrial society as the latter was from pre-industrial agrarian society. It is concerned with the production of services rather than goods, the majority of its work-force is in white-collar rather than manual occupations, and many of these workers are professional, managerial, or technical employees. The old working class is disappearing, and with it many of the class conflicts of industrial society. New alignments, based on status and consumption, are supplanting those based on work and production.

Post-industrial society is a highly educated society, and, indeed, knowledge is its central resource. But knowledge in a special sense. Industrial society ran on practical knowledge, the knowledge that comes from doing rather than from pure research. Its representative figures are inventors like Watt and Edison. Post-industrial society depends on theoretical knowledge, the knowledge that is developed in universities and research institutes. It not only looks to theoretical knowledge for many of its characteristic industries, such as the chemical and aeronautical industries; it increasingly puts a good part of its national resources into developing such knowledge, in the form of support for higher education and research and development activities. This shift of emphasis is reflected in the growth in importance of the 'knowledge class' – scientists and professionals – and of 'knowledge institutions', such as universities. These will eventually displace businessmen and business organizations as the ruling complex in society.

Bell's account of post-industrial society has been the most influential. It is based largely on generalization from American experience, but many European sociologists have found sufficient similarities in their own societies to concur: for instance, Alain Touraine in *The Post-Industrial Society* (1971), although he stressed more than Bell that conflicts in the new society will be as severe as in the old. Bell's ideas have been particularly acceptable to futurologists of both West and East, who have made the concept of post-industrial society central to their thinking. In Eastern Europe, post-industrialism has usually been given a Marxist gloss, as a 'higher' stage on the way to full socialism, but, with that necessary qualification, East European reception of the post-industrial idea has been remarkably warm.

How plausible is the post-industrial concept? Many of the changes Bell notes in the economy and the occupational structure are undoubtedly occurring. Industrial societies are to a large extent now white-collar, service societies. But that is largely because they have exported their manufacturing sectors to the countries of the Third World, without in any way giving up their control. Multinational corporations have their headquarters in the cities of the 'post-industrial' world, but set up their plants and recruit their work-force in the industrialized world, for obvious reasons of cheapness and political convenience. Hence post-industrial societies contain and continue the ethic and social purpose of industrialism, which in many cases overwhelms the striving towards the newer post-industrial ethic of social responsibility and professional commitment. The same feature is clear in the area to which great importance is attributed, white-collar and professional work. We may be (almost) all professionals now, but much professional work has been 'industrialized' by bureaucratization and the application of computer technology, thus making professional workers increasingly like the proletarians of industrial society. The bulk of research in universities and the R & D (research and development) departments of industry and government is devoted to extensions and refinements of existing products and processes, such as newer car designs or higher-definition television sets. Additionally, research is directed towards newer and more efficient ways of waging war ('defence' and 'space' research) or controlling the population (much applied social science). In neither case can we discern a new social principle at work, such as would signal the coming of a new social order.

In recent years, largely under the stimulus of the writings of Ivan Illich and E.F. Schumacher, a new concept of post-industrialism has grown. In many ways this harks back to the original usage of the term by Penty. It picks out the features of modern society which genuinely suggest a movement *beyond* industrialism, rather than, as with Bell, a continuation of it. Although nostalgia for preindustrial life plays some part in this reformulation, the more serious thinkers look to the most advanced sectors of modern technology and organization to supply the building-blocks of the new society. They are especially impressed by the capacity of modern technology to abolish work: work, that is, as paid employment. Left to itself, this process can take the disastrous shape of mass unemployment and a reversion to the social conflicts of the 1930s. But they see also an opportunity which can be seized, given the political will. Work in the highly rationalized formal economy can be reduced to a minimum and shared out equally. From the wages for such work, together with some form of minimum income guarantee, we can purchase the 'appropriate' or 'intermediate' technology needed to deliver a good deal of the goods and services we require. Work can largely be organized in the 'informal economy' around a revived local domestic or communal economy. And if such a future society contains in it the elements of a pre-industrial way of life, reversing some of the tendencies towards centralization and large-scale bureaucratic organization inherent in industrialism, it is the no less post-industrial for that.

Krishan Kumar
University of Kent

Further Reading
Garshuny, J. (1978), *After Industrial Society?*, London.
Kumar, K. (1978), *Prophecy and Progress: The Sociology of Industrial and Post-Industrial Society*, Harmondsworth.
See also: *futurology*.

Poverty

The notion of poverty and the reality of attitudes and behaviour towards those classed as poor occur and recur in many societies and at different historical periods. It is correspondingly easy to assume both homogeneity and continuity in idea and response. It is as if the poor, deserving or undeserving (to use a distinction which, despite the Webbs, dates at least from medieval times), are always with us, and it is the same poor and the same desert or blame to which we refer. Such a tendency is reinforced by the close connection between poverty, a particular response to it (that is, the Poor Laws), and the emergence of the comparatively new discipline of social administration. However, it is essential to recognize that the idea of poverty, responses to the poor and the causes of the condition of poverty vary between societies and over time. In the Apostolic age of the Christian Church, for instance, the poor were extolled as 'the temple of God', but in the early eighteenth century, the dramatist

Farquhar could write 'Tis still my maxim, that there's no scandal like rags, nor any crime as shameful as poverty' (*The Beaux Stratagem*).

The ways in which poverty has been more recently conceptualized have undergone striking changes. The 1834 Report of the Royal Commission on the Poor Laws described a long-established use when it distinguished indigence from poverty. The former was 'the state of a person unable to labour, or unable to obtain, in return for his labour, the means of subsistence', whereas poverty referred to the more general condition of 'one who, in order to obtain a mere subsistence, is forced to have recourse to labour'. The idea of mere or simple subsistence held sway throughout the nineteenth century but it came to be questioned largely as a result of attempts at the systematic measurement of poverty in order that some estimate might be formed of the proportion of the society that could be described as poor. The most important study was Charles Booth's *Life and Labour of the People in London*, but it is perhaps Seebohm Rowntree's discussion of primary subsistence poverty that most clearly demonstrated its artificial and asocial basis. 'A family living upon the scale allowed for in this estimate must never spend a penny on railway fare or omnibus . . . . They must never purchase a halfpenny newspaper . . . . They must write no letters to absent children. They must never contribute anything to their church or chapel, or give any help to a neighbour which costs them money' (*A Study of Town Life*, 1899).

Such criticism of subsistence poverty has been extended in the present century. Poverty has come to be seen as a deficiency in resources that significantly hampers or prevents participation in events and relationships that give life meaning. More recently, the idea of poverty has been closely allied with that of inequality. Townsend (1979), carrying on the tradition of measurement, attempts through the idea of relative deprivation to establish both a new and a more objective notion of poverty. In addition, he has successfully argued that poverty should now be seen and measured in a worldwide context.

Changes in conception and an increasing sophistication in measurement should be viewed within the context of the changing social significance of poverty. At different times in Western society the poor have been described and treated as making a special claim on philanthropy or as a burden to be carried by public authority, local or central (so definitions of poverty will encompass those conditions that justify the particular response of state relief). At other times the poor are treated as an affront to social justice or, particularly if they can be additionally described as 'dangerous', 'perishing' or 'undeserving', as a symbolic or actual threat to the social order.

Measures specifically adopted in response to indigence and poverty have played a significant role in maintaining social attitudes to poverty, and they reveal in their working and innovation different beliefs concerning the causes of poverty. So, emphasis has moved from belief that poverty is a consequence of individual fate or fault to the idea that it is a major feature of a shared lower-class culture, or that it results from faulty socialization that is transmitted through the generations. These and other notions of causation struggle with the more simple belief that all that is wrong with the poor is that they do not have enough money.

Historically, the Poor Laws mark the first state intervention and they merit special attention, not simply because their history stretches from medieval times, but also because the English experiences of their operation led directly to the creation of the National Health Service and indirectly to the construction of other social services precisely as an alternative to the Poor Laws. Study of the Poor Laws has undergone noticeable shifts from the massive administrative work of the Webbs through attempts to link the service more closely to the economic and social conditions of the time to the recent study of Royal Commission Reports as case-studies in the construction of social reality (Green, 1983). The most important recent systematic attempt to combat poverty was the American War on Poverty launched by President Johnson. This proceeded largely on the assumption that previous attempts had failed to tackle major problems concerning service access, service delivery and service governance.

Noel Timms
University of Leicester

References

Green, B. S. (1983), *Knowing the Poor. A Case-Study in Textual Reality Construction*, London.

Townsend, P. (1979), *Poverty in the United Kingdom*, Harmondsworth.

Further Reading

Himmelfarb, G. (1984), *The Idea of Poverty – England in the Early Industrial Age*, London.

See also: *human needs; relative deprivation; social welfare policy.*

Power

Definitions of power are legion. To the extent that there is any commonly accepted formulation, power is understood as concerned with the bringing about of consequences. But attempts to specify the concept more rigorously have been fraught with disagreements. There are three main sources of these disagreements: different disciplines within the social sciences emphasize different bases of power (for example, wealth, status, knowledge, charisma, force, authority); different forms of power (such as influence, coercion, control); and different uses of power (such as individual or community ends, political ends, economic ends). Consequently, they emphasize different aspects of the concept, according to their theoretical and practical interests. Definitions of power have also been deeply implicated in debates in social and political theory on the essentially conflicting or consensual nature of social and political order. Further complications are introduced by the essentially messy nature of the term. It is not clear if power is a zero-sum concept (Mills, 1956; Parsons, 1960); if it refers to a property of an agent (or system), or to a relationship between agents (or systems) (Arendt, 1970; Parsons, 1963; Lukes, 1974); if it can be a potential or a resource (Wrong, 1979; Barry, 1976); if it is reflexive or irreflexive, transitive or intransitive (Cartwright, 1959); nor is it clear if power can only describe a property of, or relationship between, individual agents, or if it can be used to describe systems, structures or institutions (Parsons, 1963; Lukes, 1978; Poulantzas, 1979); furthermore, it is not clear whether power necessarily rests on coercion (Cartwright, 1959) or if it can equally rest on shared values and beliefs (Parsons, 1963; Giddens, 1977). Nor is it at all clear that such disputes can be rationally resolved, since it has been argued that power is a theory-dependent term and that there are few, if any, convincing metatheoretical grounds for resolving disputes between competing theoretical paradigms (Lukes, 1974, 1978; Gray, 1983).

In the 1950s discussions of power were dominated by the conflicting perspectives offered by 'power-élite' theories (Mills, 1956), which stressed power as a form of domination (Weber, 1978) exercised by one group over another in the presence of fundamental conflicts of interests; and structural-functionalism (Parsons) which saw power as the 'generalized capacity of a social system to get things done in the interests of collective goals' (Parsons, 1960). Parsons thus emphasized power as a systems *property*, as a *capacity* to achieve ends; whereas Mills viewed power as a relationship in which one side prevailed *over* the other. Mills's views were also attacked by pluralists who argued that he assumed that some group necessarily dominates a community; rather, they argued, power is exercised by voluntary groups representing coalitions of interests which are often united for a single issue and which vary considerably in their permanence (Dahl, 1957, 1961; Polsby, 1963). Against class and élite theorists the pluralists posed a view of American society as 'fragmented into congeries of small special-interest groups with incompletely overlapping memberships, widely differing power bases, and a multitude of techniques for exercising influence on decisions salient to them' (Polsby, 1963). Their perspective was rooted in a commitment to the study of observable decision making, in that it rejected talk of power in relation to nondecisions (Merelman, 1968; Wolfinger, 1971), the

mobilization of bias, or to such disputable entities as 'real interests'. It was precisely this focus on observable decision making which was criticized by neo-élite and conflict theorists (Bachrach and Baratz, 1970; Connolly, 1974; Lukes, 1974), who accused the pluralists of failing to recognize that conflict is frequently managed in such a way that public decision-making processes mask the real struggles and exercises of power; both the selection and formulation of issues for public debate and the mobilization of bias within the community should be recognized as involving power. Lukes (1974) further extended the analysis of covert exercises of power to include cases where A affects B contrary to B's real interests – where B's interests may not be obtainable in the form of held preferences, but where they can be stated in terms of the preferences B would hold in a situation where he exercises autonomous judgement. Radical theorists of power have also engaged with structural-Marxist accounts of class power over questions of whether it makes sense to talk of power without reference to agency (Lukes, 1974; Poulantzas, 1973, 1979). Although these debates have rather dominated recent discussions of power in social and political theory, we should not ignore the work on power in exchange and rational-choice theory (Barry, 1976), nor the further criticisms of stratification theories of power which have been developed from positions as diverse as Luhmann's neo-functionalism (Luhmann, 1979), and Foucault's rather elusive post-structuralism (Foucault, 1980).

Definitional problems seem to be endemic to discussions of power. One major problem is that all accounts of power have to take a stand on whether power is exercised over B whether or not the respect in which B suffers is intended by A. A similar problem concerns whether power is properly restricted to a particular sort of effect which A has on B, or whether it applies in any case in which A has some effect on B. These two elements, intentionality and the significance of effects, allow us to identify four basic views on power and to reveal some of the principal tensions in the concept (White, 1972):

(1) This makes no distinction between A's intended and unintended effects on B; nor does it restrict the term power to a particular set of effects which A has on B. Power thus covers phenomena as diverse as force, influence, education, socialization and ideology. Failing to distinguish a set of significant effects means that power does not identify a specific range of especially important ways in which A is causally responsible for changes in B's environment, experience or behaviour. This view is pessimistically neutral in that it characteristically assumes that power is an ineradicable feature of all social relations, while it makes no presumption that being affected by others in one way or in one area of life is any more significant than being affected in any other. One plausible version

of this view is to see power as the medium through which the social world is produced and reproduced, and where power is not simply a repressive force, but is also productive (Foucault, 1980). Note that with this conception there is no requirement that A could have behaved otherwise. Although this is an odd perspective, it is not incoherent, since it simply uses power to refer to causality in social and interpersonal relations.

(2) This isolates a set of significant effects. Thus, A exercises power over B when A affects B in a manner contrary to B's preferences, interests, needs, and so on. However, there is no requirement that A affect B intentionally, nor that A could have foreseen the effect on B (and thus be said to have obliquely intended it). Poulantzas's Marxism provides one such view by seeing power in terms of 'the capacity of a social class to realize its specific objective interests' (Poulantzas, 1973). Any intentional connotations are eradicated by his insistence that this capacity is determined by structural factors. The capacity of a class to realize its interests 'depends on the struggle of another class, depends thereby on the structures of a social formation, in so far as they delimit the field of class practices' (1973). As agency slips out of the picture, so too does any idea of A intentionally affecting B. Although idiosyncratic, this view does tackle the problem of whether we can talk meaningfully of collectivities exercising power. If we want to recognize the impact which the unintended consequences of one social group's activities have over another, or if we want to recognize that some group systematically prospers while others do not, without attributing to the first group the intention of doing the others down, then we will be pushed towards a view of power which is not restricted solely to those effects A intended or could have foreseen. The pressures against this restriction are evident in Lukes's and Connolly's work. Both accept unintended consequences so as to 'capture conceptually some of the most subtle and oppressive ways in which the actions of some can contribute to the limits and troubles faced by others' (Connolly, 1974). Both writers, however, also recognize that attributions of power are also often attributions of responsibility, and that to allow unintended effects might involve abandoning the possibility of attributing to A responsibility for B's disbenefits. Consequently both equivocate over how far unintended effects can be admitted, and they place weight on notions of A's negligence with regard to B's interests, and on counterfactual conditionals to the effect that A could have done otherwise. Stressing 'significant effects' also raises problems, since the criteria for identifying such effects are hotly disputed. Thus radical theorists criticize pluralists for specifying effects in terms of overridden policy preferences, on the grounds that power is also used to shape or suppress the formation of preferences and the articulation of interests.

Again, two pressures operate, in that it seems sociologically naive to suppose that preferences are always autonomous, yet it is very difficult to identify appropriate criteria for distinguishing autonomous and heteronomous preferences. Taking expressed preferences allows us to work with clearly observable phenomena since B can share the investigator's ascription of power to A – it thus has the advantage of methodological simplicity and congruence with the dependent actor's interpretation. However, taking 'repressed' preferences or real interests can be justified, since it provides a more theoretically persuasive account of the complexities of social life and of the multiple ways in which potential conflicts are prevented from erupting into crisis. Yet this more complex theoretical account is under pressure to identify a set of real interests, and the temptation is to identify them in terms of autonomous/rational preferences; the problem with this is that it often carries the underlying implication that power would not exist in a society in which all agents pursued their real interests. Power is thus used to decribe our deviation from utopia (Gray, 1983).

(3) The second view is primarily concerned with identifying the victims of power – not the agents. The focus is on A's power *over* B. The third view, which attributes power only when A intends to affect B, but which does not place any restrictions on the manner in which A affects B, switches the focus from A's power *over* B to A's power *to* achieve certain ends (Russell, 1938; Wrong, 1979). Power is concerned with the agent's ability to bring about desired consequences – 'even' but not necessarily 'against the resistance of others' (Weber, 1978). This view has a long pedigree (Hobbes, 1651), and it satisfies some important theoretical interests. In so far as we are interested in using A's power as a predictor of A's behaviour, it is clearly in our interests to see A's power in terms of A's ability to secure high net profit from an action – the greater the anticipated profit, the more likely A is to act (Barry, 1976). Another reason for focusing on A's intention is the difficulty in identifying a range of significant effects which is not obviously stipulative. Concentrating on A's intended outcomes allows us to acknowledge that there are a number of ways in which A can secure B's compliance and thereby attain his ends. Thus force, persuasion, manipulation, influence, threats, throffers, offers, and even strategic positioning in decision procedures may all play a role in A's ordering of his social world in a way that maximally secures A's ends. But seeing power solely in terms of A's intentions often degenerates into an analysis where all action is understood in power terms, with behaviour being tactical or strategic to the agent's ends. On this view agents become, literally, game-players or actors, and we are left with a highly reductive account of social structures and institutions (Rogers, 1980).

(4) The last perspective analyses power in terms of both intentional action and significant effects. It concentrates on cases where A gets B to do something A wants which B would not otherwise do. Two sets of difficulties arise here. The first concerns the extensiveness of the concept of power and its relationship with its companion terms, authority, influence, manipulation, coercion, and force. On some accounts power is a covering term for all these phenomena (Russell, 1938); on others it refers to a distinct field of events (Bachrach and Baratz, 1974). Getting B to do something he would not otherwise do may involve mobilizing commitments or activating obligations, and it is common to refer to such compliance as secured through authority. We may also be able to get B to do something by changing B's interpretation of a situation and of the possibilities open to him – using means ranging from influence and persuasion to manipulation. Or we may achieve our will through physical restraint, or force. Finally, we may use threats and throffers in order to secure B's compliance – that is, we may coerce B (Nozick, 1969). In each case A gets B to do something A wants which B would not otherwise do, although each uses different resources (agreements, information, strength, or the control of resources which B either wants or wants to avoid), and each evidences a different mode of compliance (consent, belief, physical compliance, or rational choice). Although exchange and rational-choice theorists have attempted to focus the analysis of power on the final group of cases, to claim that the others are not cases of power is clearly stipulative. Yet it is these other cases which introduce some of the pressures to move away from a focus solely on intended effects and significant affecting. Where A's effect on B is intended, instrumental to A's ends and contrary to B's preferences, and where B complies to avoid threatened costs, we have a case which firmly ties together A's intention and the set of effects identified as significant (B's recognized costs are intended by A and functional to A's objectives). But the other cases all invite extensions, either in the direction of covering cases in which A secures his will, disregarding the nature of the effects on B, or towards cases where B's options or activities are curtailed by others, either unintentionally, or unconditionally. Also, this view of power risks focusing on A's *exercise* of power over B, to the detriment of the alternative and less tautological view (Barry, 1976) that power is a possession, that it may exist without being exercised, and that a crucial dimension of power is where A does not secure B's compliance, but is in a position to do so should he choose. Wealth, status, and so on, are not forms of power, but they are resources which can be used by A to secure B's compliance. And an adequate understanding of power in a given society will include an account of any systematic inequalities and monopolies of such resources, whether they are being used to

capacity or not. The pressure, once again, is against exclusive concentration on A's actual exercise and towards a recognition of A's potential. But once we make this step we are also likely to include cases of anticipatory surrender, and acknowledging these cases places further pressure on us to move beyond easily attributable, or even oblique, intention on A's part. These pressures are resisted mainly by those who seek to construct a clear and rigorous, if stipulative, theoretical model of power. But there is also some equivocation from those who seek to match ascriptions of power with ascriptions of moral responsibility. Part of the radical edge of Lukes's (1974) case stems precisely from the use of ascriptions of power as a basis for a moral critique. But much is problematic in this move. A may act intentionally without being sufficiently sane to be held morally responsible; A may intentionally affect B to B's disbenefit without violating moral norms (as in a chess game, competitions, some exchange relations with asymmetrical results, and so on); and it is also important to recognize that B's compliance must maintain proportionality with A's threat in order for B to be absolved of moral responsibility (Reeve, 1982).

The theoretical and practical pressures which exist at the boundaries of these four possible interpretations of power account for much of the concept's messiness. Each has its attractions. The fourth view is most promising for model or theory building, the third for the prediction and explanation of action, the second for the study of powerlessness and dependency, and the first for the neutral analysis of the strategic but non-intentional logic of social dynamics. Although meta-theoretical grounds for arbitration between competing conceptions of power seem largely absent, we can make a few comments on this issue. Although 'restrictivist' definitions of power may serve specific model and theory-building interests, they inevitably provide a much simplified analysis of social order and interaction. However, more encompassing definitions risk collapsing into confusion. Thus, while there are good theoretical grounds for moving beyond stated preferences to some notion of autonomous preferences – so as, for example, to give a fuller account of B's dependence – we should be cautious about claiming that A is as morally responsible for B's situation as when A intentionally disbenefits B. Indeed, depending on how we construe the relevant counterfactuals, we might deny that agents are liable for many of the effects of their actions. Thus, we might see social life as inevitably conflict ridden, and while we might recognize that some groups systematically lose out it might not be true that A (a member of the élite) intends to disadvantage any individual in particular, or that A could avoid harming B without allowing B to harm him (as in Hobbes's state of nature). Also, although we are free to use several different definitions of power (such as the three dimensions identified by Lukes,

1974), we should recognize that each definition satisfies different interests, produces different results and allows different conclusions, and we need to take great care to avoid confusing the results. Finally, we should recognize that although definitions of power are theory-dependent, they can be criticized in terms of the coherence of the theory, its use of empirical data, and the plausibility of its commitments to positions in the philosophies of mind and action.

Mark Philp
Oriel College, Oxford

References

Arendt, H. (1970), *On Violence*, London.

Bachrach, P. and Baratz, M. S. (1970), *Power and Poverty, Theory and Practice*, Oxford.

Barry, B. (1976), 'Power: an economic analysis', in B. Barry (ed.), *Power and Political Theory*, London.

Cartwright, D. (1959), 'A field theoretical conception of power', in D. Cartwright (ed.), *Studies in Social Power*, Ann Arbor.

Connolly, W. (1974), *The Terms of Political Discourse*, Lexington, Mass.

Dahl, R. (1957), 'The concept of power', *Behavioural Science*, 2.

Dahl, R. (1961), *Who Governs? Democracy and Power in an American City*, New Haven.

Foucault, M. (1980), *Power/Knowledge*, Brighton.

Giddens, A. (1977), '"Power" in the writings of Talcott Parsons', in *Studies in Social and Political Theory*, London.

Gray, J. N. (1983), 'Political power, social theory, and essential contestibility', in D. Miller and L. Siedentop (eds), *The Nature of Political Theory*, Oxford.

Luhmann, N. (1979), *Trust and Power*, London.

Lukes, S. (1974), *Power, A Radical View*, London.

Lukes, S. (1978), 'Power and authority', in T. Bottomore and R. Nisbet (eds), *A History of Sociological Analysis*, London.

Merelman, R. M. (1968), 'On the neo-élitist critique of community power', *American Political Science Review*, 62.

Mills, C. W. (1956), *The Power Elite*, London.

Nozick, R. (1969), 'Coercion', in S. Morgenbesser *et al.* (eds), *Philosophy, Science and Method*, New York.

Parsons, T. (1960), 'The distribution of power in American society', in *Structure and Process in Modern Societies*, Glencoe, Ill.

Parsons, T. (1963), 'On the concept of political power', *Proceedings of the American Philosophical Society*, 107.

Polsby, N. (1963), *Community Power and Political Theory*, New Haven.

Poulantzas, N. (1973), *Political Power and Social Classes*, London.

Poulantzas, N. (1979), *State, Power, Socialism*, London.

Reeve, A. (1982), 'Power without responsibility', *Political Studies*, 3.

Rogers, M. F. (1980), 'Goffman on power hierarchy and status', in J. Ditton (ed.), *The View from Goffman*, London.

Russell, B. (1938), *Power*, London.

Weber, M. (1978 [1922]), *Economy and Society*, eds G. Roth and G. Wittich, Berkeley and Los Angeles. (Original German, *Wirtschaft und Gesellschaft*, Tubingen.)

White, D. M. (1972), 'The problem of power', *British Journal of Political Science*, 2.

Wolfinger, R. E. (1971), 'Nondecisions and the study of local politics', *American Political Science Review*, 65.

Wrong, D. (1979), *Power, its Forms, Bases and Uses*, Oxford.

See also: *authority; leadership; social control.*

Pragmatics

The philosopher Charles Morris (1938) defined syntax, semantics and pragmatics as, respectively, the study of the formal relations among signs, the study of the relation between signs and their denotations, and the study of the relation between signs and their interpreters. Pragmatics is now generally defined as the theory of utterance interpretation, and contrasted with semantics, the theory of sentence meaning.

A major influence has been the philosopher H. P. Grice, whose *William James Lectures* (Harvard, 1967) are fundamental. Grice argued that many aspects of utterance interpretation traditionally regarded as conventional, or semantic, could be more explanatorily treated as conversational, or pragmatic. For Grice, the main difference betwen semantics and pragmatics was that while the semantic context of an utterance is arbitrarily stipulated and unaffected by content or background assumptions, its pragmatic content should in some sense follow from a knowledge of its semantic content together with a knowledge of the context of utterance, a set of background assumptions, and general principles of truthfulness, informativeness, relevance and clarity which speakers are normally expected to observe.

Work on utterance interpretation has been carried out in a variety of disciplines, including psychology, psycholinguistics, linguistics, artificial intelligence, sociolinguistics, philosophy and literary criticism. Two substantive issues have emerged:

(1) Many assume that there are specific principles of utterance interpretation which do not follow from more general cognitive principles. In current jargon, they assume that there is a distinct pragmatic psychological system or *module*. On this approach pragmatics is treated as an extension of linguistics, the aim being

to construct explicit rules which take semantic representations, descriptions of context and background assumptions as input and yield pragmatic interpretations as output. More recently it has been claimed that utterance interpretation is simply the result of interaction among a grammar, a logic and a memory, and that there is no distinct pragmatic module as such.

(2) This issue concerns the universality of pragmatic principles. Grice regarded his pragmatic maxims as principles which all rational human beings should observe. Many pragmatists have argued that the principles governing communication are much more culture dependent or domain dependent than Grice envisaged, and look for variation rather than uniformity of the way utterances are understood. Others maintain, following Grice, that variations in interpretation follow not from variations in pragmatic or cognitive principles, but merely from variations in the context and background assumptions to which they apply.

Because the field of pragmatics is so new and so fragmented, these issues are rarely overtly confronted. For a general survey and bibliography, see Levinson (1983). For an attempt at a unified theory, see Sperber and Wilson (1986).

Deirdre Wilson
University College London

References
Levinson, S. (1983), *Pragmatics*, Cambridge.
Morris, C. W. (1938), *Foundations of the Theory of Signs*, Chicago.
Sperber, D. and Wilson, D. (1986), *Relevance: Communication and Cognition*, Oxford.
See also: *semantics; sociolinguistics.*

Prediction and Forecasting

The periods and time horizons considered in relation to specific forecasting procedures may be short term (1 to 18 months), medium term (½ to 5 years) or long term (over 5 years). Very long-term projections (15–25 years) tend to be more in the nature of perspective plans about the social and physical infrastructure of the country and, apart from the demographic projections, more politically conjectural.

There are two basic analytical approaches to forecasting:

(1) One method tries to outline a pattern of responses by relating the variable to be predicted, such as prices or sales, to all the other significant variables such as output, wage costs, exchange rate variation, imports, that policy makers believe exert a strong influence on its behaviour. This approach rests on a view of what factors are important and the interrelationships between them. A major problem, however, is that most endogenous and exogenous variables are not, in practice, independent. Directly and indirectly the various explanatory and dependent variables react on each other. For example, interest rates in the US affect interest rates and prices in Europe which lead to exchange-rate adjustments. These influence capital flows, which in turn have repercussions on interest rates. The interaction between prices and wages is also well-known and has led to bitter disputes as to 'cause' and 'effect'. To a certain extent, however, such difficulties can be handled (or their importance recognized) in the mechanical techniques chosen. Other features of a more psychological nature, involving expectations motivated by feelings of political uncertainty and individual caution, are less easy to accommodate in any mathematical schema.

(2) An alternative approach produces forecasts on the basis of historical trends and patterns. The procedure tries to quantify and 'formalize' experience in order to replicate, reproduce and extrapolate future trends in the socioeconomic variables of interest (income, production, crime, and so on). The length of past time series, the interval of the observations and their regularity should be closely related to the time horizon considered important. The relationships are rarely of a simple linear or quadratic form and will inevitably reflect a combination of trend, cyclical, seasonal and random shock disturbances.

A particular example of a large and complex economic model of the first kind concerned with short and medium-term projections is the OECD's INTERLINK model. This adopts relatively simple techniques to try and assess the overall international impact of various policy stimuli in different countries. The system links together a large number of individual country models through their international trade relations. Although the specifications of these large-scale national models differ widely, their approach is fundamentally Keynesian and mainly expenditure oriented. They are concerned essentially with the impact of government policies on consumption, investment and the balance of payments. This means that although the INTERLINK system focuses primarily on the broad macroeconomic aggregates necessary to produce the OECD's current individual country and overall economic projections, it still retains the same basic multiplier properties of the official national models. The significance of INTERLINK is that it draws the attention of policy makers to the fact that, increasingly, other countries' policies have an important impact on their own nation's demands and the levels of activity in the domestic economies. In the highly interrelated areas of budgetary finance, interest rates and currency exchange rates, such issues assume particular importance. The model also takes into account international feedback effects such as those that occur when the imports of certain countries (for example, Britain and the US) are affected by the production and exports of another country (for example, Japan), to the extent that these adversely affect the output and exports of the importing countries (Britain and the US). This leads to lower incomes in the importing countries as well as discriminatory trade policies, so that the demand for the goods produced by the exporting country is reduced and production (in Japan) has to be cut back (unless other new markets are found). National models, however sophisticated, rarely take into account these 'echo' effects, where economic disturbances elsewhere in the international system are subsequently transmitted back to their origin through related variables.

Fluctuations in economic activity associated with expansion, contraction and recovery in production and employment regularly occur in industrial countries, and many internal and external factors have been advanced for the existence of such cycles. Whatever the reasons, it is apparent that the fluctuations touch on a wide range of statistical series: income, investment, prices, construction, share values, and so on. Some of these series appear to turn consistently a certain number of months before aggregate economic activity in general. This is not purely by chance; businessmen themselves look for various 'signs' to guide their current production, pricing and marketing strategies, and they react accordingly – often bringing about the particular outcomes they foresee.

In the area of short-term forecasting especially – the field which tends to dominate official policy concerns at the national level – systems of leading indicators are increasingly complementing the use of specified forecasting models. This is not so much because such indicators more accurately predict the values of economic variables but because they better identify when and where cyclical changes are likely to take place. Leading indicators are also a convenient and economical way of obtaining an overall perspective of an economy from a large amount of detailed and potentially interconnected data. 'Good' leading indicators should refer to variables which, historically, have had a strong and stable timing relationship with the turning points of certain economic aggregates during the phases of a business cycle. Such indicators are therefore designed to provide very specific (interval) estimates of the dates for particular cyclical turning points.

A leading indicator system is usually built around a basic economic aggregate or reference series, such as the Gross Domestic Product (GDP) or total industrial production. Other economic series are then classified as to whether they are 'leading', 'coincident' or 'lagging' with respect to this predetermined benchmark variable. Among leading indicators are stock market prices (business confidence proxy), interest rates (investment and credit), inventories and orders (sales), over-time and short-time working (employment adjustment) and the money supply. Conceptually, all such variables must satisfy the requirement of some theoretical justification for the observed relationship. As more evidence is gathered over time and the links appear more sound, confidence in certain indicators increases and some series can be further refined to become better 'predictors'.

Michael Ward
Institute of Development Studies, University of Sussex

References
OECD Economic Outlook (1979), *The OECD International Linkage Model*, Occasional Studies, Paris.
OECD (1982), *OECD Interlink System* vol. 1, *Structure and Operation*, Paris.

Further Reading
Forrester, J. W. (1971), *World Dynamics*, Cambridge, Mass.
Meadows, D. *et al.* (1972), *The Limits to Growth*, New York.
Theil, H. (1961), *Economic Forecasts and Policy*, Amsterdam.
See also: *futurology; population projections.*

Prejudice

The word prejudice means pre-judgement, implying that a prejudiced person is someone who has made up his mind about a certain topic before assessing the relevant information. This sense of pre-judgement has formed an important part of the social psychological concept of prejudice. In addition, three other features are associated with prejudiced beliefs: (1) Prejudice typically refers to beliefs about social groups; it can refer also to judgements about individuals, where an individual is evaluated on the basis of being a member of a particular social group. (2) The belief or judgement is essentially an unfavourable one. Whereas it is logically possible to be prejudiced *in favour* of a group, prejudice usually denotes a negative or hostile attitude *against* a group: racist, anti-semitic and sexist attitudes would all be considered prime examples of prejudice. (3) A prejudiced belief is assumed to be erroneous or liable to lead the believer into error. A prejudice is not based on a realistic assessment of a social group, nor is contact with the group likely to overturn the prejudices. Thus Allport, in his classic discussion of prejudice, wrote 'pre-judgements become prejudices only if they are not reversible when exposed to new knowledge' (1958).

Part of the prejudiced person's error derives from a tendency to think about social groups in terms of stereotypes. In one of the first social psychological investigations of stereotypes, Katz and Braly (1935) found amongst American college students a widespread tendency to ascribe clichéd descriptions to different social groups: thus the stereotype of Blacks included the traits of being 'superstitious' and 'lazy', that of Jews as 'mercenary' and 'grasping', that of Turks as 'cruel' and 'treacherous', and so on. By thinking in such stereotypes, the prejudiced person not only has an unfavourable concept of the groups as a whole but he also exaggerates the percentage of individuals who might happen to possess the stereotyped trait; in the case of extreme prejudice, he will believe that *all* Jews or *all* Blacks possess the unfavourable traits in question.

Early research into prejudice assumed a direct relation between holding prejudiced beliefs and behaving in a discriminatory way to members of the relevant outgroup. For example, the Bogardus Distance Scale asked respondents whether they would entertain having close relations (such as marriage) or less close relations (such as working in the same place) with particular outgroups. It was assumed that the respondent's replies would predict actual behaviour towards members of outgroups. However, research into attitude theory in general has revealed that the views expressed in attitude questionnaires do not necessarily reflect behaviour.

In consequence, it is now recognized that the relations between prejudice and discrimination are more complex than was formerly thought.

Among the many theories used to explain the psychological roots of prejudice, it is possible to distinguish between motivational and learning theories. Motivational theories have sought to relate prejudiced attitudes to personality defects or to unfulfilled yearnings within the individual. These are often called 'scapegoat' theories in that they assume that the victims of prejudice are being irrationally blamed for ills that reside within the prejudiced person. One such scapegoat theory is the frustration–aggression theory (originally proposed by Dollard *et al.* (1939) and reformulated by Berkowitz (1962)). It asserts that prejudice arises when an individual has been angered by some frustration and is unable, for some reason or other, to direct this anger back on to the source of the frustration. Instead, the anger is displaced onto an innocent target. This theory has been employed, for instance, to explain why minority groups may become targets of increased prejudice in times of economic deprivation. Another motivational theory is that of Adorno *et al.* (1950) which seeks to account for prejudice in terms of the repressed hostility of authoritarian-type personalities: such people, it is argued, direct their hostilities on to weak outgroups because of their own personal inadequacies.

Motivational theories as general theories of prejudice are limited. For example, they fail to explain why particular targets are chosen for prejudice and not others; they also tend to understate the extent to which prejudiced beliefs might be the product of learning.

Pettigrew's comparison of the different levels of prejudice in South Africa and the United States showed that personality factors were less important than the existence of cultural traditions (Pettigrew, 1958). In the case of White South Africans these traditions had resulted in prejudiced beliefs, which were so widely accepted that they had become normative and, by contrast, tolerance was regarded as socially deviant. Thus, within such a prejudiced society, children are likely to be socialized through learning into acquiring prejudiced beliefs; the displacement of underlying motivations need not feature in the process.

Much of the recent research in social psychology has concentrated upon the cognitive aspects of prejudice and investigates prejudice in terms of the ways people generally perceive and make sense of the world. This research suggests that a large degree of prejudiced thinking is not the result of 'abnormal' psychological processes. Jerome Bruner (1958) and Henri Tajfel (1981) have indicated that people are not passive recipients of information; rather, they try to make sense of incoming stimuli. Thus 'normal' perception involves a certain amount of error and simplification as information is categorized and assessed according to pre-judgements, which in turn determine what is perceived or experienced. Stereotyped thinking represents an extreme case of such processes, with the stereotype influencing what aspects of the social world are selected for attention and how these aspects are interpreted. For example, a person who views a particular group as lazy will often unconsciously seek confirmation of his stereotype and ignore contradictory evidence. In addition, ambiguous evidence will be interpreted in support of the idea that the group is lazy, and the result will be a perception of that group with a systematic distortion which appears to confirm the stereotype. If the stereotype is widely held within a society, then not only will it pass as common sense, and social pressures will promote the stereotype, but cognitive processes may prevent believers from becoming aware of their own biases.

Michael Billig
Loughborough University

References

Adorno, T. W., Frenkel-Brunswik, E., Levinson, D. J. and Sanford, R. N. (1950), *The Authoritarian Personality*, New York.

Allport, G. W. (1958), *The Nature of Prejudice*, Garden City, N.Y.

Berkowitz, L. (1962), *Aggression: A Social Psychological Analysis*, New York.

Bruner, J. S. (1958), 'Social psychology and perception', in E. E. Maccoby, T. W. Newcomb and E. L. Hartley (eds), *Readings in Social Psychology*, London.

Dollard, J. L., Doob, W., Miller, N. E., Mowrer, O. H. and Sears, R. R. (1939), *Frustration and Aggression*, New Haven.

Katz, D. and Braly, K. W. (1935), 'Racial prejudice and racial stereotypes', *Journal of Abnormal and Social Psychology*, 30.

Pettigrew, T. F. (1958), 'Personality and sociocultural factors in intergroup attitudes: a cross national comparison', *Journal of Conflict Resolution*, 2.

Tajfel, H. (1981), *Human Groups and Social Categories*, Cambridge,

Further Reading

Hamilton, D. L. (1979), 'A cognitive-attributional analysis of stereotyping', in L. Berkowitz (ed.), *Advances in Experimental Social Psychology*.
See also: *attitudes; authoritarian personality; conflict resolution; ethnic relations; labelling theory; stereotypes.*

Prestige

The word prestige comes from the medieval Latin (*prestigiae*), meaning a conjurer's tricks or deception. There still clings to the term a rich hint of illusion. Present usage covers a variety of meanings, including the conception of prestige as a fixed attribute of positions in the stratification order (Rothman, 1978), the conception that prestige is relational, based on the evaluation and recognition by the audience of the bearer's claims (Simmel, 1950; Goode, 1978), and a rarer view that prestige is the aura of success or glamour projected by the individual. On these definitions, the location of prestige could be in the social structure, or the relationship between bearer and audience, or the innate qualities of the person or group. Variations abound: for example, Eisenstadt (1968) mentions that prestige, a basic societal reward, is symbolic of the individual's status; and Goldthorpe and Hope (1972) define prestige as a form of symbolic power that eventuates in structured relationships of deference and honour. T.H. Marshall (1964) addresses the problem of using prestige interchangeably with, or in place of, status. He sees prestige as less formal and institutionalized, more dynamic and person-centred than status. Hence, he calls prestige 'personal social status', distinguishing it from 'positional social status'.

Characteristics

Prestige can be achieved through personal effort or ascribed by inherited characteristics. It is usually demonstrated by material or symbolic rewards which the bearer sports or manipulates.

Prestige can be attributed to a person, a group, or any social unit, varying along a continuum from high to low prestige; and its acknowledgement might be limited to a small circle or expanded to a larger one. Prestige is always a scarce commodity, its allocation uneven. In every society, reflective of cultural values, some groups are defined as inherently worthy, and others are perceived as incapable of prestige.

People make evaluations of whether or not prestige is deserved. Even when claims are spurious, the audience can accept and anoint the undeserving prestigious; and it can reject claims that at other times might have been seen as genuine. Important attributes of the audience are its values, size, and its commitment to the prestige object. Attributes of the bearer centre on the basis of prestige, manner of expression, and response to the audience. Benefits accrue to both sets of participants: to the bearer go direct rewards, to the audience might come a sense of identification with the mighty or the beautiful or the talented (Turner, 1964), and the possibility of community with each other.

Sources

The values which are considered worthy and which prestigious individuals come to symbolize vary from locale to locale, their number increasing with the complexity of the society. Each social hierarchy – class, status, power – can generate prestige. As C. Wright Mills tells us (1963): 'A society may, in fact, contain many hierarchies of prestige, each with its own typical bases and areas of bestowal.'

A sizeable literature testifies that occupation is perceived by many sociologists as the primary source of prestige. The landmark study (National Opinion Reasearch Center, 1946), based on interviews in which people were asked to rank occupations, yielded a prestige scale. Since then many studies have replicated and extended the findings, establishing that nationally and internationally (Inkeles and Rossi, 1956) people tend to agree on the relative prestige of occupations. However, a basic criticism has been posed (Goldthorpe and Hope, 1972 and 1974): just what do the scales *actually measure*? The facile response that they reflect prestige values is open to question.

Charlotte Wolf
Memphis State University

References

Eisenstadt, S. N. (1968), 'Prestige, participation, and strata formation', in J. A. Jackson (ed.), *Social Stratification*, Cambridge.

Goldthorpe, J. H. and Hope, K. (1972), 'Occupational grading and occupational prestige', in K. Hope (ed.), *The Analysis of Social Mobility. Methods and Approaches*. Oxford.

Goldthorpe, J. H. and Hope, K. (1974), *The Social Grading of Occupations: A New Approach and Scale*, Oxford.

Gerth, H. and Mills, C. W. (1953), *Character and Social Structure*, New York.

Goode, W. J. (1978), *The Celebration of Heroes. Prestige as a Social Control System*, Berkeley and Los Angeles.

Inkeles, A. and Rossi, P. (1956), 'National comparisons of occupational prestige', *American Journal of Sociology*, 61.

Marshall, T. H. (1964), *Class, Citizenship, and Social Development*, Garden City, N.Y.

Mills, C. W. (1963), 'The sociology of stratification', in I. L. Horowitz (ed.), *Power, Politics and People*, New York.

Reiss, A. J., Jr (1961), *Occupations and Social Status*, New York.

Rothman, R. (1978), *Inequality and Stratification in the United States*, Englewood Cliffs, N.J.

Simmel, G. (1950), *The Sociology of Georg Simmel*, trans. and ed. K. R. Wolff, Glencoe, Ill.

Turner, R. (1964), *The Social Context of Ambition. A Study of High School Seniors in Los Angeles*, San Francisco.

Further Reading

Spier, H. (1937), 'Freedom and social planning', *American Journal of Sociology*, 42.

Wolf, C. (1978), 'Social class, status, and prestige', *Social Control for the 1980's*, Westport, Connecticut.

See also: *status; stratification.*

Prices, Theory of

The theory of prices lies at the heart of neoclassical economics. Its twin components of optimization and equilibrium form the basis of much of modern economic analysis. Not surprisingly, then, the theory of prices is also a showcase for economic analysis – reflecting its strength but also exposing its weaknesses.

The neoclassical theory of prices considers a stylized economy consisting of consumers and producers and the set of commodities which are consumed and produced. The object of the theory is to analyse the determination of the prices of these commodities. Given a set of prices, one for each commodity, consumers are assumed to decide on their consumption pattern in order to maximize a utility function representing their tastes between the different commodities. They are assumed to take prices as parametric and to choose commodity demands and factor supplies in order to maximize utility, subject to a budget constraint which says that expenditure (on commodities consumed) cannot exceed income (from selling factors, which are included in the list of commodities). Producers also take prices as parametric, but they maximize profits (revenue from selling commodities minus costs of purchasing factors of production), subject to technological constraints, these profits being distributed back to consumers. Consumers' commodity demands and factor supplies can be seen as functions of the parametric prices and producers' commodity supplies, and factor demands can also be seen as functions of these prices. Given these functions, derived from utility

maximization and from profit maximization, we can ask the following question: does there exist a set of *equilibrium* commodity and factor prices, such that all markets clear, that is, the aggregate demand for each commodity and each factor equals aggregate supply?

If such a set of prices existed and if the economy tended towards these prices, then the above theory of prices (that they are determined in a manner so as to balance supply and demand) would have relevance. The existence question was settled in the early postwar period, culminating in the work of Debreu (1959) – for which he has been awarded the Nobel Prize in Economics. Mathematically, the problem is one of finding a solution to a set of non-linear equations in the price vector. The major mathematical theorem that is invoked is the Fixed Point Theorem – which says that any continuous map from a compact convex set into itself has a fixed point, that is, there is an element such that that element is mapped back into itself. The requirement that prices lie in a compact convex set is met if we notice that the entire system described above is homogeneous of degree zero in prices – scaling all prices by a given number leaves all decisions unaltered. For example, doubling all commodity and factor prices would not alter the optimal combinations of commodity supplies and factor demands – the profit at the old combinations would merely be doubled. Consumers' profit income would, therefore, double, as would their factor incomes and expenditures on commodities – the pattern of consumption and factor supply would be the same as it was before. Given such homogeneity of the system, we can in effect restrict prices to be such that they add up to unity. This, together with the fact that they are not allowed to be negative, restricts the price vector to lie in the unit simplex, which is a compact, convex set.

The next key requirement is that of continuity; we need individual demand and supply functions to be continuous in the prices which form their arguments. As shown in the diagrams below for a *single* market, a discontinuity in supply or demand functions could lead to there being no price at which supply equals demand. Continuity, along with the other assumptions of the fixed point theorem, guarantees existence of an equilibrium set of prices. But what guarantees continuity? Since the demand and supply curves are derived from

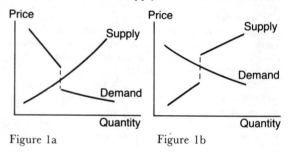

Figure 1a   Figure 1b

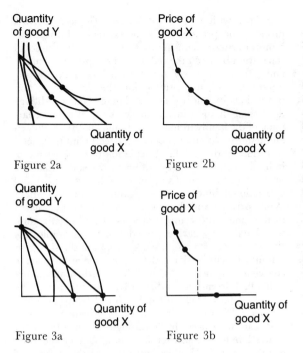

Figure 2a

Figure 2b

Figure 3a

Figure 3b

the maximization decisions of producers and consumers, the answer must lie in the objective functions and in the constraints of these problems. In fact, it is convexity of individual indifference curves that guarantees continuity of commodity demands and factor supplies as functions of the price vector. The diagrams above show convex and concave indifference curves, together with the corresponding continuous and discontinuous demand functions. A similar analysis would apply to production technology, profit maximization and the continuity of the resulting supply functions.

If the equilibrium price vector exists, then we have a theory of prices – a theory which relies on the role of prices as co-ordinating the independent demand and supply decisions of individuals, which are based in turn on quite independent optimization. But will the equilibrium price vector be attained? For this we need to consider *dynamics*, how the economy moves when it is out of equilibrium. The simple way of thinking about this is to consider what happens in a given market when the price is such that supply exceeds demand. Then, it is argued, there will be a downward pressure on prices as the excess supply makes itself felt. Similarly, when price is such that demand exceeds supply, the price will rise and reduce this gap. The limit of this process, occurring in all markets simultaneously, will be to move the price vector to its equilibrium pattern. The 'Invisible Hand' of Adam Smith leads the market to a state of rest.

If the above account were acceptable, then we would have a theory of the determination of prices – the forces of supply and demand would move the economy towards a price such that all markets clear. There are, however, at least two flies in the ointment: (1) Recall the assumption of price taking behaviour, which formed the logical basis for deriving supply and demand curves. As Arrow once remarked, if everybody is a price taker, then who changes the price? (2) If a market does not clear at the going price, some agents will be rationed – they will either not be able to purchase what they wish to purchase or to sell what they wish to sell. It then seems plausible that they will recalculate their demands on the basis of these new constraints – which, again, destroys the earlier basis for calculation of supply and demand curves.

Orthodox theory has invented the fiction of an 'auctioneer' who performs the twin tasks of adjusting prices in response to disequilibrium, along with the fiction that no trade can take place out of equilibrium, in order to overcome the above problems. But this is no more than a device to maintain the formal structure of the theory. Once the artificial construct of the auctioneer is removed, the theory breaks down. Since the theory cannot guarantee convergence to equilibrium prices within its own logical framework, it is a theory of prices only in so far as the economy is in equilibrium. This is fine for the theory, but supply and demand equilibrium has certain features which are directly at variance with observed reality – involuntary unemployment, for example. Since supply of labour equals demand for labour in equilibrium, and the theory of prices only permits considerations of supply and demand equilibrium, the theory which claims to account for the determination of prices cannot account for the phenomenon of unemployment. These features have been stressed recently by Malinvaud (1977).

The orthodox theory of prices outlined here can and has been extended to cover time, by use of the device of 'dated goods'. A commodity is now defined in terms of its consumption characteristics as well as in terms of its location in time. The number of goods is thus increased by a factor equal to the number of time periods considered in the analysis. Markets are supposed to exist *now* for all future goods, and an equilibrium set of prices is determined in exactly the same way as before. A similar device is used to introduce uncertainty. Uncertainty is captured in terms of a probability distribution over which 'state of nature' will rule at a given point in time. Goods are then distinguished according to the time and the state of nature in which they are consumed – an umbrella today if the sun shines is a different good from an umbrella today if it rains, and each of these is, in turn, different from an umbrella tomorrow if it rains, and so on. Once again, markets are assumed to exist *now* for these future 'contingent' commodities, and prices for these goods are determined by equilibrium of demand and supply. It is, of course, a major requirement of the theory that these markets for state contingent goods exist now. If they do not, then equilibrium may not exist, as shown, for example, by Hart (1975).

To summarize, the modern neoclassical theory of prices attempts to provide a rigorous basis for Adam Smith's claim that an 'Invisible Hand' leads markets to a situation in which the optimizing decisions of agents are rendered consistent with each other. The modern theory demonstrates precisely the conditions under which this must be true. In doing so in a formal and rigorous way, it shows how implausible it is that equilibrium, even if it exists, will be obtained. Of course, in conducting this analysis, the modern theory neglects institutional features of actual economics – the analysis is in an abstract setting. But it seems unlikely that if the validation of the co-ordinating role of markets is questionable in the abstract setting, it will be any more plausible once the institutional constraints have been introduced.

Ravi Kanbur
University of Essex

References
Debreu, G. (1959), *Theory of Value*, New Haven.
Hart, O. (1975), 'On the optimality of equilibrium when the market structure is incomplete', *Journal of Economic Theory*.
Malinvaud, E. (1977), *The Theory of Unemployment Reconsidered*, Oxford.
See also: *markets*; *neoclassical economics*.

Primitive Art

See Art, Anthropology of.

Privacy

Privacy as a value is often regarded as an essentially modern development, emerging out of the liberalism of nineteenth-century writers like J.S. Mill. In the Classical world, the private was associated with withdrawal from the public sphere and hence with deprivation (*privatus*), while the public arena was defined by positive values and was the social space which embraced freedom. The process of industrialization has reversed this moral evaluation, since the public domain is often regarded as artificial and constraining in contrast to the freedom of the domestic domain. The home is a private castle, behind which men enjoy rewards of labour outside the family. This cultural contrast which equates the public sphere with necessity and the private world with freedom is, from a feminist perspective, only characteristic of men. The private thus had largely negative connotations, whereas in contemporary society the notion of private is typically

associated with privilege (Williams, 1976) as in 'private property' or 'private club'. The existence of privacy as a moral criterion presupposes (1) a clear institutional separation between the public and the private domain, and (2) a system of beliefs which emphasizes the importance of the private for the cultivation and protection of individuality. These two conditions developed in the nineteenth century with the separation of the family from the economy, allocating women and children to an area characterized by intimacy and seclusion, and with the articulation of the doctrine of individual liberty in opposition to the state. Like the doctrine of individualism, 'privacy' had a critical and oppositional dimension as a critique of standardization. While privacy and the private are thus firmly located in the nineteenth-century process of industrialization, they have many earlier precedents. For example, the Protestant Reformation (Weber, 1930) of the sixteenth century, by emphasizing the importance of the private conscience in matters of doctrinal truth, isolated the individual from the authoritative institutions of the church. Alternatively, it can be argued (Hepworth and Turner 1982) that the revolution in private consciousness can be traced back through the institution of confession to the penitential handbooks of the thirteenth century. Another indication of the growth of privacy as a moral standard is the emergence of the autobiography as the dominant form of literary expression by 1800. An important turning point in this development was the retirement of Michel Eyquem de Montaigne in 1570 from public office and the publication of his *Essays*, which exhibit a modern sense of the subtlety of the interior, private person (Weintraub, 1978).

While the nineteenth-century evaluation of privacy has precursors, the liberal view of private life is distinctive in that privacy became a peculiar point of anxiety. The private world was suddenly threatened by powerful social agencies: the extension of state power, the threat of mass democracy, the surveillance of the individual by schools, factories and hospitals, the increasing documentation of the individual by bureaucracy, and the professionalization of the police and other custodial occupations. In the heyday of liberalism, Alexis de Tocqueville noted the danger to personal freedoms which was the unintended consequence of mass politics. In sociology, Max Weber saw capitalism as an *iron cage* which, through a process he called 'rationalization', would subordinate people to a new system of public domination and reduce the individual to a mere cog in the machine. More recently, Michel Foucault (1975) and Jacques Donzelot (1977) have conceptualized modern society as a network of 'disciplines' which police the individual from the cradle to the grave: society, in this view, is a system of surveillance. Within this analysis, modern society is fundamentally paradoxical. A capitalist system requires individualism because the consumption of commodities depends on private hedonism, suitably stimulated by commercial advertising. At the same time, it produces individuation, that is, the standardization of persons for purposes of taxation, registration and surveillance. In this contradiction between private individualism and public individuation the individuality of the private person is progressively undermined within an administered society. The growth of computer technology and systems of information storage and retrieval reinforces the process by which the public domain invades and undermines the privacy of individual citizens.

From a different perspective, privacy is itself treated as an ideology of capitalist society. The notion of the private individual is a facet of bourgeois ideology which legitimates private property through the doctrine of individual rights. Privacy is thus seen as a primarily conservative belief – a necessary adjunct to private appropriation. The relationship between beliefs and social structure is, however, more complex than this view would suggest. 'Civil privatism' is partly undermined by the development of complex society, because urban life requires a social infrastructure (health, transportation, education, communication systems and leisure), much of which is provided by the state (Habermas, 1976). In the language of Marxist urban sociology, there is a steady growth of collective consumption of urban facilities over private appropriation. The normative image of the private Robinson Crusoe becomes increasingly archaic with the development of capitalist society. Thus, while the disappearance of Private Man is often seen to be a direct consequence of technological advances (particularly in computer technology), the rise and fall of privacy is in fact the effect of culture and social structure. Privacy is a social principle for the division of cultural space, reflecting changes in the relationship between the person, the family and the economy.

Bryan S. Turner
Flinders University of South Australia

References
Donzelot, J. (1977), *The Policing of Families*, New York. (Original French, *La Police des familles*, Paris.)
Foucault, M. (1977(1975)), *Discipline and Punish, Birth of the Prison*, London. (Original French, *Surveiller et punir: naissance de la prison*, Paris.)
Habermas, J. (1976 [1973]), *Legitimation Crisis*. London. (Original German, *Legitimationsprobleme im Spatkapitalismus*. Frankfurt.)
Hepworth, M. and Turner, B. S. (1982), *Confession, Studies in Deviance and Religion*, London.
Mill, J. S. (1971 [1874]), *Autobiography*, London.
Weber, M. (1930 [1904–5]), *The Protestant Ethic and the Spirit of Capitalism*, London. (Original German, 'Die protestantische Ethik und der Geist des Kapitalismus', *Archiv fur Sozialwissenschaft und Zozialpolitik*.)
Weintraub, K. (1978), *The Value of the Individual, Self and Circumstance in Autobiography*, Chicago.
Williams, R. (1976), *Keywords, A Vocabulary of Culture and Society*, London.
See also: *freedom*.

Problem Solving

Problem solving is a major function of thought and has long been researched in cognitive psychology. Since the information-processing approach to cognitive psychology became theoretically dominant in the early 1960s, thinking has generally been regarded as a serial symbol manipulation process that makes use of a very limited working memory, supported by an extensive long-term memory. This approach has been fruitful and, by emphasizing both analysis and organization, largely avoids the dangers of elementarism and vagueness which had beset the earlier behaviourist and Gestalt approaches. Much of the recent research on problem solving has focused on 'move' and reasoning tasks which I discuss in this article.

Move Problems
In this class of well-defined tasks, objects or quantities have to be manipulated (in reality or symbolically) in order to change some given starting configuration into a goal configuration. Normally, the available moves or actions are specified for the would-be solver at the start. Move problems may or may not involve an adversary. Non-adversary move problems, especially small-scale, artificial puzzles, have been extensively investigated. The importance of prior experience with the problem area has clearly emerged in the study of adversary move problems. De Groot (1965) found that both amateur and grand master level chess players searched mentally to similar extents when asked to choose the best next move in a given board position; but, the grand masters always came up with a better move. A series of studies involving memory for realistic and randomly arranged chess boards showed that grand masters have developed a very extensive network of familiar patterns in terms of which they can efficiently encode new positions (De Groot, 1965; Chase and Simon, 1973). Similar results regarding expertise have also been found in the games of GO (Eisenstadt and Kareev, 1977) and Bridge (Charness, 1979).

Reasoning Problems
Deductive and inductive reasoning problems have recently been the focus of considerable attention. In the deductive area, the syllogism has been a favourite experimental task. The somewhat venerable 'atmosphere' hypothesis, according to which the presence of

particulars or negatives in the premises colours the conclusions reached (Woodworth and Sells, 1935), still seems to be *descriptively* useful in summarizing error patterns (Begg and Denny, 1969), although the explanation for these patterns is still controversial, for the following reasons:

(1) The arguments of Henle (1962) for human rationality, which stressed the discrepancies between experimenters' and subjects' interpretations of syllogistic tasks, have been very influential. (2) Phenomena that are not accounted for by the atmosphere hypothesis have been uncovered, for example, Johnson-Laird's (1975) finding that the order of the premises affects the nature of the conclusion drawn. Johnson-Laird and Steedman (1978) were able to account for this 'figural bias' effect and for other fine grain results with a computer simulation that embodied a very promising 'analogical' model of reasoning.

Inductive reasoning has been intensively studied, especially in the contexts of concept learning and Wason's 4-card task. In the case of concept learning, Bruner, Goodnow and Austin (1956) noticed a reluctance among their subjects to attempt falsification of current hypotheses, and this apparent 'set' for verification was the starting point for a long series of studies by Wason and others using the 4-card task. In this task, subjects have to say which cards need to be turned over to test a conditional rule relating the showing and the not-showing faces of the cards. For example, the rule might be 'if there is an "A" on one side there is a "4" on the other side'. Given cards showing A, B, 4 and 7, which need to be turned over? (Answer, A and 7). Most subjects do not choose the potentially falsifying '7' card. Johnson-Laird and Wason (1970) interpreted this result as showing 'verification bias'. A number of subsequent studies found improved performance if the materials were thematic rather than abstract (Wason and Shapiro, 1971; but see Manktelow and Evans, 1979, for a cautionary note). Facilitation was also found if the rules were of dubious truth-value (Pollard and Evans, 1981) or if certain ambiguities in the standard task were clarified (Smalley, 1974). While many have interpreted the above pattern of results in a manner akin to Henle's analysis of interpretation factors in syllogistic reasoning, Evans (1980) proposed that most responses to the standard form of the task are due to an unconscious, nonrational, 'matching bias'. Supporting evidence comes from the high success rates found with negative 'if-then' rules, coupled with zero transfer to positive rules.

Concluding Comments
Overall, the results of recent research on problem solving are consistent with the standard information-processing assumptions of serial processing, limited working memory and vast long-term memory. Perhaps not surprisingly, data from studies of daydreaming and creative thinking suggest, however, that more complex models will be required to explain thought in general (Gilhooly, 1982) than seem required for the special case of 'problem solving'.

K. J. Gilhooly
University of Aberdeen

References
Begg, I. and Denny, J. P. (1969), 'Empirical reconciliation of atmosphere and conversion interpretations of syllogistic reasoning errors', *Journal of Experimental Psychology*, 81.
Bruner, J. S., Goodnow, J. J. and Austin, G. A. (1956), *A Study of Thinking*, New York.
Charness, N. (1979), 'Components of skill in bridge', *Canadian Journal of Psychology*, 33.
Chase, W. G. and Simon, H. A. (1973), 'Perception in chess', *Cognitive Psychology*, 4.
De Groot, A. D. (1965), *Thought and Choice in Chess*, The Hague.
Eisenstadt, M. and Kareev, Y. (1977), 'Perception in game playing', in P. N. Johnson-Laird and P. C. Wason (eds), *Thinking*, Cambridge.
Evans, J. St B. T. (1980), 'Current issues in the psychology of reasoning', *British Journal of Psychology*, 71.
Gilhooly, K. J. (1982), *Thinking: Directed, Undirected and Creative*, London.
Henle, M. (1962), 'On the relation between logic and thinking', *Psychology Review*, 69.
Johnson-Laird, P. N. (1975), 'Models of deduction', in R.C. Falmagne (ed.), *Reasoning: Representation and Process*, Hillsdale, N.J.
Johnson-Laird, P. N. and Steedman, M. (1978), 'The psychology of syllogisms', *Cognitive Psychology*, 10.
Johnson-Laird, P. N. and Wason, P. C. (1970), 'A theoretical analysis of insight into a reasoning task', *Cognitive Psychology*, 1.
Manktelow, K. I. and Evans, J. St B. T. (1979), 'Facilitation of reasoning by realism: effect or non-effect?', *British Journal of Psychology*, 70.
Pollard, P. and Evans, J. St B. T. (1981), 'The effects of prior beliefs in reasoning: an associational interpretation', *British Journal of Psychology*, 72.
Smalley, N. S. (1974), 'Evaluating a rule against possible instances', *British Journal of Psychology*, 65.
Wason, P. C. and Shapiro, D. (1971), 'Natural and contrived experience in a reasoning problem', *Quarterly Journal of Experimental Psychology*, 23.
Woodworth, R. S. and Sells, S. B. (1935), 'An atmosphere effect in formal syllogistic reasoning', *Journal of Experimental Psychology*, 18.

Further Reading
Mayer, R. E. (1983), *Thinking, Problem Solving, Cognition*, San Francisco.
See also: *thinking*.

Production Function

A production function is a representation of the technical relationship between the rate of output of a good (measured in physical units), and the rates of inputs of the elements of production (measured in physical units) required to produce the specified rate of output. The production functions utilized in economic theory are assumed to be 'efficient', that is, for any set of values for inputs, they show the maximum possible rate of output, given technical knowledge. When presented in the form of an equation, for example $x = f(v_1, v_2, \ldots v_n)$, then only the output (x) and the variable inputs (the v_i's) are shown explicitly, while the fixed inputs (for example, the factory building and machinery) are implied in the form of the function along with the given technical knowledge. These fixed inputs determine the productive capacity of a factory, and the extent to which given increases in the variable inputs can increase output.

Many different types of production processes can be represented formally in terms of a production function. There can be joint products; some inputs may be complements while there is a degree of substitutability between others. With substitutability there is more than one efficient combination of inputs that can be used to produce a particular rate of output, and the choice of input combination to use is based on the economic criterion of least cost. The least cost of producing any given rate of output is determined by utilizing the technical information contained in a production function and the prices of the inputs. If there are no fixed inputs, then the shape of the average cost curve as the rate of output increases will indicate 'returns to scale'. Constant average costs reflect constant returns to scale, decreasing average costs reflect increasing returns, and increasing average costs reflect decreasing returns.

In neoclassical analyses, production functions are assumed to allow for some substitutability between inputs, and these functions are also often taken to be homogeneous of degree one. That is, if all inputs are varied in the same proportion, then output is also varied in the same proportion. Output would increase in a proportion greater (smaller) than the proportionate increase in the inputs if the degree of homogeneity were greater (smaller) than one. If only one input is varied, the values for all the other inputs being kept constant, then it is assumed that the marginal product of the variable input (the increase in output due to a small unit increase in the input) will eventually diminish as the rate of employment of the input is increased. These functions have an important role in the neoclassical theory of distribution. It is deduced that, in a perfectly competitive system, competition will ensure that each input will be paid its marginal product, and, further, if the production function is homogeneous of degree one, payment of all inputs according to their marginal products will exhaust the total product. The assumption of substitutability, which is required to enable marginal products to be calculated, is made to appear reasonable by use of aggregate inputs, or factors of production, such as labour and capital, each of which combine many specific elements of production. However, the attempt to explain factor payments using aggregate production functions has been shown in some *Cambridge Controversies in the Theory of Capital* (Harcourt, 1972) to lack a consistent theoretical foundation, because capital must be measured in value terms that presume a particular distribution of income. As Sraffa (1960) noted, '[There] is not an independent measure of the quantity of capital which could be used, without arguing in a circle, for the determination of prices and of shares in distribution.'

A. Asimakopulos
McGill University

References
Harcourt, G. C. (1972), *Some Cambridge Controversies in the Theory of Capital*, Cambridge.
Sraffa, P. (1960), *Production of Commodities by Means of Commodities*, Cambridge.

Further Reading
Asimakopulos, A. (1978), *An Introduction to Economic Theory: Microeconomics*, Toronto.
Frisch, F. (1965), *Theory of Production*, Chicago.
Robinson, J. (1953–4), 'The production function and the theory of capital', *Review of Economic Studies*.
Walters, A. A. (1963), 'Production and cost functions', *Econometrica*.
See also: *capital theory*; *microeconomics*.

Productivity

Productivity represents a relationship between the inputs used in a productive process and the output they generate. It is increases in productivity which make possible growth in income per head. A considerable amount of work has gone into an analysis of the historic growth process in the Western world, in an attempt to unravel the extent to which the growth in output has been achieved through growth in productivity rather than through increases in inputs. Thus Kendrick (1961) looks at the United States, Denison (1967) tries to analyse the reasons for different growth rates in different countries, and Matthews, Feinstein and Odling-Smee (1982) analyse the growth process in the United Kingdom. More recently, particularly since the oil crises of 1973–4, growth rates in many Western countries have slowed down. Attempts to find explanations for what, to a casual observer, seems to be a reduction in productivity growth are found in Denison (1979) and Matthews, ed. (1982).

The essence of productivity analysis is a production function of the type Y = f(K, L) where K, L are inputs of capital and labour respectively and Y is output. A simple notion of productivity growth would be one in which productivity grows in the same way as manna appears from heaven. Thus one may find the production function is in fact $Y = e^{at}f(K, L)$. Here output grows at the rate a, even though there need be no increase in the measured inputs. In his analyses Denison attempts to decompose this growth in productivity into changes arising from sources such as education, economies of scale, advances in knowledge, and so on. Courbis (1969) presents a clear framework showing how the index number problems of productivity measurement fit into a general scheme of index numbers.

The above production led to attempts to analyse neutral progress as that which is capital and labour saving in equal proportions. If there are constant returns to scale the above production can be written as $Y = f(e^{at}K, e^{at}L)$, and this represents Hicks's neutral technical progress (Hicks, 1965). But the above approach does not take account of the fact that capital is a produced good. Rymes (1972, 1983) argues that Harrod (1961) produced a more suitable framework in order to allow for this. In such a framework one comes close to arguing that all increases in productivity are attributable to increases in labour productivity. Finally, Bruno and Sachs (1982) make the obvious point that capital and labour are not only inputs to production. Any analysis which fails to take account of changes in raw material inputs may give misleading results.

Martin Weale
University of Cambridge

References

Bruno, M. and Sachs, J. (1982), 'Input price shocks and the slowdown in economic growth: the case of UK manufacturing', *Review of Economic Studies*.

Courbis, R. (1969), 'Comptabilité nationale à prix constants et à productivité constante', *Review of Income and Wealth*.

Denison, E. F. (1967), *Why Growth Rates Differ*, Washington, D.C.

Denison, E. F. (1979), 'Accounting for slower growth: the United States in the 1970s', Washington.

Harrod, R. F. (1961), 'The neutrality of improvements', *Economic Journal*.

Hicks, J. R. (1965), *Capital and Growth*, Oxford.

Kendrick, J. W. (1961), 'Productivity trends in the United States', *National Bureau for Economic Research*, New York.

Matthews, R. C. O., Feinstein, C. H. and Odling-Smee, J. C. (1982), *British Economic Growth, 1856–1973*, Oxford.

Matthews, R. C. O. (ed.) (1982), *Slower Growth in the Western World*, London.

Rymes, T. K. (1972), 'The measurement of capital and total factor productivity in the context of the Cambridge theory of capital', *Review of Income and Wealth*.

Rymes, T. K. (1983), 'More on the measurement of total factor productivity', *Review of Income and Wealth*.

Professions

The term profession originally denoted a limited number of vocations which were the only occupations in preindustrial Europe that enabled people with no unearned income to make a living without engaging in commerce or manual work. Law, medicine and divinity constituted the three classical professions, but officers in the army and navy were also included in the ranks of the professions.

The changes associated with industrialization brought about major changes in the structure of these older professions, and also resulted in the rapid growth of new occupational groups, many of which have subsequently claimed professional status. These changes within the occupational structure have been reflected in the sociological literature in the attempt to define the distinguishing traits or characteristics of modern professions. In their classic study, *The Professions*, (1933) Carr-Saunders and Wilson argued that 'the typical profession exhibits a complex of characteristics' and, since then, numerous sociologists have attempted to define this set of characteristics in terms of which, it was held, professional occupations could be distinguished from nonprofessional ones.

This approach – sometimes called the trait or check-list approach – has not, however, resulted in any widespread agreement as to what constitutes an adequate or useful definition of profession. Thus, for example, Millerson (1964), after a careful examination of the literature, listed no less than twenty-three 'elements' which have been included in various definitions of profession. These elements were culled from the work of twenty-one authors who have tried to define the essential characteristics of a 'true' profession and, significantly, no single item was accepted by every author as a necessary characteristic of a profession; nor were any two authors agreed about which combination of elements could be taken as defining a profession. However, the most frequently mentioned characteristics were: (1) possession of a skill based on theoretical knowledge; (2) provision of training and education; (3) testing of competence of members; (4) organization;

(5) adherence to a code of conduct; and (6) altruistic service.

During the 1950s and 1960s many sociologists used this check-list approach to examine a variety of occupations, including social work, teaching, nursing and librarianship, in order to see whether such occupations could properly be regarded as professions; those occupations which exhibited some but not all of the characteristics variously held to constitute the defining elements of a profession were termed semi-, quasi- or para-professions.

Since the early 1970s, however, this largely descriptive approach has increasingly been abandoned in the light of some telling criticisms, particularly from Freidson (1970) and Johnson (1972). It was argued that those traits held to define a profession were frequently analytically or empirically ambiguous, while the lists of defining elements appeared to be constructed in a largely arbitrary manner, with little attempt to articulate theoretically the relationships between the elements. Finally, critics felt that this approach reflected too closely the ideological image which professionals try to convey of their own work, with an uncritical acceptance of the professions' claims to such attributes as ethical behaviour, altruism and community service.

In contrast to the earlier literature, recent work has been more critical, and has tended to focus on the relation of professions to the market, and on the analysis of professional power. In relation to the former, Berlant (1975) sees professionalization as a process of monopolization, while Larson (1977) sees it as a process of occupational mobility based on securing control of a particular market. However, the dominant influence in the last decade has probably been that of Freidson and Johnson, for both of whom the central problems relate to professional power.

For Freidson, it is professional autonomy – the power of the professions to define and to control their own work – which is the single uniform distinguishing characteristic of the professions. In this perspective, specialized knowledge or altruistic behaviour are *not* seen as essential characteristics of professions. However, claims to such attributes – whether valid or not – may be important in the professionalization process in so far as they constitute the rhetoric in terms of which occupational groups seek to obtain from the state special privileges, such as a system of licensing and self-government, and a protected market situation. The professionalization process is thus seen as essentially political in character, a process 'in which power and persuasive rhetoric are of greater importance than the objective character of knowledge, training and work'.

Johnson's work centres on the analysis of practitioner-client relationships. He notes that those occupations which are conventionally labelled 'professions' have, at various times and in various places, been subject to a variety of forms of social control. Thus, in certain contexts, practitioners may be subject to control by powerful clients (patronage), or practitioner-client relationships may be mediated by a third party, such as the church or state (mediate control), The term professionalism is reserved for a particular form of occupational control, involving a high degree of self-regulation and freedom from external control which, in its most developed form, was a product of the specific social conditions in nineteenth-century Britain and America. Johnson's work represents a radical break from traditional work in the subject, for he argues that profession should be used to refer not to an occupation, but to a particular form of occupational control, while professionalization is seen as a 'historically specific process which some occupations have undergone at a particular time, rather than a process which certain occupations may always be expected to undergo because of their essential characteristics'. This point has recently been echoed by Freidson (1983), who has pointed to important differences between professions in Britain and America, and high-status occupations in continental Europe. Professionalism, he suggests, is an 'Anglo-American disease' and, like Johnson, he suggests that, 'as an institutional concept, the term "profession" is intrinsically bound up with a particular period of history and with only a limited number of nations in that period of history'.

I. Waddington
University of Leicester

References
Berlant, J. L. (1975), *Profession and Monopoly: A Study of Medicine in the United States and Great Britain*, Berkeley and London.
Freidson, E. (1970), *Profession of Medicine: A Study of the Sociology of Applied Knowledge*, New York.
Freidson, E. (1983), 'The reorganization of the professions by regulation', *Law and Human Behaviour*, 7.
Johnson, T. J. (1972), *Professions and Power*, London.
Larson, M. S. (1977), *The Rise of Professionalism*, Berkeley and Los Angeles.
Millerson, G. (1964), *The Qualifying Associations: A Study in Professionalization*, London.

Further Reading
Dingwall, R. and Lewis, P. (1983), *The Sociology of the Professions: Lawyers, Doctors and Others*, London.

Profit

In terms of business accounting, gross profit is the difference between total sales revenue and expenditure on wages and salaries, rents and raw materials, and any other outlays incurred in the day-to-day operation of the firm. Net profit is gross profit net of money costs, such as interest payable on loans and depreciation allowance. After deduction of tax, profit may be distributed amongst the firm's owners or retained to contribute to reserve and investment funds.

In economics, profit is also regarded as revenue net of cost, but the costs concerned include imputed costs, as well as expenditures on inputs to the production process. A distinction is drawn between normal and supernormal (or excess) profit. Normal profit is regarded as the income accruing to the entrepreneur. It is the return that the entrepreneur must receive to cover the opportunity costs of the inputs employed. If actual profits are less than normal profits, then the entrepreneur will be able to switch his resources to a more profitable activity. The imputed costs, referred to above, are, therefore, the opportunity costs, namely the returns that could be earned by employing or hiring out the entrepreneur's assets to gain maximum pecuniary gain. Supernormal profits are profits earned in excess of normal profits. In competitive markets these should be zero, in the long run, but in markets with elements of monopoly (or oligopoly) they may be non-zero, hence they are often called monopolistic profits. In pure, perfectly, or imperfectly, competitive markets, excess profits can be made in the short run but, given the assumption of freedom of entry into the market, these will not persist in the long run. Similarly, less than normal profits may be earned in competitive markets, in the short run, provided that variable costs are being covered, but the assumption of freedom of exit will ensure that normal profits are made in the long run. A major factor leading to the persistence of excess profits in the long run, in monopolistic markets, is therefore the existence of barriers to entry to the market.

Profit has been variously regarded as the wages paid to the entrepreneur; as the rent paid for specialist knowledge possessed by the entrepreneur; as the interest on the entrepreneur's capital; as recompense for risk taking; as payment for management skills; and as surplus value expropriated by capitalists from workers.

In connection with modern firms, the view that profit is the return to entrepreneurial risk taking is complicated by the fact that the ownership of the firm is often divorced from its control. In the simple case of an entrepreneur who is both owner and manager of the firm, this return to risk view is attractive. In a limited company, however, the problem arises that it is not easy to see how the risk is divided between the shareholders, who receive the distributed profits, and the management, which may be regarded as essentially salaried employees. The matter is further confused when some of the management holds shares, in the form of directorships, and when the management is responsive to the wishes of shareholders, expressed at shareholders' meetings. It is also to be noted that not all risks need be borne by the firm, since many of them can be converted into a known cost through insurance.

F. H. Knight (1971) distinguished between risk and uncertainty. Risk entails events that occur with known probability and which can be insured against, in principle. Uncertainty occurs due to a change in the environment and entails unforeseeable events. The existence of uncertainty creates an environment in which, even in competitive markets, excess profits may be made in the short run. In the long run, when the change is understood, profits will return to normal. If the world is such that change is continually creating unforeseen events, or shocks, then there will always be newly created profitable opportunities. Change will be signalled by movements in the market price or in quantities, such as sales or inventories, and the firm must decide how to respond to such changes in order to take advantage of profitable opportunities. In order to do this the firm must form expectations of future changes and respond rapidly once prices or quantities deviate from expectations. In a competitive market, if a firm waits until the change is fully understood it will have missed the profitable opportunity, since others will have taken it up already. Lucas (1977) has developed a theory of the business cycle based on responses, in pursuit of profit, to price changes in the presence of rationally formed expectations.

Marx (1898) took a very different view of profit and its source. He argued that labour was only paid wages sufficient to maintain its labouring power. Normal profit then resulted from selling the product at its real value, which included surplus value resulting from unpaid labour. The whole of the expropriated surplus value or 'profit' is not necessarily pocketed by the employing capitalist, however. The landlord may take one part, namely rent, and the money-lending or finance capitalist may claim a portion of surplus value, in the form of interest. The surplus value remaining in the hands of the employing capitalist may then be called industrial or commercial profit. Profit is not derived from land or capital as such, but is due to the fact that ownership of these factors enables capitalists to extract surplus value from workers. Clearly this view has had to be modified by Marxian theorists in the light of increasing ownership of capital, through direct or indirect shareholding, by workers.

Andy Mullineux
University of Birmingham

References

Knight, F. H. (1971), *Risk, Uncertainty and Profits*, Chicago.

Lucas, R. E. (1977), 'Understanding business cycles', in R. E. Lucas (1981), *Studies in Business Cycle Theory*, Oxford.

Marx, K. (1898), *Wages, Prices and Profit*, London.

Further Reading
Begg, D., Fischer, S. and Dornbusch, R. (1984),
  Economics: British Edition, London.
See also: *entrepreneurship; risk.*

Progress

See Evolution and Progress.

Project Analysis

Project analysis is the evaluation of investment proposals in terms of the balance between benefits accruing to and costs incurred by the investor. The discounting of cash flows (x) generated (the net differences between cash flows, 'with' and 'without' the project) in each year (i) over the planning horizon (n), at a rate determined by the opportunity cost of the funds involved (r), produces the net present value (NPV). Broadly, a positive net present value implies that the project should be accepted; the internal rate of return (the rate of discount which brings the NPV to zero) and the cost-benefit ratio (the ratio of discounted benefits to discounted costs) can also be used as decision criteria.

$$NPV = \sum_{i=0}^{n} \frac{x_i}{(1+r)^i} > 0$$

Further developments include: the application of an overall capital budget constraint, within which alternative projects are chosen so as to maximize the sum of their NPVs; the optimization of capacity expansion over time, maximizing NPV for a particular product line; and the application of probability distributions to uncertain cash flows to produce an 'expected' NPV.

The application of such a criterion to public investment implies a different objective function, which involves the assessment of costs and benefits to the whole economy, as well as to the state budget itself. The modern approach is derived from neoclassical welfare theory, but the first exponent was the French engineer Dupuit in 1844 (benefits of bridges to hauliers). This was further developed by the US Corps of Engineers in the New Deal years to calculate the 'indirect' benefits of hydroelectric projects in the form of increased farm yields from irrigation. In the postwar years, the methodology was again advanced in developed market economies, towards a full estimation of secondary costs and benefits. This is a complex process, involving not only partial equilibrium analysis of changes in other economic sectors (for example, the value of time savings to commuters on improved highways) in the context of 'second-best' situations (e.g. government pricing policies), but also attempts to quantify the value of non-economic factors such as loss of amenity (e.g. noise from airports), and the

inclusion of 'social' criteria such as regional balance. This 'cost-benefit analysis' remains highly controversial, because it relates to political debate.

In developing market economies, the imbalances of the industrialization process (principally foreign-exchange shortages and surplus labour) require that 'shadow prices' be used in order to reflect the true opportunity cost of inputs and net value of outputs; multilateral aid agencies such as the IBRD have been particularly influential in this respect. The dominant method at present is to value commodities at their international ('border') price if so traded, and according to costs of production if nontraded; while labour costs are revalued to reflect underemployment (the 'shadow wage rate'). The application of suitable weights to reflect income-distribution criteria, and the adjustment of the discount rate to reflect fiscal constraints on accumulation, extend the scope of such investment criteria. In socialist planned economies, the discounting criterion is closely paralleled by the 'investment efficiency index', which reflects the reduction in input costs over time for a planned output, as a result of the investment project, with the return on other investments providing the equivalent of the opportunity cost of capital. Indirect costs and benefits are simply computed in a planned economy, where production is in any case programmed; a more recent development is the evaluation of foreign trade effects at international prices. Project appraisal criteria are brought to their logical conclusion in the 'economic calculus' as the basis for decentralized state enterprise operation with centrally managed prices.

E. V. K. Fitzgerald
Institute of Social Studies, The Hague

Further Reading
Dasgupta, A. K. and Pearce, D. W. (1972), *Cost-Benefit Analysis: Theory and Practice*, London.
Little, I. M. D. and Mirrlees, J. A. (1974), *Project Appraisal and Planning for Developing Countries*, London.
Merret, A. J. and Sykes, A. (1963), *The Finance and Analysis of Capital Projects*, London.
Radowski, M. (1966), *Efficiency of Investment in a Socialist Economy*, Oxford.
See also: *cost-benefit analysis.*

Projective Methods

Projective methods encompass a wide range of approaches to the assessment of individuals and share the following characteristics: (1) stimulus ambiguity-projective techniques consist of materials that can be interpreted, structured, or responded to in a great many different plausible ways; (2) lack of any one correct or true answer – projective stimuli are not designed to represent or resemble any one specific object of experience; and (3) open-ended, complex, and individualized responses – the subject does not usually provide a simple yes-no or true-false answer, but is given the opportunity to organize or structure his response in a personal or individualized way. Projective methods represent an indirect approach to the assessment of a person. Personality characteristics are revealed while the person is ostensibly doing something else, such as telling a story about a picture, or drawing a person. Proponents of projective techniques claim that the person's subjective experience is revealed through these responses; in this manner, the mainsprings of his social behaviour are expressed.

The term projective methods was coined by Lawrence K. Frank, more than thirty years after projective techniques were introduced. Upon surveying the growing number of these techniques and trying to establish what they had in common, Frank concluded that projective methods provide 'a field with relatively little structure and cultural patterning, so that the personality can project upon that plastic field his way of seeing life, his meanings, significances, patterns, and especially his feelings' (Frank, 1939). This is accomplished by means of projection, that is, attributing one's own traits and characteristics to external stimuli. Frank also spelled out several implications of this position: (1) Projection takes place with a minimum of awareness or conscious control. The person transcends the limits of his self-knowledge and reveals more than he is capable of communicating directly. (2) The ambiguous stimuli of projective techniques serve mainly as stepping stones for self-expression. Their specific characteristics are relatively unimportant. (3) The responses to projective techniques are little influenced by the social situation in which they are presented or by the person's current psychological state; they are based on his enduring personality characteristics.

This conceptualization of projective methods is compatible with psychodynamic theories of personality, such as those of Freud and Jung, which emphasize the importance of unconscious impulses and motives. Responses to projective methods lend themselves easily to interpretation in terms of unconscious drives, intrapsychic conflicts, defences against them, and symbolic representation of these forces.

More recent theoretical formulations have attempted to look at projective techniques from other points of view. Bruner (1948) forged links between responses to projective stimuli and the principles of the 'hypothesis theory' of perception. In Bruner's view, responses to ambiguous stimuli reflect hypotheses, based on past experience and present expectations. Fulkerson's (1965) point of departure was decision making under conditions of uncertainty. Uncertainty in responding to projective methods is of two kinds: stimulus ambiguity,

amply emphasized by Frank and other traditional theorists, and situational ambiguity, somewhat glossed over in these formulations. Fulkerson stressed the conscious choices open to the person: to emit or to withhold a response and how to present or communicate it to the examiner, all on the basis of the person's subjective understanding of the context and purpose of projective examination. Epstein integrated responses to projective stimuli with conflict theory. The situation with which the person is confronted in responding to projective materials arouses a conflict of expression versus inhibition of various drive states. This conflict can result in verbal expression of the impulse in question, its suppression, or various compromise reactions, for example, expressing the drive symbolically, partially, or indirectly.

Since 1900, a multitude of projective techniques have been developed. Of these, four varieties have become prominent: inkblot tests, which require the person to impose meaning upon, and to interpret, inkblots or portions thereof; story-telling tests in which the person is asked to provide an imaginative, dramatic account of a picture; graphic techniques, in which the task is to produce a drawing, of a person, or a house, for example, with a minimum of further specifications; and completion techniques, exemplified by sentence completion in which the person is asked to complete a sentence stem, for example, 'Last summer . . .', 'Whenever I get angry . . .'. Projective techniques have preponderantly relied upon the visual modality for the presentation or production of stimuli. Auditory techniques consisting of vague sounds difficult to recognize or structure have been repeatedly proposed, but have not gained wide acceptance. The same is true of several projective techniques that require tactile exploration of stimuli.

Inkblots were introduced by Hermann Rorschach of Switzerland who developed a test consisting of 10 cards. Rorschach devised a multidimensional scoring system based on content (for example, animal, human, plant, object) as well as determinants (for example, form, movement, colour, shading) and location (for example, whole, large, small, or tiny detail). In the ensuing decades, this test was widely used in clinical and research settings; a reasearch literature came into being numbering by now several thousand studies. Not unexpectedly, the results of this work were divergent and complex; some of it supported. and some of it refuted, Rorschach's and other proponents' claims. In 1961, Wayne Holtzman at the University of Texas succeeded in developing a modern and statistically streamlined inkblot test. Consisting of two forms of 45 inkblots each, it allows only one response per card, makes possible determination of test-retest reliability, and exhibits improved objectivity in scoring. Remarkably, it has supplemented, especially as a research tool, but has not replaced, the Rorschach which its proponents continue to prefer because of its allegedly superior clinical sensitivity and ease of administration.

The most prominent exemplar of the story-telling format is the Thematic Apperception Test introduced in 1935 by Henry A. Murray at Harvard University. Twenty cards are administered to the person who is asked not only to describe what he sees, but to extend the story beyond the present into both past and future and to relate the actions, thoughts and feelings of the people depicted. The resulting imaginative production, in Murray's words, reflects person's 'regnant preoccupations', his characteristic motives, feelings and fantasies. The voluminous literature about the T.A.T. has demonstrated, but not really explained adequately, how its content relates to overt, observable behaviour.

Graphic approaches are best illustrated by the Draw-a-person and House-Tree-Person techniques. Their rationale rests on the assumption that the person's own characteristics are reflected, or projected, in response to the minimally brief instructions, such as, 'Draw a person, any kind of a person.'

In the completion techniques, more structure is provided and the person's contribution is concentrated upon a 'gap-filling' activity, as in completing an incomplete sentence or story. Despite its manifest transparency and the ease with which it can be faked, sentence completion, in light of accumulated research, has proved valuable as an auxiliary avenue for assessing personality.

After over eight decades of use, projective techniques remain controversial. In general, they stand in a nonrandom, but highly imperfect, relationship to their nontest referents. They work better in identifying broad and general tendencies of behaviour than in predicting specific acts. Their continued use and study, despite some loss of popularity in the 1970s, is linked to views which emphasize the importance of a person's subjective experience not only as a determinant of his behaviour, but also as a worthy subject of knowledge in its own right.

Juris G. Draguns
Pennsylvania State University

References

Bruner, J. S. (1948), 'Perceptual theory and the Rorschach test', *Journal of Personality*, 17.

Epstein, S. (1966), 'Some theoretical considerations on the nature of ambiguity and the use of stimulus dimensions in projective techniques', *Journal of Consulting Psychology*, 30.

Frank, L. K. (1939), 'Projective methods for the study of personality', *Journal of Psychology*, 8.

Fulkerson, S. C. (1965). 'Some implications of the new cognitive theory for projective tests', *Journal of Consulting Psychology*, 29.

Further Reading

Rabin, A. J. (ed.) (1981), *Assessment with Projective Techniques: A Concise Introduction*, New York.

Semeonoff, B. (1976), *Projective Techniques*, London.

Prostitution

Prostitution is the sale and purchase of sexual relations. While universal, its prevalence, the specific forms it takes, and how it is morally evaluated and legally dealt with, can all vary greatly. There can be homosexual prostitutes (of either sex), as well as male prostitutes who sell sexual favours to women. But it is the sale of female sexuality to men that has usually been the predominant pattern, and (at times) has given rise to the greatest social concern.

Owing, perhaps, to the influence of psychological and social-service orientations, the 'causes' of prostitution often are addressed through the study of individual prostitutes. This misleading view of prostitution, as being something 'done by' prostitutes – whilst ignoring the casual significance of male demand for their services – is itself indicative of the sexual double standard on which the phenomemon of prostitution rests. Numerous analysts have noted the hypocrisy that this standard entails, and have also drawn an analogy between the commercial sale of sex and the common exchange within marriage of sexual favours for financial security and social standing (for example, Engels, 1942 [1891]). Both patterns reflect the tendency, found to some extent in most societies, for the dominant males to treat women as their 'sexual property' (Lévi-Strauss, 1969 [1949]).

Recent feminist analyses emphasize the oppressiveness of a system that socially and legally punishes individual prostitutes, while at the same time breeding male demand for prostitution, limiting women's other means of attaining a livelihood, and encouraging girls and women generally to view their sexuality as a commodity to be 'capitalized' on in order to enhance their life chances. From this standpoint (James et al., 1975), there is no mystery regarding either the 'causes' of the individual prostitute's job choice or the prevalence of prostitution as a general social pattern. Wishing to express their solidarity with prostitute women, yet at the same time frequently considering prostitution overall to be an exploitative by-product of sexual inequality and sexist value distortions, feminists have confronted something of a dilemma in assessing public-policy measures and proposals. Historical studies have shown, furthermore, that anti-prostitution campaigns (Walkowitz 1980; Rosen 1982) often display or evoke general tendencies towards sexual repression and paternalistic control.

Laws against prostitution are usually ineffective in curbing the practice. Their administration typically involves routine harassment and minor punishment of prostitutes (while largely ignoring their customers) and efforts to restrict blatant public solicitation. Contemporary feminists assert that such laws oppress prostitute women. They tend, however, to oppose the 'legalization' or regulation of prostitution – on the ground that this confers on the practice a governmental stamp of legitimacy. An alternative policy of 'decriminalization' (eliminating laws that victimize the prostitute, but not involving the state in the regulation of prostitution) is often preferred as a short-term ameliorative. Nevertheless, most feminists also advocate the eventual elimination (or substantial reduction) of prostitution. To that end, they urge ongoing efforts to reduce the institutionalized sexism in which they believe prostitution to be largely grounded.

Edwin M. Schur
New York University

References
Engels, F. (1942 [1891]), *The Origin of the Family, Private Property, and the State*, 4th edn, New York.
James, J. *et al.* (1975), *The Politics of Prostitution*, Seattle.
Lévi-Strauss, C. (1969 [1949]), *The Elementary Structures of Kinship*, Boston. (Original French, *Les Structures élémentaires de la parenté*, Paris.)
Rosen, R. (1982), *The Lost Sisterhood*, Baltimore.
Walkowitz, J. (1980), *Prostitution and Victorian Society*, Cambridge.

Further Reading
Beauvoir, S. de (1953), *The Second Sex*, New York.
See also: *pornography; sexual behaviour.*

Psychiatry

Psychiatry is a speciality of medicine concerned with the diagnosis, treatment and study of mental diseases or disorders. Its practitioners are psychiatrists (in the United States, physicians who complete four years of approved training following their graduation from medical school). A number of professionals from other disciplines treat patients with psychiatric disorders. The most important of these are clinical psychologists, psychiatric social workers and psychiatric nurses. They commonly refer to those who seek help as 'clients' rather than 'patients'. These professionals may work in various collaborative relationships with psychiatrists or as independent practitioners. They employ the same verbal therapies as psychiatrists. Psychiatry differs from these specialities in being a medical discipline whose practitioners are physicians. As such, psychiatrists are specifically trained to (1) make precise syndromal or aetiological diagnoses, whenever possible, and distinguish one syndrome from another; (2) diagnose (or know when to refer to other physicians) those organic conditions which mimic psychiatric disorders such as brain tumour, cancer of the pancreas, and hyperthyroidism (these conditions can present as anxiety or depressive disorders); (3) treat particular psychiatric disorders with psychotropic medications or other somatic treatments; (4) manage untoward psychological reactions to medical illness; and (5) integrate the biological with the psychological and social dimensions of mental disorders. In addition, the psychiatrist's training in medicine may encourage a research career in the biology of mental disorders. American psychiatrists as a whole have a high level of expertise in psychological treatments, particularly the psychodynamic approach. This is due to the impact of psychoanalytic theory on academic psychiatry especially since 1945, when many distinguished psychoanalysts assumed the chairs of academic departments.

Psychiatry relates closely to other medical specialities such as internal medicine, family medicine, neurology and pediatrics as well as to many scientific disciplines that contribute to the understanding of mental disorders. These include psychology, epidemiology, anthropology, sociology, genetics, and biochemistry.

The Range of Psychiatric Disorders
Although abnormal states of thinking, feeling, and behaving may be studied and treated in isolation, more often they are understood as part of specific syndromes, disorders, or diseases. In the US the most widely accepted classification of psychiatric disorders is presented in the American Psychiatric Association's third edition of the Diagnostic and Statistical Manual of Mental Disorders (DSM-III). Although developed by psychiatrists in the United States, this classification is widely used by psychiatrists in other countries, and by other mental health professionals. The classification attempts to provide a comprehensive description of the manifestations of mental disorders while remaining atheoretical with regard to aetiology. A related classification of mental disorders with broad international acceptance is the ninth edition of the International Classification of Disease (ICD-9).

The following are the major categories of psychiatric disorders according to DSM-III:
– Disorders Usually First Evident in Infancy, Childhood, or Adolescence
– Organic Mental Disorders
– Substance Abuse Disorders
– Schizophrenic Disorders
– Paranoid Disorders
– Psychotic Disorders Not Elsewhere Classified
– Affective Disorders
– Anxiety Disorders
– Somatoform Disorders
– Dissociative Disorders
– Psychosexual Disorders

– Factitious Disorders
– Disorders of Impulse Control Not Elsewhere Classified
– Adjustment Disorders
– Psychological Factors Affecting Physical Condition
– Personality Disorders

The manual describes subcategories of the above major categories together with specific defining criteria for each disorder. There is a high degree of reliability for most of the disorders; that is, two observers of the same patient are likely to agree on the diagnosis. There is considerable variability in the established validity of these diagnostic categories.

Family and couple therapists criticize DSM-III on the grounds that they regard the couple or the family, not the patient, as the pathologic unit. Behaviour therapists criticize DSM-III on grounds that it is the thought, feeling, or behaviour, not the syndrome or disease, that is the pathologic unit. Psychodynamic clinicians are apt to view psychopathology as part of a continuum based on the concept of 'developmental lines', rather than as discrete disease entities. In addition, they believe that each patient can be described only by a unique and complex formulation. Diagnostic categories are regarded therefore as both conceptually incorrect as well as oversimplifications of human problems. Despite these criticisms, there is a growing consensus amongst US psychiatrists that DSM-III will prevail and continue to grow in importance through future editions.

There are two extreme and opposing positions regarding psychiatric disease: (1) that psychopathology, both social and individual, is everywhere and that therapeutic intervention may be useful for all human conditions; (2) that mental illness is a myth, and therefore lies out of the purview of medicine.

Conceptual Models in Psychiatric Thinking
There are many conceptual frameworks by which psychiatrists attempt to organize their thinking about patients with mental disorders. The presence of multiple approaches, particularly when thay are not made explicit, commonly leads to misunderstanding amongst psychiatrists and between psychiatrists and other medical professionals, mental health professionals, and patients. The four conceptual models most often used are (1) the biologic; (2) psychodynamic; (3) sociocultural and (4) the behavioural.

(1) According to the biologic model, psychiatric illness is a disease like any other. Its cause will be found to be related to disorders of genetics, biochemistry, and/or the functional anatomy of the brain. Abnormal behaviours are understood as partial manifestations of a syndrome or underlying disease process. In his relationship to the patient, the biologic psychiatrist behaves like any other physician: he elicits the history through careful questioning, establishes a diagnosis and recommends a treatment plan which the patient is expected to accept. The biologic approach, after giving psychiatry its classification of mental illness in the late nineteenth century, was generally unproductive until the 1950s. From that time until the present its contributions to psychiatry have included the development of antipsychotic, antidepressant, and antimania medications; the increased understanding of the genetic transmission of some mental illness; and metabolic studies of depressive disorders. The biologic model has been least helpful in the study of the neuroses and personality disorders.

(2) According to the psychodynamic model, it is the development deficit, fixation, regressive response to current stress, and/or conflict within the mind that leads to psychiatric symptoms. The symptom represents both an expression of an underlying conflict as well as a partial attempt to resolve it. The concept of unconscious mental processes is all important. In the relationship to the patient, the therapist assumes a nondirective posture in order to elicit meaningful associations, as well as to develop a transference reaction in which the patient reacts to the therapist as he would to other important people in his life. The psychodynamic model had its origin with Sigmund Freud in the late nineteenth and early twentieth centuries. There have been significant theoretical developments since 1950 in ego psychology, object relations theory, and self psychology. Although the psychodynamic model is a general psychology of normal and abnormal behaviour, it is most helpful in the understanding and treatment of neuroses and personality disorders.

(3) The sociocultural model focuses on the way the individual functions within his social system. Symptoms are traced not to conflicts within the mind nor to manifestations of psychiatric disease, but to disruptions or changes in the social support system. According to the sociocultural approach, symptoms, disorders, or the designation that someone is mentally ill may be seen as social phenomena: responses to breakdown or disorganization of social groupings, attempts at social communication, a cultural or ethnic expression of distress, or a message by the social group that certain behaviours are no longer acceptable. Treatment consists in helping the patient deal better with the existing social system. The sociocultural approach was reawakened in the 1950s. From that time until the present, the psychiatric ward was viewed as a social system, the relationship between social class and mental illness was established, and federal legislation was enacted to provide psychiatric care for catchment areas in the community.

(4) The behavioural model regards symptoms in their own right as the problem. Symptoms are manifestations neither of disease, intrapsychic conflict, nor social breakdown. In order to develop a treatment

strategy, the behavioural formulation takes into account conditions antecedent to and reinforcing of the pathologic behaviours. The behavioural model, like the three models previously discussed, began its period of rapid growth in the late 1950s. Behavioural therapists are hopeful of offering several possible advantages to other forms of treatment including a shorter duration of treatment and applicability to a broad range of patients.

Which conceptual approach a psychiatrist uses depends on several factors including his own training and ideology, the diagnosis of the patient, and the availability of clinical services. The use of a single approach to explain all psychopathology (including the belief that all psychopathology will ultimately be explained by biochemistry) is reductionistic. In optimal clinical practice, the psychiatrist attempts to understand the patient simultaneously by means of several conceptual approaches or frames of references, with the understanding that even the four approaches described above may not exhaust the ways in which psychopathology of people can be understood. Various attempts to integrate several conceptual frameworks have been referred to as systems theory, biopsychosocial approach, multidimensional approach, or eclecticism.

Psychiatric Treatments
Psychiatric treatments can be divided into two major categories: the biologic approaches (somatotherapy) and the psychologic or verbal therapeutic approaches. The most commonly used somatic treatments are drugs followed by electroconclusive treatments. Other somatic treatments much less used include insulin treatment and neurosurgery. Drugs may be divided into four major groups: (1) the anti-anxiety agents; (2) antidepressant agents; (3) antimanic agents; and (4) antipsychotic agents. The anti-anxiety agents such as Librium and Valium are useful in the short-term treatment of some anxiety states. Their sedative-hypnotic effect makes them also useful for the short-term treatment of insomnia. This class of anti-anxiety agents (benzodiazepines), because of their relative safety, has rendered the barbiturates virtually obsolete. Antidepressant agents such as Tofranil and Elavil (tricyclics) and Nardil (MAO inhibiter) reverse depressive symptomatology while the antimanic agents such as Lithium Carbonate reverse symptoms of mania or hypomania while sometimes functioning as an antidepressant. The antipsychotic agents such as Haldol and Thorazine are useful in managing the excitement, delusions, hallucinations, and disorientation of various psychotic states in schizophrenia, depressive psychoses, and organic psychoses. With prolonged use, the antipsychotic agents can cause tardive dyskinesia, a permanent involuntary movement disorder involving primarily the tongue, neck, and facial muscles. Electro-convulsive therapy, the passage of electrical current through the brain, is used primarily for depressed patients for whom drug therapy has failed, has or will produce serious side effects, or will take too long before exerting a therapeutic effect.

There are hundreds of psychologic treatments. They may be classified according to theoretical approach, structure of the treatment, and duration. In terms of ideology the psychodynamic approach, based on the principles of psychoanalytic theory, is the most widely used. Behaviour therapies which include the specific techniques of relaxation, cognitive restructuring, and flooding have made major inroads in clinical practice during the past twenty-five years. In addition, there are various interpersonal, existential, Jungian, Adlerian, and other therapies. To what degree specific dimensions of each ideological approach are uniquely therapeutic and to what degree there are common therapeutic dimensions of many approaches is a subject of considerable interest. As to structure, the therapist may treat the patient alone, with a spouse, as part of a family, together with a broader social network, or with a group of other patients. When therapy is provided to a couple or to a family, then the couple or family, not the individual, may be regarded as the patient. Most therapies take place once a week but may occasionally be as infrequent as once a month or as frequent as four or five times per week as in psychoanalysis. Depending on the goals of treatment, the sessions may range from one visit (evaluation), eight to twelve visits (brief or short-term therapy), one to four years (long-term therapy), or three to seven years (psychoanalysis). Treatment may take place in a private office, in a mental health centre, or in a psychiatric inpatient unit.

The therapeutic efficacy of the somatic treatments is well established. The efficacy of particular psychological treatments for designated symptoms or disorders has been receiving increasing confirmation during the past ten years. For certain depressive and schizophrenic disorders, it has been established that a combination of drug and psychological or social treatments is more effective than either used alone. Psychiatric treatment has also been shown to diminish patients' use of medical facilities.

Psychiatry – Past and Future
Psychiatric illness is not new to modern society. In the Hippocratic writings (400 B.C.) there are clear descriptions of the major psychiatric disorders. Throughout the centuries psychopathology was described, explained, and classified by the great physicians of the time. The degree of sophistication, or lack thereof, paralleled that for medicine in general. There was no autonomous discipline of psychiatry.

The historian George Mora divides modern scientific psychiatry into three overlapping periods: (1) From

1800 to 1860, the mental hospital, or asylum, was the centre of psychiatric activity. It was staffed by a new type of physician, the alienist, totally devoted to the care of the mentally ill. The major accomplishments of this period were the practice of 'moral therapy', the description and classification of mental disorders, and the study of brain anatomy. Famous names associated with this period are Esquirol, Morel, Kahlbaum, Tuke, Rush, and Ray. (2) From 1860 to 1920, the centre of psychiatry moved from the hospital to the university which could simultaneously treat patients, teach, and do research. The important names of this era include Griesinger, Meynert, Forel, Bleuler, Charcot, Jackson, Kraepelin, A. Meyer, and S. Freud. It was Kraepelin who provided a classification of mental disorders that is the intellectual precursor of DSM-III. Meyer developed the psychobiologic approach, trained a whole generation of leaders in American psychiatry and provided the fertile ground for the growth of psychoanalysis in this country. (3) The period from 1920 to the present has been referred to as the 'psychiatric explosion'. As described earlier, the greatest expansion of knowledge in psychodynamic, sociocultural, biologic, and behavioural approaches began in the 1950s.

It is anticipated that within the next one to two decades there will be important new developments in psychiatry. These will include: (1) greater sophistication in nosology with improved validity for certain diagnostic categories; at the same time there will be philosophical and empirical sophistication in understanding the limitations of the diagnostic or categorical approach to other mental disturbances; (2) significant advances in understanding the biology of mental processes in general and of the depressive and schizophrenic disorders in particular; (3) significant advances in the evaluation of psychologic therapies so that more effective matches can be made between disorder and treatment; (4) significant advances in the integration of biologic, psychodynamic, behavioural, and social approaches to the diagnosis and treatment of mental disorders; (5) advances in the integrative efforts between psychiatry and other medical disciplines such as neurology, medicine, and paediatrics.

The advances described above will further define psychiatry both as a mental health profession and as a medical speciality.

Aaron Lazare
Massachusetts General Hospital

Further Reading

American Psychiatric Association (1980), *Diagnostic and Statistical Manual of Mental Disorders (DSM-III)*, 3rd edn, New York.

Baldessarini, R. (1983), *Biomedical Aspects of Depression and Its Treatment*, Washington, DC.

Brenner, C. (1982), *The Mind in Conflict*, New York.

Gedo, J. E. and Goldberg, A. (1973), *Models of the Mind: A Psychoanalytic Theory*, Chicago.

Greenhill, M. and Gralnick, A. (1983), *Psychopharmacology and Psychotherapy*, New York.

Lazare, A. (1973), 'Hidden conceptual models in clinical psychiatry', *New England Journal of Medicine*, 288.

Lazare, A. (1979), 'Hypothesis testing in the clinical interview', *in Outpatient Psychiatry: Diagnosis and Treatment*, Baltimore.

Lishman, W. (1978), *Organic Psychiatry: The Psychological Consequences of Cerebral Disorder*, Oxford.

Papajohn, I. (1982), *Intensive Behavior Therapy: The Behavioral Treatment of Complex Emotional Disorders*, New York.

Rutter, M. and Hersov, L. (eds) (1984), *Child Psychiatry – Modern Approaches*, 2nd edn, Oxford.

See also: *biological psychiatry; DSM-111; mental disorders; mental health; psychoanalysis; psychopharmacology.*

Psychoanalysis

Psychoanalysis is a procedure for the treatment of mental and emotional disturbances. Sigmund Freud originated and developed psychoanalysis as a result of his individual researches into the causes of hysteria, one of the common forms of mental illness in Europe in the latter part of the nineteenth century (see Jones, 1953).

The unique characteristic of psychoanalysis as a therapy derives from its theory of psychopathology. The central finding of psychoanalysis is that mental and emotional disturbances result from unconscious mental life. Treatment therefore depends upon the ability of the patient, with the help of the analyst, to reveal unconscious thoughts and feelings. The formula that propelled the psychoanalytic method from its inception ('what is unconscious shall be made conscious') remains vitally significant today. The changes that have occurred in the formula have resulted from a broadened and deepened understanding of the nature of unconscious mental life and how it functions developmentally in relation to consciousness and to the environment.

According to Freud's first conception of symptom formation, morbid thought patterns occurred during a dissociated state and were prevented from normal discharge because of the altered states of consciousness. The undischarged tensions produced symptoms. The cure required some method of discharge – an abreaction or mental catharsis. By applying hypnosis, the noxious material could be brought to the surface and discharged through verbal association. This chain of inference, formulated first in collaboration with Joseph Breuer (1842–1925) who described his clinical experience in treating a female patient he named Anna O.

(Freud, 1955, Vol. II) was dependent upon a quantitative hypothesis concerning unconscious mental life and its relation to conscious states. In this prepsychoanalytic period of research, excessive excitation and the blockage of discharge were thought to produce pathological effects.

A major shift occurred both in research and in the explanatory theory toward the turn of the century. Freud recognized, largely through his self-analysis but also through careful attention to what his patients told him, that a qualitative factor was as important as the quantitative in the pathological process. The unconscious thoughts and feelings contained sexual content and meaning which was linked to arousal, or in earlier language, the quantity of excitation.

The introduction of the qualitative factor altered the theory of neurosis and the therapeutic procedure and, indeed, the method of research. Instead of managing a procedure designed to discharge quantities of noxious excitation stored within the psyche, the problem shifted to uncovering the meaning of the symptoms, and, through association, their roots in the unconscious. Hypnosis no longer served the purpose, since it was imperative that the entire treatment procedure elicit the full participation of the patient. Freud asked his patients to recline on the couch and to say whatever came to mind. This method, called 'free association', created a contradiction in terms. Freud discovered that it was difficult for the patient to carry out his request. Difficulty in associating did not seem to be a random effect, but along with the symptoms could be understood as an inherent aspect of the patient's manner of thinking and feeling and the particular form and content of the presenting symptoms. Freud visualized the difficulties of free association as *resistance* and as part and parcel of the problem of unconscious content, attempting to break through the barriers that guarded conscious mental life.

The research and treatment method, called psychoanalysis, replicated the individual's intrapsychic struggle with the unconscious. Freud's model of neurotic suffering combined both the quantitative and qualitative ideas in the concept of intrapsychic conflict. Symptoms, those alien and debilitating conditions, appear as a result of conflict within the psyche.

According to this model, the terms of neurotic conflict begin with desire; the aim is gratification. The impulse to act, to seek direct gratification of desire, is inhibited by restrictive forces within the psyche. The most familiar type of restriction arises from the individual's moral standards, which render unacceptable the direct gratification of desire. This opposition of the forces of desire and morality produces the debilitating symptoms but in forms that will allow a measure of gratification of desire, however small and costly. Symptoms, resulting from intrapsychic conflict, are the individual's best effort at compromise.

However, as Freud discovered, symptom formation, since it utilizes compromises, follows principles of mental function which apply across a broad spectrum of activity. Therefore, the dynamics of intrapsychic conflict go beyond the pathological and enter into the realm of a general psychology. Normal mental activity such as dreaming, to cite one illustration, follows the same principle as the activity that leads to symptom formation (Freud, 1955, Vols IV and V). A dream is a symptom of mental conflict since it represents a compromise among forces in the unconscious that simultaneously push toward gratification of desire while inhibiting this tendency. The symbolic content of the dream disguises the conflict but also expresses all the terms of the conflict – both desire and prohibition.

This model of intrapsychic conflict underwent a variety of modifications throughout Freud's lifetime. For example, the idea of desire shifted from a dual instinct theory of sex and self-preservation to a dual instinct theory of sex and aggression. Closer attention to the object of desire (in contrast to the aim of discharge) revealed that while its normal pathway was outward toward objects and the environment, it could turn inward, particularly during stressful episodes in the individual's life. But even where desire turned inward, the object remained important in the psychoanalytic theory of conflict because of the observation that the individual retained an internalized image of the object, while seemingly relinquishing it in its real form. Even in the case of the most severe psychological disturbances – psychoses – the individual may appear uninterested in the object world, but the internal conflict evolves around the representations of these objects both in their beneficent and malevolent forms.

The formalization of the model of conflict led to the structural hypothesis which postulates three parts of the psychic structure: id, super-ego, and ego. The id is the part of the mind which generates desire, both sexual and aggressive impulses. The super-ego is the agency that involves the conscience (the imperatives of 'thou shalt not') and the ideals (the imperatives that one must achieve in order to feel loved and to experience self-esteem). The ego is the executive apparatus that consists of a variety of functions which together mediate the terms of the conflict between id, super-ego and, finally, reality.

Several problems arise in the application of the structural hypothesis, indeed, in working with all of these superordinate hypotheses in psychoanalytic theory. The hypothesis, called the metapsychology of psychoanalysis, poses a number of problems in application, both in strict scientific research as well as in clinical work. Some of these problems can be dismissed readily, such as the use of the structural hypothesis as though it referred to 'real' agencies of the mind. The id, super-ego, and ego are abstract concepts, an attempt to organize a theory of conflict. They are not anatomical entities, nor are they especially valuable as a guide to the phenomenology of conflict. But the structural hypothesis and the concepts of id, super-ego and ego serve a number of intellectual purposes in the theory of psychoanalysis. One example is the concept of resistance, or what prevents unconscious content from direct appearance in conscious images and thoughts. The work of psychoanalysis indicates that the derivatives of unconscious mental life are omnipresent in consciousness, but in such indirect and disguised forms (except in the case of delusional thinking and hallucinations) as to stretch credulity about the idea of unconscious derivatives affecting conscious thinking and activity. The structural hypothesis organizes Freud's observations and conclusions about resistance as a part of unconscious mental life: he posited the need to broaden the term of resistance (from barriers to consciousness) to defence as an unconscious function of the ego to limit the danger that occurs when the pressure to act on impulses becomes great (Freud, 1955, Vol. XX).

Another problem with the structural hypothesis of psychoanalysis derives from the logical consequences of using this hypothesis to distinguish among and explain the forms and functions of various pathologies. Psychological conflict implies that a psychic structure exists within the individual, so that, for example, moral imperatives no longer depend upon the parents for their force. The individual has a conscience which inflicts some measure of painful anxiety and guilt when unconscious desire seeks gratification.

The classical theory of psychoanalysis presumes that psychic conflict and structure become established during the last stages of infantile development, which is called the Oedipal stage (Freud, 1955, Vol. VII). In relinquishing incestuous desire, the child of approximately age five identifies with the objects and consequently emerges from infancy with a reasonably self-contained psychic structure. The pathologies linked to conflict in psychic structure, the transference neuroses, include hysteria, obsessional neuroses and related character neuroses. These pathologies are called transference neuroses because they do not impair the patient's ability, despite pain and suffering, to establish attachments to objects. However, the attachments are neurotically based in that the patient shifts the incestuous struggle from parents to other people. In the transference neuroses, the relationship to objects is not totally determined by the persistence of neurotic disturbance. For example, a person may be able to function reasonably well with other people except that he is incapable of sexual intimacy as a result of neurotic inhibition.

Psychoanalytic investigation, especially of the post-World War II period, has given rise to doubt about some of the formulations of the structural hypothesis and some of its derivatives in the explanation of pathologies. For example, can one clearly differentiate structural conflict from earlier developmental problems which derive from the deficits of infancy? The investigation of borderline conditions (a consequence of developmental deficits) or narcissistic disturbances (the conditions of impaired self-esteem and painful self-awareness), suggest that early internalizations of objects so colour the later identifications as to minimize the effects of psychological structure (see Segal, 1964). Critics argue that to treat such patients using classical techniques will prove futile. On the more theoretical plane, the critics also dispute the distinction between transference and narcissistic disturbances because of the importance of object attachments in the latter category of disturbance. Perhaps underlying the controversies within the psychoanalytic profession are more fundamental differences than the suggestion that one or more hypotheses are open to question. After all, any scientific endeavour attempts to disprove hypotheses and to modify the theory as a result of fresh observation and experimentation.

Almost from its inception, psychoanalysis has been the centre of debate in which the contenders, more than disputing particular hypotheses, are engaged in a test of contradictory world views. As indicated earlier, a tension inherent in psychoanalytic observation and explanation pervades the field. The dialectics of quantity and quality, of mechanics and meaning, colour the evaluation and practice in the field. The tension extends into more abstract polarities: humanity between science and humanism, tragic and utopian views of humanity, and conservative versus imperialistic visions of the place of psychoanalysis in improving human relations.

Freud cautioned against abandoning points of view implicit in the quantitative and qualitative position in psychoanalysis. While he was an artist in his observation of pathology and mental function (see, for example, Freud's exquisite narrative of an obsessional illness in his case 'The Rat Man' (Freud, 1955, Vol. (X)), Freud never abandoned the theory of instincts and its grounding in biology. From early on, the disputes in psychoanalysis have resulted from attempts to frame the theories of pathology and therapy along a single dimension, what Freud called the error of *pars pro toto*, or substituting the part for the whole. Thus, in contemporary psychoanalysis, the stress on developmental deficits over structural conflict arises in part from a humanistic perspective and leads to the use of the therapist not as an object in a transference drama that requires interpretation, but as a surrogate who will use his beneficent office to overcome the malevolence of the past, particularly of early infancy. These debates within psychoanalysis have strong intellectual, as well as cultural and philosophical, foundations. Some investigators place psychoanalysis squarely in the midst of interpretive disciplines rather than the natural sciences

(Ricoeur, 1970). They link psychoanalysis to hermeneutics, linguistics and the humanities as against biology, medicine, psychiatry and the sciences. These debates also have economic and political ramifications concerning what constitutes the psychoanalytic profession and the qualifications of those who seek to enter its practice.

Psychoanalysis began as a medical discipline for the treatment of neurotic disturbances. It continues this therapeutic tradition of classical psychoanalysis in broadened application to the psychoses, borderline and narcissistic conditions through variants of psychoanalytic psychotherapy. As a result of its methods of investigation, its observations and theories, psychoanalysis has become a part of the general culture. The applications of psychoanalysis in literary criticism, history, political and social sciences, law and business are evidence of its infusion into the general culture. Writers, artists and critics, while debating the uses of psychoanalysis beyond the couch, understand the theory and experiment with its applications to the arts. Freud gave birth to a therapy and a theory and perhaps beyond his intent, to a view of the world and the human condition.

Abraham Zaleznik
Harvard University

References

Freud, S. (1953–66), *Standard Edition of the Complete Psychological Works of Sigmund Freud*, 24 vols, edited by J. Strachey, London.

Jones, E. (1953), *Sigmund Freud: Life and Work*, 3 vols, London.

Ricoeur, P. (1970), *Freud and Philosophy: An Essay on Interpretation*, New Haven.

Segal, H. (1964), *Introduction to the Work of Melanie Klein*, New York.

See also: *countertransference; defences; free association; Freud, S.; hysteria; Klein, M.; super-ego; transference; unconscious.*

Psycholinguistics

Psycholinguistics is concerned with the theoretical, experimental and descriptive study of those cognitive processes involved in the production and comprehension of language by mature speakers, and in the acquisition of language by infants. It expanded rapidly as an academic subject area during the 1960s, initially in response to claims made by Chomsky (1965) and his followers (a) that specific language-learning proclivities are innate in humans and (b) that the human infant is programmed to identify and learn a particular model of grammar (transformational grammar). Psycholinguistics now forms an essential component of most degree programmes in linguistics, psychology, cognitive science and language teaching.

Psycholinguistic studies may be grouped into five main areas:

(1) Long-term programmes designed to test claims for the unique attribution of language-learning abilities to humans and to determine the limits of what may be classified as language. These have largely involved attempts at teaching specially limited forms of 'language' to other primates, particularly chimpanzees.

(2) Studies of language acquisition and language development in children (mostly constructed as longitudinal studies, following the linguistic progress of a group of children over months or years). These have been concerned to determine the nature of the linguistic input to the human infant, and the nature of the grammar controlling the speech which the infant produces (where the 'grammar' determines not only the emergent syntactic structures and word-forming processes, but also the sound-system – vowels and consonants – produced by the child). Such studies are used to underwrite theoretical models which account for the initial output of the child, which differs radically and systematically from that of the adult, and its gradual approximation to adult forms.

(3) Studies of language processing in normal adults. These have concentrated on the processing of meaningful linguistic units – words, sentences and short texts – examined in experimental settings. Whereas some experimental research has been concerned with the processing of speech (hence with speech sounds and the role played by prosodic features like stress and intonation) and a small body of research has examined features of language production, the usual experimental paradigm in this area has involved the study of aspects of the processing of written input (which lends itself to a more controlled input and to the conventional technique of measuring reaction-time). Typically, attempts are made to test theoretical models of word-meaning, storage, retrieval, models of sentence-meaning and sentence-processing (in, for instance, ambiguous sentences, which provide test-cases for general sentence-processing models) and models of text-meaning, text-memory, and the sort of inferencing necessary to understand what is implied but not explicitly stated in a text.

(4) Studies of various types of language pathology. These have investigated 'deviant' performance, in the expectation that the malfunctioning of a mechanism (in this case some aspect of language processing) may shed light on its normal functioning. At one extreme such studies investigate transient malfunctions, like slips of the tongue (inadvertent malapropisms), which only interfere trivially with communication but reveal powerful performance constraints, and, at the other extreme, gross malfunctions which may pathologically

impede communications, as in cases of dyslexia or aphasia.

(5) Studies of the acquisition of a second language (for instance by bilinguals) and of foreign-language learning. These may incidentally illuminate language processes in general, but are usually undertaken with specifically educational aims, in the attempt to improve language teaching methods and materials.

Gillian Brown
University of Essex

Reference

Chomsky, N. (1965), *Aspects of the Theory of Syntax*, Cambridge, Mass.

Further Reading

Clark, H. H. and Clark, E. V. (1977), *Psychology and Language*, New York.
Fodor, J. A. (1976), The *Language of Thought*, Brighton.
Greene, J. (1972), *Psycholinguistics*, Harmondsworth.
See also: *bilingualism; Chomsky; language development; pragmatics.*

Psychology

Almost a hundred years ago, William James (1890) epitomized psychology as 'the science of mental life'. It is the discipline that gathers together all those who have a systematic interest in the mind and its workings, in people and the lives they lead. To say this, though, is to pose a puzzle, even a paradox. For what the visitor finds, when he enters a university department of psychology, opens a textbook of psychology, or dips into psychology's professional journals, seems both startling in its diversity, and, often, to have little to do either with the mind or with people. It is this puzzle that an account pf psychology must explain.

Looking back to James and his contemporaries, the founding fathers of psychology, one sees scarcely a trace of the diversity to follow, or of the retreat, real or apparent, from their conception of the psychologist's subject-matter. These men wrote about the mind and about people, and did so without embarrassment. Francis Galton, for instance, allowed his curiosity to range from hereditary studies of genius, the invention of rudimentary statistics and the first attempts to test intelligence, to discussions of the mind that sit comfortably beside those of the early psychoanalysts. While

Freud was still a young man, with his life's work ahead of him, Galton (1883) wrote: 'There seems to be a presence chamber in my mind where full consciousness holds court, and where two or three ideas are at the same time in audience, and an ante-chamber full of more or less allied ideas, which is situated just beyond the full ken of consciousness. Out of this ante-chamber the ideas most nearly allied to those in the presence-chamber appear to be summoned in a mechanically logical way, and to have their turn of audience.' Beyond or below this ante-chamber, Galton also discerned 'a darker basement, a storehouse from which older and remoter ideas can with greater difficulty be called up into consciousness.' Such language and assumptions were accessible not only to Galton's academic neighbours, but also to those outside psychology; Poincaré, for example, the great French mathematician, was intrigued by the source of his own mathematical insights, which seemed to arrive unbidden (Hadamard, 1945).

Without question, Galton's imagination was circumscribed by what we now see as ugly Victorian prejudices. 'It is in the most unqualified manner,' he said (1883) 'that I object to pretensions of natural equality.' He also observed that 'The mistakes the negroes made in their own matters were so childish, stupid, and simpleton-like, as frequently to make me ashamed of my own species.' Nowadays we would expect Galton to distinguish altogether more crisply between questions of diversity, essential to our evolution as a species, and questions of value. Nevertheless, he entertained the great problems of human self-awareness, and did so with unbridled energy. Thus, one morning, he decided that he would view the world around him as though being spied upon (Burt, 1961). By the time his walk was over 'every horse on every cabstand seemed to be watching me either openly or in disguise'. These 'persecutory delusions' lasted for the rest of the day, and could be revived at will three months later.

In the years after the First World War, the intellectual freedom of men like Galton was gradually abandoned. Psychology became the focus of a new enthusiasm: behaviourism. Under this influence, psychology, then establishing itself as an academic subject in universities, began to settle upon two of its abiding preoccupations: the first, with its status as a science, as opposed to a scholarly pursuit like history or a therapeutic one like medicine; the second, with the need to banish from the discipline all 'subjective' considerations, all mention of mental states, and to root psychology instead in the prediction of relationships between stimulus and response.

Gradually, throughout the 1930s and 1940s, the influence of behaviourism strengthened; to the extent that, by the early 1950s, the subject-matter of psychology itself had been redefined. Instead of being taught that psychology was the science of mental life, students were taught that it was the 'science of behaviour' (Skinner, 1953). The behaviour in question, their professors made plain, was not just that of human beings, but of all animal species, from octopus to man – and these creatures, not in their wild state, but in the artificial environment of the laboratory.

Behaviourism was to remain the dominant orthodoxy in university departments of psychology until the late 1960s, when doubts were voiced (for example, Kagan, 1967; Hudson, 1972). The mood, since, has grown more pluralistic. While behaviourism produced neither the centrally placed bodies of knowledge nor the intellectual mastery that pioneers like Watson and Skinner promised, its legacy is all round us, in that the activities of professional psychologists make less than complete sense if this influence is ignored. The anxiety over psychology's status as a science remains, scarcely abated; and so too does the distrust of any argument that cannot be tethered to objective evidence about what people, animals or, more recently, computers can be seen to do.

Worries about the scientific respectability of psychology have led, in turn, to a sense of hierarchy within psychology. Precisely controlled experimental research, designed to test a theory that is itself carefully formulated, is highly regarded; field research or research which is geared to the practical needs of the world at large have a lower status. As in the scientific community as a whole, the pure is elevated over the applied. The subject-matter of academic psychology has organized itself, too, around a variety of abstract themes: learning, memory, attention, motivation, intelligence, personality, creativity, and so on. Pursuing these, psychologists have sometimes seemed to execute a wilful retreat from questions of practical relevance.

In the 1950s, when this retreat was at its most pronounced, it seemed at times that psychological research enjoyed higher prestige the further removed from ordinary human concerns it became. Experimental studies, of course, were not always narrowly conceived; Gregory's (1966) work on visual illusions, for example, combined elegance with a wider sense of implication. But research on issues of pressing social concern was usually treated, in comparison, as suspect. McClelland's (1961) studies of the motives of the entrepreneur were accorded a certain respect, as was the work, inspired by Nazi Germany, on the authoritarian personality (Adorno, 1950), and the research by social psychologists like Asch (1955) and Milgram (1963) on social pressure and compliance. Even here, though, the lure of theory, and of the apparent rigour of tests and statistics, were sometimes to prove disruptively strong. Only rather exceptionally did psychologists study a pertinent slice of life without the protection of either, as Bronfenbrenner (1970) was to do in his comparison of Russian and American experiences of childhood.

Another feature of psychology at this stage in its growth, despite its optimism and energy, was its reliance on sources outside itself for new initiatives. Obvious instances are the impact on the discipline of the early information theorists and of a linguist like Chomsky. Another instance, more subtle, is that of Kelly (1955). His background was complex: first in mathematics and physics, then in educational sociology and psychology. He earned a living as an aeronautical engineer before settling on a career in psychology. Perhaps because of this grounding, half inside psychology, half out, his work on the semantics of everyday life has remained fertile, even though the area was one that more conventional psychologists like Osgood (1957) had already begun to develop. In the hands of the orthodox, the wider implications of a good idea were sometimes buried beneath technique that was rigorous but subtly misplaced, evidence that was copious but inconclusive. Preoccupied with questions of rigour, psychologists also allowed academic neighbours like the sociologist Goffman (1959) to pre-empt important parts of their own subject-matter, placing upon it constructions in which psychological notions played only an insignificant part.

Whatever its excesses, behaviourism helped establish a concern for rigour over questions of method. Less directly, it pointed to a source of uncertainty – and, hence, of diversity – that lies at the very heart of psychology, and which refuses to go away. For the study of the mind is based upon an unresolved, and some would say unresolvable, tension: that between human consciousness and the brain in which that consciousness is housed. At the centre of psychology, there is the baffling relation of the mind to body; of the meanings in terms of which human beings order their lives, some crisply determinate, others ambiguous, vague or half-hidden, and the central nervous system without which such meanings could not exist.

In practice, psychologists leave the mind/body problem to philosophers. The shape that their discipline takes nevertheless reflects this point of strain. Psychologists have in the past tended to form two camps: on the one hand, the 'soft', those concerned with people, the relations between them, and the meanings with which their lives are imbued; on the other, the 'hard', who are committed to the study of the brain and how it works. The 'soft' have a natural affinity with social scientists, historians, therapists, while the 'hard' have close links with brain chemists, biologists, computer scientists.

This distinction between 'soft' and 'hard', although it still enjoys wide currency, is an unfortunate one. It provides a tempting line of fissure, and it is unrepresentative, too, of the variety that the inhabitants of many psychology departments nowadays display. If you walk into a psychology department, anywhere in the Western world, and listen to what is taught, or speak to the teachers about their research, you will probably find as many instances that violate this simple distinction between 'soft' and 'hard' as conform to it. In order to make sense of psychology as it now stands, another, more complex, model or metaphor is required.

Consider the members of staff in a particular department who have joined forces to teach an introductory course in psychology to first-year students (the instance is real rather than imagined). There are four of them. The first is a young woman who usually describes herself as a social psychologist. Her special concern is with stress, and her research has carried her into the clinical world, where she studies the anxieties experienced by surgical patients, especially those with breast cancer. She works in close collaboration with surgeons, and the aim of her research is in part the practical one of reducing the distress that serious illness and surgery induce.

Her teaching partner, in the first term of the course, is, superficially, of a different stamp. He was trained in a famous physiology department rather than a department of psychology, and his research is squarely scientific: it deals with the brain's ability to assimilate information reaching it from the eye, and he conducts it in a small, electrically-screened cubicle, with a high degree of experimental refinement and control. His interests in psychology range quite widely, but what he publishes is addressed to an audience that is very specialized indeed.

In the second term, another pair of lecturers take over. The first studies the relations of young mothers to their infants, the ways in which patterns of child-raising differ from one social class to another, and, more generally, the emergence of the individual's sense of identity – the ideas and commitments around which a sense of self is hung. Her partner started out in life as a mathematician. He is an expert in the study of memory and of mental imagery; and has carried out studies, for example, of the effects on memory of the kinds of head injury sustained in traffic accidents. More recently, he has become interested, too, in methods of teaching, and in the ways in which university students learn.

These four psychologists, members of a single department, plough four distinct furrows. Next year, their places on the introductory course could be taken by others. One, whose appointment is half in psychology, half in biology, specializes in animal behaviour, and is knowledgeable about the interaction of hereditary and environmental forces. He might speak to the students about the mating behaviour of red deer, or show them films of rats running in mazes. Another deals with psychoanalytic theory and feminism. Yet another does research on the chemistry of the brain, and hopes to shed light on the causes of senile dementia. A fourth is interested in the relation of Kelly's repertory grid analysis to information technology; a fifth pays systematic attention to the skill of reading.

The diversity that these academics represent is far greater than one would find in any other discipline on the university's campus. Yet they all see themselves and are seen by others as psychologists. They combine to teach the same students, and the students they teach see themselves, in turn, as becoming psychologists.

Despite their differences, a visitor might expect all these psychologists to share a belief in the same body of theories, in the sense that physicists share a belief in the theoretical edifice that Newton, Einstein, Hiesenberg and others have built. If so, he would be mistaken. There is no commonly accepted body of psychological theory. In practice, the best theorizing in psychology has been done at the local level, and attempts to create grand, overarching theories have met with little success.

This absence of a uniting theory may come as an uncomfortable surprise. Even more uncomfortable is the discovery that psychologists of different persuasions often have little to say to one another about research, and can differ with one another quite sharply about the kinds of psychology that students should be taught. They may disagree, for example, about whether a grounding in elementary statistics is essential, or whether students ahould be exposed to the ideas of Freud. Rather than exchanging views with one another, they often find it easier and more natural to talk to academic neighbours, outside psychology. The psychologist who specializes in animal behaviour may well find that he goes to conferences where he meets ethologists and geneticists, rather than psychologists whose special interests differ from his own. And his colleagues likewise.

Not only do many psychologists lack a driving interest in one another's research; it frequently happens that they cannot understand one another's publications. Thus a psychologist working on the computer simulation of short-term memory may find it hard, even impossible, to follow a paper written by a colleague who is excited by recent critiques of psychoanalytic theory, advanced by scholars on the Continent (see, for example, Bowie, 1979). And vice versa. At this point, the visitor may well protest that psychology is not a discipline at all; simply a cacophany, a muddle. To reach this conclusion is an error, however; and it is so, because it rests on an excessively simple view of what a discipline is like.

The point is best made in terms of diagrams, as Campbell (1977) suggests. The usual assumption about a discipline like chemistry is that it consists of a common core of agreed theory, and a number of subsidiary specialities or applications. In diagrammatic terms, this might be represented as a pyramid, or as a nest of concentric circles, like the layers of an onion. Pyramids and concentric circles are not the only diagrams one can draw, though. Consider this:

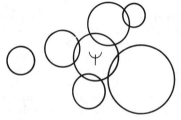

Figure 1

Psychology is represented by the centrally placed circle, marked 'Ψ'; other, related disciplines – social science, biology, computer science – by the adjacent circles. Some of the neighbouring circles overlap the 'psychological' circle, but none includes it. If the circle representing psychology is now abstracted from the rest, one sees this:

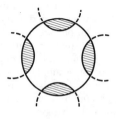

Figure 2

This diagram poses some interesting possibilities: for example, that it is in its areas of overlap with its neighbours – here, shaded – that the field of psychology is at its most exciting. It is in these zones of overlap that their interests bring the psychologist and his neighbours into contact – and, often, conflict. Thus both psychologist and computer scientist may have an interest in human memory, but very different presuppositions about how memory can best be explained. Likewise, psychologists and sociologists share an interest in crimes of violence but disagree sharply over their likely causes.

Analogous conflicts arise continually, and three or more disciplines sometimes stake a claim, as has happened in the field of sex and gender and the explanation of the psychological differences that men and women display. Those, like Kinsey, with a background in biology, have generated bodies of evidence about regularities in behaviour, although their researches, as it happened, were often informed by a libertarian, permissive system of moral values (Robinson, 1969). At the same time, evidence was drawn from anthropology, pioneers like Margaret Mead stressing the extent to which male and female patterns of behaviour were culturally rather than biologically determined (D'Andrade, 1967); and, then, from medicine and from

within psychoanalytic tradition, there evolved a further body of work stressing the confusions of gender identity that can arise, and tracing these to the relation of the infant in question to the parent of the opposite sex (Stroller, 1968; Money and Ehrhardt, 1972). Into this area, there also moved endocrinologists, interested in the impact of sex hormones on behaviour; feminists, concerned with the extent to which evidence about sex differences becomes muddled with political prejudice; and those studying abnormalities of sexual behaviour – a perversion like fetishism, for instance, which seems a male preserve.

Such areas of overlap usually arise from contact between psychologists and their academic neighbours, but, from time to time, the contact is with specialists whose concerns are more immediately practical: the doctor concerned with the care of his patients, the police superintendent worried about relations between his junior officers and the Black community. Whether academic or practical, the moral pointed by the diagram is the same: intellectually, psychology is a discipline that thrives on exchange with the worlds of expertise that surround it.

Other morals flow too. If psychology is a field in which excitement characteristically arises around the edges, its heartland will consist not so much of specific theories or bodies of evidence, as of those broader concerns which have remained unchanged since psychology's beginnings as a branch of philosophy: the relation of mind to body, the origins of knowledge, the distinction between the real and the illusory. It is in their sensitivity to these centrally placed foci of conceptual unease that psychologists of quality mark themselves out from those whose contribution is more technical. It also follows that, in the shaded areas around the edge of the field, specialized languages and techniques will evolve in response to local needs. A consequence is that, considered as a whole, psychology will tend to be a polyglot, containing a number of languages rather than a single language. The risk, plainly, is that the task of translation will be skimped, and that psychology will tend to split apart as nations do. If this were to happen, professional life in the short run might be more tranquil, but the uniting commitment to the study of mental life would dissolve, and with it would be lost the chance to resolve the more complex problems that human beings pose.

Grant such a model of psychology, more complicated than the onion with its skins or the pyramid with its layers, but down-to-earth nonetheless, and what one finds inside a psychology department fits comfortably into place. The diversity and polygot nature of psychology represent not a lapse from some simple ideal, but the consequences that flow, quite properly, from the complexities of the psychologist's subject matter. This complexity, it is important to see, is not just a question of the styles that psychologists adopt, the schools of thought they form or the methods of inquiry they find it most comfortable to use. It is inherent in the problems themselves, as the work on sex and gender shows. The direction of an individual's sexual desires, his sense of his own maleness or femaleness, his presentation of himself in terms of his interests, habits and social style as typically male, typically female or more androgynous: all this will depend on physical questions – his chromosomes and sex hormones, his anatomy – but on these overlaid with the influence of parents and contemporaries and the values implicit in the wider culture. The confusions and perplexities that characterize this aspect of human experience demand patient scrutiny; and this, in its turn, may depend as much on clinical and on literary skills (see Brown, 1966; Gass, n.d.; Barthes, 1979) as it does on those of scientific research.

This point about the multifaceted nature of the psychologist's subject-matter can equally be made elsewhere. The question of mental illness, far from seeming depressing or sordid, is the focus of keen interest among laymen and psychologists alike. Insight into its causes or cure could come from a variety of quite different directions, and these could prove to be complementary. The attraction of mental illness as a research problem is precisely its many-sidedness.

The traditional view is that mental illness – or, more specifically, schizophrenia – is congenital. In support of this, there is the evidence of genetics. This shows that the closer the kinship between two people, the more likely both are to be schizophrenic, identical twins seeming to show the highest concordance of all (Kallmann, 1953). Adjacent, but separate, there is the work of the pharmacologists and brain chemists. They point to certain substances that can be recovered from the brains of schizophrenics that are not present in the same quantities in the brains of those who are not schizophrenic. Adjacent again, but again separate, there are arguments based on the analogy with the computer: the suggestion, for instance, that the schizophrenic brain is like a computer suffering from information overload.

Such theories and speculations can be categorized broadly as 'physical'. They have been subjected to vigorous attack over the last twenty years or so. One onslaught (for example, Laing and Esterson, 1964) advanced the claim that rather than going mad, people are driven mad – and driven mad, characteristically, by parents who exert 'double binds' upon them. More sweeping still has been the argument, often attractive to students of social science, that schizophrenia is what results when a society stigmatizes, isolates and humiliates its deviants, a process in which orthodox psychiatrists are seen as playing a malign role.

The key to the problem of schizophrenia, if there is one, could emerge from any of four or five separate areas of research, or from a combination of these. Along one path, a cure might arise from better parental practices; along another, from a revolutionary new drug therapy.

At meetings between opposed camps, an air of awkwardness often reigns, and, frequently, there are displays of mutual incomprehension. More tellingly, though, rival camps also have the chance to probe the logical weaknesses in each other's positions. Thus it was quickly discovered that the genetic evidence about identical twins was less conclusive than it seemed, because identical twins share not only their genetic endowment but very similar environments too (Newman, 1937). In search of rigour, the debate was forced back from concordance in identical twins in general to concordance in those few pairs who had been separated from birth, and whose environments had of necessity been different (Shields, 1962). Inexorably logical, this step precipitated another, however. Gradually, research workers realized that, as they could not know in advance which aspects of an individual's environment might play a crucial part in causing schizophrenia, they had no means of demonstrating that the separated twins' environments were dissimilar in significant rather than trivial respects.

Step by step, in other words, the logical demands made upon the competing bodies of evidence were sharpened; and, one after another, bodies of evidence which at first sight had seemed clinching were revealed as helpful but inconclusive. More generally, it was also realized that the discussion of causes was logically separate from the discussion of cures. Many participants in the debate about the causes of schizophrenia assumed that evidence from genetics must be resisted because it was evidence that schizophrenia could not be cured. Only slowly did it dawn that schizophrenia might prove to be genetically transmitted, after all, and yet that, in one form or another, perfectly satisfactory clinical or social treatments might nonetheless be established.

While the debate about the causes of schizophrenia has recently seemed to lose a little of its intensity, another topic, eclipsed for several decades, is now moving back towards the limelight: the question of why we dream. Again, this is multifaceted. A popular view, derived from Freud (Sulloway, 1979), is that we dream in order to fulfil repressed sexual wishes. This line of reasoning, which sees dreams as pregnant with hidden meaning, did not recommend itself to behaviourists, however, who professed to believe, many of them, that dreams do not exist; or, if they did, that they were purely random. The 1950s saw the establishment of laboratories for the study of sleep and dreaming. While important discoveries were made, the theorizing within these laboratories tended to be biological in inspiration. The dream, more often than not, was seen as a by-product of some physiological or chemical process in which a balance in the brain is restored (Oswald,

1980). More recently, analogies between brain and computer have led to the suggestion that the dreaming brain is akin to a computer in its 'off-line' state, during which its programmes are up-dated or 'cleaned'.

Such biological research nonetheless faced a difficulty: that of explaining the evolutionary function that sleep and dreaming must perform. The sleeping, dreaming animal is at the mercy of its predators; and any pattern of behaviour so blatantly dangerous must have a vital adaptive function if it is to survive. One task, then, is to state what this adaptive function is. Another is to explain (rather than explaining away) the widely held and carefully substantiated view that dreams, although in code, can sometimes serve as a complement to and comment upon waking thought (Rycroft, 1979); that, as Darwin (1871) observed, dreams are an involuntary kind of poetry.

Again, four or five bodies of evidence are relevant; there are four or five circles that can in principle overlap. Adopting an evolutionary frame of reference, and drawing heavily on the computer analogy, Crick and Mitchison (1983) have proposed that animals have the dreams associated with rapid eye movement sleep in order that their brains can clear themselves of 'parasitic' patterns of response; and that, without this capability, the brain would quickly become overloaded. A corollary of this argument, as the authors point out, is that we dream in order to forget; that dreams, on the whole, neither can nor should be recalled.

Such a theory is difficult if not impossible to test directly. One would have to show that the occurrence of a thought in an unrecalled dream reduces the likelihood of that thought recurring. On the other hand, it is an error to restrict psychology to the study of theories that can be directly verified or falsified; and an error, too, to assume that the issue of the dream's meaning is closed. Einstein was not alone among scientists in treating the dream as a useful source of insight, both in its own right and as part of a more general access to intuitive or imaginative modes of thought. There is no inherent reason why a theory like Crick and Mitchison's should not be modified to allow the brain to scan its own 'parasitic' products, and to glean from them ideas that it can set to good use. If this modification were adopted, dreams would be seen less as household rubbish, more as items jumbled together on a bric-á-brac stall, most virtually worthless, a few of genuine value and richly deserving rescue.

As with research on schizophrenia, there also exists the need to specify, with detachment and precision, what it is that dream theories are seeking to explain. In research on schizophrenia, there is still uncertainty about symptoms – whether 'thought disorder' is always present, and what 'thought disorders' consist of. Similarly with dreaming. The laboratory research on sleep and dreaming makes it clear that many dreams are more 'thought-like' than had previously seemed likely.

This finding has implications that run in several directions. It brings to mind the possibility that this distinction between thought-like and dream-like dreams has its basis in the activities of the left and right cerebral hemispheres respectively. It raises once again the question of 'cognitive style' and the differences that individuals display in their access to the nonrational aspects of their own experience (Getzels and Jackson, 1962; Hudson, 1966); and it suggests that one might with profit look more closely at the dream-like states that occur while we are awake: not just reveries and fantasies, but at the dream-like states evoked in an altogether more disciplined and fastidious way in the verbal and visual arts (Hudson, 1982). As with schizophrenia, so with dreaming; a more scrupulous mapping of mental states could sharpen the pressures under which relatively simple-minded evolutionary and computer-based theories are at present placed.

Of course, not all debates in psychology appeal as directly to the layman as do those about schizophrenia or sleep and dreaming. Nor can all be contained relatively comfortably within frames of reference that are familiar. Sometimes, the discipline faces a challenge from outside, and one with implications that cannot be foreseen. One such is the computer.

While early computers were 'stupid', their descendants are showing signs of adaptability: the ability to learn from experience, and even to evolve their own instructions (Boden, 1977). Arguably, students of artificial intelligence can now learn from the adaptive systems that have evolved naturally: the brain and also the genetic mechanisms whereby inherited patterns of behaviour are passed from one generation to the next. It could be of real value to designers of artificial brains, for example, to know why natural brains dream. This new field – that of 'intelligent systems' – cuts across the established boundaries between computer science, biology and psychology, and it will be of interest to see how lively a part psychologists play in it.

The implications of the computer, though, are not tidily circumscribed. It opens a door onto an immediate future in which, to a wholly unprecedented degree, human beings will live in intimate contact with machines: not only the computer and word processor but the camera and television set – and these instruments not just as useful servants, but as devices that invade the individual's consciousness and alter it in both profound and superficial ways.

The tendency of psychology over the last half century, a period of massive professional growth and proliferation, has been somewhat inward-looking. It has addressed certain themes – ones that, over the years, have come to be seen as the 'classical' ones – and it has preserved from its formative stages a deep preoccupation with objectivity in judgement, correctness in method. Yet it seems unlikely that the human implications of information technology can satisfactorily be met from such a stance. Social change, both in this area and in others, will in all probability be too rapid and too radical.

Whether the question at issue is the human implication of the computer, or some other respect in which an advanced industrial society is subject to change – the impact, for example, of structural unemployment on the lives of those on whom idleness is imposed – the challenge is in principle the same. In order to make contributions of value, psychologists may have to recover some of the intellectual freedom and vitality (though not the ugly prejudices) that founding fathers like Galton and James enjoyed.

Liam Hudson
Brunel University, Uxbridge

References

Adorno, T. W. *et al.* (1950), *The Authoritarian Personality*, New York.

Asch, S. E. (1955), 'Opinions and social pressure', *Scientific American*.

Barthes, R. (1979), *A Lover's Discourse*, London.

Boden, M. (1977), *Artificial Intelligence and Natural Man*, Hassocks.

Bowie, M. (1979), 'Jacques Lacan', in J. Sturrock (ed.), *Structuralism and Since*, Oxford.

Bronfenbrenner, U. (1970), *Two Worlds of Childhood*, New York.

Brown, N. O. (1966), *Love's Body*, New York.

Burt, C. (1961), 'Galton's contribution to psychology', *Bulletin of the British Psychological Society*, 45.

Campbell, D. T. (1977), *Descriptive Epistemology*, preliminary draft of William James Lectures, Harvard University, unpublished.

Crick, F. and Mitchison, G. (1983), 'The function of dream sleep', *Nature*, 304.

D'Andrade, R. G. (1967), 'Sex differences and cultural institutions', in E. E. Maccoby (ed.), *The Development of Sex Differences*, London.

Darwin, C. (1871), *The Descent of Man*, London.

Galton, F. (1883), *Inquiries into Human Faculty*, London.

Gass, W. (no date), *On Being Blue*, Boston.

Getzels, J. W. and Jackson, P. W. (1962), *Creativity and Intelligence*, New York.

Goffman, E. (1959), *The Presentation of Self in Everyday Life*, New York.

Gregory, R. (1966), *Eye and Brain*, London.

Hadamard, J. (1945), *The Psychology of Invention in the Mathematical Field*, Princeton.

Hudson, L. (1966), *Contrary Imaginations*, London.

Hudson, L. (1972), *The Cult of the Fact*, London.

Hudson, L. (1982), *Bodies of Knowledge*, London.

James, W. (1890), *Principles of Psychology*, New York.

Kagan, J. (1967), 'On the need for relativism', *American Psychologist*, 22.

Kallmann, F. J. (1953), *Heredity in Health and Mental Disorder*, New York.

Kelly, G. A. (1955), *The Psychology of Personal Constructs*, New York.

Laing, R. D. and Esterson, A. (1964), *Sanity, Madness and the Family*, London.

McClelland, D. C. (1961), *The Achieving Society*, New York.

Milgram, S. (1963), 'Behavioral study of obedience', *Journal of Abnormal and Social Psychology*, 67.

Money, J. and Ehrhardt, A. A. (1972), *Man and Woman, Boy and Girl*, Baltimore.

Newman, H. H. *et al.* (1937), *Twins: A Study of Heredity and Environment*, Chicago.

Osgood, C. E. *et al.* (1957), *The Measurement of Meaning*, Urbana.

Oswald, I. (1980), *Sleep*, Harmondsworth.

Robinson, P. A. (1969), *The Sexual Radicals*, London.

Rycroft, C. (1979), *The Innocence of Dreams*, London.

Shields, J. (1962), *Monozygotic Twins Brought up Apart and Brought Up Together*, Oxford.

Skinner, B. F. (1953), *Science and Human Behavior*, New York.

Stoller, R. J. (1968), *Sex and Gender*, London.

Sulloway, F. J. (1979), *Freud, Biologist of the Mind*, London.

Psychopathic Personality

The condition of the psychopathic personality has been variously labelled by psychiatrists over the past two hundred years as 'hereditary moral insanity', 'constitutional psychopathic inferiority', 'psychopathic personality', 'sociopath', and more recently, 'antisocial personality disorder'. Each of these labels suggests a different aetiology. The aetiology remains debatable, and even the condition itself defies precise description.

Some psychiatrists regard this disorder as an unreliable category, as a 'wastebasket' condition which lacks the features of a genuine mental disorder. Critics of the psychopath label also decry the use of this term as obscuring what, in their view, is instead criminal, immoral or other situationally based behaviour. The supposed core of psychopathy includes egocentricity and lack of respect for the feelings and rights of others, coupled with persistent manipulative and/or antisocial behaviour – at times, of an aggressive, even violent, type. These core characteristics are manifested by certain criminals, but also by other, more outwardly successful, persons. As William McCord (1982) writes, 'The psychopath simply does not care, one way or another, about the communality of human beings known as society.'

While appearing superficially normal (because

cognition is intact and the individual does not manifest any obvious mental pathology) the psychopath's destructive pattern of activities is manifested over time, usually resulting in social and personal tragedies for himself and others.

The best-known modern criteria for psychopathic personality disorder were developed by Cleckley (1982). Cleckley's approach stresses the psychopath's persistent personality features such as untruthfulness and insincerity, poor judgement and failure to learn by experience, pathological egocentricity and incapacity for love, and inadequately motivated antisocial behaviour. Psychodynamically-oriented psychiatrists explain these features as attributable to pathological super-ego development, inner emptiness and compensatory impulsivity. Recent, more 'objective', non-aetiological diagnostic approaches recommended by the American Psychiatric Association (DSM III) stress a constellation of long-standing antisocial behaviour dating from childhood, and poor adult work behaviour, violation of social and interpersonal norms, and impulsivity.

The prevalence of psychopathy in normal and criminal populations is unknown. Over the centuries, the aetiology has been variously attributed to genetic predisposition or other constitutional problems and, more recently, to emotional deprivation in childhood with poor, inconsistent and sadistic parenting. Biological theories are related to the psychopath's putative brain immaturity, autonomic nervous system defects which inhibit learning of social norms, or hormonal defects. In some instances, aspects of the psychopathic syndrome may appear following brain injury. However, the aetiology of psychopathy remains obscure and controversial.

Little is known about treatment. The natural history of this disorder, however, includes attrition with age of certain diagnostic features and psychopathic behaviour. After age forty, the psychopath is said to 'burn out'. Current treatment approaches (usually not successful) include milieu therapy to promote the psychopath's identification with better-adjusted, more prosocial peers. From the psychological or behavioural perspective, consistent, limit-setting treatment approaches are advocated. Individual psychotherapeutic work directed towards uncovering and resolving inner conflicts is usually not successful. The psychopath is neither a neurotic nor a psychotic. The nature and extent of past social adjustment (not the mental status) best predict the psychopath's future adjustment.

The challenge of psychopathy, including the appropriateness of categorizing mental disorders along somewhat vague socially based criteria, will probably persist for a long time.

Loren H. Roth
University of Pittsburgh

References
McCord, W. (1982), *The Psychopath and Milieu Therapy*, New York.
Cleckley, H. (1982), *The Mask of Sanity*, New York.
See also: *character disorders*.

Psychopharmacology

The last thirty years have witnessed dramatic progress in our knowledge of drugs to treat the major psychiatric disorders. Prior to the 1950s, psychiatrists possessed only a few nonspecific sedative and stimulant drugs to treat anxiety and depression. Electroconvulsive therapy (ECT) had also been found effective for patients with depressive illness, but it proved much less useful for patients with chronic schizophrenia. For many of the half-million patients in American mental hospitals in the 1950s, and hundreds of thousands more throughout the world, no effective treatment existed.

Then, in the space of only six years – from 1949 to 1955 – three pharmacological discoveries sparked a revolution in psychiatric treatment. These were: (1) antipsychotic drugs; (2) antidepressant drugs; and (3) lithium.

(1) *Antipsychotic drugs* counteract delusions (beliefs in things which are not real) and hallucinations (seeing visions, hearing voices, and the like) – symptoms common in schizophrenia and manic-depressive illness. Within a few weeks, these drugs may bring a patient from a floridly psychotic state, in which he must be confined to a locked ward of a mental hospital, to a state of near-remission, in which he can be discharged and return to normal social and occupational life. Indeed, the introduction of antipsychotic treatment is credited with decreasing the population of American mental hospitals from 550,000 to 430,000 in the twelve years after 1955, despite a steady rise in the population.

Remarkable as their effects may seem, however, all antipsychotic drugs may have annoying side-effects: sedation, muscle stiffness, restlessness, slowed physical and mental functioning, and other problems. Perhaps as a result of these side effects, the antipsychotic drugs have often been misnamed 'major tranquillizers'. In fact, they are not tranquillizers at all; it is a serious misconception to think that they 'tranquillize' the patient into being free of his symptoms. Rather, they seem to have specific and selective effects on the psychosis itself. Any sedative or tranquillizing properties of the antipsychotic drugs appear purely accidental. In fact, if a normal person were to take even a small dose of one of the more potent antipsychotic drugs – such as fluphenazine or haloperidol – he would in all likelihood notice no tranquillization, and, indeed, might possibly experience a jumpy, restless feeling called akathisia.

Fortunately, given the wide range of available antipsychotic drugs, and the various medications developed to treat the side-effects, it is usually possible to reduce the side-effects to a tolerable level. This is important, since many patients must take the drugs for months or years to ensure protection from recurrent psychotic symptoms.

(2) *Antidepressant drugs* include the tricyclic antidepressants (such as imipramine and amitriptyline) and the monoamine oxidase inhibitors (such as phenelzine and tranylcypromine), discovered in the 1950s, together with several newer families of agents. These drugs provide relief for patients suffering from so-called major depression, or from the depressed phase of manic-depressive illness – conditions formerly responsive only to electro-convulsive therapy. The effect of antidepressants, like that of the antipsychotics, may be dramatic: a patient too depressed to eat or sleep, unable to perform even the most rudimentary tasks, and thinking constantly of suicide, may respond so well that he is completely back to normal functioning in three or four weeks.

Like the antipsychotics, antidepressants are the subject of various misconceptions. In particular, they are not 'psychostimulants' or 'mood elevators'; a normal person taking them would typically notice some sedation, lightheadedness, dry mouth, and a few other side-effects, but no increased energy or euphoria. Antidepressants appear to act by correcting some underlying chemical imbalance in the brain, rather than propelling the patient into an artificial euphoria.

(3) *Lithium* is unique among psychiatric medications in that it is a simple ion, rather than a complex molecule. For reasons still poorly understood, it counteracts the manic phase of manic-depressive illness (it appears less effective in acute depression), and, taken over the long term, protects patients against relapses of mania or depression. Since it has relatively few side-effects, it may be taken for years at a time with few problems. Such long-term prophylactic use of lithium has transformed the lives of thousands of sufferers from manic-depressive illness and related disorders. Prior to lithium, many patients were accustomed to frequent psychiatric hospitalizations for the exacerbations of their illness, with severe disruption of their personal lives and their careers. Now they often enjoy partial or total protection against such occurrences.

Other Psychiatric Drugs

Other types of psychiatric drugs continue to be introduced. Benzodiazepines, such as chlordiazepoxide and diazepam, have been found safer and perhaps more effective than barbiturates for sedation in anxious patients; other benzodiazepines, such as flurazepam and temazepam, are excellent sleeping-pills. Stimulants, such as methylphenidate and magnesium pemoline, have ameliorated the symptoms of childhood hyperkinesis or minimal brain dysfunction, now called 'atten-

tion deficit disorder'. Anticonvulsant drugs, such as carbamazepine and sodium valproate, appear effective in some cases of manic-depressive illness. Even two food substances – a fat called lecithin and the amino acid L-tryptophan, which are now used primarily for research purposes – may be helpful in mania and depression, respectively. But none of these recent discoveries has matched the impact of the introduction of the antipsychotics, the antidepressants and lithium. Not only have the latter three classes of drugs greatly reduced the ravages of schizophrenia and manic-depressive illness, but they appear helpful for a number of other disorders, among them, panic disorder and agoraphobia, some forms of drug and alcohol abuse, anorexia nervosa and bulimia, certain organic mental disorders, and others.

The discovery of these medications has not only great clinical and public-health consequences, but major theoretical implications. It is an important observation that the drugs have little psychiatric effect on normal individuals, but a profound effect on patients suffering from actual psychiatric disorders. In other words, unlike the nonspecific sedative and stimulant medications, these compounds appear specifically to correct some underlying abnormality in the brain. This specificity not only suggests that there are biological abnormalities underlying many of the major psychiatric disorders, but gives clues as to what the abnormalities may be. Studies of the action of psychopharmacologic agents have given impetus to the growing field of biological psychiatry. In time, this research may greatly enhance our knowledge of the aetiology of psychosis, depression, and other symptoms – and yield even more specific and effective treatments.

Harrison G. Pope
The Mailman Research Center
Belmont, Mass.

Further Reading

Baldessarini, R. J. (1977), *Chemotherapy in Psychiatry*, Cambridge, Mass.

Davis, J. M. (1975), 'Overview: maintenance therapy in psychiatry. I: schizophrenia', *American Journal of Psychiatry*, 132.

Davis, J. M. (1976), 'Overview: maintenance therapy in psychiatry. II: affective disorders', *American Journal of Psychiatry*, 133.

Goodwin, F. K. (ed.) (1976), 'The lithium ion: impact on treatment and research', *Archives of General Psychiatry*, 36.

Hollister, L. E. (1983), *Clinical Pharmacology of Psychotherapeutic Drugs*, 2nd edn, New York.

Jefferson, J. W. and Greist, J. H. (1977), *Primer of Lithium Therapy*, Baltimore.

Klein, D. F., Gittleman, R., Quitkin, F. and Rifkin, A. (1980), *Diagnosis and Drug Treatment of Psychiatric Disorders: Adults and Children*, 2nd edn, Baltimore.

Quitkin, F., Rifkin, A. and Klein, D. F. (1979), 'Monoamine oxidase inhibitors: a review of antidepressant effectiveness', *Archives of General Psychiatry*, 36.
See also: *biological psychiatry*.

Psychosomatic Illness

In the broadest sense of the term, all human illness is psychosomatic, since the functions of mind and body are closely interwoven. Emotional disorders are commonly accompanied by bodily symptoms, and physical illness often leads to pathological emotional responses. Clinical practice reflects this duality. Psychiatrists working in general hospitals are often called upon to evaluate and treat patients (1) whose illnesses are the response to an emotional stress, and (2) those for whom physical illness or injury is in itself a stressful precipitant of a pathological emotional reaction that, in turn, complicates the underlying physical disorder.

(1) In the first category of psychosomatic illness, emotional factors may be a major precipitator of physical illness. In many patients with a variety of chronic bodily disorders (such as peptic ulcer, hyperthyroidism, and bronchial asthma), severe emotional stress (the loss of a wife or husband, for example) appears to play a significant role in the onset and recurring episodes of the physical illness. Such patients often have major defects in their capacity to experience and express emotions aroused by stress. The arousal, barred from discharge over the psychological, emotional and behavioural channels that normally attenuate it, is shunted directly into nervous and endocrinal pathways that control the body's organs. The resulting chronic stimulation of these organs leads to pathological changes manifested as physical illness. Modern scientific investigation of the psychosomatic process is beginning to uncover a wealth of facts that shed important light on the psychological, neuronal, endocrinal and immunological mechanisms at work in stress-induced psychosomatic illnesses. The knowledge thus gained will ultimately be translated into more effective treatment measures for a host of hitherto chronic, debilitating human diseases.

(2) In the latter category of psychosomatic illness, the individual patient's characteristic personality features help to determine the response to the stress of illness. As psychiatrists see it, these personality features often not only induce complications in the course of the illness, but create problems in the medical management of the case. Dependency needs, in particular, pose a central psychological difficulty. The incapacitation resulting from a serious illness or injury compromises the patient's autonomy, independence, and self-sufficiency, and forces him into the role of an invalid who must look to others for help and care. Individuals who are fiercely independent may find it difficult to give up their autonomy. As a consequence, they deny the seriousness of their illness and refuse to comply with the treatment programme necessary for their recovery. On the other hand, in persons with strong, overt dependency needs, the symptoms of a physical disorder provide a means of gratifying those needs. As a result, both the symptoms and the incapacitation arising from the illness are intensified and often prolonged beyond the time when physical healing has taken place.

John C. Nemiah
Beth Israel Hospital, Boston
Harvard University

Further Reading
Nemiah, J. C. (1961), 'Psychological complications of physical illness', in J. C. Nemiah (ed.), *Foundations of Psychopathology*, New York.
Weiner, H. (1977), *Psychobiology and Human Illness*, New York.
See also: *anxiety; stress*.

Public Choice

Public choice, or the economic theory of politics, is the application of the economist's way of thinking to politics. It studies those areas in which economic and political forces interact, and is one of the few successful interdisciplinary topics. The behaviour of the individual is taken to be rational, an assumption which political scientists and sociologists have also found to be fruitful.

While the term public choice was coined in the late 1960s, the type of politico-economic analysis has a long history. Condorcet was the first to recognize the existence of a voting paradox: in a system of majority voting, the individual preferences cannot generally be aggregated into a social decision without logical inconsistencies. Italian and Scandinavian public finance scholars have also explicitly dealt with political processes, in particular in the presence of public goods. Another forerunner is Schumpeter, who regarded the competition between parties as the essence of democracy.

The following four areas are central to public choice:

(1) *Preference aggregation.* Condorcet's finding of a voting paradox has been generalized to all possible methods of aggregating individual preferences. The impossibility result remains in force, in particular when many issue-dimensions are allowed for.

(2) *Party competition.* Under quite general conditions, the competition of two vote maximizing parties leads to an equilibrium: both parties offer the same policies in the median of the distribution of voters' preferences. The programmes proposed differ

substantially when there are more than two parties competing, and when they can form coalitions.

(3) *Interest groups*. The product of the activity of a pressure group is a public good, because even those not participating in its finance may benefit from it. Consequently, economic interests are in general not organized. An exception is when the group is small, when members only receive a private good from the organization, or when it is enforced by government decree.

(4) *Public bureaucracy*. Due to its monopoly power in the supply of public services, the public administrations tend to extend government activity beyond the level desired by the population.

In recent years, the theories developed have been empirically tested on a wide scale. The demand for publicly provided goods and services has been econometrically estimated for a great variety of goods, periods and countries. An important empirical application is *politico-economic models* which explicitly study the interaction of the economic and political sectors. A vote maximizing government, which has to take into account the trade-off between inflation and unemployment, willingly produces a political business cycle. More inclusive politico-economic models have been constructed and empirically tested for various representative democracies: economic conditions such as unemployment, inflation and growth influence the government's re-election requirement, which induces in turn the government to manipulate the economy to secure re-election.

Viewing government as an endogenous part of a politico-economic system has far-reaching consequences for the theory of economic policy. The traditional idea of government maximizing the welfare of society has to be replaced by an emphasis on the consensual choice of the appropriate rules and institutions.

Bruno S. Frey
University of Zurich

Further Reading
Frey, B. S (1978), *Modern Political Economy*, Oxford.
Mueller, D. (1979), *Public Choice*, Cambridge.
See also: *interest groups; public goods; voting.*

Public Goods

Public goods are characterized by non-excludability (individuals not paying for the good cannot be excluded) and by non-rivalry in consumption (that is, it does not cost anything when, in addition, other persons consume the good). The supply of a public good is Pareto-optimal (efficient) if the sum of the marginal utilities (or the sum of the marginal willingness to pay) of the persons benefiting equals the marginal cost of supply. This efficiency condition differs from the one of the polar opposite, private goods, where marginal utility has to equal marginal cost of supply.

The basic problem of public goods is that the prospective consumers have no incentive to reveal their preferences for such a good and are thus not ready to contribute towards financing the provision of the good. In the extreme case this incentive to act as 'free rider' leads to no supply of the public good at all, although everyone would potentially benefit from its provision.

Public goods is one of the few theoretical concepts in modern economics often used by other social sciences. One of the most important applications is to the problem of organizing economic interests. Pressure groups largely provide a public good because all persons and firms sharing these interests benefit from the activity. For that reason, there is little or no incentive to join. The (pure) public goods conditions apply, however, only when the interests are shared by a large number of persons or firms, for example by consumers and taxpayers, and when there are no exclusive benefits offered to members only.

The incentive to act as a free rider in a market setting may (partly) be overcome by resorting to the political process. The direct use of simple majority voting does not guarantee that the resulting public-good supply is Pareto-optimal. This is only the case if the median voter (who throws the decisive vote) has a 'tax price' equal to his marginal willingness to pay. This will rarely be the case. In a representative democracy the competition between two parties leads under ideal conditions to the same outcome for public goods supply as simple majority voting. With more than two parties and/or imperfect political competition, the resulting public goods supply cannot in general be determined. Public goods should not be identified with public provision: some public goods are privately provided, and there are many non-public goods which are politically provided.

Decision-making procedures have been devised which solve the free-rider problem. These 'preference-revealing mechanisms' result in no one gaining by understating his preference for the public good. However, these proposals are difficult to understand by the participants and violate the principle of anonymity of voting.

In laboratory experiments, it appears that individuals are ready to contribute to the cost of providing a public good to some extent, even in the large number setting. Ethical considerations seem to play a significant role in the public goods context; many people appear to have moral qualms about behaving as free-riders.

Bruno S. Frey
University of Zurich

See also: *public choice.*

Public Health

The Dictionary of Epidemiology (Last, 1983) defines public health as 'one of the efforts organized by society to protect, promote and restore the people's health. It is the combination of sciences, skills, and beliefs that are directed to the maintenance and improvement of the health of all the people through collective or social actions. The programmes, services and institutions involved emphasize the prevention of disease and the health needs of the population as a whole. Public health activities change with changing technology and social values, but the goals remain the same: to reduce the amount of disease, premature death, and disease-produced discomfort and disability in the population. Public health is thus a social institution, a discipline, and a practice.'

The practice of public health is to a large extent a political activity, and its approach is coloured by the degree to which health care is a private or public matter in the community. Approaches can range from, on the one hand, the 'rats, lice and sewers' circumscription of public health which occurs where individual health care is seen as a primarily time-limited contract between (potential) healer and (potential) healee, to the broad encompassment of all the problems which may affect the health of a population (that is, practically everything), on the other. The latter approach is not new and was recognized by Winslow in 1951: 'No sound distinction . . . can be drawn between "sanitation", "preventive medicine", "curative medicine", "health medicine", "health promotion", and "improvement of standards of living". All are part of a comprehensive public-health programme in the modern sense.' The declaration of Alma-Ata (1978), endorsed by the Member States of WHO, goes even further: 'Economic and social development . . . is of basic importance to the fullest attainment of health for all . . . . The promotion and protection of the health of the people . . . contributes to a better quality of life and to world peace.'

Public health therefore is an area where traditional practitioners of medicine and healing represent only a fraction of the troupe of actors: mathematicians, engineers, sociologists, managers, educators, political scientists, theologians and others have all played a role in its development. The latest edition of *Maxcy-Rosenau's Textbook of Public Health and Preventive Medicine* (Last, 1980) stresses the degree to which 'the range and scope of the science and skills required for the practice of public health have extended since 1913', when the first edition of *Rosenau's Preventive Medicine and Hygiene* was published (note the change of title, which last occurred in the 1956 edition). This constitutes a welcome extension in scope. It must, however, be borne in mind that the main tools which support the effectiveness of public health – that is, enable it to affect favourably the health

of a community – include (1) fundamental and applied research in epidemiology in order to identify and quantify the problems of the community and to measure the impact of interventions, and (2) political decision-taking, which assists in the implementation of solutions to these problems. Physicians and other members of the health professions should be no worse than average at politics and, by virtue of their training, they are usually well prepared to take decisions. Even in the face of calls for demedicalization of the practice of medicine (see Illich, 1975), one might thus wish to retain a major role for epidemiologically-minded physicians and health professionals in the practice of public health.

M. C. Thuriaux
World Health Organization
Regional Office for Europe, Copenhagen

References

Illich, I. (1975), *Medical Nemesis. The Expropriation of Health*, New York.

Last, J. (ed.) (1980), *Maxcy-Rosenau's Textbook of Public Health and Preventive Medicine*, 11th edn, New York.

Last, J. (ed.) (1983), *Dictionary of Epidemiology*, New York.

Winslow, C. E. A. (1951), *The Cost of Sickness and the Price of Health*, Geneva.

See also: *epidemiology; health economics; medical sociology.*

Punishment

Punishment is an intended evil. At the macro-level, discussion has centred on the reasons for punishment, its effects, the acceptable forms of punishment, and the relationships between social structure and level of punishment. At the micro-level – which will not be covered here – the discussion has concerned the effects of punishments as opposed to rewards on the ability to learn.

There are two main sorts of justification of punishment: (1) The natural law position argues that we punish because we punish, or, in some formulations, we punish because it would be unjust not to do so. God or Nature demand it. Even if we live seconds before doomsday, the condemned murderer must be hanged otherwise justice would not have been done. Often implicit in this model is a sort of equilibrium theory: evil balances out evil. The tariff, however, may change over time: an eye for an eye in biblical time becomes two years of imprisonment – or 500 dollars – in our time. (2) The other major position is utilitarian: punishment has a purpose; we punish because it is necessary. Punishment is a means to get offenders (individual prevention) or potential offenders (general prevention) to obey the law. The magnitude of the pain inflicted is in this case not proportionate to the crime but to the intended social purposes. Legal philosophers often attempt to reconcile the two major positions, particularly by insisting that no more pain should be inflicted for reasons of utility than is acceptable according to just desert. The equally logical opposite position – that pain should not be inflicted if it serves no purpose – is more seldom expressed. The empirical study of punishment is closely related to these moral issues. If punishment deters, then the utilitarian position is strengthened.

Criminologists have given much thought to the effects of punishment on the offender himself. In general, they have not been able to identify any particular form of punishment that would seem to reduce the probability of relapse: no one measure (apart from death or castration, of course) appears to work better than any other. Some criminologists even claim that the only thing they have found is that punishments are likely to increase the danger of committing further crimes, because all punishments – even if they are called someting else – imply stigma.

As far as the effects of punishment on other people's behaviour is concerned (that is, the general preventive effects), results of research are more complex both to describe and interpret. These effects are evident when we contrast extreme alternatives. Capital punishment for minor and easily detected offences will reduce them, while the absence of any sanction will encourage them – as we see in situations where the police are out of action. More commonly, the choice lies between degrees of punishment, for example, between one or two years imprisonment. In such cases, there are few indications that one punishment is more effective than another. Even death penalties are not demonstrably more effective deterrents than long prison sentences.

Modern societies differ widely with respect to their penal traditions. Table 1 gives the number of prisoners per 100,000 inhabitants in selected countries. (The figures for Eastern Europe are less reliable than those for the West, and most are from the last years of the 1970s. Those for the US and Western Europe are mainly from the 1980s. In all cases, the definition of 'prison' presents problems.) Eastern-bloc countries generally have higher prison figures than Western countries. Where life is harsh and power relatively uncontrolled, a strict penal policy is likely. The personal safety of the citizens seems only slightly affected by the incarceration rate of a nation. Moscow has one form of security – and insecurity. New York has another.

Table 1

Prisoners per 100,000 inhabitants in selected industrialized countries

USSR	660
USA	280–300
Poland	220–300
DDR	222
Bulgaria	150
Czechoslovakia	142
Austria	118
Yugoslavia	101
BDR	100
Finland	99
England	86
Denmark	68
Sweden	49
Norway	44
The Netherlands	23

What are regarded as acceptable forms of punishment clearly also reflect general cultural traditions. Some countries find it acceptable to punish the whole family, others only the culprit. Some take life, some arms, some testicles, while some limit themselves to depriving the offender of time or money. Welfare states, with their emphasis on reducing suffering, face particular problems in deliberately inflicting suffering. A characteristic solution is to disguise this value-conflict by calling punishment 'treatment', 'education' and so on.

Nils Christie
University of Oslo

Further Reading

Andenaes, J. (1974), *Punishment and Deterrence*, Ann Arbor.

Christie, N. (1981), *Limits to Pain*, Oxford.

Hirsch, A. von (1976), *Doing Justice*, Report of the Committee for the Study of Incarceration, New York.

Mathiesen, T. (1974), *The Politics of Abolition*, Oxford.

Rawls, J. (1972), *A Theory of Justice*, Oxford.

See also: *capital punishment; penology; rehabilitation.*

Quesnay, Francois (1694–1774)

Francois Quesnay, the founder of the Physiocratic school, was born in Méré (Seine-et-Oise) and died in Versailles after a long and distinguished medical career, which culminated in his appointment as one of the Physicians Royal of Louis XV. His work as an economist commenced late in life for reasons still obscure (Groenewegen, 1983) and his first economic writings – the articles *Fermiers* and *Grains* for the *Encyclopédie* – appeared in 1756 and 1757. During these years he also wrote the articles *Hommes* and *Impôt*, which together formulated the basic principles of what became known as Physiocracy. Quesnay succinctly summarized them in his *Tableau économique*, the first edition of which was published in 1758 allegedly with the assistance of Louis XV himself. Most of Quesnay's later economic writings were elaborations and modifications of these principles. They were collected together by his leading disciple, Du Pont de Nemours, in a book entitled *Physiocratie*, from which the school took its name. Quesnay's economic work (which ceased in 1768) also appeared anonymously as chapters in books by his major collaborator, the Marquis de Mirabeau.

Marx described Quesnay as the founder of modern political economy because he had introduced the analysis of capital to the science, and inspired Marx's own reproduction schema. Since the 1950s, Quesnay's *Tableau* has been correctly interpreted as an early model of economic growth, of input-output analysis, of general equilibrium and of that interdependence of production, circulation and distribution in a surplus-producing economy which is the hallmark of classical political economy. Up to then, Quesnay's economics had often been ridiculed because of its excessive claims for the productivity of agriculture, the sterility of manufacturing, and his lack of value and profit analysis. Wider availability of his work, combined with the rehabilitation of classical political economy, has corrected these misinterpretations and has restored his reputation to the fame he enjoyed during his lifetime.

Peter Groenewegen
University of Sydney

References
Groenewegen, P. D. (1983), 'Introduction' to F. Quesnay, *Farmers*, Sydney.

Hecht, J. (1958), *Francois Quesnay et la Physiocratie*, Paris.

See also: *physiocratic thought*.

Questionnaires

Questionnaires pose a structured and standardized set of questions, either to one person, to a small population, or (most commonly) to respondents in a sample survey. Structure here refers to questions appearing in a consistent, predetermined sequence and form. The sequence may be deliberately scrambled, or else arranged according to a logical flow of topics or question formats. A questionnaire might, for example, commence with experiences from the subject's childhood, proceeding through time to the present. Questionnaire items follow characteristic forms: open-ended questions, where respondents fill in the blank, using an original choice of words; or the closed-response format, where responses must conform to options supplied by the interlocutor. Choices are frequently presented in the 'agree-disagree' or 'yes-no' form, or in extended multiple choice arrangements such as the Likert Scale, where several adverbs describe a hierarchy of sentiments such as agreement or favourability. Standardizing the phrasing for each question is a key phase in questionnaire design. Seemingly minor alterations in wording can substantially affect responses, a phenomenon which has generated much methodological research.

Questionnaires are distributed through the mail (perhaps the most usual method), or by hand, through arrangements such as the 'drop-off', where a fieldworker leaves the questionnaire for respondents to complete by themselves, with provision either for mailing the complete form back to the research office, or for a return call by the fieldworker to collect the questionnaire. A questionnaire administered in a face-to-face interview, or over the telephone (growing in popularity among researchers), is generally termed a 'schedule'. In deciding upon one of these methods, researchers balance off costs, probable response rate, and the nature of the questions to be posed.

John Goyder
University of Waterloo

Further Reading
Schuman, H. and Presser, S. (1981), *Questions and Answers in Attitude Surveys*, New York.
See also: *interviewing; sample surveys*.

Quetelet, Adolphe (1796–1874)

Adolphe Quetelet, a Belgian, was an astonishing polymath – poet, geometer, astronomer, meteorologist, demographer, criminologist, sociologist, statistician and more – who exercised a profound influence over individuals and organizations in many branches of science, and whose work raised questions about the role of the statistical approach in the social sciences which can still be fruitfully debated.

Quetelet's method employed an unbiased accumulation of sufficiently large and extensive data sets, their analysis in a style of remarkable neutrality, and a vivid, often inspiring, account of what might be inferred from the analysis. Embedded in a framework of ethical and humanitarian goals and unmarred by any trace of personal rancour, this method proved, in his lifetime, to be novel, irresistible and timely: the intellectual climate was eager to find a scientific basis for the social reforms that were clearly needed to deal with new economic and political forces.

Quetelet used simple cross-tabulation to reveal associations between social ills and factors that he called 'causes' or 'influences'. Where the latter were not beyond the control of man, the possibility of social amelioration was furthered in memorable sentences such as: 'It is Society that prepares the crime and the criminal is only the instrument that carries it out'; and 'There is a budget that is paid with frightful regularity, that of the prisons . . . and the scaffolds: it is that, above all, that we must try to reduce'.

A long-running controversy developed on the question of Free-will versus Determinism, misled by Quetelet's playful phrase 'frightful regularity' and like examples. These merely referred to the regularity of proportions calculated from repeated large samples of the same, stable population – a simple consequence of the laws of probability. For Quetelet, the problem, such as it was, had a straightforward solution: *individual* free-will was quite compatible with *social* determinism.

Fortunately, neither this controversy, nor the one with Comte about who had priority in coining the term *physique sociale* for their quite different theoretical structures, diminished Quetelet's influence on major thinkers. Karl Marx, for example, made use of Quetelet's methodology in his preparation of a statistical case for economic revolution, a conclusion that the liberal ameliorator in Quetelet might have queried! The eminent statistician Karl Pearson was another Quetelet beneficiary, and not just in the realm of ideas. For Florence Nightingale had admired Quetelet and his works with a religious intensity; this, in turn, probably influenced Galton to support Pearson as the first university professor of statistics *per se*, initiating the English, now worldwide, school of statistics.

Quetelet's role in the organization of nineteenth-century science was no less impressive than his influence on individuals. The landmarks were:

1825 – joint founder of the journal *Correspondance mathématique et physique*;
1826 – initiator of the Royal Observatory of Brussels;
1834 – inspirer of the new Statistical Society of London, later the Royal Statistical Society;
1841 – creator of the Belgian 'Commission Centrale de Statistique';
1853 – President of the First International Congress of Statistics.

As early as the 1820s, Quetelet had absorbed the Laplacian optimism that the exactness of mathematics could be usefully applied to the 'moral and political' sciences, and, with the illumination of a prophet, had seen how this could be done. All that remained was the long process of verification, which was fortunately accomplished before a stroke sadly impaired his faculties in 1855.

We are now free to assess whether Quetelet's optimism at the start and his measured satisfaction at the end of this process were justified. In reading his works, of which the earlier versions are the better organized, it should be possible to divorce this assessment from any prejudices induced by the 'arithmomania' and 'quantophrenia' which infected some of Quetelet's disciples, and which now appears in subdued form as an incantatory methodology in all sciences, not excluding the social.

M. Stone
University College London

Further Reading
Lazarsfeld, P. F. (1961), 'Notes on the history of quantification in sociology: trends, sources and problems', *Isis*, 52.
Lottin, J. (1912), *Quetelet, statisticien et sociologue*, Louvain-Paris.
See also: *statistical reasoning*.

R

Race

Few concepts in modern times have been less understood and few more liable to misuse than the concept
of race when applied to man.

Such powerful feelings has it aroused that its use is
sharply declining among the writers of physical anthropology textbooks in the United States. Of twenty such
textbooks published between 1932 and 1969, thirteen
(65 per cent) accepted that races of man exist, three
(15 per cent) claimed that they do not exist, while of
the remaining four, two did not mention the subject
while two stated that there was no consensus on the
subject. On the other hand, of thirty-eight such textbooks that appeared between 1970 and 1979, only
twelve, or 32 per cent, stated that races of man exist,
whereas fourteen, or 37 per cent, claimed that races
do not exist; of the remaining twelve texts, four were
non-committal on the matter, three failed to mention
race and five indicated that there was no consensus
(Littlefield, Lieberman and Reynolds, 1982).

It is of course a moot point how much we may
conclude from a study of the contents of textbooks, but
it is, to say the least, striking that, during the 1970s,
there was in the US so marked a swing away from
the earlier widespread acceptance of the existence of
human races. Critics of the study cited have raised the
question of the degree to which that change reflects
new concepts flowing from new data and novel
approaches, and the extent to which the change might
have been predicated upon extraneous factors, such as
a swing of 'fashion', political considerations, or the
composition of classes of students to which the texts
were directed. Nor is it clear whether the tendency in
the United States typifies other parts of the world of
physical anthropology.

Certainly the change tells us that, even among
experts, no less than in the public mind, the concept
of race is being critically re-examined and that no
consensus, let alone unanimity, among specialists on
the validity or the usefulness of the race concept
appears to exist at the present time. It is worthwhile
therefore to examine the meaning of race. Since race
is basically a concept of biology in general, we shall
start by examining race as a biological notion.

Race as a Biological Concept

Many, perhaps most, species of living things comprise
numbers of populations which may be dispersed
geographically and among varying ecological niches.
To impart order to the subdivisions within a species,
biologists have used several terms such as subspecies,
race and population to classify the various groupings
of communities that make up a species. Thus, in a
species within which two or more subspecies are recognized, a race comprises populations or aggregates of
populations within each formally designated
subspecies. Often the term race is qualified: biologists
recognize 'geographic races' (which may be synonymous with subspecies); 'ecological races' where, within
a species, there occur ecologically differentiated populations; and 'microgeographic races' which refers to
local populations (Mayr, 1963).

Although students of any group of living things may
differ from one another on the finer details of such
intraspecific classifications, there has for some time
been fairly general agreement that race is a valid
biological concept. Classically, the differences among
the races in a species have been identified by their
morphology, that is, their observable physical
structure.

In the last half-century, and especially since 1950,
biologists, not content with studying the morphological
make-up of populations within species, have been
studying the genetic composition of the subdivisions
within species. These studies have directed attention
to a number of non-morphological traits such as the
genes for blood-groups and for specific proteins. When
these hereditary characters are analysed, they reveal
that there are no hard and fast boundaries between
races and populations within a species. For any such
genetic marker, it is not uncommon to find that the
frequency of the trait in question is distributed along
a gradient (or *cline*) which cuts across the boundaries
of races, as delimited by morphology. Such gene clines
often do not parallel any detectable environmental
gradient; they appear to be neutral in relation to
natural selective agencies in the environment.

Different genetic markers within a species may vary
along different gradients. Thus, if one were to base
one's thinking about the subdivisions of a species on
the distribution of any one genetic marker, one would
be liable to reach a different conclusion from that which
might flow from the use of another genetic marker.

Hence, newer methods of analysis combine the
frequencies of many different genetic markers, in the
hope that the resulting sorting of populations will more

nearly reflect the objective genetic relationship of the subgroups within a species.

Character-gradients apply as well to some morphological features. That is, some structural features such as body size, ear size, or colouring, change gradually and continuously over large areas. Such gradients, unlike the genetic clines, appear to parallel gradients in environmental features and have probably resulted from the action of natural selection (Huxley, 1963). However, the frequencies of the genes governing morphological characters are less commonly used in the study of genetic interrelationships within a species, for several good reasons: (1) such traits are often of complex, difficult and even uncertain genetic causation; (2) many of them and, particularly, measurable characters are determined not by a single gene-pair, but by numbers of different gene-pairs; (3) such characters are especially subject to environmental modification: for example, if animals live in a lush area and eat more food, they would be expected to grow bigger than those of the same species living in a more arid region. This 'eco-sensitivity' of the body's metrical traits renders them less useful in an analysis of genetic affinities.

In sum, race is a biological concept. Races are recognized by a combination of geographic, ecological and morphological factors and, increasingly, in the last third of the twentieth century, by analyses of the distribution of gene frequencies for numbers of essentially non-morphological, biochemical components. As long as one focused on morphological traits alone, it was sometimes not difficult to convince oneself that races were distinctly differentiated, one from another, with clear-cut boundaries between them; the progressive application of genetic insights and analyses to the problem revealed that recognizable gene variants (or *alleles*) are no respecters of such hypothetical boundaries. Often, indeed, one race merges with the next through intermediate forms, while members of one race can and do interbreed with members of other races. Hence, the importation of genetic appraisal into the discussions on race has led to a definite blurring of the outlines of each race, and so to an attenuation of the concept of race itself.

Race in Human Biology

The biological concept of race, as just sketched, has been applied to the living populations of the human species. At least since the time of the Swedish naturalist and systematist Linnaeus (1707–78), all living human beings have been formally classified as members of a single species, *Homo sapiens*. The accumulation since the middle of the nineteenth century of fossil remains of the family of man has revealed that earlier forms of man lived which could validly be regarded as different species of the same genus, for example *Homo habilis* and *Homo erectus*. Our species, *Homo sapiens*, probably made its appearance between one-half and one-third of a million years before the present.

As *Homo sapiens* spread across first the Old World and, more latterly, the New World, the species diversified, in varied geographical zones and ecological niches, into numerous populations. At the present time we have a situation in which living humanity is divided into several major and many minor subdivisions among which the same kinds of variation are encountered as apply to other living things. Thus, the populations show morphological variation, including some gradients associated with environmental gradients, and varying gene frequencies with clines of distribution that, for individual genetic markers, breach the limits of morphologically defined groups of populations.

Physical anthropologists, relying on morphological traits, have for long divided living humankind into great geographical races (also called major races, subspecies and constellations of races). Most classifications recognized three such major subdivisions, the Negroid, Mongoloid and Caucasoid; some investigators designated other major races, such as the Amerind and the Oceanian. Within the major races, several dozen minor races (or, simply, races) were recognized, the number identified varying with the investigator. As with other living groups, historically the classification of living *Homo sapiens* was based on morphological traits, such as skin colour, hair form and body size. As genetic analysis came to be applied, in respect first of blood-groups and later of a variety of proteins, clines were found which cut across the boundaries of minor and even of major races. Moreover, it was found that the genic variation between the major races was small in comparison with the intra-racial variation. Doubts began to be expressed as to whether there was any biological basis for the classification of human races (for example, Lewontin, 1972).

The problem is compounded by the fact that, even when genetical analysis became based not just on a few traits such as the ABO, MN and Rh blood-groups, but on a number of traits, different results were obtained according to which combinations and numbers of traits were used. For example, Piazza *et al.* (1975) analysed frequency data for eighteen gene loci in fifteen representative human populations: they found that the Negroid populations were genetically closer to the Caucasoid populations than either group of populations was to those populations classified as Mongoloid. This, in turn, was interpreted as signifying an earlier phylogenetic split between Mongoloid, on the one hand, and Negroid-Caucasoid on the other, and a later (more recent) split between Negroid and Caucasoid.

However, Nei's (1978) analysis, based on eleven protein and eleven blood-group loci in twelve human populations, revealed a first splitting between Negroid and Caucasoid-Mongoloid. Subsequently, Nei (1982) and Nei and Roychoudhury (1982) used a still larger number of genetic traits, namely sixty-two protein loci and twenty-three blood-group loci, that is eighty-five gene loci in all, for which data were available for some eighteen world populations. Interestingly, while the protein data revealed a first splitting between Negroid and Caucasoid-Mongoloid, the blood-group data suggest a slightly closer affinity and therefore a slightly more recent splitting between Negroid and Caucasoid.

Clearly, at the time when this article is being written, the last word has not been said on the exact pattern of affinities among the living races. Nor is there a consensus as to whether the large size of intraracial genetic variation, compared with interracial, vitiates any biological basis for the classification of human races. As two representative recent studies, we may cite Lewontin (1972) who believes there is no basis; and Nei and Roychoudhury (1982) who disagree with Lewontin and assert that, while the interracial genic variation is small, the genetic differentiation is real and generally statistically highly significant. Furthermore, it is clear that, by the use of genetic distance estimates, Piazza *et al.* (1975), Nei and Roychoudhury (1982) and others have been enabled to study the genetic relationships among the mainly morphologically defined human races, to construct dendrograms and to impart some understanding of the pattern of recent human evolution. Thus, the latter investigators have found evidence from protein loci to suggest that the Negroid and the Caucasoid-Mongoloid groups diverged from each other about 110,000 ± 34,000 years before present, whereas the Caucasoid and Mongoloid groups diverged at about 41,000 ± 15,000 years before present. These estimates do depend on a number of assumptions and may be modified with the accretion of more data.

One further point may be mentioned here: the extent of genetic differentiation among the living races of man, as determined by the study of protein loci, is not always closely correlated with the degree of morphological differentiation. Indeed, evolutionary change in morphological characters appears to be governed by quite different factors from those governing genetic differentiation in protein-forming genes of the human races, on presently available evidence. Genetic differentiation at protein loci seems to occur largely by such biological processes as mutation, genetic drift and isolation, with migration playing an important role in the establishment of current genetic relationships among human races. On the other hand, morphological characters have apparently been subject to stronger natural selection than 'averge protein loci' (Nei and Roychoudhury, 1972; 1982).

In short, the race concept can be applied to modern man, even when one uses the most modern analytical procedures of population geneticists, and such application has been found of heuristic value. Nevertheless, irrespective of sociopolitical considerations, a number of modern investigators of human intraspecific variation find it more useful and more valid to base such studies on populations, as the unit of analysis, and to discard the race concept in these attempts.

Abuses and Aberrations of the Race Concept

Among the various misconceptions that surround the concept of race, are ideas about 'race purity', the effects of racial hybridization, 'superior and inferior races', race and mental differences, race and culture. A full review of this vast subject is not possible here: it has been dealt with in a number of studies of recent decades such as those of Tobias (1970), Montagu (1972), Mead *et al.* (1968), Kagan (1968), Jensen (1969), Bodmer and Cavalli-Sforza (1970), Scarr-Salapatek (1971), Lochlin *et al.* (1975), Scarr (1980) and Gould (1981).

Although the foregoing selection of writers adopt widely differing standpoints, especially on the subject of race and intelligence (as supposedly reflected by IQ test results), it would not be unfair to claim that the following reflect the view of a great majority of physical anthropologists, human biologists and human geneticists at this time:

(1) Race is an idea borrowed from biology.

(2) At a stage when the study of human populations was primarily, if not exclusively, morphological and its objective classificatory, the race concept helped to classify the immense variety of living and earlier human beings of the species *Homo sapiens*. With the advent of genetic analysis and the discovery that clines of genetic differentiation transcend the supposed 'boundaries' of human races, the race concept has been appreciably weakened.

(3) While some population geneticists have found that race still serves a useful purpose in the study of the genetic affinities of living populations, in the determination of the causal factors that have operated to produce genetic differentiation and in the reconstruction of the phylogenetic history of modern human diversity, others have found the concept of such negligible value in these studies as to have led them to discard race entirely. Time will tell whether we are witnessing 'the potential demise of a concept in physical anthropology' (as Littlefield *et al.*, 1982 have been speculating), or whether the concept will survive the politico-social abuses to which it has been subject and which have been regarded by some as the primary cause of its decline from favour among many investigators and writers of textbooks.

(4) If, for purposes of this analysis, we accept the existence of races of man (as of other living things), we must note that races differ not in

absolutes, but in the frequency with which different morphological and genetic traits occur in different populations.

(5) The overwhelming majority of the genes of *Homo sapiens* are shared by all mankind; a relatively small percentage is believed to control those features which differentiate the races from one another.

(6) The formation of the modern races of man is a relatively recent process, extending back in time for probably not much more than 100,000 years. As against this period of recent diversification, at least forty times as long a period of its hominid ancestry has been spent by each race in common with all other races, as it has spent on its own pathway of differentiation. This statement is based on the evidence that fossilized members of the family of man (the *Hominidae*) are known from 4 million years before the present; molecular and some other evidence suggests that the appearance of the hominids may go back to 5 or more million years before the present.

(7) Racially discriminatory practices make certain assumptions about race, some overt, some tacit. These include the assumptions that:
   (i) races are pure and distinct entities;
   (ii) all members of a race look alike and think alike, which assumption, in turn, is based upon the idea that how one behaves depends entirely or mainly on one's genes;
   (iii) some races are better than others.

(8) The scientific study of human populations has provided no evidence to validate any one of these assumptions.

(9) Genetical and morphological analysis of human populations has failed to confirm that some races are superior and others inferior.

(10) Accidents of geography and history, difficulties of terrain, physical environment and communication, are sufficient to account for the contributions which different populations have made to the varying advancement of human culture and to civilization.

(11) Culture, language and outlook are not inseparably bound up with particular morphological or genetic racial features; for example, man's very culture is today altering the direction of his evolution, as the species spreads into every corner of the world, and as cultural and racial divergence gives way over large areas to cultural and racial convergence.

(12) The myth of the pure race has been thoroughly disproved. There are no pure (genetically or morphologically homogeneous) human races and, as far as the fossil record goes, there never have been.

(13) Not only is purity of race a non-existent fantasy,

but there is no evidence to support the notion that purity of race is a desirable thing.

(14) Racial groups are highly variable entities; for many traits intraracial variability is greater than interracial variability. Intermediates exist between one race and the next.

(15) Members of all races are capable of interbreeding with members of all others, that is, all that have been put to the test.

(16) The supposed evils attendant upon race-crossing do not bear scientific scrutiny: neither sterility, diminished fertility, nor physical deterioration, has been proven to be a biological consequence of race-mixing. If there are unfortunate effects from such crossing, they are *social* (not biological) and they appear to result from the way in which other members of the populations in questions look at and treat the 'hybrids'.

(17) The study of the races of humankind has been based on physical (that is morphological, physiological and biochemical) and genetic traits; mental characteristics have not been used in the classification of the human races, nor have they been found useful for such a purpose.

(18) Scientific studies have not validly demonstrated any genetically determined variations in the kinds of nervous systems possessed by members of different human races, nor any genetically determined differences in the patterns of behaviour evinced by members of different races.

(19) The claim that genetic factors contribute as much as 75 or 80 per cent of the variance of IQ test-score results and are therefore largely responsible for Black-White differences in mean test-score results has been seriously questioned in a number of investigations. It has been shown that a heritability estimate of 0.75 does not apply to American Blacks, among whom a much smaller percentage of the variance of test-score results has been shown to be genetically determined, and a larger proportion environmentally determined. The immense literature that has accumulated since Jensen (1969) put forward his hypothesis that American Blacks are genetically inferior in intelligence to Whites has revealed many flaws that were implicit in the reasoning behind the hypothesis. The main conclusion that many of these studies have reached is that 'currently available data are inadequate to resolve this question in either direction' (Bodmer and Cavalli-Sforza, 1970). On the other hand, a number of investigations have led to the development of environmental hypotheses. For example, Scarr (1980) has found evidence in her studies to support a two-fold hypothesis: such differences as exist between comparable populations she attributes partly to environmental factors and partly to

cultural factors. On this additional cultural hypothesis, her work has led her to stress a different relevance of extra-scholastic or home experience to scholastic aptitudes and achievement: 'The transfer of training from home to school performance is probably less direct for Black children than for White children' (Scarr-Salapatek, 1971). Clearly, at this stage of our ignorance, it is unjustified to include intelligence, however tested, among the validly demonstrated, genetically determined differences among the races of mankind.

Phillip V. Tobias
University of the Witwatersrand, Johannesburg

References
Bodmer, W. F. and Cavalli-Sforza, L. L. (1970), 'Intelligence and race', *Scientific American*, 223.
Gould, S. J. (1981), *The Mismeasure of Man*, New York.
Huxley, J. S. (1963), *Evolution: The Modern Synthesis*, 2nd edn, London.
Jensen, A. R. (1969), 'How much can we boost IQ and scholastic achievement?', *Harvard Educational Review*, 39.
Kagan, J. (1968), 'On cultural deprivation', in D. C. Glass (ed.), *Environmental Influences: Proceedings of the Conference*, New York.
Lewontin, R. C. (1972), 'The apportionment of human diversity', *Evolutionary Biology*, 6.
Littlefield, A., Lieberman, L. and Reynolds, L. T. (1982), 'Redefining race: the potential demise of a concept in physical anthropology', *Current Anthropology*, 23.
Lochlin, J. C., Lindzey, G. and Spuhler, J. N. (1975), *Race Differences in Intelligence*, San Francisco.
Mayr, E. (1963), *Animal Species and Evolution*, London.
Mead, M., Dobzhansky, T., Tobach, E. and Light, R. E. (1968), *Science and the Concept of Race*, New York.
Montagu, A. (1972), *Statement on Race*, 3rd edn, London.
Nei, M. (1978), 'The theory of genetic distance and evolution of human races', *Japanese Journal of Human Genetics*, 23.
Nei, M. (1982), 'Evolution of human races at the gene level', *Human Genetics, Part A: The Unfolding Genome*, New York.
Nei, M. and Roychoudhury, A. K. (1972), 'Gene differences between Caucasian, Negro and Japanese Populations', *Science*, 117.
Nei, M. and Roychoudhury, A. K. (1982), 'Genetic relationship and evolution of human races', in M. K. Hecht, B. Wallace and C. T. Prance (eds), *Evolutionary Biology*, 14.
Piazza, A., Sgaramella-Zonta, L. and Cavalli-Sforza, L. L. (1975), 'The fifth histocompatibility workshop: gene frequency data: a phylogenetic analysis', *Tissue Antigens*, 5.
Scarr, S. (1980), *Race, Social Class and Individual Differences*, Hillsdale, New Jersey.
Scarr-Salapatek, S. (1971), 'Race, social class and IQ', *Science*, 174.
Tobias, P. V. (1970), 'Brain size, grey matter and race – fact or fiction?', *American Journal of Physical Anthropology*, n.s. 32.
See also: *ethnic groups; evolution; intelligence and intelligence testing; population genetics.*

Race Relations

See Ethnic Relations.

Radcliffe-Brown, Alfred Reginald (1881–1955)

Radcliffe-Brown was the first social anthropologist in Britain to have a full professional training, being Rivers's first undergraduate anthropology student at Cambridge. Later he carried out field research in the Andaman Islands (1906–8) where he initially interested himself in historical, ethnological questions, in the manner of Rivers. However, around 1909 he was converted to the sociology of Durkheim, and he eventually published a Durkheimian analysis of Andaman beliefs and rituals (1922). For the rest of his career he developed an essentially Durkheimian anthropology, parallel with Durkheim's nephew Mauss in Paris, and opposed the entrenched ethnological tradition. The version of Durkheimian theory which he propagated was orthodox, and less interesting than the subtler variant developed by Mauss, but he made an enduring contribution at the level of ethnographic analysis.

Radcliffe-Brown also made field studies in Australia (1910–11), and while his own ethnographic contribution was not remarkable, he was able to bring new order to the rich but confused and scattered reports on Australian social organization, demonstrating the structural uniformities which could be discerned despite various local divergences (Radcliffe-Brown, 1931). These Australian studies dealt particularly with kinship systems, and Radcliffe-Brown greatly influenced the development of kinship theory, breaking with the pseudo-historical explanations which Rivers and his predecessors had favoured, and establishing structural-functional explanations of kinship institutions.

Radcliffe-Brown held foundation chairs in social anthropology in the Universities of Cape Town and Sydney, and, from 1937 to 1946, in Oxford, and he taught also at the University of Chicago and a number of other universities in several continents. His body of publications was not large, but he became the leading influence in British social anthropology in the mid-twentieth century.

Adam Kuper
Brunel University, Uxbridge

References
Radcliffe-Brown, A. R. (1922), *The Andaman Islanders*, Cambridge.
Radcliffe-Brown, A. R. (1931), *The Social Organization of Australian Tribes*, Sydney.

Further Reading
Kuper, A. (ed.) (1977), *The Social Anthropology of Radcliffe-Brown*, London.

Radicalism

Though social theories and philosophical analyses may be termed radical, the primary modern usage of the word radicalism is to designate basic or extreme political challenges to established order. The term (with an upper-case R) came into use in the late eighteenth and early nineteenth centuries to refer to an élite political faction which sought parliamentary and other 'rationalizing' reforms, and became a key root of the Liberal Party in England. Almost immediately, a lower-case usage developed to describe all sorts of political orientations which shared either an analysis of current troubles claiming to go to their roots, or a programme deduced from first principles. Under pressure of the French Revolution and various English popular agitations, attention came increasingly to focus on actual mobilizations – radical actions – rather than merely radical ideas.

Social scientists are still divided in the extent of their emphasis on the importance of rationalistic analyses (for example Marxist class consciousness) compared to other more directly social sources of radical actions. There are two conventional views among the latter group. One, now nearly discredited, holds that social atomization and marginalization dispose those cut off from the social mainstream to engage in protests which reveal more of their psychological troubles than any serious programme for social change. The other stresses the underlying interests which a common position in relation to some external factor, such as markets or means of production, gives to individuals. Both positions are challenged by empirical findings that a great deal of organization and internal cohesion are necessary to radical collective action. Common 'objective' interests are not necessarily enough to produce concerted action. Activists can hope to achieve this coalescence through further organizational efforts, and they often see trade unions and similar organizations as way-stations on the road to class organization.

Traditional communities, however, have been the basis of more radical movements than class or any other abstract bonds and formal organizations. The popular radical movements (as opposed to élite radicals) of early industrial Britain acted on radical social roots in reaction to the disruptions of the Industrial Revolution. Though the members of these communities often lacked sophisticated radical analyses, they had visions profoundly at odds with conditions around them. Perhaps even more importantly, they had the social strength in their communal relations to carry out concerted action against great odds for long periods of time; few compromise positions were open to them, unlike the members of the 'modern' working class. These sorts of social foundations continue to be central to radical movements around the world. Peasants and other traditional farmers along with artisans and craft workers form the mainstay of these radical movements.

Social revolutions, the most radical of actual political transformations, certainly have many causes besides anti-governmental radical movements. A state structure weakened by external conflicts or internal disunity may, for example, be essential to the success of a revolutionary movement. Where revolutions succeed, and transform societies rather than only change regimes, two sorts of radical groups have generally been involved. On the one hand, there has usually been a tightly organized, forward-looking, relatively sophisticated group of revolutionaries. On the other hand, there has also generally been a broad mass of protesters and rebels acting on the basis of strong local communities and traditional grievances. The latter are essential to making the revolution happen, to destabilizing the state. The former, however, are much better positioned to seize power during the transformation.

At least in the contemporary world of states and other large-scale abstract social organizations, there is a paradox to radicalism (which may of course be of the 'right' as well as the 'left'). Most radicalism is based on local bonds and tradition, yet when successful, it both disrupts tradition and displaces power towards the centre of society and its large-scale systems of control. This is true even of radical movements aimed at less extreme goals than revolutions. The US civil rights movement could succeed in ending local intolerance and oppression only by forcing an increase of central state power and its penetration into local life. But it could not at the same time make local communities democratic and preserve their autonomy as free realms of direct participation.

Craig Calhoun
University of North Carolina, Chapel Hill

Further Reading
Calhoun, C. (1983), 'The radicalism of tradition', *American Journal of Sociology*, 88.

Moore, B., Jr (1979), *Injustice: The Social Bases of Obedience and Revolt*, White Plains, New York.
See also: *populism; revolutions; social movements.*

Random Sampling

Random sampling is the basic sampling process that underlies all more complex probability samples – stratified samples, cluster sampling, sequential sampling – as well as inferential statistics. It is based on the probability principle that a truly random selection from a population will on average provide a sample that is representative of all characterstics of it. Thus the same resources devoted to an intensive study of a sample usually yields considerably more information than a census.

The size of sample required to estimate characteristics of the population depends on the precision required and the homogeneity of the characteristics in the population, greater precision and heterogeneity requiring larger samples. Population here refers to any arbitrarily but clearly defined group. The sampling frame is an enumeration of the individuals or units of the population.

Samples are taken by using a table of random numbers to select individuals from the sampling frame. Alternatively a lottery process may be used. The only requirement is that all units must have an equal chance of being drawn with each selection. This is 'sampling with replacement'. Since we are usually concerned with large populations and, in that case, estimates of population values from formulas for replacement and non-replacement sampling are virtually identical, we usually do not replace cases once drawn.

David R. Krathwohl
Syracuse University

See also: *sample surveys.*

Rape

Rape can be defined socially or legally. The social definition includes sexual activity in which one partner is an unwilling participant. Legal definitions yield much greater variability, with victim non-consent, assailant force, and evidence of sexual intercourse often required in order to satisfy legal statutes. Historically, the crime has required a female victim and a male perpetrator. Research on rape has expanded with increased social awareness and sensitivity to rape primarily as a result of the women's movement. The research has developed in two parallel areas: (1) social research on the societal beliefs about rape and assumptions about responsibility in rape episodes; and (2) clinical research on the psychological consequences for victims and the motivation of rapists.

Social Stereotypes

Social stereotypes regarding rape include a view of the woman as responsible for preventing the rape, and yet, an assumption that many women secretly desire and would enjoy being raped. In addition, most people regard rape as a sexually motivated crime. Although these stereotypes appear to have little or no basis in reality, they are evident in the attributions people make about rape episodes. For example, when asked to provide causal explanations for the occurrence of a rape, people will assign increasing responsibility for the rape to the female victim, if she is assumed to be sexually appealing. Thus an attractive woman is likely to be judged as more responsible for the rape, as is a woman who has been sexually active or who has been raped before. The underlying belief seems to be that a woman is 'asking for it' by being sexually active or attractive. Additionally, the woman is more negatively evaluated if she is regarded as not having struggled sufficiently or as not being emotionally upset by the rape. This tendency to see the victim as playing a causal role in the attack could have serious implications for the social adjustment of the rape victim, as well as the legal disposition of rape cases.

Rapist Motivation

No single explanation applies to all rape cases. The current view, however, is that the crime is not primarily sexually motivated, nor is it routinely a manifestation of psychiatric disorder. Many rapists are married or have ongoing relationships at the time of the crime. One-third or more may experience sexual dysfunction during the attack (such as failure to achieve an erection), and many report finding little or no sexual satisfaction in the rape. The attack, particularly that of a woman by a man, is seen as an expression of power or anger. This hostile nature of the crime may contribute to the victim's psychological suffering.

Victim Reactions

The victims of sexual assault suffer psychologically in a variety of ways. Distressing emotions, particularly anger, fear and anxiety, predominate in the days immediately following the attack. Self-recrimination and guilt over being victimized are also frequent. Sexual functioning is likely to be negatively affected, specific fears may develop, and symptoms of depression (difficulty in sleeping, sadness, appetite loss, etc.) may occur. Victims may also have various other responses, including obsessional thoughts, withdrawal, nightmares and psychophysiological disorders. Psychological support and short-term crisis psychotherapy are desirable. For some victims, however, the psychological distress precipitated by the assault may last for years, requiring more extensive psychological intervention.

Arnie Cann and Lawrence G. Calhoun
University of North Carolina, Charlotte

Further Reading

Berger, V. (1977), 'Man's trial, woman's tribulation: rape cases in the courtroom', *Columbia Law Review*, 77.

Burt, M. R. (1980), 'Cultural myths and supports for rape', *Journal of Personality and Social Psychology*, 38.

Cann, A., Calhoun, L. G., Selby, J. W. and King, H. E. (eds) (1981), 'Rape', *Journal of Social Issues*, 37.

Katz, S. and Mazur, M. A. (1979), *Understanding the Rape Victim*, New York.

Rape Avoidance

There are as many myths about how to avoid rape when attacked as about rape itself. The advice that women were given was consistent with the traditional female role; passive (relax and enjoy it); manipulative ('you're so handsome – why don't we go for a drink first?'); humanistic ('I'm Mary and I don't want to do this but I care about you. Tell me your problems'), and acting 'crazy' (drooling, speaking incoherently). Women were also told not to fight back since it would only excite the assailant.

But since 1976, when the Queen's Bench (1976) study was published, a body of research has accumulated demonstrating that active strategies are more likely to deter the assailant. Talking was rarely effective by itself and the use of physical strategies by women sharply increased the possibility of stopping the rape, with little added risk of serious injury. Two of five women in Bart and O'Brien's (1984) study who were severely injured used *no* strategies and *all* the women who used no strategies were raped. Moreover, raped women who fought back were less likely to suffer depression afterwards.

Bart and O'Brien, comparing fifty-one avoiders with forty-three raped women (self-defined), found differences in socialization, demographic and situational variables, and in strategies used during the attack. While raped women were more likely to plead, avoiders yelled, fled or tried to flee, and used physical strategies. There was also more frequent environmental intervention in the latter cases. Additionally, the more types of strategies used, the higher the probability of avoidance. The avoiders generally focused on not being raped, while the raped women focused on not being killed. The researchers' demographic and socialization variables substantially supported the feminist view that traditional socialization socializes women for victimization.

Pauline B. Bart
University of Illinois, Chicago

References

Bart, P. B. and O'Brien, P. (1984), 'How the women stopped their rapes', *Signs*, vol. 10.

Queen's Bench Foundation (1976), *Rape: Prevention and Resistance*, San Francisco.

Further Reading

Bart, P. B. (1981), 'A study of women who both were raped and avoided rape', *Journal of Social Issues*, 37.

Sanders, W. (1974), *Rape and Woman's Identity*, Beverly Hills, California.

Rational Expectations

Expectations of the future play an important part in economics. Investment, for example, is affected by expectations of demand and costs. The foreign exchange rate is affected by expectations of inflation and interest rates. The rational expectations hypothesis embodies the assumption that people do not make systematic errors in using the information available to them to predict the future. Some errors in prediction are generally inevitable, due to lack of information and the inherent uncertainties of economic affairs. The rational expectations hypothesis postulates that, given the information used, the prediction errors are random and unavoidable.

Rational expectations are on average self-fulfilling, the term rational expectations equilibrium being used to describe situations in which expectations lead to actions that confirm the original expectations. For example, the expectation of a rise in stock market prices may itself generate the rise. The absence of systematic prediction errors in rational expectations equilibrium suggests that people have no incentive to change the way they make predictions, and hence that the equilibrium is likely to persist unless disturbed by outside events.

The rational expectations hypothesis is seen by some economists, including Muth, who coined the term rational expectations in 1961, as the extension to expectation formation of the assumption that people act 'rationally' in pursuit of their own self-interest, which forms the basis of neoclassical economics. In this context rational behaviour is that which achieves the highest possible level of an objective (generally utility for a household, and profits for a firm), given the constraints imposed by economic and technological conditions. People fare less well in reaching their objectives if they do not have rational expectations. This identification of the rational expectations hypothesis with the more general rationality postulate has been criticized on the grounds that although people may seek to pursue their interests, they may make systematic mistakes in predictions owing to lack of understanding of their economic environment, particularly when that environment is changing rapidly. Nevertheless the rational expectations hypothesis is more appealing to many economists than any of the available alternatives, providing as it does a relatively simple and plausible description of expectation formation which can be readily incorporated into mathematical economic models.

The rational expectations hypothesis has been very widely used in the 1970s and 1980s in both theoretical and empirical research in economics. The earliest applications were to markets for assets, such as stock and futures markets, where demand depends upon expectations of the future value of the asset. More recently, the rational expectations hypothesis has been adopted in some macroeconomic theories, which also employ the hypothesis that, in the absence of unanticipated inflation, there is a unique 'natural rate' of output and employment. The conjunction of the natural rate and rational expectations hypotheses is the basis for the controversial claim of policy neutrality, that monetary policy can have no systematic and predictable effect on output and employment, and hence that there is no long-term trade-off between inflation and unemployment.

Margaret Bray
University of Cambridge

Further Reading
Begg, D. K. H. (1982), *The Rational Expectations Revolution in Macroeconomics Theories and Evidence*, Oxford.

Rationality

See Reason, Rationality and Rationalism.

Reaction Times

For experimental psychologists, the study of reaction times is both a methodological preoccupation and a topic of intrinsic theoretical interest. It was launched when the Rev. Nevil Maskelyne, then British Astronomer Royal, discovered (in 1796) that he and his assistant David Kinnebrook produced estimates for timings of stellar transits which differed by as much as 0.8 secs. He dismissed Kinnebrook 'with regret', and the event was later mentioned in a history of the Royal Observatory. Twenty-four years later Friedrich Bessel read this account, and investigated individual differences between the timings made by careful observers who all used precisely the same method. He found that mean differences between all possible pairs of readings ranged from 0.044 secs to 1.021 secs. This was probably the first quantitative measurement made on the decision speed of human beings. It was also an elegant

insight which had important practical and theoretical results. Thenceforward individual astronomers, however eminent, calibrated themselves to obtain 'personal constants' which might be used to adjust their observations. After this moment it became impossible to sustain the romantic belief that 'nothing in the universe is faster than the speed of thought', or to retain the more prosaic fallacy that all humans can make decisions equally rapidly if only they will try hard enough. The study of individual differences had its small beginning.

The methodological study of reaction times concerns the reliability of experimental procedures involving comparisons of times taken for different types of decisions and by different individuals. Many psychological experiments involve decisions which are so easy that people make very few, or no, mistakes in any of the tasks which are compared. In such cases we can only judge which task is slightly harder by timing, preferably in milliseconds, how long people take to make these different decisions. We then assume that decisions that take longer are more difficult for the human central nervous system to make. Thus measurements of reaction times can be used to deduce the way the nervous system works. This can be illustrated by the first, perhaps apocryphal, theoretical use of reaction times made by Helmholtz (allegedly in about 1852) in which people were given electrical shocks, either on one foot or on the cheek and, in either case, responded by rapidly clenching their teeth on a response-key. Helmholtz is said to have found that response times to foot-shock were reliably longer than to cheek-shock. Dividing the differences between mean reaction times (RTs) for foot and for cheek stimulation by the mean physical distance in metres between these locations on his subjects' bodies, he obtained an estimate, quite surprisingly accurate, of the mean speed of human nerve conduction.

Later studies by Donders and by Wundt extended the use of RTs to examine latencies for otherwise unexaminable internal processes, such as the differences between the times required to identify signals and the times required to select responses to them. These studies have been extended by S. Sternberg (1969) in attempts to compare the times taken to search the contents of short-term memory, as the number of items to be remembered increases; by R. Sternberg, to obtain differences in the times taken to solve logical problems; by Shepherd and Metzler (1971) in an attempt to examine differences in the times required to rotate mentally images of complex objects, and by Neisser (1963), Rabbitt and Vyas (1970) and others in attempts to study the strategies that people use to locate objects by visual search.

Reaction times have also been a fascinating theoretical study in themselves. This is because, superficially, they seem to offer a means of studying very elementary neural processes underlying decision making. This optimism may arise from the following, naïve consideration: if healthy young people practise at a simple task in which they have repeatedly to make the same response whenever a particular signal (such as light flash or tone) occurs, their response times to particular signals average 170 msecs to 180 msecs. We know that about 40 msecs of this time is necessary for peripheral processing of the signal in the eye or the ear. We also know that a further 40 or 50 msecs is needed by muscles and joints to execute any chosen response. Thus only 90 msecs or so seems to be required by internal decision processes in the central nervous system. We also know that since no neurone can communicate with another in less than a millisecond this means that a system of not more than 90 neurones, in series, end to end, must subserve the decision process whose latency we have measured.

A few moments thought convinces us that this line of logic, tempting to the great nineteenth-century investigators such as Donders and Wundt, is simplistic. Any organism which could only react to events as soon as they occurred would lag, perpetually, from 90 to 170 msecs behind the phenomenal present. This would make it too slow to compete successfully with other organisms who manage to develop means of anticipating future events. Thus the study of simple reaction times is, essentially, the study of the way in which humans formulate and vary their anticipations of events which have not yet taken place. The study of times taken to decide which of several different events has taken place (choice reaction times) has become the study of why humans process different kinds of information at different rates (Hick, 1952), of how humans adjust their decision speeds in order to trade off accuracy to gain speed (Schouten and Bekker, 1956; Rabbitt and Vyas, 1970) and of how humans learn to anticipate selectively which of several events, of different probabilities of occurrence, will happen next and when it will occur.

In these respects the study of reaction times is both a topic of considerable practical interest (as when we need to know how much time people need to begin to apply their car brakes in response to unexpected events on motorways, or what is the minimum time within which fighter-pilots can make any of the complex decisions required of them). It is also one of the most important methodologies we have with which to deduce how the brain interprets sensory information and successfully predicts future events by relating what is currently perceived to memories of past contingencies.

Patrick Rabbitt
University of Manchester

References

Hick, W. E. (1952), 'On the rate of gain of information', *Quarterly Journal of Experimental Psychology*, 4.

Neisser, U. (1963), 'Decision time without reaction-time: experiments in visual scanning', *American Journal of Psychology*, 76.

Rabbitt, P. M. A. and Vyas, S. M. (1970), 'An elementary preliminary taxonomy of errors in laboratory choice RT tasks', *Acta Psychologica*, 33.

Schouten, J. F. and Bekker, J. A. M. (1967), 'Reaction time and accuracy', in *Attention and Performance* 1, ed. A. F. Saunders, Amsterdam.

Shepherd, R. N. and Metzler, J. (1971), 'Mental rotation of three dimensional objects', *Science*, 171.

Sternberg, S. (1969), 'On the discovery of processing stages; some extensions of Donders's model', *Acta Psychologica*, 30.

Reason, Rationality and Rationalism

Rationality is a problem shared by the social sciences and philosophy. Before considering the various issues it raises, it is best to offer provisional definitions of the three related notions of reason, rationality and rationalism.

Reason is the name of an alleged human faculty capable of discerning, recognizing, formulating and criticizing truths. Philosophic disputes about reason concern its very existence (extreme irrationalism may deny that any such faculty exists at all); the nature of its operations (for example, can it actually secure data, or can it only make inferences, how powerful are the inferences it can make; can it make discoveries or can it only check discoveries made by other means?); the areas of its operations (is it restricted to deductive reasoning, or to science, can it be applied to moral, aesthetic, political issues, can it initiate conduct?).

Rationality is a trait which individuals or collectivities display in their thought, conduct or social institutions. Various features can be seen, singly or jointly, as marks or defining features of rationality:

(1) a tendency to act only after deliberating and calculation, as opposed to acting impulsively or in obedience to unexamined intimations;

(2) a tendency to act in accordance with a long-term plan;

(3) a control of conduct by abstract and general rules;

(4) instrumental efficiency: the selection of means purely by their effectiveness in bringing about a clearly specified aim, as opposed to allowing means to be selected by custom or impulse;

(5) a tendency to choose actions, institutions, and so on in terms of their contribution to a single and clearly specified criterion, rather than by eval-

uating them by multiple, diffuse and unclear criteria, or accepting them in virtue of their customariness;

(6) a propensity to systematize convictions and/or values in a single coherent system;

(7) an inclination to find human fulfilment in the exercise or satisfaction of intellectual faculties rather than in emotion or sensuality.

Rationalism is the name of a number of doctrines or attitudes:

(1) the insistence of the authority of individual, independent, cognitive activity, as opposed to authority of some extraneous privileged sources (Revelation, Church);

(2) the higher valuation of thought or inference as against sensation, observation or experiment, within cognitive activity;

(3) the view that collectivities, or individuals, should best conduct their lives in accordance with explicit and intellectually chosen plans, rather than by custom, trial and error, or under guidance of either authority or sentiment.

It should be noted that doctrine (1) opposes the partisans of human reason, assumed to be fairly universally or evenly distributed amongst all men, to followers of privileged Authority. In other words, Rationalists in sense (1) include *both* sides of dispute (2), that is both adherents of thinking and adherents of sensing as the main source of knowledge. In other words, issues (1) and (2) cut across each other. As 'rationalism' is widely used in both senses, and the issues are cross-related in complex ways, failure to see this ambiguity leads to confusion. A key figure in Western rationalism was Descartes, who was a rationalist in both senses. On the one hand, he recommended that all traditional, inherited ideas be subjected to doubt, a kind of intellectual quarantine, and only be awarded certificates of clearance if they were found logically compelling to the inquiring mind. Though Descartes, when applying this method, did in fact eventually award just such a certificate to the theism of the faith of his birth, the sheer fact of making inner reason the first and last Court of Appeal in effect constituted and encouraged rationalism in sense (1). But he was also a rationalist in the second sense, and considered innate rational powers to be far more important than sensory information. His view of the human mind has been powerfully revived by the contemporary linguist, Noam Chomsky, notably in *Cartesian Linguistics* (1966) and supported by the argument that the amazing range of linguistic competence of most men cannot be explained without the assumption of an innate grammatical structure present in all mind, which thus corresponds to one aspect of the old 'reason'.

In the seventeenth and eighteenth centuries, the programme of Descartes's rationalism (sense 1) was implemented, amongst others, by the school of 'British empiricists', of whom the greatest was probably David Hume. However, at the same time they repudiated rationalism (sense 2). Hume (1976 [1739–40]), for instance, basically considered thinking to be nothing but the aftertaste of sensations: thinking about a given object was like having an aftertaste of a dish when one is no longer eating.

The eighteenth century is often said to have been the Age of Reason; in philosophy, however, it was also the age of the Crisis of Reason. This was most manifest in the work of Hume. His main discovery was this: if rationalism (1), the subjection of all belief to evidence available to the individual, is combined with empiricism, the view that the senses alone supply the data-base at the individual's disposal, we end with an impasse: the data-base supplied by the senses simply is not strong enough to warrant our endorsement of certain convictions which seem essential for the conduct of life – notably, the presence of causal order in the world, or continuous objects, or of moral obligation. Hume's solution for this problem was that these crucial human tendencies, such as inferring from the past to the future, or feeling morally constrained, not being warranted by the only data-base available to us, were simply rooted in and justified by habit, a kind of Customary Law of the mind.

Immanuel Kant (1929 [1781]) tried to provide a stronger and less precarious refutation to Hume's scepticism. His solution was, in substance, that the human mind has a rigid and universal structure, which compels men (amongst other things) to think in terms of cause and effect, to feel obliged to respect a certain kind of ethic (a morality of rule-observance and impartiality, in essence), and so on. So the inner logical compulsions on which Descartes relied as judges of culturally inherited ideas were valid after all, but they were only valid for the world as experienced by beings with our kind of mind; they were not rooted in the nature of things, as they were 'in themselves'. They were rooted in *us*.

It is amongst Kant's numerous intellectual progeny that the problem of reason becomes sociological. The two most important ones in sociology were Emile Durkheim and Max Weber. Each of them very obviously inherits the Kantian problem, but they apply it to society and to the diversity of human cultures in radically different, indeed almost diametrically opposed, ways. Durkheim followed Kant in being concerned with our conceptual compulsions, in holding conceptual compulsion to be central to our humanity. But where Kant was content to explain it by invoking an allegedly universal structure of the human mind, operating behind the scenes in each individual mind, Durkheim sought the roots of compulsion in the visible life of distinct communities and above all in ritual. The core of religion is ritual, and the function of ritual is to endow us with shared concepts, and to endow those concepts with a compelling authority for all members of a given community. This is the central argument of his *The Elementary Forms of Religious Life* (1915 [1912]). For Durkheim, all men are rational, rationality manifests itself in conceptual compulsion, but the form that rationality takes varies from society to society. Sharing the same compulsions makes men members of a social community.

If for Durkheim all men are rational, for Weber some men are more rational than others. He notes that the kind of rationality which Kant analysed – orderly rule-bound conduct and thought – is specially characteristic of one particular tradition, namely the one which engendered the modern capitalist and industrial society. (Weber is less explicitly concerned with Kant than is Durkheim, but the connection is nevertheless obvious.) Weber's problem is not why all men are rational (all men think in concepts and are constrained by them), but why some men are *specially* rational, quite particularly respectful of rules and capable of selecting means for their effectiveness rather than for their congruence with custom, thereby becoming apt at establishing modern capitalist and bureaucratic institutions.

Weber (1961 [1924], 1968 [1922]) noted that the kind of world codified by the great philosophers of the Age of Reason, a world amenable to rational orderly investigation and manipulation rather than propitiation, was not a world inhabited by all mankind, but only by the participants of the historical tradition which had engendered capitalism and large-scale bureaucracy. He believed that this kind of 'rational' mentality was an essential precondition of a capitalist or bureaucratic civilization, and was *not* the necessary corollary of the other preconditions of that civilization: in other words, in opposition to 'historical materialism', he did not believe that the emergence of that civilization could be explained in terms of its material preconditions alone. One further and independent necessary factor was also required. (He modified rather than inverted the materialist position, in so far as he did not claim or believe that the nonmaterial necessary condition, or any set of such conditions, could ever be sufficient.) Hence in his hands the philosophical problem of rationality becomes a sociological one – how did rationality come to dominate one particular civilization and eventually, through it, the entire world.

The Durkheimian and Weberian traditions are not the only ones through which the philosophers' concern with Reason reaches the social sciences. There are at least two others.

In Kant, the attribution of rationality to a rigid and universal structure of the human mind, but *not* to the material which that mind (or those minds) handled,

led to a tense and uncomfortable dualism: the world was a blind, amoral machine, and the intrusion of either cognitive rationality or moral conduct into it was a mysterious imposition by our minds of order onto material indifferent and alien to that order. At the core of the philosophy of Hegel lay the supposition that Reason was not merely (as Kant thought) responsible for the individual striving for consistent behaviour and explanations, but that it was also a kind of grand and impersonal Puppet Master of History. In other words, the pattern of history had an underlying principle which was not alien to the rational strivings within us, but on the contrary, provided a kind of guarantee for them. The idea is attractive, inherently and inescapably speculative, but it did seem to receive some support from the vision of history as Progress, which had become fashionable at about the same time. Marxism, whilst disavowing the mystical elements in Hegel, nevertheless took over the underlying intuition of a rational historic design. People who continue to uphold some version of this view are not normally called 'rationalists', but nevertheless their ideas are relevant to the debate about the relation of reason to life.

The other relevant tradition, in addition to the Hegelo-Marxist one, is associated with the great names of Schopenhauer, Nietzsche and Freud. Kant had identified Reason will all that was best in man. Schopenhauer (1958 [1819]) taught that men were dominated by a blind irrational Will, whose power they could not combat in the world, though they could at best occasionally escape it through aesthetic contemplation and compassion. Nietzsche (1909–13) shared Schopenhauer's views, but inverted his values: why should the 'Will' be condemned, in the name of a morality which was really the fruit of 'resentment', of a twisted and devious manifestation of that very Will which was being damned? Freud (1930) took over the insights of both thinkers (though not Nietzsche's values), provided them with an elaborate setting in the context of clinical practice and psychiatry, invented a technique purporting to alleviate at least some of the more pathological manifestations of irrational forces and set up an organization for the application and supervision of that technique. In so far as he did not applaud the dominance of irrational forces but on the contrary sought to mitigate them, he cannot (unlike Nietzsche) be accused of irrationalism; but his views of the devious and hidden control of seeming reason by hidden unreason closely resemble Nietzsche's, though as stated they are elaborated in what seems to be a far more specific form, and are linked to clinical practice.

The social scientist is likely to encounter the problem of Reason and Rationality (under a diversity of formulations) in connection with the various traditions and problems which have been specified. The main problem areas are:

(1) innate reason vs. experience as a source of cognition, the debate opposing thinkers such as Descartes and Chomsky to empiricists and behaviourists;

(2) the anchoring of inner logical compulsions either to an allegedly universal human mental equipment, or to the specific culture – in other words the opposition of (say) Kant and Durkheim;

(3) the question of a historically specific form of rationality, its roots, and its role in engendering modern civilization – what might be called the Weberian problem;

(4) the feasibility, in principle or in particular cases, of locating a rational plan in history;

(5) the debate as to whether the real driving force, and the location of genuine satisfaction, within the human psyche is to be sought in irrational drives or in rational aim, calculation, insight or restraint (or in what proportion);

(6) rationality in the sense of explicit criteria and conscious plan, as opposed to respect for tradition and continuity in the management of a polity;

(7) rationalism in the sense of favouring free inquiry as against the authority of either Revolution or Tradition.

These various issues are of course interrelated, although by no means identical, but they are often confused, and the lack of terminological consistency frequently furthers this confusion.

Ernest Gellner
University of Cambridge

References

Chomsky, N. (1966), *Cartesian Linguistics: A Chapter in the History of Rationalist Thought*, New York.

Durkheim, E. (1915 [1912]), *The Elementary Forms of Religious Life*, London.

Freud, S. (1930 [1930]), *Civilization and its Discontents*, London.

Hume, D. (1976 [1739–40]), *A Treatise on Human Nature*, 2 vols, London. (Original German edn, *Das Unbehagen in der Kultur*, Leipzig.)

Kant, I. (1929 [1781]), *Immanuel Kant's Critique of Pure Reason*, Riga. (Original German edn, *Kritik der reinem Vernunft*.)

Nietzsche, F. (1909–13), *Beyond Good and Evil* and *The Genealogy of Morals*, in O. Levy (ed.), *The Complete Works of Friedrich Nietzsche*, vols 12 and 13, Edinburgh.

Schopenhauer, A. (1958 [1819]), *The World as Will and Representation*, New York. (Original German edn, *Die Welt als Wille und Vorstellung*, Leipzig.)

Weber, M. (1961 [1924]), *General Economic History*, London. (Original German edn, *Wirtschaftsgeschichte*, Munich.)

Weber, M. (1968 [1922]), *Economy and Society*, New York. (Original German edn, *Wirtschaft und Gesellschaft*, 2 vols, Tübingen.)

Further Reading

Bartley, W. W. (1962), *The Retreat to Commitment*, New York.

Elster, J. (1978), *Logic and Society: Contradictions and Possible Worlds*, Chichester.

Hollis, M. and Lukes, S. (1982), *Rationality and Relativism*, Oxford.

MacIntyre, A. C. and Emmet, D. (1970), *Sociological Theory and Philosophical Analysis*, London.

Magee, B. (1963), *The Philosophy of Schopenhauer*, Oxford.

Wilson, B. (ed.), *Rationality*, Oxford.

Reference Groups

Reference group refers to an individual or social grouping which either sets or maintains standards for the individual, or which acts as a frame of comparison relative to which the individual compares himself.

Reference group theory and research developed out of the symbolic interactionist tradition within American social science. It was related to Charles Cooley's view that the self arises out of the ideas which others entertain of the given individual. The idea is also present in G. H. Mead's analysis of the differences between role-taking, the 'significant other' in the play stage, and the 'generalized other' in the game stage of human development. Being able to take on the role of the generalized other means that the individual is able to develop fully human characteristics, of an effective self able to look at, assess, control and direct his actions. The existence of the generalized other means that individuals can be the object of their own reflexive consciousnesses. Furthermore, Mead's discussion implies that it is because humans are able through symbols to take on the role of the other that they can refer their attitudes and behaviour to social groups with which they are not directly involved. Reference group analysis thus developed to take cognizance of the fact that people may refer for judgement to groups of which they are not and perhaps cannot be members.

H. H. Hyman first coined the term reference group in 1942 (Hyman and Singer, 1968). He distinguished two different orientations that might be taken to such a group – the *identificatory* and the *judgmental*. In the former case, this produces a normative commitment to the group in question; in the latter, it entails actors evaluating themselves with respect to income, status, education and so on by comparison with the achievements of the other group. This distinction was clarified by H. H. Kelly who distinguished between the normative and comparative function of any reference group;

this in turn developed into the now commonplace distinction between the normative reference group and the comparative reference group.

Four other points should be noted: (1) We should distinguish between different forms of the social object to which reference is made, that is, whether it is an individual, a group, a collectivity or a social category. (2) Reference to any such social object should be viewed as either positive or negative, as in the case of the normative reference group involving respectively identification with or separation from the given social object. (3) We should also distinguish audience reference groups, namely those social objects which function as a source of evaluation and appraisal for the social actor but which are not bases of normative identification or social comparison. (4) There are highly complex and variable relations possible between an individual and a given group, ranging from formal membership, psychological membership, regular interaction, intermittent interaction, to no contact at all (see Merton, 1957).

There have been a number of attempts to identify universalistic explanations of the *selection* of normative reference groups. Some writers suggest that the 'acceptance' of a reference group depends upon the ease with which satisfactory interpersonal contacts can be made. Others argue that the choice of normative references depends upon an individual's status-image and the function of the reference group in a process of status conferral. Others again argue that the selection of normative references will depend upon the degree of perceived interdependence between the individual and the group in question. And finally, it is suggested that an individual is more likely to refer to a given group the more that he is perceived to be socially valuable to the group in question. However, although these are all useful hypotheses, none has been seen to be universally valid.

The best known examination of the *consequences* of normative reference group selection is Theodore Newcomb's study of Bennington College (Hyman and Singer, 1968). He observed that during four successive years, 'junior' and 'senior' students were markedly less conservative than freshmen in terms of a number of public issues; a cohort study over the same period showed the same trend. Moreover, non-conservatism was associated with high participation, involvement and status within the college. Hence, where the college acted as a normative reference group then the student's attitudes became less conservative; where this was not the case and the home and family remained as significant normative reference groups, then attitudes stayed more conservative. However, there are difficulties in this and related studies: (1) It is often difficult to avoid circular argument, since the change of attitude both constitutes the explicandum *and* provides evidence for the patterning of normative group selection.

(2) It is necessary to analyse an actor's *interpretation* of competing normative reference groups rather than assume that particular consequences necessarily follow. (3) Changing patterns of reference group selection have to be related to the temporal development of the self and especially to changes in the life-cycle – hence reference group choices may be historically dependent one upon the other, as in Merton's analysis of 'anticipatory socialization' (1957).

Comparative reference group analysis is based on the argument that once clear physiological needs have been satisfied, then human beings require other bases by which to assess their achievements and satisfactions. In particular, it is argued, humans derive such assessments by comparing themselves with others. Many social philosophers from Aristotle onwards have noted these processes (Urry, 1973). De Tocqueville analysed how the mass of the citizenry began to compare themselves with the newly emergent middle class who 'have no conspicuous privileges, and even their wealth . . . is impalpable and, as it were, *invisible*'. Marx in turn disputed this, arguing that 'although the pleasures of the labourer have increased, the social gratification which they afford has fallen in comparison with the increased pleasures of the capitalist'. He concludes that since our wants and pleasures 'are of a social nature, they are of a relative nature'. And, from a different tradition, Max Scheler maintained that: 'The medieval peasant prior to the thirteenth century does not compare himself to the feudal lord, nor does the artisan compare himself to the knight . . . every comparison took place within a strictly circumscribed frame of reference. . . . In the "system of free-competition", on the other hand . . . aspirations are intrinsically *boundless*, for they are no longer tied to any particular object or quality.' A version of this can be found in the famous intepretation of the 'promotion finding' in the *American Soldier* study, which established that those units where there was a high rate of promotion expressed *more* dissatisfaction about future promotion chances than units where promotion rates were lower. Hence, Robert Merton argued that higher mobility rates induced excessive hopes and expectations for further promotion, and more widespread comparisons were made. This view was amplified by W. G. Runciman who also, on the basis of a national sample survey, concluded that manual workers in the UK had fairly restricted comparative reference groups, especially with regard to class dimensions of inequality. Certain nonmanual workers made wider and more class-conscious comparisons (1972). An important reason for this was that there generally has to be some kind of basis or similarity along other dimensions of social inequality, apart from the one where the comparison is occurring, in order that wide-ranging comparisons can be made. For example, the Amba in East Africa were willing to work for Europeans at a much lower price than for employers from another tribe, because 'a European is on a much higher social plane, and therefore comparisons are out of the question'. There was no other similarity or basis for the comparison.

Most research indicates that actors normally operate in terms of fairly restricted patterns of social comparison. It is only in periods of rapid social change that these established patterns may be upset. John Urry (1973) distinguished between 'conventional comparisons', those used in everyday life and structured in terms of the actor's social network, and 'structural comparisons', those feasibly made when that everyday world is disrupted, and comparisons are structured by the environing patterns of social stratification. Urry also emphasized that relative deprivation involves a number of distinct stages of development, in particular, that there are varied conditions under which revealed deprivations are deemed unjust, and blame may be attributed to the dominant groups or the wider society. Ted Gurr has likewise elaborated an integrated theory of political violence, in which the first stage, the development of discontent, stems from the perception of relative deprivation between people's value expectations and value capabilities (1970).

Overall, there is nothing which we might term 'reference group theory'. The term is, as Runciman argues, useful in describing certain processes of attitude formation within an individualistic social science, based on related notions of self, identity and role. The key idea is, as Thoreau puts it, 'If a man does not keep pace with his companions perhaps it is because he hears a different drummer.'

John Urry
University of Lancaster

References
Gurr, T. (1970), *Why Men Rebel*, Princeton, New Jersey.
Hyman, H. H. and Singer, E. (eds) (1968), *Readings in Reference Group Theory and Research*, New York.
Merton, R. K. (1957), *Social Theory and Social Structure*, New York.
Runciman, W. G. (1972), *Relative Deprivation and Social Justice*, Harmondsworth.
Urry, J. (1973), *Reference Groups and the Theory of Revolution*, London.
See also: *Mead, G. H.; relative deprivation.*

Refugees

Whether as banished exiles or in planned exodus ('anticipatory flight'), the reality of refugees and their forced flight has existed since Adam left Eden. Refugees may be typed, simplistically, according to their desire or possibility of returning to their homeland:

(1) 'Majority-identified' refugees may feel loyalty to the nation – their homeland – and to most of their compatriots, but not to the reigning government and its adherents – for example, most political refugees. In their own minds, their return is merely delayed.

(2) 'Events-alienated' refugees are reacting to intolerable forces which push them out – violence, persecution, occupation, partition of old frontiers (as in the case of India and Pakistan). They have become unwanted aliens with little hope or desire or possibility of return.

(3) 'Self-alienated' refugees are moved by personal or ideological reasons to alienate themselves beyond a point where they wish to return (Kunz, 1981). Factors related to homeland, displacement and the host country raise analytical difficulties in classifying such types as refugees, as displaced persons, or as voluntary immigrants. To say that 'refugees are pushed, immigrants are pulled' towards a host country does not catch the complexity of the migration process.

In this century of refugees, the legal concept of refugee has been gradually formulated, especially between the two world wars, initially by Western nations. Two basic statutes (UN Convention, 1951 and UN Protocol, 1967), to which by 1981 some ninety nations had adhered, extend international protection to refugees via asylum and favourable legal status in the host country. These statutes define the refugee as 'a person who, owing to a well-founded fear of persecution for reasons of race, religion, nationality, membership of a particular social group or political opinion, is outside the country of his nationality and is unable or, owing to such fear, unwilling to avail himself of the protection of that country' (UN Conference, 28 July 1951, Article 1). Previous international instruments (during the 1930s) dealt only with specific groups of refugees; in contrast, the 1951 definition has a more general application and includes the critical principle of *non-refoulement* which prohibits expulsion or forcible return of the refugee against his will. The 1951 Convention does not apply to those refugees under the care of UN agencies other than UNHCR (such as Palestinian refugees with the United Nations Relief and Works Agency) nor to those refugees who have a status equivalent to nationals in their country of refuge.

There are many *de facto* refugees who fall outside the scope of the Convention/Protocol as presently interpreted (for instance, internally displaced persons and victims of repressive military and economic policies) such that the concept of refugee tends to be defined situationally. Thus the definition has also been widened in scope (for example by the Pan African

Conference on Refugees in 1979). No comprehensive refugee policy defined by law existed in the USA until its Refugee Act of 1980, although thousands of *de facto* refugees (for example Cubans, Haitians, Indochinese) had previously been admitted there. Social, as well as legal, status, whereby refugees become the wards of the host government, is also a significant factor in their treatment by voluntary agencies. Exile is a state of mind, not just the lack of a passport.

Currently, the African continent (especially the Horn of Africa) with its five million refugees (compared with only 750,000 in 1970) accounts for about half the world's refugees. Some two million Afghan refugees are in Pakistan camps. Other large groups (such as El Salvadorians, Vietnamese) are scattered in various countries of asylum in Central America and South-East and East Asia.

Michael Kenny
Catholic University of America

Reference
Kunz, E. F. (1981), 'Exile and resettlement: refugee theory', in B. N. Stein and S. M. Tomasi (eds), *Refugees Today, International Migration Review*, 15.
See also: *migration*.

Regional Analysis

Regional analysis, pioneered by geographers (specifically by Walter Christaller who expanded upon Thünen) in the 1930s, has been increasingly appropriated by other social scientists. Before Christaller, geographers defined regions as natural systems created by topographical features, but Christaller defined them as they were organized by social relationships and organizational principles. In his major work (1966), Christaller's primary concern appeared to be analysing the relative sizes, locations and hierarchical relationships among human settlements or central places. Thus, some considered Christaller's main contribution to the social sciences to be a method for analysing the economic relations connecting urban centres to one another in patterned ways. When most people think of Christaller, in fact, they think of hexagons, the locational arrangement that Christaller found to be the most economical way for market centres to be organized on a landscape. Yet Christaller's contribution to the understanding of social and economic relations in space went far beyond his utilization of elementary principles of geometry: he showed – and regional analysis has built upon this – the variable ways in which human environments are constituted by social relationships in space.

The possibility of extending regional analysis so that it could deal directly with social and cultural phenomena was not widely appreciated until Skinner (1964–5) used locational principles, developed by both Christaller (1966) and Lösch (1954), to analyse rural marketing systems and social relations in China. Stimulated by Skinner, a number of anthropologists began applying principles of locational analysis in their work. The first to do so were students of peasant or rural marketing systems, where these principles had obvious application. Like Skinner, they began to extend their analyses beyond the economic to confront issues of society and culture on a regional scale. Regional analysis was further extended to new questions (concerning kinship, religion, ethnicity, politics and class), by considering questions of history and evolution, and by developing certain new principles of analysis (Smith, 1976).

Practitioners of regional analysis have continued working along these same lines, giving somewhat more emphasis to regions defined by cities, as opposed to those organized by peasant marketplaces. Skinner (1977) extended his analysis of Chinese society by examining relationships between cities at the higher reaches of Chinese regional systems, concentrating on political rather than economic relations. He also considered the relationship between 'natural' and socially constructed regions, arguing that the core–periphery structure of most economic regions rested upon the interaction between natural features and economic constraints. But others continue to emphasize social over natural determinants of regional-system structures.

At present, relatively few non-geographers continue to apply Christaller's original principles of regional analysis. (Archaeologists provide the main exception in that they continue to be concerned with locational analysis and principles of the space economy *per se*.) On these grounds, one could argue that regional analysis has not had a wide or lasting influence. Yet the basic principles of regional analysis have crept into the standard social science repertoire, especially that of anthropologists, so that few now ignore the regional, spatial context of their communities. Inasmuch as these scholars pay less attention to the ecological features of the regions they describe and more attention to how regional systems are socially constructed, they are indebted to regional analysis. And on these grounds, one could argue that regional analysis has become more than one of several competing paradigms or approaches in the social sciences; it has become an accepted way of dealing with complex hierarchical relationships in societies.

Carol A. Smith
Duke University

References
Christaller, W. (1966), *Central Places in Southern Germany*, trans. C. W. Baskin, Englewood Cliffs, New Jersey.
Lösch, A. (1954), *The Economics of Location*, New Haven, Conn.

Skinner, G. W. (1964–5), 'Marketing and social structure in rural China', Parts 1 and 11, *Journal of Asian Studies*, 24.

Skinner, G. W. (1977), 'Regional urbanization in nineteenth-century China', in *The City in Late Traditional China*, Stanford.

Smith, C. A. (ed.) (1976), *Regional Analysis: vol. 1, Economic Systems, vol. 11, Social Systems*, New York.

Further Reading

Thünen, J. H. von (1966), *Von Thünen's Isolated State*, trans. C.M. Wartenberg, Oxford.

See also: *ecology; social geography; spatial statistics*.

Regression

(1) In the simplest case there are two variables X and Y for which n pairs of observations (X_iY_i) are obtained $(i = 1,..,n)$. The problem of *linear regression* is to identify a solution for a and for b, in such a way that the sum of the squared differences between y_i and $(a + bX_i)$ is minimized. This solution can be calculated as follows:

   (i) calculate $D = n.\Sigma X_i^2 - (\Sigma X_i)^2$

   (ii) $b = \{n.\Sigma X_iY_i - (\Sigma X_i).(\Sigma Y_i)\}/D$

   (iii) $a = \{(\Sigma Y_i).(\Sigma X_i^2) - (\Sigma X_i).(\Sigma X_iY_i)\}/D$

Table 1

X	Y	X^2	Y^2	XY
1	4	1	16	4
1	2	1	4	2
2	5	4	25	10
4	2	16	4	8
7	7	49	49	49
Σ: 15	20	71	98	73

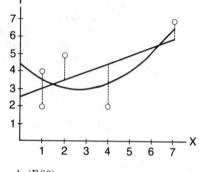

Figure 1 (R68)

A simple example with n = 5 is shown in Table 1. For this example, $D = 130$, $b = 65/130 = .5$, $a = 325/130 = 2.5$.

The figure graphs results. The solution $a + bX_i$ appears in this graph as a straight line (with intercept a and slope b). The solution guarantees that the vertical distances from observations to the line have smallest sum of square – these distances are drawn in the figure as dotted lines.

(2) A generalization is *polynomial regression* where instead of a straight line a curve is fitted to the observations, corresponding to a polynomial in X_i, defined as $a + b_1X_i + b_2X_i^2 + b_3X_i^3 + \ldots$ In the figure the thin line shows the solution for the best fitting quadratic curve.

(3) Another type of generalization is the case of *multiple regression*, where observations on a variable Y are obtained, together with values for a number of variables X_1, X_2, etc. Assuming that all variables are in deviations from their mean, multiple regression solves for *regression weights* b_j, in such a way that the sum of the squared differences between Y_i and $\{b_1X_{1i} + b_2X_{2i} + b_3X_{3i} + \ldots\}$ has a minimum. The correlation between the last form between brackets and Y_i is called the *multiple correlation*.

(4) From the statistical point of view the linear regression problem assumes that the value of X_i is fixed – not subject to random error – whereas the corresponding value of Y_i is sampled from a population of possible values; Y_i therefore will have a random error component, so that we may write $Y_i = a + \beta X_i + \epsilon_i$. The solution for a and b calculated on the basis of sampled values then becomes an estimate of the population parameters α and β.

(5) If both X and Y are subject to sampling error, the regression problem changes into a *correlation* problem. In this case there is not only a solution for regression of Y and X (as described in (1) above), but also a solution for regression of X and Y, with roles of X and Y reversed. In a graph, this results into *two* regression lines.

John van de Geer
University of Leiden

See also: *measures of central tendency and dispersion*.

Rehabilitation

Rehabilitation of prisoners may carry three distinct meanings: reform of character, reinstatement in society, and mitigating institutionalized behaviour. Apparently respectable citizens may, however, continue unapprehended with offences of a kind for which they were once imprisoned. Such ambiguity mystifies the study of the treatment not only of offenders but also of Skid Row alcoholics, the psychologically disturbed, neglected children and other members of society regarded as needing help.

There are other problems, besides those of definition, in the evaluation of rehabilitation:

(1) Rehabilitative programmes sometimes change what they claim to achieve – or even for whom they achieve it (Regier, 1979) – once their original ambitious aims meet with failure.

(2) Sociologists consider the viewpoint not only of helpers but also of the helped. Helpers may support rehabilitiation in one sense, but offenders, patients or clients may reject it in another. Thus Davies (1974) defines rehabilitation as 'overcoming the effects of incarceration', whereas a probationer says, 'It would be easier to be back inside.'

sometimes very tightly. A consideration for human rights implies that rehabilitation should not be reduced to coercion. The 'latent function' of a rehabilitative organization may be more regimented control. Goffman's analysis of 'total institutions', Foucault's critique of their insidious expansion, and a concern for phenomena like the hospitalization as mentally ill of political dissidents or troublesome relatives (Scheff, 1966) all cast doubt on the assumption that 'rehabilitation' must be intrinsically beneficial.

Maurice Glickman
University of Botswana

References

Davies, M. (1974), *Prisoners of Society: Attitudes and After-Care*, London.

Regier, M. (1979), *Social Policy in Action: Perspectives on the Implementation of Alchohol Reforms*, Lexington, Mass.

Scheff, T. (1966), *Being Mentally Ill*, Chicago.

Further Reading

Glickman, M. (1983), *From Crime to Rehabilitation*, Aldershot.

HMSO (1963), *The Organization of After-Care. Report of the Advisory Council on the Treatment of Offenders*, London.

See also: *penology; punishment*.

Reich, Wilhelm (1897–1957)

There is no more audacious figure in the history of modern psychiatry than Wilhelm Reich. Born on 24 March 1897 in an eastern province of the Austro-Hungarian empire, he died sixty years later in a US penitentiary. His various accomplishments included the development of *character analysis* (or the investigation of defensive character traits) within the framework of psychoanalysis. This work, undertaken in Vienna in the 1920s, profoundly influenced the later growth of ego psychology, especially Anna Freud's *The Ego and the Mechanisms of Defense*, (1936).

Between 1927 and 1933 in Vienna and Berlin, Reich made conceptual contributions towards the integration of psychoanalysis and Marxism. His practical 'sex-political' work during this period brought sex education and counselling to large numbers of people in a way that connected emotional issues with social concerns. These activities later influenced the new left in the 1960s and the orientation of the women's movement towards 'politicizing the personal'.

Following his expulsion from the German Communist Party in 1933 for his psychodynamic emphases, and from the International Psychoanalytic Association in 1934 for his social stance, Reich moved to Oslo. There he delineated the *muscular armour*, that is, chronic muscular spasms representing the somatic anchoring of characterological rigidities. This work provided the originating impulse for such latter-day therapies as Bioenergetics, Gestalt Therapy and Primal Therapy.

In the 1940s and 1950s in America, Reich, whose work had always been radical, began to investigate *orgone energy*, an energy which, he asserted, functioned as the life energy inside the organism and in nature at large. These ideas were dismissed by almost the entire psychiatric and psychoanalytic community. Reich subsequently invented and distributed a device, the *orgone energy accumulator*, which, he believed, had therapeutic and preventive properties for a number of illnesses. When he continued to distribute the accumulator after an injunction against it was obtained by the US Food and Drug Administration, the accumulators were destroyed, most of his publications were burned, and he was imprisoned on 11 March 1957.

Reich's extraordinary and defiant journey across scientific boundaries merits serious evaluation of both its fruitfulness and its error.

Myron Sharaf
Cambridge Hospital and Harvard University

Further Reading

Higgins, M. Boyd (1960), *Wilhelm Reich: Selected Writings*, New York.

Reich, W. (1961), *Character Analysis*, New York. (Contains translations of *Charakteranalyse*, 1933, and *Psychischer Kontakt und vegetative Strömung*, 1935.)

Sharaf, M. (1983), *Fury on Earth: A Biography of Wilhelm Reich*, New York.

See also: *gestalt therapy*.

Reinforcement

See Conditioning, Learning.

Relative Deprivation

Deprivation is relative. People experience resentment or discontent about their condition not necessarily when they are deprived in an absolute sense, but when they feel deprived relative to some standard of comparison. These are the essential concepts behind the theory of relative deprivation (RD). Because a wide range of studies on racial riots, student and feminist protest movements reveal that the participants in these events are generally not the most deprived or disadvantaged of their respective groups, the RD explanation appears to be a plausible alternative to an absolute deprivation thesis.

The first use of the term 'relative deprivation' dates from the Second World War. Samuel Stouffer and his colleagues at the Research Division of the Information Branch of the US Army (1949) employed it in *The American Soldier* as an *ad hoc* explanation for the surprising findings that some objectively better-off soldiers actually experienced greater discontent. Since then, social psychologists, sociologists and political scientists have developed a number of models of relative deprivation in order to explain various personal and collective phenomena.

Stated simply, relative deprivation refers to the negative emotion, variously expressed as anger, resentment, or dissatisfaction, which individuals experience when they compare their situation with some standard or reference. The standard might include other persons, other groups or comparisons with oneself in the past.

In examining the various existing models (see Crosby, 1976; Davis, 1959; Gurr, 1970; Runciman, 1966), it becomes readily apparent that all share some features:

(1) The basic premise of all models is that objective and subjective well-being are not isomorphically related. Every model specifies various cognitive and emotional factors which precede feelings of relative deprivation. Most models regard the two precursory conditions for feelings of relative deprivation as: the absence of some possession or right (referred to as X) and the awareness by the person experiencing RD that another person or another group has X. However, the other conditions, such as deserving X, expecting X, personal responsibility for not having X, vary from model to model.

(2) There is an assumed link between experienced relative deprivation and the attitudinal or behavioural consequences at the personal and collective levels. The various consequences of RD (depending on the theory) are stress, low self-evaluation, attempts at self-improvement, and the growth of social movements, collective violence and even revolutions.

The fundamental process of RD has now been firmly established. Current research efforts are directed at understanding some of the persistent puzzles that remain: When is it that the feeling of RD is followed by action? Why is it that more action is sometimes taken when RD is decreased? What are the distinctions, in terms of antecedents and consequences, between personal RD (a type of personal discontent that occurs when an individual compares his own situation to that of others) and collective RD (feelings of social discontent that occur when an individual compares the situation of his group as a whole to that of an outgroup)? Answers to these questions are likely to emphasize even more the need to consider psychological factors in explaining otherwise incomprehensible events.

Lise Dubé-Simard
University of Montreal

References
Crosby, F. (1976), 'A model of egoistical relative deprivation', *Psychological Review*, 83.
Davis, J. A. (1959), 'A formal interpretation of the theory of relative deprivation', *Sociometry*, 22.
Gurr, T. R. (1970), *Why Men Rebel*, Princeton, New Jersey.
Runciman, W. G. (1966), *Relative Deprivation and Social Justice: A Study of Attitudes to Social Inequality in Twentieth-Century England*, Berkeley and Los Angeles.
Stouffer, S. A., Suchman, E. A., De Vinney, L. C., Star, S. A. and Williams, R. M. (1949), *The American Soldier: Adjustment during Army Life*, vol. 1, Princeton, New Jersey.

See also: *reference groups*.

Relativism

The core proposition informing cultural relativism is that the standards which back human cognition are neither absolute nor identical in all societies. Instead, they are cultural in nature and may vary from one society to another. One prescription which relativists draw from this is that what is said and done in any society should be understood in its own terms, according to the standards current in that society. Another is that no basis exists for judgements that the institutions of one culture are superior to those of another. It is especially important to avoid ethnocentrism, that is, the practice of conceptualizing and evaluating what happens in another society against standards drawn from the observer's own society.

One source of cultural relativism is in reports of anthropologists and other travellers that people in various parts of the globe live in successful and productive social orders, although they adhere to standards of truth and morality quite different from those prevailing in the West. In addition, relativism emerged as a reaction to certain tendencies towards intolerance in Western thought. One was the evolutionism which dominated late nineteenth-century anthropology. Closely allied with the idea of progress, evolutionism held that social institutions evolve just as much as natural species do, and that it was possible to arrange the institutions from various human societies on a scale from least to most advanced. It always worked out that Western civilization perched on the top of the evolutionary ladder, while other societies were arrested at one or another of the lower rungs. Charitable Westerners perceived in this circumstance a calling to convert and uplift their less fortunate brethren; tougher-minded imperialists rejoiced in their right, by dint of evolutionary laws such as the survival of the fittest, to exploit their inferiors. In either case, very little in the way of respect, understanding or tolerance was accorded to the institutions of non-Western cultures.

Relativism also grew in reaction to the Romantic idea that people realize their humanity through culture. Stated in those terms, it is a view shared by contemporary anthropology and which is entirely in accord with cultural relativism. Certain variants, however, went on to add the corollary that some peoples are biologically equipped to produce higher levels of culture than others. The most virulent development of such racism, of course, is Nazi ideology.

Anthropology has generated two basic doctrines to combat intolerance and racism: cultural relativism and the psychic unity of mankind. The latter notion – that any normal human infant has the capacity to learn the language and customs and to function as an effective member of any society – is drawn up directly against racism. Cultural relativism counters intolerance at the institutional and cultural level by its denial that cross-cultural evaluations can legitimately be made.

Desirable as its objectives may be, serious philosophical problems have been raised about relativism. If ethical standards may vary among cultures, there is no pan-human morality. Does this commit the relativist to condoning contradictory judgements; to affirm, for example, that to kill a relative of the person who murdered your father is both an exemplary deed (in some societies) and morally wrong (in other societies)? How is the unit within which moral standards operate to be defined? Are minority ethnic groups within a larger society justified in following their separate moral imperatives? Should the same legitimacy be extended to other minorities or subcultures such as terrorist groups or organized crime?

The relativist premise that cognitive standards are culturally variable includes standards of truth and knowledge. Hence, the relativist would have to certify as true a vast collection of propositions, including that witches can kill at a distance; that there is no such thing as witchcraft; that the world is governed by impersonal natural laws; that the world is governed by the will of anthropomorphic beings; and that animals perceive one another as human beings and human beings as animals (Schieffelin, 1976). Is the world big enough, or disorganized enough, to contain a collection of truths such as these? Or is the relativist left with no other course than to conclude that people with different standards of truth inhabit different worlds? Yet precisely what that might mean is far from clear.

One thing it does seem to mean is that relativism is a self-defeating programme. Among the cognitive standards which may vary between cultures are epistemological ones: criteria for what constitutes knowledge and understanding. Presumably the internal understanding counselled by relativism entails that any culture should be understood in terms of its own epistemological standards. It is possible, however, that the epistemological standards in question are different from our own. In that event an internal understanding of the culture would not constitute proper understanding from the perspective of the anthropologist and those who read his reports. The only understanding which would make sense to them would be one that conforms to their own epistemological standards, but they are alien to the culture under examination. Relativism, in other words, appears to rule out the very kind of internal understanding that it is designed to achieve.

Problems such as these are serious enough that few, if any, scholars today defend relativism in its pure form. Some reject it entirely in favour of an absolutist position. But many anthropologists and other thinkers, finding the official disregard for cultural factors in absolutism and the clear ethnocentric tendencies of its practitioners to be at least as problematic as relativism, seek some sort of middle ground. One means of dealing with the moral problem is to attempt to articulate common denominators shared by all or most ethical systems, despite surface differences. Another is to argue that relativism does not commit one to condoning all of the practices which may be encountered. It is one thing to understand that the people who engage in a certain practice consider it to be moral because it conforms to their standards of morality. But the anthropologist's own judgement as to the morality of the practice is an entirely different matter. That depends on the relation of the practice to his own standards, and these may differ from the standards of the culture under study. Understanding, that is to say, does not entail agreeing.

Again, the variability of truth does not necessitate abandoning the notion that all humans inhabit the same world. Truth and knowledge are not contingent solely upon the state of external reality. As C.I. Lewis pointed out long ago (1929), it is inescapable that for any object to be known at all, it must be known in relation to a mind. If the mind were different – if, for example, it operated in terms of other culturally based premises – the description of the object might well be different, and yet it could still be a true description of an independently existing reality.

F. Allan Hanson
University of Kansas

References
Lewis, C. I. (1929), *Mind and the World-Order*, New York.
Schieffelin, E. L. (1976), *The Sorrow of the Lonely and the Burning of the Dancers*, New York.

Further Reading
Hanson, F. A. (1975), *Meaning in Culture*, London.
Hatch, E. (1983), *Culture and Morality*, New York.
Herskovits, M. (1972), *Cultural Relativism*, New York.
Jarvie, I. (1984), *Rationality and Relativism*, London.

Religion and Ritual

Anthropologists who specialize in the study of preliterate societies have always been faced with the difficult problem of defining what kind of phenomena can be called religious. At first sight what religion is, in those places where the world religions occur, seems fairly straightforward. There are special places for it – temples, churches, mosques – and special people to deal with it – imams, rabbis, priests. Even in these cases, however, the matter is much less simple. If we take the example of Islam, we find that such activities as sleeping, waking, eating, defecating and washing all have a religious character; thus, even here, it is not clear where religion begins or where it ends.

The problem is even more complicated in the case of traditional societies, not only because phenomena which are easily referred to by the English word 'religion' are part and parcel of activities which we would not so label, but also because people in such societies, unlike the participants in a world religion, have no concept of 'religion' as a distinct phenomenon. This has led social scientists to try a whole range of definitions, usually settling, with little conviction, on formulae such as: religion involves the belief in supernatural forces (see Goody, 1961). The problem with this type of definition is in the difficulty of distinguishing between 'natural' and 'supernatural' knowledge. For example, are we to call the belief that one should respect one's father and mother a natural or a supernatural belief, since it refers to empirical beings, but cannot be justified on purely practical grounds? Another type of definition tries to deal with such difficulties. For example, Durkheim called religious all beliefs and practices which were believed to be right of themselves, not merely right because they were the best way of doing something according to practical criteria. The first type of beliefs and practices were, according to him, 'sacred'; the second 'profane'

(Durkheim, 1915 [1912]). But in practice it is impossible to distinguish on the basis of this criterion, as it separates what is not separated in ordinary life. This point is repeatedly made by Weber, who stresses how particular religions are coterminous with particular ways of acting, particular ways of life; as a result the 'sacred' and the 'profane' are ultimately inseparable (Weber, 1930 [1905]). This, however, does not help in defining what religion is, and the only solution seems to be to abandon the notion of religion as an analytical category and to look at social reality in terms less closely tied to a particular cultural tradition. This is implicit in the work of Marx where religion is subsumed under the wider label of ideology, which also includes such ideas as the 'rightness' of competition in capitalist systems (Marx and Engels, 1939 [1845–6]).

Even if we reject the notion of religion as an analytical tool, we can retain it as a general indication of an area of study. Taking this perspective, we may ask what kinds of topics seem to recur in the discussion of religion. What these areas are is well summarized in Plato's famous theory of ideas in *The Republic*. After considering the problems of the relation of man to his environment and his biological and psychical nature, Plato argues that all we apprehend through our senses is in fact a necessarily compromised and misleading shadow of a clearer, simpler and eternal reality which we may not see but which governs what we see. He concludes that there are some men who can see the 'truth' better than others, and that therefore they can see more clearly what more ordinary men see only as distorted shadows. It follows, according to Plato, that these men should, because of their proximity to the true source of knowledge, be political leaders. We have here three of the typical ingredients of religion: (1) philosophical or intellectual speculation; (2) the denial of the validity of experience; and (3) the legitimation of authority. We shall consider these three topics in turn.

Intellectual speculation about problems surrounding the human condition seem to be typical of all known societies, and they always focus around the same particularly fundamental problem: how far is man separate or continuous with animals, plants and even geographical and cosmological events? The answer is, like any answer to this fundamental question, always unsatisfactory, and therefore such answers endlessly throw up further problems, thereby initiating an ongoing, never resolved, dialogue. Of course in most cases such speculation is not carried out in abstractions, but in terms of specific notions which seem to concretize the problem. What is the significance of cooking food as opposed to eating it raw? Is human copulation the same thing as animal copulation? What would copulation between different species mean? Does the fact that all human societies exchange – especially in marriage – finally differentiate men from animals?

What would happen to this difference if men copulated with their sisters? Are the cycles of life related to the cycles of plants, the seasons, the heavenly bodies? The continuing boldness of thought and fascination of human beings with such metaphysical questions is well illustrated by Lévi-Strauss's work on the mythology of South and North American Indians, *An Introduction to the Science of Mythology* (1970–81).

It is misleading to imagine that such intellectual pursuits are more typical of complex societies than simple ones. If anything, it is the other way round. Anthropologists' reports of the freest and boldest metaphysical speculation all relate to societies with the very simplest technology. This is because these societies are often the ones where institutionalized political inequality is least developed, and the accompanying regulation of speculation by means of authority leads to a diminution of the type of free speculative activities discussed by Lévi-Strauss for the Amerindians. When speculation does occur in more centralized society, it becomes quite separate from the main religious concerns which centre on ritual. How this happens will become clear when we consider the process by which the value of experience is denied in religion, and how this is linked with authority.

The organization of speculation by authority occurs through ritual. Ritual, like religion, is another word which has posed many problems for anthropologists. But for all anthropologists rituals are relatively fixed sequences of behaviour; as a result they are not individual and not *ad hoc*. Rituals are not legitimated in terms of an immediate instrumentality (Leach, 1954); they convey meaning by means of symbols, defined by one anthropologist as 'minimal units of ritual' (Turner, 1967). If rituals are to be seen as a means of communication, they use very peculiar means, which has led Sperber (1975) to point out how misleading it is to see them as a kind of language. Rituals use symbols which seem to refer and connote only in the vaguest of ways. Rituals employ relatively fixed sequences of language, and, above all, singing, which hinders analytical communication (Bloch, 1974). They use endless repetition (Leach, 1966), reminding us again that they convey meaning in a different, less simple, way than other statements. For all these reasons, rituals seem to be the very opposite of the free speculation characteristic of the myth that Lévi-Strauss studied. They are invariant, they are unclear, there is little possibility for individual innovation and they are anti-intellectual.

In spite of this, a surprisingly similar pattern seems to emerge in all rituals, throughout the world, and they all seem to carry much the same message. This is Plato's message: do not trust the world of appearances for there is something truer, more permanent, that lies hidden beyond. If we do not accept the truth of this message, the question we must ask of rituals is not what they reveal of the beyond, but rather how they create the image of the beyond. In other words, anthropologists reverse the platonic assertion about rituals which state that this world is a shadow of another, but see rituals as creating an image of a shadow out of the reality of this world, although a shadow which is presented as the real thing.

There are a number of suggestions in the anthropological literature as to how rituals effect this inversion. Two French authors, Hertz (1960 [1928]) and Van Gennep (1960 [1909]), noted the tripartite division that seems to occur in many rituals. Van Gennep stressed how rituals often involve the idea of a journey which illustrates a social transformation; this would be the case for initiation rituals. The rituals enact the child leaving his childhood state, then going through an intermediate stage, the liminal stage (after the Latin *limen*, meaning threshold, one of the commonest symbols of such a state) and finally entering the world of adulthood. Van Gennep called such rituals 'rites of passage' because they use the symbolism of a journey.

One of the usual ways of explaining such rituals has been to follow Van Gennep's lead and to see rites of passage as devices for the smooth transfer of social roles from individual to individual. It is clear, however, that such an explanation is insufficient, and that it ignores the religious aspects of such practices.

Other anthropologists have paid special attention to the middle 'liminal' stage, noting that this stage is governed by rules which, in a number of ways, contrast, or are even totally opposed to, those of normal life (Turner, 1967; Gluckman, 1963). The liminal stage often seems to involve inversions of authority, for example, women ruling over men, children over adults; in some cases this stage also involves the chaotic suspension of normal behaviour in orgiastic sequences. This is a common feature of all ritual, for example, the Lent carnival in the Christian calendar. The explanation of such apparently bizarre behaviour goes to the very heart of ritual and religion. Ritual is a dramatic commentary on life, which represents it as a mixture of two elements, pure and impure. The task of ritual is to separate the two so that the impure can be eliminated in order that the true – pure – can emerge. Or, looked at from an atheistic perspective, this antithetical process creates the illusion of the Other. In this light we can reinterpret the three stages of the rites of passage: the first acts out the mixed state; it is followed by the acting out of the impure chaotic state; this is then driven out and replaced by the contrasting image of the pure holy state.

We can see this three-stage schema in initiation rituals, whether they be Christian baptism or Australian aboriginal initiation ritual. The first stage is a fairly neutral representation of nonritual, birth; the second stage involves the creation of an image of birth as a horrifyingly polluting event, so that the third stage can be staged as a 'cleansing' of the child from the polluting effects of birth in order that he be 'reborn' again in a higher, purer, truer way. The same pattern can also be observed in funerary rituals, which involve stressing death as a dirty, polluting, horrifying event so that the latter part of the ritual can involve a 'victory over death' in a superior world (Bloch and Parry, 1982). This perspective enables us to understand one of the most puzzling features of religion. Although all religions proclaim the existence of a transcendental purity, which escapes the false reality of the shadows of this world (shadows which we would otherwise take for reality), they do this by emphasizing dirt, pollution, decay and corruption (Douglas, 1966). Revelling in the idea of pollution is so typical of religion because the drama which creates the transcendental requires the representation of its antithesis. This also explains the repeated presence of the notion of cleaning in all types of religion – which often takes the somewhat extreme form of bodily mutilation, such as the ritual bleedings of New Guinea or of Jewish circumcision.

The basis of religious rituals is therefore an elaborate denial of the sufficiency of nonreligious activity, especially a denial that the creative potential is in human hands. Birth is denied its creativity and death its finality, and, interestingly, these two ideas are usually closely linked in a total denial of the time-scale of human production and reproduction. Instead, and by means of the drama of ritual, a timeless order is created in which human life, birth and action are irrelevant. This image may be more or less elaborate. In the systems of ancestor worship found in many parts of Africa, an image is created of people surviving beyond their life-span, and that succeeding generations of a descent group are really the same moral entity reincarnated (Fortes, 1959). In traditional Hindu belief, an image is created of great mystical cycles, of a length totally incomparable with the biological cycles of human life. These cycles, unlike human history, are represented as the 'real' basis of the cosmos.

The religious image involves identifying this life with death and decomposition, and the Other life with the victory over death, since the religious world is sufficiently timeless and unchanging for the human life-span to be meaningless. In order to convey this message, rituals juggle endlessly with the idea of death and birth by creating the image of a life-giving death (Frazer, 1980). This appears to lie behind one of the commonest forms of ritual sacrifice, which seems to rest on the paradox that killing produces transcendental life (Robertson-Smith, 1889; Hubert and Mauss, 1964 [1899]).

The world created by ritual is, however, extremely vague. Rituals create by drama, not by exegesis. Consequently, when – as in world religions – there are also professional theologians trying to organize and systematize beliefs, their ideas seem curiously distant from the everyday religion of people (Tambiah, 1969;

Geertz, 1960). Accordingly some anthropologists distinguish between two types of religion, a folk religion and an official theological religion (Srinivas, 1952). It is partly as a result of these problems that anthropologists and sociologists have found it almost impossible to agree about the notion of 'belief' (Leach, 1966). The messages of ritual are quite specific about what is *not* the real world, as was Plato, but much vaguer about what the 'real' world is like. What seems to matter above all in religion is the declaration of the limitations, if not outright pointlessness, of conscious human action.

This last fact explains the close relation between religions and political systems. For political power to appear as more than mere coercion, but as a legitimate exercise, it must be represented as the instrument of something which transcends the here and now. This 'something' need not always be religious, but it very often is. For example, African elders appear justified in their control of others because they are the representatives of the pure, death-defying, ancestors. Medieval kings were 'Christ's representatives on earth'. In some parts of the world, rulers are actually represented as gods. In cases such as these the religion will inevitably frown on metaphysical speculation involving a challenge to authority. On the other hand, the powers that be will enforce participation in rituals. The political significance of religion in such cases depends partly on the fact that religious rituals reinterpret existence as shadows, so that the true legitimacy of power lies beyond the actions of subordinates; but it also rests on the fact that religion is a reinterpretation and a deconstruction of real life. This means that the 'other' world which religion creates is also partly the world we all know, but seen in another light, the distorting light of ritual; as a result the other world still appears to some extent true to our senses and our emotions. Religion, in order to be powerful and to perform its political role, must have this appearance of deep truth, and explanations of religion must not only explain how it maintains authority but also why it is so apparently necessary and comforting to the participants.

Yet it would be misleading to think that organized religion always supports authority. Indeed, the use of religion by those in authority means that it is likely also to be used in religious revolts. In such cases the rebels claim either that the present rulers are not the true representatives of the divine on earth, while they, the rebels, are (Ileto, 1979), or more rarely, that they have discovered a superior source of divinity which therefore renders invalid the claims of the power holders (Worsley, 1957). But victory has little to do with the specifically religious claims of either side; it is a matter of who is strongest on the battlefield.

Maurice Bloch
London School of Economics and Political Science

References

Bloch, M. (1974), 'Symbol song and dance or is religion an extreme form of traditional authority?', *European Archives of Sociology*, 1974.

Bloch, M. and Parry, J. (eds)(1982), *Death and the Regeneration of Life*, Cambridge.

Douglas, M. (1966), *Purity and Danger*, London.

Durkheim, E. (1915 [1912]), *The Elementary Forms of the Religious Life*, London.

Fortes, M. (1959), *Oedipus and Job in West African Religion*, Cambridge.

Frazer, J. G. (1980), *The Golden Bough*, New York (first published 1890–1915).

Geertz, C. (1960), *The Religion of Java*, Glencoe, Ill.

Gluckman, M. (1963), *Order and Rebellion in Tribal Africa*, London.

Goody, J. (1961), 'Religion and ritual: the definitional problem', *British Journal of Sociology*, 12.

Hertz, R. (1960 [1928]), *Death and the Right Hand*, London. (Original French edn, *Mélanges de la sociologie religieuse et folklore*, Paris.)

Hubert, J. and Mauss, M. (1964 [1899]), *Sacrifice: Its Nature and Function*, London. (Original French edn, *Essai sur la nature et la fonction du sacrifice*, Paris.)

Ileto, R. C. (1979), *Pasyon and Revolution: Popular Movements in the Philippines 1840–1910*, Manila.

Leach, E. R. (1954), *Political Systems of Highland Burma*, London.

Leach, E. R. (1966), 'Ritualisation in man in relation to conceptual and social development', in J. Huxley (ed.), *A Discussion on Ritualization of Behaviour in Animal and Man*, London.

Lévi-Strauss, C. (1970–81 [1964–72]), *An Introduction to the Science of Mythology*, 4 vols, London. (Original French edn, *Mythologiques*, Paris.)

Marx, K. and Engels, F. (1939 [1845–6]), *The German Ideology*, parts 1 and 3, New York. (Full text first published in 1932 as *Die Deutsche Ideologie*.)

Robertson-Smith, W. (1889), *Lectures on the Religion of the Semites*.

Sperber, D. (1975), *Rethinking Symbolism*, Cambridge.

Srinivas, M. N. (1952), *Religion and Society among the Coorgs of South India*, Oxford.

Tambiah, S. J. (1969), *Buddhism and the Spirit Cult*, Cambridge.

Turner, V. (1967) *The Forest of Symbols*, Ithaca, New York.

Van Gennep, A. (1960 [1909]), *The Rites of Passage*, London. (Original French edn, *Les Rites de Passage*, Paris.)

Weber, M. (1930 [1905]), *The Protestant Ethic and the Spirit of Capitalism*, London. (Original German edn, *Die protestantische Ethik und der 'Geist' des Kapitalismus*, Tubingen.)

Worsley, P. (1957), *The Trumpet Shall Sound*, London.

Further Reading

Leach, E. R. (1966), 'Virgin Birth', *Proceedings of the Royal Anthropological Institute*.

Turner, V. (1969), *The Ritual Process*, Chicago.

See also: *civil religion; ideology; rites of passage; sects and cults; secularization.*

Repertory Grid Analysis

See Personal Construct Theory.

Representation, Political

The history of political representation is that of the rise of European parliaments, through the transformation of the sovereign's councillors into a sovereign assembly.

The medieval monarch used to seek advice from persons chosen at his discretion for their competence and trust, but since he wanted them to report from all the land and then to convey his orders and tax demands back to 'their' people, he tended to pattern his selection after the actual social hierarchy, choosing those in the nobility and high clergy, whose fiefs and dioceses constituted his kingdom, and (as early as the thirteenth century in England) among important commoners.

During crises, when the king most needed their co-operation, the councillors demanded and obtained the right to be convened periodically and to be masters of their agenda; also, instead of answering individually to the king for their particular community (which was soon to be reapportioned into electoral districts), they made collective deliberations and rendered them obligatory and compelling. They were now acting as one single assembly (whose number, election, immunity and so on had to be formalized) and speaking for the people as a whole; thus the king, who had been seen as the head, and natural representative, of his people, implicitly began to speak only for himself.

Not only political legitimacy, but also power, had shifted: in the name of political representation they had in fact established their rule. For example, the slogan of the American Revolution did not mean 'no taxation without our spokesman to the king' but 'without our share of power', indeed 'without governing ourselves'. Parliament, instead of the king, was sovereign.

Whatever its constitutional formula, representative government is an awkward proposition, (1) because the more faithful the representation, the less the ability to rule, that is, to make choices or even compromises or coercions; and (2) because the demands of modern politics have both glorified government (the rise everywhere of the executive branch which executes always less and rules always more) and diminished the role of parliaments based on territorial representation. When the representational logic of the former royal councillors came to its democratic triumph with their election according to the principle 'one man, one vote', it appeared that one vote is too little to be correctly represented: every man wants to press for his multifaceted interests through specific spokesmen or organizations which will fight the suppressions, amalgamations and distortions that territorial representation implies in each electoral district and then at the legislative level, whatever the endeavours of special and minority groups to force their 'quotas' into elected or appointed bodies.

Political representation takes an ironical turn when (1) advocates of functional representation criticize parliaments for disregarding obvious demands of the people and arbitrarily imposing their idea of the common interest (much like the kings had been criticized as unrepresentative); (2) when parliamentary elections often become geared to the nomination of a government rather than of representatives; and (3) when the executive branch surrounds itself more and more formally with 'councillors' drawn from the most important interest groups in the country and whose 'advice' tends to become obligatory and compelling.

Jean Tournon
University of Grenoble

Further Reading
Birch, A. H. (1971), *Representation*, London.
Eulau, H. (1978), *The Politics of Representation*, London.
Eysenck, H. J. (1954), *The Psychology of Politics*, London.
Pennock, J. and Chapman, J. (1968), *Representation*, New York.
Pitkin, H. (1967), *The Concept of Representation*, Berkeley and Los Angeles.
See also: *democracy; interest groups and lobbying; political participation.*

Research and Development

While change in products, processes and services has always been a dimension of human experience, in recent years the pace of change itself has clearly been accelerating. One of the most important discoveries of the twentieth century is the 'invention of the art of invention' – that is, more sophisticated approaches to managing and developing new products, services or processes, specifically, research and development.

It is through research and development that ideas are discovered, developed and introduced into the market place. A large and increasing amount of money is spent on research and development by public and private sectors each year. Success in the market place for many organizations depends on managing this process well.

Despite the importance of new products or processes to the individual organization, and the high costs in many instances of development, many new ideas fail to reach the level of sales or profitability which was anticipated when they were being developed. For example, in some consumer product markets the success rate of new products can be as low as one new product in a hundred product launches.

Considerable attention has been given to the quality of research and development activity. The activities of idea generation, screening, business analysis, prototype development and testing to commercialization have all been investigated in an effort to improve the chances of success. In addition, the organization and management of research and development have been closely examined.

It is generally agreed that there is no one optimum form for organizing research and development activity. At one extreme, long-range speculative research where no immediate production process is planned appears to need a flexible or 'organic' setting, while short-term minor product modification activity requires a far more structured or 'mechanistic' setting. Moreover, the successful organization appears to be one which is capable of making a 'shift' from an organic or flexible environment in which ideas can be developed, to a mechanistic or controlled one in which these ideas can be translated into tangible products or processes.

Finally, it also appears that the customer or user of the new idea has an important role to play. Some of the most successful ideas for new products in a variety of industries in recent years have come from the customer rather than the research and development activities of the supplier.

S. T. Parkinson
Henley – The Management College

Further Reading
Parkinson, S. T. (1984), *New Product Development in the Engineering Industry*, Cambridge.

Reserve Currency

Governments hold reserves of foreign currencies to enable them to intervene in the foreign exchange markets, in order to try to influence the exchange rate of the domestic currency against foreign currencies, by buying and selling various currencies. The need for such reserves would not arise if currencies were allowed to float freely. The fixed exchange-rate system existed from 1944, following the Bretton Woods Agreement, until 1973; it was succeeded by the 'dirty' floating system in which governments frequently intervene to influence exchange rates rather than let them float freely. Both systems require governments to hold foreign exchange reserves in order to be able to influence exchange rates. Reserve currencies are currencies widely held by governments as part of their foreign exchange reserves.

Given that the Bretton Woods Agreement resulted in the major countries fixing the exchange rates of their currencies, against the US dollar, and given the significance of the US in the world economy, the US dollar became the major reserve currency throughout the world. Sterling had been a major reserve currency prior to the Second World War but its role declined significantly in the post-war period. Following the collapse of the fixed exchange-rate system in 1973, there has been a move to diversify foreign currency holdings by governments. The Deutschmark, the Swiss franc and the Japanese yen have all emerged as widely held reserve currencies.

There is some debate concerning whether this diversification of foreign currency holdings is optimal or whether some internationally created reserve asset might provide a better basis for the international monetary system, such as the Special Drawing Right or the European Currency Unit or some other specially created asset.

Andy Mullineux
University of Birmingham

Further Reading
Grubel, H. (1984), *The International Monetary System*, 4th edn, Harmondsworth.
Kenen, P. B. (1983), *The Role of the Dollar as an International Currency*, New York.
Roosa, R. V. *et al.* (1982), *Reserve Currencies in Transition*, New York.
See also: *international monetary system*.

Residential Mobility

Most social scientists investigating mobility consider it from one of two perspectives. Some are interested in it as it relates to particular geographic areas; they consider the percentage of people within an area who change residence over a given period of time; that is the *mobility rate*. Others try to quantify mobility in terms of individuals: how often people or groups move in a year, several years, or a lifetime. These data provide a *mobility history* of people and allow comparisons to be made among individuals or groups.

Information on mobility rates and mobility histories are useful, for example to urban planners, who need to anticipate changes in population distributions and housing needs. In addition, the mobility rates and histories of communities and nations can be compared. Although comparable mobility data are not available for most nations, information that is available suggests that people in the United States, Australia and Canada have very similar annual mobility rates (about 20 per cent), which are comparatively high among industrial nations, while Ireland's rate of 5 per cent is one of the lowest. Britain's and Japan's mobility rates (11.8 per cent and 12 per cent respectively) fall about midpoint between these two extremes.

Although these comparative percentages are interesting, in general mobility data are most useful when viewed within the context of other issues. For example, researchers consider why people move, and how moving (or not moving) affects their health, and also the viability of communities. Forced mobility is common, but most researchers focus on voluntary mobility. When people relocate from choice their reasons vary. Most theories of mobility are drawn from economic models and basically propose that people assess the costs and benefits of moving versus staying, and so make a decision. These costs and benefits are not merely financial, but also include such factors as satisfaction with a home (or community). Research indicates that people move for logical reasons: a change in their housing needs (for example, a growing family needs a larger home); change in their social status – upwardly mobile people often reflect their changing status by moving to better quality homes; and the desire for enhanced economic opportunities – moving to an area where there are more jobs. People also move when they are unhappy with their community or home. The reasons for moving are relevant to the movers' health and to the viability of communities. Thus, to understand mobility decisions fully, one must consider the total context of peoples' lives: their life-stage, physical and social environmental needs and their expectations regarding housing options.

A major shortcoming in existing theories and research on mobility is that they ignore the non-mobile in societies. Relocation is conceptualized as an option considered by people who are trying to improve their overall life-situation. Yet some people do not have this option available to them. For example, the poor often cannot afford to move. Members of minority groups in some societies have limited alternatives available to them. In the United States, for example, the pattern of mobility among Black and White Americans differs. Whereas Black Americans are more likely to make short moves, White Americans are more likely to move long distances. Data support the proposition that regardless of income or social status, Black Americans are severely restricted in their options for residential relocation. Similar patterns also appear to exist in Britain. These different patterns support the current view among social scientists that major relocation alternatives are limited to the advantaged within any society.

Sally Ann Shumaker
Johns Hopkins University

Further Reading

Long, L. H. and Boertlein, C. G. (1976), 'The geographical mobility of Americans: an international comparison', *Current Population Reports*, no. 64.

Michaelson, W. (1977), *Environmental Choice, Human Behavior and Residential Satisfaction*, New York.

Rossi, P. H. (1980), *Why Families Move*, 2nd edn, Beverly Hills, Calif.

Shumaker, S. A. and Stokols, D. (eds) (1982), 'Residential mobility: theory, research and policy', *Journal of Social Issues*, 38.

Speare, A., Goldstein, S. and Frey, W. H. (1975), *Residential Mobility, Migration, and Metropolitan Change*, Cambridge, Mass.

See also: *migration; urbanization.*

Returns, Laws of

Among the abstract generalizations for which economists have at some time or another claimed explanatory or predictive powers analogous to those inherent in the natural or scientific laws of the physical sciences, the laws of returns have the longest history. They describe the relationship between the rate of growth of output for an expanding industry and the rate of increase in the inputs of the required factors of production (land, labour and capital): and they provide an instructive illustration of the way so-called economic 'laws' are in practice circumscribed by the organizational and technological conditions in which they operate.

In principle there are three ways in which the output of an industry might expand as a result of the injection of additional inputs into the production process. In the case of constant returns, output increases in proportion to the increase in total inputs. In the case of increasing returns, the rate of growth of output is greater than the rate of increase in inputs. In the case of diminishing returns, the rate of growth of output will fall short of the rate of growth in inputs. In practice an expanding industry may be subject to successive phases of increasing, constant and diminishing returns. In the early stages of its growth, when all factor inputs are in elastic supply and there are economies to be gained by increasing the scale of operations, increasing returns would be the norm. Where there is an important factor of production in limited supply (for example, land in the case of agriculture), there will come a point beyond which adding equal doses of the other factors to a fixed quantity of, say, land, will yield a declining rate of return to the variable factors – unless of course there are advances in knowledge (technological progress)

compensating for the scarcity of land and possibly generating further economies of scale.

Cases of increasing returns in manufacturing were noticed by seventeenth- and eighteenth-century observers. Adam Smith, for example, explained a tendency for output to grow faster than inputs in manufacturing industry partly in terms of the scope offered for division of labour (improved organization) in factory industry, and partly in terms of what would now be classified as technological progress (advances in knowledge, improved machinery, and so on). Other eighteenth-century writers were more concerned with the evidence for diminishing returns in agriculture and its implications for an economy experiencing a rising population. Turgot, for example, pointed out that if increasing amounts of capital are applied to a given piece of land the quantity of output resulting from each additional dose of capital input will first increase and then, after a certain point, decrease towards zero.

Most English nineteenth-century classical economists readily accepted the assumption that diminishing returns prevailed in agriculture, and increasing returns in manufacturing. Few of them expected much technological progress in agriculture and were consequently pessimistic about the long-term consequences of a sustained increase in population. According to J.S. Mill, for example, 'This general law of agricultural industry is the most important proposition in political economy.' The neoclassical economists, such as Alfred Marshall, writing later in the century when it was evident that economic progress involved a high degree of industrialization, were more optimistic about the outcome of what they saw as the conflict between the two forces of diminishing returns in the primary product industries and increasing returns, reinforced by technical progress, in the manufacturing sector. Their problem, however, was that the only assumption about laws of returns which was consistent with the long-term competitive equilibrium analysis on which the neoclassical theory of value depended was the unrealistic assumption of constant returns. For as Piero Sraffa showed, in an article published in the 1926 *Economic Journal*, if increasing returns to scale prevailed, the profit-maximizing firm would be driven to expand indefinitely, thus destroying the basis for perfect competition; while the existence of diminishing returns would mean that costs and prices would be interdependent for all those industries competing for a factor in scarce supply, thus invalidating the Marshallian technique of partial equilibrium analysis.

Meanwhile, however, leading economic historians had already questioned the empirical validity of the laws of returns. In a famous article on 'empty economic boxes' published in the 1922 *Economic Journal*, Clapham had complained that, 'A great deal of harm has been done through omission to make clear that the Laws of Returns have never been attached to specific industries, that we do not, for instance, at this moment *know* under what conditions of returns coal or boots are being produced.'

Today the concept of diminishing returns is still sometimes invoked in support of Malthusian polemics by those who insist on the limits to growth, or as ready-made explanations for such events as the spectacular rise in commodity prices in the early 1970s; similarly those wishing to promote policies favouring some branch of manufacturing may justify their case by categorizing it as subject to increasing returns. However, modern economic theorists have effectively abandoned the idea that it is either useful or possible to formulate a theoretical justification for broad, generalizable laws of returns. More significant has been recent research focused on whether and when particular industries experience constant or increasing or decreasing returns to scale; these are essentially empirical issues which raise complex technical and analytical problems and yield results valid only for highly differentiated sectors of industries. In this context the laws of returns are demoted to tentative hypotheses which provide the starting point for a programme of theoretical and/or empirical research into the characteristics of a particular production function.

Phyllis Deane
University of Cambridge

Revolutions

A revolutionary crisis, or revolution, is any political crisis propelled by illegal (usually violent) actions by subordinate groups which threatens to change the political institutions or social structure of a society.

Some revolutionary crises result in great changes in politics and society, as the Russian and Chinese Revolutions; some result in great political changes but few changes in social life outside of politics, as the English Revolution; some result in hardly any change at all and are hence considered unsuccessful revolutions, as the Revolutions of 1848 in Germany.

The word 'revolution' first appeared in political writing in fourteenth-century Italy and denoted any 'overturning' of a government; such events were seen as part of a cycle in the transfer of power between competing parties, with no great changes in institutions implied. However, since the French Revolution, revolution has become associated with sudden and far-reaching change. It is this particular sense of the word that has been carried to fields other than politics, as in the Industrial Revolution, or scientific revolutions.

Revolutions have causes, participants, processes of development and outcomes. No two revolutions are exactly alike in all these respects, thus no general theory of 'revolutions' has proven satisfactory. Understanding revolutions requires theories of causes, of participants, of processes and of outcomes of revolutions that stress the variations in each element and how they combine in specific historical cases.

Many of the key issues in current studies of revolution were set out in the nineteenth century by Marx and Engels (1968). Marx viewed Europe's history since the Middle Ages as a progression through various modes of production, each one more fruitful than the last. 'Bourgeois' revolutions, exemplified by the French Revolution of 1789, were necessary to destroy the privileged feudal aristocracy and the agrarian society over which it presided. However, the resulting political freedom and material benefits would extend only to the class of professionals and businessmen who controlled the succeeding capitalist society; thus a further revolution in the name of labourers remained necessary to extend self-determination and the material benefits of modern industrial technology to all. The major elements of this view – that revolution is a necessary agent of change; that such change is progressive and beneficial; and that revolutions, in both cause and effect, are intimately related to great historical transitions – pose the articles of faith for practising revolutionaries and the chief research problems for academic analysis.

In recent years, the work of Tocqueville (1856) has assumed increasing importance. Tocqueville's analysis of the French Revolution stressed the continuity of the Old Regime and the post-Revolutionary state, and the greater centralization of state power that followed from the Revolution. Similar continuities have occurred elsewhere: The Russian Imperial bureaucracy and secret police, the Chinese Imperial bureaucracy, and the Iranian personal authoritarian state have been replaced by similar, albeit more powerful, post-revolutionary versions. Thus the extent of the historical transformation associated with revolutions appears less striking in practice than in Marxist theory.

In the last two decades, social scientists seeking the causes of revolutions first focused on changes in people's expectations and attitudes, but later moved to an emphasis on institutions and the resources of states. Gurr (1970) argued that when people's social opportunities no longer accorded with their expectations, either because expectations were rising too quickly, or welfare was falling, feelings of 'relative deprivation' would make fertile ground for popular opposition to governments. Johnson (1966) suggested that any large and sustained 'disequilibrium' between the economic, political and cultural sectors of a society – such as education increasing more rapidly than economic output, or economic organization changing more rapidly than political organization – could lead many individuals to withdraw their allegiance to the current regime. Huntington (1968) emphasized expectations in the political sphere, arguing that if popular expectations for participation in politics came to exceed a country's institutional procedures for political participation, unmet demands for political participation could lead to an explosion of popular activity directed against the current regime. However, Tilly and his collaborators (1975), in empirical studies of collective violence, found that strikes and riots did not occur most frequently during times of deprivation, such as periods of falling real wages or falls in economic output. Nor were strikes and riots especially common during times of 'disequilibrium', such as periods of rapid urbanization or industrialization. Instead workers acted to protect and defend their interests whenever the opportunity was available; those opportunities depended on shifts in the balance of power between workers and the employers and states that they faced. Tilly's 'resource mobilization' view argued that whenever conflict arose over economic or political issues, the incidence of popular protest depended chiefly on how the abilities and the range of actions open to those at odds with the current regime compared with the resources of the regime and its supporters. Recently, Skocpol (1979), emphasizing the differences between states and the importance of international competition, has led the way in developing a 'social-structural' perspective on revolutions, which views revolutions as a consequence of state weaknesses combined with institutions that provide aggrieved élites and popular groups with opportunities for effective collective action.

The origins of revolutions do not appear to reside in an exceptional level of 'deprivation' or 'disequilibrium'. Instead, revolutions occur when difficulties that are successfully coped with in other times and places – wars and state fiscal crises – occur in states with institutions particularly vulnerable to revolution. Skocpol has identified three institutional features that make for such vulnerability: (1) a state military machine considerably inferior to those of nations with which the state is normally in competition; (2) an autonomous élite able to challenge or block implementation of policies sought by the central administration; (3) a peasantry with autonomous village organization. One could also add a fourth: large concentrations of artisans and labourers in and near inadequately policed political centres. These elements, in various combinations, have played a role in the origins of the major revolutions of modern times: England 1640 (1, 2, 4); France 1789 (1, 2, 3, 4); Mexico 1910 (1, 2, 3); China 1911 (1, 2); Russia 1917 (1, 3, 4); Iran 1979 (2, 4). In recent years, peasant organization has often been supplied by a revolutionary party, rather than automonous village organization. This functional substitution has led to different, characteristically peasant-party-based, revolutions: China 1949, Vietnam 1972, Nicaragua 1979.

A military or fiscal crisis in an institutionally vulnerable state may begin a revolution; however, the process of revolution and the roles of various participants vary greatly. Certain processes appear to be, if not universal, extremely common: an initial alliance between moderates seeking reform and radicals seeking far-reaching change; involvement in international war (in part because nearby states fear the revolution spreading, in part because revolutionary leaders find the nationalist fervour generated by external wars useful); a gradual fission between moderates and radicals, with the latter triumphing; a civil war as leaders of the revolutionary parties seek to extend their control throughout the nation and eliminate opposition; the emergence of authoritarian rule by a single dominant leader. Other variables – the extent and autonomy of popular participation, the extent of civil war, the degree and permanence of radical triumph, and the duration of autocratic rule – range from high to low across revolutions, depending on the resources available to various groups, the skills of individuals, and the luck of political and military battles.

The outcomes of revolutions are equally diverse. These depend not only on the factors that caused the revolution, but also on the vagaries of the revolutionary process, the influence wielded by external countries and the problems and resources faced by the eventual victors in the revolutionary struggle. The French and English Revolutions, though differing greatly in the level of popular uprisings, resulted eventually in similar regimes: monarchies in which possession of private property was the key to political participation and social status. By contrast, the Russian and Chinese (1949) Revolutions, the former with a level of autonomous popular participation, both rural and urban, akin to that of France, the latter with a chiefly rural peasant-party revolution, both resulted eventually in socialist party-states, in which membership and rank in the state party are the keys to political participation and social status. Mexico's revolution led to a hybrid capitalist party-state, in which political participation is directed by and through the state party, but private wealth is the chief criterion of social status.

Evaluations of the material progress made under post-revolutionary regimes are also mixed. There are cases of great progress in health and literacy, such as Cuba; but the ability of post-revolutionary regimes to provide a generally higher material standard of living than similarly situated non-revolutionary regimes is yet to be demonstrated (Eckstein, 1982).

The role of ideological changes in causing revolutions and shaping their outcomes is hotly debated. Most revolutionaries have proven quite pragmatic in modifying revolutionary programmes as seemed necessary; Russia under the New Economic Plan of the 1920s, and China in the 1980s, have embarked on such pragmatic paths. At other times ideological fervour has taken precedence, as in the Jacobin years of the French Revolution, and the Great Leap Forward and Cultural

Revolution in China. Ideological programmes are thus a rather unpredictable, if far from dominant, element in shaping revolutions.

Ideology in a broader sense, as an overall cultural perspective, has been a more uniformly important factor. Eisenstadt (1978) has noted that the key to revolution lies in the coalescence, in a time of political crisis, of diverse movements – peasant uprisings, élite political revolts, religious heterodoxies – into a widespread attack on the institutions of the old regime. Thus the main role of ideologies in revolutions has been to bring together diverse grievances and interests under a simple and appealing set of symbols of opposition. For this purpose, any ideology that features a strong tension between good and evil, emphasizes the importance of combating evil in this world through active remaking of the world, and sees politics as simply one more battlefield between good and evil, may serve as the foundation for a revolutionary ideology. Thus puritanism, liberalism, communism, anti-colonialism, and, most recently, Islam, have all proved adaptable to providing symbols for revolutions. Studies of peasants' and workers' revolts have stressed that traditional ideologies – the communal ideology of 'members' against 'outsiders' of the peasant village and the craft guild – can also motivate actors in revolutionary crises. None of these ideologies of themselves brought down governments; but they were crucial in providing a basis for uniting diverse existing grievances under one banner and encouraging their active resolution.

In the past, major revolutions have occurred only in pre-industrial or early industrializing nations with small élites. If this pattern continues, the arena of major revolutions in the future will be Africa, Southern Asia and Central America. The advanced industrial democracies may see strikes and mass demonstrations, but are unlikely to witness revolutions. An enigma for which there is little historical precedent appears in the developed South American nations and the Eastern European socialist states, with developed industrial economies and small highly dominant élites. These countries have faced incipient revolutionary crises (Hungary 1956, Czechoslovakia 1968, Poland 1980) and frequent *coups d'état* (Brazil 1964, Argentina 1966), but so far they have lacked the autonomous élite groups or popular organizations that made for revolutionary vulnerability in successful revolutions of the past. This is in large part because neighbouring superpowers, by backing specific élites in these countries, have actively shaped political struggles and their outcomes. Whether these nations' future development, and future superpower actions, will render them more similar to vulnerable states will be a crucial factor in the future incidence of revolutions.

Jack A. Goldstone
Northwestern University

References
Eckstein, S. (1982), 'The impact of revolution on social welfare in Latin America', *Theory and Society*, 11.
Eisenstadt, S. N. (1978), *Revolution and the Transformation of Societies*, New York.
Gurr, T. R. (1970), *Why Men Rebel*, Princeton, New Jersey.
Huntington, S. (1968), *Political Order in Changing Societies*, New Haven, Conn.
Johnson, C. (1966), *Revolutionary Change*, Boston.
Marx, K. and Engels, F. (1968 [1848]), *The Communist Manifesto*, London. (Original German edn, *Manifest der Kommunistischen Partei*, London.)
Skocpol, T. (1979), *States and Social Revolutions*, Cambridge.
Tilly, C., Tilly, L. and Tilly, R. (1975), *The Rebellious Century 1830–1930*, Cambridge, Mass.
Tocqueville, A. (1856), *The Old Regime and the French Revolution*, New York.

Further Reading
Goldstone, J. A. (1982), 'The comparative and historical study of revolutions', *Annual Review of Sociology*, 8.
Moore, B., Jr (1966), *Social Origins of Dictatorship and Democracy*, Boston.
Wolf, E. R. (1969), *Peasant Wars of the Twentieth Century*, New York.
See also: *Marx's theory of history and society; radicalism; relative deprivation; Tocqueville.*

Ricardo, David (1772–1823)

David Ricardo, political economist and politician, was born in London on 18 April 1772, the third son of a Dutch Jew who had moved to England around 1760 and worked on the London Stock Exchange. Ricardo's education reflected his father's wish that he join him in business, which he did at the age of 14; he is reported by his brother not to have had a 'classical education', but one 'usually allotted to those who are destined for a mercantile way of life'. At the age of 21, following a period of waning attachment to Judaism, he married a Quaker, became a Unitarian and was estranged from his father. Thrown back on his own resources, he pursued a brilliant career as a Jobber, within a few years amassing considerable wealth. At this time, his leisure hours were spent studying mathematics, chemistry, geology and minerology.

In 1799, Ricardo happened to peruse Adam Smith's *Wealth of Nations*. The subject matter interested him, although it was ten years before he published anything himself on it. His first article appeared anonymously in the *Morning Chronicle*, addressed to the 'Bullion Controversy'. Briefly, he argued that the low value of the pound on the foreign exchanges and the premium quoted on bullion over paper resulted from an over-issue of paper currency. His views were elaborated in published letters and pamphlets.

The 'Bullion Controversy' brought Ricardo into contact with, among others, James Mill, Jeremy Bentham and Thomas Malthus. Mill remained a close friend, encouraging the reticent Ricardo to publish, giving advice on style, and eventually persuading him to enter Parliament, which he did in 1819 as the independent member for the pocket borough of Portarlington in Ireland; with Bentham, Mill was also responsible for tutoring Ricardo in Utilitarianism. As for Malthus, he too became an enduring friend, although his intellectual role was mainly adversarial: something which provided Ricardo with a mental stimulus which, in the sphere of political economy, his more admiring friends were largely incapable of supplying.

In 1814, Ricardo began a gradual retirement from business, taking up residence in Gatcombe Park, Gloucestershire. One year later he published *An Essay on the Influence of a Low Price of Corn on the Profits of Stock*, one of many pamphlets spawned during the 'Corn Law Controversy'. Borrowing Malthus's theory of rent – that rent is an intra-'marginal' surplus and not a component of price, itself determined at the agricultural 'margin' – Ricardo inveighed against protection, claiming it would result in a rise of money wages, a reduced rate of profit, and a consequent slackening in the pace of capital accumulation. This was predicated on a theory of profitability at variance with Adam Smith's 'competition of capitals' thesis; taking the social propensity to save as given, Ricardo argued that 'permanent' movements in general profitability would uniquely result from changes in the (real) prices of wage-goods.

These views were developed in *On the Principles of Political Economy and Taxation* (first edition, 1817). In particular, Ricardo wanted to disseminate a single proposition, that the only serious threat to the unconstrained expansion of free-market capitalism came from the less productive cultivation of domestic land.

To illustrate this proposition Ricardo had developed a 'pure' labour theory of value, with 'permanent' changes in exchange relationships between competitively produced, freely reproducible commodities, the sole consequence of altered direct or indirect labour inputs (always assuming uniform profitability). He had also discovered limitations, eventually reduced to one of differences in the time structures of labour inputs. Pressed by Malthus to justify his use of the theory in the face of problems which he had himself unearthed, Ricardo departed on his celebrated quest for an 'invariable measure of value' which, if 'perfect', would magically obviate all variations in exchange relationships not the result of 'labour-embodied' changes, and this *without* assuming identical time-labour profiles.

This futile search found expression in a new chapter 'On Value' in the third edition of the *Principles* (1821). Ironically, the impossibility of finding a 'perfect' measure of value was only recognized in a paper Ricardo was finalizing immediately before his sudden death on 11 September 1823.

Adumbration of a theory of comparative advantage in international trade (*Principles*, all editions) and of the possibility of net labour displacing accumulation (*Principles*, third edition) constitute further distinctive Ricardian contributions. Generally, he was a vigorous and fairly uncompromising advocate of *laissez-faire* capitalism: relief works schemes would be abolished, since they involved taking capital from those who knew best how to allocate it; taxation should be minimal, with the National Debt speedily paid off; the Poor Laws should be scrapped, because they distorted the labour market; and monopolies were *necessarily* mismanaged.

These views were promulgated from the floor of the House of Commons, where Ricardo also campaigned against religious discrimination and in favour of a meritocratic society. His guiding legislative principle was that it be for the public benefit and not in the interest of any particular class, with the 'public benefit' rigidly identified with the outcome of a private property, *laissez-faire* system. To this end, he favoured a gradual extension of the electoral franchise, immediately in order to weaken the legislative power of the landed aristocracy.

In his lifetime, Ricardo's political economy reigned supreme. But after his death, perhaps owing to the inability of followers such as James Mill and J.R. McCulloch to work to the same high level of abstraction, 'Ricardian' economics was rendered platitudinous and diluted to little more than free-trade sloganizing. At the same time, Ricardo's labour theory of value was used by 'Ricardian Socialists' (such as Piercy Ravenstone and Thomas Hodgskin) to justify labour's claim to the whole product – a view Ricardo would have abhorred. Later, his writings exerted a powerful influence on Karl Marx which, if only by association, had the effect of placing Ricardo outside the mainstream of economic thought: a view which Alfred Marshall (and, more recently, Samuel Hollander) attempted to rebut. Following publication of Piero Sraffa's *Production of Commodities by Means of Commodities* (1960) Ricardo again achieved prominence as primogenitor of a 'Neo-Ricardian' school of thought, this identification resting on Sraffa's interpretation of Ricardo in his Introduction to *The Works and Correspondence of David Ricardo*. Sraffa's interpretation has increasingly been challenged, and a consensus has not yet been reached. It is, however, a tribute to Ricardo's complex genius that he should still evoke controversy.

Terry Peach
University of Manchester

Further Reading

Blaug, M. (1958), *Ricardian Economics: A Historical Study*, New Haven, Conn.

Hollander, J. H. (1910), *David Ricardo: A Centenary Estimate*, Baltimore.

Hollander, S. (1979), *The Economics of David Ricardo*, Toronto.

Ricardo, D. (1951–73), *The Works and Correspondence of David Ricardo*, edited by P. Sraffa with the collaboration of M. H. Dobb, Cambridge.

See also: *Sraffa*.

Riesman, David (1909–)

David Riesman was born in Philadelphia in 1909 and was educated at Harvard University. Despite his stature as a sociologist, he was trained as a lawyer and clerked for Justice Brandeis of the US Supreme Court. His first academic position was as professor of law at the University of Buffalo from 1937 to 1941. However, between 1949 and 1958 Riesman was professor of social sciences at the University of Chicago. In 1958 he accepted the position of Henry Ford II professor of social sciences at Harvard University and has held that post ever since.

Riesman's scholarly contributions are in two related areas. The first of these is his American national character studies, the second is his writings on education. Riesman's first investigation of national character was published in his best-known book, *The Lonely Crowd: A Study of the Changing American Character* (written in collaboration with R. Denney and N. Glazer, 1950), and was then elaborated and amended in his *Faces in the Crowd: Individual Studies in Character and Politics* (in collaboration with N. Glazer, 1952), and *Individualism Reconsidered* (1954). Riesman's conception of the changing American Character from tradition, to inner- and to other-directedness associated with industrialization and growing population density is now widely and popularly recognized. Also, Riesman, with C. Jencks, early on drew attention to *The Academic Revolution* (1968) in America. In this volume he suggested that education, especially higher education, was becoming the central influential institution in American life, affecting character and life-styles and distributing persons to social classes.

Riesman's education studies encompass much more than the effects of schooling on character. He contributed important statements upon the varieties and limits of education, experimental colleges, student activism, educational politics, politics and education, educational reform, minority education, educational values and so on. His studies of character, culture and society also include the delightful *Conversations in Japan:*
Modernization, Politics and Culture (1967), written with his wife, Evelyn Thompson Riesman.

The importance and recognition of Riesman's contribution to the social sciences and to education is signified by the great number of honours and awards he has received and by the exceedingly large number of national advisory and planning councils and committees he has served upon. However, less well known of Riesman is his importance as a teacher. At Harvard his course on American society was one of the most sought-after and well-attended undergraduate courses in the college curriculum. While Riesman concentrated on teaching undergraduates he also worked closely with Harvard graduate students in American studies, sociology, literature, philosophy, government and education. His influence upon his former graduate students is now evident in their faculty teaching styles and in their scholarship.

Gerald M. Platt
University of Massachusetts, Amherst

Risk Analysis

Risk analysis originally meant the estimation of the relative likelihood and magnitude of alternatives where the outcome of a course of action is uncertain. It is now expanded to include the study of different perceptions of risk and the management techniques for determining their social acceptability. The estimation of the *probability* of alternative consequences of an event is now better conveyed by the term 'risk assessment'.

Risk assessment is the technical stage in the process of risk decision making. It is the application, usually by engineers or financial experts, of a range of formal techniques, such as Bayesian analysis, to estimate the probabilities that different courses of action will result in gain or loss. The risk assessor may also seek to calculate the probability of different magnitudes of loss or gain associated with any alternative outcome. Complex techniques, such as fault-tree analysis, may combine several of these methods to cover sequential probabilities, such as each stage in the alternative chains of events that could lead to a nuclear accident.

In addition to determining the most likely outcomes, assessors may devise worst case scenarios to assist risk managers in determining the acceptability of a risk. These are especially important where probability values are unobtainable, or known to be unreliable. Formal risk assessments are commonly expressed in terms of deaths per unit measure of activity or loss of life-expectancy.

There are two established views of the validity of such procedures: (1) The frequentist position is that straightforward data about numbers of objects and observed repeatable events unequivocably count as objective, while less clearly defined information that can influence belief about an outcome counts as subjective. This position is often favoured by engineers and technocrats. (2) The alternative position is that all probability judgements cannot be other than subjective. A probability estimate is always somebody's probability. One's degree of belief in an outcome is based on evaluation of the information available. Few, if any, events are truly repeatable; the same horse-race cannot be run twice. Even when it is contested at the level of determining numerical probabilities, the subjectivist position is particularly strong when it comes to evaluating any given probability value as high or low, and in determining and ranking utilities and costs in risk management.

Risk management involves the use of decision theory to choose between assessed probabilities and outcomes. The standard decision rule, Bayes' rule, tells us to choose the alternative that maximizes expected utility. Established techniques include the use of payoff tables and game theory for choosing between alternative courses of action involving straightforward choices between risks, decision trees for sequential choices, and cost/benefit analysis for establishing the social acceptability of costs. Where the decision maker is unable to assign reliable probabilities to the relevant possible outcomes of each alternative, the minimax criterion is often employed. This requires the risk manager to select the alternative with the best/worst possible outcome. In every case, establishing the acceptability of a risk requires the subjective ranking of perceptions of various probabilities, costs and utilities. The process of obtaining consent from relevant constituencies, monitoring sources of risk, and distributing liabilities and also aspects of risk management.

Risk perception is the field of risk analysis concerned with the psychological and sociological factors affecting the selection of some risks for concern and the unselfconscious minimizing of others. The psychometric paradigm examines individuals' abilities to make accurate estimates of probability, and the disparities between their stated attitudes to different probabilities and actual behaviour under laboratory conditions. The sociometric paradigm views perceptions of risks and their acceptability as part of a culturally determined moral order. For example, opinion polls show that industrialists perceive environmental damage as less threatening to society than do either the public or environmentalists, because such things as the discharge of effluent do not threaten their world view of wealth creation.

The sociometric paradigm does not attribute the selection of concerns simply to cynical self-interest, but to the operation of socially conditioned perceptual filters that admit concerns relevant to the perceivers' day-to-day experience, while blocking those that would make daily life intolerable. Thus, the sociometric approach seeks to identify portfolios of risk carried by various populations according to their internal social structure and their place in society as a whole.

Steve Rayner
Oak Ridge National Laboratory, Tennessee

Rites of Passage

'The life of an individual in any society is a series of passages from one age to another and from one occupation to another' (Van Gennep, 1960 [1909]). Since the publication in 1909 of Arnold Van Gennep's *Les Rites de passage*, this term has been used primarily to refer to life crisis rituals, such as those accompanying birth and death, puberty, marriage, initiation into adulthood or entry to priestly or political and other secular offices. Also included are those individual or collective rites which mark changes in the season or calendar. The common element in such rites, Van Gennep argued, is that they effect a transition from one social condition to another and, as a consequence, display a definite three-phase structure, with *rites of separation*, *transition* and *aggregation*. This pattern, though discernible to some extent in all, tends to be most fully realized in initiation rites where it may be given added force in the symbolism of death and rebirth. The *rites of separation* thus enact a symbolic 'death' which removes the individual from society and his old social status before he is transformed in the subsequent rites of *transition* and, finally, 'reborn' into a new social position and back into the community in the culminating *rites of aggregation*.

For Van Gennep the theme of passage provided the clue to the diverse symbolic devices employed in such rites. For example, the ritual movements may be represented in spatial terms, by exits and entrances, crossings and journeys, and in the general significance attached to crossroads, boundaries and thresholds. Of much current interest is Van Gennep's identification of the mid or transitional period as one of marginality or liminality (from the Latin, *limen*, meaning threshold). It represents, he writes, the point of inertia for the novices between contrary ritual movements; they are regarded as outside society, untouchable and dangerous, sacred as opposed to profane. Sharing with Van Gennep a similar concern with social classification and the cultural imposition of order on natural and social affairs, structuralist anthropologists such as Mary Douglas and Edmund Leach have argued that ideas of danger attach to any situation or object which transgresses or cannot be placed within the dominant system of social classification. Novices, betwixt-and-between defined social positions, are inherently anomalous and thus likely to be regarded as both polluted and polluting. Outside and opposed to normal social life, liminality is also given ritual expression in licence, disorder and role reversal.

From a functionalist perspective, Max Gluckman (1963) sees such inversional elements as motivated by underlying conflicts in the structure of social relations. Proposing the idea of 'rituals of rebellion', he argues that they give a voice to those usually held inferior and oppressed. For example, Zulu women, never full citizens in the villages of their husbands, dressed up as men in a first sowing rite and were given licence to behave obscenely and ape the ways of their menfolk. This interpretation has been influential but meets with difficulties in dealing with ritual situations where superiors assume the style and behaviour of inferiors. Victor Turner, taking a new approach and exploring the experiential implications of liminality, sees the key process in initiations as one of ritual 'levelling', with the person stripped of social insignia and signs of secular status, reduced to nakedness and subject to humiliation by ordeal, test and trauma. Socially invisible, dead to the normal world, the initiate is at the same time united with fellow initiates. This humbling process, he suggests, contains a revitalizing element, 'giving recognition to an essential and generic human bond, without which there could be *no* society' (Turner, 1969). In this context he asks us to consider two modalities of social experience, of 'structure' where people are differentiated by social role and position and linked in an often hierarchical political system, as opposed to what he calls 'communitas', as it presents itself in an undifferentiated community of equals who may recognize each other in an immediate and total way. 'Communitas emerges where social structure is not,' says Turner, reaffirming the bonds of essential unity upon which the social order ultimately rests. While he feels that communitas finds its most characteristic expression in the liminal period of *rites de passage* where the individual is divested of normal social attributes, he argues that it may be engendered also in role reversals in seasonal rites and be an attribute more generally of structural marginality and inferiority, exemplified by such figures as sacred clowns and holy beggars.

In contrast to psychoanalytic accounts, anthropological theory has made relatively little of the dramatic ordeals and mutilations which are commonly found in association with initiations. For example, circumcision for Van Gennep is best explained as a separation rite, while for Turner it is an aspect of ritual levelling. Such symbolism is seen as essentially arbitrary – Van Gennep (1960) writes, 'The human body has been treated like a simple piece of wood which each has cut and trimmed to suit him.' Psychoanalytic accounts of initiation, of course, take the opposed view that genital mutilation is central to the development and purpose of such rites. Neo-Freudian explanations diverge, with some regarding circumcision as a symbolic castration, while Bettelheim (1954) has suggested that it is best regarded as a mimetic menstruation, representing male envy of female reproductive powers. Seen as a response to universal problems, such explanations fail to account for the cross-cultural variability in incidence and type of such ordeals. However, a more psychologically informed anthropology seems to be developing, aiming to explore the subjective experience of initiation as this is encoded in different cultural idioms. It is perhaps no accident that interesting work here is coming from New Guinea societies with their plethora of explicit sexual symbolism (see Herdt, 1982).

To conclude, two broad approaches to the study of *rites de passage* can be distinguished. The first looks to social classification and, with Van Gennep, gives primacy to the idea of transition. This gives a unity to the category but, in so far as it portrays rituals as static dramas of form, tends to underplay the creative intent of such rites in pre-industrial society and the culturally specific ways in which this is conceived and realized. As Turner reminds us, many *rites de passage* intend an active transformation of the person. The second approach looks to the subjective effects of ritual and the concepts of personhood mediated by the ritual process. To some extent this harks back to earlier functionalist concerns with the efficacy of ritual (prefigured, for example, in Richards, 1982 [1956]), but it promises to be a far more eclectic venture, drawing freely upon other disciplines.

Suzette Heald
University of Lancaster

References
Bettelheim, B. (1954), *Symbolic Wounds*, Glencoe, Ill.
Douglas, M. (1966), *Purity and Danger: An Analysis of Concepts of Pollution and Taboo*, London.
Gluckman, M. (1963), *Order and Rebellion in Tribal Africa*, London.
Herdt, G. H. (1982), *Rituals of Manhood: Male Initiation in Papua New Guinea*, Berkeley and Los Angeles.
Leach, E. (1976), *Culture and Communication; The Logic By Which Symbols Are Connected*, Cambridge.
Richards, A. I. (1982 [1956]), *Chisungu: A Girl's Initiation among the Bemba of Northern Rhodesia*, London.
Turner, V. W. (1969), *The Ritual Process*, London.
Van Gennep, A. (1960), *The Rites of Passage*, London. (Original French edn, *Les Rites de passage*, Paris, 1909.)

Further Reading
Gluckman, M. (ed.) (1962), *Essays on the Ritual of Social Relations*, Manchester.
Turner, V. W. (1967), *The Forest of Symbols*, Ithaca.
See also: *death; life cycle; religion and ritual; Van Gennep.*

Rivers, William Halse (1864–1922)

Even in the less specialized scientific world of his day, Rivers was remarkable for the range of his professional interest. A doctor who had done research in physiology, he joined the famous Cambridge expedition to the Torres Straits in 1898 and carried out a study of vision, concluding that perception of space and colour is culturally conditioned. The expedition stimulated his interest in ethnology, and he engaged in further ethnographic research among the Todas of southwestern India in 1901–2, and in Melanesia in 1907. Yet Rivers also continued to do research in physiology and psychology, and in 1903 he conducted an influential series of experiments on sensory perception with Henry Head. During this period he taught both psychology and anthropology at Cambridge.

In the First World War, Rivers was a psychiatrist in a hospital for shell-shocked officers, yet characteristically he found time for research, and published books on instinct and on dreams.

Although Rivers wrote a dozen books dealing with a variety of issues in at least three different disciplines, he is remembered mainly for his contributions to kinship studies and for the identification of cultural influences on perception. A late interest in diffusionism cost him some influence and posthumous reputation among anthropologists, and his functionalist successors tended to underrate his contribution. His main theoretical work, *Kinship and Social Organisation* (1914), retains only an historical interest today, and his ethnographies are not among the classics of their kind; yet he is properly regarded as the leading British anthropologist of his generation, the first generation of professional fieldworkers.

Adam Kuper
Brunel University, Uxbridge

Further Reading
Slobodin, R. (1978), *W. H. R. Rivers*, New York.

Robbins, Lionel (1898–1984)

Lionel Robbins, born in 1898 (on a farm that has since disappeared beneath the approaches to Heathrow Airport) had his university education interrupted at an early stage by the First World War and did not return to it again until 1920. Then, after a couple of years working with the Labour Party (he was secretary to Arthur Greenwood when the latter was organizing the Labour Campaign for Nationalization of the Drink Trade), he entered the London School of Economics to be taught by (*inter alia*) Hugh Dalton, Edwin Cannan, Harold Laski and Graham Wallas. After graduating he worked as a research assistant to William Beveridge (updating *Unemployment: A Problem of Industry*) and in 1925 was offered a lectureship at the London School of Economics. There he remained (apart from two short spells at New College Oxford in 1924 and 1925, and his service in the Economic Section of the Offices of the War Cabinet from 1939–1946), first as lecturer, then as professor (to which he was appointed at the age of 30) and eventually, some years after he had formally retired from his chair, as chairman of the Court of Governors from 1968 to 1974.

Robbins was a dedicated and appreciated teacher, a distinguished scholar and economist and a prolific writer of elegant, lucid, analytical prose. His first book, published in 1932, made him famous among economists. This slim volume, entitled *An Essay on the Nature and Significance of Economic Science*, was a reasoned statement of the scope and scientific method of economic theory, written at a time when orthodox neoclassical doctrine was on the defensive for its apparent irrelevance to the policy problems of persistent depression. He restored the tarnished scientific credentials of mainstream theory by defining economic science as the systematic study of human behaviour in the face of manifold ends and scarce means and by drawing a firm line between the positive and the normative aspects of the discipline. The book unleashed wide debate (often based on misinterpretation of his arguments), but Robbins's vision of scientific economics as being essentially a study of individual rational choice in situations of scarcity became the orthodox textbook justification for a value-free economics; and his insistence on the subjective nature of interpersonal comparisons helped to stimulate the new research programme then developing in welfare theory.

Despite the abstract nature of his bestselling book Robbins was no ivory tower economist and most of his publications were focused on problems of applying economic theory to real-world policy problems. As he later wrote in his *Autobiography of an Economist* (1971), his claim that pure economic theory was neutral as between ends 'did not mean that economists should not have ideas of their own about ethics and policy: on the contrary I definitely stated that it is only if one knows how the machine runs or can run that one is entitled to say how it ought to run.' The young LSE professor also attracted attention in the 1930s by resisting the policy prescriptions being advocated by Keynes, then the most prestigious British economist. Later he was to concede that he had been wrong in opposing the use of Keynesian expansionist measures to counter recession, but he remained unconvinced by Keynes's arguments in favour of protectionism.

Robbins's other major book of lasting importance was *Robert Torrens and the Evolution of Classical Economics* (1958), in which he traced the development of nineteenth-century classical ideas through the eyes of an observer of the theoretical debates. In 1958 Robbins's immense personal prestige was recognized by elevation to a life peerage. It was after he had retired from his professorship that he was invited to chair a government Committee of Enquiry on the present state and future prospects of higher education in Britain. The resulting Robbins Report, supported by five statistical appendices and seven volumes of evidence, was largely accepted by the government of the day and launched an unprecedented era of growth in opportunities for higher education in Britain which lasted for over a decade. Before Robbins died, in 1984, however, he had witnessed the so-called 'Robbins principle' of providing higher educational opportunities for all who could benefit from them repudiated by a Conservative Government dedicated to ruthless cutting of public expenditures.

Phyllis Deane
University of Cambridge

Further Reading
Peston, M. (1981), 'Lionel Robbins: methodology, policy and modern economic theory', in J. R. Shackleton and G. Locksley (eds), *Twelve Contemporary Economists*, London.

Robinson, Joan (1903–83)

Joan Robinson's forebears were upper-middle-class English dissenters – her great-grandfather was F. D. Maurice, the Christian Socialist – and she carried on the family tradition with distinction. Her incisive mind made her a powerful critic; her insights and intuitions, whereby she provided logical arguments of great penetration (without the help of modern mathematical techniques), allowed her to make significant contributions across the whole spectrum of economic theory. In addition, she made a special study of the socialist countries, especially of China, which she visited frequently.

Her achievements include her contribution to the imperfect (monopolistic) competition 'revolution' of the 1930s (Robinson, 1969); the very considerable part she played in helping Keynes make his revolutionary jump from *The Treatise* to *The General Theory*, both in discussion and comments and with expository, often original, articles; and her part in bringing Marx's insights back on the agenda of modern economists. Her most distinctive personal contribution has been her own special blend of classical and Marxian-cum-Keynesian and Kaleckian theory with which she pioneered (along with Harrod, Kahn, Kaldor and Pasinetti) a generalization of *The General Theory* to the long period. Her *magnum opus* was *The Accumulation of Capital* (1956). Parallel with these developments was her sustained critique of the methods and results of orthodox neoclassical theory, ostensibly set within the bounds of capital theory but in fact an influential attack

on the whole compass of mainstream value and distribution theory.

Her views on method changed as she pondered on how best to capture the passing of time in models of economic processes. Initially she used the orthodox static method, regarding it and theory generally as a box of tools. She came later to regard this as a 'shameless fudge' and moved to a 'horses for courses' method, in part due to the influence of Keynes and Kalecki. (Joan Robinson always admired Kalecki's contributions and championed his, to some extent unrecognized, achievements.)

A stream of challenging evaluative essays, collected together in six volumes (Robinson, 1951–80), have inspired the young as much as they have irritated their orthodox elders. Never one to mince words, possessor of a civilized wit, sometimes bleakly rude, not always fair but always honest, Joan Robinson more than any other economist of this century became a model for progressive radicals, fearlessly following arguments to conclusions no matter how unpalatable they prove to be.

G. C. Harcourt
Jesus College, Cambridge

References
Robinson, J. (1969 [1933]), *The Economics of Imperfect Competition*, 2nd edn, London.
Robinson, J. (1969 [1956]), *The Accumulation of Capital*, 2nd edn, London.
Robinson, J. (1951–80), *Collected Economic Papers*, 6 vols, Oxford.

Further Reading
Eatwell, J. (1977), 'Portrait: Joan Robinson', *Challenge*, 20.
Gram, H. and Walsh, V. (1983), 'Joan Robinson's economics in retrospect', *Journal of Economic Literature*, XXI.
Harcourt, G. C. (1982), 'Joan Robinson', in P. Kerr (ed.), *The Social Science Imperialists: Selected Essays G. C. Harcourt*, London.
See also: *Cambridge School of Economics; Kalecki.*

Rogers, Carl R. (1902–)

Founder of client-centred or non-directive psychotherapy, Carl Rogers is considered part of the 'third force' in psychotherapy, a force which is characterized in opposition to psychoanalytic approaches on the one hand and behaviourist approaches on the other. Rogers himself thinks of his therapy as a 'person-centred approach' to human relationships, which can be extended to education, marriage and family relationships, intensive groups and even international relations.

Like other members of the third force, Rogers's basic premise is that every human being has an 'actualizing tendency' towards complete growth that can be mobilized in the correct therapeutic setting. Rogers's theory and therapy emphasize the actual here and now relationship between therapist and patient or client rather than the transference. The therapist is encouraged: (1) to be genuine (congruence between his or her feelings and their expression to the client); (2) to show unconditional positive regard for the client; and (3) to demonstrate empathic understanding of the client. The goal is 'to free the client to become an independent, self-directing person'. This method is in contrast to a behaviourist approach, where the therapist selects particular reinforcement techniques to modify particular behaviours.

Beginning his studies at the Union Theological Seminary in New York City, Rogers soon crossed the street to Columbia University's Teachers College (Ph.D. 1931). His early work with children, as Director of the Society for the Prevention of Cruelty to Children in Rochester, New York, led to his 1939 book, *Clinical Treatment of the Problem Child*. Challenging the medical model of psychiatric diagnosis and psychoanalysis, he chronicled the development of his client-centred approach through several books, beginning with *Counselling and Psychotherapy* in 1942. As professor of clinical psychology at the University of Chicago, he published *Client-Centered Therapy* (1951), a statement of his technique which included applications in education – as student-centred teaching – as well as group therapy, and play therapy for children.

On Becoming a Person (1961) brought together Rogers's writings from the 1950s, in which he emphasized that the therapist must be personally present to infuse the therapeutic relationship with an 'I-Thou' quality, a theme taken from the works of the philosopher Martin Buber. Carl Rogers's treatment method has had a profound effect on the practice of psychotherapy, particularly among nonpsychiatrists in their counselling of 'clients' without serious mental illness. Although Rogers himself spent several years attempting to treat patients with serious mental illness, this work was less successful. In the early 1970s, Rogers examined the encounter group movement and the changing institution of marriage. His 1980 collection, *A Way of Being*, highlights autobiographical material about his half-century as a 'practising psychologist'.

Louisa B. Tarullo
Harvard University

Further Reading
Rogers, C. R. (1967), 'C. R. Rogers', in E. Boring and G. Lindzey (eds), *A History of Psychology in Autobiography*, vol. 5, New York.
See also: *group therapy*.

Role

A role is the expected behaviour associated with a social position. A man from Outer Mongolia visiting the courts of justice in Britain and observing a series of criminal trials would not understand what he saw until he appreciated that people in court proceedings have to play particular roles: judge, prosecutor, defence advocate, accused, witness, juror, usher, spectator and so on. The interpretation of behaviour in a courtroom provides a good example of the utility, indeed the necessity, of a concept of role. Its positive features will be discussed first before considering whether the selection of some other example might not cast doubt upon the value of the concept.

Were he able to overhear conversations in various parts of the court building, the visitor would be able to discover: (1) the number and names of the positions that have to be occupied if the proceedings are to be lawful; (2) the names of the individuals occupying these positions on particular occasions; (3) how well particular individuals were thought to perform their roles. Over a long period of time the visitor could watch particular barristers pleading before various judges and taking different kinds of cases; some would advance their careers more rapidly than others. Watching a lawyer after he had become a judge, the observer might conclude that he had taken certain of the other judges as models of what to emulate and what to avoid. In such ways the observer could (4) ascertain the processes by which individuals learn to play roles according to the satisfaction or dissatisfaction of others. He would also learn (5) about the processes by which individuals come to occupy the various positions.

To start with, the observer might be surprised to notice that the barrister who had spoken for the prosecution in a case that had just been completed was appearing for the defence in the next case. He would learn (6) that it is the role of the barrister to speak for whichever client he is engaged (by a solicitor) to represent; his personal opinions of his clients' moral merits are irrelevant, while the uniform he wears (wig, gown and standardized costume) reinforce the message that his personality is subordinated to his role. Observation would also show that (7) barristers are punished for infringing the rules (one who asks leading or irrelevant questions will be rebuked by the judge) and rewarded for doing well (by being asked to take more cases, and cases bringing higher fees). Every now and again an unusual event would reveal some other kind of rule showing that (8) two roles may not be held by the same person if there is any suspicion that their obligations may conflict. A judge may not preside over a case in which he has a personal interest. A barrister may be unable to represent both of two men jointly charged with an offence, since the two may dispute with each other as to their relative culpability. Judges and barristers would be criticized were they, in their leisure time, to associate with known criminals.

The roles of judge and barrister are assumed willingly, that of the accused is usually not. Sometimes accused persons deny the authority of the court to try them, but they are still tried. However reluctant a man may be to feature as an accused, once he has been arraigned it is usually in his interest to play the expected role in the hope that he may be able to utilize it in a manner that will enable him either to escape conviction or secure a lighter sentence. Thus it may be possible to obtain a better understanding of the way such a person behaves if it is assumed that he comprehends what is expected of him and is seeking to turn those expectations to his advantage.

Court proceedings illustrate the utility of the role concept for the additional reason that they can be given a historical dimension that reveals the steady differentiation and sharper definition of the roles involved. In many societies at one stage of their history, cases were settled by *kadi*-justice (to use an expression of Arabic origin employed by Max Weber). In *kadi*-justice a politically powerful person makes an informal decision according to ethical or practical values, rather than by reference to previous decisions or to statute law. In such circumstances political and judicial roles are not distinguished. Even in the mid-seventeenth century, English criminal trials were, by modern standards, very brief: the Surrey assizes tried on average per day fourteen defendants charged with serious offences. Nowadays the proceedings are more complex. The evidence of each witness can be examined at length; there is time to evaluate the evidence in terms of the roles the witnesses were playing; while everyone in court will be conscious that the judge, the lawyers and the witnesses are taking part in a drama and interpreting their roles in a way that can be compared with actors on a stage. A higher material standard of living permits people to be more self-conscious about their behaviour.

There is, for example, a book entitled *Games People Play* (1964) by Eric Berne which describes and assigns names to the various characteristic disputes arising in families. One of them is 'Uproar', occurring most frequently between a domineering father and an adolescent daughter bidding for greater freedom. It has sexual undertones. It derives its name from the fact that the dispute is often terminated by one or both parties shouting angrily, retiring to a bedroom and slamming the door. It is possible to see Uproar as a game in which two people play distinctive roles (even though these roles are not defined by rights and obli-

gations, which has been the traditional way of conceptualizing role in anthropology and much of sociology). If, however, the players have read an analysis of the 'game', they are much more likely to recognize what is happening if they themselves are drawn into a dispute of this kind. They will have an insight into the dynamics of the relationship and the way in which they are contributing to it. Not only may they find themselves playing a role but they will be conscious of themselves as doing so, and in some circumstances they may even distance themselves from their role by signalling that their behaviour is not completely serious. This awareness is facilitated by the use of the word 'role' in ordinary language and by the availability of books analysing behaviour in role terms, a feature of European and North American culture in the second half of the twentieth century.

'Father' and 'adolescent daughter' can both be considered social positions, but the behaviour expected of people occupying these positions is much less well defined than in the case of the judge and the barrister. Until relatively recently in Britain (and in many parts of Europe), adolescent daughters were constrained much more narrowly than their brothers. When they reached marriageable age, middle-class young women put their hair 'up' to indicate their change of status. The dressing of their hair was a role sign; the alteration in it was a minor ceremonial of role-changing (as a wedding is a major ceremonial of it). An unmarried woman was not supposed to meet a man unless a chaperone was present. These role expectations have since changed, along with other changes in the social structure, but the speed and extent of their change in particular households will have been an outcome of a conflict between fathers and daughters, each seeking to impose their own definitions of expected behaviour. Indeed, changing expectations with respect to gender roles have been an occasion for intense discussion in recent years. What the sociologist or social psychologist can do is to ascertain the expectations of a role such as 'adolescent daughter' held by people in other, related, positions. An examination of these expectations and their determinants could contribute to an analysis of the more general problem and indicate ways in which it could most easily be resolved. This could be particularly relevant to the domestic problems of immigrant Muslim groups in European cities. In the father-daughter relationship within these groups, the conflicts between two value systems are brought to a head.

The two senses of the word 'expect' in English conceal a particular difficulty. Someone may expect a doctor to be male and a nurse to be female simply, because most people in these two positions are of those genders. This is a purely *statistical* expectation. Someone else may expect a doctor to be male and a nurse female because of a belief that this is right and proper (just as the office of priest in the Catholic

Church is limited to males). This is a *normative* expectation. The two kinds of expectation go together in the sense that someone growing up in a society in which all doctors are male may come to believe that all doctors should be male. Anyone who makes use of the concept of role may need to explain whether the expectations associated with a position are of the one kind or the other; both can be comprehended in role analysis.

Role as a concept in social science cannot be compared to an elementary particle in physics. It is not possible to list all the roles in a particular society, because there are no clear principles for deciding what is a social position: in the end it is a question of discovering whether it is useful in given circumstances to regard, say, pedestrian, as a role. In so far as people are conscious of themselves and others as occupying positions with generally known rights and duties, then their behaviour cannot be understood without reference to their expectations about how they should behave and others should behave towards them. The research worker may ask them what their expectations are; he may observe their behaviour and deduce their expectations from it; or he may do both and find out that when their stated expectations are not met they do not necessarily do anything about it (a serious breach will be another matter). In order to analyse actual behaviour, the concept of role is only a beginning which must be supplemented by a battery of related concepts which give it greater utility. Biddle (1979) defines 334 such concepts.

Biddle also comments upon research work showing that boys and girls are treated somewhat differently in the classroom. In the United States, boys (who are taught mostly by women teachers) do less well in reading than girls, whereas in Germany (where the teachers are more likely to be male) boys do better than girls. One possible explanation of this finding is that school children take teachers as role models. Female pupils can identify with female teachers, but male pupils experience a conflict between their masculinity and their relationship to a female role model. This conflict can stimulate them to behave in ways that the school system defines as deviant. A similar argument is heard in societies like the United States and Britain, in which Black people constitute a minority of the population. The poor performance in examinations by Black children may be ascribed to the dearth of suitable role models, such as Black teachers, Black newsreaders on television and Black popular heroes. This kind of hypothesis can be tested by the methods of social science. Evidence also suggests that the absence of good male and female role models in the home can have a negative effect upon the personality development of children.

Writers who are concerned about social harmony are readily drawn to a conception of society as a unit in which everyone has a series of roles to play and where all the main roles are clearly defined. For them the concept of role helps describe the relation between the individual and society. But for those who see society as an arena in which groups with opposed interests clash with one another, such a view is regarded as suspect; they are most inclined to picture individuals as coerced by injustifiable role expectations which exact compliance, or to maintain that the very concept of role is redundant. These are criticisms of an unimaginitive use of the concept of role (seen as a representation of social relations) rather than of a problem-solving approach to role which seeks to elucidate a particular pattern of behaviour. When the social scientist starts from a set of observations and seeks to account for what people do, he regularly has to explain behaviour in terms of people's conforming with rules. The barrister does not ask a leading question in circumstances where it is forbidden. Any explanation of why people follow rules implies a concept of role, because the rules apply to those who occupy particular social positions. Depending on the nature of the problem, it then becomes necessary to make use of other concepts from the vocabulary of role analysis particularly as it has been developed by social psychologists. By discovering which formulations are most effective in providing explanations, the present confusion about alternative definitions will eventually be dispelled.

Michael Banton
University of Bristol

Reference

Biddle, B. J. (1979), *Role Theory: Expectations, Identities and Behaviour*, London.

Further Reading

Banton, M. (1965), *Roles: An Introduction to the Study of Social Behaviour*, London.
Goffman, E. (1959), *The Presentation of Self in Everyday Life*, New York.
Jackson, J. A. (ed.) (1972), *Role*, Cambridge.
See also: *Goffman; status*.

Rorschach Test

See Projective Methods.

Rostow, Walt Whitman (1916–)

Few contemporary economists present us with broad vistas on the scale of their classical predecessors. One such, both economist and historian, is Walt W. Rostow whose grand vision of the evolutionary process, whether right or wrong, can be compared with that of Marx. In fact, Rostow describes his *magnum opus* as a non-Communist Manifesto. Very early in his development, Rostow set himself the tasks of applying neoclassical economics to economic history analysis and relating economic forces to social and political ones.

Rostow offers a sweeping generalization of economic growth universally relevant to most societies and periods. This grand design was subject to much criticism for being empty of content, tautological, and historically wrong. However, as M. M. Postan, a benevolent critic, remarked, it does not matter that historical experience of various countries diverges from the sequential order of stages postulated by Rostow, nor that the relevant quantities did not always move as Rostow postulated. Rostow's contribution should be evaluated as a treatise on the morphology of economic development (Kindleberger and di Tella, 1982). And Fishlow (1965), a not so friendly critic, suggests that though we cannot accept the whole of Rostow's explanation of economic growth, 'There is good cause to pursue his many suggestions concerning the process by which industrialization becomes rooted. Rostow, paradoxically, is at his best read as a prospectus rather than as a treatise.' Though to Fishlow the manifesto is nothing but a partial hypothesis, 'it is a rare occasion when operational, albeit partial, theories pregnant with potential are put forward. The conception of take-off is just such an event'. Rostow's pioneering work on British business cycles is regarded by many as the first breakthrough of rigorous application of economic theory to history, anticipating cliometrics.

Born in 1916, Rostow was educated at Yale University. He was a Rhodes scholar in the 1930s, beginning a life-long and fruitful on-and-off association with Oxbridge. His public service career, begun during the war, continued in the post-war years at the UN. In 1951 he joined the Massachusetts Institute of Technology faculty where he remained until 1961, when he became involved in various advisory capacities with the Kennedy-Johnson administrations. His controversial position during the Vietnam war earned him much animosity. In 1969 he returned to the academic world, to the University of Texas at Austin – an association that has proven very fruitful.

George R. Feiwel
University of Tennessee

References
Fishlow, A. (1965), 'Empty economic stages?', *Economic Journal*, 75.
Kindleberger, C. P. and di Tella, G. (eds) (1982), *Economics in the Long View: Essays in Honour of W. W. Rostow*, 3 vols, New York.

Further Reading
Rostow, W. W. (1960), *The Stages of Economic Growth*, Cambridge.

Rostow, W. W. (1978), *The World Economy: History and Prospect*, Austin, Texas.
Rostow, W. W. (1980), *Why the Poor Get Richer and the Rich Slow Down*, Austin, Texas.
See also: *cliometrics; economic growth*.

Rousseau, Jean-Jacques (1712–78)

Rousseau's contribution to the social sciences has been a paradoxical one. In his first *Discours* (Discours sur les sciences et les arts, (1964 [1750]) ['On science and art'], Rousseau argued that scientific inquiry in general tends rather to corrupt than to enlighten, and that public virtue would be better served by ignorance than by systematic knowledge. On the other hand, in his second *Discours* ('Sur l'origine et les fondements de l'inégalité parmi les hommes', 1964 [1775] ['On the origins of inequality']), Rousseau himself offered a pioneering work in social theory that generations of social scientists have considered crucial to the founding of such disciplines as sociology and social anthropology – the very sorts of theoretical inquiry that Rousseau had virtually ruled out in his first *Discours* as inimical to the public good (See Derathé, 1970; Durkheim, 1965; Lévi-Strauss, 1962.)

Furthermore, whereas Rousseau argued in the second *Discours* that man is not originally a social being and that sociability is fundamentally alien to man's nature, his argument in *Du contrat social* (1762) [*The Social Contract*, 1978], his main work of political philosophy, is that one can only conceive of a legitimate state where the members are wholeheartedly devoted to the good of the community and are able to identify their own interests with those of the whole society. It would seem that an author whose work is rooted in such basic contradictions would be incapable of producing a cogent and consistent social philosophy, and indeed many critics would dismiss Rousseau's achievement on just these grounds. However, one of the central claims of Rousseau's thought is that society itself is founded on irresolvable contradiction, and that therefore paradox may be the most appropriate medium in which to understand the essence of social life.

It is in his magnificent treatise on education, *Émile, ou de l'education* (1762) [*Émile*, 1979], that Rousseau states the basic insight of his social theory – the impossibility of reconciling the contradiction between nature and society: 'He who would preserve the supremacy of natural feelings in social life knows not what he asks. Ever at war with himself, hesitating between his wishes and his duties, he will be neither a man nor a citizen. He will be of no use to himself nor to others. He will be a man of our day, a Frenchman, an Englishman, one of the great middle class.' This insight is further developed in *The Social Contract* (published in the same year as *Émile*).

The core idea of *The Social Contract* is a very simple one: it is that no polity can be considered legitimate except in so far as its laws issue from the will of its members; that citizens are only entitled to renounce natural liberty for the sake of a superior freedom; and that the touchstones of politics based on right are law, democratic will and popular sovereignty. Rousseau managed to articulate a vision of politics as a moral community, even though he remained suspicious of all social relationships and held to the view that society as such is inevitably corrupting. His solution to the problem lay in substituting the power of law for the power of men, thus making men independent of one another by making them all equally dependent on the laws of the republic.

Although Rousseau categorically repudiated the conditions of political life in modernity, many of the fundamental ideas of liberal democracy are owed to him: the idea that the overarching function of government is legislation; the idea that political legitimacy flows from the will of the people; and the idea that formal equality and the rule of law are essential to democratic liberty.

From the first *Discours* onwards, Rousseau's work represented a lifelong battle against the assumptions and aspirations of the Enlightenment. Although Rousseau knew, and had been personally close to, many of the leading members of the French Enlightenment, his ideas led him into increasingly heated and passionate controversies with the champions of Enlightenment. Of these, the most significant product was Rousseau's *Lettre à d'Alembert sur les spectacles* (1758) [*Letter to D'Alembert*, 1968], debating the issue of whether the theatre should be introduced into Rousseau's native city of Geneva. In general, the spokesmen of the Enlightenment sought to refashion the nature of man and society by constructing scientific principles of social existence. Rousseau, by contrast, thought that man is best as he is by nature, that human nature is invariably deformed by life in society, and that such a science of society could only deepen the corruption and debasement of man. This was, in fact, the central insight of his social and moral philosophy, the foundation upon which all his political principles and psychological analyses are built.

Despite recurrent attempts to expose 'totalitarian' traits within Rousseau's political thought, the ever-present concern throughout his political writings was with republican liberty. Rousseau feared that without the sustaining nourishment of genuine citizenship and civic virtue, men in society would become slaves to social conformity, that they would (in the words of the second *Discours*) always live outside of themselves rather than within themselves, and that they would forfeit their natural liberty without attaining the higher condition of civil freedom, thus being worse off rather than better for having left nature to enter social existence. Notwithstanding the supposed romanticism attributed to Rousseau's thought, he possessed a sober and clear-headed insight into the possibility that post-Enlightenment science and technological civilization would pose an ever-greater threat to freedom and civic solidarity.

Even though Rousseau's literary and autobiographical writings have established the image of him as an unworldly and misanthropic dreamer, his political discernment is testified to by his acute diagnosis of the crumbling social order in Europe: In *Considérations sur le gouvernement de la Pologne* (1782) [The Government of Poland, 1972] Rousseau writes, 'I see all the states of Europe hastening to their doom'; in *Émile*, he predicts, 'The crisis is approaching, and we are on the edge of a revolution'; 'In my opinion it is impossible that the great kingdoms of Europe should last much longer.'

There remains, of course, the predictable complaint that Rousseau's social theory is irretrievably utopian, and cannot in any sense be applied to modern conditions. For Rousseau himself, given the conception of political philosophy that he adheres to, and steeped as he is in the classical utopianism of Plato, this does not necessarily count as a very telling objection. As he remarks in *Émile*, 'We dream and the dreams of a bad night are given to us as philosophy. You will say I too am a dreamer; I admit this, but I do what the others fail to do. I give my dreams as dreams, and leave the reader to discover whether there is anything in them which may prove useful to those who are awake.'

Ronald Beiner
University of Southampton

References

Derathé, R. (1970), *Jean-Jacques Rousseau et la science politique de son temps*, Paris.

Durkheim, E. (1965 [1953]), *Montesquieu and Rousseau: Forerunners of Sociology*, trans. R. Manheim, Ann Arbor, Mich. (French edn, *Montesquieu et Rousseau, précursors de la sociologie*, Paris.)

Lévi-Strauss, C. (1962), 'Jean-Jacques Rousseau, fondateur des sciences de l'homme', in S. Baud-Bovy *et al.*, *Jean-Jacques Rousseau*, Neuchâtel.

Further Reading

Texts by Rousseau:

(1979), *Emile, or On Education*, trans. A. Bloom, New York.

(1964), *The First and Second Discourses*, ed. R. D. Masters, trans. R. D. and J. R. Masters, New York.

(1972), *The Government of Poland*, trans. W. Kendall, Indianapolis.

(1978) *On the Social Contract*, ed. R. D. Masters, trans. J. R. Masters, New York.

(1968), *Politics and the Arts*, trans. A. Bloom, Ithaca, New York.

Other:

Masters, R. D. (1968), *The Political Philosophy of Rousseau*, Princeton, New Jersey.

Shklar, J. N. (1969), *Men and Citizens: A Study of Rousseau's Social Theory*, Cambridge.

See also: *social contract*.

Rural Planning and Development

Rural planning and rural development are ideas that have become current only since the Second World War. With the attainment of independence, countries of the Third World have all set for themselves the objective of economic and social development. It has also been widely recognized by policy makers of these countries that development would not come about on its own, but that it necessitated careful government planning, and that the rural sector, particularly agriculture, would have to be the focus of development efforts because of its all-too-evident preponderance. But policy makers have not agreed on the question of whether to give primacy to these sectors or not: some held that such primacy should attach to the rural sector because of the position it holds in the economy, while others emphasized the necessity of industrialization along modern lines with due place given to large-scale and heavy industries and sophisticated technologies, in order to reverse the dominant position held by the rural sector.

Different countries have tried to implement rural planning through different kinds of institutions set up for that purpose. At the one extreme is a purely governmental institution like the Block Development Offices of India, which take responsibility for a cluster of villages in a locality, are multipurpose in their activities and are manned by salaried employees of the government. At the other extreme are the Communes of China, largely autonomous collective bodies taking care of all economic, social and civil problems of a defined rural area including a large number of villages. These Communes are of course subject to regulatory directives from above, but they enjoy considerable freedom in the internal organization of their work, and offer much scope for spontaneous initiatives by their members. In between these two extremes lie various different kinds of institutions which incorporate a mixture of central authority and local autonomy in various kinds of co-operative and collective frameworks, for example, the Ujamaa villages of Tanzania. While the deficiencies of the first approach are by now well established, the second approach has not yet been tried out enough to assess whether it can yield much better results. There is, actually, a contradiction inherent in the very idea of local level rural planning:

planning necessarily implies consistency and optimality at an economy-wide level, which means that all decisions, however local, have to be logically connected with decisions taken centrally about various macroeconomic variables, as well as with decisions taken in other sectors like industry, trade and so on. This problem has received theoretical attention in the literature of Decentralized Planning, but has not been satisfactorily resolved at the practical level.

Ashok Rudra
Visva-Bharati, India

Further Reading

Ghai, D. *et al.* (eds) (1979), *Agrarian Systems and Rural Development*, London.

Hague, W. *et al.* (1977), 'Towards a theory of rural development', *Development Dialogue*, 2.

See also: *agricultural economics; co-operatives; development administration; planning, economic; rural sociology*.

Rural Sociology

Until recently, rural sociology has been regarded as somewhat marginal to the main theoretical interests of both sociology and anthropology. It seemed of little interest to general sociology, which was mostly concerned with the 'larger questions' of industrial and urban change or with the search for grand-theoretical schema aimed at providing a broad understanding of social behaviour. And anthropology was too committed to the investigation of the peculiarities of nonWestern societies and cultures to find much of interest in a field which focused primarily on rural situations in the industrialized West. In addition, rural sociology has frequently been criticized for its heavy empiricist and naive positivist approach and for being too ready to undertake applied research for government or agribusiness. Although these criticisms have been voiced most vehemently against the American rural sociological tradition, some traces of the same tendency and argument can be found with respect to certain types of European rural sociology. In Britain the situation was rather different, in that, apart from the early development of rural community studies (mostly in fact carried out by social anthropologists and social geographers in the 1950s and early 1960s), rural sociology has hardly developed at all as a specialism, and it was left to agricultural economists and rural planners to investigate the social problems of the countryside.

Specialized departments of rural sociology first appeared in the United States from the 1930s onwards when a number of Land Grant Colleges were set up under the auspices of the US Department of Agriculture to research rural problems and to train rural extensionists and sociologists to work closely with government agencies and farmers' organizations (see

Hightower, 1973, for a trenchant critique of this policy). This initiative was consolidated after the Second World War with the emergence of a specific style of research focusing upon such questions as the spread of technological innovations, the disparities between rural and urban life styles, educational and occupational mobility patterns, and the impact of Community Development programmes. These various dimensions were, in the main, explored employing a methodology based on questionnaires, formal interview techniques, and quantitative analysis. The dominant framework for analysing the empirical findings was the idea of a rural-urban continuum, and it sought to explain differences in social and cultural patterns by reference to the place of communities along a continuum, which ran from the most urban to the most rural type of settlement. During the 1950s and 1960s, a great deal of rural-sociological research became organized around this specific conceptual schema, so successfully in fact that it was exported to certain European and Third World countries. As Hofstee (1963) observed, this package came to Europe in the form of a kind of 'mental Marshall aid'. It was also diffused to parts of Latin America and Asia. Indeed the founding of various international associations specializing in rural sociology, such as the International Rural Sociological Association (IRSA), which currently holds a world congress every four years, is in great part due to the enthusiasm and institutional resources of senior members of the American rural-sociology tradition.

By the end of the 1960s the notion of a rural-urban continuum was theoretically bankrupt. Several studies had demonstrated that differences in social and cultural patterns did not simply coincide with spatial or ecological milieux (Pahl, 1966). Diffusion studies were becoming increasingly complex in terms of trying to isolate the critical socio-psychological factors explaining the spread and adoption rate of innovations among farmers, but these studies had failed to deal with the wider structural conditions affecting the propensity of farmers to respond to new opportunities; nor was there any analysis of the structure and content of social networks among farmers and extensionists that might also affect the adoption pattern (Rogers and Shoemaker, 1971). These limitations, together with others such as the neglect of comparative work on different forms of agricultural production (for example, family farms, capitalist enterprise and collective farms), on the effects of different government policies towards agriculture, and on questions of regional inequality, led to the beginnings of new ways of conceptualizing rural sociology.

Whereas the early tradition had assumed that there was something especially distinctive about rural locations which made them socially and culturally different from urban forms of social life, researchers increasingly took the view that rural locations were merely empirical or geographical entities in which one worked. Being 'rural' carried no special theoretical or methodological implications for the research. The significance of one's work and its relevance to other rural sociologists or to sociologists and others working in different types of empirical contexts depended essentially on the kinds of theoretical and methodological questions posed, and not merely on the fact of having had common rural experience.

In an attempt to resolve these various issues, and at the same time preserve some professional and institutional distinctiveness, several rural sociologists have recently proposed a realigning of the field in order to connect up with more general theoretical debates and to stimulate new lines of inquiry (Newby, 1980; 1981; Newby and Buttel, 1980). Several promising new directions for empirical and theoretical analysis have been suggested, each one necessitating an appreciation of developments in other fields.

Although American rural sociology was born out of an interest in agricultural policy questions, it seems that, until recently, little systematic comparison was undertaken of the characteristics, means of implementation, and social outcomes of different policies. The sociology of agricultural and rural development policy raises important problems for analysis that require sound theorization: for example, we need to be able to characterize more adequately differences in the nature and activities of different states and explain the ways in which various rural populations and classes are affected by planned development. Over the past few years a number of interesting studies have been conducted on this theme in various European and American situations (for example, Mann and Dickinson, 1980; Sinclair, 1980). But the work needs strengthening by taking fuller cognizance of existing sociological, economic and anthropological analyses of similar problems in Third World countries (Long, 1977) where a wide range of policies have been tried (for example, small-farmer, 'green revolution', large-scale settlement and land-reform programmes, and a large variety of marketing and fiscal measures).

Another related area for further research concerns the impact of world food trade and agricultural aid flows between the industrial and poorer nations on specific rural populations. New research along these lines, which simultaneously looks at both ends of the process (that is, EEC and American interests and situations as well as those of the Third World countries) has been initiated by sociologists and political economists (Friedmann, 1981) and promises to develop over the next few years into a focal point for rural sociological research. This type of interest, however, leads to a rethinking of the boundaries of so-called rural sociology, since the basic phenomena and structures lie essentially beyond the farm gate, though they clearly have a major impact on farming behaviour and on the livelihood and welfare of rural populations. Conventional boundaries of analysis are also questioned in recent work which looks at ecological and environmental pollution problems affecting rural populations. Although rural populations are not usually the worst affected by these problems, there are a number of critical situations where they are (as in the devastation brought by oil exploration and by nearby industrial pollution of water sources). The analysis of such situations requires both an understanding of broad, cumulative ecological processes, as well as the politics of natural resource use. The rural sociologist has an important role to play in such research, but any conclusions he reaches must draw upon the work of environmentalists, technologists and political scientists (Redclift, 1984).

Perhaps one of the most disquieting aspects in the history of rural sociology is, as Newby (1980, 1981) has repeatedly pointed out, the failure to develop a systematic analysis of agricultural production, at the level of either the enterprise or the overall agrarian structure. Despite the important early attempts to look at different forms of agricultural production, at contrasting patterns of land tenure and their influence on local social organization and power systems, and at the question of capitalist penetration in agriculture, it has only been since the late 1970s that this research theme has re-emerged as central to a sociology of agriculture (Harriss, 1982). Comparing the work carried out on agricultural populations within the industrialized countries with similar research in the Third World, it appears that the latter has made much more progress in understanding these dimensions. This has no doubt been partly because the sociology of development and social anthropology were quicker to respond to the new developments in Marxist theory emanating from the French structuralists (Oxaal et al., 1975). This is likewise true of the incorporation of the 'dependency' and 'underdevelopment' problematic which has generated a whole series of Third World rural studies dealing with structures of inequality and patterns of uneven development, and which has also built upon the early European debates on the development of capitalism in agriculture to lay the foundation of a comparative political economy of agriculture. This type of analysis has reawakened an interest in these questions among rural sociologists. We now have a series of new studies exploring the different ways in which capital controls and the state manages agricultural production (for example, through vertical integration and by specialized services) in different industrial countries. This work is, in turn, having a useful feedback on Third World studies.

Rural sociology has, it seems, lost the grounds for claiming to be a distinctive discipline with its own special object of investigation and mode of explanation. It has been forced to engage in a number of interchanges with other disciplines working on similar analytic problems. Its search for a new identity has, in particular, led to a closer appreciation of the theoretical and empirical findings of studies falling under peasant studies, economic anthropology, sociology of development, economic history, political economy, policy studies, and environmental studies. Some rural sociologists look upon this broadening of the theoretical and empirical concerns as evidence of the fragmentation and general disarray of the field. Others look to the future believing that they are witnessing the beginnings of a more dynamic, theoretically better-informed and more socially relevant comparative sociology of rural development.

Norman Long
Agricultural University, Wageningen

References

Friedmann, H. (1981), 'State policy and world commerce; the case of wheat, 1815 to the present', Working Paper Series, 14a, University of Toronto.

Harriss, J. (1982), Rural Development: Theories of Agrarian Change and Peasant Economy, London.

Hightower, J. (1973), Hard Tomatoes, Hard Times, Cambridge, Mass.

Hofstee, E. W. (1963), 'Rural sociology in Europe', Rural Sociology, 28.

Long, N. (1977), An Introduction to the Sociology of Rural Development, London.

Mann, S. A. and Dickinson, J. A. (1980), 'State and agriculture in two eras of American capitalism', in H. Newby and F. Buttel (eds), The Rural Sociology of Advanced Societies: Critical Perspectives, Montclair, New Jersey.

Newby, H. (1980), 'Rural sociology – a trend report', Current Sociology, 28.

Newby, H. (1981), 'Rural sociology and its relevance to the agricultural economist: a review', Journal of Agricultural Economics, vol. 12.

Newby, H. and Buttel, F. (eds) (1980), The Rural Sociology of Advanced Societies: Critical Perspectives, Montclair, New Jersey.

Oxaal, I. et al. (1975), Beyond the Sociology of Development, London.

Pahl, R. (1966), 'The rural-urban continuum', Sociologia Ruralis, 6.

Redclift, M. (1984), Development and the Environmental Crisis, London.

Rogers, E. and Shoemaker, F. (1971), Communication of Innovations: A Cross-Cultural Approach, Glencoe, Ill.

Sinclair, P. R. (1980), 'Agricultural policy and the decline of commercial family farming; a comparative analysis of the US, Sweden and the Netherlands', in H. Newby and F. Buttel (eds), op. cit.

See also: agricultural economics; co-operatives; peasants; rural planning and development.

S

Saint-Simon, Claude-Henri De (1760–1825)

Born into the nobility but an advocate of doing away with hereditary privileges, Saint-Simon was a true entrepreneur of social ideas and an early visionary of major features and trends of the modern industrial social order. Paradoxically, he later formulated principles of socialism and corporatism. Though it was his secretary Auguste Comte who coined the term 'sociology', Saint-Simon merits credit for having conceptualized a science of social organization, which he called 'social physiology' to emphasize that historical change is at the heart of human society. Saint-Simon's analyses of social classes, social stratification, and the relation between dominant ideas and social organization were taken over by later Marxism. Saint-Simon viewed conflict between classes and revolutions as explosions of social contradictions to be recurrent features of Western history, which he saw as alternating between 'organic periods' and 'periods of crises'. Still, he saw the progress of a new age, anticipated by Condorcet, as realizable through increased productivity of all sectors of society. What was needed was a new political system, based on scientific knowledge and led by a meritocracy of scientists, artists, and industrialists. The science of society would synthesize the knowledge necessary for reorganizing the polity and ending a period of crises. Saint-Simon proposed (*De la réorganisation de la société européene*, 1814; *The Reorganization of European Society*) that to facilitate the productive forces of an industrial age, a new European Parliament should replace present national bodies. A common body politic had existed in the Middle Ages, and a new one, cemented by the social teachings of a 'new Christianity', could be founded having as its mission the uplift or socialization (in the sense of full social participation) of the impoverished proletariat, the most numerous class. Thus, for Saint-Simon, economic and spiritual development would lead to the end of the exploitation of man by man.

Edward A. Tiryakian
Duke University, North Carolina

Further Reading
Manuel, F. E. (1956), *The New World of Henri Saint-Simon*, Cambridge, Mass.
Taylor, K. (ed.) (1975), *Henri Saint-Simon (1760–1825): Selected Writings*, New York.
See also: *Comte*.

Sample Surveys

The modern sample survey evolved from the Victorian social survey movement, which assembled facts about urban poverty. Other sources were the development of the statistical theory of probability, and the early attempts to carry out straw polls before elections. In the twentieth century, Bowley and others used samples in preference to attempts (on the model of Booth) to survey entire populations. Gradually (and particularly in the United States) the survey was broadened to include questions about attitudes as well as about facts. The surveys increasingly came to focus on the individual rather than on a sometimes ecletic combination of units of analysis, and today the survey normally studies people ('respondents'). Respondents may be questioned about their own lives or asked about the society around them. Information is elicited in answer to questions, often ordered in the formal structure of a questionnaire; but the information may be combined with the fieldworker's own observations. The resulting body of variables (the items of information classified by respondents) is then arranged in a matrix amenable to statistical analysis. Some writers – a minority, however – also use the term surveys for other kinds of data sets, such as aggregated statistics for organizations, social groups, or areal units. In this sense a survey is a non-experimental (*ex post facto*) analysis, to be distinguished from an experimental design.

Sample surveys are intended to provide information about a larger population. The probable accuracy of generalizations from a sample survey to its population can be calculated using the mathematics of significance testing, if certain conditions are met. The most important condition is random sampling, in other words, every member of the population sampled must stand an equal chance of being selected for the sample. For some populations, students enrolled in a school, for instance, random selection poses no obstacle, but for more diverse constituencies true random sampling is virtually impossible. In a national population, which changes constantly as individuals are born, age and die, a sampling frame (a list of all members of the population from which to sample) becomes outdated before it can be used, and it requires a massive effort to compile in the first place. In practice, shortcut approximations to random sampling are generally employed for surveying. Special procedures are then used to estimate the correction factor (termed 'design effect'), to permit the application of significance tests.

But human subjects not only complicate sampling by ageing, changing social characteristics, and shifting residence: they are sometimes not available or not willing to respond to surveys. The study of this 'nonresponse' preoccupies many survey methodologists, and is motivated by both technical and ethical considerations. Technically, only a minor inconvenience – the erosion of the sample case base – results as long as nonresponse occurs at random. Much evidence, however, shows that nonresponse to surveys follows predictable lines. Even if nonresponse derives from a simple availability factor, such as the difficulty of contacting night-shift workers at home during the conventional leisure hours, the resulting uncompleted questionnaires or interview schedules constitute a form of sampling error not accommodated in standard significance testing. An enormous literature on maximizing survey response has accumulated, particularly with reference to mailed questionnaires. Postal surveying counteracts the availability problem, to the extent that people read their mail at a time of their own choosing. Consequently, the elasticity of response due to conditioning becomes evident. Response to mailed questionnaires increases, sometimes dramatically, when follow-up mailings are carried out, or prizes or cash incentives are included with the questionnaire, or even after tests have been conducted to allow for improvements in the covering letter sent out with the questionnaire.

The pursuit of maximum response is sometimes carried to such lengths that ethical issues are raised. If people ignore calls by interviewers or solicitations through the mail by considered choice, should their wishes not be respected? This depends in part on their motives for nonresponse. Many researchers regard principled refusal as very rare, so that in their view the survey fieldworker may be justified in employing persuasive tactics – or as justified as the car salesman or the life-insurance representative. There seems, however, to be increasing sensitivity to the rights of the citizen to privacy and confidentiality, and these rights are now emphasized by the granting agencies which fund much survey research.

Despite problems of these kinds, the sample survey has developed into the dominant method of research in sociology (particularly in the US), and in several of the other social sciences. Not all methodologists applaud this development, and a substantial group prefer such alternatives as participant observation. The survey is especially useful in the collection of comprehensive information about naturally occurring social phenomena. The resultant data may be used either for detailed description or for multivariate analysis, where statistical techniques are used to weigh the influence of various factors on the dependent (to be explained)

variable. In either case, the attraction of the survey method lies in its promise to generalize from a sample to a population. A practical difficulty is that survey designs must be determined in advance, and can be altered in mid-study only with great difficulty and expense. Consequently, surveys tend to be employed largely for purposes of confirmation rather than exploration. The logic of the sample survey seems ideally suited to research topics where it is defensible to assume that every sample member's responses are of equal social importance and analytical utility.

One reason that the survey continues to attract social scientists is that it satisfies some key conditions for scientific procedures. The procedures used in a sample survey can be codified, scrutinized, and replicated with a precision denied to less formal methods. The rules for reaching conclusions about the association between variables measured in a survey can be specified in advance (as, for example, when a significance level upon which an hypothesis test will hinge is selected). Social scientists who take the second word of their title literally (too literally, some would argue) tend to be drawn to sample surveys.

John Goyder
University of Waterloo, Ontario

Further Reading
Babbie, E. (1973), *Survey Research Methods*, Belmont, Calif.
Gordon, M. (1973), 'The social survey movement and sociology in the United States', *Social Problems*, 21.
Kish, L. (1965), *Survey Sampling*, New York.
Marsh, C. (1982), *The Survey Method: The Contribution of Surveys to Sociological Explanation*, London.
See also: *marketing research*; *opinion polls*; *random sampling*.

Samuelson, Paul Anthony (1915–)

Paul Samuelson, born in Gary, Indiana, 15 May 1915 and educated at Chicago and Harvard, ranks among history-making economists. The citation of the 1970 Nobel Prize in Economic Science reads in part:

> By his many contributions, Samuelson has done more than any other contemporary economist to raise the level of scientific analysis in economic theory . . . . He has rewritten considerable parts of central economic theory, and has in several areas achieved results which now rank among the classical theorems in economics.

Samuelson's contributions cover a range of subjects almost as broad as economics itself. They range from the very esoteric, through questions in the mainstream and issues that have played an important role in the accretion of economic knowledge, to the very relevant modern problems of political economy. He played an outstanding role in the analytical revolution in economic theory. In large measure he is the architect of the modern neoclassical conception and the neoclassical synthesis. His work strives to extend the boundaries of mainstream economics. His pervasive influence on contemporary economics is also in good measure due to his role as teacher to generations of economists the world over ever since the first appearance of his masterly and controversial textbook in 1948.

During his graduate work at Harvard he came into what was then the vanguard – the three great waves of modern economics: the Keynesian revolution, the monopolistic or imperfect-competition revolution, and the creative application of mathematics to economics. It is particularly in the third wave that Samuelson made the greatest splash.

Many of the subjects on which Samuelson has written are controversial. There are clashing perceptions on fundamentals, if not on shortcomings of specific formulations. His general neoclassical approach, if not his macroeconomics and his mathematics, is under strong attack from various quarters. For instance, many of his contributions centre on neoclassical dynamics and the surrounding controversies: the sensitive pure theory of capital and growth and the conditions for efficient or optimal intertemporal allocation in the 'good society'. One of his major preoccupations is the philosophy, dynamism, *modus operandi*, and feasibility constraints of the mixed economy, perceived broadly as one where a democratic government regulates the market economy and keeps it prosperous.

In drawing up the prerequisites for a 'master-economist', Keynes (1951) suggested, 'He must be mathematician, historian, statesman, philosopher – in some degree.' This remarkable combination fits Samuelson particularly well. He is a man of intense and sparkling intellect, passion for his chosen field, scholarly versatility and eclecticism, concern for the improvement of economic welfare, and preference for the middle road.

George R. Feiwel
University of Tennessee

References
Keynes, J. M. (1951), *Essays in Biography*, ed by G. Keynes, London.
Samuelson, P. A. (1948), *Foundations of Economic Analysis*, Cambridge, Mass.

Further Reading
Brown, E. C. and Solow, R. M. (eds) (1983), *Paul Samuelson and Modern Economic Theory*, New York.
Feiwel, G. R. (1982), *Samuelson and Neoclassical Economics*, Boston.

Samuelson, P. A. (1966, 1972, 1977), *The Collected Scientific Papers of Paul A. Samuelson*, 4 vols, Cambridge, Mass.
Samuelson, P. A. (1980), *Economics*, 11th edn, New York.

Sapir, Edward (1884–1939)

Edward Sapir, born in Schleswig-Holstein, Germany, in 1884, emigrated to the United States with his parents when he was five. He was the foremost linguist among the students of Franz Boas in American anthropology. After initial training in Germanic philology, he turned to anthropology, applying Indo-European methods to the study of unwritten languages.

During his career, Sapir carried out extensive fieldwork on a wide range of American Indian languages – Takelma, Wishram Chinook, Southern Paiute, Yana, Nootka, Sarcee, Hupa and Navaho. This first-hand research was crucial to his classification of the languages of native North America into only six families, replacing John Wesley Powell's 1891 classification into fifty-five stocks. Sapir built on the fieldwork of the intervening generation, largely Boasian, but also extended the methods of comparative linguistics to uncover new levels of linguistic relationship. The six-unit classification was enthusiastically received by ethnologists as well as linguists because of its usefulness for reconstructing culture history. Indeed, Sapir's 1916 'Time perspective in aboriginal American culture: a study in method' had already argued that language had a special role in historical reconstruction because phonetic laws allowed clear identification of divergence from common ancestry.

Sapir also contributed significantly to the development of linguistic theory, being the first in North America to define the concept of the phoneme (independently of the Prague School in Europe). His emphasis on the psychological reality of sound systems for speakers of a language drew on his work in anthropological theory, particularly the relationship of psychology and culture.

In his one general book, *Language* (1921), Sapir stressed that language is symbolic expression of thought rather than merely form. He suggested that linguistic categories strongly influence habitual thought, an argument elaborated by his student Benjamin Whorf in the so-called Sapir-Whorf hypothesis. Sapir argued for 'drift' in languages changing from a common genetic base, and defined degrees of synthesis in language typology. Towards the end of his life, he turned to semantics, largely based on English.

Sapir even took advantage of an opportunity to study an African language, Gwabo. He illustrated that genetic and areal processes of linguistic change were interrelated, in his study of Tocharian, an Indo-European language of Central Asia, as influenced by borrowing and contact with Tibetan.

Sapir's influence was seminal in the development of culture and personality as a specialization within anthropology. Although his textbook was never completed, his argument that culture has its locus in the individual was elaborated in various papers from 1917 on.

In addition to his academic work, Sapir published a considerable amount of poetry and literary criticism, played the piano, attempted musical composition, and was interested in mathematics. In general, he envisioned a humanistic science which crossed disciplinary boundaries.

Sapir spent fifteen years in Ottawa as Director of the Division of Anthropology within the Geological Survey of Canada (1910–25). Later he pursued an academic career at the University of Chicago (1925–31) and Yale University (1931–39), teaching both linguistics and culture theory. He trained a cadre of linguistic students and was important in the institutional development of linguistics, anthropology and psychology/psychiatry.

Sapir's premature death in 1939 prevented completion of much of his research. He is, however, virtually unique in anthropology and linguistics for the scope of his work and for his ability to apply insights from one area of interest to another. He has often been hailed as a genius for the intuition (actually based in detailed analysis) which led him to conclusions more laboriously corroborated later by others. His work in a range of disciplines and subject areas continues to inspire current research.

Regna Darnell
University of Alberta

Further Reading
Sapir, E. (1916), 'Time perspective in aboriginal American culture: a study in method', Canada, Dept. of Mines, Geological Survey, Memoir 90, Anthropological Series, no. 13.
Sapir, E. (1921), *Language*, New York.
Sapir, E. (1949), *Selected Writings of Edward Sapir*, ed. D. Mandelbaum, Berkeley and Los Angeles.
See also: *Boas; culture and personality; language and culture*.

Sartre, Jean-Paul (1905–80)

Although not the originator of the term existentialism (Gabriel Marcel was), Jean-Paul Sartre is undoubtedly the figure who made existential philosophy one of the most powerful intellectual currents over a twenty-year period from the early 1940s onwards. A philosopher by training, he extended the existential phenomenology of Husserl and Heidegger in a landmark treatise, *L'être et le néant* (1943) (*Being and Nothingness*, 1956), and in a famous conference which marked post-war France (*Existentialism and Humanism*, 1948). Sartre was a man of letters par excellence, but for the purpose of this volume, we will gloss over his considerable contributions as a novelist, playwright, and literary critic, as well as editor of a major review (*Les Temps Modernes*). However, there is a unity and totality to his writings, the many-sided search and affirmation of freedom as the basic aspect of the human condition.

Man, for Sartre, does not have an essential or objective nature; he is what he chooses to be; he is foremost a project, or in the famous Sartrian formula, 'Existence precedes essence'. Men do not exist in the abstract but in situations. There is a duality of being in all human situations, a being 'in-itself' (*en soi*), that of fixed objects, and a transcending being which is consciousness (*pour soi*), subjectivity. Where Marx talked of 'commodification', Sartre talked of 'objectification' or the reduction of conscious being to inert, object being. The theme of alienation common to both Marxists and Sartrian analysis derives ultimately from Hegel (who influenced both Marx and Kierkegaard, the forerunner of existential thought). In Sartre's early analyses, *La nausée* (1938) (*Nausea*, 1948); *Huis clos* (1945) (*No Exit*, 1946) and other works, social relationships are sources of self-alienation (quite in contrast to G. H. Mead who viewed them as sources of self-development). Both the person and others can equate or identify the role one plays with the being of the self, that is, self is reduced to a given social role defined by others. For Sartre, this reduction of being *qua* social object is to live inauthentically, in 'bad faith'. Sartre viewed organized, institutionalized society – at least the bourgeois society that he, like his surrealist predecessors, never ceased to inveigh against – as a set of oppressive objectification of practices, what he termed 'pratico-inert'.

As a 'man of the left', Sartre was convinced that intellectual writers should be 'engaged' in causes, that thoughts and social action are one. His classroom was the Café Flore and the Café des Deux Magots on the Left Bank more than the university. He had deep involvements with Marxism (reflected in *Critique de la raison dialectique*, 1960 [*Critique of Dialectical Reason*, 1976]), with the French Communist Party and the Soviet Union (manifest in his refusal to accept the Nobel Prize), and he was in the vanguard of various protest movements: bitterly opposed to French colonialism (Indochina, and particularly Algeria) and American imperialism in Vietnam, as well as the Soviet intervention in Czechoslovakia in 1968. His existential perspective made him the champion of all whose liberty he saw as deprived by inauthentic society, whether the oppressed were homosexuals (*Saint Genet, comédien et martyr* (1952) (*Saint Genet, Actor and Martyr*, 1964), or Jews (*Anti-Semite and Jew*, 1948), or Blacks ('Black

Orpheus' in an anthology of poems edited by Senghor), or colonial victims (introduction to F. Fanon's *Wretched of the Earth*). He sided with revolutionary and protest movements (China, Cuba, the May 1968 student movement), because in their projects he saw the possibility of human freedom being realized for all. His direct influence on the social sciences was meagre, but his moral influence on a great many social scientists and on a wider public was immense. As Marcuse said of him, Sartre was 'the conscience of the world'.

Edward A. Tiryakian
Duke University, North Carolina

Further Reading
Craib, I. (1976), *Existentialism and Sociology: A Study of Jean-Paul Sartre*, Cambridge.
Hayim, G. J. (1980), *The Existential Sociology of Jean-Paul Sartre*, Amherst, Mass.
Stack, G. J. (1977), *Sartre's Philosophy of Social Existence*, St Louis.
Tiryakian, E. A. (1979), *Sociologism and Existentialism*, New York.
See also: *existential psychology*.

Saussure, Ferdinand de (1857–1913)

Although linguistics existed as a science as early as the beginning of the nineteenth century, Ferdinand de Saussure, born in 1857 in Geneva, son of an eminent Swiss naturalist, is generally regarded as the founder of modern linguistics. Saussure's *Cours de linguistique générale*, 1916 (*Course in General Linguistics*, New York, 1959) is the most important of all linguistic works written in Western Europe in the twentieth century. Yet it was first published only after his death and was an edited version of notes taken by his students of lectures he gave in Geneva between 1907 and 1911. After having spent ten productive years (1881–91) teaching in Paris (before returning to a chair at Geneva, where he remained until his death), Saussure became increasingly perfectionist, and this prevented him from presenting any treatment of linguistics in the form of a book, since he found it impossible to write anything at all, on such a difficult subject, which he regarded as worthy of publication. This combination of modesty and painful consciousness may explain why he only produced two books in his lifetime, both of them when he was still young, and both in comparative and Indo-European grammar, and not in theoretical linguistics. His first book, published in 1879, when he was only twenty-one, was written in Leipzig while he was attending the lectures of two important Neo-grammarians, Leskien and Curtius. His brilliant insights into the vexed question of the Indo-European resonants brought him immediate fame. The second book was

his doctoral dissertation (1880), and was concerned with the absolute genitive in Sanskrit.

Saussure's major contribution is to theoretical linguistics. Yet his writings on the subject are confined to the *Cours*, and then only in the introduction, in Part One 'Principes généraux', and in Part Two, 'Linguistique synchronique', the remainder of the book, albeit suggestive, not having enjoyed equivalent fame. His theory is characterized by the famous distinctions he introduced, which were adopted later by all linguists, and by his conception of the linguistic sign.

After distinguishing the study of all social institutions from semiology, as the study of sign systems, then semiology itself from linguistics, and finally the study of language in general from the study of specific human languages, Saussure arrives at the distinctions which have deeply influenced all linguistic thinking and practice in this century. These are:

(1) *Langue* versus *parole*, that is, a distinction between, on the one hand, language as a social resource and inherited system made up of units and rules combining them at all levels, and, on the other hand, speech as the concrete activity by which language is manifested and put to use by individuals in specific circumstances. Saussure states that linguistics proper is linguistics of *langue*, even though we may speak of a linguistics of *parole* and despite the fact that the use of speech alters language systems themselves in the course of history. In fact, he only considers linguistics of *langue* in the *Cours*.

(2) *Synchrony* versus *diachrony*: Saussure repeatedly emphasizes that linguistics, like any other science dealing with values (see below), must embrace two perspectives. A synchronic study is conducted without consideration of the past and it deals with the system of relationships which is reflected in a language as a collective construct. A diachronic study deals mostly with unconscious historical change from one state to another.

(3) *Syntagmatic* versus *associative* relationships: a syntagm is defined as a combination of words in the speech chain, and it ties together elements that are effectively present, whereas the relationships called *associative* by Saussure (and, later, 'paradigmatic' by Hjelmslev) unite absent terms belonging to a virtual mnemonic series. Thus, the word *teaching* has an associative relationship with the words *education*, *training*, *instruction*, and so on, but a syntagmatic relationship with the word *his* in the syntagm *his teaching*. Saussure adds that the very best type of syntagm is the sentence, but he says that sentences belong to *parole* and not to *langue*, so that they are excluded from consideration. This attitude, although

consistent, was to have serious consequences for structural linguistics, as it is the reason for its almost total neglect of syntax.

Saussure defines the linguistic sign as a double-faced psychic entity which comprises the concept and the acoustical image. These he calls the *signifié* and the *signifiant*. The sign has two fundamental material characteristics. First, it is arbitrary. There is no internal and necessary relationship between the signifié and the signifiant; if there were any, then, to take an example [ks] would be the only possible signifiant for the meaning 'ox'. Thus different languages would not exist in the world. Second, the signifiant is linear: it is uttered along the time dimension, which is a line, and it is not possible to utter more than one sign at the same time. Saussure adds that the whole mechanism of language relies on this essential principle.

Saussure then goes on to treat the notion of *'value'* (*valeur*), which is the status of a linguistic unit in relation to other units, from the very existence of which it draws its definition, so that value and identity are two notions that can be equated. Therefore, in language, as Saussure says in a formula that was to become very famous, 'there are only differences'. For example, since English *sheep* coexists, in the language, with *mutton*, whereas there is nothing comparable as far as the French *mouton* is concerned, *sheep*, although meaning *mouton*, has a different value.

Saussure's theory, despite its uncompleted form, has been very influential. The phonology of the Prague School and Hjelmslevian glossematics, to mention only two examples, owe much to it. Even some of the gaps have been indirectly useful. Thus, the absence of the sentence has been compensated for by transformational syntax, and the nontreatment of the linguistics of *parole* by the development of pragmatics.

Claude Hagège
École Pratique des Hautes Études
University of Paris

References
Saussure, F. de (1879), *Mémoire sur le système primitif des voyelles dans les langues indo-européennes*, Leipzig.
Saussure, F. de (1880), *De l'emploi du génitif absolu en sanscrit*, Geneva.
Saussure, F. de (1916), *Cours de linguistique générale*, Paris.

Further Reading
Amacker, R. (1975), *Linguistique saussurienne*, Paris and Geneva.
Culler, J. (1976), *Saussure*, Glasgow.
Engler, R. (ed.) (1968–74), *Ferdinand de Saussure, Cours de linguistique générale*, Wiesbaden.
See also: *linguistics*; *semiotics*.

Say's Law of Markets

Say's Law of Markets is named after the French economist Jean-Baptiste Say. It refers to the belief that a free, competitive market automatically creates full employment of both labour and capital. The Law states that unemployment of either labour or capital is a result of a market disequilibrium and that the unfettered operation of the forces of supply and demand will eliminate all market disequilibria.

Say's Law was accepted by most of the classical economists, particularly Adam Smith and David Ricardo, and by most adherents to the orthodox neoclassical school of economic theory (from 1870 to the present). Economists who have rejected the law include Thomas Robert Malthus, Karl Marx, and John Maynard Keynes.

Say's Law presumes that in a market economy at any point in time there is a clearly defined set of prices for all items capable of being exchanged. Within the context of this set of prices, a desire to engage in exchange by someone who owns an exchangeable commodity is defined as a supply of the commodity the individual wishes to give up and a demand for a quantity of another commodity which represents *the value equivalent* of the amount of the commodity that is being supplied (the value equivalence being defined only with respect to the existing set of prices). Therefore, each desire to exchange is simultaneously a supply and a demand of identical value magnitudes. If such desires to exchange are the only components of the social aggregate supply, it follows that aggregate demand and aggregate supply must be equal.

In this view, there can be a market disequilibrium in which an excess supply for any commodity exists or an excess supply of labour exists, but given the necessary equality of aggregate demand and aggregate supply, it follows that the value of all excess supplies in all such markets must be exactly offset by a corresponding set of markets in which excess demands exist. The problem is then seen as a wrong or disequilibrium set of prices. The prices in markets with excess supply are too high and the prices in markets with excess demand are too low.

It is argued, however, that excess supply tends to lower prices, while excess demand tends to raise prices. Therefore, the problem is self-correcting and the market tends to an equilibrium in which there is full employment of capital and labour. It follows that Say's Law tends to support the *laissez-faire* economic philosophy which generally provides an intellectual rationale for minimizing the role of government in the market place. Those who reject Say's Law (for example, the followers of Keynes) often support a more active role for government in the market place.

E. K. Hunt
University of Utah

Scaling

A social scientist may occasionally be dealing with numerical data representing counts or measurements, but more often with categorical data that can be classified according to some criterion. Categorical data can be bi-categorical (dichotomous) where only two alternatives for a response are available such as yes or no, right or wrong, agree or disagree; they are multi-categorical (polychotomous) where more than two alternatives are available, for example, strong agreement, agreement, neutral, disagreement and strong disagreement. Scaling is defined as assigning numerical values to objects of study – individuals, stimuli, response alternatives or whatever – on the basis of a so-called model of scaling which must be consistent with the data. Such a model may be deterministic or probabilistic.

The basic assumption of all models of scaling, whether deterministic or probabilistic, is that the objects in question can be arranged on one or more underlying or latent continua. In the case of a single latent continuum one speaks of a unidimensional model, and in the case of more continua, of a multidimensional model. The notion of an underlying continuum, whose reality is not directly observable but whose existence is postulated, is essential. Other types of models are conceivable and in fact exist. It may be that the notion of a continuum, though given, is directly observable, such as length measured by means of a yardstick; or it may be that rather than a continuum there exists another underlying mathematical 'object', such as a graph. In such cases one does not speak of scaling in the strict sense of the word.

Models of scaling assume at least one latent continuum, which is referred to as the scale. The objects being studied are represented by points on the scale. Two different possible relations defined upon the points are of importance. In some instances the only thing that counts is the question of whether a point is situated to the right of another point. Such a relation is called an order or dominance relation on points. But what may also be relevant is the nearness or proximity of two points. Such a relation will be called a proximity relation. These relations, whether of dominance or proximity, can also be defined upon the distances between points; however, models with a proximity relation on distances have not yet appeared in the literature. Another distinction is related to the probabilistic nature of the model. One may assume that the position of the point, representing an object on the continuum, is fixed (deterministic models) or random (probabilistic models). Depending on the specific model employed, observations can be classified according to eight kinds of data (see Coombs, 1964).

The capital Q in Table 1 is the first letter of the word quadrant. The distinction between a- and b-data

Table 1

The objects come from	Relation between points	Relation between distances
Two sets	single stimulus data: QIIa / QIIb	preferential choice data: QIa / (QIb)
One set	stimulus comparison data: QIIIa / QIIIb	similarities data: QIVa / (QIVb)

corresponds to the type of relation assumed. In the case of a-data we have an order relation. In the case of b-data it is a proximity relation. For each type of data one has deterministic and probabilistic models. Parentheses refer to data where hardly any models are available. Well-known examples are:

QIa-data:
Coomb's unfolding analysis (Coombs, 1964) which is deterministic and Zinnes and Grigg's probabilistic, multidimensional unfolding analysis (Zinnes and Griggs, 1974);

QIb-data:
no models available yet;

QIIa-data:
Guttman's scalogram analysis (Coombs, 1964), the multidimensional conjunctive-disjunctive and compensatory models (Coombs, 1964) which are deterministic, the logistic model (Lord and Novick, 1968), the normal ogive model (Lord and Novick, 1968) and the Rasch model (Fischer, 1977) which are probabilistic;

QIIb-data:
Coombs's parallelogram analaysis (Coombs, 1964) which is deterministic;

QIIIa-data:
Coombs's triangular analysis (Coombs, 1964) which is deterministic, Thurstone's Model for Comparative Judgment (see Coombs, 1964) and Luce's Choice Model (Coombs, 1964) in many texts referred to as the BTL or Bradley-Terry-Luce model, which both are probabilistic;

QIIIb-data:
the Goodman-Galanter model (Coombs, 1964) which is deterministic and Hefner's model (Coombs, 1964) which is probabilistic;

QIVa-data:
Multidimensional Scaling (Shepard, Romney and Nerlove, 1972), which is deterministic and a multidimensional extension of the model of Zinnes and Griggs mentioned above;

QIVb-data:
Pfanzagl's bisection system (1968), a deterministic model only used in psychophysics.

The models mentioned here as examples hardly represent an exhaustive survey of all the models published in the literature.

The normal ogive model, the logistic model and the Rasch model are usually referred to as ICC models (ICC = item characteristic curve). According to an ICC model the probability of a certain response R is determined by a fixed-scale position for the subject representing his 'ability' and a monotonically increasing function dependent on the item (or stimulus) representing its 'difficulty'. This requires further explanation. According to QIIa data models we have a random scale position $s(i)$ of subject i and a random scale position $s(j)$ of item j both distributed according to some probability distribution. Italicized letters will refer here to random variables. As a result the distribution of the difference $s(j) - s(i)$ also has a certain probability distribution. Usually the assumption is made that $s(j)$ and $s(i)$ are stochastically independent. The probability that subject i reacts to item j with response R is equal to the value of the distribution function of the difference $s(j) - s(i)$ at the point zero. ICC models are a special case of QIIa models under the assumption that the distribution of $s(i)$ only differs in a location parameter a_i:

$$s(i) = a_i + s.$$

Thus the distribution of s does not depend on i but may depend on j. Then the ICC coincides with the distribution function of $s(j) - s$. Let G be defined by

$$G(a_i) = P[\,s(j) - s(i) < 0\,] = P[\,s(j) - s < a_i\,]$$

then it is obvious that G represents the ICC.

Many numerical scales in psychology are not arrived at by means of a model relating a latent continuum to manifest data, but are generated instead by the subjects directly according to some specified instruction. Well-known examples are the so-called quantitative judgement methods described by Torgerson (1958). However, these methods also make assumptions concerning the numbers produced by the subjects. If these assumptions have testable consequences, then they should be tested in order to validate the procedure.

A. H. G. S. van der Ven
Catholic University of Nijmegen

References
Coombs, C. H. (1964), *A Theory of Data*, New York.
Fischer, G. H. (1977), 'Linear logistic test models: theory and application', in H. Spada and W. F. Kempf (eds), *Structural Models of Thinking and Learning*, Berne.
Lord, F. M. and Novick, M. R. (1968), *Statistical Theories of Mental Test Scores*, Reading, Mass.
Pfanzagl, J. (1968), *Theory of Measurement*, New York.
Shepard, R. N., Romney, A. K. and Nerlove, S. B. (1972), *Multidimensional Scaling, Theory and Applications in the Behavioral Sciences*, New York.
Torgerson, W. S. (1958), *Theory and Methods of Scaling*, New York.
Zinnes, J. L. and Griggs, R. A. (1974), 'Probabilistic, multidimensional unfolding analysis', *Psychometrika*, 39.
See also: *categorical data.*

Schizophrenia

The technical term for madness, psychosis, refers to a mental state in which a person perceives, thinks, and/or behaves in strange ways. Thus, the psychotic person may hear voices that other people do not perceive (auditory hallucinations), have beliefs that others would consider irrational (delusions), behave in strange ways, such as carrying around a bag with small bits of paper, or have difficulties in thinking clearly, such as having thoughts follow each other in a disorganized fashion.

Schizophrenia is one form of madness or psychosis. It is the disorder marked by a psychotic state or states and identified especially by certain characteristic symptoms. These symptoms include particular kinds of auditory hallucinations and certain delusions, such as feeling controlled by an outside force. Bizarre behaviour and formal thought disorder are also common. However, since these symptoms can also be found in other types of psychosis, the diagnosis of schizophrenia is frequently one of exclusion – having a psychosis in which affective symptoms (depression or elation) are not predominant, and where no organic origin has been identified. Another criterion often included for diagnosing schizophrenia is that the condition continue for at least several months.

Perhaps because it is such a terrifying disorder, there are many existing beliefs about schizophrenia that far outdistance the available information. Thus, for example, people who are not mental health professionals often believe that schizophrenia means a split personality, or that it involves only people who are totally 'out of touch with reality'. Such views are either incorrect and/or oversimplifications, and thus neither do justice to the complexities of the disorder nor to the basic humanity of the people afflicted with it.

Other common but distorted beliefs about schizophrenia are that it is entirely hereditary, that patients never recover, and that people who have it are totally incapacitated. Although research suggests that there may be a genetic component in the causation of schizophrenia, it is likely that those genetic characteristics make a person vulnerable to developing schizophrenia rather than causing the disorder as such. In fact, schizophrenia appears to be caused by a wide range of biological factors and life experiences, probably acting together in ways that are not currently understood.

It has often been believed that people with schizophrenia do not recover, but a group of longitudinal studies has now demonstrated the inaccuracy of this notion. While many patients have the disorder over a long period of time, about 60 per cent of people diagnosed as schizophrenic recover completely or have only limited residual impairment.

Finally, although many people with schizophrenic disorders are impaired severely, at least for periods of time, with treatment and rehabilitation it is often possible for such persons to return to the community and function effectively.

Certain hallucinations, delusions, bizarre behaviour, and 'formal' thought disorder are indicative of schizophrenia, but it is important to note that this condition is not totally different from more normal human experience. There are, for example, degrees of intermediate states between florid schizophrenia and normal behaviour, and many of these states are considered normal. The existence of these intermediate states suggests that many manifestations of schizophrenia and other psychoses may be extremes on continua of functioning, functioning that may be found in people who are normal and not psychotic. Thus, the person who has been paged by name all day on a loudspeaker system may hear his name being called at night after leaving the building where the system operates. Sometimes people believe that someone in their organization is out to ruin them when there is little evidence for this. There are particular types of religious beliefs that may or may not be based in reality. Some behaviours which appear strange may nevertheless have a purpose. A person who has just heard some shocking news or encounters some other kind of highly unusual situation may be disorganized in his thinking for a brief period.

Treatments of schizophrenia focus both on direct control of symptoms and on countering the underlying causes, although it is not certain that treatments supposedly directed at the causes do in fact operate in that way. Antipsychotic medications are pre-eminent among the treatments focused more directly on symptom reduction or elimination. These do not merely 'tranquillize' or sedate the person generally, but appear to have a more specific action tending to reduce the psychotic symptoms themselves, at least in some patients. Although the development of these medications has been an important advance in the treatment of schizophrenia, there is a growing opinion that they do not resolve the basic processes of the disorder. There has also been increasing concern about the side effects of these medications. Some of these effects, such as abnormal involuntary movements of the face and other parts of the body, may not appear until after a prolonged use and then may be irreversible.

There is evidence to suggest that certain kinds of personal or social treatments are also helpful for schizophrenia. Thus, hospitalization that temporarily provides an environment with reduced stimulation, and the more reality-oriented forms of group and individual psychotherapy appear to be helpful. The acquisition of insight and interpersonal and occupational skills may help reduce the person's vulnerability to recurrence of psychosis. If a particular stressful event or situation appears to have contributed to a recurrence of the psychotic state, it may also be helpful to assist the person to understand and/or change that circumstance.

Schizophrenia is a shocking and striking condition, causing much agony for the individual, as well as for family, friends, and co-workers. Because schizophrenia relates to the human condition more generally in so many ways, it also has much to teach us about biology, psychology and social attachments. Considerable progress has been made in understanding and treating this condition, but much remains to be learned.

John S. Strauss
Yale University

Further Reading
Kaplan, H., Freedman, A. and Sadock, B. (1980), *Comprehensive Textbook of Psychiatry*, 3rd edn, Baltimore.
Strauss, J. S. and Carpenter, W. T. Jr (1982), *Schizophrenia*, New York.
See also: *genetic aspects of mental illness; psychiatry; psychopharmacology.*

Schultz, Theodore W. (1902–)

Over a long and active life, T.W. Schultz has been scholar, teacher, research entrepreneur, intellectual catalyst, and counsellor on a world scale. Starting from an early leadership in agricultural economics that has continued for half a century, Schultz went on to spark the human investment revolution in economics, and these themes are joined in his work on economic development. Throughout his career Schultz has been motivated by policy concerns. While intellectual curiosity is always there, to him the enlargement of understanding is exciting and valued in proportion to the ultimate potential contribution of that understanding to human welfare. Recognition of the quality and breadth of his service brought him the Distinguished Fellow Award from the American Economic Association, the infrequently awarded Francis A. Walker

Medal, and a Nobel Prize in Economics (in 1979, together with W.A. Lewis).

During the depression years and the devastating droughts of the 1930s, Schultz was writing extensively on problems of adjustment in agriculture and encouraging colleagues and students to explore strategies that could smooth adjustments to economic fluctuations and vagaries of weather. In addition to Schultz's own writings, culminating in his *Agriculture in an Unstable Economy* (1945), the intellectual harvests from this leadership spread widely and continue to be garnered.

Believing firmly in the basic shrewdness and rationality alike of farm people of his native land (in mid-America) and peasants of the Third World, Schultz has always emphasized the critical importance of incentives (price and other signals) appropriate to the efficient allocation of resources to and within agriculture. He demonstrated the perverse effects of 'parity' farm programmes on distributions of income and wealth within agriculture in the United States. In more recent years, he has pointed repeatedly to the unfortunate consequences in less-developed countries of price-depressing marketing arrangements and assorted taxes that have distorted agricultural production and held back economic development generally.

Schultz's initial ideas about investment in human beings, progressively developed by him and by others over the past two decades, have spawned a remarkable diversity of research endeavours: in development economics, agricultural economics, labour economics, economic history, international economics, urban economics. His first writings on education built on economic decision theory, with the apparatus of rates of return and opportunity costs, but in applications to economic growth (Schultz, 1958; 1960; 1961). The breadth of his thinking is illustrated by the symposium he organized, bringing together many facets of investments in people (Schultz, ed., 1962).

A comparatively recent article, and one of his most famous, is Schultz's 'The value of the ability to deal with disequilibria' (1975). The emphasis is on effects of education viewed explicitly in a world of uncertainties and change, but the ideas expressed here are deeply imbedded in his approach to development and to agricultural development in particular. They were anticipated in part in his 1964 book on *Transforming Traditional Agriculture*. That book attacks systematically the 'zero marginal product' hypothesis in discussions of the role of agriculture and labour supplies in the industrialization of less-developed nations. Among those who were not participants in the 'zero marginal product' controversy, this book probably is best known for its emphasis on the efficiency of farmers in traditional agriculture given the knowledge and resources available to them. The two points are closely entwined, since he was attempting in part to break down what he saw as pervasive distortions in notions

of what 'other people', and peasant farmers in particular, are like. But this was only a first step toward his positive argument: the idea of inexpensive *new sources of permanent income streams* as the key to entry on a path of dynamic development. In a sweeping generalization, by the simple idea of turning rates of return around to get prices of future income streams and combining this twist with the 'permanent income' concept, Schultz gained powerful leverage for the analysis of economic growth. He has applied this not merely to education but also, emphatically, to the importance of research and innovation. Indeed, it is only with the latter that education can yield substantial returns through the 'ability to deal with disequilibria'.

Mary Jean Bowman
University of Chicago

References
Schultz, T. W. (1945), *Agriculture in an Unstable Economy*, New York.
Schultz, T. W. (1958), 'Human wealth and economic growth', *The Humanist*, 19.
Schultz, T. W. (1960), 'Capital formation by education', *Journal of Political Economy*, 68.
Schultz, T. W. (1961), 'Education and economic growth', in N.B. Henry (ed.), *Social Forces Influencing American Education*, Chicago, National Society for Study of Education, Yearbook 60 (2).
Schultz, T. W. (ed.) (1962), *Investment in Human Beings*. *Journal of Political Economy*, Supplement 70 (5), Part II.
Schultz, T. W. (1964), *Transforming Traditional Agriculture*, New Haven.
Schultz, T. W. (1975), 'The value of the ability to deal with disequilibria', *Journal of Economic Literature*, 13.

Further Reading
Bowman, M. J. (1980), 'On Theodore W. Schultz's contributions to economics', *The Scandinavian Journal of Economics*, 82.

Schumpeter, Joseph Alois (1883–1950)

Schumpeter, who belongs to the top layer of eminent twentieth-century economists, cannot be easily assigned to a definite school or branch of economics. His outstanding characteristics were his broad erudition, his interdisciplinary thinking, combining economic theory with sociology and history, and his immense capacity for mastering plentiful and difficult materials.

Throughout his life he was attracted by the problem which dominated the thinking of the classical economists and of Marx: the long-term dynamics of the capitalist system. He saw one of the main sources of growth (and profits) in the existence of 'risk-loving' entrepreneurs who, by pioneering new products, new production methods and so on, are destroying old structures and inducing change. This idea was already propounded in his early *Theorie der wirtschaftlichen Entwicklung*, 1912, (*Theory of Economic Development*, 1951), and then came up repeatedly, particularly in his monumental two-volume study on all aspects of the business-cycle – theoretical, statistical, historical (*Business Cycles*, 1939). The intertwining of economic, sociological and political factors and their influence on long-term trends was treated in a more popular fashion in *Capitalism, Socialism and Democracy* (1942), which became an outstanding success. After Schumpeter's death, his widow. Elizabeth Boody, edited the unfinished *History of Economic Analysis* (1954), an enormous and unique tableau of economic thought from earliest times till today.

The numerous economic and sociological publications by Schumpeter, which included seventeen books, were produced in his academic career which led him from provincial universities in the Habsburg Empire (Czernowitz, Graz) to the University of Bonn (1925), and finally to Harvard University (1932). In between he had an unlucky spell as Minister of Finance and private banker in inflation-ridden Austria just after World War I.

Kurt W. Rothschild
Johannes Kepler University, Linz

Further Reading
Frisch, H. (ed.) (1981), *Schumpeterian Economics*, Eastbourne.
Harris, S. E. (ed.) (1951), *Schumpeter: Social Scientist*, Cambridge, Mass.
See also: *Austrian School*.

Schütz, Alfred (1899–1959)

Alfred Schütz was born and educated in Vienna where he completed his university studies (with Hans Kelsen, Ludwig von Mises, Friedrich von Wieser) in 1920 with a degree in financial law. Rather than pursuing an academic career, Schütz entered the world of banking as an apprentice with Bankverein Wien moving through the ranks up to a reputed international position. After Hitler's *Anschluss* of Austria, he left with his family for Paris, and later, in 1939, emigrated to New York. Schütz perceived the societal and political dissolution of Europe as a disintegration of its social fabric. From his early studies, he turned to the work of Henri Bergson, Edmund Husserl, Max Scheler, and Max Weber. However, by personal choice and because of economic hardships consequent upon his American exile, Schütz led a double existence as a banker and philosopher aiding and assisting many to escape before the holocaust closed in upon Europe. Only in the last decades of his life did Schütz, the social philosopher, also become a teacher. The Graduate Faculty of the New School for Social Research in New York (founded as a University in Exile by Alvin Johnson and Emil Lederer in 1933) invited Schütz to teach in 1943, first as lecturer without pay, then from 1952 on as professor of sociology and social psychology. The importance of his work for the study of action, knowledge and symbols in everyday life, and his impact on contemporary theory and methodology of the social sciences unfolded in his later teaching years and especially through posthumous publications (*Collected Papers I–III*, The Hague, 1962–6).

The fabric of everyday life can neither be sustained by the warp of scientific culture nor by the woof of historical traditions. It depends on human actions. This leitmotiv of Schütz's work first emerged in *Der sinnhafte Aufbau der sozialen Welt* (1932) (*The Phenomenology of the Social World*, 1967). Schütz analysed the mundane processes constituting the world of modern man which he later defended in his famous Harvard Lecture (1940) and in the subsequent bitter dispute with Talcott Parsons (*The Theory of Social Action*, 1978). Schütz overturned the traditional opposition between common sense and theory formation, showing that the latter is just one cognitive style within multiple finite provinces of meaning, all being founded in the paramount reality of everyday life. His study, *Don Quixote, The Problem of Reality* (first published in Spanish in 1955, and reprinted in *Collected Papers II*) is considered the masterpiece on this theme.

Schütz developed his work in discourse and dialogue, reflecting most of his ideas in extensive correspondences with Eric Voegelin and Felix Kaufman, trusted friends from the Vienna days, and with Aron Gurwitsch, whom he had met in Paris, and others. This group of emigrant scholars initiated what has come to be called Social Phenomenology, a merger of Continental Phenomenology with American Pragmatist social thought.

Richard Grathoff
University of Bielefeld

Further Reading
Grathoff, R. (1978), 'Alfred Schütz', in D. Käsler (ed.), *Klassiker des soziologischen Denkens*, Vol. II, Munich.
Natanson, M. (ed.), *Phenomenology and Social Reality: Essays in Memory of Alfred Schütz*, The Hague.
Schütz, A. (1962–6), *Collected Papers*, 3 Vols, The Hague.
Schütz, A. and Luckmann, T. (1974), *The Structures of the Life World*, London.
Wagner, H. R. (1983), *Alfred Schütz: An Intellectual Biography*, Chicago.
See also: *phenomenology*.

Science, Sociology of

The practitioners of the sociology of science, as it is currently conceived, may be divided into two schools. One of these is primarily North American. It is centred around the work of Robert K. Merton (1973) and proceeds from the standpoint of structural-functionalism. The other, somewhat looser grouping, may be called 'constructivist' in its orientation and is closer to the European tradition of the sociology of knowledge. Internal differences between the members of the two schools make this a somewhat rough division, but it is accurate as a first approximation. The schools are divided by their selection of problems, their preferred research methods and theoretical style, the level of abstraction at which they work, and sometimes by the attitudes displayed towards their subject matter, namely science itself. As might be expected from this characterization, members of the two schools often experience some difficulty in understanding and sympathizing with the efforts of their counterparts. In short, we have something like two Kuhnian 'paradigms' whose adherents are struggling for mastery of the field.

The Functionalist School

The functionalist approach sees pure, or academic, science as a social institution whose 'goal' is the extension of 'certified knowledge'. This goal, which represents a 'value' for members of the institution, is assumed to give rise to certain 'institutional imperatives'. These may be codified in terms of the 'norms' of science which, with some additions and modifications, have been identified as follows: (1) The norm of *organized scepticism* enjoins the critical scrutiny of all knowledge claims. (2) The norm of *universalism* requires of scientists that, when they assess knowledge claims, they ignore all 'particularistic' factors like the race, sex, nationality and religion of the claimant, and confine themselves to rational, scholarly and technical criteria. (3) The norm of *communism* says that individual scientists do not own their discoveries. Knowledge is the common property of the scientific community. (4) The norm of *disinterestedness* enjoins the scientist to work for the sake of science and truth rather than for personal profit or fame.

This general picture is based on the idea that the success of science has been the result of its embodying these lofty ideals at the institutional level. Individual deviations, for example, lapses by scientists into the use of particularistic criteria in assessing the work of others, do not, by themselves, amount to a refutation. One reason is that individual deviations often cancel one another out. For example, 'organized scepticism' does not require every scientist to be sceptical on every occasion about every new claim. Even if every scientist were totally *unsceptical* about, say, his *own* ideas, the institutional norm would still be satisfied provided scientists were sceptical of *other* peoples's ideas, and there was sufficient diversity of opinion in the community as a whole. Furthermore, within this framework there are a number of responses available with which to analyse the more blatant deviations from the norms. The first and most obvious response is to deplore such behaviour as an impediment to the achievement of the institutional goal. In other words, it can be handled evaluatively as simply *bad* science, or *anti*-science. Thus it could be said that the Lysenko affair 'held back' Soviet genetics because it represented the intrusion of political considerations into what should have been a purely scientific question. A second, more sophisticated, response is to argue that some of the deviations are apparent rather than real and that, properly understood, the behaviour in question is 'functional'. This was the response made by Merton and others to the fact that prominent scientific careers are often marked by priority disputes, such as the famous dispute between Newton and Leibniz over the discovery of the calculus. At first glance a priority dispute seems to represent a notable lapse from the norms of communism and disinterestedness. The disputants are treating discoveries as pieces of property, and are clearly concerned with matters of reputation. It is therefore tempting to see priority disputes as no more than expressions of personal vanity. The sociological explanation that has been offered is that we should see in them the operation of the 'reward system' of science. The institution works as an exchange system in which 'gifts' of knowledge, or contributions to science, are rewarded by 'recognition'. A natural law may have the discoverer's name attached to it, or fellowships may be awarded along with prizes and medals. These are the currency of the system. A concern with priority then becomes the concern that genuine contributions receive a just reward. By keeping the exchange system unpolluted it ensures that the institution is functioning correctly in the light of its goals.

Concepts like 'recognition' and 'reward' are amenable to quantitative measure: prizes and degrees and research grants can be counted and ranked. The other term in the exchange, the 'contribution', is less easy to measure. The 'quantity' of scientific work contributed by an individual can be measured by the number of published papers and books (with due corrections for multiple authorship). 'Quality' is the problem. One operational definition that has been used is the frequency with which a published paper is cited by other scientists. Not all citations represent a positive expression of indebtedness, and some are made in the context of criticism; but these dangers are recognized by those who adopt this measure of quality and it has been put to ingenious and sophisticated use. The result has been to bring into prominence the highly stratified character of the scientific community: most scientists produce very few papers. High rates of productivity, in both quantity and quality, are the prerogative of very few scientists. The same highly skewed character applies to the distribution of reward: it is concentrated in a very few hands. This raises the question, crucial from the functionalist standpoint, of whether the two distributions are related in a 'fair' and 'rational' manner. The overall conclusion of researchers into this question is that rewards *are* 'fairly' distributed, that is, highly-cited work is highly rewarded. Furthermore, factors like the status of the institution from which the work comes seem to have only a marginal effect on recognition.

There are a number of other foci in the research of the functionalist school, for example, the 'communication system' of science, concerned with the passage of information through networks of specialists, and the 'peer review system' of science, whereby applicants for research grants are assessed by fellow specialists in the field. (The details of this research can be found in the references given below.) The aim of the present account is to sketch the broad outlines and style of the research rather than its detailed and sometimes controversial results. What it is important to know is that, despite the intrinsic interest of this work and the obvious efforts of its practitioners to proceed with scientific rigour, the reception that it has received has sometimes been cool. The reasons for this are clearly stated by the critics. The theoretical framework is vague and the level of abstraction is held to be too great. The result of these defects is that, all too often, the conclusions about the essential fairness and rationality of science seem to come a little too quickly. Critics say that there is no adequate consideration of how other underlying processes might have generated the data to be explained. For example, Mulkay (1980) has argued that the correlation of high citation and high reward might easily conceal patterns of differential access to resources and opportunities to pursue research. More generally, the complaint is that when scientific work is examined in detail the functionalist framework, especially the so-called 'norms' of science, become less and less illuminating. It is certainly noteworthy that the sociology of science, as the functionalists conceive it, is mostly the sociology of the scientist rather than the sociology of scientific knowledge. Examining the actual use of the norms of science – the occasions on which they are explicitly evoked – suggests that, rather then being determinants of behaviour, they are rhetorical resources to be used in a selective and justificatory fashion. Furthermore, the idea that scientists are 'socialized' into the norms and values of science (in the sense of 'internalizing' them), leads to the prediction that an academic training followed by a move into industrial science should lead to a 'value conflict'. Although this prediction may be weakened

by allowing for differential socialization and selective recruitment (illustrating the vagueness of the original theory), the evidence from the study of industrial scientists still does not lend much support to the hypothesis of value conflict. Findings such as these are cited by critics of Mertonian functionalism as justification of their initial scepticism.

The Constructivist School

The alternative to the functionalist paradigm has been to plunge into the detailed study of scientific activity. Contemporary and historical case studies have been used to address questions such as the following: how are theories selected and modified? How is experimental evidence assessed and brought into relation with theoretical claims? How do we create our sense of having an emerging awareness of an independent reality? Such enquiries soon reveal that there is a wealth of empirical material which has received no adequate response from the functionalists. A representative example of this style of work is the study of claims to have replicated, or failed to replicate, the experimental work of others. A functionalist would refer this to the norm of scepticism: what is replication but the form in which new experimental claims are subject to critical scrutiny? This response suffices on the general level, but the subject becomes more interesting if we enquire further. One such case is the controversy over gravity waves. What emerges is that a replication hardly ever consists in an attempt to repeat exactly what another scientist has done. In principle this would hardly be possible, and in practice there is usually an attempt to improve the experimental technique. There is therefore always a gap between the original and the replication. Thus the comparability of the results is always in principle open to dispute. It is always possible to say that the 'same' conditions do not prevail. Even if the apparatus is judged to be the same for all practical purposes, there is still the important variable of the competence of the experimenters. It transpires that these subtle problems are often decided by reasoning backwards from the outcome of the experiment. For example, if you accept the original experiment which appeared to detect gravity waves, then a failure to repeat the findings becomes an incompetent experiment, or one that must be 'different' in some crucial respect. On the other hand, if you began by doubting the original detection, then a failure to repeat the finding, even in somewhat different circumstances, becomes important evidence against the theory.

Functionalist critics sometimes dismiss such case-studies as if they were surveys with a sample size of N=1. They scoff at the allegedly 'philosophical' character of the method of argument and the conclusions drawn. In their defence 'constructivists' argue that case-studies can bring to light issues of a highly general character with profound implications for the focus of sociological curiosity. Thus the work on replication points to the important and problematic role of judgements of 'sameness'. Once noticed, this is a theme that emerges time and again. It is involved in every act of classification and identification. Since this includes the bringing of cases under general principles, it points immediately to the negotiable character of the functionalist's own 'norms' of science. More importantly it points to the 'work' that goes into unifying the fragmentary character of experience, and hence to the diversity of interests, traditions and goals that can inform the process of knowing. Sometimes these interests will be generated within the scientific community, but sometimes they have come from without, having reference to the broader political and social context of science. We therefore cannot define the 'goal' of science before we begin sociological enquiry. It is one of the virtues of the constructivist school that it has realized this, and hence treats as an empirical problem what the functionalists are tempted to settle *a priori*.

David Bloor
University of Edinburgh

References
Merton, R. K. (1973), *The Sociology of Science*, Chicago.
Mulkay, M. (1980), 'Sociology of science in the West', *Current Sociology*, 28.

Further Reading
Barnes, B. and Edge, D. (eds) (1982), *Science in Context: Readings in the Sociology of Science*, Milton Keynes.
Ben-David, J. (1981), 'Sociology of scientific knowledge', in J. F. Short (ed.), *The State of Sociology: Problems and Prospects*, Beverly Hills.
Ben-David, J. and Sullivan, T. A. (1975), 'Sociology of science', *Annual Review of Sociology*, 1.
Collins, H. M. (ed.) (1982), *Sociology of Scientific Knowledge: A Source Book*, Bath.
See also: *knowledge, sociology of*; *Kuhn*; *Merton*; *Popper*.

Sects and Cults

The sociological concepts of sect and cult usually refer to religious groups or quasi-groups – which may be large or small, with complex or simple forms of organization – that are regarded, by members and nonmembers alike, as deviant in relation to a wider cultural or doctrinal context. The deviance in question has negative connotations for non-adherents and positive connotations for adherents. It is necessary in this stipulation to mention quasi-groups as well as groups: groups regarded as sectarian tend to promote intra-group solidarity and personal identification with the group, while cultic quasi-groups do not systematically encourage group cohesion and explicit sharing of ideas.

Sects have been more frequently studied than cults, for two reasons: (1) For some purposes, it has often been found unnecessary to make a distinction between the two forms, and the more generic 'sect' has in that case been used by social scientists. (2) Even though sect has a clear history as a pejorative term (for long used within Christendom to denote heretical departures from official doctrine), sociologists in the twentieth century have used the term more or less nonjudgementally. That orientation has arisen from the scholarly view that the history of Christianity (and perhaps other major religious traditions) has been characterized by an interplay between *sectarian heterodoxy* and *churchly orthodoxy*, and from the argument that certain kinds of sectarian movement have been crucial in the development of Western notions of individualism and voluntary organization – notably Protestant sects of the seventeenth century.

In contrast, cults have not as such had an innovative impact on the wider society. They tend not to be solidary groups. Cults have typically offered particular, concrete benefits to their adherents rather than the comprehensive world-views and conceptions of salvation typical of religious sects. A complication in distinguishing between sects and cults became particularly evident in the 1970s, with the proliferation in a number of societies of controversial 'new religious movements' (many of them inspired by non-Western ideas or leaders). These became labelled as cults by journalists and leaders of movements which developed for the purpose of stimulating legal control of their activities, most notably their conversion techniques and methods of retaining recruits. But many of these new movements are, more accurately, sects from a sociological standpoint.

Yet the term *cultus* is probably much older than words linked to sect. That status derives from the fact that the traditional connotation of words linked to cult has focused upon religious *rituals and practices* (often of a magical, instrumental rather than a religious, celebratory kind), while sect has a shorter, clear-cut history because of its primary reference to deviant religious *doctrines*. The history of religious doctrines (intellectually systematized bodies of knowledge elaborated by religious specialists as orthodoxies) is confined to the period since the rise of the great world-religious traditions, such as Judaism, Christianity, Islam and Buddhism; while in periods and areas relatively untouched by the major religions of world significance, the more typical form of orientation to the superempirical world has taken the form of an emphasis on ritual practice and concrete religious action – within the context of, or in relation to, mythologies which have tended not to emphasize the notion of the salvation of the individual. In the mythological, as opposed to the doctrinal, context *a variety* of different rituals and practices – including magical ones directed at the obtaining of immediate, concrete (rather than long-term salvational) benefits – have typically arisen.

This does not mean that cultic phenomena have not appeared outside the relatively primitive contexts of predoctrinal mythology and *orthopraxis*. In fact we may illuminate an important aspect of the difference between sects and cults by pointing to the fact that while in medieval Christianity sect was used as a condemnatory way of talking about movements which were regarded officially as heretic – displaying intolerable heterodoxical tendencies – the Church could at the same time tolerate and even encourage *cults* devoted to the veneration of individuals who had been sanctified, often posthumously, as saints. Indeed the problem of heterodoxy (sectarian departure from official doctrine) was alleviated in the traditional Catholic Church by the carefully-monitored sanctioning of cultic practices – often of a more-or-less magical character – in such a way as to institutionalize heteropraxis (departure from official conceptions of religious ritual and concrete action). However, within the Christian Church of that time and within Catholicism since the Protestant Reformation of the sixteenth century, the tolerance of *orders* of priests and monks has constituted a form of institutionalized sectarianism, that is, the incorporation within the official conception of variations on and near-departures from doctrinal orthodoxy.

In the wake of the Reformation – and most particularly in those societies which became influenced by Protestantism – social and cultural circumstances arose which encouraged the flowering of a great variety of religious beliefs and practices, notably because those societies witnessed a considerable growth of religious individualism. Thus, whereas the notion of sect had developed almost entirely for the purpose of depicting violation of the dominant, official religious beliefs and values of *the church*, in societies extensively affected by Protestantism the relevance of a distinction between sect and church was greatly reduced, most notably in the US after that country achieved independence from Britain in the eighteenth century.

The modern study of deviant religious groups was initiated in Germany early in the present century by Max Weber (1930 [1922]) and Ernst Troeltsch (1931 [1908–11]). Weber, as a historical sociologist, was interested in the contribution of sectarian Christian movements to the development of modern conceptions of rationality and individualism; Troeltsch was, as a sociologically informed theologian, particularly interested in the interplay in Christian history between churchly orthodoxy and sectarian heterodoxy, with particular reference to the ways in which religion had in the past and could continue to have an impact on secular institutions. In spite of frequent references to Weber and/or Troeltsch, the typical student of religious movements during the past few decades has been interested in different kinds of question.

Much of the modern perspective can be traced to the influence of Richard Niebuhr. His book, *The Social Sources of Denominationalism* (1929), crystallized interest in the kinds of social and economic circumstances which pushed individuals into joining deviant religious movements, and in the degree to and manner in which religious sects moved away from deviant to a more mainstream position within the wider society. Under Niebuhr's influence, and with particular reference to American and British societies, the position has been characterized in terms of religious organizations of the *denominational* type. In that perspective denominations are seen as standing midway between the sect, which demands a great deal of involvement from its participants and stands in a negative relationship to the wider society, and the church, which is more central to the society and therefore does not typically demand that its members discipline themselves against the culture of the wider society (although it may do so in periods of rapid change). Sociologists, investigating these issues, concluded that sects which seek to convert as many members as possible are most likely to relinquish their original commitments, while those which emphasize esoteric doctrines are much less likely to do so (for which they 'pay' by remaining small). More recently, however, the study of sects has taken a new turn, while the study of cults – including the circumstances under which cults may become transformed into sects – has been revived.

The recent sociological focus upon sects and cults tends to be less directly concerned with the conceptual identification of sects and/or cults as distinctive types of religious organization than with the ways in which new religious movements arise, their methods of organizing their memberships and the critiques which they frequently offer with respect to modern societies. More specifically, whereas until recently the major sociological interest in sects and cults centred upon their esoteric nature and the conditions of their persistence or demise, the proliferation of many new religious movements in the early 1970s, and the rise to prominence of what are often called 'fundamentalist' religious movements in the late 1970s, has given rise to a broader set of sociological concerns about the nature and direction of change of modern societies. Among those concerns have been the relationship between religious movements and the modern state (not least because in some societies the state has sought to regulate the activities of new movements), and the extent to which the proliferation of new religious movements (and the revival of older ones) signals a global resurgence of religiosity.

Roland Robertson
University of Pittsburgh

References

Troeltsch, E. (1931 [1908–11]), *The Social Teachings of the Christian Churches*, London. (Original German edn, *Die Soziallehren der christlichen Kirchen und Gruppen*, Tübingen.)

Weber, M. (1930 [1922]), *The Protestant Ethic and the Spirit of Capitalism*, London. (Original German edn, *Die protestantische Ethik und der 'Geist' des Kapitalismus*, Tübingen.)

Further Reading

Barker, E. (ed.) (1982), *New Religious Movements: A Perspective for Understanding Society*, Lewiston, NY.

Robbins, T. and Anthony, D. (eds) (1981), *In Gods We Trust*, New Brunswick.

Robbins, T. *et al.* (ed.) (1985), *Cults, Culture and the Law*, Decatur, Georgia.

Robertson, R. (1980), *The Sociological Interpretation of Religion*, Oxford.

Wilson, B. (ed.) (1981), *The Social Impact of the New Religious Movements*, New York.

See also: *communal groups; religion and ritual.*

Secularization

Secularization refers to a displacement of religious beliefs, ritual, and sense of community from the moral life of society. Everyday experience in 'secularized' society tends to be carried on without routine invocations of the sacred. The major institutions of society become legitimated primarily by secular ideologies and formal legal doctrines rather than by religious ethics. Religious beliefs may continue to bestow a spiritual significance to basic social values (Parsons, 1974), but public moral issues are deliberated overtly within the frameworks of secular ideologies.

The rise of secularized societies in the modern era has had crucial sources within the traditions of Western Christianity itself. Christian thought of antiquity and the Middle Ages incorporated Hellenic rationalism and many of the civil and communal values of Graeco-Roman life. The inner-wordly asceticism and rationalism of the Reformation imparted a new ethical dignity to secular institutions (Weber, 1930 [1922]). The values of legal order, political freedom, individual autonomy, material well-being, and progressive reform of secular society, perhaps the key elements of modern secular ideologies, were thus synthesized and given respect within Christian doctrine.

It was, however, the philosophies of the Enlightenment that provided the pivotal impetus toward thoroughgoing secularization. They proposed that society should be founded on moral principles devised by rational inquiry into the universal nature of human social life. The rational principles of social organization were often presented as antithetical to religious traditions resting on faith (Gay, 1966). Antagonisms toward the established order were thus united with abstract hopes for a just future. A tense cultural dilemma arose over the question of whether social institutions should be legitimated in terms of moral rationalism or religious tradition. Rationalistic ideals in religion and conservative secular ideologies have since mediated the starkest alternatives. Yet, the Enlightenment established the moral authority of ideologies for evaluating economic, political, stratificational, and other social arrangements in terms independent of religious ethics. It elevated bodies of formally rational moral beliefs, designed as grounds for legitimating secular institutions, into a domain of culture functionally differentiated from religion (Lidz, 1979).

Sociologists have long debated whether or not secularized societies can maintain durable moral foundations. Some stress the difficulty of upholding strong social values and ethical principles without a basis in religious spirituality. Their starkest vision depicts secular society as caught lastingly in disorientation, anomie, absence of communal feeling, and spiritual poverty (Wilson, 1982). Others emphasize the encouragement to progress and social justice produced by moral thought devoted to the rational design of practical institutions. They portray secularization as a cognate of industrialization, democratization, urbanization, and other processes essential to the emergence of modern civilization.

Despite their rootedness in European culture, secular ideologies have taken on moral authority in many civilizations around the globe, somewhat in the manner of the world religions (Bellah, 1965). Marxism, intensely hostile to religion and established tradition, has highlighted the urgency of social change and the dignity of secular interests in societies on every continent. Liberal doctrines have promoted a variant of secular rationalism more closely tied to the workings of market economies, competitive democratic institutions, and procedurally formalized law, yet they have been more tolerant of traditionalistic 'establishments'. Our understanding of secularization will probably be much affected by the experiences of non-Western societies over the next several decades.

Victor Lidz
Haverford College, Pennsylvania

References

Bellah, R. N. (1965), 'Epilogue', in R. Bellah (ed.), *Religion and Progress in Modern Asia*, New York.

Gay, P. (1966), *The Enlightenment: An Interpretation; The Rise of Modern Paganism*, New York.

Lidz, V. (1979), 'Secularization, ethical life, and religion in modern societies', in H. Johnson (ed.), *Religious Change and Continuity*, San Francisco.

Parsons, T. (1974), 'Religion in postindustrial America', *Social Research*, 41.

Weber, M. (1930 [1922]), *The Protestant Ethic and the Spirit of Capitalism*, trans. T. Parsons, New York. (Original German edn, *Die protestantische Ethik und der 'Geist' des Kapitalismus*, Tübingen.)

Wilson, B. (1982), *Religion in Sociological Perspective*, London.

Further Reading

Martin, D. (1978), *A General Theory of Secularization*, New York.

See also: *civil religion; religion and ritual.*

Securities Markets

Securities may be distinguished by the type of issuer. *Primary securities* are issued by nonfinancial deficit-spending units to acquire real assets. *Secondary securities* are issued by financial intermediaries which issue their own secondary securities chiefly to households, typically through their retail outlets, in order to acquire primary securities from ultimate borrowers. Due to economies of scale in lending and borrowing, they are able to endow their own secondary securities with low risk, high divisibility, high liquidity, and a variety of assorted services-in-kind that make them more attractive than primary securities in the portfolios of ultimate wealth-owners. Intermediaries make a profit by lending at higher rates than they borrow. Commercial banks, savings institutions (such as building societies and savings and loan associations), insurance companies, pension funds, and mutual funds are the most important types of financial intermediaries.

Securities markets is a broad term embracing a number of markets in which securities are bought and sold. The broadest classification is based upon whether the securities they handle are new issues, or are already outstanding. New issues are sold in *primary markets;* securities that are already outstanding are bought and sold in *secondary markets.* Another classification is between fixed and variable income securities. Fixed income securities are traded in the *bond* or *bill markets.* Variable income securities are traded in organized *stock markets,* or *over-the-counter markets.* A final classification is by maturity. Securities with maturities of less than one year trade in the *money market;* those with longer maturities are bought or sold in the *capital market.*

Primary securities may be sold to lenders directly, but ordinarily, due to the high transactions costs involved in borrowers seeking out lenders, they are sold by businesses that specialize in selling securities: security underwriters (investment or merchant banks). Underwriters purchase securities directly from borrowers at one price, and sell them to lenders at a higher price. The difference is referred to as the underwriter's spread, which represents compensation for undertaking the distributional activities, and for absorbing the risk that goes along with guaranteeing the borrower a fixed price before the securities are actually placed in the hands of lenders.

New issues of common stock are sold by way of 'public offerings', that is to say, reoffered to the general public, with no one investor buying more than a small proportion of the issue. In contrast, a significant proportion of bond issues of corporations and municipalities are sold by 'direct placement' to one of a few large financial investors, usually insurance companies and pension funds. Common stock and many corporate bonds are sold on a negotiated basis, while most bonds of state and local governments and public utilities are sold on the basis of competitive bidding, in the expectation that this will lead to lower borrowing costs.

The prices and yields established in secondary markets provide the basis for the terms and conditions that will prevail in the primary markets. The yield of a bond is the return to an investor buying the bond at its current market price. If a bond sells in the market for more (or less) than its face value, the yield is less (or more) than the coupon rate which the bond bears. The return of a common stock is the dividend yield (dividend-price ratio) plus the expected capital gain, which if the dividend yield is constant will be equal to the rate of growth of the dividend stream. In addition, the existence of secondary markets permits securities to be liquidated, that is, turned into cash at relatively low cost. It is in this manner possible for the economy to make long-term commitments in real capital that are financed by savings of a short-term nature. By endowing financial assets with the characteristics of high liquidity, low risk and high marketability, secondary security markets, like financial intermediaries, enhance the attractiveness of securities for the portfolios of ultimate wealth-owners, and thus encourage saving by surplus spending units.

Secondary markets for corporate stock play an important role in guiding corporate investment decisions. Corporate managements must decide how much of their after-tax earnings they should pay out to the shareholders in dividends, and how much they should retain to reinvest in the business. In making this judgement, the expected returns from reinvestment in real assets must be compared with the return which shareholders could earn on the stock market. There is considerable evidence that mature corporations continue to reinvest internally-generated funds even when few profitable investment opportunities exist. Managers are likely to act in pursuit of their own self-interest, and their salaries and perks may be more closely related to corporate size. However, if corporate managers consistently reinvest when the expected return falls below the cost of funds, the value of the company's shares will fall on the stock markets, rendering the company increasingly attractive as a takeover candidate. This market for corporate control thus operates to ensure that overall capital allocation is efficient, by compelling inefficient managers to face the likelihood of takeover.

The stock market and the market for government bills and bonds are the most active secondary markets in terms of the volume of transactions. In contrast, the secondary markets for corporate and local government bonds are relatively inactive, even though brokers and dealers stand ready to make markets by quoting buying and selling prices for those who want to engage in exchange. For nonmarketable securities, such as bank loans, no secondary markets exist. In stock markets '*specialists*' stand ready to trade with those who demand immediate servicing of their orders, and thus improve a market's continuity and resilience or depth, by reducing the variability of transaction prices over time.

Secondary markets comprise both *organized exchanges*, and *over-the-counter* markets. Brokers operating on the floor of the exchange receive, buy and sell orders from the public, and then trade with Jobbers (specialists) who act both as agents and principals in a continuous auction process. Over-the-counter markets have no centralized location or limited number of members or 'seats'. They are characterized by freedom of access, and trading takes place through a complex system of telephone and teletype linkage, now being automated to keep a consolidated book of unfilled limit orders, and do a myriad of record-keeping and communication chores. Technology is likely to reduce the costs of search to the point where market perfection is closer at hand, so that all trades will be exposed simultaneously to all participants. What remains as yet unclear is whether computers will be used to replace dealers and specialists in the market-maker function.

As stated, market makers stand ready to provide liquidity in secondary markets by holding a buffer or inventory of securities in which they act as principals. However, in order to ensure the continuous liquidity of financial markets, a central bank must stand ready continually to purchase securities on demand in exchange for cash, in its central role of lender of last resort. Ultimately, in a crisis, the only securities which possess liquidity are those which the central bank is willing to purchase.

Basil J. Moore
Wesleyan University, Connecticut

Self-Concept

The self-concept has had a diversity of meanings, due in part to its multidisciplinary heritage. Philosophy and theology have emphasized the self as the locus of moral choices and responsibility. Clinical and humanistic psychologies have stressed the self as the basis of individual uniqueness and neurosis. Within sociology the self-concept has acquired an indelibly social character, with the emphasis on language and social interaction as the matrix for the emergence and maintenance of the self. The current popularity of self-concept within experimental social psychology places greater emphasis on its cognitive and motivational aspects, such as the self-concept as a source of motivation, as a performance aimed at managing impressions, and as a source of perceptual and cognitive organization.

At its core, the idea of self-concept or self-conception is based on the human capacity for reflexivity, frequently considered the quintessential feature of the human condition. Reflexivity or self-awareness, the ability of human beings to be both subjects and objects to themselves, can be conceptualized as the dialogue between the 'I' (for example, the self-as-knower) and the 'me' (the self-as-known), an internal conversation, which emerges (at both the ontogenetic and the phylogenetic levels) with the emergence of language – an argument extensively developed by G. H. Mead (1934). Language requires us to take the role of the other with whom we are communicating, and in the process enables us to see ourselves from the other's perspective.

Properly speaking, this process of reflexivity refers to the concept of self. The self-concept, on the other hand, is the *product* of this reflexive activity. It is the conception the individual has of himself as a physical, social, moral and existential being. The self-concept is the sum total of the individual's thoughts and feelings about himself as an object (Rosenberg, 1979). It involves a sense of spatial and temporal continuity of personal identity, a distinction of essential self from mere appearance and behaviour, and is composed of the various attitudes, beliefs, values, and experiences, along with their evaluative and affective components (such as self-evaluation or self-esteem), in terms of which individuals define themselves. In many respects the self-concept is synonymous with the concept of ego (see Sherif, 1968), although psychologists have preferred the latter term and sociologists the former. The various aspects of the self-concept can be grouped into two broad categories: (1) identities and (2) self-evaluations.

(1) The concept of identity focuses on the meanings constituting the self as an object, gives structure and content to the self-concept, and anchors the self to social systems. 'Identity' has had its own interesting and complex history in the social sciences. In general, it refers to who or what one is, to the varius meanings attached to oneself by self and others. Within sociology, identity refers both to the structural features of group membership which individuals internalize and to which they become committed, for example, various social roles, memberships, and categories, and to the various character traits that an individual displays and that others attribute to an actor on the basis of his

conduct in particular social settings. The structure of the self-concept can be viewed as the hierarchical organization of a person's identities, reflecting in large part the social and cultural systems within which it exists (Stryker, 1980).

(2) Self-evaluation (or self-esteem) can occur with regard to specific identities which an individual holds, or with regard to an overall evaluation of self. People tend to make self-evaluations on the basis of two broad criteria: their sense of competence or efficacy, and their sense of virtue or moral worth (Wells and Marwell, 1976; Gecas and Schwalbe, 1983).

Several processes have been identified as important to the development of self-concepts: reflected appraisals, social comparisons, self-attributions and role-playing. The most popular of these in sociology is reflected appraisals. Based on Cooley's (1902) influential concept of the 'looking-glass self' and Mead's theory (1934) of role-taking as a product of symbolic interaction, reflected appraisals emphasize the essentially social character of the self-concept, such as the idea that our self-conceptions reflect the appraisals and perceptions of others, especially significant others, in our environments. The process of reflected appraisals is the basis of the 'labelling theory' of deviance in sociology, and of self-fulfilling processes in social psychology.

Social comparison is the process by which individuals assess their own abilities and virtues by comparing them to those of others. Local reference groups or persons are most likely to be used as a frame of reference for these comparisons, especially under conditions of competition, such as athletic contests or classroom performance. Self-attributions refer to the tendency to make inferences about ourselves from direct observation of our behaviour. Bem's (1972) 'self-perception theory' proposes that individuals determine what they are feeling and thinking by making inferences based on observing their own overt behaviour. Role-playing as a process of self-concept formation is most evident in studies of socialization. It emphasizes the development of self-concepts through the learning and internalizing of various social roles (for example, age and sex roles, family roles, occupation roles).

The self-concept is both a product of social forces and, to a large extent, an agent of its own creation. Along with the capacity for self-reflexivity discussed earlier, the agentive aspect of the self-concept is most evident in discussions of self-motives (that is, the self-concept as a source of motivation). Three self-motives have been prominent in the social psychological literature: (1) self-enhancement or self-esteem motive; (2) self-efficacy motive; and (3) self-consistency motive.

(1) The self-esteem motive refers to the motivation of individuals to maintain or to enhance their self-esteem. It is manifest in the general tendency of persons to distort reality in the service of maintaining a positive self-conception, through such strategies as selective perception, reconstruction of memory, and some of the classic ego-defensive mechanisms.

(2) The self-efficacy motive refers to the importance of *experiencing* the self as a causal agent, that is, to the motivation to perceive and experience oneself as being efficacious, competent and con'sequential. The suppression or inhibition of this motive has been associated with such negative consequences as alienation, 'learned helplessness', and the tendency to view oneself as a pawn or victim of circumstances (see Gecas and Schwalbe, 1983).

(3) The self-consistency motive is perhaps the weakest of the three, yet it continues to have its advocates. Lecky (1945), an early advocate, viewed the maintenance of a unified conceptual system as the overriding need of the individual. Those theorists who view the self-concept primarily as an organization of knowledge, or as a configuration of cognitive generalizations, are most likely to emphasize the self-consistency motive. The self-concept as an organization of *identities* also provides a motivational basis for consistency, in that individuals are motivated to act in accordance with the values and norms implied by the identities to which they become committed.

In the past, the bulk of research on the self-concept has focused on self-esteem (see Wells and Maxwell, 1976; Wylie, 1979), that is, on the antecedents of self-esteem, the consequences of self-esteem, and the relationships between self-esteem and almost every other aspect of personality and behaviour. Much of this research focus continues to be evident. But there are noticeable trends in other directions as well. The most evident are: the dynamics of self-presentation and impression management in naturalistic and experimental settings; the development and the consequences of commitment to specific identities (especially gender, ethnic group, deviant, and age-specific); historical and social structural influences on self-conceptions (such as wars, depressions, cultural changes, and organizational complexity); and, increasingly, we find a focus on the effect of self-concept on social structure and social circumstances. The self-concept is rapidly becoming the dominant concern within social psychology (both the sociological and the psychological varieties), as part of the general intellectual shift from behavioural to cognitive and phenomenological orientations in these disciplines.

Viktor Gecas
Washington State University

References

Bem, D. J. (1972), 'Self-perception theory', in L. Berkowitz (ed.), *Advances in Experimental Social Psychology*, vol. 6, New York.

Cooley, C. H. (1902), *Human Nature and the Social Order*, New York.

Gecas, V. and Schwalbe, M. L. (1983), 'Beyond the looking-glass self: social structure and efficacy-based self-esteem', *Social Psychological Quarterly*, 46.

Lecky, P. (1945), *Self-Consistency: A Theory of Personality*, New York.

Mead, G. H. (1934), *Mind, Self and Society*, Chicago.

Rosenberg, M. (1979), *Conceiving the Self*, New York.

Sherif, M. (1968), 'Self-concept', in D. K. Sills (ed.), *International Encyclopedia of the Social Sciences*, vol. 14, New York.

Stryker, S. (1980), *Symbolic Interactionism: A Social Structural Version*, Menlo Park, Calif.

Wells, L. E. and Marwell, G. (1976), *Self-Esteem: Its Conceptualization and Measurement*, Beverly Hills, Calif.

Wylie, R. C. (1979), *The Self-Concept*, Lincoln, Neb.

Further Reading.
Gecas, V. (1982), 'The self-concept', *Annual Review of Sociology*, 8.

Rosenberg, M. (1979), *Conceiving the Self*, New York.
See also: *labelling*; *Mead, G. H.*

Semantic Differential

The semantic differential was developed by Charles Osgood and his colleagues at the University of Illinois during the 1950s as an objective method for the measurement of the connotative meaning of concepts. The aim was to produce a scaling instrument which gave representation to the major dimensions along which meaningful reactions or judgements vary, and which would allow any concept to be described in terms of those dimensions.

The method of investigation required informants to describe various concepts (for example, Psychology) on a series of scales, consisting of pairs of polar adjectives such as successful-unsuccessful, difficult-easy, or serious-humorous. This method is based on the proposition that many of these scales are essentially equivalent and represent a single dimension of meaning, and that only a limited number of dimensions are needed to define a semantic space within which the connotative meaning of any concept can be specified.

The empirical problem was to identify this limited set of dimensions, and then to demonstrate repeatedly, using different samples of concepts, descriptive scales and subjects, and different methods of data collection and analysis, that essentially the same set of dimensions appears, and appears with the dimensions having the same relationships to one another.

In the original empirical test of these propositions (Osgood and Suci, 1955) fifty-seven-step scales were used by 100 subjects to describe twenty different concepts. The ratings of each scale, averaged over both subjects and concepts, were then subjected to factor analysis to summarize the pattern of correlations of scales with scales.

The analysis produced three factors which were termed:

Evaluation (such as good-bad, beautiful-ugly, clean-dirty)

Potency (such as large-small, strong-weak, heavy-light) and

Activity (such as fast-slow, active-passive, sharp-dull).

In numerous subsequent studies, these same three factors repeatedly emerge, indicating the stability of the underlying dimensions of semantic judgement. They regularly account for some 50 per cent of the total variance, with Evaluation the major factor, accounting for double the variance of either the Potency or Activity factors. In each study the variance which remains is taken up by a number of minor factors, which are specific to particular concept areas.

Thus a semantic differential could be constructed, consisting of only a small number of scales (typically ten–twelve) chosen to represent the three principal dimensions, and yielding, when used to describe a concept, three scores describing it with respect to a three-dimensional semantic space.

Osgood, Suci and Tannenbaum (1957) reported studies of the connotative meaning of many different concept areas, including studies of attitude structure and change, the changing semantic space of a patient during psychotherapy, the description of a case of multiple personality, a study of the structure of aesthetic judgements, and investigations of the effects of the mass media. Since these original studies, an enormous number and variety of studies of affective meaning have been conducted (a selection of which are reprinted in Snider and Osgood, 1969), and variations on the procedure have become standard techniques used by social scientists in many different disciplines.

In addition, a major cross-cultural research effort has established the generality of these dimensions across thirty grossly different language-culture communities (Osgood, May and Miron, 1975) and provided an Atlas of affective meanings of over 600 diversified concepts. These results suggest that the structure of meaning may be a human universal irrespective of linguistic and cultural differences.

Guy Fielding
Sheffield City Polytechnic

References
Osgood, C. E., May, W. H. and Miron, M. J. (1975), *Cross-Cultural Universals of Affective Meaning*, Urbana, Ill.

Osgood, C. E. and Suci, G. J. (1955), 'Factor analysis of meaning', *Journal of Experimental Psychology*, 50.

Osgood, C. E., Suci, G. J. and Tannenbaum, P. H. (1957), *The Measurement of Meaning*, Urbana, Ill.

Snider, J. G. and Osgood, C. E. (1969), *Semantic Differential Technique: A Sourcebook*, Chicago.

Semantics

In logic, philosophy and linguistics the term semantics is used for the study of linguistic meaning, and also for two central aspects of that inquiry – the study of the way in which the meanings of complex expressions depend on the meanings of their parts (structural semantics) and the ways meanings are assigned to simple expressions or morphemes (lexical semantics). In the narrower usage, semantics is contrasted with syntax, the study of the structure of expressions, and pragmatics, the study of their use.

Many of the basic concepts of syntax and semantics, as well as recognition of crucial problems, stem from the work of Bertrand Russell, Gottlob Frege and Charles Sanders Peirce around the turn of the century. The distinction between syntax and semantics, the development of semantical methods, and the demonstration of their importance and power through the proof of fundamental theorems of model theory we owe to Kurt Gödel and Alfred Tarski. These logicians were mainly interested in the logical analysis of mathematics, and concentrated on artificial languages, with a straightforward structure, suited for expression of mathematical ideas. But, due in large part to the pioneering work of Richard Montague, the techniques and concepts of model theoretic semantics are now proving fruitful in the study of natural languages, and we use a simple example from natural language to hint at what a semantical theory is like.

Consider the sentence, *Mary hit Alice*: if we observe that English speakers standardly use this sentence to convey to their audience the information that Mary hit Alice, or as part of a question designed to elicit such information (*Did Mary hit Alice?*), and a wide variety of other ways connected with these, our remarks belong to pragmatics, the study of the use of language. It is natural to postulate a property of the sentence, its meaning, in virtue of which it can be used in these ways. Meaning is intimately related to use; expressions have the meaning they do because of how they have been used, and are used as they are, because of the meaning they have thus acquired. The meaning depends, among other things, on the structure of the sentence, and the things designated by its parts. The sentence *Alice hit Mary* means something different from *Mary hit Alice*, and both sentences would mean something different if *Alice* stood for Max rather than Alice, or *hitting* stood for kissing rather than hitting. Finally, it seems clear that the meaning of declarative sentences is intimately connected to whether they are true or false. If *Mary hit Alice* is true, that is because of a combination of two factors, the meaning of the sentence, and the way things are, that Mary did in fact hit Alice.

Meaning is a relation between words and the world, so a theory of meaning really presupposes an ontology, an account of what there is for words to mean. Thus semantics connects up with the deepest and most tangled regions of philosophy, and might appear hopeless at the outset. But fortunately, great progress has been made with a few simple schemes. For illustrative purposes, we use extensional semantics, whose ontology consists simply of individuals, including the truth-values truth and falsity, and sets built out of them by the devices of set theory. The semantics systematically assigns such individuals and sets to expressions as their extensions. Thus our Lexical Semantics can consist of the assignments:

The extension of *Alice* is Alice.
The extension of *Mary* is Mary.
The extension of *hitting* is the set of pairs that have hitters as the first member and their victims as the second.

Our Structural Semantics assigns sets of individuals to verb phrases, and truth-values to sentences, according to these rules:

Where A is a verb phrase consisting of a transitive verb B followed by a name C, the extension of A is the set of individuals who are the first members of pairs that (a) belong to the extension of B and (b) have the extension of C as second members.
Where A is a sentence consisting of a name B followed by a verb phrase C, the extension of A is truth if the extension of B is a member of the extension of C, falsity otherwise.

Thus our sentence is true if Alice hit Mary, which is what we want.

This example is intended to give the barest sense of what goes on in semantics. Considerable ingenuity, and a richer ontology, is required to deal with such topics as tense and other forms of context dependence, complex noun phrases (*a man, the man, every man*), expressions that embed whole sentences (*believes that Mary hit Alice*), adjuncts, anaphora, non-declarative sentences, and many more in contemporary semantics.

John Perry
Stanford University

Further Reading

Barwise, J. and Perry, J. (1983), *Situations and Attitudes*, Cambridge, Mass.

Dowty, D. R., Wall, R. E. and Peters, S. (1981), *Introduction to Montague Semantics*, Dordrecht.

Enderton, H. B. (1972), *A Mathematical Introduction to Logic*, New York.

Frege, G. (1960), *Translations from the Philosophical Writings of Gottlob Frege*, ed and trans. by P. Geach and M. Black, Oxford.

Mates, B. (1972), *Elementary Logic*, New York.

Montague, R. (1974), *Formal Philosophy: Selected Papers by Richard Montague*, ed by R. H. Thomason, New Haven.

Tarski, A. (1956), *Logic, Semantics, Metamathematics*, trans. by J. H. Woodger.

Russell, B. A. W. (1956), *Logic and Knowledge*, ed by R. C. Marsh, London.

Van Heijenoort, J. (1967), *From Frege to Gödel: A Source Book in Mathematical Logic, 1879–1931*, Cambridge, Mass.

Whitehead, A. N. and Russell, B. (1925), *Principia Mathematica*, 2nd edn, Vol. 1, Cambridge.

See also: *Peirce*; *pragmatics*.

Semiotics

Semiotics is an ancient mode of inquiry which incorporates all forms and systems of communication as its domain. Until recently, the development of semiotic theory and methods has taken place within specific fields, first in medicine, then in philosophy and, in this century, in linguistics. The rapid development of semiotics since 1950 span several fields, including sociology, anthropology, literary and cultural criticism, linguistics and psychoanalysis.

The central idea in semiotics is a particular conception of the structure of the *sign* which is defined as a bond between a signifier and a signified: for example, the bond that exists between a series of sounds (signifier) and their meaning (signified) in a given language, or the social convention that the colour red stands for danger. Semiotic research involves the study of conventions, codes, syntactical and semantic elements, and logic – in short, all the mechanisms which serve both to produce and obscure meanings, and to change meanings in sign systems. As such, semiotics is uniquely adapted to research on several questions which fall in the domain of the social sciences: communication conduct, myth, ritual, ideology, and sociocultural evolution and change. Major contributions to socio-semiotic research include Erving Goffman's studies of face-to-face interaction, Roland Barthes's critique of modern material culture, Lévi-Strauss's research on American Indian myths, and Jacques Lacan's psychoanalytic investigations.

Historical Origins
The first known synthesis of semiotic principles was accomplished in Classical Greek medicine, a branch of which dealt with the symptoms and signs of illness. It was in this applied context that the Greeks made explicit the *principle of the arbitrariness of the relationship of the signifier to the signified* that became the basis for the first accurate diagnosis of disease. The Greeks noted, for example, that a pain in the wrist may indicate a problem with the vital organs, not the wrist, and began to base their diagnosis on the pattern of *relationship between signs*. The combination of arm pains, pale skin, and difficult breathing were given a more nearly correct medical meaning in the place of the incorrect array of meanings they might have for someone operating within the primitive framework of a concrete, analogical connection between signifiers and signified. This effected a transfer of phenomena that formerly could be understood only within a religious framework into the scientific domain.

Semiotics flourishes during times, such as the present, when there is general anxiety about the capacity of Western science to solve important problems, or when there is widespread questioning of the ultimate validity of Western cultural and philosophical values. When there is an intellectual crisis, the problematical relationship of the signifier to the signified is not a secret buried deep in the heart of the sign and social consensus. Rather the signifier/signified relationship appears to almost everyone as a series of discontinuities between events and their meanings.

Peirce's Typology of Signs
The intellectual base of current semiotic activity is mainly the writings of the Swiss linguist, Ferdinand de Saussure and the American pragmatist philosopher, Charles S. Peirce. Following Peirce's synthesis of semiotic principles, there are three major types of signs based on the structure of the relationship of the signifier to the signified: icons, indices, and symbols. (1) An *iconic* sign depends on a bond of resemblance between the signifier and the signified and requires social and legal arrangements and agreements concerning authenticity and originality. (2) *Indices* are produced by the direct action of that which they represent, such as the line left at high tide, and they engage scientific, historical and other forms of curiosity and detective work. (3) *Symbols* are arbitrary and conventional (such as the words in a language) and they require community consensus on proper meanings. Since any object or idea can be represented by each of the three types of signs, the mode of representation implies the form of interpretation and specific social arrangements as well. In short, every mode of scientific and other discourse is the result of (unconscious) decisions that reflect basic, often unstated, social values. Semiotics can function as a 'metalanguage' by analysing the ways the various fields and disciplines represent their subject matter, for example, the frame of mind and form of social relationship that is implicit in experimental science or in Marxist theory.

The Semiotic Critique of 'Rational' Science
Semioticians often make a claim to be both more

rigorous and more politically engaged than their colleagues in disciplines which base their methods on Cartesian rationalism. The source of this seemingly paradoxical claim is found in the contrast of the *signifier/signified* relationship which is the basis of semiotics, and the *subject/object* relationship which is the basis of 'rational' science. According to the semiotic critique of rationalism (and its offspring, positivism), the *subject/object* opposition takes the form of an imperative to establish a hierarchy in which scientific subjectivity dominates its empirical object. This originally innocent formulation, which unleashed enormous intellectual energy, contains no safeguards against excesses and abuse. Specifically, the subject/object split is the ultimate philosophical justification for one group or class (for example, the 'West' or the 'East') to claim the right to dominate others, to assert that the *meanings* they provide are the only correct meanings from the range of possible meanings. Of course it is possible to advance scientific understanding and social thought within this paradigm by policing deviant intellectual tendencies and precisely calibrating social ideology to scientific theory, but the successes of this approach should not render it less suspect. From the perspective provided by the signifier/signified relationship, it appears more a moral or political *position* than a rigorous analytical mode.

Dean MacCannell
University of California, Davis

Further Reading
Barthes, R. (1972 [1957]), *Mythologies*, trans. A. Lavers, New York.
Baudrillard, J. (1981), *For a Critique of the Political Economy of the Sign*, trans. C. Levin, St Louis.
Burke, K. (1973 [1941]), *The Philosophy of Literary Form: Studies in Symbolic Action*, Berkeley and Los Angeles.
Eco, U. (1976), *A Theory of Semiotics*, Bloomington.
Goffman, E. (1974), *Frame Analysis: An Essay on the Organization of Experience*, New York.
Greimas, A. J. and Courtèes, J. (1979), *Sémiotique: dictionnaire raisonné de la théorie du langage*, Paris.
Lacan, J. (1966), *Écrits*, Paris. (Trans. A. Sheridan, 1977, London.)
Lévi-Strauss, C. (1976 [1958–73]), 'The scope of anthropology', in *Structural Anthropology, vol. II*, New York. (Original French, *Anthropologique structurale*, 2 vols, Paris.)
MacCannell, D. and MacCannell, J. F. (1982), *The Time of the Sign: A Semiotic Interpretation of Modern Culture*, Bloomington.
Peirce, C. S. (1940 and 1955), *Selected Writings*, selected and edited by J. Buchler, New York.
de Saussure, F. (1954 [1915]), *Course in General Linguistics*, New York. (Original French, *Cours de linguistique générale*, Paris.)
Sebeok, T. A. (ed.) (1978), *Sight Sound and Sense*, Bloomington.
See also: *Barthes; Peirce; Saussure*.

Sensation and Perception

Sensation and perception refer to the mechanisms by means of which we are aware of and process information about the external world. Aristotle classified the senses into the five categories of seeing (vision), hearing (audition), smelling (olfaction), tasting (gustation), and the skin senses. It is now commonplace to subdivide further the skin senses into separate categories of pain, touch, warmth, cold, and organic sensations. In addition, two senses of which we are not normally aware are also included – kinesthesis, or the sense of position of our limbs, and the vestibular sense which provides information regarding movement and position of the head.

Early theorists often regarded sensation as more elementary and less complex than perception, but the distinction has not proven to be useful. Physical energies such as light, sound waves, acceleration, are *transduced* by the sensory end organs so as to activate nerves which carry the signals to the central nervous system. The properties of the sense organs determine the acceptable range of physical stimuli. For example, the human ear responds to vibrations of the air only between 20 and 20,000 cycles per second. The minimum physical energy required to activate the sensory end organs is referred to as the *absolute threshold*. Thresholds for hearing depend systematically on the frequency of the vibrations, being minimal in the intermediate frequency range which involves speech sounds, and progressively higher for both lower and higher frequencies. Similarly, within the range of wave lengths which activate the eye, the visual system is most sensitive to yellow and yellow-green, and less sensitive to red and blue. Wave lengths outside of this range do not activate the visual system although infra-red radiation may be perceived as heat.

The quality of sensation – whether it is perceived as light, sound, pain, smell and so on – is not determined directly by the nature of the physical stimulus but rather by the nervous pathways being activated. Under normal conditions, light energy will typically stimulate visual pathways because the light threshold for the eyes is much lower than for any other form of physical energy. Pressure on the eyeball, however, will elicit a light sensation. Similarly, all the sense organs have the lowest thresholds for the appropriate forms of stimulus energy. The relationship between the quality of sensory experience and the specific nervous pathways activated is referred to as Mueller's doctrine of *specific nerve energies*. This concept was important in the early history of psychology because it focused attention on the role of the nervous system in mediating experience. We do not perceive the external world directly, but rather are aware of the activity of the nerves. Since awareness and knowledge depend on nervous activity, the study of the nervous system is fundamental to the science of psychology.

The intensity of sensation is not predictable from the absolute energy in the stimulus but is rather related to some multiple of stimulus energy. For example, the energy required for a light to appear just noticeably brighter than another light is closely predicted by the *ratio* of energies. An increment of a light unit which is just noticeable when viewed on a 10 light unit background will not be visible when viewed on a 100 light unit background. The just noticeable difference is closely predicted by the ratio of energies. The *differential threshold* for the 100 unit background would, in this case, be 10. To a first approximation, the ratio of the just noticeable difference to the background, historically known as *Weber's law*, is a constant. In the last century, the physicist Fechner argued, on the basis of Weber's law, that the subjective magnitude of sensation is determined by the logarithm of the stimulus energy. This relationship was viewed by Fechner as representing a quantification of the mind and the solution of the mind-body problem. The procedures devised to study sensory functions, known as *psychophysics*, provided an important methodology in support of the founding of experimental psychology as an independent laboratory science in the late nineteenth century.

Information from the senses is combined with past experience, either consciously or unconsciously, to construct our awareness of the external world and to guide our motor responses. For the most part, these perceptions are accurate, but there are instances in which they are in error. Incorrect perceptions are referred to as *illusions* which may result when normal mechanisms are inappropriately activated. When viewing two-dimensional photographs or drawings, distortions of size, shape and direction may occur because of the misapplication of sensory and perceptual mechanisms which normally subserve three-dimensional vision. Illusions should be differentiated from hallucinations, which refer to perceptions which have no basis in the external world. Hallucinations are typically associated with psychopathology, drugs, or pathology of the nervous system.

The theoretical importance of sensation and perception derives from the empirical point of view in philosophy which maintains that knowledge is mediated by the senses. In this context, limitations of sensory systems, illusions, and distortions by past experience or bias relating to motivational factors play a central role, because they determine the content of the mind. The predominance of the empirical view was responsible for the emphasis on the study of sensation and perception during the early history of experimental psychology.

Sensory systems can act independently or in conjunction with other senses. The 'taste' of food results from the combination of inputs from olfaction, gustation, the skin senses, and kinesthesis. This can be demonstrated by comparing the taste of foods when the nasal passages are blocked. In this case, taste is reduced to a less complex combination of the four basic gustatory qualities of salt, bitter, sour and sweet. The wide variety of food qualities is made possible in large part by olfactory cues. The appearance of food, its temperature, and resistance to chewing also contribute to these complex sensations.

Spatial orientation depends on the integration of visual, vestibular and proprioceptive information, all of which contribute to the maintenance of erect posture and location. The interactive nature of the sensory systems subserving spatial orientation is responsible for the fact that overactivation of the vestibular sense can lead to the illusory sensation that the visual world is moving. Similarly, if a large area of the visual environment is moved, an objectively stationary observer will experience a compelling illusory sensation of body motion (vection).

The correspondence between the physical pattern of stimulation and our corresponding perception of the world has remained a problem of major interest in perception. If two adjacent stationary lights are alternately flashed, the observer will report apparent movement between them. This phenomenon was cited by the *Gestalt* psychologists in support of their position that perception consists of more than the elements of stimulation. It is also the basis for the perceived movement in motion pictures and television. The contribution of the observer to perceptual experience is emphasized in numerous theoretical analyses of perception. In the case of *Gestalt* psychology, the organization is provided by inherent properties of the nervous system. Within the context of theories which stress the role of attention or motivation, the observer 'selects' only certain aspects of the environment for processing, in other words, we tend to see and hear what we want to see and hear and actively exclude information which is potentially embarrassing or unpleasant. The phenomenon of selective perception is illustrated by the reaction to painful stimuli which may be minimized or ignored if associated with an otherwise pleasant event such as victory in an athletic contest, but may be reported as very painful under unpleasant circumstances. Since the study of human perception frequently depends on the verbal report of an observer, it can not be evaluated directly and is therefore subject to modification by motivational states.

The active contribution of the observer to perception is also illustrated by the phenomenon of perceptual constancy. The first stage of sensing or perceiving visual stimuli is the formation of an optical image in the eye. This image is determined by geometric principles so that its size will be inversely proportional to the distance from the observer. In spite of wide variation in retinal image size, the perceived sizes of objects tend to remain constant and to correspond to their true dimensions. The tendency to perceive the veridical sizes of objects in spite of the continually changing pattern of the retinal image is referred to as perceptual 'constancy'. Other perceptual attributes also demonstrate constancy effect. The foreshortening of the retinal image resulting from oblique viewing is not perceived. Circular objects appear round even though the retinal image is elliptical, for example, shape constancy. When we move our eyes, the retinal image also moves but the perception of the environment remains stationary, for example, space constancy. A white object appears 'white' and a dark object appears 'dark' even under wide ranges of ambient illumination, for example, brightness constancy. Similarly, the colours of objects tend to remain the same even though the spectral quality of the light reflected from them varies as they are illuminated by the different wavelengths provided by natural and artificial illumination, for example, colour constancy. Perceptual constancies are essential in biological adjustment because they permit the organism to be aware of and to respond to the biologically relevant, permanent physical characteristics of objects in the environment. The eye has been likened to a camera, and they are similar, as both have an optical system for focusing an image on a light sensitive surface. However, whereas the camera is passive, the eye, as well as other sensory systems, is connected to the brain so that the final perception is a result of the active combination of physical stimuli with information from the observer's past experience, motivation and emotions.

Sensation and perception have been of interest, not only because of their central role in the acquisition of knowledge and in mediating awareness, but also because they play an essential role in many aspects of human and animal behaviour. Pain is an essential protective mechanism which is normally activated whenever the integrity of the organism is in danger. Olfaction provides warning against ingestion of poisons. Serious threats to health are a consequence of the fact that no information is provided by our sensory systems for some dangers, for example, ionizing radiation, carbon monoxide, early stages of some diseases.

Knowledge of sensation and perception is important in performance evaluation and prediction and in medical diagnosis. Many tasks in modern society place unusual demands on the individual's sensory capacities as, for example, in aviation. Consequently sophisti-

cated batteries of tests have been developed to identify those individuals with the superior visual and perceptual capacities necessary to operate high-performance aircraft. In a technologically-oriented society, the ability to acquire information from reading is indispensable and has led to the development of an extensive visual health-care system. The systematic changes in vision, balance and hearing which occur as a consequence of ageing are relevant to the design of safe environments and the successful adjustment of the elderly. Visual tests are sensitive to pathology and are used to evaluate the consequences of disease, in diagnosis, and in the evaluation of therapy.

Perceptual tests provide a methodology for evaluating group dynamics and personality. If a single stationary point of light is viewed in an otherwise dark room, it will appear to move. The extent of this reported *autokinetic* movement has been shown by Sherif to depend on the magnitude of apparent movement reported by other observers and their social status. The extent to which one's reports are influenced by others is taken as a measure of social pressure and conformity. Ambiguous stimuli are also used to evaluate personality. In the Rorschach test, subjects are asked to describe what they see in patterns formed by inkblots. It is assumed that the reports will be a reflection of the individual's personality dynamics which are attributed or 'projected' unconsciously into the ambiguous stimulus.

Herschel W. Leibowitz
Pennsylvania State University

Further Reading
Boring, E. G. (1942), *Sensation and Perception in the History of Experimental Psychology*, New York.
Boring, E. G. (1950), *A History of Experimental Psychology*, 2nd edn, New York.
Carterette, E. C. and Friedman, M. P. (eds), *Handbook of Perception*, New York (1974), Vol. I, *Historical and Philosophical Roots of Perception*; (1973), Vol. III, *Biology of Perceptual Systems*; Vol. IV, (1978), *Hearing*; (1975), Vol. V, *Seeing*; (1978), Vol. VIA, *Tasting and Smelling*; (1978), Vol. VIB, *Feeling and Hurting*; (1978), Vol. VIII, *Perceptive Coding*; (1978), Vol. IX, *Perceptual Processing*.
Held, R. H., Leibowitz, H. W. and Teuber, H. L. (1978), *Handbook of Sensory Physiology, Vol. VIII, Perception*, Heidelberg.
Kling, J. W. and Riggs, L. (eds) (1971), *Woodworth and Schlosberg's Experimental Psychology*, 3rd edn, New York.
Pastore, N. (1971), *Selective Theories of Visual Perception: 1650–1950*, London.
See also: *nervous system; sensory and motor development; vision.*

Sensory and Motor Development

In describing the stages of intellectual growth from birth to maturity, Piaget (1953) emphasized the initial and continuing importance of motor activity. In his view, the basis for later cognitive growth is constructed in the first two years by the production of physical rather than mental transformation of reality. Since this activity depends on sensory information about objects and events, the capacity to detect, discriminate, classify and integrate input from the different senses is basic to an understanding of behavioural development. Despite the motor and linguistic incompetence of the young infant, ingenious advances in technology permit a re-assessment of the origins of sensori-motor activity, the role of experience, and the manner in which information from one sensory modality is related to that of another.

Behavioural and physiological measures are used to index responsiveness to sensory stimulation. Fundamental to all aspects of pattern perception is the resolution of visual detail when contrast is varied from low to high. This capacity improves rapidly during the early months, probably as a consequence of neuronal maturation. There are, as well, changes in the structure of the eye, improvement in the control of extra ocular muscles and in visual accommodation. From birth, there is a preference to look at patterned rather than plain surfaces. An early ability to discriminate differences in brightness and colour is combined with a tendency to classify the colours of the spectrum in much the same fashion as adult humans. Colours from the one hue (for example, blue) are perceived as more similar than colours from different hue categories (for example, blue and green) although the physical difference between them is similar (Bornstein, 1981). In the auditory domain, early discrimination and classification of stimulation can also be observed. Perhaps the most striking example is the sensitivity to the acoustic properties that differentiate the phonetic segments of speech sounds (Jusczyk, 1981). This ability is not confined to sounds that are phonemic in the parental language. The discrimination and classification of consonants and vowels clearly precede and facilitate language acquisition.

Most research on sensory development has been concerned with the visual and auditory modalities. Recent findings on intermodal perception suggest that the haptic, kinaesthetic and proprioceptive senses also may not be as primitive as had previously been assumed. Although interpretation of these findings is controversial, there is a view that young infants are predisposed to recognize equivalence in the information derived from different modalities. Thus, for example, they detect the correspondence between the appearance of a speaker articulating a speech sound and the auditory characteristics of that sound, and they can match the visual appearance of an object with haptic information obtained from its oral exploration (Meltzoff, 1981). The age at which imitation first occurs is not yet clear. Nevertheless the reproduction of the facial expression of another person implies the translation of visual input into structurally similar but unseen proprioceptive output. It is clear that all these intermodal perceptions do not originate from a long period of gradual associations between the separate senses, as Piaget argues. It is equally clear that they are not the product of tuition of other senses by a primary touch sense, as classical theories maintain.

The study of early sensory and motor development has revealed a competence that was previously unsuspected. The exciting aspect of this research lies not so much in the demonstration of precocity as in the challenge to specify the nature of the relevant stimulus characteristics and the mechanisms that detect them. Recent findings have theoretical implications for normal development and clinical implications for those with sensory disabilities.

B. E. McKenzie
La Trobe University, Australia

References
Bornstein, M. H. (1981), 'Psychological studies of color perception in human infants: habituation, discrimination and categorization, recognition, and conceptualization', in L. P. Lipsitt (ed.), *Advances in Infancy Research*, Vol. 1, Norwood, NJ.
Jusczyk, P. (1981), 'Infant speech perception: a critical appraisal', in P. D. Eimas and J. L. Miller (eds), *Perspectives on the Study of Speech*, Hillsdale, NJ.
Meltzoff, A. N. (1981), 'Imitation, intermodal coordination and representation in early infancy', in G. Butterworth (ed.), *Infancy and Epistemology*, Brighton.
Piaget, J. (1953), *The Origins of Intelligence in the Child*, London.

Further Reading
Lipsitt, L. P. (ed.) (1982), *Advances in Infancy Research*, Vol. 2, Norwood, NJ.
See also: *developmental psychology*; *Piaget*; *sensation and perception*.

Separation and Loss

Separation and loss are central life events which impinge on all individuals throughout the life cycle. The significance of these common human experiences, particularly in early childhood, are viewed quite differently by psychoanalysts, learning theorists and critical period theorists. Psychoanalysts emphasize the potential for fixation and regression, with the possibility of permanent limitations in emotional vitality as a response to losses in infancy. Learning theorists suggest that, given the appropriate environmental stimulation, humans are plastic and can transfer their attachments and recover from periods of loss or deprivation. Critical period theorists believe that phase-specific development requires adequate environmental conditions and that the absence of such (for example, maternal contact) at a critical period can result in permanent developmental arrests.

Psychiatric research after the Second World War, which left many European children without parents, attempted to trace the long-term effects of orphanhood on the children. Early research relied on dubious methods and reported a wide spectrum of pathological results, the common finding being a loss of affectivity in personal relations. Since that time, there have been attempts to obtain more exact information about infants and children who have been separated from their primary caretakers through death, parental hospitalization and adoption. Rene Spitz (1946) and John Bowlby (1969; 1973) are central figures in the pioneering investigations of early childhood response to maternal separations.

Spitz is best known for his description of depressive reactions in six-to-nine-month-old infants deprived of their mothers' presence for a duration of three to five months. He called this reaction – characterized by listlessness, immobility, setbacks in psychomotor development, and profound weight loss – anaclitic depression, postulating that the loss of the love object left the dependent infant with no outlet for his aggressive and libidinal drives. But since his subjects were not provided with substitute caretakers, his research describes the results of loss of mothering rather than, as he seems to suggest, the loss of the love object.

Bowlby described separation anxiety and grief reactions in infants six months and older. He characterized the mourning process in three stages: (1) a protest stage, viewed as an angry and anxious attempt to regain the object and protest the abandonment; (2) the despair stage; and (3) the detachment or readjustment stage. This same behaviour pattern had been noted by observers of young primates separated from their mothers.

Separations and losses have also been addressed at other phases in the life cycle. Reactive stages to the knowledge that one is dying, responses to marital separations and divorce, as well as reactions to the death of a loved one in later life have also been detailed. Bowlby's triad of rage, despair and readjustment often figure prominently in clinical descriptions of response to loss.

Grief reactions are regarded as both normal and adaptive responses to separation and loss. Mourning is only viewed as pathological when the individual becomes fixated over time in the early stages of rage and despair and is unable to detach and re-acclimate.

Separation responses are pathological when the individual becomes excessively anxious, fearful and unable to initiate autonomous activity.

The impact of loss and separation from the caring parent continues to be a subject of great interest to psychotherapists. It would be fair to say that it now rivals the Oedipus complex in its psychotherapeutic significance as a critical developmental event. These are questions of great political significance as well, because they bear on the advisability of day care centres and the entry of women into the work force.

Karen Stone
Belmont, Massachusetts

References
Bowlby, J. (1969; 1973), *Attachment and Loss*, Vols I and II, London.
Spitz, R. (1946), 'Anaclitic depression', *Psychoanalytic Study of the Child*, 2.
See also: *attachment*; *bereavement*; *Bowlby*.

Set Theory and Algebra

Set theory appears in the foundations of mathematics and is indispensable in many of its branches. As such, it undergirds much of the application of mathematics in the social sciences and, moreover, it provides a natural representation for many relational social phenomena.

A set is a collection of objects, known as elements, which can be specified by a common property or simply listed. In the social sciences, the use of set theory and algebras starts with a specification of the elements in relation to some social phenomenon, data, model or theory. While the use of sets may start with some concrete representation, the concept of a set is an abstraction. Set theory is the mathematical discipline studying the general properties of abstract sets.

Sets (of interest) are taken as subsets of some universal set. Operations can be defined which operate on sets in a universal set to produce other subsets of that universe. The union of two sets A and B, written $A \cup B$, is obtained by putting together all elements of A, of B, or of both. The elements common to both A and B form the intersection, written $A \cap B$. All elements in a given universe not belonging to A form its complement, A'. Regardless of any empirical content, the operations satisfy general rules, for example, $(A \cup B)' = A' \cap B'$. This is established within set theory and is not subject to empirical verification since it follows from the definition of the operations.

The Cartesian product, $A \times B$, of A and B is the set of all ordered pairs, (a,b), with a from A and b from B. A (binary) relation, λ, between A and B is any subset of $A \times B$. If A and B are the same, we have a relation defined over a set; for example, A is the set of all societies and λ is the relation 'exports to'. These relations may have different properties: reflexive or irreflexive, symmetric or asymmetric, transitive or intransitive, and so on. Different properties define different relation types which have distinctive mathematical properties.

When a set, together with some operations, satisfy a set of specifications (axioms), an algebra results. For example, a Boolean Algebra of sets is a non-empty collection, A, of subsets where (i) if A and B belong to A so do their union and intersection and (ii) if A belongs, then A' does. By taking different sets, operators and axioms, different algebras are formed.

A homomorphism is a correspondence between algebras where some of the algebraic structure in the first is preserved in the second. Homomorphic reduction of one structure to another is a powerful tool, especially for work on structural equivalence.

One area of contemporary social science making heavy use of algebraic representations is social-networks analysis. Graph theory, matrix algebra and algebraic topology see frequent use therein. (*Social Networks* is a new journal whose articles frequently use sets and algebras.)

The art of using algebras involves a judicious matching of empirical and/or substantive problem with an appropriate algebra, and using the derived theorems of that algebra.

Patrick Doreian
University of Pittsburgh

Further Reading
Kim, K. H. and Roush, F. W. (1980), *Mathematics for Social Scientists*, New York.
Roberts, F. S. (1976), *Discrete Mathematical Models; With Applications to Social, Biological and Environmental Problems*, Englewood Cliffs, N.J.
See also: *graph theory; mathematical models*.

Sexual Behaviour

Our knowledge about human sexual behaviour has increased greatly and so has the availability of information about it. And, of course, sexual behaviour itself has changed. Although many social scientists argue that we have experienced more than just a change – perhaps a revolution – others would regard this claim as an overstatement.

Sex is defined here as anything connected with genital stimulation, sexual gratification, reproduction, and the behaviour that accompanies such stimulation, gratification and involvement. Kissing, petting, coitus and masturbation, for example, constitute forms of sexual behaviour and are referred to by the term sex and its derivatives, *sexual* and *sexuality*. Sexual behaviour, when discussed within a particular social context such as premarital, marital, or extramarital sexual behaviour, refers to those acts by an individual (either physically acted out or mentally acted out, as in the case of fantasizing) which involve another individual (imagined or real) and which centre around sexual gratification.

Procreation and Recreation
Sexual interaction has at least two distinct functions: (1) procreation, which accounts for only a tiny portion of coital activity in contemporary society, and (2) recreation, which has always accounted for most sexual interaction, although the extent of recreational sex may be different for males and females. That the extent of recreational sex outweighs that of procreational sex is suggested by the lower birth-rates for both wanted and unwanted children since a generation ago, and by the increase in the frequencies of premarital, marital and extramarital sexual behaviour throughout most of the Western world. Certainly today, recreational sex, whether inside or outside of marriage, is the rule rather than the exception.

There is evidence, however, that the increasing incidence and prevalence of sexual behaviour for purposes other than procreation has not been accompanied by an increased awareness of the consequences and ramifications of such behaviour. Research indicates that in the United States, for example, most never-married, sexually experienced teenage women have engaged in coitus without using contraception. Thus, it is easy to understand why illegitimacy rates and the number of abortions performed for unmarried women have both increased dramatically, and why a significant minority of brides are pregnant on their wedding day. It seems clear that as long as we live in societies which frown upon and are largely unsupportive of pregnancy out of wedlock, and young couples themselves do not desire such pregnancies, a thorough discussion of contraception, pregnancy, childbirth, and the consequences of sexual activity is warranted.

Revolution or Evolution?
The limited, but reasonable, evidence found throughout Western societies suggests that human sexual behaviour has undergone the following changes in recent years:

(1) An increase in the number of individuals having premarital coitus, particularly females.
(2) An increase in the number of partners with whom an individual is likely to have premarital sexual relationships.
(3) Individuals are having their first sexual relationships at earlier ages.
(4) A lesser level of commitment is necessary before individuals become involved in sexual relationships.
(5) A greater frequency of marital coitus.

(6) A greater incidence of extramarital coitus, particularly among women.

(7) A higher proportion of abortions are being given to unmarried women; there is also a higher frequency of abortions among unmarried women.

(8) An increase in the illegitimacy rate among unmarried women, particularly teenagers.

(9) Increased utilization of family-planning services and contraceptives by females of all ages.

(10) Widespread adoption of more effective methods of contraception by women of all ages, social-class levels, religions and races.

(11) More open discussion of, and exposure to, sexuality in books, magazines, films and other media.

(12) More liberal acceptance of alternative life-styles and alternative expressions of sexuality, such as homosexuality.

(13) More freedom for females in initiating informal heterosexual social contacts and sexual relations.

(14) A greater willingness to talk about sex, to tolerate different values and attitudes, and to accept sex, even in cases where another individual's standards may be different from one's own.

If it is true that these changes have occurred in recent years, then it might seem evident that, by almost any definition, a sexual revolution has occurred. But this conclusion is potentially misleading for a number of reasons.

Social scientists have usually pointed to premarital intercourse as the key indicator of sexual revolution, even though this must surely be only a part of it. If we focus, for the moment, on premarital sexual behaviour in Western societies, we find evidence that between the 1920s and the 1960s changes were minimal. In the years that coincided with the post-war baby boom, economic prosperity, television, industrialization, and the increasing impact of mass media, people began to talk and write often about 'the sexual revolution'. Respected social scientists and others have declared this revolution to be over and done with a number of times.

In retrospect, it appears that although sexuality was more frequently and openly discussed during the 1950s and early 1960s there was, in fact, no dramatic increase in sexual behaviour. It now seems as though we were misled by all the talk, since the data show only a slight change in actual behaviour.

However, when we look at data collected since the mid-1960s, we begin to see some noticeable, significant, and at times dramatic changes in the number of individuals engaging in premarital intercourse. This trend is best documented in the United States, but there is some evidence of similar trends in Europe. Indeed, the incidence has increased moderately for males during the last decade, and dramatically for females. It can be said that the females are 'catching up' – at least in

terms of the cumulative number of females who have had at least one coital experience before marriage.

Most of the available data on sexual behaviour, however, concern indicators of frequency and incidence. It is likely that the magnitude of social change must be judged not just on the basis of cumulative incidence, but rather on the nature and quality of the relationships being examined. Thus, although it appeared that females were catching up with males in terms of actual incidence, there were still dramatic differences in their reactions to, feelings about, management of, and socialization for sexual relationships.

A revolution *has* occurred if we are referring to the very significant increase in the prevalence of female sexual activity, both inside and outside of marriage. But 'revolution' is perhaps an overstatement if we consider sexual performance, values, and the attitudes that are more deeply rooted in the socialization process.

Graham B. Spanier
State University of New York at Stony Brook

Further Reading
Kinsey, A., Pomeroy, W., Martin, C. and Gebhard, P. (1948), *Sexual Behavior in the Human Male*, Philadelphia.
Kinsey, A., Pomeroy, W., Martin, C. and Gebhard, P. (1953), *Sexual Behavior in the Human Female*, Philadelphia.
Masters, W. and Johnson, V. (1966), *Human Sexual Response*, Boston.
Masters, W. and Johnson, V. (1970), *Human Sexual Inadequacy*, Boston.
Sorenson, R. C. (1973), *Adolescent Sexuality in Contemporary America*, Cleveland.
See also: *homosexuality*; *incest behaviour*; *rape*.

Simmel, Georg (1858–1918)

Lukács, a student and early admirer, who later became an important Marxist theorist and an outspoken critic of social scientists, once called Simmel the greatest 'philosopher of transition' of his day. Simmel was the only one among his academic contemporaries in Germany who was able to draw upon the conflicting schools of philosophy of the time (neo-Kantianism, neo-Hegelianism, Marxism, and Philosophy of Life) to define the starting point for analyses of a kind that probably only he was capable of carrying out. Simmel could exploit a variety of theoretical idioms, and he could also combine different disciplinary and methodological perspectives. He studied important cultural phenomena such as religion, the money economy, the rise of morality, the self-preservation of groups, using modes of analysis drawn from philosophy, psychology, sociology, economics and theology, each of which yielded specific insights. This pluralism, however, made him suspect among his colleagues, most of whom were preoccupied with gaining academic recognition, building up a following, and establishing the special claims of their disciplines. Yet today, long after his more limited critics have been forgotten, it is precisely this synthesizing approach which is Simmel's attraction for those who wish to break through the traditional disciplinary boundaries within the social sciences.

Simmel once described his work, with deliberate ambiguity, as a 'struggle for life'. He referred to the mental and physical struggle for individual survival in a sociocultural environment increasingly dominated by an expanding technology, economy, and bureaucracy, and, also, to the struggle of the educated bourgeoisie against growing 'proletarianization' of spiritual and material life, a development which was equally the consequence of industrialization, mass consumption, and modern conditions of living and communication.

This critical and conservative argument was pursued in so many domains, although at times his methodology was insufficiently developed so that his interpreters could not easily comprehend the underlying logic. Simmel himself recognized that the fate of his legacy was in doubt. His most enduring contributions have proved to be his works on Kant (including *Kant*, 1904; *Kant und Goethe*, 1906; and *Hauptprobleme der Philosophie*, 1910), his writings on the philosophy of art and culture (including *Philosophische Kultur*, 1911; *Rembrandt*, 1916; and *Zur Philosophie der Kunst*, 1922), and, above all, his analyses of capitalism and his attempt to define a distinctive sociology with its own methods, themes and theories.

Simmel was born a Jew, but he was baptised and received a Christian education. He spent most of his life in Berlin and was a thoroughly metropolitan and urban figure. As he showed in a study which is still worth reading, the metropolis provided the point of reference for his critical analyses of modern culture (*Die Grosstadte und das Geistesleben*, 1903). When his father, a businessman, died, a friend of the family supported him while he completed his studies, and enabled him to live without financial anxieties as a *Privat-dozent*, whose only income would otherwise have come from lecture fees.

Simmel had a considerable reputation in Germany and abroad, yet his academic career was not smooth. In fact, he was a victim of discrimination because of his Jewish origins and his unorthodox life and views. He was repeatedly passed over for positions in the University of Berlin, and in both 1908 and 1915 he was rejected by the University of Heidelberg, with which he had philosophical affinities, despite the support of such famous colleagues and friends as Max Weber, Rickert and Husserl.

But the failure, in conventional terms, of Simmel's career was above all a consequence of his individual-istic intellectual development. Initially, he was mainly concerned with problems of natural science, social philosophy and evolution (*Über soziale Differenzierung*, 1890). He later took up a critique of idealism, reconstructing the origins and meaning of morality, on the basis of novel psychological, sociological and historical insights (*Einleitung in die Moralwissenschaften*, 1892–3). Then, for several years, he was concerned with aspects of the Kantian theory of knowledge and with problems in the philosophy of history (*Die Probleme der Geschichtsphilosophie*, 1892) (*The Problems of the Philosophy of History*, 1977). In the process he developed a typological and interpretive approach which he then employed in a 'Marx-completing' (as he himself put it) study of the impact of a money economy on human life (*Philosophie des Geldes*, 1900) (*The Philosophy of Money*, 1978), and in other topical studies.

Simmel's analysis of capitalism and his *Soziologie: Untersuchungen über die Formen der Vergesellschaftung* (1908), which includes most of his contributions to pure sociology in this period, are now generally regarded as his main contributions to the establishment of sociology as a science. There has been particular interest in his concept of a 'formal' or 'pure' sociology, in which the forms of social life are abstracted from their historical-material context. In this way he treated topics such as power, conflict, group structure, individuality and social differentiation. These exercises have also been the object of strong, sometimes onesided, and uninformed, criticism.

At about the same time, Simmel engaged in an extensive discussion of Marxist theories of value and of alienation. Politically, he was for a while attracted by the ideology of the Social Democrats. He was a founder member of the German sociological association, served on its board, and delivered the opening lecture at its inaugural meeting in 1910, but he resigned from the organization two years later because of conflicts concerning the theory and politics of science, although giving as his reason his desire to concentrate on philosophical interests.

He now turned to philosophical questions of life and culture, under the influence of Hegelian thinking (*Lebensanchaungen*, 1918; *Der Konflikt der modernen Kultur*, 1918). These works earned him a name as a metaphysician and as an apologist for capitalism, but in a later work, *Grundfragen der Soziologie* (1917), he argued that his entire œuvre was engaged with one basic question, the limits of individuality in modern society. He died before he was able to develop the projected new social science, which was to encompass psychological, philosophical and epistemological aspects, and which would amount to a 'general' or 'philosophical' sociology. For those who share this ambition, his work remains a rewarding resource.

Peter-Ernst Schnabel
University of Bielefeld

Further Reading

A.

Works of Simmel in English translation include:

The Sociology of Religion, 1959.

Fundamental Problems of Sociology, 1950.

The Philosophy of Money, 1937.

Two valuable anthologies are:

Levine, D. N. (ed.) (1971), *Georg Simmel on Individuality and Social Forms, Selected Writings*, Chicago.

Wolff, K. H. (1950), *The Sociology of Georg Simmel*, Glencoe, Ill.

B.

Coser, L. A. (ed.) (1965), *Georg Simmel*, Englewood Cliffs, NJ.

Frisby, D. P. (1981), *Sociological Impressionism: A Reassessment of Georg Simmel's Social Theory*, London.

Simon, Herbert A. (1916–)

Herbert A. Simon is a social scientist for all seasons. He has made signal contributions to economics, psychology, political science, sociology, philosophy, computer science and business administration, but with a common theme of inquiry running throughout his work: the study of human (organizational) decision making for which he was awarded the 1978 Nobel Memorial Prize in Economics. But unlike the economic imperialists, Simon addresses his works in various disciplines in the languages of those disciplines. In 1976, Simon was nominated Distinguished Fellow of the American Economics Association and was cited, *inter alia*, for showing that a unified social science is still possible and for going far in demonstrating how to build it.

Born in 1916 in Milwaukee, Wisconsin, Simon obtained a Ph.D. in political science from the University of Chicago. After a few years of field research in municipal administration and on the faculty of the Illinois Institute of Technology, in 1949 Simon became one of the founding fathers of the Graduate School of Industrial Administration at Carnegie where he has remained a guiding light in the development of the business and psychology programmes.

Within the unifying theme of decision making, Simon's professional career can be divided into two major categories: (1) decisions in organizations and modelling of behaviour, and (2) artificial intelligence. (1) He developed two closely interrelated concepts: bounded rationality and satisficing – two ideas which he admits form the core of his entire intellectual activity (Simon, 1980). In a nutshell these concepts focus on the limits of human and organizational gathering and processing of information. These ideas challenged the dominant notion of rational economic man and gave rise to the behavioural study of organizations, but did not quite penetrate mainstream economics. His contributions to economics also include the relations between causal ordering and identifiability, the theorem on the conditions for the existence of positive solution vectors for input-output matrices, theorems on near-decomposability and aggregation, and a number of applied econometric studies. Simon is also one of the pioneers of operations research. (2) In the mid-1950s Simon and Allen Newell (1972) approached the study of problem-solving through computer simulation. They opened up and have since concentrated on the entire spectrum of artificial intelligence and human cognition.

In his autobiography Simon (1980) notes that early in his career he perceived the need to infuse into the social sciences the kind of rigour, mathematical underpinnings, and techniques of experimentation that had contributed to the success of the natural sciences and that he aims at closer relations between the natural and social scientists.

George R. Feiwel
University of Tennessee

References

Newell, A. and Simon, H. A. (1972), *Human Problem Solving*, Englewood Cliffs, NJ.

Simon, H. A. (1980), 'Herbert A. Simon', in G. Lindzey (ed.), *A History of Psychology in Autobiography*, Vol. VII, San Francisco.

Further Reading

Ando, A. (1979), 'On the contributions of Herbert A. Simon to economics', *Scandinavian Journal of Economics*, 81.

Baumol, W. J. (1979), 'On the contributions of Herbert A. Simon to economics', *Scandinavian Journal of Economics*, 81.

March, J. G. (1978), 'The 1978 Nobel Prize in Economics', *Science*, 202.

Simon, H. A. (1976 [1947]), *Administrative Behavior*, 3rd edn, New York.

Simon, H. A. (1982), *Models of Bounded Rationality*, 2 Vols, Cambridge, Mass.

Skinner, Burrhus F. (1904–)

A behaviourist and the most prominent figure in contemporary American psychology, Skinner has devoted most of his professional career to studying the effects of the consequences of behaviour on behaviour. He received his Ph.D. from Harvard in 1931, and from 1948 to 1975 was a professor there. His approach is descriptive and inductive; he is unconcerned with the physiological, mental, or affective processes taking place within organisms (see *The Behavior of Organisms*, 1938). The prototypic environment for Skinnerian (operant) conditioning is the Skinner Box, a chamber designed to give the animal being conditioned little room to move around in; it is equipped with a lever or other manipulandum which when activated produces a specific consequence (for example, food, water, avoidance of electric shock) according to a predetermined schedule. A consequence which, over trials, leads to an increase in the frequency of the response producing the consequence is referred to as a reinforcing stimulus. One of Skinner's major contributions has been to demonstrate that various schedules of reinforcement are characterized by unique response-frequency patterns. The ability to generate predictable response patterns has, in turn, found useful application in almost all areas of psychological research. Operant conditioning techniques also comprise the primary procedural foundation of behaviour modification, a set of intervention strategies which have been effectively employed in all major institutional settings, particularly in schools, mental hospitals, and care facilities for the psychologically retarded. Skinner was one of the pioneers of programmed learning. As a social critic, he has throughout his professional life advocated the reorganization of societies so that positive reinforcement (rewarding desired behaviours) rather than punishment or the threat of punishment be used to control human actions. His philosophy is detailed in two widely read books, *Walden Two* (1948), a novel about an entire society being controlled by operant techniques, and *Beyond Freedom and Dignity* (1971). Skinner's most important general contribution to the social and behavioural sciences may be to inspire methodological precision and accountability.

Albert R. Gilgen
University of Northern Iowa

Further Reading
Gilgen, A. R. (1982), *American Psychology since World War II: A Profile of the Discipline*, Westport, Connecticut.
See also: *behaviourism*; *conditioning, classical and operant*; *learning*.

Slavery

The definitions of slavery are as numerous as the societies in which slavery was to be found, and for good reason. The rights which owners had over their slaves and the duties by which they were bound constituted a bundle whose composition varied from society to society, although the slave's rights were always heavily circumscribed. Nevertheless, certain elements can probably be considered part of all these bundles: (1) The slaves were initially outsiders, brought by force to serve their new master, or they were in some way expelled from full membership of their society, for instance because of debt or as the result of a criminal trial. They might of course be the descendents of such individuals, depending on the degree to which a given society was prepared to assimilate slaves to full membership. (2) At least in the first generation, slaves were marketable commodities, at any rate where commercialization was present in any recognizable form. In other words, they were a species of property and it was this which distinguished slaves from other forms of forced labour. (3) Slaves had specific, generally inferior, occupations within the total division of labour. (4) Slaves were only held in their status by force or the threat of it, and in many ways the ending of the necessity for this marked a slave's full assimilation into the society.

Within this broad framework, the variations were enormous. This is to be expected from an institution which, in its various forms, existed all over the world – Australia is the only large and inhabited land mass where slavery never occurred – and from the beginnings of recorded human history until the twentieth century. Indeed, vestiges still survive, particularly in parts of the Islamic world and in various prostitution rackets. Nevertheless, the various slave systems may perhaps be distinguished according to two criteria, namely the degree of 'openness' and the extent to which the system of production was organized around it.

As regards the former question, particularly in societies whose social systems were organized around kinship groups, slavery could be a valued means of expanding the size of that group and the number of dependents an important individual had beyond the limits set by the natural processes of reproduction. Since slaves were by definition outsiders, and thus people without kin of their own, they and their descendants could be incorporated into their owners' group, albeit often in a inferior position. On the other hand, where there was no premium on the number of kin an individual might have, or where the rules for the division of property made it advantageous to cut down the number of co-sharers, then slaves and their descendants could rarely gain admission to the higher ranks of society. In such circumstances, slaves would only be freed as a result of a formal act of manumission. These might occur with greater or lesser frequency, but in all such cases the ex-slave began his or her life of freedom in a lowly status, often still formally dependent on his or her former owner.

With regard to the second criterion, while slavery as such has existed in an enormous number of societies, the number in which it has been crucial to the organization of production has been relatively few. Ancient Greece, Ancient Rome and in modern times, the Southern United States, the Caribbean and parts of Brazil are the best known of these, although there were a number of other parts of the world, such as seventh-century Iraq, eighteenth-century colonial South Africa, Zanzibar in the nineteenth century, and parts of the Western and Central Sudan in the same period, for which a convincing case could be made. The emergence of economies based on slave labour depended on at least three conditions: (1) private property rights, above all land, had to be established, and concentrated to the extent that extra-familial labour was required; (2) internal labour had to be insufficiently available, often as the result of the emancipation of earlier labourers, whether they were bonded peasants as in Ancient Greece or indentured servants as in colonial America – in other words, large-scale slavery was a consequence of large-scale freedom; (3) since slaves generally had to be bought, commercial market production had to be sufficiently developed. Although the demand for slaves on a grand scale may well have been logically prior to their supply, the continued existence of a slave society required the regular importation of new slaves, almost invariably through an organized slave trade, as – with the exception of the United States – slave populations were unable to reproduce themselves naturally.

In those cases where slavery was an integral part of the organization of labour, it tended to be rather towards the 'closed' pole of the assimilation continuum, even though the distinction between slave and free was nowhere as harsh as in the United States. For this reason, it was only in these societies (and not always even there) that a genuine slave culture was able to develop, as something distinct from that of the owners. Therefore, it was only in such societies that slaves were able to organize sufficiently for a large-scale rebellion to be possible, although individual acts of resistance were to be found wherever slavery existed. Very often, the major revolts were nonetheless the work of newly imported slaves, as the efficacy of repression tended to persuade second generation slaves of the futility of a rising, and led them to adopt an ambivalent attitude, which combined outward acquiescence with the effort to create a way of life for themselves that was as free and as comfortable as the circumstances permitted. In this way they tended to confirm the paternalist ideology of their masters, although this would then be rudely shattered by the general refusal of ex-slaves to remain in their former owners' service when, after the abolition of the institution, there was no longer legal compulsion for them to do so.

Robert Ross
University of Leiden

Further Reading
Miller, J. C. (1984), *Slavery: A Comparative Teaching Bibliography*, Boston.

Sleep

Sleep is an area of human behaviour which occupies a third of the total life span and occurs thoughout all societies and all of history. Despite its pervasiveness it has been largely ignored by social scientists until recently. As laboratory-based studies began in earnest in the early 1950s to describe the nature and dimen-sions of sleep as a regularly recurring behaviour (Aserinsky and Kleitman, 1953; Dement and Kleitman, 1957), it became clear that this period was far from a passive state of quiescence or non-behaviour. By recording the electroencephalogram (EEG), electrooculogram (EOG) and electromyogram (EMG) continuously throughout the time period from waking into sleep until the final reawakening, it was found that there were regular cyclic changes within sleep itself. The discovery that sleep consists of two distinct types, Rapid Eye Movement (REM) sleep and Non-Rapid Eye Movement (NREM) sleep, which differed as much from each other as each did from wakefulness, led to a series of studies detailing the properties of these two states and their interactions within the context of the whole circadian (sleep-wake) rhythm. Each hour and a half the shift from a synchronized, physiologically quiescent, NREM sleep in which motor activity is intact, to the desynchronized, physiologically active, REM state accompanied by motor paralysis, became known as the ultradian rhythm. Within NREM sleep, variations in EEG pattern were further differentiated by convention into numerical sleep stages 1, 2, 3, 4. This laid the basis for the descriptive mapping of a night's sleep by the number of minutes spent in each sleep stage across the hours of the night and by the length of the ultradian cycle. This plot is referred to as sleep architecture. Once these conventions were established (Rechtschaffen and Kales, 1968) age norms for these sleep characteristics were also established (Williams, Karacan and Hursch, 1974). Study of these developmental changes provided insight into sleep-wake relations. Individual differences in sleep parameters were also explored and related to variations in intelligence, personality and life-style. For example, although it is still a matter of some debate, long sleepers (those sleeping in excess of nine hours per night) were found to differ reliably from short sleepers (who sleep less than six hours per night) in psychological makeup, with long sleepers being more introverted, with lower energy and aggressive drive than short sleepers. It is clear that there is a selective difference in the type of sleep that is increased for these people. Long and short sleepers have the same amount of stages 3 and 4, but long sleepers have twice the amount of REM sleep and their REM sleep has increased eye movement density. Thus it is in the area of REM function that the need of long sleepers for more sleep must be explored. Other variations also occur, for example, in depth of sleep. These have been studied using the degree of auditory stimulation needed to produce an arousal as the measurement. This procedure has established that all sleep stages become progressively lighter with age, making sleep more fragile in the elderly.

Beyond the descriptive and correlational studies there has been the continuing challenge concerning the question of sleep function. This question has been approached most often by looking into the effects on waking behaviour of sleep deprivation, either total or selective. Until recently these studies have been hampered by the limits to which human subjects could be subjected. Short studies of sleep loss have produced only small and equivocal results. These have been summed up ironically as: the effects of sleep deprivation are to make one more sleepy. However, the effects on subsequent sleep are clear. After total sleep loss, sleep architecture is changed. REM sleep is postponed in favour of a prolonged period of stages 3 and 4 sleep. It appears that this synchronized sleep is preemptive and is recouped first. In fact, if the degree of sleep loss has been more than a night or two, the first night of recovery sleep may contain no REM sleep at all. This may not reappear until a second recovery night. The opposite is true of the recovery following a period of selective REM sleep deprivation. On the first night of ad-lib sleep, REM sleep appears earlier in the architectural plot and the total amount may be increased above the usual proportion when total sleep time is controlled. In other words, both NREM stages 3 and 4 and REM sleep act as if they have the properties of needs requiring they be kept in homostatic balance. Recently, a long-term sleep deprivation study using rats and employing yoked non-sleep-deprived animals as controls has established that extreme sleep loss results in debilitative organic changes and death (Rechtschaffen *et al.*, 1983). This is the first study to establish that sleep is necessary to sustain life. How much sleep of what kind is necessary at the human level to ensure well-being will probably be determined not from experimental studies, but may come from the many clinical studies currently being carried out of patients suffering from various disorders of sleep and of sleep-wake relations.

Against the background knowledge of normative sleep architecture, for each sex across the whole life span, significant deviations in amount and type of sleep can now be identified as well as differences in the distribution of sleep across the circadian cycle. Studies that have sought to relate waking psychopathology to sleep pathology have been most productive in the area of depression. Although it has been well known that most persons suffering from affective disorders also suffer from insufficient and poor quality sleep, the detailed laboratory monitoring has revealed the nature of this dysfunction to be specific to REM sleep. This is found to be significantly displaced in the overall architecture. The first REM sleep occurs too soon, at half the normal cycle length, is often abnormally prolonged on first occurrence, from a norm of ten to as much as forty minutes, and with an increase in the density of eye movements within this time period and a change in total time distribution. Instead of REM being predominant in the second half night, as in normal individuals, in the depressed the distribution in the first and second halves of the night is equal (Kupfer *et al.*, 1983). Since REM deprivation is known to increase waking appetite and sexual activity in cats and depression is associated with reduction of these behaviours, the finding of a specific REM dysfunction in these patients hints that this sleep stage is implicated in the regulation of appetitive behaviours.

Studies of sleep under time-free conditions have established that the normal human circadian rhythm is not twenty-four hours but slightly greater than twenty-five. This finding suggest that social learning has played a part in entraining sleep to a twenty-four hour cycle. Loss of these social cues or *zeitgebers* during vacation time or when unemployed, for example, often leads to later sleep onset time and longer sleep periods leading to later arousal hours. Most normal individuals have little trouble becoming re-entrained. However, some individuals with withdrawn schizoid personalities, or perhaps some neurological deficit, have no established sleep-wake rhythm. These people suffer from an inablilty to function in regular occupations due to the unpredictabililty of their time periods for active prosocial behaviours.

Nocturnal sleep studies of persons whose waking life is interrupted by uncontrollable episodes of sleep have revealed several different types of sleep disturbance that are responsible for these intrusions, including narcolepsy and sleep apnoea syndromes. The study of sleep and its interaction with waking behaviour has enlarged the capacity of the social and behavioural scientist to account for some aspects of human behaviour previously poorly understood and has changed the time frame of observation to one including the full circadian cycle.

Rosalind D. Cartwright
Rush-Presbyterian-St Luke's Medical Center, Chicago

References

Aserinsky, E. and Kleitman, N. (1953), 'Regularly occurring periods of eye motility and concomitant phenomena during sleep', *Science*, 118.

Dement, W. and Kleitman, N. (1957), 'Cyclic variations in EEG during sleep and their relation to eye movements, body motility and dreaming', *Electroencephalography and Clinical Neurophysiology*, 9.

Kupfer, D., Spiker, D., Rossi, A., Coble, P., Ulrich, R. and Shaw, D. (1983), 'Recent diagnostic treatment advances in REM sleep and depression', in P. J. Clayton and J. E. Barretts (eds), *Treatment of Depression: Old Controversies and New Approaches*, New York.

Rechtschaffen, A., Gilliland, M., Bergmann, B. and Winter, J. (1983), 'Physiological correlates of prolonged sleep deprivation in rats', *Science*, 221.

Rechtschaffen, A. and Kales, A. (eds) (1968), *A Manual of Standardized Terminology, Techniques and Scoring System for Sleep Stages of Human Subjects*, Los Angeles.

Williams, R., Karacan, I. and Hursch, C. (1974), *Electroencephalography (EEG) of Human Sleep: Clinical Applications*, New York.

Further Reading
Cartwright, R. (1978), *A Primer on Sleep and Dreaming*, Reading, Mass.

Dement, W. (1972), *Some Must Watch While Some Must Sleep*, San Francisco.

Hartmann, E. (1973), *The Functions of Sleep*, New Haven.

Webb, W. (1975), *Sleep, the Gentle Tyrant*, Englewood Cliffs, NJ.

See also: *dreams*.

Slutsky, Eugen (1880–1948)

Eugen Slutsky was a Russian mathematician and statistician who made signal contributions to economics and greatly influenced the development of econometrics. He was educated at the University of Kiev and the Institute of Technology in Munich. He taught at the Kiev Institute of Commerce, later joining the Institute for the Study of the Business Cycle in Moscow, and the Central Institute of Meteorology. From 1934 until his death he worked at the Mathematical Institute of the Soviet Academy of Sciences.

In one of those sad quirks of fate so common in science, Slutsky published in 1915 an unnoticed paper that answered Pareto's quest for the comparative statics properties of utility maximization by elaborating the substitution and income effect of price change (later known as the Hicks-Allen-Slutsky effect). Had Slutsky not written as a mathematician in an Italian journal during wartime, there would not have been a need to rediscover his basic propositions in the 1930s. As it was, one of the distinguished rediscoverers and value-added contributors, R. G. D. Allen, subsequently (1936), with true scholarly integrity, resurrected Slutsky's work. In fact, Allen (1950) considers that the contemporary theory of consumer's behaviour 'is essentially as much a development of Slutsky's work as of Pareto's'. Though Slutsky wrote before his time and as a mathematician, 'the concept of compensated price changes which he introduced has become so well established that it dominates the theory of consumer's behaviour'.

Slutsky's other important contribution to economics was originally made in the late 1920s (1937). He showed that random shocks can be easily cumulated by moving averages and other linear processes into coherent waves that imitate business cycles. His results shed light on questions as to whether a moving average

trend warps the real oscillations in a series and on the broader ones of the structure of economic time series.

In later years Slutsky's work deviated from economics into mathematical statistics and probability theory. 'It is unfortunate that, for so long before his death, Slutsky was almost inaccessible to economists and statisticians outside Russia. He opened up new areas but left them to be explored by others, and the exploration even now is far from complete. His assistance, or at least personal contacts with him, would have been invaluable' (Allen, 1950).

George R. Feiwel
University of Tennessee

References
Allen, R. G. D. (1936), 'Professor Slutsky's theory of consumers' choice', *Review of Economic Studies*, 3.

Allen, R. G. D. (1950), 'The work of Eugen Slutsky', *Econometrica*, 18.

Further Reading
Chipman, J. S. (1982), 'Samuelson and consumption theory', in G. R. Feiwel (ed.), *Samuelson and Neoclassical Economics*, Boston.

Konüs, A. A. (1968), 'Slutsky, Eugen', in D. L. Sills (ed.), *International Encyclopedia of the Social Sciences*, Vol. 13–14, New York.

Samuelson, P. A. (1947), *Foundations of Economic Analysis*, Cambridge, Mass.

Slutsky, E. (1915), 'Sulla teoria del bilancio del consumatore', *Giornale degli Economisti*, 51. (English translation in G. J. Stigler and K. E. Boulding (eds) (1952), *Readings in Price Theory*, Homewood, Ill.)

Slutsky, E. (1937), 'The summation of random causes as the source of cyclic processes', *Econometrica*, 5.

Smith, Adam (1723–90)

Adam Smith was born in Kirkcaldy, on the East Coast of Scotland, in 1723. After attending the Burgh School Smith proceeded to Glasgow University (1737–40) where he studied under Francis Hutcheson. Thereafter he took up a Snell Exhibition in Balliol College, Oxford (1740–6). In 1748 Henry Home (Lord Kames) sponsored a course of public lectures on rhetoric and Smith was appointed to deliver them. The course was successful and led, in 1751, to Smith's election to the chair of logic in Glasgow University where he lectured on language and on the communication of ideas. In 1752 Smith was transferred to the chair of moral philosophy where he continued his teaching in logic, but extended the range to include natural theology, ethics, jurisprudence and economics.

Smith's most important publications in this period, apart from two contributions to the *Edinburgh Review* (1755–6), were the *Theory of Moral Sentiments* (1759, later editions, 1761, 1767, 1774, 1781, 1790) and the *Considerations Concerning the First Formation of Languages* (1761).

The *Theory of Moral Sentiments* served to draw Smith to the attention of Charles Townsend and was to lead to his appointment as tutor to the Duke of Buccleuch in 1764, whereupon he resigned his chair. The years 1764–6 were spent in France, first in Bordeaux and later in Paris where Smith arrived after a tour of Geneva and a meeting with Voltaire. The party settled in Paris late in 1765 where Smith met the leading *philosophes*. Of especial significance were his contacts with the French economists or Physiocrats, notably Quesnay and Turgot, who had already developed a sophisticated macroeconomic model for a capital using system.

Smith returned to London in 1766, and to Kirkcaldy in the following year. The next six years were spent at home working on his major book, which was completed after a further three years in London (1773–6). The basis of Smith's continuing fame, *An Inquiry into the Nature and Causes of the Wealth of Nations*, was published on 9 March 1776. It was an immediate success and later editions (of which the third is the most important) appeared in 1778, 1784, 1786 and 1789.

In 1778 Smith was appointed Commissioner of Customs and of the Salt Duties; posts which brought an additional income of £600 per annum (to be added to the continuing pension of £300 from Buccleuch) and which caused Smith to remove his household to Edinburgh (where his mother died in 1784). Adam Smith himself died, unmarried, on 17 July 1790 after ensuring that his literary executors, Joseph Black and James Hutton, had burned all his manuscripts with the exception of those which were published under the title of *Essays on Philosophical Subjects* (1795). He did not complete his intended account of 'the general principles of law and government', although generous traces of the argument survive in the lecture notes.

The broad structure of the argument on which Smith based his system of social sciences may be established by following the order of Smith's lectures from the chair of moral philosophy. The ethical argument is contained in *Theory of Moral Sentiments* and stands in the broad tradition of Hutcheson and Hume. Smith was concerned, in large measure, to explain the way in which the mind forms judgements as to what is fit and proper to be done or to be avoided. He argued that men form such judgements by visualizing how they would behave in the circumstances confronting another person or how an imagined or 'ideal' spectator might react to their actions or expressions of feeling in a given situation. A capacity to form judgements on *particular* occasions leads in turn to the emergence of *general rules* of conduct which correct the natural partiality for self. In particular Smith argued that those rules of behaviour which related to justice constitute the 'main pillar which upholds the whole edifice' of society.

Smith recognized that rules of behaviour would vary in different communities at the same point in time as well as over time, and addressed himself to this problem in the lectures on jurisprudence. In dealing with 'private law' such as that which relates to life, liberty or property, Smith deployed the analysis of *The Theory of Moral Sentiments* in explaining the origin of particular rules in the context of four socioeconomic stages – those of hunting, pasture, agriculture and commerce. In the lectures on 'public' jurisprudence he paid particular attention to the transition from the feudal-agrarian state to that of commerce; that is, to the emergence of the exchange economy and the substitution of a cash for a service nexus.

The economic analysis which completed the sequence and which culminated in the *Wealth of Nations* is predicated upon a system of justice and takes as given the point that self-regarding actions have a social reference. In fact the most complete statement of the psychology on which the *Wealth of Nations* relies is to be found in Part VI of *The Theory of Moral Sentiments* which was added in 1790.

The formal analysis of the *Wealth of Nations* begins with an account of the division of labour and of the phenomenon of economic interdependence before proceeding to the analysis of price, the allocation of resources and the treatment of distribution. Building on the equilibrium analysis of Book I, the second book develops a version of the Physiocratic *model* of the circular flow of income and output before proceeding to the analysis of the main theme of economic growth. Here, as throughout Smith's work, the emphasis is upon the unintended consequences of individual activity and leads directly to the policy prescriptions with which Smith is most commonly associated: namely, the call for economic liberty and the dismantling of all impediments, especially mercantilist impediments, to individual effort.

Yet Smith's liberalism can be exaggerated. In addition to such necessary functions as the provision of defence, justice and public works, Jacob Viner (1928) has shown that Smith saw a wide and elastic range of governmental activity.

The generally 'optimistic' tone which Smith uses in discussing the performance of the modern economy has also to be qualified by reference to further links with the ethical and historical analyses. Smith gave a great deal of attention to the social consequences of the division of labour, emphasizing the problem of isolation, the breakdown of the family unit, and that mental mutilation (affecting the capacity for moral judgement) which follows from concentrating the mind on a restricted range of activities. If government has to act in this, as in other spheres, Smith noted that it would be constrained by the habits and prejudices of the governed. He observed further that the type of government often found in conjuction with the exchange or commercial economy would be subject to pressure from particular economic interests, thus limiting its efficiency, and, also, that the political sphere, like the economic, was a focus for the competitive pursuit of power and status.

A. S. Skinner
Glasgow University

References
Works by Adam Smith:

I   *Theory of Moral Sentiments*, ed. D. D. Raphael and A. L. Macfie (1976).
II *Wealth of Nations*, ed. R. H. Campbell, A. S. Skinner and W. B. Todd (1976).
III *Essays on Philosophical Subjects*, ed. W. P. D. Wightman (1980) consisting of:
    'The History of Astronomy'; 'The History of the Ancient Physics'; 'History of the Ancient Logics and Metaphysics';
    'Of the External Senses'; 'Of the Imitative Arts'; 'Of the Affinity between Music, Dancing and Poetry'.
    The volume also includes:
    'Contributions to the *Edinburgh Review*' (1755–6) and 'Of the Affinity between certain English and Italian Verses', edited by J. C. Bryce.
    Dugald Stewart, *Account of the Life and Writings of Adam Smith*, edited by I. S. Ross.
IV *Lectures on Rhetoric and Belles Lettres*, ed. J. C. Bryce (1983). This volume includes the *Considerations Concerning the First Formation of Languages*.
V   *Lectures on Jurisprudence*, ed. R. L. Meek, D. D. Raphael and P. G. Stein (1978). This volume includes two sets of students notes.
VI *Correspondence of Adam Smith*, edited by E. C. Mossner and I. S. Ross (1977). This volume includes:
    A Letter from Governor Pownall to Adam Smith (1776);
    Smith's *Thoughts on the State of the Contest with America* (1778); and
    Jeremy Bentham's *Letters to Adam Smith on Usury* (1787, 1790).

Further Reading
Campbell, T. D. (1971), *Adam Smith's Science of Morals*, London.
Haakonssen, K. (1981), *The Science of the Legislator: The Natural Jurisprudence of David Hume and Adam Smith*, Cambridge.
Hollander, S. (1973), *The Economics of Adam Smith*, Toronto.
Lindgren, R. (1975), *The Social Philosophy of Adam Smith*, The Hague.
Macfie, A. L. (1967), *The Individual in Society: Papers on Adam Smith*, London.
O'Driscoll, G. P. (ed.) (1979), *Adam Smith and Modern Political Economy*, Iowa.
Rae, J. (1965 [1895]), *Life of Adam Smith*, London. (Reprinted with an introduction by J. Viner, New York.)
Reisman, D. A. (1976), *Adam Smith's Sociological Economics*, London.
Scott, W. R. (1937), *Adam Smith as Student and Professor*, Glasgow.
Skinner, A. S. and Wilson, T. (1975), *Essays on Adam Smith*, Oxford.
Viner, J. (1928), 'Adam Smith and laissez faire', in J. Hollander *et al.*, *Adam Smith, 1776–1926*, Chicago.
Winch, D. (1965), *Classical Political Economy and the Colonies*, London.
Winch, D. (1978), *Adam Smith's Politics*, Cambridge.
See also: *classical economics*.

Social Anthropology

The term social anthropology came into use in the early twentieth century, to refer to studies concerned with the constitution of primitive society rather than with 'primitive mentality' or biological evolution. The substantive concern had crystallized much earlier, Tylor writing in 1865, for example, of 'that interesting, but difficult and almost unworked subject, the Comparative Jurisprudence of the lower races', and commenting that 'no one not versed in Civil Law could do it justice' (Tylor, 1865). The foundations of the subject were indeed laid by lawyers – Maine and McLennan in Britain, and Morgan in America. Their models of primitive social organization had a number of points in common:

(1) The most primitive societies were ordered on the basis of kinship relations. With the development of private property, a territorial state emerged. This was the most revolutionary change in the history of human society.
(2) The kinship organization of primitive society was based on descent groups.
(3) The descent groups were exogamous and were related by a series of marriage exchanges.
(4) The kinship terminology was a linguistic expression of the system of descent grouping and marriage alliance.

Kinship, descent and the primitive state became the central concerns of the developing speciality, the classification of kinship systems dominating social anthropological research until the mid-twentieth century. A parallel tradition, concerned with 'primitive mentality', paid more attention to religion and technology. The most important early writer in this tradition, Tylor, took little interest in the 'Comparative Jurisprudence of the lower races'. For their part, the social anthropologists were interested in religion only as an expression of social institutions. They developed the theory of totemism in the late nineteenth century, linking 'totems' to a social structure based on exogamous clans. A later theory explained 'ancestor worship' as the ideological expression of descent groups.

Social anthropology was initially committed to an evolutionist view of the development of society. Scholars aimed to reconstitute fossil types of primitive society. Information about 'contemporary savages' was analysed mainly in order to establish the type or level of society to which a particular population might be said to belong. In the early twentieth century a competitive approach, 'diffusionism', proposed by geographers, became popular. According to the diffusionists, societies changed and developed as a consequence of borrowing and migration rather than internal processes. A reconstitution of human history should stress population movements and communication. There was no regular succession of types of society. Rather, successive centres of innovation stimulated bursts of colonization and trade. Later, as more detailed field studies of particular societies became more common, the emphasis shifted to the internal constitution of particular societies. The structure of social organization – treated ahistorically – became the central concern. For the leading 'functionalists', Malinowski and Radcliffe-Brown, the key question became how the parts of the society (the institutions, groupings and practices) contributed to the organization of the whole. Some of the British functionalists became dissatisfied with the rather formal and static analyses of Radcliffe-Brown and his followers, and experimented with transactionalism, network analysis and other varieties of processual sociological theory. In the mid-twentieth century Lévi-Strauss's new structuralism became one of the dominant influences.

Despite these and other shifts in theoretical fashion, the substantive issues in social anthropology remained remarkably stable for many years. The continuities can be illustrated with reference to the major works of social anthropology in the 1940s, *African Political Systems* (1940), edited by M. Fortes and E. E. Evans-Pritchard; *The Nuer* (1940), by E. E. Evans-Pritchard; and M. Fortes's two monographs on Tallensi clanship and kinship. Like their Victorian predecessors, these anthropologists tried to reconstitute types of primitive society and to demonstrate the role of descent groupings as the basis of social organization. They also took for granted a fundamental historical break between stateless societies, based upon descent groupings, and the early states. Their view of primitive society was further developed in the monographs of the dominant British school of social anthropology in the 1950s and 1960s. Conceptual refinements were introduced. The model of segmentary-lineage society became increasingly subtle and differentiated, and local and temporary variants of this fundamental 'type of primitive society' were proposed and discussed. The evolutionist assumptions which underlay the model were played down though seldom denied outright, and they can be clearly discerned in the sophisticated variant developed by Lévi-Strauss, in which primitive societies are sorted into types according to the marriage arrangements which bind together putatively exogamous and enduring descent corporations (Lévi-Strauss, 1969 [1949]).

Despite these continuities with Victorian evolutionism, new directions were already evident by the 1930s. The wave of functionalist studies of particular societies, carried out in the Malinowskian manner by participant observation, yielded a new kind of data, recalcitrant to simple formalism. Some ethnographers began to emphasize individual variation, informal special processes, and strategies of maximization and competition. Sociology in Britain and France was at the time less active and innovative, and the anthropological descriptions of exotic societies even suggested fresh ways of studying European communities. Similar social processes were being uncovered in the most remote and technologically simple communities and in the slums of Boston or the towns of the Mediterranean. It seemed for some time as though the boundaries between sociology and social anthropology would dissolve, or that social anthropology might now become what Radcliffe-Brown had proposed, a form of comparative sociology, defined not by a special subject-matter but by a comparative perspective. This process has not, however, been consummated, and social anthropologists are still generally to be found studying exotic, small-scale, technologically-impoverished populations in the tropics, or marginal, culturally-foreign communities in Europe and America. Since there no longer seems to be any theoretical justification for this special focus of attention, it may not persist for long, although the cluster of preoccupations and technical skills associated with this ethnographic concentration is certainly distinctive.

Another development, which crystallized in the 1950s, is associated particularly with E. E. Evans-Pritchard. Discontented with the sociological formalism of Radcliffe-Brown, Evans-Pritchard argued for a more historical anthropology, allied with oriental studies, in which the goal would be not the discovery of putative sociological laws but rather the humanistic understanding of exotic cultural traditions. This development in anthropology mingled with a movement in historiography, stimulated especially by the early writers of the *Annales* school, towards a history of 'mentalities', of popular traditions and informal social institutions. One of its main successes was in the description and interpretation of witchcraft in African and medieval European societies. Another focus of interest is the history of the family, marriage and sexuality in Europe.

The divergent development of social and cultural anthropology has also come to an end. For a time 'social anthropology' was a British and French speciality. The increasing American domination of all branches of anthropology imposed a greater degree of integration of European social anthropology with American varieties of cultural anthropology. Exponents of both traditions now coexist in the major North-American departments. In Europe, partly under the influence of Lévi-Strauss's later works, there has been a shift in interest from social institutions to the study of myth, religion, systems of classification and other 'cultural' matters. The traditional social anthropological view, derived from Durkheim, that these cultural phenomena were to be understood as expressions of social relations is now less in evidence, though it characterizes, for example, the work of Mary Douglas (1973).

The integration with sociology, on the one hand, and history, oriental studies and cultural anthropology on the other have not been complete, but the independent and distinctive character of social anthropology is much less evident today than it was a generation ago. The main reason for this is a general if sometimes only implicit rejection of the notion that social anthropology has a special subject-matter, primitive society. It is now generally agreed that there is no 'type' of primitive society. The classical models of 'primitive society', notably the model of segmentary-lineage systems, are being abandoned. Contemporary preliterate, or technologically simple peoples are integrated into overarching modern societies, which radically influence their internal organization. The one distinctive field of analysis developed within social anthropology which continues to have broader relevance and to show signs of a certain dynamism is kinship studies, but as it becomes more sophisticated it is increasingly the domain of specialists.

The present fluid situation is difficult to evaluate, however, because the reorientation and redefinition of social anthropology is occurring in the context of a general shift of disciplinary boundaries in the social sciences. New disciplines, like family history, semiotics and cognitive science, are colonizing traditional social-anthropological spheres of interest. At the same time, the major traditions of sociology and historiography are fragmenting and begetting more specialized but more theoretically eclectic fields of study, to which anthropologists are sometimes attracted.

Adam Kuper
Brunel University, Uxbridge

References

Douglas, M. (1973), *Natural Symbols*, London.
Evans-Pritchard, E. E. (1940), *The Nuer*, Oxford.
Fortes, M. (1945), *The Dynamics of Clanship among the Tallensi*, London.
Fortes, M. (1949), *The Web of Kinship among the Tallensi*, London.
Fortes, M. and Evans-Pritchard, E. E. (eds) (1940), *African Political Systems*, London.
Lévi-Strauss, C. (1969 [1949]), *The Elementary Structures of Kinship*, Boston and London. (Original French edn, *Les structures élémentaires de la parenté*, Paris.)
Tylor, E. B. (1865), *Researches into the Early History of Mankind*, London.

Further Reading

Evans-Pritchard, E. E. (1951), *Social Anthropology*, London.
Kuper, A. (ed.) (1977), *The Social Anthropology of Radcliffe-Brown*, London.
Kuper, A. (1983), *Anthropology and Anthropologists: The Modern British School*, London.
Leach, E. R. (1982), *Social Anthropology*, London.
See also: *anthropology*; *cultural anthropology*; *Evans-Pritchard*; *Malinowski*; *Radcliffe-Brown*.

Social Change

Social change is ubiquitous, but most members of most societies either delude themselves into thinking that stability prevails, or, in times of particularly obvious, discontinuous and rapid change, that return to unchanging normality is desirable and possible. There is no single source of change, but almost all aspects of social life may at one time or another, singly or in combination, produce irrevocable change. Over time, however, some of the causes of change have proved particularly significant.

Ecological changes, either through changes brought about by the human population, or through short- and long-term cyclical changes in climate and topography, have contributed powerfully to social change. The permanent shift to agriculture from gathering and hunting, for example, was probably caused by a related combination of population growth and climatic shifts brought about by the waning of the most recent ice age (Smith and Young, 1972).

Population growth, even without climatic change, sooner or later provokes migration, new production techniques, serious local overcrowding, or usually some combination of these. It now seems likely that population growth in geographically circumscribed but highly productive areas produced the single greatest organizational change in human social history, the creation of the first states about 5000 years ago (Carneiro, 1970).

Ecological (including demographic) change, technological change, and political change remain the most important causes of general social change today as they have been in the past.

Cultures consist of sets of ideas, customs and rules of behaviour which guide social action. As the circumstances in which societies exist change, so will cultures adapt and change. But ideas and customs have a life of their own. People become attached to them for their own sake. It is this general ideological commitment to established ways, except when these have failed dramatically, that creates the illusion of and wish for stability. Though cultures change, the element of resistance to change, which is sometimes stronger, sometimes weaker, but always present, makes it difficult to predict adaptation to material changes in a society. Supposedly universal laws of social change based on correlations with material changes flounder on the rocks of cultural singularities. This does not mean that the ultimate causes of change are not material, but that culture, though materially derived, plays a partially independent role in determining the direction and speed of social change.

The only method for understanding social change is to study the complex interactions between ecological, political, economic and cultural histories of societies. Specific, detailed social histories can be used comparatively to establish general conclusions and uniformities, as well as to highlight unique or rare patterns of change (Steward, 1955). Abstract theories derived from superficial readings of history tell us far less. Strictly evolutionary theories that insist on forcing all change into predetermined moulds lead to sterile conclusions.

It is neither difficult nor particularly useful to define social change. Anything which regularly organized groups of people normally do or think while living their collective lives constitutes a social system. Any change in such a system, as long as it is repetitive rather than simply limited to a few episodes, constitutes social change. Such a definition does not distinguish between major and minor changes, and it is more interesting to do this by understanding how and why the most critical changes have occurred, as well as which ones are likely to take place in the future.

The most important transformations in social structure have probably been the technological revolution produced by the adoption of sedentary agriculture, the organizational revolution that accompanied the rise of states, and the much more recent, still unfolding, transformation of thought, technology and politics encompassed under the term 'modernization'. It is this latter change which poses the biggest challenge to students of change.

Max Weber devoted his career to understanding why a set of changes ranging from the Renaissance and Reformation to the Industrial Revolution occurred in a part of Western Europe rather than in the other great agrarian civilizations – China, India, the Islamic Near and Middle East, or even earlier in Rome itself.

His answer, based on the histories of each of these civilizations and on a comparison of their cultures as revealed through their religions, was that a singular drive to orderly, predictable, rational explanations of social life and the natural universe existed only in the West (Weber, 1968 [1922]).

The problem, only partially elucidated by Weber, is to find the source of this drive. Did it originate with the rational scepticism of Greek philosophy, with the orderly and comprehensive development of Roman law, or with the Christian theology and church organization, itself a product of the Jewish religion, Greek philosophy, and Roman law? Why did this rationalizing drive not take place in Islam which, after all, was influenced by the same cultural forces? Why not in the great Oriental Empires with their complex bureaucratic organizations and ancient philosophical traditions?

The answer, consistent with both Weberian and Marxist scholarship, is that the ecological and political environment of Europe in the Middle Ages was uniquely favourable to the development of strong, independent towns run by and for merchant élites. Merchants and town artisans anywhere are likely to be more rational and calculating than peasants, warriors or court officials. They deal in ponderables that can be weighed and counted, in goods that can be manipulated in predictable ways, in profits that can be foreseen, even if imperfectly. Peasants, on the other hand, face a capricious nature and an even less predictable élite of rapacious nobles and states, and have little hope of control. Superstition, reliance on magic and resignation tend to characterize peasant thought. The warrior ethic, on the other hand, emphasizes boldness, deliberate outbursts of nonrational violence, and showy grand gestures that contrast sharply with the townsman's petty and avaricious calculations. The bureaucratic élites running the great Chinese empires, however, developed a rational ethic of social responsibility and the ability to calculate and manipulate people. Church officials in the West developed some analogous ways of thinking. But because these forms of rationality dealt purely with social matters, and not with production or technical aspects of production, they were far less friendly to the practical, mechanical rationality of the bourgeois, and in the long run, to the development of experimental science. This was particularly the case among the Confucian bureaucrats of China (Weber, 1968 [1922]; Needham and Ronan, 1976).

It would take volumes to detail the events that led to the emergence of a powerful bourgeois ethic in the West, but it is possible to outline the various political and economic combinations which produced different outcomes in the various great civilizations.

In Europe the feudal anarchy of the ninth to eleventh centuries allowed more or less independent towns to emerge (Bloch, 1961 [1939–40]; Anderson, 1974). Later, kings used the economic strength and administrative expertise of the bourgeois to help them overcome feudal lords fighting royal power, and also to try to keep control over the church which provided the other source of administrative talent. By the fourteenth century, towns, along with nobles and the church, were one of the elements in the political compromise from which strong states developed. The arrangement in which the various 'estates' shared power remains to this day embodied in the English parliamentary system (Poggi, 1978). Even in France, which became an absolutist monarchy in the seventeenth century, as well as in Germany, where no central state emerged until much later, towns were important enough to maintain considerable political and intellectual weight. Only where a unified Habsburg Imperial and Papal Catholic alliance triumphed were towns fiscally ruined and intellectually forced back into orthodox stagnation. This is why Iberia became the backwater of Europe, and why Northern Italy, home of Europe's most independent and progressive cities at the time of the Renaissance, sank into Southern European poverty and intellectual irrelevance in the seventeenth and eighteenth centuries.

It is no accident that Protestantism flourished in areas with relatively weak royal power and strong towns, and that Protestantism came to be associated with later economic and scientific progress (Weber, 1968 [1922]; Merton, 1970). Nor is it surprising that in that small corner of northwestern Europe where all the right historical circumstances combined, namely the Netherlands and England, the commercial and scientific progress of the seventeenth century led to the first Industrial Revolution in the late eighteenth century.

In the Near East, on the other hand, the presence of steppe nomads who repeatedly conquered and plundered towns, stripped them of their hinterlands, and destroyed irrigation works resulted in an economically and demographically weak society (Ashtor, 1976). Cultures adapted and came to reflect the resignation and inward-looking mysticism suited to defeat rather than the rational and open attitude which had characterized Islamic thought in its earlier golden age (Hodgson, 1974).

In China, the fragmented Han Empire (third century) was reunited in the sixth century and thereafter feudal fragmentation occurred only briefly. Whenever the Empire disintegrated, it was put back together again. The Confucian literati who ran its administration developed their own rational ethic but also discouraged intellectual innovation and prevented town merchants from becoming an independent force. This both reduced the drive to expand China's commercial relations abroad, and the experimentation necessary for technological innovation. Western Europe expanded its area of economic operations throughout the world in the sixteenth to nineteenth centuries, underwent a technological and scientific revolution, and inalterably changed its social structures. China under the Ming and Qing dynasties (fourteenth to twentieth centuries) fell into a trap in which whatever limited innovations occurred were barely adequate to feed a growing population. No decisive breakthroughs took place, and China, once more advanced than the West, fell hopelessly behind (Elvin, 1973).

The same elements, though in different combinations, can be used to explain the differential dynamism of other civilizations, and to increase our understanding of the fundamental causes of change.

A social process can be partially but not entirely understood through the study of its origins. Charles Tilly (1981) has emphasized that the two major types of change in the last four centuries, which are continuing today, are the ever-increasing power of the state and the proletarianization of labour. The consequences of these changes for the ways in which people live and think have spread far from Western Europe, where they began, to the entire world. Studying them can help us understand many of the smaller-scale changes which are of interest: changes in family structures, in local political organizations, in types of protest, in work habits, and countless other areas.

Another important scholar who has worked on major social change is Barrington Moore (1966) who has been able to explain why modernization may produce different political outcomes: democracy, fascism, or communism. His thesis, in brief, is that where modernization takes place under the control of a state-noble alliance, fascism is likely to result. Where the state's power is curbed by a noble-bourgeois alliance, or by a bourgeois revolution, democracy is a more probable outcome. Finally, failed state-noble alliances permit successful peasant revolutions which result in communism. By comparing these various classes and their historical interaction in England, France, the United States (where a kind of landed nobility existed only in the old South), India, Japan, China, Germany and Russia, Moore demonstrated the utility of large-scale historical comparative analysis.

His student, Theda Skocpol, working along similar lines, has developed a temporally limited but convincing theory of revolution by comparing France, Russia and China (1979). She argues that external failure, the inability of a state to keep up with foreign competitors and intrusions, has been the single most important cause of revolutions in the last two centuries. Also, she emphasizes that Marxist class analysis has underplayed the role of what is perhaps the most important class of all, the state bureaucracy.

It is possible to discern the key issues in future social change. Will the poor parts of the world be able to experience rapid economic growth and social modernization within a framework similar to that of the West? Or will it be necessary, as Immanuel Wallerstein (1979) and other 'world-system' theorists claim, to revolutionize the entire world's social system and create a 'socialist world-economy' in order to spread the benefits of modernity more equitably? Will rich nations fight against progress in poor nations, or will they encourage it?

Is the continuing strengthening of almost all modern states likely to bring a stop to scientific and technological progress? All past historical experience suggests this may be so, but perhaps the very creation of a class of professional scientists and technical specialists has changed the social basis of innovation.

Finally, is the proletarianization of labour combined with the strengthening of states going to result in drastically reduced freedom for individuals as they become faceless cogs in huge, impersonal bureaucratic machines? Is a form of communism or fascism (which closely resemble each other in daily practice if not in their stated ideologies and historical origins) going to predominate throughout the world? What social consequences would this have?

Are ecological transformations produced by modern technology going to create difficult circumstances for future generations? There is no reason to assume that ecological change is any less powerful a cause of serious problems and change today than it was in the past.

These are the big questions. Other interesting aspects of social change follow from them. But it is only by understanding how individual lives are linked to the largest-scale political, cultural and economic changes that progress can be made in understanding past as well as future social change.

Daniel Chirot
University of Washington

References

Anderson, P. (1974), *Passages from Antiquity to Feudalism*, London.
Ashtor, E. (1976), *A Social and Economic History of the Near East in the Middle Ages*, Berkeley and Los Angeles.
Bloch, M. (1961 [1939–40]), *Feudal Society*, Chicago. (Original French, *La société féodale*, Paris.)
Carneiro, R. L. (1970), 'A theory of the origin of the state', *Science*, 169.
Elvin, M. (1973), *The Pattern of the Chinese Past*, Stanford.
Hodgson, M. G. S. (1974), *The Venture of Islam*, Vols 1 and 2, Chicago.
Merton, R. K. (1970), *Science, Technology and Society in Seventeenth Century England*, New York.
Moore, B. (1966), *Social Origins of Dictatorship and Democracy*, Boston.

Needham, J. and Ronan, C. A. (1976), *The Shorter Science and Civilisation in China*, Vol. 1, Cambridge.
Poggi, G. (1978), *The Development of the Modern State*, Stanford.
Skocpol, T. (1979), *States and Social Revolutions*, New York.
Smith, P. E. L. and Young, T. C. (1972), 'The evolution of early agriculture and culture in Greater Mesopotamia: a trial model', in B. Spooner (ed.), *Population Growth: Anthropological Implications*, Cambridge.
Steward, J. H. (1955), *Theory of Culture Change: The Methodology of Multilinear Evolution*, Urbana, Ill.
Tilly, C. (1981), *As Sociology Meets History*, New York.
Wallerstein, I. (1979), *The Capitalist World-Economy*, Cambridge.
Weber, M. (1968 [1922]), *Economy and Society*, New York. (Original German, *Wirtschaft und Gesellschaft*, Tübingen.)

Further Reading

Bell, D. (1973), *The Coming of Post-Industrial Society: A Venture in Social Forecasting*, New York.
Boserup, E. (1981), *Population and Technological Change*, Chicago.
Hobsbawm, E. J. (1969), *Industry and Empire*, Harmondsworth.
McNeill, W. H. (1982), *The Pursuit of Power*, Chicago.
Wolf, E. R. (1982), *Europe and the People Without History*, Berkeley and Los Angeles.

See also: *futurology; modernization; post-industrial society.*

Social Class

See Class.

Social Contract

The doctrine that government should be for and by the people informs the constitution of all countries claiming to be democratic, even when the precept is not observed in practice. Democratic governments today rest their claims to legitimacy and obedience on electoral consent, but the concept of consent itself derived originally from contract theory which discovered the origins of government in a primal act of consent, the social contract. The foremost exponents of contract theory, Hobbes, Locke and Rousseau, did not believe that savages had literally congregated and agreed to set up governments; contract was, rather, a hypothetical device. Its purpose was to show that governments should be viewed *as if* they had been established by the people and evaluated according to whether they served the purpose of protection for which they were instituted. In Hobbes's case the theory had illiberal implications: almost any government, however bad, would serve to keep anarchy at bay. But for Locke, the people had the right to resist a government which failed to protect their lives and property. Whether the conclusions of contract theory were reactionary or revolutionary depended on its basic assumptions.

In *Leviathan* (1651), Hobbes, fresh from the horrors of civil war, imagined men in an anarchic state of nature, living in fear of sudden death. These men would eventually make a contract to guarantee peace, for their own protection. But since none would trust their fellows, they would then appoint a sovereign, independent of the contract, to enforce it and maintain order by all necessary means, including coercion. Because Hobbes sees authorization as a blank cheque, imposing no accountability on those in authority, his sovereign would have unqualified power over those who authorized him.

Locke's contract theory (1690) was developed partly in protest against Hobbes's absolutist conclusions, partly to vindicate the revolution of 1688 which replaced the Stuarts with a constitutional monarchy. His state of nature is peaceful and orderly; people follow natural, moral laws and cultivate land and acquire property. But the absence of laws to resolve disputes leads people to establish a government by agreement. In making the contract, individuals surrender their natural rights, receiving instead civil rights and protection. The government thus created has a limited, fiduciary role. Its duty is the preservation of 'life, liberty and estate', and if it reneges, the people have the right to overthrow it. Although Locke argued that the contract enforced consent to majority rule, his was not a theory of democracy but an argument for a balanced constitution with a people's legislature, an executive monarch and an independent judiciary. This innovatory constitutionalism was a far cry from Hobbes's axiom that sovereignty was necessarily indivisible. Locke's doctrine that post-contract generations must consent to government, either actively or tacitly, later gave rise to consent theory.

Contractualism is developed in a different direction by Rousseau (1762), who argued that governments originally resulted from conspiracies of the rich to protect their property. But through an ideal social contract, individuals would freely consent to exchange their natural autonomy for a share in government. This could only be achieved by a direct, participatory democracy, which would be directed by the 'General Will'. The General Will is 'that which wills the common good', the decision which all citizens would accept if they laid aside personal interests. Dissenters from the General Will could be 'forced to be free', that is, compelled to obey laws for the public good which, if less self-interested, they would themselves freely have chosen. The General Will thus represents our 'better selves', but liberal theorists have often regarded it as a potential justification for authoritarianism or for totalitarian regimes claiming to act in the 'real interests' of the people (although undoubtedly this was not Rosseau's intention) and have therefore rejected Rousseau's contract theory.

Despite their differences, all three theories reflect the same desire to make the legitimacy of governments rest on the people's choice. The cultural environment which produced this desire was one of increasing individualism, secularization and legalism: the doctrine of individual free will dictated that nobody should be governed without his own consent, while the decline of the 'divine right of kings' dogma meant that a secular justification for political power was needed. The recourse to a contractual justification mirrored the growing reliance on contracts in the expanding commercial world, and a new, anti-feudal, legalistic attitude to public affairs.

The central fallacy of contract theories, as T. H. Green stated (1901), is that they presuppose 'savage' men with notions of rights and legality which could only be generated *within* a society. More damning for critics such as Hume, Bentham and Paine was the fact that existing governments were blatantly based on coercion, not consent, and operated largely for the benefit of the governors. History too suggested that most governments had been established through conquest and force. Such criticisms explain why contract theory was later replaced by the more plausible idea of democratic consent. However, contractarianism has recently been revived in Rawls's *Theory of Justice* (1971), which identifies the principles of justice as those to which people would consent, if deliberating in a state-of-nature-like vacuum. Rawls's work, which vindicates a broadly liberal view of justice, illustrates again how the original assumptions, especially those concerning human nature, determine the form and the contents of a hypothetical social contract. Contract theory is not abstract speculation, but a political myth tailored to prove a point.

Despite the logical and empirical shortcomings of contract theory, it deserves serious attention because of its relation to central political ideas such as 'the will of the people', legitimacy and political obligation. All these have been employed manipulatively by regimes which have no basis in the people's choice. The 'social contract' which British politicians have recently resurrected seems neo-Hobbesian, requiring unconditional compliance from citizens. To avoid such ideological manoeuvres and sleights of hand, we now need to reject the rhetorical invocation of implicit, tacit or imaginary social contracts and to develop a doctrine of meaningful and participatory choice and consent.

Barbara Goodwin
Brunel University, Uxbridge

References
Green, T. H. (1901), *Lectures on the Principles of Political Obligation*, London.

Hobbes, T. (1968 [1651]), *Leviathan*, ed. C. B. Macpherson, London.

Locke, J. (1924 [1690]), *An Essay Concerning the True Original, Extent and End of Civil Government*, London.

Rawls, J. (1971), *A Theory of Justice*, Cambridge, Mass.

Rousseau, J. J. (1913 [1762]), *The Social Contract* (trans. G. D. H. Cole, London). (Original French, *Du contrat social*, Paris.)

Riley, P. (1982), *Will and Political Legitimacy: A Critical Exposition of Social Contract Theory in Hobbes, Locke, Rousseau, Kant and Hegel*, Cambridge, Mass.

See also: *Hobbes; Locke; Maine; Rousseau.*

Social Control

Conceptualizations of Social Control

In the first book on the subject published over eighty years ago, E.A. Ross, defined social control (1901) as 'concerned with that domination which is intended and which fulfils a function in the life of the society'. The definition suggests that social control is intentional; but as Pitts (1968) observed: 'when [Ross] described social control in action, he fell back upon all the forms of the Durkheimian *conscience collective* that constrain the individual: public opinion, law, belief systems, education, custom, religion . . .' Stated otherwise, in attributing social control to institutions, Ross ignored this question: granted that institutions constrain human behaviour, in what sense are those constraints intentional or purposive? Moreover, if institutions are the loci of social control, what of control within and over institutions? Ross's conceptualization of social control is more objectionable than the questions suggest. He actually treated social control as though it is any collective activity that somehow contributes to social order. If that conception is accepted, social control cannot be a manageable notion; and this question becomes illogical: Does social control contribute to social order?

The counteraction of deviance. Writing fifty years after Ross, Talcott Parsons (1951) formulated what is now the prevailing conception of social control in sociology. 'The theory of social control . . . is the analysis of those processes . . . which tend to counteract . . . deviant tendencies . . . . Every social system has, in addition to the obvious rewards for conformative and punishments for deviant behaviour, a complex system of unplanned and largely unconscious mechanisms which serve to counteract deviant tendencies.' Parson's 'counteraction-of-deviance' conception of social control seemingly denies the relevance of intention. The denial perhaps reflects the widespread conviction in sociology that the unanticipated consequences of human behaviour are the most important; but if the purposive quality of human behaviour is ignored, then the distinction between successful and unsuccessful social control is lost. The loss is all the more important

because the distinction bears on this question: Why are some means of social control employed more than others? Finally, in light of the counteraction-of-deviance conception, it is illogical to ask: Does social control counteract deviant tendencies?

The counteraction-of-deviance conception is widely accepted in the two social-science disciplines where the conceptualization of social control receives serious attention – sociology and anthropology. Nonetheless, the conception presupposes that deviance is not an ambiguous notion, but its definition is a thicket of difficulties and controversies. The older, normative conception of deviance is now eroded because of several seemingly insoluble problems with the notion of norms, and the reactive conception of deviance is subject to four serious objections (Gibbs, 1981). Finally, because of the obvious circularity, it will not do to define social control by reference to deviance and then define deviance by reference to social control (Black, 1976).

Even if there were no problems with the notion of deviance, the counteraction-of-deviance conception of social control excludes several kinds of organized manipulations of human behaviour on a vast scale. Contemplate contemporary American advertising, where thousands of individuals attempt to manipulate the behaviour of millions; but it is not social control unless the advertisers are 'counteracting deviance'. Then contemplate the activities of Nazis in Weimar Germany and those of American abolitionists prior to the end of slavery. To say that those activities were social control because they 'counteracted deviance' only generates sterile arguments about norms; but, apart from norms or deviance, what were those activities if not social control?

One merit of the counteraction-of-deviance conception is that it does suggest an answer to an important question: What is *social* about social control? The *typical* bank robber is engaged in control but not social control (that is, not the counteraction of deviance), nor is someone when hailing a cab. Those two illustrations suggest that social control (1) has a normative quality and (2) is distinct from everyday interaction. The trick, therefore, is to conceptualize social control so as to recognize those two features but avoid reference to deviance. Unfortunately, because writers who do not explicitly endorse the counteraction-of-deviance conception (for example, Janowitz, 1975) fail to offer an alternative, there is only one distinct alternative in the current literature (Gibbs, 1981).

Social control is an attempt by one or more individuals (the first party in either case) to manipulate the behaviour of one or more other individuals (the second party in either case) through still another individual or individuals (the third party in either case) by means other than a chain of command or requests. The definition excludes *proximate* control, meaning control without a third party, as when a customer requests something or a mother physically restrains her child; and it also excludes *sequential* control, as when X orders Y to order Z. Social control is not necessarily more important; rather, proximate and sequential control are conspicuous in everyday interaction, especially in bureaucratic or military social units. Moreover, the distinction bears on this question: What happens when requests are ignored or commands disobeyed? People commonly resort to social control. Finally, as defined in the context of the third-party conception, social control is essential to manipulate behaviour on a large scale; as such, it is indispensable for the Gandhis and Hitlers of the world.

The third-party conception can be clarified by examining five types of social control: (1) Should a child say to a sibling, 'Give me back my candy or I will tell Mother!', that statement is *referential social control*. The first party (the child in this instance) attempts to manipulate the behaviour of the second party (the sibling) by making reference to a third party (the mother). But referential social control may involve millions, as when Hitler (first party) castigated Jews (third party) to gain the support of gentiles (second party). Then observe that referential social control may be a feature of adjudication, as when a trial attorney makes reference to a ruling of another court.

(2) Another type of social control – *allegative* – is conspicuous in tort law. A plaintiff cannot command a judge or jury to compel the defendant to pay damages; rather, that goal is realized by allegations about the defendant (second party) that the judge and/or jury (third party) find credible and evaluate negatively. But allegative social control transcends law. Thus, rather than resort to referential social control, a child may make allegations about a sibling to their mother.

(3) *Vicarious* social control is illustrated by an idea in the deterrence doctrine – when legal officials (the first party) punish accused criminals (third party), the punishment deters others (second party). However, a judge may impose a punishment, including an award of damages in a civil case, to placate the complainant or plaintiff; and vicarious social control is not limited to punishment or to the legal sphere. For example, an employer may ceremonially reward a very productive employee in the hope that other employees will strive for greater productivity.

(4) In so far as a *third* party influences the second party's behaviour, the first party can manipulate that behaviour by using or terminating the third party's influence; and such *modulative* social control does not entail an allegation about the second party. Thus, when an advertiser (first party) pays a celebrity (third party) to extol some product on television, the advertiser assumes that the celebrity has some influence over consumers (second party). Modulative social control in the legal sphere is common when law is used to promote class or caste interests, as when teaching

slaves to read is legally proscribed with a view to reducing the influence of 'agitators'.

(5) Without knowledge as to what and whom prospective controllees hate, fear, value, and respect, a would-be controllee cannot answer this question: Which kind of control would be most effective? The question is especially salient in controlling numerous individuals, in which case limited resources give rise to another question: Who should be subject to special efforts at control? The first party may seek an answer by using a third party to (a) gather information on prospective second parties, including surveillance; (b) conduct research on the effectiveness of alternative means of control; (c) create conditions that facilitate control; or (d) exclude particular kinds of second parties from certain social or spatial contexts, as in the case of immigration laws. Such uses of a third party are *prelusive* social control, the most highly-organized type.

Major Questions

The counteraction-of-deviance conception of social control is inconsistent with the way political scientists and economists commonly use the term (Gibbs, 1982), and the concept will not become central for all of the social sciences as long as that conception prevails. Moreover, the conception has not made social control central even to sociology or anthropology, and it has not generated substantial research or a theory. No less telling, advocates of that conception have left the major questions about social control obscure, even though there are two obvious candidates. First, why do means of social control vary among social units and over time? Second, what is the relative efficacy of the various means of social control?

The first major question. Prior to Parsons, historical and cross-cultural contrasts in means of social control received considerable attention, but writers (for example, Lumley, 1925) were largely content to describe those contrasts. Only observations on variation in the punitiveness of criminal sanctions gave rise to theories (see Sutherland and Cressey's survey, 1974); and today only Durkheim's theory receives serious attention. Since the punitiveness of criminal sanctions is only one facet of social control, it is not surprising that work on the subject has waned. Yet it is not obvious why both advocates of functionalism and advocates of Marxist-conflict sociology have largely ignored the first major question about social control. Functionalists in the Parsonian tradition view social control as important only in that it supposedly corrects mistakes or errors in socialization, and they appear indifferent to the means employed. For that matter, if one assumes that normative consensus is the basis of social order, that in itself is a tacit belittlement of social control. Since Marxist-conflict sociologists emphatically deny that normative consensus is the basis of social order, it may appear that they treat social control as more important than do functionalists. Even so, Marxist-conflict sociologists have shown little concern with demonstrating and explaining variation in means of social control. Their indifference reflects their assumption that the use of coercion by a proper-tied class is the basis of social order in all societies; hence, they are evidently loath to recognize the possibility that the character of social control varies substantially among societies and historically.

Only two extensive lines of current research have some possible bearing on the notion of social control. One line is commonly referred to in connection with 'societal reaction theory'; but that term is misleading, for it really denotes little more than a vast body of research on contingencies in reactions to deviance, especially events in the criminal justice process (such as arrest, sentencing). The research became popular in the 1960s as a reflection of the belief that the alleged causes of deviant behaviour (including crime and delinquency) received too much attention, to the neglect of this question: What determines the character of the reaction to particular deviant acts and particular deviants? The question itself reflects a tacit rejection of a belief associated with classical criminal justice – reactions to a crime are determined by strictly legal factors, the nature of the offence in particular. To the contrary, so advocates of societal reaction theory argue, reactions are determined by, *inter alia*: (1) the race, class, sex, ethnicity and demeanour of the alleged deviant; (2) characteristics of the reactors, such as racial prejudice on the part of police officers; (3) characteristics of persons allegedly harmed by the deviant act, such as crime victims; and (4) the situation or circumstances, such as the time and place of the deviant act. As the list suggests, there is no agreement as to the major contingency in reactions to deviance, and the high ratio of male to female arrests alone makes it absurd to assume that the 'power' of the deviant is decisive (that is, that women avoid arrest for armed robbery more often than do men because women have more power). A simple societal reaction theory is precluded because research findings indicate that: (1) the nature of the offence is much more a determinant of the reaction to a crime than once supposed; (2) that the contingencies are by no means the same for all steps in the reaction process (such as arrest, sentencing) or for all types of offences (for example, property crimes versus violent crimes); and (3) the extent to which legal reactions to crimes are contingent on extralegal factors may vary substantially from one social unit or period to the next (see Curran, 1983).

While several sociologists have defined social control as 'reactions to deviance', not all reactions counteract deviant tendencies, nor does a reactor necessarily believe that the reaction reduces the probability of more deviance. Hence, neither the counteraction-of-deviance conception nor the third-party conception (*supra*) justifies the identification of all reactions to deviance as social control. Even if the identification were justified, research in connection with the so-called societal reaction theory is concerned with differences in reactions to particular cases of deviance in the same social unit or jurisdiction and *not* with variation in means of social control among social units or historically. Consequently, societal reaction research must be expanded if it is to play an important role in social control studies.

The second major question. Recognition of defects in early (1950s) studies of capital punishment led a few sociologists in the late 1960s to reconsider the deterrence doctrine – the argument that legal punishments can deter criminality. An army of social scientists oppose the argument, and no major theorist (for example Merton, Sutherland) has emphasized the possibility that the crime rate is appreciably a function of legal punishments. So it is not surprising that Parsons and his disciples never identified the deterrence doctrine as a theory of social control. Indeed, in light of the counteraction-of-deviance conception, it could be argued that legal punishments are not social control without a demonstration that they do prevent crimes. Such a demonstration is not needed to identify legal punishments as social control in light of the third-party conception (*supra*). Durkheim notwithstanding, deterrence appears to be the 'primary and essential postulate' in all but one of the world's criminal law systems (Morris, 1966).

The identification of legal punishments as social control does not validate the deterrence doctrine, and there are all manner of problems in attempting to test the doctrine. The most conspicuous problem is the sheer number of possibly relevant properties of legal punishments, especially in the case of general deterrence (deterring individuals without actually punishing them). Since early research on capital punishment considered only statutory penalties for murder (that is, the presumptive severity of *prescribed* punishments), the investigators ignored eight possibly relevant properties of legal punishments (Gibbs, 1975). Deterrence research expanded in the late 1960s to encompass the objective certainty and the presumptive severity of *actual* punishments (for example, the proportion of crimes that result in imprisonment and the length of sentence served), but even today perceptual properties of punishments (for example, perceived certainty, perceived severity) do not receive sufficient attention.

Another problem stems from the recognition that legal punishments may prevent crimes through any one of several nondeterrent mechanisms (see Gibbs, 1975). For example, because a person cannot steal a car when he is in prison, imprisonment prevents repetition of that offence by incapacitating the offender. In so far as legal punishments are prescribed and/or imposed in the belief that they prevent criminality, they are means of control regardless of the preventive mechanism. However, the belief that the actual punishment of an offender deters potential offenders (that is, general deterrence) makes that punishment *social control* in light of the third-party conception.

The third and final major problem stems from an undisputed argument – that the crime rate is not a function solely of legal punishments. All manner of extralegal factors (for example, possibly the unemployment rate) could be relevant; and until those factors are held constant in comparing crime rates, an incontrovertible interpretation of findings in deterrence research will be precluded. To date, unfortunately, no truly defensible aetiological theory of crime can be used to identify relevant extralegal factors. Nonetheless, the problem has implications when viewing the deterrence doctrine as a theory of social control. The doctrine is a very narrow theory of social control because it is traditionally construed as limited to legal punishments. However, when attempts are made to hold relevant extralegal factors constant when comparing crime rates, the deterrence doctrine will become all the more relevant in the study of social control. Even though structural variables (for example, class composition, the unemployment rate) may be the most important extralegal factors in the aetiology of crime, extralegal controls over human behaviour, including social control, are also relevant (see, especially, Wilson, 1980). Accordingly, attempts to improve the quality of deterrence research will expand knowledge of both legal and extralegal social control.

Jack P. Gibbs
Vanderbilt University

References

Black, D. (1976), *The Behavior of Law*, New York.
Curran, D. A. (1983), 'Judicial discretion and defendant's sex', *Criminology*, 21.
Gibbs, J. P. (1975), *Crime, Punishment, and Deterrence*, New York.
Gibbs, J. P. (1981), *Norms, Deviance and Social Control: Conceptual Matters*, New York.
Gibbs, J. P. (ed.) (1982), *Social Control*: Views from the Social Sciences, Beverly Hills, Calif.
Janowitz, M. (1975), 'Sociological theory and social control', *American Journal of Sociology*, 81.
Lumley, F. E. (1925), *Means of Social Control*, New York.
Martindale, D. (1978), 'The theory of social control', in J. S. Roucek (ed.), *Social Control for the 1980's*, Westport, Connecticut.
Morris, N. (1966), 'Impediments to penal reform', *University of Chicago Law Review*, 33.
Parsons, T. (1951), *The Social System*, New York.
Pitts, J. R. (1968), 'Social control: the concept', in D. L. Sills (ed.), *International Encyclopedia of the Social Sciences*, New York.
Ross, E. A. (1901), *Social Control*, New York.
Sutherland, E. H. and Cressey, D. R. (1974), *Criminology*, 9th edn, Philadelphia.
Wilson, H. (1980), 'Parental supervision: a neglected aspect of delinquency', *British Journal of Criminology*, 20.
See also: *deviance; norms; punishment*.

Social Darwinism

Social Darwinism refers loosely to various late nineteenth-century applications (mostly misapplications) of ideas of biological evolution associated (often erroneously) with Darwin, to human societies. Though often associated with conservatism, *laissez-faire* capitalism, fascism and racism, Social Darwinism was, in fact, a pervasive doctrine of the late nineteenth and early twentieth centuries, especially in Britain and in North America, and its influence covered the entire political spectrum, including, for example, British Fabian socialism.

Its two leading intellectual proponents were Herbert Spencer in Britain (to whom we owe the phrase 'survival of the fittest'), and William Graham Sumner, a professor of anthropology at Yale University in the United States. To Spencer, we owe the misleading analogy that a society is like an organism (hence, the term 'organicism' sometimes used to describe his theories). Just as an organism is composed of interdependent organs and cells, a human society is made up of specialized and complementary institutions and individuals, all belonging to an organic whole.

Spencer himself was never very clear about his analogy: he claimed both that society was 'like an organism', and that it was a 'super-organism'. His central notion, however, was that the whole (organism-society) was made up of functionally specialized, complementary and interdependent parts. Thus, he is also considered to be one of the main fathers of sociological functionalism.

Sumner's concept of mores (his term, by the way), and his turgid disquisitions on morality are his most lasting contributions. What his writings have to do with Darwinism is questionable. 'Bad mores are those which are not well fitted to the conditions and needs of the society at the time . . . . The taboos constitute morality or a moral system which, in higher civilization restrains passion and appetite, and curbs the will' (Sumner, 1906). Sumner uses terms such as 'evolution' and 'fitness' to be sure, but his moralistic pronouncements and his repeated emphasis on the 'needs of the society' are the very antithesis of Darwin's thinking. Spencer was also prone to inject ethics into evolution, seeing an 'inherent tendency of things towards good'. Darwin, on the other hand, saw evolution as a random process devoid of ethical goals or trends, and natural selection as a blind mechanism discriminating between *individual organisms* on the basis of their *differential reproductive success*.

Another central theme in Sumner is that 'stateways cannot change folkways', meaning that state action is powerless to change the underlying mores. This certainly made him an apostle of *laissez-faire*. Indeed, he went so far as to contradict himself and suggest that state intervention is worse than useless; it is noxious. These propositions probably form the core of the doctrine associated with social Darwinism, namely, that the existing social order with its inequalities reflects a natural process of evolution in which the 'fitter' rise to the top and the 'unfit' sink to the bottom. Any attempt, through social welfare, for example, to reduce inequalities is seen as noxious because it allows the unfit to 'breed like rabbits'. Indeed Spencer, as a good Victorian puritan, believed that intelligence and reproduction were inversely related. Overproduction of sperm, he thought, leads first to headaches, then to stupidity, then to imbecility, 'ending occasionally in insanity' (1852).

Again, these ideas are quite antithetical to those of Darwinian-evolutionary theory. If the lower classes reproduce faster than the upper classes, it means they are *fitter*, since, in evolutionary theory, the ultimate measure of fitness is reproductive success. To say that the unfit breed like rabbits is a contradiction in terms.

Social Darwinism, in short, is a discredited moral philosophy that bears only a superficial terminological resemblance to the Darwinian theory of evolution, and is only of historical interest.

Pierre van den Berghe
University of Washington

References
Spencer, H. (1852), 'A theory of population deduced from the general law of animal fertility', *Westminster Review*, 1.
Spencer, H. (1864), *Principles of Biology*, London.
Spencer, H. (1873–85), *Descriptive Sociology*, London.
Sumner, W. G. (1906), *Folkways*, Boston.

Further Reading
Hofstadter, R. (1959), *Social Darwinism in American Thought*, New York.
Ruse, M. (1982), *Darwinism Defended*, Reading, Mass.
See also: *evolution; evolutionism and progress; Spencer.*

Social Geography

Although research and teaching in social geography have increased dramatically in the last two decades, its proponents are unlikely to agree on a definition. There is no single methodology and no generally accepted conceptual framework – perhaps little more than the common interest of a number of scholars focusing their work on social group activities in the context of the physical and social environments. Those who would enlarge the field to all human activities, and hence identify it with human geography, think it pointless to formulate a discipline. The current emphasis on processes has taken many social geographers into the much more general realms of political economy; in contrast, humanist social geographers have been drawn to the study of individual behaviour. Between the two extremes most workers in this field have identified as fundamental units of study groups which share social experiences, and a geographical approach concerning groups, interactions in space and place and region.

Historically, social geography has its roots in the French school of human geography established by Vidal de la Blache, which owed much to the French sociological tradition. The German school, exemplified by Bobek, has paid more attention to the regional expression of cultural differences, an emphasis on the works of man and on the cultural landscape of which Sauer, in the United States, was a notable proponent. Americans still work in 'cultural' rather than 'social' geography, but the difference is sometimes one of scale only. British social geography drew on the French experience, but, as in the United States, a new infusion of sociological models, particularly from the Chicago School of the inter-war period, led to an emphasis on social ecology.

The surge of research which came in the 1960s was characterized by empiricism and the search for spatial patterns, depending for their interpretation on the borrowing from the models of cognate subjects, particularly sociology and economics. The positivist basis of this work was reinforced by the rapid rise of computer science, strengthening the studies with the assurance of scientific method and its attendant academic respectability. Although this period was unusually fruitful in extending research and teaching, its limitations were the excessive emphasis on stage (patterns) and the dependence on positivist methodology: however sophisticated the latter became, it helped only to further detail areal classification and description. Scant attention was paid to process, and the methodology could not encompass parameters which were not amenable to quantification. To many, this only highlighted the need to recognize the unquantifiable – particularly values – and the way they affected human behaviour. Behaviourism engaged more and more scholars (Davies, 1972), together with the significance of human perception against which groups behaved and with which they reacted.

The French had given particular attention to the subjective environment, and more specifically to social space – that is, space created by social activity – and Buttimer (1978) was largely responsible for introducing this concept in the US and Britain, always underlining the significance of social values. At the same time, Hägerstrand (1969) was stressing the social dimension and the individual reaction as a corrective to the highly abstract analysis of space then dominating human geography in the US and Britain. He also added the time dimension to human activities, an aspect which geographers at the University of Lund have extended even further.

Empirical work stemming from the ecologist school has added vastly to the literature of social geography (Jones and Eyles, 1977). Social-area analysis attracted much research, though it was very weak on theory; segregation was another fruitful field, as was intra-city migration and, more recently, the study of criminal areas and work on the old, and on women. The behavioural point of view has added depth to many of these studies, although many of them have depended on the same methodology which underlay earlier studies. The subjective element in social geography, however, has been developed further in the direction of humanism and existentialism (Leys and Samuels, 1978), and participant observation became again an integral tool of research. The characteristics of this kind of study are its preoccupation with the philosophical bases and its emphasis on either very small groups or even on the individual. Contributions are diffuse, seemingly marginal to a geographer's interest, and defy a simple account of their part in the field as a whole. But the very considerable contributions of Tuan (1977), for example, make it clear that perception, behaviour and group values must be central to an understanding of the relationships between group and environment, particularly as the latter is also seen as an expression of social values.

There was another reaction against the scientific assumptions and the abstractions of so much work in the 1960s, and that was a concern with society itself rather than with the niceties of methodology and philosophy. Among other urban social areas identified were those of poverty and deprivation, and, here, an examination of the processes giving rise to these patterns involved the researcher in fundamental social problems. There were antecedents for such work. Aspects of Booth's famous survey of London could be hailed as social geography. French researchers in the 1880s referred to a 'socialist' geography (Dunbar, 1978). Relevance is not an American discovery of 1968. It does now mean more, however, than the 'liberal' tradition of, for example, English geographers who for generations have been involved in practical social issues by providing the raw material for social change, though not necessarily committing themselves to policy issues. 'Relevance' today suggests a commitment to changing the social system. Academically, human geography has been equated with 'welfare geography' (based on a positivist methodology): advances in research have focused entirely on processes and their

manipulation. The latter have centred on a Marxist philosophy, most explicitly put forward by Harvey (1973). Most recently, variants of a structuralist viewpoint have dominated social geography. Paradoxically, in moving away from the formal stages and patterns with which the social geographer began, the emphasis on structure and process has also made solutions to problems more remote, as well as bypassing elements of place and space which some structuralists and Marxists ignore. The response to 'concern' has become so theoretical that problems in the field are in danger of being put on one side.

The seeming confusion and the apparent contradictory nature both of aims and methodologies in social geography are mainly an outcome of rapid expansion and dramatic increase in research, and partly a reflection of the rapidly changing paradigms of geography as a whole. If it is premature to define a narrow field of study it is because of the richness of ideas and their novelty (Jones, 1980). It is likely that there will remain many strands in the academic approach to a study which is as complex as society itself.

Emrys Jones
London School of Economics and Political Science

References

Buttimer, A. (1978), 'Values in geography', *Association of American Geographers Commission on College Geography*, Resource Paper 24.

Davies, W. K. D. (1972), *The Conceptual Revaluation in Geography*, part IV, London.

Dunbar, G. S. (1978), 'Some early occurrences of the term "social geography"', *Scottish Geographical Magazine*, 94.

Hägerstrand, T. (1969), 'On the definition of migration', *Scandinavian Population Studies*, 1.

Harvey, D. (1973), *Social Justice and the City*, London.

Jones, E. and Eyles, J. (1977), *An Introduction to Social Geography*, Oxford.

Jones, E. (1980), 'Social geography', in E.H. Brown (ed.), *Geography Yesterday and Tomorrow*, Oxford.

Leys, D. and Samuels, M. (eds) (1978), *Humanistic Geography: Prospect and Problems*, London.

Tuan, Y. F. (1977), *Topuplobia*, Englewood Cliffs, NJ.

Further Reading

Eyles, J. (1974), 'Social theory and social geography', *Progress in Geography*, 6.

Gregory, D. (1978), *Ideology, Science and Human Geography*, London.

Harvey, D. (1981), 'Marxist geography', in R. J. Johnston (ed.), *Dictionary of Human Geography*, Oxford.

Herbert, D. and Smith, D. M. (eds) (1979), *Social Problems and the City*, Oxford.

Kirk, W. (1963), 'Problems of geography', *Geography*, 48.

See also: *geography; regional analysis; spatial statistics; time-space analysis.*

Social Identity

In its most general sense, social identity refers to a person's self-definition in relation to others. Within social psychology, however, it usually has a more specific connotation – namely, a self-definition in terms of one's membership of various social groups. This sense of the term owes much to G. H. Mead, who emphasized a social conception of the self, arguing that individuals experience themselves 'from the standpoint of the social group as a whole' to which they belong (Mead, 1977). It is important to distinguish this public (or *social*) aspect of identity from the more private (or *personal*) aspects. Indeed, Mead himself, in stressing the importance of the group, can be seen as contrasting his approach from the more individualistic psycho-dynamic formulations. Thus, it has become common to refer to social identity in the manner above, and to personal identity as reflecting those parts of one's self-definition which have to do with personality traits, physical attributes, interpersonal styles and the like. More recently, Brown and Turner (1981) have argued that this is not merely an abstract theoretical distinction but one which, following Tajfel (1978), may have important behavioural implications: according to whether 'personal' or 'social' identities are psychologically uppermost in any situation may determine whether people exhibit sporadic and idiosyncratic 'interpersonal' behaviours, *or* organized and socially uniform 'intergroup' behaviours.

Historically, the concept of social identity has occupied a central place in both social-psychological and sociological theorizing. For instance, Lewin (1948), whose field theory inspired a whole generation of post-war social psychologists, wrote and researched extensively on the psychological significance of group affiliations, especially for minority and marginal groups. Within a more psychoanalytic tradition, the work of Erikson (1960) on identity conflicts and identity diffusion in the individual's life cycle has had important clinical applications. Within sociology, too, social identity has not gone unnoticed. For example, in Parson's General Theory of Action it is defined as a subsystem of personality and assigned a major role in determining a person's participation in the social system (see, for example, Parsons, 1968).

Reflecting these theoretical concerns, much empirical research has attempted to measure different components of identity. The bulk of this work has concentrated on aspects of personal identity focusing on such topics as self-esteem, locus of control, and level of aspiration. These methodologies have been compre-hensively reviewed by Wylie (1974). In contrast, very few attempts have been made to measure social identity. One of the earliest, and still widely used, techniques is the Twenty Statements Test devised by Kuhn and McPartland (1954). This simply involves a respondent giving up to twenty responses to the question 'Who am I?' These responses may then be analysed to reveal the nature of that person's social and personal identity referents, the evaluative quality of the terms used, and the importance attributed to different elements. A typical finding is that social identity referents emerge earliest in response protocols, the most commonly mentioned categories being sex and occupational role. Zavalloni (1971) has proposed a technique for investigating a person's social identity idiographically. This method allows the respondent to differentiate between different subgroups within a larger category, sometimes attaching very different valence and meaning to those subgroup identifications. However, both of these techniques yield essentially qualitative data and, in the latter case, are time-consuming to administer and analyse. A simpler and more practicable instrument is suggested by Driedger (1976). This consists of a short scale in which the respondent is permitted to affirm or deny, in varying degrees of strength, different aspects of ingroup membership. Although designed to measure ethnic identity, there is no reason why the technique could not be extended to measure the strength of other group identifications also.

Despite these methodological difficulties, the concept of social identity continues to excite considerable research interest. Much of this has been stimulated by Tajfel's Social Identity Theory (for example, Tajfel, 1978), which proposes a causal link between social identity needs and various forms of intergroup behaviour. Central to this theory is the hypothesis that people's social identities are sustained primarily through social comparisons, which differentiate the ingroup from relevant outgroups. From this simple idea it has proved possible to explain the prevalence of intergroup discrimination, even in the absence of real conflicts of interest, and to provide persuasive analyses of the plight of minority groups, industrial conflicts over pay differentials, and linguistic differentiation between ethnic groups.

Rupert Brown
University of Kent

References
Brown, R. J. and Turner, J. C. (1981), 'Interpersonal and intergroup behaviour', in J. C. Turner and H. Giles (eds), *Intergroup Behaviour*, Oxford.
Driedger, L. (1976), 'Ethnic self-identity: a comparison of ingroup evaluations', *Sociometry*, 39.
Erikson, E. H. (1960), 'The problem of ego identity', in M. R. Stein, A. J. Vidich and D. M. White (eds), *Identity and Anxiety*, New York.

Kuhn, M. H. and McPartland, T. S. (1954), 'An empirical investigation of self attitudes', *American Sociological Review*, 19.

Lewin, K. (1948), *Resolving Social Conflicts*, New York.

Mead, G. H. (1977), *On Social Psychology*, revised edn, A. Strauss, Chicago.

Parsons, T. (1968), 'The position of identity in the General Theory of Action', in C. Gordon and K. J. Gergen (eds), *The Self in Social Interaction*, New York.

Tajfel, H. (1978), *Differentiation between Social Groups*: *Studies in the Social Psychology of Intergoup Relations*, London.

Wylie, R. C. (1974), *The Self Concept*, London.

Zavalloni, M. (1971), 'Cognitive processes and social identity through focussed introspection', *European Journal of Social Psychology* 1.

Further Reading

Gordon, C. and Gergen, K. J. (1968), *The Self in Social Interaction*, New York.

Tajfel, H. (1982), *Social Identity and Intergroup Relations*, London.

See also: *self-concept*.

Social Indicators

The social indicator 'movement' in the form of a dedicated body of scholars, numerous books, academic articles, national and international meetings, and a journal of social indicators research is of fairly recent origin under this name. It emerged jointly with a revival of interest in measurement of social change, social analysis and social policy in two places: in the international organizations in the early 1950s and in the United States in the mid-1960s.

Work in the United Nations and other international agencies centred upon measurement of levels of living, particularly in the developing countries. The purpose was to assess need as well as record progress in meeting need. One of the issues at the time was the extent to which concepts and methods of measurement in developed countries were applicable also to developing countries. In the United States, interest in social indicators and related concepts, such as 'social reporting' or 'national goals accounting', arose from academic curiosity and political concern about social trends, the need to consider social change as a totality, and the awareness that there was nothing on the social side corresponding to the well-established economic accounts or economic reports. There was also thought to be an immediate practical application, in the evaluation of programme benefits. Some of these hopes, for instance, to obtain social accounts to match economic accounts, have not been fulfilled for reasons that are now well known: the considerable heterogeneity of 'social' items, absence of a comprehensive social model,

lack of a common unit of measurement such as the dollar or pound in economic accounting. Since these early endeavours, use of the term has spread to the majority of developed and to some of the statistically more advanced developing countries. The United Kingdom began its periodical *Social Trends* in 1970; other national reports include *Données Sociales* (France), *Social Indicators* (Trinidad and Tobago), *Life and its Quality in Japan*, *Perspective Canada*.

The Meaning of Indicators

To make a scientific contribution, the term 'social indicators' must be defined so as to distinguish it from other, similar terms as regards both 'indicator' and 'social'. There is so far no agreed definition. Of the several in vogue only the following two-step procedure appears to give a distinct meaning which at the same time is sufficiently broad to provide for a programme of work. A first step is to define the 'fields' of conceptual items which are to be measured. These may be broad, such as 'development' or the 'quality of life of the people in Britain'; or they may be narrow, such as the 'educational status' of a specific local population or the 'health conditions of the Palestinian refugees'. They may be conventional social sectors, such as health or education, or 'domains' as used in French planning to denote problem groups or areas, of which inequality or social problems associated with the process of ageing are examples. Because few such fields or domains can be measured directly, recourse is had to 'indicators'. The second step therefore consists of selecting indicators that are conceptually related to the field, and that, using as few indicators as possible, cover it as comprehensively and precisely as possible. Thus, the health of a refugee population can be described in terms of several discrete components of which the overall level of health services, access to services, health status are examples. None of these can be fully measured directly, and selected indicators are used for each. Health status, for example, is commonly approximated by age-specific mortality rates or incidence of selected diseases.

The indicators so defined derive their meaning solely from the context in which they are used. An infant mortality rate (deaths of infants under one year per 1,000 live births) is a statistic. It becomes an indicator by virtue of being chosen to describe a specific field. Indicators are normally numeral, but attempts to force concepts intrinsically unsuited to quantification into a numeric mould should be avoided.

The conceptual part of the work is clearly important (defining what is meant by development or health; then obtaining suitable indicators). The difficulties are greatly compounded in practice, particularly in some of the less-developed countries, by a scarcity of relevant data. In the present state of the art, the indicators actually selected often substitute only very imperfectly for reality, a fact to be remembered when considering conclusions of complex analysis involving the use of indicators.

Meanwhile, work on indicators proper (as distinct from social analysis, social reporting, programme evaluation, and so on) has tended to concentrate on three aspects: (1) to improve concepts and theory, for example, through improved specification of the fields and more appropriate indicators; (2) to improve the supply of relevant data; and (3) to validate empirically selected indicators.

Other Definitions
Of the other definitions sometimes used in the literature none seems to distinguish indicators sufficiently from broader concepts, such as statistics. Thus, the term is occasionally employed in the sense of selecting a small number of key-variables (which are then called indicators) from a large number. However, deciding what is 'key' or crucial normally requires a theoretical framework involving the two-step procedure outlined above. The crucial elements are normally decided upon as part of the first step and not in the selection of indicators. Other criteria, for example, that indicators be normative, that they be part of a model, or that they take the form of time series, although commonly features of indicators, have been criticized as unnecessarily restrictive.

The Meaning of 'Social'
There is no universally accepted meaning of 'social' indicators to distinguish them from economic or other kinds of indicators. The tendency has been to define social as a residual category to include everything that is not 'economic'. Commonly included fields are health, public safety, education, employment, income, housing, leisure, recreation, population as in the United States Bureau of the Census publication *Social Indicators*, to which in the UK's report *Social Trends* has been added: households and families, resources and expenditure, transport, communications and the environment, participation, social groups. Indicators of distribution, such as income distribution, are important. Researchers interested in structural change might add indicators of social differentiation or social organization; social psychologists could include indicators of social attitudes, and demographers indicators of population change.

Wolf Scott
United Nations Research Institute
for Social Development

Further Reading
Lard, K. C. (1983), 'Social indicators', *Annual Review of Sociology*, 9.
McGranahan, D. (1972), 'Development indicators and development models', *The Journal of*

Development Studies, 8. (Special issue on development indicators, ed. N. Baster.)
Sheldon, E. B. and Moore, W. E. (eds) (1968), *Indicators of Social Change: Concepts and Measurements*, New York.

Socialism

Socialism is the name for a varied group of political theories and movements. Socialist ideas and agitation began in the early nineteenth century in England and France. The period between the 1820s and the 1850s was marked by a plethora of diverse and distinguished theorists, among them, Saint-Simon, Fourier, Owen, Blanc and Proudhon, and also many lesser thinkers. It was also marked by the foundation of co-operative societies, model utopian communities and the advocacy – and in the case of Blanc's national workshops half-hearted adoption – of schemes to be put into action by governments.

Socialism was brought into existence by the rise of industrial production and the intensification of wage labour in handicraft enterprises alongside it. Prior to the large-scale existence of workshops, factories and machines, most radical conceptions of a reorganization of society were agrarian, as in Rousseau's constitution for an imaginary republic of Corsica. Socialist doctrines sought to 'organize' society in order to replace the anarchy of the market-place and large-scale poverty with an orderly system based on greater or lesser degrees of central control, co-operation and mutuality. Organization offered a rational solution to the 'social question' – the problems of mass poverty and poor urban living conditions. Most of the early socialists were middle-class reformers, concerned philanthropists who sought to better the lot of the poor by changes in social organization rather than charitable works.

The radical and revolutionary movements in this period were nationalist in countries like Hungary or Poland or Italy under foreign domination, and popular-democratic in England and France. Such political movements were not dominated by socialist ideas. Between 1848 and 1871 the popular democratic and revolutionary traditions exhausted themselves in the European countries in a series of political defeats, at the barricades in countries like France, or through political containment in the case of the Chartists in England.

In the period between 1848 and 1871, Marx and Engels made radical attempts to recast socialist theory. They attacked the utopianism of their predecessors, refusing to promulgate schemes of social reform. In essence they argued that:

(1) the class struggle is the objective basis of socialist victory, socialism is identified with the proletariat

and its struggle to eliminate exploitation and oppression;

(2) the class struggle arises from the system of social production and that the development of the forces of production would secure the objective basis for a planned economy;

(3) the overthrow of the exploiting class and its ruling machinery, the state, would usher in a new period of popular self-government in which the domination of man by man would be replaced by the administration of things.

Marx and Engels insisted on the necessity of revolution, and the seizure of power by the working class, but they did recognize that universal suffrage might facilitate the downfall of capitalism.

Actually, it did nothing of the sort. Between 1870 and 1914 the institutional foundations of modern socialism were developed in Britain and Germany. Universal suffrage created the modern political party – a permanent machine with paid officials whose task is to mobilize the mass electorate. The SPD became the dominant force in German socialism, not because it came to treat Marx's ideas as party orthodoxy, but because it started early and effectively to compete for votes in elections for the Reichstag. In Britain and Germany, large-scale industrialism was accompanied by the growth of trade unionism. The British Labour Party was created to facilitate the parliamentary representation of the trade unions, and the links between the SPD and the unions were similarly close.

As a mass electoral party and the political representative of unionized labour, any socialist movement in an advanced industrial country had to relegate to virtual impotence the popular insurrectionary politics of the old European 'left'. Even Engels conceded as much, and Eduard Bernstein did no more than carry the conclusion to its logical extreme. Bernstein's *Evolutionary Socialism* (1899) represented the first articulate advocacy of 'social democracy' as against socialism, and it displaced the goal of 'revolution' for a never-ending struggle for attainable reforms. Others, like Karl Kautsky, argued that by parliamentary and legal means the workers could engineer a revolutionary change in the social system.

To the mass party and the labour union must be added the rise of big government as a key institutional support of modern socialist movements. In the period 1870–1914 in Britain and Germany, central state and municipal authorities came to provide, administer and organize an increasing range of activities, mass schooling, social insurance, public health, sewerage and electric light, and so on. This administration of mass needs and utilities provided another base for socialist advocacy and practice. Fabian socialism consciously sought to intervene in central and local government's provision, to provide an organizing core

of intellectuals equipped to shape the extent and character of 'big government'. The success of the Fabian position stands in stark contrast to the failure of the anti-statist doctrines of Guild Socialists and others. For all the forceful advocacy by able thinkers like G. D. H. Cole (1953–61), the Guild Socialist movement was dead by the early 1920s. Likewise, British syndicalism perished in the same period, while institutional unionism survived and flourished.

After 1914 the landscape of the socialist movement in Europe was changed by World War I, the split in socialism and the rise of Communism. The Communist Parties for a considerable period in the 1920s and early 1930s emphasized revolutionary insurrectionary politics, going so far as to stigmatize the still existent European socialist parties like the SPD as 'social fascist'. World War II, the consolidation of Soviet rule in Eastern Europe and the stabilization of parliamentary democracy in Western Europe led to a radical change in the Communist parties. Where legally permitted or successful, they became mass electoral parties and developed links with their own labour unions, as in France and Italy, for example, and sought to participate in government. The split between Communism and socialism in Europe, bitter into the 1950s, ceased to have much meaning with the rise of Eurocommunism.

Since 1945 socialist and social democratic parties have participated in government to a hitherto unprecedented degree. The post-war boom was a period of intensification of 'big government' and welfarism. In Scandinavia, the UK and Germany, socialist parties became accepted parties of government, and in the Swedish case ruled uninterruptedly for over thirty years. In this period, traditional socialist ideas, centring on publicly-owned planned production, suffered at the expense of social-democratic views of redistribution and welfare in a state-managed, full-employment, capitalist system. Anthony Crosland's *The Future of Socialism* (1964) advocated, like Bernstein, a change in British Labour Party doctrine to match the Party's practice.

Since the end of the post-war boom in 1973, social democratic ideas have had to compete with a revitalized socialist fundamentalism in the UK. At the same time throughout Europe many intellectuals have begun to rethink the goals of socialism. Many are chastened by the experience of centrally-planned production and distribution in the USSR, but also by the consequences of the growth of statist welfarism in Western Europe. Many favour the sort of anti-authoritarian, decentralizing and self-management views advocated by Cole and the Guild Socialists. The problem with much of this rethinking is the failure to provide a new political base comparable to that provided by the mass party, the union and big government. A good example of such views is André Gorz's *Farewell to the Working Class* (1982). Socialist doctrine has entered a period of diversity and productivity comparable to the 1820s–50s; its institutional supports, however, remain those developed in the period 1870–1914.

Socialism has been treated as an exclusively European phenomenon. Socialism in the United States, having grown spectacularly between the formation of the American Socialist Party in 1901 and 1912, thereafter underwent a process of decline such that in 1938 it had been reduced to a mere 7,000 members. This failure is attributable to many causes but most important is the character of American trade unionism which made it impossible to create the links between a united union movement and a socialist political party so important in Germany and England. Socialist doctrines in the Third World, where they are not modelled on those of Europe, have tried to offer a vision of social organization different from that based on large-scale industry, as in the case of 'African Socialism'. Julius Nyerere (1969) offers perhaps the most systematic version of this alternative to European ideas. Some commentators would contend that not only have such doctrines been a dismal failure in practice, but also that as a doctrine they are better conceived as a variant of agrarian populism. Socialism is an outgrowth of advanced industrialism but, as the United States shows, is by no means an inevitable one.

Paul Hirst
Birkbeck College
University of London

References

Berstein, E. (1961 [1899]), *Evolutionary Socialism*, New York.
Cole, G. D. H. (1953–61), *A History of Socialist Thought*, Vols I–V, London.
Crosland, A. (1964), *The Future of Socialism*, London.
Gorz, A. (1982), *Farewell to the Working Class*, London.
Nyerere, J. K. (1969), *Freedom and Socialism*, Dar-es-Salaam.

Further Reading

Wright, A. W. (1979), *G. D. H. Cole and Socialist Democracy*, Oxford.
See also: *communism; equality; mixed economy; welfare state.*

Socialization

Socialization has been defined as 'the process whereby the individual is converted into the person'. The study of this process forms large areas of psychology, anthropology and sociology; and it is interesting that the emergence of socialization as a field of study occurred almost simultaneously, in the late 1930s, in all three disciplines. One early school of thought, perhaps best known as the 'culture-personality' school, attempted to draw together the approaches of different disciplines by applying psychoanalytic theory to anthropological data. Abram Kardiner led a series of seminars in New York in the 1930s whose aim was to determine the personality characteristics associated with different cultural groups, and to establish their antecedents in child-rearing practices. The effort failed, probably because of the overwhelming scale and interdisciplinary nature of the task; and current studies of socialization tend to be intra- rather than interdisciplinary. Sociologists concentrate on the effects of social institutions such as the family, the school, or the media; and psychologists work on the individual level by investigating topics such as parent-child interaction, sex-role identity, play, moral thinking, and the development of the self-concept. This last topic probably has more potential for fruitful collaboration between psychologists and sociologists than any other – cognitive-developmental theory and symbolic interactionism have a good deal in common, for example – though few attempts have been made to develop the link.

In psychology, the term 'socialization' was originally used by a group of American theorists to connote a particular view of the nature of human development, a view which derived from 'behaviourism' or 'reinforcement theory'. In its purest form this tries to explain human behaviour as conditioned responses to environmental stimuli, learnt by association with different rewards and punishments. These 'neobehaviourists', including Robert Sears, Neal Miller, John Dollard and Albert Bandura, were concerned to explain development in a manner that was objective, neutral, value-free and thoroughly susceptible to scientific investigation. Whereas 'education' implies some deliberate guidance of, or intervention into, development, with a predetermined end-state or goal in view, 'socialization' was intended to convey a detached, dispassionate approach to the study of the influence of society upon the individual.

This early psychological approach ran into severe problems. It was clearly not possible to explain the full complexity of human behaviour in terms of simple learning processes. In investigating phenomena such as children's imitation of aggressive behaviour and the effects of parental discipline, for example, it became necessary to introduce concepts like *internalization* and *identification*. These are essentially cognitive, or 'internal', concepts, that is, they cannot be pinned down in terms of identifiable 'pieces' of behaviour. The less rigorous form of reinforcement theory that resulted from this kind of modification became known as 'social learning theory'.

The last twenty years has seen a radical shift away from this kind of explanation. Indeed, the changing view of the nature of socialization has transformed developmental psychology from a quiet backwater of the discipline into one of its most vigorous and active areas. Three broad characteristics of the new view can be distinguished:

(1) The reciprocal, interactive nature of the relationship between the child and its environment is stressed. The environment is not seen to condition, or 'shape', the passive child any more than the child is seen to 'shape' its own environment; rather, the two form an active, symbiotic system in which any change in one has immediate effects upon the other. This is very different from what Danziger (1971) has called the 'social problem' approach to the study of child-rearing, which is closely related to social learning theory. This approach, now largely abandoned, sought correlations between ratings of parental behaviour on dimensions such as 'punitiveness' and 'permissiveness', and of children's behaviour on dimensions such as 'dependency' and 'aggressiveness' – the best-known study being that of Sears, Maccoby and Levin (1957). The difficulties of establishing direction of causality, as well as the uncertain status of the dimensions of behaviour employed, contributed to its eventual abandonment. One alternative strategy is to carry out longitudinal studies, in which the development of a selected subject group is systematically assessed at a series of points in time. Several famous investigations of the long-term stability of different aspects of behaviour have been carried out using this technique (for example, Thomas, Chess and Birch, 1968).

(2) The second major characteristic of the new view of socialization is a shift towards what might be called a 'cognitive' approach. The revival of interest in Piaget's cognitive-developmental theory has provided considerable impetus in this respect. Piaget emphasizes the active part played by the child in imposing meaning upon its world; and these constructions of meaning are 'negotiated' with others, notably, of course, the parents in the first instance. The extremely complex patterns of mother-infant interaction being investigated in the 1970s and 1980s are seen as a developing series of 'conversations', in which the mother's interpretations of her child's intentions are reflected in the child's responses to her. The newly-coined term 'intersubjectivity' summarizes this aspect of the interaction, now regarded as a key feature of early socialization.

(3) There is a new emphasis on an 'ecological' approach. Early research took an extremely stereotyped view of family relationships, such that the mother-infant bond was studied more or less to the exclusion of all others. In recent years father-child relationships are being studied more, as well as relationships with siblings. The ecological approach argues that no single relationship (such as between mother and child) can be studied adequately without taking into account the significant others in what is a highly complex network of relationships. These others include other members of the immediate family; they may also include grandparents, babysitters, childmin-

ders and so on. Such changes in research emphasis may well relate to other changes in society; such as the greatly increased proportion of working mothers in the population, and the correspondingly greater degree of involvement of fathers in child care. There can be no doubt, when seen in this light, that socialization research has important practical as well as theoretical implications.

David J. Hargreaves
University of Leicester

References
Danziger, K. (1971), *Socialization*, Harmondsworth.
Sears, R. R., Maccoby, E. E. and Levin, H. (1957), *Patterns of Child Rearing*, Evanston, Ill.
Thomas, A. S., Chess, S. and Birch, H. G. (1968), *Temperament and Behavior Disorders in Children*, New York.

Further Reading
Cairns, R. B. (1979), *Social Development*, San Francisco.
McGurk, H. (ed.) (1978), *Issues in Childhood Social Development*, London.
See also: *culture and personality; developmental psychology; education; Piaget.*

Social Mobility

Social mobility has long been a central topic of sociological speculation, and, over the last forty years, the object of many empirical enquiries. Interest in the topic arises in part from its supposed relation to justice and efficiency in societies, and in part from the relative ease with which mobility may be quantified. Numerous hypotheses have been advanced which turn on the extent or pattern of mobility, trends in mobility over time, and comparisons of mobility across countries (Lipset and Bendix, 1966). For example, it is argued that the relative ease of upward movement in nineteenth-century America helps to explain the absence of a significant socialist movement (Sombart, 1976 [1906]). However, empirical enquiry does not unequivocally support the proposition that there was more mobility in America than in Europe. Indeed, the results of most empirical investigations are inconclusive.

Nevertheless, certain propositions have emerged with some degree of support. In recent years it has been established that among men, there is a strong, but by no means perfect, correlation between level of education attained and social standing of occupation (Blau and Duncan, 1967). It also appears that measured intelligence (IQ) in childhood is the best single predictor of both the educational achievement and the occupational level of men (Duncan, 1966). Attempts to find adequate predictors of income have been less successful.

Propositions about mobility in a society as a whole must be distinguished from propositions about movement into an élite. It has been shown that from the sixteenth to the nineteenth century there was a decline in the proportion of 'plebeian' students entering Oxford and Cambridge, whereas in 1800 the University of Glasgow drew more heavily on the working class and farmers for its intake than do many modern universities. In France, the *grandes écoles* provided an avenue of upward mobility for the *petite bourgeoisie*. During the English Industrial Revolution the entrepreneurs who established capital-intensive industries such as steel, railways and banking came from wealthier families, though some working men found openings in smaller enterprises. Dissenters were peculiarly well represented among industrial innovators. Working-class representation in the British House of Commons reached a peak after the Second World War and then declined (Kaelble, 1977, gives an excellent brief review of historical studies).

These findings, together with a few more of the same kind, constitute the sum of our knowledge of what mobility has actually occurred in recent centuries – and few of them are immune from refutation.

When, however, we turn from matters of empirical fact to matters of theoretical interpretation, we come up against problems of measurement, models and meaning which sociologists, the main investigators of social mobility, are only now tackling. One such issue is the theoretical distinction between mobility in the sense of *generalized* upward movement in a society such as nineteenth-century North America, and movement which consists of equal upward and downward flows between any two social categories. A society manifesting this latter type of bilateral equal exchange in any high degree is said to be 'open' or 'fluid' (Thernstrom, 1973). And within both generalized upward shift and fluidity (whether these are high or low in degree) we must distinguish between movement occasioned by universalistic qualities ('merit') and movement, or lack of it, based on ascriptive qualities (such as father's class).

The argument that high mobility inhibited the development of socialism in the United States is usually based on the observation that few middle-class Americans moved down into the working class, whereas many sons and daughters of farmers (and also many immigrants who started in menial jobs) moved up into the middle class. On the other hand, latter-day claims that America is a more open and meritocratic society than Britain are based on the belief that there is more bilateral exchange in America, and that those who rise in the American social scale do so because they have acquired good educational credentials and therefore deserve their mobility. In fact it would appear that British men (data for women are harder to interpret) are no less mobile than American men, when allowance is made for the relative concentration of Britons in the working class, and for the flight from the land in America. It also seems that, under the selective system of education, the able British son of a working-class father had a better chance than his American analogue of getting a good job, because he was more likely to receive a good education and to be groomed by his secondary school for the higher occupations (Hope, 1984).

In recent years, the topic of social mobility analysis has been the main arena for the development of quantitative analysis in sociology. Although interest in the technical aspects of the work has, for a time, distracted sociologists from the traditional problems of social stratification, they are considering those problems once more with a renewed interest in theory and a more sophisticated grasp of the nature of sociological explanation.

Broadly speaking, European and American writers appear to diverge on the topic of mobility. On the whole, Americans are interested in the question of how individuals take up positions in a vertical hierarchy which is mainly a matter of material advantage. And when they find that position in that hierarchy is determined, to quite a high degree, by level of education attained, they claim that their society is a 'meritocracy', where 'universalistic' rather than 'ascribed' qualities are the basis of 'achievement'. They tend to think that this model adequately describes the social structure for White males, though not for Blacks and females (Blau and Duncan, 1967; Featherman and Hauser, 1978). European researchers, by contrast, more often consider the 'life-chances' and the degree of 'class-consciousness' of 'collectivities' with a view to predicting whether these aggregates are likely to undertake 'class-action'. And they ask whether mobility disrupts class solidarity and induces alienation of one sort or another (Dahrendorf, 1959). In both Europe and the United States political scientists speculate anxiously on the relation between mobility, particularly the downward movement of whole categories of persons, and support for Fascism (Lipset, 1981).

Keith Hope
University of Oxford

References
Blau, P. M. and Duncan, O. D. (1967.), *The American Occupational Structure*, New York.
Dahrendorf, R. (1959), *Class and Conflict in Industrial Society*, London.
Duncan, O. D. (1966), 'Ability and achievement', *Eugenics Quarterly*, 15.

Featherman, D. L. and Hauser, R. M. (1978), *Opportunity and Change*, New York.

Hope, K. (1984), *As Others See Us*, New York.

Kaelble, H. (1977), *Historical Research on Social Mobility*, New York.

Lipset, S. M. (1981), *Political Man: The Social Bases of Politics*, Baltimore.

Lipset, S. M. and Bendix, R. (1966), *Social Mobility in Industrial Society*, Berkeley and Los Angeles.

Sombart, W. (1976 [1906]), *Why is there No Socialism in the United States?*, trans. P. M. Hocking, and C. T. Husbands, New York.

Thernstrom, S. (1973), 'Urbanization, migration, and social mobility in late nineteenth century America', in H. G. Gutman, and G. S. Kelley (eds), *Many Pasts: Readings in American History*, Englewood Cliffs, NJ.

See also: *élites*; *stratification*.

Social Movements

For Lorenz von Stein (1855) the social movement of the nineteenth century was the proletariat. Scholarship in the twentieth century has pluralized the term, removed its historical connotation and applied it to a variety of social phenomena, from unstructured collective behaviour, to cults and religious sects, to issue-oriented protest movements all the way to organized revolutionary groups. The only common denominators in the variety of definitions employed is that social movements are uninstitutionalized groups in some insurgent relationship to existing society, involving unmediated bonds between leaders and followers.

With so broad a focus, empirical richness has been gained but at the cost of both theoretical clarity and methodological consensus. Though organizational and statistical analyses are increasingly common, the typical research approach remains the descriptive case study. The mass of case studies available has led to a large number of typologies, based in part on the empirical properties of groups and in part on their relation to existing society.

Theoretically, the field has focused on three major questions: (1) What kind of people are recruited into social movement organizations? (2) How does the appearance of social movements relate to reversals in economic growth and changes in class relations? (3) How do relations between leaders and followers affect the outcomes of social movement activity?

Social movement theory and research have two main sources. In the conservative reaction against the French Revolution and its aftermath, a school of thought developed which emphasized the formlessness, rage and irrationality of the mob, contrasting it with the structure, calm and moderation of 'normal' (bourgeois) society (Oberschall, 1973). With less animus against mass unrest, Durkheim's concept of 'anomie' provided a theoretical rationale for such behaviour, providing a guide for the location of 'vulnerable' groups within the class structure, and connecting social movement research to the transition from traditional to industrial society.

With the rise of the Socialist movements of the late nineteenth century grew a belief in the underlying rationality, form and justice of lower-class unrest. The early twentieth century, with its institutionalization of the working-class movement, strengthened this 'rationalist' strand of research and theory. Michels shifted the theoretical emphasis to the relations between leaders and followers within movements, posing the question of the effect on unconventional movements of using conventional means. In Britain, a tradition of social history began which emphasized the rational bases of lower-class unrest and its relation to the market and the state.

The great cataclysms of the twentieth century – Fascism and the Bolshevik Revolution – had the reverse effect. Fuelled by a generation of exiles who brought with them nightmarish memories of what 'the mob' – especially when poisoned by revolutionary agitation – could become, these experiences were the source of a new generation of theories relating social movements structurally to economic decline and to psychological 'relative deprivation'. In this new synthesis, culminating in the work of Smelser (1963), social movements were regarded mainly as signs of dysfunction in the social system, and social movement recruits were once again seen as atomized individuals set adrift on the seas of social change.

The turbulence of the 1960s led to a resurgence of interest in social movements, with one group developing multivariate statistical models of violent behaviour to examine its relationship to deprivation, a second attempting to reshape and renew a Marxist interpretation of social movements, and a third blending the 'rationalist' perspective with new findings and insights from economics and political science.

The multivariate approach, best represented by Gurr's work (1980), though most innovative methodologically, was closest in spirit to the 'breakdown' theories of the past. Like the tradition, its findings about the effects of relative deprivation and the psychological sources of social movements were divided and inconclusive. The firmest findings of multivariate statistical analysis come from an area tangential to social movement research – strike waves and their relation to economic fluctuations.

Recent Marxist and Marxist-influenced schools of social movement research show great richness and internal variation. From their perspective, Touraine (1971) and his followers regard the social movement as a transcendent experience in radical rupture with existing authority and therefore as a rare form of collective action. In contrast, Tilly (1978) and his collaborators are less exclusive. Closer to the spirit of British social history than to French historical sociology, they focus on all forms of 'challenge' to the polity on the part of groups whose resources can be mobilized to gain entry to it. Though explicitly comparative, Tilly's work has been most influential in the United States, where it dovetails with a lively tradition of research on protest in political science and a reawakening interest in working-class history.

The 'resource mobilization' theories of the 1970s have blended the 'rationality' approach with insights from economics. Mobilization is generally defined as collective action by actual or prospective movement leaders to gain control of the resources of previously unmobilized population groups on behalf of their actual or perceived interests or values, much as entrepreneurs combine the factors of production (McCarthy and Zald, 1977). In contrast to theorists of breakdown or deprivation, these students focus on leaders rather than followers and view leaders' success as the result, not of changes in deprivation, but of short-term or contingent factors that enable them to find a constituency to represent. In contrast to the more structural perspective of the Marxists, they focus on the organizational innovations and political advantages that social movements can employ to mobilize a following.

An important impact of the 1960s on social movement research has been to underscore the remarkable diffusion of social movement-like activity among population groups that have been historically moderate in their behaviour – for example, the salaried middle class, regional ethnic groups, women and minorities. There has also been observed a hybrid of 'interest-group movements' combining traditional organization and membership with a capacity for unconventional or disruptive action. In these groups – visible in both environmental and the anti-nuclear movements of the 1980s – we see radical action employed on behalf of politically legitimate goals, reversing the paradox first seen by Michels that groups with politically unacceptable goals frequently use politically institutionalized forms of action.

Sidney Tarrow
Cornell University

References
Gurr, T. R. (ed.) (1980), *Handbook of Political Conflict: Theory and Research*, New York.
McCarthy, J. and Zald, M. (1977), 'Resource mobilization and social movements: a partial theory', *American Journal of Sociology*, 82.
Oberschall, A. (1973), *Social Conflict and Social Movements*, Englewood Cliffs, NJ.
Smelser, N. (1963), *Theory of Collective Behavior*, New York.
Stein, L. von (1855), *Geschichte der Sozialen Bewegung Frankreichs von 1789 bis auf unsere Tage*, Berlin.
Tilly, C. (1978), *From Mobilization to Revolution*, Reading, Mass.
Touraine, A. (1971), *The Post-Industrial Society*, New York.

Further Reading
Marx, G. and Wood, J. L. (1975), 'Strands of theory and research in collective behavior', in *Annual Review of Sociology*, A. Inkeles (ed.), vol. I.
Piven, F. F. and Cloward, R. (1977), *Poor People's Movements: Why They Succeed and How They Fail*, New York.
See also: *political participation; radicalism.*

Social Problems

Until the early 1970s the sociology of social problems had, for over fifty years, looked for the underlying causes of a long list of human miseries and conditions considered destructive to society and offensive to conventional morality. This field overlapped with the study of social disorganization and deviant behaviour. Since then a new set of questions has emerged giving the study of social problems a fresh start and a more independent existence. These questions began with the observation that many troublesome behaviours have, at various times, been defined in different ways. People who drink alcohol to excess were thought to be sinners by the temperance movement in the early nineteenth century, regarded as criminals by the prohibition movement in the early twentieth century and as diseased addicts by the medical establishment after 1940. Homosexuality used to be both a crime and a mental disorder. Now it is a life style, thanks to the decriminalization movement and a particularly dramatic official vote by the American Psychiatric Association in December 1973. Child battering, wife abuse, and sexual harrassment all used to be unnamed, uncounted and invisible; now they are firmly-fixed constellations in the universe of social services, official statistics and problem populations.

The new sociology of social problems attempts to describe and explain how new definitions of social problems emerge, how troublesome persons or social arrangements are identified, how institutions are created to deal with them. The field has largely abandoned the attempt to explain deviant behaviour and social disorganization. Rather, it is attempting to explain how society, through an essentially political process, discovers and invents its problems. Attention to these processes of creating meanings concerning disturbing and troublesome behaviours and conditions distinguishes the new from the old approach to social problems.

Many contemporary problems that address the inequitable treatment of racial minorities, women, children, the elderly, prisoners, mental patients, the developmentally disabled and the unborn have been put on society's agenda by the vigorous actions of social movements. Social movements have also created awareness of problems concerning pollution, toxic wastes, the dangers of nuclear energy production and the threat of nuclear holocaust.

The helping professions promote solutions to social problems and are another important participant in the social problems process. The leading examples are the medical profession and its subalterns and the social welfare bureaucracies, which together have assembled what Kittrie (1972) has termed 'the therapeutic state'. A large number of troublesome behaviours previously punished as crimes have become subject to treatment and are now considered diseases. 'Treatments' for psychopaths and sociopaths, such as lobotomies or psychosurgery, aversive conditioning and behaviour modification, electric and chemical shock have replaced more primitive societal reactions, like punishment. The objective effectiveness of these treatments is of less importance than their political appeal and the prestige of the disciplines on which they rest.

A new tradition of research on the mass media, drawing on the insights of ethnomethodology, has enlarged the study of social problems, describing the 'creation' and production of news, and explaining how systems of classification and new vocabulary both reflect and take part in the struggle to name and control controversial issues.

Governments respond to claims that define conditions as social problems by: funding research on solutions to problems; establishing commissions of inquiry; passing new laws, and creating enforcement and treatment bureaucracies. But governments may also be the source of new definitions of social problems, especially embattled or ambitious agencies campaigning to increase their budgets and personnel. Research in the United States shows that the problem of marijuana use and more recently the concern about teenage alcoholism were created in this way.

Malcolm Spector
McGill University

Reference
Kittrie, N. (1972), *The Right to be Different*, Baltimore.

Further Reading
Conrad, P. and Schneider, J. (1980), *Deviance and Medicalization: From Badness to Sickness*, St Louis.
Spector, M. and Kitsuse, J. I. (1977), *Constructing Social Problems*, Menlo Park, Calif.
See also: *crime and delinquency; deviance; mental health.*

Social Psychology

Many textbook authors have attempted to define the field of social psychology in a few succinct words. Their definitions focus on social influence processes as they affect the individual, or responses to so-called 'social stimuli', or on the variables that affect interactions between persons. Most would agree that social psychology is the biochemistry of the social sciences, a field lying between the study of customs and social norms on the one hand, and the study of individual personalities on the other. Although the field is in this sense interstitial, this should not demean its significance as a major social-science discipline. In its theories and research, social psychology provides vital information concerning how personalities are shaped and how cultural norms and values are translated into individual thoughts and actions.

Though there remain a number of highly resonant pockets of similar interest in sociology, most of the research literature and the recent texts in social psychology have been written by psychologists. It is also the case that social psychology, at least until recently, has been dominated by theories and research generated in America. Many of the seminal figures behind this array of contributions did, however, emigrate from Europe in the 1930s: Brunswik, Heider, Katona, Lazarsfeld and Lewin. In addition, under the stimulus of the European Association of Experimental Social Psychology (founded in 1967), there has been considerable recent momentum toward redressing the imbalance represented by America's pre-eminence.

The field of social psychology grew out of the recognition of human diversity within cultural uniformity. Essentially the field focuses on choices and behavioural decisions among the competing options that confront us all in complex contemporary societies. It has become a field that, more than any other, deals with the psychology of everyday life: the psychology of conversations, of self-presentations, of conformity, of persuasion, of winning and losing, helping and hurting, liking and avoiding.

Recent History

Gordon Allport argued three decades ago (1954) that most of the major problems of concern to contemporary social psychologists were recognized as problems by social philosophers long before psychological questions were joined to scientific methodology. Perhaps the most fundamental question was that posed by Comte: How can man be simultaneously the cause and consequence of society? But the discipline of social psychology has a more recent history than its flavouring ideas and concerns. Although many conveniently mark its birth in 1908 with the publication of influential early texts by McDougall and Ross, in a very real sense the field began to cohere and develop its own identity only in the mid-1930s and did not really take on momentum until after World War II. This coherence and subsequent momentum depended largely on the development of indigenous theories and methods, usually associated with the contributions of Kurt Lewin in the late 1930s and early 1940s. Partly through sustained advocacy and partly through example, Lewin championed the possibilities of experimentation in social psychology. His experimental studies of autocratic, democratic, and *laissez-faire* leadership atmospheres (with Lippitt and White in 1939) showed how complex situational variables could be manipulated, validated, and shown to produce distinctive but orderly consequences. Lewin hoped to solve the problems of generalizing from the laboratory to the 'real world' by advocating (a) the linkage of experimentation to theory and (b) the parallel conduct of laboratory and field experimentation on conceptually cognate problems.

Though there would be wide agreement that Kurt Lewin deserves the title of the father of *experimental* social psychology, there were many other influences gathering under the social psychology umbrella during the 1920s and 1930s in America. These included the sustained series of empirical studies on group problem solving, the ingenious attitude measurement methodologies of Thurstone (1929) and Likert (1932), and the development of respondent sampling and survey research techniques.

But the central identity of social psychology was to remain anchored in the experimental approach. One of Lewin's students, Leon Festinger, exemplified Lewin's emphasis on going back and forth between the laboratory and the field, and showed in particular how experimentation made sense only if it were wedded to theory. During the two post-war decades when he was active as a social psychologist, Festinger (1954; 1957) developed two theories that had a profound impact on the field. The first of these was a theory of social comparison processes, a detailed set of postulates and propositions concerning the consequences for social interaction of man's need for the kinds of information about himself and the outer world that only other people could provide. The second was a theory of cognitive dissonance, which portrayed the various mental and behavioural manœuvres by which people attempt to restore cognitive consistency. The power of this theory was greatly enhanced by Festinger's recognition that some cognitions are more resistant to change than others, and that behavioural commitment is a potent source of such resistance. This recognition permitted rather precise predictions concerning the form that dissonance reduction would take in different situations. In particular, changes would be observed in the least resistant cognition. The ideas informing both of these theories remain important in much of current social-psychological thinking and have become a part of our cultural wisdom. Equally important,

perhaps, the voluminous research generated by the theory of cognitive dissonance provided a clear example of coherent progress through experimental research in social science, research yielding cumulative insights that helped to refine and amplify the theory inspiring it.

A very different kind of theoretical orientation became prominent in the late 1960s, just as the enthusiasm for investigating dissonance phenomena began to wane. This was the attributional approach to social behaviour, an approach associated with Fritz Heider and identified with his seminal treatment of the *Psychology of Interpersonal Relations* (1958). The basic premise of the attributional approach is that people are motivated to understand behaviour, and readily do so by viewing it within a meaningful causal context. Our response to others, in other words, is a function of the causes we attribute to explain their behaviour. Though initially the focus of attribution theory was almost entirely on the perception of other persons, Kelley (1967) and Bem (1967) extended the attributional orientation to include self-perception. The perception of our own inner dispositions and emotions is mediated by our causal evaluations of our own behaviours, taking into account relevant features of the situational context.

As the attributional orientation flourished in the early 1970s, it fed and was fed by a broad revival of interest in social cognition. Though social psychology (at least since the subjectivism championed by W.I. Thomas) has always emphasized the cognitized social world, an emphasis on detailed analyses of information processing and social memory has become more dominant over the past five years. The heritage of the attributional approach is largely reflected in a concern with attributional biases and errors in the application of inference strategies (Nisbet and Ross, 1980), though there remains a strong current of interest in attribution of responsibility, attributional approaches to self-presentation, and attributional analyses of self-fulfilling prophecies.

While these developments in social cognition were occurring within the 'mainstream' of experimental social psychology, some social psychologists continued to concentrate on the traditional problems of social influence and group processes. Asch's (1956) classic studies of conformity and Milgram's (1974) research on obedience have become standard textbook entries. In different ways, their findings showed the remarkable sensitivity of normal adults to social influence pressures. The nature of group processes was especially informed by Thibaut and Kelley's (1959) analysis of outcome exchanges in dyads and larger groups. This analysis capitalized on the contingency matrices of game theory, as well as building on both reinforcement and social comparison theories within psychology. It provided a rich and provocative framework for dealing with power relations, roles, and the development of norms. Many publications in the 1960s and 1970s dealt with complex interpersonal conflict situations that might be resolved through bargaining and negotiation. Throughout this period, also, a steady stream of articles appeared shedding light on such social phenomena as aggression, helping behaviour, attitude change, jury decision making, crowding, social discrimination, sex-role stereotypes, the impact of television, and a variety of other applied topics. More comprehensive historical overviews – both general and within specific content areas – may be found in the *Handbook of Social Psychology* (Lindzey and Aronson, 1984).

Current Status of the Field

Any brief characterization of such a complex discipline must be arbitrary and selective in many respects. Nevertheless, it is possible to venture a few generalizations on the current state of the field that would probably recruit a sizeable consensus. The emphasis on experimentation has been buffeted by critical winds from several directions. Some critics have concluded that the problem of generalizing from laboratories (and sophomores!) is insurmountable. There is no way to extrapolate meaningfully from the historical and contextual particularities of any given experiment. Other critics have been concerned with the ethics of those deceptive cover stories which most social psychology experiments seem to require. Still others are·bothered by the treatment of subjects as manipulable objects rather than collaborators with whom one negotiates appropriate explanations for behaviour. Finally, there are those who feel that experimentation implies a highly restrictive form of linear causation, misrepresenting the normal processes of situation selection and movement through complex feedback loops in which the behaviour of actors is both causal and caused. Though many of these criticisms raise vital concerns, neither singly nor in combination are they likely to relegate the experimental approach to a secondary position in the armamentarium of social psychology. The viability of the experimental approach may be even more assured as its practitioners more clearly realize its particular strengths and its limitations. Even if the generalization problem seems insurmountable, on occasion, the design of experiments may be extremely important in facilitating and disciplining conceptual thought.

The current flowering of cognitive social psychology seems to be producing new intellectual alliances and breaking down old boundaries between general experimental and social psychology. Certainly social psychologists are borrowing paradigms from the traditions of general research on thought and memory; cognitive psychologists in turn are showing greater sensitivity to the variables of social context. In a similar fashion, social psychological theory has shed light on such clinical phenomena as depression, alcohol abuse, obesity and a range of problems associated with symptom labelling. Though social psychology may in some respects play the role of a gadfly within the social sciences, borrowing here and lending there, it is not likely to lose its special identity as the one field especially concerned with the details of interpersonal influence. At present, the pendulum seems to have swung away from a concern with social interdependence and group phenomena toward a concern with individual information processing. Here there seems to be some divergence between the more 'individualistic' Americans and the more 'groupy' Europeans. It would be interesting if the more blatantly *social* psychology of the Europeans influenced an American revival of interest in groups. This seems to be an old story in social psychology: the study of individuals must be informed by a clear understanding of the matrices of social interdependence within which they function; the study of groups must comprehend the cognitive and motivational processes of group members. The tension between these two foci, in the long run, may be what keeps the field on its relatively straight track – in spite of temporary deviations in course.

Edward E. Jones
Princeton University

References

Allport, G. W. (1954), 'The historical background of modern social psychology', in G. E. Lindzey (ed.), *Handbook of Social Psychology*, Vol. I, Cambridge, Mass.

Asch, S. E. (1956), 'Studies of independence and conformity: a minority of one against a unanimous majority', *Psychological Monographs*, 70.

Bem, D. J. (1967), 'Self-perception: an alternative interpretation of cognitive dissonance phenomena', *Psychological Review*, 74.

Festinger, L. (1954), 'A theory of social comparison processes', *Human Relations*, 7.

Festinger, L. (1957), *A Theory of Cognitive Dissonance*, Evanston, Ill.

Heider, F. (1958), *The Psychology of Interpersonal Relations*, New York.

Kelley, H. H. (1967), 'Attribution theory in social psychology', *Nebraska Symposium on Motivation*, 14.

Lewin, K., Lippitt, R. and White, R. K. (1939), 'Patterns of aggressive behavior in experimentally created "social climates" ', *Journal of Social Psychology*, 10.

Likert, R. (1932), 'A technique for the measurement of attitudes', *Archives of Psychology*, 140.

Lindzey, G. E. and Aronson, E. (1984), *Handbook of Social Psychology* (3rd edn), Cambridge, Mass.

McDougall, W. (1908), *An Introduction to Social Psychology*, London.

Milgram, S. (1974), *Obedience to Authority*, New York.

Nisbet, R. E. and Ross, L. (1980), *Human Inference: Strategies and Shortcomings of Social Judgment*, Englewood Cliffs, NJ.

Ross, E. A. (1908), *Social Psychology: An Outline and a Source Book*, New York.

Thibaut, J. W. and Kelley, H. H. (1959), *The Social Psychology of Groups*, New York.

Thurstone, L. L. and Chave, E. J. (1929), *The Measurement of Attitude*, Chicago.

See also: *attitudes; attribution theory; cognitive dissonance; conflict resolution; conformity; culture and personality; environmental psychology; loneliness; prejudice; role; social identity; socialization; social psychology of language; stereotypes; stigma.*

Social Psychology of Language

An examination of mainstream journals and influential texts in social psychology in the early 1970s and before suggests that language held at most a peripheral status within social psychology. Correlatively, a perusal of sociolinguistics demonstrated a neglect in its journals and texts of a coherent social-psychological approach. Important exceptions were apparent with regard to the study of bilingualism and forms of address, and it is true that many sociolinguists have emphasized the role of social-psychological constructs such as attitudes, identities, motivations in their analyses. Notwithstanding the reasons why a social psychology of language (SPL) has never really gelled in North America (apart from Canada), there are many indications that it has now 'arrived' as a distinctive, complementary approach to the sociology of language, anthropological linguistics and sociolinguistics. Research activity since 1977 has grown enormously. The *Journal of Language and Social Psychology* was established in 1982 as a forum for this speciality. Interestingly, an active 'interpersonal communication' branch of communication science has developed simultaneously, with an implicit social-psychological emphasis.

Given the overlap of interest in many topics studied by sociolinguists and social psychologists (for example, relationships between language and situation, sex roles, socioeconomic status), what then *is* SPL? Its distinctiveness lies essentially in two domains, the theoretical and methodological. Theoretically, researchers are interested in the ways in which the production and reception of language behaviours are mediated by processes of cognitive organization. Aspects of cognitive organization would include perceived goal structures, situational construals, cognitive monitoring, causal attributions, and the (interactive) roles they play in determining, for instance, speaking and listening strategies. Given that social-psychological theories are largely about the complexities and dynamics of cognitive organization and the representation of the social world, this perspective broadens the *explanatory* scope of language study. For example, social-identity theory proposes that we desire to belong to social categories which afford us a positive social identity; it articulates the conditions under which group members will search for, or even create, dimensions along which they are positively differentiated from relevant outgroups. This then helps us to explain why some groups maintain their own languages, dialects and nonverbal styles while others lose them and assimilate towards the communicative patterns of a more powerful group.

Methodologically, SPL utilizes for the most part the experimental method characteristic of general psychology, although, as with the latter, there are critics of it. Such a procedure is extremely useful in its potential for replication and rigorous control of extraneous variables, as well as in its capacity to allow more exact specifications of the conditions under which certain language patterns are emitted, and the types of responses people make to particular language behaviours in specific contexts. In addition, the discipline has techniques for measuring complex psychological dispositions (such as personalities or ideologies), attitudes, attributions, cognitive representations).

Given the embryonic state of SPL, exciting prospects are held out for its future. Signs already exist that greater diversification is on its way: (1) methodologically, with more naturalistic observations of language behaviours and the utilization of individuals' own language accounts and cognitive scripts; (2) theoretically, in the trend towards grander propositional formats; (3) linguistically, in the move to incorporate discourse, conversational and phonological analyses; and (4) given the appreciation amongst workers of the interdependence of language and society, we expect great advances in our knowledge as to when and why language behaviours (consciously and nonconsciously conceived) determine, and redefine, the situations in which interactants find themselves.

Howard Giles
University of Bristol

Further Reading

Giles, H., Robinson, W. P. and Smith, P. M. (eds) (1980), *Language: Social Psychological Perspectives*, Oxford.

Fraser, C. and Scherer, K. R. (eds) (1982), *Advances in the Social Psychology of Language*, Cambridge.

Ryan, E. B. and Giles, H. (eds) (1982), *Attitudes Towards Language Variation: Social and Applied Contexts*, London.

See also: *psycholinguistics; sociolinguistics.*

Social Science

Social science is the ambitious concept to define the set of disciplines of scholarship which deal with aspects of human society. The singular implies a community of method and approach which is now claimed by few; thus the plural, social sciences, seems more appropriate. As commonly understood, the social sciences include, centrally, economics, sociology (and anthropology) and political science. At their boundaries, the social sciences reach into the study of the individual (social psychology) and of nature (social biology, social geography). Methodologically, they straddle normative (law, social philosophy, political theory) and historical approaches (social history, economic history). In terms of university departments, the social sciences have split up into numerous areas of teaching and research, including not only the central disciplines, but also such subjects as industrial relations, international relations, business studies, social (public) administration.

The term, social science(s), does not sit easily in the universe of scholarship, especially not in English. *Sciences sociales* and *Sozialwissenschaften* are somewhat happier expressions, though they too have suffered from being interpreted either too widely or too narrowly. Frequently, social science is meant to define either sociology, or synthetic social theory only. Everywhere, the implied analogy to the natural sciences has been contested. In 1982, the British government challenged the name of the publicly financed Social Science Research Council, arguing *inter alia* that 'social studies' would be a more appropriate description for disciplines of scholarship which cannot justly claim to be scientific. (The Council is now called, Economic and Social Research Council.)

The history of the concept does not help much in trying to make sense of it. Today's social sciences have grown out of moral philosophy (as the natural sciences have emerged from natural philosophy). It has often been observed that their separate identity owes much to the great revolutions of the eighteenth century, the Industrial (English) and the bourgeois (French) Revolutions. Among the Scottish moral philosophers of that time, the study of political economy was always coupled with that of wider social issues (though not called social science). With the ascendency of positivism in the early nineteenth century, especially in France, positive philosophy, or social science, took the place of moral philosophy. Positivism, according to Auguste Comte (1830–42; 1844), emphasizes the factual as against the speculative, the useful as against the idle, the certain as against the indecisive, the precise as against the vague, the positive as against the negative or critical. It is thus both science in the sense of nineteenth-century materialism and prescription. Comte borrowed the term, *science social*, from Charles Fourier (1808) to describe the supreme synthetic discipline of the edifice of science. At the same time, he had no doubt that the method of social science (which he also called social physics) was in no way different from that of the natural sciences.

Five developments either stemming from Comte, or encouraged by different traditions, have helped confuse the methodological picture of the social sciences:

(1) Many of those who took the analogy to the natural sciences seriously, engaged in social research. The great factual surveys of Charles Booth in Britain, and of the Chicago School in the United States, bear witness to this trend. Frederic Le Play had started a similar tradition in France. In Germany, the *Verein für Socialpolitik* adopted the same research techniques. Such often large-scale descriptive enterprises are the precursors of modern ('Empirical') social research and analysis.

(2) Science, of course, is more than fact-finding. Thus a natural-science notion of theoretical social science has informed at least two of the heroes of sociology, Emile Durkheim (1895) and Vilfredo Pareto (1916). Durkheim in particular was impressed by the need to study 'social facts', whereas Pareto stimulated both metatheoretical insights and specific theories. They have had few followers.

(3) Instead, by the turn of the century, a methodological dichotomy was born which gave rise to a third aspect, or notion, of social science. Against the ambitions of those who tried to emulate the natural sciences in the study of social phenomena, the German school of thought gained ground, according to which social phenomena do not lend themselves to such rigid analysis, but require a different approach, one of *Verstehen*, of empathy and understanding. Max Weber (1921) straddles different approaches, but introduced into social science what were later called 'hermeneutic' or 'phenomenological' perspectives.

(4) It will readily be seen that all three approaches mentioned so far are most closely associated with the subject of sociology and its history. Indeed, economics soon began to go its own way. Ever since the decline of the German historical ('romantic') school of economists, it developed as the discipline which of all the social sciences most nearly deserves the name, science. Economic knowledge is to a considerable extent cumulative; theories are developed and tested, if not always against reality, then at least against models and their assumptions. *Verstehende* economics, even descriptive economics, have become the exception.

(5) Max Weber also insisted on another distinction which defines the fifth aspect of social science, that between knowledge, however gained, and values.

Prescription and description (or theory) belong to different universes of discourse. The distinction was explosive at the time (*Werturteilsstreit*), and continues to be that, although political theory, moral philosophy, jurisprudence have gone their own ways, and the study of social policy has shifted from the prescriptive to the analytical.

These then are the disparate methodological elements of social science today: empirical social science, descriptive in character if not in intention, increasingly sophisticated in its techniques which are themselves manifold; rare attempts at developing theories in the strict sense, attempts which are neither universally recognized nor cumulative; *verstehende Sozialwissenschaft*, perhaps best described as the historical analysis of the present, often full of empirical data as well as attempts at explanation, the bulk of today's social science; economics; and explicitly prescriptive social theory, often political in substance and intent.

Looking at the social sciences as a whole, this is quite a pell-mell, and is perceived as such. However, all attempts to produce a new synthesis have failed. The most ambitious recent examples are those by Karl Popper (1945; 1959) and Talcott Parsons (1937; 1951; 1956). Popper insists that there is one logic of scientific inquiry. It is the logic of progress by falsification: we advance hypotheses (theories), and progress by refuting accepted hypotheses through research, that is, by trial and error. Popper did not primarily have the social sciences in mind, but it is here that his language has created havoc. Everybody now 'hypothesizes', though few such projects are even capable of falsification. More importantly, Popper's logic, if misinterpreted as practical advice to scholars, leads to an arid notion of scholarly activity, especially in the social sciences. If hypothetico-deductive progress is all there is, then 99 per cent of all social science is useless. Popper's logic of scientific inquiry provides but one measure of advancement; it is not a litmus test for distinguishing between what is and what is not social science. Indeed, Popper himself has written important works of social, or at any rate social-philosophical, analysis.

Talcott Parson's attempted synthesis is even more ambitious in that it is addressed to the theoretical substance of social science. Throughout his numerous abstract analyses, Parsons has argued that the substance of social science is one, social action, and that even the incarnations of social action stem from the same general model, the social system. The social system has four subsystems: the economy, the polity, the cultural system, and the 'integrative' systems. Economics, political science, the study of culture and that of social integration (sociology) are thus related, and interdependent, disciplines. Descending from the social system, all subsystems require similar analysis.

Parson's claims have had little effect on social sciences other than sociology. Economists in particular have largely ignored them. Their central weakness may be that while society can be looked at in this way, it need not be. In any case, different social sciences have continued to go their own way. Have they progressed? It would be vain to deny this, though concepts of progress differ with different methods. At the same time, the social sciences have probably given us *multa non multum*. Perhaps, a more modest approach is indicated today. In the absence of a synthesis, it is desirable to let a hundred flowers bloom. Each of the social sciences will continue to contribute to knowledge. It is not unlikely that important developments will occur at the boundaries of different disciplines. It is also probable that most social sciences will incorporate several of the approaches which have split the subjects. Though the search for synthesis will never cease, in fact the social sciences will for some time remain a variegated and somewhat disparate group of intellectual endeavours.

Ralf Dahrendorf
Former Director, London School of
Economics and Political Science

References
Comte, A. (1830–42 [1896]), *Cours de philosophie positive*, Paris. (English translation, *The Positive Philosophy of Auguste Comte*, London.)
Comte, A. (1844), *Discours sur l'ésprit positif*, Paris. (English translation, *Discourse on the Positive Spirit*, London.)
Durkheim, E. (1895 [1938]), *Les Règles de la méthode scientifique*, Paris. (English translation, *The Rules of Sociological Method*, Chicago.)
Fourier, C. (1808), *Théorie des quatre mouvements et des destinées générales*, Lyon.
Pareto, V. (1916 [1935]), *Trattato die sociologia generale*, Rome. (English translation, *The Mind and Society: Treatise on General Sociology*, 4 Vols, London.)
Parsons, T. (1937), *The Structure of Social Action*, New York.
Parsons, T. (1951), *The Social System*, Glencoe.
Parsons, T. and Smelser, N. (1956), *Economy and Society*, New York.
Popper, K. (1945), *The Open Society and Its Enemies*, London.
Popper, K. (1959 [1934]), *The Logic of Scientific Discovery*, New York. (Original German edn, *Logik der Forschung*, Vienna.)
Weber, M. (1921 [1968]), *Wirtschaft und Gesellschaft*, Tübingen. (English translation, *Economy and Society*, New York.)

Social Skills and Social Skills Training

The Meaning and Assessment of Social Competence

A socially competent person is someone who possesses the necessary social skills to produce the desired effects on other people in social situations. These may be the professional skills of teaching, selling, interviewing, and so on, or the everyday skills of communicating effectively, being persuasive, and maintaining social relationships. Social competence can be assessed by objective measures of success, for example, in selling, or self-rating scales, for example, for assertiveness, or the amount of difficulty experienced in different situations. Interviews can find out more details about areas of social difficulty. Role-playing in laboratory or clinic can provide information about specific areas of deficit. In the case of clients for social skills training (SST), the particular goals of treatment can then be decided upon.

Social inadequacy of different degrees is widespread. Among children, some are isolated, others aggressive. Over 50 per cent of students say they often feel lonely, 15–20 per cent seriously so, and 40 per cent of students say that they are shy. Between 7–10 per cent of adults are handicapped by an inability to establish or sustain normal relationships or cope with common social situations. Among outpatient neurotics the corresponding figure is 25–30 per cent, while for hospitalized psychotics it is probably 100 per cent. Failures of social competence can lead to rejection and social isolation, and ultimately to the development of anxiety, depression and other symptoms of mental disorder.

For any particular professional social skill, such as selling, teaching, or supervising working groups, some people are far less effective than others. Some salespersons may sell 25 per cent of what the better ones sell, poor supervisors may generate four times as much absenteeism and labour turnover, and much less output than better supervisors. Among people who go to work abroad, for example, for those going to parts of the Middle or Far East for commercial firms or the Peace Corps, as many as 60 per cent may fail, and return home early.

Methods of Social Skills Training

(1) *Role-playing* is now the most widely used method. An area of skill is briefly described, such as how to combine a principle with an example (teaching), how to make someone talk more (interviewing). This is followed by a demonstration, live or on film ('modelling'). The contents of this teaching depend on the results of research into the most effective way of performing the skill, for example, which teaching methods get the best results. A trainee then role-plays in front of video cameras for 5–10 minutes, with another trainee, or with a prepared stooge. Finally there is a feedback – consisting of playback of video-

tape, and comments from the trainer. Between sessions trainees are encouraged to try out the new skills ('homework'), and report back on how they got on.

(2) *Supplementary exercises* for special aspects of social skills can also be used. These include training to send and receive nonverbal communications from face and voice, in the conduct of conversations, in appearance and other aspects of self-presentation, and the handling of particular situations and relationships. These specialized methods make use of research into, for example, nonverbal communication and conversational analysis.

(3) *Educational methods* are a valuable addition to, but not a substitute for, more active methods of training. The 'Culture Assimilator' for intercultural skills consists of instruction on the situations which have been found to cause most difficulty in the other culture. Training for situation and relations can include instructions on the rules and other basic features, and can correct common misunderstandings.

The Current Extent of Social Skills Training

SST is being increasingly used for neurotics, disturbed adolescents, depressives, alcoholics, drug addicts and prisoners, usually as part of a larger treatment package. Training usually consists of role-played sessions, once or twice a week, for one to one-and-a-half hours, in groups of four to ten with two trainers, sometimes combined with individual treatment.

Teaching skills are often taught by 'microteaching', a form of role-playing, using short practice lessons to small groups of children. Similar methods are used for industrial supervisors, managers, doctors, social workers, police and other professional groups.

Training for everyday social skills is less readily available. However, in North America there is widespread assertiveness training, mainly for women, occasional training in heterosexual skills for students with 'minimal dating' problems, and training for making friends for young people who are lonely. While Americans are very interested in assertiveness, British clients for SST are more interested in making friends.

Intercultural skills training is being increasingly widely given for people who are going to work abroad – export salesmen, diplomats, military personnel, Peace Corps members and others. A variety of methods are used, including education in the different customs of the other culture and meeting members of the culture and recently returned expatriates.

Marital therapy of various kinds is widely available, but has not prevented one marriage in three failing. American Behavioral Marital Therapy is based on increasing rewardingness, and contracts in which each partner agrees to a concession, such as to go dancing together once a week in exchange for going to football once a week. Other methods of marital therapy consist of role-playing focused on interaction between the couple, or of group therapy for two.

The Effectiveness of SST

Does it work? For socially inadequate neurotics, SST does a little better than behaviour therapy aimed to reduce anxiety: SST improves the skills, and may later reduce the anxiety. The worse the patients are, the more sessions are needed. Mental patients of all kinds can be helped by SST, preferably as part of a larger package.

Professional social skills, and intercultural skills, can be trained in quite a short course of role-playing – typically six sessions. Marital problems can be somewhat alleviated by existing forms of therapy.

However, it should be emphasized that most follow-up studies have been carried out on earlier and fairly simple versions of SST. Research has now made possible much more sophisticated training, such as that embodied in the various supplementary exercises listed earlier.

Michael Argyle
University of Oxford

Further Reading

Argyle, M. (ed.) (1981), *Social Skills and Health*, London.

Argyle, M. (ed.) (1981), *Social Skills and Work*, London.

Argyle, M. (1983), *The Psychology of Interpersonal Behaviour* (4th edn), Harmondsworth.

Argyle, M. (1985), 'Some new developments in social skills training', *Bulletin of the British Psychological Society*, 37.

Bellack, A. S. and Hersen, M. (1979), *Research and Practice in Social Skills Training*, New York.

Singleton, W. T., Spurgeon, P. and Stammer, R. B. (eds) (1980), *The Analysis of Social Skill*, New York.

Spence, S. and Shepherd, G. (1983), *Developments in Social Skills Training*, London.

See also: *group therapy*.

Social Structure

In its most general sense, social structure consists of all those relatively stable features of a social system which an acting unit would be prudent to take into account if it wishes to make rational decisions in interacting with others. 'Units' of any social system, including a society, may be either subcollectivities of it or social roles. Relevant social structure varies according to units' interests, goals and 'location' relative to other units. For certain purposes one might want to take into account the ethnic composition of a population; for others, the age composition; for still others, the composition according to generational experience, for example, of the Great Depression or the

Nazi movement. One must not reify social structure. For any given purpose of analysis, however, social structure is in principle something describable objectively.

All sociologists have at least implicitly regarded as central the *normative* aspects of social structure. Marx's conception of class structure, for instance, certainly involves several important and stable normative patterns, such as property, contract, the institutions of family and kinship, and others. Further, the normative 'order' involves a great *many* aspects of culture. Thus, if there is a tax on 'dogs' the tax collectors will not permit people to evade the tax by regarding an Irish setter as a non-dog.

The extreme importance of the normative aspect of social structure is connected with the problem of order (see, for example, Parsons, 1968b). Inherent in all social interaction are two sets of possibilities. First is the possibility of conflict, mutual interference, deceit, the use of coercion for one-sided advantage. The other set of possibilities includes direct and indirect co-operation or at least mutual non-interference of units (when they are pursuing different and unrelated goals). It has been shown that this second set of possibilities depends mainly on some 'internalized' normative order. That is, interacting units must regard conformity (not conformism) as an unvarying end in itself, not as a matter of convenience or expediency, which varies from situation to situation. In all its levels and forms, however, normative social structure must not be thought of as shaping social interaction like a cookie cutter; rather, it serves as a set of guidelines and a common basis for 'negotiating' more precise terms of interaction in myriad concrete situations (Durkheim, 1933 [1893]; Mead, 1934).

Especially important as focuses of normative order are the ways in which it is inherently possible to control the actions of others. Briefly, these ways come down to forms of *inducement* (in a positive sense), *coercion*, *persuasion* through advice or counsel (influence), and *activation of commitments* (in effect, 'promises' that have already been made) (Parsons, 1967b). These ways are subject to normative controls, that is, to rules. 'Generalized symbolic media' are the more or less institutionalized symbolic forms of these inherent bases of social control (Parsons, 1969).

'The problem of order' is part of the larger inherent problem of integration. Normative consensus is one aspect. Another is the degree of consistency in a varied complex of norms, covering family life, economic, political and religious activities, and many others. Differentiated structural content and applications have *varied* functional significance, but *all* social structure is relevant to the functional problem of integration. A closely related aspect of this larger problem of integration is the range of variation from close, diffuse solidarity (full *Gemeinschaft*), through more specific solidarities (*Gesellschaft*) and peripheral attachments, to alienation and hositility: a range of *affect* as well as obligation.

Integration is certainly problematic as viewed by the analyst or observer, but quite often it is also problematic from the 'subjective' point of view as well (that of participants in the system of reference).

As a problem and as a functional process, 'integration' has to do with normative order *and anomie*, common or compatible interests *and conflicting interests*, solidarity and alienation, mutually reinforcing solidarities and conflicting solidarities, and more or less serious conflicts with regard to normative content. At the very least, any normative order must be interpreted; and disputes over its application to concrete circumstances and over the relevant facts must be resolved if integration is to be maintained, restored, or patched up.

The outcomes of social processes, which to some extent are regulated by normative social structure, are usually only partially successful in functional terms. Outcomes sometimes generate so much strain that some units of the system in question may be alienated and may withdraw, may engage in one or another form of deviant behaviour, or may seek to change the structure of the system.

The *institutionalization* of social structure is very much a matter of degree. *Several* variables are involved, including at least the following: the firmness of legitimation; the certainty of social control (application of sanctions); the extent in the relevant population to which uninitiated members are actually socialized in the relevant patterns; and the extent to which there exist competing and incompatible patterns that also have for some persons or groups a claim to legitimacy.

Four *levels* of social structure have been distinguished (Parsons, 1959; 1960; 1967a). Societal *values* are the most general or abstract normative conceptions of what the ideal society itself would be like – of course, according to some, most, or all of the participants in the society. Values are always more or less 'sacred', thus close to religion, and may be explicitly legitimated and given a meaningful setting in religious terms.

At the next level 'down' we find *institutional patterns*. Examples include the rules of kinship obligations; the rights and obligations we call property; patterns of authority. The theoretical model is Durkheim's treatment of the institution of contract (1933 [1893]).

Differentiated institutional patterns almost directly imply the existence of collective and role units whose activities have different kinds of functional significance. Below institutional patterns, then, are specialized *collectivities* (families. firms, schools, churches, political parties, and so on). These are structural in a double sense. First, their very existence is often a relatively stable part of the social systems in which acting units are engaged. Second, their own internal normative order or organization may be and often is a more concrete or specific level of the societal normative order.

Finally, within all such collectivities we can distinguish types of *roles*. Concretely these are the *relevant performances* of their individual occupants. Functionally they are contributions to collective goal-attainment.

The four levels constitute a hierarchy of control such that if a lower level is inconsistent with a higher level, pressure will ordinarily be brought to bear to 'correct' the lower level. In so far as 'correction' is unnecessary, then social control is already operating: and we may say that the four 'levels' are also *components* of the same concrete social structures. For example, someone in the role of 'medical doctor' is controlled by a different set of institutional patterns and social values according to whether his role is a contribution to collective goal-attainment of a hospital, a big-league football team, or an insurance company processing claims against it. Social structure at any given time also includes still-operative *authoritative decisions* (exercises of 'power').

In 'advanced' modern societies especially, institutionalized universalistic *law* is an important part of social structure at all the 'levels' distinguished above (Fuller, 1968; Parsons, 1978; Lidz, 1979; Münch, 1982). Ideally it is backed up not only by coercion or actual force but by widely accepted morality (or, legitimation); by sentiments of solidarity and loyalty, on which the symbolic medium of influence is based in part; and by both vested and prospective interests, which might be regarded (broadly) as a form of inducement.

Broadly speaking, Max Weber's famous analysis of bureaucracy (1968 [1922]) applies to specialized collectivities in which formal law and unequal 'power' are characteristic, but Parsons greatly improved upon Weber's analysis by pointing out that 'formal organization' also includes types that depend much more on generalized symbolic media other than 'power' (Parsons, 1968a). Moreover, all these types of formal organization are concretely interdependent and often interpenetrating. A notable example of interpenetrating types is the modern 'bureaucracy', in which various professions, which stress fiduciary value commitments, are increasingly important.

The outcomes of all structure and process are routinely and quite expectably different for different units, depending on evaluations of their performances, the degree of their conformity to established norms, the wisdom of their decisions, and even chance variations, as well as more or less systemic or random 'injustice'. Any concrete system of social classes, for example, is determined by factors such as 'accident' of birth (actually, ascription), subcultural motivation to achieve, opportunities for achievement afforded by the educational system, and religious and ethnic discrimination. Any judgement that an element of social structure is 'dysfunctional', therefore, cannot be absolute and should be made with caution, preferably in an evolutionary and comparative perspective.

The *evolution* of social structure has been marked by an increasingly clear differentiation of the levels of social structure; by the more explicitly felt need and pressure, eventually, either to justify in functional terms any social constraints and inequalities or else to reduce or eliminate them; by greater attention to the development of the economy, science, and education; and by many other structural changes. However, social evolution in this 'progressive' sense is far from even and automatic; evolution itself and evolutionary emulation are usually accompanied by a great deal of social conflict and episodes of retrogression as well as progress.

Harry M. Johnson
University of Illinois
Champaign-Urbana

References

Durkheim, E. (1933 [1893]), *The Divison of Labour in Society*, New York. (Original French edn, *De la division du travail social*, Paris.)

Fuller, L. (1968), *The Anatomy of Law*, New York.

Lidz, V. M. (1979), 'The law as index, phenomenon and element – conceptual steps toward a general sociology of law', *Sociological Inquiry*, 49.

Mead, G. H. (1934), *Mind, Self and Society*, Chicago.

Münch, R. (1982), 'Talcott Parsons and the theory of action. II. The continuity of the development', *American Journal of Sociology*, 87.

Parsons, T. (1959), 'General theory in sociology', in R. K. Merton, L. Broom and L. S. Cottrell (eds), *Sociology Today*, New York.

Parsons, T. (1960), 'Authority, legitimation and political action', in T. Parsons, *Structure and Process in Modern Societies*, New York.

Parsons, T. (1967a and b), 'Durkheim's contribution to the theory of integration of social systems', and 'Some reflections on the place of force in social process', both in T. Parsons, *Sociological Theory and Modern Society*, New York.

Parsons, T. (1968a), 'Components and types of formal organization', in P. P. Le Breton (ed.), *Comparative Administrative Theory*, Seattle.

Parsons, T. (1968b), 'Order as a sociological problem', in P. G. Kuntz (ed.), *The Concept of Order*, Seattle.

Parsons, T. (1969), 'Theory and the polity', in T. Parsons, *Politics and Social Structure*, New York.

Parsons, T. (1978), 'Law as an intellectual stepchild', in H. M. Johnson (ed.), *System and Legal Process*, San Francisco.

Weber, M. (1968, [1922]), 'Bureaucracy', in *Economy and Society*, Vol. III, New York. (Original German edn, *Wirtschaft und Gesellschaft*, Tübingen.)

See also: *groups; norms; role; social structure, anthropological approaches.*

Social Structure: Anthropological Approaches

Within anthropology, the two leading theorists concerned with social structure have been Radcliffe-Brown and Lévi-Strauss. Radcliffe-Brown insisted that the study of society could not be reduced to individual psychology. One should study the relationships which existed between individuals. These relationships tend to assume repetitive and stable forms, the 'structural form' of the relationship. By extension, a social structure is the aggregate of such units, the sum total of social relations in a given social field. Radcliffe-Brown argued that once such structures had been described they could be compared, and that ultimately the basic laws of social structure would be discovered (see Kuper, 1977). Because he analysed social structures in terms of the rules or norms which standardize behaviour and social forms, his model has come to be known as the 'jural' or 'normative' model.

Lévi-Strauss (1963 [1958]) opposed to this the view that 'structure' cannot be directly derived from 'empirical reality'. Instead it has to do with the models we construct in order to understand empirical reality; and these models must depend on deduction rather than induction. Where Radcliffe-Brown defined social structure with reference to social relationships structured by shared norms, Lévi-Strauss's structures depended rather on systems of exchange and communication based upon shared mental operations. Their approaches differed so much because they were concerned with different aspects of social behaviour. Nevertheless, Radcliffe-Brown and Lévi-Strauss (far more than most of the leading sociologists) both derived their theoretical orientations from Durkheim, who argued that society regulated behaviour, through *conscience collective*, and generated our mental categories. Radcliffe-Brown and Lévi-Strauss shared Durkheim's concern that societies be treated as wholes, and, like him, they were less concerned with questions of change and conflict.

The individualist rationalist approach is also influential in anthropology, represented especially by the Norwegian anthropologist, Fredrik Barth (1982). For Barth, social interaction is purposive and goal-oriented, and actors seek to maintain or maximize social values by choosing the strategy which seems to offer them the best opportunities. However, choices are partly constrained by jural rules, and also by the values and moves of other social actors. The social structure is, then, a statistical outcome of individual moves governed by 'strategic rules'.

Michel Verdon
University of Montreal

References

Barth, F. (1982), *Process and Form in Social Life*, London.

Kuper, A. (ed.) (1977), *The Social Anthropology of Radcliffe-Brown*, London.

Lévi-Strauss, C. (1963 [1958]), *Structural Anthropology*, London. (Original French edn, *Anthropologie structurale*, Paris.)

See also: *Lévi-Strauss; Radcliffe-Brown; social structure.*

Social Welfare

The adjective 'economic' is perhaps more appropriate, since when it is discussed by economists, 'social' welfare encompasses goods and services but not wider social issues. The modern approach is a fusion of two earlier approaches, a rough-and-ready 'statistical' approach and a finely-honed welfare analytic approach.

The statistical approach measures social welfare in terms of just two parameters: real income and its distribution. One's overall judgement is then to some degree subjective, depending upon how real income gains (or losses) are valued as against egalitarian losses (or gains). To capture the whole income distribution in one parameter is, of course, extremely arbitrary, but for many purposes (for example, cross-country comparisons) it is reasonably safe to take some measure of real income per head and an index of inequality like the Gini coefficient. The measurement of real income itself is not unambiguous because its composition changes over time as does its distribution. The composition aspect is intimately connected with both the theory of index numbers and the theory of consumer behaviour. To use current prices as weights for the different commodities is, however, a reasonable practical approximation to changes in real income. Distributional changes are more serious, and only in the rare case where real income had increased to the same degree for everyone could they be ignored. All this is essentially an elaboration of Pigou's double criterion that real income increase without the poor being worse off *or* that the poor be better off and real income not decrease.

It was thought for some time – by Kaldor and Hicks – that it would be desirable to use real income alone, without distributional judgements, to evaluate economic policies. This is because interpersonal comparisons were said to be 'unscientific'. The 'new welfare economics' advocated the use of a compensation principle: if adoption of a policy enabled the gainers to compensate the losers and still be better off, then the policy would bring an improvement. Later, due to Scitovsky, it had to be added that the losers could not then bribe the gainers to return to the original position. Controversy arose as to whether the principle was merely a test for real income increases or a criterion for improvement. Part of the difficulty lay in whether compensation was to be actual or merely hypothetical. In the 1950s, Little insisted, successfully, that distributional considerations would have to be reintroduced. Though the attempt to jettison distribution failed, there is still a feeling that real income is somehow more important and more fundamental, especially in the longer term (it is, after all, a *sine qua non*). The compensation principle was intended to be a test of economic efficiency from which it is not desirable to depart too far.

The other, welfare analytic, approach starts from the preferences of individuals rather than from aggregate income. Individual utilities are a function of individuals' goods and services, and social welfare is a function of individual utilities (Bergson, 1938). Together with competitive theory, this construction enables one to draw out certain optimality properties of markets – this is especially so if lump-sum redistributions (almost impossible in practice) are permitted. Most of these propositions, except those to do with redistribution, are independent of distributional weights and therefore robust against distributional preferences. Whatever these preferences, efficiency requires equality of marginal rates of substitution in production and consumption. So if lump-sum redistributions are possible, social welfare is maximized under competition with distribution being a separate 'political' matter. Unfortunately the dichotomy cannot be sustained, and there are no truly simple rules for maximizing social welfare.

A second use of the welfare analytic approach which has so far proved to be strongly negative (though usefully so) is relating social choice to individual preferences. There should, it was felt, be some method for moving from the latter to the former. Arrow (1951) showed that no such transition rule was possible. Starting from individual preference orderings, it is impossible to derive a social ordering without violating at least one of a number of perfectly reasonable axioms, for example, that the ordering be not imposed, not dictatorial, not restricted in domain, and so on. To give examples, a competitive mechanism has to be rejected because the domain is restricted to Pareto-improvements on the original allocation and a Bergsonian welfare function because it would have to be imposed (by an economist?). Social choice cannot therefore be grounded in individual preferences except for relatively trivial cases.

The modern reaction to these two weaknesses of the welfare analytic approach (the impossibility of lump-sum redistributions or of acceptable transition rules) is to be very much more explicit about distributional judgements and interpersonal comparisons. Failing that, work on social choice remains barren and formal. Following Atkinson (1970) a great deal of technical work has been done on the relationships between social-welfare functions and indices of inequality.

There is scope within the approach for a whole spectrum of value judgements running from a zero preference for equality to Rawlsian emphasis on the income of the poorest. The modern approach moves away from Arrow's assumption that we have only ordinal information about individuals, without reverting to crude utilitarianism. In the same spirit it ventures to make statements about equivalence between individuals and to compare 'needs'. Social welfare can then be indexed (always provisionally) by statistical measures which certainly carry recognized value judgements with them but have good foundations in consumer theory. The measures are a compromise between statistical convenience and (possibly sterile) theoretical purity.

David Collard
University of Bath

References
Arrow, K. J. (1951), *Social Choice and Individual Values*, New York.
Atkinson, A. B. (1970), 'On the measurement of inequality', *Journal of Economic Theory*, 2.
Bergson, A. (1938), 'A reformulation of certain aspects of welfare economics', *Quarterly Journal of Economics*, 52.

Further Reading
Mishan, E. J. (1981), *Introduction to Normative Economics*, Oxford.
Sen, A. K. (1982), *Choice, Measurement and Welfare*, Oxford.

See also: *social welfare policy; welfare economics*.

Social Welfare Policy

In the long boom succeeding World War II, social welfare policy was widely seen as the state's intervention in society to secure the well-being of its citizens. This progressivist interpretation of increasing social expenditure by the state was sustained by the writings of key post-war welfare theorists such as Titmuss (1950) and Marshall (1967). The former welcomed increasing collectivism as a necessary and desirable means of enhancing social integration; the latter saw in the developing British Welfare State the extension of citizenship through the acquisition of social rights. The Beveridge-Keynes Welfare State, which had been called into existence by the exigencies of war and the balance of social forces in the post-war situation, came to assume an ideological significance, both as the exemplar against which other Welfare States were to be assessed, and also as an explanation of the development of the Welfare State itself. This ideological construction had few means of accounting for developments in other countries such as the pioneering achievements in social policy in New Zealand, nor of specifically conservative political strategies such as those of Bismarck's Germany, in which social insurance was conceived of as a mechanism to weaken the working-class movement and inhibit the spread of socialist ideas. For that matter, its emphasis on the peculiarly British nature of the achievement led to difficulties in explaining the rather better performance by most indicators of Britain's new partners when she joined the European Community, a phenomenon which was received with some shock by British political culture.

Relatively early on in the post-war period, social democratic theorists such as Crosland (1964) acknowledged the significance of social welfare policy and the achievement of the full employment economy in modifying a basically capitalist social formation. Nonetheless, redistribution was to be secured through growth, thus avoiding the political opposition of the rich – a strategy which was thrown into question as economic growth faltered and even declined. The significance of these policies for structuring sex-gender relations within the home and within the labour market was grasped very much more slowly (Wilson, 1977). Nonetheless, the achievement of the Welfare State or welfare capitalism, as it has been variously termed, was aided by the discourse and practices of social policy in which 'need' was set as morally and administratively superior to the market as the distributive principle for welfare. Thus integral to the achievement of welfare capitalism and institutional welfare was a concept of need which stood as an antagonistic value to that of capitalism with its, at best, residual welfare.

Need was at the same moment emancipatory and constrained within the dominant social relations. In its emancipatory aspect, need fostered the language of rights, not only in theoretical writing but within the popular demands of the new social movements which rose during the late 1960s and early 1970s within North America and Europe (Piven and Cloward, 1971; Rose, 1973). Aided by the 'rediscovery of poverty' in the 1960s (Harrington, 1962; Abel-Smith and Townsend, 1965), large-scale mobilization around income maintenance and housing exerted substantial pressure on governments to offer more, and more responsive, welfare provision. Thus, the new social movements shared with institutional welfare an opposition to mere residual welfare, but continuously sought to go beyond not only the level of existing provisions but also the organizational forms through which they were realized. Instead – and this tendency was to become magnified as the welfare movements were joined by the 1970s wave of feminism – existing forms of welfare were seen as coercive, inadequate and statist. In contrast, the oppositional forms developed by the movements themselves emphasized democratic accountability, and nonhierarchical ways of working. Freire's (1972) thesis of conscientization as the politically creative strategy for the poor in the Third World was shared by the new social movements as they sought to develop an alternative practice of welfare to what was usual in the old industrialized societies. At their most radical the new movements sought that society itself should be organized around the meeting of human need.

While the boom lasted, this critique of institutional welfare as statist and bureaucratic made relatively little impact on either mainstream social welfare policy thinking or on political culture: ideological support for a more or less institutional welfare overlaid the deeper antagonism between need and the market. The separation of need from market values was further facilitated by the separation between economic and social policy discourses. Social policy felt able to ignore economic policy since it was confident that Keynesian demand management techniques had delivered and would continue to deliver the precondition of the Welfare State, namely the full employment economy. Economists largely ignored the discussion of social welfare policy as of no interest to other than social ameliorists, until the crisis of the mid-1970s during which the loss of confidence in Keynesian techniques fostered a return to an endorsement of the market and an increasingly open opposition to state welfare expenditure (Friedman, 1962). Where institutional welfare had seen expanded welfare policies as socially integrative, a radical political economy had emphasized their contribution to capital accumulation and social control (O'Connor, 1973; Gough, 1979); now monetarism and the advent of a new right saw such expenditures as harming individualism and competitiveness and thus weakening the central dynamic of capitalism. With considerable populist skill the new right acknowledged the critique of the coercive character of public welfare, and offered an increase in personal liberty through rolling back the (Welfare) State, restoring the market and the family as the paramount providers of welfare.

The very depth of the current crisis which has provided the conditions for the rise of the new right, nonetheless serves as a major constraint for its remedies. Global restructuring of manufacturing is associated with widespread and foreseeably long-term unemployment in the de-industrializing countries. Unemployment, averaging around 12 per cent in the OECD countries in 1982 and with few clear indications of a significant improvement, requires, even in the most residual conception of welfare, substantial expenditure for both maintenance and control of an expanding surplus population. This situation is aggravated by the large numbers of young people among the unemployed, among whom ethnic and racial minorities are over-represented.

Despite these political constraints, since 1975 most Western governments have reduced the rate of growth of their social welfare budgets. Thus, up to 1975 the real rate of social expenditure growth in the seven largest OECD countries was no less than 8 per cent

per annum (15 per cent growth at current prices); between 1975 and 1981 the real rate was halved. While all countries have experienced difficulties in maintaining their social welfare budget in the face of the reduction of the growth of the overall economy, governments with a specifically anti-welfare ideology such as the US and Britain have made substantial inroads. Thus, in the case of Britain an institutional system of welfare moves increasingly towards a residual model, particularly in the area of social security. The Nordic countries stand apart as the last bastion of the most highly developed expression of the old Welfare State, although the mix of labour market and social policies through which they achieve this varies substantially between them. Given the double significance for women of the existence of the Welfare State, as potential provider of both employment and services, it is perhaps not by chance that those Nordic countries with a continuing commitment to welfare have also an unusually high proportion of women representatives in their parliaments and upper houses. It is noteworthy that writers from these countries, such as Himmelstrand (1981) and his co-workers, are taking an active part in the current international debate concerning the possible future direction open to a post-Welfare State society. These writers seek to develop a theory which looks beyond welfare capitalism, to a new but very much more democratically based corporatism. Such post-Welfare State theorists are typically not unsympathetic to the claims of the new social movements (Gorz, 1982). However, they seem not to have fully appreciated the significance of feminist theorizing concerning the relationship between paid and unpaid labour within the development of the Welfare State, and thus the advantage to the dominant gender of retaining the present arrangements. Thus, even though the precondition of the old Welfare State, the full employment of one gender with welfare flowing through the man to the dependent family, no longer fits the actuality of either domestic or labour market structures, the ideological defence of those arrangements persists. Faced with the growing 'feminization of poverty' (Pearce, 1978), and the profoundly segregated (by both occupation and between full and part-time employment) labour market, there is a serious question concerning the extent to which the needs of women are met by the new post-Welfare State theorizing.

These are cautious, even sceptical reflections on the debate around the Welfare State and the place of social welfare policy (Glennister, 1983). How far any of the new theories can offer to serve as the new fusion of the social and the economic, the contemporary historical equivalent of the old Welfare State of Keynes and Beveridge is not yet clear. What is clear, however, is that social welfare policy having spent its years of greatest growth relatively detached from economic policy has now been forcibly rejoined by circumstance.

Together they occupy the centre of an intensely debated political arena.

Hilary Rose
University of Bradford

References

Abel-Smith, B. and Townsend, P. (1965), *The Poor and the Poorest*, London.

Crosland, C. A. R. (1964), *The Future of Socialism*, London.

Freire, P. (1972), *Cultural Action for Freedom*, Harmondsworth.

Friedman, M. (1962), *Capitalism and Freedom*, Chicago.

Glennister, H. (ed.) (1983), *The Future of the Welfare State*, London.

Gorz, A. (1982), *Farewell to the Working Class*, London.

Gough, I. (1979), *The Political Economy of Welfare*, London.

Harrington, M. (1962), *The Other America*, Harmondsworth.

Himmelstrand, U., Ahrne, G., Lundberg, L. and Lundberg, L. (1981), *Beyond Welfare Capitalism; Issues Actors and Social Forces in Societal Change*, London.

Marshall, T. H. (1967), *Social Policy*, 2nd edn, London.

O'Connor, J. (1973), *The Fiscal Crisis of the State*, New York.

Pearce, D. (1978), 'The feminization of poverty: women, work and welfare', *Urban and Social Change Review*.

Piven, F. F. and Cloward, R. (1971), *Regulating the Poor: The Functions of Public Welfare*, New York.

Rose, H. (1973), 'Up against the Welfare State: the claimant unions', in R. Miliband and J. Saville (eds), *The Socialist Register*, London.

Titmuss, R. M. (1950), *Problems of Social Policy*, London.

Wilson, E. (1977), *Women and the Welfare State*, London.

See also: *human needs; social welfare; social work; welfare economics; welfare state.*

Social Work

It is perhaps not surprising that the term social work, combining the rich ambiguity of 'social' with the misleading and somewhat deterrent simplicity of 'work', has undergone considerable change in usage since it first appeared in England towards the end of the last century. It was then used to describe a perspective applicable from a number of different occupations rather than to announce the arrival of a particular new occupation. This perspective derived from the serious reconsideration of the role of citizen, and it can be illustrated from the dedication of a book entitled *The Spirit of Social Work* (Devine, 1911) to 'social workers, that is to say, to every man and woman, who, in any relation of life, professional, industrial, political, educational or domestic; whether on salary or as a volunteer; whether on his own individual account or as part of an organized movement, is working consciously, according to his light intelligently and according to his strength persistently, for the promotion of the common welfare'. (The fact that Devine was an American, indicates the speed with which 'social work' was exported to America and thence, eventually to many other societies, developed and developing.)

This broadly brushed backcloth has been more or less evident in the present century as social workers have attempted to claim a role that is specialized and professional. It is perhaps one reason why an agreed and satisfactory definition of 'social work' is not yet forthcoming. Other features of social work activity have also contributed to this lack of agreement about the nature of social work. The broad purposes of social work have become more ambiguous as social workers have increasingly become state employees rather than volunteers or paid workers in non-statutory agencies. Sometimes public appreciation of social work has been blunted by the large claims made on behalf of social workers (for instance, that social work can cure a considerable range of private sorrows and public ills or simply that social workers represent the conscience of society). Changes in the dominant theories said to underpin social work – economics or sociology or psychoanalytic theories – and confusion between espoused theories and those actually informing practice have created at least the impression of significant ruptures as a tradition of practice struggles to assert itself. Finally, social work, like teaching, is both an 'attempting' and a 'succeeding' term: on occasions practitioners will deny the term to activity that was not particularly successful or that infringed one of the contested maxims that figure largely in professional talk.

A rough description of the contemporary social worker is of a person (traditionally a woman but increasingly in some societies a man) who as a representative of some statutory or non-statutory agency delivers a wide range of services, from income maintenance and welfare commodities, to directive and non-directive counselling. These services are directed or offered to individuals or to groups of different kinds, based on kinship, locality, interest or common condition. For the efficient and effective delivery of such services, social workers claim to use skills of various kinds, a range of theoretical and practical knowledge, and a set of values specific to social work.

Definition or general description take us some way towards grasping social work, but a more productive approach is to examine certain key questions concerning the form and the purposes of social work that have arisen at different times in the present century. In relation to form, two questions predominate: is social work to be treated as a profession (and if so, what kind of profession); is social work to be practised as an applied science, as an art, or as some kind of ministration? Flexner's (1915) consideration of the professional nature of social work raised questions that may still fruitfully be pursued. He concluded that social work met some of the criteria for professional status, but that social workers were mediators rather than full professional agents, that they pursued no distinctive ends, and that they were required to possess certain personal qualities rather than expertise in scientifically-derived technical skills. More recently, it has been suggested that social work can most easily be viewed as a semi-profession or as a bureau-profession. The characterization of social work as part of a humanistic as contrasted with a scientific movement is best studied through the work of Halmos (1965).

Controversy within social work is somewhat rare, but important questioning concerning the purpose of social work can be appreciated through three major debates (Timms, 1983). The first, between leaders of the influential Charity Organization Society and the Socialists at the turn of the century, concerned the emphasis to be given to the individual and to his social circumstances and to preventive as opposed to curative work. The second, between two American schools of social work, the Functionalists and the Diagnosticians in the middle of the century, raised questions concerning the independence of social work as a helping process contrasted with a process of psychological treatment. The third, most immediate, controversy revolves around the possibility of a social work that is politically radical or, specifically, Marxist.

Noel Timms
University of Leicester

References
Devine, E. (1911), *The Spirit of Social Work*, New York.
Flexner, A. (1915), 'Is social work a profession?', *Proceedings of the 42nd National Conference of Charities and Correction*.
Halmos, P. (1965), *The Faith of the Counsellors*, London.
Timms, N. (1983), *Social Work Values: An Enquiry*, London.

Further Reading.
Younghusband, E. (1978), *Social Work in Britain: 1950–1975*, 2 vols, London.
Timms, N. and Timms, R. (1982), *Dictionary of Social Welfare*, London.
See also: *social welfare policy; welfare state*.

Society

Society is one of those concepts that appear to mean everything and nothing. Sociology, for example, is supposed to be the 'study of society', and indeed most textbooks usually tend to start off with this definition. In very broad terms society is conceived of as the framework or totality in which human beings engage in social relations. In its *weakest* sense, the term denotes the backdrop to individual conduct – it is like the setting for a play in which the focus of attention is on the intentions and actions of the actors. In other words, society is regarded as a social environment comprising the aggregate total of people in so far as they influence and frame this or that person's behaviour.

In its *strongest* sense, society as a totality entails much more than 'background' – it is seen as constitutive of all human behaviour. Society, from this point of view, seems to act as an overwhelming determining force. Human beings are born into a ready-made set of social relationships which completely dominate their lives. From the cradle to the grave they are moulded (socialized) by society or, more accurately, by the agents of society. Of course, this 'strong' definition is usually qualified by highlighting particular social contexts. Although we talk about world or international society, social scientists tend to concentrate on particular societies. Thus, for example, British society is the totality which is of relevance to British sociologists. Accordingly, it is particular societies that are usually given explanatory priority in social analysis.

In general, it would appear that the weak definition is associated with individualistic accounts of social life, whereas the strong definition relegates individual intentionality to a secondary status. However, if we examine past and extant views of society, we often find that some practitioners find it difficult to adopt an exclusively weak or strong stance. An instance of this is discoverable in the work of G. H. Mead (1934), who seems to fluctuate between a complete social determinism, and a form of voluntarism.

The society concept is difficult to formulate in an unambiguous manner. The history of sociology is replete with attempts to come to a satisfactory formulation of the term. Durkheim's classic discussion of 'society' as something existing external to individuals has had a long and powerful influence on a large number of sociologists. His claim that knowledge and individuality are fundamentally social in origin still tends to dominate social thought. Moreover, in recent discussions subjectivity and intentionality have been treated as though they are entirely social. The problem with this kind of thinking is that it tends to turn society into a thing – it reifies social processes by imbuing them with a life of their own.

Social theorists have employed various strategies to conceptualize society, the most important of which are:

(1) *Society as structure*. In order to concretize society, mainstream sociologists have tended to define it as structure, that is, a recognizable network of

interrelating institutions. The word 'recognizable' is crucial in this context, because it suggests that the way in which societies differ from one another depends on the manner in which their particular institutions are interconnected.

(2) *Society as recurrence.* The notion that societies are structured depends upon their reproduction over time. In this respect the term 'institution' is crucial. ('To speak of *"institutionalized"* forms of social conduct is to refer to modes of belief and behaviour that occur and recur or . . . are socially reproduced' (Giddens, 1982).) Hence, although British society is continuously changing we can recognize its main features as they are reproduced in institutionalized forms.

(3) *Society as contradiction.* While we may subscribe to the arguments that society is both structured and reproduced, it could be claimed that this does not tell us why and how it is structured and reproduced. The Marxist account attempts to provide us with a basis for understanding how particular social formations arise and correspond with particular modes of production. In this sense, society is not a static or peacefully evolving structure, but is conceived of as the tentative solution to the conflicts arising out of antagonistic social relations of production. Thus capitalist society is always in the process of being transformed by the tensions and contradictions implicit in the mode of production (Marx, 1913).

(4) *Society as culture.* Frequently, social scientists emphasize the cultural aspect of social relationships. In so doing, they see society as being made possible by the shared understandings of its members. Because human beings exist in a linguistic and symbolic universe which they themselves have constructed, the temptation is to construe society as a highly-complex symbolic and communication system. This stress on culture is associated with the notion that society is underpinned by ideas and values (Weber, 1930; Parsons, 1968). In this respect, one of the perennial problems of social analysis has been the analytical distinction between culture and society. It seems highly improbable that such a distinction is valid, except for heuristic purposes.

(5) *Society as process.* Here the emphasis is on the way in which people continuously interact with one another. The key terms are 'negotiation', 'self – other', 'reflexivity' – the implication being that society is constituted and reconstituted in social interaction. Society is not imposed upon people in the processual definition; rather it has to be accepted and confirmed by participants. Each interaction episode contains within it the possibility of innovation and change. So against the view of society which sees it as a 'structure', the

process view asserts that people 'make' structures (Mead, 1934; Goffman, 1959; Garfinkel, 1967). It is this idea of 'making' that may link the process view of society to humanistic Marxism.

All of these strategies contain implicit or explicit assumptions about human nature and the individual. Some recent theories have completely rejected the individual as a datum for social analysis (Althusser, 1969; Foucault, 1972). Nevertheless, the opposition between individual and society still remains a theme of popular and academic consciousness, especially in the context of contemporary concerns about the inroads that bureaucracy and the state have made into the personal sphere. The old distinction between the 'state' and 'society' is difficult to maintain in a period in which the state seems to penetrate every aspect of social life.

Arthur Brittan
University of York

References

Althusser, L. (1969 [1965]), *For Marx*, Harmondsworth. (Original French edn, *Pour Marx*, Paris.)

Foucault, M. (1972 [1969]), *The Archaeology of Knowledge*, London. (Original French edn, *L'Archéologie du savoir*, Paris.)

Garfinkel, H. (1967), *Studies in Ethnomethodology*, Englewood Cliffs, NJ.

Giddens, A. (1982), *Sociology*, London.

Goffman, E. (1959), *The Presentation of Self in Everyday Life*, New York.

Marx, K. (1913 [1859]), *A Contribution to the Critique of Political Economy*, Chicago. (Original German edn, *Zur Kritik der Politischen Ökonomie*.)

Mead, G. H. (1934), *Mind, Self and Society*, Chicago.

Parsons, T. (1968), *The Structure of Social Action*, 2nd edn, New York.

Weber, M. (1930 [1922]), *The Protestant Ethic and the Spirit of Capitalism*, London. (Original German edn, *Die protestantische Ethik und der 'Geist' des Kapitalismus*, Tübingen.)

Further Reading

Bottomore, T. and Nisbet, R. (eds) (1978), *A History of Sociological Analysis*, London.

Goudsblom, J. (1977), *Sociology in the Balance*, Oxford.

Held, D. (1980), *Introduction to Critical Theory: Horkheimer to Habermas*, London.

See also: *culture; institutions; social structure; sociology.*

Sociobiology

Although the term only gained wide currency after the 1975 publication of E. O. Wilson's *Sociobiology, The New Synthesis*, the theoretical roots of sociobiology go back to the mid-1960s, with publications by Hamilton (1964) and Maynard Smith (1964). Sociobiology is the study of animal behaviour, especially social behaviour, from the perspective of evolution by natural selection. As such, it is squarely in the mainstream of neo-Darwinian evolutionary theory.

The subject became intensely controversial and ideological in the late 1970s and, for that reason, many of its practitioners prefer to conduct their work under blander labels such as 'evolutionary ecology' or 'behavioural biology'. Some continue to use the older labels of 'ethology' or 'behaviourism', although sociobiology differs in emphasis from these two approaches. Behaviourism put the emphasis on the ontogeny rather than the phylogeny of behaviour, and stressed environmental conditioning to the neglect of the genetic basis of behaviour. Sociobiology insists on the equal importance of heredity *and* environment, since a phenotype is always the product of interaction between a genotype and a multiplicity of environmental variables. Ethology is more clearly an ancestral discipline of sociobiology in that it too is concerned with the evolution of animal behaviour. Until the 1960s, however, ethology tended to be heavily descriptive rather than explanatory and theoretical, and such theoretical basis as it had was rooted in group-selectionist thinking, holding that animals behaved for the survival of the group or the species.

More than any other development, it was the rejection of group selection as the main explanation for the apparent altruism of some forms of animal behaviour (such as alarm calls, the suicidal stinging of bees, or the mimicking of wing injuries by birds) which launched sociobiology as the dominant new approach to animal behaviour. Apparently altruistic behaviour was reduced to a simple model of maximization of reproductive success (or 'fitness') at the level of the individual organism, and ultimately of the gene (as popularized in Dawkins's 1976 book, *The Selfish Gene*). The central theorem of 'inclusive fitness', first presented in 1964 by W. D. Hamilton, is that an organism can be expected to favour the fitness of another, even at an apparent cost to its own fitness, if the following inequation holds:

$$k > \frac{1}{r}$$

where k is the ratio of benefits (for recipient) to costs (for 'altruist') of the interaction, and r is the proportion of genes shared by common descent between 'altruist' and recipient.

In sexually reproducing, diploid organisms, an individual shares one half of its genes with a parent, offspring, or full sibling; a quarter with a grandparent, grandchild, uncle-aunt, nephew-niece, and half-sibling; an eighth with a first cousin, great-grandparent, and so on. In an 'altruistic' transaction between parent and offspring, the benefit to offspring (in terms of fitness) has to be greater than 2, since the pair share one half of their genes; between first-cousins, the benefit-cost ratio would have to exceed 8, since they share an eighth of their genes, and so on. An individual's 'inclusive fitness' includes its own reproductive success plus the effect of its nepotism on the reproductive success of its relatives. Thus, through nepotism (favouring kin over non-kin, and close kin over distant kin), an individual can maximize its inclusive fitness better than by being ruthlessly selfish (for example, by cannibalizing its offspring when hungry).

In the last analysis, what looks like altruism is behaviour genetically programmed to maximize the replication of genes. Organisms are temporary assemblages of genes, programmed to maximize the reproduction of the very genes that do the programming. An organism is, evolutionarily speaking, a gene-carrying and gene-reproducing machine, as Dawkins (1976) so persuasively argues. Since apparent 'altruism' is reducible to ultimate genetic selfishness, the term 'nepotism' is a more accurate description of the preferential behaviour toward kin.

In species after species, ranging from social insects (bees, ants, wasps, termites), to warm-blooded vertebrates, and including· human and nonhuman primates, nepotism has been shown to be an important basis of sociality, and predictor of beneficent behaviour. Given the ubiquity of nepotistic behaviour in humans, and the universal importance of kinship in human societies, there is no *a priori* reason to exclude humans from the purview of sociobiology. Indeed, application of the sociobiological model to human systems of mating and reproduction have yielded promising results in such areas as incest avoidance, the avunculate, matrilineal descent, adoption, infanticide, polygyny and polyandry, sex roles and sexual behaviour (Alexander, 1979; Chagnon and Irons, 1979; Symons, 1979; van den Berghe, 1979).

One of the applications of the theorem of inclusive-fitness maximization has been to strategies of parental investment and mating. Females specialize in producing few, large, and therefore expensive, gametes (eggs), while males produce vast quantities of miniaturized, and therefore, inexpensive gametes (sperms). Eggs are dear; sperms are cheap. Females go for quality, males for quantity. Consequently, their reproductive strategies differ: since the females of nearly all species invest more in reproduction than the males, they maximize their fitness by selecting the best possible mates, while males are programmed for greater promiscuity.

Another consequence of this asymmetry of parental investment strategies is that nubile females are a scarce resource for males, who therefore compete with one another for access to females (sexual selection). Sexual dimorphism, in both anatomy and behaviour, is clearly linked to the range of reproduction systems in diploid animals. Monogamy, polygyny and polyandry, for example, are alternative strategies which vary both between and within species. The theory of parental investment permits a specification of the morphological correlates and environmental conditions favouring the various options. The application of this paradigm to human mating and reproductive strategies has gone a long way, not only in explaining cross-cultural uniformities in sex roles, family composition, double standards of sexual behaviour, and so on, but also in accounting for cultural variations in adaptation to different ecological conditions. Male investment strategies in putative offspring versus uterine nephews, for instance, have been linked to probability of paternity. Differential patterns of marriage (hypergyny, polyandry, monogamy, polygyny, exogamy, and so on) have been studied as situationally-variable adaptive responses tending to maximize the inclusive fitness of the actors (Alexander, 1979; Chagnon and Irons, 1979; van den Berghe, 1979).

Reciprocity is another mechanism favouring fitness maximization and another basis of sociality, besides nepotism. Although social scientists have long recognized the importance of exchange and reciprocity in the maintenance of human sociality, it was Trivers (1971) who linked reciprocity to evolutionary theory and specified the conditions for its evolution. Human systems of reciprocity are extremely complex and vulnerable to free-loading, and the evolution of increasingly sophisticated forms of cheating, and of detecting cheaters, may have been one of the principal selective forces in the rapid increase in hominid intelligence. Reciprocity, however, is not a human monopoly. Indeed, sexual reproduction is probably the oldest and the most widespread template for reciprocity.

The role of coercion as a third important basis of sociality (besides nepotism and reciprocity) has hitherto been neglected in sociobiology. Coercion, that is the use of force or threat of force to garner resources at the expense of other individuals' fitness, is not a human monopoly, but human forms of coercion and intrasocietal parasitism are uniquely elaborate, and have become increasingly so with the evolution of state-level, class-stratified societies.

One of the central theoretical issues in human sociobiology at present is the relationship between genes and culture, a relationship mediated through the human mind, as Lumsden and Wilson (1981) clearly suggest. Among evolutionary theorists, there is general agreement that human culture has some emergent properties, and that the linkages between genes and behavioural phenotypes are seldom if ever direct. Clearly, there are no genes for specific cultural traits, like playing chess or riding bicycles. Rather, our genes give us flexible programmes to adapt by learning. These programmes range in flexibility but few of them

are either completely closed and automatic, or completely open and malleable. We are predisposed to learn and to accept some cultural traits more readily than others. Thus, we learn painlessly certain very complex tasks (such as speech) that evolved sufficiently long ago to be wired into our brain, while we find it more difficult and stressful to learn much simpler tasks (such as control of excretory functions) for which probably no neural programmes exist because their selective advantage is too recent.

Human sociobiologists generally agree that culture is adaptive, and therefore interacts with genetic evolution by natural selection, since culture has fitness consequences for individual humans. Likewise, sociobiologists all agree that humans share a unique set of characteristics (as, indeed, do by definition all other species), some of which distinguish human evolution from that of infra-human species. However, the extent to which it is useful to regard genetic evolution and cultural evolution as two autonomous (though interrelated) processes, each responding to different mechanisms of selection and transmission, is hotly debated at present. Against those who argue for a co-evolutionary model of genes and culture as discrete but interacting processes, there are those who argue that culture is merely a species-specific set of proximate mechanisms of adapting fast through a high degree of ability to transmit learned behaviour socially by symbolic language.

As natural selection directly 'acts' on phenotypes, not genotypes, and as phenotypes always include an environmental component, it is, of course, fallacious to oppose genes and environment. Within this gene-environment interaction model, culture can be seen as the man-made part of the environment, preselected by the specifically human genome. The real issue is not whether culture is part of the natural world. It obviously is. Culture can have no empirical referent outside of the human organisms that invent and transmit it, and, therefore, its evolution is inevitably intertwined with the biological evolution of our species.

The issue is the degree of autonomy of the mechanisms of cultural evolution from those of genetic evolution. In the end, that question is not so much an empirical one, as one of level of analysis and of the type of question asked. Those who specialize in trying to understand human affairs attach greater importance to the unique characteristics of our species than those to whom we are but one species among millions. And, among students of human behaviour, those who delight in explaining cultural diversity and historical specificity are less concerned about our biological evolution than those who seek to understand the common nature of our humanity.

Sociobiology complements rather than threatens the traditional social sciences. It merely urges us to look at ourselves as part of a broader scheme of things which encompasses the whole of the natural world. In that sense, sociobiology is merely the latest phase of a process of scientific demystification which began with Copernicus, and successively reduced our claims to centrality and uniqueness. The price of lucidity about our place in the universe has always been a certain amount of existential discomfort. This may help explain the passion with which sociobiology is attacked.

Pierre L. van den Berghe
University of Washington

References

Alexander, R. D. (1979), *Darwinism and Human Affairs*, Seattle.

Chagnon, N. and Irons, W. (eds) (1979), *Evolutionary Biology and Human Social Behavior*, North Scituate, Mass.

Dawkins, R. (1976), *The Selfish Gene*, London.

Hamilton, W. D. (1964), 'The genetical evolution of social behaviour', *Journal of Theoretical Biology*, 7.

Lumsden, C. J. and Wilson, E. O. (1981), *Genes, Mind and Culture*, Cambridge, Mass.

Maynard Smith, J. (1964), 'Group selection and kin selection', *Nature*, 201.

Symons, D. (1979), *The Evolution of Human Sexuality*, New York.

Trivers, R. L. (1971), 'The evolution of reciprocal altruism', *Quarterly Review of Biology*, 46.

van den Berghe, P. L. (1979), *Human Family Systems*, New York.

Wilson, E. O. (1975), *Sociobiology, The New Synthesis*, Cambridge, Mass.

See also: *altruism; ecology; ethology; evolution; genetics and behaviour; population genetics; Social Darwinism.*

Sociocultural Evolution

Building on Max Weber and Emile Durkheim, Talcott Parsons showed that sociocultural evolution is not necessarily an ethnocentric delusion (Parsons, 1966, 1971; Münch, 1980). Our present 'advanced' risk of nuclear catastrophe, however, makes us sceptical about the unqualified idea of *progress*. To be sure, the world is beginning to give top priority to the integrative problems of the international social system as a whole. There is also a great deal of ideological distortion about the depravity of the modern world. In any case, overall sociocultural change is definitely not a random zigging and zagging among equally probable societal possibilities.

Nonliterate societies have relatively little control over sickness and disease and a relatively short average life expectancy. Except for small élites, people in many 'backward' societies are stuck in illiteracy, in magic, and (ironically) in relentless materialism, due to several kinds of poverty. The 'superiority' of the most advanced modern societies also includes greater dignity for the average individual: relative emancipation from class, religious and other barriers; and greater, more nearly equal educational and career opportunities. Moreover, the advantages of modern societies do not necessarily depend on greater natural resources, or on imperialistic exploitation alone; they are also based on far-reaching cultural and social-structural innovations.

All known human societies have a religion, a spoken language, a kinship system, and considerable technology. Some societies rose from the 'primitive' stage to the 'intermediate' by institutionalizing *writing*. This facilitates the deliberate cultivation of symbol systems as such, that is, of culture. The 'advanced' stage is reached when a system of *universalistic law* is institutionalized. This permits a 'higher' level of constructive harnessing of economic and political interests and better control of their inherent potentialities for injustice and disruption without common benefit.

Enhanced functional capacity may at first involve any one of the four sets of functional problems that Parsons distinguished for all 'action' systems. Broadly speaking, enhanced functional capacity tends to require more specialization (or structural differentiation), but other processes are also necessary because the four functional subsystems of a society are to some extent interdependent. However, not all attempts to bring about constructive change succeed in becoming institutionalized.

The development of culture and social structure is not the same process as the natural selection of genes, nor can sociocultural evolution be reduced to any other single factor. For instance, higher levels of science and technology have certainly depended on the nature of prevailing religious ideas and goals and on certain kinds of social organization. Innovations may be diffused to less advanced societies, in some of which they could almost certainly not have originated. Not all other societies, however, will necessarily catch up with the most advanced; but neither is evolutionary leadership likely to remain indefinitely in the same society or set of societies. The unit of 'progress' is some innovation, but in another sense it is a *society* that has achieved enhanced functional capacity. Parsons's theory of stages (and substages) has received some statistical confirmation (see Buck and Jacobson, 1968; Jacobson, 1971).

Harry M. Johnson
University of Illinois
Champaign-Urbana

References

Buck, G. L. and Jacobson, A. L. (1968), 'Social evolution and structural-functional analysis: an empirical test', *American Sociological Review*, 33.

Jacobson, A. L. (1971), 'A theoretical and empirical analysis of social change and conflict based on

Talcott Parsons' ideas', in H. Turk and R. L. Simpson (eds), *Institutions and Social Exchange: The Sociologies of Talcott Parsons and George C. Homans*, Indianapolis.

Münch, R. (1980), 'Über Parsons zu Weber: von der Theorie der Rationalisierung zur Theorie der Interpenetration', *Zeitschrift für Soziologie*, 9.

Parsons, T. (1966), *Societies: Evolutionary and Comparative Perspectives*, Englewood Cliffs, NJ.

Parsons, T. (1971), *The System of Modern Societies*, Englewood Cliffs, NJ.

See also: *evolution; evolutionism and progress.*

Sociolinguistics

Sociolinguistics has developed in recent years as a subdiscipline within the general study of language. In contrast to those scholars whose primary focus has been the internal structure of language, that is, grammar, a small group of researchers have attempted to place language in its larger social and cultural context. However, this latter view has not genuinely challenged the predominance of theoretical linguistics, which insists on the autonomy of grammar and pursues the search for explanatory principles of some depth over a limited domain of narrowly grammatical phenomena. Sociolinguists, on the other hand, question both the desirability and the feasibility of studying language divorced from its social functions. Unfortunately, the debate between the two groups has often been trivialized by the misguided criticism by some sociolinguists that theoretical linguists, particularly adherents of the generative-transformational model, because of their thesis regarding the autonomy of syntax, are thereby committed to the position that the study of syntax should remain unrelated to questions of meaning and language use.

Illustrative of the misconceptions underlying much discussion is the work done in the United States by linguists such as William Labov (1975) on Black English. No serious linguist doubts that the study of dialect variation belongs squarely within the field of linguistics. Furthermore, it is a truism among linguists that the language of the ghetto is of the same order as the language of the suburbs. What has sometimes been suggested, but not convincingly demonstrated, is that the study of the former has theoretical consequences. The importance of these studies has been to combat the prejudice of educators and others, and as such has been significant and worthwhile, but little linguistic sophistication is required to make this point, and linguistic theory is not seriously challenged by such observations.

A related and more general epistemological issue is raised by the insistence by theoretical linguists on the need for idealization of the data as a prerequisite for scientific inquiry. In linguistics, this has taken the form of an assumption regarding the grammar as a description of an ideal speaker-hearer's linguistic knowledge in a homogeneous speech community, an assumption which disregards both variation among speakers and the fact that actual linguistic behaviour (performance) is invariably an imperfect reflection of linguistic knowledge (competence). Some sociolinguists find this idealization unpalatable, and consequently argue both that variation is critical in understanding structure, and that the competence/performance distinction is itself suspect. This has led to a return among sociolinguists towards an empiricist bias, a bias which had previously characterized the autonomous linguistics of the 1940s and 1950s in the United States, prior to the impact of Noam Chomsky (1957) on the discipline.

The convergence of autonomous linguistics and sociolinguistics is not imminent. The latter, dealing with intrinsically more interesting phenomena, is not likely to achieve the rich, explanatory theories sought and to a certain extent arrived at by the former.

Sol Saporta
University of Washington

References

Chomsky, N. (1957), *Syntactic Structures*, The Hague.

Labov, W. (1975), *The Study of Non-Standard English*, Urbana, Ill.

Further Reading

Fishman, J. (ed.) (1968), *Readings in the Sociology of Language*, The Hague.

Hymes, D. (1974), *Foundations in Sociolinguistics: An Ethnographic Approach*, Philadelphia.

See also: *language and culture; pragmatics; social psychology of language.*

Sociology

Sociology is at present an unsystematic body of knowledge gained through the study of the whole and parts of society. The knowledge contained in sociology covers a very wide and differentiated range of phenomena such as the conduct of individuals in institutions like families, churches and sects, workshops, armies, civic and political associations, territorial, ethnic and national communities; the patterns of relationship among individuals; the role of structure and authority in the working of institutions and communities; the stratification of societies; communities and institutions with respect to income and status or deference; the role of cognitive and normative beliefs in the actions of individuals and in the functioning of communities, institutions and societies.

The ordering of sociological knowledge is fragmentary and of many levels of particularity, from the most abstract and most generalized or theoretical to the most concrete and descriptive. Sociological knowledge varies in the degree of reliability and precision. Sociologists have invented or borrowed from other disciplines techniques of observation and analysis which are intended to improve the veracity of sociological knowledge.

Sociological knowledge is a knowledge of causal connections, or connections of interdependence among the phenomena studied. Sociologists seek to explain phenomena in terms of motives, states of mind, 'social' conditions.

The Legitimacy of Sociology

Ever since the name of sociology was coined by Auguste Comte, sociologists have sought to be more scientific in their methods and more systematic in their interpretation of their observations. They have not been content with the occasionally profound penetrating observations about human conduct and its motives or about the varieties of forms of government, their emergence and decline such as are to be found in Aristotle's *Politics* and the *Nichomachean Ethics*, or in the works of Thucydides and Tacitus, and of Machiavelli and Guicciardini and many others. Political and moral philosophy, great historical works, great and not so great works of literature contain many deep particular insights and generalizations which in substance could well be regarded as properly sociological as that term has come to be understood. But these have not been enough for sociologists. Long before sociology became as scientific as it is now – and that is not very scientific according to the standard of the natural and especially the physical sciences by which the intellectually more ambitious sociologists have measured themselves – there was a conviction that sociology was justified only if it became more systematic and more scientific in substance and method. The ambition to become scientific and to acquire a deeper and more coherent understanding of society has not been the only motive for the cultivation of sociology. Famous sociologists have thought that the justification for doing sociological work was the illumination of the minds of rulers and of the wide public about the practical 'social problems' which needed 'remedies' or solutions. Comte's dictum *Savoir pour prévoir pour pourvoir* is still given in one form or another by many sociologists as the justification for their discipline and their own work. Although the practical application of sociological knowledge raises serious ethical problems, the belief that sociological knowledge should be applied in practical action is perfectly consistent with the belief that it should be scientific in its methods and hence in its explanations, interpretations and theories. Indeed, many sociologists have believed that it could be effectively 'applied' in practical action only if it were scientific and systematic.

It was not merely an effort to make knowledge of society and its constituent parts more reliable, more precise and more systematic that drove the forerunners of contemporary sociology in the nineteenth century to try to improve the scientific quality of their subject. They also wished to render it acceptable to prevailing intellectual opinion and, in certain countries, to the academic world. Auguste Comte and Herbert Spencer, the first two eminent philosophers who also thought of themselves as sociologists, did not think of sociology as necessarily being a subject for teaching and study in universities. By the end of the nineteenth and in the first quarter of the present century, when universities ascended to pre-eminence among intellectual institutions, and when the amateur and vocational practice of science and scholarship had diminished, it behoved the proponents of sociology to prove their academic acceptability. This was an additional motive for making their subject scientific and persuading others that it was scientific. But even if it were proved to be scientific, there would be no convincing argument for it if its subject-matters were already being dealt with adequately by disciplines previously established in universities. It was necessary to show that it had its own subject-matter.

Sociology in the nineteenth century did indeed have its own subject-matter and one, moreover, the study of which was established for many decades before sociology was considered to be worthy of academic status: it had 'the poor', the outcasts, the humble, the insulted and injured, the criminals of modern societies. These were the objects of the most important pieces of empirical research of the nineteenth and early twentieth centuries. From the surveys of Louis René Villerme, Henry Mayhew, Eiler Sundt, Charles Booth and Seebohm Rowntree up to Thomas and Znaniecki's more self-conscious sociology in *The Polish Peasant in Europe and America* (1916), the peripheral sectors of society had become accepted as meriting careful study; that careful study fell to the lot of sociologists. In peasants, in *Lumpenproletarians*, wandering journeymen, and street vendors, in the unemployed, the half-employed, the poor and the immigrants, in the prostitutes, criminals and in deserted wives, in unmarried mothers and illegitimate children, sociology found a subject all of its own which was disregarded by other academically established disciplines. Political history, with its accounts of kings and wars and the fates of empires did not write about the poor. *Staatswissenschaft* and political science which dealt with laws and political institutions did not deal with them except as objects of criminal law. Neither did *Völkerkunde*, human geography, and ethnology which dealt with remote places and primitive peoples. Economic theory, which proceeded as if men were rational, freely choosing actors seeking to maximize their incomes, had no place for those who lived under the constraints of tradition and ignorance and the constriction of poverty, who lived outside the law and who had no acknowledged impact on events except in revolutionary outbursts, short-lived riots and other outbursts of irrationality.

The argument for the legitimacy of sociology went more deeply than the practical value of knowledge of the 'dangerous debtor and dependent classes'. Sociologists contended that their 'discipline' could at least prospectively discover the laws of social life, not the laws enacted by legislatures or promulgated by rulers but the laws which were more fundamental than legislated laws. The condition of social order and conflict, of persistence and change from simplicity to complexity in the division of labour, from *Gemeinschaft* to *Gesellschaft*, from *solidarité mécanique* to *solidarité organique*, from rural to urban society, from primary groups to the larger, impersonal society became the theme of sociological interpretation. This was the profounder intellectual task which sociologists claimed for their discipline; it was one which no other discipline looked after and it performed the valuable intellectual service of laying bare and interpreting the nature of the modern age. Sociology participated in the *malaise* of the last part of the century, of the vague sense that somehow things were not right in the world, that modern society was developing in an unsatisfactory way. Sociologists claimed that it was legitimate for scholars to attempt to understand and explain what was going on in modern societies. Sociology was admitted into American and French universities at the time when it was beginning to be thought – for the first time – that universities should include the contemporary world among the subjects they taught about and investigated. Sociology seemed to meet that expectation.

The Foci of Sociology
Even though sociology is not a science in the sense of having a coherent, widely accepted body of general or theoretical propositions which rest on more particular propositions and which explain particular, reliably observed events, a vast amount of sociological knowledge does exist of varying degrees of precision, reliability and generality. Individuals who have been publicly designated as sociologists, as well as individuals who were not thought of as sociologists during their own lifetime but who have been declared retrospectively to have been sociologists, have in fact produced a very large heterogeneous and unarticulated mass of knowledge about various societies, parts of societies and kinds of actions. Despite their aspirations to be systematic, no sociologist has yet been able to systematize all this knowledge. The societies studied by sociologists have mainly been their own; they have given most of their attention to their own contemporary societies and in the quite recent past. Although sociological theories, at least programmatically, ordinarily

announce an intention of universal validity, sociological research at any given time has mostly been confined to the sociologists' own times and their own countries. 'Comparative sociology', which deals with other or several countries, and 'historical sociology', which deals with the remoter past, form only a very small part of the huge body of sociological literature. These two kinds of sociological literature have, however, increased in recent years.

There are various reasons for this temporal and territorial parochiality of sociology. The first reason derives from the long dominant, practical concern of sociology with 'social problems', in other words, with morally problematic conditions of the sociologists' own time and society. The second lies in the methods of sociology which require the use of deliberately acquired statistical data. The governmental acquisition of large quantities of information in statistical form is to a very large extent a phenomenon of the nineteenth and twentieth centuries, and sociologists wishing to have reliable evidence have perforce had to draw on such rather recently assembled information. The distrust of written, unpublished documents in archives and of printed books as evidence because of their questionable 'representativeness' has also, until recently, compelled sociologists to deal with contemporaneous situations. It is only in contemporaneous situations that sociologists could 'create' reliable data for their studies by direct observation and by interviews which by their nature can be conducted only on living persons, and by a combination of these two methods into 'participant-observation' which was for a time a much favoured procedure. This did not preclude the instigation of 'life-histories' which were also for a time among the sources used by some leading sociologists, (for example, Dollard, 1935). These instigated 'life-histories' could only be produced by living persons, and this reinforced the temporal confinement of sociologists. Recently, sociologists have discovered statistical series describing aspects of life in the earlier centuries of modern times, and at least one sociologist who is also a classical scholar (Hopkins, 1978) has even done quantitative work on ancient Roman society. An increasing number of sociologists have extended their territorial horizons and undertaken to study societies other than their own (Eisenstadt, 1963; Bendix, 1978). Still, the sociologists who study society remote from their own time and space are a relatively small minority in the profession of sociology.

The majority of sociologists who carry out research are still mainly working, although in a more sophisticated manner, on the favoured topics of the empirical sociology as it took form up to the early twentieth century, namely, 'social problems'. They study the crises and dissolution of families, conflicts in the relations of spouses with one other and conflicts between parents and their children. They study criminality and delinquency in all their forms; they study the leisure-time pursuits of young persons; they study the aged, especially the isolated aged who cannot easily fend for themselves. They study processes of social selection, the advantages of birth in higher strata and the disadvantages of birth in lower strata. They study the impediments to democracy. The condition of 'the poor' and powerless, who had sunk somewhat from the horizon of sociologists in the period after the Second World War, has returned to its former prominence. Sociologists still continue to give much of their attention to this complex of phenomena, but as their numbers increased and they became better established, they have added numerous other fields to their stock-in-trade. To some extent, these new subjects are extensions of the study of 'the poor' and of other sore-spots of modern industrial societies.

Rural studies, in contrast, once a major subject of sociological interest, have become relatively less important in the schedule of sociological activities in Western countries (see Sorokin *et al.*, 1930–2). Migration from rural areas to large cities within any single country has diminished in prominence, while international migration and immigrants have reacquired, in the sociological research on the European continent, the prominence which they once had in American sociology in the first quarter of the present century. The study of urban communities has had an upsurge, after its decline in American sociology; more prominently even than in the past, urban studies have concerned themselves with derelict areas of the 'inner city' and with suburban communities.

The relationship among ethnic groups within a single society was an almost dominant subject in American sociology for the first half of the century (see Myrdal, 1944; Dollard, 1937; Warner, 1942); it then declined, but latterly it resumed its prominence after about two decades. It is a major topic nowadays in the United States. Studies of 'ethnic prejudice' were part of this run of activity; they too receded and have not recovered their ground. Ethnic relations, and particularly the study of 'nationalities', had been a topic of sociologists in Central Europe before the First World War and then almost disappeared. Within the past decade it has again become an important field for European and American sociologists.

The study of mobility between classes of occupation had been a major subject of empirical sociological studies in France, Germany and Great Britain in the decades preceding and following the turn of the century (Michels, 1934; Glass (ed.), 1954; Sorokin, 1927). It became a subject which drew increasing interest in the United States from the 1920s onward; it has remained a substantial interest of European and American sociology since that time. It has, with the study of the past, been the most active part of sociological research in Great Britain.

Industrial sociology – the study of social relations in workshops – ascended slowly to the point where it became a major field of research in the 1930s in the United States and then again briefly after the Second World War in the United States and Great Britain, but it has diminished since then (Roethlisberger and Dickson, 1939; Mayo, 1949). On the other side, the sociological study of the management and the careers of managers of business firms which had scarcely existed before the Second World War became more interesting to sociologists after the war in the United States and Great Britain. The study of the hierarchy of social status or deference was first undertaken in small communities in the United States in the 1930s and then flourished, after the war, on a national scale, following the development of sample surveys of attitudes. It has not been developed so much in other countries.

The study of the distribution of educational opportunity, that is, of the distribution of the amount of schooling of different occupational income and ethnic groups, became a very active field in Great Britain and the United States from the early 1930s; it has continued ever since then, with some fluctuations, to occupy the attention of sociologists in many countries (Floud, Halsey and Martin, 1956; Coleman (ed.), 1969). International comparison of educational attainment in relation to the level of industrialization, economic productivity and the rate of economic growth, although developed mainly by economists and educationists, has also been taken up by educational sociologists. Investigations of the teaching profession, of the 'social atmosphere' of classrooms, of the administration of schools and educational systems were taken up by sociologists. There is now a whole specialization called 'educational sociology'.

A quite new field of sociological study is that of military institutions. This appeared after the Second World War and a considerable body of literature has been produced on the cohesion and morale of armed forces, military discipline, the recruitment of soldiers of different ranks and the relations between armed forces and civil, especially political, institutions (Janowitz, 1960).

The sociological study of scientific institutions, of beliefs about science and its legitimacy, of the careers and reputation of scientists, the distribution of status and eminence among them and of the social constitution of the growth of scientific knowledge has emerged as a small but intensively cultivated object (Ziman, 1968; Polanyi, 1964; Merton, 1973; Ben-David, 1971). This subject existed to a very small degree before the Second World War. Some sociologists have even gone so far as to declare scientific knowledge itself to be a 'social phenomenon' in which truth and validity are no more than conventions like any other social convention. A closely related field called the 'sociology of knowledge', which came into the world first in Germany with great *éclat* in the 1920s and early 1930s and which attempted to explain beliefs in political, moral and social philosophy and in theology by reference to the 'class position' or 'social location' of different kinds of intellectuals, aroused great interest among German sociologists, but it did not go much beyond the programmatic phase (Mannheim, 1936; 1952; 1956; Shils, 1972). The study of 'intellectuals', their interrelations and their social role has made some progress in a number of countries.

Political institutions, such as parliamentary bodies, parties, elections, political campaigns, had made a first appearance as sociological subjects in Germany, France and Italy before the First World War (Tingston, 1963; Lazarsfeld *et al.*, 1944; Berelson *et al.*, 1954; Lasswell, 1935, 1936). The voting behaviour and political attitudes of various occupational, religious and ethnic groups were studied in many countries in the 1920s and 1930s. It was also developing in the United States. This branch of sociological study received a tremendous impetus from the development in the United States, and then elsewhere, of the techniques of sample surveys, which first occurred outside of sociology but which was quickly incorporated into it. It has since flourished throughout the Western world in the international collaboration of sociologists and political scientists.

The mechanisms of the exercise of political and bureaucratic power and the correlates of the acquisition of roles of authority began to interest American sociologists after the Second World War (Lipset, Trow and Coleman, 1956); it has been a topic which engaged the close attention of the most important German and Italian sociologists well before the First World War.

After the Second World War, some sociologists for the first time became interested in the formation and fortunes of new states (Geertz, 1967; Almond and Coleman (eds.), 1960). They studied the new states arising in former European colonies in Asia and Africa and related phenomena in Latin America; their interests were almost entirely contemporaneous. The study of 'political development' then engaged the interests of a small number of sociologists who worked closely with political scientists and anthropologists. Few of them placed this phenomenon in a historical context. Despite the pioneering work of Max Weber in this field, and the popularity among sociologists of Max Weber's writings, only one important book has been written in the comparative study of empires and the growth of states.

The sociological study of 'formal organization' was to some extent an offshoot of the study of political power, private and public administration and of the study of industrial sociology by persons who were not academic sociologists (Simon, 1947; Barnard, 1948). This subject was scarcely studied by sociologists until

after the Second World War, although one of its major inspirations, Max Weber's study of bureaucratic authority, was written either during the First World War or shortly before. Since that time, it has become a major interest of sociologists.

Almost since its beginning sociologists had been interested in the study of social movements, including in this the labour and socialist movements and the attendant phenomena of strikes, revolutions, demonstrations, crowds and mobs, rumours and political ideologies. These subjects were already taken in hand in several European countries, especially in France and Italy, in the late nineteenth century (Michels, 1934; Sombart, 1909; Geiger, 1926; Tilly, 1948). The interest then spread to Germany before the First World War and to the United States in the 1920s and 1930s. It has continued since then, although it has since ceased to be one of the more prominent concerns of sociologists.

The sociological study of religion, especially of the study of religious sects, has long been one of the major foci of sociological interest. The two greatest modern sociologists – Weber and Durkheim – placed religious phenomena firmly at the centre of their conception of society and it has continued in a very eminent position ever since then (Weber, 1930 [1922]; 1920; Durkheim, 1915 [1912]; Mauss, 1964, 1972; Le Bras, 1955). It is one of the most international of all the activities of sociologists. French, German, Dutch, British, Italian and American sociologists have all worked in this field in relatively large numbers.

The Methods of Sociology

Proto-sociological research began in the early nineteenth century in France and Great Britain with the use of governmentally gathered statistics; much of it was done by civil servants, civic spirited amateurs and social reformers. It aimed at the description of the magnitudes of particular phenomena such as consumption patterns, housing accommodations, crimes and other infringements on law and morality (see Bulmer, 1984; König, 1967–9; Hyman, 1963). Some early proto-sociologists collected information directly from the persons whom they were writing about through conversations, casual observations, and more immediately from the use of questionnaires and specially elicited written accounts of behaviour by the persons being studied or those who were thought to be familiar with them; the use of 'informants' and of specially qualified persons, such as magistrates and clergymen, continued for a long time to be one of the devices used in 'field work'. Although such research was not at that time called 'sociological', its procedures have greatly influenced contemporary sociological research and they still persist in modified form.

In the present century, the methods of sociological research have moved towards the creation of new data and away from exclusive reliance on already existing data, such as published official statistics. Even where official statistics are still used, there is a marked disposition to go beyond what has been published in census and other governmental reports and to re-analyse the 'raw' data contained in the original protocols in which they were recorded. Except for general demographic purposes, the categories and the units of official statistics were seldom quite what sociologists thought they needed to treat their intellectual problems realistically.

The next step forward was already indicated by the British social surveys of the late nineteenth and early twentieth centuries, which used interviews with either expert 'informants' or with the subjects themselves, or both. Robert Park, one of the formative sociologists of the early part of the present century, had been a newspaper reporter, and he saw the potentialities of the interview as a device for eliciting knowledge not otherwise available. The early development of the interview in American sociology as well as the collection of 'human documents' was concomitant with the practice of an extended period of residence or participation in the community or institution being studied. Thus interviews were combined with direct observation and casual conversations which supplied information about the person engaged in the conversation. This technique of 'participant-observation' also offered the possibility of direct observation of actions and conversations in which the observer did not himself participate but which he was enabled to observe by his quasi-membership in the community or institution.

Another technique for the 'creation' of data was the elicitation of 'personal' or 'human' documents of an autobiographical kind. This produced results similar to a prolonged interview or series of interviews reconstructing the course of life of the subject and centering on a series of significant experiences and situations in the life of the individual in question. The analysis of other sorts of personal documents such as unpublished diaries and published and unpublished letters was also used by sociologists in the period when the 'life-history' was in vogue. The 'open-ended' interview which proceeded by suggesting major topics to the person being interviewed and allowing him or her to respond freely has also been widely employed. The use of 'personal documents' has now diminished, yielding to 'open-ended' and especially to 'structured interviews' or questionnaires.

These techniques all produced a very rich kind of material, very suggestive to the analyst and often very valuable for purposes of illustration of a general theme, tendency, attitude or situation. What they did not offer was precision, reliability and comparability; they were insufficient for scientific purposes. A promising solution of this difficulty was offered by 'content analysis' which was a method of analysing documents which permitted references in texts to be classified systematically, that is, to be 'coded' and enumerated, so that impressions could be supported by the exact measurement of magnitudes. Content-analysis was cumbersome and expensive; its merits were also available through the use of standardized interviews made through the filling in of questionnaires; these asked the same question of all persons interviewed and they provided for precoded alternative responses. This new technique, in combination with the sample survey which was another protection against the deceptiveness of plausible but uncontrolled impressions and insights, won the day in the competition among the various methods of sociological investigation.

Experimentation has never obtained much suffrage among the techniques of sociological research. Moral inhibitions and strictures on the manipulation of human beings, the unwillingness of human beings to submit to the manipulative designs of sociologists, and the difficulties of obtaining enough identical situations and persons sufficiently similar to provide 'experimental' and 'control groups' have had the result that the experimental procedure, which is the *sine qua non* of scientific work in the physical and biological sciences, made little progress as a technique of sociological research. The experimental method has as a result been used largely in situations in which artificially arranged small groups have been constituted, or where the 'experimental' or 'independent variable' has been trivial and entirely unlikely to have lasting or injurious consequences.

At the same time, the technique of 'controlled comparison' or what has been called the 'imaginary experiment' has been embraced as the best alternative to the impermissible and impossible experiment. With sufficient care and scale, enough instances of individuals, groups or situations can be located in which many features are identical and in which there were marked variations in the feature or features to which causal efficacy may be hypothetically imputed. Techniques of statistical correlation of varying degrees of complexity can then be applied to the data to discover whether there was in fact some degree of interdependence and hence presumably of causal relations between the 'independent' and the 'dependent variables'. This technique of correlation is equally applied to data created by the investigator through interviews (or observations), or in any other situation where sufficiently large numbers of cases or instances can be obtained.

The triumph of the sample survey, of 'created' data – in place of 'real' data observed as the events occur in the ordinary course of social life – and of the statistical correlation of variations, has not however culminated in the extinction of the techniques of 'participant-observation' and of more impressionistic analysis. The latter techniques continue to be used but they too have been affected by the increased sensitivity to statistical requirements. The great shifts in techniques of sociological research have also changed the patterns of organization of sociological research.

Well into the twentieth century, academic sociological research was primarily a 'one-man job'. The insistence, however, on the observation of many cases, and on the precoding, use, and the tabulation of a large body of data created approximately at the same time – a requirement imposed by the necessity of eliminating variations attributable to changes in variables which should be held constant if the research is to be scientific – and the complex statistical operations needed to order the data, have all contributed to turning sociological investigation from the activities of a single scholar, sometimes aided by one or several assistants, into collective hierarchical divisions of labour, acquiring and ordering data through the prescribed actions of a plurality of individuals. This change has necessitated the expenditure of large sums for the employment of staff whose remuneration is not provided for through regular salaries as university teachers and the small sums made available in regular university budgets. The change in the scale of individual investigations has been made possible by the availability of large sums of money for research from public and private patrons. Research has become a collective activity. It has become more 'institutionalized', that is, it has acquired an internal institutional structure of authority and co-ordinated division of labour and it has also become much more connected with some external institutions, which supply funds and control expenditures and others which 'use', in many different ways, the results of the investigation.

The Substance of Sociology
The multiplication in the number of sociologists creating huge quantities of data and publishing a great volume of papers, monographs and books has resulted in great increments of more or less reliable knowledge about many particular situations in many countries. The synthesis of this immense and heterogeneous amount of knowledge into a coherent body of generalized knowledge has not occurred. No one could possibly read all the sociological literature in the many languages containing the results of all this research. The task of synthesis is made even more difficult by the fact that even in studying quite similar but still different particular situations, sociologists use categories for the classification of the data which do not allow unambiguous comparisons and syntheses.

This does not at all mean that sociological investigations are wholly disjunctive *vis-à-vis* those which have preceded them in the study of similar topics and problems. Sociological investigators do indeed study 'the literature' bearing on their topics and they aim to benefit from it. But in doing so and in trying to improve upon the deficiencies of the classifications of observations in the earlier work which become apparent in

them by reflection, they change in varying degrees the classifications. When they try to improve definitions of the variables they are studying by making them more precise than they were in earlier enquiries, they thereby make more difficult the precise comparison and synthesis of their results with the results of other enquiries on the same topic.

These are not the only obstacles to synthesis. The phenomena studied by sociological research are conceived by the sociologists quite concretely, although not with the immediacy with which they are experienced by those persons who are the phenomena being studied. To move from concreteness to abstraction is always a difficult task. It is even more difficult to move into abstract categories which also summarize in abstract form the interdependence of the diverse phenomena which are reported by the sociologists investigating them. An inductive unification of the multifariousness of concrete sociological results into a coherent general theory is perhaps an impossibility. In any case it has never been done.

Nevertheless, the results of sociological research are not wholly random; they do fall into vaguely apprehended patterns in accordance with certain fundamental propositions. A sociologist brought up in the traditions of sociology as it has grown in the present century, has a number of postulates which he shares with the majority of other sociologists and which pervade most sociological research and the interpretation of its results.

The most fundamental of these postulates is that human actions are limited or determined by 'environment'. Human beings become what they are at any given moment not by their own free decisions, taken rationally and in full knowledge of the conditions but under the pressure of circumstances which delimit their range of choice and which also fix their objectives and the standards by which they make choices. The ends of their actions are determined by the influence of their previous 'environment', which limit their range of choice and to which they became habituated; their choices are determined also by their passions and their interests and they are also assimilated from the patterns presented by the 'culture' in which they have lived. The environment is also seen as consisting of the demands and resistances of the other human beings whose co-operation is necessary for the realization of any end of the acting subject. The resources of wealth, position and prestige are distributed in a determinate way in society, and the individual's shares of these goods facilitate or hamper his actions in pursuit of his own ends. The moral, cognitive and ratiocinative powers of the individual are as nothing alongside the imprinting and constrictive powers of the environment in shaping his beliefs and conduct. Thus the human being in society is both a product and victim of the society in which he lives.

When he frees himself to the extent that he can, and acts rationally, all he can do is to puruse his own 'interest'. His 'interest' lies in the maximization of his own advantages, the advantages being conceived of as wealth and power.

This complex idea is at the heart of sociological thought – if it is not inconsistent to speak of thought in a discipline which sometimes denies the reality and efficacy of rational thought. Sociology came into existence out of a variety of intentions. One of these intentions was to show the inadequacy of the conception of human beings as rational entities acting on the basis of knowledge formed by detached reflection on experience, or guided by rational deductions from ultimate or first principles. The forerunners of sociology wished to cast doubt on the dogmatic assertion and imposition of ideals by the dominant, particularly ecclesiastical, institutions of their time. They wished to weaken the argument that ideals are universally valid and that human beings act in accordance with them. The forerunners of sociology were concerned to show that there is no fixed eternal and universal human nature and that man's nature and his ideals change with circumstances. Sociology was intended as a corrective to the view that human conduct and morals are the same everywhere and that the principles of conduct pronounced by Christian moralists are natural to man.

They wished to free man from the superstitions which deformed his reason but at the same time, they were sceptical about his rational powers. The unifying theme of this dual postulate is that the human being is not a self-contained, self-determined, self-determining entity, uniform throughout the world and history, a child of God and reason.

This postulate, which long antedates sociology, is almost its touchstone. It makes sociology what it is. More refined, more differentiated, it still remains at the foundation of nearly all that is called sociology, both in theory and in research. When it leads to 'sociologism' it is a hindrance to the further development of sociology, but without it, sociology would be without its task and without its hypotheses.

The naturalistic conception of man from which sociology proceeded perceived that human beings, like all other living organisms, are dependent on their environment. The geographical environment was accorded great causal importance by certain early sociologists. Others went more directly to seek the genesis and determinants of society in the biological nature of man. The coincidence of the Darwinian ideas about the origin and evolution of species seemed to some sociologists to provide adequate accounts of the rise and fall of societies and of the success and failure of human beings. The struggles among individual human beings and groups within societies, and of societies with other societies, were explained by the niggardliness of nature and the competition for survival. This theme became less prominent in sociological studies in the present century, and the significance of natural ecological and biological qualities have been denied by sociology in favour of a conception of the environment as preponderantly, if not exclusively 'social'. 'Economic factors' have continued to have attributed to them a preponderant determinative power, but they have been separated from the realm of the natural order. One could say that the expulsion of the biological and natural ecological determinants of human existence has been one of striking features of sociological studies since the 1930s.

With all its ambiguities and limitations, the very idea of the determinative influence of the social environment remains absolutely basic to sociology. It has, moreover, sharpened sensitivity to connections between spheres of social life which at first glance seem to be utterly unconnected. This capacity to discern connections between activities or institutional arrangements which appear to be unconnected derives from the postulate of the systemic character of society. Society, according to this postulate, is a whole of interdependent parts, each of which is the 'environment' for all of the others. Although sociologists have made little progress in the delineation of whole societies, either in theory or in particular investigations, the idea of a 'society' as a whole or as a system whose parts are interconnected in many ways, is a fundamental postulate of sociology.

The postulate regarding the 'environmental' determination of conduct or of the dependence of conduct on 'social forces' outside the individual has as a corollary a dual image of two types of societies. One is the small, territorially very restricted communities whose members know each other, dwell long together, and have biological links with each other through descent and kinship; in this to some degree self-sufficient local society, there are ties of solidarity and a unity which prevents the individual members from acting solely in accordance with their own individual interests or their 'class interest'. The contrasting image is that of a large society in which individuals live together in a far-flung differentiated division of labour, do not know each other through long association, biological and territorial ties, and have little sense of unity or solidarity with each other. They are bound to each other only by the belief that the individual interest of each is served by the collaboration of many other individuals in an elaborate division of labour. In this distinction the fundamental focus of sociologists on the outcasts of modern society, the 'uprooted', the 'disorganized', the 'anomic', the victims of an urban, commercial society, is extended on the one side to the self-contained solidary village or rural community (*Gemeinschaft*), and on the other to the modern urban market economy, (*Gesellschaft*) the human costs of which formed the original subject-matter of sociology.

The attrition of the primordial determinants of conduct with the entry into the market-oriented, commercial industrial urban society, isolates individuals, makes them dependent on their own powers and resources, and compels them to organize themselves into associations aimed to realize particular, often very specific ends as defined by their interests. Modern society, having renounced solidarity around primordial things, becomes, despite all the strictures expressed in sociology about the limited powers of reason, a scene of individuals and groups purposefully pursuing their own interests.

There is in fact at the heart of sociology a fundamental moral ambivalence. On the one side, it proceeds from an abhorrence of the disorders of life of the lower classes in modern urban industrial societies, and this in turn is connected with an appreciation of the small community centred around primordial things. On the other side it believes in the scientific rational 'solution of social problems'. It conceives of modern society as rational, bureaucratic with large concentrations of power. It tends to look on modern industrial societies as inhuman, amoral, held together only by coercion and interest. Both its intellectual traditions and its political bias dispose it to this view. At the same time, common sense, empirical observation and certain strands of theoretical traditions, show the untenability of this view.

The postulate of the determinative influence of environment implies or is at least compatible with the existence of a culture of symbolic constructions, of moral rules and models. These can be represented in a commonly shared set of rules which hold in check inclinations to pursue individual interests. These common rules fix ends and assert a proper relationship between individual ends and legitimately available and usable means. If such means of fulfilment are not available, or if they become excessive, 'anomie' results; it is the infringement on the expectation of 'normal', law-bound conduct. Although the conception of *anomie* fastens attention on the traditional subject-matter of empirical sociological investigations, namely, criminality, delinquency, suicide, and other irregularities of conduct, it also points to the existence of a moral order in society.

This postulate of a moral order although contradictory to the traditional emphasis on 'social disorganization', is entirely consistent with the postulate of the power of environment. It is indeed a differentiation and elaboration of that idea. According to it, individuals, when they are introduced, voluntarily or involuntarily, as infants, as children or later in life, into a small group or other collectivity, are gradually 'socialized' or 'assimilated' into the prevailing conception of 'normal' conduct, accepting its norms and beliefs. Whole categories of individuals, removed from their former collectivities and introduced into a new collectivity, undergo a process of 'disorganization', or in other words experience 'anomie', until they become 'reorganized' or 'resocialized' into a new collectivity in which their individual 'interests' are subordinated to 'collective' interests, as long as the means or resources are available for them to realize their newly defined 'interests'.

Another closely related postulate declares that when a collectivity becomes 'disorganized' or 'anomic', a strong counter-tendency emerges to seek solidarity through the affirmation of contact with 'sacred values' or 'norms'. There is a need of individuals to generate solidarity with other individuals, or in communities or already existing or new corporate bodies. There is, moreover, a tendency in human beings, when they are placed in market situations or in societies dominated by market or large corporate bodies with bureaucratic administration and a differentiated division of labour, to seek to establish more intimate affectional relations; these are variously called 'primary groups' or 'informal groups'. Human beings cannot survive in a social 'vacuum', that is, a structure without affection or without some tangible connection with sacred things which gives meaning to human existence.

Alongside the postulate of the ordering of the conduct of individuals through pursuing their interests under environmental constraints, there is another postulate which asserts that corporate bodies and whole societies are ordered by the coercive power of the legitimate authority of small minorities of the total population. According to this postulate, authority inevitably appears in large corporate groups and in all but the smallest societies because of the need for order and co-ordination, the restraint of internal conflict within the societies and groups for the conduct of relations with external groups and societies and for the gratification of desire for power, wealth and deference.

This postulate asserts that persons in positions of authority tend to seek their own individual, dynastic or class ends which may or may not be identical with the ends of the collectivity. Bureaucrats and immediate collaborators of those in the highest positions of authority tend to be impelled by considerations of maintenance of the corporate body and the consolidation of the power of those in positions of authority. There is a tendency among the subordinated strata of the collectivity to become 'alienated' or 'anomic' *vis-à-vis* the authorities who rule over them.

Alongside those postulates, which are widely shared among sociologists, there are some about which there is less consensus. Some of these postulates are to be found in the writings of the most esteemed sociologists but, for a variety of reasons, they have not been so completely accepted. The fundamental postulate of the variability of human conduct and belief in consequence of the variations in 'environment', and the refusal to admit any autonomy to the forces of reason and ideals, has made it hard for sociologists to attribute any validity to the outlook which asserted the partial autonomy of the 'higher' powers of the human mind such as intellectual curiosity, imagination, reason and religious sensibility. The first sociological enquiries sought out the physical and physiological miseries of the poor, housing conditions, health, drunkenness, diet, clothing. They studied the misfortunes of the human animal. Their humanitarian compassion was mingled with concern to avoid the catastrophes of violent revolution, bloodshed, and the destruction and confiscation of property in material goods. The idea that human beings are primarily biological organisms living in a physical environment was readily assimilable to the popularized Darwinian view of man which emerged after the appearance of sociology. Sociology has not always been able to free itself from that standpoint.

Nevertheless, certain major figures of sociology made some partially successful efforts to do so and in consequence the breadth of the postulates of sociology has been extended. This extension is apparent in the postulate that rulers seek legitimacy and that subjects or citizens demand legitimacy of those who exercise authority over them; the postulate of the sacredness of the social order is alien to the utilitarian view which gives primacy to interests and their pursuit.

The postulates regarding 'legitimacy' and the associated one regarding a 'normal' order of society both imply the existence in society of an order of symbolic configurations, both normative and cognitive. These configurations are transmitted in traditions and they are in an unceasing process of modification and revision while having great powers of persistence through many generations. Religious belief, scientific knowledge, artistic works, philosophical outlooks and moral codes belong to this order of symbolic configurations. Some of the foregoing postulates might be contradictory to some of the others but this does not mean that they are untenable. Their contradiction points rather to the diversity of the propensities of human beings and the opposing tendencies which enter into the conduct and into the patterns of their societies.

The postulates underlie the interpretation which sociologists make of their data; they guide the choice of variables as well as of interpretations. They are not equally shared by all sociologists and, when they are formulated in more exact terms, they usually alienate many sociologists who might accept them as long as they are left vague. Nevertheless, in the present state of sociology, these postulates serve as a general theoretical orientation. They function as a general theory. There is at present no systematically articulated general theory in sociology which finds general acceptance among sociologists. The most fully developed attempt to construct a general comprehensive theory of sociology in recent years has not been well received, although in fact many of the postulates of that general theory are adhered to by many sociologists.

Even though there is no general sociological theory about which there is consensus, and although the discrete results of the huge body of results of sociological research have not been ordered into a coherent descriptive account of any particular society, sociological study has contributed much that is interesting and illuminating to the understanding of contemporary societies and of societies in general. The sociological understanding of the ties that bind human beings together and of their conflicts, of the relations between superiors and subordinates, of the relations of rulers and citizens and subjects, of neighbours and of members of different ethnic groups with one another, of one religious community and another, has become much more intimate and more richly differentiated. There is cumulativeness of sociological knowledge but it is vague and general; successive investigations do deposit a residue of better understanding but the deposit defies precise formulations.

Nevertheless, it remains a genuine intellectual deficiency that the results of sociological investigations are not clearly and precisely cumulative and that they do not contribute in a definite manner to an explicit general theory which is open to corrections and revision as research goes on, and as it is undertaken in more societies and for longer and remoter historical periods. In this very crucial respect, sociology is not a science. But neither is it a congeries of arbitrary constructions. It exists in a middle zone, sometimes moving towards the zone of science, both in theory and in research, sometimes persisting in its tendency towards the arbitrary construction of notional artifacts, again both in theory and in research.

The Development of Sociology as an Intellectual Discipline and as a Profession

The name of 'sociology' is more than 150 years old. The antecedents of sociology are much older, and in the nineteenth century a great deal of valuable research and reflection which is now called sociological was not designated as such at the time. It has required a retrospective self-discovery to reclaim this knowledge and to incorporate it into subsequent sociological theory and research (see Eisenstadt and Curelau, 1976; Schelsky, 1959; Dahrendorf, 1963; Clark, 1973; Shils, 1980). Sociology has also drawn on the achievements of scientists and scholars who were not themselves sociologists in name or practice but whose knowledge has been drawn into sociology. The writings of geneticists, philosophers, statisticians, ecologists, ethnographers, political historians, lawyers and legal historians, psychometricians, economic historians, ecclesiastical historians, theologians, historians of ideas, and economic theorists have all been, and continue to be, drawn upon by sociologists. The early propounders of the claim of sociology to be accepted as an academic discipline tried to define the boundaries of sociology and to show that it was capable of being an autonomous discipline. It was in fact never this kind of subject and it is not so at present. The boundaries of sociology are very vague and this is wholly to the advantage of the understanding of society. Sociology, before it became an academic subject taught under that name, was the work of civil servants, clergymen, philanthropic businessmen, journalists, military officers, engineers, and professors of law, education and economics, all doing their sociological work avocationally or after retirement from their life-long professions. It began to be taught in American colleges and universities as early as the middle of the nineteenth century, but acquired a standing as a 'major' undergraduate and graduate subject, taught by a fully staffed department and with the proclamation of its intention to perform and promote research, only in 1892 at the University of Chicago.

Sociology became the object of professorial teaching, but without a surrounding department of sociology, at the University of Paris in 1906 where Durkheim became professor of education and, in 1913, professor of sociology. No further professorships of sociology were created in France until after the First World War when one was established at Strasbourg. In Great Britain a chair was created at the London School of Economics in 1907, and after that date and until after the Second World War, one additional chair in 'social science' was created at the University of Liverpool. In Germany, there was no chair of sociology in any university until after the First World War. Thereafter, there was one chair of sociology at the University of Frankfurt am Main, and several chairs in which sociology was joined with philosophy or other subjects. Sociology as a subject of teaching and research was suspended or abolished in German universities during the period of National Socialism. In Italy sociology was taught, but without specially designated professorships, since early in the present century; in the Scandinavian countries there was no professorship for sociology until after the Second World War. Since 1945 sociology has flourished in the sense of the great multiplication of appointments at professorial level and at the middle and lower ranks of the academic hierarchy in nearly all countries. This has occurred in nearly all universities; new universities have had departments of sociology in their original establishment; older universities which were resistant to sociology have also accepted it.

With its institutional establishment within universities, sociology has spilled over its departmental boundaries. In university departments of political science and anthropology, even of economics, more attention and more respect are paid to sociology. Departments of literature and language, of history ancient and modern, of Chinese and Indian studies, Biblical studies and of comparative religion and the history of science draw on sociology. Indeed, there is scarcely a branch of learning in the 'human sciences' which does not turn to sociology occasionally and which does not here and there attempt to incorporate 'the sociological approach' into its work. Law and medical faculties often find places for sociologists on their staff or sponsor research which is sociological in method and substance.

While sociology has become practically universally adopted as a subject of academic study and specialization, and has entered into many other academic fields, sociological research, which once had to be done avocationally by persons who were not university teachers of the subject, has, to an increasing degree since the Second World War, become a non-academic subject once more. It is by no means that the universities are doing less sociological research; on the contrary, they do more than ever. But much more is being done by survey-research organizations, some attached to universities and some without any formal connection with universities. More of it is being done for 'customers', governmental and private, who pay to have the research done on problems which they specify in anticipation of some practical use for the results.

Sociology and the World

Sociologists, almost since the beginning, have had a distrustful attitude to the world as they saw it. They saw it as a realm of encrusted and hardened prejudices and superstitions, of irrationality of conduct, of injustice in the distribution of burdens and rewards, of the erosion of community and the uprooting of 'the people', of egotism and self-seeking, of injurious conflict and disorder. From both conservative and progressive points of view, sociologists have found fault with their own contemporary societies. The beginnings of empirical sociological research were largely aimed at disclosing to the educated public the dark sides of their society, the misery, vice and squalor of the condition of the impoverished, unemployed, dangerous, debtor and dependent 'classes' (see Lazarsfeld et al., 1967). The foundation of modern theoretical sociology had as its main theme the replacement of the small community of solidarity and mutual support by the individualistic, competitive, impersonal, even inhuman society, without a common faith. Sociologists, at least many of them, sought to cure these deficiencies by making them better known to those who were thought to be in a position to ameliorate them. The greatest sociologist, Max Weber, thought that one of the functions of sociological study and research was to enable individuals to 'face the hard facts'; he meant 'hard', not in the sense used by contemporary sociologists who use the term to describe data obtained by scientific techniques of investigation, but rather in the sense of being disagreeable because they showed the hardness of life itself.

Sociology has not deviated far from this original path. Sociologists have constantly aimed at showing where things have gone wrong. Many of the leading sociologists have had reforming intentions. They have, however, also believed that by making their methods as scientific as possible, they could be objective and dispassionate in their analysis. They have incessantly tried to see things in their society as they really are, and to hold in check while doing their research their desires, passions and ideals of a society which would be better according to their lights.

Despite this traditional critical attitude towards the existing social order in Western countries, towards the capitalistic economic system, and towards politicians, sociologists have been drawn into the service of the reigning authorities. Sociological research is now thought to be capable of producing sound knowledge which can be of practical utility. The extent to which much of this knowledge is used in the practical activities of governmental officials, politicians and businessmen may be questioned, but there cannot be any doubt that many of those persons in positions of power believe that it is potentially useful. In this respect, the earliest and enduring ambitions of sociologists have been realized to a noteworthy degree.

Sociology, partly because it has been a subject studied by undergraduates, has entered the public consciousness. The educated public generally regards sociological knowledge as offering insight about the world as it is. Although sociologists have not been accredited by governments in the way that economists have been, they stand very well with the educated public and the media of mass communication.

Sociologists have been more successful than their intellectual achievements probably merit. They have come into an age and culture which believes in the desirability of knowledge and they have been given the benefit of the doubt. They are well established in higher education and they receive much financial support from governments and private philanthropic foundations and, to a lesser extent, from private business firms. They are allowed much freedom to pursue their intellectual interests. A large part of the original programme of sociology has been achieved. The intellectual part of that programme – the discovery of the fundamental laws of social life – still remains.

Edward Shils
University of Chicago
Peterhouse College, Cambridge

References

Almond, G. and Coleman, J. S. (eds) (1960), *The Politics of the Developing Areas*, Princeton, NJ.

Barnard, C. (1948), *The Function of the Executive*, Cambridge, Mass.

Ben-David, J. (1971), *The Scientist's Role in Society: A Comparative Study*, Englewood Cliffs. NJ.

Bendix, R. (1978), *Kings or People*, Berkeley and Los Angeles.

Berelson, B., Lazarsfeld, P. and McPhee, W. (1954), *Voting*, Chicago.

Bulmer, M. (1984), *The Chicago School of Sociology*, Chicago.

Clark, T. N. (1973), *Prophets and Patrons: The French University and the Emergence of the Social Sciences*, Cambridge, Mass.

Coleman, J. (ed.) (1969), *Equality of Educational Opportunity*, Cambridge, Mass.

Dahrendorf, R. (1963), *Die angewandte Aufklaerung*, Munich.

Dollard, J. (1935), *Criteria for the Life History*, New Haven.

Dollard, J. (1937), *Caste and Class in a Southern Town*, New Haven.

Durkheim, E. (1915 [1912]), *The Elementary Forms of Religious Life*, London. (Original French edn, *Les formes élémentaires de la vie religieuse: le système totémique en Australie*, Paris.)

Eisenstadt, S. (1963), *The Political Systems of Empires*, New York.

Eisenstadt, S. and Curelau, M. (1976), *The Form of Sociology: Paradigms and Crisis*, New York.

Floud, J., Halsey, A. and Martin, F. (1956), *Social Class and Educational Mobility*, London.

Geertz, C. (1967), *Old Society and New States*, New York.

Geiger, T. (1926), *Die Masse und ihre Aktion, ein Beitrag zur Soziologie der Revolution*, Stuttgart.

Glass, D. (ed.) (1954), *Social Mobility in Britain*, London.

Hopkins, K. (1978), *Conquerors and Slaves*, Cambridge.

Hyman, H. (1963), *Survey Design and Analysis*, Glencoe, Ill.

Janowitz, M. (1960), *The Professional Soldier*, Glencoe, Ill.

König, R. (ed.) (1967–9), *Handbuch der empirischen Sozialforschung*, Stuttgart.

Lasswell, H. (1935), *World Politics and Personal Insecurity*, New York.

Lasswell, H. (1936), *Who Gets What, When, How?*, New York.

Lazarsfeld, P., Berelson, B. and Gaudet, H. (1944), *The People's Choice*, New York.

Lazarsfeld, P., Sewell, W. H. and Wilensky, H. L. (eds) (1967), *The Uses of Sociology*, New York.

Le Bras, G. (1955), *Études de sociologie religieuse*, Paris.

Lipset, S., Trow, M. and Coleman, J. (1956), *Trade Union Democracy*, Garden City, NJ.

Mannheim, K. (1936 [1929]), *Ideology and Utopia*, London. (Original German edn, *Ideologie und Utopie*, Bonn.)

Mannheim, K. (1952), *Essays on the Sociology of Knowledge*, London.

Mannheim, K. (1956), *Essays on the Sociology of Culture*, London.

Mauss, M. and Hubert, H. (1964 [1899]), *Sacrifice: Its Nature and Function*, London. (Original French edn, *Essai sur la nature et la fonction de sacrifice*, Paris.)

Mauss, M. (1972 [1904]), *A General Theory of Magic*, London. (Original French edn, 'Equisse d'un théorie générale de la magie', Paris.)

Mayo, E. (1949), *The Social Problem of an Industrial Civilization*, London.

Merton, R. K. (1973), *Science, Faith and Society*, Chicago.

Michels, R. (1934), *Umschichtengen in den herrschender Klassen nach dem Kriege*, Stuttgart.

Myrdal, G. (1944), *An American Dilemma: The Negro Problem and Modern Democracy*, New York.

Polanyi, M. (1964), *Science, Faith and Society*, Chicago.

Roethlisberger, F. J. and Dickson, W. J. (1939), *Management and the Worker*, Cambridge, Mass.

Schelsky, H. (1959), *Ortsbestimmung der deutschen Soziologie*, Dusseldorf.

Shils, E. (1972), *The Intellectuals and the Power*, Chicago.

Shils, E. (1980), *The Calling of Sociology*, Chicago.

Simon, H. A. (1947), *Administrative Behavior*, New York.

Sombart, W. (1909 [1896]), *Socialism and the Social Movement*, London. (Original German edn, *Sozialismus und soziale Bewegung im 19 Jahrhundert*.)

Sorokin, P. (1927), *Social Mobility*, New York.

Sorokin, P., Zimmerman, C. and Galpin, C. J. (1930–2), *Systematic Source Book in Rural Sociology*, 3 vols, Minneapolis.

Tilly, C. (1948), *The Vendée*, Cambridge, Mass.

Tingston, H. (1963), *Political Behavior*, Totowa, NJ.

Warner, W. L. (1942), *The Status System of an American Community*, New Haven.

Weber, M. (1930 [1922]), *The Protestant Ethic and the Spirit of Capitalism*, London. (Original German edn, *Die protestantische Ethik und der 'Geist' des Kapitalismus*, Tübingen.)

Weber, M. (1951), *The Religion of China*, Glencoe, Ill.

Weber, M. (1952), *Ancient Judaism*, Glencoe, Ill.

Weber, M. (1958), *The Religion of India*, Glencoe, Ill.

Ziman, J. (1968), *Public Knowledge: The Social Dimension of Science*, Cambridge.

Further Reading.

Durkheim, E. (1933 [1893]), *The Division of Labor in Society*, New York. (Original French edn, *De la division du travail social: étude sur l'organization des sociétés supérieures*, Paris.)

Durkheim, E. (1951 [1897]), *Suicide, A Sociological Study*, London. (Original French edn, *Le suicide; étude sociologique*, Paris.)

Durkheim, E. (1953 [1924]), *Sociology and Philosophy*, London. (Original French edn, *Sociologie et philosophie*, Paris.)

Durkheim, E. and Mauss, M. (1963 [1901]), *Primitive Classification*, London. (Original French edn, 'De quelques formes primitives de la classification', *Année Sociologique*, I.)

Lipset, S. M. and Bendix, R. (1964), *Social Mobility in Industrial Society*, Berkeley and Los Angeles.

Mauss, M. (1954 [1925]), *The Gift*, London. (Original French edn, 'Essai sur la don', *Année Sociologique*, I.)

Merton, R. (1949), *Social Theory and Social Structure*, New York.

Michels, R. (1915), *Political Parties*, Glencoe, Ill.

Park, R. *et al.* (1967), *The City*, Chicago.

Park, R. and Burgess, E. (1921), *Introduction to the Study of Society*, Chicago.

Parsons, T. (1937), *The Structure of Social Action*, Glencoe, Ill.

Parsons, T. (1951), *The Social System*, Glencoe, Ill.

Shils, E. (1975), *Centre and Periphery*, London.

Shils, E. (1981), *Tradition*, Chicago.

Simmel, G. (1955 [1908]), *Conflict and the Web of Social Relationships*, Glencoe, Ill. (Original German edn, *Soziologie: Untersuchungen über die Formen der Vergesellschaftung*, Berlin.)

Tönnies, F. (1957 [1887]), *Community and Society*, Ann Arbor. (Original German edn, *Gemeinschaft und Gesellschaft*.)

Weber, M. (1949), *Methodology of the Social Science*, A selection of and translation of his essays by E. Shils, London.

Weber, M. (1968 [1922]), *Economy and Society*, New York. (Original German edn, *Wirtschaft und Gesellschaft*, 2 Vols, Tübingen.)

Sombart, Werner (1863–1941)

Werner Sombart, a German sociologist, economist and economic historian, first taught at the University of Breslau (1890–1906) and then at a *Hochschule* in Berlin (1906–17). From 1917 to 1931 he was professor at the University of Berlin, and he died in Berlin on 19 May 1941. Sombart's most famous work is his three-volume study on the development of capitalism (*Der moderne Kapitalismus*, 1902–28) in which he presented a survey of the historical phases that capitalism could go through before being replaced by socialism: *Prae-kapitalismus* (see Rostow's traditional society) which is characterized by *das Nährungsprinzip* (food principle), *Frühkapitalismus* (or early capitalism) from the fifteenth century until 1760, *Hochkapitalismus* (or high capitalism) from 1760 until 1913, and *Spätkapitalismus* (or late capitalism) from 1914 on. The last three phases are characterized by the *Erwerbsprinzip*: a restless and rational striving after capital accumulation and profits. Sombart's theory resembles the well-known stage theories of List, Hildebrand, Knies, Bücher, and others, but his different phases are not necessarily determined by chronological succession. Sombart explicitly states that other successions, mixed forms, and even parallel forms appeared in the course of history. Initially strongly influenced by Marx, Sombart later became a pronounced anti-Marxist. He shared with Max Weber the conviction that sociology and economics must be free of value judgements. In his book *Sozialismus und soziale Bewegung im 19 Jahrhundert* (1896) (*Socialism and the Social Movement*, 1909), Sombart revealed himself to be an advocate of profound social reforms for the benefit of the working class. Although he formed no school in the strict sense of the word, he had a great influence on traditional economic history up to 1950.

Erik Aerts
Archives Générales du Royaume, Brussels

Sorel, Georges Eugène (1847–1922)

Often associated with the sociologists Mosca and Pareto, Georges Sorel, the French social philosopher, is more properly seen as an innovator in Marxist theory and the methodology of the social sciences. By temperament a *moraliste*, by training and profession an engineer in government employment (until 1892) and scientist, Sorel's work falls into two broad categories: his writings on politics (including ethics), and his examination of the philosophical problems posed by explanation in general and, more specifically, by science and religion.

Despite frequent changes in political position, the morality advocated by Sorel remained throughout a conservative one, emphasizing the values of work, the family, self-denial and heroism. His earliest writings gave little hint of radicalism, but by 1893 Sorel had espoused Marxism. From 1896 he began a reinterpretation of Marxism, which was initially perceived as a science which had discovered the 'laws' that 'determined' the development of capitalism. This culminated in 1908 in his *Réflexions sur la violence* (*Reflections on Violence*, New York, 1914). Taking the class war as the 'alpha and omega' of socialism, Sorel described the central tenets of Marxism as 'myths', as images capable of inspiring the working class to action. The most powerful of these myths was that of the general strike, which, Sorel hoped, would lead the working class to eschew the practices of parliamentary democracy, adopt the use of violence, and in the process create the ethical and material bases of socialism.

At a philosophical level Sorel sought to discredit the positivist designation of science as the sole legitimate mode of explanation. Defending science as a progressive, experimental activity, Sorel's rejection of its universalistic claims was counterbalanced by a recognition of the distinctiveness of our different forms of consciousness and by an advocacy of both an intellectual and methodological pluralism. These issues were dealt with at length in his defence of William James, *De l'utilité du pragmatisme* (1921).

Jeremy Jennings
University College of Swansea

Further Reading

Roth, J. J. (1980), *The Cult of Violence: Sorel and the Sorelians*, Berkeley and Los Angeles.

Sorel, G. (1969 [1908]), *The Illusions of Progress*, Berkeley and Los Angeles. (Original French edn, *Les illusions du progrès*.)

Sorel, G. (1972 [1914]), *Reflections on Violence*, New York.

Sorel, G. (1976), *From Georges Sorel: Essays in Socialism and Philosophy*, New York.

Stanley, J. L. (1982), *The Sociology of Virtue: The Political and Social Theories of Georges Sorel*, Berkeley and Los Angeles.

Sorokin, Pitirim A. (1889–1968)

One of this century's foremost sociologists, Pitirim A. Sorokin led a very active life: involved in radical politics in his youth in Russia, banished by the Bolshevik government, he became a controversial academic at Harvard. His stress on social dynamics in his *magnum opus*, *Social and Cultural Dynamics* (4 vols, 1937–41, abridged edn, 1957) reflects the social and historical changes he experienced. Social reality for Sorokin is everchanging, with recurrent discernible features; this entails knowledge of the historical process and of cultures other than our own Western. While Sorokin's study of the rise and fall of cultural systems may liken him to his contemporary Arnold Toynbee, he may also be viewed as a descendant of the first sociological prophet of modern society, Henri Saint-Simon. Both used their experiences of revolutions (the American and the French in the case of Saint-Simon) as stimulants for creative writing about social organization, social discontinuities, and the need for social reconstruction. Both also came to propose altruism as a necessary social force in the 'reconstruction of humanity' (the title of a work of Sorokin published in 1948).

Sorokin's career (presented in the autobiographical *A Long Journey*, 1963) may be divided into three periods. The first reads like a Dostoevsky saga. Born in a poor peasant milieu, never enjoying the care of parents, Sorokin experienced physical as much as intellectual hunger, but his exceptional intellect permitted him to complete graduate training in sociology and criminology. Politically a populist seeking major reforms for the peasantry and the working class, he later became secretary to Kerensky in the provisional government of 1917, which lost out to the Bolsheviks. Sentenced to death for anti-state activities by both the Tzarist and Leninist regimes, he was exiled in 1922. His experiences of the Russian Revolution and of the great Russian famine of 1921 provided him with many observations for materials on social behaviour in extreme situations (*Sociology of Revolution*, 1925; *Man and Society in Calamity*, 1942; *Hunger as a Factor in Human Affairs*, 1975).

The social cataclysms of World War I and the Russian Revolution led him to renounce an earlier optimistic positivism that combined with a general orientation of evolutionary progress. Coming to America in 1924 and moving from the University of Minnesota to establish a department of sociology at Harvard in 1930, Sorokin entered a period of sociological maturity marked by a spate of landmark studies in the areas of social stratification, sociological theory, rural sociology, and social change. His *Social Mobility* (1927) is still an important background work in the area of stratification and mobility, a primary field of investigation for sociology in the United States and Great Britain.

Sorokin suffered a second 'banishment' in the late 1930s, when he found himself eclipsed by a younger colleague, Talcott Parsons, who, unlike Sorokin, succeeded in establishing a major school of sociology, sometimes called the 'structural-functional' school, that drew various of Sorokin's earlier students. Parsons became head of a new department, Social Relations, and after World War II Sorokin was cut off from graduate teaching. Yet he entered a third period of creativity, publishing several works concerning altruistic behaviour (a topic rediscovered twenty years later by sociobiology), as well as critiques of both contemporary sociology (*Fads and Foibles*, 1956) and American society (*The American Sex Revolution*, 1957; *Power and Morality*, 1959). The latter anticipated by a decade the writings of 'humanistic', 'critical' sociology associated with such names as Gouldner, Birnbaum, and Friedrichs, among others. From the 1940s to the mid 1960s, Sorokin's place in American sociology was similar to that of C. Wright Mills at Columbia, both mavericks and gadflies in the profession, both critics of the concentration of military-industrial power. Fortunately, grassroots support provided vindication: Sorokin won the presidency of the American Sociological Association (ASA) in a write-in campaign at age seventy-five, and the year following his death, at the annual meetings of ASA, he was the object of a thronged testimonial session organized by students in recognition of his bitter opposition to the Vietnam war.

Given his enormous productivity, to summarize his writings is necessarily to oversimplify, and the reader should consult major volumes devoted to him (Allen, 1963; Tiryakian, 1963; Hall and Prasad, 1972). A few key emphases, however, may be useful for an initial orientation. Sorokin's 'integralist' sociology is an alternative to the two major sociological paradigms of the contemporary period, namely the 'structural-functional', on the one hand (sometimes identified with a 'consensus' view of society) and the Marxist, on the other (sometimes identified with a 'conflict' model). Unlike both, Sorokin rejected an evolutionary perspective. His major macro-unit of analysis is a *civilization*, a cluster of societies sharing similar paramount cultural orientations, which are reflected in major social institutions. Cultural orientations, or fundamental social values, have three major channels of perceiving and relating to reality: A *sensate* orientation sees truth as contained or expressing the reality of a material, physical universe, hence, stressing the value of the senses. An *ideational* orientation, in contrast, views reality as beyond the senses, transcending the physical world, and being given by faith and revelation. An *idealistic* orientation sees truth as being both in this world and beyond it, hence requiring an enriched reason, somewhat in the mode of Aristotle and Thomas Aquinas. Sorokin's comparative study of civilizations led him to find cycles of fluctuations in the cultural dominance of a given orientation, cycles of ascendancy, maturity and decline which take several centuries to complete. The twentieth century is characterized in the West by advanced industrial societies in the phase of a late sensate culture which rose to hegemony in the sixteenth century and is now marked by increasing hedonism and violence. Change is immanent to all large-scale social groupings but there are limits to the extent that a given cultural orientation can go; akin to the limits of a pendulum swing. In its decadent or declining phase, a civilization frequently experiences calamities or crises which tend to manifest a polarization of behaviour: many persons will come to behave in a rapacious, brutal, hedonistic and even criminal manner, while others will also engage in acts of altruism, charity, self-sacrifice, not found with the same frequency in 'normal times'. Sorokin, like Saint-Simon, saw the present age as one of crisis (*S.O.S. The Meaning of our Crisis*, 1951), one involving the concentration of irresponsible power and the decadence of sensate values. His denunciations of materialism, hedonism and totalitarianism are strikingly similar in tone and content to that of a later Russian exile to America, Aleksandr Solzhenitsyn. Indeed, the latter's famous Harvard address of 1978 (*A World Split Apart*) could well have been pronounced by Sorokin while he was at Harvard.

Edward A. Tiryakian
Duke University
North Carolina

References

Allen, P. J. (ed.) (1963), *Pitirim A. Sorokin in Review*, Durham, N.C.

Hall, G. C. and Prasad, R. (eds) (1972), *Sorokin and Sociology*, New York.

Tiryakian, E. A. (ed.) (1963), *Sociological Theory, Values and Sociocultural Change*, New York.

Further Reading

Coser, L. A. (1977), *Masters of Sociological Thought*, 2nd edn, New York.

Cowell, F. R. (1967), *Values in Human Society – The Sociology of P. A. Sorokin*, Boston.

Spatial Statistics

Spatial data are data collected across a set of geographical units, such as administrative or census regions, states, counties or cities. Data collected in this way are extensively used in the social sciences, and applications can be found in most issues of social science journals carrying quantitative papers. Spatial statistics is concerned with the special properties and problems of such data.

The central issue in spatial statistics is that of statistical dependence or 'autocorrelation': spatial data are structured, with neighbouring or geographically close units tending to have similar values, so that there is spatial autocorrelation within the variable. As the statistician F. F. Stephan (1934) expressed it: 'Data of geographic units are tied together, like bunches of grapes, not separate, like balls in an urn.' This dependence across space parallels that in time-series data, where there is frequently autocorrelation in time. Classical inferential statistics ignores this spatial (and temporal) structure, and assumes each observation is independent (like balls in an urn), so that spatial data tend to violate a basic assumption of classical statistics.

Time-series analysis has a long and continuous history since the early days of statistics, developing a large literature and becoming a major component of econometrics. In contrast, although there was recognition of spatial dependence as early as 1889 (in a comment by Francis Galton), spatial statistics has no continuous history of development until the 1960s. Within comparative anthropology there is a literature discussing 'Galton's problem' – the problem that spatial dependence caused by diffusion may lead to apparent, but spurious, correlations between cultural variables across societies – but it contained (until recently) only limited statistical development. Similarly, within geography there was a tradition of quantitative map analysis. In the last decade the field of spatial statistics and spatial econometrics has flourished, with work by quantitative geographers, statisticians and economists (Cliff and Ord, 1973; Paelinck and Klaassen, 1979). A major reason for this late development is that spatial problems are more complex than time-series problems: not only is one dimension (time) extended to two dimensions (space), but also the regularly-spaced observations of most time series, in which causal influences flow one way from the past into the present, give way in spatial data to irregular patterns of regions and cities which mutually interact with one another.

The recent work begins with the construction of formal statistical tests for the presence of various types of spatial dependence in data, assesses the way such dependence can bias the results of classical statistical techniques such as correlation and the t-statistic, and extends the tests to the important case of residuals from regression models. The growth of spatial econometrics is an attempt to extend (and generalize) the ideas developed in econometric theory to spatial problems in the social sciences. Recent work includes model specifications that incorporate spatial dependence directly into the model, either through error structures or through direct spatial lags or spillovers between areas, reflecting travel-to-work and spatial interaction between regions and cities.

L. W. Hepple
University of Bristol

References

Cliff, A. D. and Ord, J. J. (1973), *Spatial Autocorrelation*, London.

Paelinck, J. H. P. and Klaassen, L. H. (1979), *Spatial Econometrics*, Farnborough.

Stephan, F. F. (1934), 'Sampling errors and the interpretation of social data ordered in time and space', *Journal of the American Statistical Association*, 29.

See also: *time-space analysis*.

Spencer, Herbert (1820–1903)

Herbert Spencer was the major theorist of social evolutionism and made important and lasting contributions to sociology's methods and concepts. Born at Derby in the English Midlands, his education was haphazard and strongly inclined to scientific subjects. He never attended secondary school or university and, after some years' employment as a railway engineer and political journalist, he supported himself by his writing. Strongly marked by his provincial, nonconformist background, Spencer was active in the 1840s in radical middle-class politics and his first book, *Social Statics* (1850), attempts to justify his libertarian social ideals as the necessary outcome of a process of natural development. In the 1850s a series of essays (especially 'The development hypothesis' and 'Progress: its law and cause') drew from biology the elements of a general evolutionary *Naturphilosophie*. This was the basis of his life-work, the multi-volume *System of Synthetic Philosophy*

(1862–96) which first set forth a set of general evolutionary principles and then applied them to biology, psychology, sociology and ethics. In sociology in particular Spencer broke new ground in comparative data collection and synthesis. Several other works appeared alongside the *System*: his influential essay *Education* (1860), strongly utilitarian and anti-classical; *The Study of Sociology* (1873), an original exposition of sociological method; and *The Man Versus the State* (1884), a vigorous defence of his *laissez-faire* views.

Spencer was an evolutionist before Darwin – it was even he who coined the phrase 'survival of the fittest' – and always upheld certain pre-Darwinian views, notably the inheritance of acquired characteristics. His evolutionary sociology has a number of distinct strands. From the organic analogy came a functionalist language of societal description and a characterization of progressive or evolutionary change as a process of differentiation in social structures and functions, accompanied by higher levels of integration. Change was also represented as a movement between two distinct types of society: 'militant', where integration derives from a controlling centre (as in an army), and 'industrial', where order is the spontaneous product of individuals co-operating (as in a market). In his later writings Spencer abandoned militant/industrial as a description of process and used it purely as a typological contrast. Finally, Spencer also explained evolution as the product of a steady adaptation of the individual character to 'the social state'. In this respect his sociology rests on definite psychological foundations, despite a strain between this methodological individualism and the holism implied in the organic model of society.

Spencer's reputation reached its apogee in the 1870s and 1880s. As *the* major expression of so-called 'Social Darwinism', Spencer's work was taken up by positivist Marxists and Asian modernizers as well as by apologists for *laissez-faire* capitalism. American social science was cast in a Spencerian mould for a generation or more. However, his political ideals were coming to seem anachronistic by the 1880s, and the evolutionary paradigm, with its optimistic naturalism, lost much of its appeal after 1900. But Spencer exerted influence even on writers like L. T. Hobhouse, who rejected much of his politics, or Durkheim, who pitched his methodology against Spencer but still adapted his typology of societies from Spencer. After long neglect, a wheel came full circle when Parsons, the chief modern exponent of functionalism, revived an essentially Spencerian form of social evolutionary theory in the 1960s.

J. D. Y. Peel
University of Liverpool

Further Reading
Burrow, J. W. (1966), *Evolution and Society*, Cambridge.

Peel, J. D. Y. (1971), *Herbert Spencer: The Evolution of a Sociologist*, London.
Herbert Spencer on Social Evolution (1972), selected writings edited and with an introduction by J. D. Y. Peel, Chicago.
See also: *Social Darwinism*; *sociocultural evolution*.

Sport, Sociology of

Despite claims that a few so-called primitive tribes have nothing equivalent to sports, sport is probably among the few cultural universals of mankind, and it is one of the most important institutions in industrial societies. A large majority of the population participates in recreational or competitive sports, or in physical education, or follows sports as spectators or through the media. (Interest in sport is far more widely current than is direct involvement.) Perhaps no other event engenders more widespread international interest that the Olympic Games or the football World Cup, which are followed simultaneously by more than one thousand million people.

Scientific interest in sport as a social phenomenon is none the less rather recent. One of the earliest attempts to approach sport from a strictly sociological point of view was Heinz Risse's *Soziologie des Sports* (1921), which tried to identify the social functions of competitive sport both in antiquity and in modern industrial society. A remarkable growth of interest in the subject occurred after World War II, and especially since 1965, and according to Lüschen's estimate, over 3,000 books and journal articles on the subject had appeared by 1979.

The sociology of sport addresses a wide range of questions, determined partly by different sociological approaches, and partly by the specific problem areas. The phenomena of sport have been explained both from within, with reference to the internal structure of sport, and from without, with primary reference to other social and cultural factors. There have also been attempts to interpret other social phenomena with reference primarily to sport. Studies range from such matters as socialization patterns and value contexts to the relevance of sport to international conflicts. Some major fields of interest are the study of sport activity, for example, Olympic success, with reference to sociocultural background (Seppänen, 1968, 1981), the analysis of intersystem conflict, the structure of sports groups, analysis of games and culture, and the relationship between sport and social class. There are also solid studies of socialization and sport, social change and the relevance of sport to the position of minorities. Less work has been done on such areas as the organization of sport, careers, and professionalization; and there is surprisingly little written about the interdependence of sport and economy, law, education or politics.

Paavo Seppänen
University of Helsinki

References
Seppänen, P. (1968), *Sport Success and the Type of Culture*, Helsinki.
Seppänen, P. (1981), 'Olympic success: a cross national perspective', in G. Lüschen and G. H. Sage (eds), *Handbook of Social Science of Sport*, Champaign, Ill.

Further Reading
Lüschen, G. and Sage, G. H. (eds) (1981), *Handbook of Social Science of Sport*, Champaign, Ill.
See also: *play*.

Sraffa, Piero (1889–1983)

Piero Sraffa had a major influence on the intellectual developments of the twentieth century. He was an intimate friend of Gramsci, of Wittgenstein – he played an important role in persuading Wittgenstein to change his philosophical views as between the *Tractatus* and the *Philosophical Investigations* – and of Keynes. Sraffa was the most important critic of the orthodox theory of value and distribution. His work in the 1920s and early 1930s, especially his 1926 *Economic Journal* article on 'The laws of returns under competitive conditions', destroyed the logical foundations of Marshallian partial equilibrium analysis – though some prefer to ignore this work. His 1960 classic, *Production of Commodities by Means of Commodities*, undermined the logical foundations of the supply and demand theories of value and distribution (in so far as they were directed to answering classical questions concerning the rate of profits) – and has met a similar neglect among mainstream economists.

Between 1926 and 1960, Sraffa worked on his magnificent editions of Ricardo's works and correspondence (1951–5, ten volumes), in later years in collaboration with Maurice Dobb. They are one of the finest examples of sustained and meticulous scholarship in the discipline. In addition, the *Introduction* to Volume I of Ricardo (1951) along with the positive aspects of *Production of Commodities. . .* paved the way for a rehabilitation of classical economics, based on the contention that the surplus of commodities over those necessary for their reproduction is the central concept of economic theory around which theories of value, distribution, production, employment and growth may – and should – be set.

Sraffa also made coherent some of the insights and intuitions in Marx's work on the origin of profits in the surplus labour and surplus value extracted in the sphere of production, and their reflection in the prices of production in the sphere of distribution and exchange. As Dobb and Meek have noted, it is possible to trace a line of development in this theory from Quesnay through Ricardo to Marx, and then Sraffa's concepts of a Standard commodity and a Standard system. Sraffa's devastating review article in the 1932 *Economic Journal* of Hayek's *Prices and Production* gave Keynes the concept of own rates of interest which he used to telling effect in the key chapter 17 of *The General Theory*. Indeed, Sraffa was a universally respected – and feared – critic in Cambridge itself from the 1920s to the 1960s. Austin Robinson (1977) refers to his 'immense' contribution as 'an eliminator of mistakes and red-herrings and as a puncturer of other people's over inflated bright ideas'.

G. C. Harcourt
Jesus College, Cambridge

References
Robinson, A. (1977), 'Keynes and his Cambridge colleagues', in D. Patinkin and J. Clark Leith (eds), *Keynes, Cambridge and The General Theory*, London.
Sraffa, P. (1926), 'The laws of returns under competitive conditions', *Economic Journal*, 26.
Sraffa, P. (1932), 'Dr Hayek on money and capital', *Economic Journal*, 42.

Further Reading
Harcourt, G. C. (1982), 'The Sraffian contribution; an evaluation', in I. Bradley and M. Howard (eds), *Classical and Marxian Political Economy. Essays in Honour of Ronald L. Meek*, London.
Pasinetti, L. L. (1979), 'Sraffa, Peiro', in D. L. Sills (ed.), *International Encyclopedia of the Social Sciences. Biographical Supplement*, Vol. 18, New York.
Roncaglia, A. (1977), 'The Sraffian revolution', in S. Weintraub (ed.), *Modern Economic Thought*, Oxford.
See also: *Cambridge School of Economics; Ricardo*.

Stagflation

Stagflation is a form of inflation which occurs or persists despite the presence of a substantial or even increasing percentage of measured unemployment of the labour force. The measured inflation rate may, however, be decreasing. Stagflation is therefore not inconsistent with a substantial degree of disinflation, provided only that the residual inflation rate remains significantly positive.

The term stagflation (stagnation plus inflation) came into common usage in the United States in the late 1960s and early 1970s to describe the state of the American economy as American involvement in Indochina was reduced substantially, and the American government sought to reduce or reverse the so-called 'Vietnam' inflation by fiscal and particularly by monetary measures. But aspects of the stagflation phenomenon itself were known earlier under other names, such as 'cost-push inflation', 'sellers' inflation', 'administered-price inflation', and even 'new inflation'. The novelty was that the inflation rate seemed resistant to reductions in aggregate demand from whatever source.

Stagflation is in any case inconsistent with thorough-going price flexibility in input and output markets – in other words, with pure competition. But such flexibility had been assumed, as regards outputs though not the wages of labour, by the expository or 'textbook' Keynesianism of the immediate post-war period (1945–55). Its policy recommendation had been for fiscal and monetary expansion (particularly the former, in the form of higher public expenditures and deficits) as a remedy for unemployment, and for fiscal and monetary contraction as a remedy for inflation, which was itself assumed to arise from the excess demand of 'too much money chasing too few goods'. The uselessness and irrelevance of such recommendations in the face of unemployment with inflation (that is, of stagflation) led to widespread public, political and journalistic dissatisfaction with both Keynesian theory and macroeconomics generally, and to demands of its complete scrapping or restructuring.

Macroeconomics offers no unified counsel as to how stagflation should be dealt with. In particular, counsel which assumes low employment as the major problem, which concentrates on short-run solutions, which is not averse to 'living with inflation', differs from counsel which assumes inflation to be the major problem, which concentrates on long-run solutions to 'squeeze inflation out of the economy', and which is not averse to 'living with unemployment'. The problem, in short, is one of social and economic priorities.

In this discussion we shall deal separately with two related sorts of scenarios of stagflation. The first type begins with a failure or refusal of the monetary and fiscal systems – particularly the former – to respond to or 'accommodate' an exogenous and often external inflationary shock. The second type begins with monetary and fiscal measures – again, primarily the former – to decelerate or reverse an inflation already in progress. These two stagflation scenarios are often found together, and much of the technical analysis of the two cases is quite similar.

A standard example of Type I stagflation, the exogenous shock, begins with a rapid and unanticipated rise in the price of an imported raw material like petroleum (the OPEC oil shocks of 1973 and 1979), although a domestic catastrophe like drought or earthquake could serve as well on the supply side. (On the demand side, the US involvement in Vietnam provided a similar shock to the Canadian economy in the middle and later 1960s.) To make the analysis clearer but at considerable cost in realism, we suppose a starting position marked by both high employment and price-level stability. The price of crude oil and petroleum-intensive products (fuels, petrochemicals) rises. The reduced supply of petroleum also lowers the country's real income. Nothing, however, is done to ease either fiscal policy (by tax cutting or increased expenditures) or monetary policy (higher monetary growth rates or lower interest rates). The price increase in the economy's petroleum-intensive sector leads to inflation unless other sectors cut their prices and allow their profit margins to be squeezed, and unless labour accepts some part of the real income cost in lower money and real wages. In these circumstances, any inflation is of the stagflation variety because there is no monetary or fiscal 'validation' of the higher price level at the going high level of employment. Without such validation, the employment and capacity-utilization levels will fall.

In a pressure-group economy, a price rise in one sector does not in the short run trigger price declines in other sectors, in profit margins, or in the wages of organized labour. And as we have said, without increased purchasing power to carry the higher price level at the previous level of employment, the employment level will fall. The stagflation scenario is then largely complete. Not entirely complete, however, for we can inquire further into the reasons and rationalizations for the failure of non-oil sectors and of labour to accept price, profit and wage reductions and maintain employment despite the higher oil price and its repercussions through the economy. There are three explanations: (1) forecasting; (2) distributional considerations; and (3) a 'strike' against the monetary and fiscal policy of the government in power. These three reactions are often simultaneous, and it is difficult to distinguish between them.

(1) The 'forecasting' reaction is nothing more than a rational belief (in the light of recent history in many countries) that government monetary and fiscal policy will soon 'accommodate' higher oil prices. In which case, prices and wages lowered now would shortly rise again anyway, and patience is preferable to controversial concessions. (We should also remember that much of the initial unemployment consequent upon stagflation is concentrated upon youth not yet hired, youth employed only recently, temporary employees, and employees of concerns in financial difficulty. The bulk of the labour force is protected by 'seniority' institutions.)

(2) As for the 'distribution' reaction, it is very well to argue in the abstract for wage-price-profit concessions in non-oil sectors to maintain employment and avoid inflation, or for the equitable sharing of the

real income loss which results from reduced oil supplies. But what does all this mean in the concrete? What constitutes 'equity'? How much of the cost is to be borne by whom? What wages and profit margins are to be cut, and by how much? The purely competitive market has its own rough-and-ready, quick-and-dirty solutions for such problems, but these are solutions which, for reasons of 'fairness', 'equity', and/or 'compassion', pressure-group economics and collective bargaining are designed to avoid. The 'distribution' argument against deflationary adjustment is, in simple terms, that the group bargaining and negotiation procedures necessary to allocate the oil-shock losses are too costly in time, acrimony, nervous strain, and possible output losses through strikes and bankruptcies, to be undertaken before they have become practically necessary as well as theoretically desirable.

(3) The 'strike' reaction can be understood if we suppose a monetarist government in power, which cannot be expected to yield to group pressure or 'adjust' its fiscal and especially its monetary policies to the higher price of oil. But if we also suppose a regime of parliamentary democracy, subject to periodic elections, then there is likely to exist, or to arise if stagflation persists, an opposition party or faction which advocates accommodative policies of monetary and fiscal ease. Does it not then make good *Realpolitik* deliberately to refuse concessions to the current hard-nosed, anti-inflationist regime, and even facilitate its overthrow by making the stagflation worse and its alternative more attractive? This is what I mean by a political 'strike' against government fiscal and monetary policies, to facilitate the government's replacement by the 'accomodationist' opposition. Until the accommodationist pressure groups have faced and lost at least one general election, it is unlikely that they will themselves accept the adjustments required to end stagflation.

We turn now to stagflation of Type II (which is not fundamentally different), namely, a situation in which a government tightens its monetary and fiscal policy, particularly the former, with the aim of decelerating or reversing an inflationary process in being. We again assume initial high employment and also a situation when some prices (including wages and interest rates) have already been adjusted to next year's anticipated inflation, while others have not yet been adjusted for last year's inflation. Relative prices, wages, and interest rates, in other words, are 'wrong' from the viewpoint of the omniscient economist. In this situation stagnation results from the 'leading' prices and (especially) wage rates being too high and rigid downward. The inflation results from the 'lagging' prices and wages receiving an additional upward fillip in the interests of 'fairness', 'equity', or simply high inflationary expectations. The stagflation results, of course, from the conjunction of the stagnation and inflation factors.

Once again, competitive market forces would provide a rough-and-ready solution if unchecked. This solution would presumably feature the decline of those prices and wages that had risen too high under the influence of over-sanguinary expectations, and the rise of those which had been restrained by caution, money illusion, or long-term contracts. But once again, power or pressure economics have partially replaced market forces in the short run. The rationalizations of Stagflation Type I, which we have classified as forecasting, distributional disagreement and strikes against controls, take over just as in Stagflation Type I. There is however a minor difference, in that any distributional 'losses' to be allocated are not actual losses as in Type I but the non-achievement of the gains anticipated from outpacing inflation.

Incomes policies are advocated widely as remedies for stagflation, as well as for inflation in the large by writers fearing stagflation. Some of these involve direct controls over prices, wages, interest rates, and/or profit margins. Others are associated with tax penalties for firms raising the wages they pay or the prices they charge beyond levels approved by government agencies. (In the US, such systems are known generically as TIPs or Tax-Induced Incomes Policies.) The only reason why stagflation requires different remedies than inflation generally, is that the greater need to avoid increasing unemployment demands greater delicacy in tightening constraints. Similarly, remedies for the unemployment aspects of stagflation are no different from those for unemployment generally, except for a greater delicacy required to avoid igniting or accelerating inflation.

Martin Bronfenbrenner
Duke University, North Carolina
Aoyama Gakuin University, Tokyo

Further Reading
Cornwall, J. (1983), *Post-Keynesian Analysis of Stagflation*, London.
See also: *employment and underemployment; inflation and deflation.*

State

State refers, in its widest sense, to any self-governing set of people organized so that they deal with others as a unity. It is a territorial unit ordered by a sovereign power, and today involves officeholders, a home territory, soldiers distinctively equipped to distinguish them from others, ambassadors, flags, and so on. The inhabitable land of the world has for the last century been parcelled up into such units; before that, quite large areas had been either unclaimed and uninhabited, or inhabited by nomadic and wandering peoples who were not organized as states. Most states are now represented at the United Nations, and they vary in size and significance from China and the United States at one extreme, to Nauru and the Seychelles at the other.

More specifically, however, the term state refers to the form of centralized civil rule developed in Europe since the sixteenth century. This model has been imitated, with varying success, by all other peoples in the modern world. What most distinguishes the state as an organizational entity is the freedom and fluency with which it makes and unmakes law. The empires of the East, by contrast, were predominantly bound by custom, while in Europe in the medieval period, authority to rule was dispersed among different institutions, and in any case took long to acquire the habits of fluent legislation.

The modern European state came into being gradually, and has never ceased to evolve. Its emergence can in part be traced in each of the major European realms by way of the growing currency of the word 'state', along with its analogues in other European languages: *stato, état, estado, Reich* and so on. The idea, however, has played a varying role in different countries – much less, for example, in Britain than in some continental countries. Machiavelli in the *Prince* (1513) exhibits a clear grasp of the emerging realities of central power, but while he sometimes talks of *lo stato*, he can also use expressions like *loro stato* (your state) which suggest that he is not altogether clear about the difference between a state and a régime. In Jean Bodin's *Six Livres de la République* (1578) later in the sixteenth century, the French state was explicitly theorized in terms of the idea of sovereignty, as the absolute and perpetual power of both making and unmaking laws. The *unmaking* of laws is important, because it constitutes one reason why the growth of absolute power could be welcomed as a liberation from the dead hand of inherited rules. A weariness with the civil strife of the sixteenth and seventeenth centuries further disposed many people to welcome absolute rulers as guarantors of peace. Monarchs were, of course, far from loathe to acquire this power, and set to work diminishing the co-ordinate powers and jurisdictions inherited from earlier times. The Church was perhaps the most important of these jurisdictions, and lost power no less in realms that remained Catholic than in those which became Protestant. Parliamentary institutions fell into desuetude everywhere except in England. The nobility, which had been turbulent in the exercise of its feudal powers, were domesticated as courtiers, most famously at the Versailles of Louis XIV. Monarchy became strictly hereditary and evolved mystiques both of blood and divine right. The absolute power thus generated was often used with a ruthless cynicism typified in the motto 'canons are the arguments of princes' and exemplified in the careers of spectacularly aggrandizing monarchs like Charles XII of Sweden and Frederick the Great of Prussia. But all states alike tried to expand their power both by mobilizing the resources available and by conquering new territory. It would be a mistake, however, to think that this early modern absolutism became indistinguishable from despotism. The sovereigns remained subject to myriad customary restrictions and had to operate for the most part in terms of law, whose abstractness limits its usefulness as an instrument of pure policy. Further, as the new system settled down in the later seventeenth century, the more powerful classes, such as the nobility, clergy and the bourgeoisie in the towns, solidified into corporations which sensibly limited the freedom of action exercised by monarchs who found in Enlightenment rationalism a doctrine highly conducive to their dreams of mobilizing national power. What emerged was the *ancien régime*, a social form so immobile it needed a French Revolution and a Napoleon to destroy it.

The issues raised by the emergence of this quite new form of civil association can best be grasped by their reflection in European political philosophy. A pure theory of the state was presented by Thomas Hobbes in *Leviathan* (1651). Hobbes argued that subjection to a sovereign ruling by law was the only alternative to the incessant discord created when proud and insecure individuals jostled together. Hobbes was clear, as Machiavelli was not, that the state (or *Leviathan*) is an abstract and impersonal structure of offices conditionally exercised by particular men. Men must, as subjects, rationally consent to the absolute power of the sovereign, but this consent lapses if the sovereign cannot protect them, or if he begins directly to threaten their lives. The boldness of the Hobbesian conception, which reflects the thoroughness with which Hobbes thought the issue through, lies in the extrusion of any external limitations on the sovereign power: what the sovereign declares to be just is *ipso facto* just, and he has the right to determine religious belief, and what may be taught in the schools. Liberty is the private enjoyment of the peace brought by civil association, a peace in which alone culture and material prosperity may be garnered.

Being a philosophical work, the *Leviathan* explained but did not justify, and fragments of its argument were appropriated by both sides in the English civil war. Both sides were offended by it. The *Leviathan* was publicly burned at Oxford in 1685. Immediately after the Revolution of 1688, John Locke published *Two Treatises on Government* which softened the intolerably austere picture of the state Hobbes gave. This was an occasional work which popularized the notion that governments rested upon the consent of their subjects, and were limited by natural rights (to life, liberty and property) with which men entered civil society. Their business was to protect such rights. Locke avoided the idea of sovereignty altogether and emphasized that the rulers *represented* the ruled. The spread of liberalism in the next two centuries extended this idea, both in theory and in practice.

In the course of the eighteenth century, it became clear that the modern European state raised quite new problems, both practical and theoretical. It was a free association of individuals claiming the power to legislate for themselves, without any necessary moral, religious or metaphysical commitments. Two ideas, potentially disharmonious, consequently dominated further development: community, and freedom. The best formulation of the problem is in the sixth Chapter of Rousseau's *Social Contract* (1762):

How to find a form of association which will defend the person and goods of each member with the collective force of all, and under which each individual, while uniting himself with others, obeys no one but himself, and remains as free as before.

Rousseau's solution focused on a general will constituting a community of citizens devoted to the public interest. Such a conception clearly emerged from the ancient conception of the virtuous republic which had haunted European thought since Machiavelli's *Discourses on the First Ten Books of Livy* (1518), and which was unmistakably subversive of the European system of extended monarchies. Just how subversive it was soon became evident, both in the thought of Immanuel Kant, who argued that republics were the condition of perpetual peace, and in the French Revolution, whose protagonists adopted Rousseau posthumously as one of their own.

The problem was that the classical republic was possible only in a small city with a homogeneous population. Montesquieu had argued in *De l'esprit des lois* (1748) (*The Spirit of the Laws*) that no such thing was possible in the conditions of modern Europe. In the 1820s Hegel presented in the *Philosophy of Right* (1821), an account of the modern state as the objective embodiment of the fully-developed subjective freedom towards which the human spirit had always been tending. At the time, however, a whole group of writers emerged to emphasize the misery and repression, as they saw it, of modern life and the iniquity of the state. Marx and Engels argued that the state was an illusion masking the domination of the bourgeois class, and predicted that after a proletarian revolution, the state would wither away. A newly homogeneous mankind would be able to surpass the unity and virtue of the classical republics on a world-wide scale.

The actual history of states has been one of a continuous growth, both in their claim to regulate the lives and property of their subjects, and in their physical capacity to enforce such claims. It is, for example, possible to regulate a literate society much more completely than an illiterate one. The propensity of European states to engage in war with one another has provided frequent emergencies in which necessity

trained governments in how to regulate; and all states now have bureaucracies and other instruments of control. Yet, paradoxically, the increase in the state's range and power has produced countervailing decreases in effectiveness. When its functions were limited to guaranteeing order and security, the state was accorded immunity from some of the moral restraints binding on individuals. The doctrine called 'reason of state' authorized the breaking of treaties, deceit, and the employment of violence, when necessary. From the nineteenth century onwards, some extensions of state power (especially the redistributions of wealth which began to constitute the state as a system of welfare for all members of society) were justified on the ground that the state stood for a higher morality. Citizens thus came to believe that they had rights *against* the state. The state's claim to suspend law, to guard its own secrets, to the use of nonlegal measures in dealing with enemies who themselves resorted to terror – all the traditional apparatus of *raison d'état* – was challenged, and it was felt to be the duty of the state to represent the highest moral standards even against those who violated them. In developments such as this, and in the persistently transforming dynamism of the idea of democracy, will be found reasons for seeing the modern state, at least in its European heartland, not as an abstract idea, but as an institution ceaselessly responsive to the beliefs that move its subjects.

Kenneth Minogue
London School of Economics and Political Science

Further Reading
d'Entreves, A. P. (1967), *The Notion of the State*, London.
Mabbott, J. D. (1967), *The State and the Citizen*, 2nd edn, London.
Maritain, J. (1951), *Man and the State*, London.
See also: *government; social contract; stateless societies; state, origin of.*

Stateless Societies

All societies – whether states or stateless – may be conceived of as being made up of 'elementary' units, whose structure is ordered by two sets of forces, one emanating from the reproduction of the society, the other from the local grouping of its members. These elementary units are 'descent groups'. Their mode of reproduction in the field of kinship is fixed by rules of filiation, while rules of alliance define the modes whereby women are exchanged between them. The term 'segmentary' describes a form of social organization in which descent groups constitute the only relevant units from the point of view of social control, such that the field of politics is restricted to relationships within and between such groups, power initially being no more than simply an extension of family authority based on seniority. A 'segmentary' form of organization is not a simple consequence of the mechanism of 'segmentation'; it requires the adjustment of this segmentation (whether by processes of 'fission' or 'fusion') to practical ends. The practical and ideological regulation of the system tends to produce a permanent redefinition of the *ad hoc* segmentary unit, whose corporate character requires a certain average genealogical depth, a given breadth of collateral extension, and a roughly-fixed number of local units. The unilineal and exogamous 'lineage' provides a good model for such a unit.

Within a segmentary-lineage system, lineages are not equal, but, on the contrary, are ordered hierarchically by a principle which projects, at the level of the universe of segmentary units, the dual system of genealogical ranking by generation, and differentiation according to age. Consequently, certain lineages may be better placed to accumulate goods and services, women, land, sacred forces, and so on. As a result of the intrinsic fluidity of the segmentary units, segmentary systems vary considerably in their historical forms. The hierarchical ordering of lineages may be more or less marked – this is related to the nature of the economy – and the lineage system may or may not be associated with another mode of sociopolitical control, which may take the form of clans, age-classes, estates, or societies within or outside the field of lineage organization. Mixed systems, which result from such combinations, tend to be less segmentary in nature, and differentiate jural, political and military control clearly from domestic and social control.

The question arises, with respect to both nomadic and sedentary societies, of how the levels of segmentation are spatially fixed. The territory of a global society – the definition of which depends on the consciousness of the members that they belong to one grouping – may be envisaged simultaneously as a descent group's domain, which is divided into various localities, and as a locality, which is divided among various lineages. The term local community is used when the segments of various lineages in one locality are not simply regrouped in a single area but integrated in a coherent economic and social whole, to the degree that the unilocal character of this unit is more significant than its multilineal character. In such a local community specific functions and institutions appear – such as the function of the 'chief' or the institution of a 'council' of the community – which are clearly based on a locally-based power, which no longer coincides with segmentary forms of authority. The opposition between segmentary systems and community systems accounts for the two major orientations of stateless political systems, but this opposition is also relevant for state-based societies. In Africa, and in some other regions, there is a continuity between segmentary stateless societies and states in which the dominant group is organized on a segmentary basis, and also between stateless systems based on local communities and city-states.

Michel Izard
École des Hautes Études en Sciences Sociales

Further Reading

Bazin, J. and Terray, E. (eds) (1982), *Guerres de lignages et guerres d'états en Afrique*, Paris.
Leacock, E. and Lee, R. (eds) (1982), *Politics and History in Band Societies*, Cambridge.
Middleton, J. and Tait, D. (eds) (1958), *Tribes Without Rulers: Studies in African Segmentary Systems*, London.

See also: *descent and descent groups; political anthropology; social anthropology; state, origin of.*

State, Origin of

A specific state is defined necessarily with respect both to a territory and to a population which occupies it, and which constitutes the society of which the state is the emanation. In a state, political power is monopolized by a dominant, specialized, and numerically minority group, which disposes of the means of military force that is used for wars outside and for coercion within. Born in violence, the power of the state can perpetuate itself only by inducing a social consensus; at the very moment that it captures political power for its own profit, the dominant group is obliged to elaborate, for the society at large, an ideology which legitimates it, which serves to establish a contractual bond associating the state and the society.

The appearance of the state marks a radical break in the history of the society, from the point of view of spatial organization, the internal differentiation of the society, and the control of economic and social relations. The most evident consequence of these changes is a shift in the scale of the frame of reference of social life.

The key problem with reference to the forms of emergence of the state is whether the state is born in a process which is external to the society concerned, or in a process of evolution internal to the society. In practice, these two types of causality need not be mutually exclusive, and commonly correspond to two successive steps in the history of a single state. Historically, the passage from a stateless society to a state generally follows the conquest of a stateless society by a military force of external origin; the state then would originate in a 'transformation in the practice and the ends of the war' (Bazin and Terray, 1982). The conquest initially defines the nascent state as a territory; the initial goal is the delimitation of a 'pacified zone', which permits the reorientation of the war to external goals. Following the conquest, the real history of the new state begins, in its relation with its territory and the corresponding society. The militarily and politically dominant group progressively extends its control, for its sole benefit, through the regulation of persons and goods, the social division of labour, the circulation of goods, the manipulation of sacred symbols, and so on. The means of control is the apparatus of the state, which takes account of the emergence of a sector of civil administration within the power structure, to which the military force is subordinated. In this way, depending on the historical context, there emerge court aristocracies, despotic bureaucracies and merchant oligarchies, which assure the continuity of the state and provide it with the means for the reproduction of the system of exploitation, which is its purpose. The ideal objective of the activity of the apparatus of the state is the centralization of state power, and this is achieved when the sovereign, separated from his warlike origins, becomes simply the singular incarnation of sovereignty regarded as a system which accounts for the order of the world. The war which began it all is now no more than an imaginary point of reference for the state to which it gave birth.

Michel Izard
École des Hautes Études en Sciences Sociales

Reference

Bazin, J. and Terray, E. (eds) (1982), *Guerres de lignages et guerres d'états en Afrique*, Paris.

Further Reading

Claessen, H. J. M. and Skalnik, P. (eds) (1978), *The Early State*, The Hague.

Claessen, H. J. M. and Skalnik, P. (eds) (1981), *The Study of the State*, The Hague.

Cohen, R. and Service, E. R. (eds) (1978), *Origins of the State: The Anthropology of Political Evolution*, Philadelphia.

Krader, L. (1968), *Formation of the State*, Englewood Cliffs, NJ.

See also: *political anthropology; state; stateless societies.*

Statistical Reasoning

Statistical reasoning (SR) is a form of reasoning with probabilistic features, applicable to *inference and decision making* in the presence of an uncertainty that cannot be expressed in terms of known and agreed chance probabilities. Thus SR is not relevant to games of pure chance, such as backgammon with well-engineered dice, but is likely to be involved in guessing the voting intentions of an electorate and fixing an advantageous polling date.

Its application is usually mediated by some standard *statistical method* (SM) whose prestige and convenience, especially if computerized, can induce a neglect of the associated SR. Even when explicitly formulated, SR may be *plausible* (*or not*) in appearance and *efficacious* (*or not*) in its ultimate influence. The *evolutionary theory* of SR (Campbell, 1974) postulates that it is a genetically controlled mental activity justified by survival advantage. A related *black-box* view of the efficacy of SR may be useful in deciding between the claims of different SR schools that their respective nostrums are found to 'work in practice'. We will concentrate here, however, on the plausibility of the types of SR usually associated with particular statistical methods, and go on to consider principles that may assist in the continually required discrimination in favour of good SR. Our i^{th} example of *method* is denoted by SMi and the jth example of possible *reasoning* for it is denoted by SRi_j. Undefined terms will be supposed to have their ordinary interpretations.

SM_1: *The incorporation of an element of objective random sampling in any observations on a population of identifiable items, that ensures for each item a specified, non-negligible probability of being included in the sample.*

$SR1_1$: Without the element of random sampling, it is impossible for the sampler to justify the selection of items without reference to some systematic, comprehensive theory, which may be erroneous or, worse, subject to undeclared or subconscious bias.

$SR1_2$: With the element, it is maintainable by probabilistic argument that the unobserved items should not be systematically different from those observed. This permits tests of hypotheses about the population as a whole.

$SR1_3$: The power of such tests may be enhanced by the device of *restricted randomization* which excludes in advance the selection of samples that would only weakly discriminate among alternative hypotheses.

$SM2$: *Random manipulation of controllable independent variables in the treatment of experimental units, and the analysis of the effect of this manipulation on dependent variables.*

$SR2_1$: If the effect referred to were reliably established, this could be described as *causal*, operating either directly or through the agency of other variables. The use of an isolated random manipulator – uninfluenceable and influential only through controllable independent variables – is necessary in order to rule out the hypothesis of *spurious correlation* between the dependent variables and naturally occurring variation of the independent variables. As a bonus, it also rules out the possibility of the experimenter using 'inside knowledge' to produce such a correlation by unconscious or deliberate choice of the values of the control variables.

SR2$_2$: The extent to which such causal inference is possible in non-experimental investigation depends on the extent to which changes in the independent variables are induced by factors judged to be equivalent to an isolated random manipulator, as in *quasi-experimental studies* (Blalock, 1972).

SM3: *Evaluation of the achieved significance level* P *for the observed value* t *of a test statistic* T *whose (null) distribution is specified by a (null) hypothesis* H$_0$ *i.e.*

$$P = Pr \ (T \geqslant t | H_0).$$

SR3$_1$: When it is small, P provides a *standardized interpretable encoding* of the deviation of t from the values of T that would be expected if H$_0$ were true. Increasing values of t are encoded as decreasing values of P which induce increasing dissatisfaction with H$_0$. A small value of P forces the simple dichotomy: either H$_0$ is true and a rare event has occurred, or H$_0$ does not describe the actual distribution of T.

SR3$_2$: P is *not* the 'probability that H$_0$ is true', which probability is not definable in the set-up of SM3.

SR3$_3$: The 'dissatisfaction' in SR3$_1$ increases *smoothly*: there is no critical value, 0.05 for example, at which P suddenly becomes scientifically important.

SR3$_4$: The *provenance* of T should be taken into account in the calculation of P when, for example, T has been selected as a result of a search for any interesting feature of the data.

SM4: *Calculation, from the data* x, *of a 95 per cent confidence interval* $(\ell(x), u(x))$ *for a real-valued parameter* θ *in a statistical model defined as a set* $\{Pr_\theta\}$, *indexed by* θ, *of probability distributions of* X, *the random generic of* x.

SR4$_1$: The particular interval $(\ell(x), u(x))$ is regarded as relevant to inference about the true value θ because of the *coverage property.*

$$Pr \ (\ell(X) \leqslant \theta \leqslant u(X)) = 0.95$$

SR4$_2$: The value 0.95 is *not* the 'probability that θ lies in the particular interval $(\ell(x), u(x))$', which probability is not definable in the set-up of SM4.

SR4$_3$: Can the 'relevance' mentioned in SR4$_1$ be reasonably maintained when, as may happen, the calculated interval turns out to be (a) the whole real line, or (b) the empty set, or when it may be logically established that the interval contains θ? Such counter-examples to SR4$_1$ do not arise in the commoner applications of the confidence interval method.

SM5: *Given data* x *for a statistical model indexed by a parameter* θ, *a posterior probability distribution for* θ *is calculated by the Bayesian formula*

$$posterior \ density \ \propto \ prior \ density \ \times \ Pr_\theta(x)$$

and used freely for purposes of inference and decision.

SR5$_1$: There are now several nearly equivalent formulations of the Bayesian logic (Fishburn, 1970) whose upshot, roughly, is that any individual, willing to accept a few qualitative axioms about 'probability' and to give expression to them in a rich enough context, will discover that he has a *subjective probability* distribution over everything – or at least over everything related to x. The formula in SM5 is particularly convenient if the first fruits of the introspective process for determining this distribution are (i) the assignment of probability 1 to the assertion that data x was indeed randomly generated by the statistical model and (ii) the probability distribution of θ which is the 'prior density'.

SR5$_2$: If the 'process' in SR5$_1$ were *faithfully* undertaken by a very large number of Bayesians in a range of contexts, then, if the statistical models to which unit probability is assigned were indeed correct, it would be a consequence of the supposed randomness in the models that the data x would, with high probability, show significant departure from its associated model in a specifiable proportion of cases. This would be so, even if the Bayesians were fully aware of the features of their data at the time of their probability assignments.

It may therefore be necessary to defend the rights of Bayesians to use statistical models that would be rejected by other statistical methods.

SR5$_3$: The difficulty for the Bayesian approach just described may be overcome by the assignment of a probability of $1 - \epsilon$ rather than unity to the statistical model: awkward data can then be accommodated by reserving the prior probability ϵ for any ad hoc models.

SR5$_4$: A similar loophole may be employed in dealing with the paradox created by data that simultaneously deviates highly significantly from what is expected under a sharp subhypothesis, $\theta = \theta_0$, say, of the model, while *increasing* the odds in favour of θ_0 (Lindley, 1957). For example, suppose a 'psychic' correctly predicts 50,500 out of 100,000 tosses of a fair coin and the statistical model is that the number of correct guesses is binomially distributed with probability. For the prior that puts prior possibility ½ at $\theta = $ ½ and ½ uniformly over the interval (0,1), the posterior odds in favour of $\theta = $ ½ are 1.7/1, although the outcome has an achieved significance level of 0.0008.

SR5₅: Bayesians claim that all probabilities are subjective with the possible exception of the quantum theoretic sort. At best, subjective probability distributions may agree to assign unit probability to the same statistical model but, even then, the posterior distributions would differ, reflecting individual priors. Such differences have not succumbed to extensive but largely abortive efforts to promulgate *objective priors* (Zellner, 1980), just as attempts to formalize the apparently reasonable slogan 'Let the data speak for themselves!' have proved nugatory.

SM6: *Given are*
(i) *a statistical model* $\{Pr_\theta\}$,
(ii) *a set* $\{d\}$ *of possible decisions*,
(iii) *a loss function* $L(d,\theta)$, *the loss if decision* d *is taken when* θ *is true*,
(iv) *a set* $\{\delta\}$ *of decision rules, each of which individually specifies the decision to be taken for each possible* x.
Deducible are the 'risk functions of θ, *one for each* δ, *defined by the expectation under* Pr_θ *of the randomly determined loss* $L(\delta(X),\theta)$. *The method, not completely specified, consists in selecting a decision rule from* $\{\delta\}$ *that has a risk function with some optimal character.*

SR6₁: The ambiguity of choice of T for the 'achieved significance level' method (SM3), coupled with that method's lack of concern about its performance when H₀ does not hold, led Neyman and Pearson to treat testing a hypothesis as what may now be viewed as a special case of SM6. This has, simply, $\{d\} = \{$Accept H₀, Reject H₀$\}$, L = 0 or 1 according as d is right or wrong and, as a consequence, a risk function equivalent to a statement of the probabilities of error: 'size' and '1 - power'.

SR6₂: A difficulty with the risk function approach to inference that is implicit in the Neyman-Pearson treatment of hypothesis testing was pointed out by Cox (1958). It can be illustrated with a simple story. Two pollsters A and B wanted to test the hypothesis that no more than half the electors of a large city, willing to respond to a particular Yes-No question, would do so affirmatively (Cohen, 1969). Pollster A suggested that the poll would require only 100 randomly chosen respondents, whereas B wanted to get 10,000 responses. They agreed (i) to toss a fair coin to decide the sample size, (ii) to employ the 5 per cent hypothesis test, most powerful in detecting a Yes:No ratio of 2:1, with probabilities of error defined before the outcome of the toss is known. They check with a statistician that this test would have an overall power of 99 per cent for the alternative hypothesis that the proportion of yeses was 2/3. In the event, the sample size was 10,000 and the number of yeses was 5678. Both A and B were astonished when advised that this number was too small to reject the hypothesis by the agreed test, even though, had it been obtained in a survey with a non-random choice of the sample size 10,000, it would have had an achieved significance level (SM3) of less than 1 in a million!

The reason for this behaviour is that the Neyman-Pearson lemma, justifying the test, ignores all possibilities other than the null and alternative hypotheses, under both of which any outcome in the region of 5678 yeses has only the remotest possibility of occurring.

SR6₃: Another apparent difficulty for risk functions arose in connection with the widespread use of least squares estimates for normal models. Taking risk as mean square error, James and Stein (1961) found that improvements could be made, whatever the true values of the parameters, by means of a special estimator even when this combined the data of quite unrelated problems. This striking phenomenon may be regarded as providing a criticism of least squares estimation viewed as a form of restriction on $\{\delta\}$: a Bayesian approach whose prior insists that the problems are indeed unrelated will not allow any pooling of information – but will also not produce least squares estimates.

The above examples of SR were elicited in response to statements of representative statistical methods and are of a somewhat *ad hoc*, fragmentary character. Are there no general principles that can be brought to bear on any problem of statistical methodology of whatever size and shape? The answer depends very much on the extent to which the 'uncertainty' in the problem has been crystallized in the form of an agreed statistical model $\{Pr_\theta\}$. Given the latter, the ideas of Birnbaum (1969) and Dawid (1977) deserve wider appreciation.

In Dawid's terminology, an 'inference pattern' is any specified function $I(\xi,x)$ of the two arguments: a 'potential experiment' ξ and associated potential data x (the value of variable X). For each ξ in a specified class, a statistical model $\{Pr_\theta\}$ is provided for X, where the parameter θ indexes the supposed common uncertainty in all the potential experiments considered. These are the defining conditions under which a number of principles require that I be the same for data x in ξ and data x' in ξ':

Principle	*Conditions for* $I(\xi,x) = I(\xi',x')$
(i) 'Distribution'	ξ and ξ' have the same $\{Pr_\theta\}$ and x = x';
(ii) 'Transformation'	ξ' is given by a 1−1 transformation t of the data in ξ and x' = t(x);
(iii) 'Reduction'	$I(\xi,x)$ is a function of r(x), ξ' is given by reporting the value of r, and x' = r(x);

(iv) 'Ancillarity' a(X) has a constant distribution (independant of θ), ξ' is the experiment whose statistical model is the set of probability distributions of X given a(X) = a, a(x) = a and x' = x;

(v) 'Sufficiency' ξ' reports the value of a sufficient statistic t(x) and x' = t(x);

(vi) 'Likelihood' the likelihood functions of θ, given x in ξ and given x' in ξ', are proportional

There are implications among such principles so that if one accepts the weaker looking ones, one is then obliged to accept the stronger ones – such as the Likelihood Principle. Very many statistical methods violate the latter.

When there is no agreed statistical model, however, SR cannot receive the (occasionally doubtful) benefit of mathematical support. Perhaps as a consequence, it has not received much attention in the literature, except in the popular texts excellently represented by Huff (1973) or the occasional philosophical article (most philosophical discussions of SR are implicitly model-dependent). At this premodelling level, there is a broad consensus among the statistically-minded as to what constitutes poor SR: it is much more difficult to characterize good SR. The latter is required to avoid the elementary logical pitfalls but has to go well beyond that in constructive directions. A paradoxical snag in statistical thinking about some problems is how to recognize that the data are inadequate to support such thinking: imaginative SR is often needed to specify the kind of data needed to support the embryonic inferences being formulated.

Premodelling SR stands to gain much from the recent advances in 'descriptive statistics' largely associated with the work of Tukey (1977). The techniques of 'exploratory data analysis' and 'computer-intensive methods' (Diaconis and Efron, 1983) extend the range of statistical activity ultimately subject to SR scrutiny but, at the same time, they enhance the risks that SR will be neglected by methodologists fascinated by the complexity of such techniques.

M. Stone
University College London

References

Birnbaum, A. (1969), 'Concepts of statistical evidence', in S. Morgenbesser *et al.* (eds), *Philosophy, Science and Method: Essays in Honor of E. Nagel*, New York.

Blalock, H. M. (1972), *Causal Models in the Social Sciences*, London.

Campbell, D. T. (1974), 'Evolutionary epistemology', in P. A. Schilpp (ed.), *The Philosophy of Karl Popper*, La Salle, Ill.

Cohen, J. (1969), *Statistical Power Analysis for the Behavioral Sciences*, New York.

Cox, D. R. (1958), 'Some problems connected with statistical inference', *Annals of Mathematical Statistics*, 29.

Dawid, A. P. (1977), 'Conformity of inference patterns', in J. R. Barra *et al.* (eds), *Recent Developments in Statistics*, Amsterdam.

Diaconis, P. and Efron, B. (1983), 'Computer-intensive methods in statistics', *Scientific American*, 248.

Fishburn, P. C. (1970), *Utility Theory for Decision Making*, Publications in Operations Research, No. 18, New York.

Huff, D. (1973), *How to Lie with Statistics*, Harmondsworth.

James, W. and Stein, C. (1961), 'Estimation with quadratic loss', *Proceedings of the 4th Berkeley Symposium of Mathematical Statistics and Probability*, 1.

Lindley, D. V. (1957), 'A statistical paradox', *Biometrika*, 44.

Tukey, J. W. (1977), *Exploratory Data Analysis*, Reading, Mass.

Zellner, A. (1980), *Bayesian Analysis in Econometrics and Statistics: Essays in Honor of Harold Jeffreys*, Amsterdam.

See also: *Bayes' theorem; categorical data; measures of central tendency and dispersion; multivariate analysis; regression; stochastic models.*

Status

Difficult to conceptualize and often elusive to the empirical grasp, yet the idea of status is essential to an understanding of social stratification. It has been apparent to social scientists that members of all known societies are stratified to some extent, that sometimes the basis of this order has been relatively simple, such as sex and age, and sometimes the divisions are many and complex.

In the past, status was a juristic term connoting the individual's rights and duties as relevant to his condition and station in life. However, in the nineteenth century, after social upheavals had shaken the old order to its foundations, Alexis de Tocqueville commented that among the repercussions could be noted a quickening in the scramble for status. To people of higher status, the inherited right to privileges and honour seemed to be slipping away; and to those of lower status, there was suddenly hope of changing their lot. The sharp changes in status fortunes that emerged from the erosion of privilege could not be encompassed by the old legalistic definition of the term, yet it was some time before it was broadened sufficiently to be useful as a tool for analysis.

This came with Max Weber, who pointed out that status, class or income, and political power are the three major dimensions of social stratification. It is unclear which had priority but Weber implied that if an individual has high status, wealth would follow, although they usually overlap, both being products of the distribution of power. In saying that status is 'an effective claim to social esteem in terms of positive or negative privileges' (Weber, 1978), Weber emphasized its relational base and that a status claimant must have an audience from which to receive or to demand deferential response. More recently, Gerth and Mills (1953) emphasized that a status situation is not fixed, but tends to be played out on the uncertain grounds of claimant and audience negotiation and compromise. Harold Garfinkel (1956), in his work on status degradation, underlines the crucial role a fickle audience can play in determining the destiny of a claimant.

A different interpretation has distinguished the work of anthropologist Ralph Linton (1936). For him, status is primarily a position in a social structure, involving rights, duties, and reciprocal expectations of behaviour, none of which depends on the personal characteristics of the status occupant. Davis (1948) further developed this idea for sociology; and Merton (1957) went on to postulate that individuals have an array of social positions, forming a composite or status set. More recently, Lenski (1954) studied disjunction between the status and class positions of individuals and groups, called status crystallization, in which rewards in one do not correspond to rewards in the other. He found that when this is perceived as an inequity, it elicits dissatisfaction and responses of anger and desire to change the system, or withdrawal and apathy.

In summary, then, two major conceptualizations of status have emerged: (1) status, as seen by Weber and his followers, is relational and intersubjective; (2) status, as outlined by Linton and others, is positional and highly structured. Much of today's work takes an uneasy path between the two.

Types

Although the literature is replete with typologies of status, among the most important are those of ascribed and achieved status. Ascribed status is that which is inherited, such as sex, race, or ethnicity, or over time, age, and is crucial to defining the basic patterns of people's lives. Achieved status, on the other hand, is acquired through personal effort or chance, possibly from occupational or educational attainment. Both of these types are bases for the formation of status communities.

Status Communities

From collections of status individuals who have commonalities of occupation or education or experience, communities tend to develop. Members, becoming cognizant of their similarities, of shared styles of living and interests, come to identify with one another (Bensman, 1972). The status community organizes to defend the 'good life', to capture and monopolize whatever privileges and rewards it can, to block entry to lower-status invaders, and to press and push ever upward to higher-status heights. It is a power base eventually devolving upon its members the moral sense of *deserved* honour and superiority.

Lower-status groups, which Weber (1946) calls negatively privileged, might also cohere into an 'ethnic community'. Just as with status communities, ethnic members believe in their own dignity and honour, though perhaps necessarily rooted elsewhere than in the misery of the present; the past, perhaps, or even in a millenarian vision of the future. For many of these groups – Blacks, Jews, lower-caste Indians, women, and so on – it is the lack of social power and the marks of ascriptive status that have bound them to the wheel of ill fortune.

Status Symbols

Status symbols are those visible marks that celebrate the individual's or group's difference and superiority. Erving Goffman (1972) calls status symbols 'specialized means of displaying one's position'. Symbolic value can be lent to almost any object or situation. Language, etiquette, gestures, material objects, particularly if they are difficult to acquire, can distinguish a group and set it apart. Whatever connotes the individual's or group's place in the social order can be used to elevate it symbolically and, by reference, to demean outsiders. During periods of rapid social change or in urban settings where the individual's status is unknown, status symbols can be manipulated and fraudulently used by individuals laying claim to higher status, and indeed the bearer can gain greater deference and privilege than deserved.

A major criticism of status theory is that it is politically conservative, that the gradations of increasing or decreasing status obscure the reality of sharp class lines (Vanneman and Pampel, 1977). Yet inequality is hardly explicable by reference *only* to a class system of discrete categories, nor, for that matter, to a concept emphasizing achieved status positions. Neither adequately accounts for the continuing troubles of subordinate groups. Status analysis, which emphasizes the relations between groups and the long-term effects of ascriptive status, might more effectively explain a world piloted by organized honour, privilege, and power when used together with other stratification theory.

Charlotte Wolf
Memphis State University
Tennessee

References

Bensman, J. (1972), 'Status communities in an urban society: the musical community', in H. R. Stub (ed.), *Status Communities in Modern Society*, Hinsdale, Ill.

Davis, K. (1948), *Human Society*, New York.

Garfinkel, H. (1956), 'Conditions of successful degradation ceremonies', *American Journal of Sociology*, 61.

Gerth, H. and Mills, C. Wright (1953), *Character and Social Structure*, New York.

Goffman, E. (1972), 'Symbols of class status', in H. R. Stub (ed.), *Status Communities in Modern Society*, Hinsdale, Ill.

Lenski, G. E. (1954), 'Status crystallization, a non-vertical dimension of social status', *American Sociological Review*, 19.

Linton, R. (1936), *The Study of Man*, New York.

Merton, R. K. (1957), *Social Theory and Social Structure*, 2nd edn, Glencoe, Ill.

Vanneman, R. and Pampel, F. C. (1977), 'The American perceptions of class and status', *American Sociological Review*, 42.

Weber, M. (1978 [1922]), *Economy and Society, I and II*, Berkeley and Los Angeles. (Original German edn, *Wirtschaft und Gesellschaft*, Tübingen.)

Weber, M. (1946), *Max Weber; Essays in Sociology*, trans. and ed, H. Gerth and C. Wright Mills, New York.

Further Reading

Berger, J. M., Fiski, M. H., Norman, R. Z. and Zeldich, M. (1977), *Status Characteristics and Social Interaction*, New York.

Blumberg, P. (1974), 'The decline and fall of the status symbol: some thoughts on status in a post industrial society', *Social Problems*, 21.

Jackman, M. R. and Jackman, R. W. (1973), 'An interpretation of the relation between objective and subjective social status', *American Sociological Review*, 38.

Jackson, E. F. (1962), 'Status consistency and symptoms of stress', *American Sociological Review*, 27.

Wolf, C. (1978), 'Social class, status and prestige', in J. S. Roucek (ed.), *Social Control for the 1980's*, Westport, Conn.

See also: *prestige; stratification.*

Stereotypes

Stereotypes are usually defined as oversimplified, and often biased, conceptions of reality that are resistant to change. The term is primarily used with reference to conceptions of particular categories of people, conceptions that are often negative in tone and linked to prejudiced attitudes and behavioural discrimination.

The term derives from the Greek *stereos*, meaning solid, and *typos*, meaning the mark of a blow, impression, or model. A stereotype was originally a method of duplicate printing, but the word was adapted for its present usage by Walter Lippmann in his classic book, *Public Opinion* (1922). Lippmann stressed the important function of stereotypes as cognitive preconceptions that are essential for the management of a reality that would otherwise overwhelm us with its complexity.

The phenomena of stereotyping have become standard topics in sociology and social psychology. Early empirical studies (for example, Katz and Braly, 1933) stressed the degree of consensus in the stereotypes depicting different ethnic groups. Labelling theorists in sociology have emphasized the power of stereotypes in generating invidious emotional responses to deviant or minority persons. Frustration-aggression theory in psychology also stimulated interest in the dynamics of prejudice and emphasized the motivated nature of many of our stereotypes (Dollard *et al.*, 1939).

Two important developments in social psychology shortly after World War II accelerated interest in the processes of stereotyping. One was the general atmospheric interest in the role of motivation and past experience as determinants of our perceptions. A capstone of this development was a paper by J. S. Bruner (1957) linking perception to the concept of pre-established cognitive categories. Bruner explicitly stressed the assimilation of incoming information to the 'typical instance' of a category, thus providing a fruitful context for the discussion of stereotyping. Another influence was *The Authoritarian Personality* (Adorno *et al.*, 1950). This represented an attempt to illuminate some of the hidden dynamics of anti-Semitism and of more general predispositions toward the over-simplified thinking associated with Fascistic belief systems. Thus, stereotypic thinking was found to characterize high scorers on the various authoritarianism scales.

Gordon Allport's analysis of prejudice and stereotypy in 1954 began a general movement toward treating stereotypes as a consequence of normal cognitive functioning rather than looking at them as a by-product of frustration or pathological defensiveness. In this, and subsequent treatments, stereotypes have been viewed as the often unfortunate end-products of inevitable and even necessary strategies of information processing.

As the field of social psychology has become explicitly more cognitive, there has been renewed interest in stereotypes and the experiences and settings that contribute to them. Edited volumes by Hamilton (1981) and Miller (1982) summarize much of the recent research in the stereotyping area. Although it is still generally acknowledged that stereotypes may at times be motivated and serve as a justification for hostile or prejudiced attitudes, more stress is currently being placed on the contention that processes of prejudgement and categorization are built into every act of perception or information processing. Thus stereotypes are nothing more than cognitive categories that often satisfy emotional needs, prove quite resistant to disconfirming information, and operate as powerful cognitive magnets to which such information is assimilated. Though stereotypes are generally viewed as the maladaptive extreme of the cognitive processing continuum, and serve to perpetuate social conflict and discrimination, there is also much evidence that group stereotypes may be readily discarded when judging individual group members. Thus it appears that individuals are quite capable of having strong and rather rigid views of typical group members, but these views do not necessarily influence how a particular member is perceived or evaluated.

Edward E. Jones
Princeton University

References

Adorno, T. W., Frenkel-Brunswik, E., Levinson, D. J. and Sanford, R. N. (1950), *The Authoritarian Personality*, New York.

Allport, G. W. (1954), *The Nature of Prejudice*, Cambridge, Mass.

Bruner, J. S. (1957), 'On perceptual readiness', *Psychological Review*, 64.

Dollard, J., Doob, L. W., Miller, N. E., Mowrer, O. H. and Sears, R. L. (1939), *Frustration and Aggression*, New Haven.

Hamilton, D. L. (ed.) (1981), *Cognitive Processes in Stereotyping and Intergroup Behavior*, Hillsdale, N.J.

Katz, D. and Braly, K. (1933), 'Racial stereotypes in 100 college students', *Journal of Abnormal Social Psychology*, 28.

Lippmann, W. (1922), *Public Opinion*, New York.

Miller, A. G. (ed.) (1982), *In the Eye of the Beholder: Contemporary Issues in Stereotyping*, New York.

See also: *labelling theory; prejudice; stigma.*

Steuart, Sir James (later Steuart-Denham) (1713–80)

James Steuart was born in 1713, the son of Sir James Steuart, Solicitor-General, and Anne Dalrymple, daughter of the Lord President of the Court of Session. He attended the local school in North Berwick before entering Edinburgh University in 1725. Steuart was called to the Bar in 1735 although he did not formally practice as an advocate.

Steuart travelled on the Continent between 1735 and 1740. The Grand Tour took him to Holland, France, Spain and Italy – where he met a group of Jacobites. In 1745 when the Jacobite Rebellion reached Edinburgh, Steuart joined the 'Cause', serving mainly in France in a diplomatic capacity. In 1746 he was exiled, and although he returned to England in 1763 at the end of the Seven Years War, he was not pardoned until 1771. Steuart died in 1780 and was survived by his only son, later to become General Sir James Steuart, who died without issue.

In the manner of Adam Smith, Steuart began to write his major work, the *Principles of Political Economy*, during his sojourn abroad. Unlike Smith, he completed the major part of his 'system' in the isolation of Tübingen, Germany, where he had gone to escape the consequences of the European War. Although the first two books were completed in the late 1750s and the whole work published in 1767, the analysis is essentially prephysiocratic in character and largely innocent of the kind of macroeconomic system which was a feature of Quesnay's teaching.

A man of distinguished abilities, who made important contributions to specific areas of analysis (notably the theory of population), Steuart's work is marked by his extensive knowlege of conditions in a variety of countries. The *Principles* is dominated by a concern with a socioeconomic system in a state of transition, and by a concern with the consequences of a situation where different national economies have different growth rates. Both perspectives ensured that the book was largely concerned with matters of economic policy, and have given rise to the misleading claim that Steuart was mercantilist.

A. S. Skinner
Glasgow University

References

Steuart, Sir James (1767), *An Inquiry into the Principles of Political Oeconomy: Being an Essay on the Science of Domestic Policy in Free Nations*, London.

Steuart, Sir James (1805), *The Works, Political, Metaphysical, and Chronological, of the late Sir James Steuart of Coltness, Bart*, 6 Vols, London.

Further Reading

Chamley, P. (1963), *Economie politique et philosophie chez Steuart et Hegel*, Paris.

Skinner, A. S. (1981), 'Sir James Steuart, author of a system', *Scottish Journal of Political Economy*, 28.

Vickers, D. (1960), *Studies in the Theory of Money, 1690–1776*, London.

Stigler, George J. (1911–)

George Stigler, Nobel Prize laureate, the only child of immigrant parents, was born in Renton, Washington in 1911. He graduated from the University of Washington in 1931 and received his Ph.D from the University of Chicago in 1938. He taught at Iowa State University in 1936, and then at the Universities of

Minnesota, Brown and Columbia before settling at the University of Chicago in 1958.

In 1946, Stigler published an early work on linear programming. During the 1940s he began empirical work on price theory, starting with a test of the kinked oligopoly demand curve theory of rigid prices. In the 1950s he proposed a survivor method of determining efficient sizes of enterprises, and worked on delivered price systems, verticle integration, and similar topics. An early interest in the existence of dispersion of prices, as opposed to a single market price, culminated in an article 'The economics of information' (1961). During the 1960s he began the detailed study of public regulation. More recently, he has entered into the study of the extension of the economics of information to political behaviour. It was for his seminal studies of industrial structures, functioning of markets and causes and effects of public regulation that he was awarded the Nobel Prize in Economic Science in 1982.

Although a specialist in price theory, Stigler has maintained a continuing interest in the history of economics throughout his career. Indeed his interest in the subject intensified as the questions raised by the sociology of science became more prominent.

Vincent J. Tarascio
University of North Carolina, Chapel Hill

References
Stigler, G. J. (1941), *Production and Distribution Theories*, New York.
Stigler, G. J. (1961), 'The economics of information', *Journal of Political Economy*, June.

Stigma

The sociologist Erving Goffman is usually credited with introducing the term 'stigma' into the social sciences. He begins his influential essay (*Stigma: Notes on the Management of Spoiled Identity*) with a brief etymological summary.

> The Greeks . . . originated the term *stigma* to refer to bodily signs designed to expose something unusual and bad about the moral status of the signifier. The signs were cut or burnt into the body and advertised that the bearer was a slave, a criminal, or a traitor – a blemished person, ritually polluted, to be avoided, especially in public places. Today the term . . . is applied more to the disgrace itself than to the bodily influence of it. (Goffman, 1963)

The concern with stigma fits well into a broader and older concern with deviance and its labelling. The labelling perspective favoured by many sociologists of deviance (especially those who share the orientation of 'symbolic interactionism') emphasizes the social construction of boundaries separating the 'normal' from the 'deviant'. These boundaries serve an important symbolic function of affirming in-group values and are relevant in several different domains. Goffman distinguishes between blemishes of character (for example, mental illness, homosexuality, criminal behaviour), abominations of the body (physical deformities of various kinds), and the tribal stigma of race, nation and religion. Though it is important to note that stigma can emerge in each of these domains, it should also be recognized that the tendency to avoid disabled or deviant persons may stem from the awkwardness of not knowing how to act in their presence, rather than being a reflection of the drastic discredit usually associated with the term stigma.

Cutting across the content domains of potential stigma, a number of dimensions may be identified that affect the degree of discredit likely to result from the process. One such dimension is *concealability*. Those conditions that can be concealed under normal conditions give rise to decisions about 'passing', about whether or when to disclose the condition. Another dimension is *origin*: how did the condition come about and to what extent was the person responsible? People tend to attribute greater responsibility for alcoholism and obesity than for mental retardation or the paraplegia of a combat veteran. Other dimensions of variation include *aesthetic* concerns, the extent to which the condition actually or symbolically *imperils* others, and to which it may *disrupt* normal social interaction. Deafness, for example, is typically more disruptive than blindness, though particular interaction contexts may make blindness more salient as a disability.

In spite of these sources of variation and their important differential consequences, the stigmatizing process has a number of features that transcend the particularities of any single deviant condition. Associated with a crucial act of categorizing or labelling the deviant person, there is an arousal of emotions typically featuring a mixture of revulsion and sympathy. Recent discussions of stigma (Katz, 1981; Jones *et al.*, 1984) have made much of the ambivalence involved in stigma. The act of labelling often sets in motion a process of devastating cognitive reconstruction that gives innocent behavioural data an ominous, tell-tale meaning. Thus there are strong tendencies for stigmatizing reactions to move in the direction of stereotypes that rationalize or explain the negative affect involved. Many sigmatizing reactions, however, are initially characterized by vague discomfort and unjustified 'primitive' affect.

Edward E. Jones
Princeton University

References
Goffman, E. (1963), *Stigma: Notes on the Management of Spoiled Identity*, Englewood Cliffs, NJ.

Jones, E. E., Farina, A., Hastorf, A. Marcus, H., Miller, D. and Scott, R. A. (1984), *Social Stigma: The Psychology of Marked Relationships*, New York.
Katz, I. (1981), *Stigma: A Social Psychological Analysis*, Hillsdale, NJ.
See also: *deviance; labelling theory; stereotypes.*

Stochastic Models

The term stochastic comes from the Greek word *stochos*, meaning a target and suggesting uncertainty. Stochastic models are often used to describe mathematical models with one or more components that depend upon some random variable, that is, a *nondeterministic* or *probabilistic* model.

Deterministic models have a long history in the physical sciences going back at least to Kepler and Newton, and for a long time scientists believed that all natural phenomena should and could be described in terms of deterministic models. The pioneering work of Mendel in genetics, and of various physicists in statistical mechanics, have made the use of probabilistic models commonplace.

In the sense described above, stochastic models include all models used in the statistical analysis of data. In a more restricted sense, stochastic modelling is usually associated with the *theory of stochastic processes*, and is used to describe the probabilistic behaviour of processes evolving or developing in time and/or space. The use of stochastic modelling in the behavioural and social sciences has grown in recent years, and the following applications of general classes of stochastic process models are noteworthy:

Random walk: the movement of stock market prices.
Markov chains: learning models in psychology, social mobility; voting behaviour.
Branching processes: the extinction of family names.
Birth and death processes: the diffusion of news and numbers; demographic models for population growth.
Continuous-time Markov processes: occupational mobility; the study of graded social systems.

An introduction to these and other social science uses of stochastic models can be found in Bartholomew (1982).

Stephen E. Fienberg
Carnegie–Mellon University, Pittsburgh

Reference
Bartholomew, D. J. (1982), *Stochastic Models for Social Processes*, 3rd edn, New York.

Stock-Flow Analysis

Economic variables can be classified into two basic forms: flow variables (such as income), and stock variables (such as wealth). Other variables may be formed as a ratio between flows (such as the proportion of income saved), a ratio between stocks (such as proportion of wealth held as liquid assets), or a ratio between a flow and a stock (such as the ratio between capital and output). Clarity in economic analysis requires that a clear distinction between flows and stocks be maintained at all times. A flow should always have attached to it the relevant time period *during* which the flow occurs (to say that a person's income is $500 is meaningless until one adds 'per week' or 'per month' or whatever the relevant period). For precision, a stock variable should always have attached to it the date at which the stock existed or was valued. A change between a stock at one date and the stock at a later date will be a flow during the period covered by the dates (see Fisher, 1906).

Stock-flow analysis is concerned with the relationship between stock variables and flow variables: there are two basic branches. The first branch comprises causal stock-adjustment models in which a flow is causally related to changes in a 'desired' or 'equilibrium' stock. The second branch is concerned with valuation models in which a stream of future flows is discounted and summed to a present-value stock equivalent.

An important feature of stock-adjustment models is that adjustment to change may be spread over several time periods, so giving rise to lags, distributed variously over those time periods, in the impact on flows. Hence the analysis of distributed lags tends to be a feature of stock-adjustment models.

Examples of stock-adjustment models are, in macroeconomics, the accelerator principle in which the aggregate flow of fixed-capital formation is related to changes in the 'desired' stock of fixed capital, and, in microeconomics, the relationship of the flow of demand for new cars to the pre-existing stock of cars (partly because of replacement demand). Bringing stocks into the analysis of flows has proved a powerful explanatory device and has served greatly to elucidate the variance in flows. For example, it is likely that a full understanding of personal sector savings flows (particularly in conditions of inflation) will require more information on personal sector stocks of financial assets, and for this we will have to await the regular compilation of national and sectoral balance sheets to complement the national income flow accounts.

Valuation models, based on the operation of discounting, are a form of stock-flow analysis in which a stream of future flows is rendered into a stock-equivalent at the present date. In this way, a series of flows (or entitlement thereto) may be given a single valuation or 'price'. Accordingly, discounting is a common technique of financial analysis.

Dudley Jackson
University of Wollongong, Australia

Reference
Fisher, I. (1906), *The Nature of Capital and Income*, New York.
See also: *capital consumption*.

Stockholm School

The Stockholm School – known also as the Swedish School – refers to a group of Swedish economists who were active in the late 1920s and the 1930s. Its members were Dag Hammarskjöld, Alf Johansson, Erik Lindahl, Erik Lundberg, Gunnar Myrdal, Bertil Ohlin and Ingvar Svennilsson. Their interests centred on macroeconomic theory and its application to economic policy. (Although they did not all work in the same university, they were nevertheless a 'School' in that they all influenced one another in these two areas of economic science.) They were themselves influenced by the older generation of Swedish economists, in particular, Knut Wicksell and Gustav Cassel, who developed the cumulative process.

The School's origins can be traced back to exploration of the economists into dynamic methods and its application of macroeconomics. Dynamic method developed in four separate stages, the first of which was Myrdal's dissertation (1927) which used the concept of long-run equilibrium where anticipations had been included as a datum. The next two stages were marked by Lindahl's notion of intertemporal equilibrium (1929) and temporary equilibrium (Lindahl, 1939). The final stage represented a protracted evolution from Lindahl's temporary equilibrium to Lundberg's disequilibrium-sequence analysis (Lundberg, 1937).

The ideas of the Stockholm School concerning fiscal policy were similar to those of Keynes as contained in his *General Theory*. However, the Swedes did not develop Keynes's principle of effective demand where savings and investment are made equal via quantity changes. While the ideas of the School were still prevalent in the 1940s and 1950s, they were by this time heavily mixed with other ideas that were current at the time.

Björn Hansson
University of Lund

References
Lindahl, E. (1939), *Studies in the Theory of Money and Capital*, London.
Lundberg, E. (1937), *Studies in the Theory of Economic Expansion*, London.
Myrdal, G. (1927), *Prisbildningsproblemet och föränderligheten* (Price Formation and Economic Change), Stockholm.

Further Reading
Hansson, B. A. (1982), *The Stockholm School and the Development of Dynamic Method*, London.

Myrdal, G. (1939), *Monetary Equilibrium*, London.
Ohlin, B. (1978), 'On the formulation of monetary theory', *History of Political Economy*, 10 (Swedish original, 1933).
See also: *Myrdal; Ohlin; Wicksell*.

Stratification

Social stratification refers to the division of people into layers or strata which may be thought of as being vertically arranged, in the same way that layers of the earth are arranged above or below other layers. Although the geological metaphor which sociologists use draws attention to a striking feature of many, if not most, societies, there are limits beyond which its use becomes misleading. The arrangement of persons in a society is enormously more complex than the arrangement of the layers of the earth; and social strata are not visible to the naked eye in the way that geological strata are.

When we talk of social stratification we draw attention to the unequal positions occupied by individuals in society. Sometimes the term is used very broadly to refer to every kind of inequality, although it may be useful to restrict it to inequalities between groups or categories of persons with a definite or at least a recognizable identity. Thus we speak of stratification between manual and nonmanual workers or between Blacks and Whites, but not usually of stratification between the members of a family. The implication of this is that one may reasonably describe such simple societies as of the Andaman Islanders or the !Kung Bushmen as being unstratified although there certainly are inequalities in these societies.

There is disagreement as to whether stratification is a universal feature of all human societies (Bendix and Lipset, 1967). While some of this disagreement may be traced to divergent uses of the same terms there are also genuine differences in point of view. The so-called functional theory of stratification maintains that stratification in the broad sense is not only universally present but that it performs a definite social function. Others maintain that just as there have been societies in the past where stratification in the strict sense was absent or rudimentary, so also there can be societies in the future where it will be absent or inconsequential. It is not easy to see how societies which are at present stratified will cease to be stratified in the future or to prove that stratification has a determinate social function because it is present everywhere, or nearly everywhere.

The geological metaphor of stratification tends to obscure the fact that in a given society the same individuals may be differently ranked depending upon the criteria selected. Every society uses more than one criterion of ranking, and different societies do not give prominence to the same criteria. It requires much skill and judgement to identify the significant criteria in each case and to determine their degree of consistency. While some scholars stress the consistency between the different dimensions of stratification or even the determining role of one or another among them, others argue that, though related, these dimensions are mutually irreducible (Béteille, 1977).

The economic aspect or dimension of stratification is important in all societies and manifestly so in modern societies. But we see how complex the problem is as soon as we try to specify the nature of the economic dimension, for it may refer to either wealth or income or occupation which, although closely related, are not one and the same. Wealth and income are relatively easy to measure, but, since their distribution is continuous, there is no easy way to draw lines between people on the basis of how much of the one or the other they have. Moreover, what matters is not simply how much wealth or income people have but also how it is acquired and how it is used.

In past societies, wealth in some forms such as land was valued more than wealth in other forms such as money, and inherited wealth more than wealth acquired by trade or commerce. Capitalism reduces the significance of such distinctions but does not eliminate them altogether. And while the accumulation and transmission of wealth might be severely restricted in socialist societies, disparities of income are important there as well.

All industrial societies, whether of the capitalist or the socialist type, show a certain family resemblance in their occupational structure: (1) The occupational role acquires far greater salience in these societies than in all other societies known to history. As the separation of the occupational from the domestic domain becomes more complete, more and more people come to have definite occupations, and their social identity comes increasingly to be defined in terms of these. Much of a man's adult life is spent in the pursuit of his occupation in a factory or an office, and his early life is largely a preparation for it. (2) The occupational structure itself becomes more differentiated and more complex.

While all occupations may in some sense be equally useful, they are not all equally esteemed by members of society. The commonsensical view of this, at least in capitalist societies, is that occupations are differentially esteemed because they are unequally paid; but this leaves unexplained why some occupations are better paid than others. The ranking of occupations is in fact a very complex phenomenon, being governed partly by considerations of scarcity and partly by the values distinctive to the society concerned (Bendix and Lipset, 1967; Goldthorpe and Hope, 1974). In all modern societies occupational ranking is complicated by the variability of values among sections of the same society and by the rapid replacement of old occupations by new ones.

While there obviously is some correspondence between the esteem enjoyed by an occupation and the income it provides, this correspondence is not perfect (Cole, 1955). This is partly due to the changes continuously taking place in the modern world among the various occupations in regard to both income and esteem. But there may be other, more fundamental, reasons behind the lack of perfect correspondence. Disparities of income between manual and nonmanual occupations have been greatly reduced in most industrial societies, but manual occupations continue to be less esteemed than nonmanual ones, sometimes even when they are better paid. This is true not only of capitalist but also of socialist societies, despite the bias for the manual worker in socialist ideology.

Occupation is closely linked with education in all industrial societies but probably more so in socialist than in capitalist ones (Cole, 1955; Wesolowski, 1979). Obviously, education is valued because it provides access to well-paid occupations but it is valued for other reasons as well. Education gives people access to knowledge and to the inner meaning of life both within and outside their own occupational sphere; all of this is valued for its own sake and not merely for the financial returns it provides.

Education, occupation and income enter as important ingredients in the styles of life adopted by men and women. Social stratification manifests itself typically through differences in styles of life among members of the same society (Heller, 1969; Bottomore, 1965). Such differences relate to both the material and the nonmaterial sides of life and may manifest themselves in gross or subtle ways. Habitation, dress and food all indicate differences in styles of life and, as is well known, language divides people no less than it unites them. Groups differentiated by their styles of life, particularly when they are ranked among themselves, are generally referred to as status groups.

Popular usage does not distinguish systematically between classes and status groups, but it is useful to do so. According to a famous distinction, a class is defined by its position in the system of production, whereas what characterizes a status group is its pattern of consumption (Weber, 1978). A class is conceived of as being a somewhat larger aggregate than a status group, and classes acquire their identity in opposition to each other in the political arena. Whereas the relations between classes are typically relations of conflict, the relations between status groups are relations of emulation. Emulation by inferiors of the styles of life of their superiors provides stability to the prevailing system of stratification.

Income, occupation and education are not the only things that count in regard to status or style of life even in modern societies. Race and ethnicity have independent significance in regard to both. Although differences of race are biological in origin, how much they count in stratification depends on the value assigned to these differences in the society in question. The very existence of sharp differences of race as in South Africa and, to some extent, the United States indicates the restriction by law or custom of intermarriage between members of different races. Such restriction is usually, if not invariably, associated with feelings of superiority and inferiority between the races concerned.

Endogamy as either a rule or a tendency is perhaps the most effective mechanism for maintaining the boundaries between social strata (Ghurye, 1969; Weber, 1958). On the whole it is more strictly practised between groups based on race, caste and ethnicity than between those that are defined solely in terms of income, occupation and education. Where boundaries are strictly maintained between racial or ethnic groups through endogamy, through residential segregation and in other ways, access to higher education and employment tends to be more difficult for members of some than of other groups. In such cases 'equality of opportunity' can do very little to prevent the reproduction of the existing system of stratification.

Stratification by race is seen in its clearest and most extreme form in South Africa. There the segregation of races is not only a widespread social practice; it is also accepted as a basic social principle. Segregation or apartheid – literally meaning 'apartness' – is the official norm of South African society, and it seeks to regulate every sphere of social life from marriage to politics. The roots of apartheid, as of a great deal of stratification by race, go back to the experience of colonial rule. In South Africa what we see today is the unequal relationship between a settler and an indigenous population imposed by the former on the latter and perpetuated through the principle and practice of segregation.

Power plays a part in the maintenance and reproduction of social stratification everywhere (Dahrendorf, 1968; Béteille, 1977). First, there is the use of the apparatus of state for enforcing the privileges and disabilities of superior and inferior strata, as in South Africa. But violence may also be used for the same end outside the framework of the state as in the case of lynching, whether of Blacks by Whites in the United States or of untouchables by 'caste Hindus' in India. Whereas power is important everywhere in upholding the existing order, the extent to which force is openly used to the advantage of superior against inferior strata varies. The naked use of force becomes common where agreement breaks down in a society about the ranks to be occupied by its different members.

Race is often compared with caste, since both forms of stratification are marked by great rigidity. Indeed, the term caste has become a synonym for rigid social stratification. The caste system was found in its most characteristic form in traditional India among the Hindus, although divisions of a broadly similar kind were found also among other religious groups in India as well as in other South-Asian countries. Until recently the divisions of caste were very elaborate among the Hindus, and they were kept in place by a variety of rules and restrictions. Each caste or subcaste had in the course of time developed its own style of life through which it maintained its social identity, and Max Weber thought that castes were best characterized as status groups.

Many changes are taking place in the caste system. The division into castes in contemporary India – like the division into races in the United States – coexists with many other divisions and inequalities whose roots lie elsewhere. An important aspect of the traditional order of Indian society was that inequalities between people not only existed in fact but were accepted as a part of the natural scheme of things. To a large extent this was true also of medieval Europe where the hierarchical conception of society was supported by both law and religion. Today things have changed considerably, and in most societies inequality or stratification exists within a legal and moral environment in which equality is the dominant value. This means that stratification in most contemporary societies is far more amorphous and fluid than the division of past societies into orders or estates or castes whose hierarchy was recognized and acknowledged by most, if not all, members of society.

André Béteille
University of Delhi

References

Bendix, R. and Lipset, S. M. (eds) (1967), *Class, Status and Power: Social Stratification in Comparative Perspective*, London.

Béteille, A. (1977), *Inequality Among Men*, Oxford.

Bottomore, T. B. (1965), *Classes in Modern Society*, London.

Cole, G. D. H. (1955), *Studies in Class Structure*, London.

Dahrendorf, R. (1968), 'On the origin of inequality among men', in R. Dahrendorf, *Essays in the Theory of Society*, London.

Ghurye, G. S. (1969), *Class, Caste and Occupation*, Bombay.

Goldthorpe, J. H. and Hope, K. (1974), *The Social Grading of Occupations: A New Approach and Scale*, Oxford.

Heller, C. S. (ed.) (1969), *Structured Social Inequality: A Reader in Comparative Social Stratification*, London.

Weber, M. (1958 [1920]), *The Religion of India*, New York. (Original German edn, section of *Gesammelte Aufsätze zur Religionssoziologie*.)

Weber, M. (1978 [1922]), *Economy and Society*, 2 vols, Berkeley and Los Angeles. (Original German edn, *Wirtschaft und Gesellschaft*, Tübingen.)

Wesolowski, W. (1979), *Classes, Strata and Power*, London.

Further Reading

Jencks, C. *et al.* (1972), *Inequality*, New York.

Marshall, T. H. (1977), *Class, Citizenship and Development*, Chicago.

See also: *caste; class, social; equality; ethnic groups; hierarchy; social mobility; status.*

Stress

The breadth of the topic of stress is reflected both in the diversity of fields of research with which it is associated and in the difficulty of finding an adequate definition. Some stresses such as noise, heat or pain might best be considered as properties of the environment which represent departure from optimum and which differ only in intensity from levels which are normally tolerable. Thus, stress could be seen as a stimulus characteristic, perhaps best defined as an 'intense level of everyday life'. In contrast, it is possible to envisage stress as a pattern of responses associated with autonomic arousal. Initial impetus for this approach was provided by Selye (1956), who proposed that stress is the nonspecific response of the body to any demand made upon it. Physiologically committed, it assumed that the stress response was not influenced by the nature of the stressful event, but was part of a universal pattern of defence termed the 'General Adaptation Syndrome'. Selye demonstrated a temporal pattern in cases of prolonged stress. There were three identifiable phases: alarm, resistance and exhaustion. The capacity of the organism to survive was assumed to be a function of exposure time; resistance to further stress was lowered in the alarm phase, raised in the subsequent resistance phase and further lowered in the exhaustion phase.

Neither stimulus-based nor response-based definitions cope well with varied and complex stresses such as taking an examination, parachute jumping, surgical operations and public speaking. The problem that 'one man's stress is another man's challenge', is partly solved by a definition which presupposes that stress is the result of imbalance between demand and capacity, and, more importantly, by the *perception* that there is imbalance. The factors which create ambition and translate into intentions are as important in determining stress levels as those which affect capacity.

A number of models have been proposed which assume that the conditions for stress are met when demands tax or exceed adjustive resources (Lazarus, 1966, 1976; Cox and Mackay, 1978). In particular, Lazarus has proposed that several appraisal processes are involved in the assessment of threat. The intensity of threat depends on stimulus features, but also on the perceived ability to cope. In turn, coping may take the form of direct action or avoidance and may involve anticipatory preparation against harm, or the use of cognitive defence strategies.

Fisher (1984) has proposed that mental activity in the perception and response to stress forms the essential basis of worry and preoccupation, and is likely to be concerned with the assessment and establishment of control. The perception of personal control is not only a likely determinant of psychological response, but has been shown to determine hormone pattern. For example, applied and laboratory studies have suggested that control over the work pace dictates the pattern of noradrenaline and adrenaline balance, and may determine the degree of experienced anxiety.

Working conditions and events in life history together form an important source of potential stress and may have a pervasive influence on mental state and physical health in the long term. Stress at work is no longer thought to be the prerogative of white-collar and professional workers. Repetitive manual work is associated with high adrenaline levels; paced assembly line workers have been found to be very anxious, and computer operators who spend more than 90 per cent of their time working at the interface may be tense for 'unwind periods' after work. Depression is likely when personal discretion is reduced, when there is lack of social support, or when social communication is impaired, as in conditions of high machine noise.

A significant additional feature of life history is the adjustment required by change. Two important consequences of change are interruption of previously established activity and the introduction of uncertainty about future control. Studies of homesickness in university students have suggested the importance of worry and preoccupation as features of adjustment to change. Grieving for the previous life style is as much a feature as concern about the new, and in some individuals this may be an important prerequisite for the establishment of control (Fisher, 1984; Fisher *et al.*, 1985).

Competence is a necessary condition of the exercise of personal control, but it may be difficult to maintain in stressful circumstance. Studies of the effects of environmental stress on attention and memory have indicated changes in function in relatively mild conditions of stress. Although the changes may not always be detrimental in mildly stressful conditions, at high levels of stress, behavioural disorganization and consequent loss of control are characteristic. It has been found that performance is related to arousal level in the form of an inverted 'U' curve. Mild stresses, by increasing arousal, are likely to improve performance, whereas severe stresses are more likely to cause deterioration. However, the assumption of a single dimension of arousal has been undermined by physiological evidence suggesting that there are arousal patterns which may be stimulus or response specific. The concept of compatibility between concurrent and stress-produced arousal levels is proposed by Fisher (1984) as part of a composite model of the relationship between stress and performance. The model also takes into account the influence of worry and mental preoccupation associated with stress and the establishment of control as joint determinants of performance change.

In both occupational and life-stress conditions, the pattern of behaviour – and hence the accompanying hormone balance which features in a particular stress problem – may result from decision making about control. A critical decision concerns whether a person is helpless or able to exercise control. The mental processes involved in control assessment may involve detecting and summarizing the relationship between actions and consequences over a period of time. In dogs, prior treatment by inescapable shock was shown to produce inappropriate helplessness in later avoidance learning (Seligman, 1975), which led to the hypothesis that depression and helplessness are closely associated, and may be transmitted as expectancies about loss of control. The question 'Why are we not all helpless?' is appropriate, given the high probability that most people experience helplessness on occasions in their lives; it has been partly answered by research which suggests that normal subjects resist helplessness and depression by overestimating control when rewards are forthcoming (Alloy and Abramson, 1979). Equally, they may put more effort into a task, or find other evidence suggesting that control is possible, thus raising self-esteem (Fisher, 1984). By contrast, those already depressed assess control levels accurately, but are more likely to blame themselves for circumstances which indicate that there is no control. Therefore, lack of optimistic bias and lack of objectivity in attributing the cause of failure distinguishes the depressed from the non-depressed person.

The above considerations suggest that analysis of decisions about control in different stressful circumstances may provide the key to understanding the risks attached to long-term health changes in an individual. A person who is too readily helpless may be depressed and may incur the punishment produced by control failure. He thus experiences distress. A person who struggles against the odds of success incurs the penalty of high effort. A person who practises control by avoidance may need to be constantly vigilant, and to evolve elaborate techniques for avoidance and, if successful, will never receive the information which indicates control is effective.

The outcome of decision making about control could have implications for physical health because of the mediating role of stress hormones. Repeated high levels of catecholamines may, because of functional abuse of

physical systems, increase the risk of chronic illness such as heart disease. High levels of corticoid hormones may change the levels of antibody response, thus changing the risk associated with virus and bacterial born illness, as well as diseases such as cancer (Totman, 1979; Cox and Mackay, 1982).

S. Fisher
University of Dundee

References

Alloy, L. B. and Abramson, L. Y. (1979), 'Judgements of contingency in depressed or non-depressed students: sadder but wiser?', *Journal of Experimental Psychology (General)*, 108.

Cox, T. and Mackay, C. (1982), 'Psychosocial factors and psychophysiological mechanisms in the aetiology and development of cancers', *Society of Science and Medicine*, 16.

Fisher, S. A. (1984), *Stress and the Perception of Control*, Hillsdale, NJ.

Fisher, S., Murray, K. and Frazer, N. (1985), 'Homesickness, health and efficiency in first year students', *Journal of Environmental Psychology*, 5.

Lazarus, R. (1966), *Psychological Stress and the Coping Process*, New York.

Lazarus, R. (1976), *Patterns of Adjustment*, Tokyo.

Seligman, M. E. P. (1975), *Helplessness: On Depression Development and Death*, San Francisco.

Selye, H. (1956), *The Stress of Life*, New York.

Totman, R. (1979), *The Social Causes of Illness*, London.

See also: *activation and arousal*; *bereavement*; *pain*; *psychosomatic illness*; *separation and loss*.

Structural-Functionalism

See Functional Analysis, Parsons, Social Structure.

Structuralism

Since the 1940s the term structuralism has become generally used for a certain approach (not a school or dogma), particularly in linguistics, social anthropology and psychology. Although there is some difference between the way it is applied in these disciplines, and between American and European usage, it generally refers to types of research in which the object of investigation is studied as a system. Because a 'system' is a 'set of connected things or parts' (Oxford English Dictionary), this entails concentration on the relations between the elements which constitute the system; in the words of Dumont (1970):

We shall speak of structure exclusively . . . when the interdependence of the elements of a system is so great that they disappear without residue if an inventory is made of the relations between them: a system of relations, in short, not a system of elements.

Ferdinand de Saussure (1931), who is generally regarded as the founder of structural linguistics, makes a basic distinction between the study of language as *parole* (speech, that is, language as produced by a speaking individual) and of language as *langue*: as a system. The *system* is essential, while *parole* is 'contingent and more or less fortuitous'.

The structuralist emphasis on the relations between the elements in a system appears, for example, in Saussure's discussion of the 'value' (*valeur*) of words:

the value of words in a language which express similar ideas limit each other's scope. The value of synonyms, like 'to fear', 'to dread', 'to be afraid of' is entirely determined by their mutual opposition. If 'to dread' did not exist, its meaning would be adopted by its neighbours.

The field most developed by later linguists is structural phonetics, usually termed phonology in Europe and phonemics in the US. The aim of phonetics, as a *parole* discipline, is to give the most accurate description of speech sounds; phonology, on the *langue* level, is concerned with the question of which speech sounds function as phonemes, in other words, the smallest units which differentiate between the meanings of words. That is to say, it is not the phonologist's concern whether there is a phonetic difference between the English -p- sounds in *pin*, *prone*, *up*, etc. It is his concern that the opposition between -p- and -b-, -d-, -f- and so on makes for the distinction between words with different meanings such as *pin* and *bin*, *pin* and *din*, *pin* and *fin*, and so on, that is, that the -p- in English is a phoneme.

Roman Jakobson (1971) developed a means to specify what distinguishes each phoneme, that is, what are any phoneme's 'distinctive features': 'The inherent distinctive features which have so far been discovered in the languages of the world ... amount to twelve basic oppositions, out of which each language makes its own selection' (Jakobson and Halle, 1971). These basic oppositions are, for example, vocalic versus nonvocalic, abrupt versus continuant, voiced versus voiceless, and so on. This approach is typically structural, as it defines phonemes, as the elements in a system, by considering what distinguishes each element from the others, that is to say, by concentrating on the relations between the elements. The relations, in this case, are of the most elementary type: binary oppositions. It is not surprising that this linguistic method made an impression on the structural anthropologist Lévi-Strauss. Another aspect of the distinctive feature analysis affected Lévi-Strauss more than any other anthropologist, namely its universal applicability: it refers, as we saw, to '*the* languages of the world'.

Two other concepts which anthropology owes to structural linguistics are 'syntagmatic' and 'paradigmatic relations'. Elements in a language, for example, words in a sentence which are arranged in a certain sequence, form a syntagmatic chain. A paradigmatic (or, in Saussure's now obsolete terminology, 'associative') set comprises elements, for example, words, which are equivalent in one or more respects. For example, 'impardonable, intolerable, indefatigable ...' and 'teach, teacher, taught ...' are two paradigmatic sets (de Saussure, 1931). These concepts have been applied, again particularly by Lévi-Strauss, in the analysis of myths. The events narrated in any single myth form a syntagmatic chain, while the personages and events occurring in a myth, or a corpus of myths, can be studied as members of paradigmatic sets.

It is not unlikely that Saussure was familiar with the works of Emile Durkheim, which were very influential in his time. Durkheim can be considered as one of the founding fathers of modern sociology, but structural anthropology can also trace back its origins to him, his collaborators, united around the journal *Année Sociologique*, and his pupil and successor Marcel Mauss. The work of this school can be exemplified by Durkheim and Mauss's joint publication 'De quelques formes primitives de la classification' (1903). The opening sentences of this long article are typical.

Contemporary psychology has shown how very complex apparently simple mental operations really are, but 'this operation ... has been only very rarely applied as yet to operations which are properly speaking logical'. The authors then demonstrate such logical operations in several non-Western societies by describing systems of territorial classification:

In totemic societies it is a general rule that the tribe's constituent groups, namely moieties, clans, subclans, arrange the territorial sectors which each of them occupies in accordance with their mutual social relationships and the resemblances and differences between their social functions. (Durkheim and Mauss, 1903)

For example, when the entire Wotjoballuk tribe of New South Wales is (temporarily) united in one territory, one of the tribe's moieties must always occupy the northern, the other moiety the southern area. The two clans with the sun as their totem occupy the eastern portion of the settlement, and so on.

It was particularly this work from the French school which served as an inspiration and an example to (amateur, and later professional) anthropologists in what was to become the other consistently active centre of structural anthropology, the Netherlands. Their earlier (roughly pre-1950) works, usually based on data from Indonesia, give clear evidence of their origin. They are concerned with orderliness or system as it appears in the deeds, words and works of the members of the investigated societies – this is common to all structural anthropology. But the earlier Dutch writers, like their *Année Sociologique* exemplars, concentrated on 'ordering' rather than on 'order'; on structures of which the social participants are aware, and which they deliberately construct. In addition, the nineteenth- and early twentieth-century structuralists in both countries shared the idea that social structure serves as the model for all other classification systems. From the study of territorial classification, Dutch structural research fanned out, as it were, to the structural principles, particularly binary oppositions, in Javanese material culture, traditional theatre, and mythology. In the 1930s, however, kinship and marriage systems became the focus of interest. A major discovery was the frequent occurrence of 'asymmetric connubium', a system whereby marriages between individuals are so arranged that they conform to a regular connubial relationship between groups (clans or clan segments): one group always acts as 'bride-giver' to a second, while this 'bride-receiving' group gives women in marriage to the males of a third group (de Josselin de Jong (ed.), 1977). This brings us to more recent times, and back to France.

Claude Lévi-Strauss is the foremost exponent of structural anthropology. His first major work (1949) might be called a rediscovery of asymmetric connubium (which he terms *échange généralisé*), but he places it in a much wider and richer context: ethnographically, by using material from Siberia, China, India, South East Asia and Australia, and above all theoretically, by making the *échange* system shed light on the concepts of incest and exogamy, and on the opposition, which is to be fundamental in all his subsequent work, between nature and culture.

'In language there are only differences' (de Saussure, 1931); Lévi-Strauss applied this typically structural viewpoint in his book on totemism (1962). Totemism does not associate each clan with one animal species as its totemic ancestor, but consists of a classification of the animal world, based on the 'distinctive features' of each species, and a classification of clans on the same basis. When the two classification systems are associated with each other, the result is totemism, in which 'it is the differences which are similar' (1962). Lévi-Strauss's study of a set of cultural phenomena as a system of variations has its climax in the four volumes of *Mythologiques* (1964–71).

Myths are the purest manifestation of *la pensée sauvage* (1966 [1962]): thought which, in contrast to 'domesticated thought' does not aim at practical results, but tries to solve problems as an end in itself. The problems dealt with in the 813 myths of South and North American Indians analysed in *Mythologiques* are, principally: Why do we humans prepare our food, and animals not? Why can we take off our clothing and ornaments, and barter them with foreign groups, while the animals

can not? How did this come about? In other words, the problem of culture versus nature.

In analysing myths, a basic precept for the investigator is to avoid 'mythemology', that is, the interpretation of each single mythical personage or event in isolation (the heroine 'stands for' fertility, travelling by boat 'stands for' long life, and so on). Here again, it is not the elements, but the relations between the elements that is essential (for example: the lizard, as a land animal, stands in opposition to the aquatic crocodile; hence they are also in opposite relationships to the human hero: the hero of Myth 1 chases lizards, the hero of Myth 124 is chased by a crocodile).

By the same token, a myth can never be understood in isolation, but should be studied in its relation to other myths. All the American Indian myths studied in the book are to be considered as variant versions of each other, linked together by 'transformations'. That is to say one does not compare myths when, and because, they are similar, but because of their differences: the myth corpus, like a language, is a system of differences – sometimes even of perfect oppositions.

Lévi-Strauss uses the same method in his most recent book, *La voie des masques* (1975). A certain type of mask used by the Salish Indians of British Columbia is his starting point for a study of comparable masks in the same region: comparable, not on the grounds of similarity, but of systematic 'transformations'. Part II of the book discusses the *Dzonokwa*, a type of mask which is the opposite of the Salish mask in every respect: in form and colour, in its ritual function and performance, in the myths about its origin, and in the way it is obtained and inherited. By introducing the concept of transformation, Lévi-Strauss has added a new dimension to comparative studies in general, and revivified comparative anthropology. Also in contrast to the earlier French and Dutch structuralists, he does not confine his research to structures of which the cultural participants are aware. On the contrary, his frequent references to the *'structure inconsciente de l'esprit humain'* indicate his particular interest in not only unconscious structures, but also in basic structuring principles which are not culture-specific, but (probably) of universal occurrence.

Outside anthropological circles there is a tendency to equate structural anthropology with Lévi-Strauss; this is a popular misconception. It is striking that, while Lévi-Strauss has a tendency (stronger in some works than in others) to study the products of the 'unconscious structure of the human mind' as closed systems, the aim of many of his French congeners is to link the conceptual structures more closely to social problems. Georges Balandier demonstrates that three binary oppositions (male-female, elder-younger, superior-inferior) are frequently the basis of conflicts. Roger Bastide applies the insights of structural anthropology to the problems in developing countries. Louis

Dumont demonstrates the fundamental difference between inequality and hierarchy: the latter is exemplified by India, for 'the caste system is above all a system of ideas and values, a formal, comprehensible, rational system' (1970). Maurice Godelier remedies structuralism's neglect of economic factors, and thereby achieves a synthesis between structuralist and Marxist anthropology. Although Roland Barthes can also be mentioned in this context, as he studies the effect of 'mythologies' on modern Western societies, his principal achievement is his comparison between myth-as-language and natural language, thus making good use of the old association between structural linguistics and anthropology. Georges Condominas also closes a circuit, by directing the research of his active Centre for South-East Asian Studies to the topic of *l'espace social*, that is, territorial classification.

Among British anthropologists there are several whose works are typically structural, although they might not call themselves structuralists. In view of the British tradition of *social* anthropology, it is not surprising that the tendency, just discussed in connection with the French group, also appears in British structuralist publications, be it in a different form.

Rodney Needham's works on matrilateral cross-cousin alliance started from a position very close to Lévi-Strauss's *Les Structures élémentaires de la parenté*, but diverged sharply with the introduction of the concepts of prescriptive and preferential alliance. E. R. Leach's position has moved in the opposite direction: sharply critical of the *Structures* (which he called a 'splendid failure'), he came to be more and more in sympathy with Lévi-Strauss's views in his later publications on myths and belief systems. While one of Mary Douglas's best-known books (1966) could be called 'Lévi-Straussian', the social context (in the form of the pressure exerted on an individual by his 'group' and the society's 'grid') plays a dominant role in a later work (1970). Victor Turner's principal works are concerned with ritual. Lévi-Strauss has only very seldom dealt with this subject, perhaps because rituals, by their very nature, have also to be studied as socially operative. Turner devotes great attention to this aspect, for example, in the case of 'rituals of affliction'.

Of structuralists outside linguistics and anthropology, the most prominent are the psychologist Jean Piaget, the historian Fernand Braudel and other members of the *Annales* group. As a structuralist, Piaget is noted for his emphasis on self-regulation as a characteristic of structures. Braudel is very close to Lévi-Strauss when he recognizes 'structures' as one of the three types of history, history '*de langue durée*', of which the participants in the events are not conscious.

P. E. de Josselin de Jong
University of Leiden

References
Douglas, M. (1966), *Purity and Danger*, London.
Douglas, M. (1970), *Natural Symbols*, London.
Dumont, L. (1970 [1966]), *Homo Hierarchicus*, London. (Original French edn, *Homo Hierarchicus*, Paris.)
Durkheim, E. and Mauss, M. (1963 [1903]), *Primitive Classification*, London. (Original French edn, 'De quelques formes primitives de la classification', Paris.)
Jakobson, R. and Halle, M. (1971), *Fundamentals of Language*, The Hague.
Josselin de Jong, P. E. de (ed.) (1977), *Structural Anthropology in the Netherlands*, The Hague.
Lévi-Strauss, C. (1969 [1949]), *The Elementary Structures of Kinship*, London. (Original French edn, *Les structures élémentaires de la parenté*, Paris.)
Lévi-Strauss, (1962 [1962]), *Totemism*, London. (Original French edn, *Le totémisme aujourd'hui*, Paris.)
Le'vi-Strauss, C. (1966 [1962]), *The Savage Mind*, London. (Original French edn, *La pensée sauvage*, Paris.)
Lévi-Strauss, C. (1970–9 [1964–72]), *Introduction to a Science of Mythology*, London. (Original French edn, *Mythologiques*, 4 vols, Paris.)
Lévi-Strauss, C. (1975), *La voie des masques*, Geneva.
Saussure, F. de (1931 [1916]), *Cours de linguistique générale*, Paris.
See also: *Barthes; Braudel; Jakobson; Lacan; Lévi-Strauss; Saussure; semiotics*.

Structural Linguistics

Structural linguistics, the study of languages through observation and description of their basic units and the relationships of same, may be said to have begun with the great Sanskrit grammar of Panini (ca. 300 B.C.). This work was not known in the West until the end of the eighteenth century. The foundations of modern structural linguistics were laid in the later nineteenth century by Jan Baudouin de Courtenay, a Pole teaching in the Russian University of Kazan, and Ferdinand de Saussure, a Swiss. Baudouin, working closely with his Polish graduate student (and successor in the Kazan chair), Mikolaj Kruszewski, approached the notion of a system of basic units of sound (phonology) and form (morphology) which derive their informative power from the fact of their opposition (or contrast) to each other. It was at Kazan that the terms *phoneme* and *morpheme* were first used in approximately their present sense. Saussure, whose work was known in Kazan, was working along the same lines, and he, who knew no Russian or Polish, was acquainted with the Kazan ideas through German translations of two works by Kruszewski. Kruszewski died early and Saussure's lectures were published only after his death by devoted students. Since Baudouin de Courtenay, because of his concern for social and psychological factors in language use, came to define phonological and morphemic units as, at least in part, mental constructs, he lost touch with the main body of structuralists, who were led by Edward Sapir and Leonard Bloomfield in the US and by N. S. Trubetzkoy, Roman Jakobson and L. V. Shcherba in Europe. Shcherba remained in the Soviet Union, while Trubetzkoy (from Vienna) and Jakobson helped to found the Prague Circle, where structural linguistics was stretched to include 'structural' studies of literature. An offshoot of the Prague Group was the Copenhagen Circle, of which the leading figures were Louis Hjelmslev and Hans Uldall.

A major difference between the formulations of the Prague School (as exemplified in the work of Jakobson) and the New-World structuralists is the definition of the basic units of phonology (phonemes) as *bundles of distinctive features* by the former, and as *classes of sounds and phones* by the latter (exemplified particularly in the work of Bernard Bloch, Bloomfield's successor at Yale). An interesting development of the Prague doctrines was offered by the Frenchman André Martinet who sought, in the phonological structure of a language, the 'pressures' or impulses for future phonological development. In the Bloomfield-Sapir tradition, universals of phonological structure have been sought notably by C. F. Hockett, and of morphosyntax by J. H. Greenberg, while efforts at writing a distribution-based grammar (with minimal recourse to meaning) were made by Zellig Harris.

Much of the linguistic work ever done has been accomplished in the twentieth century as a result of the efforts of Kenneth Pike, a student of Sapir's, who has trained hundreds of missionary linguists at the Summer Institute of Linguistics. Thus, structural linguistic analysis, as a prerequisite to Bible translation, has given us excellent accounts of many languages from the preliterate world.

D. L. Olmsted
University of California, Davis

Further Reading

Hymes, D. and Fought, J. (1981), *American Structuralism*, The Hague.

Stankiewicz, E. (ed. and trans.) (1972), *A Baudouin de Courtenay Anthology: The Beginnings of Structural Linguistics*, Bloomington.

See also: *Bloomfield; Jakobson; Martinet; Sapir; Saussure.*

Subculture

In common parlance the term, subculture, is used most often to describe those special worlds of interest and identification that set apart some individuals, groups, and/or larger aggregations from the larger societies to which they belong. We speak of youth subculture(s), ethnic subcultures, regional subcultures, occupational subcultures, and the subcultures which develop among those who share special interests such as stamp collecting, bird watching, or drug use.

Yet neither membership in a particular category (race, ethnicity, age, sex, occupation, or area of residence) nor behaviour (drug abuse or bird watching) is sufficient to account for or to characterize a subculture. The critical element, rather, is the degree to which values, artifacts, and identification are shared among and with other members of a category, or those who engage in a particular type of behaviour. Such sharing is enhanced by the extent of *social separation* between members of the larger society and those who belong to a particular category, or those who engage in particular behaviours. Hair colour, for example, is prominent in descriptions of individuals, but is not a basis for social separation. The social structural characteristics noted above, and many types of behaviour, have become major bases for social separation.

Subcultures exist in relation to larger cultures and societies. The nature of these relationships is critical to the origin, development, and the status of subcultures within societies. They may be merely different, and be viewed indifferently; they may be viewed positively; or, because defined as deviant, viewed negatively. Some are not merely different, but oppositional to major cultural values, in which case they are properly termed contra- or countercultures. Definitions and experiences involving subcultural 'outsiders' and 'insiders', as well as *among* 'insiders', exert powerful, often determining, influences on subcultures. Suspicion, distrust, and fear of the different, deviant, and/or unknown, may lead to rejection by the dominant society, particularly when those who are so defined also lack power. A cycle of interaction may thus be set in motion in which those who are defined as different, and so on, are increasingly thrown on their own resources, develop their own values, beliefs, roles and status systems. Examples are delinquent and lower-class subcultures, religious sects and other groups which withdraw from the larger society. Conversely, powerful groups are able to command the resources necessary to avoid many of the negative effects, if not always the negative definitions, of their difference. 'High society', the professions, and learned disciplines come immediately to mind. As these examples suggest, organizational forms and subcultures should not be confused, though they are mutually reinforcing.

Structural differentiation of societies provides the boundary conditions for subcultural formation. Changes in structural differentiation produce subcultural changes. Subcultures thus are inevitably linked to social change, serving both as the 'engines' of social change and as resisters to it. For example, the esoteric knowledge, language, and techniques of science promote the discovery of further knowledge and its application; but the vested interests in occupations and professions – and identification with the past which is often associated with subcultures – resist change.

Subcultures vary along many dimensions: rigidity of separation, degree of exclusivity, how much of the lives of participating individuals is encompassed, the extent to which they are group centred or more diffuse among those who identify or are identified with them, and the extent to which they overlap with other subcultures. Numerous theories have attempted to account for these and other characteristics and variations of subcultures, but no general theory of subcultures has been entirely successful.

James F. Short Jr
Washington State University

Further Reading
Cohen, S. (1980), *Folk Devils and Moral Panics*, 2nd edn, New York.
Cressey, D. R. (1983), 'Delinquent and criminal subcultures', in S. E. Kadish (ed.), *Encyclopaedia of Crime and Justice*, New York.
Fischer, C. S. (1982), *To Dwell Among Friends: Personal Networks in Town and City*, Chicago.
Yinger, J. M. (1960), 'Contraculture and subculture', *American Sociological Review*, 25.
Yinger, J. M. (1977), 'Presidential address: countercultures and social change', *American Sociological Review*, 42.
See also: *communal groups; culture; gangs; sects and cults.*

Subsidies

Subsidies are negative taxes which may be put on consumption goods or investment goods or factor services. Specific examples include subsidies on welfare goods and housing, accelerated depreciation provisions for investment, general wage subsidies, wage subsidies for specific purposes such as training, deficiency payments to farmers, and payments to public utilities for providing services in sparsely-populated areas.

Whereas taxes generally reduce taxed activities, subsidies normally increase the subsidized activity and are sometimes justified because the activity concerned generates external benefits. For example, a training subsidy might be introduced to encourage a better-trained labour force. When subsidies are introduced to aid the poor, an important issue is whether the subsidy should be paid in cash or in kind – for example, through food vouchers. Payments in kind make it more likely that the subsidy is used as desired, such as on food purchases, but is open to objections on paternalistic grounds and because such payments prevent people from spending their income as they themselves prefer.

Subsidies frequently present problems of public accountability because it may be difficult to discover or control the extent of the subsidy. For example, support for a subsidy to a branch railway line does not necessarily mean unlimited support for losses on railway lines. Subsidies are of course open to all sorts of political pressures, but the force of this argument is for subsidies to be open and known. It may, for example, be difficult to discover if housing subsidies go mainly to those who live in publicly-owned housing or who have subsidized rents, or to owner-occupiers with subsidized mortgages and who escape income taxation on the implicit income from home ownership. In the absence of knowledge, both renters and owner-occupiers may feel the other group is the more heavily subsidized.

C. V. Brown
University of Stirling

See also: *taxation.*

Suicide

Social science research into the causes of suicide can be classified into five major explanatory categories: early childhood experiences and personality; cultural factors; social integration; economic conditions, and modernization.

(1) Suicide in adulthood has been linked to experiences in the family of origin and to certain character traits: loss of a parent, chronic love withdrawal, being a first-born child, and the suicidal behaviour of relatives (Lester, 1972). Personality characteristics often associated with suicide include depression, impulsiveness, pessimism, negative self-concept, passivity, introversion and dichotomous thinking. Psychologists tend to link these traits with early childhood trauma, while sociologists are more likely to associate them with events in adulthood, including divorce and unemployment.

(2) The cultural explanations of suicide stress values, cultural-role expectations, and the influence of the media. For example, male role expectations in Western society have been associated with suicide – males are expected to be 'strong', therefore they are less able than females to cope with crises. But given the recent convergence in sex roles, the differences between rates of suicide in the sexes are decreasing in most industrial nations. American studies have also found that there are cultural differences in the manner in which members of the different racial groups internalize aggression; again, with the decline of racial separation and discrimination in the US, these differences are less marked than before, and consequently suicide rates are similar in the different racial groups (Stack, 1982). Finally, in the US and Britain, suicide stories carried in the media have been found to increase slightly the suicide rate (Phillips, 1974).

(3) Suicide research continues to investigate social integration, or the degree of subordination of the individual's self-interest to the group. Its components include marital, religious and political dimensions. Researchers have found that the higher the marital integration (low divorce rate) of a group, the lower its suicide rate (Stack, 1982). However, earlier findings that Catholics had a lower suicide rate than Protestants have not been supported by recent research. Other measures of religiosity, for example, church attendance, have been shown to reduce the likelihood of suicide. Durkheim's contention that political crises such as war decrease suicide by rousing collective sentiments has recently also been seriously questioned (Stack, 1982). Multivariate research in the US indicates that it is full employment during wartime, rather than aroused collective sentiments, that is responsible for the lower suicide rates (Marshall, 1981). Migration too is positively associated with suicide. This is because migrants have to renounce close ties with friends, family and co-workers (Stack, 1980).

(4) Economically-deprived groups and the unemployed have higher suicide rates, while improvements in economic conditions appear to reduce the rate. The world-wide trend towards a lower suicide rate among elderly males has been attributed to better social security programmes.

(5) Durkheim also attributed the increase of suicide in the nineteenth century to the process of modernization. Factors such as the rise of individualism, urbanization, industrialization, and the replacement of religious authority with free inquiry in the educational system, were seen as lowering social integration. But present-day research does not find a relationship between modernization and suicide. While in some nations suicide has increased, in others it has decreased or levelled off. Other factors, for example, commitment to education, have been suggested as explanations.

There has been a most striking post-war surge in suicide in industrial nations among young people aged between fifteen and twenty-four. Some of the reasons for this are: massive unemployment and its associated frustrations, even among highly educated people; the decline of religious identification; increased tolerance of deviant behaviour in the youth subculture; and the emotional consequences of divorce on children (Waldron and Eyer, 1975; Stack, 1983).

Steven Stack
Pennsylvania State University

References
Durkheim, E. (1951 [1897]), *Suicide – A Sociological Study*, London. (Original French edn, *Le Suicide: étude Sociologique*, Paris.)

Lester, D. (1972), *Why People Kill Themselves: A 1980's Summary of Research Findings on Suicidal Behavior*, Springfield, Ill.

Marshall, J. (1981), 'Political integration and the effect of war on suicide', *Social Forces*, 59.

Phillips, D. (1974), 'The influence of suggestion on suicide', *American Sociological Review*, 59.

Stack, S. (1980), 'Interstate migration and the rate of suicide', *International Journal of Social Psychiatry*, 26.

Stack, S. (1982), 'Suicide: a decade review of the sociological literature', *Deviant Behavior*, 4.

Stack, S. (1983), 'The effect of the decline in institutionalized religion on suicide, 1954–1978', *Journal for the Scientific Study of Religion*, 22.

Waldron, I. and Eyer, J. (1975), 'Socioeconomic causes of the recent rise in death rates for 15–24 year olds', *Social Science and Medicine*, 9.

Sullivan, Harry Stack (1892–1949)

Harry Stack Sullivan was born in Norwich, New York on 21 February 1892 and died on 14 January 1949 in Paris. Helen Swick Perry's excellent biography of Sullivan records in detail the events of his life, certain aspects of which profoundly influenced his highly original and creative contributions to psychiatry.

The first and foremost is the effect upon Sullivan's view of the world of his rural, Irish, Roman-Catholic background, and growing up socially isolated because of the then current religious prejudices, as virulent as racial prejudice. It is the fact of his having been a Roman Catholic, rather than his practising the religion itself, that is of central importance in understanding some of his points of view.

The second important biographical fact is that his formal education was limited to one semester at Cornell in 1908 and his receiving his medical degree from the Chicago School of Medicine and Surgery in 1917, a school which Sullivan himself described as 'a diploma mill'. His formal academic work in both institutions can only be described at best as marginal, at worst abysmal. Obviously Sullivan, who in his prime was an intellectual of the highest versatility, was largely self-educated.

Between 1918 and 1922, the years before he began work at Sheppard-Pratt Hospital, Sullivan served in various capacities in the Army Medical Corps and in a number of federal agencies dealing with veterans' matters. This experience in the army gave structure to his life and probably saved him from a mental breakdown. But more importantly, it gave him the chance clinically, in his various roles, to become certified by the government as a neuropsychiatrist. Thus, the loose ends of his cursory medical education were brought into synthesis. He finally had clear and formal medical status in psychiatry.

These themes of social isolation stemming from his Roman-Catholic background, his avid interest in self-education and innovation, and his profound sense not only of American patriotism but of world patriotism marked his life's work.

Sullivan began to formulate his own theoretical ideas, which were stimulated and elaborated by two close friendships: with Clara Thompson, whom he met in 1923, and Edward Sapir, whom he met in 1926. To Thompson he owed the debt of being exposed to psychoanalysis in a formal sense and to Sapir, the anthropologist, he owed support for his convictions about the importance of the interaction between individuals and their cultural and family environments. Although there is no doubt that Sapir was a brilliant intellectual foil to Sullivan through their mutual interest in culture and personality, there was a common bond which probably intensified their friendship: Sullivan as a Roman Catholic and Sapir as a Jew had both suffered religious and ethnic prejudice.

It is interesting that in formulating his theoretical propositions concerning the human condition, be it normal or pathological, Sullivan never abandoned the original intellectual stance he had hoped to realize as a student at Cornell, where he had intended to become either a mathematician or a physicist. To a degree that is equalled by no other psychiatrist before or since, Sullivan was extremely aware of when he was speaking as a scientist, profoundly influenced by the operationalism of Percy Bridgeman and other scientific thinkers and philosophers, and when he was speaking as an artist in the domain of interpersonal relationships. In his own language, Sullivan, depending on the particular situation, was the 'personification' of the natural scientist, the interpersonal artist, or the poetic, imaginative, Irish, lyric thinker. It was his ability to speak in different tongues that gave Sullivan credence in academic circles as well as in the medical domain of science. Given this basic tenet of the operational, to Sullivan what went on between people was the only data admissible to psychiatry. He largely ignored dreams and what he called reverie processes, because they could not be observed. They could create behaviour which could be observed and was thus admissible as clinical data.

A second aspect of Sullivan's theory is that it is *species specific*: human beings are not part of an evolutionary chain as seen by Freud, but are to be seen in their own right. Their primate heritage gives them a capacity no other species possesses: a symbol system and a capacity to interchange symbol systems. This conceptualization was no doubt profoundly reinforced by his friendship with Sapir, whose expertise in anthropology was linguistic relativity. Thus, as Perry has remarked, the capacity to communicate or the inability to communicate is the key to the human condition. Closely related to this idea is Sullivan's assertion that our particular primate status requires us to be in interpersonal contact at all times with significant others. If that contact cannot be maintained, deterioration and mental illness are inevitable.

Corollary to these two basic ideas was Sullivan's postulation that anxiety early in life was induced by the anxious mother and thus anxiety as what he called a 'dysjunctive state' was an inevitable part of the human condition. Sullivan can thus be seen not only as an interpersonal theorist, but as an extremely provocative expositor of the place of anxiety in human affairs. Possibly one of the most interesting aspects of Sullivan's work – given the realities of his personal history – are his highly sophisticated and value-free essays on human sexuality.

One of his most important clinical contributions was the development of milieu therapy in the treatment of schizophrenics. A natural outgrowth of his emphasis on the interpersonal, it is a standard approach in modern psychiatry.

Sullivan's theoretical creativity, for practical purposes, stopped with the onset of World War II, where he became engaged, once again, in various capacities with the military. He was one of the first to see the implications of Hiroshima and, having full knowledge that to undertake a crusade on behalf of peace was to cost him his life, with implacable will he forged ahead. His attempt to set up various foundations bridging psychiatry and the social sciences, his enlisting psychiatrists and social scientists in the cause of peace, all marked the turbulent last years of his life. It can be said that he died serving the cause of humanity.

George W. Goethals
Harvard University

Further Reading
Sullivan, H. S. (1953), *The Interpersonal Theory of Psychiatry*, London.

Super-Ego

The concept super-ego is, roughly, the psychoanalytic equivalent to the more commonly-used word, conscience. It stands for the internalized value-concerns a person learns mostly in childhood, that affect the way one is accepted, approved of, and loved. They stem from the perceptions (carried out by the 'ego') about what kind of behaviour and attitudes will gain approval from the persons who provide nurturance and care, especially during the early years of life, and who will withhold such benefits when those values are not followed. They are the product of 'instrumental learning' which is to say, trial-and-error experimentation in everyday living: what gets love and approval 'works' and is therefore replicated, remembered, and for purposes of efficiency, ultimately automated (and becomes a part of the 'dynamic unconscious').

Such childhood super-ego values are not at first reasoned out or understood beyond the fact that they work to gain approval with all of its consequences. They are life-preservative. Since so many of the values become unconcious (and automated), if inquiry were made about them and why they existed, the answer would be no more profound than, 'Just because', or 'Mummy/Daddy says I should'. Punishments for breaches are by the Talion Principle: 'An eye for an eye, a tooth for a tooth, a hand for a hand'.

With growth and development, and as the child begins to wonder 'Why?', these values are explored and re-evaluated. 'Thou shalt not kill' loses its status as a categorical imperative, and reasons why this rule is needed to achieve social equilibrium are substituted for the blindly accepted dogma of the immature super-ego. The aura of God-given (parent-given) truth is progressively eroded away under the assault of more complex, social reality-based reasoning and experience. The less absolute but more reliable and flexible reality-testing process develops and becomes a manifestation and a function of the mature psyche and its super-ego. Although some residual fragments of the childhood super-ego may remain to stir restlessness throughout life, under most circumstances the considered evaluation of goals, consequences, and other people's interests and concerns will prevail and allow effective interpersonal interactions and intrapsychic satisfaction.

In order for this process to occur, it is important for the growing child to be reared in a fairly consistent and substantially constant environment. This means that both parents (as well as most members of the child-rearing surroundings) should agree upon and communicate the values they wish the child to internalize. They must all *say* the same things and then *behave* (model) the same behaviour. A failure to do so leaves images and values in confusion and can cause subsequent emotional conflict. When the child moves out into the broader world away from his immediate family, there will ideally be a continuity of values so that he does not have to make a choice between them (when they do, home usually wins). The fact that many children nowadays are reared in mobile families means that they may be forced to adapt to several highly varied environments, and thus multiple value systems, during their formative years; this can present substantial problems.

While psychiatrists (and many others long before them) have noted that the first five years of life are crucial to the formation of the super-ego, later development may also have powerful effects upon the whole or upon specific values within it. Some values are subject to little conflict and, therefore, are relatively easy to maintain. Others are more fragile and vulnerable and need some or much reinforcement throughout life.

Andrew S. Watson
University of Michigan

See also: *Freud, S.; moral development; psychoanalysis.*

Swedish School

See Stockholm School.

Symbolic Interactionism

Symbolic interactionism is the title that was awarded belatedly and retrospectively to the ideas of a group of sociologists and social psychologists once centred on the University of Chicago. As that group evolved during the 1920s, 1930s and 1940s, its members began to scatter throughout the universities of North America, bearing interactionism with them. The critical early generation of George Mead, William James, Charles Cooley, William Thomas and Robert Park was succeeded first by that of Herbert Blumer and Everett Hughes and then by third and fourth generations populated by such people as Erving Goffman, Howard Becker, Anselm Strauss and Eliot Freidson.

Interactionism itself alludes to a deliberately unsystematic and often vague method of interpreting the ways in which people do things together, a method that has flowed from the theoretical and practical work of the Chicago School (of Sociology). Because it is unsystematic, there are a number of versions of interactionism. There is no one orthodoxy, and any published account must therefore be a little partial.

Theoretically, interactionism was shaped by pragmatism. It has been framed by a series of special perspectives on the possibilities of knowledge and the limits of enquiry. It not only describes the character of social life but also suggests how it should be studied: problems of definition and method have been collapsed into one, it being argued that the sociologist and the persons whom he observes follow the same procedures. Society and sociology are produced by special processes of knowledge, and it is those processes which must be understood before sociology can proceed. Knowledge itself is described as belonging neither to the surveying mind alone nor to the world alone. On one level, interactionists contend that it is misleading to imagine that people's interpretations of events and things are free: interpretations are restrained by the capacity of those events to 'answer back'. On another level, it is claimed that knowledge is not a simple mirror of its objects: people actively create, shape and select their response to what is around them. Knowledge is then presented as an active process in which people, their understanding and phenomena are bound together in what has been called the 'knowing-known transaction'. That transaction is exploratory, emergent and situated, lending a dialectical structure to all activity. Interactionists argue that practical knowledge does not arise in seclusion. Rather, it addresses specific problems and purposes, those problems establishing distinctive questions and perspectives that illuminate some facets of the world and not others. Illumination, in its turn, will disclose new ideas which can return to transform problems and purposes, leading to another shift of question and another train of ideas. And so it goes on in an indefinite regress that will end only when exhaustion, boredom or practical satisfaction has been attained. It is evident that there cannot be a logical terminus for investigation or activity. All knowledge is destined to be provisional, liable to reformulation with the answering of just one more question. All knowledge is a novel and often unanticipated synthesis of what has gone before. Moreover, all knowledge is embedded in its own context and history of development. There are limits to generalization and abstraction.

Chief amongst the problems that confront a person is the character that he possesses. People do not always understand themselves, their past and their possible futures. Facts about the self are revealed with each new action and they cannot always be predicted or assimilated. Yet is is vital to learn what one is and what one might become. Without that knowledge, there would be no appreciation of how one's actions will affect others and how others will affect oneself. It is necessary to place oneself. Just as people observe the world about them, so they observe themselves, composing a series of running conjectures about identity. The process of self-exploration translates the subject into an examining 'I' and an examined 'me', the 'me' being an objectification of inferences made by oneself and others. Indeed, the responses of others are critical because they may be used to construct a sense of how one appears, a 'looking-glass self'. Over time, the symbolic effects worked by such responses can become relatively anonymous, depersonalized and standardized, the basis of an abstract representation called the 'Generalised Other'. This whole process is itself orchestrated and mediated by language, and most of its constituent forms have been likened to those of a conversation. Interactionists have given great emphasis to words as a means of animating, stabilizing and objectifying what would otherwise be fleeting and private experience. It is in the work done by words that people can share a community of perspectives about themselves, one another and the objects which are in their environment.

The prime vehicle of social action is the 'significant gesture', an expression or display which incorporates replies to the responses which others might make to it. In its anticipation of others' answering behaviour, the significant gesture ties people together, allowing lines of conduct to converge and unite. Society itself tends to be seen as a mosaic of little scenes and dramas in which people make indications to themselves and others, respond to those indications, align their actions, and so build identities and social structures.

The task of the interactionist is to describe that activity, and it is also thought to be emergent and anchored in its contexts. Enquiry is frequently tentative, open and exploratory, deploying a variety of strategies but leaning towards ethnography and 'participant-observation'. It is held to be the job of the sociologist to enter the social situations of his subjects, observe their conduct, understand their practices and the symbolic work that accompanies them, and then retire to report what has been seen. Those descriptions of conduct are frequently built up into larger portraits of social worlds, reference being made to the patterns which seem to organize them. There is interest in such ordering processes as the career, conflict and the division of labour. Any resulting analysis may be tested by its plausibility, its ability to provide scripts for behaviour, and by the criticism supplied by the subjects themselves.

Interactionists would maintain that sociology resides in research, not in schematic treatises about society, epistemology and methodology. All argument, including interactionism, must be rooted in the elucidation of particular problems in specific contexts. Attempts to render it universal or apart from concrete experience will deny it authenticity. The conventional interactionist territory has then been the small world of an occupation, institution or social group. And interactionism itself has been most conspicuous in those sectors of sociology which dwell on substantive areas, medicine, deviance, education and careers being instances. In the main, the approach has been closely identified with American scholars who are linked at first or second hand with the University of Chicago. Its greatest impact was probably achieved in the 1960s and 1970s when it changed the form of the sociology of deviance, Becker and Goffman acting as especially important figures.

Paul Rock
London School of Economics and Political Science

Further Reading
Becker, H. (1970), *Sociological Work*, Chicago.
Blumer, H. (1969), *Symbolic Interactionism: Perspective and Method*, Englewood Cliffs, NJ.
Goffman, E. (1959), *The Presentation of Self in Everyday Life*, New York.
Hughes, E. (1958), *Men and Their Work*, Glencoe, Ill.
Rock, P. (1979), *The Making of Symbolic Interactionism*, London.
Rose, A. (ed.) (1962), *Human Behavior and Social Processes*, Boston.

See also: *Chicago School of Sociology; ethnomethodology; Goffman; Mead, G. H.; Park; pragmatics; symbolism.*

Symbolism

The 'action' that is the concern of the social sciences, including psychology, is what has been called *symbolic interaction* (Herbert Blumer, interpreting G. H. Mead). Symbolic interaction involves communication in terms of signals and symbols; it is communication of *decisions* in a broad sense. Culture consists of symbolic codes or systems and the multifarious messages that are communicated with their aid.

Properly speaking, a symbol stands for a *concept*, general or particular. The person, thing, category, idea, or event evoked as a concept may be only imaginary but may, along with other symbolized meanings in complex messages, bring about thoughts, feelings, or intentions in the decoders of the symbol. Every symbol is thus mental or intentional in itself though its *vehicle* must of course be something physical such as marks on paper, as in writing.

Symbols should be carefully distinguished from *signals*, which are indications of past, present, or future occurrences. A signal is usually more accessible than the thing that may be said to be signalized. This fact is arranged to be so in the case of signals set up by human or animal intention to announce the presence or the past or future occurrence of the event to be signalized. However, a signal may simply be an intrinsic part of a larger complex of which the signalized event is also a part.

A map is a complex symbol or signal that in its own 'space' follows point for point (re-presents) the relations to be conceived of, and perhaps taken account of, in the represented space itself. By contrast, the words in human languages are for the most part more arbitrary, in the sense that there may be no apparent connection between symbol and symbolized other than that established by convention. Many symbols, however, such as those important in Freudian psychology, are connected with their meanings through deeply-rooted and sometimes almost universal associations.

The most useful typology of symbols for the purpose of the sciences of action takes more account of content and function than of form (Parsons, 1961). There are four types of symbolization: 'constitutive'; moral-evaluative; expressive, and cognitive.

(1) Constitutive (or religious) symbols are often-latent patterns of the most general kind in their implications.
(2) Moral-evaluative symbols are integrative.
(3) Expressive symbols have to do with goal attainment, and in their aesthetic forms express relatively 'pure' purposiveness, as Kant explained.
(4) Cognitive symbolization is largely adaptive.

Concrete symbols are often of mixed types. Thus, constitutive or religious symbols frequently have cognitive, expressive, and moral-evaluative implications or aspects, though what is distinctive about the constitutive type is the imaginary representation of ultimate reality. Such representations are cognitive in form but not in fact. Perhaps because they are not tied down, strictly speaking, to the representational, 'constitutive' symbols are sometimes capable of maintaining a reassuring pattern in action while at the same time generating and bringing to realization latent possibilities in the pattern itself. In the broad field of 'representing' ultimate reality, however, relatively new symbolization may also appear, with new possibilities, entering the competition for human commitments.

Harry M. Johnson
University of Illinois
Champaign-Urbana

Reference
Parsons, T. (1961), 'Introduction', in T. Parsons *et al.*, *Theories of Society*, Part V, New York.
See also: *Mead, G. H.; semiotics; symbolic interactionism.*

Systems Analysis

See General Systems Theory.

T

Taboo

The term taboo derives from various Polynesian languages where it has the sense of 'forbidden'. More specifically, what is forbidden and dangerous is unregulated contact between the everyday world and the sacred, which includes both the holy (for example, the person of a chief) and the unclean (for example, a corpse). Most modern anthropological thinking about taboo derives from Durkheim (1912), for whom this disjunction between profane and sacred was the cornerstone of religion – the sacred being secondarily divided between the 'auspiciously' and 'inauspiciously' sacred. Taboos have the function of keeping separate what must not be joined – of policing the boundaries between sacred and profane, and between 'good' and 'bad' sacred – while rites in general re-create the solidarity of the group. Developing this second proposition, Radcliffe-Brown (1952) argued that taboo behaviour expresses and reinforces the values and sentiments essential to the maintenance of society. More recent work, however, has taken as its starting point the notion that taboos mark the boundaries between a culture's fundamental categories.

This line of thought has been brilliantly exploited by Douglas (1966; 1975). Dirt, said Lord Chesterfield, is 'matter out of place'. It implies disorder and a confusion of cherished categories. Pollution behaviour and taboo focus on that which is ambiguous in terms of such categories. There is even a sense in which taboos entrench the categories by highlighting and defining the boundaries between them. Margins and boundaries tend therefore to be populated by anomalous creatures of various kinds, and if they don't exist they have to be invented. In myth, for example, the elephant-headed Hindu deity Ganesa often appears – in keeping with his physical character – as an ambivalent trickster. It is he who marks the boundaries between sacred and profane space and time, for he conventionally stands at the entrances to temples, and is worshipped at the beginning and end of major rituals.

Anomalies can be dealt with in various ways:
(1) They can be suppressed or eradicated. In some societies twins are destroyed for they are seen as blurring the boundary between humans (characterized by single births) and animals (characterized by multiple births). As products of the same parturition they are mystically one but physically two; and in a society which attaches much importance to the birth order of siblings they are doubly ambiguous, for there are two physical beings to occupy one structural role in the kinship system (Turner, 1969). (2) A second possibility is to regard the anomaly as filthy and unclean – as in the 'abominations' of Leviticus. Here, for example, land animals are divided into the clawed and hoofed; the latter having the linked characteristics of being ruminant and cloven-hoofed, and being rated as the only legitimate meat. Creatures like the pig (which divide the hoof but do not chew the cud), or the camel, hare and hyrax (which chew the cud but are not cloven-hoofed) are abominated and tabooed. (3) Alternatively the anomaly may be welcomed as a positive mediator between, say, the sacred and the profane, or between nature and culture. Thus, in the taxonomic system of the Congolese Lele the pangolin is a highly ambiguous creature. It is an arboreal animal with the scaly body and tail of a fish, and is credited with a number of anthropomorphic qualities, the most important of which are a sense of sexual 'modesty' and the reproduction of only one offspring at a time. It therefore stands in the same kind of relationship to humans as begetters of twins stand to animals. Both mediate between nature and culture and are the focus of cult groups which control hunting and fertility.

What the theory fails to explain, however, is why some anomalous creatures are filthy abominations while others are positive mediators. Douglas (1973) has, though not entirely satisfactorily, tried to solve this puzzle by suggesting that attitudes to boundary crossing in the social sphere are reflected in attitudes towards potential mediators in other spheres (evaluation of creatures – like pigs – which straddle the Jewish insistence on endogamy, for example, going with the negative evaluation of creatures which straddle conceptual boundaries). More plausibly she notes that that which is anomalous and marginal is not only the focus of pollution and danger, but also a source of extraordinary power. The Aghoris are a small sect of Hindu ascetics who perform austerities at, and may live on, the cremation grounds. They rub their bodies with cremation ash, use shrouds for loin-cloths, cook their food on wood pilfered from the pyres, consume it out of a human skull; and they are *supposed* to meditate while seated on top of a corpse, and to eat and drink all manner of foul substances including urine, excrement and the putrescent flesh of corpses. By such austerities the ascetic is held to acquire extraordinary supernatural powers by which he can surmount the ordinary physical limitations of the mortal condition (Parry, 1981). The categories are safe and orderly, but imply restriction. What lies outside is dangerous, but also highly potent.

J. P. Parry
London School of Economics and Political Science

References
Douglas, M. (1966), *Purity and Danger: An Analysis of Concepts of Pollution and Taboo*, London.
Douglas, M. (1973), *Natural Symbols*, Harmondsworth.
Douglas, M. (1975), *Implicit Meanings: Essays in Anthropology*, London.
Durkheim, E. (1976 [1912]), *The Elementary Forms of the Religious Life*, London.
Parry, J. P. (1981), 'Sacrificial death and the necrophagous ascetic', in M. Bloch and J. Parry (eds), *Death and The Regeneration of Life*, Cambridge.
Radcliffe-Brown, A. (1952), *Structure and Function in Primitive Society*, London.
Turner, V. (1969), *The Ritual Process: Structure and Anti-Structure*, Chicago.
See also: *Douglas; religion and ritual.*

Tarde, Gabriel (1843–1904)

Gabriel Tarde, the French criminologist, was one of the founders of social psychology and the study of collective behaviour. Born in Sarlat, east of Bordeaux, where he spent most of his life, Tarde was descended from a long line of magistrates, and he himself was a local judge for almost a quarter of a century. While working as a judge, he began to write about the role of personality and environment in crime, and became a leading spokesman for the French school of Lacassagne, and a major opponent of the Italian school of Lombroso. He published a number of articles and books in this period including *La Philosophie pénale* (1890) (*Penal Philosophy*, 1912).

Tarde was also interested in the relation between man and society. The first volume of his two-volume study on the subject, *Psychologie sociale et la logique sociale*, formed the basis for his best-known book on social psychology, *Les Lois de l'imitation* (1890) (*The Laws of Imitation*, 1903). Tarde defined the basic social-psychological realities as belief and desire, and the basic social processes as invention, imitation and opposition; it was the task of the sociologist to uncover the logical and extra-logical laws which guide them. The whole system was later summarized in *Les Lois sociales – esquisse d'une sociologie* (1898) (*Social Laws – An Outline of Sociology*, 1899). In that same year, he also published his collection, *Études de psychologie sociale*, the first book to include the term 'social psychology' in its title. Part of it was

devoted to the famous debate with his rival Durkheim about the nature of sociology. Tarde was appointed to a professorship at the Collège de France in 1900, and he died four years later before completing his work on an 'exemplary paradigm'. Durkheim, who became professor at the Sorbonne in 1902, survived him by thirteen years, and in this period developed a paradigmatic community (Lubek, 1981).

Tarde did not receive recognition in his own country for many years. It was mainly through his influence on many of the founders of American social psychology and sociology that some of his ideas survived. These can be traced in the interactionist tradition, and in later research on attitudes, opinion and communications. Recently, however, Tarde has been rediscovered in France, and several of his works have been reprinted, both in French and English.

Jaap van Ginneken
University of Leiden

Reference
Lubek, I. (1981), 'La Psychologie sociale perdue de Gabriel Tarde', *Revue Française de Sociologie*, XXXI.

Further Reading
Clark, T. N. (ed.) (1969), *Gabriel Tarde on Communications and Social Influence: Selected Papers*, Chicago.
Milet, J. (1970), *Gabriel Tarde et la philosophie de l'histoire*, Paris.

Tawney, Richard Henry (1880–1962)

R. H. Tawney, distinguished economic historian, social philosopher and passionate enemy of privilege, was born in Calcutta in 1880, the son of an Oriental scholar in the Indian Educational Service, and was educated at Rugby School and Balliol College, Oxford. The most formative experience of his early life was his work as first tutor of the Workers' Educational Association (WEA), a movement in adult education for working people; here his egalitarian Anglican beliefs found their most complete expression.

Largely through his teaching in this organization, and, after 1921, at the London School of Economics (his lifelong academic home), Tawney developed a concept of economic history as a branch of moral philosophy. In his view, the subject entailed the retrieval of the resistance of groups and individuals in the past to the imposition on them of capitalist thought and behaviour. No one could miss the presentmindedness of his history or his commitment to the British Labour movement, expressed both in his important scholarly works, such as *The Agrarian Problem in the Sixteenth Century* (1912) and in *Religion and the Rise of Capitalism*

(1926), and in his role as adviser to the Labour party on educational policy over a period of fifty years.

In effect, Tawney was the epitome of the engaged scholar in British academic life in the first half of the twentieth century. Indeed it was this very quality which made his work so attractive to a generation of students, who learned from him that the study of economic history could raise fundamental questions concerning human behaviour and moral values. The same desire to speak to major social issues and to avoid the desiccation of academic specialism can be seen in his more speculative essays in social philosophy, *The Acquisitive Society* (1920) and *Equality* (1931).

As a spokesman for Christian socialism and humane scholarship, he has had no peer in Britain, either in his lifetime or since his death in 1962.

J. M. Winter
Pembroke College, Cambridge

Further Reading
Terrill, R. (1973), *R. H. Tawney and his Times*, London.
Tawney, R. H. (1978), *History and Society*, London.
Tawney, R. H. (1979), *The American Labour Movement*, Brighton.
Winter, J. M. (ed.) (1972), *R. H. Tawney's Commonplace Book*, Cambridge.
Winter, J. M. (1974), *Socialism and the Challenge of War*, London.

Taxation

Taxes are the main source of government revenue. Amongst the OECD countries in 1981 taxes accounted for between one-fifth (in the case of Turkey) and one-half of gross domestic product (in the case of Sweden).

There is considerable variation in the relative importance of different kind of taxes. In 1981 France raised only 13 per cent of tax revenue from personal income tax, while New Zealand raised 61 per cent. Neither the United States nor the United Kingdom appear unusual either in the total amount of tax that they collect or in the composition of the tax burden, except that both raise a high share of revenue from property taxes, and the US raises a low share from taxes on goods and services.

It is assumed here that it has been decided how much total revenue the government requires. This makes it possible to concentrate on how best this revenue requirement can be met. This question is considered under three headings: allocative effects, distributional effects and administrative effects.

Allocative Effects
Taxes will in general cause people to change their behaviour. If there are two activities (or goods) A and B, and A is taxed while B is not, then, unless their incomes change, people will normally do (or buy) less

of A and more of B. An important exception is where it is not possible to do less of A. For example, a tax on each person (a head or poll tax) cannot be avoided except by dying.

If A is an activity which has harmful side effects – for example, a chimney that smokes – then reducing activity A may be desirable. In general, however, it is preferable to tax activities where the reduction in production or consumption will be small. One aspect of this concerns the effects of taxes on prices of goods. Taxes will normally raise prices (though not usually by the amount of the tax). The increase in price will cause people to reduce consumption, especially where the quantity demanded is very sensitive to price. Because high consumption is generally to be preferred to low consumption, this leads to the proposition that taxes should tend to be concentrated on goods where demand is relatively insensitive to price changes.

It is also interesting to look at an example where people's incomes are *not* held constant, for instance, a tax on income from work. A tax on the income from work will have two effects on the amount of work people will want to do. It will reduce take-home pay and thus encourage them to want to work more to maintain their real income (the 'income effect'). But it will also reduce the amount that people receive for giving up an hour of their leisure and so encourage them to work less (the 'substitution effect'). This means that an income tax distorts the work-leisure choice. If the tax base included leisure as well as income, this distortion could be avoided, as in the case of the head tax mentioned above. The difficulty with head taxes is that it is impractical to vary them in accordance with a person's capacity to earn income.

Distributional Effects
Taxes generally change the distribution of income. This is fairly obvious if we think about the distribution of income after tax, but taxes can also influence the distribution of income before tax. If, for example, income taxes change the amount of work people do, this will change the distribution of pre-tax income.

A common fallacy is that in order to redistribute income towards the poor, it is necessary to have a schedule of rates which increase as income rises. However, provided that tax receipts are used to finance a benefit which is equally available to all, there is no need for a rising schedule of tax rates.

Many people would like to see taxes make the distribution of net income more equal. 'More equal' is of course a very vague phrase, and there are clearly differences as to how far towards equality people would like society to go.

Achieving the balance between allocative and distributional effects of taxes is the subject matter of the field of optimal taxation. In the case of income tax the problem is to find the structure of rates that provides the best balance between high rates to provide revenue for redistribution and low rates to ensure that the income available for redistribution does not fall too much. More crudely, the problem is to balance the size of the cake against its distribution. It has been argued that the schedule of tax rates against income should start at zero, rise, and then at some high level of income fall again to zero. This optimal schedule thus looks rather like an upside down U, whereas the actual tax schedule in some countries is U-shaped if one includes means-tested state benefits on low incomes as well as income taxes.

Administrative Effects
Collecting taxes imposes costs on both the public and private sector which can vary widely. For example, the US and UK have very nearly the same number of people collecting income tax, but the US population is roughly four times the UK population. (It may be that private sector costs of income tax compliance are lower in the UK than in the US.)

One of the main determinants of administrative costs is the complexity of the tax law. Very often these complexities are introduced to attempt to make the law fairer, but ironically the complexities may reduce public awareness to the point where, for example, the poor do not make full use of provisions that could benefit them.

One of the most important sources of complexities is multiplicity of rates as between different kinds of income such as earnings and real capital gains. Where the rate of tax on capital gains is relatively low, there is a strong incentive for those with high earnings into capital gains. A single uniform rate on all income would be a considerable simplification. It would also be a move in the direction of the optimal schedule of income tax rates discussed above.

C. V. Brown
University of Stirling

Further Reading
Kay, J. A. and King, M. A. (1983), *The British Tax System*, 3rd edn, London.
Brown, C. V. (1983), *Taxation and the Incentive to Work*, 2nd edn, London.
Blinder, A. S. *et al.* (1974), *The Economics of Public Finance*, Washington DC.
See also: *distribution of incomes and wealth; fiscal policy; subsidies.*

Technical Assistance

Technical know-how, along with tools, has been transmitted from one society to another throughout history. The use of wind power or of a device such as the stirrup provide early examples of what amounts to a spontaneous diffusion of knowledge.

The deliberate adoption of techniques was undertaken when continental Europe strove to emulate England's early Industrial Revolution. The US subsequently relied on European expertise to initiate her industrialization; in turn, American engineers familiarized their Latin-American counterparts with the new skills.

In the late nineteenth century, Dutch officers taught the Japanese how to cast cannon; even the Chinese eventually deigned to solicit foreign technological advice (Nakaoa, 1982). In addition, merchants, pilgrims and missionaries transferred various crafts, occasionally in defiance of bans imposed by governments anxious to preserve their comparative advantage. All such instances of technical assistance were, of necessity, incidental and *ad hoc.*

But after World War II a conscious, large-scale effort was introduced to impart industrial and agricultural expertise, with the object of inducing growth of the economy of underdeveloped countries; for the work of empiricists such as Denison and Solow had made it clear that technological knowledge was a major factor in development (Mansfield, 1982). Technical assistance, accordingly, came to be looked upon as a considered strategy, whereby industrial countries transfer knowledge, skills and even complementary attitudes to economically backward nations, in order to assist them in their efforts to improve living standards. These activities were henceforth largely undertaken and financed by institutions for the disbursement of foreign aid. The Food and Agricultural Organization of the United Nations (FAO) was among the first of the agencies to implement a programme of technical assistance. Subsequently, the UN Economic and Social Council (UNESCO) was assigned the preparation of an industrial assistance policy. A resolution was carried in 1948, outlining the principles of such a strategy and calling for the training of experts and supply of the requisite equipment. The following year, the Council launched an Expanded Programme of Technical Assistance. (Vas-Zoltán, 1972). Meanwhile, President Truman delivered his 'Point Four' address, urging 'a wider and more vigorous application of modern and technical knowledge' in the interest of poor nations. Thus, the scene was set and the institutional framework provided for a new angle on the Third-World problem.

Early experience soon showed the mere transference of objective information as contained in manuals and instruction leaflets to be inadequate. For the effective operation and maintenance of sophisticated equipment, an element of 'bricolage', some sort of tinkering attitude, apparently needs to be imparted. A communication gap became apparent, and this could be bridged only by subjecting would-be recipients to an elaborate learning-by-doing process which, incidentally, conformed with the 'modernization' approach to development then prevalent (Inkeles and Smith, 1974).

Also, a suitability gap was revealed: factor proportions as embodied in modern machinery reflect the high wage levels and low capital costs prevailing in advanced industrial countries. Modes of production in these countries are geared to mass markets where substantial purchasing power is brought to bear. Transplantation to the alien economic environment of a poor country entails maladjustment: there labour is abundant and, therefore, cheap; investments funds are scarce and costly. Consumer aspirations may have been raised, but incomes as yet are low and potential markets, consequently, limited. The realization of the suitability gap has given rise to a new approach to technical assistance, advocating the adaptation of technology to conditions peculiar to the receiving economy. This has become known as the 'appropriate technology' movement.

H. J. Duller
University of Leiden

References

Inkeles, A. and Smith, D. H. (1974), *Becoming Modern – Individual Change in Six Developing Countries*, London.

Mansfield, E. (1982), *Technology Transfer, Productivity and Economic Policy*, New York.

Nakaoa, T. (1982), 'Science and technology in the history of modern Japan: imitation or endogenous creativity?', in A. Abdel-Malek, G. Blue and M. Pecujlic (eds), *Science and Technology in the Transformation of the World*, Tokyo.

Vas-Zoltán, P. (1972), *United Nations Technical Assistance*, Budapest.

Further Reading

Bradbury, F. (1978), *Transfer Processes in Technical Change*, Alphen aan den Rijn.

Duller, H. J. (1982), *Development Technology*, London.

Maddison, A. (1965), *Foreign Skills and Technical Assistance in Economic Development*, Paris.

See also: *aid; economic growth; technological progress.*

Technological Progress

The importance of technological progress for economic and social development is undeniable, but it is a field where understanding and analytical effort have lagged far behind other areas, such as short-term supply-demand analyses. This is due at least partly to the complexity of the process of technical change and the difficulty of obtaining precise definitions and measure-

ments of it. Important advances have been made in recent years, but it remains a relatively neglected field.

Schumpeter, one of the few distinguished economists to put technological progress at the centre of his analysis, stressed the importance of new products, processes, and forms of organization or production – factors which have clearly been associated with enormous changes in the economic structures of developed economies since the Industrial Revolution. The rise of major new industries, such as railways and steel in the nineteenth century, and automobiles, synthetic materials and electronics in the twentieth, depended upon a complex interaction of inventions, innovations and entrepreneurial activity, which Freeman (1982) has aptly described as 'technological systems'. Since the onset of the post-1973 recession, the idea that developed capitalist economies are subject to 'long waves' of alternating periods of prosperity and stagnation, each wave being of around fifty to sixty years' duration, has been revived: some commentators argue that new technological systems are primarily responsible for the onset of an upswing, which begins to slow down as the associated technologies and industries reach maturity. Other economists, while accepting the notion of such cycles, argue that technological progress is a consequence, rather than a cause, of them. Outside the long-wave literature, there is an ongoing debate concerning the direction of causality regarding observed statistical associations between the growth of an industry and the pace of technical innovation.

At the macroeconomic level, the traditional, neoclassical growth models treat technological progress as part of a residual factor in 'explaining' increases in output, after accounting for the effects of changes in the volume of the factors of production (capital, labour and so on). This residual is normally large, and implicitly incorporates factors such as the education of the workforce and management expertise which contribute to improvements in efficiency, in addition to technological progress. In such approaches technological change is purely 'disembodied', that is, unrelated to any other economic variables. The class of so-called vintage capital models, which have become quite widely used over the last decade or so, treat technological progress as at least partly 'embodied' in new fixed investment: plant and machinery are carriers of productivity improvements and the gains from technological progress depend on the level of investment in them. Even the latter approach, however, does not go far in capturing the processes and forces by which new techniques are absorbed into the production system; the 'evolutionary' models pioneered by Nelson and Winter (1982) attempt to explore the conditions under which entrepreneurs will strive to adopt improved techniques. Such approaches are, however, in their infancy.

Discussion of how new techniques are generated and adopted is typically conducted at a more microeconomic case-study level. An *invention* is a new or improved product, or a novel procedure for manufacturing an existing product, which may or may not become translated into an *innovation*, that is, the (first) commercial adoption of the new idea. In many cases, scientific discoveries pave the way for inventions which, if perceived as having potential market demand, are adopted commercially; in the nineteenth century, the inventor/innovator was frequently an independent individual, but in the twentieth century the emphasis has moved to scientific and technological work being carried out 'in-house' by large firms. If an innovation is successful, a period of *diffusion* often follows, where other firms adopt or modify the innovation and market the product or process. It is at this stage that the major economic impact frequently occurs. Freeman has illustrated this process in the case of plastics, where fundamental scientific research work in Germany in the early 1920s on long-chain molecules led directly to the innovation of polystyrene and styrene rubber, and indirectly to numerous other new products in the 1930s. Further innovations and massive world-wide diffusion took place after the Second World War, facilitated by the shift from coal to oil as the feedstock for the industry. In the 1970s the industry appears to have 'matured' with a slow-down in demand and in the rate of technological progress.

The measurement of inventive and innovative activity is beset with difficulties. Input measures include the manpower employed and financial expenditure, although there is necessarily a degree of arbitrariness in defining the boundary of research and development activity. Output measures of invention include patent statistics, but these need to be interpreted with caution, owing to the differences in propensity to patent between firms, industries and countries with different perceptions of whether security is enhanced by patent protection or not, and differences in national patent legislation. The use of numbers of innovations as an output measure normally requires some – necessarily subjective – assessment of the relative 'importance' of the individual innovations. Despite their limitations, however, the use of several indicators in combination can provide a basis for comparisons between industries or between countries.

Over the post-war period, governments have increasingly recognized the importance of attaining or maintaining international competitiveness in technology. The emergence of Japan as a major economic power owes much to a conscious policy of importing modern foreign technology and improving it domestically. Most countries have a wide variety of schemes to encourage firms to develop and adopt the new technologies, and policies for training or retraining the workforce in the skills needed to use new techniques. In the current context attention is, of course, focused particularly on microelectronics-related technologies; and – whatever their validity – fears that these technologies could exacerbate unemployment problems generally take second place to fears of the consequences of falling behind technologically, in the eyes of governments and trade unions alike.

Forecasts of the impact of new technologies are notoriously unreliable. The cost-saving potential of nuclear power was dramatically overstated in the early stages, while the potential impact of computers was first thought to be extremely limited. For good or ill, we can however say that technological progress shows no sign of coming to a halt.

J. A. Clark
University of Sussex

References
Freeman, C. (1982), *The Economics of Industrial Innovation*, 2nd edn, London.
Nelson, R. R. and Winter, S. G. (1982), *An Evolutionary Theory of Economic Change*, Cambridge, Mass.

Further Reading
Heertje, A. (1977), *Economics and Technical Change*, London.

Terrorism

Terrorism consists of a series of acts intended to spread intimidation, panic, and destruction in a population. These acts can be carried out by individuals and groups opposing a state, or acting on its behalf. The amount of violence is often disproportionate, apparently random, deliberately symbolic: to hit a target which would convey a message to the rest of the population. Violence perpetrated by the state or by right-wing terrorist groups is anonymous. Its goals are to shift sectors of public opinion to support the restoration of law and order and repressive measures, at the same time physically destroying political opponents and intimidating their actual and potential supporters. Violence from left-wing groups is usually 'signed'. Its goals are the awakening of public opinion to the injustices of the 'system', the 'punishment' of hated representatives of the system and their lackeys, and the expansion of political support for, and/or the defence of, their organizations. The ultimate goal is to muster enough support to overthrow the regime or, at least, to produce a revolutionary situation. An intermediate stage might be the unmasking of the 'fascist face' of the regime and the revelation to the population of its repressive reality.

Terrorism by the state or against it must be considered rational behaviour within the context of alternative options. It is suggestive of the lack of vast support both for the state and for terrorist organizations. Otherwise, both would utilize different political means. It is indeed a short cut to the problem of the creation of the necessary support. Sociopolitical terrorism may arise both in democratic and non-democratic states. It is more frequent in the former because of the relative ease with which terrorist organizations can be created in an atmosphere of freedom, when their appearance is unexpected. In non-democratic states, of course, it may be the state apparatus itself which resorts to terrorist activities. In any event, the lack of peaceful alternatives to change is likely to radicalize the situation and to push some opponents towards violent, clandestine activities.

There is not a single cause of terrorism: several conditions and determinants must be present. For state terrorism the most important conditions are the willingness and determination of the dominant groups to retain power against mounting opposition, even by violent means. For sociopolitical terrorism, it is the inability to acquire sufficient support for radical changes in the light of mass passivity and élite unresponsiveness. However, terrorism is never simply the response to socioeconomic conditions of marginality. It is always the product of a political project. Be they at the service of the state or against the state, the terrorists pursue political goals.

According to their goals, one can define and identify several types of terrorism: repressive, revolutionary, secessionist. It is also possible to speak of international terrorism – though somewhat inappropriately – for those groups staging their activities on the international scene. They want to dramatize their plight and obtain international visibility, recognition, and support (such as some sectors of the Palestine Liberation Organization (PLO), the Armenians, the Ustasha). However, most terrorist organizations are indigenous, such as the Irish Republican Army (IRA), the German Rote Armee Fraktion, the Italian Brigate Rosse and the neo-fascist Ordine Nuovo, the French Action Directe, the Basque ETA. They have roots and pursue goals that are inherently 'national', even though they might enjoy some (reciprocal) 'international' support.

On the basis of the superior technical strength of modern states and of the legitimacy of democratic ones, it is often said that political terrorism cannot win. However, terrorism by the state can achieve significant results, and political terrorism against non-democratic regimes can severely weaken them (though, in order to win, the terrorist group will have to transform itself into guerrilla bands).

Terrorism, even if it is defeated, is not without consequences. The dynamics of political competition, the structures of the state, the relationships between citizens and political-administrative bodies will be changed to an extent that has thus far not been assessed. Therefore, political terrorism will endure as the weapon of groups that have neither the capability, the possibility, nor the patience to utilize other instruments to pursue their goals and implement their strategies.

Gianfranco Pasquino
University of Bologna

Further Reading
Alexander, Y., Carlton, D. and Wilkinson, P. (eds) (1979), *Terrorism: Theory and Practice*, Boulder, Colorado.
Bell, R. (1975), *Transnational Terrorism*, Washington.
Crenshaw, M. (ed.) (1983), *Terrorism, Legitimacy and Power*, Middletown, Conn.
Eckstein, H. (1963), *Internal War*, New York.
Laqueur, W. (1977), *Terrorism: A Study of National and International Political Violence*, Boston.
Lodge, J. (ed.) (1981), *Terrorism: A Challenge to the State*, London.
Schmid, A. P. (1983), *Political Terrorism: A Research Guide to Concepts, Theories, Data Bases and Literature*, New Brunswick, NJ.
Stohl, M. (ed.) (1979), *The Politics of Terrorism*, New York.
Wardlaw, G. (1982), *Political Terrorism: Theory, Tactics, and Countermeasures*, Cambridge.
See also: *force*.

Thematic Apperception Test

See Projective Methods.

Therapeutic Community

The use of community social processes for the treatment of mentally ill and personality disordered patients has been labelled 'therapeutic community'. Factors which have led to this approach include a growing dissatisfaction with the results of individual psychotherapy, the recognition of some harmful effects of institutionalization itself, and the realization of the importance of social experiences in learning and, therefore, in therapy.

The impetus for the therapeutic community came during and after World War II with the development of therapeutic units for soldiers suffering combat fatigue. In these army centres every aspect of the soldiers' hospital life was designed to counteract the socialization experience involved in being defined as mentally ill. The success of these units in returning soldiers to full activity was in sharp contrast with previous experience, and led to efforts at their replication in the civilian community.

Procedures in therapeutic communities derive from three sources: (1) group therapy, in which patients receive continuous feedback on their behaviour as seen by others and their maladaptive use of defence mechanisms; (2) democratic traditions of self-government, including a sharing of facilities, the use of first names, and frank expressions of thoughts and feelings between patients and staff; and (3) the importance of being part of a social unit to counteract alienation and promote rehabilitation. The power of peer group pressure has long been used in self-help groups, such as Alcoholics Anonymous.

The tone of the therapeutic community is often set by a daily meeting where all patients, ward staff, and doctors openly discuss problems and psychopathology.

Problems of the therapeutic community include the blurring of roles which makes it possible for staff to evade responsibility and authority. Also, the community approach may become a vehicle for the patient's rationalizing hostility towards authority or leadership in any form.

Despite difficulties, the concept has added to the effectiveness and humanity of the psychiatric unit. Those therapeutic communities which have achieved stability have incorporated professional control while permitting patients an active voice in their own care.

Bernard S. Levy
Harvard University

Further Reading
Almond, R. (1974), *The Healing Community*, New York.
Caudill, W. (1958), *The Psychiatric Hospital as a Small Society*, Cambridge, Mass.
Cumming, J. and Cumming, E. (1962), *Ego and Milieu*, New York.
Jones, M. (1953), *The Therapeutic Community*, New York.
See also: *group therapy.*

Thick Description

Thick description is often used in the sense of the-more-data-the-better, but this is not quite what Gilbert Ryle (1980), who coined and defined the phrase, or Clifford Geertz (1973; 1983), who has made it the cornerstone concept of his interpretive anthropology, had in mind.

In doing ethnography, 'The aim is to draw large conclusions from small, but very densely textured facts; to support broad assertions about the role of culture in the construction of collective life by engaging them exactly with complex specifics' (Geertz, 1973). Geertz advocates tacking back and forth between basic questions and exceedingly extended acquaintances with extremely small matters. While not averse to temporarily 'fixing' the flow of social discourse and cultural processes as 'game', 'drama', 'template', 'web of significance' or 'text', Geertz hopes to avoid the reifications and reductionism of method-obsessed, law-seeking social science; thick description should be thought of as open-ended, a layering of meaning in which any bit of behaviour or any statement about human phenomena can always be further contexted and interpreted by the next human who comes along.

This insistence on the open and democratic determination of meaning confronts the worst biodeterminist, rationalist and élitist social engineering tendencies in social science; but it tends to gloss over the deepening division of the world into exploiters and exploited, as well as, for example, the increasing power of corporate and state-controlled media to define more and more of everyone's culture.

Geertz's chapter on 'Thick Description' opens his collected essays, *The Interpretation of Cultures* (1973); and a fine example closes the collection, 'Deep Play: Notes on a Balinese Cockfight' (see also Geertz, 1983).

Charles Keil
State University of New York at Buffalo

References
Geertz, C. (1973), *The Interpretation of Cultures*, New York.
Geertz, C. (1983), *Local Knowledge*, New York.
Ryle, G. (1980), *Collected Papers*, Vol. 2, Atlantic Highlands, NJ.
See also: *ethnographic fieldwork; Geertz.*

Thinking – Cognitive Organization and Processes

The term thinking is one of those most difficult to encapsulate in a simple definition. We learn the word long before we encounter psychological research, and our ideas about thinking are strongly influenced by commonsensical notions which may not map neatly onto the concepts which psychologists have found necessary to develop when studying cognition. We may be puzzled, for example, when psychologists argue that we are not consciously aware of much of our thinking, or that it is not really sensible to draw boundaries between thinking and perceiving, understanding and remembering. In psychology the word 'cognition' (from the Latin *cognosco*, to know) has come to be used in a wide sense, encompassing perceiving, comprehending and remembering, as well as thinking, in part because psychologists are aware of the interrelationships between all these processes.

Within philosophy, from Aristotle onwards, there was a strong tradition that thought involved a chain of associations of conscious images. This view underpinned the initial founding of experimental psychology in the late nineteenth century as the scientific study of consciousness. One of the major disputes in the early 1900s followed the frequent failure of subjects at Würzburg, when introspecting on their thought processes, to report imagery. It is easy to verify for oneself that one can think of the superordinate category of 'cat' or an example of a flower without any intervening imagery. William James had already commented that thought was like the perches and flights of a bird (1890). During the flights, we are not aware of the components which lead to the next conclusion. Subsequently, there has been general agreement that much of the processing that underlies thinking, as well as the other cognitive processes, is not available to consciousness. (Morris and Hampson (1983) discuss those processes which are not open to introspection.)

The problems which the 'imageless thought' controversy raised for the early introspective psychology encouraged the growth of behaviourism. For the founder of this school, J. B. Watson, thought was 'nothing but talking to ourselves' and since 'any and every bodily response may become a word substitute' it became difficult to separate thinking from behaviour in general; in the US the study of thinking was submerged in the rush to investigate animal learning.

In Germany, however, the reaction to the introspective psychology took another form. Gestalt psychologists argued that the mind could not be analysed into simple sensations, but actually functioned towards forming good, whole patterns. Problems arose when there was imbalance in the mental field, conceived as akin to an electromagnetic field, so that problem solutions reflected a sudden rearrangement of the field in a way analogous to the reversal of the Necker cube in perception. This change in the field corresponded to insight into the problem. One Gestalt psychologist, Kohler, produced a famous monograph on *The Mentality of Apes* (1925) claiming insight into their problem solving, which challenged many behaviourist assumptions. Others, such as Duncker and Maier, examined the conditions which aided or impeded human insight. They showed, for example, how 'functional fixity' in the way in which we think of a pair of pliers will inhibit insight into their potential use as a pendulum bob in a given problem. In a related way, the repeated use of, say, a particular order of filling and emptying jugs in successfully solving a series of problems requiring the measurement of an amount of water, will 'set' the solver to try to use this solution when a far easier one is available.

With the decline of behaviourism and the development of computer science and cognitive psychology in the 1950s and 1960s, thinking became an important research topic. The need to design computers to solve problems stimulated research on how problems were solved by humans.

It became obvious to researchers on artificial intelligence (AI) that problem solving required both a massive base of stored knowledge and suitable operators to manipulate that knowledge. Newall and Simon (1972) studied the thought processes of experts and novices while playing chess and solving other prob-

lems. By getting their subjects to 'think aloud' they produced protocols of the steps in solving their problems. They were able to show that the subjects broke the problems down into sub-goals which they tackled with various strategies until the final solution. They developed a computer program called the General Problem Solver (GPS) which was able to solve a wide range of problems. It began by identifying the initial stage, goal state, and legal operators, and broke the problem down into manageable sub-goals using the principle of means-ends analysis. This involves reducing the difference between the present state and the desired sub-goal by selecting suitable operators.

Means-ends analysis represents one way of choosing strategies. The study of AI soon showed that both computers and people need rules of thumb, known as heuristics, which they can apply to situations as a good gamble that they will lead to successful solutions. Such heuristics must often function adequately; but much of the study of thinking by psychologists has deliberately chosen problems where the normal steps to a solution will fail. By so doing, more complex problem solving can be studied and the heuristics themselves clarified.

One aspect of thinking where heuristics have been especially explored is in decision making. Tversky and Kahneman (1974) have argued that some of our decisions will be biased by the failure of the heuristics we use to estimate the probability of events occurring. They identify two common heuristics, availability and representativeness. When using the availability heuristic, we assess the likelihood of something happening, say, our having a heart attack, by recalling instances of such events happening to people of our age. If we can think of many cases, we judge a heart attack as likely. This heuristic will work well so long as the sample that we recall is not biased by the properties of our memories. Tversky and Kahneman were able to demonstrate major errors in estimates of probability, which appear to result from instances being recalled disproportionately to their real occurrence.

The representativeness heuristic appears in the gambler's fallacy. It is commonly and erroneously believed that because the red and black of a roulette wheel have equal probabilities in the long term, a run of several red wins increases the probability that the next win will be black. People expect small samples to be representative of the long-term frequency pattern and ignore the fact that each spin has the same probability of red and black. Tversky and Kahneman, and Nisbett and Ross (1980) have documented the influence of such faulty heuristics of decision making in many problems.

Attempts to make computers solve problems revealed the need for the computer already to possess a rich knowledge of the world. Schank and Abelson (1977) found it necessary to equip their computer with expectations about what should happen, for example, when using a restaurant. They called the knowledge of such events 'scripts'. The use of prior knowledge is essential not only in problem solving or question answering, but in our comprehending and making sense of our minute-by-minute experience of the world. In so far as thinking can be defined as going beyond the information given, this is common to perceiving, comprehending and remembering as well as to thinking. As the research of, for example, Bransford (1979) has shown, we are constantly going beyond the given information to construct a plausible account of, and draw deductions from, our experience. For this reason it is hard to draw distinctions among the various aspects of cognition.

There have been several attempts to model the knowledge base used in comprehension and thought. Network models (Anderson, 1976) have been the most popular. These represent the stored knowledge as nodes (or knots) representing concepts which are joined by specified relationships such as 'is the cause of', 'is an example of', to other nodes. According to such models, thinking, at least in part, involves the activating of nodes and the tracing and evaluating of the routes that are joined between them.

Another popular way of modelling the representation of knowledge has been by production systems. A production is a rule linking defined conditions to specified actions, so that if the conditions are met the actions will be carried out. It is assumed by advocates of the production system (for example, Anderson, 1980; Allport, 1979) that our knowledge and skills are represented by a vast collection of these rules which can be activated by appropriate conditions, and can modify and transform the currently active information in the cognitive system in a very flexible way.

Psychologists have long been interested in individual differences in thinking, and have recognized that being good at solving problems is an important skill, which is closely involved in the construction of intelligence tests. Since Binet was asked in 1905 to devise the first intelligence test, their use and interpretation has been controversial. Nevertheless the standard intelligence tests clearly measure individual differences in ability, even if it can be argued that these abilities are selected and limited by cultural factors.

In recent years cognitive psychologists have tried to specify what actual cognitive skills underlie the factors, such as verbal and spatial ability, which consistently emerge from psychometric studies. Hunt (1978) and Sternberg (1977) have tried to analyse in detail the sort of tasks used in intelligence tests, and to determine how individual differences in skills and strategies may contribute to the overall IQ score.

A fundamental issue in the study of thinking which divides many current researchers is the extent to which rational thought is based upon logic. Cohen (1977) argues that human thought is logical, and that appar-

ently illogical arguments result either from ignorance or misunderstandings, or the use of less familiar theories of probability. Many others (for example, Johnson-Laird, 1982; Evans, 1980) see the basis of thinking as being often alogical and not based upon the formal principles familiar to logicians. One theme of recent research has been to show that familiarity with real-world uses of particular rules means that subjects can easily solve reasoning problems, even though they fail with abstract problems based on the same logical structure (Cox and Griggs, 1982). Such research suggests that, whatever the fundamental rationality of human thinking, the reality of the quality of thinking and problem solving in the everyday world depends as much upon memory as logic. This illustrates the point made initially, that it is a mistake to try to separate thinking too much from the rest of cognition.

Peter E. Morris
University of Lancaster

References

Allport, D. A. (1979), 'Conscious and unconscious cognition: a computational metaphor for the mechanism of attention and integration', in L. G. Nilsson (ed.), *Perspectives on Memory Research*, Hillsdale, NJ.

Anderson, J. R. (1976), *Language, Memory and Thought*, Hillsdale, NJ.

Anderson, J. R. (1980), *Cognitive Psychology and its Implications*, San Francisco.

Bransford, J. D. (1979), *Human Cognition: Learning, Understanding and Remembering*, Belmont, Calif.

Cohen, L. J. (1977), *The Probable and the Provable*, Oxford.

Cox, J. R. and Griggs, R. A. (1982), 'The effects of experience on performance in Wason's selection task', *Memory and Cognition*, 10.

Evans, J. St B. T. (1980), 'Thinking: experimental and information processing approaches', in G. Claxton (ed.), *Cognitive Psychology: New Directions*, London.

Hunt, E. (1978), 'The mechanisms of verbal ability', *Psychological Review*, 85.

James, W. (1890), *The Principles of Psychology*, New York.

Johnson-Laird, P. N. (1982), 'Thinking as a skill', *Quarterly Journal of Experimental Psychology*, 34a.

Kohler, W. (1925), *The Mentality of Apes*, New York.

Morris, P. E. and Hampson, P. J. (1983), *Imagery and Consciousness*, New York.

Newell, A. and Simon, H. A. (1972), *Human Problem Solving*, Englewood Cliffs, NJ.

Nisbett, R. E. and Ross, L. (1980), *Human Inference: Strategies and Shortcomings of Social Judgement*, Englewood Cliffs, NJ.

Schank, R. C. and Abelson, R. P. (1977), *Scripts, Plans, Goals and Understanding*, Hillsdale, NJ.

Sternberg, R. J. (1977), *Intelligence, Information Processing and Analogical Reasoning*, Hillsdale, NJ.

Tversky, A. and Kahneman, D. (1974), 'Judgment under uncertainty: heuristics and biases', *Science*, 125.

See also: *artificial intelligence; cognitive science; intelligence; memory; problem solving.*

Third World

The division of the world into three categories is a very popular device among social scientists, and especially economists and sociologists of development. The distinction derives from a United Nations classification system, which distinguishes between developed, free market economies (The First World), centrally-planned economies (the Second), and undeveloped, free market economies (the Third). The criteria for this classification are an awkward mixture of economic and political indices, easier to describe than to define (or to defend). Western European countries, the United States of America and Japan, clearly fall into the First World; all socialist countries clearly fall into the Second; and the Third World is therefore a residual category which includes the very rich (such as Kuwait), the very poor (such as Bangladesh), some very complex (such as Brazil), and some starkly simple economies (such as Paraguay). Reduced to its simplest terms, the Third World consists of economies which are neither fully industrial nor centrally planned; this definition permits the inclusion of a great range, not only of economic, but also of social and political conditions.

Arbitrary as it may seem, the division has proved highly durable. All those economies which now belong to the First World were already relatively industrialized by the outbreak of World War I, when an invisible door was slammed in the face of all economies which had not yet achieved some measure of industrial sophistication. Many settler societies (notably Australia, New Zealand, Canada, Argentina, Uruguay, and perhaps Israel) have often enjoyed higher incomes per capita than Western European societies: but in spite of the availability of capital, skilled manpower, and natural resources, none has broken through to the charmed circle of industrial maturity. They commonly perceived the United States as the development model to follow, and therefore adopted essentially *laissez-faire* strategies. Japan has been the equally compelling model for several Asian governments, which have striven for industrialization through encouragement of industrial capital and the coercion of a domestic labour force. Brazil, Iran, South Africa, South Korea, and Taiwan are among the more 'arresting' instances of this strategy; and thus far the appalling human costs

have not been matched by redeeming economic performance.

The term Third World is not only arbitrary: it is also pejorative. Nobody believes that the conditions it describes ought to be permitted. Where differences of opinion occur, they are about prescribing how the conditions are to be abolished. Economists commonly emphasize specific measures which individual governments might adopt, with a view to increasing national income or promoting industrial production. Sociologists and political scientists commonly insist that political and social reforms of various kinds must precede any major transformation of economic conditions. In point of fact there must be some question as to the ability of the world's resources, however benignly controlled, to sustain the level of industrial production which universal industrialization implies. If that doubt is valid, then the transformation of the First World may be as urgent as the abolition of the Third. In any event, this arbitrary, pejorative, and thoroughly irritating term seems destined to enjoy a long life, since the conditions it describes are evidently profoundly entrenched in the political, social and economic structure of the contemporary world.

Donald Denoon
Australian National University, Canberra

Further Reading
Goldthorpe, J. E. (1984), *The Sociology of the Third World*, Cambridge.

Worsley, P. (1964), *The Third World*, London.
See also: *underdevelopment.*

Time

Like philosophers and natural scientists, psychologists have been intrigued by questions about time. How, in the apparent absence of a special sense organ, can we experience time? Is time an intuitive mode of perception, as Kant suggested, or a cognitive construction? Psychological approaches over the past century have yielded a number of important insights, not the least of which is the multiplicity of time experience.

The oldest and best developed approach is the study of time perception (Block, 1980; Michon, 1978). When deprived of clocks and other measuring devices, humans can still make remarkably accurate judgements about duration and order. Yet duration judgements can also be distorted in principled ways depending upon the properties of the stimuli and the activities of the perceiver. Experiments using discrete pairs of tones or light flashes show that separations as brief as 25–90 milliseconds still allow the detection of two separate events. However, when the separation is less than about one-fifth of a second, there is a strong tendency to perceive the events as dynamically related, an impression underlying the effectiveness of 'moving' marquee lights. A number of studies indicate that humans are most accurate in judging durations of about one-half of a second. But there is virtually no progressive under- or overestimation as durations increase up to times of several minutes. Given the considerable accuracy of duration judgements, it is not surprising that some theorists have posited the existence of an internal 'biological clock'. Yet none of the candidate physiological processes (for example, heart rate, cortical alpha rhythm) seem to be responsible for time perception. In addition, the biological clock model seems inconsistent with a number of systematic distortions of subjective time estimates.

Distortions of time estimates. like other perceptual illusions, provide clues to the processes responsible for normal experience. One time illusion, noted by William James in 1890, is that interesting experiences are subjectively shortened while they occur but are overestimated in retrospect. Conversely, empty intervals seem long as they are experienced but short when they are later remembered. Several explanations have been offered for these effects including the notion that when engaged in an engrossing task, one has little attention left over to monitor the passage of time or extraneous changes in the environment. By one account of the retrospective stretching or shrinking of experiences, the 'storage space' of the corresponding memory is used as a cue to the length of the experience. Thus, simply coded events seem briefer than elaborately coded events.

The relationship between time and memory is also central in some of the more cognitive approaches to the study of time. When thinking about past events, we often have a compelling feeling that one event was more recent than another. Laboratory studies indicate that judgements of recency are better when two events are meaningfully related (Tzeng and Cotton, 1980). One intepretation is that for related pairs (for instance two plays with the same leading actor) the first event is remembered at the time that the second is experienced. This leads to the establishment of an order code. Other studies of real world memory show that personal 'temporal landmarks' often play a key role in judging the date of past events.

The structure of memory provides information about the time of past events, but how do we know the present time? Several studies of temporal orientation show that the current day of the week can be identified more rapidly just before or after a weekend than in midweek (Koriat, Fischhoff and Razel, 1976). Apparently, current or recent activities and thoughts are tested against stored associations of different days of the week. The relative indistinctness of midweek days seems to be responsible for the delay in orienting on these days.

Relatively little attention has been given to human understanding of natural periodicities and conventional time systems. But recent studies indicate that several distinct kinds of representations or processes underlie part of this knowledge. When asked to make judgements about the order of months, subjects appear to recite covertly the names of months in some tasks and to use spatial-like images in other tasks (Friedman, 1983).

Another perspective comes from developmental research (Friedman, 1982). The ability to distinguish temporal patterns is well developed by infancy. This finding is not surprising when one considers the exquisite sensitivity to order necessary for speech production and comprehension. Other abilities show a more gradual development. Adults can infer the relative durations of two events given simultaneous starts and successive finishes. Five-year-olds under some circumstances can make similar judgements but they are easily perturbed by a variety of perceptual factors including distance and end point in the case of moving objects. Other abilities show a gradual onset, including awareness of the past-present-future trichotomy and knowledge of conventional time systems. Perhaps better than other approaches, developmental studies point to the multifaceted nature of time experience.

William J. Friedman
Oberlin College, Ohio

References
Block, R. A. (1980), 'Time and consciousness', in G. Underwood and R. G. Stevens (eds), *Aspects of Consciousness*, Vol. I, London.
Friedman, W. (ed.) (1982), *The Developmental Psychology of Time*, New York.
Friedman, W. (1983), 'Image and verbal processes in reasoning about the months of the year', *Journal of Experimental Psychology: Learning, Memory and Cognition*, 9.
Koriat, A., Fischhoff, B. and Razel, O. (1976), 'An inquiry into the process of temporal orientation', *Acta Psychologica*, 40.
Michon, J. A. (1978), 'The making of the present: a tutorial review', in J. Requin (ed.), *Attention and Performance*, *VII*, Hillsdale, NJ.
Tzeng, O. and Cotton, B. (1980), 'A study-phase retrieval model of temporal coding', *Journal of Experimental Psychology: Human Learning and Memory*, 6.
See also: *memory*.

Time-Space Analysis

All events in society take place in time and space, but time-space analysis is specifically concerned with the structuring and modelling of events and data *through* time and *across* geographical space, and especially with the quantitative, statistical analysis of time-space data. The term is mainly employed for this type of quantitative analysis, but it is also sometimes used in a broader sense for research on the structure and role of time-space constraints on individual and social behaviour in time-space budgets for the day, the week, or the year (see Parkes and Thrift (1980) for these wider contexts).

Time-space analysis requires data collected consistently across a set of regions (such as cities, administrative areas, or census units) for several (and preferably for many) time periods. Analysis of such data is important, because it allows the direct testing and modelling of phenomena such as diffusion and regional interaction, which have to be either assumed or only indirectly tested in most other analyses and data sets. Data sets suitable for time-space analysis have not been widespread – in contrast to the superabundance of pure cross-sectional data suitable for spatial statistics – but more are becoming available as government statistical data accumulate.

Time series data exhibit internal regularities, notably autocorrelation between the value of a variable at time t and its own lagged value at t-1 or t-2. Such relationships at various lags t-1, t-2, . . ., t-k define the autocorrelation function. Similarly, the cross-correlation function examines lagged relationships between two series x_t and y_t for various leads and lags, and time series econometrics offers many ways of incorporating such lags into dynamic regression models. Purely cross-sectional, spatial data also exhibit regularities, in this case the spatial autocorrelations between observations for regions at different distances apart. The time-space autocorrelation function generalizes these approaches to lags or distances apart in *both* time and geographical space. Instabilities and trends in time, and regional variations in autocorrelation, can also be detected in large data sets. Time-space cross-correlation functions can be determined and used as the basis for time-space dynamic regression models, and for the forecasting and control of time-space systems.

Applications of time-space analysis include: the diffusion of technology, innovations, and institutions; the spread of measles and influenza epidemics through cities and regions; the spread and contraction of regional economic fluctuations; and the diffusion of regional wage inflation. The methods are also useful for the specification of regional interactions in the multiregional econometric models recently constructed for the US and several European countries. Most applications have been in human geography and regional economics, but relevance in a wider social and political science context is examined by Klingman (1980).

Because of the presence of time-lags, the specification and estimation of time-space models has proved easier than that of purely cross-sectional, spatial models, and the extension of time series models and techniques to time-space analysis has been rapid. The literature is now large (see Bennett (1979) for a comprehensive survey).

L. W. Hepple
University of Bristol

References
Bennett, R. J. (1979), *Spatial Time Series*, London.
Klingman, D. (1980), 'Temporal and spatial diffusion in the comparative analysis of social change', *The American Political Science Review*, 74.
Parkes, D. N. and Thrift, N. J. (1980), *Times, Spaces and Places: A Chronogeographic Perspective*, Chichester.

See also: *spatial statistics*.

Tinbergen, Jan (1903–)

The Dutchman Jan Tinbergen was the first economist to receive the Nobel Memorial Prize for Economics (in 1969, jointly with the Norwegian Ragnar Frisch). He originally studied physics at Leiden University, but then in 1929 joined the Central Bureau of Statistics in The Hague. Economists differ in their judgements of where Tinbergen's special merit lies. Readers of his more recent books may well believe that Tinbergen is, above all, interested in income distribution. His research in this area aims to explain the trend towards greater equality in a number of Western countries, and his particular contribution is in specifying the degree of 'acceptable' inequality to an egalitarian: a man with strong feelings of justice, and not satisfied by mere proclamations of fairness, he is concerned to ensure that statistical analyses and policy measures are based on sound quantitative research.

Others will think primarily of his studies in development planning and the world economy. Tinbergen has served as an adviser to many underdeveloped countries. His research unit at the Rotterdam School of Economics, where he was professor of development planning from 1933 to 1973, attracted many visitors from the Third World, and was called Balanced International Growth.

Earlier in his career, Tinbergen was the inspired and inspiring director of the Central Planning Bureau at The Hague (1945–55), an agency which planned economic policy in collaboration with politicians. (Politicians specify the goals, while economists suggest ways of achieving these goals.) In order to do the job successfully, a precise and quantitative insight is required into the relationship between policy measures (tax rates, wage rates, exchange rates, government expenditures) and policy outcomes (prices, production, employment, balance of payments). It was Tinbergen, together with a number of other econometric pioneers, who changed the face of economic theory. When the depression of the 1930s wrecked production, income and employment, the League of Nations at Geneva invited him and Gottfried van Haberler to survey existing economic theories. Tinbergen studied the quantitative aspects, taking the view that relationships between economic variables show a certain constancy over time and lend themselves to statistical research. These relationships can be understood only if they are brought together in a model.

Tinbergen's lead was followed by other econometricians, like Lawrence Klein in the US. The theoretical basis for the early models was basically Keynesian, and they were used for prediction and for a rationalization of economic policy. The political objective was to stabilize the growing economy at a high level of employment, and because these goals were more or less attained between 1945 and 1970, the approach gained prestige. Later models, developed from Tinbergen's and Klein's were elaborately specified and were able to take account of every kind of theoretical consideration. But more recently the approach has come under criticism. Monetarist critics prefer very small models in which the quantity of money plays a dominant role. Others point to the non-constancy of the parameters. The discussion will continue, but whatever its outcome, it will be guided by Tinbergen's quest for precision and quantification.

J. Pen
University of Groningen

Further Reading
Tinbergen's publications include:
(1937), *Statistical Testing of Business Cycle Theory*, Geneva.
(1938), *An Economic Approach to Business Cycle Problems*, Paris.
(1939), *Business Cycles in the USA, 1919–32*, Geneva.
(1951), *Business Cycles in the UK*, Amsterdam.
(1952), *On the Theory of Economic Policy*, Amsterdam.
(1962), *Shaping the World Economy*, New York.
(1965), *Economic Policy: Principles and Design*, Amsterdam.
(1968), *Development Planning*, London.
(1975), *Income Distribution, Analysis and Policies*, Amsterdam.

Tobin, James (1918–)

James Tobin is one of the most outstanding of the American heirs of the Keynesian Revolution. Born in Illinois in 1918, he graduated from Harvard in 1939 and interrupted his postgraduate studies to serve in the US Navy from 1942–6, completing his Harvard Ph.D. in 1947. In 1950 he joined the Yale economics department, where he became Sterling professor in 1957 and served two stints (1955–61 and 1964–5) as

director of the Cowles Foundation for Research in Economics.

His scholarly output has been substantial and so wide-ranging in its reach and perception that it is impossible to summarize adequately. He is best known, however, for his important researches in macro-economic and monetary theory. The Nobel Prize awarded to him in 1981 was for his pioneer contributions to portfolio selection theory (where he laid the foundations for the modern theory of finance) and for his analyses of the interactions between real and financial markets, involving a path-breaking application of general equilibrium theory. His powerful influence on contemporary economic research has been partly due to the originality of his ideas, and partly to his propensity for focusing sharply and effectively on major theoretical problems of urgent immediate concern to theorists and policy makers; for example, in his analyses of the determinants of consumption and investment behaviour, or of the real/financial transmission mechanisms involved in aggregative models of economic growth and fluctuations, and in his contributions to the current controversy on stabilization theory and policy. In addition, he has developed new statistical and econometric techniques and made significant contributions to social policy debates on poverty and unemployment.

Phyllis Deane
University of Cambridge

Further Reading
Purvis, D. and Myhrman, J. (1981), 'James Tobin's contribution to economics', *Scandinavian Journal of Economics*, 84. (Also contains official citation on the Nobel Memorial Prize in Economics, 1981, and a bibliography of over 200 items listing his scholarly publications from May 1941–October 1981.)
Tobin, J., Harris, S. E. *et al.* (1956), *The American Business Creed*, Cambridge, Mass.
Tobin, J. (1966), *National Economic Policy*, New Haven.
Tobin, J. (1974 and 1975), *Essays in Economics*, vol. I, *Macroeconomics*, and vol. II, *Consumption and Econometrics*, Amsterdam.
Tobin, J. (1974), *The New Economics: One Decade Older*, Princeton.

Tocqueville, Alexis de (1805–59)

Alexis de Tocqueville, French statesman and political writer, may be considered the founder of comparative historical sociology. He was one of the first to undertake the rigorous comparison of social systems, studying France, England, America and Algeria, and collecting information also on India – his aim being to specify similarities and differences.

An aristocrat by birth, and a committed political animal, he was also a nonpositivist sociologist: his approach was closer to that of Weber than of Marx or Durkheim. 'Liberty,' he remarked, 'is the foremost of my passions.' In the hope of furthering the cause of liberty in France, he undertook the study of democracy in America, where the role of the 'equality of status' as the 'generating factor' attracted him. In America, equality could be reconciled with liberty because democracy preceded equalization and structured it. Men who enjoyed identical civil rights rejected all pressures, and the importance of associations and of local elections frustrated the development of administrative centralization – which, like the threat of social atomization, fostered despotism. In France, in contrast, the Revolution of 1789 reduced the aristocratic society to rubble. The extremely centralized state, rather than the society itself as in the US, did try to foster the equality of civil status, but the resistance to the aristocracy stimulated the development of universalistic and radical theories, unknown in the US, which legitimated the revolutionary process. From that point democracy became inceasingly vulnerable, and it confronted a state, which, while supporting its development, nevertheless remained external to the society. Moreover, both in the US and in France, democracy was threatened by a new authoritarianism, that of industrial power, whose growth it fostered.

Tocqueville's two major works, *De la démocratie en Amérique*, vol. I–IV, (1835–40) (*Democracy in America*, 1945) and *L'Ancien régime et la révolution* (1856) (*The Ancient Regime*, 1952), form a logical unity. In his prolific correspondence with Beaumont, Gobineau, and Mill, as in his *Souvenirs*, Tocqueville was always careful to distinguish the multiple variables which organize different social systems: avoiding deterministic approaches, he always emphasized the essential significance of the values specific to the actors who fashioned consensus or turned revolutionary as a consequence of disappointed hopes.

Pierre Birnbaum
University of Paris

Further Reading
Birnbaum, P. (1970), *Sociologie de Tocqueville*, Paris.
Drescher, S. (1968), *Dilemmas of Democracy: Tocqueville and Modernization*, Pittsburgh.
Lively, J. (1965), *The Social and Political Thoughts of Alexis de Tocqueville*, London.

Tönnies, Ferdinand (1855–1936).

Tönnies, German social theorist and philosopher, was born into an old North German farming family and raised in a small-town environment. He studied philology, philosophy, theology, archaeology and art history at several universities, taking his doctorate at Tübingen in 1875. In 1881 he was granted his *habilitation* for a study of Hobbes which drew on newly-discovered papers of the philosopher. This stimulated his interest in the history and philosophy of law. In the course of his study he introduced the categories of *Gemeinschaft* and *Gesellschaft* (which were to find their way into the title of his magnum opus).

Tönnies served on the staff of the Prussian statistical bureau in Berlin, and began to publish on social and political themes. His commitment to reform delayed his academic career, and he was only appointed to a chair in economics and political science in 1913, when he was nearly fifty. He retired from this post three years later, but returned to the University of Kiel as lecturer in sociology in 1920. He was one of the founders of the German Sociological Association (as was Simmel) and became its president in 1922. But he disbanded the association in 1933 in protest against National Socialism and the already obvious trend towards a 'German National' sociology.

In his principal work, *Gemeinschaft und Gesellschaft* (1887) (*Community and Association*, London, 1957), one of the classics of sociology, Tönnies adopted a position somewhere between the then dominant schools of natural law and historical jurists. *Gemeinschaft*, motivated by a 'natural will' (*Wessenwille*), was a social form characterized by an intense emotional spirit. It was constituted by co-operation, custom and religion, and its typical expressions were the family, village and small-town community. By contrast, *Gesellschaft* was a large-scale organization, such as the city, state or nation, based on convention, law and public opinion. This dualistic frame of reference resembled Durkheim's contrast between 'organic' and 'mechanical' solidarity, and Weber's distinction between *Vergemeinschaftung* and *Vergesellschaftung*, which were parallel attempts to define the social changes that followed industrialization. Using this contrast, Tönnies built up a system of pure, applied and empirical sociology, but his ambitious attempt to link psychological processes and social structure have largely been forgotten.

Peter-Ernst Schnabel
University of Bielefeld

Further Reading
Cahnman, W. J. (ed.) (1973), *Ferdinand Tönnies: A New Evaluation*, Leiden.
Jacoby, E. G. (1971), *Die moderne Gesellschaft in sozialwissenschaftlichen Denken von Ferdinand Tönnies. Eine biographische Einführung*, Stuttgart.
Mühlmann, E. W. (1957), 'Sociology in Germany: shift in alignment', in H. Becker and A. Boskoff (eds), *Modern Sociological Theory in Continuity and Change*, New York.

Totemism

As commonly defined, totemism refers to the identification of man and animal – either the identification of a social group with an animal species, or of a person with a species or individual animal.

The notion of totemism belongs to the history of anthropology and has fallen to some extent into disrepute. It was devised in the last quarter of the nineteenth century to subsume a class of phenomena which seemed associated: the identification of unilineal kinship groups with elements of the natural world, most often animals, vegetables, meteorological phenomena and cardinal points, but also a diversity of other objects. Membership of a totemic group is usually accompanied by prohibition on the consumption of one's own totem, if it is edible.

Totemism has been variously regarded as an elementary form of religion, or as a type of social organization, a form of classification or a cosmology. The extent of disagreement between authors both now and in the past suggests that 'totemism' is a blanket term for a complex arrangement of facts which seem in need of an explanation, although there is no agreement on precisely where the problem lies. Lévi-Strauss (1963) has convincingly argued that, just like the notion of hysteria in psychiatry, totemism as a concept dissolves on close examination. Nevertheless, the notion of totemism draws attention to the radical incommensurability of systems of classification such as our own, founded on visual resemblance, and other systems of classification founded on cosmological and hidden affinities. Hence totemism raises the question of whether it is possible to translate one cultural system into another.

Our difficulty when confronted with totemism is rooted in the unfamiliarity of classifications founded on essential, deep affinities between entities, as opposed to the visual, superficial resemblances which motivate our own categorizations. The identification of men and animals which led to the totemic question is the most spectacular, and to us the most counterintuitive, consequence of an alternative mode of classification. Totemism, however, can justifiably also be regarded as a religion, since, as Radcliffe-Brown (1952) observed, the assumption that specific affinities join certain entities is both the condition and the consequence of considering the world as not only a natural but also as a moral order, that is, in religious terms. In this respect, totemic classifications exhibit properties that are absent from our own classifications: a notion of the whole, and a sense of the responsibility of members of each class for the continuation of the common order.

Paul Jorion
Food and Agricultural Organization, Benin

References
Lévi-Strauss, C. (1963), *Totemism*, Boston. (French edn, *Le Totemisme aujourd'hui*, Paris, 1962).

Radcliffe-Brown, A. R. (1952 [1929]), 'The sociological theory of totemism,' in *Structure and Function in Primitive Society*, London.

Further Reading
Frazer, J. G. (1909), *Totemism and Exogamy*, London.

Trade and Markets, Anthropology of

Diverse trade patterns are found in the non-Western societies of the world. Anthropologists usually analyse these transactions quite differently from economists. For economists, trade and markets are a way of distributing goods through pricing mechanisms so that individual preferences may be satisfied. An economist is concerned to know what determines exchange rates and how closely a particular trade approximates perfect market conditions. For anthropologists, trade and markets provide an index or mirror of social organization. The anthropologist tries to show how a people organize and conceive trade and markets, and how these are linked to other activities in society.

In general, trade reflects the technological conditions in society. For example, in non-complex societies trade goods are usually small, durable and partible, while the velocity of trade is relatively low. The items traded are various, ranging from dyes and feathers used for display, to axes and knives used for productive purposes, to salt and foodstuffs which are directly consumed. Trade also may serve both material and social ends. Some trades are self-interested, immediate transactions between unrelated parties; others are based on credit, occur between kinsfolk and serve to bolster social bonds.

Anthropologists have distinguished several patterns of trade:

(1) *Silent trade* took place in neutral zones between different and often hostile cultures. Contact was minimized by placing objects on the ground and then withdrawing from the area. Transactors offered no information other than quantity of item. Silent trade has attracted attention because it provides a supposed point of origin for all material transactions. It is based on pure self-interest; it suggests that trade originates between groups as a consequence of resource differences (supply) and new tastes (demand); and it offers the prospect that hostility is mediated by economic need and interdependence. But the frequency of silent trade was slight; in fact, it seems to have been found principally between commercial or colonizing societies and native groups. It has seldom been observed between exotic societies themselves. The concept of *primitive* silent trade is primarily a myth that serves to

legitimate the universality of Western-style transactions.

(2) *Ports of trade*, found in the early Near East and the African coast, were permanent marketplaces, located in neutral zones, which functioned to promote intergroup trade. The trade within them was strictly regulated as to objects and quantities, though not necessarily prices.

(3) Under the expression *institutionalized trade* we may include a variety of non-market transactions. For example, extensive trade networks, linking individuals between and within groups, are found in aboriginal Australia and New Guinea; items pass along branching paths at irregular intervals. To participate in the chain brings material benefits as well as prestige, while social sanctions from ostracism to witchcraft ensure that lingering debts are repaid. Elsewhere 'trade partners' may provide outlets and supplies as well as a source of refuge in hostile territory. Some material exchanges occur within the context of rituals. In Western Arnhem Land (Australia) tobacco, spears and blankets are exchanged between groups only during a ceremonial dance.

(4) *Markets* are ubiquitous, being found in societies of the most diverse types. Here, too, much can be learned by examining the social context and implications of the material transactions. For example, markets usually reproduce the local system of production. Small-scale, subsistence producers sell to small-scale, low-margin traders. Neither uses capital-intensive technology. The goods which flow through a market often can be sorted into a pattern. Consumable foodstuffs flow from rural producers to urban dwellers, while manufactured tools and luxuries pass in the other direction. Market days may be staggered by location and specialization so that traders can travel from one to another; in some systems a central marketplace supplies a number of smaller, satellite markets. Such temporal and spatial hierarchies usually reflect the political organization of society. The internal patterns of markets also show variation. Haggling, for example, is not a unitary process but varies according to local custom, goods traded and times of the year. Finally, economic transactions in markets may be closely linked to other social relationships. A marketplace may be the locale for the transmission of gossip and news as well as for finding partners of the opposite sex. In addition, ties of ritual kinship or friendship may be extended to market relationships; from one perspective such permanent bonds reduce risk and provide insurance, but from another they deny the autonomy and pervasiveness of purely market principles. Overall, a market may be the only time when all segments of a diverse society are brought together physically. Within the marketplace hierarchies of goods, the physical location of traders and the style of transactions encode and display relations of prestige and power. In this respect 'pure'

market trade is like a social ritual that conveys cultural information to participants and observers.

Stephen Gudeman
University of Minnesota

Further Reading
Belshaw, C. S. (1965), *Traditional Trade and Modern Markets*, Englewood Cliffs, NJ.
Polanyi, K., Arensberg, C. M. and Pearson, H. W. (1957), *Trade and Market in the Early Empires*, New York.

See also: *economic anthropology; exchange; markets.*

Trade

See International Trade.

Trade Unions

A trade union is a combination of employees for the purpose of regulating the relationship between employees and employer so that the pay and conditions of the employees may improve. Such regulation can be brought about in three main ways: (1) unilateral regulation by the trade union; (2) bargaining with the employer by the employees collectively; (3) statutory regulation (Clegg, 1976).

Historically, unilateral regulation was used by unions of skilled craftsmen who would agree among themselves not to accept employment unless certain terms were met by the employer. Subsequently, with the extension of trade unions to cover nearly all sections of the work force, collective bargaining over pay and conditions became the major activity of trade unions in most countries, with trade union officers also acting to resolve any grievances of individual members, or of small groups, within the work-place. The process of collective bargaining now has very wide scope, and trade union officers frequently exert considerable control and management of the 'internal labour markets' of the members' employing organization (in regard to such things as recruitment, promotion, discipline, and task allocation). The state has tended to intervene both in the employee-employer relationship and also in the process of collective bargaining by legislation and through judicial or quasi-judicial procedures. Thus trade unions have developed their legal expertise and their political connections to operate (and occasionally to resist) and to influence legislation in their members' interests.

Most countries have some statutory legislation concerning the formation of a trade union and the conduct of its affairs (paralleling company or partnership legislation). Generally, a trade union is required to be registered, to have rules conforming to certain standards (for example, for the election of a governing body and the appointment of officers), and to keep and submit (audited) accounts. In return, a registered trade union may be granted certain legal immunities or privileges, the most important being the right not to be sued for breach of contract as a result of action taken in the course of collective bargaining. In some countries, deregistration (or the threat thereof) has been used by governments to influence the behaviour of trade unions.

The logic of collective bargaining (and of its corollary, that agreements must be honoured by both sides) requires that, when necessary, the employee members of a trade union will act together in a united front and that no members will break ranks either by refusing to take, say, strike action when instructed by trade union officers or by taking strike action when this has not been instructed. A trade union must, therefore, have some method of ensuring that each member does what is required of him. A trade union can usually rely on voluntary compliance based on fraternal solidarity or ideological commitment, but the use of sanctions against recalcitrant members always raises difficult questions of the rights of individuals against the needs of the collectivity.

In general, trade unions have become an integral and accepted part of the economies in which they work. This has caused controversy among those who have other views of the functions of trade unions. Marx and Engels saw trade unions as developing inevitably and together with capitalism and (optimistically from their viewpoint) as being in the vanguard of the revolutionary process to overthrow the capitalist system. Marx and Engels subsequently observed the tendency of trade unions, especially in Britain, to become 'corrupted': by concentrating on improving the condition of workers through collective bargaining, they were, by implication, accepting the capitalist system.

Although Marx and Engels observed these tendencies towards the 'embourgeoisement' of the working class, it was Lenin who argued that trade unions tended to become integrated into the capitalist system and that there was therefore a need 'to divert the working-class movement from this spontaneous, trade-unionist striving to come under the wing of the bourgeoisie, and to bring it under the wing of revolutionary Social-Democracy' (Lenin, 1902). Subsequently, Trotsky extended Lenin's thesis of trade union integration into the capitalist system to an attack on trade union leaders who used their authority actively to assist capitalism in controlling the workers, so ensuring trade unions' full incorporation into the system. Seen from another point of view, Trotsky's attack is simply a criticism of the role of trade unions in enforcing collective agreements. The view that trade unions render capitalism 'safe' by institutionalizing conflict may meet with approval or disapproval, but it is central in understanding the role of trade unions in many countries.

Given that trade unions, as an integral part of the market economy, bargain effectively, the question arises as to their economic impact. There are two broad issues of interest: their impact on the general level of wages and their impact on the structure of earnings within the labour market. In situations of full employment, the process of collective bargaining (or the 'power' of trade unions) has been blamed for causing inflation by increasing remuneration per employee by more than the increase in real output per employee, so leading to rising unit labour costs, rising prices, and loss of 'competitiveness' (at an unchanged exchange rate) in world markets with consequent loss of jobs. In response, governments have sometimes attempted to agree with (or to impose on) trade unions an incomes policy, usually comprising some limitation on collectively bargained pay increases together with other measures more acceptable to the unions.

On the issue of pay structures, there is evidence to show that (at least during certain periods – especially of high unemployment) average earnings for unionized groups of employees tend to be higher than average earnings for employees who are not unionized. Some argue that trade unions (or rather, the consequences of collective bargaining) have been at least partly responsible, in co-operation with many other influences, for creating and maintaining labour market 'segmentation'. This is the situation where employment is divided between a relatively unionized 'primary' labour market comprising well-paid jobs with good conditions of employment (short hours, holidays with pay, promotion prospects, pensions) in large firms and in the public sector, and a peripheral relatively non-unionized 'secondary' labour market with low pay and inferior conditions. This strand of criticism of trade unions has been developed both in industrial countries and also in Third-World countries where, it has been argued, trade unions serve to enhance the real incomes of an employed urban élite at the expense of the rural peasantry: incomes policies in Third-World countries have as often been aimed at this problem as at controlling inflation.

D. Jackson
University of Wollongong, Australia

References
Clegg, H. (1976), *Trade Unionism under Collective Bargaining: A Theory Based on Comparisons of Six Countries*, Oxford.
Lenin, V. I. (1902), *What Is To Be Done?*
See also: *corporatism; labour relations*.

Traits

Traits describe individual differences in personality, ability, and temperament. They refer to stable and consistent behaviour patterns and thus provide both economical descriptions of the way one person differs from another and are the basis for predicting how a person may be expected to behave.

A trait description (for example, 'She is intelligent', or 'He is kind') gives information about the standing of the individual on that characteristic relative to others, because traits are regarded as dimensions (like physical dimensions such as height or weight) along which people can be ordered. But, unlike physical characteristics, traits can never be observed directly; they are rather inferred from behavioural signs, and in this sense their existence is always hypothetical.

Traits have been studied extensively in the mapping of individual differences in personality. Trait theorists disagree about the definition of traits and about the precise number and form of traits they consider necessary for an adequate description of personality. An early personality theorist to study traits was Gordon Allport (1937), who defined them as enduring tendencies within the individual to behave in certain ways. This is a broad definition, and it raises the question of what distinguishes a trait from other kinds of inferred constructs used to describe individuals. One particularly problematic distinction is that between trait and attitude. Allport proposed a distinction which is still generally accepted: attitudes, unlike traits, have a well-defined object of reference, are often specific as opposed to general, and typically involve an evaluation of the object.

One of Allport's views which was less well received was that individuals are characterized by their own unique traits. A more commonly accepted notion is to treat traits as dimensions, which are applicable to most, if not all people, and which are able to capture the uniqueness of each individual according to their particular combinations and relative strengths. Two contemporary advocates of this approach to personality are Cattell and H. J. Eysenck. Cattell (1973) concludes that over twenty traits are needed to capture the breadth and diversity of personality, whereas Eysenck (1969) argues for a simpler picture with only three traits; extraversion, neuroticism, and psychopathy.

One important aspect in the study of traits is trait measurement, based on the assumption that a small but carefully selected sample of behaviour will indicate an individual's score on a trait, and this score may then be used to predict how that person will behave in a wide variety of contexts. Traits are inferred from three behavioural indicators: self-report questionnaires, behaviour ratings made by observers, and behavioural responses to situations created by the tester. The questionnaire is the most convenient and widely used.

The measurement of personality traits is currently in decline, because evidence of the last two decades suggests that behaviour patterns are less consistent than one would predict on the basis of traits. A person's questionnaire score for a personality trait such as extraversion is not a particularly good predictor of how that person will actually behave in another situation (Mischel, 1968). However, test scores for traits of ability and cognitive style yield more reliable behavioural predictions. Mischel's book, *Personality and Assessment*, had a major impact on trait research, causing many to abandon the use of the trait concept in personality, but it also led others to renewed efforts to discover the circumstances in which behaviour is consistent. As a result, it is now generally accepted that, while many behaviours do remain stable when they are compared across different points in time, they do not necessarily demonstrate the same degree of cross-situational stability (Mischel and Peake, 1982).

Despite psychologists' misgivings about the value of the trait concept, trait terminology constitutes at least 5 per cent of the English language, which suggests that traits must have some predictive and descriptive value. Some psychologists believe that this wealth of trait terminology is a useful source of insights into personality (Goldberg, 1982). Recent reconceptualizations go some way towards resolving the contradiction between these opposing views of the value of personality traits.

Currently, the trait concept is experiencing a reprieve, due to a transfusion of ideas from cognitive psychology. These new conceptualizations (for example, Buss and Craik, 1983; Hampson, 1982), while differing in details, share the same basic assumption: that traits are categorizing concepts which group together diverse behaviours performed in different situations and at different times. What these behaviours have in common is a family resemblance to a prototype behaviour for that trait. The major difference between this remodelled trait concept and the traditional view, such as Allport's, is that a trait is no longer regarded as being a mental structure existing within the individual. Instead, the trait is seen as a cognitive category that helps us interpret behavioural acts.

Sarah E. Hampson
Birkbeck College, University of London

References

Allport, G. W. (1937), *Personality: A Psychological Interpretation*, New York.

Buss, D. M. and Craik, K. H. (1983), 'The act frequency approach to personality', *Psychological Review*, 90.

Cattell, R. B. (1973), *Personality and Mood by Questionnaire*, San Francisco.

Eysenck, H. J. and Eysenck, S. B. G. (1969), *Personality Structure and Measurement*, London.

Goldberg, L. R. (1982), 'From ace to zombie: some explorations in the language of personality', in C. D. Spielberger and J. N. Butcher (eds), *Advances in Personality and Assessment*, vol. 1, Hillsdale, NJ.

Hampson, S. E. (1982), 'Person memory: a semantic category model of personality traits', *British Journal of Psychology*, 73.

Mischel, W. (1968), *Personality and Assessment*, New York.

Mischel, W. and Peake, R. K. (1982), 'Beyond *déjà vu* in the search for cross-situational consistency', *Psychological Review*, 89.

Further Reading

Hampson, S. E. (1982), *The Construction of Personality: An Introduction*, London.

Rorer, L. G. and Widiger, T. A. (1983), 'Personality structure and assessment', *Annual Review of Psychology*, 34.

See also: *attitudes; personality.*

Transactional Analysis

Transactional Analysis (TA), the creation of Eric Berne, is a personality theory and method of treatment which dates back to the mid-1950s. It has grown in popularity and today its concepts are applied in education, management, and other fields of human relations. It is popular partly because of its clear simple language and cleverly-turned phrases; yet research has developed increasingly complex and detailed theory and it has been employed with the most difficult psychiatric problems.

Among the fundamental concepts of TA is the *ego state*, a recurrent pattern of behaviour, feelings and thoughts. Drawing upon his psychoanalytic background, Berne identifies three basic states: *child*, the archaic qualities fixed in early childhood; *adult*, the objective qualities based on rational appraisals of reality; and *parent*, derived from qualities of parental figures.

A *transaction* is a two-person interaction in which the *ego state* of one person stimulates a corresponding state from another. Transactions are called *complementary* if they are parallel, that is, both parties behave objectively in an adult transaction; *crossed*, when ego states do not correspond; and *ulterior* when there are simultaneous manifest and latent levels of transaction.

The psychological *game* is a predictable, stereotyped pattern of behaviour, frequently complex, destructive and motivated by hidden desires. Some popular examples are 'courtroom', 'kick me', 'confession', 'yes, but. . .', 'try and catch me', and 'poor me'. As these colourful names imply, the purpose of a game is not straightforward, but designed to engage another within an intrapsychic conflict. Berne's formula for the game is

$$CON + GIMMICK =$$
$$RESPONSE \rightarrow SWITCH \rightarrow PAYOFF.$$

The term *stroke* is used for the reinforcers of behaviour provided by people – the words, glances and other symbolic recognitions that motivate. A *life script* –

conformity with some important early transaction – may be destructive in its later effects, for example, when one attempts to play out an unrealistic life plan. *Contracts* are the basic agreements of acceptable behaviour explicitly or implictly agreed upon between people. The treatment contract in TA is considered essential to effective psychotherapy, and should include the patient's goals and how he or she will know when these have been achieved.

The terms and theory, easily learned and shared, become a useful shorthand for analysis of otherwise confusing and complicated experiences. Catchy phrases invite a dimension of playfulness in otherwise ponderous analysis in a way that enhances the working alliance. Although the process is initially intellectual, powerful affects are soon liberated.

TA has been especially valuable in the clarification of communication problems. It provides a readily grasped group of tools for the analysis and treatment of communication problems between people, in groups, and between intrapsychic parts of a person.

Arnold R. Beisser
University of California, Los Angeles
Gestalt Therapy Institute

Further Reading

Berne, E. (1961), *Transactional Analysis and Psychotherapy*, New York.

Berne, E. (1964), *Games People Play*, New York.

Transference

The concept of transference was formally brought into psychiatry by Sigmund Freud, who discovered empirically that his patient's perceptions of him during analysis were coloured, distorted, and even completely fabricated in relation to the patient's early feelings toward important figures in his own past: parents, siblings, caretakers and the like.

These early, often infantile, feelings were transferred to the analyst *unconsciously*; the patient initially believed that these essentially internal perceptions were valid reflections of the therapist himself. At times, they were recognized as internal and inappropriate to the real situation; for example, a patient might say: 'This is strange, but I seem to feel toward you as I did toward my mother.'

At first it seemed to Freud that transference feelings were an obstacle and impediment to the rational progress of the analysis. However, he came to recognize that the transference was a repetition of earlier conflicts and feelings, and thus the analysis of the transference became the central task of the analyst. Modern psychoanalysts consider the transference even more important for therapeutic exploration and treatment.

Such transference feelings were later discovered to play a part in almost all human relationships, at least to some degree. A common example is a person's tendency to see various authority figures in parental terms and to experience feelings for them which are derived from childhood. To take an extreme case, love at first sight is a phenomenon almost entirely composed of transference feelings; since this sort of attachment owes nothing to the *real* aspects of the loved one, the feelings must originate from elsewhere, in the past.

A number of dynamic psychiatrists hold the view that, for operational purposes, everything that occurs within the analytic or therapeutic session may be viewed as a manifestation of transference feelings by one or the other parties. More recently, two areas relevant to this issue have become the focus of attention. The first is the so-called 'real' relationship, that is, those elements of the therapeutic relationship that are transference-free (or relatively so). The second is the idea that certain psychological entities may best be diagnosed by noting the specific types of transference formed during therapy itself (for example, narcissistic personality disorders).

The usual form of transference in therapy (and life in general) might be described as 'neurotic transference', in the sense that the feelings transferred derive from the original neurotic conflicts of the individual. One characteristic of this sort of transference is that it is 'testable'; the patient can correct his own misperception once attention is called to the nature and form of the error. Thus, a patient might say in such a situation, 'I see that I was automatically expecting you to reject me as my father once did.' On occasion, however, the transference perception is *not* testable, and resists reality testing. Such a fixed transference is called a psychotic transference, in which the patient is unalterably convinced of the reality of the transference perception: thus the patient might say, 'You *are* rejecting, there is no doubt about it; my father's nature is irrelevant to the matter.' These psychotic transferences are quite common among patients with the borderline syndrome, and contribute to the difficulty of therapeutic work with them.

It may be a safe generalization that the major source of difficulty with all parts of therapy, especially the therapeutic alliance, is the feelings that derive from the transference. This problem is balanced by the fact that the ability to work successfully with transference material is often the hallmark of the successful therapist.

Thomas G. Gutheil
Harvard University
Program in Law and Psychiatry, Boston

Further Reading
Freud, S. (1958), *The Dynamics of Transference*, London.
Greenacre, P. (1954), 'The role of transference',
  Journal of the American Psychoanalytic Association, 2.
Greenman, R. R. (1965), 'The working alliance and
  the transference neurosis', *Psychoanalytic Quarterly*,
  34.
Orr, D. (1954), 'Transference and
  countertransference: an historical survey', *Journal
  of the American Psychoanalytic Association*, 2.
See also: *countertransference; psychoanalysis.*

Transformational Generative Grammar

Transformational generative grammar (TGG) is the linguistic theory introduced by Noam Chomsky of MIT. Today it stands as the leading approach to the scientific study of language in the US and has numerous adherents in other countries as well.

The central notion of TGG is that the grammar of a language functions (and hence can be studied) as an *autonomous system*, that is, as a self-contained entity whose properties are not derivable from the society, culture, personality, beliefs, and so on of the speakers of the language. Generativists (as adherents of TGG are known) refer to this system as the 'linguistic competence' of the speaker of the language. Linguistic competence is one of many systems that interact to result in the speaker's 'linguistic performance' – the actual use of language in concrete situations.

Linguistic competence is characterized by a set of generative rules. While proposed competence models have evolved considerably over the years and exist in several versions today, most have in common the following components:

(1) *Phrase-structure rules*. These rules specify the fundamental constituent order and hierarchical structure of the language. They are essentially rules of clause expansion, and all have the form A → BC (read as 'A is composed of B and C'), where A, B, and C are grammatical categories (that is, 'parts of speech') in the given language. The output of these rules is called a 'phrase-marker'. Basic grammatical relations such as 'subject' and 'object' are defined from the structural configurations holding between the constituent elements of the phrase-marker.

(2) *Lexicon*. The lexicon consists of a list of the morphemes (word-forming units) of the language with their idiosyncratic properties. For example, the entry in the lexicon for the word 'eat' contains information denoting its phonological shape, its meaning, and its idiosyncratic properties (such as the fact that it can occur optionally with a direct object).

(3) *Rules of lexical insertion*. These rules take morphemes from the lexicon and insert them into the structure generated by the phrase-structure rules. They are stated in such a way as to ensure co-occurrence compatibility between morphemes (that is, they will

allow such sentences as *five hours elapsed* and *John read the book*, but block *five hours elapsed the book* and *John elapsed*).

The phrase-marker which results from the application of the phrase-structure rules and the rules of lexical insertion is called the *deep structure* of the sentence.

(4) *Transformational rules.* These rules map phrase-markers onto phrase-markers, each such rule corresponding to a syntactic generalization in the language. Sentences may be related, then, by virtue of their sharing deep structures, but not the full set of transformational rules. In most versions of TGG, active sentences (for example, *John saw Bill*) and passive sentences (for example, *Bill was seen by John*) have essentially identical deep structures, but differ in their derivations in that the passive transformation applies to the latter but not the former. In this way the grammar relates actives and passives.

The phrase-marker resulting from the application of the transformational rules is called the *surface structure* of the sentence.

(5) *Phonological rules.* These determine the phonetic shape of the morphemes of the language. Systematic alternations in pronunciation between words (such as that between the vowels in *sāne-sănity, vāin-vănity, profāne-profănity*) are accounted for by positing that at an abstract ('phonemic') level of representation the sounds are represented in the same way, but the words differ with respect to which phonological rules apply to them. The phonological rules apply to the morphemes in the surface structure of the sentence. The output of the phonological rules is called the *phonetic representation* of the sentence.

(6) *Semantic rules.* These rules take syntactic structures as inputs and apply to yield the interpretation of the sentence. In the view of most generativists, only a fairly limited subset of what is commonly termed 'meaning' is handled by the semantic rules – essentially those aspects of meaning that enter into determining the sentence's truth conditions. It is assumed that aspects of interpretation more directly related to belief, situational context, and so on are not part of linguistic competence *per se*, but are properties of cognitive systems that interact with it. The output of the semantic rules is called the *semantic representation*, or, more commonly today, the *logical form* of the sentence.

There are a number of questions related to the organization of the grammatical model that have engendered considerable debate among generativists. Probably the most vehement controversy has centred on the precise nature of the interaction between the syntactic and the semantic rules. Before 1970, most generativists assumed that the level of deep structure was the sole input to the semantic rules. This assumption led ultimately to the framework called 'generative semantics', which was quite influential in the early 1970s. Generative semantics rejected outright the distinction between semantic and syntactic rules (and with it the existence of a level of deep structure distinct from semantic representation). However, severe empirical difficulties resulting from generative semantic assumptions led to that model's being all but abandoned by the end of the 1970s. Today, virtually all generativists maintain the distinction between syntactic and semantic rules, and assume that both deep structure and surface structure, or surface structure alone, provide the input to the rules of semantic interpretation.

Today the major controversy centres on the need for transformational rules. Chomsky and his associates working in the 'government-binding' framework continue to posit such rules, albeit in a form vastly simplified from that of earlier work. In the framework called 'generalized phrase-structure grammar', introduced by Gerald Gazdar of the University of Sussex in 1980, there are no transformations at all – their work is accomplished by expanded phrase-structure, lexical, and interpretive rules.

Probably Chomsky's most controversial claim is that important aspects of a speaker's linguistic competence are innately determined. Chomsky believes that the overall structure of the grammar as well as a number of constraints governing its operation are part of the child's genetic endowment. He draws his evidence primarily from the 'poverty of the stimulus' presented to the child language learner. Chomsky reasons that it is implausible that any purely inductive learning strategy could explain the acquisition of the incredibly complex principles that make up a grammar, given the confusing and, to a certain degree, degenerate welter of utterances with which the child is bombarded. Therefore, it follows that the child must be born with a 'language acquisition device' that shapes its linguistic development.

While strictly behaviouristic approaches to language acquisition have few supporters any more (thanks in part to Chomsky's devastating review of B. F. Skinner's *Verbal Behavior* in 1959), the opposition to Chomsky argues that the principles that govern the child's acquisition of language are not specifically linguistic ones. Rather, they maintain, following the late Swiss psychologist Jean Piaget, that linguistic development is simply a by-product of general cognitive maturation. The matter is still far from being settled; generativists, however, have taken comfort from recent studies that indicate that there exist neurological structures apparently adapted for syntax alone, and from certain pathological cases where syntactic development has vastly outstripped general cognitive maturation, and hence cannot be based on it.

The roots of TGG are firmly in the structuralist tradition. Indeed, Chomsky was the pupil of Zellig Harris, the leading American structural linguist of the

1940s and early 1950s. In so far as the goal of TGG is to elucidate the structural properties of language and the interrelationships of linguistic elements, it is correct to refer to it as a 'structuralist' approach. However, TGG differs from other structuralist models with respect to the complexity of the structures posited and their abstractness. The revolutionary impact of Chomsky's *Syntactic Structures*, published in 1957, was due in large part to its demonstration that an account of the syntactic properties of human language demands recourse to structures and rules far removed from casual inspection. Prior structuralist analyses tended to be confined to only those patterns readily observable in the data and rarely employed abstract theoretical constructs.

The earliest work in TGG focused largely, but not exclusively, on the synchronic grammatical description of English, a fact for which generativists received much criticism. However, in the last decade generativists have broadened their scope of inquiry considerably, and have now produced syntactic and phonological analyses of hundreds of languages. In fact, on a number of occasions, proposals for 'universal grammar' (the name for the biologically-determined aspect of grammar) have been modified as compelling evidence for such modification has arisen from the intensive study of a language that had not previously been subjected to a TGG analysis. Also, in recent years, there has been increased interaction between generativists and researchers in other fields. For example, joint work with psychologists has resulted in a number of studies of child language acquisition and of speech production and perception. Along the same lines, generativists have authored, or coauthored, papers on second language learning, the representation of language in the brain, pragmatic strategies for language use, and computer applications of formal grammatical analysis.

Frederick J. Newmeyer
University of Washington

Further Reading
Chomsky, N. (1965), *Aspects of the Theory of Syntax*, Cambridge, Mass.
Chomsky, N. (1975), *Reflections on Language*, New York.
Chomsky, N. and Halle, M. (1968), *The Sound Pattern of English*, New York.
Newmeyer, F. J. (1980), *Linguistic Theory in America: The First Quarter-Century of Transformational Generative Grammar*, New York.
Newmeyer, F. J. (1983), *Grammatical Theory: Its Limits and its Possibilities*, Chicago.
See also: *Chomsky; linguistics; psycholinguistics; structural linguistics.*

Transport, Economics and Planning

Traditionally economists' interest in transport focused on the transport industries (the railways, shipping, airlines, and so on) and specifically on ways in which the market mechanism could be improved to maximize the benefits derived from public and private transport operations. The emphasis has changed in recent years, with more attention given to the environmental and distributional aspects of transport, while market efficiency is seen as only one dimension in a broader decision-making process.

The demand for transport is a derived demand since transport is seldom wanted for its own sake but rather for the benefits which can be obtained when reaching a final destination. In addition, transport provision can affect where firms locate or where people decide to live. Consequently, it is unrealistic to treat transport in isolation from the broader industrial and spatial environment in which it is provided. This interface with, for example, industrial and residential location and with economic development more generally means a practical involvement in subjects such as regional economic policy and urban land-use planning.

The expansion of urbanization poses particular problems for the transport system. The central location of many employment opportunities, the inflexible nature of much existing transport infrastructure, and the pollution and noise associated with concentrated traffic flows generate problems both of pure economic efficiency and of extensive external costs which free-market mechanisms are thought incapable of resolving. Costs of providing major new road and urban rail systems, combined with the need for co-ordinated decision making in an environment of imperfect knowledge and diverse interest groups, has further pushed policy away from free-market provision. The resultant introduction of urban transport planning has attempted both to meet wider social objectives and retain traditional economic concepts of efficiency.

Urban transport planning in the immediate post-World War II period was primarily concerned with drawing up physical plans for the utopian transport system. Modern structure planning, in contrast, is more concerned with the interaction of transport with the urban economy in general and with the operations of all modes of transport, rather than with narrow, engineering questions of infrastructure design. Such planning is co-ordinated with policies for the development of land use and the improvement of the urban environment.

Economics contributes to the modern urban transport planning process in several important ways, but two are of specific relevance: (1) It provides the theoretical economic underpinnings for travel demand forecasts which offer guidelines to the traffic impacts of alternative planning strategies. Many models in current use (especially of the disaggregate type) originate from the microeconomic work of Kelvin Lancaster on attribual demand analysis. (2) Social investment appraisal procedures, generally involving variants on the cost-benefit analysis (CBA) methodology, now form the basis for the evaluation of alternative urban transport plans. While conventional CBA approaches involve reducing all aspects of decision making to common monetary units, the specific concern with distributional implications and the diverse effects of modifications to the urban transport network have substantially changed the conventional framework. Thus, the Planning Balance Sheet methodology developed by Nathaniel Lichfield (1962) presents details of the costs and benefits associated with alternative plans in an accountancy framework. It emphasizes the specific impacts on various affected parties, while not reducing all items to monetary terms.

Inter-urban transport tends to be the subject of less control, mainly because its indirect consequences are smaller, but also because long-distance mobility is not considered to be a social necessity. Infrastructure (such as the motorway network in the UK or the Interstate Highway System in the US) does tend to be planned, but transport operations are increasingly left to market forces operating within defined legal boundaries designed for safety, fuel economy, and so on. Recently the regulatory framework built up during the inter-war period in the US and the UK has been dismantled and entry to transport markets has become much freer. But this trend is less pronounced in much of continental Europe, where inter-urban road and rail transport is treated as an input into wider, macroeconomic policies – transport efficiency in these countries is, for example, treated as secondary to regional and industrial objectives.

Political considerations necessitate a high level of capacity control in international transport fields. Capacity in international air transport, for instance, is regulated, and national planning of airport and airline policy revolves more around questions of national image than pure economic efficiency. International shipping is less regulated since much of the traffic moves outside of national waters. However, in an attempt to protect the interests of Third-World countries, there have in recent years been moves by UNCTAD to regulate and plan the growth of the shipping cartels or 'conferences' which provide much of the capacity on major routes.

Transport is regarded as very important in economic development. Substantial international aid is directed towards improving the transport infrastructure of Third-World countries, on the premise that good transport is a precondition for take-off into self sustained growth. But some economists argue that there is little evidence that improved transport per se necessarily results in economic growth and, in some instances, by allowing market penetration by competitors, it may stifle it. The role of planning in less-developed countries should, therefore, be seen not in terms of improving general mobility but rather in terms of integrating transport investment into a larger development programme designed to achieve the fastest growth in Gross National Product.

K. J. Button
Loughborough University

References
Lancaster, K. (1971), *Consumer Demand: A New Approach*, New York.
Lichfield, N. (1962), *Cost-Benefit Analysis in Urban Development*, Berkeley and Los Angeles.

Further Reading
Button, K. J. (1982), *Transport Economics*, London.
Glaister, S. (1981), *Fundamentals of Transport Economics*, Oxford.
See also: *economic planning; urbanization; urban planning.*

Tribe

The concept of tribe and its associated abstract, tribalism, live balanced uncomfortably on a divide. On the one side is straightforward empirical usage. 'Tribe' describes the social organization of peoples living (usually) in the tropics and (usually) employing little technology. But it tells more than that. The tribe is bigger than a family, but somehow not the same as a nation. It is tied together by complex bonds of kin and duty. Class or conflict-based analysis has not been commonly used when examining tribes. On the other side of the divide is a heterodox compilation of ideas about primitive mentality which associate with, and derive from, the ambiguity within a concept that is marked off from the normal stock of domestic Western social labels. From this duality arises both utility and passion.

The concept – in both dimensions – marches from its beginnings with the systematic study of ethnology. Of course, it had been used as an instrument of colonial government (in India by the British, in the East Indies by the Dutch) long before the Darwinian revolution helped create the Victorian intellectual climate which gave such visible prominence to the work of men like Frazer and Tylor. Sir Henry Maine, whose work spanned Indian government and the academic concern of the time with progress and sequence from primitive to civilized, was influential through his book *Ancient Law* (1861) in crystallizing such an approach: it sought to give more detailed interpretative salience to the descriptive foundations of Enlightenment ethnography, foundations best exemplified in the records of Cook's Pacific voyages.

The nineteenth-century ethnographers were also especially important in propelling the view that tribalism was a shorthand for the prescientific, emotional, irrational, animistic mentality of primitives. It fitted easily the contemporary sequential models of social development. The raw nerves of that association dangle into the present. In contrast were the anthropologists who embraced Malinowski's approach through participant fieldwork which Malinowski, in *Argonauts of the Western Pacific* (1922), developed on the Trobriand Islands during the First World War. During the inter-war years, those scholars produced the corpus of detailed case studies upon which most subsequent anthropology rests. They were the 'classic' generation. Their concern was greatly with a search for cross-culturally comparable regularities in social patterning. They sought thus to make anthropology 'scientific'. They used the notion of tribe unselfconsciously and to great effect, exposing the structures and functions of kin embedded in its ecological and social matrix.

This was also the golden age of European colonialism in Africa, where much of this work was done. Indirect rule, whether Lord Lugard's *de jure* British version, or the *de facto* form found in Francophone Africa, dealt in the currency of tribe. But that time has now passed, except in South Africa, where the Afrikaner discipline of *volkekundige* still keeps alive the ideal of tribal mentality or 'ethnos' as a central part of its anthropology.

The image made in Accra to commemorate the achievement of political independence by Ghana shows the fleeing agents of colonialism. Along with the District Officer is the anthropologist, clutching under his arm a copy of Fortes and Evans-Pritchard's *African Political Systems* (1940). The association of anthropologists and anthropology with the colonial regimes under which they worked was understandable. For a period of about twenty years, up to the oil crisis of the early 1970s that ended the long boom that had followed the Second World War, there was a strong trend in scholarship to reject the terms and concepts of tribe principally because of their tainted connections. The criticism arose from convictions which were anti-colonial, which supported the new nation-states and were more or less Marxian. Tribe, it was argued, was an invention of the dominator. It was a 'false consciousness' without any indigenous root, fostered in order to divide and rule. Those, like the anthropologists, who had adopted it into their perspectives, were deluded and thus became, consciously or not, the agents of oppression. In its place there should be substituted a class-based analysis, that would more effectively expose the full dimensions of exploitation upon which colonial society rested.

During the 1970s, as the problems of the new states mounted, the overstatement of the criticism became more widely appreciated. Case studies began to appear addressing the question of 'consciousness' more sensitively. It was shown that indeed there were examples of invented tribes and it was seen how the idea was central to the operation of migrant labour systems; but it was also shown how, like the prisoner, the colonized could sometimes take on and manipulate the stereotype as a way of engineering a little private space in life, free from intrusion. And there was a cooler re-examination of some of the rich cultural material of tribal life which showed how, even if the word was rendered unusable, something approximating to the concept was required. This was to re-engage the debate about modes of thought and to describe the ethnic dimension, which was one of the many shells of the Chinese box of accurate social analysis. Furthermore, whatever its origin, the fact of tribe during the colonial era was a phenomenon that could not be ignored.

Thus by the 1980s, the concept of tribe has performed several rotations of fashion over the preceding 200 years. It appears that if the record of those movements is regarded – at just the time when the truly isolated rural society to which the concept first applied is generally overwhelmed – there is a better chance than ever of grasping the dimensions of experience to which the notion of 'tribe' for so long and with such maddening imprecision applied.

Gwyn Prins
Emmanuel College, Cambridge

Further Reading
Fried, M. H. (1975), *The Notion of Tribe*, Menlo Park, Calif.
Gluckman, M. (1971), 'Tribalism, ruralism and urbanization in South and Central Africa', in V. Turner (ed.), *Colonialism in Africa*, vol. III, Cambridge.
Mafeje, A. (1976), 'The problem of anthropology in historical perspective', *Canadian Journal of African Studies*, X.
Prins, G. (1980), *The Hidden Hippopotamus*, Cambridge.
Redfield, R. (1955), *The Little Community*, Chicago.
See also: *social anthropology; stateless societies.*

Tylor, Edward Burnett (1832–1917)

Born into a well-to-do Quaker industrial family, Tylor did not attend a university. He became interested in 'primitive cultures' by chance, a casual meeting with an English archaeologist leading him to spend several months in Mexico.

Partly under the influence of Darwinian evolutionary thinking, some archaeologists had begun to argue that the remains of ancient cultures exhibited a serial progression, like the fossil varieties of contemporary animal species. German philologists claimed to have discovered a similar progression in man's intellectual productions, notably language. Tylor developed these themes in his *Researches into the Early History of Mankind and the Development of Civilization* (1865). In his second major book, *Primitive Culture* (1871), he extended the argument to the development of religion, suggesting that all religions had advanced from an original form, 'animism', which attributed the possession of spirits to inanimate natural objects. His arguments were based on world-wide comparisons, and were informed by a search for 'survivals', fossilized forms of behaviour which carried over from earlier stages of development and persisted especially in ceremonial contexts. In an important late paper (Tylor, 1889), he introduced a statistical method for the comparative study of cultural traits.

Tylor also introduced a novel, German, idea of culture into English-speaking discourse. Culture, in this usage, included not only the products of élite civilization, but the whole gamut of learnt skills, habits, modes of communication and beliefs which went to make up a particular way of life, and it was the proper object of anthropological study. Cultures progressed along uniform lines, either as a result of borrowing or by independent inventions which took similar forms at particular levels of development.

Due in part to his longevity, Tylor was the most authoritative figure in anthropology by the turn of the century, and some talked simply of 'Mr Tylor's science'. Oxford created a readership in anthropology for him in 1884, and he later became a professor by personal title. He was elected a Fellow of the Royal Society, and towards the end of his career he was knighted.

Adam Kuper
Brunel University, Uxbridge

Reference
Tylor, E. (1889), 'On a method of investigating the development of institutions', *Journal of the Anthropological Institute*, 18.

Further Reading
Leopold, J. (1980), *Culture in Comparative and Evolutionary Perspective: E. B. Tylor and the Making of Primitive Culture*, Berlin.

U

Unconscious

Perhaps the single most important idea in Freud's theory is that human beings are influenced by ideas, feelings, tendencies and ways of thinking of which they are not conscious. Freud's original 'topography' of the mind had three divisions: the conscious, the preconscious, and the unconscious. His theory can be pictured as follows: the mind is like a darkened theatre, with a single spotlight to illuminate the actors on the stage. Consciousness is equivalent to the actor in the spotlight at any moment. All of the other actors who can be illuminated as the spotlight moves across the stage are equivalent to the preconscious. To complete Freud's picture we must imagine that there are many actors who are off-stage, in the unconscious. Unless they make the transition to the stage, the light of consciousness cannot illuminate them. Seen or unseen, on-stage or off, all the actors take part in the play of psychic life. The barrier between off-stage and on-stage is removed or weakened in dreams, and by free association, which is the basic technique of psychoanalysis.

Freud understood the unconscious as dynamic. Unconscious impulses were thought to be constantly active, influencing the preconscious and conscious – sometimes in discernible ways. Freud's explanation for slips of the tongue (now commonly called Freudian errors) is the substitution of an unconscious thought for what was consciously intended. By considering these unconscious influences, Freud found meaning in what others saw as trivial mistakes – for example, when a man calls his wife by his mother's name. Freud's theory of humour is similarly based on the dynamic interaction between conscious and unconscious. The joke allows the pleasurable release of some repressed idea or feeling; aggressive sexual jokes are thus a classic example.

Freud's theory of the unconscious became more complex in the course of his writings. At first he assumed that everything which was unconscious had once been conscious and had been repressed. The paradigmatic example was the subject who under hypnosis could be given some post-hypnotic suggestion, such as to open an umbrella indoors, but told to *forget* that he had been given that instruction. When the trance was ended, the subject would comply with the suggestions and open the umbrella indoors, but be unable to explain why he had done such a silly thing. Thus his behaviour was influenced by an idea about which he had no conscious awareness. Freud believed that his patients, like hypnotic subjects, were capable of splitting off from consciousness certain ideas and feelings by a defensive process he called repression. These repressed unconscious ideas could influence the patient's behaviour, producing neurotic symptoms without his awareness.

Freud's clinical work demonstrated that the most significant repressed ideas led back to childhood experiences. The content of the unconscious seemed to be ideas and tendencies, mainly sexual and aggressive – which he thought of as instinctual and biological – which were repressed under the moral influence of the environment. But the repressed remained active in the unconscious and continued in dynamic interaction with the conscious. Thus Freud's conception of the unconscious emphasized the continuing and irrational influence of the past on the present.

The idea of the splitting of consciousness was not original to Freud, nor was that of an instinctive unconscious. These ideas in some form go back at least as far as Plato. The German philosophers of the nineteenth century, Schopenhauer and Nietzsche, had a view of human nature which, in many ways, anticipated Freud. Freud's theory of the unconscious nonetheless met with intense philosophical criticism, even ridicule. The idea that what was mental was not identical with consciousness and that the mental might be a mystery to consciousness was problematic for certain philosophical notions. Descartes had said, 'I think therefore I exist.' He used this introspective claim as the basis of a theory of knowledge. Freud's concept of the unconscious challenged the certitude of all such introspective claims about the certainty of self-knowledge. The idea of unconscious influences also called into question the notion of free will. Perhaps because Freud emphasized the sexual aspects of the unconscious, his views were easy for philosophers to ridicule. The philosopher Sartre, who was in many ways more sympathetic than most contemporary philosophers to Freud's emphasis on the importance of sex, still found it necessary to reject Freud's fundamental concept of the unconscious. He interpreted repression as self-deception; asserting that it is impossible to lie to oneself, he described repression as 'bad faith.'

Freud's concept of the unconscious derived from his study of dreaming. He viewed the unconscious (associated with the infantile, the primitive, and the instinctual) as striving toward immediate discharge of tension. Dreaming and unconscious thinking are described as primary process thought, that is, they are unreflective, concrete, symbolic, egocentric, associative, timeless, visual, physiognomic and animistic, with memory organized about the imperative drive, in which wishes are equivalent to deeds and there is a radical departure from norms of logic – for example, contradictory ideas exist side by side. Primary process thought is contrasted with the modulated and adaptive discharge of tension in secondary process. By contrast, conscious thinking is reflective or directed, abstract, specific and particular, situation oriented, logical, chronological, auditory, verbal and explanatory. Memory is organized around the conscious focus of attention; thought and actions are clearly distinguished; thinking is rational and logically oriented. Freud's view was that although the child advances from primary process to secondary process thinking, primary process does not disappear, but remains active in the unconscious. It can be revealed in dreams, in psychotic thinking, and in other regressed mental states. Preconscious thinking was characterized as intermediate between these two types. The distinction between primary and secondary process is a key development in Lacan's linguistic reinterpretation of Freud.

Carl Jung, probably the greatest figure in psychoanalysis next to Freud, was an early advocate of what he called the collective unconscious. He assumed that in addition to repressed content, there was an inherited component to the unconscious shared by the human race. He based this conception on the evidence that certain symbols and complexes endlessly recur in the history of civilization. The Oedipus myth of the Greeks is the Oedipal dream of modern times. Freud and Jung took these ideas quite literally, believing that the individual was born not just with instinctual tendencies, but with inherited complexes and symbols – for example, the serpent as a phallic symbol. Despite his eventual break with Jung, Freud maintained his own version of a collective unconscious, which also included the idea that certain moral concepts such as taboos had been inherited.

Freud subsequently reconceptualized his ideas about the unconscious in terms of the ego, the super-ego and the id. The id and the unconscious are now often used interchangeably in the psychiatric and psychoanalytic literature. While the theory of the unconscious remains controversial even today, the intuition that consciousness does not fully grasp the deeper mystery of our mental life continues to play an important role in twentieth-century thought.

Alan A. Stone
Harvard University

Further Reading
Freud, S. (1953 [1900]), *The Interpretation of Dreams*, The Standard Edition of the Complete Psychological Works of Sigmund Freud, Vol. IV, New York.
Ellenberger, H. F. (1970), *The Discovery of the Unconscious: The History and Evolution of Dynamic Psychiatry*, New York.
See also: *Freud, S.; Jung; psychoanalysis.*

Underdevelopment

The original meaning of underdevelopment was a neutral one, simply defining the condition of poorer countries which then were called underdeveloped countries. However, this term was felt to be derogatory and has since disappeared from the international vocabulary, being replaced by the more euphemistic 'developing countries'. As a result the term underdeveloped has now assumed a specific and rather different meaning. It is now closely associated with the so-called dependency school, and it indicates a belief that in the world economy there are centrifugal forces at work, strengthening the position of the already rich 'core' while keeping the 'periphery' poor and in a state of permanent underdevelopment. The chief author using and building on this term was André Gunder Frank (Frank, 1967). Frank was also the first to speak of 'development of underdevelopment', meaning the development of a rich country/poor country or core/periphery relationship which results in the impoverishment of the poor or periphery partner.

There are a number of variants within the underdevelopment school. These range from the radical wing which identifies underdevelopment with neocolonial relationships and is an outgrowth of Marxist thinking, to nonpolitical or non-ideological explanations such as the principle of 'cumulative causation' developed by Gunnar Myrdal (Myrdal, 1956). The principle of cumulative causation states that in the case of poor countries or poor groups a vicious circle is at work keeping them poor (for example, low income causing low savings and low investment, in turn causing low income in the next round; or low income leading to poor health leading to low productivity and low income). By contrast, in rich countries, or among rich groups, a reverse beneficial circle enables them to go from strength to strength and to improve their condition progressively. The strict Marxian view is perhaps best represented by W. Rodney in *How Europe Underdeveloped Africa* (1972): 'An indispensable component of modern underdevelopment is that it expresses a particular relationship of exploitation: namely the exploitation of one country by another.' This view logically also leads to the use of the concept in describing domestic relations within developing countries (as in relations between an urban élite and the rural poor), but in practice the term is now associated with an international context of relations between countries. In between these two extremes are various other schools of thought explaining that the system of international trade relations has a tendency to benefit rich countries more than poor countries. The best known of these schools is the Prebisch-Singer theory according to which the terms of trade of primary products tend to deteriorate in relation to the prices of manufactured goods (Prebisch, 1964; Singer, 1950).

The radical view that any international contact between rich and poor countries will be to the disadvantage of the latter, obviously leads to the policy conclusion that poorer countries should either try to be self-sufficient or inward-looking in their development; while in the case of smaller countries, where this is not feasible, regional groupings of developing countries are advocated. One does not have to be an advocate of the underdevelopment school, however, to support such policies; it is clear that trade, investment and other economic relations among the developing countries are conspicuously and abnormally sparse compared with relations between rich and poor countries. It can be argued that it is also in the interest of the richer industrialized countries to support such closer South-South co-operation.

The milder variation is that international contacts are advantageous for both partners, in accordance with liberal doctrine and the law of comparative advantage, but that the benefits are unequally distributed.

The belief of the more radical underdevelopment school that international relations are positively harmful to the poorer partners can in turn lead to two different policy conclusions. One is to reduce North-South contacts and instead develop South-South relations; the other is to reform the international system so that its benefits are more equally distributed. The latter approach is implied in the pressure of the developing countries for a New International Economic Order which has dominated the international discussions during the last decade, and also in such reform proposals as the two Brandt Reports (Brandt I, 1980; and Brandt II, 1983).

H. W. Singer
Institute of Development Studies
University of Sussex

References

Brandt I (1980), *North-South: A Programme for Survival*, (The Report of the Independent Commission on International Development Issues under the Chairmanship of Willy Brandt), London.

Brandt II (1983), *Common Crisis, North-South: Co-operation for World Recovery*, The Brandt Commission, London.

Frank, A. G. (1967), *Capitalism and Underdevelopment in Latin America*, New York.

Myrdal, G. (1956), *Development and Underdevelopment*, Cairo.

Prebisch, R. (1964), *Towards a New Trade Policy for Development*, New York.

Rodney, W. (1972), *How Europe Underdeveloped Africa*, Dar-es-Salaam.

Singer, H. W. (1950), 'The distribution of gains between investing and borrowing countries', *American Economic Review*.

See also: *dependency theory; development studies; Third World*.

Urbanization

The term urbanization appears in the literature of nearly every social science; within each it is used loosely when the theories of the particular field are applied to the study of urban units, their populations or individuals living in urban places. The term does, however, have two interrelated, more specific, meanings: (1) Demographers, who use it to refer to the redistribution of population between rural and urban areas, have given it its most specific meaning at a conceptual level, but the demographic study of urbanization has failed to produce an internationally accepted set of criteria defining urban. (2) In a number of other social sciences, most notably economics, geography and sociology, urbanization refers to the changing morphological structure of urban agglomerations and its development. Indeed, within the social sciences today one of the major research issues centres around the separation of the causes and consequences of urbanization as a demographic phenomena and the emergent morphology of large urban complexes in the Western world.

Population Redistribution

The demographic study of urbanization has concentrated on the movement of people between rural and urban areas on a world scale, and on the differential level, pace and pattern of this redistribution between the more and less developed countries. As late as 1950 only 28 per cent of the world's population is thought to have been living in urban sectors. At mid-decade over one half of the population in the more developed countries lived in urban areas, but only a little more than 15 per cent of the population of the less developed regions. By 1980 estimates suggest that the level of urbanization in the more developed regions reached 70 per cent, and in the lesser developed regions over 30 per cent. These redistributions are a consequence of the differential rates of increase in the rural and urban populations of the more and less developed countries. Over the 30-year period from 1950 to 1980, for example, the urban population increased by some 85 per cent in the more developed regions while the rural population actually decreased by over 10 per cent.

Among the less developed regions the urban population increased by more than 250 per cent and the rural population increased by more than 60 per cent. While the differential pace of urbanization can be directly linked to the differential rates of urban and rural growth, it is considerably more difficult to identify the differentials in the components of urban and rural population change. This is largely due to the fact that urban and rural population growth, in addition to being affected by natural increase and net migration, is also affected by changing boundaries (or area reclassification) of what are defined as urban and rural areas.

The dominant historical trend of population redistribution has been towards an increasing concentration of population in urban areas. However, within urban areas themselves, there has been movement away from urban centres towards the suburban periphery. Definitions of urban, suburban and rural vary markedly from country to country; still, strong indications are that in many Western countries this decentralization of population is occurring, and that increasingly it involves movement beyond large agglomeration (metropolitan) boundaries into the nonmetropolitan sector.

Urbanization and Urban Morphology
The link between urbanization as a strictly demographic phenomenon and urbanization as a morphological phenomenon has its roots in the early works of European economists such as Weber, Gras (1922) and Christaller (1933), and in the US intellectual tradition known as human ecology. Traditional approaches linking population redistribution to urban structure tried to account for the concentration of population in large urban agglomerations and the development of urban systems. Large agglomerations developed around a single urban centre which attracted the excess rural population and absorbed it into an economy based on production and manufacturing and the associated services and product distribution industries.

Whilst these urban centres were developing, a second area or outer ring grew up around them. This ring was increasingly dominated by the centre, as the ecological distance between previously independent communities and the centre was reduced through technological innovations in transport and communication. As the total area expands, formerly independent and quasi-independent communities lose many of their specialized functions and services to the centre where the full advantages of external economies offered by location can be had. Once economic activity and jobs are centralized in the agglomeration centre, the outer area becomes primarily a residential suburb, increasingly dependent on and oriented to the centre.

With three sources of change (other than natural change) contributing to their population growth (migration from the centre, migration from rural areas and other agglomerations, the incorporation of new territory and its population), suburban areas begin to grow at a faster rate than either agglomeration centres or rural areas. The structural limits to growth and expansion are thus set by the economy's capacity to support population and the centre's ability to co-ordinate, control and integrate wider territory, while the territorial limits to growth are determined by transportation technology and the need to be able to move people routinely to the centre.

This traditional approach depicts suburban areas and their populations as almost totally dependent on urban centres. It also focuses attention on the concentration of services and economic activity in the centre and on the decentralization of population or places of residence. Recent research has shown that population is now decentralizing beyond traditional agglomeration boundaries, while services and economic activity are reconcentrating in traditional suburban territory. These observations, which contradict the traditional approach, have led some researchers to suggest that there are limits to the size of agglomerations under the control of a single centre: once the point is reached where the cost of moving people, goods and information is too high to support continued growth of the decentralizing structure, nucleation begins and there is a return to scale, and a number of smaller centres emerge. Within each of these centres, a surrounding population can satisfy all its routine and daily needs.

Alternatively, others have argued that the reconcentration of services and economic activity within the suburban ring and the further decentralization of population is merely an extension of the traditional expansion model. It represents a new stage in the agglomeration process culminating in an urban structure dominated by a inner ring which will perform the functions and assume the characteristics of city centres in the past. This, it is argued, will facilitate greater residential expansion and make old city centres dependent on this inner suburban ring, similar to the earlier dependence of suburbs on cities. Beyond this inner ring, traditional population decentralization will continue leading to greater expansion of metropolitan territory.

David F. Sly
Florida State University

References
Christaller, W. (1933), *Die Zentralen Orte in Suddeutschland*, Jena. (Trans. C. W. Baskin, *The Central Places of Southern Germany*, 1966, Englewood Cliffs.)
Gras, N. S. B. (1922), *An Introduction to Economic History*, New York.

Further Reading
Berry, B. J. L. (1981), *Comparative Urbanization: Divergent Paths in the Twentieth Century*, New York.

Burnley, I. H. (ed.) (1974), *Urbanization in Australia: The Post-War Experience*, Cambridge.

Goldstein, S. and Sly, D. F. (eds) (1977), *Patterns of Urbanization: Comparative Country Studies*, Liege.

Hawley, A. (1981), *Urban Society: An Ecological Approach*, New York.

Sly, D. F. and Tayman, J. (1980), 'Metropolitan morphology and population mobility: the theory of ecological expansion reexamined', *American Journal of Sociology*, 86.

Sly, D. F. (1982), 'The consequences of metropolitan decentralization for personal gasoline consumption', *Population Research and Policy Review 1*.

See also: *city; migration; regional analysis; residential mobility; urban planning*.

Urban Planning

Urban planning is as old as civilization. The cities of antiquity reflected the glorification of rulers and their military and religious needs. The first working-class town was designed to provide labour for the building of an Egyptian royal pyramid. More democratic influences entered with the Greek *agora* and Roman *forum*. Hydraulic engineering was always a major influence upon urban planning from the ancient empires of Egypt and Mesopotamia, to the development of cities in The Netherlands. The planning of medieval cities was governed by their walls and fortifications. The founding of colonies and military centres produced many examples of planned towns.

From the later Middle Ages onwards, the patronage of rulers, corporations of merchants and individual landowners enabled architect-planners to create or reshape many famous cities. Examples are the work of Bernini and others in Rome, of the two Woods in Bath, of Craig in Edinburgh, and the baroque-style cities of Southern Germany and Austria.

The Industrial Revolution and the consequent growth of vast, sprawling cities changed the character of urban planning quite radically. Planning developed along three different but related lines:

(1) The detailed regulation of land uses was a feature of many old cities, but it became minimal during the earlier *laissez-faire* period of industrialization. Health and sanitary problems compelled the adoption of building codes and regulations about street widths and housing layouts. Subsequently, statutory planning schemes were introduced which separated 'incompatible' land uses, specified housing densities, and reserved land for open space and other public purposes.

This 'hygienic' type of planning has been much criticized for spoiling the 'muddled variety' of urban life. The protective effect of zoning laws has been strongest in upper-class residential suburbs. Elsewhere, planning controls have been kept more flexible by the pressures of the private land market. This was particularly true of the US, where the regular gridiron layout of cities assisted land speculation, and where the first zoning code for New York City permitted a maximum population of 365 million. By contrast, development has been controlled quite closely in The Netherlands, and some other European states, but the fragmentation of land ownership and the existence of speculative values are widespread obstacles to planning and also to participation.

Political attempts have been made to tax and control development values so as to facilitate planning; for example, there were three such attempts in the UK between 1945 and 1980. These had some success in limiting planning compensation, thus helping the protection of rural areas and green belts, but little success in collecting betterment or assisting urban renewal. Some European countries, particularly after World War II, have pooled and reallocated land holdings so as to aid redevelopment. However, the implementation of regulatory plans depends upon either private or public initiatives. To be effective, government planning requires integrated policies and complex co-ordination, and in Western societies urban change depends increasingly upon business and financial interests.

(2) The historical architectural tradition continued in new ways. Modern cities are usually no longer dominated by great public works, save in autocratic states or special cases like Brasilia. Highway planning has become more influential or even dominant over the design of cities. Haussmann's boulevards restructured Paris, largely for purposes of crowd control. The 'city beautiful' movement, exemplified in Burnham's Chicago plan, included boulevards, parks and museums, but ignored the decaying ghettoes behind the city frontage. Regional 'parkways' combined roads and parks, sometimes attractively. Robert Moses in New York built a career around linking planning with the co-ordination of public works. Monumental designs for cities of the future, such as those of Le Corbusier, belong with the historic architectural tradition, but are likely to be realized only in specialized projects.

(3) There have emerged the 'planned public developments' such as the British new towns, Canberra in Australia, and many examples of municipal enterprise. These towns represent massive exercises in public estate development, which carry on older traditions of private or corporate land management. Public land ownership is the key, when combined with the vesting of wide responsibilities for city development in the same agency. Stockholm's post-war development, when the city owned most vacant land, sponsored or

provided most of the housing, and owned and developed the transportation system, is a good example of comprehensive planning for urban growth. Many other European and British cities possessed many similar powers, although rarely so completely. Changes in the political climate, and the replacement of strong city governments by two-tier metropolitan systems, had by 1980 largely brought to an end the era of the city planning and development machines (Self, 1982). Comprehensive planning by *ad hoc* bodies like new town corporations has also proved politically vulnerable.

Planned public developments have often provided improved social and environmental standards and better access to facilities for the aged, teenagers, and working wives; but they have also imposed technocratic concepts upon a passive clientele. The failings have been most marked in redevelopment schemes, which have produced much unpopular high-rise housing, a neglect of social facilities, and in the US extensive displacement of the poor in the interests of subsidized commercial development.

The profession of town planning was dominated historically by architects but has increasingly utilized the skills of engineers, valuers, economists, sociologists and others. Regional planning, a particular interest of geographers, has grown in importance. Planning has been closely linked with other major functions, such as housing at one time and, more recently, transportation. There is much disagreement about the best education for a town planner, and about the separability of his role from the general task of urban management.

The modern development of planning has been much influenced by imaginative writers such as Geddes and Mumford (1961) and by practical idealists such as Ebenezer Howard and Sir Frederic Osborn who initiated two garden cities. Concepts of balanced growth, limitation of urban size, new communities, and rural protection were important for the major advance in town planning powers after 1940. Social ideals, although subdued by bureaucratic routine, remain important for planning and also for professional planners.

Planning systems have grown in complexity, often involving national guidelines, regional outline plans, subregional or county plans, and detailed local plans. These various plans sometimes conflict and are often outflanked by both public and private developers. Planning has built up complex techniques of forecasting and modelling, and become increasingly concerned with steering and monitoring exogenous economic and social trends.

Nonetheless, urban planning remains highly political and reflective of the dominant values of a society. In communist systems, strong public powers for planning exist, although their use is limited by administrative rivalries, and their results may be disliked. In capitalist democracies, the planner has become either a specialist in land use regulation, or a rather weak generalist articulating a 'community interest'. Much has been written about spatial inequalities in cities, and the dominance of capitalist interests (Harvey, 1973). Effective urban planning, which integrates regulation and implementation, depends upon political support for the integrated use of public powers, especially in relation to the control of land values.

Peter Self
London School of Economics and Political Science

References
Harvey, D. (1973), *Social Justice and the City*, London.
Mumford, L. (1961), *The City in History*, London.
Self, P. (1982), *Planning the Urban Region*, London.
See also: *city: urbanization*.

Utilitarianism

Utilitarianism is the doctrine that decisions should promote good consequences. It is a normative theory, meant to guide conduct and to serve as the basis of sound evaluations. It does not assume that actual decisions or judgements always satisfy that standard.

Like other important philosophical ideas, utilitarianism has many variations. The founders of modern utilitarianism, Bentham (1789) and J. S. Mill (1861), assumed that good consequences are, at bottom, desirable conditions of individuals (perhaps including animals other than humans). Bentham's 'hedonistic' utilitarianism called for the promotion of 'pleasure' and the prevention of 'pain'. Mill, who distinguished 'higher' and 'lower' pleasures, seems to have held that human good consists in the free development of individuals' distinctive, and distinctively human, capacities. 'Ideal' utilitarians believe that what is most fundamentally of value can include such things as beauty, which need not be defined in terms of human good or conscious states.

Utilitarianism in its various forms can be understood to combine a theory of intrinsic value with some notion of how stringently and directly it should be served, for example, whether good consequences must be maximized or need only be promoted to a lesser degree, and whether each and every decision should be so regulated ('act' utilitarianism) or rather that acts should conform to useful patterns ('rule' utilitarianism).

Utilitarians often claim as a virtue of their theory that it bases evaluations on ascertainable facts, such as how much 'pleasure' and 'pain' would result from alternative courses of action. But the calculations require 'interpersonal comparisons of utility', of which many are sceptical. This has led some theorists to develop normative standards in terms of less demanding notions of efficiency, as in welfare economics.

Utilitarians have generally favoured social reforms (because, for example, income transfers from rich to poor are supposed to promote welfare overall), and they have championed political rights and personal liberty (because, for example, 'paternalistic' interference is supposed to be counterproductive). Critics charge, however, that utilitarianism lacks principled commitment to all such values: it cares only how much good is produced, but not about equitable distribution, respect for personal desert, or the security of freedom and individual integrity.

Most generally, critics charge that utilitarianism distorts sound moral judgement: to promise to do something, for example, is deliberately to place oneself under an obligation, the demands of which (it is argued) are greater and more specifically directed than utilitarianism allows. They claim that utilitarianism fails to take obligations (or for that matter rights) seriously.

Utilitarianism nevertheless remains a widely accepted theory of central importance, though its status – like that of any normative principle – is uncertain. The idea that principles merely express more or less arbitrary attitudes seems largely based on an exaggerated contrast between ethics and science, which suffers from overly simple conceptions of empirical knowledge and discovery. Developments in the theory of reference and justification, along with the decline of logical positivism, have revived interest in moral realism (or cognitivism) and in the possibility of rationally defending either utilitarianism or some competing doctrine.

David Lyons
Cornell University

References
Bentham, J. (1789), *An Introduction to the Principles of Morals and Legislation*, London.
Mill, J. S. (1861), *Utilitarianism*, London.

Further Reading
Brandt, R. B. (1979), *A Theory of the Good and the Right*, Oxford.
Sen, A. and Williams, B. (eds) (1982), *Utilitarianism and Beyond*, Cambridge.
Smart, J. J. C. and Williams, B. (1973), *Utilitarianism, For and Against*, Cambridge.
See also: *Bentham; Mill*.

Utopianism

Utopianism is a form of social theory which attempts to promote certain desired values and practices by presenting them in an ideal state or society. Utopian writers do not normally think of such states as realizable, at least in anything like their perfectly portrayed form. But nor are they engaging in a merely fanciful or fantastic exercise, as the popular use of the term suggests. Often, as in Plato's *Republic*, the first true utopia, the aim is to show something of the essential nature of a concept – justice or freedom – by painting it large, in the form of an ideal community based on such a concept. At other times, as with Sir Thomas More's *Utopia* (1516), the object is primarily critical or satirical, to scourge the vices of the writer's society by an artful contrast with the virtuous people of Utopia. Only rarely – Edward Bellamy's *Looking Backward* (1888) is a good example – do utopian writers seek to transform society according to the blueprint painstakingly drawn in their utopia. Essentially the function of utopias is heuristic.

Until the seventeenth century, utopias were generally located in geographically remote areas of the globe. The European voyages of discovery of the sixteenth and seventeenth centuries killed off this useful device by making the world too familiar. From then on utopias were spatially displaced: to outer space – journeys to the moon begin in the seventeenth century – or beneath the sea, as in the frequent discovery of the sunken civilization of Atlantis, or deep below the earth's crust. But increasingly too the displacement was temporal rather than spatial, a move encouraged first by the seventeenth-century idea of progress and later by the vastly expanded notion of time offered by the new geology and biology of Lyell and Darwin. Instead of utopia being the better place, it became the better time. H. G. Wells took his Time-Traveller billions of years into the future, and Olaf Stapledon in *Last and First Men* (1930) employed a time scale of 2,000 million years to show the ascent of man to full utopian stature.

The displacement of space by time also produced a new sociological realism in utopias. Utopias were now placed in history and, however distant the utopian consummation, it could at least be presented as something mankind was tending towards, perhaps inevitably. The link with science and technology in the seventeenth century – as in Bacon's *New Atlantis* (1627) and Campanella's *City of the Sun* (1637) – strengthened this development. With the rise of nineteenth-century socialism, itself heavily utopian, utopianism became increasingly a debate about the possible realization of socialism. The utopias of Bellamy and Wells (*A Modern Utopia*, 1905) were the most powerful pleas on behalf of orthodox socialism, but William Morris offered an attractive alternative version in *News from Nowhere* (1890). An alternative of a different kind came with the invention of the 'dystopia' or anti-utopia, an inversion and a savage critique of all utopian hopes. Foreshadowed in Samuel Butler's anti-Darwinian *Erewhon* (1872), it reached its apogee in the 1930s and 1940s, especially with Aldous Huxley's *Brave New World* (1932) and George Orwell's *Nineteen Eighty-Four* (1949). Only

B. F. Skinner's *Walden Two* (1948) kept the utopian torch alight in these dark years, and there were many who saw in this utopia of behavioural engineering a nightmare worse than the blackest dystopia. Utopianism, however, revived strongly in the 1960s, in such works as Herbert Marcuse's *An Essay on Liberation* (1969), and is to be found alive and flourishing in the futurological and ecological movements.

Perhaps utopianism is inherent in the human condition, perhaps only in those cultures affected by the classical and Christian traditions; but one might well agree with Oscar Wilde that 'a map of the world that does not include Utopia is not worth even glancing at'.

Krishan Kumar
University of Kent

Further Reading
Manuel, F. E. and Manuel, F. P. (1979), *Utopian Thought in the Western World*, Cambridge, Mass.
Mumford, L. (1922), *The Story of Utopias*, New York.
See also: *futurology*.

V

Value, Labour Theory of
See Labour Theory of Value.

Van Gennep, Arnold (1873–1957)

Arnold Van Gennep, the creator of modern French folklore studies, was born in Germany but educated mostly in France. He took a degree at the École Pratique des Hautes Études in Paris, applied (without success) for a chair at the Collège de France, and actually held the first professorship in Swiss ethnography at the University of Neuchâtel (1913–15), yet he remained all his life an academic outsider, if not an outcast. His relationship with the academic ethnology of Durkheimian allegiance, then on the upsurge, was aloof. This did not prevent him from becoming a tireless and methodical collector of information on French popular culture, an efficient organizer of local data-gathering through questionnaires, the founder and publisher of several journals and book collections specializing in folklore, the compiler of a comprehensive bibliography of French folk traditions (1932–3; 1935) and, above all, a prolific author of studies on customs, beliefs and rituals in traditional France and in several European and overseas societies. Because he was linguistically so gifted and enormously well read, he was able to make a powerful contribution – through translations (of Frazer, Havelock Ellis, Westermarck and others) and scientific journalism – to the popularization of the ethnographic knowledge then available.

Van Gennep secured a measure of intellectual legitimacy for the scientific study of folklore, which had been totally neglected in Republican France. His approach was essentially empirical with limited theoretical underpinning, but with a bias towards the comparative method. *Les Rites de passage* (1909) (*The Rites of Passage*, 1960) is a classical illustration of his approach. Rituals marking various stages in the life cycle (pregnancy, birth, childhood, initiation, engagement, marriage, burial) regularly include three sequences: separation, transition, and aggregation or incorporation. Van Gennep stresses the sequential unity of all rituals, as well as their formal patterns, and suggests that rites of passage are indispensable elements of folk culture since they consecrate stages of the physical reproduction of every society.

Victor Karady
Centre National de la Recherche Scientifique, Paris

References
Van Gennep, A. (1908–14), *Essais d'ethnographie et de linguistique*, 5 vols, Paris.
Van Gennep, A. (1932–3), *Le Folklore du Dauphiné. Étude descriptive et comparée de psychologie populaire*, 2 vols, Paris.
Van Gennep, A. (1935), *Le folklore de la Flandre et du Hainaut français (département du Nord)*, 2 vols, Paris.

Further Reading
Belmont, N. (1979), *Arnold Van Gennep, The Creator of French Ethnography*, Chicago.
See also: *folklore; rites of passage.*

Veblen, Thorstein Bunde (1857–1929)

Thorstein Veblen, the son of immigrants to the United States, was brought up in isolated farming communities in Wisconsin and Minnesota. He received his doctorate in philosophy from Yale in 1884, but his agnosticism prevented his gaining an academic appointment until 1896 when he received a fellowship in economics at Chicago where he remained until 1906. Subsequently he taught at the Universities of Stanford and Missouri, and in 1918 he moved to New York where he was, for a year, an editor of *The Dial* and taught briefly at the New School for Social Research. The last years of his life were spent in self-imposed, relative isolation in California. Veblen was a true interdisciplinary scholar who possessed a wealth of economic, anthropological, sociological and linguistic knowledge, but his rejection of academic boosterism and his undisguised extra-marital affairs prevented him from gaining an academic rank commensurate with his abilities.

Veblen was a Darwinist in so far as he felt that biological and social evolution were characterized by blind, purposeless drift. In consequence, he rejected Marxism as teleological, utopian and unscientific, and condemned mainstream, orthodox economics for dealing in neat abstractions while avoiding examination of the real, and sometimes unsavoury, factors which affected the working of the economy. In Veblen's view, the metaphysical conceptions of classical economics were anachronistic in the era of machine production and served only to sanctify the economic dominance of businessmen and especially of financier-tycoons – the captains of industry – who, Veblen felt, produced little but waste, industrial disruption and paper profits for themselves.

Veblen's first two books, *The Theory of the Leisure Class* (1899) and the more specialized *Theory of Business Enterprise* (1904), provided a mordant and ironic examination of these processes. Veblen drew a sharp distinction between socially useful 'industrial' occupations and nonproductive, socially deleterious 'pecuniary' ones and depicted American society as being permeated by the spirit of business enterprise which was manifested in fraud, chicanery, self-aggrandisement and predation. *The Higher Learning in America* (1918) further documented the implications of this spirit in the 'business-like' conduct of American universities.

After 1914, Veblen's writings became more overtly political as he cast aside the guise of academic objectivity which had lightly veiled the condemnations contained in his earlier writings. In *Imperial Germany and the Industrial Revolution* (1915) and *An Enquiry Into the Nature of Peace* (1917) he analysed the emergence of Germany as an industrial and military power and pessimistically concluded that a lasting peace was unlikely, as the newly industrialized, militaristic and dynastic nations of Germany and Japan would eventually join forces and provoke a renewed and perhaps more devastating world conflict. The Russian Revolution encouraged Veblen to think that the 'vested interests' in America might similarly be overthrown, but the optimistic materialism of the 1920s dashed his hopes, and his last major work, *Absentee Ownership* (1923), represents the bitter and splenetic outpourings of a disappointed man.

Veblen's writings, which included a large number of important articles and several books in addition to those cited above, constituted an excoriating critique of capitalistic institutions and documented the dominance of 'imbecile institutions' over reason in human affairs. Personally, Veblen was taciturn, uncommunicative and resolutely unconventional. He made disciples almost inadvertently, greatly influencing the school of institutional economists who insisted on studying the sordid realities of the working of the economic system and indirectly influencing, among many others, such unconventional theorists as the economist J. K. Galbraith and the radical sociologist C. W. Mills. Veblen's reputation has declined in recent years, at least in part and rather ironically, as many of his ideas and concepts have passed into common academic parlance. In this respect Veblen has 'paid the penalty of taking the lead', a phrase he coined in the context of a discussion of Britain's failure to maintain its earlier industrial and commercial dominance.

John Whitworth
Simon Fraser University

Further Reading
Diggins, J. P. (1978), *The Bard of Savagery: Thorstein Veblen and Modern Social Theory*, New York.
Dorfman, J. (1934), *Thorstein Veblen and His America*, New York.
See also: *institutional economics*.

Vision

The principal advantages of the visual system over other senses are two in number: (1) The individual can respond to stimuli at distances that are very large as compared with his size: this makes for safety and can have competitive advantages. (2) The large ratio between the objects giving rise to visual stimuli and the wavelengths of the radiations whereby information is transmitted optimizes the quantity and quality of the information that arrives at the eye.

The description of the stimulus can be rationalized by a presentation in terms of a five-dimensional continuum. One dimension scales the spectral wavelengths of the radiation, partnered by dimension No. 2, namely stimulus intensity. No. 3 gives the size of the stimulus in angular measure: a Fourier transform (Campbell and Robson, 1968) can be shown to have parallels with the radiational spectrum, large objects being characterized by long spatial waves and vice versa. No. 4 measures contrast: a high intensity cannot make an object visible unless it can be made to stand out from its visual surround. And No. 5 represents the dimension of time.

It is feasible to view the whole of the visual system, beginning with the cornea and terminating with the locus of sensory perception, as a series of filters which operate on the five-dimensional input so as to maximize the wanted-signal/noise ratio. The use of the word 'wanted' is used advisedly because the response to a stimulus can be modified by earlier stimuli and responses, memory, and so on. Although the filters act independently they affect dimensions other than their own. For example, a change in intensity may modify apparent duration, contrast, and even spectral appearance.

Since the eye has evolved in response to sunlight its reaction to electro-magnetic radiations – the 'visible' spectrum – is easy to understand. The intensity of sunlight is maximal approximately in the spectral range to which the photo-sensors in the retina are mainly sensitive. The band seen is a window between the absorptive walls of the cornea and lens which protect the retina from noxious effects of ultra-violet light on the one hand, and the absorption of vitreous, that is, water, which fails to transmit infra-red radiations, on the other. The optics of the eye – made up essentially of cornea, contractile pupil and accommodative lens – serve to form a high contrast image on the retina where radiation triggers chemical events in the photo-receptors. These initiate an electric response that ultimately reaches the cortex and more central sensory areas. The pupil is a spatial filter providing a short-wavelength limit to the spatial spectrum transmitted by the eye. It is a characteristic of the resolving power of the retina that, in its central region called the fovea, it accurately matches the relation between contrast transmission and spatial wavelength of the ocular optics. This is more economical than is true of the spectral response of the retinal rods and cones which does not quite match the spectral distribution of natural light reaching them: the result is energy waste.

The size of the pupil is under reflex control and varies homeostatically not only with stimulus intensity but also so as to maximize retinal contrast, for example, when the ocular axes converge to a nearby visual target. This pupillary near-response is evoked alternatively by the lenticular mechanism of accommodation, another reflex that ensures that a high-contrast retinal image is formed independently of object distance.

Both the iris tissue, which determines the pupillary area, and the crystalline lens, which can accommodate its optical power as just noted, are subject to significant changes due to senescence. The pupil aperture is controlled by the interplay of the dilator and the sphincter under sympathetic and parasympathetic control respectively. Of the two smooth muscles, the former atrophies faster with age so that the pupil constricts in the old, admitting less light to the retina. A number of senescent changes occur in and around the lens which interfere with its power to accommodate. The result is presbyopia and the need for reading-glasses if a high-contrast retinal image of close objects is to materialize.

Given high contrast, the visual system can resolve normally visual angles of the order of 1 minute of arc. This high performance, inexplicable in terms of evolutionary pressures that have existed within the recent biologically significant time-scale, depends not only on optical normalcy, but also on good illumination (Davson, 1976). It tends to fall off – as in blue light – probably because contrast sensitivity is poor in this part of the spectrum.

The transduction of radiation into a nervous response takes place in the rods and cones; the former mediate vision in darkness, the latter in light. The latter also are associated with colour vision and high contrast sensitivity. Hence, if they are absent, as happens in certain diseases, vision is severely handicapped (Ripps, 1982). Rod and cone mechanisms also differ as regards temporal responses, the former being more sluggish and having the longer latent period of the two.

Considerable contrast, spatial, and temporal analysis takes place in the retina as it would be uneconomical to propagate redundancy to the cortex. It would also be difficult since the visual pathways converge onto a relatively tight optic nerve only to diverge again at the level of the optic radiation (past the lateral geniculate body) and, of course, in the cortex. At the level of the lateral geniculate body there occurs a confluence of the messages from the two eyes, but binocular cell-responses can be recorded only from inner cortical areas. Current evidence suggests that the visual field is not dissected cell by cell, but that there is provision for multiple projections specializing in different types of analysis, for example, colour, disparity (for space perception), and so on. It is unknown how the ultimate synthesis, if any, occurs.

Some attention has recently been given to the possibility that there exist significant sex differences in the sphere of vision. There is evidence that women are a little short-sighted in comparison with men, which may be due to the fact that their crystalline lenses have a higher optical power than those of men (Weale, 1983). Moreover, senescence appears to affect the two sexes differently in most of the ectodermal tissues that have been studied. Women apparently become presbyopic some five years earlier than do men (the lens, like the retina, the skin, hair, is derived from ectoderm). The visual acuity of older women is poorer than that of men by a small, but statistically significant, amount. Recent observations on squirrel monkeys show that chromatic responses recorded from the lateral geniculate body reveal highly significant sex-differences apparently related to their colour vision. Defects in the latter have, of course, been long known to be inherited on a sex-linked basis.

These observations are sufficiently weighty to point to the need to keep visual performance and related data separate for the two sexes, unless they have been shown not to differ on a statistically significant basis. Only some of the differences may be explicable in terms of different hormonal environments. However, this is unlikely to be the only explanation as the sex-linked differences in the progress of some retinal diseases are, at present, hard to envisage on this basis.

R. A. Weale
Institute of Ophthalmology
University of London

References

Campbell, F. W. and Robson, J. G. (1968), 'Application of Fourier Analysis to the visibility of gratings', *Journal of Physiology*.

Davson, H. (ed.) (1976), *The Eye, vol. 2A*, New York, London and San Francisco.

Ripps, H. (1982), 'Night blindness revisited: from man to molecules. Procter Lecture', *Invest. Ophthal. Vis. Sci.*

Weale, R. A. (1983), 'Transparency and power of post-mortem human lenses: variation with age and sex', *Exp. Eye Res.*, 36.

Further Reading

Marr, D. (1982), *Vision: A Computational Investigation into the Human Representation and Processing of Visual Information*, San Francisco.

Weale, R. A. (1982), *Focus on Vision*, London.

Weale, R. A. (1983), *A Biography of the Eye. Development, Growth, Age*, London.

See also: *colour vision; depth perception; McCollough effect; sensation and perception.*

Vital Statistics

An individual's entry into or departure from life, or change in civil status, is known as a vital event. In demographic applications the term most commonly encompasses births, marriages and deaths, while including stillbirths as well as live births, and divorces as well as marriages. An exhaustive list of such events would also contain annulments, adoptions, legitimations, recognitions and legal separations, but these latter vital events are less commonly the subject of demographic analysis. Vital statistics are the basic or derived data regarding vital events.

Christenings, marriages and burials were recorded in European parish registers as long ago as the sixteenth century. The first serious study of vital statistics, that of John Graunt in 1662, was based upon burial and christening records and presented the first crude life tables. Civil registration of vital events became compulsory in Scandinavia and some of the American colonies fairly early in the seventeenth century but in England not until 1837, although England was the first country to produce regular publications of vital statistics. In contrast, most developing countries today have either a defective system of vital registration, or none at all.

The information contained in a registration document includes the date and place of the vital event being registered, and the date and place of registration. The sex of the child and names and ages of parents are included on a birth certificate, and the cause of death, and age, marital status and occupation of the deceased on a death certificate. Other information on background characteristics is also obtained, the exact inventory varying with the type of event being registered, and from country to country.

Demographic data are of two types, 'stock' and 'flow', the stocks being population totals at a particular moment and the flows represented by movements into and out of a population over a period of time. Information on stocks is obtained from periodic population censuses or population registers, and on flows from a system of registration of vital events. The most obvious examples of flows are births and deaths, although marriage is also a flow as it represents movement from the unmarried to the married state. The most basic demographic measures incorporate both types of information, with a flow in the numerator and a stock in the denominator. Thus, for example, the crude birth rate, the simplest fertility measure, is calculated as the ratio of births which occurred during a particular year, as obtained from registration data, to the estimated mid-year population. Similarly, the total number of deaths in a particular year is related to the mid-year population in order to estimate the crude death rate.

Such measures can be made more informative by taking into account additional attributes such as age or, depending on the background information collected on the registration forms and its comparability with census information, other characteristics as well. Some examples are life tables for different occupational groups or regional age-specific fertility rates.

Most developing countries, as already noted, lack a comprehensive system of vital registration. In an attempt to compensate for this deficiency a number of techniques have been developed over the last twenty years by which vital rates can be estimated from fairly simple questions appended to a census schedule. Vital rates are also estimated, with varying degrees of success, from specially designed sample surveys.

Gigi Santow
Australian National University, Canberra

References

Shryock, H. S., Siegel, J. S. and Associates (1973), *The Methods and Materials of Demography*, Washington DC.

Spiegelman, M. (1968), *Introduction to Demography*, Cambridge, Mass.

Further Reading

Brass, W. and Coale, A. J. (1968), 'Methods of analysis and estimation', in W. Brass *et al.* (eds), *The Demography of Tropical Africa*, Princeton.

Graunt, J. (1939), *Natural and Political Observations Made upon the Bills of Mortality*, ed. W. F. Willcox, Baltimore.

Wrigley, E. A. and Schofield, R. S. (1983), 'English population history from family reconstitution: summary results 1600–1799', *Population Studies*, 37.

See also: *census; fertility; mortality; nuptiality.*

Vocational and Career Development

The field of vocational and career development concerns itself with how and why individuals develop preferences for one or another type of work, how they eventually choose an occupation and proceed in their attempts to achieve satisfaction from their work. It has produced instruments and procedures to assist individuals via education, consultation and counselling to optimize their vocational and career potential.

The field cuts across many different domains. Thus, developmental psychologists are interested in the developmental antecedents of important vocational and career decisions; test and measurement specialists create instruments to measure such domains as vocational interests, personality, and vocational maturity; sociologists study the impact of family characteristics and the sociocultural environment on careers, and counselling psychologists develop methods to intervene in the vocational and career-development process.

The most significant theories in the field of vocational and career development have been formulated since 1950, and are summarized by Osipow (1983). The first of these emphasized that vocational development is more than a single decision regarding an occupational choice. It is a process, occurring over a number of years and consisting of several distinct periods during which the individual makes successive compromises between his wishes and the realistic opportunities present.

In 1953, Super presented his self-concept theory, which viewed vocational development as being inextricably linked to the development of a person's self-concept. Super extended his developmental approach to include not only the Exploratory Stage, during which vocational exploration and tentative decisions occur, but also the Establishment Stage, during which vocational decisions are evaluated and modified, leading to mature vocational behaviours and career decisions (see Super, 1982).

A third major theory is Holland's, initially developed in 1959. The basic feature of this theory rests on the assumption that there are a finite number of different work environments which attract different personalities. If the work environment 'matches' the personality of the person choosing it, this can lead to a successful career. Most research in this area has confirmed Holland's basic conceptualization (see Holland, 1973).

Other important approaches to vocational and career development since 1950 include Tiedeman's developmental theory (see Tiedeman et al., 1978), Krumboltz's social-learning theory (see Krumboltz, 1979), and Roe's personality theory (see Roe, 1979). Interest in the field is growing rapidly, in part because of its recent attention to the vocational and career development of women and minorities, and in part because of its growing recognition of career development as a life-span process.

Fred W. Vondracek
Pennsylvanian State University

References

Holland, J. L. (1973), *Making Vocational Choices: A Theory of Careers*, Englewood Cliffs, NJ.

Krumboltz, J. D. (1979), 'A social learning theory of career decision-making' in H. Mitchell *et al.* (eds), *Social Learning and Career Decision Making*, Cranston, Rhode Island.

Osipow, S. H. (1983), *Theories of Career Development*, 3rd edn, Englewood Cliffs, NJ.

Roe, A. (1979), 'Confronting complexity', *Academic Psychology Bulletin*, 1.

Super, D. E. (1982), 'Self-concepts in career development: theory and findings after thirty years', Presented at the 20th International Congress of Applied Psychology, Edinburgh.

Tiedeman, D. V *et al.* (1978), *The Cross-Sectional Story of Early Career Development*, Washington, DC.

See also: *occupational psychology*.

Von Neumann

See Neumann.

Voting

Studies of electoral behaviour seek to account for the response of individuals and groups to, as well as their influence on, the body politic. Most of the studies have been carried out in Western democracies, where not only is voting by secret ballot but where respective governments and other political factions are thought not to interfere with the individual's vote choice. While different social science disciplines approach the study of voting from rather different vantage points, they have in common the need to interpret information obtained about a particular election within an historical or comparative framework. An historical approach relates given election results to those of previous elections, thereby seeking explanations for change in the country's, the parties' or the voters' history; a comparative approach seeks explanations across national boundaries for the rise and influence of similar voting trends or of similar political and social movements, as for example, the Women's Movement, the environmental and anti-nuclear lobbies, as well as the growth of prejudice, anti-immigrant sentiments in Britain and anti-*Gastarbeiter* sentiments in West Germany. Other comparative studies examine the impact of the recession and of unemployment on the public's vote choice and on the parties' promises and performances.

Countries differ in the role assigned to the public in political decision making. In Britain this is limited to votes cast to elect a British and, more recently, also a European Member of Parliament, and to the election of local councillors. In the United States the public participates far more. There are elections at national, state and local levels including the election of a wide range of officials, even judges. Additionally, the public is asked to vote on policy, including some budgetary proposals put forward by the officials or – and this is an important extension of the public's right – by members of the public. Thus in the US the public votes for a wide range of officeholders, a wide range of policy proposals and can also affect the political agenda. In France and in some other countries, referenda are called to allow the public to vote in important policy issues.

Because of the bewildering range of vote opportunities across countries, most comparative analyses deal with general elections only, since these occur in every country, are judged the most important by the electorate and therefore yield a higher turnout compared with other elections.

Voting practices differ across countries in a number of important ways: (1) In the frequency and variety of occasions on which the electorate's views are sought. (2) In the number of parties that participate. (3) In the minimum voting age stipulated. (4) In the ease or difficulty of registration, once eligible. While all countries have general or national elections and require an election to be called after a fixed number of years (generally four or five), in some countries the date of the election is laid down, while in others, as in Britain, the government of the day can call an election at any time within the stipulated period of office when it judges its chances propitious for re-election.

To these differences must be added two other very important differences, namely the constitutional checks on the power conferred on the leader of the government of the day, and the electoral system itself. In the United States there are constitutional checks and balances restraining the power of the President; in Britain the power of the Prime Minister is directly proportional to the size of the majority of seats held by the Prime Minister's party in the House of Commons.

The electoral system of a country profoundly affects the extent to which the legislative chamber reflects the voters' preferences. Most European countries have accepted one or other form of proportional representation, of which the direct form is used in the Irish Republic where the distribution of seats in parliament directly reflects the distribution of votes in the country for the different parties. Britain's 'first past the post' method is by now the exception and causes the most serious distortion in the representation of voters' preferences in parliament. This is because each individual casts the vote *within* his constituency in order to return one of the candidates as the constituency Member of Parliament. There are 650 constituencies. The government of the day is formed not necessarily from the party with the highest number of votes in the country, but from the party that has more Members of Parliament among the 650 than any other party. The 1983

election provides a particularly glaring example of the degree of distortion generated by this system. The figures presented below show the number of votes cast for each party, the number of seats gained and the number that would have been gained had there been proportional representation. While at present the Conservative government has a large absolute majority, with proportional representation it would not have a majority at all – a difference which, of course, has profound repercussions on the government's ability to bring about legislative changes where these are opposed by the other parties. (Or put another way, it

Other Parties	No. of votes cast	Seats allocated	Seats allocated by proportional representation
Conservatives	13 mil	396	280
Labour	8.5 mil	209	182
Alliance	7.8 mil	23	170

took 33,000 votes to elect one Member of Parliament for the Conservative party and 339,000 votes for the Alliance party. This is because the Alliance candidates in most constituencies scored a high percentage of votes but since they did not come first, their votes were wasted.)

Types of Election Studies
While all aim to explain the antecedents and consequences of election results, studies differ in the level of analysis adopted (macro- or micro-level) and in the models of electoral decision making they employ. At the macro-level of analysis, aggregate statistics across elections are used to determine trends and to isolate the rare 'critical election' one which records a significant shift in vote choices which persists in subsequent elections. Studies of trends in the electorate's preference for parties of the right or left, changes in turnout (there has been a general downward trend sufficiently pronounced in the United States that now just over half the electorate votes in Presidential elections), in the share of the vote by the two major parties (which has steadily decreased) are examples of such analyses.

At the micro-level, interest focuses on the individual voter's process of decision making, both in a particular election and across elections. This latter approach only became possible once individual voters themselves were questioned and not as in the 1930s, when inferences about vote choice had to be drawn from relating election returns to known characteristics of the electorate in that district: the only ones available being demographic data (age, sex, social class and religious affiliation). The change came in the United States with the pioneering work of Lazarsfeld and Berelson who in the 1940s carried out the first surveys of voters in particular districts, followed by the first national election surveys in 1948 conducted by the Michigan Survey Research Center, which has since then continued to undertake such surveys at every subsequent election. Similar surveys of voters were subsequently conducted in Britain and in most European countries, seeking information from individual voters about their vote choice, reasons for that choice, their images of parties and candidates, and about their knowledge of the parties' stands and their attitudes towards the policy proposals put forward. Cross-sectional studies are periodically supplemented by panel studies, where respondents are re-interviewed at the next or even subsequent general elections. The two longest panel studies were conducted in Britain, one extending over fifteen years.

Campbell and his colleagues, analysing the Michigan surveys of the 1950s, found reality to be at variance with the picture of the ideal citizen in a democracy. Voters cared little about politics, were relatively ill informed about issues and often voted for parties whose policy proposals they did not like. Campbell developed a model of vote choice in which he explained these inconsistencies by suggesting that the voter early in life, through parental example, develops a party identification (seeing himself as a Democrat or Republican) which guides both vote choice and policy evaluations. A kind of 'standing decision', as Key suggests, facilitates vote choice apart from rare occasions where attitudes to particular candidates or the strength of feelings about a particular issue proves decisive, overriding party attachment (a phenomenon that is described as the result of short-term forces but not one which basically affects long-term party attachment, which if anything grows with the years). 'An individual thinks politically as he is socially' is an apt description suggesting that it is group membership that affects party attachment.

The *rational model* of voting put forward by Downs, and elaborated since, views the voters' behaviour in making their choice as rational in this as in other decisions where the choice is made on the basis of summing preferences, a choice in this case based on evaluation of candidates, issues, and party images. A more recent elaboration of the rational model put forward by Himmelweit *et al.* (1985) is described as the *consumer model of voting*, in which the search for the best fit or less misfit between preferences and parties affects the voters' choice, tempered by the strength of party attachment and the persistent habit of voting for one rather than another party.

The consumer model does not require voters to be well informed, but does require them to have preferences for given candidates and/or policies and to perceive parties to take dissimilar stands on these policies. One further factor must be added, a factor which Lipset has developed in comparing twenty elections from 1979 into the 1980s in Western democracies. He compiled for each country a 'misery index' to do with inflation and unemployment rates and found that in countries where such an index was high, the party in office was defeated in 17 of these elections, with socialists and liberals replacing their more conservative rivals in half, while the more right-wing parties defeated left-of-centre incumbents in the other half. The point here is an extension of one made by Fiorina: that the incumbents are judged on their performance and that a change in vote may reflect simply a desire for change rather than a preference for the policies of the opposing party, a view substantiated by the increase in negative reasons of voting for a party.

The difference between the Michigan and the consumer model is not that one accords an important place to party attachment and the other does not, but that the former sees party attachment as the key to vote decision, while the latter sees it as an important factor interacting with other preferences which also affect the decision. Where voters' preferences are evenly balanced, party attachment will prove decisive, or alternatively as in the calmer period of the 1950s where few issues divided the electorate. That is, in the consumer model, the strength of party attachment in influencing the vote will have as much, if not more, to do with the characteristics of a particular election, the number of issues which divide the electorate and the degree to which parties offer alternate styles of government, as with the individuals' strength of attachment from whatever cause to one or other party.

In the last twenty years there is much evidence of the electorate's increased awareness of parties' stands, and increased readiness to evaluate policy choice. Above all, there is growing evidence of volatility in voting and of a decline, not only in the readiness to identify with one or other party but particularly in the strength of that identification and with it its influence on vote choice.

Discussions about the most appropriate model of vote choice will undoubtedly continue. With individuals in many other aspects of their lives seemingly less influenced and more critical of institutional norms than before, and with the rapid social, technological and economic changes affecting their lives, it seems likely that parties will be less and less able to rely on party loyalties, with policy proposals being accepted on trust, and will instead be judged more on past performance and on the realism of new policy proposals.

Hilde Himmelweit
London School of Economics and Political Science

Reference
Himmelweit, H. T. and Jaeger, M. (1985), *How Voters Decide*, revised edn, Milton Keynes.
Further Reading
Barnes, S. H. and Kasse, M. (1977), *Political Action: Mass Participation in Five Western Democracies*, Beverly Hills, Calif.

Budge, I and Fairlie, D. J. (1983), *Explaining and Predicting Elections*, London.
Särlvik, B. and Crewe, I. (1983), *Decades of Realignment: The Conservative Victory of 1979 and Electoral Trends in the 1970's*, Cambridge.
See also: *elections*.

W

Walras, Antoine Auguste (1801–66)

Antoine Walras was one of the first economists to perceive that value derived from marginal utility (*rareté*) rather than total utility. Born at Montpellier, he became professor of rhetoric at the College of Évreaux in 1831, where, in the same year, he published his first book on political economy, *De la nature de la richesse et de l'origine de la valuer* (Paris). In 1835 he went to Paris at the Athénée as professor of political economy. Later he was appointed as professor of philosophy and French literature at Caen.

A. A. Walras was led to the study at economics at a time when there existed a controversy regarding the nature of the value of things and its determination. Some writers equated value with cost of production, while others argued that the value of things derived from their usefulness, that is, utility to the consumer. A. A. Walras argued that value did not come from either, but from the *change* in utility associated with an incremental increase in the quantity of the good consumed. Later, the application of mathematics to this principle was to revolutionize economic science.

The direct influence of A. A. Walras on the development of economic science was less profound than his indirect influence, through his son, Marie-Esprit Léon Walras, who became one of the founders of the marginal utility theory of value in the 1860s, and whose work in General Equilibrium Theory establishes him as one of the greatest economists in the history of economics.

Vincent J. Tarascio
University of North Carolina, Chapel Hill

Walras, Marie-Esprit Léon (1834–1910)

The son of Antoine Auguste Walras, Léon Walras was born on 16 December 1834, at Evreux, in the department of Evre, France. In 1858, he decided to devote his life to the development of economic science, largely through the influence of his father, who was also his teacher.

Denied a teaching post in France, he became the first occupant of a newly-founded chair in economics at the University of Lausanne, Switzerland in 1870, where he remained until his retirement in 1892. Through his work, together with that of his successor,

Vilfredo Pareto, a new school of thought was established, which became known as the Lausanne School of Political Economy.

Walras's approach to political economy consisted of his trilogy – pure economics, applied economics, and social economics – each part constituting a particular aspect of political economy. The first was essentially developed in his *Eléments d'économie politique pure* (1874–7) (*Elements of Pure Economics*, London, 1953) when he presented the theory of general economic equilibrium, with its emphasis upon the interdependence of economic phenomena. Through a method of successive approximations, he began with the theory of exchange, then production, followed by his theory of capital, and, finally, monetary theory. In the process, he made significant contributions to each of these fields. Taken as a whole, his *Eléments* has often been recognized as one of the greatest theoretical achievements in the history of economic science.

The other two components of his trilogy – applied and social economics – dealt with economic policy and economic justice respectively. These two works did not achieve the same status as his pure economics among his contemporaries, and have all but been forgotten by modern economists, reflecting a current preference for narrow scope of economics.

Vincent J. Tarascio
University of North Carolina, Chapel Hill

Reference
Walras, L. (1874), *Eléments d'économie politique pure*, Paris.

Further Reading
Hicks, J. R. (1934), 'Leon Walras', *Econometrica*.
Jaffé, W. (ed.) (1965), *Correspondence of Léon Walras and Related Papers*, 3 vols.
Walker, D. A. (ed.) (1983), *William Jaffé's Essays on Walras*, London.

War

War, as we know it, is a relatively new phenomenon in the history of humanity. That groups of people have inflicted damage on other groups is nothing new. But, as Quincy Wright showed (1942), the most common form of war, which he called 'social war', was a ritual.

Groups might attack each other, but hostilities commonly ended when the first blood was spilt.

War waged in order to obtain economic and political goals, to rob and to dominate, is a more recent phenomenon, related to what is usually called 'civilization'. The more society is characterized by agriculture (as opposed to hunting-gathering or cattle), the more it is organized as a state (as opposed to clan, tribe, village), and the more internal division of labour there is (over and above what is found in all societies, based on gender and age), the more belligerent the societies seem to be, in the sense that they use aggressive wars to obtain economic and political goals. As these structural characteristics are typical of Western societies ('modern', 'developed'), one would expect them to be particularly predisposed to belligerence. But the significance of Western social cosmology, the deep ideological structure of Western society, should also be mentioned. There is the idea of being the centre of the world, and possessing social formulas which are valid for the whole world – expressed, for example, in the missionary command (Matthew, 28:18-20). Given such beliefs, war is not only a right but a duty. This view is shared in Islam and in the secular offspring of Christianity, liberalism, and Marxism.

War is getting more dangerous all the time. There is an increased risk for the belligerents of getting killed, and an ever-greater portion of those who are killed are civilians. No more than about 2 per cent of belligerents in war in the Middle Ages lost their lives. The proportion rose to about 40 per cent in the First World War. But, whereas only one quarter of those killed in the First World War were civilians, about half of those who died in the Second World War, and more than 75 per cent in the Indochina Wars were civilians. It should be noted that in the event of a major nuclear war there will be many casualties in nonbelligerent countries due to the new phenomenon of fall-out. In addition, there will be casualties after hostile action has ceased due to long-term effects on the environment.

In order to understand wars, it is not enough to focus on the arms used; equally or more important is the conflict formation within which the war is enacted. If we divide the world into Centre and Periphery countries depending on where they are located on the international division of labour, we get three major types of war:

1 Centre-Centre wars – the current East-West conflict would be of this type.
2 Centre-Periphery wars – the current North-South conflict is an example.
2 Periphery-Periphery wars – these are often, disparagingly, referred to as 'local wars'.

Characteristically, Centre countries, and particularly the superpowers, regard their own conflicts as the real ones, and see all other conflicts as derived from them, and not without some reason. However, in the post-Second World War period, the Centre-Periphery wars have been by far the most important. At least 70 per cent of belligerent activity in the roughly 150 wars which have been waged since 1945 can be said to fall into this category, among them all the national and people's wars of liberation. The problem has been how to escape the colonial or neocolonial grip which Centre countries have had and continue to have on Periphery countries. Typically, one Centre country is allied with a local bridgehead of economic and political élites. If one superpower or bloc is involved, the other one can usually be counted on to support the local opposition, but meticulously avoiding direct confrontation in order not to escalate the conflict into East-West confrontation with the risk of nuclear war. In terms of casualties, the sum of the modern Centre-Periphery and the Periphery-Periphery wars is already of the magnitude of a Third World War. However, it does not conform to the European formula for a world war, which is based on an action like Germany crossing the Rhine and the Oder, or a Blitz attack on one of the present superpowers (like the German Operation Barbarossa on the Soviet Union on 22 June 1941 and the Japanese on Pearl Harbor on 7 December 1941). It is this image which has disposed today's superpowers to adopt a Nevermore policy of guarding against a first strike through incessant quantitative and qualitative improvements in armaments, making arms both more destructive and less vulnerable.

If nuclear war is a *macro* war, and conventional war (without weapons of mass destruction such as nuclear, biological, chemical, environmental and radiological weapons) are termed *meso* wars, then what would be a *micro* war? Clearly such a term might be used to describe what is often referred to as terrorism (by those against whom it is directed). The target is more precise, such as selected individuals and places; the weapons have short range and small impact areas, such as handguns. Such micro wars may become part of any concrete pattern of warfare but are probably particularly important in Centre-Periphery contexts as the form of warfare chosen by the weak. Dialectically, terrorism leads to counter-terrorism, military-police action, torture, death squads, and so on. It would be artificial not to include such conflicts in the concept of modern warfare, just as the old distinction between external and internal wars ('civil wars') becomes meaningless with the internationalization of almost all major conflicts today.

There are two broad approaches in the fight against war. One is directed against the arms, the other is concerned with the conflict itself, with a view to solving its deeper-lying causes. The former approach has not been a success, as is apparent from the great number of disarmament conferences which have not reduced the total amount of destructive power, although they have sometimes possibly shifted its form, reflecting technological changes. One possibility here might be to harness technical changes for the development of purely defensive arms, which could be used to buttress a non-provocative military posture, somewhat along the lines of the policy of the Swiss, the Yugoslavs, the Austrians, and the Finns in Europe.

Conflict resolution, however, remains a basic condition, necessary, if not sufficient, for avoiding wars and warlike activities. The problem is, as a rule, that conflict resolution presupposes some kind of change, usually also some redistribution of power and privilege, and will be resisted by those interested in the status quo, a category which includes those with a generally expansionist and domineering stance in world affairs, and with material and political interests all over the world.

Johan Galtung
International Peace Research Institute, Oslo

Reference
Wright, Q. (1942), *A Study of War*, Chicago.

Further Reading
Sorokin, P. (1957), *Social and Cultural Dynamics*, Boston.
See also: *Clausewitz; conflict; conflict resolution; feud; force; military sociology; peace; terrorism; war, primitive.*

War, Primitive

In line with contemporary anthropological usage which restricts the word primitive to the technology of other cultures, primitive war may be characterized as any fighting between opposed groups using technically unsophisticated weapons (arbitrarily defined as lacking explosive devices).

When both sides are evenly matched, a common situation, fighting with these relatively ineffective weapons – bows and arrows, spears, war clubs, battle axes, knives and swords – results in few deaths, contrary to popular opinion fed by sensational and fallacious stories, and the small number of reliably documented massacres notwithstanding. Although gruesome customs like headhunting, cannibalism and scalping accompany primitive war in some regions, the bestiality and number of casualties resulting pales into insignificance compared to the horror and carnage when industrial nations fight with their technologically awesome arsenals.

Military encounters in primitive warfare take various forms: battles, raids, ambushes, duels, supernatural combats and so on. In battles, enemies confront one another and exchange fire, each dodging the other's missiles, often parrying with shields; they may engage in close combat with bludgeoning weapons. In raids, one side stealthily approaches the (sometimes fortified) settlement or territory of the other and launches a swift surprise attack, usually retreating hastily, and if successful first destroying and pillaging the routed enemy's property. In ambushes, warriors lay in wait at some frequently visited place and attack the surprised enemy who may be enticed to the spot by treachery. In duels, warriors meet in single combat, usually egged on – even supported militarily – by their respective sides. In supernatural combats, people try to manipulate other forces to strike down their enemy, using black magic called sorcery.

The military tactics that feature in the above encounters are straightforward and, customarily circumscribed, frequently predictable. Strategies are similarly limited and predictable, and they are commonly spontaneous and short-term, prompted by spur-of-the-moment events. In terms of numbers killed, successful raids and ambushes are the most effective, whereas battles lead to fewer fatalities, except in the uncommon event of one side overwhelming the other.

Anthropologists generally make an ill-defined distinction between two kinds of small-scale hostility: feud and war. A feud can be minimally defined as an aggressive relationship between two groups which never ends, the start of which, generations previously, may be forgotten. Revenge is the force that keeps these hostilities going indefinitely. When one side settles an old score, the other, losing as a consequence, incurs a blood-debt and prosecutes the feud in revenge, and so it goes on.

A war, on the other hand, is a state of hostility which may be settled peacefully at some stage. The time spent fighting varies from one place to another and is often fairly brief. A medley of motives prompt wars although, following Clausewitz, all such aggression is probably at root politically motivated. The political element is clear in densely populated state polities, which frequently go to war for gain, be it territorial annexation, political conquest or pillage of property.

The underlying political factor is less obvious in stateless societies. Here too the obligation to avenge killed relatives is a regular motivating force. The victims' relatives are supported in their quest for vengeance by a group of persons mobilizing on their behalf. The covert political reason for war in stateless societies is that revenge prevents any person subjecting another to his will, and consequently undermining the egalitarian political order. Disputes frequently spark off stateless wars, when persons confront one another over some issue and come into conflict, each trying to force a settlement in his favour and thus coming to blows. If someone gets killed as a result, the killer instantly faces a group mobilized to wreak vengeance. The killer's relatives will unite to defend themselves, not only because they think their side in the right in the homicidal confrontation, but also because they are all fair game to square the account.

Enemies are commonly related, sometimes closely, to one another in the face-to-face kin-founded societies in which primitive warfare occurs. The result is considerable pressure for a settlement, since hostility will be too disruptive for many people. They will try to act as intermediaries. The manner in which peace is effected varies from one society to another, and commonly involves a period of unstable truce that strengthens into peace, and often features some ceremony to sanction its existence.

While warfare, primitive or modern, may harness individual aggression, it is fallacious to argue that it is an unavoidable consequence of innate human bellicosity. Warfare is an artifact of human culture. All societies experience conflicts of interests, which result in disputes between individuals and groups, and the threat of war is inevitable so long as political systems countenance violence as a way of resolving deadlocks.

Paul Sillitoe
University of Durham

Further Reading

Bohannan, P. (ed.) (1967), *Law and Warfare*, New York.

Turney-High, H. H. (1971), *Primitive War*, Columbia, South California.

See also: *feud; war.*

Watson, John Broadus (1878–1958)

As the founder of behaviourism and as a publicist and popularizer of psychology, John B. Watson was perhaps the most influential American psychologist of his generation. Born in 1878 near Greenville, South Carolina, Watson grew up in a large and poor rural family. He attended Furman University, a small Baptist college near Greenville, and graduated with a Master of Arts Degree in 1899. Watson entered the University of Chicago in 1900, where he studied with John Dewey, psychologist James Rowland Angell, neurophysiologist H. H. Donaldson and biologist Jacques Loeb.

At Chicago, Angell had been instrumental in founding the functional school of psychology. Influenced by Darwin, William James and Dewey, the functionalists opposed the elementistic psychology developed by Wilhelm Wundt in Germany and espoused in America as structuralism by British-trained psychologist E. B. Titchener. Whereas structuralism attempted to discover the structure of mind by first isolating the basic elements of consciousness, functionalism was concerned with the mind in use and

held that the function of consciousness was its capacity to enable an organism to adapt to its environment.

Although a protégé of Angell, Watson was later to reject both functionalism and structuralism. Even as a student he was particularly influenced by Loeb's insistence that all life processes could be explained in physiochemical terms. Watson's own interests lay in comparative or animal psychology. He was uncomfortable with human subjects and what he considered to be the artificiality of introspective methods, which required subjects to observe and record the sensations and perceptions of their own conscious experience. His dissertation, completed under H. H. Donaldson, was a study of the correlation between the learned behaviour and the neurophysiology of the white rat. In 1903, Watson received the first Ph.D. granted in psychology from the University of Chicago. With the recommendation of Angell and Dewey, he was invited to stay at Chicago as lecturer and director of the psychological laboratory and quickly gained a reputation as a leading figure in the relatively new field of comparative psychology.

In 1908, Watson was invited by James Mark Baldwin to develop a programme in experimental psychology at Johns Hopkins University. Less than a year later, Baldwin was forced to resign, leaving Watson as chairman of the department and editor of the *Psychological Review*. At Johns Hopkins, Watson became increasingly dissatisfied with the assumptions of both structuralism and functionalism. As long as psychology considered its subject matter to be the investigation of consciousness, he argued, it perpetuated a mind-body dualism that kept it beyond the pale of current scientific assumptions. Watson believed that he could resolve this issue by simply denying the existence of mind as a distinct entity. For years he had been investigating animals without referring to purely mental categories or functions. As early as 1910, he had become convinced that psychological investigations could be conducted exclusively through the observation of behaviour without any reference to consciousness. By 1913, he was ready to make his position public. In a lecture entitled 'Psychology as the Behaviourist Views It', Watson issued an open challenge to the established preconceptions of psychological method and theory.

Watson's behaviourism not only offered a new methodological approach to psychological investigation, but attempted to redefine fundamental assumptions of the profession itself. Claiming that psychology had 'failed signally' to take its place as 'an undisputed natural science', Watson placed the blame on the use of the introspective method and its underlying assumption of the existence of states of consciousness. Watson considered 'mind' and 'consciousness' to be as unverifiable as 'soul' and refused to make any assumption that could not be observed and verified from overt behaviour. Behaviourism, Watson argued, would at once enable psychology to become a 'purely objective natural science', with its 'theoretical goal' being nothing less than the 'prediction and control of behavior'. Watson hoped to ally psychology with the positivist trend in the natural and social sciences. He also sought to bridge the gap between experimental and applied psychology by claiming that behaviourism would enable psychologists to develop techniques that would be of direct use to 'the educator, the physician, the jurist and the business man'.

In 1914, Watson was elected president of the American Psychological Association. In his presidential address the following year, he consolidated his behaviourist theory by offering the conditioned motor reflex (as described by Russian neurologist, V. M. Bechterev) as an objective methodology that could be used to measure and control sensory responses. Watson then began experiments on human subjects which culminated in 1919 which his famous 'Little Albert' experiment, by which Watson claimed to have developed techniques to condition, at will, specific emotional reactions in infants. In the midst of conducting this experiment, Watson became romantically involved with his graduate assistant, and as a result, was forced to resign from Johns Hopkins in 1920 under the cloud of a widely publicized divorce scandal.

Watson then moved to New York, where he became a successful advertising executive until his retirement in 1945. During this period, he was a tireless promoter of the use of psychological techniques in business and industry. He also continued to teach at the New School for Social Research and sponsored psychological research on infants at Columbia University. During the 1920s and 1930s, Watson promoted behaviourism to a mass audience. His widely read *Behaviorism* (1924) was followed by an enormous output of popular magazine and newspaper articles. In *The Psychological Care of Infant and Child* (1928), Watson advised parents to raise children according to a strict regimen that discouraged displays of affection. Later writings included his utopian vision of a society ordered on behaviouristic principles and governed by a hierarchy of technicians.

Although few psychologists were willing to accept Watson's abandonment of consciousness wholeheartedly and came to reject the more radical aspects of his extreme materialism, behaviourism's objective methodology had a powerful impact on the direction of American experimental psychology. Moreover, the popular reception of behaviourism in America was not only a tribute to Watson's skill as a propagandist, but reflected a national preoccupation with order and efficiency in a society that was in the process of rapid urban and industrial expansion.

Kerry W. Buckley

Further Reading

Boakes, R. A. (1984), *From Darwin to Behaviorism*, Cambridge.
Buckley, K. W. (1986), *Mechanical Man: John B. Watson and the Beginnings of Behaviorism*, New York.
Watson, J. B. (1913), 'Psychology as the behaviorist views it', *Psychological Review*, 20.
Watson, J. B. (1924), *Behaviorism*, New York.
Watson, J. B. and Watson, R. R. (1928), *The Psychological Care of Infant and Child*, New York.
See also: *behaviourism; conditioning.*

Weber, Max (1864–1920)

Max Weber, the son of a member of the Reichstag and an activist Protestant mother, grew up in Berlin in an intellectually lively home frequently visited by the Bismarckian era's leading politicians and intellectuals. After receiving an outstanding secondary education in languages, history, and the classics, he studied law, economics, history, and philosophy at the Universities of Heidelberg, Strasbourg, Göttingen, and Berlin. Although his first appointments, at the Universities of Freiburg (1894) and Heidelberg (1897), were in the faculty of economics, he is best known today as one of the major founders of modern sociology and as one of the intellectual giants of interdisciplinary scholarship. As strange as it may sound, he ranged freely across the entire palette of written history, from the ancient Greeks to the early Hindus, from the Old Testament prophets to the Confucian literati, from the economic organization of early Near-Eastern civilizations to the trading companies of the Medieval West, and from the origins of Continental law to comparative analyses of the rise of the modern state.

The diversity of these themes – only a small sampling – should not lead us to view Weber as a scholar of unlimited energies frantically leaping about for its own sake. Rather, when looked at closely, a grand design becomes visible in his writings, yet one that remained incomplete and whose inner coherence can be plotted only against the inner torments of their author. Weber and others of his generation in Germany viewed the dawning of rapid industrialization and the modern age itself with profound ambivalence rather than as a first step toward a new era of progress. While welcoming the possibilities it offered for a burgeoning of individualism and an escape from the feudal chains of the past, he saw few firm guidelines in reference to which modern man might be able to establish a comprehensive meaning for his life or even his everyday action (1946). Moreover, the overtowering bureaucracies indispensable to the organization of industrial societies were endowed with the capacity to render persons politically powerless as well as to replace creative potential with stifling routine and merely functional relationships. These developments threatened to curtail the flowering of individualism.

Just such quandries stood behind all of Weber's sociological writings, particularly those undertaken after 1903. In these studies he wished to define precisely the uniqueness of his own civilization and to understand on a universal scale the manner in which persons, influenced by social constellations, formulate *meaning* for their lives that guides action. A curiosity founded in such questions instilled in him an amazing capacity to place himself, once he had constructed a 'mental image' of another era and civilization, into the minds of persons quite unlike himself. This aim to understand how values and actions made sense to their beholders, however foreign they were to the social scientist investigating them, formed the foundation for Weber's *verstehende* sociology.

Perhaps it was this sensitivity, as well as a sheer respect for meanings formulated over centuries, that prompted Weber to construct one of his most famous axioms, one debated heatedly to this day. To him, all scientific judgements must be 'value-free': once researchers have selected their themes of inquiry, then personal values, preferences, and prejudices must not be allowed to interfere with the collection of empirical data and its 'objective' evaluation (1949). Everyone involved in scientific work should avoid an inadvertent intermixture of his values with those of the actors being studied. To Weber, even the scientist who happened to be a Calvinist was duty-bound – as long as he wished to pursue science – to describe, for example, tribal sexual practices accurately and to interpret them in reference to their indigenous 'cultural significance', however repugnant they seemed to him personally. This postulate also implied a strict division between that which *exists* (the question for scientific analysis) and that which *should be* (the realm of personal values).

In explicitly circumscribing the legitimate domain of science and denying it the right to produce norms, ideals, and values, Weber had a larger purpose in mind. He hoped to establish an inviolable realm within which individuals would be forced to confront themselves and autonomously formulate a set of personal values capable of guiding their actions and endowing them with meaning. Nothing less was required as a counter-force in an age in which bureaucratization and the scientific world view threatened to encroach upon decision making, thus upsetting the already tenuous character of individualism. Weber's own adherence to a value-free science, particularly in his studies of pre-modern and non-Western societies, the penetration of his insight into the diverse ways in which meaning could be formed and patterned action ensued, and the universal-historical scope of his investigations enabled him to write – however fragmented, incomplete, and

poorly organized – a comparative historical sociology of civilizations unique in the history of sociology.

Even though his interest focused upon comparisons between civilizations, Weber's emphasis upon individual meaning prevented him from taking the Hegelian Absolute Spirit, the Marxian organization of production and class struggle, or the 'social facts' of Durkheim as his point of departure. Nor was he inclined, due to his continuous accentuation of the conflicts between diverse 'spheres of life' (religious, political, economic, legal, aesthetic) and the centrality of power and domination, to view societies, like Parsons, as basically integrated wholes. In fact, Weber's orientation to the individual and the meaning he attaches to his action would seem to carry him dangerously close to a radical subjectivism. Two procedures guarded against this possibility:

First, in his substantive studies, it was the patterned actions of individuals in groups, and not individuals acting alone, that captured his attention. It was only this regular action that, according to Weber, proved to be culturally significant and historically powerful. Individuals tended to become knit together into collectivities primarily in five ways: acknowledgement of common material interests (as occurred when classes were formed), recognition of common 'ideal interests' (as took place when status groups arose), adherence to a single world view (as occurred in religious groups), acknowledgement of affectual feelings (as found in person-oriented groups, such as the household, the clan, and the neighbourhood), and awareness of relations of domination (as took place in the charismatic, patriarchal, feudal, patrimonial, and bureaucratic forms of domination). However massive and enduring an institution might appear, it must not, according to Weber, be understood as more than the orientations of individuals acting in common.

The second means employed by Weber to avoid lapsing into a radical subjectivism involves his major methodological tool, one that reveals his indebtedness to Kant: the 'ideal type' (1949). Indeed, this heuristic construct so effectively guarded against this possibility that a number of commentators have accused Weber – particularly in his later work – of moving away from a *verstehende* sociology and of reifying the social phenomena he studies. In part, Weber himself is to blame. Instead of discussing, for example, 'bureaucratically-oriented action', he uses the term 'bureaucracy', and rather than using 'class-oriented action', he speaks of 'classes'.

Perhaps the ideal type can be best understood against the backdrop of Weber's view of social reality. For him, when examined at its basic level, social reality presents a ceaseless flow of occurrences and events, very few of which, although repeatedly interwoven, seem to fall together coherently. Due to its infinite complexity, no investigator can expect to capture reality exhaustively, nor even to render accurately all its contours.

Weber took over a nominalistic position to confront this conundrum and propounded the use of the ideal type. This purely analytic tool enables us to acquire a purchase upon reality through its 'simplification'. Far from arbitrary, however, the procedures for doing so involve a deliberate *exaggeration of the essence* of the phenomenon under study and its reconstruction in a form with greater internal unity than ever appeared in empirical reality. Thus, Weber's conceptualization, for example, of the bureaucracy or the Calvinist does not aim to portray accurately all bureaucracies or Calvinists, but to call attention only to essential aspects. As an artificial construct, the ideal type abstracts from reality and fails to define *any* particular phenomenon. Nonetheless, it serves two crucial purposes: it allows us, once an entire series of ideal types appropriate for a theme under investigation have been formed, to undertake comparisons across civilizations and epochs; and, when used as a heuristic yardstick in comparison to which a given bureaucracy or Calvinist church can be defined and its deviation assessed, it enables an isolation and clear conceptualization of distinctive attributes. Only after a number of ideal-typical 'experiments' have been conducted can we move on to questions regarding the purely empirical *causes* for the uniqueness of the particular case. For Weber, these questions were more interesting than ones of definition alone.

Although he outlined a methodology – only hinted at above – that would allow him to investigate the manner in which individuals formulated meaning in different civilizations and epochs as well as to define precisely the uniqueness of the modern West, it must be concluded that, when viewed in reference to these broad aims, his various writings constitute mere fragments. Most, including his comparative studies on the *Economic Ethics of the World Religions* (*EEWR*) (these include *The Religion of China* [1951], *The Religion of India* [1958] and *Ancient Judaism* [1952]), and *Economy and Society* (*E&S*) were published in incomplete form. Nonetheless, the discrete elements of the whole have stood on their own and become classics in their own right. Broadly speaking, Weber's works divide into more empirical investigations on the one hand and analytical models on the other.

By far his most famous, debated, and readable book, *The Protestant Ethic and the Spirit of Capitalism* (1930 [1922]), falls into the former category. In this classic, Weber sought to understand certain origins of modern capitalism. For him, this form of capitalism was distinguished by a systematic organization of work, the replacement of a 'traditional economic ethic' among workers as well as entrepreneurs by methodical labour, and a systematic search for profit. Thus, Weber saw an attitude toward work and profit – a 'spirit of capi-

talism' – as important, and denied that the influx of precious metals, technological advances, population increases, the universal desire for riches, or the Herculean efforts of 'economic supermen' (Carnegie, Rockefeller, Fugger) were adequate to explain the origin of modern capitalism.

Religious roots, according to Weber, anchored this 'spirit', namely the doctrines of the Protestant sects and churches, particularly the seventeenth-century pastoral exhortations of Calvinism. The deep anxiety introduced by this religion's predestination doctrine in respect to the overriding question of one's personal salvation proved more than believers could reasonably bear. Gradually, worldly success came to be viewed as a *sign* that God had bestowed his favour and, thus, as evidence of membership among the predestined elect. In this way, since it allowed the devout *to believe* they belonged among the chosen few and thereby alleviated intense anxiety, worldly success itself became endowed with a religious – indeed, a salvation – incentive, or 'psychological premium'. Methodical labour in a calling (*Beruf*) proved the surest pathway toward worldly success, as did the continuous reinvestment of one's wealth – an unintended consequence of this attitude – rather than its squandering on worldly pleasures. To Weber, the medieval monk's 'other-worldly' asceticism' became, with Calvinism, transformed into an 'inner-worldly asceticism'.

In calling attention to this religiously-based cause of modern capitalism, Weber in no way sought to substitute an 'idealist' for a 'materialist' explanation (1930 [1922]). Rather, he aimed only to point out the heretofore neglected idealist side in order to emphasize that a comprehensive explanation of modern capitalism's origins must include consideration of the 'economic ethic' as well as the 'economic form'. Far from claiming that Calvinism led to modern capitalism in a monocausal fashion, Weber asserted that the rise of this type of capitalism can be explained adequately only through multidimensional models (1961 [1927]; Collins, 1980; Cohen, 1981; Kalberg, 1983). Indeed, as Weber noted in his discussion of 'backwoods Pennsylvania (1930 [1922]), and as Gordon Marshall has demonstrated in the case of Scotland (1980, 1982), a constellation of material factors must exist in a manner such that a conducive context is formulated, for without this context the 'spirit of capitalism' is powerless to introduce modern capitalism. On the other hand, once firmly entrenched, modern capitalism perpetuates itself on the basis of secularized socialization processes as well as coercive mechanisms and no longer requires its original 'spirit'.

While addressing the rise of modern capitalism in a novel manner, *The Protestant Ethic* failed to grapple with the larger, comparative issue: the distinctiveness of the Occident, Weber knew well, could be defined only through a series of comparisons with non-Western civilizations. In turning to China and India, he again took the issue of modern capitalism as his focus, though here he posed the negative question of why, in these civilizations, this type of capitalism had failed to develop. Moreover, far from attempting to assess only whether Confucian, Taoist, Hindu, and Buddhist teachings introduced or inhibited methodical economic action, these studies turned as well to the 'materialist' side and sought to discuss the economic ethics of non-Western world religions in the context of a whole series of social structural and organizational variables. This comparative procedure enabled Weber also to delineate the array of 'material' factors in the West that proved unique and conducive to the development of modern capitalism. These empirical studies, in addition to his investigations of ancient Judaism, carried him a giant step further as well in his attempt to understand the manner in which sociological configurations influence the formation of meaning.

Yet these studies remained, as Weber himself repeatedly emphasized (1972 [1920]; 1930 [1922]), drastically incomplete, especially if examined in reference to his overall goals. They are, furthermore, too poorly organized to provide us with a distinctly Weberian approach for an unlocking of the elusive relationship between ideas and interests. These empirical investigations must be read through the lens of the analytical categories and models Weber develops for the analysis of social action on a universal-historical scale in one of the genuine classics of modern social science, *E&S* (1968 [1922]).

At first glance, this tome seems to conceal thoroughly Weber's larger aims. Part One is concerned primarily with the articulation of a broad series of sociological concepts. Although empirically-based, each of these, since formulated on a universal-historical scale, remains at a high level of abstraction. Nonetheless, each one can be utilized as a heuristic yardstick that serves as a point of reference for the definition of particular cases. The ideal types in Part Two are less all-encompassing and relate generally to specific epochs and civilizations (Mommsen, 1974). This section reveals on every page how its author, in considering historical examples, extracted their essence and constructed ideal types. Just this perpetual movement between the historical and ideal-typical levels, as well as Weber's unwillingness to formulate an ideal type before scrutinizing innumerable cases, accounts for its exceedingly disjointed character. His failure to discuss his overriding themes in a synoptic fashion has also decreased the readability of *E&S*.

These problems have blinded most Weber specialists to the comprehensive 'analytic' of social action buried between the lines of this treatise and utilizable for the comparative and historical study even of entire civilizations (Kalberg, 1980, 1985). Consequently, each chapter has been read and debated apart from its broader purposes in the Weberian corpus and in an ahistorical fashion. Nonetheless, standing on their own, the separate chapters have attained classical status in a wide variety of sociology's subfields, such as the sociology of religion, urban sociology, stratification, economic sociology, modernization and development, the sociology of law, and political sociology. In each chapter, Weber lays out, in light of the specific problematic involved, a universal-historical analytic that includes a differentiated discussion of the ways in which, at each stage in each analytic, social action becomes patterned by diverse internal and external constraints and acquires its *locus* in specific status groups and organizations.

Only the typology of rulership (*Herrschaft*) can be given special attention here. (This translation has been suggested by Benjamin Nelson and appears to me preferable to either 'domination', which captures the element of force yet weakens the notion of legitimacy, or 'authority', which conveys legitimacy but downplays the component of force.) In this voluminous section Weber wished to define the major bases conceivable for the legitimation of rulership and to articulate, for each, the typical relationships between rulers, administrative bodies, and the ruled. Charismatic personalities derived a right to rule from their extraordinary personal qualities and the belief of the ruled in their transcendent inspiration; traditional rulership (patriarchal, feudal, and patrimonial) rested upon custom and the belief that 'time immemorial' itself provided a justification for continued rule; and rational-legal (bureaucratic) rulership was legitimated through laws, statutes, and regulations. Crucial for the endurance of all types is at least a minimum belief on the part of the ruled that the rulership is justified. While many interpreters have reified these concepts, Weber designed them exclusively as heuristic yardsticks.

Throughout *E&S*, as well as the *EEWR*, a subtle and dialectical view of the relationships between value-oriented, interest-oriented, and tradition-oriented action prevails. As opposed to the more empirically-based *EEWR* studies, these relationships in the *E&S* are dealt with more as models which, on the one hand, combine ideal types in relationships of 'elective affinities' and, on the other hand, chart the patterned 'relations of antagonisms' between discrete concepts and even differentiated spheres of life. At this point, Weber's sociology goes far beyond mere concept-formation and classification and moves to the level of the dynamic interaction of constellations. At this 'contextual' level, he shifts repeatedly back and forth between ideal types of varying range, all of which aim to articulate 'developmental sequences': entire series of ideal types that, on the basis of a developmental dimension as well as a focus upon spheres of life and types of rulership, seek to conceptualize epochal change. Whether the change hypothesized by these research instruments in fact took place in the history of a particular epoch and civilization remained for Weber an empirical question, one that involved, above all, the strength of 'carrier' strata, the success of new groups and organizations in establishing their rulership, and sheer power. Despite his awareness of the inflexibility of tradition and the manner in which millennia-long histories remained within civilizational 'tracks', or world views, Weber's conviction that power and unexpected historical 'accidents' could always introduce a chain-reaction realignment of configurations prevented him from constructing global formulas that promised to forecast the unfolding of societies. To Weber, the materialist interpretation of history, for example, provided a useful hypothesis rather than a scientific explanation.

This sketch of Weber's sociology has touched upon only a few of its major contours. The intensity of Weber's persistent struggle with the immense complexity, unresolved paradoxes, and even contradictory drifts of social reality, and his refusal to simplify on behalf of doctrinal or ideological positions, can be appreciated only by those who directly confront his writings. Fortunately, in turning toward systematic analyses of the major underlying themes in his corpus as a whole, the ongoing Weber renaissance in the Federal Republic of Germany (Kalberg, 1979), Great Britain, and the United States (Glassman, 1983) promises to knit together its fragments and to reveal the concerns that literally possessed one of our century's most remarkable scholars.

Stephen Kalberg
Harvard University

References
Cohen, I. J. (1981), 'Introduction to the Transaction Edition', in M. Weber, General Economic History, New Brunswick.
Collins, R. (1980), 'Weber's last theory of capitalism', American Sociological Review, 56.
Glassman, R. (1983), 'The Weber renaissance', in S. G. McNall (ed.), Current Perspectives in Social Theory, Greenwood, Connecticut.
Kalberg, S. (1979), 'The search for thematic orientations in a fragmented œuvre: the discussion of Max Weber in recent German sociological literature', Sociology, 13.
Kalberg, S. (1980), 'Max Weber's types of rationality: cornerstones for the analysis of rationalization processes in history', American Journal of Sociology, 85.
Kalberg, S. (1983), 'Max Weber's universal-historical architectonic of economically-oriented action: a preliminary reconstruction', in S. G. McNall (ed.), Current Perspectives in Social Theory, Greenwood, Connecticut.
Kalberg, S. (1986), Max Weber's Comparative Historical Sociology of Reconstruction, London.
Marshall, G. (1980), Presbyteries and Profits: Calvinism and the Development of Capitalism in Scotland, 1560–1707, Oxford.
Marshall, G. (1982), In Search of the Spirit of Capitalism, London.
Mommsen, W. (1974), Max Weber: Gesellschaft, Politik und Geschichte, Frankfurt.
Weber, M. (1972 [1920]), Collected Papers on the Sociology of Religion, London. (Original German edn, Gesammelte Aufsatze zur Religionssoziologie, vol. 1, Tübingen.)
Weber, M. (1961 [1927]), General Economic History, London. (Original German edn, Wirtschaftsgeschichte, Munich.)
Weber, M. (1930 [1922]), The Protestant Ethic and the Spirit of Capitalism, London. (Original German edn, Die protestantische Ethik und der 'Geist' des Kapitalismus, Tübingen.)
Weber, M. (1946), From Max Weber, eds H. H. Gerth and C. W. Mills, New York.
Weber, M. (1949), The Methodology of the Social Sciences, selection and translation of essays by E. Shils, New York.
Weber, M. (1951), The Religion of China, New York.
Weber, M. (1952), Ancient Judaism, New York.
Weber, M. (1958), The Religion of India, New York.
Weber, M. (1968 [1922]), Economy and Society, New York. (Original German edn, Wirtschaft und Gesellschaft, Tübingen.)

Further Reading
Bendix, R. (1960), Max Weber: An Intellectual Portrait, London.
Bendix, R. and Roth, G. (1971), Scholarship and Partisanship: Essays on Max Weber, Berkeley and Los Angeles.
Löwith, K. (1982), Max Weber and Karl Marx, London.
Nelson, B. (1981), On the Roads to Modernity: Conscience, Science and Civilizations, Totowa, NJ.

Welfare Economics

If economics is the study of how to make the best, or optimal, use of limited resources, welfare economics is concerned with the meaning of the term 'optimal' and with the formulation of statements that permit us to say that a given policy or event has improved or reduced social welfare.

Optimality is defined in terms of maximizing social welfare, so that the focus of concern is on what compromises the latter concept. Typically, it is taken to be the sum of the welfares of all members of a defined society. By adopting the value judgement that it is individuals' own judgements of their welfare that is to count in the formulation of a measure of social welfare, we have the basis for Paretian welfare economics (after Vilfredo Pareto). In this case, to say that individual A's welfare has improved is to say no more than A prefers one situation to another. To say that *social* welfare has improved requires a further definitional statement, namely that the improvement in A's welfare has occurred without any other individual being worse off. Thus social welfare has improved if, and only if, at least one individual's welfare has improved and no one's has decreased. It may be noted that while the first requirement is a value judgement, the second is a matter of definition. It is not an additional value judgement.

Paretian welfare economics is almost self-evidently sterile, since we can envision few situations in which no one is harmed by a policy. Some individuals gain and some lose. The sterility of the pure Paretian principle arises because of the alleged difficulty of comparing one person's gain in welfare and another's loss: the so-called fallacy of interpersonal comparisons of utility. If this is accepted, there are obvious difficulties for the formulation of criteria for a gain in social welfare. The principle emerging from the work of Kaldor and Hicks declares that there is a net gain in social welfare if those who gain can use part of their gains to compensate the losers and still have something left over. In other words, *if* compensation occurred, those who stand to lose would be fully compensated and their welfare would accordingly be the same before and after the policy in question. Gainers would still be better off provided the required compensation is less than their gross gains. This is the Kaldor-Hicks compensation principle.

Scitovsky (1941) pointed out that a further condition is required, since a policy may alter the distribution of income in such a way that those who lose may be able to pay those who gain sufficient to induce them back to the initial situation. The requirement that this should *not* be the case defines the Scitovsky reversal test for a state of affairs to be defined as a (modified) Pareto-improvement. Since *actual* compensation mechanisms are complex, all compensation criteria are typically formulated in terms of the potential for compensation. There is no requirement for the compensation to occur. This provides the complete separation from the Pareto principle: the compensation principle may sanction a policy that leads to a (strict) Pareto deterioration in social welfare. Scitovsky's work opened the way for an explicit treatment of the distribution of income. Little (1957) defined various alternatives whereby social welfare can be said to increase according to the fulfilment of the compensation criterion (the efficiency test) and an improvement in the distribution of income (an equity test). The seminal work of Rawls (1971), however, best defines the turning point in welfare economics, whereby there is explicit and simultaneous attention paid to both efficiency and equity through the adoption of Rawl's 'maximin' principle of benefiting the least well off in society.

The historical oddity of welfare economics remains that it has survived as an elaborate framework in itself, and as the foundation of practical techniques such as cost-benefit analysis, despite severe and arguably fatal criticism in the 1950s – notably in the work of de Graaf (1957). Arrow's famous 'impossibility theorem' (Arrow, 1963) also indicates the problems of defining any social welfare function based on the fundamental Paretian value judgement about consumer sovereignty. Tendentiously, one might suggest that the survival and health of welfare economics arises from its preoccupation with social decision rules which, if not embraced by economics, renders the science inconsistent with its own functional definition of making the 'best' use of scarce resources. 'Best' implies a criterion for judging alternative states of affairs, and this is the concern of welfare economics.

David W. Pearce
University College London

References

Arrow, K. (1963), *Social Choice and Individual Values*, 2nd edn, New York.
Hicks, J. (1939), 'Foundations of welfare economics', *Economic Journal*, 49.
Kaldor, N. (1939), 'Welfare propositions of economics and interpersonal comparisons of utility', *Economic Journal*, 49.
Little, I. M. D. (1957), *A Critique of Welfare Economics*, 2nd edn, Oxford.
Rawls, J. (1971), *A Theory of Justice*, Oxford.
Scitovsky, T. (1941), 'A note on welfare propositions in economics', *Review of Economic Studies*.

Further Reading

Ng, Y.-K. (1979), *Welfare Economics*, London.
Sudgen, R. (1981), *The Political Economy of Public Choice: An Introduction to Welfare Economics*, Oxford.
Just, R. E., Hueth, D. H. and Schmitz, A. (1982), *Applied Welfare Economics and Public Policy*, Englewood Cliffs, N.J.
See also: *Hicks; Pareto; social welfare.*

Welfare State

The term Welfare State was first used, according to some authorities, when the People's Budget of 1909 in Britain was styled the Welfare Budget, although in Germany *Wohlfahr-staat* had already been applied to the system of social insurance introduced by Bismarck in the 1980s. Welfare State only came into general use in the 1930s, however, when democratic governments in Europe and the US displayed a real concern for the welfare of their citizens suffering under the strains of economic depression. The Oxford scholar Alfred Zimmern used the phrase Welfare State to characterize the democratic states, in contrast to the states of the Fascist dictators. It gained wide currency with the publication of the Beveridge report in Britain in 1942, though Beveridge and many others objected to it and preferred the idea of a Social Service State.

The view that the Welfare State was created in Britain by the Labour Government which came to power after the Second World War in 1945 is nonsense, because for centuries in Britain, and later in Scandinavia, and, especially, New Zealand, statutory powers to provide welfare services had long been in force. The United States of America rapidly developed state welfare resources during President Roosevelt's New Deal in the 1930s. In Britain, the Beveridge report on 'Social Insurance and Allied Services', published in 1942, proposed a full and free national health service, a system of social insurance, and retirement pensions. These measures were implemented in a series of Acts passed between 1945 and 1948, and then extended by successive governments, and the Welfare State ceased to be a divisive party-political issue. The Conservative Party, which came to power in Britain in the 1970s no longer talks about dismantling the Welfare State as they once did in the 1950s.

.Welfare State could well have applied to New Zealand in the 1890s, which, because of its progressive measures of social legislation such as the provision of old-age pensions and a variety of industrial conciliation schemes, was described by one writer as the 'social laboratory of the world'. These measures were adversely affected by the depression of the 1930s, but when the Labour Party first came to power in New Zealand in 1935, it embarked on even more ambitious measures, including a comprehensive social security system to protect citizens against the ill effects of unemployment, sickness, industrial injury and old age, and the provision of an almost free national health service. The Second World War delayed their implementation, but they were fully operational after the war ended, and still are.

A Welfare State is one in which there are conscious and deliberate policies to secure at least a minimum standard of living for all, and to promote equality of opportunity. There will no doubt be shifts of emphasis in the provision of services. For example, it has been suggested in recent years in Britain that there should be more private and less state spending on health and educational services. But there is little chance of a massive reversal of welfare policies in most democratic states in the near future.

D. C. Marsh
Formerly of the University of Nottingham

Further Reading
Bruce, M. (1981), *The Coming of the Welfare State*, London.
Marsh, David (1980), *The Welfare State*, London.
Robson, W. A. (1976), *Welfare State and Welfare Society: Illusion and Reality*, London.
See also: *public goods; social welfare; welfare economics.*

Wicksell, Knut (1861–1926)

Knut Wicksell, Sweden's most prominent economist, began his academic career studying mathematics at the University of Uppsala in the 1870s. He became intensely engaged in public debate on social issues in the 1880s, earning himself a reputation as a radical pamphleteer. He promoted neo-Malthusian ideas concerning prostitution, emigration from Sweden and drunkenness. His interest in social problems, as well as the criticism he met from economists, induced him to study economics. Supported by grants, a small inheritance and an income from journalism, he spent the period 1885–90 in Great Britain, Germany, Austria and France pursuing academic work in economics. In 1889, Wicksell became familiar with the work of the Austrian economist Böhm-Bawerk, whose ideas on capital theory exerted a profound influence upon his thinking.

In the 1890s Wicksell published his major contributions dealing with the theory of production and distribution, *Über Wert, Kapital und Rente* (1893) (translated into English as *Value, Capital and Rent*), on taxation, *Zur Lehre von der Steuerincidenz* (1895), and on monetary theory, *Geldzins und Güterpreise* (1898) (translated into English as *Interest and Prices*). He became professor of economics at the University of Lund in 1901 after being required to take a degree in law, a time-consuming task, to qualify for the chair. He summarized his scientific work in two volumes in the early 1900s, translated as *Lectures I* and *II*. He continued to be active in public debate until his death in 1926, propagating neo-Malthusianism, antimilitaristic causes, women's liberation and other left-wing liberal positions.

Wicksell successfully presented a coherent picture of neoclassical economics around the turn of the century. One of the major contributions was to combine Böhm-Bawerk's Austrian capital theory with Walras's general equilibrium theory. Another major contribution was his theory of price level determination, generally termed the cumulative process. This theory has exerted a significant influence on Swedish economic thinking as well as on monetary policy.

Lars Jonung
University of Lund

Further Reading

Gårdlund, T. (1958), *The Life of Knut Wicksell*, Stockholm.

Knudtzon, E. (1976), *Knut Wicksells tryckta skrifter 1868–1950*, Lund (Knut Wicksell's bibliography).

See also: *Stockholm School*.

Witchcraft and Sorcery

Beliefs in witchcraft and sorcery are one way of explaining the inexplicable, controlling the uncontrollable, and accounting for the problem of evil. By attributing unmerited misfortune or unwonted success to the illicit use of occult powers and substances by human beings motivated by malice, greed or envy, the beliefs help to explain, not simply how something happened, but *why* it happened as it did and, thus, to provide moral and psychological theories of causation. Such beliefs may be only one explanatory mode in a cosmology which offers other (and sometimes competing) causal explanations; and recourse to diviners, oracles or 'witchdoctors' may be necessary before a particular event is attributed to witchcraft and action taken to redress the situation.

Anthropologists and others following them, such as historians (see Mair, 1969; Marwick, 1982), often distinguish between the 'witch', who possesses an innate, mystical power, and the 'sorcerer', who employs technical, external means such as destructive magic to gain his or her nefarious ends, though the distinction is not always so clear-cut. It is the 'witch' in this narrow sense who is often spoken of as the epitome of evil, the negation of the human being, the cancer within the society or the external enemy intent on destruction, whose image has been said to represent the 'standardized nightmares of the group' (Monica Wilson in Marwick, 1982) and to embody the obverse of accepted moral and physical norms. These role types derive from Evans-Pritchard's *Witchcraft, Oracles and Magic among the Azande* (1937), a seminal study in the sociology of knowledge, though he neither expected the Zande distinction to be universally valid, which it is not, nor anthropologists to use it thus; and, indeed, recently even his own interpretation of the Zande has been questioned. The definitional problems are formidable, and some would in any case regard the search for universals as a fruitless and invalid exercise (MacGaffey, 1980) and would construe the general and wide-ranging use of the terms here as misleading.

The distinction between mystical and technical means has been found useful, though again problematical. Some writers have stressed that whilst empirical, if doubtful, evidence of sorcery might be found, witchcraft powers and acts are 'all-in-the-mind', unverifiable and unbelievable to the outside observer. Therefore, confession of such powers and activities (and the search

for them) has been taken sometimes as evidence of delusion or psychopathology, as in some interpretations of the European witchhunts of the fifteenth to seventeenth centuries; but although doubt may be cast on confessions produced under torture or other forms of pressure, in some circumstances confession or self-accusation may be used as a protest, as an appeal and as a weapon, for example by subordinate and frustrated women (Mair, 1969; Wyllie in Marwick, 1982). In Western Europe and North America today, where beliefs in witchcraft are confined to the religious and occult fringe, and in rural cultures, proponents of such beliefs may be regarded generally as eccentric if not deluded, as would be anyone who attributed personal misfortunes to the occult powers of colleagues. But in witch-believing cultures the believer is rational; it is the nonbeliever who may be seen as deviant, misguided or irrational by his peers, and it is unbelief or disbelief which requires explanation (Evans-Pritchard, 1937; Hirst and Woolley, 1982).

Witch beliefs may postulate that anyone, anywhere, may practise witchcraft and sorcery, or that only persons in specified social categories or possessing specified attributes will pose a threat. The sociology of the beliefs, on the other hand, the patterns of allegations, accusations and confessions shows the selection of 'targets' (whether witch or victim) to be the outcome of quarrels, grudges and strained relations between suspect, accuser and victim. These charges are mainly made about and between people who are not separated by any great social, structural or spatial distance. However, there are some differences depending upon whether the witch-hunt is an individual or communal affair. Many such ethnographic studies of witchcraft have been in effect structural-functional studies of micropolitics, relating the beliefs and accusations to social-structural factors, showing how they contribute to the maintenance of the system and demonstrating their reactionary and conservative functions, although sometimes they have been shown to be radical forces acting as vehicles of social change (Mair, 1969; Marwick, 1982).

More recently, cognitive, symbolic, semantic and rationalist perspectives have begun to remedy some of the omissions and defects of their functionalist predecessor (Marwick, 1982). One such approach involves looking at 'witches' and 'witchcraft' as part of a wider frame of reference such as person categories and concepts of human action. MacGaffey (1980), for example, has shown how comparative analysis of religious structures is facilitated by examining the role of the witch/sorcerer as just one in a set of religious commissions associated with occult powers (such as witch-finder, diviner, magician, priest, prophet, chief). These roles may be differentiated by criteria such as means used (mystical or technical), ends sought (public or private), effects intended (death or life, destruction or protection) and legitimacy (good or bad). This approach, too, allows us more easily to take into account the 'moral ambiguity' of power, that the 'same' power may be good or bad, licit or illicit, and its deployment social or antisocial according by whom it is used and for what ends. In a different vein, witchcraft and sorcery are being analysed within the wider context of social control systems and categories of deviance, in relation to law, criminology and madness in early modern Europe and in colonial contexts (Hirst and Woolley, 1982). Yet another approach is to set witch-finding movements within the context of other religious movements and of cults explaining misfortune. Such developments require witchcraft and sorcery to be seen not as isolated elements, as empirical realities, but as aspects of wider classifications and of action systems.

Anne Akeroyd
University of York, England

References

Evans-Pritchard, E. E. (1937), *Witchcraft, Oracles and Magic among the Azande*, Oxford.

Hirst, P. and Woolley, P. (1982), *Social Relations and Human Attributes*, London.

MacGaffey, W. (1980), 'African religions: types and generalizations', in I. Karp and C. S. Bird (eds), *Explorations in African Systems of Thought*, Bloomington.

Mair, L. (1969), *Witchcraft*, London.

Marwick, M. G. (ed.) (1982), *Witchcraft and Sorcery: Selected Readings*, Harmondsworth.

Further Reading

Douglas, M. (ed.) (1970), *Witchcraft Confessions and Accusations*, London.

Favret-Saada, J. (1980), *Deadly Words: Witchcraft in the Bocage*, Cambridge.

See also: *deviance; magic; witch-hunts.*

Witch-Hunts

Witch-hunting, the search for the agent(s) responsible for individual and communal afflictions, is a corollary of beliefs in witchcraft and sorcery. In *individual witch-seeking* the cause of a particular affliction is sought from specialists such as diviners who, if witchcraft is diagnosed, may indicate the witch responsible. Whether the complainant confronts the suspect will depend on whether such an action is necessary for effecting a cure and for averting future danger, and on his (and others') assessment of the practicality and costs (social, political, economic and legal) of an overt accusation. A widespread series of misfortunes may so perturb a community that *communal witch-testing* will occur, initially directed against those thought to be responsible for the crisis-precipitating events. But should panic grow, and further evidence of witching activity appear and/or past events be reinterpreted in that light, then a small witch-hunt may develop. *Mass witch-hunting* takes three main forms: (1) the summoning of an individual witchfinder by a community or its representatives; (2) the acceptance of a peripatetic witchfinder or witch-cleansing cult, such as those of Central Africa which may recur every ten to fifteen years as their predecessor's millenarian claims are seen to have been false; and (3) a hunt organized and orchestrated by an élite primarily for its own ends. Such hunts aim to protect a community (or polity) by uncovering all witches and either neutralizing their occult powers and destroying their materials or eliminating the witches by expulsion, imprisonment or execution.

The great European witch panics of the fifteenth to seventeenth centuries exemplify the élite mass witch-hunt. Arising out of actions against heretics, those purges were perpetrated by the religious and secular educated, literate élite against a witch of their own making: the satanic witch, the agent of the Devil, was the creation of the Inquisition, of torture and of theological demonology (Cohn, 1975). Explanations for those horrific events range from collective psychopathology, to misogyny, minority persecutions and class conflict; but while such multiple explanations are necessary to a fuller understanding, particularly crucial is the fact that the persecutions were coterminous with attempts to establish and maintain Christianity as a political ideology (see Larner, 1981).

Élite witch-hunts have analogies with 'moral panics', and actions against 'deviants', 'public menaces' and 'enemies of the state/people' (such as communists, intellectuals, capitalists, Jews, heretics, 'unpatriotic subversives', and 'thought-criminals' and other social categories made scapegoats). The term witch-hunt is actually a twentieth-century American word describing the pursuit of a group for its beliefs or characteristics, or of an individual on trumped-up charges, the victimization of those selected as ideological or political enemies as occurred during McCarthyism in America, the Cultural Revolution in Maoist China, and similar political witch-hunts. Such purges may be shortlived and they, or their excesses, repudiated, but often rehabilitation comes too late for the many victims of such élite obsessions (Shils, 1956) with secrecy, subversion, conspiracy and xenophobia.

Anne Akeroyd
University of York, England

References

Cohn, N. (1975), *Europe's Inner Demons: An Enquiry Inspired by the Great Witch-Hunt*, London.

Larner, C. (1981), *Enemies of God: The Witchhunt in Scotland*, London.

Shils, E. A. (1956), *The Torments of Secrecy: The Background and Consequences of American Security Policies*, London.

Further Reading
Marwick, M. G. (ed.) (1982), *Witchcraft and Sorcery; Selected Readings*, 2nd edn, revised and enlarged, Harmondsworth.
See also: *witchcraft*.

Wittgenstein, Ludwig Josef Johann (1889–1951)

Wittgenstein was born in Vienna and though originally trained as an engineer became a pupil of Bertrand Russell at Cambridge. He returned to Austria to serve in the First World War, and in 1921 published the German edition of the *Tractatus Logico-Philosophicus*. He then became a school teacher in Lower Austria. In this, as in everything else, he was an intense and demanding man, and soon resigned his post. After that, he became involved in the design of a house which still stands in Vienna, a monument to the aesthetic austerity that he championed. Around this time he rejected the *Tractatus* and began to articulate his later philosophy. He returned to Cambridge in 1929 and held the chair of philosophy from 1939 to 1947.

In the *Tractatus* the essence of language is assumed to reside in its fact-stating function. This is said to rest on the capacity of sentences to 'picture' facts. Pictures consist of parts which correspond to the parts of the thing pictured. The parts of a picture stand to one another in a certain relation, and this says how the corresponding objects are arranged if the picture is true. In language the parts are names, and elementary sentences are arrangements of names. More complicated sentences can then be built up by using the rules of Russell's logic. Wittgenstein may have based his picture theory on the way in which systems of material points have a symbolic representation in sophisticated versions of theoretical mechanics. Certainly the conclusion he drew was that the only meaningful language was the language of science. All attempts to transcend this and express what is 'higher' – namely, ethics, aesthetics and the meaning of life – are doomed. Even the attempt to state the relation of language to the world tries to go beyond these limits, so the doctrines of the *Tractatus* itself are meaningless. Those who understand my propositions correctly, said Wittgenstein, will surmount them like a ladder, and then throw them away.

Is this an attack on everything nonscientific? Wittgenstein's friend, Paul Engelmann, tells us that it is the exact opposite. The aim is not to dismiss what cannot be said, the 'higher', but to *protect* it. The *Tractatus* is an ethical document which must be understood in terms of Wittgenstein's involvement with the great Viennese critic Karl Kraus and the influential architect Adolf Loos. Kraus exposed moral corruption which shows itself in the corruption of language. Loos conducted a campaign against aesthetic corruption which shows itself in the confusion of art with utility and the pollution of functional simplicity by needless decoration. The *Tractatus* likewise expressed the ethics of purity, separation, simplicity and the integrity of silence.

Why Wittgenstein became dissatisfied with this position is unclear, but some light may be shed by relating his shift of opinion to a broad cultural change in which he participated. If the *Tractatus* addressed the issues that exercised pre-war Viennese intellectuals, the late philosophy addressed the problems that confronted them in the post-war years. We know that the military defeats and economic and constitutional problems in Europe were accompanied by an acute sense of cultural crisis. One symptom of this was the enormous popularity of Spengler's irrational life-philosophy with its conservative pessimism. Wittgenstein is known to have been impressed by Spengler, and the later work can be seen as a brilliant expression of this form of conservative irrationalism. All the features of this style – the priority of the concrete over the abstract, of practice over norms, life over reason and being over thought – are prominently displayed.

In his later work Wittgenstein rejected the idea that language has a single essential function. It is not structured by correspondence with objects but by its role in the stream of life. There are as many ways for words to carry meaning as there are ways of organizing action. The picture theory gave way to the idea of 'language-games'. We must not theorize about language but observe its diversity as we name, count, instruct, question, promise, pray and so on. The real heart of the late philosophy, however, is the analysis of rule following. It is tempting to explain human behaviour in terms of our capacity to follow rules. In § 201 of the *Investigations* Wittgenstein argued that no course of action can be determined by rules because any course of action could be said to accord with the rule. Any non-standard interpretation of a rule could be justified by a non-standard interpretation of the rules for following the rule. Ultimately it must be said of all rules that they are obeyed 'blindly'. At every point, rules, and the application of the concepts in them, depend on taken for granted practices or customs. Wittgenstein used this insight to bring out the conventional character of all knowledge and discourse, whether it was an introspective report or a mathematical truth.

For the later Wittgenstein, then, the notion of meaning is explained in terms of *use*. Meaningless or metaphysical discourse is language 'on holiday', that is, not employed in a language game that has a genuine role in a form of life. The job of the philosopher is to inhibit our tendency to detach words from their real use. In this the philosopher is like a doctor who must bring language back to its healthy everyday life. What had to be accepted as given, said Wittgenstein, was the 'form of life'. Other than this all belief is groundless: this is the end-point of all justification. Nothing could be a clearer expression of the conservative thinker's belief in the priority of life over reason.

It is only now that this European dimension of Wittgenstein's thinking, both in its early and late phase, is beginning to emerge. This offsets the somewhat narrow readings that have been given them as forms of logical and linguistic 'analysis'. Nevertheless the full potential of the late philosophy, as the basis of a social theory of knowledge, still awaits exploitation.

David Bloor
University of Edinburgh

Further Reading

As Wittgenstein's unpublished writings gradually appear in print, the corpus of his work now stands at over a dozen volumes. Nevertheless, the main texts of the early and late philosophy, respectively, are still: *Tractatus Logico-Philosophicus*, trans. D. F. Pears and B. F. McGuinness, London, 1961; and *Philosophical Investigations*, trans. G. E. M. Anscombe, Oxford, 1953.

Bloor, D. (1983), *Wittgenstein: A Social Theory of Knowledge*, London.
Engelman, P. (1967), *Letters from Ludwig Wittgenstein · with a Memoir*, Oxford.
Janik, A. and Toulmin, S. (1973), *Wittgenstein's Vienna*, London.
Specht, E. K. (1963), *The Foundations Of Wittgenstein's Late Philosophy*, Manchester.
Winch, P. (1958), *The Idea of a Social Science and its Relation to Philosophy*, London.

Women's Studies

Women's studies as an identifiable area of teaching and research emerged in the late 1960s, although the intellectual antecedents go back further, most notably in the work of Simone de Beauvoir and Virginia Woolf. Courses on women were not unknown prior to the 1960s but they were few and far between. One of the earliest known courses in America on the status of women in the United States was offered by the Department of Sociology at the University of Kansas in 1892. There were also some early twentieth-century examples of economics courses devoted to women's labour in an industrial society. One of these, given at the University of Washington at Seattle in 1912 by Professor Theresa McMahon, was on the subject of 'Women and Economic Evolution, or the Effects of Industrial Changes on the Status of Women'. A recent review of McMahon's teaching and writing described her work as something

of an anomaly for its time, and it is noted that 'academic studies of the relationship between economics and the status of women are essentially a phenomenon of the 1960s and 1970s – there is little to bridge the gap between McMahon's essays and current attempts to analyse the subject' (Page, 1976).

The contemporary women's movement provided the impetus for the establishment and growth of women's studies across the disciplines. In 1969, feminists at Cornell University organized a conference on women which reflected the concerns of the movement and which led to a faculty seminar to examine the portrayal of women in the curriculum of the social and behavioural sciences. As a result of the seminar, an interdisciplinary course was established on 'The Evolution of Female Personality', followed in 1970 by a female studies programme that co-ordinated six courses from different departments of the University. At about the same time, across the continent, a women's studies programme started at San Diego College in California, providing such courses as 'Women in Comparative Cultures', 'Women in Literature', and 'Contemporary Issues in the Liberation of Women'. By the end of the year there were 110 courses on various US campuses. The number has continued to grow and there are now estimated to be some 30,000 courses in US colleges and universities (Boxer, 1982). The number of women's studies programmes, i.e., interdisciplinary degree programmes, is nearly 500.

The women's studies movement, for that is what it has become, is by no means limited to the United States. Similar programmes were established in other countries during the seventies in Europe and, more recently, in Asia and Latin America. Canada and the UK are well advanced in the number and scope of courses available. The UK, for example, has an MA course in Women's Studies at the University of Kent at Canterbury and also an MA in Human Rights with a specialization in Women's Rights at the University of London. However, the greatest expansion in women's studies in the UK has occurred in adult education and in non-degree granting areas of education (Klein, 1983). In Italy women's studies is taught by academic women primarily in courses sponsored by trade unions and organizations which grew out of the Italian women's movement (Balbo and Ergas, 1982).

Women's studies spread to the developing world slowly at first and then more rapidly following the U.N. Mid-Decade Conference for Women in Copenhagen in 1980. At that time, as part of the Forum of Non-Governmental Organizations, a series of women's studies seminars and workshops was conducted under the joint sponsorship of The Feminist Press and the National Women's Studies Association of the US, The Simone de Beauvoir Institute of Canada, and SNDT Women's University of India. About 500 people from 55 countries attended, most of whom formed the membership of an international network of scholars and practitioners. Women's studies is now flourishing in India and a Women's Studies Association has been formed. A Latin-American Women's Studies Association came into being in 1981. Other parts of the world are active to various degrees except for Eastern Europe, which has thus far largely ignored the subject. In some areas, as in Africa, efforts are concentrated on research rather than teaching.

An important factor in the growth of women's studies during the seventies was the formation of women's caucuses or committees within professional associations to press for more recognition of women scholars and their concerns. Although the primary purpose of these committees was to advance the professional status and career opportunities of women, they also directed attention to women as a subject of teaching and research in the disciplines. Some were more active than others, depending in part on the nature of the discipline and the number of women in it. Those at the forefront of the movement were in the fields of literature, history, sociology, and psychology. As early as 1970, the Commission on the Status of Women of the Modern Languages Association was instrumental in the publication of course syllabuses and reading lists in a 'Female Studies' series, which served as a resource for teachers in the humanities and social sciences. Similarly, the Committee on Women Historians of the American Historical Association provided the impetus for the preparation and publication of a monograph on *Teaching Women's History*, by Gerda Lerner.

Later, as the field progressed, a National Women's Studies Association (NWSA) was founded in 1977. Its stated purpose was 'to further the social, political, and professional development of women's studies throughout the country, at every educational setting'. From the beginning, NWSA drew a large and enthusiastic membership that consisted not only of scholars but also teachers in elementary and secondary schools and in community-based programmes, as well as librarians and others interested in feminist education. NWSA thus provided a mechanism for mutual support among women's studies constituencies and for the dissemination of knowledge about women's studies. It also served as a model for similar organizations in other countries or regions of the world.

Women's studies scholarship was not at first accepted as a legitimate area of academic endeavour, and was largely ignored except by the feminists who were its adherents. Most attention was negative: it was viewed as polemic or faddish and not to be taken seriously. But women's studies has continued to grow and flourish to the present day with no abatement in sight. Foundations and other funding agencies offered critical support. When the Ford Foundation initiated a fellowship programme for research on women in 1972, it served not only to support the efforts of individual scholars – men as well as women – but also to give visibility and legitimacy to the field. Foundation support also made possible the establishment of organized research centres which provided institutional resources for women's studies scholarship.

There are at the present time some forty women's studies research centres throughout the United States, nearly all of them established in the last ten years. Most are campus-based, but some are free-standing including several in Washington, DC that focus on issues of public policy concerning women. These centres supplement the efforts of individual scholars and make possible the development of large-scale and interdisciplinary research programmes. Among the best known are the Bunting Institute at Radcliffe College, the Center for Research on Women at Wellesley College, and the Center for Research on Women at Stanford University. In Washington, the Women's Research and Education Institute (WREI) functions as the research arm of the Congressional Caucus on Women's Issues. In that capacity, WREI acts as a bridge between researchers and policy makers on issues of particular concern to women. It maintains regular contact with the network of women's research and policy centres, working on the one hand to stimulate researchers to consider the broader implications of their work, especially as it affects public policy, and on the other to examine policies from the perspective of their effect on women.

In 1981, the research and policy centres joined to form a National Council for Research on Women to share resources and to promote collaborative programmes of research, curriculum development, and public information. Council programmes include a Data Base Project to co-ordinate efforts to improve the storage and retrieval of information on research about women. The project involves the construction of a comprehensive indexing system and computerized data base containing bibliographic references to published, unpublished, and non-print material about women. Through its member centres the Council links over 2,000 scholars and practitioners. The Council also works to strengthen ties with centres of scholarship in other countries, of which there are a small but growing number.

The growth of women's studies teaching and research during the seventies and since then has been accompanied by a parallel expansion in the volume of books and journals for the dissemination of the new knowledge. Academic presses now commonly have a section on women's studies along with other disciplines. Articles relating to women's roles and experience regularly appear in professional journals. In addition, a number of new journals are devoted entirely to women's studies. The most widely-known of the new journals is *Signs: Journal of Women in Culture and Society,* established in 1975 and published by the University of Chicago Press. Two other notable journals in the field are the London based *Women's Studies International Forum* and *Feminist Studies*, published in association with the Women's Studies Program at the University of Maryland.

In the current stage of the evolution of the new scholarship about women, the issue is no longer its legitimacy and further growth, but rather its place in the curriculum. A variety of programmes in recent years have attempted to integrate the new knowledge into the so-called 'mainstream' curriculum, with the purpose of enlightening all students, men and women, not only those taking women's studies courses. This is not simply a matter of adding new material to the curriculum; what is involved is the introduction of new perspectives that may challenge the assumptions and methods of the disciplines. It is now well known, for example, that periodization in history and labels such as 'The Dark Ages' and 'The Renaissance' have their conceptual basis in a distinctly male vantage point. The female experience in those eras was sharply different: 'The Dark Ages' were a period of ascendancy for women and 'The Renaissance' a period of contraction in women's roles. Similarly, in the field of economics, feminist scholars have looked at the differential labour force participation of men and women and found that the response to wage changes is considerably more complex than the textbooks had assumed. Women's studies scholars have not only influenced the content of the disciplines but also the methodologies used.

Mainstreaming projects currently under way in the United States include faculty development projects, summer institutes, and organized efforts to restructure curricula. A mark of the maturity of the field was a conference in 1981 sponsored by the Association of American Colleges, bringing together college and university administrators and women's studies scholars to consider the implications of the new scholarship on the traditional goals and assumptions of liberal education and the resulting possibilities and imperatives for curricula and institutional change.

Mariam Chamberlain
Russell Sage Foundation, New York

References
Balbo, L. and Ergas, Y. (1982), *Women's Studies in Italy*, London.
Boxer, M. J. (1982), 'For and about women: the theory and practice of women's studies in the United States', *Signs, Journal of Women in Culture and Society*, 7.
Klein, R. D. (1983), 'A brief overview of women's studies in the U.K.', *Women's Studies International Forum*, 5.

Page, A. N. (1976), 'Theresa McMahon's "Women and economic evolution", a retrospective view', *Journal of Economic Literature*.

Further Reading
Langland, E. and Gove, W. (eds) (1983), *A Feminist Perspective in the Academy: The Difference it Makes*, Chicago.
Sherman, J. A. and Beck, E. T. (1977), *The Prism of Sex*, Madison.
Spender, D. (1981), *Men's Studies Modified*, London.
See also: *women's studies in psychology; women's studies in social anthropology.*

Women's Studies in Psychology

Women as mothers have been, and continue to be, a major subject of interest to those working in developmental and abnormal psychology. Psychology's interest in women in their own right is of relatively recent origin. Prior to the late 1960s' resurgence of feminism, it was all too often assumed that generalizations about women's and men's psychology could be validly based on studies that included only male subjects. Now, however, it is generally recognized that the psychology of women may differ from the psychology of men. Indeed, some psychology journals even insist that their contributors control for the possibility of such differences.

Psychological sex differences have, in particular, been reported in the areas of aggression, visuo-spatial, mathematical, and verbal ability. Some seek to explain these differences in biological terms (Hutt, 1972). Much current research is guided by the view that men's aggressiveness is hormonally determined by the androgens and that sex-related cognitive differences are an effect of girls' brains being specialized earlier for verbal, boys' for visuo-spatial, processing.

Others seek to explain these differences, and sex-role development in general, as a consequence more of nurture than of nature. Two approaches currently dominate this perspective on gender development: (1) Social-learning theory, the approach of Walter Mischel (1966), views sex-role development as resulting from the child's imitation of those behaviours that parents, other children, education and the media convey as 'sex-role appropriate'. (2) The approach of Lawrence Kohlberg (1966) views gender development as crucially determined, not so much by external influence, as by the child's own ideas about sex and gender. These start with its ability (at about the age of two years) to categorize itself correctly by sex, then by its developing recognition that sex remains invariant through life. This process is accompanied, according to Kohlberg, by changes in the child's understanding of sex-role stereotypes which it regards first as given by biology, later as given by social convention, and which it finally comes to judge in terms of the conformity of these stereotypes with principles of equity and justice.

Social psychology has been more interested in sex differences in achievement – differences that are currently researched in terms of attribution theory. Women, unlike men, it is said, tend to attribute their successes to luck and their failures to lack of ability, and for this reason become easily disheartened from striving for educational and occupational achievement. Women's greater tendency to become disheartened and depressed has also become a focus of concern in abnormal psychology where it has been assimilated to the currently dominant behavioural model of depression, Seligman's 'learned helplessness theory'. According to this perspective the reason that women more often suffer from depression than men is that their social situation renders them less than able to control the sources of reward and reinforcement in their lives. Assertiveness training has been recommended as one way of alleviating this condition, and this technique has also been applied quite generally as a way of increasing women's self-confidence.

Behavioural approaches to the explanation and treatment of mental disorder have also been applied to other conditions that affect women more than men (such as agoraphobia, anorexia). Psychology's long-standing hostility to psychoanalysis has scarcely been affected by its recent interest in women's mental health, despite the fact that others are increasingly looking to psychoanalysis both as a means of understanding mental health problems in women and, more generally, as a means of understanding the psychological correlates of sexual divisions in society. One particularly influential theory in this context has been post-Freudian object-relations theory, according to which the infant is initially psychologically merged with the mother and only gradually comes to experience itself as individuated from her. It has been suggested by Nancy Chodorow that mothers, being the same sex as their daughters, identify more with them than with their sons and thereby foster in them a continuing sense of mergence in personal relations. On the other hand, being the opposite sex to their sons, mothers tend to relate to them as separate and different from themselves and thereby propel them relatively early into the separation-individuation process such that they grow up having a greater sense than women of their separateness in personal relations (Chodorow, 1978).

Whereas this use of psychoanalysis emphasizes psychological sex differences – women as more merged, men as more individuated in personal relations – others (for example, Juliet Mitchell, 1974) have used psychoanalysis to stress the psychological similarity between the sexes, to show that the traits associated with masculinity and femininity reside in both sexes. In this they draw on Freud's claim that girls and boys are initially 'bisexual', that they are both equally feminine and masculine in infancy, and on his view that even when girls become predominantly feminine (and boys predominantly masculine) following the Oedipus complex, masculinity remains present, albeit repressed and unconscious, within the female psyche (as femininity remains present in the male psyche).

The view that people are often psychologically feminine as well as masculine has also been propounded, although not in psychoanalytic terms, within mainstream psychology. Prior to the late 1960s it had been assumed that psychological health consisted, among other things, in conforming with the norms of one's sex – in being feminine if one was a woman, masculine if a man. The advent of the women's movement was accompanied, however, by a questioning of the adaptiveness of such sex-role conformity. And this resulted in the development by Sandra Bem of a test designed to measure the extent to which individuals adhere to masculine, feminine, or both masculine and feminine traits – a test now much used in conjunction with other measures to assess whether sex-role conformity is indeed adaptive or whether adaptiveness is instead a matter of 'androgyny', of combining both masculine and feminine traits (Bem, 1974).

Janet Sayers
University of Kent

References
Bem, S. (1974), 'The measurement of psychological androgyny', *Journal of Consulting and Clinical Psychology*, 42.
Chodorow, N. (1978), *The Reproduction of Mothering*, Berkeley and Los Angeles.
Hutt, C. (1972), *Males and Females*, Harmondsworth.
Kohlberg, L. (1966), 'A cognitive-developmental analysis of children's sex-role concepts and attitudes', in E. E. Maccoby (ed.), *The Development of Sex Differences*, Stanford, Calif.
Mischel, W. (1966), 'A social-learning view of sex differences in behaviour', in E. E. Maccoby (ed.), *The Development of Sex Differences*, Stanford, Calif.
Mitchell, J. (1974), *Psychoanalysis and Feminism*, London.

Further Reading
Sayers, J. (1985), *Sexual Contradictions: Psychology, Psychoanalysis and Feminism*, London.

Women's Studies in Social Anthropology

Women anthropologists have always been prominent, but before the early 1970s only sporadically were studies explicitly focused on women as such. Social anthropology's response to the women's movement is shown in the flood of writing by professionals within the discipline which has appeared since then. In 1979 the interdisciplinary feminist journal *Signs* published its second review of anthropology, listing over 80 English-language works for the three years 1976–8. A more selective review in 1982 added another 40 for the years 1979–81. The quickest response was theoretical – old analyses and positions were reappraised – since implementation in research strategies, especially given the nature of lengthy anthropological fieldwork, was bound to take time. Acceptance has shown the reverse pattern. Most social anthropologists today agree that studies of women are desirable, and pre-1970s naivety about the 'status of women' has gone for ever. But there is still widespread theoretical resistance to the implications of the feminist input. The process is one of challenge and containment. Many feminist anthropologists see themselves as taking on the whole of the subject; they are met with a tendency to hive off women's studies from the rest of social anthropology.

Ambiguities surrounding the anthropology of women are reflected in the variety of orientations. The four main areas are:

(1) *Women's studies*. Original impetus came from outside the discipline. Women's studies subsumes anthropology as a branch of the social sciences and thus part of the *interdisciplinary* academic effort to respond to the widely-based *Women's Liberation Movement*. Explicit political intentions underwrite the ultimate goal as reform of social conditions and the ending of the oppression of women. This concern crosscuts disciplines. Anthropologists have drawn on works produced by historians of science, philosophers, psychologists, literary critics, sociologists and so on, to illuminate their understanding of Western society. In turn anthropology has been drawn on to provide cross-cultural 'answers' to queries raised by Western feminism. Anthropological findings here have the character of a resource for both academic and non-academic students of 'women and society'. This gives it a popular status of a novel kind.

(2) *The anthropology of women*. Those seeking to understand the placement of women in Western society may assume 'women' as a universal social category. To outsiders anthropology is seen to provide documentation on the condition of women in other societies; within is an insistence that *women* are indeed a proper subject matter. One strand of feminist theory presupposes continuity of experience in the very fact of being a woman; another strand seeks to locate specific experiences within specifiable social-historical conditions. Anthropologists in addition may explicitly counterbalance male bias in ethnographic reporting by focusing on women, their lives and concerns. Women should be seen as social actors in their own right. Treating their affairs fully and seriously often yields new insights into power and prestige relations, and thus contributes to the study of society as a whole. The implications of this are developed in (3).

(3) *The study of gender* or *male-female relations*. Others insist that ideas about women are always structured in relation to those about men, and argue that the focus of study should be interaction. This may be of a social or ideational kind. Some anthropologists take as their subject matter *sexual inequality*, relations of super-subordination between men and women being so prevalent as to amount to a research focus in itself; others concentrate on *gender constructs* as social representations. Such constructs speak to and are derived from stereotypes about women and men but may also hierarchialize other values, delimiting what is considered culturally important and unimportant. A concern with the construction of inequality and differential value also informs the next orientation.

(4) *Feminist anthropology*. Society is seen as structured by the interests of some at the expense of others. Feminists may take it as axiomatic that male interests tend to define what is 'important': their subject matter is *male ideology*. Or they may look rather to *class ideology*. These share with feminists in other disciplines an awareness of class interests in the reproduction of labour power and the placement of women's domestic labour. As anthropologists, they open up the wider question of gender role ideology in modes of production of a precapitalist kind. Theoretical affinities with different types of Marxism may be claimed or disowned. Many combine the feminist criticism that orthodox academic Marxism has an impoverished grasp of the nature of sexual inequality with the anthropological criticism that noncapitalist social formations fall outside its central theoretical purview. Nevertheless Marxist-derived precepts give this orientation a theoretical strength that the others lack.

These orientations all share certain characteristics. They assume *male bias* in much previous ethnographic reporting and the double form this often takes – male bias from the ethnographer's own society informing analysis of male bias in the societies studied. Women's studies (1) sometimes looks to anthropology to counter Western bias, treating its findings as relatively unbiased. Explicit criticism of internal anthropological (male) bias is incorporated in the other approaches: that anthropology has ignored half the world (2); that the constructed nature of inequalities and stereotypes is taken for granted instead of being questioned (3); and (4) that the very notion of 'social' or 'individual' to classify interests already draws the lines of power, anthropologists being guilty of participating in the mystification of class or other relations of inequality. A radical view would be that 'doing anthropology' within the terms of the establishment is itself ideologically contaminated. In their different ways these orientations also *challenge received categories of analysis*, whether using anthropological reports to challenge Western assumptions (1) or seeing anthropology endorsing Western assumptions as an inevitable epistemological corollary of its place within Western social science (4). Western concepts such as 'family' or 'politics', 'nature' or 'culture', are scrutinized; anthropological categories of analysis are re-examined. Major areas concern what we mean by 'domination', the theoretical placement of unacknowledged or informal 'power', and the ideological structuring of the 'domestic-political' divide. These explorations are supported by a thoroughgoing *comparative approach* which looks at conditions across the world's societies. Finally, a high proportion of the anthropologists engaged in such exercises are *women*. By no means all women anthropologists mark off their studies as being 'about women', but those concerned with these issues tend to be women themselves.

What are described here as orientations cannot be matched with discrete populations of anthropologists. On the contrary the same person may adopt any of the positions, depending on context. The labels thus shift. In Britain certain 'feminist' anthropologists set themselves apart from mainstream anthropology in favour of wider feminist interests; particularly in the States, on the other hand, self-styled 'feminism' is a more inclusive category. In so far as *reformist* intentions are at issue, any one of these orientations may be seen in 'feminist' light. In so far as the goal is consciousness about the condition of 'women', any of them may be seen as a contribution. Existential continuity comes from women feeling that they can move from one position to another without losing integrity. This dimension of *experience* is theoretically justified in feminist writings. It does not mean that men cannot or do not contribute to the study of women or male-female relations, but that their motivations are often less complex. Women's sureness and confidence in slipping context may, however, also contribute to the resistance their studies still meet.

In Britain, resistance from other social anthropologists picks on the following factors. Some writings are seen as too removed from the subject's central concerns (as in 1): whereas Western urbanization or ethnicity is seen to fall within anthropology's view, attention to literary, psychological or other 'cultural' matters is treated as fringe. Women appear to write only about women (as in 2), and are evaluated as in-turned, containable, dealing with something rather less than 'society'. Even an explicit focus on male-female relations (3) may be regarded as reducible to the female element, for example women's and men's interaction within the family or household. Finally (4) feminism as such may be thought to be politically rather than intellectually motivated – in that pursuing ideological concerns of their own, women anthropologists cease to study society, frequently introducing an intrusive rhetoric that makes them blind to obvious 'facts'.

The insinuation running through these types of resistance is that studies focused on women are less than studies of *society*. Post-war social anthropology in Britain has sustained the comparative study of institutions – 'kinship', 'economics' – with relations between the sexes seen as incidental to 'society' as a set of interlocking institutions. (Concern with 'role/status', and in America with 'culture/personality', crosscuts this but is weakly theorized.) A focus on women challenges the idea of society as anthropology's subject matter – hence its containment as being concerned with 'less than' society! In fact feminist anthropologists draw on an ongoing anthropological interest in the relationship between social forms and representations of them, by arguing that 'society' cannot be taken for granted. One should not get trapped in the terms of reference set up by the ideologies of particular societies, including the self-modelling of what 'society' is, but attend rather to the ideological structuring itself. The powerful contribution that feminist anthropology has already made to the conceptualization of 'domesticity', for instance, draws on anthropological insight into kinship ideology and the economic and political functions of kinship in non-Western societies.

In the face of rich cross-cultural data is a dramatic theoretical divide, cutting across the four orientations and particularly anthropological in its formulation. There are those who take the subordination of women as axiomatic, and see the role of feminist awareness as international; there are those who reject the analytical categories ('power', 'domination') implicit in this view, and who regard the condition of women in the West as a product of the social-political forces of capitalism. In this view it is the spread of world capitalism and/or state systems that makes modern women's situation in the developing countries so precarious. A neutral position is adopted by those whose interests are rather in the grasp of what they call 'cultural' realities.

The anthropological relevance of the biology of sex differences is a separate topic, not treated here. The evolution of human behaviour has been subjected to feminist critique but lies outside the main concerns of social anthropology. Here there is general agreement that the social classification of men and women in terms of biological destiny is an artifact of (especially Western) culture. Dialogue with Western concepts has always marked anthropological endeavour – the anthropology of women belongs to this tradition in using such concepts not as explanations for why women are treated as they are but as ideas and attitudes themselves to be explained.

Marilyn Strathern
University of Manchester

Further Reading

Ardener, E. (1975), 'Belief and the problem of women', in S. Ardener (ed.), *Perceiving Women*, London.

Caplan, P. and Bujra, J. M. (eds) (1978), *Women United, Women Divided*, London.

Rosaldo, M. Z. and Lamphere, L. (eds) (1974), *Women, Culture, and Society*, Stanford.

Sharma, U. (1980), *Women, Work, and Property in North West India*, London.

Young, K., Wolkowitz, C. and McCullagh, R. (1981), *Of Marriage and the Market*, London.

See also: *division of labour by sex; marriage; women's studies.*

Work and Leisure

Work can refer to any physical and/or mental activities which transform natural materials into a more useful form, improve human knowledge and understanding of the world, and/or provide or distribute goods to others. The definition of work cannot be limited to references to activities alone, however, but most also consider the purposes for which, and the social context within which, those activities are being carried out. For some people their 'work' is to play games to entertain spectators, games such as football, tennis or snooker which many others play for their own pleasure and relaxation; to read a book for interest or amusement has a different significance from reading the same book in order to prepare a lecture. Work activities are instrumental activities: they are undertaken in order to meet certain individual needs either directly, or indirectly by providing for the needs of others so that goods and services, or the means to purchase them, are received in exchange. Work activities may also be valued for their own sake, but they always have an extrinsic purpose.

In industrial societies the most socially prominent and economically important forms of work are those activities which occur within relationships of employment, or self-employment, and provide goods and services for sale in the market in return for a wage, salary or fee. This predominance of one social context and form of organization of work is a relatively recent development; within human history as a whole the direct provision of a family's or a community's needs (as in peasant societies), or production carried out under coercion (for example serfdom, or slavery), have been much more common. Indeed the development of industrial societies necessitated not only considerable social innovation in forms of work organization (such as factories and offices) but also the emergence and internalization of new values regarding work, ones which provided the necessary sense of obligation to work hard and in a rational and regular way under the control of others (Thompson, 1967). Such a 'work ethic', whose origins were seen by Weber (1930 [1922]) as lying particularly in certain forms of Protestantism, has however coexisted with the more traditional view of work as a necessity. Whereas when work is viewed as a moral duty, of value in itself, not to work is to be 'idle'; when work is a tiresome necessity, not to work is to have 'leisure'.

The current importance of work within an employment relationship and a market context should not obscure those forms of work which are differently structured and located. Of particular importance is domestic work, which is often very time consuming and clearly makes a considerable and absolutely essential contribution to the economy, though one which is only rarely acknowledged. Also part of the so-called 'informal' economy are other household activities such as do-it-yourself home improvements and exchanges of help and services between relatives and neighbours; activities in the wider community such as voluntary work; and work in the 'hidden economy': jobs 'on the side' for pay which is not taxed, and the clearly illegal 'work' of criminals (Gershuny and Pahl, 1980).

Leisure

A definition of leisure is equally difficult. It can be used to refer to a quality of life (leisure as the mark of a 'gentleman'), or to refer to some combination of time, activity and experience: time free from work and other necessary activities such as eating and sleeping; 'play' activities which are outside normal routines; and experiences which are intrinsically rewarding (Roberts, 1981; Parker, 1971). Whilst leisure can fairly clearly be distinguished from paid employment, it may be much more difficult to separate it from other forms of work such as housework or voluntary work. Leisure is also differently experienced and unevenly available: people with jobs (especially men) have more clearly demarcated leisure time and activities than those with domestic responsibilities, such as housewives, whose 'work is never done'.

During recent years a major preoccupation has been with unemployment, the lack of paid work for all those able and willing to do it. In so far as current levels of unemployment are seen as due to structural changes in the economies of industrial societies, and especially the use of mini-computers, robots and so on to replace human labour, they have raised the question of whether we may be seeing the start of a 'leisure society', one in which it will no longer be normal for all adults to work, and where there will be far more leisure and maybe even the need to 'work' at one's leisure activities (Jenkins and Sherman, 1979, 1981). There are, of course, a lot of unresolved questions about such a future for work and leisure: (1) It is far from clear that the potential of the new technology is as great as has been claimed, and if it is, whether that potential can be realized in ways which will release people from employment. (2) There are considerable problems in ensuring that the economic benefits of the new technology are distributed in ways which reward people generally rather than just the few: existing fiscal and tax arrangements are certainly far from adequate. (3) Even if many people can be provided with a high standard of living without the need to undertake (much) paid employment, there is a motivational problem: who is going to be prepared to do the remaining heavy, repetitive, unpleasant or unrewarding jobs once pay is no longer an incentive?

Most important of all we need to consider the social and psychological functions currently filled by work, and especially paid employment, and to ask whether leisure, even if it is 'worked at', or any other activities, can provide alternatives. Can leisure structure the day as work and employment do; provide social contacts outside the immediate family and locality; link individuals to goals and purposes outside themselves; give a sense of identity and status; and enforce activity and through that some sense of control over events (Jahoda, 1982)? Work provides a sense of necessity and constrains what we can do; for this reason it is often resented and contrasted unfavourably with leisure and 'free time'; paradoxically without the constraint the sense of freedom may also be lost.

Richard K. Brown
University of Durham

References

Gershuny, J. I. and Pahl, R. E. (1980), 'Britain in the decade of the three economies', *New Society*, 3.
Jahoda, M. (1982), *Employment and Unemployment*, Cambridge.
Jenkins, C. and Sherman, B. (1979), *The Collapse of Work*, London.
Jenkins, C. and Sherman, B. (1981), *The Leisure Shock*, London.
Parker, S. R. (1971), *The Future of Work and Leisure*, London.
Roberts, K. (1981), *Leisure*, London.
Thompson, E. P. (1967), 'Time, work discipline and industrial capitalism', *Past and Present*, 38.
Weber, M. (1930 [1922]) *The Protestant Ethic and the Spirit of Capitalism*, London. (Original German edn, *Die protestantische Ethik und der 'Geist' des Kapitalismus*, Tübingen.)

Further reading

Abrams, P. and Brown, R. K. (eds) (1984), *UK Society: Work, Urbanism and Inequality*, London.
Anthony, P. D. (1977), *The Ideology of Work*, London.
Esland, G. and Salaman, G. (1980), *The Politics of Work and Occupations*, Milton Keynes.
Gershuny, J. (1978), *After Industrial Society*, London.
Hedges, N. and Beynon, H. (1982), *Born to Work*, London.
See also: *employment and unemployment, psychological aspects.*

World-System Theory

The sociologist Immanuel Wallerstein developed world-system theory in the early 1970s in an attempt to explain the origins of capitalism, the Industrial Revolution, and the complex interconnections of the 'First', 'Second' and 'Third' Worlds. The multidisciplinary research of world-system theory focuses on historical studies of the growth of the world-system and on contemporary processes within it.

The 'modern world-system' arose in Western Europe about 500 years ago (Wallerstein, 1979). It was based on capitalist trade networks which transcended state boundaries, hence it is called the 'capitalist world-economy'. The drive for capital accumulation caused increasing competition among capitalist producers for labour, materials and markets. As competition waxed and waned through repeated 'crises of overproduction' various regions of the world were incorporated into the unevenly expanding world-economy.

Uneven expansion differentiates the world into three interrelated types of societies. The central, or 'core', societies specialize in industrial production and distribution, have relatively strong states, a strong bourgeoisie, a large wage-labour class, and are heavily involved in the affairs of non-core societies. At the other extreme, in the 'periphery', societies concentrate on the production of raw materials, have weak states, a small bourgeoisie, a large peasant class, and are heavily influenced by core societies. The remaining societies form the 'semi-periphery', which shares characteristics of both the core and periphery. Semi-peripheral societies are typically rising peripheral societies, or declining core societies. The semi-periphery blocks polarization between core and periphery, thus stabilizing the system. The economic and political interrelations of the core and periphery are the presumed sources of the development in the core, and the lack of development in the periphery.

A key assumption of world-system theory is that the world-economy must be studied as a whole. The study of social change in any component of the system – nations, states, regions, ethnic groups, classes – must begin by locating that component within the system. The typical component analysed is a state. Thus world-system theory has a dual research agenda. On the one hand, it examines the consequences of dynamic changes in its components (such as states) for the evolution of the system and for the movement of various components within the system. On the other hand, it examines the consequences of dynamic changes in the world-system for the internal dynamics and social structure of its various components.

Case studies investigating the emergence and evolution of the world-system offer finer-grained analyses of various components of the system and complement global analyses. Controversy surrounds the measurement and explanation of the system and explanation of the system and its parts, and centres on two major issues: (1) to what degree and how is 'underdevelopment' in the periphery necessary to the development of the core; and (2) whether market (exogenous) factors or social-structural (endogenous) factors, especially class, are the primary agents of change.

World-system literature is complicated by a number of intertwined polemics, which focus on the role of socialist states in the contemporary world-system; the probability of a world socialist revolution; the degree to which underdevelopment is a necessary consequence of core development; the effects of various policies on the evolution of the world-system; and whether world-system theory is a useful extension or a crude distortion of Marxist theory.

Polemical debates notwithstanding, world-system theory has generated many studies of long-term social change. These studies use techniques from the various social sciences and appear in a variety of publications. In its first decade world-system theory has developed its own journal, *Review*, and has made a major contribution to the social sciences by focusing attention on the importance of both global and historical factors in understanding both changes and processes of contemporary social life.

Thomas D. Hall
University of Oklahoma

Reference

Wallerstein, I. (1979), *The Capitalist World-Economy*, Cambridge.

Further Reading

Bergesen, A. (ed.) (1980), *Studies of the Modern World-System*, New York.
Chirot, D. and Hall, T. (1982), 'World-system theory', *Annual Review of Sociology*, 8.
Nash, J. (1981), 'Ethnographic aspects of the world capitalist system', *Annual Review of Anthropology*, 10.
Wallerstein, I. (1974), *The Modern World-System*, I, New York.
Wallerstein, I. (1980), *The Modern World-System*, II, New York.
Wallerstein, I. (1984), *The Politics of the World-Economy*, Cambridge.
See also: *dependency theory; dual economy; imperialism.*

Wundt, Wilhelm (1832–1920)

Wundt, a medically-trained German academic, was a professor of philosophy at the University of Leipzig and is remembered chiefly as a pioneer of experimental psychology. His establishment of modest facilities for experimental psychological research by some of his students in 1879 is conventionally regarded as marking the foundation of the world's first psychological laboratory. Wundt's innovation attracted a large number of students from all over the world, especially during the last two decades of the nineteenth century. In many cases these students attempted to found similar laboratories after they returned to their home countries.

A further contribution to the institutionalization of experimental psychology involved Wundt's publication of a journal, *Philosophische Studien*, in which reports of experimental psychological research appeared regularly, though still interspersed with philosophical papers. However, the major source of Wundt's reputation as an experimental psychologist was probably his textbook, *Grundzüge der physiologischen Psychologie* which first appeared in 1874 and grew to a monumental three-volume work in five subsequent revised editions.

It was Wundt's belief that the experimental method, which had proved so effective in physiological research, could be employed, with some modification, in the investigation of some of the problems which had been debated by philosopher psychologists. Two sets of problems were particularly important in this context: questions about the sources of our knowledge of the external world, and questions about the nature of voluntary action. This led to systematic research in the area of sensation and perception and in the area of reaction times.

While Wundt derived his experimental methodology from physiology, he took most of his theoretical concepts from philosophy. His central concept was 'apperception', a term which has its roots in the philosophy of Leibniz, was systematically developed by Kant and applied to psychology by Herbart. These were the men whom Wundt regarded as his intellectual ancestors. The concept of apperception referred to the active and synthetic qualities of the mind which were fundamental to all its expressions.

There is a double irony in the fact that posterity remembered Wundt mainly as the 'father' of experimental psychology. In the first place, his work in this area, extensive though it was, represented only a relatively small part of an enormously productive academic career. He published major works in all the main branches of philosophy, logic, ethics, metaphysics and epistemology. For him, though not for many of his pupils, the significance of psychological research very much depended on a philosophical context. Towards the end of his life, he strongly opposed both the notion of an applied psychology and the notion that psychology should cut its ties with philosophy. These were not the outcomes he had intended.

Moreover, this 'father' of experimental psychology had never seen this branch of the subject as more than a part of psychology as a whole. It was to be supplemented by another part, called *Völkerpsychologie*, a psychology of culture which would use a comparative and historical rather than an experimental methodology. Wundt devoted the last part of his life mainly to this subject. His ten-volume text with this title did not produce anything like the echo of his text on physiological psychology. It did, however, anticipate certain developments that took place long after Wundt's death, notably in the importance it gave to psycholinguistics.

In spite of his prodigious output and vast influence, Wundt founded no school and had no real disciples. He identified his psychological system as 'voluntarism' because he regarded the dynamic and affective aspect of psychological processes as fundamental. But there were no 'voluntarists' among his students, especially not among the strict experimentalists. By the time of his death in 1920, his version of psychology had become thoroughly unpalatable to the majority of psychologists, especially in the US, who saw psychology as a practical technology of behaviour and as a natural science like any other. By contrast, Wundt's vision for psychology had been that of a bridge between the natural and the humanistic sciences.

K. Danziger
York University, Ontario

Further Reading

Bringmann, W. G. and Tweenay, R. D. (eds) (1980), *Wundt Studies*, Toronto.

Rieber, R. W. (ed.) (1980), *Wilhelm Wundt and the Making of a Scientific Psychology*, New York.

Wundt, W. (1894 [1863]), *Lectures on Human and Animal Psychology*, 2nd edn, New York. (Original German edn, *Vorlesungen über die Menschen und Tierseele*.)

Wundt, W. (1897), *Outlines of Psychology*, Leipzig.

Alphabetical List of Entries

corruption
cost-benefit analysis
countertransference
Cournot
creativity
crime and delinquency
criminology
cross-cultural psychology
crowding out
crowds *see* collective behaviour and
  crowds
cults *see* sects and cults
cultural anthropology
culture
culture and personality
culture area
cybernetics *see* general systems
  theory

death
Debreu
decision making
defences
deflation as a statistical technique
deindustrialization *see*
  industrialization and
  deindustrialization
delinquency *see* crime and
  delinquency
democracy
demographic transition
demography
dependency theory
depreciation
depressive disorders
depth perception
descent and descent groups
devaluation
development *see* development
  studies; economic development
development administration
developmental psychology
development banks
development studies
deviance
diffusion
distributions of income and wealth
distributive justice
divine kingship
division of labour by sex
divorce
Douglas
dreams
drugs *see* drug use;
  psychopharmacology
drug use
DSM III
dual economy
Durkheim
dynamics *see* economic dynamics
dyslexia

Eastern psychology
ecology
econometrics
economic anthropology
economic development
economic dynamics
economic efficiency
economic externalities
economic geography
economic growth
economic history *see* cliometrics;
  history
economics
economies of scale
education
educational psychology
efficiency *see* economic efficiency
elasticity
elections
electroconvulsive therapy
Elias
élites
emotion
empathy and sympathy
employment and
  underemployment
employment and unemployment,
  psychological factors
energy
Engel
Engels
entrepreneurship
environmental psychology
epidemiology
equality
equilibrium
ergonomics
ethics in social research
ethnic groups
ethnic relations
ethnographic fieldwork
ethnology
ethnomethodology
ethology
evaluation
Evans-Pritchard
evolution
evolutionism and progress
exchange
exchange rate
existential psychology
experimental design
externalities *see* economic
  externalities
Eysenck

factions
family
family history
family therapy
fantasy

Fascism
federalism
fertility
feud
feudalism
Feyerabend
fieldwork *see* ethnographic
  fieldwork
financial crises
financial systems
firm, theory of
fiscal policy
Fisher
folklore and myth
force
forecasting *see* prediction and
  forecasting
foreign aid *see* aid
Foucault
Frankfurt School
Frazer
free association
freedom
free trade
Freud, A.
Freud, S.
Friedman
friendship
Frisch
functional analysis
futurology

Galbraith
games
game theory
game theory, economic
  applications
gangs
GDP *see* national income analysis
Geertz
gender studies *see* women's studies
generalized media
general systems theory
genetic aspects of mental illness
genetics and behaviour
geography
gerontology, social
gestalt therapy
GNP *see* national income analysis
Goffman
Gouldner
government
Gramsci
graph theory
Greenberg
grid/group
group dynamics
groups
group therapy
Gurvitch